ENCYCLOPEDIA OF

LITERARY TRANSLATION

INTO

ENGLISH

Volume 1

BOARD OF ADVISERS

Michael Alexander
University of St Andrews

M.M. Badawi
St Antony's College, Oxford

T.H. Barrett
School of Oriental and African Studies, University of London

Susan Bassnett
University of Warwick

Rina Ben Shahar
University of Haifa

Anne Born
Translators Association, London

Barbara Bray
Translator and writer, Paris

Julia Bray
University of St Andrews

Peter Bush
University of East Anglia

Greg Clingham
Bucknell University

David Connolly
University of Athens

Edwin Gentzler
University of Massachusetts

Andrew Gerstle
School of Oriental and African Studies, University of London

Stuart Gillespie
University of Glasgow

Terry Hale
University of Hull

Theo Hermans
University College London

André A. Lefevere (died 1996)
University of Texas

Lauren G. Leighton
University of Illinois at Chicago (emeritus)

Anthony Levi
University of St Andrews (emeritus)

Bernard McGuirk
University of Nottingham

Edith McMorran
St Hugh's College, Oxford

Ian McMorran
University of Paris

Edwin Morgan
Poet and translator, Glasgow

Noël Peacock
University of Glasgow

Barbara Reynolds
Translator and critic, Cambridge

Michael Robinson
University of East Anglia

Colin Smethurst
University of Glasgow

Christopher Smith
University of East Anglia

R.H. Stephenson
University of Glasgow

Lawrence Venuti
Temple University

Anthony Vivis
Translators Association, London

ENCYCLOPEDIA OF

LITERARY TRANSLATION

INTO

ENGLISH

Volume 1
A–L

Editor
OLIVE CLASSE

FITZROY DEARBORN PUBLISHERS
LONDON · CHICAGO

Ref
PN
241
.E56
2000
V.1

Copyright © 2000 by
FITZROY DEARBORN PUBLISHERS

All rights reserved including the right of reproduction in whole or in part in any form. For information write to:

FITZROY DEARBORN PUBLISHERS
919 North Michigan Avenue, Suite 760
Chicago, Illinois 60611
USA

or

310 Regent Street
London W1B 3AX
England

C.1

British Library and Library of Congress Cataloguing in Publication Data are available

ISBN 1-884964-36-2

First published in the USA and UK 2000

Typeset by Regent Typesetting, London
Printed and bound by the Bath Press

Cover design by Sign

45749095

CONTENTS

EDITOR'S NOTE

Literary translation lies at the heart of many cultures. Over the centuries the world's literatures have absorbed in massive numbers the written treasures of foreign countries, often so thoroughly that some translated works, such as Dante's *Divine Comedy*, Cervantes's *Don Quixote* and Hans Andersen's fairy tales, have been naturalized into the receiving cultures with the status of classics or even of sacred texts.

At the same time, but slowly and intermittently, awareness has grown of the fact that the processes and products involved in the transference of a work from one language into another are neither simple in themselves nor without fundamental problems and hidden implications.

Since about the middle of the 20th century three far-reaching changes have affected attitudes towards literary translation. First, the rapid upsurge of international cultural exchanges has brought a worldwide increase in the quantity of works translated – and re-translated – and their dissemination. Second, the public is gradually becoming aware that much of its reading is mediated by translation, and more people than before are even beginning to recognize the existence and power of the hitherto "invisible" translator. Third, the phenomenon of translation has been brought under the methodical scrutiny of a scientific age; as a result, the rise in the number of professional translators and of their readers is being accompanied all over the globe by a swift expansion in the number of scholars, university courses, institutions, conferences and learned journals devoted to the study of the theory and practice of literary translation in all its interdisciplinary aspects: literary, linguistic, cultural, sociological, psychological, ideological and political. These academic developments, generating a wide but fertile diversity of opinions, amount virtually to a renaissance of the subject of translation.

The moment is opportune, therefore, for an initial mapping of the broad territory being opened up. The present work is one of the first attempts at a large-scale charting of the field of English-language literary translation. The purpose is to provide a historical and analytical survey, in more than 600 entries, of the theory and practice of literary translation into English from the principal world languages and from the works of major writers and groups of writers in those languages. The *Encyclopedia* is intended to interest and inform the general reader and to assist students and teachers of languages and literatures. It is hoped also that Translation Studies scholars and practising translators may discover in its pages helpful facts and ideas.

The terms that compose our title have several meanings in general usage. They need to be defined in their present context.

This **Encyclopedia** embraces systematically the relevant "circle of knowledge or of instruction" (Greek *egkuklios paedeia*). The scope of the enterprise is bold, wider than that of most other efforts made so far. Much of the copious factual and critical material contained here on writers, texts and topics is newly recorded, or newly interpreted in a translation-oriented sense. Even difficulties frequently encountered in the task of discovery, scrutiny and organization can be part of the overall picture each entry tries to present. For instance, the vast pool of English-translation source material is only in the process of being explored. Many interesting texts are rare or out of print. The bibliography of translations is at an early stage: in databases and library catalogues the attribution of translations can be absent, uncertain or erroneous, while publishers and reviewers do not always name individual translators, especially in the case of anthologies and selections done by several hands. As far as possible such gaps and errors have been remedied here. A large amount of the bibliographical material furnished was not readily available before now.

Delimitation of the area defined by the composite term **literary translation** is notoriously subject to debate, the significance of the whole not corresponding to the sum of its parts as diversely understood.

The noun "translation" is the easier part to circumscribe for practical purposes. We leave aside the more general acceptions of the term (as for example that in which translation is held to be the conversion of any sign into another sign, neither necessarily verbal). For the purposes of this book, the word "translation" is held to refer principally to interlingual translation, i.e. translation from one language into another, and the sense of the term includes both the process and the product of the transference of some proportion of the content, form and effects of a written source text (ST) from one language to another so as to create a so-called target text (TT).

In the commercial context and to working translators "literary translation" signifies, broadly speaking, translation of composed texts that are intended for wide or public dissemination or performance, in conventionally agreed contradistinction to "technical translation", i.e. that of texts with a scientific, technical, technological or legal function. Used colloquially, the word "literature" can denote any written text or body of texts, ranging from a given culture's established canon of famous and admired works, plus its esteemed modern ones (as in "French Literature"), to mere documentation issued for a specific but ephemeral practical purpose ("If you're interested in our new model, I'll send you our literature"). In general usage, however, which is followed here, the terms "literature" and "literary" imply aesthetic purpose, together with a degree of durability and the presence of intended stylistic effects. Literature so defined normally comprises, in the main, fiction, poetry and drama. Except in the case of certain culturally eminent texts such as the Bible, the Koran, and a few exceptional historical, philosophical and reflective writings, works produced with instruction or exhortation as their primary aim are excluded from this book. So: literary translation is for our purposes the translation principally of works of fiction, poetry and drama that have an important function, and are highly regarded, in the source culture. One of the chief intended effects of translation is to extend this important function and high regard into the target culture.

To narrow our definition further: it is current practice for those concerned with literature to distinguish between the written products of high culture and popular culture, while treating both kinds of product with due attention and interest. For the purpose of making a start in the most widely interesting area of a huge field, the content of this *Encyclopedia* is confined in the main to translation and translations of texts, mainly of fiction, poetry and drama, recognized as belonging to the cultural category of high or at least serious literature, that is, of texts actually or potentially situated in a consensually evolved or evolving and loosely defined "canon" of "great works".

English: we have cut the Gordian knot constituted by the growing worldwide diversity of types of English ("Englishes"). Here, for practical purposes, the word generally encompasses the mutually comprehensible varieties of standard English, used, as the mother tongue, mainly in England, Ireland, Scotland, Wales, the United States, Canada, New Zealand and Australia. For similar reasons, it has been necessary to confine coverage to translations into English, mainly in the sense just described; and to restrict the focus of topic entries mainly to translation history and theory as enunciated in English, with only ancillary references to non-English theorists.

This *Encyclopedia* is an instrument of record, a progress report on an emerging field of study, and it aims at neither consensus nor polemic. The Editor has been guided throughout by the spirit of inquiry. In these pages many practitioners and theorists of literary translation expound and implement respected current and past views, sometimes controversial ones. These views range from the assumption, still widespread among general readers and working translators, that the translation process principally involves linguistic skills reinforced by perseverance, chance and luck, all put to the service of the source text; through to the various more modern understandings of the process and the product as problematic and capable of involving a multidisciplinary range of specialized technical and theoretical considerations, not all of which give primary importance to source texts. But no master theory, no master narrative, dominates the *Encyclopedia*. It is too early to draw definitive conclusions about the larger tendencies of translation into English, though of course some smaller patterns and fashions do emerge already and are of great interest for the history of reception (as when certain canonical European authors are found to be sparsely translated or when on the other hand survey articles reveal ephemeral vogues for translating minor foreign authors).

It will be noticed that a large proportion of the entries, following a long academic tradition, focus on the linguistic and literary-historical aspects of source and target texts. All such entries (as well of course as those by contributors more interested in cultural transference and other functions of translation privileged by the more modern practitioners and theorists) have an advantage over the current norm of translation appraisal available to the general public: their analyses are based on thorough knowledge of both the source language and the target language. "Readability", or fluency in English, is often the only criterion applied to published translations – of necessity, when readers, reviewers, editors and publishers are frequently unable to read the work in question in the original language. The desire, sometimes the demand, of publishers for translations that sound like original English texts can result in versions that "betray" the source, either by taming and domesticating its form and content or, especially in the case of the modern, non-canon work, by giving it the benefit of (unremunerated) cosmetic improvement. It is to be hoped that by raising the general consciousness of current thinking on the issue of "fidelity" versus "freedom", as well as of the many other wider or less apparent implications of the act of translation, this book will help to enhance the status of translators and translated texts.

The communication gap that has tended in recent years to exist between practising ("working") translators and translation scholars and theorists is closing, largely because of the increased number of people operating in both areas and as a result of eclectic membership of professional translators' associations. One of the intended functions of the *Encyclopedia* is to further this rapprochement.

It must be said that interesting and instructive as academic analysis and theory are, translation and translations cannot be entirely caught in the net of method. The often solitary struggles, delights and defeats of the working translator involve elements of personality, judgement, motive and linguistic chance, interacting to produce a highly complex outcome that to a large extent eludes explanation by any system. Many of our contributors give insights into individual endeavours, triumphs and failures at the coalface that are unimagined by the general reader of translations.

Yet the translator, especially the freelancer working without academic recognition or a regular university salary, has latterly been notoriously "invisible" because frequently unnamed by publishers and reviewers. The fact that the text being read actually *is* a translation is another element obscured when a translation is not attributed. Acknowledging the translator is not only a simple act of justice: as the translator Ros Schwartz has pointed out (*The Times*, 2 December 1998), it also foregrounds the important notion that what is being offered is *a*, not *the*, translation, and that other versions may offer other insights. Many anglophone readers seem unaware of the fact that certain texts familiar to all were not originally written in English. The novelist Beryl Bainbridge is reported to have thought for years that Proust wrote in English.

An eminent translator, reflecting on long experience, finds that the status of the professional translator has improved in recent decades, even if conditions and rewards are still not ideal. Patricia Crampton, translator into English from a very wide range of languages and internationally-known official representative of translators' interests, recalls that even in the early 1970s it was possible for a noted and venerable publisher to patronize a woman from whom he proposed to commission the English version of a highly marketable title. This on the assumption that she must be an amateur, a housewife who was working to pay some small domestic bill and whose concern for proper remuneration and a contract providing translator's royalties and copyright could be brushed aside as not serious. The concern *was* serious. The individual stood her ground, her point was carried, and in the UK, with the backing of the Translators Association (TA), and abroad, through the work of International Federation of Translators (FIT) and other bodies, she saw her claims for fair terms and conditions form the basis of sustained negotiations for contractual rights for the profession. The turning point came in 1976 with the General Conference of Unesco in Nairobi. Crampton was privileged to be a member of the tiny delegation whose proposal for a translator's charter won the Conference's approval. The battle for the translator's copyright and royalty had been won.

Current developments promise to increase the already vast range and importance of translation into English. In anglophone countries, the number and quality of literary texts – including children's books – originally written in English, taken with the extra expense of translators' fees and royalties, have meant that until now translations into English are far fewer as a percentage of national publication output than are translations out of English in other countries. But English is now a global language. To the 300 or so million native speakers of English in the world and the further 200 or so million speakers of English as a second language must be added perhaps as many as a billion learners (David Crystal, *English as a Global Language*, 1997). This growing potential market, and increasing public awareness of cross-cultural interests should expand considerably the demand for literary translation, and translators, into English.

Guide for Readers

The *Encyclopedia*'s list of entries was drawn up with the invaluable help of the Board of Advisers. The standard length for essays is 1,000 words, plus bibliographical material (a list of Translations; items for Further Reading), with for writer/work entries a prefatory biographical sketch. Particularly important entries, such as general surveys and the article on the Bible in English Translation, are allotted more space, up to 6,000 words or more. The project expanded from the originally planned single volume into two. This is because the zeal and enthusiasm of contributors, as well as offers made of interesting items not originally listed, led to the decision to admit further articles and allow an increase in the length of major entries. Also, very importantly, the bibliographical material discovered in the course of contributors' research proved more voluminous and revealing than had been expected.

The editorial approach to creating the list of entries has been as eclectic as possible. At the same time, given that the field of writers and works in English translation has not yet been fully and systematically examined by scholars, the list is to some extent exploratory. It covers the translation history of major ancient and modern writers and texts in the principal world languages, insofar as they have been translated and insofar as there have been experts available to write on the translation picture in question. Gaps arise mainly where translation coverage, even in the case of some "canon" items, does not exist or where the material is sparse or has not yet been surveyed or studied; as well as defining and describing the existing translation corpus, the *Encyclopedia* also begins on the task of identifying lacunae and shortcomings in this coverage, so indicating areas that would reward further research.

Entries are arranged alphabetically. As regards content, they fall into three categories. (1) General and historical surveys of Literary Translation into English from the major world languages, classical and modern. (2) Topics related to the history, theory and practice of Literary Translation into English. (3) Writer and Work entries: these are analytical accounts of the treatment in English translation of (a) all the significant translated works by major world authors or (b) single translated works.

The general surveys of the history of translation into English from a given major language, say Chinese or Czech, begin by classifying it according to language type and giving an account of its special characteristics and resources and its principal differences from English as they affect translation. This feature should be of particular interest to the student and the general reader.

Topic entries (e.g. Children's Literature in English Translation, Feminist Translation Theory, Ezra Pound as Translator, Translation Norms) are listed alphabetically along with the survey and writer/work entries and deal with aspects of the history and theory of literary translation into English.

The aim of writer/work entries is to give an overall historical and analytical picture of the translation-into-English situation of the whole of an author's work or of a single notable text. Most writers included in the book have a single entry devoted to them, covering their best-known work or works. Others have a composite entry containing a general essay followed by essays on one or more of their works whose translation history merits special attention. Single works that are the subject of a dedicated entry within a writer entry are listed chronologically by date of original publication, and by their best-known English title. There are main entries on a number of anonymous works (or works with no established authorship): these appear alphabetically under their best-known English title, or, if there is no such English title, under their original titles.

The lists headed Translations are usually selective (these selections being the contributors'), and concentrate on the whole on the more important renderings. As a general rule, each listed translation is referred to or discussed in the essay (at points indicated by the names of translators appearing in SMALL CAPITALS), although, where this is not practical, translations may be treated in groups. These lists of Translations are arranged in alphabetical order of translators' last names (the chronological order is usually indicated in the essay part of entries), under the source text titles, which are listed in the source language in chronological order of publication, where appropriate. The date of the first edition of source texts is given wherever possible (and/or, in the case of plays, the date of first performance if it is known and important). Dates of first editions of translations are given, plus subsequent publication dates when these are of interest (in the case of revised editions, editions/reprints issued long after the first, etc.). Bibliographical and publication details of source texts are given in cases where they shed light on the translation profile (e.g. when there are several authoritative versions of a source text, as for Cellini's *Life* and the works of St John of the Cross), or when a large and important oeuvre is represented by a small number of English translations (e.g. the case of Gezelle).

The contents of collections (in lists of translations we use the term "collection" to signify the body of an author's entire works, or of his/her entire works in one genre, in English translation) and of selections are given when the information is available. Parallel texts and bilingual editions are indicated when the relevant information was obtainable; if it is known only that both source and target texts are given but not whether they are printed in parallel, the edition is described as bilingual.

Entries conclude with suggestions for further reading, except where none is available to date. Items listed under Further Reading are intended to be mainly translation-oriented and to avoid, as far as is practicable, references to purely literary information about source texts. Sometimes all there is to list for Further Reading is translators' introductions, or journal articles and critical studies that contain passages relative to translation. In accordance with the general policy of making as much as possible of the material contained in the *Encyclopedia* accessible to monolingual readers, the items listed for Further Reading are usually in the English language.

Editing of entries has been done with as light a hand as is compatible with accuracy and clarity. Where US and UK alternative spelling and punctuation practices exist, the consistent choice of the contributor is respected. Contributors' opinions and styles stand in their own right. The traditional linguistic/literary approach to translation includes at its extremes both the positive *critique des beautés* and the carping search for errors: both these evaluative methods are truthfully represented here, preferably in balance, and only with evidence provided in support of judgements. Many entries, on the other hand, reflect instead the growing awareness of cultural and political aspects of translation, and of the scientific study of spoken and written communication (grammar, semantics, contrastive linguistics, pragmatics). Differing elements in this range may be observed in certain writer entries in which several texts are dealt with by several contributors.

While the overall arrangement of entries is alphabetical, there are other aids to accessing the contents of the *Encyclopedia*:

(1) List of Writers and Works by Language (p. xxvii). This list groups writers, and those works with main entries, according to the language in which they wrote or were written.

(2) Chronological List of Writers and Works (p. xxxiii). Writers are listed in order of birthdate; works with main entries by date of composition or publication.

(3) Title Index (p. 1527). Allows readers to find an entry by the source text or target text titles cited in the Translations lists.

(4) Translator Index (p. 1567). Allows readers to find individual translators cited in the Translations lists.

(5) General Index (p. 1639). This indexes the essays and may be particularly useful for finding translators, writers or topics that do not have an entry of their own, and that do not appear in the Translations lists.

Acknowledgements

The *Encyclopedia* has had the benefit of a distinguished Board of Advisers whose generous counsels helped to give it shape and for whose work, enthusiasm and encouragement the Editor is most grateful. The Board of Advisers consists of the following: Michael Alexander, M.M. Badawi, T.H. Barrett, Susan Bassnett, Rina Ben Shahar, Anne Born, Barbara Bray, Julia Bray, Peter Bush, Greg Clingham, David Connolly, Edwin Gentzler, Andrew Gerstle, Stuart Gillespie, Terry Hale, Theo Hermans, the late André Lefevere, Lauren G. Leighton, Anthony Levi, Bernard McGuirk, Edith McMorran, Ian

McMorran, Edwin Morgan, Noël Peacock, Barbara Reynolds, Michael Robinson, Colin Smethurst, Christopher Smith, R.H. Stephenson, Lawrence Venuti, Anthony Vivis.

Some of our more than 290 contributors heroically undertook a large number of entries at the outset and/or volunteered to fill gaps against the clock. They include Salih J. Altoma, Kristine J. Anderson, Ian Hilton, the late and much missed André Lefevere, Parvin Loloi, James Partridge, Zoja Pavlovskis-Petit, Glyn Pursglove, Paul Reed, Paul Rickett, Paul Starkey, Tom Winnifrith and Yang Ye. To these, and to every one of the *Encyclopedia*'s other contributors, the Editor owes profound thanks for their scholarship, their dedication, their patience and, in cases too numerous to mention here but individually present in my mind, generous encouragement and support given to the project, going so far beyond the line of duty as to enter the realm of (sometimes, so far, largely electronic) friendship.

My special thanks are offered to Fitzroy Dearborn colleagues. From the outset, when Tracy Chevalier suggested to him the theme of translation, managing director Daniel Kirkpatrick fostered the project, and in its final stages his energy and skill turned a document into a book. Lesley Henderson, Fitzroy Dearborn's Commissioning Editor, has been an unfailing source of calm, optimism, information and expert advice. Their work and that of the rest of Fitzroy Dearborn's editorial and technical staff (especially Nina Bunton, Patrick Heenan, Winston James, Cathy Johns, Helena Lyons, Helen Rappaport, Virginia Williams and Alison Worthington), has sustained the *Encyclopedia* throughout and earned my warm gratitude.

OLIVE CLASSE
Formerly Senior Lecturer, now Honorary Senior Research Fellow,
Department of French Language and Literature,
University of Glasgow

General Reading (mainly in English or in English translation)

Arrowsmith, William and Roger Shattuck (editors), *The Craft and Context of Translation: A Symposium*, Austin: University of Texas Press, 1961

Asher, R.E. and J.M.Y. Simpson (editors), *The Encyclopedia of Language and Linguistics*, 10 vols, Oxford and New York: Pergamon Press, 1994

Bailey, Richard W. and Manfred Görlach (editors), *English as a World Language*, Ann Arbor: University of Michigan Press, 1982; Cambridge: Cambridge University Press, 1984

Baker, Mona (editor), assisted by Kirsten Malmkjær, *Routledge Encyclopedia of Translation Studies*, London and New York: Routledge, 1998

Bassnett, Susan and André Lefevere (editors), *Translation, History and Culture*, London: Pinter, 1990

Bassnett, Susan (editor), *Translating Literature*, Cambridge: Brewer, 1997

Bassnett, Susan and André Lefevere, *Constructing Cultures: Essays on Literary Translation*, Clevedon and Philadelphia: Multilingual Matters, 1998

Bassnett, Susan and Harish Trivedi (editors), *Post-colonial Translation: Theory and Practice*, London and New York: Routledge, 1999

Bassnett-McGuire, Susan, *Translation Studies*, London and New York: Methuen, 1980; revised edition, London and New York: Routledge, 1991

Benjamin, Walter, "The Task of the Translator: An Introduction to the Translation of Baudelaire's *Tableaux Parisiens*" (original article in German, 1923) in his *Illuminations*, edited by Hannah Arendt, translated by Harry Zohn, New York: Harcourt Brace, 1968, London: Jonathan Cape, 1970; and in *Theories of Translation: An Anthology of Essays from Dryden to Derrida*, edited by Rainer Schulte and John Biguenet, Chicago: University of Chicago Press, 1992

Boase-Beier, Jean and Michael Holman (editors), *The Practices of Literary Translation: Constraints and Creativity*, Manchester: St Jerome, 1998

Biguenet, John and Rainer Schulte (editors), *The Craft of Translation*, Chicago: University of Chicago Press, 1989

Brower, Reuben A. (editor), *On Translation*, Cambridge, Massachusetts: Harvard University Press, 1959

Campbell, George L., *Concise Compendium of the World's Languages*, London and New York: Routledge, 1995
Catford, J.C., *A Linguistic Theory of Translation: An Essay in Applied Linguistics*, London: Oxford University Press, 1965
Copeland, Rita, *Rhetoric, Hermeneutics, and Translation in the Middle Ages: Academic Traditions and Vernacular Texts*, Cambridge and New York: Cambridge University Press, 1991
Crystal, David, *The English Language*, London: Penguin, and New York: Viking, 1988
Crystal, David, *English as a Global Language*, Cambridge and New York: Cambridge University Press, 1997
Dalby, Andrew, *A Guide to World Language Dictionaries*, London: Library Association, and Chicago: Fitzroy Dearborn, 1998
Delisle, Jean and Judith Woodsworth (editors), *Translators through History*, Amsterdam: Benjamins, 1995
Even-Zohar, Itamar, "Polysystem Studies", *Poetics Today*, 11/1 (1990)
France, Peter, *The Oxford Guide to Literature in English Translation*, Oxford and New York: Oxford University Press, 2000
Hofstadter, Douglas R., *Le Ton beau de Marot: In Praise of the Music of Language*, London: Bloomsbury, and New York: Basic Books, 1997
Holmes, James S., *Translated! Papers on Literary Translation and Translation Studies*, Amsterdam: Rodopi, 1988
Lefevere, André (editor and translator), *Translation / History / Culture: A Sourcebook*, London and New York: Routledge, 1992
Lefevere, André, *Translation, Rewriting, and the Manipulation of Literary Fame*, London and New York: Routledge, 1992
Matthews, P.H., *The Concise Oxford Dictionary of Linguistics*, Oxford and New York: Oxford University Press, 1997
Neubert, Albrecht and Gregory M. Shreve, *Translation as Text*, Kent, Ohio: Kent State University Press, 1992
Newmark, Peter, *Approaches to Translation*, Oxford and New York: Pergamon Press, 1981
Newmark, Peter, *A Textbook of Translation*, New York: Prentice Hall, 1988
Nida, Eugene A., *Toward a Science of Translating, with Special Reference to Principles and Procedures Involved in Bible Translating*, Leiden: E.J. Brill, 1964
Nida, Eugene A. and Charles R. Taber, *The Theory and Practice of Translation*, Leiden: E.J. Brill, 1969
Nida, Eugene A., *Translating Meaning*, San Diego: English Language Institute, 1982
Nord, Christiane, *Translating as a Purposeful Activity: Functionalist Approaches Explained*, Manchester: St Jerome, 1997
Pym, Anthony, *Method in Translation History*, Manchester: St Jerome, 1998
Radice, William and Barbara Reynolds (editors), *The Translator's Art: Essays in Honour of Betty Radice*, Harmondsworth and New York: Penguin, 1987
Robinson, Douglas (editor), *Western Translation Theory: From Herodotus to Nietzsche*, Manchester: St Jerome, 1997
Schulte, Hans and Gerhart Teuscher (editors), *The Art of Literary Translation*, Lanham, Maryland: University Press of America, 1993
Schulte, Rainer and John Biguenet (editors), *Theories of Translation: An Anthology of Essays from Dryden to Derrida*, Chicago: University of Chicago Press, 1992
Shuttleworth, Mark and Moira Cowie (editors), *Dictionary of Translation Studies*, Manchester: St Jerome, 1997
Simms, Karl (editor), *Translating Sensitive Texts: Linguistic Aspects*, Amsterdam: Rodopi, 1997
Snell-Hornby, Mary, *Translation Studies: An Integrated Approach*, revised edition, Amsterdam: Benjamins, 1995
Steiner, George, *After Babel: Aspects of Language and Translation*, Oxford and New York: Oxford University Press, 1975; 3rd edition 1998
Steiner, George, *Errata: An Examined Life*, London: Weidenfeld and Nicolson, 1997; New Haven, Connecticut: Yale University Press, 1998
Toury, Gideon, *In Search of a Theory of Translation*, Tel Aviv: Porter Institute for Poetics and Semiotics, Tel Aviv University, 1980
Toury, Gideon, *Descriptive Translation Studies and Beyond*, Amsterdam: Benjamins, 1995
Van Doren, Mark (editor), *An Anthology of World Poetry*, New York: Boni, 1928; several subsequent editions
Venuti, Lawrence (editor), *Rethinking Translation: Discourse, Subjectivity, Ideology*, London and New York: Routledge, 1992
Venuti, Lawrence, *The Translator's Invisibility: A History of Translation*, London and New York: Routledge, 1995
Venuti, Lawrence, *The Scandals of Translation: Towards an Ethics of Difference*, London and New York: Routledge, 1998
Washburn, Katharine and John S. Major (editors), *World Poetry: An Anthology of Verse from Antiquity to Our Time*, New York: Norton, 1998

ADVISERS AND CONTRIBUTORS

Elza Adamowicz
Marianne J. Ailes
Michael Alexander
Roger Allen
Salih J. Altoma
Gunilla Anderman
Kristine J. Anderson
Stefania Arcara
Katherine Arens
Bernard Ashbrook
M.M. Badawi
Brian James Baer
Ehrhard Bahr
Aida A. Bamia
T.H. Barrett
John Barsby
Kevin Bartholomew
Susan Bassnett
Edward M. Batley
Petra Maria Anna Bauer
Roderick Beaton
Anthea Bell
Sheila Bell
Rina Ben Shahar
Bernard P.E. Bentley
Özlem Berk
Monica Bethe
Peter Bien
Jean Boase-Beier
Robin Orr Bodkin
Roy C. Boland
Marilyn Booth
Anne Born
Barbara Bray
Julia Bray
Karen W. Brazell
David Brookshaw
Catharine Savage Brosman
Gordon Brotherston
Sarah Annes Brown
Timothy Buck
George Bull
Glyn S. Burgess
Peter Burian
Leon Burnett
Peter Bush
Keith Cameron
John Campbell
Julie Mercer Carroll
Anthony Hood Chambers
Gertrud Graubart Champe
Chan Man Sing
Robert Chandler
Nam Fung Chang
Peggy Chaplin
Sally K. Church
Diskin Clay
Greg Clingham
Carrol F. Coates
Jenefer Coates
A.E.B. Coldiron
David Connolly
Malcolm Cook
Paul Cooke
David Cowling
Ian S. Craig
Edoardo Crisafulli
Michael Cronin
Anthony Cross
Robert Cummings
Dick Davis
John Denton
Eric Dickens
Lisa M.W. Dillman
Mark Dinneen
Jordi Doce
Chris Drake
Peter Dunwoodie
Sarah Ekdawi
Steve Ellis
Christopher English
John R.J. Eyck
Ian Fairley
Michael Falchikov
Sarah K. Farrant
Joseph Farrell

Katherine Faull
Jane Fenoulhet
Győző Ferencz
John Fletcher
Pauline Fletcher
John L. Flood
Richard Freeborn
Michael Freeman
David Frier
Raymond Furness
Marilyn Gaddis Rose
John Gatt-Rutter
Katherine Gyékényesi Gatto
Christa Gaug
Edwin Gentzler
Andrew Gerstle
Marian Giles Jones
Stuart Gillespie
Derek Glass
Barbara Godard
Karein K. Goertz
Margaret Bozenna Goscilo
Stathis Gourgouris
Katie Gramich
Peter Graves
Jane Grayson
David Groves
Harry Guest
Terry Hale
Stephen Halliwell
Gerald Hammond
Raymond Hargreaves
Nigel Harris
Celia Hawkesworth
Kenneth Haynes
Theo Hermans
Linda Hess
Leo Hickey
Ian Hilton
Andrew Hiscock
Thomas P. Hodge
Leighton Hodson
Bernard Hœpffner
David Hopkins
David Horrocks
Guiyou Huang
W. John Hutchins
Theresa Hyun
Michael P. Iarocci
Michael Irwin
John Claiborne Isbell
Catherine Jagoe
Regina Janes
Judith Jesch
Alan Jones
Paul Jordan
Alita Kelley
Judith A. Kelly
Angus J. Kennedy
Peter Khoroche
Faye Yuan Kleeman
Alexis Klimoff
David Kornacker
Andreas Kramer
Dennis M. Kratz
Katja Krebs
Christopher Larkosh
André A. Lefevere
Hera T. Leighton
Lauren G. Leighton
Michael G. Lerner
Anthony Levi
Virginia L. Lewis
Raymond S.C. Lie
John Lingard
Karin Littau
Angela Livingstone
Ernesto Livorni
Heather Lloyd
Janet Lloyd
Irving Yucheng Lo
Dana Loewy
Parvin Loloi
Susan E. Loubet
Philip Lutgendorf
Elizabeth Drayson MacDonald
Keith McDuffie
Bernard McGuirk
Richard McKane
Kathleen M. McKilligan
Paul St John Mackintosh
John Macklin
Hugh McLean
Edith McMorran
Ian McMorran
Kirsten Malmkjær
Gaetana Marrone
William Martin
Diane E. Marting
Tom Mason
Anthony Mathews
Christopher Mattison
Rachel May
Julie Scott Meisami
Christi A. Merrill
George S. Miller
John Minford
Beverly Mitchell
Olivia Mok
Elizabeth Moles
Edwin Morgan
Anthony Mortimer
Leith Morton
C.M. Naim
Robert J. Neather
Peter Newmark
Joy Newton
William H. Nienhauser, Jr
Robert Niklaus
Moses N. Nintai

Peter Noble
Alexis Nouss
Eva Núñez Méndez
Cormac Ó Cuilleanáin
Deirdre O'Grady
Riitta Oittinen
Laura J. Olson
Kyoko Omori
Cindy Opitz
Mary M. Orr
Adriana S. Pagano
Francesc Parcerisas
Stephen Parkin
James A. Parr
James Partridge
Alan K.G. Paterson
Zoja Pavlovskis-Petit
Noël Peacock
Raquel de Pedro
Chris Perriam
John Phillips
Ursula Phillips
Adrian James Pinnington
Glyn Pursglove
William Radice
Petar Ramadanović
Helen Rappaport
Judy Rawson
Nancy M. Reale
Paul Reed
Barbara Reynolds
James P. Rice
Paul Rickett
Ruth Rischin
Michael Robinson
Wendy Rosslyn
Christopher Rundle
Hélène N. Sanko
Barry P. Scherr
Henry G. Schogt
Clive Scott
J.K.L. Scott
Steven Shankman
Shing-yue Sheung
J.P. Short
Ewa Siwak
Colin Smethurst
Christopher Smith
Joseph Thomas Snow
Martin Sorrell
Robin Sowerby
Ezra Spicehandler
Patricia Springborg
Patricia Harris Stäblein
Paul Starkey
Anna Stepanova
Joanna Stephens
R.H. Stephenson
Cole Swensen
Malcolm George Taggart
Tetsuya Taguchi
Barry Taylor
Neil Thomas
Colin Thompson
Derick S. Thomson
Tanya Thresher
Lilit Žekulin Thwaites
Ursula Tidd
Michael Tilby
Richard E. Torrance
Anthony Trippett
Harish Trivedi
Carmen Valero-Garcés
Isabelle Vanderschelden
Karen Van Dyck
Lawrence Venuti
Else R.P. Vieira
Paul Vincent
Anthony Vivis
Mary B. Vogl
Véronique Wakerley
Jennifer Wallace
Mark G. Ward
Roderick H. Watt
I.A.. White
J.J. White
J.C. Whitehouse
John R. Whittaker
Mark Williams
Rhys W. Williams
Tom Winnifrith
Laurence Wong
Siu-Kit Wong
Sharon Wood
Carolyne Wright
Paul Wright
Yang Ye
Peter V. Zima

ALPHABETICAL LIST OF ENTRIES

LIST OF WRITERS AND WORKS BY LANGUAGE

African Languages
African Languages: Literary Translation into English

Akkadian
Gilgamesh

Albanian
Albanian: Literary Translation into English

Arabic
Adūnīs
Arabic: Literary Translation into English
Mahmūd Darwīsh
Egyptian Women Writers
Jamāl Ghītānī
Imīl Habībī
Tawfīq al-Hakīm
Yahyā Haqqī
Tāhā Husayn
Ibn Hazm
Yūsuf Idrīs
Ghassān Kanafānī
Idwār al-Kharrāt
The Koran
Najīb Mahfūz
Maqāmāt
'Abd al-Rahmān Munīf
Pre-Islamic Poetry
Alīfah Rifāt
al-Tayyib Sālih
Yūsuf al-Shārūnī
Hanān al-Shaykh
The Thousand and One Nights

Bengali
Bengali Women Writers
Indian/South Asian Languages, Modern: Literary Translation into English
Rabindranath Tagore

Catalan
Catalan: Literary Translation into English
Ramon Llull

Chinese
Bai Juyi
Chinese: Literary Translation into English
Confucius
The Dream of the Red Chamber
Du Fu
Han Yu
Hanshan
I Ching
Jin Ping Mei
The Journey to the West
Laozi
Li Bai
Li Qingzhao
Li Shangyin
Lu Xun
Lu You
Martial Arts Fiction in English Translation
Pu Songling
San Guo Zhi Yan Yi
Shijing
Shui Hu Zhuan
Sima Qian
Songs of the South
Su Shi
Tao Qian
Wang Wei
The Western Chamber
Xin Qiji
Zhuangzi

Czech
Karel Čapek
Czech: Literary Translation into English
Jaroslav Hašek
Václav Havel
Miroslav Holub
Bohumil Hrabal
Milan Kundera
Jaroslav Seifert
Josef Škvorecký

Danish
Hans Christian Andersen
Karen Blixen
Danish: Literary Translation into English
Jens Peter Jacobsen
Henrik Stangerup

Dutch
Hugo Claus
Louis Couperus
Dutch: Literary Translation into English
Guido Gezelle
Hadewych
Mariken van Nieumeghen
Harry Mulisch
Multatuli
Cees Nooteboom
Reynard the Fox
Jan van Ruusbroec

English
Beowulf

Estonian
Estonian: Literary Translation into English

Finnish
Finnish: Literary Translation into English

French
Alain-Fournier
Jean Anouilh
Guillaume Apollinaire
Aucassin and Nicolette
Honoré de Balzac
Jules-Amédée Barbey d'Aurevilly
Charles Baudelaire
François-Augustin Caron de Beaumarchais
Simone de Beauvoir
Samuel Beckett
Les Belles Infidèles
Tahar Ben Jelloun
Georges Bernanos
Bertran de Born
Yves Bonnefoy
André Breton
Albert Camus
Louis-Ferdinand Céline
René Char
Chateaubriand
Christine de Pizan
Sidonie-Gabrielle Colette
Benjamin Constant
Pierre Corneille
Denis Diderot
Du Bartas
Joachim Du Bellay
Marguerite Duras
Egyptian Women Writers
Paul Éluard
Georges Feydeau
Gustave Flaubert
Francophone African and Caribbean Writers
Francophone Arab and Maghrebian Writers
French: Literary Translation into English
French-Canadian Writers
André Gide
Jean Giono
Jean Giraudoux
Ivan Goll
Julien Green
Anne Hébert
José Maria de Heredia
Victor Hugo
J.-K. Huysmans
Eugène Ionesco
Max Jacob
Alfred Jarry
Milan Kundera
Louise Labé
Jean de La Bruyère
Pierre Choderlos de Laclos
Comtesse de La Fayette
Jean de La Fontaine
Jules Laforgue
La Rochefoucauld
Comte de Lautréamont
Pierre Loti
Maurice Maeterlinck
Stéphane Mallarmé
André Malraux
Marguerite de Navarre
Marie de France
Pierre Carlet de Chamblain de Marivaux
Roger Martin du Gard
Guy de Maupassant
François Mauriac
Medieval Epic
Henri Michaux
Molière
Michel de Montaigne
Montesquieu
Gérard de Nerval
Blaise Pascal
Georges Perec
Francis Ponge
Jacques Prévert
Marcel Proust
Raymond Queneau
François Rabelais
Jean Racine
Arthur Rimbaud
Alain Robbe-Grillet
Roland, The Song of
Jules Romains
Pierre de Ronsard
Edmond Rostand
Jean-Jacques Rousseau
Gabrielle Roy
George Sand

Nathalie Sarraute
Jean-Paul Sartre
Léopold Sédar Senghor
Marquise de Sévigné
Georges Simenon
Claude Simon
Madame de Staël
Stendhal
Paul Valéry
Paul Verlaine
Jules Verne
Boris Vian
Comte de Villiers de L'Isle-Adam
François Villon
Voltaire
Émile Zola

Gaelic
Gaelic, Irish: Literary Translation into English
Gaelic, Scots: Literary Translation into English

German
Ingeborg Bachmann
Gottfried Benn
Thomas Bernhard
Johannes Bobrowski
Heinrich Böll
Wolfgang Borchert
Sebastian Brant
Bertolt Brecht
Hermann Broch
Georg Büchner
Paul Celan
Adelbert von Chamisso
Alfred Döblin
Heimito von Doderer
Friedrich Dürrenmatt
Faust Book
Lion Feuchtwanger
Theodor Fontane
German: Literary Translation into English
Johann Wolfgang von Goethe
Ivan Goll
Günter Grass
Franz Grillparzer
Jacob and Wilhelm Grimm
Peter Handke
Gerhart Hauptmann
Heinrich Heine
Hermann Hesse
E.T.A. Hoffmann
Hugo von Hofmannsthal
Friedrich Hölderlin
Ödön von Horváth
Peter Huchel
Uwe Johnson
Franz Kafka
Georg Kaiser
Heinrich von Kleist
Karl Kraus
Siegfried Lenz
Gotthold Ephraïm Lessing
Heinrich Mann
Thomas Mann
Medieval Epic
Eduard Mörike
Robert Musil
Johann Nepomuk Nestroy
The Nibelungenlied
Friedrich Nietzsche
Novalis
Reynard the Fox
Rainer Maria Rilke
Joseph Roth
Friedrich von Schiller
Arthur Schnitzler
Carl Sternheim
Adalbert Stifter
Theodor Storm
Ernst Toller
Georg Trakl
Frank Wedekind
Peter Weiss
Christa Wolf
Wolfram von Eschenbach
Arnold Zweig
Stefan Zweig

Greek, Ancient
Aeschylus
Aesop
Anacreon
Aristophanes
Aristotle
The Bible
Callimachus
Demosthenes
Euripides
Greek, Ancient: Literary Translation into English
Hesiod
Homer
Homeric Hymns
"Longinus"
Longus
Menander
Musaeus Grammaticus
Pindar
Plato
Plutarch
Sappho
Sophocles
Theocritus
Theophrastus

Greek, Modern
C.P. Cavafy
Odysseus Elytis
Greek, Modern: Literary Translation into English
Greek, Modern: Women Writers
Nikos Kazantzakis

Alexandros Papadiamantis
Yannis Ritsos
George Seferis
Angelos Sikelianos

Hebrew, Ancient
The Bible

Hebrew, Modern
Hebrew, Modern: Literary Translation into English

Hindi
Indian / South Asian Languages, Modern: Literary Translation into English
Kabir
Tulsidas

Hungarian
Endre Ady
Hungarian: Literary Translation into English
Gyula Illyés
Attila József
Ferenc Molnár
Sándor Petőfi
Miklós Radnóti
Sándor Weöres

Italian
Ludovico Ariosto
Giorgio Bassani
Ugo Betti
Giovanni Boccaccio
Dino Buzzati
Italo Calvino
Giosuè Carducci
Baldassarre Castiglione
Guido Cavalcanti
Benvenuto Cellini
Gabriele D'Annunzio
Dante Alighieri
Eduardo De Filippo
Grazia Deledda
Umberto Eco
Dario Fo
Antonio Fogazzaro
Ugo Foscolo
Natalia Ginzburg
Carlo Goldoni
Battista Guarini
Italian: Literary Translation into English
Giuseppe Tomasi di Lampedusa
Giacomo Leopardi
Carlo Levi
Primo Levi
Niccolò Machiavelli
Alessandro Manzoni
Dacia Maraini
Medieval Epic
Eugenio Montale
Cesare Pavese
Petrarch
Luigi Pirandello
Ignazio Silone
Italo Svevo
Torquato Tasso
Giovanni Verga

Japanese
Akutagawa Ryūnosuke
Chikamatsu Monzaemon
Dazai Osamu
Endō Shūsaku
Hagiwara Sakutarō
Haiku
Japanese: Literary Translation into English
Kawabata Yasunari
Mishima Yukio
Murasaki Shikibu
Natsume Sōseki
Ōe Kenzaburō
Ibara Saikaku
Sei Shōnagon
Shiga Naoya
Tanizaki Jun'ichirō
Zeami

Korean
Korean: Literary Translation into English

Latin
Apuleius
Ausonius
Boethius
Julius Caesar
Catullus
Church Latin
Cicero
Claudian
Desiderius Erasmus
Horace
Juvenal
Latin: Literary Translation into English
Livy
Lucan
Lucretius
Martial
Medieval Epic
Ovid
Persius
Petronius
Plautus
Propertius
Quintilian
Seneca
Suetonius
Tacitus
Terence
Tibullus
Virgil

Latvian
Latvian Writers

Norwegian
Bjørnstjerne Bjørnson
Knut Hamsun
Henrik Ibsen
Norwegian: Literary Translation into English
Sigrid Undset

Old Norse
Egil's Saga

Persian
Farīd al-Dīn Abū Hamīd Mohammad 'Attār
Abul Qasim Firdausī
Ghālib
Shams al-Dīn Muhammad Hāfiz
Nizāmī
Omar Khayyām
Persian: Literary Translation into English
Jalāl al-Dīn Rūmī
Sa'di

Polish
Witold Gombrowicz
Zbigniew Herbert
Zygmunt Krasiński
Adam Mickiewicz
Czesław Miłosz
Polish: Literary Translation into English
Bruno Schulz
Wisława Szymborska
Stanisław Witkiewicz

Portuguese
Jorge Amado
Luís de Camões
João Guimarães Rosa
Latin America: Translation Studies
Clarice Lispector
Lusophone African Writers
Joaquim Machado de Assis
Fernando Pessoa
Portuguese: Literary Translation into English
José Saramago

Russian
Bella Akhmadulina
Anna Akhmatova
Vasilii Aksenov
Leonid Andreev
Leonid Aronzon
Isaak Babel
Andrei Belyi
Aleksandr Blok
Mikhail Bulgakov
Ivan Bunin
Anton Chekhov
Fedor Dostoevskii
Sergei Aleksandrovich Esenin
Evgenii Evtushenko
Nikolai Gogol'
Ivan Goncharov
Nikolai Karamzin
Ivan Krylov
Mikhail Lermontov
Nikolai Leskov
Osip Mandel'shtam
Vladimir Nabokov
Aleksandr Ostrovskii
Boris Pasternak
Boris Pil'niak
Andrei Platonov
Aleksandr Pushkin
Russian: Literary Translation into English
Mikhail Saltykov-Shchedrin
Mikhail Sholokov
Andrei Siniavskii
Vladimir Soloukhin
Aleksandr Solzhenitsyn
Lev Tolstoi
Iurii Trifonov
Marina Tsvetaeva
Ivan Turgenev
Andrei Voznesenskii
Evgenii Zamiatin
Mikhail Zoshchenko

Sanskrit
Buddhist Sacred Texts
Indian Languages, Ancient: Literary Translation into English
Kālidāsa
Mahābhārata
Ramayana

Serbo-Croat
Ivo Andrič
Danilo Kiš
Miroslav Krleža
Vasko Popa
Serbo-Croat: Literary Translation into English

Slovak
Slovak: Literary Translation into English

Spanish
Leopoldo Alas y Ureña
Vicente Aleixandre
Isabel Allende
José María Arguedas
Miguel Ángel Asturias
Adolfo Bioy Casares
Jorge Luis Borges
Guillermo Cabrera Infante
Pedro Calderón de la Barca
Rosario Castellanos
Camilo José Cela
Luis Cernuda

Miguel de Cervantes
Rosa Chacel
Julio Cortázar
Eduardo Galeano
Federico García Lorca
Gabriel García Márquez
Luis de Góngora
Juan Goytisolo
Jorge Guillén
José Hernández
Juan Ramón Jiménez
John of the Cross
Latin America: Translation Studies
Lazarillo de Tormes
José Lezama Lima
Antonio Machado
Medieval Epic
Pablo Neruda
Juan Carlos Onetti
Octavio Paz
Ramón Pérez de Ayala
Manuel Puig
Francisco de Quevedo
Fernando de Rojas
Juan Rulfo
Ernesto Sábato
Ramón Sender
Spanish: Literary Translation into English
Spanish: Contemporary Women Writers
Tirso de Molina
César Vallejo
Mario Vargas Llosa
Lope de Vega Carpio

Swedish
Selma Lagerlöf
Edith Södergran
August Strindberg
Swedish: Literary Translation into English

Turkish
Turkish: Literary Translation into English

Urdu
Ghālib
Indian / South Asian Languages, Modern: Literary Translation into English

Welsh
Welsh: Literary Translation into English

CHRONOLOGICAL LIST OF WRITERS AND WORKS

2nd millennium BC	*Gilgamesh*
uncertain date BC	*I Ching*
c.12th–7th centuries BC	*Shijing*
c.900 BC–c.AD 100	Bible
8th century BC	Homer
c.700 BC	Hesiod
c.8th–4th centuries BC	Homeric Hymns
c.630 BC	Sappho
6th century BC	Aesop
6th? century BC	Laozi
c.570–c.475 BC	Anacreon
c.551–479 BC	Confucius
525 or 524–456 BC	Aeschylus
c.518–c.438 BC	Pindar
c.496–406 BC	Sophocles
c.480–c.407/06 BC	Euripides
c.450–385 BC	Aristophanes
429–347 BC	Plato
c.400 BC–AD 400	*Mahābhārata*
384–322 BC	Aristotle
c.384–322 BC	Demosthenes
c.372–c.287 BC	Theophrastus
c.369–286 BC	Zhuangzi
c.342–c.292 BC	Menander
c.305–240 BC	Callimachus
c.300–260 BC	Theocritus
c.3rd century BC	*Ramayana*
mid-3rd century–c.184 BC	Plautus
184–159 BC	Terence
fl. 150 BC	Moschus
c.145–c.86 BC	Sima Qian
106–43 BC	Cicero
fl. 100 BC	Bion
100–44 BC	Julius Caesar
c.94–c.55 BC	Lucretius
c.84–c.54 BC	Catullus
70–19 BC	Virgil
65–8 BC	Horace
59 BC–c.AD 17	Livy
55/48–19/18 BC	Tibullus
c.54 BC–c.AD 2	Propertius
43 BC–AD 17	Ovid
c.4 BC–65 AD	Seneca
1st century AD	"Longinus"
c.AD 30–after 96	Quintilian
AD 34–62	Persius
AD 39–65	Lucan
c.AD 40–c.104	Martial
c.AD 50 to 65–after 130	Juvenal
c.AD 50–after 125	Plutarch
c.AD 55–120	Tacitus
died AD 66	Petronius
c.AD 69–c.125	Suetonius
2nd century AD	*Songs of the South*
c.AD 123/5–after 163	Apuleius
2nd–3rd centuries AD	Longus
c.AD 310–c.395	Ausonius
AD 365 or 372–427	Tao Qian
c.AD 370–c.404	Claudian
fl. c.AD 400	Kālidāsa
late 5th century?	Musaeus Grammaticus
c.480–c.524	Boethius
7th century	The Koran
fl. 627–649	Hanshan
699?–761	Wang Wei
8th century	*Beowulf*
701–762	Li Bai
712–770	Du Fu
768–824	Han Yu
772–846	Bai Juyi
812?–858	Li Shangyin
10th century	*The Thousand and One Nights*
c.940–c.1020	Abul Qasim Firdausī
born c.965	Sei Shōnagon
973?–1014?	Murasaki Shikibu
994–1064	Ibn Hazm
1037–1101	Su Shi
1048–1131	Omar Khayyām
1084–1151	Li Qingzhao
c.1100	*The Song of Roland*
1125–1210	Lu You
1140–1207	Xin Qiji
c.1141–c.1209	Nizāmī
c.1145–c.1221	Farīd al-Dīn Abū Hamīd Mohammad 'Attār
c.1150–c.1215	Bertran de Born

late 12th–early 13th centuries	Marie de France
13th century	*Aucassin and Nicolette*
13th century	*Egil's Saga*
13th century	*The Western Chamber*
c.1200	*The Nibelungenlied*
fl. c.1200–1220	Wolfram von Eschenbach
1207–1273	Jalāl al-Dīn Rūmī
c.1215–1292	Sa'di
1232–1316	Ramon Llull
fl. 1250	Hadewych
1255?–1300	Guido Cavalcanti
1265–1321	Dante Alighieri
1293–1381	Jan van Ruusbroec
14th century	*San Guo Zhi Yan Yi*
14th century	*Shui Hu Zhuan*
1304–1374	Petrarch
1313–1375	Giovanni Boccaccio
c.1325/26–c.1389/90	Shams al-Dīn Muhammad Hāfiz
c.1340/41–1400	Geoffrey Chaucer
1363–1443	Zeami
c.1364–c.1430	Christine de Pizan
c.1431–after 1463	François Villon
c.1448–c.1518	Kabir
1457–1521	Sebastian Brant
c.1466–1536	Desiderius Erasmus
c.1467–1541	Fernando de Rojas
1469–1527	Niccolò Machiavelli
1474–1533	Ludovico Ariosto
1478–1529	Baldassarre Castiglione
1479/1498	*Reynard the Fox*
c.1484–1553	François Rabelais
1492–1549	Marguerite de Navarre
16th century	*Jin Ping Mei*
16th century	*The Journey to the West*
1500–1571	Benvenuto Cellini
1514 or 1515	*Mariken van Nieumeghen*
1522–1560	Joachim Du Bellay
1524–1585	Pierre de Ronsard
c.1524–1580	Luís de Camões
c.1524–1566	Louise Labé
c.1532–1623	Tulsidas
1533–1592	Michel de Montaigne
1535–1601?	Sir Thomas North
1538–1612	Battista Guarini
1542–1591	John of the Cross
1544–1590	Du Bartas
1544–1595	Torquato Tasso
1547–1616	Miguel de Cervantes
c.1553–1625	John Florio
1554	*Lazarillo de Tormes*
1559/60–1634	George Chapman
1561–1627	Luis de Góngora
1562–1635	Lope de Vega Carpio
1577–1640	Robert Burton
1580–1645	Francisco de Quevedo
1580?–1648	Tirso de Molina
1587	Faust Book
1588–1679	Thomas Hobbes
1600–1681	Pedro Calderón de la Barca
1606–1684	Pierre Corneille
1608–1674	John Milton
1613–1680	La Rochefoucauld
1615–1669	Sir John Denham
1618–1667	Abraham Cowley
1621–1695	Jean de La Fontaine
1622–1673	Molière
1623–1662	Blaise Pascal
1626–1696	Marquise de Sévigné
1631–1700	John Dryden
c.1633–1685	Wentworth Dillon, 4th earl of Roscommon
1634–1693	Comtesse de La Fayette
1639–1699	Jean Racine
c.1640–1715	Pu Songling
1642–1693	Ibara Saikaku
1645–1696	Jean de La Bruyère
1653–1725	Chikamatsu Monzaemon
1688–1763	Pierre Carlet de Chamblain de Marivaux
1688–1744	Alexander Pope
1689–1755	Montesquieu
1694–1778	Voltaire
1707–1793	Carlo Goldoni
1712–1778	Jean-Jacques Rousseau
1713–1784	Denis Diderot
1729–1781	Gotthold Ephraïm Lessing
1732–1799	François-Augustin Caron de Beaumarchais
1741–1803	Pierre Choderlos de Laclos
1746–1794	Sir William Jones
1747–1813	Alexander Fraser Tytler
1749–1832	Johann Wolfgang von Goethe
1759–1805	Friedrich von Schiller
before 1763	*The Dream of the Red Chamber*
1766–1826	Nikolai Karamzin
1766–1817	Madame de Staël
1767–1830	Benjamin Constant
1768–1848	Chateaubriand
1769–1844	Ivan Krylov
1770–1843	Friedrich Hölderlin
1772–1801	Novalis
1776–1822	E.T.A. Hoffmann
1777–1811	Heinrich von Kleist
1778–1827	Ugo Foscolo
1781–1838	Adelbert von Chamisso
1783–1842	Stendhal
1785–1863	Jacob Grimm
1785–1873	Alessandro Manzoni
1786–1859	Wilhelm Grimm
1791–1872	Franz Grillparzer
1797–1869	Ghālib
1797–1856	Heinrich Heine
1798–1837	Giacomo Leopardi
1798–1855	Adam Mickiewicz
1799–1850	Honoré de Balzac
1799–1837	Aleksandr Pushkin
1801–1862	Johann Nepomuk Nestroy
1802–1885	Victor Hugo
1804–1875	Eduard Mörike

1804–1876	George Sand
1805–1875	Hans Christian Andersen
1805–1868	Adalbert Stifter
1808–1889	Jules-Amédée Barbey d'Aurevilly
1808–1855	Gérard de Nerval
1809–1883	Edward FitzGerald
1809–1852	Nikolai Gogol'
1812–1891	Ivan Goncharov
1812–1895	Lady Charlotte Guest
1812–1859	Zygmunt Krasiński
1813–1837	Georg Büchner
1814–1841	Mikhail Lermontov
1817–1888	Theodor Storm
1818–1883	Ivan Turgenev
1819–1898	Theodor Fontane
1820–1887	Multatuli
1821–1867	Charles Baudelaire
1821–1890	Richard Burton
1821–1881	Fedor Dostoevskii
1821–1880	Gustave Flaubert
1822–1888	Matthew Arnold
1823–1886	Aleksandr Ostrovskii
1823–1849	Sándor Petőfi
1826–1889	Mikhail Saltykov-Shchedrin
1828–1906	Henrik Ibsen
1828–1882	Dante Gabriel Rossetti
1828–1910	Lev Tolstoi
1828–1905	Jules Verne
1830–1899	Guido Gezelle
1831–1895	Nikolai Leskov
1832–1910	Bjørnstjerne Bjørnson
1834–1886	José Hernández
1834–1896	William Morris
1835–1907	Giosuè Carducci
1838–1889	Comte de Villiers de L'Isle-Adam
1839–1908	Joaquim Machado de Assis
1840–1922	Giovanni Verga
1840–1902	Émile Zola
1842–1911	Antonio Fogazzaro
1842–1905	José Maria de Heredia
1842–1898	Stéphane Mallarmé
1844–1900	Friedrich Nietzsche
1844–1896	Paul Verlaine
1846–1870	Comte de Lautréamont
1847–1885	Jens Peter Jacobsen
1848–1907	J.-K. Huysmans
1849–1912	August Strindberg
1850–1923	Pierre Loti
1850–1893	Guy de Maupassant
1851–1911	Alexandros Papadiamantis
1852–1901	Leopoldo Alas y Ureña
1852–1932	Lady Augusta Gregory
1854–1891	Arthur Rimbaud
1856–1924	William Archer
1858–1940	Selma Lagerlöf
1859–1952	Knut Hamsun
1860–1904	Anton Chekhov
1860–1887	Jules Laforgue
1861–1928	Italo Svevo
1861–1941	Rabindranath Tagore
1862–1921	Georges Feydeau
1862–1946	Constance Garnett
1862–1946	Gerhart Hauptmann
1862–1949	Maurice Maeterlinck
1862–1931	Arthur Schnitzler
1863–1933	C.P. Cavafy
1863–1923	Louis Couperus
1863–1938	Gabriele D'Annunzio
1864–1918	Frank Wedekind
1866–1957	Gilbert Murray
1867–1916	Natsume Sōseki
1867–1936	Luigi Pirandello
1868–1918	Edmond Rostand
1869–1951	André Gide
1870–1953	Ivan Bunin
1871–1919	Leonid Andreev
1871–1936	Grazia Deledda
1871–1950	Heinrich Mann
1871–1922	Marcel Proust
1871–1945	Paul Valéry
1873–1954	Sidonie-Gabrielle Colette
1873–1907	Alfred Jarry
1874–1929	Hugo von Hofmannsthal
1874–1936	Karl Kraus
1875–1939	Antonio Machado
1875–1955	Thomas Mann
1875–1926	Rainer Maria Rilke
1876–1944	Max Jacob
1877–1919	Endre Ady
1877–1962	Hermann Hesse
1878–1957	Alfred Döblin
1878–1945	Georg Kaiser
1878–1952	Ferenc Molnár
1878–1942	Carl Sternheim
1880–1918	Guillaume Apollinaire
1880–1934	Andrei Belyi
1880–1921	Aleksandr Blok
1880–1942	Robert Musil
1880–1962	Ramón Pérez de Ayala
1881–1958	Juan Ramón Jiménez
1881–1936	Lu Xun
1881–1958	Roger Martin du Gard
1881–1942	Stefan Zweig
1882–1944	Jean Giraudoux
1882–1949	Sigrid Undset
1883–1923	Jaroslav Hašek
1883–1924	Franz Kafka
1883–1957	Nikos Kazantzakis
1883–1971	Shiga Naoya
1884–1958	Lion Feuchtwanger
1884–1951	Angelos Sikelianos
1884–1937	Evgenii Zamiatin
1885–1962	Karen Blixen
1885–1970	François Mauriac
1885–1972	Ezra Pound
1885–1972	Jules Romains
1885–1939	Stanisław Witkiewicz
1886–1914	Alain-Fournier
1886–1956	Gottfried Benn
1886–1951	Hermann Broch

1886–1942	Hagiwara Sakutarō
1886–1965	Tanizaki Jun'ichirō
1887–1914	Georg Trakl
1887–1968	Arnold Zweig
1888–1948	Georges Bernanos
1888–1935	Fernando Pessoa
1889–1966	Anna Akhmatova
1889–1973	Tāhā Husayn
1889–1966	Arthur Waley
1890–1938	Karel Čapek
1890–1960	Boris Pasternak
1891–1940	Mikhail Bulgakov
1891–1950	Ivan Goll
1891–1938	Osip Mandel'shtam
1892–1927	Akutagawa Ryūnosuke
1892–1975	Ivo Andrič
1892–1953	Ugo Betti
1892–1942	Bruno Schulz
1892–1923	Edith Södergran
1892–1941	Marina Tsvetaeva
1892–1938	César Vallejo
1893–1984	Jorge Guillén
1893–1981	Miroslav Krleža
1893–1939	Ernst Toller
1894–1940	Isaak Babel
1894–1961	Louis-Ferdinand Céline
1894–1938	Boris Pil'niak
1894–1939	Joseph Roth
1895–1952	Paul Éluard
1895–1925	Sergei Aleksandrovich Esenin
1895–1970	Jean Giono
1895–1958	Mikhail Zoshchenko
1896–1966	André Breton
1896–1966	Heimito von Doderer
1896–1957	Giuseppe Tomasi di Lampedusa
1896–1981	Eugenio Montale
1898–1984	Vicente Aleixandre
1898–1956	Bertolt Brecht
1898–1994	Rosa Chacel
1898–1936	Federico García Lorca
1898–1987	Tawfīq al-Hakīm
1899–1974	Miguel Ángel Asturias
1899–1986	Jorge Luis Borges
1899–1972	Kawabata Yasunari
1899–1984	Henri Michaux
1899–1977	Vladimir Nabokov
1899–1951	Andrei Platonov
1899–1988	Francis Ponge
1900–1984	Eduardo De Filippo
1900–1998	Julien Green
1900–1977	Jacques Prévert
1900–1999	Nathalie Sarraute
1900–1971	George Seferis
1900–1978	Ignazio Silone
1901–1938	Ödön von Horváth
1901–1976	André Malraux
1901–1986	Jaroslav Seifert
1902–1963	Luis Cernuda
1902–1983	Gyula Illyés
1902–1975	Carlo Levi
1902–1982	Ramón Sender
1903–1981	Peter Huchel
1903–1976	Raymond Queneau
1903–1989	Georges Simenon
1904–1969	Witold Gombrowicz
1904–1973	Pablo Neruda
1905–1993	Yahyā Haqqī
1905–1937	Attila József
1905–1980	Jean-Paul Sartre
1905–1984	Mikhail Sholokov
1906–1989	Samuel Beckett
1906–1972	Dino Buzzati
1906–	Léopold Sédar Senghor
1907–1988	René Char
1908–1986	Simone de Beauvoir
1908–1967	João Guimarães Rosa
1908–1950	Cesare Pavese
1909–1948	Dazai Osamu
1909–1994	Eugène Ionesco
1909–1994	Juan Carlos Onetti
1909–1944	Miklós Radnóti
1909–1990	Yannis Ritsos
1909–1983	Gabrielle Roy
1910–1987	Jean Anouilh
1910/12–1976	José Lezama Lima
1911–1969	José María Arguedas
1911–1996	Odysseus Elytis
1911–	Najīb Mahfūz
1911–	Czesław Miłosz
1911–	Ernesto Sábato
1912–	Jorge Amado
1913–1960	Albert Camus
1913–	Claude Simon
1913–1989	Sándor Weöres
1914–1999	Adolfo Bioy Casares
1914–1984	Julio Cortázar
1914–1996	Marguerite Duras
1914–1997	Bohumil Hrabal
1914–1998	Octavio Paz
1916–2000	Giorgio Bassani
1916–	Camilo José Cela
1916–1991	Natalia Ginzburg
1916–2000	Anne Hébert
1916–1982	Peter Weiss
1917–1965	Johannes Bobrowski
1917–1985	Heinrich Böll
1918–1986	Juan Rulfo
1918–	Aleksandr Solzhenitsyn
1919–1987	Primo Levi
1920–1970	Paul Celan
1920–1959	Boris Vian
1920?–1977	Clarice Lispector
1921–1947	Wolfgang Borchert
1921–1990	Friedrich Dürrenmatt
1921–1996	Imīl Habībī
1922–1991	Vasko Popa
1922–	Alain Robbe-Grillet
1922–	José Saramago
1923–	Yves Bonnefoy
1923–1985	Italo Calvino

1923–1996	Endō Shūsaku
1923–1998	Miroslav Holub
1923–	Wisława Szymborska
1924–1998	Zbigniew Herbert
1924–	Yūsuf al-Shārūnī
1924–	Josef Škvorecký
1924–1997	Vladimir Soloukhin
1925–1974	Rosario Castellanos
1925–1970	Mishima Yukio
1925–1997	Andrei Siniavskii
1925–1981	Iurii Trifonov
1926–1973	Ingeborg Bachmann
1926–	Dario Fo
1926–	Idwār al-Kharrāt
1926–	Siegfried Lenz
1927–	Günter Grass
1927–1991	Yūsuf Idrīs
1927–	Harry Mulisch
1928–	Gabriel García Márquez
1928/9–	al-Tayyib Sālih
1929–	Guillermo Cabrera Infante
1929–	Hugo Claus
1929–	Milan Kundera
1929–	Christa Wolf
1930–	Adūnīs
1930–1996	Alīfah Rifāt
1931–1989	Thomas Bernhard
1931–	Juan Goytisolo
1932–	Vasilii Aksenov
1932–	Umberto Eco
1932–1990	Manuel Puig
1933–	Evgenii Evtushenko
1933–	'Abd al-Rahmān Munīf
1933–	Cees Nooteboom
1933–	Andrei Voznesenskii
1934–1984	Uwe Johnson
1935–1989	Danilo Kiš
1935–	Ōe Kenzaburō
1936–	Václav Havel
1936–1972	Ghassān Kanafānī
1936–	Dacia Maraini
1936–1982	Georges Perec
1936–	Mario Vargas Llosa
1937–	Bella Akhmadulina
1937–1998	Henrik Stangerup
1939–1970	Leonid Aronzon
1940–	Eduardo Galeano
1941–	Mahmūd Darwīsh
1942–	Isabel Allende
1942–	Peter Handke
1944–	Tahar Ben Jelloun
1945–	Jamāl Ghītānī
1945–	Hanān al-Shaykh

A

Acceptability

Translators need to steer a careful course between accuracy (or, as it is sometimes called "adequacy") and acceptability. They clearly have an obligation to transfer into the target language as much as possible from their source; if that was not their ambition, we might, indeed, wonder why they ever embarked on the taxing enterprise. Their efforts will, however, be largely negated if readers of their translations find the language and, in some cases, also the content of their translation off-putting and even alienating. Serving in effect as advocates for the texts they are presenting in another language, translators toil in vain if their versions are found unacceptable by the public for which they are intended. What is true in the abstract holds particularly where publishers are concerned; they know that, except in rare instances where there is an overwhelming desire to have access to the content or a key to understanding the foreign-language text, the public will not buy translations that make difficult or unpleasant reading.

This means that translators of non-literary texts often function to some extent like editors, clarifying anything that may have been left obscure in the source. They are justified in doing so, because they know well that they will be blamed if their translation, no matter what may have been found in the source, does not readily yield satisfactory sense or slip easily into whichever style is expected in the target language. Because literary works are distinguished (possibly even defined) by each author's individuality in use of language and development of theme, translators of such texts must be much more circumspect. The needs of a motor mechanic are best met by the clearest possible version of a car repair manual. It is, however, plainly no service to the author of the original or to the reading public to simplify in translation the labyrinthine plot of a Gothic tale or to demystify its characters.

Similar considerations apply to style. For practical purposes a translation correct in grammar and usage and conventional in style will generally fit the bill. But it is not good enough to make all literary authors sound the same in translation. That would be absurd. Just as we can distinguish the language of Dickens and Henry James from the everyday norms of the English of their time and can also identify the personal manner of expression of each of those novelists, so too translated authors ought ideally each to have in the target language an individual voice corresponding to their personal idiosyncrasy in relationship to the stylistic norms of the source language in which they originally wrote. Such a principle is more easily adumbrated than applied. First steps belong to comparative stylistics: identifying characteristic forms and structures in the source and the target languages generally, in order to identify the original author's significant deviations from the norms of the former so that consideration can next be given to some appropriate reflection of it in the latter. This usually will involve not exact copying, but rather doing something tending in the same direction. Two banal examples. The indefinite personal pronoun "on", very frequently found in French, is generally not well rendered as "one" in English, but when translating an author who, by French standards, employs "on" particularly insistently, "one" might well be apt more often than is usual in English. Similarly, a translation ought to convey Heinrich von Kleist's predilection for long sentences. All the same, it is enough to make them seem long by English norms, without following him clause by clause in trying to reflect his exaggeration of German tendencies towards syntactic complexity.

Thomas Gordon stands as a warning to translators who lack discretion in their efforts at mirroring the style of their author; the public simply would not accept his work in the 18th century (see the entry on Tacitus' *Annals*). Since then attitudes to style have become more elastic. Romanticism started the revelation of the values of alternative literary traditions, and there is a growing awareness that the range of possibilities within English literature is far wider than what schoolmasters used to deem "good English". All the same, there are limits, and translators who go too far in an endeavour to convey the style of their originals run the risk of being dismissed as "unreadable".

Judgment is also called for in the treatment of cultural references. Some readers may, for instance, revel in the atmosphere of Old Russia, in which the translator of Turgenev is most likely steeped as well. But for others samovars and dachas, the intricacies of personal nomenclature within the family, and allusions to geography, history and administrative offices can become a serious bar to enjoyment and appreciation. Footnotes lend an academic air to the page, and what should have become familiar inevitably seems remote. Some tactful help can often be given within the text, and it is not difficult to argue that departures from literal fidelity are justified because they make the text more acceptable to the public for which it has been prepared. First impressions are particularly important, which explains why a London theatre director was probably right when he decided that British audiences for Anouilh's *Invitation au château* would be more likely to respond in the right way to Horace if he changed his name to Hugo.

Acceptability is not an immutable concept. A translator will generally have to go further in the direction of his public's expectations with an unknown work by an author who has not been heard of than would be the case with a text that already enjoys some prestige. Perhaps interest may even have been stirred by an earlier translation that subsequently is rejected as over-domesticated, in style or reference, and is not now regarded as really true enough to the original. That does not mean, however, that the first translator has not done well. In fact being superseded can sometimes even be regarded as a mark of success; it may show a demand has been created for a new version that tips the balance between acceptability and accuracy back to the latter. Even then the first term in the equation cannot be ignored: making a translation that is not acceptable cannot but be unrewarding, in more than one sense of the word.

CHRISTOPHER SMITH

Further Reading

Toury, Gideon, *In Search of a Theory of Translation*, Tel Aviv: Porter Institute for Poetics and Semiotics, 1980

Toury, Gideon, *Descriptive Translation Studies and Beyond*, Amsterdam and Philadelphia: Benjamins, 1995

Adaptation

The term "adaptation" may, like the term "translation", be used to refer either to the product of a process, or to the process itself.

Outside translation theory, the term "adaptation" is typically used to refer to the presentation in one medium or style of a work of art originally produced in another medium or style, for example to the dramatization of a novel, to the rewriting for children and/or language learners of a novel originally intended for adult native speakers, or to the presentation in prose of a work originally written in verse.

These examples illustrate the problems one would encounter in attempting to specify the precise degree and exact type of alteration to an original that adaptation involves. Although it rarely (if ever) happens, the use of a narrator, or of text on screen, makes it possible in principle for an adaptation of a novel as film to include every word of the original while adding features that result naturally from the new medium; in the case of adaptation for children or non-native speakers, we typically find a high degree of deletion, abbreviation and alteration; while in the case of verse-to-prose adaptation, addition often predominates.

When translation is involved, these difficulties of precise definition multiply: an original work in language *a* and medium *A* may be produced in language *b* and medium *C*.

In what follows, I shall consider only translational cases of adaptation, and I shall concentrate on the written medium. But even given this delimitation of subject matter it is not possible to draw a precise borderline between "translation" and "adaptation"; indeed, it is possible to argue that to attempt to do so would be futile, as any process of producing a comprehensible text in one language on the basis of a source text in another language necessarily involves some degree of adaptation.

Translation theorists typically mean by "adaptation" a translation, or the process of producing a translation, that deploys some or all of the following characteristics: the inclusion of material for which no direct source can be found in the original text; the absence of some source-text features; and clear alteration to some features of the source text. Adaptation may be more or less extensive, and if it is applied selectively, for example to names of people and places only, the translation as a whole may not strike a reader or critic with access to the original as an adaptation.

In the case of translation of certain types of non-literary texts, including journalism, tourist brochures, advertising materials and instruction manuals, adaptation is often considered an essential part of the translation process; names, tropes, text structure, and various other text aspects may, as a matter of course, be adjusted or changed completely to accord with the conventions of the target language. Where literary texts are concerned, however, there is a tendency among some theorists to view adaptation negatively, particularly when it is extensive. For example, in *About Translation* (1991), Peter Newmark appears to suggest that adaptation is inappropriate in the case of "serious translations of serious originals", though it may be suitable in the case of "comedies, ephemeral texts and blockbusters". He considers adaptation in general to be a form of creativity gone wild: when creativity dominates a text, the result is "an adaptation, an idiosyncratic interpretation ... (or a bad translation)".

However, adaptation typically results from a clear orientation towards a group of people as recipients of the text, and translators and editors themselves tend to refer to their texts as adaptations when they have made conscious efforts to make the texts more accessible to the intended readership than a more "faithful" translation might be; and this is so independently of the extent of textual alterations involved. For example, in *Training the Translator* (1995), Paul Kussmaul discusses the Germanization of a selection of people- and place-names in Werner Lincke's translation of an Enid Blyton story, to which Lincke refers as an adaptation. An interesting example of a far more extensive adaptation is to be found in *Alitjinya Ngura*

Tjukurtjaranga (Alitji in the Dreamtime), the Pitjantjatjara version of Lewis Carroll's *Alice in Wonderland*. In her introduction to Nancy Sheppard's back-translation into English, published in 1975 by the University of Adelaide, the editor, Barbara Ker Wilson, explains that the story has been adapted to the culture and environment of the aboriginal target audience so that, for example, the White Rabbit with his fan and gloves becomes the Kangaroo with his dilly bag and digging stick. This is not because Pitjantjatjara lacks terms for rabbits, fans, or gloves, or because its speakers lack the relevant concepts; it is because a kangaroo is what an aboriginal girl would naturally dream about; as the illustrations show, Alitji is an aboriginal girl, not an English Alice, and the title indicates that the dream motif is considered an important aspect of the work.

A further example of clear adaptation is to be found in Mataira's renderings in Maori of the lyrics to four songs by Strauss. In *Pacific Quarterly Moana* (1980), these are described as "versions rather than translations because specific details of season and aspects of nature referred to in the originals have been adjusted to the landscape of Aotearoa".

As Hedges points out (in "Translation and Creative Process", 1980), there is always a danger that adaptation will lead to loss of the quality of "otherness" which attracts readers to a text originating in a foreign culture. On the other hand, it is clear that a translation that is so radical in its "otherness" that it remains incomprehensible to the average reader may quickly lose its attraction. When deciding whether and how extensively to adapt, and when judging translated literature, it is therefore necessary to bear in mind the purpose that the text is intended to serve, the readership at which it is aimed, and the literary conventions of the culture in which the text is to function.

KIRSTEN MALMKJÆR

Further Reading

Hedges, I., "Translation and Creative Process", *Pacific Quarterly Moana*, 5/1 (January 1980) pp. 87–93

Holdaway, R., "Verse to Prose: A Literary Fashion", *Canadian Journal of Linguistics*, 10/1 (1964) pp. 47–55

Kussmaul, Paul, *Training the Translator*, Amsterdam: Benjamins, 1995

Newmark, Peter, *About Translation*, Clevedon, Avon, and Philadelphia: Multilingual Matters, 1991

Adūnīs 1930–

Syrian poet and literary critic

Biography

Born ʻAlī Ahmad Saʻīd in Qasabin, Syria, in 1930. His early career in Syria was marked by political involvement (including a six-month term of imprisonment in 1955), and his early political views (heavily influenced by the Syrian nationalist Antūn Sa'āda) left an enduring mark on his early poetry. Ad?nīs is widely acknowledged as one of the most influential figures in modern Arabic literature. His importance derives not only from his poetry, but also from his extensive critical and theoretical writing and from his role as founder and editor of two literary periodicals that have provided an outlet for many younger writers: *Shi'r* [Poetry] (which he founded with Yūsuf al-Khāl in Beirut in 1957) and *Mawāqif* [Opinions] (established in 1968). Exiled from Syria, he settled in Lebanon, and later opted for Lebanese citizenship; more recently, he has lived mainly in Paris.

Translations

Poetry (selections)

Hazo, Samuel, *The Blood of Adonis: Transpositions of Selected Poems*, Pittsburgh: University of Pittsburgh Press, 1971

Hazo, Samuel, *Transformations of the Lover*, Athens: Ohio University Press, 1982

Hazo, Samuel, *The Pages of Day and Night*, Marlboro, Vermont: Marlboro Press, 1994

Al-Udhari, Abdullah, in his *Victims of a Map* (anthology; bilingual edition), London: Saqi, 1984

Other Writing

al-Shi'riyya al-'Arabiyya, 1985

Cobham, Catherine, *An Introduction to Arabic Poetics*, London: Saqi, and Austin: University of Texas Press, 1990

Although Adūnīs's poetry is less immediately accessible and appealing to the non-Arab reader than that of Mahmūd Darwīsh for example, it has been translated into a wide variety of languages, and samples of his verse appear in almost every anthology of modern Arabic poetry in translation.

It was not the first collection of his verse to be published, but there is a general consensus that it was with *Aghānī Mihyār al-Dimashqī*, 1961 (*Songs of Mihyār the Damascene*) that Adūnīs first established himself as an entirely distinctive voice in modern Arabic poetry; indeed, in the view of many critics, the lyricism and coherence of this collection, in which Adūnīs adopts the *persona* of the medieval Arab poet Mihyār to articulate his vision of the world, have never been surpassed.

In addition to its revolutionary political content, much of Adūnīs's work is marked by a mystical flavour, derived from the writings of the Sufi poets, which is fused with symbolist elements akin to those of some 20th-century French poets. Like many Arab poets of his generation, he mingles the Islamic heritage with other religious and mystical traditions, identifying Mihyār, for example, with figures from the Bible and Greek mythology such as Noah and Ulysses. His later poetry, in which he shows a growing preference for the prose poem, is also marked by an increasing complexity and fondness for experimentation, which at times approaches obscurity; one critic, indeed, has wondered whether Adūnīs's later verse does not in fact represent "a dead end, which if universally followed could spell the end of Arabic poetry" (Badawi, 1975). Throughout his development the poet has remained true to his two fundamental projects: to recreate Arab society and to transform the Arabic language – these two projects being so intertwined in his eyes that it is impossible to separate the one from the other.

The English-speaking reader is fortunate in having in COBHAM (1990) an excellently translated introduction to Adūnīs's views on the Arab cultural heritage, and the place of poetry within it. Originally delivered as four lectures at the Collège de France in 1984, and published in both Arabic and French in 1985, *An Introduction to Arab Poetics* discusses the oral tradition of pre-Islamic Arabia; the influence of the Qur'ān on Arabic poetry and poetics; the relationship between poetry and thought in the classical Arabic poetic tradition; and the concept of poetic modernity in Arab society. The last essay is of particular interest, as Adūnīs's name has been closely associated with the concept of *hadātha* (modernity), and he here touches on an essential dichotomy in contemporary Arab culture, which in his view "derives from the past in most of its theoretical aspects ... while its technique comes mainly from the West". While emphasizing the need for poetic renewal, Adūnīs stresses that both the Arabic language and Arab society reach back deep into history, and he concludes that "for an Arab poet to be truly modern his writing must glow like a flame which rises from the fire of the ancient". Catherine Cobham's translation may well strike the uninitiated reader as a little obscure at times; but the obscurities, and occasional quirks of style, are Adūnīs's, not hers, and the work remains one of the few pieces of Arabic literary criticism of this sort translated into English, an indication of the importance both of the author and of his ideas.

The poems available in English translation in HAZO (1971, 1982) and AL-UDHARI (1984) represent a cross-section of Adūnīs's verse published up to the early 1980s, including several poems from *Aghānī Mihyār al-Dimashqī*; examples of his later verse are covered by HAZO (1994). A number of bibliographical hazards await the reader here, not least the fact that the first two-thirds of *Transformations of the Lover* (Hazo, 1982) represents a republication (with minor revisions) of the poems already translated in *The Blood of Adonis* (Hazo, 1971). Appreciation of the development of the poet's art and sensibility is also hindered by the fact that, in common with most anthologies of modern Arabic verse in translation, the collections do not give references to the source texts; in the case of Adūnīs, the problem is exacerbated by his habit of constantly revising his poems for successive editions of his works.

Despite these complaints, HAZO's (1971, 1982) sensitive and resourceful attempts at "recreating [Adūnīs's] poems in American" may be strongly recommended as an introduction to Adūnīs's verse. Adūnīs's name has been particularly associated with the revival of the short *qit'a* ("fragment"), and Hazo's volumes contain several examples of this form, as well as a number of seminal longer poems, including "The Crow's Feather" and "The Funeral of New York". Hazo himself claims only a "rudimentary knowledge" of Arabic, but the results of his reworking of the literal translations provided by Mirene Ghossein and Kamal Boullata are ample proof of the potential of this method of translation. His selection is usefully complemented by AL-UDHARI's (1984) bilingual anthology of poems by Adūnīs, Mahmūd Darwīsh and Samīh al-Qāsim, which includes not only the powerful extended poem "The Desert (The Diary of Beirut Under Siege, 1982)", but also, in "The Minaret", one of the most succinct poetic comments on the predicament of contemporary Arab society:

A stranger arrived.
The minaret wept:
He bought it and topped it with a chimney.

PAUL STARKEY

Further Reading

Abu-Deeb, K., "The Perplexity of the All-Knowing", *Mundus Artium*, 1/10 (1977)

Badawi, M.M., *A Critical Introduction to Modern Arabic Poetry*, Cambridge and New York: Cambridge University Press, 1975

Jayyusi, Selma, "Modernist Poetry in Arabic", in *Modern Arabic Literature*, edited by M.M. Badawi, Cambridge and New York: Cambridge University Press, 1992

Endre Ady 1877–1919

Hungarian poet, short-story writer and journalist

Biography

Born at Érmindszent, a village in East Hungary, 22 November 1877, into a family of impoverished gentry. As a boy he was educated mainly at Calvinist schools, then studied law and began his adult career as a journalist. He spent much time in Paris between 1904 and 1911. Ady's private life was marked by illness and bohemian unconventionality. His political views, expressed in newspaper articles as well as in verse, were radical. During his time in Paris he came to admire Baudelaire and Verlaine, some of whose poems he translated, as well as the French Symbolists, though he was more concerned than they with real life. He played a leading part in the movement to modernize Hungarian society and literature at the end of the 19th century and the beginning of the 20th. From its foundation in 1908 he was associated with the literary journal *Nyugat* [West], edited by Ignotus (Hugó Veigelsberg). Ady's poetry was intense and passionate in content and innovative in technique. His first mature work, *Új versek* [New Poems] (1906), was a turning point in the development of Hungarian poetry. He died in Budapest, 27 January 1919.

Translations

Short Stories

Sollosy, Judith, *Neighbors of the Night: Selected Short Stories*, with an introduction, Budapest: Corvina, 1994 (contains translations of selected stories 1904–10: "A tízmilliós Kleopátra" ("A Cleopatra Worth Ten Million"), 1904; "Tíz forint Vőlegénye" ("Ten Forints' Bridegroom"), 1905; "Olga pofont kap" ("Olga and the Blond Danube"), 1905; "Tamás a piros kertben" ("Thomas in the Red Garden"), 1905; "A megvakított Phryné" ("The Blinded Muse"), 1905; "A legfölségesebb ajkak" ("The Man of the Charitable Lips"), 1905; "Az idegen fiú" ("The Wild Boy"), 1905; "Bond és a vénségpók" ("Bond and the Spider of Old Age"), 1905; "A némák örülnek" ("The Mute Couple"), 1905; "Az este szomszédjai" ("Neighbors of the Night"), 1906; "A halál kis négyesfogata" ("Death's Little Coach-and-Four"), 1906; "A Zenóbia faluja" ("Zenobia's Village"), 1906; "Az Óhidyak igazsága" ("The Justice of the Óhidys"), 1906; "Répakapálás" (Hoeing the Beet"), 1906; "Béni, az apostol" ("Béni the Apostle"), 1906; "Jóba, a kőtörő" ("Joba the Stone Crusher"), 1906; "A süket Flóra" ("Flora"), 1907; "Tavaszi mise" ("Spring Mass"), 1908; "Szelezsán Rákhel kísértete" ("The Ghost of Rachel Szelezsán"), 1908; "Mihályi Rozália csókja" ("The Kiss"), 1908; "A százezer forint" ("A Hundred Thousand Forints"), 1908; "Stella Morbida Párizsban" ("Stella Morbida in Paris"), 1908; "A Cirle szemei" ("Post Mortem"), 1908; "Muskétás Tanár Úr" ("Schoolmaster Barrel Gun"), 1909; "Az Érzékeny Rubek" ("The Sensitive Lieutenant"), 1910)

Poetry (selections)

Bard, Eugene, *Selected Poems*, with an introduction, Munich: Hieronymus, 1987

Bonnerjea, René, *Poems*, with an introduction, Budapest: Vajna & Bokor, 1941

Nyerges, Anton N., *A Selection of Poems from the Writings of Endre Ady*, Bloomington: Indiana University Press, 1946

Nyerges, Anton N., *Poems of Endre Ady*, with an introduction, Buffalo: Hungarian Cultural Foundation, 1969

Other Writing

Cushing, G.F., *The Explosive Country: A Selection of Articles and Studies 1898–1916*, with an introduction, Budapest: Corvina, 1977

Ever since the disappearance of the Iron Curtain in 1989, the Corvina publishing house in Budapest has produced numerous translations of Hungarian prose works into English that are of exceptional quality and also remarkably accessible. SOLLOSY's *Neighbors of the Night* (1994; short stories written by Endre Ady from 1904 to 1910) is a fine example of this welcome trend. Her selection gives readers new to Ady's prose an excellent introduction to this neglected portion of his oeuvre (few would disagree in any case that Ady's poetry is superior to his prose in terms of its literary value, and thus more deserving of translation into English). The selection is well-rounded, covering the best years of his creative output (particularly those he spent in Paris), and a broad range of topics from the dark side of *fin-de-siècle* Europe. Sollosy's introduction provides valuable information on Ady's connection to the French Symbolists and Decadents and his own sophisticated use of symbols. Her translations exhibit conscientious attention to detail and enviable skill in reproducing the author's symbolic and stylistic intentions. Readers of *Neighbors of the Night* will come away with a reliable sense of Ady's place, at least as a prose writer in the literary world of his time.

CUSHING's selection of short prose pieces (1977) represents a valuable addition to the existing corpus of Ady in translation. As Cushing points out in his introduction to *The Explosive Country*, Ady was a journalist as well as a poet. Therefore his journalistic writings represent a crucial aspect of his overall career. Those who wish to understand Ady better as poet and as individual will be anxious to read through the profusion of political, social and personal viewpoints presented in this expertly translated volume. In addition, such readers will gain valuable insight, through such articles as "Roosevelt and Paris", "The Explosive Country", "Karl Kraus in Budapest", and "The Grief of a Transylvanian", into the cultural and political issues and affairs of Ady's time, not only in Hungary but throughout Europe. The radicalism, anti-clericalism, vision and discontentment of this great poet, all hallmarks of the brightest poet of turn-of-the-century Hungary, are superbly expressed in *The Explosive Country*. Cushing has done a great service in making these articles available in such reliable and readable translations.

BONNERJEA's 1941 translation of the *Poems* begins with an informative introduction to Ady's life and career, giving readers excellent background information for a preliminary understanding of his verse. Bonnerjea translates 64 poems, arranged in chronological order and also according to the original collection in which each poem was first published. The original Hungarian titles are given below each English title. Bonnerjea's introduction includes a telling apology applicable to all those brave souls who undertake the important yet risky task of translating from Hungarian into an Indo-European language: "The difference between the two languages [i.e. English and Hungarian] constitutes the greatest drawback to a successful translation of Ady. This consideration, coupled with Ady's uncouth prosody in general and his visions of almost superhuman range, make of him perhaps one of the most difficult poets to translate in world literature". These difficulties, along with others outlined by the translator in the same introduction, prompt him to "appeal to my reader's indulgence on the grounds of the insurmountable obstacles a translator has to face and the scrupulous conscientiousness with which I have attempted to accomplish my task".

This conscientiousness is evident in Bonnerjea's at times *too perfect* renditions of the originals. Overall, he does an expert job in recreating Ady's rhyme schemes, though on several occasions his lines rhyme when those in the original do not, and the regularity of Bonnerjea's rhythm is at times a far cry from the complex freedom that characterizes Ady. The translator is often forced to make concessions in his selection of words to communicate Ady's original meaning, using complex, multisyllabic words to render the most simple Hungarian vocabulary, and creating prosody that, while it may flow rhythmically, is of exaggerated grammatical and/or lexical complexity. Bonnerjea also takes risks with the author's intentions by circumlocuting terms such as "Hortobágy" and "hetaera" rather than recording them directly as other translators often do (they could certainly be explained in simple footnotes). Bonnerjea seems to be addressing his translations to a wide audience including those utterly unfamiliar with Hungarian culture. Some readers will undoubtedly prefer such an approach, but it cannot be said to represent faithfully the poet's intentions.

These are minor criticisms, and overall Bonnerjea does an admirable job with a seemingly impossible task. His close attention to rhyme scheme and rhythm makes his translations eminently readable and, while he does not give error-free renditions of Ady's original meanings, most of the translations are remarkably faithful to the poet's intentions. His selection makes for a volume that, while slim, gives an accurate representation of the various themes and the overall thrust of Ady's poetry. His work is certainly to be recommended.

The poems translated by Antal (Anton) NYERGES (1946) number among his earlier translation efforts and, as such, are more faithful to the originals than much of his later work (e.g., his translations of Petőfi, published in 1973). The selection contains 60 poems, arranged roughly thematically, and covering several of the themes so dear to Ady: love-making, death, the Hungarian (Transylvanian) countryside, Paris, religion. The text is furnished with a useful table of contents containing a welcome listing of the original Hungarian titles of the poems translated. For the most part, Nyerges offers translations faithful to the meaning and the rhyme schemes of Ady's originals. There are some notable exceptions, however, where Nyerges gets rather carried away by his own creativity and misrepresents the author's intentions. This tendency is more pronounced in his later Ady volume (1969). Certainly there is even in this early group of translations a somewhat experimental, daring quality about Nyerges's work. But the spirit of Ady's originals is well-represented, and Nyerges is particularly successful in reproducing the original rhyme schemes and atmosphere. Nyerges also has an undeniable flair for language and often comes up with expressive, even pithy, vocabulary, giving an excellent indication of his own poetic talents.

NYERGES (1969) is the most complete collection of Ady's poems in English translation and was billed as a commemorative edition to celebrate the 50th anniversary of the poet's death. Here Nyerges offers nearly one-third of Ady's poems in skilful translation. This volume also includes a 45-page introduction to the poet's life and work that is filled with useful and cogent insights. The index is also valuable, providing as it does alphabetical lists of the poems according to Nyerges's translated titles as well as the Hungarian original titles. The organization of the poems is based on their appearance in the various collections published during (and after) Ady's lifetime and is in essence chronological. Nyerges lays great stress on the thematic organization displayed in these original volumes and does a fine job, despite the limitations of an abridged assortment of Ady's poetry, of realizing the author's often opaque thematic intentions. The quality of such a large collection of translations varies almost of necessity. Many of the original translations published in Nyerges's 1946 selection were altered by the translator, sometimes attempting improvement by omitting archaic language and simplifying wordy expressions, but at times such "improvements" merely increased the experimental nature of the translation and departed, sometimes radically, from the poet's original intentions. A good example of this is "The Ghost Got into Paris", Nyerges's 1969 translation of "Párizsban járt as ősz", which is subjected to a valuable critical analysis by Maxim Tabory in the 1988 article listed below. This type of departure from the original is, however, more unusual in this comprehensive volume than it is in the later collection of translations from Petőfi (1973). For the most part, Nyerges's translations here can be relied upon for their remarkable (especially in light of the extraordinary differences between English and Hungarian) faithfulness to Ady's poetic and symbolic intentions and achievement. *Poems of Endre Ady* represents two decades of work, a fact that the quality and thoroughness of this volume make readily apparent.

Eugene BARD's little volume of *Selected Poems* (1987) belongs in much the same class as the one by Bonnerjea. Intriguingly, Bard makes no reference to the work of his predecessors, explaining his publication simply as "a labor of love, l'art pour l'art, an experiment on what could be done with Ady in colloquial American English". In view of the difficulties inherent in any attempt to render Hungarian poetry into English, and the fact that there can be no "perfect" translation of any Ady poem, Bard's contribution is welcome, and the quality of his translations is high indeed. *Selected Poems* contains some 10 per cent of Ady's poetic production and constitutes thus an excellent introduction to his work for readers who may be overwhelmed by a volume the size of Nyerges's *Poems of Endre Ady*. Bard's volume contains a three-page introduction as well as informative notes, geared toward the literary novice, on seven of the poems he translates. His translations rival those of Bonnerjea and Nyerges in their faithfulness to Ady's intentions in terms of both meaning and form. In fact, a good number of them (though not all) represent improvements, as they succeed in conveying Ady's meaning with greater concision and simplicity, without sacrificing anything in terms of rhyme scheme or rhythm.

Bard's contribution to the translation of Ady poems is important, and not just because of the overall dearth of Ady collections in English. Readers who seek to know this important poet better and who have little or no access to Hungarian will fare best when they take the opportunity to compare and contrast *all* the existing versions of Ady's works in translation in order to round out their picture of this complex genius. *Selected Poems* would be an excellent place to start.

VIRGINIA L. LEWIS

Further Reading

Birnbaum, Marianna D., "Innovative Archaisms in the Poetry of Endre Ady", in *Hungarian Studies Review*, 11 (1984) pp. 15–34

Tabory, Maxim, "Six English Versions of 'Párizsban Járt Az Ősz' by Endre Ady" in *Translation Review*, 27 (1988) pp. 28–33

Aeschylus 525 or 524–456 BC

Greek tragic dramatist

Biography

Born in Eleusis, Attica. He was of noble family. In 490 he was wounded at the battle of Marathon, defending Athens against the Persians, and probably fought them again at the battle of Salamis, 480. He was 41 when in 484 he won his first important drama prize. He was invited to the court of Hieron I, tyrant of Syracuse, to produce plays, not long after the city of Etna was founded. He was back in Athens by 468. He returned after 458 to Sicily and died there, near Gela, 456 BC.

Aeschylus is the first of the three great 5th-century Greek tragedians; indeed, if (as Aristotle says at *Poetics*, 1449a, 15–16) he introduced the second actor to what had originally been an interchange of single actor and chorus, he may fairly be called the creator of tragedy as we know it. Aeschylus wrote some 90 to 100 plays, of which seven survive: a connected tragic trilogy, the *Oresteia*, and four isolated tragedies, *Seven against Thebes*, *Persians*, *Suppliants*, and *Prometheus Bound*. These plays, like all Greek and Roman dramas, were written in verse; spoken dialogue alternated with choral odes, sung and danced to the accompaniment of the *aulos*, a double reed instrument, and with other forms of song and chant.

Tragedy, as practised by the Greeks, may itself be called a form of cultural translation, in which the heroic legends of epic are mediated in dramatic form to the new world of the Greek polis. Aeschylus came to maturity as the institutions of Athenian democracy were being forged; he himself fought against the Persians at Marathon. His drama is part of the remarkable flowering of culture and confidence that accompanied the rise of Athens to the leadership of Greece in the aftermath of the Persian Wars.

Aeschylus is the tragic poet closest to Homer, both in language and in stylistic features such as extended catalogues, but he can also be strikingly original, for example, in the coining of compound words and intricate periphrases. Aeschylean drama does not shy away from ideas, and the ideas are often expressed in complex and demanding ways, but the language generally remains concrete and pictorial. Above all, Aeschylus' style is distinguished by its range. On the one hand, we find the grandeur and sonorous elaboration already deliciously parodied by the comic poet Aristophanes in his *Frogs*, some 50 years after Aeschylus' death. On the other hand, there is also place in Aeschylus for plain speech, sometimes strikingly simple and direct, even colloquial.

Greek tragedy presents a number of special problems for the translator, and all of them are found at their most demanding in Aeschylus. Literal translation of so conventional a form, with its highly figurative language, is almost bound to sound ludicrous. "Fragment of a Greek Tragedy", A.E. Housman's brilliant parody directed at once at the apparent vagaries of Aeschylean thought and diction and at attempts to give an overly literal account of them, is still amusing and very much to the point. On the other hand, the besetting sin of much Aeschylus in English is a tendency to stray from the intractable literal meaning into poetic cliché and Wardour Street archaism.

Perhaps in part because of the textual and interpretative difficulties that Aeschylus presents, he was the last of the Greek tragedians to be translated into English. English versions of plays by Euripides began to be written as early as the mid-16th century, but it was not until 1773 that a play of Aeschylus, *Prometheus Bound*, appeared in the translation of Thomas Morell, followed within four years by Robert Potter's version of all the extant tragedies. From early in the 19th century there has been a steady stream of translations, singly, in groups, and complete, and in both verse and prose, including versions by a number of celebrated writers (both Brownings, Henry David Thoreau, Edward FitzGerald, Louis MacNeice, Robert Lowell, Ted Hughes). Currently, numerous competing versions of all the plays are available.

Translations

Complete Plays (by various hands)

Grene, David and Richmond Lattimore (editors), *The Complete Greek Tragedies* (Centennial Edition), vol. 1: *Aeschylus*, Chicago: University of Chicago Press, 1992 (series first published 1953–59)

Oates, Whitney J. and Eugene O'Neill, Jr., *The Complete Greek Drama*, New York: Random House, 1938

Slavitt, David R. and Palmer Bovie (editors), *Aeschylus*, 2 vols, Philadelphia: University of Pennsylvania Press, 1998–99

Complete Plays (by a single translator)

Blackie, John Stuart, *The Lyrical Dramas of Aeschylus*, London: J.W. Parker, 1850 (verse)

Buckley, Theodore Alois, *The Tragedies of Aeschylus*, London: H.G. Bohn, 1849 (prose)

Campbell, Lewis, *Aeschylus: The Seven Plays in English Verse*, London: Kegan Paul, 1890; revised edition, London: Oxford University Press, 1906

Cookson, G.M., *Four Plays of Aeschylus*, Oxford: Blackwell, 1922 (contains *The Suppliant Maidens*, *The Persians*, *The Seven against Thebes*, *The Prometheus Bound*)

Cookson, G.M., *Agamemnon, Choephoroe, Eumenides*, London: Chapman and Hall, 1924

Ewans, Michael, *The Oresteia*, London: Dent, and Rutland, Vermont: Tuttle, 1995

Ewans, Michael, *Suppliants and Other Dramas*, London: Dent, and Rutland, Vermont: Tuttle, 1996 (contains *Persians*, *Seven against Thebes*, *Suppliants*, *Fragments*, *Prometheus Bound*)

Morshead, E.D.A., *The House of Atreus ... Translated into English Verse*, London: Kegan Paul, 1881

Morshead, E.D.A., *The Suppliant Maidens*, *The Persians*, *The Seven against Thebes*, *The Prometheus Bound*, London: Macmillan, 1908

Murray, Gilbert, *The Complete Plays of Aeschylus, Translated in English Rhyming Verse*, London: Allen and Unwin, 1952 (individual plays published between 1920 and 1939)

Paley, Frederick A., *Aeschylus Translated into English Prose*, Cambridge: Deighton Bell, 1864

Potter, Robert, *The Tragedies of Aeschylus*, Norwich: J. Crouse, 1777; 2nd edition with notes, London: Strahan and Cadell, 1779

Smyth, Herbert Weir, *Aeschylus* (bilingual edition), 2 vols, London: Heinemann, and New York: Putnam, 1922–26 (prose; Loeb Classical Library)

Swanwick, Anna, *The Dramas of Aeschylus*, London: Bell and Daldy, 1873

Vellacott, Philip, *The Oresteian Trilogy*, Harmondsworth: Penguin, 1956; corrected edition, 1959

Vellacott, Philip, *Promethus Bound*; *The Suppliants*; *Seven against Thebes*; *The Persians*, Harmondsworth: Penguin, 1961

Way, Arthur S., *Aeschylus in English Verse*, London: Macmillan, 1906–08

Persians

Persai, 472 BC; traditional Latin title *Persae*

The first complete tragedy by Aeschylus to survive, and the only one that deals with contemporary events, *Persians* was produced in 472 BC at Athens.

Translations

Benardete, S.G., *The Persians*, in *Aeschylus II*, Chicago: Chicago University Press, 1956

Hall, Edith, *Persians* (parallel texts), with an introduction, Warminster, Wiltshire: Aris and Phillips, 1996

Lembke, Janet and C.J. Herington, *Persians*, with an introduction, New York and Oxford: Oxford University Press, 1981

Podlecki, Anthony J., *The Persians by Aeschylus, A Translation with Commentary*, with an introduction, Englewood Cliffs, New Jersey: Prentice Hall, 1970

Persians is perhaps the least often translated of the plays of Aeschylus, and may be the most difficult to bring successfully into English. Almost all existing versions are part of complete translations of Aeschylus. For comments on a selection of these, see the article on the *Oresteia*; the four recent versions listed here were also issued as parts of series.

Persians presents special problems of several kinds. The first regards genre: this is a history play, and, since there is reason to believe that Aeschylus himself was at the battle of Salamis (480 BC), its description of the Persian defeat there is arguably the only eye-witness account to survive from the Persian Wars. On the other hand, the play mingles this account with the supernatural – dream, prophecy, a ghost rising from his tomb – and all the trappings of myth. The interpenetration of these two frames, second-nature to archaic Greece, is alien to modern sensibility. Second, the play is almost entirely devoted to anticipation, narration, and lamentation; there is essentially no action as we usually understand that word. Last, and most remarkably, the play is presented from the Persian point of view, which means among other things that much of it is given over to ritual lament, with keening choruses and an elaborate final threnody, entirely chanted or sung. Greek is very rich, English poor in the language of grief. "Ah me" and "alas" are only token translations of *otototototoi*, *io io moi*, and many other such outbursts of anguish in the Greek.

BENARDETE (1956) provides an emotionally rather undernourished but readable and accurate version, with rhythmic correspondence between matching stanzas in the lyrics, and dialogue largely rendered in blank verse. Benardete's language has a deliberately archaic flavor, but generally remains too colorless and inert to convey the grandeur of Aeschylus' conception or the power of his images.

PODLECKI (1970) is disappointingly timid. For example, at lines 104–05, where Aeschylus deploys two of his characteristic compound epithets to produce a feeling of concentrated power – "to wage towercleaving wars and horsebattling tumults" – Podlecki gives us the rather low-keyed "destruction of walls, waging of wars, / The furious cavalry charge", and in a note admits that "the English is too pale for the vigorous Aeschylean phrase." Podlecki attempts to follow the original metres, but the result is some rather crabbed writing rather than a strong sense of the musicality of the original verse. On the other hand, this version does offer a comprehensive introduction and extensive notes, which makes this translation a source of much useful information for the Greekless reader.

The translation by LEMBKE & HERINGTON (1981) is of a different kind, and their accomplishment is of a different order. This is a high modernist version in style, versification, and layout. Unlike the Benardete and Podlecki translations, if this one errs, it is on the side of boldness. Lembke & Herington emphasize the archaic strangeness of Aeschylus' text. Although their version is not always as literal as the others, it is by no means a free or impressionistic rendering, but displays consistent effort to rethink Aeschylus' drama in modern language. The introduction is a model of both scholarly and interpretative intelligence, and the notes offer, in addition to commentary on the play, interesting insights into translation issues.

HALL's prose translation (1996) is designed to facilitate reading the original text, printed *en face*, and does so successfully but at the price of smoothing out almost all the cragginess and power of Aeschylus' Greek. The interjections of grief and lament are transliterated rather than translated. The introduction and notes are learned and helpful, but in the latter some knowledge of Greek is assumed.

PETER BURIAN

Further Reading

Lembke, Janet, "Translator's Note", in *Persians*, translated by Lembke and C.J. Herington, 1981

Parker, Douglass, "Aeschylus and the New Gramarye", *Arion*, new series, 1 (1973) pp. 205–10

Seven against Thebes

Epta epi Thebas, 467 BC; *Septem contra Thebas*

The final tragedy of a connected trilogy produced at Athens in 467 BC. The first two tragedies, *Laius* and *Oedipus*, and *Sphinx*, a satyr play that followed the trilogy, are all lost.

Translations

Dawson, Christopher M., *The Seven against Thebes by Aeschylus: A Translation with Commentary*, with an introduction, Englewood Cliffs, New Jersey: Prentice Hall, 1970

Grene, David, *Seven against Thebes*, with an introduction, in *Aeschylus II*, Chicago: Chicago University Press, 1956

Hecht, Anthony and Helen H. Bacon, *Seven against Thebes*, with an introduction, New York and Oxford: Oxford University Press, 1973

Meagher, Robert Emmet, *Seven against Thebes*, Wauconda, Illinois: Bolchazy Carducci, 1996

Thoreau, Henry David, *The Seven against Thebes*, in *The Writings of Henry David Thoreau: Translations*, edited by K.P. Van Anglen, Princeton, New Jersey: Princeton University Press, 1986 (originally published 1843)

Seven against Thebes, a dramatization of the mutual slaughter of Eteocles and Polynices in fulfillment of their father Oedipus' curse, has not inspired many individual versions, although of course it forms part of the numerous complete translations of Aeschylus. (For comments on a selection of these, see the article on the *Oresteia*.) The play offers little action as such, and yet its combination of anticipation, description, and lamentation is charged throughout with high emotion and is, in its way, highly theatrical. The central event of this "drama full of Ares" (Aristophanes, *Frogs*, 1021) is the great scene in which a messenger describes the seven warriors advancing against the seven gates of Thebes and Eteocles answers by describing the seven champions he will send against them, culminating in his decision to face Polynices at the seventh gate. The translator must find a way to make clear the tension of a scene in which the power of words becomes the agency of fate, and what amounts to a recital of the heraldic devices emblazoned on the shields of the attackers and defenders brings Oedipus' curse to the point of accomplishment.

A particular problem that has prompted divergent responses from translators concerns the ending of the play, in which the magistrates who succeed the fallen kings reopen the conflict by refusing burial to Polynices, and his loving sister Antigone announces her opposition to the decree. Because of this ending, *Seven against Thebes* was long thought to be the second part of a trilogy that concluded with a play corresponding in subject to Sophocles' *Antigone*. When the ancient evidence for the composition of the trilogy was at last published in 1848, however, questions arose regarding the authenticity of the ending. Today most, but not all, scholars believe the ending to be a later addition designed to align Aeschylus' version with Sophocles' famous tragedy. Some scholars, indeed, argue that Antigone and Ismene, who are brought on in the preceding scene to lament their dead brothers, have no part at all in Aeschylus' original conception, and reassign their lines to half-choruses. The available translations reflect the entire gamut of scholarly opinion on these questions.

THOREAU's version (1843) is a draft that might well have undergone considerable revision had Thoreau found a publisher for it. The manuscript is complete but contains a considerable number of revisions and alternative readings. The translation, as Thoreau himself wrote to the editor of a New York periodical, is "in the manner of *Prometheus Bound*", his Aeschylean translation published in *The Dial* at the beginning of 1843. That is to say, it is a studiously literal version in rhythmic prose, making up what it lacks in elegance by an honest attempt to convey the directness and concision of Aeschylus' language. Thoreau goes further than most other translators in bending English syntax and word order to suggest the movement of the Greek, and unlike other versions of the period, his prefers the original Greek names for the deities to their Latin equivalents. Since Thoreau's version was written before the make-up of the trilogy became known, the authenticity of the ending was not an issue for him.

GRENE (1956) offers a version that is reliable but without special distinction. Dialogue is rendered primarily in blank verse, lyric in free verse that suggests nothing of the formal discipline or forceful diction of Aeschylean song. Oddly, Grene's very brief introduction does not mention the questions raised by the ending, and the whole text is printed without any suggestion of doubt as to its authenticity. As with the rest of the Chicago series, there are no explanatory notes.

DAWSON (1970), on the contrary, provides an exhaustive Introduction, and nearly every page of the translation has more notes than text. Dawson prints those parts of the ending that refer to Antigone and Ismene (lines 861–74 and 1005–53) in brackets, as interpolations, and he gives the remaining lines assigned to them in the manuscripts to half-choruses. Throughout, the reasoning behind his choices is explicit, and the English-speaking reader is given the evidence on which to assess those choices. The translation itself is readable while remaining sensitive to the nuances of Aeschylus' language. The dialogue can be read as iambic lines of varying length, the choral lyrics provide a sense of rhythmic responsion between stanzas. As a close version without literary pretensions, this is a decided success.

Useful as Dawson's edition is, those who want to experience *Seven against Thebes* as dramatic poetry will do well to turn to Hecht & Bacon (1973). This collaboration of a poet and a classicist makes a strong case for the play's greatness. The language is powerful, and the directness and even roughness of much of the dialogue comes through well in the short, free-verse lines that Hecht has chosen. Choral lyrics, on the other hand, are given a variety of treatments, including passages in sonorous rhymed verse that renders something of their musicality available to contemporary readers. The introduction makes the best possible case for the authenticity and integrity of the text as transmitted, and the translation succeeds in making this view of the drama believable and playable.

Meagher (1996), who has also translated a number of Euripidean plays with theatrical performance in mind, has the great merit of writing clear and speakable English that can be credibly acted. This version does not have the poetic power of Hecht & Bacon, especially in the choral odes, but it is well crafted and fluent throughout. Its only real disadvantage is that Meagher, believing the received ending to be spurious, simply omits lines 861–74 and 1005 to the end. His version thus offers an inconclusive ending, implausibly spoken by an Antigone and Ismene who appear without introduction or identification, while at the same time it denies the reader any chance to assess the merits of the deleted lines.

Peter Burian

Suppliants

Iketides, mid-460s BC; *Supplices*

The first tragedy of a tetralogy performed in the mid-460s in Athens. The remaining tragedies (*Aigyptioi* and *Danaids*) as well as the accompanying satyr play (*Amymone*) are lost.

Translations

Benardete, S.G., *The Suppliant Maidens*, in *Aeschylus II*, Chicago: Chicago University Press, 1956

Burian, Peter, *The Suppliants*, with an introduction, Princeton, New Jersey: Princeton University Press, 1991

Caldwell, Richard, *The Suppliants*, in *The Tenth Muse: Classical Drama in Translation*, edited by Charles Doria, Chicago: Swallow Press, and Athens: Ohio University Press, 1980

Friis Johansen, H., *The Suppliants* (bilingual edition), Copenhagen: Gyldendal, 1970

Lembke, Janet, *Suppliants*, with an introduction, New York and Oxford: Oxford University Press, 1975

Aeschylus' *Suppliants* presents some special obstacles to its translators. The myth on which it is based is not well known, and in the absence of the remaining tragedies there is neither downfall nor resolution, indeed no tragic conclusion of any kind. The play emphasizes lyrical reflection over dramatic action. The text is unusually corrupt and uncertain. Not surprisingly, then, few versions have been undertaken beyond those in complete translations of Aeschylus. (For comments on a selection of these, see the article on the *Oresteia.*) Nevertheless, *Suppliants* offers its translators a succession of choral lyrics that are among the glories of Greek poetry, a gripping enactment of terror, cunning, and lust in a confrontation between the sexes, and a skeletal drama of civic crisis and clashing forms of power.

Suppliants recounts the arrival in Argos of the 50 daughters of Danaus. They have fled Egypt to escape their cousins, the 50 sons of Aegyptus, who are in hot pursuit and mean to claim them as brides, even at the cost of war. The suppliants win protection in Argos, the home of their ancestor Io. Pelasgus, the Argive king, repels the men who attempt to seize them, and the play ends with the suppliants leaving to take refuge within the city. The struggle has only begun.

Until recently, *Suppliants* was widely considered the earliest of extant Greek tragedies, probably not much later than 490 BC. This conclusion was based on the play's preponderance of choral lyrics (the chorus is, in effect, the protagonist) and simplicity of action, features that Aristotle ascribes to early tragedy. In the 1950s, however, publication of a scrap of papyrus that convincingly assigns the trilogy a date in the mid-460s made this view impossible to maintain and made it possible to see many thematic and formal links between *Suppliants* and the later plays of Aeschylus, particularly the *Oresteia.*

Friis Johansen's literal prose translation (1970) is designed to accompany his Greek text, and thus reveals verbal meaning without attempting to find a language capable of reflecting the lyrical flights of the original. It does, however, honestly mirror the difficulties of interpreting a corrupt and, in a few places, apparently mutilated text.

Benardete's translation (1956) is the first of a number of modern renditions in verse. Benardete provides an emotionally rather underpowered but readable and accurate version, with rhythmic correspondence between matching stanzas in the lyrics, and dialogue largely rendered in blank verse. Benardete's language has a deliberately archaic flavor, but generally remains too colorless and inert to convey the grandeur of Aeschylus' conception or the power of his images.

Lembke (1975), writing in a high modernist vein, gives her free verse rough rhythmic correspondence between paired stanzas in the choral songs, but otherwise seems concerned more to express the raw power and depth of feeling of Aeschylus' text than to find equivalents for the formal magnificence and compact intricacy of Aeschylean verse. Her version is not always a safe guide to Aeschylus' literal meaning, for she elaborates many images and frequently provides expansions of Aeschylean ideas. Nevertheless, Lembke's vivid response to Aeschylus' verbal magic and her search for direct emotional equivalents in our own idiom gives this translation great distinction. Many of her choices, particularly when they deviate from the literal, are given illuminating discussion in endnotes.

Caldwell (1980) offers a free-verse rendition that is a disappointment in almost every way. The verse itself is undistinguished, sometimes jarringly colloquial and sometimes simply bland. Caldwell too often shades the meaning to favor his own reductively Freudian reading of the play, heightening at every point the Danaids' refusal to marry the sons of Aegyptus into complete rejection of any sexual union.

The translation by BURIAN (1991) attempts to represent the difference in register between speech and song in Aeschylus by casting the dialogue in relaxed blank verse and using strict syllabic responsion to convey the formal discipline of Aeschylus' strophic choruses. This version is closer to the literal meaning than Lembke's or Caldwell's.

PETER BURIAN

Further Reading

See the introductions to the translations by Lembke and Burian

Oresteia

Oresteia, 458 BC

The only connected trilogy of Greek tragedies to survive, consisting of *Agamemnon*, *Choephoroe* (*Libation Bearers*), and *Eumenides*. These were originally followed by a lost satyr play, *Proteus*. First performed at the Theater of Dionysus in Athens in 458 BC.

Translations

Oresteia

Fagles, Robert, *The Oresteia*, New York: Viking Press, 1975; London: Wildwood House, 1976; Harmondsworth: Penguin, 1977

Grene, David and Wendy Doniger O'Flaherty, *The Oresteia*, with introductions by the translators and by Nicholas Rudall, Chicago: University of Chicago Press, 1989

Harrison, Tony, *The Oresteia*, London: Rex Collings, 1981; reprinted in *Theatre Works 1973–1985*, Harmondsworth: Penguin, 1985

Hughes, Ted, *The Oresteia*, London: Faber, and New York: Farrar Straus, 1999

Lattimore, Richmond, *Oresteia*, Chicago: University of Chicago Press, 1953 (*Agamemnon* first published in *Greek Plays in Modern Translation*, edited by Dudley Fitts, New York: Dial Press, 1947)

Lloyd-Jones, Hugh, *The Oresteia*, 3 vols, Englewood Cliffs, New Jersey: Prentice Hall, 1970; 1 vol., London: Duckworth, 1979 (prose)

Lowell, Robert, *The Oresteia of Aeschylus*, New York: Farrar Straus, 1978; London: Faber, 1979

Meineck, Peter, *Oresteia*, with an introduction by Helene P. Foley, Indianapolis, Indiana: Hackett, 1998

Thomson, George, *The Oresteia of Aeschylus* (bilingual edition), 2 vols, Cambridge: Cambridge University Press, 1938; revised version in *Aeschylus*, edited by Robert W. Corrigan, New York: Dell, 1965

Agamemnon only

Browning, Robert, *The Agamemnon*, London: Smith Elder, 1877

FitzGerald, Edward, *Agamemnon*, privately printed, 1865; London: Bernard Quaritch, 1876

Hamilton, Edith, *Agamemnon* in *Three Greek Plays*, translated by Hamilton, New York: Norton, 1937

Kennedy, Benjamin H., *The Agamemnon ... with a Metrical Translation*, Cambridge: Cambridge University Press, 1878

MacNeice, Louis, *The Agamemnon of Aeschylus*, London: Faber, 1936

The *Oresteia*, written near the end of Aeschylus' life, shows us a dramatist and poet of genius working at the height of his powers. In three tragedies that are, in effect, acts of a single vast drama, Aeschylus enacts Clytemnestra's murder of her husband Agamemnon on his triumphant return from Troy, Orestes' revenge murder of his mother and her lover, and lastly Orestes' pursuit by the Furies and judicial absolution at Athens. The main outline of the story is Homeric, but its denouement, involving the establishment of the Athenian homicide court and the transformation of the Furies into protective deities who dwell in the Attic soil, seems to have been an Aeschylean invention based on local legend and cult.

None of the many English versions can be said to succeed in representing the trilogy in all its aspects; much of the musical splendour of its language escapes even the best efforts of the many scholars and poets who have attempted translations, and the vast majority of older versions now seem singularly inert and remote from the vivid imagery and thematic density of a dramatic text that Swinburne called "probably on the whole the greatest spiritual work of man". Nevertheless, contemporary readers (and theatrical producers) can choose from versions that offer many strengths of different kinds.

The first two complete translations of Aeschylus give a clear idea of two contrasting modes of translation that held the field until at least the 1930s. POTTER (1721–1804), a clergyman of some learning and literary ambition, published the first in 1777. His rendering of the dialogue into blank verse and the lyrics into rhymed stanzas tends, like much 18th-century verse, toward sonorous abstraction at the expense of the variety and vigor of Aeschylus' language. Potter's verse, in short, speaks fluently but without great distinction in the voice of its time. Dr Johnson, asked for his opinion of Potter's Aeschylus, replied, "I thought what I read of it *verbiage*." But to judge by its long-lived popularity, most readers seem to have agreed with one of Johnson's interlocutors, James Harris, who found it "pretty" (James Boswell, *Life of Johnson*). The flavor of Potter's verse can be gleaned from his handling of a typical Aeschylean metaphor figuring Ares, the war god, as a merchant exchanging warriors' bodies for urns full of their ashes (*Agamemnon*, lines 437–44):

> Thus in the dire exchange of war
> Does Mars the balance hold;
> Helms are the scales, the beam a spear,
> And blood is weighed for gold.
> This, for the warrior, to his friends
> His sad remains, a poor return
> Saved from the sullen fire that rose
> On Troy's curst shore, he sends,
> Plac'd decent in the mournful urn.

The adjectives of the last four lines are almost pure Potter, designed for decorum and insuring dull predictability. Despite his faults, however, Potter was regularly reprinted until 1903, and as late as 1938 Oates and O'Neill chose Potter's *Persians* for their *Complete Greek Drama*.

Only in 1849 was a complete English Aeschylus again attempted, this time "literally translated" into straightforward, if not always fluent, prose by BUCKLEY (1825–56), a short-lived but prolific writer, editor, and translator. Buckley's translation was regularly reprinted until World War I as part of the widely used Bohn series, designed in the first instance for use by students. Here is Buckley's version of the sample passage:

> And Mars, that barters for gold their bodies, and that holds the
> balance in the tug of the spears, sends to their friends some
> fragments of scorched dust from Ilion, a thing of bitter tears,
> filling the vases with light ashes instead of the man.

Buckley's prose does not hint at Aeschylean magnificence, does not particularly strive for eloquence, but it is also without pretension. Compared to Potter, Buckley is refreshingly spare and direct, although he continues the practice of substituting the more familiar Latin forms for the names of the Greek deities.

The many remaining versions of the 19th and early 20th century are almost all variations on the manner of Potter or of Buckley. The verse translations that had the widest circulation all gave the impression of Aeschylus as a minor versifier, though no doubt with a grand tale to tell. BLACKIE (1850), whose version was taken up by the Everyman's Library and reprinted often up to the time of World War II, shows Tennyson's influence more than Dryden's, but is hardly more inspired than Potter. SWANWICK, a remarkable woman who went to Berlin to learn Greek as well as German, was ranked high as a translator by her contemporaries. Her Aeschylus (1873), regularly reprinted until 1907, now seems quaint and a little fussy in its careful rhyme and prosodic clichés. Much the same must be said for MORSHEAD's translations (1881), still given pride of place in Oates and O'Neill's *Complete Greek Drama*. The blank verse dialogue and rhyming-couplet choruses of the 1890 Aeschylus of CAMPBELL, Professor of Greek at St Andrews, is somewhat less cloying, though hardly more inspiring. It, too, however, achieved notable popularity as part of the Oxford University Press World's Classics series, in which it continued to appear until well after World War II. But it took WAY (1906) to turn Aeschylus into a *fin de siècle* poetaster:

> The War-god, who exchangeth
> Men's lives for gold,
> And, where the mad spear rangeth,
> The scales doth hold,
> Sends back to hearts that yearn
> For a brave man's return,
> Filling one small sad urn
> Pyre-ashes cold.

What is perhaps more surprising is that the taste for this sort of translation of Aeschylus lasted well into the 20th century. MURRAY, the Oxford Professor of Greek whose translations did more than anyone else's to shape the popular understanding of Greek drama, had an enormous following. His versions of the plays of Aeschylus, published individually between the World Wars and collected only in 1952, serve to remind us that readers and theatergoers interested in the classics regularly preferred translations that offered the comfort of tradition rather than the innovations of modernism. Murray's greatest weaknesses are the archaisms and the rhymes that he obviously regarded as appropriately poetic, but that now seem less to give a sense of period than to make his translations into period pieces. COOKSON (1924), equally prone to archaism and even more hapless in versification, succeeded Blackie as the Everyman Aeschylus, with no appreciable gain, and in the 1950s was "canonized" as part of the Encyclopaedia Britannica's prestigious Great Books series. VELLACOTT's Penguin (1956), often reprinted and still available, while free of blatant archaisms, still employs Potter's combination of blank verse and rhymed choruses. Lifeless in rhythm and diction, this version meets the minimal requirements of verse, but not of poetry.

Of prose versions subsequent to Buckley's, three require brief mention. That of PALEY, an important editor of Aeschylus, is refreshingly and, for its time (1864) surprisingly, direct. Without poetic pretensions, it also lacks pretentious poeticism and steers clear of Wardour Street archaism. SMYTH's *Oresteia* (1926), on the other hand, although it is the work of a fine Hellenist and appears with an authoritative text *en face* in the most widely consulted classical series of the English-speaking world, can only seem a step backward with the convolutions of its faux-biblical style. Prose is, however, the vehicle for one of the most useful recent versions, that of another eminent scholar, LLOYD-JONES (1970). A readable literal translation is set out line by line, accompanied by unusually full annotation.

A few individual verse translations of *Agamemnon* stand apart. In the three-year period 1876–78, Edward FitzGerald, Robert Browning, and Benjamin Hall Kennedy published highly distinctive, although in many ways flawed translations.

FITZGERALD's version is, like his famous *Rubaiyat of Omar Khayyam*, very free. Much of the dialogue is rendered with reasonable fidelity, but particularly in the choruses FitzGerald adds, omits, and rewrites more or less at will. The result is, if anything, even more precious and winsome than the other Victorian versions of Aeschylus. Deficient as a translation, it no longer seems remotely Aeschylean in style and can be read only as a curiosity.

BROWNING's translation is notorious for the opposite excess: exasperated literalism. Where FitzGerald hoped by sacrificing the letter to recreate the effect of Aeschylus for the Greekless reader, Browning imagines such a reader requiring the translator "to be literal at every cost save absolute violence to our language" – and some have felt that Browning paid that price as well. Browning, as Reuben Brower well remarks, "attempts to defy the first condition of all translating" – finding equivalents in his own language and culture for the experience of the original. Thus, Greek word order, coined compounds that mirror Aeschylean, not English, usage, and much else, make Browning in places far more difficult than Aeschylus. There is, however, something heroic as well as quixotic in the attempt, and at moments a sense of the otherness of the Greek is coupled with a poetically illuminating phrase. The translation is a *tour de force* in more ways than one. Browning uses an 11-syllable line for dialogue, which adds to the exoticism of the effect, and he manages to remain literal while using rhymes for the choral lyrics. This is a case where rhyme seems to work to the translation's advantage, and some of the lyrics are surprisingly successful. Here is Browning's rendering of our passage:

For Ares, gold-exchanger for the dead,
And balance holder in the fight o' the spear,
Due weight from Ilion sends –
What moves the tear on tear –
A charred scrap to the friends:
Filling with well-packed ashes every urn,
For man – that was – the sole return.

No one could mistake this for original English poetry, even poetry as quirky as Browning's can be, but it nevertheless has a power that comes precisely from the shunning of Victorian prettiness.

KENNEDY, the Regius Professor of Greek at Cambridge, was no poet, but his *Agamemnon* is of some interest for the plainness that put it far ahead of its time. Its most successful aspect is the casting of the dialogue in alexandrines, the meter most like Greek iambic trimeter in its flow. The choruses, unrhymed and with rhythmic correspondence between strophe and antistrophe, are at times rather clumsy, but offer a close construe of the Greek that has none of the contortions of Browning's translation and few of the poeticisms of other Victorian versions. Unfortunately, Kennedy seems to have had little influence on subsequent translators.

Two translations of *Agamemnon* from the mid-1930s break radically with previous verse versions. MACNEICE, a classical scholar as well as a poet, produced the first truly "modern" translation of Aeschylus (1936), one widely acclaimed for its masterful control of rhythm and diction. The style, not surprisingly, is akin in many ways to that of Eliot's deliberately "Aeschylean" plays of the 1930s. Written in the first instance for the stage, MacNeice's version manages to follow Aeschylus metaphor for metaphor while remaining accessible. The result is recognizably Greek in origin, but remains believable as an English response to ancient poetry of the highest order.

HAMILTON (1937) also translates in a modernist manner, although her diction and versification have far less distinction that MacNeice's. The lineation of the choral passages seems largely to follow the structure of clauses rather than any necessity of rhythm, and the language, for all its plainness, can seem rather slack and cliché-ridden. Nevertheless, Hamilton's version is straightforward and clear, and repeated performances have proved its stageworthiness.

The following year saw the publication of THOMSON's *Oresteia*, the first of a number of translations of the entire trilogy that stand out as particularly successful. Actually, Thomson produced two versions. That of 1938 was, so to speak, caught between two worlds: still wedded to *thou* and *ne'er* and occasional "poetic" inversions, but direct and honest in its rendering of Aeschylus' thought. In the choral lyrics, Thomson unobtrusively offered rhythmic responsion between strophe and antistrophe. Auden saw fit to include this version in his widely read *Portable Greek Reader* (1950). Thomson improved it considerably, however, in a revision published in 1965, which eliminated most of the archaisms and decompressed some of the more elaborate syntactical periods, while at the same time retaining a consistent tone that, while not too remote, is not overly colloquial either.

LATTIMORE's *Oresteia* (1953) is described by Robert Lowell with admiration as "so elaborately exact", and that is a fair statement of Lattimore's accomplishment. Lattimore, poet as well as classicist, combines a high degree of literalness with unusual sensitivity to Aeschylean complexities of expression. Like MacNeice, Lattimore has found a way of giving a sense of the otherness of the original while at the same time finding an English idiom that offers a worthy representation of that original.

Robert FAGLES's *Oresteia* (1975) is freer than Lattimore's, more expansive in style, and more redolent of the traditions of English poetry. It is also wordier and at times perhaps a little too lush. Fagles's rendering of the Ares passage is representative:

War, War, the great gold-broker of corpses
holds the balance of the battle on his spear!
Home from the pyres he sends them,
home from Troy to the loved ones,
heavy with tears, the urns brimmed full,
the heroes return in gold-dust,
dear light ash for men.

One might fault here a trace of sentimentality, but in general the translator's response to the emotional implications of the text is one of his strengths, and this *Oresteia* expresses with considerable success the intensity of feeling that radiates from almost every line of Aeschylus.

The most recent versions have all been written explicitly for performance. LOWELL's (1978), unrevised at his death and published posthumously, is a theatrical version; his aim was "to trim, cut, and be direct enough to satisfy my own mind and at a first hearing the simple ears of a theater audience". The result is a compact and powerful dramatic poem but it is not a reliable guide to the literal meaning of the Greek. In addition to the substantial cuts, there are changes in everything from assignment of lines (Pylades is given a small speaking part at the beginning of *Orestes*, Lowell's *Libation Bearers*) to mythological exempla (Zeus, not Cronus, is said to have "castrated his own father"). Nevertheless, Lowell conveys most of the action and much of the imagery of the original with great immediacy.

HARRISON (1981) also wrote his *Oresteia* with performance in mind, in this case a specific production by Sir Peter Hall for which he supplied, in his own words, "a rhythmic libretto for masks, music, and an all male company". This is a translation, rather than the sort of cultural transposition Harrison successfully achieved with his *Phaedra Brittanica*; nevertheless, it is a free translation, inventively employing the resources of alliteration and rhyme. Its style, which has somewhat unfairly been dubbed "neo-*Beowulf*", also features nonce compounds that read like kennings, exotic, archaic, and anachronistic expressions, and much highly rhythmic anapaestic verse – too much, perhaps, as it inevitably produces a sing-song quality. Still, Harrison's *Oresteia* achieves powerful theatrical and emotional excitement. Here is Harrison's version of our passage:

Geldshark Ares god of War
broker of men's bodies
usurer of living flesh
corpse trafficker that god is –

give to WAR your men's fleshgold
and what are your returns?
kilos of cold clinker packed
in army-issue urns

Three more recent translations, explicitly designed for the theatre, aim not so much to reproduce the intricacies of Aeschylus' dense poetic language as to capture his dramatic artistry in words that can convincingly be spoken, and easily understood, from the stage. All of them stay as close to the literal meaning as is compatible with this goal, all strive for accessibility first and foremost. They are thus to be understood to some extent as reactions on the one hand to the relative licence of stage versions such as that of Harrison, and on the other to the difficulty of using "poetic" versions such as Lattimore's or Fagles's for theatrical production. GRENE & DONIGER O'FLAHERTY (1989) actually provide two versions, a complete text and a shortened acting version prepared for a 1986 production at the Court Theater in Chicago by Nicholas Rudall. EWANS's 1995 translation, the most accomplished of the three in its writing, reflects practical theatrical experience as well as scholarly training. Ewans also offers unusually full notes related primarily to production and arguing forcefully for his sometimes unorthodox views about performance conditions in the theatre of Aeschylus' day. MEINECK (1998), too, developed his translation through performance, and the result is a clear and forceful rendering. Its accessibility is enhanced for readers by helpful annotation, making it particularly suitable for classrooms as well as for the stage.

The two most recent poetic versions treat the text with considerable freedom, but to very different effect. SLAVITT (vol. 1 of *Aeschylus* edited by Slavitt and Palmer Bovie, 2 vols, 1998–99), attempting, as he says in his preface, to "make emotional sense" of the text for a contemporary audience, manages some passages with admirable directness, but too often succumbs to archness and odd fluctuations of tone. Metatheatrical asides of a kind never found in Greek tragedy ("We're only the chorus / We can never leave this space. It's one of the rules.") and bits of jarringly contemporary language, such as "Is this stress-related?" (the chorus to Clytemnestra after she has killed Agamemnon) seem trivializing rather than revelatory, especially in the context of Slavitt's metrically formal and emotionally rather low-keyed version. They do not produce a post-modern frisson so much as an impression of indecision about the nature of the text itself.

HUGHES's posthumously published *Oresteia*, no less free in its expansions and variations on the Greek, is far closer to the spirit of the original, and its taut free verse offers a poetic achievement of a different order. Here, for example, is Hughes's expansion / embodiment of the "untranslatable" pun Aeschylus' chorus makes on the name of Helen "destroyer of ships, destroyer of men, destroyer of cities" (*hele-nas, hel-andros, hele-ptolis, Agamemnon*, 689–90):

Not a face or name but a poison
To send whole fleets to perdition
as if their captains were madmen –
Chewing and spitting her name –
Helen. The name Helen
Not so much a name as an earthquake
To bounce a city to burning rubble.
Not a name but a plague
Spreading scream by scream from city to city,
As houses become tombs.

There is an Aeschlyean vigor and boldness of language here. As one might expect from this poet, the translation responds more vividly to the trilogy's dark, chthonian elements than to its Olympian theology, and some unevenness in the writing suggests that final revisions may have been cut short by the author's death. Taken all in all, however, Hughes's *Oresteia* is a major accomplishment and one of the most remarkable translations this great work has ever received.

PETER BURIAN

Further Reading

Brower, Reuben, "Seven Agamemnons", in *Mirror on Mirror: Translation, Imitation, Parody*, Cambridge, Massachusetts: Harvard University Press, 1974

Dover, Kenneth J., "The Speakable and the Unspeakable," in *Greek and the Greeks: Collected Papers*, vol. 1, Oxford: Blackwell, 1987 (originally published in *Essays in Criticism*, 30 (1980))

Ewans, Michael, "Aischylos: For Actors, in the Round", in *The Art of Translation: Voices from the Field*, edited by Rosanna Warren, Boston: Northeastern University Press, 1989

Green, Peter, "Some Versions of Aeschylus: A Study of Tradition and Method in Translating Classical Poetry", in *Essays in Antiquity*, London: John Murray, 1960

Housman, A.E., "Fragment of a Greek Tragedy", in *Collected Poems and Selected Prose*, edited by Christopher Ricks, London: Allen Lane, 1988 (first edition, 1883; numerous subsequent reprints)

Silk, Michael, "Words That Say What They Mean?", review of Hughes's *Oresteia*, *Times Literary Supplement* (17 December 1999)

Prometheus Bound

Prometheus Demotes, after 456 BC; *Prometheus vinctus*

This striking and audacious tragedy, of unknown date, is traditionally ascribed to Aeschylus. In recent years, some scholars have concluded that the play must be the work of a follower of the great dramatist and date from some time after his death in 456 BC. The reasons for this view, involving stylistic – above all metrical – considerations and the apparent influence of Sophistic ideas to be found in the play, are authoritatively set out in M. Griffith, *The Authenticity of "Prometheus Bound"*, Cambridge: Cambridge University Press, 1977. Other scholars accept the authenticity of the play, most regarding it as part of a trilogy written very late in Aeschylus' career. This view is reinforced by the existence of fragments of a *Prometheus Unbound* (*Prometheus Lyomenos*), also attributed to Aeschylus in antiquity and almost certainly written as a sequel to *Prometheus Bound*.

Translations

Browning, Elizabeth Barrett, *Prometheus Bound*, London: A.J. Valpy, 1833; revised version in *Poems*, London: Chapman and Hall, 1850 (this version is reprinted in most modern editions)

Grene, David, *Prometheus Bound*, in *Three Greek Tragedies*, Chicago: University of Chicago Press, 1942; reprinted in *Aeschylus*, Chicago: Chicago University Press, 1969

Hamilton, Edith, *Prometheus Bound*, in her *Three Greek Plays*, New York: Norton, 1937

Havelock, Eric, *Prometheus Bound*, in *The Crucifixion of Intellectual Man*, Boston: Beacon Press, 1951; as *Prometheus*, Seattle: University of Washington Press, 1968

Hilburn, Emily, *Prometheus Bound*, in *The Tenth Muse: Classical Drama in Translation*, edited by Charles Doria, Chicago: Swallow Press, and Athens: Ohio University Press, 1980

Lowell, Robert, *Prometheus Bound*, New York: Farrar Straus, 1969; London: Faber, 1970

Morell, Thomas, *Prometheus in Chains*, London: T. Longman, 1773

Paulin, Tom, *Seize the Fire: A Version of Aeschylus's Prometheus Bound*, London: Faber, 1990

Scully, James and C.J. Herington, *Prometheus Bound*, New York and Oxford: Oxford University Press, 1975

Thoreau, Henry David, *The Prometheus Bound*, in *The Writings of Henry David Thoreau: Translations*, edited by K.P. Van Anglen, Princeton, New Jersey: Princeton University Press, 1986 (originally published in *The Dial*, 3, 1843)

Warner, Rex, *The Prometheus Bound of Aeschylus*, London: Bodley Head, 1947

Prometheus Bound is the only Aeschylean play, apart from the *Oresteia*, to attract numerous individual translations. (For comments on a selection of complete translations of Aeschylus, see the article on the *Oresteia*.) The play's great attraction for translators and readers is no doubt its subject: Prometheus' punishment by and continued defiance of a tyrannical Zeus. *Prometheus Bound* was the first play of Aeschylus to be translated into English, and the myth of the rebellious Titan was the theme also of numerous important poems and plays, especially in the late 18th and early 19th centuries (e.g., Goethe's "Prometheus", Shelley's *Prometheus Unbound*). It is worth noting that at least 12 individual translations appeared between 1822 and 1853, and another 10 in the expansive and optimistic period between 1890 and World War I. "Prometheus", in Karl Marx's famous phrase, "is the foremost saint and martyr in the philosopher's calendar."

The first translation of *Prometheus Bound* was published (with a Greek text and Stanley's Latin version) in 1773, making it the first translation of Aeschylus to appear in English, anticipating Robert Potter's complete plays by four years. The translator, Thomas MORELL (1703–84), was a cleric, classical scholar, and poetaster who had earlier supplied Handel with a number of oratorio texts. His version, in indifferent blank verse and uninspired rhyming lyrics, "though not impregnated with the fire of Aeschylus, has been useful to schoolboys", according to Morell's younger contemporary, John Nichols.

Among the 19th-century translators of *Prometheus Bound* are two writers of great eminence, Elizabeth Barrett Browning and Henry David Thoreau. BROWNING produced two distinct versions, the first published in 1833, when she was 24, the second written in 1845 and published in 1850. It is remarkable that a woman in the England of her day had Greek adequate to this difficult task, since formal study of ancient languages was a tool for entry into the elite professions restricted to men. Like Virginia Woolf at the end of the century, Browning benefited from tutoring provided primarily for her brother. When he went away to school, she persisted in Greek studies on her own. The command of linguistic detail that she achieved is evident in the first version of *Prometheus Bound* in her sensitivity to etymology. For example, at line 241, *erruthmismai*, a verb derived from the noun *rhythmos* (regular motion, rhythm), that here means roughly "I have been brought to order" and is usually translated "I am punished" or the like, retains its musical connotation in Browning's version:

> And I who pitied man, am deem'd myself
> Unmeet for pity, but am *harp'd on thus*
> By Jove's fell hand, dishonor'd spectacle.

In the second version, the metaphor implicit in the etymology is carried even further:

> And I, who pitied man, am deemed myself
> Unworthy of pity; while I render out
> *Deep rhythms* of anguish *'neath the harping hand*
> That strikes me thus–a sight to shame your Zeus.

These passages also suggest the relation of the two versions. Both are written in the combination of blank verse dialogue and rhymed lyrics standard in verse translations of Greek drama until well into the 20th century. The earlier version is a little more straightforward and closer to the literal meaning of the Greek, the later somewhat freer and more elaborate, and willing at last to call the gods by their Greek names rather than the Roman ones long preferred in English literature. Browning herself regarded the second version as a great improvement over the first, which she called "as cold as Caucasus on the snow-peak and as flat as Salisbury plain" (*The Letters of Elizabeth Barrett Browning to Mary Russell Mitford, 1836–1854*, edited by M.B. Raymond and M.R. Sullivan, Waco, Texas: Armstrong Browning Library of Baylor University, 1983, vol. 3, p. 76). Modern readers may prefer the greater simplicity of the first version.

THOREAU (1843) offers a translation of a very different kind, written in rhythmic prose in an attempt to convey precisely the movement of the thought and the force of Aeschylus' metaphorical language. The result, although not slavishly literal, is occasionally wooden and inelegant in its bending of English syntax and word order. On the other hand, there is a sense of the spareness and directness of Aeschylean speech unusual in versions of this period. Like Browning's second version, but unlike other versions of the period, Thoreau prefers the original Greek names for the deities to their Latin equivalents. *Prometheus Bound* was published in the January 1843 issue of *The Dial*, an important American literary periodical of the period, but never republished in Thoreau's lifetime. Van Anglen's excellent edition uses the revisions that Thoreau made in his own copy of *The Dial*.

HAMILTON (1937) is the first modernist translation, in free verse like her *Agamemnon*, but comfortingly old-fashioned in its diction. An effect of noble austerity is achieved largely through simplification of syntax. At some points, Hamilton's approach is very effective – the short, abrupt lines she gives to Io, for example, effectively convey the character's confusion and dismay. Elsewhere the language and rhythms can seem rather slack. Hamilton's version has, in any case, the real merit of providing a speakable performance text.

GRENE's translation (1942), which has achieved wide circulation as part of the Chicago series, offers a reliable guide to the contents of the play but an uninspired representation of its poetry. Grene translates the dialogue into blank verse, with the exception of the opening exchange between Kratos ("Might") and Hephaestus and, inexplicably, the two great speeches where Prometheus sets forth his gifts to humankind, which are rendered as prose. The lyrics have a dignified but slightly musty air. What is missing overall is the linguistic verve appropriate to a play so given to rants and raging.

WARNER's 1947 translation is, like Grene's, readable but somewhat flat. Its virtues are simplicity and directness, its limitation a prosaic quality even where Aeschylus is spacious and grand. Warner's choice of alexandrines as the basic dialogue meter conveys gravity better than excitement, and the free verse of the lyrics feels rather textureless. Nevertheless, Warner achieves clarity and concision, and his version stays helpfully close to the literal meaning.

In the context of a series of adequate but uninspiring versions, the translation by SCULLY & HERINGTON (1975) stands out for its arresting contemporary voice as well as its scrupulous attention to Aeschylus' figurative language. This version is everywhere responsible to the Greek text, but equally loyal to an ideal of the candor and clarity of real speech. Compare, for example WARNER's version of lines 101–05:

What am I saying? I have known all before,
all that shall be, and clearly known; to me,
nothing that hurts shall come with a new face.
So must I bear, as lightly as I can,
that destiny that fate has given me;
for I know well against necessity,
against its strength, no one can fight and win.

with SCULLY & HERINGTON:

Wait, what am I saying ?
I know how it all turns out:
no unforeseen
heartbreaks for me.
I see,
I do what I'm bound to do and take the consequence
as best I can.
I know: no one
wrestles Necessity down.

Because of the shortness of many of the lines, Scully & Herington's *Prometheus Bound* counts 1670 lines to the Greek's 1090, but it is fair to say that few other versions seem more spare or concise. The typographic layout of the text may now seem a little precious, but no one who troubles to read Scully and Herington out loud can doubt that it is a milestone in the translation of *Prometheus Bound*.

HILBURN (1980) gives us version in free verse that is simpler in every way than Scully and Herington – metrically less varied, with sentences shortened and ideas also simplified to a certain extent. Lines 61–62, for example, which Scully and Herington render in American vernacular but with great precision, "He's got to learn: / intellectual that he is, next to Zeus he's stupid," in Hilburn are reduced to, "He must smart to learn from Zeus." Prometheus as sophist has disappeared from the picture. Hilburn aims less at subtlety of thought – and not at all at grandeur – but emphasizes direct communication of dramatic emotion. This is a version that might be very effective on the stage.

It remains to mention two important theatrical adaptations of *Prometheus Bound*, one American and one Irish. LOWELL's (1969) is in prose, keeping most of the structure of the original intact but cutting, adding, and altering a great deal. Lowell describes the result on the title page as "derived from Aeschylus", and in an Author's Note he specifies: "Half my lines are not in the original. But nothing is modernized. There are no tanks or cigarette lighters. No contemporary statesman is parodied. Yet I think my own worries and those of the times seep in." PAULIN's *Seize the Fire* (1990) does have tanks, if no cigarette lighters. Paulin's script, in tightly knit verse that embraces the spoken vernacular, embodies a strong reading of *Prometheus Bound* directly related to contemporary issues: feminism, authoritarianism, corruption, and – particularly in its unsparing treatment of the use of torture and brutality as a political weapon – the troubles in Ireland. *Seize the Fire* is one of a number of fine recent adaptations of Greek tragedy by Irish poets, including Paulin's own *Riot Act* (*Antigone*) and Seamus Heaney's *The Cure at Troy* (*Philoctetes*).

PETER BURIAN

Further Reading

Arnott, Peter D., *An Introduction to the Greek Theatre*, London: Macmillan, and New York, St Martin's Press, 1959, pp. 199–203

Aesop 6th century BC

Greek fabulist

Biography

The Aesop of history was a one-time slave from Thrace, a contemporary of Sappho (early 6th century BC). The Aesop author of fables in a half-legendary figure.

The earliest recension of the Fables is the Greek prose Augustana collection (so called because the manuscript was once at Augsberg), first printed by Schneider in 1812. One of the most diffused Greek redactions is the Accursiana or Planudean collection edited by Maximus Planudes at the beginning of the 14th century.

The Roman fabulist Phaedrus, a freedman of the Emperor Augustus, turned the (now lost) Greek prose Aesop of Demetrius of Phalerum (c.350–283 BC) into Latin iambic senarii (lines of six feet). In the Middle Ages Phaedrus himself was lost from sight (he was not printed until 1596) but was paraphrased in Latin prose by one "Romulus" (a pseudonym), in turn put into witty Latin elegiacs by an author known variously as Walter the Englishman and Anonymous Neveleti (named after his 17th-century editor Isaac Nevelet). This version was a medieval schoolbook: it was heavily glossed, and formed the basis for most medieval vernacular versions. In 1477 Heinrich Steinhöwel published a compendium of fables in Latin and German which added to Romulus and Walter the tales of Avianus, Remigius, Petrus Alfonsi, Poggio and others. In 1515 Martinus Dorpius (alias Maarten van Dorp) issued a Latin compilation which included fables translated or composed by humanists such as Anianus, Abstemius and Barlandus. This edition was commonly used in English schools. Aesop in Latin and later in Greek continued until recently to be part of the English school curriculum.

English translators have drawn on various Aesopic originals, and have allowed themselves to mix-and-match sources and to adapt their material to circumstances. We may discern three traditions of English Aesops: the classical (in which Aesop is regarded as one among several ancient Greek authors), the political, and the pedagogical. Different translators have focused variously on Aesop's didacticism and on his ironic epigrammatic wit, in "familiar" or lapidary style, producing versions for children and for cynics. This survey omits modern retellings for children. English versions other than those listed are to be found in bilingual or polyglot editions.

Most of the Fables are brief tales of animals, although some feature the natural elements and humans. Their subject is prudence. The animals are anthropomorphized to the extent that they speak, and that they display the character traits conventionally assigned to them (crafty fox, simple sheep). However, their concerns are strictly feral: the search for food. Until the modern period, the Fables are invariably accompanied by a moralization, either in the mouth of the character who realizes his folly *in articulo mortis*, or in the words of the narrator. The lengths of the moralizations differ considerably: modern translations, and modern reprints of older translations, often abbreviate or omit them.

Fables

Translations

In general, only versions that had more than one edition are included. Not all editions are noted: dates of subsequent editions are given only as an indication of diffusion.

Anonymous, *Aesop's Fables, with His Life, Morals and Remarks; Fitted for the Meanest Capacities*, London: C. Brown and T. Norris, 2nd edition, 1716; 11th edition, 1754

Barret, William, *Aesop's Fables, with Their Moralls, in Prose and Verse Grammatically Translated; Illustrated with Pictures and Emblems* ..., London: R.D. for Francis Eglesfield, 1651; 1st edition 1639; 19th edition, 1741

Behn, Aphra, *Aesop's Fables with His Life in English, French and Latin; Newly Translated*, London: H. Hills for Francis Barlow, 1687; reprinted 1703

Caxton, William, *Here Begynneth the Book of the Subtyl Historyes and Fables of Esope* ..., Westminster: William Caxton, 1484, and subsequent editions; modern edition, Amsterdam: Theatrum Orbis Terrarum, and New York: Da Capo, 1972

Croxall, Samuel, *Fables of Aesop and Others ... Illustrated with Cuts*, London: Jacob Tonson and J. Watts, 1722; numerous reprints

Dodsley, Robert, *Select Fables of Esop and Other Fabulists*, with an introduction, Birmingham: printed by John Baskerville for R. and J. Dodsley, 1761; several reprints

Handford, S.A., *Fables of Aesop*, illustrations by Brian Robb, Harmondsworth: Penguin, 1954; several reprints, including 1996

Jackson, John, *A New Translation of Aesop's Fables, Adorn'd with Cuts* ..., London: Tho. Tebb, 1708

James, Thomas, *Aesop's Fables*, with an introduction, illustrations by John Tenniel, London: John Murray, 1848, several reprints; selected and adapted by Jack Zipes, Harmondsworth: Penguin, 1996

L'Estrange, Sir Roger, *Fables of Aesop and Other Eminent Mythologists: With Morals and Reflexions*, London: printed for R. Sare, 1692, and subsequent editions; selections reprinted, with an introduction by Kenneth Grahame, Ware: Omega, 1984

Ogilby, John, *The Fables of Aesop Paraphras'd in Verse, and Adorn'd with Sculpture, and Illustrated with Annotations*, illustrated by Francis Cleyn, London: printed by Thomas Warren for Andrew Crook, 1651; text reprinted, with illustrations by Wenceslaus Hollar, London: printed by Thomas Roycroft for the author, 1665

Philipot, Thomas, in *Aesop's Fables, with His Life, in English, French and Latine*, illustrated by Francis Barlow, London: printed by William Godbid for Francis Barlow, 1666

Temple, Robert and Olivia Temple, *Aesop: The Complete Fables*, with an introduction by Robert Temple, Harmondsworth and New York: Penguin, 1998

Townsend, George Fyler, *Three Hundred Aesop's Fables: Literally Translated from the Greek*, with an introduction, illustrated by Harrison Weir, London: Routledge, 1867; several reprints

CAXTON (1484) translated his English prose Aesop from the French of Julien Macho (printed 1480), which followed Steinhöwel's text. There were 11 editions up to 1658. In common with his source, Caxton precedes each fable with a title that summarizes the plot and a promythium that announces the moral; the fable is recounted fully, with some typically medieval doublets ("glad and joyful"); the conclusion is given in a sentence or two. (Subsequent English Aesops title their fables only with the names of the protagonists.) Like so many Aesops before and since, Caxton's was illustrated; the 186 woodcuts were modelled on those of the French edition. However, there is no reason to assume that his Aesop was intended for children.

BARRET's version (1639) was translated from the Latin of Dorpius; Barret's choice of texts and his woodcuts derive from Boissat's French Aesop of 1631. He addresses a mixed audience, saying "To the Reader": "Let children look upon the pictures; look thou further". For the first 118 fables, story and moral are given first in prose and then in verse; for numbers 119–213 (in the 1651 edition at least), there is verse only. In its periodic structure, Barret's prose follows the Latin closely; hence the "grammatically translated" of the title page:

> An eagle having gotten a cockle, could not pluck out the fish by force or art. A crow coming unto her gives her counsell. She perswadeth her to soar aloft, and to cast down the cockle from on high, upon the stones ...

The pentameter couplets are amplifications. Reissued in an augmented edition in 1651, Barret was regularly republished in the 18th century, without his name, replacing Caxton as the standard low-cost Aesop.

The commentaries with which OGILBY glossed his 81 verse fables (1651) are the first to make topical political statements, here critical of Cromwell. His renditions are full and leisurely, with obvious ambitions to be fine writing:

> What is the crow that by a cunning plot
> a piece of cheese had got?
> Or sherking rook, or chough, or pye?
> Some bold affirm, as boldly some deny.
> But sure I am it was the draw or crow,
> And I can prove it to be so,
> that robbed the king his master of his meat;
> and now, to make his cozenage more compleat
> on man, his king's king, put the second cheat ...

The morals are brief, in two couplets. Each book has scholarly annotations appended.

PHILIPOT's English versions (1666) were published in a deluxe trilingual edition by Francis Barlow, whose engravings were doubtless the chief feature of the volume. Fable and moral are given in French and Latin prose and English verse. The English text is distinguished by its brevity and by being engraved on the plate beneath the illustration rather than set in type:

> A graine of barly and a jem did dwell
> Ith' casket of a dunghill as their cell
> Till the rude clawes of a keene hungry cock
> Did that dull cabinett of dirt unlock
> And having rak't forth with cheap disdaine
> Wa[i]ves ye bright jem to taste ye coorser graine.
> [Moral:]
> Some earthly natures choycer pleasures find
> In sordid joyes then in a vertuous mind.

In the 1687 edition of Barlow's fables, the Latin and French texts were revised and Philipot's verses were replaced by BEHN's (1687). The fable is no more than two couplets, with another for the moral. "City Mouse and Country Mouse", 14 lines in Philipot, is now compressed into an epigram:

> The city mouse invites her country guest
> To tast the daintyes of a city feast
> But oft disturbed by interrupted noys,
> They hide, and fear his appetite destroys.
> Morall:
> The great the hurry of the world endure,
> And tis the country life alone's secure.

Sir Roger L'ESTRANGE translated his prose Aesop (1692) from Dorpius, whose edition was commonly used at Oxford and Cambridge. His preface devotes much attention to the pedagogical aspect of the fable. In his edition, the fable is brief (sometimes only two sentences); the moral is brief, general and abstract; and the reflection is long and political. Although the work is in de luxe folio format, there are no illustrations. L'Estrange is a Tory writing in defence of absolute monarchy. His style typifies 17th-century Senecan style, colloquial and pithy by turns: "A certain fox spy'd out a raven upon a tree with a morsel in his mouth, that set his chops a watering; but how to come at it was the question". Dodsley (1761) found him "the grossest [example] of the indelicate and low". No subsequent version had such extensive morals.

The ANONYMOUS late 17th-century prose translation went through about a dozen editions between 1716 (the second edition) and 1800. Despite the reference on the title page to "the meanest capacities", this is not the Jackson version. Each fable comprises an illustration, the story, told economically, a very brief moral and a rather sanctimonious "Remark", slightly shorter than the story. The translator makes reference to Scripture more frequently than do other English versions.

JACKSON's (1708) translation is an answer to Barret's. It is explicitly pedagogical, and deliberately moderately priced, "fixt like the Golden Medium betwixt the courseness and grossness of the vulgate translations of Aesop, and the over-polite labour of Sir Roger". Fable and moral, in prose, are brief, in a few sentences; the verse "reflections" are two to six lines. The title page advertises a "Plain, Easy and Familiar Style, adapted to the Meanest Capacities".

CROXALL's prose translation of 1722 had 196 oval woodcuts by Elisha Kirkhall. It is dedicated to the five-year-old George, Baron Halifax, and the style is not inconsistent with a young readership. The fable and its application are of equal length. In his preface, Croxall attacks L'Estrange for his Catholicism. Townsend (1867) thought that Croxall's version was padded out and that it deviated so far from his original as to constitute a parody.

> An honest, plain, sensible, country-mouse, is said to have entertain'd at his hole, one day, a fine mouse of the town. Having formerly been playfellows together, they were old acquaintance, which served as an apology for the visit ...

DODSLEY (1761) rendered his fables at length, but relegated the one-line morals to an index, as the fable "leaves the reader to collect the moral". In his long prefatory essay he declares the style of fables "should be familiar, but it should be elegant", citing La Fontaine as an exemplar. The publisher's preface to the 1824 edition, for instance, claims Dodsley's "principal aim was to select such Fables as would make the strongest and most useful impressions on the minds of the youth", but his introduction suggests a sophisticated audience. There are illustrations.

JAMES (1848) tends to fullness in the fables and brevity in the morals. He intended to translate from the earliest known source, but allowed himself leave to conflate versions: "this method of translation – wholly without excuse if applied to a genuine classic – will perhaps be deemed admissible for a popular volume of Aesopean Fables". He acknowledges his debts to L'Estrange, Croxall and Dodsley. James's was one of the most reprinted versions of the 19th century, and is still in print.

TOWNSEND (1867) surveys previous English Aesops and presents his prose translation from the newly discovered 1st-century AD Babrius (and other sources) as possessing a modern scholarly rigour: it is "as nearly a literal translation as possible of the Greek text" which sacrifices "the smoothness and thoroughly English tone" of its predecessors for "a nearer approach to the spirit, thoughts and (in some cases) to the epigrammatic terseness of the original". His morals are limited to one line or are lacking.

HANDFORD (1954) departs from his predecessors in giving his fables titles that comment on the action: "A Lesson Learned Too Late". His style is concise but natural. Its status as a Penguin Classic has made this the most read English Aesop of the second half of the 20th century.

Handford's successors in the Penguin Classics, TEMPLE & TEMPLE (1998) translate entire the 358 Greek fables brought together from various manuscript sources by Emile Chambry in his Paris edition of 1927. The translators include the original morals, but without enthusiasm. They have made a point of rendering accurately the species of animals and birds: thus the creature that, transformed into a woman, retains nevertheless her feral instincts, is in Handford (no. 96) a cat and in the Temples (no. 251) a house-ferret. They also include a few unseemly fables, such as those of the coprophiliac camel and ass, and the bisexual hyena. Their style of translation is very much like that of Handford: the proportion between tale and moral is the same, and the expression modern but not overly colloquial.

BARRY TAYLOR

Further Reading

Alberge, Dalya, "A Talent Lost in Translation", *The Times* (2 December 1998)

Allot, Terence, " 'Brutes Turn'd Politicians': The Seventeenth-Century Fable", *New Comparison*, 7 (Summer 1989) pp. 20–32

Blackham, H.J., *The Fable as Literature*, London: Athlone Press, 1985

Daniel, Stephen H., "Political and Philosophical Uses of Fables in Eighteenth-Century England", *Eighteenth Century*, 23 (1982) pp. 151–71

Eames, Marian, "John Ogilby and His Aesop", *Bulletin of New York Public Library*, 65/2 (1961) pp. 71–88

Hale, David G., "William Barret's *The Fables of Aesop*", *Papers of the Bibliographical Society of America*, 64 (1970) pp. 283–94

Hale, David G., "Aesop in Renaissance England", *The Library*, 5th series, 27 (1972) pp. 116–25

Hobbs, Anne Stevenson (editor), *Fables*, London: Victoria and Albert Museum, 1986

Hodnett, Edward, "Elisha Kirkhall c.1682–1742: Master of White-line Engraving in Relief and Illustrator of Croxall's *Aesop*", *Book Collector*, 15 (1976) pp. 195–209

Hodnett, Edward, *Francis Barlow: First Master of English Book Illustration*, London: Scolar Press, 1978

Hodnett, Edward, *Aesop in England: The Transmission of Motifs in Seventeenth-Century Illustrations of Aesop's Fables*, Charlottesville: University Press of Virginia, 1979

Perry, Ben Edwin (editor and translator), *Phaedrus and Babrius*, London: Heinemann, and Cambridge, Massachusetts: Harvard University Press, 1965 (Loeb Classical Library)

African Languages

Literary Translation into English

Although there is a great deal of debate today over whether African writers should use their indigenous languages or European languages of colonization (English, French and Portuguese) in literary creation, it is worth noting that African literature continues to be expressed in all these African and European languages. In addition, translation between the literatures in question has developed during the 20th century as a result of colonization and contact between the peoples. This essay seeks to survey major translations from African languages into English, laying particular emphasis on the various types of indigenous languages, their special characteristics and resources, major differences from English, and a historical overview of African-language literature in English translation.

Generally speaking, British colonial policy in Africa encouraged the development of indigenous languages for literary creativity, and the translation of religious and literary works, at the outset from English into the local languages and subsequently from African languages into English. In fact, the early British missionaries, in their drive to convert Africans to Christianity, felt that their evangelization mission would be more successful if the message of God were propagated in the languages of the people. Consequently, many of the indigenous languages were transposed to writing, and vocabularies as well as grammars produced; schools were opened to educate converts and the printing press was introduced. In South Africa, for example, after the arrival of the British in 1806, the missionaries transposed one of the local languages, Xhosa, to writing, opened a school, and set up a printing press at Lovedale in 1824. Other printing presses were founded later: the Marianhill Mission press in Natal for the publication of works in Zulu and the Sesuto Book Depot in Morija in 1862 for works in Sotho. In addition, newspapers and journals were published in Xhosa and other local languages; the Xhosa-English magazine, *Ikwezi* (Morning Star), was started in 1841, to be replaced later by *Indaba* (The News) in 1862. Other South African languages were also transposed to writing; writing in Sotho started in the 1880s, while Zulu grammars, glossaries and translations appeared in 1883. This policy eventually made some Africans use their mother tongues for literary creation, while others used English; indeed, many literary works were produced in the local languages, and some of them were translated into English.

Translation was thus done for mainly religious, educational and cultural reasons. Since works in indigenous languages could be read only by a few members of specific tribes or localities, efforts were made to translate some of them into English so as to reach a wider audience of non-Africans and other Africans who wanted to know about literature in African languages other than their own. However, it is worth noting that many works in African languages were not translated until after World War II. The major African written languages that will serve as a broad basis for our study will include, in particular, Swahili, Amharic, Arabic, Hausa, Zulu, Xhosa and Yoruba.

African indigenous languages, often estimated at 800 in number, may be broadly classified as follows (Finnegan, 1970): (a) the Niger–Congo group, comprising Bantu languages (Zulu, Swahili, Luba, Xhosa, etc.) as well as sub-families such as the West Atlantic, Kwa, Gur, Mandingo, Ijaw and Central and Adama-Eastern languages; (b) the Afro-Asiatic family, made up of Arabic and languages such as Hausa spoken in most of North Africa, the Horn and East Africa, and a vast area near Lake Chad; (c) the Central Saharan group, including languages to the north and the east of Lake Chad; (d) the Click (or Khoisan) family, made up of the Bushman and Hottentot languages; and (e) the Macrosudanic group, comprising various Sudanic languages found around the Nile–Congo divide and eastwards in the Nilotic and Great Lakes region of East Africa.

Although the languages are grouped under different families and each language has its own specificity and resources as regards structure and vocabulary, there are certain features that are common to them all, a fact due perhaps mainly to long contact with one another. A major distinctive feature of African languages, excluding the Afro-Asiatic family, is tone (pitch) as an element of their structures. Tone is prominent in several West African languages and is significant, as it affects grammatical form and lexical meaning; in Yoruba, Ibo or Ewe, for example, the meanings of words with exactly the same phonetic form may differ totally according to the tone of each, while the tense of a verb, the case of a noun, even the difference between the affirmative and the negative can also sometimes vary according to the various tones used. Furthermore, nouns are commonly classified in a rather complex manner; for example, Bantu languages have systems of noun classes based on the prefixes used and it is possible to form new words from a few roots by using affixes, agglutination and internal vowel changes. In addition, the structure is based on grammatical class-gender, with concordial agreement; this means that each class of nouns has a typical prefix which, in one form or another, is repeated throughout the sentence in which the noun occurs. Sometimes by changing the prefix of a particular word, it is possible to change its class, and thereby, its meaning or connotation. In many cases, praise names and ideophones account for a significant amount of the lexical resources of African languages. Ideophones, which to some extent function in the same way as adverbs and are onomatopoeic, seem more like interjections in actual use and grammatical form; they often appear duplicated. All in all, African languages tend to have wide vocabularies and can easily adopt foreign terms. As regards verbs, although the forms for conjugation of verbs are regular, they are often complex and have a wide variety of moods, implications, aspects and tenses. It is also common to have words derived from verbs in many ways as, for example, in Zulu. The sounds, for their part, could be said to be predominantly vocalic in Bantu languages; there are no neutral or indeterminate vowels, and consonant combinations are generally avoided.

Some of the main differences between African languages and English stem primarily from the fact that most African languages are tonal while English is stress-timed. The sounds of ideophones in African languages often convey aspects that are not normally associated with sound in English; for example, colour, taste, smell, silence, etc. Moreover, the rather complex noun classifications and grammatical class-gender with concordial agreement found in the structure of many African languages do not exist in English. Generally speaking, Bantu language structure does not, as does English, follow a more or less rigid word order; consequently, there are many possible ways in which, by changing word order or terminology, various shades of meaning can be expressed precisely. In English, to express such shades of meaning, one would have to resort to emphatic stress, which is sometimes ambiguous. Furthermore, verse rhythms and metres in African languages often draw on the grammatical and syntactic possibilities of the languages, which are not, as in English, bound by a fixed word order. At the level of discourse, African languages are generally oratorical, with a large stock of proverbs, praise names, etc.

All these differences, of course, have certain implications for the translation of African language literatures into English; the translator would need to be familiar with them.

Many literary works in some written African languages have

been rendered in English. Not many African languages, however, have been translated into English. While translations have concerned a variety of literary genres (prose, drama and poetry), items from many oral traditions (tales, legends, epics, etc.) of specific tribes and languages have been translated into English under the names of individual writers or as collections and anthologies.

Translations of Swahili works into English have often been published as bilingual editions. For example, Hemedi bin Abdallah's *Utenzi wa Vita vya Wadachi Kutamaliki Mrima* (1891) was translated as *The German Conquest of the Swahili Coast, 1891 AD* in 1955 by J.W.T. Allen, and Hamad Abdallah's *Utenzi wa Abdirrahmani na Sufiyani* appeared in 1961, translated by Roland Allen, under the title *The History of Abdurrahman and Sufian*. J.W.T. Allen also translated some Swahili classical narrative verse (*tendi*) which appeared in 1971 in a bilingual edition as *Tendi*, while Ali A. Jahadhmy published a wide selection of Swahili poetry, produced by various translators, in an *Anthology of Swahili Poetry* in 1975. Similarly, Jan Knappert translated and published Swahili verse in *Traditional Swahili Poetry* in 1967, *Swahili Islamic Poetry* in 1971, *A Choice of Flowers* (UK; US as *An Anthology of Swahili Love Poetry*) in 1972, and *Four Centuries of Swahili Verse: A Literary History and Anthology* in 1979. Lyndon Harries also translated various forms of Swahili verse in *Swahili Poetry* in 1962 and the poems of Ahmad Nassir bin Juma Bhalo of Mombasa under the title *Poems from Kenya* in 1966; he rendered and published Said Bakari bin Sultani, Ahmed's chronicle of events of the 19th-century Comoros as *The Swahili Chronicle of Ngazija* in 1977.

As regards translations from Amharic (the official language of Ethiopia), it is worth noting that fiction and drama have figured largely. Translations of fiction include the first Amharic work of fiction, "Tobbya", written in 1900 by Afarawak Gabra Iyasus, which was translated in 1964 by Taddesse Tamrat under the same title; Makonnen Endalkachew's short novel rendered into English in 1955 by K.M. Simon as *The City of the Poor*; and Taddesse Liben's short story translated in 1961 under the title "Truth: A Modern Ethiopian Short Story" by Paulos Quanna. Turning now to plays, Lidj Endelkachew translated Makonnen Endalkachew's biblical drama into English in 1955 as *King David the Third, King of Gondar* while Stephen Wright rendered the same playwright's three-act drama on the Italian occupation of Ethiopia in the 1930s under the title *The Voice of Blood* in 1955. Menghistu Lemma translated his own drama into English: *The Marriage of Unequals*, a two-act play on modern Ethiopian life, was published in 1970, and his satirical drama, *Telfobekise* (1962), was rendered in English and published under the title *Snatch and Run; or, Marriage by Abduction* in 1964.

From Arabic, Mohammed Al-Maghili's essay on Moslem kingship was translated into English in 1932 by T.H. Baldwin as *The Obligations of Princes*, while A.D.H. Bivar published "A Manifesto of the Fulani *Jihad*" which contains his translation of Usuman dan Fodio's (1754–1817) *Wathigat ahl al-Sudan* [Document for the Black People] in 1961. Furthermore, Usuman dan Fodio's prose work relating to Islamic legal theory which was completed in 1806, *Bayan Wujub al-Hijrah, 'Ala 'L-'bad*, was translated in 1978 by F.H. El Masari and published in English and Arabic under the same title. Similarly B.G. Martin translated Usuman dan Fodio's early 19th-century poem, *Ta'lim al Ikhwan* ("Instruction of the Brethren") in 1967 in a study "Unbelief in the Western Sudan: Uthman dan Fodio's Ta'lim al Ikhwan", and he published his translation of two poems by al-Hajj Umar the same year in a paper "Two Poems by al-Hajj Umar" published in *Salaga: The Struggle for Power*, edited by J.A. Braimah and J.R. Goody. Another prominent translator of Arabic works into English was Sir Herbert Richmond Palmer: from 1913 to 1915, in an article "An Early Fulani Conception of Islam", published in two instalments in the *Journal of the African Society*, he translated Usuman dan Fodio's early 19th-century *Tanbih al-Ikhwan* ("Warning to the Brethren") into English; in 1931, he translated into English *In Fak el Maisuri* (1806–09), by Sultan Muhammad Bello of Sokoto, in the work *The Carthaginian Voyage to West Africa*; in 1926 Ahmed Ibn Fartua's 1583 historical document was translated by him under the title *History of the First Twelve Years of the Reign of Idris Alooma of Bornu (1571–1583)* and in 1928 the "Kano Chronicle", written in Arabic between 1883 and 1893, was published in English, along with translations of oral traditions from various languages, in *Sudanese Memoirs*.

As for translations from Hausa, Abubakar Tafawa Balewa's 1934 novel *Shaihu Umar* was translated into English in 1967 by Mervyn Hiskett, who published his translations of various Islamic verse genres in 1975 in *A History of Hausa Islamic Verse*. Furthermore, some works have been adapted into English, resulting in less than full translations: Muhammadu Bello's *Gand'oki*, a 1934 novel, was adapted in 1971 under the title *The Adventures of the Warrior Gand'oki*, while Abubakar Imam's *Ruwan Bagaja* (1934) was adapted as *Ruwan Bagaja, The Water of Cure* in 1971. Many Hausa poems have also been translated into English: R.A. Adelaye and F.H. El-Masri published "*Sifoffin Shehu*: An Autobiography and Character Study of Uhtman b. Fudi in Verse" in 1966; D.W. Arnott translated " 'The Song of the Rains': A Hausa Poem by Na'ibi S. Wali" in 1968; Stanislaus Pilaszewicz translated some of Al-Hadji Umaru's poetry in the article " 'The Arrival of the Christians': A Hausa Poem on the Colonial Conquest by Al-Hadji Umaru" in 1974 and " 'The Song of Poverty and Wealth': A Hausa Poem on Social Problems by Al-Hadji Umaru" in 1975; Neil Skinner and Kabir Galadanci translated Akilu Aliyu's *Wak'ar Soja* ("Song for the Soldiers") in an article entitled "Wak'ar Soja – A Hausa Poem of the Civil War" in 1973; and Neil Skinner translated Aliyu Na-Mangi's *Wak'ar K'azama* ("Song of the Slattern") and other poems in an article entitled "The Slattern – A Theme of Hausa Poetry" in 1971.

Translations from Zulu include historical works, epics and poetry. J. Boxwell translated John Dube's 1933 historical novel, *Insila kaTshaka*, into English in 1951 as *Jege the Bodyservant of King Tshaka*, while H.C. Lugg rendered Magema Fuze's (b. 1840) historical work, *Abantu Abamnyama Lapa Bavela Ngakhona*, into English as *The Black People and Whence They Came: A Zulu View* in 1979. Mazisi Kunene published English translations of his own works, *Anthem of the Decades: A Zulu Epic* in 1981 and *Emperor Shaka the Great: A Zulu Epic* in 1979. Florence Louie Friedman translated Benedict Wallet Vilakazi's poems, *Inkondlo kaZulu* (1935) and *Amal' Ezulu* (1945) into English verse (from the literal translations of D.M. Malcolm and J. Mandlenkosi) in *Zulu Horizons* in 1973, while Mazisi Kunene published translations of Zulu verse in *Zulu Poems* in 1970 and *The Ancestors and the Sacred Mountain: Poems* in 1982.

From Xhosa, translations into English include Enoch Guma's novel *u-Nomalizo* (1917), rendered by J. Wallis in 1928 as *Nomalizo; or, "The Things of This Life Are Sheer Vanity"*, and Samuel Edward Krune Mqhayi's fiction, *Ityala Lamawele* (1914), translated by August Collingwood under the title "The Lawsuit of the Twins" in 1966 as articles in *New Africa*. Furthermore, A.C. Jordan (with the assistance of Priscilla P. Jordan) translated his classic 1940 novel, *Ingqumbo Yeminyanya*, as *The Wrath of the Ancestors* in 1980, while Wandile Francis Kuse rendered some of Mqhayi's poetry and prose in the article "The Form and Themes of Mqhayi's Poetry and Prose" in 1977. Other poems by Mqhayi ("Ah Velile" and "A Silimela") were also translated in 1977 by Jeff Opland in an article "Two Unpublished Poems by S.E.K. Mqhayi".

Translations into English from Yoruba (a Kwa language spoken in southwest Nigeria) have been mostly of novels and drama. Wole Soyinka translated D.O. Fagunwa's 1938 novel of enchantment, *Ogboju Ode Ninu Igbo Irunamle* into English in 1968 as *The Forest of a Thousand Daemons: A Hunter's Saga*. In addition, D.O. Fagunwa's folklorist novel, *Igbo Olodumare*, first published in 1949, was translated into English by Gabriel Ajiboye Ajadi in 1984 in his doctoral dissertation entitled "A Critical Introduction for and an Annotated Translation of D.O. Fagunwa's *Igbo Olodumare* ('The Forest of God')". As regards drama, Duro Ladipo's 1964 Yoruba folk operas, *Oba Koso*, *Oba Moro* and *Oba Waja*, were translated into English by Ulli Beier as *Three Yoruba Plays* in 1964. Another drama by Ladipo, *Moremi* (1967) was also translated by Beier in *Three Nigerian Plays* in 1967. In 1972, Kole Ogunmola produced his own English operatic version of Amos Tutuola's 1952 novel, *The Palm-Wine Drinkard*, under the title *Omuti*.

Other major translations of literary works from African languages into English include Yohanna Abdallah's *Chiikala Cha Wayao* [The Olden Times of the Yaos] written in the Yao language (Malawi), translated by Meredith Sanderson and published in 1919 as *The Yaos*; some Fante (Ghana) poems translated by Robert Acquaah in 1920 under the title *Fante Classical Poems*; Okot p'Bitek's long poem in Acoli (Uganda), *Wer pa Lawino* (1969), translated by the author himself as *Song of Lawino* (1966); Sahle Sellassies's novel in Chaha (Ethiopia), translated by Wolf Leslau in 1964 as *Shinega's Village*, and Richard K.P. Pankhurst's translation of historical documents from Ge'ez (Ethiopia) into English as *The Ethiopian Royal Chronicles* (1967).

Much of African oral literature has been translated; in particular, G.P. Lestrade translated some Venda (Transvaal) stories and published them as a collection under the title *Some Venda Folktales* in 1942; Henry Callaway worked on Zulu oral tradition and published *Nursery Tales, Traditions and Histories of the Zulus* in 1868; and Sigismund Wilheld Koelle in 1854 published *African Native Literature; or, Proverbs, Tales, Fables, and Historical Fragments in the Kanuri or Bornu Language, to Which are Added a Translation of the above and a Kanuri–English Vocabulary*.

In order to help translators solve some of their problems, reference grammars and terminology books such as dictionaries, lexicons and glossaries between English and certain African languages have been published. These include *Dictionary of the Amharic Language* (1841) by Karl W. Isenberg; *Vocabulary of the Hausa Language* (1862) by James F. Schön; *Vocabulary of Six East-African Languages* (1850) by Johann Ludwig Krapf; *English-Kikuyu Vocabulary* (1904) by A.W. McGregor; and *Isizulu: A Grammar of the Zulu Language* (1859) by Lewis Grout. The usual practice nowadays is to compile dictionaries and glossaries for the African languages transposed from speech to writing.

MOSES N. NINTAI

Further Reading

Finnegan, Ruth, *Oral Literature in Africa*, Oxford: Clarendon Press, 1970

Gérard, Albert S., *African Language Literatures*, Harlow: Longman, and Washington, DC: Three Continents Press, 1981

Nintai, Moses, "Mapping Transference: Problems of African Literature and Translation from French into English" (dissertation), University of Warwick, 1993

Westley, David, "African-Language Literature in English Translation: An Annotated Bibliography", *Research in African Literatures*, 18/4 (1987) pp. 499–509

Bella Akhmadulina 1937–

Russian poet and translator

Biography

Born Izabella Akhatovna Akhmadulina in Moscow, 10 April 1937, her father a Tartar, her mother Russian. She was brought up in Moscow but was evacuated to Kazan during World War II. After graduating from high school in Moscow she attended the Gor'kii Literary Institute, Moscow, 1955–60, but was expelled for writing "apolitical" verse. In 1960 she travelled in Central Asia. She married 1) the poet Evgenii Evtushenko in 1954 (divorced); 2) Iurii Nagibin in 1962 (separated 1967); 3) Gennadii Mamlin; 4) Boris Messerer in 1974; two daughters.

Akhmadulina worked briefly for the newspaper *Metrostroevets*. She began her literary career as one of the "New Wave" poets of the post-Stalin "thaw", 1953–63. Her first published poem, "Rodina" [Homeland], appeared in 1955, her first volume of verse, *Struna* [String], in 1962. There followed the next year two long poems, "Skazka o dozhde" ("A Tale about Rain") and "Moia rodoslovnaia" [My Family Tree]. In 1967 there were two more long poems, one of which gave its name to the major collection *Oznob* (*Fever*), 1968. In 1969 came *Uroki muzyki* [Music Lessons]. After a period of near silence, Akhmadulina began to publish again in the 1970s: *Stikhi* [Poems], 1975; *Svecha* [Candle], *Metel'* [Blizzard] and *Sny o Gruzii* [Dreams of Georgia], all 1977. Akhmadulina participated in the unofficial almanac *Metropol'* with the experimental prose story "Mnogo sobak i sobaka" ("Many Dogs and the Dog"), 1979. Her readings of her own works have drawn large audiences. She has also translated, notably from Georgian. She was made a member of the American Academy of Arts and Letters in 1977 and at home received the State Prize for Literature, 1989.

Translations

Selections and Anthologies of Poetry

Carlisle, Olga (editor), in *Poets on Street Corners: Portraits of Fifteen Russian Poets* (parallel texts), with English commentary, New York: Random House, 1968 (includes 6 poems by Akhmadulina, translated by Stanley Noyes, Jean Valentine, and Olga Carlisle)

Dutton, Geoffrey and Igor Mezhakoff-Koriakin, *Fever and Other New Poems*, New York: Morrow, 1969; London: Peter Owen, 1970 (contains 22 poems; also published in *New Poems: Yevtushenko, Akhmadulina*, Melbourne, Australia: Sun, 1968)

Feinstein, Elaine, in *Three Russian Poets: Margarita Aliger, Yunna Moritz, Bella Akhmadulina*, translated by Feinstein, Manchester: Carcanet, 1979 (includes 10 poems by Akhmadulina)

Maddock, Mary, in *Three Russian Women Poets: Anna Akhmatova, Marina Tsvetayeva, Bella Akhmadulina*, translated by Maddock, with an introduction by Edward J. Brown, Trumansburg, New York: Crossing Press, 1983 (includes 19 poems by Akhmadulina)

Reeve, F.D., *The Garden: New and Selected Poetry and Prose* (parallel texts), New York: Holt, 1990; London: Marion Boyars, 1991 (contains 34 poems and 3 prose pieces)

Bella Akhmadulina's fame rose during the literary renaissance following Stalin's death (a period known as "the Thaw", 1953–63), when young poets such as Yevgeny Yevtushenko and Andrei Voznesensky began to be published freely and widely. These new poets were immensely popular and held reputations as rebellious figures. Their books sold out within a few hours, and their public readings were held before large, enthusiastic crowds in concert halls and stadiums (as Olga Carlisle describes in *Poets on Street Corners*, 1968). Responding to the new movement, American, British, and Australian translators produced anthologies of the "new wave" of contemporary Russian poetry, emphasizing the great outpouring of talent that followed when the constraints of the Stalin regime were lifted, or at least eased. Most of the anthologies of this period contain some of Akhmadulina's early poems (Carlisle, 1968, examined here, is an example).

As one of a handful of contemporary Russian women poets who has achieved recognition abroad, Akhmadulina has been extensively anthologized as a woman writer; two collections of Russian women poets are examined below (Maddock, 1983, and Feinstein, 1979). Akhmadulina's poems have also cropped up in journals such as *Russian Literature Triquarterly* and *International Poetry Review*. Only two books of translations devoted entirely to her poetry have appeared in English (Dutton, 1969, and Reeve, 1990). The latter, although named after Akhmadulina's 1987 collection *Sad* (*The Garden*), is not a translation of that volume, but rather a selection of poems from many of Akhmadulina's collections. Thus there exists no translated collection which shows the interesting way that Akhmadulina builds poems around a particular theme, as she does for example in *Taina* [The Secret] (1983), and *The Garden*. Readers are referred to Sonia Ketchian's *The Poetic Craft of Bella Akhmadulina* (1993) for an exploration of this aspect of her work. There has as yet been no translation of Akhmadulina's most recent (post-1988) work, collected in volumes entitled *Larets I kliuch* [The Chest and the Key] (1944), *Sozertsanie stekliannogo sharika* [Contemplating the Crystal Ball] (1997), and others.

Akhmadulina's lyrics incorporate elements of fantasy and humor, puns, archaic language, and folkloric motifs. Critics have spoken of the spontaneity and playfulness of her poetry, and the way in which she speaks of commonplace objects and events in uncommon, fresh terms. Prior to 1975, her poetry tended to focus on aspects of contemporary life and nature; in the middle period, 1975 to 1985, the focus was on poetry itself and the word in relation to nature; and in the later period, as Ketchian observes, the poet treats philosophical and religious themes. Akhmadulina's poems are rhymed and use conventional meters; she tends to favor iambic four-, five-, and six-foot metres. Occasionally, she varies the number of feet per line in a single poem for effect.

Because one of Akhmadulina's main devices is the image (especially the startling image), translations of her poetry, as Mary Maddock notes, can hope to be relatively successful. An example is her phrase "the rain ... crawled to me on its belly", which is likely to be striking in any language. But translators have spoken of the difficulty of rendering her other devices – plays on words, archaisms, neologisms, near rhyme, and linguistic innovations. Translators are divided about the importance of preserving Akhmadulina's use of meter and rhyme. For example, while Dutton and Reeve attempt to preserve meter and rhyme, even if meaning must be changed somewhat, Feinstein and Maddock dispense with rhyme and, to some extent, meter. The principle of "following" a poet's rhyme and meter in a translation is certainly debatable, particularly when one is dealing with a representative of a "new wave" of poetry. Akhmadulina's poetry must be viewed within the context of modern Russian poetry, in which the use of conventional rhyme and meter patterns – albeit with innovations – is commonplace. The same is not true in the British-American context. Since contemporary English-language poets have moved away from conventional rhyme and meter, would not Akhmadulina's rhymes and meters rendered in English sound trite, comic or old-fashioned to an Anglo-American audience? If Akhmadulina's and her contemporaries' innovations in rhyme, punctuation, and meter are difficult to render into English, would it not be better to render innovation in another way – say, through the *absence* of traditional rhyme and meter? Akhmadulina herself used a similar guiding principle as translator of Georgian poetry into Russian. In a 1960 essay she stated:

> I must admit that I never tried to observe the external forms of a poem: meter, type of rhyme ... I just wanted to make them contemporary Russian poems, which would feel intimate to the contemporary Russian reader.

CARLISLE (1968) includes six poems by Akhmadulina in her collection. The poems were "adapted" by English-language poets from literal versions. Stanley NOYES, Jean VALENTINE and CARLISLE herself worked on the Akhmadulina poems. The Russian originals appear on facing pages. None of these translations is rhymed or follows a conventional metrical pattern. They vary in terms of approach: Carlisle's and Noyes's are close in content to the originals, while Valentine's are quite freely – and quite skillfully – adapted.

DUTTON & MEZHAKOFF-KORIAKIN (1969) translate 22 of Akhmadulina's early poems written after the publication of her first book, *Struna* [String] (1962). They include some important longer lyrics: "Fever" and "A Tale about Rain in Several Episodes", as well as two poems addressed to Marina Tsvetaeva. Generally speaking, these translations are very close in meaning to the originals. They are accurate and do not simplify or paraphrase Akhmadulina's strange or difficult wording. The translators follow Akhmadulina's meter and rhyme schemes fairly exactly. Occasionally the rhyme sounds far-fetched, or the need to keep to the rhyme scheme forces the translators to introduce a new idea or image, but on the whole the rhymes and meter are done skillfully.

MADDOCK's 1983 collection includes 19 lyrics, mostly from Akhmadulina's early work. She does not attempt to preserve rhyme or meter, but there are some felicitous internal and external rhymes and assonances, and a general rhythmic pulse, which lend the poems coherence. Her translations can be characterized as spare: she uses few words to accomplish Akhmadulina's images, often to very good effect. Since Akhmadulina herself does not economize words, some of Maddock's rephrasings may be seen as simplifications, e.g., Akhmadulina's line "Here is the sound of rain, as if the sound of a dombra" becomes in Maddock's translation "The rain sounds like a dombra." However, these are appealing, readable, poetic translations which preserve the meaning and freshness of Akhmadulina's poetry.

FEINSTEIN (1979) translates 10 poems, including the long cycle "Twelve Lyrics from Rain". Perhaps because she used literal versions of these poems rather than working directly from the Russian, Feinstein's translations often paraphrase and explain Akhmadulina's difficult images. Sometimes her interpretations of the poems serve to make them more accessible for a non-Russian reader, e.g., in Feinstein's translation of the poem "I Swear," addressed to Marina Tsvetaeva, an oblique mention of Aleksandr Pushkin is clarified as referring to a statue of the great poet.

REEVE's 1990 book contains 34 poems from various periods and three prose pieces and thus constitutes the most complete and up-to-date collection of Akhmadulina's work in English. The original Russian is printed on the facing page for all of the poems. Reeve strives to preserve not only meaning but also measure and rhyme, with good success in many passages. Occasionally inappropriate diction or confusing phrasing is used in order to keep to a rhyme scheme, and there are a few mistranslations. In general, however, these translations are appealing and reliable.

LAURA J. OLSON

Further Reading

Condee, Nancy, "Axmadulina's Poemy: Poems of Transformation and Origins", *Slavic and East European Journal*, 29/2 (Summer 1985) pp. 176–87

Ketchian, Sonia I., *The Poetic Craft of Bella Akhmadulina*, University Park: Pennsylvania State University Press, 1993

Literaturnoe Obozrenie, 3/263 (1997): special issue on Akhmadulina

Rydel, Christine, "The Metapoetical World of Bella Akhmadulina", *Russian Literary Triquarterly*, 1 (1971) pp. 326–41

Rydel, Christine, "Bella Axmadulina's Literary Odyssey" in *Critical Essays on the Prose and Poetry of Modern Slavic Women*, edited by Nina Efimov *et al.*, Lewiston, New York: Mellen, 1998

Anna Akhmatova 1889–1966

Russian poet, essayist and translator

Biography

Born Anna Andreevna Gorenko in Bolshoi Fontan, near Odessa, Ukraine, 23 June 1889. Her father was a merchant navy officer. She was educated in Tsarkoe Selo (now Pushkin), near St Petersburg (later Petrograd, later Leningrad; where she spent most of her life), and later attended law school in Kiev. She began writing poetry at the age of 11. Her first published poetry (1907) appeared in the journal *Sirius*, founded by the poet Nikolai Gumilev, whom she met while she was at school and married in 1910 (divorced 1918). With Gumilev, Osip Mandel'shtam and others she was a member of the Acmeist literary movement, which in 1910–12 reacted with its clarity and precision against the prevailing Symbolism. In 1918 Akhmatova married her second husband, Vladimir Shileiko (separated 1920, divorced 1928). In 1920 she was a librarian at the Institute of Agronomy in Petrograd. In 1921 Gumilev was executed for alleged counterrevolutionary plotting. Until then Akhmatova had published her poetry and given occasional readings of it, but between 1922 and 1940, though she continued writing, she had no publishing outlets. The Gumilev connection counted against her and her work itself was judged to be bourgeois. During this period her only son, the writer Lev Gumilev, and her third husband, art critic Nikolai Punin (died 1953), spent time in prison. From 1940 some Akhmatova poems appeared in Soviet magazines and in 1943 she published a volume of verse in Tashkent, where she went when evacuated from besieged Leningrad. She returned to Leningrad at the end of World War II, publishing poems in periodicals and giving readings, but suffered strict censorship again from 1946, when she was expelled from the Union of Soviet Writers. For several years she earned her living translating a variety of languages, including French, Italian, Serbo-Croat and Korean, into Russian. With the Khrushchev "Thaw" in the 1950s, Akhmatova could publish again and major works appeared from 1958. She became a dominant figure in Russian poetic circles and was able to leave Russia and go to Italy to receive the Taormina Prize (1964) and to England to receive an Oxford honorary doctorate (1965). Her death in Domodedova, near Moscow, 5 March 1966, was marked by official tributes.

Her major works, ranging through personal, patriotic and religious themes, include the love poetry of *Vecher* (*Evening*), 1912, and *Belaia staia* (*White Flock*), 1917, the long narrative poem *Poema bez geroia: Triptikh* (*Poem without a Hero: A Triptych*), 1960 and later versions, and *Rekviem* (*Requiem*), 1963, an anti-Stalinist poetry cycle about the 1930s Terror.

Translations

Collection of Poetry

Hemschemeyer, Judith, *The Complete Poems of Anna Akhmatova* (parallel texts), edited by Roberta Reeder, 2 vols, Somerville, Massachusetts: Zephyr Press, 1990; expanded edition, as *The Complete Poems of Anna Akhmatova*, Boston: Zephyr Press, and Edinburgh: Canongate, 1992

Selections and Anthologies of Poetry

Arndt, Walter (editor and translator), *Selected Poems* (includes *Requiem*, translated by Robin Kemball and *A Poem without a Hero*, translated by Carl. R. Proffer), Ann Arbor, Michigan: Ardis, 1976

Berg, Stephen, *With Akhmatova at the Black Gates: Variations*, Urbana: University of Illinois Press, 1981

Bobrova, Raissa, Sergei Roy, Olga Shartse, Peter Tempest, Graham Whittaker and Irina Zheleznova, *Anna Akhmatova: Stikhi / Anna Akhmatova: Poems* (parallel texts), Moscow: Raduga, 1988

Bowra, C.M. (editor), *A Second Book of Russian Verse*, various translators, London: Macmillan, 1948; Westport, Connecticut: Greenwood Press, 1971

Campbell, David and Rosemary Dobson, in *Moscow Trefoil and Other Versions of Poems from the Russian of Anna Akhmatova and Osip Mandelstam*, edited by Natalie Staples, Canberra: Australian National University Press, 1975

Coffin, Lyn, *Poems*, New York: Norton, 1983

Davies, Jessie, *Seventy-Five Poems by Anna Akhmatova* (parallel texts), Liverpool: Lincoln Davies, 1991

Duddington, Natalie, *Forty-Seven Love Poems by Anna Akhmatova*, London: Jonathan Cape, 1927

Kunitz, Stanley and Max Hayward, *Poems of Akhmatova* (parallel texts), Boston: Little Brown, 1973; London: Collins-Harvill, 1989

McKane, Richard, *Selected Poems: Anna Akhmatova* (parallel texts), London and New York: Oxford University Press, 1969; reprinted 1989

Maddock, Mary, *Three Russian Women Poets: Anna Akhmatova, Marina Tsvetayeva, Bella Akhmadulina*, Trumansburg, New York: Crossing Press, 1983

Markov, Vladimir and Merrill Sparks (editors), *Modern Russian Poetry: An Anthology with Verse Translations* (parallel texts), with an introduction, London: Macgibbon and Kee, 1966; Indianapolis: Bobbs Merrill, 1967

Obolensky, Dimitri (editor), *The Penguin Book of Russian Verse* (parallel texts), with an introduction, Harmondsworth and Baltimore: Penguin, 1962, revised 1965; reprinted as *The Heritage of Russian Verse*, Bloomington: Indiana University Press, 1976

Shelley, Gerard, *Modern Poems from Russia*, London: Allen and Unwin, 1942; reprinted Westport, Connecticut: Greenwood Press, 1977

Thomas, D.M., *Anna Akhmatova: Way of all the Earth*, London: Secker and Warburg, 1979; Athens: Ohio University Press, 1980; republished as *You Will Hear Thunder: Akhmatova, Poems* (includes *Requiem* and *Poem without a Hero*), London: Secker and Warburg, and Athens: Ohio University Press, 1985

Thurley, Geoffrey, *White Flock* (parallel texts), London: Oasis Books, 1978

Poetry

Poema bez geroia, 1963

Hemschemeyer, Judith, *Poem without a Hero* in *The Complete Poems of Anna Akhmatova*, translated by Hemschemeyer 1990

McKane, Richard, *Poem without a Hero* in *Selected Poems*, translated by McKane, 1969

Mayhew, Leonore and William McNaughton, *Poem without a Hero and Selected Poems*, Oberlin, Ohio: Oberlin College Press, 1989

Proffer, Carl R., with Assya Humessky, "A Poem without a Hero", *Russian Literature Triquarterly*, 1 (1971) pp. 15–66; in book form, Ann Arbor, Michigan: Ardis, 1973; reprinted in *Selected Poems*, edited by Walter Arndt, 1976

Thomas, D.M., *Requiem and Poem without a Hero*, London: Elek, and Athens: Ohio University Press, 1976; reprinted in *You Will Hear Thunder*, translated by Thomas, 1985

Prose

Meyer, Ronald (editor), *My Half Century: Selected Prose*, Ann Arbor, Michigan: Ardis, 1992

There has been no lack of translators brave enough to tackle Anna Akhmatova's poems. The first was DUDDINGTON, who produced a sizeable collection in 1927, and the wartime alliance with Russia led several more translators to publish small numbers of lyrics in the 1940s. The year 1946 saw the condemnation of Akhmatova by the Soviet Communist Party, which resulted in the total absence of published translations between 1949 and 1959, but since the "Thaw" there have been few years without new translations and some, notably around the 1989 centenary, which have seen several.

Translators face an array of difficulties beyond those intrinsic to verse translation. Akhmatova writes with restraint, apparent simplicity and naturalness; she is laconic and elliptical. Padding and explanation therefore call attention to themselves (most conspicuously MADDOCK (1983) turns a stark 24-word two-stanza lyric into a self-indulgent 61 words and three stanzas), and expansion of ellipses can result in reduction of necessary ambiguity or simply in erroneous readings. Akhmatova's subtle rhythmic variations are difficult to imitate, and ternary metres and trochees, which she uses freely, have narrower functions in English than in Russian. Her rhymes are mostly exact or approximate, classical rather than inventive, and she makes extensive use of feminine and dactylic rhyme, both much more plentiful in Russian than in English. Moreover, the fact that, within the relatively conservative tradition of 20th-century Russian poetry, she is a metrically conservative poet who plays formal constraint against turbulent emotion means that translators must consider whether the contemporary English tradition of unrhymed free verse is appropriate. Furthermore, Akhmatova paid considerable attention to the arrangement of individual collections and cycles of poems, which suffer from piecemeal translation. Her evolution from poet of unhappy love to the dissident chronicler of Stalin's Russia makes the selection of poems important. And she is self-consciously a poet of intertextuality, referring extensively to Russian and Western poetry, paintings, sculpture, music, ballet, and theatre. These allusions must be taken account of, and, ideally, be indicated and/or explained.

The general tendency has been from publications of small numbers of disconnected lyrics towards extensive collections, culminating in HEMSCHEMEYER's *Complete Poems* (1990, 1992). There has also been an expansion of information conveyed in notes, essays, translations of Akhmatova's prose, and bibliography, though intertextuality is dealt with only by PROFFER, MCKANE and HEMSCHEMEYER. It is also relatively common to provide parallel texts (OBOLENSKY, MARKOV & SPARKS, KUNITZ & HAYWARD, THURLEY, DAVIES, the *Raduga* group (BOBROVA *et al.*), HEMSCHEMEYER 1990), suggesting either the assumption of semi-bilingual readers (certainly by MCKANE 1989 and DAVIES 1991 who intends her texts as visual and aural aids for understanding the original), or the urge to represent Akhmatova's musicality and strict harmonious forms.

Strategies for translating the poetry vary from the plain prose of OBOLENSKY to the three solutions equally common over the whole period: unrhymed free verse, analogies of various kinds, and mimetic metre and rhyme. Readers can, therefore, find translations that answer their own preferences as to approach. Each of the strategies has its dis/advantages. Mimesis of metre and rhyme pattern (ARNDT, BOWRA, COXWELL, DAVIES, FITZLYON, FULLER, and TEMPEST) ignores the different semantics of the metres in the two languages. Its chief defect for translation of Akhmatova is that, since Russian words are on average longer than English and exact rhyme is hard to find, it leads to padding, unnatural word order, and ingenious rhymes that attract inordinate attention. Other consequences include tautology, elisions, unnatural accentuation, and changes of register. The strategy is best suited to translation of suitable individual texts. Unrhymed free verse (CAMPBELL, DOBSON, DUDDINGTON, MCKANE, MADDOCK, THURLEY, and WEISSBORT) allows reproduction of Akhmatova's syntax and tones of voice, but at the expense of musicality, sound orchestration, and (since shorter English words result in shorter, lighter, swifter lines) of the weightiness that reads as authority, grief and resignation. It is difficult to appreciate the formal discipline of the poems, and final stanzas, lacking the cadence provided by rhyme, often end flatly and inconclusively. The third strategy (COFFIN, HEMSCHEMEYER, KUNITZ & HAYWARD, MARKOV & SPARKS, SHELLEY, ZHELEZNOVA) is to search for analogies to Akhmatova's metrics better suited to English verse. One is to loosen the rhyme pattern, rhyming even lines but not odd. Others are to admit less exact rhyme (including assonance, alliteration etc.); to substitute accentual for syllabo-tonic lines, whilst keeping the number of stresses constant; to vary the line-length. While the balance and harmony of Akhmatova's composition are lost, the line-unit can remain intact, the sense of poem-closure can be preserved, and word order is usually natural. Both second and third strategies are serviceable for large collections.

Crucial requirements are accuracy, and consistency of approach. Linguistic errors are too frequent in the work of THURLEY and of MADDOCK (who is insensitive to Akhmatova's sophisticated handling of tenses) and, to a lesser extent, in THOMAS. The *Raduga* group overestimates the flexibility of English word order and misjudges English register – the collection abounds in misleading colloquialisms and poeticisms (some Shakespearian). A few translators fluctuate unsatisfactorily between the strategies described here (CUNNINGHAM, THOMAS, *Raduga*) – though Kline considers the third of them to be itself inconsistent.

Of the collections and selections, five reflect Akhmatova's *oeuvre* as a whole. ARNDT's (1975) is extensive, including some later lyrics, KEMBALL's *Requiem* and PROFFER's *Poem without a Hero*. Arndt's metric translation meets with the usual hazards and produces verse that sounds not merely conservative but anachronistic when compared to contemporary English poetry. Not surprisingly, he does not attempt the modernist *Poem without a Hero*.

THOMAS (1979) is inconsistent, reproducing the original rhyme scheme, recasting it, or abandoning it; several poems begin with iambic lines, subsequently breaking down, but mostly he uses free verse. On occasion he idiosyncratically omits personal pronouns. There are inaccuracies, amongst them "I'm not yet cured of happiness" for "I do not cure happiness", muscat roses for musk roses, "sunburnt" for "dark-skinned" (removing the reference to Pushkin), and word order that makes Dante, instead of Florence, perfidious and base. On inaccuracies in Thomas's *Poem without a Hero* see Haight (1986).

COFFIN's translation (1983) is judiciously plain, and almost always sounds natural; this remarkable achievement is underlined by the very few occasions when the tone is slightly undignified or unreserved. Rhyme never controls the text, and rarely attracts undesirable attention. One regrets, therefore, that many cycles, including *Requiem*, are incomplete.

The *Raduga* collection (1988) (which fails to credit the translators on the title page) has some excellent translations of individual poems (notably by TEMPEST) but it is the work of several poorly coordinated hands. Most of the translators seem not to be native speakers of English.

MCKANE's 1989 translation is an almost complete collection of the later poems, with a selection of earlier poems (many more of which are in his 1969 translation). The second collection, less elliptical than the first and with more natural word order, is again accurate and perceptive in its readings and conveys the soberness of Akhmatova's poetry, though over-emphasizing its sparseness and starkness. The notes reveal familiarity with academic research, and the apparatus to the complex and allusive *Poem without a Hero* is useful.

HEMSCHEMEYER's translation (1992) is invaluable for being complete. This was an enormous project, and few Russian poets are so well served. The translations are accurate and consistent and reflect well Akhmatova's self-controlled dignity. They are less bare than McKane's, and although Hemschemeyer does not reveal Akhmatova's unobtrusive virtuosity, the reader can see her entire poetic evolution clearly. This is an academic edition with extensive and illuminating notes, and is also the most complete collection to date of the Russian texts of Akhmatova's poems.

WENDY ROSSLYN

Requiem

Requiem, 1963

Translations

Davies, Jessie, *Requiem by Anna Akhmatova* (bilingual edition), Liverpool: Lincoln Davies, 1991

Haight, Amanda and Peter Norman, *Requiem* in *Anna Akhmatova: A Poetic Pilgrimage*, edited by Haight, New York and London: Oxford University Press, 1976; reprinted 1990; pp. 92, 99–108 (Haight's quotations from the cycle on these pages in fact provide the complete text but for two sentences of "Instead of a preface" and an epigraph)

Hemschemeyer, Judith, *Requiem*, in *The Complete Poems of Anna Akhmatova*, translated by Hemschemeyer, vol. 2, 1990, pp. 94–115

Kemball, Robin, *Requiem*, *Russian Review*, 33 (1974) pp. 303–12; with minor revisions, reprinted in *Selected Poems*, edited by Walter Arndt, 1976, pp. 143–53

Kunitz, Stanley and Max Hayward, *Requiem*, (parallel texts) in *Poems of Akhmatova*, translated by Kunitz and Hayward, 1973

Lowell, Robert, *Requiem*, *Atlantic Monthly*, 214 (1964) pp. 62–65

McKane, Richard, *Requiem* in *Selected Poems: Anna Akhmatova*, translated by McKane, 1969, pp. 90–105; reprinted with minor revisions, Newcastle-upon-Tyne: Bloodaxe Books, 1989, pp. 281–88

Marshall, H., *Requiem*, *Russian Literature Triquarterly*, 2 (1972) pp. 201–13

Thomas, D.M., *Requiem* in *Requiem and Poem without a Hero*, translated by Thomas, 1976, pp. 23–32 (revised and completed version of translation first published in *The Guardian*, 19 April 1965); reprinted in *You Will Hear Thunder*, 1985

Whittaker, Graham, *Requiem* in *Anna Akhmatova: Stikhi / Anna Akhamatova: Poems*, translated by Whittaker, 1988, pp. 226–41

Requiem, a cycle of poems written between 1935 and 1961, describes the sufferings of the women whose husbands and sons were arrested during Stalin's Terror. Because its subject was taboo politically – the biblical allusions were not in themselves objectionable – the cycle could not be written down, and had to be memorized by trusted friends. The poems later circulated in manuscript and four were published in the USSR (1940–66), but the entire text could be published only abroad (Munich, 1963, without Akhmatova's knowledge) and did not appear in the USSR until 1987. The authoritative text is in Struve and Filippov's edition of Akhmatova's works (Munich-Washington, 1967–68).

The first translation, shortly after the Munich publication, was LOWELL's (1964). Akhmatova asserts that the text is woven from the "poor" words she overheard whilst waiting outside the prison with the other women, and the text balances the simplicity of the heard and the artistry of the written. Lowell's text tips too far towards fashioning the source material. Moreover, Lowell makes frequent omissions and additions, which change the relationship between the particular and the general, blunt the horrors described, diminish the psychological suffering of the heroine, and turn the poem into a commemoration of the imprisoned men rather than the waiting women. The image of the statue of the weeping Akhmatova is replaced insensitively and illogically by that of Peter the Great, who is often compared to Stalin. We have on record "Akhmatova's extreme distress at the publication of Robert Lowell's 'imitations' of 'Requiem'" (Haight, 1976, p. 108).

The next translation (omitting "Dedication") was by THOMAS (1965). His declared principle was to keep to the original metre and the pattern of feminine and masculine line-endings, using assonance as an equivalent of rhyme, but at times he substitutes new metres, mixes metres within poems, changes clausulae and stanza boundaries and attenuates rhyme severely. Omitting the dates of poems makes it appear that the cycle was written as a unitary work. Thomas has some imaginative touches, such as "wailing wall" as an equivalent for the Kremlin wall as an execution site. But also some unforgivable ones: he adds "the prison-poplar's / Tongue's in its cheek", suggesting that the deaths are laughable, and has the heroine think, as the death sentence on her son is passed, of "Summer, calling out [?] my Black Sea dress" – a gross trivialization in a poem that concentrates on the torment of the inner self and ignores the adornment of the body.

An important corrective to these first translations was MCKANE's (1969), which is linguistically accurate and respects the original text. McKane reproduces the dates and numbering of the poems (but adds footnotes on realia). This is essentially a plain prose translation which observes line and stanza divisions, but the effect of abandoning metre and rhyme is to impose an artificial uniformity on a cycle that is metrically diverse and, moreover, to tip the balance between overheard and created too far towards the overheard.

MARSHALL (1972) is the first translator to attempt to preserve the original rhyme scheme, but even without the additional constraint of imitating the original metres the English sometimes makes poor sense: "The Ennisay winds / And the Polar Star with scintillation girdles" and "the madness of wings / My spirit has half-stifled". He mistranslates Akhmatova's epigraph from the liturgy and introduces an allusion to part of the biblical narrative (not used by Akhmatova) that mitigates the suffering of the mother.

KUNITZ & HAYWARD (1973) declare that they aim to produce "a new poem sprung from the matrix of the old, drenched in memories of its former existence", and parallel texts suggest the assumption of some semi-bilingual readers. The strategy is to substitute less exact sound linkages for rhyme as necessary, but even so, pursuit of rhyme leads to padding and some of the additions are self-consciously literary and/or obscure (but not "poor"): "ah soon!", "night of stone". Akhmatova's distressingly plain "I cannot distinguish Now who is a beast and who a man, And whether it will be long before the execution" becomes confused: "I am powerless to tell / somebody brute from something human, / or on what day the word spells, 'Kill!'" One or two passages are unintentionally comic ("I hurled myself at the hangman's foot", "the blue hatband marches up the stairs"), or introduce unwarranted sexual connotations: "an inconsolable shade seeks me" is rendered as "a grieved shadow hunts my body's warmth".

KEMBALL (1974) attempts "to render as closely as possible the sense, the spirit, and the music of Akhmatova's *own* message (and *not* the translator's) while strictly retaining the *form* (metre, line-length, rhyme-scheme)". He is remarkably successful in avoiding the intrinsic dangers of padding, inversions, clichés, and poeticisms and his translation is linguistically accurate. However, the same metre has different connotations in the two literary traditions, and ternary metres (3 poems) are particularly difficult: matching Akhmatova's amphibrachs in "Epilogue II" (and matching the rhyming couplets) makes the solemn heavy ending of the cycle sound jaunty and effortless.

HAIGHT & NORMAN (1976) circumvent this trap, preferring free verse for the most part, so that the poem's origin in the spoken word is emphasized. Some poems have metrical underpinnings or rhyme or sporadic assonance, avoiding, however inconsistently, McKane's uniformity. Haight was Akhmatova's confidante and an authority on her poetry, and the text is interpreted with sensitivity.

WHITTAKER's translation (with parallel texts, 1988) is unsatisfactory on many counts: errors of register, insouciant metres, trivializing ("as if thrown down obscenely on her back" becomes "her world had been stolen from under her feet") and the stark details are often blunted, probably in accommodation to the Soviet publishers: one example – Whittaker refers to Ezhov not as orchestrator of the Terror but as "Commissar of the Interior".

DAVIES (1991) also introduces poeticisms ("knell", "neverlands afar", "lief", "harken") into a text that describes horror with almost clinical factualness. She attempts to reproduce the formal characteristics of the poems (and provides the Russian), but is less successful overall than Kemball, notably because of less natural word order.

HEMSCHEMEYER's translation (1990) is almost entirely accurate, but as she does not substitute for rhyme in its function as marker of closure, the poems tend to end flatly. However, she catches the stark simplicity of the original. She is the only translator to reveal, through notes, that the text incorporates allusions to multiple other texts, religious and secular. These notes are well justified as the only way in which the reader can hear some at least of the intertexts perceived by the first audience (readers steeped in the Russian literary tradition).

WENDY ROSSLYN

Further Reading

Haight, Amanda (editor), *Anna Akhmatova: A Poetic Pilgrimage*, New York and London: Oxford University Press, 1976; reprinted 1990

Haight, Amanda, "Anna Akhmatova in English: A Question of Translation", *Scottish Slavonic Review*, 6 (1986) pp. 119–22

Hemschemeyer, Judith, "Translating Akhmatova", *Translation Review*, 32 (1990) pp. 12–14

Kline, George L., "Seven by Ten: An Examination of Seven Pairs of Translations from Akhmatova by Ten English and American Translators", *Slavic and East European Journal*, 38/1 (1994) pp. 47–68

Kurt, Anna and John Crowfoot, "Akhmatova and Translation", *Soviet Literature*, 6/495 (1989) pp. 177–81

Meyer, Ronald (editor), *Anna Akhmatova: My Half Century; Selected Prose*, Ann Arbor, Michigan: Ardis, 1992 (Akhmatova on translators and translations)

Nayman, Anatoly, *Remembering Anna Akhmatova*, translated by Wendy Rosslyn, London: Peter Halban, and New York: Holt, 1991, pp. 151–54

Rosslyn, Wendy, "Gender in Translation: Lowell and Cixous Rewriting Akhmatova" in *Gender and Sexuality in Russian Civilisation*, edited by Peter Barta, Amsterdam: Harwood, 2000

Weissbort, Daniel, "Translating Akhmatova: A Conversation with Stanley Kunitz", in *Translating Poetry: The Double Labyrinth*, edited by Weissbort, London: Macmillan, 1989

See also translator's notes in Hemschemeyer (1990)

Vasilii Aksenov 1932–

Russian novelist, short-story writer, screenwriter, dramatist and essayist

Biography

Born in Kazan, 20 August 1932, into a Communist family; his mother was the writer Evgeniia Ginzburg; both parents spent years in Soviet prisons. In the late 1940s Aksenov visited his mother in prison and exile. He was brought up in a state home, later attending the Pavlov Medical Institute, Leningrad and graduating in 1956. He worked as a doctor in the far north, 1956–60, then in Leningrad. He became a writer in 1960. In 1962 he travelled to Poland, Japan and India, and in the same year became editor of the magazine *Iunost'*, in which had appeared his first story, in 1959, and his best-known early work, the short novel *Zvezdnyi bilet* (*The Starry Ticket*), in 1961. In 1975 he was a visiting professor at the University of California at Los Angeles. In 1979, with 22 other writers, he tried unsuccessfully to publish work in the anthology *Metropol'* without submitting it to the censor; he was banned from publishing and exiled (July 1980). He emigrated in 1980 to the US, becoming writer-in-residence at the University of Michigan and subsequently occupying other academic posts. His Soviet citizenship was restored in 1990 and he returned to Russia in the early 1990s.

Aksenov married 1) Kira Mendeleva in 1957 (divorced 1979; one son); 2) Maia Karmen in 1979.

Aksenov became famous in the early 1960s with novels, *Kollegi* (*Colleagues*), 1960, and *Zvezdnyi bilet* (*A Starry Ticket*), 1961. Since then as well as prose fiction he has written avant-garde plays, mainly in the 1960s, and essays, principally in the 1970s and 1980s.

Translations

Novels

Kollegi, 1960

Wettlin, Margaret, *Colleagues*, Moscow: Foreign Languages Publishing House, 1960

Zvezdnyi bilet, 1961

Brown, Alec, *A Starry Ticket*, London: Putnam, 1962

MacAndrew, Andrew R., *A Ticket to the Stars*, New York: New American Library, 1963

Ozhog, 1980

Glenny, Michael, *The Burn: A Novel in Three Books (Late Sixties–Early Seventies)*, New York: Random House, and London: Hutchinson, 1984

Ostrov Krym, 1981

Heim, Michael Henry, *The Island of Crimea*, New York: Random House, 1983; London: Hutchinson, 1985

Skazhi izium, 1985

Bouis, Antonina W., *Say Cheese!*, New York: Random House, 1989

Moskovskaia saga, 1993

Glad, John and Christopher Morris, *Generations of Winter*, New York: Random House, 1994

While Vasilii Aksenov's literary career has been marked by experimentation with narrative form, certain stylistic features have remained constant throughout his work, features that pose special challenges to the translator. Most notable in this regard is the author's use of dialogue saturated with bits of poetry and song, colloquialisms, slang and foreign borrowings, especially Americanisms. The speech of Aksenov's characters raised a topic that had been taboo in works of orthodox socialist realism: the fascination exerted by Western culture on many young people in the Soviet Union of the 1950s and 1960s. And so Aksenov's works could be said to be about *translation* itself, that is, the act of "carrying over", whether it be from one culture to another or from one stylistic register (street slang) to another (the lofty rhetoric of the socialist realist novel).

The quality of the translations of Aksenov's work has been a function of his popularity in the West. The translations of his early works, still under the influence of socialist realist narrative, tend to be uneven and full of inaccuracies. As Aksenov's literary experimentation attracts the attention of Western literati, the quality of the translations of his works significantly improves. His emigration to America in 1980 facilitated the active participation of the author in the translation of many of his later works.

The translation of *Colleagues* by WETTLIN (1960) is, for the most part, accurate. However, as is typical of many translations done for the Foreign Language Publishers of Moscow, the translation follows the original closely, which often results in awkward turns of phrase. Wettlin preserves in her translation terms specific to Soviet life, such as *fel'dsher* (medical practitioner lacking graduate qualifications) and *stilyagi* (young people given to uncritical display of extravagant fashions in dress and manners; teddy boys), providing explanations in footnotes. However, she also preserves the Russian underworld slang for kill, *shmaz*, which sounds more comical than threatening in the English text. Often Wettlin's translation of colloquialisms is inappropriate to the context in which they appear as, for example, when a murderous *negodiai* (scoundrel) with a knife becomes a *stinker*.

BROWN's translation (1962) of Aksenov's second novel, under the title *A Starry Ticket*, is notable for its often incongruous rendering of colloquial speech and slang expressions. Brown translates most of the slang with English and American slang equivalents taken from a variety of epochs and regions, which often results in an unnerving tension between the characters' speech and Soviet realia. An old woman in chapter 1 erupts in archaic English: "It fair makes me blood run cold." Brown often translates neutral Russian expressions with clumsy colloquialisms: drinking becomes "gurgling down"; tired of becomes "fed up to the gills with"; a grade of C becomes a "just-scraped-through". Even more curious in this translation are Brown's unwarranted additions to the text. When the narrator sits by the window to shave, Brown adds, in parentheses, "to get the light". Inaccuracies abound, including mistakes in rendering tense in English, and Brown takes great liberties in translating the chapter headings. MACANDREW's translation (1963) of

Zvezdnyi bilet appeared a year after Brown's under the title *A Ticket to the Stars*. This translation is readable and avoids the gross inaccuracies and ill-chosen turns of phrase typical of Brown's translation. MacAndrew tends consistently to choose slang equivalents from standard American slang, avoiding expressions that too vividly conjure images of the culture of the target text.

Aksenov's most famous novel, *The Burn*, is also his most challenging to translate. In this work, Aksenov adds a healthy dose of neologisms, surreal description and poetry to his slangy, colloquial dialogues. GLENNY's translation (1984) is accurate while preserving the literary effects of the source text. Glenny employs a number of translation strategies to deal with Aksenov's extensive wordplay and heavy use of foreign words and phrases. He makes conservative use of footnotes to explain wordplay and Soviet acronyms, to give historical information or to indicate that certain portions of text appear in English in the source text. Elsewhere, Glenny includes explanatory information within the body of the translation. Stylistic peculiarities that may be lost in translation are also noted within the body of the translation, as when one character's speech is described as "perfect Russian thieves' slang". English words that appear in Cyrillic characters in the source text are transliterated back into English in the translation so as to mark them as spoken in English by Russian speakers. Neologisms are typically translated piece by piece as calques.

Aksenov's *The Island of Crimea* represents challenges to the translator similar to those of *The Burn*. HEIM (1983) offers a very effective and accurate translation. The novel has a more traditional narrative than *The Burn*, but introduces a fictional creole, Yaki, described in the novel as "a mixture of Russian, Tatar, English with assorted Romance and Hellenic roots". Foreign and fictional words and phrases are italicized in the translation but Heim foregoes the use of footnotes. Heim also reworks Aksenov's dialogues so as to provide natural-sounding dialogue in English while highlighting the intrusion of foreign words and phrases.

BOUIS's translation (1989) of *Say Cheese!* was done from an unpublished manuscript and differs markedly from the Russian edition of the text. The manuscript that Bouis translated makes extensive use of footnotes to provide explanatory asides, tinged with humor and irony, some addressed directly to American readers. These footnotes are largely incorporated into the body of the published Russian text. Bouis elucidates wordplay by including both a translation and a transliteration of key words. Overall, Bouis's translation is effective and the translations of poetry contained in the novel are high-quality, respecting the rhyme scheme and meter of the original.

The first two volumes of Aksyonov's 3-volume *Moscow Saga* were published as *Generations of Winter*, a pluralized form of the title of volume 1. The translation was undertaken before the third volume had been written. The translation by GLAD & MORRIS is both readable and accurate. The snippets of song and poetry are rendered in accurate translations that preserve both meter and rhyme. Footnotes are conservatively employed to provide translations of Georgian words and expressions that appear in Cyrillic script in the source text and to give historical and cultural background information.

BRIAN JAMES BAER

Further Reading

Kustanovich, Konstantin, *The Artist and the Tyrant: Vasily Aksenov's Works in the Brezhnev Era*, Columbus, Ohio: Slavica, 1992

Whitney, Thomas P., *The New Writing in Russia*, Ann Arbor: University of Michigan Press, 1964

Akutagawa Ryūnosuke 1892–1927

Japanese short-story writer and critic

Biography

Born 1 March 1892 on a dairy farm in Tokyo. He was raised by his maternal grandparents from infancy because of his mother's mental illness. Shy and introspective, as a youth Akutagawa was fond of Edo Period (1603–1868) tales of ghosts and the macabre and he read widely in traditional Chinese romances. The young Akutagawa later ventured into translated works of Western writers, especially Nietzche, Tolstoi, Dostoevskii, Baudelaire, and Strindberg. He was drawn to English and American writers for their satire and mystery, and was greatly influenced by authors such as Swift, Poe, and Bierce. His first short story, "Rashōmon" (1915), was published when he was still attending the elite Tokyo University as an English major. The well-received story propelled him from being an unknown college student into one of the most promising young writers of his day, and gained him entry into Natsume Soseki's inner circle, the exalted literary salon *Mokuyōkai*. After graduating (his thesis was on William Morris, a fellow enthusiast of the Middle Ages), Akutagawa taught briefly at the Naval Academy, then took up a position with the *Osaka Daily News* in 1919 and supported himself as a professional writer until his suicide in Tokyo, 24 July 1927 at age 35. Akutagawa was troubled by his mother's madness and its implications for his own physical and mental well-being. Familial and financial pressure may have also contributed to his death.

As a writer, Akutagawa was blessed with an unflagging curiosity and was versatile in his approach. His broad knowledge of East and West, and past and present, was reflected in his thoughtful literary creations. Setting himself against both the autobiographical, confessional style of the Naturalist movement and the earlier Proletarian literary movement, Akutagawa sought inspiration in the tales of China's and Japan's distant past, in Buddhist anecdotes and exotic Christian parables. In this sense, he was a conscious cultural translator in the truest sense.

Translations

Novellas

Kappa, 1927

Bownas, Geoffrey, *Kappa*, with an introduction by G.H. Healey, London: Peter Owen, 1970; Rutland, Vermont: C.E. Tuttle, 1971

Kojima, Takashi and John McVittie, *Kappa* in their *Exotic Japanese Stories*, New York: Liveright, 1964, pp. 209–65

Shiojiri, Seiichi, *Kappa*, Tokyo: Hokuseido Press, 1947; revised edition, 1949; reprinted Westport, Connecticut: Greenwood Press, 1970

Aru ahō no issō, 1927

Inoue, Akio, "Life of a Certain Fool" in his *Posthumous Works of Ryūnosuke Akutagawa*, Tenri: Tenri Jihosha, 1961

Peterson, Will, *A Fool's Life*, New York: Grossman, 1970

Short Stories (selections and anthologies)

Bell, Eric S. and Ukai Eiji, in *Eminent Authors of Contemporary Japan: One-Act Plays and Short Stories*, Tokyo: Kaitakusha, 1936

Britton, Dorothy, *Tu Tze-Chun*, with an introduction by E.G. Seidensticker, Tokyo: Kodansha, and London: Ward Lock, 1965

Britton, Dorothy, *The Spider's Thread and Other Stories*, Tokyo: Kodansha, 1987

Inoue, Akio, *Posthumous Works of Ryūnosuke Akutagawa*, Tenri: Tenri Jihosha, 1961

Kojima, Takashi, *Rashomon and Other Stories*, with an introduction by Howard Hibbett, New York: Liveright, 1952, London: Prentice Hall, 1954; with an introduction by Osamu Shimizu, New York: Bantam, 1959 (contains "In a Grove", "Rashomon", "Yam Gruel", "The Martyr", "Kesa and Monto", "The Dragon")

Kojima, Takashi, *Japanese Short Stories*, with an introduction by John McVittie, New York: Liveright, 1961

Kojima, Takashi and John McVittie, *Exotic Japanese Stories*, with an introduction, New York: Liveright, 1964

Kojima, Takashi, *et al.*, *Hell Screen; Cogwheels; A Fool's Life*, Hygiene, Colorado: Eridanos Press, 1987

Norman, W.H.H., *Hell Screen and Other Stories*, with an introduction, Tokyo: Hokuseido Press, 1948; Westport, Connecticut: Greenwood Press, 1971

O'Brien, James, in *Akutagawa and Dazai: Instances of Literary Adaption*, Tempe: Center for Asian Studies, Arizona State University Press, 1988

Sasaki, Takamasa, *The Three Treasures and Other Stories for Children*, Tokyo: Hokuseido, 1944

Say, Allen, *The Nose: A Tale based on "Hana"*, Berkeley, California: Oyez, 1973

Shaw, Glenn W., *Tales Grotesque and Curious*, Tokyo: Hokuseido, 1930; 2nd edition, 1938

Shaw, Glenn W., *Rashomon and Other Stories*, annotated by Michio Tanaka, Tokyo: Hara Shobo, 1964; reprinted 1976

Akutagawa Ryūnosuke's stature as a writer in modern Japanese literature is attested by an award named after him: the Akutagawa Prize, the most prestigious literary award to be awarded to any living writer in Japan. He was also one of the first modern Japanese writers to be read outside Japan.The translation of Akutagawa's short stories into English started three years after the author's death. Except for the two novellas *A Fool's Life* and *Kappa*, the great majority of his translated works are either in the form of collections of short stories by the author or scattered through literary journals and short story collections of various authors.

SHAW's *Tales Grotesque and Curious* (1930), considered the earliest rendition of the author's works into a Western language, contains 11 short stories, including such well-known works as "Rasho Gate"("Rashōmon") and "The Nose" ("Hana"), which have been retranslated several times. Translated with the author's approval, the collection includes Akutagawa's earliest short stories, most written in 1916. "Rashomon", the first story by Akutagawa ever translated into English, was first published in 1920, three years after the author published the original in his first book. The excellent translation by Shaw, both accurate and attentive to the nuance of the original, set a high standard for later translations of Akutagawa's oeuvre.

NORMAN's *Hell Screen and Other Stories* (1948) includes four stories, an introduction and two elaborate fold-out color illustrations depicting scenes from the narrative. Norman's introduction makes use of extensive direct quotes from Shaw's introduction. He did, however, provide two full texts from the 13th-century *Uji Shūi Monogatari* which are accepted as the sources for Akutagawa's *Jigokuhen* (*Hell Screen*). Norman was inclined to leave the titles untranslated and used the Japanese terms for the official ranks, titles, and personal pronouns. He assigned names to characters in order to avoid the problem of anonymity in *Hell Screen*. Norman's *Hell Screen*, rendered in colloquial vernacular, is able to capture the oral quality of the aging narrator better than Kojima's (1961) later, more sombre, scholarly style.

Among the many translators of Akutagawa, the KOJIMA–MCVITTIE team made a considerable contribution by their superlative choice of material and the sheer number of stories they translated. KOJIMA's *Rashomon and Other Stories* (1952) contains six stories and includes an illuminating introduction by Howard Hibbett and seven full-page illustrations by M. Kuwata. Kojima's translation, rendered in facile American English prose, while on the whole truthful to the original text, often omits passages and embellishes minor details. Nevertheless, it is quite readable, and the illustrations and annotations are helpful, particularly to readers not familiar with Heian culture.

Japanese Short Stories (1961), which includes 10 stories and a detailed introductory essay by J. MCVITTIE and 15 exquisitely reproduced woodblocks print by M. Kuwata, is not merely a readable text but also a feast for the eyes. In general, the translations of Kojima, in fluent English, are very reliable. Some, however, may find them too matter-of-fact in tone.

Exotic Japanese Stories (1964), another collaboration of KOJIMA & MCVITTIE, includes 17 stories, an informative introductory essay, and 22 elaborate woodblock prints by M.

Kuwata. The reader benefits tremendously from an introductory note at the beginning of each story that provides interesting information contexualizing the multiple layers of historicity that often inform the author's works. This work is noteworthy for the abundant scholarly annotations appended at the end of the book.

As the titles in these short story collections indicate, there is in these translations an attempt to appeal to Western readers through the "exotic" and "grotesque" quality of Akutagawa's writings. These qualities are a result of his inspiration by the elegant past of the Heian court, historical accounts, medieval folk tales, and Buddhist morality tales. BRITTON's "Tu Tze-Chun" of 1965 ("Toshishua", 1920) takes full advantage of this fascinating aspect of the fable, expanding a short allegorical tale into a picture book. With an introduction by E.G. Seidensticker and gorgeous woodcut illustrations by N. Matsubara throughout the text, this translation is similar to SASAKI's *The Three Treasures, and Other Stories for Children* (1944), but aiming for a wider audience.

The author ventured into longer narrative forms in his later career, shifting from tales of the distant past to fictional works of a more immediate, urgent, and autobiographical nature. KOJIMA & MCVITTIE's *Kappa* (1964), as always readable and faithful to the original, suffers somewhat from its flat, pedantic style. BOWNAS's translation (1970), though taking a certain amount of freedom with the text, reads smoothly and successfully captures the biting Swiftian satirical touch of the parody.

A more literal testament to the author's state of mind in the twilight of his life is the fragmentary, episodic, diary style of *Cogwheels* and *A Fool's Life* (KOJIMA *et al.*, 1987). CORMAN & KAMAIKE's rendition of *Cogwheels* is beautifully executed. It conveys the anxiety and disintegration of the narrator/author's mind with a restrained and dignified eloquence. *A Fool's Life*, by PETERSON, depicts the frantic struggle of the narrator, facing impending madness and death, through the epigrammatic sketches of the author's last days.

Of the many Japanese writers whose works have been introduced into English, Akutagawa seems to be one who endures the "violence" of translation well. Some of the nuances of his lucid and thoughtful language may be lost in the act, but his rich, imaginative, and compelling story-telling comes through. Akutagawa also left behind a body of essays and literary criticism; a translation of his controversial literary debate with Tanizaki Junichirō, in particular, would surely help Western readers to understand his works better. Regrettably, translations into English still focus on his fictional works and none of these important examples of literary theory has been translated.

FAYE YUAN KLEEMAN

Further Reading

Hiraoka, Toshio, *Remarks on Akutagawa's Works: With American Student's Opinions*, Tokyo: Seirosha, 1990

Keene, Donald, "Akutagawa Ryūnosuke" in *Dawn to the West: Japanese Literature in the Modern Era*, White Plains, New York: Holt Rinehart and Winston, 1984, pp. 556–93

Lippit, Noriko Mizuta, *Reality and Fiction in Modern Japanese Literature*, New York: M.E. Sharpe, and London: Macmillan, 1980, pp. 39–69

Masuyama, Shinichi (editor), *Akutagawa Ryūnosuke Kenkyū* (A Study of Akutagawa Ryūnosuke), Tokyo: Tokyōdō, 1961

Ōoka, Shōhei, "Akutagawa Ryūnosuke o bengo suru – jijitsu to shōsetsu no aida" (In Defense of Akutagawa Ryūnosuke – Facts and Fiction), *Chūōkōron* (December 1971) pp. 50–61

Tsuruta, Kinya, "The Hell Screen / In a Grove / Kappa", in *Approaches to the Modern Japanese Short Story*, edited by Thomas E. Swann and Kinya Tsuruta, Tokyo: Waseda University Press, 1982, pp. 11–44

Ueda, Makoto, "Akutagawa Ryūnosuke" in *Modern Japanese Writers and the Nature of Literature*, by Ueda, Stanford, California: Stanford University Press, 1976, pp. 111–44

Yu, Beongcheon, "Akutagawa in English Translation" in his *Akutagawa: An Introduction*, Detroit: Wayne State University Press, 1972

Alain-Fournier 1886–1914

French novelist, short-story writer and poet

Biography

Born Henri Alban Fournier at La Chapelle-d'Angillon in central France, 3 October 1886. His early childhood was spent in Épineuil, the small country town where his father was schoolmaster. His later studies took place mainly in Paris. There followed a period of journalism for the *Paris Journal* and *L'Intransigeant*. He served in the French cavalry and infantry, 1907–09, 1911, and 1913–14. His fame rests mainly on his atmospheric, elegiac, semi-autobiographical novel *Le Grand Meaulnes* (1913) and his correspondence with his brother-in-law, the writer and critic Jacques Rivière. He was killed in action at St-Rémy, Normandy, 22 September 1914.

The Lost Domain

Le Grand Meaulnes, 1913

Translations

Davison, Frank, *The Lost Domain*, with an introduction by Alan Pryce-Jones, London: Oxford University Press, 1959;

with afterword by John Fowles, Harmondsworth: Penguin, 1968

Delisle, Françoise, *The Wanderer*, with an introduction by Havelock Ellis, Boston: Houghton Mifflin, 1928; London: Constable, 1929

Morris, Sandra, *The Lost Domain*, London and Glasgow: Blackie, 1966

Vivian, Katherine, *Le Grand Meaulnes: The Land of Lost Content*, with an introduction by Patrick Garland, London: Folio Society, 1979

Le Grand Meaulnes is one of the best-known novels in the whole of 20th-century French literature. Based on real-life events in the life of its author, it combines nostalgic evocation and reminiscence with down-to-earth descriptions of simple country life. The main themes of childhood and love are evoked in such a way that the story, involving a framework of rural communities in central France, and a chance encounter with the heroine, is endowed with a mystery and other-worldliness that have prompted comparison with a quest for the Holy Grail. Simple words have special significance for the author because they evoke nostalgia for a lost childhood and a lost love. The work is imbued with a sense of wonder, and the object of love is idealized and noble.

The arrival in a village school of Augustin Meaulnes, the novel's eponymous hero, transforms the life of the hitherto delicate narrator, François Seurel, the schoolmaster's son. An adventurous spirit leads Meaulnes, via a labyrinthine journey, to a domain of romantic fantasy where he meets a beautiful girl, Yvonne de Galais, and her exotic brother, Frantz. The encounter transforms his life. After many vicissitudes, he is reacquainted with Yvonne and eventually marries her. Their happiness is short-lived. Meaulnes is tormented by events unrevealed until the end of the book. He goes away the day after the wedding, and Yvonne dies in childbirth. The child survives, looked after by the faithful friend Seurel until, about 18 months after his abrupt departure, Meaulnes returns. Seurel imagines that it will not be long before he whisks away his daughter to embark on further adventures.

The challenge for a translator is to retain the "atmosphere" of the book, and to respect the imagery – very often connected with the sea – and the key-words. These latter encompass shadows, silence, mystery, lighting effects, desolation, wintry scenes, shipwrecks in literal as well as metaphorical senses. At the same time, elements of life in late 19th-century France – details of school life, clothing, means of transport, performances by strolling players – need to be sensibly rendered into English. Above all, the emotional quality of the narrative has to be handled sensitively. The questions to be borne in mind when judging a translation of a French novel that appeared in 1913 are the following. Is it easy to visualize the scene? Do the descriptions convey what they should? Has the rural, turn-of-the-century Frenchness been dealt with satisfactorily? Has the simplicity, in which lies the power of *Le Grand Meaulnes*, been respected?

Each of the four translations improves on the previous one. Davison's, appearing first in 1959, has been frequently reprinted, and there is little to choose between that of Morris (1966) and Vivian (1979).

DELISLE's (1928) is the least satisfactory. It is rather literal (e.g. "a cold Sunday of November"), contains errors of translation and occasionally transfers epithets, with the resultant shift in meaning. Colloquial French syntax is sometimes retained, which seems to break all the normal rules of translation: "But what can he be wanting here today, that fellow?" The conversations are often particularly stilted and the whole romantic tone is destroyed by reference to the loved one – never referred to as anything other than a girl in the French – as "dear woman".

Some of the decisions taken by Delisle are quite irritating. What possible justification is there for using "Admiral Meaulnes" every time the character is mentioned? The local farm names have been translated ("the farm of the Fair Star" sounds much more ludicrous than the French equivalent), but not the place names. The romance of the domain called *Les Sablonnières* is lost in the use of *Sand Pit House*. Details that add to the atmosphere in French are sometimes omitted.

The explanatory footnotes are useful to clarify realities such as details about schooling or the fact that members of the fire brigade have guns, and to correct the misleading impression given by words like "gypsy", "vagrant", "vagabond", and "mountebank" (all used by Davison) to convey "strolling-player". It is all the stranger, therefore, that "infants' classroom" can be used in the context of a secondary school. Several examples of inappropriate translations can be found, giving odd, if not downright wrong, impressions to the reader. Some of these derive from the fact that the translator is French and has not quite hit on the right word in English. Occasional attempts are made to translate the rare examples of rustic speech ("I be off to tell M. Seurel").

The translator keeps up the momentum of the story surprisingly well, but the rather clumsy treatment of Yvonne's death reduces the emotion that is still very much present in the other translations.

DAVISON (1959) takes a few liberties and sometimes fails to convey the reality of a situation, such as that pertaining to the French educational system. This is unfortunate, since the opening scenes of the book are firmly set in a school. To call the archives of the local Mairie a Public Records Office is to conjure up a vision in English of a much more important place, rather than a room in a school – every village school in France doubled up as the Mairie. "Quarter" is incomprehensible for "morning break".

Conveying the imagery is not easy, and identification with the images is not helped by the use of clumsy words like "adventurings". Occasionally the translation is more literary than the original ("which had in it a presage of winter"), and the translator sometimes elaborates on the original and makes his version more flowery.

Frustration arises for those who know French well, since the translation frequently adds details that do not exist in the original, in an attempt, one supposes, to interpret feelings more explicitly. A reluctance to use English cognates of French words means that the attempt to avoid them produces a less good version. The opposite also occurs. A very French-sounding word will be used when no hint of its original can be found in the text: "the furtive ebullition subsides". The result is clumsiness.

One of the perennial dilemmas of an English translator of narrative is whether or not to retain the historic present tense of the French. Davison does so; the result is somewhat artificial in English, but the problem is real.

Images are sometimes destroyed and errors of interpretation occur. Attempts are made to use old-fashioned words in English ("descried a faint glimmer of light"), where the French does not invite them.

Davison uses occasional footnotes, for example to explain why he has not translated the title *Le Grand Meaulnes* or to justify his rendering of "domaine" as "domain". Unwittingly comic translations are, fortunately, rare. This one lends an unnaturalness to children's speech and uses a French cliché to translate more ordinary French: "They've given us 'carte blanche,' haven't they?" A simple French phrase often becomes something elaborate. The most often-quoted sentences in the original are betrayed by flat, mundane translations. Meaulnes made a leap into Paradise, he did not "stray into heaven".

In spite of these reservations, the narrative, in the main, flows well in Davison. It is certainly possible to gain a clear picture of the unfolding story, and heart-rending scenes seem as moving in English as they are in French. What is difficult to determine is whether the emotion comes from the English version or from one's memory of the original.

MORRIS (1966) creates a much better initial impact because the school setting is rendered more appropriately. There are errors, however. The text does not say that Madame Seurel's "furniture would be ruined". Neither did Monsieur Seurel take the stove from the classroom to his own quarters, only the embers. Such stoves were hardly free-standing.

Morris takes liberties and tends to embroider. She also, on occasion, simply omits a metaphor that is too difficult to convey, and leaves out details, ostensibly when they are deemed not to add much to an existing epithet, for example.

The translation flows well and seems more modern than the two earlier ones. This is not to say that it has been transposed in time to another epoch, but that the language is less clumsy and more ordinary, as Alain-Fournier intended. On balance, the language is very natural and very moving with few jarring elements (and they jar only if one knows the French version and the French places particularly well). It reads, in comparison with the earlier versions, much more like something written in English and set in France than a translation of something originally written in French.

After a slightly clumsy start, VIVIAN's translation (1979) runs very smoothly. It does not try to invent English names for the places, and uses footnotes on occasion to explain French customs and buildings, as well as phrases that have no exact equivalent in English. This includes the word "grand", which is never translated here in conjunction with the name of the main character because it is a word with multiple connotations, all of which are conveyed in the French; "big" would not be adequate in English. Some lapses occur, as in chapter headings, with, for example, the clumsy "A Strange Entertainment". One of the key phrases of the book, conveying despair and anguish when the romantic adventure turns sour, sounds banal in English because of an infelicitous choice of noun: "everything is a labour as it used to be".

In summary, the impression one gains from all the above mentioned translations is that errors of interpretation or inappropriate renderings result from an attempt to tackle the translation without adequate research into the physical background of the book or Alain-Fournier's voluminous correspondence and early drafts.

MARIAN GILES JONES

Further Reading

Cancalon, Elaine D., *Fairy-Tale Structures and Motifs in Le Grand Meaulnes*, Bern: Herbert Lang, and Frankfurt: Peter Lang, 1975

Champigny, Robert, *Portrait of a Symbolist Hero: An Existential Study Based on the Works of Alain-Fournier*, Bloomington: Indiana University Press, 1954

Gibson, Robert, *The Quest of Alain-Fournier*, London: Hamish Hamilton, 1953; New Haven, Connecticut: Yale University Press, 1954

Gibson, Robert (editor), *Le Grand Meaulnes*, with an introduction and notes, London: Harrap, 1968

Gibson, Robert, *The Land Without a Name: Alain-Fournier and His World*, London: Elek, and New York: St Martin's Press, 1975 (contains translations by the author)

Gibson, Robert, *Alain-Fournier: Le Grand Meaulnes*, London: Grant and Cutler, 1986

Giles-Jones, Marian, *A Critical Commentary on Alain Fournier's Le Grand Meaulnes*, London: Macmillan, and New York: St Martin's Press, 1968

March, Harold M., "The 'Other Landscape' of Alain-Fournier", *Publications of the Modern Language Association of America*, l/6 (1941) pp. 266–79

Russell, R.B., *Le Grand Meaulnes; or, The Lost Domain*, with *Miracles*, by Alain-Fournier, translated by Adrian Eckersley, and an introduction by Eckersley, Horam, East Sussex: Tartarus, 1999

Tahourdin, Adrian, "A Bird Was Learning Its Song", *Times Literary Supplement* (21 May 1999)

Ullmann, Stephen, "The Symbol of the Sea in *Le Grand Meaulnes*" in his *The Image in the Modern French Novel: Gide, Alain-Fournier, Proust, Camus*, Cambridge: Cambridge University Press, 1960

Leopoldo Alas y Ureña 1852–1901

Spanish novelist and literary critic

Biography

Born in Zamora, Spain, 25 April 1852. In 1869 Alas moved with his family to Oviedo. He studied law in Madrid and from 1870 at the University of Oviedo. In 1883, after a year in Saragossa, he was appointed to a post as professor of law and political economy at the University of Oviedo, which he kept for the rest of his life, specializing in Roman law. In his early years Alas was influenced by the philosophical doctrine of Krausism. Alas also wrote novels, articles and literary criticism under the pen-name Clarín. He was a close friend of the novelist Armando Palacio Valdés (1853–1938). Died in Oviedo, 13 June 1901.

Alas, writing as Clarín, was one of the most influential literary critics in 19th-century Spain; and an important novelist whose reputation has only recently been recognized. The novel for which he is best known today, his early work *La Regenta* (*La Regenta*), published in 1884-85, was not well received in his own lifetime but is now acknowledged by many to be among the best Spanish naturalist novels of the period. His other important novel, *Su único hijo* (*His Only Son*), 1891, has also received much critical attention. Both novels satirize life in the fictional city of Vetusta, which Alas based on Oviedo. Alas also published collections of short stories, including *Cuentos Morales* (*The Moral Tales*), 1896, and *El gallo de Sócrates* [Socrates' Rooster], 1900. His articles on literary criticism, written from 1870 onwards, were sometimes known as *paliques* ("chit-chat") and *solos*, indicating the lightweight nature of their style and their personalized and acerbic satirical content, which attacked the decadent literary life of the Spanish Restoration period. His articles were collected in a number of volumes, including *Solos de Clarín* [Solos by Clarín], 1881; *Sermon perdido* [Lost Sermon], 1885; *Nueva campana* [New Campaign], 1887; *Mezclilla* [Melange], 1889; and *Palique* [Small Talk], 1893. He also wrote more serious essays on Baudelaire, Zola and other authors, naturalism in literature, and philosophical subjects.

Translations

Novel

La Regenta, 1884–85

Rutherford, John, *La Regenta*, with an introduction, London: Allen Lane, 1984

Short Story

¡Adios cordera!, 1892

McMichael, Charles B. (revised by the editors), "Adios Cordera" in *The Best of Spanish Literature in Translation*, edited by Seymour Resnick and Jeanne Pasmantier, New York: Ungar, 1976, pp. 248–55

Leopoldo Alas, professor of Roman law at the University of Oviedo in northern Spain, was best known during his lifetime as a discerning literary critic whose incisive views made him a number of enemies. Although he produced another novel *Su único hijo* [An Only Son] (1891) and several stories, he is finally gaining the world recognition he deserves as author of the two-volume novel *La Regenta* (1884–85), of which an English translation was not published until a hundred years after the original appeared. It is true that in 1976 one of Alas's stories, published in MCMICHAEL's English version, was ranked with "the best of Spanish literature".

John RUTHERFORD's 1984 English version of *La Regenta* took him five times longer to complete than it had taken Alas to write the original, and it is virtually impossible to fault. The irony, gentle or angry, of the original, is captured perfectly, as is the novel's ultimate bleak message. The English version even defies Nida and Taber's claim of the untranslatability of language where form is part of the content, by providing malapropisms that are, if anything, more comical than Alas's originals, while retaining their semantic value:

> "She's a Venus of Melons!" said a well born young blade named Ronzal, alias the Student, in raptures.
> "Rather than the Venus of Melos, the Venus of Medici," corrected the youthful and already wise Saturnino Bermúdez, who knew what he meant, more or less.

In the Spanish original, Ronzal had compared the buxom beauty to the "Venus del Nilo". In another instance we read:

> "He is no saint ... but ... I protest against all such slanderous aspersions."
> Ronzal made a note of the word; he had always thought that one said "nasturtiums".

In the original, Ronzal thought the word *especies* (species) should be *especias* (spices).

Rutherford's translation conveys the feeling of a time and culture without sacrificing the "textual effect" and "play of the signifier, which calls attention to the materiality of language" (Venuti) that give Alas's style its idiosyncratic tone. The title *La Regenta* is also a pun, and this time it is truly untranslatable. "Regenta" means both "the judge's wife" and also "the woman in command", and the storyline involves power play in a provincial backwater. Ana Osores, the proud, beautiful, intelligent – but decidedly humourless – orphaned daughter of a penniless upper-class intellectual and a foreign woman he met in exile, is married off to the good-natured Judge Quintanar, considerably her senior, who, on his retirement, neglects her by going hunting and designing "scientific" machines with a bachelor friend. Ana's adversary, De Pas, is a handsome priest of humble origin and boundless ambition, and the sequential storyline, set in the 1870s, concerns a struggle for control between the two, paralleled by events at all social levels involving others who vie for power in the shabby, boring town of "Vetusta", based on Alas's native Oviedo. Ana sublimates her unfulfilled sexual desire in religious, literary, and charitable activities, and only near the end of the story, after understanding the true nature of De Pas's interest in her and rejecting him, she allows herself to be seduced by the politician Mesías, who has been pursuing her throughout the novel. The irate cleric, with the help of an envious and ambitious maidservant, makes certain Ana's husband finds out about the affair. Although Judge Quintanar's favourite form of literature is the drama of avenged honour, when faced with a situation typical of such plays he would like to turn a blind eye to Ana's involvement with another man. Social pressure, mainly from De Pas, finally forces him to challenge Mesías, who is no huntsman, to a duel, and accidentally Quintanar, who is an excellent shot, is the one who is killed. Mesías must flee the town; Ana is distraught, as well as socially disgraced. De Pas cuts her; in future she can expect unwelcome advances from the men of the town, though she can always count on the respect and friendship of her late husband's hunting companion, the mild, somewhat ridiculous elderly bachelor, dilettante scientist, and unbeliever, who is also broad-minded, compassionate, and non-judgemental.

Most importantly, the English version succeeds in conveying the stylistic innovation of the original Spanish that later French critics were to call *style indirect libre*, claiming its invention for Flaubert, though Rutherford points out in his introduction that it had been exploited by Jane Austen before the author of *Madame Bovary* was born. Alas himself spoke of his style as "latent" or "the underground speaking of a consciousness", and he uses it both to explore his protagonists' inner lives and to give a panoramic view of the way of thinking of the society in which they live. There is constant switching of viewpoint from, for example, the rather laconic tone of the basic narrator to the tone of different characters in the novel or to that of the society at large, and interpreting these switches in tone demands an alertness of interpretation on the part of the reader and the translator that we think of as belonging to novels of modernity and postmodernity.

> Ana's attack of nerves was, as on the previous evening, melting into tears, into an impulsive pious determination always to be faithful to her husband. In spite of his infernal machines, Quintanar was her duty; and the canon theologian would be her aegis and protect her from all the formidable blows of temptation. But Quintanar knew nothing of this. The theatre had left him feeling awfully sleepy – he had not slept a wink the night before ...

In the above passage the first and third sentences are in the voice of the basic narrator. The rather pretentious reflection on temptation, as well as the opinion of Judge Quintanar's inventions, are Ana's thoughts, while the last sentence shows the mind-set of Quintanar himself.

The novel was not well received in its own time. It was highly immoral by the standards of those days. Critics did not know how to assess it, and it was neglected even in Spanish-speaking countries until recently. *La Regenta* belongs to a tradition that includes *Don Quixote*, *Tristram Shandy*, and *Madame Bovary* (to which it has been compared, though Alas's humour is much broader than Flaubert's); it is a tragic story told by a humorous narrator. The reader frequently laughs aloud while reading it, yet the message conveyed by the storyline is dark in the extreme; the novel deals with our human ability, or lack thereof, to control our destiny and find self-fulfillment in the face of a total lack of interest on the part of a probably non-existent God, as illustrated by the author's pointing out in the second paragraph of the novel that the very pinnacle of the cathedral spire is surmounted by an iron cross, which itself is topped with a lightning rod. Alas's psychological insight and technical mastery were decades ahead of their time.

Acting as critic, Alas had praised the styles of Galdós and Flaubert but also championed Zola's naturalism, though his own novel belongs to the realist, rather than the naturalist, school. Scientistic attitudes are ridiculed in the text, while among a plethora of petty and not so petty sinners, a religious, as well as a free-thinker, are presented as likeable characters.

All classes are depicted in a society that, in spite of the mental and physical inertia of its prominent citizens, is becoming materially "modern" but no better morally or spiritually. A degree of social mobility (in both directions) is starting to exist, thanks to emigration, commerce, human greed and unscrupulousness. The lower classes, feared by the upper, possess a vitality their betters lack. The novel is one of high moral seriousness, in fact, of a type that, prior to the advent of postmodern emphasis on the comic, Hispanic critics had found impossible to categorize and for this reason neglected. Its current popularity dates from the 1960s, when it was praised by Latin American novelists then gaining world-wide recognition, and its inclusion in the canon of Western literature is long overdue. The high quality of Rutherford's translation makes omitting it from reading lists no longer excusable.

ALITA KELLEY

Further Reading

Lefevere, André, *Translating Literature: Practice and Theory in a Comparative Literature Context*, New York: Modern Language Association of America, 1992

Nida, Eugene A. and Charles R. Taber, *The Theory and Practice of Translation*, Leiden: E.J. Brill, 1969

Rutherford, John, *Leopoldo Alas: La Regenta*, London: Grant and Cutler, 1974

Venuti, Lawrence, "Introduction" in *Rethinking Translation: Discourse, Subjectivity, Ideology*, edited by Venuti, London and New York: Routledge, 1992

Albanian

Literary Translation into English

About five and a half million people in Europe speak Albanian, with only just over half the number living in Albania itself. There are substantial Albanian populations in Kosovo, Macedonia and Montenegro. Long-standing Albanian communities live in Italy and Greece, and there has been extensive if usually temporary emigration to these two countries in the past few years. There has also been at an earlier stage emigration to the United States and Australia.

Albanian is an Indo-European language but has no particular affinity with any other tongue, although there have been borrowings from Greek and Latin and to a lesser extent from Slavonic and Turkish. These borrowings reflect Albanian history. Except in the time of the ancient Illyrians, from whom the Albanians are supposed to be descended, Albania until World War I was always under foreign domination, apart from a brief period in the 15th century under the great hero, Scanderbeg. Sometimes this domination has been only nominal, as the preservation of the language suggests, but many people of Albanian blood have found fame in other countries, Mother Teresa and Kemal Ataturk being an improbable pair of examples.

Albanian is heavily inflected, and foreigners find it hard to cope with a difficult grammar and a seemingly bizarre orthography. This is one reason why there has been so little translation from Albanian. There are two main dialects of Albanian, Gheg in the north, Tosk in the south, and it was not until 1950 that a standard literary Albanian, based largely on Tosk, evolved. More worryingly it was not until 1908 that it was agreed to adopt the Latin alphabet, and Albanian continued to be written by some in the Arabic script until well after that date, since over 70 per cent of the population is Muslim. Some Albanian literature was written in Greek letters, there being a substantial Orthodox minority in the south and a small Catholic group in the north. Illiteracy was rife until after World War II, when the Communist regime under Enva Hoxha, a former schoolmaster, did much to improve education, although they also sought to abolish religion.

Small, backward, remote and divided, Albania might seem a poor breeding ground for literature. Even the literate had temptations to write in languages other than their own or to engage in non-literary writing. It is odd that many of the great names in Albanian literature like the brothers Abdyl, Naim and Saim Frashëri (1830–92, 1846–1900, 1850–1904), Gjergji Fishta (1871–1940), Faik Konitza (1875–1942), and Fan Noli (1882–1965), both wrote in other languages and were political figures. The latter was Albania's first and almost only democratically elected prime minister, and one of the best translators of Shakespeare into any language. This latter achievement might suggest that translation between English and Albanian is not all that difficult, but in fact the creditable literary achievements of the Albanians have been very poorly represented in English versions.

Albanian is rarely studied in British or American universities. Before World War II there were few cultural links with Britain, and America was very remote. It was to Italy, France and Germany that Albanians went for higher education. Under the Communist regime Albania severed links with almost all other foreign countries, but Britain and the United States were particularly hated. Translation into English by Albanians in Tirana for the state publishing house was not particularly inspired, and was used to promote politically correct works. Thus there were translations of the novels of authors like Shevquet Musaraj (1914–86) (*Before the Dawn*, Tirana: 8 Nentori, 1981–82) and Sterjo Spasse (1914–89) (*The Awakening: A Novel*, Tirana: 8 Nentori, 1980), preaching grim socialist realism. Some poetry with the same message was translated into the English periodical *Albanian Life*, sponsored by the pro-Communist Albanian Society of Great Britain.

Writers like Ismail Kadare (1936–) (*The General of the Dead Army*, translated by Derek Coltman, London: W.H. Allen, 1971) and Dritero Agolli (1931–) (*The Man with the Gun*, Tirana: 8 Nentori, 1981) produced prose and poetry that seemed to approve of the regime, while carrying a hidden note of dissent, obscured in translation. Writers from a previous generation such as Fishta and Lasgush Poradeci (1899–1987) were frowned upon. The poetry of Migjeni, the alias of Millosh Nikolla (1911–38) with its strong hostility to religion, was regarded with favour by the Communist regime, and was translated into English before that regime fell (*Migjeni: Selected Albanian Songs and Sketches*, translated by Ali Cungu, Tirana: Naim Frashëri, 1962). Albanian writers such as Martin Camaj (1925–92) and Arshi Pipa (1920–) who managed to escape abroad were able to write about Albanian literature and language in English, but there are few translations of their own Albanian work.

Enver Hoxha died in 1985, the year that Gorbachev came to power in the Soviet Union. In Albania Communist rule gradually crumbled until in March 1992, free elections raised to power a democratic regime, headed by Sali Berisha. Kadare had defected to the west, and his novels are now freely translated, making him the one Albanian author of world standing. But there has been controversy over these translations. Some texts have been inadequately translated into English from a French translation; other versions have been unable to cope with the coded note of dissent beneath the apparently conformist message, while still others have been baffled by the almost untranslatable terms governing such institutions as the blood feud. Apart from these translations of Kadare, most of our knowledge of Albanian literature is due to one man, Robert Elsie, a Canadian living in Germany. Other translators of note include Pipa and Leonard Fox. Elsie has produced not only anthologies of folk tales and a wide range of modern poetry, but also a dictionary and a two-volume history of Albanian literature. This latter work contains English versions of many Albanian writers, including a number from Kosovo and Italy, and examines the wealth of literature before the Communist era, available previously only in a few humdrum English versions, or not at all. Much work could and should be done to bring these writers to the notice of English readers, but this work will be hard. In particular it will be hard to find translators trained in both the Albanian language and the Ottoman script. Many writers from Kosovo and Italy and among those active in the Rilindja period of national awakening in the 19th century do not use standard Albanian. Kadare's most famous novel, *The General of the Dead Army* has been translated only from the French in England and America. The history as well as the language of the Albanians is too little known, and literature has suffered as a result.

TOM WINNIFRITH

Further Reading

Camaj, Martin, *Selected Poetry* (parallel texts), translated by Leonard Fox, New York: New York University Press, 1990
Elsie, Robert, *Dictionary of Albanian Literature*, New York: Greenwood Press, 1986
Elsie, Robert, "Albanian Literature in English Translation: A Short Survey", *Slavonic and East European Review*, 70 (1992) pp. 249–57
Elsie, Robert (editor and translator), *Anthology of Modern Albanian Poetry: An Elusive Eagle Soars*, London and Boston: Forest Books, 1993
Elsie, Robert, *History of Albanian Literature*, 2 vols, Boulder, Colorado: Social Science Monographs, 1995
Hamp, E.P., entry on Albanian, in *Encyclopedia of Language and Linguistics*, edited by R.E. Asher and J.M.Y. Simpson, 10 vols, Oxford and New York: Pergamon Press, 1994
Pipa, Arshi, *Contemporary Albanian Literature*, Boulder, Colorado: East European Monographs, 1991
Vickers, Miranda, *The Albanians: A Modern History*, London and New York: Tauris, 1995
Winnifrith, Tom (editor), *Perspectives on Albania*, London: Macmillan, and New York: St Martin's Press, 1992

Vicente Aleixandre (Merlo) 1898–1984

Spanish poet

Biography

Born in Seville, Spain, 26 April 1898, the son of a railway engineer. The family moved to Malaga in 1900 and to Madrid in 1909. Aleixandre attended religious schools in Madrid, 1909–13. From 1914 he studied at the Central School of Commerce and in the Faculty of Law of the University of Madrid, obtaining in 1919 both a diploma in business administration and a degree in law, but meanwhile resolving to become a poet. After lecturing at the Central School of Commerce, Madrid, 1919–22, he worked for a railway company until 1925, when renal tuberculosis obliged him to give up his post. He now became a full-time writer, producing his first poems while convalescing. He was ill again, 1936–39. During the Spanish Civil War he sided with the Republicans and his work was banned, 1936–44. Before the war Aleixandre had won awards at home: the National literature prize, 1933; the Spanish Academy prize, 1934; and after the war official recognition resumed at home (membership of the Royal Spanish Academy in 1949; the national critics' prize 1963, 1969, 1975) and became international in 1977 when he received the Nobel Prize for Literature. In the same year he was given the Grand Cross of the Order of Carlos III. Died 13 December 1984, in Madrid.

Aleixandre published his first poems in the *Revista de Occidente* in 1926, going on to contribute to numerous other periodicals. His first volume of poems appeared in 1928 and was followed across the decades by many others, largely in free verse. Among the best known are *La destrucción o el amor* (*Destruction or Love*), 1935, and *Sombra del paraíso* (*Shadow of Paradise*), 1944.

Translations

Selections of Poetry

Barnstone, Willis and David Garrison, *A Bird of Paper: Poems of Vicente Aleixandre*, Athens: Ohio University Press, 1982
Bartman, Joeffrey, *The Cave of Night* (parallel texts), San Luis Obispo, California: Solo Press, 1976
Bourne, Louis, *The Crackling Sun: Selected Poems of the Nobel Prize Recipient 1977*, with an introduction, Madrid: Sociedad General Española de Librería, 1981
Hyde, Lewis and Robert Bly, *Twenty Poems*, Madison, Minnesota: Seventies Press, 1977
Hyde, Lewis (editor), *A Longing for the Light: Selected Poems of Vicente Aleixandre*, New York: Harper and Row, 1979

Poetry

La destrucción o el amor, 1935
Kessler, Stephen, *Destruction or Love: A Selection from La destrucción o el amor of Vicente Aleixandre*, Santa Cruz, California: Green Horse Press, 1976

Sombra del paraíso, 1944
Harter, Hugh A., *Shadow of Paradise* (bilingual edition), Berkeley: University of California Press, 1987

Mundo a solas 1934–36, 1950 (written 1936)
Hyde, Lewis and David Unger, *World Alone / Mundo a solas*, Great Barrington, Massachusetts: Penmaen Press, 1982

When Vicente Aleixandre won the Nobel Prize for Literature in 1977 his poetry was scarcely known to English-speaking readers. Despite his stature as a major figure in Spain's Generation of 1927 – the premier generation of 20th-century Spanish poets – his work had only begun to awaken the interest of translators, and it was not until the late 1970s and early 1980s, in the wake of the publicity generated by the prize, that several translations finally began to bring glimpses of his poetic world to readers unfamiliar with Spanish. Given the lengthy span of Aleixandre's career and the considerable volume of his work, the majority of his translators (BARTMAN, 1976; HYDE & BLYE, 1977; HYDE, 1979; BOURNE, 1981; BARNSTONE & GARRISON, 1982) have opted to assemble collections of representative poems from the major periods of his poetic development,whereas translations of individual books of poems have been more limited in number. (KESSLER, 1976; HYDE & UNGER, 1982; HARTER, 1987). To date, much of his writing remains to be translated.

In a broad sense Aleixandre's poetry has much to do with translation. An implicit theme throughout much of his work is the perplexing and at times paradoxical relationship between words and the ideas they convey, between language and the reality – often subconscious – that it expresses. His poetic enterprise thus shares with translation the struggle to express a content that is seemingly beyond the resources of language, and in this context it is not surprising to find that the title of his highly acclaimed volume, *Shadow of Paradise* (1944), is a most apt image to characterize translations of his poetry. In Aleixandre's cosmology, Paradise is irretrievably lost; but at the same time it is ever present in the fragmented world of its remnants, its shadow. In a similar way, Aleixandre's original poetry is, by definition, lost in the act of translation; yet it too resonates – and with considerable variety – in the poems of his various translators.

BARTMAN (1976) is a collection of 19 brief surrealist poems loosely based on Aleixandre's originals. Rather than strict translation, it is a fine example of creative writing inspired in Aleixandre. The author has used the original Spanish texts – printed on facing pages – as a starting point for his own, often very different, compositions.

KESSLER (1976) contains roughly half of the poems that appeared in the Spanish *Destruction or Love* (1933). The poems were selected in consultation with Aleixandre in order to "reflect the range of moods and thematic progressions in the work as a whole", and they do so successfully. The translations are among the most literal available, reproducing the structure of the source text (i.e. word order, repetitions, breaks in the lines, etc.) as much as possible.

HYDE & BLY (1977) reject this structural or "syntactic" approach in favor of a "vision" view of translation. Hyde explains that "with poetry this was often the poet's situation in the first place – he saw something and tried to speak the words that would recall it. The translator tries to see the thing behind the poem and then find the words in his own tongue that will lead back to it" (7). The result is a fine series of English poems that reflect the translators' particular readings of the originals. Such built-in interpretation, however, comes at the expense of the more hermetic style of the source texts. Compare, for example, the first lines of the poem "Life", as rendered literally in KESSLER (1976) to the more personal lines in HYDE & BLY (1977):

> A paper bird inside my chest
> says that the time of kisses hasn't come;
> to live, to live, the sun crackles unseen,
>
> (Kessler)

> A paper bird I have in my chest
> tells me the time for kisses has not yet come;
> To live! To live! . . . no one sees the sun crackle,
>
> (Hyde & Bly)

HYDE (1979) combines the work of 15 translators and contains a total of 68 poems as well as several prose excerpts. Despite the large number of contributors, the translations are remarkably even in style, and the breadth of the collection affords the reader a clear outline of the different phases of Aleixandre's poetic development.

BOURNE (1981) is larger in scope, with more than 90 poems and a marked scholarly focus. Of particular interest to students of Aleixandre is the book's 75-page introduction, which not only sketches the poet's creative trajectory over 50 years of writing but also offers a most lucid account of the linguistic challenges faced by the translator. Read in conjunction with the translations themselves, these comments offer the reader the most in-depth presentation of Aleixandre's poetry available in anthology form.

BARNSTONE & GARRISON (1982) also offers an extensive selection of poems and it includes a "Poet's Preface" in which Aleixandre addresses the English-speaking reader. The poems in this collection often highlight previously untranslated layers of meaning from the Spanish texts. Returning once again to Aleixandre's "Life", for example, compare the differences in nuance between Kessler's "To die, a little noise is enough, / that of another heart going silent," and Barnstone & Garrison's "To die a tiny noise will do / as when another heart is silenced".

HYDE & UNGER (1982) is the first translation of a book of poems in its entirety. Several of the poems contained in this volume can also be found in Hyde (1979), but read in their original context they acquire new shades of meaning. In this regard, the volume is particularly useful for readers interested in the poet's sense of composition at the book-level.

In a similar vein, HARTER (1987) brings to the English-speaking reader the first complete translation of Aleixandre's *Shadow of Paradise*. The translator is acutely aware of the difficulties posed by the language of this masterwork, and many of his solutions (e.g. the use of English tetrameter to approximate the rhythms of Spanish hendecasyllable verse) are impressive indeed.

MICHAEL P. IAROCCI

Further Reading

Bousoño, Carlos, *La poesía de Vicente Aleixandre*, Madrid: Gredos, 1956; 3rd edition, 1977

Cabrera, Vicente and Harriet Boyer (editors), *Critical Views on Vicente Aleixandre's Poetry*, Lincoln, Nebraska: Society of Spanish and Spanish-American Studies, 1979

Daydi-Tolson, Santiago (editor), *Vicente Aleixandre: A Critical Appraisal*, Ypsilanti, Michigan: Bilingual Press / Editorial Bilingüe, 1981

Morris, C.B., *Surrealism and Spain, 1920–1936*, Cambridge: Cambridge University Press, 1972

Schwartz, Kessel, *Vicente Aleixandre*, New York: Twayne, 1970

See also the introductory material in Barnstone & Garrison and in Bourne

Isabel Allende 1942–

Chilean novelist

Biography

Born in Lima, Peru, 8 August 1942, of Chilean parents. Her parents separated when she was a child and, as her stepfather was a diplomat, she spent much of her early life abroad. When she was still young, she returned with her mother to live in Santiago de Chile in her grandparents' home, which was to form the model of the Trueba household in *La casa de los espíritus*. In Chile, Allende took up journalism, writing for several publications including the women's magazine *Paula*, and publishing *Civilice a su troglodita* [Civilize Your Caveman], 1974, a collection of her whimsical articles on gender relations. Political events were to take over, however, and the right-wing military coup of 1973, which deposed her uncle, President Salvador Allende, brought about great changes in Chile. Isabel Allende left Chile a year after the coup, fleeing the Pinochet regime, and settled in Venezuela with her first husband, Miguel Frias, and their two children. It was while in Venezuela that she began writing fiction and published her first novel, *La casa de los espíritus*, in 1982. Isabel Allende now lives in Marin County, California, with her second husband, William Gordon, and extended family, in a house named *La casa de los espíritus*.

Translations

Novels

La casa de los espíritus, 1982
Bogin, Magda, *The House of the Spirits*, New York: Knopf, and London: Jonathan Cape, 1985

De amor y de sombra, 1984
Peden, Margaret Sayers, *Of Love and Shadows*, New York: Knopf, and London: Jonathan Cape, 1987

Eva Luna, 1987
Peden, Margaret Sayers, *Eva Luna*, New York: Knopf, 1988; London: Hamish Hamilton, 1989

El plan infinito, 1991
Peden, Margaret Sayers, *The Infinite Plan: A Novel*, New York and London: HarperCollins, 1993

Hija de la fortuna, 1999
Peden, Margaret Sayers, *Daughter of Fortune*, New York and London: HarperCollins, 1999

Short Stories

Cuentos de Eva Luna, 1990
Peden, Margaret Sayers, *The Stories of Eva Luna*, New York: Atheneum, and London: Penguin, 1991

Autobiography

Paula, 1994
Peden, Margaret Sayers, *Paula*, London: HarperCollins, 1995

Despite the upsurge of interest in Latin American writing in the past quarter century, it is noteworthy that women writers have failed to achieve the popular success and the critical acclaim of authors such as García Márquez or Vargas Llosa. There are exceptions, such as the Brazilian Clarice Lispector, whose work is highly regarded, thanks in great part to her promotion by Hélène Cixous as a major proponent of *écriture féminine*, or Laura Esquivel, whose lightweight novel *Como agua para chocolate* (*Like Water for Chocolate*) has been adapted for the screen. But the only woman writer who has been well received by both critics and readers is the Chilean Isabel Allende.

Allende's success may be attributed not only to her chosen subject matter of the family and relationships (the traditional sphere of the female author), but also to her liberal/left-wing political engagement. In this, she follows in the footsteps of her uncle, Salvador Allende, the president of Chile who was deposed and died in unclear circumstances in 1973. There is also little doubt that, for the English-speaking reader at least, the perceived exoticism of Isabel Allende's fiction, and of the woman herself, also plays a part in her appeal.

Following the publication of her first novel, *The House of the Spirits*, in which the spirit world impinges on everyday reality and little Clara moves salt cellars with the power of her mind, Allende was seemingly set to take her place in the ranks of the magical realists. However, her subsequent works show few of these early supernatural leanings. Similarly, Allende was seen as a writer of feminocentric fiction until the appearance of *The Infinite Plan* in which she traces the life of a male protagonist.

The translations of Allende's writings are generally effective but face the challenge of the author's rather ponderous narrative. Her prose style can tend towards the purple, although there are moments of stark reality, such as Alba's imprisonment in *The House of the Spirits*, translated by Magda BOGIN (1985). Inevitably, this work suffers in translation on account of its cultural specificity, notably in the case of the names of the central line of female characters: the symbolic resonance of Nívea, Clara, Blanca and Alba, each suggesting a progressive lightening/enlightenment and a move towards the *dawn* of a new age of reconciliation and understanding, goes unremarked by the English-speaking reader.

There are times when the translator can do little more than faithfully render the embarrassingly expressed original: the description of Irene and Francisco's lovemaking in *Of Love and Shadows*, accurately translated by Margaret SAYERS PEDEN (1987), comes complete with the equivalent of waves crashing on the shore and recalls the language of pulp romantic fiction. In this, Allende's choice of metaphor may have been influenced by the work of Barbara Cartland, some of whose novels she has translated into Spanish.

SAYERS PEDEN has continued to translate Allende's fiction and her work on *Eva Luna*, the tale of a modern-day Hispanic Scheherazade, and *The Stories of Eva Luna*, shows a sensitivity to the original. Allende's 1991 work of fiction, *The Infinite Plan*, represents something of a departure in that it is set mainly in the United States and centres on the life of Gregory Reeves, a "gringo" whose upbringing in a Californian *barrio* means that he is fluent in Spanish. The clash of languages is left largely unexplored in the original text but is picked up by Sayers Peden's translation, which judiciously allows a few Spanish expletives to remain in the English translation. Thus it is ironic that the English-speaking reader experiences the effect of a linguistic culture clash that is denied to those reading in Spanish.

Allende's 1994 publication, *Paula*, is her most personal, as it deals with her family history (previously fictionalized in *The House of the Spirits*) and the death of her daughter. Such emotive subjects rarely lend themselves to anything but sentimental prose, and *Paula* is no exception; the translation, again, is a faithful rendition (SAYERS PEDEN, 1995).

It is interesting to note that *The House of the Spirits* has been adapted for both stage and screen. The stage version, based on the English translation and produced in Britain, was adapted by Allende herself in collaboration with the director, Michael Batz. Running to some seven hours over two nights, it drew together an international cast and mixed critical reviews. It valiantly attempted to convey the sense of the family saga, but was hindered in terms of dramatic power by the verbatim rendering of the written text into script.

The film version was hardly more successful, although for very different reasons: here, two generations, which play an important role in the linear progression of the narrative, were conflated, with the result that the cinema audience would have difficulty in recognizing the novel. Allende's second novel, *Of Love and Shadows*, has also been made into a film.

As a female voice in the cacophony that is modern Latin American fiction, Isabel Allende is a significant figure. It is to be hoped that her visibility on the world stage will encourage readers to seek out the work of other Latin American women writers.

JANET LLOYD

Further Reading

Castro-Klarén, Sara, Sylvia Molloy and Beatriz Sylvia (editors), *Women's Writing in Latin America: An Anthology*, Boulder, Colorado: Westview Press, 1991

Coddou, Marcelo (editor), *Los libros tienen sus propios espíritus: estudios sobre Isabel Allende*, Xalapa, Veracruz: Universidad Veracruzana, 1986

Hart, Patricia, *Narrative Magic in the Fiction of Isabel Allende*, Rutherford, New Jersey: Fairleigh Dickinson University Press, and London: Associated University Presses, 1989

Jorge Amado 1912–

Brazilian novelist

Biography

Born in Ferradas, Itabuna, Bahia, 10 August 1912. After studying law and working as a journalist, Amado began his long literary career in the 1930s, with a series of social realist novels, all set in his native Bahia, which championed the struggle of the poor against exploitation and oppression. This phase culminated in 1943 with *Terras do sem fin* (translated as *The Violent Land* in 1945), one of Latin America's most powerful regionalist novels. His espousal of communist politics helped orientate those works, but with the publication of *Gabriela, cravo e canela* (*Gabriela, Clove and Cinnamon*) in 1959, his writing took a new direction, more lyrical and humorous and less overtly political, though social protest was maintained through increased use of satire and irony. This new style resulted in a number of highly popular novels, exemplified by *Dona Flor e seus dois maridos* (*Dona Flor and Her Two Husbands*) in 1966 and *Tereza Batista, cansada de guerra* (*Tereza Batista, Home from the Wars*) in 1972, which extolled the resilience and creativity of the Bahian poor through strong, colourful protagonists and vivid depiction of the region's rich popular culture. His early political activities involved many vicissitudes, including imprisonments and exile, and he has travelled widely. Amado has received numerous literary prizes and awards, and film and television versions of his work have further extended its popularity. Undoubtedly Brazil's best-known novelist of the 20th century, Amado has become a national celebrity with a strong following abroad: his novels have now been translated into some 40 languages.

Translations

Novels

Jubiabá, 1935
Neves, Margaret A., *Jubiabá*, New York: Avon, 1984

Mar morto, 1936
Rabassa, Gregory, *Sea of Death*, New York: Avon, 1984

Capitães de areia, 1937
Rabassa, Gregory, *Captains of the Sands*, New York: Avon, 1988

Terras do sem fim, 1943
Putnam, Samuel, *The Violent Land*, New York: Knopf, 1945; revised edition, London: Collins Harvill, 1989

São Jorge dos Ilhéus, 1944
Landers, Clifford E., *The Golden Harvest*, New York: Avon, 1992

Gabriela, cravo e canela, 1958
Taylor, James L. and William Grossman, *Gabriela, Clove and Cinnamon*, New York: Knopf, and London: Souvenir Press, 1962

Os velhos marinheiros: duas histórias do cais da bahia, 1961
Onís, Harriet de, *Home is the Sailor*, New York: Knopf, and London: Chatto and Windus, 1964 (translation of *A completa verdade sobre as discutidas aventuras do comandante Vasco Moscoso de Aragão, capitão de longo curso* [The Whole Truth about the Debatable Adventures of Captain Vasco Moscoso de Aragão, Master Mariner])

Shelby, Barbara, *The Two Deaths of Quincas Wateryell*, New York: Knopf, 1965 (translation of *A morte e a morte de Quincas Berro Dágua*, 1961)

Os pastores da noite, 1964
Onís, Harriet de, *Shepherds of the Night*, New York: Knopf, 1966; London: Collins Harvill, 1989

Dona Flor e seus dois maridos, 1966
Onís, Harriet de, *Dona Flor and Her Two Husbands: A Moral and Amorous Tale*, New York: Knopf, 1969; London: Weidenfeld and Nicolson, 1970

Tenda dos milagres, 1969
Shelby, Barbara, *Tent of Miracles*, New York: Knopf, 1971; London: Collins Harvill, 1989

Tereza Batista, cansada de guerra, 1972
Shelby, Barbara, *Tereza Batista, Home from the Wars*, New York: Knopf, 1975; London: Souvenir Press, 1982

Tieta do agreste, pastora de cabras, 1977
Shelby Merello, Barbara, *Tieta, the Goat Girl*, New York: Knopf, 1979; London: Souvenir Press, 1981

Farda, fardão, camisola de dormir: fábula para acender uma esperança, 1979
Lane, Helen, *Pen, Sword, Camisole: A Fable to Kindle a Hope*, Boston: Godine, 1985

Tocaia grande: a face obscura, 1984
Rabassa, Gregory, *Showdown*, New York and London: Bantam, 1988

O sumiço da santa, 1988
Rabassa, Gregory, *The War of the Saints*, New York: Bantam, 1993; London: Serpent's Tail, 1994

Children's Fiction
O gato malhado e a Andorinha Sinhá, 1976
Shelby Merello, Barbara, *The Swallow and the Tomcat: A Love Story*, New York: Delacorte Press, 1982

The majority of Jorge Amado's novels are available in English, though some of his social realist works of the 1930s and 1940s, together with some of his travel writing, still await translation. Furthermore, some of the translations are extremely difficult to obtain in the United Kingdom.

Jubiabá (1935) tells the story of a black youth whose political militancy on behalf of his fellow workers gives new meaning to his previously aimless life. The documentation of social struggle is counterbalanced with lyrical descriptions of Bahian life and popular culture. NEVES (1984) adheres to the form of the original, and manages to convey the lively, colloquial tone of the dialogue. The popular songs through which the characters articulate their struggle are skilfully translated in rhyme while still retaining their mood. A list explaining "untranslatable terms" is included, though it is minimal.

Sea of Death (*Mar morto*, 1936) and *Captains of the Sands* (*Capitães de areia*, 1937) were both translated by Gregory Rabassa in the 1980s, but neither translation is now readily available in the United Kingdom. *Sea of Death* is a lyrical narrative that extols the bravery and resilience of the seafaring community in Bahia in their constant struggle against poverty and the dangers of the sea, while *Captains of the Sands* recounts the adventures of abandoned children who live on the streets, with the acquisition of political consciousness again the central theme.

The Violent Land (*Terras do sem fim*, 1943) is a historical novel, recording the epic and violent struggle between rival cacao planters in Southern Bahia. PUTNAM's translation (1945) follows closely the form and style of the original text and largely succeeds in capturing the lyricism that gives it much of its dramatic force, as well as achieving naturalness in the dialogue. A brief glossary serves to explain regional terms italicized in the text.

Golden Harvest (*São Jorge dos Ilhéus*, 1944) picks up the story of the cacao lands from the previous novel and traces the infiltration of foreign economic interests into the region. Amado employs a more prosaic language in this work and LANDERS (1992) succeeds in capturing its tone in his translation, though his use of North American slang to translate the popular speech patterns of the characters and their popular songs, with such phrases as "But listen good, my li'l brown gal", at times jars with the regional theme and atmosphere of the work.

Gabriela, Clove and Cinnamon (*Gabriela, cravo e canela*, 1958) is a humorous novel about the daily life and customs of Ilhéus, in Bahia, in the 1920s. It focuses on the love story of Nacib, a bar owner, and Gabriela, a migrant from the interior. TAYLOR & GROSSMAN (1962) strive to convey the irony, humour and witty dialogue of the original. Some of the lyrical quality that characterizes the prose in certain sections is sacrificed for the sake of ease of reading, but the overall exuberant style of the novel, including florid subtitles and poetic epigraphs, is well captured in the translation.

Home is the Sailor (ONÍS, 1964) is a translation of one of the two novelettes in *Os velhos marinheiros* (1961), entitled *A completa verdade sobre as discutidas aventuras do comandante Vasco Moscoso de Aragão*. It is a picaresque story of a bohemian whose grandiose dreams of being a heroic sea captain are finally converted into reality. The humour and lively dialogue are preserved by ONÍS in her translation. She achieves an accurate rendition of the tone of the popular story-teller that Amado adopts, finding, for example, appropriate language to translate the hyperbolic titles and subtitles of the original.

The second novelette, *The Two Deaths of Quincas Wateryell* (*A morte e a morte de Quincas Berro Dágua*, 1963) is a short satire of bourgeois values, in which the protagonist gives up the security of his middle-class life to become a vagabond, living on the margins of society. SHELBY (1965) reproduces the relatively restrained language of the third-person narrative and concentrates on conveying the corrosive humour of the work. However, her rendition of the slang employed by the dropouts with whom Quincas associates is not always totally convincing.

Shepherds of the Night (*Os pastores da noite*, 1964) is a novel in three episodes that focuses on the life, culture and struggle of the marginalized sectors of the Bahian population. Humour and irony are again used to convey social denunciation. The chief merits of the ONÍS translation (1966) are that it successfully reproduces Amado's informal, colloquial method of narration, and achieves natural sounding dialogue. It also includes a glossary giving detailed explanations of regional terms and historical figures referred to in the text.

Dona Flor and her Two Husbands (*Dona Flor e seus dois maridos*, 1966) is a humorous novel satirizing the hypocrisy and stifling social conventions of the bourgeoisie. Flor is torn between her living spouse and the ghost of her former husband, who represent contrasting values and ways of life. Voodoo magic enables her to reconcile them, however, and she lives the rest of her life happily with both of them. It is another work characterized by colloquial language, and ONÍS (1969) again finds suitable idiomatic expressions in English and largely succeeds in reproducing the lively, amusing dialogues. She uses another glossary to explain vocabulary specific to Bahian culture.

Tent of Miracles (*Tenda dos milagres*, 1969) highlights the role of black culture and miscegenation in Brazil. The novel's hero, Pedro Arcanjo, fights against prejudice and dedicates his life to promoting Afro-Brazilian culture. The defiance of the oppressed is expressed through irony and humour, well conveyed in the SHELBY translation (1971), which also seeks an approximation of the popular, idiomatic speech employed by the characters. A glossary helps to clarify some of the regional terms used.

Tereza Batista, Home from the Wars (*Tereza Batista cansada de guerra*, 1972) tells of a picaresque heroine who fights against injustice and exploitation. The novel imitates the form, style and thematic content of Brazil's traditional popular poetry, or *literatura de cordel*. SHELBY (1975) places much emphasis on reproducing the humorous tone of the language, including the verbosity and hyperbole of the popular poet, which Amado parodies in large sections of the novel and which is particularly difficult to translate convincingly. The work includes a number of lewd passages and Shelby finds suitably ribald English equivalents for her translation.

Tieta, the Goat Girl (*Tieta do agresta, pastora de cabras*, 1977) features the adventures of another strong, independent heroine, who ends up playing a leading role in a fight to protect the environment. The imitation of *cordel* tradition is even more accentuated in the style and form of the work. The exaggerated, melodramatic tone, encapsulated in the exuberant subtitles, is captured (1979) by SHELBY MERELLO, much of whose effort is spent on reproducing the idiomatic expressions and slang of the extensive dialogues.

Pen, Sword and Camisole: A Fable to Kindle a Hope (*Farda, fardão, camisola de dormir: fábula para acender uma esperança*, 1979) is an allegory of the fight for democracy under an authoritarian regime. It is a farce set in Rio de Janeiro, about a contest for a vacant place in the prestigious Brazilian Academy of Letters. LANE (1985) follows Amado's more restrained use of language in this novel and manages to convey its humour and satire, but in places her translation of dialogue is rather too stiff and formal, as in "I had a passing affair with his daughter, a wanton young lady but rather vapid."

Showdown (*Tocaia grande: a face obscura*, 1984) examines again the historical development of the *cacao* lands of Bahia, particularly the growth of the towns in the region. It is a documentary novel, without the epic tone of the earlier works on the subject or the poetic prose or humour of Amado's most popular novels. The colloquial language of the dialogue is skilfully conveyed into English by RABASSA (1988). He omits several chapters in his translation, to abbreviate what is for many critics an excessively verbose text.

The War of the Saints (*O sumiço da santa*, 1988) brings together many of Amado's long-running concerns, emphasizing the Afro-Brazilian culture of Bahia and the magical beliefs of its population. RABASSA's extensive glossary of over 100 regional terms gives valuable guidance to the reader. He succeeds in retaining Amado's informal style of narration, and again shows his ability to find natural-sounding equivalents for idiomatic expressions and the slang frequently used in dialogues.

MARK DINNEEN

Further Reading

Brookshaw, David, *Race and Color in Brazilian Literature*, Metuchen, New Jersey: Scarecrow Press, 1986

Chamberlain, Bobby J., *Jorge Amado*, Boston: Twayne, 1990

Ellison, Fred, "Jorge Amado" in his *Brazil's New Novel*, Berkeley: University of California Press, 1954

Patai, Daphne, *Myth and Ideology in Contemporary Brazilian Fiction*, Rutherford, New Jersey: Fairleigh Dickinson University Press, 1983

Schlomann Lowe, E., "The 'New' Jorge Amado", *Luso-Brazilian Review*, 6/2 (1969) pp. 73–82

Anacreon c.570–c.475 BC

Greek poet

Biography

Born in Teos, Ionia, Asia Minor, c.570 BC. When the Persians invaded in about 540, Anacreon left for Thrace where he helped other Teians found the Greek colony of Abdera. From c.533–522 he lived at the court of Samos as tutor to the son of the tyrant Polycrates. After the death of Polycrates he was invited to Athens by Hipparchus, son of the tyrant of Athens, Pisistratus. After the assassination of Hipparchus in 514 Anacreon may have gone to Thrace, then Thessaly. A statue depicting him was erected on the Acropolis. He wrote in Ionian Greek and in lyric, iambic, and elegiac metres. Died c.475 BC, place of death unknown.

Translations

Addison, John, *The Works of Anacreon*, with *The Odes, Fragments, and Epigrams of Sappho*, London: John Watts, 1735

Aldington, Richard, *Greek Songs in the Manner of Anacreon*, London: The Egoist, 1919

Barnstone, Willis, *Greek Lyric Poetry*, New York: Bantam, 1962

Davidson, Judson France, *The Anacreontea and Principal Remains of Anacreon of Teos*, London and Toronto: Dent, 1915

Fawkes, Francis, *The Works of Anacreon, Sappho, Bion, Moschus and Musaeus*, London: J. Newbery, L. Davis and C. Reymers, 1760

Manning, F.J., *The Odes of Anacreon* (bilingual edition), London: Printed privately, 1837

Moore, Thomas, *The Odes of Anacreon*, London: John Stockdale, 1800, and many subsequent editions

Pope, P.M., *The Anacreonta: Translated into English Verse*, London: Bowes and Bowes, 1955

Richardson, Erastus, *The Odes of Anacreon*, New Haven, Connecticut: Yale University Press, 1928

Stanley, Thomas, *Poems*, London, 1651

Thurlow, Edward Hovell, *The Doge's Daughter*, in his *Moonlight; The Doge's Daughter ...*, London: White, 1814

Urquhart, D.H., *The Odes of Anacreon*, London: T. Cadell, 1787

West, M.L., *Greek Lyric Poetry*, Oxford: Clarendon Press, and New York: Oxford University Press, 1993

Willis, Francis, Abraham Cowley, John Oldham and Thomas Wood, *Anacreon Done into English*, Oxford: L. Lichfield for Anthony Stephens, 1683

Of the poems of Anacreon there were once many books, but only fragments now survive. They are poems of wine and love, their craftsmanship of the highest order, humour and emotion held in exquisite balance. Some fragments also suggest the presence of a vein of satire. Between the 1st century BC and the 6th century AD (approximately), many poets composed sympotic songs in the manner and spirit of Anacreon. They imitated his metres, and sometimes adopted his persona. These anacreonta or anacreontics were treated as genuine works of Anacreon until well into the 19th century. Indeed, they have been translated more frequently than the genuine fragments. This brief essay discusses English versions of both the genuine fragments and (mainly) the anacreontic imitations.

The anacreontic poems were much admired and imitated after their publication, by Henricus Stephanus, in 1554. They leave their mark on many Elizabethan poets – see, for example, Robert Greene's version ("Cupid abroad was lated in the night") of Poem 33 (see M.L. West, *Carmina Anacreonta*, Leipzig, 1984). Herrick is heavily influenced by the anacreontics.

The first substantial English translation was that of Thomas STANLEY (1651), who translated 55 of the anacreontics. Stanley's lively couplets are often attractive, and he resists the temptation to over-decoration. He is largely accurate, though there are instances (e.g. 15) where he silently "purifies" the original's "immorality".

The 1683 versions by WILLIS and others are far freer. The Preface (signed S.B.) tells us that this is the work of one who is "an utter Enemey to the too narrow tye of a verbal Translation". The translators work by expansion and addition – so much so that one might regard these as variations on the themes of the original rather than translations. The versions by COWLEY, here reprinted, are the most successful.

The octosyllabic couplets of ADDISON (1735) are energetic, but the search for rhyme frequently involves him in the addition of spurious adjectives and some awkward inversion. His fondness for compound adjectives is an irritating mannerism.

The version by FAWKES (1760) – which includes reprints of translations by William BROOME – has an attractive elegance, but expands and elaborates greatly; new images are added, narrative contexta are provided.

The 56 versions from the anacreontics by URQUHART (1787) are also heavily decorated by lines of his own invention, and by a varnish of dubiously poetic diction.

The versions of Thomas MOORE (1800), published before he was 20, gained him fame and the nickname "Anacreon Moore". Moore poeticizes what is simple in the original. "Give me the lyre of Homer" becomes "Give me the harp of epic song, / Which Homer's finger thrill'd along". Moore's fancies are often entertaining, his verse attractively lyrical, but the results are too diffusely free to have a very high rank as translations.

The 55 anacreontics of THURLOW (1814) are rather chaster in their language and take fewer liberties with the sense of the original. The best of them (e.g., the two versions of poem 21 – i.e. Thurlow's Ode XIX) have a neo-classical poise.

MANNING (1837) makes an extraordinary attempt to, in effect, bowdlerize the anacreontics. Endeavouring to bring the poems "nearer to purity", by "clothing the ideas in such language as will not offend the purest mind", Manning produces risibly poor results.

In DAVIDSON (1915) the notes, drawing attention to many analogies in ancient and modern literature, are more interesting than the translations, which are full of redundant adjectives and adverbs and frequently flawed by falsely poetic archaisms. The general manner is unduly pompous. There are translations of many of the fragments of Anacreon, as well as of the anacreontics.

The prose versions by ALDINGTON (1919) – of the anacreontics only – are scrupulous in their avoidance of expansion and are very attractive in their clarity. As a guide to the content of the anacreontic imitations these can be warmly recommended.

RICHARDSON (1928) is largely faithful in his 60 anacreontics in rhymed couplets. His diction, though, is sometimes rather coyly archaic.

POPE (1955) employs a variety of English metres and stanza forms; while they are largely faithful and free from decorative expansion, there is little fire or rhythmic subtlety in these workmanlike versions.

The BARNSTONE (1962) anthology offers versions both of 27 of the genuine fragments and 20 of the anacreonta. Barnstone is generally faithful and engagingly unverbose in his treatment of the originals. His unrhymed syllabics frequently correspond to (without precisely imitating) the metrical and stanzaic patterns of the Greek.

WEST (1993) translates almost all of the surviving fragments of Anacreon – some of them no more than a single line in length. He is certainly the English reader's best guide to the verse of Anacreon himself, scholarly and unflamboyantly lucid.

Some of the best translations of individual anacreontic poems are to be found outside these substantial collections, e.g. Herrick's delightful version ("*Cupid* as he lay among") of poem 35 and Dr Johnson's assured translation ("Lovely courier of the sky") of poem 15.

GLYN PURSGLOVE

Further Reading

Baumann, Michael, *Die Anakreonteen in englischen Übersetzungen: Ein Beitrag zur Rezeptionsgeschichte der anakreontischen Sammlung*, Heidelberg: C. Winter, 1974

Blessington, F., "On translating mediocrity: Anacreonta 3 and English Poetry", *Classical Bulletin*, 62 (1986) pp. 21–26

Mason, Tom, "Abraham Cowley and the Wisdom of Anacreon", *Cambridge Quarterly*, 19/2 (1990) pp. 103–37

Rosenmeyer, Patricia A., *The Poetics of Imitation: Anacreon and the Anacreontic Tradition*, Cambridge and New York: Cambridge University Press, 1992

Hans Christian Andersen 1805–1875

Danish story writer, novelist, travel writer, poet and dramatist

Biography

Born in Odense, Denmark, 2 April 1805, the son of a shoemaker. Andersen grew up in poverty, working in a factory after his father died. He attended schools in Odense until he was 14; then lived alone in Copenhagen, 1819–22, trying to be taken on at the Royal Theatre there. He was not well enough educated for this, nor did he succeed as a singer, but he had literary talent, and a director of the Theatre put him through grammar school (Slagelse, and Elsinor, 1822–27). He obtained his arts certificate in 1828 and became a freelance writer. A royal travel grant in 1833 allowed him to make journeys in Germany, Switzerland and Italy that resulted in works in several genres containing descriptions of those countries. Further extensive travels followed when Andersen became celebrated, during the course of which he met many notable people, including Charles Dickens, and was entertained by royalty. He received a pension from Frederik VI in 1838. Honours and titles were bestowed on him in Denmark and abroad. Died 4 August 1875 in Copenhagen.

Andersen became internationally known for his novels and especially his fairy tales. His travel books and autobiographical works are also of great interest. His first works, however, were poems, of which he published a volume in 1830, and he also wrote numerous plays and some libretti. His first success as a novelist, with *Improvisatoren* (*The Improvisatore*), came in 1835, the same year as the first of the series of tales and stories that brought him fame. The listing below is confined to selected writing in genres for which Andersen became well known in English.

Translations

Collection

Andersen's Works, by several translators, overseen and revised by Horace Scudder, 10 vols, New York: Hurd and Houghton, 1870–71

Novels

Improvisatoren, 1835

Howitt, Mary, *The Improvisatore; or, Life in Italy*, London: Richard Bentley, and New York: Harper, 1845

O.T., 1836; *Kun en Spillemand*, 1836

Howitt, Mary, *Only a Fiddler! and O.T., or, Life in Denmark*, London: Richard Bentley, 1845

De to baronesser, 1848

[Lohmeyer, Charles Beckwith], *The Two Baronesses*, London: Richard Bentley, 1848; Boston: Houghton Osgood, 1879

At være eller ikke være?, 1857

Bushby, Anne S., *To Be, or Not to Be?*, London: Richard Bentley, 1857

Autobiography

Das Märchen meines Lebens ohne Dichtung, 1847 (in collected German edition), Danish edition as *Mit eget eventyr uden digtning*, 1942 (written 1846)

Howitt, Mary, *The True Story of My Life: A Sketch*, London: Longman Brown Green and Longmans, 1847

Mit livs eventyr, 1855, revised and updated 1869, 1877

Jones, W. Glyn, *The Fairy-Tale of My Life*, New York: British Book Centre, 1955; reprinted New York: Paddington Press, 1975

Michael, Maurice, *The Mermaid Man: The Autobiography of Hans Christian Andersen: A New Abridged Translation*, London: Arthur Barker, and New York: Library Publishers, 1955

[Scudder, Horace], *The Story of My Life*, New York: Hurd and Houghton, 1871

Travel Writing

En digters bazar, 1842

Beckwith, Charles (i.e. Charles Beckwith Lohmeyer), *A Poet's Bazaar*, London: Richard Bentley, 1846

Thornton, Grace, *A Poet's Bazar: A Journey to Greece, Turkey, and up the Danube*, New York: Kesend, 1988

I Spanien, 1863

Bushby, Anne S., *In Spain*, London: Richard Bentley, 1864

Thornton, Grace, *A Visit to Spain and North Africa, 1862*, London: Peter Owen, 1975

Et besøg i Portugal 1866, 1868

Thornton, Grace, *A Visit to Portugal, 1866*, London: Peter Owen, 1972; Indianapolis: Bobbs Merrill, 1973

Little, Anastazia, *Travels*, Los Angeles: Green Integer, 1999 (selections)

The Improvisatore established Andersen as the leading Danish writer of contemporary novels and, together with the next two novels, made him famous throughout Europe. He broke new ground in moving beyond the Romantics' preferred Italian setting (Mylius 1993), as the main character, Antonio, a poor boy from the Roman slums, is enabled, by the support of wealthy patrons, to study and travel. HOWITT's 1845 *The Improvisatore; or, Life in Italy* was translated from Laurids Kruse's German version but follows the original closely. It was enthusiastically reviewed by William Jerdan in the *Literary Gazette* on 1, 8, and 22 March and 28 June 1845, and other critics echoed Jerdan's favourable assessment of this and subsequent Andersen publications.

The initials *O.T.* stand for Odense Tugthus (Odense Gaol), where the main character, Otto Thostrup is born. The novel depicts life in Denmark in the 1830s, and examines character psychology in more depth than had been the case in *The Improvisatore*. *O.T.* was immediately popular, and, although the novel declined in popularity during the mid-20th century, more recent critics have embraced it as a forerunner of modernist experimentalism. *Only a Fiddler* has two main characters, Christian and Naomi. Christian is a boy of humble origins whose musical gifts are eventually nourished but whose weakness of character ultimately prevents him from making good; he dies a poor village fiddler. Naomi, his childhood friend, is stronger in character, but a passionate affair-turned-sour finally leaves her boringly married to a French marquis in Paris. For this novel, Andersen was severely castigated by Kierkegaard, who accused him of being unable to form a clear philosophy of life. More recently, however, the novel has been praised for the vivacity of its landscape descriptions and for the poetic clarity of its language (Grønbech 1980, p. 68). HOWITT began translating *Only a Fiddler* and *O.T.* immediately after finishing *The Improvisatore*, using, again, German translations. Again, however, the translation (1845) follows the source closely.

LOHMEYER's *The Two Baronesses* (1848) appeared in English a month in advance of publication of the Danish original. The novel reflects a century of socio-political change and looks ahead to the new Danish constitution, "Grundloven", adopted in 1849. The translator was not named initially, and for a while many readers and critics believed that Andersen had written the novel in English himself. This and other works by Andersen appeared in translations before they were published in Danish in order to protect the publisher of the translations against piracy; had the original been published in Danish already, anyone could freely translate and market it (Mylius 1993, p. 90).

To Be, or Not to Be? was published simultaneously in Denmark and the UK. In this novel, Andersen, who was a great admirer of H.C. Ørsted's natural philosophy and of modern inventions in general, seeks to show that science and religion are not opposing forces. The novel is set in and around Silkeborg, a developing industrial town in traditionalist, rural mid-Jutland, and the main character, Niels, must adjust his own development to tradition as well as to the new town and times. BUSHBY's translation (1857) is from Danish and is generally accurate, except where Andersen makes use of marked grammatical structures ("*det snarere æder Een op*", "it rather eats one up" is rendered "for that is soon eaten up").

The True Story of My Life charts Andersen's childhood and youth through a vision of life as a fairytale and of benevolent providence taking a hand in the shaping of the writer's fate. It was not published in Danish until 1942. HOWITT's version (1847) was based on the German translation by Julius Reuscher of the manuscript introduction to an 1847 German collection of Andersen's works.

The Story of My Life (1855) was published in Danish as the last two volumes of Andersen's collected works. It was brought up to date for the publication of Andersen's collected works in the United States in 1870–71 and this addition was published in Danish as a supplement to his works, posthumously, in 1877. It is in part a careful revision of *The True Story of My Life*, and though it lacks some of the latter's spontaneity, it retains Andersen's vision of his life as a beautiful fairy tale, shaped by benevolent God. SCUDDER's translation (1871) came into being because Andersen made it a condition of permitting Scudder to publish a complete collection of his works that the Howitt translation, *The True Story of My Life* (1847), be replaced by a new translation of an updated autobiography. Glyn JONES bases his translation (1954) on the annotated edition by H. Topsøe-Jensen (1951). It does not include the extension of the memoirs up to 1867, but the account of the first 50 years of Andersen's life is complete. MICHAEL's *The Mermaid Man* (1955) is subtitled "A new abridged translation". The guiding principle for the abridgment is explained in an introductory note: to retain the essence of what Andersen wanted the world to know about himself while discarding "all that can no longer be of interest ... all petty detail which a reader to-day might well find boring". Unfortunately, this is judged to include the introductory passage where the fairy tale vision is stated, and a great deal besides: information about Andersen's use in fiction of characters (including his mother) from his childhood; all verse; and a wealth of detail and quotation which help bring to life the people and places described in the original.

A Poet's Bazar (1842) is commonly considered to be Andersen's greatest travelogue. It describes his journey from Denmark to Turkey and the Black Sea, including a trip along the Danube from Czernawoda to Vienna. LOHMEYER (1846) strives for accuracy, though he omits certain phrases that might have helped to portray Andersen's acerbic humour, for example, "The Copenhagen public has now forgotten her – it is a year since she was here." He adds explanatory intertextual glosses, which are often helpful ("the Duchies" is glossed "of Schleswick and Holstein"), though not always (*Kongens Nytorv*, a square in Copenhagen, is glossed "the King's new market, which is no market"). However, the translation is a complete, fairly accurate representation of Andersen's text. THORNTON (1988) begins at chapter 4, and omits large sections throughout, so that, but for her added diary-style dates and headings, the translation might easily give the impression of a breathless, modern-day package tour.

In Spain appeared in Danish in November 1863 as volume 24 of Andersen's collected works. While visiting Spain, Andersen found sufficient peace and anonymity to study his surroundings in depth. The opening passage contains his famous argument against those who decry the railway as the destroyer of the magic of travel. In Andersen's view, rail travel was more magical and liberating than previous modes: picture follows picture in rich succession, and travellers can either pause at their leisure or fly direct on the wings of steam towards their destination. BUSHBY (1864) follows Andersen's text closely, though there are signs of inadequate comprehension where relatively rare syntactic structures occur in the source. She translates all the poems included in the original, though the translations suggest that she may not have perceived the powerful sexual imagery in some of them. THORNTON (1975) cuts what she considers "the more repetitive prose passages" and omits all the poems. No reason is given for this omission, but it is interesting to note that when the Spain poems were included in *Nye Digte af danske Digtere* [New Poems by Danish Poets] (1863) their sensuality shocked Andersen's acquaintances (Mylius 1993, p. 152).

A Visit to Portugal was published as volume 28 of *Samlede Skrifter* [Collected Works], *Reiseskizzer og Pennetegninger* [Travel Sketches and Pen Drawings]. It covers Andersen's journey in 1866 from Copenhagen via Madrid to Lisbon, and back via Bordeaux to Copenhagen. THORNTON's annotated translation (1972) provides a wealth of information about the people, places and events that figure in the text. The translation is generally speaking a close representation of the information, and even to some extent the lexis, of the original; however, it disregards Andersen's organization of clauses into sentences to such an extent that not only the style but also emphasis and topicality are altered. Thornton includes all the source text's poems, claiming to have "retained the same verse structure and rhyme patterns as the original". No translator is likely to be able to follow such a strategy closely without having to accept distortions of other aspects of the original, and it has to be said that the verses in which Thornton abandons her stated policy almost always fare rather better than the rest as far as meaning is concerned.

KIRSTEN MALMKJÆR

Further Reading

Bredsdorff, Elias, *Hans Christian Andersen: The Story of His Life and Work, 1805–75*, London: Phaidon, 1975; New York: Noonday Press, 1994

Bredsdorff, Elias, *Hans Christian Andersen: An Introduction to His Life and Works*, Copenhagen: Reitzel, 1987

Grønbech, Bo, *Hans Christian Andersen*, Boston: Twayne, 1980

Jørgensen, Aage, "... A Rag, but of Silk", in *Norwich Papers in European Languages, Literatures and Culture*, no. 3: *Hans Christian Andersen, Translation Problems and Perspectives*, edited by W. Glyn Jones, Norwich: School of Modern Languages and European Studies, University of East Anglia, 1995, pp. 31–43

Jørgensen, Aage, *H.C. Andersen-litteraturen, 1969–1994: En bibliografi* [H.C. Andersen Literature, 1969–1994: A Bibliography], Odense: H.C. Andersens Hus, 1995

Kierkegaard, Søren, *Early Polemical Writings*, edited and translated by Julia Watkins, Princeton, New Jersey: Princeton University Press, 1990

Mylius, Johan de, *H.C. Andersen – Liv og Værk: En tidstavle, 1805–1875* [H.C. Andersen – Life and Work], Copenhagen: Aschehoug, 1993

Mylius, Johan de, Aage Jørgensen and Viggo Hjørnager Pedersen (editors), *Andersen og Verden: Indlæg fra den første internationale H.C. Andersen-konference, 25–31 august 1991* [Andersen and the World: Contributions to the First International H.C. Andersen Conference], Odense: Odense Universitetsforlag, 1993

Tales

Because the content of individual books of English translations does not generally correspond to the content of individual original Danish publications, original titles are here listed together, followed by the select list of translations.

Major Editions in Danish

Eventyr, fortalte for børn [Fairy Tales, Told for Children], 3 parts, 1835–37

Eventyr, fortalte for børn: Ny samling [Fairy Tales, Told for Children: New Collection], 3 parts, 1838–41

Billedbog uden billeder (*A Picture-Book without Pictures*), 1839–41

Nye eventyr [New Fairy Tales], 3 parts, 1843–45

Nye eventyr: Andet bind [New Fairy Tales, vol. 2], 2 parts, 1847–48

Historier [Stories], 2 parts, 1852

Nye eventyr og historier [New Fairy Tales and Stories], 4 parts, 1858

Nye eventyr og historier: Anden række [New Fairy Tales and Stories: Second Series], 4 parts, 1861–66

Eventyr og historier: Ny samling [Fairy Tales and Stories: New Collection], 1872

Eventyr og historier: Tredie række, anden samling [New Fairy Tales and Stories: Third Series, Second Collection], 1872

Translations

Complete Collections

Haugaard, Erik Christian, *The Complete Fairy Tales and Stories*, foreword by Naomi Lewis, London: Gollancz, and New York: Doubleday, 1974

Hersholt, Jean, *The Complete Andersen: All of the 168 Stories*, 6 vols, New York: Limited Editions Club, 1942–47

Selections
Blegvad, Erik, *Hans Christian Andersen: Stories and Fairy Tales*, London: Heinemann, 1993
Boner, Charles, *A Danish Story-Book by Hans Christian Andersen, with Numerous Illustrations by Count Pocci*, London: Joseph Cundall, 1846
Boner, Charles, *The Nightingale and Other Tales*, London: Joseph Cundall, 1846
Boner, Charles, *The Shoes of Fortune and Other Tales*, London: Chapman and Hall, 1846; New York: Wiley, 1852
Boner, Charles, *The Dream of Little Tuck and Other Tales*, London: Grant and Griffith, 1847
Bushby, Anne S., *A Poet's Day Dreams*, London: Richard Bentley, 1853
Bushby, Anne S., *The Sand-Hills of Jutland*, London: Richard Bentley, 1860
Bushby, Anne S., *The Ice-Maiden*, London: Richard Bentley, 1863
Chatelain, Madame de, *Tales and Fairy Stories*, London: Routledge, 1852
Dulcken, Henry William, *Stories and Tales*, London: Routledge, 1864
Dulcken, Henry William, *What the Moon Saw, and Other Tales*, London: Routledge, 1865
Dulcken, Henry William, *Hans Christian Andersen's Stories for the Household*, London: Routledge, 1866; as *The Complete Illustrated Works of Hans Christian Andersen*, London: Chancellor Press, 1983, 1994
Howitt, Mary, *Wonderful Stories for Children*, London: Chapman and Hall, 1846; New York: Wiley, 1849
Keigwin, R.P., *Eighty Fairy Tales*, Odense: Skandinavisk, 1976; with an introduction by Elias Bredsdorff, New York: Pantheon, 1982 (translation first published in Denmark, 1950)
Leyssac, Paul, *It's Perfectly True and Other Stories*, New York: Harcourt Brace, 1938
Lohmeyer, Charles Beckwith, *A Christmas Greeting to My English Friends*, London: Richard Bentley, 1847
Nisbet Bain, R., *The Little Mermaid and Other Stories*, London: Lawrence and Bullen, 1893
Peachey, Caroline, *Danish Fairy Legends and Tales*, London: William Pickering, 1846; 2nd enlarged edition, London: Addey, 1852
Spink, Reginald, *Hans Andersen's Fairy Tales*, with an introduction, London: Dent, 1958
Taylor, Meta, *A Picture-Book without Pictures*, London: David Bogue, 1847; in *A Picture-Book without Pictures and Other Stories*, New York: James Miller, 1864
Wehnert, Alfred, *Andersen's Tales for Children*, London: Bell and Daldy, 1861

Until the publication of literary fairy tales by Hans Christian Andersen, the only Danish examples of the genre were B.S. Ingemann's collection, *Eventyr og Fortællinger* [Fairytales and Tales] (1820) and a few tales by Adam Oehlenschläger and by Mrs Gyllembourg. Of these, only Ingemann's influenced Andersen (Mylius 1993, p. 20), whose chief inspiration from early on was the natural philosophy of Romanticism. The Romantic influence is perceptible in many of the tales and a few are directly inspired by earlier works within the Romantic tradition. For example, "The Little Mermaid" draws on the German Romantic writer Friedrich de la Motte Fouqué's *Undine* (1811). However, the tales also amply illustrate Andersen's originality. Andersen is often said to have written some of the earliest pieces of modern prose in Danish, and many critics note his exceptional linguistic dexterity. In translations it is clearly easier to convey Andersen's modernism than his linguistic skills, though it is fair to say that neither task is likely to have appealed greatly to Andersen's early English translators, steeped as they were in Victorian propriety.

As Zipes points out in *Victorian Fairy Tales* (1987), English translations of Andersen's literary fairy tales helped re-establish the genre in Britain. Bredsdorff's *H.C. Andersen og England* testifies to their almost universal, instant appeal to critics and reading public alike. As he points out, in the two years following the publication of Mary Howitt's selection of 1846, six different translators published nine different selections including, between them, 44 different tales. Since then, the pace of publication has slowed a little, though new translations and versions continue to appear regularly.

Discussion here is limited to major editions of the tales, though it should be mentioned that lavishly illustrated publications of one or a few tales appear regularly, and that several tales have formed the basis of Disney animated films. These latter illustrate particularly well the tendency noted by Hjørnager Pedersen in his contribution to *Norwich Papers in European Languages, Literatures and Culture* (1995) for English translators and adaptors to shorten the tales, and to approximate far more closely than Andersen himself to the folktale norm:

> Happy endings are introduced ... and social satire and person-centered sentimentality tend to be left out, together with 'literary' romantic features like descriptions of scenery ... The translations often concentrate on the surface action rather than on the deeper message.

One reason for this is that publications of individual tales are usually aimed specifically at children, which also means that any references to violence and sexuality are typically removed; another reason is lack of interest in and/or attention to Andersen's linguistic artistry.

Howitt claims that her *Wonderful Stories* (1846) were translated from Danish, although her previous novel translations had been based on German translations. Bredsdorff (1954) documents many of her inadequacies, concluding that "if we had only Mary Howitt's translation of the fairy tales, Andersen would be unreadable in English today!" (my translation).

Boner's translations (1846, 1846, 1846, 1847) were also from German translations. His style is more elaborately "literary" than Andersen's, but he does not alter the content of the stories, or add to them. Caroline Peachey's translations of 14 tales (1846) are clearly influenced by the German translations, though she claims, in the second, enlarged edition (1852), that all the stories are translated from Danish. Bredsdorff's main quarrel with Peachey is that she tones down Andersen's colloquial style, loses his humour, and constantly attempts to "improve" the stories by adding material of her own. Lohmeyer's *A Christmas Greeting to My English Friends* (1847) was published with no indication of the translator's identity. The translations are accurate in content but uniform stylistically despite the varied registers of the sources.

TAYLOR's *A Picture-Book Without Pictures* (1847) is based on the German translation by de la Motte Fouqué. It omits three "evenings" (11, 32 and 33), which deal with a wedding night, an execution and a small girl who invents her own version of the Lord's Prayer. Since Taylor otherwise stays close to her German source, it is probable that these omissions were motivated by fear of causing offence. In her preface to *Tales and Fairy Stories* (1852), CHATELAIN explains that she has altered the ending of "The Red Shoes" because she found the original "too repulsive" (in the original, Karen has her feet chopped off; in Chatelain's version, only the shoes are removed). Apart from this alteration, and some inventive titles, these translations stay close to the originals, except for a fondness for archaisms and a tendency to elaboration. There are also traces of the German translations ("little Peter Spielmann"), but the close adherence to the Danish originals suggests that Chatelain must have relied mainly on these. Bredsdorff (1954) considers her translation better than any previously produced.

BUSHBY (1853, 1860, 1863) could read Danish and had been chosen to translate Andersen's tales by the publisher, Bentley, who was dissatisfied with Lohmeyer's efforts on Andersen's other works. Unfortunately, Bushby's Danish seems to have been somewhat limited, leading to the retention of errors in earlier translations as well as some that are Bushby's very own. Bredsdorff (1954) lists a number of these, together with numerous additions, omissions, and stylistic elevations. As Bredsdorff also points out, WEHNERT (1861) adds to Andersen's tales so liberally that it is impossible to say whether his translation is based on German translations or on the originals. He considers Wehnert's translations worse than any other produced in Andersen's lifetime.

DULCKEN's translations of 1864 and 1865, together with new translations of five further tales, were published in one volume containing 111 stories in 1866. These translations have been reprinted regularly, and appear in *The Complete Illustrated Works of Hans Christian Andersen* (1983, 1994). Bredsdorff considers that whereas Dulcken, who was German, knew Danish well, he lacks "feeling" for English. However, Malmkjær argues, in "Wilde Versions of Andersen's Themes" (1995), that it is likely that Dulcken manipulated the texts deliberately in order to create a set of tales that would appeal to "the household" of his 1866 title.

In the preface to his translation, NISBET BAIN (1893) criticizes his predecessors for failing to understand Andersen's "quaint conceits", "delicate nuances", "child-like *naïveté*" and humour, suggesting that translators must "become children again" if they wish to understand Andersen. His is the first translation that comes close to Andersen's style in clarity and simplicity. According to his preface, LEYSSAC (1938) has the adult reader/listener as much in mind as Andersen did himself, but it is interesting to note that he adheres to the source no less closely than Nisbet Bain, and, like him, uses mainly colloquial language.

The most scholarly English edition of Andersen's tales – if not the most accurate from a linguistic point of view – is without a doubt HERSHOLT's complete translation in six volumes (1942–47), with notes giving origins of themes, and dates and places of first publication of the sources. Volume 1 also includes *Lucky Peer*, normally classified as a novel. The 11th "evening" of *Picture-Book Without Pictures* appears here in its first English translation, subtly adjusted to tone down the clear sexual imagery of the original. This collection is available on CD-ROM.

In his introduction (1982) to KEIGWIN's translation of 1950, Bredsdorff declares that he considers this the best version of Andersen's tales. It is devoid of additions, omissions and errors, and Keigwin's style suits the tales well. SPINK's translation (1958) was inspired by what he perceived as the lack of buoyancy in the Everyman Library's edition by Alice Lucas, which it came to replace. The original edition includes an introduction and notes by the translator, and roughly half of its 51 tales were subsequently used in an edition for children. The original edition, without the introduction and notes, has been republished in the new Everyman's Children's Classics series. Spink's aim is to reproduce Andersen's prose rhythm, and in this he is helped considerably by adhering more closely than most translators to Andersen's punctuation.

The complete edition by HAUGAARD (1974) also includes translations of Andersen's preface to his 1837 tales "For the Older Reader", and "Notes for My Fairy Tales and Stories" (1874), which provides information about how the tales came into being. Haugaard's concern to make the tales accessible to modern readers leads him to introduce "How to Cook Soup upon a Sausage Pin" with a paragraph of his own explaining what a sausage pin is, while his desire for accuracy explains the name *Inchelina* for the small creature more commonly known in English as *Thumbelina*. This is the most readable and widely available complete collection of Andersen's tales in English.

For beauty of illustrations, reader-friendliness of print size and quality of production, coupled with a reasonable degree of faithfulness to Andersen's Danish, no translation compares with BLEGVAD's (1993).

KIRSTEN MALMKJÆR

Further Reading

Bredsdorff, Elias, *H.C. Andersen og England* [H.C. Andersen and England], Copenhagen: Rosenkilde & Bagger, 1954

Bredsdorff, Elias, *Hans Christian Andersen: The Story of His Life and Work, 1805–75*, London: Phaidon, 1975; New York: Noonday Press, 1994

Bredsdorff, Elias, *Hans Christian Andersen: An Introduction to His Life and Works*, Copenhagen: Hans Reitzel, 1987

Grønbech, Bo, *Hans Christian Andersen*, Boston: Twayne, 1980

Jørgensen, Aage, *H.C. Andersen-litteraturen, 1969–1994: En bibliografi* [Literature on H.C. Andersen, 1969–1994: A Bibliography], Odense: H.C. Andersens Hus, 1995

Malmkjær, Kirsten, "What's in an Adjective?", in *Norwich Papers in European Languages, Literatures and Culture*, no. 3: *Hans Christian Andersen: Translation Problems and Perspectives*, edited by W. Glyn Jones, Norwich: School of Modern Languages and European Studies, University of East Anglia, 1995, pp. 44–54

Malmkjær, Kirsten, "Wilde Versions of Andersen's Themes", *Working Papers in English and Applied Linguistics*, vol. 2, Cambridge: Research Centre for English and Applied Linguistics, 1995, pp. 155–68

Mylius, Johan de, *H.C. Andersen: Liv og Værk: En tidstavle*,

1805–1875 [H.C. Andersen: Life and Work], Copenhagen: Aschehoug, 1993
Pedersen, Viggo Hjørnager, "Ugly Ducklings? Reflections on Some English Versions of Hans Andersen's 'Den Grimme Ælling'", in *Translation Theory in Scandinavia*, edited by Patrick Nigel Chaffey, Antin Fougner Rydning and Solveig Schult Ulriksen, Oslo: University of Oslo, 1988, pp. 229–43
Pedersen, Viggo Hjørnager, "Translating Hans Christian Andersen with Particular Reference to Phraseology and Lexis", in *Norwich Papers in European Languages, Literatures and Culture*, no. 3: *Hans Christian Andersen: Translation Problems and Perspectives*, edited by W. Glyn Jones, Norwich: School of Modern Languages and European Studies, University of East Anglia, 1995, pp. 55–68
Spink, Reginald, "On Translating Andersen", in *Norwich Papers in European Languages, Literatures and Culture*, no. 3: *Hans Christian Andersen: Translation Problems and Perspectives*, edited by W. Glyn Jones, Norwich: School of Modern Languages and European Studies, University of East Anglia, 1995, pp. 24–30
Zipes, Jack (editor), *Victorian Fairy Tales: The Revolt of the Fairies and Elves*, New York and London: Methuen, 1987

Leonid Andreev 1871–1919

Russian short-story writer, dramatist and essayist

Biography

Born in Orel, 21 August 1871. His father died when Andreev was a child, and he grew up in poverty. After attending the Orel high school (1882–91), he studied at St Petersburg University from 1891 (the year of his third suicide attempt), but failed to pay his fees and was dismissed in 1893. He then enrolled at Moscow University, graduated there in law in 1897 and practised briefly and unsuccessfully as a barrister. His first stories were published in the journal *Orlovskii vestnik* in 1895. From late 1897 he contributed court reports, satirical pieces and short stories to various newspapers, including *Kur'er*. He became a friend of Gor'kii and his circle, and the first of his volumes of short stories was published by Gor'kii's publishing house Znanie in 1901.

He married 1) Aleksandra Mikhailovna Veligorskaia in 1902 (died, to Andreev's great grief, 1906; two children); 2) Anna Il'inishna Denisevich in 1908 (three children).

In 1905 Andreev was arrested imprisoned briefly for holding an illegal political meeting, and from 1905 to 1907 he lived in exile. From 1907 to 1908 he was editor of the modernist literary almanac *Shipovnik*. He moved to Vammelsuu, Finland in 1908, living there alone until his death. Before World War I he travelled to Germany, France and Italy. During the war he was co-editor of the patriotic newspaper *Russkaia volia*, 1916–17. Though pro-revolution in earlier days, he was anti-Bolshevist after 1917 and in 1919 issued his famous *S.O.S.* appeal for allied intervention to save Russia from Bolshevism. Died suddenly in Kuokkaala, Finland, 12 September 1919.

Andreev's writing evolved into its own manner by way of several literary movements, including realism and symbolism. He enjoyed a period of very great popularity in Russia in the first years of the 20th century with stories and plays. He continued to write stories, also a novel, but in the period 1908–16 his successes in Russia and abroad came mostly from more than 20 full-length plays and some half-dozen short ones. *Tot, kto poluchaet poshchechiny* (*He Who Gets Slapped*), 1916, made an international mark. He was also a painter and a photographer.

Translations

Selections of Stories

Bernstein, Herman, *The Crushed Flower and Other Stories*, New York: Knopf, 1916; London: Duckworth, 1917, reprinted in part from the *New York Times*, the *New York World* and the *Independent* (contains "The Crushed Flower"; "A Story Which Will Never Be Finished"; "On the Day of the Crucifixion"; "The Serpent's Story"; "Love, Faith and Hope"; "The Ocean"; "Judas Iscariot and Others"; "The Man Who Found the Truth")

Carlisle, Olga Andreyev (editor), *Visions: Stories and Photographs by Leonid Andreyev*, San Diego: Harcourt Brace, 1987 (contains "The Thought", "The Red Laugh", "At the Station", "The Thief", "The Abyss", "Darkness", "The Seven Who Were Hanged")

Short Stories and Novellas

Bezdna, 1902

Carlisle, Olga Andreyev and Henry Carlisle, "The Abyss" in *Visions*, edited by Olga Andreyev Carlisle, 1987

Mysl, 1902

Cournos, John, *A Dilemma: A Story of Mental Perplexity*, Philadelphia: Brown, 1910

Vor, 1905

Carlisle, Olga Andreyev and Henry Carlisle, "The Thief" in *Visions*, edited by Olga Andreyev Carlisle, 1987

Rasskaz o semi poveshennykh, 1908

Bernstein, Herman, *The Seven Who Were Hanged*, New York: J.S. Ogilvie, 1909

Luker, Nicholas, "The Seven Who Were Hanged" in *An Anthology of Russian Neo-Realism: The "Znanie" School of Maxim Gorky*, edited by Luker, Ann Arbor, Michigan: Ardis, 1982; reprinted in *Visions*, edited by Olga Andreyev Carlisle, 1987

Osly, 1915
Bernstein, Herman, "Donkeys", *Smart Set* (December 1922); in *The Smart Set Anthology*, edited by Burton Rascoe and Groff Conklin, New York: Reynal and Hitchcock, 1934

Plays
K zvezdam, 1906
Goudiss, A., *To the Stars: A Drama in Four Acts*, *Poet Lore* 18/4 (1907)

Zhizn' cheloveka, 1907
Baring, Maurice, *The Life of Man*, *Oxford and Cambridge Review* (Midsummer 1908)
Dickinson, Thomas H. (editor), *The Life of Man* in *Continental Plays*, Boston: Houghton Mifflin, 1935
Hogarth, C.J., *The Life of Man: A Play in Five Acts*, London: Allen and Unwin, and New York: Macmillan, 1915
Meader, Clarence L. and Fred Newton Scott, *The Life of Man*, with *The Black Maskers* and *The Sabine Women*, in *Plays*, translated by Meader and Scott, London: Duckworth, and New York: Scribner, 1915; as *Three Plays*, New York: Fertig, 1989
Seltzer, Thomas, *The Life of Man by Leonid Andreyev*, with *Savva*, translated by Seltzer, with an introduction, New York: Kennerley, 1914

Tsar-Golod, 1908
Kayden, Eugene M., *King-Hunger*, *Poet Lore*, 22/6 (1911); as *King Hunger*, Boston: Badger, 1911; revised edition, Sewanee, Tennessee: University of the South Press, 1973

Liubov' k blizhnemu, 1908
Seltzer, Thomas, *Love to Your Neighbor: A Comedy in One Act*, New York: Glebe, 1914; as *Love of One's Neighbor*, New York: Boni, 1914

Anatema, 1909
Bernstein, Herman, *Anathema: A Tragedy in Seven Scenes*, New York: Macmillan, 1910; *Anathema: The Epilogue* in *The Golden Age of Russian Literature*, edited by Ivar Spector, revised edition, Caldwell, Idaho: Caxton, 1943

Moi zapiski, 1910
Bernstein, Herman, "The Man Who Found the Truth", *New York Times* (28 August 1910); also in *The Crushed Flower and Other Stories*, translated by Bernstein, 1916

Okean, 1911
Bernstein, Herman, "The Ocean", *New York Times* (22 January 1911); in *The Crushed Flower and Other Stories*, translated by Bernstein, 1916

Prekrasnye sabinyanki, 1912
Seltzer, Thomas, *The Pretty Sabine Women: A Play in Three Acts*, *The Drama*, 13 (February 1914)

Ekaterina Ivanovna, 1913
Bernstein, Herman, *Katerina: A Drama in Four Acts*, New York: Brentano, 1923; London: Brentano, 1924

Korol', zakon, i svoboda, 1914
Bernstein Herman, *The Sorrows of Belgium: A Play in Six Scenes*, New York: Macmillan, 1915

Mysl, 1914
Laurence, William L., *A Devil in the Mind: A Drama in Six Scenes*, produced 1931

Tot, kto poluchaet poshchechiny, 1916
Belov, Yuri, *He Who Gets Slapped*, produced 1997
Carlin, George A., *He Who Gets Slapped: A Novel Adapted from Andreyev's Drama and the Victor Seastrom Photoplay*, New York: Grosset and Dunlap, 1925
MacAndrew, Andrew R., *He Who Gets Slapped* in *An Anthology of Russian Plays*, edited by F.D. Reeve, vol. 2, New York: Vintage, 1963
Seastrom, Victor and Carey Wilson, *He Who Gets Slapped* (screenplay), Hollywood: Metro Goldwyn Mayer, 1924
Stambler, Bernard (libretto), *He Who Gets Slapped (Pantaloon): An Opera in Three Acts*, music by Robert Ward, New York: Galaxy Music, 1961
Zilboorg, Gregory, *He, the One Who Gets Slapped: A Play in Four Acts*, New York: Dial Press, 1921; as *He Who Gets Slapped: A Play in Four Acts*, New York and London, Brentano, 1922

Sobachii val's, 1922
Bernstein, Herman, *The Waltz of the Dogs: A Play in Four Acts*, New York: Macmillan, and London: Brentano, 1922

Samson v okovakh, 1923
Bernstein, Herman, *Samson in Chains*, New York: Brentano, 1923

Other Writing
Pis'ma o teatre, 1912–14
Kayden, Eugene M., "Letters on the Modern Theater" (excerpts), *New York Times* (5 October 1919); "Letters on the Movies", *New York Times* (19 October 1919)

Pervaia stupen', 1917
Yarmolinsky, Avrahm, "The First Step", *The Shield* (September 1917)

Derzhava Rerikh, 1919
Kaun, Alexander, "The Realm of Roerich", *New Republic* (21 December 1921)

S.O.S., 1919
Pollock, J., "S.O.S", *The Nineteenth Century and After* (June 1919)

Dnevnik Satana, 1921
Bernstein, Herman, *Satan's Diary*, New York: Boni and Liveright, 1922

Heir of Schopenhauer, Dostoevskii, and Nietszche, Leonid Andreev has been received in the West as a sceptic, who in dramas, stories and polemical essays on the tyranny of irrational human impulses and the perpetuation of flawed social institutions anticipates postmodernist writing, the works of Camus in France, and of Zinoviev and Kundera in Eastern Europe. Formalistically, however, Andreev has been viewed as a traditionalist, whose hallucinatory tales look back to Gogol' and Tolstoi, whose allegories evoke Maeterlinck, and whose social critiques speed into the 20th century along a track laid down by Turgenev, Tolstoi, Saltykov-Shchedrin, and Gor'kii.

Acknowledging Andreev as a spokesman of modernist disquiet, readers in Great Britain and America responded to his works within well defined national cultural contexts and moods. Thanks to the British tradition of giving refuge to generations of Russian political exiles and free-thinkers, Andreev's works first trickled into England in the period of the abortive 1905 Revolution: this cordiality granted Andreev a respect that continues to this day.

While America, too, first read Andreev around 1905, its reception of his art accelerated during the literary revival of the pre-World War I era. Indeed, the American cultural renaissance of the 1910s and 1920s would be unthinkable without the publication of Andreev's works in the new "little" magazines and the productions of his plays in "little" theaters across the land. America's agonizing self-scrutiny with regard to World War I, and its polarization during and after the revolutions of 1917, were quickened by translations of Andreev's writings, as these appeared in the national media and in small press publications. From the 1910s and throughout the 1920s Andreev's works were published in *The Dial*, *The Drama*, and *Glebe*, and his plays were performed by the Washington Square Players and the Theater Guild. A decade later, his tragicomedy *He Who Gets Slapped* was adapted as an experimental silent film by the great Swedish director, Victor Sjöstrom, making Andreev an MGM star. Prior to his publication in Russia, translators touted Andreev's accessibility to an American readership, while critics parsed, praised, and polemicized with Andreev's heroes. He was taken up by Tyrone Guthrie for the Theater Guild; in the 1950s, *He Who Gets Slapped* would swirl through the imagination of composer Robert Ward, inspiring a new American opera, and the Andreev revival would continue well into the 1980s.

To the Stars, Andreev's symbolist play affirming the victory of social visionaries and activists at a time of social unrest in Russia, was published in translation by GOUDISS, in 1907 in the Boston literary journal *Poet Lore*; this set the keynote for America's reception of Andreev. If the play was written under the impact of the armed insurrections of the 1905 era in Russia's towns, in it the American reader caught Andreev's representation of man, "the son of eternity, a citizen of countless worlds, a sun-snarer" (Eugene Kayden).

With the first English-language translation of *The Seven Who Were Hanged*, Herman BERNSTEIN (1909) soon brought before the American public Andreev's impassioned protest against tsarist autocracy. The translation, undertaken by Bernstein in 1908, the year of the short novel's composition, presented to Americans "the horror and indignation experienced by thinking Russia at the sight of numerous scaffolds erected by autocracy to punish political opponents" (Moisaye Olgin). *The Seven Who Were Hanged* "did more to protest the spread of universal capital punishment than Tolstoi's 'I Cannot be Silent'", claimed Alexander Kaun. Indeed, it was the universal implications of Andreev's works, their "meaning for the human conscience", that his new American readers found so compelling.

Diplomat, journalist, translator, and author, BERNSTEIN over the next 15 years translated *Anatema* (*Anathema*, 1910), *Moi zapiski* (*The Man Who Found the Truth*, in the *New York Times*, 1910), and *Okean* (*The Ocean*, in the *New York Times*, 1911), the last a recasting of Andreev's lyrical drama of unbridled individualism and chaos into a pirate story that blended Byron and Melville. In the World War I years, Bernstein translated the lyrical drama *The Sorrows of Belgium*, as well as Andreev's anti-war works, and the collection of short fiction *The Crushed Flower* (1916). In the 1920s, Bernstein translated Andreev's posthumously published writings: in 1922 *Satan's Diary* and the play *The Waltz of the Dogs*; for Mencken's magazine, the *Smart Set*, the story "Donkeys"; and in 1923, the dramas *Samson in Chains* and *Katerina*.

Publication of the drama *King Hunger* (*Tsar-Golod*), in a translation by Eugene KAYDEN for *Poet Lore* (1911) soon brought Andreev into discussions of the new American theater. In 1914 the play formed the subject of an important chapter of *The Social Significance of the Modern Drama*, written by America's best-known woman radical, Emma Goldman, in which she set Andreev squarely before the American people as one of a constellation that included Shaw, Maeterlinck, and Gor'kii. *King Hunger* explored Russia's years of famine in the early 1900s and the desperation of the general strikes that followed the 1905 Revolution. Unlike Hauptmann's weavers, claimed Kayden, "the working men of Andreev do not demolish machines, cut belts, quench boilers. Hunger leads them to collective solidarity" (*The Dial*, 1919).

During World War I Andreev was a much-prized writer in the US. The *New York Sun* in December 1914 published a scene from *The Sorrows of Belgium*, a lament for a tiny country caught in the vise of German militarism, the whole of which appeared in English in book form (BERNSTEIN, 1915) the following year with a dedication to King Albert I. On its opening bill of one-act plays for February 1915 the newly-formed Washington Square Players featured Andreev's *Love of One's Neighbor* in SELTZER's translation (1914), thereby linking Andreev to the experimental *Glebe* that had appeared on the eve of World War I and that would publish Pound, Joyce, and William Carlos Williams. Andreev soon was taken up in the midwest. In 1915 *The Pretty Sabine Women*, translated by SELTZER and published in Chicago's little magazine, *The Drama* (1914), opened at the Chicago Little Theater and would be produced in January 1916 at the Indianapolis Little Theater.

From 1914 to 1919, Andreev repeatedly spoke out against social violence in any form. *The Shield*, the miscellany produced by Gor'kii, Fedor Sologub, and Andreev carried Andreev's essay, "The First Step" (translated by YARMOLINSKY, 1917), where he argued for civil rights for the Jews of Russia. From 1915 until his death in 1919, Andreev's antiwar writings appeared in major American journals. The essay "S.O.S.", in which Andreev summons the West to save Russia from the Bolsheviks who betrayed the 1917 revolutions, was translated by POLLOCK (1919) and printed in the *Nineteenth Century*, the *Russian Review*, and the *Yale Review*.

Andreev died on the very day in September 1919 that Herman Bernstein cabled him with the completed arrangements for his US visit. Soon thereafter, in memory of Andreev, the *New York Times* carried translations by KAYDEN of his essays on the aesthetics of the theater and cinema ("Letters on the Modern Theater") and within a month, the *New Republic* followed with a selection (KAUN, 1921) from "The Realm of Roerich", Andreev's homage to the avant-garde Russian stage designer.

In America in the 1920s the mood of new freedom in the face of despair, following on the war, can perhaps account for the ascendancy of Andreev's dramatic works that so stirred "the minds of his contemporaries to discontent, to analysis, to revolt, voicing the cultural gamut of modern unrest and skepticism" (Alexander Kaun, *The Nation*, 11 October 1917).

Within this discordant tonality, one Andreev work seemingly derived its success from a congeniality to the American temperament and taste. The pre-eminent American decade of Andreev dramas opened with *He Who Gets Slapped* in a masterful translation in *The Dial* in March 1921 by Kiev-born Gregory ZILBOORG (1890–1959), the former secretary to the Ministry of Labor in the cabinets of Prince Lvov and Kerensky who in America became a noted psychoanalyst. The translation would be reissued no fewer than 17 times. Zilboorg's translation brought Andreev to the attention of one of America's leading poets, Marianne Moore, an editor of *The Dial* magazine, and to the pages of the journal that published T.S. Eliot's *The Waste Land*, thus reinforcing the diverse tonalities of postwar literary expression.

Less than a year later, *He Who Gets Slapped* opened at the Garrick Theater as a production of the Theater Guild, the former Washington Square Players. From January through the summer of that year there were 308 performances of the play, at the Garrick and the Fulton theaters in New York. Performed next in 1924 by Le Petit Théâtre du Vieux Carré, New Orleans, it was well on its way to being taken into the American national theater repertory, when it went West – and into another art form. Film critics concur that the 1924 Victor Sjöstrom (SEASTROM) silent film *He Who Gets Slapped* wrote a new chapter in American cinema history. Produced by Irving Thalberg for the recently amalgamated MGM Studios, the screen version, prepared by Carey Wilson together with the film's director, featured Lon Chaney in the role of He, and Moira Shearer as Consuelo.

A succession of Andreev dramas followed on the triumph of *He Who Gets Slapped*, each re-activating discussions of the aesthetics of the American theater. The American refusal to relinquish its optimism conditioned the response to the 1928 production of *The Waltz of the Dogs* (translated by BERNSTEIN, 1922) at New York's Cherry Lane Theater. Less than a year later, the Civic Repertory theater presented *Katerina*, the American version (BERNSTEIN, 1923) of *Ekaterina Ivanovna*. Then in May 1931 *A Devil in the Mind* was performed by Leo Bulgakov and Associates at the Fulton Theater, New York. Looking back to Tolstoi's "The Kreutzer Sonata", the play shows the degradation of a doctor who feigns insanity in order to kill with impunity his best friend, the husband of a woman he once loved. The American version, W.L. LAURENCE's adaptation of Andreev's 1914 play *Mysl* [Thought], that he had dramatized from his story of 1902, highlighted the psychological line of the action. However, it is questionable whether Andreev's plot could carry the burden that he assigned to it. Indeed, the play was Andreev's remaking of a 1902 story, also entitled "Thought", and the rewrite was intended to illustrate Andreev's theory of "Panpsychism" – namely, that the new theatre must counterpoise cinema (what Andreev had seen of it) and theatre of action: "Not hunger, not love, not ambition", he wrote in his *Letters on the Theater* (1912–14), "but thought, human thought in its sufferings, joys, and struggles" is the new hero of the drama. American viewers were not convinced.

None the less, incredulous or earnest in their desire to be presented with a brighter vision of human motivation, Andreev's American public eagerly sought out his works in print. Among the magazines introducing Andreev to American audiences in the 1920s was H. L. Mencken's irreverent the *Smart Set*, which published the witty allegory "Donkeys" in its December 1922 issue. There, in a popular fiction magazine that counted Mark Twain, Max Beerbohm, and Frank Norris among its authors, BERNSTEIN's 1922 translation confirmed Andreev's place as a nay-sayer who might not always be tolerated by his American peers, but who certainly was one of them.

If the years from 1920 to 1931 marked the high point of Andreev's popularity in the US, over the next five decades – when his work was banned in the Soviet Union – he continued to be published and produced in America, the Cold War notwithstanding. The plays that Americans tried to understand earlier and in some cases had genuinely taken to heart fared especially well, including *The Life of Man* (translated by BARING, DICKINSON, HOGARTH, MEADER & SCOTT, and SELTZER) and *Anathema*.

But it was revivals of *He Who Gets Slapped* in various adaptations (including CARLIN and MACANDREW), and in unpublished acting versions, that linked Andreev's name to successive decades of American culture. After a quarter of a century, in 1946, the Theater Guild rethought Andreev's concept and its own vision of the play. Whether or not a postwar bitter realism impelled its decision to come to terms with the real and the symbolic elements of the dramatic structure of this play, Andreev's drama was reduced from four acts to two, and, with a new literalism, the character He was renamed Funny. This "*does* reduce the [play's] potential symbolism", observed Lewis Nichols in the *New York Times* (20 March 1946). The new *He Who Gets Slapped*, in the translation by Zilboorg, opened on 20 March and played 46 times at the Garrick Theater and at the Booth.

Andreev's He next metamorphosed into Pantaloon, the hero of an American opera. Robert Ward, a promising younger composer wrote music to the libretto of Bernard STAMBLER, for a production by the Columbia University Opera Workshop; *Pantaloon* premiered 17 May 1956. A decade later, as a drama, *He Who Gets Slapped* (Zilboorg translation) played nine times in a Joseph della Sorte production at the Garrick Theater, beginning 17 November 1967. It was revived in the 1970s by the Guthrie Theater in Minneapolis, and in the 1980s it was given by Berkeley Repertory Theaters.

A 1997 production of *He Who Gets Slapped* marks yet another dazzling metamorphosis in the political and aesthetic life of Andreev's tragicomedy. Translated (though as yet unpublished) and directed by Russian expatriate clown Yuri BELOV, the drama ran at the Ivy Substation, Culver City, California, to unanimous critical acclaim. Belov brought to the new production, which succeeded as both allegory and entertainment, the amalgam of high and low theater gained in his decades of experience as artistic director of the Moscow Pantomime Clown Theater and of the Moscow State Circus, as well as of the Stanislavsky Drama Theater and the Lunacharsky University Theater.

Andreev's fiction, ranging from psychological stories to allegory and realist epic, from lyric prose to sardonic social comment, continues to be reissued in America and the UK. Since the 1980s this process has been quickened by a lively Anglo-American collaboration. Notable among the many reissues of *The Seven Who Were Hanged* is the powerful rendering (1982) of the short novel by Nicholas Luker of the University of Nottingham, England. Five years this translation was reprinted in *Visions*, a remarkable collection of Andreev stories bringing together new translations by Olga (Andreyev) and Henry Carlisle. Hopefully, the chapter of *The Seven* that Andreev personally had excluded from its first Russian edition and that now has been retrieved from Russian archives and issued in Russian (1988, 1994), will be added to reissues of Luker's splendid translation. Each of the six stories translated by the Carlisles in *Visions* transmits the taut psychological and social perceptions of the author. The collection carries an introduction by Andreev's granddaughter, in which she masterfully joins literary and social history to memoir. Finally, the growth of the Andreev archive at the Brotherton Library, University of Leeds, continues to internationalize his legacy, encouraging an Anglo-American partnership of which the Carlisle translations and books on Andreev (see Further Reading) are its most eloquent testament. "Literature, which I have the honor of serving, is dear to me, just because the noblest task it sets itself is that of erasing boundaries and distances", Andreev wrote to Bernstein in 1908. The Anglo-American translations of his works helped to bring about that erasing so prized by the great Russian writer.

Ruth Rischin

Further Reading

Bernstein, Herman, introduction to "Andreyev's Diaries and Last Letters", *New York Times* (12 March 1922)

Davies, Richard (editor), *Photographs by a Russian Writer*, London: Thames and Hudson, 1989

Goldman, Emma, *The Social Significance of the Modern Drama*, Boston: Badger, 1914; reprinted New York: Applause, 1987

Kayden, Eugene, "Leonid Andreyev, 1871–1919", *The Dial* (15 November 1919)

Olgin, Moissaye J., "A Wounded Intellect", *The New Republic* (24 December 1919)

Simonson, Lee, "An Open Letter to Gilbert Emery" [*He Who Gets Slapped*], *New York Times* (12 March 1922)

Zilboorg, Gregory, introduction to *He Who Gets Slapped*, *The Dial* (March 1921)

Ivo Andrić 1892–1975

Bosnian novelist and short-story writer

Biography

Andrić was born 9 October 1892 near Trávnik, Bosnia, went to school (1898–1912) in Višegrad and Sarajevo and studied (1912–14) at the universities of Zagreb, Vienna and Cracow, taking his Ph.D. at Graz in 1923. In World War I, as a nationalist, he was interned in Split by the Austrians. Andrić served in the Yugoslav diplomatic service 1920–41 in many cities of western and central Europe. He was Yugoslav minister in Berlin at the outbreak of World War II in 1939 and was in occupied Belgrade for the duration. He wrote full-time from 1941 to 1949. For six years from 1949 he represented Bosnia in the Yugoslav parliament.

Andrić began his literary career in 1918 with two volumes of lyrical and philosophical prose, to be followed by five novels and six volumes of short stories. He won many literary and academic awards for his writing, including the 1961 Nobel Prize for Literature on account of his famous novels *The Bridge on the Drina* and *Bosnian Story* (both 1945). He died in Belgrade, 13 March 1975.

Translations

Novels

Gospodjica, 1945

Hitrec, Joseph, *The Woman from Sarajevo*, New York: Knopf, 1965; London: Calder and Boyars, 1966

Travnička hronika, 1945

Hawkesworth, Celia and Bogdan Rakić, *The Days of the Consuls*, London and Boston: Forest, 1992

Hitrec, Joseph, *Bosnian Chronicle*, New York: Knopf, 1963

Johnstone, Kenneth, *Bosnian Story*, London: Lincoln Prager, 1958

Na Drini ćuprija, 1945

Edwards, Lovett F., *The Bridge on the Drina*, New York: Macmillan, and London: Allen and Unwin, 1959; with an introduction by William H. McNeill, Chicago: University of Chicago Press, 1977; as *The Bridge over the Drina*, with an introduction by William H. McNeill, London: Harvill, 1994

Selections of Short Stories

Hawkesworth, Celia, *The Damned Yard and Other Stories*, London and Boston: Forest, and Belgrade: Dereta, 1992

Hitrec, Joseph, *The Pasha's Concubine and Other Stories*, New York; Knopf, 1968

Short Stories

Priča o Vezirovom slonu, 1948

Willen, Drenka, *The Vizir's Elephant: Three Novellas*, New York: Harcourt Brace, 1962 (contains *The Vizir's Elephant*, *Anika's Times*, *Zeko*)

Prokleta avlija, 1954

Hawkesworth, Celia, *The Damned Yard* in *The Damned Yard and Other Stories*, translated by Hawkesworth, 1992

Johnstone, Kenneth, *Devil's Yard*, New York: Grove Press, and London: Calder, 1962

Other Writing

Hawkesworth, Celia and Andrew Harvey, *Conversation with Goya; Bridges; Signs*, London: Menard Press, 1992

The difficulties of translating Ivo Andrić concern both the specific cultural background of his works and the exemplary role of his writing in the standardization of the Serbo-Croat language. First, Andrić writes about an amalgam of Turkish (Muslim), Orthodox Christian, and Catholic cultures at the intersection between mythical and historical times, a complex compound that does not lend itself easily to a rendering into any language. Second, Andrić's style is not outright realism, but a pretension to it, so that his work can perform the function of a chronicle while remaining essentially a trope for historical changes rather than their record. Andrić's writing is thus a work of fiction of the same order as Mehmed Pasha's bridge in *The Bridge on the Drina*, a metaphorical connection between East and West. Finally, translation is all the more difficult since – as Celia HAWKESWORTH (1992) notes in the preface to her English translation of *Travnička hronika* (*The Days of the Consuls*) – Serbo-Croat dictionaries of rarely used words frequently take their illustrative examples from Andrić's writings.

His most famous work, the novel *The Bridge on the Drina*, is the four centuries long story of a bridge built in Bosnia in the 16th century, and of the human events, noble, ignoble, atrocious, that it witnesses, placed as it is at a point where empires, religions, and cultures meet and collide. In *Bosnian Chronicle / The Days of the Consuls* the implications for those, consuls and a vizier, existing at this cultural junction are explored within a shorter time-scale.

Lovett F. EDWARDS's translation of *Na Drini ćuprija* (*The Bridge on the Drina*), published in 1959, is generally an accurate rendition of the original, although the nuances of some idiomatic phrases escape the translator. It is at times overly descriptive, primarily because Edwards inserts explanations of Turkish words in the body of the text, rather than adding a separate glossary, as Andrić does in the original.

Similar broad descriptive strokes can be found in Joseph HITREC's 1963 translation of *Travnička hronika* (*Bosnian Chronicle*), and in his 1968 translation of Andrić's short stories, published in English as *The Pasha's Concubine*. The consequences of such a strategy may be more serious than they seem, because the idiomatic quality of the language is an essential part of Andrić's attempt to portray a culture of orally transmitted tradition.

Travnička hronika was retranslated by Celia HAWKESWORTH in 1992 as *The Days of the Consuls*. This translation, done in collaboration with Bosnian native Bogdan Rakić, is evidently aware of Hitrec's choices but renders Andrić more dynamic and more colloquial. For example, here is a rather simple sentence from the beginning of chapter 12:

> *Umesto onog vlažnog travničkog doba 'koje nije ni jesen ni zima' nastupila je več početkom novembra rana i jaka studen.*
>
> Instead of that humid season, "which is neither autumn nor winter", Travnik was visited by an early and bitter cold wave at the start of November. (Hitrec 1963)
>
> Instead of the damp Travnik season, "neither autumn nor winter", there was a sharp, early frost at the very beginning of November. (Hawkesworth 1992)

The weather in Hitrec's translation becomes "humid" (not simply damp, *vlazno*), it "visits" (not simply comes to, *nastupiti*) the city, and the chill (*jaka studen*) is a "cold wave". Hawkesworth, on the other hand, slightly downplays the distance of the narrator from the events and stories reported. Her translation of "*koje nije ni jesen ni zima*", lacking the pronoun (*koje*, which), is closer than the original to direct speech. The chill (*studen*) becomes "a sharp, early frost" – "sharp" would be entirely accurate if the original were "*oštra*" not "*jaka*", "frost" if the original were "*mraz*", etc.

It needs to be noted, however, that some of the distancing from the original that appears in the translations – in Hitrec's less and in Hawkesworth's more – can be justified because of the general characteristics of Andrić's style, which, on the one hand, is detached and alienated, and, on the other hand, pretends to be authentic and particular when presenting the protagonist's (often collective) speaking voice.

This brings us to the mytho-poetic aspects of Andrić's quasi-historical chronicles, the elements of which may not be entirely accessible even to the native of Yugoslavia, especially now, after the war that has brought an end to the unity Andrić has come to symbolize (despite his early nationalistic opinions). The question that the present translations of Andrić pose is whether it is necessary for a translator to choose between rendering his work as a chronicle *or* a tale, his style as realistic *or* mytho-poetic (generally, the translators choose the former), especially since Andrić himself did not make a clear decision in this regard. The reason for translators' general preferences are not entirely obvious, given that there is already a tradition for translations of various neo- or "magical" realisms from "Third World" cultures into English. In cases such as Mario Vargas Llosa and Maryse Condé, for example, idiosyncratic terms, rather than being explicated and/or translated, are left in the original form, thus allowing the reader to confront the strangeness which is (also) present in and integral to the original. That this is less the strategy of Andrić's translators may well point to certain preconceptions about the different position Balkan culture has vis-à-vis the English readership.

All the translations of Andrić into English offer an invaluable rendition of the disappeared culture(s) in the Balkans and, what might have been most important for Andrić, a bridge between East and West, mythical and historical time. This is so despite the translations' occasional shortcomings and, in some sense, because of them. For the translators – themselves engaged in Yugoslavian culture and highly knowledgeable about it and its past – reflect its views and prejudices. With Yugoslavia having disappeared, translation – in the sense of a carrying over – seems to be the future for Andrić, as he has yet to find a place in Bosnian, Croat, and Serbian literatures and their languages (permanently?) separated by the war.

PETAR RAMADANOVIĆ

Further Reading

Bergman, Gun, *Turkisms in Ivo Andrić's Na Drini ćuprija, Examined from the Point of View of Literary Style and Cultural History*, Uppsala: Almqvist & Wiksell, 1969

Hawkesworth, Celia, *Ivo Andrić: Bridge between East and West*, London: Athlone Press, 1984

Juričič, Želimir B., *The Man and the Artist: Essays on Ivo Andrić*, Lanham, Maryland: University Press of America, 1986

Mikhailovich, Vasa D. and Matja Matejić, *Comprehensive Bibliography of Yugoslav Literature in English*, Columbus, Ohio: Slavica, 1984, supplements 1988, 1992

Jean Anouilh 1910–1987

French dramatist

Biography

Born Jean-Marie-Lucien-Pierre Anouilh in Cérisole, Bordeaux, southwest France, 23 June 1910, to a poor family. His early education was in Bordeaux. His family moved to Paris when he was in his teens, and he studied law at the Sorbonne University, Paris, from 1928 to 1929. After leaving the Sorbonne he worked in Paris as a publicity and gag writer for films and as a copywriter in advertising.

Anouilh had become interested in the theatre while he was at university, and started writing for the stage; he worked as secretary to Louis Jouvet's Comédie des Champs-Elyseés, 1931–32, and his first play, *L'Hermine* (*The Ermine*), was produced in Paris in 1932. He married the actress Monelle Valentin in 1931 (one daughter). He went on to become assistant to the director Georges Pitoëff and became a full-time writer in the late 1930s after the success of his *Le Voyageur sans bagage* (*Traveller without Luggage*), produced in 1937. In 1953 he was divorced from Valentin and married Nicole Lançon, with whom he had two daughters and one son. He also worked as a film director. Anouilh's plays won many awards, including a Tony award (New York), 1955; the New York Drama Critics' Circle award, 1957; the Cino del Duca prize, 1970; the French Drama Critics award, 1970; and the Paris Critics prize, 1971. Died in Lausanne, Switzerland, 3 October 1987.

Anouilh's literary breakthrough came in 1937, when his play *Le Voyageur sans bagage* was produced, followed shortly afterwards, in 1938, *La Sauvage* (translated as *The Restless Heart*). Many of these early naturalistic plays, including *Jézabel*, *L'Hermine* and *Eurydice*, produced 1942, were termed by Anouilh his *pièces noires* ("black plays"), an indication of their pessimistic atmosphere. In contrast, a contemporary group of more optimistic dramatic works, also produced during the late 1930s and 1940s, were called *pièces roses* ("rose-coloured plays"). These plays include *Le Bal des voleurs* (*The Thieves' Carnival*), produced 1938; *Léocadia*, produced 1940; and *Le Rendez-vous de Senlis* (*Dinner with the Family*), also 1940. During the later 1940s Anouilh turned his attention to mythical and historic subjects, the best-known of these plays being *Antigone* (1944), one of his most successful productions, along with *L'Alouette* (*The Lark*), about Joan of Arc, published in 1953, and *Becket*, produced in 1959. Work of the 1940s and 1950s includes his *pièces brillantes* ("brilliant plays"), among which are *L'Invitation au château* (*Ring round the Moon*), produced in 1947; *Cecile*, written 1951; and *La Répétition; ou, L'Amour puni* (*The Rehearsal*), 1950. Anouilh's *pièces grinçantes* ("grating plays") of this period include *Pauvres Bitos; ou, Le Dîner de têtes* (*Poor Bitos*), 1956, and *La Valse des toréadors* (*Waltz of the Toreadors*), 1952. Although some of Anouilh's plays of the 1960s were considered unfashionable by the critics, his more successful work in the later 1960s and 1970s includes *Cher Antoine* (*Dear Antoine*), 1969; *Ne réveillez pas Madame* [*Don't Wake the Lady*], 1970; *Vive Henry IV*, 1977; and *La Culotte* [*The Trousers*], 1978.

Translations

Selections of Plays

Hill, Lucienne *et al.*, *Jean Anouilh: Five Plays*, with an introduction by Ned Chaillet, London: Methuen, 1987; reprinted as *Plays: One*, 1993 (contains *Léocadia*, translated by Timberlake Wertenbaker; *Antigone*, translated by Barbara Bray; *The Waltz of the Toreadors*, translated by Lucienne Hill; *The Lark*, translated by Christopher Fry; *Poor Bitos*, translated by Lucienne Hill)

John, Miriam *et al.*, *Plays*, 3 vols, New York: Hill and Wang, 1958–67 (vol. 1: *Antigone, Eurydice* (*Legend of Lovers*), *The Ermine*, *The Rehearsal*, *Romeo and Jeannette*; vol. 2: *Restless Heart*, *Time Remembered*, *Ardèle*, *Mademoiselle Colombe*, *The Lark*, translated by Lillian Hellman; vol. 3: *Thieves' Carnival*; *Medea*; *Cecile, or, The School for Fathers*; *Traveller without Luggage*; *The Orchestra*; *Episode in the Life of an Author*; *Catch as Catch Can*)

John, Miriam *et al.*, *The Collected Plays*, 2 vols, London: Methuen, 1966–67 (vol. 1: *The Ermine*, translated by Miriam John; *Thieves' Carnival*, *Restless Heart* and *Traveller without Luggage*, translated by Lucienne Hill; *Dinner with the Family*, translated by Edward O. Marsh; vol. 2: *Time Remembered*, translated by Patricia Moyes; *Point of Departure*, translated by Kitty Black; *Antigone*, translated by Lewis Galantière; *Romeo and Jeannette*, translated by Miriam John; *Medea*, translated by Luce and Arthur Klein)

Plays

Le Voyageur sans bagage, 1937

Hill, Lucienne, *Traveller without Luggage* in *The Collected Plays*, translated by Miriam John *et al.*, vol. 1, 1966

Whiting, John, *Traveller without Luggage*, London: Methuen, 1959

Antigone, 1946, produced 1944

Bray, Barbara, *Antigone* in *Jean Anouilh: Five Plays*, translated by Lucienne Hill *et al.*, 1987

Galantière, Lewis, *Antigone*, London: Samuel French, and New York: Random House, 1946

L'Invitation au château, 1948, produced 1947

Fry, Christopher, *Ring round the Moon: A Charade with Music*, London: Methuen, and New York: Oxford University Press, 1950

L'Alouette, 1953

Fry, Christopher, *The Lark*, London: Methuen, 1955

Hellman, Lillian, *The Lark*, in *Plays*, translated by Miriam John et al., vol. 2, 1959

Becket, 1959

Hill, Lucienne, *Becket; or, The Honour of God*, London: Methuen, 1961

Le Nombril, 1981

Frayn, Michael, *Number One*, London: Samuel French, 1985

In the 50 or so years of his association with the theatre Jean Anouilh wrote more than 40 plays. Of these, it is the early plays of the 1930s and the historically-based plays that have received most critical and public acclaim, as evidenced by the obituaries that appeared in *The Times* and *Le Monde*, on 5 and 6 October 1987 respectively. Jacques Chirac's tribute, for example, singled out *L'Alouette*, *Antigone* and *Becket*. Not until after World War II did the early plays filter through to English audiences, with the result that nearly all of the translations making up the Methuen collection belong to that decade. Translations of the historical plays, on the other hand, most of which belong to the same decade, followed on closely from the originals. During the 1950s, therefore, Anouilh enjoyed immense popularity in England, and it is mainly with this period that the present article is concerned. His star then suffered an eclipse on both sides of the Channel until the appearance of his last play, *Le Nombril* (1981), which was awarded the *grand prix* of the Société des Auteurs and ran for over a year in Paris. Its 1984 run in the West End, however, was relatively short.

Le Voyageur sans bagage (1937), about an amnesiac's return to what may be his long-lost family, was Anouilh's first real success. For the *Collected Plays* (1966), the original translation by John WHITING was replaced by that of Lucienne HILL (also first published 1959), the main translator of Anouilh's plays. Whiting's version contains a fair number of inaccuracies, which render certain passages inconsequential, especially the scenes involving the colloquial language of the servants, where he is linguistically out of his depth. While his English is not unidiomatic, there is a flatness of tone to his dialogue that does less than justice to the stylistic range of the original. For example, the comical theatricality of Juliette's "... bafouée dans son douloureux amour" and the caustic snobbery of the Duchess's "C'est bien une idée de paysans de venir en groupe pour mieux se défendre" become tonally indistinguishable in Whiting's "to feel herself laughed at in her tragic love-affair" and "The working classes always come in large numbers, the better to defend themselves". In contrast, Hill is never overstretched linguistically. Her version is both accurate and sensitive to tonal variation, carefully differentiating, in the case in question, between the mock-tragic tone adopted by Juliette ("...bearing the cruel pangs of thwarted love") and the Duchess's high-handed dismissiveness of the lower classes ("Safety in numbers – that's the peasant mentality all over").

Lewis GALANTIÈRE (1946) has made some concessions to his American audience with his rather free translation of *Antigone*. The play derives its power from the contrast between the extraordinary role that Antigone is called on to perform, in burying her dead brother's body against the orders of the king, and the ordinariness of everything and everyone around her, but it does so only by maintaining a careful balance between the mythical pedigree of the characters and their modernization. Galantière's version sometimes upsets this balance by overemphasizing the modern: to have Créon refer to Antigone's father as her "dad" is taking informality a little bit too far, especially when he will go on to refer to blood tests and birth-certificates, increasing still further the list of anachronisms which some critics had already found excessive in the original. Barbara BRAY's translation (for BBC Radio 3, published 1987) underscores the American flavour of Galantière's adaptation and makes it sound a little dated in comparison. She follows the French text much more closely, respecting the economy of the original and scrupulously preserving the theatrical terminology Anouilh frequently uses to underpin the life–theatre analogy. However, not all the plusses are on Bray's side: an occasional error or awkward rendering slips in which Galantière had managed to avoid.

Christopher FRY's *Ring round the Moon* (1950) did much to establish Anouilh in England and must surely count as the definitive translation of *L'Invitation au château*. He is clearly at ease with Anouilh's style of writing; his own version loses none of the sparkle of the original dialogue. He has, however, taken certain liberties with the text, cutting the more acerbic passages, such as Horace's (*alias* Hugo's) cynical reflections on the charitable deeds of the rich at the beginning of act 5 (act 3, scene 2 in Fry), and inserting, prior to Anouilh's act 2, a very witty scene of his own (the beginning of his own act 1, scene 2), that turns Madame Desmermortes into a Lady Bracknell. A noticeable tendency of Fry's translating, as distinct from his adapting, is to give a bolder touch to the humour through more concrete renderings: in the original French, Romainville's protestations of sexual disinterestedness are those of the cultured Frenchman ("Je m'intéresse à cette jeune fille comme je m'intéresse à tous les arts"); while his English counterpart invokes English eccentricity ("I'm only interested in this girl as I'm interested in butterflies and old furniture").

FRY's *The Lark* (1955) is not quite as masterly as his *Ring round the Moon*, but impressive none the less. There are, for instance, more mistranslations: some of these are minor and will go unnoticed; others are more irritating, since they introduce an incoherent note into the dialogue ("... it was more extraordinary for Him [God] ... to make Lazarus live again, than for me to thread a needle" should clearly read "... it was *no more* extraordinary ..."). On the other hand, the wider range of registers to which the more epic proportions of this play about Joan of Arc give rise are deftly handled, a more vivid touch being given to the dialogue here and there. The callousness of Charles's "J'ai horreur de cette atmosphère de prison, c'est d'un humide!", during his visit to Joan towards the end of the play, is even more effectively conveyed in Fry's version by the grotesquely comic "This prison atmosphere is deadly, so damp it would really be healthier to sit in the river". Despite this example, however, Fry has deliberately toned down Anouilh's cynicism. This is most noticeable in the way the play ends: whereas Anouilh had juxtaposed the triumph of Joan with a comment from her inglorious father: "I always said that girl would go far", Fry has chosen to omit the father's lines altogether.

Lillian HELLMAN's *The Lark* (1959), described as an adaptation, is indeed much freer than Fry's version. She has omitted quite lengthy passages and has even made additions of her own. These changes are on the whole skilfully wrought, and while they may occasionally be felt to entail a loss of subtlety there is often a gain in comic richness, as in Fry's case. When, for example, Beaudricourt describes the mental paralysis that besets him each time he has to make an important decision, we are given, in preference to a literal "... a blank. A fog", a more colourful "my head acts like it's gone some place else". Again like Fry, she alters the ending, though more radically and to different effect. She, too, gets rid of the father's comments, but still shows us the other side of the coin by conceiving an exchange of insults between Charles and Warwick. For several reasons, Hellman's ending coheres less well with the rest of the play, however, than Anouilh's.

The original French production of *Becket* left out several complete scenes and Lucienne HILL (1961) has chosen to do the same. In addition she has made several small cuts of her own. These are not always appropriate: for example, Becket's assertion that "one is only immoral if one fails to do what is necessary, when it is necessary" contributes too much to our understanding of his character to be safely omitted. Cuts apart, Hill follows the original text closely; indeed, a little too closely at times, for although one would be hard-pressed to find any inaccuracies at all, she is guilty of the occasional *calque*, such as "the King has a long arm" or "... to reduce him to powder". Small blemishes like these are to some extent offset by imaginative renderings elsewhere, as when "médusée" is translated as "like a fascinated rabbit" or "les rois, ça repousse" as "kings spring up again like weeds". In short, while Hill has done a very competent job, she also whets our appetite for a little more of the adventurousness these examples display.

Although Michael FRAYN (1985) has been fairly ruthless with the surgeon's knife in his adaptation of *Le Nombril*, the instrument in question is that of the plastic surgeon, for the scars are all but invisible and the aesthetically pleasing parts that have been spared are treated with the utmost respect and solicitude. Judging, no doubt rightly, that the English have less regard for literary figures than do the French, especially when the literary figures concerned happen, into the bargain, to be French, Frayn has cut most references to them, to their works and to literature in general. Otherwise, his version reproduces with scrupulous exactness the tone and meaning of the original text, without ever reminding us that it was once a piece of French. The most substantial cut by far is what is effectively a dig at the theatre of the absurd: an unexplained, daily delivery of boxes that turn out to be empty. The other major change is a complete rewriting of Anouilh's ending, which has Léon, the major protagonist, and his "close" friend, Gaston, come to blows in front of press photographers over the relative merits of novels and plays. Frayn himself has preferred to focus on a different theme, material greed: Léon's entire family home in on the newly successful Gaston, sensing a likely financial saviour. Elsewhere, Frayn's skill as a translator is admirable. Spurning stock equivalents, he produces an idiom that is quite distinct from, but which loses nothing of, the original. One illustration of the translation's many strengths is Léon's irreverent response to the news of a colleague's death: "Tiens! un faire-part! Il y en a encore un qui a dévissé", which effortlessly crosses the cultural divide as "Aha! Black edges! Another redskin bites the dust!".

Prominent among Anouilh's translators is the name of Lucienne HILL, whose translations have, for good reason, frequently been taken up by Anouilh's American publishers also. However, Anouilh must surely enjoy the distinction, among modern French writers, of having attracted the highest number of translators, and so it would not be feasible even simply to list all the translations of his work that have appeared. For fuller information, therefore, the Unesco *Index translationum* should be consulted.

PAUL REED

Further Reading

Delaura, David J., "Anouilh's Other *Antigone*", *French Review*, 35 (October 1961) pp. 36–41

Harvitt, Hélène, "The Translation of Anouilh's *Becket*", *French Review*, 34 (May 1961) pp. 569–71

Knepler, Henry W., "*The Lark*: A Case History", *Modern Drama*, 1 (May 1958) pp. 15–28

Guillaume Apollinaire 1880–1918

French poet, dramatist, short-story writer and critic

Biography

Born Wilhelm Apollinaris de Kostrowitzky in Rome, 26 August 1880, illegitimate son of a Polish mother and an Italian father. Wilhelm was educated in Monte Carlo, Cannes, and Nice as, abandoned by his father, his mother took her two sons round with her to the casino towns. From the age of 18 he was writing verse and prose pieces, in 1899 beginning to use the name Apollinaire. After minor office and teaching jobs he was tutor to a German family in the Rhineland, 1901[0]. From 1903 he began to move in Paris literary and artistic circles, working as a freelance writer and critic and making friends in 1904 with Picasso and other avant-garde painters. He edited several little reviews, including *Le Festin d'Ésope*, 1903, and *Les Soirées de Paris*, 1912[-14. He wrote a manifesto on Futurism and essays on Cubism (*Les Peintres cubistes*, 1913), and helped promote the work of Le Douanier Rousseau. He was imprisoned briefly on suspicion of art theft, 1911. He volunteered in 1914 and served in the artillery, then the infantry, continuing to write even at the front. In March 1916 he received a severe head wound and was invalided out of the army. His innovative verse play *Les Mamelles de Tirésias* was produced in 1917. He married Jacqueline Kolb in 1918; she and other loves figure poignantly in his poetry. He died in Paris of influenza, 9 November 1918.

Creator, theorist, precursor, Apollinaire is best known for the lyric collections *Alcools* (1913) and *Calligrammes* (1918), poems modern but grounded in tradition, with a bold, allusive texture, rich in haunting phrases and cadences. Some of the *Calligrammes* are presented in pictorial typography.

Translations

Selections

Bernard, Oliver, *Selected Poems*, Harmondsworth: Penguin, 1965; expanded bilingual edition, London: Anvil Press, 1986

Shattuck, Roger, *Selected Writings of Guillaume Apollinaire*, with an introduction, New York: New Directions, and London: Harvill Press, 1950

Poetry

Alcools, 1913

Greet, Ann Hyde, *Alcools* (parallel texts), with an introduction by Warren Ramsey, Berkeley: University of California Press, 1965

"Zone", 1913

Beckett, Samuel, *Zone* (bilingual edition), Dublin: Dolmen Press, and London: Calder and Boyars, 1972 (originally published in *Transition*, 50, 1950)

Calligrammes: Poèmes de la paix et de la guerre, 1913–1916, 1918

Greet, Ann Hyde, *Calligrammes: Poems of Peace and War, 1913–1916* (parallel texts), with an introduction by S.I. Lockerbie, Berkeley: University of California Press, 1980

Stories

Les Exploits d'un jeune Don Juan, 1907

Lykiard, Alexis, *The Exploits of a Young Don Juan*, London: W.H. Allen, 1986

Les Onze Mille Verges, 1907

Rootes, Nina, *Les Onze Mille Verges; or, The Amorous Adventures of Prince Mony Vibescu*, London: Peter Owen, 1976; New York: Taplinger, 1979

L'Hérésiarque et cie, 1910

Hall, Rémy Inglis, *The Heresiarch and Co.*, New York: Doubleday, 1965; as *The Wandering Jew and Other Stories*, London: Rupert Hart-Davis, 1967

Le Poète assassiné, 1916

Padgett, Ron, *The Poet Assassinated and Other Stories*, New York: Holt Rinehart, and London: Rupert Hart-Davis, 1968

Guillaume Apollinaire's best-known works, the verse collections *Alcools* and *Calligrammes*, have both been translated in their entirety by Ann Hyde GREET in clear, "parallel text" editions each with a substantial introduction – by Warren Ramsey and S.I. Lockerbie, respectively. Her translation (1980) of *Calligrammes* is much the more successful, taking great care to reproduce the layout of the original texts, and equally, as far as possible, paying due attention to the varying typography (such as boldface, character size and capitalization). This intention has been pursued to the extent that the actual translations seem to have been largely generated by the original topography, so that in "Paysage" ("Landscape") "UN CIGARE allumé qui fume" becomes "A LIGHTED cigar that smokes". Although when this is considered strictly as a conventional translation it may seem unpersuasively literal to retain an indicative relative clause, this must be offset against the reader's experience of pleasure in spatial recognition, wherein such renderings become much more convincing, since a certain figurative literalism is in any case invoked in the whole calligrammatic exercise. One anomaly should, however, be indicated. The original texts are uniformly placed in italics and their English counterparts in roman type, except in such cases as "Liens" ("Chains") – originally in italics – where the French texts are now transposed into roman type and revert back to the original italics only in translation in order to maintain this difference. However, the calligrammatic poems "proper" retain roman type as the "home key" in both French and English versions (indeed the handwritten effects are also duplicated in translation). This is more than a mere quibble, not only because this shift in typefaces in the verse poetry causes unnecessary complications, but more importantly because both topographical layout and typology – and their dialectical interaction – are thematized in these works as integral agents in the strategies of meaning-production. These translations do, on the other hand, respect Apollinaire's largely simple syntax and exact vocabulary, which together produce a sense of rapidity and concreteness essential to the sense of surprise that this poetry frequently strives to create.

The translation of *Alcools* (GREET, 1965) is noticeably less assured. Most strangely, there is a tendency to insert blank spaces into the verse lines to mark the syntactic hiatus created by Apollinaire's juxtaposition of semantically and referentially diverse units. Not only is this an unnecessary intrusion into the already fragmented poetic line, it also deprives the translator of the opportunity to employ this device of spacing when the original versions themselves have recourse to this practice. There is equally a tendency to indulge in a foreign romantic lyricism, such that the laconic "Nous ne nous voyons plus sur terre" of "Adieu" becomes "Never more on earth we two together". The annotation of this volume is admirably extensive but is, alas, not always limited to points of explication or clarification and becomes judgmental and interpretively interventionist: what is the function of a note informing us that lines 49 and 50 of "Le Voyageur" are "the two most beautiful lines in this poem"?

SHATTUCK's volume (1950) also includes a substantial introduction, although perversely the quotations included therein are left untranslated. He succeeds in conveying much of the pathos and beauty of the French and is substantially less verbose than many, producing the best incipit to the celebrated "Zone": "You are tired at last of this old world". Although he pays due respect to the original word order he does not do so slavishly or unidiomatically, and his diction is generally less domesticated than most, even if he does perhaps tend to err on the side of the traditional. All of these virtues allow him to recreate in English an Apollinairean voice that does not sound awkward or merely capricious.

BERNARD (1965), unfortunately, often indulges in rather wordy paraphrasing, sometimes to the extent of almost creating an incantatory effect quite alien to the abrupt reticence of the originals and thereby sacrificing any sense of Apollinairean pathos. In "Carte Postale" the line "Tandis que meurt ce jour d'été" is quite spuriously touched up into "While Summer day becomes a shade". One cannot help but feel that these translations are incarcerated in a preordained poetic language of orthodoxy almost entirely inappropriate to the sense of fragility and experimentation that are laconically manifested in Apollinaire's attempts precisely to forge a *new* poetic language.

BECKETT's (1950) translation of "Zone" ("In the end you are weary of this ancient world ...") almost too neatly falls into the stereotypical conception of his own rather grim concerns, but thankfully never becomes merely self-seeking. This is a relatively free rendering, but with little sense of inaccuracy or arbitrariness, its real achievement being cumulative. It does however share the common unwillingness to exploit fully the colloquial idiom in which the original text is couched, with a resultant loss of some vibrancy within the poetic line. Perhaps the most significant reservation about this version is that Beckett often indulges in a rewriting of the original syntactic fragmentation into relatively conventional forms (subject, verb, predicate, for instance) which not only lose the spatial disruption and fragmentation of the French text, but become also the basis for some rather baroque ornamentation: "J'ai une pitié immense pour les coutures de son ventre" becoming "The seems of her belly go to my heart".

As for the prose "fiction", HALL (1965) is rather unidiomatic in spite of having chosen a good selection of texts. She sometimes gives the impression of a certain amateurishness, while PADGETT (1968) is also a little too literal at times but is generally more convincing. ROOTES (1976) does her best with unpromising material, but why bother if one is prudishly going to avoid, or be prevented from, translating the full title of this "erotic" work? LYKIARD (1986), however, will probably long remain without peers in conveying the profound tedium and puerility of the original work whose humourless repetitiveness he inadvertently manages to make hilarious in its ineptitude and banality.

PAUL RICKETT

Further Reading

Bates, Scott, *Guillaume Apollinaire*, New York: Twayne, 1967; revised 1989

Breunig, Leroy C. (editor), *Apollinaire on Art: Essays and Reviews, 1902–1918*, translated by Susan Suleiman, London: Thames and Hudson, and New York: Viking, 1972

Carmody, Francis J., *The Evolution of Apollinaire's Poetics, 1901–1914*, Berkeley: University of California Press, 1963

Davies, Margaret, *Apollinaire*, Edinburgh: Oliver and Boyd, 1964; New York: St Martin's Press, 1965

Mathews, Timothy, *Reading Apollinaire: Theories of Poetic Language*, Manchester: Manchester University Press, 1987

Samaltanos, Katia, *Apollinaire: Catalyst for Primitivism, Picabia and Duchamp*, Ann Arbor, Michigan: UMI Research Press, 1984

Steegmuller, Francis, *Apollinaire: Poet among the Painters*, London: Rupert Hart-Davis, and New York: Farrar Straus, 1963

Apuleius c.AD 123/5–after 163

Roman novelist and orator

Biography

Lucius Apuleius was born in Madaura, a province of north Africa (now M'Daourouch, Algeria), c. AD 123/5. He was educated in Carthage, Athens and Rome. He lived in Oea (now Tripoli), where in 155 he married Aemilia Pudentilla, a rich widow. He may have had a son named Faustinus.

Apuleius was acquitted of a charge of sorcery at the town of Sabratha, a Roman colony near Oea. Later he settled, wrote, and taught rhetoric and philosophy in Carthage, lecturing also in other African towns. His success as an orator brought him a statue, the priesthood of the god Aesculepius and other honours. Died later than AD 163 (probably much later).

Apuleius wrote much, but not all his writings are extant. The principal remaining works are the satirical novel *Metamorphoses* (*The Golden Ass*), commentaries on Plato, and the *Apologia*, with which he defeated the charge of sorcery made against him.

The Golden Ass

Metamorphoses

Translations

Adlington, William, *The XI Bookes of the Golden Asse, Conteininge the Metamorphosie of Lucius Apuleius*, Oxford: University College, 1566, many reprints; a revised version available in Charles Whibley's edition, London: D. Nutt, 1893; New York: Modern Library, 1928; reprinted New York: AMS Press, 1967

Anonymous, *The Works of Apuleius, Comprising The Metamorphoses, or Golden Ass, The God of Socrates, The Florida, and His Defence, or, A Discourse on Magic*, London: Bohn, 1853

Butler, H.E., *The Metamorphoses or Golden Ass of Apuleius of Madaura*, Oxford: Clarendon Press, 1910

Byrne, Francis D., *The Golden Ass of Apuleius*, London: Imperial Press, 1905

Graves, Robert, *The Transformations of Lucius, Otherwise Known as The Golden Ass*, Harmondsworth: Penguin, 1950

Hanson, J. Arthur, *Apuleius: Metamorphoses* (parallel texts), 2 vols, Cambridge, Massachusetts: Harvard University Press, 1989 (Loeb Classical Library)

Head, Sir George, *The Metamorphoses of Apuleius: A Romance of the Second Century*, London: Longman Brown Green and Longmans, 1851

Lindsay, Jack, *The Golden Ass by Apuleius*, New York: Limited Editions Club, 1932; reprinted Bloomington: Indiana University Press, 1962

Taylor, Thomas, *The Metamorphosis or Golden Ass, and Philosophical Works of Apuleius*, London: Robert Triphook and T. Rodd, 1822

Walsh, P.G., *The Golden Ass*, Oxford: Clarendon Press, and New York: Oxford University Press, 1994

Apuleius' most outstanding work, and the only complete novel to survive from Roman antiquity, is the *Metamorphoses*, usually referred to as *The Golden Ass*, because the episodes composing it are presented by a man changed for a time by magic into a donkey. It was probably based on a Greek narrative by Lucius of Patras, and bears a strong resemblance in its essentials to Lucian's *Lucius or the Ass*. The date of *The Golden Ass* is uncertain. Because at one point in his life Apuleius stood trial for sorcery, later antiquity assumed that *The Golden Ass* was autobiographical – a supposition facilitated by the fact that the story is told in the first person.

Apuleius' language is an odd, highly stylized and often extravagant but beautiful Latin in the "Asiatic" mode, regarded by some as representative of so-called "African Latin". Apuleius' story is highly entertaining. It consists of the main narrative, which deals with the metamorphosis of the narrator, his subsequent misadventures, and his eventual return to human shape; and a number of subsidiary tales told by various characters. The best-known and the longest of these is the story of Cupid (or Amor) and Psyche, often edited and translated separately. It forms a large portion of *The Golden Ass* (book 4, chapter 28 to book 6, chapter 24) and is the prototype of one of the most popular European fairy tales, *Beauty and the Beast*. Translations that limit themselves to this story are not considered in the present review, although at least one of them is truly outstanding; that of Walter Pater, included in his novel *Marius the Epicurean*.

The Golden Ass is such good reading that almost any translation "works", but most of the 19th-century translators are ill at ease with Apuleius' ribaldry and often expurgate some of the most erotic passages. Later translations are preferable for this reason and some others.

ADLINGTON (1566) does not expurgate, but he shies away from some of the linguistically difficult passages, which also happen to be outstandingly elegant examples of "Asiatic" style. This translation continues to be reprinted, mainly because of its enjoyable Elizabethan language.

TAYLOR (1822), a notable Neoplatonist, is attracted to Apuleius because of the latter's presumed Platonism. (Apuleius wrote an essay on *The God of Socrates*.) Taylor's rather stilted style is typical of its period and actually fits the mannered Latin of the original. His copious footnotes are mainly concerned with Platonism.

HEAD (1851) has an unfortunate attitude toward his subject. Not only does he expurgate but he sees fit to apologize for the "imperfection of the Latinity of the Metamorphoses". One is puzzled why he chooses to translate an author who embarrasses him.

The ANONYMOUS translation in the Bohn series (1853) is quite precise, but it is mainly a "trot" with helpful notes on cultural peculiarities as well as stylistic and linguistic matters: the translator takes pains to quote Latin phrases and explain how and why he has rendered them into English.

BYRNE's is a very good translation (1905) but it has been largely supplanted by more modern renderings, which either are based on updated editions of the Latin or have outstanding literary merit.

BUTLER (1910) offers good style, but he expurgates and – even worse – occasionally rewrites.

LINDSAY's translation (1932) is smooth and readable. However, Graves surpasses him in the quality of his English, and Hanson and Walsh in precision. Still, this is one of the more accessible versions.

GRAVES's version (1950) is ebullient, full of life: a masterpiece. It bears all the marks of Graves's way with the English language. It is not absolutely faithful: in places it seems influenced by Adlington's, which Graves admired. However, the liberties Graves takes with the text are easy to forgive because of the excellence of the product.

HANSON's, like the other translations in the Loeb series, aims to facilitate access to the original. The translation (1989) is printed facing the Latin text. Loeb editions are very uneven, but this is one of the best in the series. The translation is highly readable and precise, and the footnotes excellent.

WALSH's translation (1994) is probably the best currently available. It is based on the best modern editions of the text and offers precision, readability, and informative notes.

ZOJA PAVLOVSKIS-PETIT

Further Reading

See the translators' introductions to Graves, Hanson, and Walsh

---

The Arabian Nights

See The Thousand and One Nights

Arabic

Literary Translation into English

The Language

Arabic is a major Semitic language widely used throughout the world by more than a billion Arabs and Muslims. Originally spoken in Arabia and adjacent areas of Iraq and Syria, it has spread with the rise of Islam (AD 610) to other regions extending between the Iberian peninsula and China. Apart from its significant role as the religious language of Muslims who belong to diverse nationalities or ethnic groups, Arabic is the national language of about 220 million inhabitants of Algeria, Bahrain, Egypt, Iraq, Jordan, Kuwait, Lebanon, Libya, Mauritania, Morocco, Oman, Palestine, Qatar, Saudi Arabia, Somalia, Sudan, Syria, Tunisia, United Arab Emirates, and Yemen. There are also several million speakers of Arabic who live elsewhere in different parts of the world, e.g. Australia, Britain, France, Germany, Iran, Israel, North and South America, and Turkey. In addition, Arabic is spoken or serves as an official language in sub-Saharan African countries including Cameroon, Chad, Comoros, Djibouti, Ethiopia, Mali, Niger, Senegal, and Tanzania.

In view of its role as the language of both the Qur'ān (Koran) and Arabo-Islamic civilization, Arabic has left its mark in numerous languages that adapted or adopted a considerable number of terms from its vocabulary, as well as its script. English, for example, has many, perhaps thousands of loan words derived from Arabic, e.g., admiral, adobe, alcohol, atlas, average, coffee, cotton, cipher, gazelle, jar, mattress, nadir, ream, rice, safari, sofa, sugar, tariff, and zero. The Arabic alphabet, on the other hand, is the second most widely used alphabet in the world's writing systems (next to the Latin alphabet) as it has been adapted by numerous languages such as Persian, Pashto, Urdu, Malay (Jawi), Ottoman Turkish and other Turkic languages. The Arabic alphabet itself consists of 28 letters corresponding to the Arabic consonants, and is written from right to left. Three of these letters stand also for the language's long vowels. The short vowels are represented not by letters but by diacritical points that are also used to indicate the three cases: nominative, accusative, and genitive. However, these signs are normally left out in writing or printed texts. The most notable exception to this norm is the Qur'ān, Islam's Holy Book, which is fully vocalized, with all the short vowels and case endings indicated. The normal absence of signs for short vowels and case endings represents a serious problem that both native and non-native speakers of Arabic have to overcome in learning Arabic and using it correctly.

There are two distinct forms or varieties of Arabic: "classical" and "colloquial", which exist side by side and perform different functions. The classical variety, known also as "written", "standard", and "literary" Arabic, maintains a high degree of uniformity and functions as the standard language in all Arab countries. It is the vehicle of formal situations, secular and religious, and is acquired through formal education. In terms of structural characteristics, classical Arabic has 28 consonants, three short vowels and three long vowels, and a complex inflectional system of case or modal endings including dual forms, indicating number and gender for verbs, nouns, and pronouns. It is noted for its rich lexicon, which reflects different periods of usage from the pre-Islamic (i.e. 6th century) until the present. The modern phase of classical Arabic includes also a great deal of colloquialism, on account of a substantially increased use of various dialects in literature and other artistic forms, while the dialects themselves exhibit a tendency toward incorporating elements from the classical language, especially in the phonological and lexical areas.

The colloquial, on the other hand, is the actual language of daily activities, mainly spoken, though occasionally written, and it varies in its sound system and structure not only from one Arab country to another but from one area to another within each country. In spite of their differences, the colloquial varieties share a simplified inflectional system almost free of case or modal endings and of the dual form except in the case of nouns. While normally relegated to folklore and popular literature in the past, the colloquial varieties have become an important component of modern Arabic literature, particularly in plays and works of fiction. This is in addition to their use as the primary medium of songs and films.

The dichotomy between the classical and colloquial dialects, their coexistence in written and oral discourse, and the long continuous literary use of Arabic may be regarded as factors responsible for the difficulty both native and non-native speakers experience in attaining competence in Arabic or translating modern Arabic literature. It is primarily because of these factors that certain English-speaking writers tend to characterize Arabic as "a hurdle", " a linguistic Iron Curtain", or a "florid language" far from easy to translate into English. While these factors may limit non-native speakers' direct access to Arabic literature, they should not be viewed as an insurmountable obstacle for truly serious students of Arabic or competent translators.

SALIH J. ALTOMA

Further Reading

Altoma, Salih J., *The Problem of Diglossia in Arabic: A Comparative Study of Classical and Iraqi Arabic*, Cambridge, Massachusetts: Center for Middle Eastern Studies, Harvard University, 1969

Beeston, A.F., *The Arabic Language Today*, London: Hutcheson, 1970

Cadora, F.J., *Interdialectal Lexical Combatibility in Arabic*, Leiden: E.J. Brill, 1979

Cannon, Garland Hampton, *The Arabic Contributions to the English Language: An Historical Dictionary*, Wiesbaden: Harrassowitz, 1994

Cantarino, Vicente, *Syntax of Modern Arabic Prose*, 3 vols, Bloomington: Indiana University Press, 1974–75

Caspari, C.P., *A Grammar of the Arabic Language*, translated from the German of Caspari and edited with numerous additions and corrections by W. Wright, 3rd edition, revised by W. Robertson Smith and M.J. de Goeje, Cambridge and New York: Cambridge University Press, 1988

Chejne, A.G., *The Arabic Language: Its Role in History*, Minneapolis: University of Minnesota Press, 1969

Doniach, N.S., *The Oxford English–Arabic Dictionary of Current Usage*, Oxford: Clarendon Press, 1972; reprinted 1979

Holes, Clive, *Modern Arabic: Structures, Functions, and Varieties*, London and New York: Longman, 1995

Wehr, Hans, *A Dictionary of Modern Written Arabic*, Wiesbaden: Harrassowitz, 4th edition, 1979

The Pre-Modern Period (the European Middle Ages to the end of World War II)

The first period of translation from Arabic, the European Middle Ages, is one of translation into Latin. It covers philosophical/theological, mathematical and medical texts, including much Arabic material translated from the Greek, together with early translations of the Koran (Qur'ān) and Petrus Alfonsi's *Disciplina Clericalis* (early 12th century), a Latin re-telling of Arabic, Persian and other Middle Eastern stories that were later taken up into various European vernaculars.

In the second period, from the Renaissance to the end of the 17th century, there were further translations of the Qur'ān (some into vernaculars, with Du Ruyer's 1647 French translation serving as a basis for English re-translations; see Beeston, 1983) and of grammatical works and other aids to the learning of the Arabic language. For this period again, Latin is the main target language of translation. From the mid-17th century direct translations into French, e.g. Du Ruyer's Qur'ān, provide the basis for some English re-translations. This period sees the full establishment of Arabic as a university discipline in the West; its concerns are theological and linguistic (and, in France, historical and anecdotal, with Barthélemy d'Herbelot's 1697 *Bibliothèque orientale*, an encyclopedic work compiled from Arabic and other Islamic sources; see Toomer, 1996).

The first period for direct English translations from Arabic comes in the first half of the 18th century, with Simon Ockley's translation (1708) of the 12th-century Andalusian Ibn Tufayl's philosophical allegory *Hayy ibn Yaqẓān* (the "Philosophus Autodidactus" of Edward Pococke's 1671 Latin translation), a possible influence on Daniel Defoe's *Robinson Crusoe*, and with George Sale's translation of the Qur'ān (1734); this latter is both a scholarly and a literary event. Sale's Qur'ān accurately follows standard Muslim readings and glosses and is designed to reproduce the effect of the Muslim scripture on Muslim readers. It is followed, towards the end of the century, by Sir William Jones's translations of pre-Islamic poetry (1782; see Franklin, 1995). Here we enter the realm of literary translation proper, with aesthetic enthusiasm, and aesthetic fidelity, the prime motive and goal of the translations, whose impact on European sensibilities was far-reaching. Meanwhile, re-translations of Galland's French "translations" from the *Arabian Nights* (1704–17) had gained a wide English readership.

The 19th century is the period in which existing and new translations from Arabic have the most immediate and easily traceable effect on English writers (such as Coleridge, Carlyle, Tennyson) and in which the *Arabian Nights* are several times translated directly from the Arabic and gain the widest general readership (see Irwin, 1994). (But French and above all German scholarship now take the lead, Rückert's literary translations of both prose and poetry being outstanding.) Scholarly translations in handsome editions paid for by private subscription are sponsored by the Oriental Translation Fund of Great Britain and Ireland (these include the first of three 19th-century English renderings of the 12th-century *Maqāmāt* of Harīrī, a virtually untranslatable philologico-rhetorical narrative-didactic *tour de force*: Theodore Preston's aptly titled *Makamat or Rhetorical Anecdotes of Al Hariri of Basra* of 1850).

At the end of the 19th century and beginning of the 20th, C.J. Lyall's verse translations of pre-Islamic poetry, and the verse translations of poetry of all periods up to the 13th century in R.A. Nicholson's *Literary History of the Arabs* (first edition 1907), represent a high-water mark in terms of literary aspiration. Technical problems of translation – language structure, prosody and cultural transposition – receive discussion. Some major medieval prose works – historical, biographical and anecdotal – are also published in book form in the years between the two world wars, when the E.J.W. Gibb Memorial Trust, together with the Royal Asiatic Society and publishers such as E.J. Brill of Leiden and Basil Blackwell of Oxford, to all intents and purposes take over the work of the Oriental Translation Fund. Before and especially after World War II, A.J. Arberry tries to recapture the heroic literary spirit of the scholars of the earlier part of the century, and is successful in finding a more general readership for some of his numerous translations, notably of the Qur'ān, of Spanish Arabic poetry and mystical poetry and prose.

So far, during the periods described, translation has gone hand in hand with scholarship; editing and translation are parallel activities, though more texts are edited than are also translated. Until the 19th century, Arabic remains a manuscript culture. Europeans are then the first to produce scholarly printed editions, and in so doing draw a new map of Arabic literature, a process to which Arab scholars begin to contribute only in the course of the century. The texts selected for editing and translation belong almost exclusively to the classical periods of Arabic; most later, and all contemporary literature is ignored by translators. The *Arabian Nights* – despised by Arabs as "low" – is the sole exception to this concern with early, "high" literature.

Some general points are to be noted. First, 19th-century English scholars and their immediate successors were rediscovering classical Arabic literature fairly randomly, on the basis of the manuscripts available. Their translations – often still the best, or the only ones we have – reflect a patchy and sometimes arbitrary picture of what actually constitutes classical Arabic literature.

Second, the translators' concerns – or, more often, those of the scholars who use their texts – are not always primarily literary, and some of the source texts are not properly "literary" works: European and Arabic definitions of literary genres, and indeed of what constitutes literature, do not always coincide. Thus McGuckin de Slane's translation (1842–71) of the 13th-century Ibn Khallikān's *Biographical Dictionary* draws attention to literary form as an intrinsic constituent of the original, but is usually treated simply as a research tool. D.S. Margoliouth's translation (1921) of the 10th-century Miskawayh's history of *The Eclipse of the 'Abbasid Caliphate* faithfully renders its combination of vigour and suspense; yet historians have largely ignored the literary sophistication of the narrative. Conversely, the ongoing translation of the 9th-century Tabarī's multi-volume and multi-source *History*, the work of several translators, generally aims to render content rather than style, although, like most histories, it contains literary set pieces. Similarly, R.B. Serjeant's 1997 translation of the 9th-century comic masterpiece, Jāhiz's *Book of Misers*, seems designed for scholarly rather than literary consumption.

Lastly, except for the *Nights* and the Qur'ān, none of the works translated into English has ever gained a wide general readership; translations of mystical poetry and Spanish Arabic poetry probably have the widest public, among students of comparative religion and comparative literature.

As a result of these factors, the picture of pre-modern Arabic literature to be derived from a discussion of English translations is necessarily uneven and unbalanced. In particular, most major medieval poets remain largely untranslated, partly because of technical difficulties, but partly also because aesthetic understanding has been slow to develop. A similar combination of factors applies to the large, miscellaneous class of literary or semi-literary writing known in Arabic as *adab*, which for medieval readers would have included works such as those of Harīrī, Ibn Khallikān, Miskawayh and Jāhiz. The absence of firm generic distinctions and especially of a clear-cut concept of fiction in pre-modern Arabic may have discouraged translators from seeking a wider public; but much straightforward storytelling has lacked translators. Thus a large literature of love stories remains almost unknown in English except for the 11th-century Ibn Hazm's *Ring of the Dove* (translated by Arberry, 1953), as does the important genre of semi-popular devotional story-telling, of which Kisā'ī's *Tales of the Prophets* (date and authorship uncertain; translated by W. Thackston, 1978) is not the outstanding example. Versions of some of the long, semi-oral romance cycles, another staple of popular literary culture, have only recently been translated, for example, by M.C. Lyons (*The Arabian Epic*, 1995).

Modern Arabic literature, initially heavily influenced by Western norms and by Western genres such as the novel, short story and play, did not gain full maturity and recognition until after World War II, but since then the ratio of modern to classical translations has been all but reversed. Translations of contemporary Arabic writing now greatly outnumber those of classical literature; this is a trend that began in the 1960s and has gained momentum since the 1980s, when university courses in Arabic began to give equality or preference to modern as against classical Arabic studies, at the same time as the number of students enrolled increased. The structure of contemporary publishing has also played its part: institutional support for classical translations has become less sustained and arguably less concerned with the literary quality of translations, while commercial interest in contemporary Arabic fiction has steadily increased, and a wide non-specialist readership demands accessible texts. Factors contributing to this development include the growth of Arab women's fiction and the award of a Nobel Prize to the Egyptian novelist Najīb Mahfūz (Naguib Mahfouz) in 1988.

In the items listed below, Beeston (1983) gives a bibliography of translations of the Qur'ān into European languages and has translations of early poetry, Ashtiany (1990) contains translations of medieval Arabic prose and poetry, Irwin (1994) analyses the literary qualities of English translations of the *Nights*, Irwin (1999) republishes a selection of translations and addresses the question of translators' literary targets, and Meisami & Starkey (1998) provides a wide-ranging guide to translations from both classical and modern Arabic literature.

JULIA BRAY

Further Reading

Ashtiany, Julia *et al.* (editors), *'Abbasid Belles-Lettres*, Cambridge: Cambridge University Press, 1990 (The Cambridge History of Arabic Literature)

Beeston, A.F.L. *et al.* (editors), *Arabic Literature to the End of the Umayyad Period*, Cambridge: Cambridge University

Press, 1983 (The Cambridge History of Arabic Literature), pp. 502–20
Irwin, Robert, *The Arabian Nights: A Companion*, Harmondsworth: Penguin, 1994, pp. 9–41
Irwin, Robert (editor and translator), *Night and Horses and the Desert: An Anthology of Classical Arabian Literature*, London and New York: Allen Lane, 1999
Meisami, Julie Scott and Paul Starkey (editors), *Encyclopedia of Arabic Literature*, 2 vols, London and New York: Routledge, 1998

Contemporary Arabic Fiction

Since 1988, the year Najīb Mahfūz was awarded the Nobel Prize for literature, contemporary Arabic fiction has experienced a steadily growing interest among Western readers and publishers. This is in marked contrast to the pre-1988 period during which the demand for, or interest in, Arabic fiction was confined, with a few exceptions, to a relatively limited audience. Reviewing in retrospect English translations of contemporary Arabic fiction, it is possible to outline their progress in three stages or phases: the preparatory or initial phase 1947–67; the phase of expanded translation from 1968 to 1988 and the post-Nobel phase, i.e. since 1988.

During the 1947–67 phase works of fiction and drama written in Arabic received marginal attention in the West whether by means of translation or in literary studies. This lack of interest can be explained in part by two facts. First the novel and the short story, like drama, have begun to evolve as genres in Arabic only since the mid-19th century, largely as a result of European influence. Second, orientalists have continued to express their reservations even as late at the 1970s about the literary value or the degree of maturation of dramatic or fictional works produced by Arab writers. H.A.R. Gibb, for example, while noting the positive progress Arab writers made in these genres, felt that their "short stories, novels, and plays remain bounded by the horizons and conventions of the Arab world" and that "when translated into other languages they are so often more interesting as social documents than as literary achievements". Similar views have been expressed by other orientalists until recent years, as LeGassick (1992) remarks. It is therefore not surprising to note that between 1947 and 1967 only a small number of works of fiction (perhaps no more than 10) appeared in English. They include *Tales from Egyptian Life* by Mahmūd Taymūr (Cairo, 1947), and an anthology of *Modern Arabic Short Stories* (London, 1967), both of which were translated by Denys Johnson-Davies. The fact that 20 years elapsed between these two translations illustrates not only "the difficulty of finding a publisher" for Arabic literary works to which Johnson-Davies himself alluded, but, more importantly, the marginality assigned to modern Arabic literature in general in Oriental or Middle Eastern studies. It was also during this phase that the first novel to appear in English by Najīb Mahfūz, the 1988 Nobel Laureate, was published in Beirut in 1966 under the title *Midaq Alley* (translated by Trevor LeGassick). Other notable titles published in the same period are Tawfīq al-Hakīm's *Bird of the East* (Beirut, 1966), Desmond Stewart's translations of Fathī Ghanīm's *The Man Who Lost His Shadow* (Boston, 1966), and 'Abd al-Rahmān al-Sharqāwī's *Egyptian Earth* (London, 1962).

As a phase of expanding, but still largely academic, interest in modern Arabic literature in general, the period 1968–88 has been associated with several positive developments. During these years a much larger number of works of fiction (exceeding 50 novels and 35 short story collections of uneven quality) appeared in English translation in both Arab and Western countries. They represent mostly Egyptian writers but include a few works by other noted Arab novelists: Tawfīq Awwād and Halīm Barakāt (Lebanon), Jabrā I. Jabrā and Ghassān Kanafānī (Palestine), 'Abd al-Rahmān Munīf (Saudi Arabia) and Tayyib Sālih (Sudan). Of all Arab writers it was Najīb Mahfūz who became the focus of successive studies and translations. However, most of his translated works were initially published in Cairo (by the American University in Cairo Press). The most notable exception is his allegorical and highly controversial novel *Children of Gebelawi* (1981), which was published in London and Washington. It is relevant to recall in this context that the original Arabic version is still banned in Egypt and other Muslim countries and that it has never been published as a book in Egypt on account of its unconventional or "heretical" presentation of religions including Islam. It is also important to note that his masterpiece, the *Cairo Trilogy*, appeared in English translation only after he was awarded the Nobel Prize in 1988.

Another positive trend that began to emerge during this period is the translation of works by Arab women writers such as Sahar Khalīfa (1985), Emily Nasrallah (1987), Alifah Rifāt (1983), Nawāl Sa'dāwī (1983, 1985, 1987, 1988) and Hanān al-Shaykh (1986). The number of translated works by these or other women writers increases as we proceed beyond the 1980s. This growing interest in women's writings can be explained by two facts. First, more talented Arab women writers have emerged and made significant contributions to Arabic literature during the last four decades. Secondly, the global orientation of feminism in the West has brought into focus the cause of Third World feminism and women's perspectives about major political or social issues in their respective countries. There is no doubt that among Arab women writers Sa'dāwī has been particularly widely received, and she has been accorded favourable reviews in feminist literature. This is due perhaps more to her radical and outspoken approach to portraying women's conditions in Egypt or in Arab societies than to the intrinsic literary values of her works. While censored or banned in Egypt and elsewhere in the region, Sa'dāwī's fiction and the non-fiction works have received circulation in the West reaching beyond the usually limited audience that Arabic literature had until 1988.

During this phase two presses in particular were noted for their active interest in the publication of literary translations from Arabic: Heinemann in London and the Three Continents Press in Washington, DC. Heinemann's series, Arab Authors, with Denys Johnson-Davies in an advisory role, was instrumental in translating and publishing more than 20 works, mostly novels and short story collections.

The post-Nobel phase (1988–) shows a marked departure from the earlier phases in several ways. The first obvious development is the relative frequency or regularity with which Arabic works of fiction are translated or reprinted in response to demand. Note, for example, the various editions or printings of works by Mahfūz, Munif, Sa'dāwī, Salih, and Shaykh. Second, a larger number of publishers (including, for the first time, major commercial publishers) and university presses have become involved in publishing and marketing contemporary Arabic works. Special reference should be made to the series that the

Three Continents Press and PROTA (Project for Translation from Arabic) continue to publish or support in the US, and the more recent series produced by several American university presses or programs (e.g. Arkansas, Columbia, Minnesota, Texas and the University of Texas Center for Middle Eastern Studies). To these must be added the effective role that the mainstream journals have exercised in expanding the audience for Arabic literature. Such journals, especially those that are library-oriented, have begun to review on a fairly regular basis Arabic works in English translation, and to recommend them for acquisition by public libraries (for more details see Altoma, 1993).

In short, by the late 1990s an extensive corpus of Arabic fiction had become accessible in English translation to an equally expanded audience. The corpus itself can be viewed as representative to a large extent of contemporary Arabic fiction in terms of major themes, trends, works, or authors. However, the corpus continues to show a skewed pattern or representation resulting from the predominance of Egyptian authors, and the glaring absence of important authors from other Arab countries, especially Algeria, Iraq, Lebanon, Morocco, Syria, and Tunisia. The emphasis on Egypt is undoubtedly justifiable given the fact that Egypt led, and still plays a leading role in the development of Arabic literature. But this emphasis should not continue to exclude other talented writers, both men and women, who have made notable contributions to Arabic fiction. What is also needed is a close evaluative study, or more than one, of the quality of the translations themselves, though they have been, on occasions, the subject of positive or negative general evaluations in published reviews.

SALIH J. ALTOMA

Further Reading

Allen, Roger, *The Arabic Novel: An Historical and Critical Introduction*, Syracuse, New York: Syracuse University Press, 1995

Altoma, Salih J., "The Reception of Najīb Mahfūz in American Publications", *Yearbook of Comparative and General Literature*, 41 (1993), pp. 160–79

Altoma, Salih J., "Contemporary Arabic Fiction in English Translation: A Chronological Survey, 1947–1996", *Yearbook of Comparative and General Literature*, 44 (1996) pp. 137–53 (lists more than 200 works of fiction and includes three indices: Authors, Translators, and Publishers)

Badawi, M.M., *A Short History of Modern Arabic Literature*, Oxford: Clarendon Press, and New York: Oxford University Press, 1993

Boullata, Issa J. (editor), *The Arabic Novel since 1950: Critical Essays, Interviews, and Bibliography*, Cambridge, Massachusetts: Dah Mahjar, 1992 (*Mundus Arabicus*, vol. 5)

Cooke, Miriam, *Women and the War Story*, Berkeley: University of California Press, 1996

Gibb, H.A.R., *Arabic Literature: An Introduction*, 2nd edition, Oxford: Clarendon Press, 1963

Johnson-Davies, Denys, "On Translating Arabic Literature: An Interview with Denys Johnson-Davies", *Alif*, 3 (1983) pp. 80–93

Kilpatrick, Hilary, *The Modern Egyptian Novel: A Study in Social Criticism*, London: Ithaca Press, 1974

LeGassick, Trevor, "The Arabic Novel in English Translation" in *The Arabic Novel since 1950*, edited by Issa J. Boullata, 1992, pp. 47–60

Moosa, Matti, *The Origins of Modern Arabic Fiction*, 2nd edition, Boulder, Colorado: Rienner, 1997

Sakkut, Hamdi, *The Egyptian Novel, 1913–1952*, Cairo: American University in Cairo Press, 1971

Zaydan, Joseph T., *Arab Women Novelists: The Formative Years and Beyond*, Albany: State University of New York Press, 1995

Contemporary Arabic Poetry

In surveying English translations of contemporary Arabic poetry, a number of central developments and issues need to be briefly identified.

First, Arabic poetry, the primary genre for the Arabs for more than 14 centuries, has been marginally represented in English translation until recent years. A quick review of more than 2000 modern poems translated into English during this century indicates that only a small fraction (about 50) of these poems was published before 1950, and in nearly all cases the translation was made by native speakers of Arabic. It is generally admitted that earlier British and American Orientalists/Arabists tended to focus in their works on non-literary aspects of Arabo-Islamic culture, and thus failed to take an active part in the translation of poetry or other Arabic literary genres. The only notable exception as far as poetry is concerned is Arthur Arberry, whose contributions to the translation of poetry (classical and modern) include his pioneering anthology (1950). As Arberry pointed out in his preface, the anthology was a joint attempt in which he and students from several Arab countries cooperated to produce a collection representative of Arabic poetry written during the years 1920–40. Arberry's versified translation strikes readers of poetry as laboured and ineffective in achieving the poetic quality of the original, but by choosing versification he raised an important issue regarding the method to be followed in translating poetry. He obviously felt that his translation should reflect the poetic styles and techniques of the original poems. Apart from its stylistic flaws, Arberry's anthology serves as a positive contribution to the translation of modern Arabic poetry for two reasons: its being the result of collaboration between Arabic and English-speaking translators, and the broad scope it has maintained in terms of the poets and the countries represented: 45 poets, 11 countries, in addition to the two Arab-American (Mahjarite) schools active in the United States and South America.

Second, following the publication of Arberry's anthology (1950) and until the early 1970s, slow but steady strides were made in the translation of Arabic poetry, particularly in the US. However, the translations were not easily accessible to the general public since they appeared mainly in journals or little magazines. During these two decades no other anthology comparable to Arberry's was published, in spite of the proliferation of Arabic studies in American or British institutions.

Finally, it is only in recent years, during the 1970s and 1980s, that we see a more significant stage in the history of literary translations from Arabic. During this period a fairly extensive and diversified corpus of contemporary Arabic poetry became accessible in English translation as a result of efforts undertaken not only in English-speaking countries (mainly the UK and US) but also in different Arab countries such as Egypt, Iraq, and Lebanon. The latter fact underlines the prominent role that

Arab translators and scholars have continued to assume to ensure that Arabic literature in general may reach a wider audience, or receive the recognition it deserves as part of world literature. Whether working alone or jointly with English-speaking translators, Arab translators (poets, scholars, and others) have contributed to most of the translations that are currently available in English (see, for example, Altoma, 1993, especially pp. 13–16, 146–49).

Apart from innumerable translated poems published in periodicals or included in studies dealing with Arabic literature, there are now numerous anthologies that represent the poetry of the postwar period. These can be classified into three categories: general/Pan-Arab anthologies, region- or country-oriented anthologies, and anthologies of poets.

In view of limitations of space, we shall briefly examine representative anthologies of the first group indicating their scope as well as their method of translation.

Khouri & Algar's bilingual anthology (1974) offers a fine and faithful translation of 80 poems by 35 poets. The poetry selected, while it includes examples from the works of leading pre-1950 poets who are known for their innovation or departure from the classical tradition, represents mostly the post-1950 free verses and prose poem movements. Issa Boullata's anthology (1976) focuses on these movements and captures, with great sensitivity, the spirit of the period (1950–75) as manifested in the works of 22 poets. Both anthologies cover countries where the new currents first emerged: Egypt, Iraq, Lebanon, Palestine, Syria, and Sudan. Khouri & Algar's collection includes in addition, a noted romantic poet from Tunisia, al-Shabbi (1909–34). However, both anthologies, useful and reliable as they are, lack the poetic quality that only creative translators in the target language can achieve. Jayyusi's Project for Translation from Arabic (PROTA) has sought to address this problem by enlisting the contribution of English-speaking poets in several of the anthologies Jayyusi has edited since the early 1980s. Her *Modern Arabic Poetry* (1987), in particular, stands out as a landmark in the history of Arabic poetry in English translation for the following reasons. First, as a leading poet and authority on the subject, Jayyusi has carefully chosen a large number of poems representative of the various phases of modern Arabic poetry, ranging from the neo-classical to works illustrating the more recent and radical transformation that Arabic poetry has undergone. The anthology includes examples (sometimes excerpts) from the works of more than 90 poets, arranged in two broadly defined sections: poets writing before, and after, the 1950s. Second, as a testament to the pan-Arab unity of culture and spirit, Jayyusi's collection provides a broader geographical representation than previous anthologies by including poets from different parts of the Arab world (from the Gulf to the Atlantic), though a majority of her poets are still drawn, for historical considerations, from Egypt and the fertile crescent region (Iraq, Jordan, Lebanon, Syria, and Palestine). Third, the anthology has succeeded in large measure in providing a truly poetic translation of the original text, thanks to the participation of 16 English-speaking poets (Charles Doria, John Heath-Stubbs, W.S. Merwin, Christopher Middleton, Desmond O'Grady, Peter Porter, Richard Wilbur, etc.). This was achieved in cooperation with a group of first translators who are competent in both Arabic and English. There is an obvious literary benefit in enlisting the help of creative translators in the target language, not only because of their rootedness in the poetics of their literary tradition or their first-hand familiarity with the literary taste of their time, but also because they are more qualified to serve as effective intermediaries between two different cultures: their own and that of the source language. Such an approach has its own potential risk, as some critics maintain, in that it may lead to inaccurate rewriting of the original poems. However, inaccuracies in Jayyusi's anthology are rare, though the original poems in some instances have been deliberately given truncated or abridged versions in English, especially in the case of traditional poetry. The translated version of "Lullaby for the Hungry", for example, by the greatest modern poet, Muhammad Madhī al-Jawāhirī (1900–97) is based on 20 lines selected from a much longer (100-line) poem. But, as Jayyusi herself stated, such neo-classical poetry presents the translator with a most onerous task in view of the fact that it relies on a rich legacy of rhetorical usages, allusions, and other devices that are not translatable. Instead of excluding the translation of traditional poetry, which still plays a central role in the Arab world, Jayyusi has wisely attempted to represent it in her anthology in abridged versions.

Other general anthologies that deserve to be noted include al-Udhari's *Modern Poetry of the Arab World* (1986), which presents in a chronological and theme-oriented scheme works of leading poets from the fertile crescent region. The selections are grouped under four headings: the Taf'ila (free verse) movement (Iraqi School), 1947–57; the Majallat Shi'r Movement (Syrian School), 1957–67; the June Experience (i.e. June War of 1967), 1967–82, and the Beirut Experience (i.e. Israel's occupation of Beirut), 1982 onwards. As the headings suggest, Udhari's anthology brings together some of the finest modernist poets, known for both their poetic innovations and their radical social and political visions. Among the poets represented are Adūnīs, al Bayātī, Darwīsh, Hāwī, Jabrā, al-Khāl, al-Māghūt, Qabbāni, al-Sayyāb and Sa'dū Yūsuf. However, Udhari's scheme of classification or periodization and of selection can be questioned on several grounds, such as its limited regional representation (despite the title) and the fact that not all of his selections belong to the periods in which they are included.

Anne Fairbairn & Ghazi al-Gosaibi's bilingual anthology (1989) represents an ambitious undertaking by two poets: an Australian, Fairbairn, and Ghazi al-Gosaibi, a Saudi poet of distinction, who is also noted for his literary studies and contributions to other works of translation including his own poetry. Intended primarily as an introduction for Australian readers, the anthology was designed with a view to providing a broad picture of 20th-century Arabic poetry. To meet this objective, Fairbairn and al-Gosaibi were guided by three criteria: to select poems from every Arab country; to represent different schools with the exception of prose poetry; and to choose poems dealing with universal themes. In spite of the obstacles that such an undertaking has to overcome, both editors/translators have succeeded in presenting a large number of poems or excerpts selected perceptively from the works of more than 90 poets. Most of the poets chosen belong to the post-1950 generation. As for the method of translation followed, Fairbairn has attempted to "trans-create" the originals on the basis of Al-Gosaibi's liberal translations and in consultation with other Arabists. It is relevant to note that the leading Australian poet A.D. Hope (1907–2000) has viewed the anthology as "a miraculous achievement" bringing together "poets from so many countries who are working in so many directions" (see his foreword).

All the anthologies cited above include the works of several women poets, but Kamal Boullata's anthology (1978) is dedicated to Arab women's contributions to the poetic revolution that has taken place in the Arab world during the last 50 years. Among the 13 poets represented are Nāzik al-Malā'ika (Iraq), Salma Khadra Jayyusi and Fadwā Tūqān (Palestine), and Fawziyya Abu Khalid (Saudi Arabia). Although not comprehensive in its coverage of women poets, Boullata's work still serves as an important guide to Arab women's creative spirit as they address personal, national, and universal problems of their time. It includes about 100 poems or extracts of poems mostly translated from Arabic, but others were translated from French or originally written in English. The English translation from Arabic, primarily by Boullata, is noted for both its artistic sensitivity and reliability. The fact that it has been used in major world anthologies of women's poetry may serve as a measure of its success.

As indicated earlier and as this survey suggests, an extensive corpus of contemporary Arabic poetry has become accessible in English translation in a variety of sources including numerous anthologies. Nevertheless, this corpus, extensive as it is, offers only a partial representation of Arabic poetry today. There are still a large number of poets who have not been adequately represented or have not been translated at all, especially those of North African countries – al-Babatin's (1995) dictionary of living poets alone lists more than 1600 poets, chosen from a much larger number of poets active in different parts of the Arab world. This is not to imply that all poets listed merit serious consideration for the purpose of translation. But it does indicate the need for a wider representation of Arabic poetry in English. In addition, no detailed evaluative assessments have been made thus far of this extensive corpus of translations to indicate their theoretical foundations or the extent of their success and other relevant issues.

SALIH J. ALTOMA

Selected Regional Anthologies

Elmessiri, A.M., *The Palestinian Wedding: A Bilingual Anthology of Contemporary Palestinian Resistance Poetry*, Washington, DC: Three Continents Press, 1982

Enani, M.M., *An Anthology of the New Arabic Poetry in Egypt*, Cairo: General Egyptian Book Organization, 1986

Jayyusi, Salma Khadra, *Literature of Modern Arabia: An Anthology*, London and New York: Kegan Paul / King Fahd University, 1988 (see pp. 41–252 for poetry in translation from Bahrain, Kuwait, Oman, Qatar, Saudi Arabia, United Arab Emirates, and Yemen)

Jayyusi, Salma Khadra, *Anthology of Modern Palestinian Literature*, New York: Columbia University Press, 1992 (see pp. 81–331 for translations of Arabic poems by 57 Palestinian poets)

Lu'lu'a, Abdul Wahid, *Modern Iraqi Poetry*, Baghdad: Dar al'Ma'mun, 1989

Selected Anthologies of Poets

Adūnīs, *The Blood of Adonis: Transpositions of Selected Poems*, translated by Samuel Hazo, Pittsburgh: University of Pittsburgh Press, 1971

Adūnīs, *The Pages of Day and Night*, translated by Samuel Hazo, Marlboro, Vermont: Marlboro Press, 1994

Adūnīs, *Transformations of the Lover*, translated by Samuel Hazo, Athens: Ohio University Press, 1982

al-Bayati, Abdul Wahhab, *Love, Death, and Exile*, translated by Bassam K. Frangieh, Washington, DC: Georgetown University Press, 1980

Darwīsh, Mahmūd, *Selected Poems*, translated by Ian Wedde and Fawwaz Tuqan, Cheadle, Cheshire: Carcanet, 1973

Darwīsh, Mahmūd, *The Music of Human Flesh*, translated by Denys Johnson-Davies, London: Heinemann, and Washington, DC: Three Continents Press, 1980

Darwīsh, Mahmūd, *Psalms*, translated by Ben Bennani, Colorado Springs: Three Continents Press, 1994

Hawi, Khalil, *Naked in Exile: Khalil Hawi's Threshing Floors of Hunger*, translated by Adnan Haydar and Michael Beard, Washington, DC: Three Continents Press, 1984

al-Haydari, Buland, *Dialogue in Three Dimensions*, translated by Husain Haddawy, London: Pan Middle East Graphics and Publishing, 1982

al-Maghut, Muhammad, *The Fans of Swords: Poems*, translated by May Jayyusi and Naomi Shihab Nye, Washington, DC: Three Continents Press, 1991

Qabbani, Nizar, *Arabian Love Poems* (bilingual edition), translated by Bassam K. Frangieh and Clementina R. Brown, Colorado Springs, Colorado: Three Continents Press, 1993

Qabbani, Nizar, *On Entering the Sea: The Erotic and Other Poetry of Nizar Qabbani*, translated by Lena Jayyusi, New York: Interlink Books, 1996

al-Sayyab, Badr Shakir, *Selected Poems*, translated by Nadia Bishai, London: Third World Centre for Research and Publishing, 1986

Further Reading

Altoma, Salih J., *Modern Arabic Poetry in English Translation: A Bibliography*, Tangier: King Fahd School of Translation, Abdelmalek Essaadi University, 1993 (for more information on other anthologies not discussed above or listed below, see pp. 13–16, 146–49)

Arberry, Arthur J., *Modern Arabic Poetry: An Anthology with English Verse Translations*, London: Taylor's Foreign Press, 1950

Asfour, John Mikhail, *When the Words Burn: An Anthology of Modern Arabic Poetry, 1947–87*, Dunvegan, Ontario: Cormorant Books, 1988; revised edition, 1992

al-Babatin's Dictionary of Contemporary Arab Poets, 6 vols, Kuwait, 1995

Boullata, Issa J., *Modern Arab Poets: 1950–75*, London: Heinemann, and Washington, DC: Three Continents Press, 1976

Boullata, Kamal, *Women of the Fertile Crescent: An Anthology of Modern Poetry by Arab Women*, Washington, DC: Three Continents Press, 1978

Fairbairn, Anne and Ghazi al-Gosaibi, *Feathers and the Horizon: A Selection of Modern Poetry from Across the Arab World* (bilingual edition), Canberra: Leros Press, 1989

Jayyusi, Salma Khadra, *Modern Arabic Poetry: An Anthology*, New York: Columbia University Press, 1987

Khouri, Mounah A. and Hamid Algar, *An Anthology of*

Modern Arabic Poetry, Berkeley: University of California Press, 1974
al-Udhari, Abdullah, *Modern Poetry of the Arab World*, Harmondsworth and New York: Penguin, 1986

Contemporary Arabic Drama

In contrast to contemporary Arabic fiction and poetry, Arabic drama is the literary form least represented in English translation. This is due largely to its own peculiar and complex historical development as a new genre in Arabic.

Introduced first in Lebanon around the mid-19th century, Arabic drama has had to overcome or cope with more obstacles than those experienced in the other genres: obstacles religious, social, political, literary, and linguistic. Three of these have constantly preoccupied, and in a sense beleaguered, Arab playwrights in their creative efforts: the absence of a well-defined and developed dramatic tradition in Arabic; the linguistic dichotomy between the unified and unifying classical language on the one hand and on the other the various naturally spoken varieties of Arabic labelled as dialects, colloquials and vernaculars; and the generally intolerant, and often repressive, political climate that restricts the playwright's freedom to present his works to the public. The latter has contributed to the prevalent use of symbolism, folklore, historical events or figures, and other dramatic tricks. Such facts explain the reason for the slow and long-drawn-out process by which Arabic drama has emerged as a serious, respectable, and authentic Arabic genre. Many have taken part in this process from Mārūn al-Naqqāsh (Lebanon, 1817–55), the first to introduce drama into Arabic, Abu Khalil al-Qabbānī (Syria, 1833–1902), Ya'qūb Sanū' / James Sanua (Egypt, 1839–1912), the leading neo-classical poet-dramatist Ahmad Shawqī (Egypt, 1868–1932), to Tawfīq al-Hakīm (Egypt, 1898–1987) and the new generation of playwrights. But the most significant of all in terms of his contributions is al-Hakīm, who was responsible, more than anyone else, for establishing Arabic drama on firm foundations. This he achieved through his remarkable and unmatched output of more than 80 plays and numerous expository writings, in which he covered a broad range of dramatic types, themes, and techniques. His masterly use of Classical Arabic as a dramatic medium has been widely acclaimed throughout the Arab world. Al-Hakīm epitomizes the Arab playwright's search for a suitable dramatic language; he used the colloquial in certain social plays and experimented, though only in one play, with the so-called "third language", a language that conforms in writing to the rules of classical Arabic, but can be, with minor modifications, turned into the vernacular on the stage. The fact that he opted for the classical variety of Arabic in most of his plays reflects a keen awareness of the need to establish drama as an integral part of the unbroken literary tradition and as a truly pan-Arab genre, capable of appealing to Arab audiences irrespective of their regional dialects.

Other Arab playwrights, particularly since the 1950s, have increasingly favored the use of the colloquial language in their works, for stylistic and ideological considerations. Being the language spoken naturally in daily activities at home, in the street, and in the place of work, the colloquial is judged to be ideally suitable for the stage as an instrument of realistic presentation, characterization, and immediate communication. It is because of such justifications, which were advanced at earlier times, that a large number of talented contemporary dramatists, in different Arab countries, have adopted the colloquial as their primary dramatic medium. There is no doubt that both intrinsic and external considerations favor such a practice, especially in the case of comedies or plays dealing with the Arab people's political and social concerns. None the less, the practice itself has its own drawbacks. It limits the play's chance of being appreciated or read as literature in the conventional sense. It may also lead to a new literary dichotomy in the form of sub-regional dramatic genres (Egyptian drama, Syrian drama, Iraqi drama etc.) that differ not only from the pan-Arabic dramatic form but also from each other. Indeed some of the same proponents of the colloquial usage, including Yūsuf Idrīs, a dramatist known for his insistence on the colloquial, have pointed to the difficulty of following plays staged in unfamiliar colloquials.

Needless to say, this division of Arabic drama into two distinct types has presented the translators with a more onerous task, which demands, among other qualifications, competence not only in the standard classical language but also in one or more of its spoken varieties. It is perhaps partly due to this fact that only a small number of Arabic or other colloquial (primarily Egyptian) plays have been translated into English.

The English translations of Arabic drama under survey include four anthologies, three collections based on al-Hakīm's writings, and about 20 individual works representing Egyptian playwrights. Plays published in periodicals or in other general sources are not covered.

Abdel Wahab's *Modern Egyptian Drama* (1974) is intended to represent important trends of the Egyptian prose drama of the 1960s which Abdel Wahab, as a drama critic, had frequently reviewed while in Egypt. It includes four plays by al-Hakīm, Yūsuf Idrīs, Mīkhā'il Rūmān and Rashad Rushdi, all of which address a general theme of a struggle against power, and an excellent introduction.

Manzalaoui's collection (1977) consists of nine plays, eight of which are by al-Hakīm, Mahmud Taymūr, Idrīs and other Egyptian playwrights. The ninth belongs to Muhammad Māghūt, a leading Syrian novelist and poet. Only three of these plays (Māghūt's and two by al-Hakīm) were written originally in the classical language. Central among the features of this collection is the team approach followed in the process of translation, which involved in every case more than one translator. The overall stylistic revision was the responsibility of Andrew Parkin, a non-Arabist scholar of Western drama and poetry. According to his statements, Parkin's focus in his revisions was on speech for the stage "in the hope of making all the lines possible to deliver convincingly from stages in the English-speaking world". Parkin's approach, meritorious as it is, cannot be assessed in view of the fact that the translations under survey have rarely been staged in English-speaking countries.

Johnson-Davies's collection of *Egyptian One-Act Plays* (1981) presents five short plays written in the colloquial by al-Hakīm, Alfrid Faraj (known also as Alfred Farag), Ali Salim and two other lesser known writers. Noted for his pioneering and leading role in translating modern Arabic literature since the 1940s, Johnson-Davies combines his fine translations with a brief introduction on Egypt's theatrical achievements, the need for more English translations, and the artistic sophistication displayed in the works he selected, as well as in the works of other authors, including Yūsuf Idrīs and Nu'man 'Āshūr. (Another anthology of *Egyptian One-Act Plays* compiled by David Woodman is noted below.)

The fourth anthology, undoubtedly broader in scope, is *Modern Arabic Drama* (1995), edited by Salma Khadra Jayyusi and Roger Allen. In an effort to present a pan-Arab view of contemporary Arabic drama, and to complement earlier translations, Jayyusi and Allen chose 12 plays of varied lengths from the works of leading dramatists in several Arab countries: Egypt, Iraq, Kuwait, Lebanon, Palestine, Syria, and Tunisia. Among the dramatists included are al-'Ani (Iraq), Ikhlasi (Syria), al-Madani (Tunisia), Mahfūz (Lebanon) and Wannūs (Syria). This is in addition to four well-known Egyptian playwrights: 'Abd-al-Sabūr, Diyab, Faraj, and Sālim. The anthology continues the same team approach followed in Jayyusi's earlier works of translation from Arabic by enlisting a group of first and second translators. The latter include Alan Brownjohn, Richard Davies, Charles Doria, and Desmond O'Grady. Apart from the preface written by the editors, the anthology includes a detailed introduction written by M.M. Badawi in which he surveys the history of Arabic drama and discusses major authors (many of whom are not represented in the anthology) and dramatic trends in different parts of the Arab world.

The three other collections of al-Hakīm's plays by Hutchins (1981–84) and Johnson-Davies (1973) cover various periods, themes and types (such as theatre of ideas and theatre of society) of al-Hakīm's output from the 1930s to the 1970s. Hutchins's volumes include also selections from al-Hakīm's introductory remarks or commentaries which he wrote in relation to his works.

Of all Arabic playwrights al-Hakīm has received understandably the greatest attention in English, whether in translation or in studies dedicated to his works. More than 30 of his plays have been translated, most of which are included in all the collections cited above, with the exception of Jayyusi and Allen's, or have appeared as separate works, including some of his best plays, such as *The Tree Climber* (regarded as his masterpiece) translated by Johnson-Davies, and some of his earliest attempts in which he adapted Islamic material or themes, as in *The People of the Cave* (Cairo, 1989) and *Muhammad* (Cairo, 1985). An incomplete translation of the former was published earlier by P.J. Vatikiotis in the journal *The Islamic Literature* (1955, 1957). It is noteworthy that some of al-Hakim's plays are available in two or more translations. There are, for example, three versions of al-Hakīm's full-length play, *The Sultan's Dilemma*, as translated by Abdel Wahab, M.M. Badawi in Manzalaoui's anthology, and Johnson-Davies (1973), and two translations of a shorter play "Song of Death" by Badawi and Johnson-Davies, in addition to other examples of multiple translations.

Other important dramatists represented in the corpus under survey are Salāh 'Abd al-Sabūr (1931–81), Yūsuf Idrīs (1927–91) and Alfrid Faraj (1929–). 'Abd al-Sabūr is noted for his verse plays, including *Murder in Baghdad* (a tragedy based on the martyrdom of al-Hallaj in Baghdad, 922, but highly relevant to the contemporary context) and *Night Traveller*, a black comedy pointing to man's helplessness in the face of tyranny. Idrīs, one of the greatest writers of fiction and drama, is highly acclaimed for his masterpiece *Farafir* (translated under the title of *Farfoors* by Abdel Wahab and as *Flipflap and His Master* by Trevor LeGassick, in Manzalaoui's anthology). A satirical and serious comedy, *Flipflap* stands out as a bold attempt not only to create a truly Egyptian drama based on Egypt's folkloric legacy, but also to tackle a variety of interrelated local and universal themes of freedom, democracy, social injustice, and the search for elusive absolute equality. Faraj has written some of the finest politically oriented plays based largely on adaptations of historical or folkloric materials from different periods. His comedy *'Ali Janah al-Tabrizi and His Servant Quffa* (included in Jayyusi & Allen's anthology but appearing also in book form in Cairo, 1989) demonstrates his ability to create out of a tale from *The Arabian Nights* a work of considerable complexity and relevance. Aside from its comic presentation, and its implications regarding the Arab world's realities, it raises, in Badawi's words, "interesting questions such as the relation between illusion and reality [and] the thin line separating the prophet or social reformer from the impostor".

Reference should be made to other translations of Egyptian plays that have been published in Cairo, mostly by the General Egyptian Book Organization. Among the playwrights included in the latter's publications are 'Abd al-Sabūr, Faraj, al-Hakīm, 'Izz al-Dīn Ismā'il, Samir Sarhan, 'Abd al-Rahmān al-Sharqāwī, and Sa'd al-Din Wahba.

As this brief survey indicates, modest progress has been made in recent years toward promoting the English translation of Arabic drama. Apart from the fact that a limited number of Arab playwrights and works have been translated, the translated texts have had, thus far, a limited appeal beyond a narrow, largely Arabist, audience. It is to be hoped that Arabic drama will receive in due course the recognition it deserves as part of world drama.

SALIH J. ALTOMA

Translations

Anthologies and Selections

Abdel Wahab, Farouk (translator), *Modern Egyptian Drama: An Anthology*, Minneapolis: Bibliotheca Islamica, 1974

Hutchins, William M. (translator), *Plays, Prefaces, and Postscripts of Tawfiq al-Hakim*, 2 vols, Washington, DC: Three Continents Press, 1981–84 (vol. 1, *Theater of the Mind*, includes *The Wisdom of Solomon*, *King Oedipus*, *Shahrazad*, *Princess Sunshine*, and *Angels'Prayer*; vol. 2, *Theater of Society*, includes *Between War and Peace*, *Tender Hands*, *Food for the Millions*, *Poet on the Moon*, *Incrimination*, and *Voyage to Tomorrow*)

Jayyusi, Khadra Salma and Roger Allen (editors), *Modern Arabic Drama: An Anthology*, with an introduction by M.M. Badawi, Bloomington: Indiana University Press, 1995

Johnson-Davies, Denys (translator) *Fate of a Cockroach: Four Plays of Freedom*, by Tawfīq al-Hakīm, with an introduction, London: Heinemann, 1973 (contains *Fate of a Cockroach*, *The Song of Death*, *The Sultan's Dilemma*, and *Not a Thing Out of Place*)

Johnson-Davies, Denys (translator), *Egyptian One-Act Plays*, London: Heinemann, and Washington, DC: Three Continents Press, 1981

Manzalaoui, Mahmoud (editor), *Arabic Writing Today: The Drama*, Cairo: American Research Center in Egypt, 1977 (nine plays by eight playwrights)

Woodman, David (editor), *Egyptian One-Act Plays*, Cairo:

American University in Cairo Press, 1974 (Published in two separate versions, Arabic and English, the anthology is based on the compiler's academic project at AUC to solicit one-act plays for possible staging at AUC's theatre. According to Woodman, a committee of prominent Egyptian scholars and writers [Suhayr al-Qalamawi, Hamdi Sakkut, Yahya Haqqi, and Ahmad Zaki] participated in the selection of the plays.)

Individual Works

'Abd al-Sabūr, Salāh, *The Princess Waits*, translated by Shafik Megally, Cairo: General Egyptian Book Organization, 1975

'Abd al-Sabūr, Salāh, *Murder in Baghdad*, translated by Khalil I. Semaan, Leiden: E.J. Brill, 1972; Cairo: General Egyptian Book Organization, 1976

'Abd al-Sabūr, Salāh, *Night Traveller*, translated by M.M. Enani, Cairo: General Egyptian Book Organization, 1980

'Abd al-Sabūr, Salāh, *Now the King is Dead*, translated by Nehad Selaiha. Cairo: General Egyptian Book Organization, 1986

'Āshūr, Nu'mān, *Give Us Our Money Back*, translated by Mahmoud El Lozy, Cairo: Elias Modern Publishing House, 1994

Faraj, Alfrid, *The Caravan, or, Ali Janah al-Tabrizi and His Servant Quffa*, translated with an introduction by Rasheed el-Enany, Cairo: General Egyptian Book Organization, 1989

al-Hakīm, Tawfīq, *A Conversation with the Planet Earth* [and] *The World is A Comedy*, translated by Riad Habib Youssef, Cairo: General Egyptian Book Organization, 1985

al-Hakīm, Tawfīq, *Muhammad*, translated by Ibrahim Hassan el-Mougy, revised by Ahmad Kamal Metwalli, 2nd edition, revised by W.M. Hutchins, Cairo: Al-Adab Press, 1985

al-Hakīm, Tawfīq, *The People of the Cave*, translated by Mahmoud El Lozy, Cairo: Elias Modern Publishing House, 1989

al-Hakīm, Tawfīq, *The Tree Climber*, translated by Denys Johnson-Davies, London: Oxford University Press, 1966; 2nd edition, London: Heinemann, and Washington, DC: Three Continents Press, 1985

el-Ramly, Lenin, *In Plain Arabic*, translated by Esmet Allouba, Cairo: American University in Cairo Press, 1994

Sarhan, Samir, *The Lady on the Throne*, translated by Mona Mikhail, Cairo: General Egyptian Book Organization, 1989

al-Sharqāwī, 'Abd al-Rahmān, *Orabi Leader of the Fellahin: A Verse Translation*, translated by Thoraya Mahdi Allam; revised edition by M. Mahdi Allam, Cairo: General Egyptian Book Office, 1989

Wahba, Sa'd al-din, *The Road of Safety*, translated by Fawzi M. Tadros and Patricia A. Kinchlow, Cairo: General Egyptian Book Organization, 1979

Wahba, Sa'd al-din, *Mosquito Bridge*, translated by Charlotte Shabrawi, revised by Samir Sarhan, Cairo: General Egyptian Book Organization, 1987

Further Reading

Allen, Roger (editor), *Critical Perspectives on Yusuf Idris*, Washington, DC: Three Continents Press, 1994

Altoma, Salih J., *Modern Arabic Literature: A Bibliography of Articles, Books, Dissertations, and Translations in English*, Bloomington: Indiana University Asian Studies, 1975

Badawi, M.M., *Modern Arabic Drama in Egypt*, Cambridge and New York: Cambridge University Press, 1987

Rudnicka-Kassem, Dorota, *Egyptian Drama and Social Change: A Study of Thematic and Artistic Development in Yusuf Idris's Plays*, Cracow and Montreal: Enigma Press, 1993

William Archer 1856–1924

British literary translator, critic, editor and journalist

Biography

Born 23 September 1856 in Perth, Scotland, eldest son of Thomas Archer, of Gracemere, Queensland, Australia, and his wife Grace Lindsay, of Muirton, Perth. Thomas Archer was Agent-General for Queensland in London, 1882–84 and 1888–90. The Archer family had connections in Australia and Norway. William attended Perth Academy and George Watson's College, Edinburgh, before studying at Edinburgh University, where in 1875, while still reading for his M.A. degree, he began writing leaders for the *Edinburgh Evening News*. Having already travelled in Scandinavia, he went around the world in 1876–77 in the course of a visit to his parents in Australia. From 1878 he lived in London. He became a barrister in the Middle Temple (1883) but did not practise law – his chief interest lay in the theatre. He was drama critic for the London *Figaro*, 1879–81, and later for other papers, including the *World* and the *Manchester Guardian*, and his reputation was established by the 1890s. *The Theatrical "World" 1893–97*, a collection of his criticism, appeared in 5 volumes (1894–98). He wrote several books on drama, notably a study of Irving and a biography of Macready; *Masks or Faces?*, on the psychology of acting; and in 1923 the influential *The Old Drama and the New*, promoting the plays of Ibsen, Galsworthy and George Bernard Shaw. As well as famously translating and editing the works of Ibsen, Archer also produced editions of Congreve (1912) and of Farquhar (1906). In 1907, with Harley Granville-Barker, he published proposals for the foundation of a National Theatre. He supported the abolition of theatre censorship and worked for the League of Nations Union. He wrote several plays, of which one, *The Green Goddess*, was staged successfully in 1923. Died in London, 27 December 1924.

William Archer's 13-volume edition of Henrik Ibsen's plays was published by William Heinemann between 1906 and 1912. According to Archer, it represented "one of the chief labours" and "one of the greatest privileges" of his life. In 1880 his translation of *The Pillars of Society* became the first Ibsen play to be performed in England; but the Ibsen campaign really began in 1889 with Archer's translation of *A Doll's House*. In 1890 he edited *Ibsen's Prose Dramas* in English in five volumes for Walter Scott; and from 1891 to 1900 he translated and published each new Ibsen play from *Hedda Gabler* to *When We Dead Awaken*. His promotion of Ibsen earned him Norway's Order of St Olaf and the dramatist's lasting friendship and gratitude.

Archer was uniquely suited to the task of Ibsen translation. He was bilingual in English and Norwegian. His grandfather had emigrated from Scotland to Norway, and Archer learned Norwegian at the family home in Larvik, not 30 miles from Ibsen's birthplace. Like Ibsen, Archer grew up in an atmosphere of Christian fundamentalism, which helped to shape his personality, if not his system of thought. Georg Brandes wrote of "a dual tendency" in Ibsen's nature: "a native propensity to mysticism and an equally inbred inclination to sharp, dry common sense". Thomas Postlewait says of Archer: "Like Ibsen, he wore the mask of rectitude and judgment over a depth of emotion ... His role as translator of Ibsen served as a vital way for expressing this masked identity: present yet simultaneously absent." Both men aimed at and succeeded in restoring a serious, literary drama to the stage.

The 12-volume edition contains all the plays Ibsen admitted to his collected works, except for *Catiline*. An assessment of Archer as translator is, at first sight, complicated by collaboration and separate authorship. Archer attributes 10 plays to himself. Five are listed as collaborations between Archer and other translators. The remaining six are attributed to separate authors. In his introduction to Volume 1, however, Archer makes the real situation clear: "For the translations of all the plays in this edition, except *Love's Comedy* and *Brand*, I am ultimately responsible, in the sense that I have exercised an unrestricted right of revision ... The revision, whether fortunate or not, has in all cases been very thorough" – most thorough, one should add, in the cycle of 12 modern plays.

The translations of Ibsen's early national romantic plays are serviceable, but suffer from Elizabethanisms and inversions. In *Lady Inger of Östråt*, for example, what is literally "more than one mocker [*spottefugl*]", becomes "Many a scurril knave"; and in *The Vikings at Helgeland*, Hiördis tells Gunnar, "Thou pratest senselessly". More successful is *The Feast at Solhoug*, where Ibsen's pastiche ballads are charmingly rendered, perhaps by Archer's collaborator Mary Morison. Archer himself gets into his stride with *The Pretenders*, Ibsen's first undisputed masterpiece. Here there are fewer archaisms, and the great speeches given to Bishop Nikolas and Earl Skule lose little of their original power.

Peer Gynt, with its virtuoso rhymes and variety of metres, is the hardest of all Ibsen's plays to turn into speakable or even readable English. The Archers, William and one of his younger brothers, Charles, reproduce Ibsen's metres, translate the play "*line for line* ... with the utmost fidelity", but, wisely perhaps, make no attempt at rhyme. The result is still the most accurate reading version, though it is no longer suitable for the stage. Archer's *Emperor and Galilean*, Ibsen's huge two-part closet drama, is also eminently readable.

Few translations have had such a wide-reaching cultural impact as Archer's of Ibsen's modern cycle. First, in James Agate's words, "the renaissance of the British theatre began with Ibsen whose sponsor was William Archer". Then, Archer's Ibsen was to have a profound effect on modern literature in the English-speaking world. James Joyce's 1900 essay on *When We Dead Awaken* bears witness to this, as does Michael Egan's reference to Henry James's "gradual assimilation of Ibsen's symbolic manner" through Archer: "the golden bowl was struck in Norway".

Archer's versions of the modern plays were on the whole well received by his contemporaries. The anti-Ibsenite faction attacked Ibsen's "scandalous" subject matter rather than Archer's style, though his use of contractions was felt to be too vulgar for the English stage. George Bernard Shaw found that "the air of Norway breathed through [Archer's] versions", and that he "understood and cared for Ibsen's imagination". Gilbert Murray found parts of Archer's *The Master Builder* and *John Gabriel Borkman* "extraordinarily beautiful as mere language". In the 1920s a reaction set in; both Ibsen and Archer were seen as advocates of dry-as-dust social realism, despite Archer's repeated assertions that it was Ibsen's emotion and poetry he wished to transmit, not "ethical, or political, or sociological doctrines". It follows that his translations came to be dismissed as too literal and "Victorian". Michael Meyer, the best Ibsen translator of the 1960s and 1970s, complains that Archer "fell back into exactly the kind of Mrs Tanqueray dialogue from which Ibsen was trying to liberate the theatre". The fact is that Archer's translations at their best achieved a remarkable fusion of accuracy and dramatic rightness. His lapses do err on the side of meaning rather than speakability. In *Ghosts*, Mrs Alving sees "the sequence of things" – a clear but awkward equivalent to "*sammenhengen*" ("the connection"); but he captures the steely quality in Judge Brack's act 4 interrogation of Hedda Gabler – "Dearest Hedda – believe me – I shall not abuse my advantage" – and the visionary power of *Little Eyolf* and *John Gabriel Borkman*. Postlewait is right to ask from late 20th-century critics of Archer "a fitting generosity of spirit, a sense of debt". Finally, we must remember that Archer's published translations for the private reader were purposefully more formal and literary than the theatre scripts, which he revised repeatedly during rehearsals to bring actors and audience closer to "Ibsen the pure poet, the creator of men and women, the searcher of hearts, the weaver of strange webs of destiny".

Archer's versions of Ibsen were performed with great frequency in Britain and the US in the 1890s and the early 20th century. As translations they were on the whole regarded for many years as unassailable. Archer eventually won the Ibsen campaign, in spite of some uniquely fierce opposition in the early days from the London critics – "uniquely fierce" in the sense that initial opposition to the plays was much stronger in England than it was in Scandinavia, Germany or France.

Archer also translated Maurice Maeterlinck's *Interior*,

Gerhart Hauptmann's *Hannele* (both, it should be noted, Symbolist plays), and Edvard Brandes' drama, *A Visit*. His finest translation apart from Ibsen, however, is his splendidly idiomatic selection of Alexander Kielland's *novelleter*, published as *Tales of Two Countries* in 1891. Kielland is an unjustly neglected master of the short story, his style somewhere between Chekhov and Joyce, and Archer's versions from the original Norwegian deserve to be reissued, even after a whole century.

JOHN LINGARD

Translations

Hauptmann, Gerhart, *Hannele: A Dream Poem*, 1894
Ibsen, Henrik, *Peer Gynt: A Dramatic Poem*, translated with Charles Archer, 1892
Ibsen, Henrik, *The Collected Works of Henrik Ibsen*, entirely revised and edited by William Archer, translated by William Archer, Edmund Gosse, Charles Archer, Frances E. Eleanor Marx-Aveling, Mary Morison, C.H. Herford and A.C. Chater, 13 vols, 1906–12
Kielland, Alexander, *Tales of Two Countries*, 1891
Maeterlinck, Maurice, *Interior*, translated by Archer, in *Three Little Dramas for Marionettes* (includes translations by Alfred Sutro), 1899

Further Reading

Archer, Charles, *William Archer: Life, Work and Friendships*, London: Allen and Unwin, and New Haven, Connecticut: Yale University Press, 1931
Archer, William, *William Archer on Ibsen: The Major Essays, 1888–1919*, edited by Thomas Postlewait, Westport, Connecticut: Greenwood Press, 1984
Baylen, Joseph O., "Edmund Gosse, William Archer, and Ibsen in Late Victorian Britain", *Tennessee Studies in Literature*, 20 (1975) pp. 124–37
Fjelde, Rolf and Sverre Arestad, "Translating *Peer Gynt*", *Modern Drama*, 10 (1967) pp. 104–10
Franc, Miram Alice, "Ibsen Translations in England" in her *Ibsen in England*, Boston: Four Seas, 1919, pp. 57–75; reprinted Folcroft, Pennsylvania: Folcroft Press, 1970
Granville-Barker, Harley, "The Coming of Ibsen" in *The Eighteen-Eighties: Essays by Fellows of the Royal Society of Literature*, edited by Walter de la Mare, Cambridge: Cambridge University Press, 1930, pp. 159–96; reprinted Great Neck, New York: Core Collection, 1978
Postlewait, Thomas, *Prophet of the New Drama: William Archer and the Ibsen Campaign*, Westport, Connecticut: Greenwood Press, 1986
Stanley, Raymond, "Ibsen and His Translator, William Archer", *Meanjin Quarterly*, 23 (1964) pp. 174–78
Whitebrook, Peter, *William Archer: A Biography*, London: Methuen, 1993
Woodbridge, Homer E., "William Archer: Prophet of Modern Drama", *Sewanee Review*, 44 (1936) pp. 207–21

José María Arguedas 1911–1969

Peruvian novelist, short-story writer, poet and ethnologist

Biography

Born in Andahuaylas in the southern Peruvian highlands, 18 January 1911. His father was an impoverished itinerant lawyer; his mother died when he was an infant and his father remarried. Before the child was old enough to accompany his father, whose work took him throughout southern Peru, he was ill-treated by his stepmother and stepbrother and raised by the servants and peasants with whom he identified thereafter; he claimed Quechua was his first language. Quechua is an Amerindian language belonging to the Andean-Equatorial group and spoken mainly in Peru, Ecuador, and Bolivia. He boarded from the age of 10 at provincial schools, in 1931 entered San Marcos University in Lima, and obtained a doctorate in ethnology in 1947, having studied while working as a postal clerk then as a schoolteacher, since his father's death in 1932 left him penniless. Although from the 1933 publication of the story, *Warma Kuyay*, Arguedas was known in Lima intellectual circles, to which his first wife Celia Bustamante belonged, it was not until 1953 that his professional and other publications brought nominations granting financial security and frequent invitations abroad. Political activity in the 1930s had led to the months in prison that inspired the novel *El Sexto* [The Sixth] (1961). But, although the brutalized condition of the Quechua people, forced upon them centuries earlier by the Spanish invasion, and the need for social change – violent if necessary – figure in all his fiction, it is the tenderness and generosity of spirit of those same people and their feeling for the natural world that was absorbed by the child Arguedas, "raised by Don Felipe Maywa's folk", that predominate. He committed suicide, Lima, 2 December 1969.

Translations

Selections (short stories, poetry, essays)
Cadillo-Alfaro de Ayres, Angela and Ruth Flanders Francis, "The Agony of Rasu-Ñiti", *Review*, 25/26 (1980) pp. 43–46
Harss, Luis, "Between Quechua and Spanish"; "Child of Sorrow" from *El zorro de arriba y el zorro de abajo*; "The

Pongo's Dream"; "Suicide Diary," *Review*, 25/26 (1980) pp. 15–17, 48–89, 50–52, 47–48
Stephan, Ruth Walgreen, *The Singing Mountaineers: Songs and Tales of the Quechua People*, Austin: University of Texas Press, 1957

Novels
Yawar fiesta, 1941
Barraclough, Frances Horning, *Yawar Fiesta*, Austin: University of Texas Press, 1985

Los ríos profundos, 1958
Barraclough, Frances Horning, *Deep Rivers*, with an introduction by John V. Murra, afterword by Mario Vargas Llosa, Austin: University of Texas Press, 1978

In the 1983 Lima edition of the collected works of José María Arguedas, photographs show covers of foreign editions of his works in many languages, but not English, in which they are sparse even today. Fortunately, *Deep Rivers*, the American translator Frances Horning BARRACLOUGH's 1978 version of his masterpiece, *Los ríos profundos* (1958), conveys remarkably well the dignity of the Quechua-inspired Spanish of the original. Barraclough, a painstaking worker, has also translated some of Arguedas's shorter fiction (*Yawar Fiesta*, 1985) and also his longest novel, *Todas las sangres* (1964), as *All the Bloods*, for which a publisher is sought. She is currently translating, under contract from Unesco for Colección Archivos, *The Fox from Above and the Fox from Below* (*El zorro de arriba y el zorro de abajo*, 1971) the highly personal, idiosyncratic, posthumous novel left unfinished by Arguedas's suicide in December 1969 during a crisis of the clinical depression that plagued him throughout his life. Translations of other short pieces have appeared in journals (see listing), but except for Ruth **Stephan**'s 1957 versions of Arguedas's Quechua songs and tales, only the texts indicated appear to be accessible in book form. A collection, in English, of major critical essays on Arguedas's work by his principal interpreters, edited by Ciro Sandoval and Sandra Boschetti-Sandoval, published in 1998, should help create a wider reading public for the writer who has come to be regarded by his admirers as an icon of alterity.

Los ríos profundos appeared at the very beginning of the period classed as "The Boom" (*el boom*) in Latin American literature, whose dates are usually given as c. 1960–70. The Boom implies a time-frame when Latin American writers gained world-wide stature, as European and Anglo-American publishers, readers, and critics became aware of the existence of modernistic/postmodern experimental fiction being written in an area of the world whose literature they had virtually ignored until that time. Prior to the publication of that novel, Arguedas's work had been interpreted by critics in his own language as being primarily of a social nature and belonging to the indigenist strain of Zolan naturalism; yet, from the very first, as William Rowe, Margot Beyersdorff, and other critics have pointed out, his expressed concerns had been to transpose the characteristics of Quechua speech to "translate" into Spanish the quiet dignity of the Indian's native language. Quechua is quite unlike Spanish and translates more felicitously into English or other Germanic-based languages than into one with Latin roots; onomatopeia is common; a noun can serve as an adjective and precede the noun qualified: while Spanish must say "Fiesta of Blood" (Fiesta de sangre), Quechua, like English, says "*Yawar* (Blood) fiesta", the title of a short novel also translated by BARRACLOUGH (1985). Complex stylistic experimentation figures throughout his work and reveals his obsession with language, and when in *Deep Rivers* the main protagonist, young Ernesto, finds his unique literary voice, he is, in Barraclough's translation, as proud "as [if] I had swum across the rivers in January, when they are laden with the heaviest, most turbulent waters."

In rendering Arguedas's Spanish into English, Barraclough faced an insurmountable problem. As the anthropologist, John Murra explains in his introduction to Barraclough's translation, Peruvian highlanders speak Spanish on Quechua grammatical underpinnings, and though every word might be Spanish, the syntax is often Quechua. English translation cannot, for cultural reasons, produce the effect of Arguedas's Spanish text on a reader whose language is Spanish; this effect can perhaps best be imagined by comparing it with the one undoubtedly produced by the first reading of works by Burns or Synge during those writers' lifetimes. Through Arguedas's language, a people scorned or mocked reveal themselves as possessing "a perception, a world view of their own ... utterly unlike the Iberian one" (says Murra in his introduction to *Deep Rivers*). To capture the dignity of the original, Barraclough opts for simple vocabulary and a slow cadence that is lyrical in its own right:

> The calm, rippling current of the river flows slowly eastward; the long boughs of the *chachacomo* bushes graze the surface of the waters, are swept under, and spring back violently on freeing themselves from the current. It looks like a river of molten steel, blue and smiling, despite its solemnity and depth ... I didn't know if I loved the river or the bridge more. But both of them cleansed my soul, flooding it with courage and heroic dreams. All of the mournful images, doubts and evil memories were erased from my mind ... thus renewed and brought back to myself, I would return to town, resolutely climbing the dreadful slope, holding mental conversations with my old distant friends ... those who had brought me up and made my heart like their own.

Arguedas's feeling for the natural world merits special mention in Mario Vargas Llosa's afterword to Barraclough's translation, and it can be pointed out that the translators of Wordsworth and Coleridge's *Lyrical Ballads* into Spanish felt it necessary to draw attention to the bucolic, even pantheistic, intensity of much English literature. This is so much less common in literature in Spanish that Arguedas's descriptions of the subject's sense of oneness with natural surroundings have been treated by some Hispanic critics almost as if the attitude is one unique to Arguedas's work.

Murra also mentions how Arguedas, at the beginning of his literary career, was persuaded there would be no future in publishing in Quechua, yet as soon as his position as a writer in Spanish was assured, he published an extraordinary poem in that language: "Tupac Amaru kamaq taytanchisman – haylli taki" [To Our Great Father, Tupac Amaru] (1942), which foretells the "rise" of the Indian through sheer ubiquitous presence in western cities, and this has, indeed, taken place since the poem was written. Critics Antonio Cornejo-Polar and Martín Lienhard have recently discussed Arguedas's pervading influence in Peru as a writer of Quechua (see Sandoval and Boschetto-Sandoval, 1998).

Arguedas's final unfinished novel states that he lived, unconditionally, to write, in order to express his faith in the redemptive force of the Quechua vision. During the Boom years such an attitude placed him in the vulnerable position of appearing to argue from the standpoint of an outmoded modernity, when postmodern parody/despair was the order of the day. In the years following Arguedas's death, a writer's perception or negation of redemptive forces have come to be seen by many critics as literary constants and, far from seeming outmoded, Arguedas appears as at the vanguard, addressing a new public of Andean immigrants who share, in Julio Ortega's words, the writer's awareness of "past misfortunes and dreams of what might be."

According to Nuala Ní Dhomhnaill, who has chosen to write in the language of another marginalized people, voices can now be heard, world wide, of those who refuse to abandon their people's "unique and unrepeatable way of looking at the world" and, consequently, offer the viable alternative to the "genuinely global ... monoculture" that threatens to engulf all societies and literatures. This is the public Arguedas foresaw and that he speaks to in all his work.

ALITA KELLEY

Further Reading

Beyersdorff, Margot, "Voice of the Runa: Quechua Substratum in the Narrative of José María Arguedas", *Latin American Indian Literatures Journal*, 2/1 (Spring 1986) pp. 28–48

Ní Dhomhnaill, Nuala, "Why I Choose to Write in Irish, The Corpse That Sits Up and Talks Back", *New York Times Book Review* (8 January 1995) pp. 3, 27–28

Ortega, Julio, *Poetics of Change: The New Spanish-American Narrative*, translated by Galen D. Greaser and Ortega, Austin: University of Texas Press, 1984

Rowe, William, *Mito e ideologia en la obra de José María Arguedas*, Lima: Instituto Nacional de Cultura, 1979

Sandoval, Ciro and Sandra Boschetto-Sandoval (editors), *José María Arguedas: Reconsiderations for Latin American Cultural Studies*, Athens: Ohio University Center for International Studies, 1998

Ludovico Ariosto 1474–1533

Italian poet

Biography

Born 8 September 1474, in the duchy of Ferrara, at Reggio Emilia, where his father was commander of the citadel. From 1489 to 1494 he read law at the University of Ferrara, then turned to the study of literature. After the death of his father in 1500, the responsibilities of eldest son forced him to find employment at the ducal court. From 1503 to 1517 he was in the service of the then duke's son, Cardinal Ippolito d'Este, for whom he travelled on diplomatic missions and military expeditions. Between 1518 and 1533 he served Alfonso d'Este, the cardinal's brother, now duke of Ferrara. For three years (1522–25), Ariosto governed the troubled mountain province of Garfagnana, before returning to Ferrara, where he married his long-term mistress and was able to lead a life of study and literary creation. He died at Ferrara, 6 July 1533.
He is famous for his great epic poem, known in English by its Italian title *Orlando Furioso*. He also wrote, besides satires, burlesques and sonnets, five plays that were significant, as vernacular imitations of Latin models, in the evolution of modern European comedy.

Orlando Furioso [Roland Demented]

Orlando furioso, 1515; 2nd revised edition 1521; 3rd revised edition 1532

Ludovico Ariosto began writing his epic in 1505. It is a continuation, in 46 cantos composed of rhyming eight-line stanzas, of the Ferrarese Matteo Boiardo's unfinished poem *Orlando innamorato* [Roland in Love], abandoned in 1494. Roland/Orlando is the legendary heroic Christian knight of Charlemagne (747–814), in the tradition dating back to the 11th-century French epic *The Song of Roland*. Ariosto takes up the story at the point where Charlemagne's men are fighting near Paris against the Muslim invaders, the Moors and the soldiers of the Saracen King of Spain. Orlando is the rival of his cousin Rinaldo for the heart of the beautiful princess Angelica. Learning that she has married a Moor, Roland goes mad from thwarted love. Cured by extra-terrestrial means, he defeats the pagans. Ariosto's poem also relates the love between the soldier Ruggiero and Rinaldo's warrior sister Bradamante, who were the supposed ancestors of Ariosto's patrons, the Estes. The texture of epic and romantic themes is interspersed with humorous elements.

Translations

Gilbert, Allan H., *Orlando Furioso*, with an introduction, 2 vols, New York: S.F. Vanni, 1954

Harington, Sir John, *Orlando Furioso in English Heroical Verse*, London: Richard Field, 1591; several modern editions
Hoole, John, *Orlando Furioso*, London: George Nicol, 1783; 2nd edition, 1785
Reynolds, Barbara, *Orlando Furioso / The Frenzy of Orlando: A Romantic Epic*, with an introduction, 2 vols, Harmondsworth and Baltimore: Penguin, 1975–77
Rose, William Stewart, *Orlando Furioso*, 8 vols, London: John Murray, 1823–31
Waldman, Guido, *Orlando Furioso*, with an introduction, Oxford and New York: Oxford University Press, 1974

HARINGTON'S *Orlando Furioso* (1591) is an acknowledged classic of Elizabethan translation. Its successes are possible partly because of the nature of the English language at the time Harington wrote, and the rich linguistic texture and melange of registers seem at times to match Ariosto's own. The overall effect is well described by W.S. ROSE, a later translator (1823–31): "His narrative is light and lively, and, in perusing it, the reader always feels as if he is swimming with the stream." Harington freely omits and adapts, and this version is more than 700 stanzas shorter than its source (though both are in octaves); this is not always advantageous, and Harington often loses Ariosto's subtleties without providing compensating gains. A work of great energy and occasional inspiration, this translation is, however, a cruder product than its source, "unable to reproduce either the linguistic elevation or the subtle oscillations of level which are found in Ariosto's text" (Kirkpatrick, 1995).

HOOLE (1783) chooses heroic couplets, paying the price in the loss of Ariosto's independent, self-sufficient stanzaic units with their own harmony and shape. This translation suffers also from the pruning of the more sensual passages throughout the poem. Hoole seems himself to have felt he came too late in time to do full justice to Ariosto: "there is", he writes in his preface, "a certain easy negligence in [Ariosto's] muse that often assumes a playful mode of expression, incompatible with the nature of our present poetry". This version does lack "playfulness", but Sir Walter Scott is unduly harsh in calling Hoole "the noble transmuter of the gold of Ariosto into lead". Scott's judgment in part reflects the prejudices of his era, for Hoole's is a thoroughgoing English "Augustanization" of Ariosto, modelled on the best of the Augustan narrative poets, John Dryden; it gives little sense of the Italian verse, but reads well enough in its own right. Hoole incorporates copious notes on historical points, literary analogues and other matters.

ROSE'S monumental eight-volume version of 1823–31 was hugely successful in its own era, so much so that it was frequently reprinted for well over a century, during which time no new complete English version appeared. Rose's friend Ugo Foscolo commended it as "one of the best models in the treatment of the English stanza". Rose's handling of his octaves is correct enough, but the overall result is flat, the diction wilfully archaic, the rhythms monotonous, and Ariosto's quirky humour often dissipated. Rose's comparative accuracy in rendering the literal meaning, and his stanza-by-stanza correspondence to his source, are insufficient compensation. Scott is more justified in mocking this version, writing in his journal that the Italian might be printed *en face* "for the sake of assisting the indolent reader to understand English"; Rose writes more than once, Scott observes, of a lady having "voided her saddle".

GILBERT'S (1954) is a prose version, with numbered paragraphs corresponding to the original stanzas so that the reader can refer back to the Italian. The introduction shows a sensitive understanding of the formal qualities of the poetry, and the translation reflects a careful reading of the Italian. Gilbert's ambitions are strictly limited: this is a guide to, rather than a replacement for, Ariosto's poetry – as prose renderings must necessarily be.

The introduction to WALDMAN'S 1974 translation is dismissive of attempts to render the *Furioso* in verse, and he embraces prose, arguing that it is possible to match Ariosto's skill as a narrator but not as a poet. Once again the result is useful as a guide for those with limited Italian (and the text, as in Gilbert's rendering, is helpfully keyed to the original), but an exclusive reliance on this version would tend to induce puzzlement as to the reasons for the poem's historically high standing. The overwhelming impression Waldman's English prose gives is that to lose the poetry is to lose nearly everything: despite a laudable intention to let the *Furioso* "reach a wide audience at last", and despite Waldman's often clever solutions to linguistic problems, strikingly little of the character of Ariosto's work comes over.

Taken all in all, REYNOLDS (1975–77) is the poem's most successful 20th-century English translator. Writing in octaves, she responds with fertile, sometimes inspired inventiveness to the challenge of Ariosto's verse. Unabashed by the strictures of previous commentators, Reynolds argues in her introduction that there is "nothing about the English language which is inherently inappropriate to the Italian of Ariosto". On the contrary, "twentieth-century English ... possesses, and is unashamed to use, a direct, unrhetorical vocabulary and style corresponding closely to the unrhetorical elements" in the *Furioso*, as well as a poetic diction inheriting Italian and Latinate elements for the poem's more heightened styles. Something of the translation's admixture of these qualities can be seen in XXXI. 87, describing Rinaldo's slaughter of the pagans at Paris:

> The crash of metal clashing, clattering,
> The rolling thunder of so many drums,
> So many thudding hoofs, the whinnying,
> The roar which from so many voices comes,
> O'er hill and plain and valley echoing,
> A tumult which all pandemoniums
> Exceeds must come from hell, so it was said,
> And that was why the pagans turned and fled.

But the pleasures of this translation, not least its sheer readability over long stretches of narrative, cannot be adequately illustrated by one short excerpt. There is also a full editorial apparatus in the much-reprinted Penguin edition, including maps, tables, notes, and a 100-page introduction.

STUART GILLESPIE

Further Reading

Brand, C.P., *Italy and the English Romantics: The Italianate Fashion in Early Nineteenth-Century England*, Cambridge: Cambridge University Press, 1957
Brand, C.P., *Ludovico Ariosto: A Preface to the "Orlando Furioso"*, Edinburgh: Edinburgh University Press, 1974
Jack, R.D.S., *The Italian Influence on Scottish Literature*, Edinburgh: Edinburgh University Press, 1972

Kirkpatrick, Robin, *English and Italian Literature from Dante to Shakespeare: A Study of Source, Analogue and Divergence*, London and New York: Longman, 1995
Praz, Mario, "Ariosto in England" in his *The Flaming Heart: Essays on Crashaw, Machiavelli, and Other Studies in the Relations Between Italian and English Literature from Chaucer to T.S. Eliot*, New York: Doubleday, 1958
Reynolds, Barbara, "The Pleasure Craft" in *The Translator's Art: Essays in Honour of Betty Radice*, edited by William Radice and Barbara Reynolds, Harmondsworth and New York: Penguin, 1987
Rich, Townsend, *Harington and Ariosto: A Study in Elizabethan Verse Translation*, New Haven, Connecticut: Yale University Press, and London: Oxford University Press, 1940
Scaglione, Aldo (editor), *Ariosto 1974 in America: Atti del Congresso Ariostesco, Dicembre 1974*, Ravenna: Longo, 1974

Aristophanes c.450–385 BC

Greek comic dramatist

Biography

Born in Athens, possibly c.450 BC, possibly as late as 444. Very little is known of his life. He may have lived or owned property on Aegina. His early plays, and a few later ones, were not directed personally by him; the first production in his own name was that of *Hippeis* (*The Knights*), 424). Most of his plays represent the Old Attic Comedy; their targets were political, literary and philosophical figures, ideas and institutions. They won at least four first prizes at the city Dionysia and Lenaia festivals. Aristophanes' son, the comic poet Araros, produced his last two plays; all three of his sons are known to have written plays of their own. Aristophanes served on the Athenian Senate in the early 4th century. Died c.385 BC.

Eleven of Aristophanes' works survive, plus 32 titles (some possibly alternative titles; four probably spurious) and nearly 1,000 fragments. The extant plays are: *Acharnes* (*The Acharnians*), 425; *Hippeis* (*The Knights*), 424; *Nephelai* (*The Clouds*), 423; *Sphekes* (*The Wasps*), 422; *Eirene* (*Peace*), 421; *Ornithes* (*The Birds*), 414; *Lysistrate* (*Lysistrata*), 411; *Thesmophoriazousai* (*Women at the Thesmophoria*), 411; *Batrachoi* (*The Frogs*), 405; *Ekklesiazousai* (*Assembly-Women*) c.392; *Ploutos* (*Wealth*), 388. The last two of these are considered to mark the transition from Old to New Comedy.

Translations

Collections

Barrett, David, *The Frogs and Other Plays*, Harmondsworth: Penguin, 1964
Barrett, David and Alan H. Sommerstein, *The Knights, Peace, The Birds, The Assemblywomen*, Harmondsworth: Penguin, 1978
Dickinson, Patric, *Plays*, 2 vols, London: Oxford University Press, 1970
Rogers, Benjamin Bickley, *The Comedies of Aristophanes*, 11 vols, London: Bell, 1902–16
Sommerstein, Alan H., *Lysistrata, The Acharnians, The Clouds*, Harmondsworth: Penguin, 1973

Selections

Frere, John Hookham, *Four Plays*, London: Oxford University Press, 1907 (contains *The Acharnians*, *The Knights*, *The Birds*, *The Frogs*; translations originally published 1839–40)
Halliwell, Stephen, *Birds, Lysistrata, Assembly-Women, Wealth*, Oxford: Oxford University Press, 1997

Plays

Nephelai, 423 BC
Arrowsmith, William, *The Clouds*, Ann Arbor, Michigan: University of Michigan Press, 1962
Stanley, Thomas, *The Clouds* in *The History of Philosophy*, vol. 1, London: Printed for Humphrey Moseley and Thomas Dring, 1655

Ornithes, 414 BC
Arrowsmith, William, *The Birds*, Ann Arbor: University of Michigan Press, 1961

Lysistrate, 411 BC
Fitts, Dudley, *Lysistrata*, New York: Harcourt Brace, 1954; London: Faber, 1955
Harrison, Tony, *The Common Chorus: A Version of Aristophanes' Lysistrata*, London and Boston: Faber, 1992

Ploutos, 388 BC
Fielding, Henry and William Young, *Plutus: The God of Riches*, London: T. Waller, 1742
Randolph, Thomas, *Ploutophthalmia, Ploutogamia: A Pleasant Comedie Entituled Hey for Honesty, Down with Knavery*, London: "F.J.", 1651

Before 1800 only three of Aristophanes' 11 surviving plays existed in any sort of English version. *Wealth* or *Plutus*, whose apparent moralism had long made it the comedian's best-known work (a verdict sharply reversed in modern times), was part translated, part adapted, possibly around 1628 (though publication was posthumous), by Thomas RANDOLPH, Cambridge scholar-playwright and adopted son of Ben Jonson. The same work was rendered by H.H.B., the Irish dramatist Henry Burnell (1659), by Lewis Theobald (1715), and by Henry FIELDING & William YOUNG (1742). *Clouds* produced four versions, the earliest (and incomplete) in Thomas STANLEY's *History of Philosophy* (1655), followed by Lewis Theobald's (1715), James White's (1759), and Richard Cumberland's (1798). A solitary rendering of *Frogs*, by C. Dunster, was published in 1785. Early in the following century (though publication did not come till 1839–40) James Hookham FRERE worked on *Acharnians*, *Knights*, *Birds*, and *Frogs*; his drafts were praised by his friend Coleridge in 1817. In keeping with gradually freer attitudes to ancient Greek culture, the 19th century saw translators eventually tackling all the plays, though never without bowdlerization. The well-known and often reprinted translations by Benjamin Bickley ROGERS, first published with his commentaries in 1902–16, represent a culmination of Victorian activity in this area.

A special configuration of difficulties helps to explain why until the mid-19th century Aristophanes was one of the least translated of major ancient authors. Among these are a huge diversity of topical and culturally specific references; a constantly shifting gamut of stylistic registers, encompassing everything from lyric poetry to colloquial raciness; an extreme fertility of linguistic play and invention; and, last but not least, a licence (part of the festive traditions of Greek comedy) for bawdy and obscenity. Only in the 20th century have attempts been made to reproduce uninhibitedly the specially Aristophanic combination of verbal virtuosity with vulgarity, formal verse structure (of various kinds) with unfettered imaginative exuberance.

Overall solutions to the challenge posed by Aristophanes cannot be separated from such basic decisions as the choice between verse and prose. Both RANDOLPH (1651) and Burnell (1659) used prose, but Randolph sometimes juxtaposed the two forms in the manner of Elizabethan-Jacobean drama, partly to convey a contrast between different registers (e.g. using verse for parody of tragedy). Despite the frequently loose relationship to the original (only half the length of the English play), Randolph clearly saw the possibility of blank verse as a serviceable approximation to the Greek poet's dialogue metre (iambic trimeters, a slightly longer line). This practice was applied consistently in STANLEY's *Clouds* (1655), which shows for the first time how neatly turned English lines could keep close step with the original. Thereafter blank verse remained common until the early 20th century. But by ROGERS's time (1902–16) the convention was so mannered that the possibility of exploiting the suppleness of blank verse to match the vigour of Aristophanic dialogue had been lost sight of. What mars Rogers's blank verse, as that of some of his predecessors (including Frere), is a generalized ethos of poetic archaism (including a liberal deployment of "ye", "erst", "methought" and the like) that makes it nearly impossible to catch the shifts and juxtapositions of tone, from the colloquial to the mock-elevation of paratragedy, that occur within the same metrical form.

Aware of the loss of comic pertness and flexibility in the rendering of Aristophanic dialogue, translators in the middle and second half of the 20th century, in both Britain and America, have typically turned either to prose (e.g. the Penguin Classics versions by BARRETT 1964, SOMMERSTEIN 1973, and BARRETT & SOMMERSTEIN 1978) or to free verse. Prose makes the control and variation of register easier, but it loses the linguistic tautness that comes from the iambic verse-form. The better free verse translations, such as William ARROWSMITH's (1961, 1962), sometimes maintain this, though the results are not always as natural or speakable as their proponents claim (witness e.g. the awkward artificiality of the short four-stress line used in some of Patric DICKINSON's renderings (1970)). There is a case to be made, as HALLIWELL (1997) attempts to demonstrate, for refurbishing and suitably modulating iambic pentameters in order to emulate the combination of vivacity and craft in Aristophanic dialogue.

On the lyrical side, where Aristophanes is the most variegated and multiform of poets, English translators have turned surprisingly often to rhyme; FRERE even referred to "the necessity of rime" in this context. Rhymed couplets or short stanzas appear in, for example, STANLEY's *Clouds* and FIELDING & YOUNG's *Plutus*, and they have proved a tenacious option, still to be found in BARRETT, SOMMERSTEIN, and most of the modern American versions. Sustained use of rhyme in this way tends to make Aristophanic lyrics too uniformly jaunty. The tradition of exercises in close metrical imitation, seen in, for example, FRERE and (above all) ROGERS, occasionally produced virtuoso effects, but only for those who could compare English with Greek. In the lyrics as in Aristophanes' so-called "recitative" metres, experimentation is both possible and desirable. ARROWSMITH's adaptation of William Carlos Williams's triplet line for a portion of *Birds* is among the more interesting modern instances. But 20th-century translators have arguably under-explored the potential of free verse to capture something of the fluidity of Greek lyric rhythms.

Cribs aside, translators of Aristophanes have regularly admitted some degree of modernization, though not always with the gusto of RANDOLPH (1651), who can turn a Priest of Zeus into the Pope, or Tony HARRISON (1992), who telescopes Lysistrata and her followers into the women of Greenham Common. But even the freer of 20th-century versions tend to retain many of the playwright's references and allusions; to do otherwise would be to shed a whole dimension of his engagement with his times. Translators have found it much easier to excise obscenity, and have even given specious reasons for doing so: Dudley FITTS (1955) suggested that sexually crude language would somehow shatter Lysistrata's persona (a point lost on Aristophanes himself). There are very few who shirk nothing in this area.

STEPHEN HALLIWELL

Further Reading

Dover, K.J., *Aristophanic Comedy*, Berkeley: University of California Press, 1972, pp. 230–37

Sommerstein, A.H., "On Translating Aristophanes: Ends and Means", *Greece and Rome* 20 (1973) pp. 140–54

See also the translator's introduction in Halliwell

Aristotle 384–322 BC

Greek philosopher

Biography

Born in Stagira, Macedonia, in 384 BC. He was orphaned young. His father, Nicomachus, had been physician to Amyntas II, king of Macedon. From the age of 17 he spent 20 years (367–347) at Plato's Academy in Athens, first as a pupil, then as a teacher. In 347, after Plato's death, Aristotle went to live with other philosophers from the Academy at Assos, in Asia Minor, where he married Pythias, niece of his friend, the local ruler Hermeias. When Hermeias was murdered by the Persians in 344, Aristotle went to Mytilene on Lesbos, and taught there. In 342 he was invited to the court of Philip II of Macedon at Pella, to be tutor to the king's son, the future Alexander the Great. In 335 Aristotle returned to Athens and established there his own school of literature, science, and philosophy, the Lyceum, whose students were known as "peripatetics". After Pythias' death, some time after the return to Athens, Aristotle lived with and had a son, also called Nichomachus, by Herpyllis. On the death of Alexander the Great in 323 Aristotle was accused of impiety and retreated to Chalcis, Euboea, leaving his school to Theophrastus. Died 322 BC, at Chalcis.

Most of Aristotle's works are lost. What remains is constituted chiefly by teaching notes, from various periods but with few indications of dates of composition. These extant works cover a range of philosophical, scientific and human subjects. The principal among them are the *Organon* (a treatise on logic); the *Physics* (on natural philosophy); biological studies such as the *History of Animals*; *On the Soul* (which can be classed as psychology); the *Metaphysics*; works on human topics, such as the two treatises on ethics, the *Nichomachean Ethics* and the *Eudemian Ethics*, the *Politics*, the *Rhetoric*; and the *Poetics*.

Poetics

Translations

Butcher, S.H., *Aristotle's Theory of Poetry and Fine Art*, London: Macmillan, 1895

Bywater, Ingram, *Aristotle on the Art of Poetry*, Oxford: Clarendon Press, 1909

Else, Gerald F., *Aristotle: Poetics*, Ann Arbor: University of Michigan Press, 1967

Golden, Leon, *Poetics*, Englewood Cliffs, New Jersey: Prentice Hall, 1968

Grube, G.M.A., *Aristotle on Poetry and Style*, New York: Liberal Arts Press, 1958

Halliwell, Stephen, *The Poetics of Aristotle*, London: Duckworth, and Chapel Hill: University of North Carolina Press, 1987

Halliwell, Stephen, *Poetics*, Cambridge, Massachusetts: Harvard University Press, 1995 (Loeb Classical Library; also includes *On the Sublime* by Longinus, translated by W.H. Fyfe; and *On Style* by Demetrius, translated by Doreen C. Innes)

Heath, Malcolm, *Poetics*, London and New York: Penguin, 1996

Hubbard, M.E., *Poetics*, in *Ancient Literary Criticism*, edited by D.A. Russell and M. Winterbottom, Oxford: Clarendon Press, 1972

Janko, Richard, *Poetics*, Indianapolis: Hackett, 1987

Pye, Henry James, *A Commentary Illustrating the Poetic of Aristotle*, London: John Stockdale, 1792

Taylor, Thomas, in *The Rhetoric, Poetic, and Nicomachean Ethics of Aristotle*, vol. 1, London: James Black, 1811

Twining, Thomas, *Aristotle's Treatise on Poetry*, London: 1789

English translations of the *Poetics* began as a late off-shoot of neo-classical interest in the work, which had developed from the late 15th century in Italy and beyond and had expressed itself first in Latin and subsequently in vernacular versions of the treatise. The very first English rendering, published anonymously in 1705, was actually made from Dacier's French of 1692; meanwhile, Latin renderings, including one made by Goulston in 1623, continued to be widely used. After two other anonymous 18th-century English translations had appeared, as well as one by PYE in 1792, Thomas TWINING's version of 1789 marked a watershed for the new degree of interpretative understanding that it deftly brought to the text and elaborated in its accompanying essays. The only translation produced during Romanticism's (qualified) reaction against the *Poetics* was that of Thomas TAYLOR (1811); but Taylor's own neo-platonist proclivities show themselves only in his preface, not in his rather dull and unreliable treatment of the text. A succession of mediocre 19th-century academic versions was superseded by two strikingly well-turned though somewhat different translations. The first, by Samuel BUTCHER and underpinning the essays in his *Aristotle's Theory of Poetry and Fine Art* (1895), allowed itself a speculative tenor that partly assimilated Aristotle to the spirit of Hegel. The second, in the edition by Ingram BYWATER (1909), managed to be both scholarly and attractively fluent.

In the wake of Butcher and Bywater, both of whom retain value, the 20th century has seen a veritable spate of English renderings, more than 20 in fact, issuing from both sides of the Atlantic. The density of this attention to such a short text perhaps betrays a persistent conviction that Aristotle's thoughts have a compression that calls for repeated attempts at decoding but never quite yields up all it might be thought to promise.

What, then, are the challenges posed by this brief yet immensely influential treatise? Above all, perhaps, the paradoxical fact that a work to which has often been ascribed, whether for good or ill, a canonical status, and many of whose ideas (especially *hamartia* and *katharsis*) have become shibboleths in critical debates on tragedy, should survive in a frequently crabbed and scrappy form. Put another way, the (supposedly) cerebral dryness of Aristotle, as philosophical analyst, is the medium for a discussion of the fundamental nature of poetry, especially tragedy and epic. A basic dilemma implicitly faces all translators of the *Poetics*, though one which post-Romantic expectations of personal commitment and engagement in literary criticism have particularly accentuated: whether to try to stick close to the choppy state of the text, and perhaps jeopardize or undercut the scope of Aristotle's critical ideas; or to smooth out the work's awkwardness into a more elegant style of discourse. The consequences of this dilemma are far-reaching, since they impinge on an important general issue in interpretation of the *Poetics*, namely the extent to which Aristotle's approach is rigorously methodical and even prescriptivist in spirit.

The neo-classical appropriation of the *Poetics* in England tended, almost involuntarily, to create a poised and refined Aristotle whose tone of voice was hard to distinguish from the decorum of contemporary literary tastes. This left its mark on both PYE and TWINING, who, while wholly aware of the often problematic nature of the Greek text, nonetheless produced polished versions that eschewed the awkwardness of the original. Twining, in his preface, cautioned against translations in "broken English", which he shrewdly explained in terms of writing "one language in the idiom of another" (1789, p. iv). By the time of BUTCHER and BYWATER, both of whom use a lucid and conceptually confident prose, a tradition had been created of allowing the *Poetics* to speak in a modern voice that is as urbane as it is academically careful. This tradition of "making coherent sense" and avoiding "slavish adherence to the actual Greek words" (HUBBARD, 1972, p. 89), has continued to predominate in the 20th century; but there have been occasional reactions against it from those who believe in a greater degree of stylistic authenticity. Most extreme in this category, which includes the deliberately rough-hewn version by ELSE (1967), is JANKO (1987), who makes profuse use of square brackets in order to expose the inner workings of conversion from Greek to English grammar: the typographically distracting and syntactically confusing results bring Twining's warning forcefully to mind. Janko also exemplifies excessively the practice, more moderately engaged in by, for example, HUBBARD, of imposing on the work an elaborate grid of sections and sub-sections. This approach leaves us with an Aristotle (the bogey of Romantics and others) seemingly obsessive about analytical itemization. More discursive translations of the work, such as HEATH's (1996), can, however, tilt the balance back towards conveying an argumentative momentum that though orderly gives the thrust of major ideas precedence over complete scrupulousness of explication.

The *Poetics* has engendered especially sharp argument over a number of specific concepts whose treatment by translators is inevitably implicated in interpretative dispute. Most prominent among these are *hamartia* (denoting the cause of the tragic hero's misfortune), whose ordinary sense is "mistake", "fault", etc. and *katharsis* (denoting one of the effects of tragedy upon the audience), which encompasses "cleansing", "purification", "purgation". A selection from the range of renderings of *hamartia* speaks for itself: "error or frailty" (Butcher), "error of judgement" (Bywater), "flaw" (GRUBE, 1958), "miscalculation" (GOLDEN, 1968), "piece of ignorance" (Hubbard). Variation in the case of *katharsis* has been more restricted, partly because of a traditional polarization between "purgation" and "purification", but also because "catharsis" itself has been in currency as a regular English noun, first medical and later (partly in the wake of Freud) psychological, since the early 19th century. Many modern versions therefore, including Bywater, Hubbard, Golden, and Halliwell, keep the original term, whether transliterated or not. A good case can be made for doing the same with *hamartia* too, since interpretative uncertainty cannot be satisfactorily resolved by the imposition of any particular word or phrase. The same policy may even be advisable, and has been adopted, for example by Hubbard, for Aristotle's central aesthetic concept, *mimesis*, whose neo-classical and Latinate conversion to "imitation" has still not become obsolete, despite its increasingly inappropriate connotations. More generally, the late 19th and 20th centuries have seen a broad trend towards standardization of terminology: e.g. the structural terms introduced in chapter 18 are now most commonly translated "complication" and "denouement", though "tying"/"involvement" and "(re)solution"/"untying" are sometimes found.

It is no accident that most translations of the *Poetics* (and the generalization would hold for languages other than English, too) have been furnished with copious annotation, a full commentary, or explanatory essays. Few translators feel that they can allow their words, where such condensed thought is concerned, to stand as self-sufficient.

STEPHEN HALLIWELL

Further Reading

Halliwell, Stephen, *Aristotle's Poetics*, London: Duckworth, 1986 (chapter 10)

Herrick, M.T., *The Poetics of Aristotle in England*, New Haven, Connecticut: Yale University Press, 1930

Matthew Arnold 1822–1888

British poet, critic and translation theorist

Biography

Born 24 December 1822, in Laleham, near Staines, Middlesex. In 1837 Arnold entered Rugby School, where his father, the famous Dr Thomas Arnold, had been headmaster since 1828. He went on to Oxford as a classical scholar of Balliol College (1841–44) and was made a Fellow of Oriel College in 1845. After teaching for a short time at Rugby, he he was private secretary from 1847 to 1851 to the president of the Privy Council. In 1851 he married Frances Lucy Wightman (four sons, two daughters) and in the same year began a career as a government inspector of schools that was to last until 1886 and take him frequently on official visits around Britain and in Germany, France, Holland and Switzerland to report on the state of education.

The first volume of poetry published under his own name came out in 1853. His most famous poems are "The Forsaken Mermaid" (1849), "The Scholar Gypsy" and "Sohrab and Rustum" (1853–54), and "Dover Beach" and "Thyrsis" (1867). His tragedy, *Merope*, came out in 1858.

As professor of poetry at Oxford, 1857–67, Arnold gave his highly influential lectures *On Translating Homer* (1861), as well as a course from which derived *On the Study of Celtic Literature* (1867).

After *New Poems* (1867), Arnold wrote mainly in prose. In his collections of essays (*Essays in Criticism*, 1865 and 1888; *Culture and Anarchy*, 1869) he propounded his seminal views: on the civilizing function of criticism, exercised on a broad and cosmopolitan range of cultural phenomena; on the high role of poetry at a time when religions were declining; on the need for true discriminating taste, based on knowledge of the best texts of the masters. He advocated "sweetness and light" and admired the "high seriousness" of classical authors, deploring and aiming to remedy the "Philistine" materialism, provincialism and cultural anarchy he found widespread in Victorian society.

Died 15 April 1888, in Liverpool.

In 1857 Matthew Arnold gave his inaugural lecture as Professor of Poetry at Oxford, "On the Modern Element in Literature". In this lecture he discussed the relationship between writing and society and established as a basic principle the fact that all literatures are interconnected. In his concluding statement, he argued that the intellectual history of one race could not be clearly understood without reference to other ages, nations and literatures, and that of all literatures Greek was of absolute and enduring interest. The literature of ancient Greece, he declared, was "even for modern times a mighty agent of intellectual deliverance ... an object of indestructible interest."

In the autumn of 1860 he gave two lectures on Homer, followed by a third lecture in January 1861. All three were published in 1861 under the title *On Translating Homer* and remain Arnold's greatest contribution to the discussion on translation. He was cheered by his student audience at the end of the third lecture, but attacked in *The Saturday Review* and criticized by some of the translators whose work he had dismissed in the lectures. In 1862 he gave a fourth lecture on the same topic, "On Translating Homer: Last Words", which also contained a tribute to his close friend, the poet Arthur Hugh Clough, who had recently died.

Arnold's views on translation were rooted in practical advice: the translator should not waste time wondering what the Greeks might have thought of his work, nor aim too hard to please ordinary English readers, nor trust his own judgment of his work. Instead, he should produce a text aimed at readers who could understand the Greek original. Homer, Arnold maintains, should be approached by a translator "in the simplest frame of mind possible," with the aim of reproducing the essential qualities of the Greek author: plain, direct speaking and plain, direct thought, matter and ideas all deriving from a fundamental stylistic nobility. Arnold criticizes some of Homer's translators for failing on several of these counts: Cowper and Wright for mistranslating the pace of Homer's verse, Pope and Sotheby for failing to represent his plainness and directness, Chapman for failing to appreciate his plainness and directness of ideas, and his own contemporary, Newman, for failing to appreciate Homer's nobility. Pope, he claimed was too artificial, Chapman introduced Elizabethan fancifulness into the Greek original and Newman was too clumsy and prosaic.

Arnold goes on to discuss his terminology and to explore what he perceives as Homer's fundamental qualities: rapid movement, plain language and style, simple ideas and noble manner. Through his critique of earlier translations, he arrives at the conclusion that not all forms of English poetry will be acceptable for the translator, bearing in mind that his ideal reader of a hypothetical translation of Homer is basically a scholar who knows the Greek source text well. By a process of elimination, Arnold arrives at the conclusion that the hexameter is the most suitable form for rendering Homer into English. Rhythm, he argues, is crucial and all translators should aim to write lines that will "read themselves". Once a translator can write lines in this way, part of the objective of rendering Homer's plainness will be achieved.

Arnold's advice to the translator seeking to reproduce the plainness and directness of Homer's language and thought is to read the Bible, which is "a grand mine of diction for the translator of Homer". The stylistic goals of the translator must take precedence over anything else, and Arnold urges the translator to sacrifice "without scruple" verbal fidelity in the interests of creating a fluid style. He also urges the translator to be bold and innovative, pointing out that when it comes to translating epithets it is important to create in the reader a sense of surprise and naturalness, rather than relying on more banal, everyday epithets. Yet it is also important not to invent strange, unfamiliar terms that might distract the reader and strike a jarring note.

Arnold's advice to translators is idealistic, as he acknowledges. His views on translation derive from the fundamental belief that all texts are created in a particular context and reflect in some way the world-view of a writer who is a product of that context. This means that there are inevitably differences between cultures, so that in the case of Homer, his grandeur is "not the mixed and turbid grandeur of the great poets of the north", of Shakespeare or Goethe, it is "a perfect, a lovely grandeur". He also believes in an aesthetic that is also moral, hence his insistence on Homer's nobility combined with his refusal to define that nobility or to lay down any rules for obtaining it. In a final comic moment, he imagines Homer thanking his English translators for doing him honour but adding the barb that they praise him too much like barbarians.

The lectures *On Translating Homer* encapsulate Arnold's theories of translation. He saw the translator as having a prime responsibility to the original author, but needing scrupulously to take into account the demands of his readers. In creating an ideal reader, someone capable of reading the original and therefore assessing the greater or lesser degree of skill shown by the translator, Arnold shows that his theory of translation was based on the maintenance of equilibrium between source and target systems. The translator's moral responsibility was therefore to balance the possibly conflicting elements and ensure that harmony prevailed.

Arnold's ideal translator would be a scholar and a poet, someone who understood all the nuances of the source text and could write in a way that would render for his readers the beauty, excitement and grandeur of Homer's original. To be successful, he argues, a translator must have both "a true sense for his subject" and a "disinterested love of it", qualities at the same time essential and extremely rare. Clough, he sustains, was one of the few poets whose life and work reflected those qualities.

Arnold's lectures are important because they offer a view of translation at variance with much of the actual translation practice of his time. He emphasized the responsibility of the translator, and rejected easy solutions. He saw the task of the translator as finely balanced between cultures, with a translator who should be neither servile nor arrogant in relation to the original author. His view on translation, like the rest of his literary criticism, was essentially a humanistic and enlightened one.

SUSAN BASSNETT

Further Reading

Arnold, Matthew, *On Translating Homer: Three Lectures Given at Oxford*, London: Longman Green Longman and Roberts, 1861

Arnold, Matthew, *On Translating Homer: Last Words. A Lecture Given at Oxford*, London: Longman Green Longman and Roberts, 1862

Leonid Aronzon 1939–1970

Russian poet

Biography

Born in Leningrad, 24 March 1939, the city where he was to spend almost all his brief life, before dying in a tragic suicidal accident in the hills outside Tashkent. He taught Russian literature at evening classes and later worked as a screenwriter for popular scientific films. In 1958 he married Rita Moiseyevna Purishinskaya, who inspired his love poems and his poems on nature. Their marriage was "made in Heaven", a friend said. He died 13 October 1970.

Translations

Beyer, Thomas R., Jr, Arkady Rovner, Susan Yates, Susan Clark and Richard McKane in *Gnosis Anthology of Contemporary American and Russian Literature and Art*, edited by Rovner, 2 vols, New York: Gnosis Press, 1982

McKane, Richard, poems in *Gnosis*, (1978), 5–6 (1979), 9–10 (1991), 11 (1995); in *Alea*, 1990, with two verse co-translations by Stephen Sartarelli; in *Literary Review* (Spring 1991); in *Modern Poetry in Translation* (January 1997); in *Acumen* (1997)

McKane, Richard, in *The Shalford Book of 20th Century Russian Poetry*, translated by McKane, with a preface by Peter Levi, London and Dallas: Kozmik Press, 1985; as *20th Century Russian Poetry*, London and Cincinnati: Kozmik Press, 1990 (contains 15 poems by Aronzon)

McKane, Richard (editor and translator), *Leonid Aronzon: Death of a Butterfly, Poems 1958–1970* (bilingual edition), Moscow and New York: Gnosis Press, and London: Diamond Press, 1998

The most striking fact about Leonid Aronzon's biography as a poet, and one that presents a huge problem for his translators, is that not a single poem of his was published in his lifetime, except for a few pieces for children. He was one of the Russian poets, along with his Petersburg colleagues Nayman, Rein, Bobyshev and Brodsky, who in the 1960s made a conscious decision not to publish, not to have anything to do with the official publishers of the time, but to circulate poems to friends and in *samizdat*. Anatoly Nayman, the poet and secretary to Anna Akhmatova, in a private conversation self-effacingly suggested to the present writer that of the numerous Petersburg School poets of the 1960s and 1970s, Joseph Brodsky, Elena Shvarts (*Paradise*, translated by Michael Molnar and Catriona Kelly, Newcastle-upon-Tyne: Bloodaxe, 1994) and Aronzon were the outstanding figures. It was indeed Shvarts who edited the supplement of the magazine *Chasy* [Hours] that was to be the first publication in Russian of Aronzon, in 1979. A selection, by Rita Aronzon, was published as a small volume by the Maler Bookshop in Israel in 1985. In 1990 the Leningrad Committee of Literators brought out another small book of selected poems by Aronzon, edited by his former friend Victor Earl, who also published a selection of Aronzon's poems, with an essay, in the magazine *Vestnik Novoi Literatury*, 3 (1991). In 1994 *Leonid Aronzon: Izbrannoe* [Selection] edited by Elena Shvarts was published in Petersburg by XXX Years. Fortunately for Aronzon, Felix Yakubson, Rita Aronzon's second husband, was able to compile a 140-poem chronological Russian manuscript of poems outside the two collections mentioned above and gave it via Arkady Rovner and Victoria Andreyeva, the editors of *Gnosis*, to the translator Richard McKane, while he was in Russia for the Pasternak Conference in 1990. This supplemented additional Aronzon poems published and commented on by K.K. Kuzminsky in his mammoth 5-volume collection of mainly Petersburg poetry, *The Blue Lagoon Anthology of Modern Russian Poetry* (Blue Lagoon, Texas: Institute of Modern Russian Culture, 1980–86). Earl adds, in his brief comments on Aronzon in the Leningrad Committee of Literators book, that he is preparing a future larger book of Aronzon's work.

During this time, *Gnosis*, the New York bilingual literary and philosophical magazine, had been publishing Aronzon's poems in the original and in translations by Richard McKane, in 1978, 1979, 1991 and 1995. Aronzon was also featured in English in the bilingual *Gnosis Anthology of Contemporary American and Russian Literature and Art* (edited by Arkady Rovner, 1982), where there were translations not only by Richard McKane but also by Thomas R. Beyer, Jr, Arkady Rovner, Susan Yates and Susan Clark, the only other translators of Aronzon. The first translations of Aronzon to appear in the UK were 15 poems in Richard McKane's [*The Shalford Book of*] *20th Century Russian Poetry* (1985 and 1990). From 1990 to 1997 magazines other than *Gnosis* on both sides of the Atlantic also published English translations of Aronzon poems.

The poems by Aronzon translated in *20th Century Russian Poetry* prompted Peter Levi, the then Oxford Professor of Poetry, to write in his Preface:

> He is a poet of great formality, sadness and sensuousness: almost as if he had fallen asleep in Paris in 1843 and woken now, and these were his waking dreams. But even his sonnets have the after-echo and the ominous tension of modern poetry at its best. One has the impression of powerful strength of spirit, as if a new and more certain age had dawned.

The few people who have read or heard Aronzon's poems in English at venues like the Troubadour Coffee House and the Pushkin Club in London or at Sheffield University have been overwhelmed by his blend of sensuousness and mysticism and his heavenly landscapes. Here is no cold cerebralism but a hot, ecstatic quality. Perhaps it is that very mysticism and sensuality that meant Aronzon had to wait for the *glasnost* years in order to be published in Russia, and to find a readership at last outside a small group of friends who kept his memory alive.

Obviously there is a fundamental initial difficulty for the translator when the poet has died without publishing: that of locating authentic texts. This is especially the case with Aronzon, as an author of the Third Literature, neither official Soviet nor dissident, both the latter two literatures being more publishable in Russia or the West. The translator of an unpublished poet is set the problem of collating texts from various sources (including friends of the poet), which he or she can do only with trust and tact: trusting in his or her instinct that the poetry is great, and proceeding judiciously because the poet is dead and there may be few people ready to promote his work. Irena Orlova, a great friend of Rita Aronzon, has an archive of Aronzon in Washington. The result of the search, in Aronzon's case, is the large book *Death of a Butterfly* (McKane, 1998), published by the Gnosis Press in Moscow and New York and by the Diamond Press in London. The editors of *Gnosis* and the translator decided that it would be a bilingual text. For many Russian readers as well as English readers Aronzon's poems will be completely new; this gives an interesting twist to Joseph Brodsky's assertion that "a translation, by definition, lags behind the original".

Aronzon is arguably the best love poet of the 1960s. Hot-blooded, passionate, at times carnal, at times infinitely tender, his love poems are written to his own wife, something which is especially unusual for the 1960s in the Soviet Union. But there is a great sadness and depression behind these poems as well. He soars to the heights and sinks to the lows: like a swing, as he put it in a prose passage, "Uncle". So translating him is a delight, but also a challenge. The translator has to be conscious of these mood swings, perhaps even to have experienced them himself or herself so as to be able to catch the lyric tone, the tonality of the words. Rhythm here too is of the essence. An extract from a nature and love poem ("Empty Sonnet") where rapture and sadness coexist, one of the first that was translated, demonstrates the point:

> Who loved you more rapturously than I?
> May God protect you, God protect you, O God protect
> you.
> The gardens wait, the gardens wait, wait in the nights
> and you in the gardens, you in the gardens are waiting too.
>
> I would like to, I would like to instil my sadness
> into you, instil it so as not to alarm
> your sight of the night grass, your sight of its stream,
> so that sadness, so that grass would become our bed.

In the Russian the poem also opens with a rhetorical question. Here is the rapturous, the solemn religious and the sad within five lines, and in between there is the word that is translated by "wait" which in Russian means "stand", which was included in an earlier version of this translation. Aronzon's repetitions are faithfully rendered and lend the poem its incantatory quality. Here the poet desires to instil his sadness into us, his readers; indeed the translator of Aronzon has to search for many synonyms of sadness, sad, anguish, anguished, grief, grave, as well as their extensions, in order to translate the word "toska": yearning, longing, nostalgia, aching.

A pair of identical sonnets of Aronzon's faces the translator and reader with the summit of erotic art (there seems to be a parallel with Baudelaire's poem "Les Bijoux"). Here the poetry is at its most physical, though endowed with an almost spiritual quality at the same time. Translators have to tread warily to achieve the tenderness of these sonnets. The second stanza again has the typical Aronzon haunting, spell-like quality, which has to be mirrored in the translation:

How it suits you, how it goes with you, it's just you:
all this day, all this Bach, all this body,
this day, and this Bach, and this plane
flying there, flying here, flying somewhere.

The final word of the poem is a *tour de force* in English that Aronzon, who knew virtually no English, could not have anticipated: the Russian "padyozhakh", which means "cases" in the grammatical sense, becomes "conjugations". Since this is a poem eminently about conjugal love it was an irresistible translation:

Not approaching one iota, not one step,
give yourself up to me in all gardens and conjugations.

All of Aronzon's poems rhyme, but most translators from modern Russian (except for some of the translators of Brodsky and Brodsky himself) agree that hunting for full rhymes can produce distortions in the translation. However, Thomas R. BEYER in Aronzon's "Couplets" (*Gnosis Anthology* ..., 1982) used some daring rhymes, and Stephen SARTARELLI successfully co-translated two translations of Richard McKane into rhyme (in *Alea*, 1990). The important element to capture in Aronzon is rhythm. An example of a solution to the rhyme-rhythm problem may be seen in a short poem where again nature floods into love, and where the translation, unlike the other Aronzon poems translated by McKane, has a rhyme or half-rhyme scheme with a flexible line length:

Scented eruption, spreading lava of flowers
flooded hill: but breaking off the bliss that comes is not in one's powers.
From every pore springs burst forth, springs of flowers and the glory of God,
and a butterfly symbol flies up as exhalation of lava's steam-cloud.

RICHARD MCKANE

Further Reading

Levi, Peter, preface to [*The Shalford Book of*] *20th Century Russian Poetry*, translated by Richard McKane, 1985 and 1990

Miguel Ángel Asturias 1899–1974

Guatemalan novelist, short-story writer, poet, journalist and dramatist

Biography

Born in Guatemala City, 19 October 1899. The son of a lawyer and a teacher, Asturias learned from a young age to speak out against the wrongs he saw around him. His thesis for graduation from law school, *Guatemalan Sociology: The Social Problem of the Indian*, 1923 (translated 1977), began a lifetime of writing about the indigenous peoples of the Americas. Asturias spent most of his life away from Guatemala, either in exile during periods of dictatorships or representing his country as a diplomat during times of reform or radical change. As a young man in Paris during the heyday of Surrealism, he knew personally many of its prominent figures, as well as Latin American émigrés like himself. The publication of *Leyendas de Guatemala* [Legends of Guatemala], 1930, and this short story collection's highly successful French translation provided him with an entrance into literary avant-garde circles. In addition to his prolific journalism (collected in a volume in the Unesco Archivos series) he maintained a constant production of novels, many of which are available in translation, and less frequently produced works in other literary genres. Returning to Guatemala in 1933, he lived there until leaving in 1944 for Mexico, where he published *El Señor Presidente* (*The President*), 1946. Begun in Paris, this novel about a dictatorship in an unnamed Latin American country is his most popular and most often taught work. *Hombres de maíz* (*Men of Maize*), 1949, is read less only because it is a more difficult work. Asturias's next three novels, called the Banana Trilogy: *Viento fuerte* (*The Cyclone*), 1950, *El Papa verde* (*The Green Pope*), 1954, and *Los ojos de los enterrados* (*The Eyes of the Interred*), 1960, are written in a style that critic Gerald Martin has called "socialist surrealism", meaning the works advocate social justice through a Surrealist poetics. Asturias was awarded the Lenin Peace Prize in 1966 and the Nobel Prize for Literature in 1967. Major books such as *Mulata de tal* (*Mulata*), 1963, *El espejo de Lida Sal* (*The Mirror of Lida Sal*), 1967, and *Maladrón* [The Bad Thief], 1969, appeared in his later years; he was able to write until his final illness. Died in Madrid, 9 June 1974.

Translations

Novels

El Señor Presidente, 1946

Partridge, Frances, *The President*, London: Gollancz, 1963; as *El Señor Presidente*, New York: Atheneum, 1964; in *Miguel Ángel Asturias, Jacinto Benavente, Henri Bergson*, New York: Alexis Gregory, and Delmar, California: CRM, 1971 (Nobel Prize Library, vol. 2)

Hombres de maíz, 1949
Martin, Gerald, *Men of Maize*, with an introduction, New York: Delacorte Press, 1975; London: Verso, 1988; revised edition Pittsburgh: University of Pittsburgh Press, 1993

Viento fuerte, 1950
Flakoll, Darwin and Claribel Alegría, *The Cyclone*, London: Peter Owen, 1967
Rabassa, Gregory, *Strong Wind*, New York: Delacorte Press, 1968

El Papa verde, 1954
Rabassa, Gregory, *The Green Pope*, New York: Delacorte Press, and London: Jonathan Cape, 1971

Los ojos de los enterrados, 1960
Rabassa, Gregory, *The Eyes of the Interred*, New York: Delacorte Press, 1973; London: Jonathan Cape, 1974

El alhajadito, 1961
Koch, Beverly, *The Talking Machine*, New York: Doubleday, 1971 (excerpt from part 4 of *El alhajadito*)
Shuttleworth, Martin, *The Bejeweled Boy*, New York: Doubleday, 1971

Mulata de tal, 1963
Rabassa, Gregory, *Mulata*, New York: Delacorte Press, 1967; as *The Mulatta and Mister Fly*, London: Peter Owen, 1967

Short Stories
El espejo de Lida Sal, 1967
Alter-Gilbert, Gilbert, *The Mirror of Lida Sal: Tales Based on Mayan Myths and Guatemalan Legends*, Pittsburgh: Latin American Literary Review Press, 1997

Other Writing
Sociología guatemalteca: el problema social del indio, 1923
Ahern, Maureen, *Guatemalan Sociology: The Social Problem of the Indian* (bilingual edition), with an introduction by Richard J. Callan, Tempe: Arizona State University, Center for Latin American Studies, 1977

"Miguel Ángel Asturias: Acceptance Speech" in *Miguel Ángel Asturias, Jacinto Benavente, Henri Bergson*, New York: Alexis Gregory, and Del Mar, California: CRM Publishing, 1971 (Nobel Prize Library, vol. 2)

Comiendo en Hungría, with Pablo Neruda, 1969
Balogh, Barna, revised by Mary Arias, *Sentimental Journey around the Hungarian Cuisine*, Budapest: Corvina Press, 1969

Maureen AHERN's translation (1977) of Miguel Ángel Asturias's 1923 thesis *Guatemalan Sociology* is accurate and reads well in English. This work won a prize in Guatemala and was immediately published; despite its straightforward prose and clear translation, it may be misunderstood by those who cannot immerse themselves in the milieu from which it comes. Richard J. Callan's introduction takes a first step toward helping contemporary English readers to understand Guatemalan attitudes toward the native Americans in that country at the beginning of the 20th century – attitudes that Asturias sought to combat.

Highly lauded by Gerald Martin as a "bedazzling translation", Gilbert ALTER-GILBERT (1997) has rendered the short stories in *The Mirror of Lida Sal* as carefully as if they were poetry. This volume would probably be the best of the translated works for an English speaker who wishes to begin reading Asturias, because the works are short and varied, and because the translator achieves much of the linguistic and creative virtuosity of the original.

In *Sentimental Journey around the Hungarian Cuisine* (1969), Barna BALOGH translated the texts by two Nobel Prize winners, Asturias and Pablo Neruda, the Chilean poet, and then her translations were revised by Mary ARIAS. Called "friends of the new Hungary" in the introduction, these famous Spanish American writers, who very much liked to eat, and to eat Hungarian food, also show in this light work their support for Eastern Bloc countries. Typical of its contents is Asturias's praise of goulash, in "The Rehabilitation of Soup", a brief prose piece sprinkled, but not too heavily, with the original Hungarian names for foods.

The first translators of *Viento fuerte*, FLAKOLL & ALEGRÍA (1967) form a writing team committed to many of the same causes as Asturias. No doubt they were attracted to the activist stance promoted by this first novel of Asturias's Banana Trilogy about the United Fruit Company. An important Central American poet and novelist in her own right, Claribel Alegría has often teamed up with her US-born journalist husband to make available testimonial and historical works about El Salvador and Nicaragua. For some reason, Flakoll & Alegría leave untranslated a song in Spanish, as well as the occasional cultural reference (e.g. *guaro*), that might have been better translated, but in general *The Cyclone* is very well done and the differences between it and Gregory RABASSA's version (1968) of the same novel are small.

Beverly KOCH (1971) has simplified the language of Asturias's "La Maquinita de hablar" ("The Talking Machine"), a section of *The Bejeweled Boy* (*El alhajadito*), in addition to adapting it substantially, in order to make this interpolated story suitable for young children. The illustrations are by a famous French illustrator, Jacqueline Duhême, and the dialogue of this story about a frog family appears on alternating pages amid colorful foliage and tropical creatures.

Hombres de maíz (*Men of Maize*) once again takes up the neo-Indigenist themes found in *Leyendas de Guatemala;* it treats the subject of an Indian rebellion from an autochthonous point of view. Gerald MARTIN has translated *Men of Maize* twice: once in 1975, then as head of a team of scholars for the 1993 critical edition in English. Not only does this second translation render the Spanish ideas better than the earlier one, but there are now extensive notes and a glossary for the curious or less informed, unobtrusively placed at the end of the novel. Given the highly allusive and referential nature of the original work, as well as the quality of the translation, Martin's Archivos critical edition is highly recommended. Martin has revised his introduction and added cultural and critical materials beyond his earlier editions of this novel (although there is less such material than in the Spanish critical edition).

Frances PARTRIDGE was one of the first to translate a novel by Asturias, and her translation (1963) of *El Señor Presidente* has survived several changes in publishers. *The President* follows the sense of the original quite closely, although one can always dispute difficult passages. The high number of onomatopoeic words and expressions makes this classic novel reverberate with poetic prose not easy to recreate in another language; Partridge has chosen to privilege meaning over form in most cases, making for a respectable, readable and informative version.

Gregory RABASSA (1967, 1968, 1971, 1974), a frequent translator of Asturias, is well known as a prize winning translator of Latin American literature from Spanish and from Portuguese. Of Asturias, Rabassa has published four books in English: the three novels of the Banana Trilogy, *Strong Wind*, *The Green Pope*, and *The Eyes of the Interred*, plus *Mulata*. The theme in the Banana Trilogy is the exploitation of the workers by the United Fruit Company on the coastal plantations of Central America. It is interesting to compare Rabassa's translation *Strong Wind* (*Viento fuerte*), with that by Flakoll & Alegría, entitled *The Cyclone*. Although very similar, Rabassa's version wins for its thoroughness and clarity. *The Green Pope*, the second in the trilogy, and *The Eyes of the Interred*, the third, are much longer novels, but they also exhibit the care and clarity for which Rabassa is known. In view of the major role the United States plays in these works, and the excellence with which they are rendered into English, it is a pity that all of them are not always in print.

The odd little book *The Bejeweled Boy*, translated well by Martin SHUTTLEWORTH (1971), has been said to be for children. The reasons given are the mythological themes, the playful and whimsical tone, and primarily the age of the young boy protagonist. The large and sometimes eschatological vocabulary as well as the occasionally mature subject matter, however, make this a book more for the child within an adult reader. Shuttleworth does not appear to be bothered by this dilemma, and reproduces the adult vocabulary and creative ferocity of the original. Comparing translations of the section called "The Talking Machine", Shuttleworth's English rendition reflects Asturias's challenging syntax and lexicon; it shares hardly a sentence with KOCH's adaptation for children (1971).

DIANE E. MARTING

Further Reading

Brotherston, Gordon, "The Presence of Mayan Literature in *Hombres de maíz* and Other Works by Miguel Angel Asturias", *Hispania*, 58 (March 1975) pp. 68–74

Callan, Richard J., *Miguel Ángel Asturias*, New York: Twayne, 1970

Diaz, Nancy Gray, "Metamorphosis as Integration in Miguel Angel Asturias' *Hombres de Maíz*", *Revista Canadiense de Estudios Hispánicos*, 12 (Winter 1988) pp. 235–52

Harss, Luis and Barbara Dohmann, "Miguel Ángel Asturias; or, The Land Where the Flowers Bloom" in their *Into the Mainstream: Conversations with Latin American Writers*, New York: Harper and Row, 1967

Martin, Gerald, "*Mulata de tal*: The Novel as Animated Cartoon", *Hispanic Review*, 41 (1973) pp. 397–415

Willis, Susan, "Nobody's Mulata", *Ideologies and Literature*, 4/17 (1983) pp. 146–62

Farīd al-Dīn Abū Hamīd Mohammad 'Attār c.1145–c.1221

Persian mystic, poet and biographer

Biography

Born in Nīshāpūr, northeast Persia (now Iran), c.1116, perhaps as late as 1145. He trained and practised as a pharmacist (*'attār*) and as a physician. However, the name *'attār* may have come from the profession of his father or grandfather. 'Attār travelled through the Muslim Middle East, India and central Asia, settling afterwards in his native town, where most of his life was spent. When he retired he became a member of the Sufi sect, writing many poems (odes, sonnets and quatrains) and compiling prose biographies of nearly 100 Sufi saints (*Tadhkarāt al-'Auliyā*). Around 20 of the works formerly attributed to him are now thought to be spurious. According to tradition, 'Attār was killed during the Mongol invasion of Persia. Died at Nīshāpūr, c.1221.

'Attār's most famous work is the *Mantiq al-Tair* (*The Conference of the Birds*), an allegory of the philosophy and practices of sufism; the birds of the poem represent the sufis.

Translations

Prose

Tadhkarāt al-'Auliyā

Arberry, A.J., *Muslim Saints and Mystics: Episodes from the Tadhkirat al-Auliya' ("Memorial of the Saints")*, with an introduction, Chicago: University of Chicago Press, and London: Routledge and Kegan Paul, 1966

Behari, Bankey, *Selections from Fariduddin 'Attar's Tadhkaratul-Aulyia; or, Memoirs of Saints: Parts 1 and 2*, Lahore: Muhammad Ashraf, 1961; 2nd edition, 1965

Poetry

Ilahi-Namah

Boyle, John Andrew, *The Ilahi-Nama, or Book of God*, with an introduction, Manchester: Manchester University Press, 1976

Mantiq al-Tair

Avery, P.W., *The Speech of Birds: Concerning Migration to the Real*, Cambridge: Islamic Texts Society, 1998

Carrière, Jean-Claude and Peter Brook, *The Conference of the*

Birds, Based on the Poem by Farid Uddin Attar, Chicago, Illinois: Dramatic Publishing, 1982
Darbandi, Afkham and Dick Davis, *The Conference of the Birds*, with an introduction, Harmondsworth and New York: Penguin, 1984
FitzGerald, Edward, *A Bird's-Eye View of Farid-uddin Attar's Bird Parliament* in his *Letters and Literary Remains*, edited by W. Aldis Wright, 3 vols, London and New York: Macmillan, 1889
Masani, R.P., *The Conference of the Birds, A Sufi Allegory, Being an Abridged Version of Farid-ud-din Attar's Mantiqut-Tayr*, London and New York: Oxford University Press, 1924
Nott, C.S., *The Conference of the Birds*, London: Janus Press, 1954
Smith, Margaret, in *The Persian Mystics: 'Attār*, London: John Murray, 1923; New York: Dutton, 1932

Farīd al-Dīn 'Attār's work arrived into the English language relatively late by comparison with translations of other major Persian poets. Indeed, most of his work has yet to appear in English translations. He is the master of long mystical narrative poems, written in the *masnavi* (rhyming couplets) form. His best known *masnavi*, the *Mantiq al-Tair*, is a Sufi (Islamic mystical doctrine) allegory in which a group of birds under the leadership of the hoopoe set off on a journey in search of their king, the *Simurgh* (Phoenix). All the birds, save 30, perish on the way. When the survivors come face to face with the *Simurgh*, they see *si murgh* (30 birds), and thus are themselves the *Simurgh*. This is a most ingenious pun in Persian poetry, and thus very difficult to convey in another language. 'Attār's *Ilahi-Namah* is, on the other hand, a great mystico-didactic poem, in which a king invites his six sons to reveal their most valued wish. They all have worldly and unrealistic ambitions. The king answers each separately by recounting appropriate stories and always concludes with the same advice – that true happiness is attained only through following a spiritual path. 'Attār's only work in prose is his *Tadhkirat al-Auliya*, in which some of the material is itself a translation of earlier Arabic works. His biographies of Muslim saints and mystics have long been important literary sources in the Muslim world.

The translation by BEHARI (1961) is a much abridged version of 'Attār's prose work. It includes only 62 entries out of 142. He concentrates on the anecdotes rather than the biographical information. His prose is accurate, though at times archaic.

ARBERRY (1966) provides a selection of 38 "memorials". His versions are more complete than Behari's. He also provides some useful biographical and bibliographical information of his own for each entry. His language is simple but elegant, reflecting the unaffected prose of the original.

FITZGERALD's version (1889) of *The Conference of the Birds* in heroic couplets – a form similar to that of the original – is, like his *Rubaiyat of Omar Khayyam*, a masterly achievement in poetical adaptation. It succeeds in conveying much of the original's sense and tone, despite being a substantially abridged and often very free version. His rendering of the *Simurgh* pun is very successful. Without actually employing the Persian word, he conveys in often beautiful verse much of 'Attār's sense of mystical union.

The simple prose version by MASANI (1924) of *The Conference of the Birds* translates only half of the poem. Another prose translation is NOTT's (1954) reworking of Garcin de Tassy's literal translation into French. Although the intervention of another language has at times obscured the meaning of some of the stories, Nott does at least succeed in conveying the word play at the end of the poem. The French translation is complete, but Nott omits a number of anecdotes and stories because they seem "repetitive", or "because the meaning is obscure". These unfortunate omissions illustrate his lack of any understanding of the nature of the Persian poem.

SMITH's book (1932) includes a selection of simple prose translations from various works by 'Attār. Unfortunately these are scattered short pieces which do not give any sense of the wholeness of their originals but do manage to capture some of 'Attār's Sufi beliefs. She includes some translations by other writers. The section from the *Mantiq al-Tair* is by Edward Browne.

The stage adaptation of 'Attār's poem by CARRIÈRE & BROOK (1982) is the result of Peter Brook's experimental theatre work at the Centre International de Création Théâtrale in Paris. In the late 1960s and during the 1970s it was taken all over the world with huge success. It was particularly well received in Africa. The script appears to have been based on Nott's translation.

AVERY (1998) presents a complete and scholarly translation in prose. He imitates the form of the original by translating each Persian verse unit (*bait*) in a couplet.

The best English version is that by DARBANDI & DAVIS (1984). Written in heroic couplets, it is the only complete translation in verse. It follows the original very closely and accurately. The language is both very lucid and elegant, and the narrative captures much of the original's sometimes ecstatic and at other times highly sarcastic tone. Their handling of the poem's serious pun is very successful.

The only translation of 'Attār's *Ilahi-Namah* is the literal version by BOYLE (1976). His translation, as he informs the reader in his introduction, is "modelled on R. A. Nicholson's masterly version of the *Mathnavi* of ... Rumi". Each Persian verse unit (a couplet) is translated into one single line, thus giving some sense of the original's form, though not its poetical quality. Detailed notes and commentaries are provided. Although Boyle's version is accurate so far as 'Attār's meaning goes, many readers are likely to find his diction rather old-fashioned.

PARVIN LOLOI

Further Reading

Loloi, Parvin, review of Darbandi & Davis, *Acumen*, 1 (April 1985)
Wickens, G.M., "Select Bibliography of Translations from Persian Literature: Classical Persian Literature", in *Persian Literature*, edited by Ehsan Yarshater, Albany, New York: Bibliotheca Persica, 1988
Yohannan, John D., *Persian Poetry in England and America: A 200-Year History*, Delmar, New York: Caravan Books, 1977
Yohannan, John D., "Persian Literature in Translation", in *Persian Literature*, edited by Ehsan Yarshater, Albany, New York: Bibliotheca Persica, 1988

See also the introductions to Arberry, Boyle and, particularly, Darbandi & Davis

Aucassin and Nicolette

Cest Daucasi et de Nicolete, 13th century

Aucassin and Nicolette is a 13th-century French adventure romance, in prose and verse, by an unknown author who refers to the work as a *chantefable* (song-story). It tells how the love of Aucassin, son of the lord of Beaucaire, in Provence, and Nicolette, a captive bought from the Saracens but revealed at length as the daughter of the king of Carthage, persists through opposition, separation, imprisonment and shipwreck until final happiness.

Translations

Anonymous, "Aucassin and Nicolette" in *Tales of the Twelfth and Thirteenth Centuries*, vol. 2, London, 1786

Bourdillon, F.W., *Aucassin and Nicolette: A Love Story* (bilingual edition), London: Kegan Paul Trench, 1887; many reprints, including London: Folio Society, 1947

Burgess, Glyn S., *Aucassin and Nicolette*, with *The Pilgrimage of Charlemagne* (bilingual edition), edited by A.E. Cobby, New York: Garland, 1988

Child, Harold, *Aucassin and Nicolete*, London: A. & C. Black, 1911

Gibb, E.J.W., *Aucassin and Nicholete: A Romance of the Twelfth Century*, Glasgow: privately printed, 1887

Goodrich, Norma L., *Aucassin and Nicolette* in *The Ways of Love: Eleven Romances of Medieval France*, edited by Goodrich, Boston: Beacon Press, 1964; London: Allen and Unwin, 1965

Hale, Edward Everett, "Nicolette and Aucassin" in his *Crusoe in New York and Other Tales*, Boston: Roberts, 1880

Henry, M.S., *This Is of Aucassin and Nicolette: A Song-Tale of True Lovers*, translated by Henry, versified by E.W. Thomson, Boston: Copeland and Day, 1896; as *Aucassin and Nicolette: An Old-French Song Tale*, Edinburgh: Schulze, 1902

Housman, Laurence, *Of Aucassin and Nicolette*, with an introduction, London: John Murray, 1902

Lang, Andrew, *Aucassin and Nicolete*, London: Nutt, 1887; East Aurora, New York: Roycroft Shop, 1899; many reprints

Macdonough, A. Rodney, *Aucassin and Nicolette: The Lovers of Provence*, with an introduction by E.C. Stedman, and a preface by Gaston Paris, New York: Fords Howard and Hulbert, 1880

Mason, Eugene, " 'Tis of Aucassin and of Nicolette" in *Aucassin and Nicolette and Other Mediaeval Romances and Legends*, translated by Mason, with an introduction, London: Dent, and New York: Dutton, 1910

Matarasso, Pauline, "Aucassin and Nicolette" in *Aucassin and Nicolette and Other Tales*, translated by Matarasso, Harmondsworth: Penguin, 1971

Moyer, E.F. and C.D. Eldridge, *Aucassin and Nicolette*, Chapel Hill, North Carolina: Linker, 1937

Way, Gregory L., "Aucassin and Nicolette" in *Fabliaux or Tales, Abridged from French Manuscripts of the XIIth and XIIIth Centuries by M. Le Grand, Selected and Translated into English Verse*, translated by Way, with preface and notes, 3 vols, London: Bulmer, 1800; revised edition, 1815

West, Michael, *Aucassin and Nicolete*, London: Harrap, and New York: Brentano, 1917

Of all the medieval French texts that have been made available to an English-speaking audience over the years, only the *Song of Roland* has been translated with the same frequency as *Aucassin et Nicolette*. Legrand d'Aussy's French prose adaptation of this tale was published in 1779, and as early as 1786 an ANONYMOUS English version appeared in a volume entitled *Tales of the Twelfth and Thirteenth Centuries*. In 1800 Gregory L. WAY provided a version that he called "a metrical translation" and he presented the text as one long poem of 769 decasyllabic lines.

The last two decades of the 19th century witnessed a remarkable crop of translations, by E.E. HALE (1880), A.R. MACDONOUGH (1880), F.W. BOURDILLON (1887), E.J.W. GIBB (1887), Andrew LANG (1887), E.J. Wilkinson (1887), and M.S. HENRY (1896). Such was the demand for translations of this text that most of these versions were frequently reissued, and if first published in Britain they were subsequently published in the US or vice versa (for details see the bibliography established by Sargent-Baur and Cook, 1981). Two of the translations, those by Bourdillon and Lang, proved particularly influential. Laurence Housman, who produced his own, excellent translation of *Aucassin et Nicolette* in 1902, comments that BOURDILLON "should be read by all scholars scrupulous of textual accuracy and a pure style of English, free from the upholstery of Wardour Street, which has marred other and perhaps better known translations". Bourdillon's translation was reissued as late as 1970. But above all it is LANG's translation (1887) that has enjoyed particular acclaim. Ezra Pound went as far as to say that "Andrew Lang was born in order that he might translate it perfectly and he has fulfilled his destiny" (*The Spirit of Romance*, 1910). This translation passed through several editions and a huge number of printings, including what seems to be a pirated edition by Thomas B. Mosher in 1895 (see Sargent-Baur and Cook, p. 35). As late as 1957 it was reprinted by the Gravesend Press (Lexington, Kentucky) and in the same year included in a volume entitled *Medieval Romances* (New York: Modern Library, pp. 246–83). This volume was edited by R.S. Loomis and L.H. Loomis, who comment that the text has been exceptionally well served by Lang: "Its sweetness has been kept but without sacrifice of its soft raillery, its whimsical juxtaposition of absurdities, even of parody, with high romance".

Translators of Old French texts normally face the problem of deciding whether to maintain the original verse form or to put the text into English prose. However, the unusual form of *Aucassin et Nicolette*, with its alternation of verse and prose, largely imposes on the translator the need to keep the original alternating pattern. The only decision in this case concerns whether or not to retain the seven-syllable line of the Old French verse. Many translators do in fact maintain this heptasyllabic line (Bourdillon, Lang, Housman, *et al.*). But it is noticeable that, even taking into consideration the date of the translations and the expectations of their public, the verse sections have caused translators to wax lyrical and to indulge in extraordinarily archaic language. Perhaps the first translator to offer a version that still reads well today was HOUSMAN (1902), but even he, in an interesting introduction, makes the point that the prose sections demanded accuracy in the translation whereas the verse sections permitted freedom, because he found passages "where a close rendering seemed absolutely damaging to all lyric quality".

The early 20th century produced several new translations of *Aucassin and Nicolette*. In 1910 Eugene MASON produced a volume for Everyman's Library in which *Aucassin and Nicolette* was followed by a number of other medieval tales. A year later there appeared what is materially perhaps the most pleasing of all English translations of *Aucassin and Nicolette*; the translation itself is by Harold CHILD (1911), but the volume is noteworthy for the high quality of its production and for the delightful illustrations by A. Anderson. In 1917 yet another translation appeared, this time by Michael WEST, one written in a style that was distinctly archaic for its time.

The interwar period is notable for the frequent reprinting of Mason's translation. In 1937 E.F. MOYER & C.D. ELDRIDGE did produce a new translation, but no further translations appeared until Norma GOODRICH's 1964 anthology, *The Ways of Love*. Goodrich's version is unusual in that it puts the entire text into prose, and in addition it offers an unsatisfactory mix of the archaic and the colloquial. In recent years the most frequently read translation has probably been the one published in 1971 by Pauline MATARASSO. This translation made the text available to the general public, but in particular it provided a useful service for the student of medieval French. In the original text of *Aucassin et Nicolette* the verse sections are in assonance rather than rhyme, and translators have normally opted for rhyming couplets. But Matarasso has "retained a semblance of assonance, while taking certain liberties". She renders the prose sections in elegant, modern English, but in the verse she has succumbed to the tendency to produce a distinctly archaic rendering. The first section, for example, begins: "Who would hear a goodly lay / Of a dotard old and grey / Parting fair young lovers twain". G.S. BURGESS, the most recent (1988) translator of this text, has adopted a different procedure, aiming to provide a more literal version of both prose and verse. This translation appears in a volume intended to cater for the needs of the scholarly rather than the general public and it is accompanied by an edition of the text by A.E. Cobby.

GLYN S. BURGESS

Further Reading

Burgess, Glyn S. and Anne E. Cobby, *The Pilgrimage of Charlemagne and Aucassin and Nicolette*, New York: Garland, 1988 (contains an introduction, bibliography and translation by G.S. Burgess and an edition by A.E. Cobby, pp. 93–116, 120–72).

Cobby, Anne E., *Ambivalent Conventions: Formula and Parody in Old French*, Amsterdam and Atlanta: Rodopi, 1995

Martin, June Hall, *Love's Fools: Aucassin, Troilus, Calisto and the Parody of the Courtly Lover*, London: Tamesis, 1972

Sargent-Baur, Barbara Nelson and Robert F. Cook, *Aucassin et Nicolete: A Critical Bibliography*. London: Grant and Cutler, 1981 (see especially pp. 34–37)

Ausonius c.AD 310–c.395

Roman poet

Biography

Decimus Magnus Ausonius was born in Burdigala (Bordeaux), and educated there and at Tolosa (Toulouse), Ausonius taught grammar and rhetoric at Burdigala for 30 years until he was appointed as tutor to the future emperor Gratian. He held various posts, including the prefecture of Gaul and the consulate, but after the murder of Gratian in 383 he retired to his native city. The literary merit of his many and varied poems is often slight, but they are of great historic interest, recording the author's wide experience, and they reflect the amiable personality of the author. The *Moselle* (*Mosella*), which has been called the first French poem, shows Ausonius at his best.

The Moselle

Mosella, c.371

Translations

Blakeney, E.H., *The Mosella* (parallel texts), London: Eyre and Spottiswoode, 1933

Brittain, Frederick, in *The Penguin Book of Latin Verse* (parallel text), Harmondsworth and Baltimore: Penguin, 1962, pp. 80–83

Evelyn-White, Hugh G., *Ausonius* (parallel texts), 2 vols, London: Heinemann, and Cambridge, Massachusetts: Harvard University Press, 1919 (Loeb Classical Library)

Flint, F.S., *The Mosella*, London: Spottiswoode, 1916

Isbell, Harold, in his *The Last Poets of Imperial Rome*, with an introduction, Harmondsworth and Baltimore: Penguin, 1971, pp. 52–64

Johnston, Sir Charles, in his *Rivers and Fireworks, including Evening Light on the Moselle as Described by Ausonius and The Demon by Michael Lermontov*, London: Bodley Head, 1980, p. 24

Lindsay, Jack, *Poems by Decimus Magnus Ausonius: Patchwork Quilt*, London: Fanfrolico Press, 1930; also in his *Song of a Falling World: Culture During the Break-up of the Roman Empire (AD 350–600)*, London: Andrew Dakers, 1948, pp. 78–82

The *Moselle*, written c.371 in praise of that river and the northeast Gaul countryside it flowed through, consists of 483 dactylic hexameters, rhetorical descriptive verse that yet shows a genuine feeling for nature quite unlike and superior to what one finds in most ancient compositions of this kind. No longer widely known yet charming and interesting, the *Moselle* fares best when the translator is imaginative and the translation relatively free.

FLINT (1916) provides a good prose translation, reliable and readable. EVELYN-WHITE (1919) performs an important service in translating all of Ausonius into English for the first time. However, although reliable and therefore useful to those interested in the period, his prose version lacks literary distinction. This is a pedestrian "trot" with some helpful notes.

LINDSAY's two very different translations (1930, 1948) display his versatility. Neither version of the *Moselle* is complete, and the excerpts are not identical. *Patchwork Quilt* contains a good selection of Ausonius's verse; so does *Song of a Falling World*, a monograph in which Lindsay manages to make a neglected period of Latin literature absorbingly interesting, for he has the novelist's gift for bringing to life the people and the period.

His earlier translation is dazzling in its choice and juxtaposition of words, while the later (also in free verse) sounds more consciously poetic (and therefore perhaps closer to Ausonius). On the whole, the 1930 translation is more interesting, especially because the meters Lindsay uses there somehow fit (although in no way approximate) the Latin, and reflect Ausonius' almost childlike delight in writing.

BLAKENEY's version (1933) appears to be the first complete translation of the *Moselle* into English verse. It is sound but somewhat pedantic. Since what is best about Ausonius' poem is the feeling it expresses rather than its poetic excellence, a stylistically humdrum translation like this one may in a way be appropriate, yet more creative efforts, such as Lindsay's, give better access to the spirit of Ausonius. Blakeney uses blank verse.

Although BRITTAIN's avowed aim is to provide "plain prose translations", in dealing with the excerpt of the *Moselle* he produces (1962) something plain indeed but quite readable.

ISBELL's (1971) is a good translation into free verse that gives some idea of the considerable charm of the original.

JOHNSTON's little book (1980) is an oddity, as is evident from its title. He translates only a brief extract from the *Moselle*, along with a few samples from Ausonius' other poems, but all are well done. These free verse translations seem based on Evelyn-White's prose but quite evidently Johnston has read the original too.

ZOJA PAVLOVSKIS-PETIT

Further Reading

See Lindsay's discussion of Ausonius in *Song of a Falling World*

B

Isaak Babel 1894–1940

Russian short-story writer and dramatist

Biography

Born Isaak Emmanuilovich Babel, in the ghetto of Odessa, Ukraine, 13 July 1894. His father was a Jewish tradesman. Babel went to the Nicholas I Commercial School in Odessa, 1905–11, and then to the Institute of Financial and Business Studies in Kiev and later in Saratov, graduating in 1915. He served in World War I from 1917 to 1918, fighting first for the Tsar and then, when the Revolution came, with the Bolsheviks. He lived in St Petersburg from 1918, working in journalism and publishing. In 1919 he married Evgeniia Gronfein, 1919 (one daughter); he also had a daughter by Antonina Pirozhkova. In 1920 he was a supply officer with S.M. Budenny's 1st Cavalry in Poland. He lived in Moscow from 1923. He was secretary of a village soviet at Molodenovo, 1930, but subsequently fell from official favour. In 1935 he visited Paris. In 1939, after being arrested, he disappeared. It is now known that he was executed 27 January 1940.

Stalin died in 1953 and Babel was rehabilitated in 1954. Babel's first stories had been published in 1916 in a monthly periodical edited by Gor'kii. His best-known works are the collections of stories *Konarmiia* (*Red Cavalry*), 1926, revised 1931, based on his own experiences in Poland, and *Odesskie rasskazy* (*Odessa Stories*), 1931. As well as his stories about Jewish life, war and revolution, Babel wrote plays: *Zakat* (*Sunset*), 1928, produced 1927, and *Mariia* (*Marya*), 1935, produced 1964.

Translations

Selections of Short Stories

Hayward, Max and Andrew R. MacAndrew, *The Lonely Years 1925–1939*, New York: Farrar Straus, 1964 (also contains letters by Babel); as *The Lonely Years, 1925–1939: Unpublished Stories and Private Correspondence*, Boston: Godine, 1995

Hayward, Max, *You Must Know Everything: Stories, 1915–1937*, edited by Nathalie Babel, New York: Farrar Straus, 1969

MacAndrew, Andrew R., *Lyubka the Cossack, and Other Stories*, New York: New American Library, 1963

McDuff, David, *Collected Stories*, Harmondsworth: Penguin, 1994

Morison, Walter, *The Collected Stories*, New York: Criterion, 1955

Yarmolinsky, Avrahm (editor), *Benya Krik the Gangster, and Other Stories*, New York: Schocken, 1948

Short Stories

Konarmiia, 1926; revised 1931

Helstein, Nadia, *Red Cavalry*, New York: Knopf, 1929

Plays

Zakat, 1928

Ginsburg, Mirra and Raymond Rosenthal, *Sunset* in *Noonday*, 3 (1960)

Senelick, Laurence, *Sundown* in *Russian Satiric Comedy: Six Plays*, edited and translated by Senelick, New York: Performing Arts Journal Publications, 1983

Mariia, 1935

Caslon, Denis, *Maria* in *Triquarterly*, 5 (1966)

Glenny, Michael and Harold Shukman, *Marya* in *Three Soviet Plays*, edited by Glenny, Harmondsworth and Baltimore: Penguin, 1966

Other Writing

Dnevnik, 1920

Willets, H.T., *1920 Diary*, with an introduction by Carol Avins, New Haven, Connecticut: Yale University Press, 1994

Benia Krik, 1926 (screenplay)

Montagu, Ivor and S.S. Nolbandov, *Benia Krik: A Film Novel*, London: Collett, 1935; reprinted Westport, Connecticut: Hyperion Press, 1973

Stroud, Nicholas, *The Forgotten Prose*, Ann Arbor, Michigan: Ardis, 1978

Isaak Babel's carefully wrought prose presents special challenges to the would-be translator. He agonized over the structure of sentences, the selection of individual words and even the placement of his punctuation marks; each choice was meaningful to Babel and too free an approach to his originals risks losing the sense of style that even appears as a subject in a couple of his works. At the same time the richly figurative narratives and the lively dialogues, often filled with dialect, rely heavily on peculiarities of the Russian language that are difficult to reproduce in English. Content is important for Babel, of course, but in his case the very quality of his writing is what distinguishes the tales from those of other writers and makes him a true master of the short form. Any successful translation has to convey the notion of stylistic virtuosity and at the same time remain as faithful as possible to the finer points of the original.

Babel tended to think of his stories in terms of cycles. While he planned several, only two were completed: *Red Cavalry*, containing more than 30 stories, and *Odessa Stories* (*Odesskie rasskazy*), with just four (although other tales are set in Odessa and are sometimes included under this heading in various Russian and English editions). Since *Red Cavalry* accounts for nearly half of his short stories, it is convenient to look at that collection separately and then at the rest of the stories as a group.

HELSTEIN (1929), the first to render *Red Cavalry* in English, makes a genuine effort to capture both the various voices in Babel's stories and the striking imagery; in individual cases, she succeeds nicely. And yet numerous sentences read quite awkwardly in English, while mistakes and omissions crop up all too frequently. Strangest of all is the decision to make several changes in the ordering of the stories; most notably, the first, "Crossing the Zbroutch [sic]", which provides an epic opening to the entire cycle, is inexplicably placed second.

MORISON (1955), rather than retranslating the *Red Cavalry* cycle for his collection, chooses to edit Helstein. He changes her unusual transliterations into a consistent and modern norm, corrects a few errors, and places the stories back into the order that Babel had intended. His greatest achievement is to improve the style to the point that the stories read quite well in English. He tends to work perhaps too hard to make the stories accessible to English readers; thus "Crossing the Zbruch" becomes "Crossing into Poland" (a translation imprecise geographically as well as linguistically) while the neologisms that characterize Sovietized Russian are often quietly eliminated (the expressive "Comdiv 6" in Helstein becomes the bland "Commander of the Sixth Division"). One senses that a lot of the editing was done directly from the English; most of the errors and omissions remain.

MACANDREW (1963) takes Helstein one stage further by ignoring Babel's ordering almost entirely. He regroups the stories thematically and omits several. The river in the first story become the "Zubrich", indicative of an occasional carelessness with details. The translations convey the sense of the original and generally seem quite accurate, but again it is possible to find phrases or sentences that are inexplicably omitted, and there is a tendency to add words in the English in order to clarify certain passages.

The most recent edition, by MCDUFF (1994), is also the most reliable. Personal and geographical names are correct for once, and he is alone in providing notes regarding some of the more obscure references in the stories as well as about textological variants in the Russian. The major jarring note occurs in some of the dialogues and first-person narratives, which sometimes fail to capture the liveliness and brilliance of the original. His insistence on accuracy can be taken to an extreme; thus he transliterates "nachdiv" from the Russian and provides a note; "Comdiv" might convey more to the native speaker of English.

A special note needs to be made of WILLETS's translation (1994) of Babel's diary; this contains the background material for many of the stories in *Red Cavalry*, and the translation reproduces faithfully the less formal (but equally noteworthy) style of these jottings. The valuable introduction and notes by Carol Avins help make this volume a significant resource.

The remaining stories have fared marginally better than those that comprise the *Red Cavalry* collection. MORISON (1955) proves to be a better translator than editor. Except, again, for a tendency to "translate" names and terms that are better left in the original, his versions of *The Odessa Stories* convey the flavor of the Jewish Odessa that Babel describes, and he is one of the few translators to limit the cycle to the four tales that Babel himself included. The translations of the semi-autobiographical childhood stories as well as of various late works contain a few small inaccuracies but are generally faithful. Under the label "Old Odessa" MACANDREW (1963) places some 14 stories, including some that have nothing whatsoever to do with that city. A similarly cavalier attitude can be found toward details; he will occasionally add words or fail to check a specific reference or name. None the less, the vigor of Babel's manner comes through with striking effect. MCDUFF offers an unusual selection of the other stories, omitting two or three well-known late works by Babel but also including several works not found in the other general collections. He once more offers reliability, at the occasional expense of fluency.

In the earliest of the more specialized collections YARMOLINSKY (1948) provides just 10 stories, mostly translated by the editor and all dealing with Jewish themes, taken from both cycles and also from the semi-autobiographical tales. His renditions are adequate but do not quite capture the rhythm of Babel's prose. HAYWARD & MACANDREW (1964) and HAYWARD (1969) both contain stories not previously available in English, along with other materials (primarily letters in the former case, journalism in the latter). The works in both collections, coming from either extreme of Babel's career, often lack the virtuosity of his best work, which helps explain a certain flatness in the English. The translations of the stories generally adhere closely to the originals and contain relatively few misreadings. STROUD (1978) renders a miscellany of early stories and journalistic pieces, concluding with excerpts from the *1920 Diary*. His versions exhibit an academic precision but do not always avoid lexical or syntactic awkwardness.

Babel's relatively descriptive screenplays contain only a minimum of dialogue; MONTAGU & NOLBANDOV (1935) cope well with the more straightforward passages, but their translation, "As They Did It in Odessa", for the title of the third reel, which bears the same name as the oft-translated Odessa story "How It Was Done in Odessa", is symptomatic of the clumsiness with which Babel's more idiomatic writing is rendered.

Translators have served Babel reasonably well in his plays, arguably better than in his stories. Both GINSBURG & ROSENTHAL (1960) on the one hand and SENELICK (1983) on the other have provided solid translations of his first play. If Senelick stays closer to an exact translation of the Russian, Ginsburg & Rosenthal occasionally arrive at the more felicitous phrasing in English. CASLON (1966) struggles at times to provide English equivalents for the elliptical Russian in Babel's second play, but GLENNY & SHUKMAN (1966) come up with a version that manages to remain faithful to the Russian while at the same time reading quite well in English. The example of the plays suggests that perhaps a team of translators will one day provide the ideal translations for the stories as well.

BARRY P. SCHERR

Further Reading

Carden, Patricia, *The Art of Isaac Babel*, Ithaca, New York: Cornell University Press, 1972
Falen, James E., *Isaac Babel: Russian Master of the Short Story*, Knoxville: University of Tennessee Press, 1974
Luplow, Carol, *Isaac Babel's Red Cavalry*, Ann Arbor, Michigan: Ardis, 1982
Rougle, Charles, *Red Cavalry: A Critical Companion*, Evanston, Illinois: Northwestern University Press, 1996
Sicher, Efraim, *Style and Structure in the Prose of Isaak Babel*, Columbus, Ohio: Slavica, 1986
Timmer, Charles B., "Translation and Censorship" in *Miscellanea Slavica: To Honour the Memory of Jan M. Meijer*, edited by B.J. Amsenga *et al.*, Amsterdam: Rodopi, 1983

Ingeborg Bachmann 1926–1973

Austrian poet, novelist, dramatist and short-story writer

Biography

Born 25 June 1926 in Klagenfurt, Austria, where she spent her childhood and attended local schools. She studied philosophy and psychology at Graz, Innsbruck and Vienna universities, gaining a doctorate in philosophy in 1950. She was influenced by Wittgenstein, also by Heidegger, the subject of her doctoral thesis.

Bachmann lived with the composer Hans Werner Henze, 1953–56, and the writer Max Frisch, 1958–62. After working as a radio script writer and editor in Vienna, 1951–53, she was a freelance writer in Ischia, Naples, Rome, and Munich, 1953–57, visiting the United States in 1955. The years 1958 to 1965 were divided between Rome, Zurich, West Berlin and Frankfurt, and from 1965 she lived in Rome.

Bachmann made her name with poetry in the 1950s: *Die gestundete Zeit* (*Time by the Hour*), 1953; *Anrufung des Grossen Bären* (*Invocation of the Great Bear*), 1956. She won the Gruppe 47 prize, 1953, and further awards, in Germany and Austria, after changing to prose. As well as plays for radio, novels, short stories, essays and translations, she wrote libretti for Henze, including *Prinz Friedrich von Homburg* (from Kleist's *Prince of Homburg*), 1960, and *Der junge Lord* (*The Young Milord*), 1965. Died in Rome 17 October 1973, in a fire.

Edition

Translations use the 1978 edition of Bachmann's collected works: *Werke*, edited by Christine Koschel, Inge von Weidenbaum and Clemens Münster, 4 vols, Munich: Piper, 1978

Translations

Poetry

Anderson, Mark, *In the Storm of Roses: Selected Poems*, Princeton, New Jersey: Princeton University Press, 1986
Filkins, Pater, *Songs in Flight: The Collected Poems of Ingeborg Bachmann*, with an introduction, New York: Marsilio, 1994

Radio Play

Der gute Gott von Manhattan, 1958
Wilding, Faith, *The Good God of Manhattan* in *German Radio Plays*, edited by Everett Frost and Margret Herzfeld Sander, New York: Continuum, 1991

Short Stories

Das dreissigste Jahr, 1961
Bullock, Michael, *The Thirtieth Year*, London: Deutsch, and New York: Knopf, 1964; Edinburgh: Polygon, 1993 (contains "Youth in an Austrian Town", "The Thirtieth Year", "Everything", "Among Murderers and Madmen", "A Step Towards Gomorrah", "A Wildermuth", "Undine Goes")

Novels

Malina: Roman, 1971
Boehm, Philip, *Malina: A Novel*, New York: Holmes and Meier, 1990

Der Fall Franza; Requiem für Fanny Goldmann, 1979
Filkins, Peter, *The Book of Franza, and Requiem for Fanny Goldmann*, with an introduction, Evanston, Illinois: Northwestern University Press, 1999

Ingeborg Bachmann is one of the few German-language authors who achieved prominence as a lyrical poet. Initially, in the 1950s, her published work involved two volumes of poetry, a few radio dramas, and libretti. But in the 1960s Bachmann gave up poetry for prose. As well as the creative work she wrote literary and philosophical essays, most notably on Ludwig

Wittgenstein, whose language philosophy greatly influenced Bachmann's vision of literature. Furthermore, Bachmann translated poems by Giuseppe Ungaretti from the Italian into German.

Bachmann's writing drew on the various discourses of post-1945 Western Europe, but also on the Austrian intellectual and literary tradition. Thus her work combines existentialism with language philosophy, typically modernist features with surrealism. Bachmann's poetry and prose thematize the horrors of World War II and the Holocaust and counter them with an utopian vision of a peaceful coexistence of different nations. This utopia is spin-off of the "felix Austria" myth, characteristic of the entire late 19th- and early 20th-century Austrian literature, especially of novels by Josef Roth and Robert Musil.

Because Bachmann throughout her work attended to issues of gender, wrote her later prose in a distinctly female voice, and insisted on the sources of violence in patriarchy, she is considered a forerunner of women's literature in the German speaking countries. Her writing helped to create and canonize feminist discourse within the entire German-language literature.

In contrast to the pattern of her career in German-speaking countries, Bachmann entered the English-language literary market as a prose writer. In Germany and Austria, Bachmann's gender shifted the reception of her writing towards a simplified and more autobiographical approach. A similar shift occurred in the English-language translations of Bachmann – they too show that the translators' knowledge of the author's gender had affected their translation work. The first book-translation of Bachmann into English is BULLOCK's *The Thirtieth Year* (1964), a volume of Bachmann's short stories. Bullock, one of the best and most productive translators of 20th-century German-language literature, renders Bachmann's stories in an accessible and fluent English prose. However, his translation shows clearly that his experience of translating male authors, among others Frisch, Dürrenmatt, and Lenz, as well as his understanding of what female authorship entails, have influenced his translation. Bullock converts Bachmann's discreet handling of female sexuality into explicit sexual references more typical of male authors or the later provocatively frank feminist writing. One of the most difficult features of Bachmann's discourse is her almost compulsive and very free use of intertextuality and allusions to literary and philosophical texts. In the story "A Step towards Gomorrah", often referred to as the female story of creation (see Bartsch), Bachmann plays on allusions to the Bible and to Nietzsche. Rather than quoting these texts, she rewrites them, offering an alternative to these artifacts of patriarchy. But Bullock's translation shifts the German source text. As a result, the English version reinstates the female-identified and female-oriented text into the patriarchal paradigm against which Bachmann is writing. Bullock's translations also efface Bachmann's attention to and preoccupation with language, her indebtedness to Wittgenstein and Kraus.

Bachmann's poetry came out in two English translations, by ANDERSON (1986) and by Filkins. Anderson's volume includes only selected poems by Bachmann. In choosing the poems, Anderson was guided by their translatability. Thus Anderson omits intricately rhymed poems, including the entire cycle "Von einem Land, einem Fluß und den Seen" from the volume *Invocation of the Great Bear*, and Bachmann's youth poems. Bachmann's poems in Anderson's translation do not always work as poems in English. However, as the result of Anderson's academic background, his rendering attends very closely to the language of Bachmann's poetry. This practice is entirely legitimate in the case of Bachmann, since her surrealist imagery often results from shifts on the linguistic plane.

FILKINS (1994) offers a complete translation of Bachmann's poetry. His translations are occasionally very free, and quite often more fluent than the source language poems. Filkins is faithful to Bachmann's meter, stanzaic form, rhyme, and lineation. While claiming to preserve the consistency of Bachmann's imagery and vocabulary, because of constraints of strophe and rhyme Filkins is frequently forced to chose between an image and its linguistic structure. Understandably, he often favors the image. In 1999 FILKINS's translation of Bachmann's *The Book of Franza, and Requiem for Fanny Goldmann* appeared.

In Germany and Austria, Bachmann's prose has suffered a complicated reception history. As a lyrical poet, together with Paul Celan, she quickly became a celebrity of the German 1950s literary market, and later was made into a cultural icon. When in the early 1960s she turned from writing poetry to prose, critics continuously rejected her prose as overtly lyrical, lacking social engagement, and therefore anachronistic. Especially her novel *Malina* (1971) came under scrutiny. Critics charged her with confessionality and insisted that she did not know how to write prose. One of the reasons for this negative reception is that as a lyrical novel, in the tradition of Rainer Maria Rilke and Jens Peter Jacobsen, *Malina* belongs to a late 19th-century genre no longer canonical in Germany, and never canonized in the United States.

BOEHM's 1990 translation of *Malina* produces a smooth, easily readable text, and therefore not at all a faithful rendering of the original. He effaces much of Bachmann's lyrical diction, the musical structure of the narrative, and Bachmann's reliance on repetition and transformation. Bachmann's feminist narrative in *Malina* is structured as a tightly woven net of repetitions, ruptures and displacements. But Boehm's concern for good style disrupts these features of her discourse and dilutes the key element of Bachmann's feminist aesthetics, metonymy and displacement. His translation weakens the novel's feminist proposition and silences Bachmann's critique of patriarchy.

EWA SIWAK

Further Reading

Achberger, Karen R., *Understanding Ingeborg Bachmann*, Columbia: University of South Carolina Press, 1995

Bartsch, Kurt, *Ingeborg Bachmann*, Stuttgart: Metzler, 1988

Bjorklund, Beth, "Ingeborg Bachmann" in *Major Figures of Modern Austrian Literature*, edited by Donald G. Daviau, Riverside, California: Ariadne Press, 1988, pp. 49–82

Modern Austrian Literature, 18/3–4 (1985): special Ingeborg Bachmann issue

Bai Juyi (Po Chu-i) 772–846

Chinese poet

Biography

Born in Xinzheng, Henan province, the son of a minor functionary. Bai Juyi was China's first popular and "professional" official-turned-poet. As a child prodigy, he mastered the rules of rhyming and prosody between the ages of five and six, but because he had to struggle against poverty his career started relatively late and he did not become an "Advanced Scholar" until he was nearly 30. Another poet, Yuan Zhen (779–831), soon became his lifelong friend. Over the years the two exchanged hundreds of poems. As an official, Bai Juyi did not achieve an eminence equal to that of his friend. Bai Juyi served for some periods at the imperial court, but at other times, owing to his honesty and outspokenness, he was exiled to administrative posts in outlying districts, where he invariably won the respect and affection of the people, whose sufferings under oppression he brought, in his poems, to the attention of the powerful. Bai Juyi's time in public service coincided with an era of great political instability and social upheaval in China, comparable only to the turmoil and chaos following the end of the Han dynasty in AD 220, though of shorter duration. During the poet's lifetime eight different emperors sat on the throne, some of them dying unnatural deaths, in their prime, after only a few years' reign.

The most prolific of writers up to his time, Bai Juyi created an oeuvre consisting of more than 3600 titles, both poetry and prose of various types. In a famous letter to Yuan Zhen, dated December 815, Bai Juyi states some of his strongest views about poetry. He believes that its highest function is "to save the world", its second "to perfect one's own character". He classifies the first two divisions of his own works under the general title of "satirical and allegorical" poems, which he valued the most, and "contemplative" poems, or poems of "quiet contentment". The third and fourth categories in his classification, by style and by content, are "elegiac or lyrical pieces as inspired by events" and "miscellaneous poems written according to strict rules of tone-pattern". The highest kind of poetry must strive to combine passionate ideals with plain speech. Plain diction is an unmistakable characteristic of Bai Juyi's style. He once boasted that his poems could be understood by any old woman from the country. While moral passion and Confucian stoicism exert the strongest influence on Bai Juyi's poetry of political and social criticism, his mind is always receptive to the other great religious traditions of China – to philosophical Taoism and to Buddhism (particularly the doctrines of the Zen school of meditation). He and his wife were converted to Buddhism in the summer of 834. He retired from public office in 842. Died at Laoyang in 846.

Edition

Ku Hsueh-chieh (editor), *Po Chu-i chi*, 4 vols, Beijing: Zhonghua, 1979

Translations

Selection

Alley, Rewi, *Bai Juyi: 200 Selected Poems*, Beijing: New World Press, 1983

Anthologies

Bynner, Witter, *The Jade Mountain: A Chinese Anthology: 300 Poems of the T'ang Dynasty*, New York: Knopf, 1929

Cranmer-Byng, L., *A Lute of Jade: Selections from the Classical Poets of China*, with an introduction, London: John Murray, 1909; New York: Dutton, 1911

Levy, Dore J., *Chinese Narrative Poetry: The Late Han Through T'ang Dynasties*, Durham: Duke University Press, 1988

Levy, Howard S., *Lament Everlasting: Translations and Essays*, Tokyo, 1962

Levy, Howard S. (vols 1–2) and H.W. Wells (vols 3–4), *Translations from Po Chu-i's Collected Works*, 4 vols, New York: Paragon, and San Francisco: Chinese Materials Center (vol. 4), 1971–78

Liu, Wu-chi and Irving Yucheng Lo (editors), *Sunflower Splendor: Three Thousand Years of Chinese Poetry*, Bloomington: Indiana University Press, 1975 (18 items)

Payne, Robert, *The White Pony: An Anthology of Chinese Poetry*, New York: Day, 1947; London: Allen and Unwin, 1949

Turner, John A., *A Golden Treasury of Chinese Poetry* (bilingual edition), edited by John J. Deeney, Hong Kong: Chinese University of Hong Kong, 1976

Waley, Arthur, *One Hundred and Seventy Chinese Poems*, London: Constable, 1918; 2nd edition, with an introduction, 1962 (59 items from earlier collections)

Waley, Arthur, *Translations from the Chinese*, New York: Knopf, 1919 (more than 100 titles by Bai Juyi in this anthology of 180 poems)

Waley, Arthur, in *Madly Singing in the Mountains: An Appreciation and Anthology of Arthur Waley*, edited by Ivan Morris, London: Allen and Unwin, and New York: Walker, 1970

Bai Juyi (in the Wade–Giles system of romanization: Po Chu-i) was a reformer-poet of the middle of the T'ang dynasty (616–907) who became probably China's best-known poet abroad. His fame reached into Korea and Japan even during his lifetime, and his works, over a millennium later, won him a large audience in the English-speaking world, thanks largely to the translations of Arthur Waley. In an introduction to the 1962 edition of his *170 Chinese Poems*, WALEY admitted that he had translated 10 times more poems by Bai Juyi than by any other Chinese poet only because Bai was "the most translatable" of all major Chinese poets. It is therefore easy to understand why this least allusive, plain-speaking, popular poet of China came to be the most celebrated abroad, at least in the English-speaking world. An index to the English translations of the works of 25 T'ang poets (Fung and Lai, 1984) devotes more than 100 pages to listing all translations by title and first-line, and cites their appearance in books, journals, and anthologies. According to their tabulation, Bai Juyi had 1,192 poems (items numbered 1,175–2,367) translated into English, as compared with only 685 for Du Fu, China's greatest poet, and 277 for Li Bai. If we include the translations published since 1984, this number could easily exceed 1200 – a number almost twice that for Du Fu and four times that for Li Bai. Rather, therefore, than trying to evaluate all the translations, we shall note the more significant contributions, or departures, among them.

WALEY's success as a distinguished translator of classical Chinese poetry is attributable to several causes, but chiefly to his erudition. His scholarship embraced the entire range of Asian tradition, including the Japanese; his command of Chinese literature spanned four millennia. His scholarship informed, guided, and enriched all his translations.

For classical Chinese poetry, in particular, Waley's success stems from a clear-cut goal he set for himself and his masterly and resolute way of achieving it. To begin with, he decided to avoid all the "untranslatables", which, naturally, include "rhyme". Rhyme occurred in Chinese poetry as early as the time of compilation of the *Songs* or *Odes*, which tradition says Confucius collected, and it continued to be used down the ages by all the poets, adhering to various kinds of restrictions depending on genre-differentiation. Later poets relied, too, on the use of a rhyme-dictionary which served as an official code to govern such uses, and it was rigidly followed, despite changes in linguistic habits from one century to the next or from one region to another. It would be quite impossible, therefore, to insist that any of the rhyme-patterns (of which there are many) in a Chinese poem must be reproduced by some sort of rhyming in English.

Then, the prosodic considerations in a Chinese poem must somehow be compensated for, if not reproduced, in a translation. In the Chinese original, the rhythm in a given line is dependent on the alternation between syllables, each unit distiguished by a different "tone" quality (whether "even" or "deflected"). English, on the other hand, is an accented language. To solve this problem, Waley adopted the "sprung rhythm" principle from the poetry of Gerard Manley Hopkins – or, it could also be said, from *Beowulf* and Anglo-Saxon poetry. In other words, he tried to have the number of stressed syllables per English line equal to the number of syllables in a Chinese line (which usually could be either five or seven), disregarding the number of unstressed syllables in between. Therefore, by taking full advantage of this breakthrough, a line in a Waley translation of Bai Juyi could be as long as "Let me with these last-left flowers in my hand come to you and have you for my guide", or as short as the opening line from the same poem: "To-day the scarlet peonies that grow in front of my steps", when both originals are heptasyllabic lines (from an early poem, "Written upon Being Moved by the Sight of Peonies").

But aside from rhyme and rhythm, the core of a poem is always the imagery, and it is to the images that Waley devotes his entire attention. But even here, sometimes as a result of differences in cultural and/or linguistic patterns of behavior, some audacious originality is called for in order to find the *mot juste* in one language as a substitute in another. For example, in the Bai Juyi poem already cited, one notes Waley's use of "last-left" to describe "flowers", which is his clever way of translating *can*, a word that means "residual" or "what remains". The same word *can* occurs in another poem, in the very common expression *canbei*, or "the left-over wine in a cup". But it receives a different treatment from Waley this time, since the entire line of seven syllables contains other kinds of challenges. The line literally translates as: "again-urge (to drink)-residual-cup-watch-sun-shadow" (*geng quan canbei kan riyin*). Now this line comes out in Waley as: "Drink at least what is left in your cups; I am watching the shadow grow." By making the person watching the sunset not the addressee of the poem but the poet himself, Waley has removed "the sun" from the line and made the line even more lyrical.

The same genius is at work when Waley translates the line "floating-life-the same as-passing-guest" (*fusheng tong guoke*) as "Life, like a passing stranger, comes and goes its way ..." (Waley, 1970), or "ruddy-cheeks-fade-not-stop" (*hongyen xiao bu xie*) as "The flush of youth will not cease to fade" (*ibid.*). But philosophical ideas can create more problems for a translator than cultural terminology. For example, two lines from another poem addressed to Bai's friend, Mr Li, are heavily laden with Taoist thought, the literal translation of which would be: entrust-shape-old-small-beyond / forget-heart's thought-life-death-midst (*wei xing laoxiao wai / wang huai shengsi jian*). But Waley's translation reads: "I have schooled my body to forget if it is young or old, / My heart to feel the same about life and death" (*ibid.*). Waley's solution is vastly superior to that of Howard S. LEVY (1971–78, vol. 1). Levy's translation reads: "I entrust myself beyond youth and old age, forget to have cherishings between life and death". Who can penetrate the mystery of what is meant by Levy's "cherishings between life and death"? On the other hand, Waley's disregard of the literal, when it happens (though rarely), may be seen as deliberate and even inspired. In a long poem written upon a visit to the Wuzhen ("Aware-of-the-Truth") Monastery – entitled by Waley "The Temple" – there occurs this marvelous line: "I peered down but could not see the dead" (1918), when the original says only: "*bujianren*", or "no one is seen". The closing passage of the same poem, where Bai Juyi expressed his desire never to return to an official's life, contains the following superb image, as translated by Waley: "Like a captive fish loosed into the Great Sea / To my marble basin I shall not ever return." These two lines read in Chinese: *chiyu fang ru hai / yi wang heshi huan*, or "Fish from the pond loosed into the sea / Once on their way, when will they ever return?". One notes that in the Chinese poem there is no mention of a marble basin or any trace of the dead. Nevertheless, such passages from Waley will be read with awe, admiration, and gratitude.

Two of Bai Juyi's poems, which he himself did not value highly, deserve a special mention. Both were popular in his own time and one of them also inspired a large body of literature in its wake. These are the two long narrative poems, the "Song of Everlasting Sorrow", "Chang hen ge" or "Ch'ang-hen ko" (sometimes translated as "Song of Eternal Remorse/Regret"), written in 806 or soon thereafter, and "Pipa xing" or "Pipa yin", or "The Ballad of the *Pipa*," sometimes translated as "Song of the Lute", or "The Lute Girl", composed in 816 – *pipa* being the name of a musical instrument generally known as the "balloon-guitar" in English. Both poems employ the seven-syllable line, and the first is 120 lines long, the second much shorter with 88 lines. Both heavily anthologized, each of them has scores of English translations, as many as 20 for "Chang hen ge".

Written only about 50 years after the events it purports to narrate, the "Song of Everlasting Sorrow" tells the story of the love of Emperor Xuanzong (684–762; reigned 715–56) for his favorite consort Yang Guifei (718–756) before, during, and after the An Lushan Rebellion. The only historically accurate fact represented in the poem is the elevation of a court lady, who became the most powerful person in Chang'an, by an old, doting emperor more than twice her age. In Bai Juyi's ballad, the central event was a coup during the An Lushan Rebellion, staged by the imperial guards, who demanded the death of the king's consort; and, accordingly, she was strangled in front of the emperor. With Consort Yang cast as a *femme fatale* and the cause of the empire's collapse, Bai Juyi devotes the entire first section of the first half to describing the splendor of the court and a pleasure-seeking monarch's infatuation with a "voluptuous" (*yen*) beauty. This section ends abruptly with the movement of the troops, and the second section tells of the unseemly death of the young, beautiful imperial consort at the roadside station of Mawei. Then follows a languid tale about the emperor's loneliness, in exile in Sichuan and after his return to a despoiled palace, mercilessly deprived of the companionship of his beloved. The song then goes on to its grand denouement of the second part, which describes the emperor's attempt to seek a meeting with his deceased spouse, with the aid of some Daoist priests acting as mediums. At such a meeting, which takes place at a magic island, between an "etherealized" ("immortalized"?) consort and the emperor's emissaries, the famed beauty recalls vows and gifts of love that she had exchanged with the emperor in the human world. And the song closes with this well-known couplet: "Heaven is eternal, earth endures, and yet someday they will end, / But this sorrow, ever self-renewing, sees no date of its surcease" (my translation). By "transform[ing] the story of the emperor and his favorite concubine from the most foolhardy intrigue of the century" into a love story, Bai Juyi has created "a legend of transcendent love" (Dore J. Levy, 1988).

While the "Song of Everlasting Sorrow" employs third-person narrative and the omniscient point-of-view, the "Song of the Pipa" is intensely lyrical, with the first-person narrator remaining in control of the action throughout. Written when Bai Juyi was serving as marshal in exile in Chiang-chou, the poem tells of the poet's chance encounter with a courtesan who is an expert player of the *pipa*. With this occasion serving as a framework, the poem immediately plunges into a minute description of her music that evening. After this opening section, Bai Juyi tells the story of the woman musician's sad life, beginning with her early days as a prize student in the Imperial Music Academy until the present, when all of her former lovers and her merchant husband have gone away, leaving her languishing and alone on a riverboat. The poet, already overwhelmed by her expert playing, is now rendered speechless and dumbfounded by her tale of woe. The concluding section returns to the narrator who, as an exiled official, suddenly realizes that, in his isolation and reduced circumstances, he has a special bond with the musician. "We are both lost wanderers at the ends of the earth; / Meeting here, what need have we to have known each other before?" (translation by Dore J. Levy, 1988) – the poet asks at a crucial break in the story. The realization of their affinity thus becomes the poem's "emotional center", according to Dore Levy, who hails Bai Juyi's ballad as "a narrative of the creation of the poem itself".

Translations of these two ballads differ quite widely, not so much in intent and in interpretation as in artistry. Perhaps the happiest overall effect is achieved by Dore J. LEVY. For example, a lyrical couplet from the "Song of Everlasting Sorrow", describing the consort's appearance as she was first startled awake to face the newly arrived messenger from the emperor from the other world, is translated by her as follows: "On her jade face from loneliness the tears trickled down, / Like pear blossoms on a branch when the spring brings down the rain." The original reads: *yurong jimo lei langan / lihua yizhi chun dai yu* (literally, jade-countenance forlorn tears balustrade / pear-blossom one branch springtime carrying rain). The earliest English translation of this poem is the one appearing in 1909, by L. CRANMER-BYNG, in *A Lute of Jade*: " ... her face is fixed and calm, / Though many tear-drops on an almond bough / Fall, and recall the rains of spring." A more smooth translation appearing in 1929, in *The Jade Mountain*, is Witter BYNNER's version: "And the tear-drops drifting down her sad white face / Were like a rain in spring on the blossom of the pear." Far less successful is Robert PAYNE's, in *The White Pony*, 1947: "Her pure face sorrowing, slowly the tears falling — / O branch of pear blossom in the spring rain!" Here is Howard S. LEVY's version, in three lines: "Her jade countenance by the balustrade, / Mournful and tear-stained; / A dew-filled pear blossom in the spring rain" (*Lament Everlasting*, 1962). John TURNER, in 1976, renders this passage as: "Her woeful countenance all streaked with tears, / —A sprig of blossom drenched with springtime dew." In 1983, Rewi ALLEY re-translates these two lines as: " ... With so much sadness, / her eyes filled with tears, and her face seemed like / A branchful of pear blossoms in the spring rain." There has been so much re-translation from Chinese poetry into English of what is only too familiar that all such efforts seem like exercises in futility; it is immensely refreshing, though, to come upon good translations.

IRVING YUCHENG LO

Further Reading

Fung, S.K. and S.T. Lai, *25 T'ang Poets*, Hong Kong: Chinese University Press, 1984

Levy, Dore J., *Chinese Narrative Poetry: The Late Han through T'ang Dynasties*, Durham, North Carolina: Duke University Press, 1988

Nienhauser, William H., Jr, "Po Chu-i Studies in English, 1916–1992", *Asian Culture*, 22/3 (1994) pp. 37–50

Palandri, Angela C.Y. Jung, *Yuan Chen*, Boston: Twayne, 1977

Pulleyblank, Edwin G., *The Background of the Rebellion of An Lu-shan*, London and New York: Oxford University Press, 1955

Waley, Arthur, *The Life and Times of Po Chu-i*, London: Allen and Unwin, 1949

Watson, Burton (translator), *Po Chü-i: Selected Poems*, New York: Columbia University Press, 2000

Honoré de Balzac 1799–1850

French novelist

Biography

Balzac (he added the noble *de* himself) was born in Tours, 20 May 1799. His father was a civil servant, working in army supplies. Honoré was sent from an early age to boarding schools in Tours, Vendôme and Paris. He then worked in a lawyer's office and attended law lectures at the Sorbonne. In 1819, with an allowance from his parents, he turned to a literary career, living in poverty, completing a tragedy and a number of pseudonymous novels with sensational plots, as well as leaving unfinished various essays and novels of a more serious nature. He then went into publishing and printing on his own account, but the ventures failed, leaving him deep in debt. He turned to journalism. In 1829 his historical novel *Les Chouans* (*The Chouans*) was published; in 1831 he had his first major success with *La Peau de Chagrin* (*The Wild Ass's Skin*). Balzac's was a life of prodigious energy and effort, devoted to creating works of literature (some 90 fiction titles united from 1842 to 1848 under the title *La Comédie humaine* (*The Human Comedy*), plus half a dozen plays), paying his debts, living high, and keeping up his many friendships and affairs with women. In 1850, after a correspondence and liaison stretching over many years, he married a widowed Russian countess, Madame Eve Hanska. He died in Paris, 18 August 1850.

The Human Comedy depicts French society, from the time of the 1789 Revolution to the end of the July Monarchy in 1848, through a wide range of characters, about 2,000 in number, some of them recurring after their first appearance. These personages are observed in the social and historical circumstances that mould their personalities and lead to their passion-driven and money-steered actions. From the last quarter of the 19th century, Balzac's fiction has been much translated into English in the UK and the US. There have been several collections (Saintsbury's the best-known), many selections and a stream of single works – novels and stories – from the *Human Comedy*. The best known in English of his vastly influential novels are *Le Père Goriot* (*Old Goriot*), *Eugénie Grandet* (*Eugénie Grandet*) and *La Cousine Bette* (*Cousin Bette*).

Translations

Collections (from *La Comédie humaine*)

Ives, G.B. *et al.*, *The Human Comedy, Now for the First Time Completely Translated into English*, 53 vols, Philadelphia: Barrie, and London: Caxton Press, 1895–1900 (This subscription edition includes a translation of the *Contes drolatiques*, by G.J. Murdoch. The first 11 volumes (*Scènes de la vie parisienne*) were published in a limited edition in London in 1895–96 by H.S. Nichols and, in a limited edition of 22 vols, in 1897–99 by Leonard Smithers.)

Saintsbury, George (editor), *The Human Comedy*, translated by Clara Bell, Ellen Marriage, James Waring and R.S. Scott, 40 vols, London: Dent, 1895–99 (omits *Physiologie du mariage*, *Sarrasine*, *La Fille aux yeux d'or*, *Une Passion dans le désert* and *Petites misères de la vie conjugale*)

Wormeley, Katharine Prescott, *The Comedy of Human Life*, 40 vols, Boston: Roberts, 1896 (A reissue of an edition that had begun publication in 1885. The first 12 volumes (containing translations of *La Recherche de l'absolu* [The Alkahest], *Les Employés*, *César Birotteau*, *Le Médecin de campagne*, *Le Cousin Pons*, *La Duchesse de Langeais*, etc., *Eugénie Grandet*, *La Peau de chagrin*, *Modeste Mignon*, *Le Père Goriot*, *Les Paysans*, *La Rabouilleuse* [The Two Brothers]) were published in England under the title *Balzac's Novels in English* (London and New York: Routledge, 1886–91). The complete edition, which does not in fact contain the entire *Human Comedy*, was never published in England. Augmented by two volumes translated by G.B. Ives for the Barrie edition (see Ives, above), Wormeley's version also went to make up the Centenary Edition (Boston: Little Brown, 1899).)

Novels (from *La Comédie humaine*)

Le Dernier Chouan, 1829; revised as *Les Chouans*, 1834

Crawford, Marion Ayton, *The Chouans*, Harmondsworth: Penguin, 1978

Saintsbury, George, *The Chouans*, London: J.C. Nimmo, 1890

Physiologie du mariage, 1829

Anonymous, *The Physiology of Marriage*, London: privately printed, 1904

Macnamara, Francis, *The Physiology of Marriage*, London: Casanova Society, 1925

See also *Petites misères de la vie conjugale*, 1846

La Peau de chagrin, 1831

Hunt, Herbert J., *The Wild Ass's Skin*, Harmondsworth: Penguin, 1977

Paul, Cedar, *The Fatal Skin*, London: Hamish Hamilton, 1948

Le Curé de Tours, 1832

Mitford, D., *The Vicar of Tours*, with *Pierre Grassou*, London: Euphorion Press, 1950

Eugénie Grandet, 1833

Anonymous, *Eugénie Grandet*, London and New York: Routledge Warne and Routledge, 1859

Crawford, Marion Ayton, *Eugénie Grandet*, Harmondsworth: Penguin, 1955

Raphael, Sylvia, *Eugénie Grandet*, with an introduction by Christopher Prendergast, Oxford and New York: Oxford University Press, 1990

See entry on *Eugénie Grandet*, below

La Duchesse de Langeais, 1834 (part of *Histoire des Treize*, 1835)

Mitford, D., *The Duchesse de Langeais*, London: Euphorion Press, 1949

Ferragus, 1834 (part of *Histoire des Treize*, 1835)

Knutsford, Lady, *The Mystery of the rue Soly*, London: Edward Arnold, 1894

La Recherche de l'absolu, 1834

Robson, William, *Balthazar; or, Science and Love*, London and New York: Routledge Warne and Routledge, 1859

La Fille aux yeux d'or, 1835 (part of *Histoire des Treize*, 1835)
Dowson, Ernest, *The Girl with the Golden Eyes*, London: L. Smithers, 1896

Histoire des treize, 1835
Hunt, Herbert J., *History of the Thirteen*, Harmondsworth: Penguin, 1974

Le Père Goriot, 1835
Anonymous, *Daddy Goriot; or Unrequited Affection*, London: Ward and Lock, 1860
Crawford, Marion Ayton, *Old Goriot*, with an introduction, Harmondsworth and Baltimore: Penguin, 1951
Krailsheimer, A.J., *Père Goriot*, Oxford and New York: Oxford University Press, 1991
Reed, Henry, *Père Goriot*, New York: New American Library, 1962
See entry on *Père Goriot*, below

Le Lys dans la vallée, 1836
Hill, Lucienne, *The Lily in the Valley*, London: Elek, and New York: Citadel Press, 1957

Illusions perdues, 1837–43
Hunt, Herbert J., *Lost Illusions*, Harmondsworth: Penguin, 1971
Raine, Kathleen, *Lost Illusions*, London: Hamish Hamilton, 1951

Histoire de la grandeur et de la décadence de César Birotteau, 1838
Buss, Robin, *César Birotteau*, Harmondsworth: Penguin, 1994
Frenaye, Frances, *César Birotteau*, London: Elek, 1956
Simpson, John Hawkins, *History of the Grandeur and Downfall of César Birotteau*, London: Saunders Otley, 1860

Splendeurs et misères des courtisanes, 1838–47
Heppenstall, Rayner, *A Harlot High and Low*, Harmondsworth: Penguin, 1970

Béatrix, 1839–44
Harcourt-Smith, Rosamond and Simon Harcourt-Smith, *Beatrix: Love in Duress*, London: Elek, and New York: Citadel Press, 1957

Pierre Grassou, 1840
Mitford, D., *Pierre Grassou*, with *The Vicar of Tours*, London: Euphorion Press, 1950

Une ténébreuse affaire, 1842
Hopkins, Gerard, *The Gondreville Mystery*, London: Elek, and New York: Citadel Press, 1953
Hunt, Herbert J., *A Murky Business*, Harmondsworth: Penguin, 1972

Ursule Mirouët, 1842
Adamson, Donald, *Ursule Mirouët*, Harmondsworth: Penguin, 1976

La Rabouilleuse, 1843
Adamson, Donald, *The Black Sheep*, Harmondsworth: Penguin, 1970
Frenaye, Frances, *The Bachelor's House*, New York: Criterion Books, 1956
Wilkins, Eithne, *A Bachelor's Establishment*, London: Weidenfeld and Nicolson, 1951; New York: Farrar Straus and Young, 1952

La Cousine Bette, 1847; in serial form 1846
Crawford, Marion Ayton, *Cousin Bette*, Harmondsworth and New York: Penguin, 1965
Raine, Kathleen, *Cousin Bette*, London: Hamish Hamilton, 1948; New York: Modern Library, 1958
Raphael, Sylvia, *Cousin Bette*, with an introduction by David Bellos, Oxford and New York: Oxford University Press, 1992
See entry on *Cousin Bette*, below

Petites misères de la vie conjugale, 1846
Tickell, Geoffrey, *Conjugal Life: Pinpricks of Married Life* (with *The Physiology of Marriage*, translation anonymous, selected and edited by Derek Stanford), London: Neville Spearman, and Westport, Connecticut: Associated Booksellers, 1957

Le Cousin Pons, 1847
Cameron, Norman, *Cousin Pons*, London: Hamish Hamilton, 1950
Hunt, Herbert J., *Cousin Pons*, Harmondsworth: Penguin, 1968
Kent, Philip, *Cousin Pons*, London: Simpkin Marshall, 1880

Selections of Short Stories
Crawford, Marion Ayton, *Domestic Peace and Other Stories*, Harmondsworth: Penguin, 1958
Kent, Philip, *The Cat and Battledore and Other Tales*, 3 vols, London: Sampson Low, 1879
Raphael, Sylvia, *Selected Short Stories*, Harmondsworth: Penguin, 1977
Walker, H.H., *The "Comédie humaine" and Its Author*, with translations from the French, London: Chatto and Windus, 1879; new edition 1881 (contains "The Purse", "Gaudissart II; or, The Selim Shawl", and *Albert Savarus*)
Wilson, William and the Count Stenbock, *Shorter Stories from Balzac*, London: Walter Scott, 1890

Short Stories
Contes drolatiques, 1832–37
Anonymous, *Droll Stories*, New York: Random House, 1948
Anonymous, *Droll Stories from the Abbeys of Touraine*, London: Comyns, 1952
Brown, Alex, *Droll Stories Collected in the Monasteries of Touraine*, London: Elek, 1958; London: Folio Society, 1961
Crawford, Robert, *Nine Tales from the "Contes drolatiques"*, London: T. Werner Laurie for private circulation, 1921
Le Clercq, Jacques, *Droll Stories*, New York: Heritage Press, 1939
Lignolles, André de, *Selections from the Droll Stories*, London: Bourbon Press, 1948
May, J. Lewis, *Ten Droll Tales*, London: John Lane, 1926
Plummer, J. *et al.*, *The Devil's Heir, and Other Tales from "Les Contes drolatiques"*, London: John Westhouse, 1945
Sims, George R., *Contes drolatiques: Droll Stories Collected from the Abbeys of Touraine*, London: Chatto and Windus, 1874
Whittling, R., *Droll Stories Collected from the Abbeys of Touraine*, London: Mathieson, 1896

Plays
La Marâtre, 1848
Saunders, Edith, *The Stepmother*, London: Wingate, 1958

Mercadet, 1851
Lawrence, Slingsby [i.e. G.H. Lewes], *The Game of Speculation*, London: Lacy, 1852 (Lacy's Acting Edition, vol. 5)

The translation of Honoré de Balzac's novels into English was slow to take place, their perceived immorality being thought to render them unsuitable for Victorian readers. As early as 1832, his work was being castigated in England for its "obscenity", and "impiety". In a celebrated article which appeared in the *Quarterly Review* in April 1836, John Wilson Croker singled Balzac out as the chief culprit in his attack on the immorality of the whole of contemporary French literature: "... a baser, meaner, filthier scoundrel never polluted society ... English ears would not bear an unreserved repetition of the prurient lessons of M. de Balsac [sic]". There was general agreement that only *Eugénie Grandet*, *Le Curé de Tours*, *Le Médecin de campagne* and certain of the early short stories could safely be placed in female hands.

In 1859 Wilkie Collins, in an article often wrongly attributed to Charles Dickens, said of Balzac's reputation in England: "he is little known because he is little translated." Although there had been more translations than Collins was aware of, the assertion was essentially true. England was certainly behind America, where, for example, a translation of *Eugénie Grandet* (1833) appeared as early as 1843. It is, however, impossible to compile a definitive list of 19th-century translations. Some that are known to have existed appeared in an ephemeral format and have disappeared without trace. There are likely to have been others. The existence of at least some translations mentioned by contemporary observers remains open to question. Collins himself could not be sure that his memory of an early translation of *La Peau de chagrin* was not an invention.

The first recorded English translation in volume form, a mediocre version of the *Scenes from Parisian Life, First Series* (1834–35) by "the translator of the *Recollections of the marquise de Créquy*", was published as early as 1834, but in Paris. In addition, during the 1830s, translations and adaptations of several of Balzac's stories, beginning with *La Grande Bretèche* (1832), appeared in the periodical press. These versions often left much to be desired. *Le Père Goriot* was reduced by *Blackwood's Magazine* to a five-page summary that succeeded in omitting all reference to the original author. A similarly cavalier attitude to literary property on the part of magazine editors was displayed in abridgements of *Gobseck* and *Maître Cornélius*. As for *Les Maraña* (1834), this minor, but usefully short, work is said to have given rise to no fewer than three separate English versions in the 1840s. In 1842 it was included as a penny-issue novel in *The Romancist and Novelist's Library*; in his introduction, W.T. Hazlitt (son of William and translator of Vigny's *Cinq-Mars*) referred to one or two previous translations of Balzac and expressed the desire to see the novelist's entire output translated and made available in an affordable format. A translation of *Un Épisode sous la Terreur* appeared in the *Monthly Chronicle* in 1841. In 1846, an adaptation of *Le Bal de Sceaux* was published in *Fraser's Magazine*.

The most successful translation (or adaptation) of a work by Balzac in this period was, however, not of a novel at all, but of his play *Mercadet* (*The Game of Speculation*). Translated by G.H. LEWES, using the pseudonym "Slingsby LAWRENCE", it was staged in 1852, to much acclaim, at the Lyceum Theatre in London. This, in spite of the fact that Lewes had earlier considered Balzac to be "a very dangerous writer".

Collins recognized the difficulty of translating Balzac, a difficulty said to be "caused by his own peculiarities of style and treatment". He warned that:

> [a] special man, not harried for time, and not easily brought to the end of his patience, might give the English equivalent of Balzac with admirable effect. But ordinary translating of him by average workmen would only lead through the means of feeble parody, to utter failure.

The difficulties were often more specific. Thirty-five years later, Saintsbury felt moved to "bespeak an unusual indulgence for the translator [Clara BELL] in regard to the technicalities" of French bankruptcy law in *César Birotteau*.

Contemporaneous with Collins's 1859 article was the first English (as opposed to American) translation of *Eugénie Grandet*. Collins, who had seen this translation announced, called for it to be accompanied by English versions of *La Recherche de l'absolu* and *Le Père Goriot*. These were duly forthcoming (under the titles *Balthazar; or, Science and Love* and *Daddy Goriot; or, Unrequited Affection*), along with versions of *César Birotteau* and, it would seem, one further novel. The publishers used extracts from Collins's article to publicize and justify their venture. When, in 1863 he came to collect his essay in volume form, Collins lamented the fact that the translations of *Le Père Goriot* and *La Recherche de l'absolu*, at least, clearly bore out his strictures concerning the translation of Balzac by "average workmen". He pronounced these two attempts to be unworthy of "critical remonstrance", and warned his reader that "the experiment of rendering the French of Balzac into its fair English equivalent still remains to be tried".

The perceived difficulty of the task seems to have been responsible for the relative paucity of translations over the following 25 years. Philip KENT translated *Le Cousin Pons* and three volumes of early short stories, *The Cat and Battledore* (*La Maison du chat-qui-pelote*) *and Other Tales*. Other works that may have been translated at this time include *Le Médecin de campagne*, *La Duchesse de Langeais*, and *La Rabouilleuse*. A "complete and unabridged" translation, by George R. SIMS, of the risqué *Contes drolatiques* (1832–37) appeared surprisingly early, in 1874. (The translator's copy containing his corrections with a view to a second edition is in Cambridge University Library.)

It was not until the 1880s and 1890s that a serious attempt was made to ensure that something approaching the totality of Balzac's work was made available to English and American readers. The period in question saw no fewer than three major new editions.

Publication of the 12 volumes of Katharine Prescott WORMELEY's *Balzac's Novels in English* began in London in 1886, a year after the American edition. The translator's name appears on only some of the title pages. The chief claim to fame of this relatively undistinguished series of translations rests on two of its volumes, *César Birotteau* and *The Duchesse de Langeais and Other Stories*, becoming the subject of a review by Oscar Wilde in the *Pall Mall Gazette*. Wilde did not mince his words: "The translations are very unequal and some of them are positively bad". As an example of the many mistranslations, he selected "Good advice is an egg [oeuf] in the hand" for "Bon conseil vaut un oeil [eye] dans la main". The best of the versions was said to be that of *The Duchesse de Langeais*, "though even this leaves much to be desired". Wilde concluded: "We fear Mr Routledge's edition will not do ... his translators [sic] do not understand French". Doubtless few translators would have relished an assessment of their work by the author of "The Critic as Artist", but the fact remains that Wormeley's translations, even where unexceptionable in terms of accuracy, are lifeless in comparison with the exuberant originals. Wormeley went on to translate many of the remaining titles of the *Human Comedy*, but the 40-volume edition published in the US appears not to have been published in England.

Wormeley's edition omitted a number of works. A subsequent American initiative, the Barrie edition (IVES *et al.*), made much of being the first "complete" translation. It was the work of a number of translators, principally William Walton and G.B. Ives, and included the *Contes drolatiques*. The Prospectus volume contained a comparison of the three versions of the *Human Comedy* now competing for attention. The first 11 volumes (*Scènes de la vie parisienne*) were published in London in a limited edition by Nichols in 1895–96 and, in an edition of 22 volumes, by Leonard Smithers in 1897–99. It was subsequently published in its entirety in London by the Caxton Press.

Neither American edition has enjoyed the success of the third of the editions stimulated by the centenary of Balzac's birth, the Dent edition of 1895–99, which was largely the work of Ellen MARRIAGE and Clara BELL but with some works translated by James WARING or R.S. SCOTT. All 40 volumes were introduced by George SAINTSBURY, who himself had been responsible for a separate translation of *Les Chouans* in 1890. (Arnold Bennett praised the learned professor's introductions for being "startlingly just".) For fear of attracting censorship or worse (this was the period in which Zola's English publisher ended up in prison), the following titles were omitted: *Physiologie du mariage*, *Sarrasine*, *La Fille aux yeux d'or*, *Une Passion dans le désert*, *Petites misères de la vie conjugale*. The fact that *La Cousine Bette* and *Splendeurs et misères des courtisanes* were translated by Waring suggests that they were thought unsuitable to be translated by a woman. (Arnold Bennett would tell the story of a famous circulating library in 1909 refusing to supply a lady friend of his with a copy of the translation of *Splendeurs et misères des courtisanes*.) For many years, it was through the Dent translations that the majority of English readers made the acquaintance of Balzac's fiction. The Dent edition provided many, though not all, of the 15 versions later used in Dent's Everyman Library. It has also been used as the basis for limited editions of several of Balzac's major works and, most recently of all, has provided David Campbell's relaunched Everyman Library with its versions of *La Cousine Bette* and *Eugénie Grandet*.

The Dent edition was highly regarded by readers of the time. The *Athenaeum* critic wrote: "we are disposed to speak highly of the merits of this new translation ... in Mrs BELL, Miss MARRIAGE and Mr WARING, [Saintsbury] has found translators whose work is at once accurate and spirited". The reviewer claimed to note a "tendency to unnecessary paraphrase in the earlier volumes, which has disappeared, with advantage, as the translators have warmed to their work". They "never err in essentials. Their rendering is always correct and often extremely happy". He therefore dismissed James Payn's claim, made in 1884, that Balzac "is not translatable, or when translated is not readable". Playing on Macaulay's quip that a bad translation resembles champagne served in decanters, he added: "one might almost say that the ideal rendering of Balzac should be to an English reader like the artistic transfusion of an old claret, which leaves behind all its sediment in the bottle".

Subsequent generations have been more inclined to find fault with these translations, though it should be remembered that they were produced at a prodigious rate. It is more than likely the Dent edition of *Le Lys dans la vallée* that Arnold Bennett castigated for being a "rotten English translation". Writing in 1950, H.O. Stutchbury maintained that "the translation of the Dent edition lacked the distinction of Scott Moncrieff's Proust". The Balzac scholar and translator Donald Adamson has observed that MARRIAGE and BELL might have brought to their work "a little more precision and elegance". In at least one case, the editor of a reprint has found it necessary to make a large number of corrections to the Dent translator's text. The flaws in the Dent versions have, nevertheless, been exaggerated. The work of Saintsbury's team represented a notable break from the literal and often stilted versions that had preceded them.

Independently of these monumental enterprises, the 1890s movement made a significant contribution to the enhancement of Balzac's reputation with the English reading public. The "Yellow Book" generation was particularly drawn to the forbidden territory of Balzac's more erotic writings, with the celebrated specialist in *curiosa*, Leonard Smithers, publishing Ernest Dowson's translation of *La Fille aux yeux d'or*, a work omitted by both Saintsbury and Wormeley.

There was no advertised attempt to produce an entire *Human Comedy* in English for the 20th-century reader (though this ambition may have been behind the translations that Elek began publishing in the late 1950s). In 1999 the bicentenary of the author's birth was not used as an excuse to repair this omission. Many individual novels have, however, been translated, often more than once. Prominent among these is the work of some well-known writers and translators: Gerard HOPKINS (*Une ténébreuse affaire*), Kathleen RAINE (*La Cousine Bette* and *Illusions perdues*), Norman CAMERON (*Le Cousin Pons*), Rayner HEPPENSTALL (*Splendeurs et misères des courtisanes*), Rosamond and Simon HARCOURT-SMITH (*Béatrix*) and Henry REED (*Eugénie Grandet* and *Le Père Goriot*). Thirteen novels and two volumes of short stories have appeared in Penguin Classics. The majority of these are exceptional in their accuracy, having been assigned to specialist scholars (H.J. HUNT, D. ADAMSON and Sylvia D. RAPHAEL). The, mainly earlier, translations by Marion Ayton CRAWFORD of some of Balzac's most important works have neither the merit of accuracy nor the ability to communicate the author's delight in linguistic display. The 1994 translation, by Robin BUSS, of *César Birotteau* is, by contrast, both nicely judged and reliable. Yet until this influential series is more comprehensive in its range Balzac's achievement is likely to remain insufficiently understood by the English-reading public. Meanwhile, Penguin's Balzacian mantle has been borrowed to good effect by the World's Classics. The three new translations it has so far made available (the work of Sylvia RAPHAEL and A.J. KRAILSHEIMER) succeed in combining accuracy and readability very well.

Outside the *Human Comedy*, the *Contes drolatiques* have attracted many publishers and translators since George SIM's bold enterprise of 1874. Some 10 separate translations have appeared, though a number of them offer only a selection of tales. The nine stories translated by Robert CRAWFORD in 1921 have the interest of being rendered in a pastiche of "14th- and 16th-century English" [sic].

MICHAEL TILBY

Further Reading

Adamson, Donald, "La Réception de la *Comédie humaine* en Grande-Bretagne au Xxe siècle", *L'Année balzacienne* 1992, pp. 391–420

Axelrod, M.R., *The Politics of Style in the Fiction of Balzac, Beckett, and Cortázar*, London: Macmillan, and New York: St Martin's Press, 1992

Bellos, David, *Balzac Criticism in France, 1850–1900*, Oxford: Clarendon Press, 1976

Butor, Michel, "Balzac and Reality" in *Inventory*, translated by Richard Howard, London: Jonathan Cape, 1970

Collins, Wilkie, "Portrait of an Author, Painted by his Publisher", *All the Year Round*, 18 June 1859, pp. 184–90, reprinted in his *My Miscellanies*, 2 vols, London: Sampson Low, 1863

Decker, Clarence R., "Balzac's Literary Reputation in Victorian Society", *Publications of the Modern Language Association of America*, 46 (1932) pp. 1150–57

Hemmings, F.W.J., *An Interpretation of "La Comédie humaine"*, New York: Random House, 1971

Herschberg-Pierrot, Anne (editor), *Balzac et le style*, Paris: SEDES, 1998

Hunt, Herbert J., "The 'Human Comedy': First English Reactions", in *The French Mind: Studies in Honour of Gustave Rudler*, edited by Will Moore, *et al.*, Oxford: Clarendon Press, 1952, pp. 273–90

Hunt, Herbert J., *Balzac's "Comédie humaine"*, 2nd edition, London: Athlone Press, 1964

Marceau, Félicien, *Balzac and his World*, translated by Derek Coltman, London: W.H. Allen, 1967

Monod, Sylvère, "La fortune de Balzac en Angleterre", *Revue de littérature comparée*, 24 (1950), pp. 181–210

Prendergast, Christopher, *Balzac: Fiction and Melodrama*, London: Edward Arnold, 1978

Pugh, Anthony, *Balzac's Recurring Characters*, London: Duckworth, 1975

Robb, Graham, *Balzac*, London: Picador, 1994

Stutchbury, H.O., "English Writers on Balzac", *Adam* (June 1949) pp.12–18

Tilby, Michael (editor), *Balzac*, London and New York: Longman, 1995

Eugénie Grandet

Eugénie Grandet, 1833

Translations

Anonymous, *Eugénie Grandet*, London and New York: Routledge Warne and Routledge, 1859

Bair, Lowell, *Eugénie Grandet*, with an introduction by Milton Crane, New York: Bantam, 1959

Crawford, Marion Ayton, *Eugénie Grandet*, Harmondsworth: Penguin, 1955

Gould, Edward S., *Eugenia Grandet*, New York: Winchester, 1843

Lawrence, Merloyd, *Eugénie Grandet*, with *The Curé of Tours*, Boston: Houghton Mifflin, 1964

Marriage, Ellen, *Eugénie Grandet*, London: Dent, 1895 (volume 4 of the Saintsbury edition of *The Human Comedy*); reprinted London: Folio Society, 1953 (the Folio Society edition incorporates a large number of corrections)

Raphael, Sylvia, *Eugénie Grandet*, with an introduction by Christopher Prendergast, Oxford and New York: Oxford University Press, 1990

Reed, Henry, *Eugénie Grandet*, New York: New American Library of World Literature, 1964

Tomlinson, May, *Eugénie Grandet*, Philadelphia: Barrie, 1895(?); London: Caxton Press, 1900(?)

Walter, Dorothea and John Watkins, *Eugénie Grandet*, with *Père Goriot*, translated by E.K. Brown, New York: Modern Library, 1946

Wight, O.W. and F.B. Goodrich, *Eugénie Grandet*, New York: Rudd Carleton, 1861

Wormeley, Katharine Prescott, *Eugénie Grandet*, London: Routledge, and Boston: Roberts, 1886

Balzac's story of a miser of Saumur and his gentle but resolute daughter Eugénie was felt by contemporary English critics to be one of the few works of his not to transgress the bounds of decency. John Wilson Croker, writing in the *Quarterly Review* in April 1836, proclaimed that it had "the almost singular merit that it can be read by a man without indignation, and by a woman without blushes". It was duly the first of Balzac's major novels to be translated into English, albeit in America, in 1843 (GOULD). It was not until 1859 that a translation appeared in England, in a cheap edition aimed at a wide audience. This ANONYMOUS version is interesting for its having taken the French text of the second (Charpentier) edition of 1839; it therefore includes both the "preamble" and the "epilogue" that Balzac later abandoned. With only minimal changes, consisting mainly of alterations to the paragraphing and the replacement of some of the French terms that the translator had seen fit to retain, but also of the omission of the "preamble" and "epilogue", this version was later adopted by the Nelson Library and continued to be reprinted for the best part of a century.

Writing in 1859 before he had had the opportunity to catch sight of the ANONYMOUS version of the same year, Wilkie Collins declared: "If the translation already accomplished of this book be only creditably executed, it may be left to speak for itself." It is not known whether subsequently he considered it to merit the opprobrium he directed against the contemporary translation of *Le Père Goriot*. It could be objected that the 1859 translator of *Eugénie Grandet* adheres too closely to the original to compete with certain later translations, his version at times appearing quite stilted. On the other hand, its period flavour is not without its attraction.

A second American translation (by WIGHT & GOODRICH) was published in 1861. Neither this, nor GOULD's *Eugenia Grandet* of 1843, which is probably the version reprinted in New York in 1878, achieved the impact of the third American translation, by Katharine Prescott WORMELEY, which appeared, though without the translator's name on the title page, in 1886. Wormeley's translation of *Le Père Goriot* had the previous year been highly praised by the reviewer of the *New York Tribune*:

> The translation ... is very good, and Balzac is not the easiest author to translate. The publishers cannot do better than to intrust the succeeding volumes in the same capable hands, and it would be only justice to the translator to put his or her name on the title-page; for it is a meritorious deed to have turned into excellent, nervous English the prose of this great Frenchman.

In fact, Wormeley's version of *Eugénie Grandet* suffers from an un-Balzacian flatness and is not redeemed by anything like total accuracy.

Both Wormeley's version and May TOMLINSON's translation for the Barrie (and Caxton Press) edition of *The Human Comedy* are eclipsed by that of Ellen MARRIAGE (1895), which was part of the Dent edition of *The Human Comedy* under the general editorship of George Saintsbury. This became the version popularized by its inclusion in Dent's Everyman Library. It was also used as the basis of two bibliophile editions that appeared in 1953 and 1960 respectively. The first of these, published by the Folio Society, boasted a "methodical revision" of the text leading to "the correction of some 120 plain mistakes, like bark for *bâillement* [yawn], and simple omissions". The Folio Society editor (N.J.A.) also saw fit to proceed to "the restoration of a few examples of Balzac's mania for pseudo-scientific diction; and an occasional touch of precision where Miss Marriage veiled her author's native sensuality". It is arguable that certain additional emendations should have been made, but the inadequacies of Marriage's translation have none the less been exaggerated. As the Folio Society editor himself recognizes, "its qualities are such as to convey to a modern reader something like the sandalwood smell of the original". Above all, it marks a monumental break with the narrow concept of literalness that hampered earlier 19th-century translators, and it succeeds in adopting an infectious story-telling idiom that the English reader recognizes as natural. Marriage provides an object lesson in the need to be ready to alter the order of words and clauses, and combine or break sentences, in keeping with the inherent rhythms of English narrative prose. The Limited Editions Club edition of 1960, while leaving Marriage's version intact, appropriately restores the chapter divisions and titles that had featured in the first edition of the source text and that were swept away by the Charpentier edition of 1839.

For at least the first half of the 20th century, almost all English readers of Balzac derived their familiarity with *Eugénie Grandet* from the versions of MARRIAGE or the ANONYMOUS Nelson Library translator. This virtual monopoly was brought to an end by the appearance in 1955 of a new translation in the Penguin Classics series. Unfortunately, Marion Ayton CRAWFORD's version does Balzac's English reader a signal disservice. Unlike the work of the other translators of Balzac in this series, Crawford's version of *Eugénie Grandet* contains many dubious interpretations, contestable renderings and odd formulations. The misunderstandings are most apparent in the superfluous explanations with which Crawford expands the original. More generally, the translation is marred by other forms of unnecessary addition that can be remarkably heavy-handed. Thus, at a point where Marriage produces a version comparable in length to the original ("they all know the exact value of sun or rain at the right moment"), Crawford expands the texts as follows: "everyone knows to a sou just how much profit a sunbeam or a timely shower is bringing him and is mentally engaged in setting down figures accordingly on the credit side of his ledger."

In his introduction to Lowell BAIR's translation of 1959, the Shakespearean scholar Milton Crane proclaims that Bair "succeeds in providing the reader with the novel his author might well have written had his language been not French but English". Bair's version indeed contains some well-chosen examples of more modern usage, but alongside the versions of Marriage and Reed (see below), it does not escape, particularly in the dialogue, a certain flatness that comes from an over-literal reproduction of the original syntax and word order. Furthermore, it contains straightforward errors of the type "trowel" for *rabot* (a plane) and "brandy" for *cassis*.

The 1964 translation by the poet and radio dramatist, Henry REED takes the text of the last version to be revised by the author (the so-called "Furne corrigé") but follows the Garnier edition of 1961 in restoring "Balzac's shapely design of the edition of 1834". It also includes the opening and closing paragraphs, to which only the reader of the anonymous 1859 translation had previously had access in English. Further emendations are discussed by Reed in a lengthy translator's note. They include, controversially, the correction of what the translator identifies as the printer's wrongly positioned insertions of Balzac's marginalia (though without apparently checking his intuitions against the manuscript or that portion of the corrected proof that survives). Reed also tidies up, as far as is possible, Balzac's own, incomplete, alterations of dates and the ages of certain of his characters. "Grandet no longer puts on a couple of decades in the space of 12 to 14 years and ... Madame Grandet does not die both in 1820 and 1822". A similiar attempt is made to substitute "a more logical time-scheme" for Balzac's "grotesque miscalculations connected with the central action".

Reed's actual translation is outstanding and is to be preferred to all its rivals. It modernizes the original in precisely the way Milton Crane claimed for Bair's version and avoids the errors and distortions that disqualify Crawford's. Consistently resourceful, it is inherently Balzacian through the translator's own relish for words. Alone of all the published English translations, it brings the characters alive through their speech, as in this case of an outburst by the Grandets' servant, offered a small glass of cassis from the bottle she was carrying when she tripped on a rickety stair: "In my place, there's plenty what would have broken the bottle. I held it up in the air and nearly broke my elbow instead".

The most recent translation of *Eugénie Grandet* is by Sylvia RAPHAEL (1990). It is based on "Furne corrigé", but follows the Limited Editions Club version in restoring the divisions into chapters with titles, and also restores some of the original paragraph divisions. If it does not quite match the Balzacian qualities of Henry Reed's version, it still succeeds in being highly readable. While avoiding the linguistic impoverishment that stems from the much narrower approach to literalness employed by some of its predecessors, it has the important merit of being the most strictly accurate of all the translations to date.

MICHAEL TILBY

Further Reading
See Prendergast's introduction to Raphael (1990)

Old Goriot

Le Père Goriot, 1835; in serial form 1834–35

Le Père Goriot was originally published in four instalments in the *Revue de Paris* between 14 December 1834 and 11 February 1835. It was published in book form by Werdet in 1835. The standard text is that of the Furne edition published in 1843 as part of *La Comédie humaine*. Pierre-Georges Castex's critical edition (Garnier, 1963) varies from the Furne edition mainly in questions of punctuation and division into paragraphs. It restores the division of the text into the original four parts (suppressed for reasons of economy by Furne).

Translations
Anonymous, *Old Goriot*, London: Caxton, 1897
Brown, E.K., *Père Goriot*, with *Eugénie Grandet*, translated by Dorothea Walter and John Watkins, New York: Modern Library, 1946
Canon, Raymond R., *Père Goriot*, with an introduction, New York: Airmont, 1965
Crawford, Marion Ayton, *Old Goriot*, with an introduction, Harmondsworth and Baltimore: Penguin, 1951
Krailsheimer, A.J., *Père Goriot*, Oxford and New York: Oxford University Press, 1991
Marriage, Ellen, *Old Goriot*, London: Dent, and New York: Macmillan, 1896
Raffel, Burton, *Père Goriot/Old Goriot*, New York: Norton, 1994
Wormeley, Katharine Prescott, *Père Goriot*, Boston: Roberts, 1897; London: Downey, 1898

As Crawford's introduction points out, "the translator of Balzac need not mourn the loss of French lucidity and grace of style, for whereas force is of the measure of his writing, lucidity is often a minor consideration and grace of little importance to him". *Le Père Goriot* does not present any major obstacles to translation, except perhaps for the problem of finding and retaining the right tone. Some of the subtleties of style (extensive use of the subjunctive, ambiguities, syntactical elegances) are not necessarily easy to render into English. Minor problems concern allusions to contemporary figures, places and events (which can be explained in footnotes or by expanding the text or simply avoided); obscurities; puns and other plays on words; the use of different registers. Translators seem to differ on the question of whether to divide the novel into its four original parts and whether to call the protagonist Old Goriot (too familiar in English?) or Père Goriot (to underline the theme of paternity).

Translations other than those listed certainly exist but are not always easy to obtain (even on interlibrary loan). The more readily available are those by Crawford (Penguin Classics), Marriage (Everyman), and Krailsheimer (World's Classics).

MARRIAGE's translation has been going strong since 1896 and was a staple of the Everyman Library from 1907 to 1991 (revised by A.J.B. Glover in 1946). It has been widely published under different imprints and is still probably the most frequently encountered translation. At times the text is rather too literal, at other times liberties are taken with the original but to little positive effect ("he of the forty years and dyed whiskers" for "l'homme de quarante ans, à favoris peints"; "to heap execrations on" for "maudir" when "condemn" would have been more appropriate). The formal style occasionally swings to the other extreme when excessively familiar or colloquial expressions are employed. Needless archaisms are introduced ("on the way thither"). The syntax is strained at times, which creates the impression of an unnatural English style.

The ANONYMOUS translation of the Caxton edition (1897) is not a bad version at all. Although the style adopted is plain, it nevertheless keeps close track of the original text. In fact it creates the effect of being a relatively modern translation since the style is more in keeping with contemporary taste. It reads well and has an authentic feel.

WORMELEY's version (1897) takes us across the Atlantic and offers us an American view of Balzac. Originally published as part of a grander enterprise, the translation of *La Comédie humaine*, Wormeley's text has over the years appeared under a variety of imprints. This particular *Père Goriot* is no doubt a product of its time but, that time being closer to the age of Balzac, the style adopted fits more comfortably with that of the original. There is little discernible American influence on the text. This translation reads well in English to the point that there is little temptation to refer back to the original to check for accuracy. A fair number of French words and phrases are retained e.g. "pension bourgeoise", "danseuse", "grande dame", "comme il faut", "toilette", "billets-doux" (sometimes also elaborated upon in English), more than in other translations, a choice that contributes to the preservation (illusion?) of local colour. Where explanatory notes are provided they are inserted into the text.

BROWN's version (1946), another American rendering, is an honest attempt at a faithful translation. The style is fairly plain and unpretentious and avoids the more outlandish expressions favoured by some translators. However, it does contain some mistakes, for example, when Bianchon drops the name of the phrenologist Gall, Vautrin enquires "Monsieur l'a connu?" (masculine third person singular pronoun); Brown gives us "You've known her, Sir?" The error is further compounded in subsequent exchanges. There are also minor omissions.

CRAWFORD's translation has featured in Penguin Classics since 1951. Despite telling insights into Balzac's style, methods and translatability, Crawford does not quite seem to strike the right tone. Although the translation is not inaccurate, the style, in common with that of Marriage, is rather formal, even stilted at times ("Isn't it strange to be able to foretell that?" from the ex-convict Vautrin). Also shared with Marriage is a taste for extremely familiar expressions, which when juxtaposed with more formal passages create a strange effect. Crawford opts for "Old Goriot" and a continuous text. Explanatory notes are worked into the text.

CANON (1965) is something of a rogue publication. Although the introduction is signed Raymond R. Canon, M.A. and the publisher has copyrighted "the special contents of this edition" the translation is in fact that of Ellen Marriage (with some minor changes). Despite the publisher's claim that the work is "complete and unabridged", there is a notable omission (of about a page) at the very beginning, where Balzac (usually) introduces his very Parisian drama.

KRAILSHEIMER (1991) has produced a generally accurate translation which is close to the original without being too literal. The style is consistent throughout and the text reads smoothly in English. The tone, especially in passages of dialogue and in casual remarks, can be more modern than the original e.g. "Perhaps I'll enjoy this one" for the more precious "Peut-etre ceci va-t-il m'amuser"; "he's a bit of lad" for "c'est un fameux gaillard". This strategy sometimes produces odd effects e.g. "tatty furnishings"; "suburban wineshops" for "cabarets de la banlieue". Krailsheimer successfully transposes puns and Madame Vauquer's famous mispronunciations and finds imaginative equivalents for nicknames such as Trompe-la-Mort (Death-Dodger rather than the usual rather strained Cheat-Death) and Docteur de droit travers (Doctor of Imprudence). Some more obscure references are bypassed e.g. "Eugène accompanied the vicomtesse to where people wait for their carriages" for "Eugène accompagna la vicomtesse jusqu'au péristyle, où chacun attend sa voiture", but most points requiring elucidation are covered by notes at the end of the text.

The latest translation to date is that of RAFFEL (1994) who, in his preface, claims that "... the only justification for a new translation of an old classic ... must be that what has come before is less satisfactory than what we are now offered ... Of course, I think I have improved upon the efforts of those who have preceded me". Unfortunately, this is far from being the case. In his desire for vividness Raffel has littered the text with inappropriate American expressions: "petty-ante poker player" (Goriot!), "dressed fit to kill" (Delphine), "the bigwigs in the police department". Rastignac takes "his B.A. and his elementary law degree", "the Countess of Restaud lived on Helder Street", Benvenuto Cellini is referred to as "that rare son of a gun" and Goriot as an "old goat" (for "vieillard"). Raffel has an irritating habit of translating street names ("New Saint Genevieve Street") yet retaining French words like "pension" and "salon" and always refers to the boarding house as "Maison Vauquer" (without the definite article). There are also omissions of whole sentences and of references: "en mettant en doute sa paternité, le Père Goriot tressaillit comme si son hôtesse l'eût piqué avec un fer". In a book so concerned with money the translator would do well to harmonize his currency since he uses francs, pounds and cents. With Borges we can complain that the original is not faithful to the translation.

MALCOLM GEORGE TAGGART

Further Reading

Little has been published about translations of *Le Père Goriot* or even about translating Balzac. The following, related more to adaptations than to translations, are worth mentioning.

Boulard-Bezat, Sylvie, "Les adaptations du *Père Goriot*", *L'Année balzacienne*, 8 (1987) pp. 167–78

James, Henry, *The Pension Beaurepas*, with *Washington Square* and *A Bundle of Letters*, 2 vols, Leipzig: Tauchnitz, 1881 (originally published in *Atlantic Monthly*, 43, 1879)

Tintner, Adeline R., "Henry James's The Pension Beaurepas: A Translation into American Terms of Balzac's *Le Père Goriot*", *Revue de Littérature Comparée*, 3 (1983) pp. 369–76

Cousin Bette

La Cousine Bette, 1847; in serial form 1846

This novel, with *Cousin Pons* (*Le Cousin Pons*, 1847), forms the *Poor Relations* group in the *Scenes of Parisian Life* section of Balzac's *Human Comedy*. The central character is Élisabeth Fischer, a middle-aged spinster of peasant origin and plain appearance, who loses her protégé, a handsome young Polish sculptor, to the daughter of her beautiful cousin Adeline, formerly also a Mademoiselle Fischer from Lorraine and now the wife of the debauched baron Hector Hulot, highly placed in Paris in the military administration. Unlike Sylvain Pons, the other *Poor Relation*, Bette does not remain a passive victim. Impelled by jealousy and envy she duplicitously plots a complex revenge for her loss, contriving, unsuspected, the downfall of her better-endowed relatives.

The novel was translated several times into English in the last decades of the 19th century, notably in the Saintsbury collection, less notably in other collections and selections (WORMELEY, 1888 and in her *Comedy of Human Life of Honoré de Balzac*, 1896–1900; IVES, for limited circulation, 1896 and in IVES *et al.*, *Honoré de Balzac ... translated into English*, 1895–1900). There are at least four 20th-century translations.

Translations

Bell, Clara, *Cousin Betty*, in *Collected Works*, edited by Saintsbury, vol.10, London: Dent, 1896

Bonner, Anthony, *Cousin Bette*, New York: Bantam, 1961

Crawford, Marion Ayton, *Cousin Bette*, Harmondsworth and New York: Penguin, 1965

Ives, G.B., *The Poor Relations: First Episode: Cousin Bette*, with *Pierre Grassou*, translated by William Walton, and *The Girl with the Green Eyes*, translated by E.P. Robins, 2 vols, in *Honoré de Balzac. . .translated into English*, translated by Ives *et al.*, Philadelphia: Barrie, 1896

Kent, Philip, *Cousin Bette*, with *Cousin Pons*, in *Poor Relations*, translated by Kent, London: Simpkin, Marshall, 1880

Raine, Kathleen, *Cousin Bette*, London: Hamish Hamilton, 1948; New York: Modern Library, 1958

Raphael, Sylvia, *Cousin Bette*, with an introduction by David Bellos, Oxford and New York: Oxford University Press, 1992

Waring, James, *Cousin Betty*, with a preface by George Saintsbury, London: Dent, 1897; New York: Lupton, n.d.; as *Cousin Bette*, London: Campbell, and New York: Knopf, 1991

Wormeley, Katharine Prescott, *Cousin Bette*, Boston: Roberts:

1888, and in *The Comedy of Human Life of Honoré de Balzac*, translated by Wormeley, Boston: Hardy, Pratt, 1896–1900, and Boston: Roberts, 1893–98

Towards the end of 1836 Balzac became the first novelist ever to publish a novel in a French daily newspaper. *La Vieille Fille* appeared in Girardin's new half-price *La Presse* in 12 instalments from 23 October to 4 November. By 1846, the date of *Cousin Bette*, and the end of Balzac's period of most intense literary activity, he was well used to writing for serialization and was perfectly aware that he was rivalling Eugène Sue in taking fiction down-market. Hulot in *Cousin Bette* is a study in geriatric eroticism. For a newly emergent literate public Balzac was not writing high art. He was purporting to purvey morality while simultaneously depicting prurience for a cut-price press. Knowing that is the key to translating him successfully.

The novel's pace is extraordinarily swift, and the tone racy. Passages of narrative mingle with brief playlets of conversation, minute descriptions, and narratorial comments of the most sweeping sort about human affairs, sometimes based on genuine insight, sometimes not. We shall consider five translations, spread across the time-range. It is instructive to compare their treatment of one of the narrator's most general assertions, as well as one of his detailed interiors. The first passage comes from a chapter (83) of "Moral Reflexions". Hulot, finding himself humiliated and blackmailed by his vicious current mistress and her husband, has again returned, again briefly penitent, to his virtuous wife. The narrator expresses his views on the difficulty of finding in one woman satisfaction of both love and lust. The second extract is from Chapter 128, in which, later, bent on a conventionally charitable errand, the baroness Hulot recognizes, in the corruptor of youth she has come to confront, her missing husband, living in squalor as a public letter-writer. Here are the passages in French:

> L'amour, cette immense débauche de la raison, ce mâle et sévère plaisir des grandes âmes, et le plaisir, cette vulgarité vendue sur place, sont deux faces différentes d'un même fait ... Certes, le mariage doit être accepté comme une tâche, il est la vie avec ses travaux et ses durs sacrifices également faits des deux côtés ... Cette réflexion n'est pas un placage de morale, elle donne la raison de bien des malheurs incompris.
>
> (chapter 83)
>
> CABINET D'AFFAIRES
> Ici l'on rédige les pétitions, on met les mémoires au net, etc.
> Discrétion, célérité.
>
> L'intérieur ressemblait à ces bureaux de transit où les omnibus de Paris font attendre les places de correspondance aux voyageurs. Un escalier intérieur menait sans doute à l'appartement en entresol éclairé par la galérie et qui dépendait de la boutique. La baronne aperçut un bureau de bois blanc noirci, des cartons, et un ignoble fauteuil acheté d'occasion.
>
> (chapter 128)

Balzac's word-choice in the first passage makes clear that he is consciously over-writing. His narrator does not wish his grotesquely exaggerated generalization to be taken with total seriousness, but the BELL translation in the Saintsbury edition of 1896 disastrously misses Balzac's self-parody. "Sur place" does not mean "upon the streets" but "on the spot". "Inordinate carousal of the reason" is too clinical a rendering of the exclamatory "immense débauche", and even the mock concession starting "Certes", trumpeting irony in French, reads in the English text like a solemn assertion: "Certainly, marriage should be looked upon as a task to be accomplished". The second passage comes out even less well. The "public scrivener" (Écrivain public") advertizes "Petitions drawn up here, Accounts adjusted, etc.," which combines over-specificity, inaccuracy and oddness. "The interior" is sanitized with references to companies and convenience, surely not intentionally omitted by the narrator, who does not give us the Saintsbury "waiting-rooms provided by the omnibus companies of Paris for the convenience of their patrons". Nor are we told in French that the apartment is let. The "cartons" (cardboard files) of the final sentence become "cards", and all Balzac's grace notes are treated as crochets. That the "shabby second-hand easy-chair" was *bought* second-hand is just one of those tiny Balzacian touches which turn his low-brow writing into an art form.

The Everyman reissue in 1991 of the 1897 James WARING translation raises questions of commercial practice. By 1991 this sort of "translation" is almost fraudulently inept. Valérie's note to Hulot beginning "Mon vieux grognard, ne va pas Rue du Dauphin, notre cauchemar est malade ..." becomes "Dear old man...our incubus is ill ..." The first of our passages is simply bulldozed into the sort of language more appropriately used for textbooks, with a paragraph break to make the lesson easier to assimilate:

> Love, which is the debauch of reason, the strong and austere joy of a lofty soul, and pleasure, the vulgar counterfeit sold in the market-place, are two aspects of the same thing ...
>
> Marriage, no doubt, must be accepted as a tie; it is life, with its duties and its stern sacrifices on both parts equally.

At the start, the second passage fares a little better. The "Écrivain public" remains in French, and accounts are not adjusted, but audited. However, "The shop was like one of the little offices where travellers by omnibus await the vehicles to take them on to their destinations", (for "... have to wait for a connection"), and "Madame Hulot saw a dirty writing-table of some light wood, some letter-boxes [i.e. a grimy deal desk, cardboard files], and a wretched second-hand chair".

Kathleen RAINE in 1948 still turns Balzac's juicy prose into dessicated fruits, as if wondering what the first passage was doing in a story at all,

> Love cuts clean across reason; the virile and austere delight of great minds, and pleasure – the vulgar commodity sold in the market-place – are two aspects of the same reality ... To be sure, marriage must be accepted as a duty; it is life, imposing its tasks and stern sacrifices ...

This translation has a tendency to paraphrase, which contributes to the destruction of the impact of Balzac's prose. On the door of the "public letter-writer", we now have "Business agency. Petitions drawn up, accounts audited", but the single words "Discrétion, célérité" grow into "All work confidential, and carried out promptly".

The Penguin Classic translation by Marion Ayton CRAWFORD published in 1965 is the only one to allow anything at all of Balzac's boisterousness to seep through, but it is not much, and unhappily our first passage emerges rewritten rather than translated:

> Love, which awakens the mind to joy and delight, the virile, austere pleasure of the most noble faculties of the soul, and sex, the vulgar commodity sold in the market, are two aspects of the same thing... Obviously, marriage must be accepted as a duty: it is life, with its toil and bitter sacrifices exacted from both partners.

The notice on the door of the italicized *Public Letterwriter* is almost identical to that of Kathleen Raine, but there are still all sorts of nuances missing from the paragraph that follows, although we do at last have "mezzanine" for "entresol":

> The interior was like the waiting-rooms where Paris omnibus passengers wait for their connexions...The Baroness noticed a blackened deal desk, cardboard boxes, and a battered, shabby, second-hand arm-chair.

Balzac does not repeat the syllable "wait"; a "bureau de transit" is a snide way of referring to a waiting-room; "font attendre" has that lingering sense of "keeps them waiting", and even Balzac needed only one other adjective for the second-hand chair.

The Oxford World Classic of 1992 is by Sylvia RAPHAEL. The series presentation tends to make the translation look more like a set of extracts than the abridgement it manages to remain. Balzac's "immense débauche" comes out somewhat pallid as "Love, when reason runs riot", but this version defers more than the others to the source:

> ... the manly, serious pleasure of great hearts, the sensual pleasure, the vulgar commodity sold on the market-place, are two different aspects of the same thing ... Clearly, marriage must be accepted as a task to be performed. It is life, with its toil and painful sacrifices to be made equally on both sides.

The public letter-writer, now hyphenated, "puts accounts in order". The second passage runs:

> Inside it was like the waiting-rooms where Paris omnibus passengers wait for their connections ... The Baroness noticed a blackened whitewood desk, cardboard boxes, and a shabby, second-hand armchair.

Where in these English versions has Balzac's ebullient energy gone? How is the inner uncertainty informing the self-conscious bombast of the first passage conveyed, or the miserable drabness of the setting described in the second? In the second passage Balzac's acute sense of the message an interior can convey about its inhabitants makes clear that he is preparing us for what turns out to be the mock-emotional climax of the meeting between Adeline and Hulot, and for Adeline's tears at the sight of the surroundings in which Hulot has been living. Balzac deserves better of his translators than the pancake prose into which they have rendered him.

ANTHONY LEVI

Further Reading

Bellos, David, *La Cousine Bette*, London: Grant and Cutler, 1980

See also Bellos's introduction to Raphael (1992)

Jules-Amédée Barbey d'Aurevilly 1808–1889

French short-story writer, novelist, essayist and critic

Biography

Born 2 September 1808 at Saint-Sauveur-le-Vicomte, Normandy, into an aristocratic Catholic and royalist family. He received his early education locally at Valognes; the Cotentin region forms the background of much of his fiction. He attended the Collège Stanislas in Paris from 1827 to 1829 and studied law at Caen, 1829–33. In 1833 he went back to Paris and for some years lived the life of a dandy. In 1851, the family fortune gone, he turned to journalism, writing on literature, the theatre, politics and fashion for several right-wing papers. His aggressive and on the whole reactionary criticism targeted Hugo and Zola, but he praised Stendhal, Balzac and Baudelaire. In 1869 he succeeded Sainte-Beuve as literary critic of *Le Constitutionnel*. After 1870, with the receipt of some legacies and the growth of his reputation, Barbey attended salons and acquired a literary following.

Among Barbey's first published works are several novels and his essay on dandyism, *Du Dandyisme et de George Brummell* (*Of Dandyism and of George Brummell*), 1845. Another, better-known novel, *Une Vieille Maîtresse* [A Former Mistress], published in 1851, was written in 1844. *L'Ensorcelée* (*Bewitched*), 1854, and *Le Chevalier des Touches* [The Chevalier des Touches], 1864, are typically sensational and picturesque adventure novels, looking back to the counter-revolutionary insurrections of the Breton and Norman "Chouans". Barbey is remembered particularly for the stories in *Les Diaboliques* (*Weird Women*), 1874. His articles on 19th-century literature and theatre were published in volume form towards the end of his life. He died in Paris, 23 April 1889.

Translations

Essay

Du Dandyisme et de George Brummell, 1845

Ainslie, Douglas, *Of Dandyism and of George Brummell*, with an introduction, London: Dent, and Boston: Copeland and Day, 1897; reprinted New York: PAJ, 1988

Lewis, D.B. Wyndham, *The Anatomy of Dandyism, with Some Observations on Beau Brummell*, London: Peter Davies, 1928

Novels

L'Ensorcelée, 1854

Willcox, Louise Collier, *Bewitched*, New York: Harper, 1928

Une Histoire sans nom, 1882

Saltus, Edgar, *Story without a Name*, New York: Belford, 1891; with an introduction, New York: Brentano, 1919

Ce qui ne meurt pas, 1883

Melmoth, Sebastian, *What Never Dies*, Paris: privately printed, 1902; in *The Writings of Oscar Wilde* (spurious attribution), New York: Keller, 1907; original reprinted London: Fortune Press, 1933

Short Stories

Les Diaboliques, 1874

Anonymous, *Weird Women: Being a Literal Translation of "Les Diaboliques" of Barbey d'Aurevilly*, London and Paris: Lutetian Bibliophiles Society (printed for subscribers), 1900

Boyd, Ernest, *The Diaboliques*, with an introduction, New York: Knopf, 1926; as *Les Diaboliques*, with an introduction by Peter Quennell, London: Elek, 1947

Kimber, Jean, *The She-Devils (Les Diaboliques)*, London and New York: Oxford University Press, 1964

Only a small portion of Barbey d'Aurevilly's substantial oeuvre has been translated into English, and that mostly his fiction. He has been fortunate in that his translators have all been conscientiously respectful of his work and kept their own textual manipulations to a minimum. The resulting English works are of varying stylistic quality, but all give a faithful reflection of Barbey's content.

Despite translators' emphasis on his fiction, his major contribution to English letters is his essay, *Du Dandyisme et de George Brummell*, which Ellen Moers has called "the last pivotal work upon which the history of the dandy tradition turns". An Anglophile himself, Barbey considered puritanism to be an essential aspect of the ideal dandy; hence his choice of an Englishman to epitomize his conception of this species of intellectual aesthete. In turn, the introductions to English translations of his works usually promote the image of Barbey himself as a dandy: his physical appearance and characteristic apparel are usually described in detail, and his translators are also often dandies or associated with decadence or aestheticism.

Those would-be 19th-century dandies who were influenced by Barbey's essay, however, had to read it in French; its first translation, AINSLIE (1897), did not appear until some 40 years after its first publication in Paris. Ainslie, who later became the aesthetic philosopher Benedetto Croce's first English translator and popularizer, claimed in his introduction that he "attempted to suggest in English as near the original as possible what must in its essential elegance almost altogether evaporate from the silver vessel". Nevertheless, he considered Barbey an idealist who "had a preconceived theory of Dandyism which he fitted on to Brummell very adroitly". Ainslie is well-written and economical, with hardly an extraneous word. The same cannot be said for LEWIS (1928), which is replete with verbiage, reflecting a conscientious faithfulness so extreme it often attempts to reproduce Barbey's French syntax. Lewis seems to be based on Barbey's third edition which included a supplementary essay, "A Precursor of the Dandies". This supplement is not to be found in Ainslie.

If *Du Dandyisme* was Barbey's most influential work, the collection of six stories titled *Les Diaboliques* has been considered his most representative. Although ostensibly about diabolical women, it is also, as Moers remarked, "a whole catalog of the dandy species". It was also Barbey's most popular work. Of the four major editions listed here, only two are original translations. The one attributed to BOYD (1926) proves on closer inspection to be a lightly revised edition of ANONYMOUS (1900). Although claiming in its subtitle to be "a literal translation", Anonymous changed the order in which the stories appeared, and renamed General Brassard of "The Crimson Curtain" "Brossard". The foreword, signed by Charles Carrington, serves to introduce Barbey d'Aurevilly but does not tell us which French edition was followed, nor give us any hints who the translator might have been. Boyd largely reproduces this version word for word, including some of its errors. His changes are minor, and sometimes for the worse. The title "Don Juan's Greatest Triumph" in ANONYMOUS becomes the more awkwardly literal "The Greatest Love of Don Juan" and "What Lay Beneath the Cards; or, A Notable Game of Whist" becomes merely "Beneath the Cards of a Game of Whist". BOYD also restores the original order of the stories. The edition published by Elek (1947) credits no translator but repeats the Knopf edition word-for-word, only substituting an introduction by Peter Quennell for Boyd's and keeping the original title completely French. KIMBER (1964), on the other hand, is completely original and succinct where the others are wordy. Seemingly less wedded to the notion of "literal translation", it comes much closer to producing an "English" work. This edition is also the only one to identify its source text: Barbey's *Oeuvres complètes* published by Francois Bernouard (Paris, 1926).

The first of the only three of Barbey's novels to be translated into English, *Une Histoire sans nom* (*Story without a Name*) relates the story of an inexplicable pregnancy and its devastating consequences. SALTUS, the translator (1891), was regarded in his time as an American decadent, straightforwardly treating shocking themes in his own novels. The extent to which he was identified with Barbey d'Aurevilly is revealed in his introduction to his 1919 edition of *Story without a Name*, where he cites a reviewer who "said I had invented Barbey and that the vile story was my own vile work". Saltus bears the mark of the translator's own style; he does not hesitate to delete phrases or to abridge subtly if he feels it is called for.

The second of Barbey's novels to be translated into English was his *Ce qui ne meurt pas*. Sebastian Melmoth was the alias Oscar Wilde adopted when he was living in France after he emerged from prison. However, Robert Ross, Wilde's literary executor, emphatically denied that Wilde translated this work. In the midst of editing the authorized edition of Wilde's collected works for Methuen, Ross became incensed upon learning that A.R. Keller in the US was also publishing an edition of Wilde's works that would include spurious works such as this translation (Maureen Borland, *Wilde's Devoted Friend*, 1990). Nevertheless, Keller proceeded with its plans and other editions of Wilde's *Works* continued to include *What Never Dies* throughout the first half of the 20th century. Who did translate it, if Wilde did not, is a mystery. In any case, Barbey's long fictional response to George Sand's *Lélia* seems an odd choice for Wilde, although the reasons for associating the fin-de-siècle dandy with the man who defined dandyism are obvious. The translation itself is respectful of Barbey's text without being awkward about it; its occasional errors of interpretation are generally done with grace.

WILLCOX, an essayist, critic and editor, devoted the latter part of her life to translating the works of contemporary French and German writers. *Bewitched* (1928) was the last translation she published before her death. It is a historical novel about the Chouans, an obsessive love story and a chilling ghost story all in one. Like the efforts of most of Barbey's other translators, Willcox is unswervingly loyal to Barbey's text, accurate and literal to a fault although more gracefully written than LEWIS (1928). The novel was reviewed favorably by several US newspapers.

KRISTINE J. ANDERSON

Further Reading

Chartier, Armand B., *Barbey d'Aurevilly*, Boston: Twayne, 1977
Moers, Ellen, *The Dandy: Brummell to Beerbohm*, New York: Viking, and London: Secker and Warburg, 1960
Rogers, B.G., *The Novels and Stories of Barbey d'Aurevilly*, Geneva: Droz, 1967
Stanton, Domna C., *The Aristocrat as Art: A Study of the Honnête Homme and the Dandy in Seventeenth- and Nineteenth-Century French Literature*, New York: Columbia University Press, 1980

Giorgio Bassani 1916–2000

Italian novelist, short-story writer, poet and critic

Biography

Born in Bologna, 4 April 1916, to a wealthy Jewish family from the city of Ferrara, where he was brought up. He studied at Bologna University under the art historian Roberto Longhi. His first book was published pseudonymously in 1940 on account of the anti-Jewish laws then in force. Bassani took part in the Resistance after 1943. He had a variety of jobs after the war before moving to Rome and pursuing a career in publishing and journalism: he was the editor of *Botteghe oscure* and *Paragone*, and was also responsible for Feltrinelli's discovery and publication of Lampedusa's *Gattopardo*. Died in Rome, 13 April 2000.

Translations

Short Stories

Cinque storie ferraresi, 1956
Quigly, Isabel, *A Prospect of Ferrara*, London: Faber, 1962
Weaver, William, *Five Stories of Ferrara*, New York: Harcourt Brace, 1971

Novels

Gli occhiali d'oro, 1958
Quigly, Isabel, *The Gold-Rimmed Spectacles*, London: Faber, and New York: Atheneum, 1960
Weaver, William, *The Gold-Rimmed Eyeglasses* in *The Smell of Hay*, London: Weidenfeld and Nicolson, and New York: Harcourt Brace, 1975

Il giardino dei Finzi-Contini, 1962
Quigly, Isabel, *The Garden of the Finzi-Continis*, London: Faber, and New York: Atheneum, 1965
Weaver, William, *The Garden of the Finzi-Continis*, New York: Harcourt Brace, 1977

Dietro la porta, 1964
Weaver, William, *Behind the Door*, London: Weidenfeld and Nicolson, and New York: Harcourt Brace, 1972

L'airone, 1968
Weaver, William, *The Heron*, London: Weidenfeld and Nicolson, and New York: Harcourt Brace, 1970

L'odore del fieno, 1972
Weaver, William, *The Smell of Hay* (includes *The Gold-Rimmed Eyeglasses*), London: Weidenfeld and Nicolson, and New York: Harcourt Brace, 1975

Giorgio Bassani was one of the first Italian post-war novelists to be translated into English: Isabel Quigly's version of *Gli occhiali d'oro* first appeared in 1960. Since that date all Bassani's fiction has been translated and most remains in print. His reputation in English-speaking countries has been helped by the well-known film versions of *Il giardino dei Finzi-Contini* (despite Bassani's outspoken repudiation of the screenplay) and the more recent *Gli occhiali d'oro*. It is not hard to understand the reasons for Bassani's popularity: while his writing can be subtle, it presents no outstanding challenges of linguistic or narrative technique for readers or, indeed, translators (in his review of *Il giardino dei Finzi-Contini* on its publication in 1962, Montale slyly remarked that part of its appeal lay in the fact that none of its characters had had the opportunity to read Robbe-Grillet or Beckett). Bassani's work is modern in its preoccupations – existential doubt, social, racial and sexual exclusion and isolation, and the ambiguous tensions underlying all relationships, themes that tend to coalesce round the determining event, as much for Bassani's own experience as for his fiction, of the introduction of the so-called "racial laws" against Italian Jews in 1938, as Mussolini's regime became increasingly drawn into Nazi Germany's sphere of influence. These contemporary concerns are unfolded, though, within a detailed depiction of provincial bourgeois life that springs directly from the 19th-century European realist tradition.

Bassani's popularity among English-speaking readers should not, however, disguise the fact that in two ways his work has been ill-served in translation. After one false start at the creation of a larger structure (*Gli occhiali d'oro* was to have been the first part of a largely autobiographical trilogy), Bassani went on to forge, after all its individual parts had been published, one complete sequence that can be said to mimic the structure of an authentic "roman-fleuve": this is *Il romanzo di Ferrara* [The Novel of Ferrara], which first appeared in 1973, and which gathers together all Bassani's fiction in one sequence, from the earliest realism of the *Cinque storie ferraresi* to the fragments of autobiographical reflection on his writing that conclude *L'odore del fieno*. Characters and places weave in and out of focus through the texts, establishing something of the veracity of a chronicle or gazetteer, and lending force and depth to the presence of Ferrara throughout, restrictive and restorative, a confined provincial backwater and a numinous source of memory. Bassani's most successful stylistic effects tend to be cumulative, and the scale of *Il romanzo di Ferrara* allows this aspect of Bassani's gift to be seen most clearly; the cycle is, besides, fundamental for the appreciation of Bassani's complete achievement; yet Bassani's work in translation is still unavailable in this form. The second shortcoming of the English versions of Bassani is connected to the first. In the creation of *Il romanzo di Ferrara*, which first appeared two years after its last part, *L'odore del fieno*, was published, Bassani began an extensive revision of all his fiction. He had always been an assiduous reviser of his own work: even by the time of the publication of *Cinque storie ferraresi* the early stories collected in the volume had undergone extensive change, and Bassani was to continue working on them: there are, for example, eight different versions (falling into two main groups) of *La passeggiata prima di cena* between its first appearance in the review *Botteghe oscure* in 1951 and its inclusion in the final 1980 publication of *Il romanzo di Ferrara*. The revisions are largely linguistic rather than structural, and translation is perhaps too blunt an instrument to capture the significance of the small but manifold changes – in verbs, adjectives, conjunctions, etc. – that Bassani introduced to compose what has been described as the deliberate "mediocrity" of his prose style. Furthermore, it is open to debate whether the author's alterations serve a clearer artistic vision or betray an essentially uncreative restlessness, yet their scale is such that the overall effect of numerous passages is subtly changed. No English translations of Bassani's works are based on the final versions of the texts (*Il romanzo di Ferrara*, 1980); this shortcoming is most serious for the early works which have undergone the most extensive changes: Isabel QUIGLY's *A Prospect of Ferrara* (1962) is based on the 1956 Italian edition of *Cinque storie ferraresi*, whereas William WEAVER's *Five stories of Ferrara* (1971) is based, despite its title, on the 1960 edition *Storie ferraresi*. All the other translations of the later novels predate the completion of the revision that Bassani began for the first appearance of *Il romanzo di Ferrara* in 1973.

All Bassani's fiction has been translated by the American translator William WEAVER; Bassani's first three works have also been published in Britain in versions by Isabel QUIGLY. It can be said that Bassani is on the whole well-served by both his translators (although it is stated on the dustjacket of Weaver's version of *Five Stories of Ferrara* that it "is the first that fully satisfied the author"). Quigly tends to naturalize Bassani's prose into English rather more than Weaver; in many cases this works well and contributes to the fluency and general readability of her translations, whereas Weaver can sound stilted, especially in the early work (e.g. "una cittadina di mezza montagna" Quigly translates as "a small town in the mountains", and Weaver as "a half-mountainous city"), but she slides over aspects of the Italian that Weaver is more careful in rendering (and Quigly's versions are not free of plain errors). Weaver can sound awkward precisely because he is so attentive to the Italian original, and more often than not, despite the idiomatic strangeness this is to his (and the author's) advantage: when the narrator in *The Garden of the Finzi-Continis* tells of his evenings spent in the company of the Milanese engineer Malnate, who is always careful to check that he returns home at the end of the evening by watching him enter his house, Bassani writes "l'ultima immagine che mi rimaneva di lui ..."; Quigly renders this unexceptionally as "My last sight of him was always the same", whereas Weaver's version, "The last image of him left to me was always the same", although strange in its echo of the Italian, shares more expressively in the concerns of the book, full as it is of lingering images that are powerful yet inexplicable, as well as being more plangent (in general Weaver is more sensitive to the rhythms of Bassani's prose). Bassani has a sensitive ear for the distinctive qualities of other people's speech, generally rendered through free indirect discourse, his preferred narrative mode; again Quigly tends to flatten these, while Weaver is more successful. The narrator of *The Garden of the Finzi-Continis* is struck by the distinctive style of speech of Micòl Finzi-Contini and her brother, which he calls "finzi-continico": when she first talks to him from the top of a ladder resting against the garden wall she remarks that she has "sotto i piedi la mia brava scala a pioli", which Quigly renders as "I'm standing on my dear old ladder", while Weaver both hears and conveys more: "My feet are on my faithful ladder" (preserving the oddity of describing the stance in this way, the self-conscious rhythm and alliteration, Micòl's instinctive – and instinctively haughty – personalization of the objects that surround her).

In this connection, it might be added that the sparing use of dialect in Bassani's work and the way it is always introduced as something extraneous to the mainstream style of the text mean that it does not present a problem for translators. Quigly tends to keep it and provide a footnote; Weaver avoids footnotes but provides an accompanying paraphrase within the text when the meaning is not clear from context. It is surely a misjudgment, however, on Quigly's part to translate the half-contemptuous, half-compassionate comment in Ferrarese Jewish dialect made by the narrator's father when he sees the wretched and besotted Fadigati on the beach in Riccione (in *The Gold-Rimmed Spectacles*): "Puvràz". Quigly translates it as "Poor chap"; Weaver keeps the dialect word – "Puvràz ... poor man". Weaver is also more respectful of the culture-specific details in the books and more imaginative in transforming them into plausible English equivalents, where this is possible.

WEAVER's most successful translations are of the two books that exist only in his versions: *Dietro la porta* and *L'airone*. The skill of his translation here matches the incisiveness and focus that Bassani displays in these works. In his *Behind the Door* (1972) Weaver is enterprising in finding sustained equivalents both for the schoolmaster Guzzo's formal and erudite sarcasms and for the schoolboy Pulga's louche and slangy gossip. In *The Heron* (1970) he renders very well the slow-motion quality of the narrative, with its dream-like intensity of detail.

STEPHEN PARKIN

Further Reading

Baldelli, Ignazio, "La riscrittura 'totale' di un'opera: da *Le storie ferraresi* a *Dentro le mura* di Bassani", *Lettere italiane*, 26 (1974)

Chiappini, Alessandra and Gianni Venturi (editors), *Bassani e Ferrara: le intermittenze del cuore*, Ferrara: Corbo, 1995

De Stefanis, Giusi Oddo, *Bassani: entro il cerchio delle sue mura*, Ravenna: Longo, 1981

Radcliff-Umstead, Douglas, *The Exile into Eternity: A Study of the Narrative Writings of Giorgio Bassani*, Rutherford, New Jersey: Fairleigh Dickinson University Press, and London: Associated University Presses, 1981

Sempoux, André (editor), *Il Romanzo di Ferrara: contributi su Giorgio Bassani*, Louvain-la-Neuve: Presses Universitaires de Louvain, 1983

See also the introductions by Jonathan Keates to the reprinted editions of Weaver's translations of *Behind the Door* and *The Heron* (London: Quartet, 1992, 1993)

Charles Baudelaire 1821–1867

French poet and art critic

Biography

Born in Paris, 9 April 1821. His father was a wealthy civil servant, who introduced his son to art and died when Baudelaire was five years old. His stepfather, colonel Jacques Aupick, whom his mother married in 1828, was an ambitious soldier who went on to become a general, and later a diplomat and senator. When his stepfather was posted to Lyons in 1831, Baudelaire attended the Collège Royal de Lyon, going later, when the family moved back to Paris in 1836, to the Lycée Louis-le-Grand. He was expelled from the school for a disciplinary matter in 1839, but obtained his baccalauréat in the same year. He was a law student at the École de Droit, University of Paris, 1839–41, living in bohemian style in the Latin Quarter of Paris, frequenting prostitutes and falling into debt. He was sent to India by his stepfather in 1841, but left the ship when it called at the Île Bourbon (now Réunion) and returned to Paris in 1842. He was able to start living on his inheritance from his father later that year, and he began writing poetry, experimenting with opium and spending extravagantly. He started a relationship with a beautiful mulatto woman, Jeanne Duval, who became his mistress, the inspiration for his poetic writing and later his financial responsibility. Deeply involved with the Paris cultural scene, he associated with the artists Delacroix, Manet and Daumier; his first writings on art criticism were reviews of the Paris *Salons* of 1845 and 1846. After 1844, Baudelaire's profligate lifestyle and debt resulted in his stepfather's legal withdrawal of access to his inheritance, and he was forced to live on a restricted allowance; this exacerbated the antagonism he felt towards his stepfather and caused periods of angry depression. Baudelaire became interested in the work of Edgar Allan Poe in 1847 and contributed translations regularly to literary journals; his collections of Poe's work in translation were published in 1856 and 1857.

The first edition of *Les Fleurs du mal* (*Flowers of Evil*), his controversial collection of poems, was published in 1857, and led to trial and prosecution for indecency. He was fined for offences against public morals; six of the poems in *Les Fleurs du mal* were banned from the book, later to be published in Belgium in 1866 as *Les Épaves* [Wreckage]. In 1859 Baudelaire went to live for a while, intermittently,with his mother in Honfleur and wrote a number of poems, including "Le Voyage" ("The Journey") and his volume of art criticism, *Le Peintre de la vie moderne* (*The Painter of Modern Life*) published in *Le Figaro* in 1863. In 1860 he published in volume form his translations of part of Thomas De Quincey's

Confessions of an English Opium-Eater (*Les Paradis artificiels*), and the following year an enlarged edition of *Les Fleurs du mal*. He attempted unsuccessfully to be admitted to the French Academy in 1861. He was further embroiled in financial difficulties after his friend and publisher, Poulet-Malassis, was declared bankrupt in 1862. He became physically and mentally ill, dependent on alcohol and opium. A sequence of 20 of his prose poems was published in *La Presse* in 1862. In 1864 he went to Brussels to try to find a publisher for his work; he became increasingly ill and financially destitute. He returned to Paris in 1866, where he collapsed; paralyzed, he spent the rest of his life in a sanatorium there. Died in Paris, 31 August 1867.

The work for which Baudelaire is best known is his poetry collection *Les Fleurs du mal*, published in part in the journal the *Revue des Deux Mondes*, June 1855, and later in volume form in 1857 and 1861. The 1861 edition contains 126 poems in six sections, including a new section, *Tableaux parisiens*. Other notable works by Baudelaire include his *Petits Poèmes en prose*, 1869, his 1847 autobiographical story, *La Fanfarlo*, his art criticism and his translations from the work of Poe and De Quincey.

Editions

Although in their fame and availability in English the *Flowers of Evil* far outstrip the rest of Baudelaire's works, his prose poems, novella (*La Fanfarlo*), art criticism and some other essays, journals and correspondence have also found anglophone translators, often of appropriate eminence and skill.

Anyone consulting the French texts should use the *Oeuvres complètes*, 2 vols, edited by Claude Pichois, Paris: Gallimard, 1975–76 (Bibliothèque de la Pléiade), for all except the letters. The authoritative edition for the letters is *Correspondance*, edited by Claude Pichois with Jean Ziegler, 2 vols, Paris: Gallimard, 1973 (Bibliothèque de la Pléiade). Benjamin's social history (see Further Reading) re-creates the underside of Baudelaire's Paris and thus supports the view of the city presented in the "Spleen" poems and the *Paris Spleen* prose poems. Readers should bear in mind that during the Restoration and the Bourgeois Monarchy, regimes Baudelaire's detested stepfather served with distinction, Paris acquired its international reputation as a capital of fashion, glamour and romance.

Translations (other than of *The Flowers of Evil*, for which see below)

Selections

Cameron, Norman, *My Heart Laid Bare and Other Prose Writing*, with an introduction by Peter Quennell, London: Weidenfeld and Nicolson, 1950; New York: Vanguard Press, 1951 (contains *The Painter of Modern Life*, *The Poem of Hashish*, 19 *Short Poems in Prose*, "Journals and Notebooks")

Charvet, P.E., *Selected Writings on Art and Literature*, with an introduction, Harmondsworth: Penguin, 1992 (originally published as *Selected Writings on Art and Artists*, 1972)

Clark, Carol and Robert Sykes (editors), selection in *Baudelaire in English*, London and New York: Penguin, 1997 (contains 14 prose poems, by eight translators)

Crowley, Aleister, *Little Poems in Prose*, Paris: Titus, 1928

Hamburger, Michael, *Twenty Prose Poems of Baudelaire*, with an introduction, London: Poetry London, 1946; revised edition (parallel texts), London: Jonathan Cape, 1968, San Francisco: City Lights, 1988

Hemmings, F.W.J., *City Blues* (selection), Melton Mowbray, Leicestershire: Brewhouse Private Press, and Coalville, Utah: Saint Bernard Press, 1977 (contains 18 prose poems)

Kaplan, Edward K., *The Parisian Prowler*, Athens: University of Georgia Press, 1989 (contains 50 prose poems)

Lloyd, Rosemary, *The Prose Poems*, with *La Fanfarlo*, translated by Lloyd, Oxford: Oxford University Press, 1991

Scarfe, Francis, *The Poems in Prose*, with *La Fanfarlo*, translated by Scarfe, London: Anvil Press, 1989

Symons, Arthur, *Poems in Prose from Charles Baudelaire* (selection), London: Mathews, 1905; Portland, Maine: Mosher, 1909

Varèse, Louise, *Paris Spleen, 1869*, New York: New Directions, 1947; London: Peter Owen, 1951

Prose Poems

Petits Poèmes en prose, 1869, later entitled *Le Spleen de Paris*

Cameron, Norman, *Short Poems in Prose*, selection in *My Heart Laid Bare and Other Prose Writing*, translated by Cameron, 1950 (contains 19 prose poems)

Novella

La Fanfarlo, 1847

Boyd, Greg, *La Fanfarlo* (bilingual edition), with an introduction, Berkeley, California: Creative Arts Press, 1986

Lloyd, Rosemary, *La Fanfarlo*, with *The Prose Poems*, translated by Lloyd, 1991

Scarfe, Francis, *La Fanfarlo*, with *The Poems in Prose*, translated by Scarfe, London: Anvil Press, 1989

Essay

Les Paradis artificiels, 1860

Cameron, Norman, *The Poem of Hashish*, in *My Heart Laid Bare and Other Prose Writing*, translated by Cameron, 1950

Diamond, Stacy, *Artificial Paradises*, Secaucus, New Jersey: Carol, 1996

Criticism

Salons, 1845, 1846, 1855, 1859

Mayne, Jonathan, *Art in Paris, 1845–1862: Salons and Other Exhibitions Reviewed by Charles Baudelaire*, London: Phaidon, 1965; 2nd edition 1981

L'Oeuvre et la vie d'Eugène Delacroix, 1863

Bernstein, Joseph M., *Eugène Delacroix: His Life and Work*, New York: Lear, 1947

Le Peintre de la vie moderne, 1863

Cameron, Norman, *The Painter of Modern Life* in *My Heart Laid Bare and Other Prose Writing*, translated by Cameron, 1950

Mayne, Jonathan, *The Painter of Modern Life and Other Essays*, London: Phaidon, 1964; 2nd edition 1995

Edgar Allan Poe, sa vie et ses ouvrages, 1852

Bandy, W.T. (editor and translator), *Seven Tales by Edgar Allan Poe together for the First Time with Their French Translation and a Prefatory Essay by Charles Baudelaire*, New York: Schocken, 1971 (includes translations of "The Black Cat", "Mesmeric Revelation", "Ligeia", "The Man in the Crowd", "The Oval Portrait", "The Fall of the House of Usher", "The Purloined Letter")

Journals
Journaux intimes, 1920
Cameron, Norman, *My Heart Laid Bare* in *My Heart Laid Bare and Other Prose Writing*, translated by Cameron, 1950; as *Intimate Journals*, with an introduction by Richard Howard, London: Syrens, 1995
Isherwood, Christopher, *Intimate Journals*, with an introduction by T.S. Eliot, London: Blackamore Press , and New York: Random House 1930 (contains *Squibs and Crackers, My Heart Laid Bare, A Selection of Consoling Maxims on Love*)

Letters
Lloyd, Rosemary, *Selected Letters of Charles Baudelaire: The Conquest of Solitude*, Chicago: University of Chicago Press, and London: Weidenfeld and Nicolson, 1986
Morini, Simona and Frederic Tuten, *Letters from His Youth*, New York: Doubleday, 1970
Symons, Arthur, *The Letters of Charles Baudelaire to His Mother, 1833–1866*, London: Rodker, 1928; New York: Haskell House, 1971

As a literary genre, the prose poem overflows demarcation and definition. However, Baudelaire's 50 "little poems in prose" have given tradition a model, subsequently used in evaluating other prose poems. His model is elusive by design, alternating irony and lyricism, embedding enigmatic anecdotes and apostrophes, these always accompanied by elliptical commentary that, again by design, apparently explains what has gone before but chiefly confuses it. The narrating persona, a man, not unlike Baudelaire himself, usually speaks *to* us but, on occasion, he speaks to someone else within our reader's earshot (18, "Invitation to the Voyage") or lets us witness a miniature drama (15, "The Cake") or speaks about himself in the third person (45, "The Shooting Range and the Cemetery"). These poems are brief, ranging from 75 to 1,500 words. Their language is charged visually (phanopeia, in Pound's terminology), aurally (melopeia) and etymologically and culturally (logopeia).

The composition of the prose poems generally paralleled that of *The Flowers of Evil*, usually taking up the same subjects after the drafting of the verse poems (indeed Claude Pichois believes there is only one exception to this pattern: number 17, "A Hemisphere in Tresses"). Usually, the prose version of the particular insight or experience involved is a little more ironic in tone than the poem version, a little more bleak in expectation. For example, in the *Flowers of Evil* "Invitation to the Voyage" the poet offers an imaginary visit to a port, recognizable as Amsterdam, where in an atmosphere of

> ... ordre et beauté
> Luxe, calme et volupté

literally, "order and beauty, luxury, calm, and voluptuousness", the couple will understand the secret language of the soul:

> Tout y parlerait
> À l'âme en secret
> Sa douce langue natale.

The – much longer – prose poem "Invitation to the Voyage" multiplies the site's accoutrements of tasteful luxury but indicates – "Des rêves! toujours des rêves!" ("Dreams, dreams ever!" SYMONS, 1905) – that not even in imagination could they hope to step into that picture.

In sum, like *The Flowers of Evil*, the prose poems promise to yield to new readings indefinitely, and in the end this inexhaustible richness qualifies them as poems, rather than vignettes or sketches. The "yield" is particularly rich when they are read in tandem with a translation. However, they have not received anything approaching the same number of translations as the *Flowers*.

No English version of the *Poems in Prose* has yet achieved the resonance that bilingual readers hear or imagine (but rarely articulate). Thus, any translation inevitably falls short of the subjective criteria being applied. However, most of the existing texts serve to prove that a good poet with good material can elicit moving and sensitive translations. It might be supposed that SYMONS (1905), who played such an important role in introducing French Symbolism and Decadence to English-speaking writers, would prove the ideal translator (like Baudelaire for Poe). But Symons was a wordsmith rather than a poet, and his translations of Baudelaire's poetry and poetic prose are less successful than those he did (SYMONS, 1928) of the letters. HAMBURGER (1946) and VARÈSE (1947) produced touching and sensitive versions from the prose poems; if these had been kept in print no subsequent translation would have been necessary. The CAMERON selection of works (1950) includes, as well as *The Painter of Modern Life*, *The Poem of Hashish*, and "Journals and Notebooks", a 19-item selection of *Short Poems in Prose*. KAPLAN's *Parisian Prowler* (1989), which won the Lewis Galantière prize of the American Translators Association in 1990, presents a unified narrative voice. This unity makes visible the links from one poem to the next; the interpretation is supported by erudition (see Kaplan, 1990).

The CLARK & SYKES anthology (1997) contains English versions, with brief editorial comments, of 14 of the 50 *Petits Poèmes en prose* and their verse epilogue, by eight different hands. This judicious selection covers a wide chronological and stylistic range: SYMONS (1905, two prose poems and the epilogue); CROWLEY (1928, three items); HAMBURGER (1946, two items); VARÈSE (1947, two items); CAMERON (1950, one item); HEMMINGS (1977, two items); KAPLAN (1989, one item); and CLARK (1997, one item). A general closeness to the original wording leads, in several of the items included, to a certain amount of word-for-word translation of French set phrases, as if these carried authorial intention, and to marked under-use of particular syntactic resources of English (for example, of the option of sometimes omitting relative *that* and *which*) where these could have helped to avoid prosiness and gallicisms and to preserve the expressive cadences of the source.

In the ironic novella *La Fanfarlo*, translated by BOYD (1986), SCARFE (1989), and LLOYD (1991), Baudelaire models his title character on the dancer Lola Montès, the triumphant wife, Madame de Cosmelly, on his sister-in-law (married to his step-brother from his father's first marriage), and the duped poet and theatre critic Samuel Kramer on himself. Madame de Cosmelly enlists Cramer, with whom she had a teenage flirtation, to ingratiate himself with the dancer (whose interest he arouses by writing hostile reviews of her performances) and thus lead her to drop Monsieur de Cosmelly from her list of lovers. Boyd's carefully annotated bilingual edition is no longer in print.

BANDY's facing-page bilingual edition (1971) of Baudelaire's essay of 1852 on Edgar Allan Poe and of seven tales Baudelaire translated from Poe's English is a treasure for translation studies. For over a quarter of a century Bandy was the doyen of US Baudelaire scholarship and a close collaborator of Claude Pichois.

Like MAYNE's renderings (1965) of the *Salons*, all the translations listed above of Baudelaire's correspondence – SYMONS (1928), MORINI & TUTIN (1970), and LLOYD (1986) – are competent; Lloyd's can be considered authoritative.

MARILYN GADDIS ROSE

Further Reading

Benjamin, Walter, *Charles Baudelaire: A Lyric Poet in the Era of High Capitalism*, translated by Harry Zohn, London: New Left Books, 1973
Derrida, Jacques, *Given Time*, vol. 1: *Counterfeit Money*, translated by Peggy Kamuf, Chicago: University of Chicago Press, 1990
Kaplan, Edward K., *Baudelaire's Prose Poems*, Athens: University of Georgia Press, 1990
Richardson, Joanna, *Baudelaire*, London: John Murray, and New York: St Martin's Press, 1994
Sartre, Jean-Paul, *Baudelaire*, translated by Martin Turnell, London: Horizon, 1949; New York: New Directions, 1950

The Flowers of Evil

Les Fleurs du mal, 1857; 2nd edition 1861

Probably the most famous and most widely influential volume produced by a modern French poet, Baudelaire's *Les Fleurs du mal* appeared on 25 June 1857. The Ministry of the Interior banned the volume in July, accusing the author of "outrage to public decency". On 20 August, the Sixth District Court fined the author 300 francs (reduced to 50 francs upon appeal) and the publishers 100 francs apiece. Six poems were withdrawn ("Lesbos", "Femmes damnées – Delphine et Hippolyte", "Le Léthé", "À celle qui est trop gaie", "Les Bijoux", and "Les Métamorphoses du vampire") and published privately in 1858. The first edition contained 100 poems (including those that would have to be withdrawn). The second edition, lacking the condemned pieces, appeared in early February 1861, with 126 numbered poems. The third edition, containing 151 poems but without the censored six, appeared posthumously in volume 1 of the *Œuvres complètes de Charles Baudelaire* (19 December 1868). Because Charles Asselineau and Théodore de Banville established the final order of poems in the third edition, the second edition is usually followed as being the latest ordering of poems by Baudelaire himself.

Translations

Complete Translations

Campbell, Roy, *Poems of Baudelaire*, London: Harvill Press, 1952
Crosby, William H., *The Flowers of Evil and Paris Spleen*, with an introduction by Anna Balakian, Brockport, New York: BOA, 1991
Duke, Francis, *The Flowers of Evil and Other Poems*, Charlottesville: University of Virginia Press, 1961
Howard, Richard, *Les Fleurs du mal*, Boston: Godine, 1982
McGowan, James, *Charles Baudelaire: The Flowers of Evil*, with an introduction by Jonathan Culler, Oxford: Oxford University Press, 1993

Selections

Dillon, George and Edna St Vincent Millay, *Flowers of Evil* (parallel texts), with an introduction by Millay, New York: Harper, 1936
Egan, Beresford and C. Bower Alcock, *Flowers of Evil: Fleurs du mal in Pattern and Prose*, London: Sophistocles Press–Werner Laurie, 1929; New York: Sylvan Press, 1947
Lappin, Kendall, *Echoes of Baudelaire: Selected Poems*, with an introduction by Greg Boyd, Santa Maria, California: Asylum Arts, 1992
Leakey, F.W., *Baudelaire: Selected Poems from "Les Fleurs du mal"*, Hexham, Northumberland: FWL Publications, 1994; 2nd edition, London: Greenwich Exchange, 1997
MacIntyre, C.F., *One Hundred Poems from Les Fleurs du mal*, Berkeley: University of California Press, 1947
Richardson, Joanna, *Selected Poems: Baudelaire* (parallel texts), with an introduction, Harmondsworth and Baltimore: Penguin, 1975
Scarfe, Francis, *Baudelaire*, with an introduction, Harmondsworth and Baltimore: Penguin, 1961 ("plain prose translations")
Shanks, Lewis Piaget, *Les Fleurs du mal*, New York: Holt, 1926
Shapiro, Norman R., *Selected Poems from Les Fleurs du mal* (parallel texts), with a foreword by Willis Barnstone, Chicago and London: University of Chicago Press, 1998
Squire, Jack Collings, *Poems and Baudelaire Flowers*, London: New Age Press, 1909
Sturm, F.P., *The Poems of Charles Baudelaire*, with an introduction, London and New York: Walter Scott, 1906; without translator's name, in *The Poems and Prose Poems of Charles Baudelaire*, edited by James Huneker, New York: Brentano, 1919; New York: AMS Press, 1981
Symons, Arthur, *Les Fleurs du mal, Petits Poèmes en prose, Les Paradis artificiels*, London: Casanova Society, 1925; in *Baudelaire, Rimbaud, Verlaine: Selected Verse and Prose Poems*, edited and with an introduction by Joseph M. Bernstein, New York: Citadel Press, 1947

Anthologies (compiling the work of various translators)

Clark, Carol and Robert Sykes (editors), *Baudelaire in English*, with an introduction, London and New York: Penguin, 1997
Laver, James and Jacob Epstein (editors), *Charles Baudelaire: Flowers of Evil*, with an introduction, London: Limited Editions Club, 1940
Mathews, Marthiel and Jackson Mathews (editors), *Charles Baudelaire: The Flowers of Evil* (bilingual edition), with an introduction, New York: New Directions, 1955; revised, with some new translations, 1963

Scarfe argues that we must see *Les Fleurs* as "a complete work, a unit with its own internal structure" (1961, introduction). The sense of Baudelaire's thematic structuration and the sequence of different poetic forms (poems in quatrains, exceptional stanzaic line groups, sonnets, and non-strophic poems) is lost in those editions where translators have seen fit to reorder the poems for chronological or thematic reasons (SYMONS, EGAN & ALCOCK, SCARFE, DILLON & MILLAY). Some translators (along with many critics) have found Baudelaire's poetic technique lacking in originality (RICHARDSON) or "traditional" (CROSBY, MCGOWAN). It is far more judicious to say that Baudelaire was a master of classical French versification and that he sets up surprising tensions between conventions of verse technique (metre and rhyme, most visibly) and other aspects of his poetic discourse. Over 100 of the 126 poems in the second edition are in traditional poetic form – 60 sonnets (with extraordinarily varied rhyme schemes), 42 poems in quatrains, and 17 non-stanzaic poems (rhyming couplets) – but Baudelaire strategically places a small number of pieces composed in unusual typographical groupings (2-, 3-, 5-, 14-line groups) throughout the volume. All of this is lost in free-verse and prose translations and in those volumes where the order of the pieces is disrupted. The approach that leaves aside rhyme and/or metre in favor of lexical fidelity and the reproduction of imagery fails to give the reader of the target language a sense of the true poetry, but attempts at exact reproduction of French versification inevitably involve a serious departure from the poetic diction of the original.

When Marthiel & Jackson Mathews state in their introduction that "no one can translate all of the poems of a great poet", they doubtless think of consistently "successful" translations. A few translators have published significant selections or complete versions of the *Fleurs* that betoken skill and reflection, even if the results may be evaluated variously.

The 50 versions published by English poet STURM (1906) still merit consideration. He respects Baudelaire's stanzaic forms and frequently the rhyme schemes, without straining for rhyme at all costs ("The Swan"). His "Contemplation" ("Recueillement") reads with a tinge of archaic eloquence: "Thou, O my Grief, be wise and tranquil still, / The eve is thine which even now drops down..." Represented only by "To a Brown Beggar-maid" in the LAVER & EPSTEIN anthology (1940), to MARTHIEL & JACKSON MATHEWS (1955) his versions appeared superior (18 poems). Although his "grief" for "angoisse" is debatable in the first stanza of "Reversibility", the second stanza is surprisingly close to the original:

Angel of kindness, have you tasted hate?
With hands clenched in the dark, and tears of gall,
When Vengeance beats her hellish battle-call,
And makes herself the captain of our fate,
Angel of kindness, have you tasted hate?

SQUIRE (1909) followed Sturm closely and was the favorite of Laver & Epstein (29 poems). Like Sturm, Squire transposes alexandrines into iambic pentameters. He follows Baudelaire's rhyme schemes, managing even to keep the tension between syntactic and metrical structure, as in the second quatrain of "The Spiritual Dawn", where the sentence stops short of the stanza (lines 5–7). The Mathews anthology still retains 10 Squire poems, although Sturm and Campbell are their favorites.

Bernstein's opinion that SYMONS (1925) offers the version "nearest the original in spirit" (Bernstein (editor), introduction) would be hard to defend. Fidelity to the original is sacrificed mercilessly in an abortive effort to reproduce Baudelaire's metre and rhyme – iambic hexameter for the French alexandrine in "To the Reader". Where "the Sun" in the poem of that name orders "harvests" to flourish in the "immortal heart" of the poet, Symons has him make "the harvest ripen as he cherishes / The immortal heart before the whole world perishes!" – a rendering that barely relates to the original. He distorts the unique 14-line stanza of "Invitation to the Journey" by expanding the first 12 lines to 13 plus the 2-line refrain, for no obvious reason.

SHANKS (1926), professor of French literature at Harvard, was, the Mathewses point out, the first American to translate the complete *Fleurs*. His "The Phantom" found favor with Laver & Epstein (who retained 18 of his translations) and with the Mathewses:

Down in the fathomless despair
Where Destiny has locked me in,
Where light nor joy descends, and where
– Sole lodger of Night's dreary inn [...]

In the source text, this and the following three sonnets, grouped under the same general title, are (along with "The Death of Lovers") written in decasyllables. Shanks has done them into the iambic tetrameter often used for the octosyllable, thus losing the metrical distinction between Baudelaire's 8-syllable and his 10-syllable lines.

The EGAN & ALCOCK versions (1929) are done into prose paragraphs with a torturous syntax. "Posthumous Remorse" is rendered in one sentence, like the original periodic sonnet. At times the translators' diction barely relates to the original, as in "The Balcony": "Fled love of all loves ..." for "Mère des souvenirs, maîtresse des maîtresses ..."

If their versions rarely stand out above all others, DILLON & MILLAY (1936) do produce original renderings while striving for the equivalent of Baudelaire's rhyme schemes and metres. Millay's clock ("L'Horloge") ticks with crisp regularity: "*Remember!* Time, the player that need not cheat to win, / Makes a strong adversary. Is thy game begun?" In Dillon's rhythmic tetrameter for "The Vampire", the poison and sword say:

"Though one of us should be the tool
To save thee from thy wretched fate,
Thy kisses would resuscitate
The body of thy vampire, fool!"

MACINTYRE (1947) ranks approximately with Squire for the Mathewses (11 poems). For the alexandrine, he uses an iambic pentameter that tends toward a dactylic rhythm, as in his version of "Sed non satiata" (he keeps Baudelaire's Latin title):

Bizarre deity, as dark as night,
Scented with musky perfume and Havana,
Work of some obi, the Faust of the savanna,
Witch with ebony flanks, child of black midnight.

He is unable to orchestrate the same two vowels, "a" and "i", throughout the "Sonnet d'Automne" as does Baudelaire. While it is true that "there is no way in which a translator ... can miraculously recreate for an English reader even the approximate aural connotations and associations that a French poem has for a French reader" (Leakey, 1994, introduction), the disappearance of obsessive sonorities is a distinct loss. In "The Ragpickers' Wine", MacIntyre maintains Baudelaire's flat rhyme scheme (aabb) configured in quatrains. In the final stanza, the mellifluous flow of the original becomes more cacophonic:

To lull these wretches' sloth and drown the hate
Of all who mutely die, compassionate,
God has created sleep's oblivion:
Man added Wine, divine child of the Sun.

The South African poet CAMPBELL (1952) is favored with 31 poems in the Mathews anthology, including some of the longer pieces – "The Seven Old Men", "The Little Old Women", and "Lesbians". He retains Baudelaire's abab quatrains, with iambic pentameter, in "The Little Old Women":

In sinuous folds of cities old and grim,
Where all things, even horror, turn to grace,
I follow, in obedience to my whim,
Strange, feeble, charming creatures round the place.

In "The Cat" (LI in the second French edition), he keeps the abba rhyme scheme with a lilting iambic tetrameter:

A fine strong gentle cat is prowling
As in his bedroom, in my brain;
So soft his voice, so smooth its strain
That you can scarcely hear him miowling.

RICHARDSON's metrical renderings (1975) mark a midpoint in the spectrum of translation strategies. She renders alexandrines by iambic pentameters and sometimes hints at Baudelaire's rhyme schemes: "The sea's your mirror; you observe your soul / Perpetually as its waves unroll..." ("Man and the Sea"). Her rhythms suggest those of the original when the mistress walks "Like a long serpent which a sorceress / Stirs into rhythmic measure with her wand" ("Clad in her undulating pearly dress ...").

For the sake of rhyme, DUKE (1961) distorts: Elvira's "faithless lover who had once been true" (Don Juan was never true). Certain versions are better: "How brightly space today is lit! / With neither bridle, spur, nor bit / Let's ride away astride of wine ..." ("Lovers' Wine").

HOWARD (1982) foregoes rhyme and the "varnish" of the individual piece in favor of "articulating a sustained structure among all the poems". He can represent Baudelaire's sustained rhythm with new sound: "Shivering dawn, in a wisp of pink and green, / Totters slowly across the empty Seine ..." ("Twilight: Daybreak"). Leakey (1992) cites his rendering of "The Murderer's Wine" as a "complete and sensational success": "My wife is dead, so now I'm free / To drink until I drop".

CROSBY (1991) has an ability to maintain Baudelaire's rhymes and at times even his diction: "When low and sullen skies lie solid as a lid / Upon the groaning spirit, prey to long ennui ..." (*en proie aux longs ennuis* – "Spleen", IV). Through use of cognates, he occasionally gives a sense of the sonorities of the original: "How far, perfumed paradise [*paradis parfumé*], how far from me, / Where only love and joy reflect an azure sky ..."

LAPPIN (1992) eschews "the rhyme-scheme entirely" and strives "for strict semantic fidelity to what the poet actually says or clearly implies, without omission or substantive addition." The result is sometimes unpoetic – "All Nature's a temple whose pillars, alive, / Sometimes utter words indistinct and unclear ..." ("Correspondences") – but occasionally reads smoothly: "For a long time I dwelt beneath vast porticoes / Which the suns and the sea tinged with myriad fires ..." ("The Previous Life").

While McGOWAN (1993) is willing to let rhyme come as it will, he remains consistently close to Baudelairean metre and rhyme. His "Murderer's Wine" equals or betters Howard's version: "My wife is dead and I am free! / And I can guzzle all I want." The combination of bi- and tri-accentual metres in his "Invitation to the Voyage" gives a rhythmically close equivalent to the French:

My sister, my child
Imagine how sweet
To live there as lovers do!

LEAKEY (1994) shares with Howard accuracy along with a sense of concise, pithy discourse. At best, Leakey offers sustained, unadorned rhythm conveying its own poetry: "My youth flashed by as one dark storm, / Lit by rare shafts of brilliant sun..." ("The Enemy"). It is difficult, however, to accept the extreme liberties he takes with Baudelaire's poetic forms. In "To the Reader", the lines fall into heteroclite typographical groups that give no hint of the original quatrains. The sonnet form is sometimes thrown to the winds through condensation ("The Phantom", I), unequal groups of lines ("Correspondences") and inverted groups (6+8 lines in "Evening Meditation" – a liberty that Baudelaire used elsewhere, but not here). The anglophone reader (of whatever nationality) who can be induced to read or hear poetry is likely to have some idea about traditional poetic form, and may be surprised in particular at this violence done to the sonnet.

SHAPIRO (1998) offers the latest significant selection of renderings from *Les Fleurs*, with parallel texts. Although he favors working with selected poems over compulsive completeness, he includes 42 of the 60 sonnets present in the second, 1861, edition. Like others before him, Shapiro uses the iambic pentameter as a conventional equivalent of the French alexandrine, and approximates other meters. He often follows Baudelaire's rhyme schemes, literally or as closely as possible. Without slavishly attempting to re-create Baudelaire's exact form, he engages in new word and sound play that approaches Baudelaire's own techniques. The first quatrain of "Sonnet d'automne" displays sustained echoes of the English long "e":

I look into your crystal eyes and see:
"Why me, strange lover? What am I, to meet
With your esteem?" Hush, and play coy, my sweet!
My heart, at odds, save with the brutal, free [...]

It is not possible to deal here with all the translators who have experimented with rendering Baudelaire in English. Laver &

Epstein, the Mathews & Mathews, and Clark & Sykes reproduce Aldous Huxley's version of "Lesbians: Delphine and Hippolyta", which Leakey praises as "the one undoubted masterpiece that the translation of *Les Fleurs du Mal* into English verse has yielded" (1992, p.102). The Laver & Epstein anthology used three versions by English composer Cyril Scott and one by Countee Cullen (poet of the Harlem Renaissance). In the Mathews anthology, among other more recent well-known poets, we find Doreen Bell, Barbara Gibbs, Anthony Hecht, Robert Lowell (8 poems), Richard Wilbur, and Yvor Winters. The 1997 anthology by CLARK & SYKES (1997) is a judicious selection of translations ranging over the gamut of efforts and contains a generally excellent introduction on Baudelaire and the history of his translators.

CARROL F. COATES

Further Reading

Burton, Richard D.E., *Baudelaire in 1859: A Study in the Sources of Poetic Creativity*, Cambridge and New York: Cambridge University Press, 1988

Burton, Richard D.E., *Baudelaire and the Second Republic: Writing and Revolution*, Oxford: Clarendon Press, and New York: Oxford University Press, 1991

Chesters, Graham, *Baudelaire and the Poetics of Craft*, Cambridge and New York: Cambridge University Press, 1988

Leakey, F.W., *Baudelaire: "Les Fleurs du Mal"*, Cambridge and New York: Cambridge University Press, 1992

Pichois, Claude and Jean Ziegler, *Baudelaire*, translated by Graham Robb, London: Hamish Hamilton, 1989

Swinburne, Algernon Charles, *"Les Fleurs du Mal" and Other Studies*, edited by Edmond Gosse, London: privately printed, 1913; New York: AMS Press, 1985

Wright, Barbara, review of Walter Martin's *Charles Baudelaire: Complete Poems* (Manchester: Carcanet, 1997), *In Other Words*, 12 (Winter 1998)

See also the editors' introduction to Clark & Sykes

François-Augustin Caron de Beaumarchais 1732–1799

French dramatist and memorialist

Biography

Born Pierre-Augustin Caron, in Paris, 24 January 1732, the third of six surviving children. He was educated at a trade school, the École des Métiers d'Alfort, 1742–45, then apprenticed to his clockmaker father; in 1753 he invented a new escapement mechanism. In 1755 he began to buy official posts in the royal household. In 1756 he married the widow of a fellow official and in 1757, the year of her death, added to his name that of a small property of hers, so becoming "de Beaumarchais". Growing popular at court, he gave music lessons to Louis XV's daughters. In 1761 he bought ennoblement with the title of secrétaire du Roi. He went to Madrid in 1764 as agent for the financier Pâris-Duverney; married again in 1768 (a rich widow who died in 1770), increasing his fortune, already augmented by speculations; was involved in several spectacular court cases in the 1770s; was a secret government agent 1774–75, arranging aid to the American insurgents; and in 1777 was involved in founding an organization for the defence of authors' rights. He married for the third time in 1786. From the three marriages one daughter survived. With the Revolution his fortunes declined. Arrested on suspicion of profiteering from arms, 1792, he fled to London, returning to France, 1793. From 1794, after more wanderings, arms deals and imprisonments, he was exiled in Holland and Germany until July 1796. Died in Paris, 17/18 May 1799.

Amid his many other activities, Beaumarchais also lived dangerously as a writer. After some early *parades*, or farcical sketches, for performance in society, and as well as three bourgeois dramas (*Eugénie*, 1767, *Les Deux Amis*, 1770, and in 1792 *La Mère coupable*, an inferior sequel to the Figaro plays) he wrote two reverberating comic masterpieces, *Le Barbier de Séville* (1775) and *Le Mariage de Figaro* (1784). There was also an opera (1787), but his other triumph as a writer was a series of four polemical *Mémoires* (1773–74).

Translations

Selections of Plays

Anderson, Graham, *The Barber of Seville, The Marriage of Figaro, The Guilty Mother: Three Plays*, with an introduction, Bath, Avon: Absolute Press, 1993

Wells, John, *The Figaro Plays*, edited by John Leigh, London: Dent, 1997 (contains *The Barber of Seville*, *The Marriage of Figaro*, *A Mother's Guilt*)

Plays

Eugénie, 1767

Griffith, Elizabeth, *The School for Rakes*, London: Beckett and De Hondt, 1769 and several further editions

Les Deux Amis; ou, Le Négociant de Lyon, 1770

C. H., *The Two Friends; or, The Liverpool Merchant,* London: Gebhart Earle and Hamet, 1800

Le Barbier de Séville; ou, La Précaution inutile, 1775
Anderson, Graham, *The Barber of Seville* in *The Barber of Seville, The Marriage of Figaro, The Guilty Mother*, translated by Anderson, 1993
Ellis, Brobury Pearce, *The Barber of Seville; or, The Useless Precaution*, New York: Appleton Century Crofts, 1966
Fawcett, John and Daniel Terry, *The Barber of Seville*, London: Thomas Hailes Lacy, 1870
Fowlie, Wallace, *The Barber of Seville* in *Classical French Drama*, edited by Fowlie, New York: Bantam, 1962
Griffith, Elizabeth, *The Barber of Seville; or, The Useless Precaution*, London: J. Chouquet, 1776
Myrick, Arthur B., *The Barber of Seville*, lyrics translated by George Allan England, London: Dent, and New York: Dutton, 1905
Wood, John, *The Barber of Seville*, with *The Marriage of Figaro*, with an introduction, Harmondsworth: Penguin, 1964

La Folle Journée; ou, Le Mariage de Figaro, 1785, produced 1784
Anderson, Graham, *The Marriage of Figaro* in *The Barber of Seville, The Marriage of Figaro, The Guilty Mother*, translated by Anderson, 1993
Gaskill, William, *The Marriage of Figaro*, songs by Pauline Melville (performed at the Crucible Theatre, Sheffield, 1988) in *Landmarks of French Classical Drama*, with an introduction by David Bradby, London: Methuen, 1991
Holcroft, Thomas, *The Follies of a Day; or, The Marriage of Figaro*, London: G.G.J. and J. Robinson, 1785; altered by John Philip Kemble, London: J. Barker, 1811
Wood, John, *The Marriage of Figaro*, with *The Barber of Seville*, with an introduction, Harmondsworth: Penguin, 1964

L'Autre Tartuffe; ou, La Mère coupable, 1794, produced 1792
Anderson, Graham, *The Guilty Mother* in *The Barber of Seville, The Marriage of Figaro, The Guilty Mother*, translated by Anderson, 1993
Wild, James, *Frailty and Hypocrisy*, London: John Hayes, 1804

Opera
Tarare, produced 1787, published in a revised version 1790
James, Mr C., *Tarare: An Opera in Five Acts, with a Prologue*, London: R. Faulder, 1787

Letters
Shewmake, Antoinette (editor and translator), *For the Good of Mankind: Pierre-Augustin Caron de Beaumarchais: Political Correspondence Relative to the American Revolution*, Lanham, Maryland: University Press of America, 1987

Such was the appeal of Beaumarchais's Figaro that English translations of *Le Barbier de Séville* and *Le Mariage de Figaro* followed within a year of their first appearance in print. All of the other plays except some early farces have been attempted, whatever their reception in the French theatre, by at least one translation. The earliest versions of the adventures of the heroi-comic barber were published in London; *The Barber of Seville* (1776) by Elizabeth GRIFFITH and *The Marriage of Figaro* (1785) by Thomas HOLCROFT. Mrs. Griffith had already translated *Eugénie* (1767) as *The School for Rakes* (1769). The third part of the Figaro trilogy, *La Mère coupable*, did not appear in London until 1804, in a version entitled *Frailty and Hypocrisy* by James WILD. The lesser known *Les Deux Amis; ou, Le Négociant de Lyon* (1770), translated by C.H. in 1800, became *The Two Friends; or, The Liverpool Merchant*. Neither the latter, nor *Eugénie*, seems to have been translated since then, but it is interesting to note the relative promptness with which Beaumarchais's works moved from the Parisian to the London stage.

Beaumarchais's reputation in the English-speaking theatre rests mainly therefore upon Figaro's exploits, and the translation history of the trilogy shows that *The Barber of Seville* has received most attention, while *The Guilty Mother* has only recently been published in one volume (ANDERSON, 1993, WELLS, 1997) with its more popular siblings. As their operatic life has been almost as long as their literary one, the librettos, notably Dent's (see Further Reading), are of interest.

Since 1987, SHEWMAKE's compilation of Beaumarchais's correspondence relative to the American Revolution has been available in English.

The idiosyncrasies of Beaumarchais's dramatic style have provided a challenge for translators. Three particular aspects of the problem may be identified. First, the dramatist's reliance on lists, usually sequences of verbs orchestrated by pauses for breath, movement, or both, loses its effect if the rhythmic phrasing is not reproduced. Second, although it has been justly observed that all Beaumarchais's characters speak in his style, they are nevertheless differentiated by register. Third, Beaumarchais's unflagging wordplay, manifested by double meanings, variants of sayings and proverbs, and his rich vocabulary, constitutes a pitfall for the unaware, if secondary meaning in the translation is to match the subtlety of the original.

MYRICK's *The Barber of Seville* (1905) is an interesting example and reminder of how the English language has changed over the past century. He refers in his brief introduction to the "dramatic ingenuity" and "nervous style" of the original, and his version successfully captures the sense of spontaneity characteristic of Beaumarchais's dialogue. He is best in scenes where the rank-marked style of the count is contrasted with the vernacular of Figaro, but this will now appear disconcertingly quaint, with the use of "'Tis" and "Faith". The deliberate archaisms of ENGLAND's lyrics evoke the age of madrigals.

Not all the 20th-century versions of *The Barber of Seville* are currently procurable (for example *The Barber of Sevilla* "translated literally into English" by E.R. Sahiar in Bombay in 1910). The select list includes three translations from the 1960s, of which two from the US, FOWLIE (1962) and ELLIS (1966), each translate *Le Barbier de Séville*, while from the UK WOOD (1964) has a volume containing *The Barber of Seville* and *The Marriage of Figaro*. All are respectful, neutral renderings, presumably designed to last as long as possible. They had, after all, been long awaited.

Fowlie's version is included in a collection of classic French plays. The accompanying introduction to the theatre of Beaumarchais refers to the timing of responses, an observation not always supported by the pedestrian, sometimes surprisingly literal text of the translation.

Ellis offers a livelier *Barber*, emulating the verve of the original by the use of freer renderings, a feature that would make it preferable for reading aloud. Although Beaumarchais tended to over-exploit his talent for the well-turned phrase, the translator must try to do it justice, and here it is respected. Figaro's definition of money as "le nerf de l'intrigue" (act 1, scene 6) appears as "gold is the sinews of intrigue" in Fowlie and Wood, whereas Ellis adds emphasis: "Money! That's what makes schemes work." Double meanings are attempted too. Figaro's self-portrait "faisant la barbe à tout le monde" (act 1, scene 2) produces "bearding everybody", less devil-may-care than the original, but more daring than most. Irrational speakers of British English may object to the Americanisms, albeit these are few.

Of the 1960s group, Wood shows the greatest sensitivity in all three aspects defined above as particularly problematic. Bazile's adapted proverbs are catchily converted: "ce qui est bon à prendre ... est bon ... à garder" (act 4, scene 1) becomes "Easy come ... easy go ... easy kept!" The social register is reproduced without excesses, and Wood is the least surprised by *faux amis* and the like. He alone assigns to the celebrated lines on drunkenness and the lower orders (act 1, scene 4) the appropriate meaning for "bonne" of "right" rather than "good". Nor does he translate literally Bartholo's allusive injunction to his sneezing servant "tu éternueras dimanche" (act 2, scene 7). Wood's *The Marriage of Figaro* is equally meticulous, and he reproduces expertly the changing moods of this more serious play, especially in the fifth act. He also differs from the rest in allowing each act to run seamlessly, having jettisoned scene divisions.

ANDERSON's version (1993) of all three Figaro plays at last enables the reader to make comparisons between them. The translator's introductory notes on his translation point out that this is certainly the first edition to be published in one volume. As an experienced translator, whose work has been commissioned for theatrical performance, Anderson recognizes the importance of writing speakable text but does not sacrifice the style of the original beyond the requirements of present-day comprehension or the substitution of one pun for another. In *The Marriage of Figaro* (act 3, scene 15), the argument between Bartholo and Figaro over the exact meaning of a written promise made to Marceline, turning upon the existence, or not, of an accent, is replaced by very acceptable wordplay in English. The translator himself acknowledges that he felt less free to adjust the text of so little-known a play as *La Mère coupable* and the result in that case is a fair rendering of the posturing heroi-tragicomic style that was and is doubtless partly responsible for the eclipse of the third part of the trilogy.

PEGGY CHAPLIN

Further Reading

Barzun, Jacques, "Racine and Beaumarchais", in *Phaedra and Figaro: Racine's Phèdre* [translated by Robert Lowell] *and Beaumarchais's Figaro's Marriage* [translated by Jacques Barzun], New York: Farrar Straus and Cudahy, 1961

Dent, Edward J. (translator), *The Barber of Seville* (libretto; from the Italian of Cesare Sterbini), London: Oxford University Press, 1940

Dent, Edward J. (translator), *Le Nozze di Figaro* (libretto by Lorenzo da Ponte), London and New York: Boosey and Hawkes, 1947 (English–Italian parallel texts, with essays in English)

Kite, Elizabeth S., *Beaumarchais and the War of American Independence*, Boston: R.G. Badger, 1918

See also translators' introductions to Anderson, Ellis, Fowlie, Wood

---

Simone de Beauvoir 1908–1986

French novelist, feminist and philosopher

Biography

Born in Paris, 9 January 1908, into an upper-middle-class family. Family fortunes dwindled and she initially became a philosophy teacher. In 1929 she formed a lifelong partnership and intellectual collaboration with Jean-Paul Sartre. Despite her talent for philosophy, her ambition was to be a literary writer. Nevertheless, much of her writing indicates her philosophical concerns.

Beauvoir's first published novel, *She Came to Stay* (*L'Invitée*, 1943, translated 1949) explores conflict in self–other relations. In her subsequent fiction of the 1940s, *The Blood of Others* (*Le Sang des autres*, 1945, translated 1948) and *All Men are Mortal* (*Tous les hommes sont mortels*, 1946, translated 1955), the existentialist aspects of *She Came to Stay* are explored further within historical frameworks. Beauvoir's realization of her own historicity resulted from her experience of the German Occupation in wartime Paris. Beauvoir wrote several significant philosophical texts, such as *Pyrrhus et Cineas* (*Pyrrhus et Cinéas*, 1944), and *The Ethics of Ambiguity* (*Pour une morale de l'ambiguïté*, 1947, translated 1948). In *The Second Sex* (*Le Deuxième sexe*, 1949, translated 1953), she offers a constructionist, materialist analysis of women's gendered identity, five years after women gained the right to vote in France. In 1954, she won the Prix Goncourt for *The Mandarins* (*Les Mandarins*, 1954, translated 1956), a portrait of the immediate post-war period in France. From the mid-1950s, Beauvoir began writing her memoirs. These offer an invaluable political and cultural account by a left-wing female intellectual of France and of the many countries which Beauvoir visited. Her late fiction, *Les Belles Images* (1966, translated with the same title 1968) and *The Woman Destroyed* (*La Femme rompue*, 1968, translated 1969), focuses extensively on women's situation. In *Old Age* (*La Vieillesse*, 1970, translated 1972), Beauvoir analysed another controversial issue – ageing. Her last book, *Adieux: A Farewell to Sartre* (*La Cérémonie des adieux*, 1981, translated 1984) describes Sartre's final years. Died in Paris, 14 April 1986.

Translations

Novels

L'Invitée, 1943

Moyse, Yvonne and Roger Senhouse, *She Came to Stay*, London: Secker and Warburg/Lindsay Drummond, 1949; Cleveland: World, 1954

Le Sang des autres, 1945

Moyse, Yvonne and Roger Senhouse, *The Blood of Others*, New York: Knopf, and London: Secker and Warburg/Lindsay Drummond, 1948; Harmondsworth: Penguin, 1964

Tous les hommes sont mortels, 1946

Cameron, Euan, *All Men Are Mortal*, London: Virago, 1995 (based on Friedman's original 1955 translation)

Friedman, Leonard M., *All Men Are Mortal*, Cleveland: World, 1955

Les Mandarins, 1954

Friedman, Leonard M., *The Mandarins*, Cleveland: World, 1956; London: Collins, 1957; with an introduction by Doris Lessing, London: Flamingo, 1993

Les Belles Images, 1966

O'Brian, Patrick, *Les Belles Images*, London: Collins, and New York: Putnam, 1968

La Femme rompue, 1968

O'Brian, Patrick, *The Woman Destroyed*, London: Collins, and New York: Putnam, 1969

Short Stories

Quand prime le spirituel, 1979

O'Brian, Patrick, *When Things of the Spirit Come First: Five Early Tales*, London: André Deutsch, and New York: Pantheon, 1982

Essays and Philosophical Writing

Pour une morale de l'ambiguïté, 1947

Frechtman, Bernard, *The Ethics of Ambiguity*, New York: Philosophical Library, 1948

Le Deuxième Sexe, 1949

Parshley, Howard Madison, *The Second Sex*, New York: Knopf, and London: Jonathan Cape, 1953; numerous subsequent reprints

La Vieillesse, 1970

O'Brian, Patrick, *Old Age*, London: André Deutsch/ Weidenfeld and Nicolson, and New York: Putnam, 1972; as *The Coming of Age*, New York: Putnam, 1972

Biographies and Autobiographies

Mémoires d'une jeune fille rangée, 1958

Kirkup, James, *Memoirs of a Dutiful Daughter*, Cleveland: World, and London: André Deutsch/Weidenfeld and Nicolson, 1959

La Force de l'âge, 1960

Green, Peter, *The Prime of Life*, Cleveland: World, and London: André Deutsch/Weidenfeld and Nicolson, 1962

La Force des choses, 1963

Howard, Richard, *Force of Circumstance*, New York: Putnam, and London: André Deutsch/Weidenfeld and Nicolson, 1965

Une Mort très douce, 1964

O'Brian, Patrick, *A Very Easy Death*, New York: Putnam, and London: André Deutsch/Weidenfeld and Nicolson, 1966

Tout compte fait, 1972

O'Brian, Patrick, *All Said and Done*, New York: Putnam, and London: André Deutsch/Weidenfeld and Nicolson, 1974

La Cérémonie des adieux, suivi de Entretiens avec Jean-Paul Sartre août-septembre 1974, 1981

O'Brian, Patrick, *Adieux: A Farewell to Sartre*, New York: Pantheon, and London: André Deutsch/Weidenfeld and Nicolson, 1984

Letters

Lettres à Sartre, 1930–1939, 1940–1963, 1990

Hoare, Quintin (editor and translator), *Letters to Sartre*, London: Radius, 1991; New York: Arcade, 1992

A major figure in post-World War II culture, Simone de Beauvoir is well-known for her pioneering study of gender, *The Second Sex*, and for her novels, memoirs and philosophical essays. She played a key role in French atheistic existentialism and worked as a founder director of the influential left-wing journal, *Les Temps modernes*.

Simone de Beauvoir's writing has posed considerable challenges for translators since the late 1940s, when the first English translations of her fiction appeared. Her dense, lucid prose is the hallmark of an intellectual trained in philosophy, who was determined to make her mark as a literary writer.

In some respects, MOYSE & SENHOUSE's *She Came to Stay* (1949) is one of the more successful translations in Beauvoir's fictional corpus. However, the omission of the Hegelian epigraph ("each consciousness pursues the death of the other"), occasional infelicities in the rendition of phenomenological lexis and value-laden overtranslations diminish the text's philosophical concerns relating to self–other relationships. The occasional rendition of free indirect speech in inverted commas is confusing for the reader.

The complex narrative and temporal structures of *The Blood of Others*, Beauvoir's second novel, are also relatively ably tackled by MOYSE & SENHOUSE (1948). However, her use of the French historic present tense to plunge the reader into the stream of the characters' consciousnesses is sometimes (and perhaps inevitably) lost. Certain terms of philosophical significance are inconsistently translated, such as "un autre" as both "another being" and as "other".

In 1995, a film version of *All Men Are Mortal*, perhaps Beauvoir's least well-known novel, prompted a highly readable British adaptation by Euan CAMERON of the original FRIEDMAN translation (1955). Yet occasional sentences are curiously omitted with no apparent compensatory purpose.

Among Beauvoir's philosophical essays of the 1940s, FRECHTMAN's *The Ethics of Ambiguity* (1948) offers a largely faithful rendition. Some Heideggerian references are obscured in terms used, such as "the genuine man" for "l'homme authentique". Moreover, the important existentialist concepts, "le pour-soi" and "l'en-soi" are confusingly translated both as "for-oneself" or "for-itself" and "in-oneself" or "in-itself" respectively.

Among Beauvoir scholars, the 1953 translation of *The Second Sex* by H.M. PARSHLEY has attracted much criticism – particularly since it is the only published translation. As Margaret Simons has noted, the Parshley text omits over 10 per cent of Beauvoir's original, including much historical material on American and European suffrage movements and the development of socialist feminism in France. These omissions are not individually indicated and make cross-referencing impossible. Furthermore, key philosophical terms either are substantially mistranslated as their diametrical opposites or are inconsistently translated, for example, "for-itself" is rendered in English as "in-itself" and the Heideggerian phrase, "la réalité humaine" translated as "the real nature of man" – a nonsensical rendition in the context of Beauvoir's existential phenomenology. Although all philosophical texts present translators with specific difficulties of terminological equivalence, the degree of mistranslation here of key philosophical terms used by Beauvoir in *The Second Sex* is striking. Several factors complicated Parshley's task as a translator: his lack of philosophical knowledge, pressure from his American publishers to produce quickly a "reader-friendly", popular translation and Beauvoir's deliberate lack of involvement in the project. The shortcomings of the English translation did not prevent *The Second Sex* from becoming a pioneering text of modern feminism, and its inadequacies were replicated because some translations into other languages were based not on the French original but on Parshley's translation. Beauvoir's reputation as a philosophical thinker has not been enhanced by this process.

FRIEDMAN's version (1956) of the Goncourt prize-winner, *The Mandarins* (1954), contains a number of infelicitous solutions, including some gendered over-translations indicating the translator's ideological attitude, for example, "Now, you're going to be a nice little girl and let me get back to my work" for "maintenant tu vas être bien gentille et me laisser travailler". Informed by her research for *The Second Sex*, Beauvoir explores the micro-politics of gender relations on many occasions in *The Mandarins*, yet certain passages dealing explicitly with the characters' sexuality are edited in the translation – perhaps as a result of publisher's constraints.

From the late 1950s, Beauvoir's memoirs were published. These quickly gained a significant readership in translation. Cordero argues that the KIRKUP translation (1959) of *Memoirs of a Dutiful Daughter* (1958) has a tendency to overtranslation, lexical errors and British colloquialisms. Existentialist terms are also rendered inaccurately, such as "mauvaise foi" as "betrayal", "angoisse" as "panic", "existence" as "fate". As Moi notes, some cultural references are inappropriately translated (for example, the "Normalien" slang, "petits camarades" as "left-wingers") and undertranslations occur, particularly in the area of education, where cultural equivalence is difficult to achieve.

Translations of Beauvoir's subsequent autobiographical volumes also contain inaccurate renditions of philosophical terms and some over-translations with added intensifiers that jar with her lucid, concise style in French. HOWARD's *Force of Circumstance* (1965) has occasional infelicitous renditions of idiom and over-translations, yet includes a useful index – unlike the other three volumes of autobiography. O'BRIAN's *A Very Easy Death* (1966), translating Beauvoir's moving narrative about her mother's death, renders the profusion of medical terminology in the original text (1964) without too much awkwardness. There is, nevertheless, a certain amount of translationese and overtranslation, for example, "bien que je vécusse dans l'erreur", a somewhat ironic reference to Françoise de Beauvoir's view of her daughter's atheism and independent lifestyle, is rendered as "although I was living in sin".

Among Beauvoir's late fiction, O'BRIAN's translation (1968) of *Les Belles Images* (1966) is a valiant rendition of a complex literary text. A significant translation problem is the extensive use of the historic present tense. This is rendered frequently by the English preterite, which unfortunately distances the reader from the characters and understates the confusion experienced by Laurence, the novel's protagonist.

A recent addition to Beauvoir's autobiographical corpus, an edited version of her letters to Sartre (HOARE, 1991), offers valuable footnotes and signals individual omissions to the reader. Beauvoir's letters to Simone Jollivet are not included and substantial cuts are made elsewhere, including much autobiographical material, amounting to one third of the original.

As Moi notes, much of Beauvoir's writing in translation suffers from publishers' perceptions and marketing of her as a popular woman writer. Consequently, the philosophical rigour of her writing is often lost, her intellectual concerns are muted and the literary qualities of her writing diminished. Much of her writing is also marked by her interest in gender and class politics. However, the frequent editing of her texts and conflicting ideological concerns on the part of translators and publishers often obscure the scope and stature of Beauvoir's contribution to 20th-century cultural capital.

URSULA TIDD

Further Reading

Bair, Deirdre, "'Madly Sensible and Brilliantly Confused': From *Le Deuxième Sexe* to *The Second Sex*", *Dalhousie French Studies*, 13 (Fall 1987) pp. 23–35

Bennett, Joy and Gabriella Hochmann, *Simone de Beauvoir: An Annotated Bibliography*, New York: Garland, 1988

Cordero, Anne D., "Simone de Beauvoir Twice Removed", *Simone de Beauvoir Studies*, 7 (1990) pp. 49–56

Heath, Jane, *Simone de Beauvoir*, Hemel Hempstead: Harvester Wheatsheaf, 1989

Moi, Toril, *Simone de Beauvoir: The Making of an Intellectual Woman*, Oxford and Cambridge, Massachusetts: Blackwell, 1994

Patterson, Yolanda, "Who Was This H.M. Parshley? The Saga of Translating Simone de Beauvoir's *The Second Sex*", *Simone de Beauvoir Studies*, 9 (1992) pp. 41–46

Simons, Margaret A., "The Silencing of Simone de Beauvoir, Guess What's Missing from The Second Sex", *Women's Studies International Forum*, 6/5 (1983) pp. 559–64

Simons, Margaret A., "Two Interviews with Simone de Beauvoir", *Hypatia*, 3/3 (1989) pp. 25–41

Stefanson, Blandine, introduction to *Les Belles Images*, London: Heinemann, 1980, especially pp. 24–39

Samuel Beckett 1906–1989

Irish dramatist, novelist, short-story writer, translator and self-translator

Biography

Born Samuel Barclay Beckett into a middle-class family at Foxrock, near Dublin, 13 April 1906. After preparatory school he atended Portora Royal School in County Fermanagh and went on in 1927 to Trinity College Dublin, graduating in French and Italian (1931), having been a *lecteur* in English at the École Normale Supérieure, 1928–30.

In the late 1920s and the 1930s Beckett met (1928) and frequented James Joyce in Paris. He published an essay on Joyce in 1929. He was lecturer in French at Trinity College Dublin, 1930–31. After a period of wandering between Ireland, Germany, France and London, he settled in Paris in 1937. In 1945 Beckett worked for the Irish Red Cross in France. He married Suzanne Deschevaux-Dumesnil in 1961. As well as being awarded the Nobel Prize for Literature (1969), he won official honours in the UK, the US, Ireland, France, Germany and Italy. Died 22 December 1989, in Paris.

After the stories *More Pricks than Kicks* (1934), came the the first of his novels, *Murphy* (1938), written in English. Most of Beckett's many works exist in both French and English versions, the translations usually done by himself, sometimes in collaboration. The novel *Watt* came out in 1953, the year in which Beckett entered into international celebrity as a dramatist of the Theatre of the Absurd with *En attendant Godot* (*Waiting for Godot*, 1954). Meanwhile he was publishing the trilogy of darkly comic novels *Molloy* (1951, written in French; translated into English under the same title, 1955), *Malone meurt* (1951; *Malone Dies*, 1956) and *L'Innommable* (1953; *The Unnamable*, 1958).

After *Godot*, the best known of his dramatic works for stage, radio and screen are *Fin de partie* (1957; *Endgame*, 1958); *Krapp's Last Tape* (1958; *La Dernière Bande*, 1959); and *Happy Days* (1961; *Oh, Les Beaux Jours*, 1963). Now world-famous, he continued to write highly original and experimental works of fiction and drama, and to assist in productions of his plays, until shortly before his death.

Samuel Beckett read French and Italian at Trinity College, Dublin, where he received a Foundation Scholarship. He graduated in 1927. As an outstanding student, he was chosen to be *lecteur* at the École Normale Supérieure from 1928 to 1930. He became fascinated also with German and spent time in Germany off and on during the 1930s. In 1950 Unesco commissioned him to collate translations to celebrate the 200th anniversary of Goethe's birth, and, although his Spanish was rudimentary, to translate Octavio Paz's *Anthology of Mexican Poetry* (1958), a task he is reported to have loathed.

In the early 1930s Beckett translated seven poems of Paul Éluard and secured a commission to translate Rimbaud's *Bateau ivre*. The versions of Éluard are lucidly faithful, although Beckett is content to sustain the charge of archaism by using "thou" in his translation of *À peine défigurée*. In the Rimbaud he is splendidly concerned more with music than mathematics, casting *dix nuits* ("ten nights") as *nine nights*. His 1950 translation of Apollinaire's *Zone* is a tour de force:

> they see a
> Nimitation of Simon Magus in Judaea.

In the 1970s he transformed some of Chamfort's cynical maxims into verse-epigrams. It must probably be said, however, that his translations of other writers, though definitely the work of a poet, are a minor aspect of his overall achievement, done, as it were, from an academic love of language, whereas, in recasting his own work, he was desperately concerned to "re-create" the total effect. This entailed complete freedom to invent, cut, adapt, and transform. Any reader confronted with the parallel texts of any work Beckett himself rendered into the other tongue can relish the heady and perhaps perilous delights of free translation. When, in 1953, he began his English version of *En attendant Godot*, he embarked on nearly four decades of the richest possible experimentation with the innate possibilities of two languages.

Beckett tackled his translation of *Godot* after its *succès de scandale* in January that year at the Théâtre Babylone in Paris. Whereas, in the original French, Estragon was *assis par terre* (sitting on the ground), the English stage-direction has him sitting on a low mound. In Act II, "the tree has four or five leaves" as opposed to being "couvert de feuilles" (covered in leaves). Estragon, asked his name by Pozzo, replies "Adam" not "Catulle". "Je me fais au goût" (I get used to the taste) becomes stronger: "I get used to the muck". The ironically religious reference to "le marché de Saint-Sauveur" is lost in the one word "fair". Lucky's age, guessed comically as 11, is new in the English. The meditation "C'est long, mais ce sera bon" (It's long but it'll be good) turns into a quotation from the Book of

Proverbs: "Hope deferred maketh the heart sick" and Beckett's love of English alliteration leads him to maintain the literal sense of "s'en prenant à la chaussure alors que c'est son pied le coupable" but to sharpen the form to give "blaming on his boots the faults of his feet". Estragon's "J'écoute" (merely "I'm listening") is exaggerated to "I find this really most extraordinarily interesting".

It is as though with these changes Beckett's intention is to work towards a greater dramatic clarity. For example, the hint that Estragon is slow on the uptake in the stage-direction, "Trying in vain to work it out", appears only in English – as does his grudging admission that the boot he refuses to accept as his own does in fact fit. The marvellous crescendo of insults leading to the winning one "Crrritic!" is new in the English.

Beckett referred to the task of translating his play *Fin de partie* (1957) (*Endgame*, 1958) as "heartbreaking work" and feared that "the loss incurred was even greater than with *Godot*". There *are* losses – the splendid pun ouïe/oui (hearing/ yes) is not attempted, no English equivalent is found for the jingle "le fanal est dans le canal" (the lantern's in the canal), merely "the light is sunk", and two pages near the end remain untranslated. Yet, if some jokes and comic effects are sacrificed, there are many tremendous gains. The play upon words when Clov mispronounces "coite" (the feminine of *coi*, doggo) as if it were the word for coitus (*coït*) is brilliantly explained by the misunderstanding *laying* for *lying*. The roguish "And a great one for the men" replaces the coarser "Et pas farouche pour un liard" (not exactly shy at a halfpenny a time). Hamm's criticism of his father's greed, "Ah, il n'y a plus de vieux" (The old aren't what they used to be) expands to "The old folks at home! No decency left!"

Interestingly, Hamm's "calotte en feutre" (felt skullcap) is now "a stiff toque". The tale of the tailor is given ribald alliteration: "Voici Pâques fleuries et il loupe les boutonnières" (Palm Sunday arrives and he makes a mess of the buttonholes) turns into "The bluebells are blowing and he ballockses the buttonholes". Prospero's "Our revels now are ended" gives the English audience a recognizably ironic reference instead of the bolder French "Finie la rigolade" (The fun's over). An added lyricism turns "Vieille fin de partie perdue, finir de perdre" (Old endgame lost, losing's over now) into "Old endgame lost of old, play and lose and have done with losing".

Asked why he wrote in French, Beckett replied "Parce qu'en français c'est plus facile d'écrire sans style" (Because in French it's easier to write without any style). Certainly, in *Malone Dies*, his 1956 translation of his 1951 novel *Malone meurt*, the plainness of the original French is elaborated – "fier de sa belle bosse" (proud of his fine hump) becomes "proud as punch of his fine hunch". Clichés lend a new colour – "tout" (everything) is "the end-all and the be-all", "périmée" (out of date) is "gone to rack and ruin" and "le temps m'est mesuré" (my time's limited) "the sands are running out".

The initial clarity of the French can be obscured – "avant de gagner les hauts rochers nocturnes" (before reaching the high rocks in darkness) is squeezed into "before night and its high crags". The English can add a cruder emphasis – "rotten crucifix" for "chicot-crucifix" (referring to the stump of a tooth which Moll had had drilled into the shape of a crucifix) and "to hell with all this fucking scenery" instead of "il s'agit bien de la nature" (what's nature got to do with it anyway).

Many problems are deftly solved. The two registers in "Tu es parmi des amis. Vous vous rendez compte" (in which the first sentence is said to Macmann, the second is an aside to the reader from Malone) are effectively rendered as "You are among friends. Friends! Well well" and "ce tutoiement torrentiel" (this torrential use of the familiar second person) turns into "this torrent of civility". The trick of repetition for wistful or ironic purposes gives "come home. Home" for the one word "rentré" (returned home), as also later in *Ill Seen Ill Said*. It is possible to wonder, just occasionally, whether the English was already hovering in Beckett's mind when he was penning the French, as "lakh ... lock" replaces "lack ... mèche" (a hundred thousand rupees ... lock of hair) and "locomotive motive" "arrière-pensée locomotive" (locomotive intent). Curiously, he alters "nonagénaire" (in his nineties) to "octogenarian". The repeated verb "nier ... nier" (deny ... deny) changes to "deny ... drown". A sly glance at Balzac's story *Louis Lambert* is given when the Louis family in *Malone meurt* are renamed Lambert in *Malone Dies*. The epitaph "Ci-gît un pauvre con, tout lui fut aquilon" (Here lies a poor sod to whom everything came as a horrible blow) is freely recast as "Here lies a ne'er-do-well, six feet under hell." The colloquial force of the original is perfectly maintained without slavish literalness.

When in 1958 he came to translate his 1953 novel *L'Innommable* as *The Unnamable*, Beckett decided to increase the bleakness by omitting the narrator's claim that he has friends: "mes amis, car moi aussi j'ai des amis quelque part, je le sens, par moments" (my friends, for I've got friends too somewhere, I'm sure of that, sometimes at any rate). He frequently elaborates: "scatter to the winds" for "supprimerai" (suppress) or adds an adjective: "stimulate the lagging discourse" for "alimenter le discours". "Les vieux" are specified as "gaffer and gammer", though, strangely, he alters "pépé" (Grandad) to "Granny". "L'heure tardive" (a late hour) is clarified as "the eleventh hour" and "l'avenir" (the future) chillingly personified as "the scytheman".

Irishisms occur in *The Unnamable* – "a darling dream", "a broth of a dream". The vocabulary is widened to include the faintly archaic "betimes" for "tôt" (soon) and "Méchante obscurité, arrière, couche, sale cabot" (wicked obscurity, get back, down, you filthy cur) is given as "Currish obscurity, to thy kennel, hell-hound."

Idiom crosses the Channel: "un percheron" gets two equivalents, "Clydesdale" and "Suffolk stallion". "Un soir de fête" (a holiday evening) becomes "a merry bank-holiday evening". At school "matheux" (good at maths) is "bright boy". "De peur d'être frappé" (for fear of a blow) becomes more colourful: "cringing from the rod". The knowing reference to candidates for the École Normale Supérieure in "propos de khâgneux" is reduced to "college quips". "Me ramenèrent rue de la Gaîté, séance tenante" (took me back to the rue de la Gaîté, there and then) is rendered as "land me back, there and then, in all the fun of the fair". "Effets de manche" is clarified as "flowers of rhetoric" – the lawyer using words (rather than flourishing gowned arms).

There are characteristic turns of phrase, relishing English alliterations: "never a mum of his mouth to me" for "il ne me jette jamais la parole": "and I still the teller and the told" for "comme il s'agissait toujours de moi". Other unmistakable Beckettisms include "off it goes on" for "premier pas va" (first step, off you go) and "like distant laughter and brief spells of hush" instead of "à confondre avec des rires, de petits silences" (just like laughter or short silences) and, letting himself go, he expands "promenades sentimentales et solitaires" (sentimental walks, alone) into "jaunts and rambles, honeymoons at home and abroad, and long sad solitary tramps in the rain". Sometimes the language gets totally recast: "à en avoir mal au cou, aux reins" (till your neck and back hurt) becomes, altering the effort: "till black and blue in the face". The idiom is replaced: "en voilà du pain sur la planche, qu'il y moisisse" (there's bread on the board [i.e. things to be done], let it stay and go mouldy) becomes "there are some irons in the fire to be going on with, let them melt". "Faisons celui qui n'y voit que des chandelles" (let's be like someone seeing stars) moves from the act of violence to its aftermath: "let's turn the black eye".

Certain aural effects are left behind: "mielleuse, fielleuse" (honeyed, bitter) becomes "honeyed and perfidious" and "dans le suaire, preuve d'avoir sué" (in the shroud – proof that you've sweated) is "bundled into my shroud". The music of "d'histoires de berceau, cerceau, puceau, pourceau, sang et eau, peau et os, tombeau" is transformed: "talks like this of wombs and cribs, diapers bepissed and the first long trousers, love's young dream and life's old lech, blood and tears and skin and bones and tossing in the grave". Beckett coins "wordy-gurdy" for "chasse aux mots" (word-game) and gives "encore une lueur de foutue" (another light buggered up) as "another gleam down the drain".

The BBC commission for the radio play *All That Fall* in 1957 prompted Beckett to compose for the first time in English since the novel *Watt* in 1942. His play *Krapp's Last Tape* (1958) had trouble with the Lord Chamberlain, as "let me in" was interpreted as an obscene imperative. The translation in *La Dernière Bande* ("m'ont laissé entrer") clarifies the issue, showing that the woman, opening her eyes, merely admitted Krapp's presence. *Oh, les beaux jours* (1963) is a freer translation of the 1961 English play *Happy Days*: Winnie's recollections of her first loves are given a French context, as are Willie's equivocal extracts: "Wanted, bright boy" is transformed into "Coquet deux-pièces calme soleil" (Attractive two-room flat, quiet, sunny). The quotation from *Cymbeline* becomes "Qu'ils pleurent, oh mon Dieu, qu'ils frémissent de honte" (May they weep, O Lord, may they tremble with shame). "Paradise enow" is "mon coin d'azur" (my little bit of blue sky). J.-J. Mayoux finds "un léger accent anglais" in "Chanter trop tôt est funeste, je trouve toujours" (To sing too soon is fatal, I always find).

The pompous language of Words in the radio play *Words and Music*, broadcast 1962, receives a corresponding pedantry in *Paroles et musique* (1966). With "voire" (nay, rather …) and "réels zou imaginés" (real or imagined). His Yeatsian lyricism: "Arise then and go now the manifest unanswerable", changes to "Oh coeur sphinx énigmes sans mot" (Oh heart sphinx insoluble riddles). The mood of "nodding … the ingle … " is more violent in "crachotant … sur les tisons" (spitting on to the embers). The poem superbly demonstrates the differing power of each language when the monosyllables *scum, hag, trash* become *immondice, sorcière, ordure*. The French also adds a memorable phrase "l'oeil nu collé au cristallin". *Cascando* (1963), another play for radio, moving again the other way, turns Molloy's friend Maunu into Woburn and gives an Irish flavour with "boreen" for "chemin creux" (sunken lane).

Beckett admitted the impossibility of capturing both senses (fois/temps) implied in the title of the play *That Time* (1976). Similarly, the pun audible in his novel *Comment c'est* (1961) is absent from *How It Is* (1964). It is sometimes necessary to consult the original to be sure of a meaning: "Luke like in outer hall" was clearer as "tiède comme dans le vestibule". Idioms are explained: "rieurs de vendredi" are "those who laugh too soon". "Tout est là les trois quarts" (everything is there, three-quarters at any rate) has a different diminuendo in "all-important most important". "Ce cinéma" is "this dumb show". A quibble on "amour peut-être au pluriel" (love maybe in the plural) becomes rather curiously "the or thee". "Increvable" (unkillable) is more actively "unbutcherable". The simple "les mots vous font voir du pays" (words take you around) is more enigmatic: "words my truant guides", "temps à venir" (time to come) more expansive: "boundless futurity", "dans leurs bagages" (in their luggage) more specific: "among their trophies".

With his French versions of *Play* and *Eh Joe* the dramatist brilliantly recasts the locutions to fit the language: "get off me, keep off me" becomes "tu me lâcheras, pour de bon", "a shade gone" "un peu dérangée" and "I smell you off him" "Vous l'avez empesté". "Blubber mouth" is seen as "bouche deux boudins" (a mouth like two black puddings/US blood puddings). Ash and Snodland are resited as Sept-Sorts et Signy-Signet. The swing of "At home all heart to heart and bygones bygones" is the colder "A la maison un seul mot d'ordre – s'ouvrir le coeur, passer l'éponge et tourner la page" (In the house a single system – have it all out, wipe the slate clean, turn over a new leaf). "Tongue still hanging out for mercy" is the starker "encore soif de pitié" (still thirsty for pity). "All grey with frozen dew" is the less lyrical "gris de givre" (grey with frost). "Hellish half-light" is "lueur infernale" in *Comédie*, and "that penny-farthing hell" in *Eh Joe* (1966) becomes "cet enfer de quatre sous" in *Dis Joe* (1972). "On and off" is rendered as "avec des trous" (with gaps). The "slut" whose terms are "penny a hoist tuppence as long as you like" becomes the "pisseuse … tant la saillie" (scrubber … so much a go). The announcement in the *Independent*, "'On Mary's beads we plead her needs and in the Holy Mass'" is clarified: "L'annonce sans plus … Innocente envolée avant l'heure … Vierge-saints-priez-âme-repos" (Just the notice … An innocent soul taken before her time … Virgin-saints-pray-soul-repose).

In the French version of the 1966 short play *Come and Go* the three exclamations "Oh!" become "Miséricorde!" "Malheur!" and "Misère!", "Chez les soeurs" (at the school run by nuns) explains "at Miss Wade's" and "one sees little in this light" contracts to the equally chilling "il fait sombre". The colloquial word order of the French title *Va et vient* (1966) reverses the implications of birth and death in *Come and Go*.

The short novel *The Calmative*, written in French in 1946 and translated into English in 1967, has in the English the harsher "fornications" for "amour" and "gallows night" instead of the possibly ironic "joyeuse nuit". The hint from Lamartine "Je suspendis mon vol" (I checked myself in flight) before the kiss is simply "My mouth stood still". "Qu'avez-vous à grimacer ainsi?" (What are you pulling a face for?) has a new twist: "What are you grinning and bearing?" There are cuts, notably the reference to "le Samaritain … ou qui sait, un salutiste" (The Samaritan … or who knows, a member of the Salvation Army).

The 13 *Textes pour rien* composed in 1950 and translated as *Texts for Nothing* in 1967 also appeared in *No's Knife*, a title taken from the 13th text: "the screaming silence of no's knife in yes's wound" adapting "le silence hurlant est plaie de oui et couteau de non" (the screaming silence is the wound of yes and the knife of no) and picking up an expression in the eighth text not present in the French: "ah if no were content to cut yes's throat and never cut its own". The erudite glance at the Greek for yellow, "ah vieux rire à la xanthine" – "rire jaune" is "to give a sickly smile" – is even obscurer as "ah old xanthic laugh". "De guerres lasses et de morts aussitôt debout" (with tired wars and corpses getting up straightaway) gains a different effect: "with arms laid down and corpses fighting fresh". "Sauf prévu" becomes "if nothing foreseen crops up". There are other new turns of phrase: "old shuttlecock sentiment", "dead and kicking", "wordshit", "a castrato scream".

The tone in the prose piece *Imagination morte imaginez* (1965) gets slightly adapted in the English version: "one glimpse and vanished, endlessly, omit" for "fixez, pff, muscade, une éternité, taisez" (see, poof, hey presto, an age, say no more). "The ring of bone" is ambiguous for "l'os sonne". The "hop" in *Bing* (1966), an even shorter prose piece, is given each time as "ping" in the English *Ping* (1967). The archaic "head haught" changes the starker "tête boule bien haute" (round head held high), like "unover" for "inachevé". The language of *Enough* (1967) is more elaborate than that of *Assez* (1966): "on his last legs", "blue bloodshot", "flat and splay". From *Sans* (1969), translated as *Lessness* (1970), "tout beau tout nouveau" (novelty has charms) is altered to "old love new love", "enfin" becomes the faintly ambiguous "long last" and "éteint ouvert" "blacked out fallen open". The active singular of *Le Dépeupleur* (1970) becomes the passive plural of *The Lost Ones* (1972). "Place" is rendered as "coign", "reprennent le collier" (get back into harness) as " buckle to anew" and "le haïssable de toujours" as "some old abomination". The sentence "Dans les feux sombres du plafond le zénith garde encore sa légende" is not translated.

In the French version, *Pas* (1978), the glance at the Crucifixion given in *Footfalls*, his play performed at the Royal Court in 1976 in honour of Beckett's 70th birthday, is amplified: "lacrosse" becomes "jeu du ciel et de l'enfer" (game of heaven and hell). The appalling "fuck life" in *Rockaby*, first performed in Buffalo in 1981, is "aux gogues la vie" (life – chuck it down the loo) in *Berceuse* (1982). Unlike the other short plays of the 1970s and 1980s, *Solo* is "adapté" not "*traduit* par l'auteur". In the 1984 English version of *Catastrophe*, the 1982 play dedicated to Vaclav Havel, "au point où nous en sommes" (the stage we're at) becomes "no harm trying".

The cool tone of the prose piece *Mal vu mal dit* (1981) is treated differently: "l'herbe la plus mauvaise s'y fait toujours plus rare" keeps its meaning but receives a tauter, more literary form as "ever scanter the rankest weed" in *Ill Seen Ill Said* (1982); "à leur guise" is "as they list", "au port dit bon" is "safe as the saying is and sound", "son pisse-légende" becomes "its drivelling scribe". For "au petit malheur" Beckett coins "mishaphazard".

The ambiguity of *Still* (a short prose piece written in English in 1973) is clarified by the French title *Immobile* (1975).

The 1976 English translation, *For To End Yet Again*, of the 1975 French prose piece *Pour finir encore* has "woe" for "tant pis" and Beckett allows himself a flourish of alliteration in "where all the footsteps ever fell can never fare nearer to anywhere nor from anywhere further away".

In the 1980 translation (*Compagnie*) of the novel *Company* (1979), "tu es né" replaces "you saw the light of day". "Bow window" is kept in the French but "a great rock" becomes "un mégalithe". "Ballyogan" and other proper names are kept, but "Croker's Acres" with its assonance and hint of death is mellowed to "les pâturages". The Shakespearean tag "upon the place beneath" becomes "sur le sous-jacent", and "withershins" is explained as "dans le non-sens des aiguilles" (in a clock-stupid direction).

In the early novel *Mercier et Camier* (written in 1946 but not published until 1970 – translated in 1974) "Je survivais en parlant" (I survived by talking) becomes "Gab was my salvation", and "retutoyez-vous" (return to using the familiar form) "be on speaking terms again". "Aux tons charmants d'extinction" (with such delightfully fading tones) is "its ghostly tartan rending to behold". Beckett alters the format of the novel slightly, numbering the sections differently and condensing whole passages into paraphrases. One more example shows this supreme commander of two languages at his inventive best: "Je suis la discrétion même. Un tombeau" (I'm the soul of discretion. Silent as the grave) turns into "I'm discretion itself. The wild horse's despair."

HARRY GUEST

Translations

Apollinaire, Guillaume, *Zone* (bilingual edition), 1972 (originally published in *Transition*, 50, 1950)
Bosquet, Alain, *Selected Poems*, translated with others, 1963
Paz, Octavio (editor), *Anthology of Mexican Poetry*, 1958
Pinget, Robert, *La Manivelle/The Old Tune* (bilingual edition), 1960
Rimbaud, Arthur, *Drunken Boat*, edited by James Knowlson and Felix Leakey, 1976

Self-Translations

French to English
Malone meurt, 1951; as *Malone Dies*, 1956
En attendant Godot, 1952; as *Waiting for Godot*, 1954
L'Innommable, 1953; as *The Unnamable*, 1958
Le Calmant, 1954; as *The Calmative*, 1967
Nouvelles et textes pour rien, 1954; as *Stories and Texts for Nothing*, 1967
Fin de partie, 1957; as *Endgame*, 1958
Fragment de théâtre I & II, 1958; as *Rough for Theatre I & II*, 1976
Pochade radiophonique, 1960; as *Rough for Radio I*, 1976
Esquisse radiophonique, 1960; as *Rough for Radio II*, 1976
Comment c'est, 1961; as *How It Is*, 1964
Cascando, 1963; as *Cascando*, 1963
Imagination morte imaginez, 1965; as *Imagination Dead Imagine*, 1966
Assez, 1966; as *Enough*, 1967
Bing, 1966; as *Ping*, 1967
Sans, 1969; as *Lessness*, 1970
Premier Amour, 1970; as *First Love*, 1973
Mercier et Camier, 1970; as *Mercier and Camier*, 1974
Le Dépeupleur, 1970; as *The Lost Ones*, 1972
Pour finir encore, 1975; as *For to End Yet Again*, 1976

Mal vu mal dit, 1981; as *Ill Seen Ill Said*, 1982
Catastrophe, 1982; as *Catastrophe*, 1984

Collaborative Translations
Molloy, 1951; as *Molloy*, with Patrick Bowles, 1955
L'Expulsé, 1954; as *The Expelled*, with Richard Seaver, 1967
La Fin, 1954; as *The End*, with Richard Seaver, 1967

English to French
Krapp's Last Tape, 1958; as *La Dernière Bande*, 1959
Happy Days, 1961; as *Oh Les Beaux Jours*, 1963
Words and Music, 1962; as *Paroles et musique*, 1966
Play, 1964; as *Comédie*, 1966
Eh Joe, 1966; as *Dis Joe*, 1972
Come and Go, 1967; as *Va et vient*, 1966
Not I, 1973; as *Pas moi*, 1975
Still, 1973; as *Immobile*, 1975
That Time, 1976; as *Cette fois*, 1978
Footfalls, 1976; as *Pas*, 1978
Company, 1979; as *Compagnie*, 1980
A Piece of Monologue, 1982; as *Solo*, 1982
Rockaby, 1982; as *Berceuse*, 1982
Ohio Impromptu, 1982; as *Impromptu d'Ohio*, 1982
What Where, 1984; as *Quoi où*, 1985
Stirrings Still, 1988; as *Soubresauts*, 1989

Collaborative Translations
Murphy, 1938; as *Murphy*, with Alfred Péron, 1947
Watt, 1953; as *Watt*, with Ludovic and Agnès Janvier, 1969
All That Fall; as *Tous ceux qui tombent*, with Robert Pinget, 1957
From an Abandoned Work, 1958; as *D'un ouvrage abandonné*, with Ludovic and Agnès Janvier, 1967
Embers, 1959; as *Cendres*, with Robert Pinget, 1959

Beckett's poems in English and French are published in *Collected Poems, 1930–1978*, 1984

Further Reading

Axelrod, M.R., *The Politics of Style in the Fiction of Balzac, Beckett and Cortázar*, New York: St Martin's Press, 1992
Bair, Deirdre, *Samuel Beckett: A Biography*, London: Jonathan Cape, and New York: Harcourt Brace, 1978
Cohn, Ruby, *Samuel Beckett: The Comic Gamut*, New Brunswick, New Jersey: Rutgers University Press, 1962
Cohn, Ruby (editor), *Casebook on Waiting for Godot*, New York: Grove Press, 1967; Basingstoke: Macmillan, 1987
Fitch, Brian T., *Beckett and Babel: An Investigation into the Status of the Bilingual Work*, Toronto: University of Toronto Press, 1988
Fletcher, John, *The Novels of Samuel Beckett*, London: Chatto and Windus, and New York: Barnes and Noble, 1964
Fletcher, John and John Spurling, *Beckett: A Study of His Plays*, London: Eyre Methuen, and New York: Hill and Wang, 1972
Friedman, Alan Warren, Charles Rossman and Dina Sherzer (editors), *Beckett Translating/Translating Beckett*, University Park and London: Pennsylvania State University Press, 1987
Harvey, Lawrence E., *Beckett: Poet and Critic*, Princeton, New Jersey: Princeton University Press, 1970
Hoffman, Michael J., *Samuel Beckett: The Language of Self*, Carbondale: South Illinois University Press, 1962
Knowlson, James and John Pilling, *Frescoes of the Skull: The Later Prose and Drama of Samuel Beckett*, London: Calder, 1979; New York: Grove Press, 1980
Locatelli, Carla, *Unwording the World: Samuel Beckett's Prose Works after the Nobel Prize*, Philadelphia; University of Pennsylvania Press, 1990
McMillan, Dougald and Martha Fehsenfeld, *Beckett in the Theatre*, London: Calder, and New York: Riverrun Press, 1988
Pilling, John and Mary Bryden (editors), *The Ideal Core of the Onion: Reading Beckett Archives*, Reading: Beckett International Foundation, University of Reading, 1992

Les Belles Infidèles

This humorous term, in which both "belles" and "infidèles" can be read as a noun, with the other word as an adjective, means on a literary register at the same time everything from "unfaithful beauties" to "elegant traducers". It was coined by the learned, if worldly, French ecclesiastic, Gilles Ménage (1613–92), member of the circles of Retz and Foucquet, close to Mme de Lafayette and on friendly terms with Madeleine de Scudéry and Mme de Sévigné. The term was directed at the work of his friend, the widely-read translator Nicolas Perrot d'Ablancourt (1606–64), who was praised by Charles Perrault in his comparison of modern authors with those of antiquity and who would have been made royal historiographer but for his Protestantism. Ménage was taken aback by the success of his *bon mot*, and tried partially to explain it away. It was said of him by the society portraitist Tallemant des Réaux that he would rather lose a friend than an aphorism.

Historians have applied the term "les belles infidèles" to the texts produced by a large group of French translators working in the second third of the 17th century. The two principal translators to have emerged from within the group are Perrot d'Ablancourt himself, and Jean-Louis Guez de Balzac (c.1597–1654), whose letters from his home in Angoulême were said to be received by Parisian addressees with the reverence normally accorded only to papal encyclicals. In his 1968 study *Les "Belles infidèles"* Roger Zuber points out that the history of translation is, like the history of literature, part of the history of taste. The particular interest of the authors of "les belles infidèles", he continues, is that they were critics as well as translators, reflecting as they translated on the theory underlying what they were doing, and, in Perrot d'Ablancourt's case, translating only in response to his critical theory. The interest of the work of those who produced "les belles infidèles" lies primarily not in whom, or how accurately, they translated, but in why they made the adaptations they did.

Essentially, it was to bring foreign, predominantly antique, authors to life again. Perrot d'Ablancourt is dismissive of his function as a mere "painter", preferring to look for the beauties of the original language rather than to achieve the literal accuracy of the copyist or to achieve the meticulous observance of minutiae, like the doctors of the law in the gospels. He regards himself partly as the friend rather than the representative of the authors he is introducing to a French readership, and partly, following in this another translator, Antoine Le Maître, as a magician, revivifying dead authors, himself invested with their spirit. Perrot d'Ablancourt goes so far as to utilize the metaphor of metempsychosis, and talks of Thucydides himself passing "into another body as by a sort of metempsychosis, from being Greek becoming French".

The presentation of translation theory in the period of "les belles infidèles" shares in the exuberant exaggerations about human physical capacity and moral potential emitted by the French novelists and moralists writing in the second third of the 17th century. The creators of "les belles infidèles" were responding to the imaginative constraints of their own culture, re-creating the texts they translated, as their original authors had projected their own vision to re-create nature in literature. Like the originals, the translations were to be creative works. They aspired to the creation of beauty, and in poetic theory translators were recurrently said, not only in their own period, but sporadically throughout the history of post-Renaissance literature from Ronsard to Rilke, to participate themselves in the creative activity of God.

Guez de Balzac's preferred metaphor for translation was the reception to be accorded to an honoured guest. The Greeks should not be treated as strangers, but made to feel at home in French, and the translators should act not as slaves or servants, but as hosts and guides. They owed it to their ancient guests to exercise their own artistic creativity. Producers of "belles infidèles" made no secret of what it was they were trying to achieve in presenting the ancient authors of Greece and Rome to their own French contemporaries, nor what principles underlay their translations and what appeared to them to be the justification for them. Since, however, the authors of "les belles infidèles" continued to use such traditional terms as "reason", "reasonable", "natural" and "good sense" to describe their norms, the real aim of their undertakings, and the relationship of what they achieved to what became the normative cadenced prose of the later 17th century in France, went largely unremarked.

They were inappropriately criticized by later 17th-century writers whose imaginative needs, drawing on critical norms that also exploited a hegemony of the rational, clashed with theirs. The confrontation of attitudes eventually produced the famous "querelle des anciens et des modernes", which pitted the victorious protagonists of modern literature and Houdar de la Motte's outrageously optimistic adaptation of Homer against the austere preferences of the protagonists of the "anciens", the authentic sensibility of Aeschylus and Euripides, and the insistence of Mme Dacier (c.1651–1720) on fidelity to the original text of the *Iliad* and the *Odyssey*. The most interesting feature of the criticisms made of "les belles infidèles" concerns their creators' consciousness that translations had to cross not only linguistic but also cultural chasms that were virtually impossible to bridge.

Guez de Balzac himself could go so far as to write that the real object of translation was not text, but the interior emotions of those who heard or read the translations. A translation has to move the reader with the same strength as the original moved the readers, listeners or audience for which it was intended. In the realm of literary judgement, unlike those of morality and theology, error can sometimes be more beautiful than truth.

"Les belles infidèles" cannot easily be identified, and still less counted. The phrase is best understood as denoting the production of a group dominated by a widespread attitude towards translation based on the principles we have noted, found in France during a limited period. Nevertheless, although the phrase was coined to denote a group of French translators, of whom Ménage considered Perrot d'Ablancourt the chief, the phenomenon of felicitous infidelity in translation, rendering tone and spirit with more accuracy than it rendered meaning, was not limited to France. Among translators into English who shared Perrot d'Ablancourt's approach to the task during the same period is Thomas Urquhart (1611–60), who published two books of Rabelais in 1653 (a third appeared posthumously in 1693). John Florio (1553?–1625) had published an eccentric but lively and hugely influential translation of Montaigne's *Les Essais* in 1603, and Roger L'Estrange (1616–1704), a royalist pamphleteer, is well known for his translations of Erasmus, Aesop, Quevedo and Josephus.

The authors of "les belles infidèles" should be taken as a group representing an identifiable tendency, even an ideal, whose theoretical exposition, often informally expressed in letters, was sometimes put in merely hyperbolic terms. This ideal was none the less a real one, wholly or partially embraced by an important handful of literary practitioners, chiefly in the second third of the 17th century, which seriously brought into prominence early in the post-Renaissance era the theoretical problems that beset literary translators even today.

ANTHONY LEVI

Further Reading

Mounin, Georges, *Les Belles infidèles*, Paris: Cahiers du Sud, 1955; Lille: Presses Universitaires de Lille, 1994

Zuber, Roger, *"Les "Belles infidèles" et la formation du goût classique*, Paris: Colin, 1968; revised edition, Paris: Michel, 1995

Andrei Belyi 1880–1934

Russian poet, short-story writer, novelist, essayist and critic

Biography

Pseudonym of Boris Nikolaevich Bugaev, born in Moscow 26 October 1880. A leading Russian Symbolist writer of prose, poetry, criticism and theory, who published his first work in 1902 while still a student of mathematics, philosophy and zoology at Moscow University, Boris Bugaev adopted the pseudonym Andrei Belyi (meaning Andrew White), to spare his father, a prominent professor of mathematics, in times of increasing political sensitivity. Belyi, like Blok, was influenced by the mystical philosophy of Solovev, and attempted to reconcile metaphysics with dialectical materialism. He travelled to Italy, North Africa and the near East (1910–12) and for two prolonged periods (1912–16 and 1921–23) to Europe, at one point living in Switzerland in a commune run by Rudolph Steiner, whose anthroposophy was to offer lifelong inspiration to both Belyi's thinking and his writing. Though at first in favour of the 1917 Revolution, Belyi was soon disillusioned by the censorship and artistic constraints introduced after the period of experimentation and in 1921 he left for Berlin where he could publish without interference. However, in 1923 he returned to Moscow, his native city, where, despite being isolated and ignored, he continued to produce a prolific stream of works until his death in 1934.

Belyi's work is difficult to characterize, lacking a clear line of progression or authorial development: he wrote and rewrote materials, changed titles, published various versions of the same text both in instalments and in complete form, each edition bearing a different emphasis; he planned series of texts that never materialized, and so on. His main works are: poetic prose: *Simfoniia (Symphonies)*, 1902–08; *Peterburg (Petersburg)*, 1916; *Serebrianii golub' (The Silver Dove)*, 1910; *Kotik Letaev (Kotik Letaev)*, 1922, and *Kreshchennyi kitaets (The Christened Chinaman)* 1927; poetry: *Zoloto v lazuri (Gold in Azure)*, 1904; *Pepel* [Ashes], 1909; *Urna* [The Urn], 1909; *Pervoe svidanie (The First Encounter)* 1921; Memoirs: *Vospominaniia o A.A. Bloke (Memoirs of Blok)*, 1922; *Na rubezhe dvukh stoletii* [At the Boundary of Two Centuries], 1930; *Nachalo veka* [The Beginning of the Century] 1933; *Mezhdu dvukh revoliutsii* [Between Two Revolutions], 1934; critical and theoretical works: *Formy iskusstva (The Forms of Art)*, 1902; *Ritm kak dialektika* [Rhythm as Dialectic], 1929; *Simvolizm* [Symbolism], 1910; *Masterstvo Gologia* [Gogol's Craft], 1934.

Translations

Short Stories

Rasskazy, 1904–18, edited by Ronald E. Peterson, Munich: Wilhelm Fink, 1979

Peterson, Ronald E., *The Complete Short Stories*, Ann Arbor: Ardis, 1979

Novels

Serebrianii golub', 1910

Reavey, George, *The Silver Dove*, New York: Grove Press, 1974

Peterburg: roman v vos'mi chastiakh s prologom i epilogom, in instalments, 1913–14 (St Petersburg); in book form, 1916 (Petrograd); 1922 (Berlin); 1928 (Moscow); 1935 (Moscow); 1981 (Moscow)

Cournos, John, *St. Petersburg*, with a foreword by George Reavey, New York: Grove Press, 1959; London: Weidenfeld and Nicolson, 1960

McDuff, David, *Petersburg*, Harmondsworth: Penguin, 1995

Maguire, Robert A. and John E. Malmstad, *Petersburg*, with an introduction, Bloomington: Indiana University Press, 1978, and Hassocks, Sussex: Harvester, 1978; Harmondsworth: Penguin, 1983

Kotik Letaev, 1922

Janacek, Gerald, *Kotik Letaev*, Ann Arbor: Ardis, 1971

Kreshchennyi kitaets, 1927

Beyer, Thomas R., *The Christened Chinaman*, with a preface and annotations, Tenafly, New Jersey: Hermitage, 1991

Poetry

Dramaticheskaia simfoniia, 1904

Keys, Roger and Angela Keys, *The Dramatic Symphony*, with *The Forms of Art*, translated by John D. Elsworth, Edinburgh: Polygon, 1986; New York: Grove Press, 1987

Zoloto v lazuri, 1904

Malmstad, John E., "Gold in Azure" in "The Poetry of Andrej Belyj: A Variorum Edition" (dissertation), Princeton, New Jersey: Princeton University, 1968

Pervoe svidanie, 1921

Janacek, Gerald, *The First Encounter* (parallel texts) with a foreword by Nina Berberova, Princeton, New Jersey: Princeton University Press, 1979

Selections of Prose

Cassedy, Steven, *Selected Essays of Andrey Bely*, with an introduction, bibliography, translator's notes, Berkeley: University of California Press, 1985

Peterson, Ronald E., *Andrei Bely's Short Prose*, Birmingham: University of Birmingham, 1980

Shein, Louis J., *Readings in Russian Philosophical Thought: Logic and Aesthetics*, The Hague: Mouton, 1973 (selections from *Symbolism as Weltanschauung* and *Forms of Art*)

Prose

Formy iskusstva, 1902

Elsworth, John D., *The Forms of Art*, with *The Dramatic Symphony*, translated by Roger and Angela Keys, Edinburgh: Polygon, 1986; New York: Grove Press, 1987

A leader of the Symbolist school and a founding Formalist, Andrei Belyi reflects in his writing a wide cosmos of poetry and science, metaphysics and spiritualism. Believing that true creativity occurs only in a state of "cerebral play", Belyi explored human cognition and perception through art. He composed ironic and allusive texts of high complexity, indulging in elaborate distortion of syntax and play on meaning. The texts work on various levels through polyphonic musicality. Sound and rhythm prevail over sense, stretching meaning to its limits. His writing is among the least transparent in the Russian language, resisting full understanding let alone easy translation. The lexicon ranges from the concrete to the abstract, while his verbal inventions are freighted with symbolism often of a purely private kind. Narrative development is subsidiary to stylistic texture, often transmuting obscure autobiographical events into a kaleidoscope of dense, wryly comic lyric images. His punctuation is idiosyncratic. Oppositions are drawn up between east and west, science and intuition, ideal and real, by means of codes and arcane references. These explorations of chaos and consciousness have labelled him a difficult experimental writer, in the manner of James Joyce, Gertrude Stein, etc. There are affinities with Gogol and Dostoevskii. Despite relentless disapproval in the Soviet Union, Belyi managed to publish a total of some 50 titles within his lifetime, and his influence has continued to resonate throughout Russian literature, especially in the work of Zamiatin, Pil'niak and Nabokov. *Masterstvo Gogolia* [Gogol's Craft] (1934) became a seminal text for formalist theory.

Belyi's oeuvre encompasses the full range of literary forms: narrative fiction, verse, essays, memoirs and articles, through all of which he explores critical and philosophical themes on art, music, mathematics and the transcendent. He does not conform to the usual conventions of genre, and characteristics tend to overlap: autobiographical elements run through fiction while fantasy and mythification suffuse more didactic discourse. All this accords with Belyi's understanding of the universe and man's place within it.

Though unlikely ever to gain popular appeal, he has attracted increasing interest from scholars and translators in the closing decades of the 20th century. His refusal to conform to the politically correct ideas of his own time placed him on the margins of the literary canon and earned him the Soviet label of bourgeois formalist. Yet he has been counted, most notably by Vladimir Nabokov, among the great literary innovators of European Modernism, with his best known novel *Petersburg* being frequently compared with *Ulysses*. Published first in serial form, in 1913–14, and rapidly translated into German, *Petersburg* reached anglophone readers for the first time only in 1959, translations into the other major European languages following over the next 20 years.

Because most other Russian writing had been rendered in safe, smooth versions such as Constance Garnett's, experimental work such as Belyi's was at first ignored. From the 1970s onwards, however, growing interest among Western scholars and specialists has prompted the English translation of Belyi's main titles. Among the numerous obstacles that have stood in the way of translation are the establishment of originality of text and difficulty in obtaining reliable Russian originals: some texts were published in several different editions under varying pressures of Soviet censorship, while others, having been printed only in small numbers, are rare, although facsimile editions have subsequently become available in Germany, England or America. But the main obstacle must be the sheer density of Belyi's style. Being rhythmic, polysemous and complex, it presents so many challenges to the translator that annotations or commentaries are mandatory to prevent the author being dismissed as merely exotic or obscurantist. Decisive courage and creative ingenuity are required to tackle the word-play and symbolism: the usual strategy of translating sense over style and information over ornament misses essential qualities of the writing. As in the case of Joyce, it has taken time for a body of scholarly comment and academic exegesis to accumulate, offering ways in to difficult texts that require a broad intercultural approach. Having been overlooked for his experimentalism, Belyi is however now gaining wider recognition and attention as Russian literary perspectives are opening up.

Petersburg: A Novel in Eight Chapters with Prologue and Epilogue, is set in the city of St Petersburg in 1905. This sophisticated novel follows a student's involvement in a revolutionary plot, involving a bomb hidden in a sardine tin, to assassinate what turns out to be his own loathsome father. A blend of detective novel and symbolic lyricism, the narrative unfolds as a hallucinatory dream: comic and cosmic merge in waves of patterned, suggestive imagery. Chaos constantly threatens order, irony undercuts pathos. Material objects evaporate into abstractions while metaphysical ideas take on concrete form. The entire city of St Petersburg, always a potent theme in Russian literature, attains spiritual dimensions.

The existence of several editions of this work raises vexing questions of intention and authority for the translator. Originally completing it in 1913, Belyi published *Petersburg* first in instalments in the periodical *Sirin* (1913–14), then in book form under the same imprint in 1916. He was prompted, perhaps while preparing a shortened version for translation into German in 1919, to publish a revised Russian version. Therefore in 1921 he left Russia for Berlin where, under constraints of time, he made further cuts and revisions to publish there a second Russian version in 1922 which is a tighter, more elliptical text, less digressive and more aesthetic. Its resulting inconsistencies are variously interpreted as deliberate obfuscation, editorial oversight or careless rewriting, but this was the only edition published without censorship or editorial interference. Later Soviet editions contain yet further revisions and cuts that are assumed to have been made by censors. In 1981, however, the longest, original, 1916 edition was reissued by the Moscow Academy of Sciences, edited by L. Dolgopolov. It is thus difficult to speak of a single original of *Petersburg*: Belyi was author both of the first, full-length, 1916 version and also of the shortened 1922 edition. Each of the three currently available translations into English is based on a different edition.

The first English translation of *Petersburg* did not appear until 1959, although its translator had been given a copy of the 1916 version in its year of publication. That it took more than 40 years to reach an anglophone readership can be partly explained by attitudes towards the Soviet Union which were dominated by political rather than literary considerations and by divergent attitudes within the reading public which focused on social rather than stylistic aspects of Russian literature.

A second translation of *Petersburg* by MAGUIRE & MALMSTAD, with extensive notes, was well received in 1978 and published in England as a Penguin Modern Classic. However, in 1995 Penguin reissued the novel in a new translation by David McDUFF, which received little critical attention. The fact that Vladimir Nabokov's famous quote of 1973, ranking Bely's *Petersburg* among the greatest masterpieces of

20th-century prose, has been prominently printed on the cover of each version thereafter should be of interest to all students of translation. This endorsement placed Belyi in a particular modernist context while harnessing him to the high reputation of the leading Anglo-Russian writer of the 20th century, and surely helped to secure Belyi's niche in the Western literary pantheon, despite many qualities of his writing being inevitably effaced in translation.

Based (probably) on the 1916 edition, COURNOS (1959) was the first English translation. Though initially applauded as a pioneer work, this version has now been widely discredited for its misreadings and unauthorized cutting of important features such as chapter headings, narrative voice and ironic asides, as well as further subtle but vital literary features. While the translator's preface draws broad comparisons between Belyi and Joyce, the text of the translation itself makes no such resemblance apparent. There are no footnotes or annotations and the translator's short introduction provides only a general context which chiefly sets Belyi in a 19th-, not a 20th-century context.

MAGUIRE & MALMSTAD (1978) is a translation of the Berlin 1922 edition, which, though shorter and more elliptical, the translators consider a stronger version than that of 1916. As stated in their comprehensive and exemplary introduction, this version aims to remove the impediments to deeper understanding and appreciation by offering a scholarly textual analysis as well as over 60 pages of annotation. Their translation does indeed offer a wider view of Belyi's artistic and intellectual concerns, but it reads pleasurably as well. Conscious of Belyi's

> highly idiosyncratic verbal texture, the translators have eschewed smooth English as deliberately as Belyi did smooth Russian ... everywhere [resisting the] urge to paraphrase or to inflict other normalizations on his style ... [The] translation is literal in the sense that [they] have tried to find the most appropriate equivalent for a given word and stuck to it throughout, bearing in mind the importance of repetition as one of Belyi's principal devices.

Similar sensitivity is shown over such textual features as soundplay, rhythm and versification as well as the multiplicity of meanings that symbolists deliberately cultivate. Strategies for coping with the unusual punctuation, paragraphing and so on are described. This translation provides a clear view of Belyi's strengths and position within Russian letters, while giving the reader an idea of the qualities that have earned him wider respect.

McDUFF's translation (1995) is based on the 1916 first edition, as reprinted in Moscow in 1981. The translator, himself a poet, provides a preface that offers biographical background information focusing particularly on the author's intellectual and spiritual interests. There are 20 pages of annotation. The translator's only comment on methodology concerns fidelity to punctuation. He chose the first and longer edition because "with its rhythmical meanderings and convolutions it would reflect the confused atmosphere of the age". Taken from an original text that is less compressed and less jerkily episodic than later editions, this version may indeed be more explicit, but with reduced focus on the complex workings of Belyi's texture – e.g. patterning and play – it is less effective in capturing the essence of a symbolist writer for whom polysemy or musicality, for example, are not merely stylistic devices but integral images of cosmological significance. Lacking vitality, this version seems more remote from Belyi's wider artistic and philosophical aims.

JENEFER COATES

Further Reading

Alexandrov, Vladimir E., *Andrei Bely: The Major Symbolist Fiction*, Cambridge, Massachusetts: Harvard University Press, 1985

Andrej Belyj Society Newsletter, Riverside, University of California, 92521

Elsworth, John D., *Andrey Bely: A Critical Study of the Novels*, Cambridge: Cambridge University Press, 1983

Janacek, Gerald (editor), *Andrei Bely: A Critical Review*, Lexington: University Press of Kentucky, 1978

Karlinsky, Simon, review of translations of *The Silver Dove* and *Kotik Letaev* in *New York Times Book Review* (27 October 1974)

May, Rachel, *The Translator in the Text*, Evanston, Illinois: Northwestern University Press, 1994

See also introductions to Maguire & Malmstad (1978) and preface to Beyer translation of *The Christened Chinaman*

Tahar Ben Jelloun 1944–

Moroccan novelist, dramatist, poet and essayist

Biography

Born in Fès (Fez), Morocco, 21 December 1944. He studied at the Collège Ibn Al Khatib and Lycée Regnault in Tangier, and in 1962 he studied philosophy at the University of Mohammed V in Rabat. He obtained a doctorate in social psychiatry, already showing the interest in the life of North African emigrants, and of other exiled or disadvantaged groups and individuals, that marks his writing. In 1968 he taught philosophy in Tétouan and then in Casablanca. He contributed to various periodicals and newspapers, and his first collection of poetry, *Hommes sous linceul de silence* [Men under the Shroud of Silence], was published in 1971. His autobiographical first novel, *Harrouda* (also 1971) is set in Fès and Tangier. Ben Jelloun turned the first of his plays, *Chronique d'une solitude* [Chronicle of Solitude] (1976) into the second of his novels, *La Réclusion solitaire* (*Solitaire*) (1976); the third novel, *Moha le fou, Moha le sage* [Moha the Fool, Moha the Wise], a satire on North African politics, was published in 1978. He is best known for his sixth novel, the immediately successful *L'Enfant de sable* (1985; *The Sand Child*, 1987) and its sequel, *La Nuit sacrée* (1987; *The Sacred Night*, 1989), which won the Prix Goncourt.

Translations

Novels

L'Enfant de sable, 1985
Sheridan, Alan, *The Sand Child*, San Diego: Harcourt Brace, 1987; London: Quartet, 1988

La Nuit sacrée, 1987
Sheridan, Alan, *The Sacred Night*, San Diego: Harcourt Brace, and London: Quartet, 1989

Jour de silence à Tanger, 1990
Lobdell, David, *Silent Day in Tangier*, San Diego: Harcourt Brace, and London: Quartet, 1991

Les Yeux baissés, 1991
Neugroschel, Joachim, *With Downcast Eyes*, Boston: Little Brown, 1993

L'Homme rompu, 1994
Volk, Carol, *Corruption*, New York: New Press, 1995

Essay

Alberto Giacometti, 1991
Sheridan, Alan, *Alberto Giacometti*, Paris: Flohic, 1991

Tahar Ben Jelloun writes in French rather than in Arabic in order to reach a larger audience, and one from a culture other than his own. When he says: "J'écris pour dire la différence" ("I write to express the difference"), he speaks for the modern intellectual Maghrebin, who attempts to bridge the gap between two cultures (French and Maghreb) on opposite sides of the Mediterranean.

A former student of Roland Barthes, Ben Jelloun is as much teacher as he is philosopher, sociologist, essayist, novelist, and playwright; he is, above all, a poet. His writings often take the linear shape of the arabesque, engulfing the reader and taking him or her into the world of the *Thousand and One Nights*, where the imaginary as well as the fantastic often invade the realm of real life. The heightened, lyrical prose of his fiction makes an exotic impression in French, and in English translation.

Being from a country where the storyteller is possessed by the demon of words, Ben Jelloun constructs and deconstructs his characters, making them appear and disappear as the story unfolds. He is the voice of all, men as well as women, yet his greatest compassion seems to turn toward women whose identity is either suppressed or brutally shaped by a strongly patriarchal Muslim society.

Although both genders appear in all his long fiction, it is possible to distinguish two series of novels: those concerning male lives and those concerning female lives. Among the writings centered on men are his essay *Alberto Giacometti* (1991) and the two novels *Jour de silence à Tanger* (1990) and *L'Homme rompu* (1994). His prize-winning novel *L'Enfant de sable* (1985), as well as *La Nuit sacrée* (1987) and *Les Yeux baissés* (1991) deal with female issues, especially those of a woman's identity, or the lack of it, and embody Ben Jelloun's determination to present women's voices.

L'Enfant de sable, translated as *The Sand Child* (SHERIDAN, 1987), and its sequel, *La Nuit sacrée*, translated as *The Sacred Night* (SHERIDAN, 1989), turned Ben Jelloun into the internationally known author he is today.

In *The Sand Child*, storytellers in Marrakech marketplaces entertain their listeners with the story of the life of Zahra, a girl raised as Ahmed, a boy. In this story Ben Jelloun deconstructs a false character, Ahmed, to reconstruct the true character, Zahra, combining poetry and dream with a meditation on Moroccan culture wherein "to be a woman is an unfortunate natural handicap".

The title *L'Enfant de sable* in French, in English *The Sand Child*, brings to mind the image of an hourglass in which the sand measures the passing of time. As Ahmed becomes an adult, time brings physiological changes which, in turn, challenge the father's initial decision to raise his eighth daughter as a male. His reason for such a cruel decision resides in the fact that in Morocco, as everywhere in the Muslim world, a father is believed to be cursed if he does not procreate a son. Helpless, the child Zahra/Ahmed acquiesces to the parental decision although "he" will have some haunting recollection of "his" mother's fears (and ultimately fall into insanity), as "his" body develops upon reaching puberty. The hourglass tips over when, at "his" father's deathbed, Ahmed/Zahra is confronted with the truth, asked for forgiveness and begged to bury all evidence of falsified circumcision papers and any traces of "his" male past. Ahmed/Zahra is 20 when "he" realizes that "he" is in fact a "she". Slowly the reawakened Zahra brings herself to deconstruct Ahmed, her imposed male identity, to bring forward the womanhood that has been so violently suppressed. As the sand fills the bottom of the hourglass, Zahra emerges with all her scars, and another ambiguous and painful life begins as she joins a group of travelling performers, posing as the "man with breasts".

In *The Sacred Night*, Zahra, formerly known as Ahmed, begins to tell her story on the "sacred night", which is the 27th day of Ramadan and also the night her father died. The narrative unfolds, shifting in and out of the past to the present. After her father's revelation, she renounces her role of son and heir and wanders off. On her journey she experiences rape; ghosts haunt her everywhere; she finds a little love with a strange sister, the Seated Woman, and the blind Consul. When an uncle threatens to expose her past, she kills him and is imprisoned and tortured. In prison she realizes that she is freer now than she has ever been in her 20 years as Ahmed, and to free herself completely she must tell her story.

The novel *Les Yeux baissés* (1991) was translated by Joachim NEUGROSCHEL as *With Downcast Eyes* (1993). The story opens in the Berber village of Imiltanout, located in the south of Morocco. In the second part of the novel, the scene shifts to the Parisian Arab neighborhood of La Goutte d'Or, where the immigrant family lives; in the last part, the family moves back to the native village and the legend begins. The title, in both French and English, is a reference to expectations imposed by the Muslim family and society on women. Humility requires that they do not look people in the eye but that they face them with "downcast eyes", a mark of respect and also a body language that conveys the message that they know their place, which is "to be" and yet to be invisible, to hear yet not be heard; in brief, to be denied any freedom and identity.

This is the story of a Moroccan girl caught between the constraints of her heritage and the discovery of a new way of life and a new set of values learned during her stay in France. The parents realize that she no longer speaks "with downcast eyes", and she realizes that she is an outcast in French society. Her inner struggle is reflected in a dream where French and Berber words are engaged in a fight. As she returns to the village, her story comes to a tragic end. Throughout this novel Ben Jelloun again presents the voice of the woman caught between two different worlds and two different cultures that remain worlds apart. The novel introduces us to a culture where murder is a tool, and a young girl bears the responsibility for an entire village. As in all his narratives, Ben Jelloun uses the real world to suggest metaphorically an inner journey.

If, on the one hand, women experience solitude because of the constraints the patriarchal society imposes upon them, men, on the other hand, experience solitude only as they grow old. Ben Jelloun dedicated his novel *Silent Day in Tangier* to his aging father. Both the novel and the essay *Alberto Giacometti* (SHERIDAN, 1991) center on solitude and absence. The sculptures of Giacometti, with their slender appearance and extended hands, reinforce the idea of loneliness.

In *Silent Day in Tangier* (LOBDELL, 1991) a bedridden old man bitterly reflects on his empty existence. He had friends but they have all passed away. He had a wife, but when was the last time he loved her? The memories of his younger years do not bring him any comfort either. His biggest mistake was to move his fabric shop from Fès to Tangier, where he never was successful. All he has left are his thoughts, so he passes judgements on the changes that have occurred in society. He feels that death is slowly creeping in. His eyes wander from one thing to another as do his thoughts. So it is a silent day in Tangier where a man dies alone without a wife or a son to hold his hand for the great journey.

L'Homme rompu (1994) was translated by Carol VOLK as *Corruption* (1995). The setting is Casablanca and Tangier. It is a story that illuminates the confrontation between personal integrity and the realities of the work ethic that face ordinary men in the modern world.

The main character is Mourad, father of two, a civil servant engineer in charge of signing building permits. His wife, Hilma, constantly belittles him because he is not as successful as his co-workers, who all take bribes. He is the last honest man in town, but family needs and Hilma's pressure are strong. Finally, he gives in and accepts the first envelope stuffed with cash. Soon after, some state auditors appear and Mourad is convinced that it is because of him; however, it is only of the theft of an old, disused Olivetti typewriter that he is (rightly) accused. After staying at home for days in a feverish state of guilty fear, he takes courage, helped by a surreal dream, and decides to go back to his office, only to discover that an old Remington typewriter has mysteriously replaced the missing Olivetti, to the satisfaction of the state auditors. The investigation is over. Mourad, his integrity compromised, is hailed by his co-workers and, with a "Welcome to the tribe", joins the ranks of the successful corruptibles.

English translations of Tahar Ben Jelloun's major novels have followed swiftly upon their publication in French. In general they have been done by translators possessing a superb command of French and English. Three additions should be considered for the next editions of these translations: an introduction explaining cultural features, an index of Arabic words found in the novels, and an appendix clarifying the historical and religious differences between cultures in the Mediterranean basin.

HÉLÈNE N. SANKO

Further Reading

Bourkhis, Rhida, *Tahar Ben Jelloun: la poussière d'or et la face masquée: approche linguistique*, Paris: L'Harmattan, 1995

Novén, Bengt, *Les Mots et le corps: étude des procès d'écrire dans l'oeuvre de Tahar Ben Jelloun*, Uppsala: Uppsala University, and Stockholm: Almqvist & Wiksell, 1996

Bengali Women Writers in English Translation

Though they write in the highly nuanced and musical language of Rabindranath Tagore, winner of the Nobel Prize for Literature in 1913, and though their language is as old as English, not many Bengali writers have been translated. Bengali literature is under-represented in English in part because its script is non-Roman, in part because it is difficult to study outside of West Bengal and Bangladesh: only a few universities in the West offer even elementary courses. Non-Bengalis learning the language are generally scholars of South Asian religions, anthropologists studying folk culture, or aid-agency and development consultants. The handful of non-Bengali literary translators usually concentrate on one major writer – almost always male.

Bengali women poets and writers were not significantly represented in English translation until the mid-1980s, yet women have participated in literary activities in Bengal since the latter half of the 19th century, when, as part of the widespread social reforms of the "Bengal Renaissance" movement, upper-caste and upper-class families began sending their daughters to newly created girls' schools or hiring home tutors. As privileged women learned to read and write, they started to question many of the socially sanctioned customs that oppressed them: *purdah* (the seclusion of women), child marriage, *sati* (the immolation of Hindu widows on their husbands' funeral pyres), and prohibitions against any career but marriage and family. Educated housewives wrote diary-like life narratives; some of these were of high literary quality and were serially published – often under pseudonyms so as not to violate *purdah*'s dictates of public anonymity for women – in newspapers and magazines.

By the early 20th century, Bengali women ventured to publish under their own names; some became so popular that a few male writers took female pen names to improve their own reputations! One of the first works available in English was, in fact, written in English by Begum Rokeya Sakhawat Hossain (1880–1932), essayist, educator, and pioneering Bengali Muslim feminist. "Sultana's Dream", a short story first published in 1905 in a Madras-based English periodical, *The Indian Ladies' Magazine*, is a fantasy satire about a utopian "Ladyland" in which men are in *purdah* – relegated to menial tasks and childrearing – while wise and powerful women govern the peaceful, prosperous nation.

Another woman who began writing in *purdah* was Jyotirmoyee Devi (1894–1988). Tutored at home, married at age 11, and widowed with six children at 25, she moved from Rajasthan to her in-laws' house in Calcutta after her husband died. Her *River Churning: A Partition Novel*, dealing with the violence and social upheaval in North India after the 1947 Partition, has been translated into English (1995). Calcutta-born Shudha Mazumdar (1899–1994) received an English-medium convent-school education and a thorough training in traditional Bengali culture before marriage at age 12 to a Indian Civil Service officer twice her age. Wherever her husband was posted, she organized efforts to improve women's health and welfare, joined the struggle for Indian independence, and wrote prose reminiscences of Bengali life. The first volume of her *Memoirs of an Indian Woman* (1989), written in English, recalls her life up to the early 1930s, against the backdrop of the Indian nationalist movement and the changing roles of women in colonial Bengal.

Heir to Begum Rokeya's legacy, Begum Sufia Kamal (1911–99) was born to a noble Muslim family in East Bengal. She was tutored in the women's quarters at home and married at age 11 to a progressive-minded lawyer. She began writing poetry after the couple transferred to Calcutta. Moving to Dhaka after Partition, she was active in social service work for women and the liberation movement for East Pakistan, now the nation of Bangladesh. Her poems of Bangladesh's 1971 freedom struggle, *Where My Darlings Lie Buried* (1975), were translated by her second husband, writer Kamaluddin Ahmad Khan, and edited by her son Sajed Kamal. Another writer who chronicled the Bangladesh Liberation War was Jahanara Imam (1929–94), whose 1971 diary-memoir, *Of Blood and Fire*, was a bestseller both in the Bengali original and in English translation.

In 1930, 16-year-old poet Maitreyi Devi (1914–90), daughter of a renowned Indian philosopher, fell in love with a Romanian student who had come to Calcutta to study with her father. When the mutual attraction was discovered, the student, future Indologist Mircea Eliade, was thrown out of the house; he eventually returned to Europe to write *Maitreyi*, a fictionalized romance about which the real Maitreyi learned with shock and consternation nearly 40 years later. Her own "reply" to Eliade's novel was *It Does Not Die* (1976, reprinted 1994), an immediate bestseller in Bengali, which the author herself translated to English. The two books, Eliade's (now titled *Bengal Nights* after the French translation of the Romanian original) and Devi's (a reprint of the first Calcutta edition), were published together in 1994 by the University of Chicago. The books created a sensation among readers for the conflicting depictions of a love affair and the cultural notions – and misreadings, especially Eliade's – on which it was based.

Most of these earlier writers wrote in English, or self-translated, or employed other Bengali native speakers to translate their work. Part of the British colonial legacy is the enduring presence of English: many educated people in the Subcontinent have at least basic fluency. Even now, most translations from Bengali to English are by English-educated Bengalis for Indian or Bangladeshi publishers. In these books, the English is sometimes awkward – demonstrating the perils of translating *from* one's native language *to* a second language studied from books, without experience of current usage or idiomatic and colloquial nuances that only native or near-native speakers can distinguish. (There is also the post-colonial, subaltern position that the various English usages of the Subcontinent are not "deviations" from some distant norm, but legitimate variants. "Indian English" is indeed a rich idiomatic variation; but many who hold such views make their points in the Oxbridge or Ivy League accents in which they have been educated, and ultimately sidestep the issue: a need for faithful and graceful translations, no matter what variant of English the target language may be.)

The finest practitioners among Bengali translators include Calcutta-based Enakshi Chatterjee who, besides Jyotirmoyee Devi's novel, has translated stories by Bani Ray (1920–) and Kabita Sinha (1931–98); Dhaka University English Professor Emeritus Kabir Chowdhury, translator of novels by Selina Hossain (1947–); Syed Manzoorul Islam, also a Dhaka University English professor; and poet Mohammad Nurul Huda. Islam and Huda have translated work by leading Bangladeshi poets. Unfortunately, most books by these translators (all of whom, except Chatterjee, happen to be men) are published in small Indian and Bangladeshi editions, almost impossible to find outside the Subcontinent.

Notable translators whose work mediating Bengali women writers is available in the West are Kalpana Bardhan and renowned post-colonial scholar Gayatri Chakravorty Spivak: both of these women are native speakers of Bengali resident for many years in the US. Both have made substantial contributions, particularly of stories by Mahasweta Devi (1926–), one of West Bengal's leading fiction writers and an energetic social activist for the rights of India's indigenous pre-Aryan tribal peoples. There are few native English speakers sufficiently fluent in Bengali to effect translations on their own, and most work with native-speaking collaborators. One American translator reasonably fluent in Bengali and focusing on women's writing is Carolyne Wright, who has so far published poetry collections by European-exiled Bangladeshi dissident writer Taslima Nasrin (1962–) and by Calcutta-based Anuradha Mahapatra (1957–).

In preparation is a comprehensive anthology of poetry and prose in translation by the leading 20th-century Bengali women poets and writers. Australian translator Marian Maddern has been working for over two decades with Bengali literature; her essay, "Translating Modern Bengali Poetry", which contains examples of work by several Bangladeshi women, appeared in 1994. She has published other books on Bengali translation in the University of Melbourne Indian Studies Series.

Some Bengali "expatriate" women writers are settled in the West but contribute actively to Bengali literary publishing in their home countries. Some, such as the poet and literary scholar Ketaki Kushari Dyson (1940–),who has lived near Oxford since finishing her postgraduate studies, self-translate and also write original work in English for non-Bengali readers; others, like Washington, DC-based Bangladeshi fiction writer Dilara Hashem (1936–), prepare preliminary versions for other translators to work from. Another rapidly evolving sub-genre consists of work by women writers of Bengali origin, settled in the West, fluent in Bengali but writing in English, chiefly about the immigrant's or cultural hybrid's experience. Such writers, including Bharati Mukherjee (1942–) and Chitra Banerjee Divakaruni (1956–), with major North American and UK publishers, are not themselves subjects for translation. Divakaruni does occasional poetry translations, however, for anthologies.

A few other young Bengali women, raised and educated in the West, but accustomed from infancy to speak – and also trained to read and write – in their parents' first language, have begun translating: theirs is the ideal balance of fluency in both source and target languages. One such translator is US resident Jhumpa Lahiri, whose special focus has been the short stories of Ashapurna Devi (1909–), one of West Bengal's most popular fiction writers.

CAROLYNE WRIGHT

See also the entry Indian/South Asian Languages, Modern

Further Reading

Devi, Jyotirmoyee, *River Churning: A Partition Novel*, translated by Enakshi Chatterjee, New Delhi: Kali for Women, 1995

Devi, Mahasweta, six stories in *Of Women, Outcastes, Peasants, and Rebels: A Selection of Bengali Short Stories*, translated by Kalpana Bardhan, Berkeley: University of California Press, 1990

Devi, Mahasweta, *Imaginary Maps: Three Stories*, translated with an introduction by Gayatri Chakravorty Spivak, New York: Routledge, 1995

Devi, Maitreyi, *It Does Not Die*, translated by the author, Calcutta: Writers Workshop, 1976; Chicago: University of Chicago Press, 1994

Imam, Jahanara, *Of Blood and Fire: The Untold Story of Bangladesh's War of Independence*, translated by Mustafizur Rahman, New Delhi: Sterling, 1989; Dhaka: Academic Publishers, 1990

Kamal, Sufia, *Where My Darlings Lie Buried*, translated by Kamaluddin Ahmad Khan, edited by Sajed Kamal, New York: Vantage Press, 1975

Maddern, Marian, *Bengali Poetry Into English: An Impossible Dream?*, Calcutta: Editions Indian, 1977 (University of Melbourne Indian Studies 1)

Maddern, Marian, "Translating Modern Bengali Poetry" in *Riding Out: New Writing From Around the World*, edited by Manfred Jurgensen, Brisbane: Phoenix-Outrider, 1994

Mahapatra, Anuradha, *Another Spring, Darkness: Selected Poems of Anuradha Mahapatra*, translated by Carolyne Wright with Paramita Banerjee and Jyotirmoy Datta, with an introduction by Wright, Corvallis, Oregon: Calyx Books, 1996

Mazumdar, Shudha, *Memoirs of an Indian Woman*, edited and with an introduction by Geraldine Forbes, Armonk, New York: M.E. Sharpe, 1989

Nasrin, Taslima, *Lajja (Shame)*, translated by Tutul Gupta, New Delhi: Penguin India, 1994

Nasrin, Taslima, *The Game in Reverse: Poems by Taslima Nasrin*, translated and with an introduction by Carolyne Wright, New York: Braziller, 1995

Rokeya, Sakhawat Hossain, *Sultana's Dream, and Selections from The Secluded Ones*, edited and translated by Roushan Jahan, New York: Feminist Press, 1988

Tharu, Susie and K. Lalita (editors), *Women Writing in India*, vol. 1: *600 B.C. to the Early 20th Century*, New York: Feminist Press, 1991 (Bengali texts from Rami, Chandrabati, Jogeswari, Bhabani, Rassundari Devi, Hannah Catherine Mullens, Mokshodayani Mukhopadhyay, Swarnakumari Devi, Sarat Kumari Chaudhurani, Binodini Dasi, Nirupama Devi, Ashapurna Devi, various translators); vol. 2: *The 20th Century*, New York: Feminist Press, 1993 (Bengali texts from Mahasweta Devi, Sulekha Sanyal, Kabita Sinha, Nabaneeta Dev Sen, Malini Bhattacharya; various translators)

Zide, Arlene R.K. (editor), *In Their Own Voice: The Penguin Anthology of Contemporary Indian Women Poets*, New Delhi: Penguin, 1993 (poems by Sanjukta Bandyopadhyay, Gita Chattopadhyay, Nabaneeta Dev Sen, Chitra Banerjee Divakaruni, Ketaki Kushari Dyson, Apabrita Lahiri, Chitra Lahiri, Anuradha Mahapatra, Vijaya Mukhopadhyay, Rajlakshmi Devi, Pratima Ray, Mallika Sengupta, Kabita Sinha; most translations by Carolyne Wright, Chitra Banerjee Divakaruni, and Paramita Banerjee)

Gottfried Benn 1886–1956

German poet, novella writer, dramatist and critic

Biography

Born in Mansfeld, 2 May 1886, Gottfried Benn, a clergyman's son, qualified and practised as a doctor, though he was interested in literature from early days. He first made a name for himself as an Expressionist writer (the important collection of poems, *Morgue und andere Gedichte*, [Morgue and Other Poems] was published in 1912), before embarking upon a relatively short-lived yet markedly sympathetic identification with Nazism which duly heaped embarrassment and opprobrium upon his head. He fell from sight and favour, and the episode hastened his return to the army as a doctor. Rehabilitation slowly followed after World War II, and Benn, who had continued penning poems and other writings over the previous decade while carrying on with his professional medical duties, saw the publication of the volume *Static Poems* (*Statische Gedichte*) in 1948. In 1944 he had written the innovative prose of his *Roman des Phänotyp* (*Novel of the Phenotype*). His influential poetological talk on "Problems of Lyric Poetry" (*Probleme der Lyrik*) at Marburg in 1951 confirmed a leading role for him in modern German poetry and attracted international attention, and not least that of T.S. Eliot in the UK. Germans both old and young bought and avidly read Benn's writings in that post-war phase – poetry, essays and experimental prose. Died in Berlin, 7 July 1956.

Translations

Selections

Ashton, E.B. (editor), *Primal Vision: Selected Writings*, with an introduction, translated by Ashton, Babette Deutsch, Michael Hamburger, Eugène Jolas, Ernst Kaiser, Christopher Middleton and Eithne Wilkins, New York: New Directions, 1960; London: Bodley Head, 1961

Becker, Reinhard Paul and Volkmar Sander (editors), *Prose, Essays, Poems*, New York: Continuum Press, 1987

Draghici, Simona, *Gottfried Benn: Poems, 1937–1947* (parallel texts), Washington DC: Plutarch Press, 1991

Ritchie, J.M., *Gottfried Benn: The Unreconstructed Expressionist*, London: Wolff, 1972 (contains translations of 5 prose pieces and 20 poems)

Self-deprecatingly, Gottfried Benn viewed his collected writings when they were published in 1922 as "not a document worth mentioning". He was also to say of himself that he was at best "a character cameo, an eccentric, a specialist", who "didn't get any big parts to fill an evening with". In fact Benn counts among the most important writers in German literature of the first half of the 20th century, and certainly one of the most controversial.

Only the occasional individual poem or piece of prose writing by Benn had been translated into English prior to the advent of Nazism (the pioneering efforts of Eugene Jolas are here to be remembered), but the republication after World War II of Benn's earlier works, as well as the appearance of new writings by him to mark the revival of his literary fortunes, now stimulated the endeavours of English scholars and translators. Michael Hamburger, who also translated a number of Benn's poems, provided early guidance for English readers with his perceptive and critical essay in *Reason and Energy: Studies in German Literature* (1957), written in Benn's lifetime.

The first substantial selection in English translation of Benn's work did not appear until some little time after Benn's death, and *Primal Vision* (1960), edited by E.B. ASHTON, arguably remains the best introduction in translation to Benn's writings. The volume begins with a 20-page introduction by the editor reflecting with objectivity and understanding the human, political and literary strengths and weaknesses of Gottfried Benn the man, the doctor, the writer. The prose translations that follow are essentially shared between ASHTON himself and the renowned translating pair of Ernst KAISER & Eithne WILKINS. The selections, covering 208 pages, comprise the bulk of the volume, and range from a piece from the cycle of *Rönne* stories, the dialogue sketch *Home Front* (also from the World War I period and dealing with the decay of reality), and essays from the 1920s and 1930s (e.g. "Primal Vision", 1929, and "The New Literary Season", 1932, here translated by Eugene JOLAS) to samples of the later prose of *World of Expression*, excerpts from *Novel of the Phenotype*, *Double Life*, a chapter from *The Ptolemaean* (*Der Ptolomäer*, 1949) and the essay *Artists and Old Age*. A scene from the dialogue *Three Old Men* rounds off the link with his early conversation piece *Home Front*. Benn saw the modern poem as monological, without belief, without hope. Of his own verse, 32 poems are presented here in this volume in the German original with facing translations, which usefully allows the reader the measure of comparison. They are arranged chronologically and range from the earliest period of creativity with examples from the *Morgue* cycle published in 1912, when Benn was 26, to the time of his death in the mid-1950s. The bulk of these translations are by the poets and Germanists Michael HAMBURGER and Christopher MIDDLETON and are of good quality overall despite – because of – certain liberties from time to time. But in his talk "On Translating Benn" in *Gottfried Benn* (Casey & Casey, 1990) Hamburger himself has spoken feelingly of the difficulties involved. He argues that the very best poems by Benn were those of the 1920s, which are certainly the most idiosyncratic and bring their own translating problems with them, and he remarks on Benn's inability or unwillingness to reconcile extremes where elements are "too cerebral": "he brings in rhymes like 'Philosophia Perennis' and 'Tennis', which is somehow too clever to go with that form of primitivism ... he is actually aiming at". Inevitably, the most easily translatable are the free verse poems, the more casual poems, and also the more realistic ones – like "Fragments"and "Chopin". The inherent difficulties ensure therefore that half-rhyme instead of full is found sometimes (as in "Gesänge", "Epilog"), on occasion rhyme is seemingly more "hit and miss" (as in "Palau") or, again, the translations are more free to get the rhymes that are essential to the sound, as in Ashton's versions of "Qui sait" and "Einsamer nie –".

Ashton's volume was printed both in America and in England, but Benn in translation has never become as well received in the English-speaking world in the popular sense as Rilke, Hölderlin or Heine. As late as 1972 Hamish RITCHIE, in *Gottfried Benn,* his introductory book on the German writer, whom he describes in the sub-title as "The Unreconstructed Expressionist" (a term he takes in fact from Ashton's introduction to his own volume), was lamenting that Gottfried Benn "still needs to be introduced to the English-reading public", and admitting that few of his 1920s poems could be rendered into English satisfactorily – these rhymed verses with their trochaic rhythms and their scientific and technological neologisms to conceal strict, classicist orthodoxy. All this despite Benn being described as"one of the most fascinating and important German poets of this century". Ritchie's monograph on Benn concludes with a modest yet reasonably representative selection of Benn's work in translation. This comprises five pieces of prose writing, including the early dramatic sketch *Ithaca* (*Ithaka*, 1919) and the first in the cycle of *Rönne* stories, *Brains* (*Gehirne*, 1916). The "Reply to the Literary Émigrés" (to be found in Ashton's volume under "Answer to the Literary Emigrants") stands here neatly beside Benn's "Address to Heinrich Mann". Strangely and notably absent from both volumes is any version of the important talk on "Problems of Lyric Poetry". (The omission seems to have been first countered in the shape of an unpublished annotated translation of Benn's talk by Marjorie N. Smith in 1970 for her thesis submitted to the South West Texas State University.) Nor does Ritchie's book contain any samples of Benn's later prose. Of the 20 poems contained there, 10 are to be found in English versions in Ashton's volume. On balance, the more felicitous phrasing is to be found in the Ashton volume (where, though, Americanisms in spelling and terminology are encountered – "colors", "center", and, inappropriately, "truck-driver" (as against Ritchie's "drayman") for "Bierfahrer". On the other hand, Ritchie does boldly assay the notoriously difficult though important "The Lost I" and "Sentence Structure" from the late poems, as well as the character study "The Young Hebbel" from the early period. Arguably, Ritchie's volume suffers by not including the German originals of the poems.

A translation (*The Voice behind the Curtain*) of Benn's second major radio play, *Die Stimme hinter dem Vorhang* (1952), which was widely discussed at the time, can be found in *New Directions in Prose and Poetry* 22 (New York: New Directions, 1970).

As the title suggests, Simona DRAGHICI's book *Gottfried Benn: Poems 1937–1947* (1991) consciously restricts itself in scope and intent.

To mark the centenary of Benn's birth, a noteworthy and sound introduction to the man and his work is provided by BECKER & SANDER's 1987 selection of the German writer's works in English translation, published in New York.

IAN HILTON

Further Reading

Adams, Marion, *Gottfried Benn's Critique of Substance*, Assen: Van Gorcum, 1969

Casey, P.F. and T.J. Casey (editors), *Gottfried Benn*, Galway: Galway University Press, 1990

Dierick, Augustinus P., *Gottfried Benn and His Critics: Major Interpretations, 1912–1992*, Columbia, South Carolina: Camden House, 1992

Hamburger, Michael, essay on Gottfried Benn in his *Reason and Energy: Studies in German Literature*, New York: Grove Press, and London: Routledge and Kegan Paul, 1957; longer revised version in his *A Proliferation of Prophets: Essays on German Writers from Nietzsche to Brecht*, Manchester: Carcanet, 1983; New York: St Martin's Press, 1984

Hamburger, Michael and Christopher Middleton, *Modern German Poetry 1910–1960: An Anthology with Verse Translations*, New York: Grove Press, and London: MacGibbon and Kee, 1962

Hilton, Ian, "Gottfried Benn" in *German Men of Letters*, vol. 3, edited by Alex Natan, London: Wolff, 1964, pp. 129–52

Manyoni, Angelika, *Consistency of Phenotype: A Study of Gottfried Benn's Views on Lyric Poetry*, New York: Peter Lang, 1983

Roche, Mark William, *Gottfried Benn's Static Poetry: Aesthetic and Intellectual-Historical Interpretations*, Chapel Hill: University of North Carolina Press, 1991

Wodtke, Friedrich Wilhelm (editor), introduction and notes to Benn's *Selected Poems* (text of poems in German), London: Oxford University Press, 1970

Beowulf: Intra-lingual Translation

The composition of the anonymous Old English poem *Beowulf* was probably complete by 900. It survives in one manuscript of c.1000 and in transcripts made in 1786–87, which preserve some readings. The major scholarly edition is that of F. Klaeber, *Beowulf and the Fight at Finnesburg*, 3rd edition, Boston: Heath, 1936. Other editions are: Michael Alexander, *Beowulf* (parallel text), Harmondsworth: Penguin, 1995; George Jack, *Beowulf: A Student Edition*, Oxford: Clarendon Press, 1994; and C.L. Wrenn, *Beowulf*, 3rd edition, revised by W.F. Bolton, London: Harrap, and New York: St Martin's Press, 1973

Translations

Alexander, Michael, *Beowulf: A Verse Translation*, Harmondsworth: Penguin, 1973

Clark Hall, J., *Beowulf and the Finnesburg Fragment* (prose

translation), new edition, revised by C.L. Wrenn, with prefatory remarks by J.R.R. Tolkien, London: Allen and Unwin, 1940; New York: Barnes and Noble, 1958
Donaldson, E. Talbot, *Beowulf: A New Prose Translation*, New York: Norton, 1966; edited by Joseph F. Turso, New York: Norton, 1975; also in the *Norton Anthology of English Literature*, 6th edition, New York: Norton, 1993
Garmonsway, G.N. and Jacqueline Simpson, *Beowulf and Its Analogues*, London and New York: Dent, 1968
Heaney, Seamus, *Beowulf: A New Translation*, with an introduction, London: Faber, and New York: Farrar Straus, 1999
Kennedy, Charles W., *Beowulf*, New York: Oxford University Press, 1940
Morgan, Edwin, *Beowulf: A Verse Translation into Modern English*, Aldington, Kent: Hand and Flower Press, 1952; Berkeley: University of California Press, 1962

Modern English derives from Old English, the language of the Anglo-Saxon settlers of Britain between the 5th century and c.1100, through the intermediate stage known as Middle English (1100–1500). The Norman Conquest of 1066 dethroned English as an official and literary language, though it was spoken and written in differing dialects in different parts of the country. But when in the 14th century, and especially at the court of Richard II, English re-emerged as an official and literary language alongside French and Latin, it had changed greatly. In this Middle stage, English words became thoroughly mixed with French, and the dialects that emerged in the provinces of England showed large differences from one another. A fundamental alteration since 1066 was the gradual loss of grammatical inflections and the consequent change from a synthetic to a more analytical language, with increased use of pronouns, articles and prepositions and the establishment of the modern subject-verb-object order of the chief elements of the sentence. Subsequently, the admixtures of Latin at the Renaissance, the stylistic changes associated with the rise of science, and the eventual development of English as an imperial, technical and business language made contemporary English a language very different indeed from Old English.

There are, however, recognizable continuities, especially in vocabulary. The first words of one Old English version of the Our Father are "Ure faeder se the eart on heofenum". In the early Modern English "Our Father who art in heaven", the relative pronoun has changed, the preposition has changed, and "heaven" has lost its dative inflection; and in contemporary English the second person singular occurs only in rare or archaic uses. Yet most of the old words are recognizably the same in modern English, and their order is the same. It is as much the similarities as the differences between Old and Modern English that create difficulties for the translator of Old English poetry into Modern English, whether into prose or verse.

Nearly all of the 30,000 surviving lines of Old English poetry are composed, without end-rhyme or stanza form, in the same metre, with a line containing four main stresses balanced by a mid-line pause, rather than the iambic pentameter, with 10 syllables of five "feet", of English poetry from Chaucer to Tennyson. Thus it is said of Grendel, the monster of *Beowulf* (in a modern version that follows the old metre): "The fell and the fen his fastness was". In this line the first three of the four stressed syllables are pointed by alliteration. (Alliteration being an essential feature of Old English poetry, the term "alliterative verse" is best kept for Middle English verse, which does not keep to the rules of Old English verse; its alliteration is wild, decorative and not functional.) The change of Old English from a synthetic to an analytic language increased the number of small words, such as prepositions, articles and pronouns, needed to express what had previously been indicated in the inflections of nouns and verbs. This loss of inflection made it increasingly difficult to compose in the Old English metre, which permits only a limited number of unstressed syllables: a difficulty found not only by writers of Middle English alliterative verse but also by modern translators of Old English verse into Modern English verse, especially for those who (like the present writer) try to reproduce the Old English metre. Synthetic languages are more condensed than analytical languages, which require more words to express an idea. This can also be seen in translations of Latin or Chinese verse into modern English.

A second source of difficulty for the translator is English literature itself: the successive mountain ranges of English poetry since Chaucer. The achievements of poets in English ever since Chaucer have been cast in a syllabic-accentual metre different in its basis to Old English verse. The music of Old English verse is thus unfamiliar. This can be part of its attraction. But a fundamental problem is caused by semantic changes in the language, not only denotative changes in meaning (OE *cniht* means "youth", not "knight"), but the associations of more complex words. The translator who wishes to reproduce, or produce an analogue for, the characteristic effects of Old English poetry has often to use English words adopted from French or Latin which have cultural associations foreign to Anglo-Saxon, or Old English words that have changed their meanings or associations. To take an example from the aristocratic vocabulary often required in translating the old poetry, the words "noble", "chieftain", "prince" and "hero" do not sound Anglo-Saxon, whereas "atheling" and "thane" are *too* Anglo-Saxon; the word "earl" is a word of Norse origin which is now a title, like duke, viscount and marquess. The translator cannot go far beyond "king", "lord", "war-leader" and "man" in rendering a poetic style rich in near-synonyms for these heroic leading roles. The first sentence of *Beowulf* is often translated in prose somewhat as follows: "Listen! We have heard of the glory of the kings of the people of the Spear-Danes, how in former days those princes accomplished glorious deeds". This modern English sentence shows a clustering of nouns of similar meaning awkwardly linked by "of the"; "glory" is too close to its echo in "glorious". The metre of Old English produced two-stress phrases, often noun-phrases, in a syntax that ran to replication and richness rather than economy.

Old English poetry was rediscovered by antiquarians in the 18th century, and substantial specimens of it began to be published early in the 19th century. It was of interest to all those in search of the origins of this nation whose language had begun to prevail over much of the world. One-tenth of the 30,000 lines of Old English verse are to be found in the major achievement of the old poetry, *Beowulf*. The poem is set in southern Scandinavia, not England, and the whole text was first published in Copenhagen by an Icelander, with a translation into Latin; its first vernacular translation was into Danish. Extracts then appeared in English, and the first English edition of the whole text was by Kemble in 1833. Anglo-Saxon was of immense interest to the Victorians. As an undergraduate, Alfred Tennyson tried his hand, in 1830, at a few lines of *Beowulf*, not published until recently: "Him the eldest / Answered. / The army's leader / His wordhoard unlocked: 'We are by race / Gothic people / And Hygelac's / Hearth ministers. / My father was / To folk known'". It is indicative of the kinds of interest in Anglo-Saxon at that time that Tennyson chose to try out such a Homeric, archaic and patriarchal passage. Tennyson much later translated the whole of the Old English battle-poem *Brunanburh*.

Traces of Anglo-Saxon influence are to be found in the diction and rhythm of many poets, including Gerard Manley Hopkins, Ezra Pound (see also his famous translation of *The Seafarer*), T.S. Eliot, David Jones, W.H. Auden, Geoffrey Hill and Tony Harrison. The 3,182 lines of *Beowulf* have attracted many translators; there are full verse versions by William Morris, Edwin Morgan and the present writer. In 1999 Seamus Heaney published a complete verse translation, which won the Whitbread Book of the Year Award. J.R.R. Tolkien's saga-romances for children are steeped in *Beowulf*. Over 100 translations of *Beowulf* have been published in English, and several are currently in print. One reason for the number of translations is that the poem has been studied as part of degree courses in English language and literature for more than a century, and thousands of students have invested millions of hours in trying to master its difficulties, linguistic, stylistic and historical. The basic story of Beowulf, concerning the epic feats of the eponymous warrior hero, is simple, but its style is rich, convoluted, rewarding. It repays study and tempts the translator.

Translations of *Beowulf* are of all sorts: prose and verse, literal and literary, modernizing and archaizing. Klaeber's edition of the source text lists and comments on the earlier translations, of which the most notable are by Kemble (1837), Thorpe (1855), Thomas Arnold (1876), Earle (1892) and Clark Hall (1901, 1911, revised edition 1950), all in prose. In verse there is the notably weird version by William Morris (and A.J. Wyatt), published by the Kelmscott Press in 1895, on which Klaeber comments: "Fine imitative measure; very archaic, strange diction". Charles Scott Moncrieff published a verse *Beowulf Translated* (London, 1921); he later translated Proust. There are more American than British verse translations of *Beowulf*, a bias towards verse also to be found in American translations of classical epic poems.

Only post-war versions are currently available outside libraries. I give the first sentence of *Beowulf* followed by translations.

> Hwæt, We Gar-Dena in geardagum,
> Theodcyninga thrym gefrunon,
> Hu tha æthelingas ellen fremedon!
>
> (Klaeber)

> Lo! We have heard of the glory of the kings of the people of the Spear-Danes in days of yore – how those princes did valorous deeds!
>
> (Clark Hall, revised by Wrenn, 1940)

> Lo! We have listened to many a lay of the Spear-Danes' fame, their splendour of old,
> Their mighty princes, and martial deeds!
>
> (Kennedy, 1940)

> How that glory remains in remembrance,
> Of the Danes and their kings in days gone,
> The acts and valour of princes of their blood!
>
> (Morgan, 1952)

> Yes, we have heard of the glory of the Spear-Danes' kings in the old days – how the princes of that people did brave deeds
>
> (Donaldson, 1966)

> We have indeed heard tell of the splendour of warrior Danes in days gone by, of the kings of that nation, and of how those high-born men achieved deeds of valour.
>
> (Garmonsway, 1968)

> Attend!
> We have heard of the thriving of the throne of Denmark
> How the folk-kings flourished in former days,
> How those royal athelings earned that glory!
>
> (Alexander, 1973)

> So. The Spear-Danes in days gone by
> and the kings who ruled them had courage and greatness.
> We have heard of those princes' heroic campaigns.
>
> (Heaney, 1999)

The prose versions mentioned here are generally very accurate, CLARK HALL's crampedly so. DONALDSON is plain, unceremonious, idiomatic, sometimes flat. GARMONSWAY is very full, dignified, nuanced and rhythmical; the best of the prose versions. Of these verse versions, KENNEDY's metre goes with too jolly a swing; MORGAN is free, rich, almost Shakespearean, inventive. ALEXANDER keeps the versification, and aims at an elevated style. HEANEY is bold and downright.

MICHAEL ALEXANDER

See also the entry Parallel Texts

Further Reading

Alexander, Michael, "Old English Poetry into Modern English Verse", *Translation and Literature*, 3 (1994) pp. 69–75

Alexander, Michael, "The Sheen on the Mere; or, Beowulf in Ulster", *Agenda*, 37/4 (Spring–Summer 2000) pp. 80–84 (on Heaney's translation)

Heaney, Seamus, "The Drag of the Golden Chain", *Times Literary Supplement* (12 November 1999)

Shippey, Tom, "*Beowulf* for the Big-Voiced Scullions", *Times Literary Supplement* (1 October 1999)

See also the translator's introduction to Morgan, and J.R.R. Tolkien's preface to the 1950 revision by Wrenn of Clark Hall

Georges Bernanos 1888–1948

French novelist and polemicist

Biography

Born in Paris, 20 February 1888. He was of remote Spanish descent. His parents were of artisan and peasant stock, but they improved their fortunes. From 1897 to 1901 he attended a Jesuit school in Paris. He continued his education at other religious-run schools and then studied law and literature at the University of Paris, going on to do military service 1909–10, subsequently serving in the French army during World War I and marrying in 1917. He sold insurance for a while and turned to journalism in 1922, living mainly from his writing after the mid-1920s, often in financial difficulties. He joined, and for a time wrote for, the Catholic and royalist Action Française group. His literary works embody his personal preoccupations with Christian spirituality and the problems of sin and salvation. From 1938 to 1945 he lived in South America. His best-known fiction titles are *The Star of Satan* (*Sous le Soleil de Satan*, 1926) and *The Diary of a Country Priest* (*Journal d'un curé de campagne*, 1936). After 1937 he published polemical essays, notably, in 1938, *Les Grands Cimetières sous la lune* (*A Diary of My Times*), which attacked Franco and the Church in Spain. He was elected to the French Academy in 1936. Died at Neuilly-sur-Seine, 5 July 1948.

Translations

Novels

Sous le Soleil de Satan, 1926

Binsse, H.L., *Under the Star of Satan*, New York: Pantheon, 1949

Lucas, Veronica, *Star of Satan*, London: John Lane/Bodley Head, 1927

Morris, Pamela, *Star of Satan*, London: John Lane/Bodley Head, and New York: Macmillan, 1940

L'Imposture, 1927

Whitehouse, J.C., *The Imposter*, Lincoln: University of Nebraska Press, 1999

La Joie, 1929

Varèse, Louise, *Joy*, New York: Pantheon, 1946; London: Bodley Head, 1948

Un Crime, 1935

Green, Anne, *A Crime*, London: Robert Hale, 1936; as *The Crime*, New York: Dutton, and London: Museum Press, 1946

Journal d'un curé de campagne, 1936

Morris, Pamela, *The Diary of a Country Priest*, London: Boriswood, and New York: Macmillan, 1937; several subsequent reprints

Nouvelle Histoire de Mouchette, 1937

Whitehouse, J.C., *Mouchette*, London: Bodley Head, and New York: Holt Rinehart and Winston, 1966

Monsieur Ouine, 1943; full text, 1946; in completed form, 1955

Dunlop, Geoffrey, *The Open Mind: A Novel*, London: John Lane, 1945

Un Mauvais Rêve, 1950

Strachan, W.J., *Night is Darkest: A Novel*, London: Bodley Head, 1953

Play

Dialogues des Carmélites, 1949; produced 1952; opera by François Poulenc, 1960

Hopkins, Gerard, *The Carmelites*, London: Fontana, 1961

Legat, Michael, *The Fearless Heart*, London: Bodley Head, and New York, Macmillan, 1952

Essays

Jeanne, relapse et sainte, 1934

Batchelor, R., *Sanctity Will Out: An Essay on St. Joan*, London: Sheed and Ward, 1947

Les Grands Cimetières sous la lune, 1938

Morris, Pamela, *A Diary of My Times*, London: Boriswood, and New York: Macmillan, 1938

Lettre aux Anglais, 1943

Binsse, Harry Lorin and Ruth Bethell, *Plea for Liberty: Letters to the English, the Americans, the Europeans*, New York: Pantheon, 1944; London: Denis Dobson, 1945

La France contre les robots, 1945

Clark, Helen Beau, *Tradition of Freedom*, London: Denis Dobson, and New York: Roy, 1950

Quantitatively, Georges Bernanos, a powerfully idiosyncratic Catholic writer, seems to have been fairly well served by the translation process. His eight novels, as well as a dramatic work and a number of his political, polemical and religious writings, have appeared in English. Nevertheless, there have been gaps – his 1927 novel *L'Imposture* remained untranslated until 1999 – some surprising and very unhelpful delays, and a distinctly unsystematic sequence of publication in Britain and the United States. The translations themselves have also been perceived as varying in quality. These factors, together with Bernanos's uncompromising and unreconstructed Catholicism and political views, have meant that he is now a neglected writer in the Anglo-Saxon world. Yet many of the original French versions of his writings attracted full, thorough, serious and on the whole very sympathetic reviews on publication in at least one prestigious English-language journal, the *Times Literary Supplement*, which provided informed and informative comment in an orderly chronological sequence. With the English translations, however, the situation was quite different. That natural and steady sequence of works was not maintained, as is shown by the list above. Thus, for example, his fourth novel *Un Crime* (1935) appeared in English only a year after its publication in Paris, but many years before his third, *La Joie*, published in Paris in 1929 came out in New York as *Joy* (1948). Although most of his later works, including his major novel *The Diary of a Country Priest* and those published posthumously, came out in English very shortly after the appearance of the French originals, the last of his imaginative works to be published in its final form in his lifetime had to wait almost 30 years for its first English edition (as *Mouchette*, 1966).

Since the English versions of both his fiction and his non-fiction represent the work of many different translators (including the present writer) and were published fairly sporadically, the simplest and most helpful approach is to note what contemporary reviews had to say about them as they appeared.

The (or *A*) *Crime* (GREEN 1936), the first of Bernanos's novels to be reviewed in translation, was perhaps not the best introduction to his work for an Anglo-Saxon readership. It was noted that readers might find the book exasperating and perplexing, but also that they might share the translator's obvious enthusiasm for it. The translation was praised both for itself and as an attempt to introduce Bernanos to a wider public. *The Diary of a Country Priest* (MORRIS 1937) was described as Bernanos's best work to date and one of the best novels to have appeared over the preceding six years. In depicting the supernatural, Bernanos was said to have given birth to a kind of fiction that had hitherto seemed inconceivable. Nevertheless, it was suggested, his thoroughly French, penetrating and difficult-to-render style and his familiarity with the French countryside and understanding of his own religion combined to create a peculiar atmosphere the translation showed too little feeling for. By far the most popular of his novels in the English-speaking world, *The Diary of a Country Priest* has been reissued many times, receiving attention in the world press on each occasion.

The first version of *Star of Satan* appeared in 1927 (LUCAS), but attracted little attention. In the review of a new translation (MORRIS 1940), the characteristics of the novel were described as elaborate irony, a generally excessive "literary quality" and a vehement and angry passion over the primal categories of Christian belief, into the mysteries of which Bernanos was said to have powerful insight. There was no comment on the quality of the translation.

Neither the translator nor the reviewer of *The Open Mind* (DUNLOP 1945) knew that they were dealing with a defective and inferior version of the novel *Monsieur Ouine*, the full French text of which was not published in Paris until a year later. Hence there were understandably objections to it on the grounds that despite its force it lacked aesthetic and intellectual coherence and conviction. There has still been no translation of the definitive text, but one is due to be published by the University of Nebraska Press in 2001.

Joy (*La Joie*, 1929) did not appear in English until 1948 (VARÈSE), the year of Bernanos's death, when what was seen as an excellent translation of a moving and mysterious work was discussed briefly as part of very full, intelligent and sympathetic literary obituaries.

Night is Darkest (STRACHAN 1953; *Un Mauvais Rêve*, 1950) was judged to be among the best of second-rate works, but one in which Bernanos threw his characters together with almost arrogant efficiency and produced immensely well-treated suspense and pieces of acute observation. The translation was described as adequate.

The permissive and dismissive cultural climate of the 1960s marked a swing away from Bernanos, at least in Britain, where his last novel (or novella) to appear in English, *Mouchette* (WHITEHOUSE 1966), was very summarily and rather condescendingly reviewed, despite being described as lyrical, compassionate and well translated. This was a far cry from the enthusiastic 1937 review of the original, where Bernanos was said to radiate an imaginative and even spiritual splendour. On the other hand, the English version was more favourably received in the United States, where the American novelist John Updike, writing in the *New Yorker*, devoted a fair, lucid, evocative and intelligent review to it, paying the author the compliment of taking him seriously on his own terms.

Shortly before his death, Bernanos was working on the dialogue for a film script, the *Dialogues des Carmélites*, which was adapted for the theatre and published posthumously in France in 1949. The first English translation, *The Fearless Heart* (LEGAT 1952), was criticized for its stiffness and awkwardness, whereas the second, *The Carmelites* (HOPKINS 1961), was praised for catching admirably the dignity and ease of the original.

The circumstances surrounding World War II, when France was occupied and Bernanos an exiled writer engaged in what his English biographer has called "controversy and contemplation" rather than fiction, produced a favourable climate for translation. *A Diary of My Times* (MORRIS 1938), an abridged version of *Les Grands Cimetières sous la Lune* (1938), was well received as a book but sharply criticized as a translation. *Plea for Liberty* (BINNSE & BETHELL New York 1944, London 1945), the translation of *Lettre aux Anglais* (1943), was praised, and the book seen as meriting a permanent place in the libraries of English-speaking readers. The brief essay on Joan of Arc, *Jeanne, relapse et sainte* (1934) was deemed to have been insulted by the vulgarity of its English title, *Sanctity will Out* (BATCHELOR 1947). *Tradition of Freedom* (CLARK 1950) was seen by the reviewer as an apt and evocative title for the translation of *La France contre les robots* (1945); in his opinion, none of the author's writing fell below the dignity of the vocation to which he had so perseveringly responded.

L'Imposture (1927), the only novel by Bernanos hitherto untranslated into English, is now available in the version by WHITEHOUSE (*The Imposter*, 1999).

J.C. WHITEHOUSE

Further Reading

Hebblethwaite, Peter, *Bernanos: An Introduction*, London: Bowes and Bowes, and New York: Hillary House 1965

Speaight, Robert, *Georges Bernanos: A Study of the Man and the Writer*, London: Collins and Harvill, 1973; New York: Liveright, 1974

Whitehouse, J.C., *Vertical Man: The Human Being in the Catholic Novels of Graham Greene, Sigrid Undset and Georges Bernanos*, New York: Garland, 1990

Thomas Bernhard 1931–1989

Austrian poet, novelist, short-story writer and dramatist

Biography

Born 9 February 1931 to an unmarried mother at a convent in Heerlen, in the Netherlands. He was brought up as a small child by his maternal grandparents, in Vienna and Seekirchen. The grandfather, the writer Johannes Freumbichler, was a strong influence on Bernhard's intellectual development. Bernhard went to school in Salzburg (1943–47) and then (1947–57) studied music and drama in Salzburg and Vienna. From 1952 he also worked as a newspaper reporter and art critic. He developed tuberculosis and spent several periods in hospitals and sanatoria; it was at a sanatorium that he met the woman who was to be his companion until her death in 1984.

He began his prolific and successful literary career in the late 1950s with three volumes of death-centred lyric poetry and some libretti, but his breakthrough came with the novel *Frost* [Frost](1963). *Frost* was followed by numerous other novels (notably *Das Kalkwerk*, 1970, translated as *The Lime Works*, 1973; *Korrektur*, 1975, translated as *Correction*, 1979; and the best-selling *Holzfällen*, 1984, translated as *Woodcutters*, 1987), and by short stories, published separately and in volumes, a large number of plays, and some biographical and autobiographical texts. Some of Bernhard's characters have real, well-known people as their model or basis. He won many awards for his work, including the Büchner prize in 1970. He died on 12 February 1989 in Gmunden, to the east of Salzburg, having forbidden in his will the performance and printing of his works in Austria for the duration of the copyright.

Translations

Novels

Verstörung, 1967
Winston, Richard and Clara Winston, *Gargoyles*, New York: Knopf, 1970

Das Kalkwerk, 1970
Wilkins, Sophie, *The Lime Works*, New York: Knopf, 1973

Korrektur, 1975
Wilkins, Sophie, *Correction*, New York: Knopf, 1979; London: Vintage, 1991

Beton, 1982
McLintock, David, *Concrete*, London: Dent, and New York: Knopf, 1984; with an introduction by Martin Chalmers, London: Quartet, 1989

Der Untergeher, 1983
Dawson, Jack, *The Loser*, New York: Knopf, 1991; London: Quartet, 1992

Holzfällen: Eine Erregung, 1984
McLintock, David, *Woodcutters*, New York: Knopf, 1987
Osers, Ewald, *Cutting Trees: An Irritation*, London and New York: Quartet, 1988

Alte Meister: Komödie, 1985
Osers, Ewald, *Old Masters: A Comedy*, London and New York: Quartet, 1989

Auslöschung: Ein Zerfall, 1986
McLintock, David, *Extinction*, New York: Knopf, 1995

In der Höhe: Rettungsversuch, 1989
Stockman, Russell, *On the Mountain: Rescue Attempt, Nonsense*, afterword by Sophie Wilkins, Marlboro, Vermont: Marlboro Press, 1991

Short Stories

Der Stimmenimitator, 1978
Northcott, Kenneth J., *The Voice Imitator*, Chicago: University of Chicago Press, 1997 (contains 104 short stories, including "Hotel Waldhaus")

Ja, 1978
Osers, Ewald, *Yes*, London: Quartet, 1991; Chicago: University of Chicago Press, 1992

Die Billigesser, 1980
Osers, Ewald, *The Cheap-Eaters*, London: Quartet, 1990

Selection of Plays

Jansen, Peter and Kenneth Northcott, *Histrionics: Three Plays*, Chicago: University of Chicago Press, 1990; London: Quartet, 1991 (contains *A Party for Boris*; *Ritter, Dene, Voss*; *Histrionics*)

Plays

Ein Fest für Boris, 1970
Jansen, Peter and Kenneth Northcott, *A Party for Boris* in *Histrionics*, translated by Jansen and Northcott, 1990

Die Macht der Gewohnheit, 1974
Plaice, Neville and Stephen Plaice, *The Force of Habit*, London: Heinemann/National Theatre, 1976

Der Präsident, 1975
Honegger, Gitta, *The President*, with *Eve of Retirement*, translated by Honegger, New York: Performing Arts, 1982

Vor dem Ruhestand, 1979; produced 1980
Honegger, Gitta, *Eve of Retirement*, with *The President*, translated by Honegger, New York: Performing Arts, 1982

Der Theatermacher, 1984; produced 1986
Jansen, Peter and Kenneth Northcott, *Histrionics*, in *Histrionics: Three Plays*, translated by Jansen and Northcott, 1990

Ritter, Dene, Voss, 1984; produced 1986
Jansen, Peter and Kenneth Northcott, *Ritter, Dene, Voss* in *Histrionics*, translated by Jansen and Northcott, 1990

Autobiographical Writing

McLintock, David, *Gathering Evidence: A Memoir*, New York: Knopf, 1985; London: Vintage, 1994 (from works published 1975–82; contains *A Child*; *An Indication of the Cause*; *The Cellar*; *Breath*; *In the Cold*)

Wittgensteins Neffe: Eine Freundschaft, 1982
Osers, Ewald, *Wittgenstein's Nephew: A Friendship*, London and New York: Quartet, 1986; New York: Knopf, 1989; London: Vintage, 1992

The work of Thomas Bernhard appears to be receiving critical acclaim in Britain and the US, judging by the number of recent translations, most of which were published during the 1980s and 1990s. Bernhard's output was prolific; between the 1950s and his death in 1989 he produced 15 novels, 18 stage-plays and six autobiographical volumes. His writing presents the translator with a difficult and peculiar task. Bernhard extracts the utmost from the possibilities of the German language, with his self-professed distinction between this and Austrian German, pushing the constraints of its grammar to the extreme. The structure of his work is based upon musical principles, the twelve-tone serialism of J.M. Hauer, which is a forerunner of Schoenberg's system. Whether this is of particular relevance to the reader is a point for conjecture, but it must not be overlooked when considering the peculiar narrative methods of his novels.

Correction (*Korrektur*, 1975) is Bernhard's most acclaimed novel, whose central character, Roithamer, is based upon Ludwig Wittgenstein. The anonymous narrator of the novel visits the garret of Roithamer shortly after the latter's suicide, to sort through his manuscripts.

Bernhard employs here a consciously contrived and distinctive style, whose most prominent features are density and exaggeration. The prose is a succession of tightly constructed complex sentences that run on for more than a page. Such complexity is impossible to render in English because of the grammatical disparity of the two languages. WILKINS's translation (1979) admirably captures this complexity, as much, perhaps, as is possible.

Monologue is the kingpin of Bernhard's work, in both the novels and the plays. The punishing cadenza of the language of *Correction* strives for abstraction and, through this abstraction, for a core of meaning that will ultimately prove unattainable. Bernhard does not capitulate to this defeatist view, but exhibits its absurdity through his complex use of language. It is this quality of abstraction that eludes Wilkins in her translation. An important aspect of Bernhard's work is constituted by his neologisms, which are both amusing and essential. Essential because of the specificity required by Bernhard to construct his philosophical argument, to show the effort of searching for such specificity and abstraction. In response to the neologisms, Wilkins relies upon more general terms. Her rendering of "to be a fool in the head" as simply "crazy" destroys the significance of the original term in relation to Roithamer's character. The translation develops a conversational and less rigorous style, with the use of short forms of words and phrases particular to the American vernacular. Wilkins's aims are geared toward an accessible translation. The style is generalized as opposed to specific and it is this that dilutes the power and particularity of Bernhard's novel. It may seem unjust to criticize Wilkins's version on such seemingly minor points, as it is a more than adequate translation, but the extremes of Roithamer's thought are lost through an attempt to be literal.

Wittgenstein's Nephew is Bernhard's account of his friendship with Paul, nephew of the more famous philosopher. In this work Bernhard writes in a lighter vein, but the usual Bernhard obsessions are still present. This text presents less of a challenge to a translator than do the dense, convoluted narratives of the novels. Ewald OSERS (1986) captures the tone of this work, and the eccentricity of Paul is conveyed fully, not least his obsessive attachment to music. There is little to criticize in this fine translation. Osers shows delicate poise in dealing with Bernhard's notorious neologisms ("coffee house-seeking disease" rendered as "going-to-cafés-disease"); his literal transcriptions contain much of the quality of the original.

The stage-plays of Bernhard have unfortunately received less attention from translators than the novels – and have received even less attention from the theatre: they mostly await production in England. Exceptions are *The Force of Habit (Die Macht der Gewohnheit*, 1974, translated by Neville and Stephen PLAICE for the National Theatre in 1976) and *Histrionics* (*Der Theatermacher*, 1984), translated in 1990 and performed in London renamed as *The Showman*.

Histrionics revolves around the central character Bruscon, an ageing actor touring in the backwoods of Austria, with his long-suffering family in tow, nightly performing his "Wheel of History". The play is virtually a monologue by Bruscon. The most striking stylistic device is the absence of punctuation, and the printed structure of the text, in which sentences and clauses are broken up to create a rich sense of ambiguity. It is this facet of the play that reflects the disordered obssesiveness of Bruscon's mind.

Any attempted translation of a play must compromise between a literal rendering, primarily concerned with readability, and a version for performance. JANSEN & NORTHCOTT (1990) have found an accomplished idiomatic style for performance in English. They have succeeded in keeping the comic rhythms of Bruscon's ranting, losing little in overall effect. The sequence of the lines is disrupted to attain this quality of rhythm, but this proves to be of little concern. The rendering of neologisms is not literal, but this would quickly become wearing in a performance text. The solution to the difficulty is to find adequate and equally amusing correlations. This version is an American one but avoids slang, though an English translator would surely have given "blood sausage" as "black pudding".

The 1990s in fact brought Bernhard's work a wider dissemination in both the UK and the US as OSERS (1990, 1991), JANSEN & NORTHCOTT (1990), DAWSON (1991), STOCKMANN (1991), MCLINTOCK (1995) and NORTHCOTT solo (1997) produced English translations of texts – novels, stories, plays and autobiographical writings – that had not previously been made available to Anglophone readers.

Bernhard's dominant themes are illness, the proximity of death, the fear of insanity, and the cruelty and absurdity of existence. His central characters are often artists or scientists unable to achieve creative fulfilment. Austrian society and culture are sharply satirized. However, the sombre negativity of Bernhard's subjects is balanced by his creative style and sardonic humour, and this latter feature is one of those used by Nicholas Lezard, in his review of NORTHCOTT's 1997 *The Voice Imitator*, to recommend that the British and United States public should sample the pleasures already appreciated by Bernhard's large European readership.

KATJA KREBS and KEVIN BARTHOLOMEW

Further Reading
Calandra, Denis, "Thomas Bernhard" in his *New German Dramatists*, New York: Grove Press, and London: Macmillan, 1983
Dowden, Stephen D., *Understanding Thomas Bernhard*, Columbia: University of South Carolina Press, 1991
Enright, D.J., "Almost Famous", *Times Literary Supplement* (9 January 1998)
Hardin, James and Donald D. Daviau, *Austrian Fiction Writers: After 1914*, Detroit: Gale, 1989
Lezard, Nicholas, "His Master's Voice", review of Northcott's translation of *The Voice Imitator*, *The Guardian*, 19 December 1998
Modern Austrian Literature, 20, (1988): special Thomas Bernhard issue

---

Bertran de Born c.1150–c.1215

French troubadour poet

Biography

Bertran de Born was a Provençal troubadour and warrior, born in the Périgord region of France into the lesser nobility. After disputes with his brother he became lord of the castle and large family estate of Altafort (Hautefort). He spent some time at the court in Normandy of Eleanor of Aquitaine and her second husband (Bertran's feudal lord) Henry II of England. Bertran was said to have incited Princes Richard (Coeur de Lion) and Henry Plantagenet, the sons of Henry II, to rebel against their father. Richard had become king Richard I of England by the time Bertran went with him to Palestine on the Third Crusade. In 1197, after years of battle and politics, this "sower of schism", as Dante called Bertran, became a Cistercian monk. He died at the monastery of Dalon, near Altafort.

As a poet Bertran de Born glorified both love and war, writing not only lyrics to several women but also provocative *sirventes*, satirical poems, concerning Languedoc's current political conflicts and Richard I's wars against Philip II of France.

Translations

Collection

Paden, William D. Jr, Tilde Sankovitch and Patricia H. Stablein, *The Poems of the Troubadour Bertran de Born*, Berkeley: University of California Press, 1986

Selections

Blackburn, Paul, in *Proensa: An Anthology of Troubadour Poetry* (parallel texts), edited and with an introduction by George Economou, Palma de Mallorca: Divers Press, 1953; as *An Anthology of Troubadour Poetry*, Berkeley: University of California Press, 1978
Bonner, Anthony, in *Songs of the Troubadours*, translated by Bonner, New York: Schocken Books, 1972
Egan, Margarita, in *The Vidas of the Troubadours*, translated by Egan, New York: Garland, 1984
Fox, John, first part of "Be. m platz lo gais temps de pascor" in *A Literary History of France: The Middle Ages*, edited by Fox, London: Benn, and New York: Barnes and Noble, 1974
Goldin, Frederick, in *Lyrics of the Troubadours and Trouvères: An Anthology and a History*, edited by Goldin, with an introduction, New York: Anchor Books, 1973
Lindsay, Jack, extracts in his *The Troubadours and Their World*, London: Muller, 1976
Pound, Ezra, in his *The Spirit of Romance*, London: Dent, and New York: Dutton, 1910; in his *Personae*, New York: New Directions, 1926, 1971, 1990; London: Peter Owen, 1952
Press, Alan R., in *Anthology of Troubadour Lyric Poetry* (parallel texts), edited by Press, Edinburgh: Edinburgh University Press, and Austin: University of Texas Press , 1971; Edinburgh: University of Edinburgh Press, 1985
Smythe, Barbara, *Trobador Poets: Selections from the Poems of Eight Trobadors*, with an introduction and notes, London: Chatto and Windus, and New York: Duffield, 1911; reprinted New York: Cooper Square, 1966

There are some 30 troubadour songbooks and fragments extant. As the earliest was assembled around 1250 in Italy, 12th-century troubadour poetry probably distinguished itself from the Latin written culture as a primarily oral art, practised by a composer-singer in tandem with a public performer or *jongleur* who presented the songs. That Bertran de Born was a major poet is evidenced by the frequency with which his songs were imitated and referred to by other contemporary poets and by the frequency with which he referred to and imitated such poets in the close network of troubadour artistry. Bertan's position at the center of this critical expansion of formalism and the development of aesthetic terminology in the new vulgar languages of Europe is also reflected in the large number of songs attributed to him that feature in the troubadour songbooks.

Bertran de Born's works have been the focus of numerous editions in French and German, but there is only one large-scale edition in English: Paden, Sankovitch and Stablein, *The Poems of the Troubadour Bertran de Born* (1986).

From the beginning, as references to Bertran and citations of his songs by other troubadours and his extensive inclusion in the songbooks attest, Bertran de Born has fascinated poets and audiences. His witty poems on contemporary politics and love evoke a wider yet deeper vision of life's moral dynamics than that of most of his fellows. Translations of his complete works can be found in French and German, but there is only one translation of his corpus in English, that of the PADEN, SANKOVITCH & STABLEIN edition (1986) mentioned above. Poets and authors in English have, however, translated a selection of Bertran de Born's works in numerous anthologies of troubadour verse. EGAN (1984) includes a photograph of Altafort, now Hautefort, and reproductions of miniatures of Bertran from songbooks (I, B.N., French 854, and K, B.N., French 12473).

Controversy has long raged about the distinct quality of Bertran's poetic voice. In the prose tales of the *Novellino*, assembled by an anonymous 13th-century Florentine, Bertran incarnates on the one hand the force of war, in his counsels to the Young King, the seditious heir to England's King Henry II, and on the other the force of love, in his advice to Saladin, the great Muslim warrior of the late 12th century. Late 13th- and early 14th-century Florence saw the emergence of a more nuanced account of Bertran's achievements. In Dante Alighieri's *De vulgari eloquentia* Bertran is a great war poet, and in Dante's *Il Convivio* he is a model of largesse, even in the company of great leaders in diverse domains. When Dante composes his *Commedia*, he shapes Bertran to a more spectacular role. In canto 28 of the *Inferno*, placed among those who created discord and used to define Dante's concept of punishment as a counterweight to transgression, Bertran stands at the foot of a bridge, in the ninth and final pit of the eighth circle of Hell, swinging his own severed head like a lantern. His punishment, separation of body from head, symbolizes his identity as one who divided a father from his son, Henry II of England from the seditious Young King. What Dante evidences here is the importance of Bertran de Born's poetry to the communication of major political and moral ideas, in a large-scale work by a Florentine poet writing two centuries after the troubadour's death.

Dante's spotlighting is not, however, based on historical fact. While Bertan de Born may have occasionally encountered members of that notoriously ill-tempered Angevin family in various ceremonial circumstances, there is no evidence to show that he promoted any discords among them that they were not capable of fomenting themselves. Bertran does, though, urge on and celebrate these strifes for his own political and ethical motives. In voicing the shape of a worthy life, he makes songs where lyric and epic diction often collide and explode with disturbing intimacy and immediacy. Although he expresses himself in the relatively brief sequences of stanzas and the subjective voice that mark lyric form, Bertran measures the dimensions in which love or war are enacted by the communal standards of moral and physical pre-eminence and sacrificial violence usually found in the lengthy and impersonal narratives of epic poetry.

For the translator, the apparent clarity and simplicity of Bertran's expression poses the greatest challenge. It is easy to make him entertain us in the topos of the *miles gloriosus*, but Bertran undercuts his evocations of war's shattering power with complex references to its liberation of the individual into the supreme moment where life and death can be experienced together in a sacrificial engagement that is salutary in an otherwise self-interested and materialist society. Ezra POUND shows his appreciation of Bertran's subtle coloring when the metempsychosis of Bertran is achieved through his own feline shape and gaze in "Near Perigord" (1915). Pound's 1926 *Personae* features Pound's translations, ventriloquisms and reflections on Bertran de Born written between 1908 and 1915. (Pound studied Old Provencal with William P. Shepard at Hamilton College; he continued this work at the University of Pennsylvania where he took a Master's degree and prepared for the doctorate.)

Ben (adverb: *honorably*; substantive: *good*) and *bel*, variously indicating pleasure and beauty, are two of the most difficult words in Bertran's poetry to convey in translation. For example, in translating the first line of a poem famously attributed to Bertran, "Be.m platz lo gais temps de pascor...", translators vary their choices from the cool irony of "The gay time of spring pleases me well," and " Well am I pleased by gay Eastertide" (PADEN, SANKOVITCH & STABLEIN, 1986; PRESS, 1971) to the dramatic tension of of "I love the joyful time of Easter" (GOLDIN, 1973) and the more fulgent enthusiasm of "I love the gay season of spring" or "I love the spring-tide of the year" (BONNER, 1972; SMYTHE, 1911). If Bertran is indeed a poet for the 20th century, as Ezra Pound would have him, the tone that his spring sounds in the translator's ear should be nearer that of Stravinsky.

In the poem in question a dominant pattern of the troubadour lyric theme – the linking of spring with song about happy or unhappy love – appears in a martial variation. Here the sights and sounds of spring rouse not the lover to tenderness but the soldier to delight in the spectacle and harsh triumphs of warfare. The poem opens:

Be. m platz lo gais temps de pascor
que fais fuolhas e flors venir
e platz mi, quan auch la baudor
des auzels, que fan retentir
  lor chan por lo boschatge;
e platz mi, quan vei sobre. ls pratz
tendas e pavilhos fermatz;
  et ai gran alegratge,
quan vei per champanha rengatz
chavaliers e chevals armatz.

Where John FOX (1974), dealing briefly with Bertran de Born, translates the passage rather flatly into prose:

Gay springtime, bringing leaves and flowers in its wake, pleases me well. It pleases me to hear the gay birdsong echoing in the woods. It pleases me to see the tents and pavilions set up on the meadows, and I feel great exultation when I see armed knights drawn up in ranks in the countryside.

POUND himself (1910) also forgoes rhyme and the combination of eight- with six-syllable lines, but he transmits the simple poetic force of the Provençal text with his short words, rhythmical measures, and deft avoidance of flatness:

Well pleaseth me the sweet time of Easter
That maketh the leaf and the flower come out.
And it pleaseth me when I hear the clamor
Of the birds, their song through the woods;
And it pleaseth me when I see through the meadows
The tents and pavilions set up, and great joy have I

When I see o'er the campagna the knights armed and horses arrayed.

His archaizing inversion and *-eth* verb endings are, in themselves, hardly of the 20th century, but they contribute to an effect that combines immediacy with cultural distance, as in his rendering a few lines later of Bertran's glee at the eternal sight of war refugees, when "the scouts set in flight the folk with their goods" with "after them an host of armed men." LINDSAY (1976) words the latter vision plainly, in prose: "I'm happy when skirmishers put to flight both men and wealth, and after them a serried mass of men in arms"; some of the other Bertran extracts in the book are translated into verse, still, apart from the rhyme-schemes, in a modern mode.

Bertran de Born's fine sensitivity to the divine comedy of human life flickers throughout his wide ranging expression, although it is seldom fully rendered in translations.

PATRICIA HARRIS STÄBLEIN

Further Reading

Pound, Ezra, *Personae*, New York: New Directions, 1971 (first published 1926)

See also the introduction, glossary and translators' notes in Paden, Sankovitch & Stablein, and the translator's notes in Goldin and Press

---

Ugo Betti 1892–1953

Italian dramatist

Biography

Born in Camerino, Italy, 4 February 1892. Betti's family moved to Parma when he was nine years old, and he later went to Parma University to study law, graduating in 1914. During World War I he served as an artillery officer until 1917, when he was captured by the Germans after the Italian defeat at Caporetto, and he remained a prisoner until December 1918. During his imprisonment he wrote a volume of poems, *Il re pensieroso* [The Thoughtful King], which was published after the war in 1922. After being repatriated, Betti carried on with his legal studies, concentrating on railway law. He was a magistrate in Parma from 1919, becoming a judge in 1923. His first play, *La padrona* [The Mistress] was produced in 1926. He moved to Rome in 1930 and worked as a judge in the Appellate Court there from that date until 1943. He married Andreina Frosini in 1930. He continued to write during this period, and published several further plays, volumes of poetry and collections of short stories. He was also a contributor to the journal *Oggi*, from 1933. He received the Mondadori Academy prize in 1932. In 1943 Betti retired to Camerino, and from 1944 was librarian at the Ministry of Justice in Rome. In his later years he wrote further works for the stage and acted as a legal adviser for the Coordinamento Spettacolo, a national association of writers and publishers. Betti was awarded the Italian Institute of Drama prize in 1949. Died in Rome, 9 June 1953.

Betti's reputation as the pre-eminent 20th-century Italian playwright after Pirandello, with whom he is often compared, evolved belatedly: he achieved little success and critical acclaim for his work in Italy until his plays were produced successfully in Paris in the 1950s and gained international acclaim. His first play, *La padrona* (1926), brought attention to his writing and drew a mixed response. Later significant dramatic works were *Frana allo scalo nord* , first performed in 1936, translated as *Landslide* in 1964; *Corruzione al palazzo di giustizia* (*Corruption in the Palace of Justice*), 1949; *Delitto all'isola delle capre* (*Crime on Goat Island*), produced in 1950; and *La fuggitiva* (*The Fugitive*), produced in 1953. Betti's short-story collections include *Caino* (1928), *Le case* [The Houses], 1933, and *Una strana serata* [A Strange Evening], 1948.

Translations

Selections of Plays

McWilliam, G.H., *Three Plays on Justice*, with an introduction, San Francisco: Chandler, 1964 (contains *Landslide*, *Struggle till Dawn*, *The Fugitive*)

Reed, Henry, *Three Plays*, London: Gollancz, 1956; New York: Grove Press, 1958 (contains *The Queen and the Rebels*, *The Burnt Flower-Bed*, *Summertime*)

Plays

Frana allo scalo nord, 1932, produced 1936

McWilliam, G.H., *Landslide* in *Three Plays on Justice*, translated by McWilliam, 1964

Il paese delle vacanze, 1937, produced 1942

Reed, Henry, *Summertime* in *Three Plays*, translated by Reed, 1956

Corruzione al palazzo di giustizia, 1944, produced 1949

Reed, Henry, *Corruption in the Palace of Justice* in *The New Theatre of Europe*, edited by Robert W. Corrigan, New York: Dell, 1962

Lotta fino all'alba, 1945, produced 1949

McWilliam, G.H., *Struggle till Dawn* in *Three Plays on Justice*, translated by McWilliam, 1964

Delitto all'isola delle capre, 1946, produced 1950
Reed, Henry, *Crime on Goat Island*, London: French, 1960; with an introduction by G.H. McWilliam, San Francisco: Chandler, 1961

La regina e gl'insorti, 1949, produced 1951
Reed, Henry, *The Queen and the Rebels* in *Three Plays*, translated by Reed, 1956

L'aiuola bruciata, 1951, produced 1953
Reed, Henry, *The Burnt Flower-Bed* in *Three Plays*, translated by Reed, 1956

La fuggitiva, 1953
McWilliam, G.H., *The Fugitive* in *Three Plays on Justice*, translated by McWilliam, 1964

Ugo Betti was the author of 25 plays written in the period between 1926 and his death. Of these, eight were translated into English but all were allowed to go out of print within a few years of the author's death. His work is now rarely performed in Italy, although the investigations by the magistrates in Milan into political corruption in the late 1980s gave his dramas on justice a renewed topicality, and *Corruption in the Palace of Justice* was reprinted in 1993.

In his lifetime, Betti was regarded as the heir to Pirandello and as a major figure in European theatre. "It is our duty", wrote McWilliam in the introduction to his *Three Plays on Justice*, "to place him where he belongs, in the company of the major playwrights of the present century: Shaw, Pirandello, Eugene O'Neill, Bertolt Brecht". However, fascism and war meant that Betti began to be known outside Italy only in the 1950s and he attained the fame he had always craved only after being diagnosed as suffering from the cancer that was to cause his death in 1953. His appearance on the stage in London, Paris and New York coincided with the emergence of Brecht and Beckett, and although their styles and subjects clashed, they were judged by many critics to be of comparable calibre.

Betti presented his translators with a set of problems that derived from the allusive, poetical style and the pervasive, multilayered symbolism he adopted to express the spiritual quest at the heart of all his drama. Although a judge, Betti had no trust in human justice, and his plays on justice, such as *Landslide*, begin with a courtroom investigation but are gradually converted into an inquiry into the futility of all merely temporal proceedings, and an assertion of the innate human need for a transcendental, divine justice. Kenneth Tynan, no admirer of Betti, mocked both the relentlessness of this process and what he dismissed as the pseudo-seriousness of his drama: "Heaven forbid that he should be caught forgetting to philosophize!" (Tynan, 1961),

The gradual switch of register in Betti's texts from the colloquial to the spiritual, aimed at reflecting a change of consciousness inside the individual and a move from the often selfconsciously sordid realism of his openings to the equally selfconscious spiritual lyricism of the concluding passage, is difficult to capture and convey in translation. The problems were aggravated by Betti's tendency toward sentimentality, particularly in his depiction of female characters. Often the process of conversion in the male characters was triggered by their nascent love for a woman of virginal purity.

Part of Betti's success in Britain and America was due to the skill of his two principal translators in finding an idiom that adhered to the sense and conveyed the authentic poetry of the original, while subduing its tendency toward a grandiloquence that could easily have seemed laboured to English-language audiences. In the closing scene of *Landslide*, the judge declines to hand down legal judgement in the case regarding responsibility for the death of workmen in an accident at a railway station, and McWilliam (1964) strikes the right blend of judicial oratory and subdued statement for the climactic announcement: "We declare that these men pronounce their just and proper sentence every day, in the lives they lead and the torment they suffer ... and perhaps from the hands of the judge they will need something else, something higher: compassion. Compassion."

The linguistic problem was not so acute in a work like *Summertime*, which was one of three plays Betti wrote in the mid-1930s purely as entertainment pieces, with none of the higher purpose of what he regarded as his central work. Reed's text (1956) was modified slightly, with the character of Maria dropped and a commercial traveller introduced, but these alterations do not change the tone of what is essentially a light love story.

On the other hand, the two "political" plays, *The Queen and the Rebels* and *The Burnt Flower-Bed*, required, and received from Reed (1956) delicate handling, since they are more correctly described as antipolitical, designed to show that any hierarchy of values founded on the purely political is inadequate for human beings, whose inner nature compels them to undertake a quest of quite a different order. Both plays have at their core an act of self-sacrifice by a young woman, the result of which is to change the immediate course of events and to alter the very code by which public affairs have been conducted. In *The Queen and the Rebels*, Argia, an ex-prostitute, is mistaken for the fugitive queen who is being pursued by a band of insurgents, but eventually she chooses to offer herself for execution and allow the terrified queen to escape. In her final speech, Argia's words in the translation move at a dignified rhythm that reproduces the tone of Betti's original: "I believe that God ... has intentionally made us, not docile, for that He would find useless ... but different from Himself and a little too proud ... so that we may stand against Him, thwart Him, amaze Him ... perhaps that is His purpose."

These themes and this idiom were already familiar to an anglophone public weaned on the religious and poetic drama of T.S. Eliot and Christopher Fry. Betti's translators had a proven style to hand, and his drama had a place of honour in the theatrical culture of that time in virtually every European country.

Joseph Farrell

Further Reading

Brown, E. Martin (editor), introduction to *Three European Plays*, Harmondsworth: Penguin, 1958
McWilliam, G.H. "Interpreting Betti", *Tulane Drama Review* (September 1963)
May, Frederick, "Drama of Reality", *Drama*, 35 (Winter 1960) pp. 15–23
Rizzo, G., "Regression: Progression in Ugo Betti's Drama", *Tulane Drama Review* (September 1963)
Scott, J.A., "The Message of Ugo Betti", *Italica*, 37/1 (March 1960) pp. 44–57

Tynan, Kenneth, *Curtains: Selections from the Dramatic Criticism and Related Writings*, London: Longman, and New York: Atheneum, 1961

See also the translators' introductions to McWilliam (1964) and Reed (1956)

The Bible in English Translation

At its most extreme, in the form of the interlinear version in which the original text and the translation are set next to each other on parallel lines, the Bible throws up the most conservative of all forms of translation, something recognized and hailed by Walter Benjamin in his seminal essay "The Task of the Translator". Benjamin argued for an ideal of translation in which the target language was profoundly influenced by the source language; and it is arguable that, even at its freest, the English Bible has brought into the target language and culture more of the Hebraic quality of the original texts (New Testament as well as Old) than is common in other translations' relation to their source.

An interlinear version represents the most mechanical form of translation possible, apart from machine translation itself. It is a mere word-for-word following of the original, with paraphrase and interpolation kept to an absolute minimum: and there tends to be an element of the mechanical in most Bible translation, if only because of the translators' mindfulness of the injunction not to take away from the text or add to it. Certainly, up to the 20th century, English translations of the Bible are faithful often to the point of literalness. And yet the influence of the English Bible upon our literary canon and upon our general culture has been profound. Its words, phrases and rhythms were familiar to the vast mass of the population for centuries, and throughout English literary history it acted as a source for images, themes, character and narrative. In effect, it was perceived as an inspired text.

The idea of inspiration has always been an important factor in the reception of Bible translations. Originally written in Hebrew and a little Aramaic, the Old Testament was translated into Greek in a version known as the Septuagint, on account of its supposedly having been produced by 70 translators. As the famous story has it, each translator worked independently of the others, but when they came to compare their translations they were identical, a sure testimony to their shared inspiration. In the early Christian era, St Jerome's Latin version of the Hebrew Old Testament and the Greek New Testament, completed in the first years of the fifth century and commonly known as the Vulgate, achieved inspired status as the official version of the Catholic Church.

Because the Vulgate embodied a later inspiration than the original, so it set the model for translations that came to be perceived as superior to the originals from which they were derived. Something of the same aura envelops the most famous and influential English translation, the 1611 Authorized Version (also known as the King James Bible), hence the hold it had on English culture for 350 years and the passion with which it has been defended in the last 50 against a flood of late 20th-century versions. Together with the Prayer Book and the works of Shakespeare, it was held to represent the idea of Englishness. An English prime minister, Stanley Baldwin, was "convinced ... that the hearing – sometimes almost unconsciously – of the superb rhythms of the English Prayer Book Sunday after Sunday, and the language of the English Bible, leaves its mark on you for life."

In fact, the Authorized Version was not an inspired new translation but a painstakingly meticulous revision of the work of successive 16th-century translators, bringing to culmination the second, and by far the most important, phase of Bible translation in England. The first phase extends from the very earliest English texts to the end of the 14th century. Indeed, the first extant piece of written English, part of Caedmon's 7th-century poem on the creation, is actually a translation of a passage of Genesis, and the Anglo-Saxon period saw translations of various parts of the Bible, ranging from close, fairly literal versions to versifications and paraphrases. Significantly, and perhaps unexpectedly, the bulk of this work was translation from the Old Testament, and it remains a peculiarity of English culture, as opposed to much of the Continental tradition, that the emphasis has been as much on Old Testament material as it is on New.

In effect, a large proportion of Old English literature is Bible translation, done either for socio-political purposes, as in Alfred's prefixing of the laws of England with the laws of Exodus, or for religious and cultural purposes, as in the metrical versifications of substantial parts of Genesis, Exodus and Daniel. But all of this first phase work was actually translation of translation, the Vulgate or other Latin versions forming the original text. The Vulgate was the source text for the major medieval translation, the first English version of the whole Bible, known as the Wyclif Bible, a Lollard version produced by followers of John Wyclif towards the end of the 14th century. This version exists in many manuscripts but in essentially two forms, one a literal translation that reproduces the Latin syntax, the other a much freer rendering. There are still strong traces of Latinate syntax in the second version, as in "And anon he coming nigh to Jesu, said, Hail master" or "And they holding Jesu, led him to Caiphas" (Matthew 26: 49 and 57). But this translation often has an impressive fluency:

> Forsooth Jesus was still. And the prince of priests saith to him, I conjure thee by quick God, that thou say to us, if thou be Christ, the son of God. Jesus said to him, Thou hast said; netheless [i.e. nevertheless] I say to you, an other time ye shall see man's son sitting at the right-half of the virtue of God, and coming in clouds of heaven.

The best hypothesis to explain the two Wyclif Bible texts is that the literal translation was not so much a version in itself as a base text from which a proper translation could be made. In essence, then, this Bible seems to have been a sophisticated work of creative translation, carefully planned and executed, and potentially a major work of literature in its own right. This impression is reinforced by its having, in a number of its manuscripts, a strikingly intelligent preface which discusses the problems and techniques of translation. The writer explains that his first principle of translation is "to translate after the sentence [i.e. the thought or meaning] and not only after the words, so that the sentence be as open or opener in English as in Latin". And he insists upon the translator's need to discipline himself: "by this manner, with good living and great travail, men can come to true and clear translating ... seem it never so hard at the beginning".

Like the Wyclif Bible itself, this preface is too little known, and yet it represents the fullest, most interesting analysis of the translator's craft produced by any English Bible translator before the 20th century. But it, and the Wyclif Bible as a whole, remained only a cultural dead-end. Because of its Lollard roots the established Church, alarmed at its undermining of Church authority, acted to proscribe it, and England became the one European nation with an express prohibition against the translating of the Bible into the vernacular, the possession of such a translation, or even the reading of one. The Bible was still a major element in English culture, providing material for songs, poems and plays, but the people's access to it was essentially second-hand.

The Reformation in England may reasonably be said to have been founded upon the idea of translating the Bible, the two translators who inaugurate this second phase being William Tyndale and Miles Coverdale. Of the two, Tyndale is by far the more significant figure. Indeed, he has claims to being described as the most influential English translator of all time. He began with the New Testament in 1526 (revised in 1534), then he translated the Pentateuch in 1530, the Book of Jonah in 1531, and the historical books of the Old Testament (Joshua–2 Chronicles), which were published posthumously in the 1537 Matthew Bible. This work forms the basis of all later English translations: so much so that it is not too fanciful to describe Tyndale as the most substantial member of the Authorized Version translation panels in spite of his having been dead for 70 years; for the 1611 text, in all of the New Testament and in the parts of the Old that he translated, is at least 75% his work, and even the freest modern versions still employ his basic vocabulary.

Tyndale's work is virtually a new start in English. He himself claimed that he made no use of English predecessors, and what scholarly work has been done on links between his versions and the Wyclif Bible has thrown up very little evidence for any continuity. His main source, as it was for all of the Reformation vernacular translations, was Martin Luther's German Bible; but Tyndale's achievement was materially different from that of most of Luther's followers because he, like Luther, had taken care to learn not only New Testament Greek but also Old Testament Hebrew. So, while Luther's German was a heavy influence, it was not an absolute one: Tyndale was quite prepared to go his own way where his interpretation of the original differed. In Exodus 32:1, for instance, where Luther had offered a fairly straightforward (and dull) rendering of the people's protests to Aaron that they needed a new god to worship, Tyndale's version captures all of their peevishness, largely by following the Hebrew word order closely: "Up and make us a god to go before us: for of this Moses, the fellow that brought us out of the land of Egypt, we wote [i.e. know] not what is become." Similarly, he captures the serpent's mockery at Eve's protestation that if they eat the fruit they will die: "Then said the serpent unto the woman, Tush! ye shall not die."

Tyndale's one recorded observation about the capacity of English to convey biblical style was designed to put the Vulgate firmly in its place:

> They will say it can not be translated into our tongue, it [i.e. the English language] is so rude. It is not so rude as they are false liars. For the Greek tongue agreeth more with the English than with the Latin. And the properties of the Hebrew tongue agreeth a thousand times more with the English than with the Latin. The manner of speaking is both one, so that in a thousand places thou needest not but to translate it into the English word for word when thou must seek a compass in the Latin and yet shalt have much work to translate it well-favouredly, so that it have the same grace and sweetness, sense and pure understanding with it in the Latin as it hath in the Hebrew. A thousand parts better may it be translated into the English than into the Latin.

This statement provides a key to Tyndale's method: mainly word-for-word translation and, wherever possible, fidelity to the word order of the original.

Like Luther's German, Tyndale's English Bible played a major part in the emergence of English as a language of expressive power. For one thing, it encouraged the growth of a literate population: people learned to read in order to read the Bible, and for the mass of the population the Bible was the only book they owned or thought of owning. Well over half a million Bibles were printed in the 16th century, this for a population that averaged less than five million. For another thing, Tyndale's Bible helped dismantle the Church's belief that there was a special holy language which was essentially untranslatable. Tyndale had the best of the argument over this matter with the Church's chief defender, Sir Thomas More. More insisted that such words as the Greek *agape* were degraded by being turned into the English word *love*, because *love* is something common to a host of things distinct from God's love, the essential meaning of *agape*. Tyndale replied that such an argument would render all translation impossible since exact equivalents could never be found. Relics of More's argument can be found in the clumsy efforts of Catholic translators to produce a vernacular version of the Vulgate later in the century, the Rheims-Douai Bible (OT 1582; NT 1610) being stuffed with such renderings as "Give us today our supersubstantial bread" or "Whatever thou shalt supererogate, I at my return will repay thee."

After Tyndale's execution (1536) on the eve of the Reformation in England, other translators completed what he had begun. The most notable of these, Miles Coverdale, produced in 1535 the first complete English Bible to be printed (Coverdale's Bible) and played an instrumental part in the translation, under Archbishop Cranmer's sponsorship, of the first authorized version, known as the Great Bible, issued in 1539–40. Coverdale knew neither Greek nor Hebrew, so he was heavily dependent upon Tyndale's work and upon Luther-based Continental versions, but he more than made up for his scholarly deficiency by his sense of style. He was the original English translator of the poetic and prophetic books of the Old Testament, and while Tyndale had forged an impressive prose to render the largely narrative or epistolary books of the Old and New Testaments, Coverdale set the pattern for the Bible's poetry. Although he was working 200 years before Robert Lowth formulated the parallelistic basis of Hebrew poetry, Coverdale clearly intuited it, with massively influential effect, for his version of the Psalms, made for the Great Bible, became the text of the Psalter as used in the first and in successive versions of the Book of Common Prayer.

The history of English Bible translation for the rest of the 16th century is one of continued revision. The chief version of Elizabeth I's reign, itself a revision of Tyndale's and Coverdale's work, was the Geneva Bible (1560), so called because the work on it was done by Marian exiles in Geneva. The Bible that Shakespeare and the whole galaxy of great Elizabethan and Jacobean writers were familiar with – the Authorized Version did not supersede it until the middle of the 17th century – the Geneva Bible offered the mass of the people, in relatively cheap editions, state-of-the-art translation. Its text was virtually swamped by marginal annotation, which included, where the original was obscure or ambiguous, literal renderings of the Hebrew and Greek and alternative translations. In addition, this translation marked off in a different script all words not in the original that had been added to make English sense. This had been an occasional practice in earlier versions, but the Geneva Bible made thorough use of it – the Authorized Version uses italics for the same purpose – so that readers could identify for themselves the true words of God.

The most striking thing about the Geneva Bible's appearance for its first readers would have been its division of the Bible into verses, an innovation that materially altered the way the Bible was read for the next 400 years. Verse division was designed to aid the nascent Puritan practice of citing chapter and verse proof texts, but its effect was to make the Bible appear on the page like no other book, whereas the earlier English versions had looked like standard narratives or poems. Only in this century has this effect been reversed, with most modern Bibles taking as their essential unit the paragraph rather than the verse.

The Geneva Bible may fairly be described as the Puritan Bible. The very language of its preface uses Puritan buzz words – *purity, edify, brethren* – to state the translators' purposes:

> We have in every point and word, according to the measure of that knowledge which it pleased almighty God to give us, faithfully rendered the text, and in all hard places most sincerely expounded the same. For God is our witness that we have by all means endeavoured to set forth the purity of the word and the right sense of the Holy Ghost for the edifying of the brethren in faith and charity.

Its notes, too, were seen as potentially subversive, by James I among others, and its popularity so worried the authorities that an official version, the Bishops' Bible, was translated and issued in 1568. But this version never began to rival the Geneva Bible in the people's affection; and even after the Authorized Version had appeared the Geneva version still dominated, particularly in Puritan communities, so that when the New Model Army went into battle in the 1640s "with their Bibles in their boots", this Bible was a specially produced soldier's Bible drawn from the Geneva translation. It was a compendium of the most warlike passages and psalms of victory, titled *The Soldier's Pocket Bible: Containing the most (if not all) those places contained in holy Scripture, which do show the qualifications of his inner man, that is a fit Soldier to fight the Lord's Battles, both before the fight, in the fight, and after the fight.*

The Geneva translators worked on the whole Bible, but their chief contribution was to improve the places where Tyndale had not translated. So, Coverdale's two attempts at Ecclesiastes 1:2, in his 1535 Bible and in the Great Bible, were "All is but vanity, saith the preacher, all is but plain vanity" and "All is most vain vanity, saith the preacher, and all is most vain, I say, and but plain vanity." In the Geneva Bible this becomes: "Vanity of vanities, saith the Preacher: vanity of vanities, all is vanity." And there is a marked tendency in this version to follow Tyndale's practice in preserving the Hebrew word order, as in Isaiah 38:19, where the Great Bible's perfectly acceptable English is "Hebraized": "But the living, yea the living acknowledge thee, like as I do this day. The father telleth his children of thy faithfulness" [Great]; "But the living, the living, he shall confess thee, as I do this day: the father to the children shall declare thy truth" [Geneva].

The one concrete achievement of the Hampton Court conference, called by the newly crowned James I with the intention of resolving the differences between moderate Anglicans and the growing Puritan movement, was the setting up of panels to work on a new translation of the Bible. These panels produced the Authorized Version, which became the official Anglican version for the next three centuries. The Authorized Version was, in spite of its use of the latest advances in scholarship in Semitic languages, still only a revision of the Tudor Bibles, a fact happily acknowledged in its preface: "we never thought from the beginning that we should need to make a new translation, nor yet to make of a bad one a good one ... but to make a good one better, or out of many good ones one principal good one." It was, accordingly, a highly archaic version. Made at the end of a century in which the English language had developed considerably, it preserved to a great extent the syntax and verbal formulas of the 1520s and 1530s, the decades when Tyndale and Coverdale had translated. While their versions must have struck their contemporary readers, such as the ploughboy whom Tyndale had wanted to sing scripture as he worked, as vigorously modern, the Authorized Version would have seemed to its readers to be somewhat detached from the language which they spoke. One famous example is the absence of *its* from its vocabulary. This form of the possessive had come into use in English in the late 16th century and was already gaining dominance in 1611, but the Authorized Version invariably uses *his* or *her*.

If we appreciate that the Authorized Version was a revision we can more readily appreciate that it was as much a literary as a scholarly enterprise. Analysis of some of the recently recovered translators' working drafts shows that while a good number of their revisions were made for theological or grammatical purposes, an equivalent number can be understood only as being prompted by their sense of style. Many of their most telling revisions were tiny, almost unnoticeable ones. For example, Hebrews 13:8 in the Geneva text reads: "Jesus Christ yesterday, and today, the same also is for ever." This becomes in the Authorized Version: "Jesus Christ yesterday, and today the same, and for ever." And any kind of comparison of the Authorized Version with a modern version, at the level of expressive power, demonstrates its superiority. Try, for instance, setting the New English Bible's translation of Proverbs 20:17 against the Authorized Version's: "Bread got by fraud tastes good, / but afterwards it fills the mouth with grit" [NEB]; "Bread of deceit is sweet to a man: but afterwards his mouth shall be filled with gravel" [AV]. Or, describing Nabal's shock at finding that he has enraged David, in 1 Samuel 25:37: "he had a seizure and lay there like a stone" [NEB]; "his heart died within him and he became as a stone" [AV].

The men who worked on this version heard John Donne preach, probably went to see Shakespeare's plays, and knew the classics well. With Tyndale, Coverdale and the Geneva translators as their bedrock, they produced an English Bible that, after the restoration of the monarchy in 1660, came to be perceived as one of the great literary achievements of the culture. From Milton to D.H. Lawrence its rhythms and its vocabulary helped weave the triple net of language, religion and nationality, to adapt Joyce's formula, that defined the high and the low cultures of England.

At this point it is worth giving some examples of what characterizes the style of the English Bible. One distinctive feature in narrative passages, particularly in the Old Testament, is the use of a coordinating rather than subordinating syntax: *and*, the English equivalent of the ubiquitous Hebrew conjunction *waw*, binds clauses and sentences together in a totally sequential manner. Not "when Abraham came he saw" or "Abraham saw on his arrival" but "And Abraham came and he saw". Another characteristic Hebrew form, what is called the "construct", lies behind the paucity of adjectives in the Authorized Version. Instead of adjective plus noun this form links together two substantives: not "holy beauty" or "the very dark valley" but "the beauty of holiness" and "the valley of the shadow of death". Linked to this is the reproduction in English of the Hebrew construct form to render the genitive: not "God's hand" but "the hand of God", and not "God's love" but "the love of God". This second example embodies the ambiguity that this form encourages, for "the love of God" may be His love for us or our love for Him. And this form is most characteristically biblical in superlatives: not "the most holy place" or "the greatest king" but "the holy of holies" and "the king of kings". Another easily identified element of biblical English, much imitated by poets, is its reproducing of the Hebrew cognate accusative: not "Jacob dreamed" but "Jacob dreamed a dream", not "made a vow" but "vowed a vow". And Hebrew narrative formulas find English equivalents: "and it came to pass" for the narrative link *wayehi* (literally "and it was"), and the use of the adverb *surely* to convey the emphasis carried by the Hebrew infinitive absolute: "the day that thou eatest thereof thou shalt surely die" (Genesis 2:17).

The Authorized Version was actually a more conservatively literal version than any of its Renaissance predecessors, reproducing more faithfully than even they did the syntax and the word order of the original. Something that exercised the translators a great deal, if their preface is reliable evidence, was the matter of verbal repetition. In what was probably a pre-emptive defence against fundamentalist Puritans, the preface argues that the translators did not think it necessary to try to achieve an exact equivalence of translation whereby the same Hebrew or Greek word would always be translated by the same English word: "that we should express the same notion in the same particular word; as for example, if we translate the Hebrew or Greek word once by *purpose*, never to call it *intent*; if one where *journeying*, never *travelling*; if one where *think*, never *suppose* ... thus to mince the matter, we thought to savour more of curiosity than wisdom, and that rather it would breed scorn in the atheist than bring profit to the godly reader." None the less, it is still noticeable that they observed more of such an equivalence than the more apparently Puritan Geneva Bible, and certainly much more of one than any later version. While a 20th-century translator is likely to provide different renderings for the occurrences of the Hebrew verb *yada* in the early chapters of Genesis, say *know* ... *realised* ... *slept with*, the Authorized Version maintains a one-for-one equivalence: *God doth know ... they knew that they were naked ... And Adam knew Eve his wife*. In part this conservatism explains the extraordinary accessibility of the 1611 version. Its deliberately limited lexical range, along with its influence upon the culture, ensures that for today's readers it offers many fewer obscurities than contemporary texts of much smaller size, for instance a Shakespeare play or Francis Bacon's essays.

That said, the third phase of English Bible translation, spanning generally the second half of the 20th century, has had as one of its major motives the provision of the Bible to a general readership in an up-to-date language. But this aim sits uneasily alongside another motive, which is to incorporate into an English version the findings of more than a hundred years of philological and textual scholarship. So much more is now known about the various Hebrew and Aramaic registers of the Old Testament and about the *koine* of the New that the Authorized Version was bound to seem unsatisfactory merely in terms of the limited knowledge of its translators, and textual scholarship has now fragmented the original to the point that no modern translator could have, as their Renaissance predecessors did, the belief that they are translating a coherent and unified text. Even within a single book of the Bible, the scholarly postulation of multiple authorship, editorial additions and textual corruption leaves a translator in a quandary. What to do, for example, with so widely and popularly known a story as the one of the woman taken in adultery? Accepted by all earlier translators as part of the coherent development of John's gospel, it opens chapter 8 and provides the first climax in the chapter with Christ's admonition that he who is without sin should cast the first stone. The chapter as a whole then reaches its eventual climax with an attempt to stone Christ himself. But the story has a very shaky claim to being part of the gospel, and modern translators find themselves trapped between the desire to include so central and powerful a narrative of Christ's teaching in action and the need to inform their readers that the story is probably a bogus one. Versions like the New English Bible (NT, Oxford and New York: Oxford University Press, 1961; OT and Apocrypha, Oxford and New York: Oxford University Press, 1970) and the Revised English Bible (Oxford and New York: Oxford University Press, 1989) print it at the very end of John's gospel, with the REB noting that this text "has no fixed place in our witnesses. Some do not contain it at all. Some place it after Luke 21:38, others after John 7:36, or 7:52, or 21:24."

One further problem for contemporary translators is the difficulty of deciding the use to which their version is to be put. Even when the choice is seen at its most simple, between a Bible for individual, private reading or a Bible to be read aloud in church services, the great impediment is the existence of the Authorized Version. That version, which had the good fortune to be made in times when the public–private divide was nothing like so great, contrived to be "all things to all men", equally adaptable to private, meditative reading or to public ritual. The somewhat desperate need to preserve its flexibility, as the culture became more complex, saw first of all, in the Revised Version (Oxford: Oxford University Press, 1885) and the Revised Standard Version (Oxford: Oxford University Press, 1946), efforts to modernize the Authorized Version's scholarship without abandoning its words. The first two principles of the Revised Version's translators were "To introduce as few alterations as possible into the text of the Authorized Version" and "To limit, as far as possible, the expression of such alterations to the language of the Authorized and earlier English versions." And the Revised Standard Version's preface describes its aim as to embody "the best results of modern scholarship as to the meaning of the Scriptures", but to express these in a language that preserves "those qualities which have given the King James Version a supreme place in English literature".

Later, when it was clear that a "new" translation was required, there developed the even more desperate ploy of appointing a panel of literary advisers to aid the main translation committees of versions such as the New English Bible. Philip Larkin's account of his involvement with the New English Bible sums up the whole enterprise: "The whole text seemed to me lacking in vitality, rhythm, distinction and above all memorability, and I found myself revising almost every sentence ... after about a year they quietly stopped sending me anything." Larkin's instincts were right, for the literary value of virtually all modern Bible translation is negligible. The reasons are obvious: partly the cumbersome process of consultation by which each version is rendered acceptable to the various constituencies for which it is designed, and partly the fact that the translators are invariably not writers but theologians and philologists.

More than anything else, the various books of the Bible are disturbing and challenging texts, often the records of visionaries, poets, storytellers and lawmakers who were writing in difficult times. The comfortably placed academics and churchmen of mid- to late 20th-century Britain and America have none of the audacity necessary to translate these writings. So, while the Wyclif Bible and the Renaissance Bible provided texts of religious and political power for the 14th-century Lollards and for 17th-century revolutionaries, all of the major new versions of the 20th century are designed to anaesthetize rather than provoke: the Authorized Version's literal "him that pisseth against a wall" becoming, in the New English Bible, "every mother's son", and "Vanity of vanities" becoming "Emptiness, emptiness". Even their attempts to meet social challenges are generally half-hearted, as in the Revised English Bible's claims to be the first "inclusive" translation, that is, one that is gender-free. It begins Psalm 1 in a gender-neutral manner, with "Happy is the one / who does not take", instead of the literal "Happy is the man who does not take"; but by verse 2 the sexism is back in place: "His delight is in the law of the Lord." Braver translators would have used the third person plural throughout.

Of the individual books of the Bible, the one of most literary interest from the point of view of translation is Psalms. In the 16th and 17th centuries literary theorists like Philip Sidney used the Psalter to argue for the superiority of poetry over philosophy and history, countering the charge that poetry was a fiction; and a succession of poets, from Thomas Wyatt to George Herbert and Milton made their own verse translations of individual psalms. At a much more basic level, metrical psalms, near-doggerel translations in a sing-song metre, epitomized by the Sternhold & Hopkins Psalter (1562), dominated Puritan worship and Puritan aesthetics for virtually 100 years in Britain and longer in America. A direct line of descent may be traced from metrical psalms to the hymn book and to American black spirituals.

Translations of other books, particularly from the Old Testament, have played a significant part in the development of high and low cultures. The Song of Songs is probably the most intriguing. An anthology of erotic poetry which was inevitably allegorized into a dramatization of the love between Christ and his church, enough of the eroticism survived in translation for its language and imagery to develop into a model for secular and religious love poetry, with a strong influence upon such poets as Donne, Shakespeare, Milton and Henry Vaughan. Coverdale, the most poetic of the English translators, had titled the book in his version "The Ballad of Ballads". Like the Song of Songs, Lamentations was repeatedly translated. It offered a more disturbing model, of poetry that recorded the annihilation of a city and fears of genocide, in a vision of increasing relevance in Europe from the Thirty Years War onwards. A fine modern version is Gordon Jackson's *Five Griefsongs over a Fallen City* (Lincoln, England: Asgill, 1980), as in this rendering of an element of the alphabet acrostic of chapter 3:

> Gall of guilt alone keeps memory alive.
> Grief is a habit of mind: my soul bends under it.
> Ground down to dirt as I am, my hope is in him who made me.

Like Jackson's work, the only good modern Bible translation comes from individual translators, not the committees that produce the official versions. *The Book of J* (New York: Grove Weidenfeld, 1990) contains David Rosenberg's translation of the supposed "fragmentary texts" of the original Old Testament, "embedded within what we call Genesis, Exodus, and Numbers", alongside Harold Bloom's speculation that the author, "J", may well have been female. Rosenberg's translation aims to get beyond the vacuities of the modern versions by recovering the ruggedness and the ironies of the original. At the least, he succeeds in conveying the Hebrew's narrative immediacy:

> Now the man knew Hava, his wife, in the flesh; she conceived Cain: "I have created a man as Yahweh has", she said when he was born. She conceived again: Abel his brother was born. Abel, it turned out, was a watcher of sheep, Cain a tiller of soil.

A similar idea lies behind Everett Fox's translation of the Pentateuch, completed in 1995 (*The Five Books of Moses*, New York: Schocken, and London: Harvill, 1995). Fox takes as his watchword Martin Buber's plea that we should read the Bible "as though it were something entirely unfamiliar". His translations are designed to read entirely differently from the "clear, smooth-reading translations of the Bible" that dominated the 20th century. Instead, Fox wants to involve the reader, who "must be prepared to meet the Bible at least halfway and must become an active participant in the process of the text." He renders the birth of Eve's children like this:

> The human knew Havva his wife,
> she became pregnant and bore Kayin.
> She said:
> *Kaniti*
> I-have-gotten
> a man, as has YHWH!
> She continued bearing – his brother, Hevel.
> Now Hevel became a shepherd of flocks, and Kayin became
> a worker of the soil.

At the other extreme – although here extremes tend to meet – are translations aimed at speaking entirely in the language of today. The Good News Bible (New York: American Bible Society, and London: Collins, 1976) is the most well-known and widely sold of such versions, designed particularly to attract the young, but as a translation it is contemptible because of its patronizing approach to its readers. Much better is P.K. McCary's in book 1 of the series *Black Bible Chronicles* (New York: African American Family Press, 1993), subtitled *A Survival Manual for the Streets*. The chapter "Cain Wastes Abel" renders the division between the two brothers like this:

> And the Almighty felt Abel's gift was right-on, but not Cain's. Cain got bent out of shape about it, and his nose was wide open with jealousy.

Tyndale would have liked the flaring nose.

GERALD HAMMOND

See also the entry Parallel Texts

Further Reading

The most convenient way of accessing and collating English Bible versions from Anglo-Saxon times to the present is to use the full-text database published on CD-ROM, *The Bible in English*, edited by Sylvia Adamson and Gerald Hammond, Cambridge: Chadwyck Healey, 1996.

Bois, John, *Translating for King James*, translated and edited by Ward Allen, Nashville, Tennessee: Vanderbilt University Press, 1969

Bruce, F.F., *History of the Bible in English: From the Earliest Version*, 3rd edition, New York: Oxford University Press, 1978; London: Lutterworth Press, 1979

Butterworth, Charles C., *The Literary Lineage of the King James Bible, 1340–1611*, Philadelphia: University of Pennsylvania Press, 1941

Coleman, Roger, *New Light and Truth: The Making of the Revised English Bible*, Cambridge: Cambridge University Press, and Oxford: Oxford University Press, 1989

Greenslade, S.L., *The Cambridge History of the Bible*, vol. 3: *The West from the Reformation to the Present Day*, Cambridge: Cambridge University Press, 1963

Hammond, Gerald, *The Making of the English Bible*, Manchester: Carcanet, 1982; New York: Philosophical Library, 1983

Hill, Christopher, *The English Bible and the Seventeenth-Century Revolution*, London: Allen Lane, and New York: Penguin, 1993

Jeffrey, David Lyle (editor), *A Dictionary of Biblical Tradition in English Literature*, Grand Rapids, Michigan: Eerdmans, 1992

Mozley, J.F., *Coverdale and His Bibles*, London: Lutterworth Press, 1953

Nida, Eugene A., "Translating a Text with a Long and Sensitive Tradition" in *Translating Sensitive Texts: Linguistic Aspects*, edited by Karl Simms, Amsterdam and Atlanta: Rodopi, 1997, part 3: "Sacred Texts", pp. 189–96

Norton, David, *A History of the Bible as Literature*, 2 vols, Cambridge and New York: Cambridge University Press, 1993

Pelikan, Jaroslav, *The Reformation of the Bible, the Bible of the Reformation*, New Haven, Connecticut: Yale University Press, and Dallas: Bridwell Library, 1996

Schwarz, W., *Principles and Problems of Biblical Translation: Some Reformation Controversies and Their Background*, Cambridge: Cambridge University Press, 1955

Weigle, Luther A. *et al.*, *An Introduction to the Revised Standard Version of the Old Testament*, London and New York: Thomas Nelson, 1952

Westcott, Brooke Foss, *A General View of the History of the English Bible*, 3rd edition, revised by William Aldis Wright, London and New York: Macmillan, 1905; reprinted New York: Lemma, 1972

Adolfo Bioy Casares 1914–1999

Argentine novelist, short-story writer and critic

Biography

Born in Buenos Aires, Argentina, 15 September 1914, into a wealthy upper-class family. He travelled with his family to Europe in 1924 and to the US in 1929. He attended the University of Buenos Aires, 1933–34, but left without completing a course. In 1932 he met Jorge Luis Borges with whom he collaborated on a number of literary works (under the pseudonyms H. Bustos Domecq, B. Suárez Lynch and B. Lynch Davis). They were close friends until Borges's death in 1986. They founded the literary magazine *Destiempo* in 1936. In 1932 Bioy Casares also began his association with the Argentine writer Victoria Ocampo, founder of the literary journal *Sur*. In 1940 he married Victoria's sister, Silvina Ocampo (one daughter). With his wife and Borges he edited anthologies of fantastic literature (1940) and Argentine poetry (1941). He also wrote film scripts with Borges. Bioy Casares has been the recipient of numerous awards, including the City of Buenos Aires Municipal prize, 1941; the National Literature prize, 1969; the Argentine Society of Writers' Grand Prize of Honour, 1975; and Spain's highest literary honour, the Miguel de Cervantes prize, 1990. He was made a member of the Légion d'Honneur, 1981. He died 8 March 1999.

Bioy Casares had already published short stories when he became well-known through his fantastic novel *La invención de Morel* (*The Invention of Morel*), 1940, which was to be the basis of Robbe-Grillet's *L'Année dernière à Marienbad*, 1961. There have been many further novels, including *Plan de evasión* (*A Plan for Escape*) 1945, *Dormir al sol* (*Asleep in the Sun*) 1973, *El sueño de los héroes* (*The Dream of Heroes*), 1954, and *La aventura de un fotógrafo en La Plata* (*The Adventure of a Photographer in La Plata*), 1985, as well as short story collections and the works produced in collaboration with Borges.

Translations

Novels

La invención de Morel, 1940

Simms, Ruth L.C., *The Invention of Morel and Other Stories from La Trama celeste* [1948], Austin: University of Texas Press, 1964

Plan de evasión, 1945

Levine, Suzanne Jill, *A Plan for Escape*, New York: Dutton, 1975

Diario de la guerra del cerdo, 1969

Woodruff, Gregory and Donald A. Yates, *Diary of the War of the Pig*, New York: McGraw Hill, 1972; London: Allison and Busby, 1989

Dormir al sol, 1973

Levine, Suzanne Jill, *Asleep in the Sun*, New York: Persea Books, 1978

Short Stories

Una muñeca rusa, 1991

Levine, Suzanne Jill, *A Russian Doll and Other Stories*, New York: New Directions, 1992

Short Stories (written with Jorge Luis Borges)

Seis problemas para Don Isidro Parodi, 1942

di Giovanni, Norman Thomas, *Six Problems for Don Isidro Parodi*, New York: Dutton, and London: Allen Lane, 1981

Cuentos breves y extraordinarios, 1955

Kerrigan, Anthony, *Extraordinary Tales*, New York: Herder and Herder, 1971

Crónicas de Bustos Domecq, 1967

di Giovanni, Norman Thomas, *Chronicles of Bustos Domecq*, London: Allen Lane, 1972; New York: Dutton, 1976

Although his fame as a writer and story teller has been indissolubly linked to that of his friend and literary partner, Jorge Luis Borges, Adolfo Bioy Casares, with his subtle play on reality and its transcendent dimensions, replicate worlds and the "uncanny", has received world attention from literary critics and editors since early on in his career. This, in turn, has resulted in his work being translated and widely read in Anglo-American literary circles, mainly from the 1970s on, when his works in co-authorship with Jorge Luis Borges were already being focused on by critics and editors.

The characters and settings introduced by most of Bioy Casares's novels and short stories are actually far from being what one might classify as strange or eerie. The people are usually ordinary, speaking a colloquial idiom, leading ordinary lives somewhere in the suburban areas of the city. This ordinariness, however, is generally disrupted by the sudden irruption of an unsettling element which challenges the very foundations of everyday reality. In *Dormir al sol* (*Asleep in the Sun*), for instance, Lucio Bordenave is a watchmaker who leads a quiet and uneventful life with his wife Diana until one day a dog trainer enters their lives and Lucio sees himself trapped in a plot devised by a group of psychiatrists to transplant souls and create exact duplicates of human beings. Similarly, in *Diario de la guerra del cerdo* (*Diary of the War of the Pig*), Don Isidoro Vidal is an old man whose everyday routine is suddenly shattered by an unexplained outbreak of murder and persecution of the elderly by a gang of young people. In both novels, the emergence of unsettling elements brings about unexpected behaviours and attitudes on the part of the characters. The strange aspect reality acquires then – be that due to ill-natured violence (*Diario* ...), illogical or unnatural processes (*Dormir al sol*) or to the results of exceptional machines (*La invención de Morel*) – is recorded by Bioy Casares's narrators, who offer a myriad of interpretations for the reality they translate in their diaries, reports, letters or stories.

As in the case of other Argentine and Latin American writers, Adolfo Bioy Casares's work has been transposed into English by literary translators and critics, such as Ruth Simms, Donald Yates, Norman Thomas di Giovanni, Anthony

KERRIGAN and Suzanne Jill LEVINE. Most of their renditions show a sensitive and careful reading of the originals, recreating the colloquial tone that characterizes most of Bioy Casares's writing. An example of this is provided by Suzanne Jill Levine's account of her work as translator and "scribe" in *The Subversive Scribe: Translating Latin American Fiction*. Levine illustrates the process of recreation of some of Bioy Casares's colloquial expressions with the formula "mi señora" in *Dormir al sol* (*Asleep in the Sun*), which LEVINE (1978) translates as "the missus", an expression a husband may use in the American cultural context to refer colloquially to his wife. More neutral choices, such as "my wife", although semantically acceptable, would no doubt transform the style used by Bioy Casares, which usually involves a confessional account by a narrator who reflects upon the facts as he narrates them to his reader.

Analogous cultural adaptations are undertaken by Bioy Casares's translators, particularly when the author makes use of popular idiomatic expressions or cultural references, such as "veranillo de San Juan" in *Diario de la guerra del cerdo*, transposed by WOODRUFF & YATES (1972) as "Indian summer" in *Diary of the War of the Pig*. More specific cultural references, especially those referring to Argentine or Buenos Aires everyday life and customs, are frequently kept in Spanish, as is the case of "truco", "empanadas", "señor", "maté" in Woodruff & Yates's *Diary of the War of the Pig*, and "yerba maté" and "Señora", a vocative deliberately maintained in Spanish, in LEVINE's transposition (1992) of the short story "Bajo el agua" [Underwater] in *A Russian Doll and Other Stories*. In some cases, however, approximate translations of culturally bound terms are used, such as "ranch" for "estancia" in LEVINE's rendering of "Encuentro en Rauch" [A Meeting in Rauch] in *A Russian Doll...*

Apart from these relatively few cultural terms, which demand a certain rewriting on the part of the translator, Bioy Casares's writing does not offer substantial difficulties of cultural adaptation or rewriting of the kind presented by the works of other Latin American authors (Alejo Carpentier, João Guimarães Rosa, Jorge Amado, among the most obvious examples). Bioy Casares's writing hallmark seems to be less an exploration of linguistic experimentation and use of cultural references than the pursuit of a narrative syntax and a colloquial style that translate and recreate the masterpiece conventions of fantastic literature and suspense narration: the figure of the double, parallel times and spaces, the subtle and gradual denouement, the ambiguous end of the game. His style, which might be characterized by simple syntax and sparing use of play on words, demands from the translator special care with the narrative rhythm of the short stories and the recreation of a narrator who remembers events as if narrating would provide a logical explanation to them. Parenthetical expressions, appositions or even isolated words convey what might be described as a dialogue between the text's narrator (Bioy Casares or a concocted voice) and the narrator in the text. This duplicity further reinforces the ambiguous character that Bioy Casares attributes to any account of events in what is conventionally called reality.

As in the case of works by other Latin American writers, who frequently theorize upon translation processes in their own fiction, novels by Bioy Casares such as *Dormir al sol* or *La invención de Morel* can be read as subtle reflections on the processes of creation and recreation and on the status of originals and copies. Morel's replicating machine or the psychiatry institute's method of transplantation of souls and recreation of human beings show no doubt the displacement inherent to all reproducing processes. Most significantly, those novels can also be read as reflections upon the textual transformations brought about by hermeneutic processes. Interestingly, Bioy Casares's *La invención de Morel* can be read as a re-creation or cultural translation of H.G. Wells's *The Island of Dr Moreau* and of some of the issues developed in Goethe's *Faust*.

ADRIANA S. PAGANO

Further Reading

di Giovanni, Norman Thomas, "An Evening with Bioy" in *The Borges Tradition*, edited by di Giovanni, London: Constable, 1995, pp. 89–107

Galvez, Raul, *From the Ashen Land of the Virgin: Conversations with Bioy Casares, Borges, Denevi, Etchecopar, Ocampo, Orozco, Sábato in Argentina*, Oakville, Ontario, and New York: Mosaic Press, 1989

Levine, Suzanne Jill, *The Subversive Scribe: Translating Latin American Fiction*, St Paul, Minnesota: Graywolf Press, 1991

Bjørnstjerne Bjørnson 1832–1910

Norwegian novelist, dramatist and poet

Biography

Born in Kvikne, Norway, to the south of Trondheim, when Norway was still united with Sweden, 8 December 1832. His father was a pastor. Bjørnson studied at Christiania University (now Oslo University) from 1852 to 1854, but turned to journalism and literature. He married Karoline Reimers, 1858. In his writings and his public life he was committed to the cause of Norway's political separation from Sweden, and to helping Norwegian language and literature move away from Danish influence and achieve an identity of their own. His first success came with the publication of stories about contemporary Norwegian peasant life; and he went on to write many novels and stories by which he became known at the time in the English-speaking world. In his native country he is also famed for his 21 plays – including historical dramas such as *Sigurd Slembe* and *Mary Stuart in Scotland* and plays that challenged the then political, social and religious conventions (*The Editor*, *The Bankrupt*, *Beyond Our Power*). He was director of the Christiania Theatre from 1865 to 1867 and also directed in Bergen. He travelled in Europe and the US and lived for considerable periods in Rome and Paris. In 1903 he was awarded the Nobel Prize for Literature. He died in Paris, 26 April 1910.

Translations

Collections of Fiction

Anderson, Rasmus B., *The Works of Bjørnstjerne Bjørnson*, 6 vols, New York: Doubleday Page, 1882

Gosse, Edmund (editor), *The Novels of Bjørnsterne Bjørnson*, 13 vols, London: Heinemann, and New York: Macmillan, 1895–1909

Novels

Synnøve Solbakken, 1857

Anderson, Rasmus B., *Synnøve Solbakken*, Boston: Houghton Mifflin, 1881; reprinted in *The Works of Bjørnsterne Bjørnson*, vol. 6, 1882

Bethell, Augusta and Augusta Plesner, *Love and Life in Norway*, London: Cassell Petter and Galpin, 1870

Howitt, Mary, *Trust and Trial*, London: Hurst and Blackett, 1858

Sutter, Julie, *Synnøve Solbakken: A Norwegian Tale*, London: Macmillan, 1881; reprinted in *The Novels of Bjørnsterne Bjørnson*, edited by Edmund Gosse, vol. 1, 1895; as *Sunny Hill: A Norwegian Idyll*, New York: Macmillan, 1932

Arne, 1858

A Norwegian [Thomas Krag] *Arne; or, Peasant Life in Norway*, Bergen: H.J. Geelmuydens widow, 1861

Anderson, Rasmus B., *Arne: Early Tales and Sketches*, Boston: Houghton Mifflin, 1881; reprinted in *The Works of Bjørnsterne Bjørnson*, vol. 1, 1882

Low, Walter, *Arne*, in *The Novels of Bjørnsterne Bjørnson*, edited by Edmund Gosse, vol. 2, 1895

Plesner, Augusta and S. Rugeley-Powers, *Arne: A Sketch of Norwegian Country Life*, London: A. Strahan, 1866; Boston: Sever Francis, 1869

En glad gut, 1860

Anderson, Rasmus B., *A Happy Boy*, Boston: Houghton and Mifflin, 1881; reprinted in *The Works of Bjørnsterne Bjørnson*, vol. 4, 1882

Archer, Mrs. William, *A Happy Boy*, in *The Novels of Bjørnsterne Bjørnson*, edited by Edmund Gosse, vol. 3, 1896

Gade, Helen R., *The Happy Boy: A Tale of Norwegian Peasant Life*, Boston and Cambridge: Sever Francis, 1870

Hjerleid, Sivert and Elizabeth Hjerleid, *Övind: A Story of Country Life in Norway*, London: Simpkin, 1869

Fiskerjenten, 1868

Anderson, Rasmus B., *The Fisher Maiden*, Boston: Houghton Mifflin, 1882; also in *The Works of Bjørnsterne Bjørnson*, vol. 3, 1882

Anonymous, *The Fisher Lass*, London, Heinemann; New York: Macmillan, 1896; also in *The Novels of Bjørnsterne Bjørnson*, edited by Edmund Gosse, vol. 4, 1896

Hjerleid, Sivert and Elizabeth Hjerleid, *The Fisher Girl*, London: Trübner, 1871

Niles, M.E., *The Fisher-Maiden: A Norwegian Tale*, New York: Leypoldt and Holt, 1871

Plesner, Augusta and Frederika Richardson, *The Fishing Girl*, London: Cassell, Petter and Gulpin, 1870

Brudeslaaten, 1872

Anderson, Rasmus B., *The Bridal March* in *The Works of Bjørnsterne Bjørnson*, vol. 2, 1882; in *The Bridal March and Other Stories*, Boston: Houghton Mifflin, 1883; London: Bickers, 1884

Anonymous, *The Bridal March* in *The Novels of Bjørnsterne Bjørnson*, edited by Edmund Gosse, vol. 5, 1896

Kaptejn Mansana, 1875

Anderson, Rasmus B., *Captain Mansana, and Other Stories*, Boston: Houghton Mifflin, 1882; also in *The Works of Bjørnsterne Bjørnson*, vol. 2, 1882

Anonymous, *Captain Mansana and Mother's Hands* in *The Novels of Bjørnsterne Bjørnson*, edited by Edmund Gosse, vol. 7, 1897

Ford, Marian, *Captain Mansana*, New York: Munro, 1883

Magnhild, 1877

Anderson, Rasmus B., *Magnhild; Dust*, Boston: Houghton Mifflin, 1882; in *The Works of Bjørnsterne Bjørnson*, vol. 5, 1882

Anonymous, *Magnhild* in *The Novels of Bjørnsterne Bjørnson*, edited by Edmund Gosse, vol. 6, 1897

Det flager i byen og på havnen, 1884

Fairfax, Cecil, *The Heritage of the Kurts*, London: Heinemann, and New York: United States Book Co., 1892; in *The Novels of Bjørnsterne Bjørnson*, edited by Edmund Gosse, vols. 11–12, 1908

På Guds veje, 1889

Carmichael, Elizabeth, *In God's Way: A Novel*, London: Heinemann, 1890; in *The Novels of Bjørnsterne Bjørnson*, edited by Edmund Gosse, vols 9–10, 1908

Mary, 1906

Morison, Mary, *Mary* in *The Novels of Bjørnsterne Bjørnson*, edited by Edmund Gosse, vol. 13, 1909

Selections of Plays

Björkman, Edwin, *Plays*, with an introduction, 2 vols, New York: Scribner, and London: Duckworth, 1913–14 (vol. 1: *The Gauntlet*, *Beyond Our Power*, *The New System*; vol. 2: *Love and Geography*, *Beyond Human Might*, *Laboremus*)

Sharp, R. Farqhuarson, *Three Comedies*, London: Dent and New York, Dutton, 1912 (contains *The Newly Married Couple*, *Leonarda*, *A Gauntlet*)

Sharp, R. Farquharson, *Three Dramas*, London: Dent and New York: Dutton, 1914 (contains *The Editor*, *The Bankrupt*, *The King*)

Plays

Sigurd Slembe, 1862, produced 1863

Payne, William Morton, *Sigurd Slembe: A Dramatic Trilogy*, Boston: Houghton Mifflin, 1888

Maria Stuart i Skotland, 1864
Sahlberg, August, *Mary, Queen of Scots*, Chicago: Specialty Syndicate Press, 1912

De nygifte, 1865
Colborn, Grace Isabel, *A Lesson in Marriage*, New York: Brandu, 1910
Hjerleid, Sivert and Elizabeth Hjerleid, *The Newly-Married Couple*, London: Simpkin Marshall, 1870
Sharp, R. Farquharson, *The Newly-Married Couple* in *Three Comedies*, translated by Sharp, 1912

En fallit, 1874, produced 1875
Sharp, R. Farquharson, *The Bankrupt*, in *Three Dramas*, translated by Sharp, 1914

Redaktøren, 1874, produced 1875
Sharp, R. Farquharson, *The Editor* in *Three Dramas*, translated by Sharp, 1914

Kongen, 1877, produced 1902
Sharp, R. Farquharson, *The King* in *Three Dramas*, translated by Sharp, 1914

Det ny system, 1879, produced 1878
Björkman, Edwin, *The New System*, in *Plays*, translated by Björkman, vol. 1, 1913

Leonarda, 1879
Hansen, Daniel L., *Leonarda* in *The Drama: A Quarterly Review of Dramatic Literature*, 3 (1911) pp. 16–76
Sharp, R. Farquharson, *Leonarda* in *Three Comedies*, translated by Sharp, 1912

En hanske, 1883
Björkman, Edwin, *The Gauntlet*, in *Plays*, translated by Björkman, vol. 1, 1913
Brækstad, H.L., *A Gauntlet*, London and New York: Samuel French, 1880
Edwards, Osmund, *A Gauntlet*, London and New York: Longman Green, 1894
Sharp, R. Farquharson, *A Gauntlet* in *Three Comedies*, translated by Sharp, 1912
Sogard, Thyge, *A Glove*, in *Poet Lore*, Boston, 4 (1892)

Over ævne I, 1883, produced 1886
Björkman, Edwin, *Beyond Our Power* in *Plays*, translated by Björkman, vol. 1, 1913
Hollander, Lee M., *Beyond Human Power* in *Chief Contemporary Dramatists*, edited by Thomas H. Dickinson, Boston: Houghton Mifflin, 1915
Wilson, William, *Pastor Sang*, London and New York: Longman Green, 1893

Geografi og kjærlighed, 1885
Björkman, Edwin, *Love and Geography* in *Plays*, translated by Björkman, vol. 2, 1914

Over ævne II, 1895
Björkman, Edwin, *Beyond Human Might* in *Plays*, translated by Björkman, vol. 2, 1914

Paul Lange og Tora Parsberg, 1898, produced 1901
Brækstad, H.L., *Paul Lange and Tora Parsberg*, London and New York: Harper, 1899

Laboremus, 1901
Anonymous, *Laboremus* in *Fortnightly Review Literary Supplement*, 75 (May 1901)
Bjorkman, Edwin, *Laboremus* in *Plays*, translated by Björkman, vol. 2, 1914

Når den ny vin blomstrer, 1909
Stahl, Bernard, *When the New Wine Blooms*, New York: Brandu, 1909

Poetry
Arnljot Gelline, 1870
Payne, William Morton, *Arnljot Gelline*, New York: American–Scandinavian Foundation, 1917

Digte og sange, 1870
Palmer, Arthur Hubbell, *Poems and Songs*, New York: American–Scandinavian Foundation, 1915

Other Writing
Vis-Knut, 1878
Stahl, Bernard, *Wise-Knut*, New York: Brandu, 1909

Breve, 1880–81
Haugen, Eva Lund and Einar Haugen, *Land of the Free: Bjørnstjerne Bjørnson's America Letters, 1880–1881*, Northfield, Minnesota: Norwegian–American Historical Association, 1978

Bjørnstjerne Bjørnson is a major figure in the history of Norwegian literature. As writer and theater director, he was a leader in the 19th-century Norwegian nationalist movement. Many of his poems have been set to music by prominent composers like Edvard Grieg and Halfdan Kjerulf, and one was chosen as the Norwegian national anthem. Nearly all of his works have been translated into English at one time or another, some by several different translators. Nevertheless, it is doubtful that anyone reads Bjørnson in English today. Burchardt has noted how difficult Bjørnson's style is to render into a foreign language: "It is so impressed with the very characteristics of his native tongue, so inseparable from the firmness of its idiom, so rich with melody and full of freshness, that even the ablest translator could not render one of its beauties without failing to give some of the rest" (Burchardt, 1920). In the latter part of the 19th century, his optimistic pastoral tales, written in the style of the Norse sagas, were quite popular among English-language readers, but his idealistic, somewhat didactic social plays did not go over at all well in either America or England, and were soon overshadowed by the growing success of Ibsen.

The first of Bjørnson's works to be translated into English was *Synnøve Solbakken*, a tale about Norwegian peasant life, translated by Mary HOWITT (1858), who titled it *Trust and Trial*. It was soon followed by a somewhat inept translation of another story about a peasant, *Arne*, by a Norwegian named Thomas KRAG (1861). In 1866 Augusta PLESNER and S. RUGELEY-POWERS published their translation of the same tale, attempting to reproduce its versification in English with some success. Throughout the remainder of the century, new translations continued to be produced of the old favorite tales.

In 1880–81, Bjørnson made a lecture tour in America arranged by Rasmus B. Anderson. A consequence of Bjørnson's American visit was the first edition of all his novels to date, published by Houghton Mifflin (1881-82). The job of translating was first offered to Sara Bull, the wife of the famous violinist Ole Bull, but she passed the job on to Anderson. Anderson in turn passed the work on to Annie Aubertine Woodward MOORE, whose skills in the Norwegian language were at that time still developing. Moore therefore called on Anderson's wife Karina, who provided oral translations of *Synnøve Solbakken* and *A Happy Boy*. Anderson himself read the proofs. Because the publisher wanted a well-known name to appear on the title-page, ANDERSON (Boston: 1881–82) was listed as sole translator. These translations, which were also published in slightly different combinations of titles under the Doubleday Page imprint as *The Works of Bjørnstjerne Bjørnson*, in six volumes (New York, 1882) drew criticism from reviewers for sounding too much like translations; Moore tried so hard to do justice to the author that she did not always choose the best English idiom. Bjørnson himself wrote on the flyleaf of their translation (1881) of *Synnøve Solbakken*, "A poet's work can be translated only by a poet, and my friend Anderson unfortunately is nothing of the kind" (HAUGEN). Nevertheless, the fact of having a foreign edition of his works published before such a project had even been considered in Norway was certainly a feather in Bjørnson's cap.

In London in the 1890s, the publisher William Heinemann launched his "International Library" with Bjørnson's novel *In God's Way* translated by Elizabeth CARMICHAEL (1890) as the first book of the series. Edmund Gosse, who was Heinemann's adviser, reader and editor for these fiction translations, later became the editor for Heinemann's English edition of Bjørnson's collected fiction, which came out in 13 volumes from 1895 to 1909. These included Julie SUTTER's *Synnøve Solbakken* (vol. 1, 1895), Walter LOW's *Arne* (vol. 2, 1895), Mrs William ARCHER's *A Happy Boy* (vol. 3, 1896), Cecil FAIRFAX's *Heritage of the Kurts* (vols 11–12, 1908) and Mary MORISON's *Mary* (vol. 13, 1909). Other volumes in this edition, whose translators were ANONYMOUS, were *The Fisher Lass* (vol. 4, 1896), *The Bridal March and One Day* (vol. 5, 1896), *Magnhild and Dust* (vol. 6, 1897), *Captain Mansana and Mother's Hands* (vol. 7, 1897) and *Absalom's Hair and A Painful Memory* (vol. 8, 1898). This edition, later and therefore able to cover subsequent titles, was more complete than Anderson's, at least as far as the novels were concerned, but again did not include any of the plays.

The plays, however, did have their faithful devotees in England. As early as 1872 the Scots poet Robert Buchanan published a long account of the first two parts of the historical trilogy *Sigurd Slembe*, which included his own translations of large sections of the play. He also made an open plea for someone whose knowledge of Norwegian was better than his to provide a complete translation. He did not get his wish, however, until William Morton Payne published his version of all three parts in 1888. Two major Bjørnson play selections appeared during the years 1912–14. One set, translated by Edwin BJÖRKMAN (vol. 1, 1913; vol. 2, 1914), comprised *The Gauntlet, Beyond Our Power, The New System, Love and Geography, Beyond Human Might* and *Laboremus*. The fact of Björkman's Swedish nationality was brought up in reviews of his English translations and blamed for his writing "his adopted tongue with great fluency rather than with a fine sense for the spirit and idiom of the language." (*The Dial*, 56 (1914), p. 507), and another reviewer noted "a marked stiffness in dialogue" (L.W. Dodd in *Yale Review*, new series 3, p. 597). The other major English edition of Bjørnson's plays was brought out, also as two volumes, in the Everyman's Library, translated by R. Farquharson SHARP. The first volume, *Three Comedies* (1912), included *The Newly-Married Couple*, *Leonarda*, and *A Gauntlet*. *Three Dramas* (1914) included *The Editor*, *Bankrupt*, and *The King*.

The musical quality of Bjørnson's poems led the Nordic composers Edvard Grieg and Halfdan Kjerluf to set many of them to music. These songs were consequently the first items of Bjørnson's poetry to be translated, during the late 19th century, as a part of these composers' works. Later, Arthur Hubbell PALMER's English translation (1915) of Bjørnson's *Poems and Songs* won the admiration of the reviewer H.A. Larson for "the adroitness with which he has surmounted the technical difficulties" and "the sympathetic loyalty with which he has adhered to the words as well as the spirit of the original." (*Yale Review*, new series 5 (January 1916), p. 430). In 1917 Bjørnson's poetic epic *Arnljot Gelline* was translated by William Morton PAYNE, who was praised in a New York weekly journal for solving the enormous difficulties presented by its metrical characteristics "with almost invariable tact and skill" (*Nation* (14 February 1918), p. 185).

KRISTINE J. ANDERSON

Further Reading

Burchardt, C.B., *Norwegian Life and Literature: English Accounts and Views, Especially in the 19th Century*, London: Oxford University Press, 1920; reprinted Westport, Connecticut: Greenwood Press, 1974

Downs, Brian, "Anglo-Norwegian Literary Relations, 1867–1900", *Modern Language Review*, 47/4 (October 1952)

Hustvedt, Lloyd, *Rasmus Bjørn Anderson, Pioneer Scholar*, Northfield, Minnesota: Norwegian-American Historical Association, 1966

Larson, Harold, *Bjørnstjerne Bjørnson: A Study in Norwegian Nationalism*, New York: King's Crown Press, 1944

Karen Blixen 1885–1962

Danish short-story writer and self-translator

Biography

Born Karen Christenze Dinesen, 17 April 1885 in Rungsted, Denmark and educated privately in Denmark, England, Switzerland, Italy and France. She married her cousin, Baron Bror von Blixen-Finecke in 1914 and they went to Kenya to manage a coffee plantation. After their divorce in 1921 she stayed on until 1931 when, the coffee market having declined, she returned to her family home, Rungstedlund. She had been contributing items to Danish periodicals since 1905 under the pseudonym Osceola, but her first two books, *Seven Gothic Tales* (1934) and *Out of Africa* (1937) were written first in English and appeared under the name Isak Dinesen. Most of the works that followed in her lifetime were published simultaneously in English and Danish, both versions usually created by her, as Karen Blixen or Isak Dinesen. Her imaginative and stylish stories won her recognition and awards in Denmark and abroad. She died at Rungstedlund, 7 September 1962.

Translations (including self-translations)

Short Stories

Syv fantastiske Fortællinger, 1935 (as Isak Dinesen)
Dinesen, Isak, *Seven Gothic Tales*, with an introduction by Dorothy Canfield, New York: Smith and Haas, and London: Putnam, 1934

Vinter Eventyr, 1942
Dinesen, Isak, *Winter's Tales*, New York: Random House, and London: Putnam, 1942

Babettes Gæstebud, 1955
Dinesen, Isak, "Babette's Feast", *Ladies' Home Journal* (June 1950); in her *Anecdotes of Destiny*, 1958

Sidste Fortællinger, 1957
Dinesen, Isak, *Last Tales*, New York: Random House, and London: Putnam, 1957

Skæbne Anecdoter, 1958
Dinesen, Isak, *Anecdotes of Destiny*, New York: Random House, and London: Michael Joseph, 1958

Skygger paa Græsset, 1960
Dinesen, Isak, *Shadows on the Grass*, London: Michael Joseph, 1960; New York: Random House, 1961

Ehrengard, 1963 (translated into Danish by Clara Svendsen)
Dinesen, Isak, *Ehrengard*, New York: Random House, and London: Michael Joseph, 1963

Efterladte Fortællinger, 1975
Mitchell, P.M. *et al.*, *Carnival: Entertainments and Posthumous Tales*, Chicago: University of Chicago Press, 1977

Novel

Gengældelsens veje, 1944 (as Pierre Andrézel), "translated into Danish by Clara Svendsen", 1944
Dinesen, Isak, *The Angelic Avengers*, New York: Random House, and London: Putnam, 1946

Other Writing

Den afrikanske Farm, 1937
Dinesen, Isak, *Out of Africa*, London: Putnam, 1937; New York, Random House, 1938

Mit livs mottoer og andre essays, 1965
Mitchell, P.M. and W.D. Paden, *Daguerreotypes and Other Essays*, with a foreword by Hannah Arendt, London: Heinemann, and Chicago: University of Chicago Press, 1979

Moderne Ægteskab og andre Betragtninger, 1977
Born, Anne, *On Modern Marriage, and Other Observations*, with an introduction by Else Cederborg, New York: St Martin's Press, 1986

Breve fra Afrika 1914–24 and *Breve fra Afrika 1925–31*, 1978
Born, Anne, *Letters from Africa, 1914–1931*, edited by Frans Lasson, Chicago: University of Chicago Press, and London: Weidenfeld and Nicolson, 1981

Karen Blixen or Isak Dinesen (the pseudonym she used, chiefly in America) translated her own works from Danish into English or from English into Danish as the occasion demanded. She wrote her first book, *Seven Gothic Tales*, not in her mother tongue, Danish, but in English. The reason for this was that she lived in an English community in Kenya at the time she was beginning to write these stories. She had as her social circle the governor and his entourage and friends – though not the notorious Happy Valley set. Among these was the man who meant most to her, Denys Finch Hatton, son of the Earl of Winchelsea, one of a number of men who elected to go abroad after their service in World War I. Their love story is well known, but perhaps less so is the fact that Finch Hatton introduced Blixen to Greek and much other literature, including poetry, and entrusted his library to her. When she was obliged to leave Africa she had it shipped home to Denmark (Finch Hatton having died in an air crash).

Not only did the emergent writer, who had composed Danish marionette plays in her youth, have a thorough knowledge of English through reading and intelligent sophisticated conversation, but she also found she could entertain Finch Hatton, the big-game hunter who came to her house for rest and relaxation, by a Scheherezade kind of storytelling, excellent practice for writing. She wrote these stories in English. (She had kept her own language alive by writing long weekly letters from Africa to her family in Denmark, and by sending her brother a monograph, *Moderne Ægteskab* (*On Modern Marriage*).) The tales were thus worked out orally in one language, English, from previous notes, then written down, also in English, and later translated into Danish. Having lived so long among English people and being aware of the wider market that publication would have in England and America, she naturally sought a publisher in the English-speaking world. The book, *Seven Gothic Tales*, was published in New York and London in 1934. The Danish press discovered that the author of the highly successful book lived near Copenhagen, and asked for a translation.

Several translators were asked to provide samples. None was, Blixen felt, satisfactory. So she decided to turn translator of her own work, which obviously she understood better than anyone else. It is not only the meaning of each word that the translator has to reproduce accurately, it is the style and in particular, in complex work such as Blixen's, the tone that must be rendered.

Blixen/Dinesen's next book was *Out of Africa* (in Danish: *Den afrikanske Farm* (The African Farm)). Begun as a series of articles, this was to be her supreme achievement. The events, losses and joys of the years in Kenya were transmuted into a pastoral, deeply moving and of tragic proportions. This, stated by the writer to be a true account of her life, was in fact a poetic, selective and mythic version, focused on the land and people she loved and understood, its vast landscapes and wild life, and her own dramatic story. The language of this book is simpler than that of *Seven Gothic Tales,* which is often convoluted and studiedly 18th-century in flavour. The writer is in full command of material and medium. The Danish version followed as quickly as Blixen could produce it.

What kind of translation did BLIXEN create? Was it literal or free? Did it keep to the original or alter it? This is a subject waiting for scholars to write theses on, with ample material for detailed comparison of parallel texts. A short indication may be given here. Blixen came from an educated background where people spoke a classical, formal Danish, and wrote likewise. This, with her preferred period setting for many of her tales, the 18th century, made for a style reminiscent, perhaps, of George Eliot's in its purity. But two things stand out: in the Danish versions there can be inserted details of specifically Danish facts such as details of food or customs not found in the English because they would not be understood or enjoyed without notes. The English stories either explain these Danish details or omit them.

As time went on Blixen's compatriots complained that her stories were too convoluted as well as "decadent". She then deliberately took subjects from Danish history or folktale and presented more easily assimilable pieces. This is especially true of the third book, *Winter's Tales.*

The second aspect to note about BLIXEN's self-translations is her command of English. We saw it was so extensive that she could write with equal ease in Danish and English. But her lack of academic training makes itself felt in a few charming details, which seem to pass unremarked by English readers. However, anyone with a knowledge of Danish will note that in the first two books, especially *Out of Africa,* certain turns of phrase and words are directly unintentional Danish forms. For instance, in *Out of Africa* we read, "So she [a bushbuck fawn] held to him [a native boy] and followed him about", where English would have "stayed close to him"; "I lay out crushed maize to her" instead of "for her"; and "However often you make the experience" for "experience it". There are many such instances throughout this book, and in *Seven Gothic Tales* and some other works, although fewer as her writing developed.

But Blixen was not always her own translator. As her fame grew and new books were expected from her hand, she needed to devote her often fluctuating energies to writing. The woman who was her secretary for most of her writing life, Clara Selborn (formerly Clara SVENDSEN, under which name she at first published), helped with the translation into English of the minor novel *The Angelic Avengers*, written by Blixen in Danish during the occupation of Denmark in World War II, under a pseudonym, Pierre Andrézel. In order to conceal the author's identity, because Denmark was then occupied by Germany, the book had had to seem to be a translation and was issued in 1944 as "translated by Clara Svendsen", who had agreed to "lend" her name. During the German occupation of Denmark, translations into English from Danish were forbidden, and the French pseudonym, indicating a French original, made it safer for Blixen and Svendsen to start on the English translation of *Gengældelsens veje* [The Roads of Retribution], which as *The Angelic Avengers* (1946) sold very well in the US and earned Blixen large royalties. Svendsen had typed Blixen's dictated translation; this was the first of many such partnerships, during which there was much discussion between author/translator and secretary. Svendsen did the Danish version of the long story *Ehrengard* (1963). Her years of experience of working with the author gave her a unique knowledge of a complex writer's mind and work, and she generously advised later translators, who benefited from her scholarly and meticulous care. *Daguerreotypes and Other Essays* was translated into English by MITCHELL & PADEN (1979).

As time went on Blixen's pre-eminence among modern Danish writers came to be recognized by English readers everywhere, and occasioned a profusion of reprints and paperback editions of translations.

The majority of the letters written by Blixen from Africa to her family in Denmark were edited and published by Frans Lasson in Denmark in 1978. The present writer (BORN) translated them in 1981, and also translated in 1986 the long essay Blixen sent to her brother Thomas in 1926, *On Modern Marriage.*

ANNE BORN

Further Reading

Juhl, Marianne and Bo Hakon Jørgensen, *Diana's Revenge: Two Lines in Isak Dinesen's Authorship*, translated by Anne Born, Odense: Odense University Press, 1985

Kure-Jensen, Lise, "Isak Dinesen in English, Danish, and Translation: Are We Reading the Same Text?" in *Isak Dinesen: Critical Views*, edited by Olga Anastasia Pelensky, Athens: Ohio University Press, 1993

Langbaum, Robert, *The Gayety of Vision: Isak Dinesen's Art*, London: Chatto and Windus, 1964; New York: Random House, 1965

Thurman, Judith, *Isak Dinesen: The Life of Karen Blixen*, London: Weidenfeld and Nicolson, 1982; as *Isak Dinesen: The Life of a Storyteller*, New York: St Martin's Press, 1982

Aleksandr Blok 1880–1921

Russian poet

Biography

Born in St Petersburg, 28 November 1880, into an upper-class intellectual family. He studied law and philosophy at university, but in 1906 chose writing as his profession. His literary activity exhibits a powerful mind joined to consuming emotionality and profound mysticism. His religiosity is individual, undogmatic, unorthodox, and akin to Gnosticism. Throughout his life the symbols he used kept changing until they culminated in the long poem "The Twelve", which celebrates (as well as criticizes) the Russian Revolution, and at the same time blasphemously adapts the story of Christ and the Apostles; but it contains other levels of meaning as well, often mutually contradictory yet harmonized into a powerful whole. Blok's ambivalence toward the Revolution alienated conservatives and radicals both. The former saw him as a traitor to the traditions and values of his class, while the latter distrusted his complexity and aristocratic refinement. However, his eminence in Russian literature is assured, and is often compared to Pushkin's. The influence he exerted on Russian prosody too is phenomenal, for he, more than anyone, laid down the foundations of modern Russian versification. In 1903 he married the daughter of L.D. Mendeleev, the Russian chemist who formulated the periodic law for the classification of the elements. Died in Petrograd, 7 August 1921.

Translations (select list: the numerous translations in periodicals are not covered)

Anthologies

Bowra, C.M. (editor), *A Book of Russian Verse, Translated into English by Various Hands*, London: Macmillan 1943; reprinted Westport, Connecticut: Greenwood Press, 1971 (17 items, 16 translated by Bowra)

Bowra, C.M. (editor), *A Second Book of Russian Verse, Translated into English by Various Hands*, London: Macmillan 1948; reprinted Westport, Connecticut: Greenwood Press, 1971 (15 items; 7 including "The Twelve", translated by Bowra)

Cornford, Frances and Esther Polianowsky Salaman, *Poems from the Russian*, London: Faber, 1943 (7 items)

Lindsay, Jack, *Russian Poetry, 1917–1955*, London: Bodley Head, 1957 (1 item)

Markov, Vladimir and Merrill Sparks, *Modern Russian Poetry: An Anthology with Verse Translations* (parallel texts), London: MacGibbon and Kee, 1966; Indianapolis: Bobbs Merrill, 1967 (17 items)

Obolensky, Dimitri (editor), *The Penguin Book of Russian Verse, with Plain Prose Translations of Each Poem* (parallel texts), Harmondsworth and Baltimore: Penguin, 1962 (11 items)

Todd, Albert C. and Max Hayward, with Daniel Weissbort (editors), *Twentieth Century Russian Poetry: Silver and Steel: An Anthology*, New York: Doubleday, 1993 (23 items, including "The Twelve" and "The Scythians": most done by Geoffrey Thurley)

Yarmolinsky, Avrahm and Babette Deutsch, (editors), *Two Centuries of Russian Verse: An Anthology from Lomonosov to Voznesensky*, New York: Random House, 1966 (16 items, including "The Twelve" and "The Scythians". This anthology is the last of a number done by Deutsch and Yarmolinsky: it is fuller than its predecessors, especially in selections from Blok's poetry)

Translations of Blok alone

Fulton, Robin, *Blok's "Twelve"*, Preston, Lancashire: Akros, 1968

Hackel, Sergei, *The Poet and the Revolution: Aleksandr Blok's The Twelve* (parallel texts), Oxford: Clarendon Press, 1975

Hollo, Anselm, *The Twelve and Other Poems*, Lexington, Kentucky: Gnomon, 1971 (4 items)

Miller, Alex, *Selected Poems*, Moscow: Progress, 1981 (242 items including "The Twelve" and "The Scythians")

Stallworthy, Jon and Peter France, *The Twelve and Other Poems*, London: Eyre and Spottiswoode, and New York: Oxford University Press, 1970 (50 items)

Vogel, Lucy E., *Aleksandr Blok: The Journey to Italy with English Translations of the Poems and Prose Sketches on Italy*, Ithaca, New York: Cornell University Press, 1973 (24 poems in addition to prose essays).

The symbols and mythopoeic images that constitute the essence of Aleksandr Blok's art can be powerfully effective even in a mediocre rendering. However, a translation runs the risk of sounding unbearably trite when it does not envelop Blok's symbols in poetic language worthy of the original. The classic purity of Blok's Russian (comparable to Pushkin's) is difficult to transfer to another language. Equally challenging is the task of doing justice to Blok's supremely inventive versification. A translator has to decide whether to aim primarily for faithful rendition of the words (in which event one will sacrifice most of the haunting music of this poetry) or attempt to transfer into English Blok's rhythms and rhymes (and as a result of this choice, resort to paraphrase to facilitate these effects). The better translations tend to make the former choice. Extremely rare is a translator who succeeds on both counts.

Anthologies

BOWRA (1943, 1948) is one of the more successful translators of Blok. He keeps close to the rhythms of the original poems and shows skill in using English rhyme – different though it is from Russian – to give the reader some idea of Blok's prosodic originality. His versions (especially in the *Second Book*) are inventive and read well, although he makes at times the unruly "The Twelve" sound too genteel.

CORNFORD & SALAMAN (1943) seek to render Blok's rhythms and (not consistently) his rhymes. The relative freedom of their translations seems to result more from inability than from inspiration: they frequently change the meaning so as to make lines come out evenly, with awkward results (e.g., "A girl in silks that gleam;" *cf.* Markov & Sparks, "The figure of a girl, by silk caressed" – still a paraphrase, but a more suggestive one, and closer to the tactile connotations of the original).

LINDSAY (1957) translates a highly important poem, "The Scythians". This is an inspired rendering, possibly the best transfer of Blok into English. Lindsay uses Blok's rhythms and makes the poem rhyme. He departs from the literal but makes excellent choices of words and phrasing. (Thus "we sweep an endless flood" for *nas – t'my, i t'my, i t'my* is excellent when compared to Deutsch's "we are multitude / And multitude and multitude" or another translator's prosy "we are an infinite number". Even so, the denotation of darkness in *t'my* is lost; no translator truly succeeds in bringing across the multilayered meanings in Blok's language.)

OBOLENSKY's prose translation (1962) is unpretentious, precise, and reliable. No better help is imaginable for someone who knows some Russian but needs help to gain access to Blok. Unfortunately, although Obolensky's choice of poems is excellent, he includes neither "The Twelve" nor "The Scythians".

YARMOLINSKY wrote prose paraphrases of Russian poems on which DEUTSCH based her rhymed English versions (1966). These are very weak translations, their only merit being that they first became available in 1921, when Russian poetry was virtually unknown to English readers.

MARKOV & SPARKS's versions (1966) keep Blok's rhythms but their rhymes sometimes descend to the banal level of "hat/that" or "hand/and". In a parallel text like this, a literal prose translation would work best, since it is assumed that the reader is to some extent able to read the Russian. Still, this is a respectable translation that cannot be disregarded or dismissed as unimportant.

TODD & HAYWARD (1993) includes some material published in previous anthologies, such as Stallworthy & France's, and Yarmolinsky & Deutsch's. THURLEY's versions are in free verse and have their own effectiveness. They are impressive as poetry, but the poetry is not recognizable as Blok's.

Translations of Blok alone

FULTON's free translation (1968) of "The Twelve" is in free verse. Fulton does not trouble with rhyme (except occasionally) but keeps up a rapidly paced rhythm similar to that of the original. Admirable though this version is technically, the sardonic quality of "The Twelve" does not come through.

STALLWORTHY, a poet, & FRANCE, a Slavicist, join forces to produce a commendable translation (1970) in which rhyme is used intelligently to carry the verse, although there is no attempt to stay very close to what Blok does with it. As Stallworthy and France say:

> in the old conflict between ... fidelity and beauty, we have taken the side of beauty ... even if this means doing violence on occasion to the patterns, the rhythms, the rhymes, and even (though not often) the meaning of the original ... still we hope to have rendered something of Blok's famous music, which is easy to enthuse about, hard to analyze ...

And so they have. (Their version of "The Twelve" is based on Bowra's more literal translation.)

HOLLO (1971) gives up rhyme and uses free verse throughout. This is not inappropriate, since Blok's poetic activity was experimental, much as free verse in Western Europe was at the same time. Yet by dismissing Blok's rhyming patterns, Hollo loses the strong echoes of the folkloric and of the proletarian that Blok uses and simultaneously subverts in "The Twelve". In fact, although Hollo uses conversational English and English slang to good effect, he omits almost everything specifically Russian from his versions, and he shortens "The Twelve", omitting much of the material (and the poetry). It is almost as if Hollo were writing a poem of his own inspired by Blok's.

HACKEL's book (1975) is primarily a detailed scholarly study; the text of the poem and a translation of it appear in an appendix. Yet this rendering deserves better visibility. It is dynamic and uses the original rhythms as well as excellent, effective rhymes. Pithy (but not slangy) English colloquialisms are imaginatively substituted for Russian ones. This translation is highly recommend.

MILLER's (1981) phraseology is often infelicitous (*e.g.*, "It's young she was") and many of his rhymes are trite (as in "A girl in the little church choir was singing" – and the word "little" changes the setting). However, when he renders the rhythm correctly yet does not seek after rhyme, as in the incomparable "The Stranger" ("Neznakomka"), he does well: we seem to hear rhyme although it is not there, and the overall effect is close to the original. Miller's version of "The Twelve" is effective, but not as good as Hackel's.

Blok was a brilliant essayist as well as poet, and VOGEL's monograph (1973) includes translations of the prose that documents his journey, as well as poems inspired by it. The translations form a necessary supplement to Vogel's scholarly study, but they have merit in themselves and offer the English reader an opportunity to sample Blok's prose. The rendition of the poems is literal, in prose that looks like verse on the page.

ZOJA PAVLOVSKIS-PETIT

Further Reading

Pyman, Avril (editor), *Selected Poems*, by Blok (not a translation), Oxford and New York: Pergamon Press, 1972 (contains exhaustive bibliographies, including one of translations of Blok into English)

See also the introduction to Stallworthy & France

Johannes Bobrowski 1917–1965

German poet, novelist and short-story writer

Biography

Born 9 April 1917 in Tilsit on the Memel, moving with his parents at the age of 11 to Königsberg. He is recognized as one of the outstanding writers of the first phase of the German Democratic Republic's existence; it is easy to forget that his earliest verse had been published in the journal *Das innere Reich* in March 1944 when he was serving as a 27 year-old soldier in the German army on the Russian Front. He had then fallen into Russian hands and remained a prisoner-of-war in camps along the Volga until 1949, when he returned to East Berlin and the nascent German Democratic Republic. There Bobrowski worked as a publisher's reader for a period – including four years at the Union Verlag – and resumed his own writings, which were to be abruptly terminated by his premature death in 1965 at the age of 48. His real literary break came with the appearance in the respected journal *Sinn und Form* in 1955 of a few of his poems, following the encouragement of the journal's then editor Peter Huchel, himself a noted lyric poet. By 1962 Bobrowski had become recognized in West Germany with the award to him of the prestigious Gruppe 47 Prize. Bobrowski remained seemingly one of the few poets to prove acceptable to both West and East Germany. Further proof of recognition of his literary talents on both sides of the border came in the form of the Heinrich Mann Prize from the East German Academy of Arts and of the Charles-Veillon Prize, both awarded in 1965. Died in East Berlin, 2 September 1965.

Translations

Selections

Bullock, Michael, *Darkness and Little Light*, in *Three German Stories*, translated by Bullock, London: Oasis, 1984

Golffing, Francis, *Boehlendorff*, Francestown: Typographeum, 1989 (translation of the short story "Boehlendorff" and 7 poems)

Hamburger, Michael (editor and translator), in his *German Poetry, 1910–1975: An Anthology*, Manchester: Carcanet, and New York: Urizen, 1977

Ives, Rich, *Yesterday I Was Leaving*, Seattle, Washington: Owl Creek Press, 1986 (includes 33 selected poems of Bobrowski)

Keith-Smith, Brian, in his *Johannes Bobrowski*, London: Wolff, 1970 (contains 20 poems and seven passages of prose including "Mouse Banquet", "Letter from America" and "The First Two Sentences for a Book on Germany")

Linder, Marc, *I Taste Bitterness*, East Berlin: Seven Seas, 1970 (selection of 19 tales taken from *Boehlendorff und Mäusefest*, 1966 and *Der Mahner*, 1967)

Mead, Ruth and Matthew Mead, *Shadow Lands: Selected Poems*, with an introduction by Michael Hamburger, London: Donald Carroll, and Denver: Alan Swallow, 1966 (selected poems from *Sarmatische Zeit*, 1961, and *Schattenland Ströme*, 1962)

Mead, Ruth and Matthew Mead, *Selected Poems*, Harmondsworth: Penguin, 1971

Mead, Ruth and Matthew Mead, in *East German Poetry: An Anthology* (parallel texts), edited by Michael Hamburger, Cheadle, Cheshire: Carcanet, 1972; New York: Dutton, 1973

Mead, Ruth and Matthew Mead, *From the Rivers*, London: Anvil Press Poetry, and Iowa City: University of Iowa Press, 1975 (further selections from *Sarmatische Zeit* and *Schattenland Ströme* and also translations from *Wetterzeichen*, 1966)

Nagel, Muska, *The White Mirror*, Orono, Maine: Puckerbrush Press, 1993

Stoljar, Margaret Mahoney, *Under the Night's Edge: A Selection of Poetry and Prose* (parallel texts), with an introduction, Canberra: Leros Press, 1989

Vennewitz, Leila, *Darkness and a Little Light*, New York: New Directions, 1994 (selection of 12 tales, including "Darkness and a Little Light", "Letter from America", "Lithuanian Story", "Mouse Feast", and "Boehlendorff")

Novel

Levins Mühle, 1964

Cropper, Janet, *Levin's Mill*, London: Calder and Boyars, 1970; London and New York: Marion Boyars, 1988

Other Writing

Das Tierhäuschen, 1967 (adaptation from the Russian by Bobrowski of Samuil Marshak's *Terem-teremok*)

Gillespie, Moya, *The House in the Meadow*, London: Chatto Boyd and Oliver, and Irvington-on-Hudson, New York: Harvey House, 1970

Johannes Bobrowski's literary output was understandably limited, with two novels, a number of short stories and four collections of verse to his name. Some of this work was to appear posthumously.

Following his death, translations into English soon got under way. Indeed already by the early 1960s Christopher Middleton, for example, in England, had been translating individual poems of Bobrowski, which appeared in the *Times Literary Supplement* (e.g. in the issues of 28 April 1961 and 21 September 1962, which latter number also carried a review of Bobrowski's lyric poetry published thus far, under the heading "The Pastoral Folkworld").

The very title of *Shadow Lands*, given to the first substantial exercise in translating Bobrowski's work into English, undertaken by Ruth and Matthew MEAD (1966), and comprising a selection of poems taken from the original German collections *Sarmatische Zeit* (1961) and *Schattenland Ströme* (1962), points to the evocation of mood, the conjuring up of visions (not so much of the future but rather of the past) that feature so markedly in Bobrowski's verse. He was not a nature poet pure and simple, though his verse breathes the language of "forest", "tree", "river", "fish", "bird", "stone". Rather he was a regional writer immediately identifiable with East Prussia. The fact, for instance, that Bobrowski could use for "crane" and "eel" the Old Prussian words "gerwe" and "angurys" respectively in the poem "Names for the Persecuted" suggests clearly enough that his real interests lie in his roots), the roots of the history of that northeastern area, where Poles, Germans, Lithuanians, Russians, Gypsies and Jews converged, in a historical age now disappeared. (A certain melancholic tone does manifest itself throughout his writings.)

This spirit of the past is strongly evoked in Bobrowski's first novel, *Levin's Mill,* translated by Janet CROPPER (1970). Subtitled *Thirty-four Sentences about My Grandfather*, the story centres on the Vistula Depression of 1874. The grandfather, a prosperous German miller, seeks to ruin his young business rival Leo Levin by breaching a dam, causing Levin's mill to be swept away. But the grandfather further alienates local people who unite to oppose him. (Emphasis is put on the community and communal activities in the story.) The grandson represents the present-day perspective and reflects the writer's moral concerns over questions of sin and guilt. The 15th Sentence provides the key to the rest.

It is noteworthy, however, that Bobrowski's second novel, *Litauische Claviere* [Lithuanian Pianos] (1966) failed to attract the attention of translators and publishers in the English-speaking world. But it is unlikely now that critics would echo John Flores (1971) in his forthright dismissal of Bobrowski's prose (with particular reference to this second novel) as being "frequently rather meagre in content and annoyingly manneristic in style". Indeed many favour Bobrowski's very richness of language and allusion and apparent liking for stylistic experimentation which they see as a counter to the sterility of language and structured conformism marking much of East German writing in those years. Bobrowski was a staunch Christian and a strong supporter of socialism. He had attended the Second Bitterfeld Conference in 1964 and represented his country at several international cultural gatherings. But in some respects he felt a rather isolated figure and it had been argued early on (e.g. *Times Literary Supplement*, 22 February 1968) that it was possible to detect a change of direction in Bobrowski's work towards the end. Certainly the sense of guilt over the German past, both under Nazism and before, had consistently – and understandably – found a strong resonance in his prose writing and in his verse (not least in the portrait-poems on Gertrud Kolmar and Nelly Sachs). But inherent criticism of the communist regime can also be discovered, for example, in the short story "The Play" (translated by Marc LINDER and included in the volume *I Taste Bitterness*, 1970), in which fun is poked at the way that constructive criticism only was permitted. A writer who wants to write a critical play to be entitled "The Mishap" finishes up with "Mishap Avoided". Other signs manifest themselves in such poems as "Estrangement" and "Answer" and "Midnight Village".

Appreciation of Bobrowski in England then had started already in the early 1960s; it came somewhat later in the US. But Ruth and Matthew MEAD's versions of selected poems of Bobrowski, *Shadow Lands*, which had been published in London in 1966 as the first volume in the new Poetry Europe series, appeared in the US that same year. A further edition of the volume came out in London the following year and indeed others at regular intervals thereafter. In fact the Meads went on to expand their original selection as more poems became available from Bobrowski's *Nachlass*. Their translations were used for the 1971 *Selected Poems* of Bobrowski in the Penguin series of *Modern European Poets*. Four years later the Meads' versions comprised the selection entitled *From the Rivers* (1975), taken again from *Sarmatische Zeit* (1961) and *Schattenland Ströme* (1962) and now *Wetterzeichen* (1966), in the series on *Contemporary Poets in Translation* published in London and the US. The overall standard and degree of accuracy of their translations is good. Differences from versions by HAMBURGER (1977) or KEITH-SMITH (1970), for instance, are generally minor. All, incidentally, try to take into account what Michael Hamburger calls the "thrusts and halts" in Bobrowski's verse.

In Michael Hamburger's anthology *East German Poetry* (1972) Bobrowski with 21 poems (in the MEADS' translation) is the most represented of the 12 selected writers. HAMBURGER himself translated a handful of Bobrowski's poems in facing German-English format in his 1977 anthology *German Poetry 1910–1975*.

In the course of the 1980s and 1990s other translators tried their hand at Bobrowski's verse and stories, particularly, most recently, in America. In addition to reissuing in 1994 the verse selection *Shadow Lands*, New Directions of New York also published that same year under the title *Darkness and a Little Light* a collection of 12 Bobrowski short stories including "Letter from America", "Lithuanian Story", "Mouse Feast" and "Boehlendorff" as well as the title story. The translator was the widely experienced Leila VENNEWITZ (1994). Four of the stories in Vennewitz's volume had already been translated by Marc LINDER in his much earlier versions – and indeed wider selection – of Bobrowski's tales published in 1970 by the now defunct East Berlin publishers Seven Seas. In 1996 New Directions reprinted in their Classics Series Janet CROPPER's translation of *Levin's Mill*. Originally appearing in 1970 under the imprint of Calder and Boyars, it had subsequently been reissued in 1988 by Marion Boyars in both London and New York. Meanwhile in 1989 in Australia a selection of Bobrowski's prose and poetry appeared in Margaret Mahoney STOLJAR's translation under the title *Under the Night's Edge*.

Bobrowski himself too was a translator – from the Czech of Konstantin Biebl and from the Russian of Boris Pasternak and Samuil Marshak. Indeed in 1970, under the title *The House in the Meadow*, an English translation by Moya GILLESPIE of Bobrowski's own German version of the verse tale by Marshak, *Terem-teremok*, came out in the UK and the US.

Bobrowski's death in 1965 had promptly stimulated a number of articles in English in various journals on both sides of the Atlantic. A very sound English introduction to Bobrowski was provided by Brian KEITH-SMITH (1970), published in London. It comprises a concise monograph of 49 pages in which he looks at the writer's life as well as examining individual poems and prose pieces, considering in the course of his analysis Bobrowski's use of nature, mythology, history, patterns of music and painting, and language; the second half of the book is constituted by 43 pages of translations (20 poems and seven passages of prose which include "Mouse Banquet", "Letter from America" and the telling piece "The First Two Sentences for a Book on Germany"). The selection translated by Keith-Smith is very representative, though the poems at least would have benefitted from the presence of parallel German text.

In the following year, 1971, there appeared John Flores's

influential study of *Poetry in East Germany*, Chapter 4 of which is devoted to Johannes Bobrowski. Almost 70 pages of passionate and incisive critical appreciation of Bobrowski's work remain – even after 25 years – one of the most compelling introductions in English to the work of the East German. Bobrowski's own *Collected Works* in German appeared in 1987 in both East and West Germany. Inevitably, he has proved a consistent subject of research theses over the years.

IAN HILTON

Further Reading

Flores, John, *Poetry in East Germany: Adjustments, Visions and Provocations, 1945–1970*, New Haven, Connecticut and London: Yale University Press, 1971
Keith-Smith, Brian, *Johannes Bobrowski*, London: Wolff, 1970
Scrase, David, *Understanding Johannes Bobrowski*, Columbia: University of South Carolina Press, 1995
Wieczorek, J.P., "New Writing on Johannes Bobrowski", *Modern Language Review*, 89 (1994) pp. 406–16

Giovanni Boccaccio 1313–1375

Italian story writer, poet and scholar

Biography

Born in Florence or Certaldo, June or July 1313. His father, a Certaldo merchant, was Italian, his mother French. He was sent to be an apprentice in his father's bank in Naples, 1327–31, then studied canon law there until 1336, staying on and working in banking until 1341, but meanwhile deciding to be a writer. While in Naples he had or imagined a love affair with a noblewoman, the "Fiammetta" of one of his works. He returned to Florence in 1341, occupied some minor official posts and was there during the Black Death, 1348. After meeting Petrarch in 1350 he devoted himself to humanist scholarship. He took minor orders (1357). From 1534 he was active in Florentine public life and in the 1350s and 1360s went to Rome, Ravenna, Avignon and Brandenburg on diplomatic missions. He gave public lectures in Florence on Dante, 1373–74. In the latter year he retired to Certaldo, where he died 21 December 1375.

Much of Boccaccio's early work in Naples was in the form of romances in prose and verse. *Il filostrato* (*The Filostrato*), of about 1335, is the story of Troilus and Cressida in *terza rima*. Later he moved away from the allegorical and figurative style of his early romances, pastorals and poems. Back in Florence, he wrote in novel form the *Elegia di Madonna Fiammetta* (*Amorous Fiammetta*) and in *ottava rima* the love story of *Il ninfale fiesolano* (*The Nymph of Fiesole*), which were soon followed by the famous collection of tales, the *Decameron*, of 1348–51. In the years following the meeting with Petrarch, Boccaccio produced mainly works of erudition in Latin and Italian.

The Decameron

Decamerone, 1348–51

Boccaccio's *Decamerone*, composed between 1348 and 1351, is a collection of one hundred *novelle* told over the course of 10 days by seven women and three men. The tales are framed by a proem, an introduction to the first of the 10 days of storytelling, and a conclusion by the author. The text also contains *canzoni* composed by some of the narrators. While the work has enjoyed enormous popularity and has been translated often, into many languages, it has suffered greatly from censorship of its anticlerical and sexually explicit passages and from translations that oversimplify Boccaccio's complex and innovative literary accomplishment.

Edition

Boccaccio, Giovanni, *Decamerone*, *Boccaccio IV*, in *I Classici Mondadori*, edited by Vittore Branca, Florence: Mondadori, 1976

Translations

Aldington, Richard, *The Decameron of Giovanni Boccaccio*, London: Putnam, and New York: Covici Friede, 1930
Anonymous, *The Decameron* ..., London, 1620; as *Boccaccio's Decameron, Translated into English anno 1620*, with an introduction by Edward Hutton, 4 vols, London: D. Nutt, 1909; reprinted as vols 41–44 of the *The Tudor Translations* series, edited by W.E. Henley, New York: AMS Press, 1967
Jacobs, Joseph, *Tales from Boccaccio*, with an introduction, London: Allen, and New York: Truslove, Hanson and Comba, 1899; reprinted Mount Vernon, New York: Peter Pauper Press, 1947
McWilliam, G.H., *The Decameron*, with an introduction, Harmondsworth: Penguin, 1972; 2nd edition, 1995
Musa, Mark and Peter Bondanella, with an introduction by Thomas Bergin, *The Decameron*, New York: New American Library, 1982
Painter, William, *The Palace of Pleasure, Beautified, Adorned and Well Furnished* ..., 2 vols, London: H. Denham for R. Tottell and William Jones, 1566–67; edited by Joseph Jacobs in *The Palace of Pleasure: Elizabethan Versions of Italian and French Novels*, 3 vols, New York: Dover, 1966
Payne, John, *The Decameron of Giovanni Boccaccio*, 3 vols, London: Villon Society, 1886; New York: Liveright, 1925

Rigg, James Macmullen, *The Decameron of Giovanni Boccaccio*, with an introduction, 2 vols, London: A.H. Bullen, 1903; New York: Dutton, 1930
Singleton, Charles S., *Decameron*, 3 vols, revised and annotated version of the John Payne translation, with an introduction, Berkeley: University of California Press, 1982
Waldman, Guido, *The Decameron*, with an introduction and notes by Jonathan Usher, Oxford and New York: Oxford University Press, 1993
Winwar, Frances [pseudonym], *The Decameron*, 2 vols, New York: Limited Editions Club, 1930; 1 vol., New York: Modern Library, 1955

The earliest known translation into English of the complete text of Giovanni Boccaccio's *Decamerone* is an anonymous work of 1620. The text is divided into two parts, each prefaced by a translator's dedicatory epistle. The David Nutt publication (London: 1909) includes Edward HUTTON's (1908) introduction and was reprinted by AMS Press (1967). This early rendering is a valuable piece of the translation history of the *Decameron*; the translator apparently worked from both the Salviati (1582) edition of the *Decameron* and Antoine Le Maçon's (1545) French version. The 1620 translation also provides a record of the uneasiness with which the English were presenting Italian *novelle* to their countrymen and amending Catholic authors for Protestant audiences. Of particular interest is the addition of moral applications interjected between the brief summaries of the tales and the *novelle* themselves. The names of some characters are anglicized or given in French forms. Generally the register of this first English text is much more consistently ornate (relying heavily on the English penchant for alliteration) than is Boccaccio's Italian original. Boccaccio's more varied use of linguistic tones is especially evident in the contrasts between the voices presented within the *novelle* and in the distinctions between these and the more formal prose of the *frame*. Hutton's introduction provides a biographical sketch of Boccaccio and some critical discussion of his works, including some references to sources, analogues, and criticism. A book-length study of this translation, by Herbert G. Wright, examines the personality, style, and technique of the translator and offers a possible attribution to John Florio, although this has been subsequently called into question.

John PAYNE's accurate Victorian translation (first privately printed by the Villon Society in London, 1886) has appeared in multiple editions, including publications by Liveright (1925) and Modern Library (1931). Payne's language is of a high register and perhaps too stylized for a modern (especially American) reader, but it sounds significantly less artificial than that of his Jacobean predecessor. SINGLETON's revised, annotated version is recent (1982); its notes are excellent for their linguistic, cultural, and historical clarification. Useful and interesting is Singleton's "A Note on the Holograph", which describes the process by which Hamilton 90 (Berlin) was authenticated by Michele Barbi and Giuseppe Vandelli in 1933.

JACOBS (1899), who acknowledges his debt to Payne but accuses him of being overly archaic, translates only four *novelle*: 10.10; 10.9; 5.9; and 4.5. Less ornate than and therefore worth comparing to Payne, he is still rather antiquated for a modern ear. Jacobs's *fin de siècle* prose is fairly accurate but rather freely breaks Boccaccio's lengthy periodic sentences into smaller, more manageable English sentences. Jacobs claims concern with what "need fall under the ban of the censor" in Boccaccio, and he choses to represent in his selection of *novelle* "the more serious aspect" of his author's work. This is consonant with Jacobs's role as editor of William PAINTER's *The Palace of Pleasure* (1566–67), which contains some Boccaccian tales imperfectly translated and purportedly selected for their didactic value.

RIGG (1903) also acknowledges Payne's translation, which he considers antiquated, and he establishes his own aim "to hit the mean between archaism and modernism and to secure as much freedom and spirit as is compatible with substantial accuracy" (xxvii). Indeed, his rendering is relatively faithful and in musical language enjoyable to read, but to a modern ear Rigg himself suffers, although to a lesser degree, from the same archaism to which he objects in Payne. Rigg sustains a tone that is quite formal, even in those passages in which Boccaccio's tone is relatively colloquial. Rigg's sentence structure is often complex, periodic, and even inverted, generally following the phrasing of the original, but not capturing Boccaccio's tonal nuances. John Addington Symonds's preliminary essay offers general biographical and critical background.

ALDINGTON's translation (1930) appears in many editions and reprintings, some illustrated. This text lacks any introduction or critical apparatus. The English is distinctly more modern and even colloquial than that of other translations already mentioned, but, as McWilliam points out, it is marred by errors. Aldington retains Boccaccio's Italian personal and place names.

Also from 1930 is Frances WINWAR's American translation, which apparently represents the first English version by a woman; Winwar, herself a novelist, is faithful to Boccaccio in the more conversational passages of the text, but she is less good at rendering the ornate portions of the work into correspondingly elaborate English. Her translation omits the *proemio*.

Wonderfully readable for a late 20th-century audience, and quite accurate, is the MCWILLIAM translation (1972), which includes an introduction by the translator, the third section of which contains an excellent summary of the English translation history of the *Decameron*. McWilliam refers to a number of 18th- and 19th-century renderings of Boccaccio's text (including the 1741 translation and W.K. Kelly's 1855 version) that have not been directly treated here; there is also an excellent account of the history of expurgation of licentious portions of the original. McWilliam's prose is sensitive to Boccaccio's tonal shifts and to variations in pacing as well as register of language.

The MUSA & BONDANELLA translation (1982) is an excellent, faithful rendering into modern American English, which uses the Hamilton 90 holograph described by Singleton and used by Branca in his Mondadori edition. The Mentor (New American Library) complete text includes, but is not overburdened by, explanatory footnotes. Bergin's introduction is largely biographical. Musa and Bondanella's translation of 21 *novelle* (differing in small details from the NAL edition) appears in a Norton Critical Edition (New York and London: Norton, 1977). That text includes contemporary and modern criticism about the *Decameron*; the translators' footnotes are nearly identical to those in the NAL edition.

Guido WALDMAN's recent translation (1993) fails to achieve the accuracy and sensitivity of McWilliam or Musa & Bondanella. Waldman notes his decision to rewrite the headings of some *novelle* "to preserve the element of surprise" (xxxiii), but he makes more alterations than necessary to accomplish his purpose. The tales themselves often suffer from connotative divergences from the original resulting from translation that is too free.

NANCY M. REALE

Further Reading

Bergin, Thomas G., *Boccaccio*, New York: Viking, 1981
Cottino-Jones, Marga, *An Anatomy of Boccaccio's Style*, Naples: Cymba, 1968
Dombrowski, Robert S. (editor), *Critical Perspectives on the Decameron*, London: Hodder and Stoughton, 1976; New York: Barnes and Noble, 1977
Jones, Florence Nightingale, *Boccaccio and His Imitators in German, English, French, Spanish, and Italian Literature*, Chicago: University of Chicago Press, 1910
Marino, Lucia, *The Decameron "Cornice": Allusion, Allegory and Iconology*, Ravenna: Longo Editore, 1979
Wright, Herbert G., *The First English Translation of the Decameron, 1620*, Cambridge, Massachusetts: Harvard University Press, 1953
Wright, Herbert G., *Boccaccio in England from Chaucer to Tennyson*, London: Athlone, 1957

See also the introductions to Anonymous (1967 edition), McWilliams, Rigg, and Singleton

---

Boethius c.480–c.524

Roman philosopher and scholar

Biography

Born Anicius Manlius Severinus Boethius in about AD 480, in Rome. What we know of Boethius' life comes from the account in *The Consolation of Philosophy*, from letters and from the manuscript *vitae*. The patrician Anicii had been Christians for about a century. Boethius' father, who was consul in 487, died while the boy was young, and he was brought up by Quintus Aurelius Memmius Symmachus, whose daughter Rusticiana he later married (two sons, who were consuls in 522). After a period of travel and study, Boethius held high offices, his career culminating at the court of the Ostrogoth emperor Theodoric, where he became powerful: in 510 he was consul and in 520 he became Theodoric's chief minister. Caught between two factions in religious and political struggles, Boethius was imprisoned on suspicion of treason, tortured, and bludgeoned to death in Pavia, around AD 524.

Apart from *De consolatione philosophiae* (*The Consolation of Philosophy*), written c.524 when he was awaiting execution, Boethius' influential writings include translations, with commentaries, of Aristotle's works on logic and of Porphyry's commentary on them, a commentary on Cicero's *Topics*, and original works on logic, mathematics, music and theology. V.E. Watts, a modern translator of Boethius, describes his writings as "the channel through whose precise and organized systematization philosophy passed from the ancient world to the academic discussion of medieval scholasticism".

The Consolation of Philosophy

De consolatione philosophiae, c.524

Translations

Alfred the Great, King, *King Alfred's Anglo-Saxon Version of Boethius' De Consolatione Philosophiae* (Anglo-Saxon and English), edited and translated by J.S. Cardale, London: Pickering, 1829; modern edition, as *Alfred's Metres of Boethius*, edited by Bill Griffiths, Pinner, Middlesex: Anglo-Saxon Books, 1991
Causton, William, *Boetius: His Consolation of Philosophy*, London: printed privately, 1730
Chaucer, Geoffrey, *Chaucer's Boece, ...*, edited (from MS Ii.3.21. in the University Library, Cambridge) by F.J. Furnivall, London: Chaucer Society, 1886; reprinted New York: Johnson, 1967
Colville, George, *Boetius De Consolationae Philosophiae: The Boke of Boecius, Called the Comforte of Philosophye*, London: John Cawoode, 1556; edited by Ernest Belfort Bax, London: D. Nutt, 1897
Cooper, W.V., *The Consolation of Philosophy*, London: Dent, 1902
Duncan, Robert, *On the Consolation of Philosophy*, Edinburgh: Printed privately, 1789
Elizabeth I, Queen, *Queen Elizabeth's Englishings of Boethius, De Consolatione Philosophiae* [1593], edited by Caroline Pemberton, London: Early English Text Society, 1899
"I.T.", *Five Bokes of Philosophicale Comfort*, London: Printed by John Windet for Mathew Lownes, 1609
James, H.R., *The Consolation of Philosophy*, London: Elliot Stock, 1897
Ridpath, Philip, *Boethius's Consolation of Philosophy*, London: C. Dilly, 1785
Tester, S.J., *The Theological Tractates of Boethius* (bilingual edition), London: Heinemann, and Cambridge, Massachusetts: Harvard University Press, 1973 (Loeb Classical Library)
Waddell, Helen, the metra in her *Medieval Latin Lyrics*, London: Constable, 1929
Watts, V.E., *The Consolation of Philosophy*, Harmondsworth and New York: Penguin, 1969

The work for which Boethius is most remembered today is *De consolatione philosophiae* (*The Consolation of Philosophy*). This composition, which chronicles his imprisonment, pointed the way for the medieval understanding of love as the motive power of the universe. Its influence on Dante in the *Divina Commedia* is evident and strong.

The *Consolation* is a blend of literary forms – philosophical dialogue, monologue, and Menippean satire, in the classical tradition of the *consolatio*, a type of moral medication. The metaphor of medication, treatment, and cure is maintained throughout as Boethius reconsiders the nature of happiness and depicts the slow return of his anguished soul from a contemplation of material pain and loss to a serene participation in wisdom, under the tutelage of the Lady Philosophy.

The *Consolation* consists of five books, each divided into several sections. With two exceptions, there is one metron for each of the prose sections. The first section of Book One contains two metra, one at the opening, in which the narrator laments to the Muses his pitiable and self-pitying state, and one at the end, in which the Lady Philosophy evicts the Muses (characterized in Watts's translation as "hysterical sluts", *scenicas meretriculas*) and prescribes the remaining metra as soothing restoratives for an ailing soul. The final book, on the other hand, ends with prose because the soul has been restored to itself and needs no remedy as it contemplates, with raised head, the sublimity of the judge who sees all things. The verses included in the *Consolation* refer to the great deposit of classical poetry in a variety of meters and tones. The fierce beat of ritualism (I: vii); reflection on seasons, animals, mythological figures; Stoic precepts for a becoming life; and the grandeur of direct address of the Creator (I: v and III: ix) are all found here as elements of the developing narrative.

Translation of the *Consolation* into English began in the early Middle Ages and continued to the present. The quality, style, and purpose of the 24 translations mentioned here vary; their number attests to unfading interest in a work that has been many different things to different readers. The three attested medieval translations are by King Alfred, Chaucer and John Walton. ALFRED wrote in Anglo-Saxon, between 897 and 901, much helped in his work by Asser. As his purpose was the enlightenment of his people, whether learned or not, it is not surprising that his version is true to his own times rather than to the original. Identifying himself with the vicissitudes of Boethius, Alfred utters thoughts quite strange to the author but familiar to his readers. His additions were historical, geographic, political, mythological and Christian. Nicholas Trevet, O.P. (1265–1335) wrote an extensive commentary on Alfred's translation, which proved to be a mainstay of CHAUCER's 14th-century rendering. Other sources were the translation into French of Jean de Meun, Boethius's Latin, in a poor edition, and the entire commentary tradition. Chaucer's highly glossed *Boece* has received criticism from some quarters, both for inaccuracy and for the relative ungainliness of his prose. However, Tim William Machan maintains that Chaucer's prose translation was a meditative, exploratory process that bore fruit in his other works, notably *Troilus and Criseyde*. In 1410, John WALTON wrote a verse translation in *ottava rima* and rhyme royal. A prologue gives a life of Boethius and speaks of the damnation of Theodoric for the murder of the philosopher. The translation has been judged to be not grand, but competent. George COLVILLE's 1556 translation contains the Latin text in the margins and is of interest for its notes and synonymic glosses. In 1563, Thomas Chaloner published translations of all the metra of Book I and the first two metra of Book II. These were so skilful that it is regrettable there were not more. The translation made by Queen ELIZABETH in 1593 is remarkable for its dogged persistence. Her widely acknowledged proficiency in Latin permitted her to complete the task (some say at the rate of half an hour per page), but the result does not indicate a deep understanding of Boethian philosophy or of the author's art.

The tradition of the *Consolation* as medicine is continued with an unpublished translation by John Bracegirdle (1604–08), entitled *Psychopharmacon*. In 1609, there appeared a remarkable translation, signed only "I.T." A majority of scholars supposes that the author was an English Jesuit who could not risk identifying himself. This translation, with its sinuous verse, remained the version used in the Loeb Classical Library edition of the *Consolation of Philosophy* until it was replaced in the edition of 1973. The urge to work with the *Consolation* persisted, producing in the 17th century four other translations, chiefly remarkable for the fact that they exist at all, an edition of the Latin text and the publication of King Alfred's translation. In the 18th century, three translations were published: William CAUSTON, 1730; Philip RIDPATH, 1785; and Robert DUNCAN, 1789. An anonymous translation of all the metra was published in 1792. In 1829, Cardale published an edition of King Alfred's version, with a translation into modern English, H.R. JAMES produced a translation in 1897 and W.V. COOPER in 1902. As always, the metra inspired translators, most felicitously Helen WADDELL and Howard Mumford Jones. S.J. TESTER's translation of 1973 was commissioned for a new edition of the Loeb Classical Library. It meets the Loeb criterion of exactitude but elicits little delight. The 1969 translation of E.V. WATTS gives the reader much greater pleasure, without sacrificing fidelity. This is the best translation for a slow and careful reading of the work for its own sake; the introduction contains an interesting account of Boethius' life and times, as well as an assessment of his works and influence. It is regrettable that we do not have a parallel edition of this translation, so as to enjoy more readily some fine solutions to Latin puzzles.

Successive English versions of *The Consolation of Philosophy* have been vehicles of the translator's intentions, figured as workshops for the hammering out of English lexicon and rhythms, served as testing grounds for many a learned pen and, finally, demonstrated the striving for faithful rendering. Diction has varied, but seldom in direct progression, from the homey didactic to Chaucer's amazing amalgam of earthiness and French, to the slightly sanctimonious, to an attractive *gravitas*. Here and there, along the way, a fortunate translator has achieved a passage of the original lofty grandeur.

GERTRUD GRAUBART CHAMPE

Further Reading

Dolson, Guy Bayley, "*The Consolation of Philosophy* of Boethius in English Literature" (dissertation), Ithaca, New York: Cornell University, 1926

Fehlauer, Friedrich, *Die englischen Übersetzungen von Boethius' De consolatione philosophiae*, Berlin: Emil Felber, 1909

Machan, Tim William, *Techniques of Translation: Chaucer's Boece*, Norman, Oklahoma: Pilgrim Books, 1985
O'Daly, Gerard J.P, *The Poetry of Boethius*, London: Duckworth, and Chapel Hill: University of North Carolina Press, 1991
Patch, Howard Rollin, *The Tradition of Boethius*, New York: Oxford University Press, 1935

See also the translator's introduction to Watts

Heinrich Böll 1917–1985

German novelist, short-story writer and dramatist

Biography

Born in Cologne, 21 December 1917, into a large Catholic family. He went to school and university in Cologne. After working in his father's joinery shop he was apprenticed to a bookseller but by 1939 had begun to study literature. In World War II he served in the German infantry from 1939 and in 1945 was taken prisoner-of-war by the Russians. He married Annemarie Cech in 1942 (three sons). He wrote full-time from 1947 and was one of the founders of the literary group Gruppe 47. His work was translated into at least 18 languages and won many honours at home and abroad, including the Nobel Prize for Literature, 1972.

His subject in fiction is post-World War II Germany and its problems and ills. Widely known in English among the novels are *Gruppenbild mit Dame* (*Group Portrait with Lady*), 1971 and *Die verlorene Ehre der Katharina Blum* (*The Lost Honor of Katharina Blum*), 1974, and among the stories *Der Zug war pünktlich* (*The Train Was on Time*), 1949, and *Wanderer, kommst du nach Spa ...* (*Traveller, If You Come to Spa ...*), 1950. He also wrote plays and a volume of poetry. Died at Langenbroich, near Düren, West Germany, 16 July 1985.

Translations

Short Stories

Der Zug war pünktlich, 1949
Graves, Richard, *The Train Was on Time*, New York: Criterion, 1956
Vennewitz, Leila, *The Train* in *Adam, and The Train: Two Novels*, New York: McGraw Hill, 1970; published separately as *The Train Was on Time*, London: Secker and Warburg, 1973, Evanston, Illinois: Northwestern University Press, 1994

Wanderer, kommst du nach Spa ..., 1950
Savill, Mervyn, *Traveller, If You Come to Spa ...*, London: Arco, 1956
Vennewitz, Leila, "Stranger, Bear Word to the Spartans, We ..." in *The Stories of Heinrich Böll*, translated by Vennewitz, New York: Knopf, 1986

Novels

Und sagte kein einziges Wort, 1953
Graves, Richard, *Acquainted with the Night*, New York: Holt, 1954
Vennewitz, Leila, *And Never Said a Word*, New York: McGraw-Hill, and London: Secker and Warburg, 1978

Haus ohne Hüter, 1954
Savill, Mervyn, *The Unguarded House*, London: Arco, 1957; as *Tomorrow and Yesterday*, New York, Criterion, 1957

Billard um halb zehn, 1959
Bowles, Patrick, *Billiards at Half-past Nine*, London: Weidenfeld and Nicolson, 1961; New York: McGraw-Hill, 1962

Ansichten eines Clowns, 1963
Vennewitz, Leila, *The Clown*, New York: McGraw-Hill, 1965; London: Calder and Boyars, 1972

Gruppenbild mit Dame, 1971
Vennewitz, Leila, *Group Portrait with Lady*, New York: McGraw-Hill, and London: Secker and Warburg, 1973

Die verlorene Ehre der Katharina Blum, 1974
Vennewitz, Leila, *The Lost Honor of Katharina Blum: How Violence Develops and Where It Can Lead*, New York: McGraw-Hill, and London: Secker and Warburg, 1975

Fürsorgliche Belagerung, 1979
Vennewitz, Leila, *The Safety Net*, New York: Knopf, and London: Secker and Warburg, 1982

Frauen vor Flusslandschaft: Roman in Dialogen und Selbstgesprächen, 1985
McLintock, David, *Women in a River Landscape*, New York: Knopf, and London: Secker and Warburg, 1988

It would be fair to say that, as a politically and socially engaged writer, Heinrich Böll focused in his fiction more on content than on form. He was primarily a realistic writer, and although his style developed and became more complicated through the years he was never avant-garde or very innovative. He has even been faulted by critics for not having known or imitated the German Expressionists who preceded him or such modernist authors as Kafka, Proust, and Joyce, but others dispute this. His very early writings before and during the war were influenced primarily by the German 19th-century realists. Eventually he developed his own style, especially as he began to read American writers, such as Hemingway, Steinbeck, and Faulkner. It should be noted that although Böll might have first read these authors in German translations he eventually reviewed their works for the German press, and together with his wife Annemarie translated them from English.

Böll's familiarity with the American short story in the original, together with his direct, realistic narrative style, contributes greatly to his accessibility for the English translator. Böll's first works were classical short stories telling of war and ruined cities ("Trümmerliteratur") from a soldier's perspective. They were characteristically concise, full of understatement, and with a final ironic twist; the dialogue and language were idiomatic and simple. Already, however, there was some experimentation with interior monologue, stream-of-consciousness, cinematic flashbacks, all of which were further pursued as Böll began developing more complex narrative strategies in his novels, into which he also introduced different points of view and a larger cast of characters.

The first four items on the above list, which is cut down from approximately more than twice this number available in English translation, were first published in the original German between 1949 and 1954 and include a novella, a short story, and two of Böll's earliest novels. They are being considered here as a group because they were all rendered into English by early translators (Graves, Savill). Although these early translations are out of print, they are still worth discussing because they introduced Böll to the English-speaking audience and because their flaws and mistakes can serve as warnings to future translators. They also serve as a contrast, when their serviceable but imperfect renderings are compared to Leila Vennewitz's superior work as a translator. Vennewitz, who received the Society of Authors award in London in 1969 for her translation, as *End of a Mission*, of Böll's 1996 *Ende einer Dienstfahrt,* retranslated the first three works on the list in the 1970s and 1980s and they are now available either as part of collections or individually. The last one, *Haus ohne Hüter*, however, was not retranslated by her. Thus Mervyn Savill's is the only translation and even that seems to be unavailable, at least in the US, and in library copies his name does not appear in the book.

The first work on the list, *Der Zug war pünktlich*, is the first of Böll's works, a short story or rather novella, to be published by him independently as a book. It has been almost universally praised by critics for its artistic perfection. The reader follows the protagonist as he boards the train for the front until he is killed in an explosion in Poland. Through the young soldier's interior monologue, the reader learns of his premonition that he will die, and the main function of the plot line (as Conard explains in *Understanding Heinrich Böll*, 1992) is to tell how this prophecy comes true. *Und sagte kein einziges Wort* has a similarly simple structure. Although a novel, it resembles a short story or novella in that it also concentrates on a single, main event and covers a short time-span in the life of the protagonist(s). The story is told from two points of view, those of a husband and wife, who take turns narrating the events of a weekend they spend separately and together. The time and place are the early 1950s, at the beginning of the economic miracle in West Germany, but here Böll emphasizes family values and faith in God.

GRAVES's problems as a translator are evident in both his listed translations. In his 1956 version of the novella *The Train was on Time*, common words are often rendered inaccurately from some misguided sense that they sound better that way in English: thus the version fails to convey subtle nuances of meaning and style. At other times, Graves seems to be at a genuine loss as to the real meaning of idiomatic expressions connected with the games the soldiers play or the songs they sing. Other translations, although accurate, sound strange, archaic, obsolete, especially to the American reader ("entrain", "chum"). More serious is the fact that he does not attempt to clarify references to German history or military equipment, as for example in the case of "Junker" (for a type of plane) or "k.u.k." "kaiserlich und königlich" (used as an adjective – "imperial and royal" – for the time of the Hapsburg empire). He also sometimes alters the original in punctuation, capitalization, and paragraphing, as in the case of the crucial word "bald" ("soon") which Böll has intentionally emphasized. Very importantly, in the last paragraph Graves fails to convey the true meaning of whether the hero is dead or alive, which is the whole point of the story.

Similar problems of awkward or inaccurate renderings are also be found in the novel *Acquainted with the Night* translated by GRAVES (1954). Since it deals with the post-war years and thus is closer to his own time, the vocabulary difficulties are perhaps somewhat lessened. In an attempt at making things easier for the reader, Graves adds the names of the persons from whose viewpoint the narrative originates at the top of each chapter, but this seems scarcely necessary since the two viewpoints alternate consistently throughout the work. Perhaps the greatest flaw is the translation of the title, which means nothing in particular in the work's context. Böll, on the other hand, deliberately took his title, the exact translation of which is "And never said a word", from a Negro Spiritual, referring to Christ's silence on the cross and pointing to the novel's theme (Conard).

SAVILL, who translated Böll's elliptical title "*Wanderer, kommst du nach Spa ...*" as "*Traveller, If You Come to Spa ...*" (1956), also, like Graves above, failed to convey the title's deeper meaning, which points to the theme of this much anthologized short story. The soldier hero or anti-hero is brought seriously wounded to a makeshift military hospital that he eventually recognizes as the site of his old high school, which he had left three months before to go into battle. The half-erased message in the title comes from an ancient Greek inscription by Simonides about the Spartans who had fallen in battle while defending their country. The dying protagonist recognizes that he himself had copied it on the blackboard he sees in front of him. It would have been helpful if the translator had given some hint of its significance in his rendering, as Vennewitz did by translating it: "*Stranger, Bear Word to the Spartans, We ...*" The early translators failed to transmit other historical references, many of them specifically German, and entangled themselves in unfortunate equivalences such as "humanistic college" for "humanistisches Gymnasium" (classical high school). In general, Savill tries to adhere as much as possible to very close translations, thus revealing his insecurity both in the language and in the work's interpretation.

The last novel of the group, apparently again translated by SAVILL (1957), although without credit, has two English titles, one in the UK, *The Unguarded House*, and one in the US, *Tomorrow and Yesterday*. The latter, again, is another unfortunate translation that changes the meaning of the original. It should have become obvious by now to translators of Böll that he did not choose his titles at random, to say the least. In this second of Böll's novels about family values the title refers to two households in which the 11-year-old protagonists grow up as half-orphans, their fathers having been killed in the war. According to Conard, this work marks a turning point for Böll in that the author moves away from strictly personal problems to themes of social justice and personal responsibility. The point of view in the novel is that of the two pre-adolescent boys, which lends a dimension of naiveté to the text and intensifies the contrast with the corrupted adult world around them. As in *And Never Said a Word*, Böll uses memories, smells, songs, propaganda, and advertising slogans as leitmotifs, but here this technique is intensified and the words in question are italicized in the German text. Although it might have been difficult at times for the translator to determine why a word had been italicized, one would expect that he or she would have rendered it faithfully anyway. Savill has, by-and-large, capitalized these words, but his accuracy is not 100 per cent. Occasionally also he totally omits words like "Amis" (slang for the American occupying forces) because he cannot find its English equivalent.

BOWLES's *Billiards at Half-past Nine* (1961) has to be considered by itself because of its uniqueness. Although it was done almost four decades ago, it continues in print as the only English translation of this novel, but the name of the translator never appears in the book. Yet this translation is quite good and accurate and does not display any of the above-mentioned flaws, despite the fact that the original novel is one of Böll's most structurally complex works, considered as constituting a new phase in his experimentation with form. Critics have traced to Faulkner's influence Böll's more complicated approach to narrative perspective, chronology, and multiplicity of characters, as well as the extensive biblical and literary references. As always in Böll's novels, there is also here a tremendous concentration of the narrative present – eight hours of a day in the late 1950s in a West German city, presumably Cologne – but the narrated past expands to cover 50 years of German and family history. It deals with the problems of overcoming the past ("Vergangenheitsbewältigung"), a favorite theme in post-war Germany. The text again abounds in set phrases and significant words that not only serve as leitmotifs but also attain symbolic significance. Although perhaps some of Bowles's equivalences in slang and idiom sound a bit dated, this cannot be considered a fault of the translator but rather a natural consequence of the passing of time and the change in the spoken vernacular.

The next group on the list includes four of Böll's novels from the early 1960s to the late 1970s, which were all translated by Leila VENNEWITZ, Böll's official translator. These are not all the works that she has translated but they constitute some of Böll's major works of the period. They all deal with contemporary problems of West German society, its politics, and religion, which although rooted in time and place have been transcended by the author to become the important issues facing individuals and societies in the latter half of the 20th century anywhere in the world. Vennewitz, who in all four instances translated the novels within about two years of their original publications, seems to feel equally at home in idiomatic German and English, current events, and the world of Böll's imagination. More specifically, in *The Clown* (1963, translated 1965), the earliest of these works, she renders the language from the source to the target with admirable ease. By adding a word here and there, as with "Gottfried" to Böll's "Benn" or "Mountains" to his "Eifel", she manages to explain a perhaps obscure reference to the English speaker.

This ability extends to all her other translations. In the case of *Group Portrait with Lady*, an unusually long work for Böll, with a complex structure, replete with religious as well as tongue-in-cheek references, and above all a multiplicity of characters, VENNEWITZ (1973) renders the (1971) original admirably in all its aspects. In order to facilitate the English-language reader's comprehension she prefaces the text with a list of characters. She has also sought expert advice for more extensive translations from older German poets cited in the text.

The Lost Honor of Katharina Blum; or, How Violence Develops and Where It Can Lead is based loosely on events related to the Baader-Meinhof group and the terrorist activities and precautions of the early 1970s. The narrator calls it a report and its tone is the result of the same technique as in *Group Portrait with Lady* (Conard). By using straightforward language, Böll creates a contrast to the sensationalism of the popular press. This report-style language is conveyed into English by VENNEWITZ (1975) in a very competent way.

In *The Safety Net*, although the author is mainly dealing with a continuation of these same political events and their consequences for individuals, the narrative style goes back to that of Böll's earlier novels, while the structure is more complex than in *The Lost Honor of Katharina Blum*. In order to clarify the multiplicity of characters, VENNEWITZ (1982) again adds a list of them at the beginning. Conard considers translating *The Safety Net* as unusually challenging and even Vennewitz seems to encounter some difficulties here. For one, there is the matter of the translation of the title, which literally means "Protective Siege" and whose connotations are not rendered fully through "Safety Net". Böll's concern with language and his attempt to see West German society through semantics make it very important that the difference in meaning between such similarly-sounding German verbs as "überwachen" ("to have under surveillance") and "bewachen" ("to have under guard") be made totally clear in English. Although Vennewitz has some awkward translations in this work, she still can be relied upon to translate the important distinctions perfectly.

Frauen vor Flusslandschaft was the last work to be published during Böll's lifetime. (In 1992 *Der Engel schwieg* was published posthumously and was translated into English as *The Silent Angel* by Breon Mitchell in 1994; since excerpts of it had appeared as short stories early in Böll's career, it might not be appropriately classified as new.) It is in the format of a play and is appropriately subtitled: *A Novel in Dialogues and Soliloquies*. The characters are presented in a prose introduction and there are chapters instead of acts. The setting is Bonn and the time the mid-1980s. All characters are involved, directly or indirectly, in the then current political situation and this is manipulated by Böll to serve again as a vehicle for his social and political criticism. This novel, which has been turned into a play by Volker Schlöndorff, was translated by MCLINTOCK in 1988 in a very satisfactory manner, from the introductory translation of a Goethe poem to the idiomatic expressions and contemporary jargon.

HERA T. LEIGHTON

Further Reading
Bassnett-McGuire, Susan, *Translation Studies*, London and New York: Methuen, 1980; revised edition, London and New York: Routledge, 1991
Conard, Robert C., *Understanding Heinrich Böll*, Columbia: University of South Carolina Press, 1992
Reid, James Henderson, *Heinrich Böll: A German for His Time*, Oxford: Berg, 1988

Yves Bonnefoy 1923–

French poet, critic and translator

Biography

Born in Tours, 24 June 1923. Bonnefoy studied philosophy and mathematics, and his metaphysical lyricism shows the influence of Hegel and Heidegger on the one hand and Valéry and Jouve on the other. From 1960 he taught in the US as a professor of French literature. In 1981, the year he was made a professor at the Collège de France, he was awarded the Académie Française's Grand Prix for poetry for the ensemble of his work.

Among the best-known of Bonnefoy's poetic productions are *Du Mouvement et de l'immobilité de Douve* (*On the Motion and Immobility of Douve*), 1953, Douve being the name of the beloved whose life and death are the subject of the poem, and *Pierre écrite* (*Words in Stone*), 1965. There are also essays on art and poetry, translations from Shakespeare and other English poets, studies of Baudelaire, Rimbaud, Breton and Jouve and a book on Giacometti (1991).

Translations

Poetry

Du Mouvement et de l'immobilité de Douve, 1953
Kinnell, Galway, *On the Motion and Immobility of Douve* (parallel texts), Athens: Ohio University Press, 1968; Newcastle-upon-Tyne: Bloodaxe Books, 1992

Pierre écrite, 1965
Lang, Susanna, *Pierre écrite/Words in Stone* (parallel texts), Amherst: University of Massachusetts Press, 1976

Poèmes, 1978 and 1982; translated in two companion volumes:
Kinnell, Galway and Richard Pevear, *Early Poems, 1947–1959* (parallel texts), Athens: Ohio University Press, 1991
Pevear, Richard, *Poems 1959–1975* (parallel texts), New York: Random House, 1985

Ce qui fut sans lumière, 1987
Naughton, John, *In the Shadow's Light* (parallel texts), Chicago: University of Chicago Press, 1991

Début et fin de la neige, suivi de Là où retombe la flèche, 1991
Naughton, John and Richard Stamelman, *New and Selected Poems* (parallel texts), edited by John Naughton and Anthony Rudolf, Chicago: University of Chicago Press, 1995; Manchester: Carcanet Press, 1996

Criticism and Art History
Naughton, John (editor), *The Act and the Place of Poetry: Selected Essays*, Chicago: University of Chicago Press, 1989
Stamelman, Richard (editor), *The Lure and the Truth of Painting*, Chicago: University of Chicago Press, 1995

In *Anti-Platon* (*Anti-Plato*), 1947, one of the first of his published works, Yves Bonnefoy establishes an attention to the particular that is to prove continuous within his later poetry: "The question is, *this* object". The polemic of this volume is directed against the pallour of "perfect Ideas". In his stridency, however, Bonnefoy betrays a longing for the same ideal realm with which he declares his disenchantment. The objects found in *Anti-Plato* are things made or fantastically assembled which, without resistance, take us beyond the given order: "a horse's head larger than life encrusted with a whole town".

The uncritical surrealism of this poetic is, it chances, placed *in question* by the English translation of Bonnefoy's too categorical opening proposition: "Il s'agit bien de *cet* objet". The poet has discussed the dilemma of his early writing in *The Act and the Place of Poetry*, believing it caught "between a kind of spontaneous materialism ... and an innate concern with transcendence". Serving as a measure of distance travelled, one of Bonnefoy's most recently translated works, *Début et fin de la neige* ("The Beginning and the End of Snow"), 1991, is concerned rather with the variousness of what is given: a single flake is already "no more / Than a drop of water, lost / In the mist of bodies moving through the snow". Several and singular, snow on the poet's glove is "like this illusion" – of a poppy, held one summer, which "Dreamed the absolute was within the world's reach". The poem's associative circuit places the material and the imaginary in series. Likeness asserts an equivalence between one object, snow, and the no less realized "illusion" of another. It follows that the poppy's dream, illusory or not, is no less continuous with the real and initiating presence of snow. In Bonnefoy's world of analogy, the absolute is intimated in what is finite and actual. The poet describes this experience in an interview appended to *Ce qui fut sans lumière* ("In the Shadow's Light"), 1987: "Dreaming, in poetry, is to stop dreaming."

The translator of Bonnefoy must navigate a similar paradox in turn. The opening lines of "The Lure of the Threshold" ("Dans le leurre du seuil") might be taken to enact the translation process: "But no, once again / Unfolding the wing of the impossible / You awaken". The first premise of such work is supplied by the poet, himself pre-eminent as a translator of Shakespeare and, among others, of Keats, Yeats and Donne: "The answer to the question, 'Can one translate a poem?' is of course no" (*The Act and the Place of Poetry*). In considering his own practice, it is characteristic that Bonnefoy should polarize so absolutely the qualities of source and target language: "As so often when we pass from the language of Shakespeare to French ... lived experience is transformed into the timeless and the irrational into the intelligible". But in attempting the passage between different linguistic orders, the translator reproduces a tension at the heart of poetic language. Just as poetry asserts the presence of "specific utterance" against, but also within, the system of language, so "the language (*langue*) of translation" threatens to paralyze "the actual, tentative utterance (*parole*)" proposed. Bonnefoy writes that the poem, as form, suspends "all relation to what is other and finite", but that every form is merely the trace of some prior and more universal "intention" toward language. Through translation, one form is brought into relation with another – a certain trace is retraced – and this process, like poetry, bears witness to "the effects of finitude on the infinite which is language".

Bonnefoy has observed that the integer of his poetry is the book rather than the lyric, and we are fortunate in having access to all of his major verse collections in parallel text. Some of his prose sequences have received their first publication in this format, and several translators testify to Bonnefoy's moral sponsorship of the labour of translation. Linguistic intimacy and distance command particular attention in these volumes. In his note to *Poems 1959–1975*, Richard PEVEAR (1985) describes the "problem of finding English equivalents of the words *sens*, *vrai* and *parole*", which announce central concerns in the poetry but "do not quite mean 'meaning', 'true' and 'speech'". Susanna LANG (1976) expands on this difficulty with regard to the images in *Pierre écrite*: "it is easy in French to stress the abstract, otherworldly aspects of Bonnefoy's writing, while in English it is more natural to visualize a particular stone in a particular place". Because the network of Bonnefoy's images constitutes "an entire ontology", Lang insists that "these terms must be as consistent in the translation as in the original". Her imperative is not inconsistent with PEVEAR's acknowledgment that, on occasion, the poet has urged a "certain freedom" on his translator, for in seeking its place and orientation in *this* world, Bonnefoy's writing claims its own freedom over and against the ideal of *poésie pure*.

In his essay on "Shakespeare and the French Poet" (*The Act and the Place of Poetry*) Bonnefoy claims that English, poetically mobilized, has "a natural affinity with the Aristotelean critique of Platonic Ideas". This may well be so, but translation is perhaps truest to Bonnefoy's own poetry in dramatizing the inquiry which each of these propositional worlds pursues, through language, into the possibility of the other. Thus LANG renders *Pierre écrite* as *Words in Stone*, whereas PEVEAR (1985) prefers *Written Stone*; the volume's opening sequence is given, respectively, as "Summer of Night" and "The Summer's Night"; and its first poem is cast in two quite different voices. In the case of the main title, each translator seeks to realize the substantive tendency of the attribute *écrite*; each in her or his own way abstracts from the poet's formula in the name of an equivalent concision or concreteness. The translations of "L'été de nuit" are of interest because they put in question just what, of night and summer, belongs to what. And two versions of the volume's initial poem show that, although some mimesis may inform a misconceived closeness to the original (for PEVEAR, as Bonnefoy, the night is "obscure"), other forms of imitation may vividly take the measure of the poem's report: "This evening it seems to me / That we have entered that garden whose door / The unreturning angel closed." LANG here observes the metrical integrity of Bonnefoy's lines even where she chooses not to follow the example of his syntax. The result is a language that preserves an astonished distance in the most intimate detail of its encounter with the world.

The sure voice that sounds through Bonnefoy's astonished writing (another reading of *Pierre écrite*) is an index of all that compels the reader of his verse in French and English. It is also the guarantor of the most consistently reissued of all Bonnefoy translations, Galway KINNELL's (1968) *On the Motion and Immobility of Douve*. The poem's fascination is driven by an unanswerable question concerning the identity of the "Douve" whom it mourns. In learning to live with the futility of this question, we come to recognize the death of Douve as an *event* within, and commensurate with, the life of Douve; and having accepted that "Douve" names this event, it becomes possible to see the life of Douve as an event within the death of Douve. Kinnell's writing neither elaborates nor explicates that of Bonnefoy:

> Presence seized again in the torch of cold, / O watcher always I find you dead, / Douve saying Phoenix I wake in this cold.

Both French and English texts approach what Bonnefoy, in *The Lure and the Truth of Painting*, calls "the realism of the improbable". Their palette is necessarily limited: just as incantation establishes its own materiality, so our sense of Douve's "presence" grows more opaque, or blank, upon each naming. Douve is encountered "at a depth where images will not take", a figure whose presence is observed as a want within language, whose true place is, in a formulation central to *Lure and Truth*, "the *beyond* of what is representable".

The poetics of representation are revisited in "Wind and Smoke", drawn from *La Vie errante* (1993), which in John NAUGHTON's translation (1995) brings *New and Selected Poems* to an end. Here the principal figure is, from first to last, subject to speculation:

> The idea, it was thought, is the measure of everything,
> From which it follows that "la sua bella Elena rapita",
> As Bellori said of a famous painting by Guido Reni,
> Might be compared to that other Helen,
> The one imagined, loved perhaps, by Zeuxis.

The Helen before us is more than once removed, already possessed by those who would picture or interpret her – artists themselves possessed by a single animating "idea" of Helen. Yet the poem, while staging various (and contested) representations of Helen, exists not to arbitrate but to celebrate her transformation. Against the determined lifelikeness of Zeuxis' creation, these Helens, as figural presences, are imagined as living a life beyond even their own possessing. Helen is a figure who escapes her own idea, vanishing "Every time that a poem, / A statue, even a painted image, / Prefers itself as form". The subject of the poem is transformed in turn: "These pages are translated. From a language / That haunts the memory that I am." This language, "Like the very first of our recollections" – memories in, as well as of, infancy – returns the poet to his present being through a sense of having, and more fully, been before. Recalled to being, he becomes that memory; and haunted by the language of being, his writing comes to haunt that language. Translation is thus vital to Bonnefoy's poetry of "presence", for it is the measure of things lost or dead as well as ransomed or reborn. The poem effectively translates from the Italian of Reni, whose "rapita" equivocates finely between rapine and rapture. The English translation is faithful to this spirit, inflecting Bonnefoy's closing proposition ("c'est à croire") with a question that sounds beyond the limit of what is said: "Must we feel: origin is a burning Troy, / Beauty is regretting, art is gathering up / By the handful nothing but absent water?"

IAN FAIRLEY

Further Reading

L'Arc, 66 (1976): special issue
Caws, Mary Ann, *Yves Bonnefoy*, Boston: Twayne, 1984
Gasarian, Gérard, *Yves Bonnefoy: La Poésie, la présence*, Seyssel: Champ Vallon, 1986
Jackson, John E., *Yves Bonnefoy*, Paris: Seghers, 1976; 2nd edition, 1979
Modern Poetry in Translation, new series, 1 (1992): special issue
Naughton, John T., *The Poetics of Yves Bonnefoy*, Chicago: University of Chicago Press, 1984
Stamelman, Richard, *Lost Beyond Telling: Representations of Death and Absence in Modern French Poetry*, Ithaca, New York: Cornell University Press, 1990
Thélot, Jérôme, *Poétique d'Yves Bonnefoy*, Geneva: Droz, 1983
Williams, Adelia V., *The Double Cipher: Encounter between Word and Image in Bonnefoy, Tardieu, and Michaux*, New York: Peter Lang, 1990
World Literature Today, 53/3 (1979): special issue

Wolfgang Borchert 1921–1947

German short-story writer, dramatist and poet

Biography

Born 20 May 1921 in Hamburg. He started on his literary career by working in a bookshop, then as an actor. He was called up in 1940 and fought on the Russian front in the infantry. His time in the army was marked by two periods in prison for criticizing Germany's Nazi leaders, and by his contracting the liver complaint from which he would die. He turned actor again after the war and also worked in cabaret. His lyric poetry was produced mainly between 1940 and 1946, the volume *Laterne, Nacht, und Sterne* [Lamp, Night and Stars] appearing in 1946, but his fame as a writer was achieved through a few works produced 1946–47. His first success was *Die Hundeblume: Erzählungen aus unseren Tagen* [The Dogflower: Tales of Our Times], 1947, and the same year saw not only two more books of stories but also his play, the *Heimkehrer* drama for which he is best known, *Draussen vor der Tür*, 1947 (*The Man Outside*, 1952), whose central character, Beckmann, is an infantryman, orphaned, abandoned by his wife, coming back from the war to seek a place in a devastated society – a symbolic outsider. Borchert died in Basle, Switzerland, 20 September 1947.

Translations

Collection

Das Gesamtwerk, 1949
Porter, David, *The Man Outside: The Prose Works of Wolfgang Borchert*, with a foreword by Kay Boyle and an introduction by Stephen Spender, London and New York: Hutchinson, 1952; reprinted London: Marion Boyars, 1996 (contains all Borchert's works except the poetry)

Play

Draussen vor der Tür, 1947
Fisher, Thomas, *Outside on the Street*, produced 1998
Porter, David, *The Man Outside* in *The Man Outside: The Prose Works of Wolfgang Borchert*, translated by Porter, 1952

Short Stories

Die Hundeblume: Erzählungen aus unseren Tagen, 1947; *An diesen Dienstag*, 1947; *Hundeblumengeschichten*, 1948
Hornsey, A.W., *Wolfgang Borchert: Selected Short Stories*, with an introduction, Oxford: Pergamon Press, and New York: Macmillan, 1964
Porter, David, the stories, in *The Man Outside: The Prose Works of Wolfgang Borchert*, translated by Porter, 1952

Die traurigen Geranien und andere Geschichten aus dem Nachlass, 1962
Hamnett, Keith, *The Sad Geraniums and Other Stories*, New York: Ecco Press, 1973; London: Calder and Boyars, 1974 (contains "The Sad Geraniums", "Late Afternoon", "The Cherries", "The Wood for Morning", "All Dairies Are Called Hirsch", "The Post Crown Tooth", "Dear, Blue-Grey

Night", "The Thunderstorm", "The Wall", "Tui Hoo", "Strange", "Prussia's Glory", "Sunday Morning", "Ching Ling, the Fly", "Mary, It's All Because of Mary", "Marguerite", "Behind the Windows It Is Christmas", "The Professors Know Nothing Too")

Poetry
Laterne, Nacht und Sterne, 1946
Fickert, Kurt J., selections in his *Signs and Portents: Myth in the Work of Wolfgang Borchert, with the Poems in Bilingual Form*, Fredericton, New Brunswick: York Press, 1980

Wolfgang Borchert's most famous work is the play *The Man Outside*. It was first performed in 1947 one day after the author's unfortunate early death. The only published translation is David PORTER's of 1952.

The Man Outside is a powerful work, essentially neo-expressionist in style, portraying the return of a prisoner-of-war to his ruined homeland. Despite the occasionally shrill tone of the play it is nevertheless a fine work of satirical nihilism that captured the mood of post-war Germany.

Porter's translation is adequate, but some factors diminish its general competency. The initial descriptions of the characters of the play are misleading; for example, the Other One becomes the "One who is no one at all" instead of the "One whom everybody knows". The song of Beckmann, the protagonist, exposes Porter's inability to translate verse. He attaches too much importance to his rhyme scheme at the expense of a meaningful rendering of the original. The clumsy effort detracts from the extreme bitterness of the song and distorts its metaphors. Porter's translation contains some rather peculiar errors. He confuses "railway" with "ice rink", and at a crucial point in the play he takes a risk with English idiom that generates obscurity: "a man hurts back" exhibits an unfortunate lack of bite in a sentence that displays Beckmann's attitude to life. Porter's translation is nearly 50 years old and a little dated. Its overall style is restrained where perhaps more freedom and energy are required.

Interest in Borchert's dramatic work was reawakened through the production of his play under the title *Outside on the Street* at the Gate Theatre in London in 1998. The new translation by Thomas FISHER won the Gate Allied Domecq Translation Award and succeeds in preserving both the quality and the faults of the original. Fisher's translation is very well suited to performance and captures the essence of the original in every sense. It is regrettable indeed that this version is not available in print.

PORTER (1952) is more relaxed when translating the short stories, also in his version of the *Gesamtwerk*, and his efforts are considerably more successful. "On That Tuesday" is his finest attempt, and he transmits the meaning nearly perfectly. This is quite an achievement, as the original contains much that is specific to the German language; for example, the storyline consisting of a young schoolgirl's misspelling the German word for "war". The only criticism to be made is of Porter's persistence in creating fluent English sentences as opposed to emphasizing the stylistic devices of Borchert.

A more recent translator of Borchert's short stories, those collected in the posthumous book *The Sad Geraniums*, is Keith HAMNETT (1973). Borchert's stories are short, plotless, and ambiguous. In "The Sad Geraniums" the deliberate lack of punctuation adds to the quality of ambiguity. Hamnett chooses to add inverted commas to indicate speech, thus losing the tension of the prose. In the original it is never clear if it is the speech or the thoughts of the characters we are reading. A similar problem occurs in "Late Afternoon", when Hamnett disrupts the rhythm of the prose by adding punctuation marks where Borchert has none. He also makes a vital mistake in his translation. In "Late Afternoon" Borchert describes a chance meeting of a man and a woman and their eventual parting. The man leaves the woman standing alone. Hamnett has "No, he did not look back" whereas the original has "No, he did look back". As a result the poignancy of the original story is absent from the Hamnett version. The tale "The Wood for Morning" contains a similar crucial mistake. The story consists of the reflections of a suicidal adolescent. On his way to the attic of his parents' house, where he intends to hang himself, he recalls how he gouged a long mark into the wooden handrail. "But I did it", the boy says. Hamnett, however, has him state "I was there when it happened". The reasons for the boy's suicidal thoughts and his feelings of guilt are thus altered considerably.

Hamnett exhibits an urge to add variety where Borchert is more specific and repetitive. "The Cherries" is about a "sick man" and Borchert continues to refer to him as such throughout the story. Hamnett switches between "sick boy" and "invalid". The former is more an interpretation than a translation and the latter has connotations different from those of the word used in the original, and frankly the change is unnecessary.

Unfortunately Hamnett undermines the simplicity of Borchert's stories. Borchert's prose is spare and sometimes even oblique. Hamnett loses this quality, as if he is trying to "sharpen the edges". His translations attempt to sound more poetic than the original, which disrupts even his more successful translation of "All Dairies are Called Hirsch". Borchert is essentially evocative but simple and precise. Yet, for instance, Hamnett uses "reek", which has a negative quality, where Borchert has just "smell" ("The Post Crown Tooth"). Hamnett's apparent analysis of the text and consequent interpretation obscure the power and fine balance of the stories – stories that are, after all, Borchert's finest achievement and surely deserve better.

Though the poems of Borchert have yet to be translated in their entirety into English, some are to be found in German and English in FICKERT's critical commentary *Signs and Portents* (1980).

KATJA KREBS and KEVIN BARTHOLOMEW

Further Reading

Herd, E.W., "Wolfgang Borchert", *German Life and Letters*, 4 (1950–51)
Popper, Hans, "Wolfgang Borchert", in *German Men of Letters*, 3, edited by Alex Natan, London: Oswald Wolff, 1964
Salmon, P.B., introduction to his edition of *Draussen vor der Tür*, London: Harrap, 1963
Warkentin, Erwin J., *Unpublishable Works: Wolfgang Borchert's Literary Production in Nazi Germany*, Columbia, South Carolina: Camden House, 1997
Weimar, K.S., "No Entry, No Exit: A Study of Wolfgang Borchert", *Modern Language Quarterly*, 17 (1956)

Jorge Luis Borges 1899–1986

Argentine short-story writer, poet and essayist

Biography

Born in Buenos Aires, 24 August 1899. He was educated privately at first and knew and used English from childhood. He lived in Switzerland with his family, 1914–21, and during World War I attended the Collège des Beaux Arts in Geneva. He visited Spain in 1918 and returned to Argentina in 1921. He was co-founding editor of two journals, *Proa*, 1924–26 and *Sur*, 1931; and was associated with a third, *Prisma*. In 1932 he met Adolfo Bioy Casares, with whom he was often to collaborate as writer and as editor, sometimes under pseudonyms. Borges had a range of occupations in Buenos Aires: columnist for the weekly journal *El Hogar*, 1936–39; literary adviser for some years to publishers Emecé; municipal librarian from 1939 until the populist Péron regime dismissed him in 1946 and appointed him poultry inspector for Buenos Aires municipal market, 1946–54. Meanwhile he was writing, editing and lecturing; he was president of the Argentine Writers' Society, 1950–53. In 1955 he lost his sight, weak since the 1920s. After Péron was deposed in 1955, Borges was made director of the Argentine National Library, 1955–73. He held several academic appointments in Argentina and the US: Professor of English Literature, University of Buenos Aires, 1955–70; Norton Professor of Poetry, Harvard University and visiting lecturer, University of Oklahoma, 1969. He also received many literary awards and national and academic honours, in Latin America, Spain, the US, the UK, France, Italy, Germany and Israel. Borges was twice married, to Elsa Millan in 1967 (separated in 1970) and in 1986 to María Kodama, with whom he wrote his last book. Died in Geneva, 14 June 1986.

Borges was first published in Spanish avant-garde magazines after World War I. When he went back to Argentina in 1921 he joined the experimental, modernist Ultraismo movement. In the 1920s he wrote essays, poems and a biography. The first of many volumes of poems, sometimes mingled with prose, was *Fervor de Buenos Aires* [Buenos Aires Fervour], 1923. Notable among his many brilliant stories, literary and philosophical essays and genre-breaking pieces are *Historia universal de la infamia* (*A Universal History of Infamy*), 1935; the *Ficciones* (*Fictions*), 1944, which contain the celebrated "Pierre Menard, autor del *Quijote*" ("Pierre Menard, author of *Don Quixote*"); *El Aleph* (*The Aleph*), 1949; and *El libro de arena* (*The Book of Sand*), 1975.

Translations

Collections of Fiction

di Giovanni, Norman Thomas, *The Aleph and Other Stories, 1933–1969*, New York: Avon, 1970

Hurley, Andrew, *Collected Fictions*, New York: Viking, 1998; Harmondsworth: Penguin, 1999

Yates, Donald A. and James E. Irby (editors), *Labyrinths: Selected Stories and Other Writings*, New York: New Directions, 1962, augmented edition, 1964; Harmondsworth: Penguin, 1970 (translations by the editors and others)

Fiction

Historia universal de la infamia, 1935

di Giovanni, Norman Thomas, *A Universal History of Infamy*, New York: Dutton, 1972; London: Allen Lane, 1973

Ficciones, 1944

Kerrigan, Anthony (editor), *Ficciones*, with an introduction, London: Weidenfeld and Nicolson, and New York: Grove Press, 1962; as *Fictions*, London: Calder, 1965

Otras inquisiciones (1937–1952), 1952

Simms, Ruth L.C., *Other Inquisitions, 1937–1952*, Austin: University of Texas Press, 1964; London: Souvenir Press, 1973

El hacedor, 1960

Boyer, Mildred and Harold Morland, *Dreamtigers*, Austin: University of Texas Press, 1964; London: Souvenir Press, 1973

El informe de Brodie, 1970

di Giovanni, Norman Thomas, *Dr Brodie's Report*, New York: Dutton, 1972

Selections of Poetry

Coleman, Alexander (editor), *Selected Poems* (bilingual edition), New York: Viking, 1999

di Giovanni, Norman Thomas (editor), *Selected Poems, 1923–1967* (bilingual edition), New York: Delacorte Press, and London: Allen Lane, 1972

Poetry

Elogio de la sombra, 1969

di Giovanni, Norman Thomas, *In Praise of Darkness* (bilingual edition), New York: Dutton, 1974; London: Allen Lane, 1975

Other Writing

Weinberger, Eliot (editor), *Selected Nonfictions*, translated by Esther Allen, Suzanne Jill Levine and Weinberger, New York: Viking, 1999

As with several writers from Latin America who have reached the English-speaking world through the voice of translators sharing a deep empathy with the author of the originals, Jorge Luis Borges has been introduced to English-speaking audiences by a select number of recurrent names, such as those of James IRBY, Donald YATES, Anthony KERRIGAN, and Norman Thomas DI GIOVANNI. From the position of careful readers and interpreters of the Argentine author's work to the performance of a task of co-creation or rewriting of both the original in a translated version and the original itself in its original language, as is the case with di Giovanni's co-translation with Borges, Borges's interpreters epitomize the threefold function of the translator, namely, as reader, critic, and creator.

No claim can be made that Borges's work took long to be translated into English, as was the case with other Latin

American writers, whose work became known in English long after their originals' publication (e.g. Ernesto Sábato's *Sobre heroes y tumbas*). In fact, Borges's texts entered the international market shortly after their consecration as masterpieces, a process that took place mainly in the 1950s and 1960s, when most of the writer's early pieces (dating from the 1920s and 1930s) began to be republished in Spanish. Actually, most of the translations are based on these second editions, which, in a sense, became inaugural as they were published in a national and international context that acclaimed Borges as a significant writer. Today, almost all of Borges's works, including his last books, are available in English translations, except for his magazine chronicles, reviews and formerly unpublished texts not included in Eliot WEINBERGER's *Selected Non-Fictions* (1999) and some of his early poems not included in di Giovanni's compilation and translation (1970) of Borges's *Selected Poems, 1923–1967* and Alexander Coleman's more recent publication *Selected Poems* (1999).

Discovered and widely acknowledged by academic circles, Borges's work was first translated into English thanks to initiatives by literary journals (e.g. *The Antioch Review*, *Encounter*, *TriQuarterly*, etc.), which published most of the short stories and essays later reproduced in books, as well as to programs and courses at universities (e.g. the University of Texas at Austin), which invited Borges to lecture on literary themes and talk about his work. Later on, the publication of the author's work, in both hard cover and paperback editions, expanded the repertoire of translated texts and contributed, through commentaries and critical introductions to the volumes, to building an image of his work and guiding the reader on the journey through the Borgesian labyrinths.

Anthony KERRIGAN's introduction (1962) to *Ficciones* perhaps summarizes best the image through which Borges's work has penetrated different linguistic and cultural audiences in the West, an image that is usually correlated with the natural and non-problematic reception of the writer's work in cultural contexts other than the Argentine one: his being a cosmopolitan writer. "The work of Jorge Luis Borges is a species of international literary metaphor", states Kerrigan in the opening remarks of his introduction, thus highlighting the so-called universal character of Borges's writing. Owing to this universalism, the reception of this Argentine author, even via a translated version, is considered to pose no difficulties for the reader who shares the western literary and philosophical traditions. Non-problematic seems to be then the translation of a great part of Borges's writings, as can be noticed in the rendition of many of the texts from *Ficciones* and *El Aleph*, especially if compared to the work of other Latin American writers (e.g. the Brazilian writer João Guimarães Rosa or the Cuban Guillermo Cabrera Infante) who make substantial use of local references and experiences as well as intricate patterns of neologisms and linguistic experimentation.

YATES & IRBY's edition (1962, 1964) of writings by Borges under the suggestive title, *Labyrinths*, the labyrinth being a key image in the Argentine writer's discourse, consists in a selection of pieces from several volumes by Borges: *Ficciones*, *El Aleph*, *Discusión*, *Otras inquisiciones* and *El hacedor*. The editors classify the writings into "fictions", a section comprising stories from *Ficciones* and *El Aleph*; "essays", that is, texts of a hybrid nature (fictional and non-fictional), in which Borges explicitly theorizes on philosophical and literary issues (extracted from *Otras inquisiciones* and *Discusión*); and "parables", short pieces that Borges himself had randomly assorted in his volume *El hacedor*. The editors themselves translated most of the writings, a task also shared by John FEIN, Harriet DE ONÍS, Julian PALLEY, Dudley FITTS, and L.A. MURILLO.

KERRIGAN's edition (1962), first published under the original Spanish title, *Ficciones*, appeared simultaneously with YATES & IRBY's *Labyrinths* and offered to the reader another version of some of the stories translated in Yates and Irby's edition. Anthony Kerrigan is the translator of most the pieces, the remaining ones being translated by Alastair REID, Anthony BONNER, Helen TEMPLE, and Ruthven TODD. A comparison of the versions in Yates and Irby's and Kerrigan's editions reveals minor stylistic differences in their renditions, none of them substantially affecting the reader's interpretation of the Borgesian texts.

A more recent translation of some of these fictions is provided by Andrew HURLEY in his *Collected Fictions* (1999). As Ilan Stavans's (1999) review points out, significant changes appear in the new renditions, some of them presumably welcome to the English reader while others may in fact be quite daring. "The fear of sounding too much like his predecessors", says Stavans, "makes him take unwonted routes sometimes, but his command of the language is enrapturing". On the other hand, Stavans points out a "needless verbosity" in the translator's style. As with cases of texts that somehow attain a certain consecration in their translated versions, the earlier translations of Borges's fictions are by now consolidated versions for some English readers, as *The Quixote* in English was, perhaps, a consolidated version for Borges, who felt the original in Spanish "sounded like a bad translation" (in Howard, 1997).

SIMMS's translation (1964) of Borges's "inquisitions", rightly called by the prefacer the first translation of the work into English, similarly reveals a careful rendition of the original, itself a clear example of Borges's most universal prose. The same is the case with BOYER & MORLAND's translation (1964) of *El hacedor* [The Maker], interestingly named *Dreamtigers* in English, as is one of the pieces in the Spanish volume. Actually, the estrangement produced by the use of "dreamtigers" in the original Spanish might be said to be recreated in English, at least partially, by the shift of that suggestive word to the title of the book.

If many of Borges's texts present no major difficulties in their transposition to the English language and, as Kerrigan points out, exemplify the universal character of Borges's creations, some of the writer's texts dealing with specific aspects of Argentine culture seem to demand a more careful approach when being recreated. This approach is the one adopted by DI GIOVANNI (1970, 1972, 1972, 1974), who works upon the so-called local specificity of Borges's work – an intricate map of historical references, family remembrances, and fictional underworlds created by Borges – and elaborates a minutely detailed method of co-translation with the Argentine author, in order to render accurately all historical and local references built into the writings. Di Giovanni is also concerned about Borges's idiosyncratic use of the Spanish language, an aspect that the joint sessions of translation contributed to elucidate.

Di Giovanni's method of translation, as he himself describes it, consists in producing literal renderings of the texts to be translated, which are later worked upon in sessions with Borges, aiming at checking the translator's interpretation of the written text against the author's intentions in choosing the linguistic resources employed. When a second draft is produced, the translator works on it to polish its style and thus obtain a final version. The joint sessions between author and translator, di Giovanni points out, have a bi-directional effect: the original text is rewritten bearing in mind the receiving language and culture, becoming thus a recreation of the text in Spanish, while the new version of the text in English prompts Borges to rewrite the Spanish version. As innumerable fictions by Borges show, original and translation are merely drafts in a never ending writing process. "So far were we from treating the Spanish originals as sacred text", states di Giovanni, "that Borges many times referred to his poems as 'mere rough drafts' for the English versions" (di Giovanni, 1969).

Out of this process of co-creation, accurate and rhythmic versions of Borges's poems in *In Praise of Darkness* were produced. This same translation project also produced English translations of *A Universal History of Infamy*, *Dr Brodie's Report*, a new version of *El Aleph*, and the translation of a compilation of Borges's poems, among them some of his earliest ones, rescued and translated within the context of the unanimous canonization of Borges as an indisputable classic of modern times.

Di Giovanni's method, however, has also been the object of harsh criticism (Howard, 1997), especially in connection with his choice of translation strategies used for the rendition of *Selected Poems* (1972). As some of the translators who took part in this venture have pointed out (see *Simply a Man of Letters*, 1982), the idea of re-creating Borges's poems out of prose versions prepared by di Giovanni himself seemed an odd and highly questionable way of working with poetry. If the method is controversial and the relationship author–translator seems to have shifted at some point in Borges's late years (Howard, 1997), di Giovanni's discursive strategies can be seen from the perspective of translation studies as an individual project of translation based on his particular view of the translation process and of what he considered as ideological constraints influencing Borges's reception by an English-speaking readership. From the perspective of Latin America studies and the dissemination of Latin America literature, di Giovanni has played a significant role in helping to make Borges's work known to English-speaking audiences.

The publication of *Selected Poems* in 1999, edited by Alexander COLEMAN, brings to the scene revised and new renditions of some of the poems published in 1972, some of them having undergone substantial change while others present a few stylistic modifications. Besides modifications of the translations, changes prompted by the revised edition of the poems in Spanish are also introduced. Both di Giovanni's and Coleman's volumes are bilingual editions.

Di Giovanni's dialogues with Borges as well as most of the statements by his other translators (in *Simply a Man of Letters*) clearly reveal one of Borges's particular approaches when dealing with the translation of his work: he was willing to negotiate most of the renditions and sometimes even suggested to his translators lexical choices he himself thought more interesting. Willis Barnstone comments (in *Simply a Man of Letters*), for example, that Borges would rather have terms of Anglo-Saxon origin used in the translation instead of the Latinate or even Spanish counterparts translators would frequently propose. Through some other commentaries we also learn that Borges would readily accept his translators' arguments when a word did not seem a particularly good choice in English. It is enlightening when criticizing the different versions of his works to consider Borges's own appraisals (in *Simply a Man of Letters*) of translations of his poems. He utilized two options: "This is a beautiful translation of a bad poem of mine" and "that is a good translation of a very good poem I once wrote".

ADRIANA S. PAGANO

Further Reading

Barnstone, Willis, *With Borges on an Ordinary Evening in Buenos Aires: A Memoir*, Urbana: University of Illinois Press, 1993

Becco, Horacio Jorge, *Jorge Luis Borges: Bibliografía total (1923–1973)*, Buenos Aires: Casa Pardo, 1973

di Giovanni, Norman Thomas, "On Translating with Borges", *Encounter*, 32/4 (1969) pp. 22–24

di Giovanni, Norman Thomas, "At Work with Borges", *Antioch Review*, 30/3–4 (1970) pp. 290–98

di Giovanni, Norman Thomas, Daniel Halpern and Frank MacShane (editors), *Borges on Writing*, New York: Dutton, 1973; London: Allen Lane, 1974

di Giovanni, Norman Thomas, "A Bad Translation", *Literary Review* (January 1999)

di Giovanni, Norman Thomas, "One Mind at Work: Translating Borges with Borges", *Times Literary Supplement* (11 June 1999)

Foster, David William, *Jorge Luis Borges: An Annotated Primary and Secondary Bibliography*, New York: Garland, 1984

Helft, Nicolás, *Jorge Luis Borges: Bibliografía Completa*, Buenos Aires: Fondo de Cultura Económica de Argentina, 1997 (includes CD-Rom)

Howard, Matthew, "Stranger than Fiction", *Lingua Franca* (June–July 1997)

Manguel, Alberto, "The World, by Jorge", *Observer Review* (3 January 1999)

Simply a Man of Letters: Panel Discussions and Papers from the Proceedings of a Symposium Held at the University of Maine at Orono, Orono: University of Maine at Orono Press, 1982

Stavans, Ilan, "The English Borges", *Times Literary Supplement* (29 January 1999)

Woodall, James, *The Man in the Mirror of the Book: Borges, A Life*, London: Hodder and Stoughton, and New York: Basic Books, 1998

Woodall, James, "Rebirth of the True Georgie", *Guardian*, Saturday Review (16 January 1999)

Sebastian Brant 1457–1521

German poet

Biography

Born in Strasburg in 1457. He studied law at Basel University, and lectured there until 1500; he held municipal positions in Strasburg from 1501. Married Elisabeth Burg in 1485. Died 10 May 1521. Brant wrote and translated much Latin verse, but is remembered for *Das Narrenschiff* (*The Ship of Fools*), 1494, which was extraordinarily popular in his own day.

The Ship of Fools

Das Narrenschiff, 1494

Translations / Adaptations

Barclay, Alexander, *The Shyp of Folys* (bilingual edition), London: Richard Pynson, 1509; edited, with an introduction by T.H. Jamieson, 2 vols, Edinburgh: Paterson, 1874; reprinted New York: AMS Press, 1966

Gillis, William, *The Ship of Fools*, with an introduction by Patricia Ingle Gillis, London: Folio Society, 1971

Watson, Henry, *The Shypp of Fooles*, London: Wynkyn de Worde, 1509

Zeydel, Edwin H., *The Ship of Fools*, with an introduction, New York: Columbia University Press, 1944

Das Narrenschiff, first published in Basel in 1494, is by far Brant's most important work. It is a didactic-satirical poem in octosyllabic rhyming couplets, and is divided into a prologue and 112 short chapters, each of which deals with a particular form of folly that Brant believed to be prevalent in the society of his day. Each chapter is accompanied by a substantial woodcut, which typically illustrates either the folly in a general sense or a specific idea, proverb or exemplum that appears in the chapter.

Das Narrenschiff has not always found favour with modern literary critics, but it was extremely popular in its own day. Already by 1500 it had appeared in Latin, French and Dutch, and no fewer than 16 editions in the original German had been printed by 1519. The first two English versions, by BARCLAY and WATSON, both date from 1509. While they both contain imitations of the original woodcuts, neither could be described as translations of the German *Narrenschiff*. Barclay's work is based primarily on an adaptation of Brant in Latin hexameters published by Jacob Locher in Basel in 1497. Locher's treatment of the *Narrenschiff* is itself free: he omits three chapters, adds some nine more, shortens and amends many, and in various ways provides the work with a specifically humanist gloss. Barclay, with occasional help from a French verse adaptation of Locher by Pierre Rivière (1497), has then proceeded to expand on his source enormously (his text has 14,034 lines as against Locher's 5,672 and Brant's 7,054). In line with his desire to reach a wide and not necessarily sophisticated audience, most of his additions are proverbs, exempla and hortatory "envois", written in Chaucerian stanzas and in generally simple English. This popular homiletic style means that, in spite of the fact that he almost certainly never read Brant's text at first hand, the spirit of Barclay's work is probably closer to that of the original German than to that of Locher's cultivated Latin.

WATSON's version is a less notable achievement than Barclay's. It is an at times almost slavishly literal prose translation of a French prose adaptation by Jehan Drouyn (1498) of Rivière's adaptation of Locher. Watson therefore knew Brant's work only via three intermediaries, each of whom had amended his immediate source in significant ways. Watson, himself, however, evinces no such originality, and the close dependence of his diction on that of Drouyn is readily apparent, for example in such French-sounding chapter headings as "Of subsanatours, colomnyatours and detractours", or indeed "Of the shyp socyale mecanycque".

Given the nature of these precursors, ZEYDEL's claim that his 1944 *Ship of Fools* constitutes the first translation of the text into English is entirely correct. Both his version and the more recent one by GILLIS (1971) seek to reflect the form of Brant's 1494 original, by reproducing both its woodcuts (superbly and at the original size in the case of Gillis) and its poetic structure. This latter, very difficult, task is managed commendably by both. Some rhymes are only approximate (already in the first chapter, for example, Zeydel rhymes "trove" with "love" and Gillis "word" with "horde"), but such infelicities are inevitable, and in any event are regularly perpetrated by Brant himself. Both also stick determinedly to the metre they have chosen. In general, however, Zeydel's verse flows rather more naturally and freely than that of Gillis: again in the first chapter, for example, Gillis's slightly cumbersome "Though I can barely read a word, / I have of books amassed a horde; / Revering them each day I just / Keep volumes free of flies and dust" is less convincing as poetry than Zeydel's "Of splendid books I own no end, / But few that I can comprehend; / I cherish books of various ages / And keep the flies from off their pages". The greater approachability of Zeydel's version no doubt derives in part also from his greater readiness to emulate the racy informality that characterizes some of Brant's own language: terms like "splurge", "I'm number one" and even "bastard" all have more sober equivalents in Gillis.

The desire of both translators to reflect the form of *Das Narrenschiff* self-evidently militates against the accuracy with which they are able to convey its content. Often redundant words are added for reasons of rhyme or metre: in the prolonged extract given above, for example, Zeydel's "pages" and "of various ages", or Gillis's "amassed", "and dust" and "each day" have no direct verbal equivalents in the original. Conversely, of course, many of Brant's words are left untranslated; and the constraints of verse lead also to unusual or archaic lexical features, such as "Dominie", "e'er" or "ay" in Zeydel's first three chapters, or "tongues learnèd", "gowk" or "pelf" in Gillis's. Actual errors resulting from misunderstandings of the original are, however, very few.

Both modern translations are accompanied by worthwhile introductions: Zeydel's is full, reliable and very well informed, whereas that of Gillis (compiled by his wife, Patricia Ingle Gillis) is slighter and less authoritative, but is able to take account of more recent scholarship. Overall, Zeydel's volume in particular still has much to commend it to the English-speaking reader; but an accurate prose translation of *Das Narrenschiff* remains an urgent desideratum.

NIGEL HARRIS

Further Reading

Fraustadt, Fedor, "Über das Verhältnis von Barclays Ship of Fools zur lateinischen, französischen und deutschen Quelle" (dissertation), University of Breslau, 1894

Pompen, Aurelius, *The English Versions of The Ship of Fools: A Contribution to the History of the Early French Renaissance in England*, London and New York: Longman, 1925; reprinted New York: Octagon Books, 1967

See also Zeydel's introduction (especially pp. 24–31) and Jamieson's introduction to Barclay

---

Bertolt Brecht 1898–1956

German dramatist, critic, novelist and poet

Biography

Born Eugen Berthold Friedrich Brecht, in Augsburg, Bavaria, 10 February 1898. His father was sales director of a paper works. He went to school in Augsburg, 1904–17, and then studied medicine at Munich University. Towards the end of World War I he was an orderly for a few months in a military hospital. He married for the first time in 1922 (Marianne Zoff; divorced 1927; one daughter); for the second time in 1929 (Helene Weigel, the actress, who was later to direct his Berliner Ensemble; one son, one daughter); and had various affairs. He began to acquire his Marxist views in the late 1920s. Between 1924 and 1933 Brecht was in Berlin, writing, and working with his own theatre group and in collaboration with the composer Kurt Weill; for a short time he was with Max Reinhardt's Deutsches Theater. Brecht produced many of his most important works, in several genres, after leaving Germany in 1933 at the beginning of the Nazi regime. He moved around in Scandinavia (1933–41) before going on via Soviet Russia and Persia to the US, where he lived from 1941 to 1947. He had been deprived of his German citizenship in 1935. In 1947 he went to Switzerland, staying until 1949. In 1949 he went to live in East Berlin, where he formed his Berliner Ensemble. In 1950 he took Austrian citizenship. In 1955 he received the Stalin Peace prize in Moscow. Died of a heart attack, East Berlin, 14 August 1956.

Brecht wrote some 36 plays for the stage and several for radio and the cinema, as well as theoretical works, fiction and verse, generally based on his Marxist views.

Brecht's great international reputation and influence come from the special form of illusionless epic drama that he evolved, aimed at the "alienation" or "distancing" of the audience ("Verfremdungseffekt") from the significant moments of time depicted on the stage, in order that the didactic message should be received objectively. Most of his important works have been translated at least once on both sides of the Atlantic. *Trommeln in der Nacht* (*Drums in the Night*), an anti-war play, was his first public success. With two other plays it won him the Kleist prize in 1922.

Brecht's best-known plays are: *Baal*, 1922 (*Baal*, 1964); *Trommeln in der Nacht*, 1922 (*Drums in the Night*, 1966); *Im Dickicht der Stadt*, 1927 (*In the Jungle of Cities*, 1957); *Mann ist Mann*, 1927 (produced 1926) (*A Man's a Man*, 1961); *Das Elefantenkalb*, 1927 (*The Elephant Calf*, 1964); *Die Dreigroschenoper*, 1929 (produced 1928) (*The Threepenny Opera*, 1958); *Aufstieg und Fall der Stadt Mahagonny*, 1929 (produced 1930) (*The Rise and Fall of the City of Mahagonny*, 1976); *Der Jasager/Der Neinsager*, 1931 (produced 1930) (*He Who Says Yes/He Who Says No*, 1977); *Die Massnahme*, 1931 (produced 1930) (*The Measures Taken*, 1960); *Die heilige Johanna der Schachthöfe*, 1932 (produced 1959) (*Saint Joan of the Stockyards*, 1956); *Die Ausnahme und die Regel*, 1938 (*The Exception and the Rule*, 1965); *Furcht und Elend des Dritten Reichs*, 1945 (produced 1938) (*The Private Life of the Master Race*, 1944); *Der kaukasische Kreidekreis*, 1949 (produced 1948) (*The Caucasian Chalk Circle*, 1948); *Mutter Courage und ihre Kinder*, 1949 (produced 1941) (*Mother Courage and Her Children*, 1941); *Herr Puntila und sein Knecht Matti*, 1950 (produced 1948) (*Mr Puntila and His Man Matti*, 1977); *Der gute Mensch von Sezuan*, 1953 (produced 1943) (*The Good Woman of Setzuan*, 1948); *Galileo*, 1955 (produced 1943) (*Galileo*); *Der aufhaltsame Aufstieg des Arturo Ui*, 1957 (produced 1958) (*The Resistible Rise of Arturo Ui*, 1976); *Die Sieben Todsünden der Kleinbürger*, 1959 (produced 1933) (*The Seven Deadly Sins of the Petty Bourgeoisie*, 1979).

Translations

Collection of Plays

Willett, John and Ralph Manheim (editors), *Collected Plays*, London: Methuen, 8 vols, 1970–89; New York: Pantheon, 9 vols, 1971–91 (these editions contain, with variations in a few titles and in the arrangement of volume contents, vol. 1: *Baal*, translated by Peter Tegel; *Drums in the Night*, translated by John Willett; *In the Jungle of Cities*, translated by Gerhard Nellhaus; *The Life of Edward II of England*, translated by Jean Benedetti; *A Respectable Wedding*, translated by Jean Benedetti; *The Beggar; or, The Dead Dog*, translated by Michael Hamburger; *Driving Out a Devil*, translated by Richard Greenburger; *Lux in Tenebris*, translated by Eva Geisel and Ernest Borneman; *The Catch*, translated by John Willett; vol. 2: *Man Equals Man*, translated by Gerhard Nellhaus; *The Elephant Calf*; translated by Gerhard Nellhaus; *The Threepenny Opera*, translated by Ralph Manheim and John Willett; *The Rise and Fall of the City of Mahagonny*, translated by W.H. Auden and Chester Kallman; *The Seven Deadly Sins of the Petty Bourgeoisie*, translated by W.H. Auden and Chester Kallman; vol. 3: *Saint Joan of the Stockyards*, translated by Ralph Manheim; vol. 4: *Fear and Misery in the Third Reich*; *Señora Carrar's Rifles*; vol. 5: *Mother Courage and Her Children*, *The Life of Galileo*, and *Mr Puntila and His Man Matti*, translated by John Willett; *The Trial of Lucullus*; vol. 6: *The Good Person of Szechuan* and *The Resistible Rise of Arturo Ui*, translated by Ralph Manheim; vol. 7: *The Visions of Simone Machard*, translated by Hugh and Ellen Rank; *Schweyk in the Second World War*, translated by William Rowlinson; *The Caucasian Chalk Circle*, translated by James and Tania Stern, with W.H. Auden; *The Duchess of Malfi*; vol. 8: *The Days of the Commune*; vol.9, Adaptations (US edition only): *The Tutor*; *Coriolanus*; *The Trial of Joan of Arc at Rouen, 1431*; *Don Juan*; *Trumpets and Drums*)

Selections of Plays

Bentley, Eric and Maja Bentley, *Parables for the Theater: Two Plays*, Minneapolis: University of Minnesota Press, 1948 (contains *The Good Woman of Setzuan*, *The Caucasian Chalk Circle*); revised by Eric Bentley, as *Parables for the Theatre*, with an introduction by Eric Bentley, New York: Grove Press, 1961, London: Penguin, 1966

Bentley, Eric (editor), *Seven Plays by Bertolt Brecht*, with an introduction, New York: Grove Press, 1961 (contains *In the Swamp (=Jungle of the Cities)*, *A Man's a Man*, *Mother Courage and Her Children*, *The Good Woman of Setzuan*, all translated by Eric Bentley; *The Caucasian Chalk Circle*, translated by Eric and Maja Bentley; *Saint Joan of the Stockyards*, translated by Frank Jones; *Galileo*, translated by Charles Laughton)

Bentley, Eric and Martin Esslin, *Baal, A Man's a Man, and The Elephant Calf: Early Plays*, New York: Grove Press, 1964

Bentley, Eric, Frank Jones and John Willett, *Plays*, vol. 2, London: Methuen, 1962 (contains *Mother Courage and Her Children*, translated by Bentley; *Saint Joan of the Stockyards*, translated by Frank Jones; *The Good Person of Szechwan*, translated by John Willett)

Bentley, Eric, *The Jewish Wife and Other Short Plays*, New York: Grove Press, 1965 (contains *In Search of Justice*, *The Informer*, *The Elephant Calf*, *The Measures Taken*, *The Exception and the Rule*)

Jones, Frank and Anselm Hollo, *Jungle of Cities and Other Plays*, New York: Grove Press, 1966 (contains *Jungle of* Cities, translated by Hollo; *Drums in the Night*, translated by Jones; *Roundheads and Peakheads*, translated by N. Goold Verschoyle)

Mueller, Carl R. *et al.*,The *Measures Taken, and Other Lehrstücke*, London: Eyre Methuen, 1977 (contains *The Measures Taken*, translated by Mueller; *The Exception and the Rule*, translated by Ralph Manheim; *He Who Says Yes/He Who Says No*, translated by Wolfgang Sauerlander)

Stern, James and Tania Stern *et al.*, *Plays*, vol. 1, London: Methuen, 1960 (contains *The Caucasian Chalk Circle*, translated by James and Tania Stern with W.H. Auden; *The Threepenny Opera*, translated by Eric Bentley and Desmond Vesey; *The Trial of Lucullus*, translated by H.R. Hays; *The Life of Galileo*, translated by Desmond Vesey)

Plays

Die Dreigroschenoper, 1929, produced 1928

MacDiarmid, Hugh, *The Threepenny Opera*, London: Methuen, 1973

Happy End, produced 1929

Feingold, Michael, *Happy End: A Melodrama with Songs*, lyrics by Brecht; music by Kurt Weill; based on an unknown original German play by a pseudonymous Dorothy Lane, London and New York: Methuen, 1982

Aufstieg und Fall der Stadt Mahagonny, 1929, produced 1930

Auden, W.H. and Chester Kallman, *The Rise and Fall of the City of Mahagonny*, Boston: Godine, 1976; with *The Seven Deadly Sins of the Bourgeoisie*, London: Methuen, 1979

Die heilige Johanna der Schachthöfe, 1932, produced 1959

Jones, Frank, *Saint Joan of the Stockyards*, Bloomington: Indiana University Press, 1970; London: Eyre Methuen, 1976

Die Mutter, 1932

Gooch, Steve, *The Mother*, London: Methuen, 1978

Die Ausnahme und die Regel, 1938

Manheim, Ralph, *The Exception and the Rule*, London: Methuen, 1977

Furcht und Elend des Dritten Reichs, 1945, produced 1938

Bentley, Eric and Maja Bentley, *The Private Life of the Master Race*, New York: New Directions, 1944; London: Gollancz, 1948

Der kaukasische Kreidekreis, 1949, produced 1948

See entry on *The Caucasian Chalk Circle*, below

Mutter Courage und ihre Kinder, 1949, produced 1941

Bentley, Eric, *Mother Courage and Her Children*, New York: Doubleday, 1955; London: Methuen, 1962

Herr Puntila und sein Knecht Matti, 1950, produced 1948

Willett, John, *Mr Puntila and His Man Matti*, London: Methuen, 1977, revised edition, 1987; New York: Arcade, 1997

Der gute Mensch von Sezuan, 1953, produced 1943

Hofmann, Michael, *The Good Person of Sichuan*, London: Methuen, 1989 (National Theatre version based on the "Santa Monica version")

Galileo, 1955, produced 1943

Brenton, Howard, *The Life of Galileo*, London: Eyre Methuen, 1980

Vesey, Desmond I., *The Life of Galileo*, London: Methuen: 1963

Die Sieben Todsünden der Kleinbürger, 1959, produced 1933

Auden, W.H. and Chester Kallman, *The Seven Deadly Sins of the Bourgeoisie*, with *The Rise and Fall of the City of Mahagonny*, London: Methuen, 1979

Selections of Poetry

Berger, John and Anna Bostock, *Poems on the Theatre*, Lowestoft, Suffolk: Scorpion Press, 1961

Hays, H.R., *Selected Poems* (bilingual edition), with an introduction, New York: Reynal and Hitchcock, 1947; London: Evergreen, 1959

Willett, John and Ralph Manheim (editors), *Poems 1913–1956*, London: Methuen, 1976; New York: Methuen, 1979 (translators include Martin Esslin, Michael Hamburger, H.R. Hays, Frank Jones, Ralph Manheim, Christopher Middleton, Stephen Spender, John Willett)

Willett, John (editor and translator), *Poems and Songs from the Plays*, London: Methuen, 1990

Poetry

Hauspostille, 1927

Bentley, Eric, *Die Hauspostille: Manual of Piety* (bilingual edition), New York: Grove Press, 1966

Selection of Stories

Knapp, Yvonne, Hugh Rorrison and Antony Tatlow, *Short Stories 1921–1946*, edited by John Willett and Ralph Manheim, London: Methuen, 1983

Stories

Der Dreigroschenroman, 1934

Vesey, Desmond I., verse translated by Christopher Isherwood, *A Penny for the Poor*, London: Hale, 1937, New York: Hillman Curl, 1938; as *Threepenny Novel*, New York: Grove Press, 1956, London: Hanison, 1958

Kalendergeschichten, 1948

Knapp, Yvonne and Michael Hamburger, *Tales from the Calendar*, London: Methuen, 1961

Other Writing

Schriften zum Theater, 1957

Willett, John, *Brecht on Theatre: The Development of an Aesthetic*, London: Methuen, and New York: Hill and Wang, 1964; 2nd edition, 1978

Dialoge aus dem Messingkauf, 1964

Willett, John, *The Messingkauf Dialogues*, London: Methuen, 1965

Arbeitsjournal, 1973

Rorrison, Hugh, *Journals 1934–1955*, London: Methuen, 1993

Tagebücher 1920–22, 1975

Willett, John, *Diaries 1920–1922*, edited by Herta Ramthun, London: Eyre Methuen, and New York: St Martin's Press, 1979

Letters

Manheim, Ralph, *Bertolt Brecht Letters*, edited by John Willett, London: Heinemann, and New York: Routledge, 1990

In the English-speaking world Bertolt Brecht's writing has often attracted such epithets as "doctrinaire", "didactic", "Teutonic", "heavy", or simply "boring". To what extent this can be blamed on the translations – rather than on ideological resistance by the audience to the challenge to draw their own conclusions from the dramatic situations – is difficult to establish, since he has been quite well served by his translators. The two waves of translation – from the 1940s to the 1960s in the US, chiefly by Eric BENTLEY, and from the 1960s to the 1980s in the UK, chiefly by John WILLETT (or under his editorship) – provide an interesting contrast, illustrating differences between the two countries and changes in socio-political context, such as that which took place between Brecht's appearance before the House Un-American Activities Committee in 1947 and the visit of the Berliner Ensemble to London in 1956, the same year as John Osborne's *Look Back in Anger*, which heralded a period of experimentation within the British theatre. Taking as an example *Mother Courage and Her Children*, possibly – after *The Threepenny Opera* – the most often performed of Brecht's plays in English, we might compare Bentley's 1955 version with Willett's 1980 translation of the play (in vol. 5 of WILLETT & MANHEIM (editors), *Collected Plays*.

The first problem that the translator encounters in dealing with Brecht's writing is the nature of the language employed. WILLETT tackles the key problem of the uniqueness of the language of the play – "the invention of a major poet who chose neither to imitate 17th-century dialogue nor to reproduce modern everyday speech" – by using "a somewhat analogous artificial diction, based this time on those north English cadences which can reflect a similarly dry, gloomily humorous approach to great events" (introduction). Willett's decision inevitably comes up against the problem of social differences between German- and English-speaking culture, in that dialect is more a geographical marker and less a social class marker in Germany than in Britain (or the US). Any English dialect would therefore tend to overemphasize the demotic aspect of the dialogue. Given that the language of the play is largely proletarian, it would nevertheless seem reasonable to translate the play into an English dialect, the only inhibiting factor being the limited intelligibility of that dialect for non-dialect speakers, particularly American audiences. A "toned-down" version of a widely known dialect would therefore seem to be called for. Typical of the "naturalistic" language employed by Willett are the clipped, elliptical sentences, the reduction of the definite article ("t' "), the use of eye-dialect ("d'you"), "me" for "my", "nowt" for "nothing" and "any road" for "anyway". The only objection that could be made to these is on the level of association. The effect of the original South German speech is one likely to summon up the image of a rural, peasant or small-town community in keeping with the first half of the 17th century, whereas the use of Northern English speech suggests the urbanized areas of the 19th century, closer to the setting for John Arden's *Serjeant Musgrave's Dance* (1959). Arden's play was probably written under the influence of BENTLEY's version of *Mother Courage and Her Children*, the only translation widely available at the time. Indeed, it is most likely that Willett in his turn was influenced by Arden's play, particularly its Northern locale, in his decision to choose dialect for his own version of Brecht's play.

Archaism by contrast is something almost entirely missing

from Bentley's 1955 translation of the play. Bentley, who had collaborated with Brecht on the production and publication of the plays in the US, chose to put his version into a sort of slang or mid-Atlantic colloquial speech. The disadvantage of this is that nothing dates quite as much as slang, e.g. Bentley's use of "riff-raff". In addition, American slang has associations with a world rather remote from 17th-century Central Europe, e.g. "a barman", "your little spiel", "smart fella", "take a slug", "sons of bitches". Such terms would be quite at home in the Chicago of Brecht's version of *Saint Joan* or *Arturo Ui*. However, to say that they do not belong in "a chronicle of the Thirty Years War" would be to deny Brecht's injunctions to make his *Lehrstücke* (didactic plays) relevant to ever wider audiences. Such "alienation effects" are after all entirely in keeping with his dramatic theory.

One of the problems that both dialect and slang versions had to grapple with is finding equivalents for the many proverbial and down-to-earth (though not always traditional) folk sayings that Brecht put into the mouths of most of his characters. An analysis of these would suggest that Bentley decided generally to follow Brecht's imagery, though there are exceptions. It could be argued that Bentley was encouraged to stick to Brecht's imagery by similarities of idiom between German and American usage, e.g. "make money like hay" (Willett: "make a mint of money"). Bentley, despite being English-born, exhibits a rather American tendency to euphemism: "you cheated me" (Willett: "you've put me in shit-creek"), but both translators come up with equally adequate equivalents to the familiar quotation from *Götz von Berlichingen* (Bentley: "Oh, shove it up!"; Willett: "Oh stuff it.").

Much of the power of Brecht's writing comes from the juxtaposition of registers: religious and profane, demotic and poetic, e.g. Mother Courage's uncharacteristic outburst when pleading against her son's recruitment (Willett: "Oh, wretched mother that I am, o pain-racked giver of birth! Shall he die? Aye, in the springtime of life he is doomed."). The intertextuality is here surely broad pastiche of classical style, which both Willett and Bentley have rendered with "equivalent" echoes from their own culture, presumably from "music-hall" Shakespeare. The allusions to other writers, from Grimmelshausen to Goethe, who may or may not be familiar to members of an English-speaking audience, present a particular challenge to the translator focused on audience response. This may seem ironic in the case of references to English-language writing whose "foreignness" within the original text needs to be "marked" in some way as "back translation". Writing about Brecht's "English Aspect", however, Willett describes how "close to us" Brecht's German is, with "its English models: Kipling, Tin Pan Alley, Waley, the great Elizabethans, and even the common-or-garden thriller, its occasional hint of Whitman". Translating "Das Lied vom Weib und dem Soldaten", Willett comes near to Kipling with the line: "So it's down to the south and then northwards once more", where Bentley's "From the north to the south I shall march through the land" is more reminiscent of Masefield than of Kipling. Brecht's songs in general – whose form in translation is often dictated by the rhythm of the well-known tunes of Kurt Weill, Hanns Eisler and Paul Dessau – benefit from his familiarity with the "catchy" quality of Anglo-American popular music.

As always, the effect of a production on a particular audience, its "performability", rather than any faithfulness to the "doctrine" of "Epic Theatre", is paramount in any consideration of Brecht either in English or in German: the text is an ongoing process, not a finished product. Right from the start there was a certain instability about the text, since the "original" *Mutter Courage und ihre Kinder* was revised several times by Brecht. Bentley was using an early edition of the play for his own translation before the standard Suhrkamp edition appeared. In the introduction to his translation (1948) of *Parables for the Theatre* he argues that: "Perhaps all good foreign plays should be published first in a very literal translation, and subsquently in various attempts at a true equivalent, even, if necessary, in 'adaptations' ". It is significant therefore that the Royal Shakespeare Company in 1984–85 used neither Bentley's nor Willett's version for their production of *Mother Courage*, but commissioned, not exactly a "literal" text, more an "adaptation" (by Hanif Kureishi but unpublished) into Cockney, the *lingua franca* of the "punk subculture". Indeed the influence of Brechtian ideas in the UK and the US has probably been less through the letter of his texts than through the spirit of his theatrical practice (disseminated for example by WILLETT's translation *Brecht on Theatre* (1964) and his numerous writings on Brecht). It is interesting by contrast to note the lack of impact in the US and the UK of Brecht's poems (variously but well translated under the editorship of WILLETT & MANHEIM, 1976). Less attractive to audiences in the English-speaking theatre than the theatrical practice and techniques has been the sought-for political impact of Brecht's writing, and one has always to be aware of the possibility of ideological "spin" in the mediation of Brecht's writing through translation as in performance, e.g. emphasis on the pathos of "Mother Courage" and omission of "and her Children" from the title. The play should now call to mind not only the two world wars, but also the question whether the "hyaena of the battlefield" is still roaming the small-scale wars of our age. The collapse of the Communist régimes in Eastern Europe, including the GDR, may well herald a renewal of interest in Brecht's writing in a period when (arguably) the naked exploitation portrayed in Brecht's plays is becoming a lived reality for millions of people, some of them in the English-speaking world.

ANTHONY MATHEWS

Further Reading

Arden, John, *Serjeant Musgrave's Dance: An Un-Historical Parable*, London: Methuen, 1960; New York: Grove Press, 1962

Bentley, Eric, "The Influence of Brecht", in *Re-interpreting Brecht: His Influence on Contemporary Drama and Film*, edited by Pia Kleber and Colin Visser, Cambridge and New York: Cambridge University Press, 1990

Esslin, Martin, "Brecht and the English Theatre" in his *Brief Chronicles: Essays on Modern Theatre*, London: Maurice Temple-Smith, 1970

Jacobs, Nicholas and Prudence Ohlsen (editors), *Bertolt Brecht in Britain*, with an introduction by John Willett, London: TQ Publications, 1977

Lyon, James K., *Bertolt Brecht in America*, Princeton, New Jersey: Princeton University Press, 1980

Willett, John, *Brecht on Theatre*, London: Methuen, and New York: Hill and Wang, 1964

Willett, John, *The Theatre of Bertolt Brecht: A Study from Eight Aspects*, London: Methuen, and New York: New Directions, 1959; 4th edition, London: Methuen, 1977

Willett, John, introduction to *Bertolt Brecht: Mother Courage and Her Children: A Chronicle of the Thirty Years War*, London: Methuen, 1980

Willett, John, "Ups and Downs of British Brecht", in *Re-interpreting Brecht: His Influence on Contemporary Drama and Film*, edited by Pia Kleber and Colin Visser, Cambridge and New York: Cambridge University Press, 1990

See also the introductions to Bentley, *Seven Plays ...*, 1961, and *Parables for the Theatre*, 1961, 1966; Hofmann, *The Good Person of Sichuan*, 1989

The Caucasian Chalk Circle

Der kaukasische Kreidekreis, 1949, produced 1948

The Caucasian Chalk Circle, generally counted among Brecht's greatest works, presents in a flash-back play within a play a complex parable on ownership, in which the fate of an abandoned child is worked out through conflict between threatening misfortunes and the persevering efforts of a peasant girl, and resolved in a sort of judgement of Solomon, a tug-of-love staged within a chalked-out ring and won by the peasant girl against the undeserving claim of the child's upper-class birth mother.

Edition

Der kaukasische Kreidekreis in *Sinn und Form: Sonderheft Bertolt Brecht*, Potsdam, 1949; in *Versuche*, Heft 13, Berlin, Frankfurt: Suhrkamp, 1954; revised edition, 1955

Translations

Bentley, Eric and Maja Bentley, *The Caucasian Chalk Circle* in *Parables for the Theater: Two Plays*, Minneapolis: University of Minnesota Press, 1948 (also includes *The Good Woman of Setzuan*); revised by Eric Bentley in *Parables for the Theatre*, with an introduction by Eric Bentley, New York: Grove Press, 1961, London: Penguin, 1966; also in *Seven Plays by Bertolt Brecht*, edited by Eric Bentley, New York: Grove Press, 1961 (includes the Prologue)

Stern, James and Tania Stern, with W.H. Auden, *The Caucasian Chalk Circle*, London: Methuen, 1963 (the last act of an earlier version was published in *Kenyon Review*, 1946)

As Eric Bentley observes in his introduction to the revised 1966 Penguin edition of *The Caucasian Chalk Circle*: "One has always to ask of a Brecht translation what German text it is based on, since Brecht himself was forever changing what he wrote". This is true generally of Brecht's prolific output and it is particularly true of his plays. There are a number of bibliographies of Brecht's work in German but there is a serious lack of a reliable bibliography of English translations of his plays that gives full details of translators, publishers and place and date of publication together with a clear indication of the original German source that is being used.

The problems created by this situation are exemplified by the case of his last major play, *The Caucasian Chalk Circle*. Brecht completed a first draft of the text in America in June 1944 and immediately proceeded to a second draft which was finished later that year. In the process a number of manuscripts and typescripts were produced. The first German publication of the play is based on the second draft of 1944. During rehearsals for the German premiere in 1954 with the Berliner Ensemble, directed by Brecht himself, he made a number of changes, albeit relatively small ones. This provides the 1954 published text. Further revisions were carried out for the 1955 edition, which is now generally regarded as the standard one. Eric Bentley obtained a manuscript in 1945 which he describes as being "in substantially the form" of the first German publication. Eric BENTLEY's first translation with MAJA BENTLEY was published in America in 1948. So, rather curiously, the first English-language version actually appeared in print before the first German one. One part of Brecht's manuscript was translated but not published in 1948. As Bentley explains in the Penguin introduction to *Parables for the Theatre*: "The only significant omission from the book at that time was that of the Prologue to *The Caucasian Chalk Circle*. For the manuscript was delivered to the publishers at about the time of Brecht's appearance before the House Un-American Activities Committee in Washington (October 1947). It was on advice from him that the appearance of this prologue was postponed". The prologue is set in a Caucasian village in the Soviet Union towards the end of World War II and presents an idealized image of Soviet society. The BENTLEY & BENTLEY translation of the prologue was first published in the *Tulane Drama Review* in 1959 and included in the 1961 Grove Press edition. Bentley's revised translation then appeared in 1966, but the changes to his first version are insignificant.

Brecht had originally wanted W.H. Auden to do a translation, and a copy of the first draft of the play was sent to him in 1944. Auden collaborated with James and Tania Stern who did a rough, preliminary version. Auden himself translated the songs and verses. In 1946 the *Kenyon Review* printed the last act. The rest of this script was never published.

In 1959 Auden and the Sterns agreed to do a completely revised translation for Methuen, who had started publishing a collected edition of Brecht's plays in English. For this purpose they used the 1955 standard German edition, and their new version was first published in 1960. Again Auden was responsible for the songs and the Sterns for the dialogue. As a result the STERN & AUDEN translation differs from Bentley in a number of respects. Most of these differences are minor but a few are more substantial. For the 1955 German edition Brecht redesignated the Prologue as Act 1, with slightly revised introductory stage-directions. Consequently the original Acts 1 to 5 were renumbered Acts 2 to 6. In his 1954 production with the Berliner Ensemble he introduced an important new episode of some five pages to illustrate the determination and inventiveness of one of the main characters, the servant-girl Grusche, whose devotion is contrasted with the snobbish greed of two rich ladies. The scene appears in Stern & Auden but is, naturally, not present in Bentley.

Probably the main challenge for translators of Brecht's dramatic work is the fact that many of them contain songs and verses. In *The Caucasian Chalk Circle* one of the major roles is that of the Singer, backed up by a Chorus of musicians. He is a prime manifestation of Brecht's famous epic theatre and

"Verfremdungseffekt" (alienation-effect). Sometimes his songs provide a linking narrative between the episodic scenes and sometimes they comment on the main action and themes of the play.

Bentley usually tries to remain fairly close to the original while Auden tends towards rather freer renderings. As Auden wrote to James Stern in a letter of October 1959, "My practice is to read the original first for its meaning (my German is much better now) and then put the original out of my head and re-create". The very first song aptly illustrates the difference. Bentley produces for the first half of the song:

In olden times, in a bloody time,
There ruled in a Caucasian city –
Men called it City of the Damned –
A Governor.
His name was Georgi Abashwili.
He was rich as Croesus
He had a beautiful wife
He had a healthy baby.

Auden writes:

Once upon a time
A time of bloodshed
When this city was called
The city of the damned
It had a Governor.
His name was Georgi Abashvili
Once upon a time.
He was very rich
He had a beautiful wife
He had a healthy child
Once upon a time.

Bentley reproduces the German text very faithfully. Auden divides the song into sections, shortens the lines and introduces the phrase: "Once upon a time". Bentley is more accurate but Auden catches Brecht's rhythmical patterns more successfully. His "Once upon a time" also appropriately reflects the aura of fairytale and legend that envelops the play.

For the needs of the general reader most translations of Brecht convey his essential dramatic qualities and the particular flavours of his work. But when, as is frequently the case, there is more than one translation available, any reader who has a scholarly or research interest should always be alert to the possibility that these versions may be drawn from different German sources, a circumstance that might help to explain apparent discrepancies.

BERNARD ASHBROOK

Further Reading

Esslin, Martin, *Brecht: A Choice of Evils*, 4th edition, London: Methuen, 1984
Willett, John, *The Theatre of Bertolt Brecht*, 4th edition, London: Methuen, 1977
Willett, John, *Brecht in Context: Comparative Approaches*, London and New York: Methuen, 1984

See also Eric Bentley's introduction to *Parables for the Theatre*, 1961, 1966

André Breton 1896–1966

French poet, novelist and essayist

Biography

Born in Normandy, 19 February 1896, to a family in modest circumstances. He grew up and went to school mainly in and near Paris. In World War I he was called up (1915) and, being a medical student, served as an auxiliary in various neuropsychiatric hospitals. For a while Breton belonged to the circle of Guillaume Apollinaire, but Apollinaire died in 1918. Breton became interested in Tristan Tzara's Dadaist group, of which he remained a member until 1922, by which time he had given up medicine for literature. He made eminent friends among writers, artists and the intelligentsia in general. In Vienna in 1921 he met Freud, whose theories would nourish the Surrealist interest in dreams and the subconscious mind. He also met the exiled Trotskii and at one time was a member of the Communist Party. During World War II he lived in the US.

In Breton's creative work the distinctions between genres and between prose and verse are not always discernible. His highly imaged language and autonomously changing forms embody themes that range from the personal (especially concerning the nature and power of love) through the aesthetic to the socio-political. Among his best-known poetic works is *Les Champs magnétiques* (1920), a collection of pieces informed by his theories on automatic writing, composed in collaboration with Philippe Soupault and published in *Littérature*, the review they and Aragon had founded in 1919. *Poisson soluble* appeared in 1924 and was followed by various collections of verse and important single poems such as *L'Union libre* (1931) and the *Ode à Charles Fourier* (1947). A prose quartet was made up of the novel *Nadja* (1928), *Les Vases communicants* (1932), *L'Amour fou* (1937) and *Arcane 17* (1944). The chief vehicles for his exposition of Surrealism were *Manifeste du surréalisme* (1924), *Second manifeste du surréalisme* (1930) and *Qu'est-ce que le surréalisme?* (1934). Died in Paris, 28 September 1966.

Translations

Selections

Cauvin, Jean-Pierre and Mary Ann Caws, *Poems of André Breton: A Bilingual Anthology*, Austin: University of Texas Press, 1982

Rosemont, Franklin (editor), *What is Surrealism? Selected Writings*, New York: Monad, and London: Pluto Press, 1978

White, Kenneth, *Selected Poems*, London: Jonathan Cape, 1969

Poetry

Les Champs magnétiques, with Philippe Soupault, 1920

Gascoyne, David, *The Magnetic Fields*, London: Atlas Press, 1985

Clair de terre, 1923; revised and enlarged edition, 1966

Zavatsky, Bill and Zack Rogow, *Earthlight*, Los Angeles: Sun and Moon Press, 1993

Fata Morgana, 1941

Mills, Clark, in *New Directions in Prose and Poetry*, 6 (1941) pp. 651–75

Novels

Nadja, 1928; revised edition, 1963

Howard, Richard, *Nadja*, New York: Grove Press, and London: Evergreen Books, 1960

Les Vases communicants, 1932

Caws, Mary Ann and Geoffrey T. Harris, *Communicating Vessels*, Lincoln: University of Nebraska Press, 1990

L'Amour fou, 1937

Caws, Mary Ann, *Mad Love*, Lincoln: University of Nebraska Press, 1987

Other Writing

Manifeste du surréalisme, 1924; revised edition, 1929 and *Second manifeste du surréalisme*, 1930

Seaver, Richard and Helen R. Lane, *Manifestoes of Surrealism*, Ann Arbor: University of Michigan Press, 1969

Le Surréalisme et la peinture, 1928; enlarged edition, 1965

Watson Taylor, Simon, *Surrealism and Painting*, New York: Harper and Row, and London: Macdonald, 1972

L'Immaculée conception, with Paul Éluard, 1930

Beckett, Samuel, "The Possessions", *This Quarter*, 5/1 (September 1932) pp. 119–28

Graham, Jon, *The Immaculate Conception*, London: Atlas Press, 1990

Qu'est-ce que le surréalisme?, 1934

Gascoyne, David, *What is Surrealism?*, London: Faber, 1936

André Breton refused to speak English during his years in New York (1941–46), and it may be ironic that so few of his texts had been translated into English until quite recently, in spite of his position as leader of the Surrealist movement and its main theorist. This may be explained by the fact that his writings are complex hybrid structures, characterized by sudden shifts in register (ranging from the lyrical to the philosophical, the dogmatic or the panegyric), wordplay (puns, alliteration), dense poetic language (baroque images, extended metaphors), intertextual echoes (collage, near-quotation, reworking of set phrases), unwieldy syntax, and frequent slippages into preciosity and pomposity. Moreover, his automatic texts, supposedly dictated by the voice of the unconscious, are essentially experimental, and hence fragmented, lacking in coherence and finish. Such texts, often obscure for the French-speaking reader, present a challenge for the translator, since they demand a poetic, critical and scholarly strategy.

Les Champs magnétiques (1920) written in collaboration with Philippe Soupault in a state of self-hypnosis, is generally considered to be the first surrealist text. These poetic-prose texts are characterized by syntactic dislocation and broken chains of sounds and images, similar to the irrational associations that occur in dreams, producing hallucinatory images. GASCOYNE's translation (1985), which claims to favour literal over literary transposition, often sacrifices the play on words in order to preserve the visual impact of the source text, as where "cache-poussière des prostituées" becomes "prostitutes' dust-coat", where the allusion to "cache-sexe" (G-string) is lost. Gascoyne is at his best when he reworks the material substance of words to produce new meanings rather than reproducing the original meaning, thus simulating Breton's own poetic process, as in "sauts de joie desséchés" translated as "jaded jumps of joy", and "papier d'étain non papier déteint" as"silver paper not paper slivers".

L'Immaculée conception (1930), written in dialogue form by Breton and Paul Éluard, explores the linguistic areas where madness and bricolage overlap. It is a heterogeneous text, part collage or ludic rewriting of the Kama Sutra, Hegel, popular scientific journals and news items, part "simulation tests" of various types of mental delirium, where the creative potential of language is explored in forms of expression freed from rational constraints. In GRAHAM's translation (1990), apart from some errors of detail (verb tenses, negatives), the creativity of the text has been brilliantly reworked: porte-manteau words have been felicitously transposed ("exaspaltère" as "exultasperates"), as have the neologisms ("Saut par gloutot" as "Bound through glughole"). In the most successful translated passages the text is transposed rather than given a faithful word-for-word rendering, as in the "simulation of dementia praecox", where linguistic coherence gives way to semantic and syntactic disarticulation and finally gibberish. Faced with the impossibility of providing a literal translation, Graham has carefully charted the linguistic disarticulation and reshuffled the elements of the text to produce an autonomous piece which equals the source text in its fragmentation, materiality and violence.

CAUVIN & CAWS (1982), for whom Breton's poems are often obscure, unharmonious and unwieldy, have brought rigorous scholarship and a sensitive understanding of Breton's syntactic and semantic distortions to their translation of his poems. While noun syntagms, as in the titles *Clair de terre* and *L'Air de l'eau*, can be concisely transposed into English in the composite forms *Earthlight* and *Airwater*, in the characteristically surrealist fusion/tension of disparate elements, the reworking of clichés is sometimes lost (yet often signalled in footnotes), as in the first title, which is an echo of the ready-made phrase "clair de lune". Such play on the signifier often demands a choice that deprives the text of its semantic richness: for example, "mort pour des prunes à l'eau-de-vie", which combines two set phrases ("mort pour des prunes" and "prunes à l'eau-de-vie") is translated "so we don't die for peanuts in a shell", which keeps the collage of clichés while missing the death/life opposition present in the original. Breton often uses the double meaning of individual words as a pivot for generating verbal associations, a feature that has been faithfully transposed in Cauvin & Caws's translation, as in "Cet instant fait dérailler le train rond des pendules": "That instant derails the clocks' round train", which is based on the double meaning of "train" in both languages. The same word is used as a sound association in the image "qu'importe mes vers le lent train / l'entrain" which becomes "no matter my verses the slow train / unrestrained", where the repetition has been preserved.

The various translations of *L'Union libre* (1931) testify to the challenge of transposing Breton's fixed syntactical structures and free baroque metaphors. The litanic repetition of the noun phrases, as in "Ma femme aux fesses de dos de cygne" is translated by the rather quaint "Woman of mine with swan's-back buttocks" (Cauvin & Caws), the literal "My woman with the buttocks of a swan's back" (Zavatsky & Rogow), the verbal construction "My woman whose rumps are shoulders of swan" (Beckett), or the more mundane "My wife with the swan's back buttocks" (White). BECKETT (1932) has rendered particularly poetically the images generated through sound and sense associations. For example, he translates "Ma femme au dépliement d'éventail des jours" as "My woman whose belly is fan of the days unfurling", where he has renewed the poetic cliché, preserving the suggestion of movement and the alliteration. ZAVATSKY & ROGOW (1993), who are themselves poets, have updated some metaphors: for example, "Aux yeux ... d'aiguille aimantée" becomes "With her eyes of ... a speedometer needle", while "[Aux hanches] De balance insensible" is oddly translated "[Her hips] An imperceptible pair of scales". In the process, they appear to have succeeded in turning Breton into an American Beat poet.

Le Surréalisme et la peinture, where the clumsy syntax, many modalized forms and sudden shifts in register, with their echoes of Lautréamont's characteristic baroque rhetoric and classical periods, runs the risk of sounding like pastiche in translation, as in WATSON TAYLOR's rendering (1972), where clumsy sentence constructions tend to weigh down the text even further.

No doubt the most successful translations into English are of Breton's prose texts, where language is more transparent, although there are also passages of metaphorical density. These include HOWARD's translation (1960) of *Nadja*, and CAWS & HARRIS's of *Les Vases communicants* (1990) and Caws's of *L'Amour fou* (1987). In her preface to *Mad Love*, Caws refers to the difficulties of translating a text that is both lyrical and stilted, romantic and classical. Her translation provides a perfect balance between the transparency of the classical and the density of the metaphorical.

ELZA ADAMOWICZ

Further Reading

Balakian, Anna, *André Breton: Magus of Surrealism*, New York and Oxford: Oxford University Press, 1971

Caws, Mary Ann, *André Breton*, New York: Twayne, 1971; revised edition, 1996

Caws, Mary Ann (editor), *André Breton Today*, New York: Willis Locker and Owens, 1989

Hermann Broch 1886–1951

Austrian novelist, philosopher, dramatist and critic

Biography

Born in Vienna 1 November 1886, the son of a textile manufacturer. He was educated at first privately and then in technical colleges, beginning his adult career as an industrial manager, and turning to writing late. He worked for the Austrian Red Cross in World War I. From 1926 to 1930 he studied mathematics, philosophy and psychology at Vienna University, returning in the 1930s, having in 1928 sold the family textile mills, to study literature. Imprisoned briefly by the Nazis in 1938 as politically suspect, Broch went to London and then to the US, where he taught German literature at Princeton and Yale universities and settled, becoming an American citizen in 1944.

Broch's works reflect the fact that he lived through times of crisis that included the end of both the Habsburg empire and the Third Reich. *Die Schlafwandler* (1930–32; *The Sleepwalkers*, 1932) is a "polyhistoric" prose trilogy, a wide-ranging account of German experiences between 1880 and 1918. Broch is best known for the prose poem *Der Tod des Vergil* (1945; *The Death of Virgil*, 1945), an evocation, in interior monologue form, with aesthetic and moral resonances, of the dying Virgil's regrets. Died in New Haven, Connecticut, 30 May 1951.

Translations

Novels

Die Schlafwandler, 1930–32

Muir, Willa and Edwin Muir, *The Sleepwalkers*, London: Secker, and Boston: Little Brown, 1932; several reprints

Der Tod des Vergil, 1945

Untermeyer, Jean Starr, *The Death of Virgil*, New York: Pantheon, 1945; London: Routledge, 1946; several reprints

The translations of Hermann Broch's two major novels, *The Sleepwalkers* and *The Death of Virgil*, share a number of common characteristics. In both cases the translators, as creative writers of established standing in the Anglophone world, could sympathetically apply genuinely creative literary skills to their task of translation. Both novels were also translated in the closest cooperation and consultation with the author; indeed, in both cases the English translations proceeded in parallel with Broch's continuing revisions of the German original. In the case of *The Sleepwalkers* this resulted in certain revisions being incorporated into the English version which could not be retrospectively added to the first German edition as it had already gone to print. Thus the motif of the "verlorene Generation" ("lost generation"), present throughout the English translation, was not introduced to the first two volumes of the German text until the 1963 printing of a special edition ("Sonderausgabe"). The Muirs (1932) corresponded with Broch for over 18 months about their ongoing translation of *The Sleepwalkers*, and Jean Starr Untermeyer (1945) devoted no less than five full years to her translation of *The Death of Virgil*, which was published simultaneously with the German version.

Broch was also acutely and uncomfortably aware of the limitations of his own English and his consequent inability to make well-founded and reliable judgements of the quality of the English translations of the two novels. One significant difference between the translators was that the Muirs had already distinguished themselves with their translations of Kafka, whereas Untermeyer, by her own admission, had very little experience of translating from German when she accepted the commission to translate *The Death of Virgil*.

In general, the translation of *The Sleepwalkers* (MUIR & MUIR, 1932) reads extremely well while remaining essentially true not just to the spirit, but also to the letter of the German original. The translation of the first part of the trilogy, *Pasenow The Romantic*, is accurate, very readable, and rarely feels like a translation at all. Where this does happen, it is less a question of idiom or register than a rather stilted word order which reproduces too closely an original, characteristically German structure. *Esch The Anarchist*, the second part of the trilogy, is also generally excellent, although some of the English idiom used has not aged well for the reader of today. A number of problematical passages occur. The problems arise in part from Broch's own style, and in part from the universally recognized difficulties of translating philosophical German, with its typically heavy reliance on verbal and adjectival substantives to render abstracts. Inevitably such passages, usually those dealing with the crucial phenomenon of "sleepwalking", sound irredeemably foreign and stilted to the English ear. The intrusive nature of these "sleepwalking" passages within the generally obtaining naturalistic style of this novel was certainly intended by Broch, but their strongly disorientating effect suggests that Broch was correct to introduce such material into *Huguenau the Realist*, the final novel of the trilogy, in clearly delineated philosophical discourses quite separate from the main narrative. *Huguenau* is very accurately translated, but the sections of poetry and philosophy are as stiff and indigestible in English as in the German.

The Death of Virgil presented a unique challenge to its translator, UNTERMEYER (1945). Author and translator alike agreed that this novel was so lyrical in style as to be regarded essentially as a poem, albeit one of almost 500 pages. The novel has a musical structure, with its four parts related to each other in the same way as are the four movements of a symphony. In this work Broch's syntax functions, by his own admission, on the principle of "one thought-one moment-one sentence" and inevitably produces some of the longest and most complex sentences ever written in German. Broch also exploits the German language's capability of rendering concentrated and multi-dimensional layers of meaning through composite words and neologisms to a hitherto unprecedented degree. Untermeyer agreed with Broch that the novel, though in many respects untranslatable, was a masterpiece that simply had to be translated into English in order to make it available to a much wider readership. Faced with this challenge, she chose to rely on her instincts as a poet and to approach the translation of *The Death of Virgil* holistically, intuitively and creatively, rather than as a purely technical exercise in translating from a foreign language.

In the extended lyrical, philosophical and descriptive passages Untermeyer's translation is remarkably successful in reproducing the structures and rhythms of the original German as closely as possible, while attempting to preserve as many layers of meaning as the normally less extensive use in English of neologisms and composite words could reasonably allow. Such passages make formidable, although ultimately rewarding, demands on the Anglophone reader. Unfortunately, she is markedly less successful with many of the passages of dialogue, where bathetic inconsistencies of register and the use of certain crass Americanisms sit uncomfortably with the self-conscious archaisms ("verily", "ye", "thou", "yea", "hereafter", "quoth", "nay", "of yore") cultivated elsewhere in the text. One dialogue reads: "Give me a love charm!" – "Yes, between the legs, and potently ... dat kinda charm you'll get from me, good and gladly delivered, you shall have it!" "Des Schreckens hörnerne Pforte" is impossibly, even embarrassingly, rendered as "the horny portal of dread". Octavian's personal physician is referred to as a "medico", and the emperor himself is once described as "hollering his complaints". "Zwischenzustand" (intermediate stage) is regularly translated as "interstate". On a few, admittedly very rare, occasions the limitations of Untermeyer's German are revealed by basic mistranslations of the original, e.g. "Absturz" is translated as "crash", one of its many meanings listed in a dictionary, when the context clearly demands "fall", "collapse" or something similar; "friedfertig" is rendered as "peacefully" instead of "peaceably". Such errors simply do not occur in the Muirs' linguistically sound translation of *The Sleepwalkers*.

Although all of Broch's novels have now been translated into English, there is currently a critical consensus that only *The Sleepwalkers* and *The Death of Virgil*, whether in German or English, are likely to find a place in the canon of European or world literature. Apart from the novels, very little of Broch's extensive oeuvre has been translated into English. Two major essays that are accessible in English are *Hugo von Hofmannsthal and His Time* (University of Chicago Press, 1984) and *James Joyce and the Present Age* (*A James Joyce Yearbook*, 1949).

RODERICK H. WATT

Further Reading

Untermeyer, Jean Starr, "Midwife to a Masterpiece" in her *Private Collection*, New York: Knopf, 1965, pp. 218–277

Watt, Roderick H., "Broch Reviewed: The Reception in the United Kingdom of the English Translations of Hermann Broch's Novels", *Modern Language Review*, 82 (1987) pp. 897–909

Watt, Roderick H., "The Reception of Hermann Broch in the *Times Literary Supplement* 1932–86", *Modern Austrian Literature*, 21 (1988) pp. 17–26

Watt, Roderick H., "A Comparative Study of the Original Reception of the English Translations of Hermann Broch's Novels in the United States and the United Kingdom" in *Romanstruktur und Menschenrecht bei Hermann Broch*, edited by Hartmut Steinecke and Joseph Strelka, New York: Peter Lang, 1990, pp. 177–209

See also the translator's note to Untermeyer

Georg Büchner 1813–1837

German dramatist

Biography

Born at Goddelau in the duchy of Hesse, 17 October 1813. The philosopher Ludwig Büchner was his younger brother. Büchner attended school in Darmstadt and while studying medicine and biology at the universities of Strasbourg and Zürich became active in revolutionary politics. To escape arrest for sedition he left Germany and from 1836 taught comparative anatomy at the Univerity of Zürich until his death at the age of 24 from typhus. The three plays (two poetic dramas and a comedy) with one unfinished short story, that he left behind, mostly unpublished, exerted a crucial influence on German Expressionism and on modern drama in general. He is best known for two of the plays. As well as his complex version of the downfall of a large historical figure, Danton, he wrote in *Woyzeck* (which became the basis for Alban Berg's 1920 opera *Wozzeck*) the tragedy of an obscure victim of social and political forces and the human condition. Died in Zürich of typhoid, aged 24, 19 February 1837.

Translations

Collections of Plays

Dunlop, Geoffrey, *The Plays of Georg Büchner*, London: G. Howe, 1927; New York: Viking Press, 1928; as *The Plays of Georg Büchner*, London: Vision Press, 1952

Hamburger, Michael, *Leonce and Lena; Lenz; Woyzeck*, Chicago: University of Chicago Press, 1972

Patterson, Michael (editor), *Büchner: The Complete Plays*, London and New York: Methuen, 1987 (contains *Danton's Death*, translated by Howard Brenton and Jane Fry; *Leonce and Lena*, translated by Anthony Meech; *Woyzeck*, translated by John Mackendrick; together with other prose writings, including *The Hessian Courier*, *Lenz*, *On Cranial Nerves*, and *Selected Letters*, translated by Patterson)

Price, Victor, *Danton's Death; Leonce and Lena; Woyzeck*, with an introduction, Oxford and New York: Oxford University Press, 1971

Reddick, John, *Complete Plays, Lenz, and Other Writings*, London and New York: Penguin, 1993

Schmidt, Henry J., *Georg Büchner: The Complete Collected Works*, New York : Avon Books, 1977

Schmidt, Henry J., *Complete Works and Letters*, edited and with an introduction by Walter Hinderer and Schmidt, New York: Continuum, 1986

Plays

Dantons Tod (first published as *Dantons Tod: Dramatische Bilder aus Frankreichs Schreckenherrschaft*), 1835, produced 1902

Brenton, Howard, from a literal translation by Jane Fry, *Danton's Death: A New Version*, London: Methuen, 1982; reprinted in *Büchner: The Complete Plays*, edited by Michael Patterson, 1987

Maxwell, James, *Danton's Death*, San Francisco: Chandler, 1961; with an introduction by Martin Esslin, London: Methuen, 1968

Rappolt, Hedwig, *Danton's Death*, with an introduction, New York: TSL Press, 1980

Schmidt, Henry J., *Danton's Death*, New York: Bard, 1971

Spender, Stephen and Goronwy Rees, *Danton's Death* in *From the Modern Repertoire 1*, edited by Eric Bentley, Denver, Colorado: University of Denver Press, 1949; reprinted in *A Treasury of theTheatre*, edited by John Gassner, vol. 1, New York: Simon and Schuster, 1963

Leonce und Lena (first published as *Leonce und Lena: Ein Lustspiel*), 1838, produced 1895

Rappolt, Hedwig, *Leonce and Lena: A Comedy*, New York: TSL Press, 1983

Woyzeck (written 1835–37; first published as *Wozzeck: Ein Trauerspiel-Fragment*), 1879, produced 1913

Bentley, Eric, *Woyzeck*, London and New York: Samuel French, 1991

Ewans, Michael, *Georg Büchner's Woyzeck: Translation and Theatrical Commentary*, with an introduction, New York: Peter Lang, 1989

Mackendrick, John, *Woyzeck*, London: Eyre Methuen, 1979

Short Story

Lenz (first published as *Lenz: Eine Reliquie*), 1839

Hamburger, Michael, *Lenz*, Buffalo, New York: Frontier Press, 1970

Since the era of Expressionism, the strong, stark, elemental, and occasionally also witty language of Georg Büchner's dramas has attracted English-speaking actors and directors alike to the 19th-century dramatist's work. Despite formal and linguistic challenges, Büchner's plays have since been performed regularly on the English stage. From the first, translation of Büchner's works into English has been spurred on by producers and actors who have wanted to perform the plays in an English translation that is as fluent or fragmentary, coherent or incoherent, forceful and lyrical as the German original. Until recently, it has been primarily the plays (above all, *Danton's Death*) that have been translated and then mostly by theatre directors or professors of theatre. Only in the last 25 years have German scholars turned to translating Büchner's theoretical works and letters (Schmidt, 1977, 1986 and Reddick, 1993).

The very first English translation of Büchner's plays appeared in 1927, almost a century after the playwright's death and almost 50 years after the first publication of the collected works in 1879. For nearly 30 years the German literary scene almost completely ignored this first complete edition, and it was not until the growing impact of Expressionism on German theatre that Büchner's work began to exert influence on modern literature. Unfortunately, the first translation (DUNLOP, 1927), although introducing Büchner to the English-speaking stage, does not transmit the elemental force of Büchner's language. Both in *Danton's Death* and *Woyzeck* the language has been purged of the crude sexual allusions of the original and is rendered into genteel historical drama. The translation of *Woyzeck* also contains many inaccuracies and mistakes. But at least a beginning had been made.

The next translation of *Danton's Death* followed after more than 20 years and is far more successful than Dunlop. Commissioned for production at the Group Theatre, SPENDER & REES's *Danton's Death* (1949) was intended to provide an historical example to young left-wing actors of a kind of political activism and revolutionary zeal that might parallel their own. As such, the translation is extremely successful: it does much to convey the mood of Büchner's original while remaining faithful to the German.

James MAXWELL's London 1968 version of *Danton's Death*, with an introduction by Martin Esslin, is more an adaptation than a translation. It was also commissioned for a specific theatre – in this case, for the 1959 production at the Lyric Theatre, Hammersmith. However, the German original is altered, compressed and embellished with extra-textual material. Arguing that the original seems too short to stage as it stands, Maxwell changes the order of scenes, adds lines from Carlyle's account of the French Revolution and words of actual historical characters, and plays fast and loose with the references to the Revolution that are already in the text. So, *caveat lector*.

PRICE's 1971 translation of *Danton's Death*, *Leonce and Lena*, and *Woyzeck* for the World's Classics series, published by Oxford University Press, continues the trend of successful translation started by SPENDER & REES. In the introduction, Price makes the observation that *Danton's Death* and *Leonce and Lena* lend themselves better to translation into the language of Shakespeare because both rely heavily on a high metaphorical linguistic register and lively punning. However, *Woyzeck* presents the translator with huge problems, not only in the reconstruction of a working text but also in the language of the play. "In the first place the language is so compressed and precise; and secondly, the play is written largely in Hessian dialect and steeped in the atmosphere of Hessian folk-songs" (Price, p. xxii). He concludes that perhaps only Robert Burns would have been able to do the play justice.

SCHMIDT (1977) was the first complete edition in English of Büchner's works and as such deserves praise for its scholarly attempt to render all of the playwright's works into English. This version forms the base for SCHMIDT's 1986 German Library edition of the translations. It is this latter version, appearing in the series that has become almost the standard source for German works in English translation, on which I should like to concentrate in comparison with PRICE and SPENDER & REES.

SCHMIDT's 1986 reworking of his earlier translation of Büchner's works is, above all else, scholarly. It incorporates the latest textual emendations of the original manuscripts and also includes all surviving letters by Büchner. The translations are prefaced by a lengthy introduction by the foremost scholar on Büchner in North America, Walter Hinderer. Here, Hinderer provides a full, scholarly treatment of Büchner's biography, aesthetics, the philosophical background to his time and analyses of the individual works. There is no doubt that this is a translation for scholars of German literature rather than theatrical performers and producers, and as such it is both important and useful. Unfortunately, Schmidt's translation does not live up to the high standard of the supporting materials in the volume. SCHMIDT's translation of *Danton's Death* is wooden and occasionally inaccurate. He frequently slips into the wrong rhetorical register and also makes misplaced attempts to provide "authentic" sounding archaisms.

On occasion, however, Schmidt is the only one to translate accurately a line that others miss. For example, in *Danton's Death*, act 3, scene 5, Schmidt translates the line "Meine Mondsichel hat Ebbe bei mir gemacht" as "my moon's brought on a low tide" – a better rendition than Spender's "my sickle moon has ebbed" and slightly more accurate than Price's "The moon's on the wane sir. My purse is at low water" – the latter certainly conveys the meaning of the line, although only by adding something. In sum, Schmidt's translation loses much of the nuance and poetry of Büchner's language although it provides an excellent reference tool (with introduction, glossary, and notes).

RAPPOLT (1980) is a small pamphlet translation of *Danton's Death*. She provides a short introduction in which she makes parallels between Danton and Robespierre and Hitler and Goebbels. The translation is for the most part accurate, with occasional mistakes, however, and stylistic anomalies. Rappolt provides a useful list of notes at the end of her translation.

The translation that by far best satisfies both the Büchner scholar and the theatrical producer is REDDICK (1993). The volume contains all of Büchner's work and correspondence, the important introduction to his inaugural lecture "On Cranial Nerves", the political pamphlet "The Hessian Messenger", notes to all the translations and a bibliography. Reddick's aim, as he states in the preface, is to produce an "actable" Büchner for the English-speaking stage. The detailed and scholarly introduction to the collection is based partly on Reddick's critical study, *Georg Büchner: The Shattered Whole* (Oxford: Clarendon Press, 1994). Reddick's translation captures well Büchner's earthy, elemental use of language. In *Danton's Death*, the language of the common people is authentically crude, violent, and sexual. However, Reddick also can switch effectively to Büchner's more lyrical register in, for example, Desmoulin's wife Lucile's speeches. Reddick is by far the most reliable translation to which both actor and scholar alike can turn.

Büchner's fragmentary play *Woyzeck* appeared in English translation (DUNLOP, 1927) at the same time as his other dramatic works. The simultaneous publication of *Danton's Death*, *Leonce and Lena*, and *Woyzeck* gave the English reader the advantage over the German reader of being able to compare three strikingly different dramatic forms. Whereas both of the former share something of the dramatic form of Shakespearean drama, the latter is an open string of scenes the order of which is still largely a matter of debate among Büchner scholars. When comparing translations of *Woyzeck* the edition upon which the translation is based has to be taken into account.

The best scholarly introduction to the textual and translation history of *Woyzeck* can be found in EWANS (1989). There are basically four *Handschriften* or manuscripts (H_1–H_4) in which the series and number of scenes differ. The standard edition (Lehmann) preferred the order H_4, 1–17, and then H_1, 14–21. Although SCHMIDT bases his translation on Lehmann's order he adds a couple of optional scenes and changes the order of other scenes. This means, for example, that Schmidt opens with a different scene from that of the Lehmann or Ewans editions. This is possible, because, as Ewans states in his introduction, "It is agreed that an edition or translation of *Woyzeck* must prefer H_4's wording where it deviates from that of the earlier drafts, simply because it presents the last version of the text that Büchner made. But there is no comparable case for the H_4 order of scenes" (Ewans, p. 10). Ewans does not accept the orthodox ordering of scenes outlined above, but rather proceeds by raising a series of questions that must be answered by any producer of the play, such as, How should the play end? Franzos, the first editor of *Woyzeck*, added for example, the stage direction "ertrinkt" (drowns) at the end of the play. Ewans seems to concur with this interactive approach to staging the play, arguing, "We could create new material to conclude the play" (Ewans, p. 18). The major obstacle to this creative solution to the fragmentary nature of the play lies, however, as Ewans comments, in the fact that no-one has yet translated the play who possesses Büchner's genius for language.

To move to the translations themselves, though, we find SCHMIDT's translations to be again flat and literal with occasional inaccuracies. For example, in Marie's first song the lines "Sing ich die ganze Nacht / Heio, popeio, mei Bu, juchhe! / Gibt mir kein Mensch nix dazu" are translated by Schmidt as "I'll sing here by your bed: / Rockabye baby, my baby are you, / Nobody cares what I do." PRICE renders the lines "All night long I'll sit and sing: / 'Rockabye, rockabye, tiny thing,' / Though nobody cares for me." EWANS offers "I will sing all through the night. / Eio popeio my boy. Oh ay! / Nobody helps me with you". SCHMIDT's last line is furthest from the sense of the original which actually none of them captures completely – perhaps "Nobody gives me anything for doing it" would be closest to the original.

Büchner's comedy *Leonce and Lena* poses less of a challenge to translators and textual editors than the other works. Written as an entry in a competition for the best comedy, but unfortunately disqualified for arriving too late, *Leonce and Lena* is a compact and tightly written commentary on the absurdity of monarchy. Much as Arthur Schnitzler's *La Ronde* provides a biting critique of Viennese society at the end of the 19th century so *Leonce and Lena* attacks in comic dramatic form the in Germany in the 1830s. Just as Büchner's 1834 pamphlet, *The Hessian Messenger*, proclaimed war on the palaces, so too this short and perfectly formed work of comic art exposes the circuitous argument that justifies the continuation of absolute monarchy. PRICE's translation of the play provides a good introduction for the British audience (many of his references would mean little to a North American one) and his translation is fluent and witty, capturing much of the punning of the original. SCHMIDT provides good textual notes but again his translation is rather pedantic.

Of the translations of *Lenz*, HAMBURGER (1972) is inaccurate whereas REDDICK (1993) is again a skillful rendering of the proto-expressionist prose of Büchner.

KATHERINE FAULL

Further Reading

See the introductions to Maxwell, Price, Reddick, and Schmidt (1986)

Buddhist Sacred Texts in English Translation

The English translation of Buddhist sacred texts, and of works on Buddhism, has a long history. The accurate rendering of Buddhist scriptures itself brings into sharp focus the eternal conflict between literal and free translation in its choice of translating strategies. In 19th-century England, the Victorian, especially the middle-class, penchant for religious literature, the ideological pluralism of the period, the Western institution of Buddhism as a textual object, etc. (Almond, 1988), all combined to produce a demand for the English translations of works on Buddhism (e.g. Oldenberg, 1881, translated 1882) and Barthélemy-Saint-Hilaire (1862, translated 1895). *The Lotus Sūtra*, one of the most important and influential of all the sūtras of Mahayana Buddhism, has been absorbed into the canon of world literature in English translation.

One of the earliest, most significant English translations of Buddhist writings is the Sacred Books of the Buddhists series, translated by various Oriental scholars and edited by F. Max Müller, published from 1895 under the patronage of King Chulalankarana of Siam.

It would perhaps be helpful to future researchers in Buddhist texts to list at the outset, chronologically, the English translations of various canons of Buddhist literature, as follows:

Canonical and Paracanonical Theravāda Literature
T.W. Rhys-Davids, *Buddhist Suttas*, 1881
Eugene Watson Burlingame, *Buddhist Parables*, 1922
Edward Conze *et al.*, *Buddhist Texts through the Ages*, 1954
Edward Conze, *Buddhist Scriptures*, 1959

The Dhammapada
F. Max Müller, *The Dhammapada: A Collection of Verses*, 1881
Sarvepalli Radhakrishnan, *The Dhammapada*, 1950
Thera Nārada, *The Dhammapada*, 1954

The Milindapanhā
T.W. Rhys-Davids, *The Questions of King Milinda*, 1890-94
I.B. Horner, *King Milinda's Questions (Milindapaña)*, 1963

The Mahāsatipatthana Sutta
Thera Soma, *The Way of Mindfulness: The Satipatthana Sutta and Commentary*, 1967

Prajnāpāramitā
E. B. Cowell and F. Max Müller (editors), *Buddhist Mahayana Texts*, 1894
Edward J. Thomas, *The Perfection of Wisdom: The Career of the Predestined Buddhas: A Selection of Mahāyāna Scriptures*, 1952
Edward Conze, *Astasāhasrikā Prajnāpāramitā*, 1958

The Srīmālādevisimhanāda Sūtra
Alex Wayman and Hideko Wayman, *The Lion's Roar of Queen Srīmāla*, 1973

The Lankāvatāra Sūtra
D. T. Suzuki, *The Lankāvatāra Sūtra: A Mahāyāna Text*, 1932

The Sukhavativyūha Sūtras
E. B. Cowell *et al.*, *Buddhist Mahāyānā Texts*, 1894

The Bodhicaryāvatāra of Shāntideva
Edward J. Thomas, *The Quest of Enlightenment: A Selection of the Buddhist Scriptures*, 1950
Marion L. Matics, *Entering the Path of Enlightenment: The Bodhicaryāvatāra of the Buddhist Poet Sāntideva*, 1970

The Lotus Sūtra (Saddharma Pundarīka Sūtra)
H. Kern, *The Saddharma-pundarīka*, 1884
W. E. Soothill, *The Lotus of the Wonderful Law*, 1930 (selections)
Leon Hurvitz, *The Scripture of the Lotus Blossom of the Fine Dharma, Translated from the Chinese of Kumrājīva*, 1976

The Vimalakīrtinirdeśa Sūtra
Robert A. F. Thurman, *The Holy Teaching of Vimalakīrti: A Mahāyāna Scripture*, 1976

The Awakening of Faith in Mahāyāna
Yoshito Hakeda, *The Awakening of Faith in Mahāyāna, Attributed to Aśvaghosha*, 1967

Platform Sūtra of the Sixth Patriarch
Philip Yampolsky, *The Platform Sūtra of the Sixth Patriarch*, 1967

The Lotus Sūtra exists in many complete English translations: H. Kern's *The Saddharma-pundarīka; or, The Lotus of the True Law* (1884); Senchu Murano's *The Sūtra of the Lotus Flower of the Wonderful Law* (1974); Bunnō Katō, Yoshirō Tamura, and Kojiro Miyasaka's *The Threefold Lotus Sūtra: The Sūtra of Innumerable Meanings; The Sūtra of the Lotus Flower of the Wonderful Law; The Sūtra of Meditation on the Bodhisattva Universal Virtue* (1975); Leon Hurvitz's *The Scripture of the Lotus Blossom of the Fine Dharma* (1976); Tsugunari Kubo and Akira Yuyama's *The Lotus Sūtra: The White Lotus of the Marvelous Law* (1991). All the above texts (and Burton Watson's *The Lotus Sūtra*, 1993), with the exception of the *Saddharma-pundarīka* (Kern), were based on the 406 Kumārajīva Chinese versions of the original, universally acknowledged as the most authoritative and most felicitous in language.

The translation into English of Buddhist sacred scriptures has, to some extent, relied on indirect translation. This is the case with extract numbers 148 and 184 in Edward Conze's edition of *Buddhist Texts through the Ages, Newly Translated from the Original Pali, Sanskrit, Chinese, Tibetan, Japanese and Apabhramsa* (1954). The former extract was rendered from the Chinese of Yüan-tsang by Arthur Waley, because Yüan-tsang had before him a more interesting recension than the one found in the Sanskrit and Tibetan, whereas the latter had to make use of Professor Lamotte's French translation from the Tibetan in the absence of a Sanskrit original (Conze, 1954). In terms of religious exegesis, such English translations are, therefore, at least at two removes from their originals.

The existence of parallel texts helps to rectify some of the inadequacies in Buddhist source-texts. For example, verses not extant in Sanskrit, supposedly the primordial language for Buddhist texts, have been translated from the Pāli or Tibetan parallel texts. Such verses, often containing recapitulations corresponding to the parallel prose passages, are, semantically and stylistically, part and parcel of the originals: their transfer is thus absolutely essential to any religious translation, a source-text-oriented mode of rendering.

Since Buddhist scriptures abound in various linguistic and cultural documents, notably Sanskrit, Pāli, Chinese and Prakrit Gaina documents, the English translator, if he had to take on himself the task of introducing representative selections from the entire canon, would, ideally, have to be a linguistic virtuoso with an intimate knowledge of the different cultural traditions behind these documents. Just to give an idea of the dazzling array of such documents: the *Divyâvadâna* and *Saddharma-pundarīka* (Sanskrit documents); the *Phû-yâo King* (Chinese documents); the *Mahâparinibbâna Sutta*, the *Tevigga Sutta*, the *Mahasudassana Sutta*, the *Dhammakappavattana Sutta*, the *Suttanipâta*, the *Mahâvagga*, the *Kullavagga*, the *Pâtimokkha* (Pāli documents); the *Akârânga Sûtra*, *Dasavaikâlika Sûtra*, *Sûtra-kritânga*, *Uttarâdhyayana Sûtra* (Prakrit Gaina documents).

In the course of the English translation of Buddhist writings, the question has often been raised as to whether they should be rendered literally or freely. This is a complex, thorny problem enmeshed with such different issues as semantic versus communicative translation, religious hermeneutics, philosophy of language, etc. Because of differences in lexis, syntax, and rhetoric between Sanskrit and English, the religious translator will have to face the dilemma between source-text truth and target-language idiom. In view of their unique, sacrosanct, nature, religious texts should, perhaps, be treated rather differently from other text-types. Buddhist writings are full of the artifices of Sanskrit rhetoric: three or four simultaneously-occurring synonyms, repetitive chunks of text, etc., serve to reiterate important religious motifs or events. Sanskrit terms, e.g. *Nirvana*, *Bodhisattva*, *Dharma*, and especially these ambiguous, multivalent ones, often prove intractable in the process of transfer of messages from the source pole to the target pole. How could a word like *Dharma*, with up to 10 contextual meanings, be conveyed to the English reader with two or three senses simultaneously intended, stylistically, within one linguistic locale? In such cases, no Buddhist messages could be transmitted without doing violence to English idiom. In his solution, CONZE (1954) decided not to translate these terms at all in the hope that "they are likely in due course to be absorbed into the English language", or if he did translate, he declared that the English equivalents adopted could be considered as makeshifts only. MÜLLER (1879) retained the Sanskrit words rather than use misleading substitutes where he could not find adequate terms in English (introduction). These solutions, except for Conze's non-translation or under-translation, sound sensible enough, and should, perhaps, be preferred to other ways in which original words, within their own religious context in Buddhist writings, are arbitrarily thrust upon the English target readership. All these cases, each with its own special circumstances, flesh out thoroughly Newmark's contention, "Tension between original and translation is at its highest in the case of a sacred text whose intent is to proselytise" (1993).

The literal, faithful rendering into English of *The Lotus Sūtra*, with its textual features of formulaic language and frequent repetitions, will impinge upon appropriateness of English discourse structures. In Ria Kloppenborg's (1973) translation of *Catusparisatsūtra* (1973), co-occurring synonyms and textual repetitions in the source language were, injudiciously, retained intact. This might, as insights from contrastive textology prove, lead to non-native, awkward, redundant, and stodgy English structures at the textual level.

Burton Watson (1993), in his English translation of *The Lotus Sūtra*, raises the problem of exact interpretation with regard to Classical Chinese, the language of the Kumārajīva *Lotus*. Unlike its Indo-European counterparts, of which the English language is one, classical Chinese does indeed lack fine grammatical distinctions in number, case, tense and subject, which makes it an "ambiguous" language in terms of textual interpretation. What explains these qualms or misgivings on the part of non-native speakers of classical Chinese is the fundamental grammatical dichotomy between English hypotaxis and Chinese parataxis. To Chinese readers, grammatical subjects are unexpressed but understood, the singularity/plurality of nouns, tenses, cases, etc., though non-inflected, are all implicit in their subconscious, inferrable from contextual background. Steiner, in *After Babel* (1975), his *magnum opus* in translation with mammoth textual apparatus and commentary, rightly addresses the importance of this context issue in linguistic interpretation, "No grammar or dictionary is of very much use to the translator; only context, in the fullest linguistic-cultural sense, certifies meaning".

RAYMOND S.C. LIE

References

Almond, Philip C., *The British Discovery of Buddhism*, Cambridge and New York: Cambridge University Press, 1988

Barthélemy-Saint-Hilaire, Jules, *The Buddha and His Religion* [1862], translated by Laura Ensor, London: Routledge, 1895; New York: Dutton, 1914

Conze, Edward (editor), in collaboration with I.B. Horner, David Snellgrove and Arthur Waley, *Buddhist Texts Through the Ages, Newly Translated from the Original Pali, Sanskrit, Chinese, Tibetan, Japanese and Apabhramsa*, Oxford: Cassirer, 1954; New York: Harper and Row, 1964

Conze, Edward, *Buddhist Scriptures*, Harmondsworth and New York: Penguin, 1959

Kloppenberg, Ria, *The Sūtra on the Foundation of the Buddhist Order*, Leiden: E.J. Brill, 1973

Müller, F. Max (editor), *The Sacred Books of the East, Translated by Various Oriental Scholars*, vol. 1, with an introduction, Oxford: Clarendon Press, 1879

Müller, F. Max (editor), *Sacred Books of the Buddhists, Translated by Various Oriental Scholars*, 23 vols, London: Frowde (and other publishers for later volumes), 1895ff.

Newmark, P., *Paragraphs on Translation*, Clevedon and Philadelphia: Multilingual Matters, 1993

Oldenberg, Hermann, *Buddha: His Life, His Doctrine, His Order* [1881], translated by William Hoey, London: Williams and Norgate, 1882

Steiner, George, *After Babel: Aspects of Language and Translation*, Oxford and New York: Oxford University Press, 1975; 3rd edition 1998

Watson, Burton (translator), *The Lotus Sūtra*, New York: Columbia University Press, 1993

Further Reading

Altick, Richard D., *The English Common Reader: A Social History of the Mass Reading Public, 1800–1900*, Chicago: University of Chicago Press, 1957

Bary, William Theodore de *et al.*, *Sources of Indian Tradition*, New York: Columbia University Press, 1958

Bary, William Theodore de *et al.* (editors), *A Guide to Oriental Classics*, 3rd edition, New York: Columbia University Press, 1989

Beal, Samuel, *A Catena of Buddhist Scriptures from the Chinese*, London: Trubner, 1871

Burrow, T., *The Sanskrit Language*, London: Faber, and New York: Barnes and Noble, 1973

Chafe, Wallace, *Discourse, Consciousness, and Time: The Flow and Displacement of Conscious Experience in Speaking and Writing*, Chicago: University of Chicago Press, 1994

Chao, Yuen Ren, *Notes on Chinese Grammar and Logic*, Honolulu: University of Hawaii Press, 1955

Collins, Steven, *Selfless Persons: Imagery and Thought in Theravada Buddhism*, Cambridge and New York: Cambridge University Press, 1982

Conze, Edward, *Buddhist Scriptures: A Bibliography*, edited and revised by Lewis Lancaster, New York: Garland, 1982

Dayal, Har, *The Bodhisattva Doctrine in Buddhist Sanskrit Literature*, London: Kegan Paul Trench and Trubner, 1932; reprinted Livingston, New Jersey: Orient Book Distributor, 1975

Dijk, Teun A. van (editor), *Discourse and Literature*, Amsterdam and Philadelphia: John Benjamins, 1985

Hearne, James William, "Classical Chinese as an Instrument of Deduction" (dissertation), Riverside: University of California, 1980

Heyck, Thomas W., *The Transformation of the Intellectual Life in Victorian England*, London: Croom Helm, 1982

Jha, J.S. (editor), *The Abhidharmakosa of Vasubandhu*, Patna: K.P. Jayaswal Research Institute, 1983

Jiang, Zhongxin (editor), *A Sanskrit Manuscript of Saddharmapundarika, Romanized Text*, Beijing: China Social Sciences Publishing House, 1988

Kawamura, Leslie S. (editor), *The Bodhisattva Doctrine in Buddhism*, Waterloo, Ontario: Wilfrid Laurier University Press, 1981

Lopez, Donald S. Jr (editor), *Buddhist Hermeneutics*, Honolulu: University of Hawaii Press, 1988

Mizuno, Kogen, *Buddhist Sūtras: Origin, Development, Transmission*, Tokyo: Kosei, 1982

Nyanaponika, Thera, *The Heart of Buddhist Meditation*, London: Rider, 1962; New York: Citadel Press, 1969

Partee, Barbara H. and Petr Sgall (editors), *Discourse and Meaning: Papers in Honor of Eva Hajicova*, Amsterdam and Philadelphia: Benjamins, 1996

Sasaki, Genjun H., *Linguistic Approach to Buddhist Thought*, Delhi: Motilal Banarsidass, 1986; 2nd edition, 1992

Steiner, George, *Extraterritorial: Papers on Literature and the Language Revolution*, New York: Atheneum, 1971; London: Faber, 1972

Warren, Henry Clarke, *Buddhism in Translations*, Cambridge, Massachusetts: Harvard University Press, 1896; reprinted New York: Atheneum, 1970 (Harvard Oriental series, vol. 3)

Willis, Janice Dean, *On Knowing Reality: The Tattvartha Chapter of Asanga's Bodhisattvabhumi*, New York: Columbia University Press, 1979

Mikhail Bulgakov 1891–1940

Russian novelist, short-story writer and dramatist

Biography

Born in Kiev, 3 May 1891. Until the dramatic and unexpected publication of the novels *Master i Margarita* (*The Master and Margarita*) in 1966–67 and *Teatral'nyi roman* (*Black Snow*) in 1967, Bulgakov was considered a minor prose writer and a gifted but unlucky dramatist. Now he ranks high among the most important and best-loved Russian writers of the 20th century. Born in Kiev, he attended medical school and served as a rural doctor before leaving medicine in 1919 to write stories, feuilletons for newspapers, and plays. Unable to publish in full his novel *The White Guard* (1924), he rewrote it into a play, *Days of the Turbins*, which opened at the Moscow Art Theater in 1926 to popular acclaim and critical censure. Two other plays, *The Crimson Island* (1928) and *Cabal of Hypocrites* (a tragedy about Molière, 1929–30) were produced but had short and ill-starred runs. In the 1930s Bulgakov came increasingly under attack from the literary and political establishment, in part because of his sympathetic portrayal of the counter-revolutionary White Guard in the eponymous early novel. A bold letter to Stalin secured him some protection from that quarter, enough to keep him employed at the Art Theater and out of prison. In the late 1930s, aware that he was dying of a brain disorder, Bulgakov concentrated on revising the most important portions of *The Master and Margarita*, which he had begun 12 years earlier. The manuscript was still in progress when he died in Moscow, 10 March 1940. Thanks to the vigilance of his wife, the work fulfilled its own famous maxim that "manuscripts do not burn" and survived to be published in the 1960s.

Translations

Short Stories

Zapiski na manzhetakh, 1920–23

Rice, Alison, *Notes on the Cuff and Other Stories*, Ann Arbor, Michigan: Ardis, 1991

Diavoliada, 1924

Proffer, Carl R., "Diaboliad" in *Diaboliad and Other Stories*, edited by Carl and Ellendea Proffer, Bloomington: Indiana University Press, 1972; 2nd edition, Ann Arbor, Michigan: Ardis, 1993

Rokovye iaitsa, 1924

Ginsburg, Mirra, "The Fatal Eggs" in *The Fatal Eggs and Other Soviet Satire*, New York and London: Macmillan, 1965

Proffer, Carl R., "The Fatal Eggs" in *Diaboliad and Other Stories*, edited by Carl and Ellendea Proffer, Bloomington: Indiana University Press, 1972; 2nd edition, Ann Arbor, Michigan: Ardis, 1993

Sobach'e serdtse, 1925

Ginsburg, Mirra, *The Heart of a Dog*, New York: Grove Press, 1968

Glenny, Michael, *The Heart of a Dog*, New York: Harcourt Brace, 1968

Glenny, Michael (translator) and Alexander Chervinsky (stage adaptation), "The Heart of a Dog" in *Stars in the Morning Sky: Five New Plays from the Soviet Union*, with an introduction by Michael Glenny, London: Hern, 1989, pp. 1–59

Pyman-Sokolov, Avril, "The Heart of a Dog", *Soviet Literature*, 7 (1988) pp. 11–83; in *The Heart of a Dog and Other Stories*, translated by Kathleen Cook-Horujy and Avril Pyman, Moscow: Raduga, 1990

Novels

Belaia gvardiia, 1924

Glenny, Michael, *The White Guard*, London: Collins, and New York: McGraw Hill, 1971

Master i Margarita, 1966–67, written 1928–40

Burgin, Diana and Katherine Tiernan O'Connor, *The Master and Margarita*, Ann Arbor, Michigan: Ardis, 1995; London: Picador, 1996

Ginsburg, Mirra, *The Master and Margarita*, New York: Grove Press, 1967

Glenny, Michael, *The Master and Margarita*, New York: Harper and Row, and London: Collins/Harvill, 1967

Pevear, Richard and Larissa Volokhonsky, *The Master and Margarita*, with an introduction by Pevear, London: Penguin, 1997

Selections of Plays

Glenny, Michael, William Powell and Michael Earley, *Six Plays*, London: Methuen, 1991 (contains *The White Guard*, *Madame Zoyka*, *Flight*, *Molière*, *Adam and Eve*, *The Last Days*)

Proffer, Ellendea and Carl R. Proffer, *The Early Plays of Mikhail Bulgakov*, edited by Ellendea Proffer, Bloomington: Indiana University Press, 1972 (contains *The Days of the Turbins*, *Zoya's Apartment*, *Flight*, *The Crimson Island*, *A Cabal of Hypocrites*)

Plays

Dni Turbinykh, 1925–26

Lyons, Eugene, *Days of the Turbins* in *Six Soviet Plays*, translated by Lyons, Boston: Houghton Mifflin, 1934; London: Gollancz, 1935

Proffer, Carl R. and Ellendea Proffer, *The Days of the Turbins* in *The Early Plays of Mikhail Bulgakov*, edited by Ellendea Proffer, 1972

Reeve, F.D., *Days of the Turbins* in *An Anthology of Russian Plays*, translated and edited by Reeve, New York: Vintage, 1963

Kabala sviatosh, 1962, produced (as *Mol'er*), 1936

Hughes, Dusty and Helen Rappaport (literal translation), *Molière; or, The Union of Hypocrites*, London: Methuen, 1983

Beg, 1962, produced 1957

Hutchinson, Ron, *Flight*, London: Hern, 1998

Notes on the Cuff, 1920–23, are autobiographical sketches about Bulgakov's early days as a writer in the Caucasus and Moscow. The work is saturated with plays on words, especially on the bureaucratic neologisms of the early Soviet era. RICE (1991) attempts to recreate these puns in English, often by highly creative means, though inevitably the satiric bite is lost. Annotations are used to explain some of the puns and wordplay. Her version appears to contain all the text of the 1981 Russian version, published by Silver Age and edited by Lev Loseff, but it structures the text differently into chapters and paragraphs.

"Diaboliad", 1924, is a satire about workers at a match factory who are paid in matches when money runs out. As in "Notes on the Cuff", the humor revolves partly around puns and grotesque acronyms. PROFFER (1972) offers equally grotesque renditions in English, and also explains the wordplay and its political implications in annotations.

"The Fatal Eggs", 1924, is a satirical novella about a scientist who develops a ray that speeds and enhances organic growth, then mistakenly trains it on reptile eggs, with disastrous results. The GINSBURG version (1965) takes some liberties with syntax and vocabulary in the interest of readability and humor. PROFFER (1972) reproduces more exactly the strange and incomplete sentences and the odd visual imagery.

In "The Heart of a Dog", 1925, the story of a scientist who turns a dog temporarily into a human being, offers a biting satire of social conditions and political attitudes in Moscow in the 1920s. The GLENNY translation (1968, 1989) achieves felicitous solutions to the problem of reproducing Bulgakov's streetwise dog-diction and compact phrasing. It alters sentence structure rather more than is called for, replacing the dog's ironical tendency to connect seemingly unrelated phenomena in single sentences with more unified and logical sentences. The play adaptation is in some ways the most successful version of the work in English, since it draws on Glenny's talent for dialogue, and the prose original did not require very substantial reworking. PYMAN-SOKOLOV (1988) is faithful to the odd sentence-structure and syntax, reproducing incomplete sentences, strange connections within sentences, and interjections. This translation is less creative than Glenny's where diction is concerned, and has a more bookish quality. GINSBURG (1968) strives for ease of reading and to reproduce the humor of the original. Her dialogue tends to be somewhat more stilted than Glenny's.

Days of the Turbins, 1925–26, a play based on the epic novel *The White Guard*, concerns a well-to-do family in Kiev after the Bolshevik Revolution and their divided loyalties between the conflicting forces of revolution, resistance, and nationalist opportunism in Ukraine in 1918–19. Bulgakov's original script underwent several revisions in his lifetime. The PROFFER & PROFFER (1972) and REEVE (1963) translations are based on a version published in the Soviet Union in 1929, "apparently from the script used at [the Moscow Art Theater]". It also corresponds to the version in the five-volume collected works of Bulgakov published in Moscow in 1990. LYONS (1934) does not identify the source of his version, which differs mainly in that it has much more extensive stage directions. Of the three translations, the Proffers's, as usual, is the most scrupulously faithful to the sense of the original. Reeve's has the most readable dialogue, relatively free of awkward or stilted phrasings (such as Lyons's "I'm so hard-lucky", or the Proffers's "Well of course it's me, may I be damned if it's not!"). The play has a number of songs and ditties, and only Lyons attempts to make them singable in English.

The HUGHES & RAPPAPORT translation (1983) of *Molière* was successfully staged by the Royal Shakespeare Company in 1982; this version stays very close to Bulgakov's original.

Into *The Master and Margarita*, 1928–40, a satirical novel about the appearance of the Devil and his retinue in Moscow in the 1920s, is intertwined the story of a beleaguered writer who has written an extraordinary novel about Jesus Christ and Pontius Pilate. The four English translations of Bulgakov's novel are based on different original redactions of the text. GINSBURG (1967) translated the first published version that appeared in the journal *Moskva* in 1966–67, based on the author's widow's typescript but with significant deletions by the censors. Very shortly thereafter, GLENNY obtained a more complete manuscript and produced a translation (1967) that claimed to have restored some 23,000 words that were missing in the *Moskva*/Ginsburg version. Glenny's version also had omissions, as well as significant mistranslations. Nevertheless, for almost thirty years these were the only available English translations of the novel. The two more recent translations, by BURGIN & O'CONNOR and PEVEAR & VOLOKHONSKY, draw on considerable textual scholarship and restoration. Both stay fairly close to the (reasonably) definitive redaction of the novel that appears in the 1990 Moscow edition of Bulgakov's collected works. If the two earlier translations were designed primarily to capitalize on the sensation the novel caused when it first appeared in print, these two represent a more sober and scholarly approach to the novel, and a far more reliable one from a textual standpoint. Indeed, Burgin & O'Connor clearly had a scholarly audience in mind; the notes and commentary and the language of the translation itself have a distinctly academic ring. Richard Pevear has also contributed notes and an introduction to his translation, but these are more succinct and aimed at a mass audience.

Stylistically, the three translations considered here differ in many ways. GLENNY's is the most exuberant in terms of colloquial vocabulary and convincing dialogue. However, his version almost entirely does away with the highly intrusive narrator, and it strives to make sense of non sequiturs and leaps in logic that account for one source of the novel's humor. GINSBURG is somewhat more demure as a writer but absolutely reliable about reproducing the illogic and nonsense of the original. BURGIN & O'CONNOR are also scrupulously faithful to Bulgakov's sense (or nonsense), but sometimes they take their task too seriously and lose the wordplay or get bogged down in turgid prose. Pevear & Volokhonsky are more accomplished stylists; they employ a rich vocabulary and idiomatic usage, although their dialogue, too, can sometimes sound strained.

Banned in the Soviet Union under Stalin, one of Bulgakov's early plays, *Beg* (written in 1926, translated as *Flight* by Mirra Ginsburg in 1969 and in GLENNY's *Six Plays*, 1991, and as *On the Run* by Averil Pyman in 1972), was performed as *Flight* "to stirring effect" at the National Theatre in London in 1998, in Ron HUTCHINSON's "colloquial but precise" adaptation of the same year (*Observer*, 15 February 1998).

RACHEL MAY

Further Reading

Curtis, Julie, "The Smell of Rose Oil", *Times Literary Supplement* (29 August 1998)

Fiene, Donald M., "A Comparison of the Soviet and Possev editions of *The Master and Margarita*, with a Note on the Interpretation of the Novel", *Canadian-American Slavic Studies*, 15 (Summer–Fall 1981) pp. 330–54

May, Rachel, "Fact vs Fiction: Two Translations of Bulgakov's *The Master and Margarita*", in her *The Translator in the Text: On Reading Russian Literature in English*, Evanston, Illinois: Northwestern University Press, 1994

Milne, Lesley, *Mikhail Bulgakov: A Critical Biography*, Cambridge and New York: Cambridge University Press, 1990

Proffer, Ellendea, *An International Bibliography of Works by and about Mikhail Bulgakov*, Ann Arbor, Michigan: Ardis, 1976

Ivan Bunin 1870–1953

Russian novelist, short-story writer and poet

Biography

Born 10 October 1870, at Voronezh, in the country south of Moscow, into an old but impoverished family. He was educated at the Gymnasium at Elets (1881–85) and then at home in Ozerki, before going to Moscow University. From 1889 to 1891 he was a provincial journalist and from 1892 to 1894 a rural administration official. He was connected with the Symbolist publishing house Skorpion and, from the early 1900s until 1909, with Gor'kii's *Znanie* group, but remained independent. Bunin's early intention was to be a painter, but his first book of poetry was published in 1901. Between 1900 and 1914 he travelled in Europe, the Middle East, North Africa and India. During the 1917 Revolution and its aftermath Bunin was in Moscow, Kiev and Odessa, emigrating in 1920, via Constantinople, Serbia and Bulgaria, to Paris (1923) and finally going to live in Grasse, north of Cannes.

Much of Bunin's work reflects his regret for the decline of the Russian countryside, but his themes also had wider contexts – he translated from Longfellow and Byron and his best-known work is the long short story *The Gentleman from San Francisco* (*Gospodin iz San-Frantsisko*, 1915). His last collection of stories, *Temnye allei* (*Shadowed Paths*), appeared first in 1943. In 1909 Bunin was made an honorary member of the Russian Academy of Sciences. He won the Pushkin Prize in 1903 and 1909, and in 1933 was awarded the Nobel Prize for Literature.

Bunin's first marriage, in 1898 to Anna Nikolaevna Tsakni (one son), ended in separation in 1900. In 1921 he married Vera Muromtseva, with whom he had been living since 1907. He died 8 November 1953 in Paris.

Translations

Selections

Guerney, Bernard Guilbert, *The Dreams of Chang and Other Stories*, New York: Knopf, 1923, London: Secker, 1924; reprinted as *The Gentleman from San Francisco*, Knopf, 1927

Shartse, Olga, *Shadowed Paths*, edited by Philippa Hentges, Moscow: Foreign Languages Publishing House, 1944

Shartse, Olga, *The Gentleman from San Francisco and Other Stories*, New York: Washington Square Press, 1963

Shartse, Olga and Irina Zheleznova, *Stories and Poems: Ivan Bunin*, Moscow: Progress, 1979

Stories and Novellas

Antonovskie iabloki, 1900

Luker, Nicholas, "Antonov Apples", in *Anthology of Russian Neo-Realism: The "Znanie" School of Maxim Gorky*, edited by Luker, Ann Arbor: Ardis, 1982

Derevnia, 1910

Hapgood, Isabel, *The Village*, New York: Knopf, and London: Secker, 1923, 2nd edition, Knopf, 1933

Sukhodol, 1912

Shartse, Olga, "Dry Valley" in *Shadowed Paths*, translated by Shartse, 1944

Gospodin iz San-Frantsisko, 1915

Guerney, Bernard Guilbert, "The Gentleman from San Francisco" in *The Dreams of Chang and Other Stories*, translated by Guerney, 1923

Lawrence, D.H., and S.S. Koteliansky, "The Gentleman from San Francisco", *The Dial*, 72 (January 1922); in *The Gentleman from San Francisco and Other Stories*, translated by Lawrence, Koteliansky and Leonard Woolf, Richmond, Surrey: Hogarth Press, 1922, New York: Seltzer, 1923

Luker, Nicholas, "The Gentleman from San Francisco" in *Anthology of Russian Neo-Realism: The "Znanie" School of Maxim Gorky*, edited by Luker, Ann Arbor, Michigan: Ardis, 1982

Yarmolinsky, Avrahm and Babette Deutsch, "The Gentleman from San Francisco", *Russian Review* 2 (6 December, 1916); with "Lazarus" by Leonid Andreev, translated by Yarmolinsky and Deutsch, Boston: Stratford, 1918

"Voron", 1944

Hettlinger, Graham, "The Raven", *Kenyon Review*, 22/1 (Winter 2000)

Novel

Zhizn' Arsen'eva, 1930–39; complete edition 1952

Struve, Gleb and Hamish Miles, *The Well of Days* (parts 1–4), London: Hogarth Press, 1933, New York: Knopf, 1934; new edition, London: Lehmann, 1946; in *The Life of Arsen'ev: Youth*, edited, with an introduction by Andrew Baruch Wachtel, Evanston, Illinois: Northwestern University Press, 1994

"Lika" (part 5 of *Zhizn' Arsen'eva*), 1939

Hillis, Heidi, Susan McKean and Sven A. Wolf, "Lika" in *The Life of Arsen'ev: Youth*, edited, with an introduction by Andrew Baruch Wachtel, Evanston, Illinois: Northwestern University Press, 1994

Shartse, Olga, "Lika" in *Shadowed Paths*, translated by Shartse, 1944; in *The Gentleman from San Francisco and Other Stories*, translated by Shartse, 1963

Poetry

"Noch' pechal'na", 1900

Grebanier, Bernard, "Night Thoughts", music by Boris Levenson, New York: Hargail, 1944

Newmarch, Rosa, "Night Is Mournful, Mournful as Are My Dreams", music by Sergei Rachmaninov, New York: Boosey and Hawkes, 1947

"Na vysote, na snegovoi vershine", 1901

Franklin, Simon, "High on a Snowy Peak" in *Twentieth Century Russian Poetry: Silver and Steel*, edited, with an introduction, by Evgeny Evtushenko, edited by Albert C. Todd and Max Hayward, with Daniel Weissbort, New York: Doubleday, 1993

Markov, Vladimir, and Merrill Sparks, "On the Heights, on a Snowy Peak" in *Modern Russian Poetry*, edited, with an introduction, by Markov and Sparks, London: MacGibbon and Kee, 1966; Indianapolis: Bobbs Merrill, 1967

"Ne slykhat' eshche tiazhkogo groma", 1901

Deutsch, Babette, "A Night in July", *Russian Review*, 2 (6 December, 1916)

"Nadpis' na chashe", 1905

Deutsch, Babette and Avrahm Yarmolinsky, "The Inscription of the Bowl", *Russian Review*, 2 (6 December 1916)

"Prisela na mogil'nike Savure" ["Len"], 1907

Deutsch, Babette, "Flax" in *Modern Russian Poetry*, edited and translated by Deutsch and Avrahm Yarmolinsky, New York: Harcourt Brace, 1921

"Sinie oboi piliniali" ["V pustom dome"], 1916

Deutsch, Babette, "In an Empty House" in *Modern Russian Poetry*, edited and translated by Deutsch and Avrahm Yarmolinsky, New York: Harcourt Brace, 1921

"L'et bez kontsa. V lesu tuman", 1923

Franklin, Simon, "Endless Downpour, Misty Wood" in *Twentieth Century Russian Poetry: Silver and Steel*, selected, with an introduction by Evgeny Evtushenko, edited by Albert C. Todd and Max Hayward, with Daniel Weissbort, New York: Doubleday, 1993

Other Writing

"Osvobozhdenie Tolstogo", 1910, 1926, 1927, 1937

Marullo, Thomas Gaiton, *The Liberation of Tolstoy*, Evanston, Illinois: Northwestern University Press, 2001

Okaiannye dni, 1935

Marullo, Thomas Gaiton, *Cursed Days: A Diary of Revolution*, with an introduction, Chicago: Dee, 1998

"Rakhmaninoff", 1950

Traill, Vera and and Chancellor, Robin, "Rakhmaninoff", as one of "Six Miniatures", in *Memories and Portraits*, by Bunin, translated by Traill and Chancellor, New York: Doubleday, and London: Lehmann, 1951

On a tense Odessa evening in late November 1918, when the Black Sea port was occupied by successive European forces, Ivan Bunin consented to read from his works. Posters were put up at the last minute, it was dangerous to go out at night, and yet once Bunin began to read, the music of his symphonic prose stilled the room; the air itself seemed to await the writer's next word. Suddenly machine gun fire startled the quiet: "Gentlemen, they are shooting on Malaia Arnautskaia Street", announced a voice from the back of the hall.

Bunin's listeners that night heard two kinds of "music" – the "music" of his prose and the "music" of his times. For more than eight decades, this duality has defined the reception of Bunin's writings by an English-language readership.

A few examples. "The Gentleman from San Francisco", the first major prose fiction of Bunin to be translated into English, is not about a Russian subject. To the reader for whom Russian literature is relatively unknown, this long work might seem to be devoid of anything Russian. It is the story of a wealthy self-made American who sails first-class across the Atlantic on the luxury liner *Atlantida*, intending to enjoy a costly grand tour due to start in Rome during Passion Week. However, because of bad weather the *Atlantida* is diverted to Capri, where the Gentleman from San Francisco suffers a fatal stroke. The rich American, who had begun his journey in luxury, is smuggled unceremoniously back on board the same *Atlantida*, his body now in an improvised coffin in the ship's hold. Bunin portrays the ship as the symbol of modern decadence and as one of modern man's many technological usurpations of nature. In the description of the super ocean-going vessel ploughing the heavy seas, readers have perceived a modern image of a Dantesque circle of Hell. In the section of the story depicting the restoration of Capri to unspoilt nature and to its native inhabitants, they have also noted the religious coloration. Cloudy when the Gentleman from San Francisco arrives, the island sky clears when his body is taken away. This moment reaches its lyrical climax as the Abruzzi mountaineers descend a path leading to a grotto where stands an old and venerated statue of the Virgin, gleaming in the morning sun.

Clearly, the spiritual malaise of the World War I years, a sense that civilization had succumbed to a process of self-destruction from which recovery was problematic, contributed to the mood that inspired Bunin's story. And it was this critique of the West that governed its choice as the first piece to be translated for an American journal. Bunin affirmed his openness to a non-Russian theme in the summer of 1915, stating that a Russian-language edition of Thomas Mann's "Death in Venice" had stirred him to write a story that he at first entitled "Death on Capri". Its content may be non-Russian, but elements of its narratology clearly look back to Tolstoi. As Thomas Mann pointed out in 1926 (*Pariser Rechenschaft*, 24 January 1926), the protagonist of the Bunin story, who has no capacity to reflect on the meaning of life, may be contrasted to Tolstoi's Ivan Il'ich. Strikingly Tolstoian in style are Bunin's syntactic constructions describing the ship's journey through the blizzard, as well as his reminiscence of the autocrat Tiberius, the latter harking back to the historical digressions in *War and Peace*.

The first translators of "The Gentleman from San Francisco" attempted to listen to the "music" of Bunin's symphonic prose, even as their selection of this text represented a response to the "music of the times". In 1916 the Russian-born writer and Slavonic librarian AvrahmYarmolinsky and his wife, the well-known poet and critic Babette Deutsch, led off the English-language translations of the story for the recently founded *Russian Review*.

YARMOLINSKY & DEUTSCH (1916) undertook the daunting task of lifting the narrative out of parable – it can be read as a modern retelling of Luke 12:16–21, the parable of the rich man who after laying up his earthly treasure, feels entitled to enjoy life without regard for his spiritual poverty – and of transmitting the story's Tolstoian syntactic rhythms and its Dantesque imagery. Theirs is a competent first translation. Six years later, the "little" magazine *The Dial* published a new translation under the names of D.H. LAWRENCE & S.S. KOTELIANSKY (1922). The Russian expatriate Samuel Solomonovich Koteliansky (better known as Kot), recently introduced to D.H. Lawrence, did a yeoman first draft that was then raised to stunning artistry by Lawrence. In its exquisite rendering of Bunin's feeling for the Italian landscape, and in particular, of the passage describing the descent to the grotto of the Abruzzi mountaineers, it has never been equalled. The same year, this translation appeared in a collection of Bunin stories put out by Leonard and Virginia Woolf's Hogarth Press, even as Knopf (New York) and Secker (London) prepared to publish a rival translation by Bernard Guilbert GUERNEY (1923). Indeed, the Guerney translation carries a statement by Bunin that it is the "authorized" English version of this work. Bunin, who could fly into a rage over an omitted comma in Russian editions of his work, misplaced his confidence, for the Guerney translation is marred by quiddities. In 1982 the gifted Slavic scholar, essayist, and editor Nicholas LUKER (University of Nottingham) brought out an anthology of Russian Neo-Realism, reintroducing the West to the authors of Gor'kii's *Znanie* group, of which Bunin for a while was one. Luker, who has an ear for the British and American reader of the 21st century (and beyond), makes Bunin's symphonic prose more compact, so that the story moves faster.

Let us quickly compare. Here is the passage describing early morning in the hotel just before the dead body of the Gentleman from San Francisco is to be brought out and transported to the pier. Italic is mine.

> A na rassvete, kogda pobelelo za oknom sorok tret'ego nomera i vlazhnyi veter zashurshal rvanoi listvoi banana, kogda podnialos' i raskinulos' nad ostrovom Kapri goluboe utrennee nebo i ozolotilas' protiv solntsa voskhodiashchego za dalekimi sinimi gorami Italii, chistaia i chetkaia vershina Monte-Soliaro, kogda poshli na rabotu kamenshchiki,

popravliavshie na ostrove tropinki dlia turistov – prinesli k sorok tret'emu nomeru dlinnyi iashchik iz-pod sodovoi vody.

> At dawn, *when* the window panes in number 43 grew white, and a damp wind rustled in the leaves of the banana tree, *when* the pale-blue morning sky rose and stretched over Capri and *the sun, rising from behind the distant mountains of Italy touched with gold the pure, clearly outlined summit of Mount Solaro, when* the masons who mended the paths for the tourists on the island went out to their work – an oblong box was brought to room number 43. (Yarmolinsky & Deutsch, 1916)

Note that the Yarmolinsky retains the syntactic parallelism and the weight of the three "whens", but provides a weakened perspective: the reader sees first the most distant object – the rising sun – rather than what is closest at hand, the peak of Mount Solaro.

> *When* the dawn grew white at the window of number 43 and a damp wind began rustling the tattered fronds of the banana tree; *as* the blue sky of morning *lifted and unfolded* over Capri, *and Monte Solaro, pure and distinct, grew golden, catching the sun which was rising beyond the far-off mountains of Italy; just as* the labourers, who were mending the paths of the island for the tourists, came out for work, *a long box* was carried into room number 43. (Lawrence & Koteliansky, 1922)

Lawrence & Koteliansky soften the rhetorical emphasis of the "whens" by varying their heavy thud with "as" and "just as". They place the scene in proper perspective, so that what is nearest, Monte Solaro, comes first, and now Bunin's painterly details emerge in full. Moreover, they deftly introduce the theme of restoration through their choice of lexicon, "lifted and unfolded". Yet, incomprehensibly, in this segment of the story, they miss Bunin's symbolism for the degradation of the body and the elevation of the soul, transmitted in the contrast between the corpse of the Gentleman, emblematic of the new civilization, being carried out in a "soda water" box and the figures of the Abruzzi mountaineers, representatives of the old civilization, descending the path to the grotto.

> And at dawn, *when* it had become light *beyond the window* of room 43, and a humid wind had begun to rustle the tattered leaves of the banana tree, *when* the blue sky of morning had lifted and spread out over the Island of Capri, and the pure and clear-cut summit of Monte Solaro had grown *aureate* against the sun that was rising beyond the distant blue mountains of Italy; *when* the *stone masons* who were repairing the tourists' paths on the island had set out to work, – *a long box that had been used for soda-water* was brought to room number 43. (Guerney, 1923)

The Guerney translation is too literal (note the light "beyond the window" – an exact translation of "za oknom"). In places it is pretentious ("aureate" for the Russian "ozolotilas'", meaning simply, "had grown golden"). However, Guerney does get right the detail of the degradation of the body being taken away in a soda-water box (bottled water being another gift of Western civilization to pagan/Christian Italy).

> At dawn *when* it grew light outside the window of room 43, a damp breeze rustled the *ragged* leaves of the banana tree, *when* the morning sky rose and spread its *light blue cloak* over the island of Capri and *when* the sharply edged, clear peak of Monte Solaro was gilded by the sun rising over the distant blue mountains of Italy, *when* the stone-masons who repaired the island's paths for the tourists set off to work – a long soda-water box was brought to room 43. (Luker, 1982)

Luker's translation is concise, less flowery, more matter-of-fact. He retains the rhetorical emphasis yet introduces fresh equivalents to the lexicon of his predecessors, such as "ragged" to describe the torn leaves of the banana tree. Luker's version tells the story well and will transmit the music and power of Bunin's prose to his readers in the years to come.

From 1922 on, critics reviewing this story by an as yet unfamiliar Russian writer, responded to the "music of the times". In an unsigned review of the Hogarth Press edition of the *Gentleman from San Francisco and Other Stories*, the London *Times* of 17 May 1922 called it " a ruthless indictment of modern civilization".

In the years of Bunin's emigration (1920–53) the need to be read, in order both to keep alive the continuities of Russian literature and to earn a living, complicated the writer's own response to his foreign readership. For instance Bunin never could understand all of the fuss over his story "The Village", which he felt misrepresented him – he was not a reactionary anti-peasant ideologue. He was irked by the enthusiasm for this work expressed on more than one occasion by André Gide. Yet, in 1923, needing a readership – and money – he permitted another "authorized" translation, in this case HAPGOOD's *The Village*.

Ten years later, at Stockholm's Presentation Hall, Russia's first Nobel laureate acknowledged his selection as a collective gesture "to a Russian diaspora, humiliated and insulted in all its sensibilities".

In that same year, 1933, the Hogarth Press brought out parts 1–4 of *The Life of Arsen'ev* (written 1927–30), claimed by many readers and critics to be Bunin's finest work. Among the first critical readers to respond both to the music of this Bunin text and to the music of the times in which it appeared were the eminent émigré Slavist, Gleb Petrovich Struve, and the writer Hamish Miles, who together produced a translation of Bunin's finest novel, as far as the author had then taken his story (STRUVE & MILES, 1933).

In the 1940s, when the Soviet embassy in Paris was actively courting Bunin in an effort to persuade him to return to his homeland, this balance of text and times was upset. In these same years, the Moscow-based Foreign Languages Publishing House began to reissue Bunin in English translation. Among these is "Dry Valley" (SHARTSE, 1944), a story that focuses not on the debauchery of the peasant in 19th-century Russia, but on the decadence of the gentry. By virtue of that motif alone, it was an appropriate work with which to reacquaint the Soviet reader with this vociferously anti-Soviet writer in exile. The irony is that in "Dry Valley" Bunin is Faulkner *avant la lettre*, showing the gentry to have been as prone to self-ruination and as debauched as the peasants whom he depicted in "The Village", and his prose is not tendentious but is an elegy with a sustained musicality.

More than 40 years would pass, after its publication in Russian, before the 1994 translation by Northwestern University Press of *The Life of Arsen'ev* would bring the complete text to the English reader, a testament to the author's place in the Modernist canon of world literature. The editor, the brilliant young Slavist Andrew Wachtel, wrote an introduction that is the best statement to appear yet on the narratology of this work. As Wachtel explains, *The Life of Arsen'ev* belongs to a specific genre. It continues in Russian letters "the pseudo-autobiographical novel devoted to childhood" (introduction, p. 3), among them Sergei Aksakov's *The Childhood Years of Bagrov's Grandson* (1858); Tolstoi's *Childhood* (1852), *Boyhood* (1854), and *Youth* (1857); Gor'kii's *Childhood* (1913); and Andrei Belyi's *Kotik Letaev* (1922). In these novels, as Wachtel reminds us, there is no identification between author and narrator – each is a work of fiction while following closely the facts of its author's life. Parts 1–4 of the 1994 version of *The Life of Arsen'ev* reprint unchanged the Struve edition; but part 5, "Lika", is a new translation of Bunin's 1933 concluding section of the novel.

In reprinting unrevised the translation of parts 1–4, a choice was made, dictated possibly by the economics of publishing, together with the respect due to the achievement of a notable predecessor. Unfortunately, STRUVE & MILES suffers from recurrent use of distracting Americanisms, such as attributes formed by the -y suffix. Ludicrous to an American ear is Struve's naïve use of the word "horsey" (normally used to designate an upper-class way of life, as in "the horsey set"). Struve translates Bunin' sentence "V koniushne zhili svoei osoboi loshadinoi zhizn'iu" as "In the stables the horses were living their own horsey life." Preferable would be "In the stables equine life reigned."

The team of translators of part 5 (HILLIS, MCKEAN, & WOLF, 1994) also introduce Americanisms of the 1960s–90s: "Nu deti moi, ia ischezaiiu" is jarringly rendered as "Well, guys, I'm out of here." A more neutral translation might have been simply: "Well, children, I'm about to leave you." Let us not quibble, however: the Northwestern University Press edition makes a major new contribution to bringing Bunin's prose fiction to an anglophone readership worldwide.

Finally, mention must be made of Nicholas LUKER's translation (1982) of "Antonov Apples" for the Ardis *Anthology of Russian Neo-Realism* and the translation of "The Raven" by Graham HETTLINGER (2000) for the *Kenyon Review*. Each of these seems to be taken out of time, so that the reader, like Bunin's listener of 1918, is bewitched by the music of the author's prose.

Translations of Bunin's poetry into English were made first by DEUTSCH & YARMOLINSKY in 1916, as an attempt to demonstrate the artistic range of the author of "The Gentleman from San Francisco". Most successful among them are Bunin's terse narrative poems, such as "The Inscription of the Bowl" and "Flax". The selections made by MARKOV & SPARKS (1966) and Evtushenko (of FRANKLIN's translations, 1993) may be of more complex lyrics, but the translations do not astonish. In the tradition of Russian classical poetry, a Bunin poem (alas, only one) has been set to music. Rosa NEWMARCH wrote an unobtrusively fine translation of "Noch' pechal'na" ("Night Is Mournful ..."). All the more disappointing is the setting by Rachmaninov. Its turgid, unrelieved harmonics seem to reflect the composer's low spirits in 1906 rather than the tender yearning of Bunin's poem. Rachmaninov and Bunin met several times in Yalta before the Russian Revolution of 1917 and Bunin ecstatically recalled those meetings in a memoir (TRAILL & CHANCELLOR, 1951). Rachmaninov's setting for "Night is Mournful" appeared after World War II, when the composer was living in the United States, and Bunin in Grasse, France, writing his final pages. Needed now for Bunin's poetry are translators with the fervor for his work of one of Bunin's earliest admirers, Vladimir Nabokov.

With the fall of communism, however, and the struggle toward the rise of a new Russia, Bunin specialists are making Bunin available to anglophone readers as a cultural critic. Thomas MARULLO has completed the Herculean task of translating (1998, 2000) two of Bunin's major nonfiction works. The first is *Cursed Days*, diaries that cover the chaos and anarchy first in Moscow in 1918, then in the south, where the writer and Vera Muromtseva, his common-law wife, lived until 1920, when they left Odessa by steamer for Constantinople and thence western Europe. The translation conveys the fury of the Bunin voice as he tries to go about his daily life in Odessa in 1919, not knowing when his quarters will be torn up by the Bolsheviks. Marullo provides a masterly introduction, comparing *Cursed Days* to the strong line of dissident writing in Russian literature from the 17th-century Archpriest Avaakum to 20th-century Solzhenitsyn.

MARULLO's second major translation (2001) is *The Liberation of Tolstoy*, the title of which leads one to expect a focus solely on Tolstoi's nocturnal flight from Iasnaia Poliana in 1910. However, such is not the case. A number of Russia's most celebrated 20th-century thinkers, from Sergei Bulgakov to Nikolai Berdiaev and Mark Aldanov, have pondered the enigma of Tolstoi as man and artist. Bunin's "biography" is unique in that it remakes the genre into a multi-voiced conversation. To the voices of Tolstoi himself and of his family members, and of Bunin, the unifier of the recollections of others, is added the voice of Marullo "heard" in the extensive footnotes in which he holds Bunin and Tolstoi and those of their circles to a high standard of historical veracity. *The Liberation of Tolstoy* also illuminates the fascination of Bunin and Tolstoi with Buddhism, a subject further illuminated by Marullo's study, *If You See the Buddha*.

These first editions of Bunin's non-fiction in English translation promise a new balance between times and text. None the less, they leave us, like the hushed listeners of 1918, waiting to hear the remainder of the reading. We now need a publisher who will bring us a multi-volume reissue in English of Bunin's fiction, poetry, and prose.

RUTH RISCHIN

Further Reading

Marullo, Thomas Gaiton (editor), *Ivan Bunin: Russian Requiem, 1885-1920: A Portrait from Letters, Diaries, and Fiction*, Chicago: Dee, 1993

Marullo, Thomas Gaiton (editor), *Ivan Bunin: From the Other Shore, 1920-1933: A Portrait from Letters, Diaries, and Fiction*, Chicago: Dee, 1995

Marullo, Thomas Gaiton, *If You See the Buddha: Studies in the Fiction of Ivan Bunin*, Evanston, Illinois: Northwestern University Press, 1998

Richard Burton 1821–1890

British anthropologist, linguist, literary translator, diplomat and explorer

Biography

Richard Francis Burton was born in Torquay, Devon, 19 March 1821. His father was an army colonel. A many-faceted personality, Burton was educated in England, France and Italy and had a colourful and adventurous life. He was dismissed from Oxford University for a minor offence without a degree and in 1842 joined the Indian Army, serving under Sir Charles Napier. He left India in 1849 and travelled widely: penetrating the holy city of Mecca in disguise (1853); from 1854 exploring in Africa, controversially, with John Hanning Speke; studying the Mormons on the spot in Utah (1860). In 1861 he married Isabel Arundell. He was posted as British consul to various far-flung spots, including Fernando Po, now Bioko, off the coast of West Africa (1861–64), Brazil (1865– 69), Syria (1869–71) and Trieste (1872[-90), and was knighted in 1886.

Among the scores of publications arising from his travels are *Goa and the Blue Mountains* (1851); *Falconry in the Valley of the Indus* (1852); *Pilgrimage to Al-Medinah and Meccah* (2 vols, 1855–56); *First Footsteps in East Africa* (1856); *The Lake Regions of Equatorial Central Africa* (2 vols, 1860); and *Unexplored Syria* (2 vols, 1870). He knew many languages and published about 30 volumes of translations, some of the erotic ones privately or secretly printed. His translation of *The Lusiads* by Camões came out in two volumes in 1880. The 16 volumes of his *The Book of the Thousand Nights and a Night* were privately printed 1885–88. With a collaborator he did an English version of the *Kama Sutra* (1883). In 1886 he translated *The Perfumed Garden* into English from a French version, and at his death left among his manuscripts an English translation of the same text from the original Arabic. He died in Trieste, 20 October 1890.

The life of Richard Burton, traveller, orientalist, translator and explorer, is full of contradictions. Burton seems to have acquired an ability to learn languages early in life, perhaps when he travelled with his parents as a child, and despite being sent down from Oxford he acquired a solid grounding in classical languages and taught himself Arabic. He was later to claim that he knew 40 languages (inclusive of dialectal variations). His linguistic skills were remarkable, but he cannot be considered as a leading translator of his day, partly because of the eclectic nature of his translation practice and partly also because he did not write particularly well in English.

After studying Arabic, Burton went to India, where he acquired several Indian languages and began to take an interest in anthropology. His earliest publications in 1851 are accounts of the seven years he spent in India, then in 1855–56 he produced a three-volume account of a journey to Mecca, in which he claimed to have been the first non-Muslim European to reach the holy city. This journey established him as a controversial public figure, and when in 1858 he and John Hanning Speke reported their discovery of Lake Tanganyika, Burton's reputation as an explorer rose even higher, only to suffer a serious blow when he and Speke quarrelled publicly and questions were asked about the financing of the expedition. In 1861 Burton was sent to Fernando Po, known as the "Foreign Office grave", as British consul. For the rest of his life he was to serve as consul in marginal posts, a clear indication of his lack of favour with the British diplomatic establishment.

Burton's writings fall into several categories: there are accounts of his diverse journeys and expeditions, anthropological studies and translations. Early in his life, Burton acquired an interest in sexology and became fascinated with sexual practices outside Europe and with writings of an explicit sexual nature. Together with a friend from the Bombay Civil Service, F.F. Arbuthnot, Burton translated the Sanskrit erotic text the *Ananga Ranga, Stage of the Bodiless One, or the Hindu Art of Love* and had it privately printed in 1873. After printing only a few copies, the printers refused to proceed for fear of prosecution, and the edition did not finally appear until 1885, and then for private circulation only. Arbuthnot and Burton then translated *The Kama Sutra of Vatsyana*, an erotic treatise on sexuality and marriage. Both these works were originally intended for readers of both sexes, but with his translation of the Arabic erotic classic, *The Perfumed Garden of the Cheikh Nefzaoui*, published privately in 1886, Burton produced a text for male readers only. He translated this work from French in the first instance, and was working on an extended annotated translation from the original Arabic when he died. His wife burned the manuscript, thereby destroying 14 years of Burton's research. The clash between Isabel Burton's piety and her husband's life-long interest in bizarre sexual practices finally came out into the open.

Burton also produced a translation of a collection of erotic Latin poetry, *Priapeia*, published in 1890, and edited two Persian texts, *The Behāristān* (*Abode of Spring*) and *The Gulistān or Rose Garden of Sa'adi*, translated by Edward Rehatsek, that appeared in 1887 and 1888, both for private subscribers only.

However, in addition to his translations of erotica, Burton also produced translations of other classic texts. In 1885 he published *A Plain and Literal Translation of the Arabian Nights' Entertainments* in 10 volumes, with a further six volumes appearing in 1886–88. This translation, with copious anthropological notes, received mixed reviews, with some critics attacking it as pornographic and others praising its energy and originality. Burton's translation strategy was not of the kind guaranteed to appeal to many readers: pointing out that the original Arabic was very varied, Burton used a hybrid English that combined the contemporary with the mock-archaic.

His fascination with oriental writing led him in 1880 to produce a pseudo-translation, *The Kasīdah (Couplets) of Hājī Abdū El-Yezdī*. This is a collection of his own original poems, which he claimed under the pseudonym of F.B. to have been given to him by his master and friend, a Persian poet. The poems are supported by Burton's usual practice of extensive footnotes, in which he states that the text has never been translated verbatim, that many stanzas have been omitted and that "a familiar European turn has been given to many sentiments which were judged to be too Oriental", a statement that illustrates his translation practice as a whole. Quite why he should have decided to produce a fake translation in this way is unclear, but the success of FitzGerald's *Rubaiyat of Omar Khayyam* that appeared in 1859 may well have stirred him to try to compete.

Besides his translations from oriental languages, Burton also translated from Portuguese. In 1880 he published a version of Camões's *The Lusiads*, followed in 1881 by a long study of Camões and in 1884 by his translation of Camões's lyric poetry. Significantly, Burton uses the term "Englished" to describe what he has done with Camões's works. Following their stay in Brazil, Burton and his wife Isabel translated texts by two Brazilian writers, José de Alencar's *Iracema, The Honey-Lips* and J.M. Pereira da Silva's *Maluel De Moraes, A Chronicle of the Seventeenth Century*, both of which appeared in 1886. After his death, posthumous translations of *Il Pentamerone*, from Giovanni Battista Basile's *Pentamerone* (1634) and *The Carmina of Gaius Valerius Catullus* were published.

Burton's interest in translation seems to have derived from his personal preference for specific authors, such as Camões, and his obsessive interest in erotica, where anthropology and prurience combine. He was primarily concerned with the source texts and culture rather than in any potential readers, and so his translation practice can be said to be source-oriented. His English style tended to be pedantic and at times uneven and his translations are not very readable. Nevertheless, his extensive linguistic knowledge and scientific attention to detail meant that he produced translations with great care and academic rigour.

SUSAN BASSNETT

Translations

Camões, Luis, *Os Lusíadas (The Lusiads)*, edited by Isabel Burton, 2 vols, 1880

The Kasīdah (Couplets) of Hājī Abdū El-Yezdī: A Lay of the Higher Law, 1880

The Kama Sutra of Vatsyana, translated with F.F. Arbuthnot, 1883; "definitive" edition 1885

Ananga Ranga (Stage of the Bodiless One); or, The Hindu Art of Love, 1885

A Plain and Literal Translation of the Arabian Nights' Entertainments, Now Entitled The Book of the Thousand Nights and a Night, 10 vols, 1885; *Supplemental Notes to the Book of the Thousand Nights and a Night: With Notes Anthropological and Explanatory*, 6 vols, 1885–88

Pereira da Silva, J.M., *Manuel de Moraes: A Chronicle of the Seventeenth Century*, translated with Isabel Burton, 1886

The Perfumed Garden of the Cheikh Nefzaoui, A Manual of Arabian Erotology, 1886

Priapeia; or, The Sportive Epigrams of Divers Poets on Priapus: the Latin Text now for the First Time Englished in Verse and Prose (the Metrical Version by "Outidanos") with Introduction, Notes , Explanatory and Illustrative, and Excursus, by "Neaniskos", 1890

Basile, Giovanni Batista, *Il Pentamerone; or, The Tale of Tales*, 1893

Catullus, *The Carmina of Caius Valerius Catullus*, translated with Leonard C. Smithers, 1894

Further Reading

Lovell, Mary S., *A Rage to Live: A Biography of Richard and Isabel Burton*, London: Little Brown, and New York: Norton, 1998

McLynn, Frank, *Burton: Snow upon the Desert*, London: John Murray, 1990

Robert Burton 1577–1640

English satirist and translator

Biography

Born in Lindley, Leicestershire, 8 February 1577. He studied at Brasenose College, Oxford, and at the age of 22 was elected a student (life fellow) of Christ Church. There, in spite of later, as a clergyman, acquiring two parishes, he lived for the rest of his life. He became a bachelor of divinity in 1614 and vicar of Thomas's Church, Oxford in 1616. His first work, the Latin comedy *Philosophaster*, was written in 1606 and performed at Christ Church in 1618. He is best known for his satirical work *The Anatomy of Melancholy*. He brought out the first quarto edition of his compendious work in 1621, under the pseudonym of "Democritus Junior". In it this new "laughing philosophy" attributed the malady of "melancholy" to all humanity, and learnedly retrieved information related to that subject from classical and medieval written sources and from folklore. The original book underwent alterations and extensions, reaching a 5th edition in Burton's lifetime. He died in Oxford, 25 January 1640.

The Anatomy of Melancholy (1621, enlarged 1621–51) is one of the great books of the end of the English Renaissance. Its author, Robert Burton, was a lover of language and knowledge, about whom George Steiner said that excepting Shakespeare, literature had known "no greater gourmand of words" ("The Retreat from the World", *Language and Silence*, 1967). This immediately becomes clear to anyone who plunges into the half-million words of *The Anatomy*, Burton's attempt to give a summary of everything that was known about humanity at the end of the Renaissance.

The first half of the 17th century, during which the six

progressively larger editions of *The Anatomy* were published, produced some of the greatest translation in English literary history; this was the golden age of Thomas North, Philemon Holland, James Mabbe, John Florio, Thomas Shelton, Thomas Heywood and George Chapman. None of these names is mentioned by Burton, though he mentions Ben Jonson, Thomas Danett and Barten Holiday, whose translations he uses.

Burton wanted to write his book in Latin: "It was not mine intent to prostitute my Muse in English, or to divulge secreta Minervæ, but to have exposed this more contract in Latin, If I could have got it printed" (*The Anatomy of Melancholy*, Oxford University Press, 1989–94, vol. 1, p. 16). His English is colloquial and fairly free of Latinisms. However, *The Anatomy* contains innumerable quotations (at least 13,000) from the works of 1,694 writers (for example, Seneca is quoted 325 times), and the great majority of these are in Latin. It is a compendium of knowledge dating from the 8th century BC (Hesiod) to Burton's contemporaries: "I have laboriously collected this *Cento* out of divers writers, and that *sine injuriâ*, I have wronged no Authors, but given every man his owne". Here, as in many other instances, Burton can be compared to Montaigne: "I am ever here and there in picking and culling, from this and that book, the sentences that please me". Both Montaigne and Burton had very large libraries; at the time of his death Burton owned 2,000 books, about the same number as the Bodleian Library at its creation in 1602.

Burton quotes in Latin, not Greek: "Greek authors, *Plato, Plutarch, Athenœus &c.* I have cited out of their interpretors, because the Originall was not so ready &c." (vol. 1, p. 19) and more often than not he adds his own translation of the quotation: "My translations are sometimes rather Paraphrases, than interpretations, *non ad verbum*, but as an Author, I use more liberty, and that's only taken, which was to my purpose: Quotations are often inserted in the Text, which make the stile more harsh, or in the Margent as it hapned" (vol. 1, p. 19).

It would be easy to pass a negative judgement on Burton's translations, to look at them from today's point-of-view, with its emphasis on faithfulness to the original text; Burton, by using the word "paraphrase", forearmed himself against modern translation cavils. To take up Antoine Berman's concept of "an essentially positive critique" of translation (*Pour une critique des traductions: John Donne,* Paris, 1995), Burton's individual acts of translation should be seen in the much larger context of his humanist intent (that of most translators of that golden age), to bring important foreign texts to a public that neither read Latin nor had access to libraries. It should also be noted that Burton's quotations are frequently faulty, as if drawn directly from his memory, and that *The Anatomy of Melancholy,* with its thousands of quotations, is primarily Burton's creation ("as an author"), and not simply an anthology of quotations.

Though his translations of Latin poetry are often extremely clumsy, especially when he tried to remain close to the original or to adapt the Latin meter to an English form, he sometimes achieves very good verse translation.

A few examples of Burton's translation system (or, more exactly, of the technique he used for incorporating sentences from ancient authors into his text – as painters use pigments) should now be analysed.

In his preface, "Democritus to the reader", Burton – apparently translating Sesellius' (Claude de Seyssell's) *De Republica Gallorum* – writes about the "kingdome of *France, a diaposon and sweet harmony of Kings, Princes, Nobles and Plebians*", where the word "sweet" is borrowed from Jean Bodin, and the word "diapason" from Gaspari Contarini (vol. 1, p. 92; from Louis Évrard's analysis of a few pages of Burton).

In "A Consolary Digression" (vol. 2, p. 195), Burton misquotes the Colonna family's motto, "*Flectimur non frangimur*" ("We bend but do not stoop"), as "*Flecti potest, frangi non potest*", subsequently paraphrasing it "to signify that he [pope Alexander VI] might breake them by force, but so never make them stoope".

In some instances, by omitting a few words, Burton bends to his purpose a sentence whose original meaning was different. A quotation from Aristotle, given (for once) in Greek as well as in Latin, is translated as "for poverty begets sedition and villainy" (vol. 1, p. 70), whereas Aristotle's text said that sedition came from inequalities *not only* in riches, *but* also in public honours.

Latin quotations are sometimes used more than once, and it is interesting to note that they are not always translated in the same way. For example Seneca's words "*Vivere nolunt, more inesciunt*", are first translated as "they cannot dye, they will not live" (vol. 1, p. 389), and, further on, as "live they will not, dye they cannot" (vol. 1, p. 431), which shows Burton's inclination to adapt his borrowings to the rhythm of his own sentences. When he discourses about love, he often quotes in Latin without a translation ("Good Master Schoolmaster, do not English this") what he considers improper; a large part of the chapter on "How love tyrannizeth over Men..." is written in Latin; Plutarch's "*vitale semen conservare*" is coyly translated as an injunction to "abstaine from verery" (vol. 2, p. 32).

Burton's use of Montaigne, who is always quoted in Florio's translation, with just a few changes, though with no mention of the translators (F.A. Yates suggested that Burton collaborated with Florio in his translation of Boccalini's *The New-Found Politicke*) is treated in Fritz Dieckow's 1902 study on Burton's indebtedness to Florio.

It is not possible, in a limited space, to analyse fully the various ways in which Burton uses Latin texts. It is certain, though, that every text was grist to his *own* mill, and that his general purpose perfectly explains the liberties taken with the authors he quotes and translates.

BERNARD HŒPFFNER

Recent Editions

The Anatomy of Melancholy, edited by Floyd Dell and Paul Jordan-Smith, 2 vols, New York: Doran, 1927

The Anatomy of Melancholy, edited with an introduction by Holbrook Jackson, 3 vols, London: Dent, 1932

The Anatomy of Melancholy, edited by Thomas C. Faulkner, Nicolas K. Kiessling and Rhonda Blair, 3 vols, Oxford: Oxford University Press, 1989–94; commentary, edited by J.B. Bamborough and Martin Dodsworth, 3 vols, 1989–2000

Further Reading

Dieckow, Fritz, "John Florios englische Übersetzung der Essays Montaignes und Lord Bacons, Ben Jonsons und Robert Burtons Verhältnis zu Montaigne" (dissertation), University of Strasbourg, 1902

Évrard, Louis (editor and translator), *L'Utopie; ou, la république poétique de Robert Burton*, Paris: Obsidiane, 1992 (extracts from *The Anatomy of Melancholy*)
Jordan-Smith, Paul, *Bibliographia Burtoniana: A Study of Robert Burton's The Anatomy of Melancholy*, Stanford, California: Stanford University Press, 1931
Simon, Jean Robert, *Robert Burton (1577–1640) et L'Anatomie de la Mélancolie*, Paris: Didier, 1965

Dino Buzzati 1906–1972

Italian novelist, journalist and painter

Biography

Born Dino Buzzati-Traverso in San Pellegrino, near Belluno, 16 October 1906. He was educated in Milan at the Ginnasio Parini (1916–24), and studied law at the University of Milan, earning his degree, 1928. Buzzati was a journalist with Italy's leading daily newspaper, *Il Corriere della Sera*, Milan, from 1928 to 1972; the newspaper first published much of his writing. His first two novels, *Bàrnabo della montagne* [Bàrnabo of the Mountains], 1933 and *Il segreto del Bosco Vecchio* [The Secret of the Old Wood], 1935 established the mountain settings and the fable-like narratives that recur throughout his works. His third novel, considered to be his masterpiece, *Il deserto dei tartari* (*The Tartar Steppe*), 1940, caught the mood of the first year of World War II; it was translated into French by Albert Camus. The Kafkaesque qualities of the novel and his other works were noted, though some critics stretched the comparison. He wrote two more novels, including a work of science fiction, *Il grande ritratto* (*Larger than Life*), 1960, but did his best work in the short story (*Sessanta racconti* [Sixty Stories], 1958, and other collections). His plays were popular in Italy: the most important was *Il caso clinico* [A Clinical Case], 1953; he also directed plays, operas and ballets. *Cronache terrestri* [Earthly Chronicles], 1972, a collection of stories and essays, and *Dino Buzzati: un autoritratto* [Dino Buzzati: A Self-Portrait], 1973, were published posthumously. He was also a painter: his first exhibition was in 1958, and he had exhibitions in Milan and Paris 1966, Rome 1971, and Milan 1972. Buzzati married Almerina Antoniazzi in 1966. He was awarded a number of prizes, including the Strega prize, 1958, and the Mario Massai prize (for journalism), 1970. Died in Rome, 28 January 1972.

Translations

Novels

Il deserto dei tartari, 1940
Hood, Stuart C., *The Tartar Steppe*, London: Secker and Warburg, and New York: Farrar Straus, 1952

Il grande ritratto, 1960
Reed, Henry, *Larger than Life*, London: Secker and Warburg, 1962; New York: Walker, 1967

Un amore, 1963
Green, Joseph, *A Love Affair*, New York: Farrar Straus, 1964; London: André Deutsch, 1965

Short Stories

Sessanta racconti, 1958 (includes *I sette messageri*, 1942; *Paura alla Scala*, 1949; *Il crollo della Balliverna*, 1958)
Landry, Judith and Cynthia Jolly, *Catastrophe: The Strange Stories of Dino Buzzati*, London: Calder and Boyars, 1965

Le notti difficili, 1971
Venuti, Lawrence, *Restless Nights: Selected Stories of Dino Buzzati*, San Francisco: North Point Press, 1983; Manchester: Carcanet, 1984

The novels and short stories of Dino Buzzati, like the plays of his compatriot Luigi Pirandello before him, exemplify those texts that transcend borders and frontiers to be given, if anything, a warmer reception abroad than at home. Buzzati's precise, concise prose with its powerful narrative pull and fluid syntax has a crystalline quality that marks him off from many of his Italian contemporaries. His enigmatic, elusive works, some of which approach the parable in form, resist easy interpretation or elucidation as historical or political metaphor, even as their sharp focus compels our intrigued attention. Buzzati's sense of irony, his refusal to align himself with the political or literary orthodoxies of his day, his adoption of a genre – the fantastic – quite at odds with either the disengaged hermeticism dominant in his youth or the political materialism of the post-war period, have resulted in a body of work outside the categorical assertions of traditional literary criticism. His work deals essentially with an anguished sense of anxiety, an ineradicable unease which is existential and moral as well as erotic.

The preoccupations that were to mark the whole of Buzzati's output – waiting, as in Beckett, in expectation of some definitive event that will give purpose to life, its failure to materialize or the disappointment it inevitably engenders, the unstoppable passage of time, the futility of existence – are touched upon in Buzzati's untranslated first novel, *Bàrnabo delle montagne* (1933), which none the less has a serenity missing from later works, a lighter note of optimism in which the smallness of man can be redeemed by the poetry of nature.

It was with his third novel, *Il deserto dei tartari* (1940), that Buzzati imposed himself on the reading public both in Italy and abroad, and began to be widely translated into English, French and German. The work is set in the military environment of a remote, almost forgotten Fortress whose function is to guard against the anticipated invasion of the Tartars across the desert. On the edges of the kingdom, the Fortress looks out into the void, inhabited by generations of soldiers whose initial eager expectation of battle and glory becomes gradually more muted, slipping inexorably into a sense of life as unsalvageable and irredeemable waste.

The protagonist, Lieutenant Drogo, begins his duty at the Fortezza in the firm belief that his posting is only temporary. The rigorous discipline, order and self-perpetuating routine of military life dramatically and inexorably mark off the passage of time as Drogo's hope of returning to the city fades: Drogo and his fellow soldiers march towards the void in order, obedience and in perfect time, a chillingly formal, aesthetic illustration of *tempus fugit*. In the absence of a final end and purpose to their lives on this forgotten frontier of space and time, the means, military discipline, becomes all-important. A soldier fails to give the correct password to be readmitted into the Fortress after a patrol, and – in accordance with regulations – is shot as an enemy.

When the Tartars do, finally, arrive, the Fortress swings into action in fulfilment of its purpose. But for Drogo it is too late: he is an old man, sick and unsteady on his feet, expelled from the Fortress by his superiors as an encumbrance, nullified by the same orders and regulations that he has until now embodied. In the distilled, rarefied temporal sphere of the Fortress, Drogo incarnates an entropic and deeply pessimistic vision of life as headlong rush towards disintegration and decay held only temporarily at bay by frenetic, senseless activity and wilful illusions. Stuart HOOD's translation (1952) renders perfectly the anxiety experienced in the face of the void articulated in lucid and exact prose, while the transposition from the original "deserto" to the translated "steppe" conveys well the wild, empty spaces against which we desperately erect our meagre defences.

Despite its apparent divergence from the previous novels and stories in terms of style and genre, *A Love Affair* (*Un amore*, 1963) transposes Buzzati's continuing preoccupations with time, desire and death from the realm of the metaphysical, the literary even, to that of the erotic, and the author's rebuttal of accusations that he was bowing to the current fashion of realism, or neo-realism, in writing, is vindicated by this fundamental continuity of theme. Neither is his style, essentially, much changed. Always precise, spare and unadorned (a result of the communicativeness and readability required of high-quality journalists) Buzzati's analytical prose is ideally suited to this clinical investigation of love not as romance but as pathology, and to the precision and clarity offered by the English language. If the title of the translation directs our gaze to the mundane "affair" of the original, GREEN's translation (1964) otherwise captures well the nuances of Dorigo's exquisite suffering.

A Love Affair is set in urban Milan during the economic boom of the late 1950s and early 1960s. The hell of the modern city is closely and explicitly identified with Laide, the youthful, unpredictable, uncontainable ballerina *cum* call girl with whom the protagonist Antonio Dorigo falls in love, and whose very intangibility offers no satisfaction but only exacerbated desire. Like Drogo in *The Tartar Steppe*, Dorigo – and the similarity of names is striking – searches for the absolute, the culminating, crowning moment that will justify and give value to life, but just as the Tartars never come, so the charmed reciprocity of love eludes Antonio. The deadening repetition of military manoeuvres here gives way to the equally senseless and futile repetition of ever more frenzied raised expectations and dashed hopes. Only with her pregnancy is Laide dramatically returned from the realm of the fantasizing and fetishizing psyche to the reality of the body, no longer the source of disorienting and disordered madness.

As a journalist, precision, concision and the need to attract and maintain the reader's interest from the opening paragraphs were clearly tools of Buzzati's trade, and his spare, unrhetorical style was particularly suited to the short story, typically exploring a situation, a mood or an event rather than psychological development. A situation – bizarre, fantastic or merely strange – is outlined in the opening lines, and is then worked out to its inexorable, precisely logical conclusion. As in the work of Franz Kafka, the initial absurdity or dislocation of reality is then subject to iron rules of mathematical progression, and the sense of existential unease and strangeness results from the juxtaposition of an initial disruption of our normal perception not with flights of imaginative fancy but with disturbingly familiar and inexorable narrative and logical processes.

Buzzati's eight volumes of short stories, some of which were translated into English in the mid-1960s by LANDRY & JOLLY and in the mid-1980s by VENUTI, are dominated by an existential preoccupation with sickness and death, the metaphysical terrain of sin (against man and against nature), pardon and guilt which, again as in Kafka, is reducible to no ideological religious system but is highly expressive of a very modern existential and ontological crisis.

In "The Seven Messengers", the story that lends its title to the first collection of 1942, a prince leaves his family and home to explore his kingdom, sending back seven messengers in turn to give and receive news. As distances and time expand, so the messages become ever more strange and bizarre, becoming, over time, incomprehensible fragments of a time and an experience already dead and buried. The messages he receives from his point of departure, like the light from stars, are of places which have already disappeared, of people now aged or dying, of desires once acute but whose immediate urgency is now forgotten. His messages, too, will be increasingly strange, irrelevant and incoherent. The story eloquently dramatizes the ravages of time on memory and experience; the story impinges less on the extension and differentiation of space than on the involution of the subject, and draws on modernist relativism in its collapsing of space and time. What the prince explores is not the kingdom but his own life: the final boundary towards which he rides is not the edge of empire but the end of life itself.

"A Drop of Water" remains a tantalizing story in its resistance to interpretation, in its evocation of a fear that has no name and that springs from no identifiable – and therfore challengeable – source. In a block of tenement flats a drop of water plops up the stairs each night, past the doors of the terrified residents. As in the drawings of Escher the water goes, terrifyingly, up and not down, defying normal laws of gravity, logic, expectation and convention. The drop of water functions as a symbol that can be endlessly reinterpreted – as an allegory, a dream of death or imminent, faceless danger, a metaphysical hypothesis, a joke even. "A Drop of Water" distils Buzzati's expressionist talent for bodying forth fears and anxieties less within the political and social realities of our lives than within the ludic realm of language itself, and in this sense many of his stories and tales can be seen as the laboratory of the unconscious mind. The formalism of his narrative only serves to make all the more disquieting the irrational laws by which we must all somehow contrive to live, and the spare tension and precision of his works have been well served by his translators.

Buzzati's 1960 novel, *Il grande ritratto* (*Larger than Life*), found a notable translator in Henry REED, and a children's story of 1945, illustrated by himself, was published in English in 1947; but most of Buzzati's works, including poetry, essays, and numerous plays for stage, radio and television, are not as yet available in English.

SHARON WOOD

Further Reading

Gian Paolo Biasin, "The Secret Fears of Men", *Italian Quarterly*, 6 (1962) pp. 78–93

C

Guillermo Cabrera Infante 1929–

Cuban novelist, critic and journalist

Biography

Born in Gibara, 22 April 1929. His parents were members of the Communist Party and were arrested and imprisoned in 1936 because of their radical political beliefs. The family lived in severe poverty and in 1941 had to move to Havana to find work. He studied at the University of Havana in 1949 and from 1950 to 1954. In 1951 with friends he set up the Cinemateca de Cuba (Cuban Film Archive). The following year the story "Balda de plomo y yerro" [Ballad of Lead and Error] was published in the weekly magazine *Bohemia*. Cabrera Infante was convicted and fined on the charge of publishing obscenities and prevented from writing under his own name. From 1954 to 1960 he wrote film reviews for *Carteles* under the pseudonym G. Caín. In 1959 he became the editor of *Lunes de Revolución* (weekly literary supplement of *Revolución*), which was closed by the authorities in 1961. The following year he was banished to Brussels as cultural attaché and in 1964 he was chargé d'affaires. He returned to Cuba in 1965 to attend his mother's funeral. He moved to Madrid but was ejected by the government for having written anti-Franco articles, and emigrated to England in 1966 when he publicly denounced the Castro regime in the Argentine magazine *Primera Plana*, 1968. He was declared a traitor. He worked as a scriptwriter for 20th Century Fox and Cupid Productions, 1966–72. The growing pressures of exile resulted in poor health and he suffered a collapse in 1972. Cabrera Infante became a British citizen in 1979. He was visiting Professor, University of Virginia, Charlottesville, in 1982. Cabrera Infante was awarded the Cervantes prize in 1998.

Translations

Stories

Así en la paz como en la guerra: cuentos, 1960

Brookesmith, John and Peggy Boyers, *Writes of Passage*, London and Boston: Faber, 1993

"Un nido de gorriones en un toldo" in *Así en la paz como en la guerra: cuentos*, 1960

Cabrera Infante, Guillermo, "Nest, Door, Neighbors", *Review* (1973); in *Contemporary Latin American Short Stories*, edited by Pat McNees Mancini, Greenwich, Connecticut: Fawcett, 1974

Novels

Tres tristes tigres, 1965

Gardner, Donald and Suzanne Jill Levine, in collaboration with the author, *Three Trapped Tigers*, New York: Harper and Row, 1971; London: Pan, 1980

Vista del amanecer en el trópico, 1974

Levine, Suzanne Jill, *A View of Dawn in the Tropics*, New York: Harper and Row, 1978; London: Faber, 1988

La Habana para un Infante difunto, 1979

Levine, Suzanne Jill, with the author, *Infante's Inferno*, New York: Harper and Row, and London: Faber, 1984

Levine, Suzanne Jill, and the author, "After the Fuck" (translation of "Casuales encuentros forzados", chapter from *La Habana para un Infante difunto*), *Salmagundi*, 82–83 (1989) pp. 185–221

Reid, Alastair, "Revelations of a List-Maker", *New Yorker*, 53 (19 September 1977) pp. 32–35

Other Writing

Un oficio del siglo XX: G. Caín, 1954–1960 (film criticism), 1960

Hall, Kenneth and the author, *A Twentieth Century Job*, London: Faber, 1991

Exorcismos de esti(l)o, 1976

Levine, Suzanne Jill, "Exorcising a Sty(le)", *Review* (1974) pp. 61–62

Reid, Alastair, "Fabulas Rasas", *New Republic*, 177 (December 1977) pp. 28–29

"Origines (Cronología a la manera de Laurence Sterne)", in O, 1975

Cabrera Infante, G. "(C)ave Attemptor! A Chronology (After Laurence Sterne's)", *World Literature Today*, 61 (1987) pp. 513–18

Mea Cuba, 1992

Hall, Kenneth and the author, *Mea Cuba*, New York: Farrar Straus, and London: Faber, 1994

There are few more explosively rewarding readerly activities than sitting down with the English and the Spanish versions of a Cabrera Infante work. Perfectly bilingual, self-translating, and collaboratively translating, Cabrera Infante doubles his collected works as he and his collaborators shift his texts from one language to another. The reader must, however, beware when only one name appears with a text: has Cabrera Infante translated himself, or did he perhaps write the text originally in English? Works originating in English include his screenplays, English-language journalism, interviews and lectures, and *Holy Smoke* (1985; on cigars in literature). While conventional translating makes the reader itch to change a word here, a phrase there (feeling superior without effort, at the hardworking translator's expense), Cabrera Infante's elaborated texts produce sparks of wonder as a new original adds, drops, happens upon, develops differences from the old original. The reader has the illicit, Shandean sense of being present in the creative act and watching invention happen: straddling languages, s/he is presiding over the space between two texts, and that is always where invention happens.

The story of the translations is also a story, yet to be told, of relationships with translators or "collaborators". Cabrera Infante's principal translators, Suzanne Jill Levine and Kenneth Hall, have second lives as commentators on his work. Working with Peggy BOYERS on a translation for *Writes of Passage* (BROOKESMITH, BOYERS & CABRERA INFANTE, 1993), Cabrera Infante produced a third work – a brilliantly comic correspondence over word choice.

Even more than the Italian *traditori/traduttori* aphorism, English "collaboration" suggests betrayal of one's language to another, conquering idiom. *Tres tristes tigres* warns in a prefatory note that it is written in Cuban, specifically the dialect spoken in Havana; at various points the text represents, contests, and succumbs to the power of Americans and American English. So it is not surprising, politically or linguistically, that Cabrera Infante tried to prevent "collaboration" from appearing on the title page of *Three Trapped Tigers* (GARDNER, LEVINE & CABRERA INFANTE, 1971), only to be foiled by his (American) publisher. Cabrera Infante wanted to designate the relationship between author and translator as "closelaboration", a distinctive portmanteau word that describes precisely what occurs when a Cabrera Infante text undergoes metamorphosis. The text is followed closely, but it is also "elaborated". New puns, new allusions, new images, new alliterations are stitched into the text, which is reinvented in translation as a more literary or "writerly" work. As Suzanne Jill Levine observes, the translation replaces the evocation of a speaking voice – the fundamental mimetic act of the original work – with "conceptual, graphic, *readerly* in-jokes" (Levine, 1991).

As detailed in Levine's *The Subversive Scribe* and Cabrera Infante's interviews, "closelaboration" creates tangential "translations". If one book is dedicated to the memory of Ricardo Vigón, "que tanto amó el cine", the other remembers Ricardo Vigón, "who loved the movies till the end". The idiom available only in English deepens the relationships between life, love, literature (movies), and their equally inevitable endings. More radically, when *Un oficio del siglo XX* becomes *A Twentieth-Century Job* (HALL, 1991), does "job" mean "legitimate work", or does it mean "illegitimate, parasitic, profitable make-work for the privileged classes" (the original English meaning)? Or does it refer to Job, a patient, biblical sufferer, protesting an other-worldly power? These differ from the multiple possibilities in Spanish, where "oficio", more reverential, less cynical, evokes a young priest rather than an elderly Job. Job's interpretive appearance is an irrelevant intrusion on the original, but the English text, produced by an older writer, develops the hint and makes Job necessary.

Thirty years later, translation adds another meditative layer to the self still changing through time, around an unrecognizable boy lost in the movies. The English *Job* adds a new epigraph from *Citizen Kane*, on movie reviews. Appearing in English at last allows the Spanish disyllable Caín (*Ca*brera *In*fante) to double as Cain, the murderous brother he always was, and Kane, the movie hero/horror, blasted by memory, that he always wanted to be. "Lot's lot" spins off English "a lot" (What is Lot's lot? a city destroyed, a wife turned to a pillar of salt, incestuous daughters). The relationship between Cain and me, originally "Caesar and Cleopatra", conquest and empire, love and death, Shaw and Claude Rains, becomes "Abelard and Heloise". Comically painful, that shift follows upon the celebration of passion, pain, memory, and impotence in the intervening *Infante's Inferno*.

The elaborate progress of Cabrera Infante's work began with *Tres tristes tigres*, first translated into English (1971) by Donald GARDNER, whose parody of Poe's "The Raven" survives intact within the elaborations of the author and Suzanne Jill LEVINE (Levine, 1991; Guibert, 1972). In this brilliant reworking, one regrets only the failure to replace black Cuban Spanish with black American English. In the 1960s Levine and Cabrera Infante lacked everyone's present familiarity with black English, so Levine fell back on the convention of phonetic spelling to suggest dialectical difference. In Spanish, phonetic spelling produces an audible difference; it does not in English. In English, almost everyone says "sez", and there is no one who does not say "duz". Phonetic spelling suggests a speaker who cannot spell, but loses what it aims for – the sound of speech. When the subject is writing – as it more often is – the translation is an unsurpassable, giddy delight, parodying Cuban writers in translations that parody writers and translators, or "translating" a story (of a Walking Stick, by Mr and Mrs Campbell, visiting from Fitzgerald's "Babylon Revisited") into multiple English-Spanishes or Spanish-Englishes.

The translation of a Cabrera Infante text will have new jokes, new images, and it may also have more or fewer chapters. The US *A View of Dawn in the Tropics* (LEVINE, 1978) adds episodes to the Spanish version (1974); the British edition (1988) adds again (Levine, 1991). *Infante's Inferno* (LEVINE & CABRERA INFANTE, 1984) is missing a chapter ("Casuales encuentros forzados", published separately as "After the Fuck") because "The Amazon" doubled in translation, significantly shifting the balance and thrust of the work.

Translating rather than "closelaborating", Alastair REID produces better Borgesian sonorities in "Revelations of a List-Maker" (September 1977) than Cabreran impudence in "Fabulas Rasas" (December 1977). The supple syntax sometimes hobbles, and the "tortuga tenaz" of the Tortoise and the Hare becomes a predictably "plodding tortoise", the "indolente liebre" a "laconic hare". With Levine or Hall, the reader would never have escaped a tenacious turtle or a joke about Sparta to justify "laconic". Yet Reid preserves a transparency that can be overlaid by mannerist elaboration. Reading Cabrera Infante is happiness in any language, but *jouissance* is reserved for couplings of two, or more.

REGINA JANES

Further Reading

Guibert, Rita, *Seven Voices: Seven Latin American Writers Talk to Rita Guibert*, New York: Knopf, 1972
Janes, Regina, "From Cuba to London: From 5 to 7: An Interview with Cabrera Infante", *Salmagundi*, 52–53 (1981) pp. 30–56
Janes, Regina, "Infante Monogatari", *World Literature Today*, 61/4 (1987) pp. 574–79 (provides parallel passages)
Janes, Regina, "Ta(l)king Liberties", *Salmagundi*, 82–83 (1989) pp. 222–39
Levine, Suzanne Jill, *The Subversive Scribe: Translating Latin American Fiction*, St Paul, Minnesota: Graywolf Press, 1991
Levine, Suzanne Jill, "Translation as (Sub)Version: On Translating *Infante's Inferno*", in *Rethinking Translation: Discourse, Subjectivity, Ideology*, edited by Lawrence Venuti, London and New York: Routledge, 1992
Levine, Suzanne Jill, "Wit and Wile with Guillermo Cabrera Infante", *Américas*, 47 (1995) pp. 24–29
Nelson, Ardis L. (editor), *Guillermo Cabrera Infante: Assays, Essays, and Other Arts*, New York: Twayne, 1999
Oviedo, Jose Miguel, "Nabokov/Cabrera Infante: True Imaginary Lives", *World Literature Today*, 61/4 (1987) pp. 559–67
Pera, Cristóbal, "*Three Trapped Tigers*; or, Literature as Translation", *Translation: Perspectives*, 6 (1991) pp. 249–57
Pérez Firmat, Gustavo, *The Cuban Condition: Translation and Identity in Modern Cuban Literature*, Cambridge and New York: Cambridge University Press, 1989
Prieto Taboado, Antonio, "Idioma y ciudadania literaria en *Holy Smoke*, de Guillermo Cabrera Infante", *Revista Iberoamericana*, 57 (1991) pp. 257–64

Julius Caesar 100–44 BC

Roman general, statesman and historian

Biography

Born in Rome in 100 BC, Gaius Julius Caesar came from a patrician family with plebeian connections. After opposing the dictator Sulla, he went into exile in Asia (82–78), and there in 81 he fought his first military campaign. Back in Rome, he went into politics, taking the side of the people in the internal conflicts of the Republic's last years.

Caesar conducted a successful campaign in Spain, where in 61 he was made governor. Returning to Rome in 60 BC, he formed the First Triumvirate with Pompey and Marcus Licinius Crassus. In 59 BC he married his third wife, Calpurnia; his first, Cornelia had died, his second, Pompeia, he divorced in 62 BC. Another victorious campaign, this time in Gaul from 58 to 50, earned him governorship of the province, the support of the army and the material for *De bello Gallico*. Pushing further north, he invaded Britain (55 and 54 BC).

Crassus died in 53, leaving Pompey, favoured by the Senate, as the obstacle in Caesar's drive to power. By his unauthorized crossing under arms of the river Rubicon, which marked the boundary between his province and Italy, Caesar set off the long Civil War, the subject of his other famous commentary. At the definitive battle of Pharsalus in 48, Caesar overcame Pompey and the senatorial army. Pompey fled to Egypt, where he was murdered. Caesar conquered Egypt and placed Cleopatra on the throne (47).

Caesar's victories were now rewarded with extraordinary honours (the title "Father of his People", his statue in temples, his image on coins) and powers: consul for 10 years, in February 44 dictator for life. He died on 15 March 44 BC, assassinated in the Roman Senate.

Translations

Commentaries

De bello Gallico; *De bello civili*

Bladen, Martin, *C. Julius Caesar's Commentaries of His Wars in Gaul, and Civil War with Pompey...*, London: Richard Smith, 1705; second, improved edition, 1706
Chair, Somerset de, *Commentaries: A Modern Rendering*, London: Golden Cockerel Press, 1951
Duncan, William, *The Commentaries of Caesar*, London: J. and R. Tonson, 1753; St Louis: Edwards and Bushnell, 1856
Macdevitt (or M'Devitte), W.A. and W.S. Bohn, *Caesar's Commentaries on the Gallic and Civil Wars...*, London: Bohn, 1851, New York: Harper, 1859; as *De bello gallico and Other Commentaries*, with an introduction by Thomas De Quincey, London: Dent, and New York: Dutton, 1915
Warrington, John, *Caesar's War Commentaries*, London: Dent, and New York: Dutton, 1958

De bello Gallico

Edmunds, Clement, *Observations on the Five First Bookes of Caesar's Commentaries...*, with a translation, London: for Math. Lownes, 1609, and several subsequent 17th-century editions
Edwards, H.J., *The Gallic War* (parallel texts), London: Heinemann, and New York: Putnam, 1917; Cambridge, Massachusetts: Harvard University Press, 1952 (Loeb Classical Library)
Golding, Arthur, *The Eyght Bookes of Caius Julius Caesar, Containing His Martial Exploytes in Gallia ...*, London: Willyam Seres, 1565

Hammond, Carolyn, *Seven Commentaries on the Gallic War, with an Eighth Commentary by Aulus Hirtius*, with an introduction, Oxford and New York: Oxford University Press, 1996

Handford, S.A., *The Conquest of Gaul*, Harmondsworth: Penguin, 1951; revised by Jane F. Gardner, with a new introduction, Harmondsworth: Penguin, 1982

De bello civili

Mitchell (afterwards Gardner), Jane F., *The Civil War*, with an introduction, Harmondsworth: Penguin, 1967, 1976

Peskett, A.G., *The Civil Wars*, with an introduction, London: Heinemann, and New York: Macmillan, 1914 (Loeb Classical Library)

The achievements of Gaius Julius Caesar as a writer tend to be overshadowed by his prowess as a general and statesman. He conquered Gaul within eight years and became the supreme ruler of the Roman Empire in the next eight years. It is of course the history of these years between 60 and 44 BC that forms the subject of Caesar's two main works, his commentaries: on the Gallic wars, in seven books, and on the Civil War, in three books. A short part of *The Gallic War* and descriptions of the campaigns in Alexandria, Africa and Spain are not by the hand of Caesar, although sometimes they appear in translations. Because of the simplicity of his style and the regularity of his diction Caesar has always been popular as a Latin text in schools. This fact has not helped his reputation as an author or been an inspiration for translators, since many of the literal translations that have appeared seem clearly intended for the indolent or backward student. Though Caesar's skill as a general and as a politician cannot but be admired at all times, imperialists and dictators are not particularly fashionable at present. Nevertheless it is significant that Caesar, as well as being one of the earliest authors to be rendered into English (the sections on Britain were translated by the Earl of Worcester in 1530), was translated at regular and frequent intervals in the next four centuries. There have been no fewer than three paperback versions of the Gallic Wars since World War II. It is also interesting that translations such as those by Golding, Edmunds, Bladen, Duncan and Macdevitt were frequently reprinted, thus reducing the number of translators of Caesar's Commentaries to about 25, although there are about the same number who have attempted individual books, usually in a literal fashion.

GOLDING's translation (1565) of Caesar is not as famous as his translation of Ovid, nor did it provide such inspiration to Shakespeare. The *Dictionary of National Biography* calls it "interesting". The next major translation was that by EDMUNDS (1609) for the edification of James I's eldest son Henry, who died before his father. BLADEN (2nd edition, 1706) in a stimulating preface is critical of this version as being both inaccurate and in unsuitable English; his own attempt is full of maps and plans of considerable ingenuity, though displaying some ignorance of geography. On the other hand he writes in a lively manner and, as his dedication to the Duke of Marlborough shows, he was clearly acknowledged in military matters. DUNCAN's version (1753) lacks these virtues, although it was popular in the early 19th century.

MACDEVITT's translation (1851) was originally written for the Bohn series of literal translations with no literary pretensions. It probably owes its inclusion in the Everyman series to the introduction by De Quincey, friend of the Lake poets and author of *Confessions of an English Opium Eater*. This introduction is a magnificent if unfashionable panegyric of Caesar. The translation is less exciting. It begins promisingly, "All Gaul is divided into three parts", but soon lapses into clumsy periphrasis, talking of "those things which tend to effeminate the mind". Historic presents and ablative absolutes do not work in English, and irritatingly this translator tends to put in square brackets words that add to the sense but do not appear in Latin.

The versions of EDWARDS (1917) and PESKETT (1914) were written at about the time that World War I brought generals and Gaul and Germans to the public attention; simultaneously (1915) Everyman reissued Macdevitt. Edwards's *Gallic War* was able to take advantage of T. Rice Holmes's 1914 commentary accompanied by a translation; Peskett did not have this aid, but in his brief introduction is perceptive about the element of special pleading in *The Civil War*. Both translations, although accurate, are curiously cumbersome and pompous. Peskett unwisely retains the present tense in an unsuccessful attempt to reproduce Caesar's vivacity. Edwards's accounts of battles are far too leisurely; thus "our man discarded their pikes and got to work with their swords" hardly conveys the excitement of the battle.

DE CHAIR's translation (1951) is a curiosity. Dedicated to Sir Winston Churchill, the volume, containing *The Gallic War*, *The Civil War* and the work of Caesar's continuators, has an impressive map of Europe and a grandiloquent preface written from the House of Commons. The translator promises modern English, but takes refuge in phrases like "upon receipt of this intelligence" and "introducing the commodities that make for effeminacy". Caesar is made to speak in the first person, and there are some tiresome geographical footnotes.

WARRINGTON's version (1958) is a clear improvement upon Macdevitt, but again he promises the vigorous language of today, not, however, delivered in the clumsy "unaffected by influences which tend to effeminate character". Like de Chair he uses "I" not "Caesar", and after condemning literal translations designed to aid the schoolboy he certainly has some surprises for that schoolboy and even the general reader when he translates "in colle" ("on the / a hill") by "at Mussy-la-Fosse".

HANDFORD (1951) begins unpromisingly with the bureaucratic "Gaul comprises three parts", but his work with its short sharp sentences is clearly suitable for the crisp style of Caesar. He is able to see the ways in which the English language can accommodate participial constructions and can convey rapid narrative without recourse to lengthy subordinate clauses. Unfortunately he not only omits parts of book 8 as being the work of Hirtius, but rearranges the order of other books. The general description of the Gauls and the Germans appears as the second book rather than the sixth, certain passages are relegated to footnotes, and Handford has his own chapters rather than Caesar's. These eccentricities are corrected in GARDNER's revised version of Handford in 1982; under her birth name of MITCHELL she also produced *The Civil War* (1967). This translator is able to take account of modern historical scholarship, as indeed is HAMMOND (1996), who has some valuable footnotes, a useful introduction on Caesar's style and the difficulties it poses for the translator, some excellent maps and some salutary reminders of how Caesar's apparent objectivity is illusory.

TOM WINNIFRITH

Further Reading

Adcock, F.E., *Caesar as Man of Letters*, Cambridge: Cambridge University Press, 1956; Hamden, Connecticut: Archon, 1969

Holmes, T. Rice, *De bello Gallico* (commentary and translation), Oxford: Clarendon Press, 1914; New York: Arno Press, 1979

Rambaud, Michel, *L'Art de la déformation historique dans les Commentaires des César*, Paris: Les Belles Lettres, 1953, 1966

Pedro Calderón de la Barca 1600–1681

Spanish dramatist

Biography

Born in Madrid, 17 January 1600. His father, a government official, destined him for the church. He attended the Jesuit Colegio Imperial and matriculated in 1614 at the University of Alcalá to study canon law, transferring in 1615 to study arts, law and probably theology at the University of Salamanca, which he left c.1621 without a degree. Having abandoned the idea of an ecclesiastical career, he was a member of the household of the constable of Castille from 1621 and in 1623 began writing plays for the court. He entered the military order of St James, 1636, and enlisted in the cavalry at the beginning of the Catalan rebellion, 1640, fighting against the rebels until invalided out in 1642. From 1645 he served the duke of Alba, probably as secretary. He became a priest in 1651 and was chaplain of the Chapel of Reyes Nuevos, Toledo, from 1653, but continued to write plays as court dramatist for Philip IV and for religious festivals. He left Toledo in 1657 to live in Madrid and was appointed chaplain to the king in 1663. He had an illegitimate son. Died in Madrid 25 May 1681.

Among Calderón's many plays the best-known include the early *El médico de su honra* (*The Surgeon of His Honour*), *La vida es sueño* (*Life is a Dream*) and *El gran teatro del mundo* (*The Great Theatre of the World*).

Translations

The translations listed are divided into four sections: (1) Selections of plays; (2) Single *comedias* (dramas); (3) *Autos sacramentales* (short religious plays); (4) Other. As with the works of other Spanish Golden Age dramatists, exact dating of Calderón's plays is difficult. Accurate dates of composition, performance and/or publication for single plays being available in few cases, their Spanish titles are listed here in alphabetical and not chronological order.

Golden Age plays were, by and large, published in *partes*, i.e. volumes containing 12 plays each, more often than not without the author's permission or collaboration. Many plays were printed as *sueltas*, i.e. singly, frequently to be included in a composite volume made up of *sueltas*. Yet others existed only in manuscript. Throughout the kingdoms of Spain, copyright was perfunctorily observed. Calderón was involved with publishing his *comedias* in the *Primera parte* (First Part) of 1640, though it is to his brother that responsibility is attributed on the title page. Ever aware of unauthorized printings, Calderón complains bitterly in the only *parte* of *autos sacramentales* that he personally supervised (1677) that the fifth *parte* of his *comedias* was pirated. The transmission of his theatre through the book owes much to his contemporary, Juan de Vera Tassis, who claimed friendship with the author and assigned himself a critical and intrusive editorial role, publishing nine *partes* in all; scholars are divided over the legitimacy of the Vera Tassis contribution. Hartzenbusch's 19th-century collection of 122 pieces in the Biblioteca de Autores Españoles probably proved the most used vehicle until the scholarly editions appear, foremost among which is *Select Plays of Calderón*, London: Macmillan, 1888, by Norman MacColl.

Selections of Plays

FitzGerald, Edward, *Six Dramas of Calderon, Freely Translated* . . ., London: William Pickering, 1853 (contains *The Painter of His Own Dishonour*; *Keep Your Own Secret*; *Gil Perez, the Gallician*; *Three Judgements at a Blow*; *The Mayor of Zalamea*; *Beware of Smooth Water*), 2nd edition, Boston: Houghton, and London: Quaritch, 1883; edited by H. Olsnoer, London: Alexander Moring, 1903

FitzGerald, Edward, *Eight Dramas of Calderon, Freely Translated* . . ., London and New York, Macmillan, 1906 (contains *The Painter of His Own Dishonour*; *Keep Your Own Secret*; *Gil Perez, the Gallician*; *Three Judgements at a Blow*; *The Mayor of Zalamea*; *Beware of Smooth Water*; *The Mighty Magician*; *Such Stuff as Dreams Are Made Of*)

Holland, Henry R.V.F., *Three Comedies Translated from the Spanish*, London: Harchard, 1807

Honig, Edwin, *Four Plays*, with an introduction by Honig and an appendix by Norman MacColl, New York: Hill and Wang, 1961 (contains *Secret Vengeance for Secret Insult*,

Devotion to the Cross, *The Mayor of Zalamea*, *The Phantom Lady*)

Honig, Edwin, *Calderón de la Barca: Six Plays*, New York: Iasta Press, 1993 (contains *Secret Vengeance for Secret Insult*, *Devotion to the Cross*, *The Mayor of Zalamea*, *The Phantom Lady*, *Life is a Dream*, *The Crown of Absolom*)

MacCarthy, Denis F., *Dramas of Calderon, Tragic, Comic, and Legendary*, 2 vols, London: Charles Dolman, 1853 (vol. 1: *The Constant Prince*, *The Secret in Words*, *The Physician of His Own Honour*; vol. 2: *Love after Death*, *The Purgatory of St Patrick*, *The Scarf and the Flower*)

MacCarthy, Denis F., *Love the Greatest Enchantment, The Sorceries of Sin, The Devotion of the Cross: Attempted Strictly in English Asonante and Other Imitative Verse*, with an introduction to each drama, and notes by the translator and the Spanish text from the editions of Hartzenbusch, Keil and Apontes, London: Longman, 1861

MacCarthy, Denis F., *Mysteries of Corpus Christi*, Dublin: J. Duffy, 1863

MacCarthy, Denis F., *Calderon's Dramas: The Wonder-Working Magician, Life is a Dream, The Purgatory of St Patrick*, London: H.S. King, 1873

MacCarthy, Denis F., *Six Plays*, revised by Henry W.Wells, New York: Las Américas, 1961 (contains *Life is a Dream*, *The Wonder-Working Magician*, *The Constant Prince*, *The Devotion of the Cross*, *Love after Death*, *Belshazzar's Feast*)

Mitchell, Adrian, *Three Plays by Pedro Calderón*, Bath: Absolute Press, 1990 (contains *Life's a Dream*, adapted from a translation by C. Bainton by Mitchell and John Barton; *The Mayor of Zalamea*, adapted from a translation by C. Bainton by Mitchell; *The Great Theatre of the World*, adapted from a translation by C. Bainton by Mitchell)

Muir, Kenneth, *Four Comedies*, Lexington: University of Kentucky Press, 1980 (contains *From Bad to Worse*, *The Secret Spoken Aloud*, *The Worst is Not Always Certain*, *The Advantages and Disadvantages of a Name*)

Muir, Kenneth and Ann L. Mackenzie, *Three Comedies*, Lexington: University of Kentucky Press, 1985 (contains *A House with Two Doors is Difficult to Guard*, *Mornings of April and May*, *No Trifling with Love*)

Single *comedias*

El alcalde de Zalamea

Colford, W.E., *The Mayor of Zalamea*, Great Neck, New York: Barron's, 1959

FitzGerald, Edward, *The Mayor of Zalamea* in *Six Dramas of Calderon*, translated by FitzGerald, 1853

Honig, Edwin, *The Mayor of Zalamea* in *Four Plays*, translated by Honig, 1961, and *Calderón de la Barca: Six Plays*, translated by Honig, 1993

Mitchell, Adrian, *The Mayor of Zalamea* in *Three Plays*, translated by Mitchell, 1990

Pierra, Adolfo, *Nobility; or, The Alcalde of Zalamea*, Philadelphia, 1885

A secreto agravio, secreta venganza

Honig, Edwin, *Secret Vengeance for Secret Insult* in *Four Plays*, translated by Honig, 1961, and *Calderón de la Barca: Six Plays*, translated by Honig, 1993

La banda y la flor

MacCarthy, Denis F., *The Scarf and the Flower* in *Dramas of Calderon*, translated by MacCarthy, vol. 2, 1853

Ticknor, George, *The Scarf and the Flower*, excerpts in his *History of Spanish Literature*, New York: Harper, 1849

Basta callar

Churton, Edward, "Hunting and Hawking" in his *Góngora: An Historical and Critical Essay on the Times of Philip III and IV of Spain*, London: Murray, 1862

Los cabellos de Absalón

Honig, Edwin, *The Crown of Absolom* in *Calderón de la Barca: Six Plays*, translated by Honig, 1993

Casa con dos puertas mala es de guardar

Hewitt, John, *A Tutor for the Beaus; or, Love is a Labyrinth*, produced 1737

Muir, Kenneth, *A House with Two Doors is Difficult to Guard*, *Tulane Drama Review* 8 (1963) pp. 157–217

Muir, Kenneth and Ann L. Mackenzie, *A House with Two Doors is Difficult to Guard* in *Three Comedies*, translated by Muir and Mackenzie, 1985

La cisma de Inglaterra

Brenan, Gerald, excerpt in his *The Literature of the Spanish People*, Cambridge, Cambridge University Press, 1951

Muir, Kenneth and Ann L. Mackenzie, *The Schism in England* (parallel texts), Warminster, Wiltshire: Aris and Phillips, 1990

Con quien vengo, vengo

Dryden, John, *The Assignation; or, Love in a Nunnery*, London: 1672

La dama duende

Bullock, Christopher, *Woman is a Riddle*, a comedy based on *La dama duende*, London, Bettesworth, 1717; further editions 1729, 1731, 1759, 1770

Holland, Henry R.V.F, *The Fairy Lady* in *Three Comedies*, translated by Holland, 1807

Savage, Richard, *Woman's a Riddle*, produced in Lincoln's Inn Fields Theatre, London; Disputed authorship with Christopher Bullock (see above)

La devoción de la Cruz

Honig, Edwin, *Devotion to the Cross* in *Four Plays*, translated by Honig, 1961, and *Calderón de la Barca: Six Plays*, translated by Honig, 1993

Longfellow, H.W., *The Devotion to the Cross*, excerpts in *North American Review* 34 (1832) pp. 299–301

MacCarthy, Denis F., *The Devotion to the Cross* in *Six Plays*, translated by MacCarthy, 1961

Trench, Richard Chevenix, *The Cross*, excerpt in his *Calderón: His Life and Genius, with Specimens of His Plays*, New York: Redfield, 1856

Los dos amantes del cielo

MacCarthy, Denis F., *The Two Lovers of Heaven: Chrysanthus and Daria*, Dublin: J.F. Fowler, and London: J.C. Holten, 1870

Eco y Narciso

Brenan, Gerald, *Eco and Narcissus*, excerpt in his *The*

Literature of the Spanish People, Cambridge: Cambridge University Press, 1951

Los empeños de un acaso
Anonymous, *Deceptio Visus; or, Seeing and Believing Are Two Things*, London, 1671
Ravenscroft, Edward, *The Wrangling Lovers; or, The Invisible Mistress*, London, 1671

En esta vida todo es verdad y todo mentira
Anonymous, *The Two Parts of Hercules and Phoces*, London, 1698

La escondida y la tapada
Bickerstaff, Isaac, *Tis Well It's No Worse: A Comedy*, London: Griffin, 1770
Kemble, John P., *The Pannel: An Entertainment of Three Acts*, London: Stalkard, 1779; reprinted 1789, 1871, 1875

El galán fantasma
Lower, Sir William, *The Amorous Fantasme: Tragicomedy*, The Hague: Ramzey, 1660

Guárdate del agua mansa
FitzGerald, Edward, *Beware of Smooth Water* in *Six Dramas of Calderon*, translated by FitzGerald, 1853

La hija del aire
Anonymous, *The Daughter of the Air: A Mythic Tragedy ... after the Idea of Pedro Calderón*, London, 1831 (from the German by E.B.S. Raupach)

El hombre pobre todo es trazas
Centlivre, Susanna, *Love at a Venture: Comedy*, London: Chanby, 1706
Cibber, Colley, *The Double Gallant; or, The Sick Lady's Cure*, London: Lintott, 1710; and numerous reprints

Luis Pérez, el gallego
FitzGerald, Edward, *Gil Perez, the Gallician* in *Six Dramas of Calderon*, translated by FitzGerald, 1853

El maestro de danzar
Wycherley, William, *The Gentleman Dancing-Master*, London, 1673

El mágico prodigioso
FitzGerald, Edward, *The Mighty Magician* in *Eight Dramas of Calderon*, translated by FitzGerald, 1906
Kaenders, P., *Her Only Love: A Drama in Four Acts*, St Louis, Missouri: Herder, 1914
J.H. [Denis F. MacCarthy], *Justina: A Play*, London: James Burns, 1848
MacCarthy, Denis F., *The Wonder-Working Magician* in *Six Plays*, translated by MacCarthy, 1961
Shelley, Percy Bysshe, "Scenes from the *Mágico prodigioso*" (scenes 1–3) in *Posthumous Poems*, London: Hunt, 1824; in *The Classic Theatre*, edited by Eric Bentley, vol. 3, New York: Doubleday, 1959

Mañanas de abril y mayo
Wycherley, William, *Love in a Wood; or, St James Park*, London: Herringham, 1671

El mayor encanto amor
MacCarthy, Denis F., *Love the Greatest Enchantment* in *Love the Greatest Enchantment ...*, translated by MacCarthy, 1861

El mayor monstruo del mundo
Ticknor, George, *No Monster like Jealousy*, excerpts in his *History of Spanish Literature*, New York: Harper, 1849

El médico de su honra
Campbell, Roy, *The Surgeon of His Honour*, with an introduction by E.W. Hesse, Madison: University of Wisconsin Press, 1960
Fox, D. and D. Hindley, *The Physician of His Honour* (parallel texts), Warminster, Wiltshire: Aris and Phillips, 1996
MacCarthy, Denis F., *The Physician of His Own Honour* in *Dramas of Calderon*, translated by MacCarthy, vol. 1, 1853
Roscoe, Thomas, excerpts in *Historical View of the Literature of the South of Europe*, edited by J.C.L. Simonde de Sismondi, London: Colburn, 1823

Mejor está que estaba
Digby, George, 2nd Earl of Bristol, *'Tis Better than It Was*, known only through mention in John Downes's *Roscius Anglicanus; or, An Historical Review of the Stage after it Had been Suppress'd by Means of the Late Unhappy Civil War ... till the time of King Charles the II's Restoration ...*, London, 1708. The Digby translation is associated with *Peor está que estaba* and *No siempre lo peor es cierto* (see below)
Holcroft, Fanny, *Fortune Mends: A Comedy in Three Acts*, *Theatrical Recorder*, 2/8 (1805) pp. 75–111

Nadie fíe su secreto
FitzGerald, Edward, *Keep Your Own Secret* in *Six Dramas of Calderon*, translated by FitzGerald, 1853
Holland, Henry R.V.F, *Keep Your Own Secret* in *Three Comedies*, translated by Holland, 1807
Roscoe, Thomas, excerpts in *Historical View of the Literature of the South of Europe*, edited by J.C.L. Simonde de Sismondi, London: Colburn, 1823

No hay burlas con el amor
Cruickshank, Don and Seán Page, *Love is No Laughing Matter* (parallel texts), with an introduction and commentary, Warminster, Wiltshire: Aris and Phillips, 1986

No siempre lo peor es cierto
Digby, George, 2nd Earl of Bristol, *Elvira; or, The Worst, Not Always True: A Comedy*, London: H. Broom, 1667 (sometimes identified with *No siempre lo peor es cierto*)

Peor está que estaba
Digby, George, 2nd Earl of Bristol, *Worse and Worse*, attributed to Digby by John Downes, in his *Roscius Anglicanus* (1708) [see endnote to *Roscius Anglicanus*, edited by J. Milhouse and R.D. Hume, London: Society for Theatrical Research, 1987, p. 114]
Holcroft, Fanny, *From Bad to Worse*, *Theatrical Recorder*, 1 (1805)
Muir, Kenneth, *From Bad to Worse* in *Four Comedies*, translated by Muir, 1980

El pintor de su deshonra
FitzGerald, Edward, *The Painter of His Own Dishonour* in *Six Dramas of Calderon*, translated by FitzGerald, 1853
Johnston, David and Laurence Boswell, *The Painter of Dishonour*, Bath: Absolute Press, 1995

Paterson, Alan K.G., *The Painter of His Dishonour* (parallel texts), Warminster, Wiltshire: Aris and Phillips, 1991

El príncipe constante

Hawthorne, Julian, *The Inflexible Prince*, excerpts in *The Literature of All Nations and All Ages*, edited by Hawthorne *et al.*, Philadelphia: Finley, 1897–98

MacCarthy, Denis F., *The Constant Prince* in *Dramas of Calderon*, translated by MacCarthy, vol. , 1853, and in *Six Plays*, translated by MacCarthy, 1961

Platt, Arthur, *El príncipe constante*, excerpts in *The Sonnet of Europe*, edited by Samuel Waddington, London: Walter Scott, 1886

Roscoe, Thomas, *The Constant Prince*, excerpts in *Historical Review of the Literature of the South of Europe*, edited by J.C.L. Simonde de Sismondi, London: Colburn, 1823

Spofford, A.R. and C. Gibbon, *The Constant Prince*, excerpts, Philadelphia: Gebbie, 1882

Ticknor, George, *The Firm-Hearted Prince*, excerpts in his *History of Spanish Literature*, New York: Harper, 1849

El purgatorio de San Patricio

Hawthorne, Julian, *The Purgatory of St Patrick*, excerpts in *The Literature of All Nations and All Ages*, edited by Hawthorne *et al.*, Philadelphia: Finley, 1897–98

MacCarthy, Denis F., *The Purgatory of St Patrick* in *Dramas of Calderon*, translated by MacCarthy, vol. 2, 1853

Roscoe, Thomas, *Purgatory of St Patricius*, excerpts in *Historical Review of the Literature of the South of Europe*, edited by J.C.L. Simonde de Sismondi, London: Colburn, 1823

Spofford. A.R. and C. Gibbon, *The Purgatory of St Patrick*, excerpts, Philadelphia: Gebbie, 1882

El secreto a voces

Bridges, R.S., *The Humours of the Court* in *The Humours of the Court and Other Poems*, London: Bell, 1893, pp. 149–81

MacCarthy, Denis F., *The Secret in Words* in *Dramas of Calderon*, translated by MacCarthy, vol. 1, 1853

Muir, Kenneth, *The Secret Spoken Aloud* in *Four Comedies*, translated by Muir, 1980

Las tres justicias en una

FitzGerald, Edward, *Three Judgements at a Blow* in *Six Dramas of Calderon*, translated by FitzGerald, 1853

La vida es sueño

Birch, Frank and J.B. Trend, *Life's a Dream*, Cambridge: Heffer, 1925

Campbell, Roy, *Life is a Dream* in *The Classic Theatre*, edited by Eric Bentley, vol. 3, New York: Doubleday, 1959

Carter, H., *Life is a Dream*, privately printed, 1928

Colford, W.E., *Life's a Dream*, Great Neck: Barron, 1958

Cowan, Malcolm, *Life is a Dream*, Edinburgh: Blackwood, 1830

FitzGerald, Edward, *Such Stuff as Dreams Are Made Of* in *Eight Dramas of Calderon*, translated by FitzGerald, 1906

Honig, Edwin, *Life is a Dream*, with a foreword and introduction, New York: Hill and Wang, 1970

Howard, Annette, *Life is a Dream*, New Haven, Connecticut: Classic Theatre for Children, 1987

Huberman, Edward and Elizabeth Huberman, *Life is a Dream* in *Spanish Drama*, edited by Angel Flores, New York: Bantam, 1964

MacCarthy, Denis F., *Life is a Dream* in *Six Plays*, translated by MacCarthy, 1961

Mitchell, Adrian and John Barton, *Life's a Dream* in *Three Plays*, translated by Mitchell, 1990

Morgan, Charles, *Life's a Dream*, London: BBC Publications, 1928

Oxenford, J., *Life is a Dream*, *Monthly Magazine*, 549, 550, 551 (1842)

Raine, Kathleen and R.M. Nadal, *Life's a Dream*, London: Hamish Hamilton, 1968; New York: Theatre Art Books, 1969

Stirling, W.F., *Life is a Dream*, Havana: La Verónica, 1942

Tarver, John Ben, *The Savage Dream*, freely adapted, Toronto: Playwrights Co-op, 1972

Trench, Richard Chevenix, *Life's a Dream*, with *The Great Theatre of the World*, London: Parker, and New York: Redfield, 1856; revised edition, London: Macmillan, 1880

Autos sacramentales

La cena del Rey Baltasar

Barnes, Richard G., *King Belshazzar's Feast* in his *The Spanish Sacramental Plays*, San Francisco: Chandler, 1969

MacCarthy, Denis F., *Belshazzar's Feast* in *Mysteries of Corpus Christi*, translated by MacCarthy, 1863

Los encantos de la culpa

MacCarthy, Denis F., *The Sorceries of Sin* in *Love the Greatest Enchantment* . . ., translated by MacCarthy, 1861

El gran teatro del mundo

Brenan, Gerald, *The Great Theatre of the World*, excerpt in his *The Literature of the Spanish People*, Cambridge: Cambridge University Press, 1951

Graves, C.J., *The Great Theater of the World*, Collegeville, Minnesota: Liturgical Press, n.d.

Mitchell, Adrian, *The Great Theatre of the World* in *Three Plays*, translated by Mitchell, 1990

Singleton, Mack H., *The Great Theater of the World*, Madison, Wisconsin: Edgewood College, 1956; and in *Masterpieces of the Spanish Golden Age*, edited by Angel Flores, New York: Rinehart, 1957

Trench, Richard Chevenix, *The Great Theatre of the World*, with *Life's a Dream*, London: Parker, and New York: Redfield, 1856; revised edition, London: Macmillan, 1880

Los misterios de la misa

Lynck, F.M., *The Mysteries of the Mass*, Techny, Illinois: Mission Press, 1933

El veneno y la triaca

MacCarthy, Denis F., *The Poison and the Antidote* (scene 1) in *Mysteries of Corpus Christi*, translated by MacCarthy, 1863

Other

El desafío de Juan Rana

Jones, Willis Knapp, *Juan Rana's Duel* in his *Spanish One-Act Plays in English*: A *Comprehensive Anthology of Spanish Drama from the 12th Century to the Present Day*, Dallas: Tardy, 1934

Actual translations of Calderón's theatre into English do not appear until the early 19th century. The Restoration theatre, however, plundered Calderón on a scale greater than the formal record shows; the experienced reader of Calderón picks up quite clear echoes in, for example, Aphra Behn, where no actual play is ostensibly being adapted. Versions and adaptations of Calderón's city comedies figure frequently in the Restoration repertoire and in the booksellers' lists. Christopher BULLOCK transfers *La dama duende* from Madrid to London and Covent Garden as *Woman is a Riddle* (1717), adapts it to a Restoration style of social comedy (with characters such as Colonel Manly, Sir Amorous Vainwit, Mr Vulture) and disputes the counter-claim to authorship made by the notorious literary fraudster, Richard SAVAGE, while overlooking a seeming debt to one Mrs Lucy Price. *Woman is a Riddle* was published with great frequency from 1717 to 1770.

The scant respect for intellectual property rights (of which Calderón himself complained, with reason, in his own country) may be tempered by a claim to have improved the product. Dryden, having composed *The Mock Astrologer* from Corneille's *Le Feint Astrologue*, compares his own play with the common source for both himself and Corneille, Calderón's *El astrólogo fingido*, and airily concludes "I will be so vain to say, it has lost nothing in my hands". Cases of plunder, plagiarism and supposed amelioration will be repeated into our own days. Shelley's confidence in a letter of December 1819, that the "ideal dramas" of Calderón "are perpetually tempting me to throw over their perfect and glowing forms the grey veil of my own words" sets an uncommon standard of modesty and respect.

The first to address the problems which the conscientious English translator must answer was Richard Chevenix TRENCH (1807–86), a Cambridge Apostle, Professor of Divinity at King's College (Strand), Dean of Westminster, Archbishop of Dublin (see *The Man of Ten Talents: A Portrait of Richard Chevenix Trench, Philologist, Poet, Theologian, Archbishop*, by J. Bromley, London: SPCK, 1959). Trench was particularly exercised by the question of how to tackle the variety of metre in the polymetric prosody of the Golden Age *comedia*. He recognizes as strange to English ears the assonating verse, with vowel rhymes rather than full rhymes, and the seven/eight syllable lines which predominate, yet he reaches an uncompromising conclusion: "For one who is deeply convinced of the intimate coherence between a poem's form and its spirit, and that one cannot be altered without at the same time most seriously affecting the other, the metrical form of a great poem being not the garment which it wears, and which as a garment may be exchanged for another of a somewhat different pattern, but the flesh and blood which the inner soul of it has woven for itself, and which is a part of its own life for ever, for him there is no choice left in translating Calderón, but to endeavour to render the Spanish trochaic assonants into English of exactly the same construction". Few have followed this counsel of perfection when faced with a play of typically 3000 lines. Trench did not approve of compromise solutions; English blank verse, with the "somewhat stately movement of the long, dramatic iambic", lost the quick lyric flow; in Trench's own vivid image, "it passes like a heavy roller over all". Nor did he approve a middle way that dispensed with vowel rhyme in favour of full rhyme. Trench was correct in his analysis of the problem, to which we may add how the present-day "English ear", at least that of its actors, has become untuned to complex sentences. If the translator goes along with the fashion for simple sentences, the consequences can be serious. Once we lose the embedded syntax characteristic of Calderón's dramatic language, we also lose the way into his characters' complex inner world of thought and feeling. Trench had great skill in Spanish (learned in his early travels in Spain) and was no mean poet in his native English. He translated only two pieces, *La vida es sueño* (fragments, linked by summaries) and the *auto sacramental*, *El gran teatro del mundo* (entire; 1856). A sample of his vigorous, Tennysonian prosody (from Segismundo's monologue, *La vida es sueño*, act 1) leads one to regret that his creative mind had not found more time for Calderón:

Segismund: Ah miserable me, ah woe, woe,woe,
Heavens, why make ye me to mourn,
More than all men else forlorn?
If my birth has been my sin,
Yet what sinned I more therein
Than others, who were also born?
Born the bird was, yet with gay
Gala vesture, beauty's dower,
Scarce it is a wingèd flower,
Or a richly plumaged spray,
Ere the aërial halls of day
It divideth rapidly,
And no more will debtor be
To the nest it hastes to quit,
But with more soul than it,
I am grudged my liberty
And the beast was born, with skin,
Scarce those beauteous spots and bars,
like to constellated stars,
Doth from its great Painter win,
Ere the instinct doth begin
Of its fierceness and its pride,
And its lair on every side
It has measured far and nigh,
While with better instinct I
am its liberty denied.
Born the mute fish was also
Child of ooze and ocean weed,
Scarce a finny bark of speed
To the surface brought, and lo!
In vast circuits to and fro
Measures it on every side
All the wastes of ocean wide,
Its illimitable home;
While with greater will to roam
I that freedom am denied.

Trench casts a critical but indulgent eye over the *Six Dramas* (1853) of his Cambridge contemporary, Edward FITZGERALD, which he judges to be written "in English of an exquisite purity and vigour", yet faults on the selection of plays and on the choice of blank verse. Trench is unfair over the matter of selection, since FitzGerald tackled *The Painter of His Own Dishonour* and *The Mayor of Zalamea*, indicating discrimination on his part. FitzGerald was aware of and defended his practice of translating freely: "the live dog better than the dead

Lion; in Drama, I say". He was an accomplished poet, as his *Rubaiyat of Omar Khayyam* confirms, but he holds back from rendering in English lyric those surges of poetic intensity that can arrest and focus attention in Calderón. The luminous description of Crespo's garden, in act 2 of *The Mayor of Zalamea*, is prosaically and timidly turned by FitzGerald:

> *Lope*: A mighty pleasant parlour this!
> *Crespo*: Oh, a little strip my daughter amuses herself with; sit down, sir. In place of the fine voices and instruments you're used to, you must put up with only the breeze playing on the vine leaves in concert with the little fountain yonder. Even the birds (our only musicians) are gone to bed, and wouldn't sing the more if I were to wake them.

Denis F. MacCarthy, barrister-at-law, Professor of Poetry at the Catholic University of Ireland and no mean Calderonian scholar, published his first volume in 1853, and Trench had the opportunity to pronounce on the translations as "sometimes meritorious, yet I cannot consider them generally successful". MacCarthy certainly outdoes any other in the quantity of translations, including two *autos sacramentales* by 1863. His archaic auxiliaries and pronouns now detract seriously from his ingenuity; as in Rosaura's opening speech in his *Life is a Dream*:

> Wild hippogriff swift speeding,
> Thou that dost run, the wingèd winds exceeding,
> Bolt which no flash illumes,
> Fish without Scales, bird without shifting plumes,
> And brute awhile bereft
> Of natural instinct, why to this wild cleft,
> This labyrinth of naked rocks, dost sweep
> Unreined, uncurbed, to plunge thee down the steep?
> Stay in this mountain wold,
> And let the beasts their Phaëton behold
> For I, without a guide,
> Save what the laws of destiny decide,
> Benighted, desperate, blind,
> Take any path whatever that doth wind
> Down this rough mountain to its base,
> Whose wrinkled brow in heaven frowns in the sun's bright face.

but in his version (1863) of the *auto La cena del Rey Baltasar* he renders gracefully the short monologue of Death that belongs unquestionably to the deepest and most beautiful poetry that has flowed from Calderón's pen.

Reprints and facsimiles extend the translations of Trench, FitzGerald and MacCarthy well into the 20th century. It cannot be said that English readers have ever had access to a standard corpus of Calderón in translation; the output was limited, the quality variable.

In the 20th century, there is no systematic programme of Calderón translation. The soaring and puckish opening notes of Birch & Trend's version (1925) of *La vida es sueño* lapse into a prose translation, a token sample of how Trench's challenge is met only in part:

> Wild as a hippogriff! Fleet as the wind!
> Whither away? –
> Flash without flame! Bird without feather!
> Fish without scale! Beast without sense!
> Bolting, plunging, headlong careering,
> Through this labyrinth of barren crags! ...
> Beast! .... I leave you to wander in the wilds, or find some Phaeton to drive you; while I, in despair, with none but fate to guide me, grope my way down the rugged slope ...

Others bring to translation their experience in poetry and theatre, like Adrian Mitchell (1990), whose *Life's a Dream* the Royal Shakespeare Company performed to acclaim in 1984, with the Medieval Players doing likewise for his *The Great Theatre of the World* in the same year. Mitchell, lacking any knowledge of Spanish, relied on "literal translations" by Cecilia Bainton. Free composition on the basis of an Englished source text is a common and deplorable practice in Britain, as is the failure to acknowledge the Englished source. Professional translators may well have been discouraged by the scant respect shown by wordsmiths, actors, directors and even major companies, in Britain at least, towards their work. In the United States the situation is better and the most fastidious versions of Calderón are often by American translators who combine scholarly knowledge with linguistic skill, such as Edwin Honig (1993). Kenneth Muir (1980; with Mackenzie 1985) published his early fine translations of Calderón in the USA, and in partnership with Ann L. Mackenzie turned later (1990) to the Hispanic Classics series by the English publisher Aris and Phillips. Aris and Phillips has encouraged a new wave of Calderón translations, providing the reader with sound English versions, mostly but not always in prose, accompanied in parallel format by trustworthy Spanish texts.

Alan K.G. Paterson

Further Reading

Morley, S.G., "The Curious Phenomenon of Spanish Verse Drama", *Bulletin Hispanique* (1948) pp. 445–62

Trench, Richard Chevenix, *An Essay on Calderón: His Life and Genius* in *Life's a Dream; The Great Theatre of the World*, translated by Trench, London: Parker, and New York: Redfield, 1856; revised edition, London: Macmillan, 1880

Wilson, Margaret, *Spanish Drama of the Golden Age*, Oxford and London: Pergamon Press, 1969

See also translators' introductions to Honig, *Four Plays*, 1961, and MacCarthy, *Love the Greatest Enchantment*, 1861

Callimachus c.305–240 BC

Greek poet

Biography

Born in Cyrene, present-day Libya, but spent most of his life in Alexandria, where he was attached to the famous library and wrote a number of scholarly works (including a catalogue, the *Pinakes*, of the library) as well as the poetry that made him the most influential of Hellenistic poets.

Translations

Banks, J., *The Works of Hesiod, Callimachus, and Theognis, Literally Translated into English Prose, with Copious Notes, to which are Appended the Metrical Translations of Elton, Tytler, and Frere*, London: Bohn, 1856

Bulloch, A.W., *The Fifth Hymn* (parallel texts), with an introduction and commentary, Cambridge and New York: Cambridge University Press, 1985

Hopkinson, N., *Callimachus: Hymn to Demeter* (parallel texts), with an introduction and commentary, Cambridge and New York: Cambridge University Press, 1984

Lombardo, Stanley and Diane Rayor, *Callimachus: Hymns, Epigrams, Select Fragments*, with an introduction, Baltimore: Johns Hopkins University Press, 1988

Mair, A.W., *Callimachus: Hymns and Epigrams* (parallel texts, in one volume with Aratus and Lycophron), London: Heinemann, and Cambridge, Massachusetts: Harvard University Press, 1921; revised edition, 1955 (Loeb Classical Library)

Trypanis, C.A., *Callimachus: Aitia, Iambi, Lyric Poems, Hecale, Minor Epic and Elegiac Poems, Fragments of Epigrams, Fragments of Uncertain Location* (parallel texts), London: Heinemann, and Cambridge, Massachusetts: Harvard University Press, 1958 (Loeb Classical Library)

Anthologies

Bing, Peter and Rip Cohen, *Games of Venus: An Anthology of Greek and Roman Erotic Verse from Sappho to Ovid*, New York and London: Routledge, 1991

Fowler, Barbara Hughes, *Hellenistic Poetry: An Anthology*, Madison: University of Wisconsin Press, 1990

Higham, T.F. and C.M. Bowra (editors), *The Oxford Book of Greek Verse in Translation*, Oxford: Clarendon Press, 1938

Jay, Peter (editor), *The Greek Anthology and Other Ancient Epigrams: A Selection in Modern Verse Translations*, with an introduction, London: Allen Lane, and New York: Oxford University Press, 1973; revised edition, Harmondsworth and New York: Penguin, 1981

Paton, W.R., *The Greek Anthology* (parallel texts), 5 vols, London: Heinemann, and Cambridge: Massachusetts: Harvard University Press, 1916–18 (Loeb Classical Library)

Poole, Adrian and Jeremy Maule (editors), *The Oxford Book of Classical Verse in Translation*, Oxford and New York: Oxford University Press, 1995

The loss of all but a fraction of Callimachus' output creates a very unfortunate gap in our knowledge of ancient literature. What survives are six hymns, 64 epigrams, and small, sometimes minute, fragments of other poems. He was known for originality, meticulous craftsmanship, and avoidance of large-scale literary forms, particularly the traditional epic, preferring instead the epyllion (miniature epic), which typically features a Baroque-like switch of perspective so that a detail dominates at the expense of the main story or characters.

Although Callimachus' influence on later classics (notably Catullus and Propertius, but almost any other Latin poet as well) was enormous, he himself has not been prominent in European literary consciousness. The epigrams owe their preservation to inclusion in the *Greek Anthology*, and can be found in translations of the entirety, or selections from, that vast collection, and have been influential as part of it. The hymns have for the most part been the domain of specialists in Hellenistic poetry or in classical myth.

It is most important for a translator of Callimachus to be concise and elegant, since he was so. Translating the epigrams demands a high degree of skill in conveying the wit – a mode of thought and expression notoriously difficult to transfer from one language to another.

BANKS's Bohn edition (1856) is antiquated, but some of his notes are still useful. His own translations are in prose, followed by H.W. TYTLER's rhymed verse versions of Callimachus, mainly of historical interest.

MAIR's Loeb edition, which first came out in 1921 (reissued in 1955), used antiquated prose (for instance, "Fairly didst thou wax, O heavenly Zeus", where Lombardo and Rayor have "You were a lovely child, Zeus; well fed, you grew tall", much better reflecting Callimachus' careful attempts to differentiate himself from the traditional epic). There are good notes, however, and it is instructive to see Callimachus in the company of two other important Hellenistic poets.

TRYPANIS's prose version (1958) includes all fragments "which make sense and can be translated". Very full annotation, conscientious and enlightening, not only shows where and in what context each fragment is found but also gives an idea of what has been lost. This is an invaluable work for the scholar.

HOPKINSON's translation (1984) of the hymn to Demeter is very much part of a scholarly edition too, except that her translation is in prose. In combination with the introduction and the commentary, it is useful to students of ancient religion, especially the Eleusinian mysteries.

BULLOCH (1985) uses verse couplets (hexameters alternating with pentameters) that read like prose. This is a scholarly edition of "The Bath of Pallas". The translation, Bulloch says, "has no literary pretensions; it is intended as a working version to convey ... some of the more important qualities of style, diction, tone and manner of the original". Hardly poetry in its own right, this version is still of value to those who use the introduction and the commentary, and to students of ancient myth.

The aim of LOMBARDO & RAYOR's translation (1988) is to write English poetry that will affect the reader as Callimachus' presumably affected his Hellenistic audience. This is a creative translation, in free verse, with some rhyme in the epigrams. Lombardo & Rayor bring out explicitly the irony that is often covert in the original. One cannot think of a more successful way of conveying what Callimachus is about.

PATON's serviceable Loeb edition (1916–18) is in prose and has notes. All of Callimachus' extant epigrams are here, but scattered through the volumes, so that one has to find them with the help of the index. This is an informative rather than an elegant translation.

HIGHAM & BOWRA's old Oxford anthology (1938) has not been replaced by the new one edited by POOLE & MAULE (1995). The two supplement each other. If one had to choose, it would be the more recent anthology, but the other is still very easy to find. Higham & Bowra include 16 items by Callimachus, Poole & Maule include four (epigrams and portions of hymns in both). Taken together, this is as good a sample as any of diverse approaches taken by translators from 1755 onward. Both contain the Victorian schoolmaster William Cory's inimitable, much-quoted version of the poem commemorating Callimachus' friend Heraclitus:

They told me, Heraclitus, they told me you were dead ...

JAY (1973, 1981) includes 20 of Callimachus' epigrams, translated into unpretentious but attractive free verse.

FOWLER (1990) includes Callimachus' hymns to Apollo, Artemis, and Demeter, the hymn to Athena (usually known as "The Bath of Pallas") and a selection of epigrams (13) and fragments (five). She uses "five-beat lines" that work as free verse. Her emotional restraint is Callimachean and the translations are simple yet graceful.

Among the anthologies BING & COHEN (1991) offer a fine translation of 13 epigrams, in free verse. Their contemporary English sounds economical and elegant.

ZOJA PAVLOVSKIS-PETIT

Further Reading

Ferguson, John, *Callimachus*, Boston: Twayne, 1980, pp. 168–70 (contains "Callimachus and Later Poetry")

See also the translators' introduction to Lombardo & Rayor

Italo Calvino 1923–1985

Italian novelist and essayist

Biography

Born in Santiago de las Vegas, Cuba, 15 October 1923. His parents were Italian scientists; the family moved to San Remo, on the Italian Riviera, in 1925, and Calvino spent his childhood there, attending the Ginnasio-liceo Cassini in the town. In 1940 he was conscripted into the Young Fascists; he left and sought refuge with his brother in the Alps. In 1941 he started studying at the University of Turin; he was at the Royal University in Florence in 1943. He took part in the Resistance movement from 1943 to 1945, fighting with *Partigiano* (Partisan) forces against the Nazis in Liguria. After the war, he continued his studies at the University of Turin, graduating in 1947. He was a contributor to the Communist newspaper *L'Unità* and other journals from 1945, including *La Nostra Lotta*, *Il Garibaldino*, and *Voce della Democrazia*. Calvino's first novel, *Il sentiero dei nidi di ragno* (*The Path to the Nest of Spiders*), was published in 1947. He took over as an editor from Cesare Pavese at the Turin publishers Einaudi in 1948, remaining there until 1984. He was a contributor to *Contemporaneo* and *Città Aperta* from 1954 and co-editor, with Elio Vittorini, of the left-wing periodical *Il Menabo di letteratura*, Milan, 1959-67. He travelled to the USSR in 1952 and the USA in 1959-60. In 1967 he moved to Paris, settling there while continuing to work for Einaudi and contributing to the newspaper *La Repubblica* from 1979. He moved back to Italy in 1980, living in Rome. He was a member of the editorial board of the publishers Garzanti from 1984. Calvino won many Italian and international awards, including the *L'Unità* prize, 1945; the Viareggio prize, 1957; the Feltrinelli prize, 1973; the Austrian State prize for European literature, 1976; and the Nice Festival prize, 1982. He was made an honorary member of the American Academy in 1975. Died in Siena, 19 September 1985.

Calvino's work, which is acknowledged as both accessible and innovative, was first acclaimed by the Italian writer Cesare Pavese, and he won international recognition for his writing during the 1950s. *Il sentiero dei nidi di ragno* (*The Path to the Nest of Spiders*), his first novel, is a child's view of the Italian resistance during World War II. His first work of fantasy, the allegorical trilogy *I nostri antenati* (*Our Ancestors*), comprises *Il visconte dimezzato* (1952; *The Cloven Viscount*); *Il barone rampante* (1957; *The Baron in the Trees*) and *Il cavaliere inesistante* (1959; *The Nonexistent Knight*). His later novels include his best-known work, published in 1979, *Se una notte d'inverno un viaggiatore* (*If on a Winter's Night a Traveller*), a novel about reading fiction, and *Palomar* (translated as *Mr Palomar* in 1985), 1983.

Translations

Novels

Il sentiero dei nidi di ragno, 1947; amended edition, 1964

Colquhoun, Archibald, *The Path to the Nest of Spiders*, London: Collins, 1956; Boston: Beacon Press, 1957; reprinted London: Jonathan Cape, 1993

Il visconte dimezzato, 1952
Colquhoun, Archibald, *The Cloven Viscount*, with *The Non-Existent Knight*, London: Collins, and New York: Random House, 1962

Il barone rampante, 1957
Colquhoun, Archibald, *The Baron in the Trees*, London: Collins, and New York: Random House, 1959

Il cavaliere inesistente, 1959
Colquhoun, Archibald, *The Non-Existent Knight*, with *The Cloven Viscount*, London: Collins, and New York: Random House, 1962

I nostri antenati (*Il visconte dimezzato*, *Il barone rampante*, *Il cavaliere inesistente*), 1960
Colquhoun, Archibald, *Our Ancestors: Three Novels*, London: Secker and Warburg, 1980 (contains *The Cloven Viscount*, *The Baron in the Trees*, *The Non-Existent Knight*)

La giornata d'uno scrutatore, 1963
Weaver, William and Archibald Colquhoun, *The Watcher and Other Stories*, New York: Harcourt Brace, 1971

Le città invisibili, 1972
Weaver, William, *Invisible Cities*, London: Secker and Warburg, and New York: Harcourt Brace, 1974

Il castello dei destini incrociati, 1972
Weaver, William, *The Castle of Crossed Destinies*, London: Secker and Warburg, and New York: Harcourt Brace, 1977

Se una notte d'inverno un viaggiatore, 1979
Weaver, William, *If on a Winter's Night a Traveller*, London: Secker and Warburg, and New York: Harcourt Brace, 1981

Selections of Short Stories
Colquhoun, Archibald and Peggy Wright, *Adam, One Afternoon and Other Stories*, London: Collins, 1957
Weaver, William and D.S. Carne-Ross, *Difficult Loves*; *Smog*; *A Plunge into Real Estate*, London: Secker and Warburg, 1983; San Diego, California: Harcourt Brace, 1984 (*Difficult Loves*, translated by Weaver; *Smog*, translated by Weaver [first published, 1971]; *A Plunge into Real Estate*, translated by Carne-Ross [first published 1964]

Short Stories
Marcovaldo; ovvero, Le stagioni in città, 1963
Weaver, William, *Marcovaldo; or, The Seasons in the City*, London: Secker and Warburg, and San Diego, California: Harcourt Brace, 1983

Le cosmicomiche, 1965
Weaver, William, *Cosmicomics*, New York: Harcourt Brace, 1968; London: Jonathan Cape, 1969; reprinted London: Sphere, 1982

T con zero, 1967
Weaver, William, *T Zero*, New York: Harcourt Brace, 1969; as *Time and the Hunter*, London: Jonathan Cape, 1970

Palomar, 1983
Weaver, William, *Mr Palomar*, London: Secker and Warburg, and New York: Harcourt Brace, 1985

Sotto il sole giaguaro, 1986
Weaver, William, *Under the Jaguar Sun*, San Diego, California: Harcourt Brace, 1988; London: Jonathan Cape, 1992

Prima che tu dica "Pronto", 1993
Parks, Tim, *Numbers in the Dark and Other Stories*, London: Jonathan Cape, and New York: Pantheon, 1995

Essays and Other Writings
Fiabe italiane, edited by Calvino, 1956
Brigante, Louis, *Italian Fables* (selection), New York: Orion, 1959
Martin, George, *Italian Folktales* (selection), New York: Harcourt Brace, and London: Jonathan Cape, 1980; as *Ten Italian Folk Tales*, Harmondsworth: Penguin, 1995
Mulcahy, Sylvia, *Italian Folk Tales* (selection), London: Dent, 1975

Una pietra sopra: Discorsi di letteratura e società, 1980
Creagh, Patrick, *The Uses of Literature: Essays*, San Diego, California: Harcourt Brace, 1986; as *The Literature Machine: Essays*, London: Secker and Warburg, 1987

Atlas de littérature potentielle / Oulipo, with others, 1981
Mathews, Harry, Iain White and Warren Motte Jr, *Oulipo Laboratory: Texts from the Bibliothèque Oulipienne*, London: Jonathan Cape, 1995

Racconti fantastici dell'Ottocento, edited by Calvino, 1983
Anonymous, *Fantastic Tales: Visionary and Everyday*, London: Jonathan Cape, 1993; New York: Pantheon, 1997

Lezioni americane: Sei proposte per il prossimo millennio, 1988
Creagh, Patrick, *Six Memos for the Next Millennium*, with an introduction by Esther Calvino, Cambridge, Massachusetts: Harvard University Press, 1988; London: Jonathan Cape, 1992

La strada di San Giovanni, 1990
Parks, Tim, *The Road to San Giovanni*, London: Jonathan Cape, and New York: Pantheon, 1993

A Turkish cannon ball slices Medardo di Terralba in two in Italo Calvino's *The Cloven Viscount* (*Il visconte dimezzato*, 1952), leaving both halves able to swash-buckle independently and even fight an implausible comic duel with each other. A creative force just like this tore into Calvino's writing in 1965 with the publication of *Cosmicomics*, tales about the creation of the universe narrated by a non-human character with a mathematical name – QFWFQ. Forty years of literature were severed with strategic accuracy into two neat decades on either side: during Calvino's lifetime it was most often the second half of the divide that drew the attention of readers in English, reflecting as it did the contemporary debates on Structuralism and Postmodernism in works like *The Castle of Crossed Destinies* and *If on a Winter's Night a Traveller*. Now that his status as one of Italy's leading 20th-century thinkers grows, his work of the 1940s and 1950s, particularly the trilogy *Our Ancestors*, which originally brought him acclaim in Italy, is receiving attention once more.

From the time of the 1956 translation of his original first novel, the neo-realist *Path to the Nest of Spiders*, less than 10 years after its appearance in Italian, almost all of Calvino's works issued in Italian have been translated as soon as they appear. Thus, recent translations have followed rapidly on the posthumous publication of the memoir *The Road to San Giovanni*, the three tales written at differing intervals for a projected anthology of the five senses that comprise *Under the Jaguar Sun*, and some interesting juvenilia and testimonial writing in *Numbers in the Dark and Other Stories*.

The watershed in Calvino's fiction is also mirrored in two men who dominate translation of his work. The early neo-realism and modern fables like *Adam, One Afternoon* and the fantastic trilogy *Our Ancestors* are mostly undertaken by Archibald COLQUHOUN (in the case of the 1957 anthology *Adam*, lack of attribution makes it impossible to distinguish Colquhoun's work from that of his collaborator Peggy WRIGHT). The prolific William WEAVER, the leading translator of contemporary Italian writers, begins with *Cosmicomics*, returns later to the realist writing of the late 1950s like *Marcovaldo, Difficult Loves, Smog* and *The Watcher* and is responsible for nearly all Calvino translation until 1988.

COLQUHOUN's *Path to the Nest of Spiders* of 1956 uses the Italian first edition, which was substantially amended in 1964. Later English editions have inexplicably kept that 1956 translation of the text Calvino himself rejected. Thus we may now read (translated by William Weaver) Calvino's important preface to the 1964 edition in which he dicusses the alterations, which are not, of course, echoed in the accompanying version of the novel. Calvino's Stevensonian influences are reflected in *The Cloven Viscount*, which borrows the coastal setting and ingenuous narrator of *Treasure Island* and the duel from *The Master of Ballantrae* and sets up the moral conflict within one man of Dr Jekyll and Mr Hyde. Although Calvino's story does not suggest the use of regional accents, COLQUHOUN (1962) does keep the flavour of Stevenson in the names of Viscount Medardo's halves. The Italian "Il Buono" (The Good One) and "Il Gramo" (The Bad One) become "Good'Un" and "Bad'Un", seemingly uttered in the West Country brogue of Long John Silver ("good'un", "wild'un", "Cap'n"). *The Non-Existent Knight* translates easily as a title from the the Italian adjectival form, but Colquhoun rightly avoids "rampant" or "climbing" for the most important text of the trilogy, capturing the essence of Calvino's visual image, a nobleman who lives in the trees.

COLQUHOUN called his own translation (1959) of *The Baron in the Trees* the best he had written, excluding his version of Manzoni's classic *I promessi sposi*. Calvino wrote to thank him for his masterful handling of the passages he considered most significant; he also, however, included an indignant reproach:

> The names of the plants are nearly all spot on; I've only made a few corrrections. As for the birds, apart from many well translated names – there are some dreadful mistakes. Several times when there should have been a sparrow we've had a swallow instead. Really! Please alter this at once. Swallows have never nested in trees. And while killing a swallow is criminal to the fiercest hunters even serious animal lovers put up with people killing sparrows. You'll have my book boycotted by all upstanding English ornithologists and set the murder of a nightingale on my conscience instead of a golden oriole, which is a far less serious violation.
>
> (Letter to Archibald Colquhoun, 27 January 1959, in *I libri degli altri*, Turin: Einaudi, 1991)

The friend and protégé of Archibald Colquhoun, William WEAVER, began translating *Cosmicomics* in 1966 and recalls that from that moment on until the author's death there was never a time when he was not engaged in translating something by Calvino. An interesting article by D.S. Carne-Ross takes Weaver to task for that first translation on many scores, such as leaving out words when they are used in an incongruous context (e.g. "cappa" meaning "hood" for the surface of the sea), careless repetition of neutral adjectives, misapprehension, ambiguity, inappropriate lexical choices. While a polemical attack, the piece usefully points out the challenges of translating Calvino, such as the difficulty of bringing out the lyrical qualities of his prose without losing too much irony and some of the more overt comedy. CARNE-ROSS, who translated (1964) *A Plunge into Real Estate* (from an abridged version where Calvino excised much socio-political background), underlines Calvino's use of colloquial diction, combined with carefully filtered elements from literary language to show how he subverts prose by giving it a rhythm suggesting "the formal poetic procedures so deeply rooted in the Italian tradition" (*Delos*, 3). If Carne-Ross thinks Calvino's poetry suffers at Weaver's hands, Calvino disagreed. In Rome in 1982 he gave a paper on the translation of Italian into English, called "Translation – the real way to read a text":

> Whatever language you are translating from or into, you have to know not only the language but how to get in touch with the spirit of the language, the spirit of both languages, to know how two languages can transmit their secret essence to each other. I have the good fortune to be translated by Bill Weaver who has a supreme understanding of this spirit of language" (*Saggi II*)

Weaver's own experience of working for Calvino is retold in his article in *Calvino Revisited* and sheds light on the resolution of certain translator's difficulties. He compares Calvino and Eco, saying that any work by Calvino is much harder to translate than even *The Name of the Rose*. Simple, neutral words like "bello" (good) and "cattivo" (bad) require careful weighing; problems of judging repetition and rhythm occur in translating *Invisible Cities* (1972, translated 1974), a very popular novel among artists and architects, extracts of which appear frequently, in conjunction with images, in English-language texts. In the masterpiece *If on a Winter's Night a Traveller*, WEAVER (1981) faced the problem of having a "lettore", the reader (male), who is addressed in the second person singular as "you" and who pursues a "lettrice", the reader (female). His ingenious "Reader" and "Other Reader" avoids the gender issues inherent in Italian syntax while making the erotic distinction necessary for the novel's romantic quest. Weaver also mentions looking at writers who are imitated in *If on a Winter's Night*: among the 10 opening chapters from imaginary texts there are pastiches of, for example, Graham Greene and Simenon. Weaver also consults the work of tranlators like Antonia White and Donald Keene and makes a point of using the "beloved" Constance Garnett translation of *Crime and Punishment* when a passage from Dostoevskii's novel appears in chapter 8 of *If on a Winter's Night*. He also tracks down, where possible, original English that has been translated into Italian, such as the text of a leaflet given to Calvino on a visit to a Kyoto temple and used in *Mr Palomar*.

Like Colquhoun, Weaver found Calvino punctilious about accuracy, especially on matters scientific, which he got checked by the author for *Cosmicomics* and *Time and the Hunter*. In turn, he checked Calvino's rare lecture texts in English, allowing him to keep *faux amis* and Italianate sentences. Calling Calvino's English "more theoretical than idiomatic", Weaver writes that "he had a way of falling in love with foreign words" like "feedback" which jarred with the elegant tone of his writing. According to Weaver, Calvino's habit of amending the galleys of translations with English words of his own could alter the meaning of his original text (*Calvino Revisited*).

Calvino and Weaver both point out the importance of a good editor to the writer and his translator, paying tribute to Helen Wolff of Harcourt Brace, but Calvino's particular gratitude to Weaver is evident: "Translating is an art: to put a literary text, whatever it may be worth, into a different language, requires a sort of miracle every time" (*Saggi II*). It should be no surprise then that William Weaver treasures a gift from Calvino inscribed "For Bill, the translator as saint".

Fiabe italiane (*Italian Fables*), 1956, was a quasi-academic project on which Calvino was engaged by Einaudi to select and retell stories from the widespread Italian oral tradition. Nowadays, Calvino's name is almost synonymous, like Grimm or Andersen, with the fairy tale (Calvino's selection of 19th-century fantasy fiction *Fantastic Tales* [ANONYMOUS, 1993] is also being marketed on this principle). The continuing importance of *Italian Folktales* to English readers undoubtedly depends on the variety of academic disciplines, such as anthropology, folklore and women's studies, and structural criticism, that study the text, as well as on the popularity of fairy tales with readers of all ages.

Italian Folktales by George MARTIN (1980) was a collaboration with Calvino and Helen Wolff, translating the full quotient of 200 stories, while Sylvia MULCAHY's edition (1975), entitled *Italian Folk Tales*, contains a selection of 28 stories. The latter is divided into sections such as "Stories for Children", in which we find "The Little Girl who was Sold with the Pears" beginning, "There was once a man who had a pear tree that gave him four great basketfuls every year" and ending with a less fable-like structure, "Then the King gave his consent to the marriage of Peardrop and his son, who was very dear to him". The Martin edition of 1980 calls the tale "The Little Girl Sold with the Pears" and uses a starker style without the traditional discourse of the fable found in Mulcahy – exaggeration and symbolic upper case letters – and also keeps the Italian character's name, "Once a man had a pear tree that used to bear four baskets of pears a year ... The king was then happy for Perina to marry his son". Calvino's text falls between the two, using no emphatic epithet before "baskets" but employing a capital letter for "Re" (King). Mulcahy's text accretes and misunderstands the end of the story, which in Italian means just what George Martin has offered. Mulcahy adds paternal affection which Calvino does not mention and misreads "il Re si contentò" ("the King was glad") as "the King consented".

Calvino's discursive writing has not been dealt with in the same way as his fiction. Patrick CREAGH's *The Uses of Literature* (1986) contained some of the essays from the 1980s *Una pietra sopra* [The Last Word], an invaluable document for Calvino as author, reader and critic. Creagh's text notably misses early manifesto essays from *Una pietra sopra* like "The Lion's Marrow", "Challenge to the Labyrinth" and "The Sea of Objectivity", although it does include the seminal "Cybernetics and Ghosts", a discussion of combinatoric literature (*Oulipo Laboratory*, MATHEWS, WHITE & MOTTE, 1995, trades on Calvino's name in this area of literary experimentation rather than those of its better-known French exponents, Raymond Queneau and Georges Perec). Strangely, too, *The Literature Machine* included many texts that were not available in Italian and that later appeared in *Perché leggere i classici* [Why Read the Classics] (1992): several of these thus remain untranslated. *Six Memos for the Next Millennium* (CREAGH, 1988) translates a series of texts that were destined for an English-speaking audience as the Harvard Charles Eliot Norton Poetry Lectures for 1985–86. Five only were written, but *Six Memos* was a working title that stuck. As the slightly different English edition of Esther Calvino's introduction states "Of course, these are the lectures Calvino would have read. Patrick Creagh was in the process of translating them". CREAGH's work, furthermore, had to be completed in the immediate aftermath of Calvino's death in September 1985. Unfortunately the English edition is without an index.

The most recent translator of Calvino is Tim PARKS, who produced *The Road to San Giovanni* (1993) and *Numbers in the Dark, and Other Stories* (1995), which was noted by a *Times Literary Supplement* reviewer for being literal and faithful, yet reading well: "He daringly – and successfully – reproduces those long, tentacular sentences favoured by Calvino which English usually abhors." An autobiographical novelist himself, Parks has tackled Calvino's fiction and non-fiction and seems an ideal candidate to work on the scattered remaining texts that have not been translated: the journalistic reviews of Parisian exhibitions in *Collezione di sabbia* [Collection of Sand], the brief yet indispensable volume of folklore essays *Sulla fiaba* [On the Fable] and the still flowing stream of Calvino's collected works that have yet to be published in Italian.

JOANNA STEPHENS

Further Reading

Andrews, Richard, "Italo Calvino" in *Writers and Society in Contemporary Italy*, edited by Michael Caesar and Peter Hainsworth, Leamington Spa, Warwickshire: Berg, and New York: St Martin's Press, 1984

Cannon, Jo Ann, *Italo Calvino: Writer and Critic*, Ravenna: Longi, 1981

Carne-Ross, D.S., "Writing Between the Lines", review of article on William Weaver's translation of *Cosmicomics*, *Delos*, 3 (1969)

Hume, Kathryn, *Calvino's Fictions: Cogito and Cosmos*, Oxford: Clarendon Press, and New York: Oxford University Press, 1992

McLaughlin, Martin L., *Calvino*, Edinburgh: Edinburgh University Press, 1998

Weaver, William, "Calvino: An Interview and Its Story", in *Calvino Revisited*, edited by Franco Ricci, Ottawa: Dovehouse, 1989

Weiss, Beno, *Understanding Italo Calvino*, Columbia: University of South Carolina Press, 1993

Luís (Vaz) de Camões (or de Camoëns) c.1524–1580

Portuguese poet and dramatist

Biography

Born in Portugal, perhaps in Lisbon, in 1524 or 1525, into a family of impoverished minor nobility of Galician origin. The circumstances of his life and death are not known for certain. He may have attended the University of Coimbra, studying for the priesthood, but did not take orders. After an unhappy love affair in Lisbon he served for two years as a soldier at Ceuta in North Africa and may have lost an eye, perhaps in combat. In 1550 he went back to Lisbon, where he lived a somewhat wild life in bad company and was imprisoned for wounding a court official. He then volunteered (1553) to go to India as a soldier, travelled there by way of East Africa and fought in Goa (1554–56). He was then sent to Macao. Two years later he was shipwrecked on the way back to Goa, where he was again imprisoned. He returned at last to Lisbon in 1570 and received a small pension from the king in 1572. Camões did not marry. Died in Lisbon, 1580.

As well as his national epic, *Os Lusíadas* (*The Lusiads*), 1572, Camões wrote plays, of which three are extant, and love-poems and sonnets in the Italian style.

The Lusiads

Os Lusíadas, 1572

Translations

Atkinson, William C, *The Lusiads*, Harmondsworth and New York: Penguin , 1952

Aubertin, John J., *The Lusiads of Camões*, London: Kegan Paul, 1878; 2nd edition, 2 vols, 1884

Bacon, Leonard, *The Lusiads*, New York: Hispanic Society of America, 1950

Bosley, Keith, selections, in his *Luis de Camões: Epic and Lyric*, with essays by Maurice Bowra and others, edited by L.C. Taylor, Manchester: Carcanet, 1990

Burton, Richard Francis, *Os Lusíadas (The Lusiads)*, edited by Isabel Burton, 2 vols, London: Quaritch, 1880

Fanshawe, Richard, *The Lusiad; or, Portugal's Historicall Poem*, London: Humphrey Moseley, 1655; edited by Jeremiah Ford, Cambridge, Massachusetts: Harvard University Press, 1940; edited with an introduction by Geoffrey Bullough, Carbondale: Southern Illinois University Press, and London: Centaur Press, 1963

Ffrench Duff, Robert, *The Lusiad, Translated into English Spencerian Verse*, London: Chatto and Windus, and Philadelphia: Lippincott, 1880

Mickle, William Julius, *The Lusiad; or, the Discovery of India: An Epic Poem*, Oxford: Jackson and Lister, 1776; reprinted New York: Garland, 1979

Mitchell, Sir Thomas, *The Lusiad of Luis de Camoens*, London: T. and W. Boone, 1854

Musgrave, Thomas Moore, *The Lusiad: An Epic Poem*, London: John Murray, 1826

White, Landeg, *The Lusiads*, with an introduction, Oxford and New York: Oxford University Press, 1997

The publication in Lisbon in 1572 of Luís de Camões's great epic poem *Os Lusíadas* has proved to be the defining moment in Portuguese cultural history. It is that country's canonical work *par excellence*, the one to which poets and historians constantly refer. Within a couple of years of its appearance it was being imitated and reworked, and up to the beginning of the 19th century, when epic poetry began to fall out of fashion, its celebration of Portugal's early history and of the heroes who, in the 15th and 16th centuries, discovered and conquered far-away places, inspired scores of other works in Portuguese in a variety of genres. It is not surprising, given the stirring nature of these tales, that the *Lusiads*, named after Lusus, the mythical father of the nation, should quickly win and maintain a lasting place in the affections of the Portuguese.

Translation of one nation's self-celebration, however moving and uplifting, into the languages of other cultures is inevitably more problematical. This is increasingly true with the passage of time. ATKINSON (1952) made the point in the introduction to his prose (and truncated) rendering of Camões's masterpiece: "Few writers illustrate better than Camõens the essential dilemma that confronts the translator in every age. Loyalty to one's author is one thing, loyalty to one's public is another and the greater the gulf between author and public the greater the conflict". He affirms that the work has something to say to a 20th-century English audience as well as to a 16th-century Portuguese one, but recognizes that the message can never be the same, nor can it be expressed in anything like the original style. One appreciates his dilemma, of course, but critics generally agree that this translation, to which generations of students (among others) have resorted, offers but a pale copy of the textual glories of the original. As much from lack of ambition as anything else, one is forced to conclude. The tone is set from the very first lines, where the reference to the Virgilian intertext ("Arma virumque cano") deliberately chosen by the Portuguese poet to underline the epic status of his own work and his heroes' spirit of adventure, as well as to lay claim on their behalf to exploits far greater than those of the Ancients, is lost. The reference to the "armas e os barões assinalados", that is to say those who left their "western Lusitanian shore" to sail uncharted seas and reach beyond the (wonderfully mysterious) Taprobana, becomes merely "the story of heroes, who leaving their native Portugal behind them, opened a way to Ceylon". Atkinson claims to wish to render "a service to the living, not pious tribute to the dead". In the event, neither would appear to have been well served.

The task of translating such an allusive work would never prove easy. Translations followed hard, however, on its publication in Portuguese. First in Spanish, then in Latin, French and Italian. The English-reading public had to wait until 1655, when Sir Richard FANSHAWE produced his version, reprinted on a number of occasions since. A minor poet who specialized in translation, Fanshawe was also a confirmed lusophile. He was at pains to inform his reader that *The Lusiad* is "Portugal's historical poem" and clearly relishes the glamorous nature of his material. A loyal supporter of the royalist cause, he was appointed after the Restoration ambassador to Portugal, and then to Spain. His vigorous translation often manages to capture the flavour (if not the detail) of its model. It should perhaps best be seen as a work of literature in its own right.

Fanshawe's translation was followed by William MICKLE's in 1776: over a dozen editions were eventually to appear of this work, which is a creative reconstruction rather than a faithful translation, by a poet whom Southey called "a man of genius". In the 19th century came translations by MUSGRAVE (1826), MITCHELL (1854), AUBERTIN (1878), Robert FFRENCH DUFF (1880). The year 1880 also saw it "Englished" (and into rather idiosyncratic English, at that) by the archetypal Victorian explorer and man of letters, Sir Richard BURTON. As wilful in his approach to his work as he was to his style of life, he offers a version concerned less with being faithful to the original than with providing a colourful and consciously archaic text. It does have its moments, although some of them are decidedly odd. Camões's heroes, for example, are shown walking "the water's vasty breadth of blue/ parting the restless billows on their way". At times it is sheer but exhilarating nonsense. He also wrote a spirited account (as one would expect) of the life of a writer and adventurer in whom he recognized a kindred spirit.

As we can see, the 19th century had witnessed an upsurge of interest in the work of Camões, with a number of translations of varying accuracy and value being produced to meet a perceived public demand. In the 20th century one does not find as many as one might have imagined, partly perhaps because the epic as a genre no longer enjoys the attention it once did. Among those worth mentioning, however, is Leonard BACON's finely wrought verse translation of 1950. More recently, Keith BOSLEY (1990), an experienced and sensitive translator, has given an accurate and readable version of selected excerpts. Camões's marvellous depiction of the moment when the Castilian bugle sounded at the Battle of Aljubarrota, striking fear into the heart of every Portuguese, is poetically rendered as: "The Douro heard, and that land beyond where/The troubled Tagus runs towards the sea/And mothers terrified by its alarms /Gathered their little children in their arms". Compare this with Atkinson's prosaic "It was heard on the Douro and across the Tagus; the Tagus itself flowed more hesitantly to sea. Mothers, hearing the terrifying sound, clasped their children to their breasts" and BURTON's splendidly fustian: "O'er Douro and Transtagan lands it drave; / Tagus sore agitated seaward sped; / while mothers trembling at the terrible storm/embraced with tighter arm each tiny form."

What no less an authority than Sir Maurice Bowra called the greatest of Renaissance epic poems, which is "in many ways the epic of Humanism" and which "in its grandeur and its universality speaks for the modern world", clearly had to be translated so that it could be shared with all those unable to read it in the original. Great poetry in praise of great deeds, *Os Lusíadas*, conceived in part as a glorification of Portugal's imperial destiny, lives on as a monument to the everlasting empire of words.

The task of doing Camões justice was, and is, an impossible one, as Atkinson saw. But attempts to do so will prove worthwhile if they introduce the English-speaking public to a poet and man who, in the words of Roy Campbell, "Wrestled his hardships into forms of beauty, /And taught his gorgon destinies to sing". In his recent translation, Landeg WHITE (1997) recognizes that it "is an illusion to believe that the verse form of Camões's epic can be replicated in English", but what can be achieved, as he has done, is to give " an inkling of the great sweep of Camões's narrative, with its endless variety of incident and description, its openness to the wonders of the natural world, its relish of the differences between human societies, its tragedy, its eroticism, its humour, its episodes of pastoral, its nostalgia for that golden age before men first fitted sails to wood and took to the sea, and underlying all, its note of elegy for achievements, already fading, already requiring the pageantry of poetry's surprise".

MICHAEL FREEMAN

Further Reading

Bowra, C.M., "Camões and the Epic of Portugal" in his *From Virgil to Milton*, London: 1945; New York: St Martin's Press, 1961

Pierce, Frank, introduction to his edition of *Os Lusíadas*, Oxford: Clarendon Press, 1973

Rebelo, Luís de Sousa,"Camões – Man and Monument" in *Luis de Camões, Epic and Lyric*, edited by L.C. Taylor, Manchester: Carcanet, 1990

Taylor, L.C. (editor), *Luis de Camões: Epic and Lyric*, Manchester: Carcanet, 1990

Albert Camus 1913–1960

French novelist, dramatist and essayist

Biography

Born in Mondovi (now Deraan), Algeria, 7 November 1913, into a poor working-class European family. He contracted tuberculosis when he was 17. He attended the lycée, then the university, in Algiers, graduating in philosophy in 1936. From 1937 he took various jobs in Algiers as clerk and salesman, and also acted and produced for a theatre group. From 1939 to 1940 he worked successively for two Algerian newspapers, then for *Paris-Soir*. He was a member of the Communist Party from 1935 to 1939. After teaching for a while in Oran, he went to France for medical treatment (1942–43) and, caught there by the Allied invasion of North Africa, joined the Resistance in the Lyon region and wrote for the Resistance paper *Combat* (1943). He was a journalist in Paris, 1943–45, before working until 1960 as reader and editor for the Paris publishing house Gallimard. He edited *Combat*, which had become a left-wing national daily, 1945–47.

In 1942 he became well known as a writer with the novel *L'Étranger* (*The Outsider* / *The Stranger*) and the philosophical essay *Le Mythe de Sisyphe* (*The Myth of Sisyphus*), portraying the absurdity, the pointlessness of existence; later he would avoid nihilism by propounding the notions of revolt and of human solidarity. He did not fully embrace either existentialism or, though he was anti-capitalist, Communism.

Other novels were *La Peste* (*The Plague*), 1947, and *La Chute* (*The Fall*), 1956. Also notable are the short stories *L'Exil et le Royaume* (*Exile and the Kingdom*), 1957, and the plays and adaptations, outstanding among the former being *Le Malentendu* (*The Misunderstanding*), 1944, and *Caligula* (*Caligula*), 1944.

Internationally known, Camus was awarded the Nobel Prize for Literature, 1957. He married twice, in 1934 (divorced) and in 1940 (twin son and daughter). Died in a car accident, Villeblevin, France, 4 January 1960.

Translations

Collection of Fiction

Gilbert, Stuart and Justin O'Brien, *The Collected Fiction of Albert Camus*, London: Hamish Hamilton, 1960

Novels

L'Étranger, 1942

See entry on *The Outsider* / *The Stranger*, below

La Peste, 1947

Gilbert, Stuart, *The Plague*, New York: Knopf, and London: Hamish Hamilton, 1948

La Chute, 1956

O'Brien, Justin, *The Fall*, New York: Knopf, and London: Hamish Hamilton, 1957

Stories

L'Exil et le Royaume, 1957

O'Brien, Justin, *Exile and the Kingdom*, New York: Knopf, and London: Hamish Hamilton, 1958

Selections of Plays

Gilbert, Stuart, *Caligula and Three Other Plays*, New York: Knopf, 1958 (contains *Caligula*, *Cross Purpose* [in later reprints entitled *The Misunderstanding*], *State of Siege*, *The Just Assassins*)

Gilbert, Stuart, Henry Jones and Justin O'Brien, *The Collected Plays of Albert Camus*, London: Hamish Hamilton, 1965; as *Caligula and Other Plays*, Harmondsworth: Penguin, 1984 (contains *Caligula* and *Cross Purpose*, both translated by Gilbert; *The Just*, translated by Jones; *The Possessed*, translated by O'Brien)

Plays

Caligula, 1944

Gilbert, Stuart, *Caligula*, with *Cross Purpose*, London: Hamish Hamilton, and New York: New Directions, 1947

Le Malentendu, 1944

Gilbert, Stuart, *Cross Purpose*, with *Caligula*, London: Hamish Hamilton, and New York: New Directions, 1947

L'Etat de siège, 1948

Gilbert, Stuart, *State of Siege* in *Caligula and Three Other Plays*, translated by Gilbert, 1958

Les Justes, 1950

Gilbert, Stuart, *The Just Assassins* in *Caligula and Three Other Plays*, translated by Gilbert, 1958

Jones, Henry, *The Just* in *The Collected Plays of Albert Camus*, translated by Gilbert Stuart, Henry Jones and Justin O'Brien, 1965

GILBERT's sound understanding (1948) of the French text of *The Plague*, and the range of his English, do much to preserve for Anglo-Saxon readers the high reputation Albert Camus enjoys in France as a writer of elegant prose. Apart from a handful of very un-English renderings, curiously confined to the opening chapters (where, for example, in a reference to Tarrou's notebooks, "datent de son arrivée" becomes "synchronise with his coming"), Gilbert's English flows naturally and easily, preserving the measured rhythms of the relatively long sentences of the original. The two most salient stylistic features of the French text, however, are linguistic restraint – the narrator's professed aim is to avoid sensationalist reporting – and a low-key irony. As the aforementioned "synchronise with his coming" suggests, the former feature is not always respected: it is doubtful whether even the anatomical preoccupations of a doctor would induce an anglophonic Rieux to refer to the sides of a hole in the ground as "the lips of the pit". As for the irony, it sometimes loses its edge in the translation: in the following example, "ugly but recorded death" does not stand out sufficiently as one of a series of (five) paired oppositions, contrasting the immediate reality of the plague in Oran with the abstract, ineffectual response of the stricken city's bureaucratic machine: "what with ... the files and fires, the panics and formalities, all alike were pledged to an ugly but recorded death ...". The loss is partly an unavoidable consequence of language-specific word order, but partly, too, the result of ill-advised choices on the part of the translator, the most obvious of these, though not the only ones, being the arbitrary inversion of "files" and "fires" and the omission of the article before the second member of the pair, a move more likely to evoke complementarity than opposition.

André Gide once wrote that he deplored "the spitefulness that tries to discredit a translation ... because here and there slight mistranslations have slipped in". Since it was Justin O'BRIEN himself who translated Gide's words into English, one hesitates to make an issue of the slight mistranslations that have slipped into his *The Fall* (1957). On the whole, O'Brien copes well with the challenge of keeping track of the narrator's devious account of his life. The register in which Clamence delivers this account is at the formal extreme of conversational French, but it has all the polish of a courtroom performance, reflecting his former profession as a barrister. The relatively literal approach adopted by O'Brien adequately reproduces the formal tone of the original, only occasionally falling short of the target ("I had the good fortune to ..." would clearly have been preferable to "I had the luck to ...") or overshooting it ("to boot" is too pompous for "avec ça"). On a number of occasions, however, the literalness is overdone. Sometimes it gives rise to awkward English: there is, for instance, a string of pluralized abstract nouns, which are common in French but, for the most part, unacceptable in English ("satisfactions", "generosities", "consolations", "mockeries", etc.). Sometimes, and more seriously, the literalness results in opacity of meaning: it is difficult to see what "the feeling of the law" (for "le sentiment du droit") or "bad words" (for "mauvaises paroles") could mean to an English reader.

In translating the short stories of *Exile and the Kingdom*, O'Brien (1958) has been faced with much greater stylistic variety, from poetic evocations of the natural world to ironic descriptions of the Parisian social world, via the technical terminology of the barrel-making industry. On the whole, Camus's compelling descriptions and his irony retain their force in the translation. Mistranslations do appear (Janine's "jambes lourdes" are "aching legs", not "thick" ones), along with unidiomatic renderings ("didn't sleep a wink" would have been more natural than "didn't close an eye") and tonal infelicities (parts of the conversation between Daru and Balducci in "The Guest"); but they occur mostly towards the informal end of the stylistic spectrum, and some of them may conceivably sound less strange to American ears. Elsewhere, O'Brien is at ease with the text.

The only edition of *Caligula* and *Le Malentendu* available to Gilbert (1947) was that of 1947. It was superseded in 1958, when Camus made fairly significant revisions to both plays for a new edition. Neither translation has been updated. Gilbert stays close to the 1947 texts, producing accurate versions of them. Although he cannot resist the occasional flourish, it works well in the case of *Caligula*, where the touch of colour added to the terse simplicity of Caligula's words in the original coheres with the excesses of his behaviour: for example, to a literal "... my life means nothing" and "fear ... that draws its nobility from the belly" Gilbert prefers "my life means no more than a speck of dust" and "fear ... that draws its patent of nobility straight from the guts". While the 1958 changes made by Camus to *Caligula* concerned the meaning of the play, *Le Malentendu* was subjected largely to a stylistic pruning; in *Cross Purpose*, therefore, Gilbert's tendency to elaborate on the original clearly runs counter to Camus's intentions. For instance, when, near the end of act 1, Martha's mother complains that her daughter's remarks are hurtful, Camus, in 1958, whittled down the "sur le ton de l'accusation" of the 1947 version to a less explicit but perfectly intelligible "sur ce ton". Gilbert, on the other hand, has moved in the opposite direction with "in that tone, the tone of an accuser", towards, then, an even greater explicitness than that of the rejected 1947 version.

Of Camus's plays, *L'Etat de siège*, based on his novel *La Peste*, presents the greatest challenge to the translator on account of its diversity of tone, ranging from the bureaucratic newspeak of the Plague to the lyrical pathos of the Chorus. Gilbert's firm command of English enables him to meet the challenge without difficulty (1958). However, having proved the least popular of the plays, *L'Etat de siège* has been excluded from the 1984 Penguin selection of plays in favour of one of Camus's adaptations, of Dostoevskii's novel *The Possessed* (or *The Devils*). In contrast, *Les Justes*, the most successful of the plays, was considered worthy not only of inclusion but of a revised translation. Jones's version (*The Just*, 1984, first published 1965) follows Gilbert's *The Just Assassins*, 1958, closely enough to suggest that the one has been deliberately based on the other. Although there is nothing seriously wrong with Gilbert's translation it does have a slightly old-fashioned ring to it, even if this doesn't jar too much, given the historical setting (1905). What Jones does, successfully, is to infuse into the dialogue a more modern idiom, producing a version closer to the original French text. Gilbert's penchant for the grandiloquent and urge to explicate sometimes got the better of him, and the excesses thus generated have been trimmed off by Jones. To take one of the more extreme cases, an over-expansive "the atmosphere of smug inertia was stifling me" has been mercifully eliminated in favour of a straightforward equivalent ("I was suffocating") of the French original ("J'étouffais"). It is only fair to add that there are also times when Jones is able to capitalize on his predecessor's inventiveness.

It is a pity that Jones's brief had not extended to incorporating Camus's revisions to the two earlier plays. A pity, too, as Jones's contribution demonstrates, that publishers allow clear cases of mistranslation to survive from one edition to the next (even Jones occasionally perpetuates Gilbert's mistakes). For while one can agree with Gide that slight mistranslations do not discredit a version, it is equally true that they do not make it sacrosanct.

Paul Reed

Further Reading

O'Brien, Justin, "From French to English" in *On Translation*, edited by Reuben A. Brower, Cambridge: Massachusetts: Harvard University Press, 1959; Oxford: Oxford University Press, 1966

The Outsider / The Stranger

L'Étranger, 1942

Albert Camus's first novel, *L'Étranger*, is also his greatest. The first work to introduce into French literature the concept of the absurd derived from Dostoevskii and Kafka, it tells of a white settler in Algiers called Meursault who gets involved with a pimp, Raymond. Raymond's mistress is an Arab girl, and when in a fit of rage he beats her up her brothers seek revenge. In the ensuing confrontations Meursault shoots one of the Arabs dead. He is tried, found guilty of premeditated murder, and, in a mood of fatalistic resignation, is awaiting execution as the novel ends.

Translations

The French text used by translators is the 1942 Gallimard edition, reprinted (without modification) many times.

Gilbert, Stuart, *The Outsider*, London: Hamish Hamilton, 1946; as *The Stranger*, New York: Knopf, 1946

Laredo, Joseph, *The Outsider*, London: Hamish Hamilton, 1982; as *The Stranger*, New York: Knopf, 1988

Two translations of this masterpiece are examined. The first is by Stuart Gilbert, a close friend of James Joyce; it appeared in Britain and the US in 1946. The second is by Joseph Laredo and was first published in Britain in 1982. As one would expect, Gilbert's is the freer, more florid, more belletristic of the two. Laredo stays close to the original, but occasionally fails to rise to the occasion when Meursault's rhetoric really takes off.

Any translator of *L'Étranger* must be capable of encompassing the whole range of Camus's prose, from the bland and banal to metaphorical elaboration. Gilbert, at his best in the highly-imaged passages, is tempted to embroider the plainer stretches. The reverse is true of Laredo: he handles the restrained sections admirably, but he has not the *souffle* required to carry off the richer paragraphs successfully.

This can be illustrated most conveniently by comparing the two translators' versions of the end of part 1. This passage is central in more senses than one. It comes almost exactly halfway through the book, and it contains Meursault's self-justification, the all-important plea in mitigation which he does not utter at the criminal trial because he feels so detached from the proceedings, but which now, near to death, he composes for the unseen tribunal of his future readers. It is crucial he persuade them that he did not kill the Arab deliberately, but that it was all a ghastly mistake, no more than a cruel accident caused by the heat and the glare. We join the text after the Arab has pulled a knife and pointed it towards Meursault.

The literal sense of the next sentence is that the light spurting from the steel was like a long shining blade hitting Meursault's forehead. Gilbert renders this "A shaft of light shot upwards from the steel, and I felt as if a long, thin blade transfixed my forehead", and Laredo "The light leapt up off the steel and it was like a long, flashing sword lunging at my forehead". Laredo sticks more closely to the syntax of the original by translating the impersonal form "c'était comme" by "it was like", where Gilbert, as is his wont, chooses to personalize the comparison by writing "I felt as if"; on the other hand, Laredo succumbs to cliché in the flashing of lunging swords, whereas Gilbert writes more arrestingly – and more faithfully to the spirit of the original – about long thin blades transfixing Meursault's forehead.

In neither version do the two sentences following this differ significantly. The next crux is

> Je ne sentais plus que les cymbales du soleil sur mon front et, indistinctement, le glaive éclatant jailli du couteau toujours en face de moi. Cette épée brûlante rongeait mes cils et fouillait mes yeux douloureux

for which we have

> I was conscious only of the cymbals of the sun clashing on my skull and, less distinctly, of the keen blade of light flashing up from the knife, scarring my eyelashes, and gouging into my eyeballs (Gilbert).

and

> All I could feel were the cymbals the sun was clashing against my forehead and, indistinctly, the dazzling spear still leaping up off the knife in front of me. It was like a red-hot blade gnawing at my eyelashes and gouging out my stinging eyes (Laredo).

The 36 words of the original are matched by Gilbert's 36, but are stretched to 46 by Laredo. This is surprising, since terseness is normally Laredo's strong point, but when, as here, he is tempted to over-write, he does so with a vengeance, Gilbert's more disciplined version being distinctly superior both as a piece of English prose and as reflecting more closely the rhythm and meaning of the original.

The same can be said of the next section. Here, famously, the whole sky opens up to rain down fire: "Le ciel s'ouvrait sur toute son étendue pour laisser pleuvoir du feu". Gilbert, as befits a sophisticatedly literate member of the Joyce circle, captures the apocalyptic tone of this far better than Laredo does: from Gilbert we have "the sky cracked in two, from end to end, and a great sheet of flame poured down through the rift", while Laredo quite fails to catch the biblical note in the dull platitudes of his version, "the sky seemed to be splitting from end to end and raining down sheets of flame".

The next passage is crucial to the novel's impact: if it does not carry conviction, Meursault's entire rhetorical enterprise will have failed to sway his readers. The translator must therefore get it right. Camus's text reads: "Tout mon être s'est tendu et j'ai crispé ma main sur le revolver. La gâchette a cédé ...", the passive connotation in the last main verb being cunningly chosen to imply that the gun went off more or less by accident. Both translators rightly render this "the trigger gave", but just before that Gilbert reinforces the passive impression by translating "j'ai crispé ma main" as "my grip closed", while Laredo is nearer to the literal meaning but further from the spirit in "I tightened my grip". The same applies to "j'ai touché le ventre poli de la crosse", the erotic undertone of which Gilbert captures in "the smooth underbelly of the butt jogged my palm" and Laredo coarsens in "I felt the underside of the polished butt".

As we have seen, Laredo fails consistently to highlight Meursault's passivity. This has to be emphasized if the last rhetorical flourish in part 1 is to carry weight with readers about to embark on the description in part 2 of Meursault's trial on a charge of first-degree murder. In French, the magnificent conceit that closes part 1 reads "j'ai tiré encore quatre fois sur un corps inerte ... Et c'était comme quatre coups brefs que je frappais sur la porte du malheur". The excuse is breathtaking, but it works: how many readers pause to reflect on the enormity that Meursault has effectively disclaimed all responsibility for killing a man in cold blood and then for continuing to fire long after it was obvious that his victim was dead? All Laredo can lamely come up with in these circumstances is "And it was like giving four sharp knocks at the door of unhappiness", whereas Gilbert, true to form, rises to the occasion with the perfectly paced "And each successive shot was another loud, fateful rap on the door of my undoing". Moreover – and crucially – Gilbert recognizes that the French word "malheur" means much more than just unhappiness; it is closer to the German word "Unglück", and as such is more tellingly rendered as "undoing".

JOHN FLETCHER

Further Reading

Fletcher, John, "Persuasive Rhetorics" in his *Novel and Reader*, London and Boston: Marion Boyars, 1980, pp. 53–72

King, Adele (editor), *Camus's L'Étranger: Fifty Years On*, London: Macmillan, and New York: St Martin's Press, 1992

Cao Xuequin

See The Dream of the Red Chamber

Karel Čapek 1890–1938

Czech novelist and dramatist

Biography

Born 9 January 1890 in the village of Malé Svatoňovice in the Podkrkonoší region of Northern Bohemia. He studied philosophy, aesthetics and art history at Charles University in Prague, and by the time he started work as a journalist (1917) his literary career was already under way. At first Čapek wrote plays and collections of short stories in collaboration with his brother Josef but soon he began to work on his own. In 1920 Čapek's love of French poetry resulted in the publication of an anthology of his translations of writers such as Apollinaire, Mallarmé, Rimbaud and Cendrars, with profound consequences for the development of Czech poetry. The year 1920 also saw the publication of his single most successful work, *R.U.R.* – the play that would give the word *robot* to the English language. From the early 1920s Čapek travelled widely in Europe and wrote about his impressions and experiences for his readers back home; his time in England was chronicled in the whimsical *Anglické listy* (*Letters from England*), 1924. Also at around this time the composer Leoš Janáček turned Čapek's play *Věc Makropulos* (*The Makropulos Case*) into the libretto for his opera of the same name. Čapek continued to produce work in a wide variety of genres with varying degrees of success: novels (notably the trilogy published 1933–34 that some like to regard as his most accomplished work), short stories such as the *Povídky z jedné kapsy*, *Povídky z druhé kapsy* (*Tales from Two Pockets*), 1929, children's books (the delightful *Dašenka*, or *The Life of a Puppy*), philosophical essays and his "interviews" with President Masaryk. In the late 1930s he saw the threat of fascism and examined its consequences in the famous novel *Válka s mloky* (*War with the Newts*), 1936, and the plays *Bílá nemoc* (*The White Plague*), 1937, and *Matka* (*Mother*), 1938. His stance brought much opprobrium on him and he became disillusioned by the Munich betrayal and exhausted by the attacks on him for his opposition to fascism. Died in Prague, 25 December 1938.

Translations

Selections

Kussi, Peter, *Toward the Radical Center: A Karel Čapek Reader*, Highland Park, New Jersey: Catbird Press, 1990

Novels

Hordubal, 1933; *Povětroň*, 1934; *Obyčejný život*, 1934 (trilogy)

Weatherall, M. and R. Weatherall, *Hordubal*, London: Allen and Unwin, 1934

Weatherall, M. and R. Weatherall, *Meteor*, London: Allen and Unwin, and New York: Putnam, 1935

Weatherall, M. and R. Weatherall, *An Ordinary Life*, London: Allen and Unwin, 1936

Weatherall, M. and R. Weatherall, *Three Novels: Hordubal, An Ordinary Life, and Meteor*, New York: A.A. Wyn, and London: Allen and Unwin, 1948

Válka s mloky, 1936

Osers, Ewald, *War with the Newts*, London: Unwin, and North Haven, Connecticut: Catbird Press, 1985

Weatherall, M. and R. Weatherall, *War with the Newts*, London: Allen and Unwin, and New York: Putnam, 1937; with an introduction by Darko Survin, Boston: Gregg Press, 1975; with an introduction by Ivan Klíma, Evanston, Illinois: Northwestern University Press, 1985

Short Stories

Povídky z jedné kapsy; *Povídky z druhé kapsy*, 1929

Comrada, Norma, *Tales from Two Pockets*, complete version, Highland Park, New Jersey: Catbird Press, 1990

Selver, Paul, *Tales from Two Pockets*, London: Faber, 1932; New York: Macmillan, 1943; with drawings by Karel Svolinský, London: Folio Society, 1962

Apokryfy; *Kniha apokryfů*, 1932–45

Comrada, Norma, *Apocryphal Tales*, with an introduction, Highland Park, New Jersey: Catbird Press, 1997

Round, Dora, *Apocryphal Stories*, London: Allen and Unwin, and New York: Macmillan, 1949

Plays

R.U.R., 1920

Novack-Jones, Claudia, *R.U.R. (Rossum's Universal Robots): A Collective Drama in a Comic Prologue and Three Acts* in *Toward the Radical Center*, edited by Peter Kussi, 1990

Selver, Paul, *R.U.R. (Rossum's Universal Robots): A Fantastic Melodrama*, New York: Doubleday, 1923; adapted by Nigel Playfair, London: Oxford University Press, 1923

Ze života hmyzu, with Josef Čapek, 1921, produced 1922

Firkušný, Tatiana and Robert T. Jones, "From The Life of Insects, Act II: The Predators" in *Toward the Radical Center*, edited by Peter Kussi, 1990

Selver, Paul, *And So Ad Infinitum (The Life of the Insects): An Entomological Review*, adapted by Nigel Playfair and Clifford Bax, London: Oxford University Press, 1923; New York: Oxford University Press, 1949

Selver, Paul, *The World We Live In (The Insect Comedy)*, adapted by Owen Davis, New York: Samuel French, 1933; as *The Life of the Insects* in *International Modern Plays*, edited by Anthony Dent, London: Dent, and New York: Dutton, 1950; as *The Insect Play*, with *R.U.R.*, London: Oxford University Press, 1961

Věc Makropulos, 1922

Graff, Yvetta Synek and Robert T. Jones, *The Makropulos Secret* in *Toward the Radical Center*, edited by Peter Kussi, 1990

Selver, Paul, *The Macropoulos Secret*, adapted by Randall C. Burrell, Boston: Luce, 1925; London: Holden, 1927

Bílá nemoc, 1937

Heim, Michael Henry, "The White Plague" in *Cross Currents: A Yearbook of Central European Culture*, 7 (1988) pp. 431–501

Selver, Paul and Ralph Neale, *Power and Glory*, London: Allen and Unwin, 1938

Travel Writing

Italské listy, 1923

Marchant, Francis P., *Letters from Italy*, London: Besant, 1929

Anglické listy, 1924

Selver, Paul, *Letters from England*, London: G. Bles, and New York: Doubleday, 1925

Cesta na sever, 1936

Weatherall, M. and R. Weatherall, *Travels in the North; Exemplified by the Author's Own Drawings*, London: Allen and Unwin, and New York: Macmillan, 1939

Other Writing

Hovory s T.G. Masarykem, 3 vols, 1928–35

Round, Dora, *President Masaryk Tells His Story*, London: Allen and Unwin, 1934; New York: Putnam, 1935; New York: Arno Press, 1971 (parts 1 and 2, abridged)

Round, Dora, *Talks with T.G. Masaryk*, revised and edited by Michael Henry Heim, North Haven, Connecticut: Catbird Press, 1995 (parts 1 and 2)

Weatherall, M. and R. Weatherall, *Masaryk on Thought and Life: Conversations with Karel Čapek*, London: Allen and Unwin, and New York: Macmillan, 1938; New York: Arno Press, 1971 (part 3)

Karel Čapek still holds a special place in the affection of Czechs. He was also the first Czech author to achieve success on a European, and even (in the case of *R.U.R*) a world scale. Most of his work was translated into English in the 1920s and 1930s: the plays by Paul SELVER and much of the prose by M. and R. WEATHERALL; other works were translated by Dora ROUND and Lawrence Hyde. For some years Čapek was easily the most popular and widely read Czech author in English translation, but his reputation waned after World War II. Since 1990 the American publishers Catbird Press have brought out new and revised translations of Čapek's work.

For the translator Čapek presents significant difficulties. He was among the first major writers habitually to use *obecná čestina* (Common Czech) in his work (see also the entry on Hašek), but at the same time he loved the richness of Czech and liked to employ a rather eclectic, old-fashioned vocabulary. Čapek's style and language is thus both simple and artful at the same time – an effect difficult to reproduce in English. This, incidentally, casts doubt on the editor and translator Peter KUSSI's approach (stated in his introduction to *Toward the Radical Center*) to revising existing translations by, amongst other things, removing "outdated expressions". Čapek himself uses such expressions with relish, greatly enhancing the verbal texture of his work, and it is hard to see how eliminating them will "do justice to the linguistic brilliance of the original," as Kussi hopes to do.

In *Hordubal*, M. and R. WEATHERALL (1934, 1935, 1936; 1948)were faced with one of Čapek's most innovative and complex books in terms of narrative technique. The internal monologue (sometimes an unusual internal "dialogue") of part 1, written in a rhythmic, evocative, rather ballad-like prose, is translated accurately while retaining much of the rhythmic quality of the original. The Weatheralls capture Juraj Hordubal's colloquial and uneducated speech but of course lose the "exotic" Americanisms that add colour to the Czech text. The Weatheralls manage the shifts of register and viewpoint in the second and third parts of the novel well, i.e., they find the appropriate language and stylistic register for the straight detective story and the courtroom drama following the novel's events.

War with the Newts: In this famous but perhaps now rather dated dystopian novel, Čapek mimics different writing styles – journalistic, scientific, poetic, old-fashioned, etc. – to produce another textually complex work that taxes the imagination and resources of the translator. The WEATHERALLS' 1937 version does have moments of stylistic clumsiness and a few words are mistranslated, but as a rule the translation is readable and accurate and they imitate the mosaic of different styles convincingly. Ewald OSERS (1985) has retranslated the work, occasionally with greater fluency in the style, but it is notable how close he stays to some of the Weatheralls' phraseology. Unfortunately the Picador edition (1991) does not reproduce the typographical devices retained in the earlier translation, which enhance the visual aspect of the book.

Apocryphal Stories: Dora ROUND (1949) is an attentive translator of Čapek who follows the Czech text closely without allowing her English to become contrived or unnatural. Along with most other translators of Čapek, her biggest problems follow from Čapek's vocabulary. In the brief story "The Five Loaves", for example, Čapek uses three words meaning "doctor" – *ranhojič*, *doktor* and *felčar* – each of which has its own distinct semantic colouring. Round translates them all as "doctor", which dilutes the idiosyncratic language of the baker / narrator of the story and diminishes the impact of having words of Czech popular or folk origin in the mouth of a baker from biblical times. Kussi's revisions of Round's version of "The Five Loaves" (in *Toward the Radical Center*) amount to changing some of Round's semi-colons into unnecessary commas, and changing "ha'pence" into "cents" (Čapek uses "groš"). This, presumably, is what Kussi means when he writes in his introduction that he has edited out "excessive use of Britishisms".

Norma COMRADA (1997) evidently follows Kussi's example, as she writes in the introduction to her new translation of all the tales that her version differs from Round's "in its use of updated language, in its corrections of error, and in its entire approach to the Tales and to Čapek's narrative voice". The problematic nature of "updating" Čapek's language has already been mentioned above, but Comrada has tried to do it consistently and her translation does read easily, leaving aside the fact that she is using an idiom completely different from Čapek's. She also keeps more closely to the original than Round does. However, the side effect of all this is that the translation is considerably duller than Round's. Whether one likes the *Apocryphal Tales* themselves or not, Čapek always has a clever and interesting, often elegant prose style. Round's prose style is also elegant and enjoyable in a rather old-school way, even when the story itself is rather dull. Comrada's updated language is "styleless", and the stories are flat and featureless as a result; but the translation is smooth and accurate.

Paul SELVER's translation of *R.U.R.* has remained the standard version in English since 1923 despite the fact that it was always known to be an "adaptation" rather than a faithful translation. Selver and Playfair have made such changes – leaving out certain speeches and the ending of the play – as must have seemed necessary to them to make the play work on stage. Čapek himself was unhappy with the play and aware of its weaknesses, but Selver and Playfair's changes weaken the texture of the play even more (see Naughton, 1984). As with most of Selver's translations there are also points where he simply mistranslates, as when he turns "People with ideas should not be allowed to have an influence on [the] affairs of this world" (Novack-Jones, p. 69) into "There's no influencing people who have ideas of their own in the affairs of this world". In fact the language of the play is not at all difficult and Claudia NOVACK-JONES (1990) carries out the useful task of translating the complete text without any cuts or adaptations. Occasionally she is a shade *too* exact (translating the common Czech exclamation "hrome!" literally as "thunder!", which it is hard to imagine any English speaker exclaiming) but otherwise her translation is perfectly reliable.

SELVER's translation of Čapek's well-known *Insect Play* has been published in two adaptations: the first, with Nigel Playfair and Clifford Bax, titled *And So Ad Infinitum* was published in 1923; a second adaptation for the American stage by Owen Davis, retitled *The World We Live In*, came out in 1933. The 1923 translation/adaptation is particularly poor and completely misrepresents Čapek's play. Large sections of the original are missed out; the Tramp's character has been completely changed, rendering his role in the play almost meaningless, and most of the satire of the original play has been blunted. In act 2 Čapek uses the full range of Czech diminutives to demonstrate and to satirize the petty-bourgeois and their aspirations (in the persons of the dung-beetle couple) quite mercilessly: none of this is retained in the English. Selver might not be entirely to blame for the defects of the published edition, however, as Owen Davis's adaptation is also based on Selver's translation and is both more complete and somewhat more faithful to the original. Nevertheless, the fact that these adaptations have survived for more than 50 years and continue to be used by, for example, amateur dramatic companies, is surprising. Tatiana FIRKUŠNÝ & Robert JONES have gone some way towards undoing the feeble impression created by the earlier editions in their recent complete retranslation of act 2. In their hands the satire is sharper, although still a little watered-down from Čapek's original. They do stick faithfully to Čapek's text, however.

HEIM's 1988 translation of *Bílá nemoc* (*The White Plague*) is greatly superior to Selver's 1938 adaptation titled *Power and Glory*. Heim, on the whole, stays faithful to the original although some lines are trimmed or left out. Occasionally his lines are awkward and unlikely, as when Father says "Holka je někde s tím svým ..." translated as "Sis is out with Heart-throb ...". Heim also makes little effort to reproduce such subtlety and word play as can be found in the original. SELVER & NEALE's version is almost worthless as a translation. They break up or leave out speeches, or occasionally add their own speeches (such as a jolly dialogue between Father and Daughter about a football match in act 1, scene 3). An unflattering reference to England is neatly excised as are the more unpleasant descriptions of the plague symptoms. What Selver has translated has been done with indifference towards the original. It is perhaps worth noting that Čapek and Selver's relations by the time of this translation were quite poor.

Letters from England: Čapek's tone in the "letters" is that of a wide-eyed foreigner in a strange and exotic land, reporting back to his fellow countrymen (not without irony) on the wonders he sees there. Čapek enhances this impression by using stylistic devices that are essentially untranslatable. He uses English words in his text, either changing them according to the rules of Czech morphology (e.g. "gentlemani", "Highlandeři", "kumpanie Highlanderù") or simply leaving them in their English forms in the Czech text (e.g. "divné uličky, wynds nebo closes" or "hodovní síně s estrádou pro masters a fellows"). Both approaches would have seemed strange and exotic to the Czech eye (see Kriaková, 1989–90). Obviously SELVER (1925) can do nothing with these but reproduce the English word and so the sense of something exotic disappears. Selver does slightly better with Čapek's habit of accumulating metaphors, again to exaggerate and "make strange", but it is not difficult to find English equivalents for these. As is often the case with Selver, words, phrases and even whole sentences are missing, but still it is one of Selver's better translations.

JAMES PARTRIDGE

Further Reading

Abrash, M., "*R.U.R.* Restored and Reconsidered", *Extrapolation*, 32/2 (1991) pp. 184–92

Fox, Mary Anne, "Lost in Translation: The Ending of Čapek's R.U.R.", *ICarbS*, 4/2 (1981) pp. 101–09
Harkins, William E., *Karel Čapek*, New York: Columbia University Press, 1962
Kriaková, Hana, "Úskalí a problémy Selverova překladu anglických listù Karla Čapka" [Pitfalls and Problems of Selver's Translation of Karel Čapek's *Letters from England*], *Sborník prací Filosofické fakulty Brněnské university*, 36–37 (1989–90) pp. 17–26
Malen, Elizabeth, "Proper Words in Proper Places: The Challenge of Čapek's *War with the Newts*", *Science-Fiction Studies*, 14/14 (1987) pp. 82–92
Matuška, Alexander, *Karel Čapek: An Essay*, translated by Cathryn Alan, London: Allen and Unwin, 1964
Naughton, James, "Futurology and Robots: Karel Čapek's *R.U.R.*", *Renaissance and Modern Studies*, 28 (1984), pp. 72–86
Osers, Ewald, "Translations of *War with the Newts*" (letter to the editor), *Times Literary Supplement* (9 October 1998)

Giosuè Carducci 1835–1907

Italian poet and critic

Biography

Born in Valdicastello in the Versilia area of Tuscany, 27 July 1835. He studied in Florence and Pisa, taught in San Miniato and was appointed professor of Italian literature at the University of Bologna in 1860. In 1867 the Minister of Education attempted to transfer him to Naples because of his republicanism and anticlericalism (most notoriously expressed in his poem "To Satan", first published in 1865) and his fierce attacks on what he saw as the pusillanimous government of Italy in its first decade of unity; but Carducci resisted and remained in Bologna until his retirement in 1904 and his death in 1907. In later life, Carducci became a strong supporter of the monarchy and of the nationalistic politician Crispi. His fame as "national bard" and as professor of Italian literature was such that he became a senator in 1890, and in 1904 was voted a government pension. The Queen bought his library, and also, after his death, his house, so that they could be preserved for the nation. In December 1906, two months before his death, the King of Sweden sent a deputation to award him the Nobel Prize for Literature. He died in Bologna, 16 February 1907.

The main collections of his poems are *Levia gravia* [Light and Serious Poems],1868; *Giambi ed epodi* [Iambics and Epodes], 1882; *Rime nuove* (*New Lyrics*), a collection that received its final form in 1887; *Odi barbare* (*Barbaric Odes*), 1st edition 1877, but revised and expanded through various stages until this collection was finalized in 1893; *Rime e ritmi* (*Lyrics and Rhythms*), 1899. Almost all the translations listed below are anthologies representing all periods of Carducci's work.

Translations

Selections

Bickersteth, G.L., *Carducci: A Selection of His Poems* (parallel texts), with notes and three introductory essays, London and New York: Longmans Green, 1913
Burkhard, Arthur, *Twenty-Four Sonnets* (bilingual edition), Yarmouth Port, Massachusetts: Register Press, 1947
Higgins, David H., *Selected Verse* (parallel texts), with an introduction, Warminster, Wiltshire: Aris and Phillips, 1994
Holland, Maud, *Poems* (parallel texts), with an introduction, London: Fisher Unwin, 1907
Rendel, Romilda, *From the Poems of Giosuè Carducci, 1835–1907*, with an introduction, London: Kegan Paul, 1929
Tribe, Emily A., *A Selection from the Poems of Giosuè Carducci*, with notes and a biographical introduction, London: Longmans Green, 1921

Single Works

Rime nuove, 1887

Gilbert, Laura Fullerton, *The Rime Nuove of Giosuè Carducci*, Boston: Badger, 1916
Smith, William Fletcher, *The New Lyrics of Giosuè Carducci*, Colorado Springs: privately printed, 1942 (book 8 and five poems of book 6 are omitted)

Odi barbare, 1877–93

Smith, William Fletcher, *Odi Barbare* (parallel texts), revised by Dino Bigongiari and Giuseppe Prezzolini, New York: Vanni, 1950 (this translation had been privately printed as *The Barbarian Odes of Giosuè Carducci*, Menasha, Wisconsin, 1939)

The verse translations of Giosuè Carducci's poems published in England offer an interesting encounter between a vigorous and frequently polemical poetry, rooted in Italian history and culture, and the Georgian literary fashions then prevalent in England, with the application of techniques derived from Tennyson, Swinburne and Bridges to solve the problems posed by Carducci's "barbarous" experimentations in classical prosody. The translations show up both the clarity and the subtlety of Carducci's metrics: the thump of dactyls and anapaests in English often sounds crude in comparison. Later translators renounced the search for equivalent rhymes and rhythms, and tried prose.

Carducci's texts necessarily attract a certain kind of complicit translator, lover of the Italian countryside, which Carducci celebrated, and the classical tradition. The weighting of political verse as against the pastoral and elegiac varies, however, according to the taste of the anthologizing translators, and almost all of them offer some excuse in mitigation of Carducci's virulent attacks on Christianity.

Maud HOLLAND's collection of just 20 poems (1907), in which the Italian originals are printed on the right-hand page, is preceded by an introduction describing Carducci's funeral in "February last". Holland defends Catholicism and the popes against Carducci's attacks: in the very first poem reproduced, the last 16 stanzas (containing "a terrible attack" on Pius IX who actually had a "kindly heart") are omitted. She opts for a minimum of footnotes, and eliminates some classical references: the long and complex "Alle fonti di Clitumno" is cut to a mere vignette. The need to rhyme frequently drives Holland to invent whole phrases and to introduce new metaphors. Decoration is the order of the day: evening becomes "star-rise", elms are "elm-grove", white is "snow-white", and there is the fondness usual in poeticizing texts for hyphenated forms – "moon-curving", "sea-deep", "wind-spread", "down-bending". It is remarkable how often the English pentameters pack in far more words than the Italian hendecasyllables. This wordiness proliferates when dactyls make their entry, with a rollicking translation of "Davanti San Guido". Holland translates three of the *Odi barbare* besides the incomplete "Alle fonti di Clitumno", and tries to imitate classical metres. The tendency to accentuate the first syllable of the line means that the dactylic rhythm becomes invasive. Despite the various shortcomings of this first anthology, not exempt from errors and howlers, it has the interest and charm of having been produced relatively near the period of the original writing in Italian.

In BICKERSTETH (1913) Carducci the professor from Bologna encounters G.L. Bickersteth the don from Christ Church, Oxford. For Bickersteth, Carducci "(with the exception of our own Swinburne) was certainly the greatest [poet] alive in Europe at the opening of the twentieth century", and the book is a labour of love and erudition. The 68 poems, offering a wide selection from all books except the *Juvenilia*, are preceded by a three-part introduction, of which the third is a still indispensable disquisition on Carducci's adaptations of classical metres. Curiously, the *Levia gravia* are referred to throughout as "Levia Grandia". Bickersteth's versions are smooth and efficient but not immune from some of the same poeticizing traits as Holland, such as the frequent addition of adjectives; and he is liable to bouts of licence on the one hand and pedantic explication on the other. Coming after the learned introduction, the rendering of the *Odi barbare* is somewhat disconcerting. For a number of the pieces, including the opening programmatic "Prelude", Bickersteth opts for rhymed stanzas based on Marvell and Tennyson. Where he does imitate the classical metres (as for instance in "By the Sources of Clitimnus") he does so in accentual verse, which appears so effortless that it forgets to be "barbarous".

It is surprising that after Bickersteth's compilation the same publisher should produce another major collection of Carducci's poems. Indeed, TRIBE (1921) states in her preface that her work was finished before World War I, but "its publication has been necessarily delayed by that event". Although exactly contemporary therefore, Tribe's anthology of 46 poems (which does not print the Italian text on the facing page) is quite different in style and spirit from Bickersteth's. In her selection of poems, Tribe does not overprivilege the lyrical and elegiac – as do Holland before and Rendel to come – but presents the reader with a good range of the political poems, each furnished with an introduction and notes. She is the only one of the translators reviewed here to take on the polemical sonnet sequence, "Ça ira", about the French Revolution. She expresses some reluctance to translate the "Hymn to Satan", but then does so with a vengeance. Something goes badly wrong with the metre in a central group of poems in which some of the lines are impossible to scan, and Tribe is clearly struggling with the earlier *Odi barbare*, but the syntactic and rhythmic awkwardness is perhaps an acceptable price to pay for versions that generally maintain a remarkable fidelity to both the spirit and the letter of the text. The translator's stated aim was "to give as literal a rendering as the exigencies of metrical forms would allow", and in this she has been successful, avoiding the wordiness of the other translators and capturing Carducci's ruggedness.

RENDEL (1929) provides the briefest of prefaces, in which she comments that the antithesis of democracy and Christianity in Carducci "has now a musty flavour" – ironic in view of the Spanish Civil War in the next decade (the book was published in the year of the treaty between Mussolini and the Catholic Church). Although the introduction praises the "pure poetry" of Carducci's later collections, this anthology of 65 mostly short poems paradoxically gives little space to Carducci's mature works and is unique in the emphasis it places on the earlier period. It is as if this were a collection partly designed to fill in gaps left by earlier translators, and then the translator ran out of steam. The translations are very variable in their fidelity: fanciful invention and omitted stanzas mean that some are variations rather than translations. The extremely strong Keatsian flavour established at the beginning is never quite shaken off. Notes are minimal, and names that might have caused difficulty simply disappear. Rendel has a go at Carducci's virtuoso poem "Alla rima", but she has no metrical subtlety. The five poems from the *Odi barbare* are rendered in plodding iambics and turn out sounding like *Hymns Ancient and Modern*. A comparison with Tribe shows Rendel's translations up as amateurish and often ludicrous.

in 1942 William Fletcher SMITH produced *The New Lyrics of Giosue Carducci*. Here is Carducci's encounter with a second translating professor, this time from Colorado College. The break with Carducci's time and culture is now complete: now, after the verse anthologies, come the prose cribs and reconstructions. This private printing of translations of one particular book by Carducci, however, has no Italian facing texts, and no notes of any kind. The literal translations are arranged in paragraphs to "facilitate the location of individual passages and the identification of rhythmical units". Despite some home-grown typographical mistakes and a light sprinkling of errors, the translations achieve their purpose. It is a relief to be rid of the extra verbiage generated by most of the previous verse translations, although it is disconcerting to read a translation of the opening poem "To Rhyme" now entirely shorn of the welter of rhymes which were what the poem was all about. An odd but interesting feature is that at the end of the book 12 of the poems are presented a second time, now in versions "arranged line for line" – in order to bring out Carducci's "lucid simplicity of style".

In 1950 two professors of Italian from Colombia University, Dino Bigongiari and Giuseppe Prezzolini "partly revised" William Fletcher SMITH's translation (1939) of *Odi barbare* "so as to bring it closer to the original". The same principles and style operate here as in the Fletcher Smith *New Lyrics*, except that the Italian text appears on the left-hand page. The translations are set out in prose paragraphs corresponding to the stanza and couplet divisions of the original. These versions make a foreignizing virtue out of being literal: they retain a poetic syntax, generally avoiding English "poetic" vocabulary such as "becomes atremble" (a rare exception). Only occasionally is the result baffling (" ... two walls that lift themselves stupendous to defiance more steep").

If Rendell's translation showed the final rupture with Carducci's times, and William Fletcher Smith's translations the limitations but not inconsiderable virtues of prose, HIGGINS (1994) wins back Carducci as a university text-book in which the 19th-century poet needs to be archaeologically reconstructed. Higgins dispenses altogether with rhyme and metre but his prose translations (facing the Italian texts) are divided into lines and retain capital letters in mid-sentence at the beginning of each "stanza" or "couplet". The translations thus actively resist their status as literal prose crib. On the one hand Higgins constantly smuggles in pedantic explanations and clarifications (so that some phrases and lines are startlingly longer than the lines they are matched against; what was "Lo, epic Ferrara" in Fletcher Smith becomes "Look, Ferrara, cradle of the epic, draws near"); while on the other he produces artful phrases and curious suspensions at the end of lines, seeming to yearn for the frisson of poetry. Despite this, word order more linear than Fletcher Smith's makes Higgins's versions the more prosaic. Thus, Higgins falls between two stools, and the overall effect is one of nostalgia for a poetic world that is lost.

DAVID GROVES

Further Reading

Scalia, S. Eugene, *Carducci: His Critics and Translators in England and America 1881–1932*, New York: Vanni, 1937

See also the translators' introductions to Higgins, to Holland and to Rendel and the introductions and notes to Bickersteth and to Tribe

---

Rosario Castellanos 1925–1974

Mexican novelist, short-story writer, poet and journalist

Biography

Born in Mexico City, 25 May 1925. She grew up in Comitán, in the state of Chiapas, far from the capital of Mexico and surrounded by indigenous and *mestizo* communities. Her family owned land, but when they lost their property after the Mexican Revolution they relocated to Mexico City, where Castellanos finished her schooling. At the university, her thesis in philosophy treated the artistic production of women and the non-objectivity of aesthetic practices prejudicial to women artists. Returning to Chiapas in the early 1950s, she devoted her time to improving the lot of the marginalized Mayans around her. Her first published writings were poems, but all her works reflect her lifelong social activism. *Balún-Canán* (1957) won the Mexican Critics' Award for 1957 and the Chiapas Prize in 1958. The writer's novels, short stories, poems and essays consistently retain a few autobiographical elements, especially when she is writing about Chiapas or feminism. Her collected poems, *Poesía no eres tú: obra poética 1948–1971*, appeared in 1972. After a time as professor of letters at the Universidad Nacional Autónoma de México (UNAM), Castellanos was appointed ambassador to Israel in Tel Aviv. Died as the result of an accident at home, 7 August 1974.

Translations

Selections

Ahern, Maureen, *Looking at the Mona Lisa*, Bradford, England: Rivelin Press, 1981

Ahern, Maureen *et al.*, *A Rosario Castellanos Reader: An Anthology of Her Poetry, Short Fiction, Essays, and Drama*, Austin: University of Texas Press, 1988

Allgood, Myralyn F., *Another Way to Be: Selected Works of Rosario Castellanos* (bilingual edition), with a foreword by Edward D. Terry, Athens: University of Georgia Press, 1990

Bogin, Magda, *The Selected Poems of Rosario Castellanos* (bilingual edition), edited by Cecilia Vicuña and Bogin, with a foreword by Cecilia Vicuña translated by Anne Twitty, and translator's foreword by Bogin, St Paul, Minnesota: Graywolf Press, 1988

Palley, Julian, *Meditation on the Threshold: A Bilingual Anthology of Poetry*, with introductions: "Feminism in the Poetry of Rosario Castellanos" by Gabriella de Beer; and "Rosario Castellanos: Eros and Ethos" by Julian Palley, Tempe, Arizona: Bilingual Press / Editorial Bilingüe, 1988

Novels

Balún-Canán, 1957

Nichols, Irene, *The Nine Guardians*, London: Faber, 1958;

New York: Vanguard Press, 1959; new edition, Columbia, Louisiana: Readers International, 1992

Oficio de tinieblas, 1962
Allen, Esther, *The Book of Lamentations*, with an introduction by Alma Guillermoprieto, New York: Marsilio, 1996; reprinted New York: Penguin, 1998

Short Stories
Ciudad real, 1960
Rudder, Robert S. and Gloria Chacon de Arjona, *The City of Kings*, with an introduction by Claudia Schaefer, Pittsburgh: Latin American Literary Review Press, 1993

The prize-winning novel *The Nine Guardians* (*Balún-Canán*, 1957) treats the relations between races and cultures in the predominantly Indian region of Chiapas. NICHOLS's translation (1958) of *Balún-Canán* is very readable, and, though leaning in the direction of overliterality, rarely makes errors. A short glossary of unfamiliar Indian and Spanish words compensates for the inclusion of cultural elements unknown to English readers, but it is unfortunate that introductory material is lacking. This early novella tells of a family's gender troubles and of Mexico's land reform in the wake of the Revolution from the point of view of a little girl.

Perhaps the way English readers will know Castellanos's work, however, is through the novel translated by ALLEN, *The Book of Lamentations* (1996; *Oficio de tinieblas*, 1962), which has recently become available in the Penguin Twentieth Century Classics series. Allen's beginning imitates well the sacred moment of Mayan prayer sliding into prose allegory that opens this unusual novel. Unlike their treatment in much commercial fiction, Latin American myth and magic in this work are given the respect due to religious belief, while at the same time the harsh life lived by the Indians is portrayed with brutal realism. Whereas magical realism uses humor and exaggeration to criticize social injustices, *The Book of Lamentations* employs allegory and allusion, both of which present considerable challenges for translators.

In the 1981 volume of poems in AHERN's translation, *Looking at The Mona Lisa*, the translator collects 17 poems she previously published in poetry magazines. All but five of these translations reappear in the largest and most important collection of Castellanos in translation, *A Rosario Castellanos Reader*, edited by AHERN (1988).

In the edition of BOGIN's well-crafted translations (1988), over 30 poems appear in Spanish as well as English. An accomplished translator of Isabel Allende, Elvira Orphee, and Salvador Espriú, Bogin has chosen to emphasize Castellanos's humor and nuanced lyric moments over her famous feminist and conversational pieces. In Bogin's note, the translator speaks of opting for an English that conveys the poet's "gently elevated, at times even heroic, feel".

In *Meditation on the Threshold*, (1988) PALLEY has published the Spanish text and a facing English translation of over 40 of Castellanos's best poems about women, society, and poetry, taken from her mature volumes and presented in chronological order. In the two prefacing essays, Beer analyzes Castellanos's development of feminist ideas in her poetry volume by volume, while Palley studies the late poetry anthologized in terms of its feminist themes, autobiographical content and unique style. The translations by Palley are quite close and finely reproduce Castellanos's breezy, prosaic language.

The first of Castellanos's three collections of stories, *The City of Kings* (*Ciudad real*, 1960) demonstrates in 10 brief, incisive narratives her critical and ironic attitude toward stereotyped, oppressive, or merely insensitive attitudes and actions of those of all races in Chiapas. RUDDER & CHACON DE ARJONA (1993) have translated well the Spanish stories in *Ciudad real*, but they have left the Mayan words and regionalisms intact to retain the flavor of the original. Apparently an edition for students (who are more likely than other readers to use a glossary), *The City of Kings* contains an introduction aimed at university-level classes. The English rendition is accurate in meaning and form, but is perhaps difficult for the casual reader. Castellanos wrote these stories of protest and critique after working to help the Native Americans in her own state of Chiapas, the site of recurrent strife between the native peoples and the government.

A large compendium of the major works by Castellanos, AHERN's *A Rosario Castellanos Reader* (1988) includes translations by six hands and is intended for the classroom or serious reader. All the poems and several of the essays and short stories are very well rendered by Ahern; the other translators have much smaller roles. Little difference in styles or philosophies is noted among the translators; editing has brought about a homogeneous style. Castellanos's quotidian, realist language verging on prose is maintained in the English poems; her irony and sarcasm is everywhere present in the feminist and neo-Realist stories and essays. The auxiliary materials are exemplary, though academic.

In the ALLGOOD translation (1990), the useful introduction is aimed at the English reader unfamiliar with the literary, historical, and cultural background of the Mexican's works. Fourteen poems, with Spanish on facing pages, are well translated here. One poem is not from *Poesía no eres tú*, Castellanos's main collection. The selection reflects the poet's thematic preoccupations and is especially strong in showing the author's concern for the marginalized Indians of Mexico, but perhaps it over-emphasizes some superficial similarities to Chile's more sentimental woman poet, Gabriela Mistral. The volume contains a bibliography of primary and secondary materials, wisely separated into Spanish and English sections.

DIANE E. MARTING

Further Reading

Dauster, Frank, "Rosario Castellanos: The Search for a Voice" in his *The Double Strand: Five Contemporary Mexican Poets*, Lexington: University Press of Kentucky, 1987
Kintz, Linda, *The Subject's Tragedy: Political Poetics, Feminist Theory, and Drama*, Ann Arbor: University of Michigan Press, 1992
Lindstrom, Naomi, *Women's Voice in Latin American Literature*, Washington, DC: Three Continents Press, 1989
O'Connell, Joanna, *Prospero's Daughter: The Prose of Rosario Castellanos*, Austin: University of Texas Press, 1995

Baldassarre (or Baldesar) Castiglione 1478–1529

Italian courtier, poet, scholar and diplomat

Biography

Born in Casatico, near Mantua, 6 December 1478, into an old aristocratic family. He studied Latin and Greek in Milan in the early 1490s under the humanist Demetrius Chalcondyles. He attended the court of Ludovico Sforza in Milan, c.1494–99, then returned to Mantua and entered the employ of its ruler, Francesco Gonzaga, as diplomat and military commissioner. Accompanying Gonzaga on his Neapolitan campaign, Castiglione took part in the battle of Garigliano, 1503. In 1504 he moved to the service and the court of Guidobaldo di Montefeltro, duke of Urbino, who charged him with diplomatic and military missions. He was sent to England by the duke in 1506 and was his ambassador in Milan, 1507. From 1508, Castiglione continued in Urbino in the service of Guidobaldi's successor, Francesco Maria della Rovere, nephew of pope Julius II; he participated with papal forces in several campaigns of conquest (1509–12) and meanwhile composing many of his minor works. In 1513 he became Mantuan ambassador in Rome at the court of the new pope, Leo X, and received the title of count of Novilara. His stay in Rome as ambassador was interrupted in 1516, when he followed Francesco Maria into exile in Mantua after the papal conquest of Urbino. Also in 1516 he married Ippolita Torelli (died 1520; one son and two daughters). In 1520, after relations between Rome and Mantua had been restored, Castiglione left his estates in Mantua, resettled in Rome as Mantuan ambassador, 1520, and continued to serve the interests of Rome and Mantua. He was sent to Spain to be pope Clement VII's nuncio at the court of the emperor Charles V in Madrid, 1525–29. Died in Toledo, 2 February 1529.

As well as his masterpiece, *Il libro del cortegiano* (*The Book of the Courtier*), 1528, Castiglione left poems in Italian and Latin, a play and correspondence.

The Book of the Courtier

Il libro del cortegiano, 1528

First published in April 1528 in Venice, by the Aldine Press (case d'Aldo Romano, e d'Andrea d'Asolo suo Suocero). Since their publication, the editions of *Il libro del cortegiano* by Vittorio Cian (Florence 1894, 4th edition 1947) and Bruno Maier (Turin 1955, 2nd edition 1964) have provided the basic text for several translations and for successive scholarly editions. Prominent among these is that from Carlo Cordié, *Opere di Baldassare Castiglione, Giovanni Della Casa, Benvenuto Cellini*, Milan: Ricciardi, 1960, with its detailed bio-bibliographical notes.

Translations

Bull, George, *The Book of the Courtier Baldesar Castiglione*, Harmondsworth and Baltimore: Penguin, 1967

Castiglione, A.P., *Il cortegiano; or, The Courtier ... and a New Version of the Same into English*, London: W. Bowyer, 1727

Hoby, Thomas, *The Courtyer of Count Baldessar Castilio*, London: William Seres, 1561; edited by Janet E. Ashbee, with an introduction by Walter Raleigh, London: Edward Arnold, 1900; reprinted London: Dent, and New York: Dutton, 1974

Opdycke, Leonard Eckstein, *The Book of the Courtier*, New York: Scribner, 1903

Samber, Robert, *The Courtier*, London: A. Bettesworth, 1724

Singleton, Charles S., *The Book of the Courtier Baldesar Castiglione*, New York: Anchor Books, 1959

Within 100 years of its publication, Baldesar Castiglione's *The Book of the Courtier* had been translated into Latin (three complete translations and one rendering of just the first of its four books); French (three versions); German (two); and Spanish (the first translation into a foreign language, by Juan Boscan, Madrid, 1534). The first translation into English, also early in the field, was from Sir Thomas HOBY, 1561; this was reprinted for the third time in 1603.

The Book of the Courtier is a complex Renaissance text worked on intermittently by its nobly-born author (a soldier and courtier, scholar, poet and diplomat) from the years when Castiglione was in service at the court of the rulers of Urbino until he despatched the manuscript to Venice, with careful instructions down to the binding and ornamentation of presentation volumes included in the 1030 copies to be printed.

It has appeared in scores of editions and translations, exercised a pervasive influence on European sensibilities generally, and on social and educational attitudes in particular – fostering, for instance a certain pride in gentlemanly amateurism but also neo-Platonic idealism – and it still stands as arguably the most representative and catholic compendium of the Italian Renaissance, mediated chiefly through the politics and culture of an archetypal yet historical Court, as well as being a literary composition of subtle, often ambivalent, psychological observation and polished Latinate style, notable for its euphony, the balance of its clauses and the clever sensitivity of its pace and pitch. In the four books of *The Book of the Courtier* a convincingly portrayed group of historical figures, some famous then and now, in the quest for truth discuss successively the choice of topic for their discourse and the proper formation and pursuits of the Courtier; the application of the Courtier's accomplishments and qualities, his permissible levity and his virtues, and those of the perfect Court Lady; the attributes and proper conduct of the latter, the *donna di palazzo*; the Courtier's relationship with his Prince, the nature of good government, and the final importance of love.

HOBY's (1561) classic translation of *The Book of the Courtier* was dedicated to The Lord Henry Hastings and carried a letter of commendation from Sir John Cheke. In his epistle to the former, Hoby proffered the translated text as being, for mature men:

> a pathway to the behoulding and musing of the minde ... To yonge Gentlemen, an encouraging to garnishe their minds with morall vertues, and their bodye with comely exercises, and both the one and the other with honest

> qualities to attaine unto their noble ende: To Ladyes and Gentlewomen, a mirrour to decke and trimme themselves with vertuous condicions, comely behaviours and honest enterteinment toward all men: And to them all in general, a storehouse of most necessary implements for the conversacion, use, and training up of mans life with Courtly demeaners.

Cheke, the Protestant scholar of Greek and Latin (who had taught Hoby at Cambridge and strongly influenced him), in stating his own preference for writing an English tongue that should be "cleane and pure, unmixt and unmangeled with borrowing of other tunges ..." added that his loving friend had used a "strange word" only scarcely and when necessary and then "so as it seemeth to grow out of the matter and not to be sought for ..." In its original unmodernized form, Hoby's translation, though inevitably rather opaque here and there and betraying a less than thorough knowledge of Italian, is broadly faithful to the original, stylistically robust, plain but pleasing, charmingly and informatively of its time, when English prose was at the start of a tremendous upsurge of adaptation, invention and ingenuity. Overall, Hoby conveys the urbane, humorous, sometimes teasing, sometimes solemn and well-honed intelligence of Castiglione's more flexible and sonorous Italian. The best accessible text of Hoby is the 1900 London edition with an introduction by Walter Raleigh that includes an informed appraisal of the result of Hoby's linguistic skill and style ("conscientious, intelligent, and able" but sometimes missing the point and sometimes betraying "the bias of the serious school of thought to which he belonged", e.g. in translating *novelle* by "triflying tales" and veering away from the (common) Italian use of *divino* for something human). The rich debate about Hoby's translation continues (see Peter Burke, Further Reading, in connection with the text's key words such as *sprezzatura*, rendered both as "disgracing" and as "recklessness"). Hoby's translation stays fustily but inspiringly in print.

OPDYCKE's translation (1903) was published with the *apologia* that Hoby's version had grown "too antiquated" to be readily intelligible to the general reader and the two other translations into English were seldom met save in large public libraries. (These rival translations by SAMBER (1724) and A.P. CASTIGLIONE (1727) had sprung from a revival of interest in *The Book of the Courtier* in early 18th-century England, as part of a general reawakening of interest in the Italian Cinquecento and perhaps as propaganda for the Court of the time; their dedications were to the Duke of Montagu and King George respectively.) The translation by Opdycke aimed to be literal, the only conscious deviations from the Italian being those "deemed necessary to make its meaning clear". Opdycke provided a succinct list of editions of *The Book of the Courtier* up to his own. With numbered paragraphs, this version is a carefully executed carrying over of Castiglione's dense prose into very formal, rather old-fashioned English, respectful to Castiglione's ornate periods and cadences. Thus Opdycke's version of an ancient simile used by Castiglione begins: "And as the bee in the green meadows is ever wont to rob the flowers among the grass, so our Courtier must steal this grace from all who possess it ..." In the same passage from the first book, Opdycke finds for Castiglione's *sprezzatura* the word "nonchalance", that "shall conceal design and show that what is done and said is done without effort and almost without thought." Opdycke's English misses a good deal of Castiglione's unaffected modernity, as when the latter's simple "Parmi ancora che ..." is given as "Methinks, too ...". He also (like Samber's) understandably, for the time, shies away from the Italian's explicit sexual language as well as his mildly indecorous jokes, relegating, for example, to his notes and leaving in Italian a long sarcastic passage from the third book about Socrates' bedding of Alcibiades and Xenocrates' drunken continence, and omitting the word naked – *ignuda* – from a comment in the third book on a model of restraint who preserved her chastity though for many nights "held in the fast bonds of her lover's arms".

Charles S. SINGLETON's translation (1959) eschews the "nays" and "verilys" used by Opdycke, though his English often contrives to suggest an earlier period of discourse than the 20th century, as when the gentlemen of Castiglione's Court of Urbino "betake" themselves to the Duchess or (in the measured last sentence of the whole book) the Italian "com'è suo costume" becomes "as is his wont ..." But Castiglione's subtleties of language and ambiguities of attitude, as conveyed through the cast of characters, are not missed, and Singleton's stolid version could claim to "adhere more faithfully to the original text of the work as Castiglione left it than any recent translation into English" had done.

Sensitive to the significance of key words in Castiglione, Singleton leaves *sprezzatura* in Italian, giving "nonchalance" as his version in brackets, and has no problem with Castiglione's in its time novel *cortegiania* (which gave Hoby – who sometimes paraphrased it – and his contemporary translators of the text into Latin some perplexity). He renders it simply by "Courtiership", which is capitalized – a faint echo of Samber's capitalization of all nouns in his version of 1724. Singleton's text also usefully numbers the paragraphs of the four books, but the scholarly apparatus to his illustrated translation is minimal.

BULL's Penguin Classics translation (1967) has been criticized adversely for shortening some of Castiglione's honorific modes of address. His rendering of the text retains the rhythms and sonorities of the original while making it read smoothly in contemporary and polished English.

GEORGE BULL

Further Reading

Burke, Peter, *The Fortunes of the Courtier: The European Reception of Castiglione's Cortegiano*, Cambridge: Polity Press, 1995; University Park: Pennsylvania State University Press, 1996

Catalan

Literary Translation into English

Catalan is one of the Romance languages, like French, Italian, Spanish, Romanian and Portuguese, that come from Latin. Originating in the south of France and the northeast of the Iberian peninsula, its position on either side of the Pyrenees and bordering the Mediterranean shaped its character, making it a bridge between Iberian and Gallic Romance. Catalan has a vocalic system more complex than that of Spanish; the j and z sounds are absent. The use of adverbial pronouns *en* and *hi* resembles that of *en* and *y* in French; and many Latin words have been reduced by apocope (*filiu* > *fill*, *oculu* > *ull*, *lacte* > *llet*). It is spoken in an area that stretches from the French department of Pyrénées-Orientales in the north to Alacant (Alicante) in the south, from Lleida (Lérida) and Andorra in the west to the Balearic Islands and Alghero in Sardinia in the east. Including the varieties spoken in Valencia and Majorca, over 9 million people speak Catalan today – more than speak Danish, Finnish or Norwegian – making it unique among Europe's non-national languages.

The evolution and varying fortunes of Catalan have been shaped by historical and political factors. At an early stage in its development the close links between the Christian counts of Barcelona and the Carolingian empire brought it into contact with Provençal, the literary language of the Catalan troubadours; the union of the Catalan counts with the crown of Aragon determined its independence from Castile and Castilian; the defeat of King Pere I while defending his Albigensian subjects at the battle of Muret in 1213 put an end to any thoughts of Catalan expansion north of the Pyrenees; and the struggle with Castile over the reconquest of Spain from the Moors led Catalan to spread south to Murcia and from there across the Mediterranean to Majorca, Corsica, Sardinia, Naples, etc. The unification of the Spanish crown under Isabella of Castile and Ferdinand of Aragon and the growth of a monolithic Spanish empire – centralist and authoritarian – caused the decline in Catalan culture from the 16th century onwards. There ensued a long period of decadence during which the language was restricted to private use among the popular classes and occasional use by the Church. It took the initiative of the 19th-century Romantics to revitalize the language. It was not by chance that the name of Renaixença (rebirth) was given to the movement that had such a tremendous cultural impact and restored linguistic and national pride to both speakers and writers of Catalan. Three outstanding literary figures – the poet Jacint Verdaguer (1845–1902), the dramatist Ángel Guimerà (1847–1924) and the novelist Narcís Oller (1846–1930) – jointly brought Catalan culture back to life.

Later, certain areas of political freedom were gradually restored (home rule for Catalonia under the Mancomunitat of 1914–25, and the Statute of Autonomy, 1932–39) and the economy benefited from a belated industrial revolution, success as a trading nation and the financial advantages of non-intervention in World War I to stage a massive recovery. All this meant that Catalan language and literature were virtually restored to normal for a few years. This is seen in the spelling reform of the *Normes ortogràfiques* of 1908 and the work of Pompeu Fabra, who unified and codified the language in his *Gramàtica* of 1923, and *Diccionari general de la llengua catalana* of 1932. The Spanish Civil War (1936–39) and the dictatorship of General Franco (1939–75) put an end to this incipient normalization by implementing a policy of cultural genocide that sent literary activity underground: people were forbidden to speak the Catalan language in public, it was no longer taught in schools or universities, and books in Catalan or translations into the language were banned.

It was only in the 1960s, against a background of steadfast resistance and the gradual dismantling of the Franco dictatorship under the pressure of economic growth – stemming largely from the foreign currency brought in by Spanish migrant workers in Europe and the advent of mass tourism – that fresh public attempts were made to normalize the Catalan language and literature.

With the return of democracy to Spain, Catalonia's new Statute of Autonomy (1979) established the co-officiality of Catalan and Castilian and the status of Catalan as Catalonia's own original language. From that date Catalan became the norm in public life (outside the law, the police and the armed forces). Two key developments were the use of Catalan in education (from primary to university level) as the means of instruction across the curriculum, and the creation of public TV channels in Catalan.

The social position held by Catalan in present-day Catalonia differs considerably from that of Galician in Spain, Breton in France, or Welsh in Great Britain. Catalan is recognized as the main language of a rich, prosperous area, an economic and political driving force within Spain. For the large numbers of immigrant workers who came to Catalonia between the 1940s and the 1960s from other parts of Spain, especially from the poor rural areas of the south, language was equated with social identity and naturalization. Wherever it is spoken, Catalan is seen as a key element of upward mobility. The importance of this situation would be hard to understand were it not for another purely objective feature, also unique to Catalan: its undoubted linguistic similarity in morphological, lexical and stylistic terms to Castilian. So those Spanish-speakers who wish to learn it and integrate into Catalan-speaking society are not faced with an insurmountable barrier, as can be the case for a speaker of Spanish or English confronted with Basque, or Irish or Welsh. At present anyone living in Catalonia with a basic level of education has few difficulties in understanding Catalan (officially, the number of people who understand it is more than 95 per cent). They are less likely, however, to use it socially, since even though speakers of Castilian may have a good passive knowledge of Catalan there is little reason for them not to go ahead and speak in Castilian: all Catalan speakers understand it and historical circumstances have accustomed them to replying in Castilian (the level of knowledge is 100 per cent).

As is the case with much Romance literature, the first written evidence of Catalan comes in the form of fragments, as in the mid-12th-century translation of the *Liber judiciorum*. Translation was always important in the literature of early Catalan, dominant in which was the 13th-century novelist, poet and philosopher Ramon Llull, who wrote in Latin, Catalan and Arabic. The influence of humanism, albeit short-lived, helped revitalize the language and literary genres; the best-known examples from the period are Andreu Febrer's translation into Catalan of the *Divine Comedy* (1429), Bonifaci Ferrer's translation of the Bible (1478), and the opening passages of Joanot Martorell's novel of chivalry *Tirant lo Blanc* (1490) inspired by the early 14th-century Middle English verse romance *Guy of Warwick*. Great interest was also shown in translation during the 19th-century Renaixença, especially among the fashionable writers of the day, who translated French, Scandinavian and Russian authors or the great figures of the Enlightenment. The normalization of the language in the first third of the 20th century was accompanied by a translation boom (an important series of Greek and Latin classics, collections of modern novels, three monumental versions of the Bible, etc). The 1930s saw the emergence of collections with a wider appeal, new translators and genres, often translated via a third language, as was common practice at the time. The translations published between 1930 and 1936 of works by Gide, Proust, Woolf, Conrad, Hemingway, Joyce and Moravia attest to the high level of interest in contemporary literature.

Translation contributed to the resistance to dictatorship by defying the bans imposed by Franco. J.M. de Sagarra's translations of Shakespeare and the *Divine Comedy* (1945–53, 1948–50) and C. Riba's version of the *Odyssey* (1948) proved – albeit on a minor scale – how high culture could survive through the prestige of translation, which was more difficult to censor. The gradual relaxation of censorship encouraged the emergence of various collections of translations (such as "Isard", "Rosa dels Vents", "El club dels novellistes") which, from the 1960s, helped create a reading public in Catalan. The cultural revival came of age with the translation of highly contemporary authors in collections that are still in existence today ("El Balancí", "A tot vent"), especially of politically committed authors such as Pavese, Pratolini, Sartre, Brecht, Dos Passos, and Sillitoe.

Barcelona is one of the main centres of translation in Spain, not only in terms of the volume of books published there, but also because the various levels of the regional administration – the Catalan Parliament, the Generalitat (the autonomous government), local councils, universities, primary and secondary schools, etc. – produce vast quantities of material in Catalan that often have to be translated into Castilian, a process that has its counterpart in the large amount of administrative paperwork generated by the government in Madrid that has to be translated into Catalan. In 1998, 6730 books were published in Catalan, of which 18.2 per cent were translations. Of these, 38.5 per cent were translated from English, 32 per cent from Spanish, and 11 per cent from French.

Since the late 1980s the traditional importance of the publishing sector plus the new demands for translators from the administration and the importance of key sectors for commercial translation, such as tourism, the media and multinational companies, have led to a widespread interest in translation and the teaching of translation. The influence of the former School of Translation and Interpreting (EUTI), founded in 1972 at the Autonomous University of Barcelona (UAB), was decisive in creating in 1991 the four-year university degree in Translation and Interpreting throughout Spain and in setting up Translation Faculties (FTIs) in several universities in the Catalan-speaking area (Alacant, Barcelona – UAB and UPF – Castelló de la Plana, Vic). The same healthy situation is found in literary translators' groups, particularly those belonging to the translation sections of the Association of Writers in Catalan (AELC) and the Professional Association of Writers in Catalonia (ACEC). Both of these are represented at the European Conference of Associations of Literary Translators (CEATL).

There are regular activities focused on literary translation, among them the seminar on translation in Catalonia at Vilanova i la Geltrú (held yearly since 1993) and the academic congresses held regularly at the Universitat Jaume I in Castelló and at Vic University (yearly) and the UAB (biannual since 1992). Through the Institute of Catalan Letters, the Catalan government awards prizes to translators and grants to translators and publishers who translate from and into Catalan.

In spite of the undoubted importance of Catalan literature from its early beginnings to the 16th century, and then again from the mid-19th century to our day, very few works have been translated into or are even known in English. Sir Thomas Grenville (1755–1846), who had in his library editions of *Tirant lo Blanc* (1490) and *Lo Carcer damor* (1493), was clearly an isolated case of such knowledge, and few readers today realize that the first modern Catalan translation of the New Testament (1832) was undertaken in London and printed by the British and Foreign Bible Society.

Until recently, translations from Catalan into English were few and far between, and tended to reflect the interest of a particular individual or group: historians, Catalanophiles, academics. Among them were the pioneering translations of King Jaume I's *Crònica* (translated by John Forster, 1883), Ramon Muntaner's *Crònica* (translated by Lady Goodenough, 1920–21), Ramon Llull's *Llibre d'Amic e Amat*, *Art de contemplació*, *Blanquerna* and *Arbre d'amor* (translated by E. Allison Peers, 1923, 1925, 1926 and 1926 respectively) and Desclot's *Crònica* (translated by L. Critchlow, 1929). There were also translations of urban and rural realist and naturalist texts, the most important of which were *La papallona* by Narcís Oller, and *Mar i cel* and *Terra baixa* by Àngel Guimerà (translated by Wallace Gillpatrick, 1916 and 1914), the latter of which was popularized in the opera *Marta of the Lowlands*. None of these has ever been reissued. The translations of plays by Santiago Rusiñol and Ignasi Iglésies have been lost completely.

It is difficult to see, for example, how Gerald Brenan's interest and insight into the 15th-century poet Ausiàs March – in his 1963 work *Literature of the Spanish People*, which still stands today as a model of comparative literature – failed to inspire any translation of this author's poems. Similarly, despite the numerous poems written on Catalonia and Barcelona by British poets during the Spanish Civil War, and George Orwell's widely-read *Homage to Catalonia* (published in 1938, although not translated into Catalan until 1965), there was no corresponding interest in translations of Catalan literature but, instead, a few travel books and memoirs. The legacy of the 1930s was to be found in the informative works written on Catalonia by E. Allison Peers, John Langdon Davies and R.D.F. Pring-Mill, describing Catalan history, politics, life and culture.

It took the exemplary and tireless efforts of Joan Gili – himself the author of *Catalan Grammar* (1974) – and his Oxford-based Dolphin Book Company to produce the first wave of modern translations from Catalan: Joan Triadú, *An Anthology of Catalan Lyric Poetry* (1953); Josep Carner, *Poems* (translated by Pearse Hutchinson, 1962); Paul Russell-Gebbett, *Medieval Catalan Linguistic Texts* (1965); Carles Riba, *Poems*, *Tannkas*, and *Savage Heart* (translated by Joan Gili, 1970, 1991, 1993); Salvador Espriu, *Lord of the Shadow* (translated by Kenneth Lyons, 1975), and *Forms and Words* (translated by Joan Gili, 1980). From the early 1960s this activity was linked to the teaching of Catalan in British universities by academics such as F. Pierce, R.B. Tate, G.W. Ribbans, A. Terry, M. Wheeler and P. Polack alongside Catalan exiles and teachers living in Britain (J.M. Batista i Roca, I. Gonzàlez Llubera, A. Turull, J.L. Marfany) or the United States (J.M. Roca-Pons, J. Gulsoy, A. Ferran, J.M. Solà-Solé, A. Porqueras, J.M. Sobrer). This led to the appearance of a new generation of translators with an academic grounding in Catalan (A. Yates, R. Archer, N. Smith, J. Willis, S. Golden, M.A. Newman, J. Eddy, A. Bath, D. Keown, S.A. Kitts, H. Gardner). Many of the translations undertaken by this generation of translators (e.g. Joan Salvat-Papasseit and Salvador Espriu) were done under the auspices of the Anglo-Catalan Society (founded 1952) or the North American Catalan Society. This atmosphere was more open to the history of Catalan literature and saw the first major translations of classics such as Ramon Llull (Anthony Bonner, *Selected Works*, 1985), or Ausiàs March (Arthur Terry, *Ausiàs March: Selected Poems*, 1976; M.A. Conejero *et al.*, *Selected Poems*, 1986–93; Robert Archer, *Ausiàs March: A Key Anthology*, 1992), or the 15th-century novel of chivalry *Curial e Güelfa* (translated by Pamela Waley, 1982), or Joaquim Ruyra (1858–1939), *The Long Oar* (translated by Julie Flanagan, 1994).

The general, non-specialist reader has also had access to Catalan literature through the translations brought out by commercial publishers, such as David H. Rosenthal's translations of Mercè Rodoreda (1983, 1984, 1986), *Tirant lo Blanc*, (1984), Josep Vicenc Foix (1988), Joan Perucho (1988), V. Andrés Estellés (1992) and Víctor Català (1992). There have been other moves to gain a wider public for a varied selection of books, authors and genres that might have international appeal. These range from L. Villalonga's *Bearn* (translated by D. Bonner, 1988) to Maria Antonia Oliver's detective story *Study in Lilac* (translated by Kathleen McNerney, 1987), or the poems of Salvador Espriu (translated by Magda Bogin, *Selected Poems*, 1989), and young prose writers such as Quim Monzò and Jesús Moncada (*O'Clock*, translated by Mary Ann Newman, 1986; *The Towpath*, translated by Judith Willis, 1994).

Special mention must be made of the American poet and critic Sam Abrams, an expert on contemporary Catalan poetry and founder of the privately published Beacon series (1984–96), in which have appeared his own translations of M. Abelló, A. Bartra, N. Comadira, P. Gimferrer, M. Manent, J. Margarit, J. Palau i Fabre, F. Parcerisas, M. Pessarrodona, J. Piera, A. Ràfols-Casamada and J. Teixidor.

If Catalan literature is to be known round the world, translation into English is now a necessity, given that English is the international language at present. But more than that, it is vital to the survival of Catalan literature in its own country. Faced with the problems any minority literature has in being recognized, especially one that lives in the shadow of a more widely-known neighbour, translation into a third language means gaining an ally and the support of another external cultural system that will help keep the immediate colonialism at bay. In political terms, it is as if the close links between a small state and a superpower stop the small state falling prey to the colonial might of their neighbour. Translation into a widely-spoken language belonging to another culture not seen as threatening creative expression in Catalan enhances the self-esteem and prestige of the cultural system of literary production in Catalan.

FRANCESC PARCERISAS

Further Reading

Memòria, Barcelona: Institució de les Lletres Catalanes (annual publication)

Panorámica de la edición española de libros, *Libros en catalán*, Madrid: Ministerio de Cultura (annual publication)

Sobrer, Josep Miquel, *Catalonia: A Self-Portrait*, Bloomington: Indiana University Press, 1992

Terry, Arthur, *Catalan Literature*, London: Benn, 1972

Translation: The Journal of Literary Translation, 16 (1986)

Catullus c.84–c.54 BC

Roman poet

Biography

Born Gaius Valerius Catullus in Verona, north Italy, c.84 BC into a rich and noble family. His father was a citizen of Verona. Catullus lived principally in Rome from c.62 and probably had a villa at Tibur, near Tivoli. He also owned property at Sirmio (now Sirmione), on Lake Garda. He was a friend of Cicero, probably of Lucretius also, and was hostile to Julius Caesar. He accompanied C. Memmius on his visit as governor to Bithynia, Asia Minor, 57–56. He returned to Rome, where he died c.54 BC.

Catullus was a major figure among the learned New Poets (Neoterics) of the late Roman Republic. As a lyric poet he is ranked with Horace. He fell unhappily in love with a married woman, referred to as "Lesbia" in the 25 poems addressed to her. There are 116 extant poems attributed to him. They include the poems to Lesbia, other short poems, elegies, some long pieces and epigrams in various registers.

Translations

Anonymous, *The Adventures of Catullus, and History of His Amours with Lesbia, Intermixt with Translations of His Choicest Poems, by Several Hands, Done from the French*, London: J. Chantry, 1707 (from Jean de la Chapelle's *Les Amours de Catulle*, 1680–81)

Gregory, Horace, *The Poems of Catullus*, with an introduction, New York: Grove Press, and London: Thames and Hudson, 1956

Lamb, George, *The Poems of Caius Valerius Catullus*, 2 vols, London: John Murray, 1821

Lee, Guy (editor and translator), *The Poems of Catullus*, Oxford: Clarendon Press, and New York: Oxford University Press, 1990

Michie, James, *The Poems of Catullus*, London: Hart-Davis, and New York: Random House, 1969

Nott, John, *The Poems of Caius Valerius Catullus in English Verse*, London: J. Johnson, 1795

Rabinowitz, Jacob, *Gaius Valerius Catullus's Complete Poetical Works*, Dallas: Spring Publications, 1991

Symons, Arthur, *From Catullus: Chiefly Concerning Lesbia*, London: Martin Secker, 1924

Tremenheere, J.H.A., *The Lesbia of Catullus*, London: Fisher Unwin, 1897; reprinted New York: Philosophical Library, 1962

Whigham, Peter, *The Poems of Catullus*, Harmondsworth and Baltimore: Penguin, 1966

Wright, F.A., *Catullus: The Complete Poems*, London: Routledge, and New York: Dutton, 1926

Zukofsky, Celia and Louis Zukofsky, *Catullus (Gai Valeri Catulli Veroniensis Liber)*, London: Cape Goliard Press, 1969

The poems of Catullus, in their articulation of the extremities of love and desire, are metrically subtle and various. In tone, too, the range is great: from the grandly mythological to the brutally naturalistic. Catullus published no collection during his lifetime. The surviving manuscripts, which arrange the poems according to length and metre, represent the views of a later editor. Any English translator is faced by more than the difficulties that his original's linguistic subtlety creates; decisions must also be taken about the order in which to re-present the poems. The frankness – in some eyes the obscenity – of some of Catullus' language has also presented its problems to some translators.

Individual poems were imitated by English poets of the 16th and 17th centuries – e.g. by Crashaw (Poem 5), Campion (8), Lovelace (13, 69) and Sidney (70). The first large collection, however, seems to be the ANONYMOUS production of 1707. This views Catullus as one of "the Galantest ... Authors of Antiquity" and the work is described as "an entertaining Explication, or Gallant Commentary upon the Verses that Catullus has wrote upon his Mistress". Fewer than 50 poems are actually translated here, mostly in rhyming couplets. Selection and arrangement are essentially narrative in intention. The whole is based on *Les Amours de Catulle* by Jean de la Chapelle.

The first complete English version, by NOTT (1795) is poetically flat, and necessarily euphemistic in many places, but interesting for its notes.

LAMB (1821), too, resorts frequently to euphemism, "making", in his own words, "every attempt to veil and soften before entire omission could be justified". A few poems are left out, but what is translated is generally elegant, presented in a variety of rhymed stanzas. Lamb is at his best in the light-hearted, at his weakest when Catullus is most passionate.

TREMENHEERE (1897) arranges the poems translated to make a narrative, with the aid of somewhat novelettish prose links. He translates (very stiffly) fewer than 50 poems which, he believes, "trace the course of that ill-fated passion which wrecked the tenderest of Roman poets".

In SYMONS (1924) are far superior versions of 28 poems; the control of tone is, for the most part, assured, and in his variety of rhymed metres Symons gives to Catullus a plausible English voice. It is unfortunate that Symons made so relatively few translations from Catullus.

The volume by WRIGHT (1926) is interesting both for the best of Wright's own workmanlike translations (e.g. 3, 17) and for the reprinted selection of versions by earlier translators.

GREGORY (1956) employs a kind of unrhymed and free verse which, in his words, seeks to "approximate" the metres of the original Latin text. Combined with another approximation (to the English of our own century) the results are not happy; too often there is no equivalent to the concision and shape of the original.

WHIGHAM (1966), working in the tradition of Pound, is less attentive to detail than many translators, but only in the cause of ensuring that what he offers actually "works" as a poem in English. For the most part his are lively and attractive versions; the free verse is sensitively and intelligently handled. Poems 13 and 66, in their very different ways, show him at his best.

MICHIE (1969) is more exactly faithful than Whigham and his verse-forms are more traditional. His rhymes and his traditional metres sometimes lead him into redundancy, but many of his versions are attractive and lively. A certain coyness dissipates the intensity of some of the original's more outspoken moments, but there are enough successes (e.g. 41) to deserve attention.

The version by Celia and Louis ZUKOFSKY (1969) is a remarkable tour-de-force, though it is only a translation in a rather special sense. Most translators give priority to the meaning of the original; the Zukofskys give primacy to the *sound* of the Latin – "this translation ... follows the sound, rhythm and syntax of [the] Latin". Sometimes this concern is so skilfully reconciled with attention to the meaning (as in 34) that the result is masterly and beautiful. Elsewhere the results are often rather grotesque.

LEE (1990) is altogether more staid. Fidelity to the poet's meaning is here the chief priority and Lee is scrupulous in the avoidance of amplification. His verse rhythms are not always as lively or various as one might desire, but his is a reliable and highly competent version, particularly successful in the more "public" poems.

In RABINOWITZ (1991) Catullus is resolutely "modernized". Allusions are updated, the idiom is long-lined and slangy, with echoes of Ginsberg and Burroughs. This Catullus is, we are told, a "fucketeer playboy ... roughly the equivalent of a rock-star". The results are likely to shock classicists, but do at least offer evidence of the continuing immediacy of Catullus' concerns.

Many other interesting versions of Catullus have – for reasons of space – had to be left undiscussed here. They include the complete translations by Lindsay (1948), Sisson (1966), Raphael and McLeish (1978) and Goold (1983). Good versions of individual poems, or of smaller groups of poems, can be found in the works of Flecker, Hardy, Landor and Pound, as well as in those of the Renaissance poets mentioned above.

GLYN PURSGLOVE

Further Reading

Booth, Joan, *Latin Love Elegy: A Companion to Translations of Guy Lee*, London: Bristol Classical Press, 1995

Raffel, Burton, "No Tidbit Love You Outdoors Far As A Bier: Zukofsky's Catullus", *Arion*, 8/3 (1969) pp. 435–45

Super, R.H., "Landor and Catullus", *Wordsworth Circle*, 7 (1976) pp. 31–37

Whigham, Peter, "Notes on Translating Catullus" in *The Translator's Art: Essays in Honour of Betty Radice*, edited by William Radice and Barbara Reynolds, Harmondsworth and New York: Penguin, 1987

See also prefatory material to the translations listed, especially those by Lee, Whigham and Wright

---

C.P. Cavafy 1863–1933

Greek poet

Biography

Born Konstantinos Petrou Kavafis in Alexandria, Egypt, 17 April 1863, into a Greek merchant family. Cavafy never lived in Greece. He spent most of his life in Alexandria, though after his father's death his mother took the child to live in England, 1872–79, and he spent three years in Constantinople, 1882–85. He spoke English and wrote some of his poems in English. He earned his living as a civil servant. In 1888 he worked at the Egyptian Stock Exchange and from 1892 to 1922 was a clerk in the irrigation service of the Egyptian Ministry of Public Works. Died 29 April 1933 in Alexandria.

Cavafy had one pamphlet of his verse published privately in 1904, when he was 41, and reissued it, slightly enlarged, five years later. After that he compiled notebooks of verse for distributing to friends, and the world reputation of his poems grew after posthumous publication. The best known among them were written before World War I: "Perimenontas tous varvarous" ("Waiting for the Barbarians"), "Polis" ("The Town"), and "Ithaki" ("Ithaka"). A noted later poem is "En megali Elliniki apoikia, 200 BC" ("In a Large Greek Colony, 200 BC"), written 1928.

Translations

When Cavafy died in 1933 no edition of his poems had ever been published. The Greek text used by translators before 1963 was the 1935 edition of Rika Sengopoulou, containing only the 154 poems collected and circulated by the poet himself. Subsequently, translators have used the 1963 edition of G.P. Savidis for the "canon", and the 1977 *Unpublished Poems* and 1983 *Disowned Poems*, also edited by G.P. Savidis (all published by Ikaros, Athens).

Poetry

Dalven, Rae, *The Complete Poems of Cavafy*, New York: Harcourt Brace, and London: Hogarth Press, 1961; enlarged edition, 1976

Keeley, Edmund and George Savidis, *Passions and Ancient Days: Twenty One New Poems*, New York: Dial Press, 1971; London: Hogarth Press, 1972

Keeley, Edmund and Philip Sherrard, *C.P. Cavafy: Collected Poems*, Princeton, New Jersey: Princeton University Press, and London: Hogarth Press, 1975; revised edition, Princeton University Press, 1992

Kolaitis, Memas, *The Greek Poems of C.P. Cavafy*, New Rochelle, New York: A.D. Caratzas, 1989

Mavrogordato, John, *The Poems of C.P. Cavafy*, London: Hogarth Press, 1951

C.P. Cavafy is unusual – perhaps unique – among translated poets in that translations of his poems into English first began to appear at the same time as the poems themselves. He had a lifelong interest in seeing his poems translated into English, a language in which he was fluent and had been partly educated. In the early stages of his poetic career, Cavafy worked on English translations of his own poems with his brother, John. At a much later stage, with the assistance of E.M. Forster, Cavafy cooperated with the translator Valassopoulou in the ambitious project of translating all his acknowledged poems for the English-speaking public. Valassopoulou, however, worked extremely slowly and baulked at translating the "lurid" love poems, so the project culminated in the publication of only a handful of translations in English-language journals.

Apart from his eagerness to be translated into English, Cavafy drew on English sources for his poetry, "translating" contemporaries or near-contemporaries such as Browning and Wilde into a Greek poetic idiom, and actually working, in his youth, on short translations of French and English poetry. The latent "Englishness" of some of his writings, which is traceable to his English sources as well as to his familiarity with the English language (it has even been claimed by contemporaries that Cavafy spoke Greek with an English accent), coupled with his understated use of metre, rhyme and poetic ornament, have contributed to the false impression that Cavafy's poetry is both prosaic and easy to render in English. In fact, the complex economy of Cavafy's syntax, his occasional use of rhyme and his subtle, polished iambics are extremely difficult to reproduce. Today, Cavafy is one of the modern poets most published in English translation.

John MAVROGORDATO (1951) was Professor of Byzantine and Modern Greek Literature at Oxford and a published poet in his own right. His book of Cavafy translations was the first to appear in English and was completed in 1937, only four years after the poet's death. Publication was delayed, however, until 1951. Although influenced by the same English poetic currents as Cavafy himself, Mavrogordato produced stilted translations which sacrifice much to strictly formal features, including rhyme. The translation is restricted to the 154 poems of the "canon", since the unpublished poems were not available at the time of going to press.

Rae DALVEN (1961), an American of Greek extraction, produced a translation recommended for publication, and prefaced, by W.H. Auden, but criticized by D.J. Enright, who quotes "deviate erotic drunkenness" (for Mavrogordato's "lawless intoxication"), as an example of Dalven's insensitivity to the originals. The title is also misleading, as Dalven translated only the 154 poems of the canon with the addition of 33 (of 75) hitherto unpublished ones. These translations are less mannered than Mavrogordato's but also a great deal less memorable, with no clear guiding principle observable. However, they introduced many readers to Cavafy until they were superseded by the Keeley & Sherrard versions.

The authors KEELEY & SHERRARD (1975; revised 1992) both held academic appointments in Modern Greek, Keeley at Princeton and Sherrard at King's College London, and both published original literary works, as well as being prolific translators of and writers on modern Greek literature. Their long collaboration ended with Sherrard's death in 1995. Their translation contains 175 of Cavafy's poems and is supplemented by *Passions and Ancient Days: 21 New Poems by C.P. Cavafy*, a work undertaken by Keeley and G.P. Savidis, the poet's editor (1971). Thus the 23 "disowned" poems (which Cavafy published in periodicals c. 1886–1900, but later excluded from his collections) and 33 of the unpublished poems are excluded. The translations adopt a middle course between slavish translationese and risk-taking attempts to produce equivalent poems in English. As a result, they have been useful to generations of students but are also sufficiently accessible to have served as an introduction to Cavafy for many English-speaking readers. Since, in this writer's view, the Keeley & Sherrard translations do not stand up as poems in their own right, their continued popularity is a testament to the arresting content, rather than the subtly beautiful form, of the originals.

Memas KOLAITIS (1989) now lives in California but was originally from Alexandria, where he knew Cavafy. He is not a native speaker of English, but his translations of Cavafy are not collaborative. He is the only translator to have undertaken the task of translating all of Cavafy's poems, including the unpublished poems (some of which are little more than fragments) and the "disowned" poems. His translations combine sensitive attention to much-neglected features of the originals, such as word order, with some bizarrely un-English locutions, such as "'S Took" (for "it has been taken") and "He opened the windowshut" (for "he opened the shutter"). The translations are insufficiently literal to be useful to the student of Greek and of insufficient artistic merit to be read with true pleasure. Yet they have the merit of representing a brave attempt to render the originals into an equivalent English idiom.

SARAH EKDAWI

Further Reading

Liddell, Robert, *Cavafy: A Critical Biography*, London: Duckworth, 1974; as *Cavafy: A Biography*, New York: Schocken, 1976

Pinchin, Jane Lagoudis, "Cavafy and his Translators" (Appendix A) in her *Alexandria Still: Forster, Durnell, and Cavafy*, Princeton, New Jersey: Princeton University Press, 1977

Raizis, M. Byron, "Cavafy and His English Translators", *Balkan Studies*, 18/1 (1977) Ricks, David, "Cavafy Translated", *Cambridge Papers in Modern Greek*, 1 (1993)

Robinson, Christopher, *C.P. Cavafy*, Bristol: Bristol Classical Press, and New Rochelle, New York: Caratzas, 1988

Guido Cavalcanti 1255?–1300

Italian poet

Biography

Born in Florence, possibly in 1255. He belonged to a Guelph family and supported the White faction of the Guelph party in the violent feudings in the city. He was banished to Sarzana in June 1300 with the leaders of both Whites and Blacks, although his friend Dante was on the council that gave the order. In August he was recalled to Florence but, already ill, he died there later in the month and was buried on 29 August.

Cavalcanti wrote 50 or so canzoni, ballads and sonnets and was an exponent of the *dolce stil novo*, the 13th-century "sweet new style" in Italian love poetry.

Translations

Collections of Poetry

Cirigliano, Marc, *Guido Cavalcanti: The Complete Poems* (parallel texts), with an introduction, New York: Italica Press, 1992

Nelson, Lowry, Jr, *The Poetry of Guido Cavalcanti*, with an introduction, New York: Garland, 1986

Selections of Poetry

Anderson, David (editor), *Pound's Cavalcanti: An Edition of the Translations, Notes, and Essays*, Princeton, New Jersey: Princeton University Press, 1983

Pound, Ezra, *The Sonnets and Ballate* (bilingual edition), with an introduction, Boston: Small Maynard, and London: Swift, 1912; reprinted Westport, Connecticut: Hyperion Press, 1983

Pound, Ezra, *Guido Cavalcanti: Rime*, Genoa: Marsano, 1932

Pound, Ezra, "Cavalcanti Poems" (parallel texts), in *The Translations of Ezra Pound*, introduction by Hugh Kenner, London: Faber, 1953; New York: New Directions, 1963

Pound, Ezra, *Cavalcanti Poems*, Milan: Vanni Scheiwiller, and New York: New Directions, 1966

Rossetti, Dante Gabriel, in his *The Early Italian Poets from Ciullo d'Alcamo to Dante Alighieri (1100–1200–1300) in the Original Metres, Together with Dante's Vita Nuova*, London: Smith Elder, 1861; edited by Sally Purcell, Berkeley: University of California Press, and London: Anvil Press, 1981

It is Ezra POUND (1912, 1932, 1953, 1966), rather than Dante Gabriel ROSSETTI (1861) who is truly responsible for the proper re-evaluation of the medieval poet Guido Cavalcanti. Cavalcanti's *Rime* was for Pound what *La vita nuova* was for Rossetti, with one significant difference which the American poet emphasizes from the beginning of his literary career (*The Spirit of Romance*, London: Dent, and New York: Dutton, 1910): "Rossetti is substituting verse in one language for verse in another, while the translations in this book are merely exegetic". This is also one of the few instances in which Pound explicitly refers to translations as such, preferring later on in his writings the usage of such terms as "traduction". If this is already a telling sign for understanding the importance of the act of translating for Pound, it becomes one of the pivotal factors in the hermeneutics of *The Cantos*, in which translations of the Cavalcanti poems frequently play a central role. Pound never realized his dream of publishing Cavalcanti's *Complete Works* with two translations, one by Rossetti and the other his own. Furthermore, since the years of his most intense engagement with the poems of Dante's friend, Pound had intended that his translations be accompanied by an essay and notes explaining his poetic renderings. The American poet is not interested in translating the text literally, but in offering the images, the rhythm, and the tone of the original poem to the reader: the value of the "exegetic" translation depends on the translator's ability and sensibility. As he wrote in the notes prepared for the never accomplished *Complete Works* edition ("Postscript (1927)"), in ANDERSON, 1983), "Rossetti had already made a poetic translation, and my English began with the intention of serving as a gloze". It is Pound who proceeds to offer us several translations of the canzone-manifesto by Cavalcanti, "Donna me prega", which was and still is the subject of many philological and philosophical debates; whereas Rossetti, fully aware of the importance of that text, praises it without attempting a translation himself. Pound's lifelong dedication to Cavalcanti's poems had a turning point in the 1931 edition of *Le Rime, edizione rappezzata fra le rovine* ("patched together amid the ruins") which marks Pound's pursuit of the impossible dream of a critical edition of the collected poems.

It took a renowned scholar such as Lowry NELSON, Jr (1986), whose expertise ranged from the Provençal and *stil novo* poetry of the Middle Ages to Modernism, to undertake the difficult task of translating the entire corpus of Cavalcanti's poetry. In his informed introduction Nelson draws on his own scholarly appreciation of the poetry of Cavalcanti, but he also pays necessary homage to Pound's effort as he, "alongside his lifelong *Cantos*, celebrated Dante's first friend in essays and translations beginning in 1910 and continuing to 1966". The scholar, however, has no intention of following the path of the American poet as far as the rendering of Cavalcanti's poems into English is concerned: "In my English versions I have tried to avoid both flatness and quirkiness and to honor 20th-century standard idiom in both syntax and lexis. [...] In my own mind and practice I make a complete distinction between a poetic and a prose translation, and feel great discomfiture reading versions that zigzag between the two". The allusion to Pound's attempt is veiled, but unequivocal. Thus, Nelson's translations (based not only on the 1527 Giunta – also known as Giuntina – edition, but also on the Favati–Contini critical edition) rely on a slim and efficacious apparatus of "Textual and Explanatory Notes", in which the meter and the scheme of the rhymes is offered (relieving the translator of the burden of rendering them) along with an appreciation of the historical depth of the philosophical meaning of many terms in Cavalcanti's poetry.

The translation by Marc CIRIGLIANO (1992) reveals in the introduction the different aims of his new complete enterprise. Any intention of offering a poetic translation falls short, notably in the sequence of sonnets XV to XVIII and the canzone "Donna me prega", and mistakes such as "la versa" for the correct "il verso" are not encouraging to the reader who is engaging with Cavalcanti's *Rime*. Cirigliano comments in his introduction on the translations by Dante Gabriel Rossetti and Ezra Pound and their common "biggest mistake" of using "an English that was deliberately archaic". Furthermore, Pound's "work is replete with inaccurate translations". Finally, Cirigliano looks for "modern analogues to Cavalcanti" and he finds them in T. S. Eliot and Tristan Tzara. The affinities that the two artists present with respect to the medieval poet are, however, extrinsic, so much so that Eliot's "Ash Wednesday" is mentioned and quoted at length with no reference at all to the very first line of that poem, "Because I do not hope to turn again", which is indeed the translation of the first line of the ballata XXXV: "Perch'io no spero di tornar giammai".

ERNESTO LIVORNI

Further Reading

Anderson, David, "Prolegomena to an Edition of Pound's Cavalcanti's Translations", *Paideuma*, 8 (1979) pp. 223–26

Bailey, John, unsigned review of *Sonnets and Ballate of Guido Cavalcanti*, in *Times Literary Supplement*, 567 (21 November 1912); reprinted in *Ezra Pound: The Critical Heritage*, edited by Eric Homberger, London and Boston:

Routledge and Kegan Paul, 1972, pp. 89–93

Del Re, Arundel, review of *Sonnets and Ballate of Guido Cavalcanti*, *Poetry Review* (July 1912); reprinted in *Ezra Pound: The Critical Heritage*, edited by Eric Homberger, London and Boston: Routledge and Kegan Paul, 1972, pp. 86–88

Gilson, Etienne, review of *Guido Cavalcanti Rime*, *Criterion*, 12 (October 1932–July 1933) pp.106–12; reprinted in *The Criterion, 1922–1939*, edited by T.S. Eliot, London: Faber, 1967

Hayatt Mayor, A., "Cavalcanti and Pound", *Hound and Horn*, 13 (April–June 1932) pp.168–71

Praz, Mario, "Due note su Ezra Pound" in *Cronache letterarie anglosassoni*, vol. 1, Rome: Edizioni di Storia e Letteratura, 1950, pp. 175–83

Shaw, J.E., *Guido Cavalcanti's Theory of Love: The Canzone d'Amore, and Other Related Problems*, Toronto: University of Toronto Press, 1949

Wilhelm, James J., *The Cruelest Month: Spring, Nature, and Love in Classical and Medieval Lyrics*, New Haven, Connecticut: Yale University Press, 1965

Wilhelm, James J., "Guido Cavalcanti as a Mask for Ezra Pound", *PMLA*, 89 (1974) pp. 332–40

Camilo José Cela 1916–

Spanish novelist, short-story writer, travel writer and essayist

Biography

Cela was born 11 May 1916, in Iria Flavia, a village in the township of Padrón (province of La Coruña), in Galicia, northwest Spain. He spent his adolescence in Madrid where, after three years at university, the outbreak of the Spanish Civil War caught him in 1936. As he had suffered from tuberculosis he was declared unfit for military service, but he managed to find his way to the National Zone, served in Franco's Nationalist Army, and ultimately was wounded. After the conflict ended in 1939, he worked where he could, and he wrote. Author of almost 100 works, including novels, poetry, travel books, short stories, plays, essays, translations and dictionaries, Cela has received, as well as very many other awards and honours, the Nobel Prize for Literature (1989), and the Spanish equivalent, the Cervantes Prize (1995).

Instead of following the old realistic manner, revealing social consciousness without social protest and infused with religious themes, Cela's writing has been bold and disruptive, rousing Spain from its much-desired tranquillity in order to re-establish its cultural identity. His first two novels (*La familia de Pascual Duarte,* 1942, and *La colmena*, 1951) are the most reprinted and translated ones. The majority of the others remain untranslated into English.

Translations

Novels

La familia de Pascal Duarte, 1942

Briffault, Herma, *The Family of Pascual Duarte* (parallel texts), New York: Las Américas, 1965

Kerrigan, Anthony, *The Family of Pascual Duarte*, with an introduction, Boston: Little Brown, 1964; London: Weidenfeld and Nicolson, 1965; reprinted Boston: Little Brown, 1990

Marks, John, *Pascual Duarte's Family*, with an introduction, London: Eyre and Spottiswoode, 1946; reprinted 1983

Pabellón de reposo, 1943

Briffault, Herma, *Rest Home*, New York: Las Américas, 1961

La colmena, 1951

Cohen, J.M., in consultation with Arturo Barea, *The Hive*, with an introduction by Barea, London: Gollancz, and New York: Farrar Straus, 1953; New York: Ecco Press, 1990; London: Sceptre, 1992

Mrs Caldwell habla con su hijo, 1953

Bernstein, J.S., *Mrs Caldwell Speaks to Her Son*, Ithaca, New York: Cornell University Press, 1968

San Camilo, 1936: Vísperas, festividad y octava de San Camilo del año 1936 en Madrid, 1969

Polt, John H.R., *San Camilo, 1936: The Eve, Feast and Octave of St Camillus of the Year 1936 in Madrid*, Durham, North Carolina: Duke University Press, 1991

Mazurka para dos muertos, 1983

Haugaard, Patricia, *Mazurka for Two Dead Men*, New York: New Directions, 1992; London: Quartet, 1993

Travel Writing

Las botas de siete leguas: Viaje a la Alcarria, 1948

Lopez-Morillas, Frances M., *Journey to the Alcarria*, Madison: University of Wisconsin Press, 1964; Cambridge: Granta in association with Penguin, 1990

Camilo José Cela is undoubtedly the finest writer of fiction remaining in Spain after the Civil War and the Spanish Exodus. The sense of revolt and protest – manifested not only in content but also in the use of language – that his first two novels transmitted, as well as the problems he had with Franco's censorship, may well be the main causes for the early international interest in Cela.

His first novel, *La familia de Pascual Duarte,* published in

December 1942, made him instantly famous. The story is in the grimmest tradition of Spanish realism. It is narrated in the first person singular by Pascual Duarte, a murderer awaiting execution. The murderer's life is filled with senseless violence that sickens the reader. The novel came as a shock at a time when literature was expected to celebrate the blessing of Christian civilization that the Nationalist victory had supposedly guaranteed.

It also caused a great sensation in Spanish literary circles as, for years, no novel as authentic and disturbing had appeared in print. It was expected to win the national literary prize due to be awarded early the next year, but the prize went instead to an excellent novel about the Civil War, *The Faithful Infantry*, by Rafael García Serrano, which seemed to be more in keeping with the current political context. A second edition of Cela's book was published in November, 1943. However, the work was banned by the authorities and withdrawn from circulation by the police. The official reason given for its suppression, which came after the book had been passed for publication, printed, distributed, reviewed, and widely sold, read, and discussed, was the alleged immorality of the sexual encounter in the cemetery (Chapter V) between Pascual and Lola, when his brother Mario has just been buried.

A third edition was then published in Argentina, the new home of Spanish works (e.g. of *La colmena* by the same author) and of translated foreign ones that for one reason or another were prohibited by the manifold censorship exercised by the regime in Spain.

A transfer of control over printed matter in Spain from a Falangist Under-Secretariat for Press and Propaganda to the reputedly more liberal Ministry of National Education might explain the authorities' granting of permission for a fourth edition of the novel to be published in Barcelona with an introduction by the doctor-historian Dr Gregorio Marañón, member of the Spanish Royal Academy, in 1946. In some respects, however, the change of policy did not go as deep as many Spanish writers might have hoped.

La familia de Pascual Duarte was written in a brutally direct style, uncovering hideous realities at a time when most prose works dealt with conventional subjects and were in no way conducive to rebellious thought. It had an electrifying effect on those who got hold of it – relatively few, for the editions were small and book prices were prohibitive – for all but a small minority. When the book was forbidden, copies of the Argentine edition began to circulate in Spain, and a new edition was allowed to appear. Cela dedicated this fourth edition to "my enemies who have given me so much help in my career". It was soon translated into several languages, but nowhere did it, nor could it, achieve the impact it had in Spain.

Meaning survives in most of the English translations, but the effect on readers is distorted or diminished. Part of the information in the original text is implicit. Cela relies on the knowledge shared by himself and the Spanish reader when he evokes the brutish poverty in which Pascual was reared, his blind, crazy outbreaks, and the piled-up horrors in the starved villages of Extremadura from which Pascual Duarte has sprung. Part of this implicit meaning is lost in the translated versions, and that world of hunger and misery is difficult for a foreign reader to understand. Add to this the allusions to tradition and customs, plus a narrative style full of slang terms and obscure double meanings too local to admit translation, and an idea emerges of the barriers in the way of the translators.

MARKS's *Pascual Duarte's Family* (1946) must have followed one of the first three Spanish editions, not the first official one, the 4th edition, of 1946, since he does not include Cela's dedication and shows some small differences in dates, places and proper names with respect to this official edition. Marks's wording maintains the linked themes of moral monstrosity and instinctual impulses, but he is not consistent when translating proper names and he seems to have some difficulty in understanding and transmitting the value and meaning of tradition and culture. As a journalist – he was a reporter in Spain for *The Times* – Marks's style sounds natural and forceful. His translation is close and accurate, although at some points it lacks the electrifying effect that the text has for its Spanish readers.

KERRIGAN's translation (1964) is the closest one, in form and content, to the source text. It is based on the Spanish edition of 1962, the definitive text revised by Cela for the *Obra Completa de Camilo José Cela* (Barcelona, 1962), and it is also the only one to have been done in collaboration with the author, as Kerrigan points out in his introduction and as Cela corroborated in an interview (October 1995). Kerrigan undertakes a cultural translation through improvisation, and through paraphrases based on an excellent knowledge of Spanish tradition and customs as well as on Cela's advice. His excessive consciousness of being the vehicle of transmission for a new readership leads, at some points, to over-translation (as when he defines "flamenco"). In an interview with Michael Scott Doyle (1987), he remarks with truth that he always used the best language, the richest possible selection of words, avoiding cheap effects. The result is a vigorous and convincing close translation of many of the original's key passages. A few weaknesses at moments of intense feeling (e.g. Estirao's death, Chapter XVI) do not prevent this from being the most accurate and respectful translation.

BRIFFAULT's translation (1965) was published in parallel texts. The translator, having previously rendered another work by Cela into English *(Rest Home,* 1961), was familiar with the author. The content is respectful of the source, but neither its style nor the effect produced in the reader is fully achieved. Some of the idioms and colloquial expressions are the same as in Marks's translation, the dedication is again omitted, and some of the misinterpretations in the earlier translation are maintained, as well as some details (dates, places) that were changed by Cela for the Spanish edition of 1962. Some cultural details are dropped, and the language wavers between the excessively colloquial (e.g. the use of "Pa" and "Ma" for "Father" and "Mother") and some nice touches (Estirao's death). Briffault translates erroneously as "Note by the Editor" the "Nota del Transcriptor" ("Note by the Transcriber").

La colmena, 1951, was rejected in Spain by the same censors that in 1946 had authorized the fourth edition of *La familia de Pascual Duarte*, and it was published in Argentina. This was not surprising, as *The Hive* depicts a slice of life in the Madrid of 1942 in which every one of the values in whose name the Civil War had supposedly been fought and won has been abandoned or perverted. It was not only the content but also the style that caught the censors' attention. They considered the novel to be of "scant literary value", but in fact it was written in the most luminous, fresh and colloquial Spanish in contemporary writing, intermixed with cruel irony and bitter humor. Cela was one of the few writers remaining in Spain who dared to speak boldly. Twelve years passed before *La colmena* could appear in Spain, but many translations were made. Since then, it has been constantly reprinted and also been made into a film (as has *Pascual Duarte*).

Other works by Cela had been translated into English before the boom in Cela's reputation started by the award to him of the Nobel Prize in 1989 (*Rest Home*, 1961; *Journey to the Alcarria*, 1964; *Mrs. Caldwell Speaks to Her Son*, 1968); after the prize came new translations (*San Camilo, 1936*, by POLT, 1991; *Mazurka for Two Dead Men*, by HAUGAARD, 1992) and reissues of some earlier ones.

COHEN's translation of *La colmena* was published in 1953. It is based on the Argentine edition. Despite the difficulties presented by the original's local color, deep roots in Spanish tradition, and use of slang and colloquial expressions, Cohen's translation is respectful to the source text. The translation is preceded by an introduction by Arturo Barea, who considers himself an anti-Franco refugee and comments that Cela's own way of telling a fraction of the disturbing truth about Spain in 1942 is an act of revolt and faith that deserves a response, which the translation of the novel into English when it was still prohibited in Spain undoubtedly was.

Cela's style and narrative method are barriers to the translator. He moves back and forth between time levels to offer the same incident from different angles, changing from the present tense to the imperfect to describe actions performed by the characters within a past-time framework. In Cohen's translation, only the present tense is used. Cela also uses double meanings and current Madrid slang terms, which make the translator's task more difficult. The translator tries to convey the same meanings in English through standard English, an equivalent slang expression, explanation, or at times, omission.

Cela is also a poet, and his prose has certain mannerisms, especially repetition, a rhetorical device that contributes to his text, giving it patterned sound and rhythm as well as psychological emphasis when necessary. Cohen succeeds in reproducing this aspect, as well as Cela's realistic technique and half-colloquial style. *The Hive* is also full of references to historical proper names and events that Cohen renders into English sometimes through literal translation and sometimes through expansion, as for example in: "No creo que haga falta ser un Romanones para fumar esos puros", translated as "I don't think one's got to be *a millionaire* like Romanones to smoke this sort of cigar." Footnotes are avoided (there are only two or three in the target text). When dealing with institutional and cultural terms, the same strategies are used, more successfully in the translation of the first aspect than of the second. As for the slang terms and colloquial expressions used by Cela to represent the language of the slums, Cohen tries hard to translate as much as possible of them, and of the idioms and proverbs frequent in the source. He is successful in most cases, although we observe a diminution of the variety of expressions used and more than once some information implicit in the source text is lost in the translation. However, the work shows command of both the language and the culture. At some points, he does find it difficult to bring thematic details, institutional terms, cultural references or some of the many, often obscure, slang expressions from Madrid's slums into the new culture. Then Cohen becomes more literal and less effective, but he makes a great effort to translate everything in the text. Through a complicated game of strategies such as compensation, modulation, adaptation, or expansion, with some footnotes – and a few omissions – he produces a close and accurate translation.

CARMEN VALERO-GARCÉS

Further Reading

Doyle, M.S., "Anthony Kerrigan: The Attainment of Excellence in Translation" in *Translation Excellence: Assessment, Achievement, Maintenance*, edited by Marilyn Gaddis Rose, Binghamton, New York: American Translators Association, University Center at Binghamton, 1987

Evans, Jo, "*La familia de Pascual Duarte* and the Search for Gendered Identity", *Bulletin of Hispanic Studies*, 71/2 (1994) pp. 197–216

Flascher, J., "Aspects of Novelistic Technique in Cela's *La Colmena*", *West Virginia University Philological Papers*, 60 (1959)

Foster, David William, *Forms of the Novel in the Work of Camilo José Cela*, Columbia: University of Missouri Press, 1967

Kerrigan, A., "Camilo José Cela and Contemporary Spanish Literature", *Western* Review, 22 (1958)

Kirsner, Robert, *The Novels and Travels of Camilo José Cela*, Chapel Hill: University of North Carolina Press, 1963

See also the introductions to Marks, Kerrigan, and Cohen

Paul Celan 1920–1970

Romanian-born German-language poet

Biography

Born Paul Antschel in Czernowitz, capital of the Bukovina, then in Romania, on 23 November 1920. His family belonged to a strong Jewish community. In 1944 northern Bukovina, including Czernowitz, was annexed by Soviet troops to the Ukraine, of which it remains part. Celan went to school in

Czernowitz and visited France as a medical student in 1938, returning to Czernowitz in the summer of 1939 and taking up the study of Romance languages and literatures after the outbreak of war. In 1942 both his parents were deported to the Ukraine, where they died. Celan was conscripted into a series of Romanian labour camps between 1942 and 1944.

After the war Celan emigrated to Bucharest, where he worked as a translator from Russian into Romanian, and in his poems first adopted the name Celan. He escaped from Bucharest to Vienna in December 1947 and in 1948 issued his first collection of verse, *Der Sand aus den Urnen* [The Sand from the Urns]. In the same year Celan settled in Paris, where he later taught German literature at the École Normale Supérieure. He married the graphic artist Gisèle de Lestrange in 1952. In 1958 he was awarded the Bremen Literature Prize, and in 1960 the Georg Büchner Prize, Germany's highest literary award; the speeches made on each occasion constitute Celan's principal statements on his poetry. On 20 April 1970 he committed suicide by drowning himself in the Seine.

Celan published seven major volumes of verse: *Mohn und Gedächtnis* [Poppy and Memory], 1952; *Von Schwelle zu Schwelle* [From Threshold to Threshold], 1955; *Sprachgitter*, 1959 (*Speech-Grille*, 1971); *Die Niemandsrose* [No-One's-Rose], 1963; *Atemwende*, 1967 (*Breathturn*, 1995), *Fadensonnen* [Sunthreads], 1968 and *Lichtzwang* [Lightforce], 1970.

Translations

Selections of Poetry

Felstiner, John, *Paul Celan: Poet, Survivor, Jew*, New Haven, Connecticut and London: Yale University Press, 1995

Hamburger, Michael, *Poems of Paul Celan* (parallel texts), with an introduction, London: Anvil Press, 1988, New York: Persea, 1989; revised edition, Anvil Press, 1995; as *Paul Celan: Selected Poems*, London: Penguin, 1996

Kirkup, James, "*Sunthreads*: Fourteen Poems by Paul Celan" in his *Strange Attractors*, Salzburg: Institut für Anglistik und Amerikanistik, Universität Salzburg, 1995

Lynch, Brian and Peter Jankowsky, *Paul Celan: 65 Poems*, Dublin: Raven Arts Press, 1985

Washburn, Katharine and Margaret Guillemin, *Paul Celan: Last Poems* (parallel texts), San Francisco: North Point Press, 1986

Poetry

Sprachgitter, 1959 (with poems from *Mohn und Gedächtnis*, *Von Schwelle zu Schwelle*, *Die Niemandsrose*, and *Atemwende*)

Neugroschel, Joachim, *Paul Celan: Speech-Grille and Selected Poems* (parallel texts), New York: Dutton, 1971

Atemwende, 1967

Joris, Pierre, *Paul Celan: Breathturn* (parallel texts), Los Angeles: Sun and Moon Press, 1995

Prose

Billeter, Walter and Jerry Glenn, *Paul Celan: Prose Writings and Selected Poems*, Carlton, Victoria: Paper Castle Press, 1977

Waldrop, Rosmarie, *Paul Celan: Collected Prose*, Manchester: Carcanet Press, 1986; New York: Sheep Meadow Press, 1990

Paul Celan presents the translator into English with a particular set of challenges. As the work of a German-speaking Jew who, having fled Bucharest for Vienna in 1947, chose not to settle in a German-speaking land, Celan's writing is marked by loss and by displacement. In *After Babel*, George Steiner claims that, besides his many translations from the major European languages, "all of Celan's own poetry is translated *into* German". Celan is itself an anagram of Ancel, the Romanian form of the poet's family name, Antschel. In his writing, words make literal a dislocated world. As if to test, if not attack, the coherence and sufficiency of its own linguistic order, Celan's verse takes to an extreme the inherent capacity of German for lexical generation and syntactical complexity. It is possible to expand Steiner's remark and propose that Celan translates "*out of* and *into* German". His poetry enacts a process of unhousing and inhabiting. In his "Bremen Speech" of 1958, Celan declares that "only one thing remained reachable, close and secure amid all losses: language" (*Collected Prose*). It is in German, "through the thousand darknesses of murderous speech", that Celan himself elects to speak, an existential choice which enables him to "find a direction" on otherwise unsigned territory. This essay will consider how translation into English accommodates this project.

Celan's German speaks back to the conditions of being Jewish in the 20th century. Because of its direct voicing of Holocaust experience, the first of his poems to receive international notice was "Todesfuge", from *Mohn und Gedächtnis* [Poppy and Memory]. The poem has been translated a number of times since the 1950s, but no version is more striking than that given in John FELSTINER's *Paul Celan: Poet, Survivor, Jew* (1995). This account of Celan's life and work commands attention in itself as an exercise in translation. "Deathfugue" is one of many complete texts presented within a commentary that combines analysis of the original with an account of the translation process. Spoken by the Jewish internees of a death camp, the poem describes a repetitive, brutalized and inverted world where some are ordered to strike up a tune and sing while others "shovel a grave in the air". "Deathfugue" exposes the fractured legacy of German-Jewish culture; at the heart of its "fugue", the voice of the camp commander is ventriloquized by his victims, setting the officer's mixture of viciousness and sentiment against the lament of "his Jews". The resonances established in this doubling of voice, and extended through repetition and variation, confirm for Felstiner the poem's "resistance to translation". In his version, two key refrains are thus progressively returned to German: "death is a master from Deutschland" becomes, in its fourth incarnation, "der Tod ist ein Meister aus Deutschland"; and "your golden hair Margareta / Your ashen hair Shulamith" concludes the poem as "dein goldenes Haar Margarete / dein aschenes Haar Sulamith". Celan's simple phrases sound with complex echoes: "*Meister* can designate God, Christ, rabbi, teacher ... labor-camp overseer, musical maestro, 'master' race, not to mention Goethe's *Wilhelm Meister* and Wagner's *Meistersinger von Nürnberg*". Margarete, the officer's sweetheart, recalls the ruined heroine of Goethe's *Faust*; Sulamith is indissociable from the "black and comely" maiden of the *Song of Songs*.

It takes Felstiner's blend of translation and critical gloss to make these overtones audible for the untutored reader. And while such a method can lend itself to apology for certain translational choices, in this case it simply returns us to the singularity of the original. The convergence of Felstiner's "Deathfugue" with Celan's "Todesfuge" confounds any notion of parallel translation based on cultural and linguistic equivalence; the poem is indelibly marked by the murderous ("todbringender" or "deathbringing") speech that it inflects. Yet far from rendering translation either impossible or an inevitable act of bad faith, "Todesfuge" compels it. Felstiner notes that the poem was first published in Romanian, translated in collaboration with Celan and bearing the title "Tango of Death". Conceived as it was in some part "under the sign of translation", we may "hear the poem back to its own state in German" through the medium of translation. This is the logic of Felstiner's otherwise unnecessary "Englishing" of the poem's proper names – names that insist on an absolute identity of sign and referent. His returning of the poem to German is itself an act of translation. It is as if the first condition in translating Celan is recognition of what cannot be translated in his verse.

Introducing his *Poems of Paul Celan* – the most extensive selection available in English – Michael HAMBURGER (1988) invokes the admonition that Celan once addressed to him: "ganz und gar nicht hermetisch". The implications of this "absolutely not hermetic" are considerable. Were Celan's poetry in fact hermetic (its reputation as such registers a stock response to his difficulty), its singularity would offer nothing to translate. It would prove untranslatable because already translated, as it were, out of the inadequate language of lived experience and into a closed version of the one universal or self-sufficient tongue. Truly hermetic writing would be "less difficult" than Celan's in not requiring us "to make the kind of sense of it that we know [his] can yield". His work engages an unredeemed existence in a language that, through literalism and neologism, strives both to realize and to test the limits of its condition. Hamburger cites "Einmal", the last poem in *Atemwende* (*Breathturn*), whose translational crux turns upon its speaker's relation to the redemptive event and presence he has witnessed:

Once
I heard him,
he was washing the world,
unseen, nightlong,
real.

But a middle paragraph represents the negation of transcendental agency: "One and Infinite, / annihilated, / ied." ("Eins und Unendlich, / vernichtet, / ichten.") The sense made of Celan's "ichten" determines our understanding of the poem as a whole, which is completed by the paradoxical affirmation "Light was. Salvation." By analogy with "vernichten" (to annihilate), "ichten" was translated as the present tense "ihilate" by an anonymous reviewer in the *Times Literary Supplement*. Correcting this, however, Celan told Hamburger that it signifies the past imperfect third-person plural of "ichen" (to declare I). Both readings are supported by Grimm's *Wörterbuch*. "Ihilate" intimates creation *ex nihilo*, linking annihilation and salvation through the "ich" which passes from "vernichtet" to "Licht" in the final line. "Ied" suggests that the speaker's very testimony, as a first-person singular, repeats the annihilation of a transcendent "One and Infinite" into multiple "I"s. To say "I" may be to witness, as a survivor, salvation in eclipse. Confounding time in its possible senses, "ichten" opens a singular moment of salvation to more than one reading, summoning this past event into the present as a question yet to be answered.

Hamburger observes that, from *Sprachgitter* (*Speech-Grille*) onwards, translation founders on the increasingly fissured and condensed nature of Celan's language. For this reason, he has not translated any volume in its entirety; nor does he provide "prose elucidations", which might simply beleaguer the poems. The only other text to translate from the full range of Celan's work is designed to complement an earlier version of Hamburger's survey. LYNCH & JANKOWSKY (1985) do, however, offer one work in its totality – *Atemkristall* [Breath-Crystal], which became the first section of *Atemwende* – together with brief notes on 20 of the 65 poems translated. The most intriguing of their glosses point toward but stop short of critical analysis. On this margin it is difficult to know where to stop with any certainty. A certain threshold is, by comparison, crossed in Pierre JORIS's "Commentaries" to his complete translation (1995) of *Atemwende*, notwithstanding that such "*minimalia* function more as a map of ignorance than as a showcase for knowledges regarding Celan's late poems". An alternative strategy is found in Joachim NEUGROSCHEL's translation (1971) of the entire *Sprachgitter* and selected poems up to and including *Atemwende* (clearly the volume best represented in English). The economy and purpose of Neugroschel's versions stand without either introduction or annotation. The three last-mentioned texts might be said to move beyond the hesitations expressed by Hamburger, but it is more accurate to see them as venturing *into* hesitation. They are joined by WASHBURN & GUILLEMIN's *Last Poems* (1986), a selection that recognizes that syntactical dislocation in Celan's poems applies also to his treatment of the poetic sequence as a unit of composition. As syllable and breath come to dictate lyric articulation, and relations of syntax are in that measure distended (a quality strenuously reproduced by Joris), so mutation and permutation govern relations between the poems. Each of Celan's collections consists of a series of sequences, named in the early work and, from *Sprachgitter*, numbered. But recent critical editions reveal that Celan presented most of his late work – much as a daybook – in order of writing, while additional issues of reconstruction attend the "posthumous" volumes from which Washburn and Guillemin translate. Hence a certain contingency prevails within these larger forms of coherence. System-building in effect realizes a powerfully anti-systematic drive in Celan's poetry. The same is, of course, true of "Deathfugue"; in the later poetry, however, compositional pattern is rendered unpredictable and lyric integrity wholly untranslatable by rule or formula.

Among the "Conversational Statements on Poetry" reported in *Prose Writings* (BILLETER & GLENN, 1977), Celan claims that "The poem is voiceless and voiced at the same time. It is between the two. It must yet become voice." Something of this project is bequeathed to his translators. Bifurcation of voice is evident in the different translational choices annotated by JORIS on the one hand, and LYNCH & JANKOWSKY on the other. Commentary is generated by an idiom that resorts to the arcane in order to produce its own form of demotic; witness, for example, Celan's fascination with the synchronicity of Yiddish and Middle High German, or his compulsion to borrow from and compound specialist vocabularies in theology and the natural sciences. Joris notes how, for Celan, "the work of poetry is to be done on the word itself" through the combination and disarticulation of discrete lexical elements: units of meaning. Celan's linguistic extremism invariably answers to an extreme situation. Within the uncertain yet intimate context of the poem's speech-act – most are directed to an unspecified but familiar second person – the root sense of otherwise remote words may yield a lore that reorients their address. A poem from *Atemwende* begins: "Harnischstriemen, Faltenachsen, / Durchstich- / punkte: / dein Gelände." Joris gives "Slickensides, fold-axes, / rechanneling-/ points: / your terrain", glossing the geological context of the first two terms, which refer to rock striation and folding, and the possible geological sense of the third, which may also indicate pinpricks in a map or chart. For lines one to three Lynch & Jankowsky prefer "Armour-weals, fold-axes, / penetration- / points". They acknowledge that Celan's language is "scientifically meaningful", but consider that a technical equivalent of "Harnischstriemen" would occlude the pain and struggle which that word literally records. Celan's German performs both kinds of work. Armed against what it exposes, the poem painstakingly maps the "terrain" of its addressee in order to discover as "legible", in its second paragraph, "your banished word" (*65 Poems*). The authenticity of such words is – Joris quotes Steiner – "quarried from far and stony places".

Celan's mining of etymology engages words, or parts of words, in dialogue and dispute. Translation is, in this aspect, very literally a "gloss" on the verse; "slickensides", for example, contributes a *dialectal* inflection of Celan's idiolect. The translator always speaks back to an original but, more so than most, translations of Celan are directed "return to sender". Celan's major critical statement, "The Meridian", announces (in Rosmarie WALDROP's translation, 1986) that poems are at once "paths on which language becomes voice" and "paths from a voice to a listening You". The translator is perhaps one person intended by "zu einem wahrnehmenden Du": someone who asks, in his or her own tongue, "have I heard you correctly?" Yet even Celan's "Du" is translationally fraught, obscuring in its familiarity the creaturely or divine nature of the "you" or "thou" addressed. On the threshold of what is, to his or her ear, audible and conceivable, Celan's translator listens for what may be just out of hearing. This demands that one think laterally both about Celan's literalisms and about what might constitute "literal translation" in his case. The forking paths of English etymology in turn complicate relations of kinship with the poet's German. "The Meridian" speaks of poetry's "detours [*Umwege*] from you to you", suggesting that translation is to be conducted less as a direct exchange between two languages and more as a passage through intermediate points on the circuit that connects them. Equally, beyond the immediate example of modernist *bricolage*, a more apposite model of inter- and intralingual English might be found in John Clare's mixing of dialect and archaism, or in John Milton's profound sense of the fallen word.

Celan shares with Milton an inquiry into catastrophe lived out in language. That condition is registered in the conflicted and prepositionally unfixed nature of what Joris calls Celan's "verbal grafts". Controversion within the word may be most acutely realized in "Deine Augen im Arm", one of the poems from *Fadensonnen* presented in James KIRKUP's *Sunthreads* (1995). This selection consistently translates "du" as "thou", naturalizing a now unfamiliar form of address within its own idiom. But the person invoked by "Thine eyes in arms" resists location in or by the poem. These eyes, burnt asunder ("auseinandergebrannten") yet still cradling their apostrophized "du", are constant to a presence consumed by ashes. In response to the "Wo?" or "Where?" that follows this affirmation – a question whose direction is itself in question – there comes a line that describes the limit of translational possibility: "Mach den Ort aus, machs Wort aus." Kirkup offers "Put the place out, put the word out." Asserting the presence of "place" within "word", the German also plays on two meanings of "ausmachen": to put out, or extinguish; and to make out, or distinguish. The word that would contain these senses – as "Wort" contains "Wo?" – surely could not survive them. By the same token, words cannot circumscribe a presence whose place, "verortet, entwortet", is eventually determined as "entwo". Kirkup translates these permutations as "misplaced, unphrased, // miswhither". Celan's prefixes describe both cancellation ("ver-") and passage out of a former state ("ent-"). The "where?" at the core of "word" is answered by "whereout". Subject to such translation, Celan's words announce their necessarily ectopic construction.

Translation is, we might conclude, a construction of this sort. Celan declares as much in his version of Shakespeare's Sonnet 107. Where death "subscribes" to the poet, "Since spite of him I'll live in this poor rhyme", Celan translates "Ich lebe, ihm zu Trotz, im Reim, den ich gebaut". Rhyme is, Celan insists, a "built" structure, a place that, in displacement, recollects word of home: "Heim". Translation thus reenacts the founding gesture of Celan's poetry, an address that gathers "a 'you' around a naming and speaking I" ("The Meridian"), and that is itself glossed by Sonnet 107: "And thou in this shalt find thy monument". In a letter concerning his translations of Mandel'stam (cited by Olschner, 1985), Celan writes that his aim is "bei grösster Textnähe das Dichterische am Gedicht zu übersetzen". Keeping "as close as possible to the text", he intends "to translate the poetry in the poem". His "Textnähe" describes the margin of the "near" in which translation builds. To build – as to dwell – near, is to neighbour. Celan's translation of Shakespeare neighbours its original, building in its shelter in order to give shelter in its turn. Here we may recognize the embrace of "Thine eyes in arms". Here too, for Celan, the work of translation is continuous with the work of poetry.

IAN FAIRLEY

Further Reading

Chalfen, Israel, *Paul Celan: A Biography of His Youth*, New York: Persea, 1991

Colin, Amy D. (editor), *Argumentum e Silentio: International Paul Celan Symposium*, Berlin and New York: de Gruyter, 1987

Colin, Amy D., *Paul Celan: Holograms of Darkness*, Bloomington: Indiana University Press, 1991

Del Caro, Adrian, *The Early Poetry of Paul Celan: In the Beginning Was the Word*, Baton Rouge: Louisiana State University Press, 1998

Fioretos, Aris, *Word Traces: Readings of Paul Celan*, Baltimore: Johns Hopkins University Press, 1994

Gadamer, Hans-Georg, *Gadamer on Celan: "Who Am I and Who Are You?" and Other Essays*, Albany: State University of New York Press, 1997
Glenn, Jerry, *Paul Celan*, New York: Twayne, 1973
Hollander, Benjamin (editor), "Translating Tradition: Paul Celan in France", *ACTS: A Journal of New Writing*, special double issue 8–9 (1988)
Olschner, L.M., *Der feste Buchstab: Erläuterungen zu Paul Celans Gedichtübertragungen*, Göttingen: Vandenhoeck & Ruprecht, 1985
Samuels, Clarisse, *Holocaust Visions: Surrealism and Existentialism in the Poetry of Paul Celan*, Columbia, South Carolina: Camden House, 1994
Steiner, George, *After Babel: Aspects of Language and Translation*, Oxford and New York: Oxford University Press, 1975; 3rd edition 1998
Szondi, Peter, "The Poetry of Constancy: Paul Celan's Translation of Shakespeare's Sonnet 105" in his *On Textual Understanding and Other Essays*, translated by Harvey Mendelsohn, Manchester: Manchester University Press, and Minneapolis: University of Minnesota Press, 1986

Louis-Ferdinand Céline 1894–1961

French novelist

Biography

Born Henri-Louis Destouches in the Paris suburb of Courbevoie, 27 May 1894. His father was a clerk and his mother a shopkeeper. He went to school mainly in Paris, with short periods in Germany and England. After working at various jobs, he eventually qualified as a doctor in 1924. His health and his outlook had been badly affected by his experiences as an NCO in the French cavalry in World War I. He had been badly wounded in 1914 and invalided out of the army in 1915. He practised as a doctor in working-class Paris, West Africa and the US, and at the same time produced literary works under the pseudonym Céline. His first novel, *Voyage au bout de la nuit* (1932; translated 1934 and 1988 as *Journey to the End of the Night*), for which he is best known, brought immediate fame and notoriety, won both by its violent, subversive content and by the vigour and naturalistic crudeness of its style and tone. Through the semi-autobiographical misfortunes of the narrator, Bardamu, in World War I and during subsequent travels and sojourns, the first-person narrative attacks human nature, war, capitalism, industrialization, bourgeois institutions, and the system in general and in particular, with bitter and often comic verve. The book won the Renaudot Prize for 1933. After trying writing for the theatre, Céline published another novel, *Mort à crédit* (1936, translated in 1938 by John H.P. Marks as *Death on the Installment Plan* and in 1966 by Ralph Manheim as *Death on Credit*). His subsequent writing, little of which is available in English, continued in the same aggressive manner, manifested in the anarchistic and anti-semitic pamphlets *Bagatelles pour un massacre* [Bagatelles for a Massacre] (1937) and *L'École des cadavres* [School for Corpses] (1938). In World War II, though he himself did not collaborate actively, he continued to publish, including pamphlets, and his work was used in propaganda by the occupying Nazis. After the Liberation, he was sentenced to death, in his absence (in Denmark), as a collaborator. He was amnestied in 1951 and went back to France where he continued to propagate his pacifist and anti-semitic views and to practise medicine. Though when he continued writing essays and memoirs he did not strike a new vein, his mark as a great stylist was already made. He was married three times. Died at Meudon, near Paris, 1 July 1961.

Journey to the End of the Night

Voyage au bout de la nuit, 1932

Translations

Manheim, Ralph, *Journey to the End of the Night*, London: Calder, 1988
Marks, John H.P., *Journey to the End of the Night*, Boston: Little Brown, and London: Chatto and Windus, 1934; Harmondsworth: Penguin, 1966

Louis-Ferdinand Céline's first novel depicts the wanderings of 20th-century man, from the World War I battlefields of Flanders to the squalid, poverty-stricken suburbs of Paris, via a malaria-ridden colonial outpost in Africa and a bewildering sojourn in two of capitalism's emblematic cities, New York and Detroit. The hero's apprenticeship of life leads from the madness of mechanized mass slaughter (where darkness, at least, makes him less of a target) back to the comfort of a lunatic asylum (where, like mad Hamlet in England, there is safety in numbers). The journey through the mayhem of contemporary life is thus, simultaneously, a metaphorical inner journey into the maelstrom of the self; as his elusive alter ego, Robinson, concludes: "I had tried in vain to lose myself so as not to confront my own life ... I was returning to myself".

Like Céline's other novels, *Journey to the End of the Night* is a "novel of delirium" (Thiher, 1972), and the challenge for its two English-language translators was to render the tensions, deformations and elucubrations that articulate that delirium – a challenge significantly complicated by the *range* of linguistic devices exploited by Céline (albeit less extensively here than in his later novels): spoken and popular French; slang (of Paris or the army, for instance); outmoded literary and medical expressions; neologisms; caricatural onomastics; lexical, syntactic and morphological innovation. In the closing decades of the 19th century, Balzac, Hugo (*Le Dernier Jour d'un condamné*), Eugène Sue, Zola (*L'Assommoir*) and Jules Vallès had enhanced the realism of their novels by introducing popular French, a strategy reinforced in the post-1914 novels of Henri Barbusse or Roland Dorgelès but, in *Journey*, the comforting inverted commas that had served as protective barriers between such long-censored forms of French and established literary French disappear, and the radical diversity of the liberated language invades the entire text. Its jocular, popular iconoclasm and inventiveness is encapsulated in the novel's first pages in the symptomatic neologism *rouspignolles*, forged from three already-colourful slang terms for testicles: *roubignolles*, *roustons* and *roupettes* (Godard, 1985). The difficulties faced, and the differences in the solutions adopted, by MARKS and by MANHEIM stem primarily from that diversity, but also from the horizons of expectation and possibility available to the English translator in 1934, the American translator in 1988. In short, whereas Marks calls upon a 1930s English generally not far removed from the (more traditional aspects of the) French original, but skirts around the text's cruder, often scatological elements. Via euphemism or, not infrequently, by simply cutting them, Manheim is able to render the obscenities but cannot always avoid recourse to language (slang, in particular) that actually post-dates the novel's publication. "Baiser", for instance, is systematically rendered as "fuck" by Manheim, while Marks tones down the crudeness with "having a good time", "to have a woman", "jumping into bed" or, indeed, "embrace". Similarly, expressions such as "he didn't give a shit" or "head on fire and so was her cunt", in Manheim's version, retain the crude familiarity of "il s'en foutait" and "le feu au coeur et puis au cul", while Marks prefers a more restrained, socially acceptable rendering, "it left him quite cold" and "hot in the head and somewhere else too". One should note, however, that the sexual/scatological is not the only category in which Marks edulcorates the expressiveness of the original, as these examples from the opening wartime episode show: "une balle en plein bidon" / "a bullet hit him slap in the pan" [Manheim: "a ball tore open his guts"]; "Et puis du sang encore et partout, à travers l'herbe, en flaques molles et confluentes" / "And then, too, there was blood everywhere, softly flowing through the grass" [Manheim: "Blood and more blood, everywhere, all over the grass, in sluggish confluent puddles"].

So 1930s good taste clearly corsetted the exuberance of the original – in a translation of which Céline himself approved – but, just as obviously, the novel's linguistic shock value was less effective in the context of post-1960 liberalism. The real challenge for both translators, however, lay less in their response to such lexical brutality, eulogized or excoriated by critics both on publication and since, than in their ability to transpose the dynamic rhythms of the much-reworked spoken French in Céline's writing, the ellipses, repetitions and syntactic distortions to which it is subjected. The commonest of these distortions is generated by the co-presence of noun syntagm and substitute, since one of the two elements is not merely redundant but intrusive, disruptive. It is a distortion that English finds hard to duplicate, as we see in this famous passage on words: "Avec les mots on ne se méfie jamais suffisamment, ils ont l'air de rien les mots ... On ne se méfie pas d'eux des mots et le malheur arrive". For this Marks provides a typically stiff rendering, which reorders the sentence, drops the distortion, modifies the punctuation, abandons the repetition and mistranslates the first verb: "One can never be sufficiently defiant with words; words don't seem to be saying anything much ... One's unsuspicious about words ... and some misfortune ensues". Manheim's version avoids most of these errors, yet fails to render the distortion and the balance of the phrasing: "We're never suspicious enough of words, they look like nothing much ... We're not suspicious enough of words, and calamity strikes". Given that there are over one thousand occurrences of this key device in the novel, neither translation can be said to replicate in English the radical reworking to which the French was subjected, the defiant untying of syntactic links that rigid convention – *le bon usage* – had long imposed.

In an interview in the 1960s, Céline – who always claimed that he was, first and foremost, a *styliste* – took pride in having "made words move ... the place of words", in a dual process of semantic and syntactic disruption. The translations of Marks and Manheim only partly succeed in duplicating that process.

PETER DUNWOODIE

Further Reading

Godard, Henri, *Poétique de Céline*, Paris: Gallimard, 1985

Juilland, Alphonse, *Les Verbes de Céline*, Saratoga, California: ANMA Libri, 1985

Luce, Stanford, *A Glossary of Céline's Fiction, with English Translations*, Ann Arbor, Michigan: University Microfilms International, 1979

McCarthy, P., *Céline*, London: Allen Lane, 1975; New York: Viking, 1976

Matthews, J.H., *The Inner Dream: Céline as Novelist*, Ithaca, New York: Syracuse University Press, 1978

Noble, Ian, *Language and Narration in Céline's Novels: The Challenge of Disorder*, London: Macmillan, 1986; as *Language and Narration in Céline's Writings: The Challenge of Disorder*, Atlantic Highlands, New Jersey: Humanities Press International, 1987

Scullion, R., Philip H. Solomon and Thomas C. Spear (editors), *Céline and the Politics of Difference*, Hanover, New Hampshire: University Press of New England, 1995

Solomon, Philip H., *Understanding Céline*, Columbia: University of South Carolina Press, 1992

Thiher, A., *Céline: The Novel as Delirium*, New Brunswick: Rutgers University Press, 1972

Thomas, Merlin, *Louis-Ferdinand Céline*, London: Faber, 1979

Benvenuto Cellini 1500–1571

Italian goldsmith, sculptor and autobiographer

Biography

Born in Florence, 3 November 1500, the third child of a musician. The boy was apprenticed to a goldsmith in Florence and studied music. Involved in 1516 in a brawl, he was banished from the city and went to Siena, and from there to Bologna and Pisa and on to Rome, where he worked for a goldsmith. He returned to Florence in 1521 but two years later, after being involved in more violence, he was condemned to death. He fled to Rome, where he exercised his metalworking skills, executing commissions for notable citizens, including pope Clement VII. He also continued his musical studies. Cellini claimed to have played a decisive part in the 1527 siege of Rome by shooting and killing the Connétable de Bourbon in defence of Clement VII, who was imprisoned by the Connétable in the Castel Sant'Angelo. In 1529, after more quarrelling had resulted in a death and a wounding, Cellini took refuge briefly in Naples. He then went to live in Florence, making coins and medals. His travels and colourful vicissitudes continued. In 1537 he was himself imprisoned in Sant'Angelo for some audacious act of disrespect towards Clement VII's successor, pope Paul III. He was released in 1539. Another of his noble patrons was the French king Francis I, at whose courts in Paris and Fontainebleau Cellini worked and for whom he produced the famous gold saltcellar. In Florence he created for Cosimo de' Medici the equally famous statue of Perseus. Cellini took minor orders in 1558 and married in 1565 (he had three legitimate children and several others). Died 13 February 1571 in Florence.

Apart from the celebrated autobiography, begun in 1558, he also wrote poems, mostly sonnets, collected in 1565 as *Rime* [Poems], and treatises on the art of the goldsmith and on sculpture.

Memoirs

La Vita di Benvenuto Cellini, begun 1558

Autobiography, in two parts. First published by Antonio Cocchi in Naples in 1728, with false imprint of Cologne.

Translations

Since its publication in 1901, the critical text edited by Orazio Bacci (Sansoni, Florence) has provided the basic text for translations and for successive scholarly editions, notably from Paolo D'Ancona (Milan: Cogliati, 1925), Bruno Maier (Milan: Edizioni per il Club del Libro, 1959) and Carlo Cordié (*Opere di Baldassare Castiglione, Giovanni Della Casa, Benvenuto Cellini*, Milan: Ricciardi, 1960)

Bull, George, *The Autobiography of Benvenuto Cellini*, Harmondsworth: Penguin, 1956; Baltimore: Penguin, 1966

Cust, Robert H., *The Life of Benvenuto Cellini*, with an introduction, 2 vols, London: Bell, 1910

Macdonell, Anne, *The Life of Benvenuto Cellini*, 2 vols, with an introduction, London: Dent, and New York: Dutton, 1903; reprinted New York: Dutton, 1968

Nugent, Thomas, *The Life of Benvenuto Cellini*, 2 vols, London: (printed for) T. Davies, 1771; Philadelphia: Desilver, 1812

Roscoe, Thomas, *Memoirs of Benvenuto Cellini*, with notes by G.P. Carpani, 2 vols, London: Henry Colburn, 1822; New York: Wiley and Putnam, 1845

Symonds, John Addington, *The Life of Benvenuto Cellini*, with an introduction, 2 vols, London: Nimmo, and New York: Scribner and Welford, 1888; as *Autobiography of Benvenuto Cellini*, 1 vol., with an introduction by John Pope-Hennessy, Oxford: Phaidon, 1951

Benvenuto Cellini's partly dictated *Vita*, whose many translations include a revealing version by Goethe, published in 1796, directly illuminates the psychology and history of the Italian Renaissance and indirectly through its diversity of successive translations has proved a litmus test of changes in attitudes towards both the nature of the text and the acceptability of its moral stance and linguistic explicitness.

Recently the text of Cellini's *Life* has been regarded more as a carefully contrived literary *apologia* for a fateful life than an artless outpouring, and the 998-page manuscript in the Laurenziana as a *bella copia*, a complex narrative whose ideas had been worked out in perhaps several earlier drafts. The *Life* was originally divided into two parts by the insertion of a long poem; most English translators have respected the (thematically important) division into two books, and several (e.g. Symonds, Macdonell) have followed the Italian text of Bianchi (Le Monnier, 1852) in dividing each book into numbered paragraphs.

NUGENT'S (1771 and much reprinted) translation of Cellini's life reflected the responsiveness of a scholar primarily versed in French literature (and especially, as translator, in the work of Montesquieu, Voltaire and Rousseau) to the fully developed English interest in Florence and sense of the existence of a "great age" of Renaissance Italy. (The first truncated English translation of Vasari's *Lives* had appeared in 1685.) Dedicated to Sir Joshua Reynolds (great advocate of the study of Cellini's exemplar, Michelangelo), Nugent's still very readable version is seriously flawed by errors of translation and omissions, but retains period charm and vitality.

ROSCOE'S (1822) "revised and corrected edition" of the *Memoirs* paid lip service to the notes of Gio. Palamede Carpani from a then recent Italian edition of the *Life* but was a shameless plagiarism of the Nugent translation, with the same virtues and defects: instead of being "riddled with the French pox", for example, one of Cellini's young rivals in love is said to be "very ill with a certain disease".

SYMONDS'S monumental translation (1888) was inspired and challenged by the premises (1888 introduction) that Cellini had written "one of the world's three or four best autobiographies", had been "the most eminent exponent of later Italian Renaissance in craftsmanship of several kinds", and lacking any literary training had written "precisely as he talked, with all the sharp wit of a born Florentine, heedless of grammatical construction, indifferent to rhetoric effects, attaining unsurpassable vividness of narration by pure simplicity". Condemning "the English version which bears the name of Thomas Roscoe" as "grossly inaccurate" and as misrepresenting "whole passages which he deemed unfit for ears and eyes polite", Symonds, disclaiming the possibility of matching Cellini's "vast vocabulary of vulgar phrases and technical terminology", produced a still rather bowdlerized, (e.g. "lubberly lumber" for *coglionerie*, as Cellini described a rival goldsmith's work), misleadingly mannered translation, which yet manages to command and hold the reader's attention through its polished eloquence and pace. Symonds's stylistic conceits, under-estimation of Cellini's artistic genius and timidity over his voracious bisexuality inevitably coloured his fine – like Nugent's very apologetical – introduction to the *Life* as well as the painstaking translation itself. But the translation still holds the reader intent with its good renderings of Cellini's story telling and impressive descriptive prose.

MACDONELL (1903) sought in her translation to get closer than Symonds to Cellini's bluntness of language and reproduce his "people's speech", not always accurately, in her own undistinguished English. Interestingly, her introduction digressed to compare Goethe's translation of Cellini into German with "full-bodied" artistic (rather than scientific or philological) work from the age in England "that gave us Florio's *Montaigne* and North's *Plutarch*", with its "individuality well-nigh as strong as, if not identical with, the original".

Robert CUST's competent and generally accurate translation of the *Life* (1910) is still of value for its copious footnotes and its overall success in conveying "the force and vividness of the original narrative ... heightened rather than diminished by the wild confusion of detailed thought in the thread of it". Even so, Cust decided that the Tuscan slang words of the "very coarsest signification" – *bordellerie* and *coglionerie* – were "quite untranslatable".

BULL's Penguin Classics translation (1956 and successive editions) is less inhibited than previous translations, basing its rendering of the original into standard English on a more generous appreciation of Cellini's genius as sculptor and artistry as an instinctively powerful writer shaping his work for well-defined purposes of apologia and self-projection.

GEORGE BULL

Further Reading

See introductions to Cust and to Symonds (1888 and 1951)

Luis Cernuda (y Bidón) 1902–1963

Spanish poet and critic

Biography

Born in Seville, Spain, 21 September 1902, the son of an army officer. He went to school in Seville, 1914–18, and in 1919 went on to the University of Seville, graduating in law in 1925, having done his military service in 1923. After a year teaching Spanish literature at the teacher training college in Toulouse, 1928–29, Cernuda worked for a Madrid bookshop, for several newspapers and as a government teacher, with a spell in Paris in 1936 as secretary to Spanish ambassador. During the Spanish Civil War (1936–39) he supported the Republic and when he was in England in 1938, employed as a Spanish assistant at Cranleigh School in Surrey, he toured the country giving lectures to raise support for the Republican cause. There followed a series of teaching appointments in higher education in the UK and the US: in the Spanish department of Glasgow University, 1939–43, at Cambridge University, 1943–45, at the Spanish Institute in London, 1945, and at Mount Holyoke College, Massachusetts, 1947–52. He moved to Mexico in 1952 and from 1954 to 1960 was professor of Spanish at the Autonomous University of Mexico, Mexico City. Died in Mexico City, 5 November 1963.

Cernuda belonged to Spain's "Generation of 1927" but his work was not fully appreciated until much later in the 20th century. His first book of poems, *Perfil del aire* [Profile of the Air] came out in Málaga in 1927. Numerous other volumes followed, the best known of which is the characteristically entitled *La realidad y el deseo* (*Reality and Desire*), published in 1936 and subsequently reissued in several enlarged editions. The increasingly sombre tone of his later work is evidenced in the title of his last book, *Desolación de la quimera* [The Disconsolate Chimera], 1962. Cernuda also published a volume of three stories, some essays on Spanish and English literature and a translation of Shakespeare's *Troilus and Cressida*.

Edition

The Spanish text used by translators is that of the 1970 edition of Luis Cernuda's *La realidad y el deseo*, published in Mexico City, Mexico, by the Fondo de Cultura Económica.

Translations

Poetry

Edkins, Anthony and Derek Harris (editors), *The Poetry of Luis Cernuda*, New York: New York University Press, 1971

Gibbons, Reginald, *Selected Poems of Luis Cernuda*, Berkeley: University of California Press, 1977

St Martin, Hardie (editor), *Roots and Wings: Poetry from Spain, 1900–1975: A Bilingual Anthology*, New York: Harper and Row, 1976, pp. 246–63 (7 items)

The single volume in which Luis Cernuda gathered his collected poems, *La realidad y el deseo* (*Reality and Desire*), represents one of the major literary achievements in Spanish, and should be read as, to all intents and purposes, Cernuda's poetic autobiography. It is made up of 11 separate collections, from the adolescent *Perfil del aire* (1927) – later retitled *Primeros poemas* – to *Desolación de la Quimera* (1962), some of which had no autonomous editions outside this larger body of work. After the Civil War, exile, censorship, the lack of editorial support and interest and, it has to be added, his own fastidiousness and astringency in his dealings with friends, critics and publishers alike, prevented his work from being widely known and distributed around the Spanish-speaking world. *Reality and Desire* grew in three successive editions during his lifetime, in 1936, 1940 and 1958, until, in 1974, 11 years after the poet's death, the Spanish publisher Barral Editores published his definitive *Poesía reunida*. This superseded the Mexican edition of *Reality and Desire* (Fondo de Cultura Económica, 1970), and included juvenilia, uncollected poems, versions from Hölderlin and some English poets – notably Blake and Keats – and his translation of Shakespeare's *Troilus and Cressida*. If the response to the 1936 and 1940 editions was marred by the tragic events of civil war and exile, the 1958, 1970 and 1974 editions witness the growing esteem in which Cernuda's work came to be regarded by Spanish and Latin American writers of later generations. A number of tributes from such Spanish poets as Jaime Gil de Biedma or José Angel Valente, as well as an extremely intelligent and perceptive essay by Octavio Paz, all published in the early 1960s, did much to ensure Cernuda's reputation as a key figure in modern Spanish poetry. The influence of his mature work on the rising poets coming of age in the late 1970s and early 1980s has been immense and pervasive, almost to the point of asphyxia. His thorough knowledge of English poetry and poetic tradition, which he acquired during his 10-year stay in Britain, had a direct bearing on his later work, setting it apart from that of other members of his generation, and widening the tonal repertoire of Spanish poetry. In Cernuda's view, there were three main features of interest in English poetry: first, its plainer poetic diction, removed from the traditional baroqueness of Spanish; second, the objectivizing of personal experience through the use of dramatic monologue as perfected by Browning; and, thirdly, the use of a recognizable and explicit narrative line underlying the poem. All these features, together with a number of Cernuda's perceptive, if at times intolerant, critical insights, have been readily adopted by younger Spanish poets belonging to the so-called new school of narrative poetry, which has been dominant in recent years. This ever-growing admiration for his work has culminated with the critically acclaimed edition of his collected prose and poetic work (Madrid, 1994–95).

Cernuda's admiration for English poetry is evident in his translation of Shakespeare's *Troilus and Cressida* (*Troilo y Crésida*, Madrid: Ínsula, 1953), which he started in 1946 as a "labour of love" and completed four years later, in 1950. Given Cernuda's lack of theatrical experience, it is clear that his version, while linguistically and poetically exciting, is not meant for the stage, lacking the vivacity and agility of the original. His version, though punctilious and faithful, ultimately fails because of its stiffness and dismissal of dramatic conventions.

In view of Cernuda's interest in English poetry, it may be seen as an irony that only two volumes of Cernuda's poetry in English translation have appeared so far, both published in the United States and both lacking a wide circulation among the reading public. It would seem that the very qualities of his poetry that have secured him a central place in the Spanish poetic canon would have facilitated the job of translation and ensured an immediate response on the part of the English reader. This, however, has not been the case. A number of reasons, none very clear, may account for this: it is possible that his poetry lacks the apparent *otherness* that has so attracted the English reader to Lorca's or Guillén's achievements; it may be that only recently has his work found an attentive audience in the Spanish-speaking world. In any case, his poetry, still widely unknown to the English reader, deserves a chance to be quietly read and appreciated.

EDKINS & HARRIS (1971) constitutes, as the editors claim in the Preface, the "first attempt to put before an English-speaking audience a representative selection of Cernuda's poems". As co-editor of the 1974 Spanish edition of Cernuda's *Poesía reunida*, Harris is an authority on Cernuda's work and a faithful and trustworthy guide through the complexities of the poetry. However, the selection, in its effort to give a balanced view of Cernuda's different poetic stages, leaves out a number of extremely important pieces like "Unos cuerpos son como flores", "Remordimiento en traje de noche", "A Larra, con unas violetas" or "*Birds in the night*", to name but a few. The majority of translations, signed by the editors themselves, tend to be fairly literal, sticking close to the originals. Nevertheless, Cernuda's idiosyncratic and archaic use of syntax, which relies heavily on hyperbaton, syntactic inversion and the use of relatives, is lost in the English, which displays a rather flat and unimpressive narrative diction. The danger of overemphasizing the tone of the original is also present in many passages: thus, "hoy cuerpo en pena" turns into "today a body of torment" (p. 127), "en mala hora fuera vuestra lengua" is made into "I curse your tongue" (p. 169) and "Precipitó en la nada" is recast into "Hurled into the abyss" (p. 167). Where the syntax of the original is at pains to be subtle and tentative, the translation relies on a much more direct approach: thus, the repetition of the pronoun in "Sending their verses ... to me, demanding attention to me", or the positioning of "nothing" at the end of a poem in "To hold but tears. Silence; / Darkness trembling; nothing" (p. 9), where the original has "nada" at the end of the penultimate line. Edkins & Harris have included three of Edward R. Wilson's versions, which he did in the 1940s with the help of Cernuda himself. Although it is difficult to judge to what extent Cernuda had a part in them, these versions rate among the volume's best: a bit prosaic at times, they nevertheless convey a distinct anglified tone and diction.

GIBBONS (1977) has much to recommend it. He has rightly noted the modernity and excitement that Cernuda's phrasing offers to a Spanish reader and has tried to create a equivalent effect in English. He avoids Edkins & Harris's shortcomings, departing from Cernuda's syntax as he sees fit, cutting sentences, inserting extra pauses and doing away with a number of relatives. He tends to shorten the lines and to adjust the syntactic structure of the sentence to the line structure, following in this the example of Pound in his *Cathay* poems. The diction has Modernist overtones, and the resulting rhythm is generally brisk and lively, with hints of alliteration, as at the beginning of the poem "Common Sense": "The dark rain drums. / The attenuated fields / Tip their thick treetops / Toward winter" (p. 93). A clear example of Gibbons's expertise is to be found in the short lyric "Desire" (p. 111), a triumph of both delicacy and intensity. The occasional blunder, as in the first stanza of "He did not speak words" or in a number of lines from "*Apologia pro vita sua*", for instance, should not make us forget its numerous merits. Like Edkins & Harris's, the selection is not altogether representative, leaving out significant poems ("Mozart", "Díptico español", "El poeta y la bestia", among others) but it takes more risks, concentrating mainly on poems from the 1930s and 1940s, periods when Cernuda was most productive. In the long run, Gibbons's dexterity is more clearly seen in the meditative, narrative and self-exploratory pieces of Cernuda's mature phase; it is for this reason the reader is left wishing an ampler selection of poems from that period had been made.

It is difficult to give a fair account of ST MARTIN's selection of Cernuda's work included in the 1976 anthology of Spanish poetry *Roots and Wings*, as it contains only seven pieces, rendered into English by five different translators. Of the five, Robert BLY and James WRIGHT stand out with some finely wrought versions, while Timothy BALAND does Cernuda little justice with his work on "Remordimiento en traje de noche" and "No decía palabras". A brief comparison between his versions and those in Gibbons or Edkins & Harris is extremely revealing: Baland tends to overread and to overwrite, as a rule ending up with slow, heavy lines. To Gibbons's "Anguish makes its way through the bones" as translation of "La angustia se abre paso entre los huesos", Baland responds with an ill-formed "Despair opens a passage for itself between the bones". As elsewhere in the anthology, there is little consistency and coherence between the work and strategies of the different translators, which makes for confusing and contradictory readings.

JORDI DOCE

Further Reading

Bellver, C.G., "Luis Cernuda and T.S. Eliot: A Kinship of Message and Motifs", *Revista de Estudios Hispánicos*, 17/1 (1983) pp. 107–24

Bruton, K.J., "Luis Cernuda's Exile Poetry and Coleridge's Theory of Imagination", *Comparative Literature Studies*, 21/4 (1984) pp. 383–95

Kirkup, J., "Translating Penna and Cernuda: Working Papers" in *Translating Poetry: The Double Labyrinth*, edited by Daniel Weissbort, Iowa City: University of Iowa Press, 1989

Paz, Octavio, "Luis Cernuda: The Edifying Word" in *On Poets and Others*, translated by Michael Schmidt, New York: Seaver, 1986; Manchester: Carcanet, 1987

See also the editors' introductions to Edkins & Harris, Gibbons, St Martin

---

Miguel de Cervantes (Saavedra) 1547–1616

Spanish novelist, dramatist and poet

Biography

Cervantes was born in Alcalá de Henares, Spain in October 1547. His life was harassed and vagabond, and his early forays into the world of letters were not well received. He turned to soldiering and fought for Spain against the Turks at the battle of Lepanto, 1571, where he was badly wounded in the left arm. Returning later to Spain, he was captured by pirates and held prisoner in Algiers for five years until ransomed. He then occupied various official posts. Between 1596 and 1600 he lived mainly in Seville and moved to Madrid in about 1606. Only when he brought out his second lengthy prose work in 1605 (*Don Quixote 1*), at the age of 57, did Cervantes receive the acclaim he had been denied in his preferred genres of poetry and drama. He published a long pastoral narrative in 1585 (*La Galatea*), a collection of what he called "Exemplary Novels" in 1612, and put the finishing touches to a rambling Byzantine narrative (*Persiles y Sigismunda*) on his deathbed. He wrote several full-length plays, but his best efforts here are in the one-act *entremeses*. He died in Madrid, 23 April 1616.

Don Quixote

El ingenioso hidalgo don Quijote de la Mancha, 1605–15

Don Quixote (*Don Quijote*) is an extended satire, with elements of novel and romance, originally published in two parts. Part 1 appeared in 1605, part 2 in 1615. The complete 1605 title is *El ingenioso hidalgo don Quijote de la Mancha*, and it contains 52 chapters. The 1615 continuation is modified to *El ingenioso caballero don Quijote de la Mancha*, and that volume contains 74 chapters. Both parts were published in Madrid by Juan de la Cuesta. The number of subsequent editions in Spanish is legion.

Translations

Cohen, J.M., *The Adventures of Don Quixote de la Mancha*, Harmondsworth: Penguin, 1950

Jarvis, Charles, *The Life and Exploits of the Ingenious Gentleman Don Quixote de la Mancha*, London: J. and R. Tonson and R. Dodsley, 1742; edited with an introduction by E.C. Riley, Oxford: Oxford University Press, 1992

Motteux, Peter, *The History of the Renown'd Don Quixote de la Mancha*, 4 vols, London: Buckley, 1700–12; *Don*

Quixote: Ozell's Revision of the Translation of Peter Motteux, New York: Random House, 1930 (John Ozell's revisions date from 1719)

Ormsby, John, *The Ingenious Gentleman Don Quixote of La Mancha*, London: Smith Elder, and New York: Macmillan, 1885; edited and revised by Joseph R. Jones and Kenneth Douglas, New York: Norton, 1981

Putnam, Samuel, *The Ingenious Gentleman Don Quixote de la Mancha*, with an introduction, New York: Viking Press, 1949; London: Cassell, 1953

Raffel, Burton, *The History of That Ingenious Gentleman, Don Quijote de la Mancha*, New York: Norton, 1995

Shelton, Thomas, *The History of the Valorous and Wittie Knight-Errant Don Quixote of the Mancha*, London: printed for Blounte Barret, 1612; as *The History of Don-Quichote*, 2 vols, 1620; with an introduction by James Fitzmaurice-Kelly, 4 vols, London: David Nutt, 1896

Starkie, Walter, *Don Quixote of La Mancha*, abridged, with an introduction, London: Macmillan, and New York: St Martin's Press, 1954

Miguel de Cervantes is one of three luminaries of the Golden Age of Spanish letters who succeeds in transforming a major genre for his time and place: Lope de Vega does this in drama; Luis de Góngora in verse; Cervantes in prose narrative. Cervantes's narrative style is impossible to reproduce in English, as his most recent translator acknowledges (Burton Raffel, 1995). While the renderings of *Don Quixote* into English are several, those that are reliable are few, and only two offer sufficiently close approximations to the texture of the original to merit serious consideration. One is that of Charles JARVIS (1742), corrected, annotated, and provided with an up-to-date bibliography by Edward C. RILEY (1992), professor emeritus of Spanish at the University of Edinburgh. The other represents an original, systematic approach by an American professor of English and professional translator, Burton RAFFEL (1995).

The Riley update of Jarvis displays a charming, archaic English that is reasonably close linguistically to Cervantes's Spanish of the previous century. It is also rather British, and may therefore be more appealing to readers of that heritage. Raffel resorts to what he calls syntactic tracking, in addition to the customary attention to lexical equivalencies, and produces a text that is also close to the original, not in its archaism, but in rhythm and rhetoric, in length of sentences, patterning, and colloquial dialogue. He is also able to capture certain subtleties better than most of his predecessors – although at times this becomes a quest for innuendo, leading him astray. His version may be more appealing to North American readers.

The juxtaposition of three passages should serve to convey the flavor of Riley's revision of Jarvis and Raffel's rendering, while at the same time calling attention to certain problems. I give the original Spanish first in each instance, citing from my own edition (with Salvado Fajardo, Asheville, North Carolina: Pegasus Press, 1998). The first gives the narrator's disparaging editorial comment on Don Quixote's disjointed and misdirected speech on the Golden Age (1, 11):

> Toda esta larga arenga (que se pudiera muy bien escusar) dijo nuestro caballero, porque las bellotas que le dieron le trujeron a la memoria la edad dorada, y antojósele hacer aquel inútil razonamiento a los cabreros, que, sin respondelle palabra, embobados y suspensos, le estuvieron escuchando.

Jarvis/Riley:

> Our knight made this tedious discourse (which might very well have been spared), because the acorns they had given him put him in mind of the golden age, and inspired him with an eager desire to make that impertinent harangue to the goatherds; who stood in amaze, gaping and listening, without answering him a word.

Raffel:

> Our knight delivered himself of this copious oration – which could just as well have been omitted – because the acorn-nuts they'd given him made him remember the Golden Age, and so he was stirred to address such a useless harangue to the goatherds, who never said a word, but simply listened to him, enthralled and astounded.

Jarvis/Riley's "tedious discourse" comes closer to the tone of Cervantes's "Toda esta larga arenga" than does Raffel's "copious oration", while "made" is more like "dijo" than is the high-sounding "delivered himself of". Here Raffel loses at his own game of syntactic tracking. One doesn't know what to make of "they'd". Also, there is an appreciable difference in tone between "in amaze, gaping and listening" and "enthralled and astounded". In brief, Raffel puts a positive spin on the tone of the passage, by choosing words like "enthralled" and "copious", that is simply not evident in the original. Jarvis has captured that negative tone, and the underlying tension between narrator and character, quite admirably.

Here is a brief passage that tests basic knowledge of syntax; the duchess is speaking to Sancho:

> "... levantaos, amigo, y decid a vuestro señor que venga mucho en hora buena a servirse de mí y del duque mi marido, en una casa de placer que aquí tenemos". (2, 30)

Jarvis/Riley:

> "... rise, friend, and tell your master, he may come and welcome; for I and the duke, my spouse, are at his service, in a country seat we have here hard by".

Raffel:

> "... – rise, my friend, and inform your lord that he is most welcome to be my guest, and that of the duke, my husband, in a pleasure home we maintain here".

Both versions are quite acceptable. What is interesting, however, is that Raffel's 1995 reading corrects a monumental misunderstanding of a certain reflexive verb ("servirse de") evidenced in the version he committed to print in 1993 in the journal, *Cervantes*. There we read:

> "... – rise, my friend, and inform your lord that he is most welcome to take advantage of me, and of the duke, my husband, in a pleasure home we maintain here".

Finally, one of the most problematical passages in all of

Cervantes is the beginning of *Don Quixote* 2, 44:

> Dicen que en el propio original desta historia se lee que llegando Cide Hamete a escribir este capítulo, no le tradujo su intérprete como él le había escrito, que fue un modo de queja que tuvo el moro de sí mismo....

Jarvis/Riley:

> We are told that in the original of this history, it is said, Cid Hamet coming to write this chapter, the interpreter did not translate it, as he had written it: which was a kind of complaint the Moor made of himself....

Raffel:

> It is said that, in the true original of this chapter, one can read how, when Sidi Hamid came to write this chapter (which his translator only partially rendered into Spanish), the Moor penned a kind of complaint against himself....

Here Raffel captures much better the play on orality and literacy, involving the seemingly nonsensical assertion that the true original, which has never been mentioned until now, somehow seeks grounding in oral tradition. Moreover, this "true original" is prescient, for it alludes to a translator who will not appear until well after the completion of Cide Hamete's Arabic version, in order to inform us of nonfeasance, well before the fact, on the part of that same translator. The only fault I find here is that Raffel, with his parenthesis, attempts to improve upon Cervantes by making the illogical sound plausible – always a temptation for the translator of *Don Quixote*.

The samples presented above are mainly problem passages and do not necessarily typify the entire translation. On balance, Raffel uses a more modern idiom and tries to tease out subtleties while remaining as faithful to the original as possible. The paradox is that putting Cervantes into 20th-century American English, no matter how faithfully and accurately, may in itself be a falsification. Riley's updating of Jarvis is excellent. There are no egregious errors – as indeed there are in all other versions – and it has the merit of capturing the archaic expression of an earlier day. Ultimately, the choice centers on taste.

JAMES A. PARR

Further Reading

Allen, John J., "Traduttori Traditori: *Don Quixote* in English", *Crítica Hispánica*, 1/1 (1979) pp. 1–13

Parr, James A., *"Don Quixote": An Anatomy of Subversive Discourse*, Newark, Delaware: Juan de la Cuesta, 1988

Paulson, Ronald, *Don Quixote in England: The Aesthetics of Laughter*, Baltimore: Johns Hopkins University Press, 1998

Raffel, Burton, "Translating Cervantes: Una vez más", *Cervantes* 13/1 (1993) pp. 5–30

Riley, E.C., *Don Quixote*, London and Boston: Allen and Unwin, 1986

Russell, P.E., *Cervantes*, Oxford and New York: Oxford University Press, 1985

Rosa Chacel 1898–1994

Spanish novelist, short-story writer, poet and essayist

Biography

Born in Valladolid, 3 June 1898. She attended art classes as a child in Valladolid, then studied painting and sculpture in Madrid, 1908–18, but was forced to abandon her art studies through ill health and turned to literature. In the 1920s she began writing articles and essays on artistic, literary, and cultural topics for a variety of periodicals. She married the painter Timoteo Pérez Rubio in 1921 (one son), and they lived in Italy, where they studied art, until 1927. Returning to Spain, Chacel became a contributor to the Republican *Hora de España*. She continued to support the government on the outbreak of civil war in 1936. After periods in Germany, France and Greece in the later 1930s, she emigrated to Brazil in 1940. Until her husband's death in 1977 she remained in South America, living in Brazil with spells in Argentina, where her son was at school, and visits to New York and Spain. During the years abroad she was twice awarded the Spanish National Critics' prize (1970 and 1976). On her return to Spain she settled in Madrid, receiving the National Literature prize in 1987. She died in Madrid, 27 July 1994.

Though a member of the "generation of 1927", Chacel was little known before the Civil War. Her first novel, *Estación, ida y vuelta* [the title has a double meaning: Station, Round Trip and Return of the Seasons] written in Rome, appeared in 1930. In 1936 she published a small collection of sonnets, *A la orilla de un pozo* [At the Well's Edge]. Growing recognition began in 1970, when her 1960 novel *La sinrazón* [Unreason] was reprinted in Barcelona with her then complete works.

A historical novel, *Teresa* [Teresa], 1941, about the mistress of the 19th-century Romantic poet J. de Espronceda, had been followed by *Memorias de Leticia Valle* (*Memoirs of Leticia Valle*), 1945, in which a young girl exercises her sexual power over her male teacher. *Sobre il piélago* [On the High Sea], 1952 was one of Chacel's several collections of short stories. Back in Madrid, she went on writing short and long fiction, poetry and essays. Like *La Sinrazón*, *Barrio de Maravillas* (*The Maravillas District*), 1976, won the National Critics' prize. Prominent non-fictional prose works include *Saturnal* [Saturnalia], 1972, and *Los títulos* [Titles], 1981, and a number of autobiographical writings, notably *Desde el amanecer* [Since Dawn], 1972. In 1980 Chacel published a book on her husband's paintings. She also translated Racine and Camus into Spanish.

Translations

Novels

Memorias de Leticia Valle, 1945

Maier, Carol, *Memoirs of Leticia Valle*, with an afterword by Carol Maier, Lincoln: University of Nebraska Press, 1994

Barrio de Maravillas, 1976

Démers, D.A., *The Maravillas District*, with an introduction by Susan Kirkpatrick, Lincoln: University of Nebraska Press, 1992

The two translations into English of novels by Rosa Chacel have in one way or another been framed by the concern of a publisher and translators to make visible in the English-speaking world fiction by Spanish women. Both translations appear in the European Women Writers series published by the University of Nebraska; both come packaged with commentaries refracted through the prism of critical discussions of how to approach writing variously described as exilic, of the Generation of 27, or non-phallologocentric, or even best not described as feminist at all. For introducer and editorial board member, Susan Kirkpatrick, Chacel is the writer of non-patriarchal language, the silences and suggestions of intimate self-narration, subjectivities that almost absorb or drown out the disruptive noises of history. For Carol Maier, the labelling of Chacel becomes a site for the interrogation of predictability and of the translator's role in the interpretative presentation of an author, an exemplary experiment in the recovery of writing lost for half a century. The translations of Rosa Chacel's novels reveal a major Hispanic author and underpin a visible North American tradition of translation.

Rosa Chacel's words stream out in long monologues or dialogues where the reader is often unsure of their origins: Ariadne, threads, labyrinths, the patient plotting of the play of light on a Madrid staircase, an "inconceivable" act, a death in Sarajevo – loose but interwoven states of consciousness invite intellectual, woman-identified commentary that denies essentializing notions of feminine and masculine.

They also demand a close attention to words in a sensitive translatorly strategy. It is not easy to describe or evaluate literary translations without full access to drafts, editorial corrections and changes, correspondence between translators and authors, the many interactions that go into the making of a translation. The two Nebraska translations reveal two very distinct translating strategies: one implicit, the other articulated.

The Maravillas District is translated by D.A. DÉMERS (1992), who consistently shortens the long sentences and omits the suspension points that mirror the states of mind of the two girls growing up in Madrid on the eve of World War I. As there is no comment by Démers on his translation strategy, we can only infer that he is opting to make the text more readable, domesticated in accord with the conventional English literary transformation of "over-long" Latinate originals into short bursts of pragmatic American English. On the other hand, it also reflects an editorial policy or lack of policy that did not challenge what may have been an implicit strategy which should have been challenged. Two sentences will suffice as example:

> Más compleja la luz, más indefinible en el cuarto de la izquierda. Tiempos muy diversos, escalonados, no jerárquicamente, sino efectivamente – por lo tanto, creadores de efectos muy diversos en la luz – un tiempo femenino, no maternal, sino matronil, de ahí la jerarquía temporal avasallada, en parte, por la efectividad de los otros tiempos, más que avasallada, frustrada en las dos viejas hermanas ...

> The light is more complex and more hard to define in the room to the left. Very different times are arranged, not according to hierarchy, but according to effect – and thus they create very different effects of light. There is a feminine time – not maternal but matronly. This accounts for the partial subjugation, or frustration, of the hegemony of present time in favor of the nominal rank of former times by the two old sisters.

The translation adds verbs and conjunctions, chops up the stream of consciousness and ignores the repetition of key words: it seems to assume that the original rhythm of Chacel's idiosyncratic Spanish cannot be found in an experimental English. The effect is to create a more rational, logical prose whose form is at odds with the notions of complexity and indeterminacy it is supposed to communicate and at the same time it injects a flavour of a more modern political discourse. The Spanish has no verbs, the movement arising from the use of repetition, "luz", "más", "muy", "efectivamente", "efectos", "efectividad", past participles such as "escalonados", "avasallada". The linchpin word is "creadores" and the idea of the creation of different light effects is central to the feminine space of the novel: creation and movement within apparent stasis. The introduction by the translator of the concepts of "hegemony" and "nominal rank" overdetermines the sense of the final words, precludes the possible ironies of "frustrated, rather than subjugated" temporal hierarchy.

The Memoirs of Leticia Valle comes with an afterword by Carol MAIER in the form of 13 glosses that combine historical and literary background, textual analysis, and discussion of the difficulties of describing, fixing in words the elusive acts of writing, reading and translating. As Rosa Chacel said of her first novel, "I try for the impossible, to make the reader understand what I do not even mention." The strategy leads to a translation that responds closely to the style of the Spanish and and reacts with sensitivity to key words so that they breathe their freshness into the English. Generally, this earlier novel also suggests rather than states, but there is a more strongly defined dialogue and sense of narrative than in *The Maravillas District*. An example of the translation of one long sentence will make apparent what could be called the writing of the translation.

> Y creí sentir algo parecido a esas veces que me había puesto a buscar entre la hierba del pinar los piñones caídos y no había podido al principio distinguir nada de la monotonía de las briznas, hasta que descubría el primero y en seguida iban apareciendo más por todas partes, porque ya conocía las características de claroscuro que los delataban.

What I felt reminded me of those times in the pine grove when I started to look for pine cones in the grass and at first could not make out anything in the sameness of so much green; after I spotted the first one, though, pine cones would immediately start turning up everywhere, because then I could see the chiaroscuro that gave them away.

Maier's translation captures the immediacy of Leticia's reactions by making small changes to the structure of the sentence as in the opening words, "What I felt", "spotted" for "descubrí" and the colloquial "would ... start turning up everywhere" for "iban apareciendo más por todas partes". These quiet interventions by the translator surround the powerful transformation of the phrase "y no había podido al principio distinguir nada de la monotonía de las briznas" (literally, "I hadn't been able at first to distinguish anything from the monotony of the blades of grass"), which becomes "and at first I could not make out anything in the sameness of so much green". The bold brilliance of "the sameness of so much green" marks out the translator as a writer, letting go imaginatively from the original, to create a text that is originally recovered in another language, that communicates the feel of Leticia's shaping of her experience.

Both novels attracted numerous reviews that commented on the respective translations. For Lynda Hoffman-Jeep the source text of *The Maravillas District* "is dense like pudding-thick Spanish hot chocolate" and the translation offers "perhaps a glass of chocolate milk by comparison" (*Review of Contemporary Fiction*, Fall 1993). In the *Village Voice* (19 February 1993), James Marcus remarked on the Spanish text's density of style, the "resulting magnificence of such verbal magma" making for "tough sledding, even in D.A. Démers's fine translation". In her review of the *Memoirs of Leticia Valle* Kathryn Davis draws attention to the "informative afterword provided by the adept and sensitive translator" (*New York Times Book Review*, 13 March 1994). Bill Marx concludes that both books are "a treat for those who like their fiction crammed with intellectual and stylistic brio" (*Boston Phoenix*, March 1994), underlining the obvious fact that translations are there to be enjoyed by those who cannot read the original texts. On the other hand, Sheila Kohler spends most of her lengthy review of Maier's *Leticia Valle* (*Boston Sunday Globe*, 28 May 1995) commenting on parallels with Dostoevskii and Nabokov in a round of literary sleuthing.

PETER BUSH

Further Reading

Brown, Joan L. (editor), *Women Writers of Contemporary Spain: Exiles in the Homeland*, Newark: University of Delaware Press, 1991

Lee Six, Abigail, "Perceiving the Family: Rosa Chacel's *Desde el amanecer*" in *Feminist Readings on Spanish and Latin-American Literature*, edited by L.P. Condé and J.M. Hart, Lewiston, New York, and Lampeter, Wales: Mellen Press, 1991

Maier, Carol, "Recovering, Re-covering, and the Translation of Work by Rosa Chacel and María Zambrano" in *Feminism in Multi-Cultural Literature*, edited by Antonio Sobejano-Morán, Lewiston, New York: Mellen Press, 1996

Massardier-Kenney, Françoise, "Towards a Redefinition of Feminist Translation Practice", *The Translator*, 3/1 (1997) pp. 55–69

Adelbert von Chamisso 1781–1838

German poet, short-story writer and botanist

Biography

Louis Charles Adelaide de Boncourt, son of Louis-Marie, comte de Chamisso, was born at Boncourt, in Champagne, 27(?) January 1781, and brought up there in the family chateau. In 1792 his parents left France to escape the Revolution, going first to Belgium and in 1796 settling temporarily in Berlin, where Chamisso learned German at the French *Gymnasium*. He served for some years in the Prussian army, travelled in France and Switzerland, and frequented several literary circles, including that of Madame de Staël. He studied medicine in Berlin, 1812–13. At different periods, in his youth and in his last years, he co-edited the literary *Musenalmanach*. His novella, *Peter Schlemihls wundersame Geschichte*, appeared in 1814, and a volume of poems, *Gedichte*, in 1831.

From 1815 to 1818 Chamisso sailed round the world with Otto von Kotzebue as naturalist to the expedition, becoming on his return a curator of the Berlin Botanical Gardens.

Chamisso is best known now to the world as the author of the poems set to music in Schumann's 1840 song-cycle *Frauenliebe und -leben* (*Woman's Love and Life*) and the creator of Peter Schlemihl and his lost shadow. His literary works treat typical German Romantic themes in typical Romantic forms, but with his own humour, realism, psychological insight and compactness. He died in Berlin, 21 August 1838.

Translations

Play

Faust: Ein Versuch, 1803

Phillips, Henry, Jr., *Faust: A Dramatic Sketch*, Philadelphia: printed privately, 1881

Novella

Peter Schlemihls wundersame Geschichte, 1814

Anonymous [Sir John Bowring], *Peter Schlemihl*, London: G. and W.B. Whittaker, 1823, 1824; London: R. Hardwicke, 1861 (under the name Sir John Bowring); as *The Shadowless Man*, London: Chatto and Windus, and New York: Warne, 1910

Howitt, William, *The Wonderful History of Peter Schlemihl* (parallel texts), London: Longman Brown Green and Longmans, and Nuremberg: J.L. Schrag, 1843; reprinted London: Rodale Press, 1954

Loewenstein-Wertheim, Leopold von, *Peter Schlemihl*, London: John Calder, 1957

Rouillon, Emilie de, *Peter Schlemihl*, London: J. Souter, and Norwich: J. Fletcher, 1838

Steinhauer, Harry, *The Strange Story of Peter Schlemihl*, in *Twelve German Novellas*, edited by Steinhauer, Berkeley: University of California Press, 1977

Poetry

Aikman, C.M., "The Crucifix: An Art-Legend", *Publications of the English Goethe Society*, 7, Transactions 1891–92 (1893) pp.144–50

Lentzner, Karl, *Chamisso: A Sketch of His Life and Work with Specimens of His Poetry and an Edition of the Original Text of "Salas y Gomez"*, London and Edinburgh: Williams and Norgate, 1893

Sams, Eric, in his *The Songs of Robert Schumann*, 3rd edition, Bloomington: Indiana University Press, 1993

Strangways, A.H. Fox and Stuart Wilson, *Schumann's Songs Translated: A Selection*, 2 vols, London: Oxford University Press, 1929

Other Writing

Bemerkungen und Ansichten in *Entdeckungs-Reise in die Süd-See und nach der Berings-Strasse*, by Otto von Kotzebue, vol. 3, 1821; and in *Reise um die Welt mit der Romanzoffischen Entdeckungs-Expedition in den Jahren 1815–18 auf der Brigg Rurik*, by Otto von Kotzebue, 1836 (includes Chamisso's *Tagebuch*)

Kratz, Henry, *A Voyage around the World with the Romanzov Exploring Expedition in the Years 1815–1818 in the Brig Rurik*, by Otto von Kotzebue, Honolulu: University of Hawaii Press, 1986

Lloyd, Hannibal Evans, *Remarks and Opinions of the Naturalist of the Expedition* in *A Voyage of Discovery into the South Sea and Beering's Straits*, vols 2–3, by Otto von Kotzebue, London: Longman Hurst Rees Orme and Brown, 1821

Über die hawaiische Sprache, 1836

Chapin, Paul Gipson, *On the Hawaiian Language*, Honolulu: Department of Linguistics, University of Hawaii, 1973

Primarily known in the English-speaking world as the author of the story *Peter Schlemihl* and of a series of Romantic poems set to music by Schumann, Adelbert von Chamisso was also a distinguished botanist. The record of his Pacific voyage of discovery on the *Rurik* (1815–18), as well as constituting an accomplished piece of travel literature, has rightly attracted the attention of translators on account of the material's botanical and ethnological interest. Chamisso's resultant *Remarks and Opinions* are also not without significance for an understanding of *Peter Schlemihl*.

It is regrettable that PHILLIPS's *Faust* translation (1881) exists only in an obscure edition of 100 copies, for he handles the material well. Although some liberties are taken, this remains essentially faithful to the original in meaning, tone and verse-forms. The moods are appropriately captured in both soliloquy and the exchanges of the dialogue.

In the preface to the 1861 edition of his translation of *Peter Schlemihl*, BOWRING remarks that "several English translations have since occupied the field", but his, "as the first-born, naturally claims its own heritage". Part of that original patrimony was the advantageous assumption that the story was, as the 1823 title page proudly announced, "From the German of Lamotte Fouqué". (Fouqué was then one of the most popular of the German Romantics in England.) Even more auspicious was the inclusion of eight illustrations by George Cruikshank, which so pleased Chamisso that he had six of them added to the German second edition as supporting "evidence" of Schlemihl's shadowless condition. Bowring deserves credit as one of the few translators to include the prefatory letters and poems so vital to the story's effect. In an introduction to the 1993 Camden House reprint of the first English translation, Koepke (see Further Reading) presents Bowring's rendering as "reliable and good", arguing that its period English comes closest to Chamisso's early 19th-century German, but Violet Stockley is nearer the mark with her "not always quite accurate". Indeed, Bowring's printer seems to have had considerable problems with the translator's handwriting, leaving the names of people and places mangled at times beyond recognition (Erasmus becomes Crasimus, Spikher masquerades as Spekhin, Nennhausen is read as Neunhausen, etc.): unfortunate blemishes in a work so reliant on documentable authenticity. In a singularly spirited translation capturing the story's larmoyance and religious introspection with some verve, Bowring nevertheless nods off on occasions and shows himself not always up to the niceties of Chamisso's German. With the exception of the authorial misassignation, none of the factual errors in the 1823 translation is corrected in later editions.

It is a tribute to the quality of ROUILLON's (1838) version that it reappeared (although never under the translator's name) in numerous editions or collections of short stories throughout the 19th and early 20th centuries. This translation conveys the flavour of the original in its accurate renderings and its capturing of Chamisso's tones. In its unforced fluency, unencumbered by the heaviness that at points mars the work of Bowring and Howitt, this translation can still be recommended to modern readers.

HOWITT's text (1843) is a bilingual one, with German and English versions on adjacent pages. It offers an admirably accurate translation, but in the idiom and syntax of the 19th century. The elegance and flow of Chamisso's sentences are burdened with an all too often cumbersome quality.

Given that it appeared in 1957, LOEWENSTEIN-WERTHEIM's version of *Peter Schlemihl* has a strangely anachronistic ring, starting with the reference to the "Hausknecht" who receives the protagonist in the first paragraph as the "Boots". Despite the translator's promising name, many of the finer points of the

German are lost: the legendary Faffner's "Hort" (or "Taffner's stronghold", as Bowring would have it) becomes a "lair", the key moment where we are told that an event has taken the place of an action on Schlemihl's part simply registers that "the unexpected intervened". Biblical overtones are repeatedly lost (God becomes "inspiration", "get Thee hence" is reduced to "leave me") and the religiously inspired ostracizing of Schlemihl is on the whole misrepresented. The result sits uncomfortably between period style, modishness (the "lovely Fanny" described as "the girl of the moment") and frequent failure to respond to the story's nuances.

STEINHAUER's translation (1977), preceded by a useful bio-bibliographical note, is undoubtedly one of the most faithful, although it too omits both preliminaries and illustrations. The use of "strange" in the English title may fail to capture the sense of "wundersam" (Loewenstein-Wertheim comes closer with "wondrous"), but it represents one of the few attempts at doing justice to a deliberately intriguing title, calculatingly less explicit than *The Shadowless Man* (Bowring, 1910 edition) or *The Man Who Lost His Shadow* (Gertrude G. Schwebell, New York, 1974). There are a few lapses (plants in a botanist's study should be "dried" not "wilted", clocks have "hands" not "handles" and some of the Latin, albeit helpfully translated, is misquoted in the original). Overall, Steinhauer has produced a good readable translation for the latter part of the 20th century. Where modernization arguably sometimes sells the source-work short is in its abandoning of the text's rhetorical tropes and word plays, and of the intertextual and stylistic registers of Chamisso's style.

AIKMAN's verse translation (1893) of "Das Kruzifix" is far from trustworthy; while adhering to Chamisso's sense, it is not bound by the poetic expressions employed and it is often far too inventive.

LENTZNER (1893) combines an effusive biographical study of Chamisso's life and work with a welcome introduction to his poetry (i.e., virtually half his oeuvre). Selected poems – in parallel German and English versions – are scattered throughout the "Sketch", with the intention of bringing out Chamisso's range: from the sentimental and patriotic to comedy (the "Melancholy Story" of a man vexed by his pigtail's always being at the back of his head, twist and turn as he may) to a series of maudlin, sometimes socially conscious ballads in the Victorian tradition. The ballad of a shipwrecked mariner, "Salaz y Gomez", singled out as the author's "grandest work", is nevertheless only partially translated, yet the original is reproduced in toto. Though informative as a biographer, Lentzner can be a somewhat cavalier translator, often inclined to sacrifice fidelity for the sake of rhyme (although he abandons the poem's original terza rima), or surrendering Chamisso's freshness to the nearest cliché and suffering from a penchant for hyperbole and the falsely poetical.

SAMS (1993) includes the eight (of nine) poems from "Frauenliebe und -leben" (A woman's love and life) which Schumann set, and nine others, among them Chamisso's own translations, in particular of Hans Christian Andersen. Sams aims at conveying meaning above all, producing literal, accurate translations in poetic prose.

STRANGWAYS & WILSON (1929) include only "Frauenliebe und -leben". Their translations, which are in verse and follow Chamisso's rhyme schemes, are printed beneath the music of the vocal part, the emphasis lying on the provision of a song-version for Schumann's music. While the spirit and ideas of the original are largely retained, these (unlike Sams's) are not faithful renditions. Many concessions are made to the demands of the music and verse and considerable liberties are taken.

I.A. WHITE and J.J. WHITE

Further Reading

Koepke, Wulf, introduction to *Peter Schlemihl* by Chamisso (Bowring's translation), Columbia, South Carolina: Camden House, 1993

Rath, Philipp, *Bibliotheca Schlemihliana: Ein Verzeichnis der Ausgaben und Übersetzungen des Peter Schlemihl nebst neun unveröffentlichten Briefen Chamissos und einer Einleitung*, Berlin: Breslauer, 1919

Schweizer, Niklaus R., *A Poet among Explorers: Chamisso in the South Seas*, Bern and Frankfurt: Lang, 1973

Stockley, V., *German Literature as Known in England, 1750–1830*, London: Routledge, 1929; Port Washington, New York: Kennikat Press, 1969

George Chapman 1559/60–1634

English poet, dramatist and literary translator

Biography

Born near Hitchin, Hertfordshire, 1559 or 1560. The details of his early life are not known for certain. He probably studied at Oxford, perhaps also at the Inner Temple in London. Between 1585 and 1591 he was in Europe, and between 1599 and 1608 in London again. From 1603 to 1612 he served in the household of Henry Prince of Wales, elder brother (died 1612) of the future king Charles I, spending some time imprisoned in the Tower of London (1605) for an anti-Scottish allusion to the king (James I of England and VI of Scotland) in his, Ben Jonson's and John Marston's comedy *Eastward Hoe*.

After some early poems (e.g. *The Shadow of Night*, 1594; *Ovid's Banquet of Sence*, 1595) Chapman wrote plays for more than 10 years before turning to translation. Seven of his comedies survive, together with five tragedies, including two about Bussy d'Ambois, and some pieces written in collaboration.

Although he also translated other authors, Chapman's fame now rests chiefly on his Homer. In 1598 Chapman brought out his version of seven books of the *Iliad*. His full translation of the *Iliad* came out in 1611. In 1616 it was published together with his translation of the *Odyssey* in *The Whole Works of Homer, Prince of Poets*. Chapman died in London, 12 May 1634.

It is on his translation of Homer that George Chapman's reputation as a translator must stand or fall. Work on this translation occupied almost 30 years of Chapman's life. Chapman's command of Greek was only basic; he worked, chiefly, from the Greek text of Spondanus (Jean de Sponde) with its parallel Latin translation by Andreas Divus. It is clear that he made more use of the Latin than of the Greek itself.

Chapman's Homer has great vigour and energy. It is particularly effective read aloud – it should be noted that although Keats's famous sonnet is entitled "On First *Looking* into Chapman's Homer" it goes on to declare "Yet did I never breathe its [Homer's "wide expanse"] pure serene / Till I *heard* Chapman speak out loud and bold" (my italics).

Chapman was an inveterate enemy of what he called "a most asinine error", that translators "must attempt it as a mastery ... to doe it in as few words, and the like order" (Preface to *Juvenal*). Such translations were, in his eyes, "vulgar and verball expositions" (Preface to *Hesiod*); in his own work "the words are utterly altered; it should be so, to avoid verball servitude". The method of literal paraphrase (to use Dryden's later terms) is a denial of "free and honest poesie" (*Juvenal*). We need not be surprised, then, by the liberties Chapman takes in translating Homer. These are at their most extreme in the *Odyssey*, which might be better described as an imitation than as a translation. The 12,150 lines of the original become 16,663. The expansions are often observations of Chapman's own, or elaborations of images he finds interesting. More fundamentally, Chapman is quite prepared to depart from the original text in the furtherance of his interpretation of Homer's poem. Homer's "whole argument", according to Chapman, is "the information or fashion of an absolute man", a man exemplary of wisdom and piety. Downplaying any sense of the deviousness of Odysseus (or Ulysses, as Chapman refers to him), Chapman makes many minor changes to emphasize moral values more Christian than Homeric. In his version of the *Iliad* Chapman is generally more faithful; at times, indeed, there is a doggedly clumsy fidelity which prevents him from writing English poetry. This is part of a general unevenness of achievement – in both translations there are moments of wonderfully resonant writing and there are moments of dullness, and of crabbed obscurity almost impossible to understand. The *Iliad* is translated into rhymed fourteeners (here 14,416 lines correspond to the 15,703 of the original); for the *Odyssey* Chapman uses heroic couplets. What they have in common is what Alexander Pope called "a daring fiery Spirit that animates his Translation" (Pope's *Iliad*, 1715). Passionate involvement characterizes Chapman's Homer; it is very much a poet's translation, combatively re-creative, scornful of mere scholarly accuracy.

That fiery spirit finds less to work on in the version of the *Batrachomyomachia* published in *The Crowne of all Homers Workes*; perhaps not surprisingly a persuasively mock-heroic tone eludes Chapman. There are things in the Homeric Hymns that one would have expected to appeal to Chapman, but his versions are generally rather humdrum.

Chapman's other translations from Greek (though again he is likely to have worked with a Latin gloss close at hand) are similarly various in quality, but all are of interest in the contribution they make to our picture of this remarkable literary mind. His Hesiod, in heroic couplets and with characteristically dogmatic marginal notes, is, as its title page promises, "translated elaborately". The original is frequently elaborated by moralizing additions, both within the text and in the notes. There is much that is typically clotted and opaque but also much that reads well and attractively – e.g. the opening of the second book. (This translation too has inspired poems – both Ben Jonson's commendatory verses in the original volume and, in our own time, Peter Porter's "On First Looking Into Chapman's Hesiod" (*Living in a Calm Country*, 1975).)

The version of Musaeus contains fewer successful passages. There is often an intrusive oddity of phrasing, a needless syntactical complexity (not to mention an excessive use of parentheses); the result is decidedly uninviting to the reader.

Rather happier is the version of Juvenal's 10th satire. This has a forceful, rugged manner, which often achieves a telling sharpness in making satirical points. Juvenalian anger finds a ready echo in Chapman and it is perhaps for this reason that, while characteristically free, this translation finds him unusually restrained where the intrusion of his own views is concerned.

Another – but related – side of Chapman's complex personality found it easy, one suspects, to sympathize with the sentiments of Petrarch's seven Latin Penitential Psalms. The lyric forms (inventively handled) serve to discipline Chapman's verbosity, and these are amongst Chapman's most immediately attractive translations. An interesting oddity is the provision of a second version of the first Psalm, described as "more strictly translated".

For all its flaws, Chapman's work as a translator is never less than fascinating. Having no interest in any kind of "neutral" transcript (assuming that to be possible), his translations are imaginative interpretations of an original, re-creations which produce rewarding dialogues between two poetic personalities.

GLYN PURSGLOVE

Translations

Hesiod, *The Georgicks of Hesiod*, 1618
Homer, *Seaven Bookes of the Iliades*, 1598
Homer, *Achilles Shield ... Out of the Eighteenth Booke of Iliades*, 1598
Homer, *The Iliads of Homer*, 1611
Homer, *Homer's Odysses*, 1614(?)
Homer, *The Whole Works of Homer*, 1616
Homer, *The Crowne of All Homer's Works: Batrachomyomachia, or the Battle of Frogs and Mise, His Hymns and Epigrams*, 1625
Juvenal, *A Justification of a Strange Action of Nero ... Also a Just Reproof of a Romane Smell-Feast, Being the Fifth Satyre of Juvenall*, 1629
Musaeus, *The Divine Poem of Musaeus: First of All Books Translated According to the Original*, 1616

Petrarch, *Petrarchs Seven Penitentiall Psalms, Paraphrastically Translated*, London: Matthew Selman, 1612

Further Reading

Blessington, F., "Homer Transported: Chapman's Method", *Classical Bulletin*, 63 (1987) pp. 1–6
Chapman, George, *George Chapman's Minor Translations: A Critical Edition of His Renderings of Musaeus, Hesiod and Juvenal*, edited by Richard Corballis, Salzburg: Institut für Anglistik und Amerikanistik, University of Salzburg, 1984
Lord, George de Forest, *Homeric Renaissance: The Odyssey of George Chapman*, New Haven, Connecticut: Yale University Press, and London: Chatto and Windus, 1956
MacLure, Millar, *George Chapman: A Critical Study*, Toronto: University of Toronto Press, 1966
Sühnel, R., *Homer und die englische Humanität: Chapmans und Popes Übersetzungskunst im Rahmen der humanistischen Tradition*, Tübingen: Niemeyer, 1958

René Char 1907–1988

French poet

Biography

Born in L'Isle-sur-la-Sorgue, Vaucluse, 14 June 1907. He attended the Lycée d'Avignon and the École de Commerce in Marseilles. He did his military service in the artillery at Nîmes, 1927–28. He moved to Paris in 1929 and there met Louis Aragon, Paul Éluard and André Breton and took part (1930–34) in the second period of the Surrealist movement (he contributed in 1930 to the review *Le Surréalisme au service de la Révolution*), breaking with it in 1935. In World War II Char served with the artillery in Alsace (1939–40), and was decorated for dangerous missions carried out later for the Resistance. From 1944 he was a friend of Camus. After the war he returned to Provence.

Char wrote prolifically, producing from 1928 to 1988 scores of collections of poems, prose poems, free verse and aphorisms, written in an elliptic and allusive style considered "difficult" by many. Notable titles are *Le Marteau sans maître* (*The Hammer with No Master*), 1934; (*Seuls demeurent* [Only These Remain], 1945; *Le Poème pulvérisé* (*The Pulverised Poem*), 1947; *Fureur et mystère* (*Furor and Mystery*), 1948; *Les Matinaux* (*The Dawn Breakers*), 1950. He also wrote some plays and a war journal, *Feuillets d'Hypnos* (*Hypnos Waking*), 1946. Char was preoccupied by the role of poetry and the poet in inspiring proper responses to the constantly changing human condition. He was much influenced by philosophy (he corresponded with Heidegger) and painting. His work was honoured by awards in France and abroad. He married twice, in 1933 (divorced 1949) and 1987. Died in Paris, 19 February 1988.

Edition

Oeuvres complètes, Paris: Gallimard, 1983

Translations

Selections of Poetry

Caws, Mary Ann and Jonathan Griffin, *Poems of René Char* (parallel texts), Princeton, New Jersey: Princeton University Press, 1976

Hartley, Anthony, in *The Penguin Book of French Verse*, vol. 4, edited by Hartley, Harmondsworth: Penguin, 1959; expanded edition, 1966; revised volume incorporating all four earlier volumes, 1975

Leary, Paris and Peter Hoy, *Blue Beacon*, Leicester: Toni Savage and Duine Campbell, 1967

Rees, William, in *French Poetry, 1820–1950, with Prose Translations*, translated by Rees, Harmondsworth and New York: Penguin, 1990

Poetry

Les Matinaux, 1950

Worton, Michael, *The Dawn Breakers / Les Matinaux* (parallel texts), with an introduction, Newcastle-upon-Tyne: Bloodaxe, 1992

René Char maintained his steady and substantial output of poetry right up until his death in 1988 and, sadly, his last two collections, *Les voisinages de Van Gogh* (1985) and *Éloge d'une soupçonnée* (1988), appeared too late for inclusion in the French Complete Works. Poems from these two works remain unavailable to English speakers without access to the French originals. However, the above selection of translations manages to cover all the phases of Char's work from the early *Arsenal* (1927–29) to *La Nuit talismanique* (1972) and other works from the 1970s, even if it is the poetry of the 1930s to the 1950s that has unsurprisingly received most attention.

One of the principal merits of the CAWS & GRIFFIN volume (1976) is just such a wide-ranging inclusivity, comprising the full corpus of Char's work available at that time. This is particularly gratifying, as this collection is perhaps the most generally recommendable of all those listed, albeit with several significant reservations. CAWS's translations of the earlier poems, such as those taken from *Le Marteau sans maître* (1934; rendered as *The Hammer with No Master*), display a pleasing simplicity and minimal inaccuracy or fussiness. These translations convey a sense of a certain Charian voice emerging into the English through an admirable lack of paraphrasing and an avoidance of both domestication and pretension. Caws generally respects both the layout and the punctuation of the original French (placed opposite as "parallel texts" throughout) and retains the feeling of necessity that typifies Char's best poetry, particularly the early, Surrealist works. However, when it comes to the later texts, Caws seems regrettably to indulge in a sort of "tidying up", as these translations are forced to conform to a doubly alien English classicism. For example, the poem "Les Inventeurs" contains the line: "Nous avons dit merci et les avons congédiés" which becomes "We said our thanks and bade them leave". This lack of responsiveness to the improvised banality of the French, couched in the "unliterary" perfect tense of speech, opens up a rhetorical gap between the reported act of speech which is the content of the line and the performative act of poetic speech formally conveying this – a gap repudiated by the French in favour of a spontaneous immediacy. Caws's reluctance in the later poems to capture the improvisatory and often violent nature of Char's tone paradoxically sometimes leads equally to bathetic disruption of the texts' cadences. The "... pèsent moins qu'un mort" of "Invitation" is translated as "...weigh less than a dead man", the last word undermining the rhythmic unity and "dying" force of the sonority of this line, when perhaps a more graphic and laconic word such as "corpse" rather than "dead man" would have preserved both violence and delicacy – qualities so typical of the Charian style. Similarly, GRIFFIN's rather less numerous translations do Char much the same disservice: the French is dressed up into well-mannered English, hesitations are elided and the rather Cubist syntax of works such as "Avec Braque, peut-être, on s'était dit..." ("With Braque We Used Perhaps to Say..."), which exploits a typically French stylistic abruptness, becomes completely lost in the English. One final reservation: the annotation of which the cover boasts is so sparse as to be virtually non-existent.

WORTON's (1992) translation of the complete text of *Les Matinaux* (1950) opens with a thorough and helpfully contextualizing introduction to Char and his work, although it can at times be a little rambling, even downright moralizing. These are generally impressive and reliable versions, if occasionally prone to slight flabbiness and a tendency to "padding-out" which overstates the causality within lines such as "À trop attendre / On perd sa foi" which becomes "Waiting too long / Makes one lose faith". There is often a resultant loss of emotional directness and elliptical beauty. Overall, Worton is rightly happy to retain Char's often consciously banal diction and grammar without producing pseudo-English renderings or displaying signs of the inevitable compromises that are inherent in the whole project of translation. This too is a well-presented "parallel text".

HARTLEY (1959) produces plain prose translations that make a notoriously difficult poet even more difficult, as they quite inelegantly display flatness of style while completely ignoring the layout of the original French, obliging the punctuation to carry too much weight. There is also evidence of a degree of literal-mindedness in word selection, which misses the dialectical impulses between banality and metaphysical speculation that words such as "maison" are made to bear; ironically this creates a (false) impression of poetic caprice. Hartley has space to translate only three poems, all taken from the collection *Fureur et mystère* (1948; *Furor and Mystery*). The successor to Hartley's book, that of REES (1990), is generally more recommendable: it is better presented and includes a more substantial, if of necessity still modest, selection of poems. These translations are perhaps also a little too innocuous on the whole, failing to convey much of the fragility and grace of the originals and equally displaying a common tendency to translate into a finely-wrought classical style that is rather too anodyne and homely to capture the foregrounded paradoxes of this complex poet.

In this view at least, LEARY & HOY's (1967) translation of a single poem "Blue Beacon" – the first part of "Les Trois sœurs", which opens *Le Poème pulvérisé* (1947; *The Pulverised Poem*), offers something radically different. This is an extremely free rendering that would perhaps be most advantageously read as a poem *inspired* by the original, from which it departs to the extent of virtual unrecognizability at times. However, it brilliantly reproduces the disruptive patterns of Charian syntax and presents suitably elliptical "flashes" of coherence, hovering between lightness and obscurity, in a very beautiful and moving way. Even if this single, short translation does little to respect the actual letter of Char's text it does immeasurably more than any other to convey its spirit. Finally, mention should also be made of Pierre Boulez's three settings of Char texts – *Le Visage nuptial, Le soleil des eaux* (incompletely) and *Le Marteau sans maître* – which equally have much to say about these works through "translations" into another creative medium not limited to French speakers alone.

PAUL RICKETT

Further Reading

Caws, Mary Ann, *The Presence of René Char*, Princeton, New Jersey: Princeton University Press, 1976

Cranston, Mechthild, *Orion Resurgent: René Char, Poet of Presence*, Madrid: Turanzas, 1979

La Charité, Virginia, *The Poetics and the Poetry of René Char*, Chapel Hill: University of North Carolina Press, 1968

Lawler, James R., *René Char: The Myth and the Poem*, Princeton, New Jersey: Princeton University Press, 1978

World Literature Today (1977): "Focus on René Char"

See also the translator's introduction to Worton

Chateaubriand 1768–1848

French novelist, memorialist, political journalist and diplomat

Biography

François-René, vicomte de Chateaubriand. Born in Saint-Malo, 4 September 1768, into an old Breton family. Chateaubriand spent most of his childhood at the family chateau of Combourg. He was educated at schools in Saint-Malo, Dol, Rennes and Dinan, 1777–84. He went into the army in 1786 but his military career was interrupted by the Revolution. He travelled extensively in North America in 1791. The next year he was wounded while serving in the forces of the emigré princes. Escaping to England, he earned a hard living from 1793 to 1800 in London and Suffolk, doing translations and teaching French, while writing works to be published later. In 1800 he returned to France. In 1803, after the success of his 1802 *Génie du Christianisme*, Napoleon appointed him secretary to the French embassy in Rome; he resigned 1804. He became hostile to Napoleon and made friends with the subversive Madame de Staël. He contributed articles to the *Mercure de France*, 1800–14. From 1806 to 1807 Chateaubriand travelled to Greece and the Near East, returning to live at his house near Paris and write. He was elected to the Académie-Française in 1811 and became a peer of France, 1815, ambassador to Berlin, 1821, and ambassador to London, 1822. He played an official part at the Congress of Verona, 1822, and in 1823 became a successful minister for Foreign Affairs.

After the July Revolution of 1830 Chateaubriand retired to his house in Paris and edited his memoirs for posthumous publication. In the course of his life he had numerous women friends, including Madame Récamier. He died in Paris, 4 July 1848, and was buried on an island near Saint-Malo; his wife, whom he married in 1792, had died the year before.

In a lyrical, picturesque style Chateaubriand established themes and moods that would characterize the Romantic movement: passion, melancholy, introspective reverie, religion, love of nature. The best-known of his many works are the novel *Atala* (*Atala*),1801; his apologia for Catholicism, *Le Génie du Christianisme* (*The Genius of Christianity*), 1802, which included the immensely famous novel *René* (*René*); the prose epic *Les Martyrs* (*The Martyrs*), 1809, a story of two Greek Christians under the Roman emperor Diocletian; and the monumental *Mémoires d'outre-tombe* (*Memoirs*), 1849–50.

Translations

Fiction

Atala, 1801

Anonymous, *Atala*, London: G. and J. Robinson, 1802

Bingham, Caleb, *Atala*, Boston: Caleb Bingham, 1802; edited by William Leonard Schwartz, Stanford, California: Stanford University Press, 1930

Gerard, *Atala, A Love Tale in Six Cantos of Verse*, London: Longmans Green, 1873

Harry, James Spence, *Atala*, illustrated by Gustave Doré, London: Cassell Petter and Galpin, 1867

Heppenstall, Rayner, *Atala and René*, London: Oxford University Press, 1963

Marshall, Richard, *Atala*, St Petersburg: Alexandre Pluchart, 1817

Putter, Irving, *Atala, René*, Berkeley: University of California Press, 1952

René, 1802

Anonymous, *René: A Tale*, London: T. Hamilton, 1813

Heppenstall, Rayner, *Atala and René*, London and New York: Oxford University Press, 1963

Putter, Irving, *Atala, René*, Berkeley: University of California Press, 1952

Les Aventures du dernier Abencérage, 1826

Anonymous, *Aben-Hamet, The Last of the Abencerages*, London: Treuttel and Würtz, Treuttel Junger, and Richter, 1826

Carter, H.W., *The Adventures of the Last Abencerrage*, London: William Freeman, 1870

Hill, Isabel, *The Last of the Abencerages*, London: Richard Bentley, 1835

Nuttall, Edith, *The Last Abencerage*, London: Arthur H. Stockwell, 1922

Other Writing

Le Génie du christianisme, 1802

O'Donnell, E., *Genius of Christianity; or, The Spirit and Beauties of the Christian Religion*, Paris: E. Thunot, 1854

Shoberl, Frederic, *The Beauties of Christianity*, 3 vols, London: Henry Colburn, 1813

Stork, Emma B., *The Spirit and Beauty of the Christian Religion*, Philadelphia: Lindsay and Blakiston, 1958

White, Charles I., *The Genius of Christianity; or, The Spirit and Beauty of the Christian Religion*, 2nd revised edition, Baltimore: John Murphy, 1856

Mémoires d'outre-tombe, 1849–50

Anonymous, *Memoirs of Chateaubriand Written by Himself*, London: Henry Colburn, 1848–49

Anonymous, *An Autobiography*, London: Simms and McIntyre, 1849

Baldick, Robert, *The Memoirs of Chateaubriand*, London: Hamish Hamilton, and New York: Knopf, 1961

Texeira de Mattos, Alexander, *The Memoirs of François-René, Vicomte de Chateaubriand*, 6 vols, London: Freemantle, 1902

Atala (1801), the work which won Chateaubriand a sudden reputation on his return from exile, quickly attracted the attention of a translator on each side of the Atlantic, whose versions were published within a year. The ANONYMOUS translator of *Atala from the French of Mr De Chateaubriant* (sic) (1802) declares that "The simplicity of this affecting story, and the lively interest kept up throughout, have induced me to think that a translation of it might be acceptable to the English reader". Nevertheless, it was considered "necessary to alter, suppress or soften some parts, which no doubt escaped the author in the warmth of composition". Though quite accessible, the English here presents the modern reader with a number of distracting archaisms, not least in the spelling. BINGHAM's *Atala* (1802) undoubtedly served as a benchmark for subsequent translations, and achieved a wider circulation through the Stanford University Press edition of 1930. Despite some awkward renderings, its strength remains in its fidelity to the original sense. The translator's preface to MARSHALL's *Atala* (1817) claims that it had been undertaken more than 12 years previously. "Just as it was compleated, and ready for publication in England, a translation by another person appeared". He continues, "To translate well is very difficult. Many of the beauties of the original vanish in translation. I have endeavoured to go hand in hand with my author, and to make him write as he would have done, if he had written in English". It is a clear and effective translation, and the style appears remarkably modern. HARRY's *Atala* (1867) tends to struggle with the more ornate elements of expression, but is generally thorough and competent. GERARD's *Atala, a Love Tale in Six Cantos of Verse* (1873) takes an unconventional form, though it enjoys a fair measure of success. It appears that its main purpose was recreational, the translator having produced it in "the few leisure moments of an occupied life". He admits to adding "a line or two ... in keeping with the local colour and not unsuited for the mouth of an Indian narrator", also "omitting the least necessary and characteristic detail". The foreword to PUTTER, *Atala, René* (1952), laments the unavailability of a translation since Bingham's went out of print, and this is the first 20th-century version. It combines fidelity to Chateaubriand's text with a resolutely modern style. HEPPENSTALL, *Atala and René* (1963), reads quite smoothly, though some curious renderings derive from the complexities of Chateaubriand's language.

Both *Atala* and *René* were included in *Le Génie du Christianisme* (1802), which brought Chateaubriand resounding fame. The ANONYMOUS *René, A Tale* (1813) was accompanied by a note deriving its motivation from "The favourable reception which [attended] the other productions of M. Chateaubriand, and the peculiar interest which is attached to everything that bears his name, hitherto ... unknown to English readers" and claiming to avoid " extremes of literal translation and redundant amplification". SHOBERL, *The Beauties of Christianity* (1813), is the work of the reputable translator of a number of Romantic authors and is secure and readable. During Chateaubriand's lifetime it remained the only major English version. O'DONNELL makes the following observation in the preface to his *Genius of Christianity; or, The Spirit and Beauties of the Christian Religion* (1854):

> To translate *Le Génie du Christianisme* into another language in a style equal to the original, is next to an impossibility. It is more than a presumption to attempt it, and more than vanity to expect it. The name of the Author inspires too much terror and veneration.

The translator's preface to WHITE, *The Genius of Christianity* (1856), finds fault with both Shoberl and O'Donnell, the former having "taken unwarranted liberties with the original ... omitting innumerable passages ... which gave the author's argument its peculiar force in favour of Catholicism", and in the case of the latter, "Nearly one half of the original production has been omitted, and the order of the contents has been entirely changed". Nevertheless, comparison with Shoberl shows only minor differences in certain common passages, indicating an unacknowledged debt. STORK, *The Spirit and Beauty of the Christian Religion* (1958), treats selections from the original text, and succeeds in conveying the majesty of Chateaubriand's style in modern language.

Les Aventures du dernier Abencérage (1826), a story of chivalry and fidelity set in 16th-century Spain, was first translated in the ANONYMOUS *Aben-Hamet, The Last of the Abencerages* (1826). Though it is a faithful rendering of the sense, this does not prevent Chateaubriand's distinctive style from reading rather oddly in English. HILL's *The Last of the Abencerages* (1835) is better, and often avoids problems by choosing a phrase that is simple and direct. Nevertheless, there remain some fairly awkward patches. Unlike the other three versions, which call the heroine Blanca, this retains the original name of Bianca. CARTER, *The Adventures of the last Abencerrage* (1870), is both clear and accessible. A comparative weakness is that it tends to understate the passionate complexity of certain major scenes, to the extent of making them appear almost dull. NUTTALL, *The Last Abencerage* (1922), restores the necessary fire and is a modern rendering that retains much of the spirit of the original.

The *Mémoires d'outre-tombe* (1849–50), Chateaubriand's memoirs intended for posthumous publication, would represent a lengthy task for the translator if taken in their entirety. The first two translations represent only a fraction of the whole. The ANONYMOUS *Memoirs of Chateaubriand Written by Himself* (1848–49) were "to be completed in 10 parts", but only three volumes were finished. The translator worked from the version "revised December 1846", and her/his work is efficient enough, though more would be needed to make it really useful. ANONYMOUS, *An Autobiography* (1849), consists of four volumes containing nearly half the work. Its selection offers a broader perspective of the whole, and the translation is adequate. A more complete translation is that by TEIXEIRA DE MATTOS, *The Memoirs of François-René, Vicomte de Chateaubriand* (1902), and we are told that the decision to undertake it came from a conversation with Pierre Louÿs. One wonders if it was under the guidance of the latter that the translator chose to omit certain passages which "seemed to contain a little too much of the *esprit gaulois* to prove acceptable to English taste", as well as sections dealing with Bonaparte's career and the Journey to Jerusalem. Sometimes the translator holds too close to the French sense, at the expense of the English, yet he claims "too great a respect for this great man to take liberties with his writing". BALDICK's *The Memoirs of Chateaubriand* (1961), later published by Penguin, is clear, accessible and efficient, conveying the writer's thoughts in the language of the later 20th century.

JOHN R. WHITTAKER

Further Reading

Barthes, Roland, "Chateaubriand: Life of Rancé" in his *New Critical Essays*, translated by Richard Howard, New York: Hill and Wang, 1980

Painter, George D., *Chateaubriand: A Biography*, vol. 1, London: Chatto and Windus, 1977; New York: Knopf, 1978

Sieburg, Friedrich, *Chateaubriand*, translated by Violet M. MacDonald, London: Allen and Unwin, 1961; New York: St Martin's Press, 1962

Smethurst, Colin, *Chateaubriand: Atala and René*, London: Grant and Cutler, 1995

Switzer, Richard, *Chateaubriand*, New York: Twayne, 1971

Geoffrey Chaucer c.1340/41–1400

English poet

Biography

Born in about 1340 or 1341 in London, the son of a vintner. After attending school, possibly in Southampton (1347–49), and later in London, he was page (1357–58) to the wife of the duke of Clarence. He fought for Edward III in France in 1359; in 1360, after being taken prisoner and ransomed, he returned to England and entered the service of the king. It is probable that at about this period he studied for a while at the Inner Temple in London and possible that he was also a student at Oxford University. In 1366 he married Philippa de Roet; with whom he probably had three children. She was a connection, later a sister-in-law, of Chaucer's lifelong patron John of Gaunt, duke of Lancaster and fourth son of Edward III. Between 1370 and 1378 Chaucer was sent on official missions to Italy, Flanders and France. In 1374 he was appointed a controller of customs in the port of London and took a house in Aldgate. A justice of the peace, 1385–88, he was elected knight of the shire for Kent in 1386. His fortunes then declined for a time, but with Henry Bolingbroke, son of his deceased patron, becoming Henry IV in 1399, he returned to favour. He died in London, 25 October 1400, and was buried in the part of Westminster Abbey known as Poets' Corner.

Chaucer produced many of his major poetic works (incorporating material borrowed or translated from many sources) between 1369 and 1387: *The Book of the Duchess*, written on the death of John of Gaunt's wife; *The Parliament of Fowls*, a dream poem; *The House of Fame*, another dream poem, this one unfinished; *Troilus and Criseyde*; the unfinished *Legend of Good Women*; and some of the *Canterbury Tales*. Chaucer's prose works include his translation of Boethius (*Boece*). The *Canterbury Tales* were completed about 1390.

One of the most important areas of Chaucerian scholarship is the study of Geoffrey Chaucer as a translator. A substantial portion of the Chaucer corpus consists in miscellaneous translations: fictional compilations, secular lyrics, religious translations, etc. That this should be so may come as a surprise to posterity, which critically acclaims him as the "father of English poetry". The reason for this lies in the contrast between the modern concept of translation (one common at least before the pre-linguistic, philological age) as servile reproduction of ideas and that of the term in its various broad, medieval senses. Against the backdrop of the 14th-century literary topoi and in the then current literary, cultural and philosophical milieux, Chaucer the writer is perceived to be largely synonymous with Chaucer the translator. And the various translation processes employed in the exercise of this Chaucerian poetic genius are characteristically creative, interpolative, interpretative, intensifying and transformative.

Chaucer was distinguished as a medieval translator into Middle English, extolled as "grand translateur, noble Geffroy Chaucier" by Eustache Deschamps. He was, however, rather selfconscious about his own translations. There are some that he describes as "my translacions and enditynges of worldly vanitees", e.g. the *Canterbury Tales*, *Troilus and Criseyde*, the *Parliament of Fowls*, the *House of Fame*, the *Legend of Good Women*, the *Book of the Duchess*. To counterbalance them, there are others that he ascribes to himself as works of "holynesse" or "besynesse", e.g. Boethius' *De Consolatione Philosophiae*, Origen "Upon the Maudeleyne", a life of St. Cecilia and pope Innocent III's *De contemptu mundi*.

The 14th century was an age of vernacular compilation, and translating, in its broad, medieval sense, was inseparable from compiling from various sources. Thus, his *Treatise on the Astrolabe* Chaucer characterizes as a "lewd compilation of the labour of olde astrologiens". His English verse translation of the story of Griselda in the *Clerk's Tale* is based on both Petrarch's Latin and an anonymous French prose rendering of Petrarch, *Le Livre Griseldis*. Much of the matter and many lines of the *Book of the Duchess* derive from French poetry and from Statius and Ovid. The *Troilus* is indebted to Boccaccio's Italian poem, the *Filostrato*, for many of its stanzaic verbal echoes. The *Parliament of Fowls* reproduces some of the actual phraseology and imagery of Cicero's *Somnium Scipionis* through Macrobius's commentary.

To the diversity of sources that Chaucer typically works from, the *Boece* bears witness. Chaucer creates, theoretically, his own sources by translating, or compiling from, the disparate aspects of the *Consolation* tradition – i.e. Nicholas Trevet's commentary on the *Consolatio*, Jean de Meung's French translation, and some of the so-called Remigian glosses, a textual procedure that he describes as creating from these "olde bokes" a "newe science". Sometimes, however, Chaucer does not like to draw our attention to the sources of some of his translations (e.g. "The Knight's Tale" or "The Man of Law's Tale").

To these various sources, Chaucer may, only rarely, remain steadfastly faithful, but more often he introduces his own extensive imaginative reworking and supplementing: e.g. interpolations, insertions and other distinctly Chaucerian touches. The resultant Chaucer inventory is thus a rich one. It consists of various forms of translations, ranging from fairly close translations (the *Boece* and the *Romaunt of the Rose*), through re-tellings ("The Physician's Tale"), amalgamations and abridgements ("The Parson's Tale"), to gross adaptations and compilations (the *Troilus* and the *Parliament*) and variations on the same theme, ("The Monk's Tale"). In Chaucer's hands, translation becomes a magic wand invariably producing an intensification, a "thickening" of the texture of language and idea. For example, whereas Boccaccio will use some "indescribability topos" (like saying how the Italian Troiolo is overcome by griefs), Chaucer will instead describe how the English Troilus is torn to pieces by his woe.

Other Chaucerian touches include extensive borrowings from classical poets and historical and literary sources. For instance, Chaucer is heavily indebted to Ovid: to the *Heroides* for some passages, to the *Ars Amatoria* and the *Remedia Amoris* for added allusions and amatory lore, and to the *Metamorphoses* for much of that texture of allusions to mythological figures. For narrative enrichment in the *Troilus*, Chaucer has evidently gone back beyond his main source, Boccaccio's *Il Filostrato*, to consult and appropriate material from the earlier versions of the story of Troilus in Benoît de Sainte-Maure's *Roman de Troie* and Guido de Columnis's *Historia Destructionis Troiae*. Chaucer has also gone, for some "historical" thickening of his narrative and details, to the Latin "Dares" of Joseph of Exeter, borrowing the descriptions of Diomede, Criseyde and Troilus, and to Benoît for the account of Hector's death, etc. Some of Chaucer's borrowings derive through indirect, or intermediate, literary sources: in the *Troilus* we find Boccaccio's echoes of Dante's *Vita Nuova* and of the *cantari*, popular romances.

From these freewheeling translation practices – augmenting and supplementing, etc. – arise several interesting observations. In his translation of the *Boece*, Chaucer used both Jean de Meung's French prose translation, for his direct source, and the Latin text (a copy of a late-medieval "vulgate" version of Boethius). Whenever in doubt about the accuracy and inordinate metrical freedom of Jean's translation, Chaucer would return to the Latin. Some of the charges of "mistakes" in understanding Latin brought against Chaucer are caused by misreadings in the Latin text he used. Other charges of "crudity and awkwardness" against him can perhaps be similarly excused. For the *Complaint of Venus*, Chaucer even transposes the sex of the speaker from male to female when he translates the first, fourth and fifth *balades* in Oton de Graunson or de Grandson's *Les cinq balades ensievans*. Chaucer's intervention in *sententia* matters, and in the original narrative sequence, will alter the thrusts and significance of the original works, through the manipulation of our perception biases as a result of so-called "phenomenological hermeneutics" (Ferster, 1985). Given the prevailing literary and cultural climate of the medieval period, which valued the *intentio auctoris* of ancient authors, Chaucer found insufficient vent for his unbounded poetic imagination. This tension was resolved in his conception of his own status as both a vernacular writer, "who is incapable of true poetic invention" (Machan, "Chaucer as Translator", 1989), and a translator compiling creatively from different sources, thus exercising his unique literary genius, and thereby reclaiming his denied authorial status.

RAYMOND S.C. LIE

Further Reading

Copeland, Rita, *Rhetoric, Hermeneutics, and Translation in the Middle Ages: Academic Traditions and Vernacular Texts*, Cambridge and New York: Cambridge University Press, 1991

Donner, Morton, "Derived Words in Chaucer's *Boece*: The Translator as Wordsmith", *Chaucer Review*, 18 (1984) pp. 187–203

Ellis, Roger (editor), *The Medieval Translator: The Theory and Practice of Translation in the Middle Ages*, Woodbridge, Suffolk: Brewer, 1989

Ellis, Roger and Ruth Evans (editors), *The Medieval Translator 4*, Exeter: University of Exeter Press, and Binghamton, New York: Medieval and Renaissance Texts and Studies, 1994

Ferster, Judith, *Chaucer on Interpretation*, Cambridge and New York: Cambridge University Press, 1985

Kendrick, Laura, "'The Canterbury Tales' in the Context of Contemporary Vernacular Translations and Compilations" in *The Ellesmere Chaucer: Essays in Interpretation*, edited by Martin Stevens and Daniel Woodward, San Marino, California: Huntingdon Library, 1995

Lipson, Carol, "'I n'am but a lewd compilator': Chaucer's 'Treatise on the *Astrolabe*' as Translation", *Neuphilologische Mitteilungen*, 84 (1983) pp. 192–200

Machan, Tim William, "Scribal Role, Authorial Intention, and Chaucer's Boece", *Chaucer Review*, 24/2 (1989) pp. 150–62

Machan, Tim William, "Chaucer as Translator" in *The Medieval Translator: The Theory and Practice of Translation in the Middle Ages*, edited by Roger Ellis, Woodbridge, Suffolk: Brewer, 1989

Martin, Carol A.N., "Mercurial Translation in 'The Book of the Duchess'", *Chaucer Review*, 28/2 (1993) pp. 95–116

Meier, Hans H., "Middle English Styles in Translation: The Case of Chaucer and Charles" in *So Meny People Longages and Tonges*, edited by Michael Benskin and M.L. Samuels, Edinburgh: Middle English Dialect Project, 1981, pp. 367–76

Minnis, A.J., *Medieval Theory of Authorship*, London: Scolar Press, 1984

Minnis, A.J., "'Glosynge is a glorious thyng' Chaucer at Work on the *Boece*" in *The Medieval Boethius: Studies in the Vernacular Translations of De Consolatione Philosophiae*, edited by Minnis, Cambridge: Brewer, 1987, pp. 106–24

Oizumi, Akio, "The Romance Vocabulary of Chaucer's Translation of Boethius's *De Consolatione Philosophiae*", *Jimbungaku*, 108 (1968) pp. 57–78; 109 (1969) pp. 64–95

Patterson, Lee, *Chaucer and the Subject of History*, London: Routledge, and Madison: University of Wisconsin Press, 1991

Reames, Sherry L., "The Sources of Chaucer's 'Second Nun's Tale'", *Modern Philology*, 76 (1978) pp. 111–35

Schwarz, Werner, "The Meaning of *Fidus Interpres* in Mediaeval Translation", *Journal of Theological Studies*, (1944) pp. 73–78

Shoaf, R.A., "Notes toward Chaucer's Poetics of Translation", *Studies in the Age of Chaucer*, 1 (1979) pp. 55–66

Thompson, N.S., *Chaucer, Boccaccio, and the Debate of Love: A Comparative Study of The Decameron and The Canterbury Tales*, Oxford: Clarendon Press, 1996

Windeatt, B.A., *Geoffrey Chaucer: Troilus and Criseyde*, London and New York: Longman, 1984

Anton Chekhov 1860–1904

Russian dramatist and short-story writer

Biography

Born in Taganrog, 29 January 1860, the son of a shopkeeper. He went to local schools in Taganrog from 1867 to 1879 and then studied at Moscow University Medical School, graduating in 1884. While he was at university, Chekhov wrote articles for humorous magazines. He worked as a doctor in Moscow from 1884 to 1892. He wrote for St Petersburg daily newspapers, including *Peterburgskaia gazeta*, from 1885, and his first book of stories, *Pestrye rasskazy* [Motley Stories] was published in 1886 to critical acclaim. He was awarded the Pushkin prize in 1888. From the late 1880s onwards he devoted himself to writing, practising as a doctor only intermittently. He travelled through Siberia to study conditions in the penal colony on the remote Sakhalin Island in 1890, and published the results of his research as *Ostrov Sakhalin* (*The Island: A Journey to Sakhalin*), 1895. During the great famine in Russia of 1891–92 Chekhov worked as a doctor and medical administrator. In 1892 he moved with his parents to a country estate at Melikhovo, about 50 miles south of Moscow. He continued to write comic sketches and more serious short stories for a number of magazines, and had also started (1886) to write for the stage. His play *Chaika* (*The Seagull*), was written in 1896 and became his first successful work for the theatre on its production by Stanislavsky with the Moscow Art Theatre. Chekhov contracted tuberculosis during the 1890s: after a severe lung haemorrhage in 1897 he built a home in the Crimean resort of Yalta, where he spent most of the rest of his life, apart from periods in the south of France and other European resorts, from 1899 onwards. During this last period of his life, although he continued to write short stories, Chekhov's literary energies were channelled principally into writing the major dramatic works on which his reputation largely rests. Chekhov was a member of the Russian Imperial Academy of Sciences from 1900 to 1902: he resigned from the Academy when his friend Maxim Gor'kii's membership was withdrawn for political reasons. In 1901 Chekhov married the actress Olga Knipper, who performed leading roles in his plays at the Moscow Art Theatre both before and after his death. Chekhov died in Badenweiler, Germany, 15 July 1904.

Chekhov is one of the most popular and influential Russian dramatists and short-story writers of the late 19th century, and a leading exponent of the Russian realist school of the period. His best known plays were written mostly towards the end of his life: *Chaika* (*The Seagull*), 1896; *Diadia Vanya* (*Uncle Vanya*), 1899; *Tri sestry* (*TheThree Sisters*), 1901; and *Vishnyovy sad* (*The Cherry Orchard*), 1904. Chekhov's most important short stories are "Lady with Lapdog", "The Bishop" and "Ward No. 6". His plays and later short stories, set in contemporary Russian society, are marked by their evocation of a lyrical atmosphere which seemingly effortlessly reveals deep and sympathetic characterizations, often portraying tragic and hopeless lives.

Translations

Collection

Hingley, Ronald, *The Oxford Chekhov*, 9 vols, Oxford: Oxford University Press, 1965–80 (vol. 1: *Short Plays*; vol. 2: *Platonov*, *Ivanov*, *The Seagull*; vol. 3: *Uncle Vanya*, *Three Sisters*, *The Cherry Orchard*, *The Wood-Demon*; vol. 4: *Stories, 1888–1889*; vol. 5: *Stories, 1889–1891*; vol. 6: *Stories, 1892–1893*; vol. 7: *Stories 1893–1895*; vol. 8: *Stories, 1895–1897*; vol. 9: *Stories, 1898–1904*

Selections of Short Stories

Constantine, Peter, *The Undiscovered Chekhov: Thirty-Eight New Stories*, New York: Seven Stories Press, 1999 (contains "Sarah Bernhardt Comes to Town", "On the Train", "The Trial", "Confession; or, Olya, Zhenya, Zoya: A Letter", "Village Doctors", "An Unsuccessful Visit", "A Hypnotic Séance", "The Cross", "The Cat", "How I Came to be Lawfully Wed", "From the Diary of an Assistant Bookkeeper", "A Fool; or, The Retired Sea Captain: A Scene from an Unwritten Vaudeville Play", "In Autumn", "The Grateful German", "A Sign of the Times", "From the Diary of a Young Girl", "The Stationmaster", "A Woman's Revenge", "O Women, Women!", "Two Letters", "To Speak or Be Silent: A Tale", "After the Fair", "At the Pharmacy", "On Mortality: A Carnival Tale", "A Serious Step", "The Good German", "first Aid", "Intrigues", "This and That: Four Vignettes", "Elements Most Often Found in Novels, Short Stories, etc.", "Questions Posed by a Mad Mathematician", "America in Rostov and on the Don", "Mr Gulevitch, Writer, and the Drowned Man", "The Potato and the Tenor", "Mayonnaise", "At a Patient's Bedside", "My Love", "A Glossary of Terms for Young Ladies")

Dunnigan, Ann, *Selected Stories*, with a foreword by Ernest J. Simmons, New York: New American Library, 1960

Dunnigan Ann, *Anton Chekhov: Ward Six and Other Stories*, with an afterword by Rufus W. Mathewson, New York: New American Library, 1965 (contains "Ward Six", "The Duel", "A Dull Story", "My Life", "The Name-Day Party", "In the Ravine")

Fell, Marian, *Stories of Russian Life*, London: Duckworth, 1914; New York: Scribner, 1915

Fell, Marian, *Russian Silhouettes: More Stories of Russian Life*, London: Duckworth, and New York: Scribner, 1915 (contains *Stories of Childhood*: "The Boys", "Grisha", "A Trifle from Real Life", "The Cook's Wedding", "Shrove Tuesday", "In Passion Week", "An Incident", "A Matter of Classics", "The Tutor", "Out of Sorts", *Stories of Youth*: "A Joke", "After the Theatre", "Volodia", "A Naughty Boy", "Bliss", "Two Beautiful Girls", *Light and Shadow*: "The Chorus Girl", "The Father of a Family", "The Orator", "Ioniten", "At Christmas Time", "In the Coach House", "Lady N...'s Story", "A Journey by Cart", "The Privy Councillor", "Rothschild's Fiddle", "A Horsey Name", "The Petcheneg", "The Bishop")

Garnett, Constance, *The Tales of Tchehov*, 13 vols, London:

Chatto and Windus, 1916–23; selection, as *The Chekhov Omnibus: Selected Stories*, revised, and with an introduction by Donald Rayfield, London: Dent, 1994

Hinchliffe, Arnold, *The Sinner from Toledo and Other Stories*, Rutherford, New Jersey: Fairleigh Dickinson University Press, 1972

Hinchliffe, Arnold, *Anton Chekhov: The Crooked Mirror and Other Stories*, New York: Kensington, 1992

Magarshack, David, *Lady with Lapdog and Other Stories*, with an introduction, Harmondsworth and Baltimore: Penguin, 1964 (contains "Grief", "Agafya", "Misfortune", "A Boring Story", "The Grasshopper", "Ward 6", "Ariadne", "The House with an Attic", "Ionych", "The Darling", "Lady with Lapdog")

Makanowitzky, Barbara, *Seven Short Novels*, with an introduction by Gleb Struve, New York: Bantam, 1963 (contains "The Duel", "Ward No. 6", "A Woman's Kingdom", "Three Years", "My Life (The Story of a Provincial)", "Peasants", "In the Ravine")

Miles, Patrick and Harvey Pitcher, *Chekhov: The Early Stories, 1883–1888*, London: John Murray, 1982; New York: Macmillan, 1983

Payne, Robert, *The Image of Chekhov: Forty Stories in the Order in Which They Were Written*, with an introduction, New York: Knopf, 1963, reprinted as *Forty Stories*, New York: Vintage, 1991

Ross, Paula P., *Stories of Women*, Amherst, New York: Prometheus, 1994 (12 of the stories never before translated)

Ross, Paula, P., *Stories of Men: Anton Chekhov*, Amherst, New York: Prometheus, 1997 (13 of the stories never before translated)

Wilks, Ronald, *The Kiss and Other Stories*, with an introduction, Harmondsworth and New York: Penguin, 1982 (contains "The Kiss", "Peasants", "The Bishop", "The Russian Master", "Man in a Case", "Gooseberries", "Concerning Love", "A Case History", "In the Gully", "Anna round the Neck")

Wilks, Ronald, *The Duel and Other Stories*, with an introduction, Harmondsworth and New York: Penguin, 1984 (contains "The Duel", "My Wife", "Murder", "The Black Monk", "Terror", "The Two Volodyas")

Wilks, Ronald, *The Party and Other Stories*, with an introduction, Harmondsworth and New York: Penguin, 1985 (contains "The Party", "A Woman's Kingdom", "My Life", "An Unpleasant Business", "A Nervous Breakdown")

Wilks, Ronald, *The Fiancée and Other Stories*, with an introduction, Harmondsworth and New York: Penguin, 1986 (contains "The Fiancée", "On Official Business", "Rothschild's Fiddle", "Peasant Women", "Three Years", "With Friends", "The Bet", "New Villa", "At a Country House", "Beauties", "His Wife", "The Student")

Selections of Plays

Dunnigan, Ann, *Chekhov: The Major Plays*, New York: New American Library, 1964 (contains *Ivanov*, *The Sea Gull*, *Uncle Vanya*, *The Three Sisters*, *The Cherry Orchard*)

Fell, Marian, *Plays*, with an introduction, New York: Scribner, and London: Duckworth, 1912 (contains *Uncle Vanya*, *Ivanoff*, *The Sea-Gull*, *The Swan Song*)

Fen, Elisaveta, *Three Plays*, with an introduction, Harmondsworth: Penguin, 1951 (contains *The Cherry Orchard*, *Three Sisters*, *Ivanov*)

Frayn, Michael, *Chekhov: Plays*, with an introduction, London and New York: Methuen, 1988 (contains *The Evils of Tobacco*, *Swan Song*, *The Bear*, *The Proposal*, *The Seagull*, *Uncle Vanya*, *Three Sisters*, *The Cherry Orchard*)

Gans, Sharon and, Jordan Charney, *A Chekhov Concert: Duets and Arias from the Major Plays of Anton Chekhov*, conceived and composed by Gans and Charney, from a literal translation by Erika Warmbrunn, New York: Applause, 1997

Garnett, Constance, *The Plays of Tchehov*, 2 vols, London: Chatto and Windus, 1922–23; New York: Selzer, 1924

Hulick, Betsy, *Uncle Vanya and Other Plays*, New York: Bantam, 1994 (contains *The Seagull*, *Uncle Vanya*, *The Three Sisters*, *The Cherry Orchard*, *The Anniversary*, *The Bear*, *The Proposal*)

Magarshack, David, *Four Plays*, London: Allen and Unwin, and New York: Hill and Wang, 1969 (contains *The Seagull*, *Uncle Vanya*, *The Three Sisters*, *The Cherry Orchard*)

Rocamora, Carol, *Chekhov: Four Plays*, Lyme, New Hampshire: Smith and Kraus, 1996 (contains *The Seagull*, *Uncle Vanya*, *The Three Sisters*, *The Cherry Orchard*)

Schmidt, Paul, *The Plays of Anton Chekhov*, New York: HarperCollins, 1997 (contains *Swan Song*, *The Bear*, *The Proposal*, *Ivanov*, *The Seagull*, *A Reluctant Tragic Hero*, *The Wedding Reception*, *The Festivities*, *Uncle Vanya*, *Three Sisters*, *The Dangers of Tobacco*, *The Cherry Orchard*)

van Itallie, Jean-Claude, *Chekhov: The Major Plays*, New York: Applause, 1995

Plays

Platonov [untitled by Chekhov, generally known under this title], 1923 (written c.1881–83)

Anonymous [Dmitri Makaroff], *Platonov: An Abridged Version of an Untitled Play in 4 Acts*, with an introduction by George Devine, London: Methuen, 1961

Cournos, John, *That Worthless Fellow Platonov*, London and Toronto: Dent, and New York: Dutton, 1930

Frayn, Michael, *Wild Honey: The Untitled Play*, London and New York: French, 1984

Griffiths, Trevor, *Piano: A New Play for the Theatre Based on the film "Unfinished Piece for a Mechanical Piano"* by A. Adabashyan and N. Mikhalkov [based on *Platonov*], London and Boston: Faber, 1990

Magarshack, David, *Platonov: A Play in Four Acts and Five Scenes*. London: Faber, and New York: Hill and Wang, 1964

Ivanov, 1887

Covan, Jenny and Marian Fell, *Ivanov*, London: Brentano's, 1924 (Moscow Art Theatre Series of Russian Plays)

Gielgud, John, *Ivanov*, based on the translation by Ariadne Nicolaeff, London: Heinemann, and New York: Theater Arts, 1966

Hare, David, *Ivanov: A Play in Four Acts*, London: Methuen, 1997

Harwood, Ronald, *Ivanov*, Charlbury, Oxfordshire: Amber Lane Press, 1989

Leshii, 1890, produced 1889

Hingley, Ronald, *The Wood Demon* in *Uncle Vanya, The*

Cherry Orchard and The Wood Demon, translated by Hingley, London and New York: Oxford University Press, 1974

Koteliansky, S.S., *The Wood Demon: A Comedy in Four Acts*, London: Chatto and Windus, and New York: Macmillan, 1926

Chaika, 1896, produced 1897

Frayn, Michael, *The Seagull*, London and New York: Methuen, 1986

Gems, Pam, *The Seagull*, London: Royal National Theatre / Nick Hern, 1994

Kilroy, Thomas, *The Seagull: After Chekhov*, with an introduction, Oldcastle, Co. Meath: Gallery, 1981

Mulrine, Stephen, *The Seagull*, with an introduction, London: Nick Hern, 1997

Diadia Vania, 1897, produced 1899

Frayn, Michael, *Uncle Vanya*, London and New York: Methuen London, 1987

Gems, Pam, *Uncle Vanya*, London: Nick Hern, 1992

Guthrie, Tyrone and Leonid Kipnis, *Uncle Vanya*, Minneapolis: University of Minnesota Press, 1969

Lan, David, *Uncle Vanya: A New Version*, from a literal translation by Helen Rappaport, London: Methuen, 1998

Mamet, David, *Uncle Vanya*, adapted from a literal translation by Vlada Chernomordik, New York: Grove Press, 1989

Mitchell, Julian, *August*, from a translation by Tania Alexander, Charlbury, Oxfordshire: Amber Lane Press, 1994 (script of the film adaptation of *Uncle Vanya*, directed by Anthony Hopkins)

Mulrine, Stephen, *Uncle Vanya*, with an introduction, London: Nick Hern, 1999

Tri sestry, 1901

Frayn, Michael, *Three Sisters*, London: Methuen, 1983

Friel, Brian, *Anton Chekhov's Three Sisters: A Translation*, Dublin: Gallery Press, 1981; reprinted as *Three Sisters: A Translation of the Play by Anton Chekhov*, Oldcastle, Co. Meath: Gallery, 1992

Guthrie, Tyrone and Leonid Kipnis, *The Three Sisters*, New York: Avon, 1965

McGuinness, Frank, *Three Sisters*, from a literal translation by Rose Cullen, London: Faber, 1990

Mamet, David, *The Three Sisters*, adapted from a literal translation by Vlada Chernomordik, New York: Grove Weidenfeld, 1990

Mulrine, Stephen, *Three Sisters*, London: Nick Hern, 1994

Vishnevyi sad, 1903, produced 1904

Frayn, Michael, *The Cherry Orchard*, London: Eyre Methuen, 1978

Gems, Pam, *The Cherry Orchard*, from a literal translation by Tania Alexander, Cambridge: Cambridge University Press, 1996

Gill, Peter, *The Cherry Orchard*, from a literal translation by Ted Braun, London: Oberon, 1995

Griffiths, Trevor, *The Cherry Orchard: A New English Version*, from a translation by Helen Rappaport, London: Pluto Press, 1978

Guthrie, Tyrone and Leonid Kipnis, *The Cherry Orchard*, Minneapolis: University of Minnesota Press, 1965

Lan, David, *The Cherry Orchard*, from a new literal translation by Helen Rappaport, forthcoming

Mamet, David, *The Cherry Orchard*, with an introduction, adapted from a literal translation by Peter Nelles, New York: Grove Press, 1987

Mulrine, Stephen, *The Cherry Orchard*, with an introduction, London: Nick Hern, 1998

Letters and Notebooks

Benedetti, Jean, *Dear Writer, Dear Actress: The Love Letters of Anton Chekhov and Olga Knipper*, London: Methuen, 1996; Hopewell, New Jersey: Ecco Press, 1997

Friedland, Louis S., *Letters on the Short Story, the Drama and Other Literary Topics*, New York: Minton Blach, 1924

Garnett, Constance, *Letters of Anton Tchehov to His Family and Friends*, London: Chatto and Windus, and New York: Macmillan, 1920

Garnett, Constance, *Letters of Anton Pavlovitch Tchehov to Olga Leonardovna Knipper*, New York: Doran, 1924; London: Chatto and Windus, 1926

Heim, Michael Henry, with Simon Karlinsky, *Letters of Anton Chekhov*, New York: Harper and Row, 1973; reprinted as *Anton Chekhov's Life and Thought: Selected Letters and Commentary*, Evanston, Illinois: Northwestern University Press, 1997

Koteliansky, S.S. and Leonard Woolf, *The Note-Books of Anton Tchekhov, Together with Reminiscences of Tchekhov by Maxim Gorky*, London: Hogarth Press, 1921; as *Note-Book of Anton Chekhov*, New York: Huebsch, 1921

Koteliansky, S.S. and Philip Tomlinson, *The Life and Letters of Anton Tchekhov*, New York: Doran, 1925; London: Cassell, 1928

Lederer, Sidonie, *The Selected Letters of Anton Chekhov*, edited by Lillian Hellman, New York: Farrar Straus, 1955

McVay, Gordon, *Chekhov: A Life in Letters*, London: Folio Society, 1994

Yarmolinsky, Avrahm *et al.*, *Letters of Anton Chekhov*, New York: Viking Press, 1973

Son of a shopkeeper and grandson of a serf, well-educated, doctor by profession, incomparable observer and compulsive traveller, a man of widest interests and profound yet totally unsentimental sympathies – more than any other Russian writer Chekhov has continuously appealed to readers and theater audiences around the world. Tolstoi compared Chekhov's literary art to Impressionist painting; the analogy goes far to explain his popularity. The general reader no less than the sophisticated critic cannot fail to be captivated by Chekhov's economic, suggestive, and convincing use of ordinary detail and ordinary speech. Joined to this supreme realism is the inimitable Chekhovian sensibility, a fusion of pessimism and tolerance, love of humanity, and recognition of the hopelessness of the human condition.

Although Chekhov's plays are a mainstay of the Russian theater to this day, in Russia he tends to be even more loved for his stories; elsewhere, it is the playwright who is more in the public eye. To meet and satisfy the changing demands of producers and theatergoers, Chekhov's plays keep being adapted, sometimes very freely and occasionally almost past recognition.

Translations of Chekhov's works "have been published so

profusely as to make an attempt at a systematic, complete bibliography meaningless" (Leighton). The small selection reviewed here has been influenced by availability.

Opinions on Chekhov's translatability range from:

> To translate Chekhov adequately, one should have a vast knowledge of church ritual, the social customs of the 19th century, the dialects of Moscow and half a dozen other towns in Russia. Ideally, he should be translated by a group of churchmen, sociologists, and experts on dialect, but they would quarrel interminably and the translation would never be done. (Payne)

to

> Chekhov's art is almost always highly structured, requiring, for a full understanding, a response to the way detail is organized in an overall pattern ... These formal properties ... survive translation intact ... Secondly, the prevalence of simile rather than metaphor in the language of the original means that poetic effects ... are more easily and readily translatable ... (Hahn).

Generally speaking, compared to some other Russian authors (for instance, the virtually untranslatable Leskov or Ostrovskii) Chekhov is relatively easy to turn into English, especially since his characters and situations, although rooted in their native soil, are universal and carry the translation.

Renderings of Chekhov's plays outnumber those of the stories, but they are more problematic. To be stageworthy, translations of plays have to be frequently updated, if not completely redone, so as to speak to the audience in a language they recognize as their own idiom. The stories (and the plays when merely read) can more easily tolerate a noticeable aura of a very different time and place. Critical opinions pertaining to translations of stories address themselves to the reliability and readability of Chekhov in English, while reviews of translated plays often reflect only upon their excellence or shortcomings as theater in English, rather than as Russian works made available to a non-Russian public.

In addition to stories and plays, Chekhov's letters too have attracted a large number of translators. Chekhov was a remarkable writer even in his voluminous private correspondence, which is interesting in itself (it brings us closer to this complex but highly amiable man) and also gives insight into the Russia of his time, the countries he visited, and the contemporary literary and theatrical issues. Since no reliably complete edition of the letters is available in Russian, any translator of this material must contend not only with the difficulties of the Russian language, of private idiom, and of selection, but also with frequently daunting problems of textual criticism.

Collected Works

HINGLEY's heroic undertaking (1965–80) in translating the complete mature works of Chekhov is not as satisfactory as one would want it to be. This is a work of a painstaking scholar; the title of each piece is followed by the original Russian title, and all variants and early drafts are translated. Each volume contains in its bibliography a section on "Translations into English of the ... [works] in this volume" – a huge undertaking in itself. Yet despite being a talented writer, Hingley can irritate by his excessive use of British idiom and his tendency to anglicize at every opportunity. This practise extends to Chekhov's Russian onomastics, with the translator employing English counterparts of Russian names, omitting patronymics and simplifying or dispensing with nicknames and diminutives, and the like. What is perhaps even worse, Hingley sometimes tends to edit the great stylist Chekhov. For instance, he changes the wonderfully spontaneous *bessmertie liudei* into formulaic "eternal life", while *govorili drug drugu nepriiatnosti* loses the characteristically Chekhovian concern with pettiness when it becomes "abused each other" ("The Black Monk").

Short Stories

Numerous translations of selected Chekhov stories have been published on both sides of the Atlantic, and in some cases reissued many times, since the second decade of the 20th century.

FELL (1914, 1915) is a good example of a bad translator. She is included here for contrast with her contemporary Garnett. The way Fell treats her material (even extending to the titles of stories) shows that she regards it as quaintly alien rather than universally human.

Opinions on GARNETT (stories, 1916–23; plays 1922–23; letters 1920, 1924) are divided. She often misses Chekhov's humor and allusiveness, yet indisputably she played a capital role in introducing practically all the important Russian writers to English-speaking countries. She reveals love and respect for her material, and most of her translations read quite well. Compared to other early translators of Russian, she stands out. "Despite occasional misreadings she manages to convey both the tone ... with ... resourcefulness and fidelity ... " (Heim, about her translation of Chekhov's letters). A good example of this resourcefulness at work when she is dealing with dialogue is "You're such a sweet pet ... You're such a pretty dear!" – admirable use of English idiom to catch *Kakoi ty u menia slavnen'kii...Kakoi ty u menia khoroshen'kii!* ("The Darling"). Her versions of Chekhov have never gone out of print and have been recently reissued once more, by the Ecco Press, Hopewell, New Jersey. She has "attained something of the status of an English classic" (Hahn). Still, a reader can do better than limit him/herself to Garnett; Dunnigan, Magarshack, Payne and Wilks are preferable, but none of them covers as much territory.

DUNNIGAN (1960, 1965), sometimes accused of blandness, is faithful to the text of the stories. She makes sensible choices and steers admirably clear of translating colloquialisms with slang. She succeeds in rendering many typically Russian expressions appropriately and convincingly.

The title of MAKANOWITZKY (1963) takes one aback – did Chekhov write novels? He did not; this is a selection of his longer stories, such as "Peasants" and "The Duel". The translation is frequently awkward – one is uncomfortably aware of reading a translation (for instance, "he fell with a tray of ham and green peas" is grotesque and betrays Chekhov's expressive simplicity).

MAGARSHACK (1964) is a master translator. Accused of pedantry by some, he is yet remarkably inventive, understands Russian better than any other translator covered here, and writes a natural, simple, and direct English. Thus – to draw an example from his version of *The Cherry Orchard* – when Pishchik uses a proverb (*Kak govoritsia, popal v staiu, lai ne lai, a khvostom viliai*), Magarshack uses appropriately short words and simple idiom and even achieves an illusion of rhyme "as the saying goes, if you're one of a pack, wag your tail, whether you bark or not").

HINCHLIFFE (1972, 1992) is valuable because he offers some very early stories otherwise unavailable in English.

MILES & PITCHER (1982) strive to make Chekhov understandable to the modern English-speaker. This translation is relatively free, with uneven results, but readable.

By contrast, PAYNE (1963) says in his introduction that "to modernize [Chekhov] ... is to destroy him completely". Payne shows sensitivity and intelligence in this important, excellent translation, although he sometimes takes liberties with the material in amplifying it.

WILKS (1982, 1984, 1985, 1986) is one of the best translators of Chekhov. His versions of selected stories are very readable, occasionally pedestrian perhaps; but they do avoid the dangerous extremes of misrepresentation and oddness. One can hardly do better than to give these Penguins to anyone who wants to do some really good reading.

ROSS's versions (1994, 1997) are typically academic: they err on the side of literalness. The earlier collection "focuses on the plight of women"; the later "focuses on the peculiar existence of the Russian male". Both volumes obviously grow out of the present trend towards Gender Studies.

Plays

FELL's translations of the plays (1912) show how much matters have improved over time. They are full of errors and sound unnatural but are of some historical importance.

A vigorous defence of GARNETT's work can be found in Hahn's book. Garnett's translations of the plays (1922–23) are certainly serviceable despite mistakes and frequent awkwardness, and many readers are devoted to them.

FEN's translation (1951) can be considered superseded. It is plodding and yet not faithful: she tends to cut the text without any warning or indication.

DUNNIGAN (1964) has a tendency to be too literal. On the whole, however, she is very good, and what is said above about her translations of Chekhov's stories applies here to the plays as well.

GUTHRIE & KIPNIS (1965, 1965, 1969) collaborated on these versions meant for, and much used in, performance. Not the best translations, they are effective on stage.

MAGARSHACK (1969) can scarcely be improved upon for the plays as for the stories. His and SCHMIDT's (1997) are probably the best translations for reading and studying the plays; Schmidt may have an edge on Magarshack so far as actability goes. ROCAMORA (1996) is another good choice.

MAMET's adaptations (*The Cherry Orchard*, 1987; *Uncle Vanya*, 1989; *The Three Sisters*, 1990) are vivid and demonstrate some good decisions in linguistic and stylistic matters. Still, this is not Chekhov. A fashionable playwright recreates the classic in his own image, and the result is bald and bare, with most of the Chekhovian penumbral suggestiveness gone. There are too many omissions, too many additions. Already in his introduction to *The Cherry Orchard* he adopts a superior attitude: "Why, *Hell*. If I wanted to save *my* cherry orchard and *my* adopted daughter was in love ... " To support his interpretation of the play he puts sexual allusions where they do not appear in the original (thus Charlotta says both her parents died, and then a German lady took care of her; Mamet makes her say "Mama died. My father met a certain German lady who taught me"), etc.

HULICK (1994) is idiomatic and actable, but surpassed in both regards by some of the others.

Although VAN ITALLIE's versions (1995) are frequently performed, he cannot be the choice of anyone who seeks to get close to Chekhov. He takes as many liberties with the text as Mamet, yet with less overall harm. He adds and omits, and all the characters sound the same. Still, we feel we are dealing with Chekhov.

The aim in ROCAMORA's *Four Plays* (1996) is "to preserve the poetry and music of the language ... to preserve the period flavour of the language". She succeeds to a notable extent. Her versions are readable and actable, precise and lively.

The collaboration between GANS & CHARNEY (1997) is an oddity. It consists of excerpts from the major plays, with additional material taken from Chekhov's stories and letters. The whole "tapestry" is arranged thematically. The translation is indifferent, but the piece has a strangely moving effect and has been very successful in production in the US.

Reviewers commended SCHMIDT (1997) for arriving at "the gold standard in Russian-English translation" and pointed out that "slang and modern idiom are woven almost seamlessly into the script". This is an outstanding version, both in accuracy and in actability. An additional advantage is that Schmidt includes 12 of Chekhov's 16 plays; the minor works make our experience of the four great plays richer and deeper. (Before publishing this volume, Schmidt had for a long time been providing literal translations for notable adapters such as Randall Jarrell in *The Three Sisters*, New York: Macmillan, 1969.)

Over the last 30 years, the extraordinary and universal appeal of Chekhov and the versatility of his grammatically simple yet highly subtle texts has tempted many English-speaking playwrights in Britain and Ireland to attempt new "versions" not only of the four great plays (*The Seagull*, *Uncle Vanya*, *Three Sisters*, *The Cherry Orchard*) but also of Chekhov's three acknowledged failures (*Platonov*, *Ivanov*, *The Wood Demon*). With many of the long-standing translations of Chekhov's plays seeming increasingly stilted and unplayable at a time when the British subsidized theatre was hungry for new interpretations of old texts, the trend was probably sparked off with Edward Bond's new version of *Three Sisters* at the Royal Court in the late 1960s (a controversial production which starred the pop singer Marianne Faithfull). Since then playwrights such as Trevor GRIFFITHS (1978, 1990), Pam GEMS (1992, 1994, 1996), Brian FRIEL (1981), Frank MCGUINNESS (1990), Peter GILL (1995), Thomas KILROY (1981) and David LAN (1998) have produced often stimulating and frequently revelatory readings of the plays, in all cases thanks to the services of literal translators. But this is to list only the cream of the new translations staged over the last 30 years; many more new versions of Chekhov's plays have been undertaken, but remain unpublished, and their translators little known.

Michael FRAYN, a playwright who during his long association with the National Theatre has done so much to bring refreshing new Chekhov translations to a modern-day audience, is alone among his UK contemporaries in actually translating Chekhov himself, having learnt Russian during his time in the army doing National Service.

A more academic and straightforward approach to Chekhov's plays has been continued with the scholarly work of translator Stephen **Mulrine**, who has maintained the tradition of producing solid texts, suitable for A-level and other students, where the old stalwarts, Garnett (1920s), Elisaveta Fen (1950s), Magarshack and Hingley (1960s), left off.

As such, however, the British passion for "new versions" of Chekhov's plays continues unabated. Despite the inevitable translation problems associated with the specific Russian social and historical context, English-speaking playwrights have been drawn to the idea of investing the original Russian texts with their own contemporary cultural responses. Irish playwrights in particular have reflected a growing trend towards transplanting Chekhov's plays to a different environment and in so doing lending them new linguistic resonances. Brian FRIEL, Thomas KILROY, and Frank MCGUINNESS have all offered their own particular "Irish take" on Chekhov, with Kilroy in particular producing (1981) an overtly Irish version of *The Seagull*. The trend, or some might more pejoratively say, fashion, was taken further in 1994 with Michael Blakemore's film adaptation of *Uncle Vanya*, set on a sheep-station in the Australian outback; in 1996 Julian Mitchell produced a film adaptation of *Vanya*, set by director Anthony Hopkins in Wales.

In 1999–2000 Janet Suzman was touring a version of *The Cherry Orchard* transposed to modern-day South Africa. Such free departures from the original inevitably add fuel to the growing debate over the divide between legitimate play "translation" and the production (often by writers and directors unfamiliar with the source-language) of much freer "versions". It also underlines the moral and artistic issue at the root of all play translation: to what extent does a dramatist have the right, if any, to "hijack" the work of someone writing in another language? And while successful stage productions of Chekhov ride on the name of the director and/or playwright who have set their stamp on them, it is also too often the case that the role of the literal translator involved in bringing Chekhov's language to them in the first place is sadly under-appreciated.

Letters and Notebooks

GARNETT's translations of Chekhov's letters (1920, 1924) read well but are unreliable because of numerous omissions and abridgements.

KOTELIANSKY & TOMLINSON (1925) offer a large selection arranged chronologically, with some of the letters abridged. The translation is much too literal and quite lifeless.

KOTELIANSKY & WOOLF's volume (1921) "consists of notes, themes, and sketches for works which Anton Chekhov intended to write, and are characteristic of the methods of his artistic production". This is absorbing reading not elsewhere available in translation, and most valuable for anyone interested in the author.

FRIEDLAND (1924) is disappointing. The letters are not included in their entirety, and the resulting extracts are often close to incomprehensible. The commentary is not much help.

LEDERER's selection (1955) is quite slim by comparison with the others. The translation is imprecise and uses cuts injudiciously; yet it reads well and is currently more widely available than other versions of Chekhov's letters (aside from Benedetti).

HEIM's selection from the correspondence (1973) gives a good picture of Chekhov. It is arranged chronologically under chapter headings that indicate milestones in the author's life. There are good introductions and explanatory footnotes.

YARMOLINSKY (1973) has helpful footnotes but, as is true of most collections of Chekhov's letters, here too the text is chopped up so that the reader can sometimes form no clear idea of what is being communicated. The presence of several translators makes for unevenness of style.

MCVAY's selection (1994), generally of high quality, is difficult to obtain, being an exclusive offering of a book club.

BENEDETTI's entrancing edition (1996) of Chekhov's correspondence with Olga Knipper uses "linking passages" derived from Knipper's *Memoir* and at the same time omits material not pertinent to the development and vicissitudes of their relationship. Unlike other translations, which include only letters written by Chekhov himself, Benedetti's selection reveals the interplay and the reciprocity of their love and marriage. The translation is utterly natural and does not read like one.

ZOJA PAVLOVSKIS-PETIT and HELEN RAPPAPORT

Further Reading

Bristow, E.K., "On Translating Chekhov", *Quarterly Journal of Speech*, 52 (1966) pp. 290–94

Hahn, Beverly, "A Note on Translations" in her *Chekhov: A Study of the Major Stories and Plays*, Cambridge and New York: Cambridge University Press, 1977, pp. ix–xiii

Leighton, Lauren G., "Chekhov in English" in *A Chekhov Companion*, edited by Toby W. Clyman, Westport, Connecticut: Greenwood Press, 1985, pp 291–309

Rayfield, Donald, *Anton Chekhov: A Life*, London: HarperCollins, 1997; New York: Holt, 1998

Sendich, Munir, "Anton Chekhov in English: A Comprehensive Bibliography of Works about and by Him (1889–1984)" in *Anton Chekhov Rediscovered: A Collection of New Studies with a Comprehensive Bibliography*, edited by Savely Senderovich and Munir Sendich, East Lansing, Michigan: Russian Language Journal, 1987, pp. 189–340

Worrall, Nick, *The File on Chekhov* , London: Methuen, 1986 (includes lists of all the English translations of Chekhov's plays to date of publication, as well as listing seminal productions both in London and on the Continent and quoting from contemporary reviews)

See also Frayn's "Note on the Translation" in his *Chekhov: Plays*, 1988, for a discussion of the particular difficulties of translating Chekhov for an English-speaking audience

Chikamatsu Monzaemon 1653–1725

Japanese dramatist

Biography

Born Suigimori Jirokichi (adult name Nobumori) into a samurai family, in Echizen Province (now in Fukui district), Japan, in 1653. Little is known of his early life. The family moved to Kyoto in about 1667. Chikamatsu was in the employ of the nobleman Ichijo Zenkakuekan until about 1671 or 1672. The first professional Japanese dramatist, Chikamatsu wrote mainly for the puppet stage but also, from 1684, for the kabuki theatre. His first plays were for Uji Kadayū and other chanters of the jōruri (puppet) theatre. From 1686 he wrote for the chanter Takemoto Gidayū's theatre, Takemoto-za, in Osaka. He was house writer for Sakata Tōjūrō I's theatre, Miyako-za, in Kyoto, 1695–1703. In about 1703, after Tōjūrō's retirement, Chikamatsu returned to Osaka and to his successful collaboration with Gidayū at the Takemoto-za. He married and had two sons; his wife died in 1734. Chikamatsu died in Osaka, 6 January 1725.

Chikamatsu wrote historical romances (*jidaimono*) and domestic tragedies (*sewamono*), the latter often involving love suicides. Among his best-known plays are, in the first of these categories, the *Kokusenya kassen* (*The Battles of Coxinga*), 1715, and in the second *Sonezaki shinjū* (*The Love Suicides at Sonezaki*), 1703.

Translations

Selections of Plays

Brandon, James, *Kabuki: Five Classic Plays*, Cambridge, Massachusetts: Harvard University Press, 1975 (contains Chikamatsu's *Love Letter from the Licensed Quarter*, based on *Yūgiri awa no naruto* 1712)

Brazell, Karen, *Traditional Japanese Theater: An Anthology of Plays*, New York: Columbia University Press, 1998 (contains selections from *The Battles of Coxinga* (*Kokusen'ya kassen*, 1715), *Love Suicides at Amijima* (*Shinjū ten no Amijima*, 1720), *The Heike and the Island of Women* (*Heike nyogo no shima*, 1719))

Gerstle, C. Andrew, *Chikamatus: Five Late Plays*, New York: Columbia University Press, 2000 (contains *Twins at the Sumida River* (*Futago sumidagawa*, 1720), *Lovers Pond in Settsu Province* (*Tsu no kuni meoto ike*, 1721), *Battles at Kawa-nakajima* (*Shinshū kawa-nakajima kassen*, 1721), *Love Suicides on the Eve of the Kōshin Festival* (*Shinjū yoigōshin*, 1722), *Tethered Steed and the Eight Provinces of Kantō* (*Kanhasshū tsunagi-uma*, 1724))

Keene, Donald, *Major Plays of Chikamatsu*, New York: Columbia University Press, 1961 (contains *The Love Suicides at Sonezaki* (*Sonezaki shinjū*, 1703); *The Drum of the Waves of Horikawa* (*Horikawa nami no tsuzumi*, 1707); *Yosaku from Tamba* (*Tamba Yosaku*, 1707); *The Love Suicides in the Women's Temple* (*Shinjū mannensō*, 1710); *The Courier for Hell* (*Meido no Hikyaku*, 1711); *The Battles of Coxinga* (*Kokusen'ya kassen*, 1715); *Gonza the Lancer* (*Yari no Gonza*, 1717); *The Uprooted Pine* (*Yamazaki Yojibei nebiki no kadomatsu*, 1718); *The Girl from Hakata; or, Love at Sea* (*Hakata kojorō namimakura*, 1718); *The Love Suicides at Amijima* (*Shinjū ten no Amijima*, 1720); *The Woman-killer and the Hell of Oil* (*Onna-koroshi abura no jigoku*, 1721)); selection as *Four Major Plays of Chikamatsu*, 1961

Leiter, Samuel, *The Art of Kabuki: Famous Plays in Performance*, Berkeley: University of California Press, 1979 (contains Chikamatsu's *Shunkan* (one act of *Heike Nyogo no shima*, 1719))

Lombard, Frank, *An Outline History of the Japanese Drama*, London: Allen and Unwin, 1928, Boston: Houghton Mifflin, 1929 (contains Chikamatsu's *The Soga Revenge* (*Soga kaikeizan* 1718))

Matisoff, Susan, *Semimaru* (1693) in her *The Legend of Semimaru, Blind Musician of Japan*, New York: Columbia University Press, 1973

Miyamori Asataro, *Masterpieces of Chikamatsu: The Japanese Shakespeare*, with an introduction, revised by Robert Nichols, London: Kegan Paul Trench Trubner, and New York: Dutton, 1926 (contains *The Almanac of Love* (*Koi hakké hashiragoyomi*, a later Kabuki revision of Chikamatsu's original *Daikyōji mukashi-goyomi*, 1715); *Fair Ladies at a Game of Poem-cards* (*Kaoyo uta karuta*, 1714); *The Courier for Hades* (*Meido no hikyaku*, 1711); *The Love Suicide at Amijima* (*Shinjū ten no Amijima*, 1720); *The Adventures of the Hakata Damsel* (*Hakata kojorō namimakura*, 1718); *The Tethered Steed* (*Kanhasshū tsunagi-uma*, abridged 1724))

Mueller, Jacqueline, *A Chronicle of Great Peace* (*Goban taiheiki*, 1710), in *Harvard Journal of Asiatic Studies*, 46/1 (1986)

Shively, Donald, *Love Suicide at Amijima*, Cambridge, Massachusetts: Harvard University Press, 1953

Chikamatsu Monzaemon is the most famous popular dramatist in the Japanese tradition. He wrote more than 100 plays for Kabuki and Jōruri (Bunraku) puppet theatres. Complete Kabuki texts were not published until the late 19th century, but from as early as the 1600s plays written for the urban commercial puppet theatre were published in full, complete with a code of musical notation used for professional and amateur chanters. In the theatre one chanter usually performed all the roles, including that of the third-person narrator. The plays were published in authorized editions with both the senior chanter's name (verifying the notation) and the playwright's (verifying the content) by a specialist publisher in Kyoto and Osaka. We, therefore, have quality texts from the period of the author. These plays were performed also as Kabuki, and were widely read throughout Japan. Further, they continued to be influential in later Kabuki and fiction. New plays were written for the puppet theatre until the post-World War II period, but the bulk of the repertoire was first performed in the 18th century, during which as many as 700 plays were performed and published.

Chikamatsu produced two kinds of puppet plays: long, full-day, five-act works called *jidaimono* (history or period plays) and *sewamono* (contemporary-life plays) which were shorter three-scene plays filling the latter part of a full-day production. In the modern period, Japanese scholars have praised the *sewamono* for their realistic depiction of the tragedies of commoners and low-level samurai. As a consequence, from even early this century fully annotated editions of the 24 *sewamono* have been available. This has been a great aid to translators and has influenced their choices. Only recently have scholars begun to annotate in detail the more difficult *jidaimono*, of which there are about 70.

The earliest book-length collection of Chikamatsu translations into English is *Masterpieces of Chikamatsu: the Japanese Shakespeare* (1926) by MIYAMORI ASATARO. This contains a 60-page introduction and six plays, two of which are history plays; it is in a prose fiction format (close to the form of the original), rather than presented as a play script. This translation appeared soon after the 200th anniversary of Chikamatsu's death. Another early work is by Frank LOMBARD, *An Outline History of the Japanese Drama* (1928), which contains *The Soga Revenge* (*Soga kaikeizan*, 1718).

The first widely read and acclaimed translation, however, was by Donald KEENE, *Major Plays of Chikamatsu*, first published in 1961 and regularly reissued; this contains 11 of Chikamatsu's most famous works. Only one, however, is a *jidaimono*. A shorter version, *Four Major Plays of Chikamatsu* (1961), is also in print. Keene's work has been influential in the choice of plays for translations into other languages. We have a scholarly translation by Donald SHIVELY of *Love Suicide at Amijima* (1953). Recently René Sieffert has completed a translation of all 24 of Chikamatsu's *sewamono* into French, *Chikamatsu: Les Tragédies bourgeoises* (4 vols, 1992). Two other *jidaimono* are *Semimaru* (1693) found in MATISOFF (1973) and *Goban taiheiki* (1710) translated by MUELLER (1986). Since we have so few English translations of Chikamatsu's mature history plays, the present writer is completing a project to translate five late works, four of which are *jidaimono* (GERSTLE, 2000).

Translation of Chikamatsu's plays involves some concerns common to all dramatic texts created for performance. The West has developed a tradition of reading plays as literature removed from the stage, from the classic Greeks, through Racine and Shakespeare and Ibsen. Japan, however, is distinctly different on this point. Nō, Bunraku and Kabuki texts are considered by most Japanese to be "incomplete" removed from performance. Nō and Bunraku in particular are built upon musical, rhythmic structures. It was common from pre-modern times for connoisseurs to take lessons from professionals in elements of performance: chanting, dance or music. Therefore Chikamatsu's texts were published with a notation code for voice, both for these amateurs to use as practice texts and for aficionados to savour the performance, which they are expected to imagine or even chant aloud. Translators are faced with a question of what kind of translation to produce: for the (imagined) stage or the study. The present writer, in his own study of Chikamatsu's plays, *Circles of Fantasy* (1986), argues for the use of the printed notations to help the reader to understand the rhythms of performance and the structure of the text. Chikamatsu, however, is certainly the most literary of the many playwrights, and his works were widely read as literature even after they ceased to be performed. Students, from my experience in teaching texts in translation, have always found the plays accessible and interesting in Keene's translations. Chikamatsu's style is extremely rich, his vocabulary enormous and his range of subjects vast, from distant history to the intricacies of contemporary fashion and crime. A particular difficulty is his delineation of characters by literary style, from aristocrats and samurai to merchants, farmers and thugs. His range of allusion is impressive. A reference work in Japanese of 771 pages, *Chikamatsu goi* (1930), lists the large number and range of works he has referred to, such as Chinese and Japanese classics, Buddhist works, popular songs, and contemporary writings.

Several famous post-Chikamatsu puppet/Kabuki plays are now translated in *Chūshingura* by Donald KEENE (1971) and in *Sugawara and the Secrets of Calligraphy* (1985), and *Yoshitsune and the Thousand Cherry Trees* (1993), both by Stanleigh JONES (see Further Reading list for these publications). James BRANDON's *Kabuki: Five Classic Plays* (1975) which contains five plays, including Chikamatsu's *Love Letter from the Licensed Quarter*, is notable for its attempt to present plays for use in performance. Samuel LEITER's *The Art of Kabuki: Famous Plays in Performance* (1979), which includes Chikamatsu's *Shunkan* among four plays, is also aimed at translating plays for the stage by including considerable commentary on stage action, music and props. *Theater as Music* (1990) by Gerstle, Inobe and Malm is a study and translation of one play by Chikamatsu Hanji (1725–83) and is published with an audio cassette of a performance. Karen BRAZELL's *Traditional Japanese Theater* (1998) contains selections from some of the translations cited above as well as many other plays.

Japanese Literature in Foreign Languages, 1945–1990, issued by the Japan PEN Club, contains a list of translations of Chikamatsu's plays into the languages of the world. A recent work by Benito Ortolani, *Japanese Theatre: From Samanistic Ritual to Contemporary Pluralism*, contains a full bibliography, including translations. *Asian Theatre Journal* regularly contains translations of plays from the Japanese as well as other Asian traditions. James Brandon and Samuel Leiter are editors of a multivolume project of translations from Kabuki theatre to be published by the University of Hawaii Press.

ANDREW GERSTLE

Further Reading

Gerstle, C. Andrew, *Circles of Fantasy: Convention in the Plays of Chikamatsu*, Cambridge, Massachusetts: Harvard University Council on East Asian Studies, 1986

Gerstle, C. Andrew, Kiyoshi Inobe and William P. Malm, *Theater as Music: The Bunraku Play, "Mt. Imo and Mt. Se: An Exemplary Tale of Womanly Virtue"*, Ann Arbor: University of Michigan Center for Japanese Studies, 1990

Japan PEN Club, *Japanese Literature in Foreign Languages, 1945–1990*, Tokyo: Japan Book Publishers Association, 1990

Jones, Stanleigh H., *Sugawara and the Secrets of Calligraphy* (1746), New York: Columbia University Press, 1985

Jones, Stanleigh H., *Yoshitsune and the Thousand Cherry Trees* (1747), New York: Columbia University Press, 1993

Keene, Donald, *Chūshingura: Treasury of Loyal Retainers* (1784), New York: Columbia University Press, 1971

Ortolani, Benito, *Japanese Theatre: From Shamanistic Ritual to Contemporary Pluralism*, Leiden and New York: E.J. Brill, 1990

Children's Literature in English Translation

Literature designated as "children's" is either adapted from works originally intended for adults or written directly for an audience of children. Because it is not generally taken seriously as literature but is filtered through adults for its pedagogical possibilities, the translation norms that apply to it are quite different from those applied to adult literature; in fact, they often resemble the norms used in adapting adult works for children. For example, the notion that a translation should be "faithful to its original" is usually abandoned or reinterpreted in favor of rendering the text suitable for children in the target culture. The results of this practice are deplored by Göte Klingberg in *Children's Fiction in the Hands of the Translators*. Klingberg carefully studied translations from English to Swedish and from Swedish to English of well-known children's works done by highly regarded translators. He then classified the changes made to the originals as "cultural context adaptations", "modernization", "purification", "language adaptation", "abridgement", and "localization". His terminology reflects the kinds of manipulations to which children's texts are customarily subject in translation. Such manipulations are also performed in the adaptation of adult texts for children. In interviews and other articles, prominent English-language translators Patricia Crampton and Anthea Bell have described how children's texts are chosen for translation by publishers and have discussed their own translating practices, thereby supporting these observations.

Since children's literature is both marginal to "high" literature while at the same time a microcosm of it, polysystems theory has provided an enlightening approach to its complexities, helping to explain the phenomena noted by Klingberg. In turn, translations of children's literature have offered a number of interesting case studies contributing to the development of polysystems theory. Zohar Shavit's *Poetics of Children's Literature* offers a comprehensive portrait of children's literature as a polysystem, pointing out its peculiar status in relationship to other systems, including "serious", or "high", literature and the educational system; these factors must be taken into account when discussing the cultural and linguistic transfer of any particular work from one national or linguistic system into another. Despite its low status, the task of writing or translating children's literature is a complex one requiring the simultaneous appeal to two audiences: adults, who are in a position to make judgements about the work's quality, and children, the implied readers. Children's literature is also caught between two semiotic systems: the educational one, which judges the work according to its pedagogical values, and the literary, which applies aesthetic values. Although it does not belong to the canon of "high" literature, it has its own canon, determined by adults, and its set of disapproved non-canonical literature which nevertheless often competes quite successfully for children's attention. Although Shavit provides quite an elegant explanation for the seeming vagaries of children's literature translation, others have asserted that her observations are less valid outside the Western tradition. Reinbert Tabbert, for example, maintains that in the German Democratic Republic children's writers and illustrators were taken as seriously as those whose productions were intended for adults. Furthermore, he adds, youngsters there were considered young adults, not a "separate consumer market".

According to Shavit, the manipulation of children's texts in translation is usually motivated by the following requirements: (1) The original text must conform to a model already existing in the target literature. (2) The text must be commensurate with whatever the target culture deems forbidden or permitted to children. (3) The complexity of the text must be brought down to the level of the child, disambiguating subtleties and simplifying it in general. (4) The text must be used as a didactic instrument for a system of values or a certain ideology. (An example of this is Joachim Campe's German translation of Defoe's *Robinson Crusoe*, which adapted the novel to Rousseau's pedagogical system; this entailed deleting Defoe's bourgeois ethos and colonialist values. As a result, Crusoe arrives on the island naked instead of well equipped with all the symbols and technologies of Western culture he has with him in Defoe's original. Later translations for children into other languages used Campe's version and spawned an entire sub-genre: the robinsonnade.) (5)The text must be written in the style valued by the target culture, often with little or no regard for the original author's style. In the case of Hebrew literature, which provides most of Shavit's examples, that style is highly literary because of the desire to teach "correct language" to children. Any attempt by a translator to reflect a foreign author's linguistic portrayal of slang or other realistically childish expressions is carefully corrected by the publisher's copy editor, as Basmat Even-Zohar shows in regard to her own Hebrew translations of Astrid Lindgren's Pippi Longstocking books.

Despite the conservatism of the children's literary system, which affects the very selection of works to translate, translations have nevertheless influenced its history. For example, England was one of the first nations to develop a self-conscious independent children's literature, and the translation of works from other languages has been key to its development from the very beginning. The first translated children's book may very well be the lavishly illustrated *Fables of Aesop* published by Caxton in 1483, based on a French text taken from the German of Heinrich Steinhöwel, although, strictly speaking, the concept of children's literature did not yet exist at the time. Nevertheless, its simple language and coordination of illustration and text made it extremely useful as a school text. The next important English translation for children is John Amos Comenius's methodically pedagogical *Orbis Sensualium Pictus*, 1658, with pictures and text coordinated to teach children both the vernacular language and Latin. It was translated from German in 1659 by Charles Hoole (*Comenius's Visible World*).

Although useful for teaching and learning, didactic texts such as these did not satisfy the child's quest for reading pleasure. Instead, the much despised popular romances and beast fables marketed to the poorer classes in the form of chapbooks fulfilled this need. Translations and adaptations were also to be found among these. It was the inspiration of John Newbery, often credited as the first publisher of children's literature, to combine "instruction" with "delight", by borrowing the most successful aspects of the chapbook to use for morally pedagogic purposes, and he thus achieved great commercial success. Newbery published a verse translation of Aesop's *Fables* in 1757; his heirs, who continued the business, published the seventh edition of Robert Samber's translation of Perrault's *Histories, or Tales of Past Time* in 1777. In some editions this work was titled *Mother Goose's Tales*, a translation of *Contes de ma mere L'Oye*, which appeared on Perrault's frontispiece. In this way Mother Goose emigrated to England, where she lent her name to *Mother Goose's Melodies*, a collection of nursery rhymes also published by the Newbery company. Around 1791 another Newbery, Elizabeth, published the first English selection from the *Thousand and One Nights* made specifically for children. Translated by Richard Johnson, who expunged everything that could possibly cause offense and added his own moral reflections, it was titled *The Oriental Moralist; or, The Beauties of the Arabian Nights Entertainments*.

The didactic, realistic norm prevailing in canonical English children's literature was challenged in the 19th century by a flood of fairy-tale translations, beginning with the works of the Grimm brothers in 1823–26 and soon dominated by the works of Hans Christian Andersen. (Andrew Lang's series of *Fairy Books*, from 1889, also included translations from many other languages.) These translations turned the critical tide in favor of the fantasy genre and stimulated the production of native grown fantasies like Thackeray's *The Rose and the Ring* (1855) and Kingsley's *The Water-Babies* (1863), culminating in Lewis Carroll's *Alice's Adventures in Wonderland* (1865). The latter work has become part of both the children's and the adult canon and has posed an alluring stylistic challenge to translators worldwide; Vladimir Nabokov, for example, translated it into Russian.

Fate has not been as kind to Andersen, who has been ghettoized in the Anglo-American nursery despite the objections of Danish scholars, nor to Jules Verne, whose works have been so bowdlerized in English that even the pedagogical passages intended by Verne to teach his readers science have been deleted. Changes such as these, some of which are documented in the edition of *20,000 Leagues Under the Sea* annotated by Walter James Miller, have so tarnished Verne's English language reputation that he is regarded simply as a boys' adventure writer, or the "father" of science fiction, a non-canonical genre. The English fates of Andersen's and Verne's works reflect a common consequence of translation: often the crossover is between literary systems as well as linguistic systems. The growth of another non-canonical genre, the children's detective story, was stimulated by the highly successful translation of Erich Kästner's *Emil und die Detektive* (1929), (*Emil and the Detectives*, 1960) which itself, however, remains part of the children's canon. Kästner's plot about a group of children who outwit hardened criminals provided the model for books like the Nancy Drew and Hardy Boys series in the US, and the novels by Enid Blyton in England.

Collodi's *Pinocchio* (1883) has also been adapted to fulfil target culture social needs through its various English translations, particularly in the US. Richard Wunderlich has examined these, beginning with the Ginn Company's revision of Walter S. Cramp's translation for the Lynn, Massachusetts school board, and ending with the Walt Disney version and its numerous book adaptations. According to Wunderlich, the evolution of the American vision of Pinocchio can be attributed to social changes brought on by the Great Depression and its consequent stress on family values. Thus Collodi's mischievous Italian puppet, who originally wanted to grow up, now wants only to be an obedient boy safe in the bosom of his loving family.

In the 20th century, various associations were established to encourage the translation of children's literature. The International Board on Books for Young People, founded by Jella Lepman after World War II, established the Hans Christian Andersen award in 1956 and its biennial list of honor books, which, since 1978, has included a category for translations. It also publishes a journal, *Bookbird*, which reviews and recommends books for translation. The American Library Association established the Mildred Batchelder award in 1968, to be given to the publisher of the most outstanding translated children's book. Despite these efforts, publishers are still reluctant to publish translations.When they do, they select only texts that can be made to fit a "niche", and then often insist on numerous changes to the text to make the item sellable. These changes are invariably oriented to the target culture, as we have seen above. Nevertheless, some advocates of children's literature translations, like Klingberg, for example, feel that their pedagogical purpose should be to acquaint children with other cultures, and that adaptation to the target culture should therefore be kept to a minimum. Others are disturbed by the fact that far more translations from English into other languages exist than translations of foreign works into English, which they see as another symptom of the imperialism of the English language and Anglo-American culture. Furthermore, the foreign works that do get translated into English are predominantly from other Germanic languages. If we accept Shavit's explanation, however, the reason for the latter problem may be found in the lack of models in English that can accommodate non-Germanic works. And the process can work in the other direction as well; a recent dissertation by Ali Azeriah (*Translated Children's Literature in Arabic: A Case Study of Translational Norms*, 1994) maintains that children's literature translated into Arabic is only of peripheral interest for educators because the Islamic educational system does not rely on written works to inculcate values in children.

KRISTINE J. ANDERSON

Further Reading

Bell, Anthea, "Translator's Notebook" in *The Signal Approach to Children's Books: A Collection*, edited by Nancy Chambers, Harmondsworth: Kestrel Books, 1980; Metuchen, New Jersey: Scarecrow Press, 1981

Ben-Ari, Nitsa, "Didactic and Pedagogic Tendencies in the Norms Dictating the Translation of Children's Literature: The Case of Postwar German-Hebrew Translations", *Poetics Today*, 13/1 (Spring 1992) pp. 221–29

Carpenter, Humphrey and Mari Prichard, *The Oxford Companion to Children's Literature*, Oxford and New York: Oxford University Press, 1984

Even-Zohar, Basmat, "Translation Policy in Hebrew Children's Literature: The Case of Astrid Lindgren", *Poetics Today*, 13/1 (Spring 1992) pp. 231–45

Jobe, Ronald A., "Profile: Patricia Crampton", *Language Arts*, 65/4 (April 1988) pp. 410–14

Jobe, Ronald A., "Profile: Anthea Bell", *Language Arts*, 67/4 (April 1990) pp. 432–38

Klingberg, Göte *et al.* (editors), *Children's Books in Translation: The Situation and the Problems*, Stockholm: Almqvist & Wiksell, 1978
Klingberg, Göte, *Children's Fiction in the Hands of the Translators*, Malmö: Gleerup, 1986
O'Sullivan, Emer, "Does Pinocchio Have an Italian Passport? What is Specifically National and What is International about Children's Literature" in *The World of Children in Children's Books / Children's Books in the World of Children*, Munich: Arbeitskreis für Jugendliteratur, 1992
Shavit, Zohar, "Translation of Children's Literature as a Function of Its Position in the Literary Polysystem", *Poetics Today*, 2/4 (1981) pp. 171–79
Shavit, Zohar, *Poetics of Children's Literature*, Athens: University of Georgia Press, 1986
Tabbert, Reinbert, "The Surprising Career of Wolf Spillner's *Wild Geese*: A Case Study of East German Literature", *Poetics Today*, 13/1 (Spring 1992) pp. 248–58
Verne, Jules, *The Annotated Jules Verne: Twenty Thousand Leagues under the Sea*, translated by Mercier Lewis, edited by Walter James Miller, New York: Crowell, 1976
Wunderlich, Richard, "The Tribulations of Pinocchio: How Social Change Can Wreck a Good Story", *Poetics Today*, 13/1 (Spring 1992) pp. 197–219

Chin P'ing Mei

See Jin Ping Mei

Chinese

Literary Translation into English

The Language

Of all the scripts in current use in the world the Chinese is that with the longest continuous history. Inevitably, over three millennia, its structure and vocabulary have evolved to such an extent that Chinese schoolchildren now need special instruction in order to understand most of what was written during imperial times (206 BC– AD 1911), and direct access to the writings of their earliest ancestors is available only to those who go on to study epigraphy.

Two factors that operate here are the radical distinction that was traditionally observed between the written and the spoken languages, and the official promulgation of simplified forms of Chinese characters in the People's Republic of China since the 1950s, which has widened the linguistic gap between past and present.

Throughout imperial Chinese history all serious writing – from official edicts to private journals, and including history, philosophy, essays, poetry and private correspondence – was done in what is loosely known as the "Classical" or "literary" language. Classical Chinese, which differs from colloquial Chinese much as Latin differs from modern Italian, was the regular medium of written communication between members of the educated classes that dominated Chinese society up until the revolution of 1911. A limited amount of literature in the colloquial language took the form of novels, short stories and plays for popular consumption, but was little esteemed, despite the emergence during the Ming dynasty (1368–1644) of the first great Chinese novels. Not until the early 20th century and the New Culture Movement did the colloquial language begin to attain its present status as the model for all writing, whether literary or commonplace.

Of course, as in other languages, there are still significant stylistic differences between spoken and written Chinese, but they are no longer much greater than those observed in English. One should, however, note that, in this respect, the highly successful promotion by both Nationalist and Communist governments of "mandarin", which is based on the speech of northern Han Chinese and spoken naturally by about three-quarters of the population, as the standard spoken language has been an important unifying factor.

Classical Chinese is characterized by its lack of inflection and a strong tendency towards monosyllabism. Modern Chinese shows the same lack of inflection, but possesses a greater number of compounds and polysyllabic expressions. Consequently, where English may express case, gender, number, tense, person, etc., through inflection, Chinese relies on the subtleties of linguistic context, word order and a certain range of particles and suffixes. Thus, in Classical Chinese the sentence *jun bu jian lu hu* may mean "Have you not seen a deer, sir?"(i.e. "Haven't you ever seen a deer, sir?"), or "Don't you see the deer, sir?" (i.e. "Don't you see the deer, now?"). The tense is clear in the context. As for the deer, whether it is a case of one or more deer is clear – as in English – from the context. But in Classical Chinese all nouns are invariables like the English *deer*, *sheep*, etc. In addition, Chinese, particularly Classical Chinese, frequently leaves the subject unexpressed, as in such phrases as *si hu* "Are (you) going to die?" (Classical), or *laile meiyou* "Has / have (he / she / it / they) come or not?"(modern).

As far as the nature of the language is concerned, the commonly held misconception that all Chinese characters are pictograms or ideographs has had unfortunate consequences in the translation and interpretation of Chinese poetry. Of course, the form of several common simple characters, such as those for sun, moon, man, above and below, is visibly derived from a single pictographic or ideographic element, and combinations of such elements certainly indicate the meaning of many others. It is, however, quite wrong to assume on this basis that all, or even most Chinese characters are pictographs or ideographs, although this has become an established myth outside sinological circles.

The notions of E.F. Fenollosa (1853–1908), as eventually set out in his essay "The Chinese written character as a Medium for Poetry" (1936), which grossly exaggerated the pictorial as opposed to the phonetic element in Chinese characters, did much to further this myth, and his collaboration with Ezra Pound influenced the latter's translations of poetry, as it did those of Amy Lowell and Florence Ayscough. The results are frequently ridiculous. It is, of course, possible to break down a Chinese character into its constituent parts and view each of them as contributing "pictorially" to the meaning of the whole. However, even where this "deconstruction" may be etymologically justified, the Chinese reader is not normally conscious of it. Thus, while the character *jia* meaning "home" consists of a pig under a roof, its "pictorial" elements (which are, in any case, highly stylized forms of the original pictograms) make no more impact on a Chinese reader (ancient or modern) than the etymology of a word like holiday does on his English counterpart. Any implied "visual" appeal was not part of the Chinese poet's stock-in-trade. Unfortunately, because certain compound characters, such as *ming* (bright) and *chou* (sad) *appear* to be composed of significant pictorial elements, the likes of Ayscough and Lowell have been seduced into believing that Chinese in general, and Chinese poets in particular, read and write their script as a series of compound images. In fact, the form of *ming* (bright), which is now written by juxtaposing "sun" and "moon", is etymologically an evolution from that combining "window" and "moon". As for *chou* (sad), which consists of elements meaning "heart" and "autumn", it has nothing to do with autumnal feelings : the element "autumn" is purely phonetic. It is perhaps worth pointing out that as the phonetic elements in Chinese characters also exist as separate, independent characters with their own meanings, the potentiality for misunderstandings of the "autumnal feelings" kind is boundless. (Indeed, one early 20th-century poetess did, exceptionally – there is always an exception to any general rule that one tries to apply to Chinese! – play on the apparent semantic link between autumn and sadness.) Occasionally, one may hit upon a happy coincidence of meaning and form, but most of the time the enterprise is rather like producing false etymologies for such English words as bandage (band-age), firkin (fir-kin), butterfly (butter-fly) and ladybird (lady-bird).

Literary Translation from Chinese

The history of translation from Chinese into English is closely linked to the development of the diplomatic and missionary activity that accompanied British commercial and military intervention in 19th-century China. Of course, in the early days, the emphasis was on translation into Chinese, particularly of the Bible and religious tracts. Joshua Marshman and Robert Morrison both published complete translations of the Bible, in 1822 and 1824 respectively. Nevertheless, as early as 1761 an anonymous translation of a romantic Chinese novel had appeared, and another translation of the same novel by J.F. Davis (later to become the second governor of Hong Kong), was published in London in 1829 under the title *The Fortunate Union*. In the same year Davis also published *Poeseos sinensis commentarii: On the Poetry of China*. Generally, however, when missionaries turned their hands to translating from the Chinese, they tackled the Confucian classics. Thus Medhurst produced a translation of *The Shoo King* or *Historical Classic* (*pinyin=Shujing*) (Shanghai, 1846), and Morrison's *Horae Sinicae* (London, 1812) included a version of the *Ta hio (pinyin=Daxue)*, or *Great Learning*, one of the *Four Books* of Confucianism. In this respect, Samuel Beale (1825–89) was something of an exception. A naval chaplain in China in the 1850s, Beale later concentrated on translating various Buddhist works. He was eventually appointed professor of Chinese at University College, London, in 1877.

Two of the pioneers of literary translation from the Chinese, James Legge (1814–97) and Herbert Giles (1845–1935) were a missionary and a member of the Consular Service, respectively. Legge eventually became the first professor of Chinese at Oxford University (1876), while Giles succeeded to the chair that had been founded in 1888 at Cambridge and occupied by Thomas Wade. Wade was the creator of the system, subsequently modified by Giles, for transcribing Chinese into Roman letters that was generally used by English and American sinologists until recently,when the so-called "Wade–Giles" system began to give way to the *pinyin* transcription officially sponsored by the People's Republic of China since 1953.

Even before the emergence of the *pinyin* system, there was not complete uniformity of practice in transcribing Chinese, but now the situation is still more confusing for the reader of translated literature, because the Wade–Giles and *pinyin* systems differ markedly. The famous Tang dynasty poet Tu Fu (Wade–Giles) becomes Du Fu (*pinyin*), while the hero of *Dream of the Red Chamber* becomes Jia Baoyu instead of Chia Pao-yü. Contemporary usage further "transforms" the Tang poets Po Chü-i and Li Po into Bai Juyi and Li Bai, respectively. At present, all mainland as well as most British and American publications employ the *pinyin* system, which has imposed itself internationally, while the use of Wade–Giles is more frequent the further one goes back in time.

James Legge spent almost the whole of his missionary life in

Hong Kong, where he arrived in 1843 with the London Missionary Society, of which he was the principal. There, he began translating all the major Confucian classics. He eventually completed translations of the *Confucian Analects, The Great Learning, The Doctrine of the Mean, The Works of Mencius, The Shoo King* (*pinyin=Shujing*) or *The Book of Historical Documents, The She King* (*pinyin=Shijing*) or *Book of Poetry, The Ch'un Ts'ew* (*pinyin=Chunqiu*) with *The Tso Chuen* (*pinyin=Zuozhuan*), *The Yi King* (*pinyin=Yijing*), *The Li Ki* (*pinyin=Liji*) or *Collection of Treatises on the Rules of Propriety* and *The Book of Rites*. This Confucian canon includes, of course, works of history and literature as well as philosophy, and Legge later also set about translating the ancient poetry of southern China known as *Chu ci* (*Songs of the South*). Indeed, he was still working on this when he died. Nor was his interest in Chinese philosophy confined to Confucianism. He went on to make translations of *The Texts of Taoism*, which included the *Daode jing* or *Laozi* and the *Zhuangzi*. All Legge's translations are extremely sound, take into account traditional Chinese scholarship (he was, moreover, assisted by an erudite Chinese scholar), and are couched in good, clear Victorian English. His transcription of Chinese, however, was influenced by Cantonese pronunciation, and is very different from both Wade–Giles and *pinyin*!

Giles, for his part, was responsible for a great variety of translations, ranging from philosophy (e.g. *Chuang Tzu* (*pinyin= Zhuangzi*) *Mystic, Moralist and Social Reformer*) to poetry (e.g. *Chinese Poetry in English Verse*) and Classical prose (e.g. *Strange Stories from a Chinese Studio*, and *Gems of Chinese Literature*).

The early 20th century saw the flowering of Chinese poetry in translation. It received considerable impetus from the Imagist movement, in particular, from Ezra Pound's *Cathay* (1915), which was followed by Arthur Waley's *One Hundred and Seventy Chinese Poems* (1918), and Amy Lowell's *Fir Flower Tablets* (1921).

The translation of Chinese poetry into English presents several problems that are linguistic in origin. In the first place, there is the problem of rhythm: it is well-nigh impossible to reduplicate the terseness of the original meter. The ancient poems of the *Book of Poetry* (*Shijing*) consist mostly of lines in which there are four words that amount to four syllables. Later poetry is dominated by five-word and seven-word lines. Thus a wistful poem of the 9th century reads:

Qunian jinri ci men zhong
Ren mian tao hua xiang ying hong
Ren mian bu zhi he chu qu
Tao hua yi jiu xiao chun feng{

By cheating slightly, one can translate as follows:

This day last year at this gate,
Her face, peach flow'rs, red on red,
Her face, don't know where it's gone,
Peach flow'rs, as then, smile spring wind.

But even such a clumsily contrived monosyllabic version involves reducing flowers to "flow'rs", translating the Chinese *ren*, "some-one", as "her", omitting the "I" (not expressed in the Chinese) before "don't know", and rendering as "red on red" what in the original reads rather "reflecting red on each other". A fuller – if unpoetic – translation might read:

A year ago today, at this same gate
A girl's face and peach blossoms shone red on red,
I don't know where her face is now,
But the peach blossoms still smile in the spring breeze.

As for any notion of recapturing the sound of the original, it should be borne in mind that Chinese phonology has changed markedly over the course of the centuries, and that when contemporary Chinese recite the poems of the Tang dynasty (618–907), the golden age of Chinese poetry, they generally do so using the modern Mandarin pronunciation. (Only a few specialists pretend to chant poetry according to the reconstructed Tang sounds.) A further difficulty confronting the translator of Chinese poetry is its allusive nature. And the influence of the great poets of the Tang dynasty has been so powerful that, in addition to direct or oblique reference to a general culture of legend, history and mythology, there is even allusive use of imagery and expressions from earlier poetry. Thus mention of moon and fans evoke an abandoned mistress, while willows are associated with taking leave of a friend or lover. And one might mention here that scholar-officials frequently adopted the role of a poetic lover when writing to a distant male friend.

In responding to the above problems, the translators of Chinese poetry have created something of a genre of their own. Writing in 1928, T.S. Eliot asserted that "Chinese poetry, as we know it today, is something invented by Ezra Pound." And one might make a similar claim, with greater justification, for Arthur Waley, whose translations are not only poetic but accurate in a way that Pound's are not. Waley's solution to the problem of dealing with Chinese prosody was to use sprung verse, with English stresses corresponding to the number of Chinese words in a line. He has had many imitators since, but few have been as successful. Nevertheless, several valuable poetic contributions have been made. Witter Bynner, the American poet, aided by a Chinese scholar, rendered the famous collection of *Three Hundred Poems of the T'ang Dynasty* into English under the title *The Jade Mountain* (1929). Robert Payne edited a comprehensive anthology of ancient and modern poetry entitled *The White Pony* (1949). William Hung produced a two-volume work on *Tu Fu: China's Greatest Poet* (1952), fitting his translations into an account of the life and times of the poet, much as Waley had done in his *The Life and Times of Po Chü-i* (1949) and *The Poetry and Career of Li Po* (1950). David Hawkes published a complete translation of the ancient *Chu ci* under the title *Ch'u Tz'u: The Songs of the South* (1959). Hawkes also produced *A Little Primer of Tu Fu* (1967), which provides an excellent introduction to the art and appreciation of the translation of Chinese poetry. Not all translations of Chinese poetry have had poetic pretensions, however. Bernhard Karlgren's complete and authoritative translation of the classic *Shi jing* under the title *The Book of Odes* (1950) simply provides a literal version of the Chinese text.

In the period between the two world wars, translations of Chinese literature of all kinds continued to appear, although traditional poetry and ancient philosophy enjoyed the lion's share of translators' attention. In a broadening of philosophical horizons, H.H. Dubs produced a translation of the unorthodox Confucian thinker Xunzi, *The Works of Hsun tzu* (1928), Y.P. Mei translated *The Ethical and Political Works of Motse (pinyin=Mozi)* (1929), a utilitarian thinker of the 5th century BC, and J.J.L. Duyvendak published his translation of the writings of the 4th-century BC legalist Gongsun Yang, *The Book of the Lord Shang* (1928). Fung Yu-lan brought out a translation of the first seven "inner" chapters of the Taoist *Zhuangzi* (1931), and Waley published a translation of the *Daode jing*, *The Way and Its Power* (1934). On the other hand, translations of the major Chinese novels also began to appear, although these were not always complete translations. The *Sanguo yanyi* was translated by C.H. Brewitt-Taylor under the title *San Kuo, or, Romance of the Three Kingdoms* (1925), the *Shuihu zhuan* was translated both by Pearl Buck under the title *All Men are Brothers* (1937), and by J.H. Jackson as *The Water Margin* (1937), in a somewhat abridged version, while the erotic *Jin Ping Mei* appeared in a complete translation by C. Egerton (aided by the Chinese novelist Shu Qingchun), with the more sexually explicit passages rendered into Latin (1939).

The end of World War II and the founding of the People's Republic of China heralded a new era in Chinese studies in general and in the translation of things Chinese in particular. One important element in this development was the number of Chinese scholars who emigrated to the West, particularly to the United States , where, as university teachers and researchers, they published in English themselves, and formed a new generation of western sinologists. Another element was American political resolve to understand what had happened in China, and to confront the phenomenon of Chinese Communism. Despite problems during the McCarthy era, the overall result has been that the United States became the real powerhouse for Chinese studies in the second half of the 20th century. At the same time, in China itself there has been an enormous effort to make its culture known abroad, even if at times this effort has taken the form of fairly crude political propaganda. In terms of translation, the Chinese contribution has been spearheaded by the Foreign Languages Press in Peking, which has produced a veritable spate of English translations ranging from traditional literature, philosophy and history to modern and contemporary works, including popular fiction, drama, and, inevitably, the writings of such political leaders as Mao Zedong and Deng Xiaoping. Indeed, the Chinese socialist experiment is reflected not only in the choice of works for publication in translation by the Foreign Languages Press, but also in terms of western participation in the translation enterprise. Principal translators for the Foreign Languages Press, the Anglo-Chinese couple, Gladys Yang and her husband Yang Hsien-yi, have been responsible for a vast number of translations of all sorts, and various English academics have also contributed translations for publication by the Foreign Languages Press. The Yangs alone have set their names to translations of such great Classical Chinese novels as *The Scholars* (1957), 20th-century fiction such as *Selected Stories of Lu Hsun* (1954) and Chao Shu-li's *Changes in Li Village* (1953), the Peking opera *The White Snake* (1957), *Poetry and Prose of the Tang and Song* (1984), and *Poetry and Prose of the Ming and Qing* (1986), as well as works of a historical nature.

In the United States, to some extent centred on Columbia University, there has been a considerable advance in both the quantity and the quality of translation of philosophical works from all periods of Chinese history. In addition to new versions of the writings of early philosophers in the Basic Writings series, the Columbia College Program of Translations from the Oriental Classics has also included a translation of the first overall history of China, Sima Qian's 1st-century BC *Shi ji*, by Burton Watson under the title *Records of the Grand Historian* (1961), *Instructions for Practical Living and Other Neo-Confucian Writings by Wang Yang-ming (1472–1529)* translated by Chan Wing-tsit (1963), and *Sources of Chinese Tradition*, an anthology of writings on religion, philosophy and the realm of ideas in general from the earliest times up until the 20th century, edited by W.T. de Bary (1960).

In Britain, the Penguin Classics series has made available new translations of the Confucian philosophical canon as well as an important new translation by David Hawkes and John Minford of the 18th-century novel usually known as *The Dream of the Red Chamber* under its alternative title *The Story of the Stone* (5 vols, 1973–).

IAN MCMORRAN

Further Reading

Chan Sin-wai and David E. Pollard (editors), *An Encyclopaedia of Translation: Chinese–English, English–Chinese*, Hong Kong: Chinese University Press, 1995

DeFrancis, John, *The Chinese Language: Fact and Fantasy*, Honolulu: University of Hawaii Press, 1984

Graham, A.C., "The Translation of Chinese Poetry" in *Poems of the Late T'ang*, Harmondsworth and Baltimore: Penguin, 1965

Hawkes, David, *A Little Primer of Tu Fu*, Oxford: Clarendon Press, 1967

Karlgren, Bernhard, *Sound and Symbol in Chinese*, London: Oxford University Press, 1946; revised edition, Hong Kong: Hong Kong University Press, 1962

Liu, James J.Y., *The Art of Chinese Poetry*, London: Routledge and Kegan Paul, 1962; Chicago: University of Chicago Press, 1966

Ramsey, S. Robert, *The Languages of China*, Princeton, New Jersey: Princeton University Press, 1987

Christine de Pizan c.1364–c.1430

French (Italian-born) poet and historian

Biography

Born in Venice, c.1364. Her father, Thomas de Pizan, physician and astrologer to the French king Charles V, took her to the French court in 1368; there she became well read in Latin, French and Italian. In 1379 she married a court secretary, Étienne du Castel, who died in 1390, leaving her with three children. She began writing to support herself and her young family. She also worked as a copyist. Her patrons included Louis, duke of Orléans, Philip II of Burgundy and Queen Isabel of Bavaria. Her first poems were love ballads. Other early works included pre-feminist writings in defence of women, recently under attack, notably by Jean de Meun(g) in the 13th-century *Romance of the Rose*: these included the prose *Livre de la cité des dames* (*Book of the City of Ladies*) 1405; and the *Livre des trois vertus* (*Book of Three Virtues*), 1405. Later came prose and verse precepts for men, too, on politics, chivalry and warfare. Christine's prolific writings also include patriotic histories such as the 1404 commissioned life of Charles V, the *Livre des faits et bonnes moeurs du sage roi Charles V* (*Book of the Deeds and Good Morals of the Wise King Charles V*), and her last extant work, the poem *Ditié à la louange de Jeanne d'Arc* [Composition in Praise of Joan of Arc], 1429. In about 1418 Christine retired to a Dominican convent at Poissy to escape from the continuing Hundred Years' War. Died c.1430.

Translations

Selections

Blumenfeld-Kosinski, Renate and Kevin Brownlee, *The Selected Writings of Christine de Pizan*, New York: Norton, 1997

De Silva-Vigier, Anil, *Christine de Pisan: Autobiography of a Medieval Woman, 1363–1430*, London: Minerva Press, 1996

Willard, Charity Cannon, *The Writings of Christine de Pizan*, New York: Persea, 1994

Texts Combining Poetry and Prose

Epistre d'Othea, 1400

Babyngton, Anthony [c.1477–1537], *The Epistle of Othea to Hector: A "Lytil Bibell of Knyghthod" edited from the Harleian Manuscript 838*, edited by James D. Gordon, dissertation, University of Pennsylvania, Philadelphia, 1942

Chance, Jane, *Christine de Pizan's Letter of Othea to Hector*, Newburyport, Massachusetts: Focus Information Group, 1990

Scrope, Stephen, *The Epistle of Othea* (c.1440–59), edited by Curt F. Bühler, London and New York: Oxford University Press, 1970 (Early English Text Society)

Wyer, Robert, *The .C. Hystoryes of Troye*, London: Robert Wyer, 1530?

Livre du duc des vrais amants, 1405

Fenster, Thelma S., with lyric poetry translated by Nadia Margolis, *The Book of the Duke of True Lovers*, with an introduction by Fenster, New York: Persea, 1991

Kemp-Welch, Alice, with the ballads translated by Laurence Binyon and Eric R.D. Maclagan, *The Book of the Duke of True Lovers*, with an introduction by Kemp-Welch, London: Chatto and Windus, 1908; New York: Cooper Square, 1966

Poetry

Epistre au dieu d'amours, 1399

Fenster, Thelma S. and Mary C. Erler (editors), *Epistre au dieu d'amours* in their *Poems of Cupid, God of Love* (bilingual edition), Leiden: E.J. Brill, 1990 (also contains Thomas Hoccleve's translation made in 1402)

Prouerbes moraux, 1400–01

Woodville, Anthony, Earl Rivers, *The Moral Proverbes of Christyne*, Westminster: William Caxton, 1478; facsimile edited by William Blades, London: Blades East and Blades, 1859; recent facsimile, Amsterdam: Theatrum Orbis Terrarum, and New York: Da Capo, 1970

Dit de la rose, 1402

Fenster, Thelma S. and Mary C. Erler (editors), *Dit de la rose* in their *Poems of Cupid, God of Love* (bilingual edition), Leiden: E.J. Brill, 1990

Quinze Joyes Nostre Dame, 1402–03

Wall, Glenda, "Christine de Pizan: The XV Joys of Our Lady", *Vox Benedictina*, 2 (1985) pp. 134–47

Ditié de Jehanne d'Arc, 1429

Kennedy, Angus J. and Kenneth Varty (editors), *Ditié de Jehanne D'Arc* (bilingual: English and Middle French), Oxford: Society for the Study of Medieval Languages and Literature, 1977

Prose

Epistres sur le Roman de la rose, 1402

Baird, Joseph L. and John R. Kane (editors), *La Querelle de la Rose: Letters and Documents*, Chapel Hill: University of North Carolina Department of Romance Languages, 1978

Avision-Christine, 1405

McLeod, Glenda K., *Christine's Vision*, New York: Garland, 1993

Livre de la cité des dames, 1405

Anslay, Brian, *The Boke of the Cyte of Ladies*, London: H. Pepwell, 1521; facsimile in *Distaves and Dames: Renaissance Treatises for and about Women*, edited by Diane Bornstein, Delmar, New York: Scholars' Facsimiles and Reprints, 1978

Brown-Grant, Rosalind, *The Book of the City of Ladies*, Harmondsworth: Penguin, 1999

Richards, Earl Jeffrey, *The Book of the City of Ladies*, New York: Persea, 1982

Livre des trois vertus, 1405

Lawson, Sarah, *The Treasure of the City of Ladies; or, The Book of Three Virtues*, Harmondsworth and New York: Penguin, 1985

Willard, Charity Cannon, *A Medieval Woman's Mirror of Honor: The Treasury of the City of Ladies*, edited by Madeleine Pelner Cosman, New York: Persea, 1989

Epistre à la reine, 1405

Wisman, Josette A., *The Epistle of the Prison of Human Life, with An Epistle to the Queen of France and Lament on the Evils of the Civil* War, New York: Garland, 1984

Livre du corps de policie, 1407

Anonymous, *The Body of Polycye*, London: John Skot, 1521; facsimile, Amsterdam: Theatrum Orbis Terrarum, and New York: Da Capo, 1971

Bornstein, Diane, *The Middle English Translation of Christine de Pisan's Livre du corps de policie*, edited from MS C.U.L. Kk.1.5, Heidelberg: Winter, 1977 (edition of 15th-century translation attributed to Anthony Woodville, Earl Rivers; text includes variants from 1521 printed edition)

Forhan, Kate Langdon, *The Book of the Body Politic*, Cambridge and New York: Cambridge University Press, 1994

Lamentacion sur les maux de la France, 1410

Wisman, Josette A., *The Epistle of the Prison of Human Life, with An Epistle to the Queen of France and Lament on the Evils of the Civil War*, New York: Garland, 1984

Livre des fais d'armes et de chevalerie, 1410

Caxton, William, *The Book of Fayttes of Armes and of Chyvalrye*, London: William Caxton, 1489; edited by A.T.P. Byles, London: Oxford University Press (for the Early English Text Society), 1932, corrected edition, 1937; *The Fayt of Armes and of Chyualrye*, Amsterdam: Theatrum Orbis Terrarum, and New York: Da Capo, 1968 (facsimile of Caxton's 1489 edition)

Willard, Sumner, *The Book of Deeds of Arms and of Chivalry*, University Park: Pennsylvania State University Press, 1999

Epistre de la prison de vie humaine, 1416–18

Wisman, Josette A., *The Epistle of the Prison of Human Life, with An Epistle to the Queen of France and Lament on the Evils of the Civil War*, New York: Garland, 1984

Given that Christine de Pizan was herself a translator and that she lived at a period that was ideologically committed to the importance of the *translatio studii*, it is appropriate that a good proportion of her own prolific output can be accessed in a variety of languages, English being the most significant, simply in terms of potential readership and of the number of works translated. Translations of her work can be divided into two main groups: those made during her lifetime or within 100 years of her death, and those made in the 20th century (reflecting the current revival of interest in France's first professional female author). This second group has of course played a significant part in Christine's restoration to the literary canon after centuries of neglect. Translators, ancient or modern, have had to confront virtually identical problems: the availability (or otherwise) of a reliable base text, the unique features of Middle French language (inflections, omission of subject pronouns, which pose particular problems for translations into verse), the difficulty of engaging with hybrid forms combining verse and prose, the challenges presented by Christine's often convoluted prose style and the linguistic inventiveness and technical virtuosity of her verse.

The group of texts translated into Middle English (*Epistre au dieu d'amours*, *Epistre d'Othea, Proverbes moraux*, *Cité des dames*, *Livre du corps de policie* and the *Livre des fais d'armes et de chevalerie*) is important for a variety of reasons. First, the texts have interesting and often unexpected light to shed on the dissemination and popularity of Christine's work in the late mediaeval and early Renaissance period, and the cultural priorities of the reading public (HOCCLEVE's abridgement printed in Fenster & Erler exploits a contemporary taste for debate poems; and translators were clearly catering for a public appreciative of overtly didactic works such as the *Epistre d'Othea*, made available in no fewer than three separate translations by SCROPE, BABYNGTON and WYER, and the *Proverbes moraux* published by Caxton). Second, as linguistic and literary documents in their own right, they reflect the impact of the so-called "curial style" of the chancelleries on the development of English prose (legalistic phraseology, asymmetric and elaborate sentence structure modelled on the Latin period, the proliferation of subordinate clauses, the extensive use of doublets at the level of individual words and whole phrases (e.g. translators enriched their own language by juxtaposing native and borrowed words: "mordrers and occisions", "poys and weight"). Third, for much of the 20th century, the Middle English translations have paradoxically provided (and indeed still provide) access to some of Christine's key works pending the publication of new or better modern critical editions of the original French texts.

Though the second (i.e. modern) group of translations concentrates, as one might expect, on Christine's status as a specifically female author and issues associated with this e.g. the defence of women, the debate on the *Roman de la Rose*, her response as a woman to the doctrines of courtly love (see translations by BROWN-GRANT, RICHARDS, LAWSON, WILLARD & COSMAN, BAIRD & KANE, KEMP-WELCH, FENSTER & ERLER, FENSTER & MARGOLIS, KENNEDY & VARTY), it also includes other texts that shed light on Christine as a writer of autobiography (see MCLEOD) and allegory (see CHANCE), as a political commentator (see FORHAN, WISMAN), as a religious poet (see WALL) or as an exponent of military strategy (see Sumner WILLARD, 1999). Pride of place among the modern translations must be given to Charity WILLARD's remarkable anthology, which provides a reliable and elegant introduction to Christine's writings. The anthologies by DE SILVA VIGIER (aimed at the general reader) and BLUMENFELD-KOSINSKI & BROWNLEE (aimed at both new and specialist readers) also provide invaluable selections of material.

Among the most successful verse renderings of source verse (or partly verse) texts are those by BINYON & MACLAGAN (in Kemp-Welch), FENSTER & ERLER, and FENSTER & MARGOLIS. The incomplete Binyon & Maclagan version of the intercalated poems in the *Livre du duc des vrais amans* has an engaging archaic charm, while Margolis (in the Fenster/Margolis version of the same text) displays extraordinary ingenuity in reproducing (while trying to avoid archaisms) the complicated formal patterns and ludic qualities of Christine's verse. (The main verse narrative, it should be noted, is admirably translated into prose by Fenster.) Equally innovative and equally successful is Fenster's translation (in Fenster & Erler) of the *Epistre au dieu d'amours* and the *Dit de la rose,* rendered respectively into unrhymed lines of iambic pentameter and iambic tetrameter.

With regard to prose translations of source texts wholly or primarily written in prose, probably the most influential to date has been RICHARDS's translation (1982) of the *Cité des dames,* which (in the absence of an easily available Middle French edition) has opened up one of Christine's central texts to specialists and non-specialists alike (a remarkable number of articles and books on the *Cité des dames*, written by scholars working in a variety of disciplines, followed in the wake of the Richards translation). The equally impressive BROWN-GRANT translation (which wisely simplifies syntactic complexity, but retains the legalistic register and polemical tone of the original) is likely to ensure that the *Cité des dames* remains the most easily accessible of Christine's texts. Equally accurate and elegant translations of its sequel, the *Livre des trois vertus*, were published by LAWSON (1985) and WILLARD & COSMAN (1989). The translations of the *Epistre d'Othea* and the *Livre du corps de policie* by CHANCE (1990) and by FORHAN (1994) respectively are interesting, in that they have been produced by scholars attracted to Christine who are not themselves specialists in Middle French (Chance is an English specialist, Forhan a political scientist). Chance has provided a gist translation (verse into blank verse, prose into prose) that will be of use in the classroom (at which her translation is indeed aimed); mistranslations could be cleared up in a revised edition. Forhan has produced an engaging rendering which deliberately does not attempt to reproduce the tortuous complexity of Christine's style; mistranslations, some of which are certainly attributable to the imperfections of the 1967 Lucas edition, could (as in the case of Chance) be eliminated in a revised edition. Finally, reliable translations of three of Christine's letters, the documents on the debate on the *Roman de la Rose*, and Christine's autobiography have been produced by WISMAN (1984), BAIRD & KANE (1978), and MACLEOD (1993) respectively. All of these translations, whatever their merits or deficiencies, are culturally important in that they bear eloquent, collective witness to Christine's current posthumous fame (which Dame Opinion had indeed predicted for her in the *Avision-Christine*).

ANGUS J. KENNEDY

Further Reading

Christine de Pizan Newsletter, 1991–96

Kennedy, Angus J., *Christine de Pizan: A Bibliographical Guide*, London: Grant and Cutler, 1984, and *Supplement 1*, 1994

Willard, Charity Cannon, *Christine de Pizan: Her Life and Works*, New York: Persea, 1984

Yenal, Edith, *Christine de Pizan: A Bibliography*, 2nd edition, Metuchen, New Jersey: Scarecrow Press, 1989

See also introductions and notes to editions and translations

Chuang-tzu

See Zhuangzi

Chuci

See Songs of the South

Church Latin in English Translation

Church Latin is to be understood here primarily as that used in the Latin liturgy of the Christian church. Biblical, patristic and theological texts are therefore excluded from consideration except in so far as they are incorporated into the church's formal liturgy, as, for instance, is the whole of the Old Testament Book of Psalms. The corpus of liturgical Latin incorporates material from the beginning of the Christian era. It comprises chiefly those texts used in the official liturgical books such as those used for the celebration of Mass, for the bestowal of the sacraments, in other rites and ceremonies, and those contained in the canonical hours of the "divine office": matins, lauds, prime, terce, sext, none, vespers and compline. A small part of what is here regarded as Church Latin was originally translated from Greek.

Church Latin immediately raises for the vernacular translator at its most acute point the fundamental problem of reproducing the linguistic register of the original language. What for centuries has been at stake has been the formal and often public expression of the most intimate and intense of private feelings. In addition, the most important translations from Church Latin, which are those designed for liturgical usage, also involve questions of theological orthodoxy. It is further necessary not only to resolve the problems of translating the immensely venerable poetic texts of such liturgical hymns as the *Dies irae* (*Day of Wrath*), with its short rhyming lines and opening vocative case, but to find a way to render something of the majestic prose cadences and complicated syntax of the beautifully balanced ancient collects, "Deus qui dedisti ... : quaesumus ut, sicut ... , ita ..." ("O God, who hast granted ...: grant that, as ... , so ... "). Since, literally understood, these collects request God to change his mind, the language used has tried as far as possible to circumvent any such direct implication. The result of all these constraints, enhancing by quantum leaps those generally felt by all translators, has been the creation of a new hieratic linguistic register, often signalled by stilted, obsolescent English, in which the words do not mean what they would mean outside any liturgical context.

Liturgical translation has been further constrained by time-consecrated usage. Formulae have inevitably lost the force with which they were originally endowed. The name central to Christianity is the foremost case in point. Christ in Greek means "the anointed one". It may still today just be possible to recognize behind the Latin prayer "Domine Jesu Christe, qui dixisti apostolis tuis ... : Qui vivis et regnas Deus per omnia saecula saeculorum" (O Lord Jesus, the Christ, who said to your apostles ... : who live and reign God for ever) the theological affirmation that Jesus is the scripturally foretold anointed one, the Christ. But the ordinary English formula removes the theological statement, and the traditional official translation runs "O Lord Jesus Christ, who didst say unto thine apostles ...: who livest and reignest God for ever and ever". Even the hieratization indicated by the "O", "didst", "unto", "thine", "livest and reignest" and the formulaic but meaninglessly ritualistic "for ever and ever" does nothing to remove the impression given by the English that Jesus Christ is a composite name, rather like Karl Marx. That is a difficulty that does not exist in French, in which the second person singular is still in current use, and in which *Jésus* is "*le* Christ".

The official English version of the Roman missal contains time-honoured mistranslations which render elements of what it printed actually unintelligible. The resulting incomprehensibilities have always enhanced the process of sacralization with which the whole text has been invested, increasing its sense of mystery and disguising the relationship that the "canon" of the mass bears to the most solemn form of ecclesiastical blessing found elsewhere in the liturgy. The missal was issued by Pius V in 1570 and remained in force, supplemented but substantially unchanged, until the mid-20th century. The word *praefatio* is used for the variable first part of the sentence whose second part, starting "Te igitur ... rogamus ac petimus" (Wherefore ... we do pray and beseech thee), opens the canon of the Roman mass. It does not mean "preface", its traditional translation, but something nearer to "that which is spoken out".

The heading "infra actionem" was translated "within the action", but appears to derive from a misreading and to signify nothing, while the phrase *orationes secretae* for the prayers immediately preceding the *praefatio* does not mean "secret prayers", the standard translation, but "prayers over those things [offerings] that are set apart". The erroneous renderings have, however, now been embedded in textbooks and manuals for centuries, and reinforce the signal that the register of liturgical Latin is not that of ordinary communication. The printed Latin text, allied to its accompanying printed chant, does not conform even to normative liturgical usage at the beginning of what is known as the canon of the mass. The "preface" appears to start ("It is truly meet and just ... ") with what is clearly the end of the preceding prayer ("It is meet and just"), before moving on to the greeting invariably preceding a blessing, and the *praefationes* misplace the commas in what should be "Domine, sancte Pater, omnipotens aeterne Deus ... ", giving "Domine sancte, Pater omnipotens, aeterne Deus", rendered in English as "O holy Lord, Father almighty, eternal God".

But the arcaneness lent to the Latin usage, both by its mistakes and its formally balanced chiasmi, patterns and rhythms in both the variable and the invariable text of the mass, establishes a special and unique register of liturgical discourse. Millions have for centuries been enabled by the remoteness of the literary register from the literal meaning of the text, a remoteness that the traditional English translation enhances, to take part in the church's principal act of worship. Only on account of elevation of literary register above that of literal meaning have many found it possible to commit themselves to the Nicene creed, part of the liturgy of the mass, with its affirmations that the "one Lord Jesus Christ ... ascended into heaven ... sitteth at the right hand of the Father", and its inclusion of the statement, "I await (look for) the resurrection of the dead". "Sit" and "right hand" must be metaphors. The presumption is that an acceptable theological meaning can be found for "the resurrection of the dead".

Liturgical translation is of peculiar importance in the Latin, as opposed to the Greek, Christian tradition because of what is not so much a theological principle as a useful rule of thumb, "lex orandi, lex credendi" (the law of prayer is the law of belief). This implies that the belief of the church is embedded in its liturgy, and cannot be at variance with it. However, Christian theology was at first formulated primarily in Greek. While the English theology vernacular is still sufficiently Latinate to allow a one-for-one equivalence between such theologically semi-technical terms as *persona*/person and *natura*/nature, the Latin itself betrays the much richer Greek to an extent that has seriously affected the development of the theology of western Christendom. It was relatively easy in Greek to affirm that Jesus, the Christ, was fully divine and fully human, and even that he was wholly equal in divinity to the Father.

Those doctrines were Latinized in the assertion that Christ, as it had become usual to refer to him, possessed two natures, divine and human, in a single person, but that there were in God three persons with a single nature. Starting out from the English, which transliterates the Latin as developed most importantly by Augustine in his major theological work, the *De trinitate* (*On the Trinity*), we have trinitarian and christological doctrines whose meaning it is impossible to understand without recourse to the original Greek vocabulary. The theological Latin of the major councils and the scholastics is couched in terms belonging to a literary register to which the ordinary rules of logic cannot without heterodoxy be applied.

The formidable difficulties of conveying the meaning of Church Latin in a modern vernacular can be overcome only with the use of massive circumlocutions, virtually describing what is intended by such terms as Scotus's *haecceitas* ("thisness"), and his *distinctio formalis a parte rei* (formal distinction objectively based). The difficulty is not the same as that endemic to the translation of technical terms like "byte" or "modem", generally simply adopted in their original form by host languages. Scotus's terms are easily translated, but their meaning can be conveyed in translation only where knowledge of a whole context of intellectual debate conducted in Latin can be assumed. The analogy is rather with Kant's distinction between *Vernunft* (intelligence) and *Verstand* (reason) or the use of *Phänomenologie* in Hegel and Husserl. Translation is simple. The conveyance of uncontextualized meaning is virtually impossible.

What can be called chancery Church Latin, the language of bulls, briefs, admonitions, and letters, calls for little comment. The vernaculars had their effect, so that Roman admonitions often start with the formula "Miramur quod" (We are surprised that ...) instead of the more seemly classical accusative and infinitive construction. It is the liturgy, and in particular hymns like the *Vexilla regis*, the *Stabat mater*, the *Veni creator*, and the breviary hymns with their often heavily accentuated rhythms, strong rhymes, and short sometimes octosyllabic lines, that create problems requiring for their resolution rare degrees of linguistic virtuosity and poetic skill. If the failure of all attempts to render the poetry of the *Dies irae* into English is understandable, it should none the less have been possible in prose to improve on the official "May the gift of this divine sacrament which we have offered, cleanse and defend us, we beseech thee, O Lord", in exchange for the assonances and rich candescence of the Latin "Mundet et muniat nos, quaesumus, Domine, divini sacramenti munus oblatum".

ANTHONY LEVI

Cicero 106–43 BC

Roman orator, rhetorician, letter writer and political figure

Biography

Marcus Tullius Cicero was born 3 January 106 BC in Arpinum (Italy) into a wealthy equestrian family, but as a statesman he built a career mainly by his own ability and skill, since he was a *homo novus* – a man without inherited standing in Roman politics. After a life of full involvement in the events around him, and fertile activity as a writer, he was killed 7 December 43 BC by the henchmen of Mark Antony, with the knowledge of the future emperor Augustus.

In addition to being an astute yet honest politician and administrator, Cicero practised law. Both his political speeches and those delivered in court are masterpieces of oratorical skill. His treatises on rhetoric are also extraordinary; in both theory and practice he influenced Western rhetoric and oratory more than any other ancient did. Since Cicero was a prolific letter writer (his are real letters, unlike Pliny's epistolary essays), he is known to us much more fully and intimately than anyone else from the classical period. Aside from affording a portrait of a remarkable man and an impression of a turbulent period in Roman history, the letters are outstanding in their command of the Latin language – as are all of Cicero's preserved writings. Finally, although Cicero was not an original philosopher, his knowledge of all the Hellenistic schools of thought was encyclopedic, and it was he who moulded Latin into an instrument for philosophic discourse. (Many important words and concepts, such as *humanitas* and *urbanitas*, were coined – and often exemplified – by him.) His numerous philosophic works show a Roman concern with the pragmatic rather than the abstract but are not at all superficial; many of the subsequent centuries found them instructive and comforting. What Emerson said about Cicero's essay *De senectute* (*On Old Age*) can be applied to his literary activity in general: "charming ... uniform rhetorical merit; heroic with stoical precepts; with a Roman eye to the claims of the state ... and rising ... to a lofty strain". Perhaps no other ancient writer except Plutarch (with his *Lives*) exerted as great an influence on European thought and letters.

Translations

Translations of historic interest

"A Gentleman" [W.H. Main], *The Tusculan Disputations of Marcus Tullius Cicero. In five books. A New Translation*, London: John Whiston and Benjamin White, 1758

Anonymous, *Certaine Epistles of Tully verbally translated: Together with a short Treatise, containing an order of instructing Youth in Grammer, and withall the use and benefite of verball Translations*, London: The Company of Stationers, 1611

Anonymous, *Cicero's Three Books Touching the Nature of the Gods Done into English: With Notes and Illustrations. Setting Forth, (from All Antiquity) What Perceptions, Man, by the Only Light of Reason, may Entertein, concerning a Deity!* London: Joseph Hindmarsh, 1683

Anonymous, *Here begynneth the prohemye vpon the reducynge ... in to our englyssh tongue of the polytyque book named Tullius de senectute*, London: Caxton, 1481; as *Tulle of Olde Age: Textuntersuchung mit literarischer Einführung*, edited by Heinz Susebach, Halle: Max Niemeyer, 1933

E.C.S., *Scipio's Dreame; or, The States-Man's Extasie. Wherein is contayned an Epitomie of all the Sciences, Naturall, Morall, and Supernaturall. Tending to proue the Immortalitie of the Sovle, as the proper merit of Ivstice*, London: printed by B.A. and T. Fawcett for L[awrence] C[hapman], 1627

Grimalde, Nicolas, *Marcus Tullius Ciceroes thre bokes of duties, to Marcus his sonne, turned oute of latine into english*, London: Richard Tottel, 1556 (frequently reprinted)

Jones, E., *Cicero's Brutus; or, History of Famous Orators: also, his Orator; or Accomplished Speaker. Now first translated into English*, London: B. White, 1776

Logan, James, *Cato Major; or, A Treatise on Old Age, by M. Tullius Cicero, with Explanatory Notes from the Roman History*, with an introduction by Benjamin Franklin, Philadelphia, 1744

"T.R." [Thomas Rhymer], *Cicero's Prince. The Reasons and Counsels for Settlement and Good Government of a Kingdom. Collected out of Cicero's Works*, London: S. Mearne, 1668

Tiptoft, John, *Tullius de amicitia, in Englysh. Here after ensueth a goodly treatyse of amyte or friendship compyled in latyn by the most eloquente Romayne Marcus Tullius Cicero and lately translatyd in to Englyshe*, London: W. Rastell, 1530(?)

Collections

Translations of most of the works of Cicero were published in the mid- to late 19th century by Henry G. Bohn, subsequently George Bell & Sons (both London). They represent the efforts of several translators.

Translations of all the surviving works of Cicero are published in the 20th century by Loeb Classical Library (Cambridge, Massachusetts), older versions being gradually replaced by more modern ones. The entire set comprises 28 vols (parallel texts).

Selections

Grant, Michael, *Cicero: Selected Works*, revised edition, Harmondsworth and Baltimore: Penguin, 1965 (contains *Against Verres I*, *Twenty-three Letters*, *The Second Philippic against Antony*, *On Duties III*, *On Old Age*; original edition, 1960)

Grant, Michael, *Cicero: On the Good Life*, with an introduction, Harmondsworth: Penguin, 1971 (contains *Discussions at Tusculum* 5, *On Duties* 2, *Laelius*: *On Friendship*, *On the Orator* 1, *The Dream of Scipio*)

Hadas, Moses (editor), *The Basic Works of Cicero*, New York: Modern Library, 1951 (contains *On Moral Duties* 1, *Tusculan Disputations* 1, *On Old Age*, *Scipio's Dream*, *On the Character of the Orator* 1, *Against Catiline* 1 and 4, *For Caelius*, *Philippic* 2, and a selection of letters)

Oratory and Rhetoric

Bailey, D.R. Shackleton, *Philippics* (parallel texts), Chapel Hill: University of North Carolina Press, 1986

Bailey, D.R. Shackleton, *Back from Exile: Six Speeches upon His Return*, Atlanta, Georgia: Scholars Press, 1991 (contains *Speech of Thanks in the Senate*, *Speech of Thanks to the Citizens*, *On His House*, *On the Answers of the Haruspices*, *In Defense of Publius Sestius*, and *Examination of the Witness Publius Vatinius*)

Grant, Michael, *Selected Political Speeches of Cicero*, revised edition, Harmondsworth: Penguin, 1973; with new bibliography, London and New York: Penguin, 1989 (contains *On the Command of Cnaeus Pompeius*, *Against Lucius Sergius Catilina* 1–4, *In Defence of the Poet Aulus Licinius Archias*, *In Defence of Marcus Caelius Rufus*, *In Defence of Titus Annius Milo*, *In Support of Marcus Claudius Marcellus*, *The First Philippic against Marcus Antonius*)

Grant, Michael, *Murder Trials*, with an introduction, revised edition, Harmondsworth and New York: Penguin 1990 (contains *In Defence of Sextus Roscius of America*, *In Defence of Aulus Cluentius Habitus*, *In Defence of Gaius Rabirius*, *In Defence of King Deiotarus*; original edition 1975)

King, John R., *The Fourteen Philippic Orations of Marcus Tullius Cicero*, Oxford: James Thornton, 1878

Lacey, W.K., *Second Philippic Oration* (parallel texts), Warminster, Wiltshire: Aris and Phillips, 1986

Mitchell, T.N., *Verrines* 2.1 (parallel texts), Warminster, Wiltshire: Aris and Phillips, 1986

Watson, J.S., *Cicero on Oratory and Orators*, part of the *Landmarks in Rhetoric and Public Address* series, with an introduction by Ralph A. Micken, Carbondale: Southern Illinois University Press, 1970 (a reprint of a Bohn edition of 1848, as reprinted by Harper, New York, 1878)

Letters

Bailey, D.R. Shackleton, *Cicero's Letters to Atticus* (parallel texts), 7 vols, Cambridge: Cambridge University Press, 1965–70; translations in one volume, Harmondsworth: Penguin, 1978

Bailey, D.R. Shackleton, *Cicero's Letters to His Friends*, Harmondsworth: Penguin, 1978; Atlanta, Georgia: Scholars Press, 1978

Bailey, D.R. Shackleton, *Cicero: Selected Letters*, Harmondsworth and New York: Penguin, 1986 (selections from the above)

Wilkinson, L.P., *Letters of Cicero: A New Selection in Translation*, London: G. Bles, 1949; revised edition, *Letters of Cicero: A Selection in Translation*, London: Hutchinson University Library, and New York: Norton, 1966

Willcock, M.M., *The Letters of January to April 43* BC (parallel texts), Warminster, Wiltshire: Aris and Phillips, 1995

Philosophy

Copley, Frank O., *On Old Age, and On Friendship*, Ann Arbor: University of Michigan Press, 1967

Dingus, G.W., *The Best of Life: A Streamlined Translation of Cicero's Essay on Old Age*, San Antonio, Texas: Naylor, 1967

Douglas, A.E., *Cicero: Tusculan Disputations* 1 (parallel texts), Warminster, Wiltshire: Aris and Phillips, and Chicago: Bolchazy-Carducci, 1985

Edinger, Harry G., *Cicero: De officiis / On Duties*, with an introduction and notes, Indianapolis: Bobbs Merrill, 1974

Griffin, M.T. and E.M. Atkins, *On Duties*, Cambridge and New York: Cambridge University Press, 1991

Higginbotham, John, *On Moral Obligation: A New Translation of Cicero's "De officiis"* with introduction and notes, London: Faber, and Berkeley: University of California Press, 1967

McGregor, Horace C.P., *The Nature of the Gods*, Harmondsworth: Penguin, 1972

Powell, J.G.F., *Laelius: On Friendship (Laelivs: De Amicitia), and The Dream of Scipio (Somnivm Scipionis)* (parallel texts), with an introduction and commentary, Warminster, Wiltshire: Aris and Phillips, 1990

English translations of Cicero could easily form the subject of a book. His conservatism and moderation, his fundamental decency and love of clarity seem to have had special appeal to the British, although other Western countries and literatures were also greatly influenced. The present survey limits itself to a small selection of translations, mainly of philosophic works, that are representative of earlier periods, when Cicero was a real moral force; followed by an appraisal of a limited number of modern versions, arranged as to the particular kind of writing to which they belong.

Cicero uses different kinds of style for his oratory, his philosophic works, and his letters. It is very difficult not to let all these sound similar in translation. Another challenge comes from the virtual impossibility of transferring satisfactorily into English Cicero's remarkable command of periodic sentence structure – and even more difficult – his masterly use of prose rhythms. English has an advantage over Latin in its enormous vocabulary (the number of Latin vocables is relatively small); but although the period has been skilfully employed by great stylists such as Samuel Johnson, Cicero's virtuosity with prose rhythms is impossible to express in English.

Modern readers may find their progress impeded by the topical and historical allusions in his works. A translator's best stratagem is to use footnotes – but with a light hand, so that reading may proceed smoothly. Good translators provide informative introductions as well as maps and indices of various kinds, so that it is not necessary to have recourse to reference works while reading.

Translations of historic interest

Most of the titles included here speak for themselves. A large number of early translations of Cicero (up to and including the 18th century) are anonymous, or virtually so. One can only speculate why. Many translations are compendia of selections put together to serve some religious or philosophical purpose; that they were expected to be effective shows how revered Cicero's authority was, especially in the 17th century. Also worthy of note is the pedagogic aim of numerous translations: not only to help a student master Latin but to teach him how to think in a clear and disciplined way, and to write English after the Latin (and specifically Ciceronian) model.

All the early translations listed here possess considerable antiquarian charm. Some features of several of them deserve mention. The ANONYMOUS *Certaine Epistles* of 1611 is prefaced by an early treatise on translation. The "T.R." *Prince* of 1688 is intended as a counterpoise to Machiavelli, constructed out of material drawn from Cicero: "It hath in it Maximes, which void of all Stains, and flaws of *Machiavillian* Interest, are raised only upon principles of Honor and Vertue ... " The ANONYMOUS *Cicero's Three Books* of 1683 makes the Roman writer into a natural Christian: at the end of the polemical preface the translator declares: "*what Greater* Honour, *than for him* [Cicero] *to be joyn'd with* Christ ... " LOGAN's elegant translation (1744) of *Cato Major* (*De senectute*), frequently reprinted in Britain, is of particular interest to Americans. It exemplifies the classical, and especially Republican Roman, orientation of the colonies and the early United States. Franklin (who in subsequent editions erroneously appears to be the translator) speaks in the introduction of his "hearty wish, that this first translation of a classic, in this western world, may be followed with many others, performed with equal judgment and success; and be a happy omen, that Philadelphia shall become the seat of the American Muses".

Collections

The Bohn translations (with the possible exception of Watson, see below) have outlived their usefulness and are superseded by the Loeb series. The style of most of the Bohn volumes possesses a rather attractive stateliness, and there are useful notes, but the books are based on old editions of the source texts that are no longer satisfactory. Certainly they are not intended for the specialist, but rather reflect the cultural aspirations of the Victorian middle class. Because of their literalness they have been much valued by generations of school children, as "trots".

Considering how many translators have been, and are, involved in the Loeb series, the quality of these complete works of Cicero in English is predictably uneven, but the overall level is very high. Many volumes stand out, for instance, R. Gardner's and N.H. Watts's translations of some of the speeches. Harry Caplan's scholarly edition and translation of the pseudo-Ciceronian *Rhetorica ad Herennium* (with footnotes that amount to a commentary) are indispensable for any student of rhetoric. In general, readers should choose the more recent Loeb versions over the older ones (thus C. Macdonald's 1977 translation of some of the speeches over L.E. Lord's 1937, revised

1946). (It should be noted that several of the newer volumes are basically reworkings of previous ones.)

Selections

GRANT's selection (1965, 1971) offer the best possible introduction to Cicero's varied talents. They are scholarly yet lively and accessible to the general reader. HADAS's collection (1951) takes second place; also attractive, it is not as easily obtainable.

Oratory and Rhetoric

The introduction by R.A. Micken (1970) points out that WATSON's *Cicero on Oratory and Orators* (1848) "still remains an excellent source ... The language is quite clear and thoroughly understandable .. textual and historical notes ... still pertinent and reliable ... useful to the person who is not able to read the Latin." The Southern Illinois reissue of Watson is intended not for the classicist but for the student of rhetoric, and the introduction and bibliographies are aimed at such a person. Watson bases his version of *De oratore* on George Barnes's (1762) and appends E. Jones's version of *Brutus* (1776). A volume useful in its way, but the corresponding Loeb editions are preferable.

Although most 19th-century translations can no longer be recommended, KING's *Philippics* (1878) exemplify the best of them and are well worth reading.

GRANT's two selections (1973, 1990) of Cicero's speeches supplement very well his two general selections from Cicero (see above). Grant manages to offer the reader a most attractive variety within any of these volumes, and his introductions, notes, lists of terms, genealogical tables, tables of dates, maps, and indices, as well as the brief but well-chosen bibliographies, are models of informative conciseness.

Editions of classical texts published by Aris and Phillips are intended mainly for those many present-day students who have no, or very little, Latin and Greek and thus are able to study the classics only in translation, with perhaps sporadic and uncertain glances at the original text; or who at best make their way through the original with the help of translation. Not all the Aris and Phillips editions are covered here. LACEY's (1986) and MITCHELL's (1986) stand out in their usefulness, although because of their aims the quality of translation falls short of Bailey's or Grant's.

BAILEY's admirably scholarly editions and translations (1986, 1991) are well supplied with notes, appendices, indices of various kinds, and similar helpful materials. He is one of the most outstanding Ciceronian scholars of this century; all his publications are reliable and show profound learning, as well as excellent style.

Letters

BAILEY's work (1965–70, 1978, 1986) on Cicero's letters is as magisterial as that on the speeches (see above).

However, Bailey does not have the field entirely to himself. WILKINSON's selection of Cicero's letters (1966) is very attractive, and the translation shows great sensitivity to Latin style.

WILLCOCK (1995) offers the student an edition of "thirty-three letters exchanged between Cicero and various correspondents ... all the letters surviving from ... the beginning of the final and decisive stage in the change from Roman republic to Roman empire ..."

Philosophy

COPLEY's versions (1967) of what may be Cicero's most humane and universally appealing works, *On Old Age* and *On Friendship*, show this master translator at the top of his form. A reader can do no better than to choose these translations. Despite the breezy subtitle, DINGUS's translation (1967) is very attractive. She slightly abridges the essay *On Old Age*. The "author's" personal commentary is really the translator's. POWELL (*Laelius: On Friendship and The Dream of Scipio*, 1990) compares favorably with the other editions published by Aris and Phillips.

HIGGINBOTHAM's *On Moral Obligation* (1967) is a fine translation; EDINGER's version (1974) of *De officiis* (he also translated *De senectute* and *De amicitia*, as *On Old Age* and *On Friendship*) reads easily and smoothly; but Griffin & Atkins's is preferable. GRIFFIN & ATKINS's translation (1991) of what is probably Cicero's most influential work (*De officiis* was standard reading in the Renaissance and left a deep imprint upon the Enlightenment) is excellent. It is thorough, reliable, elegant, and has copious notes, critical bibliographies, and helpful indices. If the Latinless reader has the leisure, one may recommend parallel reading of the three translations of *De officiis* reviewed here. If only one can be chosen, it should be Griffin & Atkins.

MCGREGOR (*The Nature of the Gods*, 1972) offers a good modern translation of *De natura deorum*, not the most popular philosophic work of Cicero, but still an important one. He includes an "Imaginary Continuation of the Dialogue" (by J.M. Ross), which puts in dramatic form the later reception of this work.

DOUGLAS's excellent translation of the *Tusculan Disputations* (1985) compares very well with other Aris and Phillips editions (see above).

ZOJA PAVLOVSKIS-PETIT

Further Reading

Rolfe, John C., *Cicero and His Influence*, Boston: Marshall Jones, 1923; reprinted New York: Cooper Square, 1963

See also Douglas's appendix, Grant's introduction to *On the Good Life*, Griffin & Atkins's notes on translation and Lacey's introduction – the latter especially good on problems of translation

Classic Translations

The notion that translations die, age, fade or disappear is one that regularly appears in writing on translation. George Steiner, for example, with characteristic appreciation of the translator's humble role, states in *After Babel*: "A true translator knows that his labour belongs 'to oblivion' (inevitably each generation retranslates) or 'to the other one', his occasion, begetter and precedent shadow".

Some translations, however, succeed in avoiding "oblivion". Their existence, historical value and artistic merits continue to be recognized, and remembered – even if they are seldom, if ever, read. What happens is that they become "classic translations".

Classic translations are those that, with the passage of time, have ceased to be read, but that we remember as having been important; either because they brought an important original to the attention of the target culture, or because they were particularly good when they were published – most probably a combination of both these reasons, in that often the former is in part a result of the latter.

When the term classic is applied to a translation that is still in print, still being read, then in effect, all that is being said is that this is a translation that will become a classic in the sense described above (a prophecy by no means always fulfilled). *No one ever doubts that a classic translation, no matter how great, will eventually cease to be read and be replaced by a newer version.*

André Lefevere, in *Translating Poetry*, has described this as the translation becoming "a literary work in its own right". This is true to the extent that the translator acquires the status of an author, his work the status of an original, but the fact remains that they will be read only very rarely.

There are a number of translations into English that have achieved this sort of status and the after-life that comes with it, such as Chapman's Homer, Urquhart's Rabelais, or more recently, Constance Garnett's translations of Russian literature, particularly Dostoevskii. But an outstanding example is the case of Henry Cary, who in 1814 published a translation of Dante's *Divina commedia* that became an overnight classic – in part because of the enthusiastic reviews it received from Coleridge and Foscolo. Cary was thought to have achieved the impossible; to have succeeded in *englishing* Dante and at the same time producing a work that was worthy of the original. His blank verse was thought to be "Miltonic": a label that was a recognition of the degree of his success. Cary's is one of the most successful translations in English, as it remained in print, *unaltered*, for almost 100 years. This despite the countless other translations of Dante that were published in the meantime, and despite the accusation levelled at him by many of his successors that he had departed unduly from the original text. Cary's fame was such that when he died he was buried in Poet's Corner in Westminster Cathedral, his tomb bearing the inscription "Translator of Dante". Very few authors have achieved such consecration, let alone translators.

Here then, is a translation that has been out of print for four generations, but that we still remember as a classic. Nevertheless, no amount of success seems to be able to produce a "definitive" translation; one that can indefinitely withstand the passage of time.

Some translations, however, are particularly resistant, and may yet rival the success of Cary. FitzGerald's translation of Omar Khayy?m, for example, is still in print nearly 150 years after it was first published. Khayy?m is not a canonical figure in English literature, however, so FitzGerald's translation has not had to withstand the same degree of scrutiny as translations of the great European canonical figures have been subjected to – with the inevitable revisions and attempts at new and better translations that then follow.

The success of C.K. Scott Moncrieff's translation of Proust's *À la recherche du temps perdu* is more comparable to that of Cary. The history of this translation is perhaps an example of the most that any translator can hope to achieve in the way of status as an original, for so far, despite a number of revisions and two important changes in the source text, Scott Moncrieff has not yet been replaced. As we shall see, however, this is not an undiluted success, and has involved some severe compromises being made with Scott Moncrieff's original "authorial" translation.

Scott Moncrieff's *Remembrance of Things Past* is one of the few translations that people read knowing who the translator is, appreciating his achievement and often praising it – affording him, in short, some of the status of an author and his translation the status of an original.

The status of his translation as an original is made clear by the respect with which it was treated by those who revised it. Its status as a translation is confirmed by Scott Moncrieff's personal fame and by the fame that his translation enjoys. In Britain, for example, the Translators Association, which is part of the Society of Authors, instituted two yearly translation prizes in 1964: the Scott Moncrieff Prize and the Schlegel/Tieck Prize, for the best translation from French and German respectively, thereby placing Scott Moncrieff on a par with one of the great European translations.

Scott Moncrieff began translating *À la recherche* when Proust was still alive and did not actually complete the work himself. The last book, *Time Regained*, was translated by Sidney Schiff under the pseudonym of Stephen Hudson, in a spirit of humility and great respect towards Scott Moncrieff. This translation, published in 1941 by Chatto and Windus, remained the standard version for 40 years, unchallenged by any new translations.

However, in 1954, a new Pléiade edition of the French original was published, establishing itself immediately as a milestone and completely replacing the *Nouvelle Revue Française* edition, which seems to have been universally unpopular. Because of the considerable changes made, the Proust text was now very different from the one on which Scott Moncrieff worked.

In 1981 Chatto and Windus published a new edition of Scott Moncrieff's translation with the heading "translated by C.K. Scott Moncrieff and Terence Kilmartin" – which includes Andreas Mayor's translation of *Time Regained* ("with minor emendations") and no longer Stephen Hudson's (though no mention is made of Mayor on the title page). This same edition was then revised by D.J. Enright (Kilmartin had died) in 1993 following the publication of a second Pléiade edition.

Both the 1981 and the 1993 "Kilmartin" Editions contain Kilmartin's "note on the translation". In this note he writes extensively on both the merits of Scott Moncrieff's version and the need to revise it. What is interesting is the way in which he tries to keep a foot in both camps: he wants to reassure those who feel attached to the version they know and love that his intention is simply to bring Scott Moncrieff's translation into line with the new original; while at the same time he wants to satisfy those who find Scott Moncrieff dated, or are critical of his approach, that he has in fact intervened to *improve* the translation.

The title pages of both editions confirm this contradictory editorial approach. On the one hand, Scott Moncrieff's name is still a selling-point, causing the revised versions to hang on to it despite the many changes that have been made to the text. On the other, Kilmartin has been elevated to the rank of translator, and not simply reviser, in order to show how important are the changes he has made to the text, that in effect the translation is also his work. This double crediting is emblematic of the whole operation, which aims to be all things to all men: the same well-loved translation to admirers of Scott Moncrieff, a new more "correct", stylistically more contemporary, version for those who for one reason or another are unsatisfied with Scott Moncrieff.

Which, if either, of the two objectives is actually achieved is a much debated point, and there does not appear to be any general agreement. It is probably fair to say that those who appreciate Scott Moncrieff feel that Kilmartin and Enright have shown considerable tact and sensitivity and have succeeded in "modernizing" the translation and giving it a new lease of life. Others, who for whatever reason are dissatisfied with Scott Moncrieff, feel that it would simply have been better to produce a new translation.

To conclude, then, we might argue that Scott Moncrieff has been treated with an exceptional degree of deference. Even when his translation has been revised twice, extensively corrected, and when the original he worked on has been re-edited twice, he retains his position as *the* translator of Proust for another generation.

Yet this classic translation, this recognized masterpiece, has been re-written and reorganized; it has had its style corrected and brought into line with tastes different from those of the translator. So that if we look at it another way, we might argue that Scott Moncrieff's "original" has been more effectively eradicated than if someone had simply produced a new version that eventually became the standard. Those who want to read the original Cary can simply do so, but those who wish to read the "original" Scott Moncrieff are faced with the difficulty of having to decide which of the three Scott Moncrieff translations *is* the original.

The first volume of a new translation of Proust's novel, in seven volumes each by a different hand, is due to be published by Penguin in autumn 2002.

CHRISTOPHER RUNDLE

Further Reading

Adams, Robert M., "A Clear View of Combray", *Times Literary Supplement* (12 June 1981) (review of Kilmartin's first revision of Scott Moncrieff)

Benjamin, Walter, "The Task of the Translator" in *Illuminations*, translated by Harry Zohn, edited by H. Arendt, New York: Harcourt Brace, 1968; London: Jonathan Cape, 1970

Bernstein, Richard, "Howard's Way", *New York Times Magazine* (25 September 1988) pp. 40–44 (article on Richard Howard's Proust translation)

Corn, Alfred, "Time to Read Proust", *Hudson Review*, 35/2 (1982) pp. 298–305 (includes criticism of Kilmartin's first revision of Scott Moncrieff)

Craig, George, "fine-Tuning Proust", *Times Literary Supplement* (22 October 1993) (review of D.J. Enright's revision of the Scott Moncrieff-Kilmartin translation)

De Sua, William J., *Dante into English*, Chapel Hill: University of North Carolina Press, 1964

Grieve, James, "On Translating Proust", *Journal of European Studies*, 12/1 (1982) pp. 55–67 (review of Kilmartin's first revision of Scott Moncrieff)

Howard, Richard, "From *In Search of Lost Time*", *Paris Review*, 31/3 (1989) pp. 14–33 (interview with Richard Howard on his translation of Proust; includes an excerpt from the first chapter)

Kilmartin, Terence, "Translating Proust", *Grand Street*, 1/1 (1981) pp. 134–46

Lefevere, André, *Translating Poetry: Seven Strategies and a Blueprint*, Amsterdam: Van Gorcum, 1975

Lefevere, André, *Translation, Rewriting, and the Manipulation of Literary Fame*, London and New York: Routledge, 1992

Steiner, George, *After Babel: Aspects of Language and Translation*, Oxford and New York: Oxford University Press, 1975; 3rd edition 1998

Tapscott, Stephen, "Proust Retrouvé", *Yale Review*, 71/4 (1982) pp. 612–22 (review of Kilmartin's first revision of Scott Moncrieff)

Toynbee, Paget, "English Translations of Dante in the Eighteenth Century", *Modern Language Review*, 1 (1905–06) pp. 9–24

Toynbee, Paget, *Dante in English Literature: From Chaucer to Cary (c. 1380–1844)*, 2 vols, London: Methuen, 1909

Venuti, Lawrence, *The Translator's Invisibility: A History of Translation*, London and New York: Routledge, 1995

Claudian c.AD 370–c.404

Roman poet

Biography

Claudius Claudianus, the last major figure in the history of classical Latin literature, was born in Alexandria c.370. His earlier poems were written in Greek, but after going to live in Rome (395) he became a great Latin stylist. He was a courtier, possibly a Christian, although his work shows no evidence of Christianity. It is permeated with strong political feeling very much in the Roman mode, akin in spirit – and in sonority of expression – to Cicero and Sallust. His poems are rhetorical, but the rhetoric is virile, brilliant and powerful, although on occasion he becomes prolix. His greatest talent is for description and for intense invective, in which he rivals the great Roman satirists. The unfinished *De raptu Proserpinae* (*The Rape of Proserpina*) has real feeling for nature and for the Eleusinian myth.

Translations

Barr, William, *Claudian's Panegyric on the Fourth Consulate of Honorius* (parallel texts), with an introduction, Liverpool: Francis Cairns, 1981

Brittain, Frederick, in his *Penguin Book of Latin Verse* (parallel texts), Harmondsworth and Baltimore: Penguin, 1962, pp. 84–85

Digges, Leonard, *The Rape of Proserpine*, London: Edward Blount, 1617; edited by H.H. Huxley, Liverpool: Liverpool University Press, 1959

Gruzelier, Claire, *De Raptu Proserpinae* (parallel texts), Oxford: Clarendon Press, and New York: Oxford University Press, 1993

Hawkins, A., *The Works of Claudian* (parallel text to several of the poems in vol. 1), 2 vols, London: Porter and Langdon, 1817

Howard, Henry, *Translations from Claudian*, London: John Murray, 1823

Isbell, Harold, in his *The Last Poets of Imperial Rome*, Harmondsworth and Baltimore: Penguin, 1971, pp. 72–117

Lindsay, Jack, in his *Song of a Falling World: Culture During the Break-up of the Roman Empire* (AD 350–600), London: Andrew Dakers, 1948, pp. 135–60

Platnauer, Maurice, *Claudian* (parallel texts), with an introduction, 2 vols, London: Heinemann, and Cambridge, Massachusetts: Harvard University Press, 1922; reprinted 1972–76 (Loeb Classical Library)

Pope, R. Martin, *The Rape of Proserpine* (parallel texts), London: Dent, 1934

Strutt, Jacob George, *The Rape of Proserpine, with Other Poems from Claudian*, London: Longman Hurst Rees Orme and Brown, 1814

Gibbon's appraisal of Claudian deserves quoting: "He was endowed with the rare and precious talent of raising the meanest, of adorning the most barren, and of diversifying the most similar topics". Modern literary taste has a lower opinion of raising, adorning, and diversifying than did the 18th century; consequently Claudian is much less popular than he used to be. Often modern translations form but a part of a scholarly edition and are intended to show the editor's grasp of the difficult text rather than aimed at the general reader. The panegyric is no longer part of the literary scene, and invective has taken on forms other than poetry. Hence, access to Claudian is difficult, yet some of the translations discussed here do facilitate it. Claudian's short early Greek poems are included in the translations of his complete works.

DIGGES (1617) is mainly notable in English letters for his contribution of verses to the first Folio, as well as the 1640 edition, of Shakespeare. His version of *The Rape of Proserpine* is in rhymed verse; it is more interesting as an Elizabethan poem than as a translation of Claudian. Digges not only expands the wording of the original (a procedure quite unnecessary with so ample a poet) but even adds passages to the text, for instance, he inserts the story of Narcissus. Huxley's notes enable the reader to assess where Claudian ends and Digges begins.

STRUTT (1814) includes *The Rape*, *Rufinus*, and some of the shorter poems such as "The Phoenix" and "The Old Man of Verona". His verse gives little idea of the brilliance of the original and his use of rhyme is rather crude and intrusive.

HAWKINS's (1817) is the first complete translation of Claudian into English. Done in rhymed verse, it bears a resemblance to the poetry of Alexander Pope, yet this English Augustan tone rather fits the self-conscious formality and the vigor of the original.

HOWARD (1823) includes Book One of *Against Rufinus, The Third Consulate of Honorius, The Marriage of Honorius and Maria, Epithalamium on the Marriage of Honorius and Maria, The Gildonic War*, and *The Consulate of Mallius Theodorus*. While Hawkins sounds like Pope, Howard seems more Miltonic. His rhymed verse is energetic and he offers copious notes, with parallels from the Bible – of interest to the English reader, especially of Howard's time, but somewhat misleading in view of Claudian's entirely non-Christian frame of reference and approach to his material.

POPE (1934) uses rhyme in his translation of the prefaces to *The Rape* and beautifully cadenced unrhymed verse for the rest of the poem. He also includes the poem on the Saviour (which is probably not the work of Claudian) and an effective rhymed rendering of "The Old Man of Verona".

LINDSAY's study (1948) of late Latin literature is reliable, engaging, and helpful. This is an interesting period, but few people aside from specialists know much about it. One can think of no better introduction than *Song of a Falling World*. Lindsay's discussion is interspersed with effective, very readable translations, rhymed and unrhymed. He offers generous and varied selections from Claudian's longer poems, including samples of panegyric and invective, as well as *The Rape*, and a number of the short poems.

BRITTAIN (1962) includes in his anthology Claudian's short poem on the old man of Verona as "The Stay-at-Home". This is a plain prose translation, close and reliable.

ISBELL (1971) includes in his anthology *The Rape of Proserpine* and *Epithalamium for Honorius Augustus and*

Maria, Daughter of Stilicho (identical with the epithalamium mentioned in the paragraph on Howard). These are simple but excellent verse translations of Claudian's mythological poems (the epithalamium mixes current events and myth.) Isbell is idiomatic and readable, and anyone who is interested in myth and looking for a rewarding treatment of the story of Proserpina (in addition to that found in the Homeric hymn of Demeter) should probably turn to this version.

PLATNAUER (1922) is the first to translate all of Claudian into English prose. The purpose of the Loeb series is to facilitate access to the original, and Platnauer fulfils it. He is reliable and readable, although the poetry is lost. There is a good general introduction and some notes.

BARR's prose translation (1981) is part of a scholarly edition, with introduction and commentary. Not the most important portion of this book, the translation is extremely literal and makes for uncomfortable reading.

GRUZELIER's prose rendering (1993), like Barr's, is not meant for the general reader. It is less a literary achievement than a proof of the editor's mastery of the text. However, this is a precise and quite readable translation of *The Rape*.

ZOJA PAVLOVSKIS-PETIT

Further Reading
See the prefaces to Isbell and Platnauer

Hugo Claus 1929–

Flemish novelist, short-story writer, poet, dramatist, and stage and film director

Biography
Born Hugo Maurice Julien Claus in Bruges, Belgium, 5 April 1929. He attended schools in Belgian Flanders (at Eke, Aalbeke, Courtrai, Deinze, Ghent), including a convent boarding school. Before becoming a full-time writer he was housepainter, agricultural worker and actor. From 1949 to 1955 he edited *Tijd en Mens* and *Nieuw Vlaams Tijdshrift*. In the 1950s he lived for a time in Paris, moving in advanced artistic circles. His first novel, *De metsiers* (*The Duck Hunt*), about life in rural flanders, appeared in 1950. He married Elly Overzier in 1955 (one son).

Claus has been awarded literary prizes in Belgium and abroad; these include the Krijn prize, 1951; the Lugné-Poë prize (France), 1955; the Triennial Belgian State prize several times from 1955 on, for drama and for verse; the Huygens prize, 1979; and the Prize for Dutch Letters, 1986.

Translations
Fiction

De metsiers, 1950
Libaire, George, *The Duck Hunt*, New York: Random House, 1955; as *Sister of Earth*, London: Panther, 1966

Het verlangen, 1978
Knecht, Stacey, *Desire*, New York and London: Viking, 1997

De verzoeking, 1981
Willinger, David and Luc Deneulin, *The Temptation*, New York: Center for Advanced Study in Theatre Arts, 1984; reprinted in *Four Works for the Theatre by Hugo Claus*, edited by David Willinger, New York: City University, 1990

Het verdriet van België, 1983
Pomerans, Arnold J., *The Sorrow of Belgium*, New York: Pantheon, and London: Viking Penguin, 1990

De zwaardvis, 1989
Levitt, Ruth, *The Swordfish*, with an introduction, London: Peter Owen, 1996

Plays

Vrijdag, 1969
Claus, Hugo and Christopher Logue, *Friday*, London: Davis Poynter, 1972
Willinger, David and Lucas Truyts, *Friday*, New York: Center for Advanced Study in Theatre Arts, 1986; reprinted in *Four Works for the Theatre by Hugo Claus*, edited by Willinger, New York: City University, 1990

Het leven en de werken van Leopold II, 1970
Willinger, David and Lucas Truyts, *The Life and Works of Leopold II* in *An Anthology of Contemporary Belgian Plays, 1970–1982*, edited by Willinger, Troy, New York: Whitston, 1984

Thuis, 1975
Willinger, David and Lucas Truyts, *Back Home* in *An Anthology of Contemporary Belgian Plays, 1970–1982*, edited by Willinger, Troy, New York: Whitston, 1984

Het haar van de hond, 1982
Willinger, David and Lucas Truyts, *The Hair of the Dog*, New York: Center for Advanced Study in Theatre Arts, 1988; reprinted in *Four Works for the Theatre by Hugo Claus*, edited by Willinger, New York: City University, 1990

Serenade, 1984
Willinger, David, and Lucas Truyts, in their *The Hair of the Dog*, New York: Center for Advanced Study in Theatre Arts, 1985; reprinted in *Four Works for the Theatre by Hugo Claus*, edited by Willinger, New York: City University, 1990

Winteravond, 1994
Charters, Paul, Katheryn Ronnan Bradbeer and Paul Vincent, *Winter Evening*, *Modern Poetry in Translation*, new series 12 (Winter 1997) pp. 224–41

Selection of Poetry
Hermans, Theo, Peter Nijmeijer and Paul Brown, *Selected Poems, 1953–1973*, edited by Hermans, Portree, Skye: Aquila, 1986

Poetry
Het teken van de hamster, 1963
Claes, Paul, Christine D'haen, Theo Hermans and Yann Lovelock, *The Sign of the Hamster* (parallel texts), with an introduction by Claes, Leuven: Leuvense Schrijversaktie, 1986

The literary output of Hugo Claus, which to date comprises over a hundred volumes of fiction, drama and poetry, is daunting for its complexity and diversity as much as for its size. Just as the man himself is both the *enfant terrible* of contemporary Dutch-language literature and its most prized and fêted author, so his work ranges across genres and styles. He varies and combines literary modes and linguistic registers with astonishing ease, and freely mixes elemental passion with political satire, unabashed naturalism with allusive erudition, and Oedipal imagery with burlesque humour. A daringly experimental streak runs through his entire oeuvre.

Most of Claus's work is firmly set in his native Flanders. For the translator, major problems result from this. Many of the novels and plays exploit the spoken Flemish variant of Dutch, contrasting it with the standard language and using intermediate sub- or quasi-standard forms to great effect. Topical references abound, as they serve to evoke or caricature the social background and intellectual horizons of individual characters. Flanders being a traditionally Catholic region, references to Catholic rituals and customs are especially pervasive, and may be played out ironically in combination with Classical mythology or Freudian symbols. Claus's penchant for working patterns and fragments of other texts garnered from his vast reading into his own writing further complicates an already complex picture.

In a survey of Claus's literary output in relation to the English translations of his work, two things are striking. First, while several of his major books of fiction and drama have appeared in translation, other works regarded in the Low Countries as equally outstanding remain untranslated. This is the case, for example, with such early novels as the multi-layered and brooding *De verwondering* [Wonderment] (1962) and *Omtrent Deedee* [About Deedee] (1963) – even though Claus himself also adapted the latter for the stage (*Interieur*, 1974) and subsequently made it into a film (*Het sacrament*, 1989) – and, among the plays, with the early key work *Suiker* [Sugar] of 1958, a study of raw power.

Second, the translations clearly fall into two periods. Claus's first novel *De Metsiers*, written in a Faulknerian mode when he was just 18 and published in 1950, was translated five years later (Libaire, 1955, reissued 1966). The romantic play *A Bride in the Morning* (*Een bruid in de morgen*, 1955) appeared in English in 1960, and Claus himself collaborated with Christopher Logue on a translation of *Friday* (1972), which was staged in a fringe theatre in London. It seemed a promising enough beginning, but it petered out. It was not until the mid-1980s that interest was revived. Together with Dutch native speakers the American translator David WILLINGER brought out a number of plays in quick succession (Willinger, 1984, 1985, 1986, 1988). Coincidentally, a selection of Claus's early poems and his long, Poundian verse autobiography appeared in English around the same time (CLAES, 1986; HERMANS, 1986). All of these translations however were published by relatively marginal publishers and failed to reach a wide audience. The breakthrough came in 1990 with the translation of Claus's prose masterpiece *The Sorrow of Belgium* (POMERANS, 1990), which appeared in both New York and London, was reviewed widely and enthusiastically and went into a paperback edition. Since then the novella *The Swordfish* has come out in London (LEVITT, 1996), and a translation of the novel *Het verlangen* was published in New York and London (Knecht, *Desire*, 1997).

The *Selected Poems 1953–73* (HERMANS, 1986) was brought out by a Scottish poetry publisher with a list of both original and translated verse. Three translators were involved. No fewer than four translators collaborated on the complex and highly allusive *The Sign of the Hamster* (CLAES, 1986), which appeared in bilingual form, with detailed textual notes.

Among the drama translations, *The Temptation* (WILLINGER & DENEULIN 1984), *Friday* (CLAUS & LOGUE 1972 and WILLINGER & TRUYTS, 1986) and *The Life and Works of Leopold II* (WILLINGER & TRUYTS, 1984) may be singled out for comment. *The Temptation*, a dramatic monologue by a 100-year-old nun, was originally published in Dutch as a work of prose fiction, although Claus himself also staged it. The translation was expressly written for stage performance and employs American spoken idiom, while retaining the Flemish setting. The translation highlights the intense pathos of the situation, at once grotesque and pitiful, and makes only limited efforts to capture wordplay or make historical references intelligible. This is also largely true of *Friday*, a play about adultery, incest and guilt. *Leopold II*, full of biting satire and knockabout comedy, contains rhyming passages which are preserved in translation, as are the numerous references to Belgian history of the time. In the preface to the anthology in which this play appeared, the translator makes it clear that retaining "the tenor, intention, and language" as well as topical references was indeed the main aim, leaving theatre directors free to adapt the texts for performance. The translations are not meant as playtexts but as providing the basis for a playtext.

In translating the large and complex novel *The Sorrow of Belgium*, Arnold POMERANS (1990) had to find slang and idiomatic expressions acceptable to both American and British readers. As he explains in the preface, he decided to keep a European flavour in line with the nature of the book, which traces the growth to maturity and an artistic calling of a young Flemish boy in a small-town family of collaborators in the years before, during and after World War II. Claus's flexible, earthy style is there in the translation, but the range of registers and idioms is inevitably reduced along with their humour and ideological significance. The setting and historical context remain those of the original work, with the translator explaining some – but by no means all – of the topical references in a separate glossary. In translation the novel comes across as rather more conventional than in its original form.

THEO HERMANS

Further Reading

Bousset, Hugo, "The Far North and the Deep South: Contemporary Fiction in the Netherlands and Flanders", *Review of Contemporary Fiction*, 14/2 (1994)

Claes, Paul, "Claus the Chameleon", *Low Countries*, 1 (1993–94)

Goedegebuure, Jaap and Anne Marie Musschoot, *Contemporary Fiction of the Low Countries*, Rekkem: Flemish–Netherlands Foundation, 1993

Ross, Julian, "The Translation of *Het verdriet van België*" in *Translation and the (Re)production of Culture*, edited by C. Robyns, Leuven: CERA Chair, 1994

Todd, Richard, "The Apostles and the Hottentots", *Times Literary Supplement* (29 June 1990)

Sidonie-Gabrielle Colette 1873–1954

French novelist, short-story writer, autobiographer and dramatist

Biography

Born in Saint-Sauveur-en-Puisaye, Burgundy, 28 January 1873. Her father, wounded at the battle of Magenta, 1859, was a local tax inspector. Colette (she used her family surname to sign her works) inherited her admired mother's special rapport with the natural world. She was educated locally to the age of 16. In 1893 she married the writer Henry Gauthier-Villars ("Willy"; divorced 1910) and was exploited for a while as a member of a team of writers whose works Willy signed and spiced (the four *Claudine* novels, 1900–03, underwent this process). Leaving Willy, Colette entered into a bohemian existence, earning a living as an actress and music-hall performer (1906–27) and now writing independently. In 1912 she married Baron Henry de Jouvenel (divorced 1925; one daughter). In World War I she lived in Italy. Her third marriage, to Maurice Goudeket, took place in 1935. In World War II she was in Paris, writing in various genres. In her last years she lived in an apartment in the Palais-Royal in Paris, internationally known and honoured (she was member, 1945, and president, 1949, of the Académie Goncourt; honorary member of the American Academy, 1953; Chevalier, 1920, Officer, 1928, Commander, 1936, and Grand Officer, 1953, of the French Legion of Honour).

Between 1910 and 1939 Colette was a columnist, literary editor and drama critic for prominent newspapers and reviews, and she wrote some plays and adaptations, but she is best known for her fiction – notably the *Claudine* novels; *Chéri* and *La Fin de Chéri* (*Chéri*; *The Last of Chéri)*, 1920 and 1926; *Le Blé en herbe* (*The Ripening Corn*), 1923, *La Chatte* (*The Cat*), 1933; and *Gigi* (*Gigi*), 1944 – and for her autobiographical works and pieces about animals, e.g. *La Maison de Claudine* (*My Mother's House*), 1922; *L'Enfant et les sortilèges* (*The Boy and the Magic*), 1925, with music by Ravel; *Sido* (*Sido*) (1929); *Le Fanal bleu* (*The Blue Lantern*), 1949. She died in Paris, 3 August 1954.

Translations

Selections

Flanner, Janet (editor), *Seven By Colette*, with an introduction, New York: Farrar Straus, 1955 (contains *Gigi*, *Chéri* and *The Last of Chéri*, translated by Roger Senhouse; *The Cat*, translated by Antonia White; *My Mother's House*, translated by Enid McLeod and U.V. Troubridge; *Chance Acquaintances*, translated by P. Leigh-Fermor; and *The Vagabond*, translated by Enid McLeod)

McLeod, Enid, *Six Novels*, London: Secker and Warburg, 1988 (contains *The Vagabond*, translated by Enid McLeod; *Chéri*, *The Last of Chéri*, *Gigi*, and *The Ripening Seed*, translated by Roger Senhouse; *The Cat*, translated by Antonia White)

Phelps, Robert (editor), *Earthly Paradise: An Autobiography, Drawn from Her Lifetime Writings*, London: Secker and Warburg, and New York: Farrar Straus, 1966; Harmondsworth: Penguin, 1974 (translators Helen Beauclerk, H. Briffault, D. Coltman, Enid McLeod, U.V. Troubridge, Antonia White, and Roger Senhouse)

Phelps, Robert (editor), *The Collected Stories of Colette*, with an introduction, New York: Farrar Straus, 1983; London: Secker and Warburg,1984 (translators Matthew Ward, Antonia White, Anne-Marie Callimachi, and others)

Westcott, Glenway (editor), *Short Novels*, with an introduction, New York: Dial Press, 1951 (contains *Chéri*, translated by Janet Flanner; *The Last of Chéri* and *The Other One*, translated by V.G. Garvin; *Duo*, and *The Indulgent Husband*, translated by Frederick A. Blossom; *The Cat*, translated by M. Bentinck)

White, Antonia (editor), *The Stories of Colette*, London: Secker and Warburg, 1958; as *The Tender Shoot and Other Stories*, New York: Farrar Straus, 1958 (selections from *Bella-Vista*, *Chambre d'hôtel*, *Le Képi*, and *Gigi*)

White, Antonia *The Complete Claudine*, New York: Farrar Straus, 1976; as *The Claudine Novels*, Harmondsworth: Penguin, 1987

Novels

Claudine à l'école, 1900

Flanner, Janet, *Claudine at School*, New York: Boni, and London: Gollancz, 1930

White, Antonia, *Claudine at School*, London: Secker and Warburg, 1956; New York: Farrar Straus, 1957

Claudine à Paris, 1901

Whitall, James, *Young Lady of Paris*, New York, Boni, 1931; as *Claudine in Paris*, London: Gollancz, 1931

White, Antonia, *Claudine in Paris*, London: Secker and Warburg, and New York: Farrar Straus, 1958

Claudine en ménage, 1902

Blossom, Frederick A., *The Indulgent Husband*, New York: Farrar and Rinehart, 1935

White, Antonia, *Claudine Married*, London: Secker and Warburg, and New York: Farrar Straus, 1960

Claudine s'en va, 1903

Blossom, Frederick A., *The Innocent Wife*, New York: Farrar and Rinehart, and London: John Long, 1934

White, Antonia, *Claudine and Annie*, London: Secker and Warburg, 1962; New York: Penguin, 1963

La Vagabonde, 1910

McLeod, Enid, *The Vagabond*, London: Secker and Warburg, 1954; New York: Farrar Straus, 1955

Remfry-Kidd, Charlotte, *The Vagrant*, London: E. Nash, 1912; as *Renée la Vagabonde*, London: Nash and Grayson, and New York: Doubleday, 1931

Chéri, 1920

Flanner, Janet, *Chéri*, New York: Boni, 1929; London: Gollancz, 1930; San Francisco: Black Stone Press, 1983

Senhouse, Roger, *Chéri*, with an introduction by Raymond Mortimer, London: Secker and Warburg, 1951; with *The Last of Chéri*, New York: Farrar Straus, 1951

Le Blé en herbe, 1923

Mégroz, Phyllis, *The Ripening Corn*, London: Gollancz, 1931

Senhouse, Roger, *Ripening Seed*, London: Secker and Warburg, 1955; New York: Farrar Straus, 1956

Zeitlin, Ida, *The Ripening*, New York: Farrar and Rinehart, 1932

La Fin de Chéri, 1926

Garvin, V.G., *The Last of Chéri*, New York: Putnam, 1932; London: Gollancz, 1933

Senhouse, Roger, *The Last of Chéri*, London: Secker and Warburg, 1951; with *Chéri*, New York: Farrar Straus, 1953

Other Writing

Journal à rebours, 1941, and selections from *De ma fenêtre*, 1942 and 1944

Le Vay, David, *Looking Backwards*, London: Peter Owen, and Bloomington: Indiana University Press, 1975

In the 1920s and 1930s, American translations of Colette were far more plentiful than British ones, with some 15 homegrown translations published in New York between 1929 and 1937, compared with only four in London, although London made up the same total by publishing a dozen of the American versions. FLANNER, who started the wave of American translations with *Chéri* in 1929, is described by Phelps (1966) as "one of her [Colette's] earliest and best translators into English", but regrettably these early American translations are now very hard to procure in the UK.

Thereafter translating activity ceased until after the publication in Paris in 1949 of Colette's *Oeuvres complètes*, which was the impetus for a major new translating initiative in the UK. Between 1951 and 1964, Secker and Warburg undertook a 17-volume Uniform Edition of translations of Colette, which made most of Colette's works, and in particular her fiction, readily available in English, especially as many were later reprinted in the UK as Penguin paperbacks. All but one were also published shortly after in New York, making this series the most widely available, as well as the most comprehensive, to date. Roger Senhouse, Antonia White and Enid McLeod were the main contributors to this series, accounting for 14 volumes between them.

The first volume in the collection, *Chéri*, translated by SENHOUSE, has an introduction by Raymond Mortimer which laments the lack of "tolerable" translations of Colette while pointing out that she is a particularly awkward author to translate: "The difficulty of translating her is more nearly desperate than anyone can know who has not tried his hand at it". It is of course the very language that makes Colette hard to translate which creates her unique style: her frequent use of direct speech, notoriously liable to sounding dated; the authenticity of her narrators' *récits*, specific to their milieu, whether that of the village school or of backstage in the music hall; and the exuberance of her descriptions of nature, which can so easily sound overdone if not treated with sensitivity.

WHITE, who translated the four *Claudine* novels for the Uniform Edition (1956–62), keeps the very French atmosphere of the tales while producing an acceptable rendering, although with inaccuracies such as "passing [exams]", instead of "trying (or sitting) [exams]" as a translation of the French "passer". White is prone to lapses of this type, translating "ces demoiselles", in a formal allusion (*Claudine at School*) to two single women, as "those ladies, our mistresses", suggesting a surprising lack of close familiarity with French – and a very insensitive use of the word "mistress", one which might indeed be considered rather tongue-in-cheek given the lesbian relationship of the "ladies" referred to – while FLANNER (1930) more accurately has "the two teachers", which on this occasion is all that is required. Worse still, the reader may well be puzzled when White has a pupil borrow a corkscrew (*tire-bouchon*) from Claudine to help her get her shoes on, but Flanner fortunately recognizes the (very similar) French word for "buttonhook" (*tire-bouton*). Flanner's translation is more competent, and remains very readable despite its greater age.

MCLEOD (1954) in translating *La Vagabonde* has an easier task, since the narrator here is more sober of language than the exuberant and irrepressible Claudine. The remarks of Brague, her partner in mime, sometimes appear a little odd, but this seems acceptable given his character and lifestyle, and the fact that colloquialisms, to which he is prone, date quickly. McLeod's translation captures well the regretful inevitability of the conclusion: "She [my dog] is waiting for someone who will not come again. I can hear Blandine shifting the casseroles, I smell the smell of ground coffee; hunger gnaws sullenly at my stomach". But here too, "saucepans" would be a more accurate word for the French "casseroles", and "I smell the smell" is far clumsier than the original inoffensive "je sens l'odeur". A certain amount of clumsiness is to be found in most of the Uniform Edition translations, but they are mostly quite readable nevertheless. The fact that the language has dated somewhat is not necessarily a disadvantage, since this can sometimes help the reader recreate the world of the author.

One of the best-known of Colette's novels is *Le Blé en herbe*, a celebrated tale of awakening adolescent sexuality that was abruptly terminated in mid-serialization by *Le Matin* in 1923 as being unsuitable for its readers. Set in Brittany, it has long been a favourite in the English-speaking world, with different translations published in London and New York in 1931 and 1932 respectively. SENHOUSE's 1955 translation for the Uniform Edition has a tendency to follow too closely the original French, which leads to some strange expressions. Thus "en bas de la plage déclive" becomes "beyond the sandy declivity", instead of "at the foot of the sloping beach", and we hear of "a Breton afternoon suffused with vaporised saline", uncomfortably close to the original French "un après-midi breton chargé de vapeur saline". More seriously, the occasional error can significantly change the sense of the text. When Phil and Vinca discuss how soon the holidays must end, and the latter mentions the new clothes she has to shop for before school starts, the first of three essential items mentioned is "une robe pour aller au cours", namely a dress to wear to school, but Senhouse translates this as "my new party dress". The error is repeated a couple of pages further on, when "ta rentrée, ton cours" is transformed into "babbling about going home, about your party dresses". Far from being obsessed with parties and fashion as Senhouse implies, Vinca is merely preparing for back-to-school routine, which shows her in a very different light.

Colette is famous for her memories of the German occupation of France as seen from her flat in the Palais-Royal, and substantial selections from *De ma fenêtre* form the second half of *Looking Backwards* (1975), one of several volumes of reminiscences translated by LE VAY in the 1970s. While it is good to have these works available in English, the reader who wishes to sample a wide range of Colette's autobiographical writings could not do better than acquire *Earthly Paradise* (1966), a selection by PHELPS from works dealing with her entire lifespan, some taken from previously published translations, but the rest specially translated for this edition, with a total of seven different translators involved.

COLTMAN in this collection translates part of *De ma fenêtre* in less stilted fashion than Le Vay. Where Colette comments on people who enjoy the night hours, Coltman's "We know there are some flowers that bloom only at night" will become as formal as an old-fashioned textbook in the hands of Le Vay: "One knows that there are flowers which bloom nocturnally". The chatty atmosphere of Colette's recollections is likewise far better captured by Coltman: when Colette reminisces about well-to-do old ladies who used to show her mother their treasured possessions when she was a child, both translators use the same expression "relics of their youth", but there the similarity ends. Le Vay talks of "a nuptial night-dress, the stockings for ancient balls" – the latter a particularly infelicitous expression – whereas Coltman is more explanatory but finds an expression that encapsulates the value these objects hold for their owner: "a nightgown worn on a wedding night, stockings donned for long-past cotillions". When the ladies hand over the treasured stockings for the visitor to admire, Le Vay bluntly writes: "'Weigh them!' they would say proudly". Coltman however manages to access the nuances of female chat: "Feel the weight of them!' they would say with pride". In the work of such an intensely personal and observant writer as Colette, it is the capacity of the translator to recreate such nuances that is all-important.

KATHLEEN M. MCKILLIGAN

Further Reading

Gibbard, Eleanor Reid, "A Chronology of Colette in Translation", *Philological Papers*, 23 (January 1977) pp. 75–93

Holmes, Diana, *Colette*, London: Macmillan, and New York: St Martin's Press, 1991

Jouve, Nicole Ward, *Colette*, Brighton: Harvester, and Bloomington: Indiana University Press, 1987

Marks, Elaine, *Colette*, New Brunswick, New Jersey: Rutgers University Press, 1960; London: Secker and Warburg, 1961

Mitchell, Yvonne, *Colette: A Taste for Life*, London: Weidenfeld and Nicolson, and New York: Harcourt Brace, 1975

Sarde, Michèle, *Colette, Free and Fettered*, translated from the French by Richard Miller, London: Michael Joseph, and New York: Morrow, 1980

Stewart, Joan Hinde, *Colette*, Boston: Twayne, 1983

Thurman, Judith, *Secrets of the Flesh: A Life of Colette*, New York: Knopf, and London: Bloomsbury, 1999

Comic Texts: Translating into English

The traditional normative concept of translation, currently giving way to one that sees the act as cultural negotiation, in no way facilitates the task of the translator of a comic text. As de Man illustrated in his *Allegories of Reading*, 1979, irony in any text can never be affirmed categorically. Official Western culture, as if afraid our civilization might erode should the voice of the subversive Other turn out to be that of the Transcendent Humorist, has traditionally granted the carnavalesque less than its critical due; even today the laughter of the reader is usually subordinated to critical consideration of any social and/or metaphysical elements that can be teased out of a text; translation is also be affected by such considerations.

Borges in his essay "Palabrería para versos", in *El tamaño de mi esperanza*, 1926, affirmed that the (humorous, tragic, didactic, etc.) nature of any writing lies at the textual, as opposed to the thematic, level. It is at textual level, with language always viewed as communicative (*parole*), never theoretically (as *langue*), that translation takes place (as Lefevere, in *Translating Literature*, 1992, and other proponents of the new paradigm of translation point out). Earlier (1969) Nida and Taber had stated in *The Theory and Practice of Translation* that anything that can be said in one language can be translated into another unless form constitutes part of the message; now suprasegmentals that do not appear on the printed page are seen to affect translation as intrinsically as form.

Walter Nash writing in *The Language of Humour* (1985) emphasizes that no joke is funny unless all parties see the point, yet there is no infallible way to ensure that the reader of any text will "see the point", and translation compounds the problem. We cannot know, for example, if Ecclesiastes was speaking tongue-in-cheek since we do not know how Bronze Age Hebrews bantered with each other. When Derrida finds that the narrator who tells of Pierre Menard's academic achievements sounds more *French* in Borges's original Spanish text than in French translation, we begin to wonder about the adequacy of translations of Derrida's own self-described critical Menippean satire (1985). If Kafka laughed aloud as he read *Metamorphosis* to friends (as reported by Olsen in *Circus of the Mind in Motion*, 1990), does the original contain something that is missing in translation?

Given the arbitrary connection between signified and signifier, the translator and target-language reader can never be entirely certain what elusive cultural allusions might be contained in the source text, even though equivalency of translation at word level between source and target text may well have been achieved. Semantic significance implied by the writer's narrative voice in the source text is open to varying interpretations by the translator, and the translator's chosen interpretation is in turn open to further varying interpretation by the reader of the target language text. A brief example illustrates the insurmountable problems facing the translator in this regard. Alfredo Bryce Echenique's novel *Un mundo para Julius* (1970) begins with what appears to be a straightforward statement: "Julius nació en un palacio de la avenida Salaverry frente al antiguo hipódromo de San Felipe." Word for word English equivalency turns this into "Julius was born in a palace on Avenida Salaverry [Salaverry Avenue] facing [in front of, across from] the old [disused, former] San Felipe racetrack." Lima readers smile or laugh on reading this because they already know that there are no "palaces" there, only pretentious houses belonging to a land development of around 1930. In this first sentence the register constitutes an important part of the encoding for the Lima reader, which might include the pronunciation of the plosive of "palacio", imagined facial expression, perhaps a hand gesture. In order to balance two contextual focuses at the same time and fit words around a world view only readers from Lima can share, the translator, according to Lefevere, might "smuggle in" by some stratagem a way to have the target-language reader "see the point". This could mean adding a few words; for example: "Julius was born in *one of those* palaces ..." (readers do not usually envisage palaces collectively). The American translation by Gerdes in 1992 opts for semantic equivalency, "palacio" being translated as "mansion". The French translation by Bensoussan (titled simply *Julius*, 1973) gives us "Julius naquit dans un palais ...", losing the orality of the original Spanish through use of a verb tense that never figures in French conversational discourse; Bryce's narrator "talks", he does not *write*. Problems of register are compounded when the narrative voice uses the word "palacio" within the servants' streams of consciousness. They were raised in daub and wattle huts and probably think the house *is* a palace; this causes another shift in the register of the narrative voice that should, ideally, be reflected in the translation. The French and American translations contain no misreadings of the first sentence at word level; both amply comply with any possible norms of verbal equivalency, yet the Spanish original said much more than is relayed in the other languages.

Steiner in *After Babel* alludes to translation as taking place within the realm of the impossible; this is doubly so when humour is involved. The best the translator can hope to achieve is a temporary broaching of the boundaries that separate human beings, as s/he *attempts* to elicit in the target language reader an emotion (laughter) *suspected* of having been engendered in the source language text, but that often can be confirmed only by consultation with the living author.

Were humour entirely untranslatable, however, *Don Quixote* could not have been a universal bestseller, and it should be remembered that the type of humour preempted for the English by Sir William Temple in *Of Poetry* (1960) was called by Fielding and Sterne, its practitioners, "Cervantic" or "Cervantene", and its provenance was Spain. Nor is "Rabelaisian" humour restricted to 16th-century France. In addition to comedy that depends on situation, which is the literary equivalent of slapstick humour, innuendos exist that can be understood by persons of different cultures, and some comic wordplay can be adapted to the target language and perhaps make the reader laugh. The following felicitous examples are from Suzanne Jill Levine's *The Subversive Scribe* (1991), in which she discusses her collaboration with the Cuban post-modernist writer Cabrera Infante on the translation of his novel *Tres tristes tigres*. In English Levine calls it *Three Trapped Tigers*, rather than "sad" (*tristes*) tigers, thus preserving the alliteration and alluding to the novel's punning protagonists. British children chant "three thumping tigers taking tea" in a tongue-twister game and "thumping" might have been closer to the original effect of the Spanish, though losing, perhaps, its tragi-comic element. In the novel one of the protagonist's verbal jokes involves a list of pseudo-texts combining local scatological/sexual humour and multilingual allusions to world culture. The translator's equivalent list in English contains *Under the Lorry* by Malcolm Volcano; *Remembrance of Things Past Translation*; *Crime and Puns* by Bustrofedor Dostowhiskey; *In Calso Brodo* by Truman Capone; *Comfort of the Season* by Gore Vidal Sassoon. No comic text can guarantee that every reader will laugh, but translators in attempting the impossible can, on occasion, come close to succeeding.

ALITA KELLEY

Further Reading

Bensoussan, Albert, *Julius*, a translation into French of *Un mundo para Julius*, by Alfredo Bryce Echenique, Paris: Calman Levy, 1973

Borges, Jorge Luis, "Palabrería para versos", in his *El tamaño de mi esperanza*, Buenos Aires: Proa, 1926

de Man, Paul, *Allegories of Reading: Figural Language in Rousseau, Nietzsche, Rilke and Proust*, New Haven, Connecticut: Yale University Press, 1979

Derrida, Jacques, *The Ear of the Other: Otobiography, Transference, Translation*, edited by Christie V. McDonald, based on the French edition edited by Claude Lévesque and McDonald, translated by Peggy Kamuf, New York: Schocken, 1985

Gerdes, Dick, *A World for Julius*, a translation into English of *Un mundo para Julius*, by Alfredo Bryce Echenique, Austin: University of Texas Press, 1992

Lefevere, André, *Translating Literature: Practice and Theory in a Comparative Literature Context*, New York: Modern Language Association of America, 1992

Levine, Suzanne Jill, *The Subversive Scribe: Translating Latin American Fiction*, St Paul, Minnesota: Graywolf Press, 1991

Nash, Walter, *The Language of Humour*, London and New York: Longman, 1985

Nida, Eugene A. and Charles R. Taber, *The Theory and Practice of Translation*, Leiden: E.J. Brill, 1969

Olsen, Lance, *Circus of the Mind in Motion: Postmodernism and the Comic Vision*, Detroit: Wayne State University Press, 1990

O'Neill, Patrick, *The Comedy of Entropy: Humour, Narrative, Reading*, Toronto: University of Toronto Press, 1990

Steiner, George, *After Babel: Aspects of Language and Translation*, Oxford and New York: Oxford University Press, 1975; 3rd edition 1998

Communication Theory and Literary Translation

There exists a certain degree of scientific relation between communication theory and literary translation. Postulated in terms of a general communication model, the literary translator is the transmitter (coder) transforming, from the source, an input message, i.e. the ST (source text) author's literary topoi, into a signal, i.e. the translator's textual rendering, for sending over the channel. The signal may possibly be interfered with by different noises along the way. Then the signal (together with the noises) gets decoded into equivalent literary themes by the receiver (decoder), i.e. the target readership, becoming the final linguistic message to be deciphered by the neurological structure of the reader's brain.

The transmitter in the above model performs two functions: (a) it produces a signal whose characteristics are suitable for transmission. In this case, the produced signal is the literary translator's own textual rendering, a written configuration of linguistic marks intended for book-form transmission; or if the channel is some electronic medium, e.g. a computer, it is the literary translator's own textual rendering converted into some computer-readable form for transmission; (b) it encodes the message into a form as little liable as possible to be misinterpreted at the receiving end through the effects of noise. The form referred to here is the complex totality of the literary translator's rendering, with all its safety nets, intended to achieve the equivalence and/or other literary effects to be produced on the target readership, against all such potential noises as misinterpretation by the literary translator himself or the receivers, and unintended effects of rhetorical elements (e.g. puns, metaphors, rhetorical questions, etc.). It is a fundamental tenet of communication theory that noise immunity, namely the achievement of the equivalence and/or other literary effects in the case of literary translation, is to be gained at some price, that of the complex totality of the literary translator's rendering. Some of the noises may come from the receivers, namely the target readership. Such noises include their presuppositions, inadequate knowledge of language and/or literary conventions, differences in cultural background, etc.

The emphasis on the role of the receiver in the communication model coincides with the recent development of literary reception theory, to examine the reader's role in literature. And despite the counterclaims of pessimistic philosophers of language, the hard-nosed I.A. Richards (1953) was sympathetic to the idea of proper decoding of original (literary) messages and their recoding into a TL (target language) (Gentzler, 1993).

Eugene Nida's theory of dynamic equivalence (Nida and Taber, 1969) in Bible translation suggests that the message of the original text can be translated so that "its reception will be the same as that perceived by the original receptors" (Gentzler,

1993). In this sense, Bible translation, as a sub-genre of literary translation, is perfectly possible, the source message communicable and translatable. In this connection, Nida (1960) recommends that Bible translators employ all the resources of communication theory to aid in their work.

Toury (1995) observes that literary translation involves the imposition of "conformity conditions" on "norms which are deemed literary at the target end", thus yielding "more or less well-formed texts from the point of view of the *literary* requirements of the recipient culture, at various possible costs in terms of the reconstruction of features of the source texts". This involves an unavoidable distortion in the content and form of the literary ST (source text). Literary translation requires considerable knowledge of transfer strategies of linguistic and literary compensation, and this comes in where the reformulation of an equivalent literary message, for equilibrating reception by the receivers, is concerned.

The informativeness of the literary source is intimately related to literary translation. To calculate the information of a source, Shannon's equation for information (cf. Shannon, 1948; Shannon and Weaver, 1949)

$$-\sum_{i=1}^{n} pi\ log2\ pi$$

can be used. Shannon's information theory has been the dominant paradigm for communication research (cf. Severin and Tankard, 1979, 1997). According to the equation, where n is the number of possible alternatives and pi is the probability of each alternative being chosen, the amount of information varies proportionally with entropy, the amount of uncertainty in a choice situation; in other words, the lower the negative entropy, the more informative is a literary text. The less likely something is to happen the more informative it is when it does, so low negative entropy positively impinges upon literariness and the unpredictability of the subject-matter of literary translation. In statistical terms, the more literary translator's version can be constructed so as to carry the minimal negative entropy, that is to say, to allow the greatest leeway in interpretation on the part of receivers, the more successful it will be considered to be. In such a reader-oriented theory of literary translation, the functions of literary texts in communication are stressed, variously classified as "de-automatization", "polyphonic harmony", "indeterminacy", "polyfunctionality", and "polyvalence" (de Beaugrande, 1980). In communication terms, what a bad literary translator does, as a mediator between the ST author and the target readership, is "block(s) off any other responses besides his or her own", thereby sacrificing "the most essential function of literary communication–the multiplicity of meaning resulting from indeterminacy and openness".

Poetry, having a low level of redundancy (presence of unnecessary or repeated elements), communicates large quantities of information in a relatively small number of signs. This will, therefore, give rise to many valid interpretations, since the readers "need to supply more out of their individually variable supply of knowledge and experience" (de Beaugrande, 1978). This precisely makes poetry translation very difficult, if not impossible. On the contrary, drama translation is highly possible, because it is an oral mode of literature with a high level of redundancy-tolerating noises.

In comparison with the production and perception of LSP (Language for Special Purpose) texts, which are largely recipient-independent and, therefore, generally subject to no misinterpretation by the transmitter and the receiver as recipient of the ST and the translator's text respectively, literary translation is not so lucky. The literary translator occupies the peculiar position of a communicator not only as a reader of the ST but also as a writer of the translation. Hence there will occur a certain amount of recipient-related variability in the reception and production of literary texts.

The issue of redundancy (the basis of cryptanalysis in information theory) further impinges upon the questions of the translator's interpretation of the ST and of the receivers' interpretation of the translated literary text. Since high redundancy is conducive to effective interpretation of texts, and the degree of redundancy increases with the availability of texts, the corollary would be that the literary translator's and the receivers' knowledge of the intertextuality of the ST will help (cf. Rose, 1993). One of the essential qualities with which intertextuality is associated is the literary use of language within a "'discursive space' which is occupied by cultural codes, rhetorical practices, and all other existing texts" (Bjornson, 1980). In terms of literary theory, intertextuality in literary translation has a parallel in the process of the so-called "hermeneutical circle", revolving from part to whole, and back to part.

Weaver (1949) suggests that Shannon's engineering theory of communication is applicable to the semantic problem, namely how precisely the transmitted symbols convey the desired meaning. Here the transmitted symbols refer to the translator's textual rendering, and the semantic problem boils down to the question of how accurately such rendering reproduces the ST author's themes. However, the existence of a reader in an interlingual communication makes the understanding of text partly of an objective, partly of a subjective nature (Wilss, 1993), a fact that complicates the accurate transmission of semantic symbols and renders intersubjectivity theoretically impossible (cf. Gadamer, 1975).

Holmes (1988) suggests that the translation of (literary) texts takes place on two planes: "a serial plane, where one translates sentence by sentence, and a structural plane, on which one abstracts a 'mental conception' of the original text, then uses that mental conception as a kind of general criterion against which to test each sentence during the formulation of the new, translated text". On this suggestion, the linear, non-interactive, nature of Shannon's model of communication is perhaps of limited applicability to literary translation, though its other scientific concepts are extremely valuable. Instead, with the transition to a text-oriented research paradigm in modern linguistics (Wilss, 1993) comes the emphasis on text-rank translation, "a gradual shift of emphasis from focusing on interlingual relationships to centring upon intertextual relationships" (Ivir, 1969; Koller, 1978). In view of this, Holmes's suggestion about a structural plane is eminently appropriate to the translation of literary texts, particularly that of serial works of literature, or complex literary works like James Joyce's F*innegans Wake* or Joseph Conrad's *Nostromo*, etc.

RAYMOND S.C. LIE

References

Beaugrande, Robert de, *Factors in a Theory of Poetic Translating*, Assen: Van Gorcum, 1978

Beaugrande, Robert de, "Toward a Semiotic Theory of Literary Translating" in *Semiotik und Ubersetzen*, edited by Wolfram Wilss, Tubingen: Narr, 1980

Bjornson, Richard, "Translation and Literary Theory", *Translation Review*, 6 (1980) pp. 13–16

Gadamer, Hans-Georg, *Truth and Method*, London: Sheed and Ward, and New York: Seabury Press, 1975; 2nd revised edition, New York: Continuum, 1993

Gaddis Rose, Marilyn, "Textuality, Intertextuality, and Reception: Claude Simon in English" in *La Traduction dans le développement des littératures/ Translation in the Development of Literatures*, edited by José Lambert and André Lefevere, Bern and New York: Peter Lang, 1993

Gentzler, Edwin, *Contemporary Translation Theories*, London and New York: Routledge, 1993

Holmes, James S., *Translated! Papers on Literary Translation and Translation Studies*, Amsterdam: Rodopi, 1988

Ivir, V., "Contrasting via Translation: Formal Correspondence vs. Translation Equivalence" in *The Yugoslav Serbo-Croatian–English Contrastive Project, Studies 1*, edited by Rsim Filipovic, Zagreb: Zagreb University, 1969, pp. 13–25

Koller, W., "Äquivalenz in kontrastiver Linguistik und Übersetzungswissenschaft" in *Theory and Practice of Translation*, edited by Lillebill Grahs, Gustav Korlen and Bertil Malmberg, Bern: Peter Lang, 1978, pp. 69–92

Nida, Eugene A., *Message and Mission: The Communication of Christian Faith*, New York: Harper, 1960

Nida, Eugene A. and Charles R. Taber, *The Theory and Practice of Translation*, Leiden: E.J. Brill, 1969

Richards, I.A., "Toward a Theory of Translating" in *Studies in Chinese Thought*, edited by Arthur F. Wright, Chicago: University of Chicago Press, 1953

Severin, Werner J. and James W. Tankard, Jr, *Communication Theories: Origins, Methods, Uses*, New York: Hastings House, 1979; 4th edition, New York: Longman, 1997

Shannon, C.E., "A Mathematical Theory of Communication", *Bell System Technical Journal*, 27 (1948) pp. 379–423, 623–56

Shannon, Claude E. and Warren Weaver, *The Mathematical Theory of Communication*, Urbana: University of Illinois Press, 1949

Toury, Gideon, "Communication in Translated Texts: A Semiotic Approach" in *Semiotik und Übersetzen*, edited by Wolfram Wilss, Tubingen: Narr, 1980

Toury, Gideon, *Descriptive Translation Studies and Beyond*, Amsterdam and Philadelphia: John Benjamins, 1995

Weaver, W., "Recent Contributions to the Mathematical Theory of Communication" in *The Mathematical Theory of Communication*, edited by Claude E. Shannon and Warren Weaver, Urbana: University of Illinois Press, 1949

Wilss, Wolfram, *Übersetzungswissenschaft: Ein Reader*, Darmstadt: Wissentliche Buchgesellschaft, 1981

Wilss, Wolfram, "Translation Studies: The State of the Art" in *The Art of Literary Translation*, edited by Hans Schulte and Gerhart Teuscher, Lanham, Maryland: University Press of America, 1993

Further Reading

Adams, Robert M., *Proteus, His Lies, His Truth: Discussions on Literary Translation*, New York: Norton, 1973

Bang, Gonie, "The Imagination of the Writer and of the Literary Translator", *Babel*, 32/4 (1986) pp. 198–201

Bassnett-McGuire, Susan, "Specific Problems of Translation" in her *Translation Studies*, London and New York: Methuen, 1980

Blahut, Richard E., *Principles and Practice of Information Theory*, Reading, Massachusetts: Addison-Wesley, 1988

Blodgett, E.D., "Translated Literature and the Literary Polysystem: The Example of Le May's *Evangeline*", *Meta*, 34/2 (1989) pp. 157–68

Dornic, Stanislav, "Information Processing and Language Dominance", *International Review of Applied Psychology*, 29/12 (1980) pp. 119–40

Eagleton, Terry, "Translation and Transformation", *Stand*, 19/3 (1977) pp. 72–77

Ervin, S.M., "Information Transmission with Code Translation" in *Psycholinguistics*, edited by C.E. Osgood and F.A. Sebeok, Bloomington, 1967, pp. 185–92

Even-Zohar, Itamar, "The Position of Translated Literature within the Literary Polysystem" in *Literature and Translation: New Perspectives in Literary Studies*, edited by James S. Holmes, José Lambert and Raymond van den Broeck, Leuven: ACCO, 1978, pp. 117–27

Frawley, William (editor), *Translation: Literary, Linguistic, and Philosophical Perspectives*, Newark, New Jersey: University of Delaware Press, and London: Associated University Presses, 1984

Haghighi, Manouchehr, "Supra-lingual Aspects of Literary Translation" in *Teaching Translation and Interpreting 2: Insights, Aims, Visions*, edited by Cay Dollerup and Annette Lindegaard, Amsterdam: John Benjamins, 1994, pp. 47–50

Headland, Thomas N., "Information Overload and Communication Problems in the Casiguran Dumagat New Testament", *Notes on Translation*, 83 (1981) pp. 19–27

Ivir, Vladimir, "The Communicative Model of Translation in Relation to Contrastive Analysis" in *Kontrastive Linguistik und Ubersetzungswissenschaft*, edited by W. Kuhlwein, Gisela Thome and Wolfram Wilss, Munich: Fink, 1981, pp. 209–18

Lambert, José and André Lefevere, "Translation, Literary Translation and Comparative Literature" in *La Traduction, une Profession/ Translation: A Profession*, edited by Paul A. Horguelin, Ottawa: Canadian Translators and Interpreters Council, 1978, pp. 329–42

Nelson, Lowry Jr, "Literary Translation", *Translation Review*, 29 (1989) pp. 17–30

Popovič, Anton, "The Contemporary State of the Theory of Literary Translation", *Babel*, 24/3–4 (1978) pp. 111–13

Pym, Anthony, *Epistemological Problems in Translation and Its Teaching*, Calaceit: Caminade, 1993

Wonderley, William L., "Information-Correspondence and the Translation of Ephesians into Zoque", *The Bible Translator*, 4 (1953) pp. 14–21

Verdu, S, "The First Forty Years of the Shannon Theory", *IEEE Information Theory Society Newsletter*, 1/4–10/9 (1990)

Comparative Literature and Literary Translation

The complex (and in some ways paradoxical) relationship between the relatively young academic discipline of comparative literature and the very old practice of literary translation continues to evolve. In the 19th century, early comparative critics did not need to attend carefully to literary translations, since they could assume that polyglot readers would meet texts chiefly in their original languages rather than in translation. As polyglot readership decreased and monolingual readership increased in the 20th century, and as the number and exoticism of texts added to the canon of Western comparative studies have expanded to include Asian, African, and other works in less-studied languages, critics have reasonably begun to assume that many more readers would meet works in translation and only in translation. Yet comparatists have tended to make this assumption and this absorption of translations silently, without much attention to the phenomenon of translation as a very real filter through which comparative studies are now largely taking place. This silently absorptive relationship is changing because of the entrance of semiotic, reader-response, cultural-studies, and post-structuralist critical notions into the mainstream. The result has been an acknowledgment of translation as a literary and critical act in its own right and the understanding that certain theoretical features of "originals" are even more noteworthy in translations. Signifiers and signifieds detach and play doubly in translation; literary values are doubly contingent (Barbara Herrnstein Smith); if a text is "always already read" (Fredric Jameson) a translation is more evidently so; if any text is an interpretation, the more so is any translation. When readers construct or "produce" literary texts, they do it through the medium of language; translators thus doubly produce meaning. Cultural-studies critics continue to remind comparatists of the cultural differences embedded in language and the possibilities in translation for cultural appropriation, oppression, suppression, or denial of difference (Lawrence Venuti). Historicists are beginning to track translations as possibly powerful indices of historical difference. Recent critical practices, then, offer new possibilities for seeing translations as special junctures of culture and language, and so invite a happy conjunction of comparative literature and literary translation. (André Lefevere charted a brief history of the relationship between the two areas in introducing the Winter 1995 *Comparative Literature* (47/1: 1–10), a special issue devoted to translation.)

Yet there is perhaps a fundamental mismatch between comparative criticism and translation criticism. Studies of translation, acutely aware of the disjunctions between languages and between literatures, focus not on cross-cultural similarities but instead on the analysis of difference. Comparatists have tended to focus first on syncretism and similarity: on themes, tropes, or traditions shared even across cultures, languages, and periods. (After all, we do not call ourselves contrastivists.) Some comparative work, especially that which takes place in the monolingual comparative-literature classroom, is handled as if a given text (now likely to be a translation) is in fact its named author's work. This, plus the comparatist's general focus on similarity, can elide and render invisible the very translations that make the texts accessible for study. Here, even beyond the very serious matter of justly crediting the labor of translators, arise what we could call "translation-fundamentalist" issues, which comparatists address variously or ignore: Is it a particular kind of imperialism not to read Egzi'abeher's poetry in Amharic? Are we really reading Goethe's work when we read a text not in German and not written in the 19th century? If we don't study the literary effects of translation, are we reducing works to their mere content? Such "fundamentalist" questions are in part a legacy of older discussions of translation that focused on evaluating a translation's accuracy or fidelity to a source, but other questions, too, render delicate the connections between comparative literature and translation. For instance, since any translation is an act of interpretation, really itself an act of criticism, is it not risky for comparatists to base study or teaching of a work on what is a mediated critical production of it without heavily factoring that mediation – and thus difference, rather than similarity – into the comparative study? We ignore translation at our peril, it seems; comparatists may examine, usually as auxiliary matters, omissions or alterations in a translation, but the main thrust of comparative studies has not always suited the study of translation as a bicultural literary phenomenon in its own right.

However, the critical study of translation owes much, methodologically and canonically speaking, to the discipline of comparative literature. Comparative literature scholars have helped gain wider acceptance of cross-cultural studies; they have helped open for literary translation studies (as one kind of cross-cultural study) at least a playing space at the current critical table. And comparatists continue to encourage the entry of foreign works into the English canon. As one result of canonical paths blazed by comparatists, studies of translation have become increasingly descriptive rather than prescriptive or evaluative, and are no longer directed only towards linguistics or translation pedagogy; literary translation is increasingly viewed from a comparatist's perspective, i.e. as contact between two literary-cultural traditions. Some of us translation critics may perceive our work as a subset of cultural studies, or of comparative studies, or of strictly literary studies; some think our work is distinct from each of these but draws upon all. Some examine translations in terms of influence in the receiving culture and literature; some take translation as a genre *per se*; I also view it as a revealing, multifaceted index of difference between authors, literary traditions, periods, and cultures. Comparative literature is the elder academic field, but strengths of the young discipline of literary translation criticism (in addition to the ancient practice of the art on which we can base our work) include the latitude, variety, and flexibility we enjoy in conceiving the endeavor.

Translation critics, like comparatists, have found scholarly voice in various critical venues: festschrifts, essay collections, and special issues of mainstream journals treat comparative literature or translation, and several academic journals are devoted to each. Influential critics who consider both disciplines in their work include André Lefevere, George Steiner, Douglas Robinson, Willis Barnstone, Reuben Brower, Gerald Hammond, Susan Bassnett, and a growing number of others. Both comparative literature and translation studies, however, are in a precarious position at the moment, since what are considered more esoteric topics are often the first dropped from university course lists during times of budgetary pressure. Like comparatists, translation critics often exist between two departments and two traditions of scholarship, orphaned yet blessed with a diverse extended family. In American universities, at least, students often come to comparative literature courses without language skills sufficient to read works in their original languages, so they read translations. Even if the professor points out the interpretive effects of translation, fewer and fewer students are able to measure or engage with those effects. On the other hand, the wave of acceptance for a more multicultural canon may buoy both comparative literature departments and translation critics. Comparatists, translation critics, and foreign language departments may wish to work together for our common benefit: to improve our students' language skills, to support foreign language and literature requirements in our curricula, to design more joint courses, and to give greater attention to the critical value of translation in literary and cultural studies.

A.E.B. COLDIRON

Further Reading

Bassnett, Susan, "Un ripensamento sul rapporto tra la letteratura comparata e la scienza della traduzione" in *Bologna: La cultura italiana e le letterature straniere moderne*, 3 vols, edited by Vita Fortunati, Ravenna: Longo, 1992

Budick, Sanford and Wolfgang Iser (editors), *The Translatability of Cultures: Figurations of the Space Between*, Stanford, California: Stanford University Press, 1996

Guillén, Claudio, *The Challenge of Comparative Literature*, translated by Cola Franzen, Cambridge, Massachusetts and London: Harvard University Press, 1993

Lefevere, André, "Translation and Comparative Literature: The Search for the Center", *TTR Traduction Terminologie Redaction*, 4/1 (1991) pp. 129–44

Lefevere, André, *Translating Literature: Practice and Theory in a Comparative Literature Context*, New York: Modern Language Association of America, 1992

Journals devoted to translation

Translation and Literature; *Translation Review*; *Target: International Journal of Translation Studies*; *TTR: Traduction Terminologie Redaction*

Journals devoted to comparative literature

Comparative Literature; *Comparative Literature Studies*; *The Comparatist; Canadian Review of Comparative Literature* (especially friendly to translation criticism); *Yearbook of Comparative and General Literature*; *Revue de la littérature comparée*; *Proceedings of the International Comparative Literature Association*

Confucius c.551–479 BC

Chinese philosopher and political theorist

Biography

Confucius (K'ung-fu-tsu; Kong-zi) was born in the feudal state of Lu, in east central China (in modern Shandong province), in about 551 BC. Little is known reliably about his life, though there is much apocryphal material. He probably belonged to an impoverished noble family, was orphaned young and grew up poor and largely self-taught. He left Lu aged in his 50s, in about 495, and travelled to various states of China seeking influential political office in order to try to remedy the political wrongs and harsh social conditions he observed about him. Unsuccessful (he only ever held minor governmental posts), he returned in 484 to Lu, at the request of his disciples anxious to progress in his Way (*tao*) to right conduct, and taught them again until his death there in 479 BC.

The *Analects* (*Lun Yu*) constitute a collection of Confucius's sayings and dialogues, assembled after his death.

The Analects

Lun Yu

Translations

Lau, D.C., *The Analects* (*Lun Yu*), Harmondsworth and New York: Penguin, 1979; 2nd edition, Hong Kong: Chinese University Press, 1992

Legge, James, *The Confucian Analects* (bilingual edition), in *The Four Books: Confucian Analects, The Great Learning, The Doctrine of the Mean, and the Works of Menius*, vol. 1 of *The Chinese Classics*, London: Trübner, 1861; reprinted New York: Paragon, 1966

Pound, Ezra, *The Analects*: part 1 (book 1–book 10), *Hudson Review*, 3/1 (Spring 1950) pp. 9–52; part 2 (book 11–book 20), *Hudson Review*, 3/2 (Summer 1950) pp. 237–87

Soothill, William Edward, *The Analects of Confucius*, Yokohama: printed privately, 1910; as *The Analects, or The Conversations of Confucius with His Disciples and Certain*

Others, edited by Dorothea Hosie, London: Oxford University Press, 1937; reprinted 1958

Waley, Arthur, *The Analects of Confucius*, with an introduction, London: Allen and Unwin, and New York: Vintage, 1938; reprinted London: Allen and Unwin, 1971; New York: Vintage, 1989

"Analects" ("things gathered") as a standard term for Confucius's *Lun Yü* was first used by James Legge, a 19th-century English translator of classic Chinese texts; since then it has remained a definitive usage. An ancient copy of *The Analects* was discovered around 150 BC in a wall of the house that Confucius inhabited, and another copy was found in a neighboring state. The differences between these two versions are not great, however. According to Arthur Waley, all existing translations of *The Analects* rely entirely on the "scriptural" interpretation of Chu Hsi (Zhu Xi, 1130–1200), who spent his entire life interpreting and teaching Confucianism.

LAU's translation of *The Analects* (1979) is one of the most recent, and, in the judgement of the present writer, one of the most faithful and fluent translations ever undertaken of the founding work of Confucianism. Lau's rendering was clearly based on close reading and meticulous research of the original text, paying attention to the minutest details in the text. Lau's work starts off with a substantial introduction to *The Analects*, discussing in depth the essential Confucian ideas from a historical perspective. The translation displays a solid understanding of Confucius the man and the philosopher, as portrayed in his own sayings and the sayings of his disciples recorded in *The Analects*. In places where the text is corrupt, the translator has made every effort to re-create the most probable meanings appropriate to the context.

As a Chinese translator of English, Lau demonstrates the kind of knowledge that average English translators do not possess of Chinese cultural codes and social customs. One prominent example is his translation of "jun" as "ruler" while most other translators adopt "prince", which evidently is a rather literal but somewhat twisted rendition. An even more illustrative instance is his handling of the proper term "the River". Most English translators, such as James LEGGE and Arthur WALEY, ignorant that the Chinese term "he" in ancient times specially referred to the Yellow River, represent the word merely as a river. Lau recognizes this and correctly renders it "the Yellow River" or "the River" rather than "a river" or "the river". To make his prose flow well, Lau sometimes adds to his translation words absent from the original. In chapter 1 of book 17, where Confucius is to meet with Yang Huo, Lau adds "Confucius had someone keep watch on Yang Huo's house" to bridge otherwise unclear ideas. In chapter 25 of the same book, Lau, like some other translators, supplies "In one's household" before "it is the women and the small men that are hard to deal with". Still another strategy Lau adopts to make his text culturally accessible is his use of valuable footnotes, which provide information of all types helpful in comprehending the text.

Lau not only presents a highly readable and reliable English translation, he also provides three appendixes, "Events in the Life of Confucius", "The Disciples as They Appear in *The Analects*", and "The *Lun Yü*", a close textual study that provides an overview of the reception history of *The Analects*. All in all, if one wishes to read a resourceful and faithful English translation of the Confucian text, D.C. Lau's version is the place to start.

LEGGE's rendition of *The Analects* (1861) is important and influential because it is perhaps the first English translation of the quintessential Confucian text. His initial application of the term "Analects" to the collected Confucian sayings sets the standard title for all subsequent translations. His version is accompanied by the Chinese text, followed by detailed, erudite notes, including minute explications of Chinese characters. While keeping the pithy and laconic nature of the original text, Legge produced fluent prose that reads well in English.

Confucius's standing among the Chinese, very much like that of Jesus Christ among Christians, seemed to make Legge believe that Confucius was not only the Chinese Sage but also a god. With this preconception in mind, Legge made his translation into a bible of the Chinese. Indeed, many places in his translation read like passages taken from the Christian Bible. Chapter 3 of book 20 stands out as an illustrative example:

> *T'ang* said, "I, the child Li, presume to use a dark-coloured victim, and to announce to Thee, O most great and sovereign God, that the sinner I dare not pardon, and thy ministers, O God, I do not keep in obscurity. The examination of them is by thy mind, O God. If, in my person, I commit offenses, they are not to be attributed to you, *the people of* the myriad regions. If you in the myriad regions commit offenses, these offenses must rest on my person".

There are also uncertain moments, in the translation, when original meanings are twisted or distorted. For instance, for the widely quoted sentence in chapter 24, book 4, Legge offers these terms: "The superior man wishes to be slow in his speech and earnest in his conduct". "Earnest" deviates considerably from the sense of the original. Also, in chapter 21, book 7, where Confucius shows modesty about his own learning, Legge translates, "When I walk along with two others, they may serve me as my teachers". A Chinese reader would probably understand Confucius to mean that when walking with three people, one of them may serve as his teacher, not two as Legge interpreted.

All things considered, the importance of Legge's pioneering effort cannot be overestimated; it has served as a fairly faithful and reliable source of consultation for later translators of *The Analects*. For examples, William Edward SOOTHILL and Arthur WALEY both benefited from his work. Dawson lauds Legge's as one of the most referred-to translations which, while "heavily Victorian in tone", remains a useful source (*Confucius*, p. 92).

POUND's translation (1950) is certainly not among the best known nor is it culturally very accessible, but it is a unique and creative work. Though Pound translated a number of Chinese classics, his translations are never acclaimed as accurate and faithful, but Poundian scholars and readers agree almost unanimously on his originality. In rendering *The Analects*, a work that influenced his own thinking profoundly, Pound set himself a very modest aim (which he calls "moderate"): to give "the flavour of laconism and the sense of the live man speaking". And by all standards, Pound succeeded in this aim. He is so laconic that he often omits the subject though it can generally be understood. To make for easier understanding, Pound occasionally inserts brief notes in parentheses. He may be said to emphasize the translation of the spirit more than that of the letter; his handling of the famous opening sentence is illuminating: "He said: Study with the seasons winging past, is not this pleasant?". Pound, as is his habit, looking deeply – and often obsessively – into individual ideograms, comes up with findings that surprise the reader, such as his "the seasons winging past", a meaning he digs up from explicating the ancient character "xi" for "study and review".

Pound consulted Pauthier's French translation and Legge's English version of the Chinese text, using R.H. Mathews's *Chinese–English Dictionary* for reference. Pound the creative and original poet no doubt also contributed to the translation; that in turn resulted in a colorful blending of translation and re-creation. And because he did not gloss terms or provide notes, the translation is in places very to the point, but in other places hard to follow. One intriguing sentence in chapter 12, book 2, becomes in Pound "The proper man is not a *dish*" (Legge, Soothill, Waley, and Lau respectively use "an implement", "a utensil", "a machine", and "a vessel"). Pound's creativeness manifests itself in many passages. One such example is his rendition of "de bu gu, bi you lin", which originally means that virtue is never lonely and always has neighbors. Pound's interpretation of these terms is however both interesting and provocative: "candidness is not fatherless, it is bound to have neighbours". Such instances are not rare. However, the essential Confucian ideas in this translation are not to be missed – they are loud and clear. In addition to learning of Confucian ideas, the reader can certainly get a fair taste of Confucian humor and the terseness of the original prose style. It may also be appropriate to add that no other translator of *The Analects* has followed the original's structure as closely as this American disciple of Confucius.

SOOTHILL's *The Confucian Analects* was first published in 1910; in the World's Classics it was published in 1937, with an introduction by his daughter, Lady Dorothea Hosie. The translation eventually underwent a number of reprints. Soothill was one of the earlier translators of *The Analects* after James Legge, whom he succeeded in the Chair of Chinese Language and Literature at Oxford University. Apart from Lady Hosie's conversational introduction, the translation is accompanied by a chronology of Confucius's life and by a concise description of the 36 Confucian disciples; finally, useful notes are also provided. With this apparatus, the translation functions well as a learned work for both lay audience and specialists. The English text flows smoothly and there are no major misrepresentations or misunderstandings. However, for one central term, "junzi", denoting Confucius's ideal man of virtue, that many conveniently translate "gentleman", Soothill alternately uses "true philosopher", "true gentleman", or "the higher type of man", which in turn creates inconsistency and confusion. Besides, controversial sentences in the original continue to be controversial in his rendition. Again, the famous or perhaps notorious assertion of Confucius's on women, still quoted by some Chinese today, goes thus in Soothill's translation: "Maids and servants are hardest to keep in your house". The original literally refers to two types of people that are hard to deal with, "women" and "mean persons".

As those of a major 20th-century sinologue and translator, WALEY's translations are almost always scholarly. His *Analects* (1938) is preceded by a long, useful introduction, and followed by additional and textual notes. Waley considers his own work "somewhat dry and technical in character". In the course of translation he follows the Manchu readings which he believes are authoritative. While conceding that translations by Legge, Soothill, Couvreur, and Richard Wilhelm have their own values, Waley asserts that his own version could be justified because it "attempts to tell the European reader not what the book means to the Far East of to-day, but what it meant to those who compiled it". Raymond Dawson calls Waley's work "stylish", applauding his introduction as having "stood the test of time quite well" (*Confucius*, 1981). There is no doubt that Waley's rendition is one of the most influential and most consulted, but I should like to point out that his translation is better appreciated by Western scholars, which is altogether appropriate, because Waley was after all translating for an English-reading audience. In his attempt to translate both the spirit and the letter he consulted Legge's and other translators' work. He can be highly faithful, as is evident in his handling of the very thorny sentence in chapter 25 of book 17, where the Master is most sexist and male chauvinistic: "Women and people of low birth are very hard to deal with". Almost all translators, writes Waley, "soften the saying by making it apply to 'maids and valets'". The audacity and candidness Waley shows is rarely found in other interpretations of the Confucian text. On the other hand, from a Chinese perspective, the English translation would not be easily accessible without his extensive footnotes, endnotes, and textual notes.

GUIYOU HUANG

Further Reading

Bahm, Archie J., *The Heart of Confucius: Interpretations of Genuine Living and Great Wisdom*, New York: Walker/Weatherhill, 1969

Cleary, Thomas, *The Essential Confucius: The Heart of Confucius' Teachings in Authentic I Ching Order: A Compendium of Ethical Wisdom*, San Francisco: HarperSan Francisco, 1992

Dawson, Raymond, *Confucius*, Oxford: Oxford University Press, 1981; New York: Hill and Wang, 1982

Hughes, E.R. (editor and translator), *Chinese Philosophy in Classical Times*, London: Dent, and New York: Dutton, 1942

Ku Hung Ming (translator), *The Discourses and Sayings of Confucius*, Shanghai: Kelly and Walsh, 1898; reprinted Taipei, Taiwan: Overseas Chinese Affairs Commission, 1982

Lin Yutang (editor and translator), *The Wisdom of Confucius*, New York: Modern Library, 1938

Smith, D. Howard, *Confucius*, New York: Scribner, and London: Temple Smith, 1973

Waley, Arthur, *Three Ways of Thought in Ancient China*, London: Allen and Unwin, 1939; reprinted Stanford, California: Stanford University Press, 1982

Ware, James R. (translator), *The Sayings of Confucius: A New Translation*, New York: New American Library, 1955

Benjamin Constant 1767–1830

French novelist, politician and historian

Biography

Born Benjamin Constant de Rebecque in Lausanne, 25 October 1767, into an old Calvinist family of French origin (Constant claimed French citizenship in 1798, when France annexed Switzerland). His father was an officer in the Dutch service. His mother died shortly after his birth. The young Constant was taught by tutors before going to the universities of Erlangen (1782–83) and Edinburgh (1785). For several years from 1788 he was chamberlain to the duke of Brunswick. Constant was married twice, in 1789 to Wilhelmina von Cramm (divorced 1794, the year he left Brunswick) and in 1808 to Charlotte von Hardenberg. He also had many complicated love affairs, of which the most important was that with Madame de Staël, whom he met in 1794 and left finally in 1811. He was in one-sided love with Madame Récamier in his later years.

Travelling frequently, mainly between Switzerland, Germany and France, Constant published many political pieces from 1795 and stood in French and Swiss elections, sometimes successfully, for political office. For many years he was an opponent of Napoleon, like his lover Madame de Staël, with whom he went into exile in 1803, travelling in Sweden and in Germany, where he met Goethe, Schiller and Friedrich and August Wilhelm Schlegel. In 1815, during the Hundred Days, he was won over briefly by Napoleon. Siding with the liberal opposition under the Restoration (1815–30), he was elected deputy for Sarthe in 1819, for Paris in 1824 and for Bas-Rhin in 1827. In 1830 was appointed to the Council of State. When he died in Paris, 8 December 1830, he was given a state funeral.

As well as being a founder of liberal politics and journalism in France, Constant was among the first to study comparative religion. *De la Religion* (*On Religion*) appeared in five volumes in 1824–31. It is, however, as the author of the exquisite *Adolphe* (*Adolphe*), 1816, that Constant is famous. Other notable literary works, published posthumously, are the autobiographical story *Cécile* (*Cecile*), 1951; *Le Cahier rouge* (*The Red Notebook*), reminiscences, 1907; and the *Journaux intimes* [Intimate Journals], 1952.`

Adolphe

Adolphe, 1816

A short novel, published in 1816, complete with the standard 18th-century device of "editorial" remarks on the accidental finding of the manuscript. The second (1816) and third (1824) editions included authorial prefaces.

Translations

The best French editions are Paul Delbouille's (Paris: Belles Lettres, 1977) and the *Oeuvres* volume edited by Alfred Roulin (Paris: Gallimard, 1957 [Bibliothèque de Pléiade]), both with manuscript variants.

Hookham, Paul, *Adolphe: A Narrative Found among the Papers of an Unknown Person*, London: Philpot, 1924; New York: Knopf, 1925
Lalor-Barrett, W., *Adolphe: An Autobiographical Novel*, New York: Dial Press, 1933
Murry, John Middleton, *Adolphe* in his *The Conquest of Death*, London: Nevill, 1951
Tancock, Leonard W., *Adolphe*, Harmondsworth and New York: Penguin, 1964
Walker, Alexander, *Adolphe*, London: Colburn, 1816; Philadelphia: Carey, 1817
Wildman, Carl, *Adolphe*, in *Adolphe, and The Red Note-Book*, with an introduction by Harold Nicolson, London: Hamish Hamilton, 1948; New York: New American Library, 1959 (*The Red Note-Book* translated by Norman Cameron)

The first translation of *Adolphe* was contemporaneous with its initial French publication in 1816: a friend of Constant's, Alexander WALKER, produced an English version under authorial supervision. This compact novel has been retranslated frequently since its mid-20th-century recognition by critics as a masterpiece of French literature.

Adolphe presents a psychologically complex study of a doomed passion in the pellucidly clear, stately, and balanced prose of high French classicism. Its measured cadences and restraint in language are consistent with Constant's admiration for Racine. Constant's elevated style resides mostly in his syntax and his formal deployment of a circumscribed vocabulary. Yet translators tend to break up both his accretions of simply balanced clauses and his intricate formulations of psychological penetration. To varying degrees, they convey his imposing simplicity even when they replace the original colons and semicolons with periods; but the elegant exfoliation of his involved, layered phrasings does not withstand such sentence division quite as well. As if to compensate for this loss, some translations further deviate from the original by dressing up the diction, making it more ponderous, varied, and colorful than that of Constant.

All the translations preserve the original's main image patterns: heat and cold, storm.

HOOKHAM (1924) follows the original quite closely and handles much of its neo-classical dignity with finesse. But he also tends to poeticize or elaborate on simple expressions. Thus, for example, "toutes les femmes de sa classe" (all the women of her class) becomes the moralistic "whole sisterhood of frailty", "beaucoup" becomes "a seasoning", "timidité" becomes "an outgrowth of diffidence", "défendre" becomes "taking up the cudgels in defence". Hookham further tampers with his source by insistently varying identical terms – including the thematically resonant "lien" (bond, tie, fetter) – and by relying on melodramatic archaisms ("held under espial", "empoison", "worldlings"). Inaccuracies include a misplaced subordinate clause; indifference to past perfect sequence; in chapter 1, when the mature narrator Adolphe is somberly analyzing in retrospect the snares of social intercourse, the reversal of the psychologically revealing "pour d'autres que pour moi" (for others, not for myself) into "for others as well as for myself"; and in chapter 8 a diminution of "Why did I not throw myself into the grave before she came to hers?" to "Why did I not throw myself at her feet?"

LALOR-BARRETT's version (1933) takes the most liberties with the original. His outright omissions range from numerous phrases to a one-sentence speech in chapter 2 through to the "Letter to the Editor / Publisher" and his "Response" that close the book. Although Lalor-Barrett then imports a short passage from each dropped section into the "Editor/Publisher's Foreword", he entirely loses the classical balance of the dual moral framing. His sentences likewise often diminish the original's structure. He repeatedly breaks up accumulated parallel clauses or, worse, casts one long convoluted sentence of analysis into three or four short ones. His mistranslations include reversals of meaning, senseless expressions such as "In our surprise, we alone are surprised", and even a *faux ami* error in which he takes "sol protecteur" for "sole protector" instead of "ground offering sanctuary". Furthermore, he adds his own metaphors, embellishes neutral phrasing ("unpardonable weakness" for "faiblesse", "a past that enthralls its victims" for "un passé ... nous entoure"), glosses over the past perfect, and formulates such unidiomatic English as "We would better not talk" or "one only passion". He does, however, eliminate archaisms found in later translators ("vassals", "leagues").

WILDMAN (1948) is more reliable and precise in transmitting meaning than either Hookham or Lalor-Barrett. He also comes closer to preserving the original's stately modulations, thanks partly to his retention of the semicolons integral to Constant's style. The least inclined to add color or metaphor to the sparing language, Wildman nevertheless relies on some archaisms: "Woe betide", "coming into my ken", "envenom".

MURRY (1951) likewise rarely departs from the French syntax; in fact, he even *adds* semicolons, colons, and adverbial anaphora to enhance some parallel structures. A striking exception to his accuracy is his distortion of the emphatic apostrophe to love in chapter 4; by changing pronouns and adding a negative, he both flattens and reverses the original into "He who has *not* known *it* [love] cannot describe *it*." Nor does Murry wholly resist poetic flourishes, as when "le coeur s'ouvrait" becomes "heart was budding into" and the straightforward "l'incertitude sur l'époque de la séparation" somehow evolves into "The uncertainty in which I had contrived to wrap the time of separation". There is also the occasional oddity in English phrasing, as in "We were hounded against each other by Furies".

The least felicitous aspect of TANCOCK's version (1964) is his approach to many of the insistently short, parallel clauses, set off by semicolons, in which Constant concentrates and balances actions and reactions. By substituting conjunctions for semicolons, Tancock disperses a staccato intensity into a loosely mellow formation. But otherwise his translation is gracefully accurate and respectful of the original, with only a few lapses – for instance, the same switch of pronoun as Murry's in the apostrophe to love, a gratuitous reference to Ovidian "art of love" for "une théorie de fatuité", the over-interpretation of "diverses" as "devious".

Tancock includes Alexander WALKER's (1816) translation of the author's prefaces to the second and third editions. The unmatched meticulousness of these prefaces in following Constant's language makes it especially regrettable that Walker's version of *Adolphe* is no longer readily available. Translating virtually word for word, nuance for nuance, changing syntax only for acceptable English usage, Walker conveys fluidly and compellingly the original's Latinate complexities. Therefore, whereas the other translations omit the chiasmus in the opening of chapter 4, Walker faithfully mirrors the one in the second preface: "He suffered by her from want of sentiment; with sentiment more ardent, he would have suffered for her". Whereas most other translations play some obscure or redundant variations on the phrase "une théorie de fatuité" in chapter 3, Walker renders clearly a similar phrase in the preface, "doctrine de fatuité", as "system of unfeeling vanity". He steadily favors English cognates for the original's vocabulary and varies its identical words less frequently than his successors.

MARGARET BOZENNA GOSCILO

Further Reading

Fairlie, Alison, *Imagination and Language: Collected Essays on Constant, Baudelaire, Nerval, and Flaubert*, edited by Malcolm Bowie, Cambridge and New York: Cambridge University Press, 1981

Wood, Dennis, *Benjamin Constant: Adolphe*, Cambridge and New York: Cambridge University Press, 1987

See also Murry's *The Conquest of Death* (1951)

Contrastive Linguistics and Translation

Contrastive Linguistics (CL), despite some critical voices, has developed tremendously since 1980 in keeping with general developments in contemporary linguistics (e.g. Sociolinguistics, Pragmatics, and Discourse and Cross-Cultural Studies). Since CL works with pairs of languages, as does translation, connections between the two disciplines are easy to find. To understand CL's basic theoretical principles, methods and applications and the specific connections between CL and translation theory and practice, it is useful first to consider the nature of this area in general before going into its relevance to translation.

CL can be defined as a branch of Applied Linguistics aimed at producing inverted (i.e. contrastive, not comparative) descriptions of the languages involved. It is founded on the assumption that languages can be compared, and, as the term "contrastive" implies, it is more interested in differences between languages than in their similarities. Before going on, let us note that the term "Contrastive Analysis" (CA), although it belongs to a specific theory, has for a long time been used as a synonym for Contrastive Linguistics, and is still so used by some researchers.

CL has usually been attached to the contrastive-analysis hypothesis, originally formulated by Robert Lado (1957), which can be summarized as follows: When learning a second language (L2), those structures of L2 that coincide with native language (L1) structures will be learned with ease thanks to positive transfer, while contrasting structures will cause difficulty and give rise to error because of negative transfer. CA was, then, initially concerned with the way in which L1 affected L2, that is with "interference". Negative transfer being traditionally associated with the making of error, it was then (in the 1960s) considered useful for predicting errors on the basis of a contrastive analysis of the two languages involved. Also, on the assumption that a study of learners' errors is of significant importance for knowing how a language is learned, Error Analysis (EA) (Stephen Pit Corder, 1967) was conducted by many researchers in the late 1960s and early 1970s – and is still used as a complementary tool in Second Language Acquisition (SLA) – aimed at the study of error-making in the learner's performance in order to develop appropriate materials for SLA. It was, however, soon outdated, as it was claimed to be concerned with only one side of L2 learning.

Since its heyday in the 1960s, different methods of CA – CA and EA being often related – have been developed. They offer us different approaches to interlingual identifications and distinct ways of looking across linguistics systems, following the main tendencies in Linguistics. Contrastive grammars, or parts of grammars, were started for a number of language pairs following the structural or taxonomic model (Stockwell *et al.*, 1965); the Transformational-Generative model (Whitman, 1970; Nickel and Wagner, 1968); the Contrastive Generative Model (Krzeszowski, 1971, 1974, 1976); or the Case Grammar model (Di Pietro, 1971), to name some of the most relevant ones. In Carl James's relevant book *Contrastive Analysis* (1980) a good survey of both the "microlinguistics" (or "code-oriented" CAs) and the "macrolinguistics" ("communicative competence oriented" CAs) contrastive perspective is provided.

As we have seen, until the 1980s both pedagogical and descriptive contrastive studies tended to be exclusively concerned with language systems as opposed to language use, and therefore generally to restrict themselves to sentence syntax. A shift of emphasis from language as a self-contained system to language as a means of communication has taken place since then, and a new approach to CL is evinced, as mentioned before, giving rise to valuable new contrastive ventures which could be grouped into three loose categories: contrastive pragmatics, contrastive rhetoric, and contrastive text linguistics.

Other areas of research activities in CL are: (1) traditional contrastive descriptions of languages, i.e. contrastive grammars or portions of grammars, to gain insights into similarities and differences between two languages; (2) cross-language studies with the aim of validating general linguistic hypotheses or hypotheses concerning a given language on the basis of a general linguistic theory with the help of comparative/contrastive data; (3) theoretical and metatheoretical issues; (4) applications of language pedagogy, translation, bilingual lexicography and bilingual education.

Thus, with the movement of CL during the last decades to more communicative positions, CL may account for the processes of intertextual, intercultural and interlingual transfer. CL may, then, be considered as a discipline of interlingual competence, as is translation. And new links, both in theoretical and practical terms, between these two disciplines have been established through research, in addition to the traditional relationship of translation to Linguistics, which is commonly accepted.

For a quick overview of these relationships, we can say that both CL and Translation Theory are concerned with the transition from one language to another. The first has traditionally had as the object of inquiry the means whereby a monolingual individual learns to be bilingual. As for Translation Theory, it is concerned with the study of how texts from one language are transformed into comparable texts in another language; the emphasis here being on the process of text-replacement, not on learning. However, the broader scope adopted by CL has led to more researchers coming from different areas to conduct studies on their relationships above the purely linguistic level, looking for communicative competence in SLA, and for acceptability of translated texts in Translation Studies (House and Blum-Kulka, 1986; Weizman, 1988). In other words, although behaviorist views of transfer are largely defunct, the central notions that they gave rise to – "difference" and "difficulty" – are still very much alive.

As for the activity of translating, translation is done on existing texts, and a text is a group of written signs that the translator must analyse and break into pieces in order to understand. Then s/he must put all the pieces into written signs of the second language. As CL studies languages in contact, it seems obvious that it may provide the translator with the necessary tools to know how the two languages s/he is working with function. Thus, theoretically, an exhaustive contrastive description of the languages involved is a precondition for any systematic study of translation, and, on the discipline level, a developed CL seems to be a necessary precondition for translation studies. Through the intermediate level of translatability, which itself finds its place as a component of the theory of translation – as Toury points out (1980) – contrastive studies form part of the basis for accounting for the first type of relationship exhibited by translations, that is, the target text (TT)–source text (ST) type.

From the point of view of teaching translation, Kiraly (1995), when suggesting models for change in Translation Pedagogy, agrees with most researchers in SLA that interlanguage theory (the study of the emergence of a second language, considering that the learner, in progressing towards mastery of L2, develops a series of approximate systems or transitional dialects that are successive and intersecting) raises fundamental questions about the nature of foreign language learning, but he also emphasizes that it sheds considerable light on the underlying causes of student error, particularly persistent student error (or "fossilization" in Selinker's terminology (1972)). He suggests that an investigation of students' translation errors might be useful for developing instructional approaches and would indicate the way in which translation students attempt to internalize translation skills. The use of "parallel texts" as a method, that is, working with texts that are not related though translation but comparable from the standpoint of text thematics and text pragmatics, is a useful tool in both pragmatically oriented foreign language courses and translation courses.

Translation Studies has also been very influential on CL in the past few years through the use of TT–ST comparative analysis as a method for the establishment of a contrastive description of the pair of languages underlying them. Two main tactics have been suggested for using the "translation method" for CL: (1) to start with existing STs, in either one of the languages involved or in both of them, and to translate them into a certain target language (TL or L2); (2) to use existing translations, though not every text in TL presented and/or regarded for one reason or another as a translation; but not to use every portion of such a text as a suitable source of data for the contrastive study, or at least not to regard every such text (or portion of it) as suitable in the same manner and/or to the same extent.

Summing up, Contrastive Linguistics and Translation Studies are two distinct disciplines, having different practitioners and (almost) independent lines of development. In both areas there are studies in theoretical, methodological, descriptive and applied problems, but connections can be established between all of them. Contrastive Linguistics and Translation Studies can be considered as two levels of phenomena involving interlingual relationships and, as a result, two disciplines, two scientific frameworks are necessary, but cooperation is unavoidable.

CARMEN VALERO-GARCÉS

Further Reading

Fisiak, Jacek (editor), *Further Insights into Contrastive Analysis*, Amsterdam: Benjamins, 1990
House, Juliane and Shoshana Blum-Kulka (editors), *Interlingual and Intercultural Communication: Discourse and Cognition in Translation and Second Language Acquisition Studies*, Tübingen, Narr, 1986
James, Carl, *Contrastive Analysis*, London: Longman, 1980
Kiraly, Donald C., *Pathways to Translation: Pedagogy and Process*, Kent, Ohio: Kent State University Press, 1995
Selinker, L., "Interlanguage", *International Review of Applied Linguistics*, 10 (1972) pp. 209–31
Toury, Gideon, *In Search of a Theory of Translation*, Tel Aviv: Porter Institute, 1980, pp. 19–32
Weise, G., "Contrastive Studies and the Problem of Equivalence in Translation", *Papers and Studies in Contrastive Linguistics*, 22 (1988) pp. 187–94

Pierre Corneille 1606–1684

French dramatist

Biography

Born in Rouen, 6 June 1606; son of a lawyer and elder brother of Thomas Corneille, author of the successful tragedy *Timocrate* (1656). Pierre Corneille was educated at the Jesuit college in Rouen, 1615–22, then studied law. In 1624, for further legal training, he entered the Rouen *parlement*, of which he was a member from 1629 to 1650. In 1628 his father bought him two official posts that brought him income and some administrative duties. He married in 1641 (seven children). He was elected to the Académie Française, 1647. He lived in Paris after 1662 and died there, 1 October 1684.

Corneille, the most prolific and versatile of the three great French Classical dramatists, wrote his first poems in 1625. His first play was the successful comedy, *Mélite (Melite)* (season of 1629–30). At close intervals in the early 1630s there followed a tragi-comedy, *Clitandre* [Clitander], and several more comedies. The year 1635 saw the performance of his first tragedy, *Médée (Medea)* and his inclusion (he soon deserted) in Cardinal Richelieu's group of five authors writing to the minister's precepts. In 1636 came the comedy *L'Illusion comique* (*The Theatrical Illusion*), whose theme and form have been of particular interest to modern critics. In the 1636–37 season the tragi-comedy *Le Cid* (*The Cid*), a great success with court and public, gave rise to a prolonged critical dispute about the play's conformity with the rules and conventions of drama. The Corneille family was ennobled in 1637. *Le Cid* began the period of Corneille's greatest achievement, with a series of tragedies between 1640 and 1651, including *Horace* (*Horatius*), *Cinna* (*Cinna*), *Polyeucte* (*Polyeuctus*), *La Mort de Pompée* (*Pompey the Great*), *Rodogune* (*Rodogune*) and *Nicomède* (*Nicomede*), now in the canon of French literature. The comedy *Le Menteur* (*The Liar*) also belongs to this period.

Corneille withdrew from the theatre in 1651, returning in 1659. The plays of the late period still contain fine things, and some consider his last tragedy, *Suréna* (*Surenas*), 1674, worthy to stand beside those of Racine, whose fame overshadowed that of Corneille from about 1667.

Translations

The French text used by most translators is the edition by Charles Marty-Laveaux in the Grands Écrivains de la France series, itself based on the 1682 edition, the last published in the lifetime of Corneille.

Selections of Plays

Bolt, Ranjit, *The Liar*, *The Illusion: Two Plays*, Bath: Absolute Press, 1989

Cairncross, John, *The Cid, Cinna, The Theatrical Illusion*, Harmondsworth: Penguin, 1975
Cairncross, John, *Polyeuctus, The Liar, Nicomedes*, Harmondsworth and New York: Penguin, 1980
Clark, Noel, *Le Cid, Cinna, Polyeuct: Three Plays*, Bath: Absolute Press, 1993
Lockert, Lacy, *The Chief Plays of Corneille*, Princeton, New Jersey: Princeton University Press, 1952 (contains *The Cid, Horatius, Cinna, Polyeucte, Rodogune, Nicomedes*)
Lockert, Lacy, *Moot Plays of Corneille*, Nashville, Tennessee:Vanderbilt University Press, 1959 (contains *Pompey, Heraclius, Don Sanche, Sertorius, Otho, Attila, Pulcheria, Surenas*)
Solomon, Samuel, *Seven Plays*, New York: Random House, 1969 (contains *The Cid, Horatius, Cinna, Polyeucte, The Liar, Rodogune, Surenas.*

Plays

Le Cid, tragi-comédie, 1637
Rutter, Joseph, *The Cid, a Tragicomedy*, London: printed by John Haviland for Thomas Walkly, 1637
Mongan, Roscoe, *The Cid*, Dublin: James Cornish, 1880

Horace, tragédie, 1641, produced 1640
Mongan, Roscoe, *Corneille's Horace*, London: James Cornish, 1881

Cinna; ou, La clémence d'Auguste, tragédie, 1643, produced 1641
Cibber, Colley(?), *Cinna's Conspiracy: A Tragedy*, London: Bernard Lintott, 1713
Mongan, Roscoe, *Cinna*, London: James Cornish, 1878

Polyeucte, tragédie chrétienne, 1643, produced 1642
Lower, Sir William, *Polyeucte; or, The Martyr*, London: printed by Thomas Roycroft for G. Bedell and T. Collins, 1655

La Mort de Pompée, tragédie, 1644, produced 1643
Phillips, Katherine, *Pompey*, London: John Crook, 1663

Rodogune, princesse des Parthes, tragédie, 1647, produced 1644
Aspinwall, S, *Rodogune; or, the Rival Brothers: A Tragedy*, with an introduction, London: printed privately for Dodsley, 1765

Héraclius, empereur d'Orient, tragédie, 1647
Carlell, Lodowick, *Heraclius Emperour of the East: A Tragedy*, London: printed for John Starkey, 1664

There is no complete English translation of all the works of Corneille. One can count 17 plays translated, which is roughly half his output. Some of these have been translated many times, with *Polyeucte* and *The Cid* being easily the favourites, followed by *Cinna, Horatius* and *The Liar*. Of the remaining 12, six have been translated only once in the 300 years that have elapsed since Corneille's death. *Heraclius, The Illusion, Nicomedes, Pompey, Rodogune* and *Surenas* have attracted the attention of more than one translator, but the following plays exist only in a single translation: *Attila, Don Sanche, Melite, Otho, Pulcheria* and *Sertorius*. The reader who would like to know the early comedies will not find it possible to read them in English, with the exception of *The Illusion*. The translation of *Melite* mentioned above is a rare 18th-century version. Many plays now considered well worth the trouble of study remain untranslated as yet, and this is a pity because a full picture of the complexity of Corneille's dramatic works can be appreciated only by taking them all into account. Corneille's language is not easy to translate because he was dealing with the problems that arise in human relationships when public and private loyalties clash. The language used to express these problems is often complicated, and great skill is necessary if the sentiments portrayed are to be adequately translated into an English that is neither artificial nor unreal.

Translation of Corneille's plays started early and seven of his plays were already available in English in the 17th century. These versions are not without merit. Most of them were intended for performance and were, indeed, performed. Pepys saw performances of *The Cid, Horatius, Pompey* and *Heraclius* which he much enjoyed. The mark, then, of these translations is that they were done with the stage in mind. RUTTER's *Le Cid* (1637) omits most of the soliloquies and reduces in length speeches that presumably he thought boring. He uses iambic pentameters but does not hesitate to vary the length of line if he is seeking effect. LOWER's *Polyeuctes* (1655) is also in iambic pentameters; it follows the original quite closely but manages to impart its own flavour to the language. Katherine PHILLIPS's *Pompey* (1663) is enlivened by the introduction of song and dance into the interludes after each act. The intention is to give some relief from the seriousness of the tragedy and, indeed, the aim of the translation seems to be to take the tragic out of the tragedy. CARLELL's *Heraclius* (1664) uses heroic couplets, but very little attempt is made to convey the fire and vividness of Corneille's verse. The highly complicated play is reduced drastically in length by shortening many of the speeches and omitting much background material. The result of this process is to give a sharper focus to the action, although it does not make it very much more comprehensible. There is a charm about these 17th-century translations springing from their closeness in time to the original plays.

There are not many translations of Corneille from the 18th century. Two are perhaps worth looking at. In 1713 was published *Cinna's Conspiracy*, a translation or rather adaptation attributed to Colley CIBBER, although there is no firm evidence that it is by him. It is an interesting but in many ways infuriating version. The translator deems it necessary to supplement Corneille with quite a number of his own inventions. The intention is to make clear what to him appears obscure, but the result is not happy. What is taunt and tense in Corneille is loose and slack here. ASPINWALL's *Rodogune* (1765) is remarkable by the very fact of this play being chosen to translate. It is a good translation with many original touches. The introduction by the translator is of interest as it points up the difference between the expectations of an English audience and those of a French one. The former likes "show and bustle" while the latter is more attracted by "heightened distress".

The 19th century did not see a great number of translations of the plays of Corneille. A translation of *The Cid* was published in 1802 but then there is silence until the 1870s and 1880s when Roscoe MONGAN published translations of three tragedies in the Kelly's Key to the Classics series. His *Cinna* is dated 1878, *The Cid* 1880 and *Horace* 1881. It is impossible to say anything good of these translations. It is true that no claim is made for them other than that they are literally translated and this is indeed the case. The translation is in prose, not in itself necessarily a bad thing, but the prose here is banal and pedestrian. The word-for-word method reduces Corneille's verse to absurdity. The themes of the plays, dealing as they do with lofty and intense issues of personal relationships and public duty, need the most sensitive handling if they are to retain their power of moving. This is what they do not get in these translations. Thus Pauline's poignant question addressed to Polyeucte and Felix in Act V of *Polyeucte* becomes "Which of you two is to slay me today? Both together or each in his turn?" This is indeed what the French says but its rendering thus is ludicrous and destroys the whole effect of pathos. If prose is to be used it must be better than this. Corneille is ill-served by these translations whose only use, presumably, would be as an aid to schoolchildren trying to make sense of the French text.

The 20th century was well advanced before translations of Corneille began to appear. In 1952 LOCKERT published *The Chief Plays of Corneille* and in 1959 *Moot Plays of Corneille*. Credit is due to Lockert for bringing these latter plays to the attention of the English speaker. It is not possible, however, to give these translations wholehearted approval. The irritation caused by the value judgements implied in the choice of titles for the two collections is not dissipated by a reading of the simplistic and superficial discussion of Corneille in the introductions to the volumes. Blank verse is used for the translation, with occasional rhyming lines, and no fault can be found with this; but the language used is that of an outmoded concept that words never used in ordinary speech are, on that account, poetic. This results in a tortuousness and artificiality of language which, after a while, makes reading the plays almost a penance. The use of "thou" and "thy" for *tutoiement* is not successful and only adds to a sense of unreality. Such lines as "I am no whit surprised by what astounds thee" or "I nowise think thee base" or "O duteousness my ruin and my despair" give the flavour of these translations and show up their weakness. When one adds that scene divisions are done away with (except in cases where, in the original, there was no *liaison de scène*) one realizes that much of the dramatic force of the plays is lost. The stilted, would-be poetic language betrays Corneille. His language is sometimes complicated, sometimes convoluted and sometimes involved but it is never artificial and never consciously archaic. Thus to translate it into archaic English is wrong. It must be said, however, that the enterprise of making plays such as *Don Sanche*, *Sertorius*, *Otho*, *Attila* and *Pulcheria* available in English, however imperfect the translation, is to be welcomed.

In 1969 SOLOMON published translations of seven plays. The medium used is iambic pentameters with mingled rhymed and unrhymed lines. These versions are carefully crafted and the strength of Corneille's verse is well brought out. Solomon uses plain language and makes no attempt to create a "poetic" style but does, in fact, frequently write lines of a very high quality. The translations are accurate and this, together with the genuine "feel" for Corneille that they convey, gives them a shine Lockert never achieves.

The six translations published by CAIRNCROSS in 1975 and 1980 are excellent. In a foreword the translator acknowledges the difficulty of translating Corneille and declares that his aim is to make the plays accessible in modern English with more or less the same effect as that which the original French would have for a Frenchman. While it might be argued that this is something impossible to know, the fact that this is what is in his mind keeps the translation from veering off into artificiality and unreality. The medium used is blank verse and it is wielded with skill and sensitivity. The language used is not commonplace but neither is it pretentious, and it manages to convey something of the swell and dignity of Cornelian verse. The decision to translate *The Theatrical Illusion* is interesting because it reflects the attention this play now attracts after centuries of neglect. Here the translation keeps the fast-moving pace of the original, and all the fantasy and comedy is maintained but never falls into absurdity. It is a pity that only six plays are available in these translations.

In 1989 BOLT published translations of *The Liar* and *The Illusion*. The former is, as the translator says, more an adaptation than a translation and he takes many liberties. One character is removed altogether and lines of the translator's own invention are added. This is a racy version of the play and eminently actable. Is it Corneille? The problem is that there is very little of Corneille's concept of comedy here, as the whole shift of the comic emphasis is towards the modern. There is much to be said for this as it keeps the play alive and makes it available for modern audiences. The translator has opted to use rhyming couplets as his medium; he manipulates these with great virtuosity and they add immeasurably to the verve of the translation. In *The Illusion* the translator has remained closer to the original. This is because he found the play weird enough as it was and did not need to add new touches. The result again is fresh and bright, with the same virtuosity in producing rhymes as in *The Liar*.

CLARK's translations of *The Cid*, *Cinna* and *Polyeuct* (sic) were published in 1993. These too are translations with the stage in mind, and one at least, *Polyeuct*, has been performed. One can only applaud these attempts to make the tragedies, as distinct from the comedies, of Corneille available to the modern stage. Like Bolt, Clark opts for rhyme and the heroic couplet. Far from inhibiting him the choice seems almost to have freed his imagination. The verse runs easily and with fluidity and there is no sense of the need for rhyme hindering the development of the thought. The verse manages to preserve the seriousness and dignity necessary for tragedy, but it does so with a spark that prevents it from becoming heavy and stilted. For instance, the lyric passages in *The Cid* are excellently served. The whole translation is lively and yet disciplined, which is itself a very fine achievement. These efforts to make the plays of Corneille available in a modern guise are to be commended.

The problems of translating Corneille are manifold, as a survey of what has been attempted demonstrates. The 17th and 18th centuries tried to make a few of the best known plays available for the English stage, but the 19th century concentrated simply on giving versions to be read. The 20th century has tried both with varying success, but it is good to see that the last years of this century are turning back to Corneille for good stage plays. His complexity is not easily conveyed in translation, but some of the attempts that have been made are praiseworthy. It can only be a matter of regret that all his plays are not available for the English-language speaker.

J.P. SHORT

Further Reading
Barnwell, H.T., *The Tragic Drama of Corneille and Racine: An Old Parallel Revisited*, Oxford: Clarendon Press, and New York: Oxford University Press, 1982
Canfield, Dorothea Frances, *Corneille and Racine in England: A Study of the English Translations of the Two Corneilles and Racine*, New York: Columbia University Press, 1904; reprinted New York: AMS Press, 1966
Lough, John, *Seventeenth-Century French Drama: The Background*, Oxford: Clarendon Press, and New York: Oxford University Press, 1979
Nurse, Peter H., *Classical Voices: Studies of Corneille, Racine, Molière, Mme de Lafayette*, London: Harrap, 1971

See also the translators' introductions to Cairncross, Clark and Solomon

---

Julio Cortázar 1914–1984

Argentine novelist and short-story writer

Biography

Born in Brussels, 26 August 1914, but brought up and educated in Argentina, where he later taught French literature to school and university students. From 1948 to 1951 he worked as a translator in Buenos Aires. He settled in Paris in 1951 and earned his living in France as a writer and as a freelance translator for Unesco. He travelled in South America and lectured in the US. A current of work for human rights ran through his life and writing. In his technically innovative novels deep humanistic and literary themes mingle with social realism and fantasy. He is famous as the author of the experimental novel *Hopscotch* (*Rayuela*) and of the short story on which the film *Blow-Up*, directed by Michelangelo Antonioni, was based. He acquired French nationality in 1981. Died in Paris, 12 February 1984.

Translations

Novels

Los premios, 1960
Kerrigan, Elaine, *The Winners*, London: Souvenir Press, and New York: Pantheon, 1965

Rayuela, 1963
Rabassa, Gregory, *Hopscotch*, New York: Pantheon, 1966; London: Collins Harvill, 1967

La vuelta al día en ochenta mundos, 1967; *Último Round*, 1969
Christensen, Thomas, *Around the Day in Eighty Worlds*, San Francisco: North Point Press, 1986

62: Modelo para armar, 1968
Rabassa, Gregory, *62: A Model Kit*, New York: Pantheon, 1972; London: Marion Boyars, 1976

Libro de Manuel, 1973
Rabassa, Gregory, *A Manual for Manuel*, New York: Pantheon, 1978; London: Harvill Press, 1984

Selections of Short Stories

Blackburn, Paul, *End of the Game and Other Stories*, New York: Pantheon, 1967; London: Collins Harvill, 1968; retitled as *Blow-Up and Other Stories*, New York: Collier, 1968
Blackburn, Paul, *Cronopios and Famas*, London: Marion Boyars, and New York: Random House, 1969
Levine, Suzanne Jill, *All Fires the Fire and Other Stories*, New York: Pantheon, 1973; London: Marion Boyars, 1979
Manguel, Alberto, *Unreasonable Hours*, Toronto: Coach House Press, 1995
Manguel, Alberto (editor), *Bestiary: Selected Stories by Julio Cortázar*, translated by Paul Blackburn, Suzanne Jill Levine, Manguel, Clementine Rabassa and Gregory Rabassa, London: Harvill Press, 1998
Rabassa, Gregory, *A Change of Light and Other Stories*, New York: Knopf, 1980; London: Harvill Press, 1984
Rabassa, Gregory, *We Love Glenda So Much and Other Tales*, New York: Knopf, 1983; London: Harvill Press, 1984

Short Stories

Historia de cronopios y de famas, 1962

Poetry

Salvo el crepúsculo, 1982
Kessler, Stephen, *Save the Twilight: Selected Poems*, San Francisco: City Lights, 1997

Other Writing

La vuelta al día en ochenta mundos, 1967; *Último round*, 1969
Christensen, Thomas, *Around the Day in Eighty Worlds*, San Francisco: North Point Press, 1986

Un tal Lucas, 1979
Rabassa, Gregory, *A Certain Lucas*, New York: Knopf, 1984

Like his fellow countryman, Jorge Luis Borges, Julio Cortázar is one of the main representatives of the so-called "Boom" of Latin American literature, a significant publishing movement which launched a great number of Latin American novels into the American and European book markets during the 1960s and

1970s. Unlike Borges, whose work was actually rediscovered by the Boom's publishers, Cortázar published most of his celebrated novels and short stories during this movement. This may account for the fact it did not take long for his work to be translated into English and other languages.

Cortázar's writing, comprising experimental novel techniques, as in the case of *Hopscotch*, and short stories easily classifiable under the magical realism heading, enjoyed a wide reception in the Anglo-American market. Most of his fiction has been translated into English, the three main translators being Gregory RABASSA, Suzanne Jill LEVINE, and Paul BLACKBURN. Awaiting transposition into English are some of Cortázar's books of essays and the recently published correspondence.

Gregory RABASSA, also a translator of Gabriel García Márquez, Mario Vargas Llosa, José Lezama Lima, José Donoso and Clarice Lispector, among others, is the author of the English version of *Rayuela – Hopscotch*, winner of the 1966 National Book Award for Translation. Rabassa's rendition admirably captured the fluent narrative style of the novel's narrator, a feature that applies to most of Rabassa's translations.

LEVINE's translations of Cortázar's stories (1973, 1998) also capture the Argentine author's style, although in a manner different from Rabassa's. Her versions convey what could be called the "mood" one feels in the original, especially the subtle, nostalgic tone of some of Cortázar's stories, such as "The Other Heaven" in *All Fires the Fire* ... "Having collaborated with such polyglots as Guillermo Cabrera Infante, Julio Cortázar ...," states Levine (1991), "I have been able to observe a symbiotic if not parasitic relationship between translation and original composition." This symbiosis permeates Levine's translations, which re-create the originals through the careful choice of words and syntax.

The identity Levine establishes between creation and translation is well illustrated by Cortázar's work. Himself a translator of Chesterton, Bremond, Defoe, Gide, Poe and Stern, among others, Cortázar theorized about translation throughout his fiction and some of his essays. Among the pieces in which the protagonist is a translator, *62: Modelo para armar* offers perhaps the most challenging problematization of the so-called transparency and equivalence of the translation process. In an unforgettable initial scene, the novel depicts a Latin American in Paris who mistranslates a restaurant order in a complex mixture of the anthropophagic and historical discourses.

The re-creating potential of translation highlighted by Cortázar himself and LEVINE is also stressed by another of Cortázar's translators, Paul BLACKBURN, who, as Venuti (1995) points out, advocates linguistic experimentalism and a foreignizing intervention in the translation process. This is best illustrated, according to Venuti, by Blackburn's rendition of Cortázar's famous "Continuidad de los parques", a very short story which plays on the idea of the intermingling of reality and fiction, literature and fact, author and reader. The choice of a specific personal pronoun, where no clue is provided by the original text, together with the addition of some asides to the translated text, characterizes Blackburn's re-reading of Cortázar's textual puzzle in "Continuity of Parks".

The blurred borderlines between reality and fiction, original and translation, that permeate Cortázar's stories usually involve different semiotic codes, such as literature, music, the theatre and the cinema. As in the case of Manuel Puig, Cortázar's own work provides insightful reflections on intersemiotic transpositions, a process that transcends his fiction and can further be seen in the translation of his short stories into films. *Blow-Up*, the film by Michelangelo Antonioni based on Cortázar's "Las babas del diablo" [The Devil's Drool] is the best example of the creative reading opened up by translation. In this short story, a translator tries to translate reality into photographs, the images captured showing the different view of reality focused by the camera. The film translates the short story into moving pictures that portray a photographer's attempt at interpreting the facts caught by his camera.

When transposed into English, Cortázar's books of short stories are frequently compiled into selections of stories taken from different volumes. This is the case with BLACKBURN's *End of the Game and Other Stories*, LEVINE's *All Fires the Fire and Oher Stories*, and RABASSA's *A Change of Light and Other Stories* and *We Love Glenda So Much and Other Tales*. One of the more recent Cortázar translations, *Unreasonable Hours* (1995), is a selection of some of the stories in *Deshoras* (1982), interestingly transposed by the Argentine-Canadian critic and translator Alberto MANGUEL, who makes subtle syntactic changes in Cortázar's style and overcomes lexical challenges such as the play on words in the short story "Satarsa", re-created by him as "Tara". The same selective process can be seen in Stephen KESSLER's *Save Twilight* (1997), a selection and translation of some of the poems in *Salvo el crepúsculo* (1984).

Cortázar's work has undergone other kinds of editorial changes. After Antonioni's successful film *Blow-Up* (1966), BLACKBURN's volume *End of the Game and Other Stories* was renamed *Blow-Up and Other Stories*, even though the original story upon which the film was based has a different title. In this case, the intersemiotic transposition of the story into a film shows a bi-directional movement between original and translated text, since the original ("Las babas del diablo") produces a re-created reading, a translation (*Blow-Up*, the film), which, in turn, transforms the original by Cortázar: "Las babas de diablo" [The Devil's Drool] becomes "Blow-Up". The displacement of signifiers in the short story's title no doubt resembles the slippages and acts of mistranslation Cortázar likes playing with in his fiction. Furthermore, the transformation operating in this case also brings into play an important feature of translation processes: the role of market and mass media in cultural communities' readings of the written word.

ADRIANA S. PAGANO

Further Reading

Alazraki, Jaime and Ivar Ivask (editors), *The Final Island: The Fiction of Julio Cortázar*, Norman: University of Oklahoma Press, 1978

Axelrod, M.R., *The Politics of Style in the Fiction of Balzac, Beckett and Cortázar*, New York: St Martin's Press, 1992

Cortázar, Julio, "Bibliografia" in *Rayuela*, edited by Andrés Amorás, Madrid: Cátedra, n.d., pp. 95–107

Levine, Suzanne Jill, *The Subversive Scribe: Translating Latin American Fiction*, St Paul, Minnesota: Graywolf Press, 1991

Lo, Sara de Mundo, *Julio Cortázar: His Work and His Critics: A Bibliography*, Urbana, Illinois: Albatross, 1985

Maclean, Anne, review of *Bestiary: Selected Stories by Julio Cortázar*, edited by Manguel, in *In Other Words*, 12 (Winter 1998)

Rabassa, Gregory, "No Two Snowflakes are Alike" in *The Craft of Translation*, edited by John Biguenet and Rainer Schulte, Chicago: University of Chicago Press, 1989, pp. 1–12

Stavans, Ilan, "Translation and Identity", *Michigan Quarterly Review*, 35/2 (Spring 1996) pp. 280–95

Venuti, Lawrence, *The Translator's Invisibility: A History of Translation*, London and New York: Routledge, 1995

Louis Couperus 1863–1923

Dutch novelist, short-story writer and poet

Biography

Born Louis Marie Anne Couperus 10 June 1863 in The Hague. He spent a large part of his childhood in the Dutch East Indies (now Indonesia), where his father and grandfather were involved in the colonial administration. He came back to the Netherlands in 1877. After 1891, the year of his marriage, he lived for a long time in France and Italy, as well as spending another year in the Dutch East Indies, the setting of one of his best-known novels, *De stille kracht* (1900; *The Hidden Force*). After publishing some unsuccessful poetry the young Couperus turned to fiction. His first novel *Eline Vere* (1889) was very well received and was followed by many others. The novels deal largely with middle-class Dutch characters of sensitive feelings and sometimes rebellious or "decadent" leanings, on whom fate in the form of character or heredity presses in a sinister fashion. Couperus also wrote historical novels containing long exotic descriptions and rich evocations of sensory impressions. In the latter part of his life his writing was mainly in the field of journalism, the essay and travel stories. Couperus's fiction combines pessimistic naturalism and a delicate, even mannered, prose style, with skilful narrative serving as vehicle for psychological portraiture and social criticism. He was a major figure in Dutch literature and at one extended period his novels were translated into many European languages, well over a dozen appearing in English on both sides of the Atlantic. He died at De Steeg, 16 July 1923.

Translations

Novels

Eline Vere, 1889
Grein, J.T., *Eline Vere*, London: Chapman and Hall, and New York: Appleton, 1892

Noodlot, 1890
Bell, Clara, *Footsteps of Fate*, London: Heinemann, 1891; New York: Appleton, 1892

Extaze, 1892
Teixeira de Mattos, Alexander and John Gray, *Ecstasy: A Study of Happiness*, London: Henry, 1892, New York: Dodd Mead, 1919; reprinted London: Pushkin Press, 1998

Majesteit, 1893
Teixeira de Mattos, Alexander and Ernest Dowson, *Majesty*, London: Unwin, 1894; New York: Appleton, 1895

Psyche, 1898
Berrington, B.S., *Psyche*, London, Alston Rivers, 1908

De stille kracht, 1900
Teixeira de Mattos, Alexander, *The Hidden Force: A Story of Modern Java*, New York: Dodd Mead, 1921; London: Jonathan Cape, 1922; revised by E.M. Beekman, Amherst: University of Massachusetts Press, 1985; London: Quartet, 1992

Langs lijnen van geleidelijkheid, 1900
Teixeira de Mattos, Alexander, *The Inevitable*, New York: Dodd Mead, 1920; as *The Law Inevitable*, London: Thornton Butterworth, 1922

De kleine zielen, 1901
Teixeira de Mattos, Alexander, *The Small Souls*, London: Heinemann, 1914; New York: Dodd Mead, 1919

Het late leven, 1902
Teixeira de Mattos, Alexander, *The Later Life*, London: Heinemann, 1915; Dodd Mead, 1923

Het heilige weten, 1903
Teixeira de Mattos, Alexander, *Doctor Adriaan*, London: Heinemann, and New York: Dodd Mead, 1918

Zielenschemeringen, 1903
Teixeira de Mattos, Alexander, *The Twilight of the Souls*, New York: Dodd Mead, 1917; London: Heinemann, 1918

Van oude menschen, de dingen die voorbijgaan, 1906
Teixeira de Mattos, Alexander, *Old People and the Things that Pass By*, New York: Dodd Mead, 1918; London: Butterworth, 1919; New York: House and Maxwell, 1963

Antiek Toerisme, 1911
Teixeira de Mattos, Alexander, *The Tour: A Story of Ancient Egypt*, London: Butterworth, and New York: Dodd Mead, 1920

Short Stories

Korte arabesken, 1911
Kooistra, F., *Eighteen Tales*, London: F.V. White, 1924

De komedianten, 1917
Wilson, J.H., *The Comedians. A Story of Ancient Rome*, London: Jonathan Cape, and New York: Doran, 1926

Xerxes, 1919
Martens, Frederick H., *Arrogance: The Conquests of Xerxes*, New York: Farrar and Rinehart, 1930

Travel Writing
Oostwaarts, 1923
Menzies-Wilson, J. and C.C. Crispin, *Eastward*, London: Hurst and Blackett, and New York: Doran, 1924

Nippon, 1925
Valette, John de la, *Nippon*, London: Hurst and Blackett, 1926

Louis Couperus's talent as a storyteller, unparalleled among his Dutch contemporaries, won him many admiring readers in English translation at the turn of the 20th century, and provoked favourable comparisons with both John Galsworthy and Henry James. The preoccupation of many of his generation with linguistic expressionism and experiment leaves only a residual trace in an occasional tendency to over-lush, "purple" description. More important narrative influences on Couperus are Tolstoi's short-chapter technique and the Wagnerian *motif* (*The Twilight of the Souls*, the title of the third volume of his tetralogy, *The Books of the Small Souls* (1901–03), is an obvious *hommage* to his model).

Taken up first by the circle around Oscar Wilde and *The Yellow Book*, and by the influential critic Edmund Gosse (whose brother-in-law, the painter Lawrence Alma-Tadema, later introduced him to the author), Couperus's evocative studies of heredity, conditioning, guilt and sexuality won extravagant praise from such respected voices as John Cowper Powys and particularly Katherine Mansfield, who wrote memorably of *The Books of the Small Souls*, the four-novel cycle published 1901 to 1903 and comprising *The Small Souls*, *The Later Life*, *The Twilight of the Souls*, and *Dr Adriaan* (translated by *Texeira de Mattos*, 1914, 1915, 1917, 1918): "We do not know anything in English literature with which to compare this delicate and profound study of a passionately united and almost equally passionately divided family ... The real head of the family, the grim, ghostly shadow whose authority they never question, is Fear." On this his broadest canvas Couperus plots the disintegration of a great colonial clan, the Van Lowes. The first volume, *The Small Souls*, deals with the return from the wilderness and ostracization of Constance van der Welcke, who had scandalized her family by eloping with the "outsider" she loved. *The Later Life* chronicles Constance's flirtation with social reform and trade unionism, while in *The Twilight of the Souls* madness strikes one of the seemingly most solid members of the family, her brother Gerrit. In *Doctor Adriaan* Constance's son Addy attempts to escape the legacy of the past by committing himself as a doctor to the alleviation of human suffering, but the author leaves us in doubt whether the attempt is totally successful.

The peak in Couperus's popularity was in the years preceding and following World War I. As late as 1921 the critic A.W.G. Randall expressed the hope that "today, when Louis Couperus is again beginning to be translated and admired ... he may yet produce [an effect] on the development of English fiction." In the event, after a brief surge of interest in his shorter fiction and in his travel writing, the revival petered out. J. Kooij has sought to explain the decline in Couperus's fortunes in translation by the demise of the three-volume novel as the staple of the subscription libraries. While this may be a contributing factor, it is at most a partial explanation. Ian Buruma finds the writer's international eclipse equally puzzling: "... he has been largely forgotten outside Holland. I don't know why. The translation [*The Hidden Force*], first published in 1922, is not great, but Couperus's precious, elaborate, sometimes quite bizarre prose seems less dated in English than in the original Dutch. The reason is not just that the translator was unable to reproduce the luxuriance of Couperus's style, but that the Dutch language has changed far more than English has since 1900."

While much of Couperus's most significant work is available in English translation, thanks in large part to the dedication of a single translator, the Dutch émigré Alexander TEIXEIRA DE MATTOS, who worked closely with the author, the omissions are equally telling: neither *Iskander* (1920), the study of the disillusion and decadence of Alexander the Great (De Mattos did not live to complete his version) nor *De berg van licht* [The Mountain of Light], (1905–06), with at its centre the tragic figure of the androgynous boy-emperor Heliogabalus, found English publishers. Both were probably too outspoken for an industry still smarting from clashes with the moral establishment over "indecent" literature such as that of Zola. BEEKMAN's 1985 edition of *The Hidden Force*, a study in the "East is East ..." tradition quite worthy of comparison with a work like Forster's *A Passage to India*, retained TEIXEIRA DE MATTOS's contemporary version, while restoring many explicit passages previously bowderlized or omitted, such as sex scenes and the graphic description of red betel juice streaming mysteriously down the naked limbs of the Dutch district commissioner's promiscuous wife in her shower.

None of Couperus's other translators was as dedicated or as gifted as De Mattos.

PAUL VINCENT

Further Reading

Buruma, Ian, "Revenge in the Indies", *New York Review of Books* (11 August 1994) pp. 30–32
Mansfield, Katherine, "The Books of the Small Souls" in *Notes on Novelists*, London: Constable, 1930
Meijer, Reinder P., *Literature of the Low Countries: A Short History of Dutch Literature in the Netherlands and Belgium*, Cheltenham: Thornes, 1978, pp. 251–55
Russell, James Anderson, *Romance and Realism: Trends in Belgo-Dutch Prose Literature*, Amsterdam: H.J. Paris, 1959, pp. 108–20

Abraham Cowley 1618–1667

English poet, essayist and translator

Biography

Abraham Cowley was born 24 July 1618 in London and educated at Westminster School and at Trinity College, Cambridge. He was something of a child prodigy: his earliest volume of poems, *Poetical Blossoms*, was published when he was only 15 years old. During the Civil War he followed the queen to Paris, carried on her correspondence in cipher with the king, and undertook some missions on behalf of the royalist cause – on account of which he was briefly imprisoned in 1655. After the Restoration he retired, provided for by noble patrons, first to Barn Elms in Surrey and then to Chertsey where he died 28 July 1667. He is buried in Westminster Abbey, London.

Cowley's important works as a translator were his *Pindarique Odes, Written in Imitation of the Stile and Manner of the Odes of Pindar* (together with a short but influential preface); *Anacreontiques; or, Some Copies of Verses translated Paraphrastically out of Anacreon*, included in his *Miscellanies* (1656); the versions of Catullus, Claudian, Horace and Virgil included in *Verses Lately Written upon Several Occasions* (1663); and the translations from Horace, Martial, Persius, Propertius, Seneca, Tibullus and Virgil, scattered in his *Several Discourses by way of Essays in Verse and Prose*, which were included in the posthumously published *Works of Mr Abraham Cowley* (1668).

In the present century the general reader is likely to know Cowley only by unflattering hearsay as a "decadent metaphysical", or by a few anthology pieces. His considerable influence on English poetic translation, however, was a by-product of the general esteem in which he was held in the later 17th and early 18th centuries – when he was seen as the equal and true heir of his Roman predecessors. Sir John Denham's praise of Cowley seems to have been representative:

> To him no author was unknown,
> Yet what he wrote was all his own;
> *Horace*'s wit, and *Virgil*'s state,
> He did not steal, but emulate!

Samuel Johnson, in his *Lives of the Poets*, maintained that Cowley was "the first who imparted to English numbers the enthusiasm of the greater ode and the gaiety of the less" and that "he was among those who freed translation from servility, and, instead of following his author at a distance, walked by his side". Cowley was not, strictly speaking, the first poet to imitate or translate the "greater" odes of Pindar, or the "lesser" odes of Anacreon. Johnson's point is that Cowley, being himself "equally qualified" for "lofty flights" and "sprightly sallies", was the first to capture the "enthusiasm" of the one and the "gaiety" of the other in his own English versification. More than this, he had "imparted" his discoveries – created the means by which both Pindar's peculiar "enthusiasm" and Anacreon's peculiar "gaiety" could now be suggested in English by succeeding English poets.

In claiming that Cowley had freed translation from "servility", Johnson may have been recalling some of Cowley's own remarks in the preface to his *Pindarique Odes*, where he had argued that "exact Imitation" was a "vile and unworthy kind of servitude" which is "incapable of producing any thing good or noble". Cowley's theory was based on his appreciation of the extent of historical change between his and Pindar's times, "betwixt the Religions and Customs of our Countrys, and a thousand particularities of places, persons, and manners, which do but confusedly appear to our Eyes at so great a distance". Something *must* be forfeited in all translation, and it is therefore the English poet's duty to make good that deficiency from his own store. Since "verbal Traduction" could only diminish the original, translators should repair inevitable "losses" by adding from their own "wit or invention", and should seek "to supply the lost Excellencies of another Language with new ones in their own". (Wordsworth was to call this the principle of "substitution".) Accordingly, Cowley claims for himself the liberty allowed to one who is "Something Better" than a literal translator:

> I have left out, and added what I please; nor make it so much my aim to let the reader know precisely what [Pindar] spake, as what was his *way* and *manner* of speaking.

The success of Cowley's example and precept as an imitator of Pindar was repeated in the case of his *Anacreontiques*. Again, Johnson's testimony is as typical as it is striking. As Johnson saw it, despite the fact that Cowley had lost some of the "simplicity" of the Greek originals, his versions of Anacreon gave the same pleasure in the 1780s as they had done in the 1650s. It seems that many poets and readers had some of the *Anacreontiques* by heart and paid Cowley the compliment of poetical emulation. "SB", the author of *Anacreon Done into English out of the Original Greek* (1683) had two reasons for translating Anacreon. One was to reveal the "hidden Sweets" of his original. The other was the "tempting Pattern set by the unimitable Mr. Cowley", who had "rendered part of this Author so lively in an English dress" that his disciple "began to esteem it of almost equal Beauty with the Original". Any reader who thinks the 1683 poems are the "too licentious play of a Poetical Mind" is reassured that "'tis nothing but what is authorized by Mr Cowley, nothing but what is adapted to his Model". The poet, critic and historian John Oldmixon considered that "Mr Cowley succeeded better in his Anacreontiques, than in his other Poems" and that his "Ode upon Age" was so much "a master-piece" that "whoever pretends to give us a Translation of Anacreon must set that for his Pattern".

Cowley, it seems, had for many years no rival as a free translator of Greek odes. His versions set the model and the pattern that others followed as best they could. This was less clearly the case with his versions of Latin poetry. For example, in the early years of the 18th century Cowley's versions of Horace appeared in collections alongside versions by Dryden and one version by Milton. Milton's version of the fifth ode of Horace's first book represented an approach to translation almost exactly opposite to that propounded by Cowley, in that it was "*Rendered almost Word for Word without Rhyme according to the Latin Measure, as near as the Language will permit*". Cowley's version of the same ode was represented as a poem in which Horace's original has been "imitated". If Milton's version gives the impression of a monumental language, Cowley's speaks with a rueful English voice in an easy dance of words and images.

Opinion seems always to have been divided over the merits of these two methods of translation. Johnson thought parts of Cowley's poem beneath the dignity of the original. Some readers have found Milton's version profoundly un-English. But Dryden's translations show that for the immediately succeeding generations it was the example of Cowley rather than that of Milton that was dominant. Dryden (most noticeably in his version of the 29th ode of Horace's third book) adopted much of the freedom of Cowley's Horatian translations, and developed (in his own opinion "perfected") the metrical experiments of Cowley's translations of Pindar. It seems to have been Cowley's example, too, that convinced succeeding poets that the heroic couplet (and the occasional Alexandrine) provided the most suitable and flexible tool for translation – as used in his delightful version of Horace's "Country Mouse", or as used in part of the first Epistle of the second book (which Johnson considered to contain "an example of representative versification, which perhaps no other English line can equal"):

... Sapere aude,
Incipe, vivendi qui recte prorogat horam
Rusticus expectat dum labitur Amnis, at ille
Labitur, & labetur in omne volubis aevum.

Begin, be bold, and venture to be wise;
He who defers this work from day to day,
Does on a Rivers Bank expecting stay,
Till the whole stream, which stopt him, should be gon,
That runs, and as it runs, forever will run on.

TOM MASON

Further Reading

Cowley, Abraham, Translations, in volume 2 of *The Complete Works in Verse and Prose of Abraham Cowley*, edited by Alexander B. Grosart, 2 vols, New York: AMS Press, 1967 (reprint of 1881 edition)

Hopkins, David, "Cowley's Horatian Mice", in *Horace Made New*, edited by Hopkins and Charles Martindale, Cambridge and New York: Cambridge University Press, 1993, pp. 103–26

Martindale, Charles, "Unlocking the Word-Hoard: In Praise of Metaphrase", *Comparative Criticism*, 6 (1984) pp. 47–72

Mason, H.A., "Horace's Ode to Pyrrha", *Cambridge Quarterly*, 7 (1976) pp. 27–62

Mason, Tom, "Abraham Cowley and the Wisdom of Anacreon", *Cambridge Quarterly*, 19 (1990) pp. 103–37

Crime Fiction in English Translation

The first problem facing anyone attempting a review of the genre of crime fiction is that of deciding exactly what that genre actually is. Just as defining the novel is notoriously difficult, so the term "crime fiction" can cover such a wide range of texts as to be worse than useless. As Julian Symons writes in *Bloody Murder*, a full review of the field could (and arguably should) examine the entire span of texts dealing with criminality, from the tale of Daniel and the priests of Bel to Robbe-Grillet's *The Erasers* (first translated into English 1964), taking in on the way *Crime and Punishment*, *The Name of the Rose* and Voltaire's *Zadig* (one of the first works to present a central character with apparently supernatural powers of observation, subsequently shown to be based on methodical deduction, a clear precursor of both Sherlock Holmes and Poe's "tales of ratiocination"). For the purposes of this study, the term "crime fiction" will be taken to mean those works that appear on the shelves so labelled in any reputable bookshop. It also seems difficult to offer anything other than the most cursory of comments on the abilities (or lack of same) of the many translators; what is attempted here is a brief overview of the subject, in order to give some idea of the range of translations available and, in the words of Major Renault in *Casablanca*, "round up the usual suspects".

Compared to what may best be termed the woeful state of availability of other literatures in translation, the enthusiast of crime fiction is faced with an embarrassment of riches. It would seem that for as long as there has been writing in any language on any subject from card-sharping to toxicology, someone has been ready to translate it into English. Among the important early influences on the evolution of the crime novel in English were the splendidly self-aggrandizing *Memoirs* of Eugène Vidocq (1775–1857), the former criminal who (rather like "Thieftaker General" Jonathan Wild) rose to become Chief of the Sûreté. His stories (translated by H.T.R., i.e. W. Maginn, in 1828) of meticulous detective work and fantastically successful disguises were to inspire several generations of British and American detectives (he is also the model for Balzac's Vautrin). We could also cite the works of Émile Gaboriau (1833–73), whose *L'Affaire Lerouge* (1863, translated 1887 by an unnamed translator as *The Widow Lerouge*) introduced the detective Lecoq, denounced by Sherlock Holmes in *A Study in Scarlet* as "a bungler", while others would focus on the adventures of the enigmatic arch-criminal Fantômas who appeared (1911–62) in a seemingly endless series of novels by Pierre Souvestre and Marcel Allain, translated into English by various hands from 1915 for Stanley Paul & Co. of London.

These early examples are fascinating for those who wish to trace the development of the crime story, but for the reader who simply wants to read a crime novel, it can safely be said that they have never been so fortunate as now. In particular, they have cause to be grateful to the British publishers Serpent's Tail, who have issued translations by Ed Emery of several of contemporary Manuel Vázquez Montalbán's "Pepe Carvalho" detective stories set in and around Barcelona, and two translations of novels by the French writer Didier Daeninckx. These latter two works (*Meurtres pour mémoire* (1984), translated by Liz Heron, 1991, as *Murder in Memoriam*, and *Der des ders* (1984), translated by Sarah Martin, 1994, as *A Very Profitable War*) are quite simply magnificent, and their translators have done them justice. *A Very Profitable War* deals with political cover-ups and profiteering in the aftermath of World War I, while *Murder in Memoriam* is both a gripping detective story and an indictment of officially sanctioned mass murder, linking the brutal quashing of a peaceful demonstration by Algerian immigrants in Paris in 1961 with the internment and deportation of Jews from wartime France. This is a chilling novel, all the more so because it is firmly based in fact; Daeninckx turns the detective story into a means of investigating hidden chapters in his country's history, and gives final proof, if proof were needed, that a popular genre need not inevitably be devoid of serious content.

Daeninckx represents one way in which the hackneyed figure of the detective can be used to do something new; another wildly different example is the work of Haruki Murakami, whose novel *Hitsuji o meguri boken* (1982) has been translated with great brio by Alfred Birnbaum as *A Wild Sheep Chase* (1989). Perhaps best described as a postmodern Japanese version of Raymond Chandler, this work presents a view of Japan that will come as a surprise to Western readers whose knowledge of the country begins and ends with *Shogun*, *The Seven Samurai* and *Black Rain*.

It may seem from the above that there are no translations available of what the reader may term "normal" crime fiction. This is very definitely not the case; Daeninckx and Murakami simply represent two fascinating departures from the mainstream. Fans of the "police procedural" should look for the translations by Thomas Teal, Joan Tate and Alan Blair of the books of Maj Sjöwall (b.1935–) and Per Wahlöö (1926–75), the Swedish duo who chronicle the investigations of the lugubrious Inspector Martin Beck (perhaps to be read as fictional precursors of the Danish writer Peter Hoeg's phenomenally successful *Miss Smilla's Feeling For Snow*, 1992, translated 1993), or the Grijpstra and DeGier novels by Janwillem van der Wetering (b.1931–), probably the only Dutch Zen Buddhist crime writer. Those who prefer the private eye tradition should turn to the Pan editions of the late Léo Malet's adventures of Nestor Burma, even if inevitably a certain degree of Malet's linguistic *élan* is lost in translation. Lastly, Arturo Pérez-Reverte's *The Flanders Panel* (1990, translated 1994) combines features of the classic "Golden Age" puzzle with the psychological acuity of a Patricia Highsmith or a P.D. James.

Finally, it should again be emphasized that a survey such as this will inevitably leave out more than it covers; as Julian Symons notes, this genre can embrace writers as different as Georges Simenon, Friedrich Dürrenmatt and Jorge Luis Borges. All that can really be said is that while Maigret's adventures are excellent (and generally very well translated), they are by no means the be-all and end-all of the field.

J.K.L. SCOTT

Further Reading

Black, Joel, *The Aesthetics of Murder: A Study in Romantic Literature and Contemporary Culture*, Baltimore: Johns Hopkins University Press, 1991

Hawkins, Harriet, *Classics and Trash: Traditions and Taboos in High Literature and Popular Modern Genres*, Toronto: University of Toronto Press, and London: Harvester Wheatsheaf, 1990

Hoeg, Peter, *Froken Smillas Fornemmelse for Sne*, Copenhagen: Rosinante / Munksgaard, 1992; as *Miss Smilla's Feeling for Snow*, translated by F. David, London: Harvill, 1993; as *Smilla's Sense of Snow*, translated by Tiina Nunally, New York: Farrar Straus, 1993

Murakami, Haruki, *Hitsuji o meguri boken*, Tokyo: Kodansha, 1982; as *A Wild Sheep Chase*, translated by Alfred Birnbaum, Tokyo: Kodansha, 1989

Pérez-Reverte, Arturo, *La tabla de Flandres*, Madrid: Alfaguara, 1990; as *The Flanders Panel*, translated by Margaret Jull Costa, London: Harvill, and New York: Harcourt Brace, 1994

Symons, Julian, *Bloody Murder: From the Detective Story to the Crime Novel*, London: Faber, 1972; 3rd revised edition, New York: Mysterious Press, 1993

Winn, Dilys (editor), *Murder Ink: The Mystery Reader's Companion*, Newton Abbot, Devon: Westbridge, and New York: Workman, 1977; revised edition, Workman, 1984

Cultural Contacts and Literary Translation

Whereas written history has arisen from the sedentary (Deleuze and Guattari, 1980), translating, "carrying over" (Latin "traducere", German "übersetzen"), sites us in the nomadic context of displacements entailing an encounter of cultures. "Nomadology" as an umbrella term subsumes translation and such cultural contacts as migration, colonization, education, the media, telecommunications, and the globalized economy.

The particularity of cultures as signalled by semantic voids constituting an obstacle to translation (e.g. several words for "snow" in Eskimo) has been emphasized, as has the same word that carries different connotations in different cultures (cf. Bassnett-McGuire's discussion of the international term "democracy", for which readers will apply concepts based on their cultural context, 1991).

A shift away from the word as the operational unit and from a normative pedagogy opened the way in the mid-1970s for the incorporation of culture as an operational unit in translation studies and for a methodology drawing upon cultural history and cultural interaction through translation. Such a move evolved from Even-Zohar's polysystem theory (1979) and stemmed from Leningrad Formalism (Yakubinskii, Shklovskii, Eikhenbaum, Zhirmunskii, Tynianov, Tomashevskii, etc.), Czech Structuralism, Russian semiotics of culture, mainly Lotman, and recent systems theory. Elaborations are associated with Toury (1980) and Lefevere. The move was later labelled the Cultural Turn of Translation Studies by Snell-Hornby, who also draws attention to scholarship in Germany oriented towards cultural rather than linguistic parameters (1988) and stresses the importance of translation today in furthering rapid exchange of information and improving cultural contacts (ibid). If culture(s) become(s) the operational "unit", the object of study is the text embedded within a network of both source and target cultural signs (Bassnett and Lefevere 1990).

The lineage of Formalism from Leningrad to Tel Aviv stresses that the function of each work is its correlation with other works, with the whole of literature and, in turn, with other cultural series. It is to highlight dynamism, heterogeneity and multiplicity that Even-Zohar coined the term "polysystem" (1979). Relations can be intra- or inter-systemic, in conjunction with adjacent systems, either within the same or with other communities (ibid.). He conceives of translated literature not only as a system in its own right, but as one fully participating in the history of the polysystem of culture (1978). It can be high, low, innovative, conservative, simplified, stereotyped, and participate (or not) in changes. Translated literature can be an integral part of innovative forces, introducing new models of reality, poetic language, matrices, techniques, etc. It has a notable primary role when a literature is either peripheral or weak or both, or in turning points, crises or literary vacuums. In secondary position, it has no influence on major processes, is modelled according to norms already conventionally established by a dominant type and thus becomes a major factor of conservatism (1978).

The impact of the polysystem theory was remarkable, and illuminating case studies stressing cultural contacts via translation proliferated. Hallmark publications include the Even-Zohar & Toury collection of essays (1981) and Theo Hermans's *The Manipulation of Literature: Studies in Literary Translation* (1985). Tymoczko has demonstrated that translation played a decisive innovative role in the 12th-century shift from epic to romance in France, associated with rapid transitions in the medieval ethos from a warrior to a courtly code and the celebration of romantic love; moreover, translation was a mechanism working against provincialism (1986). Paker studied the role of translated European literature for the birth of modern Turkish literature in the second half of the 19th century, following the Westernization of Turkey in the late 18th century and involving the simplification of the prose style and the introduction of the novel and the short story as new genres (1986). Toury, who holds that a literary translation is an empirical phenomenon that acquires its identity by virtue of its position within the target literary system (1980), demonstrates the primary position of translated literature into Hebrew between 1930 and 1945 in the transition of the centre of Hebrew literature from Europe to Palestine (ibid.); also during the first period of the revival of Hebrew for secular writing, from the end of the 18th century, serious weaknesses and lacunae (e.g. certain genres) arising from its lack of non-interrupted previous tradition, were compensated by Hebrew writers' translating texts from surrounding European literatures (ibid.).

Lefevere subscribes to the heuristic construct of systems as a starting point, but he adds the cultural slant of language games, after Wittgenstein, as well as the dimensions of power, authority and ideology, after Foucault. He claims that translation, a form of refraction (and later "rewriting"), creates images of foreign texts, writers and cultures, inasmuch as it builds intercultural canons. Texts are "known" through a series of adaptations and versions within a cultural system, and "foreign" texts are refracted through translation, whereby a writer's work gains exposure and achieves influence (1982). It is through the combination of translation and critical refractions (introductions, notes, commentary, articles on it) that a work of literature produced outside takes its place inside the "new system" (ibid.). As for the "home" literature, if the receiving literature has a positive self-image, it will tend to naturalize the foreign texts by dictating the terms; conversely, it might accept the source literature as a potentially liberating influence (1985). Translation, a visible sign of "openness", potentially subverts and transforms, not in isolation, but with other forms of rewriting – hence the attempts to regulate translation even after normative poetics disappeared from Western literature (ibid.). Subversive translators may rely on the authority of a writer considered great to go against the dominant constraints (ibid.). Lefevere has expanded on the role of translations as forms of intercultural contacts. Translation fills a need, as the audience can read the previously unavailable text; forces the target language to expand and bestows authority on it; introduces new devices into the literatures by which it is received; can be a threat to the identity of a culture; can be used to subvert by usurping the authority of texts belonging to a culture alien to the target culture; can play an important part in the struggle between rival ideologies or rival poetics; can award some kind of impunity in that attacks on the dominant poetics often pass themselves off as translations; can bestow the authority inherent in a language of authority, e.g. Strindberg's dramas would not belong to world literature if they had not been launched in French, a language of authority (1990).

A key publication with case studies anchored in Lefevere's theories is *Translation, History and Culture*, edited by himself and Susan Bassnett in 1990. Tymoczko, for example, highlights the contact of literary and oral cultures via translation, elaborating on a study by Laura Bohannan of the translation of *Hamlet* for a group of tribal elders in Africa, that includes the audience's cultural responses, e.g. their remark that Claudius and Gertrude did well to marry a month after the funeral. Lefevere himself published in 1992 *Translation, Rewriting, and the Manipulation of Literary Fame*, including a chapter on changing images of Africa created by 12 anthologies of African writers designed for European and American liberal white audiences and made possible when Africa was "in the news", thus pointing to the interrelatedness of diverse forms of cultural contacts and the underlying ideology.

Post-colonial contributions are associated with, among others, Niranjana in India (1992) and Vieira in Brazil (1994 et seq.); both add the further dimension of historicity in cultural encounters. Niranjana, following Said, claims that, in a post-colonial context, the problematic of translation becomes a significant site for raising questions of representation, power and historicity. Contesting and contested stories account for and recount asymmetries and inequalities of relations between peoples, races, languages. She stresses the role of translation and education in India as weapons for British colonial domination. A parallel is presented by Bassnett who has stressed the ambiguous role of La Malinche, Cortés's mistress/interpreter, in order to describe the process of violation of a culture through colonization and, indirectly, translation (1993). For a recent collection of essays on post-colonialism and translation, see Bassnett & Trivedi (1999).

Vieira has proposed a revised heuristics of translation in the specifity of modernism and postmodernism in Latin America, as a movement of mental decolonization and redistribution of power relations. Colonialism and translation both "carry across" cultures and histories, entailing the delinearization of the local history and the creation of new configurations. Following Latin American thinkers, she claims that Latin America, *qua* displaced history and culture, begins as a metaphor of translation, an argument that gains in complexity in the successive waves of transplantation of cultures. The denial of an identity to both translator and colonized, and unequal power relationships, further pave the way for the mental decolonization of Brazilian Modernism in the 1920s and its rereading in the 1970s. In turn, the cultural climate enabled the development of translation projects decolonizing two spaces traditionally deemed marginal: translation and a colonized culture. This vanguard movement combines cultural openness to foreign contributions and the preservation of cultural identity, inasmuch as it redistributes conventional dichotomies and power hierarchies used in connection with translation and other forms of cultural contacts, such as local/foreign, superior/inferior, etc. (see the entry Latin America: Translation Studies).

The interconnection between colonialism, translation and self-discovery has also been studied. Mukherjee argues that, given the diversity of languages in India, English and translation into English continue to be the medium of literary exchange and discovery (1994). Tymoczko also argues that the Irish were cut off from apprehending their native culture in the original and that translation into English was one means by which they came to understand their identity, culture and literary forms (1983:18). Along similar lines, Homel & Simon have stressed the role of literary translation also as culture mediation in bilingual Canada, especially in moments of political tension, in that the novel in particular expresses the aspirations of French-speaking Quebec society (1988).

ELSE R.P. VIEIRA

Further Reading

Bassnett, Susan and André Lefevere (editors), *Translation, History and Culture*, London and New York: Pinter, 1990

Bassnett, Susan, *Comparative Literature: A Critical Introduction*, Oxford and Cambridge, Massachusetts: Blackwell, 1993

Bassnett, Susan and Harish Trivedi (editors), *Post-colonial Translation: Theory and Practice*, London and New York: Routledge, 1999

Bassnett-McGuire, Susan, *Translation Studies*, London and New York: Methuen, 1980; revised edition, London and New York: Routledge, 1991

Deleuze, Gilles and Felix Guattari, *Mille Plateaux*, Paris: Éditions de Minuit, 1980

Even-Zohar, I., "The Position of Translated Literature within the Literary Polysystem" in *Literature and Translation: New Perspectives in Literary Studies*, edited by James S. Holmes, José Lambert and Raymond van den Broeck, Leuven, Belgium: Acco, 1978

Even-Zohar, I. "Polysystem Theory", *Poetics Today*, 1/1–2 (1979) pp. 287–310

Even-Zohar, I. and Gideon Toury (editors), *Theory of Translation and Intercultural Relations*, Tel Aviv: Porter Institute for Poetics and Semiotics, Tel Aviv University, 1981

Hermans, Theo (editor), *The Manipulation of Literature: Studies in Literary Translation*, London: Croom Helm, and New York: St Martin's Press, 1985

Holmes, James S., José Lambert and Raymond van den Broeck (editors), *Literature and Translation: New Perspectives in Literary Studies*, Leuven, Belgium: Acco, 1978

Homel, David and Sherry Simon (editors), *Mapping Literature: The Art and Politics of Translation*, Montreal: Véhicule Press, 1988

Lefevere, André, "Mother Courage's Cucumbers: Text, System and Refraction in a Theory of Literature", *Modern Language Studies*, 12 (1982) pp. 3–20

Lefevere, André, "Why Waste Our Time in Rewrites? The Trouble with Interpretation and the Role of Rewriting in an Alternative Paradigm" in *The Manipulation of Literature: Studies in Literary Translation*, edited by Theo Hermans, London: Croom Helm, and New York: St Martin's Press, 1985

Lefevere, André, "Translation: Its Genealogy in the West" in *Translation, History and Culture*, edited by Susan Bassnett and Lefevere, London and New York: Pinter, 1990

Lefevere, André, *Translation, Rewriting, and the Manipulation of Literary Fame*, London and New York: Routledge, 1992

Mukherjee, Sujit, *Translation as Discovery and Other Essays*

on Indian Literature in English Translation, New Delhi: Allied, 1981; London: Sangam, 1994
Niranjana, Tejaswini, *Siting Translation: History, Post-Structuralism, and the Colonial Context*, Berkeley: University of California Press, 1992
Paker, Saliha, "Translated European Literature in the Late Ottoman Literary Polysystem", *New Comparison*, 1 (Summer 1986) pp. 57–66
Snell-Hornby, Mary, *Translation Studies: An Integrated Approach*, Amsterdam: Benjamins, 1988
Toury, Gideon, *In Search of a Theory of Translation*, Tel Aviv: Porter Institute for Poetics and Semiotics, Tel Aviv University, 1980
Tymoczko, Maria, "Translating the Old Irish Epic Táin Bó Cúailnge: Political Aspects", *Pacific Quarterly Moana*, 8/2 (1983) pp. 6–21
Tymoczko, Maria, "Translation as a Force for Literary Revolution in the Twelfth-Century Shift from Epic to Romance", *New Comparison*, 1 (Summer 1986) pp. 7–27
Tymoczko, Maria, "Translation in Oral Tradition as a Touchstone for Translation Theory and Practice" in *Translation, History and Culture*, edited by Susan Bassnett and André Lefevere, London and New York: Pinter, 1990, pp. 46–55
Vieira, Else R.P., "A Postmodern Translational Aesthetics in Brazil" in *Translation Studies: An Interdiscipline*, edited by Mary Snell-Hornby, Franz Pöchhacker and Klaus Kaindl, Amsterdam: Benjamins, 1994, pp. 65–72
Vieira, Else R.P., "Towards a Minor Translation" in *Inequality and Difference in Hispanic and Latin American Cultures*, edited by Bernard McGuirk and Mark I. Millington, Lewiston, New York and Lampeter, Wales: Edwin Mellen Press, 1995
Vieira, Else R.P., "A Interação do Texto Traduzido com o Sistema Receptor: A Teoria dos Poli-sistemas" in *Teorizando e Contextualizando a Tradução*, edited by Vieira, Belo Horizonte: Programa de Pós-Graduação em Letras da UFMG, 1996
Vieira, Else R.P., "André Lefevere: A Teoria das Refrações e da Tradução como Reescrita" in *Teorizando e Contextualizando a Tradução*, edited by Vieira, Belo Horizonte: Programa de Pós-Graduação em Letras da UFMG, 1996

Cultural Misrepresentation

Interlingual translation involves not only the conversion of the linguistic component of the source text into the target language, but also a transference from the source culture to the target culture. The main task literary translators have to face is that of bringing distant or unknown cultures closer to audiences all over the world. As a rule, the bigger the cultural gap to be bridged, the more difficult the translation process will become.

The school denominated Translation Studies has been criticized in anthropological treatises, particularly those in the colonial context, for ignoring the power relations that inform translation. However, in recent times (1992), the late André Lefevere (a representative of this school) acknowledged that there may be a threat in translation, since the target culture is confronted with a different approach to the world, an approach that can be perceived as potentially subversive.

No literary work ever appears in a vacuum. The cultural frame in which a given piece is conceived and created will necessarily have an effect on that piece, in terms of both form and content. The genre chosen to convey the literary message exemplifies the way in which culture affects form. The problems that content poses go beyond textual semantics, for they are rooted in a context that is alien to the reader of the translated text: the links between the source text and other texts that preceded it in time are instances of culture-bound supratextuality.

In the same way, no translation is produced or received in a vacuum. A translation will target an audience that belongs to a cultural frame different from that of the original text. The figure of the translator cannot be seen as a neutral conduit through whom the transformation of source text into target text takes place. Even when the translator tries to be as objective and accurate as possible, the adjustments all translation involves will necessarily imply decision-making that will often be alien to the author of the source text. The changes arising from this process carry the imprint of the translator, who is conditioned by his/her own socio-cultural context.

Lefevere used the phrase "universe of discourse features" for elements strongly linked to the national idiosyncrasies and lifestyles of the source culture, and described them as being "almost by definition, untranslatable or at least very hard to translate". The terms that refer to the institutions, fauna and flora, geographical characteristics, climate, items of clothing, food and drink, etc. (an extensive classification can be found in Newmark, 1988), that are specific to the source culture fall into this category.

The much debated "Sapir–Whorf thesis" (which originated in the 1930s and was developed in the 1940s) postulates that the language spoken by a community conditions and shapes that community's vision of the world. According to the strong version of this theory, different societies live in different worlds. Under these circumstances, translation is extremely difficult, or even impossible: misrepresentation is unavoidable.

A long tradition of successful interlingual translation seems to prove, however, that there is a common core of human knowledge and experience that allows for the possibility of communication between the members of two distinct cultural groups. On the other hand, it has to be borne in mind that each literary work is a unique example of expression, and its extraction from the linguistic and cultural context in which it was conceived and created will always result in a certain disfigurement.

Cultural differences may obstruct or block the channel for satisfactory communication between the authors of the source texts and the readers of their translations. Thus the concept of cultural untranslatability arises. There are two main approaches to this issue: one is linguistic (represented by Catford, 1965), and the other involves a theory of literary communication (as formulated in Popovic, 1976).

The strategies that the translator can follow in order to transfer the contents of the source text into a new context, i.e. the target culture, vary according to the kind of focus that prevails: the translation can be source-text oriented or target-text oriented. If it is source-text oriented, the cultural differences will be clearly signalled in the target text. If it is target-text oriented, there will be a tendency to minimize cultural differences, "altering" the source text so that it fits more naturally into the target culture. There is a greater risk of cultural misrepresentation in those translations that deviate from the source text, but there are occasions when such deviation is necessary.

Hervey & Higgins use the term "cultural transposition" to describe the different alternatives to a source-language-biased literal translation, in their book *Thinking Translation* (1992). These transpositions appear on a scale that ranges from exoticism (cultural features are imported from the source text into the target text with minimal adaptation — "geisha" from the Japanese, "gazpacho" from the Spanish, and "sauna" from the Finnish, are common exoticisms) to cultural transplantation at the other end (features of the target culture are substituted for those that originally appeared in the source text). These two procedures are normally avoided in translation, and intermediate, less drastic, alternatives are preferred.

Closest to exoticism, Hervey & Higgins list cultural borrowing (a source-text expression is transferred verbatim into the target text: the Spanish "guerrilla", the German "Schadenfreude", or the French "laisser faire", for example). Then comes calque ("an expression that consists of TL [target language] words and respects TL syntax, but is unidiomatic in the TL because it is modelled on the structure of a SL [source language] expression"; for instance, transforming the French "cherchez la femme" into "look for the woman" in English). And finally, closest to cultural transplantation, we have communicative translation, which substitutes a cultural equivalent for an idiom, cliché or proverb that appears in the source text. For instance, the Spanish "sordo como una tapia", literally "deaf as a wall", would be communicatively translated into English as "deaf as a post".

An interesting development in the study of cultural (mis)representation in translation was brought to the fore by Venuti, who denounces "domesticating" translation, characterized by target-culture-oriented strategies, as a form of cultural imperialism (1992). He proposes "foreignising" translation as an alternative (1995), in order to avoid the acculturation resulting from fluent, transparent strategies.

The closer translators stay to the source text, the more their readers will learn about the source culture. The farther they depart from the original, the more easily understandable the target text will be in the target culture. Finding the appropriate balance to avoid cultural misrepresentation is rarely easy, but always necessary.

RAQUEL DE PEDRO

Further Reading

Catford, J.C., *A Linguistic Theory of Translation: An Essay in Applied Linguistics*, London: Oxford University Press, 1965

Hervey, Sándor and Ian Higgins, *Thinking Translation: A Course in Translation Method: French to English*, London and New York: Routledge, 1992

Lefevere, André, "Why Waste Our Time on Rewrites? The Trouble with Interpretation and the Role of Rewriting in an Alternative Paradigm" in *The Manipulation of Literature: Studies in Literary Translation*, edited by Theo Hermans, London: Croom Helm, and New York: St Martin's Press, 1985

Lefevere, André (editor and translator), *Translation/History/Culture: A Sourcebook*, London and New York: Routledge, 1992

Newmark, Peter, *A Textbook of Translation*, New York: Prentice Hall, 1988

Niranjana, Tejaswini, *Siting Translation: History, Post-Structuralism and the Colonial Context*, Berkeley: University of California Press, 1992

Popovič, Anton, *A Dictionary for the Analysis of Literary Translation*, Edmonton: University of Alberta, 1976

Venuti, Lawrence (editor), *Rethinking Translation: Discourse, Subjectivity, Ideology*, London and New York: Routledge, 1992

Venuti, Lawrence, *The Translator's Invisibility: A History of Translation*, London and New York: Routledge, 1995

Cultural Studies and Literary Translation

> The written text is a social situation. That is to say, it has its existence in something more than the marks on the page, namely in the participations of social beings whom we call writers and readers, who constitute the writing as communication of a particular kind, as "saying" a certain thing. When these participants exist in different cultures, two issues quickly come to the forefront: can writing in one language convey the reality of a different culture? and can a reader fully understand a different cultural reality being communicated in the text? (Ashcroft, 1995)

An initial response to the question of a relationship between literary translation and cultural studies may be to assert that the two are more than synergistic, that, indeed, translation is the vehicle for cultural studies, as it allows for its movement across boundaries of time, geography, and language. At the very heart of the West's Judeo-Christian system is a dependence on the Bible, on the writings of the Greeks and Romans, on the philosophies of the great European thinkers (Kant, Hegel, and Nietzsche; Descartes, Voltaire, and Kierkegaard), texts available to almost all of their English-speaking readers only in translation. Underlying much of what defines the West's thinking individual is a reverence for texts originating in Greek or Latin, translated texts, to the point that Greek and Latin terms are used in contemporary writings to elevate the level of diction. It has been suggested that the popularity of Freudian theory, for example, among its English-language readers is due to the use of the Greek terminology (ego, id, etc.) in the English translation. The original German, which features no such culturally enhanced terminology, gained far fewer supporters. In fact, many believe that the Greeks exhausted the possibilities of plastic and verbal expression, and all that follows them is nothing more than alternative versions (Steiner, 1975). The desired translation, itself, is based upon the Platonic notion of the ideal, an ideal that Walter Benjamin decries as an impossible standard, "a hopeless pursuit of a one-to-one correspondence between interpretation and its object, between translation and foreign text" (Venuti, 1992). Unattainable as this perfect correspondence between original and translation may be, the imperfect alternatives support the Western thinker who sees, as Edward Said writes in *Culture and Imperialism*, that "the history of all cultures is the history of cultural borrowings" (1993).

Study of translation in the light of cultural studies reveals more than the power of the translated text over its target language audience; such a study also reveals the perceived dangers inherent in transmitting texts to a receiving, but perhaps not receptive, culture. The core of any act of translation holds in tension an explicit desire to embrace and re-create the foreign text and an implicit quest to assimilate the new message without risk to the integrity of the receiver. Just as the translation opens up new vistas of knowledge and cultural awareness, so also it threatens an audience that seeks to affirm its own superiority through a comparison with the "Other" met in translation. As André Lefevere pointed out in his *Translation/History/Culture*, translation is "one of the strategies cultures develop to deal with what lies outside their boundaries and to maintain their own character while doing so ...". Victor Hugo's suggestion that a nation that is offered a translation "will almost always look on the translation as an act of violence against itself" underscores the vulnerability implicit in this transfer of knowledge and ideas.

Earlier cultures, those of the 16th century, for example, differed from those of today in their enjoyment of multiple language versions of a single text, seeing no threat in the variety and alternatives offered by translation. As Antoine Berman suggests in *The Experience of the Foreign*, the 16th-century reader was not concerned with notions of "fidelity and treason", watchwords of contemporary translation, because this readership "did not hold its mother tongue sacred". When a culture does not seek to maintain its position of superiority it can be much more open to the ideas and cultural concerns of others. But for the culture that must remain superior, translations (or "rewritings", to use André Lefevere's term in *Translation, Rewriting, and the Manipulation of Literary Fame*) reflect a certain ideology and poetics and as such manipulate literature to cause it to function in a given society in a given way. Rewriting is manipulation, undertaken in the service of power, and in its positive aspect can help in the evolution of a literature and a society. Perhaps it is this desire for cultural self-preservation, this service of power, that leads translators, who claim to aspire to invisibility, to re-evaluate their methodologies in the threatening face of cross-cultural communication. While they may claim that they seek a "true semantic equivalence", their work instead "imprints the foreign text with a partial interpretation, partial to target-language cultural values, blinded by a metaphysical concept of meaning that excludes the very difference translation is called on to convey" (Venuti, 1992). Indeed, "to make a foreign work acceptable to the receiving culture, translators will often adapt it to the poetics of the receiving culture" (Lefevere, *Translation, Rewriting* ...). In doing so, these translators are making evident their particular cultural biases. When Dorothy Sayers, for example, made choices that many critics perceive to have sacrificed meaning for a strict adherence to Dante's *terza rima* in her translation of *The Divine Comedy*, she did so out of allegiance to the cultural standards of her own time and audience. All translation decisions must be based in the time of their translation, in the locus of their translator, in the cultural context of their translator. "Translators," as André Lefevere makes clear in *Translation, Rewriting* ..., "function in a given culture at a given time. The way they understand themselves and their cultures is one of the factors that may influence the way in which they translate".

Certain realities govern the world of the translation's move toward its audience, realities that establish hierarchies of texts, determining which are worthy of publication and, ultimately, what cultures are dominant. Currently the English-speaking world holds sway, and translation does its part to maintain this status quo. According to Talal Asad in his "Concept of Cultural Translation in British Social Anthropology" (1986)

> because the languages of Third World societies – including, of course, the societies that social anthropologists have

traditionally studied – are "weaker" in relation to Western languages (and today, especially to English), they are more likely to submit to forcible transformations in the translation process than the other way around. The reason for this is, first, that in their political-economic relations with Third World countries, Western nations have the greater ability to manipulate the latter. And, second, Western languages produce and deploy *desired* knowledge more readily than Third World languages do.

The English-language society and its texts are deemed superior, as are its products, its ideas, even its peoples. Those of the Third World, the post-colonial world of cultural studies, rank far behind those of the English speakers in today's Eurocentric world. As George Steiner states in *After Babel*, "English is become the world language – it carries with it the 'feel' of hope, of material advance, of scientific and empirical procedures". Not surprisingly, if this is how the language is perceived, messages depending upon it for communication will garner respect simply from their syntactical form. The publishing world reinforces this cross-cultural inequality by promoting the dominance of English-language texts and, simultaneously, subjugating the writings of non-English-speaking peoples. "Ideology is often enforced by the patrons, the people or institutions who commission or publish translations" (Lefevere, *Translation, Rewriting* ...). Post-colonial African literature is especially subject to interpretations that emphasize the weakness of Third World writing versus the strength of European work.

> In much western writing about African literature, theorizing about "progression" of narrative forms is replaced by discussion of "derivation". The journey from "traditional" to "modern" African literature, for this mentality, was due entirely to contact with Arabic and European cultures, the adoption of writing systems, and, most significantly, the transcription of African languages to European writing conventions. (Snead, 1990)

At this point, one might expect the literary translation to step into the equation, to make the other literatures accessible and so build a bridge between cultures. That, many would aver, is the aim of translation, after all: to make available to readers of one language the writings of another language, ideally, to re-create in the new language the text its original author would have created had his/her language been that of the new audience. However, doesn't this goal devalue the original culture? How meaningful is the original text if it can be transformed into a new cultural situation without being disfigured? Is there so little in the original text that depends on its own cultural situation? Can the meaning of any text exist outside of culture?

The translator's response to this conundrum has always been that a perfect translation is impossible, as unattainable as Plato's cave-bound absolutes. That culture-specific element of the text, which Walter Benjamin in his "Task of the Translator" sees as sacred, will always impede a totally successful transference of a text across language and/or cultural boundaries. Ironically, what may be most impossible to translate successfully may be those impurities in language, those traces of other cultures that have strayed across cultural/linguistic boundary lines. How, for example, Jacques Derrida asks, can the quirky Frenchness of Borges's "Pierre Menard" be carried into the French translation (Derrida, 1985)? Translation theory, as it acknowledges its limitations, illuminates the many obstacles that hinder cross-cultural communication.

The further one investigates the relationship between translation and cultural studies, the more numerous these obstacles seem. An investigation of anthropology's ethnography, for example, highlights several problem areas. The ethnographer seeks to convey the reality of another culture without imposing his/her cultural bias on that representation, just as the literary translator desires invisibility while facilitating the movement of a text across cultural boundaries. The ethnographer is doomed to failure in the same way and for the same reasons as is the translator. While both seek a method of embracing the foreign, neither can escape subversion (whether purposeful or accidental) as the foreign population or text is put through the impossible process of simultaneously being rendered familiar (and thereby accessible) and being allowed to maintain that strangeness that was its initial attraction (Crapanzano, 1986). Goethe's definition of a translator as a "man who tries to be a mediator in this general spiritual commerce and who has chosen it as his calling to advance the interchange" (Lefevere, *Translation, Rewriting* ...) ennobles the task of translation by elevating it to the spiritual plane, while others wonder at its corruptive force, its possible indication that a culture in need of translation may be a culture that is lacking something in its own character.

In any case, it is clear that the impact of translation on cultural studies has been profound, that the relationship between the two is powerful and far-reaching, and that much of what defines the English-speaking world can be found only in translation.

BEVERLY MITCHELL

Further Reading

Asad, Talal, "The Concept of Cultural Translation in British Social Anthropology" in *Writing Culture: The Poetics and Politics of Ethnography*, edited by James Clifford and George E. Marcus, Berkeley: University of California Press, 1986

Ashcroft, Bill, "Constitutive Graphonomy" in *The Post-Colonial Studies Reader*, edited by Ashcroft, Gareth Griffiths and Helen Tiffin, London and New York: Routledge, 1995

Benjamin, Walter, *Illuminations*, translated by Harry Zohn, edited by Hannah Arendt, New York: Harcourt Brace, 1968; London: Collins, 1973

Berman, Antoine, *The Experience of the Foreign: Culture and Translation in Romantic Germany*, translated by S. Heyvaert, Albany: State University of New York Press, 1992

Crapanzano, Vincent, "Hermes' Dilemma: The Masking of Subversion in Ethnographic Description" in *Writing Culture: The Poetics and Politics of Ethnography*, edited by James Clifford and George E. Marcus, Berkeley: University of California Press, 1986

Derrida, Jacques, *The Ear of the Other: Otobiography, Transference, Translation*, translated by Peggy Kamuf, edited by Christie V. McDonald, New York: Schocken, 1985

Lefevere, André (editor and translator), *Translation/History/Culture: A Sourcebook*, London and New York: Routledge, 1992

Lefevere, André, *Translation, Rewriting, and the Manipulation of Literary Fame*, London and New York: Routledge, 1992
Said, Edward W., *Culture and Imperialism*, New York: Knopf, 1993; London: Vintage, 1994
Snead, James, "European Pedigrees / African Contagions: Nationality, Narrative and Communality in Tutuola, Achebe, and Reed" in *Nation and Narration*, edited by Homi K. Bhabha, London and New York: Routledge, 1990
Steiner, George, *After Babel: Aspects of Language and Translation*, Oxford and New York: Oxford University Press, 1975; 3rd edition 1998
Venuti, Lawrence, "Reviews", *Textual Practice*, 6/2 (1992) pp. 316–24

Cultural Transference

Located at the crossroads of different languages, cultures and histories, the act of translation can be properly viewed as an act of cultural transference. Transference, transportation, transplantation, that is, transcendence of a work of art that is *borne* across a space and therefore *born* in a new context thanks to the midwife translator (for the midwifery metaphor used to describe the act of translation see Risset 1978 and Ward Jouve 1991). In fact, in the transferring process, whereby the original text is re-created in a new language for a new readership sharing a new cultural tradition, the translator may be said to perform the role of intercultural mediator, essential to the processes of cross-cultural interaction.

When the translator passes through the boundaries of his own culture in order to experience a direct contact with the alienness of the Other (Talgeri and Verma, 1988) represented in the foreign text, he can be said to be located in an in-between space, from which he will attempt to transport the sense of alterity of the foreign text to the receivers of that text in his home culture. For the original text to be received in a different culture and history, the translator will have to take a series of decisions concerning the transformation demanded by the intercultural transfer which will ultimately determine the dialogue the translated text will establish with the potential new readers.

Sometimes referred to as "cultural recontextualization" or "re-textualization" of the original text, the process of cultural transference performed by the translator is governed not only by personal choice on the part of the translator but also by other factors that play a significant role in the production of translations and rewritings in general. As Lefevere (1992) explains, translations are produced within the constraints of "patronage" (i.e. the editorial structure that demands and controls the translation), of the "poetics" favoured and accepted by the literary standards of the moment, and of the "ideology" or ideological principles prevailing at the historical time when the translation is written.

A classical description of how transference is mediated by the translator was proposed by George Steiner in the chapter "The Hermeneutic Motion" of his *After Babel* (1975). Probing into the psychological processes that may be said to govern the relationship between the original text and the translator, Steiner identifies four moves or moments in the translator's relationship with the foreign text. There is first an "initiative trust", an impulse that leads the translator to believe in the comprehensibility of the original, in its potential for meaning, when read from a different cultural site. The initial trust is followed by an "incursive and extractive" move, in which the translator advances towards the foreign text and formulates an interpretation of it. After this act of interpretation, the translator, in an "incorporative" move, brings the text into the cultural milieu of the receiving culture. The degree to which the original text will be assimilated in the new soil will vary along a cline of shadings, from a "complete nativization" of the foreign work to the maintenance of the intrinsic strangeness of that text. The last move in this process, the "restitution" or "compensation" of the forces disturbed by the act of translation, is for Steiner a relevant moment in the dynamics of intercultural contacts. After the transfer of energy from the original to the translated text, Steiner explains, the former is left in a condition of apparent loss, which upsets the balance between the cultures and traditions involved. An effort to "equalize" what has been taken and what has been added needs to be made.

Steiner's account of the translator's encounter with the foreign has generated substantial criticism by theorists concerned with gender and translation and with postcolonial perspectives of translation. The movements described by Steiner can be read as paraphrasing male sexual advances and reflecting the ideology of colonization and plundering that has governed most of the intercultural encounters in history. Also, Steiner's hermeneutic motion actually entails a unidirectional movement, in which the translator seems to get prepared in order to later invade the realm of the foreign text, take something from it and bring it home. Even the compensatory movement results from a decision utterly controlled by the translator.

More recent accounts of the dynamics of intercultural contacts, however, point to the bidirectionality of the interaction between the home and the foreign cultures as well as to a revision of the translator's role and power in those situations. Significant insights have been gained through the analysis of intercultural encounters, particularly the study of colonization, migration, exile and other forms of displacement. Translation

Studies has established enriching dialogues with other disciplines exchanging and debating perceptions of translation. Cultural transference is an issue of particular concern for postcolonial and poststructuralist studies, two areas that have elaborated on translation and drawn on Walter Benjamin's seminal essay "The Task of the Translator" in order to account for displacement and difference in the process of translation.

In his text, Benjamin problematizes views of translation that define this task as having an essentially communicative function, that is to say, the transmission of content. Benjamin defines translation as "a mode", which implies that translatability is possible and is actually what allows the original work's transcendence or "afterlife".

Translatability for Benjamin implies change due to the "transformation and renewal of something living" inherent to a work of art's afterlife. Most important, translatability entails for Benjamin the very element of untranslatability, aptly illustrated by one of the author's metaphors. "The language of the translation, " says Benjamin, "envelops its contents like a royal robe with ample folds". It is precisely at those spots where the robe flows loosely over the contents that difference can be enunciated. This disjunction pointed out by Benjamin is taken up by several poststructuralist and postcolonial critics who theorize on meaning as being produced "across the bar of difference and separation between the signifier and the signified" (Bhabha, 1990). Among these theorists, Bhabha points out the relevance of translation as an operation that leads to "a displacement within the linguistic sign" and allows for a repetition of the sign that is always "different and differential". In this sense, the notion of hybridity is closely connected to that of cultural transference. Transference can only be partial and different every time the foreign is transplanted to a new cultural site. The ample folds enveloping the original's content help us visualize the concept of opacity of the sign, the perpetual displacement giving birth to the "third space which enables other positions to emerge" (Bhabha).

Both poststructuralist and postcolonical readings of transference problematize the notion of origin and original and emphasize the dynamics of perpetual re-creation and transformation that intercultural encounters, such as translation, allow for. The movement that takes place within the linguistic sign is associated with metaphoric and metonymic displacements, essential for the production of different cultural practices. This has profound political implications for discussions of unequal encounters such as those brought about by colonialism and other asymmetrical power relationships. Also, from the perspective of translation studies, postcolonial and poststructuralist interpretations of Benjamin have allowed for a reconsideration of issues such as fidelity and the so-called derivative or lower status of the translated text.

ADRIANA S. PAGANO

Further Reading

Benjamin, Walter, "The Task of the Translator", translated by Harry Zohn, in *Theories of Translation: An Anthology of Essays from Dryden to Derrida*, edited by Rainer Schulte and John Biguenet, Chicago: University of Chicago Press, 1992

Berman, Antoine, *The Experience of the Foreign: Culture and Translation in Romantic Germany*, translated by S. Heyvaert, Albany: State University of New York Press, 1992

Bhabha, Homi, "The Third Space" in *Identity: Community, Culture, Difference*, edited by Jonathan Rutherford, London: Lawrence and Wishart, 1990

Bhabha, Homi, "Dissemination: Time, Narrative and the Margins of the Modern Nation" in *The Location of Culture* by Bhabha, London and New York: Routledge, 1994

Lefevere, André, *Translation, Rewriting, and the Manipulation of Literary Fame*, London and New York: Routledge, 1992

Risset, Jacqueline, "Traduire", *Femmes en Mouvement* (4 April 1978)

Steiner, George, *After Babel: Aspects of Language and Translation*, Oxford and New York: Oxford University Press, 1975; 3rd edition, 1998

Talgeri, Pramod and S.B. Verma (editors), *Literature in Translation: From Cultural Transference to Metonymic Displacement*, Bombay: Popular Prakashan, 1988

Ward Jouve, Nicole, *White Woman Speaks with Forked Tongue: Criticism as Autobiography*, London and New York: Routledge, 1991

Cultural Transposition

Walter Benjamin has suggested that the translated text is a transplant into another time and linguistic space, where it begins an independent existence, conditioned by its own requirements (1982). In another context, Octavio Paz views translation as signs in movement (1973). For Bassnett the discipline Translation Studies explores the process whereby texts are transferred from one culture to another" (1991), its research involving linguistic, textual, historical and socio-political aspects (1991). Snell-Hornby problematizes the concept of linguistic equivalence and stresses the orientation in Germany towards *cultural* transfer and the *function* of the prospective translation, also quoting the major contributor to this approach, Vermeer, for whom the translated text emerges in a new situation and under changed functional, cultural and linguistic conditions, e.g., different marketing conventions and strategies in the case of advertisements (1990). Vieira claims that translation changes the ontology and thus the continued existence of a work by transposing it to another history; her work on the semiotics of the perigraphy of translated books stresses that this doubly signed, dated, edited, liminal space allows the ritual function of transfer of authority, authorship, cultures, history, property relations, etc. (1992). Translating – transposing, transferring, transplanting – conveying to another place, is a spatial and temporal displacement that in itself entails ontological transformations.

Beyond this notion of transformation arising from the fact of displacement, intentionality in cultural transpositions remains to be considered. The intended audience plays an important role in strategies of cultural transposition. In the extreme example of the translation of *Hamlet* for an oral culture in Africa, the audience's oral formulas were adopted, and the tale was transposed to their material culture: Hamlet speaks with Gertrude in her "sleeping hut" and fights Laertes with machetes (Tymoczko, 1990). Immediacy of understanding and apprehension and impact are thus parameters for cultural transposition related to the potential of a translation to communicate to the reader/audience (cf. Newmark's category of communicative translation, geared towards the reader, as opposed to semantic translation, geared towards the aesthetic value of the original, 1988). Toury introduces other parameters: adherence to models set up in the target pole determines the acceptability of a translated text in the target literary polysystem and its status and position within it, whereas adherence to the norms of the source text determines its adequacy (1980), a dichotomy that has not passed unquestioned (Zlateva, 1990).

Newmark has labelled "approximate translation" the case of a cultural word from the source language being translated by a cultural equivalent in the target language for intelligibility, e.g., "A level" for the French "baccalauréat"; the same applies to terms related to the political and social life of a country, e.g. German "Bundestag", that may be glossed for a general readership as "West German Parliament" (1988); functional cultural equivalents, he claims, are important for the purpose of creating an immediate effect, as in the translation of drama bearing the potential spectator in mind (1988). Attention is drawn to the problem of literal translation in the case of oaths, curses and insults; e.g., a hapless husband in English is likened to the victim of the European cuckoo (who, Rabassa further claims, lays eggs in other birds' nests) and has no resonances for a Latin American speaker of Spanish, who resorts to the cultural equivalent billy goat, ironically the symbol of male sexuality (1989). Cultural transpositions are also frequent with culture-specific popular sayings and proverbs.

Moving to broader operational units and to the volume of information the audience can be expected to recognize and respond to, Lefevere relates translational strategies to the notion of universe of discourse. The conservative translator will retain all the local and personal peculiarities and will provide explanatory notes for allusions to contemporary persons, events or usages and for special connotations of words (1992); conversely, the "spirited" translator works on the level of a culture as a whole and the functioning of the text in that culture, as has been the case of Douglas Parker translating Aristophanes into American English, changing fields of metaphor, adding jokes in compensation for jokes lost, neglecting useless proper names (ibid.). Translators' attitudes to universe of discourse are further influenced by the status of the original, the self-image of the target culture and the type of texts this culture deems acceptable, as well as by cultural scripts (accepted patterns of behaviour) that the target audience is willing to accept (ibid.).

Cultural transposition is particularly associated with translation for the theatre, for which Bassnett introduces the parameter of playability, stressing that, in the theatre, text and performance are closely linked, the text being only one element in the totality of theatre discourse (1991); thus the translator has to transfer linguistic and other codes, yet the theatre-text is time-bound and the problem of form merges with the question of speech rhythms (1985). Kelley stresses the cognitive import of the comic text, in that humour supposes factual knowledge to be shared between humorist and audience, which means that the translator must be at home in at least two cultures, literatures and languages (1995); on the textual level, she mentions the example of the parodies of different Lima conversation styles of both sexes and several classes, which translate into American but not into British English, because in England different styles relate mostly to class distinction (ibid.).

Cultural transposition as a strategy can be a remedy and a poison (cf. Jain on the loss of local colour, below). In the case of dramatic texts this tension has been discussed in connection with *Werk zum Leser* (the work towards the reader) approaches to Brecht's translations in Portugal. Castendo analyses Brandão's translation of *Furcht und Elend des Dritten Reiches*, in which the institutions were nationalized into the equivalent Salazarist ones, the names were translated (Karl becoming Carlos) or phonologically approximated (Frau Ruh becoming Senhora Ruas) and the result was the subtraction of the specificity of national-socialism in Brecht; Hörster notes that Brandão's translation strategies in *Herr Puntila und sein Knecht Matti* (diluting dialectical oppositions such as master/servant, regulating the style to the potential Portuguese audience, approximating it to the popular music hall) ended up eliminating the distancing effects Brecht had in mind (in Dellile, 1986).

In the introduction to the proceedings of a conference held in India dedicated to literary translation and cultural transference, Talgeri and Verma elaborate the parameter of cultural sensibility in literary translation. The encounter with an alien culture may imply a confrontation of heterogeneous sensibilities, evoke a consciousness of rupture in identification, set in motion a disorienting process in which the subject experiences a sense of displacement from its stable position in the native cultural tradition; the role of the translator is to obliterate these demarcations of alienness though his "intercultural mediation" and to convey the sense of alterity of the source-language culture (1988). Talgeri and Verma further stress the participatory function of literary translation; if the individual reader shares the experience of social participation by reading literature, the translator has to create this experience by recontextualizing it in the target-language culture (ibid.). Contributions in the volume range from the problems of expressing a national identity in an alien language, through the translation of classics insofar as they reveal a temporally and spatially distant alterity, to translations of *Othello* in India, some maintaining the social and political milieu of the original, others indianizing the characters and setting, etc. (ibid.). Jain, in the same volume, stresses the role of the translator's creativity in solving the tension between the need both to convey the local colour and to be understood by an audience outside the cultural and lingual situation, especially when cultural meanings are intricately identifiable with language (ibid.).

Tymoczko highlights the political dimension of cultural transposition, as for example in translations into English of the Irish *Táin Bó Cúailnge* (1983). She argues that the re-creation of Irish culture through translation was ancillary to the Irish patriotic movements in the 18th and 19th centuries, with the aim of making Ireland's cultural heritage public and to change the English stereotype of the Irish (ignorant, irrational, musical, happy, drunken, incapable of culture); but how could nationalist claims be made, images be dignified in the eyes of Victorian culture and this monument of early Irish literature be translated accurately if the chief hero squats naked in the snow picking lice off his shirt, if a woman urinates or menstruates three lakes, if the "epic" is about a raid to steal cows, etc? Diverse translators' strategies thus involve suppression – avoidance of burlesque and of sexual and scatological episodes, glossing over indelicate elements, understatement of offensive passages – the use of an archaizing high style reminiscent of Tennyson, and filling the tale with noble or tragic stories from other parts of the cycle, etc. (Tymoczko, 1983; cf. the cognitive bias of her later discussion of the metonymics of translation to make the information load manageable, 1995).

Taking up political and historical dimensions, Benn-Ibler analyses cultural transposition as a weapon, more specifically Buarque's translation/rewriting of Gay's *The Beggar's Opera* and Brecht's *Threepenny Opera* into the *Ópera do Malandro* [The Trickster's Opera] in Brazil. Buarque's text (1978) was launched when censorship was just beginning to relax, yet years of political and social repression during the military regime left a traumatic fear of expression. In this context, Buarque introduces himself as the fictitious producer of the opera and transposes Brecht's themes of authoritarianism and corruption to criticize with impunity the socio-economic situation of Brazil; the beggar is transposed into the national figure of the trickster, the beggar's world is recast in the prostitutes' and smugglers' world, which Buarque ironically links to the prostitutes' march for health benefits and retirement pensions, etc. (Benn-Ibler, 1998).

Bassnett exemplifies equivalent social functions in cultural translation with the advertisements for Martini in Italy and Scotch in Britain – as both are long-established products in their country of origin, emphasis lies on quality and purity; conversely, when Martini is advertised in Britain and Scotch in Italy, the products are the same but the values are different, so emphasis lies on trendy living and the fashionable status consumption of the products confers (1991).

Cultural transposition as an innovative operational procedure in Brazilian postmodernism is associated with the brothers Haroldo and Augusto de Campos and with Silviano Santiago, *inter alia*.

ELSE R.P. VIEIRA

Further Reading

Bassnett, Susan, "Ways Through the Labyrinth: Strategies and Methods in Translating Theatre Texts" in *The Manipulation of Literature: Studies in Literary Translation*, edited by Theo Hermans, London: Croom Helm, and New York: St Martin's Press, 1985

Bassnett-McGuire, Susan, *Translation Studies*, London and New York: Methuen, 1980; revised edition, London and New York: Routledge, 1991

Benjamin, Walter, "The Task of the Translator" in his *Illuminations*, edited by Hannah Arendt, translated by Harry Zohn, New York: Harcourt Brace, 1968; London: Jonathan Cape, 1970

Benn-Ibler, Veronika, "Textos – leitores – contextos: Brecht no Brasil, uma leitura peversa da história" in *Discorsos de tradicion y contemporaneidad*, edited by Horacio Crespo, Córdoba, Ediciones del Centro de Estudios Avanzados, 1998

Delille, K., M.A. Hörster, M.E. Castendo, M.M. Delille and R. Correia, *Problemas da Tradução Literária*, Coimbra: Livraria Almedina, 1986

Heylen, Romy, *Translation, Poetics and the Stage: Six French Hamlets*, London and New York: Routledge, 1993

Jain, Jasbir, "Problems of Cultural Transference in Literary Translation" in *Literature in Translation: From Cultural Transference to Metonymic Displacement*, edited by Pramod Talgeri and S.B. Verma, Bombay: Popular Prakashan, 1988, pp. 12–20

Kelley, Alita, "Translation as Cultural Translation", *Ways of Working in Latin American Studies, King's College London, 5–7 April 1995* (unpublished paper)

Lefevere, André, *Translation, Rewriting, and the Manipulation of Literary Fame*, London and New York: Routledge, 1992

Newmark, Peter, *A Textbook of Translation*, New York: Prentice Hall, 1988

Paz, Octavio, *El signo y el garabato*, Mexico City: Joaquín Mortiz, 1973

Rabassa, Gregory, "No Two Snowflakes Are Alike" in *The Craft of Translation*, edited by John Biguenet and Rainer Schulte, Chicago: University of Chicago Press, 1989, pp. 1–12

Snell-Hornby, Mary, "Linguistic Transcoding or Cultural Transfer? A Critique of Translation Theory in England" in *Translation, History and Culture*, edited by Susan Bassnett and André Lefevere, London and New York: Pinter, 1990, pp. 79–86

Talgeri, Pramod and S.B. Verma (editors), *Literature in Translation: From Cultural Transference to Metonymic Displacement*, Bombay: Popular Prakashan, 1988

Toury, Gideon, *In Search of a Theory of Translation*, Tel Aviv: Porter Institute for Poetics and Semiotics, Tel Aviv University, 1980

Trejo, E. Caracciolo, "Octavio Paz, Traductor", *Siglo XX / 20th Century*, 10/1–2 (1992) pp. 195–210

Tymoczko, Maria, "Translating the Old Irish Epic *Táin Bó Cúailnge*: Political Aspects", *Pacific Quarterly Moana*, 8/2 (1983) pp. 6–21

Tymoczko, Maria, "Translation in Oral Tradition as a Touchstone for Translation Theory and Practice" in *Translation, History and Culture*, edited by Susan Bassnett and André Lefevere, London and New York: Pinter, 1990, pp. 46–55

Tymoczko, Maria, "The Metonymics of Translating Marginalized Texts", *Comparative Literature*, 47/1 (Winter 1995) pp. 11–24

Vieira, Else R.P., "Por uma teoria pós-moderna da traduçáo " (dissertation), Belo Horizonte: Universidade Federal de Minas Gerais, 1992

Zlateva, Palma, "Translation: Text and Pre-Text 'Adequacy' and 'Acceptability' in Crosscultural Communication" in *Translation, History and Culture*, edited by Susan Bassnett and André Lefevere, London and New York: Pinter, 1990, pp. 29–37

Czech

Literary Translation into English

Czech, along with Slovak and Polish, belongs to the West Slavonic language group. Czech is closely related to Slovak and speakers of each are able to converse without serious linguistic obstacles. Like the other languages in the group, Czech uses the Roman rather than the Cyrillic alphabet.

The spelling of Czech is largely phonetic. Note the consonants c (pronounced like English *ts*), ch (like Scottish lo*ch*), j (like English y), and several letters with a diacritic known as the *háček* or hook: č (like *ch*urch), ř (roughly "rzh"), š (like *sh*ort) and ž (like plea*s*ure). The consonants d, n, and t can be "softened" to ï, ò and ž (rather like British English *du*e, *ne*w, *tu*ne). The basic vowels a, e, i or y, o, u can be lengthened to á, é, í or ý, ó, ú / ù. This vowel lengthening is especially important in Czech as it is semantically distinctive (compare *dal* "he gave" and *dál* – "further, come in").

A characteristic feature of Czech prosody is that the stress in any word falls invariably on the first syllable (although when a preposition comes before a noun the stress always shifts onto the preposition). This is one reason why verse metres such as iambic and trochaic have different effects when compared with English (see Alfred French, 1973.). Another relevant factor is that vowel length is independent of syllable stress, i.e. a long syllable in a word is not stressed unless it is the first syllable. The resulting syncopated rhythmic interplay is a crucial feature of Czech poetry, and one hardly possible to convey in English translation. Czech also shows a characteristic occurrence of sporadic consonant clusters (*hřbitov*, *stvrzenka*) and vocalic r, l (*čtvrž*, *plný*), e.g. the oft-cited tongue twister *strč prst skrz krk* – "stick (your) finger through (your) neck". One factor affecting verse translation in particular is the absence of definite and indefinite articles (the, a).

From the translator's point of view another significant difference from English is that the Czech noun system is highly inflected, i.e. marked by endings for function in the sentence (subject, object, etc.) and thus Czech, unlike English, word order can be exceptionally free. Inflexion also gives Czech much greater rhyme resources. The Czech case system is similar to that of Latin (in fact there are *seven* cases). There are three genders of nouns – masculine, feminine and neuter – with masculine further divided into animate and inanimate types. The verb system, as with other Slavonic languages, is aspectual: pairs of verbs (called imperfective and perfective) work in tandem, using prefixes and suffixes to distinguish ongoing activity from completed acts. Prefixes and suffixes are also used lexically to create large groups of related verbs, nouns and other parts of speech. A rich and complex system of diminutives can cause particular difficulties to the translator because not only are tonal nuances lost in translation but they almost invariably sound banal in English.

Despite the well-documented links between Bohemia and England going back to the 10th century, it appears that no work in the Czech vernacular was translated into English before 1820, when an émigré Pole, Krystyn Lach-Szyrma, translated several texts from the pseudo-early-medieval Dvùr Králové Manuscript – later proved to be a 19th-century forgery. Before this time Bohemia appears in English literature only indirectly through references to certain historical figures or events.

The influence of John Wyclif on the Hussite movement of the early 15th century is well known, but the influence was mostly one-way. The image of Bohemia as heretical, disordered and seditious, which sprang up after the collapse of Hussitism, undoubtedly had something to do with the English lack of interest in (and even distaste for) Bohemia that lasted until the Reformation, when a more positive interest reawakened in Hus and the Hussite reforms. The only story of Bohemian origin to have appeared in English during the 15th and 16th centuries was John Capgrave's retelling of the legend of Saint Wenceslas (Václav) in 1470.

John Foxe's *Acts and Monuments* (1554) contained the "History of Master John Hus", after which Hus and Jerome of Prague passed into Protestant martyrology. Even so, there seems to have been no attempt to translate their works (those in Latin being already accessible to scholars). A further decline in the already poor relations between Bohemia and England occurred during the Counter-Reformation which followed the Czech Protestants' defeat in 1620, although the eminent exiled Czech educationalist Jan Amos Komenský (Comenius) did find a sympathetic audience (spending the years 1641–42 in England) and his copious Latin writings were published. The state of Bohemia during and after the Thirty Years' War was commented on in the occasional travel book and general history during the 17th and 18th centuries, but it was only during the decades of the Czech National Revival in the late 18th to early 19th century that some interest in Czech literature began to grow in England.

A milestone in Anglo-Bohemian literary relations came with the Benthamite Sir John Bowring's *Cheskian Anthology* of 1832, which contained translations ranging from early Hussite battle hymns to the work of contemporary writers Čelakovský, Kollár, Jungmann and others. Bowring deserves credit for his pioneering work if not for the purity of his translations. He actually worked from German versions of the texts and his translations are rather free, though occasionally lively; they met, however, with virtually no public success. Bowring's literary successor was the Reverend Albert Wratislaw, headmaster of Bury St Edmund's Grammar School. His *Lyra Czechoslovanská: Bohemian Poems, Ancient and Modern* was published in 1849, but despite Wratislaw's greater scholarly knowledge of Czech his literary taste and choice of texts were weaker than Bowring's and again the book failed to excite interest. Wratislaw was more successful with his versions of older Czech literature (e.g., *Příhody Václava Vratislava z Mitrovic: The Adventures of Baron Wenceslas of Mitrowitz*, c.1600), and in his 1878 book of lectures *The Native Literature of Bohemia in the Fourteenth Century* he included translated extracts from many of the finest works of medieval Czech literature including the *Alexandreis* (*Alexander Legend*), *Tkadleček* (*The Weaver*) and Tomáš Štítný's outstanding devotional prose.

Perhaps the first successful translation from Czech in terms of reader response was made by Count Francis Lützow, whose version of Komenský's *The Labyrinth of the World and the Paradise of the Heart* was published in 1901. Lützow, a member of an aristocratic family from Eastern Bohemia, did much to present Czech history and culture to the British, including writing a *History of Bohemian Literature*. The virtually unknown English eccentric Sir Walter William Strickland, 9th Baronet, of Malton, Yorkshire, is also of interest. Sir Walter was a traveller and free-thinker with a taste for anarchism and Buddhism, but he managed to find time to learn Czech and to translate poems and several stories by Vitězslav Hálek, Svatopluk Čech's mock-epic poem *Hanuman*, and plays by the now forgotten Emanuel Bozděch. The quality of the translations is rather good but again the impact on the British public was nil and they are long out of print.

Among the few famous works of 19th-century Czech literature that clearly transcend the bounds of provincialism, three in particular deserve special mention: Karel Hynek Mácha's *Máj* (*May*), Božena Němcová's *Babička* (*Grandmother*) and Karel Jaromír Erben's *Kytice* (*Bouquet of National Legends*). *Máj* has much the same status in Czech literature as Pushkin's *Evgenii Onegin* in Russian. Mácha's poem is a masterpiece of European subjective Romanticism, but its musical richness, the allusiveness and interrelation of language and imagery, make it particularly difficult to translate. It was first attempted in 1932 by Roderick Ginsburg. Canto II was translated by Stephen Spender and Karel Brušák in 1943 with somewhat greater success. Hugh Hamilton McGoverne produced an overly elaborate rendition of the whole poem in 1949, turning Mácha's lyrical, allusive Czech and his tightly controlled rhythms into a charming but inappropriate late Victorian English. *Máj* was subsequently translated by Edith Pargeter (better known in England as Ellis Peters, the author of medieval whodunnits) in an edition published by Artia of Prague. In 1987 the American Bohemist William E. Harkins published a rather flat version in the annual *Cross Currents* 6. The most recent complete translation, by James Naughton, is still unpublished (apart from one Canto in the Prague magazine *Yazzyk*). Naughton does not overstep the boundaries of Mácha's own terms and images for the sake of rhymes and he allows some of Mácha's ambiguities to remain as such instead of resolving them as the other translators tend to do.

A translation of Němcová's *Babička* by Edith Pargeter was published in 1962. Apart from the unfortunate title – *Granny* instead of "Grandmother" – Pargeter's translation is one of the finer attempts at turning Czech 19th-century prose into English. She captures the idyllic quality and often the easy uninterrupted rhythmic flow of Němcová's prose without losing sight of the darker undertones of the book. Pargeter was less successful with her earlier translation of Jan Neruda's (1834–91) *The Little Quarter* (1957), as her graceful literary style does not really suit the journalist Neruda's ironic stories and there are occasional misunderstandings of sense. A new translation by Michael Henry Heim, retitled *Prague Tales*, came out in 1993. The raciness and pace of his translation are not unlike Jan Neruda, but Heim's language is sometimes too slick and he makes slips that blunt the irony of the stories. Both translators make Neruda into a much less subtle writer than he really is. Many of Pargeter's other translations have appeared in the notable anthology of Czech and Slovak writing *The Linden Tree*, 1962.

If Mácha resists translation, Erben defies it almost completely. Examples of his terse but resonance-packed, ballad-like poems have appeared in various anthologies, the earliest of which was *An Anthology of Czechoslovak Literature* (1929) by the first 20th-century translator whose work met with any real public success: Paul Selver. His *Anthology* contains translations from poets such as Otokar Březina, Antonín Sova and J.S. Machar, as well as examples of the work of Erben, Jan Neruda and others. Selver also includes a short story by the important novelist K. Čapek-Chod and, incongruously, extracts from the medieval authors Jan Hus and Petr Chelčický, as well as Komenský. The quality of Selver's translations is sometimes impressive and sometimes irritatingly bad: Sova's delicate poetic flowers wilt in his hands, but he is also one of the only translators to have attempted to turn Březina's grandiloquent, metaphysical poetry into good, even grand, English.

Selver was also the first translator of Hašek's classic *The Good Soldier Švejk*, as well as of Karel Čapek's play *R.U.R.* (which in his translation gave the word *robot* to the English language); Selver subsequently fell out with the author. Čapek's work enjoyed a brief popularity in England in the 1920s and 1930s, continuing to be regularly translated, notably by Robert and Mica Weatherall. At this time F.P. Marchant tackled the brilliant mid-19th-century satirist Karel Havlíček Borovský (whose *Křest Sv. Vladimíra – The Baptism of St Vladimír* – was later entertainingly translated by William Harkins) as well as the major figure of Czech historicism Alois Jirásek (1851–1930). Also notable in pre-war translation is Lynton A. Hudson's courageous attempt at Jaroslav Durych's massive, often termed neo-Baroque, novel of the Counter-Reformation *Bloudění* 1929; (translated as *The Descent of the Idol*, 1935). In the late 1940s and 1950s there was some interest in the contemporary novelist Egon Hostovský, resulting in translations of several books (the work of Fern Long, Philip H. Smith and an early appearance by Ewald Osers).

The most important Czech poets of the first half of the 20th century have not been well represented in English. Of the occasional translations of František Halas's mordant and bleak poetry only two are in book form: *Staré ženy* (*Old Women*), impressively translated by Karel Offer in 1947, and a selection of poems translated by Václav Svěrák (1981); neither book seems to have made any impression. The prolific translator from several languages Ewald Osers (a German Bohemian resident in England since the war) has provided some samples of Vítězslav Nezval's work in the Penguin *Three Czech Poets* (1971). Osers also translated the attractive selection of Jaroslav Seifert's poetry that was published after Seifert won the Nobel Prize for Literature in 1985, but Seifert and the collection were both promptly forgotten. A much trickier task was faced by Ian and Jarmila Milner when they tackled Vladimír Holan's important but difficult poetry. Holan's work ranges from delicate lyric poetry to long narrative poems; his language is densely metaphorical, allusive and cryptic. The Milners translate Holan's words often without quite seeming to grasp their meaning. A collaborative effort by two American translators, Clayton Eshleman and František Galan, produced a more convincing version of Holan's long poem *A Night with Hamlet*, again without any discernible wider impact, (although samples of his shorter, simpler poems continue to appear in anthologies of 20th-century Czech poetry). The Milners, together with Ewald Osers and George Theiner, were later instrumental in bringing Miroslav Holub's poetry to an English audience, and he has since become the contemporary Czech poet best known to English readers.

Apart from Holub, favoured among poetry readers, it is only the small group of high profile Czech ex-dissident writers – Milan Kundera, Václav Havel, Josef Škvorecký, and to a lesser extent Ivan Klíma and Ludvík Vaculík – who have achieved any kind of readership in English. Kundera's work has had a chequered history in translation after inexcusable liberties were taken with the English version of his first novel *The Joke*: chapters were rearranged and text altered. Since then, Kundera has insisted on absolute control over translations, collaborating with and revising the work of Peter Kussi and Michael Henry Heim. Since his last Czech novel *Nesmrtelnost* (*Immortality*, 1992) Kundera has written only in French. The playwright Havel has been translated by various hands, including Vera Blackwell and George Theiner; Škvorecký has been well served by Jeanne Němcová (*The Cowards*), Káca Poláckova-Henley and the Canadian Paul Wilson. Bohumil Hrabal's work seems to have some popularity and has been translated by Wilson, Pargeter, Naughton, and the ubiquitous Michael Henry Heim. Arnošt Lustig's novels of the Jewish experience of World War II, mostly translated by Jeanne Němcová, have likewise achieved a certain readership.

Other interesting individual works have occasionally come into English: Edith Pargeter translated one of Vladislav Vančura's brilliant and linguistically challenging novels *Konec starých časů* (1934) as *The End of Old Times* (1965); Jiří Mucha (son of the Art Nouveau painter Alphonse Mucha) wrote a fascinating book *Půlnoční slunce* (*Midnight Sun*) whilst doing forced labour as a coal-miner from 1951 to 1954, and this was well translated by Ewald Osers as *Living and Partly Living*; Eva Kantůrková's prison memoirs *Přítelkyně z domu smutku* (translated as *My Companions in the Bleak House*) received some attention in 1989; other examples can be found. In general, however, apart from a couple of recent writers at particular times, Czech literature has not captured the imagination of the English audience as much as, say, Czech music has, and occasionally Czech film. Some might argue that this has as much to do with the quality of the literature itself as with the quality of the translators, but this is surely too harsh a judgment. In short, too few of the really fine works of Czech literature have been well enough translated to engage the general reader.

JAMES PARTRIDGE

See also the entry Slovak

Further Reading

Auty, Robert, "Some Unpublished Translations from Czech by A.H. Wratislaw" in *Gorski Vijenac: A Garland of Essays Offered to Professor Elizabeth Mary Hill*, edited by Auty *et al.*, Cambridge: Modern Humanities Research Association, 1970

Auty, Robert, "Czech" in *The Slavic Literary Languages: Formation and Development*, edited by Alexander M. Schenker and Edward Stankiewicz, New Haven, Connecticut: Yale Concilium on International and Area Studies, 1980, pp. 163–82

French, Alfred, "Problems of Translating Czech Verse", *Melbourne Slavic Studies*, 8 (1973) pp. 20–30

Homel, David, "Solving the Difficulties: A Panel Discussion", *Translation Review*, 20 (1986) pp. 9–14 (includes Paul Wilson on translating Czech)

Kovtun, George J., *Czech and Slovak Literature in English: A Bibliography*, 2nd edition, Washington, DC: Library of Congress, 1984; reprinted 1988

Kundera, Milan, "Three Contexts of Art: From Nation to World" in *Cross Currents: A Yearbook of Central European Culture*, 12, New Haven, Connecticut and London: Yale University Press, 1993

Milner, Ian, "Česká poezie v anglických překladech 1970–1990 (knižní vydání)" [Czech Poetry in English Translations 1970–1990 (book editions)], *Literarní měsíčník*, 18 (1989) pp. 115–17

Naughton, James, "The Reception in Nineteenth-Century England of Czech Literature and of the Czech National Revival" (dissertation), Cambridge University, 1977

Naughton, James, "Morfill and the Czechs", *Oxford Slavonic Papers*, new series, 17 (1984) pp. 62–76

Naughton, James, "Czech Literature in Britain from Bowring to Strickland" in *Grossbritannien, die USA und die böhmischen Länder 1849–1938*, edited by Eva Schmidt-Hartmann and Stanley B. Winters, Munich: Oldenbourg, 1991, pp. 107–17

Naughton, James, "The Czech Republic" in *Traveller's Literary Companion: Eastern and Central Europe*, edited by Naughton, Brighton: In Print, 1995

Novák, Arne, *Czech Literature* [1946], translated by Peter Kussi, edited by William E. Harkins, with a supplement, Ann Arbor, Michigan: Michigan Slavic Publications, 1976

Pfaff, Ivo, "Česká literatura v Anglii před stopadesáti lety" [Czech Literature in England over 150 years ago], *Svědectví*, 69 (1983) pp. 157–71

Polišenský, J.V., *Britain and Czechoslovakia: A Study in Contacts*, Prague: Orbis, 1966; revised, 1968

Short, David, "Czech and Slovak" in *The Major Languages of Eastern Europe*, edited by Bernard Comrie, London: Routledge, 1990, pp. 101–24

Short, David, "Czech" in *The Slavonic Languages*, edited by Bernard Comrie and Greville G. Corbett, London and New York: Routledge, 1993, pp. 455–532

Součková, Milada, "Poetic Transposition" in *For Roman Jakobson: Essays on the Occasion of His Sixtieth Birthday*, edited by Morris Halle *et al.*, The Hague: Mouton, 1956, pp. 488–91

Vašek, Dorina K., "Czech Literature in the English-Speaking World: A Survey of Translations and Critical Reactions to Them, 1821–1978" (dissertation), University of Toronto, 1985

Vočadlo, O.,"The Wratislaws" in *Gorski Vijenac: A Garland of Essays Offered to Professor E.M. Hill*, edited by Robert Auty *et al.*, Cambridge: Modern Humanities Research Association, 1970

Wellek, René, *Essays on Czech Literature*, edited by C.H.Van Schonneveld, The Hague: Mouton, 1963

D

Danish

Literary Translation into English

The Language

Like English, Danish is a Germanic language. It evolved from the Common Scandinavian spoken throughout the territory now occupied by Norway, Sweden and Denmark AD 550–1050. Old Danish became a separate language diverging from East Scandinavian in about 1300; its major traits as a literary language were fixed by the translation of Luther's Bible in 1550. The evolution of modern Danish has tended to simplify Old Danish, reducing the number of noun genders to two and eliminating all case differences except the genitive. From about 1400 to 1900, Danish also served Norwegians as a literary language.

The Danish alphabet is the same as the English, but with three more letters: æ, ø, and å. Modern Danish nouns have two genders, common and neuter, and two cases, a nominative and a genitive formed by adding an s. Danish uses the genitive case in many instances where English employs a preposition and noun combination. The Danish verb system is simpler than the English, with two simple tenses: present and preterite, or past, and no progressive tense; continuity of action is indicated by the insertion of another verb indicating position or motion. Danish uses the active verb with "man" ("one") in many instances where English employs a passive construction. Danish subtleties difficult to translate include a number of frequently used particles which influence tone. The Danish lexicon, much smaller than the English, is also more expandable because of its greater flexibility in forming compound nouns.

Literary Translation from Danish

Today only three Danish authors are part of the English literary canon: Hans Christian Andersen (1805–75), Søren Kierkegaard (1813–55), and Karen Blixen (1885–1962). Andersen's reputation rests almost exclusively on his fairy tales; his adult novels and plays are virtually unknown outside Denmark. Kierkegaard, now studied assiduously by philosophers internationally, had to wait nearly a century to be translated into English. Blixen, better known as Isak Dinesen to English speakers, avoided the whole translation problem by writing most of her original works directly in English and then translating them back into her native Danish, thereby establishing a solid reputation in England and the US before achieving recognition in Denmark. From the viewpoint of Danish literary historians, the selection of Danish works translated into English seems haphazard, to say the least. Authors deemed pivotal by the Danes are often either undertranslated or not translated at all. N.F.S. Grundtvig (1783–1872), for example, whose influence on Danish culture has been profound, has had only a few fragments of his voluminous works translated into English. The great romantic poet, Adam Oehlenschläger (1779–1850), is represented by only a few translated poems in anthologies. Danish drama has also been undertranslated: Denmark's greatest acknowledged playwrights, such as Ludvig Holberg (1684–1754) and Kaj Munk (1898–1944) have not had all their major plays published in English. Even the Danish Nobel Laureates, Henrik Pontoppidan (1857–1943) and Johannes V. Jensen (1873–1950), have had surprisingly few of their works translated. Although this phenomenon is understandably disappointing to the Danes, it is easily explained if we follow the polysystem theorists in taking the target language point of view. It then becomes evident that the choices made from Danish literature for English translation have been motivated by a variety of reasons having more to do with cultural currents in England and the US than with Danish literature itself.

With the two countries separated geographically only by the North Sea, Britain's relationship with the Danes goes back to the Danish invasion and occupation of England in the 9th century. Because the earliest written Danish literature was in Latin, however, it was accessible to the English without the need of translation. Thus the *Gesta Danorum* by Saxo Grammaticus, a 12th-century historian, was available to the educated English long before it was translated by Oliver Elton in 1894. The first nine volumes of this work contain legends and heroic epic poetry from the ancient Danish oral traditions, rendered in highly literate Latin. It provided a source for Shakespeare's *Hamlet*. Other important literary works from the Danish Middle Ages were the folk ballads, which probably passed orally back and forth between England and Denmark long before seeing print. None of this medieval Danish literature was translated into English, however, until it attracted the attention of 19th-century romantics.

The first Danish-language work to be translated into English was a pamphlet written by Christiern Pederson (c.1480–1533), the Danish translator of Luther's Bible. His pamphlet was translated by John Gau, a Scottish priest, in 1533, as "The richt vay to the Kingdome of Heuine". Other Danish works to be translated into English during the 16th century were written in Latin and include pamphlets by the theologian Niels Hemmingsen and a travel book. Throughout the 16th and 17th centuries, Danish scientists and scholars continued to write in Latin, and hence were available to English scholars despite the paucity of English translations.

During the 16th and 17th centuries, many Danish scholars came to England to study at the Bodleian Library. Among them was Ludvig Holberg, often credited as the father of the Danish theater. The only one of his works to be translated into English during his lifetime, however, was not one of his Danish plays, but his imaginary voyage, *Niels Klim* (1741), inspired by Swift's *Gulliver's Travels* and written in Latin. Its English and Danish translations appeared the same year, 1742. Throughout the 17th and 18th centuries, more Danish to English translations gradually appeared; but the output did not begin in earnest until the 19th century, when anthologies including Danish short works and extracts from longer ones, began to emerge. A volume by William Herbert containing some ballads and some poetry by Johannes Ewald was published in London in 1804; and a collection by Robert Jamieson published in Edinburgh in 1806 contained Danish poetry translated into Lowland Scots dialect. In 1852, Mary and William Howitt collaborated on a history of the literature of Sweden, Denmark, Norway and Iceland for which they liberally translated specimens from Danish literature to use as illustrations.

Some prominent 19th-century writers, most notably George Borrow in England and Henry Wadsworth Longfellow in the US, acquired a knowledge of Danish and an interest in Denmark's poetry, particularly the medieval ballads. Borrow's *Romantic Ballads* was published in 1826. All his translations were later gathered and published in three volumes under the title *Songs of Scandinavia* as part of his *Works* (1914). They included translations from the poems of Oehlenschläger, Ewald, Edvard Storm (1749–94), Thomas Kingo (1634–1703), Jens Baggesen (1764–1826) and B.S. Ingemann (1789–1862). Although Longfellow's translations are few in number – five poems and a fragment of another – they have been considered among the most successful in English. They include Johannes Ewald's "King Christian", and Jens Baggesen's "Childhood", and the ballad, "The Mother's Ghost". Some of these, plus translations of ballads from other hands, were published in Longfellow's anthology *The Poets and Poetry of Europe* (1845). William Morris also included four translations of Danish ballads in his *Poems by the Way* (1891).

Hans Christian Andersen is by far the most translated Danish author. Ever since *Danish Fairy Legends and Tales*, translated by Caroline Peachey, was published in 1846, Andersen translations of varying quality have been published every year, usually adapted or rewritten exclusively for children. Other 19th-century writers who were known beyond the borders of Denmark in their own time include the Jewish writer, Meier Goldschmidt (1819–87), who resided in England for a time and translated his own *Homeless* (1861). His masterwork, *En Jøde* (*The Jew of Denmark*), was published in two different translations in 1852. Another Danish Jew, Georg Brandes (1842–1927), was enormously influential on the course of literary study during the 19th century, both in Denmark and abroad, promoting the "breakthrough" of realism in the 1870s. A true comparatist, Brandes lived in several European countries and strove to ignore the barriers of national languages to write about European literature as a whole. Early in his career he translated John Stuart Mill's *On the Subjection of Women* into Danish. The first translations of his own work into English began to emerge in 1878; his *William Shakespeare*, which appeared in Danish in 1896, was published in English translation only two years later, to become for a time one of the most popular works on Shakespeare in England.

Søren Kierkegaard, who is second only to Andersen among fellow Danes in the numbers of translations his works have received, had to wait nearly a century to be translated into English. *Selections from the Writings of Kierkegaard* translated by L.M. Hollander appeared in 1923 and was largely unnoticed; the flow of Kierkegaard translations did not really begin until 1939 with the publication of *Christian Discourses and Lilies of the Field* by Walter Lowrie, who then dedicated much of his life to translating Kierkegaard's works. Other important Kierkegaard translators include David Swenson, Howard V. and Edna H. Hong, and Alistair Hannay. In the 1940s, Kierkegaard began to be perceived as a Christian existentialist and extracts of his work appeared in existentialist anthologies, which undoubtedly contributed to his popularity.

In the 20th century, translations from the Danish continued to be produced but in diminishing numbers, dropping from 49 hardbound and trade paper volumes in 1989 to 14 in 1993. Their audience is composed largely of academics and of Americans of Scandinavian descent who wish to get in touch with their roots but do not have the language skills to read the originals. Since its establishment in 1910, the American Scandinavian Foundation has been responsible for the publication of a number of translated Danish works, either in its journal, *American-Scandinavian Review*, or as individual monographs. The latter include *A Book of Danish Verse* (1922), *A Second Book of Danish Verse* (1947), and *Denmark's Best Stories* (1928), all of which served to introduce to an English-speaking audience poets such as Ingemann, Grundtvig, J.L. Heiberg (1791–1860) and F. Paludan-Müller (1809–76), and fiction-writers such as Henrik Pontoppidan and Herman Bang (1857–1912). This foundation also was the first to publish in English two works by Jens Peter Jacobsen, the great 19th-century naturalist: *Marie Grubbe* in 1917 and *Niels Lyhne* in 1919, both translated by Hanna Astrup-Larsen. The Foundation has also awarded a translation prize every year since 1980; several Danish works have been recipients.

Other Danish novels translated in the early 20th century include Martin Andersen-Nexø's proletarian novels *Pelle the Conqueror* (1906–10, translated 1913–16) and *Ditte: Towards the Stars* (1917–21, translated 1920–23). Karin Michaelis (1872–1950) was also very well known, especially in the US. Her daring novel *The Dangerous Age*, published in English translation in 1911, sold over a million copies, had three movie versions and inspired Rose Macaulay's *Dangerous Ages*, 1921. It was thereupon forgotten until recently revived and republished by Northwestern University Press in 1991 as a result of feminist interest in recovering and reevaluating women authors.

Other Danish women writers who have profited from this reawakening of interest include Tove Ditlevson (1918–), Elsa Gress (1919–) and Dea Trier Mørch (1941–). Feminist publishers, such as Seal Press, as well as other small presses, have followed suit. In 1987 *No Man's Land*, an anthology of modern Danish women's literature, was published by Norvik Press, edited by Annegret Heitmann and including shorter works and extracts by Inger Christiansen, Dorrit Willumsen, Kirsten Thorup and others.

In recent years the task of publishing Danish works in English translation has largely fallen to small presses and a few university presses, some of which specialize in Scandinavian Literature. Curbstone Press has a Danish series; the University of Nebraska's Modern Scandinavian Literature in English Translation series has included several Danish titles. Steven T. Murray and Tiina Nunnally, the editors of Fjord Press, are also prolific translators of Danish literature; a recent Fjord catalog listed new translations of previously translated classics such as Martin Andersen-Nexø's *Pelle the Conqueror* and Jacobsen's *Niels Lyhne*, as well as first translations of newer fictions such as Tove Ditlevson's *The Faces* and Villy Sørensen's (1929–) *Another Metamorphosis*. In England, Marion Boyars, a publisher of avant-garde foreign writers, recently published the contemporary Henrik Stangerup's *The Seducer*, translated by Sean Martin and *Brother Jacob*, translated by Anne Born. Norvik Press, founded by the Scandinavian scholar James MacFarlane, has also produced a number of translations from Danish, including Brandes's *Selected Letters* translated by W. Glyn Jones. The 1990s Danish success story, however, is Peter Hoeg's *Smilla's Sense of Snow* (in the UK *Miss Smilla's Feeling for Snow*), translated by Tiina Nunnally, which became a bestseller with sales exceeding 100,000 in 1993.

Quite a number of introductory, multi-author anthologies appear in this brief survey of the English translation of Danish literature, but few "collected works". As we might expect, works have been selected for translation on the basis of translators' enthusiasms, such as the 19th-century romantic enthusiasm for medieval Danish ballads, and the 20th-century interest in recovering women authors. Danes who have spent time living and lecturing in England or America, such as Brandes and Michaelis, have sometimes managed to improve their exposure there for a time; however, their reputations have not endured in these countries except among specialists. Despite the conscientious hard work of Scandinavian scholars, translators, and publishers, English-language literature has taken only the Danish works that could be fitted into one of its own particular genres or movements – Andersen into children's literature, Kierkegaard into existentialism – and let the rest go; even Hoeg's phenomenally successful *Smilla* fits into the female detective genre.

KRISTINE J. ANDERSON

Further Reading

Bredsdorff, Elias, "Danish Literature in English Translation", *Orbis Litterarum*, 5 (1947) pp. 13–257

Bredsdorff, Elias, *Danish Literature in English Translation with a Special Hans Christian Andersen Supplement: A Bibliography*, Copenhagen: Munksgaard, 1950

Haugen, Einar, *The Scandinavian Languages: An Introduction to Their History*, Cambridge, Massachusetts: Harvard University Press, and London: Faber, 1976

Hilen, Andrew, *Longfellow and Scandinavia: A Study of the Poet's Relationship with the Northern Languages and Literature*, New Haven, Connecticut: Yale University Press, 1947

Jones, W. Glyn and Kirsten Gade, *Danish: A Grammar*, Copenhagen: Gyldendal, 1981

Jones, W. Glyn, "Søren Kierkegaard in English Translation", *Yearbook of Comparative and General Literature*, 35 (1986) pp. 105–11

Mitchell, P.M., *A History of Danish Literature*, Copenhagen: Glyndendal, 1957; 2nd edition, New York: Kraus Thomson, 1971

Schroeder, Carol L., *A Bibliography of Danish Literature in English Translation, 1950–1980*, Copenhagen: Det Danske Selskab, 1982

Seaton, Ethel, *Literary Relations of England and Scandinavia in the Seventeenth Century*, Oxford: Clarendon Press, 1935; New York: Benjamin Blom, 1972

Gabriele D'Annunzio 1863–1938

Italian novelist, dramatist and poet

Biography

D'Annunzio was born 12 March 1863 in the seacoast town of Pescara in the southeast of Italy; his parents belonged to the newly emergent bourgeoisie. His first collection of poetry was published when he was only 16 and his first prose collection two years later. In 1881, D'Annunzio arrived in Rome, where he soon began writing for the daily and weekly newspapers. A collection of poetry from this period, *Intermezzo di rime* (1883), provided him with an early *succès de scandale* – the book describes the conquest of his future wife. Indeed, D'Annunzio's career was assisted throughout by the succession of women with whom he conducted love affairs, and late in 1889 the first of a sequence of novels appeared that made use of such autobiographical material: *Il piacere*. The novel concerns a few months in the life of the dashing Count Andrea Sperelli. This was followed by *L'innocente* (1892), the story of an infanticide. D'Annunzio explored the pathology of perversion still further in *Il trionfo della morte* (1894). These novels were intended by their author – for whom the rose was a symbol of sensual pleasure – to constitute a loosely constructed trilogy entitled *I romanzi della rosa* [Romances of the Rose]. Other novels of note include *Giovanni Episcopo* (1892), an experiment at writing a psychological novel within naturalist conventions, and *Il fuoco* (1900), a scandalous if not always accurate account of the author's relationship with Eleonora Duse. In 1897, D'Annunzio entered politics and, perhaps not entirely coincidentally, began writing for the theatre. D'Annunzio's theatre is one of brutal and savage forces (in *Francesca da Rimini*, for example, Malatestino brings the freshly decapitated head of his enemy onto the stage). Three of D'Annunzio's plays were translated into English by Arthur Symons: *La Gioconda*, 1899 (translated 1901); *Francesca da Rimini*, 1901 (translated 1902); *La Città morta*, 1898 (performed 1918; the translation remains unpublished). D'Annunzio engaged in several patriotic exploits that attracted considerable publicity during World War I, and in 1919 was responsible for seizing the city of Fiume, an action that some commentators claim pointed the way to the later Fascist seizure of power in Italy; D'Annunzio became a supporter of the Fascists in office. His retirement was spent near Lake Garda; he died at Gardone Riviera, 1 March 1938.

Translations

Novels

Il piacere, 1889

Harding, Georgina, *The Child of Pleasure*, with an introduction and verse translation by Arthur Symons, London: Heinemann, 1898, Boston: Page, 1910; reprinted New York: Fertig, 1990, Sawtry, Cambridgeshire: Dedalus, 1991

L'innocente, 1892

Harding, Georgina, *The Intruder*, London: Heinemann, 1897; as *L'innocente (The Victim)*, Sawtry, Cambridgeshire: Dedalus, and New York: Hippocrene, 1990

Il trionfo della morte, 1894

Harding, Georgina, *The Triumph of Death*, London: Heinemann, 1896; reprinted Sawtry, Cambridgeshire: Dedalus, 1990

Il fuoco, 1900

Bassnett, Susan, *The Flame*, with an introduction, London: Quartet, and New York: Marsilio, 1991

Vivaria, Kassandra (pseudonym of Magda Sinici), *The Flame of Life*, Boston: Page, 1900; reprinted New York: Fertig, 1990

Selections of Short Stories

Rosenthal, Raymond, *Nocturne and Five Tales of Love and Death*, Marlboro, Vermont: Marlboro Press, 1988; London: Quartet, 1993 (contains "The Virgin Orsola", "The Vigil", "The Sea-Going Surgeon", "Giovanni Episcopo", "Leda without Swan", "Nocturne")

Short Stories

Giovanni Episcopo, 1892

Jones, M.L., *Episcopo and Company*, Chicago: Stone, 1896

Rosenthal, Raymond, "Giovanni Episcopo" in *Nocturne and Five Tales of Love and Death*, translated by Rosenthal, 1988

Notturno, 1921

Rosenthal, Raymond, "Nocturne" in *Nocturne and Five Tales of Love and Death*, translated by Rosenthal, 1988

Plays

La Gioconda, 1899

Symons, Arthur, *La Gioconda*, London: Heinemann, and New York: R.H. Russell, 1901

Francesca da Rimini, 1901

Symons, Arthur, *Francesca da Rimini*, London: Heinemann, and New York: Stokes, 1902

Poetry

Alcione, 1903

Nichols, J.G., *Halcyon*, with an introduction, Manchester: Carcanet, 1988

A Cherbourg philosophy teacher named Georges Hérelle, who came across *L'innocente* (1892) while on holiday in Italy and put it into French (1893), became D'Annunzio's principal translator, and it was the commercial and critical success of this work that marked the beginning of D'Annunzio's considerable fame outside Italy.

Although it was the concluding volume of the *Romanzi della rosa* trilogy, *Il trionfo della morte*, 1894 (*The Triumph of Death*, 1896) was D'Annunzio's first novel to be translated into English. It recounts a love affair conducted by Giorgio Aurispa with his sexually demanding but infertile mistress, Ippolita Sanzio. This novel also demonstrated an ideological shift in D'Annunzio's prose writing, which now assumed a more overtly misogynistic and anti-Christian stance. The English translation, by Georgina HARDING, tends to soften these elements. Thus, the prefatory epigraph drawn from Nietzsche, which provides a clue to the intellectual source of Giorgio Aurispa's lack of interest in guilt and redemption, is omitted. More damagingly, the sensuality of the novel is toned down to such an extent that a number of the key themes of *fin-de-siècle* decadence (e.g. sterility) become entirely blurred. D'Annunzio employs the word "orgasmo" (i.e. "orgasm") several times in the course of the novel; this is paraphrased in English as "nervousness" or the reference is entirely omitted. Although it is hinted in the English translation that Ippolita suffers from some specifically feminine disorder, the exact nature of her illness is not vouchsafed – though D'Annunzio clearly identifies it as "isteralgia". A number of Italian names would seem to be misspelled in the English translation and Italian dialects are normalized throughout.

In the second volume of the *Romanzi della rosa* trilogy, *L'innocente* (1892), infanticide is committed by a well-to-do landowner when his wife gives birth to another man's child. The book was translated as *The Intruder* in 1897. HARDING, who was again the translator, would seem to have been familiar with Hérelle's French translation (as *L'Intrus*), since the English edition eschews the more obvious title, imposed on the 1990 reprint (*The Victim*). D'Annunzio's novel was considerably bowdlerized for newspaper serialization in French and by no means all of the suppressed passages were restored when the French version came out in book form. The English translation is also bowdlerized, especially with regard to passages describing sexual encounters.

Ostensibly, HARDING would seem to have taken the largest liberties in her translation of the first volume of the *Romanzi della rosa*: *Il piacere*, 1889 (*The Child of Pleasure*, 1898) and it seems likely that her translation is based on the French translation (again by Georges Hérelle). The Italian text relates Count Andrea Sperelli's sexual relations with the ardent Elena Muti and the more spiritually inclined Maria Ferres; eventually, he attempts unsuccessfully to combine both types of woman in a mental composite. The French version was modified and reshaped by the author at the insistence of the editor of *La Revue de Paris* where the novel began serialization under the title *L'Enfant de volupté* in December 1894. As Giovanni Gullace has shown (1966), this reshaping of the architecture of the novel allows for the narrative to proceed in chronological order; moreover, D'Annunzio himself eliminated passages that he considered too affected or licentious. Gullace further suggests that some of the omitted passages were plagiarized from the French author Joséphin Péladan.

Kassandra VIVARIA's serviceable though somewhat outdated translation of D'Annunzio's sixth novel, *Il fuoco* (1900), as *The Flame of Life* (1900) also tended to coyness. It has now been entirely superseded by Susan BASSNETT's reliable contemporary translation: *The Flame* (1991).

D'Annunzio's novella *Giovanni Episcopo*, which had been translated as *Episcopo and Company* by M.L. JONES (1896), was translated by Raymond ROSENTHAL in 1988 in a collection including five other D'Annunzio short stories. Rosenthal's translation is both accurate and lively.

J.G.NICHOLS's atmospheric but accurate translation (1988) of D'Annunzio's 1903 *Alcione* (generally considered the author's most successful collection of poetry) follows the various verse forms of the original (including dithyrambs, elegies, sonnets and free verse).

Arthur SYMONS's version (1902) of *Francesca da Rimini* is a literal, blank verse translation. Though D'Annunzio's drama was admired in its day, all his work in this field now seems ponderous and, in the words of Philippe Jullian (1972), "weighted down by interminable monologues and by a rhetoric which does not bear translation".

TERRY HALE

Further Reading

Gullace, Giovanni, *Gabriele D'Annunzio in France: A Study in Cultural Relations*, Syracuse: Syracuse University Press, 1966

Jullian, Philippe, *D'Annunzio*, translated by Stephen Hardman, London: Pall Mall Press, 1972

Klopp, Charles, *Gabriele D'Annunzio*, Boston: Twayne, 1988

See also the introductions to Bassnett and Nichols, and the preface to Rosenthal

---

Dante Alighieri 1265–1321

Italian poet

Biography

Born in Florence in 1265, probably in late May. His father was Alighiero di Bellincione d'Alighiero, a lawyer or possibly a money-lender, whose family was loyal to the Guelph faction in Florentine politics. Little is known about Dante's early life, which was spent in Florence. Details of his education are conjectural, but he was brought up as a gentleman, and probably studied at schools in Florence; he was taught philosophy by Brunetto Latini and learned to write poetry. Dante probably also studied for a year at the University of Bologna. His friendship with the poet Guido Cavalcanti influenced his early writing, and he associated with the group of *dolce stil nuovo* poets around Cavalcanti. In 1274, at the age of nine, he met Beatrice Portinari (born c.1265) for whom he developed an idealistic, Platonic passion, despite her marriage at a young age to Simone de' Bardi. Beatrice died in 1290. Dante was betrothed to Gemma di Maretto Donati, from an important Guelph family, in about 1283, shortly after Dante's father's death; they married in about 1294 and had at least four children. Dante served in the Florentine army cavalry in its campaign against the Ghibellines and fought in battle of Campaldino in 1289. He was involved in Florentine civic affairs during the 1290s, serving on people's council from 1295–96 and other councils in 1296 and 1297. He was registered as a poet in the Apothecaries' guild of Florence at this time. Dante was sent on diplomatic missions to San Gimignano in 1300, and in the same year he became one of the six priors governing Florence. He was in charge of road works in Florence, probably in preparation for a siege, in 1301. While Dante was on a mission to pope Boniface VIII in Rome in 1301, the Guelph faction to which Dante was loyal, the Bianchi (Whites), were defeated in Florence; he was exiled from the city and sought refuge at the courts of various Ghibelline lords in northern Italy. In 1302 he was in San Godenzo, and he was under the protection of the Scala family at Verona in 1303. His patron, Bartolommeo, died in 1304. Around this time, Dante broke with other White exiles, and probably went to Bologna. He was an agent in the court of Franceschino Malaspina in the Lunigiana, 1306, and travelled to Lucca around 1306–08. While in exile, around 1306, he started writing his *Divina Commedia*. Dante was a strong supporter of the holy Roman emperor, Henry VII of Luxemburg, from 1309 until the emperor's death in 1313, and wrote his *De monarchia* at this time. After the death of Henry VII, Dante gave up hope of returning to a position of importance in Florence, returning to Lucca around 1314. He was refused a conditional amnesty from Florence in 1316. He stayed again at the court of Can Grande della Scala in Verona, in 1317, and lived at the court of Guido Novello da Polento in Ravenna from about 1317 until his death. He went on a diplomatic mission to Venice on behalf of Guido in 1321. Dante died in Ravenna on 14 September 1321.

Dante's reputation as one of the major writers in European literary history rests mainly on his celebrated philosophical epic poem, *La Commedia*, later known as *La divina commedia* (*The Divine Comedy*), which he wrote in exile from around 1306 onwards. This work has been widely acclaimed for its spiritual and emotional resonance and breadth of theological and philosophical awareness. The poem takes the form of a poet's allegorical journey to God through hell and purgatory, finally reaching salvation. *La divina commedia* was written in vernacular Italian rather than Latin, Dante thereby also exerting influence on the subsequent significance of the Italian language in European literature. Dante's first important work, *La vita nuova* (*The New Life*) (1292–1300), is a narrative account, in prose and poetry, of his early life and love for Beatrice Portinari. *Il convivio* (*The Banquet*) (c.1304–08) is a collection of poems, with prose commentary, on philosophy, politics and ethics; and *De monarchia* (*On World-Government*) (c.1313) is a political treatise written in Latin.

The New Life

La Vita Nuova

A series of sonnets, ballete and canzoni following the course of Dante's love for Beatrice, written from the early 1280s onwards and brought together with a prose commentary by Dante at some point in the early or mid-1290s.

Translations

Anderson, William, *The New Life*, Harmondsworth and Baltimore: Penguin, 1964

Boswell, Charles Stuart, *The Vita Nuova and Its Author*, London: Kegan Paul Trench Trubner, 1895

De Meÿ, Frances, *The Vita Nuova; or, New Life*, London: Bell, 1902

Emerson, Ralph Waldo, *Dante's Vita Nuova* [1843], edited by J. Chesley Mathews, Chapel Hill: University of North Carolina Press, 1960

Garrow, Joseph, *The Early Life of Dante Alighieri, Together with the Original* (parallel texts), with an introduction, Florence: Le Monnier, 1846

Martin, Theodore, *The Vita Nuova of Dante*, London: Parker and Bourn, 1862

Musa, Mark, *La Vita Nuova*, New Brunswick, New Jersey: Rutgers University Press, 1957; revised edition, Oxford and New York: Oxford University Press, 1992

Norton, Charles Eliot, *The New Life of Dante Alighieri*, Boston: Ticknor and Fields, 1867; reprinted Boston: Houghton Mifflin, 1920

Okey, Thomas, *The Vita Nuova and Canzoniere of Dante Alighieri*, London: Dent, 1906 (*Canzoniere* translated by Philip H. Wickstead)

Reynolds, Barbara, *La Vita Nuova; Poems of Youth*, Harmondsworth and Baltimore: Penguin, 1969

Ricci, Luigi, *The New Life* (parallel texts), London: Kegan Paul Trench Trubner, 1903

Rossetti, Dante Gabriel, *The New Life* in *The Early Italian Poets from Ciullo d'Alcamo to Dante Alighieri (1100–1200–1300) in the Original Metres*, London: Smith Elder, 1861, many subsequent reprints; edited by Sally Purcell, Berkeley: University of California Press, and London: Anvil Press, 1981

Interest in the *Vita Nuova* does not start to manifest itself in England until the 1830s and 1840s, after the Romantic near-obsession with the Gothic glooms of the *Inferno* had given way to a new interest in the figure of Beatrice and in Dante's early life, an interest stimulated by the discovery of the so-called portrait of the young Dante in the Bargello in Florence in 1840. Although the poems of the *Vita Nuova* had previously appeared in translation (in Charles Lyell's *The Canzoniere of Dante*, 1835), GARROW's (1846) is the first complete version. Sensible, reasonably accurate and self-confessedly literal, its use of the dash as the main means of punctuation makes for a rushed and disordered rhythm. It tends towards a novelettish treatment of Beatrice in its various translations of "gentilissima" as "lovely", "handsome", "charming", "beauteous", "fair", indicating the desire (as explained in the introduction) to assert her reality in the face of contemporary allegorical interpretations (such as those of Gabriele Rossetti, D.G. Rossetti's father), and to see the work as the forerunner of the modern romance novel.

D.G. ROSSETTI's translation (1861) held sway for a hundred years or so as the best-received and most reprinted version, and may have been completed as early as 1846. It counters any novelettish element by emphasizing the "sacred-text" aspect of the work, through a markedly biblical phrasing – "speaking unto", "bear witness to", "it behoved her" – mingled with plentiful archaisms – "whereof", "mine ears", "somewhat thereof", "I would fain". In this, it elevates the mystical and esoteric character of the text in a manner commensurate with the Pre-Raphaelite Brotherhood's self-created identity as a circle of initiates, and with the treatment of the Dante–Beatrice story in many of Rossetti's own paintings and poems. Its appealing fluency and rhythmical control is achieved, particularly in the poems, at the cost of the addition of whole phrases of Rossetti's own; thus "s'io son d'ogni tormento ostale e chiave" ("if I am the hostel and key of every torment") becomes "if my case / Be not a piteous marvel and a sign", in keeping with the biblical cast described above. In his preface, Rossetti noted how "literality of rendering" in translation is secondary to the "commandment" that "a good poem shall not be turned into a bad one", though he also confessed in a letter to his brother, William Michael Rossetti (who produced the translations of the "divisioni", or poem-analyses), that "I should very much wish that the translation were more literal."

NORTON (1867) was the first translation to be published in the US. The most literal of versions, it follows Dante's syntax and sentence construction almost word for word, especially in the prose, indicating, perhaps, that Norton was the first recognized scholar to publish a translation (a critical essay with part-translation preceded the full version in 1859). Thus individual phrases – "a lady young and of exceeding gentle aspect" ("una donna giovane e di gentile aspetto molto"), "as do the others our peers" ("come stanno li altri nostri pari") – frequently mirror the Italian almost entirely. In spite of this, Norton's version is surprisingly readable, and the poems, where he allows himself more freedom, show some skill in handling rhyme and metre.

Of the other Victorian and Edwardian versions, those by BOSWELL (1895), DE MEŸ (1902) and RICCI (1903) made little impact. MARTIN's version (1862) had some contemporary success, and that by OKEY (1906) (all of it in prose, including the poems of the original) formed part of the serviceable Temple Classics edition of Dante's works that circulated widely as the means of introduction to Dante for many readers (including T.S. Eliot). Separate mention should be made of EMERSON, produced as early as 1843 though not published until 1957 (and with complete commentary in 1960). His aim of a simple literalism (in his own words "keeping lock step with the original") extends to a word-by-word reproduction of the poems, with no attempt at metrical organization; the "divisioni" are also omitted. This omission (and the plentiful mistakes) are in part explained by Emerson's editor as the responsibility of the inferior edition of Dante he was using (Sermartelli, Florence, 1576), though it is clear Emerson regarded the translation as in need of further revision.

Of the three modern versions, that by ANDERSON (1964) has found little favour. That by REYNOLDS (1969) is a very readable version that avoids archaisms and inversions of word order (especially in the prose) to achieve a straightforward, functional English; Dante's lengthy periods are often broken down into shorter, main-clause sentences that again facilitate comprehension. The poems combine an avoidance of elaboration and a closeness to the grammar and construction of the original with much metrical smoothness; some padding is occasionally evident to maintain the rhyme-scheme. Though the diction throughout remains quite formal, eschewing colloquialisms and contractions, there is a briskness of pace and a use of some "everyday" phrasing – "my senses reeling", "hit on the idea", "I know quite a number" – that helps counteract Victorian "dreaminess".

As distinct from Reynolds, MUSA feels the primary obligation to reproduce the complexities of Dante's sentence structure, the fact that, as he puts it in his prefatory "Note", "the reader always seems to be in the midst of a dependent clause", and that Dante's main concern is with the detail of exposition, rather than with narrative "flow". Musa's version can thus sound stilted and cumbersome; this manner is emphasized by his preference for a more orotund and even archaic diction than in Reynolds, as in phrasing like "dealing in those things wherein such advice would profitably be heeded". Though the poetry in Musa dispenses with Dante's rhyme and metre and is, indeed, much closer to the rhythms of prose, it departs from Dante's text in imagery and diction much more than do many rhymed versions, thus contrasting with the declared intention of the prose passages, that track Dante's involved clause structure.

STEVE ELLIS

Further Reading

Caesar, Michael (editor), *Dante: The Critical Heritage, 1314(?)–1870*, London and New York: Routledge, 1989

Corrigan, Beatrice (editor) *Italian Poets and English Critics, 1755–1859: A Collection of Critical Essays*, Chicago: University of Chicago Press, 1969

De Sua, William D., *Dante into English*, Chapel Hill: University of North Carolina Press, 1964

Ellis, Steve, *Dante and English Poetry: Shelley to T.S. Eliot*, Cambridge and New York: Cambridge University Press, 1983 (especially chapter 4)

La Piana, Angelina, *Dante's American Pilgrimage: A Historical Survey of Dante Studies in the United States*, New Haven, Connecticut: Yale University Press, 1948

Reynolds, Barbara, "Translating Dante in the 1990s", *Translation and Literature* 4/2 (1995), pp. 221–37

Toynbee, Paget, "English Translations of Dante in the Eighteenth Century", *Modern Language Review*, 1 (1905–06), pp. 9–24

Toynbee, Paget, *Dante in English Literature: From Chaucer to Cary (c. 1380–1844)*, 2 vols, London: Methuen, 1909

The Divine Comedy

La Commedia, written c.1307–21

Translations

Bickersteth, Geoffrey L., *The Divine Comedy*, Aberdeen: Aberdeen University Press, 1955

Binyon, Laurence, *Dante's Inferno*, London: Macmillan, 1933; *Dante's Purgatorio*, London: Macmillan, 1938; *Dante's Paradiso*, London: Macmillan, 1943; in one vol. as *The Divine Comedy, Complete*, with an introduction by Paolo Milano, New York: Viking, 1947

Boyd, Henry, *The Divina Commedia of Dante Alighieri*, 3 vols, London: T. Cadell Jr. and W. Davies, 1802

Carlyle, John A., *Dante's Divine Comedy: The Inferno: A Literal Prose Translation*, London: Chapman and Hall, 1849

Cary, Henry F., *The Vision: Or, Hell, Purgatory, and Paradise of Dante Alighieri*, London: privately printed, 1814; reprinted London: William Smith, 1844 (last revised edition; only slightly different from the 1814 edition, mainly in terms of punctuation)

Cary, Henry F., *The Divine Comedy. The Vision of Dante*, edited by Ralph Pite, London: Everyman, 1994 (based on the 1814 edition)

Ciardi, John, *The Divine Comedy*, New York: Norton, 1977 (first published in 3 vols, 1954–70)

Ellis, Steve, *Hell*, London: Chatto and Windus, 1994

Halpern, Daniel (editor), *Dante's Inferno: Translations by Twenty Contemporary Poets*, Hopewell, New Jersey: Ecco Press, 1993

Longfellow, Henry Wadsworth, *The Divine Comedy*, 3 vols, Boston: Ticknor and Fields, and London: Routledge, 1867

Mandelbaum, Allen, *The Divine Comedy* (parallel texts), 3 vols, Berkeley: University of California Press, 1980–84; translation only, with an introduction by Eugenio Montale, New York: Knopf, and London: Everyman, 1995
Musa, Mark, *The Divine Comedy*, 3 vols, Harmondsworth and New York: Penguin, 1984–86 (*The Inferno* first published Bloomington: Indiana University Press, 1971)
Phillips, Tom, *The Divine Comedy of Dante Alighieri: The Inferno*, London: Talford Press, 1983; reprinted as *Dante's Inferno*, London: Thames and Hudson, 1985
Pinsky, Robert, *The Inferno of Dante: A New Verse Translation*, New York: Farrar Straus, 1994
Sayers, Dorothy L. with Barbara Reynolds, *The Divine Comedy*, 3 vols, Harmondsworth and Baltimore: Penguin, 1949–62
Sisson, C.H., *The Divine Comedy*, Manchester: Carcanet New Press, 1980; Chicago: Regnery, 1981

The approach of this article is descriptive and target-oriented. The categorization into historical periods is taken from De Sua (1964) and the framework of the analysis (with its attendant terminology) is based on Holmes (*Translated! Papers on Literary Translation and Translation Studies*, Amsterdam: Rodopi, 1988) and Venuti (*The Translator's Invisibility*, London and New York: Routledge, 1995). From Holmes comes the idea of the three main types of verse form: mimetic (*terza rima* in English), analogical (a form, such as blank verse, having the same cultural significance in the target tradition as the original had in the source tradition), the organic (a form, such as free verse, that has no relationship with the original one). From Holmes also: the distinction between different large-scale policies: (a) exoticizing (e.g. retaining *terza rima* and source language syntax) vs. naturalizing (e.g. blank verse and target-language syntax); (b) historicizing (e.g. use of archaisms) vs. modernizing (e.g. use of modern English). From Venuti the seminal notion of transparency (the dominant canon in the English tradition of translating), i.e. a policy domesticating the foreign elements and achieving easy readability and fluency, as opposed to a foreignizing policy (synonymous with Holmes's exoticizing policy).

As far as the Italian text is concerned, the early translators in particular made their choices by comparing a variety of textual editions. It was not until 1921 that the Società Dantesca established the canonical edition of Dante's *Comedy*, later to be replaced by that of Giorgio Petrocchi (1966–67). Petrocchi's critical edition is now the authoritative edition used by the most recent 20th-century translators of Dante.

A multitude of translators and poets, from Chaucer to Seamus Heaney, have tried their hand at rendering single episodes or entire canticles of the *Comedy* (e.g. Count Ugolino, XXXII–XXXIII), which have always aroused interest in the English literary tradition. There are a great number of rewritings of Dante's poem into English (perhaps more than into any other language, cf. De Sua 1964): Dante is (together with Horace) the most widely translated poet into English (cf. De Sua 1964 and Reynolds 1995). In 1854, there were in English seven translations of the entire *Comedy* and six of *Inferno*. In the following century, up to 1954, the interest in Dante grew steadily: British and American translators produced a further 32 *Comedies*, plus 20 *Infernos*, 11 *Purgatorios* and six *Paradisos* (Cunningham, 1965).

In the 1970s and 1980s three high-quality translations of the entire *Comedy* appeared (Musa 1971, 1984–86; Sisson 1981; Mandelbaum, 1980–84) together with one more *Inferno* (Phillips, 1983). In the 1990s the poets rewriting Dante have focused on *Inferno* (Halpern edition, 1993; Ellis, 1994; Pinski, 1994).

The Neo-classical Age

BOYD's (1802) (British) is the first complete translation of the *Comedy*. His version (in pentameters arranged in six-line stanzas rhyming aabccb) is clearly a part of the 18th-century modernizing and naturalizing tradition of translating (cf. Dryden and Pope): Boyd takes great liberties in rewriting the original and makes no effort to reproduce Dante's tercets. However, his imagination has a Romantic vein, since he grasps the significance of the redemption of man in the *Comedy* and stresses Dante's "sublime genius" (critics in the late 18th and early 19th centuries found in Dante elements of a Barbaric age such as "terror", "pathos" and "sublimity"). Boyd follows a radically domesticating policy: in order to make the source text acceptable to current taste he expands, freely modifies and makes additions to it, and he shows no hesitation in altering some facts of the narration; the conviction being that the original must be purified (stylistically) of its faults (e.g. coarse language). Boyd's naturalizing policy is based on an extensive use of literary borrowings (from Shakespeare, Dryden and Pope but especially from Milton and Spenser). Contemporary critics praised Boyd's translation, though it was never as successful as Cary's later version. In fact, post-18th-century critics, who had a stricter notion of fidelity entailing a greater respect for the source text, were somehow dismissive of Boyd's translation, which they considered, at best, a loose paraphrase. Moreover, the Romantics and the Victorians found fault with Boyd's grandiose tone and elaborate diction. The 20th-century climate (especially after Pound and Eliot) enabled some critics to appreciate Boyd's domesticating policy. At any rate, whether or not Boyd produced a translation of note, it is an undeniable fact that as the first translator of the *Comedy* he rescued Dante from neglect.

The Romantic Age

H.F. CARY's (1814, 1844) (British) version of the *Comedy* was one of the most successful translations ever published in the English-speaking world. Its initial success was secured by the intervention of Coleridge and Ugo Foscolo, both of whom praised Cary's use of blank verse (analogical), seen as having the same aesthetic effect as the original *terza rima* had on the Italian public (blank verse is in keeping with the English literary tradition of religious or heroic verse, cf. *Paradise Lost*), besides which the iambic pentameter was thought to be the exact equivalent of Dante's hendecasyllabic line. Cary's choice of metre gave rise to one of the main debates among Dante translators of all times: whether or not *terza rima* (aba, bcb, cdc, ded, etc.) should be translated in rhyming tercets (the other main issue among translators of Dante revolves around the level of diction).

Cary's success was also due to his notion of fidelity, which was in harmony with the Romantic attitude: it was held that the *Comedy* was to be recreated in such a way as to preserve both its style and its content (the most influential English poets – among them Byron, Shelley, Macaulay, Tennyson and Browning – were increasingly turning to the *Comedy* for inspiration). However,

Cary is not always consistent with his declaration of intent: although he translates the source text more closely than Boyd does, his taste in terms of diction and imagery is still largely neoclassical: the language of the target text is embellished with literary expressions (mainly from Elizabethan poets and Milton), besides the fact that (rather as in Boyd) Dante's realism (or vernacular language) is considerably toned down. In fact, Cary (echoing Coleridge) openly criticizes Dante's grotesque imagery and those images that "excite bodily disgust", of which there is no example in the "more sublime" Milton (not to mention the instances of taboo language in *Inferno* which are expunged by Cary). On the whole, therefore, Cary follows a domesticating policy. His stylistic choices, however, are not always consistent: on the one hand, he aims at readability (transparency) (e.g. most of the numerous Latin expressions in the *Comedy* are rendered into English); on the other he envelops the target text in an archaic patina (historicizing policy) and frequently uses inversions and convoluted syntax. Thus, neither Dante's constant switch of registers (or mingling of styles) nor the quick flow of the original is recreated. However, Cary produced an extremely significant translation that played an important part in spreading Dante's fame abroad. Contemporary reviewers praised Cary's style for its "variety", whereas some (especially 20th-century) critics find his version monotonous and excessively deferential towards the source text. Cary, an Anglican clergyman, was influenced by his religious outlook: *The Vision* exhibits manipulations pointing to an Anglican (or Protestant-like) interpretation of the *Comedy*. In fact, in the early 19th century Dante was seen as a defender of religious liberty against Roman Catholicism (the poets Ugo Foscolo and Gabriele Rossetti, both of whom had settled in England, considered Dante to be a proto-Protestant, i.e. a forerunner of the Reformation).

The Victorian Age

CARLYLE's (1849) (British) translation of *Inferno* exemplifies the Victorian tradition, which focused on literal renderings. He employs prose, thereby allegedly reproducing the original semantic content (which is believed to be separable from poetry or aesthetic effects: unlike the Romantics, the Victorians were inclined to believe in the separation of form and content), though he is not always in accord with that intention, since he wavers between a literal prose rendering and a more idiomatic one. Carlyle's purpose was to publish a correct edition of the source text with a commentary. His version was well received by contemporary critics.

LONGFELLOW (1867) (American) uses blank verse (analogical) and divides the verse into paragraphs which closely follow (line-by-line) the source text. He shares Carlyle's approach in renouncing any attempt to reproduce the poetic quality of the original: Longfellow makes it clear that he intends to convey only "exactly what Dante says, and not what the translator imagines he might have said if he had been an Englishman". This leads to a mildly foreignizing policy as regards diction: Longfellow draws on Latinate (polysyllabic) vocabulary in order to keep close to the source, so making his text obscure at times; in his desire to produce a line-for-line rendering, he also uses frequent inversions, which again hamper readability. Well received by some critics (probably influenced by the translator's fame), Longfellow's was an influential translation at the time, especially in America. However, his quasi-literal method inevitably limits the range of poetic expression, so that his version did not attract much interest from later generations of critics and translators (apart from the few prose translators in the 20th century who inevitably followed in his footsteps).

The 20th Century

The 20th century is characterized by a variety of conflicting methods, from the quasi-literalists to the advocates of a poetic version, that has given birth to a wealth of different translations. As regards metre, for example, the advocates of *terza rima*, a mimetic (exoticizing) verse form, gain ground, though they are still opposed by a conspicuous group of more traditional proponents of analogical (naturalizing) blank verse. However, a unifying theme may be detected in a move towards colloquial English (modernizing policy). Eliot's critical influence is paramount (he emphasized Dante's simplicity and clear visual images, though Dante's style is characterized by a range of tones or different registers). Both Eliot and Pound break new ground by focusing on form, which is seen as constituting an organic unity with content. Moreover, they see the translator as a creative agent whose rewriting is triggered off by an interpretative act singling out and reproducing one (quintessential) aspect of the original (usually the simplicity and vigour of Dante's language or the burlesque, etc.). Pound's and Eliot's critical-interpretative approach will not be fully accepted until the end of the century, though Ciardi's innovative version (1977) paves the way for the acceptance of this approach. In the 1990s, interesting developments breathe new life into the practice of translating Dante: in America Pinski (1994) proposes an inventive use of *terza rima*, while in Britain Ellis (1994) modernizes diction radically and employs an organic verse form.

BICKERSTETH (*Paradiso* 1932, *The Comedy* 1955) (British), is the first important 20th-century translator to oppose the Victorian literal method of translation: Bickersteth expresses views similar to those of the Romantics (he too intends to mirror the aesthetic effects of the source text), though his attitude to verse form is quite modern, since he chooses *terza rima* (foreignizing). Yet the fact that he started to translate at the beginning of the 20th century (i.e. before the modernist revolution in poetry) accounts for his traditional stylistic choices: Bickersteth's archaisms betray Victorian leanings, though it should be noted that he also modernizes slightly the language of the Victorians.

BINYON (1947) (British), produces a mildly foreignizing version quite similar to Bickersteth's in many respects: he too adopts *terza rima*, employs archaic expressions and syntactical inversions (besides the fact that most of the original Latin expressions are preserved). There is no real mingling of styles because of the lack of vernacular language. Binyon, however, is quite creative at times (e.g. he translates Dante's evocative names in *Inferno*). Binyon has a Romantic attitude since he intends to recreate a poem in English (he stresses the importance of poetic rhythm), while at the same time being faithful to the original. Interestingly, Pound praised this translation, though he was also critical of its archaic diction. In fact, the American poet suggested in his reviews and personal letters that Binyon should try to approximate to "normal speech" (conversational English) in terms of both word order and lexical choices, but the translator did not incorporate this suggestion.

SAYERS (1949–62) (British) (the last 12 cantos of *Paradiso* translated by Barbara Reynolds) is an extremely interesting version of the *Comedy* which mirrors the transition from Romantic and Victorian ideas to the critical-interpretative approach. Sayers follows a foreignizing policy in terms of verse form by employing (quite successfully) Dante's *terza rima* in English (but also incorporates the naturalizing iambic pentameter). Sayers's use of perfect rhymes constrains the range of lexical choices available, and thus makes it difficult for her to keep close to the source text (she sternly opposes the literal method of the Victorians). Sayers is also one of the first translators of Dante to modernize diction slightly by introducing conversational English, though she is conditioned by the idea of decorum and so avoids slang and taboo language. In fact, in her version there are still literary (and rare) words which are removed from everyday English, and a Victorian influence can be detected in the limited use of archaism (traces of the historicizing policy). Sayers's greatest achievement (despite her toning down of slang and the informal) lies in the fact that she is the only translator to go some way towards reproducing Dante's mingling of styles: she retains the original Latin expressions and blends formal, archaic and colloquial English (an exoticizing policy). On the other hand, readability is greatly enhanced by eliminating the convoluted syntax and inversions favoured in the pre-19th-century tradition. Moreover, the Sayers version is highly creative (i.e. unfettered by a narrow view of fidelity) in terms of both wordplay (besides reproducing some original puns, she is one of the few translators to reproduce Dante's inventive use of evocative names in *Inferno*) and literary devices (e.g. enjambment and alliteration), all of which combine to make it a lively version. Sayers's theory of translation is ambivalent: she adopts the Romantic view (her aim is to reproduce the aesthetic effects of the source text), but she is also influenced by the critical-interpretative approach (she is influenced, in particular, by Dante's humour or burlesque). Her reception reflects the variety of 20th-century approaches. Praised by some, but attacked by others for the liveliness of her style (characterized by an "excessive" use of literary devices – such criticism reflecting the canon of transparency: the translator must keep a low profile so that his/her voice cannot be heard), she is also censured for her departures from the original and especially for forced or unnatural rhymes. Some later translators feel that Sayers's reform of diction was not fully achieved, because the language she employs is not vernacular enough for a 20th-century reader. This perspective is partly justifiable from the point of view of the 1980s and 1990s, but not if allowances are made for the fact that Sayers translated in 1949.

CIARDI (1977) (American) is another mildly foreignizing version of the *Comedy*: besides using *terza rima*, Ciardi retains most of the original Latin expressions. He also shows creativity in dealing with Dante's imagery. Ciardi's originality lies in the fact that he is the first 20th-century translator to adopt consistently the critical-interpretative approach (he appears to be influenced by Pound's views on translation). In fact, Ciardi is sceptical about the possibility of translating faithfully. Hence, rather than attempting to produce a mimetic text, he intends to recapture a few select qualities of the source text such as its poetic rhythm and idiomaticity (an outlook that sometimes leads him to rewrite the source text freely). Ciardi is more resolute than Sayers in breaking away from Victorian diction: his English is completely modern and idiomatic and, unlike the great majority of translators before him, he does not feel the need to tone down the impact of the obscene language appearing in *Inferno*. Ciardi's bold move towards the demotic and vernacular bridges the gap between the world of poets and that of translators: he is the first 20th-century translator to reform diction in keeping with modern theories of poetry (cf. Pound and Eliot). Hence, the following generations of translators, Pinski (1994) and Ellis (1994) in particular, are indebted to Ciardi for his original example.

MUSA (1971) (American) is the heir of the Victorian literal method, but rather than prose he employs iambic pentameter which, in his opinion, also facilitates literalness. Despite the fact that Musa claims to believe in two purposes of translation – producing aesthetic effects (to please and convince) and achieving fidelity – in actual fact he focuses only on the latter and thus strives to convey the original content. Musa is also a radical advocate of transparency: in his opinion the language of the target text must be simple (Sayers's diction is to be revised in terms of both syntax and diction, as he rejects any kind of ornate style) and must feature current usage (modernizing stance). Musa employs very few foregrounding effects (being again highly critical of Sayers's use of literary devices, especially when they create new effects not present in the source text): since a literary translation cannot be a poem, its language must not call attention to itself; Musa does not play with language creatively. Interestingly, he explicitly opposes free verse, which is only adequate, he claims, for poetic transposition. Musa's style accommodates the few taboo words shunned by Sayers and yet does not reproduce Dante's violent mingling of styles: rather, Musa achieves a balanced tone. Hence his version has been criticized for being flat and monotonous, but this is the price he had to pay for his theory of translation. It is to Musa's credit that he developed Sayers's and Ciardi's modernizing policy.

SISSON (1981) (British) uses iambic pentameter (naturalizing); he is critical of Sayers's diction and thus follows in Musa's footsteps by adopting the same modernizing stance. Sisson is a forceful advocate of transparency: he emphasizes Dante's clarity (cf. Eliot) and readability and creates a balanced tone (slang is avoided and no mixing of styles appears). Although Sisson stresses fidelity to the source text (which is why he does not employ *terza rima*, despite his arrangement of the verse in three-line stanzas), he differentiates himself from Musa by being less literal: Sisson contends that the translator's voice should be faintly heard so that it may balance the voice of the source-text writer. Aesthetic effects are still few (Sisson does not aim to produce a highly creative-poetical version) and there is little, if any, wordplay in his translation, but he takes some liberties with sounds (rhymes, etc.). He also introduces some variation in metre and rhythm (the length of lines varies between 13 syllables and nine). Sisson has been criticized for being static and flat (he keeps Dante's full stops at the end of each three-line unit, and does not make use of contractions) and for failing to produce a poetic version. Another criticism levelled against him is that he did not include explanatory notes and a fully-fledged commentary (a criticism reflecting the preconception that a translator must contribute to Dante scholarship). Like Musa, Sisson has the merit of modernizing Dante.

MANDELBAUM (1980–84) (American) shares some basic views with Sisson but produces a version quite different from his. Like Sisson he adopts the iambic pentameter, varying the number of syllables. Moreover, Mandelbaum's declaration of intent emphasizes two aspects of the source text's style: simplicity and violence of speech, though he does not replicate the latter in his version: there is no violent mingling of styles – he tends to create a middle tone not unlike Sisson's. Despite the fact that the Latin expressions are retained, Mandelbaum's version is highly readable (transparent) since it draws on current usage. However, the affinities with Sisson end here: Mandelbaum is keener on breaking away from Musa's literal stance and produces a more poetic version than Sisson's: Mandelbaum obviously has a different concept of translating: although fidelity remains his main objective he feels entitled to use any literary device available (without, however, adding to the original); moreover, Mandelbaum does not play with words, yet he manages to produce a "close phonic packing" by employing pure rhymes, pararhymes, assonance, alliteration and consonance, and thereby creates a varied rhythm, anticipating Pinski's use of sounds. Unfairly criticized for not being very exciting, Mandelbaum's version deserves attention in its own right.

PHILLIPS (1983) (British) is a naturalizing and quite traditional blank verse rewriting of *Inferno*, despite its retention of some foreignizing lexical items. In fact, Phillips is another 20th-century heir of the Romantic method: fidelity is his declared intent, but he also strives to mirror some of the aesthetic effects of the original. Phillips strikes a good compromise between these two intentions: his version is quite close to Dante's text, but it also gives life to a distinctive poetic rhythm. Some reviewers regard Phillips's blank verse as being of a higher quality than Sisson's. However, Phillips's style is far from being racy (e.g. wordplay and literary devices are used sparingly): its balanced tone, which makes this version highly readable, inevitably leads to the loss of Dante's vast range of styles. Phillips's translation, however, is fascinating in view of the fact that he illustrates it with 139 pictures which, besides amusing the reader, have the function of providing a commentary on the text. These pictures are extremely original: Phillips experiments and plays with images and colours in such a way that he succeeds in his intent of "pointing the reader to unexpected connections", a task facilitated by the translator-illustrator's own detailed notes to the pictures. Phillips makes a noteworthy contribution to the tradition of illustrating Dante (cf. Blake and Gustave Doré).

HALPERN (editor) (1993) assembles a version of *Inferno* by a group of contemporary English-speaking poets (Seamus Heaney, Mark Strand, Daniel Halpern, Galway Kinnell, Cynthia Macdonald, Amy Clampitt, Jorie Graham, Charles Wright, Richard Howard, Stanley Plumly, C.K. Williams, Robert Pinski, Susan Mitchell, Carolyn Forch, Richard Wilbur, W.S. Merwin, Alfred Corn, Sharon Olds, Deborah Digges, Robert Hass). A variety of methods is used: some translators, being deeply influenced by the critical-interpretative approach, use free verse (organic) and thus produce cantos in keeping with current trends in poetry; other translators have a more traditional stance and adopt either blank verse or *terza rima*, though their rewritings are also interesting. The Halpern edition develops Ciardi's diction much further: in some cantos not only is colloquial English used, but even informal expressions appear. The fact that many translators favouring different solutions present their efforts in a single volume explains why the Halpern edition reproduces Dante's range of styles and rhythms in an unprecedented manner.

ELLIS (1994) (British) has produced one of the most engaging and daring translations of *Inferno*. He employs free verse (organic) but imposes a degree of metrical regularity in terms of both number of words (seven–eight) and stresses per line. Clearly influenced by Eliot, Ellis has the merit of providing an alternative to *terza rima* and blank verse, thereby placing his work firmly in the critical-interpretative sector: he focuses on what he perceives to be the main qualities of the original: "liveliness and vigour". Although not even Ellis follows in Sayers's footsteps as regards the mingling of styles, he is one of the few translators (cf. Ciardi and Halpern edition) to bring Sayers's partially fulfilled task of modernizing Dante to its extreme and logical consequences. His version features highly idiomatic English ("the language of the 1980s and 1990s"), the emphasis being on spoken language. Monosyllabic words such as "get" and "got" are employed extensively together with contractions, while polysyllabic Latinate vocabulary tends to be avoided. Despite the fact that Ellis does not create a range of tones, he produces a lively version in which not only taboo language but even slang appears occasionally, though he is not as creative as Sayers where wordplay is concerned. Moreover, besides aiming at achieving fluency (transparency), Ellis also aims at reproducing the original's onward movement. He is, together with Pinski, the first translator after Sayers to address this question of the onward movement provided by Dante's use of *terza rima* and enjambment, by being concise (another essential aspect of Dante's style in Ellis's opinion) in terms of the number of words per line. Reviewers are at times unfairly critical of Ellis's modernizing stance, which indicates that a translator adopting a critical-interpretative approach is bound to meet considerable resistance whenever s/he makes large-scale choices at odds with mainstream or traditional ways of rewriting Dante.

PINSKY (1994) (American) develops Mandelbaum's ideas further and produces a poetical version of *Inferno*. Pinski is influenced by the critical-interpretative approach and thus focuses on one aspect of the source text: the musicality of its sound patterns. The main interest of Pinski's contribution consists in his alternative to a radically exoticizing *terza rima*: Pinski uses rhyme with a great deal of flexibility, since he is aware of the nature and constraints of the English language (which is poorer in perfect rhymes – the argument put forward by the opponents of *terza rima* in English) and therefore plays with sounds very skilfully in "faintly echoing rhymes". In fact, Pinski starts with a new definition of rhyme as "same consonant sounds at the end of words", though he also includes pure rhymes. Moreover, he tends not to translate closely line-for-line or tercet-for-tercet. Hence, Pinski can be placed in the same tradition as Ellis. Both aim at creating poems in their own right that do not simply convey the content of the source text (though both their versions are accurate and not loose paraphrases) but focus on form and are bent on reproducing the quick flow (or onward movement) of the original. In fact Pinski exploits a wide range of literary devices, though he is less creative than Sayers when it comes to wordplay. Pinski's version, praised and well received, is not as vernacular as Ellis's but still features colloquial English.

EDOARDO CRISAFULLI

Further Reading

Caesar, Michael (editor), *Dante: The Critical Heritage, 1314 (?)–1870*, London and New York: Routledge, 1989

Crisafulli, Edoardo, "Dante's Poems in English and the Question of Compensation", *The Translator*, 2/2 (1996) pp. 259–76

Crisafulli, Edoardo, "The Translator as Textual Critic and the Potential of Transparent Discourse", *The Translator*, 5/1 (1999) pp. 83–107

Cunningham, Gilbert F., *The Divine Comedy in English: A Critical Bibliography*, vol. 1: *1782–1900*, vol. 2: *1901–1966*, Edinburgh: Oliver and Boyd, 1965–66; New York: Barnes and Noble, 1965–67

De Sua, William J., *Dante into English: A Study of the Translation of the Divine Comedy in Britain and America*, Chapel Hill: University of North Carolina Press, 1964

Eliot, T.S., "Dante", reprinted in *Selected Essays*, 3rd edition, London: Faber, 1951, pp. 237–77 (1st edition, 1932)

Ellis, Steve, *Dante and English Poetry: Shelley to T.S. Eliot*, Cambridge and New York: Cambridge University Press, 1983

Friedrich, Werner P., *Dante's Fame Abroad, 1350–1850*, Chapel Hill: University of North Carolina Press, 1950

Musa, Mark, "On Translating Dante", *Yearbook of Comparative and General Literature*, 19 (1970) pp. 28–38

Pite, Ralph, *The Circle of Our Vision: Dante's Presence in English Romantic Poetry*, Oxford: Clarendon Press, and New York: Oxford University Press, 1994

Reynolds, Barbara, "English Fashions in Translating Dante", *Forum for Modern Language Studies*, 1/2 (April 1965) pp. 117–25

Reynolds, Barbara, "Translating Dante in the 1990s", *Translation and Literature*, 4/2 (1995) pp. 221–37

Tinkler-Villani, V., *Visions of Dante in English Poetry: Translations of the Commedia from Jonathan Richardson to William Blake*, Amsterdam: Rodopi, 1989

Wallace, David, "Dante in English" in *The Cambridge Companion to Dante*, edited by Rachel Jacoff, Cambridge and New York: Cambridge University Press, 1993, pp. 237–58

Mahmūd Darwīsh 1941–

Palestinian poet and prose writer

Biography

Born in al-Birwa, near Acre, Palestine in 1941. From 1948 to 1949 he was a refugee in the Lebanon. Attended Arab elementary and secondary schools in Galilee. He was the editor of the newspaper *Al-Ittiḥād* [Unity] in Haifa. From the early years of his poetic career he devoted his poetic talent to the cause of Palestine. Member of the Israeli Communist Party, 1961–71. His first collection of poetry, *'Aṣāfīr bilā ajniḥah* [Sparrows without Wings], was published in 1960 and he was arrested and imprisoned the following year. His next three books of poems were published between 1965 and 1967 and on each occasion he was again arrested and imprisoned. When he was released he was subject to long periods of house arrest. He moved to Egypt in 1970 and to Beirut the following year where he remained until the Israeli invasion of Lebanon in 1982. He currently lives in Paris.

Translations

Selections of Poetry

Bennani, B.M., *Splinters of Bone*, New York: Greenfield Review Press, 1974

Kabbani, Rana, *Sand, and Other Poems*, New York: KPI, 1986

Johnson-Davies, Denys, *The Music of Human Flesh*, with an introduction, London: Heinemann, and Washington, DC: Three Continents Press, 1980

Wedde, Ian and Fawwaz Tuqan, *Selected Poems*, with an introduction, Cheadle, Cheshire: Carcanet Press, 1973

Anthologies

Elmessiri, Abdelwahab M., *A Lover from Palestine and Other Poems: An Anthology of Palestinian Poetry* (bilingual edition), Washington, DC: Three Continents Press, 1970

Al-Udhari, Abdullah, in his *Victims of a Map* (bilingual edition), London: Al Saqi Books, 1984

Other Writing

Dhākira lil-nisyān, 1985

Muhawi, Ibrahim, *Memory for Forgetfulness: August, Beirut, 1982*, with an introduction, Berkeley: University of California Press, 1995

The best known of the so-called Palestinian "resistance poets" outside his native country, Mahmūd Darwīsh is almost certainly also the most frequently translated, selections of his poetry having appeared in at least 20 languages. Translations of his verse are to be found not only in the volumes listed above, but also in almost every anthology of modern Arabic poetry in translation. His writing, like that of his fellow "resistance poets", is marked by his personal experience as a refugee and exile not only outside his own country but also within it, an experience that mirrors that of the Palestinian people as a whole. Like most contemporary Arabic verse, his poetry is written in various forms of free verse, heavily influenced on a formal level by 20th-century Western poetry, with the occasional excursus into the prose poem. It is particularly notable for the vividness of its imagery, which at times involves also the use of a rich symbolism: images directly relevant to the Palestine situation (wounds, martyrdom, death, etc.) are linked with images whose power derives from the natural environment of the Middle East (water, rain, sand, desert, etc.); allusions to the classical Arabic literary heritage rub shoulders with references to contemporary Palestinian politics. Like many contemporary Arab poets, Darwīsh has no compunction about mingling Islamic and Christian symbolism, the suffering of Christ providing a particularly appropriate set of imagery for a Palestinian poet. Other images have an erotic flavour, the poet's homeland at times being equated with the "beloved" of mystical tradition.

Although some commentators have played down Darwīsh's poetry as subservient to his political "message", branding him a "one-subject" poet, his best poems succeed in conveying a powerful sense of the Palestinian plight through the use of vivid imagery that has a universal appeal. This imagery has become less straightforward as Darwīsh has developed as a poet, but his language has never reached the obscurity of contemporaries such as Adūnīs. WEDDE & TUQAN (1973) draw attention in their introduction to some of the difficulties of translating Darwīsh, referring in particular to the danger of trying to copy Arabic rhyme or metre too closely, but these problems are inherent in the translation of modern Arabic poetry generally, rather than Darwīsh in particular: as JOHNSON-DAVIES (1980) suggests, the main problem for the Western reader is likely to lie less in Darwīsh's poetical style than in his subject-matter.

Most anthologies of Darwīsh's poetry in translation contain a selection of poems culled from several volumes of the original Arabic, and a number of poems have been published in versions by different translators. A comparison of the different versions often reveals remarkable similarities of both approach and effect, to the extent that individual lines not infrequently appear identically in different translators' versions. Less agreement appears to be found on the extent to which the translator should help the reader by providing notes to explain the context of a poem or an obscure allusion. In contrast to both Johnson-Davies and Wedde & Tuqan, for example, who supply the occasional note of this kind, KABBANI (1986) provides no notes at all, presumably on the grounds that she does not wish to come between the poem and the reader. Although this sentiment may generally be commended, the novice reader, faced with the classical allusions of "Al-Mutanabbi's Voyage into Egypt", or the contemporary references to the killer of Robert Kennedy in the extended poem "Sirhan drinks his coffee in the cafeteria", is arguably in need of some guidance. AL-UDHARI's (1984) bilingual anthology of poetry by Darwīsh, Adūnīs and Samīh al-Qāsim is an interesting venture, though the format is unlikely to hold special appeal, except to readers reasonably fluent in both languages.

It is perhaps ironic that one of the most powerful works to emerge from the pen of a writer universally known as a poet should be, at least nominally, in prose. Perhaps best viewed as an extended prose-poem, *Dhākira lil-nisyān*, written in a three-month frenzy of creativity in 1985, is an autobiographically based account of 6 August (Hiroshima Day) 1982, when the Israeli bombardment of Beirut reached a searing climax. Darwīsh's memoir begins with the author awakening from a dream to reflect at length not only on the Israeli siege of Beirut itself, but also on the Palestinian destiny, the Palestinian experience of Beirut, Arab nationalism, and more generally on the meaning of identity, exile and the place of the writer in history. Many of the images familiar from Darwīsh's poetry reappear here in a new guise. Texts from the Arab classical heritage, including the historian Ibn Kathīr's *al-Bidāya wa-al-nihāya* ("The Beginning and the End") and Usāma ibn Munqidh's *An Arab-Syrian Gentleman and Warrior in the Period of the Crusades*, are quoted in support of Darwīsh's bleak vision. The Israeli invasion of Lebanon was a seminal event for many Arab intellectuals, prompting the poet Khalīl Hāwī to take his own life, an event referred to by Darwīsh himself; the author's concluding words ("I don't see a shore. I don't see a dove") suggest that his vision of the future does not include an end to the Palestinians' long exile.

The problems posed for the translator by this tour de force of Arabic literary expression are discussed at some length by MUHAWI (1995), who draws attention, *inter alia*, to the differences between the Arabic and English tense systems, and notes, disarmingly, that Darwīsh's practice of writing "long ambiguous sentences, with multiple levels of meaning" produces a text that is "difficult to translate". In fact, Muhawi's version more than does justice to the power of the original Arabic, demonstrating a sensitivity to the rhythms of the English language that fully matches the subtly ironic flavour of the original. The footnotes, which combine an introduction to the political context with an explanation of Darwīsh's more obscure literary and cultural allusions, strike a finely judged balance between spoon-feeding the reader and letting the literary text speak for itself, and as such, may well be considered a model of their kind.

PAUL STARKEY

Further Reading

Elmessiri, Abdelwahab M., *The Palestinian Wedding: A Bilingual Anthology of Contemporary Palestinian Resistance Poetry*, Washington, DC: Three Continents Press, 1982

Jayyusi, Salma Khadra, *Anthology of Modern Palestinian Literature*, New York: Columbia University Press, 1992

Sulaiman, Khalid A., *Palestine and Modern Arab Poetry*, London: Zed, 1984

See also translators' introductions to Johnson-Davies, Mahawi, and Wedde & Tuqan

Dazai Osamu 1909–1948

Japanese novelist and short-story writer

Biography

Born Tsushima Shūji, 19 June 1909 in Kanegi, Aomori, northern Japan, into a prominent land-owning family. His first short story was published in his school magazine when he was nearly 16. In 1927 he began to neglect his studies. He made the first of several suicide attempts in December 1929. In 1930 he went to Tokyo Imperial University, where he studied French literature but did not complete his degree. He married twice, in 1931 and 1939, and had children. His involvement with the illegal Communist Party, his illness-induced abuse of drugs, his drinking and his generally dissolute life led to estrangement from the rest of the family.

In the story "Train", published 1933 under the pseudonym by which he became famous, Dazai experimented with the first-person semi-autobiographical form associated with his influence on Japanese fiction. His work became popular after World War II and he was awarded the Kitamura Tōkoku prize in 1939. His masterpiece is the novel *Shayō* (1947; translated as *The Setting Sun*, 1956). His writing is marked by pessimism and admired for the beauty of its style.

Dazai died 13 June 1948, when, with a woman companion, he drowned himself in the Tamagawa Canal in Tokyo.

Translations

Novels

Shayō, 1947

Keene, Donald, *The Setting Sun*, with an introduction, Norfolk, Connecticut: New Directions, 1956; London: Peter Owen, 1958

Ningen shikkaku, 1948

Keene, Donald, *No Longer Human*, with an introduction, Norfolk, Connecticut: New Directions, 1958; London: Peter Owen, 1959

Selections of Short Stories

Lyons, Phyllis I., *The Saga of Dazai Osamu: A Critical Study with Translations*, Stanford, California: Stanford University Press, 1985 (contains the novel *Tsugaru* and 5 stories: "Recollections", translation of "Omoide", 1933; "Eight Views of Tokyo", translation of "Tokyo Hakkei", 1941; "Going Home", translation of "Kikyōrai", 1943; "Hometown", translation of "Kokyō", 1943; "An Almanac of Pain", translation of "Kunō no nenkan", 1946)

McCarthy, Ralph F., *Run, Melos! and Other Stories*, Tokyo: Kodansha, 1988

McCarthy, Ralph F., *Self Portraits: Tales from the Life of Japan's Great Decadent Romantic*, with an introduction, Tokyo and New York: Kodansha, 1991 (contains "Train", translation of "Ressha", 1933; "Female", translation of "Mesu ni tsuite", 1936; "A Promise Fulfilled", translation of "Mangan", 1938; "One Hundred Views of Mount Fuji", translation of "Fugaku Hyakkei", 1939; "I Can Speak"; "A Little Beauty", translation of "Bishōjo", 1939; "Canis familiaris", translation of "Chikukendan", 1939; "Seascape with Figures in Gold", translation of "Ōgon Fūkei", 1939; "No Kidding", translation of "Zakyō ni arazu", 1940; "My Elder Brothers", translation of "Anitachi", 1940; "Thinking of Zenzō", translation of "Zenzō o omou", 1940; "Eight Scenes from Tokyo", translation of "Tokyo Hakkei", 1941; "Early Light", translation of "Hakumei", 1946; "Garden", translation of "Niwa", 1946; "Two Little Words", translation of "Oya to iu niji", 1946; "Merry Christmas", translation of "Merii Kurisumasu", 1947; "Handsome Devils and Cigarettes" translation of "Bidanshi to tabako", 1948; "Cherries", translation of "Ōtō", 1948)

McCarthy, Ralph F., *Blue Bamboo: Tales of Fantasy and Romance*, Tokyo, New York, and London: Kodansha, 1993 (contains "On Love and Beauty", translation of "Ai to bi ni tsuite", 1939; "Cherry Leaves and the Whistler", translation of "Hazakura to mateki", 1939; "The Chrysanthemum Spirit", translation of "Seihintan", 1941; "The Mermaid and the Samurai", translation of "Ningyo no umni", 1944; "Blue Bamboo", translation of "Chikusei", 1945; "Romanesque", translation of "Romanesuku", 1934; "Lanterns of Romance", translation of "Roman dōrō", 1940–41)

O'Brien, James, *Dazai Osamu: Selected Stories and Sketches*, with an introduction, Ithaca, New York: Cornell University China–Japan Program, 1983 (contains 16 stories)

O'Brien, James, *Crackling Mountain and Other Stories*, Rutland, Vermont: Tuttle, 1989; London: Peter Owen, 1990 (contains 8 of the 16 stories from O'Brien 1983: "Memories", translation of "Omoide", 1933; "Undine", translation of "Gyofukuki", 1934; "Monkey Island", translation of "Sarugashima", 1935; "On the Question of Apparel", translation of "Fukusō ni tsuite", 1941; "The Monkey's Mound", translation of "Saruzuka", 1944; "A Poor Man's Got His Pride", translation of "Hin no iji", 1944; "Taking the Wen Away", translation of "Kobutori", 1945; "The Sound of Hammering", translation of "Tokatonton", 1947; and 3 new ones: "Crackling Mountain", translation of "Kachikachiyama", 1945; "Melos, Run", translation of "Hashire Merosu", 1940; "Heed My Plea", translation of "Kakekomi uttae", 1940)

Short Stories

"Shin'yū kōkan", 1946

Morris, Ivan, "A Visitor", in *Modern Japanese Stories*, edited by Morris, London: Eyre and Spottiswoode, 1961, Rutland, Vermont: Tuttle, 1962; as "The Courtesy Call", in *The World of Japanese Fiction*, edited by Yoshinobu Hakutani and Arthur O. Lewis, New York: Dutton, 1973

"Viyon no tsuma", 1947

Keene, Donald, "Villon's Wife", in *Modern Japanese Literature: An Anthology*, edited by Keene, New York: Grove Press, and London: Thames and Hudson, 1956

The Setting Sun and *No Longer Human* are Dazai's two major postwar novels. Both of them were translated by KEENE as early as the 1950s, and his versions have been reprinted several times. Both novels were published in the US by James Laughlin's New Directions, which set the course of the new American literature in the 1950s and 1960s. Dazai was fortunate to have such an eminent publisher, and such a reliable translator as Keene, who posed the standard for the translators who followed.

Dazai inherited the form of the "I-novel" (*watakushi shōsetsu*), the dominant form of modern Japanese fiction, in which it is understood that the novelist's life is often equated with the novel. One group of Dazai's short stories also represents this peculiar Japanese form of autobiographical fiction; in fact, most of his best-known stories are based on his self-destructive and suicidal life. Dazai attempted suicide at least four times before he finally succeeded in "love suicide" (double suicide) in 1948. He was a drug addict, a heavy drinker, and a notorious womanizer.

It was Dazai's mastery of narration that distinguished him from many other "I-novelists", who were apt to indulge in the monotonous description of trivial everyday life. The best part of his fiction lies in his charming narrative voice, which is in most cases first-person and manipulated with rare dexterity. Dazai's translators will be evaluated by how they emulate his virtuosity with language. KEENE (1956, 1958) is generally successful in rendering Dazai's tone in English. Dazai's narrative style is often based on colloquial Japanese, so the translator must understand not only the language but also the culture from which the language emerges. Like many other intellectuals of his time, Dazai read a great amount of Western literature in translation, and his style was much influenced by Western idiom, which, in theory, should make the translator's job easier. Yet though his style is relatively plain, his way of thinking is deeply rooted in the Japanese language. For those who are not familiar with "Japanese stream-of-consciousness", Dazai's discourse looks simply confounding. In addition, the translator confronts obstacles such as honorific language, dialects, the speech differences between classes and genders. Keene was concerned less with meticulously following the original texts than with capturing the spirit of Dazai's highly synthesized narrative voice. The result intrigued English-speaking readers, who were struck by an utterly different narrative form. Keene's pioneering translations remain readable and creative even today. The two novels have translator's introductions that offer valuable information on Japanese culture.

MORRIS's translation (1961) of the story "Shin'yū kōkan" is similarly masterly; it almost seems as if Dazai had switched from his native tongue to English. It is a pity that neither Morris's work nor Keene's translation of "Viyon no tsuma" is easily available to general readers.

Dazai, as well as being a novelist, was also a good and prolific short story writer. In the 1960s and 1970s a considerable number of his stories were translated into English by various hands, but they remain scattered in periodicals (for details see Lewell, 1993). However, the 1980s saw two landmarks in the history of the translation of Dazai's works into English. One is O'BRIEN's 1983 selection, which contains 16 stories and an informative introduction, notes and a glossary of certain Japanese words, mostly for clothes, that occur in the source texts. The other one is LYONS's 1985 book, of which the first half is dedicated to a comprehensive scholarly discussion and the other half consists of her translations of the novel *Tsugaru* (1944) and five short stories. O'Brien gives the date of the publication of "Omoide" as 1934, but, as Lyons states, it was first published in the coterie magazine *Kaihyō* in 1933 before appearing in Dazai's *Bannen* [The Declining Years] in 1934.

The emergence of these two translators was a major breakthrough. Lyons in particular deserves praise not only for her critical insight but also for her translation of the novel *Tsugaru*. Nevertheless, their works seemed to be addressed to academics rather than to the general public. It was not until the 1990s that volumes of short stories began to be published that seemed more geared to the general reader. At least three collections are available. There are some others, including McCarthy's *Run, Melos! and Other Stories* (1988), but at present they are not available in the UK. O'BRIEN's *Crackling Mountain and Other Stories* (1989) developed from his earlier book, from which eight stories were dropped and three were added for this edition. O'Brien endeavored to retain Dazai's idiosyncrasies, such as his frequent omission of quotation marks for apparently direct quotations; this violates standard English practice, but the result is generally successful. Each story in this volume is furnished with a brief but helpful note.

The translator's introduction to MCCARTHY (1991, *Self Portraits*) is mainly biographical, and features numerous photographs of Dazai from his childhood to the very end, which are hard to find in other English editions. MCCARTHY's 1993 collection contains as the subtitle suggests, romantic tales, fantastic allegories, and fables, and offers readers another side of Dazai. Thus thanks to McCarthy's efforts today's readers may investigate a range of Dazai's literary output that was inconceivable a decade ago.

TETSUYA TAGUCHI

Further Reading

Chia, Joseph, *Dazai Osamu: Life and Art*, Singapore: National University of Singapore, 1988

Lewell, John, *Modern Japanese Novelists: A Biographical Dictionary*, Tokyo and New York: Kodansha, 1993, pp. 69–72

Miyoshi, Masao, *Accomplices of Silence: The Modern Japanese Novel*, Berkeley: University of California Press, 1974

O'Brien, James, *Dazai Osamu*, New York: Twayne, 1975

O'Brien, James, *Akutagawa and Dazai: Instances of Literary Adaptation*, Tempe: Arizona State University Press, 1988

Wolfe, Alan Stephen, *Suicidal Narrative in Modern Japan: The Case of Dazai Osamu*, Princeton, New Jersey: Princeton University Press, 1990

Deconstruction and Literary Translation

In order to understand the importance of Deconstruction for literary translation it is necessary to take into account the history of translation theory which has, since Roman times, been oscillating between two extremes: the text-oriented or literal and the reader-oriented or free translation. The latter was particularly favoured by Roman writers such as Cicero and Pliny, by Renaissance translators, and by Nicolas Perrot d'Ablancourt (1606–64), and systematically practised during the European Enlightenment: by Dryden in England and Gottsched in Germany. The authors of the Enlightenment believed that it was both possible and desirable to render the gist of a text in the target language and to neglect the idiosyncrasies of the source language. They took the view, semiotically speaking, that the literary text is a *structure of signifieds* and that the peculiarities that appear in the source language on the *level of the signifiers* (the *expression plane*) can safely be neglected. For didactic reasons they were primarily interested in translating for the general public and therefore preferred the reader-oriented or free translation, thus tending to reduce the text to a message considered to be the same in all languages.

Unlike the rationalist writers of the Enlightenment, Romantics such as Chateaubriand (1768–1848) and Friedrich Schleiermacher (1768–1834) adopted a text-oriented point of view, attempting to reproduce the particularities and idiosyncrasies of the original. Schleiermacher, for example, believed in the necessity of reproducing the *strangeness* of the original and the source language in the target language and was strongly opposed to all rationalist attempts to find a conceptual equivalent of the original in the target language, an equivalent that would make the foreign text more readable, more acceptable in its new cultural context.

The Romantic tradition was later revived by Walter Benjamin (1892–1940) in his well-known essay "The Task of the Translator" (1968; "Die Aufgabe des Übersetzers", 1923) and by deconstructivist authors such as Jacques Derrida (1930–) and Paul de Man (1919–83). In spite of their divergent views on politics, philosophy and literature (Benjamin was one of the founders of critical theory of the so-called Frankfurt School, de Man represented one of the more extreme brands of American literary Deconstruction, while Derrida introduced the word "Deconstruction" into the philosophical debate in France), these three authors agree on one essential point: that a French or German literary or philosophical text has no conceptual equivalent in English or Spanish, and that what matters in translation is not the conceptual level of the signified, but the level of the signifiers (the expression plane) which has no equivalent in another language.

In his essay, Benjamin puts forward two crucial ideas: he argues that art and literature are not produced for the listener, the spectator or the reader, because art and literature serve their own purpose; he denies that the task of the translator consists in reproducing the conceptual content of a text and instead insists on the incommunicable form of the text, on its "way of saying" ("die Art des Meinens"). It is the well-nigh impossible task of the translator to render this incommunicable form of the original in the target language.

It is hardly surprising that the two most important deconstructivists – Derrida and de Man – were fascinated by Benjamin's essay "The Task of the Translator" and commented on it in great detail. Like the Romantics, like Benjamin, the authors of Deconstruction reject the rationalist idea that there exists a one-to-one correspondence between signifier and signified, that synonyms can be treated as equivalents and that the words of a source language have equivalents or synonyms in a target language. Derrida for example holds that the repetition of a word (within one and the same language) cannot be viewed as a reproduction of the same, the identical or the synonymous, for whenever a sign is repeated it (re-)appears in a different context and the shift in context alters its meaning. He calls this process *iterability (itérabilité)* and tries to show how repetition in the sense of *iterability* leads not to the consolidation but to the disintegration of textual meaning.

It goes without saying that translation is also a form of repetition or iterability, since each translated word, sentence or idiom moves from one linguistic and cultural context into another. In this new context the signifiers of the original are replaced by new signifiers, which acquire new connotations, new meanings and new cultural values. Considering this shift in meaning that inevitably accompanies each translation process, Derrida concludes that translation is aporetic: it is at the same time necessary and impossible.

In his article "Des tours de Babel" (1980) he tries to illustrate the impossibility (the aporetic character) of translation by pointing out that the God of Babel ordered and at the same time prohibited translation by imposing on the people of Babel his unique and untranslatable *name*. God thus condemned them to the impossible task of translation: to the task of finding linguistic equivalents which according to Romanticism and Deconstruction do not exist – or rather, cannot exist, because each signifier is unique.

In some respects Paul de Man continues Derrida's argument when he insists on the aporetic character of translation (as necessary but impossible) and points out that Benjamin's "Aufgabe" does not only mean "task" but also, and possibly primarily, giving up – capitulation before a sheer impossible task. (The word *Aufgabe* can mean both *task* or *giving up*.) Referring to an "aporia between freedom and faithfulness", de Man asserts that the original does not contain a meaning (a *signified*) that could be translated, for it is merely a collusion of polysemic signifiers that have no equivalent in another language. Eve Tavor Bannet aptly points out (1993) that in the deconstructive context literary criticism and translation "kill the original to supplant it". They replace it by creating their own meaning, which may or may not be that of the original.

From a semiotic point of view, the deconstructive approach appears not only as radical but as rather one-sided: how do we *recognize* in Dorothy Bussy's *Strait is the Gate* (1924) André Gide's *La Porte étroite* (1909)? As long as we adopt de Man's and Derrida's deconstructivist point of view, there is no reason why we should *recognize* Gide's original in Bussy's translation, why we should be able to *identify* the English text as being Gide's novel. Although the deconstructivists may be right in assuming that the English translation produces substantial shifts in meaning for cultural and linguistic reasons, the semioticians are also correct in assuming that we recognize Gide's original in the English version, because the latter reproduces certain fundamental semantic, syntactic, and narrative structures of the original. These structures are at least as important as the iterabilities and aporias discovered by Benjamin and the deconstructivists, for they explain why – in spite of all the aporias – literary translation has been reasonably successful in the past.

PETER V. ZIMA

See also the entry Structuralism & Post-structuralism and Literary Translation

Further Reading

Benjamin, Walter, "The Task of the Translator", translated by Harry Zohn, in *Illuminations*, by Benjamin, edited by Hannah Arendt, New York: Harcourt Brace, 1968; London: Collins, 1973

de Man, Paul, *The Resistance to Theory*, Minneapolis: University of Minnesota Press, 1986

Derrida, Jacques, "Des tours de Babel" in his *Psyché: Inventions de l'autre*, Paris: Galilée, 1987

Gentzler, Edwin, "Deconstruction" in his *Contemporary Translation Theories*, London and New York: Routledge, 1993

Tavor Bannet, Eve, "The Scene of Translation: After Jakobson, Benjamin, de Man and Derrida", *New Literary History*, 24 (1993)

Zima, Pierre V., *La Déconstruction: Une critique*, Paris: Presses Universitaires de France, 1994

Eduardo De Filippo 1900–1984

Italian dramatist, actor-manager and director

Biography

Born Eduardo Passarelli, 24 May 1900, in Naples. He was the illegitimate son of the actor-manager and playwright Eduardo Scarpetta and Luisa De Filippo. He went to school at the Istituto Chierchia in Naples and as a child acted with his father's theatre company, the Scarpetta troupe, making his stage debut in 1904. He performed with the Vincento Scarpetta company from 1914 to 1920, and then served in the Italian army for two years. He wrote his first comedy, *Farmacia di turno*, in 1920. He married the actress Dorothy Pennington in 1928. He worked with a number of other companies until 1932, when he formed the Teatro Umoristico di Eduardo De Filippo con Titina e Peppino with his brother Peppino and his sister Titina. He toured with the company, writing prolifically and directing his own plays for the company until 1945, when Peppino left to work separately, and Eduardo set up Il Teatro di Eduardo with Titina. This became a successful touring company until 1954, De Filippo producing and directing many of his own and other writers' plays for the company. From 1954 the company was based in the Teatro San Ferdinando in Naples, which De Filippo renovated, and of which he became director and owner. From the 1950s, De Filippo also directed and acted in films of his plays. He separated from his first wife in 1952 and married Thea Prandi in 1956, having had two children before marriage. They separated in 1959; she died in 1961. His last marriage was to Isabella Quarantotti in 1977. De Filippo toured Austria, Belgium, Hungary, Poland and Russia with the company in 1962. He was awarded the Institute of Italian Drama prize in 1951 and 1968, the Feltrinelli prize in 1972, and the Pirandello prize in 1975. He was named Senator for Life of the Italian Republic in 1981. Died in Rome, 31 October 1984.

De Filippo was a major figure in Italian theatre of the 20th century and a prolific writer for both the stage and screen. His works, set in Naples and written in Neapolitan dialect, are in the *commedia dell'arte* tradition of popular theatre. His writing is often compared with that of Luigi Pirandello, with whom he collaborated and whose writing often inspired De Filippo's own work. His best-known plays are *Sik-Sik, l'artefice magico* (1929; *Sik, Sik, the Masterful Magician*); *Napoli milionaria!* (*Napoli Milionaria*), 1945, which was made into a film in 1950; *Questi fantasmi!* (*Oh, These Ghosts!*), 1946; *Filumena Marturano* (*Filumena*), 1946; *La grande magia* (*Grand Magic*) 1948 ; *Sabato, domenica e lunedì* (*Saturday, Sunday, Monday*), 1959, which was produced successfully in an English version in London in 1973; and *L'arte della commedia* (*The Art of Comedy*), 1965.

Translations

Selections of Plays

Ardito, Carlo, *Three Plays*, London: Hamish Hamilton, 1976 (contains *The Local Authority*, *Grand Magic*, *Filumena Marturano*); augmented as *Four Plays: Eduardo De Filippo*, with an introduction, London: Methuen, 1992 (includes *Napoli Milionaria*, translated by N.F. Simpson, adapted by Peter Tinniswood)

Plays

Sik-Sik, l'artefice magico, 1932, produced 1929

Blander, Robert G. *Sik-Sik, The Masterful Magician*, in *Italian Quarterly*, 11/43 (Winter 1967)

Napoli milionaria!, 1946, produced 1945
Simpson, N.F., adapted by Peter Tinniswood, *Napoli Milionaria*, in *Four Plays: Eduardo De Filippo*, translated by Carlo Ardito, 1992

Filumena Marturano, 1946
Ardito, Carlo, *Filumena Marturano* in *Three Plays*, translated by Ardito, 1976
Bentley, Eric, *Filumena Marturano* in *The Genius of the Italian Theater*, edited by Bentley, New York: New American Library, 1964
Waterhouse, Keith and Willis Hall, *Filumena*, London: Heinemann, 1978
Wertenbaker, Timberlake, *Filumena*, London: Methuen, 1998

La grande magia, 1948
Ardito, Carlo, *Grand Magic*, in *Three Plays*, translated by Ardito, 1976

Le voci de dentro, 1948, produced 1949
Smith, James, *Inner Voices*, *Italian Theater Review*, 6/2 (1957)

Natale in casa Cupiello, 1959, produced 1931, revised version produced 1942
Stott, Mike, *Ducking Out*, produced 1982

Sabato, domenica e lunedì, 1959
Waterhouse, Keith and Willis Hall, *Saturday, Sunday, Monday*, London: Heinemann, 1974

Il sindaco del Rione Sanità, 1961, produced 1960
Ardito, Carlo, *The Local Authority*, in *Three Plays*, translated by Ardito, 1976

From the outset, Eduardo De Filippo has had champions of the highest calibre in the English-speaking world, all fulsome in their praise of his work, but united in their unhelpful belief that it would suffer as much damage in the move from one culture to another as would vintage wine.

Thornton Wilder, Harold Acton and Eric Bentley were all familiar with De Filippo's work in the original, and agreed that it was better left there. "Eduardo's best plays defy the translator's exertions", wrote Acton, while Wilder, himself a playwright of considerable ability, refused to attempt a translation on the grounds that it would be easier to create a new play than to enter into "the labyrinths of Eduardo's Neapolitan characters and language".

The crux of the problem lay in that specifically Neapolitan culture and theatrical tradition to which De Filippo belonged. It makes no more sense to describe him as "Italian" than to describe Dylan Thomas as "British". De Filippo was Neapolitan to the marrow. His first name was always given the dialect spelling (Eduardo, instead of Edoardo) and once he attained fame he was invariably referred to by that name alone. Naples was as much a character in his plays as any of the inquisitive, mystified, dignified little men whose dramas he wrote and performed.

De Filippo was a "*figlio d'arte*", born to the theatrical profession, the illegitimate son of Eduardo Scarpetta, another great Neapolitan actor-author, and his theatre demonstrates what it means to live inside a tradition. He was himself an actor-author, son, brother and father of actor-authors. For a hundred years, from the middle of the 19th century, Naples produced a vibrant theatre of its own, a theatre that may have cheerfully plundered French boulevard farce or *commedia dell'arte* for its plots but that was rooted in the spirit of tragic comedy exemplified by Pulcinella, the *commedia dell'arte* character identified with the city.

Wilder and Acton feared that the very strength of these roots would be a weakness if they were torn from the ground in which they had been planted, but it is more often the case that glibly cosmopolitan works have less international appeal than those that are firmly grounded in a culture. De Filippo wrote his early works in Neapolitan dialect, and if dialect was employed much less frequently in his later plays, it was never wholly eliminated. His language acquired much of its distinctive rhythmic flow, its unique blend of poetry, imagery and directness, its brutal humour, from its reliance on dialect usage. Any potential translator is faced with the problem of attempting to find some equivalent of the Neapolitan dimension, or at least of finding some means of not flattening the language, leaving it bereft of its life and sense of place.

The problem was initially avoided by having De Filippo himself perform his own work in the original. His first contacts with the English-speaking world occurred when he was invited to participate in the World Theatre Season at the Aldwych Theatre, London, in 1972. His own performance as Gennaro in *Napoli milionaria!* astounded critics precisely because his acting was so subdued and lacking in the histrionics that were conventionally associated with Italian acting, and the play itself aroused enormous enthusiasm.

In 1973 the National Theatre in London produced *Saturday, Sunday, Monday*, with a cast that included Lawrence Olivier and Joan Plowright, directed by Franco Zeffirelli. The translation was executed in an unusual style. Zeffirelli dictated a line-by-line version in his faltering English, and this was then turned into a performance text by WATERHOUSE & HALL, both noted playwrights and scriptwriters. The text was in standard English, but the cast, in a decision taken by them without the knowledge of the director, whose ear was not adequately attuned to English cadences, performed with Italian accents. Presumably this was some attempt to reproduce the colour they felt indispensable to the piece, and to convey a sense of identification with one place. The London success was not repeated in New York, where the work was taken off after a few performances.

This production was followed in 1977 by *Filumena Marturano*, with the same director, Zeffirelli, and translators, Waterhouse & Hall. The play focuses on the plight of Marturano, a woman from the slums of Naples who, after a lifelong relationship with the wealthy Domenico Soriano, discovers that he plans to abandon her now that she is no longer in her prime. The original had moved between dialect and standard Italian, but the translation is in standard English throughout, and this must be counted a loss. The earthiness, the spiciness, the bite of the dialect are lost, as is the sense of precarious movement between social classes. However, the writers have a flair for offhand humour and a capacity for pathos that match De Filippo's own gifts, and their idiom is sensitively chosen. A good example is their rendering of Filumena's powerful speech describing how, when still a young teenager but pregnant and abandoned on the streets of Naples, she addressed the Virgin Mary at a street shrine:

"You tell me. What can I do? You know everything – you know as well as I do why I'm living this dreadful life. Tell me what to do." But she said nothing. "Why don't you answer me?" Not a word. (...) And then I heard a voice, "A child is a child." I was frozen to the spot. Like stone.

This last line, which has attained the status of proverb in Italy, is one of those deceptively simple sentences that can never be adequately rendered so as to make clear the impact of the original, but the words convey something of the bite of the Neapolitan original.

De Filippo's principal English translator is Carlo ARDITO, some of whose versions have been performed on several occasions. He has been assisted by Isabella Quarantotti, De Filippo's third wife and a fluent English speaker, who has collaborated on several recent translations. Ardito, a professional translator and author with several original plays and adaptations to his credit, has declined to search for any regional voice to match De Filippo's Neapolitan, leaving that task to individual companies. At times the register can seem inappropriate, but Ardito has a good ear for rhythm and the spoken word, and his texts reproduce the energy, the occasional whimsy and the devastating change of tone of De Filippo's original. The two plays mentioned are the most "Pirandellian" of De Filippo's output, and the mixture of emotion and philosophy requires, and receives, sensitive handling.

The need to reproduce the identification of writer and city, or the associations with one city, has dogged all efforts to translate De Filippo into English. Mike STOTT transported *Natale in case Cupiello* (1942) into a North of England setting, renaming it *Ducking Out* (1982). Nothing remained of Naples. Perhaps the most successful attempt was the 1991 production at the National Theatre in London of *Napoli Milionaria*. The translation had been done earlier by N.F. SIMPSON (who had made his name in the 1960s as a writer of English Absurd drama), once again with the help of Isabella Quarantotti. He was given very little credit for his efforts, either on the programme or in the later published version. Full credit was given to the adapter, Peter TINNISWOOD. In reality, the adaptation was very faithful to the structures and plot lines of the original, and Tinniswood's main contribution was the successful choice of a regional voice to parallel De Filippo's Neapolitan. Himself a Liverpudlian, Tinniswood produced a version written "in the accents of my native city", but not, he wrote "in its dialect". It was a masterstroke. There is a swagger, an electric power to his language that is far removed from standard translator-speak. The idiom adopted gave De Filippo a context but maintained the spirit and flavour of the original work. The play is set in Naples in the immediate postwar period, when the city was on its knees and the Allied armies were in command. To change the setting would have made no sense, but the use of a language style with a lilt and rhythm of its own provided the ideal solution.

The lengthy speech delivered by Gennaro on his return from the labour camp in Germany demonstrates the sinewy strength and swing of the language.

Where was I? God knows. ... after a couple of days this German sergeant came up and asked me what my trade was. I thought suddenly: "Dear Christ, if I tell him I'm a tram driver, he's going to say: 'We've no use of tram drivers here, pal. So you're no use to us are you?' Rattatattatattatat. Good-bye, Gennaro. Good-bye, old son."

De Filippo is now routinely regarded in Britain as one of the European masters of this century, but it may be the fact that no American translator has found an idiom that does justice to his idiosyncratic language that is responsible for his failure to make comparable headway in North America.

JOSEPH FARRELL

Further Reading

Acton, Harold, "Eduardo De Filippo" in *The Genius of the Italian Theater*, edited by Eric Bentley, New York: New American Library, 1964

Bentley, Eric, "Introduction to Filumena Marturano" in *The Genius of the Italian Theater*, edited by Bentley, New York: New American Library, 1964

Cole, Toby and Helen Krich Chinoy, "Eduardo De Filippo" in *Actors on Acting*, revised edition, New York: Crown, 1970

D'Aponte, Mimi, "Encounters with Eduardo De Filippo", *Modern Drama*, 16 (December 1973) pp. 3–4

Mignone, Mario B., *Eduardo De Filippo*, Boston: Twayne, 1984

Definitions of Translation

According to *The Oxford Dictionary of English*, translation is "the action or process of turning from one language into another; also, the product of this; a version in a different language." Given that the concept of interlingual translation seems to be a straightforward one, it could be asked why there have been so many different theories and schools in this field. The answer to this question seems to be that the experts have tried to explain not so much what translation is as how to do it.

Many theoreticians give preceptive definitions of translation, i.e they attempt to describe what translations should be like, rather than defining the concept itself. The most famous is probably the one proposed by Alexander Fraser Tytler (who was accused of plagiarism by George Campbell) in his essay *The Principles of Translation* (1790), which stated that a translation should provide a complete transcript of the ideas of the original, and retain the style and manner of writing, as well as all the ease, of that same original.

The concept of translation has changed because of differences in focus in the various stages of its history. George Steiner distinguishes between four such stages, or "epochs", in *After Babel* (1975, 1st edition). His division was revised by Michel Ballard in *De Cicéron à Benjamin* (1992).

The first of these epochs is characterized by an empirical focus. Translation is defined in terms of what Steiner calls "primary statement and technical notation". Cicero, in *De optimo genere oratorum* (46 BC), and Horace, in *Ars Poetica* (c. 13 BC), lay the foundations of translation theory by not regarding word-by-word interlingual transcriptions as translations. Pliny the Younger, in his *Seventh Letter* (AD 100) defined translation as "an exceptional exercise in rhetoric".

Quintilian (AD ?35–?96) differentiates for the first time between translation and paraphrase. These two terms, however, would be frequently equated in centuries to come. John Dryden expressed in his 1680 Preface to Ovid's Epistles his preference for the middle way between word-for-word translation (or "metaphrase") and the excesses of translations whose fidelity to the original was so slight as to make them "imitations". He called this middle way "paraphrase".

Dryden felt the need to establish this balance in the light of the new trends. In the Renaissance, the love of original creation was the inspiration behind many translations. Gilles Ménage (1613–92) is said to have coined the metaphor "belles infidèles", utilized to refer to those 17th-century translations that were not such but, rather, went beyond paraphrase and became imitations of the original works. Abraham Cowley (who translated Pindar's *Odes* in 1656) defies the traditional concept of translation and attempts to re-define it:

> It does not at all trouble me that the *Grammarians* perhaps will not suffer this libertine way of rendring foreign Authors, to be called *Translation*; for I am not so much enamoured of the *Name Translator* as not to wish rather to be *Something Better*, though it want yet a *Name*.

This first epoch reached its conclusion in the early years of the 19th century, with the works of Friedrich Hölderlin. Other authors who belong to this empirical stage include St Jerome, Bruni, Luther, Montaigne, Ben Jonson, Huet, Cowley, Pope and Rochefort.

The second epoch was inaugurated by Tytler, mentioned above. It is characterized by a hermeneutic approach, which investigates what *understanding* a piece of speech means. Translation is defined in philosophical terms. Its nature is questioned in the framework of theories of language and mind. Friedrich Schleiermacher's *Über die verschiedenen Methoden des Übersetzens* (1813) signals the end of this period in translation theory. Schlegel, Humboldt, Goethe, Schopenhauer, Matthew Arnold, Valéry, Ezra Pound, I.A. Richards, Ortega y Gasset and Walter Benjamin figure among the authors who supported this approach.

The third epoch is characterized by an approach nurtured by Formalism. The Russian and Czech scholars who were heirs to this movement, with Andrei Fedorov in the lead, applied linguistic theory and statistics to translation. J.C. Catford defined translation in purely linguistic terms in his seminal work *A Linguistic Theory of Translation* (London: Oxford University Press, 1965): "Translation is an operation performed on languages: a process of substituting a text in one language for a text in another". Roman Jakobson, in his 1959 essay "On linguistic aspects of translation", states: "*Translation proper*, or interlingual translation, is an interpretation of verbal signs by signs in some other language." (Steiner, 1975).

This view would be contested in the late 1970s and the 1980s, when progress in textual linguistics and the application of other related disciplines, such as anthropology, would highlight the insufficiency of linguistics with regard to the study of translation.

The fourth epoch constitutes a return to the principles advanced in the second one. Walter Benjamin's "Die Aufgabe des Übersetzers" (1923), aided by the influence of Heidegger and Gadamer, brought on a reversion to hermeneutic inquiries. Benjamin, like Goethe a century before, viewed translation as metamorphosis. He defines translation as the passage from one language to another, through a series of continuous modifications. For Benjamin, the translation is a prolongation of the original text, an intimate relation between the languages.

The *Oxford English Dictionary* definition quoted above provides a useful insight into contemporary trends in translation studies. Some schools understand translation as a result. This is the case of the Polysystem Theory sympathizers (Even-Zohar, Toury, Ivir, etc.), the Manipulation School (Lambert, Delabastita, Hermans, Lefevere, etc.), the Leipzig School (Neubert, Wilss, etc.), and of those theoreticans who adopt a socio-cultural approach (Snell-Hornby, Vermeer, Holz-Mänttäri, etc.). Other scholars, with a more empiric approach, define translation as a process (Harris and Séguignot, Krings and Lörscher, etc.). There is a third trend, which defines translation as an intercultural communication function, and takes over the hermeneutic postulates (M. Gaddis Rose, CRIT/TRIP, Binghampton).

Two of the most recent definitions of translation pronounce that "Translation is a process by which the chain of signifiers that constitutes the source-language text is replaced by a chain of signifiers in the target language which the translator provides on the strength of an interpretation", and "Translation is the forcible replacement of the linguistic and cultural differences of the foreign text with a text that will be intelligible to the target-language reader" (Venuti, 1995). They demonstrate the long road that has been travelled in the endeavour to define translation since classical times.

RAQUEL DE PEDRO

Further Reading

Ballard, Michel, *De Cicéron à Benjamin: Traducteurs, traductions, réflexions*, Lille: Presses Universitaires de Lille, 1992

Nida, Eugene A., *Toward a Science of Translating*, Leiden: E.J. Brill, 1964

Steiner, George, *After Babel: Aspects of Language and Translation*, Oxford and New York: Oxford University Press, 1975; 3rd edition 1998

Venuti, Lawrence, *The Translator's Invisibility: A History of Translation*, London and New York: Routledge, 1995

Grazia Deledda 1871–1936

Italian novelist and short-story writer

Biography

Born in Nuoro, Sardinia, 27 September 1871, into a middle-class family. Educated in Sardinia up to the age of 11, she developed an interest in the literature of the 19th century, particularly the work of Balzac, Tolstoi and other Russian novelists. Deledda started to write short stories set in her native Sardinia in the late 1880s when she was 17. She published her first novel, *Sangue sardo* [Sardinian Blood] in 1888. She was also a regular contributor to the periodicals *L'Ultima Moda* and *Il Paradiso dei Bambini,* from 1888, and *Rivista di Letteratura popolare,* from 1893 to 1895. Deledda moved to Cagliari in 1899. In 1900 she married Palmiro Modesani and settled with him in Rome. She had two sons. Deledda lived in Rome for the rest of her life, making frequent visits to Sardinia. She wrote more than 40 works of fiction after 1900, including her significant novels *Dopo il divorzio* (*After the Divorce*), 1902; *Elias Portolu*, 1903; *Cenere* (*Ashes*), 1910; and *La Madre* (*The Mother*), 1920. Deledda published a volume of her poetry, *Paesaggi Sardi* (*Sardinian Landscapes*) in 1897. She also translated Balzac's *Eugénie Grandet* and adapted her work for the theatre. Her fictional autobiography, *Cosima*, was published posthumously in 1937. Deledda was awarded the Nobel Prize for Literature in 1926. She died in Rome, 15 August 1936.

Deledda was a prolific writer, and achieved wide critical acclaim for her novels and short stories, which are convincing portrayals of family and individual passions and conflicts set in her native Sardinian landscape and society, and include vivid descriptions of Sardinian customs and traditions often drawn from her childhood memories. Her novels are written in a naturalistic narrative style often compared with the "verism" of Giovanni Verga.

Translations

Novels

Elias Portolu, 1903

King, Martha, *Elias Portolu*, London: Quartet, 1992; Evanston, Illinois: Northwestern University Press, 1995

Dopo il divorzio, 1902; as *Naufraghi in porto*, 1920

Ashe, Susan, *After the Divorce*, with an introduction by Sheila MacLeod, London: Quartet, 1985; Evanston, Illinois: Northwestern University Press, 1995

Lansdale, Maria Hornor, *After the Divorce*, New York: Holt, 1905

Cenere, 1904; revised edition, 1910

Colvill, Helen Hester, *Ashes: A Sardinian Story*, London and New York: John Lane, 1908

La madre, 1920

Steegmann, Mary G., *The Woman and the Priest*, London: Jonathan Cape, 1922; as *The Mother*, with an introduction by Steegmann, New York: Macmillan, 1923, with an introduction by D.H. Lawrence, London, Jonathan Cape, 1928; as *The Woman and the Priest; or, The Mother*, with a foreword by D.H. Lawrence and an introduction by Eric Lane, London: Dedalus, 1987

Cosima, 1937

King, Martha, *Cosima*, New York: Italica Press, 1988

Short Stories

Chiaroscuro, 1912

King, Martha, *Chiaroscuro and Other Stories*, with an introduction, London: Quartet, 1994

Grazia Deledda was a prolific and gifted writer. At a very young age she claimed that she wanted to become a novelist in order to create a body of work entirely devoted to her native Sardinia, an island where dreams and myths lived on as realities. For over 50 years, the goal of Deledda's literary ambitions was to tell the story of a place of rigid conventions, of barbarism, and violent instinctive actions, as D.H. Lawrence described it in his introduction to *La madre*. Rich in ethnic lore and in obscure tales of passion, the world of Deledda's novels presents the old Sardinia of the turn of the century, at the time when the feudal gentry was beginning to yield its power to a new middle class. Her savage settings derive as much from fiction as from empirical reality; truth remains elusive and illusory, a victim of the tissue of legendary memories woven by the author's strange and yet traditional storytelling. Initially published in 1900 in a literary journal (and in 1903 in book form), like most of Deledda's early work *Elias Portolu* establishes the boundaries of her artistic inspiration in terms of religion, superstitious beliefs, and long-held fascinations, existing in a stationary universe of infinite age. Presenting the uncontaminated mountainous region of Barbagia with pictorial verve, she dramatizes the clash between lust and moral codes, using the archaic language embedded in a primitive society. In her first major novel, Deledda articulates her plot in a lyrical atmosphere, and encompasses realist and post-realist elements. *Elias Portolu* appeared in English only in 1992. KING's adaptation is done with as much precision and directness as the original Italian permits. The apparently simple structure of Deledda's style is rendered into a language that conserves the characteristics of a natural novelist.

Only six of Deledda's 33 novels and numerous collections of short stories have been translated into English. The widespread resurgence of interest in her work in the past decade is due to modern feminist critics.

Martha KING also translated (1994) *Chiaroscuro and Other Stories*, which depicts with biblical undertones the life of an inland community, and (1988) the posthumous fictional diary *Cosima*. King's rendering is light-handed and clear. It evokes the anthropological distinctiveness of the self-styled Italian writer. The cadences of the vernacular and the spoken dialogue are well measured, and Deledda's characters reveal their deceptions and secret dreams in verbal and gestural forms. King captures the psychological atmosphere at the core of Deledda's storytelling: isolation, the passions of revenge and retribution, and the fear of a mysterious past are transformed into a plain language that needs no literary enrichment. As King explains in her translator's note to *Chiaroscuro and Other Stories*, Deledda's phrases and sayings, so directly expressive of the Sardinian dialect, cannot always be translated into English. Instead she reconstructs the etymological sense of the word in question.

The most accomplished of King's translations is *Cosima*, Deledda's last novel. This unfinished book evokes a young woman's growing self awareness – Cosima was Deledda's middle name – as she strives to leave her remote birthplace in eastern Sardinia. Recollecting her past, the narrator frames her uneventful days with poignant details. King's translation brings to life the vivid images and vibrant colours of the Sardinian landscape and its people.

Deledda's work came to the attention of the English-speaking reader of Italian fiction at the beginning of the 20th century. The first book to be translated, in 1905, was *After the Divorce*. It tells the story of Costantino Ledda, a man convicted for a crime of which he claims to be innocent, and how he accepts his sentence as if to make amends for an ineffable sense of guilt. LANSDALE (1905) and ASHE (1985) bring little understanding to the textual problems connected with the linguistic choices Deledda makes in her own writings. As Sheila MacLeod remarks in her introduction to Ashe, the Sardinian writer, in the English version, appears to execute no definite stylistic strategy. One significant accomplishment of King's translation method remains its focus on the lyrical quality of Deledda's figurative prose, which Ashe largely overlooks. Also the opening passage quoted from Luke, 18:34 is omitted, depriving the reader of a critical thematic allusion. These two translations synthesize Deledda's style into an unimaginative technical process. While the original novel works with phrases and sentences that are stretched to convey the characters' actions and emotions, the English abruptly cuts the peculiar flow of Deledda's descriptive language.

COLVILL's translation (1908) of *Ashes: A Sardinian Story* falls into a similar pattern. It aims at a contemporary literary style, somewhere between quotidian speech and select archaism. This tale of incest, which inspired a popular film starring Eleonora Duse in 1916, presents a typical Deledda conflict between desires and prohibitions, which triggers a regression to a primal childhood where atemporal realities unfold in all their mysterious opacity.

The author's fascination with her protagonists' fatal bondage to a clan returns in *The Mother*, Deledda's best-known work in English. STEEGMANN's translation (1922), originally titled *The Woman and the Priest*, is an unfailingly accurate attempt at retaining the mood and rhythm of the Sardinian writer. An engaging and comprehensive introductory essay by D.H. Lawrence was added to the 2nd edition in 1928. This authoritative voice made an exceptional contribution to the study of Deledda abroad. It should be mentioned that the 1987 Dedalus reprint is full of inaccuracies, including the misspelling of the translator's name.

In the figures of the transgressive priest and his troubled mother, Deledda embodies the clash between superstition and established religion. In her preface the translator places Deledda's prose in the context of her career, and also draws on personal observations when exploring the inhibitions against which Deledda had to struggle to assert herself as a writer. Steegmann makes a persuasive case for the importance of understanding the aesthetic and moral values of Deledda's work. Immensely pleasing, yet rendered with great delicacy and lightness of touch, this translation stresses the meaning of each word, as it conveys a sense of the instinctual life of the characters. Undoubtedly the vocabulary of the English version is more intellectual than that of the Sardinian. What D.H. Lawrence called the instinct-word, which defines Deledda's sensorial language and syntax, is more expressive in the original text. Steegmann remains an expert in the difficult but important task of communicating Deledda's universe. Her translation conveys and attests the enduring magic of one of the most significant voices in 20th-century Italian narrative.

GAETANA MARRONE

Further Reading

See the translator's note in King (1994) and MacLeod's introduction to Ashe

---

Demosthenes c.384–322 BC

Greek orator

Biography

Born in Athens c.384 BC. Having been deprived of his inheritance, he studied rhetoric and law and became a constitutional lawyer, using his skills at first as a speech-writer and teacher. He went into politics when he was 30, to convince the Athenians of the danger threatening them from Philip II of Macedon. As well as forming an anti-Macedonian party (346–340 BC), and although he suffered from a speech impediment, he made a series of masterly orations attacking Philip (*Olynthiacs*, 349 BC; *Philippics*, 351, 344 and 341 BC). When it was proposed that Demosthenes should be honoured with a gold crown for his services to the city, the Athenian supporters of Macedon, led by Aeschines, accused him of treacherous pride. He defeated the accusation in his speech *On the Crown*. He was accused again, this time of theft of money from the treasury of Philip II's son, Alexander the Great, that had been brought to Athens in 324 by a deserter. He was fined and went into exile. When Alexander died in 323, Demosthenes was called back to direct the Greek rebellion against Macedon, but the action ended in failure (battle of Crannon, 322). Sentenced to death by Demades, who was in favour of Macedonian rule, Demosthenes took poison and died in 322 BC, on the island of Calaureia.

Translations

Collections and Selections

Francis, Rev. Philip, *Orations of Demosthenes*, 2 vols, vol. 2 entitled *Orations of Demosthenes and Aeschines*, London: Millar, 1757–58

Kennedy, Charles Rann, *The Orations of Demosthenes*, with an introduction, 5 vols, London: Bohn, 1852–63; selection, as *The Crown, the Philippics and Ten Other Orations of Demosthenes*, London: Dent, and New York: Dutton, 1911

Pickard-Cambridge, A.W., *Public Orations of Demosthenes*, with an introduction, 2 vols, Oxford: Clarendon Press, 1912; in 1 vol., London: Dent, and New York: Dutton, 1963 (contains translations of *Olynthiacs* 1–3, *Philippics* 1–3, *On the Crown*, *De pace*, *De Chersoneso*, *De classibus*, *De Rhodiorum libertate*, *Pro megalopolitos*, *De falsa legatione*)

Saunders, A.N.W., various orations in *Greek Political Oratory*, translated by Saunders, Harmondsworth: Penguin, 1970

Somers, Lord John (editor), *Several Orations of Demosthenes*, by several hands (the Earl of Peterborough, Lord Lansdowne, *et al.*), London: J. and R. Tonson, 1702; new edition, 1744

Vince, C.A., J.H.Vince, A.T. Murray, N.W. DeWitt and N.J. DeWitt, *Demosthenes*, 7 vols, London: Heinemann, 1926–49 (Loeb Classical Library)

Individual Works

De corona

Brougham, Henry, Lord, *The Oration of Demosthenes Upon the Crown*, London: Charles Knight, 1840; London: Routledge, 1893

Holland, Otho Lloyd, *The Speech on the Crown*, Bournemouth: Mate, 1926

Usher, Stephen, *Demosthenes on the Crown / De corona* (parallel texts), with an introduction and commentary, Warminster, Wiltshire: Aris and Phillips, 1993

In Midiam

MacDowell, Douglas M., *Against Meidias*, Oxford: Clarendon Press, and New York: Oxford University Press, 1990

Olynthiacae; *Philippicae*

Leland, Thomas, *All the Orations of Demosthenes Pronounced to Excite the Athenians against Philip, King of Macedon*, Dublin, 1756 and many reprints

Wylson, Thomas, *The Three Orations of Demosthenes ... in Favour of the Olynthians ... with Four Orations against King Philip of Macedon ...*, London: Henry Denham, 1570; reprinted New York: Da Capo Press, 1968

Demosthenes is generally recognized as one of the world's greatest orators, if not the greatest. Cicero, another claimant for the title, modelled himself on Demosthenes, and his speeches against Antony were known as Philippics because of their resemblance to his predecessor's speeches against Philip of Macedon. Like Cicero, Demosthenes was eventually on the losing side after a long career in which he was involved in private as well as public actions. Demosthenes' most famous speech, *On the Crown*, is in a way both public and private; it combines a justification of his political career and a memorable attack on his principal rival and political opponent, Aeschines.

Sadly Demosthenes, both in the original and in translation, has fallen out of favour with English readers. In Evelyn Waugh's *Brideshead Revisited* the hero is urged when an undergraduate at Oxford to attend lectures on Demosthenes as if it were the done thing to go to these lectures even if one were not studying classics. Even after World War II students of the classics at schools and universities were encouraged to read Demosthenes if only to improve their skill in Greek prose composition. Many such students first make the acquaintance of English orators such as Pitt and Burke by having to translate these orators into Greek. Such a task was made easier by the fact that Pitt and Burke had also read their Demosthenes. But with the decline in the study of prose composition Demosthenes became less popular. Classical studies and the study of literature in translation were not a bad substitute for the old classical training, but Demosthenes is hardly a reliable source for 4th-century history, and his rhetorical power is difficult to convey in translation. Alone among major or even minor classical authors, Demosthenes does not appear in the Penguin Classics series except in selections from a collection of Attic orators.

Oddly, Demosthenes has not been translated all that frequently into English. The sheer quantity of his surviving speeches and the web of complex political and legal allusions in them demand considerable dedication. Early translators such as WYLSON (1570), the aristocratic translators working for SOMERS (1702), and then FRANCIS (1757–58) and LELAND (1756) do not attempt more than a selection of speeches, although they do supply copious and not wholly accurate historical notes. Leland's map of Greece and Macedonia provides a remarkable insight into 18th-century geographical ignorance. This edition was frequently reprinted. BROUGHAM's translation of *Upon the Crown* (1840) is described in the *Dictionary of National Biography* as unfortunate, and it was bitterly attacked in *The Times*. But Brougham, like Demosthenes a man with many enemies and a man of extraordinary versatility, pays in his preface and in himself a good tribute to the close link between English and Greek oratory. Early versions of Demosthenes make up in dignity what they lose in accuracy. The 19th century produced some boring literal cribs.

KENNEDY (1852–63), the brother of the famous author of Kennedy's Latin grammar, was in his own right a considerable classical scholar and also a lawyer. His complete translation of Demosthenes appeared in both the Bohn and the Everyman series. It contains an interesting introduction on the difficulties of conveying Demosthenes' rhetorical power without sacrificing too much of the literal meaning. There are some useful remarks on Demosthenes' strengths and weaknesses as an orator and on the failings of other translators. Kennedy's translation of the final passage in *On the Crown* is worthy of note. Demosthenes is comparing his life to that of Aeschines. Unlike politicians of today, Demosthenes is at pains to stress his good education in contrast to the low origins and squalid upbringing of his opponent. Kennedy renders this passage, imitating Milton as he mentions in a footnote, as follows: "You taught reading, I went to school: you performed imitations, I received them: you danced in the chorus, I furnished it: you were assembly clerk, I was a speaker: you acted third parts, I heard you."

HOLLAND's versions (1926) are extraordinary. He attempted to reproduce not only the sense but also the rhythm of the original. This results in some bizarrely perverted syntax, all Greek to the average reader. Thus the passage from *On the Crown* so elegantly rendered by Kennedy is prefaced by the baffling sentence "Of the two lucks which would he choose, each for his own?" Holland continues: "You were taught the rudiments, I was the scholar; were acolyte, I catechumen; were dancer, but I called the tune; were clerk, but I was a member; had the part of Third Player, I of spectator." He also translated *Olynthiacs* and *Philippics* on the same principle.

VINCE, VINCE, MURRAY & the two DEWITTS (1926–49) conscientiously translated the whole of Demosthenes for the Loeb series. Their rendering is literally accurate but consistently misses the point. Thus the passage in *On the Crown* becomes "You were an usher, I a pupil: you were an acolyte, I a candidate: you were a clerk at the table, I addressed the House: you a player, I a spectator." With the slightly derogatory term "usher" borrowed from Brougham, this version tries to indicate the inferiority of Aeschines, but the other three comparisons fail. Acolyte/candidate is an obscure opposition; players win more praise than spectators; and in the House of Commons the clerk at the table earns more money than most members of Parliament.

PICKARD-CAMBRIDGE (1912) was an adequate scholar, principally famous for his work on Greek drama, a subject fairly close to Greek oratory. His version is slightly more literal than Kennedy's and yet not lacking in rhetorical force. In the key passage he is trying to convey Aeschines' inferiority and not quite succeeding: "You taught letters, I attended school. You conducted initiations, I was initiated. You were a clerk, I a member of the assembly. You a third-rate actor, I a spectator of the play."

Among modern translators SAUNDERS (1970) follows the Penguin tradition of speaking in ordinary language, and this is sensible because Demosthenes is not an orator of obscure grandiloquence. But less than half of this slim volume is devoted to Demosthenes and we do not find the fourth Philippic or *On the Crown*. Saunders was a schoolmaster; USHER (1993) and MACDOWELL (1990) are university lecturers, and though their editions are models of scholarly accuracy, their translations make no concessions to literary grace or popular taste. Thus MacDowell has a sentence that runs as follows: "First the man who hit the thesmothetes has these excuses: drink, love and inability to recognize him because the incident happened at night and in the dark." This is hardly the way to bring Demosthenes to the common reader.

TOM WINNIFRITH

Further Reading

Jaeger, Werner, *Demosthenes: The Origin and Growth of His Policy*, translated by Edward Schouten Robinson, Cambridge: Cambridge University Press, and Berkeley: University of California Press, 1938

Pearson, Lionel, *The Art of Demosthenes*, Meisenheim am Glan: Hain, 1976

Pickard-Cambridge, A.W., *Demosthenes and the Last Days of Greek Freedom, 384–322 BC*, New York: Putnam 1914; reprinted New York, Arno Press, 1979

Sir John Denham 1615–1669

English poet and translator

Biography

Remembered in English literature for just one poem, his *Cooper's Hill* of 1642, that helped make the closed rhyming couplet a normal form for poets of the next generation, Sir John Denham lived as a courtier. He supported the Royalist cause at home and on the continent. His reward came when Charles II appointed him Surveyor of the Works, a position which he held, though scantily qualified, in succession to Inigo Jones, and in which he was followed by Christopher Wren. A less fortunate consequence of frequenting court was the madness that afflicted him after the scandal of his second wife's liaison with the Duke of York. Born in Dublin, educated at Oxford and trained for the law at Lincoln's Inn, Denham had always had a marked tendency towards dissipation, and composing verses and writing about translation seem to have occupied no more than some of his leisure hours. None the less, his contribution to the debate on the best way to translate is noteworthy, though its significance may to some extent have been enhanced by his ability to crystallize his views in pithy formulations. Died in London, 19 March 1669.

More than half of Denham's literary production is translation, mainly from Latin but also from Greek (a short excerpt from the *Iliad*) and French (the final act of Corneille's *Horace*, completing the task begun by Mrs Phillips). In 1656 Denham brought out his *Destruction of Troy*, a version of Book Two of the *Aeneid*; this was only part of the more extensive translation of Virgil's epic that he had undertaken some 20 years earlier. Though there is evidence to show that Dryden recalled Denham's work when he in his turn was working on Virgil, Denham's versification is slack, with some poor rhyming, but the preface reveals that the translator had thought about what he was doing. Addressing himself to those who, thanks to "youth, leisure and better fortune" may be able to out-do him, he starts, in characteristically striking fashion, by remarking that "there are so few translations which deserve praise that [he] scarce ever saw any which deserv'd pardon". He adds that if even the worst authors suffer at the hands of incompetent translators, the best are injured even more. Playing on the Horatian concept of the *fidus interpres* he declares roundly that whilst a close verbal version may properly be demanded in "matters of fact or matters of faith", which would, of course, cover sacred texts as well as theology, poetry requires different treatment from the translator. Describing the translator's task, he writes:

> It is not his business alone [only] to translate language into language, but poesie into poesie; and poesie is of so subtile a spirit that in pouring out of one language into another, it will all evaporate, and if a new spirit be not added in the transfusion, there will remain nothing but a *Caput mortuum*, there being certain graces and happineses peculiar to every language, which gives life and energy to the words.

"Transfusion", whether taken to refer to alchemy or alcohol, may be a picturesque image that does little to clarify the argument. Denham is, however, making an important distinction, arguing that "poesie" and factual discourse may call for different translation strategies. Unfortunately he does not go on to make it clearer that the issue does not really centre on the differences between translating verse and prose, but rather between translating literary and non-literary texts.

Borrowing from the Renaissance rhetoricians the concept of language as the dress in which thoughts are clothed, Denham goes on to argue that, just as fashions in garments change from time to time and from place to place, so too translators must take care that their versions do not appear archaic or outlandish. Therefore, he opines, "if Virgil must needs speak English, it were fit he should speak not only as a man of this nation, but as a man of this age". Objections may be raised to such a theory of translation, but Denham is voicing here what in France had already become the doctrine of the *belles infidèles* and would become the ruling orthodoxy in Britain in the time of Dryden and Pope.

A lapidary expression of one of the melancholy eternal verities of translation makes a striking opening to Denham's epistle to Sir Richard Fanshawe, even if the implied compliment is not entirely merited.

> Such is our Pride, our Folly, or our Fate,
> The few but such as cannot write, translate.

Fanshawe's version of Giovanni Guarini's *Pastor Fido* (1585) was first published in 1648, but the encomium was most likely written around half a decade earlier. Denham comments on the difficulty of what we should call cross-cultural transfer, and argues that translator need to possess a "genius" on a par with that of the author of the original. Otherwise:

> In vain they toil, since nothing can beget
> A vital spirit, but a vital heat.

Fortunately Fanshawe does not only possess the gift; he has also chosen the new, correct method. The courtier Denham picks his qualifiers when he praises him for "nobly" eschewing the "servile path" of "slavish" word-for-word translators who are content with "cheap vulgar arts" that allow "no flight for thoughts" because they "poorly" prefer literalism. Fanshawe is lauded because he has done more than just preserve Guarini's sense: he has been "truer to his fame". This he has achieved by boldly improving weaknesses where they occur in the original and by:

> Wisely restoring whatsoever grace
> Is lost by change of Times, or Tongues, or Place.

He has also contrived to avoid the danger of betraying Guarini's music "to unhappy rhymes".

In old age Denham contributed to the pronounced vogue for psalm translations, but with no particular success, though he took pains to adopt a metrical form that would suit the chants then in use. In his *The Lives of the English Poets* Dr Johnson's appraisal of Denham's achievement in the field of translation is judicious and balanced: "he saw the better way, but has not pursued it with great success", adding that "his versions of Virgil are not pleasing; but they taught Dryden to please better".

CHRISTOPHER SMITH

Further Reading

Denham, Sir John, *Poems and Translations*, London: printed for H. Herringman, 1668

Denham, Sir John, *A Version of the Psalms of David, Fitted to the Tunes Used in Churches*, London: Bowyer, 1714

Denham, Sir John, *The Poetical Works*, edited by Theodore Howard Banks, New Haven, Connecticut: Yale University Press, and London: Oxford University Press, 1928; 2nd edition, Hamden, Connecticut: Archon, 1969

Johnson, Samuel, *Lives of the English Poets*, with an introduction by L. Archer Hind, 2 vols, London: Dent, 1925 (first published 1779–81)

Dialects

See Sociolects & Dialects and Literary Translation

Denis Diderot 1713–1784

French philosopher, novelist, dramatist and art critic

Biography

Diderot was born in Langret on 5 October 1713, the son of a master cutler. He was educated by the Jesuits (1723–28) and obtained the degree of master of arts at the University of Paris in 1732. He became a close friend of Rousseau, of the abbé de Condillac and later of d'Holbach and his group.

Diderot married Antoinette Champion in 1742; only their daughter Angélique survived infancy.

He began his career by translating Temple Stanyans's *The Grecian History* and, in collaboration with others, Robert James's *A Medicinal Dictionary*. In 1747 he was appointed, together with the mathematician Jean Le Rond d'Alembert, as editor of the *Encyclopédie; ou, Dictionnaire raisonné des sciences, des arts, et des métiers* (1751–80), at first envisaged as a translation of Ephraim Chambers's *Cyclopaedia*, but destined to become one of the great undertakings of the century, bringing together a dedicated team of contributors, including Diderot, most of whom shared the ideals of the Enlightenment. In 1745 Diderot published a very free translation of the earl of Shaftesbury's *An Inquiry Concerning Virtue and Merit*, seizing, however, on the salient features of the book and providing personal notes. His first original work, *Pensées philosophiques* (1746; *Philosophical Thoughts*), was still greatly influenced by Shaftesbury. The *Lettre sur les aveugles* (1749; *Essay on Blindness*) paved the way for Louis Braille, while stressing our dependence on our senses but also foreshadowing Diderot's atheism and materialism. The *Lettre sur les sourds et muets* (1751; *Letter on the Deaf and Dumb*) followed, and the *Pensées sur l'interprétation de la nature* (1753) promoted an experimental method side by side with inspired speculation. The final expression of his monistic determinism and energetistic materialism is to be found in *Le Rêve de d'Alembert* (written in 1769 but first published in 1830), a work based on the new biological sciences, genetics and a clear expression of transformist or evolutionary theories presented with dialectical brilliance. His chief subsequent works were shown only to a few intimates, or published in his friend Friedrich Melchior Grimm's *Correspondance littéraire*, which was addressed to heads of foreign states and a few, mostly titled, subscribers outside France. His two plays, apart from *Est-il bon? Est-il méchant?* (1777, published 1781), are less interesting than his dramatic theories, in connection with which he translated Edward Moore's *The Gamester*. The *Paradoxe sur le comédien* (a first draft of which is entitled *Garrick ou les acteurs anglais*) argues that the great actor must remain constantly in full possession of his craft and never experience what he is required to perform.

In 1759 he began his first formal art criticism with commentaries on the biennial *salons* (1759–81). Diderot missed only the *salon* of 1773. His novel, *La Religieuse* (*The Nun*), was written in 1760, but published only in 1796. A copy of his satirical dialogue *Le Neveu de Rameau*, begun in 1761 and frequently revised up to 1774, was purloined from the Diderot collection of papers sent to St Petersburg after his death and came into the hands of Friedrich Schiller. He was so impressed that he sent it to Goethe who proceeded to translate it into German (1805); in 1823 the work was badly retranslated into French and passed off as the original. The definitive manuscript, at first mistakenly attributed to Jacques-André Naigeon, was accidentally found in 1891 among the books sold on the banks of the Seine. *Jacques le fataliste* (*Jacques the Fatalist*), a philosophical *conte* after the fashion of Cervantes and Sterne begun in 1771, and the *Supplément au Voyage de Bougainville*, which advocates a free society and sexual liberty, begun in 1772, were both published in 1796. In 1778 Diderot published *Essai sur les règnes de Claude et de Néron*, known as *Essai sur la vie de Sénèque* (2nd edition, 1782) and from 1779 he contributed substantially to the abbé Guillaume Raynal's *Histoire des deux Indes*. His daughter Angélique, now Mme de Vandeul sent his library and a number of manuscripts to Catherine the Great in 1785. These documents have only recently been made available to scholars and the manuscripts kept by Diderot's descendants were rescued and inventoried by Herbert Dieckmann in 1950 and subsequently presented to the Bibliothèque Nationale in Paris. The basic text of all 19th- and 20th-century editions published prior to access to these manuscripts, apart from some of his early published works, is unsatisfactory and all early translations flawed.

Diderot died 31 July 1784 in Paris.

Editions

Correspondance, edited by Georges Roth, 16 vols, Paris: Minuit, 1955–70
Oeuvres philosophiques, edited by Paul Vernière, Paris: Garnier, 1956
Salons, edited by Jean Seznec and Jean Adhémar, 4 vols, Oxford: Clarendon Press, 1957–67; reprinted with a new introduction, 1975–79
Oeuvres esthétiques, edited by Paul Vernière, Paris: Garnier, 1959
Oeuvres romanesques, edited by Henri Bénac, Paris: Garnier, 1962
Oeuvres politiques, edited by Paul Vernière, Paris: Garnier, 1963
Oeuvres complètes, edited by Roger Lewinter, 15 vols, Paris: Club Française du Livre, 1969–73
Oeuvres complètes, edited by Herbert Dieckmann, Jean Fabre and Jacques Proust, Paris: Hermann, 1975–

Translations

Selected Works or Extracts
Barzun, Jacques and Ralph H. Bowen, *Rameau's Nephew and Other Works*, New York: Doubleday, 1956; reprinted Indianapolis: Bobbs Merrill, 1964 (contains *D'Alembert's Dream*, *A Supplement to Bougainville's Voyage*, *The Two Friends from Bourbonne*, *A Conversation between a Father and His Children*, *The Encyclopedia* [extracts], *Regrets on Parting with My Old Dressing Gown*)
Birrell, Francis, *Dialogues by Denis Diderot*, with an introduction, New York: Brentano, and London: Routledge, 1927
Coltman, Derek, *Selected Writings*, edited, with an introduction and notes by Lester G. Crocker, New York: Macmillan, and London: Collier Macmillan, 1966
Jackson, Emilie (Mrs Wilfred Jackson), *Rameau's Nephew and Other Works*, with an introduction by Compton Mackenzie, London: Chapman and Hall, 1926
Jourdain, Margaret, *Diderot's Early Philosophical Works*, Chicago: Open Court, 1916; reprinted, with a new introduction by Jules Paul Seigel, New York: AMS Press, 1973
Stewart, Jean and Jonathan Kemp, *Diderot, Interpreter of Nature: Selected Writings*, edited by Kemp, London: Lawrence and Wishart, 1937, New York: International, 1943; 2nd edition 1963

Story
Jacques le fataliste et son maître, 1796
Coward, David, *Jacques the Fatalist*, Oxford and New York: Oxford University Press, 1999
Loy, J. Robert, *Denis Diderot: Jacques the Fatalist and His Master*, with an introduction, New York: New York University Press, 1959; revised edition, New York: Collier, 1962

Novel
La Religieuse, 1796 (written 1760)
Birrell, Francis, *Memoirs of a Nun (La Religieuse)*, London: Routledge, and New York: Brentano, 1928; reprinted London: Elek, 1959
Sinclair, Marianne, *The Nun (La Religieuse)*, with an afterword by Richard Griffiths, London: New English Library, 1966
Tancock, L.W., *Denis Diderot: The Nun*, with an introduction, London: Folio Society, 1972; Harmondsworth: Penguin, 1974

Dialogues
Le Neveu de Rameau, 1823 (written 1761–74)
Berc, Shelley and Andrei Belgrader, *Rameau's Nephew*, New York: Theatre Communications Group, 1988 (adaptation in two acts)
Hill, Sylvia M., *Rameau's Nephew*, London: Longman, 1897
Tancock, L.W., *Rameau's Nephew*, with an introduction, with *D'Alembert's Dream*, Harmondsworth and Baltimore: Penguin, 1966

Le Rêve de d'Alembert, 1830 (written 1769)
Tancock, L.W., *D'Alembert's Dream*, with an introduction, with *Rameau's Nephew*, Harmondsworth and Baltimore: Penguin, 1966

Letters
France, Peter (editor and translator), *Diderot's Letters to Sophie Volland: A Selection*, London: Oxford University Press, 1972
Loy, J. Robert, *That Infernal Affair*, edited by Phyllis Brooks and Basil Guy, New York: Peter Lang, 1999

Other Writing
Prospectus, 1750 (of the *Encyclopédie*, 1751–80)
Schwab, Richard N. with Walter E. Rex, "Prospectus" in *Jean Le Rond d'Alembert: Preliminary Discourse to the Encyclopedia of Diderot*, with an introduction and notes, Indianapolis: Bobbs Merrill, 1963; reprinted Chicago: University of Chicago Press, 1995

Plan d'une Université pour le Gouvernement de Russie, 1796 (written 1778–80)
Fontainemarie, François de la, "Diderot (1713–1784) and His Plan for a Russian University", in his *French Liberalism and Education in the Eighteenth Century: The Writings of La Chalotais, Turgot, Diderot, and Condorcet on National Education*, New York: McGraw Hill, 1932

"Paradoxe sur le comédien", 1830 (written 1773)
Pollock, Walter Herries, *The Paradox of Acting*, with a preface by Henry Irving, London: Chatto and Windus, 1883

Denis Diderot, the leading encyclopedist, is, with Voltaire and Jean-Jacques Rousseau, one of the three most important French thinkers who straddle the 18th century, and since 1950 his standing has grown.

Most of Diderot's works are in the form of dialogues, written in the vivid, colloquial style of the practised conversationalist. The translator is faced with the problems of the dramatist. Diderot's dialogues, philosophical and moral discourses, are between known persons, but Diderot mischievously attributed to them some of his own opinions, as in the case of d'Alembert and Mlle de Lespinasse in *Le Rêve de d'Alembert*, and his brand of humour requires explanation as also do his references to contemporary persons or events. Rayner Heppenstall once declared that we had a precise record of an actual conversation held in a French salon. This is not so, as we know now from Diderot's emendations over the years, but something of the realism and vitality of the original needs to be preserved. Diderot's style may be colloquial, but it is characteristic of the 18th century and it is surely a mistake to modernize the text by using present-day colloquialisms. A literal and clear rendering is to be preferred, for it is the meaning that is significant. In the case of *Jacques le fataliste* a preliminary reading of Sterne would seem indicated, with his digressions, interruptions and humour. At times Diderot indulges in a lyrical, at others in an expostulatory style. Since Diderot's works have not been translated in their entirety, reference needs to be made to the French editions cited above.

Many of Diderot's works remain untranslated into English or exist in 18th-century versions only, as for instance his plays, his *Entretiens sur le Fils Naturel*, *De la poésie dramatique*, *Eléments de physiologie* and his political works, *Principes de politique des souverains*, *Entretiens de Diderot avec Catherine II*, *Observations sur le Nakaz*, but there is a rendering of Diderot's *Plan d'une université pour le gouvernement de Russie* (first published in an abridged form in 1813–14) in a compilation of works on education (FONTAINEMARIE, 1932). Although extracts from works are not truly satisfactory, and in view of the absence of translations of important works, the Further Reading list includes studies that incorporate quotations in English.

The texts chosen by Margaret JOURDAIN (1916) are of works published during Diderot's lifetime and the translation accordingly still has validity. Some of the views expressed are open to question. Jules Seigel's introduction to the 1973 reprint takes into account the fruits of more recent research.

The French text on which BIRRELL's translations (1927) are based is that provided by Jules Assézat and Maurice Tourneux's edition of Diderot's complete works (20 vols, Paris: Garnier, 1875–77) which is discredited since the availability of the manuscripts, copies of manuscripts, and autograph emendations on the Fonds Vandeul and those in the National Library of Russia, St Petersburg. The French texts selected by Birrell, however, are for the most part still valid and the translation is satisfactory.

STEWART & KEMP's translation (1937) of Diderot's most important philosophical works shows the development of his materialism, emphasizing his work in genetics and dialectics. This is one of the most useful translations of Diderot, and is based on a good selection, but Kemp may have overstated Diderot's modernism, for, while Diderot suggests chromosomes as the source of life we cannot be certain of the precise meaning of the terms he uses.

BARZUN & BOWEN (1956) are invaluable for their translations of short texts otherwise unavailable in English. Their work supersedes that by JACKSON (1926), which, however, has an interesting introduction by Compton Mackenzie.

The basic text used by COLTMAN (1966) is that of Assézat and Tourneux, but some more recent critical editions have been used in this selection of 23 widely different works. L.G. Crocker's introduction and notes are particularly useful. The volume supplements Crocker's 1954 (revised 1966) account of Diderot's life and works, which includes relevant quotations in English with particular stress on Diderot's philosophy and ethics.

LOY (1959) is an excellent translation with a scholarly introduction. He has devoted a whole volume to *Jacques the Fatalist* (Loy, 1950) which he has studied in depth, attempting to clarify the philosophical, ethical and literary problems it poses. Geoffrey Bremner's 1985 book is a further illuminating study that shows how the dialogue between Jacques and his master, the narrator and the reader demonstrates the impossibility of moral judgements in view of the complexity of human behaviour and the dichotomy between our intentions and the form our lives take. Diderot's pessimism, he convincingly argues, should not be allowed to blind us to his humour and sense of fun. LOY (1999) is a posthumously published translation that reproduces all the letters relevant to the breakup of the relationship between Diderot and Rousseau.

The great stage success in 1963 of a French adaptation of *Rameau's Nephew* in the form of a dialogue between two characters, may have prompted the English adaptation by BERC & BELGRADER (1988). They adhere closely to the French text but suffer from an attempt to transpose the essentially 18th-century dialogue into the contemporary American idiom. Thus we find expressions such as "crap" and further on "Nada, Zip, Zilch, Bupkis" immediately followed by "goddam". Such inconsistency is scarcely acceptable and would not commend this version for presentation outside the US.

TANCOCK (1966) is a welcome translation of two of Diderot's most important works, *Rameau's Nephew* and *D'Alembert's Dream*. The translator conveys the dialogue form adopted by Diderot in both works extremely well even if something of the vivacity of the French has been lost; this translation marks a definite improvement on earlier ones. HILL's 1897 translation of Diderot's autographical *Le Neveu de Rameau* was for long the only authoritative one, but has been advantageously replaced. For an introduction to the complexity and multiplicity of interpretations of the play see Falvey's 1985 study, which provides a close analysis of the text, its structure, the dialogue form adopted and its key themes.

TANCOCK (1972) is a moving and meticulous translation of one of Diderot's most significant and popular novels, *The Nun*. Tancock was a scholar who relished the work of translation and is widely considered as the best translator from the French in the team assembled by Penguin Books. The work examines the fate of a nun obliged to lead a conventual existence against her will and the torture inflicted on her successively by three Mother Superiors, each in her own selfish way monstrously cruel. The condemnation of celibacy as a crime against nature is forcefully conveyed. This translation supersedes BIRRELL (1928) and SINCLAIR (1966).

FRANCE (1972) has translated 47 letters of the 550 Diderot wrote over 20 years (1755–75) of which 189 have survived. The choice is excellent, although a second volume would be highly desirable. Diderot's correspondence ranks with that of Voltaire and Rousseau as the most significant in the French 18th century. The world of the bourgeoisie and that of the society of the baron d'Holbach, Grimm, Mme d'Épinay, Mme d'Houdetot, the abbé Galiani, and Damilaville stand out, and the letters illuminate his close relationship with Sophie Volland. This is a sound, faithful translation.

SCHWAB & REX (1963) are well known for their work on the *Encyclopédie*. To their translation of d'Alembert's *Discours préliminaire* has been appended Diderot's earlier *Prospectus*. The two editors, Diderot and d'Alembert, share the same conception of their joint enterprise, but it is interesting to note differences in emphasis in their presentation of the work.

FONTAINERIE (1932) has provided the only translation of the plan Diderot drew up for Catherine the Great, which gives concrete expression to the necessary reforms in education required to meet the aspirations of the encyclopedists.

ROBERT NIKLAUS

Further Reading

Blum, Carol, *Diderot: The Virtue of a Philosopher*, New York: Viking, 1974
Bremner, Geoffrey, *Diderot: Jacques le Fataliste*, London: Grant and Cutler, 1985
Crocker, L.G., *Diderot, The Embattled Philosopher: A Biography*, East Lansing: Michigan State College Press, 1954; revised edition, New York: Free Press, and London: Collier Macmillan, 1966
Diderot Studies, 1949–
Falvey, J.L., *Diderot: Le Neveu de Rameau*, London: Grant and Cutler, 1985
Fellows, Otis, *Diderot*, Boston: Twayne, 1977
France, Peter, *Diderot*, Oxford and New York: Oxford University Press, 1983
France, Peter, "*Jacques the Fatalist*", *Times Literary Supplement* (15 October 1999)
Furbank, P.N., *Diderot: A Critical Biography*, London: Secker and Warburg, and New York: Knopf, 1992
Loy, J. Robert, *Diderot's Determined Fatalist: An Appreciation of Jacques le fataliste*, New York: King's Crown Press, 1950
Mason, John Hope, *The Irresistible Diderot*, London and New York: Quartet, 1982
Morley, John, *Diderot and the Encyclopedists*, 2 vols, London: Chapman and Hall, 1878; numerous reprints, including Ann Arbor, Michigan: Plutarch Press, 1971
Recherches sur Diderot et sur l'Encyclopédie, 1986–
Strugnell, Anthony, *Diderot's Politics: A Study of the Evolution of Diderot's Political Thought after the Encyclopédie*, The Hague: Nijhof, 1973
Wilson, Arthur M., *Diderot*, New York: Oxford University Press, 1957; reprinted 1972

Isak Dinesen

See Karen Blixen

Alfred Döblin 1878–1957

German novelist

Biography

Committed socialist, assimilated Jew, literary innovator and Catholic convert, Alfred Döblin is best known for his epic novel *Berlin Alexanderplatz*. Although his popularity dwindled after World War II, Döblin was one of Germany's most important writers between the wars, and he continues to rank as a key representative of German modernism. Born 10 August 1878 in Stettin (now Sczcecin), on the Baltic coast, he moved at age 10 with his mother and siblings to Berlin, studied psychiatry, and published his first book, a collection of short stories, in 1913. Alongside his social-critical feuilletons, published under the pseudonym "Linke Poot", Döblin wrote a number of experimental epic novels throughout the 1920s, characterized by their anti-realist montage style and depiction of individuals in conflict with society. With his family, Döblin went into exile in 1933, first to France, where he became a French citizen, then to Hollywood, where he worked for a time as a screenwriter. He returned to Germany in 1945 as a member of the occupying French military government, but left in 1951 and spent his last years in Paris. While his work after he left Berlin is marked by an increased realism and attention to spiritual concerns, an ambivalent, politically attuned spirituality may be recognized even in his first novel (1915), *The Three Leaps of Wang Lun*. Döblin's conversion to

Catholicism in 1941 was none the less considered an aberration by the post-war German intelligentsia. His last novel, *Tales of a Long Night*, found no publisher in West Germany (although it appeared to general acclaim in East Berlin), and Döblin died in Emmendingen, 26 June 1957, all but forgotten by his public. Ignited perhaps by Fassbinder's monumental film adaptation of *Berlin Alexanderplatz* (1983), a resuscitation of Döblin and his work has been taking place since the 1980s.

Translations

Novels

Die drei Sprünge des Wang-lun, 1915

Godwin, C.D., *The Three Leaps of Wang Lun: A Chinese Novel*, with an introduction, Hong Kong: Chinese University Press, 1991

Berlin Alexanderplatz, 1929

Jolas, Eugène, *Alexanderplatz, Berlin: The Story of Franz Biberkopf*, New York: Viking Press, and London: Martin Secker, 1931; as *Berlin Alexanderplatz*, New York: Ungar, 1961; Harmondsworth: Penguin, 1978

Pardon wird nicht gegeben, 1935

Blewitt, Trever and Phyllis Blewitt, *Men Without Mercy*, London: Gollancz, 1937; New York: Howard Fertig, 1976

November 1918: Eine Deutsche Revolution, 1948–50 (original vol. *Bürger und Soldaten 1918*, 1938; vol. 1[2], *Verratenes Volk*, 1948; vol. 2[3], *Heimkehr der Fronttruppen*, 1949; vol. 3[4], *Karl und Rosa: Eine Geschichte zwischen Himmel und Hölle*, 1950)

Woods, John E., *A People Betrayed*, New York: Fromm, 1983; London: Angel Books, 1986 (translation of *Verratenes Volk* and *Heimkehr der Fronttruppen*)

Woods, John E., *Karl and Rosa*, New York: Fromm, 1983; London: Angel Books, 1983

Hamlet; oder, Die lange Nacht nimmt ein Ende, 1956

Kimber, Robert and Rita Kimber, *Tales of a Long Night*, New York: Fromm, 1984

Autobiography

Reise in Polen, 1926

Neugroschel, Joachim, *Journey to Poland*, edited by Heinz Graber, London: I.B. Tauris, and New York: Paragon House, 1991

Schicksalsreise: Bericht und Bekenntnis, 1949

McCown, Edna, *Destiny's Journey*, edited by Edgar Pässler, with an introduction by Peter Demetz, New York: Paragon House, 1992

Alfred Döblin's first novel, *The Three Leaps of Wang Lun*, is a fictionalization of a religious uprising in 18th-century China by the Wu Wei sect, and an important work of German Expressionism. GODWIN's translation (1991) occasionally waxes more lyrical than the original, which was written in what Döblin called his "stone style", but it is consistently faithful to his headstrong, often dislocated syntax. Additionally, Godwin includes as a prologue the unpublished original first chapter from Döblin's manuscript, and provides an informative critical introduction, covering the history of the Wu Wei sect, Döblin's early engagements with sinology and Futurism, and a brief discussion of the translation.

Incited by a surge of anti-Semitism in Berlin in the early 1920s, Döblin traveled to Poland in 1924 to uncover the unassimilated roots of his assimilated Jewishness. His account, *Journey to Poland*, is an engaging, at times biting, commentary on social and political conditions and ethnic relations in post-Partition Poland. NEUGROSCHEL's very readable translation (1991) captures the personal urgency, laconic tone, and lyricism of the original, while maintaining its rough, stenographic syntax. It includes as an introduction Heinz Graber's afterword from the *Ausgewählte Werke* edition (1968), and appends most of Graber's editorial notes at the end of the text, while accommodating others into the translation itself.

Döblin's epic masterpiece, *Berlin Alexanderplatz*, presents in its energetic, expressionistic manner the story of the newly released convict Franz Biberkopf and his unsuccessful attempts to reintegrate into life in his old "'hood" in Berlin. Like Joyce's *Ulysses*, to which it is inevitably compared (and which Döblin reviewed shortly before writing his own greatest novel), *Berlin Alexanderplatz* does not make things easy for the translator, with its turgid montage of fractured dialogue, quick shifts between omniscient narration and inner monologue, Berlin slang and Yiddish, neologisms, advertising jingles, and "bureaucratese". The story proceeds as much through a constant layering-on and unpeeling of narrative styles and perspectives as it does through its hero's perambulations. With its depiction of a society fragmented between competing social and political groups, the book hit a raw nerve in Weimar Germany, and became an instant bestseller upon publication in 1929. JOLAS's 1931 translation was the first of Döblin's works to appear in English. Aside from toning down some of the more ribald moments, he imaginatively reproduces puns and wordplay, and is careful to maintain the paratactic syntax and place-names of the original. His attempts to convey dialect and slang into a 1920s American parlance may seem dated now, but that is perhaps only appropriate. Jolas nevertheless avoids embedding the translation into its target language: this is the only reasonable approach, considering the novel's intensive involvement with varieties of German, which Jolas preserves in the form of a subtle and stable estrangement from the English.

Written in exile in France in 1933–34, *Men Without Mercy* narrates the familial and political conflicts of its would-be-revolutionary turned industrialist hero, Karl. A curious shift to psychological realism, it represents an unexpected development in Döblin's montage style away from the volatile disjunctions of language in his earlier works to a modest polyphony of narrative perspectives. The BLEWITTS's translation (1937) is faithful to the original sentence structure and occasionally quite elegant, but it archaizes unnecessarily ("Karl addressed him, whereat he raised his eyebrows"), and lacks a strategy for dealing with the work's careful interface of different voices.

In *November 1918: A German Revolution*, a multi-volume work written mostly in Hollywood in the 1930s and 1940s, Döblin expands the subject matter and realistic polyphony of *Men without Mercy* to depict five different narrative levels and a number of characters (major and minor, fictional and real) involved in the quelled revolution of 1918. The publication history is rather complicated, as not all volumes were published at the same time, or in the same edition. The original first book,

Bürger und Soldaten [Citizens and Soldiers], appeared in 1938, a decade before its successors. It was left out of the first full edition of the work (1948–50), but restored to the second German edition of 1978, only to be excised once again in the English translation (1983). WOODS's version (1983) combines into one volume (*A People Betrayed*) the original second and third books, *Verratenes Volk* (*A People Betrayed*) and *Heimkehr der Fronttruppen* [The Troops' Return from the Front]; while the much longer fourth book, *Karl and Rosa*, which dramatizes the activities of the revolutionaries Karl Liebknecht and Rosa Luxemburg, is retained on its own as the second. Döblin may have intended for the original second and third books to comprise one volume in the original. Nevertheless, the English version entirely leaves out one narrative level and its central character – a significant move, as David Dollenmayer (1988) points out, inasmuch as the character is an author and may represent Döblin himself. A preface would have been the place to alert the reader to these changes, but this too is missing. While Woods's translation reproduces well the melodramatic dialogue and rushed, expository prose of the original, he unnecessarily and capriciously subdivides many of the longer sentences. The translation also presents numerous lexical inconsistencies, especially with regard to Berlin place-names (e.g. "Wilhelmstrasse" remains, but "Hallesches Tor" becomes "Halle Gate"; Tiergarten, the city district, is mistaken in at least one instance for the zoo; etc.).

Destiny's Journey is an autobiographical account of Döblin and his family's flight from France in 1940, during the German invasion, to Hollywood, and their return to Europe after the war. Döblin's narrative is informed not only by historical circumstance but, significantly, by his conversion in 1941 to Catholicism. MCCOWN (1992) is consistent and conscientious in reproducing Döblin's straightforward, concise diction. The translation is based not on the first published version (1949) of the work, but on the *Ausgewählte Werke* version of 1966, edited by Edgar Pässler, which restored into print the original organization of chapters in Döblin's manuscript; it includes as well Pässler's notes and an introduction by Peter Demetz.

Combining elements of both *Hamlet* and *The Thousand and One Nights*, Döblin's last novel, *Tales of a Long Night*, presents the story of Edward Allison, an English soldier who returns home after the war to find that something is rotten in the state of his parents' marriage (the novel nevertheless ends on an oddly optimistic note). Döblin's terse sentences and taut narrative are easily reproduced in the KIMBERS's deft and, appropriately, English-sounding translation (1984).

WILLIAM MARTIN

Further Reading

Detken, Anke, Döblins *Berlin Alexanderplatz übersetzt: Ein multilingualer kontrastiver Vergleich*, Göttingen: Vandenhoeck & Ruprecht, 1997

Dollenmayer, David B., *The Berlin Novels of Alfred Döblin*, Berkeley: University of California Press, 1988

Dollenmayer, David, "'Wessen Amerikanisch?' Zu Eugene Jolas' Übersetzung von Döblins *Berlin Alexanderplatz*" in *Jahrbuch für Internationale Germanistik*, edited by Werner Stauffacher, Bern: Peter Lang, 1993

Heimito von Doderer 1896–1966

Austrian novelist, short-story writer, essayist and poet

Biography

Born in Weidlingau, near Vienna, 5 September 1896. He was educated at the Landstrasser Gymnasium until 1914, then began to study law at the University of Vienna, but in 1915 was drafted as a reserve officer into an Austrian dragoon regiment. Taken prisoner in 1916 by the Russians, he was repatriated from Siberia in 1920 and returned to the University of Vienna 1921–25, leaving with a doctorate in history. His first marriage took place in 1930 and ended in divorce, 1934. He was a member of the National Socialist Party, 1933–38; but converted to Roman Catholicism in 1940.

Doderer was conscripted into the German Air Force in 1940 and taken prisoner by the British in Norway, 1945. On his release in 1946 he returned for good to Vienna and worked as a publisher's reader; he was banned until 1950 from publishing his own works. He married for the second time in 1952. His pre-World War II writings did not meet with great success, but recognition and honours came in Austria and Germany from the 1950s. Among his best-known works are the novels *Ein Mord, den jeder begeht*, 1938 (*Every Man a Murderer*, 1964); *Die Strudlhofstiege*, 1951 (*The Strudlhof Steps*, 1974), and its sequel *Die Dämonen*, 1956 (*The Demons*, 1961); and *Die Wasserfälle von Slunj*, 1963 (*The Waterfalls of Slunj*, 1966), which was intended to be the first part of a trilogy. Died in Vienna, 23 December 1966.

Translations

Novels

Ein Mord, den jeder begeht, 1938

Winston, Richard and Clara Winston, *Every Man a Murderer*, New York: Knopf, 1964

Die Strudlhofstiege oder Melzer und die Tiefe der Jahre, 1951

Kling, Vincent, "From: *The Strudlhof Steps, or Melzer and the Depths of the Years*", *Chicago Review*, 26/2 (1974) pp. 107–38

Die Dämonen: Nach der Chronik des Sektionsrates Geyrenhoff, 1956
Winston, Richard and Clara Winston, *The Demons*, 2 vols, New York: Knopf, 1961

Roman No. 7, Erster Teil: Die Wasserfälle von Slunj, 1963
Wilkins, Eithne and Ernst Kaiser, *The Waterfalls of Slunj*, New York: Harcourt Brace, 1966

Short Stories
"Die Posaunen von Jericho" (Divertimento no. 7), 1958
Kling, Vincent, "The Trumpets of Jericho", *Chicago Review*, 26/2 (1974) pp. 5–35

"Unter schwarzen Sternen", 1961
Kling, Vincent, "Under Black Stars", *Chicago Review*, 26/2 (1974) pp. 36–54

"Meine neunzehn Lebensläufe", 1966
Kling, Vincent, "My Nineteen *Curricula vitae*", *Chicago Review*, 26/2 (1974) pp. 79–85

Heimito von Doderer is one of the few German-language writers who was not in exile and who still managed to span World War II in his literary production; he is also one of the few post-war writers coming to prominence outside the sphere of Germany's Group 47 (which included Günter Grass, Heinrich Böll, and most names in post-war German literature). His voice and aesthetics are therefore outside the mainstream of contemporary fiction. His long novels are considered by some as distinctly Austrian, yet following in the tradition of Thomas Mann as an old master of irony. Because of his own mastery of a distinctive (mature and ironic) prose style, a lobby arose in the decade before his death to put Doderer forward as a Nobel Prize candidate. The attempt failed, not least because of his brief membership of the German Writers' Union early in the Nazi period (he had gone to Munich as a career move, then quickly returned to Austria and retreated from all politics). The translations of three of his seven major novels were produced in this lobbying climate.

Comparisons with Mann are appropriate in terms of the novels' lengths, but by no means in terms of narrative stance or structure – these translations represent a failed attempt at canonization in terms of a modernist aesthetics. Doderer's work is actually of another line of descent. As a trained historian-turned-novelist, he has readapted the social criticism characteristic of the realist/naturalist novel, in light of the scientific humanism of expressionism (especially under the influence of Albert Paris von Gütersloh). His social criticism is not that of the socialist or socio-political critic more familiar in Germany and exemplified in Grass's *Tin Drum*. Instead, Doderer concentrates on individuals' comprehension (or lack thereof) of a large historical picture, and on their conflicting experiences of everyday life. He professes to account for the morality of historical perception while avoiding large-scale or partisan politics. This leads him, for instance, to ignore World War II in *The Demons*, thus leaving himself open to charges of not taking a clear moral stance on one of the greatest events in European history.

Today, his prose structure seems an attempt at a postmodern narrative, in the sense that his narrators are all unreliable, and his characters are explicitly at odds with each other in experiencing the significance of the historical events in their lives; his novels call official history into question by showing how individuals fail to understand their day-to-day lives. Helen Wolff points out (*Books Abroad* Seminar, 1968) that he attempts to throw light on the dark spots in local understanding, and that his attention to emplotment is incidental, at best. Instead, he tries to "reproduce the quality of time at a certain suspended moment in history", and forces his readers to read "interlinearly" and fill gaps that the characters themselves are unable to. In this sense, his narrative is postmodern, since it acknowledges the readers' experience of the text as more important than the author's or narrator's authority.

There is, therefore, no clear narrative equivalent to Doderer's nuanced prose in English, since it relies on an unstable interweaving of regional languages, sociolects, and authorial intrusions (including irregular shifts of tense and mood) that force the reader to construct the narrative out of unclear truth claims. By no means does the narrative structure convey finished meaning; usually concentrating on the 1920s, it meanders within the contours of a historical moment (*The Demons*, which builds up to the burning of the Parliament in 1927, or *Every Man a Murderer*), or a place (*The Strudelhof Steps*, *The Waterfalls of Slunj*). Translations of such shimmering surfaces are difficult at best, and then are complicated by Doderer's command of the formidable range of sociolects and regional variations of even "standard" bourgeois speech that existed in the last days of the Austro-Hungarian empire and persisted into the 20th-century's successor states; he also plays with narrative control in a way more suggestive of Umberto Eco than of Thomas Mann.

WINSTON & WINSTON started on arguably the most complex novel, *The Demons*, before turning back to the simpler "detective story", *Every Man a Murderer*. Their complete and straightforward translations (1961, 1964) render the texts as readable standard English in a modernist vein. In *The Demons*, they add a list of characters, and point out its connection to Dostoevskii's *The Possessed*. They omit the subtitle, which calls the book a "Chronicle", betraying under-sensitivity to the play of historical authority on which the book rests (three major characters are a chronicler, a medieval historian, and a historian in training). The work's fulcrum is the fact that only in retrospect did the Palace of Justice conflagration seem a turning point in history, since the main characters almost overlooked the day it happened. The shifts within sentences and paragraphs from speculation to reportage, from indirect speech to authorial comment, are thus not always strictly observed, since the translators are focused on the narrator's authority, rather than the decenteredness of his world which is arguably Doderer's point.

This straightforward approach to the narrative voice, however, replicates admirably the narrative style of *Ein Mord, den jeder begehrt* (*Every Man a Murderer*), which demonstrates narrators' unreliability by having the main character uncover a completely different (and perhaps more historically "true") version of a decisive moment in his life. Thus each narrative line, characterizing the narrator syntactically rather than undercutting him, is coherent in a way that those in *Demons* are not.

WILKINS & KAISER (1966) take a more aestheticizing approach to *The Waterfalls of Slunj*, replicating Doderer's twists of syntax as twists of human understanding about a group of loosely affiliated individuals. Doderer's idiosyncratic sentence rhythms and switches of register, the ambiguous music contrasting direct and indirect discourse with his narrative intrusions, could thus be considered more successfully transmitted here than in the translations of earlier novels.

As one of a set of translators who have undertaken a handful of Doderer's shorter works, KLING used his competent translations (1974) of important short stories to lobby for a complete translation of *The Strudelhof Steps* (and says as much in the *Chicago Review*), a proposition that to date has not been taken up.

KATHERINE ARENS

Further Reading

Bachem, Michael, *Heimito von Doderer*, Boston: Twayne, 1981

Hannemann, Bruno, "Heimito von Doderer" in *Major Figures of Modern Austrian Literature*, edited by Donald G. Daviau, Riverside, California: Ariadne Press, 1988

Kling, Vincent, "Doderer in English", *Chicago Review*, 26/2 (1974) pp. 3–4 (introduces Kling's translations of other short stories and essays)

Larsen, M. Deen, "Heimito von Doderer: The Elusive Realist", *Chicago Review*, 26/2 (1974) pp. 55–69

Various authors, "An International Symposium in Memory of Heimito von Doderer (1896–1966)", special issue of *Books Abroad: An International Literary Quarterly*, 42/3 (Summer 1968) (see especially Martin Swales, pp. 371–75, and Helen Wolff, pp. 378–79)

Fedor Dostoevskii 1821–1881

Russian novelist, short-story writer and journalist

Biography

Dostoevskii was born in Moscow, 30 October 1821 (old style). His father was a retired military surgeon who subsequently earned a nobleman's title. Dostoevskii was educated at home and later at a day school and then boarding school. He entered the Military Engineering Academy in St Petersburg in 1838, graduating as a War Ministry draughtsman in 1843. He resigned his commission as an engineering lieutenant in 1844 and started a literary career. His first published work was a translation of Balzac's *Eugénie Grandet*. His first novel, *Bednye liudi* (*Poor Folk*) appeared in 1846, and was an immediate critical success. Dostoevskii published more than a dozen other works during the later 1840s. The 1850s were for Dostoevskii years of politically motivated imprisonment and exile, which began with his arrest for reading a banned public letter by Belinsky at a meeting of the socially radical Petrashevskii circle, in 1849. After being reprieved by tsar Nicholas I just prior to execution, he was sentenced to imprisonment in Siberia, which he endured between 1850 and 1854, and which was followed by military service in internal exile until 1859 (the year of Alexander II's accession), when he left the army once again and was allowed to return to St Petersburg. On his return to writing, he founded with his brother the journal *Vremia* (1861–63) and in 1864–65 he edited *Epokha*. In 1857 he married Mar'ia Dmitrievna Isaeva, but her death and that of his brother, Mikhail, both in 1864, undermined him emotionally, and he inherited debts from both families. During the mid-1860s Dostoevskii conducted an erratic and unhappy relationship with Apollinaria Suslova, and turned increasingly to gambling. In 1867 he married Anna Grigorievna Snitkina, the stenographer to whom he had dictated *Igrok* (*The Gambler*) in 1866; they had four children, two of whom died before reaching adulthood. With the support of Snitkina and the responsibility of children, his personal and professional lives assumed much greater structure and stability. His greatest novels stem from the period after 1866. Debtors remained a problem, however, and partly motivated the family's extended stays in western Europe in the years 1867 to 1871. Dostoevskii sufferered from emphysema and periodically sought treatment at the German spa town of Ems. He died as a result of the disease in St Petersburg, 28 January 1881 (old style).

Dostoevskii is acknowledged as one of the major figures of 19th-century literature. The literary innovation and psychological approach of his fiction exerted a profound influence on the development of the novel in the 20th century, as well as attracting significant critical and popular acclaim in his own time. Dostoevskii wrote four major novels, *Prestuplenie i nakazanie* (*Crime and Punishment*), 1866; *Idiot* (*The Idiot*), 1868, *Besy* (*The Possessed*), 1871–72; and *Brat'ia Karamazovy* (*The Brothers Karamazov*), 1879–80. His novella, *Zapiski iz podpol'ia* (*Notes from the Underground*) was published in 1864.

Translations

Novels

Zapiski iz mertvogo doma, 1861–62

Coulson, Jessie, *Memoirs from the House of the Dead*, London and New York: Oxford University Press, 1956; edited by Ronald Hingley, Oxford and New York: Oxford University Press, 1965

Edwards, H. Sutherland, *Prison Life in Siberia*, from the French version of Neyroud, London: Vizetelly, 1887; as *The House of the Dead, or, Prison Life in Siberia*, London: Dent, and New York: Dutton, 1911

Garnett, Constance, *The House of the Dead*, London: Heinemann, 1915; reprinted New York: Limited Editions Club, 1982

McDuff, David, *The House of the Dead*, Harmondsworth and New York: Penguin, 1986
Thilo, Marie von, *Buried Alive; or, Ten Years of Penal Servitude in Siberia*, London: Longman, and New York: Holt, 1881

Zapiski iz podpol'ia, 1864
Coulson, Jessie, *Notes from Underground*, with *The Double*, Harmondsworth and Baltimore: Penguin, 1972
Garnett, Constance, *Notes from Underground*, in her *The Novels of Fyodor Dostoevsky*, London: Heinemann, 1918; revised by Bernard Guilbert Guerney for *A Treasury of Russian Literature*, New York: Vanguard, and London: Bodley Head, 1943; revised by Ralph E. Matlaw for *Notes from Underground*, with *The Grand Inquisitor*, New York: Dutton, 1960
Ginsburg, Mirra, *Notes from Underground*, New York: Bantam, 1974
Hogarth, Charles James, *Letters from the Underworld*, London: Dent, 1913
Katz, Michael R., *Notes from Underground*, New York: Norton, 1989
Kentish, Jane, *Notes from the Underground*, with *The Gambler*, Oxford and New York: Oxford University Press, 1991
MacAndrew, Andrew R., *Notes from Underground*, with *White Night*, *The Dreams of a Ridiculous Man*, and selections from *The House of the Dead*, New York: New American Library, 1961; London: New English Library, 1968
Magarshack, David, *Notes from the Underground*, in his *The Best Short Stories of Dostoevsky*, New York: Modern Library, 1956; reprinted New York: Harper and Row, 1968
Pevear, Richard and Larissa Volokhonsky, *Notes from Underground*, New York: Knopf, and London: Vintage, 1993
Shishkov, Serge, *Notes from Underground*, New York: Crowell, 1969

Prestuplenie i nakazanie, 1866
Coulson, Jessie, *Crime and Punishment*, London: Oxford University Press, 1953; New York: Norton, 1964; with an introduction by Richard Peace, Oxford and New York: Oxford University Press, 1995
Garnett, Constance, *Crime and Punishment*, London: Heinemann, 1914; New York: Macmillan, 1923
Hapgood, Isabel, *Crime and Punishment* (dramatization performed in New York, translated from the French and published in Orleneff's Russian Lyceum series), 1905
Irving, Laurence, *The Unwritten Law* (stage adaptation of *Crime and Punishment*), 1910
Katzer, Julius, *Crime and Punishment*, Moscow: Raduga, 1985
Kropotkin, Princess Alexandra, *Crime and Punishment* (revised translation "arranged for modern reading"), New York: International Collectors Library, 1953
McDuff, David, *Crime and Punishment*, Harmondsworth: Penguin, 1991
Magarshack, David, *Crime and Punishment*, Harmondsworth and New York: Penguin, 1951
Monas, Sidney, *Crime and Punishment*, New York: New American Library, 1968
Pevear, Richard and Larissa Volokhonsky, *Crime and Punishment*, New York: Knopf, 1992; London: Vintage, 1993
Ussher, Percy Arland, *The Mines of Siberiay: A New Ballad of Rooshian Rodie and Pawnbroker Liz* (adaptation), Glenageary, Co. Dublin: Dolmen Press, 1956
Whishaw, Frederick, *Crime and Punishment*, London: Vizetelly, 1886; reprinted anonymously, London: Dent, and New York: Dutton, 1911

Idiot, 1868
Carlisle, Henry and Olga Carlisle, *The Idiot*, New York: New American Library, 1969
Garnett, Constance, *The Idiot*, London: Heinemann, 1913; New York: Macmillan, 1917; revised by Avrahm Yarmolinsky, New York: Limited Editions Club, 1956
Gray, Simon, *The Idiot* (adaptation), London: Methuen, 1970
Katzer, Julius, *The Idiot*, Moscow: Raduga: 1971, revised edition, 1985–86
Magarshack, David, *The Idiot*, Harmondsworth and New York: Penguin, 1955
Martin, Eva M., *The Idiot* ("newly revised version"), London: Dent, 1914; New York: Dutton, 1916
Myers, Alan, *The Idiot*, Oxford and New York: Oxford University Press, 1992
Whishaw, Frederick, *The Idiot*, London: Vizetelly, and New York: Brentano, 1887

Besy, 1871–72
Garnett, Constance, *The Possessed*, London: Heinemann, 1914; revised to incorporate "Stavrogin's Confession", 1923; 2 vols, London: Dent, and New York: Dutton, 1931
Katz, Michael R., *Devils*, Oxford and New York: Oxford University Press, 1992
Koteliansky, S.S. and Virginia Woolf, *Stavrogin's Confession* (first English translation of the "missing chapters" that had been found in manuscript in 1921), Richmond, Surrey: Virginia and Leonard Woolf, 1922
MacAndrew, Andrew R., *The Possessed*, New York: New American Library, 1962
Magarshack, David, *The Devils (The Possessed)*, Harmondsworth: Penguin, 1953; reprinted with "Stavrogin's Confession" 1971
O'Brien, Justin, *The Possessed: A Play in Three Parts* (translation of Albert Camus's French adaptation), London: Hamish Hamilton, and New York: Knopf, 1960
Pevear, Richard and Larissa Volokhonsky, *Demons*, New York: Knopf, and London: Vintage, 1994

Brat'ia Karamazovy, 1879–80
Avsey, Ignat, *The Karamazov Brothers*, Oxford and New York: Oxford University Press, 1994
Garnett, Constance, *The Brothers Karamazov*, London: Heinemann, 1912; 2 vols, London: Dent, 1927; revised by Avrahm Yarmolinsky, 3 vols, New York: Limited Editions Club, 1933; revised by Princess Alexandra Kropotkin, Philadelphia: John C. Winston (abridged), 1949; revised by Ralph. E. Matlaw, New York: Norton, 1976
Hapgood, Isabel, *Brothers Karamazov* (dramatization performed in New York, translated from the French, and published in Orleneff's *Russian Lyceum Series*), 1905

Ivan, Rosalind, *The Brothers Karamazov* (from theatrical adaptation *Les frères Karamazov* by Jacques Copeau and Jean Croué, 1911), London: Heinemann, 1927
Katzer, Julius, *The Karamazov Brothers*, 2 vols, Moscow: Progress, 1980
MacAndrew, Andrew R., *The Brothers Karamazov*, New York: Bantam, 1970
McDuff, David, *The Brothers Karamazov*, Harmondsworth and New York: Penguin, 1993
Magarshack, David, *The Brothers Karamazov*, Harmondsworth and Baltimore: Penguin, 1958
Pevear, Richard and Larissa Volokhonsky, *The Brothers Karamazov*, with an introduction by Pevear, London: Quartet, and San Francisco: North Point Press, 1990

Autobiography
Dnevnik pisatel'ia, 1876–81
Brasol, Boris, *The Diary of a Writer*, 2 vols, New York: Braziller, 1949
Lantz, Kenneth, *A Writer's Diary*, 2 vols, London: Quartet, 1994–95

Letters
Lowe, David, with Ronald Meyer in vol. 1, *The Complete Letters*, 5 vols, Ann Arbor: Ardis, 1988–91

Fedor Dostoevskii wrote four "major" novels – *Crime and Punishment*, *The Idiot*, *The Devils* (or *The Possessed*) and *The Brothers Karamazov* – and some 30 other creative works (according to the authoritative 30-volume edition of the complete works, *Polnoe sobranie sochinenii v tridtsati tomakh*, Leningrad: Nauka, 1972–90).

The list of translations contains six representative titles. In addition to what are generally agreed to be the four major novels in his oeuvre, two shorter works have been included: *Notes from the House of the Dead*, and *Notes from Underground* (the former chosen for its unique status as the first text of the author to be translated into English, and the latter because of the extensive attention it has received as a seminal work or "sounding board" for the more complex novels that were to follow). Mention should be made of two other translations of Dostoevskii that fall outside the generally accepted confines of the creative, but that are essential reading for an appreciation of the author behind the text (and its translations). The journal publication *Dnevnik pisatelia* has been twice translated in its entirety into English, in the first instance as *The Diary of a Writer* (New York: Braziller, 1949) by Boris Brasol, and more recently as *A Writer's Diary* (London: Quartet, 1994–95; 2 vols) by Kenneth Lantz, with an "Introductory Study" of 117 pages by Gary Saul Morson. (Passages from this work were translated as early as 1916 by S.S. Koteliansky and J. Middleton Murry under the title, *Pages from the Journal of an Author*.) Then there are Dostoevskii's letters. An edition of *The Complete Letters* in five volumes (Ann Arbor: Ardis, 1988–91) is available in English, translated by David Lowe (collaborating with Ronald Meyer in volume 1). Several selections of the letters have also been published in translation.

One problem that faces the compiler of a list of translations of Dostoevskii's works is variation in the spelling of the Russian author's names. The choice of form in English is determined either by what is considered current usage (e.g. Fedor Dostoïeffsky in some early translations, Fyodor – but also Thedor and Feodor – Dostoevsky in 20th-century translations from Garnett to Pevear-Volokhonsky, and Fyodor Dostoyevsky in two generations of Penguin translations), or by bibliographical convention in following one of the recognized transliteration systems (e.g. F.M. Dostoevskii). In the present volume the Library of Congress modified system of transliteration (without diacritics) is followed for Russian names.

More significant, however, is the issue of the English title by which a particular work is generally known. There is little or no variation in the cases of *Crime and Punishment*, *The Idiot* and *The Brothers Karamazov*. Tradition has played its part in the canonization of these three titles. Russian has no definite or indefinite articles, so there is a degree of leeway in rendering each of the titles. Nevertheless, *Crime and Punishment* in the abstract rather than a more declarative *The Crime and the Punishment* has taken hold, just as *The Idiot* is universally preferred to *An Idiot*. Slightly less stable is the reversal of common usage in the literary translation of *Brat'ia Karamazovy* as *The Brothers Karamazov*, where the influence of the word order in the source title is evident. Katzer and Avsey, in the list above, have attempted to break the mould by opting for the adjustment of *The Karamazov Brothers* in conformity with the expectation engendered by the normal sequence in English. The greatest difficulty among the four major novels is how to translate the shortest of the titles, *Besy*. The persistence of what might be called the "GARNETT effect" is well illustrated by the history of the translation of this title. Although it had been referred to in the critical writing of the 19th century as "The Demons", Garnett resolved upon *The Possessed* for her title in order to bring out the Dostoevskiian subtext (Matthew 8:28) "there met him two possessed with devils"). (It should be noted, however, that she was far from being innovative in this choice, for Derély's French translation of 1886 was entitled *Les Possédés* and the German translation of Putze, published in Dresden in 1888, was *Die Besessenen*.) In England, when MAGARSHACK attempted to restore a more literal equivalent in the title of his translation, the publishers of the Penguin edition felt the need to acknowledge (and implicitly to honour) Garnett by publishing hers in parenthesis on the title page. In 1994, the circle was squared when the PEVEAR & VOLOKHONSKY translation came out as *Demons* and, what is more, in an Everyman's Library edition (the series having been acquired and relaunched by Knopf in 1991). The two shorter works in the list above have enjoyed greater liberty in their English incarnations, thereby obscuring the fact that the first word of both titles in Russian is the same: *Zapiski* (cognate with the verb *zapisat'*, to write down, and associated with the titles of significant, earlier works of Russian literature that include Gogol's *Diary of a Madman* and Turgenev's *Sportsman's Sketches*, to quote them under their most common English translations).

Errors in dating, title or attribution of translator occur in *all* the authorities consulted for bibliographical information (listed in Further Reading). Some errors seem to have been reproduced in unverified transmission from one source to another, while others have resulted from typographical misprints or unwarranted assumptions. The entries in the list of translations have whenever possible been checked against the actual items cited.

In his essay on "Tradition and the Individual Talent" (1919), T.S. Eliot introduced the idea of the *historical sense* as a critical principle by stating that: "No poet ... has his complete meaning alone. His significance, his appreciation is the appreciation of his relation to the dead poets ... You cannot value him alone; you must set him, for contrast and comparison, among the dead." Translators of Dostoevskii are required to perform an analogous, albeit diametrically opposed, office, in setting a 19th-century author among the *living*. If an "appreciation" of a foreign novelist in English translation inevitably involves what Eliot calls "contrast and comparison", then for such an *individual* talent as that of Dostoevskii it is the former that is always more likely to act as the translator's imperative. In the methodology of literary translation, contrast implies the revitalization of the literary resources of the target culture through an introjection of the outlandish, whereas comparison makes more of the attempt to accommodate the unfamiliar within a native tradition. In Dostoevskii's case, direct comparisons – whether they have been of his genius with that of Shakespeare, of his characters with those of Dickens, of his psychological realism with that of Poe, or of the consistency of his style (in Henry James's unflattering image) with that of a "fluid pudding" – have tended to be superficial and unhelpful. The problems of identifying the uniqueness of Dostoevskii and finding him an appropriate anchorage in the target culture are compounded by the fact that critical considerations of his place within the context of *Russian* literature (the more so when seen from abroad) have tended to be based upon a presumption that he must in all particulars be contrasted with Tolstoi.

The first sustained treatment (in English) of the Dostoevskii–Tolstoi thematic appeared in Dmitri Merezhkovskii's *Tolstoi as Man and Artist with an Essay on Dostoievski* (1902; the essay is reprinted as "Dostoievsky and Tolstoy" in *Russian Literature and Modern English Fiction: A Collection of Critical Essays*; edited by Donald Davie [Chicago: University of Chicago Press, 1965]). According to Merezhkovskii, Dostoevskii's "mastery of dialogue" in which "all is revealed and unrevealed" marked his writing as different from Tolstoi's, where the "language of all the characters ... is the same". Merezhkovskii's study, which itself had been translated from the Russian, presented a detailed antithesis in the lives, natures, philosophies, artistic methods and literary significance of the two authors. Dostoevskii's "sacred and demoniacal sickness" stood in contrast to "the not less divine and demonic superflux of bodily carnality, strength and health" in Tolstoi. In consequence of this opposition, Dostoevskii's characters were depicted as "living souls", Tolstoi's as "overgrown beef". *War and Peace* and *Anna Karenina* were "really novels, original epics", but Dostoevskii's major works were "not novels nor epics, but tragedies" (See Muchnic, 1969; Davie, 1965). These oppositions were to be repeated – and elaborated – by others (notably Georg Lukács in the conclusion to his *Theory of the Novel*, 1920; Thomas Mann in his essay on "Goethe and Tolstoy", 1922; revised 1925; Erich Auerbach in the penultimate chapter of *Mimesis*, 1946; and, more recently, Joseph Brodsky in *Less Than One*, 1987), until they achieved the status of *idées reçues*. Thus it came about that Dostoevskii was defined largely by his deficiencies: he was *not* English; he was *not* Tolstoi; he was *not* even a novel-writer. The exclusive, and sometimes oppressive, sense experienced by those who entered into the fictional world of the Russian author was summed up in D.H. Lawrence's laconic pronouncement (in a letter to Lady Ottoline Morrell, conjecturally dated as 24 March 1915) that Dostoevskii was "not nice". Dostoevskii, then, has always been re-constructed in English as an alien author, and translations of his novels must acknowledge this cliché.

No translations of Dostoevskii's novels into English were published in his lifetime. Since his death, however, Dostoevskii has made, and continues to make, a remarkable impact upon English literature. The history of Dostoevskii's English reception falls into three distinct phases, which may be associated, on the one hand, with the work of specific translators and, on the other, with conspicuous shifts in critical and theoretical approaches to the literary text. Dostoevskii's reputation, then, has undergone significant modification since the appearance of the very first translation, by Marie van THILO, of *Notes from the House of the Dead*, in 1881, the year of his death. This translation, published by Longmans and entitled *Buried Alive; or, Ten Years of Penal Servitude in Siberia*, added a new name to the list, dominated at the time by Turgenev and Tolstoi, of Russian authors in English translation. Like Turgenev's (whose *Notes of a Hunter* was translated as *Russian Life in the Interior; or, The Experiences of a Sportsman* as early as 1855), Dostoevskii's début came in the form of an imaginative prose work that could easily be mistaken, by a foreign, and poorly informed, readership, for factual representation. The second text to be translated, however, altered the English perception of the author. In 1886 *Crime and Punishment* came out in a translation by Frederick WHISHAW (who went on to translate half-a-dozen of Dostoevskii's works in the next two years for titles in Vizetelly's Russian Novels series). His translations of *Crime and Punishment* and *The Idiot* (1887), both bearing the same subtitle – "a realistic novel", helped to establish a stereotype (which has persisted) of Dostoevskii as a transcendental – or "fantastic" – realist with the visionary capacity to utter (as Dostoevskii himself had expressed it) a *new* word. In the course of the 20th century, Dostoevskii has evolved from his initial casting as a prophet to being taken as an example of a psychologist who has mastered a *creative* language of his own, eventually to become identified as the leading exponent of the *dialogic* voice. While the critical consensus was being regularly re-negotiated, each generation of readers discovered Dostoevskii afresh through translations that had been re-issued, revised or newly commissioned.

The first phase in the history of Dostoevskii translation culminated in the translation by Constance GARNETT of all the Russian author's fictional works as part of an ambitious attempt to bring the prose giants of Russian literature (Turgenev, Chekhov, Gogol, Tolstoi and Dostoevskii) to the notice of the English public. Her translations of Dostoevskii were brought out by Heinemann in London (and subsequently by Macmillan in New York) in a succession of volumes, from 1912 to 1920. Garnett's decision to start the series at the end with the publication of Dostoevskii's last novel first, *The Brothers Karamazov* (in 1912), to work through the other major novels next – *The Idiot* (1913), *Crime and Punishment* and *The Possessed* (1914) – and to conclude with the minor works, testified to a sense of urgency as well as priority. *The Brothers Karamazov* had not previously been translated into English (although that other indefatigable female translator of the Russian Classics, Isabel HAPGOOD, had produced a stage version for performance in New York in 1905, which was published in Orleneff's *Russian*

Lyceum Series) and those who, like Arnold Bennett or John Galsworthy, could not wait for it to come out had had to rely upon one of the *two* French versions that were already available by 1906. (When the new, English *Brothers Karamazov* did eventually appear, Joseph Conrad wrote to Edward Garnett on 27 May 1912 to tell him that "your wife's translation is wonderful. One almost breaks one's heart thinking of it. What courage! What perseverance! What talent of – interpretation, let us say. The word "translation" does not apply to your wife's achievements. But indeed the man's art does not deserve this good fortune" (quoted by Muchnic, 1969 and May, 1994).

It was through Constance Garnett's initiative that Dostoevskii was made available in his novelistic entirety to an English readership that included not only a disapproving Lawrence and a critical Conrad, but also an enthusiastic Middleton Murry and a troubled Virginia Woolf who herself was to collaborate with S.S. Koteliansky in 1922 for the Hogarth Press on a translation of newly discovered manuscript passages from Dostoevskii's fictional writings (*Stavrogin's Confession* and *The Plan of the Life of a Great Sinner*). The subsequent, critical judgement of Garnett's accomplishment has proved to be just as mixed as that which originated from her friends and contemporaries, the main difference being that whereas, in the earlier part of the 20th century, most commentators tended to focus (for better or for worse) on the Russian author and his ideas, attention has turned more recently to the efficacy of the translator and her language. Joseph Brodsky, for example, lamented the fact in his essay "Catastrophes in the Air" (*Less Than One*, London: Penguin, 1987) that both Dostoevskii and Tolstoi "were translated by the same hand", since the Western reader of Garnett thereby loses the means to distinguish between the mimetic prose of a Tolstoi "who took the idea of art reflecting reality a bit too literally and in whose shadow the subordinate clauses of Russian prose are writhing indolently till this day" and a Dostoevskii, whose style is marked by "feverishly accelerating sentences conglomerating, in their rapid progress, bureaucratese, ecclesiastical terminology, *lumpen* argot, French utopists' mumbo-jumbo, the classical cadences of gentry prose – anything! all the layers of contemporary diction". Of course, not everyone would look upon the sensuous qualities of Dostoevskii's style with Brodsky's poet's-eye view, nor would they wish to censure the translator for her promiscuous infidelity. Victor Terras, for example, prefaces his Twayne Masterworks monograph on *The Idiot* with a vote of confidence for the Garnett translation, which he describes as "the best translation from a stylistic point of view" (*The Idiot: An Interpretation*, Boston: Twayne, 1990). Others have acknowledged the excellence of what has generally come to be regarded as the "standard" translation, yet have nevertheless felt it to be in need of revision. Ralph MATLAW (writing an afterword to the Norton Critical Edition translation of *The Brothers Karamazov*) noted that as a result of lapses that are "sometimes trivial, sometimes quite crucial" the original English translation is "deficient in certain respects (here remedied)". Moreover, there is the matter, as he observed obliquely, of a "discrepancy between her literary talents and those of the authors that she has translated". (It is not altogether clear from his commentary whether Matlaw considered that this particular "discrepancy" had been "remedied" in his revision!) Whatever the verdict on Garnett, the shift of focus from the novelty of Dostoevskii's thought to the literary qualities and stylistic range of the translator is a mark of an altered emphasis on the role that translation plays in the acculturation of "strange" literary works. Constance Garnett's achievement continues to be the subject of detailed discussion and analysis. The interested reader is referred to the works listed in the section on Further Reading under Nikoliukin and May. Nikoliukin provides a checklist of differences between the English and Russian in what he calls "a comparative analysis", ranging from the broadly stylistic ("Garnett has not given due significance to the narrator as a structural principle in Dostoevskii's prose") to the narrowly numismatic ("The 'two twenty-copeck coins' ... become 'forty copecks'"); May offers an assessment of Garnett that is methodologically determined by an acceptance of the new paradigm of Translation Studies "with the translator redefining the nature of ... ownership at every level".

The second phase in the history of the translation of Dostoevskii's works into English is linked to a radical change in the perception of what language, and hence literature, is. "Language", as Ernst Cassirer observed in a lecture on "Language and Art" (1942), "cannot be regarded as a copy of things but as a condition of our concept of things" (*Symbol, Myth, and Culture: Essays and Lectures of Ernst Cassirer, 1935–1945*, edited by Donald Phillip Verene, New Haven and London, Yale University Press, 1979). Cassirer's statement acknowledges the post-Romantic rejection of a Platonic view of language in favour of a neo-Kantian perspective. The eventual repercussions of this shift for literary composition of all kinds, including translation, are summed up in Archibald Macleish's celebrated maxim that "A poem should not mean / But be". In this light, the status conferred on literary translation is that of a productive, rather than simply a reproductive, activity. The translator is not so much a servile labourer "in another man's plantation" (as Dryden had expressed it in the dedication to his 1697 translation of the *Aeneid*) as a collaborator, who bears the responsibility of introducing an alien "concept" into his own culture. To fulfil this task adequately the translator must *alter* his source model, however heretical this requirement may once have sounded (and to some still sounds). In 1816, Humboldt spoke for a much later generation when, writing in defence of his metrical translation of Aeschylus, he made the bold assertion that "the more a translation strives for fidelity, the more deviant the translation becomes ... [it can] do little more than match each peculiar trait with a different one" (Dryden and Humboldt are quoted in *Translation/History/Culture: A Sourcebook*, edited and translated by André Lefevere, London and New York: Routledge, 1992, pp. 24, 136). What, essentially, a successful translation of a work by an author belonging to an earlier age achieves is a triumph of literary resurrection (rather than a work of mere excavation and restoration) that results in a new addition to the living language of the receiving culture. Randolph Bourne, an American critic writing in *The Dial*, 63 (1917), opened his review of the latest instalment in the Garnett translations to appear, by stating that "it is impossible not to think of Dostoevskii as a living author". What readers of Dostoevskii encountered, according to Bourne (who never once mentions Garnett's name in his review), was a "superb modern healthiness", breaking down artificially erected divisions in such categories as normal-abnormal and sane-insane. After Dostoevskii's modernism, he claimed, it was impossible to return to older classical fiction. *The Brothers Karamazov* was an "epic of frustrated aspiration" and an early work, *The Double*, a "deep poem of the human spirit". Another American, James Huneker, bestowed a seal of approbation upon Dostoevskii, long before Coca Cola received the same accolade, by asserting that (compared with Tolstoi) he was "the *real thing*" (Muchnic, 1969).

Liked or loathed, the gallery of fictional characters ranging from tormented intellectuals like Rodion Raskolnikov or Ivan Karamazov to saintly misfits like Sonia Marmeladov or Alesha Karamazov, introduced through the Garnett translations, found their appointed niche in the world of English letters as a creative presence. In the period that intervened between the Garnett era and the advent of Translation Studies as a self-proclaimed independent discipline in the 1980s, Dostoevskii experienced the fate that awaits all authors who become established as (foreign) classics of world literature: he had to be translated afresh. It is a tenet for a particular school of theorists (and one eagerly endorsed by the publishing industry) that all great works of literature need re-translation for each new generation of readers.

After World War II, David MAGARSHACK emerged as Penguin's answer to Heinemann (and to Dent, since by the late 1920s, Garnett's translations had also begun appearing in the Everyman's Library edition, which had already brought out an anonymous translation of *Crime and Punishment* as early as 1911). If Garnett's Dostoevskii was, on the one hand, not to be discriminated from her Tolstoi and, on the other, too Victorian (or Edwardian) in treating the more sordid passages in the author's prose, then Magarshack offered a remedy in both respects. In the world of Penguin, he became the translator of Dostoevskii and *not* Tolstoi (although promiscuous with other Russian authors), and – for a new generation of readers – his language was couched in a contemporary English idiom. What is more, in the subliminal world of the intertextual, beyond what the reader-in-translation could perceive, Magarshack met with the approval of those who could read the original Russian text, in that his versions were considered closer to Dostoevskii in a literal sense. Unfortunately, the *consolidated* Dostoevskii, as one might call him in this second phase of the translation history, suffered from a serious shortcoming. The new translator had certain "blind spots" when it came to the matter of style. The attempt at assimilation went a stroke too far. His decision, for example to call Raskolnikov "Roddy", in an attempt to solve the tricky problem of how to render Russian diminutives in English, was too much for one exasperated critic. (Such travesties are, of course, more acceptable if the original work is adapted and set to music as in Percy Arland Ussher's *The Mines of Siberiay: A New Ballad of Rooshian Rodie and Pawnbroker Liz*, published in 1956 by the Dolmen Press in Ireland.) At a time when the creative role of translation was coming to the fore, there was a flat-footedness about the Penguin Dostoevskii. The sense of excitement that some of Garnett's early readers had apparently felt upon encountering an uncouth guest in the library had been replaced by a comfortably bourgeois feeling of familiarity in the presence of an interesting, but domesticated, foreigner in the drawing room. (Belatedly, the bland cohesion of Magarshack's English has been tacitly acknowledged in the decision by Penguin to commission a new series of translations from Dostoevskii mainly by David MCDUFF, an out-and-out literalist, whose versions are to be commended for their uncompromising determination to convey every stylistic peculiarity and lexical repetition found in the Russian.) The shortcomings of the original Penguin enterprise left open the opportunity in the post-World War II period for others to compete for the title of the new "standard" Dostoevskii, but none of Magarshack's more assiduous rivals – especially Jessie COULSON in England, Andrew MACANDREW in the United States and Julius KATZER in the Soviet Union – managed to attain the canonized status of a Garnett. A revolution in literary theory was needed before a radically different kind of translator would surface to impersonate Dostoevskii in the English language.

The symbiosis that exists between the creative and the critical is nowhere better illustrated in the history of Dostoevskii translation than in the "discovery" of Mikhail Bakhtin by the Western literary world following the translation of his critical study, *The Problems of Dostoevsky's Poetics*, in 1973 (and its re-translation in 1984). In the words of one critic, following the widespread availability of this book, "many of [Dostoevskii's] so-called faults have become virtues" (France, 1997). Bakhtin's central concerns – with the dialogic, with polyphony, with thresholds, and with double-voiced discourse – not only established Dostoevskii's reputation as innovative in his use of language as well as in his ideas, but they also ran parallel to issues that were gaining prominence for a new generation of translation theorists: difference, re-writing, visibility and the stylistics of living speech. In the last two decades, Bakhtin has achieved something of the same "cult" status that Dostoevskii experienced in the Garnett years.

One side-effect of the Bakhtinian revolution significant for new translators of Dostoevskii's novels is a recognition of the need to accommodate that distinctive clash and clamour of ideologies in the making, as they compete for dominance, which defines the *dialogic*. In the 1990s Richard PEVEAR & Larissa VOLOKHONSKY have embarked upon a project of translating the major works of Dostoevskii so as to bring out this aspect of the text, and commentators, such as Caryl Emerson and Rachel May, have praised them for capturing what the latter refers to as the "saturated ambivalence of the original text" (May, p. 53). (Peter France has remarked upon a similar enterprise in respect of the French versions being produced by André Marcowicz.) Paradoxically, insofar as the contemporary Pevear-Volokhonsky translations succeed in communicating the immediacy of event and the actuality of character, they foster an awareness of *the historical sense*, which according to Eliot "involves a perception, not only of the pastness of the past, but of its presence". Indeed, Pevear seems to ratify Eliot's statement when he remarks in the introduction to the new translation of *The Brothers Karamazov*,

> The comedy of style in the novel embodies movement and joy; it reveals the limits of language but also the freedom of language, one might almost say the freedom from language. ... The community of speech is simultaneous: the words of the dead are heard by the living; the words of the past are heard in the present.

If Pevear may be said to echo what Eliot has written, then this simply reinforces Bakhtin's insistence that the word is inter-individual and cannot be assigned to a single speaker. One of the most fascinating aspects of the reception of a literary text in translation, when a multiplicity of versions has been produced over a long period, is the simultaneous presence of different historical layers of interpretation. All the translations of Dostoevskii now *co-exist* alongside the original in what Yury Levin has called a "total complex ... in all its dynamism" (Nikoliukin, p. 226). It is only by investigating this total complex, Levin goes on to argue, that we can "define and evaluate the universal meaning and significance" of the Dostoevskiian novel. Far from cavilling about what has been lost in translation, those sceptics who question the merits of reading Dostoevskii in translation should reflect upon this claim and consider how much has been gained in the process.

Postscript: the Internet. This essay has offered a chronological survey of the reception of Dostoevskii in English. Constance GARNETT introduced Dostoevskii to the English-reading public as a new author; the translations by MAGARSHACK (and others) consolidated his reputation; and it was only in the run-in to the millennium in the post-Bakhtinian era of Translation Studies that the dialogic potential of such novels as *Crime and Punishment*, *The Idiot* and *The Brothers Karamazov* was at last being realized – and released – in the PEVEAR-VOLOKHONSKY translations. In the 21st century, technological advances will inevitably offer new, hyper-textual aids for dialogic readings-in-translation. Already it is possible to use the Internet to access Dostoevskii "on-line". The number of sites making translations of Dostoevskii available electronically is increasing at an exponential rate, yet, as the most cursory of web-searches will demonstrate, most of the novels currently available from the newest of the new media are in the old "standard" translations by Constance Garnett. An agreeable irony, and a confirmation of the dialogic pertinacity of the "historical sense".

LEON BURNETT

Further Reading

Bakhtin, Mikhail, *Problems of Dostoevsky's Poetics*, edited and translated by Caryl Emerson, Manchester: Manchester University Press, 1984 (Russian original published as *Problemy poetiki Dostoevskogo*, 1963)

Beebe, M. and C. Newton, "Dostoevsky in English: A Selected Checklist of Criticism and Translations", *Modern Fiction Studies*, 4 (1958) pp. 271–91

France, Peter, "Dostoevskii Rough and Smooth", *Forum for Modern Language Studies*, 33 (1997) pp. 72–80

Matlaw, Ralph E., "Afterword: On Translating *The Brothers Karamazov* in *The Brothers Karamazov*, translated by Constance Garnett, revised and edited by Matlaw, New York: Norton, 1976, pp. 736–44

May, Rachel, *The Translator in the Text: On Reading Russian Literature in English*, Evanston, Illinois: Northwestern University Press, 1994

Muchnic, Helen, *Dostoevsky's English Reputation (1881–1936)*, New York: Octagon Books, 1969 (originally published in *Smith College Studies in Modern Languages*, 20/3–4 (1938–39))

Nikoliukin, A.N., "Dostoevskii in Constance Garnett's Translation" in *Dostoevskii and Britain*, edited and translated by W.J. Leatherbarrow, Oxford and Providence, Rhode Island: Berg, 1995 (originally published in Russian in *Russkaia literatura*, 2 (1985))

Terry, Garth M., "Dostoyevsky Studies in Great Britain: A Bibliographical Survey", in *New Essays on Dostoyevsky* edited by Terry and Malcolm V. Jones, Cambridge and New York: Cambridge University Press, 1983

Drama: Translating into English

Underlying any translation is the attempt to recreate – rather than reproduce or reinterpret – a text written in a language other than the target language. The translation stands for the original, conveying its essential qualities – independent of it whilst interdependent with it. This means that the translation must stand alone as a piece of writing, as well as being an accurate and convincing mediation of the original.

As well as translations intended for performance in the theatre or on radio, television or film, some translations (usually of canon works) are intended for non-performance reading by students of literature, whether as an aid to deciphering, or as a substitute for, the source text. In these cases the translator will seek to follow what Nida and Taber call "formal correspondence", that is, "... a translation in which the features of the form of the source text have been mechanically reproduced in the receptor language" (*The Theory and Practice of Translation*, 1969). Other translations, intended for performance, seek to achieve "dynamic equivalence", whereby "the message of the original text has been so transported into the receptor language that the RESPONSE of the RECEPTOR is essentially that of the original receptors" (ibid; the authors' capitalization).

In dramatic translation for performance, re-creation must convey the sense of a text, whatever its origin, happening in the present and in the target culture, since an audience watching in the theatre, listening on the radio, or seeing and hearing on a screen will want to concentrate on the performance, not on a printed text. To evoke this sense of immediacy, varying methods are used. In translating a drama the translator may opt to recreate those historical references that locate a play in its original period – what Franz H. Link has called "historicism" (in *The Languages of Theatre*, edited by Ortrun Zuber, 1980). Alternatively, a translator may modernize or update references and language so that the audience experiences what Link calls "actualization" (ibid), a process Craig Raine adopted when transposing Racine's *Andromache* (published as *1953: A Version of Racine's Andromaque*, 1990) and Tony Harrison followed in his versions of English cycles of mystery plays (*The Mysteries*, 1985). A translator makes similar choices about whether to use archaic or contemporary language for the target text. Some translations of plays are widely performed although they are made in an idiom quite other than that of the original. For example, the frequently staged translations of Shakespeare plays by A.W. Schlegel, Ludwig and Dorothea Tieck and Graf Baudissin bear many stylistic hallmarks of 19th-century Romanticism, especially when compared with the translations made by Johann Heinrich Voss at much the same period, or those made in the 20th century in a more modern style by Erich Fried.

Sometimes translators transpose an original drama into a different place, time and idiom in order to illuminate aspects of their own language and society through the prism of the source text, as Tony Harrison did in his adaptation of Racine's *Phèdre* (published as *Phaedra Britannica*, 1975).

For performance a translation must not only accurately mediate the original but also recreate it in dialogue as dramatically alive and speakable as the original. As Max Beerbohm wrote: "... there is a great difference between what looks well in type and what sounds well on a pair of lips ..." ("Advice for Those about to Translate Plays", *Saturday Review of Politics, Literature, Science and Arts*, 18 July 1903). Conveying dialect or local speech convincingly is essential to re-creating the colour and immediacy of dramatists such as Franz Xaver Kroetz, who express their characters' states of mind and feelings, as well as their social positions, by these means. The danger, however, in making a dialect translation too specific is that the target translation will be able to play effectively only to a localized audience, a reservation that applies to *The Cracked Pot*, a Yorkshire dialect version by Blake Morrison of Heinrich von Kleist's *Der zerbrochene Krug*, directed in 1995 by Barrie Rutter (published 1996).

In some cases, an effective translation can rescue for performance a play not originally destined for the theatre, as with Ted Hughes's adaptation of Seneca's *Oedipus*, staged by Peter Brook in 1968 (published 1969). Similarly, a prose translation of a play originally written in verse may make the play more readily accessible. A prose adaptation might attempt to recreate full rhyme by means of assonance, alliteration and slant or half-rhymes. Whether translating prose or verse, a translator must recreate effects of subtext, ambiguity or incomplete statement in the original.

Another choice a translator must make in re-creating a source text is whether to foreignize or domesticate. The first approach makes no attempt to conceal the fact that the play has originated in a time or culture different from those in which the target audience receives the translation. For domesticated reception, a text will have been transposed or adapted to such an extent that it seems like a play written originally in the target language.

Other considerations of formal transposition apply if one adapts and translates from one genre to another. When a source novel is turned into a target drama, some narrative elements will be dramatized. For film or television some verbal messages in the source text must be re-expressed in audio-visual terms, and for radio they will be reinterpreted in narrative, music or sound effects. Dubbing and subtitling can help to make a source text comprehensible to a target audience, though equivalence here is more likely to be formal than dynamic. Dubbing transforms not only the sense but also the sound of actors performing the source text. Subtitling re-edits the source text's verbal patterns, usually abbreviating them, and this may alter emphasis and meaning.

In dramatic translation a translator must be aware of the totality of experience in a theatre. As Ortrun Zuber writes: "A play depends on additional elements such as movements, gestures, postures, mimicry, speech rhythms, intonations, music and other sound effects, lights, stage scenery ... In the process of translating a play, it is necessary for (the translator of a play) to mentally direct, act and see the play at the same time" (*The Languages of Theatre*, 1980).

Let us move from general considerations to the process. A translator of drama, as of any other text, should regard reading as part of the process of translation. Reading is a painfully acquired skill, as important to a translator as working drawings are to an architect. One should first try to get an overall impression of the style, idiom, themes and attitude – the Gestus (as the Brecht collective put it) of the play as a whole. Who are the characters, how do they relate to each other and the audience, who are strangers to them? How important is each character to the action – when on the stage or off? How important is the subtext? Is what the characters say or do always to be taken at face value?

In the early stages of a dramatic translation the source text should speak as directly as possible. Many essential decisions are made during the first stage, the so-called literal translation. Often direct literal renditions are – or later turn out to be – the best, as there is sometimes an exact equivalent between source and target languages; at other times a harsh, abrupt translation of a word or phrase jolts us into a new awareness because the translation is unexpected.

The first draft is best written down as quickly as possible. To allow breathing space for future drafts, one can write alternatives – a different adjective, noun or tense, say – over and below the "real" line. Far from being confusing, this three-way choice can be trebly helpful. From the second draft onwards, it is important not to be too draconian in crossing out, or improving upon, earlier ideas. Sometimes, fortunate choices in the first draft, when one is less inhibited, turn out to be best and should be retained. By the third or fourth draft, which will probably have been printed out in rough, to live with and work on, one should be near a reading draft – i.e. a draft plausible enough to show someone else for their comments.

Ideally, after the reading draft has been submitted, a face-to-face meeting follows between the translator and the person commissioning the translation – to discuss in detail where the work goes next. If there has been a reasonable gap since the submission, it is advisable to go back now to the translation and rework where necessary, being careful not to assume that only new ideas, only changes, are preferable.

If the translator is invited to rehearsals, it is helpful to attend as often as possible without disturbing the separate creative process of production. At rehearsals, it is important not to be too willing to change a phrase or line unless it fails to convey the passage in the source text (which one should have with one) or is so difficult to say that the director and actors dismiss it as unsayable.

In the theatre, the translator must be totally visible. He or she has to write the dialogue that the actors act, the director directs, and the critics criticize. A translator must therefore approach the translation in the way a writer would. With two differences. Basic dramaturgical decisions have already been made by the original dramatist. This is a freedom. Yet the translator is limited to a mode of expression he or she can at most recreate, not originate. This is a responsibility.

Both the responsibility and the freedom are greater if one translates work by playwrights new to the target country, new to the target language perhaps. In these cases, there is no groundwork of reception to build on. There again, a translator is not restricted by expectations of style, fashion or reputation. The writer *is* the translation.

In piecing together a method of dramatic translation for performance, some basic practical questions are helpful. What period is the play set in? In what location? Is the dialogue a localized idiom or specific dialect? Does one need to consult special dictionaries or a local native speaker, or to send queries to the author (assuming he or she is still alive) or agent? Is the cast size in the source text realistic for a production of the translated play in the target country? If the cast is too large, can roles be doubled or trebled without damaging the play's integrity? Is the theme potentially interesting to an audience in the target country? Are references in the text best left specific to their context, i.e. foreignized, or do they need transposing, i.e. domesticating? What are the author's instructions or recommendations on this?

Crucial to a successful translation of drama – if not to all literary forms – is the discovery or invention of an appropriate rhythm. The rhythm of dramatic dialogue, of which most but not all plays mostly consist, is a complex, living organism. Rhythm is the motive force, the energy, the heartbeat of language. Variations in rhythm alter emphasis, pace and through them, at times, meaning. Not only must the rhythm place the words in the most effective sequence and balance, but it must also operate between speeches, within scenes and between one scene and another.

Translating colloquial language or dialect offers special challenges. If some characters in the source text are predominantly urban in their speech patterns and others predominantly rural, the translation must register the difference clearly for a target audience. The same applies to social differences. Completely reinventing "upper-class", regional or demotic language is likely to be less productive than stylizing, using a formal vocabulary and grammar to denote "upper-class" speech and an informal, looser, "incorrect" language to indicate demotic or regional speech normally indicative of "lower-class" characters, and then leaving it to director and actors to differentiate further with appropriate accents and rhythms.

While new translations or adaptations of classic works – in Britain at least – attract more money and attention, they are generally used for one production only. Translations of contemporary plays, whilst more difficult to place and less well funded, often have a longer production life. Publication can help multiply productions.

Radio performance in the target language – at least in BBC productions – is likely to retain and possibly enhance the dramatic qualities of a source text. Some adaptation will always be needed. Often it is possible to make one of the characters a narrator-protagonist who moves the play forward as a narrative whilst also being central to the dramatic action. If a source text is very visual, it may help when translating it for radio to incorporate stage directions into dialogue rather than simply have them read out, which slows down dramatic pace and is intrusive.

Motives for commissioning dramatic translations include the wish to stage a classic, offer a certain actor a lead part, introduce a new writer to the repertoire, improve on an existing translation or create publicity by finding a striking new angle on a well-known source play. Translators of drama, as of literary works in general, will almost certainly need to be subsidized by other work until commissions come. In the case of contemporary playwrights, translations will almost certainly subsidize the original authors until they become better known. In other words, part of a translator's satisfaction in re-creating a source drama needs to lie in discovering and nurturing new work previously unknown – or little known – to the target audience.

Translators of dramatic works should also be aware of the contractual complications involved in translating drama, especially drama still in copyright. My own recommendation is to employ the services of an authors' representative or agent for this work, or, failing that, to seek advice from an appropriate professional body.

ANTHONY VIVIS

Further Reading

Johnson, David (editor), *Stages of Translation*, Bath: Absolute Press, 1996 (essays and interviews on translating for the stage)

Nida, Eugene A. and Charles R. Taber, *The Theory and Practice of Translation*, Leiden: E.J. Brill, 1969

Törnqvist, Egil, *Transposing Drama: Studies in Representation*, London: Macmillan, 1991

Vivis, Anthony, "The Stages of a Translation" in *Stages of Translation*, edited by David Johnston, Bath: Absolute Press, 1996

Zuber, Ortrun (editor), *The Languages of Theatre: Problems in the Translation and Transposition of Drama*, Oxford and New York: Pergamon Press, 1980

The Dream of the Red Chamber

Hong lou meng, written by Cao Xueqin (Hsueh-Ch'in) c.1716–c.1763

Few facts are known about the life of Cao Xueqin. His family had been rich but lost its wealth, and Cao was poor when towards the end of his life he wrote his famous novel. Generally believed to be an autobiography of Cao, and threaded with the tragic love story of Jia Baoyu and Lin Daiyu, the 120-chapter novel depicts the prosperity and decline of an aristocratic clan in the early years of the Qing (Ch'ing) Dynasty (1644–1911). It was regarded as an "obscene book" when it first appeared in the 19th century, but soon gained wide recognition as a great naturalistic love story – indeed, at times, as *the* Chinese novel. While remaining secure in its canonized position, it was reinterpreted in the Maoist era as a love story in appearance but an anti-feudalist politico-historical novel in essence.

The first 80 chapters of the work are by Cao Xueqin; it is believed that the last 40 were written wholly or partly by others.

Translations

Hawkes, David and John Minford, *The Story of the Stone: A Chinese Novel*, 5 vols, Harmondsworth: Penguin, 1973–86; Bloomington: Indiana University Press, 1979–87 (vols 1–3 translated by Hawkes; vols 4–5 translated by Minford)

Joly, H. Bencraft, *Hung lou meng; or, The Dream of the Red Chamber: A Chinese Novel*, 2 vols, Hong Kong: Kelly and Walsh, 1892–93

Wang, Chi-chen, *The Dream of the Red Chamber*, New York: Twayne, 1958; London: Vision Press, 1959 (first published in abridged form, New York: Doran, 1929)

Yang, Hsien-yi and Gladys Yang, *A Dream of Red Mansions*, 3 vols, Beijing: Foreign Languages Press, 1978–80

Translations into English of short excerpts of *Hong lou meng* appeared from 1830 onwards. Larger-scale translations began with JOLY (1892–93), which stopped at chapter 56. This was followed by WANG, published as a very much abridged translation in 1929 and then in an enlarged version in 1958 – the same year that Florence and Isabel McHugh published their *The Dream of the Red Chamber: A Chinese Novel of the Early Ching Period* (New York: Pantheon), which is an indirect translation, from Franz Kuhn's abridged German version. Then, in the 1970s and 1980s, complete translations were produced by two teams of translators. The first comprised a teacher at Oxford University, David Hawkes, and his pupil John Minford. HAWKES translated chapters 1 to 80 (1973–80), and, sharing the opinion of many scholars that the remaining 40 chapters were by an anonymous author rather than Cao, left them to the able hand of MINFORD, who completed volume 4 in 1982 and volume 5 in 1986. The second team consisted of a couple in Beijing, Hsien-yi YANG & Gladys YANG, native speakers of Chinese and English respectively.

JOLY (1892–93), a British consul in China in the late 19th century, could not help producing a work that bore the stamp of the language habits and morals of his class and time. The following passage, the translation equivalent of a speech uttered by a little page ("women cao pigu bu cao pigu, guan ni jiba xianggan, hengshu mei cao ni die qu ba le!"), is a typical example of Joly's style: "What we do, whether proper or improper ... doesn't concern you! It's enough anyway that we don't defile your father!" Whereas the original, strewn with taboo words, is the most vulgar and racy speech in the novel, a speech that would have made a Victorian lady faint if transferred intact, the translation is pompous and prudish.

WANG (1958), a native speaker and university professor of Chinese, also tends to be restricted in the target language to the formal levels of the stylistic ladder. This results in his characters speaking a more or less neutral language, thus blurring their individuality. Moreover, in the process of abridgement, Wang has taken the liberty of removing what he may have considered vulgar in the novel, as can be seen in his translation of the same passage: "Hey, you son of the Kin clan, what business is it of yours whatever we choose to do? You should be glad we haven't violated your own father." Readability is further reduced by his practice of resorting frequently to transliteration, not only of forms of address but also of interjections.

The first complete translation, by YANG & YANG (1978–80), two very prolific professional translators of Chinese literature into English, known for their faithful approach, gives the reader a full and generally adequate account of the story. Yet it is limited in stylistic range, especially with regard to its dialogue, and the translators have taken it upon themselves to cleanse the novel of its "obscenities", distilling the speech discussed above into "What *we* do is no business of yours".

Making a point of reproducing in English Cao's variations of style, HAWKES (1973–80) never balks at vulgarity. Only in his translation of the passage in question can the reader get a true taste of the original's raciness: "Whether we fuck arseholes or not, [...] what fucking business is it of yours? You should be bloody grateful we haven't fucked your dad." If Hawkes ever "errs", he tends to do so on the side of what Gideon Toury would call acceptability. He explains and amplifies within the text when he detects a cultural gap, and occasionally leaves out certain pieces of information for fear of overloading. Sometimes he puts in vivid details or jokes to add to the humour or comic effect of the original, as is the case with the following passage, where the italicized parts are entirely his invention: "Several of the servants ... overpowered him, and throwing him *face downward* on the ground, *frogmarched* him off to the stable."

In the light of the above discussion, one may conclude that HAWKES's is, so far, the English version that is the most worthy of Cao's masterpiece and, arguably, the most faithful in terms of literariness and of its appeal to the contemporary reader. At the same time, however, one should note that, in a sense, all four versions bear the mark of their time.

JOLY had to observe the Victorian proprieties, otherwise he would have risked raising the eyebrows of his peers and even being censored by his publisher. Translating between the 1920s and the 1950s, when works such as D.H. Lawrence's *Lady Chatterley's Lover* were banned, WANG had to toe a similar line. Hence his expurgation of taboo words. On the other hand, working as "propagandists" (in the good sense of the word) under the patronage of the authorities in Beijing, YANG & YANG were obligated to sanitize their translation for their target readers.

Finally, one should note that the influence of ideology is also detectable in the translating of the title. The Chinese words "hong lou" in *Hong lou meng* may mean either a grand building or the room of a rich lady. The decision made by most translators in the West to use "Red Chamber" signifies a concurrence with the traditional interpretation of the novel as a love story, whereas the choice of "Red Mansions" in Yang & Yang's version is a deliberate attempt to suggest class struggle.

Hawkes has cleverly avoided this problem by choosing *The Story of the Stone*, an alternative title that Cao Xueqin once considered using. Hawkes's translation is not however entirely exempt from the constraints of his time, for his preservation of the original's earthiness does not result from a free choice – if he had done otherwise, reviewers and readers of the day would have accused him of bowdlerizing. The very fact that we praise his work is proof that he has conformed to the dominant translational norms of *our* age – that translated literature should read like original literature and have a life of its own. However, these norms may change with time, and, when they do, critics may find flaws of every kind in Hawkes's translation, just as we do in versions with a temporo-cultural setting other than our own. When this happens, a new translation may be needed to satisfy the expectations and requirements of these critics as Hawkes's has satisfied ours.

NAM FUNG CHANG and LAURENCE WONG

Further Reading

Chang, N.F., "The Implications of Hawkes's *The Story of the Stone* to Translation Theorists", *Foreign Languages*, 3 (1991) pp. 53–60

Eoyang, Eugene, review of *The Story of the Stone*, vol. 1: *The Golden Days*, by Cao Xueqin, translated by David Hawkes, *Journal of the Chinese Language Teachers Association*, 10/2 (1975) pp. 83–87

Hawkes, David, "*The Story of the Stone*: A Symbolist Novel", *Renditions*, 25 (1986) pp. 6–17

Levy, André, review of vols 1–3 of *The Story of the Stone*, translated by David Hawkes, *T'oung Pao: Revue Internationale de Sinologie*, 70/4–5 (1984) pp. 298–302

Shen, Dan, "Objectivity in the Translation of Narrative Fiction", *Babel*, 34/3 (1988) pp. 131–40

Soong, Stephen C., "Two Types of Misinterpretation – Some Poems from *Red Chamber Dream*, *Renditions*, 7 (1977) pp. 73–92

Wang, John C.Y., review of vol. 1 of *The Story of the* Stone, translated by David Hawkes, *Journal of Asian Studies*, 35/2 (1976) pp. 302–04

Wong, Laurence K.P., "A Study of the Literary Translations of the *Hong lou meng*, with Special Reference to David Hawkes's English Version" (dissertation), University of Toronto, 1992

See also the introduction to Hawkes and the publisher's note in Yang & Yang

---

John Dryden 1631–1700

English poet, dramatist, critic and literary translator

Biography

Born 9 August 1631, at the vicarage of Aldwinkle All Saints, Northamptonshire, where his mother's father was rector. After attending Westminster School in London, Dryden studied at Trinity College, Cambridge until 1657, when he left for London. Dryden's family were Parliamentarians on both sides, and on Cromwell's death in 1658 the young poet wrote *Heroic Stanzas* in the late Protector's praise. By 1660 his *Astraea Redux* would be lauding the restoration of the monarchy. In 1663 he married Lady Elizabeth Howard, eldest daughter of the earl of Berkshire. Dryden's first successful play, in heroic verse, was *The Indian Emperor* (1665; the last was *Aurung-Zebe*, 1676) and in 1667 he published his patriotic poem *Annus Mirabilis: 1666*. In 1668 he was made Poet Laureate; in 1670, Historiographer Royal. He died in London, 1 May 1700 and was buried in Westminster Abbey.

Among the best known of Dryden's many works (poems, heroic plays, comedies, tragi-comedies, criticism, translations), are the tragi-comedy *Marriage-à-la-mode* (1672); *All for Love* (1678), a blank verse tragedy adapted from Shakespeare's *Antony and Cleopatra*; the 1680 verse satire *Absalom and Achitophel*; the pro-Anglican poem *Religio Laici* of 1682; and, after his conversion to Rome in 1685, the pro-Catholic poem *The Hind and the Panther* (1687); the important critical works, including prefaces, prologues and epilogues to some of his works, and the essay *Of Dramatic Poesy* (1668); and of course the translations. It was after the Revolution of 1688 and the loss of his poet laureateship that Dryden turned for a living to the theatre again and to the masterly translation of texts from ancient Greek and Latin, from Italian and from Chaucer's English.

Dryden as Translator

John Dryden's translations, from the classical poets Homer, Horace, Lucretius, Ovid, Virgil and Theocritus, and from the medieval writers Chaucer and Boccaccio, constitute about two-thirds of his non-dramatic verse, and were, for well over 100 years after his death, widely regarded as the crown of his poetic achievement. In these versions, composed in the last two decades of his life, Dryden was thought to have brought English verse to a new level of freshness, vigour and melodiousness, and to have recreated for English readers some of the supreme masterpieces of the classical and medieval past with a perceptiveness and vitality that made his versions equally appealing to readers acquainted with the works in their original form and to those who were dependent on translation.

Dryden was, by inclination, an "occasional" translator who liked to select poems and passages that had "affected" him with a particular vividness or urgency "in the reading", or to whose authors he felt he had a "soul congenial". (The exception that proves the rule is *The Works of Virgil* (1697), Dryden's single attempt to render an author's entire oeuvre: for all his responsiveness to the exuberant animism of the *Georgics*, and to the *Aeneid*'s vision of the glory and cost of Empire and the pains of human existence, this was the only translation that Dryden seems to have felt had strained his resources to a wearying degree.) His normal translating activity can be seen as an act, simultaneously, of self-surrender and self-exploration, with the poet (in T.S. Eliot's words) "giving the original through himself, and finding himself through the original". In this respect Dryden was perfectly suited to translation by temperament, since he was a poet for whom the discovery of truth was a matter not of espousing a single, monolithic or univocal source of wisdom, but of perceiving, and allowing vivid and powerful expression to, life's mighty oppositions and paradoxes. His extensive imaginative communion with, and inhabiting of, the souls and minds of poets very different from himself (and from one another) can thus be seen as a natural expression of the vigorous and searching comprehensiveness of his poetic and human sympathies.

Dryden's translating career got off to something of a false start with *Ovid's Epistles* (1680), a speculative venture into the translation market by the young publisher, Jacob Tonson, to which Dryden contributed a lengthy preface and three rather stiff and prurient versions. The volume's weaknesses were instantly perceived and shrewdly parodied, but it was, nevertheless, an outstanding commercial success and led to the series of miscellanies and volumes of translation (single-author and collaborative) that Tonson produced during the 1680s and 1690s, in which Dryden featured centrally as author, editor and general source of leadership and inspiration.

It was in the second of Tonson's miscellanies, *Sylvae* (1685), that Dryden published his first unqualifiedly masterly translations: of passages from Lucretius' *De Rerum Natura*, and of three odes and an epode by Horace. These poems, in which Dryden finds a vibrantly convincing English voice to express Lucretius' "noble pride and positive assertion" and Horace's "briskness", "jollity" and good-humoured insouciance, are exhortations to reject the delusions, vain desires and false hopes with which human life is normally beset, and to achieve a momentary freedom of soul by "enjoying the present hour", not in a spirit of facile hedonism, but as the result of a wise and steady survey of "Nature's laws".

In *The Satires of Juvenal and Persius* (1693) Dryden recruited a team of collaborators to render two densely allusive and topical Roman satirists whose earlier English translators had been notable only for their pedantry and crabbed obscurity. In this volume, Dryden's principal achievement was to find a viable English equivalent for the scurrilously hyperbolic "wit" which, he thought, characterized Juvenal's scoffing denunciations of the human condition, and which gave Juvenalian satire an exhilarating and "purgative", rather than merely depressing, effect ("Juvenal", he wrote, "gives me as much pleasure as I can bear").

In the third Tonson miscellany, *Examen Poeticum* (1693), Dryden returned to Ovid, of whose *Metamorphoses* he was now planning a complete, collaborative version. In his prose criticism, Dryden often reiterated the age-old criticisms of Ovid: that the Roman poet had trivialized his depictions of serious situations by prolixity, by a callous impassivity and by displays of tastelessly inappropriate verbal wit. But in the translations from the *Metamorphoses* that he included in *Examen Poeticum* and *Fables Ancient and Modern* (1700), he responded with active relish to Ovid's "turns on the words and thought", conceiving them as rhetorical devices for achieving a distinctive perspective on the world: a weirdly satisfying blend of involvement and distance, pathos and near-humour, psychological precision and extravagant fancy, discretion and daring.

In *Fables*, the voice of Ovid blends and contrasts with those of Chaucer, Homer and Boccaccio in a sequence of interconnected narratives whose imaginative world is presided over by a series of powerful gods – figures who embody or concentrate the (often competing) forces, principles or laws that hold sway both within the breast and mind of man and in the outside world, and who can ennoble, demean or baffle humanity at will, imbuing life with wonder and dignity or divesting it of all apparent meaning, purpose or coherence. In these versions, Dryden shows himself equally responsive to the turbulent wrath of the Homeric Achilles, to the paradoxical predicament of Ovid's Myrrha, simultaneously impelled and repulsed by her incestuous passion for her father, to the comic antics of Chaucer's vainglorious farmyard hero, the cock Chanticleer, to the bold and dignified speech in which Boccaccio's Sigismonda defends her sexual rights, and to the grand vision of nature's perpetual flux and renewal celebrated by Ovid's Pythagoras and Chaucer's Theseus. In the *Fables*, long regarded as the culmination of his translating career, Dryden was thought to have fused, miraculously, the "fiery" vitality of youth with the sober wisdom of old age, and to have combined a profound interpretive insight into his originals with "the skilled ease, the flow as of original composition" (John Wilson, 1845).

David Hopkins

Translations

Ovid, *Ovid's Epistles*, translated with others, 1680
Sylvae, translated with others, 1685
Juvenal, *The Satires of Juvenal, Together with the Satires of Persius*, translated with others, 1693
Examen Poeticum, translated with others, 1693
Fables Ancient and Modern, 1700
Virgil, *The Works of Virgil, Containing His Pastorals, Georgics and Aeneis*, 1697

Further Reading

Dryden, John, *The Works of John Dryden*, general editors Edward Niles Hooker and H.T. Swedenberg, Jr, 20 vols, Berkeley: University of California Press, 1956–96

Frost, William, *Dryden and the Art of Translation*, New Haven, Connecticut: Yale University Press, 1955

Gillespie, Stuart, "The Early Years of the Dryden–Tonson Partnership: The Background to their Composite Translations and Miscellanies of the 1680s", *Restoration*, 12 (1988) pp. 10–19

Gillespie, Stuart, "Horace's *Ode* 3.29: Dryden's 'Masterpiece in English'" in *Horace Made New: Horatian Influences on British Writing from the Renaissance to the Twentieth Century*, edited by Charles Martindale and David Hopkins, Cambridge and New York: Cambridge University Press, 1993

Hammond, Paul, "The Integrity of Dryden's Lucretius", *Modern Language Review*, 78 (1983) pp. 1–23

Hammond, Paul, "John Dryden: The Classicist as Sceptic", *The Seventeenth Century*, 4 (1989) pp. 165–87

Hammond, Paul, "The Translator: 1680–1700" in his *John Dryden: A Literary Life*, London: Macmillan, and New York: St Martin's Press, 1991 (chapter 7)

Hopkins, David, "Nature's Laws and Man's: The Story of Cinyras and Myrrha in Dryden and Ovid", *Modern Language Review*, 80 (1985) pp. 786–801

Hopkins, David, "New Directions: Religion and Translation in the 1680s", "'Studying Nature's Laws': The *Juvenal* and *Virgil*", and "'An Improving Writer to His Last': The *Fables*" in his *John Dryden*, Cambridge and New York: Cambridge University Press, 1986 (chapters 4–6)

Hopkins, David, "Dryden and Ovid's 'Wit out of Season'" in *Ovid Renewed: Ovidian Influences on Literature and Art from the Middle Ages to the Twentieth Century*, edited by Charles Martindale, Cambridge and New York: Cambridge University Press, 1988; reprinted in *Ovid: The Classical Heritage*, edited by William S. Anderson, New York: Garland, 1995

Hopkins, David, "Dryden and the Garth–Tonson *Metamorphoses*", *Review of English Studies*, 39 (1988) pp. 64–74

Hopkins, David, "Dryden and the Tenth Satire of Juvenal", *Translation and Literature*, 4/1 (1995) pp. 31–60

Jones, Emrys, "Dryden's Sigismonda" in *English Renaissance Studies: Presented to Dame Helen Gardner in Honour of Her Seventieth Birthday*, edited by John Carey, Oxford: Clarendon Press, and New York: Oxford University Press, 1980

Jones, Emrys, "A 'Perpetual Torrent': Dryden's Lucretian Style" in *Augustan Studies: Essays in Honor of Irvin Ehrenpreis*, edited by Douglas Lane Patey and Timothy Keegan, Newark: University of Delaware Press, 1985

Mason, H.A., "Dryden's Dream of Happiness", *Cambridge Quarterly*, 8 (1978) pp. 11–55; 9 (1980) pp. 218–71

Mason, H.A., "Living in the Present: Is Dryden's 'Horat. Ode 29. Book 3' an Example of 'Creative Translation'?", *Cambridge Quarterly*, 10 (1981) pp. 91–129

Mason, H.A., "The Hallowed Hearth: Some Reflections on Dryden's Version of the Ninth Ode in Horace's First Book", *Cambridge Quarterly*, 14 (1985) pp. 205–39

Mason, Tom, "Dryden's Version of *The Wife of Bath's Tale*", *Cambridge Quarterly*, 6 (1975) pp. 240–56

Reverand, Cedric D. II, *Dryden's Final Poetic Mode: The Fables*, Philadelphia: University of Pennsylvania Press, 1988

Sowerby, Robin, "The Freedom of Dryden's Homer", *Translation and Literature*, 5/1 (1996) pp. 26–50

Dryden as Translation Theorist

John Dryden's main discussions of the principles of translation are to be found in a series of prefaces and dedicatory epistles prefixed to poetical miscellanies and verse translations published between 1680 and 1700: *Ovid's Epistles* (1680), *Sylvae* (1685), *The Satires of Juvenal and Persius* (1693), *Examen Poeticum* (1693), *The Works of Virgil* (1697), and *Fables Ancient and Modern* (1700). These discussions focus on a number of recurring questions and preoccupations: the kinds of knowledge (linguistic, artistic, historical, human) that any successful translator must possess; the degree and kind of fidelity with which a translator should follow the "words" and "thoughts" of his chosen author; the problems involved in preserving the distinctive "character" of an original in translation; the ways in which poetic translators might claim to possess deeper insight into their originals than academic commentators; the extent to which a translator might legitimately "update" the "customs" depicted in an ancient text; the larger contributions translation might make to a nation's language and literary tradition. Dryden's treatment of such matters, however, does not form a static or monolithic body of doctrine but is presented in a series of "occasional" reflections, composed over a long period and continuously modified by fresh discoveries in the field and by shifting artistic and personal circumstances and priorities.

Dryden's first, and most famous, discussion of translation was published before any of his major achievements in the genre itself. In the preface to *Ovid's Epistles* (1680) the poet proposed his celebrated tripartite division of translation into "metaphrase" ("or turning an author word for word, and line by line, from one language into another"), "paraphrase" ("or translation with latitude, where the author is kept in view by the translator so as never to be lost, but his words are not so strictly followed as his sense, and that, too, is admitted to be amplified but not altered") and "imitation" ("where the translator – if he has not lost that name – assumes the liberty not only to vary from the words and sense, but to forsake them both as he sees occasion; and taking only some general hints from the original, to run division on the ground-work, as he pleases"). "Metaphrase" and "imitation" are both rejected, the former on the grounds that it produces renderings that are both unidiomatic and obscure and thus altogether fail to convey the "spirit" of their originals, the latter because it allows the translator so much freedom that the results are more properly thought of as original compositions than translations. "Paraphrase", the chosen method of Dryden and his fellow-contributors to *Ovid's Epistles*, is offered as an ideal *via media* between the two unacceptable extremes.

The preface to *Ovid's Epistles* established a number of sound principles to which Dryden broadly adhered for the rest of his translating career, but the details of its argument are sometimes disingenuous and self-contradictory, and its over-neat categorizations can sometimes give the impression of a rhetorically adroit piece of salesmanship (on behalf, moreover, of a somewhat mediocre volume), rather than a fully serious attempt to do justice to the complexities of its subject matter.

The cool elegance of the *Ovid's Epistles* preface certainly does not prepare one for the excited exuberance of Dryden's next essay on translation, the preface to *Sylvae*, written in the immediate afterglow of the intense creative engagement that produced his first translated masterpieces, the versions from Lucretius and Horace. Dryden has, he says, been recently possessed by a "hot fit" of translation, which has resulted in a series of versions in which he has, to his delight and surprise, "found something that was more pleasing" than his "ordinary productions". Dryden's main emphasis in this preface is on a translator's need to convey, above all, "the spirit which animates the whole" of each of his originals – Lucretius' "noble pride and positive assertion of his opinions", Horace's "briskness", "jollity" and "good humour", etc. To this end, and buoyed up by confidence in his own recent achievements, he is prepared to allow a translator far greater freedom than before. In the *Sylvae* translations, he says, he has "added and omitted" such details to and from his originals "as no Dutch commentator will forgive me" – his excuse being that he has, "perhaps", "discovered some beauty yet undiscovered by those pedants, which none but a poet could have found". His additions will, he hopes, be thought to be "secretly in" his original, or "fairly deduced from him". If all else fails, he hopes that his own thought "is of a piece with his, and that if he were living, and an Englishman, they are such as he would probably have written" (an argument he had previously, and disapprovingly, attributed to the "libertine" advocates of "imitation").

Dryden's experiences while preparing the translations included in *The Satires of Juvenal and Persius* (1693) clearly convinced him that even further freedoms were legitimate (or, at least, unavoidable) when rendering such densely allusive, topical and difficult writers as the Roman satirists. His method in this volume, he says, has been "a kind of paraphrase – or somewhat yet more loose, betwixt a paraphrase and imitation", in which he and his collaborators have even allowed themselves, occasionally, to make Juvenal "express the customs and manners of our native country rather than of Rome". While such a procedure may not, he realizes, be fully defensible, it might nevertheless be excused on the grounds that it creates both understanding and pleasure: an obscure and inelegant version of Juvenal, like those of Holyday and Stapylton, Dryden's predecessors, can, after all, give an English reader no sense whatever of the invigoratingly splenetic wit that is such a distinctive characteristic of the Roman poet's writing.

The "Dedication of the *Aeneis*" is, of all Dryden's writings on translation, the one that dwells most extensively on the problems and difficulties (even, perhaps, in the last resort, the hopelessness) of the translator's task. In this essay, Dryden shows himself constantly aware of the supreme challenge involved in finding an English diction and versification adequate to the task of rendering, in their entirety, the works of a poet peculiarly renowned for the euphonious elegance, sweetness and conciseness of his style in Latin – a language Dryden believes to be inherently superior to English in its economy, harmoniousness and variety.

The preface to *Fables*, Dryden's last volume, marks a striking return to the exhilarated and exhilarating confidence of the preface to *Sylvae*. In composing his versions from Chaucer, Ovid, Homer and Boccaccio for *Fables*, Dryden has, he says, been struck by the patterns of artistic lineage, consanguinity and congeniality that link these writers together, and with himself. Dryden has moved far beyond merely generic and technical considerations: the translator's art is now conceived as a kind of spiritual "transfusion" or metempsychosis, in which the souls of earlier poets, like the constituent elements of individual human beings (according to Ovid's Pythagoras, in Dryden's rendering), live on after death, and "some other body make; / *Translated* grow, have sense, or can discourse".

DAVID HOPKINS

Further Reading

Amos, F.R., *Early Theories of Translation*, New York: Columbia University Press, 1920
Frost, William, "Theory of Translation" in *Dryden and the Art of Translation*, New Haven, Connecticut: Yale University Press, 1955 (chapter 2); reprinted in *John Dryden: Dramatist, Satirist, Translator*, New York: AMS Press, 1988
O'Sullivan, Maurice J. Jr, "Running Division on the Groundwork: Dryden's Theory of Translation", *Neophilologus*, 64 (1980) pp. 144–59
Steiner, T.R., "Precursors to Dryden: English and French Theories of Translation in the Seventeenth Century", *Comparative Literature Studies*, 7 (1970) pp. 50–81
Steiner, T.R., *English Translation Theory, 1650–1800*, Assen: Van Gorcum, 1975 (Approaches to Translation Studies 2)

Du Fu (Tu Fu) 712–770

Chinese poet

Biography

Du Fu has generally been regarded as the greatest Chinese poet in the Chinese tradition (*shiseng*, "sage of poetry"). In 744 he met Li Bai (Li Po), a powerful influence on him. In his forties he lived through the turmoil of a rebellion from which the Tang empire never completely recovered. He served briefly in the exiled court, but soon began a life of wanderings along the Yangzi river in southwest China, living under the patronage of local officials or on support from relatives and friends, until he fell sick during a boat trip and died shortly afterwards. He was said to have written some 6000 poems, but only some 1400 survived. Du Fu was known as the "poet-historian", and his poetry, wide-ranging in form and subject, documented not only his own life but also the social upheaval of 8th-century China.

Translations

Selections and Anthologies

Alley, Rewi, *Tu Fu: Selected Poems*, selection compiled by Feng Zhi, Peking: Foreign Languages Press, 1962 (140 poems of Du Fu)

Ayscough, Florence and Amy Lowell, *Fir-Flower Tablets: Poems Translated from the Chinese*, Boston: Houghton Mifflin, 1921 (13 poems of Du Fu)

Bynner, Witter and Kiang Kang-hu, *The Jade Mountain: Being Three Hundred Poems of the T'ang Dynasty, 618–906*, with an introduction by Kiang, New York: Knopf, 1929 (36 poems of Du Fu)

Cooper, Arthur, *Li Po and Tu Fu*, with an introduction, Harmondsworth: Penguin, 1973 (26 poems of Du Fu)

Giles, Herbert A., *Chinese Poetry in English Verse*, London: Quaritch, 1898; as *Gems of Chinese Literature*, Shanghai: Kelly and Walsh, 1923 (11 poems of Du Fu)

Graham, A.C., *Poems of the Late T'ang*, Harmondsworth: Penguin, 1965 (19 poems of Du Fu)

Hamill, Sam, *Facing the Snow: Visions of Tu Fu*, Fredonia, New York: White Pine Press, 1988 (94 poems of Du Fu)

Hinton, David, *The Selected Poems of Tu Fu*, with an introduction, New York: New Directions, 1989 (more than 230 poems of Du Fu)

Kizer, Carolyn, *Knock upon Silence*, New York: Doubleday, 1965 (20 poems of Du Fu); the same poems of Du Fu are reprinted in Kizer's *Carrying Over: Poems from the Chinese, Urdu, Macedonian, Yiddish, and French African*, Port Townsend, Washington: Copper Canyon Press, 1988

Liu, Wu-chi and Irving Yucheng Lo (editors), *Sunflower Splendor: Three Thousand Years of Chinese Poetry*, with an introduction by Lo, Bloomington: Indiana University Press, 1975 (50 poems of Du Fu)

Owen, Stephen (editor and translator), *An Anthology of Chinese Literature: Beginnings to 1911*, New York: Norton, 1996 (47 poems of Du Fu)

Payne, Robert, *The White Pony: An Anthology of Chinese Poetry*, with an introduction, New York: Day, 1947 (24 poems of Du Fu)

Rexroth, Kenneth, *One Hundred Poems from the Chinese*, New York: New Directions, 1959 (35 poems of Du Fu)

Seaton, J.P. and James Cryer, *Bright Moon, Perching Bird: Poems by Li Po and Tu Fu* (parallel texts), Middletown, Connecticut: Wesleyan University Press, 1987 (68 poems of Du Fu)

Underwood, Edna Worthley and Chi Hwang Chu, *Tu Fu: Wanderer and Minstrel under Moons of Cathay*, Portland, Maine: Mosher Press, 1929 (nearly 300 poems of Du Fu)

Wu, Juntao, *Tu Fu: A New Translation*, Hong Kong: Commercial Press, 1981 (104 poems of Du Fu)

Yip, Wai-lim, *Chinese Poetry: Major Modes and Genres* (bilingual edition), Berkeley: University of California Press, 1976 (17 poems of Du Fu)

Young, David, *Wang Wei, Li Po, Tu Fu, Li Ho: Four T'ang Poets*, Oberlin, Ohio: Oberlin College Press, 1980; enlarged edition as *Wang Wei, Li Po, Tu Fu, Li Ho, Li Shang-yin: Five T'ang Poets*, 1990 (29 poems of Du Fu)

Despite the numerous translations of his poems in many languages, Du Fu is a translator's nightmare. The difficulty is due to his rich diction, copious allusions, and inclination towards prosodic complexity, as well as to the kaleidoscopic variety of his work, which make him one of those poets who lose the most in translation.

Among the numerous anthologies that include selections of Du Fu, GILES, also the author of the very first history of Chinese literature in the world (1901), should be given credit for having provided the earliest English translation of Du Fu with the 11 poems in his anthology (1898). However, he attempts to reincarnate Chinese poetry in Victorian rhyme and rhythm and iambic meter, so his translation reads today as archaic and outdated, and it is further marred by not infrequent errors of interpretation.

AYSCOUGH & LOWELL's *Fir-Flower Tablets* (1921), one of the early collaborations by a Chinese specialist and a western poet, includes 13 Du Fu poems. The English texts of the American Imagist poet Amy Lowell (1874–1925) sound delightful and refreshing, but as translation they suffer from Ayscough's limited knowledge of Chinese, especially from what may be called the "Orientalist fallacy" of her generation, best known from the case of Ernest Fenollosa and Ezra Pound, in considering all Chinese characters as pictograms and ideograms. After Lowell's death Ayscough published two volumes (1929 and 1934) on Du Fu's life, which consist primarily of her own translation of hundreds of poems, interwoven into a sketch of the events that form a background to these poems. Her English is not as readable as Lowell's, and she has carried her blind enthusiasm for Chinese etymology to further extremes. Richly decorated with illustrations and maps, they are nevertheless of little value except as collectors' items, having been superseded in terms of scholarship by Hung's monumental study (1952) which, incidentally, contains prose renditions of hundreds of Du Fu's poems, though these are not intended as translations.

BYNNER & KIANG's *The Jade Mountain* (1929) is a translation of the popular Chinese anthology of Tang poetry, *Three Hundred Tang Poems* (actually 311 poems), often compared to Palgrave's *Golden Treasury* in English poetry. It contains 36 of Du Fu's most frequently anthologized poems. The collaboration of Bynner with Kiang, who was not only native Chinese, unlike Ayscough, but also more learned than she, greatly reduced the number of potential errors lying in wait for a translator like Bynner who did not know Chinese. The anthology is rearranged in alphabetical order of the poets' family names, and included in appendices are a historical chronology, a chronology of the poets, topography, notes on the poems, and indexes of titles and first lines. Kiang has also written a fine general introduction on traditional Chinese poetry. Although misinterpretation still occurs on a number of occasions, the book has delighted generations of both general readers and students of Chinese literature, and remains today a highly commendable text for classroom use. Bynner (1881–1968), a Harvard graduate and an American poet in his own right, has succeeded in rendering most of the Chinese poems in powerful and stylish English, full of color and musical sound, and the Du Fu selection is no exception.

UNDERWOOD & CHU (1929), the result of a similar

collaboration, is the earliest collection devoted exclusively to Du Fu and includes nearly 300 of his shorter poems. Underwood avoids free verse in her translation whenever she can, and some of it sounds graceful, but the book is generally unreliable as translation. Several poems have been translated more than once and placed in different parts of the book, some are extracted and mixed up, and a few are not even based upon Du's original, but rather on the French pseudo-translation of Chinese poetry by "Judith Walter" (the poet Théophile Gautier's daughter) in her popular anthology, *Le Livre de jade* (Paris: Lemerre, 1867).

In *The White Pony* (1947), PAYNE collaborates with a number of Chinese scholars, and primarily with Professor Pu Hsiang-hsing in the Du Fu selection, which begins with an introduction, in which the Chinese poet is compared with Virgil and Baudelaire, and includes 24 well-chosen poems. Payne claims to have played the role only of editor and reviser, and announces the general aim of an attempt, wherever possible, "to translate a line of Chinese into simple, accurate and rhythmic English prose", which seems to have been faithfully executed throughout the book. The anthology is generally free from errors but lacks the sparkle of Lowell's freshness or Bynner's strength.

The American poet REXROTH, who does not have any first-hand knowledge of the Chinese language, calls Du Fu "the greatest non-epic, non-dramatic poet who has survived in any language", placing him in the company of western poets like Sappho, Catullus, and Baudelaire. The first part of his anthology (1959) consists of 35 short poems of Du Fu, for which he has worked on the basis of earlier renditions of Ayscough, Hung, and Erwin von Zach's *Tu Fu's Gedichte* (Cambridge, Massachusetts: Harvard University Press, 1952), the complete German translation of Du Fu's poetic oeuvre. The second part is a selection of some 80 poems from the Song (Sung) dynasty. Rexroth's translations vary in terms of accuracy and sometimes can be very free, but they are mostly pleasant to read.

ALLEY's collection (1962), published in Mao's China, contains 140 of Du Fu's poems. The selection is based upon an annotated Chinese collection compiled by the contemporary Chinese poet and scholar Feng Zhi (Feng Chih), who also wrote a preface for the translation. The selection reflects a strong Marxist bias, trying to demonstrate Du Fu's status as "a poet of the people". Alley's translation, with a tendency to rearrange the originals loosely, and sometimes simply to paraphrase, is in general flat and pedestrian.

GRAHAM's anthology (1965) in the Penguin Classics series, now a little classic in terms of both accuracy and style among the numerous translations of Chinese poetry, contains only 19 of Du Fu's poems in regulated octaves. Chinese literary historians, traditionally obsessed with periodization, may be puzzled to find Du, a poet of the "High Tang" era, placed in an anthology of "Late Tang" poetry. Graham, however, justifies this peculiarity by announcing his guiding principle for his selection, which is to trace the course of development in simile and metaphor, and more specifically, the advance in metaphorical concentration from the poems of Du's old age to its climax in Li Shangyin. The Du Fu selections, all from the last four years of the poet's life, "illustrate the beginnings of some of the tendencies which transformed the poetic language in the 9th century". Incidentally, the anthology contains Graham's important essay, "The Translation of Chinese Poetry", which discusses the charm and challenge of the enterprise, using lines from Giles, Lowell, Arthur Waley and Ezra Pound as illustrations. At the end of the essay Graham also makes the blunt assertion that the translation of Chinese poetry can hardly be left to the Chinese themselves, "since there are few exceptions to the rule that translation is best done into, not out of, one's own language". Graham's greatest achievement lies in his conscious effort to give each poet an individual voice – a great challenge for any translator. In this little anthology he has indeed succeeded in finding the various patterns of imagery among the different poets, and the Du Fu selection, especially the famous octaval sequence of *Autumn Meditation*, triumphantly conveys the sober dignity of the poet's voice in his last years.

KIZER's *Knock upon Silence* (1965) consists of her own poems as well as what she calls *imitations* (à la Robert Lowell), and translations. Some 20 of Du Fu's poems (one of which is here entitled "Déjeuner sur l'herbe", after Manet's painting) are included in the last category. These are reprinted, along with poems she claims to be by poets of other cultures, in her *Carrying Over* (1988), which skillfully avoids using either generic term (imitation/translation) by inserting the preposition *from* in the title. Kizer, a Pulitzer Prize-winning poet, acknowledges that she has read Waley since her childhood and has always been interested in foreign cultures. Despite having spent a year in China, however, she does not have adequate proficiency in the language. It is intriguing, none the less, to see how much of the spirit of the 8th-century Chinese male poet has been transmitted into the voice of a contemporary American female poet, and her Du Fu is fine poetry indeed, succulent, vigorous, and free from sentimentality, although perhaps it should not be judged as translation.

COOPER's anthology (1973) is the first joint collection of the two most famous High Tang poets in English. It contains only 26 poems by each poet, with commentaries and notes, but takes up nearly half of the book's space with a rambling introduction to Chinese poetry aimed at the general reader with little or no knowledge of the topic. Cooper's translation inclines to deviate from the original diction and syntax, and the anthology, also in the Penguin Classics series, pales beside that of Graham's.

The Du Fu selection in *Sunflower Splendor* (1975), which remains to date the most comprehensive English anthology of Chinese poetry in traditional forms, contains 50 of Du Fu's most representative poems, from the hands of 13 people, including eminent scholars such as LIU & LO (the co-editors), the late James J.Y. Liu, Eugene Eoyang, William H. Nienhauser, and Hugh Stimson, among others. Lo's 11-page introduction to Chinese poetry is one of the most concise and polished essays of its kind written for the western reader. The translations, understandably, display great variety in English style, but in general they are free from misinterpretation thanks to the strict editorial policy of the co-editors, which is to have every translated text checked against the Chinese source by at least three different readers.

YIP, a leading contemporary writer of vernacular Chinese poetry and a scholar as well, has produced single-handedly his anthology (1976) of Chinese poems ranging from the ancient *Book of Songs*, all the way to the Mongol Yuan (Yüan) dynasty, in various traditional poetic forms. Yip, the author of a perceptive study of Ezra Pound's *Cathay*, is himself greatly influenced by, if not totally converted to, the views and practices of Pound and William Carlos Williams. His aim for this anthology, however, is to alert western readers to "the inadequacy and the distortion" of most English translations of its contents, and, through his own practice of translation as the manifestation of his beliefs, to what he calls "the unique mode of presentation" in Chinese poetry, as implied in Chinese poetics and made possible by the syntactical freedom of the Chinese language. The original Chinese texts are printed in front of the English translations, and in the case of shorter poems also accompanied by word-for-word English annotations. Yip argues that the Chinese language is essentially asyntactical, and in his translations, which include 17 poems by Du Fu, he attempts to remove all sense of person, tense and other grammatical connections from the lines, and accordingly produces lines of English in which words are placed more or less in the same order as in the original. The result is uneven. On occasions, especially in the case of some Tang quatrains, the translations shine with originality, but on others, despite his Procrustean choice of originals to accommodate his theory, they sound broken and fragmentary, and frequently not unlike pidgin English.

YOUNG, a poet, a scholar of English poetry, and also a translator of Rilke, has included 29 (one in part only) of Du Fu's poems in his anthology (1980). He obviously has little knowledge of the Chinese language himself. In his preface he acknowledges that all the poems included have been extensively translated previously, and that he has worked from those renderings, as well as from literal versions prepared by friends. He is critical of most translations by specialists of Chinese and announces his admiration for Pound, Rexroth, Gary Snyder, and Arthur Waley (the only scholar "who translated like a poet"). His free translation in simple colloquial English, usually in very short lines and with a quick tempo, is lively and pleasant to read, though he often misses Du's trademark "sober virility" (*xionghun*), and tends to strip the original of its rich ambiguity.

In his foreword WU justifies his *New Translation* (1981) by comparing the works of a great poet to beautiful scenery which "invites different painters to paint". The selection is not as politically oriented as Alley's, and the 104 poems included cover a wide range of forms and periods. A believer in rhyme, rhythm and meter, Wu returns to the pre-modernist mode in his translation, which often sounds affected and stilted to today's post-modernist reader.

SEATON, one of the 13 translators of Du Fu featured in *Sunflower Splendor*, continues his work on the poet in *Bright Moon, Perching Bird* (1987), the second joint collection of Li and Du in English, in collaboration with Cryer, who has translated the Li Bai (Li Po) part. All English translations are placed side by side with the Chinese texts, written in various styles by a contemporary Chinese calligrapher. The selection of 68 poems includes some of the poet's less anthologized texts, in the more lively and relaxed mode, which heralded later poets like Bai Juyi (Po Chü-i). Seaton's facile colloquial American English works well with most of the pieces, but less so with several of the poet's more profound and stately poems included in the selection. Seaton's translation is in general free from mistakes, though he tends to rearrange the text, adding a line or two to the quatrain or octave in originals. A scholar of Chinese literature of the younger generation, Seaton is strangely still under the influence of the Fenollosa/Pound fallacy, and in terms of style he seems, unannouncedly though, to have followed in the footsteps of Yip, but without the extremes of the latter's asyntactical practice.

HAMILL's *Facing the Snow* (1988) contains 94 of Du Fu's poems, including some of the longer texts. Hamill, a contemporary American poet, apparently has little or only very limited knowledge of Chinese, so he has studied, wherever available, existing translations by Ayscough, Hung, Rexroth, Owen, and others. In principle he claims to agree with Dryden that translation is primarily an act of sympathetic harmony, and so sets his aim "to make accurate versions of the poems as *poems* in contemporary American language". In general he has chosen to respect the basic structure of line and couplet of the original, and to some extent the parallelism as well, but tends to be free with diction and imagery. With the help of Lo and Seaton, who read his manuscript, he has kept his translation relatively free from outright errors of interpretation.

HINTON's anthology (1989) is a chronologically arranged collection of more than 230 of Du Fu's poems, both the shorter and the longer ones, in various forms and genres. It is divided into six sections, each representing a different stage of the poet's career, and complete with appendices which include a short biography, 30 pages of notes, a finding list, a select bibliography, and an index of titles and first lines. This volume marks the beginning of Hinton's commitment to translating Chinese poetry; since then he has published fine renditions of Tao Qian, Li Bai, the late Tang poet Meng Jiao (Meng Chiao), and the contemporary poet Bei Dao, and won the 1997 Harold Morton Landon Translation Award from the Academy of American Poets. Hinton declares in his introduction that his primary concern is to recreate Du Fu as a compelling voice in English, and accordingly he has tried to remain faithful to the content but has made little attempt to mimic the formal linguistic characteristics of the originals. This is one of the few Du Fu translations that really capture the spirit of the Tang poet, and it should have its place alongside the eminent works of Bynner and Graham.

OWEN's 1212-page anthology (1996), by far the most comprehensive anthology of traditional Chinese literature in English translated almost single-handedly, continues the definitive scholarship and long-time work on the Chinese literary tradition, especially on Chinese poetics and Tang poetry, of this leading scholar in the field. Forty-seven representative poems by Du Fu in various forms and genres are included, 35 of which are in the 28-page section devoted to the poet, chronologically arranged in stages and interspersed with Owen's informative and zestful commentaries. As a translator Owen generally avoids archaisms, and in this anthology he has also tried to use various levels of English style to demonstrate the generic, periodic, and personal differences in the originals. Thus for the Du Fu selections, as for all classical Chinese, he has avoided Americanisms (which he uses only for vernacular Chinese texts), and the translations are superb both in accuracy and in style.

For further knowledge of the poet, besides those already mentioned above, one should read Hawkes's *Little Primer* (1967), which contains the Chinese text, line-by-line *pinyin* romanization, word-for-word literal rendition, and thorough exegesis, of 35 Du Fu poems from Bynner & Kiang's *Three Hundred Tang Poems*. He strangely misses one, "A View of the Wilderness", from the list, and seems to have ignored Bynner's translation. This primer is meant for people with little or no knowledge of Chinese, who can learn something about Chinese language, Chinese poetry and the poet if they work carefully through it.

It has been a perennial delight and inspiration for translators, especially for those without expertise in the language. Davis's monograph (1971) remains a useful critical biography, with readable translations of many poems. Anyone who wants to know more about Du Fu in the context of Tang poetry should read Owen's important book (1981). Among the more recent studies, McCraw (1992) presents the translation and *explication du texte* of 115 regulated octaves written during the last and most productive decade of the poet's life, Chou (1995) considers Du Fu's legacy in two separate but related aspects, as a cultural icon and as a great and original poet, and Ye's treatise on Chinese poetic closure (1996) devotes a chapter to Du Fu's closures in the context of Chinese literary tradition.

YANG YE

Further Reading

Ayscough, Florence, *Tu Fu: The Autobiography of a Chinese Poet*, vol. 1: AD 712–759, London: Jonathan Cape, 1929
Ayscough, Florence, *Travels of a Chinese Poet: Tu Fu, Guest of Rivers and Lakes*, vol. 2: AD 759–770, London: Jonathan Cape, 1934
Chou, Eva Shan, *Reconsidering Tu Fu: Literary Greatness and Cultural Context*, Cambridge: Cambridge University Press, 1995
Davis, A.R., *Tu Fu*, New York: Twayne, 1971
Hawkes, David, *A Little Primer of Tu Fu*, London: Oxford University Press, 1967
Hung, William, *Tu Fu: China's Greatest Poet*, Cambridge, Massachusetts: Harvard University Press, 1952
Kao Yu-kung and Mei Tsu-lin, "Tu Fu's 'Autumn Meditations': An Exercise in Linguistic Criticism", *Harvard Journal of Asiatic Studies*, 28 (1968) pp. 44–80
McCraw, David R., *Du Fu's Laments from the South*, Honolulu: University of Hawaii Press, 1992
Owen, Stephen, *The Great Age of Chinese Poetry: The High T'ang*, New Haven, CT: Yale University Press, 1981
Ye, Yang, *Chinese Poetic Closure*, Bern and New York: Peter Lang, 1996

Du Bartas 1544–1590

French poet and diplomat

Biography

Guillaume de Salluste, seigneur Du Bartas was born in 1544 in Montfort, near Auch, in the Armagnac region of Gascony, into the minor Gascon nobility. He studied law at Toulouse. In 1566 he inherited the title that had recently been conferred on his father and took service in the religious wars under the then Protestant Henri de Navarre. He was sent on embassies, notably to the court of James VI of Scotland, future James I of England, and to Denmark. He died at Condom of wounds, soon after fighting for the Protestant victory over the Catholic League at the battle of Ivry, which had taken place 14 March 1590.

After some earlier religious poems, he published in 1578 the work for which he is best known, *La Semaine*, an epic in alexandrine couplets, in which he described the seven days of the creation of the world, assembling much of the scientific knowledge current in his time. Between 1584 and 1603 he followed this with the uncompleted *Seconde Semaine*, an account of religious history from the Garden of Eden, covering four more days. In the Sylvester translation, these two *Divine Weeks* influenced Milton's *Paradise Lost* and won praise from Goethe. The original, widely read in France by Catholics as well as Protestants, was translated into several other European languages.

After a long eclipse, Du Bartas, reappraised in the light of 20th-century interest in "Baroque" aesthetics, has attracted new attention.

Translations

Selections

James VI, King of Scotland, translations of *La Seconde Sepmaine* and *Les Furies* in *His Maiesties Poeticall Exercises at Vacant Houres*, Edinburgh: Robert Waldegrave, n.d. [1591]; in vol. 1 of *The Poems of James VI of Scotland*, edited by James Craigie, Edinburgh: Blackwood/Scottish Text Society, 1955
L'Isle of Wilburgham, William, *Part of Du Bartas, English and French, and in His Owne Kinde of Verse* ... (bilingual edition), London: printed by John Havilland, 1625 (contains translations of *La Seconde Sepmaine*, *Les Artifices*, lines 591–728: "L'Arche", "Babilone", "Les Colonies", and "Les Colomnes")
Sylvester, Josuah (or Joshua), *The Triumph of Faith* (i.e. *Le Triomphe de la Foy*, 1574), with "The Sacrifice of Isaac", "The Ship-wrack of Jonas" and *A Song of the Victorie Obteined by the French King, at Yvry* ..., London: printed by Richard Yardley and Peter Short, 1592
Winter, Thomas, *The Third Dayes Creation* (i.e. *Le Troisiesme Jour*), London: Thomas Clerke, 1604

Poetry

La Judit(h), 1574
Hudson, Thomas, *The Historie of Judith in Forme of a Poeme*, Edinburgh: Thomas Vautroullier, 1584; edited by James

Craigie, with an introduction, Edinburgh: Blackwood/ Scottish Text Society, 1941

La Sepmaine, ou Création du Monde, 1578; *La Seconde Sepmaine, ou Enfance du Monde*, 1584

Sylvester, Josuah (or Joshua), *Bartas: His Devine Weekes and Workes*, London: printed by Humfrey Lownes, 1605; edited by T.W. Haight, with an introduction, Waukesha, Wisconsin: Youmans, 1908; facsimile, edited by Francis C. Haber, with an introduction, Gainesville, Florida: Scholars' Facsimiles and Reprints, 1965; edited by Susan Snyder, with an introduction, Oxford: Clarendon Press, 1979

For many years Du Bartas has been often quoted but seldom read. Recent scholarly interest has highlighted his importance as a Gascon soldier-poet at the end of the 16th century. Best known for his unfinished epic poem describing the creation of the world day by day (*La Sepmaine, ou Création du Monde*, Paris: Michel Gadoulleau, 1578; *La Seconde Sepmaine, ou Enfance du Monde*, Paris: Pierre l'Huillier, 1584), he wrote other poems of a Christian and biblical nature (*La Judit(h)*, *L'Uranie*, *Le Triomphe de la Foy*, published in *La Muse chrestienne*, Bordeaux: Simon Millanges, 1574) as well as circumstantial verses (*Poème à la Royne de Navarre*, in *La Sepmaine*, Ville Franche: Claude du Mont, 1579; *Cantique de la Victoire obtenue par le Roy, le quatorziesme de mars 1590 à Yvry*, Caen: Jacques le Bas, 1590). James VI of Scotland, a poet himself, greatly admired Du Bartas and the Gascon poet and he translated and exchanged their respective works, *Uranie* and *Lepanto*. As a diplomatic representative of Henri de Navarre, Du Bartas spent several months in England and Scotland during the summer of 1587 and James tried in vain to get him to stay at the Scottish court. Both during his own lifetime and in the first quarter of the 17th century, Du Bartas enjoyed considerable popularity, and many editions of his works were published.

Josuah SYLVESTER (1605) undertook the translation of *La Semaine* and produced a work of literary merit in its own right; Thomas HUDSON's translation of *La Judith* was first published separately (1584) and then included with Sylvester's work. Thomas WINTER (1604) produced a rendering of *The Third Dayes Creation* and JAMES VI of Scotland translated the *Uranie*. William L'ISLE in 1625 published in a bilingual edition a translation of four books of *La Seconde Semaine* ("L'Arche", "Babilone", "Les Colonies" and "Les Colomnes").

The translators of Du Bartas have conveyed into 17th-century English something of the flavour of the 16th-century French. The translations are reasonably accurate, sometimes with expansion and contraction, often the result of the constrictions imposed by the rhyming couplets.

SYLVESTER has been accused of free adaptation in places: he writes in a simple English that does not always convey the provincial Gascon's inventive use of French. Following the licence of the poetic adaptor, he replaces on occasion France with England, Paris with London, and takes the liberty of adding a few English names to the list of the Great. He attempts to transpose the poetic techniques of the original – compound words and alliterative phrases – perhaps more so than in the original. His poetic genius can be appreciated when compared with that of Thomas WINTER in the opening lines of *Le Troisiesme Jour*:

Mon esprit, qui voloit sur ces brillantes voutes
Qui vont tout animant de leurs diverses routes,
Qui commandoit aux vents, aux orages souffreux,
Aux esclairs flamboyans, aux images affreux ...
(Du Bartas)

My sacred Muse, that lately soared high
Among the glist'ring Circles of the Skye
(Whose various dance, which the first-Mover drives
Harmoniously, this Univers revives)
Commanding all the Windes and sulphry Stormes,
The Lightning Flashes, and the hideous Formes
Seene in the Aire ...
(Sylvester)

My Muse that whilome over-topt each spheare,
Whose course life-giving influence doth beare;
That in so brave a stile discours'd of Winds,
And ayrie meteors frighting silly minds ...
(Winter)

HUDSON's translation of *La Judith* is in a mixture of Scots and English. He has, it is opined, concentrated more on the meaning and the rhyme, which has allowed him to keep to a rigorous decasyllabic metre by occasionally using paraphrase. Nevertheless, he does succeed in giving his rendering a certain vitality and poetic rhythm; compare the following, taken from book 5 (lines 87–90):

Vous, filles d'Achelois, dont la vois charmeresse
Fait souvent naufrager la plus fine jeunesse:
Vous, Circes, qui mués par vos enchantementz
En troncs ou en porceaus vos plus accords amans ...
(Du Bartas)

Ye fearfull Rocks, ye ymps of Achelois,
who wracks the wisest youth with charming vois:
ye Circes, who by your enchantment straunge,
In stones and swine, your lovers true do chaunge ...
(Hudson)

These translations were fated to follow the fortunes of Du Bartas, at first admired, then ridiculed, and, finally, forgotten. With the revived interest in a re-evaluated Du Bartas, they may find a new life.

KEITH CAMERON

Further Reading

Ashton, H., *Du Bartas en Angleterre*, Paris: Larose, 1908; reprinted Geneva: Slatkine Reprints, 1969

Prescott, Anne Lake, *French Poets and the English Renaissance: Studies in Fame and Transformation*, New Haven, Connecticut: Yale University Press, 1978

Taylor, George Coffin, *Milton's Use of Du Bartas*, Cambridge, Massachusetts: Harvard University Press, 1934; reprinted New York: Octagon, 1968

Weller, Philipp, "Josuah Sylvesters englische Übersetzungen der religiösen Epen des Du Bartas" (dissertation), Tübingen: Kaiser-Wilhelms-Universität Strassburg, 1902

See also the introduction to the Craigie edition of Hudson's translation of *La Judit* (1941) and to the Haber facsimile edition of Sylvester's *Bartas* (1965)

Joachim Du Bellay 1522–1560

French poet

Biography

Born at the Château de la Turmelière, Liré, Anjou, probably in 1522, into a family of churchmen, soldiers and diplomats. Little is known of his childhood. Orphaned by the age of nine and delicate in health, he passed into the care of an older brother. In the mid-1540s he studied law at the University of Poitiers, where he began writing poetry. At some point he took minor clerical orders. He joined Ronsard in the academic year 1547–48 at the Collège de Coqueret in Paris, studying under the humanist and poet Jean Dorat, and was second in importance after Ronsard among the seven poets constituting the reforming literary group, the Pléiade, whose manifesto, *Deffense et illustration de la langue françoyse* (*Defence and Illustration of the French Language*) (1549) he drew up, enjoining the abandonment of medieval French forms for the enriching imitation of classical and Italian models. In 1553 he went to Rome as secretary to his cousin, Cardinal Jean Du Bellay, returning to France in 1557.

Du Bellay had published *L'Olive* [Olive], Petrarchan love sonnets, in 1549. While in Rome he had prepared the sonnet sequences for which he is best known as a witty, elegiac, touching poet: *Les Antiquitez de Rome* (*Ruines of Rome*) and *Les Regrets* (*The Regrets*), both published in 1558, in which he satirizes modern Rome and its inhabitants and praises France and his native Anjou. Also in 1558 appeared his collected Latin poems and the *Divers Jeux rustiques* [Rustic Games]. He died 1 January 1560 in Paris.

Translations

Selections of Poetry

Daniel, Samuel, *Sonnets to Delia*, nos 14, 18, 22, in *Poems and A Defence of Ryme* [1592], edited by Arthur C. Sprague, Cambridge, Massachusetts: Harvard University Press, 1930; London: Routledge and Kegan Paul, 1950 (translations of *Olive* 10, 91, 92)

Gorges, Sir Arthur, *Poems* [1580s], edited by Helen Estabrook Sandison, Oxford: Clarendon Press, 1953

Grimald, Nicholas, in *Tottel's Miscellany (1557–1587)*, edited by Hyder Edward Rollins, 2 vols, Cambridge, Massachusetts: Harvard University Press, 1928–29; revised edition, 1965 (poem no. 137, vol. 1, p. 99)

Poetry

Les Antiquitez de Rome; Songe, 1558

Spenser, Edmund, *Sonets*, in *A Theatre for Voluptuous Worldlings* by Jan van der Noot, 1569, facsimile edition by Louis S. Friedland, Delmar, New York: Scholars' Facsimiles and Reprints, 1936; in *The Works of Edmund Spenser: A Variorum Edition*, vol. 2: *The Minor Poems*, edited by Charles G. Osgood and Henry G. Lotspeich, Baltimore: Johns Hopkins Press, 1947 (includes sonnets from the *Theatre*; *Ruines of Rome: By Bellay*; *Visions of Bellay*); and in *Joachim Du Bellay: Antiquités de Rome*, edited by Malcolm C. Smith, Binghamton, New York: Center for Medieval and Renaissance Studies, 1994

Les Regrets, 1558

Sisson, C.H., *The Regrets* (parallel texts), with an introduction, Manchester: Carcanet, 1984

Other Writing

Deffence et illustration de la langue françoyse, 1549

Turquet, Gladys M., *The Defence and Illustration of the French Language*, London: Dent, 1939

Joachim Du Bellay is for modern readers (and translators, see Sisson, 1984) primarily the poet of the *Regrets*; for English poets of the 16th century, however, the focus of interest lay elsewhere. While it would probably be an exaggeration to speak of "English indifference" to the *Regrets* in this period (see Elcock, 1951), English poets preferred to imitate and translate Du Bellay's love poetry, principally the sonnets of the *Olive*, and his meditations on the mutability of earthly power in the *Antiquitez de Rome*. Edmund Spenser's translations of the *Antiquitez* and *Songe* exemplify the difficulties inherent in evaluating the wide range of 16th-century translation and adaptation work that has been brought to light by scholars such as Prescott (1978). The perceived deficiencies of Spenser's translations may represent simple misreadings of the French original, or, on the other hand, a creative adaptation of Du Bellay's writing in a new cultural context; similarly, in the case of the other English poets who drew on Du Bellay's work, it is difficult to draw the line between creative translation, that is, the attempt to render the effects of the source text in English, and adaptation, in which the primacy of the source text is abandoned. For the purposes of this essay, I shall be as inclusive as possible in my treatment of 16th-century responses to Du Bellay.

The first English attempt to translate Du Bellay illustrates the problem. GRIMALD (1557) renders fairly closely the quatrains of Du Bellay's sonnet "Face le ciel" (*Olive* 19), but diverts the praise contained in the tercets from the lady ("ô ma Déesse") to Virgil's *Aeneid*. He also establishes the pattern for future translations of sonnets by substituting the Shakespearean form of three quatrains and a final rhyming couplet for the two quatrains and two tercets of the Petrarchan original.

SPENSER's engagement with Du Bellay dated from his youth and was sustained throughout his career. His translation of 11 sonnets from the *Songe* first appeared in a context of anti-Roman religious propaganda (van der Noot, 1569), and was probably written to order, certainly in some haste. In his subsequent revision of these pieces, republished under the title *Visions of Bellay* in the *Complaints* of 1591, the poet added the four sonnets omitted in 1569, replaced the blank verse with rhyming lines and made a number of corrections. The *Complaints* also contains a translation of the *Antiquitez de Rome* (*The Ruines of Rome: by Bellay*), to which Spenser added a sonnet in praise of Du Bellay as the "first garland of free Poësie", probably in order to compensate for his removal of Du Bellay's culturally specific exordial piece "Au Roy". Spenser's versions have been heavily criticized: sonnet 2, for instance, betrays a shaky knowledge of antiquity, confusing Babylon with

Babel and Olympia with Olympus; sonnet 17 contains two obvious mistranslations. Yet the interest of Spenser's versions lies in his treatment of the themes of the decadence of earthly power and the potential for rebirth explored further in his mature English works (especially *The Ruines of Time* and *The Faerie Queene*).

GORGES in the 1580s derives a number of poems, chiefly sonnets, from Du Bellay: a range of works are represented, including the *Olive*, *Regrets* and *Antiquitez*. Changes to the originals, extending to the replacement of whole stanzas, are freely made. The force of Du Bellay's *pointe* (pointed ending) (which is frequently ironic) is often lost. The same can be said of DANIEL (1592), whose three translations from the *Olive* consistently modify the sense of the final lines, replacing the pessimism of the original by expressions of hope and entreaties to the lady. This tendency may be in part attributable to the difficulty of adapting Du Bellay's sonnets, where tension is retained until the final line, to the structure of the Shakespearean form (see Rees, 1964).

After a long pause, English interest in Du Bellay is sporadic in the 19th century (see Elcock, 1951). In the 20th century, whole works are again translated. TURQUET's rendering (1939) of the *Deffence et Illustration de la langue françoyse* is prefaced by a biographical sketch. The English text is archaizing and frequently gallicized; the intended audience, "English students who might be rebuffed by the 16th-century French", are deemed to understand "misprized" as a translation for "deprisée", or "damosels" rendering "damoizelles". There are occasional errors (e.g. the omission of a negative on p. 22 reverses the sense of the original), and the syntax of the English frequently betrays the strain of reproducing the original too closely.

SISSON's introduction (1984) makes it clear that he views his translation of the first 130 sonnets of the *Regrets* as more than an exercise in antiquarianism. His intention is to enable the modern reader to become acquainted "with the mind of a man who survives the differences of centuries and speaks to us directly". Sisson succeeds admirably in rendering the freshness and often conversational tone of the original; rhyme is sacrificed, but the 14-line structure is retained. The facing-page layout reproduces the edition of Jolliffe and Screech, with occasional misprints. Despite the immediacy of Du Bellay's translated voice, however, the absence of explanatory material (there is a single footnote) often means that the poet's barbs go astray, despite the translator's efforts to incorporate interpretation into his version (see sonnet 23, where Du Bellay's playful allusiveness is interpreted out). Sisson's versions occasionally err on the side of informality, which can sound flippant (see sonnet 31), and some lines are misconstrued, but overall his translation is sensitive and effective. Perhaps the "indifference" has now, finally, been laid to rest.

DAVID COWLING

Further Reading

Dorangeon, Simone, "Spenser, traducteur de Du Bellay" in *Du Bellay: Actes du Colloque International d'Angers du 26 au 29 mai 1989*, edited by Georges Cesbron, Angers: Presse Université d'Angers, 1990

Elcock, W.D., "English Indifference to Du Bellay's *Regrets*", *Modern Language Review*, 46 (1951) pp. 175–84

Ferguson, Margaret W., "Joachim Du Bellay" in *The Spenser Encyclopedia*, edited by A.C. Hamilton *et al.*, Toronto: University of Toronto Press, and London: Routledge, 1990, pp. 83–85

Prescott, Anne Lake, *French Poets and the English Renaissance*, New Haven, Connecticut: Yale University Press, 1978

Prescott, Anne Lake, "Du Bellay in Renaissance England: Recent Work on Translation and Response", *Oeuvres et Critiques*, 20/1 (1995) pp. 121–28

Rees, Joan, *Samuel Daniel: A Critical and Biographical Study*, Liverpool: Liverpool University Press, 1964

Marguerite Duras 1914–1996

French novelist, dramatist, screenplay writer, short-story writer and journalist

Biography

Born Marguerite Donnadieu, 4 April 1914 in Gia Dinh, near Saigon, in French Indo-China (now Vietnam). Her parents were teachers; the father died when Marguerite was four, leaving his widow to bring up three children with considerable financial difficulty. The young Duras was educated at the Lycée de Saigon and spoke Vietnamese. There were some visits to Gascony, and Duras moved to France for good in 1932, taking degrees in law and in political science at the Sorbonne in 1935, then working at the French Colonial Office, Paris, until 1941, when the city had been occupied by the Germans. She was involved in the Resistance, though the details are not clear; the stories in *La Douleur* (*The War*), 1985, refer to this period. She had married Robert Antelme in 1939 (divorced 1946; one son) and had another son in 1942, this time by Dionys Mascolo, whom she later married. In 1943 she became a freelance writer. She was a member of the French Communist Party in the 1940s, but was expelled from the Party in the early 1950s, though her views continued to be left-wing in their way.

Her first novels, *Les Impudents* [The Impudent Ones], 1943, and *La Vie tranquille* [A Quiet Life], 1944, are set in the French provinces. She was spoken of in the 1950s and 1960s in connection with the *nouveau roman* (New Novel) but her experimental forms and subjects were, like their author, original and independent. Many of her plays and films are adaptations of or from her novels or stories, e.g. *Des Journées entières dans les arbres* (*Whole Days in the Trees*) appeared as fiction in 1954, then as a play in 1965. International fame came with her screenplay *Hiroshima mon amour* (*Hiroshima Mon Amour*), 1960. Duras was the most prominent French woman writer of the second half of the 20th century. Her work in the genres of fiction, theatre and cinema won many honours, notably prizes at the Cannes Film Festival in 1962 and 1975; the Académie Française grand prize for theatre, 1983; and the Goncourt prize, 1984, for the semi-autobiographical *L'Amant* (*The Lover*). She died in Paris, 3 March 1996.

Translations

Selection of Novels

Pitt-Rivers, Sonia *et al.*, *Four Novels*, with an introduction by Germaine Brée, New York: Grove Press, 1965; London: Calder and Boyars, 1966 (contains *The Square*, translated by Pitt-Rivers and Irina Morduch; *Moderato Cantabile*, translated by Richard Seaver; *Ten-Thirty on a Summer Night*, translated by Anne Borchardt; *The Afternoon of Mr Andemas*, translated by Morduch)

Novels

Les Petits chevaux de Tarquinia, 1953

DuBerg, Peter, *The Little Horses of Tarquinia*, London: John Calder, 1960

Le Square, 1955 (adapted for the theatre in 1965)

Pitt-Rivers, Sonia and Irina Morduch, *The Square*, New York: Grove Press, and London: John Calder, 1959; in *Four Novels*, translated by Pitt-Rivers, *et al.*, 1965

Moderato cantabile, 1958

Seaver, Richard, *Moderato Cantabile*, New York: Grove Press, 1960; London: Calder and Boyars, 1966; in *Four Novels*, translated by Pitt-Rivers, *et al.*, 1965

Dix heures et demie du soir en été, 1960

Borchardt, Anne, *Ten-Thirty on a Summer Night*, London: John Calder, 1962; New York: Grove Press, 1963; in *Four Novels*, translated by Pitt-Rivers, *et al.*, 1965

L'Après-midi de Monsieur Andesmas, 1962

Borchardt, Anne, *The Afternoon of Monsieur Andesmas*, with *The Rivers and the Forests*, translated by Barbara Bray, London: John Calder, 1964; in *Four Novels*, translated by Pitt-Rivers, *et al.*, 1965

L'Amante anglaise, 1967

Bray, Barbara, *L'Amante Anglaise*, London: Hamish Hamilton, 1968

Yann Andréa Steiner, 1992

Bray, Barbara, *Yann Andréa Steiner: A Memoir*, London: Hodder and Stoughton, and New York: Scribner, 1993

Autobiographical Writing

L'Amant, 1984

Bray, Barbara, *The Lover*, New York: Pantheon, and London: Collins, 1985

La Douleur, 1985

Bray, Barbara, *The War*, London: Collins, and New York: Pantheon, 1986

L'Amant de la Chine du nord, 1991

Hafrey, Leigh, *The North China Lover*, New York: New Press, 1992

C'est tout, 1995

Howard, Richard, *No More*, New York: Seven Stories Press, and London: Turnaround, 1998

Selections of Plays

Bray, Barbara, *Suzanna Andler, La Musica, L'Amante Anglaise*, London: John Calder, 1975

Bray, Barbara and Sonia Orwell, *Three Plays*, London: Calder and Boyars, 1967 (contains *Days in the Trees* and *The Square*, translated by Bray and Orwell; *The Viaducts of Seine-et-Oise*, translated by Bray)

Bray, Barbara, *Marguerite Duras: Four Plays*, with an introduction, London: Oberon Books, 1992 (contains *La Musica*, *Eden Cinema*, *Savannah Bay*, *India Song*)

Plays and Film Writing

Hiroshima mon amour, 1960

Seaver, Richard, *Hiroshima Mon Amour*, New York: Grove Press, 1961; with *Une Aussi Longue Absence*, translated by Barbara Wright, London: Calder and Boyars, 1966

Une Aussi Longue Absence, 1961

Wright, Barbara, *Une Aussi Longue Absence*, with *Hiroshima Mon Amour*, translated by Richard Seaver, London: Calder and Boyars, 1966

Le Square, 1965, early version produced 1957

Bray, Barbara, *The Square* in *Three Plays*, translated by Bray and Sonia Orwell, 1967

La Musica (*La Musica Deuxième*), 1965 (adapted for the cinema in 1966)

Bray, Barbara, *La Musica* (*La Musica Deuxième*) in *Marguerite Duras: Four Plays*, translated by Bray, 1992

India Song, 1973 (play and film script)

Bray, Barbara, *India Song* in *Marguerite Duras: Four Plays*, translated by Bray, 1992

L'Eden Cinéma, 1977

Bray, Barbara, *Eden Cinema* in *Marguerite Duras: Four Plays*, translated by Bray, 1992

Savannah Bay, 1982, produced 1984

Bray, Barbara, *Savannah Bay* in *Marguerite Duras: Four Plays*, translated by Bray, 1992

One of the most prolific of all modern French authors, with more than 70 publications to her credit, and certainly, through intensive translation coverage, one of the best known to anglophone readers, Marguerite Duras was first and foremost a novelist, but also a film writer and a playwright. Her work in the media of the cinema and the theatre often led her to collaborate with others (with Alain Resnais, for instance, in the making of *Hiroshima mon amour*), and so it is perhaps not surprising that she adopted an unpossessive attitude towards the adaptation and translation of her texts. This absence of proprietoriality in Duras is all the more impressive in that hers is an oeuvre inspired by an intensely personal set of preoccupations. Love and sexuality, madness and death, in particular, are interconnecting themes with strong autobiographical resonances that weave themselves into the fabric of all her writing, traversing boundaries of time and genre.

Barbara BRAY was the first person to translate any of Duras's work into English, starting with the text of a production of *The Square* for the BBC in the late 1950s, and she has translated much of her output since. In her introduction to *Four Plays* (1992), Bray identifies this author's oddness and intensity of style as the greatest problems that face the translator of her writing into English – an oddness of vocabulary and syntax which results from her scrupulous avoidance of all stereotypes, and a particularly heightened tone which does not work well in a language given to under- rather than over-statement. For Bray, then, the translator must dare to take risks with meaning, according priority to linguistic and cultural context. In this bold approach to the job of the traditionally self-effacing translator, Bray appears to have the author's explicit support, quoting Duras's warning that the importance of meaning should not be over-emphasized in any translations of her work. Given the cultural specificity of all languages, no translation, for Duras, can ever be an exact equivalence of the source text, and so each must be a different and autonomous work, the product of a personal reading of the original. Duras, in fact, advocates a musical approach, whereby the sound of the text takes precedence over its sense. The translator thus becomes a musician, freely interpreting each composition, so that it may continue to live and breathe. Bray finds two kinds of music in Duras: that which inheres in the language in which the text was written and which is more or less resistant to translation (colloquialisms, repetitions, telegraphic style), and the writer's own "music", which must take priority over meaning. This more personal music is Duras's idiosyncratic voice, and Bray is right to respect it, since it is this voice that gives the writing its originality and poetic force. Those readers who expect every sentence, if not every word, to have a Durassian origin may find that, in seeking to transpose the rhythms and the harmonies intact, Bray occasionally travels too far from the source text. Such readers should note, when comparing source and target texts, that Duras did not consider her published French versions in every respect perfect or definitive. She would sometimes make alterations between editions; also, when consulted on occasion by Bray about certain obscurities, Duras would say that she did not recall her original intention and would authorize the enhancement in English of the sense and effects of the words or passages in question.

Among the novels, *The Square* is an early text (1955) which is therefore comparatively straightforward in style, and PITT-RIVERS & MORDUCH's rendering (1959) is both highly readable and unproblematically faithful to the original.

BORCHARDT's translation (1962) of *Ten-Thirty on a Summer Night* is equally accessible, and keeps close to the French text, though this tactic occasionally has unfortunate consequences, as in the faulty syntax and mixed metaphors of "Plastered on his face, he had at times a chalky laugh".

In her 1964 *The Afternoon of Monsieur Andesmas*, too, BORCHARDT's tendency towards over-literalness frequently produces stilted English vocabulary and syntax: "interrupt with a mark of comfort", "medical siestas", "under new eyes" are unEnglish syntagms, while "You're so old, you can hear anything?" leaves the interrogative structure of spoken French unchanged and ineffective in English.

In contrast, BRAY's privileging of the music over the meaning of the text leads her away from the woodenness of over-literal renderings, but towards the dangers associated with too much licence. In her *Yann Andréa Steiner* (1993), for instance, she inserts sentences here and there that have no counterpart in the source text, to the extent of appending no less than four lines apparently of her own composition to the end of the novel, though, as we have seen, such modifications could have authorial origins.

The more cautious approach adopted by BRAY in trans lations of earlier novels produces a happier medium. Her work on Duras's first overtly autobiographical text, *The Lover* (*L'Amant*, 1984; translated 1985), for example, manages to avoid gallicisms while successfully transposing the idiosyncrasies of the French into idiomatic English, preserving the poetry of Duras's disjointed style without flattening it into colourless prose. The award, jointly to Bray, of the Scott Moncrieff Prize for this translation was a well deserved tribute to her achievement.

Leigh HAFREY's highly Americanized translation (1992) of *The North China Lover* (*L'Amant de la Chine du nord*, 1991) has a directness that seems well suited to the deadpan tones of this less nostalgic re-telling of Duras's adolescent love affair, previously narrated in *The Lover*. Hafrey's American idiom can be irritating for the English reader, but it is accurate where Bray occasionally is not – *jouissance*, for example, is correctly translated by Hafrey as "orgasm", in contrast to Bray's misleading euphemism, "pleasure" (*The Lover*).

Among Duras's film-scenarios, SEAVER's *Hiroshima mon amour* (1961) and WRIGHT's *Une aussi longue absence* (1966), published together in the same volume in 1966, are both well-crafted versions, although the simplicity and economy of Duras's dialogue arguably presents the translator with fewer problems than her narratives.

The same is true of her writing for the theatre. *Four Plays* (1992), translated by BRAY, are rendered in a largely faithful style, although, in her translation of *La Musica* (*La Musica Deuxième*), commissioned by the Hampstead Theatre, London, the subtle shades of meaning created by alternation in the French dialogue between "tu" and "vous" are signalled rather clumsily in the stage-directions (were the actors supposed to reflect these subtleties in their performance?). This untranslatable feature of syntax might have been more effectively conveyed by use of language. With this single reservation, however, Bray's success in deftly transposing the Durassian voice of *La Musica* into a performable English idiom is admirable. *Eden Cinema*, *Savannah Bay* and *India Song* are similarly well rendered. Bray has a talent for capturing the quirky syntax of Duras's terse one-liners without producing too stilted an effect, and dialogue offers the translator far fewer reasons than narrative to make additions that might jeopardize a fragile yet all-important sub-text.

JOHN PHILLIPS

Further Reading
Cismaru, Alfred, *Marguerite Duras*, New York: Twayne, 1971
Harvey, Robert and Hélène Volat, *Marguerite Duras: A Bio-bibliography*, Westport, Connecticut: Greenwood, 1997
Hill, Leslie, *Marguerite Duras: Apocalyptic Desires*, London and New York: Routledge, 1993
Resnick, Margery and Isabelle de Courtivron, *Women Writers in Translation: An Annotated Bibliography 1945–1982*, New York: Garland, 1984, pp. 38–42
Tison-Braun, Micheline, *Marguerite Duras*, Amsterdam: Rodopi, 1985
Willis, Sharon, *Marguerite Duras: Writing on the Body*, Urbana: University of Illinois Press, 1986

See also the translator's introduction to Bray (1992)

Friedrich Dürrenmatt 1921–1990

Swiss dramatist, novelist and critic

Biography

Born in Konolfingen, near Bern, Switzerland, 5 January 1921, the son of a pastor. He studied literature, philosophy and natural science at the universities of Bern and Zürich, 1941–45. He married first Lotti Geissler, in 1946 (died 1983; one son, two daughters), and second Charlotte Kerr, in 1984. He was a painter before becoming a writer and later illustrated some of his own texts.

His first play, *Es steht geschrieben* [It is Written], was produced with some controversy in Zürich in 1947. While continuing to write plays, mostly subversive dark or grotesque comedies, he was drama critic for Zürich's *Die Weltwoche*, 1951–53, and began producing fiction, notably *Der Richter und sein Henker* (*The Judge and His Hangman*), 1952. A first collection of theatre essays, *Theaterprobleme* (*Problems on the Theatre*), appeared in 1955. He was co-director of the Basel Theatre, 1968–69, and co-editor of the *Zürcher Sonntags-Journal*, 1969–71. Dürrenmatt latterly wrote essays on political and philosophical subjects. World famous, he lectured and received awards at home and abroad, including in the UK and the US. Died of heart failure, 14 December 1990, at Neuchâtel, Switzerland.

The best-known, at home and internationally, of his many plays (he wrote for stage, cinema and radio) are *Romulus der Grosse* (*Romulus*), 1949, *Der Besuch der alten Dame* (*The Visit*), 1956, and *Die Physiker* (*The Physicists*), 1962. His three psychological detective novels, *Der Richter und sein Henker* (*The Judge and His Hangman*), *Der Verdacht* (*The Quarry*), 1953, and *Das Versprechen* (*The Pledge*), 1958, are also highly regarded by anglophone readers.

Translations

Plays

Der Besuch der alten Dame, 1956
Bowles, Patrick, *The Visit*, London: Jonathan Cape, and New York: Grove Press, 1962

Romulus der Grosse (2nd version), 1958, produced 1957 (earlier version 1956, produced 1949)
Nellhaus, Gerhard, *Romulus the Great* (2nd version) in *Four Plays, 1957–62*, London: Jonathan Cape, 1964; New York: Grove Press, 1965

Die Physiker, 1962
Kirkup, James, *The Physicists*, London and New York: Samuel French, 1963

Novels

Der Richter und sein Henker, 1952
Brooks, Cyrus, *The Judge and His Hangman*, London: Jenkins, 1954

Der Verdacht, 1953
Morreale, Eva H., *The Quarry*, London: Jonathan Cape, and Greenwich, Connecticut: New York Graphic Society, 1962

Das Versprechen, 1958
Winston, Richard and Clara Winston, *The Pledge*, London: Jonathan Cape, and New York: Knopf, 1959

Friedrich Dürrenmatt was a prolific writer. To mark his 60th birthday in 1981 a new edition of his collected works to that date was published. It contained 30 volumes. These volumes include more than 20 stage plays, several radio plays and a series of short stories, novels and essays on theatre, politics and philosophy. Much, though by no means all, of this writing has been translated into English. A striking aspect of this translation work is the diversity of the hands that have been involved in the task; at least eight translators have engaged themselves with the stage plays, and Dürrenmatt's bestselling novels were translated by another three people. Here we shall focus on a small selection of his best-known work.

Dürrenmatt's favourite dramatic form is what he termed "Die Komödie" (comedy) and his characteristic mode is comedy of the grotesque, an idiosyncratic blend of irony, satire and savage caricature that often carries disturbing and unsettling undercurrents. The tone of his dramatic dialogue moves abruptly between terse exchanges, comic exaggerations and elevated rhetoric in which the serious issues that underlie his plays come to the fore.

The translations of the three plays chosen for consideration have all succeeded in capturing the particular flavour of his work. *Romulus the Great* centres on the figure of the last emperor of Rome who, while the invading Teuton army nears the capital, ignores the threat and concentrates all his attention on looking after his chickens. Romulus seems to combine the outlook of a Swiss peasant with the trappings of an imperial ruler. NELLHAUS (1964) aptly captures this incongruity when Romulus proposes a new battle cry to rally the troops:

Romulus Personally, I'm more in favour of a practical slogan, a proposition that can be realized. For example: "For better agriculture and bigger chickens".

But it gradually emerges that Romulus' attitudes are calculated. He is deliberately sabotaging the resolve of his advisers; he wants to see the Roman Empire destroyed because of the crimes it has committed:

Romulus I didn't betray my empire; Rome betrayed herself. Rome knew the truth but chose violence. Rome knew humaneness but chose tyranny. Rome doubly demeaned herself: before her own people and before the other nations in her power.

Here Nellhaus accurately reflects the eloquence with which Romulus denounces his empire. He is willing to die to bring it to an end. His readiness for noble self-sacrifice is thwarted by the fact that the leader of the Teutons turns out to be an equally passionate chicken-breeder who packs Romulus off into tedious suburban retirement.

The Physicists exhibits a pattern similar to that of *Romulus the Great*. Three nuclear physicists are confined to a lunatic asylum. One of them has just strangled a nurse and the police are investigating. The police inspector claims that this would not have happened if male nurses had been appointed:

Sister Boll Do you really think so?
Inspector I do.
Sister Boll Nurse Moser was a member of the League of Lady Wrestlers and Nurse Straub was Ladies' Champion of the National Judo Association.
Inspector And what about you?
Sister Boll Weightlifter.

Like Nellhaus, KIRKUP (1963) catches the comic exaggeration in this exchange. Similarly, when the central figure, Möbius, reveals that there has been method in his madness the register changes gear and the translation faithfully records the note of high-minded earnestness:

Möbius There are certain risks which one may not take: the destruction of humanity is one. We know what the world has done with the weapons it already possesses; we can imagine what it would do with those which my researches make possible. And it is these considerations that have governed my conduct.

But Möbius too is frustrated. His manuscripts have been copied by the psychiatrist in charge of the asylum, who will use their terrible potential to set up a world dictatorship. Möbius is condemned to impotent incarceration.

Dürrenmatt's most successful play was *The Visit*. Claire Zachanassian, the richest person in the world, returns to her impoverished home town and offers its inhabitants a fortune if they kill her former lover who had seduced and abandoned her. Gradually they succumb to collective temptation. BOWLES (1962) reproduces the sinister ironies of the language and he is equal to the task of dealing with a particular problem raised by the text. It is a parody of Greek tragedy. The citizens of Güllen imitate the role of the Greek chorus. To begin with, this role is clearly comic as they lament their poverty:

Man One The whole thing's a Freemasons' plot.
Man Two Conspired by the Jews.
Man Three Backed by High Finance.
Man Four International Communism's showing its colours.

By the conclusion of the play the register has changed as they celebrate their new-found prosperity. Bowles successfully conveys the savage irony that their choral incantation betrays:

Priest Now let us pray to God
All To protect us
Mayor In these hustling, booming, prosperous times:
All Protect all our sacred possessions,
Protect our peace and our freedom,
Ward off the night, nevermore
Let it darken our glorious town
Grown out of the ashes anew.
Let us go and enjoy our good fortune.

Dürrenmatt's most popular works are his detective stories, which present a different kind of problem. The first two, *The Judge and His Hangman* and *The Quarry*, originally appeared in fortnightly instalments in a Swiss magazine. They were written hurriedly and they show much evidence of Swiss-German usage, which can deviate markedly from standard German. BROOKS (1954) and MORREALE (1962) deal with this difficulty in the same – and probably the most sensible – way: they translate the stories into standard English. It might be argued that the novels thereby lose some of the Swiss colouring present in the originals. However, they were written with a specifically Swiss readership in mind and any attempt to find an English equivalent not only would be extremely difficult, but could all too easily sound artificial. The novels deal with themes such as crime and punishment, guilt and justice, which are also central to many of Dürrenmatt's plays. For English-speaking readers there can be little doubt that it is the treatment of these themes and the suspense of the narrative that are of primary interest and that the loss or at least the considerable dilution of the particular Swiss linguistic flavour is not significant.

The Pledge is Dürrenmatt's finest novel. This story of a master detective reduced to a drunken wreck by his failure to capture a child murderer is carefully constructed and tautly written, with few of the Swiss-German features of the earlier novels. The version by Richard and Clara WINSTON (1959) is exemplary in its attention to detail and the precision of its language.

The conclusion must be that Dürrenmatt's work has been generally well served by the variety of translators who have tackled it. In particular, the spirit of irony and the grotesque that pervades his plays has found its appropriate expression in English.

BERNARD ASHBROOK

Further Reading

Tiusanen, Timo, *Dürrenmatt: A Study in Plays, Prose, Theory*, Princeton, New Jersey: Princeton University Press, 1977

Whitton, Kenneth S., *Dürrenmatt: Reinterpretation in Retrospect*, Oxford: Oswald Wolff, and New York: Berg, 1990

Dutch

Literary Translation into English

The Language

Dutch is spoken by approximately 21 million people, mainly in the Netherlands and in Flanders, the northern half of Belgium (the southern half of Belgium, Wallonia, is French-speaking). Like English, Dutch is a Germanic language. With the exception of Frisian (spoken in the province of Friesland, in the northern Netherlands), Dutch is the language most closely related to English. Typologically it stands roughly halfway between English and German. While it shares with both English and German a large stock of vocabulary of Germanic origin, Dutch has fewer cases and inflections than German, but more than English. Thus although Dutch does not know a case system along the lines of German, adjectives have inflected as well as uninflected forms, there is more variety than in English in the formation of plural nouns, and verb forms are more similar to German than to English. Word order is generally SVO (Subject-Verb-Object), but, as in German, inversion is common, whether for emphasis or in subordinate clauses. Unlike German, however, Dutch does not generally favour long, complex sentences. Among features peculiar to Dutch, and sometimes hard to translate, are diminutives of adverbs (e.g. *zachtjes* [softly]) and a wealth of modal particles, often used in combination (*wel*, *toch*, *'ns*, *even*, ... [indeed, yet, just, ...]).

Literary Translation from Dutch

From the Middle Ages to the present day, despite geographical proximity and numerous economic and cultural contacts, Dutch literature translated into English has been a very minor presence. From the 18th century onwards most of the cultural traffic has been in one direction: from the English-speaking world to the Low Countries. The literary influence of Walter Scott in the 19th century, and of contemporary Anglo-American culture more generally, can serve to illustrate the point. However, the contemporary perspective, which casts Dutch as a minor language compared with English, is misleading. In the 16th and 17th centuries, for example, English was a relatively unknown language on the Continent and Dutch was known rather more widely than it is now.

During the Middle Ages, Latin literary and learned writings originating in the Low Countries did not need to be translated abroad because Latin was the international language of intellectual commerce throughout Europe. The written tradition in (pre-1100) Old Dutch, preserved only in a few fragments, need not concern us here. Of the vernacular literary writings in Middle Dutch virtually nothing was translated into English at the time. Most translations from Middle Dutch have been done in the 19th and especially 20th century. The few exceptions date from the very end of the medieval period. However they include the best-known work of medieval Dutch literature, the animal epic *Reynard the Fox*, by the otherwise unknown "William who made Madoc". It was translated and printed in 1481 by William Caxton, who himself had learned the art of printing in Bruges.

Although the relation between the English *Everyman* and the 15th-century *Elckerlijc* attributed to Petrus Dorlandus of Diest (near Louvain) was the subject of protracted scholarly debate, it is now generally thought that *Everyman* is a translation of *Elckerlijc* rather than the other way round. The argument was finally settled in favour of *Elckerlijc* as the source on the basis of a detailed analysis of rhyming words. The anonymous play *Mariken van Nieumeghen* (c.1500, first printed c.1515), in verse and prose, appeared in English as *Mary of Nemmegen*, printed in Antwerp by Jan van Doesborch in 1518. More than a third of Van Doesborch's output was in English, including a number of translations from Dutch (among them the popular *Tyll Howleglass*, printed c.1520–30, the Dutch source of which goes back to a German original); several of the English books published by Van Doesborch were translated by Lawrence Andrewe, who afterwards settled in London as a printer.

In the late 16th century the Antwerp Renaissance poet Jan van der Noot published *Het theatre* in London (1568). The collection, a cycle of sonnets followed by an anti-Catholic prose commentary, was translated in 1569 as *Theatre of Voluptuous Worldlings* by the then 17-year-old Edmund Spenser and printed by Henry Bynneman, who himself hailed from the Low Countries. Spenser later incorporated some of the translations into his *Complaints* of 1591. The major anti-Catholic satire, in prose by Philips van Marnix van Sint-Aldegonde (1569), was translated as *The Beehive of the Romish Churche* (1578) by

George Gilpin the Elder and reprinted several times (1580, 1598, 1623, 1636).

In the 17th century the Dutch Republic emerged as a world power, if only for a short time. Its "Golden Age" culture saw the likes of Rembrandt and Vermeer. Although the first English–Dutch/Dutch–English dictionary was produced in this period (by Henry Hexham, 1658), very little vernacular writing was being translated into English. This is in contrast with the neo-Latin writings from the Low Countries. Here the tradition begun with translations of Erasmus (1466?–1536) in the 16th century was continued in the 17th; for example, several of the political, legal and theological works of Hugo Grotius (1588–1645) were translated into English, as were his Latin plays (*Christ's Passion*, by G. Sandys, 1640; and *Sophompaneas*, by F. Goldsmith, 1652). The Latin treatise on women's right to advanced study, by Anna Maria van Schurman (1641), appeared in English as *The Learned Maid* (1659).

Among the very few translated authors writing in Dutch was Jacob Cats (1577–1660). Thomas Heywood's "Emblematical Dialogue", in his *Pleasant Dialogues* of 1637 was given as "interpreted from ... I. Catzius", and Cats himself had brought out a trilingual edition of some of his emblems at the end of the 1620s, with the English versions probably by Joshua Sylvester, the translator of Du Bartas. But despite the fact that both Cats and Constantijn Huygens (1596–1687) were knighted by Charles I, and Huygens became the first foreign translator of John Donne, Dutch literature remained largely untranslated and hence unknown in the anglophone world. The first English translations of the leading Golden Age dramatist and "prince of poets" Joost van den Vondel (1587–1679) appeared in the early 19th century, and the first complete play by Vondel (*Lucifer*, translated by Charles van Noppen) had to wait until the end of that century.

Other Anglo-Dutch contacts involving translation in one form or another during this period include the large numbers of English and Scottish students attending Leiden University, and regular exchanges and translations of Puritan, Pietist and Quaker writings. Several religious works by Willem Teellinck appeared in English translation in the early 1620s; he best-known figure here is the bilingual William Sewell, author of a history of the Quakers but also of a Dutch–English bilingual dictionary (1691) and of a Dutch grammar in English in the early 18th century. Generally, however, it would appear that knowledge of English was spreading more rapidly among the Dutch than knowledge of Dutch among the English. With English mercantile supremacy beginning to assert itself, the pattern of one-directional translation became established in the 18th century with the massive influence of English spectatorial writings in the Netherlands. Although it has been argued that Daniel Defoe derived the material for his *Robinson Crusoe* in part from Hendrik Smeek's *Krinke Kesmes* (1708), the evidence has remained inconclusive. The *Poetry for Children* by the popular Hieronymus van Alphen, published in 1778–82, was translated by F.J. Millard as late as 1856.

In the early 19th century the opening words of the introduction to the *Batavian Anthology: or, Specimens of the Dutch Poets* (1824), edited by John Bowring and Harry van Dyk, summed up the state of English literary translation from Dutch: "There is a country almost within sight of the shores of our island whose literature is less known to us than that of Persia or Hindostan ... it is indeed most strange, that while the poets of Germany have found hundreds of admirers and thousands of critics, those of a land nearer to us in position – more allied by habit and by history with our thoughts and recollections – should have been passed by unnoticed". The translator and later Member of Parliament and diplomat John Bowring (1792–1872) translated poetry from Eastern Europe and Spain as well as the Netherlands, and produced also a *Sketch of the Language and Literature of Holland* (1829), the first more or less systematic presentation of Dutch literature in English. Bowring's example as a poetry translator would be followed later in the 19th and in the early 20th century by Edmund Gosse and Jethro Bithell, then by Herbert Grierson, James Russell, Adriaan Barnouw and Theodoor Weevers, and in recent decades by James Holmes, James Brockway, Manfred Wolf and Francis Jones.

Although the 19th century saw rather more translations from Dutch into English than the preceding centuries, they were still few and far between. The work now regarded as the most important Dutch novel of the century, Multatuli's *Max Havelaar* (1860), was rendered into English by Alphonse Nahuijs in 1868; two further translations would follow in the 20th century. The genre attracting most attention was the historical novel which fitted the mould created by Walter Scott. Thus E.E. Hoskin translated Jacob van Lennep's *The Adopted Son* in 1847 (Dutch: *De pleegzoon*, 1833), and F. Woodley *The Rose of Dekama*, also by Van Lennep, in 1846 (*De roos van Dekama*, 1836). A.L.G. Bosboom-Toussaint's *Majoor Frans* (1874), however, translated by James Akeroyd as *Major Frank* (1885), is a sketch of contemporary life. The most widely translated 19th-century author was the Flemish Hendrik Conscience (1812–83), who wrote numerous historical novels and romances. Not only individual works were brought out in translation in Britain and the USA from the 1840s onwards – collections of novellas and multi-volume editions also appeared throughout the latter half of the 19th century. Very soon however Conscience came to be seen as a writer of popular rather than serious literature, a fate that also befell his work in other countries and in his native Flanders.

At the end of the 19th and first few decades of the 20th century, Louis Couperus (1863–1923) became the best-known Dutch novelist in English translation, thanks largely to the efforts of his translator Teixeira de Mattos. His popularity ended abruptly in the 1930s. The most frequently translated authors in the first half of the 20th century were popular writers like Jo van Ammers-Küller (1884–1966) and Johan Fabricius (b.1899), followed by a second league made up of more literary figures including, apart from Couperus, the novelists Arthur van Schendel (1874–1946), Frederik van Eeden (1860–1932) and Madelon Lulofs (1899–1958), the playwright Herman Heijermans (1864–1924) and the essayist and historian Johan Huizinga (1872–1945). Even so, literary translations from Dutch into English in the first half of the century numbered fewer than 250 titles, including reprints.

After World War II this situation seemed set to continue, despite the phenomenal success worldwide of Anne Frank's *Diary of a Young Girl* (1947). Translations of major works by some of the most prominent Dutch and Flemish postwar novelists (*The Dark Room of Damocles* by W.F. Hermans, 1962, and *Chapel Road* by L.P. Boon, 1972) sank without trace. However, thanks in large measure to the efforts of the Foundation for the Production and Translation of Dutch Literature (Amsterdam) and its predecessor (set up in 1954), the last decade or so has witnessed a rapid and sizeable increase in the number of English translations of modern Dutch literature. Although the increase is not as spectacular as the current vogue for Dutch fiction in Germany, for example, it is nevertheless unmistakable. As a result, leading contemporary Dutch and Flemish writers are now available in English translations. Among the most translated literary authors of the postwar generation are J. Bernlef, Hugo Claus, Marga Minco, Harry Mulisch and Cees Nooteboom.

THEO HERMANS

Further Reading

Arents, Prosper, *De Vlaamse schrijvers in het Engels vertaald, 1481–1949*, Ghent, 1950

Bense, J.F., *Anglo-Dutch Relations from the Earliest Times to the Death of William the Third*, The Hague: Martinus Nijhoff, 1925

Davies, D.W. *Dutch Influences on English Culture, 1555–1625*, Ithaca, New York: Cornell University Press, 1964

Dorsten, Jan van (editor), *Ten Studies in Anglo-Dutch Relations*, Leiden: Leiden University Press, 1974

Forster, Leonard, "Literary Relations between the Low Countries, England and Germany, 1400–1624", *Dutch Crossing*, 24 (1984)

Goedegebuure, Jaap and Anne Marie Musschoot, *Contemporary Fiction of the Low Countries*, Rekkem: Flemish–Netherlands Foundation, 1993

Haley, K.H.D., *The British and the Dutch: Political and Cultural Relations Through the Ages*, London: G. Philip, 1988

Hermans, Theo, "Postwar Dutch Fiction in English Translation since 1980: A Checklist", *Review of Contemporary Fiction*, 14 (1994), pp. 175–85

Hermans, Theo, "A Checklist of Postwar Dutch and Flemish Poetry in English Translation, 1977–1997", *Modern Poetry in Translation*, new series 12 (Winter 1997) pp. 269–78

Kooper, Erik (editor) *Medieval Dutch Literature in Its European Context*, Cambridge and New York: Cambridge University Press, 1994

Meijer, Reinder P., *Literature of the Low Countries*, Assen: Van Gorcum, 1971; new edition, Cheltenham: Thornes, 1978

Morel, P.M., "Translations of Dutch Literature 1900–57" in *Bibliographia Neerlandica*, The Hague, 1962

Raan, E. van, *Het Nederlandse boek in vertaling / The Dutch Book in Translation*, 5 vols, The Hague: Staatsuitgeverij, 1958–77

Russell, James A., *Dutch Poetry and English: A Study of the Romantic Revival*, Amsterdam, 1939

Schenkeveld, Maria A., *Dutch Literature in the Age of Rembrandt: Themes and Ideas*, Amsterdam and Philadelphia: Benjamins, 1991

Vanderauwera, Ria, *Dutch Novels Translated into English. The Transformation of a "Minority" Literature*, Amsterdam and Atlantic Highlands, New Jersey: Humanities Press, 1985

Vries, T. de, *Holland's Influence on English Language and Literature*, Chicago: Grentzebach, 1916

E

Umberto Eco 1932–

Italian novelist and semiotician

Biography

Born 5 January 1932 in Alessandria in Piedmont, Umberto Eco graduated at the University of Turin with a thesis on the aesthetics of Thomas Aquinas. Eco has worked in television, publishing and journalism and has taught aesthetics and then semiotics at the universities of Turin, Milan, Florence and Bologna. Since 1975 he has been Professor of Semiotics in the Faculty of Letters and Philosophy at the University of Bologna, residing in Milan, and travelling widely abroad; he has spent considerable time as visiting professor at a number of universities in the United States. He has been a leading figure in, and Secretary General of, the International Association for Semiotic Studies, and translations of *Il nome della rosa* (*The Name of the Rose*),1980, which won the Strega prize for fiction in Italy, popularized him as the world's most famous semiotician. Theorist, virtuoso translator of Queneau's *Exercices de style*, autotranslator both from and into Italian, translator of his more abstruse works "into language accessible to all" (introduction to *Travels in Hyper Reality*), and writer of novels involving translators and acts of translation, Umberto Eco provides a most intriguing contemporary case of interlingual and intercultural exchange.

Although the following list, referring only to publications in book form, divides Eco's prolific output into theoretical and critical works, journalism and fiction, the division between academic work and journalism is not a hard and fast one: each of the two categories feeds into the other. A number of the Italian titles are collections of previously published articles, and the English titles make their own selections of articles, some previously published, others not, and correspond only in part to the Italian book titles to which they are here related.

Translations

Theoretical and Critical Writings

Il probelema estetico in Tommaso d'Aquino, 1956; revised edition 1970

Bredin, Hugh, *The Aesthetics of Thomas Aquinas*, Cambridge, Massachusetts: Harvard University Press, 1988 (based on Italian 1970 edition)

"Sviluppo dell'estetica medievale" in *Momenti e problemi di storia dell'estetica*, vol. 1, 1959

Bredin, Hugh, *Art and Beauty in the Middle Ages*, New Haven, Connecticut and London: Yale University Press, 1986

L'opera aperta, 1962; 3rd revised edition 1967

Cancogni, Anna and Bruce Merry, *The Open Work*, with an introduction by David Robey, Cambridge, Massachussetts: Harvard University Press, 1989 (contains six of the seven chapters of the third edition of *L'opera aperta*, together with one from *Apocalittici e integrati*, 1964; one from *La struttura assente*, 1964, plus three others from various sources; Merry is responsible for two chapters)

Le poetiche di Joyce, 1966

Esrock, Ellen, *The Middle Ages of James Joyce: The Aesthetics of Chaosmos*, Tulsa: University of Tulsa Press, 1982; London: Hutchinson Radius, and Cambridge, Massachusetts: Harvard University Press, 1989 (the Italian essay originally featured as the last chapter of *L'opera aperta*)

Trattato di semiotica generale, 1975

Eco, Umberto with David Osmond-Smith, *A Theory of Semiotics*, Bloomington: Indiana University Press, 1976

Lector in fabula, 1979

Merry, Bruce, John Snyder, Natalie Chilton, R.A. Downie and Umberto Eco, *The Role of the Reader: Explorations in the Semiotics of Texts*, Bloomington: Indiana University Press, 1979; London: Hutchinson, 1981 (contains versions of Italian texts appearing in a number of Italian publications, including *Le forme del contenuto*, *Il superuomo di massa* and *Lector in fabula*)

Sugli specchi e altri saggi, 1983

Eco, Umberto, Juliann Vitullo, Guy Raffa and Gino Rizzo, *The Limits of Interpretation*, Bloomington: Indiana University Press, 1990 (this compilation of pieces written between 1968 and 1988 contains four chapters based on *Sugli specchi*; Vitullo, Raffa and Rizzo are responsible for only two of the 15 chapters)

Eco, Umberto, Lucia Re and Christopher Paci, *Semiotics and the Philosophy of Language*, Bloomington: Indiana University Press, and London: Macmillan, 1984 (contains a later version of the title essay of *Sugli specchi*, as well as a translation of a chapter in *Lector in fabula*, and of other writings – particularly entries written for the *Enciclopedia Einaudi*, 1984)

Postille a Il nome della rosa, 1983
Weaver, William, *Reflections on "The Name of the Rose"*, San Diego: Harcourt Brace, 1984; London: Secker and Warburg, 1985

La ricerca della lingua perfetta nella cultura europea, 1993
Fentress, James, *The Search for the Perfect Language*, Oxford and Cambridge, Massachusetts: Blackwell, 1995

Sei passeggiate nei boschi narrativi, 1994
Eco, Umberto, *Six Walks in the Fictional Woods*, Cambridge, Massachusetts: Harvard University Press, 1994 (the "six walks" make up Eco's six Charles Norton Lectures of 1993)

Kant e l'ornitorinco, 1997
McEwen, Alastair, *Kant and the Platypus: Essays on Language and Cognition*, London: Secker and Warburg, 1999; New York: Harcourt Brace, 2000

Travel Writing and Journalism
Diario minimo, 1963
Weaver, William, *Misreadings*, San Diego: Harcourt Brace, and London: Jonathan Cape, 1993 (contains 15 of the 16 items in the source text, in a slightly rearranged order)

Apocalittici e integrati, 1964
Lumley, Robert, Jenny Condie, William Weaver, Liz Heron (from French) Geoffrey Nowell-Smith, in *Apocalypse Postponed*, edited, with an introduction by Lumley, Bloomington: Indiana University Press, and London: British Film Institute, 1994 [contains two chapters from *Apocalittici e integrati* and two appearing in *Sette anni di desiderio* – see below – together with articles from *L'Espresso* and other sources; the bulk of the translations are by Condie, seven chapters, and Lumley, five; for three chapters no translator is named.]

Sette anni di desiderio: Cronache 1977–1983, 1983
Weaver, William, Christine Leefeldt and Umberto Eco, *Travels in Hyper Reality*, San Diego: Harcourt Brace, and London: Secker and Warburg, 1986; as *Faith in Fakes*, 1986 (this book, published under two titles, contains translations of a number of items to be found in *Sette anni di desiderio*, as well as from *Sugli specchi* and other sources)

Il secondo diario minimo, 1994
Weaver, William, *How to Travel with a Salmon and Other Essays*, New York: Harcourt Brace, and London: Secker and Warburg, 1994

Novels
Il nome della rosa, 1980
Weaver, William, *The Name of the Rose*, San Diego: Harcourt Brace, and London: Secker and Warburg, 1983

Il pendolo di Foucault, 1988
Weaver, William, *Foucault's Pendulum*, San Diego: Harcourt Brace, and London: Secker and Warburg, 1989

L'isola del giorno prima, 1994
Weaver, William, *The Island of the Day Before*, San Diego: Harcourt Brace, and London: Secker and Warburg, 1995

Stories for Children
La bomba e il generale; I tre cosmonauti, by Eco and Eugenio Carmi, 1988
Weaver, William, *The Bomb and the General*, San Diego: Harcourt Brace, and London: Secker and Warburg, 1989
Weaver, William, *The Three Astronauts*, San Diego: Harcourt Brace, and London: Secker and Warburg, 1989

Umberto Eco does not devote much space in his academic writings to interlingual translation, and "translation" hardly figures in any subject index to his books. When used, the words "translate" and derivatives are applied matter-of-factly to acts of intersemiotic transfers between a wide range of systems. Although he himself is a virtuoso linguist, his lectures about texts to foreign audiences tend not to focus on discourse but on story and plot "which are not functions of language but structures that can nearly always be translated into another semiotic system" (*Six Walks in the Fictional Woods*).

In the few pages devoted specifically to interlingual translation in his *The Search for a Perfect Language*, Eco theorizes its feasibility on the basis of the American philosopher Pierce's notion of "unlimited semiosis": each natural language constitutes a "quite rigid way of seeing, organizing and interpreting reality", but it also provides a metalanguage to itself; an English word that has no direct equivalent in Italian may be understood (and hence translated) by reference to other English words that interpret it. In other works Eco develops another Piercian concept – that of "encyclopedia". A natural language is a vastly complex system of sign-functions, with meaning located in cultural units; individuals' competence relates to their knowledge not of a semantic "dictionary" but rather of the collective "encylopedia" that pragmatically defines each cultural unit.

Eco's own books require as translator a reader possessing that internalized encyclopedic competence in the semiotic sense, and also armed with dictionaries and encyclopedias in the usual sense, since almost all his books, including his novels, contain a plethora of erudite references and technical terms. He teasingly inserts obscure terms into even his most popularizing texts. Beyond the immediate problems of lexis there lies the more complicated shift between cultural codes across languages. Eco's works in their twinned versions offer a parable of the fraught encounter between European and American cultures. As for the novels, they also pose their translator the stylistic problems connected with pastiche. All three mimic and quote philosophical and aesthetic texts from historical periods in which the bibliophile Eco is deeply versed.

In Eco's teeming books and articles there is considerable overlap and repetition, as he floats and develops his ideas through various stages, and articulates them in different countries and contexts, genres and styles. Thus the texts appear to be always on the move. Eco himself is often involved in the process of translation, which more frequently than not provides the occasion for a substantial rewriting. He has had native speakers revise his English for publication, but in his turn has intervened to revise his revisers' or translators' English. In addition, because of his frequent contact with English-language universities, Eco has increasingly written directly in English (as well as in other languages), with an Italian text appearing subsequently to an English (or German or French) text. Translation in relation to Eco's works means a collaborative and creative process, and the story of the encounter between Italian texts and the English language constitutes an intriguing and at times confusing whodunnit.

There follow brief comments on a few key moments in this history, set out now in the chronological order of the translations, and combining fictional and non-fictional works in one narrative.

It took more than two decades for Eco's earliest theoretical writings, on medieval aesthetics (Bredin 1988 and 1986) and on the "open text" (CANCOGNI & MERRY, 1989) to be translated into English. *A Theory of Semiotics* (1975, translated by ECO & OSMOND-SMITH, 1976), however, which forms the cornerstone of Eco's whole production, is the product of a clash of languages. The foreword recounts the evolution of the book through various stages, influenced by Eco's "working for two years on the French, German, Spanish and Swedish translations". After "unsatisfactory attempts" at an English version of the evolving text, Eco states he re-wrote the book directly in English with the help of an English speaker. Nevertheless it is legitimate to treat the Italian text *Trattato di semiotica generale*, published a year earlier, as the source text of this English version, if only because various passages are difficult to understand without recourse to an Italian original. The English text is identical in its structure to the Italian one, although there are very many cuts and additions in the English version. The introduction in the English of the first personal singular pronoun disrupts the impersonal presentation of the Italian version, and there is a frequent oscillation in style and tone. Seen in hindsight the translation represents an interesting but laborious early stage in Eco's relationship with English-speaking and particularly transatlantic audiences, and shows among other things the first approach to the problem of cultural transfers. Peanut butter substitutes for chocolate. Of the proper names that remain, the autotranslator revels in his freedom: some he retains, some he drops, some he cunningly or arbitrarily changes. Giovanni hits Giuseppe in the Italian, but John hits Mary in the translation.

The Role of the Reader (MERRY *et al.*, 1979) is a collection of essays based on source texts from 1959 to 1971, supplemented by three items from 1976 to 1977, written after *Trattato di semiotica generale*. The title emphasizes what may now be seen as a common thread running through Eco's works. From the point of view of translation it shows Eco moving from being the reviser of others' translations of his works to being author in English. Four of the chapters are presented as "revised versions" of translations by three different translators; one is "an extensively revised version" of a translation by a fourth; only one is presented as a translation of an Italian pre-text by a fifth, reprinted "with minor alterations". Where it is possible to make close comparisons with a source text, there is a general tendency to clarify the Italian through a simplification of phrasing and syntax, some radical cutting and much shorter paragraphing, but this does not prevent some cumbersome turns of phrase being chosen to translate expressions quite straightforward in the originals.

When he prepares English translations of works long after their publication in the original version, Eco's impulse to update is resisted by his competing desire not to exercise "afterwit". This problem, which relates to the rapidly changing fashions in critical terminology in the last 40 years, is briefly referred to by Ellen ESROCK (1982) in her translator's note to *The Middle Ages of James Joyce*, where she states her aim as to "maintain the original 1960s perspective" while "[recapturing] the trajectory" of a text that was "written with an impulse towards the future". *The Role of the Reader* is not exempt from "afterwit".

The Name of the Rose (1980, translated by WEAVER, 1983) is the novel that became an unlikely publishing phenomenon and made Eco famous. The translator of this, as of Eco's other two novels, is the doyen of Italian contemporary literature translators, William Weaver. Faced with the fabulous but unremitting accumulations of lists, descriptions, philosophical debate, historical explanations, someone – editor, translator, author – decided to anticipate the empirical reader's impulse to skip, by operating quite a number of cuts, some quite substantial. As for the abundant Latin, much is cut or translated. In translating a work that feigned to be an Italian version of a 19th-century French version of a 17th-century version of a story written in Latin by a medieval German monk, featuring characters from all over Europe speaking Latin rather than their native tongue, the skilled translator must have felt unusually covered against accusations of "translationese", since that is precisely what the source text frequently required. Some of the translator's choices surprise; there are small inconsistencies. Weaver's translations of the speeches of the character Salvatore are an interesting example of Eurobabble operating from a different home base.

The film adaptation of *The Name of the Rose* (1986) had a French director, Jean-Jacques Annaud, but obeyed the dictates of Hollywood in producing an intersemiotic translation of a novel that on one level seemed to be expressly designed to be unreproduceable in film, and at another offered an action-packed murder mystery. Rumour was that the script went through 15 versions before reaching the final committee of four scriptwriters. In terms of story, the film is notable for its ludicrously happy ending, with the comeuppance of both arch-villains and the rescue of the beloved.

Travels in Hyper Reality / Faith in Fakes (1986), the translations of assorted articles, form an essential stage in the on-going collaboration between ECO and William WEAVER, Weaver translating most of the pieces and acting as reviser for four, with Christine LEEFELDT translating one other. The adaptation by Eco of a revised lecture, "Dieci modi di sognare il medioevo" (reprinted in *Sugli specchi*, 1983), shows Eco revelling in the freedom of the autotranslator and calculating which of the Italian and European learned references to drop or playfully transpose (the Italian source-books have lengthy indices of proper names that the translation omits). The translation of a subtitle, "Dieci tipi di medioevo", as "Ten Little Middle Ages" is a sign that the translation itself is not immune to that kitsch that both appalls and fascinates Eco. Weaver, although staying much closer to the Italian source texts, obviously enjoys balancing the erudite and the colloquial. While frequently brilliant, Weaver takes a number of short cuts, and quite a lot of lines are dropped.

Il pendolo di Foucault (*Foucault's Pendulum*) (1988), Eco's second novel, is a spoof on over-interpretation. The novel contains among other things a "translation" into fiction of the Brazilian episode recounted in *Travels in Hyper Reality*. William WEAVER's translation (1989) is fluent once more, and often brilliant. The short snippets of a variety of other European languages, ancient and modern, and including some Piedmontese vernacular expressions, remain intact (except that some English is translated into French). Apart from the abstruse learning – flaunted in Eco's characteristic and daunting lists – contemporary cultural references are mostly international, and only a handful of Italian proper names are changed to American ones. Any references deemed too Italian are omitted. Weaver takes acrostics, rhyming slogans, onomatopeia and the kaleidoscopic learning in his stride, and hits off the conversational style that keeps the novel moving. His expertise makes the few elementary lapses and the divergences from the source text all the more puzzling. The fact that the epigraphs do not always correspond with those in the Italian text betrays the presence of the author. Granted that Eco's most successful non-fictional works in English are the result of a collaborative translation process that involves editing and expansion, it is nevertheless odd to find in the translation of a novel a continual series of small adjustments, cuts, additions – passages that are bafflingly or quite provocatively different from the original. The result is unsettling.

In *L'isola del giorno prima* (*The Island of the Day Before*) (1994) we again have a novel by Eco that feigns to be a loose "translation" – intralingual this time – from an old manuscript. In the source text, the 17th-century Italian of the diary of the hero Roberto della Griva is occasionally quoted directly and spills over to colour the style of narration. The translation (1995) is a splendid and faithful piece of work by William WEAVER: a welcome translator's postscript, acknowledging the help of a number of people on both sides of the Atlantic, including "first of all" the author, is an indication of what it takes to translate an Eco novel, this one packed more than ever with erudition displayed in descriptive, listing and argumentative passages of great complexity. As usual Weaver likes to retain the odd unusual word, and is not averse to adding a flourish of his own. Occasionally an item slips from a list, presumably by mistake. There is no attempt made to render poetry metrically (but then, Eco did not do so in translating Donne into Italian in the source text), and in Weaver's translation the quotations from Roberto's journal do not mimic the period spelling of the Italian. Far from cutting any Latin, which is not extensive in this text, the translation adds a few extra tags. The most obvious divergence from the source text, attributable no doubt to the author, lies in the renaming of a number of chapters: several headings are transposed into Latin and others are changed. In the language of the German Jesuit Father Caspar, Eco and Weaver both produce another example of Eurobabble.

The Search for the Perfect Language (FENTRESS, 1995) was one of the first in the Blackwell series "The Making of Europe", whose titles are published in five European languages. In this case, the English translation was the last to appear and it is not clear what was happening in the interval. This, the only one of Eco's major non-fictional works not to have an author's preface, is the worst translated of all his works: while some of the mistakes seem to be those of a translator not fully understanding the source text, others seem generated by someone not completely idiomatic in English. There are cuts three or four lines long – the omission of a Rimbaud quotation at the very beginning is an unpromising start – but also additions. The Italian is couched in a rather simplified style as if deliberately written to be translatable; but the already shortish sentences are obsessively subdivided in the translation. A lot of clauses are transposed, which does not make for a more logical text. The translator seems convinced that the source text needs simplification, helpful glosses and the minimum of technical vocabulary.

Eco has pursued his interest in perfect languages and the relations between words and things in *Kant and the Platypus* (MCEWEN, 1999). The English translation does not include the quite lengthy appendices, cuts some of the notes, and most significantly omits, as untranslatable, the last section of chapter 6 of the Italian source, which is an Italian picture puzzle.

Only rarely in studies of Eco has the fact of translation rated attention. Reviews in the *Times Literary Supplement* of other English titles discussed here contain brief but acute observations on the merits and demerits of the translations. Robert LUMLEY's introduction (1994) to *Apocalypse Postponed* is particularly valuable; while not saying a great deal about translation as such, Lumley provides a corrective to the excessive internationalization of Eco: observing that "It is certainly difficult to imagine Eco as an Englishman or an American", he stresses the fact that Eco is an Italian, indeed Piedmontese, writer. The fourth of the five objectives of *Apocalypse Postponed* is "to include material written about Italy and for Italians which has tended not to be translated for that reason". Peter Bondanella (1997) is alert to translation issues, and his bibliography is valuable not least for identifyingthe sources of chapters in English books which are compilations.

DAVID GROVES

Further Reading

Bondanella, Peter, *Umberto Eco and the Open Text: Semiotics, Fiction, Popular Culture*, Cambridge and New York: Cambridge University Press, 1997

Collini, Stefan (editor), *Interpretation and Overinterpretation*, by Eco and others, Cambridge and New York: Cambridge University Press, 1992

Inge, Thomas M. (editor), *Naming the Rose: Essays on Umberto Eco's The Name of the Rose*, Jackson: University Press of Mississippi, 1988 (with an extensive bibliography of articles)

Lepschy, Giulio, review of *A Theory of Semiotics*, *Language*, 53/3 (1977) pp.711–14

Robey, David, in *Writers and Society in Contemporary Italy*, Leamington Spa: Berg, and New York: St Martin's Press, 1984, pp. 63–87

See also Lumley's introduction to *Apocalypse Postponed* (1994)

Economics and Politics of Choice: What Gets Published

The current Anglo-American publishing marketplace features three distinct kinds of publishers – major trade houses, university presses, small independents – that approach deciding what to translate, and why, in three distinct if somewhat overlapping ways. Major trade houses publish few literary translations and generally seek either books they deem to have substantial commercial potential (e.g. Laura Esquivel's *Like Water for Chocolate*, Jostein Gaarder's *Sophie's World*) or authors of Nobel Prize stature (the publishing programs in translation of Farrar Straus and of Knopf). University presses with the resources to commission translations (the 10–15 largest in the US, Oxford and Cambridge in the UK) along with the major scholarly independents – Polity, Verso, Routledge, Blackwell, Athlone – focus on works they see generating interest among scholars in more than one field, as for example the writings of French critical theorists such as Jacques Derrida, Michel Foucault, and Roland Barthes, and, more recently, fiction of literary merit that is neither sufficiently commercial nor sufficiently canonical to interest the major trade houses. Finally, dozens of small independent houses in the US and UK (e.g. Harvill, Quartet, Serif, Serpent's Tail in the UK; New Press, Dalkey Archive Press, Marlboro Press, 4 Walls 8 Windows, Seven Stories, David Godine, Graywolf, Sun and Moon, Mercury House, City Lights, Coach House, New Directions, and Exact Change in the US) take on a wide range of generally highly literary projects. This article will discuss how each of these three kinds of press evaluates potential translation projects, what role translators play in that evaluation process, and how each kind of press typically finds its translators and funds its translations.

Major Anglo-American trade houses typically learn of potential translation projects from their foreign counterparts either at international publishing gatherings such as the annual Frankfurt Book Fair or from submissions made to them by foreign publishers' foreign rights managers. These submissions are then evaluated either by in-house staff with competence in the source language or by outside readers commissioned by the house to provide a so-called reader's report (a 500–1000 word synopsis along with a 150–250 word commentary). In either case, the primary criterion for evaluation of the work's potential "publishability" in the Anglo-American market tends to be its being able to be likened to or linked with a work well known for having succeeded in that market. The present writer, for example has recently placed with major American publishers a French novel he likened to Donna Tartt's *The Secret History*, another that he described as a "*Bonjour tristesse* for the 90s" by the "new Françoise Sagan", and a work of French non-fiction on the role of virtue in everyday life presented as being of interest to readers of William Bennett's *The Book of Virtues*.

In cases such as these, translators are not infrequently the outside readers commissioned to prepare a reader's report, but unless the translator happens also to have experience working in publishing, or a particularly close relationship with the editor commissioning the report, the translator's own opinion of the work under consideration will not tend to be taken much into account; rather, the synopsis portion of the report will be used by those inside the publishing house to reach their own conclusions about the work's potential in translation. On the other hand, if a major trade house does in fact decide to acquire a work for publication in translation after commissioning a reader's report from a translator, that translator is likely to be the leading candidate to do the translation as well. Finally, in cases where the reader of the work under consideration is not also a translator, the acquiring publisher will typically do all it can to find a translator who seems familiar by virtue of either having done translations for that publisher in the past or coming recommended by someone known to the acquiring editor.

University presses and scholarly independents go through quite a different process. They too receive a certain number of proposals at international publishing gatherings and from submissions made to them by foreign publishers' foreign rights managers, but they also request works for review based on the advice of outside series editors. Whether submitted on the initiative of a foreign press or at the request of the potential acquirer, virtually all works deemed worthy of serious consideration by a scholarly press will be sent to experts in the field for review as to the work's quality, what it contributes to the corpus of works already available in that field, and what sort of readership might exist for the work in translation rather than in its original language. Unlike major trade houses, scholarly presses typically take their readers' opinions very seriously and base their translation acquisition decisions primarily upon them.

If those opinions are favorable, the press will then look into the costs of paying for a translation, an issue that major trade houses tend not to explore in detail until after acquiring a work, since their printings are generally larger, making the cost of translation easier to absorb. Scholarly presses often seek to minimize those costs by finding translators with academic affiliations, who do not count on translation income to be a significant portion of their total income and are therefore more likely to accept a small fee that amounts to a kind of honorarium. Sometimes these translators are well known to the press as translators, but often they are selected on the basis of their expertise in both the source language and English-language scholarship in the field, even if they have no significant translation experience.

Scholarly presses also tend to seek out possible sources of translation funding available from both source-language related agencies (e.g. the French Ministry of Culture and Germany's Inter Nationes) and Anglo-American ones (e.g. the US National Endowment for the Humanities). The availability of translators willing to work for reduced fees and of at least partial translation funding is crucial to the viability of most scholarly translation projects and many potential translation projects deemed of interest by scholarly presses can only be undertaken successfully if one or both of these elements is present.

Small independents typically have more limited resources than commercial houses or scholarly presses and therefore often limit themselves to considering works of evident literary merit but limited commercial appeal that someone has chosen to translate into English without benefit of any support from a publisher, for such translations can generally be used at little or no cost. In the case of such translator-initiated projects, translators obviously play a central role in deciding what is worthy of being published in translation, but may well pay for that centrality by receiving very little money for their efforts unless they themselves have successfully applied for grant money, as for example from the US National Endowment for the Arts which, through 1995, offered grants paid directly to translators for projects of literary merit.

While the broad outlines of this tripartite system have remained relatively stable over the past several decades, each of its constituent elements has gone through changes that affected or probably will affect the place of translation in its domain. The major trade houses have all tended to become international entities; for example, the four largest in the United States – Simon and Schuster / Macmillan, HarperCollins, Random House, Penguin USA – all have substantial book publishing holdings in the UK as well. The international marketing and distribution muscle of these behemoths generally makes them the most important English-language publishers in other anglophone countries such as Canada and Australia, and their sheer size tends to make them uninterested in "small" books (defined as those with first printings in hardcover of fewer than 10–50,000 copies, depending on whom you ask). Furthermore, these large houses seem to feel less and less need to justify themselves culturally by translating works produced by the "Old World".

Certain kinds of culturally interesting foreign books that might once have been published by major trade houses have been picked up by scholarly presses, some of which are now publishing contemporary fiction in translation, as well as by small presses, but in each of these sectors, new pressures are being felt that may ultimately diminish the number of translations such presses undertake. For scholarly presses, the pressure comes from reductions in library budgets throughout the US that have cut the number of copies of each new scholarly press book typically sold to libraries from approximately 1,500 to approximately 500 and from cuts in operating subsidies that American university presses have traditionally received from their parent universities. Result: scholarly presses increasingly focus their publishing programs generally and their translation choices specifically on works likely to be assigned for courses and/or with appeal to an audience broader than experts in some one scholarly field. For small presses, similar pressures come from recent cuts in public spending for the arts in the US which mean fewer grants available both to small presses themselves and to the translators who initiate many of their projects. Analogous economic pressures are also felt by scholarly and small presses in the UK.

Ultimately, then, translation finds itself in a precarious place in the current Anglo-American book world with no immediate prospects of moving to a more secure one.

DAVID KORNACKER

Egil's Saga

Egils saga Skallagrímssonar, 13th century

Poised between the *Íslendingasögur*, which fictionalize the feuds of early Iceland, and the *konungasögur*, histories of the kings of Norway, *Egils saga* has characteristics of both genres, with a strong biographical element centring on the eponymous hero, a noted 10th-century warrior and poet. The saga is the main source for most of Egil's idiosyncratic and innovative poetry. The anonymous saga was written in the 13th century and has been ascribed by some to Snorri Sturluson (1179–1241), Icelandic historian, politician and poet, and descendant of Egil.

Translations

Eddison, E.R., *Egil's Saga*, Cambridge: Cambridge University Press, 1930; reprinted New York: Greenwood Press, 1968

Fell, Christine and John Lucas, *Egils Saga*, with an introduction, London: Dent, 1975

Green, W.C., *The Story of Egil Skallagrimsson, Being an Icelandic Family History of the Ninth and Tenth Centuries*, London: Elliot Stock, 1893

Jones, Gwyn, *Egil's Saga*, with an introduction, New York: Twayne, 1960

Morris, William, *The Story of Egil the Son of Scaldgrim* in *William Morris: Artist, Writer, Socialist*, vol. 1, by May Morris, Oxford: Blackwell, 1936; reprinted New York: Russell and Russell, 1966

Pálsson, Hermann and Paul Edwards, *Egil's Saga*, with an introduction. Harmondsworth: Penguin, 1976

The colloquial style of Icelandic sagas, heavily paratactic and affecting an oral tone, challenges translators, for it can sound naive and tedious if rendered too literally into English. The prosimetrum of *Egils saga*, in which highly wrought skaldic verses counterpoint the prose, poses a double challenge to which different translators have found different solutions.

Although the English reception of Old Norse poetry begins in the 17th century, the translation of sagas happens in earnest only in the 19th. Several brief summaries of *Egils saga* (resulting from its historical interest, as some of its action takes place in England) were published earlier in that century, but the first full translation of the saga is GREEN (1893). MORRIS had begun a translation of the saga in the 1860s, but never got beyond chapter 40.

Green's intention is to make the saga available to a general reading public already familiar with the genre, and he produces an eclectic text based on three different editions. His rendering is robust and, syntactically, quite close to the Icelandic, yet surprisingly readable. He softens the relentless parataxis, but keeps the many inversions and the distinction between singular and plural in the second person, both of which are normal in Old Icelandic but sound archaic in English. His vocabulary is only mildly archaizing, and not as programmatically Germanic as some (notably Morris in his many saga translations). In the poems, he jettisons many of the elaborate periphrases ("far-fetched kennings"), concentrating instead on finding an English equivalent to the skaldic rhythms. By allowing himself some latitude in the syllable-count and greater variety in stress patterns, and by reproducing the alliteration as far as possible, Green manages verse translations that evoke the sound of the originals.

EDDISON (1930) positions himself in opposition to Green's "flaccid paraphrasing", but his pedantry produces an unreadable translation that makes maximum use of cognate words (even if they are incomprehensible) and follows Old Icelandic syntax slavishly. Compare his "Nowise liked him well of that. He was somewhat frowning" with Green's "But he did not like it, and he wore a frowning look." Eddison is a follower of Morris, but without the latter's lightness of touch. Typical of Eddison is the very literal "King Audbiorn let shear up the war-arrow and fare a host-bidding through all his realm". Morris is similar but more comprehensible: "So King Audbiorn let shear up the war arrow, and send the war bidding throughout all his realm", while Green's "Audbjorn ... bade cut the war-arrow and send the war-summons throughout his realm" keeps the exotic method of summoning troops while making clear what is happening. To Eddison the saga is "curiously English" because "we have grown accustomed to regard as distinctively English many qualities that have come down to us through the Norse strain in our ancestry". Even in 1930 his translation can hardly have sounded "English" to anyone.

Eddison had the "general reader in mind" and thought he or she needed a full apparatus of notes, bibliography and index. JONES (1960) and FELL (1975) similarly provide a host of reader's aids, but by 1960 the audience seems to be the university student rather than the lay reader. Both translators have long, interpretative introductions that supplement the relative dearth of critical comment on the sagas in English. Fell's solution to translating the verses also accommodates the student's need for a crib. Her own literal, prose translations, with full explanation of the kennings, appear in the notes, while the poet John LUCAS has provided more readable versions in the main text. These are direct and modern, paying little attention to the form of the originals (although the important end-rhyme of *Höfuðlausn*, Egil's "Head-Ransom" poem, composed at York, is retained). In the prose, both Jones and Fell are workmanlike and modern, eschewing obvious archaisms and strange syntax. While both are readable, Fell manages to combine readability with fidelity to the Icelandic text. Thus, Fell renders the sentence quoted above as "King Audbjorn had the war-arrow despatched, and the summons to war sent out through all his kingdom", while Jones's version is "King Audbjörn had the war-arrow dispatched and sent a summons to war the length and breadth of his kingdom". Jones is the only translator to preserve the strangeness of Icelandic and Norwegian names, by keeping diacritics on the vowels (though he does replace *þ* and ð with *th* and *d*).

In the Penguin Classics series, PÁLSSON is famous for producing readable translations of sagas with a number of collaborators. This combination of an Icelander with a native English speaker usually ensures accuracy, but all of his translations take liberties with the syntax and style of the originals. The English versions are fluent, even colloquial, capturing the spirit of the sagas for the general reader, but they frequently have only a notional relationship to the original text, as in "So King Audbjorn mustered his forces, sending the war-arrow right through his kingdom". Like all translators, PÁLSSON & EDWARDS (1976) ensure that *Höfuðlausn* has end-rhyme, but otherwise their verses are simple and direct, giving little or no sense of the form or diction of the originals – for example their use of alliteration would strike the untutored ear as no more than haphazard. Also, there is a very general introduction and little other apparatus, in keeping with the aim of making the saga as directly accessible to the general reader as possible.

JUDITH JESCH

Further Reading

Hreinsson, Viðar *et al.* (editors), *The Complete Sagas of Icelanders*, Reykjavik: Leifur Eiríksson, 5 vols, 1997 (contains translations of 40 sagas and 49 tales)

Johnston, George, "Translating the Sagas into English" in *Bibliography of Old Norse-Icelandic Studies*, 1972

Kennedy, John, "The English Translations of *Völsunga saga*", in *Northern Antiquity: The Post-Medieval Reception of Edda and Saga*, edited by Andrew Wawn, London: Hisarlik Press, 1994

See also the translators' comments in Eddison, Fell and Green

Egyptian Women Writers in English Translation

Although modern Arabic literature from Egypt began to appear in English translation before the middle of this century, translated works by women are of recent vintage. Indeed, although Arab women – ancient and modern – have known literary renown, before the 1980s published male writers far outnumbered female writers throughout the Arabic-speaking world, and Arab women met the same kinds of resistance to their writing locally that writing women have encountered in just about every time and place.

Writers from the Arab world, women and men, have faced resistance to publishing and distributing their works in English translation (far more than in French), especially in North America's vast publishing market. This neglect is in great part attributable to hostile political attitudes and stereotypes of the region's peoples long dominant throughout western societies (and shaped by intersections of orientalist thinking and imperialist goals). For Arabic literature is the last world literature to become accepted as an equal on the world stage. While the exertions of a few translators and publishers gradually resulted in a body of works by major Arab male writers becoming available in translation, it was probably the interest and commercial power of western feminisms that first drew publishers to contemplate works by Arab women; and then it was the growing interest in "third-world feminisms" and the critique of western feminisms as hegemonic that increased the demand, in the US especially, for works by Arab and/or Muslim women. A few presses in England had already begun to make translations available, which US publishers were able to acquire inexpensively. Nawal El Saadawi's success at launching her feminist fiction and non-fiction in English and other European languages, beginning with her collection of non-fiction essays *The Hidden Face of Eve* (1982), may have played an equivocal role: commercially successful, her works quickly became the symbolic representative of Arab women as oppositional writers, and competition to publish her works has rarely extended to interest in other female writers.

Alifah Rifāt's short story collection *Distant View of a Minaret and Other Stories* (1983) was a first step in opening the arena to other Egyptian female voices. Rifāt's stories, translated by Denys Johnson-Davies (whose steady dedication to translating modern Arabic literature has been important to its visibility and acceptance in English), are similar to El Saadawi's in treating forthrightly the subject of female sexual desire and its social repression. Yet Rifāt focuses more on the inner worlds of women, and her literary style differs markedly from El Saadawi's.

Aside from these two, it was Arab women *outside* of Egypt whose translated works introduced readers of English to the rich variety of writing by women in Arabic. Translations of works by Egyptian women have been slower to appear, and have not attracted the attention from trade publishers (especially in the United States) that the works of the Lebanese writer Hanān al-Shaykh, for example, have done. Yet this is changing.

Short story writing has been popular among women writers in Egypt, and two anthologies of stories in translation came out in the early 1990s: *My Grandmother's Cactus: Stories by Egyptian Women*, with 19 stories by eight writers of the "80s generation", selected and translated by Marilyn Booth (1991); and *A Voice of their Own: Short Stories by Egyptian Women*, which covers a longer period of time, edited and introduced by Angela Botros Samaan (1994), a project of the Egyptian Ministry of Culture's Foreign Cultural Relations section. Featuring 15 fiction writers, this anthology also gave a voice to Egyptian women as translators. Collections of stories by individual Egyptian women of a younger generation than that of El Saadawi and Rifāt have come out too: by Salwa Bakr, *Such a Beautiful Voice* (1992, translated by Hoda El Sadda) and *The Wiles of Men and Other Stories* (1992, translated by Denys Johnson-Davies); and by Sahar Tawfiq, *Points of the Compass: Stories by Sahar Tawfiq* (1995, translated by Marilyn Booth). Anthologies of the Egyptian or Arabic short story sometimes include a story or two by women, as in Mahmoud Manzalaoui's *Arabic Writing Today: The Short Story* (1968; reissued as *Arabic Short Stories 1945–1965*, 1985; stories by Suhayr al-Qalamawi and Ihsan Kamal), Denys Johnson-Davies' *Modern Arabic Short Stories* (1967; one story by Latifa al-Zayyat), and Gamal Abd El-Nasser's *Modern Egyptian Stories* (1989; stories by Etidal Osman and Sekina Fouad). William M. Hutchins's *Egyptian Tales and Short Stories of the 1970's and 1980's* (1987) is a happy exception, with eight stories by well-known women writers in Egypt. Another type of anthology collects fiction, non-fiction, and poetry by Arab women over the past century or several; there is a good selection of short stories by women from Egypt in in Margot Badran and Miriam Cooke's anthology *Opening the Gates: A Century of Arab Feminist Writing* (1990), and there are two stories in *Women and the Family in the Middle East: New Voices of Change* (edited by Elizabeth Warnock Fernea, 1985). Still, as Fatma Moussa-Mahmoud comments, "the few women's stories which have appeared in English translation hardly represent the sheer quantity of stories which have been produced over a period of more than fifty years" ("Turkey and the Arab Middle East", in *The Bloomsbury Guide to Women's Literature*, edited by Claire Buck, p. 214).

It is notable in the 1990s that a number of women short story writers have turned to the novel. A measure of the heightened interest of English-language publishing houses in translating Arab women is the speed with which recent novels by women in Egypt (and elsewhere in the Arab world) are being sought for English translation: Salwa Bakr's *The Golden Chariot* (1995), which came out in a new series published by Garnet (UK), Arab Women Writers; and Latifa al-Zayyat's last novel, *The Owner of the House*. This latter work will come out with Quartet Books (UK), a small house that has consistently produced beautiful editions of contemporary Arabic fiction in translation despite the commercial vagaries of such an endeavor. The American University in Cairo Press has published the first novel of an outstanding writer of the younger generation, Miral al-Tahawy's *The Tent*, and the same press is publishing al-Zayyat's landmark first novel, her 1960 *The Open Door*, which chronicles a young middle-class woman's coming of age in parallel with her nation's struggle for freedom.

Although poetry has been the Arabic literary art par excellence since before the founding of Islam, and although women have been among leading poets throughout the history of Arabic cultural production (albeit in far smaller numbers than men), poetry by Egyptian women remains sparse in anthologies of Arabic poetry in English, while a few other Arab women poets important to the history of modern Arabic poetry (Nazik al-Mala'ika from Iraq, Salma al-Jayyusi and Fadwa Tuqan from Palestine) have been translated but not as widely as their male compatriots. Out of 18 anthologies of Arabic poetry in English translation, I have located seven poems by Egyptian women, three of them by the romantic poet Malak 'Abd al-'Aziz. The French-Egyptian writer Andrée Chedid, who writes in French, has had one poem translated in the poetry anthology *Women of the Fertile Crescent* (edited by Kamal Boullata, 1978). (Chedid's fiction has been translated from the French: her 1960 novel *The Sixth Day* appeared in 1962 and was reissued in 1987; her 1985 *The Return to Beirut* appeared in 1989 and her 1989 novel *The Multiple Child* in 1995.)

As poetry in an Egyptian colloquial register has come to be considered more respectable, women colloquial poets have emerged – although the difficulties women have faced in gaining a foothold in the literary arena may have deterred many women from choosing the "less respectable" realm of colloquial poetry, for the percentage of women as opposed to men in that arena is far smaller than that of women writing in "literary" Arabic. Just a few of these poems have been translated, one indication of a growing interest among English-language scholars in Arabic dialect poetry. Two poems by Najwa al-Sayyid are translated in Clarissa Burt's "Awake Shahrazade!" (1987–88).

As Fatma Moussa-Mahmoud has noted, drama has not been an area to which women writers have gravitated. Nihad Gad and Fathiyya al-Assal are among Egypt's notable contemporary playwrights, however, and both have been translated in Egypt, one of many indications that Egyptian institutions such as the General Egyptian Book Organization, the Mass Culture Department, and the Higher Council for Culture are devoting increasing resources to translating Egyptian literature into English and French.

As scholars delve into the history of women's writing in the Arab world, anthologies that fill in the historical background have been one result. Badran and Cooke's anthology has already been mentioned; *Middle Eastern Muslim Women Speak* offers some personal narratives from Egypt (1977, edited by Elizabeth Warnock Fernea and Basima Qattan Bezirgan). Both feature earlier as well as contemporary women; some of these "grandmothers" have been translated at greater length, offering a look at autobiographical and non-fictional writing. A volume of early feminist leader Huda Shaarawi's memoirs have appeared as *Harem Years: The Memoirs of an Egyptian Feminist, 1876–1924* (1986), and a volume of writings by another early feminist, Mayy Ziyadah, is in preparation. Ziyadah was one of many turn-of-the-20th-century writers who emigrated from Ottoman Syria to Egypt, and matured and wrote there. *Opening the Gates* features writings by these and other early feminists. Out el Kouloub's autobiographical novel *Ramza*, written in the 1950s about an earlier period, and her 1947 *Zanouba*, published in free translations by Nayra Atiya (1994, 1996), offer another layer of context for this early period. Recent autobiographies are appearing, too: Latifa al-Zayyat's *The Search: Personal Papers*, which chronicles the history of a leftist political activist, is in press, while Islamist activist Zaynab al-Ghazali's memoirs have recently made an appearance.

If Egyptian women's writing has been slow to appear in English translation, the past decade has begun to reverse that. And these works can be read alongside an emerging body of writing in English by Arab women; Ahdaf Soueif's *In the Eye of the Sun* renders an Arabic idiom beautifully in English while offering a fine *Bildingsroman* of one female experience.

MARILYN BOOTH

Translations

Badran, Margot and Miriam Cooke (editors), *Opening the Gates: A Century of Arab Feminist Writing*, Bloomington: Indiana University Press, and London: Virago, 1990

Bakr, Salwa, *Such a Beautiful Voice*, translated by Hoda El Sadda, Cairo: General Egyptian Book Organization, 1992

Bakr, Salwa, *The Wiles of Men, and Other Stories*, translated by Denys Johnson-Davies, London: Quartet, 1992; Austin: University of Texas Press, 1993

Bakr, Salwa, *The Golden Chariot*, translated by Dinah Manisty, Reading, Berkshire: Garnet, 1995

Booth, Marilyn (editor and translator), *My Grandmother's Cactus: Stories by Egyptian Women*, London: Quartet, 1991 (includes 19 stories by 8 writers)

Boullata, Kamal (editor and translator), *Women of the Fertile Crescent*, Washington, DC: Three Continents Press, 1978, new edition, 1994 (includes poem by Andrée Chedid)

Burt, Clarissa, "Awake Shahrazade! An Egyptian Ammiya Poet and Her Works", *Newsletter of the American Research Center in Egypt*, 140 (Winter 1987–88), pp. 7–10 (two poems by Najwa al-Sayyid)

Chedid, Andrée, *The Sixth Day*, translated by Isobel Strachey, London: A. Blond, 1962

Chedid, Andrée, *The Return to Beirut*, translated by Ros Schwartz, London: Serpent's Tail, 1989

Chedid, Andrée, *The Multiple Child*, translated by Judith Radke, San Francisco: Mercury House, 1995

El-Nasser, Gamal Abd (editor and translator), *Modern Egyptian Stories*, Cairo: General Egyptian Book Organization, 1989 (includes stories by Etidal Osman and Sekina Fouad)

Fernea, Elizabeth Warnock and Basima Qattan Bezirgan (editors), *Middle Eastern Muslim Women Speak*, Austin: Unversity of Texas Press, 1977

Fernea, Elizabeth Warnock (editor), *Women and the Family in the Middle East: New Voices of Change*, Austin: University of Texas Press, 1985

Hutchins, William M. (editor), *Egyptian Tales and Short Stories of the 1970's and 1980's*, Cairo: American University in Cairo Press, 1987 (includes 8 stories by Egyptian women writers)

Johnson-Davies, Denys (editor and translator), *Modern Arabic Short Stories*, London: Oxford University Press, 1967; Washington, DC: Three Continents Press, 1981 (includes story by Latifa al-Zayyat)

Manzalaoui, Mahmoud (editor), *Arabic Writing Today: The Short Story*, Cairo: American Research Center in Egypt,

1968; as *Arabic Short Stories 1945–1965*, Cairo: American University in Cairo Press, 1985 (includes stories by Suhayr al-Qalamawi and Ihsan Kamal)
Out el Kouloub, *Ramza*, translated by Nayra Atiya, Syracuse, New York: Syracuse University Press, 1994
Out el Koloub, *Zanouba*, translated by Nayra Atiya, Syracuse, New York: Syracuse University Press, 1996
Rifāt, Alifah, *Distant View of a Minaret and Other Stories*, translated by Denys Johnson-Davies, London: Heinemann, 1983
Saadawi, Nawal El, *The Hidden Face of Eve: Women in the Arab World*, London: Zed Press, 1980; Boston: Beacon Press, 1982
Samaan, Angela Botros (editor), *A Voice of Their Own: Short Stories by Egyptian Women*, with an introduction, Cairo: Egyptian Ministry of Culture, 1994 (includes stories by 15 writers)
Shaarawi, Huda, *Harem Years: The Memoirs of an Egyptian Feminist*, edited and translated by Margot Badran, London: Virago, 1986; New York: Feminist Press at the City University of New York, 1987
Soueif, Ahdaf, *In the Eye of the Sun*, London: Bloomsbury, 1992; New York: Pantheon, 1993
al-Tahawy, Miral, *The Tent*, translated by Anthony Calderbank, Cairo: American University in Cairo Press, 1998
Tawfiq, Sahar, *Points of the Compass: Stories*, translated by Marilyn Booth, Fayetteville: University of Arkansas Press, 1995
al-Zayyat, Latifa, *The Search: Personal Papers*, translated by Sophie Bennett, London: Quartet, 1996
al-Zayyat, Latifa, *The Owner of the House*, translated by Sophie Bennett, London: Quartet, 1997
al-Zayyat, Latifa, *The Open Door*, translated by Marilyn Booth, Cairo: American University in Cairo Press, 2000

Further Reading

Badawi, M.M. (editor), *Modern Arabic Literature*, Cambridge and New York: Cambridge University Press, 1992 (The Cambridge History of Arabic Literature)
Badran, Margot and Miriam Cooke, introduction in *Opening the Gates: A Century of Arab Feminist Writing*, edited by Badran and Cooke, Bloomington: Indiana University Press, 1991
Booth, Marilyn, introduction in *My Grandmother's Cactus: Stories by Egyptian Women*, London: Quartet, 1991; Austin: University of Texas Press, 1993
Cooke, Miriam, "Arab Women Writers" in *The Cambridge History of Arabic Literature*, edited by M.M. Badawi, Cambridge: Cambridge University Press, 1992
Farid, M.S., "A Bibliography of Modern Egyptian Literature in English Translation" in *The Comparative Tone: Essays in Comparative Literature*, edited by M.M. Enani, Cairo: General Egyptian Book Organization, 1995
Moussa-Mahmoud, Fatma, "Turkey and the Arab Middle East," pp. 210–16, and associated entries, in *The Bloomsbury Guide to Women's Literature*, edited by Claire Buck, London: Bloomsbury, 1992

Paul Éluard 1895–1952

French poet

Biography

Eugène-Émile-Paul Grindel was born 14 December 1895 in Saint-Denis, just north of Paris, and educated at state schools. He served in the French army in World War I and was gassed. He was a friend of André Breton and Louis Aragon and with them founded the Surrealist movement of the 1920s and 1930s. He was politicized by the Spanish Civil War, during which he supported the Republican side. From 1942 he was a member of the Communist Party.

From 1916 onwards he wrote prolifically in verse and prose. Love was the main theme; the poems include innovative Dadaist and Surrealist pieces. After 1938 his poetry was politically committed. During World War II he worked for the French Resistance and was, with Louis Aragon, its poetic voice, being the author notably of the famous, at first clandestine, *Poésie et vérité* (1942; *Poetry and Truth*, 1944).

Éluard was married three times. After the war he travelled widely in Europe as a cultural ambassador. He died in Charenton-le-Pont, to the southeast of Paris, 18 November 1952.

Edition

Oeuvres complètes, 2 vols, Paris: Gallimard, 1968

Translations

Selections of Poetry

Alexander, Lloyd, in *Selected Writings*, translated by Alexander, with an introduction by Claude Roy, New York: New Directions, 1951; London: Routledge and Kegan Paul, 1952
Beckett, Samuel, Denis Devlin, David Gascoyne, Eugène Jolas, Man Ray, George Reavey and Ruthven Todd, *Thorns of Thunder: Selected Poems*, edited by Reavey, London: Europa Press and Stanley Nott, 1936
Bowen, Gilbert, *Selected Poems*, with an introduction, London: Calder, and New York: Riverrun Press, 1987

Hartley, Anthony, "Paul Éluard" in *The Penguin Book of French Verse*, vol. 4, edited by Hartley, London: Penguin, 1959; expanded edition, 1966; revised edition incorporating all four volumes, 1975

Rees, William (editor and translator), "Paul Éluard" in *French Poetry 1820–1950, with Prose Translations*, Harmondsworth and New York: Penguin, 1990

Poetry

Poésie et vérité, 1942

Penrose, Roland and E.L.T. Mesens, *Poésie et vérité, 1942 / Poetry and Truth, 1942*, London: Gallery Editions, 1944

Le Dur Désir de durer, 1946

Spender, Stephen and Frances Cornford, *Le Dur Désir de durer / The Dour Desire to Endure*, Philadelphia: Grey Falcon Press, and London: Trianon Press, 1950

One of the most invidious problems confronting a translator of Éluard's poetry is that the very precision and seeming reticence of this verse merely displace the difficulty of translation. While there are relatively few of the complex syntactic or verbal games typical of French post-Symbolism to be encountered here, there results a sense in which a certain quasi-natural rendering might impose itself upon the translator in the form of a mere transposition of the French vocabulary into its English counterpart. But doing this only makes the exactness of the original cadential and rhythmic effects of the French ever more elusive. One way of avoiding this problem is that adopted by HARTLEY (1959) in the handful of Éluard poems in his collection: that is, to produce unaffected prose translations that have no pretension to independence from the French texts. These versions function most effectively when taken as suggested "decodings" of the French (printed above the translations with considerably more prominence) for the English-speaking reader who can also appreciate the sound-patternings that subtly hold the original texts together as poetic units. For instance, the lines from "Par une nuit nouvelle" ("On a New Night"): "On ne peut me connaître / Mieux que tu me connais" become: "I cannot be known better than you know me". Were this a translation *from* prose, and not merely into it, this would be highly effective in its unobtrusive simplicity. However, the sense of hesitation engendered by the layout of the text as verse, with its orthodox practice of initial capitalization to introduce the second line – which both continues the first and enacts a new start of its own as a verse unit – is sadly lacking in the prose form, which thereby underplays the pathetic ambivalence of conjunction and schism that so enriches the French.

A similar problem confronts the reader of ALEXANDER's highly accurate – and never gratuitous – renderings (1951), which in any case come as a great relief after Claude Roy's rather gushing and dated introduction to this volume. In a poem such as "À Pablo Picasso" the jolting syntax is rather sanitized so that the initial agrammaticality is completely lost, with the result that the possible imitative aspect of the verse – duplicating the discontinuities so characteristic of Picasso's own painterly language – is completely collapsed into a well-integrated, if specious, linearity. These translations are, however, generally commendable, the main drawback being their rather staid, excessive fidelity to the French, preserved paradoxically at the cost of not fully conveying the Surrealist love of excessive spontaneity and invention, which can ironically produce such a feeling of inevitability and beauty.

BECKETT *et al.* (1936) offer a very heterogeneous collection of translations reflecting the diversity of the contributors, of whom there are too many to be considered individually. Despite Herbert Read's preface praising the daring irrationalities of Éluard, many of the translations are rather tame, the title of Éluard's most famous collection, *Capitale de la douleur*, rather weakly becoming *The City of Sorrow*. This is particularly problematic, since with no French texts provided (not even an acknowledgement of the original titles), there is a risk of creating an unrepresentative impression of these works to any reader unfamiliar with the French. REAVEY's attempts are frequently unconvincing and work best when he has least opportunity for lyrical self-indulgence. He does occasionally, however, present versions that depart so far from their original incarnations that they approach the point of mutual contradiction: in "Le Jeu de construction" ("The Game of Construction") the final line – "Mais pour ça, ça et ça" somehow gets turned into "O because of something or other", whose very off-hand tone directly denies the acute pain of the French. GASCOYNE is generally much more accurate and persuasive, whereas BECKETT himself largely captures the strange understatement of Éluardian Surrealism that abounds in poems such as "L'Amoureuse" (curiously translated as the more passive "Lady Love") and the delicate "Seconde nature"; he does commit, on the other hand, a grave error of judgement in employing the "thou" form in poems like "À peine défigurée" ("Scarcely Disfigured"), which is symptomatic of a general trend in Éluard translation of attempting to be seen at all costs as "literary".

SPENDER & CORNFORD (1950) likewise often disrupt the poise of the original texts by interpolating articles and auxiliary verbs omitted in the French for definite stylistic and semantic reasons. At times the desire to make Éluard speak with a stereotypically "safe" poetic voice verges on linguistic vandalism. In "Par un baiser" ("Through an Embrace") the haunting simplicity of "Sous le ciel noir nous voyons clair" is completely obscured by the bathos of "Black the sky but we see plain".

This rather monotonous preciosity is self-consciously repudiated by BOWEN (1987), who presents an extremely partial view of Éluard by obsessively making his selections from the political and war poetry, while placing these works in a rather trivialized context of history and biography, even then without any substantial attempt to relate them to the rest of the corpus of which they are far from fully representative. To make matters worse, we are told in the introduction that "[Éluard's] poetry is that of the real world". Such statements dogmatically asserted not only seem fatuous, to other poets pernicious even, but ironically utterly deradicalize Éluard's poetic project, especially given the ideological slant tacitly assumed in this assertion. This attitude is sadly reflected in a general lack of poetic sensibility in the translations themselves, which operate a general process of embarrassed simplification.

PENROSE & MESENS (1944), in contrast, pay commendable attention to the internal playings-out of the poetic verse while retaining a high degree of accuracy. They manage to convey the strangely elliptical emotional directness of the poems of *Poetry and Truth* without seeking to impose an alien coherence and continuity from the outside, the understated rhythmic effects being very nicely rendered. REES's (1990) prose versions, largely – though not exclusively – of the more numerous love poems, are not quite so successful in operating this dialectic between elliptical motion and static simplicity, but are generally more than competent and supply something like a quintessential taste of Éluard's most popular work.

PAUL RICKETT

Further Reading

Éluard, Paul and André Breton, *The Immaculate Conception*, translated by Jon Graham, London: Atlas Press, 1990

Whitting, Charles, "Éluard's Poems for Gala", *French Review*, 41 (1968)

Odysseus Elytis 1911–1996

Greek poet

Biography

Born in Heraklion, Crete, 2 November 1911, of parents from Lesbos. He published his first poems in 1935 and became one of the leading figures in the so-called "Generation of the Thirties", which also included Greece's other Nobel laureate, George Seferis. He travelled widely and, during the post war years, lived in France for extended periods, associating with leading poets and artists of his generation. He published 18 collections of poetry, a number of translations of ancient Greek and modern European poets and two large volumes of critical essays. He was awarded the Nobel Prize for Literature in 1979. Died 18 March 1996. The poetry collections are *Prosanatolismi* [Orientations] (1939); *Ilios o Protos* [Sun the First] (1943); *Asma Iroiko ke Penthimo ya ton Hameno Anthypolohago tis Alvanias* [Heroic and Elegiac Song for the Lost Second Lieutenant of the Albanian Campaign] (1945); *To Axion Esti* (*The Axion Esti*) (1959); *Exi ke Mia Typseis ya ton Ourano* (*Six and One Remorses for the Sky*) (1960); *To Photodentro ke i Dekati Tetarti Omorphia* [The Light Tree and the Fourteenth Beauty] (1971); *O Ilios o Iliatoras* (*The Sovereign Sun*) (1971); *To Monogramma* [The Monogram] (1972); *Ta Ro tou Erota* [The Rs of Eros] (1972); *Ta Eterothali* [The Stepchildren] (1974); *Simatologion* [Book of Signs] (1977); *Maria Nepheli* (*Maria Nephele*) (1978); *Tria Poeimata se Simaia Efkerias* [Three Poems under a Flag of Convenience] (1982); *Imerologio enos atheatou Apriliou* (*Diary of an Unseen April*) (1984); *O Mikros Naftilos* (*The Little Mariner*) (1985); *Ta Elegeia tis Oxopetras* (*The Oxopetra Elegies*) (1991); *Ditika tis Lipis* [West of Sorrow] (1995); *Ek tou Plision* [From Close By] (1998).

Translations

Selections of Poetry

Anagnostopoulos, Athan, *Maria Nephele: A Poem in Two Voices*, with an introduction, Boston: Houghton Mifflin, 1981

Broumas, Olga, *What I Love: Selected Poems* (bilingual edition), Port Townsend, Washington: Copper Canyon Press, 1986

Broumas, Olga, *The Little Mariner*, Port Townsend, Washington: Copper Canyon Press, 1988

Broumas, Olga, *Eros, Eros, Eros*, Port Townsend, Washington: Copper Canyon Press, 1998

Carson, Jeffrey, *Six and One Remorses for the Sky and Other Poems*, Helsinki: Eurographica, 1985

Carson, Jeffrey and Nikos Sarris, *The Collected Poems of Odysseus Elytis*, with an introduction by Carson, Baltimore: Johns Hopkins University Press, 1997

Connolly, David, *The Oxopetra Elegies* (bilingual edition), Amsterdam: Harwood, 1996

Friar, Kimon, *The Sovereign Sun: Selected Poems*, with an introduction, Philadelphia: Temple University Press, 1974; Newcastle upon Tyne: Bloodaxe Books, 1990

Keeley, Edmund and George Savidis, *To Axion Esti / The Axion Esti* (bilingual edition), Pittsburgh: University of Pittsburgh Press, 1974; in English only, London: Anvil Press, 1980

Keeley, Edmund and Philip Sherrard (editors), *Selected Poems*, with an introduction by Keeley and Sherrard, New York: Viking Press, and London: Anvil Press, 1981 (translations by Keeley, Sherrard, George Savidis, John Stathatos, Nanos Valaoritis)

Poetry

Imerologio enos atheatou Apriliou, 1984

Connolly, David, *Diary of an Unseen April* (bilingual edition), Athens: Ypsilon, 1999

Selections of Prose

Broumas, Olga and T. Begley, *Open Papers*, Port Townsend, Washington: Copper Canyon Press, 1995

Connolly, David, *Carte Blanche: Selected Writings*, Amsterdam: Harwood, 1999

Together with Cavafy, Seferis and Ritsos, Odysseus Elytis has been variously and repeatedly translated into English, particularly since receiving the Nobel Prize for Literature. This, in itself, is not surprising unless one is aware of Elytis's own views concerning the virtual untranslatability of his type of poetry. It should be noted, however, that Elytis himself translated ancient Greek lyric poetry and French, Spanish, Italian and

Russian poetry and has expressed firm views on translation method.

Greek poets are fortunate in being able to draw on an unbroken poetic tradition dating back to Homer, and Elytis made full use of a vocabulary deriving from Homer, Pindar, Sappho, the Pre-Socratics, the Bible, the Byzantine Hymnographers, traditional folk poetry, the 19th-century Greek Romantics and 20th-century Greek Surrealists. The English translator is immediately at a disadvantage in not having this same range of linguistic keys to work with. Elytis was a poet who worked from within language and his poetry is intrinsically linked with the Greek language and with the sounds and images that a particular word or group of words produces. He said of his own poetry that he did not think of something and then translate it into words, but that the ideas in his poetry were born at the same time as their verbal expression. Such poetry leads to often insurmountable translation problems.

Very few of Elytis's translators provide any useful or detailed statement of approach to the particular translation problems involved in rendering his highly innovative poetry into English. The translations as a rule contain an introduction to the poet and his poetry, but no statement of the translator's aims or methods, essential to any critical evaluation. Although translations of his work first began to appear in periodicals and anthologies as early as 1952, it was not until 1974 that two books appeared in the English-speaking world that were entirely devoted to his work. The first of these, by FRIAR, contained a generous selection of Elytis's poetry from *Orientations* to *The Sovereign Sun*; the second, by KEELEY & SAVIDIS, was a translation of Elytis's long composite poem *The Axion Esti*.

Friar, who has written elsewhere on the problems of translating poetry and on the particular problems of translating from modern Greek, makes no reference to his aims or method in his introduction to his translations of Elytis. Keeley & Savidis, in their brief preface, refer to the translation problems arising from the poem's many cultural allusions and variety of diction, and to the difficulty of finding a corresponding poetic idiom in English for Elytis's highly idiosyncratic voice. They also state that they have not engaged in what they consider to be a "doomed attempt" to reproduce the intricate formal patterns used by Elytis in parts of the poem.

Both books constitute an important contribution to the promotion of Greek literature in English by presenting to the English-speaking world a Greek poet who is without doubt one of the most original poetic voices of the 20th century. Friar's translation is singularly impressive for its poetic creativity and succeeds in conveying much of the lyrical quality of Elytis's verse. It is perhaps not without significance that it was this translation that was instrumental in Elytis being awarded the Nobel Prize. Keeley & Savidis's translation of *The Axion Esti* is more prosaic, though not always more referentially accurate for being so. Its weakness is that it lacks the impressiveness and lyrical quality of the original, largely as a result of the translators' decision to ignore the poem's stylistic elements, but also because of their choice of a contemporary Anglo-American idiom in which to render a type of poetry that, according to Elytis, lies at the opposite end of the spectrum of poetic expression.

The translations, by various hands, in *Selected Poems* (1981), chosen and introduced by Edmund Keeley and Philip Sherrard, constitute a collection of previously published translations from *Orientations, Sun the First, The Axion Esti, Six and One Remorses for the Sky, The Sovereign Sun* and *Maria Nefeli*. The translations are the work of competent translators and are generally reliable, though are not all equally successful as poems in English. Those by KEELEY & SHERRARD are, as always, referentially accurate though they tend to normalize Elytis's language, which intentionally stretches and often goes beyond the norms of the Greek language. For example, where Elytis in one of his early, more surrealistic, poems has "a sailor atop the highest mast waving (or flapping) a song", Keeley & Sherrard normalize the image by having him "whistling a song". Similarly, they often opt for a prosaic translation of words that have a particular aesthetic value in the original, when a more poetic equivalent could be found; for example, they translate the Greek word "archipelagos" as "network of islands" though this word has passed into English as "archipelago" and is arguably more appropriate for evoking Elytis's poetic landscape. STATHATOS & VALAORITIS, both Greeks by birth and both poets in their own right, provide equally accurate but more creative renderings of selections from *The Light Tree* and *Maria Nefeli*. Valaoritis, in particular, shows how Elytis's poetry can be translated both closely and poetically by a skilled translator.

A complete translation of *Maria Nephele: A Poem in Two Voices* was produced by Athan ANAGNOSTOPOULOS (1981). This collection of 45 poems, comprising two monologues on facing pages by a "young girl of today" and the antiphonist (the poet), follows a fairly complex arrangement in keeping with most of Elytis's works in his second and third periods. In contrast, however, with his other works, this poem departs from his usual lofty style, making use of a colloquial and familiar diction common to everyday language as being more appropriate to the content, which, again in contrast to Elytis's other works, takes precedence here over lyrical expression. As Elytis himself remarks: "Maria Nefeli is more amenable to translation as the weight falls elsewhere and not on the linguistic transubstantiation". Written primarily in free verse, several of the poems are composed in traditional metrical forms. Others contain intricate rhyming schemes that, according to Anagnostopoulos, "make them impossible to render accurately in English translation". Elytis has also employed alliteration and rhymed couplets in several poems, as well as internal and slant rhymes. Anagnostopoulos's translation is referentially accurate and, in view of the emphasis on the poem's content, has perhaps justifiably made little or no attempt to account for the poem's formal aspects. He provides a fairly comprehensive introduction to the poem and detailed notes on its historical and cultural allusions, but, unfortunately, not a word on his translation approach or aims.

BROUMAS (1986), in her bilingual selection *What I Love*, includes a very limited number of poems from Elytis's early work, the whole of *The Monogram* and a larger selection from *Maria Nefele*. She explains in her translator's note that she has attempted to "give Elytis's voice in English" and that "being true to his voice is to create an English with an accent, idiosyncratic". Elytis's voice is idiosyncratic even in Greek though it is certainly not infelicitous as many of Broumas's translations are. She also claims, unabashedly, that "line by line the poems nearly match the original". This may be true, but what in Greek, with its far greater linguistic flexibility, may be a slight deviation from the norm, becomes totally unacceptable in normal English usage so that Elytis's phrasing appears more awkward than idiosyncratic. She makes numerous errors in decoding the original, together with some very questionable interpretations of lines, with the result that the translation is often a parody of the original.

BROUMAS has also translated (1988) *The Little Mariner*, a work that presents often insuperable translation difficulties with its abundance of metalingual pyrotechnics where Elytis focuses on the sound and form of specifically Greek letters and words. In this long composite poem of some 120 pages, Elytis made use of lists of words (chosen, for example, for their vowel sounds), of capital letters, of words not separated by punctuation, of words split into their component parts and continued on another line, etc., giving rise to multiple readings and focusing on the signifiers themselves without reference to their signified content. Broumas's uninspired rendering of the semantic content of the poems in this collection provides the English-speaking reader with no indication of Elytis's mastery of the Greek language or of how the poems function in Greek.

The Oxopetra Elegies, translated by David CONNOLLY and published in a bilingual edition (1996), is one of Elytis's late collections. The 14 two- and three-page poems deal with all those themes that have always concerned him: our mystical relationship with nature, the senses as a form of knowledge and their analogies in the spirit, the reconciliation of opposites, the power of eros, the teaching of the insignificant, the exact moment, etc. In many ways, this collection is a summing-up of his entire work and is considered by many Greek critics to contain some of the finest and most important poems he ever wrote. The volume contains a foreword in which the translator explains his aims and approach, an introduction to Elytis's poetry (which is, in fact, a translation of Elytis's speech to the Swedish Academy on receiving the Nobel Prize), the collection in Greek with English translation *en face*, notes to the poems and biographical and bibliographical information concerning Elytis.

Elytis has not been as fortunate as other Greek poets in English translation largely because his poetry is intrinsically linked with language itself. He used language *as* poetry rather than as a means to fashion poetry. As Beaton (1994, p. 364) points out: "The power of a language freed from reference is a recurring, perhaps the dominant, preoccupation in Elytis's poetry, which may also help to account for the bafflement with which it has sometimes been received in translation".

DAVID CONNOLLY

Further Reading

Beaton, Roderick, *An Introduction to Modern Greek Literature*, Oxford: Clarendon Press, 1994

Ivask, Ivar (editor), *Odysseus Elytis: Analogies of Light*, Norman: University of Oklahoma Press, 1981

Endō Shūsaku 1923–1996

Japanese novelist and short-story writer

Biography

Born in Tokyo, 27 March 1923. He grew up in Dalian, in occupied Manchuria and returned to Japan with his mother when his parents divorced. After the divorce he and his mother joined the Roman Catholic church. After a brief period at Waseda University where he intended to study medicine, he studied French literature at Keiō University in Tokyo and graduated in 1949. The following year he attended the University of Lyons until 1953, being one of the first Japanese students to be awarded a government scholarship to study abroad. He edited the literary journal *Mita Bungaku*. He served as chairman of the Bungeika Kyōkai (Literary Artists' Association) and was elected to the Nihon Geijutsuin, the Japanese Academy of Arts in 1981. Endō married Junko Okada in 1955, and had one son. He received numerous literary awards including the Akutagawa prize in 1955 for *The White Man*. He died of pneumonia in Tokyo, 29 September 1996.

Translations

Novels

Ryūgaku, 1965
Williams, Mark, *Foreign Studies*, London: Peter Owen, and New York: Linden Press, 1989

Chinmoku, 1966
Johnston, William, *Silence*, Tokyo: Sophia University, and Rutland, Vermont: Tuttle, 1969

Samurai, 1980
Gessel, Van C., *The Samurai*, London: Peter Owen, and New York: Harper and Row, 1982

Sukyandaru, 1986
Gessel, Van C., *Scandal*, London: Peter Owen, and New York: Dodd Mead, 1988

Fukai kawa, 1993
Gessel, Van C., *Deep River*, London: Peter Owen, and New York: New Directions, 1994

With some 12 full-length novels and two short story collections currently available in English translation and with his work published in at least 28 countries (including translations into all the major European languages), the Japanese author Endō Shūsaku represents arguably the most accessible of all Japanese novelists to a Western audience. The name may not yet have acquired the recognition abroad of the likes of Mishima Yukio and Tanizaki Jun'ichirō, but this can be viewed more as a result of the universality of the themes addressed in Endō's literature – of the lack of a certain "Oriental exoticism" that attracts a devoted, if limited, readership – than as a sign of inherent lack of appeal.

Endō is a perfect example of an author whose international reputation was sealed with the appearance of the first of his novels to be translated. When William JOHNSTON's translation of Endō's acknowledged early masterpiece, *Silence*, was published in 1969, the novel was widely hailed as a "classic ... a profound and moving book" (*The Times*). Not only did the subject matter (the 17th-century Japanese response to the arrival of the Jesuit missions) strike a responsive chord with a Western audience, but the translation succeeded in capturing Endō's free-flowing style while avoiding the charge of over-fidelity to the original. For all this, the translation elicited criticism similar to that received by the original from the orthodox Catholic community, troubled by the work's apparent condonation of the act of apostasy performed by the protagonist, Rodrigues. Indeed, such an interpretation is encouraged by the translation of the crucial words with which God breaks His physical silence – in exhorting Rodrigues to "trample" on the crucifix that has been placed before him by the shogunate authorities determined to extract another apostasy – with the imperative "Trample!" rather than the words of empathy represented by the original, "*fumu ga ii*" (literally "it would be good to trample"). And the author himself has frequently expressed concern at the misunderstandings induced by one seemingly minor mistranslation in the diary extracts included as an appendix to the work. The problem centres on the translation of one word, the *shomotsu*, which Okada San'emon (the Japanese name adopted by Rodrigues following his apostasy) is depicted as writing in the extract dated "the Second Year of Enpō". According to Endō, in rendering this one term simply as a "book" (the standard translation of the word) as opposed to the more specific "document of apostasy" that the author claims to have had in mind, Johnston has reduced the intended impact of the portrayal of Rodrigues as continuing to waver with regard to his apostasy, and has succeeded rather in depicting the fallen priest simply as following in the footsteps of his lapsed mentor, Ferreira.

The distinction may be crucial but, judging from the generally favourable reviews accorded the novel both at home and abroad, the author's fears appear unfounded. And certainly, in the ensuing years, there followed a series of translations of Endō's early works (including the play *The Golden Country* (1966; translated 1970) and the novels *The Sea and Poison* (1957; translated 1972), *Wonderful Fool* (1959; translated 1974), *Volcano* (1960; translated 1978) and *Foreign Studies* (1965; translated by WILLIAMS, 1989) designed to bring the author's previous publications to a wider English-reading audience. These translations were completed by several different scholars and are consequently by no means uniform. In general, however, all have striven for a successful conversion to the target language with a consequence that the reader is rarely distracted by unwieldy phrases translated directly from the Japanese without being "transposed" (to cite Endō's own depiction of the art of literary translation) into English. In certain instances, this has involved the careful removal of certain redundant phrases, but in all cases this appears justified by the greater prevalence of repetition and ambiguity as literary devices in Japanese than in English.

By this stage, Endō's international reputation was assured, his name increasingly put forward as candidate for the various international literary prizes (including the Nobel Prize for Literature, for which he was widely tipped once news of a Japanese laureate in 1994 became public knowledge, right up to the confirmation that the award had gone instead to Endō's colleague in Japanese literary circles, Ōe Kenzaburō). Thereafter, this reputation was enhanced by publication and subsequent rapid translation of his three most recent works of "serious fiction". (Endō was always at pains to stress the distinction in his work between those works of *junbungaku* ["serious" or "pure" fiction] and works of "entertainment" – with very little of the latter having attracted the attention of potential translators.)

The first of the three, *The Samurai* (1980; translated 1982), represents a landmark in Japanese literary translation. The English version by GESSEL retains the lucidity and elegant tempo of Endō's original and betrays little evidence of the "painful but necessary changes" that the translator cites in his translator's note as inevitable when "a piece of literature is forcibly uprooted from its natural environment and thrust into strange surroundings". The events depicted in the work itself can hardly be described as fast-moving: the novel portrays the four-year journey via Nueva España and Spain to Rome, undertaken by a low-ranking samurai at the behest of his feudal lord who sought thereby to ensure trading privileges for his northern domain. Through skillful compression of his material and focus on the evolving rapport that develops between the samurai and his Western missionary guide Velasco, however, Endō succeeds in creating an atmosphere of tension and drama that belies the leisurely pace of the physical journey on which they are engaged. Such drama is adroitly captured in the English translation.

GESSEL followed up the success of this translation with English versions of *Scandal* (1986; translated 1988) and *Deep River* (1993; translated 1994), both benefiting from the consistency born of reliance on a single translator. This is particularly true of *Scandal*, a work that purportedly represents a radical change of novelistic approach (from the overt focus on the Japanese response to Christianity that had occupied so much of Endō's attention up to that time to a concentration on the shadow side of human nature), but which, with its profound consideration of the realm of the human unconscious, is more convincingly portrayed as a logical progression from the examinations of characters struggling to come to terms with their own complex beings that populate so much of his earlier work.

To some, the translated version (GESSEL, 1994) of *Deep River*, Endō's last novel, is "not quite convincing" (*Sunday Telegraph*, 12 June 1994). To a certain extent, such a reaction may be an inevitable response to the excessive expectations generated by the popularity of the earlier novels in general and by the issues left, by the author's own admission, "unanswered and awaiting a sequel" at the end of *Scandal*. For all such reservations, however, the novel reveals the extraordinary psychological dramas that lurk within the essentially unremarkable people who populate this work, and few of Endō's readers will have remained unmoved at the author's final attempt to address in his fiction questions which, though born of an intensely personal journey of faith, nevertheless mirror concerns of a universal nature.

MARK WILLIAMS

Further Reading

Boscaro, Adriana, "Man in the Novels of Endō Shūsaku", *Man and Society in Japan Today* (1984)
Gessel, Van C., "Voices in the Wilderness: Japanese Christian Authors", *Monumenta Nipponica*, 37/4 (1982)
Gessel, Van C., "Salvation of the Weak: Endō" in his *The Sting of Life: Four Contemporary Japanese Novelists*, New York: Columbia University Press, 1989
Mathy, Francis, "Endō Shūsaku: White Man, Yellow Man", *Comparative Literature*, (Winter 1967)
Mathy, Francis, "Shūsaku Endō: The Second Period", *Japan Christian Quarterly*, 40/4 (Fall 1974)
Mathy, Francis, "Shūsaku Endō: Japanese Catholic Novelist", *Month* (May 1987)
Williams, Mark, *Endō Shūsaku: A Literature of Reconciliation*, London and New York: Routledge, 1999
Wills, Elizabeth, "Christ as Eternal Companion: A Study in the Christology of Shūsaku Endō", *Scottish Journal of Theology*, 45 (1992)

English

General History of Literary Translation

The Language

The English language, one of the six official languages used by the United Nations Organization, is the most international of languages. Its geographical spread is enormous. It is the sole official language not only in the United Kingdom but also in more than 30 other countries, including Liberia, Nigeria, Uganda, Ghana and the Bahamas. It also shares official status with one or two other indigenous languages, for a variety of public and personal functions, in Singapore, India, Tanzania, the Philippines and other countries. Most of these countries are former British territories. The language has developed to the extent that there are, besides the two major national standards of British and American English, new regional varieties, such as Australian English, Indian English, African English, Singaporean English, Philippine English, Hong Kong English, aptly described by the new plural *Englishes*.

The internationalism of English contributes to its being one of the world's most important languages. The role of English as an international language has gathered momentum since the end of World War II through the economic and military global dominance of the United States. English, besides being a mother tongue for millions of its native speakers, has always served as an international language for communication. It is the official language of air-traffic control and the *lingua franca* of international business and academic conferences, of scientific and technical literature, of diplomacy and for speakers of English as a second or foreign language. It is now spoken daily in some form by an estimated one thousand million people. The choice of English as an international language is, therefore, based on political, economic and demographic criteria rather than on linguistic or aesthetic ones.

English derives from the West Germanic branch of the Indo-European language family, and is most closely related to the Low German dialects in northern Germany and to Dutch and Frisian. The Indo-European family of languages is characterized by complex inflectional and declension systems for conveying the fine distinctions in grammatical meaning. An inflectional system is a grammatical apparatus based on modifications in the form of words to indicate such grammatical functions as case, person, tense, number, mood, aspect, etc. Old English relied more than does Modern English on inflectional morphology to indicate the grammatical relations among sentence constituents.

Modern English has, in the great historic flux of changes, been stripped of many of the inflectional categories of Proto-Germanic, developing into a largely isolating morphological language, or an analytical language, like Chinese. The inflections that have remained in present-day English comprise a small number of productive inflectional suffixes for nouns, verbs and adjectives, with no inflectional prefixes or infixes. The moulded ethos of the language thus contributes to its characteristic brevity, clarity and emphasis (the qualities that led Otto Jespersen to describe English metaphorically as "masculine"), its freedom in the handling of the parts of speech, its preference for coordinate constructions in loose series, etc.

The first outstanding characteristic of Modern English, then, looked at from the diachronic standpoint, is its reduced inflections and its relatively fixed word order. The historic developments of English, from Old (or Anglo-Saxon) English through Middle English to Modern English, have been marked with continual reductions in its inflectional categories. For example, nearly all case distinctions in the noun phrase have disappeared; the distinction between mood categories (indicative, subjunctive, imperative) have largely disappeared in the verb morphology; and articles and adjectives are invariant. Modern English indicates grammatical relationships between words in sentences with the minimum of variation in their form. The loss of precise morphological indication of grammatical meanings is compensated for by the use of a relatively fixed word order, S.V.O. (subject, verb, object).

The corollary to the above simplification of inflections – and the second characteristic of English – is the growth of the use of periphrastic structures and of the use of prepositions to replace the lost case-endings. The use of periphrases and of compound tenses made with auxiliary verbs replaces the past elaborate tense systems. In its spoken mode, English has also developed a parallel in its use of new varieties of intonation to express shades of meanings formerly indicated by inflectional differences. English has also adopted natural rather than grammatical gender.

The third quality of Modern English is its extraordinary linguistic receptiveness and adaptable heterogeneity. This accounts for its cosmopolitan lexicon, enriched through the ages by other languages. It has imported many loan-words not only from French and other Romance languages but also from Hebrew, Hungarian, Arabic, Hindi-Urdu, Bengali, Malay, etc., and shares with German, Flemish, Dutch, Danish and Swedish many lexical items and grammatical structures. This makes for a marked degree of linguistic and cultural receptivity to translation from these other source languages to which it is indebted linguistically.

One of the major resources of Modern English is its syntactic flexibility. The syntactic process allowed by this reduces isomorphism between surface syntactic structures and underlying semantic structures, creating an infinity of stylistic variations. Stylistically, even within the constraints of normal English word order, changing factors such as rhythm, balance and focus of attention often dictate a conscious choice for the disposition of sentential elements. The spectrum of linguistic features thus generated may range from highly contrived syntactic structures to anacoluthon and aposiopesis. The linguistic resources of English further manifest in its vigorous expressiveness, which resides in such syntactic traits as the predominance of transitive verbs, the shift of intransitive ones into transitive, the preference for personal over impersonal constructions, and the replacement of simple verbs by phrases.

The question of the varying degrees of English receptivity to translation from other languages can be examined in terms of the transfer of typological affinities among languages. The similarities shared by members of the same language family will, theoretically, facilitate the re-packaging of linguistic structures with the concomitant transfer of meanings, whereas members of a particular language family will be relatively incompatible with members of another family in such a process of semantic transfer.

The membership of the subgroups of the Indo-European language family open to modern languages includes modern Persian (Iranic of the Indo-Iranian branch); Russian, Ukrainian (East Slavic of the Balto-Slavic branch); Portuguese, Spanish, French, Italian, Romanian (the Italic branch); Danish and Swedish (the North Germanic branch); English is a member of the West Germanic branch (it will therefore be expected to have linguistic affinity with, and hence theoretically a greater degree of receptivity to translation from, Frisian, its closely related member of the same branch). Among typical members of the non-Indo-European language family are modern languages such as Finnish, Hungarian, Estonian, Lappish (all Finno-Ugric of the Ural-Ataic branch). Languages can be further classified on the basis of isolating, agglutinative, incorporative and inflective types, each being exemplified, respectively, by Chinese, Turkish, Eskimo and Latin. English will be expected to have a high degree of translatability from its co-members of the Indo-European language family by virtue of their common linguistic-genetic background.

French, though a member of the (Italic branch of the) Indo-European family of languages, is considered one of the most difficult European languages to render into English. First, there is the problem of so-called illusory correspondence between the English and French lexicons; second, English, with its heterogeneous vocabulary, does not, when translated, attain the same degree of broad clarity and precision of expression as French. The difficulty increases if the translation is to be made to the highest standards of both accuracy and literary quality; French poetry is one of the most untranslatable forms of European literature.

Modern Standard German, a "cognate" language of English, belonging to the Netherlandic-German of the West Germanic branch, would seem to lend itself to more compatible translating into English at the lexical, syntactic and discourse levels than, say, French or Japanese and Chinese. This translation susceptibility can allow the processes of linguistic restructuring entailed by translating to be described as "mere shifts in expression". At least, the problem of "deceptive resemblance" rarely exists for English translation of German literary texts at the lexical level; and this, allegedly, reduces the risk of errors in such rendering. This is not to say, however, that translation from other languages is impossible if English differs more considerably from them in terms of syntactic structures: more complex reshuffling in sentential form may be necessary in such cases.

On the cultural plane, the degree of English receptivity to translation from other languages varies proportionally with the distance between the source and target cultures. A common Eurocentric cultural background behind English and other European languages would, therefore, make for easier, relatively straightforward transfer of cultural meanings – whether they relate to abstract concepts or concrete artefacts – from the latter to the former. Conversely, the gap existing between English culture and, say, Chinese culture presents considerably more pitfalls into which the unwary English literary translator may well fall. On this issue, the question of cultural untranslatability "due to the absence in the TL [target language] culture of a relevant situational feature for the SL [source language] text" in Catford's sense (1965) does exist, as in the case of the English translation of terms denoting culture-bound ornaments or trinkets worn by the characters in many classical Chinese novels. Even if there is present in the TL culture a situational feature relevant for the SL text, the feature in question must never be equated with the SL equivalent *in toto* because both features are context-sensitive in their respective environments. Indeed, many English literary translators have the misguided view that equivalence at the cultural level can be achieved simply by substituting so-called "relevant situational features" for the SL text.

The present world context of translation into English is ever more hospitable. During the period 1986–90, for example, there was a profusion of published English translations of poetry, fiction, drama and literary essays from Yugoslav literatures, e.g.

Tom Lozar's translation *At the Door at Evening* (1990). The translation of contemporary Korean poetry has been undertaken by Jaihiun J. Kim (1974, 1980, 1994) and others. The English translation by Paul St. John Mackintosh and Maki Sugiyama of *Nip the Buds, Shoot the Kids* (1995) by Kenzaburo Oe, winner of the 1994 Nobel Prize for Literature, has been among the most recent English translations of Japanese literary works. Stephen Owen's edition and translation of *An Anthology of Chinese Literature* (1996) gathers texts in a wide variety of genres – anecdotes, poetry, political oratory, traditional literary theory, all translated with great clarity and sense of the original. Many other literary translators around the world have also dedicated themselves to the English translation of their own national literatures, e.g. Sumerian and Akkadian, Islamic, Arabic, Bengali, Portuguese and Brazilian, Catalan, Hellenistic Greek, Hebrew, Malayan and Indonesian, modern Persian, Sanskrit, French-Canadian, etc.

As the individual histories of literary translation into English from the major languages are studied in survey entries elsewhere in this encyclopedia, the following brief conspectus of the history of literary translation in English makes no pretense to comprehensiveness, its aim being to introduce some of the salient epochs and events in the making of translated literature in English through the ages.

To 1400

English literary translation during the medieval period is characterized by, among other things, a lack of interest in the textual sources of originals and by the treatment of original texts as sources "for literary exploitation by the devices of amplification proper to the literary tradition and the idiom of the target language" (J.D. Burnley, 1989). The translations were often at two or more removes from their originals.

Literary translators before the Renaissance period, especially those medieval translators, were primarily working from rich cultures and advanced languages into English, a vernacular language that was still developing, for a readership that was discovering past literary treasures through the translated works. *Remaniement*, the reworking of given subject-matter, was one of the hallmarks distinguishing medieval literary translating activities from those in the other historic periods. Literary translators like Chaucer and Gower seek both to replicate the authority of their *auctoritates* and to substitute in their place their own authoritative texts. During King Alfred's reign (871–99), translation became a medium for creating a sense of national unity and laying the foundations for English prose. The translators' approach oscillated between free and literal translation. Notable accomplishments in the early and medieval periods were: Aldhelm (c.640–709) translated the Psalms; the Venerable Bede (c.673–735) dictated a translation of the Gospel of St John; during King Alfred's reign a programme of translating great prose works from Latin into Anglo-Saxon was initiated (Augustine's *Soliloquies*; Boethius' *The Consolation of Philosophy*; the *Anglo-Saxon Chronicle*; Bede's *Ecclesiastical History*; Pope Gregory I's *Cura pastoralis*; Orosius' *Historia Adversum Paganos*); much literature was translated into the Wessex dialect of English; 993–98: the Benedictine monk Ælfric translated *Lives of the Saints* and *Homilies* into Old English; Geoffrey Chaucer (c.1340–1400) translated Boethius; Anon. translated *"Mandeville's" Travels*, c. 1375; 1387: John of Trevisa translated Higden's *Polychronicon*, prefixing it with a statement of his principles of translation.

15th and 16th Centuries

There was a flowering of literary translating activities in the Renaissance period. The motivation for translating was in part utilitarian: translating was viewed as a means of enriching the English language (primarily its lexicon), which was considered then ineloquent in comparison to classical and some contemporary languages. During this period, translations were made from foreign prose writers, almost at the expense of original composition, e.g. Thomas Hoby's translation of Castiglione's *Il Cortegiano* (1561). Elizabethan translators rendered texts to suit the ethos of their own times: for example, one major characteristic of 16th-century English literary translation was the affirmation of the present through the use of contemporary idiom and style. This is demonstrated by, for example, the frequent replacement of indirect discourse by direct discourse in North's translation of Plutarch (1579), a device that adds immediacy and vitality to the translated text. An interesting phenomenon of Renaissance literary translation is the existence of female translators. The social climate of the Renaissance, or even medieval periods was such that translation, or at least religious translation (which is a form of literary translation), was one of the socially sanctioned ways of writing open to women. For example, Mary Herbert, countess of Pembroke (1561–1621), translated Petrarch's *Triumph of Death*, as well as Robert Garnier's *Marc-Antoine*, creating the first English translation of a secular play. And most translations made by women are more literal, since literalism afforded a certain kind of sexist protection.

Fifteenth-century landmarks include: William Caxton (c.1422–91) rendered European works into English, e.g. in 1490 his translation, *Eneydos*, of Virgil's *Aeneid* via French; Lord Berners (1467–1553) translated the *Chronicles* of Froissart, the 13th-century French romance of *Huon of Bordeaux*, and *The Golden Book of Marcus Aurelius* from the Spanish of Antonio de Guevara. The first book printed in English had been Caxton's translation (1473–74) of Le Fevre's *The Recuyell of the Historyes of Troye*. In 1470 Malory translated *Le Morte D'Arthur*.

In the 16th century, Sir Thomas Wyatt (1503–42) translated sonnets from Petrarch and his Italian followers; he also produced some longer verse translations, including the Penitential Psalms, in Dante's *terza rima*; 1509: Alexander Barclay translated Brandt's *The Ship of Fools*; 1510: Sir Thomas More translated the Latin biography by Pico's nephew, *The Life of John Picus, Earl of Mirandula*; before 1512: Gavin Douglas translated *Eneados*, the first complete vernacular translation of Virgil's *Aeneid* and the first translation of any great classical poet into English (or, rather, "Scottis"); Henry Howard, Earl of Surrey (1517–47) translated poems chiefly from Latin and Italian: he did versions of Books II and IV of Virgil's *Aeneid*; 1520: Alexander Barclay translated Sallust's *Chronicle of the War Which the Romans Had against Jugurtha*; Sir Thomas Wyatt translated Plutarch's *Quiet of Mind*; 1530: William Tyndale translated *The Pentateuch*; 1533: Tyndale translated the Latin translation of Erasmus' *Enchiridion Militis Christiani*; Lady Jane Lumley (1537–76) produced the first extant English version of Euripides' *Iphigenia*; 1542: Nicholas Udall's *Apophthegms of Erasmus*; 1553: publication of Gavin Douglas's translation of Virgil's *Aeneid*; 1559: Jasper Heywood translated Seneca's *Troas*; 1560: Heywood translated Seneca's *Thyestes*; 1561: Sir Thomas Hoby translated Castiglione's *The Courtier*; 1563: Alexander Nevile translated Seneca's *Oedipus*; 1565: Arthur Golding translated *Caesar's Exploits in Gallia*; 1566, 1567, 1575: William Painter translated Boccaccio, Bandello, Margaret of Navarre and others in his *The Palace of Pleasure*; 1566: William Adlington translated *The Golden Ass* of Apuleius; George Gascoigne translated Dolce's *Jocasta* and Ariosto's *Supposes*; John Studley translated Seneca's *Hercules, Agamemnon, Medea*; 1568–69: Thomas Underdown executed the whole of Heliodorus; 1575: Golding translated *Abraham's Sacrifice* from the French of Théodore de Bèze; 1578: Margaret Tyler translated a Spanish romance as *A Mirrour of Princely Deeds and Knighthood*; 1579: Sir Thomas North translated *Plutarch's Lives of the Noble Grecians and Romans*; 1581: Thomas Newton translated Seneca's *Thebais*; Jasper Heywood and others translated *Seneca His Ten Tragedies*; Thomas Watson translated Sophocles' *Antigone*; 1585: John Bullokar translated Aesop's *Fables*; 1587: Bartholomew Young translated Boccaccio's *Amorous Fiametta*; Abraham Fraunce translated Thomas Watson's Latin version of Tasso's *Lamentations of Amyntas*; 1590: Anthony Munday translated *Amadis of Gaul*; Sir John Davies and Christopher Marlowe wrote *Epigrams and Elegies*, with translations of Ovid; 1591: Sir John Harington translated Ariosto's *Orlando Furioso in English Heroical Verse*; 1592: William Warner translated Plautus' *Menaechmi*; Joshua Sylvester translated *La Semaine* of Du Bartas; 1593: Christopher Marlowe translated book 1 of Lucan's *Pharsalia*.

17th Century

The 17th century, especially the period after 1650, was an important era of English literary translation. John Dryden's Virgil, one of the greatest English translations of the classics, together with his many translations of Roman and Greek authors, was produced during this time. Literary translation was considered as a worthy activity in its own right, almost an art, with critical discourse about translation, notably in Dryden's prefaces, being considerably expanded and codified. In the long list of English translations from the classics in the early 17th century, the works of ancient historians and moralists together far outweigh other kinds of literature. While the perennial favourites were still Ovid and Virgil, some of the lesser translators turned to such comparatively neglected classics as Lucan, Persius, Martial and Juvenal. Philemon Holland (1552–1637), whose output includes Plutarch's *Moralia* (1603) and Suetonius' *Historie of the Twelve Caesars* (1606), was famous for the quality and scholarship of his translations. Verse translations, e.g. Dryden's *Aeneis* (1697), flourished, with an exceptional amount of fine prose translation, including Sir Thomas Urquhart's translation of Rabelais's works (1653), also being produced. This burgeoning of English literary translating activities was prompted in part by the insatiable appetite of a larger, more educated readership for classical and European works in the vernacular.

1600: Edward Fairfax produced *Godfrey of Bulloigne*, which was a translation of Tasso's *Jerusalem Delivered*; Philemon Holland translated Livy's *Romane Historie*; 1601: Holland translated Pliny's *Natural History*; 1602: Thomas Lodge translated *The Famous and Memorable Works of Josephus*; 1603: Sir John Florio translated Montaigne's *Essays*; Holland translated Plutarch's *Moralia*; 1605: Joshua Sylvester translated *Du Bartas: His Divine Weeks and Works*; 1606: Holland translated Suetonius' *Historie of the Twelve Caesars*; 1608: Thomas Heywood translated Sallust; 1610: Holland translated from Latin Camden's great antiquarian work, *Britannia*; 1616: George Chapman published *The Whole Works of Homer, Prince of Poets* and translations from Hesiod; 1618: Chapman translated Hesiod's *Georgics*; 1626: George Sandys translated *Ovid's Metamorphoses*; 1627: Thomas May translated the *Pharsalia* of the Latin poet Lucan; 1629: Thomas Hobbes translated *The Peloponnesian War of Thucydides*; 1631: James Mabbe produced *The Spanish Bawd*, which was a translation of Fernando de Rojas's *Celestina*; 1636: George Sandys translated *Paraphrase upon the Psalms*; 1640: James Mabbe translated Cervantes's *Exemplarie Novells*; 1648: Sir John Denham translated Cicero's *Cato Major: Of Old Age*; 1652: John Hall translated *Longinus of the Height of Eloquence*; Henry Vaughan translated Archbishop Anselm's *The Mount of Olives; or, Solitary Devotions*; 1653: Sir Thomas Urquhart translated *The First Book of Mr Francis Rabelais, Doctor of Physic, Translated into English*; 1656: Denham translated Virgil's *The Destruction of Troy*; Abraham Cowley produced *Poems* containing *Miscellanies*, which include excellent translations, in irregularly stressed octosyllabic couplets, of the Greek lyric poet Anacreon; 1668: Denham produced *Poems and Translations*; 1674: Hobbes translated Homer's *Odyssey*; 1680: Sir Roger L'Estrange translated *Select Colloquies of Erasmus*; Dryden with collaborators translated *Ovid's Epistles*; Roscommon translated *Horace's Art of Poetry*; 1683: John Oldham produced *Poems and Translations*; 1684: Gilbert Burnet translated More's *Utopia*; 1685–86: Charles Cotton translated Montaigne's *Essays*; 1688: Aphra Behn translated De Brilhac's *Agnes de Castro; or, The Force of Generous Love*; 1693: Dryden translated with collaborators *The Satires of Juvenal and Persius*; 1694: Laurence Echard, with collaborators, translated Plautus and Terence; 1695: Dryden translated Du Fresnoy's *De Arte Graphica*; 1697: Dryden's *The Works of Virgil*; 1698: Vanbrugh translated Dancourt's *The Country House*; 1699: Dryden's *Fables Ancient and Modern*, a partly translated miscellany of narrative poems.

18th Century

The 18th-century English literary translator was considered as painter/imitator with a moral duty both to the original writer and to his target readership. Despite the translator's meticulous attention to source text details, however, almost all complexities and digressions in the original works were still pruned away, and naturalization was the dominant paradigm for the theory and practice of English language translation in every literary genre. This practice stemmed from the translator's impulse to clarify the essential spirit of a source text. Earlier texts were rewritten on a large scale to fit them to contemporary standards of language and taste, hence the restructuring of Shakespearian texts and the reworkings of Racine. Many competent prose translations were produced during this century. Alexander Pope's multi-volume Homer and William Cowper's *Iliad* and

Odyssey represent the major efforts to put the Greek epic poet into English verse.

Eighteenth-century translators, imitators and adapters favoured ancient classical texts, first and foremost Homer and the writers of the Roman Augustan age, particularly Virgil, Horace and Ovid; but the tradition of translation from the Bible and from French, Italian and Spanish continued, and the century as a whole saw a widening of horizons, with translations into English not only from Welsh and German but also from Arabic, Persian and Sanskrit (George Sale; Sir William Jones). Serious interest in translation theory and criticism was maintained, notably by Alexander Tytler (*Essay on the Principles of Translation*, 1791). An indication of the range of these activities is given by the following brief list of publications:

1717: Sir Samuel Garth edited *Ovid's Metamorphoses, Translated by the Most Eminent Hands* (including Addison, Congreve, Dryden, Gay and Tate); 1718: Nicholas Rowe translated Lucan's *Pharsalia*; 1719: Isaac Watts translated *The Psalms of David*; 1720: Pope completed his translation of Homer's *Iliad*; Thomas Tickell published Book I of his rival version; 1725–26: Pope translated Homer's *Odyssey*; 1733–38: Pope's series of *Imitations* of Horace's *Satires*; 1734: George Sale's translation of the Koran; 1738: Charlotte Smith translated Prévost's *Manon Lescaut*; 1747: Philip Francis translated *A Poetical Translation of the Works of Horace*; 1749: Tobias Smollett translated Le Sage's *Gil Blas*; 1755: Smollett translated Cervantes's *Don Quixote*; 1756: Christopher Smart published his prose translation of Horace; 1758: Goldsmith translated Marteilhe's *Memoirs of a Protestant, Condemned to the Galleys of France*; 1760: James Macpherson translated *Fragments of Ancient Poetry Collected in the Highlands of Scotland, and Translated from the Gallic or Erse Language*; 1764: Evan Evans translated *Some Specimens of the Poetry of the Ancient Welsh Bards*; 1765: Smart translated *The Psalms of David*; 1767: Smart published his verse translation of Horace; 1775: John Nott translated Johannes Secundus Nicolaius; 1777: Nott translated Petrarch; 1782: Nott produced the first book-length translation of Propertius; 1787; Nott translated Hafiz; 1789: Sir William Jones's *Sacontala*; 1791: William Cowper translated Homer's *Iliad* and *Odyssey*; 1795: Nott produced the first book-length translation of Catullus; 1797: Nott's translation of Bonefonius; 1799: Nott's translation of Lucretius.

19th Century

Antiquarianism was one of the central characteristics marking 19th-century literary translations in English. The recurrent concern of Victorian translators to convey the temporal and geographical remoteness of the source texts led to the production of consciously archaic literary translations full of deliberately contrived foreignness of form and language. F.W. Newman (1805–97), for example, declared that the translator should retain every peculiarity of the original wherever possible, "with the greater care the more foreign it may be". From Germany, Friedrich Schleiermacher (1768–1834) had also proposed the use, in translated literature only, of a separate translation language, to which suggestion many 19th-century English translators, e.g. Thomas Carlyle and William Morris, responded enthusiastically. During this century many great English translations were produced, e.g. Edward FitzGerald's rendering of *The Rubaiyat of Omar Khayyam* (1859), which still enjoys undiminished popularity today, and Carlyle's translation of Goethe's *Wilhelm Meister* (1824). Another feature of the age was the translation of poetry by poets such as Longfellow, Byron and Shelley.

In the 19th century, with surging progress in communications and travel, in scholarship and general education, and in the technology of publication (paper-making and printing), the number of translations into English of literary texts increased greatly, in America now as well as in Britain. The stream of versions from Greek and Latin classics continued strongly, alongside an increasingly eclectic range of ventures into lesser known languages and cultures, ancient and modern.

1800: Thomas Moore translated *Odes of Anacreon*; 1803: Nott translated Horace; 1808: Robert Southey (with Frere) translated *The Chronicle of the Cid*; 1809: Byron produced *Imitations and Translations from the Classics, with Original Poems*; 1814: Henry Francis Cary translated *Dante's Divine Comedy*; Sir Charles A. Elton translated *Specimens of the Classic Poets*, a three-volume anthology of verse translations from Greek and Latin; 1821: George Lamb translated Catullus; 1824: Thomas Carlyle translated *Goethe's Wilhelm Meister's Apprenticeship*; 1833: Elizabeth Barrett Browning translated Aeschylus' *Prometheus Bound*; 1840: P.B. Shelley's *Essays, Letters from Abroad, Translations and Fragments* were published posthumously; 1846: George Eliot translated Strauss's *Life of Jesus*; 1853: F.W. Newman translated Horace; Edward FitzGerald published six plays of Calderón in English translation; 1856: F.W. Newman produced a foreignized *Iliad*; 1861: D.G. Rossetti translated *Early Italian Poets*; 1862: C.S. Calverley translated *Verses and Translations*; 1875: William Morris translated *The Aeneid* and, with Eiríkr Magnússon, *Three Northern Love Stories from Iceland*; 1879: S.H. Butcher and Andrew Lang produced the prose *Odyssey*; 1880: B.H. Chamberlain published *The Classical Poety of the Japanese*, which contains English translations of the farces *Honekawa* and *Zazen*; 1884: J.A. Symonds translated *Wine, Women and Song* from medieval Latin; 1885: Sir Richard Burton translated *The Arabian Nights* (completed in 6 volumes by 1888); 1887: William Morris translated Homer's *Odyssey*; 1888: H. E. Watts translated Cervantes's *Don Quixote*.

20th Century

The 20th century witnessed a second efflorescence, another Renaissance, in the history of English literary translation, with significant translations flowing from the pens of many scholars and praiseworthy translators. These translations were often re-translations of the great classical works, targeting a new audience. Unlike their predecessors, however, these literary translators privileged in their translating strategy the primacy of prose meaning and textual interpretation, often neglecting the imitation of literary form. Their translated works were plain, accurate versions eminently appropriate for academic exegesis. Among the outstanding practitioners of this new "plain prose" method were E.V. Rieu, Robert Graves, Michael Grant, *et al.* Deserving a mention are, perhaps, the English translations that the Penguin Classics series has brought out to popularize classics, mutating many of the Greek epics into proto-novels. A couple of interesting observations can be gleaned from the state of English literary translation during the 20th century. Some of the most admired, influential English translations relate to remote languages and to cultures radically alien to English. And Ezra Pound's rendering, with his unique genius of mimicry and self-metamorphosis, from Ernest Fenollosa's manuscript notes, of the Li Po poems in *Cathay* typifies, in a phenomenal way, some of the most persuasive translations made by writers ignorant of the source language from which they were translating.

Notable among early 20th-century translations from modern canon texts are the influential series by Constance Garnett (1862–1946) of the great 19th-century Russian novelists (Chekhov, Dostoevskii, Gogol, Tolstoi, Turgenev) and of the works of Thomas Mann by the equally indefatigable Helen Lowe-Porter (1876–1963). The Garnett and Lowe-Porter texts have been the focus in recent years of some hostile re-evaluation. Literary-historical and linguistic criteria continue to be used very frequently in the description, and often the evaluation, of translations into English but, since the rapid expansion of translation theory and academic Translation Studies in the later decades of the 20th century, some translators into English, especially those targeting the general reader or assuming a post-colonial stance, have exhibited liberal, liberated and creative approaches, sometimes privileging the target text and culture over the source.

While the enduring interest of world canon texts is indicated in the following brief list of landmarks, a large proportion of English translations published in the second half of the 20th century consists of contemporary fiction, poetry and drama from all quarters of the globe (with an impressive expansion since the 1960s of Anglo-Saxon interest in Latin American writing in translation). The texts concerned are too numerous to list here individually, but the most important of them are treated in separate Writer and Topic entries elsewhere in these pages.

1900: Samuel Butler translated Homer's *Odyssey* into prose; 1906–12: William Archer produced his complete version of Ibsen; 1912: Pound translated from Old English part of *The Seafarer*; 1915: Pound's *Cathay*; 1916: Ernest Fenollosa and Ezra Pound published *Noh*, with translations by Fenollosa and adaptation by Pound; 1921: Waley published his English translation of *The Nō Plays of Japan*; 1931: Ezra Pound published a final version of Guido Cavalcanti's *Rime*; 1935: Henry W. Wells's modernization of Langland's *Vision of Piers Plowman*; 1937: Waley published his English translation of *The Book of Songs*; 1942: Waley published his English translation of *Monkey* by Wu Ch'eng-en; 1946: E.V. Rieu translated the *Odyssey* into contemporary English prose; 1951: Richmond Lattimore translated the *Iliad* and Neville Coghill translated Chaucer's *The Canterbury Tales*; 1951: Roy Campbell's complete version of the poems of St John of the Cross; 1952: Campbell's translations of Baudelaire and of Lorca; C. Day Lewis translated *The Aeneid*; 1953: Pound reprinted his latest versions of Guido Cavalcanti and Arnaut Daniel, *The Seafarer* and *Cathay*, with a miscellany of other poetry translations mainly from Latin, Provençal, French and Italian; 1953–59: David Grene and Richmond Lattimore produced their edition of *The Complete Greek Tragedies*; 1957: David Wright produced a prose translation of *Beowulf*; 1958–69: Celia and Louis Zukofsky produced a homophonic translation of the extant canon of Catullus' poetry; 1959: J.F. Goodridge translated Langland's *Piers the Ploughman*; 1961: Robert Fitzgerald translated the *Odyssey*; A.E. Watts translated *The Poems of Sextus Propertius*; 1964: David Barrett translated Aristophanes' *The Frogs and Other Plays*; 1966: Peter Whigham translated Catullus into English; 1967: Robert Graves and Omar Ali Shah translated *The Rubaiyat of Omar Khayyam*; 1969: C. M. Bowra translated *The Odes of Pindar*; 1971: Betty Radice translated Erasmus's *Praise of Folly*; 1972: Philip Vellacott translated Euripides' *Orestes and Other Plays*; 1973: Michael Alexander translated *Beowulf*; 1976: Edward G. Seidensticker translated Murasaki Shikibu's *The Tale of Genji*; 1983: Robert Fitzgerald translated *The Aeneid*; 1990: Robert Fagles translated *The Iliad*.

English literary translation beyond the 20th century may be expected to thrive, should there be no dramatic reversals of fortune in the fate of the English language as an international language. Today, with English still showing every sign of robust survival, the centripetal tendency of major or minor national literatures around the globe to become part of the canon of world literature in English translation may be expected to continue. The recent electronic age has, additionally, ushered in a cheerful and sophisticated atmosphere for the continued expansion of literary translation in English in the international context.The process will be facilitated by the computer industry in its various applications: the Internet, databanks, electronic glossaries, etc. With the advent of teletranslation, the literary translation operator and the literary publisher can be brought together in a global network which in turn links worldwide language expertise. English literary translation within a truly internationally technical context will soon become a reality. Practitioners of English literary translation will tend to take an increasingly multidisciplinary approach, integrating methods of cognitive psychology, sociolinguistics, philosophy of language, etc., to their art or craft in the years to come, because translating is so complex a phenomenon that it can be fully understood only through a wide range of disciplinary perspectives. The establishment of Translation Studies has given the translator's awareness in this direction an added impetus. Continuing through in the backwash of a 20th-century scientific, pragmatic ethos, the 21st century will still probably slant towards accuracy in meaning at the expense of aesthetics and structural form. After all, the search for structural identity, as for many other possible objectives of literary translation, such as stylistic replication, is illusory: only meaning is real.

RAYMOND S.C. LIE

Further Reading

Bassnett, Susan, *Translation Studies*, London and New York: Methuen, 1980; revised London: Routledge, 1990

Budick, Sanford and Wolfgang Iser (editors), *The Translatability of Cultures: Figurations of the Space Between*, Stanford, California: Stanford University Press, 1996

Catford, J.C., *A Linguistic Theory of Translation: An Essay in Applied Linguistics*, London: Oxford University Press, 1965

Cohen, J.M., *English Translators and Translations*, London: Longmans Green, 1962

Copeland, Rita, *Rhetoric, Hermeneutics, and Translation in the Middle Ages*, Cambridge: Cambridge University Press, 1991

Crystal, David, *The English Language*, London: Penguin, and New York: Viking, 1988

Crystal, David, *English as a Global Language*, Cambridge and New York: Cambridge University Press, 1997
Delisle, Jean and Judith Woodsworth (editors), *Translators through History*, Amsterdam and Philadelphia: Benjamins, 1995
Duff, Alan, *The Third Language: Recurrent Problems of Translation into English*, Oxford and New York: Pergamon Press, 1981
Farrar, Clarissa P. and Austin P. Evans, *Bibliography of English Translations from Medieval Sources*, New York: Columbia University Press, 1946
Gramley, Stephan and Kurt-Michael Patzold, *A Survey of Modern English*, London and New York: Routledge, 1992
Harris, William J., *The First Printed Translations into English of the Great Foreign Classics*, London and New York: Routledge, 1909; New York: Norwood, 1977
Hussey, Stanley, *The English Language: Structure and Development*, London and New York: Longman, 1995
Knox, R.A., *On English Translation*, Oxford: Clarendon Press, 1957
Lathrop, H.B., *Translations from the Classics into English from Caxton to Chapman, 1477–1620*, New York: Octagon Books, 1967
Leask, Nigel, *British Romantic Writers and the East: Anxieties of Empire*, Cambridge and New York: Cambridge University Press, 1992
Lefevere, André, "Translation: Its Genealogy in the West", in *Translation, History and Culture*, edited by Lefevere and Susan Bassnett, London and New York: Pinter, 1995
Lewanski, Richard C. (editor), *The Literatures of the World in English Translation*, vol. 2: *The Slavic Literatures*, New York: New York Public Library / Ungar, 1967; revised 1971
Lewanski, Richard C., *The Literatures of the World in English Translation*, vol. 4: *The Celtic, Germanic, and Other Literatures of Europe*, New York: New York Public Library / Ungar, 1967
Lewanski, Richard C., *The Literatures of the World in English Translation*, vol. 5: *The Literatures of Asia and Africa*, New York: New York Public Library / Ungar, 1967
Matthiessen, F.O., *Translation: An Elizabethan Art*, Cambridge, Massachusetts: Harvard University Press, 1931
Nash, Walter, *An Uncommon Tongue: The Uses and Resources of English*, London and New York: Routledge, 1992
Niranjana, Tejaswini, "Translation, Colonialism and the Rise of English", in *Rethinking English: Essays in Literature, Language, History*, edited by Svati Joshi, New Delhi: Trianka, 1991
Pratt, Karen, "Medieval Attitudes to Translation and Adaptation: The Rhetorical Theory and the Poetic Practice", in *The Medieval Translator* 2, edited by Roger Ellis, London: Centre for Medieval Studies, Queen Mary and Westfield College, University of London, 1991
Radice, William and Barbara Reynolds (editors), *The Translator's Art*, Harmondsworth and New York: Penguin, 1987
Rener, F.M., *Interpretatio: Language and Translation from Cicero to Tytler*, Amsterdam and Atlanta: Rodopi, 1989
Robinson, Douglas, *The Translator' s Turn*, Baltimore: Johns Hopkins University Press, 1991
Steiner, George, *After Babel: Aspects of Language and Translation*, Oxford and New York: Oxford University Press, 1975; 3rd edition 1998
Steiner, T.R., *English Translation Theory, 1650–1800*, Assen: van Gorcum, 1975
Venuti, Lawrence, *The Translator's Invisibility: A History of Translation*, London and New York: Routledge, 1995

Equivalence: Formal and Dynamic

The concept of equivalence has been widely debated by the theoreticians of translation. Although the concept of equivalence is a basic one in a linguistic theory of translation, the question of how the correspondence between the source text and the target text can be assessed as to their equality or interchangeability (the primary definitions of "equivalence") remains unclear.

Susan Bassnett and André Lefevere, two of the foremost figures in the Translation Studies school, propose an etymological explanation for the dissension between scholars aligned into different theoretical trends: the German term *Äquivalenz* was introduced into translation science in central Europe from mathematics and/or formal logic in the 1970s, and conveyed a component of reversibility, which is absent from the English *equivalence*. Hence the controversy among the German-speaking experts, and the divergence from the situation in the Anglo-Saxon milieu (1990).

The dichotomy formal vs. dynamic equivalence was most famously postulated within modern translation theory by Eugene A. Nida in his seminal work *Toward a Science of Translating* (1964). This distinction has caused considerable controversy. Arguments arise even around the terminology: some scholars refer to this opposition in terms of formal vs. functional equivalence, but this is a less wide-spread posture. According to the most extensively used nomenclature, however, functional equivalents do appear within dynamic equivalence.

Formal equivalence is source-text oriented: it focuses on the reproduction of the form and contents of the message itself.

Meanings are reproduced, in Nida's words, "in terms of the source context". Dynamic equivalence, on the other hand, is very much target-text and target-culture oriented: it is based on the so-called "principle of equivalent effect", and aims at producing in the readership of the target text an effect similar to that which the original text produced in its own readers.

A translation of dynamic equivalence will, therefore, communicate less about the cultural frame in which the source text belongs than a translation of formal equivalence. In the former, differences between cultures are minimized, so that the readers can achieve a good understanding of the message without necessarily having or acquiring a knowledge of the source culture. The latter will not attempt to reduce the gap between the two cultural contexts involved, and will hence convey more information about the source culture, at the same time that it keeps closely to the nuances of the source language (idioms, proverbs, verbal systems, etc.).

From the distinction above, it is easy to see that formal equivalence may lack in intelligibility, whereas dynamic equivalence will give as a result not only a more easily comprehensible text but also a more natural-sounding one. In Nida's own words, dynamic-equivalent translation is "the closest natural equivalent to the source-language message" (1964). He was, nevertheless, aware of the restrictions on dynamic equivalence, as well as of the areas of tension between formal-equivalence and dynamic-equivalence translation.

The opposition formal vs. dynamic equivalence appears related to the age-old separation between literal and free translation. Horatius and Cicero before the Christian era, and Quintilian and Jerome in its early centuries, were the pioneers who advocated "sense for sense" translations, rather than "word for word" ones. Dynamic equivalence involves varying degrees of freedom in translation, whereas formal equivalence implies literalness of form. However, not all "free" translations aim at an equivalence of effect between the source and target texts.

It is not always possible to reproduce formal features as they appear in a given source text: certain rhetorical figures are difficult to reproduce, and the formal equivalents of elements such as puns or idioms are frequently meaningless or absurd. The deficiencies of formal equivalence translation are obvious in cases like those.

However, a number of objections can be also raised against the principle of dynamic equivalence, the most important of them being the actual impossibility of knowing how the original text affected its readers. If we focus on this question from a diachronic perspective, the unfeasibility of dynamic equivalence becomes more apparent, since a translator that followed its principles would be set to produce in the readers of the target text the same effect that the original caused decades, centuries, or even millennia ago in a readership that belonged to an entirely different cultural frame.

The issue of the distinction between dynamic and formal equivalence can be traced back to the early years of the 18th century, when Perrot d'Ablancourt (whose translations, it is worth remembering, were the first to deserve the denomination of "belles infidèles") described his method as being based on an elementary form of the principle of equivalent effect. In 1813, Friedrich Schleiermacher also referred to the fact that producing an impression similar to that which the original text produced in its readers should be the ruling principle for translators and interpreters. He also distinguishes, in his own terms, between source-text oriented and target-text oriented translations.

In the 20th century, many experts have subscribed, implicitly or explicitly, to a differentiation between formal and dynamic equivalence: Alexander Souter, Vladimir Procházka, Ronald A. Knox, C.W. Orr, Oliver Edwards, Leonard Forster, Edmond Cary and the aforementioned E.A. Nida, among others. Others proposed alternative models (Otto Kade's distinguishes between total, facultative, approximative, and nil equivalence; Anton Popovic between linguistic, paradigmatic, stylistic and textual equivalence; Albrecht Neubert proposes that translation equivalence should be considered a semiotic category, which embraces a syntactic, semantic and pragmatic dimension).

On the other hand, others have challenged the significance of any such approach: Vladimir Nabokov abhorred any translation method beyond what he called "clumsy literalism". Sándor Hervey and Ian Higgins proposed as recently as 1992 an alternative interpretation of "equivalence" as a term for "not dissimilar in relevant respects", if such a concept was to be used in a methodology of translation. The prevailing posture in Translation Studies is that of denying the validity of a differentiation between formal and dynamic equivalence: instead, an emphasis is laid on the problems of transferring the semantic content from the source language into the target language, and on the exploration of the issue of equivalence of literary texts.

RAQUEL DE PEDRO

Further Reading

Bassnett, Susan and André Lefevere (editors), *Translation, History and Culture*, London and New York: Pinter, 1990

Bassnett-McGuire, Susan, *Translation Studies*, London and New York: Methuen, 1980; revised edition, London and New York: Routledge, 1991

Hervey, Sándor and Ian Higgins, *Thinking Translation: A Course in Translation Method, French to English*, London and New York: Routledge, 1992

Lefevere, André (editor and translator), *Translation / History / Culture: A Sourcebook*, London and New York: Routledge, 1992

Nida, Eugene A., *Toward a Science of Translating*, Leiden: E.J. Brill, 1964

Nida, Eugene A. and Charles R. Taber, *The Theory and Practice of Translation*, Leiden: E.J. Brill, 1969

Venuti, Lawrence, *The Translator's Invisibility: A History of Translation*, London and New York: Routledge, 1995

Desiderius Erasmus c.1466–1536

Dutch (Neo-Latin) humanist, theologian and satirist

Biography

Erasmus was a supremely erudite and prolific scholar and a brilliant stylist. He was born in Rotterdam c.1466, but active in many countries, including England, though for the most part he chose to be independent and turned down offers from many illustrious patrons, including Henry VIII, Francis I and the Archduke Ferdinand. His rationalistic inquiry into the Scriptures and his antagonism toward the abuses of the Church paved the way for Luther; however, Erasmus refused to take a stand either for or against Luther at the Diet of Worms. Although he never joined the reformers, he was regarded with suspicion by Catholics, and many of his writings were placed on the Index of forbidden books.

The Praise of Folly (*Moriae Encomium*, 1509, dedicated to Thomas More) is the best-known work of Erasmus. Although satire is difficult to understand outside the context of the culture that gives rise to it, understanding and enjoyment of the *Praise* is facilitated by the way it is firmly grounded in the two traditions that have been the core of Western education: the Bible and the Graeco-Roman classics. Much of the pleasure in reading the *Praise* comes from awareness of the author's virtuoso command and use of both. But the main source of this work's greatness is its incomparable irony which, complex, playful, yet ultimately never unclear, serves as masterly counterpoint to the bitter denunciation that is the main purpose of the *Praise*.

After the *Encomium*, Erasmus's best-known works are the *Enchiridion militis Christiani* (1503; *Handbook of the Militant Christian*) and the *Colloquia familiaria* (1518; *Colloquies*). He died in Basel, 12 July 1536.

The Praise of Folly

Moriae encomium, 1509

Translations

Chaloner, Sir Thomas, *The Praise of Folie: Moriae Encomium, a booke made in latine by that great clerke Erasmus Roterodame*, London: Thomas Berthelet, 1549; modern edition, edited by Clarence H. Miller for the Early English Text Society, Oxford: Oxford University Press, 1965

Copner, James, *The Praise of Folly*, London and Edinburgh: Williams and Norgate, 1878

Dean, Leonard F., *The Praise of Folly: A New Translation*, Chicago: Packard, 1946

Dolan, John P., *The Praise of Folly*, in *The Essential Erasmus*, edited, with an introduction by Dolan, New York: New American Library, 1964

Hudson, Hoyt Hopewell, *The Praise of Folly*, New York: Modern Library, 1941

Kennett, White, *Witt against Wisdom; or, A Panegyric upon Folly*,Oxford: printed by L. Lichfield for Anthony Stephens, 1683; 2nd edition, as *Moriae Encomium; or, A Panegyrick upon Folly*, London: J. Woodward, 1709; frequently reprinted without acknowledgement of the translator; modern edition, as *Erasmus in Praise of Folly*, edited by Horace Bridges, Chicago: Pascal Covici, 1925

Miller, Clarence H., *The Praise of Folly*, New Haven, Connecticut: Yale University Press, 1979

Radice, Betty, *Praise of Folly, and Letter to Martin Dorp 1515*, with an introduction and notes by A.H.T. Levi, Harmondsworth: Penguin, 1971

Wilson, John, *Mori Encomium; or, The Praise of Folly*, London: William Leak, 1668; frequently reprinted, notably with alterations and introduction by Mrs P.S. Allen, as *The Praise of Folly*, Oxford: Oxford University Press, 1913

Erasmus's Latin prose is inferior to none. Unlike humanists who modelled their style on ancients such as Cicero, he developed an unimpeachably correct Latin that was all his own. Elegance, clarity and wit are qualities a translator of Erasmus should aim for, as well as awareness of, and ability to mirror, his many sources, whether quoted directly or indirectly. In the *Praise*, Erasmus's device of putting the discourse in the mouth of Folly herself expresses different aspects of her ambiguous character and gradually allows her to undergo a profound change. This affects the tone of the satire and presents an additional challenge to the translator. Another factor is that the Latin of the discourse is economical, yet Folly sounds garrulous; a translation should be concise but talkative. Finally, there is the need to achieve readability for the general public, along with accuracy for the ever increasing number of scholars who do not read Latin.

The older translations retain historic interest. They are part of the world in which Erasmus was a living force rather than a remote "classic".

CHALONER'S (1549) is the first English translation of the *Praise*. It is "a pleasure to read, but only if one appreciates pre-Elizabethan language and is not discouraged by rather inchoate sentences" (Hudson, *Praise*). Miller's edition of Chaloner is magisterial.

WILSON (1668), a Restoration playwright, has an affinity for Erasmus's wit: his own comedies, *The Cheats* and *The Projectors*, also depict varieties of ridiculous or contemptible behavior. Wilson translates Erasmus into lively, imaginative English that is a pleasure to read. However, this is not an exact translation and should be enjoyed for its own sake rather than as an aid to scholarship. Readers ought to beware of Allen's edition: the corrections are far outbalanced by expurgations.

KENNETT'S version (1683) is so free and idiosyncratic that it is altogether unreliable. Bridges's edition makes only a few corrections. This translation should be avoided, although it was widely used in the 18th and 19th centuries.

Copies of COPNER (1878) are extremely rare. There is one in the British Museum and one in the Bodleian Library. None seems to be obtainable in the United States.

HUDSON (1941) uses Jean Le Clerc's edition of the Latin, (1703) and that of I.B. Kan (1898). He acknowledges his use of Wilson's translation. The text is followed by a helpful outline and an analysis of the *Praise* in terms of classical rhetoric.

Hudson divides the text into 40 sections, thus facilitating orientation and reference. The translation is for the most part plodding, occasionally effective.

DEAN's version (1946), prepared for instructional purposes, also uses Le Clerc's edition, and acknowledges dependence on Hudson's as well as Chaloner's, Kennett's, and Wilson's translations but is not slavishly dependent on them. It can be recommended because of its sprightly tone, which brings across the good-humored aspect of Folly's character. This is not the best translation, but enjoyable.

DOLAN's version (1964) is annoying. There is a claim on the cover that the book includes the full text of *The Praise of Folly*, but if one reads the introduction one finds at the end a statement that there are "paraphrases and deletions to accommodate the modern reader". The chief advantage of this volume is that it enables the general reader to evaluate the *Praise* in the context of a number of other Erasmian writings, but the omissions and adaptations border on falsification. The style of the translation is readable, and Folly's *bonhomie* quite apparent.

RADICE's translation (1971) is to be commended for its charm and elegance: Folly is made to sound appropriately conversational yet learned too – as she should. Radice primarily uses Kan's edition, with some others, and the notes (compiled by A.H.T. Levi, who also is the author of the introduction) incorporate the commentary of Erasmus's contemporary Gerard Lijster, which was based on Erasmus's own comments. Radice uses division into chapters first adopted in the 18th century, which, although no part of the text as Erasmus wrote it, facilitates finding one's place and referring to passages. She includes a translation of Erasmus's letter to Martin Dorp, essential for a fuller understanding of the *Praise*.

MILLER's translation (1979) is conscientious, scholarly, and reliable. It is based on the most sound and thorough modern edition of the Latin, prepared by Miller himself (in *Opera Omnia Desiderii Erasmi Roterodami*, vol. 4.3, Amsterdam: North-Holland Publishing Company, 1979). The letter to Martin Dorp is included, and the excellent notes are built around Lijster's commentary. Italics are used to designate the use of Greek within the Latin text. This version should be any scholar's choice, although Radice makes for better reading.

ZOJA PAVLOVSKIS-PETIT

Further Reading

Devereaux, E.J., *English Translations of Erasmus to 1700*, Oxford: Oxford Bibliographical Society, 1968

Hudson, H.H., "Current English Translations of *The Praise of Folly*", *Philological Quarterly*, 20 (1941) pp. 250–65

Miller, Clarence H., "Current English Translations of *The Praise of Folly*: Some Corrections", *Philological Quarterly*, 45 (1966) pp. 718–33

Erotica in English Translation

Erotica, the pejorative term for which is pornography, may be considered as a literary genre concerned with the depiction of human sexuality, frequently for the purposes of sexual stimulation. Like other genres, it has its own history, acknowledged masterpieces, bibliographies and critical studies. Unlike other genres, it is one whose existence has, for obvious reasons, generally been clandestine. It is also a literary form that has relied, at times extensively, on translation.

The best-known author of erotic literature in Renaissance Europe was Pietro Aretino (1492–1556). Paradoxically, Aretino is primarily remembered for a work in which he played merely a subsidiary role: a series of 16 erotic engravings, commissioned to order by Giulio Romano from Marcantonio Raimondi in 1524, which earned the disapproval of Pope Clement VII. Aretino's connection with the affair is that he was responsible for the composition of a series of sonnets, the *Sonetti lussuriosi* (1527), intended to accompany the engravings which quickly became known as the "Postures of Aretino".

However, although knowledge of the "Postures of Aretino" was reasonably widespread in Britain throughout the 17th century, there would not seem to have been any serious attempt to translate the *Sonnetti lussuriosi* until the late 19th century. Wayland Young refers to an unidentified English translation attributed (almost certainly incorrectly) to Oscar Wilde. Samuel Putnam's translation of *The Works of Aretino* (1926) is now considered periphrastic and inadequate.

The earliest trace of Aretino's work in English is *The Crafty Whore; or, The Misery and Iniquity of Bawdy Houses Laid Open* (London: Henry Marsh, 1658). This is a free rendition of the third dialogue of the first part of his *Ragionamenti* (originally published in Venice between 1534 and 1536). Since this particular dialogue deals with prostitution, it has frequently been translated and published independently.

The dialogue form adopted by Aretino in the *Ragionamenti* exerted a strong influence on subsequent erotic writing whether in Italian, French or English. In 1655, *L'École des filles* (attributed to Michel Millot) – described by Samuel Pepys in his diary in January 1668 as the "most bawdy, lewd book that ever I saw" (though this did not prevent him from succumbing and purchasing a copy) – followed the same form. As with Aretino's *Sonetti lussuriosi*, the absence of an immediate translation (though one, no longer extant, would seem to have been forthcoming around 1680) would perhaps indicate that the English-speaking readership for such works tended to be an educated one.

However, *Vénus dans le cloître; ou, La Religieuse en chemise* (attributed to Jean Barrin), which also adopts the dialogue form, was translated into English, as *Venus in the Cloyster; or, The Nun in Her Smock*, the same year as it was published in France (1683). A single copy of this translation has survived. A later version, again as *Venus in the Cloister; or, The Nun in her Smock*, attributed to Robert Samber, is generally considered a good, workmanlike translation. Published in 1725 by Edmund Curll, this book was the object of a prosecution that brought into existence the concept of obscene libel.

These two works – *L'École des filles* and *Vénus dans le cloître* – are indicative that, despite Aretino's celebrity, 17th-century England looked to France rather than Italy for its most popular items of erotic literature. This was a tendency that would continue throughout the 18th and 19th centuries – and, indeed, into the 20th. However, mention should also be made of Nicolas Chorier's *Satyra sotadica*, originally published under the Latin title of *Aloisiae Sigeae Toletanae Satyra sotadica de arcanis amoris & veneris* (c.1660) and itself purporting to be a translation. Translated into French in 1680 as *L'Académie des dames* and into English two years later as *The School of Women* (a version that would seem to be lost), this collection is considered by Foxon to be the most pornographically advanced – it contains scenes of lesbianism, seduction, sodomy and various forms of sadism – of the three sets of dialogues considered here.

By the mid-18th century, the translation of French erotic texts was standard practice. Thus, Gervaise de Latouche's *Histoire de Dom B ..., portier des Chartreux* (c.1741–42) was available to English readers as early as 1743. With its new emphasis on sexual fulfilment, some commentators claim this to be the most important pornographic novel in the period immediately prior to John Cleland's *Memoirs of a Woman of Pleasure* (1748–49). Another erotic tradition, the licentious "oriental" tale (deriving from Galland's translation of the *Arabian Nights*), is to be seen in Crébillon fils's *Le Sopha* (1742, translated 1742) and Diderot's *Les bijoux indiscrets* (1748, translated 1749). By 1801, the English translation of *Le Sopha* had gone through some 18 editions. (Since 1927, Bonamy Dobrée's elegant translation, *The Sofa*, has generally been regarded as the standard English version.)

Some recent historians, notably Robert Darnton, have further argued that erotic texts of this period may have served a wider purpose than simply providing sexual stimulation. Indeed, with their tendency to de-legitimize the status quo and open the way to radical change, it could be that such texts served to ferment the French Revolution. Boyer d'Argens's *Thérèse philosophe* (1748) – a strange mixture of traditional pornography and metaphysical dialogue – is considered by this school as a key text in the transformation of the intellectual topography of France in the mid-18th century. An English translation, as *The Philosophical Theresa*, was reputedly published in 1750; and there were a number of 19th-century editions. More recently, Darnton provides substantial extracts in a modern translation in his 1996 study.

Although he was largely neglected during the 19th century, the name of the Marquis de Sade has nowadays become synonymous with erotic writing. The re-evaluation of Sade's oeuvre – which is generally considered today to be not only the first and most extensive study of *psychopathia sexualis* but also essential reading for those who wish to understand the political and intellectual background of the late 18th century – began in the late 1920s and early 1930s. Notable in this context are Maurice Heine's authoritative editions of *Historiettes, contes et fabliaux* (1927); *Les Infortunes de la vertu* (1930); and *Les 120 Journées de Sodome; ou, L'École du libertinage* (1931–35). There is a detachment, a lack of sentimentality, and a cruelty about Sade's writing on sex, however, that makes it entirely different from the mass of erotic fiction. Indeed, so closely does the author associate violence and pain with the erotic act that some commentators consider it to have an anti-aphrodisiac effect.

Chanover's bibliography of Sade's writing lists only two 19th-century translations into English. However, although enjoying a lower profile in Britain than elsewhere in Europe, Sade was not entirely unknown: the publisher George Cannon presumably considered that there were sufficient readers in London to justify a French-language edition of *Juliette* in 1830 (and was promptly jailed for six months for his trouble). According to Coward, strict censorship laws in Britain prevented the importation even of severely bowdlerized American translations of Sade's work until 1983.

Although British booksellers were unable to benefit from it, there was an explosion of Anglo-Saxon interest in Sade's work in the US during the second half of the 1960s. Thus, Grove Press of New York reissued (earlier editions were published in Paris in the 1950s) *The Complete Justine, Philosophy in the Bedroom and Other Writings,* compiled and translated by Richard Seaver and Austryn Wainhouse in 1965; this was followed by *The 120 Days of Sodom and Other Writings* (including seminal essays on Sade by Simone de Beauvoir and Pierre Klossowski) by the same editors and translators in 1966; and *Juliette*, translated by Austryn Wainhouse alone, in 1968. Highly acclaimed at the time, not only for the accuracy, comprehensiveness and readability of the translations but also for the scholarly academic apparatus that accompanied them, these three collections of Sade's most substantial writings are unlikely to be superseded for some time to come.

Given the strict censorship laws in operation in the UK at this time, the works by Sade brought out by British publishers have considerably less erotic interest. Thus, Margaret Crosland has edited a number of collections, also reliably translated, of Sade's shorter fiction for the publisher Peter Owen. These include: the *De Sade Quartet* (1963; reissued as *The Mystified Magistrate*, 1986), drawn from the author's *Contes et fabliaux d'un troubadour provençal du XVIII siècle*; *The Gothic Tales* (1965; reissued 1990) and *Crimes of Love* (1996), which together reproduce eight of the 11 stories included by Sade in his four-volume collection *Les Crimes de l'amour: Nouvelles historiques et tragiques*, published in 1800. The same publisher has also issued a volume of *Selected Letters* edited by Margaret Crosland and translated by W.J. Strachan (1965; reprinted 1992). Finally, David Coward's *The Misfortunes of Virtue and Other Early Tales* (Oxford: Oxford University Press, 1992) presents the title story (the first of Sade's increasingly sadistic reworkings of the story of Justine) together with a selection of tales from Sade's *Contes et fabliaux d'un troubadour provençal du XVIII siècle*. Coward's work as a translator is always meticulous, as are his annotations and other critical materials.

The close links between the French and English clandestine book trade continued throughout the 19th century. Indeed, by the end of the century, such legendary "under-the-counter" publishers as Leonard Smithers (who brought out arcane editions of Catullus, the *Priapeia* and Sir Richard Burton's translation of the *Arabian Nights*), Charles Hirsch and Charles Carrington all carried on business from Paris at one time. Carrington, for example, was responsible for the first English translation – or rather translation and adaptation, since the story is updated and the setting relocated, surprisingly, to Sheffield – of Restif de la Bretonne's *L'Anti-Justine; ou, Les Délices de l'amour* (1798) as *The Double Life of Cuthbert Cockerton* (1895). Only one copy of this work is known to exist, and the identity of the translator is open to speculation.

This tradition of publishing clandestine or semi-clandestine works out of Paris was continued through the 1930s by Jack Kahane's Obelisk Press and further continued by his son, Maurice Girodias, who founded the Olympia Press in 1953. The first batch of Olympia titles announced the future editorial direction of the firm: a two-volume edition of Henry Miller's *Plexus* accompanied by a raft of translated erotic and sado-erotic French classics, including the first translation of Sade's *La Philosophie dans le boudoir* (as *The Bedroom Philosophers*); Guillaume Apollinaire's *Les Exploits d'un jeune Don Juan* (*Amorous Exploits of a Young Rakehell*) and Georges Bataille's *L'Histoire de l'oeil* (*Tales of Satisfied Desire*). Indeed, Girodias's contribution to the dissemination of major erotic texts in English translation should not be under-emphasized. Austryn Wainhouse's translations of Sade's *120 Days of Sodom* (translated 1954), *Justine* (translated 1953) and *Juliette* (translated 1958–65) were all published by Olympia, the last two in the Traveller's Companion series, as was a new translation by him of Restif de la Bretonne's *L'Anti-Justine* under the title of *Pleasures and Follies of a Good-Natured Libertine* (1955). Among more contemporary works, Alex Trocchi, under the pseudonym Oscar Mole, translated Guillaume Apollinaire's *Les Onze Mille Verges* as *The Debauched Hospodar* (1953); Austryn Wainhouse translated Georges Bataille's *Madame Edwarda* as *The Naked Beast at Heaven's Gate* (1956) and there was an anonymous translation of Cocteau's homosexual vignettes *Le Livre blanc* as *A White Book* (1957). Maurice Girodias in collaboration with Jean-Jacques Pauvert was also involved in the simultaneous publication of the first English and French editions of the pseudonymous *Histoire d'O* in 1954.

Underlying much of this activity was the growing interest in Sade's thought and writing. Apollinaire had demonstrated that the erotic and the avant-garde had much in common towards the end of the first decade of the new century. In 1907, he published two extraordinary erotic texts of his own: *Les Exploits d'un jeune Don Juan* and *Les Onze Mille Verges*. The former is a novel of juvenile sexual initiation, a common theme in erotic writing, in which the hero successively copulates with his mother, aunt, sisters and various servants. Francis Steegmuller, Apollinaire's biographer, cannot help wondering if the novel is not also one of the author's anti-Symbolist parodies, the target being in this case Henri de Régnier. If this is so, *Les Onze Mille Verges* presumably is having some fun at the expense of the Marquis de Sade. In any event, the principal actors are motivated only by sensations that compel them to participate in the most extreme activities. Both novels by Apollinaire are available in a more recent translation by Alexis Lykiard under the title *Flesh Unlimited* (London: Creation Books, 1995). The year following their original publication, Apollinaire became editor for Georges and Robert Briffaut's widely diffused "Maîtres de l'Amour" collection of erotica, which included anthologies of writings by authors such as Sade, Aretino and John Cleland.

The Surrealists were also fascinated not only by Sade but by sexuality in general. Robert Desnos's *La Liberté ou l'amour!* of 1927 (translated by Terry Hale as *Liberty of Love!* in 1993) is not only the last automatic text of early Surrealism but an erotic quest of unparalleled proportions. This was followed in 1928 by two very different surrealist erotic texts: *Le Con d'Irène* (generally attributed to Louis Aragon) and Georges Bataille's terrifying *Histoire de l'oeil*. Aragon's voyeuristic fantasy has been translated by Alexis Lykiard under the less direct title of *Irène* (1986; an earlier translation by Lowell Bair was published by Grove Press in 1969), while Joachim Neugroschal's 1979 translation of Bataille's *Story of the Eye* has effectively superseded the Olympia Press edition.

The vast activity in the field of the publication of erotic texts during the past 100 years or so continues to make its presence felt by means of the numerous re-editions of earlier works and translations. At the time of writing, for example, all three Grove Press editions of Sade's writing mentioned earlier are in print: *The 120 Days of Sodom and Other Writings* (Aldershot: Arena, 1989); *Juliette* (Aldershot: Arena, 1991); *Justine* (London: Arrow, 1991). In some cases, new translations are also being commissioned by niche publishers such as the London-based Delectus Books, which specializes in fin-de-siècle texts. There would also seem to be signs of growth in the area of gay and lesbian fiction in translation.

TERRY HALE

Further Reading

Chanover, E. Pierre, *The Marquis de Sade: A Bibliography*, Metuchen, New Jersey: Scarecrow Press, 1973

Coward, David, introduction to *The Marquis de Sade: The Misfortunes of Virtue and Other Early Tales*, translated by Coward, Oxford and New York: Oxford University Press, 1992

Darnton, Robert, *The Forbidden Best-Sellers of Pre-Revolutionary France*, New York: Norton, 1995; London: HarperCollins, 1996

Foxon, David, *Libertine Literature in England, 1660–1745*, New Hyde Park, New York: University Books, 1965

Kearney, Patrick J., *The Private Case: An Annotated Bibliography of the Private Case Erotica Collection in the British Library*, London: Landesman, 1981

Kearney, Patrick J., *A History of Erotic Literature*, London: Macmillan, 1982

St Jorre, John de, *The Good Ship Venus: The Erotic Voyage of the Olympia Press*, London: Hutchinson, 1994

Steegmuller, Francis, *Apollinaire: Poet among the Painters*, London: Hart-Davis, and New York: Farrar Straus, 1963

Thompson, Roger, *Unfit for Modest Ears: A Study of Pornographic, Obscene and Bawdy Works Written or Published in England in the Second Half of the Seventeenth Century*, London: Macmillan, 1979

Wagner, Peter, *Eros Revived: Erotica of the Enlightenment in England and America*, London: Secker and Warburg, 1988

Young, Wayland, *Eros Denied: Sex in Western Society*, New York: Grove Press, 1964; London: Weidenfeld, 1965

Sergei Aleksandrovich Esenin 1895–1925

Russian poet

Biography

Born in the village of Konstantinovo, Riazan' province, 3 October 1895, the son of a peasant family. He attended local schools from 1904 until 1912, when he moved to Moscow. He worked at Sytin's printing house, occasionally attending lectures at Shaniavskii University. He lived with Anna Izriadnova from 1913 to 1915, and had one son. Esenin had his first poetic work published in Moscow journals by 1914. By 1915 he was living in Petrograd, where his poetry began attracting national critical acclaim, and where he met Aleksandr Blok, Sergei Gorodetskii and the peasant poet Nikolai Kliuev, with whom he formed a close friendship and literary alliance. Esenin spent 1916–17 in military service in Tsarskoe Selo; he deserted from the army after the 1917 February Revolution. In 1917 he married Zinaida Raikh, whom he divorced in 1921, and had one daughter and one son. He moved back to Moscow in 1918 and formed a close friendship with the poet Anatolii Mariengof. In early 1919 Esenin was a founder member of the avant-garde Imaginist movement. He frequented the literary cafés of Moscow during this period, giving readings of his work and drinking heavily. He issued several volumes of his own verse, critical theory, and a play (often under the imprint "Imazhinisty"), and contributed to numerous Imaginist collections between 1919 and 1922. Esenin married the dancer Isadora Duncan in 1922 and travelled with her on a dance tour of western Europe and the United States from 1922 to 1923. He returned to Russia in 1923 and wrote prolifically, including poems espousing pro-Soviet sentiment. His controversial poetic cycle *Moskva kabatskaia* [Moscow of the Taverns], written after his return to Russia, was published in 1924; Esenin separated from the Imaginists at this time. He left Isadora Duncan in 1924, but they did not divorce. He travelled in the Caucasus in 1924 and 1925. He had a son in 1924 from a relationship with Nadezhda Vol'pin, and married Sof'ia Tolstaia in 1925. Towards the end of his life he became increasingly depressed, rootless and alcoholic, and took cocaine. He was admitted to hospital in 1925 having suffered a nervous breakdown. He died, evidently from suicide by hanging, in a Leningrad hotel, 28 December 1925.

Esenin was a prolific poet, and his work, which spoke essentially from a peasant viewpoint, achieved popular success during his lifetime and afterwards, despite official disapproval of his work by the communist Soviet authorities for many years. His first collection of poems, *Radunitsa* (*All Souls' Day*) was published in 1916; there were two subsequent editions of the collection, in which Esenin made different selections of poems, in 1918 and 1921. Of his mature work, his *Ispoved' khuligana* [Confessions of a Hooligan], 1920, and the verse cycle *Moskva kabatskaia*, 1924, both describing city low-life of the period in Russia, are the best-known examples.

Translations

Anthologies

Bowra, C.M. (editor), *A Book of Russian Verse*, various translators, London: Macmillan, 1943; reprinted Westport, Connecticut: Greenwood Press, 1971 (includes 3 items, 2 by Bowra)

Bowra, C.M. (editor), *A Second Book of Russian Verse*, various translators, London: Macmillan, 1948; reprinted Westport, Connecticut: Greenwood Press, 1971 (includes 5 items, 4 by Bowra)

Carlisle, Olga Andreyev and Rose Styron, in their *Modern Russian Poetry*, New York: Viking Press, 1972 (4 items, most by Styron)

Deutsch, Babette and Avrahm Yarmolinsky, in their *Modern Russian Poetry: An Anthology*, New York: Harcourt Brace, 1921; London: John Lane, 1923 (4 items)

Deutsch, Babette and Avrahm Yarmolinsky, in their *Russian Poetry: An Anthology*, revised edition, New York: International Publishers, 1927 (6 items, 4 of which duplicate the 4 included in *Modern Russian Poetry*)

Deutsch, Babette, in *Two Centuries of Russian Verse: An Anthology from Lomonosov to Voznesensky*, edited by Avrahm Yarmolinsky and Deutsch, New York: Random House, 1966 (10 items). This anthology is a revised and expanded version of their *An Anthology of Russian Verse, 1812–1960*, New York: Doubleday, 1962, which in turn is revised and expanded from their *A Treasury of Russian Verse*, New York: Macmillan, 1949. The latter was revised from their *Russian Poetry: An Anthology*, New York: International Publishers, 1927: see above.

Glad, John and Daniel Weissbort (editors), *Twentieth-Century Russian Poetry*, Iowa City: University of Iowa Press, 1992 (6 items, all by Nigel Stott); this is an expanded edition of the editors' *Russian Poetry: The Modern Period*, Iowa City: University of Iowa Press, 1978)

Lindsay, Jack, in his *Russian Poetry 1917–1955*, with an introduction, London: Bodley Head, 1957 (3 items)

Markov, Vladimir and Merrill Sparks, in *Modern Russian Poetry: An Anthology with Verse Translations* (parallel texts), edited with an introduction by Markov & Sparkes, London: MacGibbon and Kee, 1966; Indianapolis: Bobbs Merrill, 1967 (8 items)

Obolensky, Dimitri, in *The Penguin Book of Russian Verse* (parallel texts), edited, with an introduction by Obolensky, Harmondsworth: Penguin, 1962 (7 items)

Reavey, George and Marc Slonim, in their *Soviet Literature: An Anthology*, London: Wishart, 1933; New York: Covici Friede, 1934 (4 items); reprinted Westport, Connecticut: Greenwood Press, 1972

Todd, Albert C. and Max Hayward, with Daniel Weissbort (editors), *Twentieth Century Russian Poetry: Silver and Steel: An Anthology*, selected, with an introduction by Evgeny Estushenko, New York: Doubleday, 1993 (15 items, translated by Weissbort and Geoffrey Thurley)

Selections

Davies, Jessie, *Sergei Esenin: Selected Poems* (uses Russian titles), with an introduction, Bakewell: Hub, 1979 (144 items)

Davies, Jessie, *Esenin: A Biography in Memoirs, Letters and Documents, with Previously Untranslated Prose Works and Correspondence*, Ann Arbor: Ardis, 1982

Tempest, Peter, *Selected Poetry* (parallel texts), Moscow: Progress, 1982 (86 lyrics and the long poems "Anna Snegina" and "The Man in Black", as well as excerpts from other works)

Thurley, Geoffrey, *Confessions of a Hooligan: Fifty Poems*, with an introduction, Cheadle: Carcanet Press, 1973 (50 items)

Poetry

Radunitsa, 1916

Davies, Jessie, *All Souls' Day / Radunitsa, 1916: In Parallel Text* (includes photo-reproduction of first edition), Liverpool: Lincoln Davies, 1991 (the 33 poems of Esenin's first published book)

Goluben', 1920

Davies, Jessie, *Azure / Goluben'* (parallel text; photo-reproduction of first edition), Liverpool: Lincoln Davies, 1991 (the 34 poems of the original collection)

The most popular Russian poet since Pushkin, quoted by intellectuals and factory workers, grandmothers and adolescents, despite his extraordinary accessibility Sergei Esenin is subtle and original in his use of imagery as well as rhyme and rhythm. Many of his poems are notable for their heartrending confrontation of suffering and empathy with nature. His poetry is rooted in Russian folklore and folk idiom combined with the elevated language and mysticism of Eastern Orthodoxy; yet his sense of alienation is thoroughly modern, as is his self-loathing and insistence on experiencing extreme degradation. The sect of the Old Believers – the most traditionally-minded of all Russians – forms his native background; the highly self-conscious and sophisticated literary movement of Imagism his chosen milieu. Finally, his deep love of the Russian village (Esenin was known as a Peasant Poet) and his ambivalence in the face of the Russian Revolution make this tender and abusive "poet of youth and death" unique in Russian, and world, literature.

Esenin is extremely difficult to translate. His remarkable combinations of idiom have no equivalent in English, and thus the rich resonance of his vocabulary, with its multiple layers of folk, Church, literary, and etymological allusion, readily recognizable in the original, is almost entirely lost in translations. For instance, the title of the collection *Goluben'*, that DAVIES (1991) adequately but insufficiently renders as *Azure*, is a word made up by the poet on the basis of the ordinary Russian for "light blue" (*goluboi*). In English "azure" is a literary word and part of the existing vocabulary. Furthermore, Esenin's *goluben'* bears similarity to the related word for "dove" (*golub'*) and thus connects with nature and also carries Christian connotations. "Azure" conveys none of this. Esenin's extraordinary musicality too defies transfer, for it depends on seemingly simple but actually remarkably varied and effective use of rhyme and rhythm. In modern English verse, rhyme is mistrusted. Yet translators realize they must be faithful to Esenin's constant use of it and at the same time preserve the accessibility of Esenin's vocabulary. As a result, they fall upon trite rhyme schemes. Worse still, so as to make the translation rhyme at all and the rhythm come out even, they tamper with the arresting imagery, they condense or expand, ruin the effect, and arrive at results that sound banal.

DEUTSCH & YARMOLINSKY (1921, 1927) have done much to familiarize English readers with Russian poetry. (Yarmolinsky wrote prose paraphrases of the Russian texts; Deutsch turned these into rhymed English.) However, there is a sameness about their translations; poets of diverse gifts and epochs all sound like third- or fourth-rate Victorians. Esenin himself had a low opinion of their collection, *Modern Russian Poetry* (see McVay's survey). The same criticism applies to YARMOLINSKY's *Two Centuries of Russian Verse* (1966) as it does to his and Deutsch's other anthologies. Some of the translations in this relatively late collection are different from their earlier versions but hardly better.

REAVEY & SLONIM (1933) are uneven. They seek to replicate rhythm but not rhyme; at best, their use of rhythm is so skilful that one seems to be reading rhymed poems. At other times the rhythm breaks down and then the results are clumsy. The best poem here is "The Tramp". In "Tavern Moscow", one of Esenin's most important pieces, the lack of rhyme, which in the original carries much of the cynicism, makes the translation merely a string of vulgarities, all the powerful poetry gone.

BOWRA's translations (1943, 1948), unfortunately few, are the best. He succeeds in not making Esenin sound like Burns or Housman. The "Song about a Bitch" (1948, *A Second Book of Russian Verse*), although the title sounds odd in English (cf. Weissbort's shortened but more effective "The Bitch"), comes as close as can be to Esenin's emotion and his poetic effects. This is a powerful translation of a heartbreaking poem. Bowra used rhymed, rhythmical verse. However, he does not succeed with what he calls "Last Lines", the poem Esenin wrote before killing himself; this simple but wrenching poem tests a translator as none other. Bowra's collaborator, R.M. HEWITT, is markedly inferior to him.

The multi-talented, imaginative LINDSAY (1957) comes up with fairly free rhymed versions. He succeeds better than some others because he allows himself to depart to some extent from Esenin's rhythms. This gives him more freedom and incidentally conveys something of Esenin's occasional gaucherie.

OBOLENSKY's literal renderings (1962) are in prose. They are unimaginative and only of value as a "trot" for students.

MARKOV & SPARKS (1966) employ both rhyme and rhythm, although for the most part they make only even lines rhyme. The overall effect is awkward: to facilitate what rhyme they do put in, they squeeze words into syntax unnatural for English, and some of the vocabulary too is contrived (for instance, "I have no regrets, retreats or weepings" for one of Esenin's best known lines, "Ne zhaleiu, ne zovu, ne plachu").

The free verse renderings in CARLISLE & STYRON's anthology (1972) are prosy, awkward, and often imprecise.

THURLEY (1973) tries to render Esenin's rhymes and rhythms but does not achieve consistently rhymed effects. Lack of distinction in this translation is especially regrettable because Thurley's introduction shows he understands this poetry and loves it.

Although DAVIES (1979, 1982, 1991, 1991) claims that her translations are only a teaching aid, they are clearly a labor of love. Her introduction to the *Selected Poems* shows excellent understanding of the poet and his world, as well as his technique. However, the translations (in partly rhymed verse and in rhythms approximating the originals) are syntactically contrived. The second stanza of Esenin's last poem (in *Selected Poems*) receives the best rendition imaginable, but the first stanza is below par. Still, for any reader ignorant of Russian, Davies is indispensable, and one hopes she will continue to work on these supremely difficult texts.

TEMPEST (1982) uses rhythm and rhyme. The quality ranges from indifferent to worse (as in "Au revoir, my friend, au revoir, / Dear fellow, you're here in my breast" for the beginning of the grippingly confessional final poem). To facilitate the indispensable rhyme, Tempest resorts to vagueness and to padding. Moreover, he seems to lack sensitivity to Esenin's loss of identity in empathizing with nature. (For instance, where Tempest has "Ever blest was I to be accorded / Time for blossoming before I died", Weissbort manages much better to obscure the self: "May you be blessed for evermore / That you came – to flourish and to die".)

The pallid unrhymed verse of STOTT in GLAD & WEISSBORT's anthology (1992) reads like prose. The aroma and color of the original are lost. Since rhyme and rhythm are not observed, there is no justification for imprecision (for instance, "headgear" for *shapka*, "cap").

TODD & HAYWARD's anthology (1993) promises much: the introduction is written by Evtushenko, who is also responsible for the selection of poems. The translations of Esenin, by WEISSBORT and THURLEY, are in free verse, some poems partly rhymed. They are prosy but precise and often more effective than the more "poetic" versions. (THURLEY's renditions here are not identical with the ones in *Confessions of a Hooligan*; they are improved.)

ZOJA PAVLOVSKIS-PETIT

Further Reading

McVay, Gordon, "S.A. Esenin in England and North America", *Russian Literature Triquarterly*, 8 (1974) pp. 518–39

See also translator's note in Davies, *Selected Poems* (1979), and the introduction to Thurley

---

Estonian

Literary Translation into English

In the area of the present-day Estonian Republic (*Eesti Vabariik*), Estonian has been spoken since around the 12th century. Estonian is a Finno-Ugrian language, closely related to Finnish and more tenuously to Hungarian. While Estonian has no structural links with German and Swedish, it contains many loanwords from these languages owing to the Baltic German class of landowners once prominent in the region and to Estonia's occupation by Sweden (1721–1920). Many shipping terms are Dutch, because of Hanseatic links with the parts of the Baltic littoral where Dutch and Low German are spoken. Also a much smaller number of loanwords have entered the language from Russian during the Soviet era. Present-day loans come from Finnish and English. Estonian is not connected to the Baltic languages, Latvian and Lithuanian, which form a group of their own, distantly related to the Slavonic languages.

Although the Bible was translated into Estonian as far back as the 16th century, literature as we know it did not emerge until around the turn of the 20th century. However, the 19th century saw a great interest among the German- and Estonian-speaking educated classes in folk poetry, echoes of which can still be found in even the most modernist works of contemporary literature today. The folk epos, the *Kalevipoeg*, was translated into German at the time it was published in the original Estonian in the 1860s.

Literary translation into Estonian increased significantly at the beginning of the 20th century when, for instance, one book by the Nobel prizewinner of the year was translated into Estonian from 1901 through to 1939, the last year of independent Estonia. Symbolism and Modernism made their influence felt, mainly coming from Germany, Scandinavia and Russia, but also from France thanks, paradoxically, to two Francophiles and Modernist poets in their own right, Johannes Semper (1892–1970) and Johannes Vares "Barbarus" (1890–1946) who, after translating French and Belgian poetry in the 1930s, were persuaded to become members of Zhdanov's Soviet puppet government in 1945. The main Anglophile of the 1930s was Ants Oras, who had studied at Cambridge, and a glance at issues of the literary magazine *Looming* [Creation] dating from the interwar years will reveal articles familiarizing Estonians with such authors writing in English as Galsworthy, Poe, Wilde, Eliot, Forster, D.H. Lawrence, Virginia Woolf, James Joyce and many others. George Meri, father of the present president, translated 32 Shakespeare plays into Estonian. Since 1990, translation into Estonian follows the pattern of translation into most West European languages, except that the advent of a new capitalist economy has allowed market forces to play a role, causing a larger proportion of works of doubtful literary value to be translated.

On the other hand, not a great deal of Estonian material of literary significance was translated into English before World

War II. Because of the presence of the educated classes of Baltic German landowners and a number of German-educated Lutheran clergymen, German had long been the language in which most translations from Estonian appeared.

After World War II, Estonian literature was rent down the middle. Many established writers escaped the Soviet and German occupations by fleeing to Sweden, North America and elsewhere. They continued to write for a few tens of thousands of potential readers and were blithely ignored by the publishing world of their host countries. One collection of the poetry of Bernard Kangro (1910–94), *Earthbound*, was published in English translation (1951) in Lund, Sweden.

At the same time, the Soviet Union sought to improve its image abroad by translating "Soviet Estonian" literature into English, now the most powerful *lingua franca* of the world. Virtually everything translated from Soviet Estonian literature thus remained under the scrutiny of the censor, who did, admittedly, let through good literature where this was not contrary to Soviet values. The only large-scale independent translation of Estonian literature into Western languages was into Finnish and, by the 1980s, Swedish, mainly thanks to a handful of individual translators in both countries, such as Juhani Salokannel, Eva Lille, Juokko Vanhanen and Ivo Iliste.

Between 1953, when W.K. Matthews, then Professor of Russian at the University of London, published his representative but linguistically idiosyncratic *Anthology of Modern Estonian Poetry* with the University of Florida Press, and 1991, when Estonia once again became independent, virtually everything published in English translation was thus of Soviet origin, sometimes even translated via the Russian. One example is the theme issue of *Soviet Literature* (8/1972) which does none the less introduce the reader to such names as the historical novelist Jaan Kross (1920–), poets Jaan Kaplinski (1941–) and Hando Runnel (1938–) and the then anthropological writer Lennart Meri (1929–), now the president of Estonia. Also Endel Nirk's survey of Estonian literature was published in English translation in two editions in the 1970s and 1980s, but this added to the frustration of the English-speaking reader who, so to speak, could look in the shop window but was not allowed to enter the shop and examine the goods. The many and interesting reviews in *Books Abroad* (later *World Literature Today*), edited by Ivar Ivask (1927–92), himself an exiled Estonian poet, only added to this frustration.

A very few reasonably representative collections of short stories did appear in English in Soviet Estonia, but these were not available through the normal Western bookselling channels. They nevertheless introduced the reader to, among others, Symbolist Friedebert Tuglas (1886–1971), psychological writer Mari Saat (1947–), zany Modernist Mati Unt (1944–), countryside writer Mats Traat (1936–) and absurdist Arvo Valton (1941–).

Not until around 1990 did English-language publishers begin to discover Estonian literature, partly because awareness had begun to seep through via contacts made with Finnish, Swedish and German publishing houses at the Frankfurt Book Fair. Since that time, the two novels and one book of stories by Jaan Kross have been published, as well as a number of stories by Mati Unt and Arvo Valton, this time in British periodicals and occasional publications such as *Leopard II* and *Passport*, and in the anthology of Scandinavian and Baltic stories *Baltic Shores*. A couple of collections by Jaan Kaplinski have also appeared with American university presses. Prose by Viivi Luik (1947–) and Rein Tootmaa (1957–) and poetry by Doris Kareva (1957–) have also appeared in anthologies of Eastern European writing. As yet, no periodical exists in the English-speaking world devoted exclusively to Estonian literature in translation as is the German quarterly *Estonia*.

ERIC DICKENS

Translations

Eelmäe, August, *The Sailors' Guardian: Estonian Short Stories*, Tallinn: Perioodika, 1984

Kangro, Bernard, *Earthbound: Selected Poems*, translated by W.K. Matthews, Lund, Sweden: Tulimuld Press, 1951

Kross, Jaan, *The Czar's Madman*, translated from the Finnish edition by Anselm Hollo, London: Harvill Press, and New York: Pantheon, 1993

Kross, Jaan, *Professor Martens' Departure*, translated by Anselm Hollo, London: Harvill Press, and New York: New Press, 1994

Kross, Jaan, *The Conspiracy and Other Stories*, translated by Eric Dickens, London: Harvill Press, 1995

Matthews, W.K. (editor and translator), *Anthology of Modern Estonian Poetry*, Gainesville: University of Florida Press, 1953

Moros, Elvina (editor), *The Love that Was*, Moscow: Progress, 1982

Poom, Ritva, *Estonian Short Stories*, edited by Kajar Paul and Darlene Reddaway, Evanston, Illinois: Northwestern University Press, 1996

Puhvel, Eduard (editor), *Estonian Short Stories*, Tallinn: Perioodika, 1981

Ruber, Vera, *et al.*, *The Glade with the Life-Giving Water*, Moscow: Progress, 1981

Soviet Literature, special issue, 8 (1972)

Valton, Arvo, *et al.*, *The Play: Short Stories by Young Estonian Writers*, Tallinn: Perioodika, 1984

Euripides, c.480–c.407/06 BC

Greek tragic dramatist

Biography

Euripides belonged to an Attic family and was born at Salamis, c.480 BC. He was well educated and knew the foremost philosophers of the time, but he did not take much part in public affairs, living quietly in Salamis. He won his first victory in a tragic contest in 441: he won only five such victories. The dramatic innovations of his 92 plays, concerning 80 of which we have some information and 18 of which survive complete, disconcerted the audiences of his day. The 18 extant texts are: *Alcestis*, *Medea*, *Hippolytus*, *Hecuba*, *Andromache*, *The Suppliant Women*, *The Children of Heracles*, *The Trojan Women*, *Helen*, *The Phoenician Women*, *Orestes*, *The Bacchae*, *Iphigenia in Aulis*, *Ion*, *Heracles*, *Iphigenia in Tauris*, *Electra* and *Cyclops*. In 408 or 407 BC Euripides went to live at the court of king Archelaus of Macedon. He died at Pella, in Macedon, c.407/06 BC.

Translations

Collections

Grene, David and Richmond Lattimore (editors), *The Complete Greek Tragedies* (Centennial Edition), vols 3–4: *Euripides*, Chicago: University of Chicago Press, 1992 (first published 1958–59)

Potter, Robert, *The Tragedies of Euripides Translated*, 2 vols, London: J. Dodsley, 1781–83

R[eynolds], V.R. (editor), *The Plays of Euripides in English*, with an introduction, 2 vols, translated by P.B. Shelley, Henry Hart Milman, Robert Potter and Michael Wodhull, London: Dent, and New York: Dutton, 1906

Vellacott, Philip, *The Plays of Euripides*, 4 vols (*Three Plays*, 1953; *The Bacchae and Other Plays*, 1954, revised 1972; *Medea and Other Plays*, 1963; *Orestes and Other Plays*, 1972), Harmondsworth and Baltimore: Penguin, 1953–72

Way, Arthur S., *The Tragedies of Euripides in English Verse*, 3 vols, London and New York: Macmillan, 1894–98 (Loeb Classical Library)

Wodhull, Michael, *The Nineteen Tragedies and Fragments of Euripides*, 4 vols, London, 1782

Selections

Davie, John, *The Alcestis and Other Plays*, with an introduction by Richard Rutherford, London and New York: Penguin, 1996 (contains *Alcestis*, *Medea*, *The Children of Heracles*, *Hippolytus*)

Davie, John, *Electra and Other Plays*, with an introduction by Richard Rutherford, London and New York: Penguin, 1998 (contains *Andromache*, *Hecabe*, *The Suppliant Women*, *Electra*, *The Trojan Women*)

Hadas, Moses, and John McLean, *The Plays of Euripides*, New York: Dial Press, 1936; as *Ten Plays*, New York: Bantam, 1960 (contains *Alcestis*, *Medea*, *Hippolytus*, *Andromache*, *Ion*, *The Trojan Women*, *Electra*, *Iphigenia among the Taurians*, *The Bacchants*, *Iphigenia at Aulis*)

Kovacs, David, *Cyclops, Alcestis, Medea* (parallel texts), Cambridge, Massachusetts: Harvard University Press, 1994 (Loeb Classical Library)

Kovacs, David, *Children of Heracles, Hippolytus, Andromache, Hecuba* (parallel texts), Cambridge, Massachusetts: Harvard University Press, 1995 (Loeb Classical Library)

Kovacs, David (editor and translator), *The Suppliant Women, Electra, Heracles* (parallel texts), Cambridge, Massachusetts: Harvard University Press, 1998 (Loeb Classical Library)

Kovacs, David (editor and translator), *The Trojan Women, Iphigenia among the Taurians, Ion* (parallel texts), Cambridge, Massachusetts: Harvard University Press, 1999 (Loeb Classical Library)

Murray, Gilbert, *The Plays of Euripides ... Translated into English Rhyming Verse*, 2 vols, Newtown, Wales: Gregynog Press, 1931 (vol. 1: *Hippolytus*, *The Bacchae*, *The Trojan Women*, *Electra*; vol. 2: *Medea*, *The Iphigenia in Tauris*, *Alcestis*, *The Rhesus*)

Euripides was paradoxically the least successful of the three great Athenian tragedians in his lifetime and is the most popular in post-classical times, if survival can be taken as an indication of popularity. He produced 92 plays but won only five victories in tragedy contests. Eighteen of these plays survive; there is some doubt about the authorship of the 19th, the *Rhesus*. His hatred of war, sympathy with women and foreigners, and hostility to conventional religion did not win him support with a conservative Athenian audience. Aristophanes in *The Frogs* mercilessly parodies the flatness of his dialogue and the vacuousness of his choral odes. Later generations found his ordinary language more comprehensible than that of Aeschylus and Sophocles, and his characters, ordinary men and women, more easy to relate to than their heroic figures.

It might seem that these qualities, whether faults or virtues, would make Euripides easy to translate, but other difficulties ensue. The playwright uses a bewildering variety of styles. The chorus pronounces odes in a high-flown fashion, sometimes, as Aristophanes saw, with little relevance to the action. They also frequently engage in dialogue with the actors. Speeches have surprising force and vigour; messengers and other humble people like Electra's labourer husband are made to speak with clear dignity. Arguments, though perhaps over-weighted with rhetoric, are intense and savage. Gods appear in the prologue and to solve problems at the end of the play; they address the audience in a formal manner, but we are uncertain of the theology behind their appearances.

In addition, the quality and variety of the 18 or 19 plays make a uniform translation unsuitable, and in fact few translators have attempted the whole of Euripides. The following account attempts to show the virtues and faults of those who have translated all or most of the plays and gives a detailed account of the *Alcestis*, the *Medea*, the *Hippolytus*, and the *Bacchae*. With exact numbers of translations into English being hard to calculate owing to the reduplication of editions, it would seem that the *Alcestis* was the individual play far more frequently translated than any other, with nearly 30 titles listed in the pre-1975 British Library Catalogue. The *Medea* has about half this number, the *Bacchae* and *Hippolytus* about a third. Equally popular are the *Hecuba* and *The Trojan Women*, two plays that depict the savagery of war and may owe part of their fame to this fact, although *Hecuba* was the first Euripides play to be translated (1746). Of the remaining plays the *Rhesus* and the *Cyclops* clearly stand outside the main canon, because the former may not be by Euripides and the latter is a satyr play. *Andromache* and the two *Heracles* plays are rarely read or translated; *Ion* and *Iphigenia in Aulis* are problem plays difficult to interpret. Equally difficult are *Helen* and *Iphigenia in Tauris*, with their foreign setting and fairy-tale atmosphere. Euripides' two plays on the story of Agamemnon, the *Electra* and *Orestes*, cannot compare with those of Aeschylus, nor can *The Suppliant Women* or *The Phoenician Women* stand up against Sophocles' handling of the Theban cycle.

Potter and Wodhull compete for the title of the first translator of Euripides in his entirety, Wodhull's version appearing in the year between Potter's two volumes. The first Everyman edition (V.R.R., 1906) combined Wodhull and Potter, adding the *Cyclops* of SHELLEY and the *Bacchae* of MILMAN. POTTER (1781–83) was a country schoolmaster and curate, an industrious versifier and a poor scholar; he was attacked by Dr Johnson for writing sheer verbiage, and his Euripides was thought to be inferior to his Aeschylus. His translations at the tail end of the 18th century show all the faults of his age and none of its virtues. His rhymes in the chorus are forced, his blank verse in the dialogue is plodding. He seems particularly fond of the word "dames", an unsuitable word for Hecuba or Helen.

WODHULL (1782) was an old-fashioned scholar and gentleman. The editor of the first Everyman edition says little is known of him and duly spells him incorrectly as Woodhull. Wodhull's version is correct but uninspired.

Although Byron is contemptuous of translation in general and the translation of Greek drama in particular, the Romantic movement was good for translation of some of Euripides' more inspired passages. SHELLEY's version of the *Cyclops* was attacked by Swinburne for its scholarship but praised for its unapproachable beauty, strength, ease, delicate simplicity and sufficiency.

We can contrast a semi-chorus in Shelley with a similar passage in WAY (1894–98), whose late Victorian translation, accurate and unreadable, was adopted by both the Everyman and the Loeb editions. Way was a good scholar but had no ear for the nuances of ordinary speech. Thus, where Shelley has

> Listen! Listen! He is coming
> A most hideous discord humming
> Drunken, museless, awkward, yelling,
> Far along his rocky dwelling.

Way, who did not translate the *Cyclops* originally, including it in the Loeb edition only, has in *The Madness of Herakles*

> Yea – in a slumber of bane,
> who hath slain his wife, hath his children slain
> With the string that sang them the bow's death strain.

It is easy to dismiss MURRAY (1931) as too Victorian, and to pour scorn on the way his facile rhymes sometimes obscure the sense, but some of his versions of Euripides' more tragic plays have real force in them. Thus in his *Trojan Women*, published separately in 1915, we can see the full horror of modern war: "O thou hast drawn thy breath from many fathers, madness, hate, red death, and every rotting poison of the sky."

HADAS & MCLEAN (1936), in prose, contains 10 of the plays in reliable literal translations that suit the strongest of the source texts. Hadas & McLean's approach is discussed below in the entry on *Medea*.

VELLACOTT (1953–72) also writes largely in prose, interspersing some blank verse for solemn passages and some rather flat rhyme for the choruses. He writes a stern preface praising ordinary language, preferring to tear clothes rather than to rend garments. This battle has largely been won, and after 50 years it is Vellacott who, like the New English Bible, seems a little old-fashioned. Here is Helen to Aphrodite: "You traffic in lust and falsehood, crooked intrigue and secret drugs are your instruments of death. Were there but measure in your power, no other gives gifts so sweet as yours."

KOVACS's new Loeb (1994, 1995, 1998, 1999) is now the one to consult by readers wanting parallel text versions of Euripides. So far he has translated 13 plays; a complete version is promised. GRENE & LATTIMORE as editors have in a sense provided a complete version, with different translators for individual plays, and there are recent Penguin versions of individual plays by DAVIE (1996, 1998).

TOM WINNIFRITH

Further Reading

Goldhill, Simon, *Reading Greek Tragedy*, Cambridge and New York: Cambridge University Press, 1986
Grube, G.M.A., *The Drama of Euripides*, London: Methuen, 1941; New York: Barnes and Noble, 1961
Vellacott, Philip, *Ironic Drama: A Study of Euripides' Method and Meaning*, London and New York: Cambridge University Press, 1975
Webster, T.B.L., *The Tragedies of Euripides*, London: Methuen, 1967

Alcestis

Alkestis, 438 BC

Translations

Arrowsmith, William, *Alcestis*, Oxford and New York: Oxford University Press, 1974
Banks, Joseph, *The Alcestis of Euripides, Translated into English Verse*, London, 1849
Beye, Charles Rowan, *Alcestis*, Englewood Cliffs, New Jersey: Prentice Hall, 1974
Browning, Robert, *Balaustion's Adventure*, London: Smith Elder, and Boston: Osgood, 1871
Conacher, D.J., *Alcestis* (parallel texts), Warminster, Wiltshire: Aris and Phillips, 1988
Fitts, Dudley and Robert Fitzgerald, *The Alcestis of Euripides*, London: Faber, and New York: Harcourt Brace, 1936

Alcestis is almost certainly the earliest of Euripides' plays to survive. Equally certainly it is the play most often translated into English. It still brings comfort to those with sick wives. It is usually seen as a story of female self-sacrifice rewarded by a happy ending. This is the plot of many 19th-century novels, including *Persuasion* and *Jane Eyre*.

A translation by the Rev. Joseph BANKS (1849), in blank verse with rhyme for the chorus, is not without merit, although rather exaggerating the purity of everybody's motives. Among other 19th-century translators we may note the fine adaptation of most of the play by Robert BROWNING (1871) in *Balaustion's Adventure*. Balaustion reports on an actual performance: she is a female character, and Admetus, the husband of Alcestis, appears in an unsympathetic light. The 20th century begins somewhat unpromisingly with a version adapted and arranged for amateur performance in girls' schools by Elsie Fogarty, but we can also note the more famous Richard Aldington as a translator (1930). Details of more modern readings follow.

FITTS & FITZGERALD's translation (1936) is a pioneer effort. The commentary at the end fights long-won battles against long-lost victims of archaic translators, like "meseems" and "forsooth". The resulting version is crisp and efficient, but solves a great many difficulties by the simple process of omission. Thus Apollo's opening speech is about half the length of the original and omits almost all proper names.

ARROWSMITH (1974) is one of the great names in translation. He, Grene and Lattimore keep on appearing in Greek drama (not unlike Aeschylus, Sophocles and Euripides), dealing with the same stories in a way that is both impressively similar and disconcertingly different. It is therefore sad that Arrowsmith's *Alcestis* is not one of his successes. He talks about rendering the spirit rather than the letter, but his version of Apollo's opening speech is full of ponderous phrases like "He doomed me to this duress".

BEYE's translation (1974) was part of an ambitious series, edited by the famous if controversial classical scholar Eric Havelock and the even more famous English expert, Maynard Mack. The general introduction on Greek tragedy and Greek metre is, however, a fairly elementary one; but there is a good preface to the *Alcestis*, stressing the way in which different editors and translators of the play have seen the main characters in different lights, with, for instance, Browning regarding Heracles as the only good person in the play, while others see him as a drunken buffoon. There then follow two versions of the play, identical except for the fact that the second version has copious footnotes designed to explain innuendos and ambiguities. These notes are excellent, but the actual translation, with an even but not iambic 12-syllable line for the dialogue and speeches, and baffling rather literal free verse for the choruses, is flat and unexciting.

CONACHER (1988) contains a valuable guide to recent scholarship on the play. A debt to Dale's 1954 edition is acknowledged, but there are differences of interpretation. The translation, accurate but not wholly literal, is particularly effective in dialogue.

TOM WINNIFRITH

Further Reading

Dale, A.M., *Euripides: Alcestis*, edited with an introduction and commentary, Oxford: Clarendon Press, 1954

Medea

Medeia, 431 BC

Translations

Arnott, P.D., *Medea* in *Three Greek Plays for the Theatre*, translated by Arnott, Bloomington: Indiana University Press, 1961

Coleridge, Edward P., *Medea* in *The Plays of Euripides*, translated by Coleridge, vol. 1, London: Bell, 1891

Egan, Desmond, *Medea* (parallel texts), Laurinburg, North Carolina: St Andrews Press, and Newbridge, County Kildare: Kavanagh Press, 1991

Elliot, Alistair, *Medea*, London: Oberon, 1993

Hadas, Moses and John McLean, *Medea*, in *The Plays of Euripides*, translated by Hadas and McLean, New York: Dial Press, 1936; as *Ten Plays*, New York: Bantam, 1960

Jeffers, Robinson, *Medea, Freely Adapted*, New York: Random House, 1946

Kovacs, David, *Medea* in *Cyclops, Alcestis, Medea* (parallel texts), translated by Kovacs, Cambridge, Massachusetts: Harvard University Press, 1994 (Loeb Classical Library)

Lucas, D.W., *The Medea of Euripides*, with an introduction and notes, London: Cohen and West, 1949

Murray, Gilbert, *The Medea of Euripides*, New York: Oxford University Press, 1906; London: G. Allen, 1907

Roche, Paul, *Medea* in *Three Plays of Euripides*, translated by Roche, New York: Norton, 1974

Townsend, Michael, *Medea*, San Francisco: Chandler, 1966

Trevelyan, R.C., *Medea*, Cambridge: Cambridge University Press, 1939

Vellacott, Philip, *Medea and Other Plays*, Harmondsworth and Baltimore: Penguin, 1963

Warner, Rex, *The Medea*, London: Bodley Head, 1944

Way, Arthur S., *Medea* in *The Tragedies of Euripides in English Verse*, translated by Way, vol. 1, London and New York: Macmillan, 1894 (Loeb Classical Library)

Euripides' unsurpassed treatment of the mythic figure of Medea established her among the greatest figures in all of tragedy. One of the playwright's "bad" women, she towers over the other characters in the play because of her powerful personality and her ability to determine the course of events as only Fate does in other tragedies. Yet she is understandable as a human being: abandoned wife, betrayed ally, distrusted foreigner, she is driven to crime even as she understands how wrong her actions are – and still goes through with them. In recent years she has become a figurehead of feminism.

Translating Euripides presents special problems. In his own time he was notorious for using a diction less dignified than was held to be proper for tragedy, and for making much of low-life characters. Yet his plots and characters are mythic not only because they are derived from traditional heroic stories but also because their significance is universal. The translator must strive not to debase the text in the direction of trite colloquialism and yet make it sound realistic, immediate and accessible to the common reader. Most of the translations considered here are good except when they fall into either of two excesses, modernizing too much or else trying to be too elevated.

COLERIDGE's prose version (1891) sounds awkward and antiquated. It cannot be recommended, but is included in the present survey because it is part of *The Complete Greek Drama*, edited by W.J. Oates and Eugene O'Neill, Jr (New York: Random House, 1938), an important collection largely superseded by the *Complete Greek Tragedies* published by the University of Chicago (see below under Warner).

WAY (1894) employs a rather tortured "high" style and uses archaic locutions inappropriate for the directness of Euripides' idiom. His combination of rhymed verse with iambic pentameters is dated. He compares unfavourably with his contemporary Murray, who also sounds old-fashioned but displays genuine poetic talent.

MURRAY's *Medea* (1906), in rhymed verse, is lushly Victorian but undeniably passionate and dramatic.

HADAS & MCLEAN's prose translation (1936) is mainly notable for its reliable literalness. *Medea* is so powerful a play that it is not diminished by this treatment, but a more imaginative rendition is preferable. It is a mark of the prosiness of this version that it indicates the more poetic quality of choral passages by having them printed in italics.

TREVELYAN (1939) uses iambic pentameters and rhythmic free verse. This rendering avoids both extremes of over-simplification and inappropriate elevation. However, it borders on the archaic and is not quite the equal of the best verse translations.

WARNER's translation, in free verse (1944), is excellent and will be the choice of many readers, especially since it is part of the admirable *Complete Greek Tragedies* (edited by Grene and Lattimore, University of Chicago Press; 1958 and 1959 for Euripides, and many reprints, including 1992). Warner is more free and more formal than Vellacott (see below) and his understanding of the play puts an individual cast upon it; for instance, he uses the word "love" when it does not appear in the Greek and thus underemphasizes Medea as an outraged former ally of Jason's, giving instead additional emphasis to her character as a woman in love. The use of the article in the title is odd, as if Medea were a generic figure.

JEFFERS's version (1946) is an adaptation rather than a translation. Its masterly use of free verse expresses the spirit of the play, although much is omitted or rewritten. The changes are in the interests of modernization: thus the prolonged debate between Medea and Jason at the end of the play – fascinating to ancient Greeks, who were enamoured of disputation – is shortened, and the dragon chariot in which Medea makes her escape is dispensed with. The latter change deprives her of physical superiority on stage over her vanquished husband. Jeffers's version of *Medea* is remarkably dramatic, but Euripides' original remains unequalled.

LUCAS's prose translation (1949) is sound and reliable, but of the available prose versions Kovacs's (see below) is the best.

ARNOTT's free verse (1961) is exemplary. His skilful use of modern English idiom makes this version suitable for performance. The energetic language manages to convey the strong simplicity and directness of Euripides' dialogue.

VELLACOTT's concise and powerful version (1963) combines iambic pentameters and free verse. This is probably the best translation available: faithful to the original and forceful and dramatic in its use of English. The dialogue appropriately sounds more conversational than do the long speeches and the choral passages, and the language throughout has a fine poetic ring to it.

Like several of the other translators, TOWNSEND (1966) addresses theatrical needs. His use of free verse is informal and conversational, but frequently too much so, creating bizarre effects, as when Medea's nurse says: "Oh, lordie me, / It isn't the kiddies' fault" (compare with Egan's "No no no no! Ah me, poor unfortunate woman – / why should your children be blamed"); or when Medea's outcry "come, flame of the sky" (Vellacott) becomes "Oh, blast, the ruddy lightning". One cannot recommend this version.

ROCHE (1974), a notably intelligent translator of classical works, pays special attention to the sound effect of his lines. He uses "freewheeling iambic", with some skilful, unobtrusive rhyme. This translation is notable for its elaborate stage directions (no part of the ancient text), which even incorporate Roche's interpretation of the choral passages. It can be of considerable instructional value, putting the play before the student's eye and facilitating access to the basically alien choral material.

EGAN (1991), a prominent Irish poet, uses vigorous, passionate free verse. His purpose is to make *Medea* accessible as literature and as playscript, and he succeeds on both counts. Especially admirable is his rendition of the choral passages – a stumbling block to many translators because nothing in modern experience corresponds to the Greek dramatic chorus. Egan preserves the open-endedness and allusiveness that frequently characterize these passages without, however, sacrificing the lucidity that is an equally important quality of the Greek.

ELLIOT's translation (1993) is intended for performance. This version of the play is slightly abridged: details not easily understandable to a modern audience are omitted, and there are other cuts as well, although none major. Still, any Greek tragedy is quite short compared to modern ones, and *Medea* in particular is tightly written. A reader (or a director) should opt for the complete text. Even more objectionable is Elliot's use of rather obvious rhyme in the choral passages while the body of his rendition employs free verse – especially since rhyme was disapproved of by ancient poets and is largely absent from modern English literature as well.

KOVACS's new Loeb edition (1994) completely replaces the previous one (1912), which used Way's translations (see above). Kovacs employs unpretentious clear prose that cannot be improved upon as an aid to readers who need help to gain access to the Greek text.

ZOJA PAVLOVSKIS-PETIT

Further Reading

See the introductions to Kovacs, Lucas, and Roche; Kovacs's succinct summary of the special problems of translating Euripides is particularly noteworthy

Hippolytus

Hippolytos, 428 BC

Translations

Davie, John, *Hippolytus* in *The Alcestis and Other Plays*, translated by Davie, Harmondsworth and New York: Penguin, 1996

Grene, David, *Hippolytus* in *The Complete Greek Tragedies* (Centennial Edition), edited by Grene and Richmond Lattimore, vol. 3, Chicago: Chicago University Press, 1992 (first published 1958)
Hailstone, Herbert, *The Hippolytus of Euripides*, Cambridge: E. Johnson, 1888
Halleran, Michael R., *Hippolytus* (parallel texts), with an introduction, Warminster, Wiltshire: Aris and Phillips, 1995

The *Hippolytus* is unique in Greek drama in that it was the second attempt by Euripides at the same story. Fragments of the first play survive. In it Phaedra is like Potiphar's wife, a wicked seductress, or, as Racine, and most modern readers, would think, a normal woman. The tortured heroine of Euripides' second Hippolytus play is a less sympathetic character, although one who found favour with Victorian audiences, as did the austerely chaste Hippolytus. All commentators have noticed the structural balance of the play, with Artemis opposed to Aphrodite, the action beginning with the sick Phaedra and ending with the dying Hippolytus, and these two characters opposed to each other and contrasting with the normal but equally important Theseus and nurse. Translators have been less successful in coping with the switches from the high-flown idealism of Hippolytus and Phaedra to the coarse practicalities of Theseus and the nurse, with the choruses wavering in between.

HAILSTONE's (1888) is an average literal Victorian translation, not very explicit on sexual desire, and rather too keen on vague neuter plurals like "dreadful things", "shameful things", and "honourable things". Euripides' most famous (or infamous) line, spoken by Hippolytus, comes through rather dully as "The tongue hath sworn, but the mind hath not sworn".

GRENE (1992 [1958]) is able to bring Euripides' poetry to life. Admittedly he rather fails with "my tongue swore but mind was still unpledged", but there is many a memorable phrase such as "Women! This coin which men find counterfeit!" He is particularly strong in blending ordinary words into startling juxtapositions.

HALLERAN (1995) provides an accurate translation and an up-to-date account of recent research, better on scholarship than on literary criticism. There is a strange tendency to mix the colloquial and the archaic. Thus Phaedra tells her nurse to shut her mouth and says her soul is well tilled by passion. On the other hand "My tongue is sworn, my mind unsworn" has a certain pithiness about it.

DAVIE (1996), in a new Penguin edition that includes the *Alcestis*, the *Medea* and *The Children of Heracles* as well as the *Hippolytus*, presumably concentrating on the theme of sons and lovers, does try to produce some ordinary language, particularly in speeches by the nurse. This is an improvement on other single translations and on the Penguin version of Vellacott, although in making the mind the heart in Hippolytus' statement about his oath Davie does alter the sense.

TOM WINNIFRITH

Further Reading

Barrett, W.S., *Euripides: Hippolytos*, edited with an introduction and commentary, Oxford: Clarendon Press, 1964; New York: Oxford University Press, 1992

The Bacchae

Bakchai, c.406 BC

Translations

Arrowsmith, William, *The Bacchae*, in *The Complete Greek Tragedies* (Centennial Edition), edited by David Grene and Richmond Lattimore, vol. 4, Chicago: Chicago University Press, 1992 (first published 1959)
Kirk, Geoffrey S., *The Bacchae of Euripides*, Englewood Cliffs, New Jersey: Prentice Hall, 1970; with an introduction, Cambridge and New York: Cambridge University Press, 1979
Milman, Henry Hart, *The Agamemnon of Aeschylus and the Bacchanals of Euripides*, London: John Murray, 1865
Seaford, Richard, *Bacchae* (parallel texts), with an introduction and commentary, Warminster, Wiltshire: Aris and Phillips, 1996

The Bacchae (c.406 BC) is Euripides' last and oddest play. It was written outside Athens at the court of Archelaus, king of Macedon, but first performed in Athens. Previous plays, although using gods as mechanical devices, seemed either to deny their power to influence mortals or to deplore their effect on human affairs. Dionysus in *The Bacchae* is a real presence, and it seems that Pentheus is both wicked and foolish to resist him. No commentator has really been able to solve the problem of this apparent recantation, but translators who have found the sudden switches in other plays from prose to poetry difficult to manage have coped better with *The Bacchae*, where horror and terror and splendour are never very far from the surface even at the most mundane moments.

MILMAN (1865) was a figure of the Victorian establishment, professor of poetry at Oxford and dean of St Paul's. The *Agamemnon* and *The Bacchae* seem rather disturbing plays for such a comfortable figure to translate, although both illustrate the theme of divine vengeance, and this aspect of *The Bacchae* comes through strongly in this version, a mixture of blank verse and rhyming choruses.

KIRK (1970) aims, as he says in his preface, at a close line-by-line translation that does not seem too stilted. He finds this easier in the chorus than in the speeches and dialogue, but the tension in *The Bacchae* means that odd-sounding remarks such as "And will you equip me with anything else beyond all this", uttered by Pentheus in the temptation scene, have a sinister quality about them.

ARROWSMITH (1992 [1959]), because of the speed and the savagery of the action, succeeds in the *Bacchae* where he failed in the *Alcestis*. He cuts corners for the sake of the drama, and the cumbrous line of Euripides and Kirk becomes "Yes? Go on". His account of Pentheus' death is as horrifying as the original.

SEAFORD (1996) provides the first commentary since Dodds and a rewarding account of modern scholarship, marred by the pretentious jargon of poststructuralism and metatheatricality. Pentheus is a bit of a bore in the early part of the play, but there is no need for him to speak against "pernicious initiation rituals". But, as with all Aris and Phillips editions, this translation is essentially accurate.

TOM WINNIFRITH

Further Reading
Dodds, E.R., *Euripides: Bacchae*, 2nd edition, Oxford: Clarendon Press, 1960

Winnington-Ingram, R.P., *Euripides and Dionysus: An Interpretation of the Bacchae*, Cambridge: Cambridge University Press, 1948

Evgenii Evtushenko 1933–

Russian poet

Biography

Born in Stantsiia Zima (Zima Junction), Irkutsk region, Siberia, 18 July 1933. His father, Aleksandr Gangnus, was a geologist and an intellectual who introduced Evtushenko to the work of many European writers, including Dumas, Schiller and Dante. As a young boy, after his parents' separation, Evtushenko went to Moscow with his mother, Zinaida Yermolayevna Evtushenko, and adopted her surname. He returned to Zima Junction in 1941, after the outbreak of World War II, and started to write poetry. He accompanied his father on geological expeditions to Kazakhstan, 1948, and the Altai, 1950. Evtushenko returned to live permanently in Moscow in 1944. He attended the Gork'ii Literary Institute in Moscow in the early 1950s. He considered becoming a professional soccer player, but decided instead to devote himself to writing after the success of his early poems, which appeared in a number of Moscow newspapers and journals. He published his first book of poetry in 1952, *The Prospectors of the Future*. He married the poet Bella Akhmadulina in 1954; they divorced subsequently. He became well known as a precocious Thaw-period poet after Stalin's death in 1953. His important long poem *Stantsiia Zima* (*Zima Junction*) was published in the journal *Oktyabr* in 1956. In 1957 he was expelled from Komsomol, the Communist Party's youth organization, for his hostility to orthodox Stalinism; after he was reinstated in 1959 he became secretary of its unit in the Gork'ii Literary Institute. His work was controversial in Russia, and he travelled abroad widely throughout the Khrushchev and the Brezhnev periods. His poem describing the World War II massacre of Ukrainian Jews, *Babi Yar*, appeared in 1961. He married Galina Semenova Sokol in 1962 and had one son. His work *Autobiografia* (*A Precocious Autobiography*), published in 1963 in Paris, was denounced by the Soviet authorities as sensationalist. He was refused official permission to travel abroad from 1963 to 1965. His poetic cycle *Bratskaia GES* (*Bratsk Station*), 1965, received official Soviet approval. He was awarded the USSR Committee for Defence of Peace Award in 1965. Despite his public opposition to the invasion of Czechoslovakia in 1968 he was appointed to the governing board of the Soviet Writers' Union in 1971, of which he became secretary from 1986 to 1991, and vice-president in 1991. He expressed support for Solzhenitsyn on his arrest in 1974. His third marriage in 1978 was to the English translator Jan Butler, with whom he had two sons. Evtushenko appeared as an actor in the 1979 film *Flight* (*Ascent*; or *Take-off*). He wrote his first novel *Iagodnye mesta* (*Wild Berries*), a thriller set in Siberia, in 1981. He published three books of photographs and directed two films, *Kindergarten* (1983), about his childhood, and *Stalin's Funeral* (1987). He married Maria Novika in 1986, and had two further sons. Evtushenko was a member of Congress of People's Deputies of USSR from 1989 to 1991. He became vice president of Russian PEN in 1990. He received the Badge of Honour of the Order of Red Banner of Labour and the USSR State prize, 1984. He was made an honorary member of the American Academy of Arts and Sciences in 1987.

Evtushenko became one of the best-known Russian writers in the West during the 1950s and early 1960s for his poetry questioning the socialist realism current in Soviet literature at that time and reflecting the political atmosphere in the Soviet Union before and after Stalin's death. His major poems of this period are the narrative work *Stantsiia Zima*, published in 1956, which describes a return to his native town in 1953, and *Babi Yar*, 1961. His collection of love poems, *Tretii sneg* [Third Snow], was published in 1955. Later collections of his poems include *Flowers and Bullets, and Freedom to Kill*, 1970, and *Stolen Apples*, 1971.

Translations

Selections of Poetry

Boyars, Arthur and Simon Franklin, *The Face Behind the Face: Poems*, with an introduction by Evtushenko, New York: Marek, and London: Marion Boyars, 1979 (64 items)

Dickey, James, *et al.*, *Stolen Apples: Poetry by Yevgeny Yevtushenko* (Russian originals in an appendix), New York: Doubleday, 1971; London: W.H. Allen, 1972 (56 items)

Evtushenko, Evgenii [no translator credited], *From Desire to Desire*, New York: Doubleday, 1976 (54 items)

Marshall, Herbert, *Yevtushenko: Poems* (parallel texts), New York: Dutton, and Oxford: Pergamon Press, 1966 (35 items)

Milner-Gulland, Robin and Peter Levi, *Selected Poems*, with an introduction, New York: Dutton, and Harmondsworth: Penguin, 1962 (22 items)

Reavey, George, *Early Poems* (parallel texts), London and New York: Marion Boyars, 1989 (62 items; replaces his *The Poetry of Yevgeny Yevtushenko 1953–1965*, New York: October House, 1965)

Todd, Albert C. (editor), with Evtushenko and James Ragan, *The Collected Poems, 1952–1990*, New York: Holt, and Edinburgh: Mainstream, 1991 (282 items)
Tupikina-Glaessner, Tina, Geoffrey Dutton and Igor Mezhakoff-Koriakin, *Bratsk Station, and Other New Poems by Yevgeny Yevtushenko*, New York: Praeger, and London: Hart-Davis, 1967 (26 items in addition to the Bratsk cycle)
Weissbort, Daniel, *Ivan the Terrible and Ivan the Fool*, with an introduction, London: Gollancz, and New York: Richard Marek, 1979

Other Writing
Avtobiografiia, 1963
MacAndrew, Andrew R., *A Precocious Autobiography*, New York: Dutton, and London: Collins and Harvill, 1963

Iagodnye mesta, 1982
Bouis, Antonina W., *Wild Berries*, New York: Morrow, and London: Macmillan, 1984

Ardabiola, 1984
Wason, Armorer, *Ardabiola: A Fantasy by Yevgeny Yevtushenko*, London: Granada, and New York: St Martin's Press, 1984

Pochti v poslednii mig, 1988
Bouis, Antonina W. and Albert C. Todd, with the author, *Almost at the End*, New York: Holt, and London: Marion Boyars, 1987 (23 items)

Ne umirai prezhde smerti, 1992
Bouis, Antonina W., *Don't Die Before You're Dead*, New York: Random House, and London: Robson, 1995

Evtushenko the poet and Evtushenko the political figure are indissolubly linked. It is impossible to evaluate his art without constant consideration of his life and activity. He is the first to have spoken up against Stalinism and against anti-Semitism in Russia; he protested the Soviet invasion of Czechoslovakia; he continues being active in Russian politics and keeps up the ties he has established outside Russia during his many tours abroad. Perhaps Evtushenko's most laudable accomplishment as poet is that he has resurrected the political ode – a genre largely neglected in the contemporary world.

Evtushenko is a "popular" poet: he is direct and accessible, and his energy, the strength of his convictions, his civic courage and sense of responsibility can appeal to anyone. He has produced a large body of work, and new translations keep coming out. The present survey does not consider periodicals and anthologies, only a selection of volumes entirely devoted to Evtushenko.

The problems of translating Evgenii Evtushenko are well expressed by TUPKINA-GLAESSNER & DUTTON (1967) in their "Translators' Note on *Bratsk Station*":

> It is extremely difficult to give any true impression in English of the range and quality of Yevtushenko's poetry. He uses every sort of idiom, from classical poetic diction to the colloquialisms of the different times about which he is writing. He uses a very wide variety of forms of versification, and his rhymes are so subtle that it is better not to risk trying to copy them in English, which in any case has different facilities for rhyme from Russian. Yevtushenko also writes in the style of popular songs, and parodies the solemn efforts of amateur poets (which he admires none the less, for the genuine feeling behind them) ... He loves to play with the multiple meaning of words ...

In short, his message and the narration of which he is fond do come through, but the poetry is largely lost.

The eight translators whose work appears in *Stolen Apples* (DICKEY, 1971) are DICKEY, DUTTON, FERLINGHETTI, Anthony KAHN, KUNITZ, REAVEY, UPDIKE, and WILBUR. The introduction is written by the poet. The translators for the most part use excellent free verse.

> Yevtushenko asked each of the poets involved in this project to assume the most demanding freedom: to translate only poems he liked; and to be fully himself in his work. For some ... that meant working on an intimate lyric, for others a narrative ... fluid and far-flung ... For everyone it meant riding the impulse the original voice set off, as long and in such a way as he wished. The result, ... interchanges between one poet and another.

Highly recommended.

From Desire to Desire (1976) is also made up of versions by a number of translators. It is basically a compilation of poems previously published in Marshall's, Milner-Gulland's, Reavey's, and Tupkina-Glaessner's collections.

The large volume of more than 600 pages edited by Todd (1991) contains the work of 25 translators, including such notables as James DICKEY, Lawrence FERLINGHETTI, Ted HUGHES, Stanley KUNITZ, John UPDIKE, and Richard WILBUR. The selection is Evtushenko's own and includes many of his poems about America. Many of the translations included were published previously; some appear here in a revised form. (See also under DICKEY (editor), *Stolen Apples*.)

MILNER-GULLAND, a Slavicist, & LEVI, a poet, join forces (1962) in a free verse translation. They say they:

> produce versions that may make sense as English poetry (even where this has meant abandoning an exact imitation of the rhythm, rhyme, or metaphor of the original ... we have of course tried to keep as close as possible to the original sequence of ideas, without additions or subtractions ...

MARSHALL (1966) sacrifices precision to an attempt to use at least some rhyme. Since extremely few translators of Evtushenko try to meet this challenge, Marshall's translation is noteworthy. The preface is by the poet, subtitled "To My American Readers".

TUPKINA-GLAESSNER, DUTTON, & MEZHAKOFF-KORIAKIN (1967) use free verse that reads like prose. On the whole, this is a good translation; the translators are well aware of the problems they face and discuss these in their preface. There is a preface by the poet as well.

BOYARS & FRANKLIN (1979) use free verse with rather prosy results. The introduction is by the poet.

WEISSBORT (1979) translates a long poem the original title of which literally means *Calico from Ivanovo*. Weissbort comes up with forceful free verse and makes imaginative choices. He appends notes to clarify historical and cultural references.

REAVEY's free verse (1989) opts for plain, rather than imaginative, translation. The translator's aim here is to facilitate access to the parallel text. Included is a new preface by the poet.

Almost at the End (BOUIS, TODD & EVTUSHENKO, 1989) is a representative sample of Evtushenko's recent work in poetry and prose. It is well rendered in a mixture of free verse and prose.

Evtushenko's prose seems to be easier to translate than his poetry. The forthright directness and honesty of the man come through in *A Precocious Autobiography* (MACANDREW, 1963) and the autobiographic *Don't Die Before You're Dead* (BOUIS, 1995) of which Evtushenko says: "This novel is my confession, both intimate and political." *Ardabiola* (WASON, 1984) and *Wild Berries* (BOUIS, 1984) also are interesting; the translations are smooth and readable.

ZOJA PAVLOVSKIS-PETIT

Further Reading

See translators' introductions to Milner-Gulland & Levi and Weissbort, and Tupikina-Glaessner & Dutton's translators' note

F

Faust Book of 1587

Historia von D. Johann Fausten, 1587

For a facsimile of the first edition of the German original see *Historia von D. Johann Fausten: Nachdruck des Faust-Buches von 1587*, with an afterword by Peter Boerner, Wiesbaden: Sändig, 1978. The best edition of the German text is *Historia von D. Johann Fausten: Text des Druckes von 1587 [Kritische Ausgabe. Mit den Zusatztexten der Wolfenbütteler Handschrift und der zeitgenössischen Drucke]*, edited by Stephan Füssel and Hans Joachim Kreutzer, Stuttgart: Reclam, 1988

Translation

P.F. Gent[leman], *The Historie of the damnable life, and deserued death of Doctor Iohn Faustus, London. Newly imprinted, and in conuenient places imperfect matter amended: according to the true Copie printed at Franckfort*, London: Thomas Orwin, 1592 (oldest surviving complete text of the translation); facsimile of the copy in the British Library, with afterword by Renate Noll-Wiemann in the series *Deutsche Volksbücher in Faksimiledrucken*, Hildesheim: Olms, 1985

Jones, John Henry (editor), *The English Faust Book: A Critical Edition Based on the Text of 1592*, Cambridge and New York: Cambridge University Press, 1994

Other reprints and editions, of varying utility and reliability, include:

Logeman, Henry (editor), *The English Faust-Book of 1592*, with an introduction and notes, Ghent: Engelcke, 1900

Palmer, Philip Mason and Robert Pattison More, in their *The Sources of the Faust Tradition: From Simon Magus to Lessing*, New York: Oxford University Press, 1936; reprinted 1966, pp.134–236

Rose, William (editor), *Histories of the Damnable Life and Deserved Death of Doctor John Faustus*, Notre Dame, Indiana: University of Notre Dame Press, 1963 (modernized)

Further editions of the English translation appeared in 1608, 1610, 1618, 1622, 1636, 1648, 1674, 1677?, 1682, 1690, 1696?, 1700? For details see Jones, *The English Faust Book*, pp. 246–49

The German Faust book, *Historia von D. Johann Fausten*, an anonymous, essentially didactic treatise designed to serve "arrogant, curious and godless men as a terrible example and warning", but enlivened with various entertaining episodes, was an immediate success when it was published at the Frankfurt book fair in 1587. Before the end of 1588 at least nine editions had appeared, and the book was soon translated into several languages. Of these translations the English version by a certain "P.F. Gent[leman]", was – with hindsight – undoubtedly the most important, for it provided the basis for Christopher Marlowe's *The Tragical History of Doctor Faustus*, a play that in turn was to help determine the further development of the Faust theme in Germany itself.

All modern editions of the English Faust Book, including Jones's (1994), must necessarily be based on Thomas Orwin's text of 1592, the oldest surviving complete version of the translation though, as the title page implies ("Newly imprinted"), not the earliest. However, Jones is also able to take into account a fragment (one sheet) of a previously unknown edition of apparently slightly earlier date, printed by Edwarde Allde of London, which has recently been discovered at Shrewsbury School. Examining this in conjunction with Orwin's text and the editions of 1608 and 1610 in particular, Jones concludes that the Allde and Orwin texts must derive from the superior of two (lost) manuscript versions while the editions of 1608 and 1610 go back, indirectly, to the inferior one, He argues, with some force, that the *editio princeps* was probably the work of the London printer Abel Jeffes, at a date earlier than 1592, possibly as early as 1589, which means that 1592 need no longer be regarded as the earliest possible date at which Marlowe could have written his play.

The identity of "P.F." has always been, and still remains, a problem. In 1910 Rohde sought – improbably – to identify him with the astrologer and alchemist John Dee, while Kocher, in 1940, argued that the translation was the work of the Cambridge scholar Peter Frenche; both of these men are known to have travelled extensively in Germany in the 1580s. In his recent "critical edition" (so-called – really it is a "reading edition", for he has modernized and tampered with the text in various ways), Jones puts forward a completely new candidate, though explicitly without making any "extravagant claim" for him – everyone recognizes that the initials P.F. were not uncommon even in 16th-century England. Consideration of such innovations in the English Faust Book as references to the "brazen [i.e. brass] virgin" of Breslau and detailed factual knowledge of Leipzig and especially the arcane reference to "Don Spiket Jordan" (p. 139 in Jones's edition), i.e. Spytek Wawrzyniec Jordan, *starost* (Captain) of Sandetz (Nowy Sacz) from 1584 to 1590, leads him to conclude that the translator had himself been in Cracow, as well as in Leipzig and other places, in 1587 or 1588. Jones draws attention to a certain Paul Fairfax, arraigned by the Royal College of Physicians in London for quackery in 1588–89, who had travelled in those parts and laid claim to a doctorate from Frankfurt an der Oder. At the very least there is a strange affinity between Paul Fairfax and Doctor Faustus, and Jones's thesis seems eminently plausible while remaining unproven. If he is right, the thesis has important implications for the dating of the translation. Fairfax might well have acquired a copy of the *Historia* in Germany in 1587 or 1588 (the English translation is certainly based on recension A of the German, which was not printed again after 1588) and have translated it as early as 1588, which in turn would help to explain the incidence of various English allusions to Faustus that antedate the 1592 Orwin edition. Jones rightly contends that evidence for the existence of a Faust ballad in England in February 1589 suggests that P.F.'s translation was already available; ballads are, after all, generally secondary reflections of something that has already caught the popular imagination. Furthermore Jones shows that there are strong grounds for believing that the prose romance of *Friar Bacon*, used as a source by Robert Greene for his *Honourable History of Friar Bacon and Friar Bungay*, written in 1589 or 1590, was modelled on the English Faust Book, even though the earliest surviving edition of this is of later date.

Various critics (such as Butler, Noll-Wiemann, D'Agostini and Silvani, and Jones) have analysed the precise differences between the English translation and its German source, drawing attention to the qualities of the English version and discussing omissions, additions and shifts of emphasis, and praising the English translator's greater linguistic felicity, variety and freedom of expression. Butler, for instance, says "A certain high-handed carelessness is one of P.F.'s most obvious characteristics, not unmixed with intellectual arrogance: and although a mere translator, his personality emerges more vividly than that of the original author" and she regards him as having "a more unshackled mind, a livelier curiosity and a perhaps more haphazard but wider education". Jones, for his part, credits P.F. with three qualities notably lacking in the German author: a flair for pungent expression and the felicitous phrase, a vivid visual imagination, and a taste for ironic humour. In some respects P.F. undoubtedly improved on the original, which in many ways resembles a patchwork created from a motley variety of sources. He certainly took many liberties with his source, omitting certain passages (notably chapter 65 in which Mephistopheles mocks Faustus with proverbs, one of the wittiest chapters in the original), replacing or adding others. Whereas in the German original the emphasis is on Faustus's overriding sin of *superbia*, there is a shift in the English version in the direction of "speculation, devilish cogitation and contempt for a pious vocation". The English version is rather more forward-looking than the German. Not only has P.F. added what amounts to a paean of praise for the Renaissance spirit, he shows more awareness of the 16th-century world: whereas for the German author the "whole world", even nearly a century after Columbus, comprised only Europe, Asia and Africa, the English Faust book has Faustus travel to the New World too.

JOHN L. FLOOD

Further Reading

Butler, E.M., *The Fortunes of Faust*, Cambridge: Cambridge University Press, 1952

D'Agostini, Maria Enrica and Giovanna Silvani, *Analisi comparata delle fonti inglesi e tedesche del Faust dal Volksbuch a Marlowe*, Naples: Tullio Pronti, 1978

Deats, Sara Mumson, "*Doctor Faustus*: From Chapbook to Tragedy", *Essays in Literature*, 3 (1976) pp. 3–16

Empson, William, *Faustus and the Censor: The English Faust-Book and Marlowe's Doctor Faustus*, edited by John Henry Jones, Oxford and New York: Blackwell, 1987

Goldstein, Leba M., "An Account of the Faustus Ballad", *The Library*, 5th series, 16 (1961) pp. 176–89

Herford, Charles H., *Studies in the Literary Relations of England and Germany in the Sixteenth Century*, Cambridge: Cambridge University Press, 1886; reprinted London: Cassell, and New York: Octagon Books, 1966

Kocher, Paul H., "The English Faust Book and the Date of Marlowe's *Faustus*", *Modern Language Notes*, 55 (1940) pp. 95–101

Rohde, Richard, *Das englische Faustbuch und Marlowes Tragödie*, Halle: Niemeyer, 1910

Schirmer-Imhoff, Ruth, "Faust in England", *Anglia*, 70 (1951) pp. 150–85

Smeed, J.W., *Faust in Literature*, Oxford and New York: Oxford University Press, 1973

Feminist Translation Theory

Feminist translation theory is grounded in what the linguist Deborah Cameron has called "the feminist critique of language". This critique maintains that language is androcentric, expressing the male point of view and silencing the female "other". Through sexist grammar rules and vocabulary which either denigrates women or represses reference to them, languages have become inadequate tools for the expression of female subjectivity; when speaking, a woman must either pose as a man, or "translate" her feminine perspective into the foreign "male" tongue. All languages privilege male expression, but each does so in its own way. Feminist linguistic theories come in many variations, from the Anglo-American scholarship of linguists like Cameron to the French psychoanalytic theories of Luce Irigaray and the *écriture feminine* of Hélène Cixous. Feminist translation theory is, in part, a response to the difficulties of translating literature "written in the feminine", that is, feminist discourse that deconstructs masculine language and makes a place in it for the feminine.

The major work in feminist translation theory has emerged from Canada, where the bilingual environment encourages both the practice and the theory of translation as well as permitting access to both French theory and Anglo-American scholarship. Nicole Brossard, a prominent francophone practitioner of "writing in the feminine", employs numerous grammar-defying strategies such as routinely adding the mute "e" to masculine gendered words. These practices inevitably pose problems for her translators; English, for example, does not have masculine and feminine genders to the extent French does; therefore the shock-effect of feminized masculine nouns is completely lost in English translation. Such translation problems as these have served to emphasize the active role of feminist translators, who have come to be recognized as co-creators with the authors. Two of Brossard's translators, Barbara Godard and Susanne de Lotbinière-Harwood, have been the most active in developing a feminist translation theory that not only explains their own role but also produces strategies for their translation practice. Godard's articles "Theorizing Feminist Discourse / Translation"(1984) and "Translating and Sexual Difference"(1990) clarify the connections between feminist linguistic theories and feminist translation; her "Translating (With) the Speculum" (1991) draws on Irigaray and other postmodern theorists. Susanne de Lotbinière-Harwood explicates the relevance of feminist theories of language to her practice as a translator in her book, *Rebelle et Infidèle / The Body Bilingual* (1991). Written half in French and half in English, it includes many anecdotal examples from Lotbinière-Harwood's own life and work. The book's subtitle, "Translation as a Rewriting in the Feminine", emphasizes the active role of the translator as woman writing from a female body and relating differently to each of her languages, each of which expresses a different aspect of her feminine identity. Brossard's novel, *Le Désert mauve* (1987), translated by Lotbinière-Harwood as *Mauve Desert* (1990), also serves as a contribution to feminist translation theory, for it describes the translation process undergone by a female translator-protagonist, who begins by being seduced by a "source text" and after many detailed travails ends by producing the "target text". Canadian feminist translation theory thus emphasizes feminine difference and the creative role of the translator, promoting collaboration between writer and translator and linguistic revisionism.

Other significant contributions to feminist translation theory are produced by feminists who base their arguments on Jacques Derrida's philosophy of difference / différance and his discussions of translation. These include Gayatri Chakravorty Spivak, translator of Derrida's *De la grammatologie* into English (*Of Grammatology*, 1984), Lori Chamberlain and Christina Zwarg. In her article "The Politics of Translation" (1993), Spivak considers feminist translation in a postcolonial context. In "Gender and the Metaphorics of Translation" (1988), Chamberlain argues that the metaphorical system with which translation has been represented throughout the history of English literature equates translation with "reproduction", a "feminine" activity as opposed to "production" of the original, a male prerogative. In "Feminism in Translation: Margaret Fuller's *Tasso*" (1990), Zwarg's complex argument maintains that Fuller's translations from German are based on a pedagogical model similar to Derrida's understanding of translation as a marriage contract in the form of a seminar.

Another body of feminist translation theory revolves around the usage of inclusive language when translating the Bible. It is generally agreed that biblical language is not only androcentric, but patriarchal and racist as well; the debate centers around the extent to which inclusive language may be instituted without violating the Bible's historicity. In some cases, the translation or even the very writing of the Bible has obscured the role of women. For example, the gospel of Mark does not specifically mention the women apostles until after the death of Christ, when the men all flee; it then becomes clear that the women followers of Christ have been there all along. A feminist translation would make their presence visible much earlier in the story. Some feminist critics, however, fear that mere inclusive language may become simply cosmetic, lulling the faithful into a false sense of acceptance without addressing the real issue of structural patriarchy. These issues are discussed in the "Special Section on Feminist Translation of the New Testament" in *Journal of Feminist Studies in Religion* (1990), which includes articles by Elizabeth A. Castelli and Clarice J. Martin, and three responses to them. In recently published works, both Sherry Simon (*Gender in Translation*) and Luise von Flotow (*Translation and Gender*) address the theoretical issues outlined above, locating them in historical and cultural contexts.

KRISTINE J. ANDERSON

See also the entry Gender and Gender Politics in Literary Translation

Further Reading

Brossard, Nicole, *Mauve Desert*, translated by Susanne de Lotbinière-Harwood, Toronto: Coach House Press, 1990

Cameron, Deborah, *Feminism and Linguistic Theory*, London: Macmillan, and New York: St Martin's Press, 1985; 2nd edition, New York: St Martin's Press, 1992

Cameron, Deborah (editor), *The Feminist Critique of Language: A Reader*, London and New York: Routledge, 1990
Castelli, Elizabeth, "Les Belles Infidèles / Fidelity or Feminism? The Meanings of Feminist Biblical Translation", *Journal of Feminist Studies in Religion*, 6 (1990) pp. 25–39
Chamberlain, Lori, "Gender and the Metaphorics of Translation", *Signs*, 13/3 (1988) pp. 454–72
Godard, Barbara, "Translating and Sexual Difference", *Resources for Feminist Research / Documentation sur la Recherche Feministe*, 13/3 (November 1984) pp. 13–16
Godard, Barbara, "Theorizing Feminist Discourse / Translation" in *Translation History and Culture*, edited by Susan Bassnett and André Lefevere, London and New York: Pinter, 1990
Godard, Barbara, "Translating (with) the Speculum", *TTR: Traduction, Terminologie, Rédaction*, 4/2 (1991) pp. 85–118
Lotbinière-Harwood, Susanne, *Re-Belle et infidèle: La traduction comme pratique de reécriture au feminin / The Body Bilingual: Translation as a Rewriting in the Feminine*, Montreal and Toronto: Remue-ménage / Women's Press, 1991
Martin, Clarice J., "Womanist Interpretations of the New Testament: The Quest for Holistic and Inclusive Translation and Interpretation", *Journal of Feminist Studies in Religion*, 6 (Fall 1990), pp. 41–85
Simon, Sherry, *Gender in Translation: Cultural Identity and the Politics of Transmission*, London and New York: Routledge, 1996
Spivak, Gayatri Chakravorty, "The Politics of Translation" in her *Outside in the Teaching Machine*, New York and London: Routledge, 1993
von Flotow, Luise, "Feminist Translation: Contexts, Practices and Theories", *TTR: Traduction, Terminologie, Rédaction*, 4/2 (1991) pp. 69–84
von Flotow, Luise, *Translation and Gender: Translating in the "Era of Feminism"*, Manchester: St Jerome, 1997
Zwarg, Christina, "Feminism in Translation : Margaret Fuller's *Tasso*", *Studies in Romanticism*, 29 (Fall 1990) pp. 463–90

Lion Feuchtwanger 1884–1958

German novelist and dramatist

Biography

Feuchtwanger was born in Munich in 7 July 1884 into a Jewish family. He had started writing plays and short stories as early as 1903. His first novel was published in 1910, but he had to wait another 15 years before, following on from the success of his novel *The Ugly Duchess (Die hässliche Herzogin Margarete Maultasch*, 1923), he took the literary world by storm with the appearance of the novel *Jew Suss* (*Jud Süss*, 1925).

After Hitler came to power Feuchtwanger became a victim of Nazi rule. He was on the first list of proscribed writers deprived of their German citizenship by the Ministry of the Interior. He sought refuge in the south of France, vowing to continue highlighting in his work "the reincursion of barbarism in Germany and its temporary victory over reason". In 1940 Feuchtwanger's position in France became precarious. Interned (for the second time in his life by the French – he had been briefly interned in Tunisia at the time of World War I) at Les Milles, he managed to escape and by the October reached, via Spain and Portugal, America, where he was to spend the rest of his life. He died in Los Angeles, 21 December 1958.

The Institute for Exile Studies at the University of Southern California, named after Lion Feuchtwanger, is a fitting testimony to a writer obliged because of his religious beliefs and left-wing political persuasions to seek sanctuary outside of Germany and whose international literary reputation was sustained in Britain and America long before he was eventually accepted in Germany towards the end of his life. This recognition at home – even then primarily in the Democratic Republic – came with the awarding to him of the National Prize in 1953, the start of the publication of his collected works and the establishment of a Feuchtwanger Archive in the old East Berlin Academy of Arts.

Translations

Novels

Die hässliche Herzogin Margarete Maultasch, 1923

Muir, Willa and Edwin Muir, *The Ugly Duchess: A Historical Romance*, London: Martin Secker, 1927; New York: Viking Press, 1928; several subsequent editions

Jud Süss, 1925

Dukes, Ashley, *Jew Suss* (play, adapted from Feuchtwanger's novel), London: Martin Secker, 1929; New York: Viking Press, 1930

Muir, Willa and Edwin Muir, *Jew Suss*, London: Martin Secker, 1926; as *Power*, New York: Viking Press, 1926; several subsequent reissues

Rawlinson, Arthur Richard and Dorothy Farnum, *Jew Suss* , a scenario for the film *Jew Suss* (Gaumont–British Film Corporation Ltd) of 1934 from the novel by Lion Feuchtwanger, London: Methuen, 1935; facsimile edition, New York: Garland, 1978

Erfolg: Drei Jahre Geschichte einer Provinz, 1930
Muir, Willa and Edwin Muir, *Success: Three Years in the Life of a Province*, London: Martin Secker, and New York: Literary Guild, 1930; New York: Carroll and Graf, 1984

Der jüdische Krieg, 1932
Muir, Willa and Edwin Muir, *Josephus: A Historical Romance*, London: Martin Secker, and New York: Literary Guild, 1932; several subsequent editions

Die Geschwister Oppenheim, 1933; as *Die Geschwister Oppermann*, 1948
Cleugh, James, *The Oppermanns*, London: Martin Secker, 1934; New York: Viking Press, 1934; several subsequent editions

Die Söhne, 1935
Muir, Willa and Edwin Muir, *The Jew of Rome: A Historical Romance*, London: Hutchinson, 1935; New York: Viking Press, 1936

Der falsche Nero, 1936
Muir, Willa and Edwin Muir, *The False Nero*, London: Hutchinson, 1937; as *The Pretender*, New York: Viking Press, 1937

Exil, 1940
Muir, Willa and Edwin Muir, *Paris Gazette*, London: Hutchinson, and New York: Viking Press, 1940

Der Zauberer, 1943; as *Die Brüder Lautensack*, 1944
Oram, Caroline, *The Lautensack Brothers*, London: Hamish Hamilton, 1943; as *Double, Double, Toil and Trouble*, New York: Viking Press, 1943

Simone, 1944
Hermann, G.A., *Simone*, London: Hamish Hamilton, and New York: Viking Press, 1944
Hecht, B., *Simone* (playscript based on Feuchtwanger's novel), New York: Studio Duplicating Service, 1962
Mueller, Carl Richard, *The Visions of Simone Machard*, translation of Bertolt Brecht's *Die Gesichte der Simone Machard* (play adapted in collaboration with Feuchtwanger from the latter's novel), New York: Grove Press, 1965

Der Tag wird kommen, 1945
Oram, Caroline, *The Day Will Come*, London: Hutchinson, 1942; as *Josephus and the Emperor*, New York: Viking Press, 1942

Waffen für Amerika, 1947; a dramatized version, *Die Füchse im Weinberg*, 1947
Firth, Moray (pseudonym of William Rose), *Proud Destiny*, New York: Viking Press, 1947; London: Hutchinson, 1948

Goya; oder, Der arge Weg der Erkenntnis, 1951
Lowe-Porter, H.T. and Frances Fawcett, *This is the Hour*, New York: Viking Press, 1951; London: Hutchinson, 1952

Narrenweisheit; oder, Tod und Verklärung des Jean-Jacques Rousseau, 1952
Fawcett, Frances, *'Tis Folly to be Wise'; or, Death and Transfiguration of Jean-Jacques Rousseau*, New York: Messner, 1953; London: Hutchinson, 1954

Die Jüdin von Toledo, also as *Spanische Ballade*, 1955
Wilkins, Eithne and Ernst Kaiser, *Raquel, the Jewess of Toledo*, New York: Messner, and London: Hutchinson, 1956

Jefta und seine Tochter, 1957
Wilkins, Eithne and Ernst Kaiser, *Jephta and His Daughter*, New York: Putnam, 1958; as *Jephthah and His Daughter*, London: Hutchinson, 1958

Short Stories
Marianne in Indien, und sieben andere Erzählungen, 1934
Creighton, Basil, *Little Tales*, London: Martin Secker, 1935; as *Marianne in India and Seven Other Tales*, New York: Viking Press, 1935; also in *Stories from Far and Near*, New York: Viking Press, 1945 (no translator credited); also in *Odysseus and the Swine and Other Stories*, London: Hutchinson, 1949 (no translator credited)

Poetry
PEP: J.L. Wetcheeks amerikanisches Liederbuch, 1928
Thompson, Dorothy, *PEP: J.L. Wetcheek's American Song Book*, New York: Viking Press, 1929

Selections of Plays
Ashton, Emma, *Three Plays*, London: Martin Secker, and New York: Viking Press, 1934 (contains *Prisoners of War*, *1918*, *The Dutch Merchant*)
Muir, Willa and Edwin Muir, *Two Anglo-Saxon Plays*, London: Martin Secker, 1927; New York: Viking Press, 1928 (contains *The Oil Islands*, *Warren Hastings*)

Plays
Warren Hastings, Gouverneur von Indien, 1916; subsequently adapted in collaboration with Brecht as *Kalkutta, 4. Mai*, 1925
Muir, Willa and Edwin Muir, *Warren Hastings* in *Two Anglo-Saxon Plays*, translated by Willa and Edwin Muir, 1927

Die Kriegsgefangenen, 1918
Ashton, Emma D., *Prisoners of War* in *Three Plays*, translated by Ashton, 1934

Neunzehnhundertachtzehn, 1919 (the stage manuscript of the "dramatic novel" *Thomas Wendt*, 1920)
Ashton, Emma D., *1918* in *Three Plays*, translated by Ashton, 1934

Der holländische Kaufmann, 1923
Ashton, Emma D., *The Dutch Merchant* in *Three Plays*, translated by Ashton, 1934

Die Petroleum-Inseln, 1927
Muir, Willa and Edwin Muir, *The Oil Islands* in *Two Anglo-Saxon Plays*, translated by Willa and Edwin Muir, 1927

Memoirs
Moskau 1937, 1937
Josephy, Irene, *Moscow, 1937: My Visit Described for My Friends*, London: Gollancz, and New York: Viking Press, 1937

Unholdes Frankreich: Meine Erlebnisse unter der Regierung Pétain, 1942; as *Der Teufel in Frankreich*, 1954
Blewitt, Phyllis, *The Devil in France: My Encounter with Him in the Summer of 1940*, New York: Viking Press, 1941; London: Hutchinson, 1942

Essays
Das Haus der Desdemona; oder, Grösse und Grenzen der historischen Dichtung, 1961
Bisilius, Harold A., *The House of Desdemona; or, The Laurels and Limitations of Historical Fiction*, Detroit: Wayne State University Press, 1963

Lion Feuchtwanger's most famous novel was first published in 1925, though there had been a drama version of the subject published in 1918. The story of *Jew Suss* traces the rise and fall of Joseph Suss, the Jew who became finance minister to the Duke of Württemberg in the mid-18th century, gaining prominence through flattery, fraud and treachery. The novel, with its "rebarbative title"and written "by an unknown unpronounceable foreign author" (the London publisher Martin Secker was to recall) was immediately translated into English by the formidable team of Willa and Edwin MUIR, their version published in late November 1926 in Britain as *Jew Suss* and in America under the title *Power*. Arnold Bennett reviewed it enthusiastically in the London *Evening Standard*: "It entertains, it enthrals and simultaneously it teaches: it enlarges the field of knowledge". The *Times Literary Supplement* (*TLS*) critic thought the novel had been "beautifully translated". The English version proved to be Secker's most successful individual publishing venture. By the time of the first cheap popular edition in 1928, the 27th English printing had been reached, with 88,000 copies on the market. With the Viking Press in New York sales were similarly buoyant. Ashley Dukes's "play in five acts", *Jew Suss* (1929), which was adapted from Feuchtwanger's novel and found favour with the German author, was premiered in England on 19 September, 1929, with Matheson Lang in the lead role and Peggy Ashcroft as his daughter. With Feuchtwanger in exile, a film version of the novel, with Conrad Veidt in the name part, was made in 1934 by the Gaumont–British Film Corporation (with even more significant timing Veit Harlan made his notoriously anti-semitic film of the work for the Nazis in 1940). Since World War II further reprints of the novel, originally considered to be one of the most remarkable historical novels of recent times, have steadily appeared on both sides of the Atlantic.

The same team of Willa and Edwin MUIR promptly followed up that first translation with their version of Feuchtwanger's 1923 novel under the title *The Ugly Duchess. A Historical Romance* (London 1927 and New York 1928). The story with its 14th-century setting is a study of pitifulness and frustration as the heroine, alas, no physical beauty, seeks to establish her authority and position by sheer force of character. This involved jealousy and ruthlessness, deception and murder, excommunication and fire, flood and plague. Feuchtwanger was praised for a remarkable piece of historical reconstruction by the *TLS* and *Saturday Review* alike. The latter thought too that the characters were alive and intense. The *TLS*, on the other hand, felt that neither period nor person in this novel were generally so compelling as in *Jew Suss*. Indeed the reviewer was even to remark that "excellent as Mr and Mrs Muir's translation is, the language is of an almost startling sobriety, at times quite lifeless". Nevertheless the English version was reissued in both Britain and America during the post-war decades. *The Ugly Duchess* incidentally was adapted for the London stage and premiered on 15 May 1930.

Yet again in that year of 1927 the MUIRS themselves had turned their attentions to Feuchtwanger's own dramatic talent and Secker published their English translation of *Two Anglo-Saxon Plays*, comprising *The Oil Islands* and *Warren Hastings*. The former in its German original version of *Die Petroleum-Inseln* had been premiered at the end of October 1927 in Hamburg and is based on his novel *The Ugly Duchess*. Once more we find a strong, gifted but ugly woman in Miss Deborah Gray, President of the Oil Islands Company. Greed, ambition, exploitation again provide the motivating force. Consisting of numerous scenes whose subtitles displayed on the curtain seemingly bear little relevant or cumulative connection, the play reflects Feuchtwanger's penchant for expressionistic techniques then popular in the German theatre, and a sense of detachment and alienation that would be of interest to Brecht. *Warren Hastings*, less of an experimental piece, had originally appeared in 1916 as *Warren Hastings, Gouverneur von Indien*, but was subsequently adapted in collaboration with Bertolt Brecht in 1925 as *Kalkutta 4. Mai*. The action centres on the last few days of April and the beginning of May 1775, when the Governor General thwarts attempts of the East India Company to control his actions. The first English production of the play, at the Festival Theatre, Cambridge, in October 1930, had Flora Robson as Lady Marjory Hicks, Hastings's mistress.

Collaboration between Feuchtwanger and Brecht in Germany and later during the Californian exile is of course on record; also worth mentioning is a possible point of contact between the two that would have been provided by Feuchtwanger's sole poetic endeavour (with the English allusion in its title to his own surname), *PEP; J.L. Wetcheeks amerikanisches Liederbuch* (1928), translated by Dorothy THOMPSON, as *PEP: J.L. Wetcheek's American Song Book*, published the following year in New York for the first and only time. The volume contains satirical songs very recognizable to those familiar with Brecht's similar usage in his own work.

In the very year, 1930, that Feuchtwanger's first part of a planned cycle of novels (*Der Wartesaal. Zyklus aus dem Zeitgeschehen* [The Waiting-Room. Cycle on Current Events]) had appeared in Germany as *Erfolg. Drei Jahre Geschichte einer Provinz*, the MUIRS' English version was published on both sides of the Atlantic under the literal, ironical title *Success: Three Years in the Life of a Province*. Feuchtwanger may well have been writing the original with an eye to its reception in Britain and America. The lengthy work (the original was in two volumes) provides a satirical, entertaining look at contemporary history, namely the first three years of the 1920s in Bavaria, which include the time of inflation and, towards the end of the novel, the *Hitlerputsch*. The political fortunes (and misfortunes) of the province have of course an underlying relevance to those of Germany as a nation. Actual historical figures such as Hitler, Ludendorff, Brecht are thinly disguised in an elaborate and ingenious mix of fact and fiction.

For the second part of the cycle, a new translator in James CLEUGH was on hand to deliver his version of *Die Geschwister Oppenheim* (1933, and now published in Amsterdam rather than Germany; it was to be reissued in 1948 as *Die Geschwister Oppermann*, with Feuchtwanger's apparent reluctant agreement to the change). Cleugh's version, under the title *The Oppermanns*, was published in 1934, once again by Secker in London and the Viking Press in New York. The period under the spotlight covers the events immediately prior to Hitler's assumption of power and the following months, with the Jewish boycott, the Reichstag fire and the establishment of the first "corrective" concentration camps. The position of Jews at the time is mirrored in the portrayal of the Oppermanns – three middle-aged, middle-class brothers: Gustav, Martin and Edgar, all driven from prosperity to ruin and exile.

During the 1930s Feuchtwanger regularly spoke out at public and private meetings in America and England and elsewhere in Europe against the tide of events in his own country He contributed to the *Brown Book on the Hitler Terror* (London: John Lane, 1934); and, with W.H. Auden and others, to *In Letters of Red* (London, Michael Joseph, 1938) on the subject of fascism, war and world politics; and, with Heinrich Mann, Sigrid Undset, Ivan Goll, Andre Maurois, Hans Habe, Alfred Neumann and Jan Masaryk, to the volume *The Torch of Freedom* (New York: Farrar and Rinehart, 1943). In 1937 Feuchtwanger had undertaken a 10-week visit to Russia in connection with the publication of the journal *Das Wort*. The literary product of that journey was a short book that was immediately translated by Irene JOSEPHY (1937) and published in London under the title *Moscow, 1937: My Visit Described for My Friends*. The work constitutes a straightforward account of the trip and its experiences (including an interview with Stalin). The tone is generally enthusiastic, though not uncritical in places. Reviewers on this occasion, however, were not uncritical of the quality of translation. The *TLS* reviewer was particularly severe on the translator's evident ignorance of famous Russian names and her apparent lack of access to a map of Russia, the consequences of which were "a rich and ridiculous crop of original spellings".

Feuchtwanger's experiences in Pétain's France are recounted in a book of memoirs translated by Phyllis BLEWITT under the title *The Devil in France: My Encounter with Him in the Summer of 1940*, published in New York in 1941 and in London the year after.

The MUIRS made their swan-song translation of Feuchtwanger with their version of *Exil* (1940), the third novel in the *Wartesaal*-cycle. The English translation was immediately produced and published on both sides of the Atlantic under the title *Paris Gazette* (1940). Fictional distancing gives way more to a direct account of the tragic consequences of persecution and banishment, using authentic material drawn from real events in the daily lives of exiles in Paris who have fled from National Socialism, only to feel its presence still through the German Embassy and the party offices.

Associated too with the *Zyklus aus dem Zeitgeschehen* is the unusually compact short novel *Simone*, translated by yet another hand in G.A. HERMANN (London, 1944). Past and present history merge in the story that centres on the French collapse in 1940 and on the courageous reactions to it of Simone, a 15-year-old Burgundian girl. (Brecht collaborated with Feuchtwanger in 1941–43 in California to produce eventually Brecht's own dramatized version, *Die Gesichte der Simone Machard*, English translation 1965.)

Alongside the *Wartesaal*-cycle of novels, the other major literary undertaking in prose fiction by Feuchtwanger must be rated the Josephus trilogy, his excursion into distant history to examine the plight of the Jews in Roman times. Already in 1932 the MUIRS had immediately translated the first part of the planned trilogy, the novel *Der jüdische Krieg* (The Jewish War), that appeared in English under the title *Josephus: A Historical Romance*. Against a vast backcloth of camp and court and a host of characters, Feuchtwanger concentrates on the five years of early manhood (circa AD 66) of Josephus Flavius, Jewish warrior and budding historian, and the part he played at that point in the age-long conflict between Jew and Gentile. Three years later the Muirs produced the English version of the second part of the trilogy under the title *The Jew of Rome. A Historical Romance* (1935 in London, 1936 in New York). The Emperor Vespasian is dying, Titus is waiting in the wings. For his part, Josephus is now over 40. He has written seven volumes on the Jewish War and enjoys a reputation as a writer and interpreter of Jewish life, but he is a victim of his own conscience. Once again, the relationship to the situation of the Jews in the Germany of the 1930s is clearly suggested. The concluding part of the translated trilogy, *The Day Will Come*, was published in London and New York in 1942. Given the time of publication and the circumstances of the war, the English title is arguably more effective than the prosaic though accurate title given to the American edition: *Josephus and the Emperor*. Caroline ORAM is now the new translator for this volume. Incidentally the original German version, written while Feuchtwanger was interned at Les Milles, did not appear until 1945, when it was published in Sweden as *Der Tag wird kommen*. Josephus is 50 by this time, living in semi-retirement in Rome, a city now identified with militarism, excessive orderliness and secret police. His conscience is still troubling him in his great task of writing the universal history of the Jews. As an appeaser, he is expected to dampen the ardour of his people who want to rise up to deliver Judaea from Rome. The novel becomes a psychological study of Josephus, who is symbolically contrasted with Domitian, the embodiment of power and of the denial of the spirit. The relevance of this clash of "Macht" and "Geist" to contemporary times is clear enough. "The Day Will Come" is the battle cry of the Zealots.

Whatever the circumstances during his exile, Feuchtwanger never paused in his prolific literary output. Writings in German had to be published in France and Holland, then Sweden, Mexico and America, but English translations of them appeared in Britain and the US with great frequency and usually immediacy. In 1934 Martin Secker in London and the Viking Press in New York published Emma D. ASHTON's version of *Three Plays*. These are considerably later translations of earlier dramas (*1918*, *Prisoners of War*, *The Dutch Merchant*), written before Feuchtwanger gained recognition and success as a novelist.

Among his voluminous prose fiction, Feuchtwanger did write some telling short stories. In 1934, for example, *Marianne in Indien. Und sieben andere Erzählungen* had been published, and these were quickly translated by Basil CREIGHTON and published the following year in London under the title *Little Tales* and in New York as *Marianne in India, and Seven Other Tales*. (In 1945 the Viking Press issued *Stories from Far and Near*, a selection of 15 tales, most of which had already appeared in the original *Marianne in India* and in British and

American magazines, while in 1949 the collection of stories bore the title *Odysseus and the Swine*.)

In the meantime the novels continued unabated. In 1936 Willa and Edwin MUIR were busy on their translation of Feuchtwanger's *Der falsche Nero*, published the following year in London under the title *The False Nero* and in New York as *The Pretender*. This typically long and carefully contrived story, rich in historical detail, relates the close of the reign of Titus and an impersonation of Nero by the potter Terence at the instigation of the Roman senator Varro. Again, the interpretation of the past allows for modern parallels.

Feuchtwanger returned to contemporary history for the novel *Die Brüder Lautensack*. The American edition appeared as *Double, Double, Toil and Trouble*; the British one was prosaically entitled *the Lautensack Brothers* (both published 1943). The translator is Caroline ORAM. Feuchtwanger, once more back on familiar terrain, sets his tale in the Bavarian / Bohemian border area against the backcloth of the development of the Nazi movement from 1931 to 1934.

The resumption of peace after 12 years of National Socialism brought no diminution of Feuchtwanger's literary resolve. His interest in America and in freedom drew him to Benjamin Franklin and the latter's ambassadorial trip to France in the 18th century. The outcome was the long novel *Waffen für Amerika* (i.e. Arms for America), 1947. Now there was yet another translator in Moray FIRTH (the pseudonym of William Rose) who produced an English version under the title *Proud Destiny*, published in New York in 1947 and in London in 1948.

LOWE-PORTER & FAWCETT combined to produce their English version of Feuchtwanger's study of Goya (1951). Their translation was published in 1951 in New York and the year following in London, as *This is the Hour*.

Frances FAWCETT (1953) was the sole translator for Feuchtwanger's next novel, published in 1952, about Jean-Jacques Rousseau's last days and the rise of the despots of the Terror. The English version was entitled *'Tis Folly to be Wise: or Death and Transfiguration of Jean-Jacques Rousseau*.

In his 70s, Feuchtwanger remained creatively active with a further play (*Die Witwe Capet* [The Widow Capet], 1956), on the subject of Marie Antoinette, and two novels, both of which were translated – and both by yet another new team of translators, the well-respected duo WILKINS & KAISER. The compact and exciting *Raquel, the Jewess of Toledo* (1955, translated 1956) concentrates on the tragic entanglement of King Alphonso VIII of Spain with Raquel Ibrahim, the Jewess of Toledo, set against the backcloth of medieval Spain. Feuchtwanger's skilled imagination in story-telling is maintained to the end in the depiction of one of the famous tragedies in antiquity in *Jefta und seine Tochter* (1957). WILKINS & KAISER's translation (1958) appeared in the US as *Jephta and His Daughter*, in Britain as *Jephthah and His Daughter*.

Feuchtwanger then was a major literary figure in the first half of the 20th century. The popularity of his writings, notably between 1923 and the end of World War II, was manifested through the numerous translations of his works, some of which too were turned into films – from Russia to America, Britain to Germany. His international reputation was assured most of all in the English-speaking world. *The Ugly Duchess, Jew Suss* and *Success* had been among Germany's outstanding publishing successes up to the start of the 1930s and have remained essentially so in the English-speaking world. Translation of his works ran to many editions in some instances, with revivals of interest in Feuchtwanger shown through reissues of a few novels on both sides of the Atlantic in the three decades following his death. One potential problem for translators, during the years of exile, but particularly after the end of World War II, would have been the gradual emasculation of Feuchtwanger's language through "separation from the living stream of the mother tongue", which could lead to an artificiality and abstractness. As Hans Mayer observed:"His was a German literature made in California; literature in a language that had ceased to be living German".

IAN HILTON

Further Reading

Hofe, Harold von and Sigrid Washburn (editors), *Feuchtwanger Today: Thoughts and Reflections on His 100th Birthday*, Feuchtwanger Institute for Exile Studies, University of Southern California, 1984

Kahn, Lothar, *Insight and Action: The Life and Work of Lion Feuchtwanger*, Rutherford, New Jersey: Fairleigh Dickinson University Press, 1975

Spalek, John M., *Lion Feuchtwanger – The Man, His Ideas, His Work: A Collection of Critical Essays*, Los Angeles: Hennessey and Ingalls, 1972

Yuill, W.E., "Lion Feuchtwanger", in *German Men of Letters*, vol. 3, edited by Alex Natan, London: Wolff, 1964

Georges Feydeau 1862–1921

French dramatist

Biography

Born in Paris, 8 December 1862, Georges Feydeau was the son of Ernest Feydeau, stockbroker and then writer, author of the well-known but controversial realist novel *Fanny* (1858). Georges fell in love with the theatre as a child and wrote a play in 1869. After leaving his Paris boarding-school in 1878 he worked briefly as a lawyer's clerk, then began writing monologues and one-act plays. He scored a great success in 1887 with a full-length play, *Tailleur pour dames* (*A Gown for His Mistress*, 1969), written during his year's military service, 1883–84. He married in 1889. Though his early success was not repeated for some time, his career as the well-known author, sometimes in collaboration, of getting on for 40 light farces of varying lengths took off for good in 1892 with *Champignol malgré lui* (*A Close Shave*, 1974). He made large amounts of money from his plays but lost most of it speculating on the stock exchange. In 1909 he left his wife and family and moved into a Paris hotel, where he continued to live until in 1919 he had to be moved into the mental home at Rueil-Malmaison, west of the capital, where he died, 5 June 1921.

The comically contrived situations, skilful plotting and droll and witty dialogue of Feydeau's plays have led to successful runs of some of them in English translation, and to their creator's name becoming synonymous with "French farce". Some titles (e.g. *Le Dindon*, produced 1896; *La Dame de chez Maxim*, 1899; *La Puce à l'oreille*, 1907; *Occupe-toi d'Amélie*, 1908) exist in several English versions.

Translations

Selections of Plays

Brahms, Caryl and Ned Sherrin, *Ooh! La-La!*, London: W.H. Allen, 1973 (contains *A Good Night's Sleep / Feu la mère de Madame, Before We Were So Rudely Interrupted / Gibier de potence, Keep an Eye on Amelie / Occupe-toi d'Amélie, A Little Bit to Fall back On / Les Pavés de l'ours, St Shrimp / La Dame de chez Maxim, Call Me Maestro / Amour et Piano*)

Brahms, Caryl and Ned Sherrin, *After You, Mr Feydeau!*, London: W.H. Allen, 1975 (contains *Paying the Piper / Le Dindon, Caught in the Act / La Puce à l'oreille, The Chaser and the Chaste / Monsieur Chasse, On a String / Un Fil à la patte*)

Marcoux, J. Paul, *Three Farces*, Lanham, Maryland: University Press of America, 1986 (contains *Love by the Bolt / Tailleur pour dames, All My Husbands / Le Mariage de Barillon, That's My Girl / Occupe-toi d'Amélie*)

Marcoux, J. Paul, *Five by Feydeau*, New York: Peter Lang, 1994 (contains *Brothers in Crime / Gibier de potence, The Dressmaker / Tailleur pour dames, All My Husbands / Le Mariage de Barillon, That's My Girl / Occupe-toi d'Amélie, Nothing but the Tooth / Hortense a dit: "Je m'en fous!"*)

Meyer, Peter, *Three Farces*, London: BBC, 1974 (contains *Fitting for Ladies / Tailleur pour dames, A Close Shave / Champignol malgré lui, Sauce for the Goose / Le Dindon*)

Mortimer, John, *Three Boulevard Farces*, Harmondsworth and New York: Penguin, 1985 (contains *A Little Hotel on the Side / Hôtel du Libre Échange, A Flea in Her Ear / La Puce à l'oreille, The Lady from Maxim's / La Dame de chez Maxim*)

Shapiro, Norman R., *Four Farces*, Chicago: University of Chicago Press, 1970 (contains *Wooed and Viewed / Par la fenêtre, On the Marry-Go-Wrong / Le Mariage de Barillon, Not by Bed Alone / Un Fil à la patte, Going to Pot / On purge bébé*)

Shapiro, Norman R., *Feydeau, First to Last: Eight One-Act Comedies*, Ithaca, New York: Cornell University Press, 1982 (contains *Ladies' Man / Notre Futur, Wooed and Viewed / Par la fenêtre, Romance in A-flat / Amour et piano, Fit to be Tried / Gibier de potence, Mixed Doubles / C'est une femme du monde, The Boor Hug / Les Pavés de l'ours, Caught with His Trance Down / Dormez, je le veux, Tooth and Consequences / Hortense a dit: "Je m'en fous!"*)

Plays

La Dame de chez Maxim, 1899

Brahms, Caryl and Ned Sherrin, *St Shrimp* in *Ooh! La-La!*, translated by Brahms and Sherrin, 1973

Feist, Gene, *The Lady from Maxim's*, New York: Samuel French, 1971

Mortimer, John, *The Lady from Maxim's*, London: Heinemann, 1977; also in *Three Boulevard Farces*, translated by Mortimer, 1985

La Puce à l'oreille, 1907

Anderson, Graham, *A Flea in Her Ear*, London: Oberon Books, 1993

Brahms, Caryl and Ned Sherrin, *Caught in the Act* in *After You, Mr Feydeau!*, translated by Brahms and Sherrin, 1975

Mortimer, John, *A Flea in Her Ear*, London and New York: Samuel French, 1960; also in *Three Boulevard Farces*, translated by Mortimer, 1985

Shaw, Barnett, *A Flea in Her Ear*, New York: Samuel French, 1966

Occupe-toi d'Amélie, 1908

Brahms, Caryl and Ned Sherrin, *Keep an Eye on Amelie* in *Ooh! La- La!*, translated by Brahms and Sherrin, 1973

Cogo-Fawcett, Robert and Braham Murray, *Keep an Eye on Amelie*, London and New York: Samuel French, 1991

Coward, Noel, *Look after Lulu*, London: Heinemann, 1959

Frei, Nicki and Peter Hall, *Mind Millie for Me*, Bath: Absolute Press, 1996

Marcoux, J. Paul, *That's My Girl* in *Three Farces*, translated by Marcoux, 1986

The instant appeal of a Feydeau play belies the many hurdles it can contain for the unwary translator. A mere glance at the translated titles will show that there is a risk of falling at the very first fence. *A Flea in Her Ear*, for example, is plainly wrong as a translation of *La Puce à l'oreille*, an idiom that can refer only to "aroused suspicions" in French. As for *Occupe-toi d'Amélie*, the text makes it quite clear that Marcel has been asked to ensure that Amélie doesn't get bored, not that she doesn't misbehave, however closely the two may be connected psychologically. And anything based on "turkeys" is totally inadequate as a translation of *Le Dindon*, since, unlike the French title, it will not have, for an English audience, the figurative meaning of "victim", "dupe". Furthermore, the challenge presented by the highly idiomatic French of the indigenous characters is compounded by the colourful solecisms of a sizeable foreign contingent (such as Van Putzeboum's "Tu ne l'as pas encore mariée, ta femme, et tu profites déjà sur!" in *Occupe-toi d'Amélie*), and by a number of proper names which, rather improperly, conflate identification and description (as Raymonde, the suspicious wife, remarks of Montretout – literally, "Shows everything" – the location of the shady Ferraillon establishment in *La Puce à l'oreille*, "the name says it all". But, alas, only in French!).

The three plays discussed below (out of a possible 35) have, between them, attracted a dozen different translators, not counting Feydeau's contemporaries, or Jerome Kern, who collaborated on a musical adaptation of *La Dame de chez Maxim* in 1912. There are, of course, other, equally popular, full-length plays that might have been included, such as *Le Dindon*. However, that play alone would have added four more translations and two new translators to the list. And ought one to omit a one-act play like *Feu la mère de Madame*, which has received the accolade of the Comédie Française? It is as well to accept the fact that, in the case of Feydeau, coverage is doomed to be perfunctory.

Gene FEIST's adaptation (1971) of *La Dame de chez Maxim* is based on a literal translation by Catherine M. Perebinossoff and Mierre. The primary function of the literal version would appear to have been to forestall any random occurrence of similarities between Feydeau's play and Feist's own, an occurrence rendered all the more unlikely by the extreme flimsiness of the American text, which is not so much a slimmed down version of *La Dame* ... as an anorexic one (though the padding provided by several musical numbers does its best to disguise the fact).

BRAHMS & SHERRIN, too, have taken liberties with Feydeau, by introducing a narrator into their television adaptations (*St. Shrimp*, 1973; *Caught in the Act*, 1975), which displaces the comedy from a showing to a telling. However, the device is well suited to the intimacy of the small screen, and although their banter can occasionally wear a little thin over three acts the net result is very entertaining. The pair have exercised sound judgement in *The Lady from Maxim's*, cutting the less plausible scenes, such as Madame Petypon's endless enquiries in act 2 of *St. Shrimp* about the identity of the interloper, Môme Crevette. But, at the same time, they are not always respectful of Feydeau's characterization, which, most cynics would agree, is surprisingly true-to-life. When, for instance, their Madame Petypon mistakes Môme's dress for the one she herself is expecting from her dressmaker, she too wittily remarks: "I admit this is a dress of many colours. Madame Montelimar must be in one of her scriptural moods". This is a far cry from the down-to-earth "C'est un peu clair, c'est vrai!" of the original ("I suppose it is a little bit on the light side").

Interestingly, John MORTIMER (1977) has also seen fit to inject a little more humour into the text of the same play at this same point. More plausibly, however, he gives the line to Madame Petypon's husband: "I know your taste. This is no good to you. You couldn't go near a Mass in this!". Apart from amusing touches like this, Mortimer's version closely follows the original. It invariably strikes the right note and is an impressive piece of translating that perfectly matches Feydeau's intentions.

MORTIMER's *A Flea in her Ear* (1960) contains rather more errors than his version of *La Dame* ..., but it nevertheless displays the same qualities. He again adds a little zest to the humour, making more of Ferraillon's "military" past and giving to Madame the all-too-revealing mannerism of filing the hotel's correspondence in her garter (an allusion to her equally glorious past as the Copper-bottomed Contessa, alias Culotte de peau). Rugby, the Englishman, has, more meaningfully, been converted into a German called Schwartz.

Of the three American translations of *La Puce* ..., only Barnett SHAW's (1966) is readily available in England (the other two are by Carol Johnston [Chicago: Dramatic Publishing, 1968] and Frank Galati [New York: Dramatists Play Service, 1989]). It has a number of flaws. Not only is Shaw's knowledge of French rather shaky but his English dialogue is often unconvincing, though some allowance must, of course, be made for American English. He also makes some questionable decisions, such as retaining Rugby, the English client of the Pretty Pussy Inn (the Hôtel du Minet Galant). There is little point in this, for now that everyone else speaks the same language as Rugby himself the comedy generated in the original by his inability to communicate gets completely lost.

The mock-serious tone typically adopted by BRAHMS & SHERRIN gives a nice period flavour to their version (*Caught in the Act*, 1975) of *La Puce* ... In addition, their handling of the foreign characters is very successful. Rugby has become a Russian (with a "suggestion of snow on his boots") and a friend of Chekhov's! And they have matched Feydeau's own efforts in giving to Homenidès's speech a suitably Spanish flavour. Further evidence of their translational expertise is given by their title, which makes theirs the only version to combine a parting reference to the play's title with complete intelligibility.

Though something of a contrast, in that it follows Feydeau very closely but not slavishly, Graham ANDERSON's *A Flea in Her Ear* (1993) is equally good, preserving all the pace and humour of the original. Anderson has a thorough knowledge of French, and shows his flair as a translator when, for example, he nicely catches Lucienne's linguistically spurious "qui est-ce qui te dit qu'il est pinçable?" with "how do you know there's any 'it' to catch him at?". His Rugby becomes a German, with the suitably geographical name of Lüneberg. However, not even Anderson can satisfactorily resolve the difficulties created by the French title.

Noel COWARD has chosen to replace the more extravagant stage action with some quick-fire repartee in his adaptation (*Look after Lulu*, 1959) of *Occupe-toi d'Amélie*, including some amusing understatement (like Lulu's "I didn't expect you to be quite so informally dressed", on arriving late for her rendezvous with her over-zealous Prince and finding him already stripped down to his underwear). The result is vintage Coward rather than Feydeau, and set against the more spontaneous flavour of Feydeau's own satirical humour Coward's wit appears rather too contrived. The adaptation also loses some of the satirical verve of the original through its downgrading of the role of Pochet (now Gigot), one of Feydeau's most memorable creations. Nevertheless, it is Coward who has produced the best title, although a translation by Nicki FREI & Peter HALL has the ingenious title *Mind Millie for Me* (1996). One has, too, to admire the deftness with which Coward circumvents the more intractable linguistic problems. In *La Puce à l'oreille*, a joke that exploits the double meaning of "bouledogue" ("type of dog" and "type of handgun") doesn't survive in any of the English translations. *Occupe-toi d'Amélie* features a similar joke, based on the fact that Amélie's first lover was a "Danois" ("type of dog" and "type of Scandinavian"). While both Marcoux and Cogo-Fawcett will struggle, doggedly, to make great Danes sound like Great Danes (a suitably ambiguous "German shepherd" would, it is true, have been a little too exotic, even for a woman of Amélie's catholic tastes), Coward shows just how resourceful an adapter he can be:

Lulu:	He came from Copenhagen – my friends used to call him the Great Dane.
Claire (alias Irène):	How charming! I had a Great Dane once – he used to jump onto my bed every morning.
Lulu:	So did mine.

BRAHMS & SHERRIN (*Keep an Eye on Amélie*, 1973) can find no room on their small screen either for "Great Danes" or for the army of Amélie's friends. As a result, the canine joke disappears, along with the very first scene of the play. Similarly, the wedding ceremony, which should have taken up half of act 3, is reduced to about a tenth of its original length. Like Coward, they have toned down the broader elements of farce and satire: Marcel, for instance, is no longer unnerved by Amélie's trick with the eiderdown, nor does the Prince flirt with Charlotte.

Paul MARCOUX confesses to having taken "substantial liberties with the settings" and also with the number of characters in *That's my Girl* (1986). The reasons are purely economic, the adaptations having served for American college productions. Other changes, however, are less comprehensible. Like the title. Or again, when Pochet reminds the General "You won't forget my little medal, will you?", and goes on to add "When I say 'little', that's not to say I'd refuse a big one", Marcoux inappropriately replaces this pushful hint with a naive "Perhaps a nice ribbon?"

Although the title page of COGO-FAWCETT & MURRAY's *Keep an Eye on Amélie* (1991) reads "Translated and adapted by ...", this version follows the original text much more closely than any of its predecessors. The only major departure is the omission of the quarrel between Amélie and her brother, right at the beginning. Otherwise, deviations tend to be confined to the addition of one-liners designed to spice up the text, such as Koschnadieff's "All the parts" in reply to Pochet's enquiry as to the Prince's intentions towards his daughter ("Pardon me but is this a request for her hand?"). There are, however, a few mistranslations that ought not to have slipped through, but they in no way overshadow the undeniable merits of the translation, which is funny, has pace and puts the farce back into Feydeau.

In spite of having sacrificed coverage of plays to coverage of translators, this survey has still omitted two prominent names: Norman SHAPIRO and Peter MEYER. Each is the very able translator of a number of Feydeau plays, though, on the whole, less well-known ones. However, *Un Fil à la patte* and *Le Dindon* are sufficiently popular to have tempted other translators besides the two in question. SHAPIRO's translation of the former (*Not by Bed Alone*, 1970) is, if anything, better than Frederick Davies's *Get out of My Hair!* (in *Three French Farces*, Harmondsworth: Penguin, 1973). And MEYER's version of *Le Dindon* (*Sauce for the Goose*, 1974) does not compare unfavourably with a more recent translation by Nicki Frei & Peter Hall (*An Absolute Turkey*, Absolute Press, 1994). Shapiro and Meyer have also come up with some good titles to match, demonstrating once again that if one cannot judge a Feydeau translation by its cover, its title, at least, seldom lies.

PAUL REED

Further Reading

See Shapiro's preface to *Four Farces*

Finnish

Literary Translation into English

Although Finnish literature has been translated into English since the turn of the 20th century, it was not until the late 1980s that Finnish-English translation really began to make headway. Since its founding in 1977, the Finnish Literature Information Centre in Helsinki, headed by Marja-Leena Rautalin, has actively promoted Finnish literature outside Finland's borders. *Books from Finland*, published by the Helsinki University Library, plays an important role here: it is a quarterly journal of writing from and about Finland, and it is distributed worldwide.

Finland, a small country with a population of 5 million, gained independence in 1917, and in 1995 became a member of the European Union. Situated between east and west and sharing borders with Sweden, Norway, and Russia, Finland is also quite close to Estonia, across the Gulf of Finland. During 600 years of Swedish rule (1216–1809) and 100 years of

Russian rule (1809–1917), Finland's tradition of exposure to other cultures was established. This may be one reason for our special interest in translation: translation studies as well as translations as such.

Measured in the number of translations published, the situation in Finland is very different from that in the English-speaking countries, where 2–3 per cent of books published annually are translations. Half of the 1,163 new titles of fiction (1994) published yearly in Finland are translations (figures relate to the books published by the members of the Finnish Book Publishers Association). Literature from the anglophone countries slowly gained popularity in the 1870s, although "the Anglo-American orientation" began in earnest only after World War II (Urpo Kovala, 1992). Today about 70 per cent of the translations published in Finland are from the English language.

Finnish literature is written in three different languages: Finnish, Swedish and Sámi, which is the language spoken in the far north of the country. Finnish and Swedish are the official languages of Finland, and the Sámi language is on its way to gaining legal recognition. For instance, the opportunities for native-language education are improving and the language laws are changing (see Béla Jávorszky in *Books from Finland*, 1992/3).

In the Finno-Ugric sub-family of the Uralic family of languages, Finnish is the chief in the Finnic group, which includes Estonian and Sámi (Lappic). Finnish is spoken by some 5 million people, mainly in Finland, but also in neighbouring parts of Sweden, Norway, Estonia, and Russia and, as the result of immigration, in the United States and Canada. Finnish proper exists in two main dialects, Karelian (Eastern) and Tavastland (Western). The vocabulary of Finnish has been strongly influenced by word-borrowings from Scandinavian languages and Russian. Its grammatical structure is marked by a highly developed system of agglutination, in which for example negation can be denoted by the addition of a suffix to the stem of the verb, and possession is indicated by adding a suffix to the noun. In Finnish, words are accented on the first syllable. Vowels and consonants can be long or short. Adjectives are declined and agree with the corresponding noun. In the declension system there are 12 principal cases, with others in more restricted use. Compound tenses are formed with auxiliary verbs.

The Finns are enthusiastic and critical readers. Despite the dominance of translations, Finnish literature is full of vitality and originality. On the one hand, the otherness, the special feature of Finnish literature, is a treasure to be cherished; on the other hand, the "originality" of language and culture causes major problems for translators. As Herbert Lomas, the prolific translator of Finnish prose and poetry, has pointed out, "translating from a – very – foreign language is slow and painful work" (*Books from Finland*, 1991/1).

The Finns are often described as a people who live close to nature. The traces of this as well as "shamanism" and "being different" are all found in Finnish literature. For instance, the works by Nobel Prize winner Frans Eemil Sillanpää (1888–1964; see *People in the Summernight* [1934], translated by Alan Blair, 1966) are characterized by the relationship between man and nature, rural life and social problems.

No one type of Finnish literature tends to be translated more than others. Of course, classics such as the Finnish epic *The Kalevala*, are always being translated and retranslated. This collection of 50 poems or cantos boasts five English translations, three of them published in Great Britain and two in the United States. (The epic has been translated into more than 30 languages.) *The Kalevala*, collected and edited by Elias Lönnrot (first published in Finnish in 1835 and 1849), first appeared in English in 1907 (translated by W.F. Kirby); the newest version, Keith Bosley's translation, was published in 1989.

The growing interest in women's studies probably inspired Bosley to translate another Finnish folk classic *The Kanteletar*, which is the lyric sister of *the Kalevala*. This collection of 50 mainly women's ritual poems, songs, and ballads was published in English in 1992. *The Kalevala* largely influenced Eino Leino's collection of *Whit Songs* (1903 and 1916), also translated into English by Bosley in 1978. Leino (1878–1926) was author, poet, critic, journalist, and translator, and he is still considered a central figure in Finnish cultural life.

Aleksis Kivi (1834–72) is among the first modernists in Finnish literature: he turned everyday speech into poetry. Kivi's main work, the narrative *Seven Brothers* (1870) was first translated into English in 1929; in 1991 Richard A. Impola retranslated the work. A selection of Kivi's poetry under the title *Odes* was translated by Keith Bosley in 1994.

Finnish literature in translation also includes success stories like Mika Waltari (1908–79) and his historical novels, which are international best-sellers and have become part of world literature. Waltari's *Sinuhe the Egyptian* (translated by Naomi Walford in 1949) is a story about Sinuhe, the Egyptian doctor, in the times of the great pharaohs such as Akhnaton. The book is by far the most renowned Finnish novel. In the 1950s the book became a best-seller almost overnight in the United States, and a Hollywood spectacle was made of the story. The book has also been described as Finland's post-war calling card.

Väinö Linna (1920–92) was Waltari's one rival as the representative of Finnish literature in the United States in the 1950s. His *Unknown Soldier* (1954) was published in 1957 both in London and in New York (translator unknown). The book portrays Finnish soldiers in the Finno-Soviet war of 1941–44. Linna's other great work, *Täällä pohjan tähden alla* [The Northern Star Trilogy] (1959–62), depicting the civil war in Finland in 1918 and the years afterwards, has not yet been translated into English.

In the Finland of the 1950s modernist criticism began its breakthrough, with such authors as Paavo Haavikko (1931–), Pentti Saarikoski (1937–83), and Veijo Meri (1928–). Anselm Hollo has translated poems by Paavo Haavikko (*Paavo Haavikko: Selected Poems*, 1991) and Pentti Saarikoski (*Poems 1958–1980*, 1983). A lovely piece of writing, *Dances of the Obscure*, by Saarikoski as well, was translated by Michael Cole and Karen Kimball in 1987. Ritva Poom has also translated Haavikko's *Audun and the Polar Bear* and *Münchhausen*, both in 1986. Veijo Meri's *The Manila Rope* was translated by John MacGahern and Annikki Laaksi in 1967 and *Private Jokinen's Marriage Leave* by J.R. Pitkin in 1973.

Finland has also produced many other interesting poets and prosaists whose works have been translated into English. This list includes Risto Ahti, Eeva Joenpelto, Eeva Kilpi, Leena Krohn, Leena Lander, Rakel Liehu, Rosa Liksom, Eeva-Liisa Manner, Aila Meriluoto, Kalle Päätalo, Pentti Saaritsa, Kirsti Simonsuuri, Eira Stenberg, Ilpo Tiihonen, Sirkka Turkka, Antti Tuuri, Arto Paasilinna, and several others. From this group, I shall focus on three of my favourites: Krohn, Manner, and Paasilinna.

In her books, Leena Krohn (1947–), the Finlandia Prize-winner of 1993, deals with large, fundamental issues such as mortality, existence, and philosophy. Her books are strange and yet familiar combinations of fact and fiction. *The Eyes of the Fingertips Are Opening*, a collection of prose and poetry, which appeared in 1993, has been translated by Herbert Lomas.

Eeva-Liisa Manner (1921–95) was also among the writers who brought modernism to Finnish poetry in the 1950s. Two of her most important collections of poetry, *Fahrenheit 121* and *Burnt Orange*, were published in 1968. (Part of *Burnt Orange* appeared in *Books from Finland*, 1992/3, in Lomas's translation.) Manner wrote poems of silence and space, and she is described as "utterly Finnish". In 1986, Ritva Poom translated Manner's collection of poems *Fog Horses* (1956–77).

As Finland's best-loved humorist, Arto Paasilinna (1942–) has been described as "a rural cosmopolitan with a far-reaching pen" (*Books from Finland*, 1993/3). His books, like *The Year of the Hare* (1975, translated in 1995 by Lomas), are full of wit and humor, which is certainly why they are so warmly received and why they have become such steady sellers in Europe.

Moreover, many Finnish authors writing for children, like Mauri Kunnas (1950–) and Kristiina Louhi (1950–), are known throughout the world. Kunnas's *The Canine Kalevala* (translated by Tim Steffa in 1992) is a comic cartoon version of *The Kalevala*. Louhi is mainly known for her *Aino* series, stories about a little girl named Annie, e.g., *Annie's Year* translated by David Mitchell in 1986.

Yet by far the best known and most widely translated Finnish author (who writes in Finnish-Swedish) is Tove Jansson (1914–), the creator of the Moomin stories. Outside Finland her Moomin stories are mainly considered children's books, but in Finland their profound wisdom and anarchic humour "have made them into something of a national institution" (*Books from Finland*, 1994/4). All the Moomin books, and many of Jansson's stories for adults (like *The Summer Book* and *Sun City*), are available in English. Jansson's stories have also appeared in many different forms, including picture books and films. Jansson has been translated into English by Kingsley Hart, Elizabeth Portch, Thomas Teal, and Thomas Warburton.

In this context, I need to mention a Finnish poet and translator who has not been properly introduced in English: Kirsi Kunnas (1924–), a master of verse, rhythm, and nonsense. Herbert Lomas's translations of extracts from two of her books, *Tiitiäisen satupuu* ("The Tumpkin's Story Tree", 1956) and *Tiitiäisen pippurimylly* ("The Tumpkin's Pepper Mill", 1991), have appeared in *Books from Finland*, 1979/2, and 1992/2); some of her poems have also been published in English-language anthologies, but none of her books has been translated in full into English.

Many vanguard Finnish-Swedish authors have also been translated into English, including Bo Carpelan, Tua Forsström, Annika Idström, Christer Kihlman, Oscar Parland, Gösta Ågren, and the children's author Irmelin Sandman-Lilius. The Finnish-Swedish modernist Edith Södergran (1892–1923; *Complete Poems* translated by David McDuff in 1992) is considered to be among the most important Swedish-language writers in the world. In 1994, a second, enlarged edition of *Poems by Edith Södergran* was translated by Ralph Salisbury, Lars Nordström, and Harald Gaski, who have also translated Sámi-language literature like Nils-Aslak Valkeapää's *Trackways of the Wind*. This collection of poems, drawings, and notes was published in 1994. Valkeapää (1943–) is a well-known, influential figure in the Sámi culture.

Several major collections available in the English language offer a good overview of Finnish poetry. *Contemporary Finnish Poetry* (1991) is translated and edited by Herbert Lomas. The book contains 21 post-war poets, including Aaro Hellaakoski, Tiina Kaila, Eeva-Liisa Manner, Arto Melleri, Kirsti Simonsuuri, Jari Tervo, Ilpo Tiihonen, and Lauri Viita, to mention a few. In 1989, Joan Tate and David McDuff translated and edited *Ice Around Our Lips*, an anthology of Finnish-Swedish poetry.

Translators are in a key position. It is up to them to take into account the many complex issues involved in translation, from situation and function to culture and individual viewpoints. Without translators – Keith Bosley, Hildi Hawkins, Anselm Hollo, Herbert Lomas, David McDuff, Seija Paddon, Ritva Poom, Joan Tate, and several others – cross-cultural communication, in this case between the Finnish and non-Finnish speaking world, would be impossible.

To make the translator's work possible, financial support is of primary importance. Since 1974, the Finnish Ministry of Education has been awarding translation grants, with the goal of advancing Finnish literature abroad. These grants are available to publishers, translators, authors and editors. The Finnish government also awards prizes for translation of Finnish literature.

As literature becomes more international in its focus, interest is growing in small nations and their literatures. This trend, as well as Finland's membership of the European Union, is raising the profile of Finland and Finnish literature throughout the world. Today, "Finnish literature travels to all corners of the world" (Erkka Lehtola in *Books from Finland*, 1990/1)

RIITTA OITTINEN

Further Reading

Finnish National Bibliography (annual volumes), Helsinki: Helsinki University Library

Haanpää, Eeva-Liisa and Marja-Leena Rautalin, *Bibliography of Finnish Literature in Translation 1976–1992*), Helsinki: Finnish Literature Society, 1993

Kanerva, Arja, Kaisa Lange and Maria Laukka, *Mielikuvia: Suomalaisia lastenkirjakuvittajia* [Images: Finnish Illustrators of Children's Books], Lasten Keskus / Finnish Institute for Children's Literature, 1989 (contains English summary)

Kovala, Urpo, *Väliin lankeaa varjo: Angloamerikkalaisen kaunokirjallisuuden välittyminen Suomeen 1890–1939* [The Shadow Between: The Mediation of Anglo-American Literature in Finland 1890–1939], Jyväskylä: Nykykulttuurin tutkimusyksikkö, University of Jyväskylä, 1992 (contains English summary)

Oittinen, Riitta, *I Am Me – I Am Other: On the Dialogics of Translating for Children*, Tampere, Finland: Tampere University, 1993

Oittinen, Riitta, *Translating for Children*, New York: Garland, 2000

Venuti, Lawrence, *The Translator's Invisibility: A History of Translation*, London and New York: Routledge, 1995

Abul Qasim Firdausī c.940–c.1020

Persian epic poet

Biography

Also Firdusi, Ferdowsi, Ferdosi, Fardusi. Little is known of his life. He was born at Tus, Khorasan c.940, where his family owned some land. His poem, the *Shāhnāmeh* [Book of the Kings], is an extremely long retelling (some 50,000 double lines) of the mythical, legendary and "historical" past of Persia, from the creation of the world to the Arab conquest in the 7th century AD. It is considered one of the major epics of world literature. It was completed in about 1010. Various legends concerning Firdausī's relations with the poem's dedicatee, sultan Mahmud of Ghazni, exist, but it is impossible to verify which, if any, of them is true. A romance on the subject of Joseph and Potiphar's wife, once attributed to Firdausī. is now considered to have been written some 300 years after his death.

Shah-nama / The Epic of the Kings

Shāhnāmeh, completed c.1010

Translations

Complete version

Warner, Arthur G. and Edward Warner, *The Shah-nama of Firdausi, Done into English*, 9 vols, London: Paul Trench Trübner, 1905–25

Incomplete versions and extracts

Atkinson, James, *Soohrab: a Poem Freely Translated from the Original Persian of Firdousee*, Calcutta, 1814

Atkinson, James, *Firdausi: Shahnameh*, London: Oriental Translation Fund, 1832

Champion, Joseph, *The Poems of Ferdosi*, vol.1, Calcutta, 1785; London: Cadell and Debrett, 1788

Clinton, Jerome W., *The Tragedy of Sohrab and Rostam* (parallel texts), Seattle: University of Washington Press, 1987; revised edition, 1996

Davis, Dick, *The Legend of Seyavash*, with an introduction, Harmondsworth and New York: Penguin, 1992

Levy, Reuben, *The Epic of the Kings: The National Epic of Persia by Ferdowsi*, London: Routledge and Kegan Paul, 1967; several reprints including, with an introduction by Dick Davis, Costa Mesa, California: Mazda, 1996

Robinson, Samuel, *Sketch of the Life and Writings of Ferdusi*, Manchester: Transactions of the Literary and Philosophical Society of Manchester, 1819; printed separately for the author, 1823; revised version, London: privately printed, 1876

Rogers, Alexander, *The Shah-Namah of Fardusi*, London: Chapman and Hall, 1907

Weston, Stephen, *Ferdoosee: Episodes from Shah-Namah*, London: for the author, 1815

Along with Sa'dī, Firdausī was one of the first Persian poets whose name was known in the West, and both he and *The Shāhnāmeh* are mentioned by travellers and savants from the mid-17th century onwards. However, it was only with the writings of William Jones (1746–94) that he became more than a name. Jones's extraordinarily fertile mind was drawn to Firdausī's work, and he claimed that it was while reading *The Shāhnāmeh* that he intuited the existence of an Indo-European family of languages that included Persian, Sanskrit, Latin and Greek. Jones's projected drama on the tragedy of Suhrāb and Rostam (a section of *The Shāhnāmeh*) did not go beyond the planning stage; he did, however, translate parts of the poem into Latin.

The first substantial translation into English was carried out by Joseph CHAMPION; the first volume of his projected complete translation, published in 1785, was also the last. The cessation of his work on Firdausī seems to have been a result of the collapse of his mental health. Champion's translation is into the standard 18th-century narrative form of heroic couplets; this was certainly because of the prestige of the form when Champion was writing, but as *The Shāhnāmeh* itself is also in rhymed couplets it was an appropriate choice. The diction and tone of the translation are clearly imitated from Pope's versions of Homer; the verse is studied, laboured and fairly accurate to the (defective) text from which Champion worked. It lacks virtually all sense of the elemental vigour and power of the original, but then much the same could be said of its model.

James ATKINSON published his *Soohrab* in 1814. Like Champion's, his version is into heroic couplets. Despite its date (more or less coincident with the triumph of romantic poetry in England) Atkinson's verse sounds even more like Pope's Homer than Champion's does. It has considerable charm and grace and in its best moments is both elegant and eloquent; Atkinson seems most comfortable with pathos and sentiment, an indication of the influence of romanticism on his sensibility if not on his technique. As with Champion's version, the main fault is the absence of all sense of archaic epic strength. The relative success of his version of the Suhrāb story led Atkinson to issue, in 1832, a "complete" version of *The Shāhnāmeh*. In fact this version stops short at the advent of "Sikander" (Alexander the Great), i.e. about two-thirds of the way through the poem. Most of the translation is into prose; considerable portions are omitted, and these are presented in summary form. There are occasional passages in verse. The prose is quite lively and readable; it is accurate to its text, but as with all 19th- and early 20th-century versions of Firdausī the text used was very defective. Both Atkinson's verse version of Suhrāb's story and his prose version of the "whole" poem remained the standard translations throughout the 19th century and were often reprinted.

Atkinson's Suhrāb eclipsed the privately printed extracts from *The Shāhnāmeh* by Stephen WESTON (1815); Weston's preface shows a deepening understanding of the poem, in terms both of its Asian milieu and of the conventions of its genre, but his translations do not match Atkinson's verbal skill and empathetic response.

Samuel ROBINSON brought out a small book of translations of episodes from *The Shāhnāmeh* (1819; revised and reissued 1876). His translations are lineated as verse but are not metrical.

Their model would seem to be that of the poetry of the Old Testament as it is rendered in the King James Bible.

Alexander ROGERS's "complete" version of *The Shāhnāmeh* was published in 1907. It is into heroic couplets; as verse the translation is very inferior to that of Atkinson's Suhrab, and is at times barely competent. As with Atkinson's "complete" *Shāhnāmeh* a great deal is omitted; these portions are narrated in summary form in prose. As the poem proceeds there is more and more prose until it predominates.

Between 1905 and 1925 Arthur G. and Edmond WARNER issued the nine volumes of their blank verse translation of *The Shāhnāmeh*. This is the only truly complete version of the poem in English. The Warners worked from Persian but also clearly utilized to good effect Mohl's fine mid-19th-century French version of the poem. The blank verse is not inspired but it is in general accurate and the Edwardian poeticisms are not intolerably intrusive. For a reader without Persian or French this version gives a better idea of the poem *as a whole* than any other.

Much more easily available, however, is Reuben LEVY's prose version of the poem, first published in 1967 and frequently reprinted since. Levy omits and summarizes a great deal. His choices as to what to omit sometimes seem bizarre, and his prose, while competent, is not often inspired. He can make the poem seem tedious, which it almost never is in the original. He is at his best in the late "Sasanian" sections of the poem, a part of the work often ignored or treated very summarily by previous translators.

There are two recent blank verse versions of single episodes of the poem: *The Tragedy of Sohrab and Rostam* (1987), by Jerome CLINTON, a version that conveys, especially in its closing pages, a sense of tragic grandeur close to that of the original, and *The Legend of Seyavash* (DAVIS, 1992) by the present writer. These are the only versions of parts of the poem to have been made from critical texts prepared by modern textual scholars, texts that differ, often considerably, from those used by earlier translators.

DICK DAVIS

Further Reading

See introductions to Davis (1992) and to Levy (1996 edition)

Edward FitzGerald 1809–1883

British poet and translator

Biography

FitzGerald was born, on 31 March 1809, into a wealthy Anglo-Irish family, and brought up at the family house, Bredfield Hall, in Suffolk. The conditions of his apparently rather unhappy childhood (he found his mother very difficult to get on with, and relations with women remained problematic for him throughout his life) improved when he was sent to King Edward VI Grammar School in Bury St Edmunds, Suffolk. From there he went on to Trinity College, Cambridge. His time at Cambridge was not distinguished by academic success, but it was here that he met and became friends with both Tennyson, who was to be the leading poet of Victorian England, and Thackeray, one of the period's most important novelists.

After graduation FitzGerald returned to Suffolk, where (despite his wealth) he lived in relatively simple circumstances for the rest of his life. In 1856 he married Lucy Barton, the daughter of a Suffolk poet; the couple separated within months of the marriage, almost certainly because of FitzGerald's homosexuality; FitzGerald provided generously for Lucy's upkeep on condition that she never attempt to see him. In later life he became friends with George Crabbe, the son of the poet of the same name, and it was while on a visit to Crabbe that he died in his sleep, at Merton Rectory, Norfolk, 14 June 1883.

Edward FitzGerald is best known as the translator, from the Persian, of *The Rubaiyat of Omar Khayyam* (1859); he also made other translations from Persian, including a version of Jāmī's *Salaman and Absal* as well as one of 'Attār's *Mantiq al-Tair*. In addition to his translations from Persian he produced translations, from Spanish, of dramas by Calderón; his versions from Greek include Aeschylus's *Agamemnon* and *The Choephori* (the latter unfinished) and Sophocles's two Oedipus plays.

In 1844 he became friends with a much younger man, Edward Cowell (Cowell was then 18, FitzGerald was 35). Cowell was very good looking, a brilliant linguist, and relatively poor. FitzGerald's generosity and intellectual curiosity (and probably his sentimental feelings too) soon focused on Cowell and the two became firm friends. Cowell married and it is unlikely that he reciprocated, or was perhaps even aware of, Fitzgerald's homosexual feelings.

Cowell taught FitzGerald Spanish and suggested that he read Calderón. The friendship bore fruit in 1853, when FitzGerald's *Six Dramas of Calderón, Freely Translated by Edward FitzGerald* was published. The word "Freely" in the title is indicative of FitzGerald's translation methods generally. It was his habit to cut and rearrange the original, sometimes quite drastically. This he did in the service of what he called "readability", that was, attunement to the Victorian reading public's tastes. All his translations were inspired by a strong instinctive sense of fellowship with the original work, coupled with a feeling that only he could make the work comprehensible and acceptable to his own time and culture; to facilitate this comprehension and acceptance he was ready to prune and rearrange what he saw as incidentals in order to bring across the essence of what had moved him.

In 1852 Cowell started teaching FitzGerald Persian. The first book they read together was Jāmī's allegorical love poem *Salaman and Absal* (a strange choice for a teaching text as Jāmī is one of the most abstruse and difficult of Persian poets; the poem's fairly blatant misogyny may have been attractive to FitzGerald). In 1856 FitzGerald published a verse translation of the work; as with the Calderón dramas, his version contains many cuts and much rearrangement of the original material. In the same year, despite FitzGerald's strenuous objections, Cowell left England for India; his parting gift to FitzGerald was a copy he had made of a manuscript of quatrains by the 11th-century Persian poet Omar Khayyām. FitzGerald's work on the quatrains was his main means of keeping in touch with Cowell; he sent him many lengthy letters full of questions about the poems and their author, and reporting progress on the translation.

Taking a hint from Louisa Costello, a previous translator of a number of poems by Khayyām, FitzGerald arranged the poems into a narrative (in the Persian each quatrain is an entirely separate entity). The themes that particularly interested FitzGerald, and that he emphasized by his choice of quatrains, were those of religious scepticism, and "carpe diem" – seize the day, for life, pleasure and beauty perish all too quickly. FitzGerald's very free handling of his Persian original has been much criticized, but no other translation of Persian poetry (including FitzGerald's own other attempts) brings the anglophone reader so close to the atmosphere of Persian medieval verse. Four (anonymous) editions of the poem were published in FitzGerald's lifetime, and for each reissue he made extensive revisions. The work's later extraordinary popularity was just beginning to be felt around the time of FitzGerald's death.

Between 1856 and 1862 FitzGerald worked on a version (in heroic couplets) of the *Mantiq al-Tair* (*The Conference of the Birds*) by the12th-century Persian poet 'Attār. Again he cuts drastically; his dissatisfaction with his version is indicated by the fact that he never attempted to publish it, though it was included in the collected edition of his works brought out after his death. In the 1860s he turned his attention back to Spanish (Calderón again) and thence to Greek, producing a distinctive and powerful version of Aeschylus's *Agamemnon* and a draft of the same author's *Choephori*. He also translated Sophocles's two Oedipus plays, typically compressing them into one play by making numerous cuts. With the possible exception of his rather unjustly neglected *Agamemnon*, none of his other translations has even remotely the aphoristic force and charm of his *Rubaiyat of Omar Khayyam*, which became one of the best-loved and most widely influential poems of 19th-century English literature.

DICK DAVIS

See also the entry Omar Khayyām

Translations

Aeschylus, *Agamemnon*, 1865
Calderón de la Barca, Pedro, *Six Dramas of Calderon*, 1853
Calderón de la Barca, Pedro, *The Mighty Magician, and Such Stuff as Dreams are Made Of: Two Plays*, 1865
Calderón de la Barca, Pedro, *Eight Dramas of Calderon*, 1906
Omar Khayyām, *The Rubaiyat of Omar Khayyam*, 1859 (three more editions were brought out in FitzGerald's lifetime, for each of which he made alterations to the text, and a fifth was printed from a marked-up copy of the fourth edition, which was found in his papers after his death; innumerable editions have appeared since)
Sophocles, *Downfall and Death of King Oedipus*, 2 vols, 1880–81

Further Reading

Arberry, Arthur J. *FitzGerald's Salaman and Absal: A Study*, Cambridge: Cambridge University Press, 1956 (includes FitzGerald's translation of Jāmī's poem, as well as a version by Arberry)
FitzGerald, Edward, *Letters and Literary Remains of Edward FitzGerald*, edited by William Aldis Wright, 7 vols, London: Macmillan, 1902–03
Martin, Robert Bernard, *With Friends Possessed: A Life of Edward FitzGerald*, London: Faber, 1985

Gustave Flaubert 1821–1880

French novelist

Biography

Born in Rouen, 12 December 1821, at the hospital where his father lived as principal surgeon. While attending the Collège Royal in the town 1831–39 he was already writing stories. He studied law in Paris from 1841, but in 1844, after suffering epilepsy-type symptoms, he gave up these studies and devoted himself to literature, residing at Croisset, outside Rouen, with his mother and his orphaned niece. He lived withdrawn from public life, but travelled from time to time, notably in 1850–51 to Egypt, the Middle East, Greece and Italy and in 1858 to North Africa, and had valued friendships with other writers, including Louis Bouilhet, Maxime Du Camp, George Sand, the

Goncourt brothers, Maupassant and Turgenev. A stormy affair with the poet Louise Colet lasted from 1846 to 1854.

In his maturity Flaubert was preoccupied with the creative function of literary form, and his writings were the result of long gestation. His most famous work, *Madame Bovary* (1856–57), was more than five years in the making. His other main works are the novels *Salammbô* (1862), *L'Éducation sentimentale* (1869), *La Tentation de Saint Antoine* (1872, begun 1848), plus the unfinished *Bouvard et Pécuchet* (1881), and the three long short stories, *Trois Contes* (1877). He died at Croisset, 8 May 1880.

Translations

Collection

Anonymous, *Complete Works of Gustave Flaubert*, with an introduction by Ferdinand Brunetière, New York and London: M. Walter Dunne, 10 vols, 1904

Novels

Madame Bovary, 1857; in serial form 1856

Anonymous, *Madame Bovary*, vols 1 and 2 of *Complete Works*, New York and London: M. Walter Dunne, 1904

Bair, Lowell, *Madame Bovary*, edited and with an introduction by Leo Bersani, New York: Bantam, 1959

Blaydes, W., *Madame Bovary*, with an introduction by Henry James, New York: Collier, 1902

Hopkins, Gerard, *Madame Bovary: Life in a Country Town*, London: Hamish Hamilton, and New York: Oxford University Press, 1949; with an introduction by Terence Cave, London and New York: Oxford University Press, 1981

Man, Paul de (editor and translator), *Madame Bovary*, a "substantially new translation" based on the version by Eleanor Marx-Aveling, New York: Norton, 1965

Marmur, Mildred, *Madame Bovary*, with a foreword by Mary McCarthy, New York: New American Library, 1964; New York: Doubleday, 1997

Marx-Aveling (or Marx Aveling), Eleanor, *Madame Bovary: Provincial Manners*, London and Edinburgh: Vizetelly, 1886; New York: Modern Library, 1927; with an introduction by George Saintsbury, London: Dent, 1928; New York: Watts, 1969; and numerous reprints

May, J. Lewis, *Madame Bovary: A Story of Provincial Life*, with an introduction, London: John Lane / Bodley Head, and New York: Dodd Mead, 1928; with an introduction by Jacques de Lacretelle, Avon, Connecticut, Heritage Press, and London: Nonesuch Press, 1950

Russell, Alan, *Madame Bovary: A Story of Provincial Life*, with an introduction, Harmondsworth: Penguin, 1950 and numerous reprints

Steegmuller, Francis, *Madame Bovary: Patterns of Provincial Life*, New York: Random House, 1957; with a new introduction, New York: Modern Library, 1982; with an introduction by David Campbell, London: David Campbell, and Boston: G.K. Hall, 1993; with an introduction by Victor Brombert, New York: Knopf, 1993

Wall, Geoffrey, *Madame Bovary: Provincial Lives*, with an introduction, Harmondsworth and New York: Penguin, 1992

Salammbô, 1862

Anonymous, *Salammbô*, vols 3 and 4 in *Complete Works*, New York and London: M. Walter Dunne, 1904

Chartres, J.S., *Salambo*, London and Edinburgh: Vizetelly,1886; London: Dent, and New York: Dutton, 1931

Krailsheimer, A.J., *Salammbô*, with an introduction, Harmondsworth and New York: Penguin, 1977

Mathers, E. Powys, *Salambo*, Waltham St Lawrence, Berkshire: Golden Cockerel Press, 1931; New York: Rarity Press, 1932; reprinted London: Pushkin Press, 1947; New York: Berkeley, 1955

Matthews, J.W., *Salammbô*, with an introduction by Arthur Symons, New York: Doubleday Page, 1901; London: Greening, 1908

Sheldon, M.F., *Salammbô*, New York: United States Book Co., 1885

L'Éducation sentimentale, 1869

Anonymous, *A Sentimental Education*, vols 5 and 6 of *Complete Works*, New York and London: M. Walter Dunne, 1904

Baldick, Robert, *Sentimental Education*, with an introduction, London and New York: Penguin, 1964

Burlingame, Perdita, *The Sentimental Education*, New York: Signet, 1972; reprinted New York: New American Library, 1984

Goldsmith, Anthony, *Sentimental Education*, with an introduction, London: Dent, and New York: Dutton, 1941

Hannigan, D.F., *A Sentimental Education: A Young Man's History*, with an introduction, London; Nichols, 2 vols, 1898

Parmée, Douglas, *A Sentimental Education: The Story of a Young Man*, with an introduction, Oxford and New York: Oxford University Press, 1989

Bouvard et Pécuchet and *Dictionnaire des idées reçues* (unfinished), 1881

Anonymous, *Bouvard and Pécuchet*, vols 9 and 10 of *Complete Works*, New York and London: M. Walter Dunne, 1904

Barzun, Jacques, *Dictionary of Accepted Ideas*, with an introduction, Norfolk, Connecticut: New Directions, 1954

Earp, T.W. and G.W. Stonier, *Bouvard and Pécuchet*, with an introduction by Stonier, London: Jonathan Cape, 1936; with an introduction by Lionel Trilling, Norfolk, Connecticut: Laughlin, 1954

Hannigan, D.F., *Bouvard and Pécuchet*, London: Nichols, 1896

Krailsheimer, A.J., *Bouvard and Pécuchet*, Harmondsworth and Baltimore: Penguin, 1976 (includes *Dictionary of Received Ideas*, translated by Robert Baldick)

Wall, Geoffrey, *Dictionary of Received Ideas*, with an introduction by Julian Barnes, London: Syrens, and New York: Penguin, 1994

Stories

Trois Contes, 1877

Anonymous, in *Complete Works*, London and New York: M. Walter Dunne, 1904 ("Herodias" and " A Simple Soul" in vol. 4; "St Julien the Hospitaller" in vol. 8)

Baldick, Robert, *Three Tales*, with an introduction, Harmondsworth and New York: Penguin, 1961 ("A Simple Heart", "The Legend of St Julian the Hospitator", "Herodias")

Cobb, Walter F., *Three Tales: A Simple Heart; The Legend of St Julian the Hospitaler; Herodias*, with a foreword by Henri Peyre, New York: New American Library, 1964

Ives, George Burnham, *Gustave Flaubert: A Simple Heart; The Legend of St Julian the Hospitaller; Herodias*, with an introduction by Frank Thomas Marzials, New York and London: Putnam, 1903

Krailsheimer, A.J., *Three Tales*, with an introduction, Oxford and New York: Oxford University Press, 1991 ("A Simple Heart", "The Legend of Saint Julian the Hospitaller", "Herodias")

McDowell, Arthur, *Three Tales*, London: Chatto and Windus, 1923; with an introduction by Harry Levin, Norfolk, Connecticut: New Directions, 1944 ("A Simple Heart", "The Legend of Saint Julian the Hospitaller", "Herodias")

Play

La Tentation de Saint Antoine, 1872

Anonymous, *The Temptation of St Anthony*, in vol. 7 of *Complete Works*, New York and London: M. Walter Dunne, 1904; New York: Fertig, 1978

Hannigan, D.F., *The Temptation of Saint Antony*, London: Nichols, 1895

Hearn, Lafcadio, *The Temptation of Saint Anthony*, Seattle: Alice Harriman, 1910

Mrosovsky, Kitty, *The Temptation of Saint Anthony*, with an introduction, Ithaca, New York: Cornell University Press, and London: Secker and Warburg, 1980; Harmondsworth and New York: Penguin, 1983

Early Writings

Garman, Douglas, *The First Sentimental Education*, with an introduction by Gerhard Gerhardi, Berkeley: University of California Press, 1972

Griffin, Robert, *Early Writings*, with an introduction, Lincoln: University of Nebraska Press, 1991

Jellinek, Frank, *November*, New York: Roman Press, 1932; with an introduction by Francis Steegmuller, New York: Serendipity Press, 1967

Steegmuller, Francis, *Intimate Notebook, 1840–1841*, with an introduction, New York: Doubleday, 1967 (contains a translation of *Souvenirs, notes et pensées intimes*)

Letters

Beaumont, Barbara, *Flaubert and Turgenev: A Friendship in Letters*, London: Athlone Press, and New York: Norton, 1985

Cohen, J.M., *Selected Letters: Flaubert*, with an introduction by Richard Rumbold, London: Weidenfeld and Nicolson, 1950

McKenzie, Aimee L., *The George Sand–Gustave Flaubert Letters*, with an introduction by Stuart P. Sherman, New York: Boni and Liveright, 1921

Steegmuller, Francis, *Selected Letters: Flaubert*, with an introduction, New York: Farrar Straus and Cudahy, and London: Hamish Hamilton, 1954

Steegmuller, Francis, *The Letters of Gustave Flaubert*, 2 vols, Cambridge, Massachusetts: Harvard University Press, 1980–82

Steegmuller, Francis and Barbara Bray, *Flaubert–Sand: The Correspondence*, New York: Knopf, and London: Harvill, 1993

The landmark novel *Madame Bovary* has a plot so credible, characterizations so recognizable, an interwoven social setting so authentic yet unobtrusive that it would have transcended slipshod translations. However, it has elicited highly competent renderings. Translators have managed Flaubert's style surprisingly well. This deceptively straightforward text actually works through a system of metonymy, requiring translators to weigh carefully the balance between literal and free. Once readers make the intuitive leap between the "something," i.e. this apparently realistic narrative, to the "something else", i.e. what is really at issue, they discover as much range for symbolic interpretation as in symbolist works. Extant English translations, including the oldest and anonymous, do not significantly lessen this quality.

Although its daring is disguised by metonymy (the cinema cliché of the storm in the sky signifying lovemaking on the ground begins here), in 1857 the author and publisher were accused of corrupting public morals. They were acquitted. After all, if Emma Bovary destroys herself, ruins her husband, and blights her daughter, adultery is clearly risky behavior – for a woman. Her lovers, however, are not punished, and the conniving, half-educated local pharmacist whose shop provided the poison for her suicide is rewarded by government recognition.

Long classified as the epitome of realism, extraordinary metonymy of Madame Bovary derives from descriptions that invite multi-layered explications; from dialogues on which we seem to be eavesdropping; and from a disarming recording of characters' thoughts. These thoughts, however, are not in the first-person, like stream-of-consciousness, but subtly editorialized third-person narration, i.e. Flaubert's *style indirect libre*. For all these reasons, the novel could just as well be classified as Romantic or Symbolist.

Further, perhaps as much for Flaubert's irony and ambivalence as for his artistry, the novel has withstood innumerable schools in literary criticism. Just as each reader – each Western reader at any rate – knows an Emma Bovary, each school of criticism uncovers its own *Madame Bovary*. For example, a traditional literary historian like Benjamin Bart published a biography in 1967 that made Flaubert larger than life and avoided *ad hominem* comments. Sartre in *The Family Idiot* deplores Flaubert's reducing a love affair to an outside description of a cab ride, but his indignation has elicited some of his most moving literary criticism. Marxist critics can focus on the effect of the characters' social conditioning; psychoanalytic critics, on Emma's neuroses and reality problems, exacerbated by her milieu; feminists, on her complicitous victimization in a patriarchal setting, and so on . Emma and the supporting characters have a life in the world of collective readership, like Hamlet or Don Quixote. Perhaps this is why we still read with interest Emma's "side" of the story in *Lui, A View of Him* (1869) by Flaubert's longtime lover Louise Colet.

Madame Bovary will undoubtedly remain the novel that establishes the norms for the "traditional novel", i.e. the novel by which we evaluate novels and assess their originality and/or conventionality.

For the French text of *Madame Bovary* readers should use either the six-volume *Oeuvres complètes* (Paris: Club de l'Honnête Homme, 1971–75) or a good single-volume edition like that by Bernard Ajac (Paris: Flammarion, 1986). (Any edition from the 1873 Charpentier edition onwards contains Flaubert's subsequent corrections.)

The three most striking translations are those by Marx-Aveling (1855–98), daughter of Karl Marx, Hopkins (1892–1961), and Steegmuller (1906–1996).

The translation by MARX-AVELING (1886) went through more than 30 editions prior to 1927 with a prestigious reprinting in 1969, and she is the most likely "ANONYMOUS" of 1904). She undoubtedly identified with Emma. She follows Flaubert's lexicon and syntax as closely as the two languages permit and while this gives her translation a somewhat choppy rhythm, it lets her convey also the sympathy implicit in Flaubert's ambivalence. It would appear also that wherever a shading of sympathy was possible, Marx-Aveling, herself to be a suicide, chose that sympathetic rendering.

HOPKINS (1949) does much editorializing and chooses the route of rhythm. With him, Flaubert's submerged alexandrine iambs become anapests. STEEGMULLER (1957), whose translation rivals BAIR's (1959) in availability and price, translates nearly as closely as Marx–Aveling but wherever a shading of antipathy was possible chose that. His Emma comes across to readers as more responsible for her fate. In as much as he was the doyen of Flaubert studies in the United States and, additionally a superb English stylist, his is likely to remain the preferred translation for some time to come.

DE MAN's copious critical apparatus (1965) includes translated extracts from early versions of the French source text as well as some of Flaubert's letters about *Madame Bovary* and analyses of the book by eminent scholars and critics. MARMUR (1964) appends, an English translation of the main documents from the 1857 trial.

The spirit in which translators approach this awe-inspiring text varies through the spectrum of possibilities. In his introduction, although admitting that the task "requires an effort which parallels the author's own labor" and is subject to his own human fallibility, STEEGMULLER takes it for granted "as a kind of postulate" that whatever ideas, emotions, subtleties and shadings have been expressed in French can all be re-expressed in English. For MAY, in contrast, "any attempt to render Flaubert, of all the writers, in another idiom, is foredoomed to failure". It is instructive to compare the degree to which translators of *Madame Bovary* into English do succeed in transmitting Flaubert's insights and visions and the concerted verbal textures that embody them.

In a crucial passage of part 1, chapter 7, Emma realizes that her marriage to Charles has been a terrible boring mistake:

> Puis ses idées peu à peu se fixaient, et, assise sur le gazon, qu'elle fouillaient à petits coups avec le bout de son ombrelle, Emma se répétait:
> – Pourquoi, mon Dieu! me suis-je mariée?

The mood and the rhythm come through variously, different sacrifices having been made:

> Little by little her ideas grew more definite; and as she sat on the grass and dug her parasol here and there into the turf, she kept repeating to herself, "Why did I marry him?"
> (Marx-Aveling, 1886)

> Then her thoughts would start to crystallize. She would sit on the grass into which she would dig the point of her parasol with brief thrusts and would ask herself: "My God, why did I get married?
> (Marmur, 1964)

> Then gradually her ideas took definite shape, and, sitting on the grass that she dug up with little pricks of her sunshade, Emma repeated to herself: – Why, for Heaven's sake, did I marry?
> (De Man, 1965; here he diverges considerably from Marx-Aveling. Though he presents it as "a substantially new translation", an "extensively revised version" of Marx-Aveling, for much of the time De Man's translation follows hers word for word.)

> Then her ideas gradually came together, and, sitting on the grass, poking at it with the point of her sunshade, Emma kept saying to herself
> – Oh, why, dear God, did I marry him?
> (Wall, 1992)

Nearly at the end of the book, in part 3, chapter 11, when Emma has poisoned herself and the widowed Charles comes face to face with her lover, he is too desolate to express anger:

> – Je ne vous en veux pas, dit-il.[...]
> Il ajouta même un grand mot, le seul qu'il ait jamais dit:
> – C'est la faute de la fatalité!
> Rodolphe, qui avait conduit cette fatalité, le trouva bien débonnaire pour un homme dans sa situation, comique même, et un peu vil.

Again, readings and rhythms vary in the English, for example:

> "I'm not angry with you," he said. [...]
> Then he said a great thing, the only great thing he ever said in his life,
> "It's fate must bear the blame!"
> Rodolphe, who had directed the course of this same Fate, thought him very civil for a man in his position; rather comic, indeed, and a trifle cheap.
> (May, 1928)

> "I'm not angry with you," he said. [...]
> And then he delivered himself of the one large utterance he ever made: "It is the fault of Fate."
> Rodolphe, who had directed "Fate" in this instance, thought him pretty easy-going for a man in his position, rather comic, in fact, and a bit abject.
> (Russell, 1950)

> "I don't hold it against you," he said.[...]
> And he added a bit of rhetoric, the only such utterance that had ever escaped him:
> "No one is to blame. It was decreed by fate".
> Rodolphe, who had been the instrument of that fate,

thought him very meek indeed for a man in his situation – comical even, and a little contemptible.

(Steegmuller, 1957)

Madame Bovary is by far the most read of Flaubert's works and has been much translated, but his other major titles have also been made available in several English versions since the end of the 19th century.

In *Salammbô*, Flaubert the archivist and documentary journalist reconstructed the rebellion, after the first Punic War, of Carthaginian mercenaries, 242–238 BC. In the company of photographer Maxime Du Camp, he had toured Egypt, Palestine, Syria, Turkey, and Greece, from November 1849 to April 1851. As he got into the drafting of *Salammbô*, he toured Tunisia and Algeria, from April to June 1858.

The title character is the Carthaginian general Hamilcar Barca's daughter, a virgin priestess and cult object whose sexuality is satisfied by a cult serpent. Although she is briefly kidnapped by the infatuated mercenary leader Mathô after the opening celebration banquet at the palace in Carthage, neither romance nor lust is as important in this novel as the vicissitudes of Hamilcar Barca's pacification campaign. Flaubert closes the novel by bringing the scene back to the palace to celebrate Salammbô's betrothal to the treacherous Numidian Narr'Havas at a ceremony of torture for Mathô. Mathô has a fatal collapse from the torture, and she dies from the shock of seeing him die. Readers are supposed to remember that Hamilcar Barca saved his son Hannibal from the sacrifice of male children required by Moloch so that Carthage will have a respite of glory before the triumph of wholesome Roman paganism. (Readers are supposed also to feel gratified by the implicit exaltation of major religions of the modern era.)

The critical response rested on the book's perceived authenticity and accuracy. Literary history has for the most part accommodated Flaubert's composite paganism as well as his presumed psychological authenticity. These characters are not Westerners reared in the Judeo-Christian tradition; thus, their inner lives, which seem convincing, are not such as readers of the past 150 years can identify with. Flaubert's forte has been a cinematic rendering of scene.

Students using French should use the Club de l'honnête homme *Oeuvres complètes* referred to above. However, Edouard Maynial's 1961 edition (Garnier Frères) is reliable.

Although the US Library of Congress lists 15 English translations of *Salammbô* after 1892, it is rarely read in translation. CHARTRES (1886), MATHERS (1931), and KRAILSHEIMER (1977) are complete and barely distinguishable one from another.

Less read than *Madame Bovary* but preferred by specialists, *L'Éducation sentimentale* is a *tour de force*. Flaubert adroitly exposes the wasted life of Frédéric Moreau, a good-looking but shallow scion of the provincial upper middle class, as he proceeds to learn little of value during his emotional education. Frédéric is a political spectator and luckless speculator during the final years of Louis–Philippe's bourgeois monarchy (1830–48), the brief republic, and Napoleon III's coup d'état bringing about the Second Empire. As the novel comes to a close, roughly at the time Flaubert was writing it, Frédéric seems headed toward the same grim keeping up of appearances in which he was reared.

As in *Madame Bovary*, the novel is multiply self-reflective and self-reinforcing. Frédéric's pursuits of women and pleasure parallel historical developments while depictions of one social class parallel developments in another social class and every prop suggests a mental attitude.

Recommended for students of French: the *Oeuvres complètes* mentioned above or the one-volume edition by P.M. Wetherill (Paris: Garnier, 1984).

GOLDSMITH (1941), BALDICK (1964), and BURLINGHAME (1972) are accurate and competent.

Two proficient translators of Flaubert have provided successive versions of his *Three Tales* for Penguin Classics – BALDICK (1961) and KRAILSHEIMER (1991). "A Simple Heart", which has been much used to teach post-secondary students advanced French, follows a farm girl Félicité through her life as the maid for a small town widow. (The lifestyle for Madame Aubain is very much like Madame Moreau's in *Sentimental Education*.) After many disappointments, her affection centers on her parrot Loulou, that she has stuffed after its death. When she dies during the May Mary processions, Loulou and the Holy Spirit merge in her expiring consciousness.

Both "St Julian the Hospitaler" and "Herodias" follow the iconography of Rouen cathedral. Both are cinematic in presentation. "St Julian" evokes the saint's life, "Herodias" the final days of John the Baptist.

Students of French have the choice between the *Oeuvres complètes* as above and a one-volume edition: *Trois Contes*, edited by Jacques Suffel (Paris: Garnier Flammarion, 1965).

A preferred Flaubert work among *aficionados*, the novel *Bouvard and Pécuchet*, if completed would have been the apotheosis of Flaubertian irony vis-à-vis contemporary life (counterpointing *The Temptation of Saint Anthony*, the apotheosis of Flaubertian credulity *vis-à-vis* exoticism). Even unfinished, it contains comic scenes and sarcastic narrations interspersed with lyrical passages. An inheritance allows two incredulous white-collar workers to retire to the country and expend their energies in every field of knowledge. Every chapter is a new domain – and a new fiasco. Meanwhile, the same series of historical events as in *Sentimental Education* occur, interfering with their lives at the periphery. The unfinished status of this novel has presumably discouraged translation, though there are several English versions, including again KRAILSHEIMER (1976). The small associated *Dictionary of Received Ideas* is sometimes translated on its own. The *Oeuvres complètes* as above or Claudine Gothot-Mersch's edition (*Bouvard et Pécuchet*, Paris: Gallimard, 1979) offer reliable versions of the source text.

Flaubert had pretentions to being a dramatist and composing spectacles. The seven-part "armchair" drama *The Temptation of Saint Anthony* is cinemascope before the fact, although concert readings have elicited thoughtful and thought-provoking criticism. Flaubert's initial inspiration was the Breughel painting he saw while travelling with his family in Italy in 1845. He thought about it off and on until 1869 when he finally made it his main project. He fastidiously researched the religions and heresies competing with early Christianity. If staged or filmed, this drama would make visible (via the saint's acted-out fantasies and hallucinations) the life of Saint Anthony of Egypt (AD 250–355), known as the first Christian monk.

The French text is available in the Club de l'Honnêt Homme

Oeuvres complètes as above and Jacques Suffel's one-volume edition (Paris: Flammarion, 1967). MROSOVSKY (1980) comes after several elderly English versions.

Most early Flaubert texts published since his death have been translated into English (see ANONYMOUS, *Complete Works*, 1904; JELLINEK, 1932); *Early Writings* (GRIFFIN, 1991) contains 11 embarrassing pieces that reveal Flaubert's undisguised hatred for humanity at the time he wrote them; STEEGMULLER'S *Intimate Notebook, 1840–41* (1967) is an exquisite rendering of *Souvenirs, notes et pensées intimes* (published 1965), with helpful notes.

MARILYN GADDIS ROSE

Further Reading

For *Madame Bovary*

Bart, Benjamin, *Flaubert*, Syracuse, New York: Syracuse University Press, 1967

Colet, Louise, *Lui! A View of Him*, translated by Marilyn Gaddis Rose, Athens, Georgia: University of Georgia Press, 1987

Sartre, Jean-Paul, *The Family Idiot*, translated by Carol Cosman, 5 vols, Chicago : University of Chicago Press, 1981–93

Steegmuller, Francis, *Flaubert and Madame Bovary: A Double Portrait*, New York: Viking, 1939; new edition, London: Collins, 1947; revised, with a new author's note, Chicago: University of Chicago Press, 1977

See also the introductory material in the translations listed above

For *Salammbô*

Green, Anne, *Flaubert and the Historical Novel: Salammbô Reassessed*, Cambridge and New York: Cambridge University Press, 1982

Rousset, Jean, "Positions, distances, perspectives dans *Salammbô*", in *Travail de Flaubert* by Raymonde Debray-Genette, *et al.*, Paris: Seuil, 1983, pp. 79–92

For *Sentimental Education*

Goncourt, Jules and Edmond de, *The Goncourt Journals, 1851–70*, translated, with an introduction, by Lewis Galantière, New York: Doubleday Doran, and London: Cassell, 1937

Lottman, Herbert, *Flaubert: A Biography*, Boston: Little Brown, and London: Methuen, 1989

Marx, Karl, *The Eighteenth Brumaire of Louis Bonaparte*, translated by Eden and Cedar Paul, New York: International Publishers, 1926; London: Allen and Unwin, 1939

Paulson, William R., *Sentimental Education: The Complexity of Disenchantment*, New York: Twayne, 1992

For *Bouvard and Pécuchet*

Kenner, Hugh, *Flaubert, Joyce and Beckett: The Stoic Comedians*, Boston: Beacon Press, 1963; London: W.H. Allen, 1964

Richard, Jean-Pierre, "Variations d'un paysage", in *Travail de Flaubert* by Raymonde Debray-Genette *et al.*, Paris: Seuil, 1983: pp. 169–80

For *Three Tales*

Barnes, Julian, *Flaubert's Parrot*, London: Jonathan Cape, 1984; New York: Knopf, 1985

Debray-Genette, Raymonde, "Du monde narratif dans les *Trois Contes*" in *Travail de Flaubert* by Debray-Genette *et al.*, Paris: Seuil, 1983

Grimaud, Michel, "Saint Julian Hospitalier", in *Saint/Oedipus: Psychocritical Approaches to Flaubert's Art*, edited by William J. Berg, Ithaca, New York: Cornell University Press, 1982

Stein, Gertrude, *Three Lives: Stories of the Good Anna, Melanctha, and the Gentle Lena*, New York: Grafton Press, 1909; Harmondsworth and New York: Penguin, 1990

Willenbrink, George A., *The Dossier of Flaubert's "Un Coeur simple"*, Amsterdam: Rodopi, 1976

For *The Temptation of Saint Anthony*

Foucault, Michel, "La bibliothèque fantastique" in *Travail de Flaubert*, by Raymonde Debray-Genette *et al.*, Paris: Seuil, 1983

John Florio c.1553–1625

English translator and lexicographer

Biography

Born in London to Italian Protestant parents. The family, originally from Siena, had come to England as refugees just before the reign of Edward VI. Florio may have received his early schooling on the Continent. By 1576 he was tutoring private pupils at Oxford; he himself matriculated there at Magdalen College in 1581. A professional modern linguist specializing in Italian, English, French and Spanish, he made a reputation as teacher and writer and was in the employ of noble patrons, including Anne of Denmark, wife of King James VI of Scotland and I of Great Britain. He is best known as the translator of Montaigne and for his Italian–English dictionary. He died at Fulham in August or September 1625.

Given the dominant cultural emphasis throughout the Renaissance on the unearthing, translating and refreshing of texts for wider consumption, it is not surprising that an irrepressibly enthusiastic linguist such as John Florio should attract increasing attention within courtly, aristocratic and diplomatic circles in Elizabethan and Jacobean England. A leading figure in the vibrant and competitive society of language teachers at the turn of the 17th century, Florio was clearly continuing a path that had been at least partially pioneered by his father, Michael Angelo Florio. The latter had been an eminent linguist and tutor (the erudite Lady Jane Grey was numbered among his many pupils), who had translated Bishop Ponet's catechism into Italian and, indeed, some of his manuscripts survive, detailing his account of the rules of Italian grammar.

His son's first venture into print was in 1578 with *Florio his firste fruites: a perfect induction to the Italian and English tongues*. Here were to be found 44 dialogues in question-and-answer format, arranged with parallel texts in Italian and English. In the 16th century, dialogue texts such as, for example, the *Colloquies* of Erasmus, were employed in schools for the teaching of Latin; and French textbooks of the period frequently favoured the usage of parallel texts (sometimes including rhyme) which focused on the details of everyday life. None the less, Florio made the most significant step in Britain towards the wider dissemination of Italian with this work, and extended the potential of such devices. He has his characters exploring a much wider range of topics than was common for such primers: "Familiar speeche with man or woman"; "To speake with a Gentleman"; "To Speak of England"; "Three hundreth fyne proverbes"; "Reasonynges upon Fortune and what Fortune is". It is in this collection (31st dialogue) that the phrase appears which *may* have had an influence on Shakespeare: "it were labour lost to speake of Loue". Given the topics of this sequence of texts (carefully ordered in terms of difficulty), it is clear that Florio is targeting the gentleman, rather than the trader, for his reader. He seems to wish not only to stimulate more interest in Italian (and thus recruit more clients), but to affirm the superiority of the language and culture of Italy. As the reader of his dialogues explores apparently everyday situations in Elizabethan England, sometimes wandering the London streets with the characters, he or she is confronted, on occasions, with patronizing and satirical reflections. Florio goes on to express what he considers to be the weaknesses of English itself, with its impure origins and susceptibility to loan words and borrowings. Incorporating citations from Guicciardini and from Guevara (translated from the Spanish by da Trino), Florio may appear like a refugee Castiglione embarking on a *mission civilisatrice* for his "friendly, curteous, and indifferent Reader". To consolidate the educational enterprise, he makes space at the end of the volume for a section, composed again in dialogue form, devoted to Italian grammar and pronunciation.

In 1578 Florio leaves the capital for Oxford, penetrates the academic world of Magdalen College and makes the acquaintance of Matthew Gwinne. Speculation continues over the degree of the translator's engagement with colonial debates of the time; however, by 1580, there appears, translated into English from a French version, *A Shorte and briefe narration of the two Navigations and Discoueries to the North weast partes called Newe Fravnce*. Within a couple of years, Florio is once again drawn back to the capital and, from 1583 onwards, he is employed in various capacities at the French Embassy. It is during this period that he once again turns to translation to promote interest in all things Italian: *A Letter lately written from Rome, by an Italian Gentleman, to a freende of his in Lyons in Fraunce* ... (1585).

Much more significant than either of these minor productions, however, is the publication in 1591 of *Florio's second frutes*, another collection of instructional dialogues in Italian and English. These and the earlier "fruits" became two of the most popular guides to Italian of the period. In *Second Frutes* (in which he signs himself for the first time "Resolute Iohn Florio"), the translator adopts a much less moralizing tone than he had previously in his *First Frutes* and regards his adopted land with much less *hauteur*. He once again employs the format of parallel texts that focus upon contemporary modes of behaviour. However, the subject matter of this later volume resembles much more that of a courtesy book: it is more lively, vigorous and focused on the business of love than *First Frutes* and this perhaps reflects the hedonistic temper of his aristocratic patrons. Conventional subjects of discussion ("of rising in the morning, and of things belonging to the chamber") are subsequently extended to more robust cultural discourse ("Between James, & Lippa his man, wherin they talk of many pleasant and delightsome iestes, and in it is described an unpleasant lodging, an ill-favoured old woman, also the beautiful partes that a woman ought to have to be accounted faire in all perfection, & pleasantly blazoned a counterfeit, lazy, and nought worth servant"). In both of these manuals, Florio's English translation can become maladroit because he remains too close to the original Italian, and this weakness, together with its opposite, a propensity for extravagantly liberal translation, remain with him throughout his career. *Second Frutes* comes to a close with the "Gardine of Recreation, yeelding six thousand Italian proverbs". These latter are arranged approximately alphabetically and constitute an example of Florio's enthusiasm for rhetoric: he will continue to view the deployment of the proverb as a device with which the student may master and enrich his or her knowledge of a given language.

Florio now turned to lexicography and in 1598 published *A Worlde of Wordes, Or Most copious, and exact Dictionarie in Italian and English*. This production, containing definitions of over 46,000 words, was dedicated to his eminent pupils: Shakespeare's patron, the Earl of Southampton; the Earl of Rutland; and "my most-most honored, because best-best adorned Madame", Lucie, Countess of Bedford. Throughout this work, Florio continues to celebrate the wealth of the Italian language; however, elsewhere, he seems to have moved a step nearer to appreciating the "sweete-mother-toong" of his adopted land. This dictionary represented yet another pioneering venture for Florio, for he appears to have had no tradition to build upon apart from a slim vocabulary primer for Italian authors. Clearly, he did wish this *Worlde of Wordes* to assist his pupils, and others, on their journeys through the works of such figures as Petrarch, Dante, Castiglione and Guazzo: "The retainer doth some service, that now and then, but holds your Honors styrrop, or lendes a hande ouer a stile, or opens a gappe for easier passage, or holds a torch in a darke waie" (*Epistle Dedicatorie*). Nevertheless, most innovatively, he determines to include words from an enormous range of contexts: legal, commercial and artisanal, for example. In his prefatory remarks, he asserts that the idea for this work has been germinating for some 20 years, and a growing confidence in his linguistic abilities is in evidence at the very beginning of the dictionary: "If any man aske whether all Italian wordes be here? I answere him, it may be no: and yet I thinke heere may be as many, as he is likely to finde (that askes the question) within the compasse of his reading; and yet he may haue read well too".

Having become Italian tutor to the queen herself in 1603, Florio publishes *Queen Anna's NEW WORLD of Words or DICTIONARIE of the Italian and English tongues.* In this "braine-babe" of 13 years' gestation there are over 74,000 entries, and his list of consulted authors has expanded from 72 in the earlier dictionary to 249. In what is more than a dictionary, Florio provides his reader not only, once again, with a detailed account of Italian grammar ("to avoide the many errors that diuers commit, namely my countrey men the English ..."), he also displays an encyclopedic knowledge and his undying enthusiasm for words. Florio can contain himself with relatively conventional entries; but his imagination is clearly excited by the possibilities of finding cultural equivalents or providing cultural contexts for given words:

> *Lámia*, a beast that hath a face like a man, and feete like a horse. Also a sea-dogge, or dog fish. Also a kinde of fish with so great a iaw, and is so rauenous, that is will deuoure an armed man. Also women that were thought to haue such eyes as they could at their pleasure pull out and put in againe, or as some describe them, certaine Diuels in a counterfeit shape that with flatterings allured faire yoong springals or boyes, and taking vpon them the likenesse and fashion of women were thought to deuoure them and bring them to destruction. Some thought them to be Ladies of the Fairies, or such as make children affraid, or such witches as sucke childrens blood and kill them. Vsed also for any kind of hag, witch or sorceresse. Vsed also for an impudent whore or shame-lesse strumpet. Vsed also for an high arched vault or such hollow place in roofed buildings.
>
> *Zóccoli Zóccoli*, as we say in mockery, Tush-tush, away, in faith Sir no, or yea in my other hose. Also when speaking of any body in secrecy the party by chance commeth in, as the Latins say, Lupus est in fàbula, so the Italians say, *Zóccoli Zóccoli.*

This magnificent work marks an outstanding achievement in Florio's colourful career, but his most notable claim to fame is his *magnum opus*, the translation of Montaigne's essays published in 1603. This great achievement reaffirms his long-held belief, voiced in the dedicatory remarks, that "Translata proficit". It is with this work that he may claim a place among the ranks of eminent Early Modern translators: this was a culture that produced North's *Plutarch*, Golding's *Ovid*, Harington's *Ariosto* and Hoby's *Courtier*, to name but a few. Clearly responding to contemporary tastes for contemplative, sceptical writing, Florio appears to have engaged on his enormous task with the help of another Italian Protestant, Theodore Diodati, for the more difficult French passages, and Matthew Gwinne, to trace Montaigne's classical quotations. The work was dedicated to six notable patronesses. Given that "all translations are reputed femalls, delivered at second hand; and I in this serve but as Vulcan, to hatchet this Minerva from that Iupiter's bigge braine", it was deemed appropriate that the dedicatees, many of whom had been Florio's pupils, should be female. They were addressed in three separate prefaces: Anne Harington and her daughter Lucie, Countess of Bedford; Elizabeth, Countess of Rutland, and Penelope Rich; Mary Neville and Elizabeth Grey. Along with many other translators of the period, Florio in this work is clearly challenging the remnants of scholastic belief, still current in his culture, that assigned learning to academic elites: "Shall I apologize translation? Why but some holde (as for their free-hold) that such conversion is the subversion of Universities. God holde with them, and withholde them from impeach or empaire. It were an ill turne, the turning of Bookes should be the overturning of Libraries". His undertaking is not only to render Montaigne more accessible to a wider readership but, in addition, to award him an anglicized identity furnished with the details of English cultural referents: e.g. "les miens se sont aultrefois surnommez Eyquem, surnom qui touche encores une maison cogneue en Angleterre" is rendered by Florio as "my Ancestors have hereto-fore beene surnamed *Higham*, or *Eyquem*, a surname which also belongs to a house well knowen in England" (*De la gloire*).

Florio's insatiable delight in words contrasts starkly with Montaigne's often incisive, piquant and pared-down style. The Elizabethan fondness for copia finds an all-too-willing exponent in Florio who, unlike Montaigne, equates fine writing with ornamentation, poetic complexity and the deployment of rhetoric. Such elaborative techniques may, on occasions, be justified, for they allow him to secure a place for foreign words in English, and, indeed, may even offer an outlet for self-expression. In order to give emphasis, to qualify, to concretize an image or simply to establish an emotional tone not found in Montaigne, Florio adds words, clauses and even collections of sentences to realize fully his desired text:

> Tout ce qu'ils me dient et font, ce n'est que fard, leur liberté estant bridee de toutes parts par la grande puissance que j'ay sur eulx: je ne veois rien autour de moy, que couvert et masqué.
>
> Whatsoever they say, all they doe unto me, is but a glosse, and but dissimulation, their libertie being every where brideled, and checked by the great power I have over them. I see nothing about me, but inscrutable hearts, hollow mindes, fained lookes, dissembled speeches, and counterfeit actions.
>
> (*De l'inequalité qui est entre nous*)

Many readers have identified the influence of Lyly's euphuism in Florio's fondness for addition, paraphrase, symmetry, alliteration and parallelism; however, equally convincingly, Frances Yates draws attention to the possible influence on him of the Arcadian style, with its extravagantly meandering phrases and liking for repetition and alliteration. The latter device, for example, may be exploited for no reason at all in the translated text except for the powerful pleasure it holds for the translator. However, elsewhere Florio wishes to exploit the rhythms of Montaigne's own language, replacing in the following example the latter's assonance with his own alliteration: "La raison nous ordonne bien d'aller tousjours mesme chemin, mais non toutesfois mesme train" becomes "Reason doth appoint us ever to walke in one path, but not alwaies to keepe one pace" (*Du dormir*).

In the listing of linguistic influences on Florio, Matthiessen points to the contemporary popularity of the style of the Huguenot poet Du Bartas, especially his fondness for creating compound words and ornate constructions. Indeed, Du Bartas is referred to in the work's second dedication. It is obvious that Florio delights in converting "la grandeur de courage de cet homme" into "this mans unmated-haughty heart" (*Du dormir*), and the "doulx son de cette harmones" into "the sweet-alluring and sense-entrancing sound of this harmonie" (*De la vanité des paroles*).

Nevertheless, this whole debate over influences also feeds the larger discussion concerning Florio's cultural engagement with Montaigne's texts. Many readers have noted, for example, that for the translator "les erreurs de Wiclef" become "Wickliff's opinions"; and, on occasions, Florio will depart from his usual practice of translating classical quotations if he esteems the content vulgar or morally dubious. Montaigne's citation in book 3 of Juvenal's sixth satire, for example, ("adhuc ardens rigidoe tentigine vulvae / Et lassata viris, nondum satiata recessit") is left to stand alone, while subsequent French editors have been less circumspect ("Brûlante encore de volupté, elle se retira enfin, plus fatiguée qu'assouvie"). The reader will sometimes find Florio imitating French constructions too closely or pursuing the complexities of wordplay too fervently, and so inaccuracies become inevitable: "Pensons nous que les enfants de choeur prennent grand plaisir à la musique?" can become "Thinke wee, that high-minded men take great pleasure in musicke?" (*De l'inequalité qui est entre nous*). He was often clearly working at great speed and this prevented him from identifying mistranslation, baffling punctuation and the nonsensical phrase. None the less, while Montaigne's text may on occasions appear too richly adorned, the vivacity, intimacy and innovativeness of Florio's translation bring with them an inexhaustible pleasure to the reader: "les farces des bateleurs nous resjouïssent; mais aux joueurs elles servent de corvée" becomes "Enterludes and commedies rejoyce and make us merry, but to players they are tedious and tastelesse" (*De l'inequalité qui est entre nous*).

Florio's translation was enormously influential in the educated circles of Early Modern Britain: Jonson, Shakespeare, Ralegh, Bacon and Burton, to name but a few, were clearly exposed to his rendering of Montaigne's essays. Indeed, Jonson's signed copy remains in the British Museum collection. Florio's translation enjoyed such popularity that it went to a second edition in 1613. This appears to have marked the pinnacle of his career, and the latter part of his life was characterized by poverty. It is in this period that he translated James I's *Basilikon Doron* and this constitutes the only example of his work into Italian. He also translated sections from Boccalini's *Ragguagli di Parnaso*, published in 1626 (the year after his death) in *The New-found Politicke*. In his will, the translator left the manuscript of a third enlarged edition of his dictionary, which was only to appear in print much later in 1659. Subsequently, another revision of this text by one John Davis was published in 1688.

ANDREW HISCOCK

Translations and Writings

Florio, his firste fruites: a perfect induction to the Italian and English tongues, 1578

A Shorte and Briefe Narration of the two Navigations and Discoueries to the North Weast Partes called Newe Fravnce, 1580

A Letter Lately Written from Rome, by an Italian Gentleman, to a Freende of His in Lyons in Fraunce, 1585

Florio's second frutes, 1591

A Worlde of Wordes, Or Most copious, and exact Dictionarie in Italian and English, 1598

Montaigne, Michel de, *The Essayes; or, Morall, Politike and Militarie Discourses*, 1603

Queen Anna's New World of Words or Dictionarie of the Italian and English tongues, 1611; facsimile edition, 1968

Boccalini, Traiano, *The New-Found Politike*, 1626 (part 1 contains translations by Florio)

Further Reading

Bossy, J., "Surprise, Surprise: An Elizabethan Mystery", *History Today*, 41 (September 1991) pp. 14–16

Burt, Richard and John Michael Archer (editors), *Enclosure Acts: Sexuality, Property and Culture in Early Modern England*, Ithaca, New York: Cornell University Press, 1994

Hannay, Margaret P., *Philip's Phoenix: Mary Sidney, Countess of Pembroke*, Oxford and New York: Oxford University Press, 1990

Matthiessen, F.O., *Translation: An Elizabethan Art*, Cambridge, Massachusetts: Harvard University Press, 1931

Pooley, Roger, *English Prose of the Seventeenth Century, 1590–1700*, London and New York: Longman, 1992

Rosenberg, Eleanor, *Leicester, Patron of Letters*, New York: Columbia University Press, 1955

Starnes, DeWitt T. and Ernest W. Talbert, *Classical Myth and Legend in Renaissance Dictionaries*, Chapel Hill: University of North Carolina Press, 1955

White, H.O., *Plagiarism and Imitation During the English Renaissance: A Study in Critical Distinctions*, Cambridge, Massachusetts: Harvard University Press, 1935

Yates, Frances A., *John Florio: The Life of an Italian in Shakespeare's England*, Cambridge: Cambridge University Press, 1934

Dario Fo 1926–

Italian dramatist and actor

Biography

Born in San Giano, Lombardy, 24 March 1926. Fo studied architecture at the Academy of Fine Arts, Milan, and the Brera Art Academy. His early career was as a stage designer and author for small cabarets and theatres, including the Piccolo Teatro of Milan. He then went on to work for the Italian national radio and television networks, including writing and performing the radio programme *Poer nano* [Poor Dwarf] in 1951. He was the founder of the I Dritti revue company in 1953, and was a screenwriter in Rome, 1956–58. He moved from writing social satire to overtly political material during the 1960s, after his marriage to the actress Franca Rame in 1954 and their founding of the radical theatre group Campagnia Dario Fo–Franca Rame in 1959. They went on to found the Nuova Scena theatre cooperative, which was associated with the Italian Communist Party. He performed comic sketches with Rame on the television programme *Canzonissima* in 1962. He left the Communist Party in 1962, and founded La Comune theatre collective in Milan in 1970, which started performing in factories, parks and other public spaces.

Fo achieved international recognition with his play *Gli arcangeli non giocano al flipper* (*Archangels Don't Play Pinball*), first produced in Milan in 1959. After official censorship was abolished in Italy in 1962 his work reflected a more political outlook, seen in plays such as the satirical and anti-American *La Signora è da buttare* [Throw the Lady Out], produced in Milan in 1967, and his best known plays, *Morte accidentale di un anarchico* (*Accidental Death of an Anarchist*), 1970, and *Non si paga, non si paga!* (*Can't Pay, Won't Pay!*), 1974, which employ traditional comic techniques to create political theatre. Later work by Fo includes his hugely successful and widely-performed solo theatre performance *Mistero Buffo* (*Comic Mystery*), 1969, which involves mime, imaginary dialect and material from medieval mystery plays. Plays from the 1980s include *Tutto casa, letto e chiesa* (*Female Parts*), 1978 (written with Rame); *Coppia aperta* (*The Open Couple*), 1983; and *L'uomo nudo e l'uomo in frak* (*One Was Nude and One Wore Tails*), 1985, also written with Rame.

Translations

Selection of Plays

Hood, Stuart (series editor), *Plays: One*, with an introduction by Hood, London: Methuen, 1992 (contains *Mistero Buffo*, *Accidental Death of an Anarchist* and *One Was Nude and One Wore Tails* all translated by Ed Emery; *Trumpets and Raspberries* translated by R.C. McAvoy and A-M. Giugni; *The Virtuous Burglar* translated by Joseph Farrell)

Plays

Mistero buffo, 1969

Emery, Ed, *Mistero Buffo: Comic Mysteries*, London: Methuen, 1988

Morte accidentale di un anarchico, 1970

Cumming, Alan and Tim Supple, *Accidental Death of an Anarchist*, edited and introduced by Christopher Cairns, London: Methuen, 1991

Emery, Ed, *Accidental Death of an Anarchist* in *Plays: One*, edited by Stuart Hood, 1992

Hanna, Gillian, adapted by Gavin Richards, *Accidental Death of an Anarchist*, London: Pluto Press, 1980; revised edition, London: Methuen, 1987

Non si paga, non si paga, 1974

Davis, R.G., *We Won't Pay! We Won't Pay! A Political Farce*, New York and London: French, 1984

Pertile, Lino, adapted by Bill Colvill and Robert Walker, *We Can't Pay? We Won't Pay!*, London: Pluto Press, 1978; revised as *Can't Pay? Won't Pay!*, 1982, with introduction by Stuart Hood and Franca Rame, London: Methuen, 1987

Tutta casa, letto e chiesa, with Franca Rame, 1978

Kunzle, Margaret and Stuart Hood, adapted by Olwen Wymark, *Female Parts: One Woman Plays*, London: Pluto Press, 1981, revised as *A Woman Alone and Other Plays*, edited by Hood, London: Methuen, 1991 (contains *Waking Up*, *A Woman Alone*, *The Same Old Story*, *Medea*)

Clacson, trombette e pernacchi, 1981

McAdoo, Dale and Charles Mann, *About Face*, in *New York Theater* , 4/3 (Summer–Fall 1983)

McAvoy, R.C. and A-M. Giugni, *Trumpets and Raspberries*, in *Plays: One*, edited by Stuart Hood, 1992

Coppia aperta, quasi spalancata, with Franca Rame, 1983

Hood, Stuart, *The Open Couple*, *New York Theater* 17/1 (Winter 1985); with *An Ordinary Day*, translated by Joe Farrell, London: Methuen, 1990

Il ratto della Francesca, 1986

Lowe, Rupert, adapted by Steven Stenning, *Abducting Diana*, London: Oberon, 1994

Una giornata qualunque, 1986

Farrell, Joseph, *An Ordinary Day*, with *The Open Couple*, translated by Stuart Hood, London: Methuen, 1990

Il papa e la strega, 1989

Emery, Ed, adapted by Andy De la Tour, *The Pope and the Witch*, London: Methuen, 1992

Dario Fo has attained a level of international celebrity that few playwrights in the postwar era can match. Throughout the 1980s, no other living playwright was performed more frequently, in more languages, but the international accessibility implied by the sheer volume of editions and productions of his work must seem at first glance surprising. Fo belongs unequivocally to the theatrical tradition specific to Italy, and the post-1968 political plays with which his name is most readily associated take as their subjects problems that affected Italian society. *Mistero buffo* (1969), a collection of one-man pieces first written and performed by medieval Italian *giullari* (approximately "minstrels"), is an act of homage to a figure from Italy's past, while *Clacson, trombette e pernacchi* (1981) *Trumpets and Raspberries* (McAvoy & Giugni, 1984), featuring the confusion ensuing from the kidnapping of the Fiat boss, Giovanni Agnelli, and one of his workers, is a farcical investigation of its present. Fo makes no concessions to cosmopolitan tastes.

The question must also be asked, to what extent the Fo known abroad coincides with the Fo celebrated in Italy. The precise nature of the divide between translation and adaptation, especially in the theatre, has been the subject of much debate, but in the case of Fo the adapter has often totally superseded the translator. Few of his works have been seen in English-speaking countries in the same form and structure as in Italy. The reasons for this disparity are complex. In part, it is a response to the Italian-ness of the original, and reflects a desire on the part of theatre directors and adapters to find equivalents for events, which would have been wholly familiar to Italian audiences but could not have the same resonance elsewhere. At a different level, it reflects the idiosyncratic nature of Fo's texts. Fo belongs to the quintessentially Italian tradition of the actor-author, and all his plays undergo continual modification in performance as Fo the actor registers the reaction of the audience to Fo the author. His scripts, which customarily rely heavily, if not on improvisational skills, at least on the comic brio of the performer, are more similar to the *canovaccio* (outline script) employed by *commedia dell'arte* performers than to the completed text more conventionally written by a playwright. On the page they very often appear disappointingly uninspired and lacking in comic inventiveness.

To ensure his work the same comic force, the same kind of political impact, in translation as in the original, theatre directors have normally preferred to mount more or less free adaptations rather than anything that could reasonably be termed a translation. However appropriate this policy may be for individual productions, it is harder to justify the fact that only these adaptations, sometimes surprisingly far in content and in spirit from the original work written by the author whose name they continue to bear, have found their way into print. The consequence is that there are two Fos treading international stages – Italian Fo and foreign Fo.

The most evident case is provided by his most popular work, *Accidental Death of an Anarchist*, which has become an all-purpose protest play. Fo himself attended the London premiere (Hanna & Richards, 1980), staged by the London-based, left-wing troupe, Belt and Braces, whose leading figure was Gavin Richards, and was appalled. Although a political radical, Fo is very much a theatrical conservative, who has consciously cultivated his links with an Italian theatrical tradition. In *Accidental Death*, the part of the Maniac, originally played by Fo himself, was the main vehicle for the satirical assault on the power structures that caused an innocent man to be arrested, but it also incorporated the wiles, mischief, slyness and underhand subtlety of the traditional Harlequin. These overtones were lost in the English-language version. The Richards version took liberties with the text, introducing the anarchist hymn at the end of Act 1, eliminating totally the part of the "bishop" and thus undermining Fo's assault on the Church for its part in the cover-up of the affair in question, and finally introducing an equivocal, two-tier ending that did not correspond to any of the various endings Fo had employed at different times in the original Italian. More fundamentally, the play was transformed into an exercise in zany, knockabout farce, which could not give expression to the elements of the tragic vision present in Fo's own work. Some years later, a new translation was commissioned from an anonymous translator and adapted by Cumming & Supple (1991) for the production starring Cumming and directed by Supple. This version was closer to the original but was still an adaptation. Where the Richards version had contained references to the Anthony Blunt spy scandal, the newer version updated these to contain a denunciation of police conduct, much discussed in the press at that time, in the case of the Irish citizens wrongly imprisoned for the bombings in Guildford and Birmingham. Only with the Emery translation in 1992 was a faithful rendering of the original, which respected its context and its denunciation of the political manoeuvres that led in 1969 to the defenestration of the anarchist Pinelli while he was being held in connection with the bombing of a bank in Milan, made available to an English-speaking public.

The dilemma that prevents the Fo case from being a simple one of the author's wishes being subverted by translators or directors, is that Emery's faithful translation has not yet been staged. In itself, the Richards version, for all its distortion of the original, remains a most effective piece of theatre. Richards operated a total conversion of the play, finding in farce and music-hall slapstick an equivalent in British popular culture for the Italian *commedia* forms underlying Fo's plays. It may be that Fo's work requires comprehensive imaginative intervention if the vivacity of the original is to be maintained.

Other plays have been dismantled by adapters to make them conform to their *a priori* notion of what farce should be. *Abducting Diana* started life as *Il ratto della Francesca* [Abducting Francesca] (1986), but in Lowe & Stenning (1994) was converted into a limp comedy in which an English princess called Diana is kidnapped, and all reference to banking systems and revolutionaries was suppressed. The political element is frequently the first victim of adapters who believe, often unconsciously, that their task is to provide the laughs the author has inexplicably omitted. The process is clear in Emery's *The Pope and the Witch* (1992). Where the original, *Il papa e la strega* (1989), had combined concern over the drug problem with a denunciation of financial malpractice in the Catholic Church, the English version, in De la Tour's free adaptation, was a pantomime-style romp set in the Vatican palace, focusing on the mystery surrounding the death of Pope John Paul I, which had been a topic in the film *Godfather 3*. In an effort to heighten the farce, the Cardinals were given the names of the Italian football team in the 1990 World Cup.

The problem has been less acute for the one-person, one-act feminist plays, such as *A Woman Alone*, which Fo and Franca Rame starting producing in the late 1970s. These works have never been subjected to any process of parallel rewriting (see Kunzle, Hood & Wymark, 1981). Hood's *The Open Couple* (1985) and Farrell's *An Ordinary Day* (1990) are both translations rather than adaptations. It may be that the problems affecting women in Western society are similar from country to country.

A different balance was struck with Emery's *Mistero buffo* (1988), which was published in a form that reproduced both the individual, medieval sketches and Fo's original introductions, but staged with freshly written introductory material that set the context for an audience unfamiliar with the source culture. The translation did not attempt to find an English-language equivalent of the *padano* dialect in which this work was written, but the dialect problem is only one of several raised by Fo's work and not yet satisfactorily resolved.

JOSEPH FARRELL

Further Reading

Dario Fo and Franca Rame: Theatre Workshops at Riverside Studios, London: Red Notes, 1983

Fo, Dario, *The Tricks of the Trade*, translated by Joe Farrell, edited by Stuart Hood, London: Methuen, and New York: Routledge, 1991

Hirst, David L., *Dario Fo and Franca Rame*, London: Macmillan, and New York: St Martin's Press, 1989

Mitchell, Tony, *Dario Fo: People's Court Jester*, London and New York: Methuen, 1984; revised edition 1999

Mitchell, Tony (editor), *File on Fo*, London: Methuen, 1989

Pertile, Lino, "Dario Fo" in *Writers and Society in Contemporary Italy*, edited by Michael Caesar and Peter Hainsworth, Leamington Spa: Berg, 1984

Antonio Fogazzaro 1842–1911

Italian novelist and poet

Biography

Born in Vicenza, 25 March 1842. He was taught at school by the poet, scholar and translator Giacomo Zanella. After graduating from university in 1864 he moved to Milan and married. His work aroused controversy in both the religious and the secular sphere. Though he was a devout Catholic he was interested in modern scientific thought, and several of his works were placed on the Church's Index of prohibited books. In 1896, mainly because of the enormous success of *Piccolo mondo antico*, he was made a senator. With its sequels, *The Man of the World* and *The Saint*, *The Little World of the Past* forms a trilogy of novels exemplifying the current of decadence strong in Italian literature of the period. Died 7 March 1911 in Vicenza.

Translations

Fiction

Malombra, 1881

Dickson, F.T., *Malombra*, London: Fisher Unwin, 1896; retitled as *The Woman*, London: Fisher Unwin, 1907

Daniele Cortis, 1885

Simeon, Steven Louis, *Daniele Cortis*, London: Remington, 1890

Tilton, I.R., *Daniele Cortis*, New York: Holt, 1887

Il mistero del poeta, 1888

MacMahon, Anita (verses rendered by Algernon Warren), *The Poet's Mystery*, London: Duckworth, 1903

Piccolo mondo antico, 1895

Prichard-Agnetti, M., *The Patriot*, with an introduction, London: Hodder and Stoughton, 1906; New York: Putnam, 1907

Strachan, W.J., *The Little World of the Past*, London: Oxford University Press, 1962

Waldman, Guido, *A House Divided*, London: New English Library, 1963

Piccolo mondo moderno, 1901

Prichard-Agnetti, M., *The Man of the World*, London: Hodder and Stoughton, 1907

Il Santo, 1905

Prichard-Agnetti, M., *The Saint*, with an introduction, London: Hodder and Stoughton, New York: Putnam, and New York: Grosset and Dunlap, 1906

Leila, 1910

Prichard-Agnetti, M., *Leila*, London: Hodder and Stoughton, and New York: G.H. Doran, 1911

Poetry

Valsolda, 1876

Greene, G.A., selections in his *Italian Lyrists of Today*, London: E. Mathews and John Lane / Bodley Head, 1893, pp. 109–18

Antonio Fogazzaro is the most prolific and gifted historical novelist belonging to the group of writers now known as the "Manzonian school". Following in the wake of the author of *I promessi sposi*, he provides an intellectualization of character and event in a reconciliation of social and moral conflict. In a marriage of opposites (*Piccolo mondo antico*), the encounters between active and contemplative life, reason and revelation, passion and restraint are played out against a backdrop of natural beauty. Symbolic figures and events develop chronologically in the trilogy *Piccolo mondo antico*, *Piccolo mondo moderno* and *Il santo*. The Manzonian device whereby the text takes the form of an anonymous manuscript is reproduced in *Il mistero del poeta*. Fogazzaro is a master-creator of female figures on both a grandiose and a miniature scale. Stylistically the works bear the stamp of an age of romantic realism, yielding to sophisticated decadence.

The translations selected reflect the English popularity of a writer whose works have now lost their appeal for the general reader. The STRACHAN and WALDMAN translations attempt to cultivate a new readership a half-century after his death. All are the works of scholars drawn to the content of fiction that reflects the unease marking the end of an era, and the inauguration of a new century.

F. Thorold DICKSON's *Malombra* (1896) is a literal, as opposed to a literary translation. Although the lyrical and prosaic sections in the novel are precisely reproduced, a critical and stylistic assessment of the work does not appear to have evolved before the translation was undertaken. The function of the literary devices does not appear to have been understood. As the connections between internal correlatives are not highlighted, the sense of the fantastic, central to the novel, is lost. This is particularly apparent in chapter 1, where the atmosphere is set: "mostruoso" (monstrous) is rendered by "huge"; "sconosciuto" (unknown) becomes "strange", while "viaggiatore fantastico" is merely an "eccentric traveller". The protagonist herself is not accorded the "superwoman" proportions intended by the author.

Both the SIMEON (1890) and the TILTON (1887) translations of *Daniele Cortis*, Fogazzaro's second – controversial but successful – novel, highlight the emotional dimension of the tale of extra-conjugal love. Although the English occasionally reads as slightly archaic, particularly for the modern reader, each word still conveys the restlessness of the original. These are literal translations that recreate the turmoil of a decadent figure in search of a "super-ideal".

The Poet's Mystery by MACMAHON (1903) demonstrates a conscious acknowledgement of the two separate media contained in the original: the prosaic and the poetic. The verses are rendered by WARREN. As in the original, the poetic element provides a commentary on the main themes. This work is most successful in the descriptive passages in which objects are clearly defined and image is piled upon image. The conversational passages are, however, laboured, and lose the naturalness of exchanges that characterizes Fogazzaro's prose.

PRICHARD-AGNETTI's *The Patriot* (1906) is the first translation into English of Fogazzaro's best-known novel *Piccolo mondo antico*, the story of a married couple of contrasting temperaments and beliefs, set in the 1850s in Risorgimento Italy. The translator is obviously drawn to the work on account of its historical and moral content, the latter felicitously reflected in the struggles between the sun and the fog witnessed by Uncle Piero, Franco's journey across the mountains in total darkness, and his newfound optimism at sunrise. These passages are highly successful in translation. The enthusiasm of the translator is reflected in her ability to convey the emotional sincerity of the author while adhering at all times to his text. Prichard-Agnetti succeeds in producing her text in approximately the same number of words as the original. In addition, she provides a lengthy translator's introduction, and footnotes explaining untranslatable local terms such as *breva* (north wind) and *tarocchi, matto* and *bagatto* (card games in vogue at the time of writing). In later translations of Fogazzaro's novels, Manzoni's influence will continue to be acknowledged. Here the contrasting protagonists are identified with English and American literature. "Had Fogazzaro been influenced by certain works which had already excited much comment and discussion in England and America?" (translator's introduction).

STRACHAN's *The Little World of the Past* (1962) ranks as an academic translation, as does WALDMAN's *A House Divided*, which appeared the following year (1963). Both were produced as a tribute to the author, half a century after his death. Both are precise, close translations aimed at the general reader and the student. Strachan successfully recreates, by means of contained and refined prose, the aura of an age gone by. As his title suggests, Waldman, through word choice, communicates the contrasting fortunes in the novel and highlights its domestic dimension.

The remaining novels of the cycle that began with *Piccolo mondo antico* are translated lovingly by Mary PRICHARD-AGNETTI. *The Man of the World* (translated 1907) abounds with descriptions of nature, which do not merely form an attractive setting for the work but assume a central role as an active force. These passages are reproduced in language that today ranks as gushing and sentimental. Yet the spirit of the original is interpreted without the linguistic restraint shown by Strachan in his *The Little World of the Past*.

The source text of PRICHARD-AGNETTI's *The Saint* (1906) is seen by the translator as a novel of suspense and religious debate. These are the features stressed in her introduction and consequently the guiding forces of her translation. A sense of movement towards victory is conveyed in the racy prose employed. The occasional emotional outburst appears overcharged to the modern reader.

Fogazzaro's last novel, *Leila*, which appeared just months before his death, was also translated by PRICHARD-AGNETTI (1911). In the course of the five-year period spent in translating Fogazzaro, she had perfected her craft. The final work is a literal translation which succeeds in reconciling the contrasting and conflicting features of the author's style.

The selections of verse from *Valsolda* by GREENE (1893) are rendered by means of rhymed translation. Although Fogazzaro's impressionist use of light and shade, his projection of sound and an over-riding atmosphere of gloom are preserved, such rhymes as room / gloom, misty light / sea at night, convey a simplistic impression. In the short "All the Bells", the use of repetition communicates the sense of echo of the original:

> Peace to the wave, to the hill
> These voices too, be still:
> O beat o' the bronze, be still!
> Peace!

Rhyme thus serves to highlight effect, but can at times rob the version of the detail of the original.

DEIRDRE O'GRADY

Further Reading

Bassnett-McGuire, Susan, "Translating Prose" in her *Translation Studies*, revised edition, London and New York: Routledge, 1991

Ingarden, Roman, *The Literary Work of Art: An Investigation on the Borderlines of Ontology*, translated by George G. Grabowicz, Evanston, Illinois: Northwestern University Press, 1973

Theodor Fontane 1819–1898

Prussian novelist, poet and journalist

Though of French extraction, Fontane was born 30 December 1819 in Neuruppin, Brandenburg, and spent his youth on the Prussian North Sea coast. He trained and worked as a pharmacist in different German cities, 1836–49. Turning full-time to writing when 30 and just married, he was to become belatedly recognized as one of the major writers in European literature of the later 19th century, Alongside a string of novels, the first of which, *Before the Storm*, he published at the age of 59, he is known for his poetry – he was a ballad-writer of note – and for the four-volume account of travels in his native province (*Wanderungen durch die Mark Brandenburg*, 1862–82). The work by Fontane most widely read in English is the sombre, atmospheric novel *Effi Briest*, published in 1895. His own interest in and knowledge of English and Scottish life and culture stemmed from his several years as a journalist based in London in the 1850s. Died in Berlin, 20 September 1898.

Translations

Selections

Demetz, Peter (editor), *Short Novels and Other Writings*, New York: Continuum, 1982 (contains *A Man of Honor*, *Jenny Treibel*, *The Eighteenth of March*)

Francke, Kuno (editor), *German Classics of the Nineteenth and Twentieth Centuries*, vol. 12, New York: German Publication Society, l913–14, reprinted New York: AMS Press, 1969 (includes *Effi Briest*, "Sir Ribbeck of Ribbeck", "The Bridge by the Tay", *My Childhood Years*, all translated by William Alpha Cooper)

Novels and Novellas

Vor dem Sturm, 1878

Hollingdale, R.J., *Before the Storm: A Novel of the Winter of 1812–13*, with an introduction, Oxford: Oxford University Press, 1985

L'Adultera, 1882

Annan, Gabriele, *The Woman Taken in Adultery*, with *The Poggenpuhl Family*, in her *Two Novellas*, with an introduction by Erich Heller, Chicago: University of Chicago Press, 1979; Harmondsworth and New York: Penguin, 1995

Schach von Wuthenow, 1883

Demetz, Peter (editor), *A Man of Honor* in *Short Novels and Other Writings*, 1982

Valk, E.M., *A Man of Honor*, New York: Ungar, 1975

Cecile, 1887

Radcliffe, Stanley, *Cecile*, London: Angel Books, 1992

Irrungen, Wirrungen, 1888

Anonymous, *Trials and Tribulations*, in *German Fiction*, New York: Collier, 1917

Bowman, Derek, *Entanglements: An Everyday Berlin Story*, Bampton, Oxfordshire: Three Rivers Books, 1986

Demetz, Peter (editor), *Delusions, Confusions*, with *The Poggenpuhl Family*, with a foreword by J.P. Stern and an introduction by William L. Zwiebel, New York: Continuum Press, 1989

Morris, Sandra, *A Suitable Match*, Glasgow and London: Blackie, 1968

Unwiederbringlich, 1891

Parmée, Douglas, *Beyond Recall*, with an introduction, London and New York: Oxford University Press, 1964

Frau Jenny Treibel, 1892

Zimmermann, Ulf, *Jenny Treibel*, New York: Ungar, 1976; also in *Short Novels and Other Writings*, edited by Peter Demetz, 1982

Effi Briest, 1895

Cooper, William Alpha, *Effi Briest* in *German Classics of the Nineteenth and Twentieth Centuries*, vol. 12, edited by Kuno Francke, 1913–14

Parmée, Douglas, *Effi Briest*, with an introduction, Harmondsworth and Baltimore: Penguin, 1967

Rorrison, Hugh and Helen Chambers, *Effi Briest*, London: Angel, 1995

Wallich, Walter, *Effi Briest*, London: New English Library, 1962

Die Poggenpuhls, 1896

Annan, Gabriele, *The Poggenpuhl Family*, with *The Woman Taken in Adultery*, in her *Two Novellas*, with an introduction by Erich Heller, Chicago: University of Chicago Press, 1979; Harmondsworth and New York: Penguin, 1995

Der Stechlin, 1898

Zwiebel, William L., *The Stechlin*, Columbia, South Carolina: Camden House, and Woodbridge, Suffolk: Boydell and Brewer, 1995

Poetry

Bell, Anthea, *MacRibbeck of Ribbeck of Havelland*, London: Neugebauer Press, 1990; as *Nick Ribbeck of Ribbeck of Havelland*, Saxonville, Massachusetts: Picture Book Studio, 1990

Cooper, William Alpha, "Sir Ribbeck of Ribbeck" and "The Bridge by the Tay" in *German Classics of the Nineteenth and Twentieth Centuries*, vol. 12, edited by Kuno Francke, 1913–14

Harvey, T. Edmund, *Ribbeck of Ribbeck in Havel-Land*, Ditchling, Sussex: St Dominic's Press, 1918

Shub, Elizabeth, *Sir Ribbeck of Ribbeck of Havelland*, New York: Macmillan, 1969; London: Abelard-Schuman, 1971

Other Writing

Bilderbuch aus England, 1860

Harrison, Dorothy, *Journeys to England in Victoria's Early Days 1844–1859*, London: Massie, 1939

Jenseits des Tweed, 1860
Battershaw, Brian, *Across the Tweed: A Tour of Mid-Victorian Scotland*, Phoenix House, 1965

Meine Kinderjahre, 1894
Cooper, William Alpha, *My Childhood Years* in *German Classics of the Nineteenth and Twentieth Centuries*, vol. 12, edited by Kuno Francke, 1913–14

For someone who retained a genuinely warm affection for England and English life, deriving from his own first-hand experiences, and who drew occasionally on some of those experiences for episodes in his own fiction (to say nothing of the numerous journalistic pieces he wrote with an English slant), Theodor Fontane had to wait a long time before gaining proper recognition in the English-speaking world. Indeed even as recently as the end of 1995 the Fontane scholar Alan Bance bemoaned the fact that the German writer seemingly needed to be "constantly reintroduced to the English-speaking world".

The English-speaking world's interest in Fontane as reflected in translations of his work got under way at the time of World War I. Volume 12 of *German Classics of the Nineteenth and Twentieth Centuries*, published in 1913–14 in New York, contains selections from Fontane translated by William Alpha COOPER, including his best known novel, *Effi Briest*, as well as the poems *Sir Ribbeck of Ribbeck* and *The Bridge by the Tay*, and *My Childhood Years* (the autobiographical *Meine Kinderjahre*). There was a subsequent reprint in 1969 (with neat timing to commemorate the 150th anniversary of Fontane's birth).

In fact *Ribbeck of Ribbeck in Havel-Land*, Fontane's delightful and popular poem wherein the title figure takes a pear with him to his grave to ensure the continued sharing of the produce of his pear trees even after his death, had been translated by T. Edmund HARVEY and privately printed in England as early as 1902 and, at the end of World War I, "set forth again in thankfulness for the coming of peace, Christmastide, AD 1918". Subsequently, in a new, free translation by Elizabeth SHUB, and complete with illustrations, it was published in 1969 in New York and two years later in London. Anthea BELL's version appeared in 1990, also both in America (under the title *Nick Ribbeck of Ribbeck of Havelland*) and in England (entitled *MacRibbeck of Ribbeck of Havelland*).

Towards the end of World War I, a translation of Fontane's *Irrungen, Wirrungen* (the German original published in 1888) appeared as *Trials and Tribulations* in the anthology *German Fiction* (1917) in New York. Another 50 years were to elapse before Blackie published Sandra MORRIS's version, now under the title *A Suitable Match*, in 1968, in their Chosen Books from Abroad series. The German text, with its theme of the irreconcilable conflict of duty and inclination, in the form of the inevitably thwarted love of two persons drawn together from different ends of the social spectrum, continued to attract a readership, prompting further printing of the anonymous translation (e.g. in the series The German Library, published in New York in 1989 (DEMETZ, editor) now with the title *Delusions, Confusions*) as well as a new translation by Derek BOWMAN (1986), with yet a different title – *Entanglements: An Everyday Berlin Story*.

At a politically fraught time in Anglo-German relations, Dorothy HARRISON's translation (1939) of Fontane's record of his English experiences, *Bilderbuch aus England* (1860), was published in London under the title *Journeys to England in Victoria's Early Days 1844–1859*. That it was described as "an entertaining and enlightening footnote to history" perhaps insufficiently suggests Fontane's perceptions and understandings of English ways, conveyed with sensitivity, humour and irony.

But we have to wait until the 1960s for the first full wave of translations. In 1962 the New English Library, London published in their Four Square Classics series a somewhat shortened version of *Effi Briest* in Walter WALLICH's translation. The first complete English version of Fontane's tale of human relations on the merry-go-round of love, boredom and duty, in a marriage that ultimately brings tragedy to two of the three protagonists and that reflects the changing patterns in Prussian society at the time, is that provided by Douglas PARMÉE in 1967 under the imprint of the Oxford University Press. The translation did not escape criticism, but it was subsequently reprinted, again on both sides of the Atlantic, in 1976 by Penguin in their World Classics series, following the successful film version of the novel in 1974 by Fassbinder. An entirely new translation of Fontane's novel was undertaken by RORRISON & CHAMBERS (1995). Their version, which came out in London, is deemed very faithful to the original in tone and has been widely welcomed.

Douglas PARMÉE had already tackled Fontane before *Effi Briest* with his version of *Unwiederbringlich*, another story of marital tensions and human flaws. The result, again published by Oxford University Press, was *Beyond Recall* (1964). The translation was described by the *Times Literary Supplement* reviewer, arguably over-enthusiastically, as "a minor masterpiece of translation". Certainly, Parmée succeeded in capturing the sensitivity and irony of the original in a generally accurate version. Also appearing in the 1960s for the first time was *Across the Tweed: A Tour of mid-Victorian Scotland*, Brian BATTERSHAW's translation (1965) of Fontane's record of a journey undertaken in 1858, originally published in 1860 as *Jenseits des Tweed*.

Increased American interest in Fontane manifested itself in the 1970s as other texts received attention. In 1975 E.M. VALK translated *Schach von Wuthenow* as *A Man of Honor*. Set in 1806, the short historical novel examines – via the private life of the key character, a Prussian army officer – the nature of Prussian life and society just prior to Prussia's catastrophic defeat at the hands of Napoleon. One year later, in 1976, Ulf ZIMMERMANN brought out in New York his *Jenny Treibel*, a translation of another of the Berlin novels, that briefly and wittily reflects on the nature of true values in human relations. Both texts appeared in their English versions in a selection of Fontane's works published in 1982 by Continuum, New York, again in their series The German Library, under the title *Short Novels and Other Writings*. Yet again in America, Chicago University Press published in 1979 Gabriele ANNAN's translations *The Woman Taken in Adultery* and *The Poggenpuhl Family*. The title of the former suggests clearly enough the theme, once more, of entangled human relations (without, on this occasion, ultimate tragedy); the latter depicts, with a modicum of irony and considerable sympathy, the lives of a genteelly poor family in Berlin, which reflect the social changes irrevocably underway in Prussia towards the close of the century. Annan's versions remain among the most readable of Fontane's fiction in translation. The volume also benefits enormously from a valuable introduction by Erich Heller, full of shrewd insights into, and evaluations of, Fontane's life and writings.

The 1980s marked the appearance at last of Fontane's first and major novel *Vor dem Sturm* (1878) in English translation. R.J. HOLLINGDALE's version, *Before the Storm*, published by Oxford University Press in 1985, makes for admirable reading of the long historical tale centred on the period Christmas 1812 to the end of March 1813, hence on the retreat of the Napoleonic forces from Moscow into Prussian territory prior to the War of Liberation in 1813 (the "Storm" of the title), but focused essentially on the lives and (strength of) character of a host of "ordinary" Prussian people.

Besides the reappearance of the Gabriele Annan translations, the 1990s also saw the first English version of Fontane's novel *Cecile* (1887) in Stanley RADCLIFFE's translation published in 1992 in London. The reader is on familiar territory – a triangle of human relations that ends with the death of two of the protagonists. Three years later, William L. ZWIEBEL's *The Stechlin* (1995) duly appeared in America. The origins of the translation are evident, but it is good to have available now Fontane's last novel, a typically drawn study of individual lives in a Prussian environment in the process of social and political change within the Second Empire. With the centenary of Fontane's death being marked in 1998, a translation by Russell Jackson of some of Fontane's London articles was published (*Shakespeare in the London Theatre 1855–58*, London: Society for Theatre Research, 1999). Further reissues and/or new translations of his writings may reasonably be expected.

IAN HILTON

Further Reading

Bance, Alan, Helen Chambers and Charlotte Jolles (editors), *Theodor Fontane; The London Symposium*, Stuttgart: Hans-Dieter Heinz / Akademischer Verlag, 1995

Ugo Foscolo 1778–1827

Italian poet and novelist

Biography

Born 6 Febuary 1778 on the island of Zante (Zákintos) and studied in Spalato (Split) and Venice. His patriotic novel *Le ultime lettere di Jacopo Ortis* (1802) was inspired by the author's bitterness when by the Treaty of Campoformio (1797) Venice was ceded to Austria. He served in the French armies, hoping they would free Italy from Austrian rule but, disappointed in Napoleon, returned to Milan, where in 1807 he published his famous poem *Dei sepolcri* (*On Tombs*). In 1816, when his hopes that France would bring liberation ended with the entry of the Austrians into Milan, Foscolo went to live in London, where he continued writing, working on his long poem *Le grazie* (*The Graces*), which remained unfinished, and producing in Italian essays and papers on Italian literature. Some articles by him appeared in British literary reviews. Earlier, he had written a few plays and translated Sterne's *Sentimental Journey* into Italian. He died in poverty in London, 10 October 1827.

Translations

Selections of Poetry

Kay, George, 6 sonnets, 1 ode, *On Tombs*, and a selection from *The Graces*, in *The Penguin Book of Italian Verse*, edited by Kay, Harmondsworth: Penguin, 1958; Baltimore: Penguin, 1960, pp. 233–63

May, Frederick (editor), *The J.C. Translations of Poems by Ugo Foscolo* (4 sonnets and *Dei Sepolcri*), Leeds: Pirandello Society, 1963

Poetry

Dei sepolcri, 1807 (the title means On Tombs or Concerning Tombs; in Italian the title is often abbreviated to *I sepolcri* and the work alluded to as *i Sepolcri*)

Anonymous, *I sepolcri* (part of poem), *European Review* (June 1824); *I sepolcri* (entire poem), signed S.C., published c.1820; the translation of the entire poem attributed to Sinclair Cullen, reprinted with an essay by Giovanni Calabritto, as *Sulla fortuna dei "Sepolcri" in Inghilterra*, Malta: Empire Press, 1932

Cullen, Sinclair, *The Sepulchres*, London, c.1820 (see preceding item)

Grillo, Ernesto, *I sepolcri* (bilingual edition), London and Glasgow: Blackie, 1928

Kay, George, "On Tombs" in *The Penguin Book of Italian Verse*, edited by Kay, Harmondsworth: Penguin, 1958; Baltimore: Penguin, 1960, pp. 244–58

May, Frederick, *Dei Sepolcri* in *The J.C. Translations of Poems by Ugo Foscolo*, edited by May, Leeds: Pirandello Society, 1963

Novel

Le ultime lettere di Jacopo Ortis, 1802

Radcliff-Umstead, Douglas, *Ugo Foscolo's Ultime lettere di Jacopo Ortis*, Chapel Hill: University of North Carolina Press, 1970

Although the Italian writer Ugo Foscolo resided in London from 1816 until his death in 1827, he failed to achieve the popularity among the British reading public enjoyed by his contemporaries, Manzoni and Leopardi. His poetic eloquence, latinized constructions and restlessness of spirit are not easily translatable into English, and this accounts for the fact that there are fewer English versions of his works than one might expect. The epistolary novel *Le ultime lettere di Jacopo Ortis* and the *carme Dei sepolcri* derive their inspiration from the Treaty of Campoformio (1797) and the Edict of Saint-Cloud (extended to Italy in 1806) respectively. His idealized social vision is projected through an association of history and myth, and it captures the attention of the specialist rather than the general reader.

The novel *Le ultime lettere di Jacopo Ortis* consists of a series of letters from a young idealist Jacopo, to his friend Lorenzo, with comments from the latter. Thus the subjective and objective are present, with the use of first person for declamatory and narrative purposes. The work, in addition to its function as an historical and psychological novel, also stands as a statement of the superiority of art over the artist.

Douglas RADCLIFF-UMSTEAD, one of today's leading scholars in the field of neo-classic literature stresses the abovementioned features in a translation (1970) that is both literal and literary. It recaptures the emotional dimension, carrying forward the concept of "revolution of mind" present in the text. Immediacy of statement, political rhetoric and the despair of the second section of the novel are most successfully communicated.

The translation of *Dei sepolcri* by Sinclair CULLEN (c. 1820) ranks as an attempt by Foscolo's loyal friend and travelling companion to introduce the poet's greatest achievement to the British aristocratic and literary circle in which he moved. It is little more than a paraphrase, with some inaccuracies. It is however, of historical importance as the first attempt to translate Foscolo's poetry in his adopted country. The work is reproduced in *Sulla fortuna dei "sepolcri" in Inghilterra*, Empire Press, 1932, alongside an English translation of part of the poem, signed S.C.

The most interesting translations of *Dei sepolcri* are those of Ernesto GRILLO (1928) and George KAY (1958), both academics at the University of Glasgow. Grillo had intended the translation to coincide with the centenary of the death of the poet "when the *Duce of Fascismo* had the happy thought to present a specially printed volume, containing a selection of the poet's verses" (translator's preface).

GRILLO's is a prose translation. His control of the English language is impressive. He succeeds in maintaining the rhetorical tone of the original and its juxtaposition of concepts and images pertaining to life/death, memory/forgetfulness, light and shade. While these are largely communicated by Foscolo in terms of word placement in the line, Grillo relies on alliteration to recreate the effect and poetic imagery achieved by the Italian poet:

> All'ombra de'cipressi e dentro l'urne
> confortate dal pianto è forse il sonno
> della morte men duro? (lines 1–3)

> Beneath the shade of cypress and in tear-
> solaced urns will perchance the sleep of death
> appear less loud?

These lines reveal the triumph of death and darkness. Grillo highlights the effect throughout with the use of alliteration: "mesta armonia" / "mournful melodious song" (line 9), "fugge i sepolcri" / "shuns the sepulchres" (line 17), "i delitti" / "a career of crime" (line 77). In order to accentuate the atmosphere of darkness created in the first 20 lines of the poem, "l'obblio nella sua notte" (line 18) becomes "into black night oblivion ...". Foscolo's constant use of repetition to drive home a message and image is avoided by Grillo in his translation. He opts for a more direct statement: at line 29 he omits the repetition of *celeste*; "celestial is this loving communion with the departed, a holy place and precious gift to us"; likewise at line 33 the repetition of *l'estinto*: "we often live with our dead friends and *they* with us".

Grillo's translation acts as a clarification of the text. The reference to Alfieri, through his first name *Vittorio*, (line 189) becomes "to these monuments often did Alfieri come in quest of inspiration." Further clarification is achieved at line 155: "quel grande" becomes "that immortal"; "l'arca di Colui" (line 159) becomes "the arch of the genius"; "Te beata" (line 165) is translated as "how happy art thou, O Tuscany." Finally, in the reference to Homer "il sacro vate" (line 288), Grillo provides "the sacred poet", allowing the reader to make the association of *vate* / prophet and poet.

The title page of *The Penguin Book of Italian Verse* includes the words "with plain prose translations of each poem". Thus the reader is prepared for a word-for-word rendering of the originals.

George KAY's literal translation of *Dei sepolcri* stands as a simpler and less eloquent approach than Grillo's. It reveals clear comprehension and maintains a poised, even tone throughout. Of great value to the student of Italian, it does not gain the status of a work in its own right. At all times it serves the poet. The only concession to the reader takes the form of footnotes that explain references to Nelson, Machiavelli, Michelangelo, Galileo, Newton, Dante, Petrarch, Alfieri and the Muses.

KAY's selection of poems by Foscolo is representative of the poet's versatility of style and topic: "Di se stesso", "Alla sua donna lontana", "Il proprio ritratto", "Alla sera", "A Zacinto", "In morte del fratello Giovanni", a selection from *Le grazie*. Contents vary from Foscolo's well catalogued obsession with self to his celebration of his birthplace, from his sense of predestined exile to the celebration of the triumph of Beauty. As in the case of *Dei sepolcri*, the translations are literal and accurate and allow the reader to follow the original line by line. In "A Zacinto" / "To Zante", the translator may be accused of a slightly simplistic approach: "bello di fama" is translated as "lovely with fame", "tu non altro" as "you will not have more". Yet in the interest of comprehension the selection is valuable.

DEIRDRE O'GRADY

Further Reading

Franzero, Carlo Maria, *A Life in Exile: Ugo Foscolo in London, 1816–1827*, London: W.H. Allen, 1977

Sante, Mateo, *Textual Exile: The Reader in Sterne and Foscolo*, New York: Peter Lang, 1985

Vincent, E.R., *Ugo Foscolo: An Italian in Regency England*, London: Cambridge University Press, 1953

Francophone African and Caribbean Writers in English Translation

The 20th century witnessed the rapid development of African and Caribbean literatures, and their exposure to the rest of the world. Although the literatures remain largely oral and are expressed in Creole and indigenous languages, they are also written in European languages of colonization such as English, French, and, in Africa only, Portuguese. An ever-growing interest in these literatures, coupled with the writer's need for a wider audience, have contributed to the translation of many works from French into English.

Our cursory survey of francophone African and Caribbean writers in English translation will centre around early manifestations of translation, some significant trends in translation as indicated by major translated works, some prominent translators and how they have coped with certain problems, and the foremost publishing companies involved. Francophone writers south of the Sahara and those in the French-speaking Caribbean (Martinique, Guadeloupe, Haiti) will be placed in special focus.

The arrival of the French and English as colonial masters in Africa and the Caribbean naturally marked the introduction of their languages to these areas, and their subsequent use in creative writing there. While the English encouraged the development of indigenous languages for literary creativity and, in most cases, the translation of religious and literary works between English and the local languages, the French pursued a policy of cultural and linguistic assimilation, actively discouraging the use of indigenous languages both in education and in creative writing. In areas under French domination, therefore, writers were encouraged to use only French, and translation was virtually insignificant. Thus their literary history was from the beginning closely linked to French ideas and values, and drew on them, conforming primarily to French norms in matters of themes and formal features. However, the publication in 1921 of the Martinique-born René Maran's novel *Batouala*, which exposed the effects of colonization and portrayed African life and its environment, marked the start of a new trend that was to influence later African and Caribbean writers and flourish to the present day. Indeed, négritude as a literary movement has often constituted the link between francophone writers of Africa and the Caribbean such as René Maran (1887–1960), Léopold Sédar Senghor (1906–, Senegal), Aimé Césaire (1913–, Martinique), Léon Damas (1912–78, Martinique), Mongo Beti (1932–, Cameroon), Tchicaya U Tam'si (1931–, Congo), Birago Diop (1906–89, Senegal), and others.

In contrast to the rapid development of literary creativity, however, the situation of the translation of African and Caribbean literatures from French into English, before the 1960s (the decade of independence for most of Africa) was rather bleak. Very few works were translated, and those few mainly by Europeans for their domestic audiences. Ade Ojo (1986) attempts to explain this state of affairs in terms of the educational policies of the colonial masters:

> Under the colonial education system, every educated indigene was restricted to the learning of the colonizing language and the classics: Latin and Greek. This meant that no educated African, trained especially in his native country, could be proficient in two languages of colonization. Furthermore, the choice of originals often reflected the interests of the target readership as well as the translator's ability to understand and convey the texts. This is mainly because even though European translators were well acquainted with the languages in question, they usually lacked an adequate grasp of the world and themes portrayed in African and Caribbean literary works. On the other hand, although the colonized people could understand the socio-cultural setting of the works, their education was not remotely geared towards translation between the languages. This difficult situation, as Ojo (1986) further stresses, was compounded by the attitude of the European publishers; for them

> Encouraging literary works to move beyond their original geo-political and linguistic sources, through translation, would have meant helping to internationalize or globalize the African cause. It would also have sensitized educated and articulate Africans from the other linguistic groups and [made] them become more fully aware of the predicament of the African.

Early translations included *The Dark Child* (1954), which is James Kirkup, Ernest Jones and Elaine Gottlieb's English version of Camara Laye (1928–80) of Guinea's autobiographical novel *L'Enfant noir* (1953); *The Radiance of the King* (1956), which is James Kirkup's English version of Camara Laye's novel *Le Regard du Roi* (1954); and *Mission Accomplished* (UK, 1958) or *Mission to Kala* (US, 1958), which is Peter Green's English version of another novel, Mongo Beti of Cameroon's *Mission terminée* (1957).

The works chosen for translation were often those that fell within the ideological and political framework of the colonial masters. For example, Ade Ojo has argued that Camara Laye's *L'Enfant Noir* was the first to be selected in the mid-1950s particularly because of "its thematic perspective which among others shows the European self-arrogated civilizing mission as having an enduring and seductive impact on the impressionistic mind of a young African." On the other hand, the definitive edition of the first African novel, *Batouala*, was translated by Barbara Beck and Alexandre Mboukou and published only in 1972 (Washington DC and London).

After independence, education systems received new orientations, enabling many Africans and Caribbeans to learn French and English in universities both at home and abroad. Although translations have increased since then, such evolution could be attributed more to international interest in the literatures than to the involvement of African and Caribbean translators. Indeed, today only very few Africans and Caribbeans seem to be interested in or to do literary translation. The vast majority of professional translators in these areas work for government services, international organizations and private companies; most translators are reluctant to take up literary translation, since it is not usually lucrative, permanent jobs are hard to come by, and contracts are few and far between. Besides, many translators have received very little training in literary translation, given that most professional schools concentrate on non-literary translation. The few Africans and Caribbeans who have already translated literary works from French into English include Modupé Bodé-Thomas (*So Long a Letter*, 1981, from Mariama Bâ's 1980 novel, *Une si longue lettre*); Simon Mpondo (*Hammer Blows*, 1973, from David Diop's poems *Coups de pilon*, 1956); and Guillaume Oyono Mbia (*Three Suitors, One Husband*, 1968, from his own 1964 comedy *Trois Prétendants, un mari*). Although Africans and Caribbeans are becoming increasingly involved in translation, the field is still dominated by the British and Americans. This means, therefore, that most translations have so far been done by non-Africans. Very often, these translators are university scholars and critics specialized in African or Caribbean literary studies, who are quite familiar with French and English and have developed an interest in translating the literatures; they engage in literary translation only in addition to their professional activity as lecturers and critics. In such cases, since translation is considered merely as a subsidiary activity or hobby, they do it during their spare time – hence the very few translations. Dorothy Blair, Clive Wake, James Kirkup, Richard Bjornson, Langston Hughes, and Mercer Cook, among others, fall within this group. The needs and interests of the large readership in Europe and America continue to play a decisive role in determining which works are translated. Moreover, publishers are often guided by market forces, publishing only translations they feel will satisfy their readers and be economically profitable.

Although a good number of works have been translated since the 1960s, translators have been scarcely able to keep pace with the writers. In fact, Ade Ojo indicates that less than five per cent of African literary works have been affected by translation. A close look at translated works reveals certain trends in translation, especially the preponderance of novels and prose fiction. To a large extent, this seems to reflect the taste and preferences of readers as well as the fact that African and Caribbean writers have produced more prose fiction than any other literary genre. Besides, as Dorothy Blair points out: "Publishers have so far been cautious about bringing out translations of dramatic literature, claiming that there is not sufficient readership, as compared to the large public interested in the novel, or even poetry." Oyono Mbia's plays and Seydou Badian's *La Mort de Chaka* (1961) are among the very few dramatic works that have been translated into English. As for poetry, selections of poems by one or more poets have been translated and published together in anthologies; for instance, John Reed and Clive Wake have published a translated anthology of poems by different poets (*French African Verse with English Translation*, 1972) while Melvin Dixon has published a collection of Senghor's poems (*The Collected Poetry*, 1991) and Clayton Eshleman and Annette Smith have translated and introduced Césaire's poems in a collection, *Aimé Césaire: The Collected Poetry*, (1983).

Some translators also prefer to translate the works of a specific author or authors; for example, James Kirkup has more or less specialized in the works of Camara Laye (translating *The Dark Child*, 1954; *The Radiance of the King*, 1956; *A Dream of Africa*, 1968; *The Guardian of the Word*, 1980), while John Reed has focused on those of Ferdinand Oyono (*Houseboy*, 1966; *The Old Man and the Medal*, 1967). This is probably because the translators have become quite familiar with the themes and styles of the writers in question. On the other hand, certain translators work on a wide range of authors; for instance, Dorothy Blair has translated works of varied authorship – her translations include the works of Birago Diop (*Tales of Amadou Koumba*, translated 1966), Olympe Bhely-Quénum (*Snares Without End*, 1981), Aminanta Sow Fall (*The Beggars' Strike*, 1981), Alioum Fantouré (*Tropical Circle*, 1981), Nafissatou Diallo (*A Dakar Childhood*, 1982), and Myriam Warber-Vieyra (*As the Sorcerer Said …*, 1982).

In certain cases, writers have translated their own works into English. Guillaume Oyono Mbia translated his plays *Trois prétendants … un mari*, 1964, and *Le Train spécial de son Excellence*, 1979 (*Three Suitors, One Husband*, 1968; *His Excellency's Special Train*, 1979).

Furthermore, some translations have been subsequently expanded to contain other works of the same writer; for example, Richard Bjornson's English version of René Philombe's *Lettres de ma cambuse* (1964), published as *Tales From My Hut* in 1977, was expanded to contain other stories, still by Philombe (four short stories from *Histoires queue-de-chat*, 1971) and reissued in 1984 under the title *Tales from Cameroon: Collected Short Stories of René Philombe*. This practice is more common with poetry, where collections are often expanded to contain all the other poems of a given poet; for example, Eshleman and Smith's translation of Césaire's work mentioned above.

Translators have generally encountered certain problems, most of which relate to cultural references and the source authors' peculiar use of French, especially in dialogue and imagery. In fact, in fiction and drama, "français petit nègre" and creole are often used by African and Caribbean writer respectively in their effort to create speech that reflects the peasant environment of their works, while being accessible to a wide and varied francophone audience. Many writers provide footnotes, endnotes and glossaries for terms and expressions that they feel might not be understood by readers. With regard to such culture-bound terms and expressions, as well as proverbs, translators have, on the whole, maintained those that have no English equivalents and rendered the peculiar imagery and proverbs literally. For instance, Katherine Woods has retained "tabala", "chahâda", etc., in her English version (*Ambiguous Adventure*, 1963) of Cheikh Hamidou Kane's *L'Aventure ambiguë* (1961), while Langston Hughes and Mercer Cook, in their translation of Jacques Roumain's *Gouverneurs de la Rosée* (1944) under the title *Masters of the Dew* (1947, new edition 1978) maintained creole words such as "coumbite" and "houngan" as well as the names of deities which cannot be rendered in English, and provided a glossary at the end to define and explain them. However, most of the creole words, such as "mabouya", rendered as "lizard", and "maringouin", rendered as "mosquito", are translated into standard English. In the translation of poetry, difficulties are often related to poetic use of language, repetition, rhythm and, in some cases, neologisms; for instance, Césaire's disjointed syntax, frequent use of homophony and echo effects, creation of new words, and punctuation are some of the problems with which the translators have had to cope.

As regards publication, the bulk of the translations have been published (and in most cases requested) by companies in Europe and America such as Heinemann (African Writers Series and Caribbean Writers Series), Longman, and Macmillan in Britain, and Three Continents Press in the United States, as well as university presses such as the University of California Press and the University Press of Virginia, etc.

At the present stage, therefore, the translation of African and Caribbean literary works could be said to be in its infancy. Besides, studies and publications on the translation of African and Caribbean literatures, especially from French into English, are still cursory, fragmentary, and limited to research papers, articles, and reports scattered in learned journals and reviews. Although some laudable work is being done by some commercial publishers and university presses, government policies in many countries have yet to attach any importance to literary translation. Measures to encourage the reading of translated works and the inclusion of such works in school and university syllabuses and the public examinations could go a long way to improve the situation.

MOSES N. NINTAI

Further Reading

Nama, Charles, "A Critical Analysis of the Translation of African Literature", *Language and Communication*, 10/1 (1990) pp. 356–69

Nintai, Moses, "Mapping Transference: Problems of African Literature and Translation from French into English" (dissertation), University of Warwick, 1993

Noss, Philip, "Translation and the African Tale" in *Black Culture and Black Consciousness in Literature*, edited by Chidi Ikonné *et al.*, Ibadan: Heinemann, 1987

Ojo, Ade, "The Role of the Translator of African Written Literature in Intercultural Consciousness and Realtionships", *Meta*, 31/ 3 (1986) pp. 291–99

Packman, Brenda, "Some Problems of Translation in African Literature", in *Perspectives on African Literature*, edited by Christopher Heywood, London: Heinemann, and New York: Africana, 1971

Timothy-Asobele, Jide, "Literary Translation in Africa: the Nigerian Experience", *Babel*, 35/2 (1989) pp. 65–86

Francophone Arab and Maghrebian Writers in English Translation

When one considers the relative paucity of translations of Arabic literature as a whole that are available to the general reader, it comes as no real surprise to discover an equally regrettable state of affairs with reference to those writers from North Africa or of Arabic descent who choose to write and publish in French. The reasons for this are, it could be argued, largely cultural and historical; the Maghreb (that area of North Africa now bounded by Algeria, Tunisia and Morocco) was never a region in which the British played a great role. It is not racism but simply lack of awareness that has denied anglophone readers access to the francophone equivalents of Chinua Achebe, Derek Walcott and (more contentiously) Salman Rushdie and Hanif Kureishi. However, the situation is slowly beginning to change. A growing interest in postcolonial writing, driven by the works of such figures as Homi Bhabha and Edward Said, and a reanalysis of the British Empire, are leading to a corresponding curiosity about writing from all former colonies. It is to be hoped that, in coming years, more works will be translated into English, both as aids to the continual process of the re-evaluation of our own history and, more importantly, as works of worth in themselves. That said, there is still a long way to go; the general reader probably has as much knowledge of Franco-African writing as they had of non-Peninsular Hispanic literature before the publication in English of the Colombian Gabriel García Márquez's *One Hundred Years of Solitude* in 1970. There is a desperate need for a British or American publisher to play a role analogous to that of L'Harmattan in Paris, making these works freely available in large print runs (although an honourable mention must be made of Quartet Books in London, who have published extremely good translations of several novels by the Moroccan Tahar ben Jelloun and the Algerian Assia Djebar, and Abacus, who have brought out paperback editions of several novels by the Lebanese writer Amin Maalouf, including his 1993 Goncourt Prize winner, *The Rock of Tanios*). The monoglot English reader is still unable to gain anything but the most superficial knowledge of this large and ever-growing field of literature. The March 1988 edition of *Magazine littéraire*, devoted to contemporary Arab writers, notes that since 1973 between 10 and 20 francophone novels a year had been published, taking no account of plays, poetry or volumes of short stories. This may not seem like a large figure, but when we consider that among this number are works by writers of the importance in their culture of Borges and Fuentes in the Hispanic world, then the need for translation becomes clear.

The phrase Francophone Arab and Maghrebian literature, while useful as a shorthand description, neglects the fact that there are two very distinct groups of writers to whom it can be applied. The first group includes such authors as Tahar ben Jelloun, Rachid Boudjedra and Kateb Yacine (both the latter Algerian, the last a figure of towering importance to Franco-Arabic literature, whose work is completely unknown in English), who write in French, but who are still resident in Arab countries or at least able to return there at regular intervals; in other words, they are products of a predominantly Arab culture. The second group have only begun to write and publish within at most the last 20 years. Children of the North Africans who emigrated to France after World War II, their experiences are of the *bidonvilles* or shanty towns in which they were initially housed, then the HLMs or tower blocks that ring the outskirts of most major French cities (it should be noted that for the French, the word "suburb" evokes an image of urban deprivation rather than domestic comedy). They have become known as "second generation" immigrants, a term they have rejected as insulting and inaccurate (and rightly so; born in France for the most part, mainly French-speaking, they are *not* immigrants), choosing instead a term drawn from slang – *Beur* (*verlan* or "backchat" for *Arabe*). *Beur* writing is a very young school at present, consisting largely of autobiographical fiction, of which the most famous example is Mehdi Charef's 1983 novel, *Le Thé au harem d'Archi Ahmed* (translated as *Tea in the Harem*, 1989). This story of teenagers drifting into a life of petty crime and drug abuse in a hellish estate on the outskirts of Paris is not simply about the plight of *Beurs*, but about the dispossessed as a whole; however it is clearly based on Charef's own experiences, with the central character Madjid a thinly-veiled "portrait of the artist as a young man". Ed Emery's translation of the text captures the vigour of Charef's argot-ridden original, but it should be noted that this is a text of sociological rather than literary interest. *Beur* writing is capable of great subtlety and stylistic innovation, exemplified by Farida Belghoul's 1986 novel *Georgette!* Both a depiction of a young Arab girl who tries to deny her parental culture and an excellent picture of the world through a child's eyes, this is a masterpiece, and it is a tragedy that it has as yet not been translated into English.

Any analysis of Francophone Arab literature in translation is going to run up against one inevitable obstacle; as should have become abundantly clear, there is really very little of it. In the edition of *Magazine littéraire* mentioned above, there is a list of 20 novels that are seen as central to the field; only two are listed by the British Library as ever having been available in English translation (Assia Djebar's *Fantasia: An Algerian Cavalcade* and Albert Memmi's *The Pillar of Salt*). Once more, it can only be hoped that this situation will continue to improve.

J.K.L. SCOTT

Translations

Ben Jelloun, Tahar, *The Sacred Night* [*La Nuit sacrée*], translated by Alan Sheridan, San Diego: Harcourt Brace, and London: Quartet, 1989

Ben Jelloun, Tahar, *State of Absence* [*L'Ange aveugle*], translated by James Kirkup, London: Quartet, 1994

Charef, Mehdi, *Tea in the Harem* [*Le Thé au harem d'Archi Ahmed*], translated by Ed Emery, London: Serpent's Tail, 1989

Djebar, Assia, *A Sister to Scherezade* [*Ombre Sultane*], translated by Dorothy S. Blair, London: Quartet, 1988

Djebar, Assia, *Fantasia: An Algerian Cavalcade* [*L'Amour, la fantasia*], translated by Dorothy S. Blair, London: Quartet, 1989

Maalouf, Amin, *The Rock of Tanios* [*Le Rocher de Tanios*], translated by Dorothy S. Blair, London: Quartet, and New York: Braziller, 1994

Memmi, Albert, *The Pillar of Salt* [*La Statue de Sel*], translated by Edouard Roditi, New York: Criterion, and London: Elek, 1956

Further Reading

Dejeux, Jean, *Littérature maghrébine de langue française: Introduction générale et auteurs*, Paris: Naaman, 1973

Hargreaves, Alec G., "Resistance and Identity in *Beur* Narratives", *Modern Fiction Studies*, 35/1 (1989) pp. 87–102

Hargreaves, Alec G., *Voices from the North African Immigrant Community in France: Immigration and Identity in Beur Fiction*, Oxford: Berg, 1991

Jack, Belinda, *Francophone Literatures: An Introductory Survey*, Oxford and New York: Oxford University Press, 1996

Magazine Littéraire, 251 (March 1988): special issue "Ecrivains Arabes d'aujourd'hui"

French

Literary Translation into English

The Language

It is usual to divide the history of the French language into three periods: Old French (9th to 13th centuries), Middle French (14th to 15th or 16th centuries), Modern French (16th or 17th century to the present). French is a Romance language, having developed out of colloquial provincial Latin during the second half of the first millennium and absorbed substantial material, introduced direct from classical sources by the literate clergy, between the 12th and 15th centuries. The form of the language spoken around Paris has become standard, at the expense of other regional dialects, under the influence of centralized political institutions and of the Académie Française, founded in 1635, whose *Dictionnaire*, periodically republished, is generally regarded as the primary arbiter of correct usage. There is little regional variation among educated users of modern French.

This pattern of development has led to a distinction between colloquial and educated forms of the language. Already in the 17th century Molière and Racine were making use of bathetic descents into the colloquial for comic and dramatic effect, and many writers have followed them, although in modern usage it is more often the rare excursion into high style that creates the desired contrast. Similar possibilities exist in English, but there the distinction between Anglo-Saxon and Norman French vocabulary and sentence structure is much greater, so that the English-speaker may find the contrast offered in French relatively pale, and underestimate its literary effect, while the French speaker may find English crude in comparison with the subtlety he recognizes in his own language.

Spoken French has no significant tonic stress. Words are often run together, so that a whole phrase becomes a single unit of sound offering little possibility of variation of emphasis within it. Relatively inflexible rules on word order are similarly constraining. Effects of emphasis, which in English are often obtained through variations of intonation, tonic stress and word order, must be achieved in French through techniques of syntax and of vocabulary. Such stress as exists falls on the final syllable of a word or a phrase, often accompanied by a rising intonation, giving the language a rhythm clearly distinct from that of strongly front-stressed English.

In its evolution from Latin, French has eliminated many consonants, especially from the spoken language. There are thus many homophones among the older word-stock, and care is sometimes needed to avoid ambiguity. Modern French possesses the usual basic back vowels, an alveolar [R], and a series of distinctive nasals ([ɛ̃], [ɑ̃], [ɔ̃], [œ̃] and front rounded vowels ([o], [u], [y], [ø]). The pursed lips that the latter require cause many speakers to develop a recognizably French facial shape around the mouth. There are relatively few diphthongs, no aspirate or dental fricative [th], and consonantal clusters are rare.

These substantial differences in phonetic resource mean that in any context where the sheer sound of the language is important French and English differ widely. The translation of verse is a particularly thankless task – the standard metrical forms of the two languages, and their patterns of emphasis, are necessarily quite distinct – and similar difficulties arise with all oral material, for example that intended for the theatre or for public speaking, and with all written representation of spoken dialogue.

Two of three Latin genders have survived in French (with rules of concord regarding number and gender, not found in English) and are sufficiently free from sexual connotations that certain feminine nouns may be used for male persons, and vice versa, without apparent incongruity, except as regards the names of professions, where new feminine forms are increasingly being adopted. The major medieval additions to the French language are primarily in the form of abstract nouns, while the complex Latin system of verbs has atrophied progressively, leaving in common use only four simple indicative tenses, a vestigial subjunctive mood, and, in most tenses of most verbs, no distinction in sound between the first, second and third persons singular and the third-person plural. A modest number of compound tenses are also in use. The tendency towards Latinate nouns has thus been encouraged by the decline of alternative verb-based forms. No equivalent exists to the powerful English compound formulation of verb-plus-adverb. The French translation of an English text is typically longer than the original, while a translation from French that simply reproduces in English the syntax of the original will sound verbose.

Modern French presents in normal discourse certain syntactic and lexical features that in English would mark a formal register: obligatory presence of relative pronoun or relative conjunction to introduce subordinate clauses; tendency towards complex sentence structures; frequent occurrence of relatively new Latin- and Greek-derived "learned" words and of surviving subjunctive structures. English and French share a basic SVO (subject, verb, object) word order, but in French object-pronouns usually precede the governing verb in a prescribed order, and most adjectives follow their nouns.

Modern French is spoken as a first language throughout metropolitan France, in several overseas French territories, parts of Switzerland and Belgium, the province of Quebec, and several countries of Africa. It is widely spoken as a second language, and still retains some of its historical role as a language of diplomacy. In recent years, France has experienced significant immigration, mainly from North and West Africa, and much increased contact with the English language, through the rapid development of international communications. The resultant exposure to non-Latin sources, to which French has been historically resistant, and which is chronologically recent in terms of language development, seems to be producing a more rapid rate of linguistic change than hitherto. In particular, North African elements are appearing in urban slang, and anglophone elements in the jargon of certain industries and social groups, while the historical tendency towards long, latinate words has led to a reaction, in the dropping of the final syllables to produce apocopated forms, and the construction of new acronyms from the initial letters of compound nouns. In the second half of the 20th century there is a widespread feeling that French is under threat, primarily from English, and, formal legislation has been introduced in an attempt to preserve its purity.

Nevertheless, French possesses relatively few elements of vocabulary or syntax drawn from sources other than Latin. It has changed little over the last three centuries, and remains highly resistant to new formations, particularly of verbs – most new forms admitted are nouns, even when the original was not. English, in contrast, which benefits from the Germanic as well as the Latin traditions, favours flexible verb-related structure over substantival ones, is highly receptive to new formations, and continues to evolve rapidly (for better or for worse): perhaps as a result, it offers a substantially wider range of linguistic resource.

George S. Miller

Up to the Renaissance

During the Middle English period the concept of *translatio* was one of transference of texts from one culture to another, rather than the modern concept of translation meaning a close rendition of the sense of the original text into another language. Thus all translations involved adaptation but some translations kept more closely to their source text than others. This is perhaps best described as forming a continuum of adaptation-translation with the "cut-off" point between the two difficult to determine. Although French literature had great influence on Middle English literature, translations of only a few genres exist. Thus medieval hagiographic texts seem to depend directly on Latin *vitae*, and the genres of drama and, to a lesser extent, chronicle, either derive from Latin texts or are what we would describe as original compositions. Translators focused largely, though not exclusively, on religious and moral texts. The main areas of translation are:

1. English Charlemagne romances. These are translations of the French *chansons de geste* and constitute a distinct genre of Middle English literature. Relatively few *chansons de geste* seem to have been translated into English. Those that have been are religious in character, concerned with conversion and/or relics. They fall into two main groups, the Ferumbras group, derived from the French text *Fierabras*, and the Otuel group, derived from the epic *Otinel*. There is also a fragment of a translation of the *Chanson de Roland* and a Middle English text derived from the *Pseudo-Turpin Chronicle* (see also the entry on *The Song of Roland*).

The Ferumbras group consists of three texts, each surviving in only a single MS. *Firumbras*, Fillingham MS, BL Additional 37492 (*Firumbras*, edited by M. Sullivan, E.E.T.S. [Early English Text Society], Extra Series CXCVIII, London, 1935), dates from the second half of the 15th century. Approximately the first 3,000 lines of the Old French text are lacking. *Sir Ferumbras*, Bodley, Ashmole 33 (*Sir Ferumbras*, edited by S.J.H. Herrtage, E.E.T.S., Extra Series, 34, London, 1879), is from the end of the 14th century. *The Sowdone of Babylone* (*The Sowdone of Babylone*, edited by E. Hausknecht, E.E.T.S., Extra Series 38, London, 1881), has been dated c.1450. The last of these texts is unique in that it combines in one text two Old French poems, *Fierabras* with *La Destruction de Rome*, the post-dated "preface" to *Fierabras*, found preceding it in two MSS.

Of the three Middle English texts *Sir Ferumbras* is the closest to its Old French source. *The Sowdone of Babylone* is derived, not from the French Vulgate version, but from an Anglo-Norman adaptation contained in a single MS in the British Library, BL Additional 3028 Egerton MS, and is the most free translation of its source.

The Otuel group, *Otuel a Knight* (Auchinleck MS, edited by S.J.H. Herrtage, London, E.E.T.S., E.S., 1882), *Otuel and Roland* (Fillinham MS, edited by M.I. O'Sullivan, London, E.E.T.S., O/S. 198, 1935), *Roland and Otuel* (Thornton MS, edited by S.J.H. Herrtage, London, E.E.T.S., E.S. 39, 1882) are derived from the French *chanson de geste*, *Otinel*. Again, all three texts are independent translations, and extant in single MSS. *Roland and Otuel* is preceded in the MS by *The Sege of Melayne*, one of only two English Charlemagne romances with no known French source. *The Sege of Melayne* is sometimes seen as an introduction to *Roland and Otuel*.

The original French texts *Fierabras* and *Otinel* are closely related. The English translations are faithful to the narrative but may, by apparently small changes, alter the depiction of the characters, generally losing many of the nuances of the French. Descriptions are often abbreviated. The main gain is narrative pace and, in some texts, an increased emphasis on the religious aspects of the text, with a simpler moral perspective.

The two English texts dealing with the matter of the *Chanson de Roland*, the fragment, *The Song of Roland* (edited by S.J.H. Herrtage, E.E.T.S., E.S., 35, 1880) and *Roland and Vernagu* (edited by S.J.H. Herrtage, E.E.T.S., E.S., 39, 1882) are not derived uniquely from the Oxford version of the *Chanson*. *The Song of Roland* contains some elements drawn from the *Pseudo-Turpin Chronicle*, which is the main source of *Roland and Vernagu*.

Some scholars have considered that there once existed a cyclic "Charlemagne and Roland", composed of four parts: the journey of Charlemagne to the Holy Land; the beginning of the wars in Spain, including the combat between Roland and Vernagu; *Otinel*; the conclusion of Turpin's chronicle (see G. Paris, *Histoire poétique de Charlemagne*, Paris: Libraire Émile Bouillon, 1905, reprinted Geneva: Slatkine, 1974, p. 156; R.N. Walpole, *Charlemagne and Roland: A Study of the Source of Two Middle English Metrical Romances*, University of California publications in Modern Philology, vol. 21, Berkeley: University of California Press, 1944, and "The Source MS of Charlemagne and Roland and the Auchinleck Bookshop", *Modern Language Notes*, 60, 1945, pp 22–26; Judith Weiss, "The Auchinleck MS and the Edwardes MSS", *Notes and Queries*, 214, 1969, pp. 44–49, does not agree with all Walpole's conclusions.)

2. Non-Charlemagne romances. These fall into several groups. Of those texts which, like the Charlemagne romances, are translations of French *chansons de geste*, the most important is *Ami and Aminloun*, which exists in continental French, Anglo-Norman and Middle English versions, the last two closely related (M.E. text edited by F. Lesaux, Exeter Medieval English Texts, 1995). Others are translated from French romances, or *lais*. Only one translation of a Chrétien de Troyes romance exists, the 14th-century *Yvain and Gawain*, derived from *Yvain*. *Sir Tristrem* has as its source Thomas's version of the romance of Tristan and Yseut. The mid-13th-century *Floris and Blancheflor* is a version of the early 13th-century *Florie et Blancheflor* (see H.G.E. Veldhoen, "Floris and Blanchflour: To Indulge the Fancy and to Hear of Love", in *Companion to Early Middle English Literature*, edited by H.G.E. Veldhoen and H. Aertson). Two of Marie de France's *lais* survive in Middle English translations: *Sir Launfal*, from *Lanval*, and the *Lai de Fresne*. The author of *Launcelot of the Laik*, derived from the French prose, acknowledges that his is a "paraphrase" rather than a translation of the whole of the French text, because "to translait the romans of that knycht / it passith fare my cunyng and my mycht". A similar admission could have been made by some of the other "translators", as many texts contain mistranslations, yet generally the understanding is sufficiently good to convey the general sense. *Ipomedon* survives in three versions, two in verse and one in prose. *William of Parlene* is part of the 14th-century alliterative revival. Where the original text is of insular origin it is not always easy to ascertain whether the French has been translated into English or the English text translated into French. *Havelok the Dane*, *Guy of Warwick*, *Beves of Hampton* and *King Horn* are all insular texts. (See R.M. Wilson, *Early Middle English Literature*, London: Methuen, 1968, pp. 215–25 for one theory on the way Middle English texts depended on Old French texts.)

Two translations also survive of *The Romance of the Rose*, one by Chaucer, the other, a fragment, is anonymous.

The best known Middle English text derived from an Old French source is probably Layamoun's *Brut*, written in alliterative verse and perceived as history rather than romance. Although its links with the version by Wace are quite clear, the adaptation probably goes beyond what today would be classed as "translation". This is also true of Malory's *Morte D'Arthur*.

3. Didactic literature. French didactic literature seems to have known considerable popularity in medieval England. Certain treatises were translated a number of times. The most famous of all Middle English didactic texts, Robert Mannying of Brunne's

Handlying Synne (1303) was a translation of William of Waddington's *Manuel des Péchéz*, also translated as *Manuel of Sin* by Englysche (c.1425). Several translations were made of Guillaume de Deguileville's allegorical *Pèlerinage de la vie humaine*. John Lydgate used the second recension for his (1426–30) verse translation (*Pilgrimage of the Life of Man*, edited by F.J. Furnivall and Katherine B. Locock, E.E.T.S., E.S., 77, 83, 92, 1899–1904; see Derek Pearsall, *John Lydgate*, London: Routledge and Kegan Paul, 1970), while the first recension was used for the anonymous prose *Pilgrimage of the Lyfe of the Manhode* (edited by Avril May, E.E.T.S., 288 and 292, 1985 and 1988). There are no less than nine English translations of the *Somme des Vices et des Vertus*, otherwise known as the *Somme le Roy*, written by the 13th-century Dominican friar, Lorens d'Orléans. These include the 14th-century *Book of Vices and Virtues* (edited by W.N. Francis, 1942) and Dan Michel's close translation (1340), *Ayenbite of Inwit* or *Remorse of Conscience* (edited by R. Morris, E.E.T.S., Original Series, 23, 1866, reissued 1965). The treatise *Livre pour l'enseignement de ses filles*, written c.1372 for his daughters by the Chevalier de la Tour Landry, was translated twice. The anonymous translation of c.1480, *The Book of the Knight of La Tour Landry* (E.E.T.S., O.S. 21, 1868, revised 1906), is less close than that published by Caxton.

With William Caxton, who translated and published a number of Old French texts, both narrative and didactic, we come to a different concept of translation. His sometimes slavish translations mark the beginning of a more modern concept of translation.

MARIANNE J. AILES

Further Reading

Anderson, George K., *Old and Middle English Literature from the Beginnings to 1485*, London: Oxford University Press, 1950; New York: Collier, 1962

Beston, John, "How Much Was Known of the Breton Lai in Fourteenth-century England" in *The Learned and the Lewed: Studies in Chaucer and Medieval Literature*, edited by Larry D. Benson, Cambridge, Massachusetts: Harvard University Press, 1974, pp 319–36

Cowan, Janet, "The English Charlemagne Romances" in *Roland and Charlemagne in Europe*, edited by Karen Pratt, London: King's College London Centre for Late Antique and Medieval Studies, 1996

Crane, Susan, *Insular Romance: Politics, Faith, and Culture in Anglo-Norman and Middle English Literature*, Berkeley: University of California Press, 1986

Loomis, R.S., *Arthurian Literature in the Middle Ages*, Oxford: Clarendon Press, 1959

Metlitzki, Dorothee, *The Matter of Araby in Medieval England*, New Haven and London: Yale University Press, 1977

Pearsall, Derek, *Old English and Middle English Poetry*, London and Boston: Routledge and Kegan Paul, 1977

Severs, J.B. (editor), *A Manual of the Writings in Middle English, 1050–1500*, vol. 1, New Haven: Connecticut Academy of Arts and Sciences, 1967

Spearing, A.C., "Marie de France and her Middle English Adaptors", *Studies in the Age of Chaucer*, 12 (1990) pp. 117–56

15th and 16th Centuries

Fifteenth- and 16th-century translations from French span the manuscript and print ages in both poetry and prose; we can usefully divide these translations, according to some main factors affecting them, into three general sub-periods: before print (pre-1476); after print until around mid-16th century, which is to say, a time of flux during the Tudor religious controversies and changing relations with France, but before Tottel (1558) and the Elizabethan flourishing of letters; and during the Elizabethan age, when court contexts, international relations, and English letters, language, and print industry had found clearer directions. Some further distinctions occur between prose and verse and between sacred and secular translations; yet across these categories and across the three sub-periods of 15th–16th century translation, certain continuities persist.

Fifteenth-century prose manuscript translations tend to be religious, moral, or philosophical in nature: a few saints' lives, three translations of Guillaume de Deguileville's *Pèlerinages*, books of morals, battle, and hunting (e.g. Edward, second Duke of York's c.1406 translation of Gaston de Foix's *Livre de la chasse*). Several translations of French versions of the pseudo-Aristotelian *Secreta secretorum* indicate its continuing appeal as a French source (*Governaunce of Prynces* [titles vary], translated by James Yonge c.1440, by John Shirley c.1460, by Gilbert de la Haye 1456, and anonymously, c.1460, printed Copland 1528). This work, like the translations of the *Dicts moraulx des philosophes* (those for example by Stephen Scrope c.1450, and by Anthony à Woodville c.1476), reminds us that translation was an important instrument for the serious literary project of advising nobles and princes (see Green, 1980) andthat a chief topos and purpose in medieval translating, *translatio studii* (transferral of [discourse about] learning), was still closely connected with its cousin *translatio imperii* (transferral of [discourse about] power). Fiction titles translated include many romances (the *Knight of La Tour Landry*, *Merlin*, *Kynge Ponthus*, and others). Scrope's c.1444–50 translation of Christine de Pizan's 1401 *Epistre d'Othea* was a preview of several of her works Englished in the print age (Campbell, 1925). Workman (1940), whose appendices list early prose translations, thinks translation "may have provided 15th-century England with a body of prose ... more advanced than the native prose [in certain ways]. If a large amount of such prose had been accumulating through the century, it must have affected the cultural concepts, conscious or unconscious, of both writers and readers".

However, the case for translation's effect on writers and readers is clearer for prose than for pre-print poetry. Julia Boffey (1985) proves the predominance in 15th-century England of poetry written in French. Given a continuing English audience for poetry in French, one might suspect that demand for poetic translation into English would not increase. From John Gower's *Cinkante Ballades* and *Traitié pour enssemplez les amantz mariez*, for example, one infers that English poets still found French a proper medium for poetry; R. Quixley's translation of the *Traitié* into English (c.1402, for his daughter's marriage) seems to have served an occasional rather than a primarily literary purpose. Thus the largest poetic translation into English from this period, the lyric sequence of Charles d'Orléans (BL Harley MS 682, more than 6,500 lines), stands out from the English literary landscape in a number of ways (Arn, 1995;

Spearing, 1990; Coldiron, 2000). It stands out, that is, from what little we can really see of it: it is as hard to draw tenable conclusions about these poetic translations as about this period's shorter poetry in general, and for the same reasons (relatively little extant evidence, poems copied into miscellaneous books in scattered fashion, a fair amount of partial, miscopied, misattributed, or unattributed poetry).

The situation is clearer after 1476 because of one crucial fact: the early printers' houses were also thriving centers of translation from French to English. There is good continuity between the manuscript and print translations from French; after 1476, Caxton, for example, brought to print a number of early manuscript translations from French as well as adding many new ones. Caxton (who printed at least 20 titles translated from French) and Wynkyn de Worde were chief among these early francophile printers, and their successors Pynson and R. Copland (see Erler's edition of Copland) found translation, especially translation from French, an important source of material for publication. Principal French-translators of this middle sub-period between Caxton and Elizabeth include John Bourchier (Lord Berners), translator of Froissart's chronicles, of *Arthur*, of *Huon de Bordeaux*; Henry Watson; Alexander Barclay; Anthony à Woodville, Earl Rivers; Andrew Chertsey, productive translator of French religious material; and the ever-thriving Anon.

Ringler (1988) notes that of translated verse between 1501 and 1558, 30 per cent came from French (as opposed to 5 per cent from Italian). Much of it, like the early and mid-period prose, was instructive, even didactic in character – the primers, *horae*, and shepherd's calendars that guided the daily lives of early 16th-century English readers were frequently translated from French or included verse translated from French. (The first shepherd's calendars have an interesting history in this regard: Paris printer Antoine Vérard tried to enter the English market with shepherd's calendars crudely translated from French; it took English houses and more skillful English translators to make the books succeed.) Georgic, philosophical, historical, political, romance, and religious titles continued to be translated in the middle period; these translations were still heavily content-oriented. Highlights: Lydgate's *Fall of Princes* from Laurent de Premierfait's, *Blanchardin et Eglantine*; Chrétien de Troyes's *Perceval*; the *Roman de la Rose*; and translations from Marie de France, Antoine de la Sale, Robert de Balsac, Guillaume Alexis, Octavien de Saint-Gelais, and others.

In this early print period the medieval effort at faithful import of an authoritative source's message was, judging from the translators' prefaces and practice, still a chief goal (even if, as Rita Copeland argues, the effort had been a rhetorical or hermeneutic one). The script and early print translations offer clues about the changing states of literacy in the two languages and about the audiences for works in each language (Bennett, 1952–70; Boffey, 1985). One of Caxton's first issues is a French–English vocabulary; an increasing number of French–English grammars and dictionaries may indicate an increasing number of English-only readers and perhaps a niche for French–English translation activity in this period. Beyond the probable influence of the translations' carefully rendered content, and beyond the apparent participation of translators in religious controversies, the prose translations from French may have expanded English prose style and rendered it firmer and less paratactic (Workman, 1940). Early translation from French shows us some late manifestations of *translatio studii*, reveals linguistic and literacy patterns in flux, and points out new ways to think about literary change across cultures and periods. It is rich, insufficiently studied ground.

After the mid-16th century, with printing well established, Richard Tottel's *Miscellany* (1557) in vogue, and religious controversies temporarily calmed by Elizabeth I's accession, came a third age in early-modern translation. Instead of mostly serious prose translations, largely from French with some "French filtered" material previously in Latin (Workman, 1940), and nearly all careful to reproduce a source's content, *sentence*, and *auctoritas*, translations now exploded into variety. While translators continued to rely on French sources, they added an increasing number of translations from Italian, Dutch, Spanish, Latin, and Greek (these often via Latin and/or French); French continues to be a filter through which prior materials reach English, but translations from French, predominant in the earlier sub-periods, now compete with translations from other continental literatures in an age during which imitation, translation, and the enrichment of the national language and letters were paramount concerns (Greene, 1982). Furthermore, translators continue to reproduce full sources but now increasingly incorporate select translated fragments into new English material, sometimes invisibly naturalizing the material.

Prescott details the foundational place of five French poets (Marot, Du Bellay, Ronsard, Desportes, and Du Bartas) in the English Renaissance; older studies of Tudor translation tend to look mainly at influences in poetry (Upham, 1908; Lee, 1910; Scott, 1929), interpreting the translations from French as an alternative source of Petrarchism in England (which it was, in the case of Daniel translating certain Desportes sonnets, for example). After Wyatt's translations of Marot, poetic highlights from French include Spenser's three non-Petrarchan sonnet sequences from French (1569, 1591); Thomas Combe's c.1593 *Theatre of Fine Devices* (edited by Silcox), an emblem book translated from G. de La Perrière's *Théâtre de bons engins*; John Soowthern's *Pandora*; and scattered poems in the work of Gorges, Spenser, Samuel Daniel, Drayton, Thomas Lodge, and in most sonnet sequences after Thomas Watson's 1582 *Hekatompathia*. Even in the poetry, English translators clearly do not restrict themselves to importing French Petrarchism.

Further examples: translations from Chartier (1566, 1596), from AMADIS DE GAULE (1567, 1573), of *Arthur of Britain* (1555, 1582), for example, keep alive in Renaissance England a sort of late French medievalism. Also beyond French-refracted Petrarchism is a certain subtle Hellenism, both Pindaric and Anacreontic (see Silver, 1981), and the indirect effects of a body of Greek texts translated in France (H. Estienne's Latin works and their French spin-offs being chief). The French filter for translations was not now so exclusively for Latin sources; English translators began using French versions of Italian and Spanish works, translation practices here again reflecting England's expanding sense of vernacular cosmopolitanism. Bandello's *Romeo & Juliet*, for example, came to us via Belleforest and Boiastuau (1567, 1579); Pedro Mexía, like the durably popular Diego de San Pedro before him (1540, 1549, 1560, 1575, 1597, 1608, 1639) was translated into English via French; S. Guazzo's and R. Nannini's prose came through versions by Gabriel Chappuys (1586; 1600–1); finally, Gervase

Markham brought us Ariosto via Desportes (1601, *Rodomanth's Infernall*).

Religious literature from France was still important. Aside from psalm translations mediated through French versions, there were the many translations of Du Bartas's poetry (including James's 1584 version of the *Uranie*; for details see Prescott, 1978 and *A Short Title Catalogue of Books* ... edited by A.W. Pollard and G.R. Redgrave, 1926–). Other religious translations from French include one from Innocent Gentillet (1579), those from and about Calvin (1561, 1564, 1578), and the *Stage of Popish Toyes* (1581). At least 11 English translators, some of them prominent authors (Mary, Countess of Pembroke; Sidney; Golding), rendered various works of Philippe de Mornay after 1576. In this period translation cannot be thought of separately from "original" authorship, as imitation theory and this sort of practice show; nor can religious and philosophical prose be thought of as somehow separate from these English writers' practice of letters. English translators continue to bring a great deal of French instructive, historical, and philosophical prose to English readers: a life of Catherine de Medici; many editions of Pierre de la Primaudaye's conduct book, the *French Academie*; Hoby's 1586 *Politique Discourses on Truth and Lying*, translated from Coignet; translations from François de la Noue and Philibert de Vienne; Golding's translation from Hurault (*Politicke, Moral, and Martial Discourses*, 1575); translations of Philippe de Commines's history.

As for the drama, the earlier English drama tended not to take much of its force from French drama (notable exceptions: John Heywood's farce translations in the 1520s and 1530s). But during this latter period, Golding translated de Bèze's *Abraham*, in 1577, and several of Robert Garnier's works were brought into English around the end of the century (Kyd's *Pompey the Great*, 1594; Mary, Countess of Pembroke's *Tragedie of Antonie*, 1590; Daniel's *Cleopatra*, 1594, and *Philotas* 1595), perhaps anticipating the 17th- and 18th-century translations of French classical drama.

Dictionaries and grammars continue to appear in this period, frequently in multilingual versions that perhaps reflect the new vernacular cosmopolitanism in England. Theoretical statements about translation in the period are not as numerous as we might wish (Smith, 1904; Kuhn, 1974), but most theorists agreed that English letters needed enrichment and advised doing as the Romans had done by translating older classics into our native tongue. Some included discussion of other vernaculars, and it seems to have been assumed that translation – like imitation, or perhaps an instrument or subclass of imitation – was a primary literary activity. Some theorists chided bad translators for various reasons. "Inkehorn terms", or words from other languages used in English that seemed unnatural, forced, or flamboyant, were especially scorned. (The attitude towards bad translators may itself be a piece of French influence: cf. Du Bellay's 1549 *Deffence et illustration*, 1.6, 1.7). But translation from French – poetic, political, historic, religious – flourished in the 15th and 16th centuries. Re-editions and reissues of translations from each of these sub-periods testify to their continuing viability for an English readership well into the 17th century. They open the way for later translations from Marguerite de Navarre, Montaigne, Descartes, Corneille, and other major French authors.

A.E.B. COLDIRON

Further Reading

Arn, Mary-Jo (editor), *Fortunes Stabilnes: Charles of Orleans's English Book of Love: A Critical Edition*, Binghamton, New York: Medieval and Renaissance Texts and Studies, 1995

Bennett, H.S., *English Books and Readers*, 3 vols, Cambridge: Cambridge University Press, 1952–70

Boffey, Julia, *Manuscripts of English Courtly Love Lyrics in the Later Middle Ages*, Cambridge: Brewer, 1985

Campbell, P.D.C., "Christine de Pisan en Angleterre", *Revue de Littérature Comparée*, 5 (1925)

Coldiron, A.E.B., *Canon, Period, and the Poetry of Charles of Orleans: Found in Translation*, Ann Arbor: University of Michigan Press, 2000

Copeland, Rita, *Rhetoric, Hermeneutics, and Translation in the Middle Ages: Academic Traditions and Vernacular Texts*, Cambridge and New York: Cambridge University Press, 1991

Copland, Robert, *Poems*, edited by Mary Carpenter Erler, Toronto: University of Toronto Press, 1993

Ellis, Roger (editor), *The Medieval Translator 2*, London: Queen Mary and Westfield College, 1991

Ellis, Roger and Ruth Evans (editors), *The Medieval Translator 4*, Exeter: University of Exeter Press, and Binghamton, New York: Medieval and Renaissance Texts and Studies, 1994

Green, Richard Firth, *Poets and Princepleasers: Literature and the English Court in the Late Middle Ages*, Toronto: University Press of Toronto, 1980

Greene, Thomas M., *Light in Troy: Imitation and Discovery in Renaissance Poetry*, New Haven, Connecticut: Yale University Press, 1982

Hieatt, A. Kent, "The Genesis of Shakespeare's Sonnets: Spenser's *Ruines of Rome: by Bellay*", *PMLA*, 98/5 (1983) pp. 800–14

Kuhn, Ursula, *English Literary Terms in Poetological Texts of the Sixteenth Century*, Salzburg: Universität Salzburg, 1974

La Perrière, Guillaume de, *Theater of Fine Devices*, translated by Thomas Combe and edited by Mary V. Silcox, Aldershot, Hampshire: Scolar Press, 1990

Lee, Sir Sidney, *The French Renaissance in England: An Account of the Literary Relations of England and France in the Sixteenth Century*, Oxford: Clarendon Press, and New York: Scribner, 1910; reprinted New York: Octagon, 1968

Prescott, Anne Lake, *French Poets and the English Renaissance: Studies in Fame and Transformation*, New Haven, Connecticut: Yale University Press, 1978

Ringler, William A. Jr, *Bibliography and Index of English Verse Printed 1476–1558*, London: Mansell, 1988

Satterthwaite, Alfred, *Spenser, Ronsard, and Du Bellay: A Renaissance Comparison*, Princeton, New Jersey: Princeton University Press, 1960

Scott, Janet G., *Les Sonnets élisabéthains: les sources et l'apport personnel*, Paris: Champion, 1929; reprinted Geneva: Slatkine, 1978

Silver, Isidore, *Ronsard and the Hellenic Renaissance in France*, vol. 2, parts 1–3, Geneva: Droz, 1981

Smith, Gregory G. (editor), *Elizabethan Critical Essays*, Oxford: Clarendon Press, 1904; reprinted 1967

Spearing, A.C., "Marie de France and Her English Adapters", *Studies in the Age of Chaucer*, 12 (1990) pp. 117–56

Spearing, A.C., "Prison, Writing, Absence: Representing the Subject in the English Poems of Charles d'Orléans", *Modern Language Quarterly*, 53/1 (1992) pp. 83–9

Upham, Alfred H., *French Influence in English Literature: From the Accession of Elizabeth to the Restoration*, New York: Columbia University Press, 1908

Workman, Samuel K., *Fifteenth Century Translation as an Influence on English Prose*, Princeton, New Jersey: Princeton University Press, 1940

1600 to the Present

In the very early 17th century, links between French and English cultures were still relatively close. Francis Bacon (1561–1626), although not translating, took the inspiration and title of his ten *Essays or Counsels, Civill and Morall* (1597–1625) from Montaigne (1533–92). The closeness of the two cultures is shown by the vigour and accuracy with which John Florio (c.1553–1625) reproduced Montaigne's *Les Essais* in 1603, and subsequently in 1613 and 1632. It is true that his lively language is more extravagant than that of Montaigne himself, and that his mannerisms show through, but he understood his author better than subsequent generations of scholars, who had to make conscious efforts to understand the text and were not always successful.

Florio knows, for instance, as subsequent scholars have not known, that in the longest of Montaigne's chapters the repudiation of those of Raymond Sebond's critics who put their trust in their own arguments was in fact prefaced by the statement that what Montaigne, no doubt incorporating already existing material, was considering, was the impotence of the human mind only when unaided by grace. Florio not only correctly translates Montaigne, but he understands his theology, and for the most part exactly conveys his down-to-earth conversational tone:

> Let us now but consider man alone without other help, armed but with his owne weapons, and unprovided of the grace and knowledge of God, which is all his honour, all his strength, and all the ground of his being. Let us see what hold-fast, or free-hold he hath in this gorgeous and goodly equipage.

Sir Thomas Urquhart (1611–60) was more distant from Rabelais (c.1494–c.1553) in date than Florio from Montaigne. Rabelais probably published his first three books in 1532, 1535, and 1546. Urquhart translated the first two in 1653, and the third in 1693, leaving the last two volumes to be translated by Peter Le Motteux in 1694. Despite the passing of more than a century, Urquhart is again vigorous and lively as well as accurate. He, too, understands his author better than most subsequent scholars. He makes, for instance, no effort to suggest that the famous letter of Gargantua to Pantagruel, inserted as chapter 8 into the second book, is any less heavily ironic than the rest of the narrative. Only later critics have suggested that Gargantua's letter is a straight-faced and serious insertion into a comic book. Urquhart knew that Rabelais was writing parody:

> Now it is that the mindes of men are qualified with all manner of discipline, and the old sciences revived, which for many ages were extinct: now it is, that the learned languages are of their pristine purity restored, viz Greek (without which a man may be ashamed to account himself a scholar), Hebrew, Arabick, Chaldæan and Latine. Printing likewise is now in use, so elegant, and so correct, that better cannot be imagined, although it was found out but in my time by divine inspiration, as by a diabolical suggestion on the other side was the invention of Ordnance.

After the end of the French religious wars in 1594, French culture took on a euphoric buoyancy, as literary texts explored a confidence in human nature that had already become established in cultivated English circles. There was little call for the French texts of the early 17th century to be translated into English, although *Le Cid* of 1637 was translated in the same year, when it was still clear – the French text was modified later – that Rodrigue would eventually marry Chimène, even though he had just killed her father in a duel. It was first played in England the year after its first performance and publication in France. D'Urfé's powerfully optimistic pastoral romance *L'Astrée* (1607–27), hugely popular in the rest of Europe, was not apparently translated into English, but the revolutionary optimism of François de Sales (1567–1622), who built his whole spirituality on the natural instinct to love God, did ensure the translating both of his *Introduction à la vie dévote* (1609, translated 1613) and of his *Traité de l'Amour de Dieu* (1616, translated 1630).

By the mid-17th century the tide of optimism in France had begun to turn, and the psychological focus of interest of such mid-century novelists as Madeleine de Scudéry (1607–1701) attracted the translation into English of her *Le Grand Cyrus* (1649–53, translated 1653–77) and *Clélie* (1654–60, translated 1655–61), whether in spite or because of their heroization of such military heroes as Condé and the portraits of the influential women who were active in refining the manners of the French court and those parts of French society whose refinement already allowed them to despise the court of Louis XIV. On the whole, however, French writers were plundered, imitated and discussed in England rather than translated into English. The critical canons of 17th-century French authors were seriously discussed, and Boileau (1636–1711) was translated, the *Lutrin* (1674) in 1682 and *L'Art poétique* (also 1674) in 1683, while Dryden (1631–1700), Wycherley (1641–1715), and Vanbrugh (1664–1726) borrowed from the relatively unsubtle plots of Molière (1622–73). Racine (1639–99) was translated, but mostly not until the early decades of the 18th century, although many works of his contemporaries, including *Les Passions de l'âme* of Descartes (1596–1650), the *Pensées* as well as the *Lettres provinciales* of Pascal (1623–62), *Les Caractères* of La Bruyère (1645–96), and the *Maximes et Sentences morales* of La Rochefoucauld (1613–80), had already been translated, as had the *Lettres* of Guez de Balzac (1594–1654) and Voiture (1598–1648), and parts of Scarron (1610–60).

With the revocation of the edict of Nantes in 1685, a close association developed between England and important groups of exiled French Huguenots. Bayle's relativist *Dictionnaire historique et critique* of 1696 appeared in English translation in 1710 and again in its augmented form in 10 volumes from 1734 to 1741. Saint-Évremond (1613–1703) lived in London from his exile in 1661 until his death, and was regarded as an arbiter on matters of literary taste. Early in the 18th century there was much translating in each direction, for example John Locke's refutation of Descartes inspired Voltaire (1694–1778), who himself visited England, publishing his *Lettres philosophiques* in both Paris (1734) and London (in English, 1733). Voltaire never understood the English constitution, but his use of English life, thought, religion and literature as weapons with which to batter the French establishment from the safety of London, Lorraine, Prussia and Switzerland ensured a wide English interest in his liberal and tolerant outlook on society.

Montesquieu (1689–1755), the most important political philosopher of the 18th century in any country, derived much of the inspiration for *De l'Esprit des lois* from England, which he had visited in 1729. The work appeared in French in 1748, and in English two years later. Jean Jacques Rousseau (1712–78) was different. Although he had tried to base the political theory contained in *Du contrat social* (1762) on Locke's English liberalism, he did not succeed, providing in what he himself regarded as an unsatisfactory book only a blueprint for tyranny. When he did visit England, he was already subject to fits of paranoia. He quarrelled violently with Hume, who in 1766 had found him a retreat in Derbyshire where he wrote the *Confessions* (1782 and 1789, translated 1783–91). *La Nouvelle Héloïse* (1761) had largely been inspired by Richardson and, like *Du contrat social,* was immediately translated into English.

The central figure of advanced French thinking, Diderot (1713–84), never visited England, but his plays, novels and philosophically important *Lettre sur les aveugles* (1749) were all immediately translated into English. The inspiration for the French *Encyclopédie* (1751–80), which Diderot edited, had come from Chambers's English work, and as a young man Diderot had scraped a living translating into French from English. It was during the late 18th century that the two cultures were closest to one another and that the translations flowed most freely in both directions, but the coverage was still patchy, and it is only when the major figures of the French Enlightenment had been made by cultural historians into established classics that translations of their works into English were more systematically undertaken.

The revolution of 1789 and the subsequent Napoleonic wars sundered the relationship, and not much interest was to be shown in England in the French Romantic authors, although the works of such earlier "pre-Romantic" authors from the anti-Napoleonic opposition as Constant (1767–1830) and Chateaubriand (1768–1848) were translated. Both these writers admired the British constitution, found shelter in England, and were eagerly and immediately translated into English. The pre-Napoleonic French works on history and its philosophy were notably to influence Edward Gibbon (1734–94), and the works of Rousseau and those with a literary affinity to him, such as Jacques-Henri Bernardin de Saint-Pierre (1737–1814), whose work was instantly translated into English, were clearly to influence Coleridge (1772–1834), Wordsworth (1770–1850), Burns (1759–96) and Shelley (1792–1822). After the Napoleonic wars and the introduction of serialized novels in the *feuilleton* section of the new cheap press in France, it was the great trio of suppliers of serials, the elder Dumas (1802–70), Eugène Sue (1804–75) and George Sand (1804–76), who were promptly translated into English in a development reflecting the increased demand for artistically down-market novels following on the general increase in literacy. Translations of Honoré de Balzac (1799–1850) came only later, and after delay.

Among the English authors heavily indebted to French models, and instrumental in creating the demand for translations around the middle of the 19th century, were Matthew Arnold (1822–88) and George Meredith (1828–1909). Jules Michelet (1798–1874), with his romantic periodization of French history, inaugurated a new form of historical writing, and his work, too, quickly appeared in England after its original French publication. Baudelaire's prose poems, though not the *Fleurs du mal,* were immediately translated, but there were delays before translations of Stendhal (1783–1842) appeared, and it was the same with most of Flaubert (1821–80). Of the Naturalist school, Zola (1840–1902) and Maupassant (1850–93) were both speedily translated, but the Goncourt brothers (Edmond, 1822–96; Jules, 1830–70) were not, and the non-Naturalist work of Huysmans (1848–1907), Bloy (1846–1917) and Péguy (1873–1914) had to wait for considerable periods before appearing in English. Gautier's *Mademoiselle de Maupin* of 1835 had been published quickly in English translation, but not Murger's 1848 *Scènes de la vie de Bohème.* In spite of increased literacy, most 19th-century French authors of fiction made much more money from stage adaptations of their novels than from their publication as fiction, whether serialized or not. It is noticeable that very few of the plays based on the novels, however successfully performed in Paris, were translated into English.

In spite of his influence, Gide (1869–1951), like his opponent and friend Claudel (1868–1955), was not immediately translated, and although many English writers derived inspiration from the late 19th-century Symbolist movement in France, cultural transmission had now become more ordinarily direct, based on visits to Paris and the reading of French originals. As access to France became easier, cultural inspiration and derivation becomes more complex, and the incidence of literary translation less predictable. By the time we reach World War I, it is not easy to define the content of any canon of French literature, and since then translation has increasingly been the sometimes haphazard consequence of commercial success in France or the product of educational demand in the anglophone world. Successful French novels and plays are now translated into English as a matter of course, so that an anglophone readership had not long to wait for translations of Proust (1871–1922), or even of Anouilh (1910–87), Giraudoux (1882–1944), Bernanos (1888–1948), Giono (1895–1970) and François Mauriac (1885–1970).

The most important development is probably the spread of translation outside imaginative works pretending to some literary interest or value. Sartre (1905–80), Beauvoir (1908–86), Michel Foucault (1926–84) and Barthes (1915–80) have all been translated for the content of their thought, as have important historians such as Fernand Braudel (1902–85) and Emmanuel Le Roy Ladurie (1929–), religious writers such as Teilhard de Chardin (1881–1955) and anthropologists such as Claude Lévi-Strauss (1908–). Hand in hand with this development has gone the process of filling in gaps in the catalogue of French classics from earlier periods. Two series in particular, Penguin Classics and the Oxford University Press's World Classics, have made certain that the acknowledged literary achievements in French and other literatures from past periods are for the most part readily and cheaply available in English. There are still important gaps. There is no English version of more than a handful of the letters of Madame de Sévigné (1626–96), and no version at all of Tallament des Réaux's *Historiettes* (completed c.1659).

Copyright problems have inhibited the profitability of publishing translations of fiction, apart from clear literary achievements, prize-winners and blockbusters, more than is the case for translations of non-fiction, where the demand is more easily predictable. Sometimes copyright ownership by an anglophone publisher can ensure the suppression of a translation that might compete with one that, although inferior, is newly commissioned. More often the difficulties derive from the need to purchase translation rights from owners of the copyright of the French text. Sometimes, as is currently the case with some works of Gide, the owners of translation rights cannot be identified with certainty. Occasionally, as with some works by Sade (1740–1814) and Diderot, translations have been made of a French text that the authors did not write for publication, and did not want others to read.

The immense success in English of the *Astérix* comic strip books (1959–; by René Goscinny and Albert Uderzo) makes clear that the market for good children's books is virtually inexhaustible, and that sometimes children's humour can cross cultures and work in other languages. The works of Saint-Exupéry (1900–44), especially *Le Petit Prince* (*The Little Prince*), remain popular in translation among anglophone young people, and the success in translation of such writers as Simone Weil (1909–43) point to what is perhaps an unexpected buoyancy in the market for religious works. Neither Saint-Exupéry's texts nor Weil's are without serious literary interest. The novels of Simenon (1903–89), also not without their own literary value, have achieved a wide following in their English versions, and there are periodic revivals on the English stage of works by Scribe (1791–1861), Labiche (1815–88) and Georges Feydeau (1862–1921).

Beckett (1906[–]89) preferred to translate his own plays, and translations of his works, including the novels, constitute a special case. English was his mother tongue, but it is noticeable that, when writing about those matters that touched his personal neuroses most deeply, he needed at first to use a tongue other than his own. Beckett wrote out some of the tensions in his own personality in his imaginative works in French, but they translate well into English, and *Fin de partie* (1957), although written in French, was actually played in English before its first staging in France; the ambiguous French title is translated *Endgame*, as in chess.

The demand for literary translation from French into English has varied greatly over time. There have been periods of history subsequent to 1600, as in the second half of the 18th century, during which French culture has been largely dependent on English, and has generated a corresponding need for translations out of English into French. There have similarly been periods, as in the early 17th and later 19th centuries, when the flow has been in the other direction – English culture was more dependent on French than the other way round, and translations from French originals into English were consequently in greater demand. The level of demand for translation between the languages, its predominant direction, and the dates, are important signposts in the cultural history of western Europe. In more recent times, things have altered. The pace of change is accelerating as the market in England for literary translations from French has become increasingly distorted by forces other than the literary value of the texts.

Alongside the market for translations into English of works of literary importance has grown a specifically educational demand which has more and more dominated the commercial market for literary translation. The US has always known enclaves of different European cultures, German, Italian and Jewish, while influxes of Spanish-speaking immigrants have lessened the dependence of US culture on French literary texts. In England and some other anglophone countries, such as Australia and New Zealand, French has been the traditional first foreign language taught in schools, generating a strong demand for translations, increasingly important as the study of Latin and Greek has decreased.

Education in the UK has always preserved the link between French language and French literature, with the consequent creation of what might be called an English canon of French literary texts required for educational purposes. As a result the demand has intensified for translations of short literary texts, especially short stories and plays, suitable for examination syllabuses at the secondary level, favouring relatively uncomplex authors such as Molière, Maupassant and Alphonse Daudet. It is at least arguable that the distortion imposed by educational demand has led to literary over- and undervaluations which in turn help to explain the pattern of demand for literary translations, particularly for modern texts.

The market has also been heavily affected by recent changes in national and European copyright law, generally tending to extend copyright for a longer period after publication, or after the author's death, and by changes in the value of translation rights as the cost of labour-intensive translating increases relative to the overall cost of books.

Demand for translation from French comes too from a whole spectrum of individual disciplines whose anglophone practitioners generate a market for English translations. While literary quality might count for very little, this demand for translations into English of non-literary specialist works, as for instance books on art history, does keep the publishers in contact with, and ensure the availability of, a good pool of translators, some of whom are full-time professionals, and from whom individuals can be selected for their sympathy with certain sorts of text, perhaps feminist, or non-metropolitan. Looking towards the future, it seems therefore likely that even strictly literary translation into English from French is likely to increase in volume, especially if the works short-listed for fiction prizes in France can be considered automatically to have some literary interest. Given the predominant position that English has already achieved in the worlds of finance and aviation, it seems likely that it will establish itself as the first foreign language to be learned in most non-anglophone countries, and that calls for translation into English can only increase.

Finally, it should be noted that, just as Puccini, Verdi, Bizet, Rossini and Mozart drew on libretti adapted from well-known major French classics, so Hugo's *Les Misérables*, first translated into English in the year of its appearance in France, 1862, has now been adapted into a highly popular musical with an English text. Pagnol (1895–1974) and Cocteau (1889–1963), are known for their plays and novels in English translation, but far better through the English versions of their screenplays. If the concept of "literary translation" is widened into "artistic adaptation", the future for the transference of French originals into anglophone art forms does indeed look bright.

ANTHONY LEVI

Further Reading

Harris, Geoffrey (editor), *On Translating French Literature and Film*, Amsterdam: Rodopi, 1996

Hervey, Sándor and Ian Higgins, *Thinking Translation: A Course in Translation Method: French to English*, London and New York: Routledge, 1992

Keenoy, Ray *et al.*, *The Babel Guide to French Fiction in English Translation*, London: Boulevard, 1996

Vinay, Jean-Paul and Jean Darbelnet, *Comparative Stylistics of French and English: A Methodology for Translation*, translated by Juan C. Sager and M.-J. Hamel, Amsterdam: Benjamins, 1995

French-Canadian Writers in English Translation

Translation was the first profession practised in Canada after the arrival of the Europeans, notes Jean Delisle, exercised by Amerindians whom Jacques Cartier kidnapped in 1534. Translation produced contact with North America literally – as recorded in Richard Hakluyt's *Principall Navigations* (vol. 3, 1600), compilations of "exploration" narratives, including Cartier's "Third Voyage of Discovery" (from the French text of 1541–42), which promoted settlement of the Americas – and figuratively, in that the "new world" came into being in a troping overwritten by the "old", whose perceptions framed the new world's inhabitants under the universalizing figure "Indian", as a resource for exploitation and an object for conversion. From this translation-as-violation during the colonial encounter, through to today's complex linguistic transactions in government and business mandated by official bilingualism, translation has always been an important feature in Canadian politics and culture.

The history of literary translation in Canada is more recent, dependent on growth of literary institutions in Quebec and English Canada following the establishment of the Canada Council in 1957. That three-quarters of the translations into English occurred between 1972 and 1985, twice as many as in all the years before, gives substance to Philip Stratford's contention that the history of literary translation in Canada begins in 1972 with the inauguration of the Canada Council translation grants programme. Such official sanction and financial stimulation give a special status to literary translation in Canada, both protecting it from the exclusive demands of the marketplace and engaging it in the service of nation-building through reciprocal translation that seeks to redress the imbalance of a colonial situation that necessitates the translation of a subordinate language (French) into a dominant language (English). When Canada is conceptualized in English, then translated into French, asymmetries shape translation differentially: the volume of translation into French is much greater in the fields of government documents, children's literature, and non-fictional prose, while translation into English is greater in the canonical literary fields of poetry, fiction, and drama. This unequal traffic between law and pleasure reinforces Quebec's self-perception as a translated (dominated) culture. Influences of a specifically literary nature are few, as in the dialogue between Quebec and English-Canadian feminist writing on language and power in the collaborative translation of Daphne Marlatt and Nicole Brossard (*Mauve*, 1985, and *Characters/Jeu de Lettres*, 1986) and in the bilingual journal *Tessera* (1982–).

Given the recentness of this high volume of translation activity, translation was not a frequent object of cross-cultural studies in Canada, such focus being limited to scattered speculations in translators' prefaces. This situation has radically changed in the wake of the 1969 Official Languages Act legislating bilingualism, which stimulated the development of translation programmes in universities, the establishment of translators' associations – professional (Literary Translators' Association of Canada / Association des traducteurs et traductrices littéraires du Canada [LTA/ATL], 1975) and scholarly (Canadian Association of Translation Studies / L'Association canadienne de traductologie, 1987) – and of specialized academic periodicals such as *Meta* and *TTR: Traduction, Terminologie, Rédaction*. An annual review of literary translations is published in "Letters in Canada", *University of Toronto Quarterly* (1977–). Special issues on translation have appeared in other periodicals: *Texte* 4. (1985), *Canadian Literature*, 117 (1988), *Tessera*, 6 (1989), *Meta*, 45/1 (2000). Translation achieved official recognition with the establishment in 1974 of two Canada Council, then the Governor General's awards for translation, parallel to those for poetry, fiction and drama. The John Glassco prize of the ATL/LTA (1982–) for a first translation into French or English offers encouragement to beginners. The practice of translating French-Canadian literature into English has required innovative responses to matters of cultural difference on the part of translators, as evident in recent essays and books which outline a theory of translation as conflict and displacement. Translation is understood as a double-voiced discourse or re-enunciation, a transformative practice of rewriting informed by contingencies of context that create hierarchies of value among languages. This focus on relations of power in the contact of languages shifts the emphasis but maintains the predominantly cultural cast of the long-established problematics of translation in Canada, wherein translation exposes the uneasy political relations between the two "founding" linguistic groups. Charles G.D. Roberts summarized this "cultural" turn in his 1890 preface to *Canadians of Old*: "We, of English speech, turn naturally to French-Canadian literature for knowledge of the French-Canadian people." A century later, at the height of the separation crisis, Philip Stratford noted in "French-Canadian Literature in Translation" (1969) that the publication of translations of Quebec literature had become "news from the front". "Translation is a bridge between people and we in Canada desperately need more and better bridges of this kind." Although separation is still on the political agenda, there is currently less interest in learning "what Quebec wants" and more debate about the status of unofficial languages under the Canadian Multiculturalism Act (1987). A decline in the annual number of translations from French halved the number of 1986 to 16 in 1995.

The long pre-history is punctuated by an uneven rhythm of translation. Accounts of contact published in Europe are the earliest examples, commencing with John Florio's 1580 translation of Cartier's first two voyages (from the Italian of Ramutius, since the French original was lost). While some reports from New France appeared in English simultaneously with their French publication – Marc Lescarbot's *Nova Franci; or The Description of that part of New France which is one Continent with Virginia* (1609) – many important texts had to wait till the late 19th century for translation and then by American scholars such as Reuben Gold Thwaites, who edited and translated from French, Latin and Italian the 73-volume *Jesuit Relations* (1896–1901). Translations of Champlain, the French founder of Quebec (1608), and others were published by the Canadian Champlain Society early in the 20th century. It was not until 1967, however, and then only in a selection of 68 letters privileging historical high points in the settlement of New France, that Mère Marie de l'Incarnation's *Lettres* from the 17th century were translated by Joyce Marshall as *Word from New France*.

With the British conquest of New France in 1760, the translation of government documents became a necessity and the arrival of a printing press enabled the development of literatures. The convergence favoured translation into French, the language of government translators. This activity was not matched in English, where the rare translation was most likely a sensationalist memoir of the 1837 Rebellion such as Félix Poutré's *Escaped from the Gallows* (1862). However, no fewer than three translations were prepared of Philippe Aubert de Gaspé's celebrated historical novel of the Conquest, *Les Anciens Canadiens* (1863), rendered as *The Canadians of Old* by Georgiana M. Pennée (1864), then under the same title by Charles G.D. Roberts (1890, reprinted as *Cameron of Lochiel* 1905), and as *Seigneur d'Haberville* in a 1929 revision of Pennée by Thomas G. Marquis. No other novel in Canada has been translated so many times. Roberts's version is the most famous, and established as model a practice of naturalization that omitted details, anglicized cultural references and emphasized action under the humanist imperative of self-knowledge through encounter with an other. Roberts was also the translator of Louis Fréchette's *Christmas in Canada* (1900). *Canadians of Old* (1995), Jane Brierley's revisionary translation, restores de Gaspé's annotations and reproduces his conversational style to foreground Québec specificity. W.H. Blake was also active, translating both Louis Hémon's *Maria Chapdelaine* (in 1921) and Adjutor Rivard's *Chez Nous: Our Old Quebec Home* (1924). Blake's invented words, awkward dialogue and archaicization of the *habitant*, reminding the reader of the strangeness of another culture, offer another model of translation, celebrating French-Canadian difference. From the turn of the 20th century to the 1960s, literary translations appeared at a rate of about one a year. Works translated fell into the category of historical fiction, like Laure Conan's *The Master Motive*, translated by an American (1909), or of novel-of-the-land, like Frère Marie-Victorin's *The Chopping Bee and Other Laurentian Stories*, translated by James Ferres (1925). Both advanced a view of Quebec as a traditional, hierarchical rural society of docile peasants. These models of naturalizing to the target language and of difference as subordination were current in the post-Confederation (i.e. post-1867) period, when anglophones were arrogating the designation "Canadian", relegating others to hyphenated status as "French-Canadian". An archaizing ideology guided the selection of texts for translation, including 17 collections of folklore and works by authors such as Félix-Antoine Savard (*Boss of the River*, translated by Alan Sullivan 1937), Germaine Guèvremont (*The Outlander*, translated by Eric Sutton 1950), even Ringuet (Philippe Pannton), whose elebrated 1938 critique of the rural idyll, *Thirty Acres*, was translated by Felix and Dorothy Walter (1940). Like 60 per cent of translated works prior to 1970, including most of the best-known titles, this latter work was published in the US. While publication abroad was the general pattern of Canadian authors in the period, this produced particular problems when translators lacked familiarity with the specificities of Quebec French used in local colour-realism. Particularly problematic was Hannah Josephson's 1947 translation of Gabrielle Roy's novel of Montreal in the Depression. Though *The Tin Flute* was awarded the Governor General's award for best novel in English and has become the most widely read Quebec novel in translation, with its many errors it failed to create a recognizable Montreal. Moreover, it worked from the first, not the revised edition. Unreliable too was Jean-Charles Harvey's 1934 *Les Demi-civilisés*, as bowdlerized by Lukin Barette in *Sackcloth for Banner* (1938), retranslated more felicitously by John Glassco as *Fear's Folly* (1982).

Although four times as many works were translated from French-Canadian texts between 1920 and 1960 as during the previous 350 years, this pace accelerated during the 1960s, when the number almost tripled, with an average rate of six titles per year. Political change in Quebec incited quick translation of contemporary texts on the Quiet Revolution, particularly novels about separatist terrorists such as Claude Jasmin's *Ethel and the Terrorist*, translated by David Walker (1965), Hubert Aquin's *Prochain épisode* (1965; French title retained in the translation, 1967) and Jacques Godbout's *Knife on the Table* (1968), both translated by Penny Williams (who also translated separatist Pierre Vallière's manifesto *Choose!*, 1972, while his important essay, *White Niggers of America*, appeared in Joan Pinkam's 1971 translation in the US); equally swiftly translated were novels about the existential angst and alienation of *Québécois*, by writers such as Robert Elie, André Langevin, Gérard Bessette, and Marie-Claire Blais. A particular problem for translators was *joual*, especially when the entire novel was written in this urban dialect: Jacques Renaud's *Le Cassé* was translated with two different strategies by Gérard Robitaille as *Flat, Broke and Beat* (1964) and by David Homel as *Broke City* (1984), and Marie-Claire Blais's *Un Joualonais, sa joualonie* was rendered as *St. Lawrence Blues* by Ralph Manheim (1974). These latter two translations adopted a similar tactic of transposing Quebec regional speech into American slang, a strategy that masks the specificity of challenges to the French literary establishment posed by *québécois* and contrasts with the awkward literal strategies of Robitaille, which also neglected to signal in translation the disruptive mix of English within the French. Translations were produced of other novels whose generic innovation was read allegorically as a sign of the profound social changes under way in Quebec, e.g. Yves Thériault's *Agaguk*, about the transformation of an Inuit man, translated by Miriam Chapin (1963) and Rejean Ducharme's *nouveau roman*, *The Swallower Swallowed* (1968), translated (abroad) by Barbara Bray.

An imperative to stop the break-up of the country through the mutual understanding generated by translation produced a flood of English versions of works of cultural and intellectual history, such as Philip Stratford's translations of essays by Jean LeMoyne and Claire Martin, as well as position pieces from both sides of the separation question, including the mutually translated *Dear Enemies: A Dialogue on French and English Canada* (1963) by Gwethelyn Graham and Solange Chaput-Rolland, and academic analyses and reference works that informed anglophones of the historical roots of the constitutional crisis. Political concerns also motivated translations of the emerging Quebec theatre, especially the plays of Gratien Gélinas, as in Mavor Moore's version of *Yesterday the Children Were Dancing* (1967).

Poetry, however, was the genre in which the most innovative translation activity occurred during this period. Primarily the work of anglophone Quebec poets who responded to the threat of separatism with an attempt to establish a dialogue with their francophone peers, translation was characterized in "The Translation of Poetry" (1977) by Jacques Brault as "effective communion" rather than "efficient communication" between two peoples, and by D.G. Jones as "an act of love". Trying to "bridge" the gap between two cultures in order to prevent a political split, translation imposed an interpretation of one culture upon another. The knowledge of the other culture was partial, the result of chance encounters, such as those informal ones among Montreal poets fostered by F.R. Scott in the 1950s and 1960s. The Quebec of their translations was struggling against the repressive hold of a stultifying seigneurial order. Pioneers in translating poetry, Jean Beaupré and Gael Turnbull produced a series of mimeographed pamphlets for Contact Press in the 1950s of Modernist poets in the Symbolist and Surrealist traditions – Saint-Denys-Garneau, Roland Giguère, Gilles Hénault, and Paul-Marie Lapointe. Poets themselves, these translators sought out the work of contemporaries with whom they had affinities. Indeed, John Glassco, one of Canada's major translators, considered his work "poetic translations rather than translations of poetry", as he described his *Poetry of French Canada in Translation* (1970), 200 poems translated by practising poets, with some 73 poems by 38 poets, translated by himself. Considered a milestone in Canadian translation, this anthology made available to an anglophone audience work in the most critically esteemed genre of Quebec writing, omitting, though, the formalist and politically radical texts of the 1960s. Glassco's acknowledged masterpieces are the *Journal* (1962) and the *Complete Poems* (1975) of Saint-Denys-Garneau. He also translated fiction by Monique Bosco, *Lot's Wife* (1975) and by Jean Yves Soucy, *Creatures of the Chase* (1979).

Hailed by Glassco as "Canada's first artistic translator of poetry", from whom he "pillaged" lines and phrases for his translation of Garneau, Frank Scott none the less held to an antithetical model of translation. Whereas Glassco felt that translation should be "faithful but not literal", no substitute, but an equivalent text manifesting the translator's personality in the interests of a "poetic truth", Scott was a "literalist" who aimed for one poem in two languages, not two poems. Although he translated only a few dozen poems by his contemporaries, Scott's influence was considerable because of his *Dialogue sur la traduction* (1970) with poet Anne Hébert about the process of revising his translation of her "Le Tombeau des rois". The first sustained Canadian theorizing of the act of translation, this exchange posited translation as interpretation rather than assimilation of an other, and demonstrated Scott's fidelity to the structure and language of the source text. Responding to Hébert's comments, he made changes to keep features of French vocabulary and syntax, reworked into new English poetic tensions that retain the poem's lyric power. While Scott's ethics of alterity set a standard for other translators – particularly D.G. Jones in his translation of Paul-Marie Lapointe's *The Terror of the Snows* (1976), where colloquial terms nevertheless produce high lyricism; Ray Ellenwood in his translation of Claude Gauvreau's *Entrails* (1982), where the poet's nonsense is transposed not translated; and Barbara Godard in her version of Nicole Brossard's *Lovhers* (1986), where fidelity to the syntax and sound play in French is accompanied by greater semantic freedom of invention – his particular foreignizing strategies of awkardness were most evident in Marc Plourde's translation of Gaston Miron's *The Agonized Life* (1979).

Anthologies by Fred Cogswell, *One Hundred Poems of Modern Quebec* (1970), *A Second Hundred Poems of Modern Quebec* (1971), and *The Poetry of Modern Quebec* (1976) made available a much wider selection of Quebec poetry. In these volumes, as in *The Complete Poems of Émile Nelligan* (1983), Cogswell sometimes sacrifices rhythm to rhyme and period diction. Translation activities were extended with the founding at the Université de Sherbrooke of *Ellipse* (1969–), whose issues focus on paired anglophone and francophone poets translated by a number of people, with occasional shifts in format as in no. 21 (which covered the 1977 conference Traduire notre poésie / The Translation of Poetry) or no. 50 (1994) (in which 25 translators rendered into English Anne Hébert's "Etrange capture" and 25 translators turned into French Gwendolyn MacEwen's "The Music"). Translation as interpretation has become a playground for comparative linguistics and post-structuralist disseminations. Although there have been a number of exciting monographs of poets over the years, such as D.G. Jones's Governor General's award-winning translation of Normand de Bellefeuille's *Categorics, One, Two, Three* (1992), the number of poetry books translated declined from a high of 10 in 1986 to zero in 1995.

In the decade following the establishment of the Canada Council grants, announced by Secretary of State Gérard Pelletier in 1971 in the wake of the October events, translation into English flourished, with a total of 220 literary titles published, which included fiction (83), poetry (20), drama (27), anthologies (17), literary criticism (11), early travel accounts (4), children's books (31), and folklore (8). Special consideration by the Canada Council given to editors who published translations made many small presses eager to participate. Payment by the Canada Council made freelance translating an occupational possibility. Although most translators were amateurs, academics, or writers translating for the pleasure of it, each translated a number of books, so that it became possible to recognize individual translating styles and textual preferences. The importance of the translator's signature was also addressed in legal terms in the struggle over copyright and contracts engaged by the ATL/LTA.

The story of translation since 1972 becomes one of presses and translators, in an increasingly diversified production within the established paradigm of cultural translation. In its French Writers of Canada series, Harvest House initiated a revisionist translation programme countering Quebec's agriculturist myth. While publishing contemporary fiction, it produced a number of translations of neglected earlier ironic fictions such as Conrad Dion's version of Albert Laberge's naturalist fiction of 1918, *Bitter Bread* (1977), Yves Brunelle's translation of Claude-Henri Grignon's *Un Homme et son péché* (1933) as *The Woman and the Miser* (1977) and Irène Currie's unfortunate rendering of the bowdlerized edition of Rodolphe Girard's 1904 *Marie Calumet* (1976). There were retranslations of some earlier works, including Richard Howard's version of Savard's *The Master of the River* (1976). David Carpenter's translation of Georges Bugnet's *The Forest* (1976) extended the field to francophone writers in Western Canada. Including Yves Brunelle's translation of Laure Conan's important psychological novel *Angeline de Montbrun* and Sheila Fischman's translation of Jules-Paul Tardivel's separatist utopia *For My Country* in its reprints of 19th century monuments (1975), the University of Toronto Press also filled in gaps. More than 100 novels were translated into English between 1972 and 1984. The work of the most important Quebec novelists was quickly made available in English: 10 new novels by Marie-Claire Blais appeared during this period, seven by Roch Carrier, six by Jacques Ferron, five by Anne Hébert, four each by Hubert Aquin and Victor-Lévy Beaulieu, and three each by Gilles Archambault, André Major, Jacques Poulin, Gabrielle Roy, Yves Thériault, and Pierre Turgeon. This outpouring of translations made possible the inclusion of books by Quebec authors in courses established to promote the institutionalization of Canadian literatures in the educational systems, the practice aided by anthologies of Quebec short stories, plays and literary criticism in translation. Publishers McClelland and Stewart favoured translations of established writers such as Gabrielle Roy or best selling authors such as Yves Beauchemin and Michel Tremblay; Talonbooks and Simon and Pierre specialized in drama; Coach House (a collective of poets inspired by the Pound tradition of translation as writing) specialized in experimental fiction/theory or "textes", a highlight being the collective translation of an anthology edited by Nicole Brossard, *Les stratégies du réel/The Story So Far 6* (1979); and Guernica (publishing trilingually in Italian too) and Exile focused on poetry.

Sheila Fischman's name is popularly synonymous with translation in Canada: her more than 60 translations have been twice awarded the Governor General's award and the Félix-Antoine Savard prize of Columbia University's Translation Centre. The "Letters in Canada" review of 1979 began with five prose works she translated that year by Roch Carrier, Jacques Poulin, Hubert Aquin, Naim Kattan and Marie-Claire Blais. From her beginning with Roch Carrier's 1968 *La Guerre, Yes Sir!* (1970) to her publication of Georges Sioui's *For an Amerindian Autohistory* (1995), her work has exhibited unusual versatility. Her range extends to the page-long sentences of Marie-Claire Blais (*Anna's World*, 1984), the Joycean exuberance of Victor-Lévy-Beaulieu (*Don Quixote in Nighttown*, 1978), the condensed poetic prose of Anne Hébert (*The First Garden*, 1990), the sensuous humour of Michel Tremblay (*The Fat Woman Next Door Is Pregnant*, 1981) and the complex poetic images of Roland Giguère (*Mirror and Letters to an Escapee*, 1976). Largely through her efforts, the work of a new generation of Quebec novelists – François Gravel, Jacques Savoie, Elise Turcotte, Lise Bissonnette, and Hélène Lebeau – is becoming known in English Canada. Her choice in 1970 not to translate Carrier's cursing signaled an attentiveness to cultural difference and preference for literalism. Her recent handling of English in the texts of Blais and Hébert indicates a greater concern for meaning or readability. This oscillation is symptomatic of contradictory ideologies about the translation of Québec difference, arbitrated by English-language editors who favour naturalizing strategies.

Betty Bednarski, concentrating on a single contemporary author, posits translation as encounter. Following three translations of Jacques Ferron's work, beginning with *Tales from an Uncertain Country* (1972), she published *Autour de Ferron: littérature, traduction, altérité* (1989). Conceptualizing translation in terms of Bakhtin's dialogical ethics of response-ability, she analyzes the problem of translating the English in Ferron's texts. Concerned less with the visibility of the words' original Englishness than with their creative Quebecizing in Ferron's phonetic transcription, she has not signaled the anglicisms in her text through italics or footnotes. This favours an exploration of meaning – the problematics of alterity – within Ferron's work. Conceptualizing language as multi-layered and translation as incomplete, she reformulates her position in relation to a posthumous text of Ferron where his gallicized English has a negative potential of tragic loss rather than the victory through re-creation of his earlier texts. Bednarski's ideology of language differs from that of Ray Ellenwood, another translator of Ferron, who in *The Penniless Redeemer* (translated 1984) both italicizes anglicisms and adds a phrase to signal the use of English in the French text and the political stakes of "speaking white" in the 1960s with Quebec's awareness of her colonized status. Ellenwood comes to Ferron through an interest in the textual experimentation of the *automatiste* movement (with which Ferron was associated): among Ellenwood's many translations is the group's manifesto, *Total Refusal/Refus Global* (1985), though his range extends to *Vanishing Spaces* (1980) by *métis* writer Guillaume Charette.

Differences frame approaches to Antonine Maillet, too, whose work presents the additional complication of Acadian French. Consciously avoiding Newfoundland English, translators' strategies have ranged from Douglas Mantz's phonetic transcription to create the shock and novelty of Acadian as literary language, to Barbara Godard (*The Tale of Don l'Orignal*, 1978) and Philip Stratford's creation of a synthetic language to stand for the writer's idiolect – "Mailletois" into "Stratfordese" with *Pélagie* (1982). Retaining the accent in this title to mark linguistic difference, and exercising his creative powers to produce rhyming sacrilegious songs in English, Stratford straddles foreignizing and naturalizing tendencies. In contrast, Ben Shek's translation of *Mariaagélas* (as *Maria, daughter of Gélas*, 1986) retains many Acadianisms, with an interpolated paraphrase on their first introduction in English, to insist on linguistic difference as textually and culturally significant.

In the last decade, feminism has supplanted cultural nationalism as a major motivator for translation within Canada. Translations of feminist writers exhibit more consensus in approaches because of Quebec feminism's "language-centred" writing, with implications outlined in Susanne de Lotbinière-Harwood's *Re-belle et infidèle/The Body Bilingual* (1991). Among the translators of Nicole Brossard, Barbara Godard in *These Our Mothers* (1983) and *Picture Theory* (1991), and Susanne de Lotbinière-Harwood in *Under Tongue* (1987) and *Mauve Desert* (1990), foreground the work of gender in a feminization of diction and retention of sound images as connectives to disrupt syntax. Language here is the writer's/translator's subject. So too Patricia Claxton's translations, *Turn of a Pang* (1976) and *French Kiss; or, A Pang's Progress* (1986), are highly inventive in their use of punning to foreground the materiality of language as meaning-making. Rather than emphasizing "mothertongue" as exploration/embrace in a feminist interpretation, Claxton highlights *Québécois* specificity, researching historical quotations, inserting details about Montreal history and geography, using typography to signal English in the French text, which narrates the voyage of two women through city streets to occupy the heart of anglophone territory in its west end. A prolific and varied translator, Claxton has, significantly, translated many works of history. She won the Governor General's award for her translation of Gabrielle Roy's *Enchantment and Sorrow: The Autobiography of Gabrielle Roy* (1987) and François Ricard's *Gabrielle Roy: A Life* (1999).

Surprisingly, a concern with racial difference in anglophone Canada has had little impact on translation, despite the ethnic diversity of Quebec. Almost alone are translations of Dany Laferrière's Creole, the ground over which *québécois* French lays its palimpsest, and that sends David Homel through the market and Spanish dictionaries to find precise terms for Caribbean food. Not the least of Homel's problems is how to translate *nègre*, which he treats contextually according to the political violence of the utterance. None the less, Homel rewrites *How to Make Love to a Negro* (1987) as an American novel, his colloquial, slangy translation taking considerable semantic liberties to match the frenetic rhythms of Laferrière's prose and situate it within the jazz beat of *American* Black writing. In *Dining with the Dictator* (1994) and *Why Must a Black Writer Write about Sex?* (1994, winner of the Governor General's award) this produces major contradictions, since the former novel (*Le Goût des jeunes filles*) is a rewriting under a different political regime, that of *tontons macoutes* not of Dreyfus, of Proust's remembrance of youthful desire, while the latter is a critique of US culture by a Black man from another America. Americanization camouflages the thrust of Laferrière's challenge to the salient literary institutions, narrowing identification to Blackness, from the more contradictory Caribbean-Québécois. Recent works by Asian immigrants writing in French as a second language are Ying Chen's *Ingratitude* translated by Carol Volk (1998) and Aki Shimazaki's *Tsubaki* translated by Fred Reed (2000).

Though critics claim that theatre is currently the most dynamic part of the Quebec literary institution, the volume of theatrical production has not been matched in translation which, with a few exceptions, is limited to John VanBurek and Bill Glassco's versions of Michel Tremblay and to Linda Gaboriau's more than 40 translations which, beginning with her involvement in the exchange programme of Montreal's Centre d'essai des auteurs dramatiques, have included some of Quebec's most prominent playwrights. Gaboriau's translation of Michel Marc Bouchard's *Lilies* was short-listed for the 1991 Governor General's award for translation and won the 1991 Dora Mavor Moore award for outstanding new play and the 1992 Chalmers award for an outstanding Canadian play. As these awards indicate, naturalization is the norm in theatrical translation, where the demands of immediate intelligibility by an audience constrain choices, privileging the values of the target culture. While not as excessively ethnocentric as Quebec theatre adaptations (analysed by Annie Brisset in *Sociocritique de la traduction*) – these translations retain Quebec topographical referents – they condense the wordiness and rhetorical flight of French theatrical discourse into the action-oriented English theatrical discourse. They also shift the register of swearing from the highly creative wordplay on the sacred in French into conventionalized sexual epithets in English, eliding cultural difference of taboos. Gaboriau's translations are more attentive to linguistic difference. Especially in her translations of feminist plays, in the extended monologues of the 1976 *La Nef des sorcières* (*Clash of Symbols*, 1979) and the sustained lyricism and metaphysical reflection of Jovette Marchessault's *The Magnificent Voyage of Emily Carr* (1992), Gaboriau has struggled against the demands for naturalism in anglophone theatre to stage the colour and rhythms of *québécois*.

The future of translation of French-Canadian literature is unclear. Changes in aesthetics, with an emphasis on globalization, as well as a deepening crisis in English language publishing in Canada following major cuts in state support to the arts after more than a decade of decreases and stagflation, leave many small publishers on the verge of bankruptcy. The branch plants of English and American publishers have rarely published translations. After a long silence, Anansi recommenced publishing with a translation of Acadian France Daigle's *Real Life* (1995), translated by Sally Ross and subsidized by the New Brunswick government. Translating the dynamic regional French-language literatures would be a new venture. Aside from translations of Antoine Maillet occasioned by her international eminence as winner of the Prix Goncourt (with *Pélagie-la-Charrette*, 1979), little interest has been shown in Acadian literature outside Fred Cogswell and Jo-Anne Elder's anthology *Unfinished Dreams: Contemporary Poetry of Acadie* (1990) and their translation of Herménégilde Chiasson's *Climates* (1999). No Franco-Ontarian texts have been translated. Gabrielle Roy, like Maillet, has been more easily naturalized within the English-Canadian literary system than Quebec writers, but this has not produced an increase in translations of Franco-Manitobans, Franco-

Albertans or Fransaskois from western Canada. Likewise, the many small anglophone presses focusing on the creative work of racial minority groups have not noticed the outpouring of Quebec "migrant" writing, with the exception of Homel's translations of Laferrière, only one among many Québécois-Haitian writers: the one, moreover, whose work engages the struggle of Black with White in New York and is accessible within an ideology of the Americanness of Quebec culture. The ultimate irony in this narrative of diminished expectations is that in the current period of increased theoretical reflection on the political specificities of translating from *Québécois*, most of the translations published during the last 25 years in small runs, quickly out of print, are now buried in the archives.

BARBARA GODARD

Further Reading

Bednarski, B., *Autour de Ferron: Littérature, traduction, altérité*, Toronto: GREFF, 1991
Brisset, Annie, *Sociocritique de la traduction: Théâtre et altérité au Québec*, Longueuil, Quebec: La Préambule, 1990
Delisle, Jean, *La Traduction au Canada, 1534–1984*, Ottawa: University of Ottawa Press, 1987
Godard, Barbara, preface to her translation of *Lovhers*, by Nicole Brossard, Montreal: Guernica, 1986
Godard, Barbara, "Theorizing Feminist Discourse/Translation", in *Translation, History and Culture*, edited by Susan Bassnett and André Lefevere, London and New York: Pinter, 1990
Godard, Barbara and Agnes Whitfield (editors), *Translation Studies in Canada: Discourses, Institutions, Practices, Texts*, Ottawa: University of Ottawa Press, 2001
Hébert, Anne and Frank Scott, *Dialogue sur la traduction: A propos du Tombeau des Rois*, Montreal: HMH, 1970
Homel, David and Sherry Simon (editors), *Mapping Literature: The Art and Politics of Translation*, Montreal: Véhicule, 1988
Jones, D.G., "Grounds for Translation" and "The Translation of Poetry", *Ellipse*, 21 (1977) pp. 58–91
La Bossière, Camille R. (editor), *Translation in Canadian Literature: Symposium 1982*, Ottawa: University of Ottawa Press, 1983
Lotbinière-Harwood, Susanne de, *Re-belle et infidèle: La Traduction comme pratique de ré-écriture au féminin / The Body Bilingual: Translation as a Re-Writing in the Feminine*, Montreal and Toronto: Revue-menage/Women's Press, 1991
Mantz, D., "Acadjen, Eh? On Translating Acadian Literature", *Canadian Drama*, 2/2 (1976) pp. 188–195
Mezei, Kathy, "The Scales of Translation: The English-Canadian Poet as Literal Translator", *Revue de l'Université d'Ottawa*, 54/2 (1984) pp. 63–84
Mezei, Kathy, "A Bridge of Sorts: The Translation of Quebec Literature into English", *Yearbook of English Studies*, 15 (1985) pp. 202–26
Mezei, Kathy, *Bibliography of Criticism on English and French Literary Translations in Canada, 1950–1986: Annotated*, Ottawa: University of Ottawa Press, 1988
Paratte, H-R., "Discovering Two Literatures: Some Remarks about Translations of the Two Major Literatures of New Brunswick" in *A Literary and Linguistic History of New Brunswick*, edited by Reavley Gair, Fredericton, New Brunswick: Fiddlehead Poetry Books/Goose Lane Editions, 1985
Simon, Sherry, *Le Trafic des langues: Traduction et culture dans la littérature québécoise*, Montreal: Boreal, 1994
Simon, Sherry (editor), *Culture in Transit: Translating the Literature of Quebec*, Montreal: Véhicule, 1995
Stratford, Philip, "French-Canadian Literature in Translation", *Meta*, 13/4 (1969) pp. 180–87
Stratford, Philip, *Bibliography of Canadian Books in Translation, French to English and English to French/Bibliographie de livres canadiens traduits*, Ottawa: HRCC, 1977

G

Gaelic: Irish

Literary Translation into English

Around the year 300 BC a tribe called the Gaels invaded Ireland. The language they brought with them was part of the Celtic branch of the Indo-European family of languages. Other members of the branch are Cornish, Breton and Welsh. The Celtic languages are divided into p-Celtic (Breton, Welsh, Cornish) and q-Celtic (Irish Gaelic, Scots Gaelic, Manx). The difference stems from different consonantal evolution in the two groups. In Irish Gaelic, for example, the word for "four" is *ceathair* (initial consonant sounded [k]) whereas in Welsh it is *pedwar* and in Breton *pevar*. The languages in the two groups are nowadays mutually incomprehensible. The variety of Celtic that the Gaels spoke spread later to Scotland and the Isle of Man. Modern Irish Gaelic, Manx and Scottish Gaelic, though they are now treated as separate languages, are still often commonly referred to as "Gaelic". Irish Gaelic is a highly inflected language with inflection for nouns, verbs and adjectives. There are morphological changes for the genitive, dative and vocative cases and the nouns have five different declensions. There are three declensions for adjectives. A basic difference between Irish Gaelic and English is word order: SVO (subject, verb, object) in English but VSO (verb, subject, object)in Irish Gaelic. Initial mutations such as lenition and eclipsis are used to express a number of grammatical relationships and the language has a palatal and velar sound system. Although there has been a substantial number of lexical borrowings in Irish Gaelic from English in the 20th century, the radically different structure and sound of the language mean that it cannot be understood by an English speaker without special language training.

For centuries translation activity in Ireland was concerned with rendering text into, not out of, Irish Gaelic. The first traces of translation in Irish Gaelic are to be found in the glosses of sacred and secular texts that were kept in the monasteries of Milan, Würzburg, St. Gall, Carlsruhe, Turin, Vienna, Berne, Leyden and Nancy. The translations were of Greek or Latin words and phrases, helping to explain them for the Irish teacher or student. Irish monastic presence on the European continent was extensive from the 6th century onwards and Irish monastic scholars made an important contribution to safeguarding Classical tradition in the period following the collapse of the Roman Empire. Ireland was not evangelized until the 5th century, so that religious conversion was not accompanied by Roman political and cultural domination as had happened in Gaulish France. The result was a preoccupation with and a pride in the vernacular language evidenced by the production of a grammar (*Auraicept na nÉces*) and a comparative dictionary (*Sanas Chormaic*), a linguistic self-reflexivity that was not always to be found in other European vernaculars.

There were two groups of translators in Irish Gaelic in the medieval period. The first group were translators attached to monasteries, who concentrated mainly, though not exclusively, on devotional translation. The second group were drawn from the *filid* or learned class in Gaelic society, who after a long period of study acquired an in-depth knowledge of Gaelic language and lore. A number of these *filid* specialized in the study of native law or medicine. These *filid*, men like Nicól Ó hÍceadha and Cormac Mac Duinntshléibhe in the 15th century, were largely responsible for the extensive translation of texts that were neither literary nor devotional. The Irish Gaelic translations of medico-philosophical texts like Johannes Anglicus's *Rosa Anglica* or Bernard of Gordon's *Lilium Medicinae* circulated widely in medieval Ireland. The medieval translations of religious, philosophical, medical and scientific texts were mainly for use as textbooks or for private study. Latin rather than English was the main source language for Irish Gaelic translators.

The Anglo-Norman invasion of Ireland in the 12th century did not adversely affect the standing of Gaelic in the long term, as many Norman families became increasingly hibernicized and English continued to decline in influence throughout the 14th and 15th centuries. An attempt to impose the English language in 1366 in the Statutes of Kilkenny proved a dismal failure.

The Tudors, however, were to prove much more thoroughgoing in their cultural subjection of the Gaelic Irish than their Norman predecessors. This was partly because of the concern with linguistic purity that characterized the body politic in England in the 16th century and partly because of the religious difference between the Protestant English and the Catholic Gaelic Irish. In 1537 the Act for the English order, habite and language imposed the use of the English language on the Gaelic-speaking Irish (which included Anglo-Norman families now known as the Old English). In the initial period, though, the Reformation insistence on the use of the vernacular in Church services would assist translation into Gaelic, and the very first printed book in Gaelic was a translation by Seon Carsuel of the *Book of Common Order* that was published in April 1567 in Edinburgh as *Foirm na nUrrnuidheadh*. The translation was in Classical Gaelic, which was the standard literary language for Ireland and Scotland at the time. Elizabeth I, who attempted to learn Gaelic, ordered characters to be made so that books could be printed in that language. In 1602, the New Testament appeared in a Gaelic translation, the translation of the *Book of Common Prayer* appearing in 1609. In 1640 the translation of the Old Testament into Irish Gaelic was completed, though it was not published until 1685. But in 1601, the rebellion led by the traditional Gaelic-Irish leaders Hugh O'Neill and Hugh O'Donnell was defeated by the English at the Battle of Kinsale. Their defeat, and the departure into exile of the remaining leaders of the Gaelic aristocracy after the English victory of 1607, meant the end of a system of patronage that had ensured for centuries the existence of a learned class schooled in the language and traditions of the Gaelic Irish. The other source of translators, the monasteries, were under severe pressure in Ireland as a result of Henry VIII's decision to dissolve the monasteries in the 16th century. Thus, translation into Irish Gaelic in the 17th century was increasingly the work of translators belonging to continental religious orders such as the Franciscans based in Irish colleges in Louvain, Rome, Prague and elsewhere. Yet if the 17th century saw the collapse of the political structures that sustained Irish Gaelic language and culture, it paradoxically represented a period of liberation for the language, the work of the translators at the Irish College of Saint Anthony in Louvain showing a decisive shift from bardic orthodoxy and the emergence of a simpler, more direct form of written Gaelic that would become Modern Irish.

The next period, lasting roughly until the last quarter of the 19th century, would witness a fundamental change in the direction of translation in Ireland. The consolidation of power of the new colonists meant that English became the language of trade, professional advancement and political power in Ireland. The support that was now available for translation came from Anglo-Irish patrons with an antiquarian interest in Irish language and history. Most translations would henceforth be from Irish Gaelic into English and only rarely vice-versa. The first English translation of an Irish Gaelic poem is to be found in the addenda to the *Calendar of State Papers Relating to Ireland (1601–1603)*. The translator was a clergyman, Meredith Hammer. But literary translation from Gaelic was a rare event in the 17th century, when most translation activity was in the area of interpreting and generally related to the business of warfare and diplomacy. The 18th century in this respect was markedly different, and two translation events gave impetus to the Gaelic–English translation movement. The first was the publication in 1723 of Dermot O'Connor's translation of Geoffrey Keating's hugely influential history of Ireland (*Foras Feasa ar Éirinn*). The second was the publication of James Macpherson's *Fragments of Ancient Poetry Collected in the Highlands of Scotland and translated from the Gaelic or Erse Language* in 1760. The subsequent revelation that the Ossianic translations were largely bogus did little to diminish the enthusiasm of native and foreign scholars and writers for Ireland's Gaelic literature. Charlotte Brooke's translations of Irish Gaelic poetry, which appeared in 1789 as *Reliques of Ancient Irish Poetry*, were one result of the Celtic fervour of the age. Brooke believed that translation was in essence conciliatory and that translations would promote cultural understanding and cordial union between Britain and Ireland.

This was a belief shared by other unionist translators, in the 19th century, such as Samuel Ferguson. Other translators in the century, such as J.J. Callanan, James Hardiman and Mathew Moore Graham, took a decidedly different view. They believed that translating from Irish Gaelic would be means of re-establishing a link with a glorious past and strengthening the claims of Irish people to a separate political existence. Hardiman edited an influential collection of English translations of Irish Gaelic poems that was published in 1831 under the title *Irish Minstrelsy; or, Bardic Remains of Ireland with English Poetical Translations*. The translations in Hardiman's collection were very much beholden to the literary conventions of the period and tended to be flaccid where the original Gaelic was taut and concise. Samuel Ferguson, an Ulster translator, published a series of articles in the *Dublin University Magazine* in 1834 that were extremely critical of the translations in Hardiman's collection. His own translations from Irish Gaelic, accompanying the last of the four articles in the *Dublin University Magazine*, were sober and more literal. They were subsequently published in book form in 1864 under the title *Lays of the Western Gael*. As translations they have fared much better than most of the translations in Hardiman's collection, and William Butler Yeats, in particular, acknowledged the debt of Irish poets in the English language to the pioneering work of Ferguson. Two other translators from the 19th century that figure prominently in the poetic pantheon are James Clarence Mangan and George Sigerson. Mangan, poet, polyglot and occasional mystic, produced a series of memorable translations in English for the nationalist newspaper *The Nation* in the 1840s. Mangan himself had little knowledge of Irish Gaelic and relied on cribs supplied to him by the eminent Celtic scholar Eugene O'Curry. Mangan's considerable ability as a poet in his own right resulted in highly effective and compelling translations. George Sigerson did know Irish Gaelic, and his two collections of English-language translations, *The Poets and Poetry of Munster* (1860) and *Bards of the Gael and Gall* (1897), won instant praise on their first appearance and continued to influence English-language poetry in Ireland well into the 20th century.

The single most important collections of translations in the 19th century were undoubtedly the two volumes produced by Douglas Hyde, a founding member of the Gaelic League and future president of Ireland. In 1890 *Beside the Fire* appeared, containing translations made by Hyde of Irish folk tales. He decided, however, not to use Standard British English in his translations but the English vernacular of the Irish countryside. Hyde adopted a similar approach to the English prose translations of Irish Gaelic poems in his 1893 publication *Abhráin Grádh Chúige Chonnacht / The Love Songs of Connacht*. The translations were crucial founding texts for the end-of-century Irish literary renaissance. For William Butler Yeats, Lady Gregory and John Millington Synge, Hyde's translations showed that there existed a variety of English that was both distinctly Irish and a suitable vehicle for literary expression, a fact borne out by the quality of the translations. Lady Gregory would later call this Hiberno-English "Kiltartan" and her own 1902 translation *Cuchulain of Muirthemne* did much to popularize the new literary vernacular. The vernacular would find its most spectacular expression in the plays of Synge, who was himself an active translator from Irish Gaelic, French and Italian.

It was also at the end of the 19th century that a movement emerged that explicitly championed the translation of works into rather than from Irish Gaelic. In the course of the 19th century the situation of Irish Gaelic had changed dramatically for the worse. At the beginning of the century the majority of Irish people had been either Gaelic-speaking or bilingual. On the eve of the Great Famine, there had been more Irish Gaelic speakers than at any other time in the country's history. The failure, through blight, of the potato crop from 1845 onwards had had catastrophic consequences for the native population and language. Over a million people died and another million emigrated as a result of the Famine, which mainly affected poor, Gaelic-speaking regions. In addition, the main destinations for Irish emigrants, the US, Britain and Australia (Canada was an exception) were predominantly anglophone, a circumstance offering a further incentive to change language. The free primary education system set up under the 1834 Education Act forbade the teaching of Irish Gaelic in Irish schools, and the Catholic Church, which had supported French in Quebec, was largely indifferent and in some cases actively hostile to the preservation of Irish Gaelic as the language of the people in Ireland. The main nationalist movements of the 19th century, with the exception of the Young Irelanders in the 1840s, were primarily concerned with political or military separation from Britain and considered cultural and linguistic questions to be of secondary importance. They conducted their political business almost exclusively through English. The combination of all these factors led the Irish to commit what was in effect linguistic suicide, so that by the end of the 19th century less than 10 per cent of those still living in Ireland were Gaelic-speaking. In 1877 the founders of The Society for the Preservation of the Irish Language declared one of their aims to be the production of a modern Irish literature, whether original or in translation. The establishment of Conradh na Gaeilge or The Gaelic League in 1893 gave further impetus to the movement for the restoration of the Irish language, and most of the leaders of the 1916 rebellion that led to the foundation of an independent Irish state (1922) were or had been active in the Gaelic League. Therefore it was not surprising that, partly inspired by Welsh and Flemish examples, the Irish Free State initiated a translation scheme in 1928 which was designed to encourage the translation of literature into Irish Gaelic. By 1937 a total of 214 works had been put into Irish Gaelic by translators, some of them very distinguished writers in modern Irish, working for the Publications Branch of the Irish Department of Education known as An Gúm. The works were an eclectic mixture, but the strong bias towards English as a source language condemned the scheme to failure. A situation of diglossia in Ireland meant that readers were unlikely to read an An Gúm translation, no matter how accomplished, when they could read the original in English. The lack of popular success of the literary translation scheme caused the Irish government to abandon it during the World War II years. An Gúm concentrated on the translation into Irish Gaelic of textbooks for schools and children's books, a function it fulfils to this day. The scheme was important, however, in demonstrating the generic possibilities of modern Irish Gaelic (i.e. the language could handle any genre in contemporary literature) and in revitalizing publishing in Irish. The post-war period saw an important literary renaissance in modern Irish Gaelic literature and the appearance of a number of independent publishers who provided writers and translators with an important outlet for their work. These publishers were assisted by Bord na Leabhar Gaeilge, the Irish Books Board, which gave and continues to give grant-aid for translations. More significantly, the source languages for Irish Gaelic literary translation were diversified, notably to include German, French, Italian and Spanish, so that translators were no longer imprisoned in the double bind of post-colonial linguistic dependency. The volume of literary translation into Irish Gaelic has in fact been consistently greater over the last decade than the volume of literary translation into English published in Ireland. The ultimate effect of literary translation into Irish Gaelic is both to extend the possibilities of the language and to liberate it from an aesthetic defensiveness that always threatens minority languages in difficult circumstances.

Translation into English from Irish Gaelic in post-independence Ireland has been dominated by scholars and poets. The scholars based in the universities and the Institute of Advanced Studies in Dublin published extensively annotated translations of texts from the Gaelic literary tradition under the auspices of the Irish Texts Society. Austin Clarke, Frank O'Connor and Brendan Kenneally, to name but a few translators, produced well-received anthologies of Irish Gaelic poetry translated into English. These anthologies, however, did not include the work of modern Irish Gaelic writers. In 1984, two translators, Douglas Sealy and Tomás Mac Síomóin, produced a collection of translations of poems by the distinguished Irish Gaelic poet, Máirtín Ó Díreáin. The collection was entitled *Tacar Dánta / Selected Poems*. In 1985, the Arts Council / An Chomhairle Ealáion agreed to promote bilingualism in its literary policies. Through direct publication assistance and the authors' royalty scheme, publishers were enabled to recoup costs incurred in the translation of Irish-language literary works into English. Raven Arts Press in 1986 published *An Tonn Gheal / The Bright Wave*, an anthology of English-language translations of contemporary Irish Gaelic poetry. The translators were English-language poets based in Ireland; it was the first time a project of this nature had been undertaken. The publication was highly successful and encouraged a number of similar ventures in subsequent years. The translation of Irish Gaelic prose fiction into English has, however, been scant, despite the considerable volume of novels and short stories that have been produced in Irish Gaelic, particularly in the post-World War II period. Of those translations that did appear, the most notable were Eoghan Ó Tuairisc's masterly translations of Máirtín Ó Cadhain's short stories published as *The Road to Brightcity* by Poolbeg Press in 1981. Translation has been and will continue to be an inescapable feature of the interaction between the two languages of Ireland, Irish Gaelic and English.

MICHAEL CRONIN

Further Reading

Cronin, Michael, *Translating Ireland: Translation, Languages, Cultures*, Cork: Cork University Press, 1996

Flower, Robin, *The Irish Tradition*, Oxford: Clarendon Press, 1947
Kiberd, Declan, *Synge and the Irish Language*, London: Macmillan, and Totowa, New Jersey: Rowman and Littlefield, 1979
Lloyd, David, *Nationalism and Minor Literature: James Clarence Mangan and the Emergence of Irish Cultural Nationalism*, Berkeley: University of California Press, 1987
Ó Cuív, Brian (editor), *Seven Centuries of Irish Learning 1000–1700*, Dublin: Stationery Office, 1961
Ó Siadhail, Mícheál, *Modern Irish: Grammatical Structure and Dialectical Variation*, Cambridge and New York: Cambridge University Press, 1989
Welch, Robert, *A History of Verse Translation from the Irish, 1789–1897*, Gerrards Cross, Buckinghamshire: Smythe, and Totowa, New Jersey: Barnes and Noble, 1988

Gaelic: Scots

Literary Translation into English

Scottish Gaelic belongs to the Goidelic branch of the Celtic language family, the other members of this branch being Irish Gaelic and Manx Gaelic. In Scottish Gaelic the normal word order is VSO (verb, subject, object). Adjectives, apart from a few exceptions, follow nouns rather than preceding them. Nouns are either masculine or feminine, and inflected cases survive (vocative, genitive, dative), watered down drastically in some dialects. Adjectives are similarly inflected. A once-complex verbal conjugation has been largely simplified, but strong traces survive in the so-called irregular verbs. Initial lenition and nasalization are strong characteristics of the language, often disconcerting to those unfamiliar with the system. The vocalic range of the language is unusually wide and complex: this is reflected in widespread use of rhyme and assonance, including internal rhyming, which appears even in free verse, and these features are at times hard to replicate in translation.

The ancestral form of the Irish, Scottish and Manx Gaelic languages made its first main home in Ireland, but began to infiltrate into Scotland probably as early as the 3rd century AD with a stronger thrust in the 5th and 6th centuries AD. Over the next six centuries or so it spread over much of Scotland, displacing Pictish and Brythonic (i.e. early Welsh-type) languages. In turn, Gaelic was gradually displaced by early forms of English, which came to acquire a Scots identity and be known first as Inglis and then as Scots. There was also a more temporary replacement by, or cohabitation with, Norse, especially in the Western Isles. The Norse period is roughly 800–1300 AD. By the 14th and 15th centuries a strong linguistic divide had been established between Gaelic and Scots, although Gaelic survived in areas such as Galloway and Ayrshire until at least the 17th century, and kept a peripheral existence in parts of Aberdeenshire into the 20th, and a stronger presence in Perthshire and other areas bordering on the Highlands, its heartland.

The public status of Gaelic was undermined in a number of ways, e.g. through royal influence and the influx of English and Norman nobles, through the setting up of burghs of commerce, and later through parliamentary and official intervention in the early 17th century. A strong Gaelic base was maintained by some Gaelic nobles such as the MacDonalds of the Isles, and this was fostered by literate and learned professionals (historians, lawmen, medics and poets). This particular Gaelic base was crumbling by the 17th century, and had largely gone by the 18th, but the 18th century saw a revival to some extent, based now more on literary and political ideas than on clan nobility and their power-bases.

In the pre-18th century history of Gaelic there was a long tradition of translation *into* Gaelic but not *from* Gaelic. The medics translated and adapted texts from classical and Arabic sources, the clerics translated lives of saints and ecclesiastical works, and there were adaptations from Continental religious verse, and influences from Lowland Scottish song and folklore. The *Iliad* was not translated into Gaelic until the early 19th century, and the *Odyssey* had to wait until the mid-20th century. There has been on-going translation of European poetry into Gaelic in the 20th century, including an anthology of some 3000 lines published in 1990 (*Bàrdachd na Roinn-Eòrpa an Gàidhlig*).

One of the great turning-points in translation came with James Macpherson's "Ossianic" exploits of the early 1760s. Initially motivated by some ambition to emphasize Gaelic identity after the disaster of the 1745 Rising, Macpherson published his *Fragments of Ancient Poetry* in 1760, *Fingal* in 1761–62, and *Temora* in 1763. He was originally influenced by the publication of a loose translation of a Gaelic heroic ballad. This was made by Jerome Stone and appeared in the *Scots Magazine* in 1756. Macpherson used a good range of Gaelic heroic ballads, only occasionally translating closely from them, but spuriously claiming to have translated, in *Fingal* and *Temora*, epic works dating from about the 3rd century AD. These ballads have origins going back to medieval times, sometimes to the 12th century, but Macpherson's works weave a romantic and wind-blown tapestry round some ancient names and exploits. Rousing great controversy in Britain regarding their authenticity, in Europe these works were embraced more positively, and were in turn translated into many languages.

Macpherson's work stimulated further translation and adaptation in Gaelic circles, as in the publications of the Rev. John Smith – *Gaelic Antiquities* (1780) and *Sean Dàna* [Ancient

Poems] (1787) – and other related bogus works were produced in Gaelic and English in this period. The flood of Ossianic publications, with so-called translations, continued in the 19th century.

In the second half of the 19th century the large influx of Gaelic-speaking settlers in Lowland Scotland, especially in the central belt, produced cultural contacts between Gaelic and Scots/English, and this is reflected in translations and adaptations of Gaelic song. This process was taken a stage further with the publication of a series of volumes called *Songs of the Hebrides*, edited by Marjory Kennedy Fraser and the Rev. Kenneth MacLeod (1909). Some of the song-texts have an element of fabrication, but many are genuine. There had been serious collection of song and various kinds of lore in the later 19th century, notably by Frances Tolmie (in the *Journal of the Folk-Song Society*, 1911) and Alexander Carmichael (1832–1912). Carmichael in his work *Carmina Gadelica* published a large collection of runes, hymns, incantations, charms, working songs, etc., and these had accompanying translations. Collections of folksong, published with English translations, were made and/or edited by John Lorne Campbell and Margaret Fay Shaw (e.g. *Folksongs and Folklore of South Uist*, 1955) and *Hebridean Folksongs*, 1969–81, and in Nova Scotia by Calum MacLeod in *Gaelic Songs in Nova Scotia*, 1964). In the late 19th century and the early 20th a number of books on Gaelic literature appeared, and these included many translations, mainly of song and poetry, but also on a more limited scale, of prose, especially folktales. These translations of verse were virtually all made in metrical formats, some of them quite convincing. Notable translators from this period were Peter Thomas Pattison, born in Islay in 1828 and author of a posthumous work *The Gaelic Bards* (1866), and Professor John Stuart Blackie. Two of the early books on Gaelic literature are Nigel MacNeill's *The Literature of the Highlanders* (1892) and Magnus Maclean's *The Literature of the Highlands* (1904). The most recent works in this field are Derick Thomson's *An Introduction to Gaelic Poetry* (1974, 1990), which includes a wide range of translations from all periods and in a variety of styles, and his *Gaelic Poetry in the Eighteenth Century* (1993). Ian Grimble's *The World of Rob Donn* (1979) has copious translations of the work of this 18th-century Sutherland poet.

It was not until the early 20th century that editions of Gaelic poetry with accompanying translations began to appear. One of the earliest of these was *The Gaelic Songs of Duncan Macintyre*, edited and translated by George Calder and published in 1912. Macintyre was one of the most famous 18th-century Gaelic poets, but Calder's verse translations make his work seem rather pedestrian, failing to capture the linguistic exuberance of his best work. The most remarkable Gaelic poet of the 18th century was Alexander MacDonald or Alasdair Mac Mhaighstir Alasdair, and his works were edited with translations by the Revs A. and A. MacDonald in 1924. Here too rhyming translation is used, rather more skilfully than by Calder, but not matching the originals.

The Scottish Gaelic Texts Society was founded in the mid-1930s, and a series of some 20 texts has appeared since then, usually with translations of poetry but not of prose. The poetry ranges from the classical/bardic works of medieval times, collected by the Dean of Lismore in the early 16th century to 19th century verse. Most of the editors chose to make prose translations, while some matched their translations line for line with the original Gaelic, more often than not failing to capture the rhythm and poetic timbre of the original poems.

There has been a good deal of published translation of traditional Gaelic folktales, notably J.F. Campbell's *Popular Tales of the West Highlands* (1860–62), and John G. MacKay's *More West Highland Tales* (1940, 1960), while a selection of such tales from Cape Breton is published in *Tales until Dawn*, told by Joe Neil MacNeil and edited by John Shaw (1987).

A very different scenario begins to emerge in the middle of the 20th century, with contemporary Gaelic poetry changing radically in style and content, and becoming part of the international world of poetry. There are early indications of this shift in the poetry of World War I poets, such as John Munro and Murdo Murray, and the movement is very clear by mid-century, in the work of Somhairle MacGill-Eain (Sorley Maclean), Deòrsa Caimbeul Hay (George Campbell Hay) and Ruaraidh MacThòmais (Derick Thomson). By the 1950s free verse is beginning to assert itself strongly, and that tendency grows in the following decades. A split appeared in the public for poetry, with the traditional type strongly favoured at first by the older public, while the non-traditional verse appealed to a younger and more cosmopolitan readership. A trickle of English translations began to appear in collections of the new poetry, and gradually fairly comprehensive translations became the norm, as the new collections were also accepted by non-Gaelic readers. The quality of the translations varies, but there is a strong tendency to reproduce the rhythms of the original poems, and often to suggest some at least of their metrical subtleties. Influential younger recruits to this movement in the 1950s were Dòmhnall MacAmhlaigh (Donald MacAulay) and Iain Mac a' Ghobbainn, the latter under his English name of Ian Crichton Smith establishing a separate reputation as a writer of English poetry and fiction. He made a good many translations of earlier Gaelic poetry, using rhyme and regular metres. Younger poets, such as Maoilios Caimbeul, Christopher Whyte, Meg Bateman and Anna Frater continued these traditions in the 1980s and 1990s. A number of Scottish literary periodicals, notably *Lines Review* and *Chapman*, regularly publish Gaelic verse with English translations.

There is a significant volume of translation of contemporary Gaelic verse into Welsh (translated by John Stoddart), Irish, Italian and French, and Derrick McClure published in 1996 an anthology of four Gaelic poets translated into Scots (*Scotland o Gael an Lawlander*), but naturally English is the main outlet for translation. It is sometimes felt that this tendency has become too automatic and ubiquitous, and could well be undermining a lasting Gaelic verse authenticity.

DERICK S. THOMSON

Further Reading

In addition to the books referred to above, the following editions and anthologies will help to define the range of modern translations in particular.

Clancy, Thomas Owen (editor), *The Triumph Tree: Scotland's Earliest Poetry, AD 550–1250*, Edinburgh: Canongate, 1998

Frater, Anna, *Fon t-Slige / Under the Shell*, Glasgow: Gairm, 1996

Hay, D.C., *O na Ceithir Airdean*, Edinburgh: Oliver and Boyd, 1952

Hay, D.C., *Mochtàr is Dùghall*, Glasgow: University of Glasgow, Department of Celtic, 1982
Mac a'Ghobhainn, Iain (Iain Crichton Smith), *Bìobaill is Sanasan-reice*, Glasgow: Gairm, 1965
MacAulay, Donald (editor), *Modern Scottish Gaelic Poems: A Bilingual Anthology*, Edinburgh: Southside, 1976, 1995
MacGill-Eain, Somhairle (Sorley Maclean), *Dàin do Eimhir*, Glasgow: William McLellan, 1943
MacGill-Eain, Somhairle (Sorley Maclean), *O Choille gu Bearradh / From Wood to Ridge*, Manchester: Carcanet, 1989; London: Vintage, 1991
MacThòmais, Ruaraidh (Derick Thomson), *An Dealbh Briste*, Edinburgh: Serif, 1951
MacThòmais, Ruaraidh (Derick Thomson), *Creachadh na Clàrsaich / Plundering the Harp*, Edinburgh: Macdonald, 1982
MacThòmais, Ruaraidh (Derick Thomson), *Meall Garbh / The Rugged Mountain*, Glasgow: Gairm, 1995
Whyte, Christopher, *An Aghaidh na Sìorraidheachd / In the Face of Eternity* (bilingual edition), Edinburgh: Polygon, 1991

Eduardo Galeano 1940–

Uruguayan novelist and political writer

Biography

Born in Montevideo, 3 September 1940, into a middle class Catholic family with European origins. His early work experience involved him with trade unionism and socialism. Galeano came into prominence at the end of the 1960s as a lucid and combative political journalist and cartoonist. During this time he was also the editor of a number of left-wing newspapers and magazines, such as *Marcha* and *Crisis*, with a pervasive influence on the political and cultural life of both his home city, Montevideo, and Buenos Aires, where he moved in 1973, at the beginning of his exile years. It is in this context that he published one of his most famous books, *Las venas abiertas de América Latina* (1971), translated into English as *The Open Veins of Latin America* (1973), a well-documented study that reviews the history, society and economy of the American continent from a hard-line Marxist perspective. After the 1976 military coup in Argentina, Galeano went to Spain, returning to Uruguay in 1984. In 1999 he was awarded the Lannan Prize for Cultural Freedom.

Translations

Guatemala: clave de Latinoamérica, 1967; as *Guatemala, país ocupado*, 1967
Belfrage, Cedric, *Guatemala: Occupied Country*, New York: Monthly Review Press, 1969

Las venas abiertas de América Latina, 1971
Belfrage, Cedric, *The Open Veins of Latin America: Five Centuries of the Pillage of a Continent*, New York: Monthly Review Press, 1973

Días y noches de amor y de guerra, 1978
Brister, Judith, *Days and Nights of Love and War*, New York: Monthly Review Press, and London: Pluto Press, 1983 (includes *In Defense of the Word*, translated by Bobbie S. Ortiz)

Memoria del fuego (3 vols: *Los nacimientos*; *Las caras y las máscaras*; *El siglo del viento*), 1982–86
Belfrage, Cedric, *Memory of Fire* (3 vols: *Genesis*, *Faces and Masks*, *Century of the Wind*), New York: Pantheon, and London: Quartet, 1985–88

El libro de los abrazos, 1989
Belfrage, Cedric with Mark Schafer, *The Book of Embraces*, New York: Norton, 1991

Las palabras andantes, 1993
Fried, Mark, *Walking Words*, New York: Norton, 1995

The Open Veins of Latin America (1971, translated 1973) is an eloquent and sustained attack on Western colonialism and capitalism, especially that of the United States: its argument springs from Galeano's conviction that Latin America has always, in the division of labour among nations, "specialized in losing", working as a menial and serving as a source and reserve of raw products for rich countries "which profit more from consuming them than Latin America does from producing them". The book was published at a time (the early 1970s) of broad social and political unrest, not only across the continent but also in Europe, and in the United States, where the Vietnam War and the Civil Rights Movement were in full swing. It is, in this sense, the product of a very specific era, but has also become a touchstone of left-wing political writing. If the language and rhetoric of Galeano, spiced with Marxist commonplaces, seem at times rather dated, his main points and arguments are still considered valid, and have exercised a great influence on political discussions about Latin America in the past 25 years. Cedric BELFRAGE, who has become in a way the official introducer of Galeano's work into English, brilliantly translated this book, as well as the 1967 chronicle *Guatemala: Occupied Country* (translated 1969), for the Monthly Review Press. This last work is another, less well-known piece of political journalism, dealing with the fight of left-wing guerrillas against the military dictatorship that ruled Guatemala during most of the second half of the 1960s. The book takes the form of both a chronicle and a work of denunciation: stemming from a number of magazine articles that were subsequently "reworked and much amplified", it recounts, among other things, Galeano's own involvement with the guerrillas, and includes interviews with key figures of the military regime. The Guatemalan experience was extremely important for the 27-year-old journalist, still in his formative years: characters and events from this period of his life were to appear repeatedly in his mature fiction, especially in *Days and Nights of Love and War* (*Días y noches de amor y de guerra*, 1978), imbuing his work with ideological zeal and inspiring a desire to retell the hidden and manipulated history of the South American subcontinent in his own words: "The aim of [*Guatemala, país ocupado*] is to break down as best it can the wall of deceptions and omissions which blocks the view of the public in many countries ... Latin America is the victim of a conspiracy of silence and lies". It should be stressed, perhaps, that Galeano has never ceased to be a political writer: rather, it is his literary strategies that have changed, the former journalist taking a secondary role in favour of the still *engagé* but more sophisticated creative author.

In this sense, Galeano's reputation as a writer rests mainly on a body of work that he initiated in 1978 with *Days and Nights of Love and War*, and that reached its high point with the trilogy *Memory of Fire* (*Memoria del fuego*, 1982–86). Although he had published the occasional novel in the 1960s, it is not until *Days and Nights of Love and War*, translated in 1983 by BRISTER, that the formal and thematic qualities of Galeano's literary prose are established. This volume in particular works as a transition between the early journalistic writings and the literary exuberance of *Memory of Fire*. It is built as a succession of fragments, sometimes no longer than half a page, belonging to different genres and written in different tones; these fragments may be parts of a larger fiction or of the writer's biography, they may take the form of a chronicle, a short story or an aphorism, and they may deal with either the public or the intimate world of the writer. The voice covers a wide range of tones, from the expressionism of "The Universe as Seen Through a Keyhole" to poetic lyricism or the plainly journalistic. Sometimes these fragments link up in a bigger unity, related mainly to the broad themes of "love" and "death" that give the book its title. This conception of the book as a rag-bag of fragments allows for a variety of responses and critical interpretations: if, on one level, the combination of different registers, dictions and textual sources seems particularly fit for a postmodernist approach, on another it evokes the strategies of folklore and of the traditional oral storyteller, who may combine songs, puppetry and the telling of tales for the amusement of the audience. In this sense, Galeano's apparent simplicity of diction is highly deceptive: each fragment is an achievement of high linguistic distillation and condensation, the product of endless correction and revision. Brevity is Galeano's watch word: the reader is left many times with the essential, the mere bones of the story.

For all these reasons, it seems clear that Galeano's language presents a number of difficulties for the translator, but Judith BRISTER does on the whole a good job. Her prose is flexible and able to accommodate the different styles and generic conventions of the original, and she translates with a clear and consistent diction, following Galeano's choice of simple vocabulary and a deceptively simple syntax, although at times she seems rather our of touch with some of the colloquialism in the dialogues, along the lines of the following example: "hay que joderse" rendered literally as "You have to screw yourself", where a contextually appropriate communicative equivalent is called for.

Memory of Fire is Galeano's most splendid achievement, securing him a place among the foremost Latin American writers of the last 50 years. It comprises three books, respectively entitled *Genesis*, *Faces and Masks*, and *Century of the Wind*, all translated into English by Cedric Belfrage (1985, 1987, 1988). It sets out to retell the hidden history of Latin America, to rescue, as the author himself declares, "the kidnapped memory of all America". His main concern is not only to recount the "between-the-lines" history of the continent, to retrieve the everyday history of the American Everyman, but also to give his version or subjective view of the main episodes that make up official history, which "boils down to a military parade of bigwigs in uniforms fresh from the dry-cleaners". Prefaced by a section that retells, much as Neruda does in *Canto general*, the mythic origin of the different physical elements of the continent, *Memory of Fire* covers the five centuries from 1492, year of the Discovery, to the political events taking place in the different Latin American countries in the 1970s and 1980s.

Galeano's fragmentary technique is here mastered and perfected. Each fragment is based on a solid documentary foundation, but onto this Galeano imposes his own style and manner. As in *Days and Nights of Love and War*, different fragments are written under different generic conventions, creating a mosaic of styles and literary strategies: traditional Indian stories and myths are mixed with Spanish popular songs and *conquistadores*' chronicles; statistical fact is mixed with legend; the memory of big official events is interspersed with that of individuals. Galeano is forthright in the preface to his trilogy about the subversive nature of this fragmentary combination. Although *Memory of Fire* is clearly a literary work, Galeano makes a point of quoting his bibliographical sources and referring the reader to them, allowing the book to be read as history or faction.

BELFRAGE's translation generally manages to convey the power and flexibility of the original. He is able to achieve a similar concentration and condensation of meaning, and a syntactic simplicity close to Galeano's, and also to move through different registers, thanks to an intelligent use of archaisms and modern idioms, when needed. Likewise, he transposes cultural references with a keen and alert eye, drawing from a rich lexical store. In short, the three volumes read extremely well, and are witness to a rigorous and consistent dedication on the part of the translator.

Galeano's fortunes in English, however, are not subject to his political stance. In recent volumes like *El libro de los abrazos* and *Las palabras andantes*, political preoccupations seem to have receded a little, and the fact that these works have been promptly translated (in the US) seems to suggest that Galeano's faithful English-speaking audience is capable of appreciating his work by literary as well as political criteria. *El libro de los abrazos* (1989) was translated by BELFRAGE & SCHAFER as *The Book of Embraces* (1991); *Las palabras andantes* (1993) appeared in 1995 as FRIED's *Walking Words*. This is a significant continuity, accommodating the fact that in his latest work Galeano has moved to a richer more contradictory view of the world, that encompasses political matters in a wider thematic and ideological framework. He has effected this by turning to a more truly imaginative mode of fiction and storytelling, latent rather than exposed in his earlier work.

JORDI DOCE

Further Reading

Lovell, W. George, "Memory of Fire", *Queens Quarterly*, 99/3 (1992) pp. 609–17

Federico García Lorca 1898–1936

Spanish poet and dramatist

Biography

Born in Fuente Vaqueros, near Granada, 5 June 1898. García Lorca's early years were spent on his father's farm; his mother was a teacher, and started teaching him the piano from a young age. The family moved to Granada and he went to school at the Jesuit Colegio del Sagrado Corazón de Jesús. He started studying law at the University of Granada in 1914, abandoning the subject later for courses in music, art and literature. He studied music at Granada Conservatory, becoming a successful performer and composer. He travelled around Spain, 1915–17, and published his first prose writing, *Impresiones y paisajes* (*Impressions and Landscapes*), after visiting Castile. He moved to Madrid in 1919, where he lived until 1929, meeting artists and writers, including Salvador Dalí and Luis Buñuel, and starting to write experimental poetry which was often read aloud in public before publication. He also began writing for the theatre, his first successful work being *Mariana Pineda*, produced in 1927, which had scenery by Dalí. In 1922 he worked with the composer Manuel de Falla on the folk music festival Fiesta de Canto Jondo in Granada, which inspired his interest in the art form and resulted in his *Primer romancero gitano* (*The Gypsy Ballads*), published in 1928. He was editor of the artistic review *El Gallo*, 1928. In the midst of an emotional crisis he travelled to Paris, London, New York and Havana, from 1929 to 1930. On his return to Spain he lived in Madrid and became further involved in writing for the theatre: he was the founder and director of an itinerant government-sponsored student theatre group, *La Barraca*, which was subsidized by the Ministry of National Education until 1935. He visited Buenos Aires in 1933. At the outbreak of the Spanish Civil War in July 1936 he fled from Madrid to Granada. He was arrested there, however, because of his loyalist sympathies, and shot by supporters of general Franco on the night of 18/19 August 1936.

García Lorca is considered one of the major poets and playwrights in the Spanish language. His work was highly successful during his lifetime, and its popularity was enhanced by the dramatic nature of his death; it has been consistently read and widely appreciated since. His major dramatic work is the trilogy of folk plays comprising *Bodas de sangre* (*Blood Wedding*), produced 1933, *Yerma*, produced 1934, and *La casa de Bernarda Alba* (*The House of Bernarda Alba*), completed 1936. Of his poetry, the best known works are his *Primer romancero gitano*; *Poema del canto jondo* (*Poem of the Deep Song*), written in 1922 and published in 1931; and *Poeta en Nueva York* (*Poet in New York*), which was written after his visit to the US in 1929–30 and reflects his reaction to modern urban life in New York.

Plays

Translations

Selections

Dewell, Michael and Carmen Zapata, *The Rural Trilogy*, New York: Bantam, 1987; revised edition, as *Three Plays*, with an introduction by Christopher Maurer, Harmondsworth: Penguin, 1992, New York: Farrar Straus, 1993 (contains *Yerma*, *The House of Bernarda Alba*, *Blood Wedding*)

Edmunds, John, *Federico García Lorca: Four Major Plays*, with an introduction by Nicholas Round, London and New York: Oxford University Press, 1997 (contains *Blood Wedding*, *Yerma*, *Doña Rosita the Spinster*, *The House of Bernarda Alba*)

Edwards, Gwynne and Peter Luke, *Three Plays*, London and New York: Methuen, 1987 (contains *Blood Wedding* and *Doña Rosita the Spinster*, translated by Edwards; *Yerma*, translated by Luke)

Edwards, Gwynne, *Plays: Two*, London: Methuen, 1990 (contains *The Shoemaker's Wonderful Wife*, *The Love of Don Perlimplín and Belisa in the Garden*, *The Puppet Play of Don Cristóbal*, *The Butterfly's Evil Spell*, *When Five Years Pass*)

Edwards, Gwynne and Henry Livings, *Plays: Three*, London: Methuen, 1994 (contains *Mariana Pineda* and *Play without a Title*, translated by Edwards; *The Public*, translated by Livings)

Graham-Luján, James and Richard L. O'Connell, *From Lorca's Theatre: Five Plays*, New York: Scribner, 1941 (contains *The Shoemaker's Prodigious Wife*, *The Love of Don Perlimplín*, *Yerma*, *Doña Rosita the Spinster*, *If Five Years Pass*)

Graham-Luján, James and Richard L. O'Connell, *Three Tragedies*, New York: New Directions, 1947; revised edition New Directions, 1955, London: Secker and Warburg, 1959 (*Blood Wedding*, *Yerma*, *Bernarda Alba*)

Graham-Luján, James and Richard L. O'Connell, *Five Plays: Comedies and Tragicomedies*, Norfolk, Connecticut: New Directions, 1963; London: Secker and Warburg, 1965 (contains *The Billy-Club Puppets*, *The Shoemaker's Prodigious Wife*, *The Love of Don Perlimplín and Belisa in the Garden*, *Doña Rosita*, *The Butterfly's Evil Spell*)

Graham-Luján, James and Richard L. O'Connell, *Collected Plays of Federico García Lorca*, with a prologue by García Lorca, London: Secker and Warbug, 1976 (includes the texts of the same translators' *Three Tragedies* and *Five Plays*)

Honig, Edwin, *Four Puppet Plays, Divan Poems, and Other Poems, Prose Poems, and Dramatic Pieces; Play without a Title*, Riverdale-on-Hudson, New York: Sheep Meadow Press, 1990 (includes *The Girl Who Waters the Basil*, *The Billy-Club Puppets*, *In the Frame of Don Cristóbal*, *Play without a Title*)

Logan, William Bryant and Angel Gil Orrios, *Once Five Years Pass and Other Dramatic Works*, New York: Station Hill Press, 1989 (contains *Once Five Years Pass*; *Buster Keaton's Outing*; *The Maiden, the Sailor and the Student*; *Chimera*)

London, John (translator and editor), *The Unknown Federico García Lorca: Dialogues, Dramatic Projects, Unfinished Plays and a Filmscript*, London: Atlas Press, 1996

Oliver, William I., "A Translation and Critique of Six Plays by Federico García Lorca" (MA thesis), Ithaca, New York: Cornell University, 1955

Single Plays

There is considerable confusion about how to date García Lorca's plays. In general, this list gives for each the date of completion of the manuscript, with the date of first performance according to the most reliable modern sources. Often there was a substantial gap between the two, and some of the plays were not performed until long after García Lorca's death.

El maleficio de la mariposa, finished 1919, produced 1920

Edwards, Gwynne, *The Butterfly's Evil Spell* in *Plays: Two*, translated by Edwards, 1990

Oliver, William I., *The Spell of the Butterfly* in "A Translation and Critique of Six Plays by Federico García Lorca", 1955

Los títeres de cachiporra: Tragicomedia de don Cristóbal y la seña Rosita, finished 1922, produced 1931(?)

Anonymous, *The Slapstick Puppets: A Tragicomedy of Don Cristobal and the Lady Rosita*, Ithaca, New York, 1967

Graham-Luján, James and Richard L. O'Connell, *The Billy-Club Puppets* in *Five Plays*, translated by Graham-Luján and O'Connell, 1963

Honig, Edwin, *The Billy-Club Puppets* in *Four Puppet Plays ...*, translated by Honig, 1990

Oliver, William I., *The Tragi-Comedy of Don Cristóbita and Doña Rosita* in *New World Writing: Eighth Mentor Selection*, New York: New American Library, 1955

La niña que riega el albahaca y el príncipe preguntón, finished and produced 1923

Honig, Edwin, *The Girl Who Waters the Basil and the Inquisitive Prince* in *Four Puppet Plays ...*, translated by Honig, 1990

London, John, *The Basil-Watering Girl and the Prying Prince* in *The Unknown Lorca*, edited and translated by London, 1996

Mariana Pineda, 1928, produced 1927 (finished 1925)

Blodgett, Anne K. and Marion L. Miller, *Mariana Pineda*, *Chicago Review*, 16/4 (1964) pp. 5–56

Edwards, Gwynne, *Mariana Pineda* in *Plays: Three*, translated by Edwards and Henry Livings, 1994

Graham-Luján, James, *Mariana Pineda*, *Tulane Drama Review*, 7 (1962) pp. 18–75

Havard, Robert G., *Mariana Pineda* (bilingual edition), Warminster, Wiltshire: Aris and Phillips, 1987

La zapatera prodigiosa, finished 1926, first version produced 1930, final version produced 1933

Anonymous, *The Shoemaker's Prodigious Wife*, Ithaca, New York, 1967

Edwards, Gwynne, *The Shoemaker's Wonderful Wife* in *Plays: Two*, translated by Edwards, 1990

Graham-Luján, James and Richard L. O'Connell, *The Shoemaker's Prodigious Wife* in *From Lorca's Theatre*, translated by Graham-Luján and O'Connell, 1941; revised version in *Five Plays*, 1963

Quimera; El paseo de Buster Keaton; La doncella, el marinero y el estudiante (short dialogues), 1928

Blodgett, Anne K., *Skits*, Ithaca, New York, 1969

Logan, William Bryant and Angel Gil Orrios, *Buster Keaton's Outing; The Maiden, the Sailor and the Student; Chimera* in *Once Five Years Pass ...*, translated by Logan and Orrios, 1989

London, John, *Chimera*, *Buster Keaton's Outing* and *The Maiden, the Sailor and the Student* in *The Unknown Lorca*, edited and translated by London, 1996

Oliver, William I., *Chimera; The Lass, the Sailor and the Student; Buster Keaton's Constitutional* in his "A Translation and Critique of Six Plays by Federico García Lorca", 1955

Sawyer-Lauçanno, Christopher, *Chimera*, *Buster Keaton's Stroll* and *The Maiden, the Mariner and the Student* in *Barbarous Nights: Legends and Plays from the "Little Theatre"*, translated by Sawyer-Lauçanno, San Francisco: City Lights, 1991

Amor de don Perlimplín con Belisa en su jardín, finished 1928, produced 1933

Blodgett, Anne K. and Marion L. Miller, *The Love of Don Perlimplín with Belisa in Her Garden*, Ithaca, New York, 1967

Edwards, Gwynne, *The Love of Don Perlimplín* and *Belisa in the Garden* in *Plays: Two*, translated by Edwards, 1990

Graham-Luján, James and Richard L. O'Connell, *The Love of Don Perlimplín* in *From Lorca's Theatre*, translated by Graham-Luján and O'Connell, 1941; revised version in *Five Plays*, 1963

Johnston, David, *The Love of Don Perlimplín for Belisa in the Garden*, with *Yerma*, London: Hodder and Stoughton, 1990

El público, finished 1930, produced 1978
Bauer, Carlos, *The Public*, with *Play without a Title*, New York: New Directions, 1983
Blodgett, Anne K. and Marion L. Miller, *The Audience*, Ithaca, New York, 1967
Livings, Henry, *The Public* in *Plays: Three*, translated by Gwynne Edwards and Livings, 1994

Así que pasen cinco años, finished 1931, produced 1954
Edwards, Gwynne, *When Five Years Pass* in *Plays: Two*, translated by Edwards, 1990
Graham-Luján, James and Richard L. O'Connell, *If Five Years Pass* in *From Lorca's Theatre*, translated by Graham-Luján and O'Connell, 1941
Logan, William Bryant and Angel Gil Orrios, *Once Five Years Pass (Legend of Time)* (bilingual edition) in *Once Five Years Pass ...*, translated by Logan and Orrios, 1989

Retablillo de don Cristóbal, finished 1931, produced 1934
Blodgett, Anne K. and Marion L. Miller, *Little Picture of Don Cristóbal*, Ithaca, New York, 1967
Edwards, Gwynne, *The Puppet Play of Don Cristóbal* in *Plays: Two*, translated by Edwards, 1990
Honig, Edwin, *In the Frame of Don Cristóbal: A Farce* in *Four Puppet Plays ...*, translated by Honig, 1990
Oliver, William I., *El retablillo de Don Cristóbal: A Farce for Puppets* in his "A Translation and Critique of Six Plays by Federico García Lorca", 1955

Bodas de sangre, written and produced 1933
Blodgett, Anne K. and Marion L. Miller, *Blood Wedding*, Ithaca, New York, 1969
Chambers, Alan, in "Federico García Lorca's *Blood Wedding*: Preparation for and Documentation of a Production" (MFA thesis), edited by Jennifer Sue Ross, Austin: University of Texas, 1988
Dewell, Michael and Carmen Zapata, *Blood Wedding* in *The Rural Trilogy*, translated by Dewell and Zapata, 1987; revised version in *Three Plays*, 1992
Edmunds, John, *Blood Wedding* in *Federico García Lorca: Four Major Plays*, translated by Edmunds, 1997
Edwards, Gwynne, *Blood Wedding* in *Three Plays*, translated by Edwards and Peter Luke, London: Methuen, 1987
Graham-Luján, James and Richard L. O'Connell, *Blood Wedding* in *Three Tragedies*, translated by Graham-Luján and O'Connell, 1947
Hughes, Langston, *Blood Wedding*, with *Yerma* (translated by W.S. Merwin), edited with an introduction by Melia Bensussen, New York: TCG Translations, 1994 (originally written by Hughes as *Fate at the Wedding*, 1938)
Johnston, David, *Blood Wedding*, London: Hodder and Stoughton, 1989
Kennelly, Brendan, *Blood Wedding*, Newcastle upon Tyne: Bloodaxe, 1996
Neiman, Gilbert, *Blood Wedding*, Norfolk, Connecticut: New Directions, 1939
Oliver, William I., *Blood Wedding* in "Spanish Theatre: A Study in Dramatic Discipline" (dissertation), Ithaca, New York: Cornell University, 1959
Weissberger, José A., *Bitter Oleander*, 1940 (first produced Lyceum Theatre, New York, 11 February 1935)

Yerma, finished and produced 1934
Dewell, Michael and Carmen Zapata, *Yerma* in *The Rural Trilogy*, translated by Dewell and Zapata, 1987; revised in *Three Plays*, 1992
Edmunds, John, *Yerma* in *Federico García Lorca: Four Major Plays*, translated by Edmunds, 1997
Graham-Luján, James and Richard L. O'Connell, *Yerma* in *From Lorca's Theatre ...*, translated by Graham-Luján and O'Connell, 1941; revised version in *Three Tragedies*, translated by Graham-Luján and O'Connell, revised edition, 1955
Johnston, David, *Yerma*, with *The Love of Don Perlimplín for Belisa in the Garden*, London: Hodder and Stoughton, 1990
Luke, Peter, *Yerma* in *Three Plays*, translated by Gwynne Edwards and Luke, 1987
Macpherson, Ian and Jacqueline Minett, *Yerma*(bilingual edition), Warminster, Wiltshire: Aris and Phillips, 1987
Merwin, W.S., *Yerma* [1966], with *Blood Wedding* (translated by Langston Hughes), edited with an introduction by Melia Bensussen, New York: TCG Translations, 1994

Doña Rosita, la soltera; o, El lenguaje de las flores, finished and produced 1935
Anonymous, *Doña Rosita, the Spinster*, Ithaca, New York, 1967
Dewell, Michael, and Carmen Zapata, *Doña Rosita the Spinster; or, The Language of Flowers*, New York: Theatre Communications Group, 1990
Edmunds, John, *Doña Rosita the Spinster* in *Federico García Lorca: Four Major Plays*, translated by Edmunds, 1997
Edwards, Gwynne, *Doña Rosita the Spinster* in *Three Plays*, translated by Edwards and Peter Luke, 1987
Graham-Luján, James and Richard L. O'Connell, *Doña Rosita, the Spinster* in *From Lorca's Theatre ...*, translated by Graham-Luján and O'Connell, 1941; revised version in *Five Plays*, translated by Graham-Luján and O'Connell, 1963

La casa de Bernarda Alba, finished 1936, produced 1945
Dewell, Michael and Carmen Zapata, *The House of Bernarda Alba* in *The Rural Trilogy*, translated by Dewell and Zapata, 1987; revised in *Three Plays*, 1992
Edmunds, John, *The House of Bernarda Alba* in *Federico García Lorca: Four Major Plays*, translated by Edmunds, 1997
Graham-Luján, James and Richard L. O'Connell, *The House of Bernarda Alba* in *Three Tragedies*, translated by Graham-Luján and O'Connell, 1947

Comedia sin título (unfinished in 1936)
Bauer, Carlos, *Play without a Title*, with *The Public*, New York: New Directions, 1983
Edwards, Gwynne, *Play without a Title* in *Plays: Three*, translated by Edwards and Henry Livings, 1994
Honig, Edwin, *Play without a Title* in *Four Puppet Plays...*, translated by Honig, 1990

Federico García Lorca's theatre is extraordinarily diverse. He is best known for his tragedies of doomed love set in rural Andalucía, but he also wrote farces, puppet plays, a verse fable for insects, a historical drama, and surrealist plays. The latter are so staggeringly innovative and so challenging to stage that

García Lorca referred to them as his "impossible theatre", but he personally regarded them as his best work. His uniqueness as a playwright lies in his iconoclastic fusing of genres and movements, combining poetry and drama, comedy, tragedy and symbolism, the avant-garde and the popular, the realistic and the fantastic. The tragedies portray generic figures designed to illustrate the mythic clash between passionate desire, the force that drives all life in García Lorca's cosmos, and the equally powerful mechanisms of societal repression. The characters' speech is simple, spare, and powerful, with a great sense of rhythm, and it is laced with startlingly beautiful images from the natural world. It is a challenge to translate because it is ordinary, not elevated diction, but stripped of banality and given haunting lyrical intensity. García Lorca frequently switches from prose to poetry and popular song in his plays to signal transitions beyond the everyday into a deeper, ritualistic dimension, in which he explores feelings about death, time, love, and destiny. Like the tragedies, the comedies, puppet shows, and experimental works also explore the terrain of the erotic and the non-rational, but here the humorous, playful elements are much stronger.

While García Lorca is one of the few Spanish authors whose name is widely known in the English-speaking world, productions of his plays in English were not well-received until recently. In part, this is due to resistance to non-realist drama, and in part also to the strategy chosen by GRAHAM-LUJÁN & O'CONNELL, who first translated many of the plays. Their different collections (1941, 1947, 1963, 1976) were reprinted numerous times, and were the only versions officially authorized for publication until the 1980s. Their approach is based on fidelity to García Lorca's precise words rather than a search for equivalence of sense or effect. The literalism of these translations heightens the potential for audience alienation, because the poetic quality of the commonplace is lost in laboured, unnatural syntax, and the humour and eroticism are blunted.

The first performance of a García Lorca play in English took place, with the playwright's collaboration, in New York in 1935, but reviewers attacked WEISSBERGER's translation, *Bitter Oleander* (*Bodas de sangre*), as too overwrought, and complained that García Lorca's flower imagery was ridiculous. British reviewers later in the century attested to an abiding sense that García Lorca's work was strange, awkward, and somehow culturally unassimilable to the anglophone stage. After the boom in new, more actable translations of García Lorca in the 1980s, subsequent performances in the United States and Britain, such as *Yerma* at the Edinburgh Festival in 1986 and *Doña Rosita* in London at the Almeida Theatre in 1997, have been more enthusiastically received.

Two strongly contrasting translations of *Blood Wedding* were written in the late 1930s. NEIMAN's version (1939) is so literal as to be almost a word-by-word gloss, studded with inaccuracies. HUGHES (1938), a distinguished author associated with the Harlem Renaissance, brings an African-American cadence to the work and a poet's feel for the rhythm of the dialogue. It is a great pity this translation was not published for more than half a century.

The new generation of García Lorca translators whose work began appearing in print in the 1980s complained that GRAHAM-LUJÁN & O'CONNELL's versions were lifeless transcriptions, and aimed instead, with varying degrees of success, for receptor-oriented, idiomatic translations. DEWELL & ZAPATA applied their acting and producing experience and solicited extensive input on the script from their own actors during rehearsals for their *Three Plays* (1992). They use rhyme effectively in the verse segments, but overall their tone is uneven; there are still moments where literalism intrudes. EDWARDS's numerous translations (1987, 1990, 1994) go further in the direction of colloquialism. She stresses rhythm and naturalness, and her rhyming sections capture García Lorca's lyricism without being trite; KENNELLY's version (1996) of *Blood Wedding* similarly foregrounds the poetic force of the play.

GRAHAM-LUJÁN & O'CONNELL's revised version of *Yerma* (1955) brings the work closer to natural speech than their first attempt; but Merwin's translation of *Yerma* (1966) improves considerably on that goal. He does not attempt to use rhyme. MACPHERSON & MINETT (1987) claim they want to preserve the work's Spanishness and avoid making the language too ordinary, but their bilingual version is highly colloquial. LUKE (1987) has a great feel for English dialogue, and his *Yerma* is full of pithy, popular speech and sayings. He boldly omits material deemed unnecessary and adds clarification, including swear words, elsewhere. JOHNSTON (1990) is the most adventurous and idiomatic of all *Yerma* translators. He adds images, based on material in the poems, and makes sexual innuendo explicit. He uses cultural transference, sometimes questionably.

OLIVER's *Tragi-Comedy of Don Cristóbita* (1955) brings out the fun of the original but is marred by some false cognates and other mistakes; these are remedied by HONIG's sensitive and creative translations (1990). BAUER's translation (1983) of the extremely difficult play *The Public* (*El público*) is a little stiff verbally, but accurate. LOGAN & ORRIOS (1989) are billed as ridding *Once Five Years Pass* of literalism, but don't quite live up to their intent compared to EDWARDS (1990), though their bilingual edition is thoroughly researched and documented. The register in BLODGETT & MILLER's *Mariana Pineda* (1964) is so high it sounds inordinately stuffy, and they have not reproduced the verse. HAVARD (1987) renders the assonantal rhyme of the original in iambic pentameter and blank verse, and privileges meter and poetic quality over word fidelity. His bilingual edition is heavily footnoted with useful background information.

CATHERINE JAGOE

Further Reading

Anderson, Andrew A., "Bibliografía lorquiana reciente", regular listing in *Boletín de la Fundación Federico García Lorca* (1987–)

Anderson, Andrew A., García Lorca entry in *Twentieth-Century Spanish Poets*, 1st series, edited by Michael L. Perna, Detroit: Gale, 1991 (Dictionary of Literary Biography, vol. 108)

Anderson, Reed, *Federico García Lorca*, London: Macmillan, and New York: Grove Press, 1984

Edwards, Gwynne, "Saura's *Bodas de sangre*: Play into Film" in *Hispanic Studies in Honour of Geoffrey Ribbans*, edited by Ann L. Mackenzie and Dorothy S. Severin, Liverpool: University of Liverpool Press, 1992

Gibson, Ian, *Federico García Lorca: A Life*, London: Faber, and New York: Pantheon, 1989

Higginbotham, Virginia, *The Comic Spirit of Federico García Lorca*, Austin: University of Texas Press, 1976

Honig, Edwin, *García Lorca*, Norfolk, Connecticut: New Directions, 1944, London: Editions Poetry London, 1945; revised edition, 1963
Johnston, David, "La gramática del traductor (un acercamiento al teatro de Lorca en inglés)", *Insula*, 4/510 (1989) pp. 26–27
Klein, Dennis A., *Blood Wedding, Yerma and The House of Bernarda Alba: García Lorca's Tragic Trilogy*, Boston: Twayne, 1991
Lima, Robert, *The Theatre of García Lorca*, New York: Las Américas, 1963
London, John, "Translating Lorca: The Case of *Bodas de Sangre*", *ACIS: Journal of the Association for Contemporary Iberian Studies*, 3/2 (1990) pp. 55–59
MacCurdy, Grant G., *Federico García Lorca: Life, Work, and Criticism*, Fredericton, New Brunswick: York Press, 1986
Maurer, Christopher, "Traduciendo a García Lorca", *Boletín de la Fundación Federico García Lorca*, 10 (1992) pp. 15–17

See also the introductions to Edwards & Luke's *Three Plays*; Edwards's *Plays: Two*; Dewell & Zapata, *Three Plays* (the revised edition); and Macpherson & Minett's *Yerma*

Poetry

Translations

Selections

Bly, Robert, in *Lorca and Jiménez*, translated by Bly, Boston: Beacon Press, 1973
Cohen, J.M. (editor), *The Penguin Book of Spanish Verse*, 3rd edition, Harmondsworth: Penguin, 1988
García Lorca, Francisco and Donald M. Adams (editors), *The Selected Poems*, New York: New Directions, 1961
Gili, J.L., *Lorca Selected and Translated* (bilingual edition, poems and prose translations), London: Penguin, 1961
Lloyd, A.L., *Lament for the Death of a Bullfighter, and Other Poems* (bilingual edition), London: Heinemann, 1937
Maurer, Christopher (editor), *Selected Poems: Federico García Lorca* (parallel texts), with an introduction by Maurer, translated by Maurer and 10 others, New York: Farrar Straus, 1995; Harmondsworth: Penguin, 1997
Maurer, Christopher (editor and translator), *A Season in Granada: Uncollected Poems and Prose*, London: Anvil Press, 1998 (contains 16 previously uncollected poems and 2 essays)
Skelton, Robin, *Songs and Ballads*, Montreal: Guernica, 1992
Spender, Stephen and J.L. Gili, *Selected Poems*, with an introduction by R. Martín Nadal, London: Dolphin, 1939
Williams, Merryn, *Selected Poems: Federico García Lorca* (bilingual edition), Newcastle upon Tyne: Bloodaxe, and Chester Springs, Pennsylvania: Dufour, 1992

Single Works

Libro de poemas, 1921

Brown, Catherine, *Book of Poems* (selection) in *Selected Poems: Federico García Lorca*, edited by Christopher Maurer, 1995

Canciones, 1927

Trueblood, Alan S., *Songs* (selection) in *Selected Poems: Federico García Lorca*, edited by Christopher Maurer, 1995

[Primer] romancero gitano, 1928

Campbell, Roy, 12 ballads in his *Lorca: An Appreciation of His Poetry*, New Haven, Connecticut: Yale University Press, 1952
Cobb, Carl W., *Lorca's Romancero gitano: A Ballad Translation and Critical Study*, Jackson: University Press of Mississippi, 1983
Havard, Robert G., *Gypsy Ballads* (parallel texts), Warminster, Wiltshire: Aris and Phillips, 1990
Hughes, Langston, *Gypsy Ballads*, Beloit, Wisconsin: Beloit College, 1951
Humphries, Rolfe, *The Gypsy Ballads of Federico García Lorca*, Bloomington: Indiana University Press, 1953
Kirkland, Will, *The Gypsy Ballads* (selection) in *Selected Poems: Federico García Lorca*, edited by Christopher Maurer, 1995
Williams, Merryn, selection in *Selected Poems: Federico García Lorca*, translated by Williams, 1992

Poema del cante jondo, 1931

Bauer, Carlos, *Poem of the Deep Song*, San Francisco: City Lights, 1988
Franzen, Cola, *Poem of the Deep Song* (selection) in *Selected Poems: Federico García Lorca*, edited by Christopher Maurer, 1995

Diván del Tamarit, 1940

Brown, Catherine, *The Tamarit Divan* (selection) in *Selected Poems: Federico García Lorca*, edited by Christopher Maurer, 1995

Poeta en Nueva York, 1940

Belitt, Ben, *Poet in New York* (bilingual edition), New York: Grove Press, 1955
Humphries, Rolfe, *The Poet in New York, and Other Poems of Federico García Lorca*, New York: Norton, 1940
Simon, Greg and Steven F. White, *Poet in New York* (bilingual edition), edited by Christopher Maurer, New York: Farrar Straus, 1988; Harmondsworth: Penguin, 1990; in *Selected Poems: Federico García Lorca*, edited by Maurer, 1995

Federico García Lorca's poetry is less well known in English translation than are his major plays. In Spain, though, he became popular as a poet before his main dramatic works won wide admiration. His first published volume of verse, the *Libro de poemas* (*Book of Poems*), appeared in 1921, but he had already been writing and reciting his verse and publishing poems in magazines. (In fact, much of his literary work was composed considerably earlier than it was printed.) The main volumes of poems – the *Libro de poemas*, already mentioned; *Canciones* (*Songs*)1927; the *Primer romancero gitano* (*Gypsy Ballads*), 1928; the poems based on Andalusian folk music, the *Poema del cante jondo* (*Poem of the Deep Song*), 1931; those of Arabic affiliation, the ghazals and qasidas of the *Diván del Tamarit* (*Divan of the Tamarit*), 1940; the fruits of witnessing urban alienation, *Poeta en Nueva York* (*Poet in New York*), 1940 – and outstanding single poems such as the *Llanto por Ignacio Sánchez Mejías* (*Lament for Ignacio Sánchez Mejías*), 1935, have all been translated, in whole or in part, some of them many times, on both sides of the Atlantic, as interest in Lorca's work, at first enhanced by the consternation following his violent premature death, progressively became international.

García Lorca's poetry draws on popular and classical Spanish literary traditions, and on the Arab and Gypsy heritage permeating the national culture, as well as on his own wide knowledge of the European canon and contemporary writers. It was therefore appreciated in Spain both by the people and by the highly educated; but even in Spanish it combines a vivid acuity of perception with a densely metaphorical, elliptic, dramatic, and allusive style to produce an often surreal and Surrealist strangeness. When to that is added the fact that violence of subject and a sustained lyrical and elegiac tone are not easily reconciled in English, the achievement of CAMPBELL (1952), the team of translators (BROWN, KIRKLAND, SIMON & WHITE, TRUEBLOOD, *et al.*) supporting Maurer (1995, 1998), and the tribute of other translating poets such as SPENDER (1939) and BLY (1973) are the more to be appreciated.

The difficulties and rewards of the task may be observed in English versions of the *Romancero gitano*, the volume that with the *Canciones* and the *Poema del cante jondo* brought Lorca popular fame.

Gypsy Ballads (*Romancero gitano*, 1928)

To read the *Romancero gitano* of Federico García Lorca is to encounter the world of the early 20th-century writer who reacts against the influences of preceding generations (the Castilian Generation of '98 in García Lorca's case) at the same time as he evokes the influences of Góngora, Cervantes, and 15th-century Flemish painting. To read García Lorca is to encounter the Andalusian's everyday usage of imagistic language, the mythology underlying the Andalusian culture, the reverence of the Andalusian culture for Christian iconography, the ambivalent attitude of the Andaluz toward the Gypsies, the censorious attitude of the Andaluz toward the homosexual. It is to observe García Lorca's struggle in a society that both rejects and embraces him and to watch him enter the magical world of his fellow outcasts, the Gypsies.

How to recreate the meaning, the sound quality, the historical underpinnings (which do not interfere with the poetry's strong sense of immediacy), the ever-present impact of the poet-dramatist, the mythology and symbolism of the Andalusian countryside – in English, a rhyme-poor language used by those distant from Andalusia's cultural resonance? Clearly, any study of the translations of García Lorca's *Romancero gitano* into English will evolve (devolve?) into a study of compromise and compensation. Translators who answer the siren call of these poems are to be praised, even for what might be seen as their failures, for the *Romancero gitano* offers every linguistic problem, every cultural dilemma, every contextual nightmare that can be found in the craft of translation.

In the opening poem of the work, "Romance de la luna, luna" ("Ballad of the Moon") the translator/reader need progress no further than the first four lines to meet the poem's challenges.

La luna vino a la fragua
con su polisón de nardos.
El niño la mira mira.
El niño la está mirando.

(Literally: The moon came to the smithy / With her
spikenard [or tuberose] bustle. / The boy looks, looks at
her / The boy is looking at her.)

The rhyme, the rhythm, the sonorous quality are established. The personification of the moon builds on a piece of regional folklore empowering the moon to carry away children whose gaze lingers upon it. Its "polisón de nardos" feminizes the moon and accentuates its magical character. The repetition in the final two lines of the passage creates an incantatory quality that will be carried through the poem. Additionally, this repetition enhances the child's vulnerable transfixion and provides an opportunity for the verb tenses to play, giving the poem an anchor in the past as well as enforcing its presence in the here-and-now.

The commentaries of Robert G. HAVARD (1990), noted for his scholarly approach to García Lorca and the *romances*, indicate his awareness of the complexity of García Lorca's motivation, influences, and intentions, and his translations demonstrate his effort to transfer into English all the strengths of the original. He maintains a scheme of assonance and slant rhyme in the English, providing such combinations as spikenard/hard, moon/two, up/shut. A look at lines 17–20 in Havard's translation of "Romance de la luna, luna" reveals some of the successes and failures of this version.

Huye luna, luna, luna,
que ya siento sus caballos,
Niño, déjame, no pises
mi blancor almidonando.

Run away, moon, run away, moon, moon,
for I can hear their hooves.
Boy, let me be. Don't tread upon
my whiteness starched so spruce.

While Havard's line 17 would appear to fail in its recreation of the succinct and incantatory power of the Spanish, it does, none the less, provide the original's repetition. The choice of "hear" for "siento" ("I feel" or "I sense") in the next line corresponds with the Andalusian accepted usage of that word for "oír", and "let me be" nicely captures the familiar "déjame". What is problematic is the rhyme-directed choice of "hooves" for "caballos" and "spruce" for "almidonando" ("starching"). By substituting "hooves" for horses, Havard creates an unfortunate suggestion that the hooves belong to the Gypsies, for he never mentions any horses to whom the hooves might belong. Also, the decision to use the adjective "spruce" is troublesome to the English reader who may have an association of spruce with the green color of the spruce tree, an association not found in the Spanish. In effect, Havard has imported a completely new image in a grammatically incorrect manner for the sake of a half-rhyme.

Repetition and rhyme again create a translation problem in the final two lines of the poem:

El aire la vela, vela.
El aire la está velando.

The breeze wraps her in a veil.
It wraps and wraps her does the breeze.

So reminiscent of lines 3 and 4 (quoted above), these few words provide a powerful ending to the poem through a combination of personification, repetition, assonance, unexpected use of verb tenses, and foreshadowing of the image of "el aire", a central and magical figure of the book's next poem, "Preciosa y el aire" ("Preciosa and the Wind") (as noted by Ramsden, 1988). Havard is able to transfer some of this complexity to the English, especially the personification of the "breeze" and repetition of "wraps", but these successes are again balanced with failures, a situation common to all translations. The choice of "breeze" for "aire" loses the connection to the following poem, "Preciosa y el aire". The words, "wraps her in a veil", seem at first to be an example of awkward, rhyme-directed translation, for an earlier line ends in "wails". On closer examination, however, Havard's choice may be felicitous, as it does provide more of the poetic connotations of the Spanish "velar" ("to veil", also "to protect") than do the more obvious choices of "watches" and "watching". But the verb tense shift is absent, and, even more damaging, the inversion of the final line provides a weak ending for the poem in English.

Merryn WILLIAMS's translation of the Gypsy poems (1992) offers a poetry that closely resembles the original in its line length and that successfully renders the mythical and imagistic qualities of the original. Williams occasionally uses a slant rhyme that is very comfortable for the contemporary reader: shameless/necklaces, come/stone, sings/gypsies. These are unexpected rhymes that delight, rather than forced rhymes that hammer the sound quality into the English reader's unwilling ear.

It is quite common in any translation for a certain word very aptly chosen for one reason to prove quite inappropriate for another. Williams's use of "shameless", shown above as an example of rhyme, is also an example of her failure to convey an important element of the original: a shift in the level of language. Line 7 of the Spanish contains the word, "lúbrica," which Ramsden (1988, p.137) underscores in *Romancero gitano* as a "learned word of complex meaning ... suggesting sinuous, almost snake-like fascination and seduction". Williams's "shameless" does provide a pleasing rhyme, but it does not convey the sense of the original word, or its tone, which may be the graver error, as any alteration in tone and level of language is essential to an understanding of the poet's methodology and intent. Havard offers a more successful choice, the rather rare "lubricous."

Where Williams is most successful is in her ability to convey García Lorca's lyricism in simple, straightforward language. She offers "white roses" to the reader rather than "spikenards" or "nards" (line 2). Williams's moon "moves her arm" while Havard has his "spin" (line 6). When the child of Williams's version warns the moon to flee from the Gypsies, he is concerned that they may "twist your heart to necklaces / and rings of white stone" (lines 11–12), suggesting directly the metallic composition of the moon. Perhaps Williams is able to maintain this direct language because she does not attempt Havard's ambitious rhyme scheme. The "blancor almidonando" that was transformed for the sake of rhyme by Havard to "my whiteness starched so spruce" is closer to the original in Williams's "my starchy whiteness" (line 20). The signature simplicity of García Lorca's hard images is transferred in Williams's translation.

Interestingly, both Havard and Williams begin the poem with "The moon came to the smithy". Will KIRKLAND (in MAURER, 1995) offers, instead, "The moon came into the forge". It may be a matter of personal taste whether one prefers forge to smithy, but the line is unquestionably enriched by the small word, "into", which immediately delivers the moon and the poem into the here-and-now. When this moon comes "into the forge" the child waiting there is suddenly seen as imperiled and vulnerable. Further, the little boy's reaction in the Kirkland version maintains García Lorca's repetition and shifting tenses.

The little boy stares at her, stares.
The boy is staring hard.

Kirkland's rhyme varies from the pure, nard/hard, to such pairings as run/come and high/eyes. With "lubricious" (line 7), he conveys the original's shift in tone. His word choices, while not as austere as Williams's, do transfer the sense of hard image of the Spanish. In all, Kirkland's successes outnumber his failures; by his choices, he is able to create an English poem that carries the resonance of the original. In the second stanza, Kirkland captures the original's strong sense of immediacy and tension.

El jinete se acercaba,
tocando el tambor del llano,
Dentro de la fragua el niño
tiene los ojos cerrados.

Por el olivar venían
bronce y sueño, los gitanos,
Las cabezas levantadas,
y los ojos entornados.

Closer comes the horseman,
drumming on the plain.
The boy is in the forge
his eyes are closed.
Through the olive grove
come the gypsies, dream and bronze,
their heads held high,
their hooded eyes.

It is unclear why Kirkland combines what were two distinct stanzas in the Spanish (the second beginning with "Por el olivar ..."). Perhaps his goal is to increase the suspense in the English by emphasizing the boy's helpless position between two advancing parties / potential threats.

Kirkland's response to the power of the poem's final two lines is, again, a mixture of triumph and defeat:

The air is viewing all, views all.
The air is at the viewing.

The repetition is there, as is the shift in verb tense from "is viewing" to "views". The choice of the cognate, "air", however, echoes Havard's failure to provide a connection to the wind in the *Romancero's* following poem, "Preciosa y el aire". (Of these three translators, only Merryn Williams has offered "wind" for "aire".) Additionally, Kirkland's move of "viewing" from verb to noun, while linguistically clever, diminishes the strength of García Lorca's use of "velar".

The works of these three translators demonstrate the validity of a suggestion commonly attributed to John Ciardi: that translation is the art of failure. Havard, Williams, and Kirkland all make evident that there is art in translation, and, just as clearly, they show its proclivity to failure. The poetry of Federico García Lorca provides numerous opportunities for both.

BEVERLY MITCHELL

Further Reading

Campbell, Roy, *Lorca: An Appreciation of His Poetry*, New Haven, Connecticut: Yale University Press, 1952

Cobb, Carl W., *Lorca's Romancero gitano: A Ballad Translation and Critical Study*, Jackson: University Press of Mississippi, 1983

Forman, Sandra and Allen Josephs, *Only Mystery: Federico García Lorca's Poetry in Word and Image*, Gainesville: University Press of Florida, 1992

Honig, Edwin, *García Lorca*, New York: New Directions, 1944, revised 1963; London: Jonathan Cape, 1968

Nims, John Frederick, analyses of 5 poems in *The Poem Itself*, edited by Stanley Burnshaw, New York: Holt Rinehart, 1960; Harmondsworth: Penguin, 1964

Ramsden, H., *Lorca's Romancero gitano: Eighteen Commentaries*, Manchester: Manchester University Press, 1988

Gabriel García Márquez 1928–

Colombian novelist, short-story writer and journalist

Biography

Born in Aracataca, in the northern, Caribbean, region of Colombia, 6 March 1928. Until the age of eight he was brought up by his maternal grandparents: his grandfather, colonel Nicolas Márquez, fought with the Liberals in the civil war known as the War of a Thousand Days. At the age of nine he was reunited with his parents and they settled in the town of Sucre. García Márquez studied law and journalism at the National University of Colombia, in Bogotá, and the University of Cartagena, from 1947 to 1949. He began writing fiction in 1946, and worked as a journalist for *El Espectador*, spending a period as a European correspondent in Rome and Paris. He lost his post when this newspaper was closed down by the Colombian dictator Rojas Pinilla. He then became a journalist for *El Heraldo*, Barranquilla, 1950–54. His first book of fiction, *La hojarasca* (*Leaf Storm*), was published in 1955. He married Mercedes Barcha in 1958, and had two sons. He developed close contacts with Cuba, and supported the Cuban Revolution: he was a founder of the Prensa Latina, the Cuban press agency, in Bogotá. He worked in the Prensa Latina office in Havana from 1959 and New York from 1961. During the 1960s he worked in Mexico City as a screenwriter, publicist and journalist. He subsequently lived in Venezuela, Cuba, the US, Spain and Mexico. He founded a film school near Havana. García Márquez returned to Colombia in 1982 at the invitation of the recently-installed president, Belisario Betancur, who offered him official positions, which he refused. From 1982 onwards, García Márquez lived principally in Mexico City, maintaining residences in Bogotá and Cartagena. García Márquez has won numerous awards, including the Colombian Association of Writers and Artists award, 1954; the Concurso Nacional de Cuento (Short Story) prize, 1955; the Italian Chianciano prize, 1968; the Foreign Book prize, France, 1970; the Rómulo Gallegos prize (Venezuela), 1972; the Neustadt International prize, 1972, and the Los Angeles *Times* prize, 1988. In 1982 García Márquez won the Nobel Prize for Literature.

García Márquez is among the most celebrated of modern Latin American writers and one of the major exponents of "magical realism". Much of his writing has been influenced by both his childhood experience of rural popular culture, through the stories he heard from his grandmother, and his unequivocal left-wing political views. His best-known novel is *Cien años de soledad* (*One Hundred Years of Solitude*), 1967, which features García Márquez's famous imaginary city of Macondo. Other well-known novels include *El coronel no tiene quien le escriba* (*No-One Writes to the Colonel*), 1957; *El otoño del patriarca* (*The Autumn of the Patriarch*), 1975, a novel about dictatorship in Latin America; the short novel *Crónica de una muerte anunciada* (*Chronicle of a Death Foretold*), 1981; *El amor en los tiempos del cólera* (*Love in the Time of Cholera*), 1985, a love story; and his novel about Simon Bolivar, *El general en su laberinto* (*The General in his Labyrinth*), 1989. Later work includes *Del amor y otros demonios* (*Of Love and other Demons*), 1994, a novel set in 18th-century Colombia.

Translations

Selections of Stories and Novellas

Bernstein, J.S., *No One Writes to the Colonel and Other Stories*, New York: Harper and Row, 1968; London: Jonathan Cape, 1971 (contains "No One Writes to the Colonel", "Big Mama's Funeral: Tuesday Siesta", "One of These Days", "There Are No Thieves in *This* Town", "Balthazar's Marvelous Afternoon", "Montiel's Widow", "One Day after Sunday", "Artificial Roses", "Big Mama's Funeral")

Rabassa, Gregory, *Leaf Storm and Other Stories*, New York: Harper and Row, 1972 (contains "Leaf Storm", "The Handsomest Drowned Man in the World", "A Very Old Man with Enormous Wings", "Blácaman the Good, Vendor of Miracles", "The Last Voyage of the Ghost Ship", "Monologue of Isabel Watching It Rain in Macondo", "Nabo")

Rabassa, Gregory, *Innocent Eréndira and Other Stories*, New York: Harper and Row, 1978; London: Jonathan Cape, 1979 (contains "The Incredible and Sad Tale of Innocent Eréndira and Her Heartless Grandmother", "The Sea of Lost Time", "Death Constant Beyond Love", "The Third Resignation", "The Other Side of Death", "Eva Is inside Her Cat", "Dialogue with the Mirror", "Bitterness for Three Sleepwalkers", "Eyes of a Blue Dog", "The Woman Who Came at Six O'Clock", "Someone Has Been Disarranging These Roses", "The Night of the Curlews")

Novels and Novellas

La hojarasca, 1955

Rabassa, Gregory, "Leaf Storm" in *Leaf Storm and Other Stories*, translated by Rabassa, 1972

El coronel no tiene quien le escriba, 1957

Bernstein, J.S., "No One Writes to the Colonel" in *No One Writes to the Colonel, and Other Stories*, translated by Bernstein, 1968

La mala hora, 1962

Rabassa, Gregory, *In Evil Hour*, New York: Harper and Row, 1979; London: Jonathan Cape, 1980

Cien años de soledad, 1967

Rabassa, Gregory, *One Hundred Years of Solitude*, New York: Harper and Row, and London: Jonathan Cape, 1970

El otoño del patriarca, 1975

Rabassa, Gregory, *The Autumn of the Patriarch*, New York: Harper and Row, 1976; London: Jonathan Cape, 1977

Crónica de una muerte anunciada, 1981

Rabassa, Gregory, *Chronicle of a Death Foretold*, New York: Knopf, and London: Jonathan Cape, 1982

El amor en los tiempos del cólera, 1985

Grossman, Edith, *Love in the Time of Cholera*, New York: Knopf, and London: Jonathan Cape, 1988

El general en su laberinto, 1989

Grossman, Edith, *The General in His Labyrinth*, New York: Knopf, 1990; London: Jonathan Cape, 1991

Del amor y otros demonios, 1994

Grossman, Edith, *Of Love and Other Demons*, New York: Knopf, 1995; Harmondsworth: Penguin, 1996

Short Stories

Los funerales de la Mamá Grande, 1962

Bernstein, J.S., "Big Mama's Funeral" in *No One Writes to the Colonel and Other Stories*, translated by Bernstein, 1968

Ojos de perro azul, 1972

Rabassa, Gregory, "Eyes of a Blue Dog" in *Innocent Eréndira and Other Stories*, translated by Rabassa, 1978

La increíble y triste historia de la cándida Eréndira y de su abuela desalmada, 1972

Rabassa, Gregory, "The Incredible and Sad Tale of Innocent Eréndira and Her Heartless Grandmother" in *Innocent Eréndira and Other Stories*, translated by Rabassa, 1978

Todos los cuentos, 1947–1972, 1975

Rabassa, Gregory and J.S. Bernstein, *Collected Stories*, New York: Harper and Row, 1984; revised edition, London: Jonathan Cape, 1984, Harmondsworth: Penguin, 1996 (contains 26 stories, in chronological order of their original publication in Spanish. Translated by Rabassa, from *Ojos de perro azul*: "The Third Resignation", "The Other Side of Death", "Eva Is inside Her Cat", "Bitterness for Three Sleepwalkers", "Dialogue with the Mirror", "Eyes of a Blue Dog", "The Woman Who Came at Six O'Clock", "Nabo", "Someone Has Been Disarranging These Roses", "The Night of the Curlews", "Monologue of Isabel Watching It Rain in Macondo". Translated by Bernstein, from *Los funerales de la Mamá Grande*: "Tuesday Siesta", "One of These Days", "There Are No Thieves in *This* Town", "Balthazar's Marvelous Afternoon", "Montiel's Widow", "One Day after Sunday", "Artificial Roses", "Big Mama's Funeral". Translated by Rabassa, from *La increíble y triste historia de la cándida Eréndira y de su abuela desalmada*: "A Very Old Man with Enormous Wings", "The Sea of Lost Time", "The Handsomest Drowned Man in the World", "Death Constant Beyond Love", "The Last Voyage of the Ghost Ship", "Blácaman the Good, Vendor of Miracles", "The Incredible and Sad Tale of Innocent Eréndira and Her Heartless Grandmother")

Doce cuentos peregrinos, 1992

Grossman, Edith, *Strange Pilgrims: 12 Stories*, New York: Knopf, and London: Jonathan Cape, 1993; as *Bon Voyage Mr President, and Other Stories*, Harmondsworth: Penguin, 1995

Other

Relato de un náufrago que estuvo diez días, 1970

Hogan, Randolph, *The Story of a Shipwrecked Sailor*, New York: Knopf, and London: Jonathan Cape, 1986

La aventura de Miguel Littín, clandestino en Chile, 1986

Zatz, Asa, *Clandestine in Chile: The Adventures of Miguel Littín*, New York: Holt, 1987; London: Granta, 1989

Has Gabriel García Márquez's prose become more mannered over the years, or have his translators begun to allow his idiosyncratic Spanish syntax to seep through their English prose? Or is it that only Gregory Rabassa is able to render the looping line of a meandering sentence so that it sounds naturally English as well as uniquely Marquesian? Or is it all three?

The relationship between García Márquez's books and his translations was tangled until his reputation was established by *Cien años de soledad* (1967, translated into English 1970). The first works translated into English were the novella *No One Writes to the Colonel* (1957, translated 1968) and the stories of *Big Mama's Funeral* (1962, translated 1968), mature writings that immediately preceded *Cien años* and introduced some of its characters, settings, and situations. After the phenomenal success of *One Hundred Years of Solitude*, a selection of earlier works ("Leafstorm", "Monologue of Isabel", "Nabo") was combined in RABASSA, 1972, with four post-*Solitude* stories (first collected in Spanish in *Eréndira*, 1972: "The Handsomest Drowned Man in the World", "A Very Old Man with Enormous Wings", "The Last Voyage of the Ghost Ship",

"Blácaman the Good, Vendor of Miracles"). Finally the English translation, *Innocent Eréndira* (RABASSA, 1978), included two of the seven stories published in the Spanish *Eréndira* collection ("Sea of Lost Time", "Death Constant Beyond Love") and nine stories of juvenilia from *Eyes of a Blue Dog*. *Collected Stories* (RABASSA & BERNSTEIN, 1984), omitting two novellas (*Leafstorm* and *No One Writes to the Colonel*), arranged the stories by original volume of publication. The English reader now has the writings in chronological order; the order in which García Márquez was presented to English readers was his best work first, then sweepings combined with new mature work, and then the career in orderly progression ever since.

Suggesting that linguistic variety is a mixed curse, García Márquez once remarked that *One Hundred Years of Solitude* reads better in English than in Spanish. Certainly the incommensurability of languages brings out different strengths and emphases. The title of the novella so warmly praised by Irving Howe for its stoical firmness and understated, heroic resolve, *No One Writes to the Colonel*, communicates an inverse message in Spanish. In J.S. BERNSTEIN's English, the Colonel is a firm object who absorbs the brunt of faceless, bureaucratic inaction, yet still stands firm at the end of the sentence, a hero before a firing squad, unshot. In Spanish, internal rhymes tease and mock a hapless, passive colonel who is presented as a defective, loss-ridden victim: *El coronel no tiene quien le escriba* / the colonel has no one who writes to him. Sardonic, faintly supercilious, the lilting rhythms taunt an inactive, bereft subject. In both stories / languages, mockery and opacity, heroism and irony appear, but the reader enters each with different expectations and will leave with different experiences.

The great achievement of Gregory RABASSA's translations is in large part rhythmic, though his diction is often so inspired as to obscure his mastery of omitted "ands", shifted "theres", and phrases turned to clauses. Reproducing Bernstein's heroicizing firmness, Rabassa gave us "Leafstorm" rather than an equally neologistic, more accurate, but considerably less grand "Leafscraping". He works against the occasional bottom-heaviness of the Spanish sentences and often invents brilliantly. The first sentence of *One Hundred Years of Solitude* is a case in point. "Frente al pelotón de fusilamiento" becomes a clause, "as he faced the firing squad", that (like Bernstein's title mentioned above) balances more squarely. (In the next sentence, "diáfanas" becomes the more sober "clear".) To end the sentence, Rabassa "finds" a word that exceeds the original. The colonel's father originally took him "a conocer el hielo", to meet, know, encounter ice. In Rabassa he "discovers" ice. English alliteration replaces Spanish assonance, and the new word intensifies the sense.

Sometimes incommensurability presents insurmountable problems. Correcting Rabassa's translation of *One Hundred Years of Solitude*, Gene Dilmore (1984) missed perhaps the most important error possible in a book about translating one manuscript into another. The ghost of Melquíades appears to Aureliano Segundo, studying the manuscripts, and tells him, in Rabassa's translation, that "No one must know their meaning until he has reached one hundred years of age". In this sentence, "no one" is the reader, and the reader must be one hundred years old. In Spanish, it is the manuscripts that must be one hundred years old. (This sentence has produced a surprising number of critics who proudly "do their own translations" and then, unzipped, comment on the hundred-year-old reader.) Melquíades says, "Nadie debe conocer su sentido mientras no haya*n* cumplido cien años"; literally, "No one must know their meaning until they have reached one hundred years of age". The problem derives from a conflict between idiomatic English and English rules. The English reader understands "they" as referring, incorrectly but idiomatically, to "no one", for English is inherently ambiguous in the number it assigns to "no one". Only by making the pronoun singular can the sentence be disambiguated, but that disambiguates it in the wrong direction and introduces a translation error at the heart of the issue of translating.

Unlike Rabassa, BERNSTEIN and GROSSMAN often communicate the sound of another language in their translations. In Bernstein's "Tuesday Siesta", for example, the Spanish syntax is audible in the imbalanced "They were both in severe and poor mourning clothes". Edith Grossman, who replaced Rabassa as García Márquez's principal translator with *Love in the Time of Cholera* (1985, translated 1988), similarly produces a ghostly effect, as if the English sentences were being shadowed by an obscure figure in archaic dress. The oddity is that the Spanish, simpler and more direct, lacks the accent Grossman introduces. Florentino Ariza's mother was terrified because his condition "did not resemble the turmoil of love so much as the devastation of cholera" ("no se parecía a los desórdenes del amor sino a los estragos del cólera"), and Dr. Juvenal Urbino never accepted the public positions that were offered to him "with frequency and without conditions . . . ." ("a menudo y sin condiciones"). Such locutions have a charm of their own, but they are quite unlike the magisterial equivalents to the Spanish novels that Rabassa offers up in his masterworks, *One Hundred Years of Solitude*, *The Autumn of the Patriarch*, and "The Last Voyage of the Ghost Ship".

REGINA JANES

Further Reading

Dilmore, Gene, "*One Hundred Years of Solitude*: Some Translation Corrections", *Journal of Modern Literature*, 11 (1984) pp. 311–14

Gonzalez, Anibal, "Translation and Genealogy: *One Hundred Years of Solitude*" in *Gabriel García Márquez: New Readings*, edited by Bernard McGuirk and Richard Cardwell, Cambridge and New York: Cambridge University Press, 1987

Gonzalez, Anibal, "Translation and the Novel: *One Hundred Years of Solitude*" in *Gabriel García Márquez*, edited by Harold Bloom, New York: Chelsea House, 1989

Hensey, Fritz G., "Differential Stylistics and Alternate Versions of a García Márquez Story" in *Language and Language Use: Studies in Spanish*, edited by Terrell A. Morgan, James F. Lee and Bill VanPatten, Lanham, Maryland: University Press of America, 1987

McIntyre, John, "The English Translation of G. García Márquez's *Cronica de una muerte anunciada*: Aspects of Castilian Grammar and Idiom", *Professional Translator and Interpreter*, 2 (1990) pp. 5–8

Peden, Margaret Sayers, "The Arduous Journey" in *The Teller and the Tale: Aspects of the Short Story*, edited by Wendell M. Aycock, Lubbock: Texas Tech Press, 1982

Constance Garnett 1862–1946

British translator

Biography

Born Constance Black, 19 December 1862, in Brighton, Sussex, one of eight children. Her coroner father had lived as a child in Russia, where his father worked as a naval architect to Tsar Nicholas I. From the age of six, Constance attended Brighton High School. She was an exceptional student who at 17 won a scholarship to Newnham College, Cambridge, where she finished with first class honours in the Classical tripos, though actual degrees were not yet awarded to women. Her husband Edward Garnett was the son of the Keeper of Printed Books at the British Museum and himself a writer and critic of note. Their only child was the future novelist, David Garnett (1892–1981). Constance Garnett died 17 December 1946 in Edenbridge, Kent.

Constance Garnett was the most prolific and influential translator of Russian prose into English. She translated at least 62 books between 1894 and 1928, including most of the classics of Russian realism. Garnett was largely responsible for the enormous popularity of Russian literature in England from the 1890s to the 1920s. In particular, her translations of the works of Turgenev, Dostoevskii, and Chekhov helped elevate each writer, in turn, to cult status in England and made them nearly as popular in the United States. In many cases her translations are still the canonical ones, serving as the bases for many Norton Critical Editions and mass-market paperbacks.

The Garnetts' circle of friends included leading writers and intellectuals, such as J.A. Hobson, John Galsworthy, Ford Madox Ford, D.H. Lawrence, and Joseph Conrad. In the 1890s they became acquainted with several Russian émigrés, including the writer and terrorist Sergei Stepniak. Stepniak encouraged Constance Garnett to learn Russian and consulted on her early translations. Her first translation, of Goncharov's *A Common Story*, was published by Heinemann in 1894. The publisher proceeded to commission translations of Tolstoi's *The Kingdom of God is within You* and then the collected works of Turgenev. Garnett produced 15 volumes of Turgenev's novels and stories between 1894 and 1899, with a 16th in 1921. She then translated Ostrovskii's play *The Storm*, Tolstoi's *Anna Karenina*, *The Death of Ivan Ilyich*, and *War and Peace*. The latter brought her a fee of a mere £300 and ruined her already weak eyesight. From then on she worked with a bilingual secretary, usually Natasha Ertel Duddington, who read the Russian originals to her and took down her dictated translations and who may have advised her as to language as well.

In 1912 Heinemann reluctantly published Garnett's translation of Dostoevskii's *The Brothers Karamazov* (1880). The novel had never appeared in English before, and though the French version had gained it some popularity among English literati, Edward Garnett was so convinced that the British reading public would reject it that he persuaded his wife to take a flat fee, rather than royalties. In fact, the novel's immense success and the ensuing "Russian craze" led Garnett to translate all the author's major novels, novellas, and stories, including *The Idiot* in 1913, *The Possessed* and *Crime and Punishment* in 1914, *The House of the Dead* and *The Insulted and Injured* in 1915 and *Notes from Underground* in 1918. Given the length and complexity of most of these works, this feat of endurance earned the translator praise for "heroism" and "yeoman service" to English culture, in addition to the general acclaim for her clear style and fidelity to the originals.

In spite of the popularity of Russian literature and of Garnett's translations, Heinemann refused to publish her versions of Chekhov's stories, considering the short story genre to be a publishing risk. These were picked up instead by Chatto and Windus, which brought out 13 volumes of Chekhov's stories between 1916 and 1923, two volumes of his plays (1922–23), and one volume of his letters (1926 [US edition 1924]), all of which achieved enormous popular success. Garnett finished her translating career with six volumes of Herzen's memoirs (1924–27) and a six-volume *Works of Gogol* (1922–28).

Garnett was a gifted writer of English and experts acknowledged the relative accuracy of her translations, but much of the praise for her work centered on its extraordinary volume. It was, in part, her ability to bring out multiple volumes of a writer's work in quick succession that allowed Russian literature to maintain its popularity in England for decades at a time. Her name came to be synonymous with Russian literature; her translations elicited such comments as "Turgenev for me is Constance Garnett and Constance Garnett *is* Turgenev" (Joseph Conrad, 1917) and "Chekhov, for us, is Mrs. Garnett, and Mrs. Garnett is Chekhov" (Edward Crankshaw, 1947). Among the writers who paid homage to Garnett's translations and found them influential in their own work were Arnold Bennett, Katherine Mansfield, and Virginia Woolf.

People so admired her beautiful prose and her "heroic" dedication to the task of bringing Russian literature to the English-speaking world that they reacted uncritically to her translations. Indeed, few people in England or the United States knew Russian well enough to provide informed criticism. Only later, on more sober reflection, did many critics recognize Garnett's flaws as a translator, including her tendency to smooth out the language of the originals, toning down racy language, eliminating repetitions and narrative intrusions, and generally homogenizing the voices of the different authors whose works she translated. Carl Proffer wrote of her version of *Dead Souls*, "Gogol's style becomes indistinguishable from that of Turgenev, Tolstoi, Dostoevskii, or Chekhov." Vladimir Nabokov called her translations of Gogol "dry and flat, and always unbearably demure", and Kornei Chukovskii, the dean of Russian translators, called all but her Turgenev translations "insipid, pale, and – worst of all – trivial". In the case of her Dostoevskii translations, these flattening effects were not entirely inadvertent. The publisher Heinemann asked Garnett to "tone down such passages as might be thought offensive in this country", and she herself wrote of the need to "clarify" Dostoevskii's "obscure" and "careless" writing. As a result, her versions of his novels read fluidly, but anyone who is searching in them for subtle psychological contradictions or Bakhtinian polyphony is likely to be disappointed.

RACHEL MAY

Translations
Chekhov, Anton, *The Tales of Tchehov*, 13 vols, 1916–23
Chekhov, Anton, *The Plays of Tchehov*, 2 vols, 1922–23
Chekhov, Anton, *Letters of Anton Tchehov to His Family and Friends*, 1920
Chekhov, Anton, *Letters of Anton Pavlovitch Tchehov to Olga Leonardovna Knipper*, 1924
Dostoevskii, Fedor, *The Brothers Karamazov*, 1912
Dostoevskii, Fedor, *The Idiot*, 1913
Dostoevskii, Fedor, *The Possessed*, 1914; revised to incorporate "Stavrogin's Confession", 1923
Dostoevskii, Fedor, *Crime and Punishment*, 1914
Dostoevskii, Fedor, *The House of the Dead*, 1915
Dostoevskii, Fedor, *The Insulted and Injured*, 1915
Dostoevskii, Fedor, *Notes from Underground*, 1918
Gogol, Nikolai, *The Works of Nikolay Gogol*, 6 vols, 1922–28
Goncharov, Ivan, *A Common Story*, 1894
Herzen, Aleksandr, *My Past and Thoughts*, 6 vols, 1924–27
Ostrovskii, Aleksandr, *The Storm*, 1899
Tolstoi, Lev, *The Kingdom of God is within You*, 2 vols, 1894
Tolstoi, Lev, *Anna Karenin*, 1901; frequently reprinted as *Anna Karenina*
Tolstoi, Lev, *War and Peace*, 3 vols, 1904
Tolstoi, Lev, *The Death of Ivan Ilyitch and Other Stories*, 1915
Turgenev, Ivan, *The Novels of Ivan Turgenev*, 15 vols, 1894–99
Turgenev, Ivan, *Three Plays*, 1934 (contains *A Month in the Country*, *A Provincial Lady*, *A Poor Gentleman*)

Further Reading
Garnett, Constance, "Russian Literature in English", *The Listener* (30 January 1947) p. 195
Garnett, Richard, *Constance Garnett: A Heroic Life*, London: Sinclair Stevenson, 1991
Heilbrun, Carolyn G., *The Garnett Family*, London: Allen and Unwin, and New York: Macmillan, 1961
May, Rachel, *The Translator in the Text: On Reading Russian Literature in English*, Evanston, Illinois: Northwestern University Press, 1994
Moser, Charles A., "The Achievement of Constance Garnett", *American Scholar* (Summer 1988) pp. 431–38
Rubenstein, Roberta, "Genius of Translation", *Colorado Quarterly*, 22/3 (1974) pp. 359–68
Tové, Augusta L., "Konstantsiia Garnet – perevodchik i propagandist russkoi literatury", *Russkaia literatura*, 4 (1958) pp. 193–98

Gender and Gender Politics in Literary Translation

One of the major innovations in translation studies since the late 1970s has been the debate initiated by feminist scholars, writers, and translators on the problems of gender and language. The recognition that gender is implicated in the production of meaning, and so a matter for analysis in the human and social sciences, has transformed many fields of knowledge since the 1960s. The decisive impact of feminist analysis on translation theory and practice has been to establish the ideological dimensions of any translation activity and hence the politics of cultural transmission. The encounter between gender and translation has furthered the "cultural turn" in translation studies toward a socio-semiotic (culturally bound theory of meaning) and stimulated translations that have helped create new feminist intellectual and cultural communities across linguistic and national boundaries.

Gender Theory Meets Translation Studies

Translation studies inherited questions of language and gender raised first by linguists and literary scholars who demonstrated that language as a site of contested meanings was crucial in the struggle for women's liberation. Critiques of the dominance in the literary canon of misogynist texts (Kate Millett, *Sexual Politics*, 1970) and of "phallic criticism" in reviews of women's writing (Mary Ellman, *Thinking about Women*, 1968) pointed out the "double standard" of gender politics in the determination of literary value, which produced an absence of women's writing in school curricula and among translated texts. Pioneering studies in linguistics noted differences in the language use of women and men that were the consequence of a power differential between them (*Language and Sex: Difference and Dominance*, edited by Nancy Thorne and Barrie Henley, 1975; Louky Bersianik, *L'Euguélionne*, 1976, translated as *The Euguelionne*, 1981). This socio-linguistic focus on gender differences in vocabulary was primarily American. In France, theories of the constitution of the subject in language as subjected to dominant social relations, regulated by the Oedipal contract that inscribes woman as lack (Lévi-Strauss, Lacan), were rewritten by feminists who critiqued such an economy of binaries and "solids" that exchanged women as signs to establish sociality only for masculine subjects. Instead, they advanced a theory of unbounded meaning, an economy of "fluids" (Luce Irigaray, *Ce sexe qui n'en est pas un*, 1977, translated as *This Sex Which Is Not One*, 1985) "infinitely dynamized by an incessant process of exchange from one subject to another", according to Hélène Cixous, in a writing "working (in) the in-between" ("The Laugh of the Medusa", *L'Arc*, 1975). Such unfinalizability or loss of certainty has conventionally been considered "feminine".

In 1978, the first discussions of gender and translation emerged from these concerns with language and desire. The April issue of the French feminist magazine *Femmes en mouvement* includes a text "Traduction, transgression? transfert? trahison?" [Translation, transgression? transfer? treachery?] with statements and interviews by two translators, Eugénie Luccioni and Jacqueline Risset, and representatives of the magazine. The interviewers summarize: instead of the model of castration and lack conventionally regulating theories of meaning and of gender, there is substituted a model of excess, characterized by "doubling", "syncopation", "multiplying", "*ex-stase*", in which difference and variation are valued over an unchanging universal. Such theories of enrichment, of proliferating versions that subvert the traditional privileging, in translation, of unity of either source or target text, have developed in recent feminist translation theory to emphasize the contradiction and complexity of translation as a creative textual process.

The two texts that emerged at this stage from American feminist reflections on translation exemplify its power of diversification. The first of the two, "Splitting the Mother Tongue: Bengali and Spanish Poems in English Translations" (*Signs*, 1978) combines an analysis by Barbara Stoler Miller, who translates Sanskrit erotic poetry, with the reflections of two contemporary feminist bilingual poets whose texts she translated into English. Stoler Miller outlines the means she used to translate the erotic language of Nabaneeta Dev Sen and the sensual sound-play of Agueda Pizarro de Rayo, textual strategies she links to their risk-taking in order to undo the authority of "their fathers' tongues". The authors' reflections underline the gendered codes of authorship and public authority in different languages, which lead them to write kinds of texts in English that differ from those they write in their other languages. The relations between eroticism, (self-)censorship and translation are changing, Dev Sen observes, with the transformation in social psychology brought about by feminism. This textual collage is completed with Stoler Miller's translations of their poems.

The third discussion of feminist translation, and the second of the two crucial American texts, aimed to redress the gender imbalance in the literary institution by expanding the canon to include more women writers. Translation was seen as a means of such cultural change by the Division of Women's Studies in Language and Literature of the Modern Language Association. The Division put together a panel on translation for the annual conference in 1978, and for several years following, to encourage academic work on translation and to facilitate preparation of research tools; these efforts resulted in *Women Writers in Translation: An Annotated Bibliography, 1945–1982* (New York, 1984), edited by Margery Resnick and Isabelle de Courtivron, and involved more than 50 women bibliographers and annotators in the United States and Canada. Comments on the translations were brief and evaluative rather than descriptive, and overlooked some practices deemed sexist by later feminists (see M. Simons, "The Silencing of Simone de Beauvoir", *Women's Studies International Forum*, 1983 and A. Antonopoulos, "Simone de Beauvoir and the Différance of Translation", *Institut Simone de Beauvoir Bulletin*, 1994). At this point, gender was not a category for the analysis of translation strategies but a factor in the devalued status of translation both inside the academy, where the interest of women scholars in translation is not taken into account for promotion nor supported with research grants, and outside, where financial survival as a translator is precarious. So, the editors conclude, "[a]s in most other areas of Women's Studies, translation is yet another volunteer activity, dependent on the good will of those committed to retrieving creative women from historical silence and absence".

To the projects of subverting textual unity and authority, overturning the psycho-symbolic order, opening new forms of textuality for women writers, and critiquing the double standard of value negatively linking women's work and the practice of translation, the editors' introduction to *Women Writers in Translation* adds the expansion of the canon and the documentation of women's activities as translators. All remain pertinent issues today, though they have been supplemented by new questions since the expansion of the field of gender and translation in the mid-1980s.

Notable in the three texts mentioned above is their collective authorship. Implicitly this advances collaboration as a model of feminist translation, collaboration in both senses of the word, as double-voiced utterance and as subversive project, involving cooperation and confrontation. The texts in question foreshadow a movement to theorize gender and translation as ordered not by the "double standard" and a discourse of fidelity to the one True, but by a "double bind" within the paradox of "*plus d'une langue*" (Derrida), "this language which is not one", which highlights the complexity of texts, languages and translation, where the bilingual translator, both outside and inside and at the border of cultures and languages, produces continuous exchange and change.

Queering Translation

If gender in the above paragraphs seems synonymous with feminist critique of sexism, this has been the case in translation studies generally, despite the importance of the concept of gender in the emergence of lesbian and gay studies and queer theory. Gender is a system of social relations by which power captures subjects as bodies and sexualizes them by establishing classifications and taxonomies to make distinctions among them. Judith Butler insists that gender is discursively constituted. There is no "authentic" female sexual identity that has been repressed: rather, identity categories are "*effects* of institutions, practices, discourses with multiple and diffuse points of origin". Both "woman" and "female" are unstable terms that gain their "significations only as relational terms" (*Gender Trouble*, 1990). Gender is historically and culturally variable and so manifests itself diversely at different times and in different places.

One might anticipate that such a theory would foster analysis of gender differences in the translation of lesbian and/or gay texts; however, this has rarely been the case. Differences in the strategies of feminist and non-feminist translators of Nicole Brossard's writing have been noted (Godard, "Translations", *University of Toronto Quarterly*, 1987) but not those between the practices of lesbian and straight translators of her work. In a pioneering paper on the "*dérive*" or difference of translation, which considers differences between poet and non-poet translators of poetry as well as those between men and women translators' versions of women's writing, Evelyne Voldeng points out the need to be alert to a paralingual context and "intertexte féministe" in translating lesbian poetry, which otherwise might become "a hymn to heterosexual love" (1980, published 1984 as "La Traduction poétique comme duplication ou dérivation textuelle d'une langue à une autre" [Poetic Translation as Duplication or Derivation of a Text from One Language to Another] and "Translata/latus", *Tessera*, 1). That such has been the case in translations of Sappho, with major consequences for the history and theory of poetics, has been compellingly demonstrated by Joan DeJean in "Fictions of Sappho" (*Critical Inquiry*, 1987). Myriam Diaz-Diocaretz provides further evidence of such neutralization in her pathbreaking study, *Translating Poetic Discourse: Questions on Feminist Strategies in Adrienne Rich* (1985), where she comments on the problems she confronts in making visible the relations of address between two women when translating Rich's poetry. Alice Parker, in the only text to focus entirely on lesbian translation, characterizes the lesbian as cultural outsider or foreigner speaking with "forked tongue" to negotiate with the terms of the dominant social order in a "double translation", where she "plays with codes" and opts to write bilingually in English and French to signify her "dislocation" ("Under the Covers: A Synesthesia of Desire (Lesbian Translations)", 1993). Such code-switching is the focus of a study of homosexual translation practices. Peter Bien considers the function of different strategies, as responses to diverse readerships, that establish differing lines of transmission for Cavafy's work. "Are there specifically homosexual or heterosexual ways to translate Cavafy?" he asks ("Cavafy's Homosexuality and His Reputation outside Greece", *Journal of Modern Greek Studies*, 1990). Some translators have used "sexual code-language" in their versions to differing degrees, he notes, but he concludes that translating in a "specifically homosexual way" is not advisable, since Cavafy was "preoccupied with the modern perception of the reality of loss" for which "unfertile" homosexual love is "a perfect emblem". The analytical power of Bien's approach for reading specific translations suggests on the contrary its productivity for translation studies.

Translating Grammatical Gender

The focus in translation studies on the difference between men's and women's practices is the consequence of two important aspects of the problem of gender and translation. On the one hand there is the significance of grammatical gender, which poses particular dilemmas for translation when the marks of gender or the "sexuation du discours" [sexing or gendering of discourse] (Irigaray) operate in diverse ways, or not at all, according to the languages paired in translation. On the other hand, there is the gendering of translation itself, conceptualized as a secondary activity in the binaries of production/reproduction, creation/procreation, which are metaphorically linked to male and female sexuality.

Grammatical gender is frequently what first draws attention to the question of gender in translation. "Does it matter [that the writer was a woman]?" asks Adrian Room in response to an anonymous text published in Russian. A single feminine ending of a past participle alerted him to the writer's gender. While Russian has grammatical gender, English does not. To indicate this in translation, he recommends the "addition of a feminine attribute" relating to the body or an item of clothing. "Don't Keep Sex Out of It", he urges (*Journal of Russian Studies*, 56, 1989). But many do. Difference in grammatical gender between languages is treated as an instance of the limits of translatability by Maurice Friedberg, discussing the problems for Russians translating from German (*Literary Translation in Russia: A Cultural History*, 1997; see also J. Sadan,"Vine, Women and Seas: Some Images of the Ruler in Medieval Arabic Literature," *Journal of Semitic Studies*, 1989, p. 140, footnote).

For feminists, however, grammatical gender is central to the struggle for language change, which has been an important issue of feminist politics. Feminist theoreticians draw attention to the ways gender-markers produce meaning, for they see gender differences in language as one of the powerful but unquestioned ideological presuppositions of culture. Grammatical gender is generally considered to be a formal property of language, dividing nouns into classes of masculine, feminine and neuter in the Greek from which this term is derived, and establishing the rules of agreement for adjectives, articles, and pronouns. Grammarians claim this classification is conventional. Feminist linguists detect a hierarchy of power operating in languages, such as the Romance langages, with grammatical gender that gives priority to the masculine. In French, for example, reference to 300 women and one man would require the use of the masculine plural form. This is taken as evidence of a slippage between formal and so-called "natural" gender that is referential and establishes meaning. Dale Spender terms this "he-man" language, when abstractions or general human traits are linked specifically to those considered biologically male (*Man Made Language*, 1980). "Metaphorical gender" creates this slippage: grammatical gender takes on symbolic meaning and produces coherent gender sequences for a wide range of attributes. This has a powerful effect on the way we apprehend and organize the world. In an experiment, people classified objects perceived as passive or weak as "feminine" and those seen as active or strong as "masculine" (Deborah Cameron, *Feminism and Linguistic Theory*, 2nd edition, 1992). Relational terms, these classifications work to sexualize objects and concepts and naturalize a binary distinction between genders to the advantage of the masculine.

Critiques of Phallic Translation

Such classification is ideological, not conventional, according to feminists, and consequently has become a significant issue for feminist translation studies. Analysis of the shifts in meaning produced by translators not attentive to the resonances of grammatical gender, or feminist discourse, or the realities of women's lives, was a major focus of feminist translation studies in the early 1980s, especially in Canada. Following Voldeng's observation that a man translating Nicole Brossard replaced an ambiguous possessive pronoun with the masculine "his" rather than either "its" or "hers", and her experiment with men and women translators working on the same text, which demonstrated that the female sexual body figures more explicitly in translations by women, who opt for concrete rather than abstract terms, a number of studies of Quebec texts in English translation supported her conclusion that translators are influenced by their ideological positions (Kathy Mezei, "The Scales of Literal Translation: The English-Canadian Poet as a Literal Translator", *University of Ottawa Review*, 1984; Barbara Godard, "Translating and Sexual Difference", *Resources for Feminist Research*, 1984). This led to the converse question, posed by Howard Scott: can a man translate a feminist text? In his 1984 thesis "Louky Bersianik's *L'Euguélionne*: Problems of Translating the Critique of Language in New Quebec Feminist Writing" Scott relates how he decided not to provide an explanation of sexism in the French language for an English-speaking reader but to find examples of gender-marking in English that would give an equally political message.

Feminizing Translation Strategies

Turning from the critique of sexism in men's translations, feminists concentrated on a third facet of gender difference, the translation of feminist texts by feminist translators. "The Translator as She", Barbara Godard's presentation on the panel "Translation: The Relationship between Writer and Translator" at the Women and Words Conference, 1983 (*In the Feminine*, 1985; *Meta*, 1989) highlighted the new visibility of the feminist translator, who aimed not only to advance the feminist political project of a more inclusive language in English but, in the words of Susanne de Lotbinière-Harwood, to "*resex* language", to put the feminine into discourse where it has been neutralized (*Re-belle et infidèle: la traduction comme pratique de réécriture au féminin / The Body Bilingual: Translation as a Rewriting in the Feminine*, 1991). Following the writing practice of Quebec feminists Nicole Brossard and Michèle Causse, de Lotbinière seeks out every case of gender marking to "eroticize" language by feminizing normally neutral English nouns, and feminizing titles, as "auth*er*" for the French "*auteure*", or roles, as "she-love" for the French "*amante*", to make visible the feminine. This practice extends to the creation of neologisms. "Woman-handling" the text is how Barbara Godard characterized this strategy in the preface to her translation of Brossard's *Amantes* as *Lovhers* (1986). Such "feminization strategies" make it possible for English readers to "identify the lesbian in the text", de Lotbinière-Harwood claims. She extends these assertive practices to the translation of texts by women that are not explicitly feminist, introducing italics to make visible the feminine *her* in "ot*her* "and specifying both "her and his" in plurals to avoid "generic malespeak".

Sexism shapes texts in ways other than androcentric grammar, as American women translators of Latin American writing steeped in *machismo* wryly observe in their influential essays. Their assertive translation practices are a transgressive re-appropriation of texts in a strategy of "hijacking", as Luise von Flotow terms it ("Feminist Translation", *TTR*, 1991), that characterizes a fourth position in relation to gender difference: feminist intervention to correct phallocentrism. This changes not only traditional views about translation but also the "habitual 'missionary' position" assigned to the translator (von Flotow; see also Suzanne Jill Levine's "Translation as (Sub)Version", in *Sub-Stance*, 1983, on her translation of Cabrera Infante's *Inferno*). Carole Maier too notes a shift from "submissive" to "resisting" to "antagonistic" reader and translator of the Cuban poet Octavio Armand in her essay "A Woman in Translation, Reflecting", included in the landmark issue of *Translation Review* (1985), which moved discussion of gender issues in translation from women's studies debates into translation studies. Translating "in an Age of Feminism" has heightened Maier's sense of the conflicting relation between feminist translator and male author, complicating the translator's task "to give voice" and necessitating "women translators get[ting] under the skin of both antagonistic and sympathetic works". This image of the doubleness of the translated text becomes a figure for the supplementing practices of the feminist translator. Maier uses her craft to work with and against Armand's image of "female treachery" in the "tongue's double talk". Such transformative translation working on both language and meaning functions as literary creation.

Gender Debates in Bible Translation

Debates over sexist language have been particularly intense in the field of Bible translation, where they take the same (op)positions as in translation of secular texts. The political stakes are higher though. A foundational text of Western culture, the Bible has been retranslated by different denominations who recognize the ideological basis of all interpretation. It has frequently been translated in missionary work with the political aim of conversion. In that the Bible's truth depends on its divine authorship, biblical translation has demanded a commitment to respect the renderings of predecessors so as to convey truth in conformity to a tradition of religious doctrine. Challenges to interpretation of the Bible have been launched by feminist scholars both religious and secular, who have reacted strongly to its masculinist bias and the way it has long been used to constrain women. Elizabeth Castelli writes on the radical implications of feminist translations of the Bible ("Les Belles Infidèles / Fidelity or Feminism? The Meanings of Feminist Biblical Translation", *Journal of Feminist Studies in Religion*, 1990). For some feminists, the Bible is irredeemably androcentric: the project of retranslating it from a feminist perspective risks obscuring the patriarchal quality of biblical texts and so further reifying sexism. However, Elizabeth Cady Stanton produced *The Woman's Bible* in 1895–98, and the US National Organization of Women thought the issue so important that in 1972 they approached translators working on the *Revised Standard Version* to pressure them to re-examine the androcentric language and find more inclusive terms.

Heated controversy is directed at conventional translations of the Hebrew *bene-ha-adam* and the Greek *anthropos*, which in earlier versions were translated "sons of men" and "mankind." In the process, they underwent a slippage from inclusive to gender-specific masculine language. New inclusive language translations replace these with "humankind" or "human beings". The arguments for doing so are made on differing grounds. Orlinsky and Bratcher, in *A History of Bible Translation and the North American Contribution* (1991), argue that the Hebrew and Greek terms were inclusive and so to replace "men" with "everyone" is to respect philological tradition. Arguments for more inclusive language have also been made from a reader-response perspective, which claims that a translation should bring out the universality of the Bible for contemporary readers (Paul Ellingworth, "Translating the Bible Inclusively", *Meta*, 1987). Translators such as Eugene Nida (in a paradoxical move) have retorted that this "distort[s]" the text by imposing "anachronistic" standards (Castelli, 1990). Replacement of sexist with neutral or inclusive language is not sufficient for many feminists. Joann Haugerud's 1983 translation of sections of the Bible is a more assertive project: while "Lord" is replaced by "Sovereign" and "Son of Man" is translated as "Human One", "Father" (for God) is replaced by "Father and Mother". The hope that such an affirmative-action feminist translation project would restore a hidden women's reality to the Bible is sharply challenged by other feminists. Peggy Hutaff warns that it may make women "feel more at home in patriarchal religion" ("Response [to Castelli]", *Journal of Feminist Studies in Religion*, 1990). The effects of changes in gendered language, though, are limited without radical transformation of the religious institutions that channel its transmission. This dilemma, however, raises the crucial question of the relation of language to socio-cultural practices.

Translation as a Gendered Practice: Metaphors and Models

The gendering of translation itself as a textual practice perceived as a derivative, hence "feminine", activity became a significant issue with the proliferation of translation theory in the late 1980s. The theoretical turn in translation studies was part of a more general focus on theory induced by the paradigm shift to post-structuralism with its questioning of the subject's identity and of language's certainty. Particularly influential was the deconstruction of Jacques Derrida, whose formulation of the paradox of language, which makes meaning always provisional, was translated into English by a number of feminists, especially Gayatri Spivak, Barbara Johnson, and Barbara Harlow, who subsequently extended his theory to analyse the power imbalances in gender and cross-cultural relations. "Des Tours de Babel" (1980), Derrida's important contribution to translation theory, much cited by feminist translation theorists, underlines the double bind of the Babelian text characterized by "*pas de sens*" – no meaning beyond language – which signifies not the poverty of language but the untransferability of meaning outside of language. He frames this paradox as a "virtual" or "interlinear" translation making visible the languageness of language. Translation became one more metaphor for deconstruction, along with the "supplement" and "*différance*". Fidelity, long the major criterion of "good" translation, was undermined by this generalized instability of meaning.

Feminist translation theory exposed the gendered imbalance of power in the sexualized foundational metaphors of translating activity. "Fidelity", for instance, both produces translation as an activity particularly suitable for women, "the second sex", and reproduces the hierarchy of genders and textual practices in the social. One of the first feminists to expose the implications of this sexualization was Barbara Johnson, who pointed out that underlying the metaphor of fidelity was not the marriage bond but the oedipal contract and castration ("Taking Fidelity Philosophically" in *Difference in Translation*, edited by Joseph F. Graham, 1985). The translator, loyal to two languages, is a "faithful bigamist", undermining sexual and textual unity. Johnson introduces a figure of translation as radical ambiguity and excess, exteriorizing the foreign at the heart of every text.

The single most influential essay on the gendering of translation is Lori Chamberlain's "Gender and the Metaphorics of Translation" (*Signs*, 1988), which analyses the persistence of a gender-based paradigm, regulating cultural value, in a distinction between productive and reproductive work that establishes a hierarchy between writing and translation. Originality and creativity of production are associated with paternity and authority, while the feminine is linked to repetition and procreation. This representation of the work of translation has significant consequences in material terms, affecting matters of copyright, royalties, and academic tenure. Central to this difference in value between writing and translation is a struggle for the legitimacy of the translated text and the translating subject. Chamberlain develops the argument of deconstruction regarding the interdependence of writing and translation, to advance a model of translation as creative subversion.

Chamberlain's essay is important for its historical examination of the "metaphorics of translation". A discourse analysis, it demonstrates the persistent representation of an aesthetic problem in terms of the family romance. The concept of fidelity is used to guarantee legitimacy of the offspring as the production of the father, reproduced by the mother. In translation, it is used to certify the lineage and copyright of a translation through a proper contract. This attitude manifests considerable anxiety about paternity. The most familiar formulation of this engendered theory is the phrase *les belles infidèles,* coined in the 17th century, which implies that if beautiful, a translation must be unfaithful. Under this double standard, the husband/original cannot be guilty. The sexualization of translation takes other more graphic metaphorical forms. In the 16th century, Thomas Drant compared "English[ing]" a Roman author to subduing a captive woman to make her a proper wife. This image of the text as wild woman to be tamed dates back to St Jerome (Castelli). Such violence is central to the hermeneutic model of George Steiner, for whom translation involves an "appropriative penetration", succeeded by a "capture" and "naturalization" producing "rapture", which must be balanced by an act of "restitution" or reciprocity (*After Babel*, 1975, 3rd edition 1998). The coding of translation as rape extends back to Herder in the 18th century.

Though theories of intertextuality and deconstruction reverse the conventional hierarchy to take translation as a model for writing and to advance theories of creative misreading and of the unbounded text open to interpretive completion, they none the less continue to make use of gendered metaphors for the process. Derrida refers to the paradox of translation that is both original and secondary as a *hymen*, the sign of both virginity and consummation of marriage. Some feminists, however, have taken issue with Derrida, as well as with Walter Benjamin (translation a matter of "seed" and "birth pangs" of language) for continuing to locate the task of the translator within the terms of "patriarchal imagery", which leave little room for the woman translator.

Chamberlain prophesies, in concluding, a day when women will have written their own metaphors of cultural production, and translation will no longer be legitimated through acts of engendering. Any feminist theory of translation, she suggests, will be "utopic". With or without her urging, feminists have been theorizing translation and producing new metaphors. "U-topia" (no place) is one of them. As "no-man's land", it figures translation as "working (in) the in-between" in Nicole Ward Jouve's *White Woman Speaks with Forked Tongue* (1991) and Susan Bassnett's "Writing in No Man's Land" (*Ilha do Desterro*, 1992), where they endorse Cixous's concept of writing as the "undoing of death". Bassnett also notes this focus on life-giving as enabling for the woman translator. She advances Kathy Mezei's theorization of translation as a "compound act of reading and writing" (*Tessera*, 1985) to refigure translation as a complex interaction rather than as binary privileging of either source or target text to the exclusion of the other. This rejection of hierarchy offers a notion of translation different from that of "appropriative penetration", an "idealistic" theory of translation as "*orgasmic*". Rosemary Arrojo advanced a strong critique of this theory with the argument that it is merely a reverse-image of masculinist figurations, which produces equal violence ("Feminist, 'Orgasmic' Theories of Translation and Their Contradictions", *Tradterm*, 1995).

Many feminists have attempted to reconfigure translation outside the conventional sexualized discourse. Legitimation of the translator's authority shifts to *politicized* relations with the literary institution. For this reason, Susan Bassnett stresses the innovations of women theorists in the "cultural turn" in translation studies. Feminists criticize the conventional paradigms of translation for their insistence on the singularity of languages and the irreparable loss of meaning, and locate new paradigms in metaphors of complexity and narratives of creative transformation. Central to many of these formulations is the translator's bilingualism, which may indeed give her "no place" (Maggie Humm, "Translation as Survival", *Fiction International*, 1987; Norma Alarcón, "Traduttora, Traditora: A Paradigmatic Figure of Chicana Feminism", *Cultural Critique*, 1989; Françoise Lionnet, *Postcolonial Representations: Women, Literature, Identity*, 1995). Crucial in all these new models is a critique of translation considered as loss of meaning.

To replace the venerable Tower of Babel, Karin Littau turns to another narrative of origins, that of Pandora, in order to articulate a theory of translation as constant variation. She adopts a theory of "refraction" or adaptation, where texts develop from other texts in "numerous transformations" and adapt "to a certain ideology or a certain poetics" ("Refractions of the Feminine: The Monstrous Transformations of Lulu", *Modern Language Notes*, 1995). The potential for perpetual transformation is contained in the principle of translation as production, not reproduction. Translating by "lapse and bounds" is how Barbara Godard conceptualizes this figure of continuous transformation, invoked by the principle of metonymic recombination theorized in Irigaray's work ("Translating (with) *The Speculum*", *TTR*, 1991). "Re-writing" – "Rewording" or "double-voiced discourse", introduced by Mikhail Bakhtin for reported speech (a form of "dialogic" utterance), is another term used by Barbara Godard ("Theorizing Feminist Discourse / Translation", *Tessera*, 1989) and by Kaisa Koskinen ("Between the Word of the Self and the Word of the Other; or, Translation: The Invisible Link", *XIII FIT World Congress*, 1993) for translation as perpetual transformation where language undergoes a process of ideological re-evaluation and is "refracted" when directed to a new audience of a different gender and/or language.

Gender in Translation History

Only when historical scholarship on women translators has been carried out, suggests Lori Chamberlain, will it be possible to formulate alternatives to the oedipal model of struggle over reproduction that has dominated translation theory. Analysis of the problems of translating explicitly feminist texts, one facet of this scholarship, has been a major feature of contemporary feminist theorization in the context of American translations of French feminist theory and of English-Canadian translations of Quebec feminist writing. Both these areas of translation have produced a flurry of translators' prefaces and manifestory essays on translating Cixous, Irigaray, Brossard and others, which present the strategies used for translating neologisms and word play that are central to the feminist project of linguistic change, strategies analysed by Sherry Simon as well as by Jean Delisle ("Traducteurs médiévaux, traductrices féministes: une même éthique de la traduction?" [Medieval Translators, Feminist Women Translators: The Same Translation Ethic?], *TTR*, 1994). However, the examination of the historical role of translation in women's writing in different periods and cultures, a second facet of this needed scholarship, has not been undertaken in any systematic way. Scattered essays show this to be a rich field for analysis with regard to the legitimation of the translator's discourse and practice through rhetorical strategies that establish complex links between language, culture, and the translated text, issues Delisle considers central to the political project of Canadian feminist translators. He compares their strategies of "transformance" (Godard, "Theorizing Feminist Discourse/Translation", *Tessera*, 1989) to the practices of medieval male translators who sought to improve the French language.

Historical work, a major focus in the 1990s, has centred on the medieval and Renaissance periods, when translation was more valued as a textual practice and there were few women writers. Expanding the canon by finding evidence of women's literary activities in the past constitutes a tradition to legitimate the practices of today's women translators. Frequently anonymous, the translations by medieval women into Anglo-Norman corroborate Delisle's evidence of strong translation practices. Working within the constraints of the *translatio*, these women none the less made significant changes to advance what Michelle Freeman terms "a feminine conception of poetic articulation and creativity" ("Marie de France's Poetics of Silence: The Implications for a Feminine *Translatio*", *PMLA*, 1988). In her analysis of the *Lais* as translations of Celtic material, she emphasizes as a strong assertion of authorship the late 12th-century Marie's choice of silence in her refusal to quote the source texts directly, as was customary, and her decision instead to paraphrase and gloss this unspoken word in her writing. Marie also rejects the dominant *translatio imperii* (transferral of [discourse about] power), translating not the heroic or monumental histories of Thebes or Aeneas, but more private love conversations. Analysis of the versions of saints' lives, also translated in the 12th and 13th centuries by Anglo-Norman nuns, reveals a similar reworking of the rhetoric of legitimation, to emphasize the woman translator's creative work. As Jocelyn Wogan-Brown points out (in "Wreaths of Time: The Female Translator in Anglo-Norman Hagiography", 1994), their particular variant on "the clerkly narrator as translator" continued the model of *translatio studii* (transferral of learning), in which the audience and translator are inscribed in a Christian textual community, here the female community of a convent. Wogan-Brown highlights, as crucial factors legitimizing women's authorship, patronage (the nuns at Barking were from royal and aristocratic families), the prestige of the text translated, and the text's importance in constituting or sustaining a community.

Recovery of the work of Renaissance English women translators reveals a predominance of religious texts and the model of *translatio studii*. The translation of scriptural passages, especially the psalms, was a religious discipline considered particularly suitable for women, notes Mary Ellen Lamb (in *Silent but for the Word: Tudor Women as Patrons, Translators and Writers of Religious Works*, edited by Margaret Hannay, 1985). Most circulated in manuscript and have long since disappeared. Texts surviving in print were translated by women belonging to families of some of England's most powerful courtiers. Many of these works were, like the translation of John Jewel's 1562 *Apologia ecclesiae anglicanae*, undertaken in 1564 by Anne Cooke Bacon, one of four translator daughters of Edward VI's tutor, of great political import in articulating the Protestant position on the religious question, their legitimacy secured through the Anglican textual community they constituted. Replacing an earlier inadequate version, Cooke's translation of this official document of the Church of England was still considered very precise and graceful in the 20th century. A "line-by-line transliteration", it is typical of the strict translation of Renaissance women, in contrast to the creative expansion in translations of Renaissance men. While the doctrinal and institutional importance of the text prohibited adaptation, such literal strategies were also dictated by the limits placed on women's learning, suggests Lamb. Men selected the texts to be translated. The subordination of Cooke's voice in her translations contrasts greatly with the personal tone, forceful pleading and rhetorical skill in Latin and Greek exhibited in her correspondence.

This contradiction between evidence of exceptional linguistic skills and subservience to models of female decorum, shown in the extensive use of the modesty topos by these women translators, is probed by contributors to Hannay's book. They focus primarily on the selection of text and on patronage to demonstrate how, even within this double bind, women's creative power is manifest. Rita M. Verbrugge shows the daughter of Thomas More, Margaret Roper, translating the *Precatio Dominica* of her father's celebrated friend, Erasmus, with "the care and concern for a responsible translation" of the early humanists, steering a middle course between excessively free and too literal translation. While she sometimes lost Erasmus's rhetorical effects of repetition, she enhanced his themes of living in harmony and gentleness through her word choice. She also introduced her own interjections to personalize the petition. Such personalizing is a feature of young Elizabeth Tudor's translation of Marguerite de Navarre's 1531 *Miroir de l'âme pécheresse*, where she not only toned down the religious fervour of the French queen's text but also altered the image of God as a loving father to that of a loving mother and so legitimated her translation as creation within the model of *translatio imperii* (power transmitted from one queen to another along with piety) as well as of *translatio studii*.

The translations of Mary Sidney, Countess of Pembroke, the most important woman translator of the period, offer spiritual gifts but also facilitate the transmission of power. It is the conciseness of her translation of the Huguenot leader Philippe de Mornay's *Discours de la vie et de la mort* that Diane Bornstein highlights, still in Hannay: though Sidney preserved the parallel structure and repetition of the French text, she favoured a plain syntax that shortened double to single terms. Her additions were more concrete and specific, yet made the text more metaphorical. Compared to a contemporary translation by a man, her version is at once more lively and more accurate. Claims for the importance of Sidney's translations in relation to both politics and poetics are advanced in two other essays about her translation of the *Psalmes*. Hannay points out how Mary Sidney's own dedicatory and epitaph poems for the presentation copy for Elizabeth I (1599) implicitly positions Mary as her brother Philip's successor in the partisan role of leader of militant Protestantism and this as *translatio imperii*. Beth Fisken's analysis of Mary Sidney's translation strategies makes a case for the impact of her experimentation with stanzaic forms and metrical patterns on the development of English poetics. As Hannay claims (*English Literary Renaissance*, 1994), Mary Sidney and other women translators, such as Anne Lok or Locke, found authorization for their own speech by identifying with the voice of the psalmist as a recipient of God's grace who is obliged to teach others. Anne Cooke used a similar explanation to justify her translation from the Italian. Such a prophetic stance has affinities with the emotional appropriation of Christ by medieval nuns to legitimate their translation. However, Mary Sidney had an additional authorizing voice in her brother, Philip, who not only had begun the translation of the poems but had praised them as the highest form of poetry. Her translation project is thus legitimated by the fusion of familial, religious, and political alliances. That her *Psalmes* are dedicated to Elizabeth I positions these bonds within the context of an exchange of signs between women. In similar fashion, Anne Cooke dedicates her translation from the Italian to her mother, who has been responsible for her education, and Princess Elizabeth offers her translations to her stepmother, the notable patron Catherine Parr. These English women sought to legitimate women's intellectual work through interaction with predecessors and patrons who would constitute a community of learned women to channel the transmission of knowledge.

The need to establish credibility was perhaps more acute for women translators of secular texts, those "oppositional voices" analyzed by Tina Krontiris in *Oppositional Voices: Women as Writers and Translators of Literature in the English Renaissance* (1992). Questions of conventional gender roles and power are more consciously challenged in texts sympathetic to women's sexual love. In selecting for translation (as *Antonie*, 1592) the neo-Senecan *Marc-Antoine* (1578) by French playwright Robert Garnier, Mary Sidney exacerbated the split between private and public expression, continuing her "self-effacing" literal strategies to convey the author's meaning exactly, though Garnier's themes of political corruption and women's roles as agents of justice, and his glorification of adulterous sexual love, are at odds with such models of fidelity.

The most radical departure from feminine silence and invisibility during this period was Margaret Tyler's pathbreaking translation (1578) of the chivalric romance, the *Espejo de príncipes* as *The Mirrour of Princely Deedes and Knighthood*. The first version of a complete romance from Spanish, and the only one rendered directly rather than through French, Tyler's translation set a vogue that lasted throughout the 17th century. The romance as genre was generally considered immoral in Renaissance England. Spanish literature was thought to be very liberal in its attitudes to women: men translators often altered texts to make them conform to standards of sexual modesty. Tyler does not, so her selection and rendering of the text may be considered "oppositional". She introduced into English a narrative that, in its tension between Renaissance realities and an idealized tradition of courtly love with its ideology of masculine homage, examined the restrictions on women's sexuality and encouraged the choice of passionate reciprocal love. Tyler's assertiveness may result from her relative freedom from the aristocratic codes, since she appears to have been a servant in the household of the aristocratic Roman Catholic Howard family. It most certainly is a consequence of her age, since she indicates in her dedication to the duke of Norfolk that she is past her youth. Krontiris terms Tyler's preface "a kind of feminist manifesto".

Douglas Robinson, analysing three rhetorical strategies adopted in prefaces by women translators of the 16th and 17th centuries, also emphasizes the innovation of Tyler's "deconstructing" the rhetoric of patronage ("Theorizing Translation in a Woman's Voice: Subverting the Rhetoric of Patronage, Courtly Love and Morality", *The Translator*, 1995). Tyler, Robinson claims, makes "a frontal attack on the binary logic" that limits women to the role of passive muses.

The rhetoric of morality became more significant in the 17th century with the decline of patronage and the rise of a middle-class readership interested in self-advancement. Translator Suzanne du Verger, in her version (*Admirable Events*, 1639) of Jean-Pierre Camus's 1628 *Les Événements singuliers*, takes on the role of censor in the name of bourgeois morality, excising fabulous elements and paring away stylistic decoration to improve the reader indirectly, in what Robinson terms "a feminine manner", through education. Education is emphasized in Aphra Behn's translations later in the century. She introduces into her 1688 version of Fontenelle's *Entretiens sur la pluralité des mondes* (1686) a female character, "a fair Lady to be instructed in Philosophy". Demystifying "masculine learning" for middle-class women, Behn intervenes in the text, adding a character not unlike herself to make the text more accessible for a woman reader, a move to legitimate the text through the constitution of a social community engaged in self-transformation through learning. It is no longer the prestige of a patron, but the reputation of the translator and the social value of her project that authorize translation. Robert A. Day is a forceful advocate of Behn's originality as a theorist of language and translation ("Aphra Behn and the Works of the Intellect", *Fetter'd or Free*, 1986). Her strong stance as a translator was fostered by her experience as a creative writer before turning to translation to support herself at the end of her life. Among her translations from the French is the first English version of La Rochefoucauld's *Maximes* (a free and witty adaptation of his aphorisms in "Seneca Unmasq'd", 1685), as well as two works of philosophy by Fontenelle. Twentieth-century critics judge her version of the *Entretiens* superior to those of John Glanvill (1688) and William Gardiner (1715).

It is tempting to read here, in translations by women, a persistent pattern of creative innovation and feminizing intervention, a continuing emphasis on translation as creative production. To date, however, the translation activity of only a few exceptional women has been documented and only that of women in the Renaissance systematically analysed. Douglas Robinson includes in his *Western Translation Theory* (1997) prefaces and letters by the women discussed in his article mentioned above, as well as those of Elizabeth Tudor, Elizabeth Carter (18th-century translator of Epictetus from Greek), and French translators Anne Dacier (1654–1720) and Germaine de Staël (1766–1817). Only nine among 90 theorists, these women have hitherto been excluded from histories of translation. Their introduction highlights the fact that women began to theorize translation long before the 1980s. While the inclusion of these texts is an important corrective to the history of translation, their identification has been the result of feminist rather than of translation scholarship. Betty Travitsky (1981) and Moira Ferguson (1985) first anthologized a number of these prefaces and letters. Janet Todd published all the author's translations and the "Essay on Translated Prose" in the *Works of Aphra Behn*, vol. 4 (1993), as well as giving information about translation in her *British Women Writers: A Critical Reference Guide* (1989). Similar information is included in *The Feminist Companion to Literature in English: Women Writers from the Middle Ages to the Present* (Virginia Blain *et al.*, 1990), which also has an independent entry on translation. Beatrice Slama's research on 19th-century French women of letters documents their translations (*Annales*, 1992). Even these reference works list only those translators who wrote in other genres. Locating and analysing the translating practices of women who have focused exclusively on translation will perhaps now be easier since the 20th-century publication of biographies and autobiographies of Jean Starr Untermeyer, Willa Muir, Constance Garnett, Helen Lowe-Porter, Hazel Barnes, and others, and the sustained reflections on practice since the 1980s by feminist translators such as Suzanne Jill Levine, Carole Maier, Catherine Porter, Nicole Ward Jouve, Susanne de Lotbinière-Harwood, Luise von Flotow, Barbara Godard, and others.

Much research remains to be done with regard to historical perspectives on gender and translation, especially the type of contextual descriptive study of a particular period and culture advocated by translation studies. Such analysis might take into account both the roles played by women as translators and the influence of their translations, as well as how works by women have fared in translation.

One pattern that might be traced I would term "feminism through translation". This is a particularity of translations into English from the French during the 18th century, when the ferment of Enlightenment theories of universal equality, absorbed through translations by blue-stockings such as Frances Brooke or radical republicans such as Mary Hays, Helen Maria Williams, and Mary Wollstonecraft, inspired a programme for women's sexual and political equality most forcefully stated in Wollstonecraft's *A Vindication of the Rights of Woman* (1792). Williams's rendering (1795) of Bernardin de Saint-Pierre's 1787 *Paul et Virginie* is the only one of these translations to have attracted critical notice, and that of a purely bibliographic nature (Paul Robinson, *Revue d'histoire littéraire de la France*, 1989). Her preface to this translation justifies her considerable interventions in the text – shortening the philosophical dialogue – on the grounds of the reader's lack of interest, so indicating the increasing force of the marketplace in legitimating translations, a focus on consumption that favours target- or reader-oriented theories. The insertion of eight sonnets of her own composition, attributed to one of the women characters, points to an understanding of translation as creative production. Her translation was the most popular of those available, and was reprinted repeatedly through the first half of the 19th century. Another significant moment is constituted by the 19th-century English translations of Scandinavian texts advocating women's sexual independence, as exemplified in the practice of Mary Howitt (feminist novelist Fredrika Bremer's *Neighbours*, 1842, translated 1843), Eleanor Marx (Ibsen's *An Enemy of the People*, 1882, translated 1888) and George Egerton [Mary C. Dunne]

(Knut Hamsen's *Hunger*, 1890, translated 1899), which presented the "new woman" to a resistant English public.

In contrast to these instances of cultural transmission via translation is another rich field of intertextual relations advancing feminism, which transformed translation theory through dissemination of the idealism of German Romanticism. At its centre is Germaine de Staël, whose theoretical work on gender, and on translation in cross-cultural interaction emphasizing cultural difference, has been overlooked by comparative literature and translation studies. Her translation theory and practice have received only brief analysis outside feminist circles ("Théorie et pratique de la traduction au sein du Groupe de Coppet" [Theory and Practice of Translation in the Coppet Group], in the proceedings of the 1974 colloquium on *Le Groupe de Coppet*, edited by Simone Balaye and Jean-Daniel Candaux). In her renderings of Goethe's lyrical poems in her *De l'Allemagne* (1810), considered her most important work of theory, she translates literally, neglecting the syntax and metrics that give Goethe's verse the rhythm and musicality he judged central to language. Goethe advocated neither free nor faithful translation, but a third kind of synthesis through an etymological literalness in which the translation would itself become an original. A scandal to poetic convention, Staël's translations exemplified the foreignizing, extroverted theory of translation she favoured along with Goethe, where one recognizes the foreign language and culture in a "reciprocal", not "exclusive", valorization. Translation serves to innovate, dynamize, and stimulate creativity, Staël affirmed in "De l'esprit des traductions" (1816); she considered translation a commerce necessary for every country to keep its national literature vital: translations of rare works of genius of "the human spirit" were needed to sweep away obsolete conventions. Central to this idealist theory, which she advocated against the materialism of the French and their introverted or naturalizing practices, where they contain foreign works monotonously in the circle of French conventions, is the need to avoid the uniformity of lines and rhymes of French classicism. Varying Goethe's lines and rhyming with no fixed pattern, de Staël effectively broke with French prosody, but without, however, working on language to make the translations into poems. Her translations did produce cultural difference, ironically through their privileging of content over music. Her oeuvre is a valorization of the process of translation over original "uncontaminated" texts.

Staël's writing had a decisive impact on feminism, particularly through her comparative analyses of the disparate status of women in different cultures. *Corinne, ou l'Italie* (1807), her fiction analysing the contingencies for women writers, launched "the myth of Corinne" or "the sovereign independence of genius" as intellectual freedom for women (Ellen Moers, *Literary Women*, 1977), and lent its name to feminist theorist Margaret Fuller (1810–50), "the Yankee Corinna". Fuller's translations were acts not of modesty but of creative affirmation and feminist resistance. Though she was fluent in a number of languages, her early translations were mainly from German, the one language she taught herself. Her translations, which preceded her through the door of Ralph Waldo Emerson, were influential in transmitting the theories of German Romanticism to American Transcendentalists. Salient among texts translated by Fuller are two dialectically opposed: on the one hand Goethe's *Torquato Tasso* (1807, translated 1833), a play about power, poetics, and gender, outlining the tragedy of seduction along an axis of power, and on the other Bettina von Arnim's *Günderode* (1840, translated 1842), an epistolary novel in the form of the correspondence between two women, on the model of "conversation", with its concept of reciprocal relations that is central to Fuller's feminism (Christina Zwarg, "Feminism in Translation: Margaret Fuller's *Tasso*", *Studies in Romanticism*, 1990).

The controversial novel *Goethe's Conversations with a Child* was self-translated (1839) by von Arnim, who taught herself English for the purpose. As translator, she both protected her work and gave birth to it over again. Such control over her text is a forceful move of "self-promotion", affirms Marjanne Goozé ("A Language of Her Own: Bettina Brentano-von Arnim's Translation Theory and Her English Translation Project", *The Reception of Bettina Brentano-von Arnim*, 1984). This move occurred in a particular historical context, Goozé points out, when Romantic theorists sought to constitute translation as a productive, masculine practice. Translation in Germany in the 18th century had been a field dominated by women who came to authorship through translating: Luise Kulmus Gottsched, Dorothea Schlegel, Caroline Schlegel-Schelling, Sophie Mereau, Henriette Schubart. Though von Arnim remained within the prescribed gendered reproductive role in translating her book, this held a different meaning within the changed "masculine" values for translation in the 19th century. She undertook this translation partly to implant Goethe on foreign soil – "to find a new fatherland for this book of love" – but also out of frustration with her English translators. Relying in Romantic fashion on "the unconscious and genius" (Goozé), her translation is source-text oriented, and germanizes the English language. She produces numerous neologisms. "My new English language", as she calls it, was deemed too "exotic" by English reviewers who were particularly disturbed by the erotic element in the imaginative enthusiasms and "strange etymologies" of the text.

This doubly-signed and scandalous translation contrasts greatly with the more self-effacing practices of most English female translators from German during the 19th-century. Sarah Austin, the foremost of these, was a less self-confident translator than von Arnim. Though she argued for the estranging mode of translation that moved the reader towards the author and attributed to the translator the status of creative writer, she expressed her uneasiness in a review where she wrote of having to secure herself "behind the welcome defence of inverted commas" (Susanne Stark, "Women and Translation in the Nineteenth Century," *New Comparison* 1993). George Eliot [Marian Evans], the most famous of the women translators from German, began her literary career with translations of theological works by Strauss (1846) and Feuerbach (1854), to which she appended no signature or preface. Stark probes the contradiction between the professional and creative demands of translation – requiring entrepreneurial skills, as well as study and travel, much less compatible with domestic duties than creative writing – and the hesitant stances of translators such as Lucy Duff-Gordon (Sarah Austin's daughter), the sisters Susanna and Catherine Winkworth, Edith Simcox, Mary Howitt, Elizabeth Eastlake, Mathilde Blind, and Anna Swanwick, as revealed in their prefaces, letters,and other texts published and unpublished. She concludes that for this group of women "translation was a specifically female flight from public recognition". Cultural as well as historical differences in the articulation of gender are highlighted by these discrepancies in German–English translation relations in the 18th and 19th centuries.

Gender in the Geopolitics of Translation

Gender is not the only system by which power captures subjects. Racial taxonomies are other effects of power imbalances in the wake of imperialism that valorize bodies differently. The relative might and capital of nations creates unequal relations between languages in the international arena. In its concern to expose complex relations of power, contemporary feminism has focused considerable attention on the specificities of racialized inequalities as these intersect with gender. The single most important book in the field of gender and translation (*Translating Slavery: Gender and Race in French Women's Writing, 1783–1823*, edited by Doris Kadish and Françoise Massardier-Kenney, 1994) addresses the intertwined strands of gender and race in the translation of anti-slavery writings produced by a complex translating network in which Germaine de Staël is again a central figure, embodying "the ideal of translator", according to Massardier-Kenney. *Translating Slavery* is a collaborative work of translation theory and practice. Arguing that any translation theory is embedded in a specific translation practice, the editors present a complex interweaving of French texts, English translations, theoretical essays, historical analyses, and dialogues between translators. The contributors stage the dynamics of translating across historical periods and between cultures in their renderings of texts by Olympe de Gouges (1748–93), Germaine de Staël and Claire de Duras (1778–1828), produced in relation to the rapidly shifting political positions on race and gender equality following the French revolution. The 20th-century feminist translators adopt Staël's foreignizing model of translation, emphasizing her idea of culture based on differences and cross-influences where translation functions as an agent of change. Contextual analysis provides detailed illustration of the ideological nature of translation and of the complex positioning of the three French authors' mediation between the contradictory paradigms of their class allegiances and their emancipatory attitudes to gender and race. Resisting the temptation to translate for coherence or 20th-century "political correctness", while making the text "culturally fluent", requires a translation strategy attentive to the traces of historicity. Translation is understood in this book as "linguistic mediation", a significant component of cultural hegemony: it may contribute to the repression of difference as part of a process of domination or function to valorize difference or resistance to dominant cultural forms. This collaborative project is directed to redressing the power imbalances that subordinated Africans and women in the 18th century and opposing discourses of racism and sexism today.

In its careful enfolding of the text in many texts that contextualize all the voices – of Africans, French women writers, and American and African American women translators – *Translating Slavery* exemplifies the ethical translation advocated by Gayatri Spivak in "The Politics of Translation" (*Destabilizing Theory: Contemporary Feminist Debates*, edited by Michèle Barrett and Anne Phillips, 1992). Situating translation as a critical project within the parameters of changing political relations between cultures has been Spivak's singular achievement. Her formulation of the centrality of translation to counter-hegemonic resistance to imperialism directed feminist translation studies in the 1990s to post-colonial discourse. Spivak has persistently challenged the universalist claims of feminist solidarity. Critiquing the exclusive focus on sexual difference that would relate women only in their difference from men, she urges feminism to attend to the differences among women. "First World feminists" must learn enough about "Third World women" to understand the "immense heterogeneity of the field". Spivak has shown how translation, with its sensitivity to linguistic difference, might foster anti-imperialist critique. Translation of non-European languages into English, working "across an epistemic divide", is a "different political exercise" from translation between European languages. Crucial here is the prestige of the languages paired in translation within the unequal cross-cultural relations in the wake of imperialism. Spivak advocates an estranging model of translation to reverse the hierarchy, in a deconstructive move that brings the First World reader to the Third World text. Translation would then revise the terms of cultural exchange that have advantaged the colonizing First World. Spivak's emphasis on the relations of address enacts a further deconstructive move to place the social context before the rhetorical forms in meaning-making and so make a case for translation as social action.

Spivak's materialist theory of translation as politicized address informs her practice in *Imaginary Maps* (1995), her English translation of the Bengali writer Mahasweta Devi. A complex text, consisting of an interview with Devi, a preface by Spivak, three translated stories of Devi, and an afterword on translation, it is framed rhetorically to critique political debates on minority cultures in both India and the United States, where it is jointly published. Spivak reshapes Bengali literature into both an Anglo-American and an Indian frame, but changes the terms of cultural reception by means of a dual counter-hegemonic strategy. Her abrupt syntax and "Afterword" draw attention to linguistic difference. The "Translator's Preface" argues for *différance* or contamination, against the claims of ethnic purity that would produce a binary opposition between the US and India, and counters criticisms that her English is not accessible to Indian readers. Her "American-based" idiom, where slang terms such as "chick" and "what a dish" defamiliarize the "subcontinental idiom", challenges Indian cultural nativism. The tribals, as Devi points out, have paid the heavy price of decolonization in being oppressed by that nationalism too. Spivak's translation strategy challenges the norms of cultural fluency in both US and Indian Englishes. Spivak's translation should be compared with the translations of Devi's work in process at the Bengal-based Seagull Foundation by a number of translators, including Parameeta Banerjee, to see whether these turn Devi into a Bengali "cultural exhibit" or further her anti-hegemonic project.

Concern is voiced by Susie Tharu and other editors of *Women Writing in India* (1991) over the political effects of their translations into English, language of imperialism, from a variety of regional languages. How to produce local knowledge in a global language is a problem the editors tackle in their preface. This preface provides a framework for conceptualizing the translation acts of minority groups in other multilingual countries.

The anthologizing and translating project of *Women Writing in India* has stimulated African feminists to plan a similar anthology that would gather items representing the historical range and regional variety of women's textual productions in Africa to make them available for other African readers as well as an international audience. Scrupulous attention to the rhetorical effects of translation in the context of globalization is necessary to prevent assimilation and the erasure of socio-political particularity. Spivak's injunction to present subaltern women as agents of history offering resistance within the inequities of imperialist hegemonies has furthered the question of translation in post-colonial studies. American critics Humm and Alarcón's interest in La Malincha, the Amerindian woman interpreter for Cortés in Mexico, is evidence of how the subaltern speaks through and against translation. Feminist scholars examining the translating activities of Amerindian women in Canada focus on the problem of reading through the colonial archive to locate such acts of resistance as exemplified in Julia Emberley's " 'A Gift for Languages': Native Women and the Textual Economy of the Colonial Archive" (*Cultural Critique*, 1990) and Barbara Godard's "Writing between Cultures" (*TTR*, 1997).

Historical analysis of gender and translation, and *Women Writing in India*'s influence in Africa, demonstrate the critical importance of the convergence of a lively feminist discourse and an active culture of translation for the dissemination of feminist translation theory and practice. Important too are institutions for channelling women's transmission of knowledge outside the dominant lines of tradition. Since the 1970s, feminist periodicals and publishing houses have provided a radical context from which to challenge established structures of knowledge and power and constitute other instances of legitimation in the production of cultural value. Much of the active debate on gender and translation has been stimulated by practices of translating women's creative and intellectual texts for the cross-cultural publications that have been of increasing interest to women's studies courses in the academy and to feminist presses such as the Feminist Press, co-publisher with Kali for Women of *Women Writing in India*.

Evidence of the necessity for the conjuncture of feminist centres and a translating culture in the geopolitics of translation may be found in the different significance accorded translation within feminist approaches to post-colonialism in Australia and the Caribbean in contrast to India and Canada. Translation has received almost no attention in the former instances. In the latter countries, problems of linguistic authority and dominance of one linguistic group over another highlight translation's role as politicized utterance in the making and crossing of intra-national boundaries. The participation of a Canadian feminist translator at a conference on Feminist Cultural Production in Australia (1986) had no lasting effect in a country that produces few translations. Translation has figured in the Caribbean context only in the case of multilingual Surinam, where there are few women writers (Petronella Breinburg in *Framing the Word: Gender and Genre in Caribbean Women's Writing*, edited by Joan Anim-Addo, 1996).

The institutional structures organizing translation also have a major impact on the development of a theorized reflection on the ideological dimensions of gender in translation. In the United States and Canada, the emergence of feminist theory and analysis of translation was prompted by the major role played by academics in literary translation, especially in the translation of linguistically experimental texts. Translation in this case belongs to a restricted field of production, in contrast to the large-scale market- and profit-oriented production of translation that characterizes the cultural field in countries with a high volume of translation such as Japan, Sweden, and Germany, where full-time translators assigned texts to translate have a limited self-consciousness of authorship. Canadian feminist translators have created contexts for feminist translation, participating frequently together in periodicals, at conferences, and on panels, and this networking has extended to feminist translators and theorists in Europe, where there have been few such communities legitimating work in gender and translation. Like traditions, communities for the transmission of knowledge need to be created. While resident in Germany, Canadian translator Luise von Flotow initiated such encounters, organizing a panel on gender and translation for the EST Congress in Prague (1995) that included the feminist translation theorists Jane Batchelor, Karin Littau, Eithne O'Connell, and Beate Thill. This involved a group different from that gathered by Myriam Diaz-Diocaretz at a mini-conference on gender and translation within the context of "The Politics of Feminist Theory" at Dubrovnik (1988), which brought together women such as Nicole Ward Jouve, Alice Parker, Rada Ivecovic, Liana Borghi, Marina Camboni, and Barbara Godard. That two of these translators were Italian should come as no surprise, given the convergence of theory and translation in the dynamic Italian feminist community.

The reworking of translation theory shows how textual meaning is continually being re-evaluated from a different historical or ideological position. Translation as the mediator of continuity and change has increasingly become the vehicle through which social crisis is negotiated. Considered as a category of thought, translation has become a figure for movement or transformation. As such, it is a sign of cultural force fields. Since the 1970s, gender has been one of the social practices in crisis and in turn a significant force in the field of translation studies. That entries on gender and translation are being included in encyclopedias of translation, that two major works of synthesis have appeared outlining – albeit with differing orientations – the history and theoretical contributions of gender to translation studies (Sherry Simon's *Gender in Translation: Cultural Identity and the Politics of Transmission*, 1996, with a section on the translation of French feminism into English; and Luise von Flotow's *Translation and Gender: Translating in the "Era of Feminism"*, 1997, with a focus on contemporary translation practices in Germany) would seem to indicate that questions of gender, and with them those of cultural difference, have changed the terms of exchange and meaning in translation studies.

BARBARA GODARD

Further Reading

Allen, Beverly, "Paralysis, Crutches, Wings: Italian Feminisms and Transculturation", *Surfaces* (electronic journal: www.pum.umontreal.ca/revues/surfaces/home.html), 3/4 (1993) pp. 1–25

Flotow, Luise von, *Translation and Gender: Translating in the "Era of Feminism"*, Manchester: St Jerome, and Ottawa: University of Ottawa Press, 1997 (with bibliography)

Godard, Barbara, *Gender and Translation: A Bibliography*, Ottawa: CRIAW, 2001

Simon, Sherry, *Gender in Translation: Cultural Identity and the Politics of Transmission*, London and New York: Routledge, 1996 (with bibliography)
Stark, Susanne, *'Behind Inverted Commas': Translation and Anglo-German Cultural Relations in the Nineteenth Century*, Clevedon: Multilingual Matters, 1998

Special Issues of Periodicals
Journal of Feminist Studies in Religion, 6/2 (1990): "Feminist Translation of the New Testament"
Journal of Modern Greek Studies, 8 (1990) pp. 169–244: "Translation and Deterritorialization"
Signs: Journal of Women in Culture and Society, 7/1 (1981): "French Feminist Theory"
Tessera, 6 (1989): "La Traduction au féminin / Translating Women"
Translation Review, 17 (1985): "Women in Translation"
TTR: Traduction, Terminologie, Rédaction, 4/2 (1991): "Translating Theory"
Yale French Studies, 62 (1981): "Feminist Readings: French Texts/American Contexts"
Yale French Studies, 87 (1995): "Another Look, Another Woman: Retranslations of French Feminism"

German

Literary Translation into English

The Language

The earliest records written in German (more properly called High German, to distinguish this variety from the Low German group of languages, such as English and Dutch, which went unmarked by the so-called High German consonant shifts c.500 AD) come down to us from the 8th-century AD in a variety of dialects (Franconian, Bavarian, Thuringian, Alemannic and others). Notions of a standard German arose only in the 16th century when the religious reformer Martin Luther used the variety known as "East Central German" as the medium for his celebrated Bible translation (1522–45), an immensely influential literary monument later used as a storehouse of idioms by writers as diverse as Goethe and Brecht. It was a modernized, Leipzig variety of the East Central German used by Luther that emerged as the modern standard when it was endorsed by the critic, author, lexicographer and translator J.C. Gottsched in his *Grundlegung einer Deutschen Sprachkunst* [Principles of the Art of Good German] (1748) and used creatively by Goethe, Schiller and Lessing in the later 18th century.

Modern German is an inflected language with fixed syntactical rules governing clausal word order and a non-logical gender system. These basic characteristics of German do not present unusually severe problems for the translator into English, though the compactness of meaning and structure achieved in German by such features as nouns formed by composition or preceded by complex adjectival phrases may sometimes be difficult to match in the target language.

Like English, German is a "pluricentric" language, with several national varieties. Besides the almost 80 million inhabitants of the recently united German state the main German-speaking populations are in: Austria (7.5 million German speakers); Switzerland (4.2 million German speakers, representing 74 per cent of the population, the rest of whom speak either French or Italian or Rhaeto-Romansh); Luxembourg (330,000 citizens who are "triglossic" in German with French and Luxembourgish); Liechtenstein (15,000 German speakers). German also has an important role in Eastern Europe as a lingua franca between Poles, Czechs and Hungarians, and is spoken in certain parts of Italy (Tyrol), Belgium and France (Alsace). In some cases German exists in a state of tension with other languages spoken in the same state. This is especially likely to be the case in areas affected by the 20th-century world wars such as Alsace-Lorraine (the French *départements* of Haut-Rhin, Bas-Rhin and Moselle) where German-teaching was banned after 1945. Meanwhile in Switzerland a *modus vivendi* between the four language communities has traditionally been forged out of the desire to defend Swiss identity against external threats, while the inhabitants of trilingual Luxembourg play the language card with some political skill and much tactical code-switching.

In theory, all the distinct national varieties above have equal status, but in practice the language of Germany itself forms the standard among them. (This can be observed in the way that, when people from different German-language countries wish to communicate, they tend to converge with the federal German standard.) Since, then, Germany exercises considerable power through its own national variety, other German-speaking countries are apt to interpret this as cultural imperialism and (with memories of the period 1933–45 in mind) to remain wary of the reunited Germany.

No other European vernacular has been so widely or so unfortunately "politicized" as German in the 20th century. The classical standard established by Goethe and Schiller (together with the whole humane legacy that it had encoded) was, in the opinion of many, terminally tainted by the linguistic mendacities of the Nazi propaganda machine, an effect further exacerbated by what was referred to at the height of the Cold War as the "linguistic division" (*Sprachspaltung*) between the two German states in the period 1945–90. It was widely contended that the Iron Curtain separating the communist East Germany (German Democratic Republic) and the capitalist West (Federal Republic of Germany) was also a form of semantic curtain. That is, East German was taking all manner of Russian loan words and Communist discourse into its lexicon (so it was charged), while West German was becoming excessively influenced by Americanisms (held by many in the East to be a regrettable linguistic homage to the Cold War enemy). It appears, even after the unification of 1990, that these erstwhile attempts to demonize the political discourse of "the other side" are doing lasting damage to the attempts presently being made to forge a truly unified German state.

Such political factors have led many German writers and intellectuals, in the course of the 20th century, to a radical distrust of their own language (*Sprachskepsis*). Post-war poets such as Paul Celan typically made an "attempt to deform, estrange and rejuvenate a language that had, so many felt, become stale and soiled" (Siegbert Prawer), by a use of non-existent or bizarre punctuation or by breaking up received sentence structures – all as a studied counterblast to the easily assimilable disinformation of the Nazis or of any other groups of "hidden persuaders". In and since the 1990s – a legitimately sceptical time that has progressed far beyond the Enlightenment certainties from which the proclamation of a standard language had originally proceeded – fewer German literary intellectuals are willing to entertain the notion of an "ideal" German (in either the grammatical or the philosophical sense of that term) than was ever the case heretofore. On the practical level, on the other hand, prospects seem to be good for German playing an important role as an international language of trade and communication in the next century within the expanded European market – a precedent for which was provided by the Hanseatic League of the later Middle Ages.

NEIL THOMAS

Further Reading

Barbour, Stephen and Patrick Stevenson, *Variation in German: A Critical Approach to German Sociolinguistics*, Cambridge and New York: Cambridge University Press, 1990

Blackall, Eric A., *The Emergence of German as a Literary Language, 1700–1775*, Cambridge: Cambridge University Press, 1959; 2nd edition, Ithaca, New York: Cornell University Press

Clyne, Michael G., *Language and Society in the German-Speaking Countries*, Cambridge and New York: Cambridge University Press, 1984

Good, Colin, "The Linguistic Division of Germany: Myth or Reality?", *New German Studies*, 2 (1974) pp. 96–115

Leopold, W.F., *English Influence on Postwar German*, Lincoln: University of Nebraska, 1967

Stern, J.P., *Hitler: The Führer and the People*, London: Collins, and Berkeley: University of California Press, 1975

Thomas, Neil, *The German Language in Europe: Historical and Political Dimensions*, Durham: Publications of the Centre for European Studies, 1994

Weinreich, Uriel, *Languages in Contact: Findings and Problems*, with a preface by André Martinet, New York: Linguistic Circle of New York, 1953

Wells, C.J., *German: A Linguistic History to 1945*, Oxford: Clarendon Press, and New York: Oxford University Press, 1985

16th and 17th Centuries

While a sustained awareness of a German literary culture begins in the English-speaking world only in the last decades of the 18th century, the history of translation can be traced back to the publication in 1509 of two versions of Sebastian Brant's satirical *Narrenschiff* (1494). Admittedly, Alexander Barclay's *Shyp of Folys* freely adapted an already free Latin rendering by Jakob Locher (1497), and the version by Henry Watson was based on a French redaction. Dutch or Low German might be known to Englishmen through trade relations, but not the "speche of hye Almayne", unless, like fugitive English reformers, they spent protracted periods in Germany. Lutheran treatises, indeed, make up a high proportion of 16th-century translations from the German, from the mid-1530s onwards. Several were translated by Miles Coverdale, who also drew in part on Luther for his Bible translation, while his *Goostly Psalmes and Spiritual Songs* (1539) derived substantially from Luther's hymns.

The secular literary works translated or adapted from the vernacular belonged essentially to the robust "Volksbuch" tradition of popular narratives, which had an international appeal with their emblematic figures of the jester, the trickster, the necromancer. Earliest extant are the jest-book *The Parson of Kalenboroue* (from an original of c. 1475) and an English version of the Till Eulenspiegel material, both printed by Jan van Doersborch in Antwerp, c.1519. Most resonant of all such narratives is the *Faust*-book printed in German by Johann Spiess in 1587, rapidly anglicized by one "P.F., gent." as *The Historie of the damnable life, and deserued death of doctor John Faustus* (very likely by 1589). Later comes the romance of *Fortunatus*, in a first extant edition of 1640, though Thomas Dekker had already drawn on the material in his *Pleasant Comedie of Old Fortunatus*, printed 1600, possibly based on a Dutch version of the German folk-book.

English knowledge of German literature would long be confined to tales of Faust and Fortunatus and Eulenspiegel, their enduring popularity evident from reprintings well into the 18th century. Nothing was transmitted of the 17th-century literature that turns its back on such rough-hewn traditions and finds inspiration in Classical, especially Latin, literature and the Renaissance poetry and poetics of France, Italy and Spain. Translations from German in this era comprise works of scholarship, books of travel, or theosophical and medico-alchemical treatises by Paracelsus (1493–1541), to whose early fame references in Shakespeare and Jonson attest. Most striking are the 25 and more volumes of mystical writings of Jakob Böhme (1575–1624) that appeared between 1645 and 1665, predominantly in translations by the lawyer and mystic John Sparrow or his associate John Ellistone. The one great novel of the age, Grimmelshausen's picaresque *Simplicissimus* (1669), was first translated into English in 1912. Only in respect of the hymn and spiritual song are there relatively early traces of the poetry that otherwise yields the finest achievements of the century. Poems by Angelus Silesius or Paul Gerhardt, Simon Dach or Friedrich von Spee trickle into English hymnals, partly mediated by German Pietist circles in London: the *Lyra Davidica* (1708), the *Psalmodia Germanica* (1722), compiled by Johann Christian Jacobi and Isaac Watts, and collections by John and Charles Wesley (*Psalms and Hymns*, 1737; *German Hymns*, 1742). The first truly representative anthology of 17th-century poetry derives from modern scholarship: George Schoolfield's *The German Lyric of the Baroque in English Translation* (1961).

18th Century

Translations of Gellert's Richardsonian novel *The Swedish Countess* (1747–48, translated 1752) and G.W. Rabener's *Satirical Letters* (1751–55, translated 1757) are the first halting responses to a newly emergent German literature in the mid-18th century. Wide attention was first engaged by the Swiss pastoralist Salomon Gessner (1730–88), already a cult-figure in France: by his *Idylls* and especially his religious epic *The Death of Abel*, which in Mary Collyer's prose version (1761) was continually reprinted in England and America until well into the 19th century. *The Death of Abel's* much greater model, Klopstock's *Messiah* (1748–73), had much less success, being long known only in a distortive, arbitrarily augmented prose rendering of the first 16 cantos by Joseph Collyer (translated 1763–71). By contrast, Wieland (1733–1813), the other author then frequently translated, appealing by his urbanity and eclectic openness to English, French and Classical influences, elicited the most accomplished translations of the age: his novels *Agathon* and *Reason Triumphant over Fancy* (translated 1773), both rendered by John Richardson, whose preface to *Agathon* displayed a grasp of German literary developments exceptional for a time when command of the very language was still a rarity; and William Sotheby's translation (1798) of the verse narrative *Oberon*, commended by Wieland himself as "a genuine masterpiece", with "all the grace and delicacy of the original" (praise that led John Quincy Adams to withdraw his own fine translation, done while the future sixth President of the US was on diplomatic service in Berlin).

Goethe's *Werther* (1774) reached England in 1779. Even in a truncated version of an already incomplete French rendering, it excited a feverish reaction of praise or denunciation and spawned a host of "Wertheriana": dramatization (Frederick Reynolds, 1785), poems, prose "sequels", prints, porcelain, a waxwork display. Five more translations appeared by 1802. Despite this – or perhaps because the process of absorption detached the work from its German context – its reception remained "self-contained", stimulating little curiosity as to other works of Goethe (1749–1832) and no increase in the number of German works translated; rather, the number declined in the 1780s, before an upsurge in the 1790s.

An interest in drama, focus of the most progressive energies in German literature of the 1770s and 1780s, was sparked by Henry MacKenzie's "Account of the German Theatre", first delivered to the Royal Society of Edinburgh in 1788 and based on French sources, chiefly Friedel and de Bonneville's *Nouveau Théâtre allemand* (12 vols, 1782–85). Singled out by Mackenzie as "one of the most uncommon productions of untutored genius that modern times can boast", *The Robbers* (1781), by Schiller (1759–1805), was then translated in 1792 by Alexander Tytler. "My God, Southey, who is this Schiller, this convulser of the heart? ... I tremble like an aspen leaf", wrote Coleridge on his first encounter with the play in 1794. There followed *Cabal and Love* (1784, translated 1795; also adapted by M.G. "Monk" Lewis as *The Minister*, 1797), *Fiesco* (1783, translated 1796), and four versions of *Don Carlos* (1787, translated 1795–1801). English publishers had so caught up with Schiller's output that both Coleridge's celebrated translation (1800) of *The Piccolomini* and *The Death of Wallenstein* and J.C. Mellish's *Mary Stuart* (translated 1801) even appeared before the first German book editions of these plays. Goethe was overshadowed, though some translations did appear: a minor piece *The Sisters* (1776, translated 1792), then *Iphigenia in Tauris* (1787, translated 1793), both done by William Taylor of Norwich, the most dedicated champion of German literature before Carlyle, and belatedly his "Sturm und Drang" dramas *Clavigo* (1774) and *Stella* (1776), both translated 1798, and at last *Götz von Berlichingen* (1773, translated 1799), its spirit caught by Walter Scott, if not the letter.

But British readers sooner thrilled to Bürger's (1774) ballad *Lenore*, of which there were five rival versions in 1796 (those by Taylor and Scott among them), or consumed popular fiction, be it sentimental "family" tales or more likely lurid "Germanico-terrifico" romances by such as Julius Grosse (*The Genius* and *The Dagger*, translated 1796), and tales of Romantic brigandry like Vulpius's *Rinaldo Rinaldini* (translated 1800) or Zschokke's *Abällino*, adapted as *The Bravo of Venice* (1804) by M.G. "Monk" Lewis, a particularly active mediator and imitator of these fictions. For a while, "a German story" meant to English readers a promise of thrills and frissons, not a threat of pedagogic earnestness; "from the German" became a catchpenny tag for many a confection of doubtful origin. And to theatre-goers in London or New York German drama meant overwhelmingly the comedies and melodramas of August von Kotzebue (1761–1819). Precipitants of his success were *The Stranger* (translated 1798), adapted by Sheridan from a literal translation of *Menschenhass und Reue*, and *Lovers' Vows*, similarly adapted by Elizabeth Inchbald. Between 1798 and 1801 at least 27 of Kotzebue's plays were translated or adapted, several in multiple versions. The year 1799 alone yielded more than 25 separate renderings. *Pizarro*, Sheridan's adaptation (one of six) of *Die Spanier in Peru* played continuously at Drury Lane and went through 20 editions in that one year. The most prolific translator was William Dunlap, whose New York company mounted 14 plays by Kotzebue in the season 1799–1800, accounting for more than half of all performances on the New York stage. Apart from the pioneering work of scholars such as William Bentley of Salem, American reception of German literature had hitherto been shaped by imported British translations and journal articles; Dunlap's astute adaptations of Kotzebue thus constitute the first substantial body of American translations from German.

19th Century

Kotzebue lingered in the repertoire, but a critical backlash disparaged German literature wholesale for excess of sentiment or sensation. In a political climate increasingly fearful of continental radicalism, the *Anti-Jacobin Review* branded German writers morally and politically subversive, "vauntcouriers of French anarchy", adding ridicule to invective, as in Canning and Frere's *The Rovers*, which mocks Kotzebue's *Stranger*, Goethe's *Stella* and Schiller's *Robbers*. Altogether, interest in German literature waned in the first decade of the 19th century, except for the dogged enthusiasms of individuals like William Taylor or Henry Crabb Robinson.

Madame de Staël's *De l'Allemagne*, suppressed in France and first published in London in 1813, stimulated renewed interest, offering a more sympathetic picture of the conditions of German social and intellectual life than any before, and a survey of German literature that was judiciously focused on major writers – Klopstock, Wieland, Lessing, in more detail Schiller, and at the centre Goethe – and characterized works barely heard of yet in Britain: *Egmont*, *Tasso*, *Die Wahlverwandschaften*, *Wilhelm Meister*, *Faust*, and not least Goethe's poetry, hitherto little noticed. De Staël's attention to the qualities of German education served too as a further stimulus to American scholars such as George Ticknor and Edward Everett, the first to travel to German universities and on their return highly influential mediators of German culture in America.

De Staël portrays a land of "poets and thinkers", not mere purveyors of meretricious sensation; and the prestige of German critical intelligence was further enhanced by the publication in 1815 of A.W. Schlegel's *Lectures on Dramatic Art and Literature*, translated by John Black. Welcomed far beyond the circles of "Germanists", these exerted a huge influence on subsequent discussion of drama, of Shakespeare especially. The year 1818 brought Friedrich Schlegel's *Lectures on the History of Literature, Ancient and Modern*. Their translator, J.G. Lockhart, having heard Fichte lecture and visited Goethe in Weimar, typified a new generation of mediators, whose specialist knowledge, moreover, was enlisted by new journals like *Blackwood's Magazine*, that provided a vital medium of informed discussion and transmission.

There is a surge in translation in the 1820s. Regular articles by R.P. Gillies in *Blackwood's* brought analyses and samples of contemporary dramatists: Müllner, Werner, and Grillparzer (1791–1872). Belated first translations of *The Maid of Orleans* (in 1824) and *William Tell* (1825; 1829), new versions of *Mary Stuart* and *Wallenstein*, and in 1828 two separate renderings of his *History of the Thirty Years War*, consolidate the re-evaluation of Schiller – no more the "untutored genius" and "Jacobin" – begun by Madame de Staël and reinforced by Carlyle's *Life of Schiller* (1823–24), with its emphasis on his "nobility and aspiring grandeur". Tokens of an interest in German lyric poetry, hitherto largely neglected, included *Specimens of German Lyric Poets*, translated by Benjamin Beresford and J.C. Mellish (1821). A renewed taste for German fiction brought first encounters with the German Romantics. None was more popular than Fouqué (1777–1843), whose *Undine* (translated 1818; for Southey "the most graceful fiction of modern times") and romances of knight-errantry, such as *Sintram* (translated 1820, by J.C. Hare) and *The Magic Ring* (translated 1825), were to make him the most frequently published German writer of fiction during the 19th century after the Brothers Grimm. The tales of Jacob Ludwig and Wilhelm Karl Grimm (1785–1863; 1786–1859) were first translated in a selection by Edgar Taylor as *German Popular Stories* (1824–26), illustrated by Cruikshank. E.T.A. Hoffmann (1776–1822) was represented by his novel *The Devil's Elixir* (translated by R. Gillies, 1824), and by stories such as *The Entail* and *Mademoiselle de Scudéry* in Gillies's *German Stories* and Richard Holcraft's *Tales from the German*, two of four substantial collections that appeared in 1826 alone.

Much the most influential mediator was Thomas Carlyle. His *German Romance* (4 vols, 1827) offered further texts by Fouqué, Hoffmann, Tieck (1773–1853) and Jean Paul Richter (1763–1825), whose influence is apparent in the narrative mode of Carlyle's *Sartor Resartus*; and it brought the second volume of his translation (1824–27) of Goethe's *Wilhelm Meister*. In imperious articles, notably his "State of German Literature" (1827), Carlyle confronted the charges of "mysticism" and "bad taste" still levelled against that literature. Above all, when Goethe's work was still little known beyond *Werther* and widely impugned as immoral, Carlyle championed him as both "a new Poet for the World" and a sage, "Instructor and Preacher of Truth to all men", who "loves and has practised as a man the wisdom which, as a poet, he inculcates". This view of Goethe as spiritual mentor decisively shaped English perceptions for long after, and shifted the image of German literature as a whole ever more in the direction of a literature of ideas.

The "author of *Werther*" now becomes pre-eminently "the author of *Faust*". Abraham Hayward's prose rendering (1833) of *Faust*, part 1, the first reliable basis for comprehension of a text hitherto available only in extract or travesty, was followed in the 1830s alone by a further seven translations and two early attempts at part 2. By the end of the 19th century there would be some 35 different versions, the most successful being those by Anna Swanwick (part 1, 1849; part 2, 1879) and Bayard Taylor (parts 1 and 2, Boston 1871), recycled since in countless British and American editions. Amid the controversies that attended American Goethe-reception in the 1830s and 1840s there appeared notable pioneering translations such as J.S. Dwight's *Select Minor Poems of Goethe and Schiller* (1839), the Goethe–Schiller correspondence (translated 1845, by G.H. Calvert), Goethe's autobiography (translated by Parke Godwin *et al.*, 1846), and Eckermann's *Conversations with Goethe*, translated in 1839 by Margaret Fuller, Goethe's staunchest Transcendentalist champion in the face of an enduring puritan objection to his alleged moral delinquencies, even from otherwise admiring commentators like Emerson.

In mid-century came a group of translations absorbed into or commissioned for Bohn's Standard Library series; cumulatively, the Goethe volumes in this series (14 by 1890) became in effect, and *faute de mieux*, the "standard" select edition. They included John Oxenford's translations of the autobiography (1848–49) and *Conversations with Eckermann and Soret* (1850), which owed much to Godwin and Fuller; a volume *Dramatic Works* (1850), with Swanwick's translations of *Iphigenie*, *Egmont* and *Tasso*, beside her *Faust 1*; and *Novels and Tales* (1854), which included a much improved *Werther* (by R.D. Boylan) and at last an *Elective Affinities*, done anonymously by J.A. Froude. Most of Goethe's major writings were thus accessible to the English-reading public by 1855, when G.H. Lewes's *Life of Goethe* sealed his integration within the cultural horizons of the educated Victorian.

Until mid-century, Schiller matched Goethe in the attention of commentators and translators, enjoying in America especially an uncontroversial prestige, being played up by some as an icon of integrity against the "licentious" Goethe. Not just as a dramatist: up to 1860 Schiller's poems and ballads were more widely translated than those of any other German poet (some 30 versions of his "Song of the Bell" had appeared in Britain by 1850), and had been comprehensively translated by Edward Bulwer-Lytton (1844). Schiller too is enshrined in Bohn's Standard Library with his *Works, Historical and Dramatic* (1846–49), in which new translations by such as Boylan (*Don Carlos*), Swanwick (*The Maid of Orleans*) and Theodore Martin (*William Tell*) were added to the fine earlier work of Coleridge and Mellish.

Such was the focus on Goethe and Schiller in the 1830s and 1840s that few other writers engaged sustained attention during that time. One was Jean Paul Richter, who, after De Quincey's and Carlyle's earlier advocacy, was much admired and discussed by Margaret Fuller and other Transcendentalists; some of his major novels, e.g. *Siebenkäs* and *Flegeljahre* (translated 1846 as *Walt and Vult*), appeared in English or American translation in the 1840s; others followed in the 1860s (*Titan*, *Hesperus*). Novalis (1772–1801) was similarly admired, but little translated, though belated first complete versions of his *Hymns to the Night* and his novel *Heinrich von Ofterdingen* appeared in 1841 and 1842. Of major Romantic writers, Brentano (1778–1842) and Eichendorff (1788–1857) remained barely known. Hölderlin (1770–1843) was quite unknown, and scant attention was paid to Kleist (1777–1811) (notwithstanding an extract from *The Prince of Homburg* by Gillies, 1827, and the inclusion of *Michael Kohlhaas* in John Oxenford's *Tales from the German*, 1844), but then neither writer was yet adequately recognized in Germany itself.

Heine (1797–1856), by contrast, assumed a status second only to Goethe in English perceptions, once early hostility yielded in the mid-1850s, at the painful end of his life, to celebration of "a surpassing lyric poet" (George Eliot, 1856), an artist "who has shown even more completely than Goethe the artistic possibilities of German prose"; for Matthew Arnold he was in his "intense modernism" heir to Goethe as "dissolvent" of inherited dogmas and traditions. Individual poems appeared in innumerable versions in journals and the now proliferating anthologies; selecting the "best" renderings (1887), Kate Freiligrath-Kroeker drew upon 32 different translators, including Longfellow, James Thompson and Elizabeth Barrett Browning. A purportedly "complete" edition of his poetry was published in 1859 by the tireless, if uninspired, Edgar Bowring, after his comprehensive volumes of Goethe's and Schiller's poetry. Far superior versions came soon from America (where a pirate first collected edition in German sold in some 18,000 sets by 1864): Charles Godfrey Leland's *Book of Songs* (translated 1864) and Emma Lazarus's *Poems and Ballads of Heine* (1881). Having already in 1855 translated the *Pictures of Travel*, Leland would later contribute all eight volumes of prose in the 12-volume *Works of Heine* issued between 1892 and 1905. The American tradition has since been sustained by Louis Untermeyer (*The Poems of Heinrich Heine*, 1916, augmented 1938), and Hal Draper, whose *Complete Poems of Heinrich Heine* (1982) is one of the outstanding achievements in recent translation of German literature.

Except in response to Heine – or Wagner (there are numerous versions of his libretti and his treatises) – there is little trace in the second half of the century of the fervour and spirit of discovery that had animated earlier critics and translators in Britain and America. Victorian intellectual interests, formerly engaged by a broadly philosophical focus on German literature, were moving by mid-century to other areas of German intellectual life: to historiography (Sarah Austin, for one, turned from Goethe to translation of Ranke, Raumer, Niebuhr), to philosophy or to theology and the higher criticism (George Eliot translated D.F. Strauss's *Life of Jesus*, in 1846, and Feuerbach's *The Essence of Christianity*, in 1854).

In purely quantitative terms, none the less, translation of German literature into English continued to increase until the late 1880s. There were ever more editions of Goethe and of the Grimms' tales, many still of Schiller. Contemporary fiction was routinely reviewed in leading periodicals and more extensively translated than might be inferred from the scarce translations of the writers now most prized: an early collection of stories by Adalbert Stifter (translated 1850–51), Theodor Storm's *Immensee* (translated 1863, 1881), a handful of tales by Gottfried Keller, two novels by Wilhelm Raabe (*Abu Telfan*, translated 1881; *The Hunger Pastor*, translated 1885), and none of Theodor Fontane's novels in the US before 1914, in Britain before 1964. But this, and the converse, reflected patterns of reception in Germany itself. Widely translated from the 1850s to the 1870s were, instead, the "village tales" of Berthold Auerbach (1812–82) and the adventure stories of Friedrich Gerstäcker (1861–72), their appeal enhanced by their American settings. Gustav Freytag's *Debit and Credit* (1855) generated three rival versions in 1857–58; subsequent decades brought novels by Friedrich Spielhagen (1829–1911) and Paul Heyse (1830–1914) and, prolifically translated in the 1880s and 1890s, the voluminous historical fiction of Georg Ebers (1837–98). In America, additionally, there was a vogue, assiduously promoted, for the sentimental romances of Luise Mühlbach and the family magazine sorority of Eugenie Marlitt, E. Werner, and W. Heimburg (pseudonyms all).

Yet here was little to sustain serious interest, let alone compete with the urgent claims of Zola or Ibsen or the Russian literature in the process of discovery from the mid-1880s on.

20th Century

In the 1890s and early 1900s, when in addition political tensions engendered a climate of increasing suspicion, the number of British translations from German fell steeply. If the new generation of writers were translated, it was primarily in the United States, much appearing in the Boston journal *Poet Lore*. Nietzsche (1844–1900), first translated in 1896, was the one writer to have a substantial following in Britain, celebrated as "transvaluer" of values for the modern age or, come 1914, demonized as war-mongering "German monster Nietzsky". An 18-volume collected edition, edited by Oscar Levy, was completed by 1913. Otherwise, the dramatists Hauptmann (1862–1946) and Sudermann (1857–1928) were the new writers most extensively translated before World War I, and they could number Edith Wharton and the young James Joyce among their translators. A blend of Naturalistic "daring" and *pièce bien faite* routine ensured Sudermann the wider currency on stage – his *Magda* (*Heimat*, first translated 1896) played in London and New York variously with Sarah Bernhardt, Mrs Patrick Campbell, Eleonora Duse – while Hauptmann won the greater critical respect, culminating in 1912 with the Nobel Prize and the launch of Ludwig Lewisohn's edition of his *Dramatic Works* (9 vols, 1912–29).

Other important new writers were first translated around 1910. Granville Barker's "paraphrase" of *Anatol* (1893, translated 1911) encouraged a wider interest in Schnitzler (1862–1931). Plays by Hofmannsthal (1877–1929) were explored in the wake of his celebrity as librettist after *Elektra* (1909) and *Der Rosenkavalier* (1912). From *Spring Awakening* (1891, translated 1909) to *Pandora's Box* (1895, translated 1918), the major plays of Wedekind (1864–1918) appeared in American translation. All these authors are represented in the Harvard-based series *The German Classics of the Nineteenth and Twentieth Centuries*, edited by Kuno Francke (20 vols, 1913–15), which both consolidated a familiar canon of Classical and Romantic texts and offered a more judicious representation of later 19th-century writing than any before. Here were the first English translations of novellas that are classics of the genre: Droste-Hülshoff's *The Jew's Beech* (1842), Mörike's *Mozart on his Journey to Prague* (1855), Storm's *Rider of the White Horse* (1888), and the first renderings of a Fontane novel (*Effi Briest*, 1895, albeit sorely abridged) and of Thomas Mann (*Tonio Kröger*, 1901). It was an important stock-taking, in part an expression of German-American cultural pride, even as its historical context lends it an air of leave-taking too. American entry into World War I in 1917 was to bring, no less than in Britain, an hysterical anti-German sentiment: teaching of the very language, that by 1915 was studied by some 24 per cent of all high-school pupils (as against 9 per cent studying French, and 2 per cent Spanish), was proscribed in almost half the states of the US until 1923.

Translation during the inter-war period focused overwhelmingly upon contemporary writers and upon the novel. As literary relations were slowly re-established, the *Tristan* (1901, translated 1922) and *Death in Venice* (1913, translated 1925) of Thomas Mann (1875–1955) were translated by Kenneth Burke for the New York *Dial*. His *Buddenbrooks* (1901) appeared at last in 1924, translated by Helen Lowe-Porter, who then with *The Magic Mountain* (1924, translated 1927) consolidated her position as "official", if latterly much criticized, mediator of Mann's work, continuing in the 1930s with *Stories of Three Decades* (1936), collected essays, and the first three volumes of *Joseph and His Brothers* (1933–36, translated 1934–38). Döblin's *Alexanderplatz, Berlin* (1929, translated 1931) was put into English by Eugene Jolas, who also figures as the first English translator of Kafka (1883–1924), publishing *The Sentence* in his journal *transition*, 1928. The celebrated Kafka translations by Willa and Edwin Muir began with *The Castle* (1926, translated 1930) and proceeded via the collection *The Great Wall of China* (1931, translated 1933) to *The Trial* (1925, translated 1937) and *America* (1927, translated 1938). Meanwhile they had translated, with remarkable speed for so complex a work, Broch's *The Sleepwalkers* (1931, translated 1932).

But at this time Mann's English readership lagged behind his prestige, and Kafka, let alone Hermann Broch (1886–1951), was known to but a few initiates. To focus only on the enduring monuments obscures the surge of interest in German fiction at the end of the 1920s, at its peak from 1929 to 1932, from when until 1939 more translations from German literary sources than from French were published in Britain. Many were published within months of the original issue, most in both Britain and America, with such houses as Secker (London) and Knopf (New York) prominent among the numerous publishers vying for rights.

Interest extended far beyond those few intellectuals, like Auden and Spender, for whom not Paris but Weimar Germany, Berlin especially, came to stand for regeneration in the arts, or liberation in the personal sphere. Complex patterns of fascination and recoil are traceable in contemporary reviews, but at its simplest the influx of German books reflected a widespread concern "to understand our former enemies" (*Times Literary Supplement*, 18 April 1929) – or indeed to confront shared experience, as witness the impact of the German war novels: Arnold Zweig's *The Case of Sergeant Grischa* (1927, translated 1928), Unruh's *The Way of Sacrifice*, Renn's *War* (translated 1928), Ernst Jünger's *Storm of Steel* (1920, translated 1929), above all Erich Maria Remarque's *All Quiet on the Western Front* (published and translated 1929), an unprecedented bestseller, famously filmed by Lewis Milestone in 1931. Topical social novels, read or misread as "documentary" evidence of the political and economic convulsions of postwar Germany, engaged a similar "concern to understand": examples include Lion Feuchtwanger's *Success* (published and translated 1930), Vicky Baum's bestselling *Grand Hotel* (translated 1930, dramatized 1931), Erich Kästner's *Fabian* (1930, translated 1932) and Hans Fallada's *Little Man, What Now?* (1932 translated 1933), besides novels by Leonhard Frank (1882–1961), Anna Seghers (1900–1983), Heinrich Mann (1871–1950) and Franz Werfel (1890–1945). At the same time, the runaway success of Feuchtwanger's *Jew Süss* (1925, translated by Willa and Edwin Muir, 1926) encouraged translation of further historical novels, by Feuchtwanger himself (1889–1958) and Bruno Frank (1887–1945), Ricarda Huch (1864–1947) and Alfred Neumann (1895–1952). There was keen interest too in biographies, or *vies romancées*, by Stefan Zweig (1881–1942) and the prolific Emil Ludwig (1861–1948). The growing interest in psychoanalysis revitalized interest in Schnitzler, and drew readers to the fiction of Jakob Wassermann (1873–1933) (e.g. *World's Illusion*, translated 1920) and Zweig (e.g. *Amok*, translated 1932), or to Hesse's *Steppenwolf* (translated 1929).

An era of innovative drama and theatrical practice in Germany found no comparable echo in a mainstream British or American theatre wedded to naturalistic conventions. Ashley Dukes championed Expressionist drama, translating Georg Kaiser's *From Morn to Midnight* (1916) in 1920 and Ernst Toller's *The Machine Wreckers* (1922) in 1923, but his versions were perforce constrained by their "little-theatre" stagings, by the Stage Society and at the tiny Gate Theatre in a Covent Garden loft. Kaiser's play had a modest success and later revivals, but only his *Gas* trilogy (1917–20, translated 1924–29) was otherwise translated. Toller's *The Machine Wreckers* and *Masses and Man* (1921, translated 1923), however, were frequently staged or read by socialist drama groups; subsequent plays were promptly translated and later collected as *Seven Plays*, 1935, by which time his outspoken opposition to Nazism had made him a celebrated public figure. Auden adapted the lyrics of his *No More Peace* for its world premiere in London, 1937; Stephen Spender co-translated *Pastor Hall* (1939). Dukes meanwhile enjoyed West End successes with the more conventional dramaturgy of his adaptations of Ferdinand Bruckner's *Elizabeth of England* (1931) and Alfred Neumann's *Such Men are Dangerous* (1928). The German rediscovery of Georg Büchner (1813–37) found its first English echoes at this time, with his *Plays* (1835–37, translated by Geoffrey Dunlop, 1927), and a second rendering of *Danton's Death*, by Spender and Goronwy Rees (1939), but not yet performances.

In their *Contemporary German Poetry* (1923), Babette Deutsch and Avrahm Yarmolinsky offered a rare glimpse of Expressionist poetry, with some of the earliest translations of Benn (1886–1956), Goll (1891–1950), Heym (1887–1912), Stadler (1883–1914), Trakl (1887–1914) and others, while pleading that the German poetry most expressive of these "times out of joint" was "too broken and obscure to bear translation" into a then acceptable English poetic idiom. This important anthology also marked an advance in the hesitant Anglo-American reception of Rilke (1875–1926), all but unknown here before the translation in 1930 of his novel *The Notebook of Malte Laurids Brigge* (1910), and the first rendering in 1931 of *Duino Elegies* (1923), by Edward and Victoria Sackville-West. By 1939 translations by J.B. Leishman, Rilke's most dedicated English mediator, had encompassed most of the poet's major work, including *Sonnets to Orpheus* (1923, translated 1936) and, with Stephen Spender, a new version of *Duino Elegies* (1939). In the same year, Auden could write of "the growing influence of Rilke on English poetry"; indisputably, he had already been more extensively translated and discussed in Britain and America than any German-language poet since Heine.

The coming of World War II meant inevitably a precipitous fall in the rate of translation, but not the same blanket hostility to German-language culture as during the 1914–18 War. Some threads of continuity are traceable: in the ever-growing interest in Rilke and Kafka during the war and throughout the 1950s; in Thomas Mann's celebrity in the United States, where his addresses and broadcasts made him widely perceived as the very embodiment of German culture in exile. Most of the exiled writers struggled in obscurity, but some, with a well-established popular following – Feuchtwanger, Remarque (1899–1970), Stefan Zweig – continued to be widely translated. Franz Werfel (1890–1945), in 1935 a bestselling author in America with his novel *The Forty Days of Musa Dagh* (translated 1934), enjoyed still greater success with *The Song of Bernadette* (1941, translated 1942). Most remarkable was the "discovery" of Hölderlin's poetry after over a century's neglect (only in 1923 had an authoritative German edition of his work been completed). David Gascoyne's *Hölderlin's Madness* (1938) mixed his own poems with adaptations of Hölderlin based on French translations; then the centenary of the poet's death inspired in 1943–44 volumes by J.B. Leishman, Frederic Prokosch and, most influentially, Michael Hamburger, who has gone on constantly to revise and extend his rendering of Hölderlin's work, a project culminating in the magisterial edition *Poems and Fragments* (1966, 3rd edition 1994).

Major translations of the first post-war decade included some of the great novels of Austro-German modernism: Thomas Mann's *Doctor Faustus* (1947, translated 1949), Broch's *The Death of Virgil* (translated 1945), rendered by Jean Starr Untermeyer in five years of symbiotic collaboration with the author, Canetti's *Auto-da-fé* (1935, translated C.V. Wedgwood, 1946), and Musil's *The Man without Qualities* (translated 1953–54, vol. 3, 1965). Hesse's *Magister Ludi* (translated 1950), like other novels translated after his 1947 Nobel Prize, had as yet little impact.

No writer, however, was more extensively translated in the first post-war decades than Goethe. His bi-centenary in 1949 stimulated notable new versions such as Louis MacNeice's BBC-commissioned *Faust*, and served as a focus of willed reconnection with the best of German cultural traditions. Altogether, the 1950s and 1960s brought many, mostly American, renderings of German classics of the 18th and 19th centuries that had been ignored by translators between the wars. Most appeared under academic auspices, catering to an expanding student market, with translations by Germanists such as B.Q. Morgan or Charles E. Passage; many were published by Frederick Ungar, who, like Kurt and Helen Wolff (Pantheon Books), exemplifies the vital role played by Austrian and German refugees, in the publishing world and beyond, in the dissemination of German literature. Scholarly interests and the expansion of comparative literary studies also underlie the numerous translations of medieval literature from the late 1950s on, though the major masterpieces were also presented to a wider readership via paperback series, e.g. A.T. Hatto's versions of Gottfried von Strassburg's *Tristan* (1960), the *Nibelungenlied* (1965) and later Wolfram von Eschenbach's *Parzival* (1980), for Penguin Classics.

Amid this re-exploration of the canon, belated "discoveries" were also made: a first complete English edition of Kleist's stories, as late as 1960, the translator drawn by references in Kafka's diaries; Büchner's *Lenz* (translated by M. Hamburger, 1947); Keller's novel *Green Henry* (1856, translated 1960); Fontane's *Effi Briest* (translated 1962, 1967) and *Beyond Recall* (translated 1964), the first British translations of his novels.

After the austerities of the 1950s, there was in Britain in the 1960s a cultural climate altogether more receptive to stimulus from abroad, particularly in a revitalized theatre. Crucial to a new interest in German theatre was the impact of Bertolt Brecht (1898–1956), after the revelatory London visit of the Berliner Ensemble in 1956 and the first publication in Britain (1960–62) of readily accessible collections of plays previously available only in American editions of the pioneering translations by H.R. Hays and Eric Bentley. Numerous stagings of Brecht's major plays promptly followed, and by 1960 plans were already made for the complete translation of his writings, under the general editorship of John Willett and Ralph Manheim. Publication began in 1970 and has continued to this day.

As Brecht was being explored in Britain, there came a series of striking works by the leading "post-Brechtian" dramatists, notably Dürrenmatt's 1956 *The Visit*, staged in London in 1960 after a successful New York run, and *The Physicists* (1962, translated 1963), and Frisch's *Fire Raisers* and *Andorra* (1958 and 1962, translated 1962). Hochhuth's *The Representative* (translated 1963; as *The Deputy*, 1964), more Schillerian than Brechtian, was internationally controversial because of its subject matter. Peter Brook's production of Peter Weiss's *Marat / Sade* was the sensation of 1964, ensuring further interest in his later plays (*The Investigation*, 1965, translated 1966). With Martin Esslin as Controller of Drama, BBC radio broadcast some 30 contemporary German plays between 1958 and 1970. At the end of the decade came the provocative early texts of Peter Handke (*Offending the Audience* and *Kaspar*, translated 1969), while Calder issued an ambitious series of Expressionist drama.

Such concentrated interest in new German drama has not been matched since. More interest was aroused in the 1970s and early 1980s by the "New German Cinema" of Fassbinder, Wenders and Herzog. No contemporary playwright since Handke (1942–) has won a distinct reputation in Britain, though individual works by such as Botho Strauss (1944–), Manfred Karge (1938–), and most recently Klaus Pohl (1952–) (*Waiting Room Germany*, translated 1995) have been staged, and in the United States, where he is known for his collaborations with the director Robert Wilson, most of the plays and performance texts of Heiner Müller (1929–) have been translated since *Hamletmachine* (translated 1984). Nevertheless, the older German and Austrian repertoire has been extensively explored in the last two decades, whether at London "fringe" venues such as the Gate Theatre in Notting Hill or at the National Theatre (NT), where adaptations have commonly been commissioned from leading British dramatists (working as necessary from prior literal translations): Tom Stoppard (Schnitzler's *Undiscovered Country*, 1980; Nestroy's *On the Razzle*, 1982), David Hare (Brecht's *Mother Courage,* 1995) and Howard Brenton (Büchner's *Danton's Death*, 1982, and, for the Royal Shakespeare Company, Goethe's *Faust*, 1994). Christopher Hampton's translations of Ödön von Horváth (1901–38) beginning with the NT production of *Tales from the Vienna Woods* (1931, translated 1977), established in the repertoire a writer previously quite unknown to British audiences. Elsewhere, Schiller's plays have been cultivated by the Glasgow Citizens Theatre, and plays by J.M.R. Lenz were produced at the Edinburgh Festival in 1992, marking the bicentenary of his death.

The 1960s and early 1970s were notably receptive to German poetry too. Volumes of Hölderlin, Goethe and Heine in the Penguin Poets series offered German texts with English prose translations, as had earlier Leonard Forster's *Penguin Book of German Verse* (1957), the most comprehensive anthology yet available to the English-reading public in its range from the *Hildebrandslied* (c. 800) to Brecht. Penguin's Modern European Poets series included, from 1968 to 1972, volumes of poetry by Enzensberger (1929–), Grass (1927–), Nelly Sachs (1891–1970), Celan (1920–70) and Bienek (1930–90), as well as by Johannes Bobrowski (1917–65), whose oracular lyricism had excited particular interest in the mid-1960s via translations by Ruth and Matthew Mead (*Shadowlands*, translated 1966). Bobrowski was also the first writer from the former GDR (after Brecht) to command significant attention in Britain, and lyric poetry, as a medium for the personal, sceptical, critical voice, was to remain the genre of GDR literature of greatest interest to translators. Interest in contemporary poetry had in turn been vitally stimulated by Michael Hamburger and Christopher Middleton's bilingual anthology *Modern German Poetry, 1910-1960* (1962), which with its accent on Trakl and Expressionist writers revealed a modernist tradition of German poetry barely known to English readers. Scholars and substantial poets in their own right, both editors have been prolific translators, and since 1945, or probably in the 20th century, German literature had no more accomplished and influential mediator in Britain than Michael Hamburger. Hölderlin and latterly Celan have been the central preoccupations of his work – his *Poems of Paul Celan* (1988) has been described by fellow-poets as one of the great English translations, in turn an inspiration to other artists, as in the Celan settings of Harrison Birtwistle's *Pulse Shadows*, which juxtapose the original texts and Hamburger's renderings. But Hamburger has also published volumes of Brecht, Enzensberger, Goethe, Grass, Heissenbüttel (1921–96), Huchel (1903–81), Kunert (1929–), Nelly Sachs, and Franz Baermann Steiner (1909–52), and the further important anthologies *German Poetry 1910-1975* (1976), translated single-handedly, and *East German Poetry* (1972).

Anglo-American reception of modern German fiction has focused primarily on those authors who came to prominence in West Germany in the late 1950s and early 1960s, and whose writing confronted the issues of Nazism and its post-war consequences without the evasions characteristic of the preceding decade. Ever since the eruptive impact of *The Tin Drum* (1959, translated 1961), especially in the USA, Günter Grass has been the dominant figure, his work comprehensively translated (mostly by Ralph Manheim), including the political speeches and writings that have reinforced perceptions of him abroad as the "representative" voice, albeit a critical, admonitory and controversial voice, of post-war German literature. While the fiction of Heinrich Böll (1917–85) had been steadily translated since the mid-1950s, comparable recognition came more gradually, essentially after the award of the Nobel Prize in 1972 and the success of *Katharina Blum* (1974, translated 1975); much of his earlier work was then reissued, in some cases retranslated by Leila Vennewitz, his regular translator since *The Clown* and *Absent without Leave* (translated 1965). The novels of Alfred Andersch (1914–80), Max Frisch (1911–81), Uwe Johnson (1934–84), Siegfried Lenz (1926–), and, belatedly, Martin Walser (1927–) have been extensively translated, though to a generally more muted reception. But even the best-selling Grass was overshadowed in the late 1960s and early 1970s by the retrospective cult that made of Hermann Hesse (1877–1962) a guru-figure of American counter-culture, appealing both to its activist strand by his pacificism and anti-authoritarianism, and to turners-on and droppers-out as "poet of the interior journey". Forty-five translations were issued (or reissued) between 1963 and 1980, selling, on one estimate, some 14 million copies in the USA, with *Siddharta* and *Steppenwolf* in greatest demand.

No novelist since has won an international reputation comparable to that of Böll or Grass, though from the mid-1980s on a substantial corpus of the fiction of Thomas Bernhard (1931–89) has appeared in English, eliciting some outstanding translations by David McLintock and by Ewald Osers. Otherwise few contemporary writers – Handke, Gert Hofmann, Christa Wolf are some – have been represented by more than the occasional title. Some individual works have been strikingly successful: Patrick Süskind's *Perfume* (translated 1986), and most recently, Bernhard Schlink's *The Reader* (translated 1997). Yet the very fact that such bestsellers as these had appeared in several other languages before English may also illustrate an aversion to risk on the part of major publishers, such as prompted in 1996 the Austrian, German and Swiss cultural institutes to launch a joint programme for the promotion of German books in the UK (*New Books in German*). From 1986 to 1995 the translation rights of German literature sold to England numbered on average only half of those sold to France, Italy or Spain. Smaller presses have been more enterprising: Serpent's Tail, for instance, has published several novels by Elfriede Jelinek (1946–) (e.g. *Lust*, translated 1992). Most adventurous of all has been the University of Texas journal *Dimension*, which from 1968 to 1994 presented in parallel German texts and English translation original work by some 500 German-language authors.

While transmission of the new has been sporadic, much energy has gone into rediscovery and retranslation. This is partly a response to perceived deficiencies of earlier versions, as for instance with new renderings of Thomas Mann's short stories (translated by David Luke, 1990), *Buddenbrooks*, *The Magic Mountain* and *Doctor Faustus* (translated by John E. Woods, 1994–97); or it may reflect advances in textual scholarship, as with new versions of Kafka (*The Transformation and Other Stories*, translated by Malcolm Pasley, 1992, or *The Trial*, translated by Idris Parry, 1994) and of Musil's *Man without Qualities* (translated by Sophie Wilkins and Burton Pike, 1995). Joseph Roth (1894–1939) has been revealed by new translations since the early 1980s as one of the major novelists of his age. Re-exploration of the 1950s has yielded belated "discoveries"' in Wolfgang Koeppen's *Death in Rome* (1954, translated by Michael Hofmann, 1992), and, beginning with *Nobodaddy's Children* (1951–53, translated 1996), the early fiction of the exuberantly experimental Arno Schmidt (1914–79), translated by John E. Woods, whose 1980 version of Schmidt's *Evening Edged in Gold* (1975) was one of the most resourceful translations and boldest publishing ventures (by Marion Boyars) of recent years. Particularly striking has been the resurgent interest in Rilke's poetry, extensively re-translated by Stephen Cohn, Stephen Mitchell, Edward Snow and others.

Retranslation or consolidation has been the essence of two notable large-scale enterprises. A 12-volume *Collected Works* of Goethe (1983–89), offers at last a coherently planned and executed English edition, in new translations that are in many instances the best available versions. The most ambitious of current undertakings, finally, is The German Library, edited by Volkmar Sander (New York: Continuum), steadily progressing since 1980 towards its goal of 100 volumes of German literature, aesthetic theory, and social and philosophical thought, from medieval times to the present, using both established and newly commissioned translations.

DEREK GLASS

Further Reading

Ashton, Rosemary, *The German Idea: Four English Writers and the Reception of German Thought, 1800–1860*, Cambridge and New York: Cambridge University Press, 1980

Davis, Garold N., *German Thought and Culture in England 1700–1770: A Preliminary Survey*, Chapel Hill: University of North Carolina Press, 1969

Goodnight, Scott Holland, *German Literature in American Magazines prior to 1846*, Madison: University of Wisconsin, 1907

Haertel, Martin Henry, *German Literature in American Magazines, 1846 to 1880*, Madison: University of Wisconsin, 1908

Halkin, Ariela, *The Enemy Reviewed: German Popular Literature Through British Eyes Between the Two World Wars*, Westport, Connecticut: Praeger, 1995

Hathaway, Lillie V., *German Literature of the Mid-Nineteenth Century in England and America as Reflected in the Journals 1840–1914*, Boston: Chapman and Grimes, 1935

Herford, Charles H., *Studies in the Literary Relations of England and Germany in the Sixteenth Century*, Cambridge: Cambridge University Press, 1886; reprinted London: Cass, and New York: Octagon, 1966

Keenoy, Ray *et al.*, *The Babel Guide to German Fiction in English Translation: Austria, Germany, Switzerland*, London: Boulevard, 1997

Kopp, W. LaMarr, *German Literature in the United States, 1945–1960*, Chapel Hill: University of North Carolina Press, 1967

Kreuter, Uta, *Übersetzung und Literaturkritik: Aspekte der Rezeption zeitgenössischer deutschsprachiger Literatur in Grossbritannien, 1960–1981*, Frankfurt: Lang, 1985

Morgan, Bayard Quincy and A.R. Hohlfeld (editors), *German Literature in British Magazines, 1750–1860*, Madison: University of Wisconsin Press, 1949

Morgan, Bayard Quincy, *A Critical Bibliography of German Literature in English Translation. 1481–1927*, 2nd edition, reprinted New York: Scarecrow Press, 1965; supplement, *1928–1955*, 1965; 2nd supplement, *1956–1960*, edited by Murray F. Smith, Metuchen, New Jersey: Scarecrow Press, 1972

O'Neill, Patrick, *German Literature in English Translation: A Select Bibliography*, Toronto: University of Toronto Press, 1981

Oppel, Horst, *Englisch-Deutsche Literaturbeziehungen*, 2 vols, Berlin: Schmidt, 1971

Pochmann, Henry A., *German Culture in America: Philosophical and Literary Influences, 1600–1900*, Madison: University of Wisconsin Press, 1957

Rectanus, Mark W., *German Literature in the United States: Licensing Translations in the International Marketplace*, Wiesbaden: Harrassowitz, 1990

Sander, Volkmar, "Zum deutschen Buch in Amerika: Produktion und Rezeption", *Deutsche Vierteljahresschrift für Literaturgeschichte und Geisteswissenschaft*, 60 (1986) pp. 484–95

Schirmer, Walter F., *Der Einfluss der deutschen Literatur auf die englische im 19. Jahrhundert*, Halle: Niemeyer, 1947

Stockley, V., *German Literature as Known in England, 1750–1830*, London: Routledge, 1929; reprinted Port Washington, New York: Kennikat Press, 1969

Vogel, Stanley M., *German Literary Influences on the American Transcendentalists*, New Haven, Connecticut: Yale University Press, 1955

Guido Gezelle 1830–1899

Flemish poet

Biography

Born 1 May 1830 in Bruges. As well as a profound, powerful and innovative poet, he was a philologist, a journalist and a priest, ordained in 1854 and serving in parishes as well as teaching in religious schools. He was impelled in his writings by a strong Catholic and Flemish nationalist inspiration. The art and skill of his early volumes of poetry (*Vlaemsche Dichtoefeningen* [Flemish Poetry Exercises], 1858; *Kerhofblommen* [Graveyard Flowers], 1859; *Gedichten, gezangen, gebeden* [Poems, Songs, Prayers], 1862) foreshadowed the high achievements of his maturity (e.g. *Tydkranz* [Garland of Time], 1893, *Rijmsnoer* [Rhymestring], 1897). In spite of the beauty of his work and his eminence at home as national poet, little of what he wrote has been translated into English. Died in Bruges 27 November 1899.

Editions

The Dutch texts are to be found in *Volledige Werken* [Complete Works], edited by Frank Baur, Amsterdam: L.J. Veen, 18 vols, 1930–39 and *Verzameld Dichtwerk* [Collected Poetry], edited by Jozef Boets, Antwerp and Amsterdam: De Nederlandse Boekhandel & Pelckmans, 8 vols, 1982–86.

Translations

Selections

Claes, Paul and Christine D'haen, *The Evening and the Rose*, Antwerp: Guido Gezellegenootschap, 1989

D'haen, Christine, *Guido Gezelle: Poems – Gedichten*, Deurle: Colibrant, 1971

It is an amazing fact of literary life, and literary translation, that Guido Gezelle has not been translated more often, the more so since he is rightly regarded by speakers of Dutch as one of the greatest, if not the greatest poet in that language.

Twenty-five poems have been published in anthologies and literary journals (by C. and F. Stillman, *Lyrica Belgica* I, 1960 and A. van Eyken, *Dutch Crossing*, 35, 1988), but the two translations listed above are the only translations of Gezelle available in book form to readers of English. Then again, "available" may be somewhat of an overstatement; on closer inspection, the two books turn out to be basically the same book twice, and both versions of the book have been published not in an English-speaking country but in Belgium. Moreover, both versions have also been issued by publishing houses whose obscurity is, unfortunately, more than relative. It is no exaggeration to say, therefore, that the work of Guido Gezelle, one of the great poets of the 19th century, remains by and large inaccessible to educated readers of English who are not specialists in literary studies and who would not be able to find the two translations mentioned above for themselves.

Before commenting on the quality of the translation(s), it might be appropriate to hazard a guess as to why Gezelle should have been translated so little, either by translators who use English as their mother tongue, or by translators who use Dutch as their mother tongue, but feel an obligation to render one of their greatest poets into English.

The answer is to be found in two words: "incredibly difficult". Gezelle is such a good poet mainly because, at his best, he makes the Dutch language do what it never did before he touched it. In the poems that are most highly valued today, he creates a very intricate and highly playful text, which relies heavily on its musical qualities to address and move the reader. Because the poems rely to such a great extent on their musicality, they are not really "about" anything much. Two of the most famous describe respectively the way the wind plays in the leaves of a certain kind of tree he often encountered on his walks through rural west Flanders, and the impression the singing of the nightingale makes on him.

It is this ethereal mastery that makes translators stay away from Gezelle's work, even though they will fully acknowledge its great quality and lament that it ought, indeed, to be translated, and translated extensively. It is no exaggeration to say that translators who write English as their mother tongue find it hard to understand the full meaning of many of the poems, not least because Gezelle tended to rely heavily on the vocabulary of his own west Flemish region, which makes his poems also relatively hard to understand in present-day Amsterdam. As a philologist, Gezelle also knew Middle Dutch well, and incorporated elements from its vocabulary into his poetry, because he saw himself and the writers of his generation as the heirs to the literature in Middle Dutch that had been centered around medieval Flanders and Brabant, not Holland and Amsterdam. Translators who write Dutch as their mother tongue tend not to have mastered the different registers of English to the extent that they can really render most of the nuances of the original – all of the nuances would be utterly impossible.

The translators who have produced the existing translations are, unfortunately, no exception to that rule. This statement is in no way meant to detract from their moral courage and zeal, just to describe a fact. Christine D'HAEN, a Flemish poet in her own right, first published her volume of Gezelle translations in 1971. She revised them, together with the translator and writer Paul CLAES, and a new edition, still relatively closely based on the 1971 translation, was published in 1989. Both translations are at their best with the more musical poems, because Gezelle did not really write those in any traditional meter, making up his own as he went along. Whereas they do not always capture the full implications of the original, enough comes through for the reader to realize its masterful craftsmanship, and to suspect that the poet at work here is in the same league as Gerald Manley Hopkins, at least.

Being a priest, as Hopkins was, Gezelle also wrote poems celebrating his faith, or rather, going back to the medieval concept of nature as the "visible words" of God, and therefore celebrating his faith by celebrating nature. Since Gezelle's reception became inevitably mixed up with the evolution of the movement for the recognition of the Flemish identity and the Dutch language within the Belgian state, some of these poems have become "local classics" in their own right, and they are to be found in all anthologies, which is why the translations include a representative sample of them, even though they travel considerably less well than the poems of the more musical type. The translations are considerably less successful in rendering poems of the latter, spiritual sort. These are often disfigured by archaisms and abstractions, and the translations fall willing victims to the – to them imperious – demands of rhyme. The results are lines like: "how oft, how oft did I recede", where the original says something like: "how very often did I sit". In the translations the Gezelle who writes the second type of poetry comes across as Browning on an off-day, not as the master craftsman he always remained.

It remains to add that the selection from Gezelle's work offered in these translations is rather meager, a mere 30 poems in all, so that the reader who reads him in English is not exposed to the great variety of his original output.

André A. Lefevere

Further Reading

van Nuis, Hermine J., *Guido Gezelle: Flemish Poet and Priest*, Westport, Connecticut: Greenwood Press, 1986

van Roosbroeck, Gustave, *Guido Gezelle: The Mystic Poet of Flanders*, Vinton, Iowa: Kruse, 1919

Ghālib 1797–1869

Indian poet

Biography

Born Mirza Asadullah Khan in Agra, Uttar Pradesh, India, in 1797. He lost his father when he was five, his guardian and estates at the age of nine. He learned Arabic and was interested in philosophy and astrology. He married in 1810. He wrote first in Urdu, but after 1847 mainly in Persian, in which language he was appointed in 1850 to write the official history of the Mughals. His poetic fame was long in coming, but his complex thought and lively sensibility, expressed in dense, imaged, elliptic language, have since the latter half of the 20th century aroused interest and admiration beyond the subcontinent. Ghālib lived through a chequered period of Indian history; his letters and journals contain accounts of the Mutiny of 1857–58. Died in Delhi in 1869.

Translations

Poetry

Ahmad, Aijaz (editor), *Ghazals of Ghalib: Versions of Urdu*, New York: Columbia University Press, 1971 (translated by Ahmad, W.S. Merwin, Adrienne Rich, William Stafford, David Ray, Thomas Fitzsimmons, Mark Strand and William Hunt)

Ali, Ahmed, *Ghalib: Selected Poems*, with an introduction, Rome: Istituto Italiano per il Medio ed Estremo Oriente, 1969; also in his *The Golden Tradition: An Anthology of Urdu Poetry*, New York: Columbia University Press, 1973

Husain, Yusuf, *Urdu Ghazals of Ghalib*, with an introduction, New Delhi: Ghalib Institute, 1977

Kamal, Daud, *Ghalib: Reverberations*, Karachi: Golden Block Works, 1970

Kaul, J.L., *Interpretations of Ghalib*, Delhi: Atma Ram, 1957

Lakhanpal, P.L., *Ghalib: The Man and His Verse*, Delhi: International Books, 1960

Mujeeb, M., *Ghalib*, New Delhi: Sahitya Akademi, 1969

Naim, C.M., *Twenty-Five Verses by Ghalib*, Calcutta: Writers Workshop, 1970

Naim, C.M., *Ghalib's Lighter Verses*, Calcutta: Writers Workshop, 1972

Raina, B.N., *Raina's Ghalib: A Transcreation of Mirza Ghalib's Selected Verse*, Calcutta: Writers Workshop, 1984

Sadullah, Sufia, *Hundred Verses of Mirza Ghalib*, edited by Suraiya Nazar, Karachi: Sadullah, 1975

Zakir, Mohammed, *Distracting Words* (bilingual edition), Delhi: Idara-e Amini, 1976

Letters

Rahbar, Daud, *Urdu Letters of Mirza Asad'ullah Khan Ghalib*, Albany: State University of New York Press, 1987

Russell, Ralph and Khurshidul Islam, *Ghalib: Life and Letters, 1797–1869*, London: Allen and Unwin, 1969; Delhi and Oxford: Oxford University Press, 1994

Mirza Asadullah Khan, by far the most widely admired Urdu poet, adopted Ghālib ("Dominant") for his *takhallus* or literary name. He wrote poetry in both Persian and Urdu. A certain intellectual edge – a combination of a delightful wit and a questioning mind that favors paradoxes – and the kinetic energy of his images mark his verse, and make it very attractive even now. Since very little of his Persian poetry has appeared in translation, the remarks below deal only with the Urdu.

Ghālib's fame is due to his ghazals (lyric poems), and ghazal is an extremely difficult genre to translate into English. It consists of a certain number of distichs, all in the same meter and conforming to the same scheme (aa, ba, ca, da, etc.) of single or double rhymes. Usually, each distich is a complete semantic unit, independent of other distichs, and each line in a distich is grammatically self-contained. These restrictions combine to produce a remarkably compact, almost terse, poetic statement, demanding that the reader bring to it much from his life as well as his literary experience. The ghazal's symbolic language, its manifold cultural references and allusions, the music created by the choice and placement of words, all must be recognized and responded to – a difficult task for any translator.

Probably the first full-length book to make the attempt was J.L. KAUL's *Interpretations of Ghālib* (1957). As the title indicates, Kaul sought to communicate to the reader *all* that the original two lines in Urdu communicated to him, often in much more numerous English lines. He also chose to "interpret" some 300 or so selected verses, rather than entire ghazals – a common practice in Urdu in the context of ghazals. An Urdu ghazal is most often a collection of discrete couplets – "pearls at random strung" – which the poet need not always publish or orally present in its entirety, or even in some fixed order. Kaul's interpretative mode was also employed by Daud KAMAL (1970) and B.N. RAINA (1984), but on a smaller scale. Other translators, however, have tried to match the two lines of the Urdu with two to four short lines in English – focusing on the exact words of Ghālib, and leaving interpretation to the imagination and literary experience of the reader.

The centenary of Ghālib's death in 1969 brought forth a spate of books, including translations. Ahmed ALI's *Ghālib: Selected Poems* (1969) contains a short but succinct introduction and some 80 selections of varying length in elegant and lucid translation. Often employing four or five short lines for each distich, Ali maintained the verbal economy of Ghālib's verse, while accurately communicating its ideational impulse. Aijaz AHMAD's *Ghazals of Ghālib* (1971), on the other hand, was an unusual enterprise. Ahmad prepared prose translations of 37 ghazals, reduced to only five distichs each. These he gave, with a minimum of explanatory comments, to seven American poets – W.S. MERWIN, Adrienne RICH, William STAFFORD, David RAY, Thomas FITZSIMMONS, Mark STRAND and William HUNT. The latter then prepared their own "versions" of the ghazals they felt nearest to, these versions ranging from close approximations to free-wheeling exercises. The book makes exciting reading, not for what it makes available of Ghālib, but for the fascinating creative engagement of seven modern poets of one tradition with the high classical verse of another, quite different tradition. Here is an example; first Ahmad's literal version, then three poetic versions:

In my night of loneliness, owing to the ferocity/grief of the
fire in my heart,
The shadow eluded me like a waft of smoke.
(Aijaz Ahmad)

In the lonely night because of the anguish
of the fire in my heart
the shadow slipped from me like smoke
(W.S. Merwin)

Through the bonfire my grief lit in that darkness
the shadow went past me like a wisp of smoke
(Adrienne Rich)

That lonely night fire inhabited my heart
And my shadow drifted from me in a thin cloud of smoke.
(Mark Strand)

And here is Ali's translation of that verse:

With the savagery of the fire
Of thought on lonely nights
My shadow abhorred my presence
And avoided me like smoke.

Ghālib built his couplet around a nominal construct – "the *vahshat* of heart's fire" – and through the witty process of providing a cause where none was needed: "[All shadows disappear in the dark of a night, but] my shadow stayed away from me because ...". By particularizing night as "the night of loneliness" – when the poet-lover's heart is conventionally "afire" – Ghālib makes a shadow theoretically possible. Next he gives that fire an attribute: *vahshat* – a word that allows for "intensity" – as in the case of the three "versions" – and "ferocity" – as in Ali's translation. But *vahshat* also contains a third sense: "avoidance of human contact as by a wild animal". In other words, there were both qualitative and quantitative "reasons" for the shadow to flee from its "reality" – whom it (the shadow) also defined, for only spirits, not humankind, do not cast shadows or reflections.

Since then many other selections have appeared, mostly of 100 or so verses each. These are all of indifferent quality as translations. One, however, is more ambitious in scope. Yusuf HUSAIN's *Urdu Ghazals of Ghālib* (1977) translates in their entirety not only the 234 Urdu ghazals and fragments that Ghālib himself chose to publish, but also selected verses from the ghazals that were discovered in manuscripts later. It also contains a learned introduction to Ghālib's thought. Here is the verse alluded to above in Husain's translation:

In the night of loneliness, my own shadow
Takes fright at the frenzied fire of my heart,
And runs away from me
Like smoke drifting from the flames.

A very different attempt is made in my (C.M. NAIM)'s two small books (1970, 1972). Modeled on Stanley Burnshaw's *The Poem Itself* (New York, 1960), they seek – through transliterations and extensive explanatory notes – to make the Urdu original itself available to the English reader.

Ghālib's importance in Urdu literature also lies in the letters he wrote to his friends and the younger poets who sought his advice on poetry. Most were published in his lifetime and influenced the development of modern Urdu prose. Free of conventional artifice, they contain vivid descriptions and witty dialogues, literary and lexicographic insights, political commentary and more – all in a simple and supple language. There are two translations in English. The more comprehensive and useful is *Ghalib: Life and Letters* (1969) by RUSSELL & ISLAM, who have pieced together a biography of the poet by translating portions of an Urdu biography by Altaf Husain Hali, and extensive selections from Ghālib's own Persian and Urdu letters and his Persian diary of the revolt of 1857. A delightfully readable book, it is an autobiography as much as a biography. (Russell & Islam have also finished a translation of Ghālib's selected Urdu and Persian ghazals which is expected to be published soon.)

Daud RAHBAR's *Urdu Letters* (1987) is an annotated translation of 170 selected Urdu letters in their entirety; thus the contents are more diverse. Particularly interesting are various literary and lexicographic opinions that Ghālib offered to his correspondents. Rahbar's translation is also quite literal; his English tries to retain much of what may seem quaint now even in Urdu. While Russell & Islam try to communicate only the spirit in which Ghālib wrote his words, Rahbar also offers the surface quality of those words.

C.M. NAIM

Further Reading

Naim, C.M., "The Ghazal Itself: Translating Ghālib", *Yale Journal of Criticism*, 5/3 (Fall 1992) pp. 219–32

Russell, Ralph, "On Translating Ghālib", *Mahfil* (now *Journal of South Asian Literature*), 5/4 (1968–69) pp. 71–87 (the issue also contains other relevant notes and examples)

Jamāl al-Ghītānī (Gamal Ghitany) 1945–

Egyptian novelist and short-story writer

Biography

Born in Upper Egypt in 1945, al-Ghītānī moved to Cairo with his family as a child, and later studied carpet design in Cairo, working as a designer from 1962 to 1968. In 1963 he published a short story in *al-Adīb*, a Lebanese journal. He started writing novels in the late 1960s, the first of which, *al-Zaynī Barakāt* (*Zayni Barakat*), published in 1971, was based on the story of a historical figure, al-Zaynī Barakāt ibn Mūsā, and set in Cairo in the early 16th century. His second novel, which used contemporary working-class Cairo as a backdrop, was *Waqā'i' Hārat al-Za'farānī* (*Incidents in Za'farani Alley*). It appeared in 1976. Later work includes his novel *Khitat al-Ghītānī* and his most ambitious work, the three-volume *Kitāb al-Tajalliyāt*, 1983-86, based on material by the mystical writer Ibn 'Arabī. Al-Ghītānī later became the editor-in-chief of the avant-garde Cairo-based Egyptian literary review *Akhbar Al Adab*, founded in 1993.

Translations

al-Zaynī Barakāt, 1971

Abdel Wahab, Farouk, *Zayni Barakat*, London and New York: Viking, 1988

Waqā'i' Hārat al-Za'farānī, 1976

O'Daniel, Peter, *Incidents in Za'farani Alley*, Cairo: General Egyptian Book Organization, 1988

Jamāl al-Ghītānī is among the most talented of the Egyptian so-called "generation of the sixties" – a group of writers who began publishing in the 1960s and who, though they do not form a "school" as such, share a number of common experiences and attitudes. Their work is permeated by the feeling of disillusion that followed the optimism of the early years of the Nasser regime, and is reflected in the works of social realism by 'Abd al-Rahmān al-Sharqāwī, Halāh 'Abd al-Habūr and others.

Within the group, al-Ghītānī's prose style is none the less quite distinctive, owing something (so it has been suggested) to his early training as a carpet weaver. Among its characteristics (found also in other authors of the "generation of the sixties") is the use of so-called "intertextuality" – the advancing of a narrative through the incorporation of texts from outside the main text itself; the texts themselves may be contemporary or historical, "real" (i.e. the product of another author) or "fictional" (i.e. the product of the author himself). This technique poses particular problems for the translator, who is faced not only with the usual linguistic and cultural problems of translating from Arabic but also with the task of translating from a mixture of styles, some of which may involve complex historical allusions.

These problems are exemplified in different ways by the two full-length novels of al-Ghītānī that have so far been translated into English. *Al-Zaynī Barakāt* revolves around the historical al-Zaynī, a mysterious figure who never appears in the novel itself but whose character – at once ruthless and puritanical – imposes itself on all the other characters of the novel. The work is structurally complex, being divided into a number of sections of two main types – memoirs, and *surādiqāt* ("pavilions") – and the picture of al- Zaynī is conveyed largely through the views of the other characters, including a fictitious Venetian traveller. The intertextuality of the work is manifested in the incorporation into the text of passages from *Badā'i' al-Zuhūr fī Waqā'i' al-Duhūr* by the medieval historian Ibn Iyās (1448–1522?), while at other points al-Ghītānī deliberately imitates Ibn Iyās's style. The work also incorporates a number of fictional texts (both written and oral) in medieval style, including decrees, proclamations, letters and reports. Although the Arabic of these "documents" is, by comparison with some classical Arabic texts, generally straightforward, it gives the novel at times a distinctively "archaic" ring, which has to be conveyed sensitively in any translation.

Despite the setting, however, this is in no sense a "historical" work. Rather, al-Ghītānī is using the period as a metaphor for contemporary Egypt. In his almost puritanical obsession with reform, al-Zaynī has been held to mirror President Nasser, and his survival of the Mamlūk defeat of 1517 parallels Nasser's survival of the defeat in the Six Day War of 1967; at the same time, the book's interlocking network of informants and spies is the perfect symbol for the contemporary police-state of Nasser's Egypt. In this respect the book is a good illustration of a common strategy among modern Arab authors for avoiding the attentions of the censor – the use of a historical period as an analogy for the present.

ABDEL WAHAB (1988) copes with the problems involved in translating this complex work very successfully. His elegant and polished version captures well the changes in linguistic register of the original Arabic, introducing a suitable measure of "archaic" language, for example in the formulaic announcements to the people of Egypt: "We enjoin what is right and forbid what is wrong". The brief translator's note that serves as a preface gives an informative account of the Mamlūk period of the setting, though it rather ignores the modern parallels; this omission is to some extent corrected by Edward Said's brief foreword.

Despite its contemporary setting, *Waqā'i' Hārat al-Za'farānī* shares certain features, both structural and thematic, with *al-Zaynī Barakāt*; indeed, the official reports and memoranda used to advance the narrative here may perhaps be seen as a modern equivalent of the decrees and public proclamations that fill the medieval world of *al-Zaynī Barakāt*. *Waqā'i'* begins with the realization that all the men of Za'farānī Alley have become impotent – an impotence that quickly emerges as the will of the central character, Shaykh 'Ahiyya, whose aim is to create a new kind of society based on different relationships. A series of orders is announced to the inhabitants of the alley, progressively regulating their lives in greater detail, and ending with the segregation of men from women. Eventually they rebel; but as news of the alley begins to spread outwards through the medium of the press, "Za'faranism" takes on the status of an international cult; the Shaykh acquires disciples all over the world and the novel closes with a series of dispatches from world capitals, where outbreaks of impotence have now become commonplace.

The novel gives us a portrayal of the characters of a working-class Cairene neighbourhood and at the same time a parody of the Islamic fundamentalist groups active in Egypt during the 1970s, together with, in Hasan Anwar, a cruel but prophetic caricature of President Sadat. O'DANIEL's (1988) English version is a good deal less attractive, however, than the English version of *al-Zaynī Barakāt*, both in terms of the translation itself (which, though generally competent, lacks polish) and of its presentation: both the author's and the translator's names, for example, appear on the title page in a spelling different from that on the cover. It is worth recalling that *al-Zaynī Barakāt* was the first modern Arabic novel to appear as a Penguin paperback, with all the resources of one of the world's leading paperback publishers behind it; the Egyptian government publishing house has failed to achieve a similar standard of presentation.

With the exception of a few short stories, Jamāl al-Ghīṭānī's other works remain so far untranslated. His later novels continue many of the thematic and stylistic characteristics of *al-Zaynī Barakāt* and *Waqa'i' Hārat al-Za'farānī* – the most ambitious among them being the trilogy *Kitāḅ al-Tajalliyāt* (1983–86), which uses the mystical writer Ibn 'Arabī's *al-Futūḥāt al-Makkiyya* as a source-text for a work that mingles personal and mystical elements with social and political criticism of contemporary Egypt. Less immediately attractive to the Western reader than either of the novels so far translated, it is difficult to imagine this as a likely candidate for translation into English, despite the obvious brilliance of parts at least of the text.

PAUL STARKEY

Further Reading

Draz, Ceza Kassem, "In Quest of New Narrative Forms: Irony in the Works of Four Egyptian Writers", *Journal of Arabic Literature*, 12 (1981) pp. 137–59

Guth, Stephan, *Zeugen einer Endzeit: Fünf Schriftsteller zum Umbruch in der ägyptischen Gesellschaft nach 1970*, Berlin: K. Schwarz, 1992

Hafez, Sabry, "The Egyptian Novel in the Sixties", *Journal of Arabic Literature*, 7 (1976) pp. 68–84

Mehrez, Samia, *Egyptian Writers Between History and Fiction: Essays on Naguib Mahfouz, Sonallah Ibrahim and Gamal al-Ghitani*, Cairo: American University in Cairo Press, 1994

André Gide 1869–1951

French novelist, dramatist, critic, essayist and diarist

Biography

Born in Paris, 22 November 1869, into a Protestant family, his father a professor of law from the south of France, his mother from a rich middle-class background in Normandy. A delicate only child, Gide was educated at the École Alsacienne in Paris, the Lycée de Montpellier and privately; he was devoted to literature and music. He travelled to North Africa for the first time in 1893, discovering there his capacity for sensual pleasures. In 1895 he married his cousin Madeleine Rondeaux, to whom he had long been attached. Living on his private means, he spent much of the period 1896–1906 travelling in Italy, Switzerland and North Africa. During the first three years of World War I he worked for the Red Cross. He had a daughter with Elisabeth Van Rysselberghe in 1923. In 1926 he went to the Congo and Chad with Marc Allégret, recording the experiences in travel diaries. In the early 1930s Gide was sympathetic to Communism, but visiting the USSR in 1936 he was repelled by Stalinism and he abandoned the Communist ideology. After the fall of France in 1940 Gide wrote against collaboration with the German victors and in 1942 he moved to North Africa and lived there until the end of the war. In 1947 he was awarded the Nobel Prize for Literature. He died in Paris, 19 February 1951.

Gide kept his *Journal*, later to be one of his major publications, from the age of 15. His first work of fiction, *Les Cahiers d'André Walter* (*The Notebooks of André Walter*), appeared in 1891. In 1909 Gide helped found the *Nouvelle Revue Française*. The early part of his prolific output was influenced by Symbolism. From 1896 to 1914 his work reflects a reaction against his Protestant upbringing and the French literary establishment and other conventions. In the period after World War I he was a leading figure in modern French letters.

Gide's output includes fiction, plays and works on aesthetic, literary, cultural and social subjects, also travel writings and numerous volumes of correspondence. He is best known for the short fictions *L'Immoraliste* (*The Immoralist*), 1902, *La Porte étroite* (*Strait is the Gate*), 1909, *Les Caves du Vatican* (*The Vatican Cellars*), 1914, and *La Symphonie pastorale* (*The Pastoral Symphony*), 1919; for his only long novel, *Les Faux-Monnayeurs* (*The Counterfeiters*), 1926, and for his collected *Journal*, 1939–50. In a spare, limpid style he pushed back the limits of self-analysis, renewed narrative techniques, and raised, not without scandal, public consciousness of current aesthetic and moral issues.

Translations

Selections

Bussy, Dorothy, *The Return of the Prodigal, Preceded by Five Other Treatises, with Saul*, London: Secker and Warburg, 1953

Mathews, Jackson, *My Theater: Five Plays and an Essay*, New York: Knopf, 1952

Fiction

L'Immoraliste, 1902

Bussy, Dorothy, *The Immoralist*, New York and London: Knopf, 1930

La Porte étroite, 1909

Bussy, Dorothy, *Strait is the Gate*, London: Jarrolds, and New York: Knopf, 1924

Isabelle, 1911

Bussy, Dorothy, *Isabelle*, with *The Pastoral Symphony*, in *Two Symphonies*, translated by Bussy, London: Cassell, and New York: Knopf, 1931

Les Caves du Vatican, 1914

Bussy, Dorothy, *The Vatican Swindle*, New York: Knopf, 1925; as *Lafcadio's Adventures*, New York and London: Knopf, 1927; as *The Vatican Cellars*, London: Cassell, 1952

La Symphonie pastorale, 1919

Bussy, Dorothy, *The Pastoral Symphony*, with *Isabelle*, in *Two Symphonies*, translated by Bussy, London: Cassell, and New York: Knopf, 1931

Macauley, Thurston, *The Pastoral Symphony*, in *Great Short Novels of the World*, edited by Barrett H. Clark, London: Heinemann, and New York: R.M. McBride, 1927

Les Faux-Monnayeurs, 1926

Bussy, Dorothy, *The Counterfeiters*, New York and London: Knopf, 1927; as *The Coiners*, London: Cassell, 1950

See entry on *The Counterfeiters*, below

L'École des femmes, 1929

Bussy, Dorothy, *The School for Wives*, New York and London: Knopf, 1929

Robert, 1930

Bussy, Dorothy, *Robert* in *The School for Wives; Robert; Geneviève, or, The Unfinished Confidence*, translated by Bussy, New York: Knopf, 1950; London: Cassell, 1953

Geneviève, 1936

Bussy, Dorothy, *Geneviève; or, The Unfinished Confidence* in *The School for Wives; Robert; Geneviève, or, The Unfinished Confidence*, translated by Bussy, New York: Knopf, 1950; London: Cassell, 1953

Thésée, 1946

Russell, John, *Theseus*, London: Horizon, 1948; New York: James Laughlin, 1949

Other Imaginative Writings

Les Cahiers d'André Walter, 1891

Baskin, Wade, *The Notebooks of André Walter*, New York: Philosophical Library, London: Peter Owen, 1968

Le Traité du Narcisse, 1891

Bussy, Dorothy, *Narcissus* in *The Return of the Prodigal* . . ., translated by Bussy, 1953

La Tentative amoureuse, 1893

Bussy, Dorothy, *The Lovers' Attempt* in *The Return of the Prodigal* . . ., translated by Bussy, 1953

Le Voyage d'Urien, 1893

Baskin, Wade, *Urien's Voyage*, New York: Philosophical Library, and London: Peter Owen, 1964

Paludes, 1895

Painter, George D., *Marshlands*, with *Prometheus Misbound*, London: Secker and Warburg, and New York: New Directions, 1953

Les Nourritures terrestres, 1897; *Les Nouvelles Nourritures*, 1935

Bussy, Dorothy, *Fruits of the Earth*, including *New Fruits of the Earth* (US edition) and *Later Fruits of the Earth* (UK edition), New York: Knopf, and London: Secker and Warburg, 1949

El Hadj, 1899

Bussy, Dorothy, *El Hadj* in *The Return of the Prodigal* . . ., translated by Bussy, 1953

Le Prométhée mal enchaîné, 1899

Painter, George D., *Prometheus Misbound*, with *Marshlands*, London: Secker and Warburg, and New York: New Directions, 1953

Rothermere, Lilian, *Prometheus Illbound*, London: Chatto and Windus, 1919

Autobiographical and Other Personal Writings

Si le grain ne meurt, 1926

Bussy, Dorothy, *If It Die*, New York: Random House, 1935; London: Secker and Warburg, 1950

Journal, 1939–50
O'Brien, Justin, *Journals*, 4 vols, New York: Knopf, and London: Secker and Warburg, 1947–51; 1-vol. edition, Harmondsworth: Penguin, 1967

Et nunc manet in te, suivi de Journal intime, 1951
O'Brien, Justin, *Et nunc manet in te, and Intimate Journal*, London: Secker and Warburg 1952; as *Madeleine*, New York: Knopf, 1952
Wallis, Keene, *The Secret Drama of My Life*, Paris: Boar's Head Books, 1951

Ainsi soit-il; ou, Les Jeux sont faits, 1952
O'Brien, Justin, *So Be It; or, The Chips are Down*, with an introduction, New York: Knopf, and London: Chatto and Windus, 1960

Plays and Other Dramatic Works
Philoctète, 1899, produced 1919
Bussy, Dorothy, *Philoctetes* in *The Return of the Prodigal* ..., translated by Bussy, 1953

Le Roi Candaule, 1901
Mathews, Jackson, *King Candaules* in *My Theater*, translated by Jackson, 1952

Saül, 1903, produced 1922
Bussy, Dorothy, *Saul* in *The Return of the Prodigal* ..., translated by Bussy, 1953
Mathews, Jackson, *Saul* in *My Theater*, translated by Jackson, 1952

Le Retour de l'enfant prodigue, 1907, produced 1928
Bussy, Dorothy, *The Return of the Prodigal* in *The Return of the Prodigal* ..., translated by Bussy, 1953

Bethsabé, 1912
Bussy, Dorothy, *Bathsheba* in *The Return of the Prodigal* ..., translated by Bussy, 1953

Oedipe, 1931
Russell, John, *Oedipus* in *Two Legends: Oedipus and Theseus*, translated by Russell, London: Secker and Warburg, and New York: Knopf, 1950

Perséphone, 1934
Mathews, Jackson, *Persephone* in *My Theater*, translated by Jackson, 1952
Putnam, Samuel, *Persephone*, New York: Gotham Book Mart, 1949

Travel Writing
Amyntas, 1906
David, Villiers, *Amyntas*, London: Bodley Head, 1958
Howard, Richard, *Amyntas*, New York: Ecco Press, 1988

Voyage au Congo, 1927; *Retour du Tchad*, 1927
Bussy, Dorothy, *Travels in the Congo*, New York and London: Knopf, 1929

Social and Political Commentary
Souvenirs de la cour d'assises, 1914
Wilkins, Philip A., *Recollections of the Assize Court*, London: Hutchinson, 1941

Retour de l'URSS, 1936
Bussy, Dorothy, *Back from the USSR*, London: Secker and Warburg, 1937; as *Return from the USSR*, New York: Knopf, 1937

Retouches à mon Retour de l' URSS, 1937
Bussy, Dorothy, *Afterthoughts: A Sequel to "Back from the USSR"*, London: Secker and Warburg, 1938; as *Afterthoughts on the USSR*, New York: Dial Press, 1938

Writings on Literature and Music
Oscar Wilde, 1903
Frechtman, Bernard, *Oscar Wilde*, London: William Kimber, 1951
Mason, Stuart [C.S. Millard], *Oscar Wilde: A Study*, Oxford: Holywell Press, 1905
Pollard, Percival, *Recollections of Oscar Wilde*, London and Boston: J.W. Luce, 1905

Prétextes, 1903; *Nouveaux Prétextes*, 1911; *Incidences*, 1924; *Divers*, 1931
Bertocci, Angelo P. *et al.*, *Pretexts: Reflections on Literature and Morality*, edited by Justin O'Brien, New York: Meridian and, London: Secker and Warburg, 1959 (contains a selection from the above French titles)

Dostoïevsky, 1923
Anonymous, *Dostoevsky*, with an introduction by Arnold Bennett, London: Dent, 1925; New York: Knopf, 1926

Journal des Faux-Monnayeurs, 1926
O'Brien, Justin, *Journal of "The Counterfeiters"*, with *The Counterfeiters*, translated by Dorothy Bussy, New York: Knopf, 1951; as *Logbook of the Coiners*, London: Cassell, 1952

Essai sur Montaigne, 1929
Bussy, Dorothy, *The Living Thoughts of Montaigne*, Philadelphia: McKay, and London: Cassell, 1939
Guest, Stephen H. and Trevor E. Blewitt, *Montaigne*, New York: Liveright, and London: Blackamore Press, 1929

Notes sur Chopin, 1938
Frechtman, Bernard, *Notes on Chopin*, New York: Philosophical Library, 1949

Interviews imaginaires, 1943
Cowley, Malcolm, *Imaginary Interviews*, New York: Knopf, 1944

Feuillets d'automne, 1949
Pell, Elsie, *Autumn Leaves*, New York: Philosophical Library, 1950

Other Writing
Corydon, 1924
[P.B.], *Corydon*, London: Secker and Warburg, 1952
Gibb, Hugh, *Corydon*, New York: Farrar Straus, 1950
Howard, Richard, *Corydon*, New York: Farrar Straus, and London: Gay Men's Press, 1985

The translation of André Gide into English was, in the case of the translator of the majority of his works, literally a labour of love. During his lengthy sojourn in Cambridge in the summer of 1918, Gide had met a younger sister of Lytton Strachey, Dorothy BUSSY the future author of *Olivia*. (Bussy's novel would later be translated into French by Gide's friend and fellow writer Roger Martin du Gard, in collaboration with the author.) Bussy gave Gide English lessons, became hopelessly smitten with the homosexual novelist, and subsequently helped him with the near-impossible task of making tolerable Lilian, Lady Rothermere's translation of his early *sotie*, or satirical farce, *Le Prométhée mal enchaîné*. (This, only the second work of Gide's to be translated into English, received a justified mauling at the hands of E.M. Forster in the *Daily News*.) With the express intention of rescuing Gide from other Lady Rothermeres, Bussy went on to translate, though in secret, *La Porte étroite*. Although it took five years to find a publisher for *Strait is the Gate*, Bussy in the meantime became Gide's official translator, and as such was responsible for the English versions of virtually all his major writings.

Bussy's translations were seen by her as a means of possessing the man who was not available to her physically ("I can't bear the thought of anyone else translating you"). Her frequent meetings with him and, above all, the voluminous correspondence they exchanged over 30 years, gained her unrivalled access to the author's views and opinions. Lists of queries were submitted (they could often be long, as in the case of his Central African travelogues). Author and translator would often revise the translation together. The roles were, at least partially, reversed when it came to discussions of Gide's translation of *Antony and Cleopatra*.

Gide, to the annoyance of friends (such as André Ruyters) who considered themselves better equipped linguistically, did not allow a restricted knowledge of the English language to prevent him from translating such varied authors as Conrad, Whitman, Tagore and Shakespeare, and he held strong views on the aims of translation. The translator's task was to produce a work that was intrinsically French rather than a version that represented maximum fidelity to the original. It was a precept he sought to encourage, though without any discernible effect, in his own translator.

In contrast to the position in Germany and certain other European countries, Gide's reputation in England in 1918 was restricted to a small francophone circle. The only work of his to have been translated into English at this time was his slim volume of memories of Oscar Wilde. In the mid-1920s Bussy's translations of *La Porte étroite* and *Les Faux-Monnayeurs* were, therefore, instrumental in ensuring for him the makings of a substantial, if belated, reputation in the English-speaking world, though in the case of *Les Faux-Monnayeurs* there was at least one other would-be translator ready to devote himself to the task.

The quality of Bussy's translations of Gide has been the subject of controversy. Reviewers were routinely laudatory. Gide was able to report praise for her work on the part of a number of readers he felt were qualified to pass judgement. How perfect a judge he was himself may be open to doubt, but he did not hesitate to pay tribute to Bussy's ability to penetrate to the heart of *La Porte étroite*, pronouncing her translation "excellent". The wife of his American publisher, Blanche Knopf, none the less waged a persistent, if ultimately unsuccessful, campaign against Bussy's translations, maintaining in conversation with Gide that there was a need to recast many of Bussy's phrases out of respect for grammatical conformity. (Bussy was forced, however, to accept titles for the American editions that went against the grain: *The Vatican Swindle* – Gide himself having objected to *The Vatican Cellars* as being "too domestic and bourgeois", *The Counterfeiters*, and, despite undue faith in the ability of her own chosen title to convey the notion of a change of heart, *Return from the USSR*.) Significantly, American readers have been less inclined than their English counterparts to lavish praise on Bussy's versions, though the reviewer in the *New Republic* thought that *Strait is the Gate* captured the "sober charm of the French" supremely well. (Some 20 years later, Joe Ackerley would liken Bussy's translation to "the shadow on the ground of some swan in flight".)

For all Gide's readiness to defend Bussy's translations against Blanche Knopf, and for all his willingness to submit for her assessment translations of his work by other hands, it is clear that he himself entertained doubts about her achievement, principally on account of her commitment to literalness. Bussy was aware of this – "You have often told me (very politely) that you don't think I am free enough" – but remained steadfast, claiming: "I am least unsuccessful when I stick the closest to your text". The terms in which she defined her method, however, went far beyond the specialized context of literary translation, her chief merits being defined by her as "comprehension and then respect, fidelity, and abnegation".

Gide's refusal to allow Bussy to translate *Thésée* (1946) on the grounds that "a woman's vocal chords were ill-suited to so deep a voice" provoked a crisis that involved not just the work in question, but the whole of their professional relationship. Bussy had reason to doubt Gide's confidence in her, in that he had employed a similar argument, albeit less insistently, with regard to both *Les Caves du Vatican* (he had Ernest Rhys lined up) and *Robert* ("You are free to refuse if you judge that, given the particular tone of the piece, a masculine voice would be more suitable"). In Gide's memory, doubtless, was the accusation his "general editorship" of the Conrad translation programme had attracted from the author of *Lord Jim*: "If my writings have a definite characteristic, it is their virility ... You are abandoning me to the women!". It was in vain that Bussy pointed out the paradox of Gide having successfully assumed the voice of his female characters or insisted that she considered Robert's narrative easier to do than Eveline's. On the other hand, it was she herself who had initially questioned her ability to tackle Gide's autobiography.

Respected Gidean scholars have declared Bussy's translations to be "excellent". Of her finest translations (Bussy herself felt that it was her version of *Les Nourritures terrestres* that had given her most satisfaction), George Painter has said that they form "a series comparable in its potential for the English reader's enjoyment and revelation only to the Scott Moncrieff-Kilmartin Proust". Yet there are others, such as the Australian scholar James Grieve, who have dissented from such a view. In addition to maintaining, in a letter to the *Times Literary Supplement*, that Bussy's versions are written in "a form of Frenglish ... All the words (of a sort), the shapes of the sentences are French", he charges them with "squeamishness, omissions, elementary blunders and queerspeak". Examples to support such a view can indeed be adduced, as in the case of the ambivalent feelings of Michel in *L'Immoraliste* as he watches his wife die: the phrase "plein d'angoisse et d'attente" (anguished and expectant) is travestied by Bussy's rendering of it as merely "sick at heart". In a small number of cases, however, the possibility of editorial interference on the part of Bussy's publishers cannot be discounted.

In the final analysis, the success or otherwise of Bussy's translations must be decided in terms of a still more fundamental question. Bussy recognized that the apparent straightforwardness of Gide's use of language is deceptive, yet this insight was used by her merely to bolster her commitment to literalness: "when a word is altered, when the order is disarranged by a hair's breadth, the whole spirit of the things seems to vanish". Her literalist approach has the undoubted merit of not imposing on the original an alien voice. Yet it may also be regarded as erasing the crucial sense Gide communicates of the limitations or inadequacy of all the narrative voices he adopts. It is arguable that the greatest weakness of Bussy's translations is indeed to have failed to grasp that the significance of Gide's consistently ironic writings resides not so much in the substance of what is said but in the implications of the manner in which it is said, and that its successful re-creation in another language depends, as Gide himself realized, on a much freer notion of equivalence.

Gide has been well served by the translators of the major works not undertaken by Dorothy Bussy. George PAINTER's translation (1953) of *Paludes* and *Le Prométhée mal enchaîné*, which he dedicated to "Gide's incomparable translator", is a work of great elegance and supreme readability. The lyrical beauty of John RUSSELL's translation (1948) of *Thésée* is deeply moving. The unique quality of the *Journal* has been well captured by its American translator, Justin O'BRIEN (1947–51), who has also, in 1960, translated *Ainsi soit-il*; it is possible to regret that more of Gide's major works did not fall to his lot. Villiers DAVID's translation (1958) of *Amyntas* has also attracted praise. Bussy herself was ready to pay tribute to the work of both O'Brien and Russell, as well as to Elsie PELL's translation (1950) of the *Feuillets d'automne*. On the other hand, she was not slow to point out the errors made by Bernard FRECHTMAN, translator (1951, 1949) of *Oscar Wilde* and *Notes sur Chopin*.

Gide's most often translated works have been his treatise on homosexuality, *Corydon* (of which the most recent version, by Richard HOWARD (1985), is to be preferred), and his slim volume on Wilde, the first English translation of which, by "Stuart MASON" [C.S. Millard] in 1905, reveals significant editorial interference by Lord Alfred Douglas.

MICHAEL TILBY

Further Reading

Delay, Jean, *The Youth of André Gide*, abridged and translated by June Guicharnaud, Chicago: University of Chicago Press, 1963

Goulet, Alain, *Fiction et vie sociale dans l'oeuvre d'André Gide*, Paris: Minard, 1985

Hytier, Jean, *André Gide*, translated by Richard Howard, New York: Doubleday, 1962; London: Constable, 1963

Ireland, G.W., *André Gide: A Study of His Creative Writings*, Oxford: Clarendon Press, 1970

O'Brien, Justin, *Portrait of André Gide: A Critical Biography*, New York: Knopf, and London: Secker and Warburg, 1953; New York: McGraw Hill, 1964

Painter, George, D., *André Gide: A Critical Biography*, London: Weidenfeld and Nicolson, and New York: Atheneum, 1968

Pollard, Patrick (editor), *André Gide et l'Angleterre*, London: Birkbeck College, 1986

Segal, Naomi, *André Gide: Pederasty and Pedagogy*, Oxford and New York: Oxford University Press, 1999

Sheridan, Alan, *André Gide: A Life in the Present*, London: Hamish Hamilton, 1998

Steel, D.A., "Escape and Aftermath: Gide in Cambridge 1918", *The Yearbook of English Studies*, 15 (1985), pp. 125–59

Tedeschi, Richard (editor), *Selected Letters of André Gide and Dorothy Bussy*, Oxford and New York: Oxford University Press, 1983 (the correspondence in its entirety has been published in French)

Walker, David H., *André Gide*, London: Macmillan, and New York: St Martin's Press, 1990

The Counterfeiters

Les Faux-Monnayeurs, 1926

Gide's narrative interweaves literal and figurative forms of counterfeiting as his many characters, children and adults, practise forgery, deceit, inauthenticity and betrayal. One of the protagonists, Édouard, is, like his creator, writing a novel called "Les Faux-Monnayeurs" and keeping a diary of its progress. Alongside its colourful fictions Gide's texts contains reflections on the processes of writing.

Translation

Bussy, Dorothy, *The Counterfeiters*, New York and London: Knopf, 1927; as *The Coiners*, London: Cassell, 1950

In Gide's definitive classification of his works of prose fiction, *Les Faux-Monnayeurs* was the only one to which he was prepared to attach the label of *roman*. His distinction between *roman* (novel), *sotie* (farce), and *récit* (account, narrative) was an indication of both the unprecedented scope of *Les Faux-Monnayeurs* and its function as a summa of the manifold themes pursued in his numerous compositions of the previous 25 years. Only one English translation of this key text in European modernism has been published, by Gide's "official" translator Dorothy Bussy. In contrast to her translation of *La Porte étroite*, it was begun with the full knowledge and consent of the author. Gide neglected, however, to inform his publisher, Gaston Gallimard. In the absence of Gide from Paris, Gallimard gave encouragement to another would-be translator, the American novelist Waldo Franck, in the expectation that his action would meet with the author's approval.

Bussy's chosen title for her translation was *The Coiners*, but, much to her indignation, Knopf, who published both the English and the American edition of her translation, insisted on the title *The Counterfeiters*. More than 10 years later she still regarded this latter choice of title as a "hideous hybrid", something she would "never ... get over", and "a sore point in my professional career". Gide had clearly failed to placate his devoted translator with his observation "if the word does not exist, it soon will". Bussy managed to impose her original title on the volume in the Standard Edition of Gide's works, but, after her death, her paperback publishers adopted Knopf's original title and it is as *The Counterfeiters* that the novel is generally known in the English-speaking world.

In translating *Les Faux-Monnayeurs*, Bussy enjoyed an unrivalled privilege. She had been in on Gide's project from the beginning and remained privy to the author's intentions and emphases throughout the long drawn-out process (1919–1925) of the novel's composition. Part of the work was actually read aloud to her before it was serialized in *La Nouvelle Revue Française*. Aware of the particular importance Gide's "only novel" held for its author, she went as far as to upbraid him for contemplating going to Africa before it was finished. In March 1925, she gave him notice of the series of questions she had prepared for him relating to his text. Her translation was finished in November 1926.

Les Faux-Monnayeurs was a work Bussy admired for its being both "rich and spare". Her description of it as possessing "a magnificent bone-structure, no fat, just muscle" may be taken as an indication of the quality she strove to emulate in her English version. Gide expressed considerable approval of her translation, claiming that it was superior, for example, to the none the less perfectly acceptable German version. Suppressing momentarily his reservations with regard to literal translation, and doubtless encouraged by the comments of reviewers on both sides of the Atlantic, he praised the "subtle precision of her interpretation", maintaining that she had captured "every twist, insinuation, and nuance of [his] emotions and thinking". He pointed out, however, that the table of contents of the first edition erroneously gave the title of part 2, chapter 3, as "Édouard explains his theory to La Pérouse", instead of "Édouard explains his theory of the Novel". (The error is corrected in subsequent editions.) He also pointed out "a little 'contresens'" [sic] in Bussy's translation of the music teacher La Pérouse's reference to "un accord parfait", which, he clarified, is a technical term in music, a "common chord", rather than a "perfect chord". The co-publisher of the Standard Edition (Cassell) later allowed Bussy to insert an explanatory footnote by way of a corrigendum ("as the author pointed out to me ..."); the footnote was carried over into the Penguin edition, but American editions continue to feature the original mistranslation. Already in the first edition, Bussy had had recourse to the occasional footnote, for example drawing attention in chapter 17 of part 1 to the untranslatability of Passavant's pun on *dessalé*, which, in addition to meaning "unsalted" ("desalinated") has a slang meaning of "sharp", "unscrupulous".

A certain timorousness on the part of Bussy's original publisher led to the expurgation of the reference to the bloodstained handkerchief discovered by Armand after the young Bernard has taken Armand's sister's virginity. The cut was never restored. It may, on the other hand, have been Bussy herself who felt it more decorous to describe Laura as *enceinte*, rather than "pregnant".

The echo of Flaubert's Emma Bovary remains accessible to Bussy's reader through her readiness to translate Laura's words literally: "A lover! A lover! I've got a lover". But a further literary allusion is inadvertently obscured when Bussy renders Bernard's address to the suitcase, which is an echo of Rastignac's famous challenging address to Paris at the end of Balzac's *Le Père Goriot* ("À nous deux maintenant!"), as "now suitcase, a word with you". A minor irritation is the inconsistent approach to characters' French forenames: Olivier remains Olivier but Georges becomes George.

More generally, Bussy fails to communicate a sufficiently sharp impression of the narratorial intrusions and other self-conscious devices that are designed to ironize the narration and draw attention to the willed artificiality of the composition. It is arguable that her translation of the opening sentence as "'The time has now come for me to hear a step in the passage'", fails to convey the original emphasis on Bernard's self-conscious role-playing, which would seem to require something along the lines of "'This is where I hear ...'". Gide's original text is adept at instant communication of the different kinds of falseness present in his characters' modes of expression. It is here, in its attempts to render the often subtly stylized conversations and interior monologues, that Bussy's literalist translation is at its least successful: the English reader is denied the experience of "hearing" the falseness. Gide's remarkable lightness of touch is transformed into a seemingly faithful but ultimately wooden form of expression that is not so much an absence of style as a failure to direct the English reader's responses with the sureness experienced by the reader of the original.

For all that, Bussy undoubtedly remains faithful to the spareness she admired in the original. Her version is often unexceptionable. It can thus be said to provide an excellent illustration of both the advantages and the limitations of her approach to translation. Duly conscious of the need to avoid elaboration, she does not always avoid the deadening effect of the banal. Her failure is, however, instructive, in that it reveals the extent to which Gide's art depends on the ironization of language rather than on any commitment to the *mot juste*.

There was no plan to accompany *The Counterfeiters* with a translation of the *Journal des Faux-Monnayeurs*, a work which was denied the English reader until Justin O'Brien's translation of 1951.

MICHAEL TILBY

Further Reading

Goulet, Alain, *André Gide, "Les Faux-Monnayeurs": Mode d'emploi*, Paris: SEDES, 1991

Idt, Geneviève, *André Gide, Les Faux-Monnayeurs: Analyse critique*, Paris: Hatier, 1970

Tilby, Michael, *Gide: Les Faux-Monnayeurs*, London: Grant and Cutler, 1981

Gilgamesh first half of 2nd millennium BC

This epic poem is a collection of stories and myths concerning the exploits, shared with his friend the hero Enkidu, of the demigod Gilgamesh, identified with the ruler of Uruk/Erech (Babylonia) in the 3rd millennium BC. As well as several elements resembling features in classical and medieval legends, there is a description in *Gilgamesh* of a flood and ark episode resembling the account of the Deluge in the Old Testament Book of Genesis.

Translations

Bridson, D.G., *The Quest of Gilgamesh*, Cambridge: Rampant Lions Press, 1972

Dalley, Stephanie, in her *Myths from Mesopotamia: Creation, The Flood, Gilgamesh, and Others*, with an introduction, Oxford and New York: Oxford University Press, 1989

Ferry, David, *Gilgamesh: A New Rendering in English Verse*, with an introduction by William L. Moran, New York: Farrar Straus, 1992; Newcastle upon Tyne: Bloodaxe Books, 1993

Gardner, John and John Maier, with the assistance of Richard A. Henshaw, *Gilgamesh, Translated from the Sî-leqi-Unninni? Version*, with an introduction, New York: Knopf, 1984

George, Andrew, *The Epic of Gilgamesh*, Harmondsworth: Penguin, 1999

Jackson, Danny P., *The Epic of Gilgamesh, Verse Rendition*, with an introduction by Robert D. Biggs, Wauconda, Illinois: Carducci, 1992

Jacobsen, Thorkild, in his *The Harps that Once ...: Sumerian Poetry in Translation*, New Haven, Connecticut: Yale University Press, 1987

Kovacs, Maureen Gallery, *The Epic of Gilgamesh*, with an introduction, Stanford, California: Stanford University Press, 1985; revised edition, 1989

Sandars, N.K., *The Epic of Gilgamesh: An English Version with an Introduction*, Harmondsworth: Penguin, 1960; revised edition, 1972; episode of *Gilgamesh and Enkidu*, Harmondsworth: Penguin, 1995

Shabandar, Sumaya, *The Epic of Gilgamesh: Translated from the Arabic*, Reading, Berkshire: Garnet, 1994

Temple, Robert, *He Who Saw Everything: A Verse Translation of the Epic of Gilgamesh*, London: Rider, 1991

Thompson, R. Campbell, *The Epic of Gilgamesh: Text, Transliteration and Notes*, Oxford, Clarendon Press, 1930

The oldest extant literary work, the epic of Gilgamesh poses many difficulties for the would-be translator. What has come to be known as "the standard Babylonian version" dates back to the 7th century BC. The poem is written in the Akkadian language on 12 tablets, and on each tablet are three to six columns of unequal length. This version itself is a synthesis of many older versions, of which the Sumerian, and the Old Babylonian are the oldest, dating from the first half of the second millennium BC. Fragments of the epic have been found in a wide area of the Near and Middle East – from ancient Mesopotamia to Anatolia, Egypt, Syria, Palestine and Elam (now in northern Iran). These fragments are written in five different cuneiform languages, understanding of which is still not complete. Since the poem belongs to the oral tradition, there are many variations, even of the same episode of the story. The fragmentary nature of these tablets, with frequent missing lines, as well as the lack of precise dates for their composition, presents major obstacles to the construction of a continuous narrative. As more fragments are discovered, and as our knowledge of these ancient languages improves, the constant updating of translations becomes necessary. Scholarly works written on the Gilgamesh epic or on the Mesopotamian myths in general contain many translations of the various fragments.

One of the first translations of the Babylonian version was that by THOMPSON (1930). He provides a scholarly edition of the original cuneiform text with transliterations and a prose inter-linear translation. His notes offer useful information on textual difficulties.

One of the most enduring and popular translations has been that by SANDARS (1960). Her continuous narrative in lucid and lively prose is based on earlier scholarly translations of Babylonian, Assyrian and Sumerian texts.

BRIDSON's elegantly literary translation (1972) is based on earlier translations. A slightly shortened version of it was broadcast by the BBC's Third Programme on 29 November 1954; it was published only in a limited edition of 125 copies.

Campbell Thompson's literal translation of 1930 forms the basis for GARDNER & MAIER's translation (1984), although they also took into account new material published after 1930. The emphasis in this verse rendering is on the form of the Standard Babylonian Version. The translators, therefore, have not only kept the 12-tablet format but also sought to represent, in English, the division into different segments on each tablet. Seventy-two distinct poetical units are translated. Profuse notes and a good introduction accompany this useful version of *Gilgamesh*.

Another translation from the Standard Version is by KOVACS (1985). The second edition is based on new materials published prior to the autumn of 1988. It is a literal line-by-line translation of 11 of the tablets. The 12th is ignored because it "shows much evidence of being a secondary addition onto an original eleven-tablet series" (introduction). To preserve a continuous narrative, Kovac has inserted passages from the Old Babylonian texts, and some variants from different versions are also noted.

JACOBSEN translates only one episode of the Gilgamesh epic in his book (1987). Based on the Sumerian text, his "Gilgamesh and Aga" gives a fine presentation of the epic form in English verse.

TEMPLE's interest in the Gilgamesh epic lies in its "concealed meanings" as an ancient religious text. He has, as a consequence, exercised a good deal of freedom in his version (1991). In places where the original is obscure or missing, he has inserted his own "daring" guesses, in order "to make life easier for the reader". He has not scrupled to mix Sumerian and Akkadian names in his translation, which includes 11 of the tablets, in generally elegant verse. Notes at the beginning of each tablet are informative as to both the state of the tablet and its contents.

DALLEY (1989) includes translations of both the Standard and the Old Babylonian Versions in her book. Providing line-by-line translations in very readable prose, her book offers scholarly notes and introduction. The missing parts and lines are left empty, which, while making good scholarly sense, can lead to difficulties in following a continuous narrative.

JACKSON's reworking of the Gilgamesh story (1992) is a free rendering in verse. It is an attempt "to translate the spirit rather than the word" of the epic. Jackson tries to clarify the sacred nature of the epic in his version.

Modern Arabic is one of the more appropriate languages for a version of the Gilgamesh epic to be written in. SHABANDAR's version (1994), in simple prose, is based on the fourth edition of Taha Baqer's Arabic translation.

FERRY (1992) re-creates, in well-made English couplets, the story of Gilgamesh. The Standard and the Old Babylonian texts are employed. In contrast to the literal translations already considered, his version tries to present some of the poetical qualities of this ancient epic in clear and energetic verse. A new verse translation of *Gilgamesh* by Andrew GEORGE was published by Penguin in 1999.

PARVIN LOLOI

Further Reading

Maier, John R., "Translating Gilgamesh", in *Translation Perspectives: Selected Papers*, edited by Marilyn Gaddis Rose, Binghamton: State University of New York Press, 1984

Tigay, Jeffrey H., *The Evolution of the Gilgamesh Epic*, Philadelphia: University of Pennsylvania Press, 1982

See also translators' introductions, especially William L. Moran's introduction to Ferry

---

Natalia Ginzburg 1916–1991

Italian novelist, short-story writer and dramatist

Biography

Born Natalia Levi in Palermo, Sicily, 14 July 1916, into a middle-class family, Jewish on one side, Catholic on the other. In 1919 they moved to Turin. She was educated in Turin, entering the university there in 1935, but leaving before taking a degree. In 1938 she married the Italian writer and patriot Leone Ginzburg; they had three children. When he was exiled by the fascist regime the couple lived in the Abruzzi (1940–43); arrested as an anti-fascist activist, he died in prison in 1944.

After World War II, Ginzburg, who already, before and during the war, had had short stories printed in the periodical *Solaria* and published a novella, *La strada che va in città* (*The Road to the City*), became an editorial consultant at her late husband's publishing firm Einaudi, first in Rome and then in Turin. In 1950 she married Gabriele Baldini, an academic (died 1969). From 1952 she lived in Rome but from 1959 to 1961 was in London where her second husband was in charge of the Italian Cultural Institute. In 1983 she was elected as an independent left-wing member to the Italian parliament.

Ginzberg's best-known novels include *Tutti i nostri ieri* (*Dead Yesterdays*), 1952; *Le voci della sera* (*Voices in the Evening*), 1961; *Lessico famigliare* (*Family Sayings*), (1963); and *La città e la casa* (*The City and the House*), 1984. Her fiction tends to centre on the problems of women in the modern world. She wrote a fictionalized biography of the 19th-century novelist Alessandro Manzoni (*La famiglia Manzoni* (*The Manzoni Family*), 1983; several plays, including *Ti ho sposato per allegria* (*I Married You for the Fun of It*), 1966; and a number of collections of critical essays, notably *Mai devi domandarmi* (*Never Must You Ask Me*), 1974. She translated Proust's *Du côté de chez Swann* and Flaubert's *Madame Bovary* into Italian (1953 and 1983). From the late 1940s onward her work won numerous literary awards in Italy. Died in Rome , 7 October 1991.

Translations

Novels and Novellas

La strada che va in città, 1941 (written under the name of Alessandra Tornimparte)

Frenaye, Frances, *The Road to the City: Two Novelettes* (also contains *The Dry Heart*, a translation of Ginzburg's *È stato così*), New York: Doubleday, 1949; London: Hogarth Press, 1952

Tutti i nostri ieri, 1952

Davidson, Angus, *Dead Yesterdays*, London: Secker and Warburg, 1956; as *A Light for Fools*, New York: Dutton, 1956; as *All Our Yesterdays*, Manchester: Carcanet, 1985

Le voci della sera, 1961

Low, D.M., *Voices in the Evening*, New York: Dutton, and London: Hogarth Press, 1963

Lessico famigliare, 1963

Low, D.M., *Family Sayings*, New York: Dutton, and London: Hogarth Press, 1967; Manchester: Carcanet, 1984

Woolf, Judith, *The Things We Used to Say*, Manchester: Carcanet, 1997

Caro Michele, 1973

Cudahy, Sheila, *Dear Michael*, London: Peter Owen, 1975

Famiglia, 1977
Stockman, Beryl, *Family: Two Novellas*, Manchester: Carcanet, and New York: Seaver, 1988

La città e la casa, 1984
Davis, Dick, *The City and the House*, Manchester: Carcanet, 1986; New York: Seaver, 1987

Natalia Ginzburg's novels, stories and plays offer a minute and ironic analysis of almost 50 years of Italian life, capturing the minimal ebb and flow of personal and family life from the alienating hypocrisy of Italian society under Mussolini's regime to the brash 1980s and the collapse of any moral and social bedrock. Ginzburg's work, humorous and compassionate, exposes with the lightest of touches humanity adrift on the currents of history. As she moved from the short story form to the novel, her ability to convey complex emotion with clarity of prose commanded a wide audience in Europe with swift and regular translations into English. That her later work in the 1970s as a playwright did not enjoy the same international success is perhaps a comment on Italian theatre generally as well as on the quality of her own production. While almost all of her prose works have been translated into English, her theatre is almost unknown in that language.

Ginzburg's work emerges from a background of socialism and anti-fascism (her family name was Levi, and she married the anti-fascist intellectual Leone Ginzburg, but she refuses to align herself fully with the orthodoxies of politics, feminism or, in the cultural sphere, neo-realism. As she weaves stories and novels out of the minutiae of human experience, her prose style, with both lexis and syntax indicating a move away from the Italian obsession with "high" culture, is sober and unrhetorical. Her translators have required an ear similarly fine-tuned to the subtle nuances of everyday speech and language.

Ginzburg began publishing in 1941 (*The Road to the City*) and her early work (*È stato così*, 1947, translated by FRENAYE as *The Dry Heart*, 1949) melodramatically questioned women's lives, constrained and confined by the expectations both of society and of themselves. The short story "La madre" (1948; translated as *The Mother* by Isabel Quigley, 1965) shows the dangerously tragic limitations of women's lives in the immediate post-war period, where a rigid, traditional social code denies the woman sexual and emotional independence. The woman's vitality and sexuality earn her the disapproval not only of her parents but also of her children: this volatile mother who stays out late, plucks her eyebrows, puts yellow powder on her face and smokes in bed, earns the contempt and mistrust not only of her parents but also of her children. This sober, austere story offers no solution to the tension between woman as sexual being and woman as mother within a rigid family and social structure, and ends, after a disappointment in love, with suicide.

All Our Yesterdays (*Tutti i nostri ieri*, 1952), Ginzburg's first long novel, an account of the impact of history on individual human destiny, is set in the period of anti-fascist struggle and the fight for the liberation of Italy from the Nazis. Ginzburg takes a worm's eye view of history: Anna is both protagonist and victim, caught up in events which are much bigger than herself and which she barely comprehends. For the writer, human motivation and action never have the clarity attributed to them by politicians or ideologues. The dubious motivation of the three self-proclaimed anti-fascists is contrasted with the spontaneity and warmth of Cenzo Rena, who generously marries the pregnant Anna and who is one of the most positive characters in the whole of Ginzburg's work. Rena, eventually shot by the Germans, is no idealized martyr but, like Thomas Keneally's portrait of Oscar Schindler, a man whose faults and failings are redeemed by his generous and spontaneous courage.

With *Family Sayings* (*Lessico famigliare*, 1963), her best-known novel, Ginzburg completes her journey from the third to the first person, from a desired "masculine" objectivity to "feminine" autobiography, from description or free indirect discourse to dialogue. In this re-creation of her family through language, snatches of rhyme, family stories, idiosyncratic expressions, language becomes the connective tissue which unites the members of this very modern Jewish family, scattered in a new kind of Diaspora: "all it takes between us is a word. Just a word, a single sentence, one of those old old sentences heard and repeated any number of times when we were children".

Family Sayings is a humorous, affectionate, nostalgic portrait of Ginzburg's family, traced from the early years of fascism through to the years after World War II, and remains her most consistently popular novel. Eccentricities are lovingly depicted: her father, university professor, anti-fascist, passionate, intolerant, despotic, temperamental, given to loud rages interspersed by moments of clumsy tenderness and disarming innocence; his wife Lydia, with her snatches of opera and her sudden enthusiasms just as soon forgotten; her sister and brothers with their childish pranks and chatter, later to become actively involved in anti-fascism – some of the leading opponents of Mussolini's regime were friends of the family. It is this environment of convinced public political positions and chaotic private relationships that is evoked through recollections of fragments of language, "sayings", a mixture of mispronunciations, childish rhymes, incorrect usages or dialect words, difficult to convey in any translation into English, where differences tend to reflect class rather than region. LOW's mixed approach to the translation (1984), sometimes translating and sometimes substituting comparable if not equal expressions, is reasonably successful but cannot convey the rich cultural and historical complexity of the original. The sayings are humorous, idiosyncratic, frequently without referential meaning, and their function is less to give information than to reinforce and confirm an almost tribal sense of community. The characters depicted in *Family Sayings* had everything in common because they had language in common, however far apart and dispersed they were. By one of those intuitions that occur in a state of grace, Ginzburg connected the reciprocal recognition of different members of a Jewish family to a poetic perception of life, to a sense of "belonging". Monumental events of recent Italian history are undercut by the family lexis, thus avoiding both private sentimentality and public melodrama.

The one character largely missing from the text is Natalia herself. She tells us only elliptically of her marriage to Leone Ginzburg, the Communist intellectual avoided by the bourgeoisie of Turin as a dangerous conspirator. Ginzburg's venture into pure autobiography could not be more stripped of the sentimentalism she so despised but is none the less poignant for its reserve, as when she describes the fatal return to Rome and Leone's death in prison. Ginzburg achieves dramatic effect by dramatic understatement: as in Primo Levi's accounts of Nazi prison camps, horror is conveyed not through hyperbole but through restraint, through what remains unsaid. Judith WOOLF's 1997 translation (*The Things We Used to Say*) of *Lessico famigliare* was highly commended by the judges of the 1998 John Florio prize for translation from Italian into English.

SHARON WOOD

Further Reading

Bullock, Alan, *Natalia Ginzburg: Human Relationships in a Changing World*, New York and Oxford: Berg, 1991

Soave-Bowe, Clotilde, "The Narrative Strategy of Natalia Ginzburg", *Modern Language Review*, 68 (1973), pp. 42–47

Wood, Sharon, "Memory, Melancholy and Melodrama in Natalia Ginzburg (1916–1991)" in *Italian Women's Writing from 1860–1994*, London: Athlone Press, 1995

Jean Giono 1895–1970

French novelist and dramatist

Biography

Born in Manosque, Provence, 30 March 1895, and spent most of his life there. He went to local schools, leaving at the age of 16. He began his working life as a bank clerk in Manosque, 1911–14, then served in the Alpine infantry until 1919, going back to the bank until 1928, when he turned to writing. He married in 1920 (two daughters). An active pacifist after World War I, at the beginning of World War II he was imprisoned briefly in Marseille for refusing to obey the call-up (1939). He was then released and demobilized. In 1944 he was again imprisoned, on a flimsy charge of collaboration, soon dropped. In the 1950s he travelled in the UK, Italy, Switzerland and Austria. In 1958 he started a film company, for which he wrote screenplays. His health began to weaken in the late 1960s and he died in Manosque, 9 October 1970.

Giono had published a few poems in the early 1920s but his first success was the novel *Colline* (*Hill of Destiny*), 1929, part of a regional trilogy, set mainly in Provence, completed by *Un de Baumugnes* (*Lovers Are Never Losers*), 1929, and *Regain* (*Harvest*), 1930. More novels (some of which were made into films) followed at close intervals, the best-known internationally being *Que ma joie demeure* (*Joy of Man's Desiring*), 1935, and *Le Hussard sur le toit* (*The Hussar on the Roof*), 1951. The post-World War II novels tended to have historical instead of regional settings. His last novel, *L'Iris de Suse* [The Iris of Suse], was written in 1970. There were also autobiographical and polemical works, as well as plays, but it was for his fiction that he received honours, including the Brentano prize, 1929; the Northcliffe prize, 1930; the Monaco prize, 1953; and election to the Académie Goncourt, 1954.

Translations

Novels

Colline, 1929
Le Clercq, Jacques, *Hill of Destiny*, New York: Brentano, 1929

Un de Baumugnes, 1929
Le Clercq, Jacques, *Lovers Are Never Losers*, preface by André Maurois, New York: Brentano, 1931; London: Jarrolds, 1932

Regain, 1930
Fluchère, Henri and Geoffrey Myers, *Harvest*, London: Heinemann, and New York: Viking Press 1939

Le Grand Troupeau, 1931
Glass, Norman, *To the Slaughterhouse*, London: Peter Owen, 1969

Le Chant du monde, 1934
Fluchère, Henri and Geoffrey Myers, *The Song of the World*, New York: Viking Press, 1937; London: Heinemann 1938

Que ma joie demeure, 1935
Clarke, Katherine Allen, *Joy of Man's Desiring*, New York: Viking Press, 1940; London: Routledge and Kegan Paul, 1949

Le Hussard sur le toit, 1951
Griffin, Jonathan, *The Hussar on the Roof*, London: Museum Press, 1953; as *The Horseman on the Roof*, New York: Knopf, 1954

Le Bonheur fou, 1957
Johnson, Phyllis, *The Straw Man*, New York: Knopf, 1959; London: Redman, 1961

Angélo, 1958
Murch, Alma E., *Angélo*, London: Peter Owen, 1960

Other Writing

Jean le bleu, 1932
Clarke, Katherine Allen, *Blue Boy*, New York: Viking Press 1946; London: Routledge 1948

L'Homme qui plantait des arbres, 1980 (written 1953)
Bray, Barbara, *The Man Who Planted Trees*, London: Harvill, 1995

Jean Giono is not particularly easy to translate. His prolific output is original in content and style, expressing a personal view of the world about which he wrote. His abundant imagination produced a dense metaphorical element. The personification of natural phenomena is everywhere present, and the language is very expressive.

Because of the geographical setting in which almost all the works are placed, there are many examples, especially in the earlier works, of "provençalismes". Giono claims for himself a great number of neologisms, relatively few of which are genuinely new words. A translator needs to be familiar with the "oddities" of Giono's language, although, ironically, personal or deliberate modifications made to standard French impinge less on the reader of a translation than on a French reader. The syntax of the early works is generally colloquial, but his peasants often speak more like the author than like peasants. Great freedom is exercised in constructing sentences, which frequently reflect the spontaneous thoughts of the characters.

The exuberant imagery, too much of which can smother the storyline, is much less in evidence in the later, more historical works, but the sensual element remains. These works contain a vast amount of detail and, often, technical vocabulary. Metaphors suited to the subject matter (often macabre) may not present as much difficulty as the more flamboyant and personal earlier ones. The result is a greater consistency in the quality of translation of the later, postwar works.

The original of *Lovers Are Never Losers* (1929, translated 1931 with an over-elaborate choice of title) faces the translator with the challenge of reproducing the speech of country folk, since the narrator is a casual seasonal farm worker. Although the French text uses a great many colloquial structures, some slang, and words and expressions deriving from a combination of geographical location and Giono's imagination, only an oral narration would give an indication of accent. One problem of trying to reproduce peasant speech in another language is the number of choices offered to the translator. Whatever choice is made will inevitably be the wrong choice for many readers, because it imposes on them one type of peasant, who may be jarringly unfamiliar. It would be much more sensible to adopt a neutral tone, as in the original French, and let the reader invent an accent. LE CLERCQ's (1931) translation (he also put Giono's first novel, *Colline*, 1929, into English) is especially irritating because he has made a decision on behalf of the reader that risks ruining the whole emotional climate of the novel. The reader needs to be able to appreciate the humanity of the narrator, the lofty ideals (based on ancestral religious persecution) of the hero, and the very moving scenes at the end of the book when the hidden (almost umbilical) cord between them is severed. Such emotion, although still present in the English version for a reader who is familiar with the original French, is rendered very difficult to capture by the jargon adopted by Le Clercq. To get to the emotion one needs to battle one's way through his style.

The jargon that has been adopted has been systematically sustained but feels very artificial and is sometimes inconsistent. The following examples will give an idea of the English text: "yer" for "your"; "asweatin'"; "there be"; "thenatime"; "tryin' to help 'un"; "the head of me"; "the hair of her"; "'E felt the hurt of the family cruel hard"; "a ball of forcemeat asplutterin'"; "birds were achirrupin'"; "where be it, that Douloire farm of yers?" Particular problems of comprehension arise from the mixture of British and American slang, although most of the time the meaning can be deduced: " the bloody gowk of a frigglin' mash-head".

Apart from the constant irritation of the adopted style, there are definite errors of interpretation and unnecessary additions to the dialogue which embroider on the simplicity of the original. Altogether this translation is very heavy going.

Compared with *Lovers Are Never Losers* FLUCHÈRE & MYERS's translation (1939) of *Regain* (1930) is much more natural and smooth, although the problem of conveying the title accurately is not quite overcome by the word *Harvest*, which fails to carry the essential metaphorical meaning of "renewal", or a "second harvest". The translation respects the economy of Giono's text. Emotion is generated by succinctness. The conversations are natural and convincing and convey the exact meaning of the original. The same translators are responsible for *The Song of the World* (1937), the English version of *Le Chant du Monde* (1934).

GLASS's (1969) choice of title *To the Slaughterhouse*, together with his use of the word "War" in the title of chapter 1, where Giono uses the much more cryptic pronoun "It", plunges the reader of the English translation into the underlying symbolic significance of Giono's title *Le Grand Troupeau* [The Big Flock] (1931). Was this necessary so soon in the story? Giono's book, described by Redfern (1967) as "turgid", is a series of tableaux alternating between home in Provence and the battle front in Flanders. The superficially reasonable translation reveals, in a detailed comparison with the original, many defects, some serious. The narrative flows well throughout. However, it soon becomes apparent that an attempt has been made to simplify it. Similes, for example, felt to be too difficult to put into English, have been systematically omitted. One has the feeling that the translator thinks that some of the rustic imagery sounds idiotic in English. He also puts in conversation where it does not exist or transposes sentences from one part of the page to another if he thinks it will aid comprehension. The repetitious quality of some of the French conversations has not been retained.

The number of lexical errors and Glass's apparent ignorance of slang expressions is surprising, leading to totally erroneous versions: " even if you bring your wife" is translated as "if you want a regular life", which is meaningless in the context and pure invention. Details of images are left out: "the blood trickled down his chin" makes no reference to the foamy quality of the blood. Little effort has been made to tackle the neologistic elements, or Giono's translations into French of Provençal words: "attacks of dizziness" is weak for "epilepsy". Crucial comparisons between men and animals, surely the whole metaphorical basis of the book, are omitted. This is a betrayal of Giono's purpose. Similarly, the poetic turns of phrase with which Giono endows some of his characters are also omitted. Glass seems unable to cope with anthropomorphism. Neither is he faithful to the rhythm of Giono's prose. Inappropriate translations occur. Would an Army major use a term like "my little one" in English to one of his men? Surprisingly, the graphic descriptions of death in the trenches come over very well. However, the only way to appreciate this translation is to be ignorant of the original – stylistically, topographically and metaphorically.

CLARKE's *Blue Boy* (1932, translated 1946) makes a good job of conveying the episodic nature of this semi-autobiographical and fanciful book. The translation respects the fragmentation well, and is faithful, too, to the metaphoric element prominent in all Giono's early work. The anthropomorphism dear to Giono's heart might strike an odd note in English, in spite of being faithful to the French: "an inn with its door wide open and lighted to the back of its throat"; "the street could still be heard rubbing against the shop". The wind is a person with hair, fingers, arms and shoulders. Giono's very vivid imagination, where, as a boy, he sees faces in mouldy, crumbling walls, or where he evokes the effects on him of a Bach polonaise, are very well translated, transporting the reader into the child's mind. Clarke, by whom *Que ma joie demeure* (1935) was also made available in English (CLARKE, 1940), is very faithful to the original (*Jean le bleu*). People are graphically evoked, as well as the more sordid elements in the tale – wounds, filth, rats. Parts of the book depict pain, cruelty, degradation and death, and these descriptions come over well. Compared to the earlier novels, there are few words really difficult to translate because there are fewer "provençalismes" in this book. The translation conveys emotion well. It is not, however, without its errors, especially of syntax and occasionally of lexis.

The novels loosely collected under the title *Chroniques* comprise *Le Hussard sur le toit* (1951), *Le Bonheur fou* (1957) and *Angélo* (1958), among others. Although the themes are linked, notably by the central character, Angélo, each book has its own distinctive narrative style. They are dense historical novels, with very long and somewhat convoluted chapters, often flashbacks. The metaphoric quality of the earlier work is present, but less flamboyant. Conversations frequently have a modern feel about them.

GRIFFIN (1953) is faithful to the French in *The Horseman on the Roof*, even when a resulting phrase sounds odd in English: "this burning plaster weather". Some clumsiness is present in the narrative, but the conversations run more smoothly and the macabre humour comes over well. Several words used in the context of the historical setting are left in French when it is not certain that they are sufficiently part of the English language to be easily understood. The detailed descriptions of death, illness, convulsions, and putrefaction, mingled with an ironic and buffoon-like element, are transmitted competently.

JOHNSON (*The Straw Man*, 1959) has chosen not to respect the original title *Le Bonheur fou*, although happiness is an important theme. She conveys the tempo of the book, as well as the irony and the sensuous descriptive passages. The descriptions of food are particularly well conveyed and the visual impact is good. The sentences are no more convoluted than in the original. Not unnaturally, the conversations sound rather more American than British. Explanatory footnotes are generally historical rather than lexicographical. The idiom comes over oddly at times, and sections can be too literal. Words left in French are often italicized but will not be easily understood by the general reader. Odd lapses occur: " she had been a carbonari." Some of the stranger "inventions" of Giono are dealt with by omission. The translator's foreword furnishes the reader with a useful historical background to the novel.

MURCH's translation (1960) of *Angélo* reads well. Giono's narrative form here, less dense than in earlier works, is better suited to translation. The wry humour is transmitted to the reader. The descriptions of scenery are evocative. The whole translation runs smoothly and sounds natural, with due consideration given to rendering correctly 19th-century terms. Many words are left in French. This causes no problem for the commonly known ones like *château*, *salon*, and *fête*, but others might have deserved a footnote. Some clumsiness exists: "the mountain Sainte Victoire"; "the habit still makes the monk" and some phrases are incomprehensible without some research: "she is like a little fer-de-lance".

With a few reservations, all the above three translations from the *Angélo* series convey the spirit of the originals.

BRAY's excellent translation (1995) of *The Man Who Planted Trees* – a pleasure to read – conveys well the beauty of this short fable of the regeneration of a tract of land through the efforts of one man. It contains much that is typical of Giono, thematically and from the point of view of imagery, but without exaggeration.

MARIAN GILES JONES

Further Reading

Brée, Germaine and Margaret Guiton, *An Age of Fiction: The French Novel from Gide to Camus*, New Brunswick, New Jersey: Rutgers University Press, and London: Chatto and Windus, 1958

Clarke, Katherine A., "Interview with Jean Giono", *French Review*, 33/1 (October 1959)

Giles Jones, Marian, "Jean Giono and Provençal" (dissertation), University of Wales, 1976

Gilman, Wayne C., "The General Neologisms of Jean Giono", *French Review*, 33/5 (April 1960)

Goodrich, Norma L., *Giono, Master of Fictional Modes*, Princeton, New Jersey: Princeton University Press, 1973

Peyre, Henri, *French Novelists of Today*, New York: Oxford University Press, 1967 (chapter 5 on Giono)

Redfern, W.D., *The Private World of Jean Giono*, Oxford: Blackwell, and Durham, North Carolina: Duke University Press, 1967

Saunders, F.W., "Giono's World of Words", *Forum for Modern Language Studies* (October 1968)

Scott, M., "Giono's Song of the World: The Theme of Language and its Associations in Giono's Pre-War Writings", *French Studies* (July 1972)

Smith, Maxwell A., "Giono's Use of the Ulysses Concept", *French Review*, 31/1 (October 1957)

Smith, Maxwell A., "Giono's Cycle of the Hussard Novels", *French Review*, 35/3 (January 1962)

Smith, Maxwell A., *Jean Giono*, New York: Twayne, 1966

Starr, W.T., "Jean Giono and Walt Whitman", *French Review* (December 1940)

Vial, Fernand, "Jean Giono at the Académie Goncourt", *American Society of Honor Magazine* (Spring 1955)

Walker, Hallam, "Myth in Giono's *Le Chant du Monde*", *Symposium* (Summer 1961)

Jean Giraudoux 1882–1944

French dramatist and novelist

Biography

Giraudoux, born in Bellac in the Limousin region of France, 29 October 1882, was a brilliant student at the local schools and Paris *lycée* he attended and at the École Normale Supérieure, where he took his *licence* in 1905. He taught for a while in Germany and travelled in central Europe and the US before a spell in journalism. In 1910 he became a civil servant. He served in the French army in World War I and was twice wounded. From 1917 he was a career diplomat as well as a prolific writer. During World War II he was for a time head of the French government's information service, but he retired in 1940. His reputation suffered somewhat from suspicions about his connections with the German administration in France, though his political principles, reflected in his writing, were pacifist and anti-Nazi. He died in Paris, 31 January 1944.

Giraudoux first caught the attention of the French literary world with a collection of short stories, *Provinciales*, published in 1909, which charmed and intrigued by the elegance and originality of their fanciful, not to say precious style. There followed, between 1911 and 1939 a dozen densely written, loosely structured novels, but it was not until 1928 that he came to prominence as a major writer, when he adapted for the stage one of his own novels, *Siegfried et le Limousin* (1922) as *Siegfried*. His best-known works for the theatre include *Amphitryon 38* (1929; translated as *Amphitryon 38*, 1938); *La Guerre de Troie n'aura pas lieu* (1935; as *Tiger at the Gates*, 1955); *Ondine* (1939; as *Ondine*, 1958); and *La Folle de Chaillot* (1945; as *The Madwoman of Chaillot*, 1947).

Translations

Selections of Plays

Fry, Christopher, *Plays, Volume 1*, with an introduction by Harold Clurman, London: Methuen, and New York: Oxford University Press, 1963 (contains *Judith*, *Tiger at the Gates*, *Duel of Angels*)

Gellert, Roger, *Plays, Volume 2*, London: Methuen, and New York: Oxford University Press, 1967 (contains *Amphitryon*, *Intermezzo*, *Ondine*)

La Farge, Phyllis and Peter H. Judd, *Three Plays*, New York: Hill and Wang, 1964 (contains *Siegfried*, *Amphitryon 38*, *Electra*)

Valency, Maurice, *Four Plays*, New York: Hill and Wang, 1958 (contains *The Madwoman of Chaillot*, *The Apollo of Bellac*, *The Enchanted*, *Ondine*)

Plays

Amphitryon 38, 1929

Behrman, S.N., *Amphitryon 38*, New York: Random House, and London: Hamish Hamilton, 1938

Gellert, Roger, *Amphitryon* in *Plays, Volume 2*, translated by Gellert, 1967

La Farge, Phyllis and Peter H. Judd, *Amphitryon 38* in *Three Plays*, translated by La Farge and Judd, 1964

Judith, 1931

Fry, Christopher, *Judith* in *Plays, Volume 1*, translated by Fry, 1963

Savacool, J.K., *Judith* in *The Modern Theatre*, vol. 3, edited by Eric Bentley, New York: Doubleday, 1955

Intermezzo, 1933

Gellert, Roger, *Intermezzo* in *Plays, Volume 2*, translated by Gellert, 1967

Valency, Maurice, *The Enchanted*, New York: Random House, 1950; in *Four Plays*, translated by Valency, 1958

La Guerre de Troie n'aura pas lieu, 1935

Fry, Christopher, *Tiger at the Gates*, London: Methuen, and New York: Oxford University Press, 1955; in *Plays, Volume 1*, translated by Fry, 1963; revised as *The Trojan War Will Not Take Place*, London: Methuen, 1983

Électre, 1937

La Farge, Phyllis and Peter H. Judd, *Electra* in *Three Plays*, translated by La Farge and Judd, 1964

Smith, Winifred, *Electra* in *From the Modern Repertoire*, vol. 2, edited by Eric Bentley, Denver: University of Denver Press, 1952; revised in *The Modern Theatre*, vol. 1, edited by Bentley, New York: Doubleday, 1955

Ondine, 1939

Gellert, Roger, *Ondine* in *Plays, Volume 2*, translated by Gellert, 1967

Valency, Maurice, *Ondine* in *Four Plays*, translated by Valency, 1958

Sodome et Gomorrhe, 1943

Briffault, Herma, *Sodom and Gomorrah* in *The Makers of the Modern Theater*, edited by Barry Ulanov, New York: McGraw Hill, 1961

Novels

Elpénor, 1919

Howard, Richard and Renaud Bruce, *Elpénor*, New York: Noonday Press, 1958

Suzanne et le Pacifique, 1921

Redman, Ben Ray, *Suzanne and the Pacific*, New York and London: Putnam, 1933

Siegfried et le Limousin, 1922

Wilcox, Louis Collier, *My Friend from Limousin*, New York and London: Harper, 1923; New York: Fertig, 1976

Bella, 1926

Scanlan, J.F., *Bella*, New York: Knopf, 1927

La Menteuse, 1958

Howard, Richard, *Lying Woman*, London: Gollancz, and New York: Winter House, 1972

Jean Giraudoux's novels, despite their poetic charm, were likely to appeal only to a small minority of readers (and translators) who could combine the mental agility of a chess Grand Master with the stamina of a long-distance runner. While translators virtually queued up to produce English versions of the plays, of his novels only five appeared in English translation: *Elpénor* (1919) translated by HOWARD & BRUCE as *Elpénor* (1958); *Suzanne et le Pacifique* (1921) translated by REDMAN as *Suzanne and the Pacific* (1933); *Siegfried et le Limousin* (1922), translated by WILCOX as *My Friend from Limousin* (1923); *Bella* (1926), which retained the same title in the version by SCANLAN (1927); and *La Menteuse* (1958), translated by HOWARD (1972) as *Lying Woman*. When, with *Siegfried*, the constraints of dramatic composition curbed the excesses of the novelist, Giraudoux quickly became, under Louis Jouvet's influence, the most successful French dramatist of the inter-war years and much translated into English.

BEHRMAN's *Amphitryon 38* (1938) is considerably shorter than the original play. It foregrounds the comic at the expense of the poetic, so that the end product is amusing but much less sophisticated. And as Eric Bentley once said, in this very case: "If you paid your money to see Giraudoux, you may not be willing to settle for Mr. Behrman." In contrast, the translations by LA FARGE & JUDD (1964) and by GELLERT (1967) adhere closely to the original in both intention and achievement. Whereas Behrman's apparently limited knowledge of French forces him to rely on some inspired guesswork, both of the later versions are sensitive to the linguistic nuances of the source text. There is little to choose between them: both successfully avoid turning Giraudoux's stylized prose into unnatural English, though Gellert opts for a rather more idiomatic English.

While *Judith* has been the least successful, theatrically, of Giraudoux's plays, it is linguistically the most dense and for that reason of particular interest to the translator. Both of the translations have made cuts. SAVACOOL (1955), as if to compensate, rather irritatingly makes the text over-explicit. In addition, he has decided to tone down the ornateness of Giraudoux's style, an operation that tends to diminish the play's impact as a tragedy. Whereas the French Judith "suffers" on seeing her "mission" become a matter of public election rather than personal initiative, Savacool's Judith, somewhat prosaically, "objects" to being pushed into ... [an] adventure" with Holofernes. In contrast, FRY's translation (1963) preserves the dignity of Giraudoux's heroine: his Judith does not "object" to public election, it "racks her spirit". As this example suggests, Fry's version is more successful in capturing the eloquence and rhythms of the original text. It nevertheless falls down at times on accuracy. One particularly unfortunate mistranslation concerns the blow suffered by Judith's pride, the focus of the drama, when divine and civic election prevent her from becoming the *self*-appointed saviour of her race: Judith's "Why should God have wanted to take away from me all personal merit by showering me with glory?" becomes in Fry's version an opaque "Why should God have wanted to lift me beyond myself and overwhelm me with glory?"

Both versions of *Intermezzo* are translations of quality. VALENCY (1950) has a good feel for the giralducian idiom, particularly the playwright's sense of humour. Unlike Behrman, he adapts his text with discretion, injecting just a little more pace into the dialogue and making the comic effects a touch bolder. GELLERT (1967) gives a more faithful rendering of the French text, but the satirical humour has less bite. When it comes to ridiculing the bureaucratic mentality of the school inspector, for example, Gellert's "you are supposed to be concentrating on your examinations, not shrieking with laughter" sounds a little flat in comparison with Valency's "I know of nothing in the school regulations that requires children to be gay. But there is a good deal about their being orderly." While there are few inaccuracies in either text, Gellert's mistranslation of "les enfers" as "hell" (only in the singular can it mean this) does give an odd twist to Isabelle's fascination with what Valency more correctly renders as "the other world".

Tiger at the Gates does not present quite as formidable a challenge to the translator as *Judith*. Nevertheless, despite the text's greater linguistic transparency, the tone is more varied, ranging from the flippancy and sexual innuendo surrounding the old men of Troy and Paris's affair with Hélène to the solemnity of Hector's Speech to the Dead. FRY's Hector (1955) has the same power to move us as his French counterpart. The more satirical scenes, however, can sound a little stilted, and greater variation of register would not have come amiss; even if, ultimately, it is Giraudoux himself who must face the charge of stylistic uniformity, and Giraudoux whom we've paid to see. Again, there are reservations to be made about Fry's grasp of idiomatic French. More than once the text is made to say the opposite of what is intended: instead of deliberating on whether to "risk the destruction of the city", the council considers whether to "give the city a public holiday". More surprising, however, in a writer of Fry's stature, is a failure, at one of the high-points of the play, to sustain Ulysses' analogy between the lines that crisscross the globe and the lines on Hector's palm: Fry substitutes for the linear shapes in the original text (rivers, the flightpaths of birds and the wakes of ships), shapes that in two cases out of three are not linear at all.

In SMITH's revised *Electra* (1955) two howlers persist in the very first scene –"prétendre" (to claim) is still "pretend", "oronge" (a kind of mushroom) still "orange" – suggesting a strong case for a re-revision. But although there are more mistranslations to come, the meaning of this complex play is reasonably well preserved. The translation is, none the less, ponderously literal: the "grande nouvelle" announced by Aegisthus on discovering that the son of the man he has murdered is still alive becomes a misleadingly optimistic "great news". In strong contrast, the version by LA FARGE & JUDD (1964) is much more successful in reproducing the tone of the original and does so in acceptable English. While not totally free of errors it shows a much better understanding of, and respect for, the linguistic subtleties of the text. Whenever the density and the economy of Giraudoux's French require expansion, this is achieved with intelligence and elegance. Typical of the translators' attention to detail is their rendering of the quip about Égisthe's womanizing: "Égisthe n'aime pas beaucoup les visages d'hommes inconnus. / Il ne déteste pas assez les visages de femmes connues". The force of the irony, which depends, of course, on the symmetry, and which is lost in Smith's "strange faces/well-known women's faces", is simply but effectively preserved by La Farge and Judd's "men he doesn't know / women he does know".

Visible in VALENCY's adaptation (1958) of *Ondine* is an effort to make it more theatrically effective for his American audience. He speeds up the tempo, lightens the tone and even redistributes speeches. As in *The Enchanted* (*Intermezzo*), the satirical dimension is skilfully handled, the Chamberlain being as memorably pompous as the Inspector. On the other hand, the freedom with which he approaches the more poetic elements of the play allows him to avoid the main translational challenges, though it must be said, in fairness, that one is not left with the impression that this is his objective. GELLERT's translation (1967), on the other hand, scrupulously follows the original. It is particularly impressive in its colourful rendering of the vernacular speech of the humbler characters, and reliable also in conveying meaning and register in the case of the principal ones.

Giraudoux wrote four other full-length plays: *Siegfried* (1928), *Sodom and Gomorrah* (*Sodome et Gomorrhe*, 1943), *The Madwoman of Chaillot* (*La Folle de Chaillot*, 1945) and *Duel of Angels* (*Pour Lucrèce*, 1953). They are not so firmly established in the repertoire as those discussed above, with the exception, perhaps, of *The Madwoman*. Three of the four feature in the selections of Giraudoux plays listed and, by and large, they reflect the strengths and weaknesses of the translators in question. The fourth, *Sodom and Gomorrah*, is very ably translated by Herma BRIFFAULT (1961), who had the privilege of seeing the original Paris production in 1943.

PAUL REED

Further Reading

Bentley, Eric (editor), *The Modern Theatre*, vol. 1, New York: Doubleday, 1955

Johann Wolfgang von Goethe 1749–1832

German poet, dramatist and novelist

Biography

Born into a well-to-do middle class family in the city of Frankfurt, 28 August 1749. He studied law, first at Leipzig University (1765–68), and then in Strasbourg (1770–71). From 1771–72 he practised law in Frankfurt and Wetzlar. He became famous first as a novelist all over Europe with *Die Leiden des jungen Werthers* (*The Sorrows of Werther*). His literary fame attracted the interest of the young Duke Carl August of Saxe-Weimar, who in 1775 invited him as a cabinet minister to his court. With the exception of a two-year journey to Italy from 1786 to 1788 Goethe lived all his life in Weimar. While in the first decade of his professional life he was involved in the administration of mining, industry, highway construction and the recruiting of soldiers in the duchy of Saxe-Weimar, after 1788 he was able to limit his administrative attention to the theatre, museums and the University of Jena and to devote more of his time to creative writing. The final version of *Wilhelm Meister's Apprenticeship* was written during the years after his return from Italy, from 1794 to 1796. He died in Weimar, 22 March 1832.

Translations

Collection

Middleton, Christopher and Stuart Pratt Atkins (editors), *Goethe's Collected Works* (bilingual edition), 12 vols, Cambridge, Massachusetts: Suhrkamp / Insel, 1983–89

Selections

Boyle, Nicholas (editor), *Selected Works of Goethe*, London: David Campbell, 1999 (contains *The Sorrows of Young Werther*, translated by Elizabeth Mayor and Louise Bogan; *Elective Affinities*, translated by David Constantine; *Italian Journey*, translated by W.H. Auden and Bogan; *Novella*, translated by Mayer and Bogan; *Faust*, translated by Barker Fairley; *Selected Poems*, translated by Christopher Middleton and Michael Hamburger; and *Selected Letters*, translated by M. von Herzfeld and C. Melvil Sym)

Luke, David, *Selected Poetry by Goethe*, with an introduction, London: Libris, 1999

The Sorrows of Werther

Die Leiden des jungen Werthers, 1774; revised edition, 1787

A mostly epistolary novel in two parts, including an "Editor's" preface. First published in 1774 (Leipzig: Weygand) and significantly revised in 1787. For the 50th-anniversary edition Goethe amended the title, replacing the more archaic "Werthers" with the more modern "Werther".

Werther falls passionately in love with his friend Albert's beautiful fiancée, Charlotte, second mother to her orphaned siblings. When Charlotte, married to Albert, tries to distance herself from Werther, he kills himself.

Translations

Boylan, R. Dillon, *The Sorrows of Young Werther*, with an introduction, London: Bohn, 1854

Hulse, Michael, *The Sorrows of Young Werther*, with an introduction, Harmondsworth: Penguin, 1989

Hutter, Catherine, *The Sorrows of Young Werther*, with an introduction, in *The Sorrows of Young Werther and Selected Writings*, translated by Hutter, with a foreword by Hermann J. Weigand, New York: New American Library, 1962

Lange, Victor, *The Sorrows of Young Werther* in *The Sorrows of Young Werther, The New Melusina, Novelle*, edited by Lange, with an introduction, New York: Rinehart, 1949; reprinted in *The Sorrows of Young Werther, Elective Affinities, Novella*, edited by David E. Wellbery, Cambridge,

Massachusetts: Suhrkamp / Insel, 1988 (*Goethe's Collected Works*, edited by Middleton and Atkins, vol. 11)
Malthus, Daniel (published anonymously; also ascribed to Richard Graves), *The Sorrows of Werter*, London: Dodsley, 1779 and many subsequent editions; 1789 edition reprinted Oxford and New York: Woodstock Books, 1991
Mayer, Elizabeth and Louise Bogan, *The Sorrows of Young Werther*, with *Novella*, translated by Mayer and Bogan, with a foreword by W.H. Auden, New York: Random House, 1971; in *Selected Works of Goethe*, edited by Nicholas Boyle, London: David Campbell, 1999
Morgan, Bayard Quincy, *The Sufferings of Young Werther*, New York: Ungar, and London: Calder, 1957; reprinted in *The Sufferings of Young Werther and Elective Affinities*, edited by Victor Lange, with forewords by Thomas Mann, New York: Continuum, 1990
Pratt, Samuel Jackson, *The Sorrows of Werter*, 2nd edition, London: Tegg, 1809
Render, William, *The Sorrows of Werter*, London: Phillips, 1801; Boston: Andrews and Cummings, 1807
Rose, William, *The Sorrows of Young Werther*, with an introduction, London: Scholartis Press, 1929; without its introduction, in *The Permanent Goethe*, edited by Thomas Mann, New York: Dial Press, 1948
Steinhauer, Harry, *The Sufferings of Young Werther*, with an introduction, New York: Bantam, 1962

If any translated work of literature epitomizes the notion of translation as rewriting, then it is certainly *The Sorrows of Young Werther* by Goethe. Perhaps no other work by any other German-speaking author has appeared in quite so many languages, not to mention forms. In his native Germany and then throughout Europe, Goethe gained virtual overnight celebrity with this sentimental story. Appearing toward the end of the Enlightenment, young Werther rebelliously cried out with heartfelt emotion against the cold-blooded, dogmatic droning of the Age of Reason. Rewriting of the piece actually began with Goethe himself, who produced a more pointed restatement of his text following the first round of *Werther*-mania. Subsequent waves of interest in *Werther* have seen the tale versified, collected in German and world literature anthologies, imitated and parodied – often through sequels or answers to the original – and rendered into versions for stage, opera and screen. Werther even succeeded in crossing over from word into image in a series of Chinese paintings based on the story – and all this in spite (or possibly on account) of its contemporary reception at the end of the Enlightenment and Goethe's own reticent attitude toward authorship of the piece.

Feeling rather uncomfortable with his creation, Goethe later credited *Werther*'s success simply to its timely publication. To be sure, the work was a clear sign of its times. The irony is that a work so representative of late 18th-century sentimentalism should have such staying power, given that that literary movement experienced a rise and fall as meteoric as did the character Werther himself. Well beyond the sentimentalist craze, 20th-century rewritings include Thomas Mann's "sequel" *Lotte in Weimar* (1939) and Ulrich Plenzdorf's dramatized "parody" *Die neue Leiden des jungen W.* (1972). That both these works have been translated into English – as *Lotte in Weimar* by H.T. Lowe-Porter (New York and London, 1940) and as *The New Sufferings of Young W.* by Kenneth P. Wilcox (New York, 1979) – further testifies to *Werther*'s position in the world literary canon – should recent translations of the original itself not provide evidence enough.

Much as *Werther* betokens the spirit of its age, its rewritings reflect the way their own ages interpreted the tale. If, for example, one accepts Goethe's justification for his story's good fortune, one might then rewrite *Werther* with replication of the sentimentalist sphere surrounding the work in mind. Naturally, the earliest translations especially manifested this concern. Notwithstanding their inaccuracies, they took the context of British sensibility into account when reworking German sentimentalism. With MALTHUS (1779), the French translation actually served as the model, because of its omissions of the more offensive portions of the original. By foregrounding neither creator nor creation, these versions avoided the sort of criticism that "absurdly ascribed to [the author] the erroneous sentiments which he has given to his principal character", as Malthus wrote in his preface. Particular interest in the context can be found, too, in those translations that somehow sought to answer the pathologically self-involved sentimentalism which had, in the extreme case depicted by Goethe, resulted in suicide. In RENDER (1801) and PRATT (1809), incorporating copious explicative footnotes to mark the true circumstances found in Goethe's fiction provides one contextual solution. Render further expunges all subjective sentimental ambiguity inherent in Goethe's text by fixing the context with a dialogue that supposedly took place between him and the "real" Werther. Moreover, editions of the versions by Malthus and Pratt often contained William James's antidotal *The Letters of Charlotte during her Connexion with Werter* (1786). The wealth of information these works provide about the sentimentalist situation make them inestimably valuable for an accurate view of the 18th-century reception of Werther. Their ability to extend the 20th-century hermeneutic horizon surely accounts for the re-publication (1991) of one of them, namely a 1789 edition of Malthus.

Itself another form of rewrite, William Makepeace Thackeray's satirizing "Sorrows of Werter" (1853) fairly well chronicles the point when Werther's sentimental context was no longer taken seriously. Thereafter translators began to regard the creation or its creator (in varying degrees) as the focus for their rewritings, as their acknowledgement of the German spelling of the main character's name reveals. In recognizing the intrinsic merits of the piece as a work of art or of the artist as genius, translators meant to distill the aesthetic qualities from the story's sentimental stock. However, these versions are generally written in an idiom that exposes the translator's, rather than the author's or the work's generation. The result often amounts to a creation, which never reads quite like the original but always like a fine English novel. Indeed the accessibility of these artistic versions has ensured them all numerous editions with only the most superficial revision over the years.

Witness in this regard the translations of Boylan (1854), Morgan (1957), Lange (1949), and Mayer & Bogan (1971). Though in his preface BOYLAN argues for the translator's obligation to the work, it becomes clear from his rewriting of, say, the curse "Devil" to "Deuce" that the translation should be a work of proper English. MORGAN continues this tradition with his colloquial "pshaw!" and "for shame!" even though he is the first to correct the title from "Sorrows" to "Sufferings" –

remedying a flaw Goethe himself once noted. As a subsequent editor of Morgan, LANGE curiously discloses all these translations' modernist and one might say elitist tendencies by coupling the work to Thomas Mann, who is said to show the "high degree of literacy of a practicing writer" in his "approach to the intellectual and formal substance" of Goethe's *Werther*. A similarly arrogant tone pervades Lange's own translation, which, for example, overlooks connotations of social and economic status, thereby effacing *Werther*'s often radical political commentary: "titles" become merely "phrases," the "bourgeois" a "citizen". In MAYER & BOGAN, W.H. Auden condescendingly introduces the protagonist to readers as "a horrid little monster" and a "spoiled brat". Like Boylan, though published some hundred years later, Mayer & Bogan thoroughly sanitizes Werther's messy end: Werther's brains are not "driven out", but instead "laid bare"; nor do the bereaved "hang on his lips until forcibly ripped away", but rather cling "to him till the bitter end". More recently, HULSE (1989) takes up their approach, as demonstrated by his translation of that same "bourgeois" as a "happy man" and "manual laborers" as "guildsmen". In Hulse the aim to "isolate the novel from the original events and see Goethe's artistry on its own terms" typifies these translations' tendencies toward creative whims attempting to evince artistic genius equivalent to Goethe's.

The translations of Rose (1929), Hutter (1962), and Steinhauer (1962) are concerned with portraying the artist rather than his artistry. Their introductions particularly emphasize the biographical and psychological dimensions of Goethe in *Werther*. ROSE's interest in maintaining Goethe's initial emotional outlook prompts him to return to the original edition of 1774. HUTTER supplements her edition with portions of Goethe's memoirs, and STEINHAUER prefaces his version with perhaps the most thorough attempt at such biographical introductions. Furthermore, in their consideration of Goethe as creator, Hutter and Steinhauer deserve special note since they recognize the importance of the Ossian passages in *Werther*: Hutter by actually translating Goethe's translation of Ossian, and Steinhauer by providing a dual-language edition that demonstrates how *Werther* strays from the "original" *Songs of Selma*. Since Goethe himself acknowledged the significance of these translated passages and their connection to Werther's ever-widening downward spiral, the fact that almost all translators have chosen to infuse their texts with *Songs of Selma* from English is amazing. Above anyone else, translators ought to be acutely aware of what the act of translation reveals about the inner workings of the mind. To neglect – as many have – the product of Goethe's (or, as Goethe presents it: Werther's) translation nearly obliterates critical insights into the character of Werther as well as the overall nature of the story. How they have resolved this issue tellingly marks the approach of all these translators.

JOHN R.J. EYCK

Further Reading

Herrmann, Hans Peter (editor), *Goethes Werther: Kritik und Forschung*, Darmstadt: Wissenschaftliche Buchgesellschaft, 1994

Long, Orie W, "English Translations of Goethe's *Werther*", *Journal of English and Germanic Philology*, 14 (1915) pp.169–203

Long, Orie W., "English and American Imitations of Goethe's *Werther*", *Modern Philology*, 14 (1916) pp. 193–216

Morgan, Bayard Quincy (editor), *A Critical Bibliography of German Literature in English Translation*, 2nd edition, Stanford, California: Stanford University Press, 1938; supplemented New York: Scarecrow Press, 1965 and, edited by Murray F. Smith, Scarecrow Press, 1972 (these volumes comprise arguably the most extensive listing in English of *Werther* translations and imitations as well as their innumerable editions)

Swales, Martin, *Goethe: The Sorrows of Young Werther*, Cambridge and New York: Cambridge University Press, 1987

Vincent, Deirdre, *Werther's Goethe and the Game of Literary Creativity*, Toronto: University of Toronto Press, 1992

See also translators' introductions to Rose, Steinhauser, and Hulse

Wilhelm Meister's Apprenticeship

Wilhelm Meisters Lehrjahre, 4 vols, 1795–96

The German text used by translators is based on the 1795/96 edition of the novel. The punctuation and spelling have been modernized where necessary by subsequent German editors. An earlier version of the novel was found in 1910 and identified as a copy of Goethe's manuscript made by one of his women friends and her daughter. This version was published under its original title *Wilhelm Meisters theatralische Sendung* (*Wilhelm Meister's Theatrical Mission*) in 1911. An English translation of this version, by Gregory A. Page, was published in 1913; a new translation by John R. Russell under the title *Wilhelm Meister's Theatrical Calling* was published in 1995.

Translations

Blackall, Eric A., with Victor Lange, *Wilhelm Meister's Apprenticeship*, Cambridge, Massachusetts: Suhrkamp / Insel, 1989 (*Goethe's Collected Works*, edited by Middleton and Atkins, vol. 9)

Boylan, R. Dillon, *Wilhelm Meister's Apprenticeship*, London: Bohn, 1855; and several subsequent editions

Carlyle, Thomas, *Wilhelm Meister's Apprenticeship*, Edinburgh: Oliver and Boyd, 1824, Boston: Wells and Lilly, 1828; revised edition as *Wilhelm Meister's Apprenticeship and Travels*, London: Fraser, and New York: Burt, 1839; and numerous subsequent editions of *Wilhelm Meister's Apprenticeship*, with or without the *Travels*; *Wilhelm Meister's Apprenticeship*, with a new introduction by Franz Schoenberner, New York: Heritage Press, 1959

Waidson, H.M., *Wilhelm Meister's Years of Apprenticeship*, 3 vols, London: John Calder, and Dallas: Riverrun Press, 1977–79

While Goethe's poetry and his verse dramas, especially his *Faust* tragedy, are difficult to translate, his novels do not present such problems, with the exception of a few poems inserted into his prose – among them some of his most famous.

Goethe wrote four novels, *The Sufferings of Young Werther* (1774, revised version 1787); *Wilhelm Meister's Apprenticeship* (1795–96); *Elective Affinities* (1809); and a sequel to *Wilhelm*

Meister's Apprenticeship, Wilhelm Meister's Journeyman Years (1821, enlarged and revised definitive version 1829). While *Werther* triggers numerous translations, adaptations and imitations in English, *Wilhelm Meister's Apprenticeship* was not as successful, but attracted the attention of Thomas Carlyle, who was eager to introduce this novel to the British public, although not with great success. In Germany, *Wilhelm Meister's Apprenticeship* became known as the first *Bildungsroman* ("novel of self-realization") and as the model for this genre in German literature. Although Goethe had not planned to write such a novel – the term *Bildungsroman* was coined in the 19th century – *Wilhelm Meister's Apprenticeship* had a great influence on the history of the German novel through the 20th century. The story centres on Wilhelm, a young man living in the second half of the 18th century who strives to break free from the restrictive world of his merchant class background and its business concerns and seeks fulfilment as an actor and playwright, but ends up in marrying into the nobility. The marriage to a woman of the nobility was seen by Goethe's contemporaries as a symbolic response to the French Revolution.

Wilhelm Meister's Travels (or *Journeyman* Years, with the subtitle *or, The Renunciants*), Goethe's sequel to the *Apprenticeship*, is now admired as a formal experiment. The first version, which was incomplete, appeared in 1821, and the final and complete version in 1829 as volumes 21–23 of *Goethes Werke, Ausgabe letzter Hand*. Thomas Carlyle's translation of 1827 under the title *Wilhelm Meister's Travels* was based on the first version, since the final version had not yet appeared in German. The first edition of Carlyle's translation was reprinted in 1991 (Columbia, South Carolina: Camden House). An accurate and excellent translation of the final version by Krishna Winston is available under the title *Wilhelm Meister's Journeyman Years; or, The Renunciants*, in *Goethe's Collected Works*, vol. 10 (Cambridge, Massachusetts: Suhrkamp/Insel, 1989). A main text concerned with Meister's further development frames numerous other narratives and documents; by the end Meister will leave Europe for North America.

There has been a recent resurgence of the *Bildungsroman* with a female protagonist at its centre (as in novels by Doris Lessing, Mary McCarthy, and Christa Wolf), but in spite of earlier claims to "English kinsmen" of Goethe's novel, *Wilhelm Meister's Apprenticeship* did not have a great resonance in the English-speaking world. Although the interest in translating Goethe increased after the bicentennial of his birth in 1949, Carlyle's translation still dominated the market. There was no demand for a modern translation for university instruction for a long time, because *Wilhelm Meister's Apprenticeship* did not have a firm place on college reading lists outside German departments. It took another 40 years until the standard translation by Eric A. BLACKALL (1989) in cooperation with Victor LANGE became available. All Goethe's novels are now available in modern English translations, singly and collectively in the edition of *Goethe's Collected Works*, edited by Victor Lange, Eric A. Blackall, and Cyrus Hamlin and now distributed by Princeton University Press (originally by Suhrkamp Publishers, New York, 1983–89).

CARLYLE's *Wilhelm Meister's Apprenticeship* (1824) is the first translation of the novel into English. It is not always reliable and is bowdlerized when Wilhelm Meister's sexual adventures are described, especially in book 5, chapters 12–13, or when sexual and religiously sensitive topics are discussed in book 6. Apparently Carlyle tried to allay his own moral and religious scruples or those of his audience by deleting passages from his translation in the original that appeared offensive to him. Carlyle's translation remains historically important for the reception of Goethe in England, but it cannot be considered a close or accurate rendition of the original. The reprint in paperback by Macmillan did not satisfy the need for an accurate and modern standard translation.

BOYLAN (1855) became competition for Carlyle during the second half of the 19th century, but Carlyle's translation won out at the beginning of the 20th century. WAIDSON (1977–79) is a modern translation that is close and accurate. It responded to the need for a modern translation during the 1970s, but the three-volume edition never became popular. BLACKALL (1989) is a most reliable and modern version with notes; it also quotes other translations of the poetry in *Wilhelm Meister's Apprenticeship*. This must be considered the academic standard translation. Its availability in cloth and paperback will close a gap that existed for a long time.

EHRHARD BAHR

Further Reading

Bahr, Ehrhard, *The Novel as Archive: The Genesis, Reception, and Criticism of Goethe's Wilhelm Meisters Wanderjahre*, Columbia, South Carolina: Camden House, 1998

Blackall, Eric A., *Goethe and the Novel*, Ithaca, New York: Cornell University Press, 1976

Bruford, W.H., *The German Tradition of Self-Cultivation*, Cambridge and New York: Cambridge University Press, 1975, pp. 29–57, 88–112

Lillyman, William J. (editor), *Goethe's Narrative Fiction*, Berlin and New York: de Gruyter, 1983

Reiss, Hans, *Goethe's Novels*, London: Macmillan, and New York: St Martin's Press, 1969

Shaffner, Randolph P., *The Apprenticeship Novel: A Study of the "Bildungsroman" as a Regulative Type in Western Literature*, New York: Peter Lang, 1984

Elective Affinities

Die Wahlverwandschaften, 1809

This complex work follows, through a narrator, the effects upon a wealthy married couple, Edward and Charlotte, of the presence in their household of his friend, the Captain, and her niece, Ottilie. Passion and reason, instinct and conscience, conflict long and painfully. A martyr to abnegation, Ottilie dies, followed by Edward, and they are buried side by side.

Translations

Constantine, David, *Elective Affinities*, with an introduction, Oxford and New York: Oxford University Press, 1994; in *Selected Works of Goethe*, edited by Nicholas Boyle, London: David Campbell, 1999

Froude, James Anthony, *Elective Affinities*, in *Novels and Tales by Goethe*, translated chiefly by R. Dillon Boylan, London: Bohn, 1854; published separately, with an introduction by Frederic Ungar, New York: Ungar, 1962

Hollingdale, R.J., *Elective Affinities*, with an introduction, Harmondsworth: Penguin, 1971
Mayer, Elizabeth and Louise Bogan, *Elective Affinities*, with an introduction by Victor Lange, Chicago: Regnery, 1963
Waidson, H.M., *Kindred by Choice*, London: John Calder, 1960

Perhaps surprisingly, Goethe referred to this as "my best book". Written in 1808 in the familiar German literary form of the *Novelle*, it was originally designed to be included within the format of *Wilhelm Meisters Lehjahre* (*Wilhelm Meister's Apprenticeship*), but outgrew that setting and was published separately in 1809. Three years earlier, under the pressures generated by the occupation of Weimar by French troops, Goethe had finally married his long-time mistress, Christiane Vulpius. The book draws heavily on his own emotional experiences at various stages of his life to examine the effects upon a marriage when each of the partners experiences a strong attraction towards another person: one of the new couples so formed resists the attraction with greater success than the other.

The German title is a normal dictionary word, a main entry taking up almost a page in the *Deutsches Wörterbuch* of the brothers Grimm. It is a technical term used in chemistry: "the tendency of a substance to combine with certain particular substances in preference to others". In the German, that sense is immediately apparent, and its wider implication in terms of human relationships is also self-evident. The straightforward English equivalent (in the plural used by Goethe) might well be "Preferential Affinities".

However, the origins of the German word lie in Latin. *Affinitas* was first used in this sense by Albertus Magnus in the 13th century. Many others followed him, and in Goethe's own time a work by the Swedish chemist Torben Bergman, *De attractionibus electivis*, had been translated into German as *Die Wahlverwandtschaften*. In 19th-century English, the Latinate term "elective affinities" also enjoyed a vogue (the *Oxford English Dictionary*, whose definition, in a small sub-entry, is quoted above, offers an 1831 source to this effect), and it is perhaps inevitable that this should be the title by which Goethe's work has become known in the English-speaking world. It is, nevertheless, unfortunate because the phrase has become at best meaningless, and at worst positively misleading: even if "affinities" is correctly understood as a scientific term, "elective" normally means "pertaining to the exercise of choice", whereas Goethe's usage means "incapable of choosing otherwise". None of the translators has dealt with this difficulty effectively.

FROUDE (1854), writing at a time when the English phrase was still current, has in this respect a perfect justification for his choice of title. Froude was a Tudor historian in the mould of Carlyle who later became Regius Professor of Modern History at Oxford; his version was published anonymously (it was attributed only after his death). He writes comfortably in a homogeneous style entirely consistent with Goethe's own, and there are few linguistic anachronisms to distract the reader. There are occasions, however, when he follows German sentence structure too closely – particularly in passages of spoken dialogue – and he makes a poor job of the important chapter 4 of part 1, in which the implications of the chemical allusion in the title are explained. There are also moments when he seems actually to misunderstand (when Charlotte, speaking to Edward, refers to "dein Mütterchen", it is not his mother she has in mind but his first wife, who was much older than Edward, so that Froude's "your poor mother" is not a good version). His modern reputation as a historian is that of an enthusiast and a popularizer, whose skills in these areas occasionally led him to display a less than punctilious regard for accuracy. His translation is entirely in this character, but survived honourably as the sole English version for over a century.

It was only in 1960 that WAIDSON, no doubt troubled by Froude's Victorian style and occasional inaccuracies, published an alternative, replacing the by now almost meaningless title with the immediately comprehensible, but totally wrong, "Kindred by Choice": it is not a scientific term, "kinship" is neither the human nor the chemical relationship in question, and the element *Wahl-* does not mean "by choice", but "preferential". His decision falsifies the main theme of the novel, leads to many specific complexities in the text and makes chapter 4 particularly difficult to understand. In addition, Waidson's literary style is not consistent. Current forms such as "I'll" and "we'll", and phrases such as "playing for time" sit uneasily together with Germanic formulations such as "She remembered her earnest resolution to forswear an attractive and inspiring inclination that was not without fineness and nobility". Lack of stylistic homogeneity makes this version unacceptable.

MAYER & BOGAN (1963) returned to an alternative classicism, only just recognizable as American, and somewhat reminiscent of Henry James – the formal tradition persisted longer in America than in Britain. Their version of the sentence quoted above is "She did not relax her determination to renounce her affection for the Captain, however pure and noble she knew it to be", which demonstrates their readiness to adapt Goethe's sentence form to the requirements of modern English linguistic usage (expanding the noun "affection" by including its object, and elucidating Goethe's psychological meaning by adding the phrase "however ... she knew it to be"). Perhaps they could have been more radical still. The application of the possessive "her" to two successive abstract nouns is clumsy, and an even better version would have been "She was still determined to renounce ...", but overall this is a successful translation. The only serious criticism to be made is that its slightly old-fashioned but still mid-20th-century style is not totally apposite to the preoccupations of a novelist who was writing more than 150 years previously. Curiously, however, their chapter 4 is not up to the standard of the rest of the work – Mayer & Bogan are clearly more at home with literature and human relationships than with science.

HOLLINGDALE (1971) shows the reverse characteristics. His chapter 4 is excellent – he is the first translator to realize that Goethe's *Kalkerde* is neither of the mysterious substances "calcareous earth" or "lime-earth", but the familiar "calcium oxide" – and his whole version gains from the clarity of the scientific exposition around which Goethe constructed his plot. However, Hollingdale has not found a homogeneous writing style in which he is personally comfortable: "She was conscious always of how earnestly she had resolved to forswear her affection, fair and noble though it was", is representative of much of his text. As a result, his many good and accurate modern formulations, where the other translators offer old-fashioned or inaccurate turns of phrase, seem simply anachronistic in a general context which, in spite of his efforts, remains stubbornly Victorian. As a result, this version is noticeably less comfortable to read than Froude or Mayer & Bogan.

CONSTANTINE (1994), like Hollingdale, is excellent in parts, not always the same ones as Hollingdale. He, like Hollingdale, retains much of the deliberate formality of the source text, again sometimes smoothly mediated by 20th-century phrases and rhythms, if with an uneven effect overall and occasional inelegancies. Charlotte's state of mind at the end of part 1, chapter 13 is rendered thus: "She harboured the earnest intention to renounce her affections, beautiful and noble though they were." Where Hollingdale's introduction has very helpful observations on the generalizing conventions of the *Novelle* form of narrative chosen by Goethe, Constantine's goes further in interpretation, and his translation is followed by some explanatory notes.

It is doubtful whether any of the subsequent translations offers sufficient advantages to justify turning away from Froude's.

GEORGE S. MILLER

Further Reading

Reiss, Hans, *Goethe's Novels*, London: Macmillan, and New York: St Martin's Press, 1969; revised edition, Coral Gables, Florida: University of Miami Press, 1971

Tanner, Tony, *Adultery in the Novel: Contract and Transgression*, Baltimore: Johns Hopkins University Press, 1979

See also the translators' introductions to Constantine and Hollingdale

Faust

Faust, part 1, 1808, produced 1819; *Faust*, part 2, 1832, produced 1854

From the 1770s until the year of his death, Goethe worked intermittently on his much-revised two-part verse drama, *Faust.* Loosely based on Marlowe's prose and blank verse "tragical history" *Dr Faustus* (1604), itself a treatment of a medieval legend, Goethe's play traces the vividly varied experiences of a scholar who, aspiring to know durable satisfaction, common humanness and, ultimately, moral nobility, makes a pact, and continues to consort, with the devil Mephistopheles, and profits from the devil's magic powers. By the end of part 1, Faust's seduction and desertion of his young lover Margarete had brought about her disgrace and death, followed by his own despair. In part 2, Faust, still accompanied by Mephistopheles, meets with and learns from figures and experiences at the highest levels of history and legend. Grown old, he realizes that achievement and understanding are gained not through supernatural power but by human striving.

Translations

Arndt, Walter, *Faust: A Tragedy: Backgrounds and Sources, the Author on the Drama, Contemporary Reactions, Modern Criticism*, with an introduction, edited by Cyrus Hamlin, New York: Norton, 1976

Fairley, Barker, *Faust*, Toronto: University of Toronto Press, 1970; in *Selected Works of Goethe*, edited by Nicholas Boyle, London: David Campbell, 1999

Greenberg, Martin, *Faust, a Tragedy: Part One*, with an introduction, New Haven, Connecticut: Yale University Press, 1992

Kaufmann, Walter, *Faust* (parallel texts), with an introduction, New York: Doubleday, 1961

Luke, David, *Faust*, with an introduction, 2 vols, Oxford and New York: Oxford University Press, 1987–94

MacNeice, Louis, *Faust: Parts I and II: An Abridged Version*, London: Faber, 1951; New York: Oxford University Press, 1952

Passage, Charles, *Faust, Part I and Part II*, with an introduction, Indianapolis: Bobbs Merrill, 1965

Priest, George Madison, *Faust: Parts One and Two*, with an introduction, New York: Covici Friede, 1932

Salm, Peter, *Faust: Part I* (parallel texts), New York and London: Bantam Books, 1962; reprinted 1967; revised edition, 1985

Taylor, Bayard, *Faust*, New York: Stroefer and Kirchner, and Boston: Houghton Mifflin, 1870; reprinted Houghton and Mifflin, 1946

Wayne, Philip, *Faust*, with an introduction, 2 vols, Harmondsworth and New York: Penguin, 1949–59; numerous subsequent reprints

Goethe's *Faust* has been known historically as the most important work of the most important writer in German literary history, so that many translators have tried their hand at rendering it into English. Since new translations appear so frequently, the history they tell reveals much about reigning theories of translation since the mid-19th century.

Earlier translations (19th and early 20th centuries) reveal the prevailing sense that verse itself, the art of creating perfectly metered and rhymed texts, was of the utmost importance. Bayard TAYLOR's translation (1870) serves as an example. He even reproduces the dactylic and the feminine rhymes; and he notes that when he did leave a line or two unrhymed, he made up for it by rhyming lines that the author had left unrhymed! Taylor's version is technically impressive, though many recent translators (Greenberg, Luke, Kaufmann, Wayne) have noted that in such "Victorian" (Kaufmann) translations, "the Gothic plainnesses, irregularities, and homely detail, all the popular movement to be found in *Faust*" (Greenberg's introduction) are lost. Such meticulously rhymed and metered renderings have an overall more elaborate, more elevated effect than the model.

George Madison PRIEST's translation of 1932 is interesting for historical (but not for aesthetic) reasons. His introduction clearly indicates that he sympathizes with Nazism and its appropriation of German cultural history. He suggests that it is well for scholars the world over, not just in Germany, to remember that such a man as Goethe once trod this earth – a validation, by the translator, of the fascists' brand of hero-worship, and an indication that he considered the Third Reich a legitimate heir of Goethe's cultural tradition. His text exhibits many of the faults that more accomplished translators have overcome. Most significantly, his frequent use of archaisms conflicts with his loose treatment of the meter, which often in his version comes close to iambic pentameter.

Philip WAYNE (1949–59) was still addressing an audience who expected an elevated, smooth, strictly rhymed text. He seeks to prepare the reader for unpoetic passages by suggesting that German is homelier than English overall, and he remarks that Goethe not only wrote in doggerel, but revelled in it. He makes the important point that the quality of the verse depends on who is speaking the lines: for instance, he argues, the Spirit's lines simply must be reproduced in verse, for they are "incantation", while the devil's lines are fittingly colloquial and plain. Wayne's translation is an improvement over earlier ones insofar as he attempted to reproduce the wide range of voices in the original, though it is still very uniform compared to more recent translations.

Louis MACNEICE's (1951) abridged version (8,000 of the original 12,000 lines) is hardly to be compared with Wayne's in terms of technical agility, but serves as a good counterpoint to illustrate how considerations of audience and medium make an infinite number of good translations possible. It is not wholly rhymed, although he did reproduce end rhyme for the most part, and in doing so he was going against contemporary inclinations toward free verse. He felt that the rhyme was essential to the meaning and that Goethe used it again and again to make his points. It is a colorful version, unique in that it was intended for radio broadcast and thus had to be intelligible without the visual element of stage drama. Note also that this translation was composed very quickly – he was first approached by the BBC in spring 1949, and the first broadcast took place on 30 November.

KAUFMANN (1961), PASSAGE (1965) and ARNDT (1976) all managed to create strictly rhymed and metered translations that are still intelligible to the modern student of German. Each avoided the "tortuous inversions of word order, painful archaisms, and solemn affectations" (Kaufmann, introduction) of earlier verse translations, and each succeeded in creating versions in comparatively simple, natural word order. More of Goethe's wit comes across in these versions, when the translators sought to recreate the rhythm of the lines as it sounds to a German, rather than according to each detail of metrical foot, line and rhyme.

Peter SALM's free verse translation of 1962 represents a different contemporary school of thought. Salm wrote that "[b]y relinquishing rhyme and strict meter, except in the interspersed songs and ballads, I gained the freedom to be more faithful to sense and spirit than I could otherwise have been". Yet in comparison with Kaufmann, which was also a bilingual edition, one wonders what Salm gained, for Kaufmann is as intelligible as Salm, but with the added virtues of end rhyme and precise meter.

Barker FAIRLEY's prose translation of 1970 epitomizes the attempt to make the work accessible to the modern reader and to counteract the overly elevated effect of early translations. Fairley's version is easily understandable for a modern reader with little knowledge of German language and literature. It is wonderfully readable and actable, but it suffers, as all prose and free verse translations do, from the lack of rhyme, which in the original punctuates important lines and lends significantly to the meaning.

David LUKE's translation for Oxford University Press (part 1, 1987; part 2, 1994) is superior to all others in both intelligibility and melody. The back cover claims (justifiably) that "[i]t is as near an 'equivalent' as has yet been achieved." Luke's "absolute requirements" included that *Faust* must be translated into rhymed verse, and into an English of the 20th century. In his introduction he wrote: "Half the point of what Goethe says is lost if it lacks the musical closure and neatness of the way he said it." This is precisely what free verse and prose translations (Salm, Fairley, Greenberg) lack, and what the older translations, adhering strictly to meter and rhyme, obscured – the "neatness", the clever simplicity of the original. Luke takes liberties with rhyme sequence and line length; he often substitutes masculine rhymes for feminine; and he has fewer end-stopped rhymes. The latter feature results sometimes in overrunning, and, while it is awkward in some places, in each of these instances one can easily imagine how an actor might pronounce the line splendidly. Luke's translation is pleasingly uniform in terms of register and current usage of the English language: nowhere does he rely on terms evoking a period of time, or a cultural context, that detracts from the clarity of the text. His translation is highly intelligible to the modern reader, and at the same time a faithful reproduction of the original in terms of its overall effect, if not of its exact meter and rhyme scheme.

Martin GREENBERG's 1992 translation for Yale University Press appeared shortly after Luke, but where Luke can be grouped with Wayne, Passage, Kaufmann, and Arndt, Greenberg belongs in the category of prose and free verse translations with Salm and Fairley. Greenberg praises Fairley's prose and derides all previous free-verse translations as lifeless and flat. In his introduction he stresses the importance of the vernacular in Faust, and toward this end, he treats meter and rhyme loosely, employing half-rhymes, assonance, and consonance, and using full rhymes only occasionally. Greenberg is more lively than Salm, but in foregoing end rhyme to the degree that it does, his translation gives little indication of the "neatness" of the original that Luke referred to. Both Greenberg and Luke convey more of the wit and the depth of character of the original than their predecessors in their respective genres had, but in the final analysis, Luke brings these across, as well as the rhyme and meter, more faithfully; and without sacrificing intelligibility.

JULIE MERCER CARROLL

Further Reading

Bennett, Benjamin, *Goethe's Theory of Poetry: Faust and the Regeneration of Language*, Ithaca, New York: Cornell University Press, 1986

Brown, Jane K., Meredith Lee and Thomas P. Saine (editors), *Interpreting Goethe's* "Faust Today", in *Goethe Yearbook*, Columbia, South Carolina: Camden House, 1994

Fairley, Barker, *Goethe's Faust: Six Essays*, Oxford: Clarendon Press, 1953

See also the introductions to Arndt, Greenberg, Kaufmann, Luke, Passage and Wayne

Nikolai Gogol' 1809–1852

Russian short-story writer, novelist and dramatist

Biography

Born at Sorochintsy, Poltava, Ukraine, 19 March 1809, and raised in the Ukraine. Themes from Ukrainian folklore and history feature widely in his first two collections of stories, *Village Evenings near Dikanka*, published in 1831–32, and *Mirgorod*, published in 1835. After school, Gogol' moved to St Petersburg, studying fine art and entering the civil service. His Petersburg experiences supplied the background and material for the stories conventionally gathered together under the title *Petersburg Tales*, published at various dates between 1835 and 1842.

While in St Petersburg Gogol' made the acquaintance of the leading writers of his day, notably the poets Zhukovskii and Pushkin, and frequented literary and artistic society. After resigning from the civil service in 1831, and a short and disastrous interlude as a history professor at St Petersburg University, Gogol' started travelling extensively abroad, spending long periods in Germany and Italy, largely in the company of Russian artists. Apart from a few essays and the incomplete story *Rome*, however, he remained preoccupied with Russian themes in his writing, and commenced work on a planned three-part major composition, *Dead Souls*, in 1837. His comedies *The Government Inspector* and *Marriage* were written during these years, and first performed in 1836 and 1842 respectively.

During the latter part of his life Gogol' became increasingly drawn to religious themes and in these years produced the works *Selected Passages from Correspondence with Friends*, an apologia subsequently entitled *Author's Confession*, and *Meditations on the Divine Liturgy*. After completing only the first two parts of *Dead Souls*, he passed his final months under a gathering cloud of religious introspection, subjecting himself to an overly severe regime of fasting and self-denial which undermined his already precarious health. On 11 February 1852 he burned the manuscript of part 2 (only fragments have survived), and died 10 days later, 21 February 1852, in Moscow.

Translations

Gogol' reworked his texts extensively for successive editions and some of his works consequently exist in widely differing versions. Recent translations tend to be based on the USSR Academy edition, in 14 volumes, published in Moscow and Leningrad between 1937 and 1952. The first version of *The Portrait*, which differs significantly from later revisions, can be found in the translation of *Arabesques*.

Collection

Garnett, Constance, *The Works of Nikolay Gogol*, 6 vols, London: Chatto and Windus, 1922–28; revised by Leonard J. Kent, as *The Collected Tales and Plays*, New York: Pantheon, 1964

Selections of Short Stories

Anonymous, *Evenings near the Village of Dikanka*, edited by Ovid Gorchakov, Moscow: Foreign Languages Publishing House, 1957

Anonymous, *Mirgorod, Being a Continuation of Evenings in a Village near Dikanka*, edited by Ovid Gorchakov, Moscow: Foreign Languages Publishing House, 1958

English, Christopher, with Angus Roxburgh, *Nikolai Gogol: A Selection*, Moscow: Progress, 1980

English, Christopher, with Angus Roxburgh, *Christmas Eve, Stories from Village Evenings near Dikanka and Mirgorod*, Moscow: Raduga, 1991

English, Christopher (editor and translator), *Village Evenings near Dikanka and Mirgorod*, with an introduction by Richard Peace, Oxford and New York: Oxford University Press, 1994

English, Christopher (editor and translator), *Petersburg Tales; Marriage; The Government Inspector*, with an introduction by Richard Peace, Oxford and New York: Oxford University Press, 1995

Field, Claud, *The Mantle and Other Stories*, with an introduction by Prosper Merimée, New York: Stokes, and London: Laurie, 1916

Garnett, Constance, *The Complete Tales of Nikolai Gogol*, 2 vols, edited by Leonard J. Kent, Chicago: University of Chicago Press, 1985

Hapgood, Isabel F., *St John's Eve, and Other Stories from "Evenings at the Farm" and "St Petersburg Stories"*, New York: Crowell, 1886; reprinted Freeport, New York: Books for Libraries, 1971

Hapgood, Isabel F., *Taras Bulba; also St. John's Eve, and Other Stories*, London: Vizetelly, 1887

Hapgood, Isabel F. *et al.*, *The Overcoat and Other Short Stories*, New York: Dover, and London: Constable, 1992

MacAndrew, Andrew R., *The Diary of a Madman and Other Stories*, New York: New American Library, 1960

Magarshack, David, *Tales of Good and Evil*, with an introduction, London: Lehmann, 1949; New York: Doubleday, 1957; as *The Overcoat and Other Tales of Good and Evil*, New York: Norton, 1965

Miller, Alex, "Sorochintsy Fair" and "The Carriage", *Soviet Literature*, 4/433 (1984)

Portnova, Rosa, *Tales from Gogol*, London: Sylvan Press, 1945

Tolstoy, George, *Cossack Tales*, London: Blackwood, 1860

Tulloch, Alexander, *Arabesques*, Ann Arbor, Michigan: Ardis, 1982

Underwood, Edna Worthley and William Hamilton Cline, *Evenings in Little Russia*, Evanston, Illinois: Lord, 1903

Wilks, Ronald, *Diary of a Madman and Other Stories*, with an introduction, London: Penguin, 1972

Short Stories

"Taras Bul'ba", 1835; revised 1842

Baskerville, B.C., *Taras Bulba*, London and Felling-on-Tyne: Walter Scott, 1907

Curtin, Jeremiah, *Taras Bulba: A Historical Novel of Russia and Poland*, New York: Alden, 1888

Gorchakov, Ovid, *Taras Bulba*, Moscow: Foreign Languages Publishing House, 1957
Roxburgh, Angus, "Taras Bulba", in *Nikolai Gogol: A Selection*, translated by English and Roxburgh, 1980

"Zapiski sumasshedshego", 1835
Mirsky, Prince, *The Diary of a Madman*, London: Cresset Press, 1929
Scott, Beatrice, *Diary of a Madman; Nevski Prospect*, London: Lindsay Drummond, 1945
Voynich, Ethel Lilian, *A Madman's Diary* in her anthology *The Humour of Russia*, London: Scott, and New York: Scribner, 1895

"Nos", 1836
Cowan, Catherine, *The Nose* (retold), New York: Lothrop Lee and Shepard, 1995
Daglish, Robert, *The Nose*, *Soviet Literature*, 4/433 (1984)
Struve, Gleb and Mary Struve, "The Nose" in *The Overcoat and Other Short Stories*, translated by Isabel Hapgood *et al.*, 1992

"Shinel'", 1842
Shoenberg, Zlata and Jessie Domb, *The Greatcoat* (bilingual edition), London: Harrap, 1944; New York: Transatlantic Arts, 1945

Selection of Plays
Ehre, Milton and Fruma Gottschalk, *The Theater of Nikolay Gogol: Plays and Selected Writings*, edited, with an introduction by Ehre, Chicago: University of Chicago Press, 1980 (contains *The Government Inspector*, *Marriage*, *The Gamblers*, writings on the theatre)

Plays
Revizor, 1836
Anderson, John, *The Inspector General: A Satiric Farce in Three Acts* (acting version), London and New York: Samuel French, 1931
Byrne, John, *The Government Inspector*, London: Oberon, 1997
Campbell, D.J., *The Government Inspector*, London: Sylvan Press, 1947
Cooper, Joshua, *Government Inspector and Other Plays*, by Gogol' and others, Harmondsworth: Penguin, 1990 (other plays are all by other Russian authors)
Dolman, John Jr and Benjamin Rothberg, *The Inspector-General (Revizór): A Russian Farce-Comedy* (translated and adapted for US production), Boston: Baker, 1937
English, Christopher and Gordon McDougall, *The Government Inspector*, Moscow: Raduga, 1989
Goodman, W.L., *The Government Inspector*, dialogue and adaptation by Henry S. Taylor, London: Ginn, 1962
Hart-Davies, T., *The Inspector: A Comedy*, Calcutta: Thacker Spink, 1890
Ignatieff, Leonid, *The Government Inspector*, adapted by Peter Raby, Minneapolis: University of Minnesota Press–Guthrie Theater, 1972
Mandell, Max S., *Revizór: A Comedy*, New Haven, Connecticut: Tuttle Morehouse and Taylor, 1908; as *The Inspector-General*, New Haven, Connecticut: Yale University Dramatic Association, 1910
Marsh, Edward O. and Jeremy Brooks, *The Government Inspector*, London: Methuen, 1968
Mitchell, Adrian, *The Government Inspector*, London and New York: Methuen, 1985 (adaptation)
Seltzer, Thomas, *The Inspector-General*, New York: Knopf, 1916
Seymour, John Laurence and George Rapall Noyes, *The Inspector*, in *Masterpieces of the Russian Drama*, edited by Noyes, New York: Appleton, 1933
Sykes, Arthur A., *The Inspector-General (or "Revizór"): A Russian Comedy*, London: Scott, 1892

Zhenit'ba, 1841, produced 1842
Berkman, Alexander, *Marriage*, with *The Gamblers*, translated by Berkman, New York: Macaulay, 1927
Costello, Bella, *Marriage (written in 1833): An Absolutely Incredible Incident in Two Acts*, Manchester: Manchester University Press, and New York: Barnes and Noble, 1969
English, Christopher, *Marriage* in *Petersburg Tales ...*, translated by English, 1995
Voynich, Ethel Lilian, *Marriage* in her anthology *The Humour of Russia*, London: Scott, and New York: Scribner, 1895

Igroki, 1842, produced 1843
Berkman, Alexander, *The Gamblers*, with *Marriage*, translated by Berkman, New York: Macaulay, 1927
Daglish, Robert, *The Gamblers*, *Soviet Literature*, 4/433 (1984)

Teatralnyi raziezd posle predstavleniia novoi komedii, 1842
Heaman, Isabel, *Leaving the Theater after the Presentation of a New Comedy* in *Hanz Kuechelgarten, Leaving the Theater, and Other Works*, edited by Ronald Meyer, Ann Arbor, Michigan: Ardis, 1990

Gogol''s early stories, with their Romantic themes of Cossack history and characters from Ukrainian folklore, quickly caught the attention of English translators and, as can be seen from the list above, a considerable amount of his work was translated, or at least adapted in English versions, even before the end of the 19th century. Gogol''s preoccupation with these topics, however, coupled with his predilection for taxonomy (his notebooks abound with jottings of dialect words and phrases, lists of the names of dogs and dishes, etc.), render him particularly challenging for the translator, and most of these early translations fail to do him justice. Gogol''s language is by turns quirky and familiar, awkward and mellifluous – but always fresh and lively. Some of his outlandish names and phrases have entered the common stock of the Russian language and remain in frequent use today. In his book on Gogol', Nabokov – whose own fascination with the possibilities of the Russian language places him in Gogol''s direct line of succession – warns:

> If you are interested in "ideas" and "facts" and "messages", keep away from Gogol'. The awful trouble of learning Russian in order to read him will not be repaid in your kind of hard cash. Keep away, keep away ... His work, as all great literary achievement, is a phenomenon of language and not one of ideas.

That "awful trouble" is no longer so necessary for the English-speaking reader, as interest in Gogol' continued throughout the 20th century, and at present all his major works and much of his juvenilia, letters and other secondary writings are available in readable and, by and large, accurate English translations. Even Hollywood has been caught by Gogol''s spell, and a swashbuckling version of *Taras Bulba* was filmed in Argentina in 1962, with Yul Brynner in the title role. Some of the best-known stories and plays have been tackled by numerous different translators; thus *The Government Inspector* appears no fewer than 15 times in the above list, which does not claim to be exhaustive. It may be difficult to defend the need for such multiplicity of translation, yet it remains true that, while Gogol''s own language has not aged – his prose reads as freshly and vigorously today as it did in the early 19th century – that of his translators has. It is therefore a mistake to believe that the earlier translations, because of their closer proximity in time to the original, are also closer to its spirit.

Constance GARNETT (1922–28, etc.), at one time the doyenne of English translators of the Russian classics, also turned her hand to the works of Gogol'. While her versions of the stories have an undeniable grace and elegance, shared by all her translations from Russian, they fail to do justice to the sometimes tortured and always vigorous language of the original, and her imperfect knowledge of Russian resulted in a large number of inaccuracies. The translations, originally published in the 1920s, were revised and reissued by David Garnett in the 1950s.

These translations were further corrected and revised by Leonard KENT in 1964, and reissued with further revisions in 1985 by the University of Chicago Press. The editor's decision to use the Constance Garnett translation is based on his (not universally shared) belief that her versions are closest to the spirit of the original. The errors of the original have been set right, much – although not all – of the sometimes stilted quality of the language has been removed, and useful footnotes have been added.

The English – as opposed to the American – reader of Gogol''s stories is probably more familiar with the versions by Ronald WILKS, published in 1972 in the Penguin Classics series. The translations are fresh and fluent and endeavour to preserve the stylistic variety and to capture the distinctive flavour of the original Russian. It is only a selection, however, containing a mere five stories drawn from all the main cycles with none represented in its entirety.

It is generally accepted that Constance Garnett's mantle passed to the shoulders of David MAGARSHACK, and he too turned his attention to Gogol', translating the stories (1949) and *Dead Souls* (1961). The Norton edition of Gogol''s stories contains an introduction by the translator and a selection of stories from the three cycles. The translations are generally accurate and based on authoritative versions, but there is an occasional wooden cast to Magarshack's language. At the same time, he has a tendency – when Gogol' is at his most deliberately awkward and illogical – to smooth out some of the roughness and apparent inconsistencies of the original.

The most recent translations are to be found in a new collection commissioned by Oxford University Press for its World's Classics series, translated by Christopher ENGLISH. These two collections, *Village Evenings near Dikanka and Mirgorod* (1994) and *Petersburg Tales; Marriage; The Government Inspector* (1995), together contain all Gogol''s completed stories (including "The Carriage", which does not belong to any of the three major groups), and the editions come with useful introductions by a leading Gogol' scholar, Richard Peace, as well as extensive endnotes and other useful apparatus, such as maps and the Petrine Table of Ranks.

Gogol''s plays also have long translation histories. Numerous acting versions of *The Government Inspector* have been prepared, which take greater or lesser liberties with the text, the names and the arrangement of scenes. Various attempts ranging between the ingenious and the excruciating have been made to render Gogol''s baroque names into English: thus, for Judge Liapkin-Tiapkin we find Slapkin-Dashkin and Slappen-Catchit; for the constables Pugovitsyn and Derzhimorda: Fistikov and Bruzov, or Holdmuzzle; for Postmaster Shpekin: Snoopin or Mr John Pry; for the locksmith's wife Poshlepkina: Slapcheekina; for Triapichkin: Trashkin and so forth. Of all Russian plays, *The Government Inspector* is perhaps the most "translatable", in that its characters and situations can easily be transposed culturally and geographically to most places and times. Notable among such transpositions is the translation commissioned by the Royal Shakespeare Company for its critically acclaimed Aldwych production in 1966, with Paul Scofield in the title role and directed by Peter Hall. The translation was prepared by Edward MARSH & Jeremy BROOKS (1968). In places it is fairly free, with the insertion of new text and the dialectal siting of the action in East Anglia. Consequently, while the play reads well, it is far from a meticulous reflection of the original and should therefore be viewed more as an entertaining adaptation than as a scholarly translation.

In their translation Milton EHRE & Fruma GOTTSCHALK (1980) include, besides Gogol''s two completed plays *The Government Inspector* and *Marriage*, the uncompleted *Gamblers* and a valuable collection of Gogol''s own writings on the theatre. These translations succeed in capturing the energy and humour of the original without sacrificing accuracy, although, uncharacteristically, the translators depart from the original in substituting more familiar names of writers, operas, etc., for allusions in the text that they believe might be obscure to the English-speaking reader, and in correcting apparent errors in the author's own chronology. The edition contains substantial endnotes and a valuable introduction by Milton Ehre.

The Government Inspector and *Marriage* are also included in the compilation of Gogol''s work translated (1995) by Christopher ENGLISH and described above. In this series, Oxford University Press undertake to provide fresh translations that balance accuracy and elegance and come complete with scholarly introductions and annotations. The translator's intention in this version of the plays, as also with the stories, has been to reflect the original as closely as possible (thus retaining the Russian forms of names and all the references, if necessary with glosses in the endnotes), without forfeiting readability or losing the vigour of Gogol''s Russian.

CHRISTOPHER ENGLISH

Further Reading

Fanger, Donald, *The Creation of Nikolai Gogol*, Cambridge, Massachusetts: Belknap Press of Harvard University Press, 1965

Fusso, Susanne, *Designing Dead Souls: An Anatomy of*

Disorder in Gogol, Stanford, California: Stanford University Press, 1993
Gippius, V.V., *Gogol*, edited and translated by Robert A. Maguire, Ann Arbor: Ardis, 1981; revised, with a new introduction, Durham, North Carolina: Duke University Press, 1989
Jensen, Hal, "Backwater Adrift", review of Byrne's *The Government Inspector*, *Times Literary Supplement* (9 January 1998)
Karlinsky, Simon, *The Sexual Labyrinth of Nikolai Gogol*, Cambridge, Massachusetts: Harvard University Press, 1976
Maguire, Robert A. (editor and translator), *Gogol from the Twentieth Century: Eleven Essays*, Princeton, New Jersey: Princeton University Press, 1974
Maguire, Robert A., *Exploring Gogol*, Stanford, California: Stanford University Press, 1994
Nabokov, Vladimir, *Nikolai Gogol*, Norfolk, Connecticut: New Directions, 1944; London: Editions Poetry, 1947
Peace, Richard, *The Enigma of Gogol*, Cambridge and New York: Cambridge University Press, 1981
Proffer, Carl R., *The Simile and Gogol's Dead Souls*, The Hague: Mouton, 1967
Setchkareff, Vsevolod, *Gogol: His Life and Works*, translated by Robert Kramer, New York: New York University Press, 1965
Yelistratova, Anna, *Nikolai Gogol and the Western European Novel*, translated by Christopher English, Moscow: Raduga, 1995

Dead Souls

Mertvye dushi: Poema, 1842

This unfinished novel is a satire on officialdom and the Tsarist system of serfdom. The "dead souls" are deceased peasants whose names, still on the census list, are used by the central character, Chichikov, as the means to a tax swindle.

Translations

Anonymous, *Home Life in Russia*, 2 vols, London: Hurst and Blackett, 1854
English, Christopher, *Dead Souls: A Poem*, with an introduction by Robert Maguire, Oxford and New York: Oxford University Press, 1998
Garnett, Constance, *Dead Souls: A Poem*, 2 vols, London, Chatto and Windus, and New York: Knopf, 1922
Guerney, Bernard Guilbert, *Chichikov's Journeys; or, Home Life in Old Russia*, New York Readers Club, 1942; as *Dead Souls*, revised by Guerney, New York: Modern Library, 1965; as *Dead Souls*, revised by Susanne Fusso, New Haven, Connecticut: Yale University Press, 1996
Hapgood, Isabel F., *Tchitchikoff's Journeys; or, Dead Souls: A Poem*, 2 vols, New York: Crowell, 1886; revised edition, with an introduction by Stephen Graham, London: T. Fisher Unwin, 1915
Hogarth, D.J., *Dead Souls*, London: Dent, and New York: Dutton, 1915
MacAndrew, Andrew R., *Dead Souls*, New York: New American Library, 1961
Magarshack, David, *Dead Souls*, Harmondsworth: Penguin, 1961
Michailoff, Helen, *Dead Souls*, New York: Washington Square Press, 1964
Pevear, Richard and Larissa Volokhonsky, *Dead Souls*, New York: Pantheon, 1996
Reavey, George, *Dead Souls*, New York: Pantheon, 1948; in *Dead Souls: The Reavey Translation, Backgrounds and Sources, Essays in Criticism*, edited by George Gibian, New York: Norton, 1985
Senelick, Laurence, *Dead Souls: A Comic Epic in Two Parts* (stage play), New York: Broadway Play Publishing, 1984
Siscoe, John and Jean Sherrard, *Dead Souls: An Audio Dramatization of the Novel by Nikolai Gogol*, Seattle: University of Washington Press, 1987

Russia's great prose writer was recognized in English criticism as early as 1841, and the first English translation (of his story "Portret", rendered by Thomas Budge Shaw) appeared in 1847 (Lefevre, 1949).

Gogol worked on his satiric masterpiece from 1835 to 1852. Volume 1 of *Mertvye dushi* was published in Moscow in 1842 (2nd edition 1846), though Gogol was obliged by the Imperial censors to alter the title (to *The Adventures of Chichikov; or, Dead Souls: A Narrative Poem*) and to replace the original "Tale of Captain Kopeikin" in chapter 10 with a rewritten version. As early as 1836, Gogol had planned to continue the novel in volumes 2 and 3, which would portray the redemption of the fallen denizens of volume 1, but he abandoned this project and there survive only drafts of the first four chapters of volume 2 and of a later chapter; these materials were first published in 1855. Altogether, over 600 pages of Gogol's variants and cancelled drafts have been published in Russian. Gogol's rhapsodic, playful, poetically earthy, often very colloquial language is extremely difficult to translate into English.

Though *Mertvye dushi* had been openly translated into German as early as 1846, its first appearance in English, in 1854 (ANONYMOUS), took the form of "an arrogant and vicious forgery, involving the grossest omissions and interpolations ... not intended to be literature in any serious sense, but [Crimean] War propaganda, pure and simple" (Lefevre). The novel is presented in two volumes by its editor (Krystyn Lach-Szyrma, a Polish colonel) in the guise of the factual account by an unnamed Russian nobleman who has taken a great political risk in translating, exporting, and publishing his exposé of Russian vice. The 11 chapters of volume 1 of Gogol's novel are chopped up into 26 chapters and subjected to scandalous indignities: abridgement, wholesale rearrangement (to imitate the *Bildungsroman*), ludicrous interpolation (Chichikov is said to have enjoyed *Uncle Tom's Cabin*) and outrageous alteration (Chichikov is caught and murdered by a sinister "imperial messenger" to conclude the story). Several articles denouncing this anti-Russian travesty soon appeared in Britain, and the quality of Gogol's original was publicly asserted.

Though HAPGOOD (1886) contains serious mistranslations and decorous omissions, the first edition of this version is actually superior to its later editions and to HOGARTH (1915). Volumes 1 and 2 of the novel are presented in separate bindings, and nearly all textual gaps in volume 2 are noted; this is also the only English version before GUERNEY (1996) to include both of

Gogol's own footnotes (chapters 4 and 5). Diverging from the original format, Hapgood provides titles and detailed conspectuses for all chapters. The brilliant "Captain Kopeikin" is, unfortunately, given in its censored version. Numerous, sometimes erroneous footnotes explain a variety of transliterated Russian terms in the text. Hapgood ill-advisedly emulates Ernest Charrière's French translation of the novel (*Les Âmes mortes*, Paris: Hachette, 1859) by tacking on a 50-page "conclusion" concocted by Vashchenko-Zakharchenko (Kiev, 1857); she shares her misgivings about this decision in a conscientious footnote. Though they are presented with no mention of Hapgood's name, the editions introduced and edited by Stephen Graham are in fact faultily revised versions of HAPGOOD (1886). Graham seriously alters the novel's original structure by failing to demarcate the two volumes, retaining titles for the chapters (he omits Hapgood's summaries), and numbering them continuously from I to XVII. Without warning, he replaces "Captain Kopeikin" with a one-sentence summary.

D.J. Hogarth (known as *C.J.* Hogarth in all other books from the same translator) supplies a translation of Gogol's 1846 preface to the 2nd edition, refrains from contriving titles for the chapters and offers an effectively comic British style. Hogarth takes such liberties with the original text, however, that the result verges on abridged adaptation rather than translation: Gogol's lengthy digressions are systematically removed, the censored redaction of "Captain Kopeikin" is employed, many words are left in (inconsistent) transliteration, and earthy language is masked (e.g. references to haemorrhoids are deleted). In volume 2, for the first time, gaps in the extant source-manuscripts are noted by the translator, though inconsistently.

As Proffer has shown (1964, pp. 425–27), GARNETT provides a generally accurate translation, avoids abridgements, and employs the more compact, later version of volume 2. Unfortunately, she offers the censored version of "Captain Kopeikin" and writes in a style more or less indistinguishable from that of her many translations of other 19th-century Russian authors.

The sportive, variegated American-English style of GUERNEY (1942) has been widely praised for reproducing the humorous effect of Gogol's Russian. Guerney's renderings are generally accurate, though Gogol's anti-Semitic remarks are neutralized, and colloquialisms are often overspiced: e.g. "horse's twat" instead of "dawdler" or "grumbler" for Russian *fetiuk* in chapter 4. For the 1942 edition only, nervous publishers misguidedly imposed the same title demanded by Russian censors in 1842 and ridiculously combined it with a secondary title based on Anonymous. The most serious flaw, however, is Guerney's "unconscionable textual juggling" (Proffer, p. 422): with no annotated warning he chooses and inserts passages from the vast fund of material Gogol chose to leave out, and even interposes an entire 10-page chapter (chapter 10 in Guerney, 1942, 1965). The original uncensored version of "Captain Kopeikin" too is adulterated with material from a cancelled draft of that episode. Though these distortions were convincingly denounced by Proffer in 1964, they are none the less preserved in the revised edition that appeared the following year (Guerney, 1965). Happily, in GUERNEY (1996) the editor Susanne Fusso removes all these ill-advised intercalations (which are banished to an appendix), tones down the racy colloquialisms (e.g. *fetiuk* becomes "horse's tail"), preserves Gogol's own footnotes, adds numerous annotations of her own and appends Gogol's relevant correspondence. More questionably, Fusso omits volume 2 (though excerpts from it are offered in an appendix) and (avowedly) preserves Guerney's whitewashing of Gogol's anti-Semitism. In sum, Fusso ensures that Guerney (1996) will now vie with REAVEY and PEVEAR & VOLOKHONSKY for pride of place.

Though the REAVEY (1948) version contains a number of mistranslations, it lacks the serious structural and textological flaws of previous translations, and the English style captures Gogol's humour and lyricism without the overripe archness of Guerney (1942, 1965). Reavey follows Garnett fairly closely, but introduces the comic flair lacking in her translation. The annotated Norton Critical Edition (Reavey, 1985) makes an attractive textbook.

Marred by numerous elisions, distortions and mistranslations, MACANDREW (1961), as Proffer has demonstrated, is a non-starter.

Because of its careful literality and textual integrity, MAGARSHACK (1961) was Proffer's first choice in 1964, and it remains a good alternative. The chief disadvantage here is that the English style, like Garnett's, is much more pallid than that of the original.

MICHAILOFF (1964) offers a generally accurate version in animated English prose. Frequent omissions of various adverbs and modifiers, however, tend to shear away Gogol's "important stylistic mannerisms" (Proffer, p. 428) and, like Garnett, Michailoff has opted for the early, discarded drafts of surviving chapters for her translation of volume 2. The censored "Captain Kopeikin" is given in an appendix.

The PEVEAR & VOLOKHONSKY team has produced a textually sound, literal version (1996) in rather understated English. Annotations are helpful, and textological problems are diligently pointed out. Though the Pevear & Volokhonsky translation equals the faithfulness of Magarshack, their style, which is more American, is also more effectively comic.

ENGLISH's translation (1998) for Oxford World's Classics – actually a completely revised version of an earlier translation he had undertaken for the Raduga publishing house, Moscow – takes its place at the top of the list. English gives us volumes 1 and 2, complete with carefully noted textual variants for volume 2; all censor's alterations are removed. Instead of avoiding the numerous difficulties of translating *Mertvye dushi*, English addresses them directly and cogently in a translator's foreword and numerous explanatory endnotes. There are also scores of enormously helpful endnotes elucidating key aspects of 19th-century Russian culture, politics and history. The style of the translation itself is an admirable blend of appropriately arcane vocabulary and convoluted British English in a humorously playful register. The eminent Gogol scholar Robert Maguire has furnished a superb introduction, and the translation is accompanied by a wealth of useful apparatus in addition to the aforementioned notes and prefatory material: a chronology of Gogol's life, a table of Russian civil-service and military ranks, and a map of "Chichikov's Russia". This meticulously prepared edition deserves to become the standard textbook edition of Gogol's novel, but is also ideal for less formal reading.

Two adaptations merit comment. The goal of SENELICK's stage adaptation (1984) was "to integrate ... the character of Gogol into the action" (p.iii). So, in this thoroughly rearranged, rethought, rewritten version of volume 1 (with no clear evidence of one particular translation having been used), Gogol himself becomes the most important character, and all the action takes place as he sits in a Rome café imagining the plot of *Mertvye dushi*. An adaptation of Guerney (1965), the SISCOE & SHERRARD radio play (1987) offers more than four hours of very droll, professionally produced scenes from the novel, on five audio cassettes. This enjoyable, elaborate production – which boasts incidental music and 34 cast members – is enhanced by insightful commentary from Donald Fanger and Willis Konick.

THOMAS P. HODGE

Further Reading

Frantz, Philip E., *Gogol: A Bibliography*, Ann Arbor, Michigan: Ardis, 1989, pp. 24–31

Lefevre, Carl, "Gogol and Anglo-Russian Literary Relations during the Crimean War", *American Slavic and East European Review*, 8 (April 1949) pp. 106-25

Lewanski, Richard C., *The Literatures of the World in English Translation*, volume 2: *The Slavic Literatures*, New York: New York Public Library / Ungar, 1967, pp. 243-46

Nabokov, Vladimir, *Nikolai Gogol*, New York: New Directions, 1944, pp. 61-63

Proffer, Carl R., "Dead Souls in Translation", *Slavic and East European Journal*, 8/4 (Winter 1964) pp. 420-33

Wiener, Leo, "Nikoláy Vasílevich Gógol" in *Anthology of Russian Literature*, part 2: *The Nineteenth Century*, New York: Putnam, 1903, pp. 185–86

See also the translators' introductions to Magarshack, Guerney (1965), Guerney (1996) and Pevear & Volokhonsky

---

The Golden Lotus

See Jin Ping Mei

Carlo Goldoni 1707–1793

Italian dramatist

Biography

Born in Venice, the theatrical capital of 18th-century Europe, 25 February 1707, but in 1762 the squabbles and rivalries that divided the city drove him into exile in Paris, where he died in poverty after the Revolution (on 6 February 1793). In the course of his life he produced well over 100 plays in every genre that found favour in his century – Aristotelian tragedy, opera libretto, melodrama, intermezzo, oriental extravagance, *commedia dell'arte* script and comedy. Only his comedies are known in the English-speaking world.

Translations

Selections of Plays

Baldini, Gabriele (editor), *Three Comedies*, London: Oxford University Press, 1961; Westport, Connecticut: Greenwood Press, 1979 (contains *Mine Hostess*, translated by Clifford Bax; *The Boors*, translated by I.M. Rawson; *The Fan*, translated by Eleanor and Herbert Farjeon)

Davies, Frederick, *Four Comedies*, Harmondsworth: Penguin, 1968 (contains *The Venetian Twins*, *The Artful Widow*, *Mirandolina*, *The Superior Residence*)

MacDonald, Robert David, *Carlo Goldoni*, 2 vols, London: Oberon, 1994–99 (vol. 1: *Mirandolina*, *The Housekeeper*; vol. 2: *Don Juan*, *Friends and Lovers*, *The Battlefield*)

Plays

I due gemelli Veneziani, 1750, produced 1748

Bolt, Ranjit, *The Venetian Twins*, with *Mirandolina*, Bath: Absolute Press, 1993

Davies, Frederick, *The Venetian Twins* in *Four Comedies*, translated by Davies, 1968

La locandiera, 1753

Bolt, Ranjit, in *Mirandolina*, with *The Venetian Twins*, Bath: Absolute Press, 1993

Davies, Frederick, *Mirandolina* in *Four Comedies*, translated by Davies, 1968

Gregory, Lady Augusta, *Mirandolina*, London and New York: Putnam, 1924
MacDonald, Robert David, *Mirandolina* in *Carlo Goldoni*, translated by MacDonald, vol. 1, 1994

Il servitore di due padroni, 1753, produced 1745
Dent, Edward J., *The Servant of Two Masters*, Cambridge: Cambridge University Press, 1928, 2nd edition 1952; in *Six Italian Plays*, edited by Eric Bentley, New York: Doubleday, 1958 (*The Classic Theatre*, vol. 1)

Don Giovanni Tenorio, o sia il dissoluto, 1754, produced 1736
MacDonald, Robert David, *Don Juan* in *Carlo Goldoni*, translated by MacDonald, vol. 2, 1999

Il campiello, 1758, produced 1756
Graham-Jones, Susanna and Bill Bryden, *Il Campiello*, London: Heinemann, 1976

La donna di governo, 1761, produced 1758
MacDonald, Robert David, *The Housekeeper* in *Carlo Goldoni*, translated by MacDonald, vol. 1, 1994

I rusteghi, 1764, produced 1760
Rawson, I.M., *The Boors* in *Three Comedies*, edited by Gabriele Baldini, 1961

Carlo Goldoni was the supreme theatrical professional, writing not for posterity but for performance with companies to whom he had contractual obligations and whose precise make-up and skills were known to him. His inspiration came not from the muse but from observation of those "twin books of the Theatre and the World".

"It is not language that makes a comedy", wrote Goldoni in his introduction to one of his plays, *The Wily Widow* (*La vedova scaltra*, 1750), replying to his contemporary and rival, Piero Chiari. Goldoni may have had little patience with squabbles among the academies of 18th-century Venice over refinements of linguistic usage, but the assertion does not imply that Goldoni was slapdash over the language employed in theatre.

He inherited – even if his own theatrical reforms were to terminate – the traditions of *commedia dell'arte*, including the tradition that allocated to each of the stock characters the dialect of one particular city. His own dialect was that of his native city, and his writing is based on a continual act of translation. He wrote in three languages – Venetian dialect, the Tuscan which was well on the way to being viewed as standard Italian and, in later life, in French. Sometimes more than one register is employed in the same play, with Arlecchino continuing to speak in Venetian as tradition dictated. Several of his works started life in one form only to be later rewritten in another idiom. He was aware that his command of "languages" other than Venetian was imperfect, and admitted in another preface that there were errors of grammar that could offend "delicate spirits", but he wanted it known to posterity that his "books were not language texts but collections of his comedies". He added as justification that "the whole world can understand the Italian style I have employed", using for the last verb, presumably as a deliberate provocation, the mistaken form "*mi ho servito*", where grammar would dictate "*mi sono servito*".

Many of the most frequent problems in translating playwrights are not present in Goldoni. The mainsprings of his comedy are to be found in the slick momentum of his plots, the vividness of the individual scene, the rumbustiousness of the visual gag, the presentation and manipulation of established comic characters and the command of the situation rather than in any purely linguistic elements. There are few puns in his work, few attempts to arouse laughter by the cut and thrust of verbal humour. Further, his dialogue is brief and snappy, without the sentimentality or lengthy inner monologues or disquisitions on feeling that make other playwrights of his century, like Marivaux, sound today so forced and incongruous.

While it is not unduly difficult to find equivalents for the specific styles of speech of characters such as the fawning, flattering Fabrizio of *The Lovers*, the rustic, uncouth Zanetto of *The Venetian Twins*, or the lecherous old men who appear in several comedies, the subtlety required to render Goldoni's distinctive style is greater than might appear at first sight. Robert David MacDonald is surely right to insist that "Goldoni's language looks deceptively easy". Goldoni's words and phrases are carefully honed, even when the plays were being turned out, as in the year 1750–51, at the rate of 16 in one season. There is a musical, melodious, rhythmic quality to his dialogue that might owe something to his apprenticeship with libretto and melodrama but, perhaps paradoxically, it is less evident in those works written in verse and most apparent in the dialect works such as *I rusteghi* or *Il campiello*. There is in this latter play no single predominant character, and no speech longer than a couple of sentences. The work requires a delicate touch, fluidity and snappiness, both for production and translation, all of which it received in Giorgio Strehler's classic version for the Piccolo-theatre in Milan and in the translation prepared by GRAHAM-JONES & BRYDEN (1976) for Bryden's production at London's National Theatre.

Only a handful of Goldoni's many plays have been admitted to the established European canon. It is impossible to find any justification for this situation, and no reason can be adduced for the international popularity of *La locandiera* as against the neglect of a dark masterpiece like *Gl'innamorati* which, in its depiction of tormented human relations, foreshadows Strindberg. *La locandiera* has always fared better. Perhaps it is the portrayal of Mirandolina, a strong, unconventional, independent-minded woman in total charge of her own destiny, that has given this play a wider international currency than any other by the author. It was certainly this aspect that attracted GREGORY, one of the moving spirits of the Irish literary revival, to do her own idiosyncratic translation (1924), although this remains a work of more interest to readers of Lady Gregory than to those of Goldoni. DAVIES's translation (1968) has the advantage of clarity but is unlikely to be of much value to intending producers. BOLT's version (1993) was commissioned for production and has, like his even better version of *The Venetian Twins* (1993), a sparkle and comic charge that explain the success the work had on stage.

The most accomplished version, however, was done by MACDONALD (1994–99). Indeed, it could he said that in the English-speaking world, MacDonald and Goldoni are now as intimately linked as twins, Siamese rather than Venetian. MacDonald is himself a playwright, actor and director as well as a translator of unusual talent and range, who has produced translations of plays from some eight languages, all of which he speaks. It is with Goldoni he excels, having translated 15 of his plays, all staged but not all published. In *Don Juan* (1999) he retained the verse of the original, although he dropped it for *The Housekeeper* (1994). Drawing on his own knowledge of Goldoni, he took the risk of producing works such as *La guerra* (*The Battlefield*) or *Il vero amico* (*Friends and Lovers*), which are rarely staged even in Italy.

Few translators deserve the title co-creator, but perhaps an exception could be made for MacDonald. His versions of Goldoni are translations and not adaptations, but he has the inventiveness to maintain the verve, zest and vitality that distinguish Goldoni, and the serendipity to introduce playful quotations from English authors where the text warrants it. He invariably retains titles and stray expressions in the original to remind audiences that the works being seen do after all belong to another culture. These qualities are apparent in the words spoken by the misogynistic Cavaliere in *La locandiera* (*Mirandolina*, MACDONALD 1994), when he comes to feel he may have been bested by Mirandolina:

> *Stefano*: Shall I serve the dessert now?
> *Cavaliere*: Serve every man after his deserts and who shall escape whipping? Including you. Get out! "... There's the cause why my eyes do the same as yours." What the devil is that supposed to mean? I know you, you little villain! You want to be the ruin, the death of me ... Where the devil is ashamed to go, he sends a woman. Damn all women – without women, there would be no such thing as damnation.

MacDonald is establishing a stock of quality translations worthy of the original, and perhaps in time he will secure for Goldoni the place on the English-language stage he deserves.

JOSEPH FARRELL

Further Reading

Emery, Ted, *Goldoni as Librettist*, New York: Peter Lang, 1991
Steele, Eugene, *Carlo Goldoni: Life, Work and Times*, Ravenna: Longo, 1981
Symons, Arthur, "Carlo Goldoni" in *The Genius of the Italian Theater*, edited by Eric Bentley, New York: New American Library, 1964

Ivan Goll 1891–1950

French-German poet, dramatist and novelist

Biography

Born Isaac Lang in Saint Dié, Vosges, 29 March 1891, of Jewish Alsace-Lorraine parents. He went to school in Metz and read jurisprudence at the universities of Strasbourg (1912–14) and Lausanne (1915–18). In 1914 he founded the publishing firm Rhein Verlag in Zürich. A pacifist, he moved to Switzerland in 1915 after the outbreak of World War I. He was married to Claire Studer (Claire Goll, the poet), with whom he went to live in Paris 1919–39, associating with Picasso, Chagall, Breton and Éluard, moving then to New York, where he was founding editor of the Franco-American quarterly poetry review *Hémisphères*, 1943–46. He was diagnosed as suffering from leukaemia in 1944. In 1947 he returned to Paris. Died at Neuilly, northwest of Paris, Paris, 27 February 1950.

Goll's early works were influenced by his pre-World War I associations with Expressionist, Dadaist and Surrealist writers. His first major achievement was *Poèmes d'amour* (*Love Poems*), 1925, written to his wife. He is best known for the poem cycle *La Chanson de Jean sans Terre* (*Landless John*), 1936. Goll was also a translator from French and German into those languages and into English, and while in the US he published English poems of his own (*Fruit from Saturn*, 1946).

Editions

Dichtungen: Lyrik, Prosa, Drama, edited by Claire Goll, Darmstadt: Luchterhand, 1960
Oeuvres, edited by Claire Goll and François Xavier Jaujard, 2 vols, Paris: Éditions Émile-Paul, 1968–70
Jean sans Terre / Johann Ohneland, edited by Kristian Wachinger (parallel text; critical edition), Munich: Langewiesche-Brandt, 1990

Translations

Selections of Poetry
Bly, Robert, George Hitchcock, Galway Kinnell and Paul Zweig, *Selected Poems*, edited by Zweig, San Francisco: Kayak, 1968
Exner, Richard and Marianne Exner, "Five Poems by Yvan Goll" ["Alasam", "Morgue", "Bloodhound", "Phosphorus and Salt", "Hours"], *German Life and Letters*, 8 (1954–55)
Hamburger, Michael, "Electric", "Bloodhound", "The Salt Lake", "The Rain Palace", "The Dust Tree" in *German Poetry 1910–1975: An Anthology*, edited by Hamburger, New York: Urizen, 1976; Manchester: Carcanet New Press, 1977
Jolas, Eugène, "Ivan to Claire", *Transition*, 19–20 (June 1930)
Middleton, Christopher, "Moon", "Journey into Misery", "The Rain Palace" in *Modern German Poetry, 1910–1960:*

An Anthology with Verse Translations, edited by Michael Hamburger and Middleton, London: MacGibbon and Kee, and New York: Grove Press, 1962

Reid, Madeleine, "Caravan of Longing", *Transition*, 7 (October 1927)

Reid, Madeleine, "Ivan to Claire", *Transition*, 10 (January 1928)

Poetry

Chansons malaises, 1934

Mills, Clark, *Songs of a Malay Girl*, Albuquerque, New Mexico: Swallow Press, 1942

La Chanson de Jean sans Terre, 1936; revised 1957

Abel, Lionel, William Carlos Williams, Clark Mills and John Gould Fletcher, *Jean sans Terre / Landless John* (parallel texts), with a preface by Allan Tate, San Francisco: Grabhorn Press, 1944

Abel, Lionel, Leonie Adams, John Peale Bishop, Louise Bogan, Babette Deutsch, John Gould Fletcher, Isabella Gardner, Claire and Yvan Goll, Paul Goodman, Galway Kinnell, W.S. Merwin, Clark Mills, Robert Nurenberg, Kenneth Patchen, George Reavey, Kenneth Rexroth, Eric Sellin, William Jay Smith, Robert Wernick and William Carlos Williams, *Jean sans Terre*, with a preface by W.H. Auden, New York: Yoseloff, 1958

Le Mythe de la roche percée, 1945

Bogan, Louise, *The Myth of the Pierced Rock*, Kentfield, California: Allen Press, 1962

Élégie d'Ihpétonga suivie de Masques de cendre, 1949

Deutsch, Babette, Louise Bogan and Claire Goll, *Elegy of Ihpetonga and Masks of Ashes*, New York: Noonday Press, 1954

Les Cercles magiques, 1951

Goll, Claire and Eric Sellin, *The Magic Circles*, in *Four Poems of the Occult*, edited by Francis Carmody, Kentfield, California: Allen Press, 1962

Multiple femme, 1956

Carmody, Francis, "Multiple Woman" in *Four Poems of the Occult*, edited by Carmody, Kentfield, California: Allen Press, 1962

Élégie de Lackawanna, 1973

Kinnell, Galway, *Lackawanna Elegy* (bilingual edition), Fremont, Michigan: Sumac Press, 1970

Plays

Die Chapliniade, 1920

Atkinson, Clinton J. and Arthur S. Wensinger, *The Chaplinade: A Film Poem*, *Massachusetts Review*, 6/3 (1965)

Die Unsterblichen: zwei Possen (*Der Unsterbliche* and *Der Ungestorbene*), 1920

Sokel, Walter H. and Jacqueline Sokel, *The Immortal One*, in *An Anthology of German Expressionist Drama: A Prelude to the Absurd*, edited by Walter H. Sokel, New York: Doubleday, 1963; revised and abridged, Ithaca, New York: Cornell University Press, 1984

Mathusalem; oder, Der ewige Bürger, 1922, produced 1927

Ritchie, J.M., *Methusalem; or, The Eternal Bourgeois*, edited by Ritchie, in *Seven Expressionist Plays: Kokoschka to Barlach*, translated by Ritchie and H.F. Garten, London: Calder and Boyars, 1968

Wensinger, Arthur S. and Clinton J. Atkinson, *Methusalem; or, The Eternal Bourgeois*, in *Plays for a New Theater: Playbook 2*, New York: New Directions, 1966

Other Writing

Knoblauch, Mary, *Archipenko: An Appreciation*, New York: Société Anonyme, 1930

A native of Lorraine, Ivan Goll wrote with equal facility and success in French and German, often producing versions of his own works in the other language. A bilingual writer, he was fitted also to become a prolific translator of modern French writing into German (Claudel, Duhamel, Éluard, Fargue, Mallarmé, Rolland, Romains, Soupault, Supervielle) and modern German writing into French (Benn, Brecht, Heinrich Mann, Trakl). In 1921 he translated a small anthology of modern Russian verse into German, and in the following year he edited and translated into French much of an ambitious world anthology of modern poetry entitled *Les Cinq Continents*.

Goll was also active in bringing English-language writing to his native languages. In 1918 he translated into German a selection of letters by Walt Whitman; in the late 1920s he assisted the German translator of Joyce's *Ulysses* and the group of French writers who were translating the "Anna Livia Plurabelle" section of *Finnegans Wake*. During his exile in America from 1939 to 1947, Goll, unlike other exiled poets, engaged in numerous literary activities, many of which were directly related to translation. He edited *Hémisphères*, a French-American poetry magazine (1943–46); translated contemporary American poetry into French (Louise Bogan, T.S. Eliot, Archibald MacLeish, Clark Mills, Kenneth Patchen, Carl Sandburg, Edna St Vincent Millay); translated into English, at times assisted by fellow poets, some of his own work and work of others such as Aimé Césaire; and wrote poems in English, e.g. "Atom Elegy" (1945), *Fruit from Saturn* (1946) and, with his wife Claire Goll, *Love Poems* (1947).

In the English-speaking world Goll is known mainly as a poet. During the 1940s and 1950s, translators focused on *Jean sans Terre*, the cycle of poems that Goll was working on at the time, which portray the modern poet as a rootless wanderer between continents. These efforts resulted in a small bilingual edition in 1944 and a comprehensive translation in 1958, a joint venture that drew together an illustrious circle of American poets (ABEL *et al.*, 1944; ABEL *et al.*, 1958). In the 1960s, attention was given to other periods of Goll's poetry and a more balanced picture emerged. The *Selected Poems* (BLY *et al.*, 1968) introduced Goll's early expressionist and late surrealist poetry, written predominantly in German, as did the translations of his work in representative poetry anthologies. Goll's dramatic works, written between 1918 and 1923, have been given little attention, but of the four extant translations two are of *Methusalem*, which was rediscovered in the 1960s as a forerunner of the theatre of the absurd. As yet, none of Goll's prose works, which are currently being given renewed attention in France and Germany, has been translated into English.

The translation of *Jean sans Terre* was made difficult by a number of facts. First, the cycle was a work in progress, with Goll often producing alternate versions of poems, sometimes recasting a poem by selecting quatrains from several versions. Second, Goll oversaw many of the translations made for the 1944 edition, sometimes even going so far as to alter the French in order to help solve the translators' problems. And finally, the cycle posed formal and lexical challenges, with the poems written in Europe before 1939 being more strictly versified (the rhymed quatrain with five-syllable lines) than the ones written in America, which move towards freer patterns and sometimes approximate popular forms, yet have a more mythological, esoteric lexicon than the poems written before 1939. Hence, in both the 1944 and the 1958 volumes, the translations of the poems written after 1940 are generally better, because of the less formal character of the originals, which lend themselves more easily to English speech patterns. Still, Goll's combination of the highly charged tone of German expressionism and the surrealist imagery of the French avant-garde, along with the occult themes and the esoteric lexicon, tend to make for awkward reading in English. The 1958 edition is more comprehensive than the 1944 selection and contains 70 poems in translation, some from the 1944 volume, a few of those revised; some previously published in little magazines; and some published for the first time. The best translations are by fellow poet, William Carlos WILLIAMS, who perfectly captures the mood and tone of the original in seemingly effortless poems (some of them revised between 1940 and 1958) that despite the occasionally intricate versification, do not at all appear to be translations. Like Williams, FLETCHER and REXROTH largely abandon Goll's metric scheme and use the "variable foot", whereas KINNELL and PATCHEN preserve the strict meter. ABEL and BISHOP prefer a rendition in contemporary colloquial language, as do NURENBERG, REAVEY, WERNICK and, with less precision, MERWIN. Uneven results come from ADAMS, BOGAN, DEUTSCH, GOODMAN and MILLS, who use archaic registers and force the rhyme. SELLIN's translations are often laboured and eccentric, so that in one instance Claire and Ivan GOLL can surpass them.

Whereas Richard and Marianne EXNER (1954–55) render a selection of Goll's last poems in the spiritual language of high poetic modernism, both Christopher MIDDLETON (1962) and, to a larger extent, Michael HAMBURGER (1976) choose for sometimes identical poems a less charged, everyday language. Also, their versions are not marred by syntactical inversions, which renders them more accessible.

The most successful translations to be found in BLY *et al.* (1968) are those by George HITCHCOCK and Paul ZWEIG, the former presenting versions from the German poems written in the late 1940s, the latter lexically fluent and rhythmically attractive renditions from the French love poems to Claire Goll. Zweig is more literal, Hitchcock more audacious, especially in his translation of "Der Salzsee" ("The Salt Lake"), Goll's final poem and also the final poem of the volume. Transcribing dying as lying down in a metaphorical bed, the German original holds precisely the middle between active and passive voice, whereas Hitchcock chooses to make the speaker of the poem an active subject. Both translators manage to make the surrealist imagery work in English, benefitting from the expansion of the English poetic lexicon through the surrealist "deep image". KINNELL's translation of the "Lackawanna" elegies (in the 1968 *Selected Poems* and separately, in 1970) clearly benefits from the free verse of the original and employs changes in rhythm while trying to preserve the lexicon. Bly's liberal translations (in *Selected Poems*, 1968) modify rhythm and the number of syllables, but is guilty of a number of lexical mistakes.

In their translation of *Methusalem*, WENSINGER & ATKINSON (1966) and RITCHIE (1968) largely preserve the satiric tone and the wit of the original. ATKINSON & WENSINGER also translated (1965) the brief scenario-poem *The Chaplinade*, an early portrayal of the consequences of media stardom written as a montage of loosely connected scenes, as is *The Immortal One* translated by Walter H. and Jacqueline SOKEL (1963), who capture the expressionist pathos as well as the absurdist *Verfremdung* (alienation) in the contemporary language.

ANDREAS KRAMER

Further Reading

Parmée, Margaret A., *Ivan Goll: The Development of His Poetic Themes and Their Imagery*, Bonn: Bouvier, 1981

Phillips, James, *Yvan Goll and Bilingual Poetry*, Stuttgart: Heinz, 1984

Profit, Vera B., *Interpretations of Iwan Goll's Late Poetry*, Bern: Peter Lang, 1977

Witold Gombrowicz 1904–1969

Polish novelist, playwright and diarist

Biography

Born 4 August 1904 in Maloszyce, Poland. He attended Warsaw University 1922–26 and the Paris Institut des Hautes Études Internationales 1926–27. Gombrowicz, along with Bruno Schulz and S.I. Witkiewicz (Witkacy), is among the most important Polish writers to emerge from the 20 years of Polish independence between 1919 and 1939. Gombrowicz's first novel *Ferdydurke* (1937) was a literary event, and seemed to ensure him a promising career in Warsaw's effervescent literary milieu; during this period he also published his first play *Iwona, Księżniczka Burgunda* (1935; *Princess Ivona*, 1969), wrote a number of short stories later collected under the title

Bakakaj, and published in a Radom newspaper a Gothic serial novel entitled *Opętani* (1939; *Possessed*, 1980). In August of that year 1939, however, Gombrowicz boarded the Polish transatlantic liner *Chrobry* to write a journalistic account of its maiden voyage to Buenos Aires, and when the Germans invaded Poland a few weeks later he opted to remain in Argentina, beginning an almost 24-year stay there, characterized by poverty and a struggle to survive as a writer by publishing his works in translation.

These attempts at storming the Buenos Aires literary scene in Spanish translation were largely ignored by the Argentine literary elite, and it was only through the intervention of the Polish émigré journal *Kultura*, published by the Paris-based Instytut Literacki, that Gombrowicz's works began to receive international attention; a short period of cultural liberalization in Poland in 1957–58 allowed his works to be published there, and the French translation of *Ferdydurke* in 1958 granted him his first real exposure to an international readership. In 1963 he left Argentina on a Ford Fellowship to West Berlin, and then continued on to France, where he met his future wife, the young French-Canadian doctoral student Rita Labrosse. Increasing international recognition, enhanced by the staging of his plays in Paris and Venice by the Argentine director Jorge Lavelli, resulted in additional translations into numerous European languages: the novels *Pornografia* (1960; translated under the same title 1966) and *Kosmos* (1965; *Cosmos*, 1967), and his *Dziennik* (1953–69; *Diary*, 1988–93). Since Gombrowicz's death in Vence, France, 25 July 1969, his widow, Rita, has been instrumental in preparing further translations of his works, especially those into English.

Translations

Novels

Ferdydurke, 1937
Mosbacher, Eric, *Ferdydurke*, London: MacGibbon and Kee, and New York: Harcourt Brace, 1961

Opętani, 1939
Underwood, J.A., *Possessed; or, The Secret of Myslotch*, from the French translation by Albert Mailles and Hélène Wlodarczyk, with an introduction, London and Boston: Marion Boyars, 1980

Trans-Atlantyk, 1953
French, Carolyn and Nina Karsov, *Trans-Atlantyk*, with an introduction by Stanisław Barańczak, New Haven, Connecticut: Yale University Press, 1994

Pornografia, 1960
Hamilton, Alastair, *Pornografia*, from the French translation by Georges Lisowski, London: Calder and Boyars, 1966; New York: Grove Press, 1967

Kosmos, 1965
Mosbacher, Eric, *Cosmos*, from the French translation by Georges Sedir and the German translation by Walter Tiel, London: MacGibbon and Kee, and New York: Grove Press, 1967

Plays

Iwona, Księżniczka Burgunda, 1935, produced 1957
Griffith-Jones, Krystyna and Catherine Robins, *Princess Ivona*, London: Calder and Boyars, 1969; as *Ivona, Princess of Burgundia*, New York: Grove Press, 1970

Ślub, 1953, produced 1964
Iribarne, Louis, *The Marriage*, with an introduction by Jan Kott, New York: Grove Press, 1969; London: Calder and Boyars, 1970

Operetka, 1966, produced 1969
Iribarne, Louis, *Operetta*, London: Calder and Boyars, 1971

Other Writing

Dziennik, 1953–69
Vallee, Lillian, *Diary*, 3 vols, edited by Jan Kott, Evanston, Illinois: Northwestern University Press, 1988–93

Interviews

Hamilton, Alastair, *A Kind of Testament*, edited by Dominique de Roux, London: Calder and Boyars, and Philadelphia: Temple University Press, 1973

The most important translations for the international dissemination of Gombrowicz's literary oeuvre and for studies in translation theory have been those into Spanish and French; English translations, in contrast, have been slow in appearing, and then often they have been translations from the already-existing French and German versions. This trend seems to be changing, however, with the long-awaited appearance of seminal works such as the *Diary* and *Trans-Atlantyk* and recent plans to retranslate many of his best-known novels.

The best-known example of Gombrowicz's own Spanish versions of his work was the 1947 translation of *Ferdydurke*, undertaken in the Café Rex on the Avenida Corrientes, Buenos Aires, by a "Translation Committee" that included the Cuban writers Virgilio Piñera and Humberto Rodríguez Tomeu, and Adolfo de Obieta, son of the Argentine writer Macedonio Fernández; Gombrowicz's knowledge of Spanish was nowhere near perfect, his committee knew no Polish, and there existed no Polish–Spanish dictionary to aid in the translation, yet the finished translation is the document of a literary event that prompts an inquiry into the institutions through which literary translations are produced and disseminated. Equally important, yet not as well known, was Gombrowicz's own translation and publication in Spanish of his play *Ślub* (*El casamiento*, 1948; *The Marriage*, 1969), completed in collaboration with his roommate of seven years, the young philosophy student Alejandro Rússovich, between sessions at the Rex and long walks along the Costanera Sur, a city park on the banks of the Río de la Plata, in which they would perform the work bilingually as they walked.

The English translations of Eric MOSBACHER (1961; 1967) and Alastair HAMILTON (1966) are of the well-known novels *Ferdydurke*, *Pornografia* and *Cosmos*. Despite the importance of these works, not one of them is translated directly from the Polish original, which gives them at times a sort of disembodied feel with respect to the works' source language. One might contend that this is a fitting rendering of Gombrowicz's own aesthetic of deformation; after all, the original translation of *Ferdydurke* into Spanish was made to Latin-Americanize the work, inventing neologisms to test the boundaries of the target language, its system of reference often completely autonomous and away from that of the original. In this case, however, the result is rather infelicitous; as Beth Holmgren states, "predictably enough, these works do not reflect the style – specifically, the syntactic rhythm and intonation – of the original texts. They read like ponderous paraphrases". What is more, Hamilton or his editors do not even deem it necessary to give credit to the French translator – Georges Lisowski – on which Hamilton's English version of *Pornografia* is based.

The first translation into English from the Polish original was the play *Princess Ivona*, 1969, republished a year later in New York under the more complete title *Ivona, Princess of Burgundia*. The translators, Krystyna GRIFFITH-JONES & Catherine ROBINS, are lauded, with good reason, for having "caught the ironic flavour and the conversational style of the original." Next came the fine translations of *The Marriage* (in 1969) and *Operetta* (in 1971) by Louis IRIBARNE, a renowned translator of other works from Polish, most notably the novel *Insatiability* (1930; translated 1977) by S.I. Witkiewicz. Gombrowicz states in the commentary that "the text of the modern play is becoming less and less suitable for reading. It is like a musical score that comes to life only on the stage in its performance." Iribarne does well to recognize that his work as translator must be left, in a sense, incomplete, and passed on "to the discretion of directors and actors" to add the finishing touches to this translation-in-progress through their performance.

The J.A. UNDERWOOD translation of the novel *Opętani* (1980) from the French (*Les Envoûtés*, translated by Albert Mailles and Hélène Wlodarczyk, 1977) seems to signal a return to the limited cultural horizons of Mosbacher and Hamilton, in which knowledge of the language of the original is not necessary for translation; what is more, "the approval of the author's widow, Mme Rita Gombrowicz", is invoked in the translator's introduction as a means of legitimizing this second-hand method.

The long-overdue translation of Gombrowicz's *Diary* by Lillian VALLEE (1988–93) marks a turning point in the translation of his work into English, a trend happily continued in Carolyn FRENCH & Nina KARSOV's rendition of *Trans-Atlantyk*, arguably his most difficult novel to translate because of its "mongrel" style, based in part on the Polish baroque genre called *gawęda*. These are excellent translations; here the problem is by no means that of an insufficient knowledge of the source language culture. Ironically enough, however, these two works are the ones that deal most with the author's experiences in Argentina, and the cultural complexity of the source text that results raises the question: to what extent is knowledge of the Spanish language and 20th-century Argentine culture also fundamental for a more complete translation of Gombrowicz, a writer who manifests himself, both in the original and in translation, not only as the Polish writer, but also the Argentine immigrant Witoldo? It is precisely in the moments when Argentina, and its language and culture, are evoked in Gombrowicz's work that these translations, undertaken by specialists in Slavic Studies, seem to falter. Gombrowicz, as an emblematic figure of multilingual migrant writing in the 20th century, evades the limits of national traditions, making the prospect of translation contingent upon a knowledge of language beyond that of the source language. Here the source culture is double, if not multiple, a phenomenon that ideally should be reflected in the translation.

CHRISTOPHER LARKOSH

Further Reading

Holmgren, Beth, "Witold Gombrowicz in the United States", *Polish Review*, 33/4 (1988)

Larkosh, Christopher, "Teaching / Translation / Theory: Communicative Horizons for Critical Practices" in *Teaching Translation and Interpreting*, vol. 3, edited by Cay Dollerup and Vibeke Appel, Amsterdam: Benjamins, 1996

Larkosh, Christopher, "Reading In / Between: Gombrowicz, Latin American Translations, Immigrant Bodies" in "The Limits of the Translatable Foreign: Translation, Migration and Sexuality in 20th-Century Argentine Literature" (dissertation), Berkeley: University of California, 1996

Longinovic, Tomislav Z., *Borderline Culture: The Politics of Identity in Four Twentieth-Century Slavic Novels*, Fayetteville: University of Arkansas Press, 1993

Thompson, Ewa M., *Witold Gombrowicz*, Boston: Twayne, 1979

See also the introductions and afterwords in Iribarne (1969), Underwood, Vallee, and French/Karsov; these translations include respectively introductions by Jan Kott, Czesław Miłosz, Kott and Stanisław Barańczak

---

Ivan Goncharov 1812–1891

Russian novelist

Biography

Goncharov was born in Simbirsk, 18 June 1812 into a prosperous merchant family. After his father's death in 1819, Goncharov was brought up by his godfather Nikolai Tregubov, a liberal-minded artistocrat. He attended a local boarding school, 1820–22; Moscow Commercial School, 1822–31; and studied at Moscow University, 1831–34. After graduating he entered the civil service and served for almost 30 years. From 1852 to 1855 he was secretary to Admiral Pitiatin on a trip to the Far East, and travelled to England, Africa and

Japan. He worked as an official censor in St Petersburg, 1856–60, and was a member of the committee of review of Russian censorship groups, 1863–67. He retired from the civil service as Actual Councillor of State in 1867.

Goncharov's literary fame rests on his three novels. The first, *Obyknovennaia istoriia* (*A Common Story*) was published in 1847, and was praised by Vissarion Belinskii as the best example of the new realism in fiction. His second and most famous novel, *Oblomov*, was begun in the late 1840s but the work was interrupted by his voyage to the Far East, which resulted in the publication of his travel book *Fregat Pallada* (*The Voyage of the Frigate Pallas*) in 1858. *Oblomov*, published in book form in 1859, was a critical success and the subject of much controversy. The character gave his name to the Russian term *oblovshchina* (oblomovism), meaning inertia. Goncharov's final novel *Obryv* (*The Precipice*) was published in 1869 but was not a critical success and he withdrew from public life. He died in St Petersburg, 27 September 1891.

Oblomov

Oblomov, 1859

A novel in four parts, written 1847–58; published in the first four issues of *Otechestvennye zapiski* (Notes of the Fatherland) for 1859, and as a separate two-volume edition later that year.

Translations

All translators to date have used Russian editions based on the original serial publication of the novel in 1859. A new authoritative Russian edition of the novel appeared only in 1987; it uses the second edition of 1862, in which Goncharov made about 600 corrections.

Duddington, Natalie, *Oblomov*, London: Allen and Unwin, 1929; New York: Dutton, 1932
Dunnigan, Ann, *Oblomov*, New York: New American Library, 1963
Hogarth, C.J., *Oblomov*, New York: Macmillan, and London: Allen and Unwin, 1915
Magarshack, David, *Oblomov*, Harmondsworth and Baltimore: Penguin, 1954

By common agreement, *Oblomov* is Ivan Goncharov's greatest achievement, the one work that ensures his reputation as a minor classic of 19th-century Russian literature. The novel is deceptively quiet, as may be expected when the main figure spends the entire first part, well over 100 pages, in a vain attempt to get out of bed one day. Similarly, the book appears deceptively easy to translate: Goncharov's manner lacks both the lexical and the syntactic complexities that are to be found in such contemporary figures as Gogol' or Dostoevskii. And yet a plain style is not the same as an absence of style. Essential to Goncharov's writing are the rhythmic effects he achieves by his sentence structures, the parallels through which he underlines key ideas, the shifts in manner as he describes different characters, and the subtle choices of words to convey linkages within passages; the translator who fails to convey these fails to convey *Oblomov* as well.

HOGARTH (1915), the first to translate the novel, abridged it severely. While he does include much of part 1 (which goes on to occupy virtually half of this edition), he provides what amounts to only a skimpy synopsis of part 2 (just 35 large-print pages, as opposed to about 150 pages with smaller print in other versions). Parts 3 and 4 fare only slightly better. What is more, the cuts and contractions affect even those sections that are presented more fully, time and again doing away with effects that Goncharov struggles to create in the original. The most famous passage in the novel, the extended "Oblomov's Dream" in part 1, is here, symptomatically, numbered chapter 5 instead of 9. Hogarth renders this passage more completely than most, but even here he starts by rewriting the chapter's first few sentences into a bland declarative statement, eliminating a pair of questions meant to draw in the reader. This is more efficient than Goncharov, but it is not *Oblomov*. Other sections in this chapter do somewhat better, but frequently throughout the novel Goncharov's carefully crafted prose is simply ignored for the purposes of conveying the general flow of the plot more rapidly. More startling still, with three other adequate translations available from which to choose, is the decision to reprint this outdated and inadequate version as late as 1979.

The first attempt to translate the entire novel, that of DUDDINGTON (1929), has been republished frequently over the years. The version has a charming old-fashioned air to it. The transliteration of proper names sometimes reflects an older norm, and characters are often referred to by their first name and patronymic – an accurate reflection of the Russian, but a form of address that is often confusing to readers of English. The characters, too, sometimes speak a language that seems dated and occasionally just plain stilted. A few of the more subtle effects are glossed over; the translation does not always pick up on shifts in verb tense, and Goncharov's short, pointed paragraphs are frequently lumped together. However, the more purely descriptive passages generally catch the rhythms of Goncharov's Russian, and good English equivalents are provided for individual words describing objects that are native to Russia. If not always graceful, and though marred by what appear to be simply careless omissions of occasional phrases, the translation is none the less on the whole accurate and sensitive to much of what Goncharov was attempting to convey. Duddington has clearly served as a model for subsequent translators.

MAGARSHACK (1954) essentially offers an updated and improved version of Duddington. The transliteration fits modern norms, he avoids use of the first name and patronymic (usually substituting last names or just a pronoun), and he occasionally catches minor omissions or errors on the part of his predecessor. Individual sentences often follow Duddington's closely, with the changes intended to make the English read more naturally or smoothly. Magarshack too has a tendency to combine several paragraphs into one, but for the most part he is more sensitive to Goncharov's writing manner in this regard. And he works hard to provide exact equivalents for words or phrases that are translated only loosely by Duddington. Also, the dialogue generally reads more naturally in Magarshack's version; he is better at finding modern equivalents for colloquial Russian. For all of these improvements, the translation still falls short of the ideal: the style at times seems a bit bland and the effort to remain so close to the original can create a certain ponderousness. If the dialogues are improved, they still do not always read as naturally as they might; the liveliness of the exchanges between Oblomov and his servant Zakhar, responsible for much of the work's comic verve, suffer particularly in this regard.

The most recent translator, DUNNIGAN (1963), has learned from both her predecessors. In terms of language, transliteration, and using more modern turns of speech, she makes the translation accessible in a manner similar to that of Magarshack. At the same time she adheres closely to Goncharov's paragraph structure and to the rhythms with which his descriptions are presented or his characters express ideas. She goes back to using first names and patronymics with some regularity, as a (debatable) way of keeping some of the Russian "flavor". While many passages show her own turn of phrase, one senses that she looked carefully at the earlier works, sometimes accepting an emendation made by Magarshack, sometimes going back to Duddington, and at other times rejecting both. On the whole her choices in this regard seem judicious, and while many might prefer a given phrase or paragraph in one of the two earlier full translations, both of which, it needs to be stressed, are quite adequate, hers is the most consistently accomplished. Of the three she has the best ear for dialogue, and the crucial exchanges between characters read most effectively in this version. A few of Goncharov's more subtle grammatical effects seem to escape her detection as well, but readers of this version will experience much of the flavor of the original. Thus the history of *Oblomov* offers a classic instance of three serious translators creating incremental improvements in the text available to readers of English.

BARRY P. SCHERR

Further Reading

Diment, Galya (editor), *Goncharov's Oblomov: A Critical Companion*, Evanston, Illinois: Northwestern University Press, 1998

Ehre, Milton, *Oblomov and His Creator: The Life and Art of Ivan Goncharov*, Princeton, New Jersey: Princeton University Press, 1973

Lyngstad, Alexandra and Sverre Lyngstad, *Ivan Goncharov*, New York: Twayne, 1971

Peace, Richard, *"Oblomov": A Critical Examination of Goncharov's Novel*, Birmingham: Department of Russian, University of Birmingham, 1991

Setchkarev, Vsevolod, *Ivan Goncharov: His Life and His Works*, Würzburg: Jal, 1974

Luis de Góngora 1561–1627

Spanish poet

Biography

Born in Córdoba, 11 July 1561. He was educated at a Jesuit school in Córdoba and from 1576 to 1580 studied at the University of Salamanca. He took minor orders at university, and deacon's orders in 1586. Having served as prebendary of Córdoba Cathedral, 1586–1617 he was ordained a priest in 1617. He was Royal Chaplain in Madrid, 1617 to 1625. He acquired a reputation as a writer of fine sonnets and ballads on the strength of the publication of his poems in a general anthology in 1605. In 1614 copies of his *Solitudes* (*Soledades*) were circulated at court and caused a major literary controversy that centred on Gongóra's style, which became known as *gongorismo* or *culteranismo*. His reputation declined in the 18th and 19th centuries, to be revived in the 1920s. He died in Córdoba, 23 May 1627.

Translations

Selections of Poetry

Churton, Edward, *Góngora: An Historical and Critical Essay on the Times of Philip III and IV of Spain, with Translations*, 2 vols, London: John Murray, 1862

Fanshawe, Richard, *Il Pastor Fido the Faithfull Shepherd, with an Addition of Divers Other Poems, Concluding with a Short Discourse of the Long Civill Warres of Rome: To His Highnesse the Prince of Wales*, London: Printed by R. Raworth for Humphrey Moseley, 1647

Poetry

Soledades, 1613–14

Cunningham, Gilbert F., *The Solitudes of Luis de Góngora y Argote* (bilingual edition), Alva, Scotland: privately printed, 1964; Baltimore: Johns Hopkins University Press, 1968

Manning, Hugo, *Then People May Laugh*, London: Village Press, 1973

Stanley, Thomas, *Excitations* in his *Anacreon; Bion; Moschus; Kisses by Secundus; Cupid Crucified by Ausonius; Venus' Vigils . . .* , London, 1651

Wilson, Edward Meryon, *The Solitudes of Don Luis de Góngora*, Cambridge: Minority Press, 1931; revised edition Cambridge: Cambridge University Press, 1965

Fábula de Polifemo y Galatea, 1613

Cunningham, Gilbert F., *Polyphemus and Galatea* in *Polyphemus and Galatea: A Study in the Interpretation of a Baroque Poem*, by Alexander A. Parker, Edinburgh: Edinburgh University Press, and Austin: University of Texas Press, 1977

Upton, John, *Polifemo-Luis de Góngora*, Sooke, British Columbia: Fireweed Press, 1977

Luis de Góngora's famed "culterano" style created a seemingly insurmountable task for the translator. The introduction of lexical novelties into the poetic vocabulary, intense use of metaphor and extended metaphor, rejection of the normal Spanish word order in favour of the rhythms and syntax of Latin verse, and the use of exaggerated hyperbole combined with dense musicality presents a daunting prospect. In addition to the rigours, obscurity and innovatory nature of Góngora's poetic form, the content was often based on the metaphorical conceit, used in the "conceptista" style to connect things widely separate in their natures, by virtue of an intellectual act (catachresis). Extreme concision of expression is combined with enigmatic meaning. There is also an insistence on verbal melody, and Góngora wrote in a wide range of traditional metres, including ballads, carols, *letrillas* and sonnets, as well as his major narrative poems, the *Fábula de Polifemo y Galatea* (1613), the *Soledad primera* (1613) and the unfinished *Soledad segunda* (1614).

In spite of the enormity of the task, translations of Góngora's works do exist, dating from the 17th to the 20th centuries. In contrast with his great impact on poets in Spain itself, the influence of Góngora in 17th-century England has been generally discounted. His poetry could have been known to very few English speakers at that time. However, Thomas STANLEY (1625–78), a classical scholar at Cambridge who wrote a history of philosophy, attempted a translation of the first *Soledad* in 1651. His note to the translation states that it was "never further intended than as private exercises of the language from which [it] was deduced". His effort was probably more gallant than successful. The first *Soledad* (*Solitude*) was more than 2,000 lines long and written in an irregular hendecasyllable known as the "silva". It is a pastoral poem about the adventures of a young man who is shipwrecked and washed ashore on an unknown coast. Although Stanley's original version was in free rhyme, he perhaps inadvisedly changed it to a decasyllabic rhyming couplet. The Spanish poem uses extremely artificial language, with systematic inversion of normal word order. Stanley tries to follow this inverted order, unsuccessfully, producing a clumsy, inaccurate and at times incomprehensible rendering into English. He did not finish the translation, completing only about one sixth of the original.

Perhaps Stanley's undertaking was too ambitious. Sir Richard FANSHAWE (1608–66), who read law at Cambridge and worked at the English embassy in Madrid, had greater success with his translation of seven of Góngora's sonnets. Fanshawe also produced a famous translation (1655) of the Portuguese epic, *The Lusiad*. His translations of the sonnets (1647) are remarkably accurate in meaning, yet retain the overall complexity of structure fairly well. He uses an "abab" rhyme, instead of Góngora's "abba".

No further attempts to translate Góngora's work were made until 1862, when a major essay on Góngora was published by archdeacon Edward CHURTON, which contained a wide range of translations, among which are sonnets, odes, songs, historical verse, ballads and the *Fábula de Polifemo y Galatea* (*Fable of Polyphemus and Galatea*). He made no comments on his translations, merely expressing the hope of contributing to "the stock of bright-eyed fancy and generous mirth". In comparison with Fanshawe, Churton's sonnet translations, though elegant and well-rounded, are far from the meaning of the originals, often bearing just a token resemblance, using the basic idea and re-inventing it.

His version of the *Fábula de Polifemo y Galatea* was the first to appear in English. This poem consists of 63 stanzas in "octavas", and tells Ovid's story from the *Metamorphoses* of the love of the nymph Galatea for the faun Acis, who is crushed to death by a rock hurled by the jealous giant Polyphemus. It is a carefully woven tapestry of colour and light, but Churton unfortunately deemed the original too long, translating it "with some omissions and abridgments, reducing it to little more than half the original". Churton chose to concentrate on telling the story, which is disappointing, as it was of comparatively little importance to Góngora, except to allow the development of his rich, musical descriptions. Churton's version is quite a fine poem in terms of rhythm and imagery, but it is a re-creation rather than a translation.

The next translation of Góngora's poetry appeared more than a century later in 1965, when Edward WILSON, Professor of Spanish at Cambridge University, published *The Solitudes of Don Luis de Góngora*. He used Damaso Alonso's 1927 edition of *Las soledades*, with the aim of producing "as concentrated and faithful version as I could, to reproduce the style of the original and use archaic expressions to indicate the gap in time between Góngora and ourselves and to imitate his deliberate rejection of the commonplace and colloquial". Wilson adhered to these intentions, using "thee"/"thou" forms, inversion, contraction, and preserving the strange and archaic vocabulary in examples like "canorous", "raiment", "lustrum", "remora" and "nacre". Athough tending to follow punctuation where he could, Wilson was clearly unable to retain the extreme dislocation of the original syntax. Similarly, he tries to maintain the rhyme scheme but often finds this impossible. There are considerable departures from the original meaning. The translator was only too aware of the colossal problem of remaining faithful to both style and meaning, and felt his initial version was "clotted and turgid". Yet the archaisms work surprisingly well, and the translation is a fine one, if a little ponderous.

A verse translation by Gilbert F. CUNNINGHAM is included in Alexander Parker's study of *Polyphemus and Galatea* (1977). Cunningham was a remarkably gifted translator, though not a linguist as such. He manages to make the formal Gongorine construction sound quite natural, while maintaining an astonishing fidelity to the meaning of the original. He translated the *Polifemo* in *ottava rima*, Góngora's stanza, and manages to reproduce much of the formal structure of the Spanish, in particular the bi-partite balance where noun and verb or noun and adjective are repeated in each part. Cunningham also shows extraordinary skill in conveying the poem's musicality. No less successful is his translation entitled *The Solitudes of Luis de Góngora y Argote* (CUNNINGHAM, 1964). In his introduction, Cunningham says that all translation of poetry is foredoomed to at least partial failure, and although adhering to the same rhyme scheme and line lengths as the original, he acknowledges the impossibility of conveying Góngora's classical syntax effects in an uninflected language like English. It is nevertheless a virtuoso translation.

John UPTON translates the *Fabulad de Polifemo y Galatea*

(1977), using Damaso Alonso's 1967 edition of the text, which is the Lacon manuscript in the National Library in Madrid. The translation is fresh, with a modern feel and Americanized spelling. Upton effectively conveys the violent contrast between beauty and monstrosity well, and also the richness of evoked textures – gold, pearls, ivory, coral, snow. The *Polifemo* was written in *ottavas reales* (eight line stanzas rhyming "abababcc") using an iambic hendecasyllable. Upton tends to use an eight-syllable line in English, with only sporadic rhyme. There are some very felicitous lines, for example "Where Sicily's sea flings silver foam" (stanza 4), and he retains some unusual words, like "caliginous" and "adust", without creating an archaic effect. There is the odd small error, such as "grass" instead of "hay" (heno) (stanza 10), and considerable licence on occasion, but these are compensated for by the splendid rhythm and sympathetic interpretation.

It is worthy of note that Hugo MANNING's poem *Then People May Laugh* (1973) is adapted from "the Spanish of Luis de Góngora". It is a four-stanza poem on the virtue and simplicity of the pastoral life, echoing the theme of the *Soledad primera*, which is the happiness of the simple life of village and countryside, provided it is free from the corrupting motive of gain. Any links with Góngora's style are tenuous.

ELIZABETH DRAYSON MACDONALD

Further Reading

Beverley, John R., *Aspects of Góngora's "Soledades"*, Amsterdam: Benjamins, 1980

Calcraft, R.P., *The Sonnets of Luis de Góngora*, Durham: University of Durham, 1980

Forster, Leonard, *The Icy Fire: Five Studies in European Petrarchism*, London: Cambridge University Press, 1969

Parker, Alexander A., *Polyphemus and Galatea: A Study in the Interpretation of a Baroque Poem*, with verse translation by Gilbert F. Cunningham, Edinburgh: Edinburgh University Press, and Austin: University of Texas Press, 1977

Juan Goytisolo 1931–

Spanish novelist, essayist and journalist

Biography

Born in Barcelona, 5 January 1931. He studied at the universities of Madrid and Barcelona, 1948–52. He was a co-founder of the Turia anti-Franco writers' group with Ana María Matute and others in Barcelona, 1951. His boldly experimental fiction makes him a leader of his literary generation, inviting comparison with other trail-blazers such as Joyce and Beckett. From 1956 he travelled frequently in Europe, Russia and the Middle East. He now divides his year between Paris and Marrakesh.

Translations

Novels

Juegos de manos, 1954
Rust, John, *The Young Assassins*, New York: Knopf, 1958; London: MacGibbon and Kee, 1960

Duelo en el Paraíso, 1955
Brooke-Rose, Christine, *Children of Chaos*, London: MacGibbon and Kee, 1958

Fiestas, 1957
Weinstock, Herbert, *Fiestas*, New York: Knopf, 1960; London: MacGibbon and Kee, 1961

La isla, 1961
Yglesias, José, *Sands of Torremolinos*, New York: Knopf, and London: Jonathan Cape, 1962

Fin de fiesta, 1962
Yglesias, José, *The Party's Over: Four Attempts to Define a Love Story*, London: Weidenfeld and Nicolson, and New York: Grove Press, 1966

Señas de identidad, 1966
Rabassa, Gregory, *Marks of Identity*, New York: Grove Press, 1969; London: Serpent's Tail, 1988

Reivindicación del conde don Julián, 1970
Lane, Helen R., *Count Julian*, New York: Viking Press, 1974; London: Serpent's Tail, 1989
See entry on *Count Julian*, below

Juan sin tierra, 1975
Lane, Helen R., *Juan the Landless*, New York: Viking Press, 1977; London: Serpent's Tail, 1990

Makbara, 1980
Lane, Helen R., *Makbara*, New York: Seaver, 1981; London: Serpent's Tail, 1993

Paisajes después de la batalla, 1982
Lane, Helen R., *Landscapes after the Battle*, New York: Seaver, and London: Serpent's Tail, 1987

Las virtudes del pájaro solitario, 1988
Lane, Helen R., *The Virtues of the Solitary Bird*, London: Serpent's Tail, 1991

La cuarentena, 1991
Bush, Peter, *Quarantine*, London: Quartet, and Normal, Illinois: Dalkey Archive Press, 1994

La saga de los Marx, 1993
Bush, Peter, *The Marx Family Saga*, London and Boston: Faber, 1996

Autobiography
Coto vedado, 1985
Bush, Peter, *Forbidden Territory: The Memoirs of Juan Goytisolo 1931–1956*, London: Quartet, and San Francisco: North Point Press, 1989

En los reinos de Taifa, 1986
Bush, Peter, *Realms of Strife: The Memoirs of Juan Goytisolo 1957–1982*, London: Quartet, and San Francisco: North Point Press, 1990

Other Writing
Disidencias, 1977; *Crónicas sarracinas*, 1981; *Contracorrientes*, 1985
Lane, Helen, *The Saracen Chronicles: A Selection of Literary Essays*, London: Quartet, 1992

Juan Goytisolo's work can be divided into two distinct phases, with the publication of *Señas de identidad* in 1966 marking the transition between the earlier and later periods. In his early works, comprising both novels and semi-fictional travelogues, Goytisolo portrays the devastation wrought on Spanish society by the Civil War and by the inept and repressive government that resulted from it. Using a disengaged narrative style variously described as "objectivist", "behaviourist" or "photographic" realism, Goytisolo testifies to the brutalization of the post-war generation of children, the nihilistic *ennui* of bourgeois youth, the contradictions between traditional machismo and ultramontane Catholicism, and the all-consuming vacuity of life under the regime.

Goytisolo's early works are not as unproblematic for the translator as they may seem. Although their tone is generally laconic, they include lyrical descriptive flourishes that may appear to be mere poetic embellishments but often tap into a rich subtextual vein of implicit denunciation of the reality described. Moreover, Goytisolo is a master of free indirect discourse, shifting seamlessly between spare third person narration and more emotionally charged interior monologue. Relatedly, Goytisolo indulges his passion for the rhythms of the spoken language, especially that of the lower social strata, though this feature is more fully developed in the later period. All these characteristics place demands on the translator, if the full effect of the original is to be conveyed.

Señas de identidad marks a radical stylistic departure in Goytisolo's work. The detached, realist approach of the earlier works is largely abandoned in favour of an intensely personal, formally experimental approach which draws on multiple extraneous discourses including obituaries, the diary of a Catalan worker, a tourist guide, parodic versions of politico-religious diatribes and of pompous reviews of his own work, and stream-of-consciousness interior monologue. In *Reivindicación del conde don Julián*, Goytisolo's experimentalism becomes still more radical, as the author takes revenge on his native land by undertaking a radical subversion of its language. Multiple registers and voices combine with numerous intertextual references and eccentric punctuation to form a highly idiosyncratic whole. Goytisolo has continued to employ such avant-garde techniques, to a greater or lesser degree, in most of his writings to the present day. Later works also include explicit sexual descriptions and often obscure references to Sufi mysticism and other aspects of the Arab culture in which the author has latterly made his home.

Translation, both interlinguistic and intercultural, has been a vital factor in Goytisolo's evolution as a writer. During his formative years, it constituted a crucial cultural lifeline, providing intellectual sustenance in the culturally starved climate of early Francoism: "It is very significant that the books I would soon rush upon", he writes of his university days, "would be almost without exception by foreign authors. I read the novels that I devoured between 18 and 25 either in French or in the second-rate translations that were smuggled in from Buenos Aires" (*Forbidden Territory*). Later, translation in part rescued Goytisolo's own novels, often censored by the Spanish regime, from languishing in obscurity. In an interview in the late 1970s, however, the author admitted that, further on in his career, he had consciously sought to disappear from the publishing world, because, "when I wrote novels which took me only a few months to complete, they were immediately translated into more than 10 languages, and I could live exclusively off my copyright". Goytisolo felt that this commercial success, which was partially dependent on the translatability of his writings, compromised his artistic integrity, and he therefore turned to deliberate obscurity in his later works.

Somewhat paradoxically, as Goytisolo's works have become more cosmopolitan, reflecting the author's broadening knowledge of the world and particularly of Arab culture, so they have become less accessible, and harder to translate. Precisely because the original texts are more demanding, however, the latter translations are of greater interest to the theoretician and translation scholar.

The English translations of Goytisolo's first two novels were both published in 1958. John RUST's 1958 *The Young Assassins* has a markedly colloquial and American feel, using words and expressions such as "guys", "a bunch of bums" and "I'll find a man for you, sweetie". Such idioms, redolent of the sleazy underworld of detective fiction or *film noir*, are well suited to the style of the novel, which explicitly conjures up such an ethos. Rust chooses to retain some culture-bound elements untranslated, however, providing an explanatory footnote. In the case of the word "chulo", defined as "equivalent of the British teddy-boy" in the British edition, this strikes the contemporary reader as both incongruous (given the generally American feel) and archaic. The frequent use of "gay" in its old sense, also a feature of José YGLESIAS's translations of Goytisolo discussed below, is also archaic, but not incongruous, since Goytisolo's often colloquial Spanish also contains lexical items that have lost currency or shifted in nuance.

Interestingly, Goytisolo later acknowledged that the style of *Juegos de manos* was seriously affected by his love affair, at the time, with the French language. This precipitated the unusual circumstance of a work that seemed to realize its fullest expressive potential in translation (English versions of Borges's anglicized Spanish constitute a less extreme example of the phenomenon), as Goytisolo himself observed: "my first novel, magnificently translated afterwards into French by Maurice Edgar Coindreau, read much better in this language than in the original defective Spanish: when I had to revise it some years ago to be included in some pompous Complete Works, the continuous difficulties I met in revising the text convinced me that the only satisfactory way to erase them would be to retranslate the novel scrupulously from the language in which it was unconsciously conceived" (*Forbidden Territory*).

The *Times Literary Supplement* reviewer of *Children of Chaos* strikes a note of censure, which was to become familiar in reviews of Goytisolo's novels and which the author savagely parodies in later works, against the demands the novel's structure places on the reader, while the translator is praised: "The episodic and 'flashback' style of the narration does not help the reader, although the English, in Miss Christine BROOKE-ROSE's translation, is admirably clear" (*Times Literary Supplement*, 1959, p. 57). While it is true the translation reads well overall, this is sometimes at the expense of precision and significant detail. Thus where the translation has the child protagonist feeling "lonely and cold", Goytisolo definitely has him feeling "a curious sense of detachment" ("una curiosa sensación de despego"). It is the dulling of normal childish sensibilities by the Civil War, and their replacement with a brutalized outlook, that the original implicitly conveys. The novel's subtextual denunciation is not well served generally by such "normalization" of the affectless childish responses described in the original, nor by the omission or distortion of significant detail, such as descriptive metaphors relating to the plastic arts, which subtly convey a grim sense of inhumanity and unreality in the original.

The confusion of "perjuicios" ("harm", "detriment") with "prejuicios" ("prejudices"), and of "maniobra" ("manoeuvre") with "manubrio" ("crank", "handle"), which produces two improbable sentences in the translation, suggests an imperfect grasp of the language on the part of the translator, and perhaps reflects a not uncommon practice in the translation of Spanish novels before the Latin American Boom pushed standards up in the 1960s: the task has been given to an inexpert translator of Spanish. The book has been understood only as a gripping psychological yarn of children turned to tribalism, a kind of *Lord of the Flies* without that novel's allegorical depth.

Goytisolo's third novel, *Fiestas*, a characteristically bleak account populated by an assortment of social misfits, was translated by Herbert WEINSTOCK (1960). As with *The Young Assassins*, the overall flavour is American, though Weinstock goes further than Rust in retaining an "exotic" feel by not translating elements such as "señor", "don/doña" and the word "fiesta(s)" itself, and by translating dialogue rather more literally ("I know that your life is a Way of the Cross"). This latter feature causes the translation to be stilted in places where the original is not: although Goytisolo later acknowledged his early novels were written in a "bookish, stilted style" because of his "impoverished" Barcelona Spanish (*Forbidden Territory*), this does not apply to his use of colloquial speech, for which he has always had an unerringly precise ear.

José YGLESIAS (1962, 1966), the translator of the remaining two early Goytisolo novels available in English, is generally more successful in choosing an appropriately jaunty colloquial idiom, though his dialogue occasionally also seems to fall between the two stools of American slang and "exotic" literalism: "Jesus, what a bender. The sommelier – and he's a guy who's been around – told me: 'I've seen some crazy guests in my day, but none like this couple'. And he's got more sense than a saint" (*The Party's Over*).

Yglesias was taken to task by the *Times Literary Supplement* reviewer of his translation in a way that reveals more about contemporary British reviewers' prejudices against American English than it does about Yglesias's alleged deficiencies: "whatever interest there might have been in the original has been slaughtered in an irritatingly American translation ... It is a pity that Señor Goytisolo has been presented to us in such unpalatable form, for he is the best novelist of his generation in Spain" (*Times Literary Supplement*, 1966, p. 853).

The reviewer seems to detect that the fault is not entirely the translator's, however, for he points out that "Goytisolo runs the risk that any novelist who writes on stupid people must run, that his novel will be stupid". Goytisolo had perhaps come to the same conclusion, for *The Party's Over* – the title is ironical in retrospect – marked the end of his career as a prolific and commercially successful author of orthodox realist novels.

From an average of one or two books a year, Goytisolo's publication rate drops after *Fin de fiesta* to an average of around one work every three years. The author's more assiduous approach to his work as a writer is reflected in greater intensity and minute attention to the details of formal experiment in his later works.

Gregory RABASSA's *Marks of Identity* (1969) suffers from the translator's inconsistent approach to the problem of Goytisolo's obscurity. The difficulty is that the reader is often less inclined to be forgiving of obscure or dense writing in a translation, since s/he may suspect that this is merely the result of ineptitude on the part of the translator. Rabassa seems undecided as to whether he should ease the reader's passage – he translates sections of French – or assume knowledge of culture-bound references and other languages – he does not explicate the "Nodo" (propagandistic Francoist news bulletin) or "Miura" (renowned breed of fighting bull), and leaves some Catalan exclamations untranslated but not others. Moreover, some of Rabassa's translations of colloquialisms, and especially invective, are alarmingly literal: "she hasn't got any hairs on her tongue" and "shitting on Catalan mothers" are direct transpositions of highly idiomatic Spanish expressions that require equally idiomatic equivalents (British English versions might be "she doesn't mince her words" and "slagging off Catalans").

Goytisolo's next five novels were translated by Helen R. LANE (1974, 1977, 1981, 1987, 1991), also a noted translator of Portuguese and French. Lane clearly felt what George Steiner termed "elective affinity" (*After Babel*, 1975) towards Goytisolo's experimental, iconoclastic later works, for her translations consistently capture their tripping rhythms and mischievous tone. Lane takes Goytisolo's formal experiments and self-conscious obscurity in the spirit they are intended: just as the Spanish author delights in verbal pyrotechnics and esoteric intertextual reference, so Lane seems to relish the challenge of forging ingenious English equivalents for highly idiomatic colloquialisms and culture-bound references.

LANE's brilliant debut as Goytisolo's translator (1974), with *Count Julian*, is discussed in detail below. Remarkable though *Count Julian* is, Lane's translation of Goytisolo's next work, *Juan the Landless*, is more accessible to English-speaking readers, since Goytisolo shifts his sights from the fraudulent cultural construct of "Sacred Spain" to wider cultural targets such as eurocentric arrogance and hypocritical prudery, psychoanalysis and literary criticism. Lane gives a convincing phoneticized rendition of the black American English of the Deep South to translate the effect of Goytisolo's Cuban slave speech, provides a witty version of German-accented English to simulate Goytisolo's Teutonic-Castilian original, and, most notably, offers an ingenious sequence of clichés and idiomatic expressions to match Goytisolo's tricky original, in which a patient obstinately responds to the literal meaning of such expressions in an encounter with his analyst.

In her versions of Goytisolo's next two novels, LANE's virtuosity is particularly evident in her renderings of Goytisolo's playful sexual evocations, which include borrowed discourses such as erotic letters and witty contact advertisements. Thus Goytisolo's "tío alto, recio, viril superiormente dotado ofrece lecciones de equitación a tiorra cachonda, de abundantes arrobas, ansiosa de cabalgar y ser cabalgada" becomes "tall, strong, virile, well-hung stud offers riding lessons to a hefty filly in heat who's hot to trot". Lane's version, with its extra alliteration (a prevalent rhythm-generating device in her translations of Goytisolo) and the inspired felicity of the idiom "hot to trot", perhaps even surpasses the wit of Goytisolo's original.

LANE is similarly bold elsewhere, particularly in *Landscapes after the Battle*, where she judiciously alters obscure title headings and other culture-bound elements in order to recreate the directness of impact required by Goytisolo's witty allusions. Thus Goytisolo's parodic glance at the trivial preoccupations of the press, "¿una conferencia de prensa del Gaffo? ¿un amor contrariado de Julio Iglesias?" is replaced by references that return an instant echo throughout the English-speaking world: "A Woody Allen press conference? A star-crossed love affair of Prince Andrew's?".

The Virtues of the Solitary Bird once again demonstrates the confluence, in both LANE and Goytisolo, of scholarly thoroughness and delight in verbal play. The British edition of the translation helpfully includes an English version of St John of the Cross's *Spiritual Canticle*, an important source, but the relative obscurity of the subject matter – an involved dialogue between Goytisolo and the 16th-century mystic, with parallel allusions to Sufi mysticism – make the work difficult, perhaps, in any language.

Peter BUSH's *Quarantine* employs a judicious approach to the problem of making the translation accessible without patronizing the reader or over-simplifying: a useful translator's prologue elucidates the more abstruse allusions and justifies features of the translation that might otherwise have been identified as stylistic infelicities. The translation contains deft touches in response to some awkward problems and, like Lane's versions, it is clearly the result of thorough preparation on the part of the translator. Though the allusions to Sufi mysticism show Goytisolo to be unrepentant of his predilection for "destabilizing the reader by multiplying the levels of interpretation and registers of voice" (*Quarantine*), his powerful interweavings of Dante's *Inferno* with descriptions of the Gulf War, skilfully rendered in the translation, constitute an easier point of reference for the English-speaking reader.

Goytisolo's virtuoso novel-chronicle-drama-satire-debate, *La saga de los Marx* (1993), with its gymnastic range of registers and linguistic devices, also receives a vigorous, ingenious translation from Peter BUSH (*The Marx Family Saga*, 1996; awarded the Valle-Inclán Prize for translation from Spanish, 1997).

Three works of non-fiction by Goytisolo, far less stylistically idiosyncratic, are also available in English. *The Saracen Chronicles*, translated by Helen LANE (1992), is somewhat misleadingly titled, since it draws from two other collections, *Disidencias* and *Contracorrientes*, as well as the *Crónicas sarracinas*. Lane demonstrates her customary ingenuity.

Reviewing *Coto vedado* in the *Times Literary Supplement*, John Butt accurately characterizes the style of both of Goytisolo's volumes of autobiography: "Goytisolo's relationship with the language is uneasy: his childhood straddled Castilian and Catalan, and he is now a polyglot; and this may have blocked his spontaneity in his native tongue. Like most of his recent novels, *Coto vedado* is written in a quaintly academic, slightly parodic Spanish, full of archaic pluperfects, ponderous relative clauses and Latinate vocabulary which, as usual, holds the reader well away from the sometimes shocking, usually painful experiences described. As a result the text has an impersonal quality, intensified by the author's passion for addressing himself in the second person."

Clearly, Goytisolo's subtly parodic use of his native tongue cannot be conveyed in a text not written in Spanish. Peter BUSH's translation (1989, 1990) of the two books of memoirs, however, succeeds in reflecting the author's penchant for adopting incongruously academic prose when making intimate observations – and for inserting discordant colloquialisms into lyrical pronouncements.

IAN S. CRAIG

Count Julian

Reivindicación del conde don Julián, 1970

Lane, Helen R., *Count Julian*, New York: Viking Press, 1974; London: Serpent's Tail, 1989

Reivindicación del conde don Julián (1970) completed Goytisolo's literary metamorphosis, begun with *Señas de identidad*, from realist to avant-garde experimentalist. The author continued to wage war on Spain's fraudulent myths of origin and identity, but his former weapons of denunciation – the detached tone and testimonial content of the early novels and travelogues – were replaced by a campaign of radical linguistic subversion.

Don Julián is the historical figure who allegedly betrayed Spain by assisting the Moorish invasion of 711 in order to take revenge on the Visigoth king Rodrigo, who had raped his daughter. Spanish historians ever since have sustained the myth of an idealized Roman and Visigoth Spain, surrendered to the barbarous Moorish hordes by a single, spiteful act of betrayal. Goytisolo seeks to exorcize a number of demons in the novel: the prejudices of European ethnocentrism that the myth of Don Julián has served to perpetuate in Spain, whose official historiographers were still refusing to acknowledge the cultural debt owed to the country's African and Jewish populations; the entire spurious culture of "Castilianism" that this blinkered view of history had given rise to; and the deeply ingrained sexual repression that derived from the religious cult of the Virgin. Goytisolo felt that the myth of the Spanish national essence, based on a paranoid fear of cultural heterogeneity, could be most effectively debunked by an assault on its language.

A central feature of the novel, therefore, is constituted by its parodies of the grotesquely pompous Spanish of the Real Academia. As well as parodying such language, Goytisolo also attempts to replace this "ultra-Castilian" with a revivified form of Spanish literary discourse. To this end he incorporates colloquial voices, from both Spain and Latin America, and revels in colourful sexual description.

Another characteristic of the novel that complicates the work of the translator is its use of intertextuality. The number of allusions, both implicit and explicit, to the works of other writers, from Virgil, Cervantes and Lope to Freud, Sade and Stevenson, is vast. The novel incorporates numerous quotations of well-known (and less well-known) couplets worked into the text, and even whole poems from the Spanish literary pantheon are summoned from the past to take their place in Goytisolo's catalogue of denunciation. Nor does Goytisolo restrict himself to high-cultural sources: the novel contains allusions to films, the idiom of the popular magazine, recipes, tourist brochures and public signs.

The implications of this very eclectic mode of discourse for the translator are many. The impact of the intertextual allusions is inevitably considerably lessened in English, since most of these are simply not recognizable. Many of the other features that contribute to the work's power are, however, transferable. Helen LANE, in her first attempt at translating Goytisolo, judiciously seizes on the single stylistic element of the novelist's later prose that most distinguishes it from both his own earlier work and that of other more conventional writers, namely its insistent rhythmic texture. In order to reproduce the crescendo effect of the set-pieces that form the nucleus of the work, Lane consistently and courageously departs from a safe literalism in order to clarify idioms, incorporate extra alliterations and generally remove obstructions to the discursive flow. This is not to say that Lane simplifies in the service of an easier read, for this is not the case. Rather, she has appreciated that it is the overall effect of Goytisolo's markedly declamatory prose, the rhythm of which builds steadily, rises to a climax, subsides and resumes throughout the text, that must take precedence over the exact rendering of individual words and images.

Occasionally, Lane seems to take liberties by embellishing Goytisolo's text with extra nuances. Thus for the Spanish "simultáneamente a la erección musical de un ritmo negro que brota con fuerza" in the James Bond passage, Lane has "accompanied by the musical erection of a throbbing negro rhythm". Here "throbbing" seems a more ingenious means of linking the musical and sexual contexts than Goytisolo's "brota con fuerza", but the "liberty" is surely justified in order to compensate for those deficiencies of rhythm and clarity inevitably incurred elsewhere in translating a densely stylized passage of this kind.

Goytisolo's decisive rejection of realism in favour of a more exuberantly imaginative, purely aesthetic kind of fiction moved him closer, artistically speaking, to the Latin American writers of the Boom, and away from the majority of his own compatriots. He particularly admired those writers who had seen the vital importance of language in the struggle of the Latin American nations to throw off their colonial pasts and find their true identities. In his largely ironical "Advertencia" ("Notice") at the end of the novel, Goytisolo therefore includes a genuine note of gratitude to three Latin Americans, Guillermo Cabrera Infante, Julio Cortázar and Carlos Fuentes. It was with their aid that Goytisolo produced a celebrated section of the novel, in which he phonetically transcribes witty colloquial outpourings in the idiom of the three writers' respective countries, Cuba, Argentina and Mexico.

Lane's version, wisely abbreviating the robust original fairly considerably, employs the idiom of Hispanics in North America, which retains the bluff, *machista* style of certain Mexican or Puerto Rican Spanish speakers:

> ... hombre, what the fuck's gotten into those spics! the sonsabitches got it into their thick heads that their gift of the gab's the living end. Ain't none of their fuckin' business how I sling their damned lingo, and that Lope-cat, or whatever his name is, don't cut no ice with me, man. He probly a limp-dick bastard like all the rest of 'em, couldn't get it up if you shoved a red-hot chili up his ass, hombre! I'd like to see them fancypants fairies try to make out with the pieces of tail we got around here: it'd be a *noche triste*, that's for sure! I know a couple of whores who'd turn 'em to tiger-butter in no time. We maybe little black sambos, but we've got 'em comin' and goin' in the hotlay department hey, senor, you lookin' for fucky-fucky? virgin pussy, senor? I got a sister, nice clean girl, good manners, very cheap, hot stuff, special deal, okay, senor?

It is clear that this version contains elements of pastiche: "couldn't get it up if you shoved a red-hot chili up his ass, hombre!" is clearly an attempt to parody Latino machismo by exaggeration. As usual, however, Lane turns out to have a subtle grasp of the effect of the original. Although Goytisolo is using these voices as a foil to "castellanismo" (the archetypal Spanish character and language), his original passage also taps into a rather different vein of denunciation running throughout the novel, namely that of sexual repression. Goytisolo celebrates the full life of the body permitted in Moorish culture, contrasting it with the terror of sex in Catholic Spain. By focusing on the stereotype of Hispanic machismo here, Goytisolo seems to be suggesting that although Latin Americans may appear to have broken their sexual shackles, the weight of their heritage burdens them with simply another form of self-repression: the necessity to conform to absurd *machista* values. Lane's heavy dose of pastiche is therefore fully justified as an attempt to reproduce the spirit of the original.

Count Julian fully merits Abigail Lee Six's characterization as "a masterpiece in itself, rendering more of the multiple meanings and flavour of the original than might have seemed possible". For it Helen Lane was awarded the PEN Translation prize in 1975.

IAN S. CRAIG

Further Reading

Lee Six, Abigail E., "Sterne's Legacy to Juan Goytisolo: A Shandyian Reading of *Juan sin tierra*", *Modern Language Review*, 84 (April 1989) pp. 351–57

Ugarte, Michael, *Trilogy of Treason: An Intertextual Study of Juan Goytisolo*, Columbia: University of Missouri, 1982

Günter Grass 1927–

German novelist, dramatist and poet

Biography

Born in Danzig, Germany (now Gdansk, Poland), 16 October 1927, partly of Polish descent through his mother. He went to local schools but left early. He was in the Hitler Youth Movement and from 1944, when he was 16, served in World War II. He was wounded, taken prisoner and held at Marienbad, Czechoslovakia (1945–46). In 1947 he was apprenticed to a stonemason, working then at various manual jobs until he went to study sculpture and graphic design at the Academy of Art, Düsseldorf, 1948–52, and the State Academy of Fine Arts, Berlin, 1953–55. He has illustrated some of his own works. He married in 1954 (three sons and one daughter) and again in 1979. From 1956 to 1960 he lived in Paris, where his internationally known *Die Blechtrommel* (*The Tin Drum*) was written. In 1960 he settled in Berlin, going abroad frequently to lecture (he was writer-in-residence at Columbia University, New York, 1966). In the 1960s he was an active supporter of Willy Brandt and the Social Democratic Party. In the 1990s he opposed the reunification of Germany.

Grass has been writing prolifically since he began to publish fiction, plays and poetry in the 1950s, with the encouragement of the literary Gruppe 47. As well as an author, Grass is a journalist and editor, and as well as the literary and graphic works there are books and articles on politics, art, music and other subjects. His literary creativity has won awards and honours in Germany and abroad, including the Süddeutscher Rundfunk lyric poetry prize, 1955; the Gruppe 47 prize, 1958; the Berlin Critics prize, 1960; the Foreign Book prize (France), 1962; an honorary doctorate at Harvard University, 1976; the Mondello prize (Palermo), 1977; the International literature prize, 1978, and numerous others; culminating in the Nobel Prize for Literature, 1999. The novel *Unkenrufe* (*The Call of the Toad*), 1992, aroused criticism. Grass's activity and reputation as a graphic artist has grown latterly. He now lives near Lübeck.

Translations

Novels and Novellas

Die Blechtrommel, 1959
See entry on *The Tin Drum*, below

Katz und Maus, 1961
Manheim, Ralph, *Cat and Mouse*, New York: Harcourt Brace, and London: Secker and Warburg, 1963

Hundejahre, 1963
Manheim, Ralph, *Dog Years*, New York: Harcourt Brace, and London: Secker and Warburg, 1965

Örtlich betäubt, 1969
Manheim, Ralph, *Local Anaesthetic*, London: Secker and Warburg, 1969; New York: Harcourt Brace, 1970

Aus dem Tagebuch einer Schnecke, 1972
Manheim, Ralph, *From the Diary of a Snail*, New York: Harcourt Brace, 1973; London: Secker and Warburg, 1974

Der Butt, 1977
Manheim, Ralph, *The Flounder*, New York: Harcourt Brace, and London: Secker and Warburg, 1978

Das Treffen in Telgte, 1979
Manheim, Ralph, *The Meeting at Telgte*, New York: Harcourt Brace, and London: Secker and Warburg, 1981

Kopfgeburten; oder, Die Deutschen sterben aus, 1980
Manheim, Ralph, *Headbirths; or, The Germans Are Dying Out*, New York: Harcourt Brace, and London: Secker and Warburg, 1982

Die Rättin, 1986
Manheim, Ralph, *The Rat*, San Diego: Harcourt Brace, and London: Secker and Warburg, 1987

Unkenrufe, 1992
Manheim, Ralph, *The Call of the Toad*, New York: Harcourt Brace, and London: Secker and Warburg, 1992

Short Stories

Mein Jahrhundert, 1999
Heim, Michael Henry, *My Century*, New York: Harcourt Brace, and London: Faber, 1999

Selection of Plays

Manheim, Ralph and A. Leslie Willson, *Four Plays*, New York: Harcourt Brace, 1967; London: Secker and Warburg, 1968 (contains *Flood*; *Only Ten Minutes to Buffalo*; *The Wicked Cooks*; *Onkel, Onkel*)

Plays

Hochwasser, 1957
Manheim, Ralph, *Flood* in *Four Plays*, translated by Manheim and A. Leslie Willson, 1967

Noch zehn Minuten bis Buffalo, 1957
Manheim, Ralph, *Only Ten Minutes to Buffalo* in *Four Plays*, translated by Manheim and A. Leslie Willson, 1967

Die bösen Köche, 1957
Willson, A. Leslie, *The Wicked Cooks* in *Four Plays*, translated by Ralph Manheim and Willson, 1967

Onkel, Onkel, 1965
Manheim, Ralph, *Onkel, Onkel* in *Four Plays*, translated by Manheim and A. Leslie Willson, 1967

Die Plebejer proben den Aufstand, 1966
Manheim, Ralph, *The Plebeians Rehearse the Uprising*, New York: Harcourt Brace, 1966; London: Secker and Warburg, 1967

Selections of Poetry

Hamburger, Michael and Christopher Middleton, *Selected Poems* (parallel texts), New York: Harcourt Brace, and London: Secker and Warburg, 1966

Hamburger, Michael, selection in *New Poems* (bilingual edition), New York: Harcourt Brace, 1968

Hamburger, Michael, *Selected Poems, 1956–1993* (parallel texts), New York: Harcourt Brace, 1996; London: Faber, 1998

The demands made of the translator by Günter Grass's prose fiction have if anything increased with each work he has produced since his first, highly successful novel *Die Blechtrommel* (1959). Ranging historically from the Stone Age to the present day and geographically from a variety of regions of Germany to China, India and Indonesia, his narratives call for an almost encyclopedic knowledge. Often this is highly specialized knowledge too, whether of cookery and foodstuffs, which feature obsessively in every work, or of German literature from the Baroque age to the Adenauer era, or of countless varieties of a given animal species, be they snails or toads. An increasing engagement with contemporary German political issues, even the minutiae of party politics, presents an additional challenge, especially in those works like *From the Diary of a Snail* and *Headbirths*, where fiction is mingled with opinion, polemic and autobiographical fact.

Handling the frequently abrupt changes of register in such hybrid works is just one of the many stylistic problems the translator faces everywhere in Grass's oeuvre. A penchant for wordplay, evident sometimes even in a work's title, is another. "Unkenrufe", literally "toad-calls", are also "jeremiads", a conceit crucial to an understanding of the long story of that title. The lengthy first section of *Dog Years* is divided not into chapters but into "Frühschichten" – "early shifts" – since the scene is set in a former potash mine. At the same time, however, what is being excavated are the "early *layers*" or "strata" of the protagonists' lives. Another major problem of style is posed by Grass's frequent recourse to dialect, ranging from differing varieties of Low German to Berlin, Hessian and Swiss German, as well as to older forms of the language (from the 13th and 17th centuries, for instance, in *The Flounder*) or the jargon of particular groups (women's liberationists) or generations (former 1968 student activists).

Faced with these and many other intractable difficulties of content and style, Ralph MANHEIM has in general, though one may quibble about details, produced translations admirably true to the letter and spirit of the originals. Fully aware of and honest about the problems involved – in a note prefacing *The Flounder* he acknowledges the help of others in translating a book that "called for a range of knowledge that I cannot lay claim to" – he occasionally seeks refuge in explanatory footnotes. Rightly or wrongly, he usually ignores the dialect problem, except in *From the Diary of a Snail*, where some of the Berlin, Swiss and Jewish German is retained in the original. Now and then he makes cuts, sometimes dictated by the libel laws (as acknowledged in *From the Diary of a Snail*, but not, in the case of passages concerning Franz Josef Strauss, in *Headbirths*), sometimes, one suspects, either to avoid difficulties of style or because the content is deemed too abstruse or localized for the non-German reader. Otherwise, however, little of substance gets lost and the level of accuracy, except in *The Call of the Toad*, Manheim's last, and possibly over-hurried translation, is consistently high.

His versions (MANHEIM, 1963 and 1965) of the two early works – *Cat and Mouse* and *Dog Years* – which, together with *The Tin Drum*, make up the so-called Danzig Trilogy, are particularly good. Outstanding in the novella *Cat and Mouse* are the two long speeches made by the fighter pilot and the U-boat commander at their former grammar school, where Manheim nicely captures both the jargon and the style of Grass's excellent parodies. He also copes well with the clipped delivery of the Nazi headmaster Klohse, although the full sense of some of the laconic allusions in his speeches (e.g. that to the battle of Thermopylae) gets lost. In the enormously long and demanding novel *Dog Years*, he finds ingenious solutions to problems like the two lengthy passages that run through the alphabet from A to Z, managing to retain most of the original by re-ordering the elements to fit English spelling. His versions of the catalogues Grass often indulges in – notably the long variations, rich in wordplay, on the colour brown, or the list of slang terms for venereal disease – are veritable *tours de force*. The extended parodies of Heidegger are as crude, and as amusing, as the originals but, perhaps inevitably, less easy to carry off in English.

From the Diary of a Snail is an unqualified triumph, MANHEIM (1973) handling with great aplomb the book's complex mixture of fictional narrative, election-campaign report and essayistic reflection. Even more impressive is that monster of a novel *The Flounder*, where the additional challenge of the idiosyncratic poems that frequently dot the narrative meets with a response (MANHEIM, 1978) that is always skilful and at times superb, as in the moving "Plaint and Prayer of the farm cook Amanda Woyke". Among the many qualities of this translation, the skill of Manheim's rendering into Chaucerian English of the 14th-century German of Dorothea von Montau deserves a special mention. His handling (MANHEIM, 1981) of the many quotations from 17th-century German poetry in *The Meeting at Telgte* is equally accomplished, although he makes little or no effort to reproduce the archaisms Grass employs in many passages of direct speech.

Manheim's translations of Grass's prose works from the 1980s onwards, while generally sound, never reach quite such heights. In *Headbirths* (MANHEIM, 1982) some of the dialogue between the husband and wife Harm and Dörte Peters is rendered in very stilted English, and the already dated jargon of their politically active student days is occasionally misconstrued. "Die Grünen" (The Greens), a well-established party by 1979, are referred to vaguely as "the environmentalists" throughout, and basic inaccuracies, previously rare, now mar the text. "Geschäfte" is rendered as "shops" when the context clearly demands "business deals"; "Limonensaft" becomes "lemonade" rather than "lime-juice"; and – most careless of all – the central character of the earlier *Local Anaesthetic*, already translated by MANHEIM (1969), is referred to as suffering much with "headaches" rather than "toothache" ("Zahnschmerzen"). A similar carelessness is evident at times in *The Call of the Toad*, most unfortunately in one passage of dialogue where a negative has been missed, totally distorting the sense of a key political point made by the speaker.

As these instances show, Manheim is not without his faults. Two more general weaknesses might also be mentioned. One is an occasional tendency to stick too closely to the original German, for example by rendering "Leichtathletik" as "light athletics" rather than simply "athletics", or "Leibarzt" as "body" rather than "personal" physician. The other is a habit of sometimes opting for unnecessarily wordy equivalents of perfectly simple expressions in the German. Thus "schlucken" (to swallow) becomes "ingurgitate", or the straightforward heading of a section in *The Flounder*, "Kleidersorgen" (worries about clothes) is pompously transformed into "vestimentary preoccupations". But set against Manheim's overall achievements these are quibbles. He will not be easily replaced when it comes to finding an English translator for Grass's latest novel, the again long and demanding *Ein weites Feld* (1995). It was Michal Henry HEIM who translated the *Mein Jahrhundert* stories in the year of their publication in German, 1999.

The MANHEIM translations (1966, 1967, 1967, 1967) of Grass's far less substantial or demanding early plays are perfectly competent, though *Flood* and *Only Ten Minutes to Buffalo* both contain the odd puzzling addition or change to the originals. Why, for instance, transform Lake Constance and Lake Lucerne into the North Sea and Lake Geneva? A. Leslie WILLSON's *The Wicked Cooks* (1967) is far less reliable, being marred by omissions and by some really basic howlers involving confusion of the personal pronouns "Sie" and "sie", or failure to observe either punctuation or plural form as when rendering "Wie, Kinder ...?" (What, boys ...?) as "Like a kid".

Grass's poetry is very well served indeed by the versions of Michael HAMBURGER & Christopher MIDDLETON (1966), both of whom convey especially well the quirky play of imagery in the earlier poems, while rightly resisting the temptation to interpret by introducing unwarranted coherence. HAMBURGER (1968) also succeeds wonderfully with some of the later poems from the collection *Ausgefragt*, above all in his virtuoso rendering of Grass's cookery recipe cum political manifesto in verse "The Jellied Pig's Head". Elsewhere, however, his sureness of touch sometimes deserts him, as when he fails to find the best equivalent for a word in its clearly political context, opting for "voiceless" rather than "voteless" for "stimmlos" ("The Epilogue") and "cleanses" instead of "purges" for "säubert" ("New Mysticism").

DAVID HORROCKS

The Tin Drum

Die Blechtrommel, 1959

Translation

Manheim, Ralph, *The Tin Drum*, New York: Pantheon, and London: Secker and Warburg, 1962

Günter Grass's first novel, *Die Blechtrommel*, the book that established his reputation on a world scale and with which even today he is most readily associated, makes enormous demands on the translator. Its often minutely detailed coverage of the years 1899 to 1954 requires a wide-ranging historical and cultural familiarity with the period, not just in the German-speaking world generally, but also in the narrower confines of Danzig / Gdansk, the city in which two-thirds of the book is set. Stylistically too, with its passages of virtuoso wordplay, its use of dialect, its subtle exploitation of recurring motifs and its frequent switches of narrative mode (including mock-fairy tale, burlesque drama and children's song), it constitutes a massive challenge.

In almost every respect, Ralph MANHEIM's response (1962) to this challenge is admirable, which probably explains why his version of *The Tin Drum* has remained the only translation in English, and why all Grass's subsequent prose works were entrusted to Manheim until his death in 1992. Not surprisingly, in a novel stretching to almost 600 pages, the odd inaccuracy creeps in: "Trachten einmottende Landsmannschaften", for instance, are not "moth-eaten provincial students' associations in costume" but rather "associations of expellees [from Germany's former Eastern territories] who keep their traditional local costumes in moth-balls". Such errors are, however, extremely rare, and far outweighed by Manheim's many felicities.

Foremost among his translation's strengths is the ability to capture the often complex mixture of naïveté and knowingness in the tone of Grass's eccentric narrator/protagonist, Oskar Matzerath, who has deliberately arrested his physical growth, if not his mental development, at the age of three, and is now drumming up the past from the vantage-point of a bed in a mental hospital in the post-war West Germany of the early 1950s. Crucially to the ironic and satirical impact of the novel, this tone is counterbalanced by passages that are more elegiac in nature, as Grass conjures up the memory of the Danzig of his youth, often by the straightforward device of naming, whether streets, buildings or individual people. Manheim rightly resists the temptation to cut such catalogues, or to avoid Grass's deliberate repetitions, which have the effect of litanies.

With only the odd (careless or deliberate?) omission, he also retains – and renders with appropriate panache and humour – the many Rabelaisian passages, dealing with Oskar's bizarre sexual exploits, that provoked cries of "obscenity" when the novel first appeared in Germany. Elsewhere, faced with the near impossibility of rendering Grass's wordplay, as for example in the chapter where he juggles with the Pauline trinity of Faith, Hope and Love in a parody of Hitler's advent to power, Manheim demonstrates great ingenuity in coming up with English expressions like "Old Faithful", "Cape of Good Hope" and "six love" to match the untranslatable compound formations of the original. Naturally, such substitutions entail a degree of loss, but it is difficult to see how this can be avoided. Few would quibble, for example, with Manheim's choice of "black witch" to designate the ominous figure in the repeated children's rhyme that continues to haunt Oskar and seems to personify all the destructive forces at work in recent German history, although in the original she is "die schwarze Köchin" ("the black cook").

Grass's ironically distorted portrayal of that recent history, especially his habit of juxtaposing major events with the seemingly banal and trivial experiences of his characters' private lives, often in one and the same sentence, is on the whole successfully realized in the translation. The only unfortunate thing is that Manheim somewhat garbles one key passage where Grass, unusually, offers the reader direct insights into the thinking behind this approach. To distinguish between the random, disconnected nature of history as people actually experience it and the attempts historians make to trace meaningful patterns after the event, Grass uses the image of a highly mobile piece of thread, the front end of which is darting about uncontrollably in all kinds of directions, while at the back end it is assiduously being knitted into shape. Unprocessed history, history "raw", as it were, he calls "Geschichte" – the German word that, like French "histoire", also means "story". For the "knitted" product of historians, on the other hand, he uses the latinate term "Historie". Sadly, both the conceptual distinction and the clarity of the image get lost in Manheim's version.

Another arguably avoidable loss stems from the translator's decision virtually to ignore the flavour of the Low German dialect spoken by Oskar's grandmother, and other examples of non-standard speech such as that of Markus, the Jewish owner of a toy shop. This is to be regretted. So too is the occasional unaccountable omission of odd phrases in the original text. One such is the ironic reference to some of the crowd joining a Sunday morning Nazi rally in Danzig as having previously attended early Mass but having come away from the church dissatisfied – a point important to Grass's whole critique of Nazism as a surrogate religion.

However, isolated lapses like this scarcely detract from the overall achievement. Nor should the fact that Manheim's version is clearly written for the American market make it any less impressive for British readers. Some might be puzzled by expressions such as "smudge" in the sense of "smoky fire" or "it was raining all getout", where "like the devil" would have been closer to the the grandmother's "wie Deikert komm raus", but like readers of English everywhere they can count themselves fortunate in having access to so accomplished a version of what is undoubtedly a major work of post-1945 German and world literature.

DAVID HORROCKS

Further Reading

Butler, G.P., "'Übersetzt klingt alles plausibel': Some Notes on *Der Butt* and *The Flounder*", *German Life and Letters*, 34 (1980) pp. 3–10
Butler, G.P., "A Tall Story of Some Size: *Die Rättin* and *The Rat*", *German Life and Letters*, 4 (1988) pp. 488–93
Butler, G.P., "'*The Call of the Toad* and the Szczepan Phenomenon", *German Life and Letters*, 47 (1994) pp. 94–103
Cunliffe, W. Gordon, *Günter Grass*, New York: Twayne, 1969
Forster, Leonard, "Ralph Manheim 1907–1992", *German Life and Letters*, 46 (1993) p. 105
Hayman, Ronald, *Günter Grass*, London and New York: Methuen, 1985
Hollington, Michael, *Günter Grass: The Writer in a Pluralist Society*, London and Boston: Marion Boyars, 1980
Leonard, Irène, *Günter Grass*, Edinburgh: Oliver and Boyd, 1974
Reddick, John, *The Danzig Trilogy of Günter Grass*, London: Secker and Warburg, 1975
Thomas, Noel L., *Grass: Die Blechtrommel*, London: Grant and Cutler, 1985

Greek, Ancient

Literary Translation into English

The Language

Greek is a member of the Indo-European language family, and within that family it is most closely related to the Italian languages, including Latin – there are many analogies between Latin and Greek in etymologies and inflections. Homer calls the Greeks variously Achaeans, Argives or Danaans, but in historical times they are divided into Ionians, Dorians and Aeolians, each of these groups having its own dialect. Almost all ancient Greek verse is composed in a mixture of these dialects, but each branch of poetry has one or other as its basic element. For example, Old Ionic is the medium of the Homeric poems and of Hesiod's work, the earliest literature in Greek (a later form of Ionic is found in Herodotus). Doric is used by many lyric poets, including Pindar. Aeolic is found in the Lesbian lyric writers Sappho and Alcaeus, and in Theocritus' *Idylls*. There is no literary prose in Aeolic or Doric.

From the 5th century BC onwards the political centrality of Athens lent authority to Attic Greek, defined simply as the dialect of Athens during the city's period of literary preeminence from about 500 to 300 BC. Cultivated throughout this period, Attic Greek became a language of precision and beauty. This is the language of the Greek tragedians, of the Athenian orators, of Aristophanes, of Thucydides and Xenophon, of Isocrates and Plato. The spread of Attic Greek led to its contamination by various local influences; the universal Greek which results from this process by the 3rd century BC is known as the "Koin?", or Common Dialect.

Greek is often considered the ideal language for the expression of thought. Fine distinctions can be communicated, and hypothetical or abstract notions easily entertained, for example through the use at the beginning of sentences of a particle to indicate an attitude towards the proposition about to be advanced. Written Greek seems to have some of the expressiveness only achieved in the spoken versions of English and other languages. The language's richness in verb forms also contributes much to its clarity. A middle voice expresses personal interest in an action; an optative form expresses a future condition more tentatively than the indicative or the subjunctive.

The use of past, future, aorist, and perfect infinitives and participles allows shades of expression unavailable in other languages. The development of the definite article, lacking in Latin, much increases the usefulness of these possibilities, since modifiers of the verb idea can be placed between article and noun so as to show their exact relationship. It is the existence of the definite article which makes Greek more like English than Latin is; this encourages logical, straightforward syntax.

Translation to 1600

In Chaucer's Britain knowledge of Greek was practically non-existent, as in most of Europe in the 14th century. It had almost died out during the Dark Ages, and those Greek authors who were read at all were read in Latin translation. The early Renaissance scholars, starting with Petrarch in 1339, learned Greek from Byzantine visitors to Italy. Byzantine Greek, however, was not the same as classical Greek, and its oral and written forms were distractingly different; one effect was that early printing of Greek was based on complex Byzantine handwriting.

A start is made on translation from classical Greek works in Britain in the first half of the 16th century. The first literary Greek text to be translated into English is usually said to be Lucian's *Necromantia*, in 1520; the first version of a Greek tragedy, by Lady Lumley from Euripides' *Iphigenia at Aulis*, is made about 1550. This is the beginning of Britain's rediscovery of Greek, involving major intellectual battles fought by reformers like Desiderius Erasmus (1466–1536) who wanted it to be used as a corrective to traditional Latin translations of the Bible. Many of the most innovative moral and critical ideas now began to come from Greek sources, as the New Learning sponsored by the early humanists made its way via translations by such figures as John Rastall (Lucian, c.1520), Gentian Hervet (Xenophon, c.1532), William Barker (Xenophon, ?1560), John Sandford (Epictetus, 1567 – from a French version), Christopher Watson (Polybius, 1568), Thomas Wilson (Demosthenes, 1570), and Abraham Fleming (Aelianus of Praeneste, 1576). The diplomat and writer Thomas Elyot (1490–1546), trained by Thomas More, translated Isocrates and Plutarch, and in his treatise *The Governour*, 1531, collected "the sayings of the most noble authors (Greeks and Latins)". Many excerpts from Greek writers were made known by Erasmus' Latin *Adages* and *Apophthegms*. The emphasis in this first phase of translation is on history and rhetoric. There is also the first long stretch of Homer in English in Arthur Hall's *Iliad* I-X, 1581, though Hall knew no Greek, translating from French instead.

17th Century

By 1600, however, the English language still possessed no Aeschylus, no Plato, scarcely any Aristotle – and inevitably, many poor and unreliable translations of other Greek texts. Familiarity with Greek was still rare, meaning that those texts of which English (and Latin) translations were available assumed disproportionate importance. Hence, for instance, the influence of Plutarch on Shakespeare, in Sir Thomas North's complete translation (1579), done from the French of Amyot. Another reason why Latin classics retained their priority over Greek was widespread ignorance of the Roman debt to Greek literature; thus Horace was considered a more important literary theorist than Aristotle, Seneca a more significant philosopher than Plato. Even Homer was overshadowed by Virgil, though several writers were drawn to attempt English versions of the former. But they were soon outdone by George Chapman (1559–1634), the first really major figure in verse translation from the Greek. He was responsible for renderings of Hesiod and a completion of Christopher Marlowe's version (not a translation) of Musaeus' *Hero and Leander*, but his finest work is his rendering of Homer involving an *Iliad* (completed 1611), an *Odyssey* (1616) and the Homeric hymns and other minor pieces (1624). These translations constitute the first complete version of both Homeric epics to appear from a single hand in any European language. It was Chapman's boast that he translated the second half of the *Iliad* in under four months; he says that as he worked on this section he saw "the clear scope and contexture of [Homer's] work, the full and most beautiful figures of his persons" for the first time. His rough-hewn but vigorous verse is well able to express, for instance, the cruel exultation of Achilles as he faces Hector in Book XXII:

"Dog", he replied, "urge not my ruth by parents, soule,
  nor knees.
I would to God that any rage would let me eate thee raw,
Slic't into peeces, so beyond the right of any law
I tast thy merits."

A generation after Chapman, the preponderance of Latin authors among classical texts being translated was much reduced. Greek epigram and lyric come to the fore, perhaps most fruitfully in the phenomenon of Anacreon, a poet who is in effect a creation of the European literary imagination, since, as we now know, the so-called "Anacreontea" contain no more than fragments by any writer of that name. By the 17th century Anacreon was seen, along with Sappho, Alcaeus and the Greek Anthology, as representing a new lyric model. Thomas Stanley (1625–78) published in 1651 a volume of translations of Anacreon, Bion and Moschus. Robert Herrick produced versions of Anacreontic poems which are better known today. But the Anacreontic tradition climaxes in Abraham Cowley's delightful collection of *Anacreontiques* in 1656:

Why do we precious oyntments shower,
Nobler wines why do we pour,
Beauteous flowers why do we spread,
Upon the monuments of the dead?
Nothing they but dust can show,
Or bones that hasten to be so.

The very different lyric tradition represented by Pindar was also much augmented by both translated and new verse in the Pindaric mould, and here Cowley was even further in the vanguard. His *Pindarique Odes* (1656) contain imitations of Pindar as well as original poems in "Pindarics", and it is arguable that Cowley thus created the "imitation" in English verse. (He wrote that "if a man should undertake to translate Pindar word for word, it would be thought that one mad man had translated another".) Robert Fleming translated another four of Pindar's odes in 1691; later versions appeared in the middle of the 18th century, by Ambrose Philips (1748) and Gilbert West (1749). By this time Ambrose Philips and later John Addison had also translated Sappho, their example being followed by others as the 18th century went on.

For the Restoration era (1660–1700), Greek epigram and lyric are by no means the only focus of translation from Greek. Publication records, including those for dictionaries, grammars and editions of Greek texts, establish that Greek studies in general had arrived at something of a heyday. This is by no means the almost exclusively Latin-based culture it is often represented, and some of the leading names in "Augustan" letters are the most prominent translators of Greek. The Poet Laureate John Dryden (1631–1700), for example, has interests extending to Greek history, drama and philosophy as well as poetry; he collaborates with Nathaniel Lee on a version of Sophocles' *Oedipus* in 1678, uses Greek sources in several of his own plays, and translates Theocritus (four idylls) and Homer (*Iliad*, Book I, 1700, and other selections). Translations of Homer into the 18th century call for further comment in the next section.

18th Century

John Ogilby and the philosopher Thomas Hobbes publish, respectively, verse and prose texts of the *Iliad* in the 1660s and 1670s. Dryden's version of *Iliad* I in 1700 is far more poetically successful, but it was left to Alexander Pope (1688–1744) to make his name with a complete Homer – *Iliad*, 1715–20, and *Odyssey* (with collaborators), 1725–26. Pope's translations were by no means the only ones of his own time: other selections of Homer were appearing regularly, and Pope was directly competing with Thomas Tickell, whose *Iliad* book 1 was published two days after the first part of his own version. But Pope's work is the only 18th-century English Homer still read today. His *Iliad*, in particular, is an outstanding attempt to interpret Homer to his own age – to show Homer to be a contemporary, the *Iliad* a modern work based on universal Nature. Neither is Pope (as is sometimes said) unable to perceive qualities that lie outside the norms of Augustan decorum, or unprepared to recognize the uncivilized alienness of the Homeric world. He asks at one point in his notes, for example:

> Who can be so prejudiced in their favour as to magnify the felicity of those ages, when a spirit of revenge and cruelty, join'd with the practice of rapine and robbery, reign'd thro' the world ... ?

Complex developments in taste over the remainder of the 18th century involve Homer in a new series of adventures. With the discovery of the "primitive" poetry of the balladists, especially "Ossian" in the 1760s, comes a fashion for the uncultivated, the unsophisticated, in poetry. Thomas Blackwell's *An Enquiry into the Life and Writings of Homer* (1735) is significant here. Homer now begins to be presented as an untaught bard, the product of the society he depicts – the climax of this school of thought being an influential treatise of 1795 by the German classicist Friedrich Wolf on the elements of oral tradition in Homer. Accordingly, William Cowper's admired blank-verse *Odyssey* (1785–91) offers a less studied and artificial language than Pope's, though with a strong element of Miltonic diction even so:

> Then, girding up his rags, Ulysses sprang
> With bow and full-charged quiver to the door;
> Loose on the broad stone at his feet he pour'd
> His arrows, and the suitors thus bespake ...

By the early 19th century Pope's Homer looked vulnerable to a range of criticisms. Cowper himself dismissed it with the words "I never saw a copy so unlike the original", and Charles Lamb described why he found Pope wanting in these terms:

> What certainly everybody misses in Pope, is a certain savage-like plainness of speaking in Achilles – a sort of indelicacy – the heroes in Homer are not half-civilized, they utter all the cruel, all the selfish, all the *mean thoughts* even of their nature, which it is the fashion of our great men to keep in.

Apart from a long and varied engagement with Homer, the 18th century sees many new translations of other Greek classics, some appearing for the first time in English. From 1700 to 1750 there is renewed interest in drama, for example (the translations sometimes made through intermediate French texts): Lewis Theobald's *Electra*, *Oedipus* and *Clouds* (1714–15), and George Adams's and Thomas Francklin's versions of Sophocles (respectively 1729, verse; 1759, prose). Henry Fielding and Edward Young commenced (but discontinued) a complete Aristophanes with their *Plutus* (1742). In 1758 Oliver Goldsmith was taking John Burton's collection of five translated Greek tragedies sufficiently seriously to publish a commentary on them. James Thomson had a strong interest in Aeschylus and translated the *Agamemnon* in 1738. True, this and many of the other versions just mentioned are remarkably unlike their source-texts in many respects; the point is that the attempt to translate these difficult works is being made, often for the first time. Nor are these efforts confined to drama. There were translations – of sorts – of Sappho, Bion, Moschus; many more of Pindar (Gilbert West's won the admiration of Samuel Johnson); of Demosthenes and Lysias. One prose work, Longinus' *On the Sublime* (*Peri Hypsous*), was a formative influence on English taste for several generations. This treatise was translated several times in the second half of the 17th century; then more popularly in 1712 by Leonard Welstead via Nicolas Boileau's French version; eventually in the 1739 William Smith rendering which became standard and was often reprinted.

Historical and archaeological work made a real difference to understanding of the ancient Greek world in the middle of the 18th century; it also helped to emphasize the primacy of Greek culture over Roman. By 1800, Pausanius' guide to Greece had been translated into English (Thomas Taylor's version is 1793), and other new literary material (from, for example, the Greek tragedians) was being recovered through translation in the same spirit as the physical terrain was being investigated. Knowledge of the Greek language is still a relatively rare accomplishment – Samuel Johnson observes that "Greek is like old lace": everyone acquires as much as they are able. Johnson himself translated a good deal of epigram from the Greek Anthology (as did Cowper), passages of Euripides and Anacreontic lyric.

19th Century

It is in the context of the rediscovery of the physical *place* Greece still was that some aspects of Romantic Hellenism can best be understood. For the Romantics, Greece is the land where the Mediterranean sun never ceases, the soil on which Homer trod, as if the past could *almost* be brought to life – as in Byron's song "The Isles of Greece" from *Don Juan*:

The isles of Greece, the isles of Greece!
Where burning Sappho loved and sung,
Where grew the arts of war and peace,
Where Delos rose, and Phoebus sprung,
Eternal summer gilds them yet,
But all, except their sun, is set.

English Romantic Hellenism is a well-enough known episode in literary history. But translation from Greek by the English Romantics, and their contemporaries, is a miscellaneous phenomenon about which it is difficult to make clear generalizations. It is certainly less significant for English writers than the more general influence upon them of Greek literature, including philosophy and political thought. Many of the relevant translations are reflections, but not embodiments, of the importance of Greek literature for these writers; they would not have happened without serious interest in that literature, but the important outcome of the creative contacts lies elsewhere, in non-translated writing. Here, a genuinely new movement is in operation; the broad Enlightenment appeal to antiquity had concentrated on Rome, but now the Greeks began to absorb European intellectuals as never before.

But some indication of the kinds of Greek–English translation going on at this date is appropriate, starting with work by the major Romantic writers. Shelley, the product of a good classical education, is responsible over the years 1818–22 for interesting translations of Plato's *Symposium*, for versions of parts of Theocritus, of the *Homeric Hymns*, of Bion's lament for Adonis and Moschus' for Bion, and of Euripides' *Cyclops*, as well as the disastrous Aristophanic adaptation *Oedipus Tyrannus; or, Swellfoot the Tyrant*. Leigh Hunt produced a partial version of Theocritus in his *Foliage* (1818). The young Wordsworth translated the ancient Athenian revolutionary Harmodius-song. Byron translated parts of Euripides' *Medea*; his friend Tom Moore began his literary career with translations of the *Anacreontea*, a collection quarried also by Leigh Hunt. John Hookham Frere published lively and still readable verse translations of Aristophanes. Beyond these better-known figures, a large range of minor translators is at work. The various series of practical Greek/Latin and English texts for students, with interlinear or parallel translations, should not be overlooked: there is, for instance, the Classics on the Hamiltonian System series, 1828 onwards. There are no major new Homers: it is Chapman's version that resurfaces and appeals famously to Keats ("On First Looking into Chapman's Homer"), less famously to Coleridge, Lamb, Shelley and Blake. To the Romantics, Chapman's Homer was "thoroughly invested and penetrated with the sacredness of the poetic character" (William Godwin).

Some of these developments clearly anticipate the Victorians' sense of the spiritual value of the ancient Greeks. That sense is nowhere more apparent than in Elizabeth Barrett Browning's poem *Wine of Cyprus* (1844). All the Greek poets she mentions were enormously popular subjects for translations by her contemporaries, including no less than 60 19th-century English versions of Aeschylus and at least 120 of Euripides. What is striking is that so very few of these translations are readable today:

Oh, our Aeschylus, the thunderous,
How he drove the bolted breath
Through the cloud, to wedge it ponderous
In the gnarlèd oak beneath!
Oh, our Sophocles, the royal,
Who was born to monarch's place,
And who made the whole world loyal
Less by kingly power than grace!
Our Euripides, the human,
With his droppings of warm tears,
And his touches of things common
Till they rose to touch the spheres!
Our Theocritus, our Bion,
And our Pindar's shining goals! –
These were cup-bearers undying
Of the wine that's meant for souls.

What are the reasons for the limited appeal of so many Victorian Greek translations? One way of answering is simply to display the texts – Robert Browning's *Agamemnon* (1877), for instance, self-consciously striving to reproduce an "Aeschylean" alienness:

But when he underwent necessity's
Yoke-trace, – from soul blowing unhallowed change
Unclean, abominable, – thence – another man –
The audacious mind of him began
Its wildest range.

The very popular C.S. Calverley's Sophocles is not tortuous, merely stilted (this is his *Ajax*, 1862):

But, for these things, they shall be well. Go thou,
Lady, within, and there pray that the Gods
May fill unto the full my heart's desire.
And ye, my mates, do unto me with her
Like honour: bid young Teucer, if he come,
To care for me, but to be *your* friend still.

More popular, perhaps more representative, and certainly more bearable, is Calverley's Theocritus:

Then I can pipe as ne'er did Giant yet,
Singing our loves – ours, honey, thine and mine –
At dead of night: and hinds I rear eleven
(Each with her fawn) and bearcubs four, for thee.
Oh come to me – thou shalt not rue the day –
And let the mad seas beat against the shore!

But while acceptable work is found, and even memorable work can be discovered, Victorian translation of Greek poetry and drama is usually very disappointing. (In prose, and in utilitarian translations acting as mere cribs, the results are different: to go no further than the historians, A.H. Clough's Plutarch (1864) or E.S. Shuckburgh's Polybius (1889) both repay attention.) The ultimate explanation lies in the very prestige of the classics, Greek poetry and drama above all, in the Victorian era, with correspondingly excessive respect or reverence for them. This did not inhibit translators from setting out to render the Greek classics (what enterprise could be more noble?); it did tend to prevent them from hearing their originals as contemporaries, or as "men speaking to men".

More of the obstacles can be seen at work in the disputes over translation of Homer, in most ways the central Greek cultural figure for the Victorians. Homer's translators are many: a 20-year period in the mid-19th century sees 12 complete verse renderings of the *Iliad*. Homer's Victorian translators include Lord John Russell; Lord Derby; Charles Trevelyan; John Henry Newman; Andrew Lang; William Morris; and Samuel Butler. None of their translations is read today; their significance is as episodes in a series of cultural battles rather than as works of art. Newman's Homer of 1856 is still the folk-poet of the late 18th century; for Newman Homer was "direct, popular, forcible, quaint, flowing, garrulous, abounding with formulas, redundant in particles and affirmatory interjections" – and hence "similar to the old English ballad". Newman included a glossary of his own quaint terms, such as "bulkin" ("calf"), "bragly" ("proud and fine"), "hurly" ("hubbub"). The result is a painful incongruity attacked by Matthew Arnold in the most famous Victorian document on translation, Arnold's Oxford lecture series published as *On Translating Homer* (1861). Arnold himself experimented with an alternative form of Homeric translation, in English hexameters, of which he gave specimens in these lectures. Tennyson, who experimented similarly, observed that those who had "endeavoured to give us the *Iliad* in English hexameters ... have gone far to prove the impossibility of the task". He held that blank verse was the only suitable equivalent. William Morris's folksy *Odyssey* of 1887 did nothing to disprove his contention:

> But when the Mother of Morning, Rose-fingered Day-Dawn, shone,
> Then all the rams of the cattle fared out to the field to begone,
> While the ewes unmilked and bleating about the folds must go,
> For their udders were swollen to bursting.

The last Victorian translations of Homer are Samuel Butler's *Iliad*, 1898, and *Odyssey*, 1900. Virtually accepting defeat at the outset, these plain prose versions contain only what Butler thought essential: plot, characters, dialogue.

20th Century

Because they go deservedly unread today, it is perhaps not always remembered how very popular many Victorian translations from the Greek were in their time. A mass readership for the classics in English had certainly been created, a fact which perforce had consequences for the translators. This situation persisted into the 20th century: a good example is Gilbert Murray's series of verse translations of almost every extant Greek drama, published from 1902 to 1951. But this example tends to raise the issue of quantity versus quality in modern Greek translation. T.S. Eliot asked about the possibilities for the future survival of the classics in his "Euripides and Professor Murray" (1920). For the classics to survive, Eliot argued:

> ... we need a number of educated poets who shall at least have opinions about Greek drama, and whether it is or is not of any use to us. And it must be said that Professor Gilbert Murray is not the man for this. Greek poetry will never have the slightest vitalising effect upon English poetry if it can only appear masquerading as a vulgar debasement of the eminently personal idiom of Swinburne.

Eliot is right about Murray's translations, datedly late Romantic and emptily "poeticized" as they are. But Eliot himself translated no Greek literature. Presumably something more like his ideal is represented by Ezra Pound's remarkable, and to many Greek scholars unpalatable, version of Sophocles' *Trachiniae*, titled *Women of Trachis*. (A less well known Pound translation is now available of Sophocles' *Elektra*, first published as recently as 1989.) Pound certainly strives for a poetic and dramatic idiom in which he can determine whether or not Greek tragedy is "any use to us", whether, that is, it can speak home to 20th-century man. Rather less can be said of most of the other Greek dramatic translation in that century, even by distinguished writers: Robert Lowell's *Prometheus Bound* is merely prose, while Louis MacNeice's *Agamemnon* is written in nobody's idiom. But Greek tragedy has always been difficult.

Some tendencies in 20th-century Greek translation are clear enough. One of the most famous examples is also the shortest, running thus:

> Spring ......
> Too long ....
> Gongula ......

This is Ezra Pound's version of a fragment of Sappho, written while significant archaeological discoveries were being made of literary Greek texts in the sands of Egypt. It is evocative, enigmatic, "foreign"; it is also short. Pound himself was the 20th-century's arch-magpie in the ruins of Western culture, appropriating fragments to new purposes, but many poets who have translated Greek have been attracted to short forms such as epigram and elegy. Those writers who have translated from the Greek Anthology, for example – a less than popular activity in other centuries – include Ezra Pound, Edmund Blunden, Robert Bridges, Dudley Fitts, Richmond Lattimore, Kenneth Rexroth, Clive Sansom, Edwin Morgan, Alistair Elliot, Peter Porter, Fleur Adcock and Tony Harrison. It might be added that Sappho is more translated, and probably more successfully, in the last 100 years than at any other period: there is work by, among others, Thomas Hardy, Guy Davenport and Mary Barnard, and a small gem by A.E. Housman from Fragment 168B:

> The weeping Pleiads wester,
> And the moon is under seas;
> From bourn to bourn of midnight
> Far sighs the rainy breeze:
>
> It sighs from a lost country
> To a land I have not known;
> The weeping Pleiads wester,
> And I lie down alone.

Another well-recognized modern tendency is towards adaptation, "modernization", something other than strict rendering. The watershed here, as in other aspects of modern translation, is Pound's *Homage to Sextus Propertius* (published in parts from 1917 onwards); and the tendency is strongly related to Pound's notion of translation as a "making new", an art of creative refashioning or re-enactment instead of a humble, secondary craft. Derek Walcott's and Christopher Logue's Homers are contemporary examples: the former (*Omeros*, 1990) transposes the *Odyssey* to the West Indies; the latter is an ongoing "free adaptation" of the *Iliad*, based less on the Greek than on more conventional translations used as guides, sometimes taking many lines over a few words in Homer:

> Dust like red mist.
> Pain like chalk on slate. Heat like Arctic.
> The light withdrawn from Sarpedon's body.
> The enemies swirling over it.
> Bronze flak.

Distinctions between translation and "adaptation" or "imitation" can never be absolute, but cases like this certainly go well beyond the bounds of what a classics teacher could offer a class as an aid to the understanding of meaning. For such purposes, more conventional and more popular work by translators such as the American Richmond Lattimore (a prolific translator of much Greek literature including the tragedians, Hesiod and the lyric) is likely to be adopted; but such translations tend to be very prosaic, altogether stripped of rhythm and melody, like this specimen from the episode of Hector and Andromache in Lattimore's *Iliad*:

> "but may I be dead and the piled earth hide me under before I
> hear you crying and know by this that they drag you captive."
> So speaking glorious Hector held out his arms to his baby,
> who shrank back to his fair-girdled nurse's bosom
> screaming ...

As in most eras, the avant-garde in translation attracted censure; but the most widely read Greek literary translators of the 20th century, such as Murray and Lattimore, looked out of date well before it ended.

The number of translations of Greek literature made available in English each decade continues to grow – even if the number of readers for them does not (or declines). Is it a bumper harvest of appetizing new varieties, or only a bland and mediocre cash crop for publishers? The truth lies somewhere in between, though we are too near to this material to know exactly where. We have already seen that the Victorians produced far more Greek translations than are remembered (let alone read) today: it is no surprise if the threshing-floor shows a preponderance of chaff at the beginning of the 21st century too. Yet it can be argued that the last hundred years, under the pressure generated by Ezra Pound's leadership and example in the 1910s and 1920s and increasing ever since, has become a major era of English classical translation (perhaps not primarily in England: latterly the signs are of very significant activity in the US, Scotland and Ireland). Given the precarious condition of the Ancient Greek language in the English-speaking world, it is at least clear that if classical Greek literature is, as Eliot has it, "of any use to us", translations are necessary now as at no time since the Renaissance. Nor is the extensive history of Greek translation described above any impediment to continued efforts into the future. One of the implications of the notion of the "classic" is that such a work will always elude definitive capture in translation. It follows that there is always more to be done.

STUART GILLESPIE

Further Reading

Bolgar, R.R., *The Classical Heritage and Its Beneficiaries*, Cambridge: Cambridge University Press, 1954

Bolgar, R.R. (editor), *Proceedings of an International Conference on Classical Influences*, 3 vols, Cambridge: Cambridge University Press, 1971–79

Bush, Douglas, *Classical Influences in Renaissance Literature*, Cambridge, Massachusetts: Harvard University Press, 1952

Buxton, John, *The Grecian Taste: Literature in the Age of Neo-Classicism, 1740–1820*, London: Macmillan, 1978

Clarke, Graeme, *Recovering Hellenism*, Cambridge: Cambridge University Press, 1989

Clarke, M.L., *Greek Studies in England, 1700–1830*, Cambridge: Cambridge University Press, 1945

Gillespie, Stuart, *The Poets on the Classics: An Anthology of English Poets' Writings on the Classical Poets and Dramatists from Chaucer to the Present*, London and New York: Routledge, 1988

Greene, Thomas M., *The Light in Troy: Imitation and Discovery in Renaissance Poetry*, New Haven, Connecticut: Yale University Press, 1982

Highet, Gilbert, *The Classical Tradition: Greek and Roman Influences on Western Literature*, Oxford and New York: Oxford University Press, 1957

Jenkyns, Richard, *The Victorians and Ancient Greece*, Oxford: Blackwell, 1980

Lord, George deF., *Classical Presences in Seventeenth-Century English Poetry*, New Haven, Connecticut: Yale University Press, 1987

Madison, Carol, *Apollo and the Nine: A History of the Ode*, London: Routledge, 1960

Pfeiffer, Rudolf, *History of Classical Scholarship from 1300 to 1850*, Oxford: Clarendon Press, 1976

Sowerby, Robin, *The Classical Legacy in Renaissance Poetry*, London and New York: Longman, 1994

Spenser, T.J.B., *Fair Greece, Sad Relic: A Study of Literary Philhellenism from Shakespeare to Byron*, London: Weidenfeld and Nicolson, 1954

Stern, Bernard H., *The Rise of Romantic Hellenism in English Literature 1732–1786*, New York: Octagon Books, 1969

Turner, Frank M., *The Greek Heritage in Victorian Britain*, New Haven, Connecticut, and London: Yale University Press, 1981

Webb, Timothy (editor), *English Romantic Philhellenism, 1700–1824*, Manchester: Manchester University Press, and New York: Barnes and Noble, 1982

Greek, Modern

Literary Translation into English

As Odysseus Elytis remarked in his address to the Swedish Academy on receiving the 1979 Nobel Prize for Literature, the Greek writer is dealing with a language that is spoken by only a few million people (a total of some 15 million in Greece proper and the diaspora) and yet it is a language that has been spoken for over 2500 years without interruption and with a minimum of changes. There was not one century when poetry was not written in Greek, a fact that indicates the great weight of tradition borne by the Greek language and the great weight of responsibility for the modern writer.

The language used by the modern writer is tested against a linguistic heritage that remains an unbroken, living tradition in the sense that aspects of all the major stages in that tradition survive and coexist in the modern language. Thus the language of the Homeric epics (7th and 8th century BC), the Classical Greek of the 4th and 5th centuries BC, the Koin? Greek of the New Testament, the Byzantine Greek of the 4th to 15th centuries AD and the popular language of folk literature throughout the 400 years of Turkish Rule (1453–1821) are, to varying degrees, still accessible to Greeks today in a way that Anglo-Saxon or even Middle English is not accessible to speakers of modern English. With the birth of the modern nation and the growth of a national consciousness following the War of Independence (1821–29), the question of language became a national issue. What came to be known as "The Language Question" was primarily a debate about the correct or desirable form of the written language. Very briefly, this debate polarized into a contest between the popular spoken language (demotic) and its adherents (demoticists) and those who advocated a "purified" form of the language (katharevousa), a language that was a compromise between demotic and ancient Attic Greek and one cleansed of foreign (mainly Turkish) words. This strange "diglossia" became a national and political issue and cut across education, literature and, not least, the question of translation, provoking sometimes violent confrontations. It was not until 1976 that demotic was finally established as the official language of education and, consequently, of the State.

Greek literature written in various degrees of katharevousa, particularly prose writing in the 19th century, presents special difficulties for the translator into English, in which no corresponding idiom exists. Writers admired in Greek as much for the beauty of their language as for the content of their writings appear very ordinary when translated into contemporary English. So major 19th-century Greek writers such as Alexandros Papadiamandis, Yorgios Vizyinos and Emmanouil Roïdis are perhaps not so notable in English translation. The same is true, however, of contemporary Greek writers, who are able to use an admixture of popular and purist forms of the language to produce literary effects ranging from the officious and pompous to the ironic and hilarious. It is virtually impossible for the translator to reproduce this admixture of language in English. Cavafy (1863–1933), perhaps the best-known of all Greek poets in the English-speaking world, uses just such an admixture of the popular and purist language, yet in most English translations he is presented in the common poetic idiom of post-war Anglo-Saxon poetry, which may also account to some extent for his success in the English-speaking world.

Translations from Modern Greek literature began to appear systematically immediately after World War II. No doubt Greece's part in the war, and the experiences of English soldiers who had served there, sparked an interest in modern Greece and its literature at a time when most Westerners' knowledge of Greece went no further than its ancient past. The first collection of Seferis's (1900–71)work in English, *The King of Asine and Other Poems*, appeared in 1948 and the first collection of Cavafy's work, translated by John Mavrogordato, in 1951. This period also coincided with the discovery of modern Greek literature by two of its most notable translators. Kimon Friar, born of Greek parents, grew up in the United States. He returned to Greece in 1946 and from that time began a life-long collaboration with Greek poets which resulted, apart from numerous individual works, in two large anthologies of Greek poetry, *Modern Greek Poetry: From Cavafis to Elytis* (1973) and *Contemporary Greek Poetry* (1985). Mention should also be made of his much-acclaimed translation of Kazantzakis's (1883–1957) monumental poem (33,333 verses; 1938), published in English as *The Odyssey: A Modern Sequel* (1958). The other major translator of modern Greek literature in this period was the American author and scholar, Edmund Keeley. Keeley's interest in modern Greece goes back to his early childhood which was spent in Greece. His fruitful collaboration with Philip Sherrard produced what are generally regarded as the definitive translations of Cavafy and Seferis, together with several anthologies containing poems by Odysseus Elytis, Nikos Gatsos and Angelos Sikelianos among others. Together with George Savidis, he published a translation of Elytis's major work, *The Axion Esti* (1959; translated 1974), and he has also published translations of Yannis Ritsos and Vassilis Vassilikos. Other translators who did much to help the cause of Greek literature in this period include Nanos Valaoritis, Rae Dalven, Peter Bien, Rex Warner and Peter Levi. It must be said, too, that this first generation of translators was fortunate in finding such fertile and untouched ground as modern Greek literature was in this period. It is perhaps also noteworthy that such a small number of translators are responsible for translating nearly all the major 20th-century Greek writers.

However, despite all this activity in the first decades after the war, Greek literature, with the notable exception of Cavafy, had little impact on the English-speaking world. Writing in 1962, Colin Wilson remarked that Kazantzakis's name remained almost totally unknown despite five of his major works having been published in translation in England, and even more in America. He attributes this curious situation to the fact that Kazantzakis wrote in Greek, and that modern readers do not expect to come upon an important Greek writer. Wilson remarks, somewhat ironically, that if Kazantzakis had written in Russian and been called Kazantzovsky, his works would no doubt be as universally known and admired as Sholokov's. Thirty years later, Kazantzakis's international reputation is now established, partly due, no doubt, to the success of film versions of his works by Cacoyannis, Dassin and Scorsese. It is doubtful whether the average reader in the English-speaking world could name any other Greek novelist. After Kazantzakis, the most translated novelists in English are Stratis Myrivilis, Pandelis Prevelakis,Vassilis Vassilikos and Andonis Samarakis (the two latter also benefitting from film versions of their novels). This is a lamentably small number when one considers the tremendous output of creative literature in Greece, particularly of prose fiction, since the 1960s.

The same, however, is not true of Greek poetry, which has always enjoyed a higher international profile thanks to the work of poets such as Constantine Cavafy, the two Nobel Prize-winning poets, George Seferis and Odysseus Elytis, and Yannis Ritsos. It is interesting that while prose enjoys a wider readership and, in general, its translation presents fewer difficulties, the acknowledged standing of the foremost Greek poets has led to there being probably more translations of poetry than of prose, while modern Greek drama has been particularly neglected. So, apart from Kazantzakis, it is Cavafy, Seferis, Elytis and Ritsos who remain the most translated Greek authors. Many other important Greek poets and novelists have received only minimal attention. Dionysios Solomos (1798–1857), the Greek national poet, Costis Palamas (1859–1943), Angelos Sikelianos (1884–1951) and Nikiforos Vrettakos (1911–)are virtually unknown in the English-speaking world, as indeed are a whole group of Surrealist poets who constituted one of the most important Surrealist movements outside France. Similarly, 20th-century novelists such as Yorgos Theotokas, Cosmas Politis, Stratis Myrivilis, Pandelis Prevelakis, Angelos Terzakis, Stratis Tsirkas, Costas Tachtsis and Yorgos Ioannou have fared no better. The case of Tachtsis and Tsirkas is indicative. English translations of their works were published by major publishing companies (Tachtsis remains the only Greek novelist to have been published by Penguin) yet met with little or no success.

It is difficult to account for this lack of success. A great deal of Greek literature has been translated, but it has failed to make any impact in the English-speaking world and Greek writers of today are conspicuous by their absence from major literary periodicals and the shelves of bookstores. As always it would be easy to put the blame on bad translations, but perhaps one should look to other factors such as distribution and marketing, and also to the thematic content of much post-war Greek fiction, which often presupposes a fairly detailed knowledge of recent Greek history and politics.

Apart from the significance of a work in the literary canon of a particular country, many other factors are influential in the success of the work in translation. Interest in translated works is often influenced by the political situation in the country at the time. For example, during the dictatorship in Greece (1967–74), there was a general climate of goodwill towards Greece favourable for translations, particularly of the more politically committed writers. International awards such as the Nobel Prize also lead to a sharp increase in translation activity, as happened in the case of Seferis and Elytis. In the case of Greek literature, however, these individual successes were not exploited for promoting other Greek writers. The "international presence" of the writer, particularly in the country where his or her work is being translated, would also seem to be conducive to the success of the translations. Seferis, for example, was Greek ambassador to Britain (1957–62) and his work had attracted the interest of other internationally-known writers such as Lawrence Durrell and Henry Miller. Recognition by other major writers in the language into which a writer's work is to be translated is undoubtedly another important factor. Cavafy's importance was recognized and his work promoted in Britain by, among others, E.M. Forster and W.H. Auden. Elytis, too, associated with and was known by leading European poets of his generation. It is also worth noting that the work of Cavafy, Seferis and Ritsos, at least as presented in English translation, conforms to the Anglo-Saxon poetic sensibility and is perhaps familiar to the English-speaking reader in a way that other modes of Greek writing are not.

Many contemporary Greek writers who have failed to make any impact in English translation have undoubtedly suffered from the legacy of the ancient past and of a particular perception of Greece by Westerners. The absence in their works of references to antiquity or of folkloric images of Greece conflicts with what the English-speaking reader has come to expect. In contrast, poets like Seferis and Cavafy filtered their reflections on modern Greece and their personal response to modern man's predicament through the known prism of ancient Greek history and mythology. Ritsos, too, in later period makes liberal use of the themes and characters of ancient Greek myths. Elytis, who consciously avoids any reference to ancient myth, nevertheless uses images from the Aegean world as a recurring motif in his poetry and these images are familiar to the foreign reader.

Kazantzakis is perhaps a special case in that he wrote more for an international public than a narrowly Greek one, and exploited a folkloric image of Greece with Zorba-like characters, an image consciously rejected by most Greek writers today. It is interesting, however, that successful novels by foreign authors set in Greece tend to emphasize either the ancient Greek past or Greek folkloric stereotypes. In contrast, the contemporary Greek novel is often concerned with the writer's personal response to or experience of specific historical events and the political and social situation in Greece since World War II and is set against a background of a very mundane Greek reality. This is difficult, however, for the foreign reader to relate to, and is in sharp contrast with the novels of Kazantzakis, where folkloric realism acts as a backdrop for the juxtaposition of universal philosophical and metaphysical ideas.

It is not insignificant, however, that translations of Kazantzakis were published by large publishing houses: Simon and Schuster in the United States and Faber in the United Kingdom. In the United States, the university presses, particularly Princeton and Johns Hopkins, have helped to promote Greek literature, as have several small presses, notably Nostos Books and Pella Publishing, which are concerned more or less exclusively with Greek literature. Particularly active in the United Kingdom is Anvil Press, though it should be noted that many publications in the United Kingdom in recent years are in fact re-publications of translations first published in the United States. Mention should also be made of the Greek publisher, Kedros, which in recent years has published a whole series of Greek novels in English translation, albeit with limited success. English translations of novels and short stories published in Greece and translations of scattered poems or stories in academic journals dealing specifically with Greek scholarship do little to help the cause of Greek literature in the English-speaking world, as they fail to reach a general readership. Having failed to take advantage of Kazantzakis's success, Greek writing is still awaiting a landmark publication that might effect a breakthrough into the English-speaking world.

DAVID CONNOLLY

Further Reading

Beaton, Roderick, *An Introduction to Modern Greek Literature*, Oxford: Clarendon Press 1994
Friar, Kimon, *Modern Greek Poetry: From Cavafis to Elytis*, New York: Simon and Schuster, 1973
Philippides, Dia M. L., *Census of Modern Greek Literature: Check-list of English-Language Sources Useful in the Study of Modern Greek Literature (1824–1987)*, New Haven, Connecticut: Modern Greek Studies Association, 1990
Stavropoulou, Erasmia-Louiza, *Vivliografia Metafraseon Neoellinikis Logotechnias* [Bibliography of Translations of Modern Greek Literature], Athens: Greek Literary and Historical Archive Society, 1986

Greek, Modern: Women Writers in English Translation

Numerous critics of Greek literature consider songs and folk tales the founding texts of Modern Greek literature. In presenting Greek women's literature in translation, one might begin by noting how this oral tradition is divided along gendered lines. While heroic ballads about history have been composed for the most part by male rhapsodes, laments for the dead and songs revolving around emotions have been most often composed by women. With its roots in this rich oral tradition, Modern Greek literature has always been half women's. For translations of this body of literature one can turn to the many excellent studies of women's role in this oral tradition. Translations of important texts by women are embedded in Margaret Alexiou's pioneering study, *The Ritual Lament in Greek Tradition* (Cambridge University Press, 1974) and in more recent studies such as Nadia Seremetakis's *The Last Word: Women, Death, and Divination in Inner Mani* (Chicago University Press, 1991), Gail Holst-Warhaft's *Dangerous Voices: Women's Laments and Greek Literature* (London and New York: Routledge, 1992), and Janet Hart's analysis of women's oral histories *New Voices in the Nation: Women and the Greek Resistance, 1941–64* (Ithaca, New York: Cornell University Press, 1996).

If one chooses to separate literary and oral traditions it is still clear that women have played a crucial part. For the past two centuries women have always written and been published in Greece (see Varikas 1993), though anthologists and critics have only recently begun to recover and analyse this body of literature as "women's literature". Similarly, only in the past three decades have some of these texts become available in translation. The introduction and translation of Elisavet Moutzan-Martinengou's fascinating autobiography, written in the early 1800s, is noteworthy in this respect. It is an important alternative view of the same period that the more famous *Memoirs* of General Makriyannis chronicles. The best general guide to translations of Modern Greek literature is Philippides (1986). Coriolano-Likourezos (2001) will usefully include excerpts and reviews of available translations. Below is a first attempt to survey translations of women's writing.

Since the dictatorship (1967–74) women writers have been setting literary trends in Greece. Quite a few novels by women have been translated and acclaimed by critics in England and the United States. Margarita Karapanou's *Kassandra and the Wolf* is a landmark in the recent rise of Greek women's writing. Maro Douka's novel *Fool's Gold* actually grounds the possibility of women's writing in the historical conditions of growing up under the dictatorship. The Kedros series of Greek writers in English includes this as well as other novels by important contemporary women writers such as Alki Zei's *Achilles' Fiancée*, Eugenia Fakinou's *Astradeni*, and Margarita Liberaki's *Three Summers*, a classic tale of three sisters growing up outside of Athens. Rhea Galanaki's *The Life of Ismail Ferik Pasha* was chosen for the Unesco Collection of Representative Works in 1996.

Translations of the poetry of C.P. Cavafy, George Seferis, Odysseus Elytis, Yannis Ritsos and other male poets of the generation of the 1930s have had a profound influence on the English-speaking world, much greater than that of Greek prose, which is often thought of by Greek and foreign critics alike as the poor relative. It is striking, therefore, that women's poetry remains less translated and less known than the Greek women's novels mentioned above. The pathbreaking work of poets such as Zoe Karelli and Maria Polydouri has yet to be translated. Mellisanthi's poems have recently been published in English but are difficult to obtain outside of Greece. Collections by Eleni Vakalo and Katerina Anghelaki-Rooke, the best represented Greek women poets in English, though published by important small presses are now out of print. The only real source for contemporary Greek women's poetry by these and other poets are anthologies (Barnstone, Connolly, Dalven, Friar, Fourtouni, Ricks, Siotis, Siotis / Chioles and Van Dyck). These anthologies for the most part offer individual, representative poems, though Van Dyck's includes three complete collections of poetry by Rhea Galanaki, Jenny Mastoraki and Maria Laina. The 1996 English selection of two of Kiki Dimoula's collections was very welcome.

If the translation of women's poetry has lagged behind that of women's prose slightly, the translation of women's drama has even more catching up to do. Plays by women dramatists such as Loula Anagnostaki and Margarita Liberaki have been performed with great success in France but are virtually unknown to English-speaking audiences. Although the 1980s and 1990s have witnessed a wave of interest in translating Greek women's writing, there is still a long way to go to making this literature available and vital in English.

In discussing the translation into English of the work of Greek women writers, it would be misleading not to include Greek women writers of the Diaspora since in many ways they have paved the way for an interest in and translation of Greek women's writing from Greece. From the work of the popular writer and translator Demetra Vaka-Brown in the early part of this century to the short stories and novellas of Kay Cicellis, one of Greek literature's best translators today, through the anthologies of Fourtouni, herself publisher and translator as well as poet, to the more recent literary success of Greek lesbian writers such as Spanidou and Broumas (Broumas is also a translator), Greek writing in Greece is only part of the story. The reader is particularly referred to Vaka-Brown's *A Child of the Orient* (Boston: Houghton Mifflin, 1916), Cicellis's *The Easy Way* (New York: Scribner, 1950), *The Way to Colonos* (New York: Grove Press, 1961) and her short story "Translation", published in *Shenandoah* (30/4, 1979), Thalia Cheronis Selz's "The Education of a Queen" published in the *Partisan Review* (5–6, 1961), Olga Broumas's *Beginning with O* (New Haven: Yale University Press, 1977), and Irini Spanidou's *God's Snake* (New York: Norton, 1986). In England, and, perhaps most strikingly, in Australia, similar trends are evident.

Since the translation of Greek women's writing is a relatively new endeavor, the critical literature on issues of translation and gender is still an open field. The list of Further Reading includes exemplary texts that introduce the issue of women's writing in Greece, even if the topic of translation is not explicitly addressed in all of them. Hart's and Seremetakis's accounts of women's oral history and laments, referred to above, also involve interesting self-conscious attempts to address the problem of translating this tradition of women's texts. Anthropology, generally, has been more attentive to the question of gender and translation in Greece than has literary criticism. For an initial attempt to address questions of the sexual politics of translation and the authority of the translator with regard to translating contemporary Greek women's poetry, however, see Van Dyck 1990, 1998 and 1998. If the recent interest in Greek women's literature and in translation studies continues, we can look forward in the next decade to more studies by feminist literary critics on the issue of translation.

KAREN VAN DYCK

Translations

Anagnostaki, Loula, "The City: A Trilogy of One-Act Plays", translated by George Valamvanos and Kenneth MacKinnon, *Charioteer*, 26 (1984) pp. 37–88

Anghelaki-Rooke, Katerina, *The Body is the Victory and the Defeat of Dreams*, translated by Philip Ramp, San Francisco: Wire Press, 1975

Anghelaki-Rooke, Katerina, *Beings and Things on Their Own: Poems*, translated by Jackie Willcox and the author, Brockport, New York: BOA Editions, 1986

Barnstone, Aliki and Willis Barnstone (editors), *A Book of Women Poets from Antiquity to Now*, New York: Schocken Books, 1980

Connolly, David (guest editor), "Greek Poetry: New Voices and Ancient Echoes", special issue of *Agenda*, 36/3–4 (Spring 1999)

Dalven, Rae (editor), *Daughters of Sappho: Contemporary Greek Women Poets*, Foreword by Andonis Decavalles, preface by Karen Van Dyck, Rutherford, New Jersey: Fairleigh Dickinson University Press, 1994

Dimoula, Kiki, *Lethe's Adolescence*, translated and introduced by David Connolly, Minneapolis: Nostos, 1996

Douka, Maro, *Fool's Gold*, translated by Roderick Beaton, Athens: Kedros, 1991

Fakinou, Eugenia, *The Seventh Garment*, translated by Ed Emory, London: Serpent's Tail, 1991

Fakinou, Eugenia, *Astradeni*, translated by H.E. Criton, Athens: Kedros, 1991

Fourtouni, Eleni (editor and translator), *Contemporary Greek Women Poets*, New Haven, Connecticut: Thelphini Press, 1978

Fourtouni, Eleni (editor and translator), *Four Greek Women: Love Poems*, New Haven, Connecticut: Thelphini Press, 1982

Fourtouni, Eleni (editor and translator), *Greek Women in Resistance: Journals, Oral Histories*, New Haven, Connecticut: Thelphini Press, 1986

Friar, Kimon (editor and translator), *Modern Greek Poetry*, New York: Simon and Schuster, 1973

Friar, Kimon (editor and translator), *Contemporary Greek Poetry*, with an introduction, biographies and notes, Athens: Ministry of Culture, 1985

Galanaki, Rhea, *The Life of Ismail Ferik Pasha: Spine nel cuore*, translated by Kay Cicellis, London: Peter Owen, and Paris: Unesco, 1996

Gogou, Katerina, *Three Clicks Left*, translated by Jack Hirschman, San Francisco: Night Horn Books, 1983

Karapanou, Margarita, *Kassandra and the Wolf*, translated by N.C. Germanacos, New York: Harcourt Brace, 1976

Liberaki [Lymberaki], Margarita, *The Other Alexander*, translated by Willis and Halle Tzalopoulou Barnstone, New York: Noonday Press, 1959

Liberaki [Lymberaki], Margarita, *Three Summers*, translated by Karen Van Dyck, Athens: Kedros, 1995

Melissanthi, *Hailing the Ascending Morn: Selected Poems*, translated by Maria Voelker-Kamarinea, Athens: Prosperos, 1987

Moutzan-Martinengou, Elisavet, *My Story* [1881], translated by Helen Dendrinou Kolias, Athens: University of Georgia Press, 1989

Siotis, Dinos and John Chioles (editors), *Twenty Contemporary Greek Poets*, introduction by Nanos Valaoritis, San Francisco: Wire Press, 1979

Siotis, Dino (editor), *Ten Women Poets of Greece*, introduction by Katerina Anghelaki-Rooke, San Francisco: Wire Press, 1982

Vakalo, Eleni, *Genealogy*, translated by Paul Merchant, Exeter: Rougemont Press, 1971; revised edition, Egham, Surrey: Interim Press, 1977

Vakalo, Eleni, "Selected Poems", translated by Kimon Friar, *Journal of the Hellenic Diaspora*, 9/4 (Winter 1982) pp. 28–43

Van Dyck, Karen, *The Rehearsal of Misunderstanding: Three*

Collections of Contemporary Poetry by Greek Women, Middletown, Connecticut: Wesleyan University Press, 1998
Zatelli, Zirana, "Birds", translated by Kay Cicellis, *Translation*, 14 (Spring 1985) pp. 28–37
Zei, Alki, *Wildcat Under Glass*, translated by Edward Fenton, London: Gollancz, and New York: Holt Rinehart and Winston, 1969
Zei, Alki, *Petros' War*, translated by Edward Fenton, New York: Dutton, and London: Gollancz, 1972
Zei, Alki, *The Sound of the Dragon's Feet*, translated by Edward Fenton, New York: Dutton, 1979
Zei, Alki, *Achilles' Fiancée*, translated by Gail Holst-Warhaft, Athens: Kedros, 1991

Further Reading

Anastasopoulou, Maria, "Awakening and Self/Redefinition in Greek Women Writers", *Modern Greek Studies Yearbook*, 7 (1991) pp. 259–85
Anghelaki-Rooke, Katerina, "Sex Roles in Modern Greek Poetry", *Journal of Modern Greek Studies*, 1/1 (1983) pp. 141–56
Bohandy, Susan, "Defining the Self through the Body in Four Poems by Katerina Anghelaki-Rooke and Sylvia Plath", *Journal of Modern Greek Studies*, 12/1 (1994) pp. 1–36
Chioles, John, "Poetry and Politics: The Greek Cultural Dilemma" in *Ritual, Power, and the Body: Historical Perspectives on the Representation of Greek Women*, edited by C. Nadia Serematakis, New York: Pella, 1993
Coriolano-Likourezos, Marina (editor), *Babel Guide to Modern Greek Literature*, London: Babel, 2001
Farinou-Malamatari, Georgia, "The Novel of Adolescence Written by a Woman: Margarita Limberaki" in *The Greek Novel: AD 1–1985*, edited by Roderick Beaton, New York and London: Croom Helm, 1988
Faubion, James D., "The Works of Margharita Karapanou: Literature as a Technology of Self-Formation" in his *Modern Greek Lessons: A Primer in Historical Constructivism*, Princeton, New Jersey: Princeton University Press, 1993
Friar, Kimon, "Eleni Vakalo: Beyond Lyricism", *Journal of the Hellenic Diaspora*, 9/4 (Winter 1982) pp. 21–27
Kakavoulia, Maria, "Telling, Speaking, Naming in Melpo Axioti's *Would You Like to Dance, Maria?*" in *The Text and Its Margins: Post-structuralist Approaches to Twentieth-Century Greek Literature*, edited by Margaret Alexiou and Vassilis Lambropoulos, New York: Pella, 1985
Kalogeros, Yiorgos, "A Child of the Orient as an American Storyteller: Demetra Vaka Brown", *Working Papers in Linguistics and Literature* (1989) pp. 187–93
Kolias, Helen Dendrinou, "Greek Women Poets and the Language of Silence" in *Translation Perspectives IV: Selected Papers, 1986–87*, Binghamton, New York: National Resource Center for Translation and Interpretation, 1988
Philippides, Dia M.L., *Checklist of English-Language Sources Useful in the Study (CENSUS) of Modern Greek Literature (1824–1987)*, New Haven, Connecticut: Modern Greek Studies Association, 1990
Robinson, Christopher, "The Comparison of Greek and French Women Poets: Myrtiotissa, Maria Polydure, Anna de Noailles", *Journal of Modern Greek Studies*, 2/1 (1984) pp. 23–38
Robinson, Christopher, "'Helen or Penelope?' Women Writers, Myth and the Problem of Gender Roles" in *Ancient Myth in Modern Greek Poetry*, edited by Peter Mackridge, London: Frank Cass, 1996
Van Dyck, Karen, introduction (as guest editor) and "The Sexual Politics of Babel", *Journal of Modern Greek Studies* (special translation issue), 8/2 (1990) pp. 169–71, 173–82
Van Dyck, Karen, "Reading between Worlds: Contemporary Greek Women's Writing and Censorship", *PMLA* (special censorship issue), 109/1 (1994) pp. 45–60
Van Dyck, Karen, "Bruised Necks and Crumpled Petticoats: What's Left of Myth in Contemporary Greek Women's Poetry" in *Ancient Greek Myth and Modern Greek Poetry*, edited by Peter Mackridge, London: Frank Cass, 1996
Van Dyck, Karen, *Kassandra and the Censors: Greek Poetry since 1967*, Ithaca, New York: Cornell University Press, 1998
Van Dyck, Karen, introduction in *The Rehearsal of Misunderstanding: Three Collections by Contemporary Greek Women Poets*, translated by Van Dyck, Middletown, Connecticut: Wesleyan University Press, 1998
Varikas, Eleni, "Gender and National Identity in fin de siècle Greece", *Gender and History*, 5/2 (1993) pp. 269–83

Julian Green 1900–1998

French novelist, short-story writer, dramatist and diarist

Biography

Born in Paris, 6 September 1900, the youngest of the eight children of American Protestant parents from the south living in Paris, where the father worked in the US Chamber of Commerce. Julian (as he was baptized) was bilingual in French and English but published mainly in French as Julien Green. Most of his life was spent in France. As a boy he attended the Lycée Janson-de-Sailly in Paris. From 1919 to 1922 he studied at the University of Virginia. Green served in both world wars: in 1917 as an ambulance driver for the French Red Cross, then in the French army; during World War II he worked in various capacities for the US army in the US, returning to France in 1945.

Green turned to writing in the early 1920s. His novels, such as *Adrienne Mesurat* (1927; *The Closed Garden*, 1928), *Minuit* (1936; *Midnight*, 1936), *Moïra* (1950; *Moira*, 1951), are characterized by their sombre psychological studies of men and women violently torn between spiritual and sexual urges. From his adolescence Green kept a diary, which appeared in 16 volumes from 1938. From 1963 he also published several volumes of autobiography. His best-known play is *Sud* (1953; *South*, 1991, performed 1955). In 1971 he was elected to the French Academy. He continued to write journals, poetry, drama and fiction to the end of his life. He died in Paris, 13 August 1998.

Translations

Short Stories

"Christine" (1924), "Le Voyageur sur la terre" (1926), "Les Clefs de la Mort" (1927), "Leviathan, une traversée inutile" (1928)

Bruerton, Courtney, *Christine and Other Stories*, with an introduction, New York: Harper, 1930; London: Heinemann, 1931 (contains "Leviathan", "Christine", "The Keys of Death", "The Pilgrim on Earth")

Novels

Mont-Cinère, 1926; revised editions, 1928, 1984

Best, Marshall A., *Avarice House*, New York: Harper, 1927; London: Benn, 1928; with an introduction by Tom McGonigle, London: Quartet, 1991

Adrienne Mesurat, 1927

Stuart, Henry Longan, *The Closed Garden*, New York: Harper, and London: Heinemann, 1928; as *Adrienne Mesurat*, revised by Marilyn Gaddis Rose with author's preface of 1973, New York: Holmes and Meier, 1991

Léviathan, 1929

Holland, Vyvyan, *The Dark Journey*, New York: Harper, and London: Heinemann, 1929

Épaves, 1932; revised edition, 1978

Holland, Vyvyan, *The Strange River*, New York: Harper, 1932; London: Heinemann, 1933

Le Visionnaire, 1934

Holland, Vyvyan, *The Dreamer*, New York: Harper, and London: Heinemann, 1934

Minuit, 1936

Holland, Vyvyan, *Midnight*, New York: Harper, and London: Heinemann, 1936; with an introduction by Green, London: Quartet, 1992

Varouna, 1940; revised edition, 1979

Whitall, James, *Then Shall the Dust Return*, New York: Harper, 1941

Si j'étais vous ... 1947; revised edition, 1970

McEwen, J.H.P., *If I Were You*, New York: Harper, 1949; London: Eyre and Spottiswoode, 1950

Moïra, 1950

Folliot, Denise, *Moira*, New York: Macmillan, and London: Heinemann, 1951; with an introduction by Stephen Pickles, London: Quartet, 1988

Le Malfaiteur, 1955; revised edition, 1974

Green, Anne, *The Transgressor*, New York: Pantheon, 1957; London: Heinemann, 1958

Chaque Homme dans sa nuit, 1960

Green, Anne, *Each in His Darkness*, New York: Pantheon, and London: Heinemann, 1961

L'Autre, 1971

Wall, Bernard, *The Other One*, New York: Harcourt Brace, and London: Collins / Harvill, 1973

Les Pays lointains, 1987

Beaumont, Barbara, *The Distant Lands*, London and New York: Marion Boyars, 1990

Les Étoiles du Sud, 1989

Buss, Robin, *The Stars of the South*, London and New York: Marion Boyars, 1995

Autobiography

Journal, vol. 1: *Les Anneés faciles, 1928–1934*, 1938, revised edition as *Les Anneés faciles, 1926–1934*, 1970; *Journal*, vol. 2: *Derniers Beaux Jours, 1935–1939*, 1939 (also published as *Entends la douce nuit, 1935–39*, 1939)

Godefroi, Jocelyn, *Personal Record 1928–1939*, New York: Harper, and London: Hamish Hamilton, 1939

"Souvenirs (Quand nous habitions tous ensemble)", *Les Oeuvres nouvelles*, with short works by others, 2 (1943)

Green, Julian, *Memories of Evil Days*, Charlottesville: University of Virginia, 1976 (contains "A Experiment in English" and "My First Book in English")

Journal III 1940–43 ("Devant la porte sombre"), 1946; *Journal IV 1943–45* ("L'Oeil de ouragan"), 1946; *Journal V 1946–50* ("Le Revenant"), 1951; *Journal VI 1950–54* ("Le Miroir intérieur"), 1955; *Le Bel Aujourd'hui* (Journal VII 1955–58), 1955–58

Green, Anne, *Diary 1928–57*, edited by Kurt Wolff, New York: Harcourt Brace, 1964

Partir avant le jour, 1963; revised edition, 1984

Green, Anne, *To Leave before Dawn*, New York: Harcourt Brace, 1967; London: Peter Owen, 1969

Green, Anne and Julian Green, *The Green Paradise, 1900–1916* (Autobiography 1), London and New York: Marion Boyars, 1993 (roughly the first half of *Partir avant le jour*)

Mille Chemins ouverts, 1964; revised edition, 1984

Cameron, Euan, *The War at Sixteen, 1916–19: Autobiography* (Autobiography 2), London and New York: Marion Boyars, 1993 (contains the sections *To Leave before Dawn* and *Mille Chemins ouverts*, bearing on Green's experiences in World War I)

Terre lointaine, 1966; revised edition, 1984

Cameron, Euan, *Love in America: Autobiography* (Autobiography 3), London and New York: Marion Boyars, 1994

Jeunesse, 1974; revised edition, 1984
Cameron, Euan, *The Apprentice Writer* (Autobiography 5), with an introduction, London and New York: Marion Boyers, 1993
Cameron, Euan, *Restless Youth* (Autobiography 4), London and New York: Marion Boyars, 1996

Play
Sud, 1953
Green, Julian, *South* (produced London 1955), London and New York: Marion Boyars, 1991

Other Writing
Paris, 1983
Underwood, J.A., *Paris* (bilingual edition), with photographs by Green and an introduction by Underwood, London and New York: Marion Boyars, 1991

Le langage et son double, 1985
Green, Julian, *The Language and Its Shadow* (self-translated parallel texts on language), Paris: La Différence, 1985

Frère François, 1983
Heinegg, Peter, *God's Fool: The Life and Times of St. Francis of Assisi*, San Francisco: Harper and Row, 1985; London: Hodder and Stoughton, 1986

Letters
Une grande amitié: Correspondance, 1926–1972 (Julien Green and Jacques Maritain), 1979
Doering, Bernard, *The Story of Two Souls: The Correspondence of Jacques Maritain and Julien Green*, New York: Fordham University Press, 1988

Venerable and vulnerable, Julian Green outlived all members of his generation, the *moralistes* of the *entre-deux-guerres*. Once he settled into writing in French and English, but mainly French, as a full-time, creative professional outlet – because painting was an option also – he wrote systematically and published regularly, finding time also to keep a diary that for many readers makes him his most appealing protagonist. This appeal is a credit partly to his skill as an extremely conservative stylist. As an American from an English-speaking family living in France, he considered himself ill-placed to be an innovator, although he was an early enthusiast of James Joyce. He appeals partly also because, as a Franco-American writer, US citizen and lifetime expatriate, even with military service in both world wars, he chose to be a thoughtful spectator of the 20th century.

Moreover, his nurture of his bilingual, bi-cultural background makes his corpus highly literate data for socio- and psycholinguistics. For example, *Memories of Happy Days* (1942) and "Souvenirs (Quand nous habitions tous ensemble, 1943)" (the latter translated by Julian GREEN, 1976, as *Memories of Evil Days*) began as the "same" reminiscence. However, Green soon discovered that his language behavior was determined by the language he was using. These two works cover the years of the first four volumes of his *Journal* but viewed from the norms of Anglo-American behavior.

Related to his conception of his dual heritage is the time warp of his US, the ante-bellum South of his parents. Religion and gender orientation also interacted with this heritage. He converted twice to the Roman Catholic Church, in 1916 and 1939. Finally he thought he should conceal his homosexuality from the American side of his family and constantly found his gender orientation colliding with his religious fervor. These inner struggles are expressed with consummate verbal control, giving them a power that a more open expression might not have achieved.

Because of his bilingualism and his frequent US settings, other French-English bilinguals can hear US Southern English through the French.

Curiously, when Green or his sister Anne Green translates his work, the discourse sounds like English acquired via schooling. The English translations made by others ring much more authentically, and Green has been fortunate in the translators assigned to his work. Vyvyan HOLLAND (1929, 1932, 1934, 1936), the son of Oscar Wilde, had a distinguished career as a translator. CAMERON, one of Green's most recent translators, (1993, 1993, 1994, 1996) is quite successful in making the doubly transcribed speech sound authentic. Green, who was the only native French speaker in his immediate family, transcribed as French speech that occurred in English, which Cameron then had to "back-translate". (Cameron also provides helpful translator's notes.) Anne GREEN, Julian's sister, translator (1957, 1961, 1964, 1967) and co-translator (1993), was born in the US; for most of her novels she used English, her first language.

Green was baptized Julian because he was named after his grandfather. Many English-language publications use that spelling. However, when English-language publications consider him a French writer, as does the annual PMLA Bibliography, Julien is used.

For Green's work up to 1970 translators should use the five-volume *Oeuvres complètes* (edited by Jacques Petit, Paris: Gallimard (Pléiade), 1972). Green's extensive publications subsequent to this date (competing in volume with his work prior to age 70) have received neither editing nor attention from the scholarly community. These works of Green's third and fourth age, while not necessarily problematic, lack the depth of the work of his prime. For example, his ante-bellum novels of the 1980s are of interest only because of Green's authorship. Other recent publications include juvenilia (e.g. *Histoires de vertige: nouvelles*, presumably found in the papers of his companion, the late Robert de Saint-Jean); translations into French of essays published originally in English (e.g. *L'Homme et son ombre*, 1991); and the inevitable miscellany of a surviving elder statesman.

Given the large proportion of Green's writing that has been put into English, it is puzzling that *L'Autre Sommeil* (1931), a sensitive work of fiction, possibly his very best, remains untranslated.

Green's copious autobiography is the most authoritative source of information on his writing and translating. Upon his death his uncensored diary became available to scholars; also helpful are the studies by his sister Anne and his longtime companion Robert de Saint-Jean.

MARILYN GADDIS ROSE

Further Reading

Gaddis Rose, Marilyn, *Julian Green: Gallic-American Novelist*, Bern: Lang, 1971
Green, Anne, *With Much Love*, New York: Harper, 1948

Saint-Jean, Robert de, *Julien Green par lui-même*, Paris: Seuil, 1967

Saint-Jean, Robert de, *Passé pas mort: souvenirs*, Paris: Grasset, 1983

Weightman, John, "Sex and the Devil", *New York Review of Books* (5 December 1991) pp. 53–56

See also the translator's notes in Cameron

Lady Augusta Gregory 1852–1932

Irish translator and dramatist

Biography

Born Isabella Augusta Persse, 5 March 1852, at Roxborough, Co. Galway. In 1880 she married Sir William Gregory of Coole Park (1817–92), a former governor of Ceylon. Lady Gregory helped found the Irish National Theatre Society. She was director of the Abbey Theatre in Dublin, for which she also wrote plays. She died at Galway, 2 May 1932.

Lady Gregory was one of the leading figures of the Irish Literary Revival. As the author of over 30 plays, a founding member of the Irish Literary Theatre, a collector of folklore and a close collaborator of William Butler Yeats and John Millington Synge she played a decisive role in the emergence of a new English-language literature in Ireland at the turn of the century. Lady Gregory was also an accomplished translator whose translations from Gaelic, French, German and Italian helped consolidate Hiberno-English as a mode of literary expression and made suggestive links between indigenous aesthetic forms and the dramatic literature of Europe.

In 1902 *Cuchulain of Muirthemne* appeared. This was a version in Hiberno-English of the mythological stories of the Red Branch Knights. Lady Gregory had chosen the language of English speakers in rural Ireland to translate the stories from Irish to English, a language that became known as "Kiltartan". Yeats in his preface to *Cuchulain* claimed that Lady Gregory was the first to demonstrate the literary use of distinctive Hiberno-English speech in English, but this judgement needs to be qualified. Douglas Hyde in his prose translations of Gaelic love poetry that appeared in *The Love Songs of Connacht* in 1893 had already anticipated the choice of Hiberno- rather than British English in translation. Although J.M. Synge, Standish J. O'Grady and Douglas Hyde expressed reservations about certain scholarly shortcomings in the translation and the tendency to bowdlerize, Synge would claim in a letter to Lady Gregory two years later that "*Cuchulain* is still a part of my daily bread." Her approach to translation as described in the "Dedication of the Irish Edition to the People of Kiltartan" recalls the target-oriented preoccupations of Irish translators from the medieval period: "I left out a good deal I thought you would not care about for one reason or another, but I put in nothing of my own that could be helped, only a sentence now and again to link the different parts together." In the "Dedication" she criticizes the indifference of the scholars of Trinity College Dublin to Ireland's cultural past but also foregrounds the issue of gender and translation, questioning her right to translate as opposed to remaining in the strictly domestic sphere:

> And indeed if there was more respect for things Irish among the learned men that live in the college at Dublin, where so many of these old writings are stored, this work would not have been left to a woman of the house, that has to be minding the place, and listening to complaints, and dividing her share of food.

In view of Lady Gregory's formidable energy and unstinting activity in Irish literary life, the disclaimer in the "Dedication" seems more the artifice of *persona* (Lady Gregory as an old countrywoman telling stories) than a genuine expression of her doubts as to the appropriateness of a woman translating texts.

On 20 August 1904 a patent was granted to the Abbey Theatre in the name of Lady Gregory for six years. The Abbey Theatre was the successor to the Irish Literary Theatre founded in 1899. One of the clauses in the patent restricted the Abbey to performances of contemporary Irish dramas and continental masterpieces. The clause was inserted to reassure the proprietors of other Dublin theatres that the Abbey would not encroach on their traditional territory. The constraint proved liberating as the Abbey became the focal point of the new revolution in Irish drama and a showcase for distinctive translations by Lady Gregory among others. The idea of performing Molière had first been considered in August 1905, but as Lady Gregory remarked in *Our Irish Theatre*, "when one translation after another was tried, it did not seem to carry, to 'go across the footlights'." She agreed to translate *Le Médecin malgré lui* and worked on the translation through the autumn and the New Year. She sent the typescript to Synge, who received it 15 February 1906, and the play was produced on the Abbey stage two months later. *The Doctor in Spite of Himself* was a popular and critical success and Lady Gregory did a translation of *Les Fourberies de Scapin* that was premiered as *The Rogueries of Scapin* 4 April 1908, and a translation of *l'Avare*, whose premiere as *The Miser* took place 21 January 1909. Lady Gregory's description of the first three Molière translations as "adaptations" has often led to a certain critical confusion. The translations were, in fact, careful, fastidious translations of the French texts. The translator's task was facilitated to some extent by the similarities between Gregory's own short comedies and the work of the French dramatist, similarities that George Bernard Shaw had been among the first to note. In addition, both Yeats and Gregory saw affinities between the theatre of Molière and the Irish folk drama that the Abbey sought to encourage. When the Abbey company produced the Molière plays they scrupulously adhered to the stage business of the Comédie française prompt-scripts. The last Molière play that Lady Gregory translated was *Le Bourgeois gentilhomme*. She began the translation 28 October 1924 at the age of 72, at the request of the Abbey actor Barry Fitzgerald, who had seen a production of the French play in Paris. Lady Gregory finished the translation in two months and *The Would-Be Gentleman* had its premiere in the Abbey on 4 January 1926. The combination of ballet and comedy in *Le Bourgeois gentilhomme* meant more extensive changes than for the earlier Molière plays as the translation was adapted to the theatrical capabilities of the Abbey company. The ballet was eliminated, certain scenes were cut, Gregory incorporated her own versions of songs and she occasionally transferred lines from one character to the other. However, Gregory still went to great lengths to capture specific nuances of the French text and retain the dramatic integrity of the play. Lady Gregory's translation work was primarily an act of cultural self-confidence. Tudor England and Romantic Germany had embarked on the translation of Greek and Roman classics as part of the process of nation-building. Translating Molière into Hiberno-English celebrated the national distinctness and the poetic possibilities of a language that would no longer be the parodic utterances of the Stage Irishman but a fitting vehicle for the classics of world literature. The translations of Lady Gregory, alongside those of John Millington Synge and Douglas Hyde, would radically alter the destiny of Irish literature in the English language in the 20th century.

MICHAEL CRONIN

Translations

Cuchulain of Muirthemne: The Story of the Men of the Red Branch of Ulster, 1902

Goldoni, Carlo, *Mirandolina*, 1924

Molière, *The Kiltartan Molière: The Miser; The Doctor in Spite of Himself; The Rogueries of Scapin*, 1910

Molière, *The Would-Be Gentleman* in *Three Last Plays*, by Lady Gregory, 1928

Sudermann, Hermann, *Teja* in *The Translations and Adaptations of Lady Gregory and Her Collaborations with Douglas Hyde and W.B. Yeats*, edited by Ann Saddlemyer, vol. 4 of Lady Gregory's, *Collected Plays*, 1970 (vol. 4 of the *Collected Plays* also contains the Molière and Goldoni translations)

Further Reading

Adams, Hazard, *Lady Gregory*, Lewisburg, Pennsylvania: Bucknell University Press, 1973

Coxhead, Elizabeth, *Lady Gregory: A Literary Portrait*, New York: Harcourt Brace, and London: Macmillan, 1961; revised edition, London: Secker and Warburg, 1966

Gregory, Lady Augusta, *Our Irish Theatre*, London: John Murray, 1913; revised and enlarged edition, Gerrards Cross, Buckinghamshire: Smythe, 1972

Gregory, Lady Augusta, *Seventy Years*, edited by Colin Smythe, Gerrards Cross, Buckinghamshire: Smythe, 1974; New York: Macmillan, 1976

Gregory, Lady Augusta, *Irish Myths and Legends*, Philadelphia: Running Press, and London: Courage, 1998

Kohfeldt, Mary Lou, *Lady Gregory: A Biography*, New York: Atheneum, 1984; as *Lady Gregory: The Woman Behind the Irish Renaissance*, London: Deutsch, 1985

Mikhail, E.H., *Lady Gregory: An Annotated Bibliography of Criticism*, New York: Whitston, 1982

Saddlemyer, Ann, *In Defence of Lady Gregory, Playwright*, Dublin: Dolmen Press, 1966

Saddlemyer, Ann and Colin Smythe, *Lady Gregory, Fifty Years After*, Gerrards Cross, Buckinghamshire: Smythe, 1987 (see especially Mary Fitzgerald, "Four French Comedies: Lady Gregory's Translations of Molière", pp. 277–90)

Franz Grillparzer 1791–1872

Austrian dramatist and novella writer

Biography

Born in Vienna, 15 January 1791, the son of a lawyer. Grillparzer went to school at the Anna-Gymnasium, Vienna, 1800–07, then studied law at the University of Vienna, graduating in 1811. On the death of his father in 1809 he took over responsibility for the family. In 1812 he was employed as a private law tutor and in 1813 embarked, as an assistant librarian, on a career in the imperial civil service. In 1818, after the success of his tragedy *Die Ahnfrau* (*The Ancestress*), 1817, he was appointed playwright to the state theatre. From 1823 until he retired in 1856 he was keeper of the imperial archives.

Grillparzer's character was depressive. His mother and brother both committed suicide, his career was hindered by political censorship (he had liberal views, though he was loyal to the monarchy, which did not always favour him) and he was several times frustrated in love. With one long interruption he lived in the house of his fiancée from 1826 to his death, but they did not marry.

As well as the verse tragedies – notably *Sappho* (*Sappho*), 1819 (written 1817); the trilogy *Das goldene Vlies* (*The Golden Fleece*), 1822 (written 1820); *Des Meeres und der Liebe Wellen* (*The Waves of Sea and Love*), 1839 (written 1829) – Grillparzer produced comedies; a wide range of poetry; two prose novellas, of which *Der arme Spielmann* (*The Poor Fiddler*), 1848, is much the better known; travel writing and a biography. He was the first Austrian writer to win international recognition. He was a founder member of the Austrian Academy of Sciences (1847) and received an honorary doctorate from the University of Leipzig (1859). After his retirement from the civil service he was made a member of the upper house of the Austrian parliament (1861), and in 1871, on the occasion of his 80th birthday, was honoured by the Empress Augusta of Germany. Died 21 January 1872 in Vienna.

Translations

Selection of Tragedies

Solomon, Samuel, *Plays on Classic Themes*, New York: Random House, 1969 (contains *Sappho*; *The Golden Fleece: The Guest*, *The Argonauts*, *Medea*; *The Waves of Sea and Love*)

Tragedies

Die Ahnfrau, 1817, produced 1817 (written 1816)

Spahr, Herman L., *The Ancestress*, Hapeville, Georgia: Tyler, 1938

Sappho, 1819, produced 1818 (written 1817)

Bramsen, John, *Sappho*, London: Black, 1820

Burkhard, Arthur, *Sappho*, Yarmouth Port, Massachusetts: Register Press, 1953

Frothingham, Ellen, *Sappho*, Boston: Roberts, 1876

"L.C.C." [Lucy Caroline Cumming, later Smith), *Sappho*, Edinburgh: Constable, 1855

Middleton, Edda, *Sappho*, New York: Appleton, 1858

Solomon, Samuel, *Sappho* in *Plays on Classic Themes*, translated by Solomon, 1969

Das goldene Vlies, 1822, produced 1821 (written 1820); trilogy: *Der Gastfreund* (1 act); *Die Argonauten* (4 acts); *Medea* (5 acts)

Burkhard, Arthur, *Medea*, Yarmouth Port, Massachusetts: Register Press, 1941

Burkhard, Arthur, *The Guest-Friend* and *The Argonauts*, 2 vols, Yarmouth Port, Massachusetts: Register Press, 1942

Lamport, F.J., *Medea*, in *Five German Tragedies*, translated by Lamport, with an introduction, Harmondsworth and Baltimore: Penguin, 1969

Solomon, Samuel, *The Golden Fleece* (*The Guest*, *The Argonauts*, *Medea*) in *Plays on Classic Themes*, translated by Solomon, 1969

Thurstan, F.W. and Sidney A. Wittmann, *Medea*, London: J. Nisbet, 1879

König Ottokars Glück und Ende, 1825 (written 1823)

Burkhard, Arthur, *King Ottocar: His Rise and Fall*, Yarmouth Port, Massachusetts: Register Press, 1962

Stevens, Henry H., *King Ottocar: His Rise and Fall*, Yarmouth Port, Massachusetts: Register Press, 1938

Ein treuer Diener seines Herrn, 1830, produced 1828 (written 1827)

Burkhard, Arthur, *A Faithful Servant of His Master*, Yarmouth Port, Massachusetts: Register Press, 1941

Des Meeres und der Liebe Wellen, 1839, produced 1831 (written 1829)

Burkhard, Arthur, *Hero and Leander*, Yarmouth Port, Massachusetts: Register Press, 1962

Solomon, Samuel, *The Waves of Sea and Love* in *Plays on Classic Themes*, translated by Solomon, 1969

Stevens, Henry H., *Hero and Leander*, Yarmouth Port, Massachusetts: Register Press, 1938

Der Traum ein Leben, 1839, produced 1834 (written 1833)

Stevens, Henry H., *A Dream is Life*, Yarmouth Port, Massachusetts: Register Press, 1946

Libussa, 1872, produced 1874 (written 1847–48)

Stevens, Henry H., *Libussa*, Yarmouth Port, Massachusetts: Register Press, 1941

Die Jüdin von Toledo, 1872 (written 1851)

Burkhard, Arthur, *The Jewess of Toledo*, with *Esther*, Yarmouth Port, Massachusetts: Register Press, 1953

Danton, George Henry and Annina Perian Danton, *The Jewess of Toledo*, in *German Classics of the Nineteenth and Twentieth Centuries*, vol. 6, edited by Kuno Francke, New York: German Publication Society, 1913–14; reprinted New York: AMS Press, 1969

Ein Bruderzwist in Habsburg, 1873, produced 1874 (written 1848)

Burkhard, Arthur, *Family Strife in Hapsburg*, Yarmouth Port, Massachusetts: Register Press, 1940

Comedy

Weh dem, der lügt!, 1840, produced 1838 (written 1837)

Stevens, Henry H., *Thou Shalt Not Lie*, Yarmouth Port, Massachusetts: Register Press, 1939

Novella

Der arme Spielmann, 1848 (written 1847)

Henderson, Alexander and Elizabeth Henderson, *The Poor Fiddler*, New York: Ungar, 1967

Aside from some spasmodic interest in the course of the 19th century, the translation of the works of Franz Grillparzer is, in the modern period, largely the story of two men and one press. The men in question are Henry H. Stevens and Arthur Burkhard, and the press is the Register Press at Yarmouth Port, Massachusetts. Between them the two men provided versions of all the major dramatic works with the exception of *Die Ahnfrau*, and in the case of both *König Ottokars Glück und Ende* and *Des Meeres und der Liebe Wellen* Burkhard offers new versions in 1962 of Stevens's 1938 renderings of both texts. Regrettably, as with much 19th-century German material, difficulty of access to these translations remains a serious problem.

BURKHARD's version (1953) of *Sappho* is not totally devoid of preciousness and on occasion stiltedness, particularly when handling the voices of the youthful lovers, Melitta and Phaon. Nevertheless, the pride and hurt in Sappho's experience of jealousy come across well as the ageing woman faces failure and loss. SOLOMON (1969) also offers a reasonably successful translation of *Sappho* which manages to retain much of the original imagery. There is sometimes an overly archaic feel but, for all that, good fluency is maintained.

SOLOMON (1969) also includes a translation of *Das goldene Vliess* and is clearly much happier handling the action and movement of this trilogy. The sombre brooding mood is well conveyed by the translation. BURKHARD (1941) offered initially a translation of *Medea*, to be followed the next year by the first two parts of the trilogy, *The Guest-Friend* and *The Argonauts*. Since Grillparzer essentially wrote the trilogy starting with the final part, *Medea*, it is perhaps fitting that his translator should follow suit, although curiously there is nothing in Burkhard to indicate that the works belong together as a trilogy. As in Solomon's version, the action is well conveyed, as are the sarcasm and bitterness of Medea. LAMPORT (1969) maintains a nice balance between readability and a period sense in the language. The earlier parts of the trilogy are glossed in the introduction to his volume of translations.

BURKHARD's version (1962), *King Ottocar: His Rise and Fall,* is dedicated to Henry H. Stevens, the earlier translator. Burkhard's rendering is best described as dignified. The central speeches by the Holy Roman Emperor Rudolph I in Act 3 and King Ottokar II of Bohemia in Act 5 remain true to the original and retain close fidelity to the structure of the imagery. Equally, the enigmatic and Machiavellian Zawisch comes over well.

The key to any translation of *Ein treuer Diener seines Herrn* lies in the ability to accommodate the complexity of the central character, Bancban. In this BURKHARD (*A Faithful Servant of His Master*, 1941) is in large measure successful. Bancban's quiet certainty, composure and sense of duty as co-regent of Hungary, to King Andreas, are captured well in the opening scenes, as is the dignity of his closing speech. Slightly less convincing is the treatment of the anarchic figure of Duke Otto, brother of the queen, particularly in the menacing scenes with Bancban's young wife, Erny. Overall, however, Burkhard does justice to the original text.

Perhaps the greatest test in translation comes with *Des Meeres und der Liebe Wellen* [The Waves of the Sea and of Love] based on the story of Hero and Leander. SOLOMON's version (*The Waves of Sea and Love*, 1969) is the most awkward of the three on offer. Such awkwardness is exemplified by his rendering of line 55: "So early, since, however late, you're not." There are errors, including the translation of "unverwandt" ("fixedly" or "steadfastly") as "vaguely", a crucial error in the Priest's central speech of act 3 dealing with the concept of "Sammlung" ("composure"). Equally, there are breaks in idiom, with movement from high level language to the colloquial. The key nexus and weave of imagery are partially lost, for example when "umnachtet" is rendered as "blinds" in line 1181: "What is it that so blinds a human being?", where the sustaining contrast of light and dark is suppressed (cf. Burkhard: "benight"). STEVENS (*Hero and Leander*, 1938), which clearly influenced the later Burkhard translation, reads fluently and the Priest's key speech is well treated. The network of metaphor is also reasonably reliably conveyed. BURKHARD (*Hero and Leander*, 1962) is not free of stylistic infelicities such as "jene muntre Hero": "merry little Hero". There are questionable renderings such as "halb bewusst": "half dreaming", and the full impact of "Hier also, hier!" is not fully captured by "Here, it is here." As with Stevens, the central speech by the Priest is well handled.

STEVENS (*Thou Shalt Not Lie*, 1939) gives a version of *Weh dem, der lügt!* that copes well with the faster pace of this comedy turning on a trial of strength between Christian Gallo-Romans and Germanic heathen. Caveats regarding the translation would have to include a word such as "durance" (line 420) which cannot reasonably be construed as part of Leon, the cook-hero's, normal vocabulary. Nevertheless, the slightly anarchic yet constrained figure of Leon, the centrepiece of the work, comes across well.

BURKHARD's translation (*Family Strife in Hapsburg*, 1940) of *Ein Bruderzwist in Habsburg* is a valiant attempt to render this complex and confusing work. Burkhard manages well the changing tempi as reflection alternates with action, rapid dialogue with monologue. The translation remains largely faithful to the original, retaining the linguistic parallels that bind together the spheres of public and private action. The ambiguities surrounding the figure of Emperor Rudolph II – passive, withdrawn, despairing, idealistic – are well communicated, as is the impending certainty of chaos with the appearance of Wallenstein and the anticipation of a war lasting 30 years.

As always, BURKHARD (*The Jewess of Toledo*, 1953) maintains a high degree of accuracy in his version of *Die Jüdin von Toledo*, but on balance this is one of his less successful translations. While the later acts convey King Alphons's repentance for the neglect of his country's interests and his sense of submission to higher duty, the earlier acts are less persuasive in conveying the quasi-daemonic aspect of Rahel as temptress. Equally the comic touches of a highly politically incorrect nature relating to Rahel's father Isaak seem laboured.

On reading *Sappho*, Byron remarked that while the name of Grillparzer presented difficulties of pronunciation, the world would nevertheless have to learn to pronounce it. It was a prediction that time has proved to be largely false. While Stevens, Burkhard and a few others have tried to make the works available to a wider public, the contribution of this major writer to the literature of the first half of the 19th century remains, outside the German-speaking area, essentially unknown beyond academic circles.

MARK G. WARD

Further Reading

Burkhard, A., *Grillparzer in England and America*, Vienna: Bergland, 1961

Jacob Grimm 1785–1863 and Wilhelm Grimm 1786–1859

German philologists, literary scholars and editors of folk tales

Biography

Jacob and Wilhelm Grimm were born in Hanau, Germany, Jacob 4 January 1785 and Wilhelm 24 February 1786. They both attended the Kassel Lyceum (Jacob 1798–1802; Wilhelm 1798–1803) and studied law at the university of Marburg (Jacob 1802–05; Wilhelm 1803–06). In 1806 Jacob entered the Hessian civil service in Kassel; two years later he became librarian of King Jérôme Bonaparte of Westphalia's private library at Wilhelmshöhe. He was legation secretary for the Hessian delegation at the Congress of Vienna, 1814–15. Jacob and Wilhelm both had librarians' posts in Kassel from 1815/16 to 1829. Both brothers received an honorary doctorate in 1819 from the University of Marburg. Both were professors at the University of Göttingen, 1830–37, and both, like five other professors, were dismissed from the university for their liberal political opinions (1837). They then went to live in Kassel from 1837 to 1841, the year in which both became members of the Berlin Academy of Science. In 1848 Jacob was elected to the Frankfurt parliament. Wilhelm married in 1825 (one daughter and three sons); Jacob did not marry but lived with Wilhelm and his family.

Though they are universally remembered for collecting and editing the *Kinder- und Haus-Märchen* [Tales for Children and the Home] (*Tales*), 1812–15, their main concerns were more austerely academic. Together and separately they produced and edited numerous texts on German language and literature. Jacob notably published a history of the German language (*Geschichte der deutschen Sprache*, 1848) and a pioneering historical grammar (*Deutsche Grammatik*, 1819–37) and formulated the celebrated Grimm's Law on Germanic consonantal mutations. Wilhelm edited many medieval texts. Together they started on a German dictionary (*Deutsches Wörterbuch*, 1854, eventually completed 1961). They died in Berlin, Wilhelm, the younger, first, 16 December 1859, Jacob 20 September 1863.

Tales

Kinder- und Haus-Märchen, 1812–15

Translations

For the translation history of the Grimms' *Kinder- und Haus-Märchen* several of the early editions of the German text are important. The first edition was published in two volumes by G. Reimer at Berlin in 1812–15, with subsequent editions, successively enlarged and revised by Wilhelm Grimm, in 1819–22, 1837, 1841, 1843, 1850, 1856–57 (the last to appear during the brothers' lifetime) and 1864. The "small edition", first published in 1825 and reissued in 1833, 1836, 1839, 1841, 1844, 1847, 1850, 1853, 1858, and 1864, is also important. The best among the many modern German editions are: *Kinder- und Hausmärchen der Brüder Grimm*, edited by Friedrich Panzer, Wiesbaden and Berlin: Vollmer, 1963, 1975, new edition with an afterword by Peter Dettmering, Eschborn: Klotz, 1999 (based on the first edition of 1812–15); *Brüder Grimm, Kinder- und Hausmärchen: Nach der zweiten vermehrten und verbesserten Auflage von 1819*, edited by Heinz Rölleke, 2 vols, Cologne: Diederichs, 1982 (based on the second edition of 1819); and *Brüder Grimm, Kinder- und Hausmärchen: Ausgabe letzter Hand*, edited by Heinz Rölleke, 3 vols, Stuttgart: Reclam, 1980, revised 1982 (based on the seventh edition of 1856–57).

Alderson, Brian, *Popular Folk Tales*, New York: Doubleday, and London: Gollancz 1978

Anonymous [Edgar Taylor *et al.*], *German Popular Stories, Translated from the Kinder und Haus Märchen, collected by M.M. Grimm, from Oral Tradition*, 2 vols, London: C. Baldwyn, 1823–26; 2nd edition, 1829; reprinted London: 1904; Harmondsworth: Penguin, 1971; facsimile of the 1823 and 1826 volumes, London: Scolar Press, 1977; reprinted 1979

Crane, Lucy, *Household Stories from the Collection of the Brothers Grimm*, illustrated by Walter Crane, London: Macmillan, 1882; numerous subsequent editions

Hunt, Margaret, *Grimm's Household Tales with the Author's Notes*, with an introduction by Andrew Lang, 2 vols, London: Bell, 1884; numerous subsequent editions, in whole or in part, sometimes under the name of the translator, sometimes anonymously, in many guises, e.g. *Grimm's Fairy Tales: Complete Edition*, translated by Margaret Hunt, revised by James Stern, New York: Pantheon, 1944; reprinted with an introduction by Padraic Colum, with a folkloristic commentary by Joseph Campbell, New York: Pantheon, 1975; *Household Tales by the Brothers Grimm*, illustrated by Mervyn Peake, London: Eyre and Spottiswoode, 1946; reissued London: Bibliophile, 1984

Luke, David, *Selected Tales*, Harmondsworth and New York: Penguin, 1982

Manheim, Ralph, *Grimms' Tales for Young and Old: The Complete Stories*, New York: Doubleday, and London: Gollancz, 1977

Paull, Mrs H.H.B., *Grimm's Fairy Tales*, London: Warne, and New York: Scribner, 1868

Taylor, Edgar, *Gammer Grethel; or, German Fairy Tales, and Popular Stories, from the Collection of MM. Grimm, and Other Sources*, London: John Green, 1839; as *German Popular Stories and Fairy Tales as Told by Gammer Grethel*, 3rd revised edition, London: Bell, 1878

Taylor, John Edward, *The Fairy Ring: A New Collection of Popular Tales, translated from the German of Jacob and Wilhelm Grimm*, London: John Murray, 1846; Philadelphia: A. Hart, 1854

Wehnert, Edward H., *Household Stories*, 2 vols, London: Addey, 1852–53

Zipes, Jack, *The Complete Fairy Tales of the Brothers Grimm*, New York: Bantam, 1987

For a tentative bibliography of early translations, including selections and adaptations, into English see:

Morgan, Bayard Quincy, *A Critical Bibliography of German Literature in English Translation 1481–1927; Supplement 1928–1955*, New York: Scarecrow Press, 1965 (see items 3133–3501, and in *Supplement*, S3133–S3501–64)

The Brothers Grimm are known throughout the world for their collection of tales, although they themselves – especially Jacob – regarded this as only a minor aspect of their work. The printed catalogue of the British Library lists some 300 translations (excluding adaptations) of the collection, that of the Library of Congress over 500, and more – whether translations of the whole collection or only of a single story – are added each year. The most extensive collections of German editions and foreign translations in Germany are probably those at the Brüder-Grimm-Museum, Kassel, and at the Deutsche Bücherei, Leipzig. There is no comprehensive bibliography of editions, selections and adaptations of the *Tales*. The picture is made more complicated by books that mingle the Grimms' texts with tales from other sources such as Hans Christian Andersen's *Eventyr og Historier* [Tales and Stories], published between 1835 and 1872, which have rivalled the Grimms' *Tales* for popularity.

Jacob and Wilhelm Grimm began collecting their material in 1806/07 in order to document folklore. It was an enterprise characteristic of the Romantic age, for it was stimulated by current scholarly and antiquarian interest in traditional folk poetry fostered by men like Johann Gottfried Herder and Ludwig Tieck and encouraged not least by Achim von Arnim's and Clemens Brentano's collection of folk poems, *Des Knaben Wunderhorn* (1805–08). The initial appeal of the tales in Germany must also be seen against the background of the transmission of fairytales from France (Charles Perrault) and the Orient (*The Arabian Nights*), and indeed the Grimms themselves were fully aware that many of their tales represented no more than German variants of widespread folktale types. Other factors conducive to their success were the emergence in Germany of a narrative literature for children; and the imaginative use of fairytale themes and structures in the contemporary Romantic novella or other literary genres. Nor must the political dimension of the Grimms' enterprise be overlooked: like other aspects of their work, their collecting and publication of folktales and songs proved to be a powerful element in the development of national consciousness.

The translation history of the *Tales* is complicated by the fact that the Grimms' own collection underwent continuous revision and expansion. The first volume of their collection, entitled *Kinder- und Haus-Märchen* [Tales for Children and the Home], published by Georg Andreas Reimer at Berlin in 1812, contains 86 items, the second volume, published in 1815, a further 70. The brothers continued to add to the collection, though it was to Wilhelm that almost the entire responsibility for textual and stylistic revisions of the work fell from the time of the second edition (1819) onwards. By the time of the seventh edition (1856–57), the last to appear during their lifetime, the book comprised 200 numbered items (though no. 151 occurs twice and no. 105 contains three separate short stories), plus 10 *Kinderlegenden* ("Children's legends"), thus making 213 items in all. No two of the Grimms' seven editions are identical, for they sometimes used different variants of the same tale and frequently changed the tales stylistically. Consequently there is very little uniformity among the ensuing translations, not least because translators and editors have made different selections from the German material.

The earliest translation of any of the *Tales* from German was that of a small selection into Danish in 1816. In 1820 twenty of them were translated into Dutch. The first English translation did not come out until 1823. This was followed by versions in Swedish (1824), French (1830), Hungarian (1861) and Russian (1862). To date, the Grimms' *Tales* have appeared in some 70 languages, but in many cases these translations are themselves based on the English or French versions.

Grimms' *Tales* are often referred to in English as "fairytales" but such a designation is misleading, since very few of them involve creatures such as those in *A Midsummer Night's Dream*, though wish-fulfilment and magic events are a feature of the majority of them. The Grimms themselves replaced the word *Fee* ("fairy"), a foreign word in German, by the native *Zauberin* ("enchantress") in the later editions. The term "fairytale" frequently occurs in the titles of English versions, but "tales", "popular tales" and "popular stories" are regular alternatives. The first English translation, entitled *German Popular Stories, translated from the Kinder und Haus Märchen, collected by M.M. Grimm, from Oral Tradition* (1823), appeared anonymously, but it was the work of the London solicitor Edgar TAYLOR (1793–1839) and his collaborator David Jardine. As his source Taylor used not the first edition of the *Kinder- und Haus-Märchen* but the second edition of 1819, comprising 161 tales and 9 *Kinderlegenden*. From these Taylor selected only 57, plus one that he extracted from the notes in the Grimms' third volume of their second edition, which appeared in 1822. Thus he made use of little more than a third of the material the Grimms had so far published, and in several instances he combined two or more tales into one. Taylor's second volume (1826) included four tales that do not form part of the Grimms' collection at all. In making his selection he carefully eliminated any tales with a religious dimension. He also avoided references to the Devil, either by omitting the tales concerned or by altering them in some way. There was too a tendency to avoid stories that were too horrifying. He recoiled from sexuality as well: thus "Rapunzel" is not translated at all and "The Frog Prince" is drastically altered. Overall, Taylor was clearly at pains to make the stories more reassuring and less disturbing to the children whom he envisaged as readers. Thus the first English translation has a tone markedly different from that of the Grimms' text. Perhaps heeding Jacob Grimm's advice that story-tellers should avoid being "dry and pedantic", Taylor translated rather freely, rearranging plots and characters in the process, but otherwise the style and spirit are good, though perhaps inevitably in a translation from a written source one misses the authentic oral tone. Nevertheless Taylor does succeed in capturing the true rhythms of English prose, and the Grimms themselves recognized that they were well served by him.

An important feature of Taylor's book is that, unlike the German original, it was illustrated. No less an artist than George Cruikshank (1792–1878) provided 12 etchings for the first volume and 10 for the second. These contributed greatly to the book's popularity, and indeed the Grimms themselves were so impressed that they encouraged their brother Ludwig Emil Grimm to provide illustrations for the *Kleine Ausgabe* ("Small Edition") which came out in 1825. It was this edition, prepared entirely by Wilhelm Grimm, that established the *Tales* as a children's book in Germany. George Cruikshank's illustrations and Taylor's translation were reissued as a Puffin Book by Penguin as recently as 1948. In general it may be said that many of the English editions of Grimms' *Tales* are at least as remarkable for their illustrations as for the translations: those illustrated by Walter Crane (CRANE, 1882) and Mervyn Peake (HUNT, 1946) are cases in point.

In 1839 TAYLOR's translation came out again, under the title *Gammer Grethel; or, German Fairy Tales, and Popular Stories, from the collection of MM. Grimm, and Other Sources*. The new title is appropriate, since this is in fact quite a new book, most of the translations having been substantially revised. But beyond that, the selection and arrangement of tales are different too: there are 42 stories grouped into 12 "evenings". Cruikshank's etchings have been replaced by wood-engravings based on them by John Byfield. This new text was reprinted in 1849 in Bohn's Illustrated Library and reissued in 1888 and 1897 by George Bell and Sons.

Meanwhile Taylor's original translation continued to be reprinted. The first American version (1828) copied from it betrays the publisher's woeful ignorance of German: his printer misreads Taylor's subtitle as *Rinder und Hans Marchen* (which would mean "Cattle and Hans tales"!). In England Taylor's version appeared with stereotype reproductions of Cruikshank's illustrations, with a 10-page introduction by John Ruskin (London: John Camden Hotten, 1869; reissued by Chatto and Windus, 1884). Taylor's translation, even when reprinted without his name, is easily recognizable by the characteristic titles of several tales, e.g. "Rose-bud" ("Dornröschen", generally known today as "Sleeping Beauty"), and "Snowdrop" ("Schneewittchen", more familiar – not least thanks to Walt Disney – as "Snow White").

Edgar Taylor's translation was made long before the *Kinder- und Haus-Märchen* had taken their final shape. In 1846 John Edward TAYLOR, a cousin of Edgar and a London printer, published a further selection of 43 tales under the title *The Fairy Ring*, basing his translation on the fifth German edition of 1843. The translation takes various liberties with the text. Between them the two Taylors ensured that the Grimms' *Tales* became established as a favourite of the English-reading public.

All the early English translations offered only a selection from the Grimms' collection. Much fuller than the Taylors' was the two-volume *Household Stories*, apparently translated by the illustrator Edward H. WEHNERT (1852–53); this comprised 191 tales and five of the children's legends, the text being taken from the sixth German edition of 1850, the few texts omitted being mostly ones with a religious dimension, for as the preface puts it: "The mixture of sacred subjects with profane, though frequent in Germany, would not meet with favour in an English book". This edition was lavishly illustrated with 240 pictures (including 36 full-page ones) by Wehnert, remarkable for the sentimentality and reassurance they exude. These illustrations were later reissued in colour by George Routledge and Co. Mrs H.H.B. PAULL's *Grimm's Fairy Tales* (1868), with 130 stories, may well have been "specially adapted and arranged for young people", but the translator takes unwarrantable liberties. Lucy CRANE's translation (1882) contains only 52 tales. The 1884 translation by Margaret HUNT, published with an introduction by the eminent folklorist Andrew Lang, has long been considered the best in English, since it was more complete and more accurate than most, even though one misses again a genuine oral narrative style. Hunt's edition also included a selection of the Grimms' notes, which made it valuable to scholars with insufficient German to read the original. Hunt's translation provided the textual basis for many later editions and selections well into the mid-20th century, which, however, has not deterred others from trying their hand. Other translators, now mostly forgotten, include A. Gardiner (1889), Mrs Edgar Lucas (1900), Beatrice Marshall (1900), N.J. Davidson (1906), L.L. Weedon (1910), Ernest Beeson (1916), Marian Edwardes (1922), Eleanor Quarrie (1949), Virginia Haviland (1959), F.P. Magoun Jr and Alexander Krappe (1960), Lotte Baumann (1966), Lore Segal and Randall Jarrell (1973).

More recent translators such as Ralph MANHEIM, Brian ALDERSON, David LUKE, and Jack ZIPES have striven not only to provide an accurate translation but also to recapture the authentic oral tone of the original. MANHEIM's *Grimms' Tales for Young and Old* (1977), which follows the 1819 text, was the first complete rendering into 20th-century English. While ZIPES (1987) used colloquial American style in his version, ALDERSON, who published 33 of the stories as an illustrated children's book in 1978, gave some of Grimms' dialect tales a regional English colouring, an idea taken up by LUKE whose 1982 selection of 65 tales (based on the 1857 text) includes Gilbert MCKAY's renderings of six of the Grimms' Low German tales (such as "Von den Fischer un siine Fru") into northeast Lowland Scots and Philip SCHOFIELD's translations of two Austrian and Swiss tales into an Irish idiom.

JOHN L. FLOOD

See also the entry Children's Literature in English Translation

Further Reading

Alderson, Brian, "The Spoken and the Read: *German Popular Stories* and English Popular Diction" in *The Reception of Grimms' Fairy Tales: Responses, Reactions, Revisions*, edited by Donald Haase, Detroit: Wayne State University Press, 1993, pp. 59–77

Blamires, David, "The Early Reception of the Grimms' *Kinder- und Hausmärchen* in England", *Bulletin of the John Rylands University Library of Manchester*, 71/3 (1989) pp. 53–77

Bottigheimer, Ruth B., *Grimms' Bad Girls and Bold Boys: The Moral and Social Vision of the "Tales"*, New Haven, Connecticut and London: Yale University Press, 1987

Briggs, Katharine M., "The Influence of the Brothers Grimm in England" in *Brüder Grimm Gedenken 1963. Gedenkschrift zur 100. Wiederkehr des Todestages von Jacob Grimm*, edited by Gerhard Heilfurth, Ludwig Deneke and Ina-Maria Greverus, Marburg: Elwert, 1963 (especially informative about Edgar Taylor)

Crane, T.F., "The External History of the *Kinder- und Hausmärchen* of the Brothers Grimm", *Modern Philology*, 14 (1916–17) pp. 577–610, and 15 (1918–19) pp. 65–77 and pp. 355–83

Haase, Donald (editor), *The Reception of Grimms' Fairy Tales: Responses, Reactions, Revisions*, Detroit: Wayne State University Press, 1993

Hand, Wayland D., "Die Märchen der Brüder Grimm in den Vereinigten Staaten" in *Brüder Grimm Gedenken 1963*,

edited by Ludwig Denecke and Ina-Maria Greverus, Marburg: Elwert, 1963
Hartwig, Otto, "Zur ersten englischen Übersetzung der KHM der Brüder Grimm", *Centralblatt für Bibliothekswesen*, 15 (1898) pp. 1–16 (on Edgar Taylor's first edition)
Hearne, Betsy, "Booking the Brothers Grimm: Art, Adaptations, and Economics" in *The Brothers Grimm and Folktale*, edited by James M. McGlathery *et al.*, Urbana: University of Illinois Press, 1988
Kamenetsky, Christa, *The Brothers Grimm and Their Critics: Folktales and the Quest for Meaning*, Athens: Ohio University Press, 1992
McGlathery, James M., *Grimms' Fairy Tales: A History of Criticism on a Popular Classic*, Columbia, South Carolina: Camden House, 1993
Michaelis-Jena, Ruth, *The Brothers Grimm*, London: Routledge and Kegan Paul, 1970
Michaelis-Jena, Ruth, "Edgar and John Edward Taylor, die ersten englischen Übersetzer der Kinder- und Hausmärchen" in *Brüder Grimm Gedenken 2*, edited by Ludwig Denecke, Marburg: Elwert, 1975
Sutton, Martin, *The Sin-Complex: A Critical Study of English Versions of the Grimms' Kinder- und Hausmärchen in the Nineteenth Century*, Kassel: Brüder-Grimm-Gesellschaft, 1996
Sutton, Martin, Elglischsprachige Rezeption der Grimmschen Märchen im 19. Jahrhundert" in *Brüder Grimm Gedenken 12*, edited by Ruth Reiher and Berthold Friemel, Stuttgart and Leipzig: Hirzel, 1997
Sutton, Martin, "Ein neu bearbeitetes Inhaltsverzeichnis der ersten englischen Übersetzungen der Kinder- und Hausmärchen von Edgar Taylor" in *Brüder Grimm Gedenken 13*, edited by Berthold Friemel, Stuttgart and Leipzig: Hirzel, 1999
Tatar, Maria, *The Hard Facts of the Grimms' Fairy Tales*, Princeton, New Jersey: Princeton University Press 1987
Zipes, Jack, *The Brothers Grimm: From Enchanted Forests to the Modern World*, New York and London: Routledge, 1988
Zirnbauer, Heinz, "Grimms Märchen mit englischen Augen. Eine Studie zur Entwicklung der Illustration von Grimms Märchen in englischer Übersetzung von 1823 bis 1870" in *Brüder Grimm Gedenken 2*, edited by Ludwig Denecke, Marburg: Elwert, 1975 (on Cruikshank's illustrations)

Group Translation

To many, the phrase "group translation" may at first seem like a contradiction in terms, for, like all kinds of writing, the act of translation is traditionally a solitary act, seeming to demand a depth of concentration and reflection that one can achieve only alone. But after participating in several group translation projects, the present writer was surprised to find that they actually work quite well. The experience is certainly very different from that of working alone and it is not suggested here that group efforts could or should replace the more familiar approach, but, for both process and product, group translation has some valuable differences to offer.

The group project in which I have most often been involved began at the Foundation Royaumont, just north of Paris, some 15 years ago. With two or three workshops a year, the program has resulted in the publication of French translations of about 40 books from at least eight languages. Started, and still run by Rémy Hourcade, the director of the Centre de Poésie et Traduction at Royaumont, and poet and translator Emmanuel Hocquard, the project originated in the desire to see texts available in foreign languages while they were still fresh news in their original. Hocquard, in particular, felt that the time lag, often as much as a generation or more, was hindering attempts at a true cross-cultural conversation and ultimately preventing contemporary poetry from attaining an internationalism that could have positive effects beyond the field of literature itself. Translating in a workshop format, he felt, would greatly diminish this time gap.

The format of the Royaumont program brings the original poet together with four to six poet/translators bilingual in French and the source language of the relevant text for four days, during which the group goes through a chosen text line by line. One person suggests an initial translation of a line; another suggests a modification – sometimes of a word or phrase, sometimes of the entire line; another modifies that, and so on, with frequent questions addressed to the original writer, until a consensus is reached.

Positive group dynamics is obviously crucial; a general sense of goodwill must exist or nothing gets done, but, as it has turned out, that is very rarely a problem, for two reasons. One, everyone involved is aware of the process before it begins and realizes that it requires a lot of compromise, and, two, the process is, at its base, about decentering authorship.

Translation by any means is at one remove from the individual investment of creative writing; the translator is always necessarily sharing his or her voice. And in this case, because all the translators involved are poets themselves, it can be assumed that they are exercising their needs for personal expression elsewhere, but in any case, translation by group takes the investment to yet another remove – no one feels the responsibility of authorship, with all its problems of pride and image, because, ultimately, no one's voice is individual. At any moment, there are three or four voices in the air, so that after a few hours, a truly communal voice begins to emerge.

Also, the various voices are usually speaking some combination of both the target and the original languages, releasing communication from the limits of a single language and letting it float in a more open "between". Thus Walter Benjamin's "laws of fidelity in the freedom of linguistic flux" take over; the group must recognize and depend on a constancy of sense and sensation in the midst of two languages thrown into a state of constant motion, a kind of continual construction. As a result, participants move their focus from the end product to the process required to create it. In general, the group format makes the process of translation more apparent, which has benefits for the workshop's target texts, but also for the individual translators, who return to their private work with a heightened attention to the interesting and important moments between the original and their translation.

Group translation also has the advantage of making available more alternatives to any given line than a single translator could produce. Often, a given suggestion may not be useful in itself, but will allow another person to start thinking in a useful direction. It is as simple as working with more raw material. With several people thinking and suggesting and replacing together, the text can effectively go from a first to a third or fourth draft in a single session. And though it is untraceable and intangible, the energy created by such exchange does seem to emanate from the final version.

There are two other "rules to the game" that play a large part in its success: one, the writer of the original always has the final say (a right exercisable, clearly, only to the degree that he or she knows the target language) and, two, a single member of the group is chosen at the end to take charge of the translation – to polish it, make it internally consistent, and prepare it for publication.

The Royaumont project has inspired poets in other countries to establish similar centres; at present, they form a network with projects running regularly in Portugal, Ireland, Romania, Greece and Turkey. A slightly different program, also inspired by Royaumont, has been running in the United States at Louisiana State University in Baton Rouge under the direction of Nathaniel Wing.

One of the most important aspects of these group translation projects has been their contribution to the notion of an international poetic community. In direct opposition to the isolation of the lone writer and lone translator, they bring poetry from various countries together in a single room and encourage an exchange of ideas, not only about poetry and translation, but also about aesthetics in a wider sense and about practical issues such as funding, project administration and other logistical concerns. On an individual level, these projects encourage friendship, offering a basis for a human community that reminds the translator that he or she is not alone but is connected to others with similar affections and goals.

Though the practice of group translation is not, at the moment, widespread, the opportunities it offers to examine the translation process in more depth, to foster greater literary exchange and to encourage a sense of community among translators and writers makes it a valuable aspect of contemporary translation practice.

COLE SWENSEN

Battista Guarini 1538–1612

Italian poet and diplomat

Biography

Born in Ferrara, 10 December 1538. Guarini came from an educated and distinguished Veronese family, and probably studied at Padua. By 1557 he was professor of rhetoric at Ferrara. He was a member of the Accademia degli Eterei in Padua from 1564, and in 1567 he became a courtier and diplomat in the service of Alfonso II, duke of Ferrara. He met Torquato Tasso, the court poet of the duke, and formed a close friendship with him. When Tasso was dismissed by the duke in 1579, Guarini took over his role as court poet in Ferrara. He lived at the family estate, the Villa Guarini, from 1582, where he wrote his most famous work, *Il pastor fido* (*The Faithful Shepherd*). Guarini was involved in diplomatic and secretarial work for the duke until 1588, travelling to Venice and Poland, and later Rome and Florence, on ambassadorial missions. In later life he was in service at the courts of Tuscany, Mantua and Urbino. His last years were spent studying and in feuds and litigation with his family, critics and others. Died in Venice, 7 October 1612.

Guarini's major work, and the one for which he became famous throughout Europe, is his pastoral tragicomedy *Il Pastor Fido* (*The Faithful Shepherd*), written during the 1580s and published in 1590. It was first performed in 1595 in Crema. Set in Arcadia, it was written in imitation of Tasso's play *Aminta* (1573), and was an immediate success: along with *Aminta*, it helped to establish the pastoral drama as a literary form and was widely performed and translated. Other work by Guarini includes his comedy *La Idropica* (*The Dropsical Lady*), 1583.

The Faithful Shepherd

Il pastor fido, 1590

A pastoral drama/tragicomedy very popular in Western Europe in the 17th century. It is often referred to by anglophone writers under its Italian title.

Translations

Anonymous [Clapperton, W.], *Il Pastor Fido ... Attempted in English Blank Verse*, Edinburgh, 1809

Dymoke, John, *Il Pastor Fido; or, The Faithful Shepheard*, London: [T.Creede] for S. Waterson, 1602

Fanshawe, Sir Richard, *Il Pastor Fido, the Faithful Shepheard*, London: R. Raworth for Humphrey Moseley, 1647; edited with an introduction by J.H. Whitfield (parallel texts), Edinburgh: Edinburgh University Press, 1976

Grove, W., *The Faithful Shepherd, A Dramatic Pastoral, Translated into English from the Pastor Fido of the Cav. Guarini, Attempted in the Manner of the Original*, London: Francis Blyth for G. Robinson, 1782

Settle, Elkanah, *Pastor Fido; or, The Faithful Shepherd: A Pastoral*, London: for William Cademan, 1677

Sheridan, Dr Thomas, *The Faithful Shepherd: A Translation of Battista Guarini's "Il Pastor Fido"*, edited and completed by Robert Hogan and Edward A. Nickerson, Newark: University of Delaware Press, and London: Associated University Presses, 1989

Sidnam, J., *Il pastor fido; or, the faithfull sheapheard*, 1630 (British Library, Add MS. 29493)

Battista Guarini's tragicomedy *Il pastor fido* (1590) owed much to Torquato Tasso's *Aminta* (1573). Like the earlier play, it is a pastoral drama set in Arcadia. Its plot is loosely based on a source in Pausanias and explores the consequences of a curse that Diana has placed upon the land because of the infidelity of a nymph. Guarini's play is much longer than *Aminta*, and its language is altogether more elaborate. On the whole *Il Pastor Fido* lacks the sheer beauty of Tasso's play, but it has new elements to add to the genre – notably a greater humour and a fuller understanding of human sensuality. The play's juxtaposition of elements from comedy and tragedy was seen as an affront to classical ideas of decorum, and provoked heated debate – Guarini's own contributions to which were gathered in his *Compendio della poesia tragicomica* (1601).

The identity of the first English translator of *Pastor Fido* is not certain. The anonymous translator appears – from the prefatory material – to have been a relation of Sir Edward Dymoke, and was probably John DYMOKE (1602). This first translation is frequently inaccurate and omits as much as a third of the original – most frequently the translator ignores passages of particular difficulty. It is sadly pedestrian and graceless in manner, and does no justice to the stylistic sophistication of the original. In ponderous blank verse, for the most part, it offers no response to Guarini's metrical variety.

Altogether more attractive is the translation by Jonathan SIDNAM (1630), which regrettably remains unpublished, and a manuscript of which is in the British Library, dated 1630. While attempting to reproduce something of the metrical variations of Guarini, Sidnam is generally accurate and his verse is more attractive than that of his predecessor; at his best (e.g. in Corisca's soliloquy in act 1) he achieves a very plausible dramatic idiom. Following (largely) the metrical patterns of Guarini sometimes involves some rather irritating padding.

The version by Sir Richard FANSHAWE (1647) is undoubtedly one of the finest of all English translations from the Italian. Metrically, Fanshawe makes no attempt to imitate his original. Guarini's unrhymed mixture of 11 and seven-syllable lines is replaced by rhymed iambic couplets, mostly in pentameters, occasionally in octosyllabics. He also makes considerably lighter use of rhetorical elaboration than is to be found in the original. In reducing the rhetorical mannerism of their language, Fanshawe perhaps makes the characters more obviously human than they are in Guarini himself. Partly as a consequence of his decision not to imitate Guarini's metres, Fanshawe is able to write with concision. Sir John Denham's well-known poem "To the Author of this Translation", which is prefaced to Fanshawe's version, is right to observe that "the nerves of his [Guarini's] compacted strength" are not "stretch'd and dissolv'd into unsinnewed length", since there are few wasted or redundant words here. Denham assures the reader that Fanshawe confines his "spirit" to Guarini's "circle", and it is, indeed, notable that in a translation that disdains "the servile path ... of tracing word by word, and line by line" there should be so striking a fidelity to the larger spirit of the original.

SETTLE's is an adaptation of Fanshawe for the public theatre – it was performed at the Duke's Theatre, London, in 1677. Settle confesses that he knows no Italian, and seems to have been entirely dependent on Fanshawe's translation. He omits the prologue and the choruses at the end of each act; he abbreviates considerably and omits the character of the Satyr entirely (while adding Sylvano, a shepherd, and his attendant Dorco). Settle's text retains some of Fanshawe's lines and rewrites others. While interesting as a document in the history of theatrical taste, Settle's version has no independent significance as a translation of Guarini.

The translation by Thomas SHERIDAN (1989), friend of Swift and grandfather of Richard Brinsley Sheridan, was probably written in the first half of the 1730s. The manuscript is in Dublin Central Library, and remained unpublished until 1989. In the surviving manuscript, part of act 3 scene 5, the whole of scene 6, and the greater part of scene 7 are lacking. Hogan and Nickerson, as well as modernizing the spelling and punctuation of Sheridan's manuscript, supplied their own version (in imitation of Sheridan's manner) of the missing scenes (these additions are clearly marked). Sheridan uses blank verse for the play's main scenes of dialogue, and rhymed stanzas for the choruses. Sheridan's blank verse is assured and clear, his rhymed choruses occasionally a little clumsily marred by awkward inversions.

GROVE (1782) endeavours to imitate what the translator calls "the unfettered Versification" of the original. Grove's own versification does effectively mimic the range of Guarini's, but his translation is seriously undermined by the employment of coyly archaic and self-consciously poetic diction.

CLAPPERTON (1809) – like Grove – omits Guarini's prologue, which is dismissed as "tedious and uninteresting", and he tells the reader (somewhat oddly) that the "Argument" has also been omitted since it is "prejudicial to the interest of the fable". The bulk of Clapperton's translation is in blank verse (mostly very flaccid); rhyme is employed only in the choruses, where the translator's difficulties are often evident. Clapperton's blank verse is unpretentiously lucid (but quite devoid of Guarini's sparkle); his choruses are often banal.

GLYN PURSGLOVE

Further Reading

Bullough, G., "Sir Richard Fanshawe and Guarini" in *Studies in English Language and Literature presented to Karl Brunner on the Occasion of His Seventieth Birthday*, edited by Siegfried Korninger, Vienna: Braumüller, 1957, pp. 17–31

Neri, Nicoletta, *Il Pastor Fido in Inghilterra*, Turin: Università di Torino, 1963 (includes facsimile of Fanshawe's translation)

Pursglove, G., *The Poets of Ferrara in Renaissance Britain*, Ferrara: Deputazione Provinciale Ferrarese di Storia Patria, 1992

Staton, Walter F. Jr and William E. Simeone (editors), *A Critical Edition of Sir Richard Fanshawe's 1647 Translation of Giovanni Battista Guarini's Il Pastor Fido*, Oxford: Clarendon Press, 1964

Whitfield, J.H., "Sir Richard Fanshawe and the Faithfull Shepherd", *Italian Studies*, 19 (1964)

Lady Charlotte Guest 1812–1895

British translator, diarist and collector

Biography

Born Charlotte Elizabeth Bertie, 19 May 1812, at Uffington, Lincolnshire. She was the only daughter of Albemarle Bertie, 9th earl of Lindsey, an English gentlewoman who nevertheless gained renown primarily for her translation into English of a *Welsh* literary text, the *Mabinogion*, of seminal import to Welsh culture. Lady Charlotte became acquainted with Wales and the Welsh language following her first marriage, in 1835, to Sir Josiah John Guest, the ironmaster of Dowlais, Merthyr Tydfil. They had 10 children. She was an influential figure in Merthyr during the decades of her residence there, involving herself in educational, philanthropic and cultural projects. She became passionately interested in the Welsh language and literature, ensuring that her children were taught the language as well as setting about the task herself. Her first husband died in 1852 and in 1855 she married Charles Schreiber, former M.P. for Cheltenham and Poole. She died at Canford Manor, Dorset, 15 January 1895.

Given the fact that Lady Charlotte had been resident in Merthyr only some three years before she undertook the task of translating the medieval Welsh tales taken from the *Red Book of Hergest*, many commentators believe that her command of the language would not have been sufficient for her to have accomplished the task of translation single-handed. It has been suggested that "her part in the venture was the rendering into graceful English of her collaborators' literal translation" (see Stephens, 1998). She appears to have collaborated with two scholars and native Welsh speakers, namely John Jones, known by his bardic name of "Tegid", and Thomas Price, known as "Carnhuanawc". The former certainly provided her with a transcript from the *Red Book of Hergest*, source of the tales of the *Mabinogion*, which he had copied while a student at Jesus College, Oxford, where the manuscript was housed. "Tegid" was also an experienced translator in his own right. "Carnhuanawc" was a clergyman and a Celtic scholar, well versed in Breton as well as his native Welsh; like Lady Charlotte, he was an active champion and promoter of Welsh culture.

There is no doubt, however, that it was Lady Charlotte who was responsible for the elegant English style of the translation; evidence of this is afforded by the many pages of the manuscript in her own hand that may still be examined in "Lady Charlotte's Deed Box" currently held at the National Library of Wales, Aberystwyth. Comparison with the translation that is today regarded as the most accurate and scholarly, namely that by Gwyn and Thomas Jones, first published in 1949, shows that Lady Charlotte is generally a faithful translator. Nevertheless, she does occasionally bowdlerize her text to accord with Victorian ideas of morality. In *Branwen, Daughter of Llyr*, for example, she consistently renders the Welsh for "slept with her" or "took her to bed" as "became his bride". Surprisingly, however, Lady Charlotte's text can often be more succinct and can sound more contemporary than the translation written a century later; for instance, in the same tale, where Gwyn and Thomas Jones have "'Aye, lord,' said one, 'insult has been wrought upon thee, and it is intended that such be done thee'", Lady Charlotte has simply: "'Verily, lord,' said one, 'it was an insult unto thee, and as such was it meant'."

One of the reasons for the slight bowdlerization was that Lady Charlotte envisaged some of the recipients of the tales as being children; indeed, she undertook the translation, at least partly, because she was eager to inculcate an enthusiasm for Welsh literature in the minds of the young. This included her own, increasingly numerous, offspring: the first complete published text of the *Mabinogion* collection, which appeared in 1849, was dedicated to her sons, Ivor and Merthyr, with the words, "Infants as you yet are, I feel that I cannot dedicate more fitly than to you these venerable relics of ancient lore, and I do so in the hope of inciting you to cultivate the literature of 'Gwyllt Walia', in whose beautiful language you are being initiated, and amongst whose free mountains you were born."

These words announce clearly that Lady Charlotte performed her translating labours under the influence of English Romantic images both of "Wild Wales" and of medieval culture, for she goes on to recommend to her sons the "chivalry" and "sense of honour" that she detects in the tales. Her translation includes not only the tales of the so-called Four Branches of the *Mabinogion* proper, namely *Pwyll, Branwen, Manawydan* and *Math*, but also the Arthurian and other romances found in the *Red Book of Hergest,* such as *The Lady of the Fountain* and *The Dream of Rhonabwy.*

The title *Mabinogion* is notoriously a mistake on the part of Lady Charlotte, who wrongly adopted, perhaps because *-ion* is a common Welsh plural ending, what seems to have been a scribal error which occurs only once in the whole of the original text. The correct form is, in fact, *Mabinogi.* The meaning and origin of the term itself is still in dispute by Welsh scholars, but it seems to indicate the story of a hero's maturation, the word obviously being cognate with *mab*, the word for son, boy or youth.

The tales of the *Mabinogion* are tales of wonder and fantasy, which have their origin in a long oral tradition. Though the *Red Book of Hergest* dates from the late 14th century, the tales are certainly of much earlier origin, perhaps the mid-11th century, while the tale entitled *Culhwch and Olwen* is earlier still. Apart from their enduring fascination as literature, these tales are also remarkable in the canon of medieval literature for being couched in prose, rather than verse, which would have been the normal medium for imaginative expression.

Lady Charlotte's translation was highly influential during the Victorian period. It was a direct and acknowledged source of inspiration both for Tennyson's *Idylls of the King* (1856) and for Matthew Arnold's *Lectures on Celtic Literature* (1865). Lady Charlotte undertook no further translations, however. In later life, after her second marriage in 1855, when she became Lady Charlotte Schreiber, she concentrated her manifold energies on her extensive collections of art objects, publishing two books inspired by these. She also kept a lively and fascinating journal throughout her life, leaving a record of a formidable Victorian Englishwoman who performed a valuable service to the culture of Wales in her time.

KATIE GRAMICH

Further Reading

Bessborough, Earl of (editor), *The Diaries of Lady Charlotte Guest*, London: John Murray, 1950

Bessborough, Earl of (editor), *Lady Charlotte Schreiber 1853–1891*, London: John Murray, 1952

Bromwich, Rachel, "The Mabinogion and Lady Charlotte Guest", *Transactions of the Honourable Society of Cymmrodorion*, 1986

Davies, Sioned (translator), *The Four Branches of the Mabinogi*, Llandysul: Gomer Press, 1993

Ford, Patrick K. (translator), *The Mabinogi and Other Medieval Welsh Tales*, Berkeley: University of California Press, 1977

Gantz, Jeffrey, *The Mabinogion*, Harmondsworth and New York: Penguin, 1976

Guest, Lady Charlotte, *The Mabinogion: From the Llyfr Coch o Hergest and Other Ancient Welsh Manuscripts*, 3 vols, London, 1849; 2nd edition London: Quaritch, 1877

Guest, Charlotte, *Mabinogion Tales*, with illustrations by Jo Nathan, and an introduction by Owen Edwards, Felinfach: Llanerch, 1990

Guest, Revel and Angela V. John, *Lady Charlotte: A Biography of the Nineteenth Century*, London: Weidenfeld and Nicolson, 1989

Ifans, Dafydd and Rhiannon Ifans, *Y Mabinogion* (version in modern Welsh), Llandysul: Gomer Press, 1980

Jones, Gwyn and Thomas Jones, *The Mabinogion,* London: Dent, and New York: Dutton, 1949

Mac Cana, Proinsias, *The Mabinogion*, Cardiff: University of Wales Press, 1977

Stephens, Meic (editor), *The New Companion to the Literature of Wales*, Cardiff: University of Wales Press, 1998

Jorge Guillén 1893–1984

Spanish poet

Biography

Born in Valladolid, 18 January 1893. He was first educated in Valladolid; he spent two years after secondary school in Switzerland (1909–11), was a student in the Faculty of Philosophy and Letters at Madrid University (1911–13) and received his first degree from the University of Granada in 1913. He spent the next year in Germany, then returned to live in Spain until 1917. He taught Spanish as a lector at the Sorbonne in Paris (1917–23) and at Oxford University (1929–31). In 1936 he had political problems arising from the circumstances of the Spanish Civil War; Guillén found it impossible to compromise with dictatorship and finally was imprisoned in Pamplona. After his release the Ministry of Education prevented him from holding teaching posts of any kind – so in 1938 he left Spain for North America, where he taught Spanish literature until 1958, with frequent trips to South America and Europe. After receiving many literary prizes, awarded by both European and American bodies, and after his second marriage (1961; his first wife had died in 1947) he returned to Spain. In 1976 he was awarded the Cervantes Prize (1977). He died in Málaga, 6 February 1984.

Translations

Poetry (selections and anthologies)

di Giovanni, Norman Thomas, *Cántico: A Selection*, with an introduction by Guillén, London: Deutsch, and Boston: Little Brown, 1965

Gibbons, Reginald and Anthony L. Geist, *Guillén on Guillén: The Poetry and the Poet*, with an introduction, Princeton, New Jersey: Princeton University Press, 1979

Guillén, Jorge, in his *Language and Poetry: Some Poets of Spain*, Cambridge, Massachusetts: Harvard University Press, 1961

Matthews, Elizabeth, *The Structured World of Jorge Guillén*, Liverpool: Cairns, 1985 (contains 12 poems from *Cántico* and *Clamor*)

Palley, Julian, in his *Affirmation: A Bilingual Anthology, 1919–1966*, with an introduction by Guillén, Norman: University of Oklahoma Press, 1968

Turnbull, Eleanor L., in her *Contemporary Spanish Poetry: Selections from Ten Poets* (bilingual edition), Baltimore: Johns Hopkins University Press, 1945

The poets of Jorge Guillén's generation were concerned with achieving exact forms of expression: technical ability was sought after, for it was necessary to express ideas with clarity and precision. Guillén was careful to make clear, however, that here was no "empty formalism". His use of Spanish metres did not arise through mere imitation but was the result of detailed study and comprehension of the significance of certain verse forms and literary devices. In particular, the cultivation of the metaphor was of supreme importance in Guillén's poems. He had a strong faith in the power of words, not merely to give aesthetic pleasure but to communicate. He always rejected "pure poetry" in favour of "el poema con poesía y otras cosas humanas" (the poem with poetry and other human things) and it is this human dimension and his positive attitude to the world that are characteristic of the whole of his work. There is little or nothing of conventional religious belief in his poetry, but there is notable reference to both the natural world and to human beings.

His basic poetic production consists of *Cántico* [Canticle], eventually subtitled "Fe de vida" (i.e. a document that proves one is alive – a proof of existence), which took him about 30 years to complete and was published in 1928, with enlarged editions in 1936 and in 1945, and a complete edition in 1950; *Clamor* [Clamor], with the subtitle "Tiempo de historia" [Time of History], in three volumes published in 1957, 1960 and 1963; and *Homenaje* [Homage], subtitled "Reunión de vidas" [Reunion of lives] (1967). These three were published together in 1968 as *Aire nuestra* [Our Air]. His last two major volumes were *Y otras poems* [And Other Poems] (1973) and *Final* [Finale] (1981). After 1936 Guillén's work was published outside Spain, but in the late 1970s, with the involvement of the Barral publishing house of Barcelona not only in *Final* but in the re-publication of the four previous main volumes of Guillén's poetry, full recognition of the great poet began. In 1976 (Franco had died in 1975) the first official Spanish homage to the internationally honoured Guillén was paid, with the award to him of the Cervantes Prize.

Canticle has been the most translated volume of Guillén's poetry. Italian translations are very numerous in comparison with those in French, English and German. *Canticle* is a hymn of praise, of joy, to the natural world of creation and its essential goodness. There is a "dialogue" between man and the world and man uses his senses and intellect to participate creatively in that dialogue. Guillén exalts man and his relationship to the natural world. If the vision of man in *Canticle* is ideal, the vision of man in *Clamor* is realistic but positive; here chaos and disorder appear as part of man's existence. The principal theme of the poem is embodied in an exhortation "to be human"; in being human we find our salvation. *Homage*, as the title implies, is a homage to the creative writers and philosophers who have contributed to man's existence by means of the written word.

None of Guillén's volumes of poetry has been translated in its entirety; translations are based on anthologies and selections of his poetry. In *Language and Poetry* (GUILLÉN, 1961) the author himself provides the reader with comments on and translations of his poems and gives an excellent summary of his poetic aims. He also wrote an introduction to the translation of the selection from *Canticle* by DI GIOVANNI (1965) and to the *Anthology* by PALLEY (1968).

TURNBULL's translation (1945) of a selection from *Canticle* is close and accurate, respectful of the source text; it has Spanish originals and reminiscences of the poets by Pedro Salinas.

GIBBONS & GEIST's *Guillén on Guillén* (1979) was assembled out of several hours of tape recordings of Guillén reading an anthology, selected by himself, of poems from the books then available, with commentaries by him. The Spanish text of both poems and commentaries is translated into English with a succinct and stimulating introduction.

MATTHEWS's translation (1985) of 12 major poems from *Canticle* and *Clamor* provides the reader with a substantial example of these two first books of poetry. She does not introduce unnecessary interpretation, seeking always to render the Spanish as directly as possible, with occasional changes in word order according to the requirements of English syntax. She does not translate the titles.

EVA NÚÑEZ MÉNDEZ

Further Reading

Bates, M., "Notes on a Translation of J. Guillén's Primavera delgada" in *Linguistic and Literary Studies in Honor of Helmut A. Hatzfeld*, Washington, DC: Catholic University of America Press, 1964

Debicki, A.P., "Jorge Guillén's *Cántico*", *PMLA*, 81 (1966) pp. 439–45

Havard, R.G., "The Early décimas of Jorge Guillén", *Bulletin of Hispanic Studies*, 48 (1971) pp. 111–27

Havard, Robert, *Jorge Guillén: Cántico*, London: Grant and Cutler / Tamésis, 1986

Havard, Robert, *From Romanticism to Surrealism: Seven Spanish Poets*, Cardiff: University of Wales Press, 1988

Ivask, Ivor and Juan Marichal (editors), *Luminous Reality: The Poetry of Jorge Guillén*, Norman: University of Oklahoma Press, 1969

MacCurdy, G. Grant, *Jorge Guillén*, Boston: Twayne, 1982

Morris, C.B., *A Generation of Spanish Poets, 1920–1936*, Cambridge: Cambridge University Press, 1969

Pleak, Frances Avery, *The Poetry of Jorge Guillén*, Princeton, New Jersey: Princeton University Press, 1942

Young, H.T., "Jorge Guillén and the Language of Poetry", *Hispania*, 46 (1963) pp. 66–70

João Guimarães Rosa 1908–1967

Brazilian novelist and short-story writer

Biography

Born in Cordisburgo, Minas Gerais, 27 June 1908. Guimarães Rosa's fiction represented a vital turning point in 20th-century Brazilian literature. Breaking out of the confines of the social realism that prevailed in the 1920s and 1930s, he explored deeper levels of human experience in his writing while radically renovating form and language. His knowledge of the life and culture of the backlands or *sertão* of the region, acquired while working there as a young doctor, provided him with much of the material for his work. His first collection of stories, for example, entitled *Sagarana* (1946), examined the life and emotions of the *sertão* inhabitants. Highly innovative, it had an enormous impact on Brazilian writing, but it is for his only novel, *The Devil to Pay in the Backlands* (1956; translated in 1963), that he is best known.

From the mid-1930s he worked as an official in government ministries and in the Brazilian diplomatic service, residing in Paris 1949–51. He died in Rio de Janeiro, 19 November 1967.

Translations

Novel

Grande sertão: veredas, 1956

Taylor, James L. and Harriet de Onís, *The Devil to Pay in the Backlands*, New York: Knopf, 1963

Short Stories

Sagarana, 1946

Onís, Harriet de, *Sagarana: A Cycle of Stories*, New York: Knopf, 1966 (contains "The Little Dust-Brown Donkey", "The Return of the Prodigal Husband", "The Straw-Spinners", "Duel", "Mine Own People", "Woodland Witchery", "Bulletproof", "Conversation among Oxen", "Augusto Matrogo's Hour and Time")

Primeiras estórias, 1962

Shelby, Barbara, *The Third Bank of the River and Other Stories*, New York: Knopf, 1968 (contains "The Thin Edge of Happiness", "Tartarum", "My Boss", "Substance", "Much Ado", "A Woman of Good Works","The Audacious Navigator", "Honeymoons", "A Young Man", "Gleaming White", "The Horse that Drank Beer", "Nothingness and the Human Condition", "The Mirror", "Cause and Effect", My Friend and the Fatalist", "No Man, No Woman", "Hocus Psychocus", "The Third Bank of the River", "The Dagobe Brothers", The Girl from Beyond", "Soroco, His Mother, His Daughter", "Notorious", "Treetops")

Many of João Guimarães Rosa's novellas, short stories and poems have yet to be translated into English. There are, however, translations of his most important work: *The Devil to Pay in the Backlands*, and two collections of his stories. One of the latter, however, *Sagarana*, 1946, by the translator Harriet de ONÍS, is not readily available in the United Kingdom. It consists of nine stories set in the rural interior of central Brazil, exploring the life, culture and problems of the region. Already evident in the work is the experimental use of language that would characterize the rest of his writing.

The Devil to Pay in the Backlands (*Grande sertão: veredas*, 1956) is a multidimensional novel written in the form of a monologue. It is undoubtedly one of the greatest literary achievements in the Portuguese language. The *sertão* again provides the setting, though it is a work that far transcends the regional, with its engagement with complex philosophical and moral issues, and its radical linguistic experiments. It is Rosa's concern with matters of language and style that is perhaps the dominant feature of the short stories he subsequently wrote. If the creation of a highly personal, dynamic literary language was one of Rosa's greatest achievements, it also makes his work particularly challenging for the translator.

The first-person narrator of *The Devil to Pay in the Backlands* is Riobaldo, a former bandit of the interior, who struggles to come to terms with his past life. He meditates constantly on good and evil and whether or not the devil exists, while always at the centre of his thoughts is his former companion, Diadorim, a comrade in arms whom he loved and who, after death, was discovered to be a woman. The existential dimension to the work becomes increasingly apparent as Riobaldo's thoughts lead him on a search for the meaning of his life.

Radical linguistic innovations permeate the text, making it perhaps the most difficult novel ever written in Portuguese to translate. In addition to numerous neologisms, words borrowed from other languages and syntactical experiments, the work also assimilates elements of the popular ballad and story-telling traditions of the *sertão*, which have their roots in the medieval chivalric romance. Much of the lyrical quality that results, with rhythmical prose and a range of poetic devices, has to be sacrificed by TAYLOR & ONÍS (1963) for the sake of clarity and ease of reading. They convey the sense and tone of the original in a sentence such as "At this, suddenly and clearly, there sprang up within me a powerful protest! No. Not Diadorim", but Rosa's alliteration emphasizing negation – "Num nú, nisto, nesse repente, desinterno de mim um nego forte se saltou; não. Diadorim, não!" – is inevitably lost. The translators are sometimes able to find broad equivalents in English for the onomatopoeia that is so common in the novel, using "whizzing" to translate Rosa's "pispissiu", imitating the sound of a bullet in the air, but frequently the clear description of events is prioritized over the attempt to capture the poetic force of the language. Thus, Rosa's "bala dava, zaque-zaque, empurrando o couro", referring to the bullets striking cattle hides hung up as a protective barrier, is rendered simply by "a bullet would strike and knock the hide inward".

Rosa's lexicon presents particular problems to the translators, for it is largely a personal creation, often using the roots of regional and popular terms from Brazilian Portuguese, or of words from other languages, to create neologisms. Taylor and de Onís are quite inventive in finding suitable phrasing to express the essential meaning of such words. They also use a brief glossary to explain some of the specifically Brazilian terms employed in the novel. Alterations to sentence structure, frequently linked to oral language, are perhaps the most striking feature of the novel's narrative style. Some are retained in the translation, but again the imperative for clarity and smooth reading generally necessitates restructuring and a more conventional syntax. Nevertheless, Taylor and de Onís are creative in the solutions they find for the problems posed by Rosa's highly unorthodox language. The overall result is a translation that, though inevitably unable to convey the full force, richness and originality of Rosa's writing, reads naturally in English, is remarkably free of awkward phrasing, and does succeed in conveying much of the intensity and vividness of the prose of the original. The difficulties with which the translators had to contend are discussed on pages 71 to 75 of Vincent's 1978 study, listed below.

The Third Bank of the River and Other Stories (*Primeiras estórias*, 1962) consists of 22 short stories, varied in theme, but whose protagonists generally undergo extraordinary experiences that pass beyond the bounds of social convention and, at times, rational explanation. The quest for a sense of fulfilment and of meaning to life is again a central theme, and the highly original language used, with radical changes to traditional syntax and the creation of new words, is the most striking feature of the prose. SHELBY (1968) follows the source text closely but is at times adventurous in her attempts to translate Rosa's inventive phrasing or invented words, with, for example, "hangdog head hanging down" translating the single word "cabismeditado". The results are mixed, but overall the English reads naturally, and she achieves a good balance between the need for clarity and the clear desire to convey some of the originality and colour of Rosa's prose. From her version of a story like "The Girl from Beyond", for example, the reader can well appreciate the vitality and creativity of Rosa's experiments with language. Rosa uses a range of different narrators for his stories, and Shelby expends considerable effort on capturing the specific narrative tone that results in each case. She is also adept at producing a convincing rendition of dialogue, appropriate for the varied characters concerned – children, educated professionals or poor workers from the backlands.

MARK DINNEEN

Further Reading

Coutinho, Eduardo de Faria, *The Process of Revitalization of the Language and Narrative Structure in the Fiction of João Guimarães Rosa and Julio Cortázar*, Valencia: Albatros Hispanofila, 1980

Coutinho, Eduardo de Faria, *The Synthesis Novel in Latin America: A Study of João Guimarãs Rosa's "Grande Sertão: Veredas"*, Chapel Hill: University of North Carolina Press, 1991

Perrone, Charles, "João Guimarães Rosa: An Endless Passage" in *Modern Latin American Fiction: A Survey*, edited by John King, London: Faber, 1987

Vincent, Jon S., *João Guimarães Rosa*, Boston: Twayne, 1978

H

Imīl Habībī (Émile Habiby) 1921–1996

Palestinian novelist, short-story writer, politician and journalist

Biography

Habībī was born in 1921 into a Christian family in Haifa, and attended schools in Haifa and Acre. In 1940 he became an announcer with the Palestinian Broadcasting Corporation. He was a founder member of the Palestine Communist Party, stayed in Israel after the founding of the Jewish state in 1948 and was elected several times to the Knesset. for the Israeli Communist Party, 1952–65. With others he founded the Jewish–Arab New Communist List (Rakah), 1965, and represented Rakah in the Knesset, 1965–72. He was on the editorial board of major communist publications. He began creative writing late, in reaction to the June War of 1967, in order to help preserve Palestinian identity and culture. His main works include: a 1969 short-story cycle about the June War; his most famous novel, published in 1974 and translated in 1982 as *The Secret Life of Saeed, the Ill-Fated Pessoptimist*; a play, *Luka' bin Luka'* [Luka, Son of Luka], 1980; and the 1992 novel *Sarāya bint al-Ghūl* [Saraya, the Ogre's Daughter], the second part of a trilogy. Habībī was awarded the Jerusalem Medal from the Palestine Liberation Organization in 1990, and the Israel Prize (Israel's leading cultural prize) in 1992. He died in May 1996.

Translations

Novel

al-Waqā'i' al-gharība fī ikhtifā' Sa'īd Abī al-Nahs al-mutashā'il, 1974

Jayyusi, Salma Khadra and Trevor LeGassick, *The Secret Life of Saeed, the Ill-Fated Pessoptimist: A Palestinian Who Became a Citizen of Israel*, New York: Vantage Press, 1982; London: Zed Books, 1985

Short Stories

"al-Kharaza al-Zarqā' wa-'Awdat Jubayna" in *Sudāsiyyat al-ayyām al-sitta*, 1969

Kassem, Céza and Saneya Shaarawi Lanfranchi, "The Blue Beard and the Return of Jubayna" in *Flights of Fantasy: Arabic Short Stories*, edited by Kassem and Malak Hashem, Cairo: Elias, 1985

Shaheen, Mohammad, "The Blue Charm and the Return of Jubaynah", *Journal of Arabic Literature*, 15 (1984) pp. 114–20

"Umm Rūbābīka" in *Sudāsiyyat al-Ayyām al-Sitt*, 1969

Allen, Roger and Christopher Tingley, "The Odds-and-Ends Woman" in *Anthology of Modern Palestinian Literature*, edited by Salma Khadra Jayyusi, New York: Columbia University Press, 1992

Coming from one of the most prominent Palestinian authors to continue writing from within Israel rather than in exile, Imīl Habībī's contribution to modern Arabic fiction was characterized by an unusual focus. Thematically, much of his writing derived from the situation of Arabs living in Israel, or around their relationships with their fellow-Arabs beyond the Israeli border. His style and treatment of these themes, however, is entirely distinctive: although suffused with the same underlying political commitment that also underlay his position as a Communist Arab member of the Israeli Knesset, Habībī's work is marked by a very personal brand of irony and humour, which at the same time owes a considerable amount to the Arabic classical tradition. It is this quality of humour (a feature generally poorly developed in modern Arabic literature) which has served to mark off his work from that of other Palestinian writers such as Ghassān Kanafānī and Mahmūd Darwīsh, and which probably accounts for his popularity among a wider audience. Habībī's distinctive qualities as a writer were publicly recognized in 1992 when he was awarded the Israeli Prize for Literature; criticized by many of his fellow Arab writers for accepting it, he donated the money to a Palestinian medical centre.

The complexity of the constituents of Habībī's work are well illustrated by the title of his best-known work, *al-Waqā'i 'al-gharība fī ikhtifā' Sa'īd Abī al-Nahs al-mutashā'il* (literally, "Strange events concerning the disappearance of the ill-starred Sa'īd, the Pessoptimist"), which incorporates not only a play on the name "Sa'īd" ("happy"), but also an invented word *mutashā'il*, made up from the Arabic equivalents for "optimist" and "pessimist" (*mutashī'im* and *mutafā'il* respectively) – an invention nicely captured by the "Pessoptimist" of the English version. The work itself is divided into three sections, the first and third of which are labelled "Yu'ād" (a girl's name incorporating the Arabic root meaning "to return"), while the middle section bears the title "Bāqiya" ("remaining"); in the context of the Palestinian situation, these titles have clear political overtones.

Within these three sections, Habībī's work is structured in a number of short scenes – a technique that, together with the picaresque nature of the narrative, recalls the Arabic classical literary genre of the *maqāmāt* (rhyming prose short story) perfected by al-Hamadhānī and al-Harīrī. Unlike that in many later *maqāmāt*, Habībī's language is in general fairly straightforward, though the presence of many literary, historical and contemporary allusions, and the frequent use of Palestinian words and proverbs to give local flavour to the text, pose a considerable challenge for any translator. His overall purpose is to present an account of the situation of the Palestinians under Israeli rule, which he does through the adventures of his "anti-hero" Sa'īd (a sort of Palestinian "Everyman"); the work deliberately avoids the direct appeals of much politically inspired literature, preferring instead to mix tragedy with comedy, and relying on the reader's sense of irony and humour.

JAYYUSI & LEGASSICK's translation (1982) effectively combines the talents of two distinguished scholars – native speakers, one of Arabic, the other of English – to convey in English the unique vision of Habībī's work. Although the use of two translators in this way has been criticized as the first step on the road to "translation by committee", the results in practice have been generally successful and the technique has become something of a hallmark of Professor Jayyusi's "Project of Translation from Arabic", which now runs to several dozen volumes. LeGassick and Jayyusi's translation of Habībī's novel captures well the author's humour and sense of fun, although some of the allusiveness of the original text will almost inevitably elude the "ordinary" reader, despite the provision of a substantial number of helpful endnotes.

With the exception of *The Secret Life of Saeed*, none of Habībī's major works has yet been translated into English in its entirety. The remaining works listed above comprise sections of his *Sudāsiyyat al-Ayyām al-Sitta* [Sextet on the Six Days], a work whose title carries an obvious allusion to the Arab–Israeli War of 1967 and which describes a series of reunions (following the introduction of the Israeli "open bridges" policy) between the Arabs of Israel and those Palestinians who had been dispersed to neighbouring Arab states following the establishment of Israel in 1948. "Al-Kharaza al-Zarqā' wa-'Awdat Jubayna" is an account of a Palestinian woman's return to her village from Lebanon, interwoven with a traditional Palestinian folktale, while "Umm Rūbābīka" (a corruption of the Italian "roba vecchia" – "old things", "junk") tells the story of an old woman who has spent the period between 1948 and 1967 pilfering second-hand furniture, searching in the sofas for hidden treasures – love letters, poems, diaries and the like; now that their owners have returned, she feels needed for the first time in 20 years. Both stories end on an unresolved note, reflecting the political limbo in which the Palestinians continued to find themselves following the Six Day War of 1967.

"Al-Kharaza al-Zarqā' wa-'Awdat Jubayna" presents us with a phenomenon comparatively rare in English translations of modern Arabic literature – two independent versions of a single work. Although both are generally accurate, that by SHAHEEN (1984) has the edge in terms of English idiom, KASSEM & LANFRANCHI's (1985) translation being not infrequently awkward in its rendering of the Arabic tense system into English. ALLEN & TINGLEY's (1992) translation of "Umm Rūbābīka" reads smoothly and easily, and is provided with just the right degree of annotation to smooth the path of the novice reader.

Although Habībī was not a prolific author, his sardonic brand of humour has ensured him a lasting place in the history of Palestinian prose literature. Compared with the coverage in some other languages (German, for example), his work remains poorly represented in English translation. It is greatly to be hoped that his work will attract more attention from English translators in the future, enabling his unique insight into the situation of the Israeli Arab population to reach a wider audience.

PAUL STARKEY

Further Reading

Allen, Roger, *The Arabic Novel: An Historical and Critical Introduction*, Manchester: University of Manchester Press, and Syracuse, New York: Syracuse University Press, 1982

Boullata, Issa, J., "Symbol and Reality in the Writings of Emile Habībī", *Islamic Culture*, 62 (1988) pp. 9–21

LeGassick, Trevor, "The Luckless Palestinians", *Middle East Journal*, 34 (1980) pp. 215–23

Hadewych fl.1250

Flemish mystic

Biography

Little is known about Hadewych's life. She may have been of aristocratic family and possibly lived in Brabant. Her spirituality was influenced by that of the Flemish William of St Thierry and of the French mystics Hugo and Richard of St Victor. Her works, apparently intended for reading, or in some cases singing, to a female lay community perhaps connected with a *béguinage*, consist of stanzaic poems, letters, prose Visions and poems in couplets. Her writings, using themes, images and verse forms in the courtly love tradition, express the neo-Platonic experience of human love felt and thought as a way of apprehending divine love.

Editions

All the above-mentioned groups of texts have been edited by Josef van Mierlo: *Visioenen* [Visions], Leuven, 1924–25; *Strophische Gedichten* [Stanzaic Poems], Antwerp, 1942; *Brieven* [Letters], Antwerp, 1947; *Mengeldichten* [Poems in Couplets], Antwerp, 1952

Translations

Collection

Hart, Mother Columba, OSB, *Hadewych: The Complete Works*, New York, Ramsey and Toronto: Paulist Press, 1980

Apart from some scattered selections in a few anthologies of medieval writing, or of medieval women's writing, the work of the 13th-century Flemish mystic Hadewych is available in English in only one translation. That translation (HART, 1980) offers Hadewych's complete works to the English-reading audience. As such, it is a good introduction to her work.

Hadewych wrote in four genres popular in the Middle Ages. Her collected works consist of Poems in Stanzas, Letters (in prose), Visions (also in prose), and Poems in Couplets. The main difference between the poems in stanzas and the poems in couplets is that the former are more lyrical, the latter more narrative in character.

The translation of the Visions is the most successful of all the translations contained in the *Hadewych* volume. The text flows in English, mainly because the translator has regularized the syntax of the Dutch original, which is considerably more choppy, probably not by accident but by design. Yet even in the translation of the Visions the translator is faced with one of the insoluble problems that arise in any attempt to translate mystical texts from the tradition that flourished in Flanders and Brabant from the 13th to the 16th century: the somewhat amazing fact that the mystical writers tend to use very basic, everyday vocabulary to describe their experiences. Where the translation has something like "fruition", for example, the original has "ghebruken", an infinitive used as a noun, which simply means "use," and also carries distinct sexual overtones.

The translation of the letters goes even farther in smoothing out the syntax of the original, while ignoring (or rather, being forced to ignore by the nature of the English language) one of the obvious stylistic characteristics of Flemish mysticism: the play on the same root in different words. When Hadewych writes: "verclaren metter clare claarheit" [make clear with clear clarity], the translation has: "enlighten you by the pure resplendent radiance with which he shines". The original is more concise, and its effect on the reader is stronger. In the letters the translation also occasionally exhibits short additions that make the text more explicit, presumably for theological purposes, to make Hadewych's sense if not clearer, at least more orthodox. Phrases like "the Son" or "the three Persons" are therefore added with some regularity. Finally, the register is occasionally more abstract than Hadewych's, defeating the purpose of her writing, as when she writes "hulpen" [to help], and is translated as "raise me to it".

The Poems in Stanzas are the most difficult part of Hadewych's oeuvre to read, and therefore also to translate. Their difficulty resides in the combination of their subject matter, which consists of extended meditations on, and occasional descriptions of, the mystical union, and their form, which is very intricately crafted in strict metrical patterns borrowed from the poetry of the Provencal *trobadors* and the Northern French *trouvères*. That combination is lethal for any translator, which also helps to explain why no more than one person has ever attempted to translate the complete Hadewych. To express what she wants to express, Hadewych not infrequently creates neologisms that are attested only in her works, and whose exact sense therefore remains in some doubt, as does that of the terms taken from the world of chivalry, suchas "aventure", which Hadewych integrates into her mystical writings.

All of these factors taken together explain why the translation of the Poems in Stanzas constitutes the weakest part of the translation discussed here. In addition, the translator not infrequently tends to weaken the power of the original expression, as in "niet en roeken", which basically means "not give a damn", and which is translated as "seek not", or as in "ontpluuct die ogen" [pluck open the eyes], which is merely translated as "open". This makes for a more decorous Hadewych, but the original Hadewych was a more tormented woman than the one who speaks to the reader in the translation.

Neither the Poems in Stanzas nor the Poems in Couplets are translated as either poetry or prose. Rather, they appear as something approximating cut-up prose, with an occasional nod to meter, the result of the translator's avowed strategy of having "the poems printed in lines as far as possible identical with Hadewych's". Needless to say, this strategy detracts to no small extent from the obvious poetic power of the original, especially in the translation of the intensely lyrical Poems in Stanzas.

The translation is somewhat more successful at rendering the Poems in Couplets, even though the same basic strategy is pursued throughout, with the same predictable results. Occasionally the syntax is construed in ways that do not always seem warranted by that of the original text, but it should be added, in all fairness, that the syntax of the original is sometimes so tortuous as to allow for different interpretations.

The only translation of the complete works of Hadewych available in English introduces its readers to a somewhat "sanitized" Hadewych, perhaps because the original reason why Hadewych had to be so radical in her writings is no longer there. Women who wanted to write about religious matters in the Middle Ages had to pretend to be a little unhinged, since the only way they could have access to God, or the problems of the religious life, was supposed to have been through direct experience, as they were not allowed to study these matters the way male theologians could.

The text is supplemented by notes, sometimes rather copious, which are of a uniformly high quality and greatly assist readers in coming to terms with Hadewych's variant of mysticism, which tends to be at once more exalted and more down to earth than the varieties they may be more familiar with in other traditions.

ANDRÉ A. LEFEVERE

Further Reading

Gooday, Frances Amelia, "Mechtild von Magdeburg and Hadewych of Antwerp: A Comparison", *Ons Geestelijk Erf*, 48 (1974) pp. 1–362

Guest, Tanis M., *Some Aspects of Hadewijch's Poetic Form in the "Strofische Gedichten"*, The Hague: Martinus Nijhoff, 1975

Hart, Mother M. Columba, OSB, "Hadewych of Brabant", *American Benedictine Review*, 13 (1962) pp. 1–24

Lucas, Elona K, "Psychological and Spiritual Growth in Hadewych and Julian of Norwich", *Studia Mystica*, 9/3 (1986) pp. 3–20

Vanderauwera, Ria, Hadewych entry in *Medieval Women Writers*, edited by Katharina M. Wilson, Athens: University of Georgia Press, 1984

Shams al-Dīn Muhammad Hāfiz c.1325/26–c.1389/90

Persian lyric poet

Biography

Born in Shiraz, where he spent most of his life except for a few visits to neighbouring courts, from his youth Hāfiz moved in the court circles first of the Īnjuvid rulers of Shiraz and then of their successors the Muzaffarids. Little is known about the circumstances of his life, although he appears to have been involved in court intrigues and rivalries and to have spent some time in prison. His *Dīvān* (collected poems) consists chiefly of *ghazals*, a brief lyric form of which Hāfiz is the acknowledged master, which is characterized by monometre (this metre, however, chosen from a wide range) and monorhyme (aa ba ca etc.) and the poet's self-naming (*takhallus*) in the final or penultimate line, and which is generally devoted to topics of love, with which Hāfiz incorporates panegyric and sagely musings. The text of the *Dīvān* has long been the subject of scholarly debate, with successive, and different, "critical" editions seeking to establish an "authentic" text of the *ghazals*; no edition, however, can be considered totally reliable.

Translations

Poetry (collections and selections)

Dīvān (collected poems)

Arberry, Arthur J., *Fifty Poems of Hāfiz*, Cambridge: Cambridge University Press, 1947

Aryanpur Kashani, Abbas, *Odes of Hafiz: Poetical Horoscope* (bilingual edition), Lexington, Kentucky: Mazda, 1984

Avery, Peter and John Heath-Stubbs, *Hafiz of Shiraz: Thirty Poems*, London: John Murray, 1952

Bell, Gertrude Lowthian, *Poems from the Divan of Hafiz*, London: Heinemann, 1897, 2nd edition, 1928; reprinted as *The Teachings of Hafiz*, London: Octagon Press, 1979

Bicknell, Hermann, *Hafiz of Shiraz: Selections*, edited by A.S. Bicknell, London, 1875

Boylan, Michael, *Hafez: Dance of Life* (bilingual edition), from prose translations by H. Wilberforce Clarke, Washington, DC: Mage, 1988

Clarke, H. Wilberforce, *Hāfiz: The Dīvān*, 3 vols, Calcutta: Government of India Central Printing Office, 1891; reprinted, London: Octagon Press, 1974

Hindley, John, *Persian Lyrics; or, Scattered Poems from the Diwani-i-Hafiz* (bilingual edition), London, 1800

Jones, Sir William, in his *Poems*, Oxford: Clarendon Press, 1772; London: Conant, 1777

Leaf, Walter, *Versions from Hafiz: An Essay in Persian Metre*, London: Grant Richards, 1898

Le Gallienne, Richard, *Odes from the Divan of Hafiz*, privately printed, 1903; London: Duckworth, 1905

Payne, John, *The Poems of Shemseddin Mohammed Hafiz of Shiraz*, 3 vols, London: Villon Society, 1901

Richardson, John, *A Specimen of Persian Poetry; or, Odes of Hafez* (bilingual edition), London, 1774, 2nd edition, 1802

Smith, Paul, *Dīvān of Hāfiz*, 2nd edition, Melbourne: New Humanity, 1993

Hāfiz was introduced to English-speaking readers through Sir William Jones's version of one of his *ghazals*, titled "A Persian Song", published in his *Grammar of the Persian Language* (1771; reprinted in JONES's *Poems*, 1772). Jones, who admired the poem's "wildness and simplicity", translated it into verse, wishing to imitate, as he said, "as nearly as possible ... the cadence and accent of the Persian measure". The "Persian Song" was part of Jones's project to introduce new sources of inspiration into European poetry, a project that influenced the work of the English Romantic poets. His presentation of Hāfiz as a "natural" or "primitive" poet whose verses were the product of congenial natural surroundings (see Jones, *Poems*, 2nd edition, London, 1777, especially pp. 163–73, 177–82) reflected his own conception of the true poet (one shared, moreover, with the Lake Poets). But while other versions of Hāfiz soon followed Jones's, early enthusiasm gradually gave way to growing unease at the problems encountered in translation, and to controversies over the value of the poetry itself.

While some, e.g. Hindley and Richardson, compared Hāfiz's poems to those of, for example, Anacreon, others objected to such comparisons. Walter Savage Landor, in the preface to his *Poems from the Arabic and Persian* (1800), contrasted "the delicacies of Athens and of Rome" with "the heady spirits and high-seasoned garbage of Barbarians", and expressed his astonishment "that the gazel has ever been preferred to the pure and almost perfect, though utterly dissimilar, pieces of Anacreon and Tibullus" (quoted in Pursglove, 1983). As translation was increasingly pressed into the service of British colonial interests, it was seen as having merely an instrumental or pedagogical function; and while Persian had once been essential for those involved in India, its disestablishment in 1834 as the official language of that country contributed to the decline of interest in Persian, and in Hāfiz. While literary translations continued to appear, the conviction was growing that Oriental literatures were fundamentally untranslatable, and that this justified any licence on the part of the translator.

Around the 1870s a new interest in Eastern literatures began to develop, motivated both by efforts at poetic experimentation and by an attraction to the "wisdom of the East". Translations of Hāfiz came to focus on the one hand on the formal nature of the poet's art, and on the other on the spiritual content of his poetry.

The view advanced by some philologists concerning the "atomistic" nature of Eastern poetry found little argument among translators; and the resulting debate over the "incoherence" of Hāfiz's *ghazals* – whose adherents often quoted Jones's image, in the "Persian Song", of the poem as a string of "Orient pearls at random strung" – continues to the present day. Whereas RICHARDSON (1774) had stressed the importance of knowledge of the Persian poetic tradition, and HINDLEY (1800) had refuted the notion of "incoherence", later translators have tended to be less generous. But philological rigor was not a distinguishing feature of English translation, which was largely the province of the amateur.

Some translators attempted to reproduce the form of Hāfiz's *ghazals*: BICKNELL (1875) imitated the metres of the originals, though not the monorhyme; later, LEAF (1898) and PAYNE (1901) imitated both metres and rhyme schemes. Others employed English forms such as the sonnet, or blank verse or prose. Many commented on the "shortcomings" of Persian poetry – its conventions of monometre, monorhyme, and the poet's self-naming – or contrasted the *ghazal*'s apparent "disunity" with the "unity" of classical poetry (see, e.g., Leaf, Bicknell, and Le Gallienne). Richard LE GALLIENNE (1903) – who knew no Persian, and relied on the translations of Clarke and Payne – also observed: "So distasteful to English ideas are the metrical devices and adornments pleasing in a Persian ear that the attempt to reproduce them ... can only result in the most tiresome literary antics".

Other translators were more concerned with Hāfiz's "spirituality", reflecting a growing interest in Persian Sufism. This interest is reflected in CLARKE's prose rendering of the entire *Dīvān* (1891), comprising some thousand pages of translation and commentary, and Gertrude BELL's verse adaptations of 53 lyrics (1897). Clarke's translation is redolent with Sufistic allegoresis; Bell was more reticent in this regard, and admitted: "I am very conscious that my appreciation of the poet is that of the Western. Exactly on what grounds he is appreciated in the East is difficult to determine, and what his compatriots make of his teaching it is perhaps impossible to understand." Bell's response to Hāfiz was both an enthusiastic and a poetic one; and she produced translations that stand as fine lyric poems in their own right.

The 20th century saw an increase both in translations of Hāfiz and in criticism of them. A.J. Arberry (1946) surveyed a number of English translations and upheld Le Gallienne's view that Hāfiz should be made to speak like an English poet while preserving his own "spirit". Eric Schroeder (1948), reviewing ARBERRY's (1947) and several other translations, asked, "What kind of an English poet shall we make of Hāfiz?" and insisted: "There is an appropriate level for the verse translation of any poet ... and in the case of Hāfiz that level is ... a very high one ... To reprint Jones's or Le Gallienne's versions [as did Arberry] implies ... that they are in a sense held up as possible models. And with this implication my quarrel is mortal". While one might ask, as does Pursglove (Loloi) (1983): "Why, after all, should a Persian poet be made to sound like an English poet? Is not the peculiar 'foreignness' of his music as much a part of his attraction as the 'foreignness' of his subject matter?", Schroeder's suggestion that there are historically and stylistically appropriate models for translation (he finds Donne's register close to that of Hāfiz), and criteria involved beyond those of linguistic expertise, enthusiasm, or attempting "to make the foreign poet a poet of one's own country" (Le Gallienne, 1905), attempts to put translation on a firm theoretical and practical basis.

Unfortunately, few translators have heeded this advice, and Hāfiz's poetry continues to be obscured by translations more concerned with the poet's "spiritual message" than his art. An exception is AVERY & HEATH-STUBBS (1952), who rendered some 30 poems into unrhymed couplets in verse (generally six-stressed); but while stripping the poems of the accretions and inflations typical of some other translations, they often also strip them of their density and musicality, and their practice of introducing some poems with a brief prose paraphrase meant to clarify the meaning does not allow the poems to speak for themselves, but forces one specific interpretation as the "correct" one among many possibilities.

ARYANPUR KASHANI (1984) adverts to the Persian tradition of drawing auguries from Hāfiz's *Dīvān*; his translations combine stilted attempts at verse, conveyed in a turgid and ungrammatical English, with often flagrant distortions of meaning. This effort to place the poet in a rigidly overdetermined segment of his own cultural tradition further separates poet from text. The claim of the publishers of BOYLAN (1988) was that they wished to present translations "that corresponded to our Iranian image of Hafez". Each of Boylan's free renderings of 12 *ghazals* is accompanied by CLARKE's prose version, by an elegant calligraphic presentation of the Persian text and by an impressive illumination combining calligraphy with abstract design. It includes a guide to transliteration "for using the English alphabet to recite the poems in Persian"; notes on each *ghazal* (including some of Clarke's), with, occasionally, parallel verses by other poets in Persian script, and, on the facing page, the *ghazal*'s text, in Persian calligraphy, and its transcription; a selection of anecdotes about the poet; a scholarly afterword designed to place Hāfiz in the larger context of the Persian literary tradition; and a brief bibliography of works in Persian and English. The poems themselves become obscured by a multiplicity of "versions", each curiously discrete, the relationships between them (and to the originals) unclear. The translator, it appears, knows no Persian, and has often simply reworded Clarke's versions in dubious verse which is at best uneven, at worst doggerel, and replete with inappropriate Anglicisms and colloquialisms. Like many other translators, he provides (often misleading) titles for poems that are (like all Persian lyrics) untitled, substituting a spurious concreteness for the *ghazal*'s customary abstraction; he routinely designates the "beloved" as female (whereas, by convention, the beloved of Persian lyric is male). And what justifies presenting Boylan's lame paraphrases of Clarke, along with Clarke's stilted and obsessively glossed prose versions, not only together, but at all?

Inappropriate titles are also a conspicuous feature of SMITH's translation of the entire *Dīvān* (1986; 2nd edition, 1993). Dedicated to Meher Baba, it relies on previous translations (including those of Meher Baba himself), on augury, and on meditation; Smith knows no Persian, and sees the poems as representing stages on Hāfiz's Path to Realization, to the discovery of God in himself and his attainment of the status of God-Man. He attempts to imitate the rhythms and rhyme-schemes of the originals, with results that are, to say the least, infelicitous.

That Hāfiz is the most widely translated Persian poet in English (for a complete survey of translations see Pursglove (Loloi) 1983, currently in preparation for publication) has not ensured him adequate translators: each translator has given us his or her Hāfiz, and all too often the Hāfizian text is merely an adjunct to other agendas. Hāfiz has not yet found his translator: one who can grapple with the poems as poems.

JULIE SCOTT MEISAMI

Further Reading

Arberry, A.J., "Hafiz and His English Translators", *Islamic Culture*, 20 (1946) pp. 111–249

Browne, E.G., *The Press and Poetry of Modern Persia*, Cambridge: Cambridge University Press, 1914; reprinted Los Angeles: Kalimat Press, 1983

Even-Zohar, Itamar, "Polysystem Studies", special issue of *Poetics Today*, 11/1 (1990)

Hewitt, A.S., "Harmonious Jones", *Essays and Studies by the English Association*, 228 (1942) pp. 42–49

Jacquemond, Richard, "Translation and Cultural Hegemony: The Case of French-Arabic Translation" in *Rethinking Translation: Discourse, Subjectivity, Ideology*, edited by Lawrence Venuti, London and New York: Routledge, 1992

Jazayery, M.A., "Ahmad Kasravi and the Controversy over Persian Poetry" (parts 1 and 2), *IJMES* (*International Journal of Middle East Studies*), 4 (1973) pp. 190–203, and *IJMES*, 13 (1981) pp. 311–27

Jones, Sir William, "On the Mystical Poetry of the Persians and Hindus" in his *Works*, vol. 4, London: G.G. and J. Robinson, 1807, pp. 211–35

Lefevere, André, "That Structure in the Dialogue of Men Interpreted", *Comparative Criticism*, 6 (1984) pp. 87–100

Lefevere, André, "Translation: Its Genealogy in the West" in *Translation, History and Culture*, edited by Susan Bassnett and Lefevere, London: Pinter, 1990

Meisami, J.S., "Hāfiz in English: Translation and Authority", *Edebiyat*, new series, 6 (1995) pp. 55–79

Menocal, Maria Rosa, *The Arabic Role in Medieval Literary History: A Forgotten Heritage*, Philadelphia: University of Pennsylvania Press, 1987

Pursglove (Loloi), Parvin, "Translations of Hāfiz and Their Influence on English Poetry since 1771: A Study and a Critical Bibliography", D.Phil. thesis, University College of Swansea, 1983

Rehder, Robert, "Persian Poets and Modern Critics", *Edebiyat*, 2 (1977) pp. 91–117

Schroeder, Eric, "Verse Translation and Hāfiz", *Journal of Near Eastern Studies*, 7 (1948) pp. 209–22

Shabistari, Mahmud, *Gulshan i raz / The Mystic Rose Garden*, edited and translated by E.H. Whinfield, London: 1880; reprinted Islamabad: Iran Pakistan Institute of Persian Studies, and Lahore: Islamic Book Foundation, 1978

Stetkevych, Jaroslav, "Arabic Poetry and Assorted Poetics" in *Islamic Studies: A Tradition and Its Problems*, edited by Malcolm H. Kerr, Malibu, California: Undena, 1980

Venuti, Laurence, "The Translator's Invisibility", *Criticism*, 28(2), 1986, pp. 179–212

Hagiwara Sakutarō 1886–1942

Japanese poet

Biography

Born 1 November 1886 in Maebashi, a large town northwest of Tokyo; he was the eldest son of a doctor. All his life Hagiwara strove to impress upon his father the extent of his poetic gifts. The literary world recognized them from early in his career, but he remained oppressively indebted to his father's wealth for his livelihood. Hagiwara was indulged in his every whim by his family; even after his marriage in 1919 he and his wife Ineko were housed in the family mansion. His undisciplined lifestyle and habit of dropping out of virtually every school he attended made him unemployable. He was dominated by his mother Kei; she also made life such a misery for his wife and two children that Ineko eventually left Hagiwara for a younger man. In 1939 Kei's jealous behaviour drove away Hagiwara's second wife before they had been married a year. Hagiwara led a dissolute life, indulging in drugs, drink and bouts of infidelity. He made a stunning debut with his first collection, *Tsuki ni Hoeru* [Howling at the Moon] (1917), and his mastery of the contemporary poetry scene was confirmed by the publication of his second collection, *Aoneko* [Blue Cat] (1923), where his inner chaos is revealed in a startling kaleidoscope of disturbed images: it could be said that, in poetry at least, he invented the haunted, claustrophobic and melancholic landscape of Japanese modernism. His poetry is populated by visions of decay: biological, urban and, ultimately, moral decay. Two more collections quickly followed: *Chō o Yumemu* [Dreaming of a Butterfly] (1923) and *Junjō Shōkyokushū* [Pure Lyrics] (1925). The latter contains some of the finest Japanese lyrics written in the 20th century. His last collection was *Hyōtō* [Isle of Ice] (1934), by far his darkest collection, written in a forbidding classical style considered by some to be untranslatable. Soon after his death (11 May 1942 in Tokyo), Hagiwara began to be translated into English, and translations have continued to appear with increasing frequency.

Translations

Selections of Poetry

Epp, Robert, *Rats' Nests: The Collected Poetry of Hagiwara Sakutarō*, with an introduction and notes, Stanwood, Washington: Yakusha, 1993 (contains translations of *Tsuki ni Hoeru, Aoneko, Chō o Yumemu, Junjō Shōkyokushū, Hagiwara Shishū, Hyōtō*)

Sato, Hiroaki, *Howling at the Moon: Poems of Hagiwara Sakutarō*, with an introduction, Tokyo: University of Tokyo Press, 1978

Wilson, Graeme, *Face at the Bottom of the World and Other Poems*, with an introduction, Tokyo and Rutland, Vermont: C.E. Tuttle, 1969 (contains translations of *Tsuki ni Hoeru, Aoneko, Chō o Yumemu, Junjō Shōkyokushū, Hyōtō*)

Poetry

Tsuki ni Hoeru, 1917

Epp, Robert, in *Rats' Nests*, translated by Epp, 1993

Sato, Hiroaki, *Howling at the Moon: Poems of Hagiwara Sakutarō*, with an introduction, Tokyo: University of Tokyo Press, 1978

Wilson, Graeme, in *Face at the Bottom of the World*, translated by Wilson, 1969

Aoneko [Blue Cat], 1923

Epp, Robert, in *Rats' Nests*, translated by Epp, 1993

Sato, Hiroaki, in *Howling at the Moon: Poems of Hagiwara Sakutarō*, with an introduction, Tokyo: University of Tokyo Press, 1978

Wilson, Graeme, in *Face at the Bottom of the World*, translated by Wilson, 1969

Chō o Yumemu [Dreaming of a Butterfly], 1923

Epp, Robert, in *Rats' Nests*, translated by Epp, 1993

Wilson, Graeme, in *Face at the Bottom of the World*, translated by Wilson, 1969

Junjō Shōkyokushū [Pure Lyrics], 1925

Epp, Robert, in *Rats' Nests*, translated by Epp, 1993

Wilson, Graeme, in *Face at the Bottom of the World*, translated by Wilson, 1969

Hagiwara Shishū, 1928

Epp, Robert, in *Rats' Nests*, translated by Epp, 1993

Hyōtō [Isle of Ice], 1934

Epp, Robert, in *Rats' Nests*, translated by Epp, 1993

Nekomachi, 1935

Saitō, George, *Cat Town: A Fantasy in the Manner of a Prose Poem*, with an introduction, Tokyo: Jūjiya Press, 1948

Hagiwara is generally regarded as one of the greatest Japanese modern poets, if not the greatest, and is held to be the father of modern Japanese poetry. He himself claimed in the preface to his first collection, *Howling at the Moon* (1917), that "all new poetic styles [and] ... all the rhythms of the lyric poetry of our era derive from it." His poetry varies greatly over the years in which it was written. The poet experimented with a variety of forms, and with various metrical schemes, virtually inventing a new type of poetry in the strict classical form (*bungo*) handed down by tradition. Thus his language presents translators with a number of complex problems.

The source texts have been conveniently made available in a number of collected works published in Japanese dating from immediately after the poet's death. What is considered the definitive edition of Hagiwara's collected works (*zenshū*) was published by the Chikuma Shobō company between 1975 and 1986 in 16 volumes (edited by Itō Shinkichi and Satō Fusayoshi). There was and is no shortage of reliable editions of the source texts available to the translator.

Translators have taken a variety of approaches to Hagiwara since the first volume appeared in translation in 1948. It is debatable whether the short piece (*Nekomachi*, 1935) translated by George SAITŌ (1948) is actually poetry. The original Japanese of the word Saitō translates as "fantasy" (in the subtitle of the text) normally means "novel" or "fiction" in Japanese, and a number of leading Japanese critics have categorized the work as fiction rather than poetry. However, Saitō's creative reading of Hagiwara's text can be justified on the grounds that the rest of the subtitle certainly states that it is a prose-poem. Saitō's translation has been acclaimed by one Japanese scholar of translation as a splendid example of a work cleaving to the American tradition, but the extracts that I have read do not seem excessively American in style. If Saitō's rendering is to be read as embodying the virtues of the literary over the literal (the Japanese scholar in question, Yonekawa Iwao, argues that this is the case) then he can be seen as foreshadowing the approach of the dominant school of post-war translators: the US military-trained scholars (or scholars who joined the military to work as translators and interpreters during World War II) who follow in the footsteps of Arthur Waley in stressing the primacy of translation as literature in English. But Saitō is by no means free, if free is to be interpreted as making wilful departures from the source text.

WILSON's 1969 volume presents a selection of translations that strive to be consciously "literary" when sometimes the original texts do not. We find heavy use of rhyme and alliteration by the translator, when Hagiwara himself wrote in a colloquial free-verse style as a deliberate alternative to the much more formal and rigid style inherited from the tradition of classical Japanese poetry. In his introduction, the English translator Wilson compares Hagiwara to Lorca in his use of modernist imagery, but his translations add imagery in the form of additional stanzas that reflect nothing originating in the source text. Creative additions such as these have given this volume a reputation for inaccuracy. In the introduction it is not stated explicitly that Wilson's versions are frequently original poems loosely based on the source text, although we are told that the poems are translations "only in the sense that FitzGerald's *Rubaiyat* is a translation of the work of Omar Khayyam". However Wilson makes plain his dislike for "literal translation".

SATO (1978) made the first complete versions of the two most famous of Hagiwara's collections: *Howling at the Moon* and *Blue Cat*. Sato's careful scholarship in the introduction accompanying his translations sets the tone of the volume. Sato comments on Hagiwara's verbal infelicities and oddities and declares his own intention not to smooth them out in the name of music. In other words, he intends to remain as close to the original as possible by focusing on singular and precise images. It is true that in places Sato's English is infelicitous and odd, and in that sense he is faithful to his source or at least to his interpretation of it, but in other places his adherence to a program of literalism produces angular, formal lines that imitate Hagiwara's modernist dislocation. One criticism might be that in some poems Sato is more mystifying than Hagiwara; another would be that Hagiwara, though perhaps not musical (as Sato admits in his introduction), is at least melodious, something Sato rarely is. However, Sato's avoidance of elegant paraphrase sets up sharp repetitive rhythms that capture the characteristically distorted cadence of modernist verse, and Hagiwara's visceral strength – "the sharpness that Wilson spoke of but never achieved" – comes through transparently in hard, clear imagery that points to the bent, expressionist world of Hagiwara's tormented psyche.

EPP (1993) has a mass of scholarly apparatus that allows readers to identify source-poems by title, collection and date. He also provides copious notes and a detailed introduction that displays evidence of many years spent working on Hagiwara. Epp's great achievement is to have translated the entire corpus of Hagiwara's poetry, producing the first complete translation of any modern Japanese free-verse poet.

Reviews of Epp's work have been mixed, possibly because, to avoid compromising his own poetic vision, he has chosen not to publish with a university press. Epp says little about his principles of translation but notes that English renditions need to create bridges between the original and its shadow.

Yet in attempting to make the poems work, Epp's translations strive for a wholeness that may not be there. He sacrifices the formal distortions of Sato's rigid line for a more colloquial and flexible rhythm. At times this may well be closer to the source, but the naturalization of Hagiwara into an English blank verse that is tamed of its clumsy oddness also reduces the poetic scope of the translation: it is not as shocking as the original and thus something is lost. What is gained is an element that emerges for the first time in English: the sad, elegiac tone of the rural Maebashi poet, a kind of quiet beauty all but blotted out by the strong, angular diction of the previous translators. The soft, colloquial mode, and the plaintive, haunting quality of the narrator's voice in many of the lyrics, come through more strongly in Epp's renderings than in either Sato or Saitō.

Translation is a question of loss and gain, perhaps of an imagined source, as Hagiwara's Japan in all its cultural, historic and linguistic fullness is lost to us forever. In the case of the three major translators who have sought to recreate Hagiwara in English (as opposed to Wilson who sought to recreate himself in Hagiwara but, unlike Pound with Chinese poetry, lacked the poetic resources to do it convincingly), we can glimpse shadows, smells and sights of the fading landscape that is the source text. Saitō, Sato and Epp are all close in their own way, and their renderings illuminate corners and tableaux in different fashions, but much remains to be uncovered by future translators of this complex and elusive poet.

LEITH MORTON

Further Reading

Keene, Donald, *Dawn to the West: Japanese Literature in the Modern Era*, 2 vols, New York: Holt Rinehart, 1984

Morton, Leith, "Translating Japanese Poetry: Reading as Practice", *Journal of the Association of Teachers of Japanese*, 26/2 (1992) pp. 141–81

Ueda, Makoto, *Modern Japanese Poets and the Nature of Literature*, Stanford, California: Stanford University Press, 1983

Yonekawa, Iwao, "Hagiwara Sakutaro 'Nekomachi' no Eiyaku ni tsuite", *Shōwa Bungaku Kenkyū*, 31 (1995) pp. 40–51

Haiku in English Translation

Translations

Blyth, R.H., *Haiku*, 4 vols, Tokyo: Hokuseido Press, 1949–52

Bowers, Faubion (editor), *The Classic Tradition of Haiku: An Anthology*, New York: Dover, 1996

Chamberlain, B.H., "Basho and the Japanese Poetical Epigram", *Transactions of the Asiatic Society of Japan*, 30/2 (1902)

Henderson, Harold Gould, *The Bamboo Broom*, London: Kegan Paul Trench Trübner, 1933; Boston: Houghton Mifflin, 1934

Porter, William N., *A Year of Japanese Epigrams*, London: Oxford University Press, 1911

Sato, Hiroaki and Burton Watson, *From the Country of Eight Islands: An Anthology of Japanese Poetry*, Seattle: University of Washington Press, 1981

Stryk, Lucien, *On Love and Barley: Haiku by Basho*, Honolulu: University of Hawaii Press, and Harmondsworth: Penguin, 1985

Yuasa, Nobuyuki, *The Narrow Road to the Deep North and Other Travel Sketches*, by Matsuo Basho, Harmondsworth: Penguin, 1966

Literary translation presents in an extreme way the double demand inherent in all acts of translation: (1) that the translation should be faithful to the original; and (2) that it should "work" in the target language. The difficulties this involves are perhaps paradigmatic of those involved in all our encounters with other cultures or times. From the point of view of 2), the translation of haiku in the 20th century must be considered a great success, for it engendered a new poetic genre in English, with its own anthologies, journals and conferences. Moreover, looked at from the point of view of English-language "haiku", it is evident which style of translation has "worked" best. Haiku have been translated in a great variety of ways: in one line (SATO & WATSON), two (CHAMBERLAIN), three (most translators) or four (YUASA); with rhyme (PORTER; HENDERSON) and without (most translators); in syllabics, stressed lines of prose (see BOWERS for a good anthology of translations of all periods and styles). In general, at all stages we can distinguish two tendencies: the "maximalist", in which the translator expands the original, either to approximate to more traditional English poetic forms or to convey the unexpressed overtones of the original; and the "minimalist", in which the original is translated as literally as possible or even abbreviated. The same haiku by Bashō can become:

Breaking the silence
of an ancient pond,
A frog jumped into water –
A deep resonance.

(Yuasa)

or:

The old pond.
A frog jumps in –
Plop!

(Blyth)

From the point of view of English haiku, however, it is clearly the latter, "minimalist" style that works better. It is not only more literal, it is also more literary.

By far the most translated and discussed haiku poet in English is Matsuo Bashō (1644–94) (see Chamberlain, Stryk, Yuasa and Sato for translations and discussions of his work). Often considered the greatest poet in Japanese literature by the Japanese themselves, he wrote not only *hokku* and *haikai no renga* (see below), but also short essays, diaries and accounts of his journeys through Japan. He is usually credited with having single-handedly given the haiku the dignity and seriousness of a major literary form by providing it with a philosophical and literary dimension it had previously lacked, and connecting it closely to the great tradition of Japanese literature and arts. Japanese interpretations of his work, however, themselves vary widely, as do English-language accounts.

The success of haiku outside Japan, however, can seem puzzling or even perplexing to the Japanese, who often feel that it is the most difficult form of their literature for foreigners to comprehend. This raises the question of whether the translation and reception of haiku in the West can also be considered a success in terms of 1) above, fidelity to the original. This is a difficult question to answer, not only because of the sheer artistic variety of the form (a point insufficiently stressed), but also because Japanese understanding of the form has changed dramatically over time. As is well known, the term *haiku* first gained currency in the late 19th century, when the poet Masaoka Shiki undertook the "reform" of the genre. The origin of the haiku is to be found in the *hokku* or "starting poem" of *renga*, the medieval art of linked verse. *Renga* were composed by one or more poets at a sitting, who followed increasingly elaborate rules concerning imagery, diction and the linking of each verse to the text. The form, which itself split into "serious" and "comic" genres, was closely tied to the aesthetic of traditional court poetry, and, like much of that, had something of the quality of a ritual and something of that of a game. Shiki, influenced in part by Western conceptions of literature, rejected *renga* and its rules, and developed the more expressive notion of the haiku. Like most such literary reforms, this was also retrospective, in that it altered and influenced the ways in which older *hokku* were read. At the same time, Shiki retained the requirement of a season-word, a word that indicates the season in which the haiku is written, and so a vital link with the traditional form. Moreover, the *hokku* had in fact been treated as an independent poem from much earlier times; the richly ambivalent relationship to tradition in Shiki's reform in fact harboured a certain instability, and this century has seen in Japan "free verse haiku", "haiku without season-words", "proletarian haiku" and the like. Indeed, it would be false to suggest that there is any one understanding of haiku in Japan; rather, competing interpretations jostle together.

Victorian Japanologists found haiku intriguing but essentially trivial. For CHAMBERLAIN (1902), who considered the *renga* to be a "paltry game", haiku could be redeemed only if they could be moralized, and here he drew on an older tradition of Japanese interpretation that seems to have vanished with Shiki. In fact, haiku have seemed important to English-language poets twice in the 20th century. The first time was when the group of poets in London based around T.E. Hulme were experimenting with *vers libre* before World War I, a movement which, with the help of Ezra Pound, issued in Imagist poetry. Influenced by French symbolist poetry, they wrote many haiku and tanka, understanding them to be, in F.S. Flint's words, "brief fragments of the soul's music". The rejection of rhyme and poetic diction and the emphasis upon the image naturally fostered a taste for minimalist translations of haiku.

The second time was following World War II, when R.H. BLYTH's works (1949–52) in particular had a strong influence on the Beat Poets, J.D. Salinger, Richard Wright and others. The English haiku movement also began at this time. Blyth saw the haiku as the expression of a Zen "moment", a moment of perception in which the "suchness" of things becomes evident. This was not only an expressive view of haiku, but it also had the advantage that the traditional and conventional dimension of the images used in haiku became largely irrelevant to their meaning. Blyth was also a brilliant translator, who saw the aim of a translation as a re-enactment of the original moment of perception. As well as leading to minimalist translation, this also brings his translations at times close to a kind of concrete poetry, where the shape and arrangement of the lines in English carry the meaning across to the reader. It is this sense of haiku, whether it is associated with Zen or not, that has been carried over into English haiku. The Blyth tradition of translation has been carried on by writers such as Lucien STRYK (1985).

Scholarly writing on the haiku, on the other hand, following the lead of Japanese specialists, has come increasingly to stress the traditional and conventional dimension of the form, especially in the case of Matsuo Bashō. There has also been increasing interest in *renga*. Thus, in English now as well as Japanese, there is an increasing gap between what one might call the scholarly and the literary understandings of the form. It seems likely that this gap will henceforth grow wider.

ADRIAN JAMES PINNINGTON

Further Reading

Higginson, William J. with Penny Carter, *The Haiku Handbook: How to Write, Share, and Teach Haiku*, New York: McGraw-Hill, 1985

Jones, Peter (editor), *Imagist Poetry*, Harmondsworth: Penguin, 1972

Kodama, Sanehide, *American Poetry and Japanese Culture*, Hamden, Connecticut: Archon Books, 1984

Miner, Earl, *The Japanese Tradition in British and American Literature*, Princeton, New Jersey: Princeton University Press, 1958

Pinnington, A.J., "R.H. Blyth (1898–1964)" in *Britain and Japan: Biographical Portraits*, edited by Ian Nish, Folkestone, Kent: Japan Library, 1994

Sato, Hiroaki, *One Hundred Frogs: From Renga to Haiku to English*, New York: Weatherhill, 1983

Tawfīq al-Hakīm 1898–1987

Egyptian novelist and dramatist

Biography

Born Husay Tawfīq Ismail Ahmad al-Hakīm in Alexandria, Egypt, 9 October 1898, into a well-to-do family. He was educated at schools in Cairo and at the University of Cairo, where he read law, but he failed to gain an appointment on graduating in 1925. His father encouraged him to study for a doctorate and he went to Paris to study law at the Sorbonne. There he became acquainted with Western culture, attending the theatre avidly and reading widely among European authors; this experience stimulated the interest in the relationship between the cultures of East and West which was to become crucial to his own writing. He met and married a Frenchwoman in Paris. He returned to Egypt in 1928 and served as an apprentice public prosecutor in Alexandria, from 1929 working as a public prosecutor in small towns in Egypt. He published his first play, *Ahl al-kahf* (*The People of the Cave*) in 1933. From 1934 he worked as director of the Investigation Bureau, part of Egypt's Ministry of Education. Because of his literary activities, which caused conflict in his government position, he was transferred to a post as director of social guidance at the Ministry of Social Affairs in 1939. He retired from government service to become a full-time writer in 1943. He contributed to the journals *Akhbar al-Yawm* and *Al-Ahram*, and became director-general of the Egyptian National Library in 1951. In his mature years he achieved much literary acclaim and official recognition for his work. He remained politically independent, receiving many honours; he was head of the theatre committee of Egyptian Higher Council of the Arts, Literature and Social Sciences from 1956 to 1959 and a member of the Academy of the Arabic Language from 1954. He was the Egyptian representative to Unesco,1959–60. Al-Hakīm was awarded the Cordon of the Republic in 1958 and received the State literature prize for his writing in 1961. However, in the later 1970s his work became unpopular with Muslim fundamentalists in Egypt, because of his liberal religious position. Died in Cairo, 26 July 1987.

Al- Hakīm has been called the founder of contemporary theatre in Egypt and occupies a significant position in modern Arabic writing. He was a prolific dramatist, writing more than 50 plays, and also wrote a number of novels. His first notable play was *Ahl al-kahf*, based on the story of the Seven Sleepers of Ephesus, which brought him immediate success and fame. The plays that followed this were *Sharazād* (*Shahrazad*), 1934, its theme taken from the story of *The Thousand and One Nights*; *Muhammad*, 1936, which was never performed; *Al-Malik Ūdīb* (*King Oedipus*), a version of the Oedipus legend, and *Pygmalion*, 1942, one of his "philosophical" plays. His later work deals with social themes, and includes the group of plays he called *Masrah al-mujtama'* [The Theatre of Society]. After living in Paris as a Unesco representative in 1959-60, he wrote a number of plays that show the influence of the Theatre of the Absurd, such as *Yā tāli' as shajara* (*The Tree Climber*), 1962. His later plays include *Al-Dunya riwaya hazaliyya* [Life Is a Farce], 1974 and *Ashab al-sa'ada al-zawjiya* [Happily Married], 1981. Hakīm's autobiographical *Yawmiyāt nā'ib fī al-aryāf* (*Maze of Justice*), 1937, a satirical view of Egyptian bureaucracy, is his best internationally known novel.

Translations

Novels

'Awdat al-Rūh, 2 vols, 1933

Hutchins, William, *Return of the Spirit*, with an introduction, Washington, DC: Three Continents Press, 1990

Yawmiyyāt Nā'ib fī al-Aryāf, 1937

Eban, Abba S., *Maze of Justice*, London: Harvill Press, 1947; reprinted, as *Maze of Justice: Dairy of a Country Prosecutor*, with new preface by P.H. Newby, London: Saqi, and Austin: University of Texas Press, 1989

'Usfūr min al-Sharq, 1938

Winder, R. Bayly, *Bird of the East*, with an introduction, Beirut: Khayats, 1966

Selection of Plays

Johnson-Davies, Denys, *Fate of a Cockroach: Four Plays of Freedom*, London: Heinemann, 1973; Washington, DC: Three Continents Press, 1980 (contains *Fate of a Cockroach*, *The Song of Death*, *The Sultan's Dilemma*, *Not a Thing Out of Place*)

Plays

al-Sultān al-Hā'ir, 1960

Abdel Wahab, Farouk, *The Sultan's Dilemma* in *Modern Egyptian Drama: An Anthology*, edited by Abdel Wahab, 1974

Johnson-Davies, Denys, *The Sultan's Dilemma* in *The Fate of a Cockroach: Four Plays of Freedom*, edited and translated by Johnson-Davies, 1973

Yā Tāli' al-Shajara, 1962

Johnson-Davies, Denys, *The Tree Climber*, London: Oxford University Press, 1966; Washington, DC: Three Continents Press, 1985

Other Writing

Sijn al-'Umr, 1964

Cachia, Pierre, *The Prison of Life: An Autobiographical Essay*, Cairo: American University of Cairo Press, 1992

Of Tawfīq al-Hakīm's four major full-length novels (all autobiographically based), the last – *al-Ribāt al-Muqaddas* (1944) – remains so far untranslated into English. The other three, however, each of which relates to a different period of the author's life, provide a fascinating portrait of the intellectual and emotional development of an Egyptian intellectual in the first half of the 20th century. The narrative sections of the works are written in an easily flowing classical Arabic; but the author makes effective use of colloquial Egyptian in the dialogue between the Egyptian characters of the two novels set in Egypt, *'Awdat al-Rūh* and *Yawmiyyāt Nā'ib fī al-Aryāf*.

The first part of *'Awdat al-Rūh* revolves around the frustrations of an adolescent, Mushin (obviously al-Hakīm himself), whose infatuation with the girl next door – like that of his uncles with whom he shares a flat in Cairo – is brought to an abrupt end when she marries a more promising suitor. In the second part, set in the Egyptian Delta, the tone becomes more philosophical, as al-Hakīm launches, through his characters, into a discussion of the "Egyptian spirit", which the author sees as surviving in its purest form among the *fallāhīn*. The work ends with the outbreak of the 1919 revolt on the streets of Cairo.

The considerable problems posed for the translator by this sprawling novel (marred, like many of Tawfīq al-Hakīm's works, by a lack of artistic unity) are not always satisfactorily solved by HUTCHINS (1990), who tries to keep too closely to the original. As a result, the translation, though generally accurate, is marred by some unidiomatic and infelicitous expressions which sometimes impede the flow of the narrative. Despite this, it generally succeeds in presenting a "realistic depiction of life in Egypt" (translator's introduction, p. 19). Hutchins's introduction discusses the novel as an example of the *Bildungsroman* and draws some interesting parallels with the European literary tradition.

In *'Usfūr min al-Sharq*, we find an older Muhsin studying in Paris in the 1920s. As in *'Awdat al-Rūh*, the author fails to integrate the "dialectical" parts of the novel – which here revolve around Muhsin's conversations with the Russian émigré Ivan – with the more down-to-earth narrative of his unsuccessful love affair with Suzy. A link between the two levels is provided, however, by the "East / West" theme, played out in the work on both an intellectual and a practical level; as such, *'Usfūr min al-Sharq* occupies a crucial position in the development of the modern Arabic novel, for this theme – in one guise or another – is a recurrent one in modern Arabic literature.

As the novel is set in a French-speaking environment it is perhaps not surprising that the dialogue of *'Usfūr min al-Sharq* – unlike that of *'Awdat al-Rūh* – is entirely in standard, rather than colloquial Arabic. Although this eases the translator's problems, the philosophical rambling that mars the original language of the novel can only increase the challenge. A further problem is that al-Hakīm's novel includes a large number of quotations from other writers, ranging from the poetry of Umar al-Khayyām to Beethoven's Heiligenstadt testament. WINDER (1966) generally copes successfully with these problems and, if his translation seems a little wooden at times, this is usually no more than a reflection of the original. In making his translation he has taken advantage of a French version, closely supervised by the author (Paris: Nouvelles Éditions Latines, 1960), and his introduction includes an interesting discussion of the textual divergences between the original, the French translation, and a second Arabic edition published in 1964.

Yawmiyyāt Nā'ib fī al-Aryāf is the most successful of al-Hakīm's four novels from a structural point of view, being free from the tendency to ramble apparent in the two works discussed above. Cast in diary form, the work revolves around a murder investigation, in the course of which al-Hakīm presents a damning picture of conditions in the Egyptian countryside and of the Egyptian legal system, based on the Napoleonic Code, implemented with few concessions to the *fallāhīn* to whom it was being applied. The novel, which again contains a strong autobiographical element, successfully unites a bitter humour with a biting sense of social criticism. As in *'Awdat al-Rūh*, the immediacy of the action is enhanced by a lively use of colloquial Egyptian for the dialogue passages.

The translation by EBAN (1947) successfully captures the pace and rhythm of al-Hakīm's original text, which also makes effective use of the "cliffhanger" device. More polished than Hutchins (1990) and less wooden than Winder (1966), it is by far the most successful of the three English translations of al-

Hakīm's novels to date and has recently been deservedly re-issued, with a new introduction.

Al-Hakīm's career as a dramatist covers a longer period than his career as a novelist, extending from five plays written for the popular theatre in the early 1920s to plays published in the last decade of his life. They fall into a number of different categories, depending on the particular blend of their "intellectual" content with the dramatic techniques employed. Although many were written to be read rather than acted, from the early 1960s al-Hakīm began to experiment with techniques derived from the Theatre of the Absurd and other avant-garde Western theatre. A distinctive category of his drama is formed by the series of plays on social themes which he published in the late 1940s and early 1950s.

Although early "intellectual" plays such as *Ahl al-Kahf* (1933) and *Shahrazād* (1934) remain among the most interesting of al-Hakīm's plays, recent translators have tended to focus on his later works. Outstanding among his "social" plays is the one-act *Ughniyat al-Mawt*, which revolves around the conflict between traditional and modern values – a theme that recalls the setting of the earlier novel *Yawmiyyāt Nā'ib*. The play takes its inspiration from the family feuds widespread in the Egyptian countryside, centring on the return of a young man, 'Ulwān, to his native village after an absence of several years. His purpose in returning is to preach a programme of social reform, but his family believe that he has come to avenge the killing of his father. A series of misunderstandings ensues, leading to his death at the hands of his family. This plot allows al-Hakīm considerable scope for fast-moving dialogue between characters talking at cross-purposes. JOHNSON-DAVIES (1973) – the most reliable as well as the most prolific translator of modern Arabic literature into English – captures the mood of the play well, although the wide cultural gap between the play's setting and the intended audience creates some problems and at times his rendering seems a little stilted.

From this point of view, *Yā Tāli' al-Shajara* – the first play by al-Hakīm to show the influence of the Theatre of the Absurd – presents fewer problems, for although the play contains some "Eastern" elements, it depends for its effect entirely on the vigour of its dialogue. Central to the play is the relationship between a man and his wife and the investigation that follows her disappearance; eventually the wife reappears, but her obstinate refusal to disclose her whereabouts drives her husband to kill her. Communication between the couple appears to have broken down, as each is entirely wrapped up in his or her own concerns; but by picking up the other's phrases and applying them to their own fixations, they succeed in understanding each other. JOHNSON-DAVIES (1966) well captures the freshness and lively tone of al-Hakīm's play, and his translation has been successfully produced on the English stage.

Al-Sultān al-Hā'ir presents the unusual phenomenon of a modern Arabic dramatic work available in English in two independent translations. Set in the Mamluke period, the play revolves around the system by which slaves from the bodyguards of the sultans were granted freedom and brought up to rule the country. Despite the historical setting, al-Hakīm's main purpose is to raise a question he regards as crucial for the world today: should it seek a solution to its problems in law or in force? Although the play is marred by some turgid passages, the clarity of al-Hakīm's Arabic means that the translator is faced with few serious problems. With little to choose between JOHNSON-DAVIES (1973) and ABDEL WAHAB (1974) in terms of accuracy (though Johnson-Davies's professionalism occasionally shows through in his more idiomatic phraseology), one may surmise that neither translator would have embarked on his translation had he known of the other's efforts.

Like most Egyptian authors, al-Hakīm, in addition to his fictional and dramatic works, produced much non-fictional material, mostly in essay form. Although much of this is ephemeral, his autobiographical *Sijn al-'Umr* – which covers roughly the first 30 years of his life, is of interest, not only for presenting an intimate portrait of an Egyptian family at the beginning of the century, but also (and more importantly) as a source of information on the development of the Egyptian theatre in the 1920s. Although written in a straightforward and unaffected structure, the work poses problems for the Western translator because of its occasionally rambling style and because of the number of literary and other allusions unlikely to be recognized by the average reader. CACHIA's readable translation (1992) successfully overcomes these problems by a judicious mixture of condensation and expansion in the text, and a lucid set of endnotes which could well serve as a model of its kind.

PAUL STARKEY

Further Reading

Badawi, M.M., *Modern Arabic Literature and the West*, London: Ithaca Press, 1985

Badawi, M.M., *Modern Arabic Drama in Egypt*, Cambridge and New York: Cambridge University Press, 1987

Badawi, M.M. (editor), *Modern Arabic Literature*, Cambridge and New York: Cambridge University Press, 1992 (The Cambridge History of Arabic Literature)

Cachia, Pierre, "Idealism and Ideology: The Case of Tawfiq al-Hakim", *Journal of the American Oriental Society*, 100 (1980)

Fontaine, Jean, *Mort-résurrection: Une lecture de Tawfiq al-Hakim*, Tunis: Éditions Bouslama, 1978

Kilpatrick, Hilary, *The Modern Egyptian Novel: A Study in Social Criticism*, London: Ithaca Press, 1974

Starkey, Paul, *From the Ivory Tower: A Critical Study of Tawfiq al-Hakīm*, London: Ithaca Press, 1987

Knut Hamsun 1859–1952

Norwegian novelist, dramatist and poet

Biography

Born Knut Pedersen in Lom, Norway, 4 August 1859. His family were peasants, and he had no formal education, spending his childhood in the Lofoten islands working with his uncle, a fisherman. He was apprenticed to a cobbler in Bödo, and subsequently travelled around Norway, working in a number of different occupations, including coal mining and road work. In 1882 he moved to the United States, where he worked as a streetcar conductor in Chicago and as a farmhand in North Dakota, among other things. He returned to Norway in 1884 but did not stay: after returning to the United States in 1886 he lectured and worked as a secretary in Minneapolis and later settled in Newfoundland as a fisherman. He published a fragment of his novel *Sult* (*Hunger*) in a Danish magazine in 1888, the success of this work encouraging him to devote himself to writing. He lived in Paris during the early 1890s, and travelled in Finland, Russia and Denmark during the 1890s and 1900s. Hamsun married Bergliot Goepfert in 1898 and had one daughter. In 1909 he divorced Goepfort and married Marie Andersen, with whom he had two sons and two daughters. They settled in a farm in Hamarøy, where Hamsun had lived as a child. In 1911 he moved with his family to an estate near Grimstad, southern Norway, where he wrote and farmed until his death. Hamsun openly supported Quisling's pro-German party during World War II, and was indicted, fined, and briefly confined to a mental institution after the war. He was awarded the Nobel Prize for Literature in 1920. Died in Grimstad, 19 February 1952.

Hamsun's best-known works are his novels, the earliest of which, *Sult* (*Hunger*), 1890, a psychological portrait of an impoverished writer, brought him immediate literary acclaim and recognition as the first Modernist voice in Scandinavian literature. He went on to write the important novels *Mysterier* (*Mysteries*), 1892, and *Pan*, 1894. His most significant work is generally acknowledged to be the semi-autobiographical novel *Markens grøede* (*The Growth of the Soil*), 1917: shortly after its publication Hamsun was awarded the Nobel Prize. His last major work, written after he received psychoanalytic treatment in the 1920s, is the "August" trilogy, *Landstrykere* (*Wayfarers*), 1927, *August*, 1930, and *Men livet lever* (*The Road Leads On*), 1933. Hamsun also wrote poems, short stories and plays. He published a memoir, *På gjengrodde stier* (*On Overgrown Paths*), in 1949.

Translations

Novels

Sult, 1890

Bly, Robert, *Hunger*, introductions by Bly and Isaac Bashevis Singer, New York: Farrar Straus, 1967

Egerton, George, *Hunger*, London: Smithers, 1899; New York: Knopf, 1920

Lyngstad, Sverre, *Hunger*, Edinburgh: Rebel, 1996; New York: Penguin, 1998

Mysterier, 1892

Bothmer, Gerry, *Mysteries*, New York: Farrar Straus, 1971; London: Souvenir Press, 1973

Chater, Arthur G., *Mysteries*, New York: Knopf, 1927

Pan, af løitnant Thomas Glahns papirer, 1894

McFarlane, James, *Pan: From Lieutenant Thomas Glahn's Papers*, London: Artemis Press, 1955; New York: Farrar Straus, 1956

Worster, W.W., *Pan*, with an introduction by Edwin Björkman, New York: Knopf, 1921

Victoria, 1898

Chater, Arthur G., *Victoria: A Love Story*, New York: Knopf, and London: Gyldendal, 1923

Stallybrass, Oliver, *Victoria: A Love Story*, New York: Farrar Straus, 1969

Sværmere, 1904

Geddes, Tom, *Dreamers*, New York: New Directions, 1996

Worster, W.W., *Dreamers*, New York: Knopf, 1921; as *Mothwise*, London: Gyldendal, 1921

Benoni, 1908

Chater, Arthur G., *Benoni*, New York: Knopf, 1925

Rosa, 1908

Chater, Arthur G., *Rosa*, New York: Knopf, 1925

Lyngstad, Sverre, *Rosa*, Los Angeles: Sun and Moon Press, 1997

Markens grøde, 1917

Worster, W.W., *The Growth of the Soil*, London: Gyldendal, 1920; New York: Knopf, 1921

Konerne ved vandposten, 1920

Chater, Arthur G., *The Women at the Pump*, New York: Knopf, 1928

Stallybrass, Oliver and Gunnvor Stallybrass, *The Women at the Pump*, New York: Farrar Straus, 1978

Landstrykere, 1927

Gay-Tifft, Eugene, *Vagabonds*, New York: Coward McCann, 1930

McFarlane, James, *Wayfarers*, New York: Farrar Straus, 1980

På gjengrodde stier, 1949

Andersen, Carl L., *On Overgrown Paths*, with an introduction, New York: Eriksson, 1967

Other Writing

Fra det moderne Amerikas aandsliv, 1889

Morgridge, Barbara Gordon (editor and translator), *The Cultural Life of Modern America*, with an introduction, Cambridge, Massachusetts: Harvard University Press, 1969

Knut Hamsun's early Romantic works from the 1890s are considered his greatest literary achievements, and were translated into English relatively quickly after their original publication. Hamsun's prose is difficult to evoke accurately in English on account of the rhythmic, vivid style and his frequent shifting of tenses. The use of the present tense to render past action more immediate is common in Norwegian and is a device often used in Hamsun's early works, which concentrate on an individual consciousness and its wanderings. This usage is not normal in English. Thus some of the immediacy of the original will inevitably be lost in translation.

Hunger has been seen as the classic Hamsun novel, not only because it was his first great work, but also on account of its historical setting and its careful balance of naturalism and romanticism, humour and despair. This description of an experiment in living, which uses innovative first-person narration, is full of realistic detail related in such a way as to show the ability of a youthful temperament, starving for food and for freedom, to be a writer and his own strange self. There is an emphasis, difficult to translate adequately, on rhythm and local colour, and irony infuses scenes that may otherwise seem pathetic or theatrical. EGERTON's translation (1899) preserves the meaning of the original but fails to evoke the rhythmic intensity of Hamsun's text and deletes all the explicitly erotic passages. Egerton's rather archaic prose, which makes the style awkward, retains some of the tense shifts essential in portraying this irrational individual. The protagonist's invented words are untranslated, as are some of the geographical locations within the city of Christiania (now Oslo). The author does provide footnotes to clarify the importance of these locations, however. BLY's flowing translation (1967) is relatively successful in conveying the mood of the original text, but there is both confusion over the geography of Christiania and some serious inaccuracies. For example, Bly translates one character's occupation as "lady-killer" when it is in fact gynecologist, or "lady's doctor" as in Egerton. This leads to misinterpretations of character. Bly fails to shift tenses, and thus the narrative loses the erratic nature of the protagonist's wandering mind and effaces Hamsun's technique and style. Many of the nuances in the original are lost and Bly is freely explicit in some areas where Hamsun was oblique. Although this translation is highly readable, its minor inaccuracies do an injustice to the Hamsun original. George Steiner (*The Observer Review*, 26 January 1997) finds Sverre LYNGSTAD's 1996 English version "far more scrupulous and informed" than the two earlier ones, and that it "restores to the English-speaking reader one of the cold summits in modern prose literature". Lyngstad retains Hamsun's idiosyncratic shifts between past and present tenses and thus successfully portrays the recurrent changes in point of view. Textual accuracy is paralleled with close attention to nuances and allusions, in particular Hamsun's irreverent parodic biblical ones. Lyngstad also provides useful textual notes outlining the alterations made from Hamsun's original 1890 text to his revised 1907 version.

Along with *Pan* and *Hunger*, *Mysteries* is a work central to Hamsun's most productive literary period. In spite of its difficulty it is highly readable and full of magical language which turns even the most distressing events into song. CHATER's *Mysteries* (1927) loses much of the mood evoked in the original Norwegian and contains inaccuracies that adversely affect both the irony and the symbolism so fundamental to the text. Chater does not translate the name of the protagonist's alter ego, which renders the symbolism in this name defunct for the English reader. He has also omitted some of the original text. BOTHMER's translation (1971) of the same novel evokes the passion and intensity with which Hamsun assailed the conventional values of his period, and is an accurate, more mood-conscious rendering of Hamsun's prose. The symbolism of the original remains intact, although it is over-emphasized by a liberal translation of the title of the only titled chapter in the book as "White Nights". The original refers merely to the light nights of midnight sun in northern Norway.

Pan has been widely regarded as Hamsun's most beautiful novel, largely because of the protagonist's eloquent declaration of his love of northern Norwegian nature, made in a style reminiscent of both Nietszche and Rousseau. A first-person narrative of the events of one summer, the prose is heavily imbued with a dithyrambic mood. The language of the protagonist, Lieutenant Glahn, assumes the rhythms of nature, which is challenging for any translator. The second part of the novel has a new narrator whose hatred of Lieutenant Glahn is sharply juxtaposed with Glahn's romantic musings in Part 1. WORSTER's translation (1921) (which omits the subtitle "From Lieutenant Glahn's Papers") succeeds in rendering the parataxis evident in Hamsun's evocative style. The short sentences so characteristic of Hamsun's lofty manner are upheld, but Worster changes some of the paragraph breaks, thus giving the prose the appearance of a more fluid continuity than it actually has. There are some minor inaccuracies in the translation, and some omissions, and much of the original poetry is lost. Worster does, however, successfully juxtapose the tense shifts so essential to the original. The MCFARLANE translation (1955) is far more successful in sustaining the dithyrambic mood of the original and the overtly pedantic style, so obviously, and consciously, unlike that in other Hamsun works. The English prose is rhythmic and flowing and highly accurate in rendering both the meaning and the mood of the original. The intensity of the descriptions of the natural world and the romantic poeticism of the original are intact in this translation. Parataxis is as a bundant as in the original, along with asyndectors and polysyndectors that characterize this prose and make it reminiscent of the Bible's lofty style. McFarlane maintains the essential tense shifts and accurately mirrors the emotional turmoil and joy of life felt by the protagonist.

Victoria is the quintessential Hamsun love story, a tale of mood, colour and allegory. Hamsun called it "just a little poetry" and it is a lighter and more sentimental kind of literature than previous Hamsun works. CHATER's translation (1923) is accurate and highly readable. It closely translates the original and upholds the original syntax. STALLYBRASS is freer in his translation (1969) and has added some clarifying phrases to the original text. This leads to a more readable, consistent translation.

Dreamers introduces a series of comical stories from northern Norway and makes use of a more colloquial language. "Dreamers" is not an adequate translation of the original title "Sværmere" as this word has multiple meanings in Norwegian. It means both "moth" and "dreamers", and also evokes romance and passion, "something pleasantly futile and deliciously unprofitable – foolish lovers hovering like moths around a lamp", as WORSTER indicates in the foreword to his translation (1921). Worster's version contains some minor inaccuracies and changes orthography unnecessarily for emphasis. A mistranslation of "Laban" and "Adam" into "Old Mick" and "Old Nick" respectively is out of place. GEDDES's (1996) is much more fluent and does not contain the inaccuracies of Worster. The colourful action, racy dialogue and comical style, reminiscent of an 18th-century comedy of manners, is eloquently rendered in this highly readable piece.

CHATER's rendering of *Benoni* (1925) is a literal translation of Hamsun's humorous regional novel written in a low style. Chater fails to evoke the folksy mood of the original, as the northern Norwegian dialect is not mirrored. Rather Chater mistranslates colloquialisms into nonsensical phrases, giving characters an air of stupidity rather than rural amicability. CHATER's *Rosa* (1925) is more successful in this respect, as this text is more poetical than *Benoni* in the original, but Chater's style remains rather stilted.

The Growth of The Soil, Hamsun's strongly polemical pioneer novel, is written in a low style full of local dialect. WORSTER (1920) merely renders the local dialect with archaisms and thus loses much of the flavour of the original. The meaning is intact, but the prose is stilted. Many words specific to a Norwegian rural environment have not been translated or paraphrased, and this necessitates, for understanding, some knowledge of Norwegian culture on the part of the English reader.

CHATER's *The Women at the Pump* (1928) is a literal translation of the original and provides the reader with useful footnotes relating to cultural concepts specific to Norway. The STALLYBRASS flowing translation (1978) is less literal, but it does maintain more of the sardonic humour and originality of style and technique so representative of Hamsun's later works. Oliver and Gunnvor Stallybrass also include footnotes where applicable.

The Wayfarers is the first volume of the *August* trilogy and the longest book Hamsun ever wrote. The text has the quality of a play in that it has brief stage directions used as introductions to characters and scenes, and dialogue is indicated by a character's name and an adverb. Both MCFARLANE (1980) and GAY-TIFFT (1930) have kept these aspects of the text intact. Hamsun's underlying theme of tragic displacement is glossed over by his humorous language, but much of the humour is inevitably lost in translation. The original is written in an antipoetic low style interspersed with poetic passages, and both translations are relatively successful in reflecting this. Gay-Tifft loosely translates the meaning of the text but fails to transmit the humour or mood of the original. McFarlane's flowing version mirrors both mood and the meaning, and his translation of the title as "Wanderers" is more appropriate to the themes of the original. The second and third parts of the *August* Trilogy (*August*, 1930, and *Men livet lever*, 1933) were translated by Gay-Tifft as *August* and *The Road Leads On* in 1931 and 1934 respectively.

ANDERSEN's translation (1967) of Hamsun's last book, *On Overgrown Paths*, is not entirely successful. The novel was written as a fragment of an autobiography, and each phrase in the original is in measured prose cadences which convey the diminished quality of a resilient and precise mind during a stay at the Psychiatric Clinic in Oslo. The translation does not keep these qualities intact, and where the cadence of Hamsun's original prose survives it has been slowed down to a literal and uncertain progress where sentences do not contain the rhythm. There is a slackness and timidity of phrase which, in spite of conveying the physical events, undercuts the inner ones that make up the substance of the book. In spite of the limited range, it is still a highly readable translation and the translator has included useful explanatory notes concerning the historical context of the work.

The Cultural Life of America is full of the prose rhythms so common in Hamsun's works and shows his rhetorical style better than any other work. It is a diatribe against America, and MORGRIDGE's translation (1969) contains an excellent introduction and footnotes which place the work in its social and historical context. The translation is a literal rendering of the original edition that maintains the oratorical style of this lecture.

TANYA THRESHER

Further Reading

Ferguson, Robert, *Enigma: The Life of Knut Hamsun*, New York: Farrar Straus, and London: Hutchinson, 1987

McFarlane, J.W., "The Whisper of the Blood", *PMLA*, 71 (1956) pp. 563–94

Næss, Harald, *Knut Hamsun*, Boston: Twayne, 1984

Næss, Harald and James McFarlane, *Knut Hamsun: Selected Letters*, volume 1: *1879–98*, Norwich: Norvik Press, and Chester Springs, Pennsylvania: Dufour, 1990

Han Yu 768–824

Chinese prose writer and poet

Biography

Born at Nanyang in the north of China, in what is now Honan Province. Orphaned at the age of three, he was brought up by a literary cousin. Han Yu travelled in the Empire, occupying various official government posts. He is famous for his pamphlets defending Confucianism against Buddhism. He also aimed at bringing back to prose, to replace the then current ornateness, the simple style of early Confucian writers.

Editions

The standard work for Han Yu's prose is *Han Changli wen ji jiaozhu*, with notes by Ma Tongbo, Shanghai: Gudian Wenxue Chubanshe, 1957. For the poetry, consult the chronologically arranged *Han Changli shi xinian jishi*, compiled by Qian Zhonglian, Shanghai: Shanghai Guji Chubanshe, 1984.

Translations

Prose

Giles, H.A., *Gems of Chinese Literature*, London: Bernard Quaritch, and Shanghai: Kelly and Walsh, 1884; revised edition, Shanghai: Kelly and Walsh, 1922; London: Bernard Quaritch, 1923 (contains 8 pieces)

Liu Shih Shun, *Chinese Classical Prose: The Eight Masters of the T'ang-Sung Period* (bilingual edition), Hong Kong: Chinese University Press, 1979 (contains 16 pieces)

Rideout, J.K., "Prose Essays: Han Yü", in *Anthology of Chinese Literature*, edited by Cyril Birch, vol. 1, New York: Grove Press, 1965; Harmondsworth: Penguin, 1967 (contains 6 pieces)

Spring, Madeleine Kay, *A Stylistic Study of Tang "Guwen": The Rhetoric of Han Yu and Liu Zongyuan*, dissertation, University of Washington, 1983 (contains 11 pieces)

Yang, Hsien-yi and Gladys Yang, "Han Yu: Prose Writings", *Chinese Literature*, 2 (1959) pp. 64–87 (contains 12 pieces)

Poetry

Graham, A.C., *Poems of the Late T'ang*, Harmondsworth and Baltimore: Penguin, 1965 (contains translations of four poems, one of them an extract from the *Nanshan shi*)

Liu, Wu-chi and Irving Yucheng Lo (editors), *Sunflower Splendor: Three Thousand Years of Chinese Poetry*, with an introduction by Lo, Bloomington: Indiana University Press, 1975 (includes translations of Han Yu by Kenneth O. Hanson and Charles Hartman)

Owen, Stephen, *The Poetry of Meng Chiao and Han Yü*, New Haven, Connecticut: Yale University Press, 1975 (contains a number of translations)

The translations of Han Yu's prose reveal two broadly opposite approaches. GILES's (1884, 1922) and YANG & YANG's (1959) translations both, in their very different ways, make significant economies with the original texts. RIDEOUT (1965), LIU (1979), and SPRING (1983), by contrast, attempt, with varying success, to provide less "doctored" versions whilst still avoiding the problems of a wordy, cumbersome, and repetitive style to which "faithful" versions of Han Yu's work can too easily be prone.

GILES (1884–1923) attempts to maintain accuracy, but acknowledges that he must make sacrifices for an audience still unfamiliar with China. Thus Chinese names are often dispensed with, while elsewhere the text is reworked for Western sensibilities, as when the phrase "shang can" (literally "I present my offering [to your spirit]"), is rendered "Heaven bless thee!" Some longer phrases are omitted altogether; and in those passages that do remain "uncut" there are sometimes unfortunate errors. However, these translations are still worth reading today; the Victorian rhetoric often works well, both in serious works such as "In Memoriam", and in "The Crocodile", where hyperbole perfectly captures a sense of comic *gravitas*.

YANG & YANG's free translations (1959) adopt an economical style, which shows frequent evidence of paraphrasing as well as involving the omission of whole phrases. But here the purpose, unlike that in Giles, is to play down the original rhetoric and create a sparer, more readily accessible English version, without sacrificing the fundamental content. "In Memory of my Nephew" illustrates this well: after "Heaven's will is hard to fathom ...", the next phrase, "The Gods are truly difficult to understand", is left out, since it is essentially a rhetorical repetition; yet a detail stating that the author "later found a livelihood south of the Yangtze" is retained, where Giles omits it. The approach works well and is consistently sustained, and the translators are sensitive to the shifts and nuances of the text.

Less economical with the original text, RIDEOUT's translations (1965) are more faithful, though they retain a considerable freedom of expression. The style tends towards an elegant rhetoric, involving a certain amount of archaic syntax, which sometimes also serves well to mirror the Chinese sentence structure. Though sometimes now a little dated, these translations are still often engaging.

By contrast, LIU (1979) often stays much closer to the original: in "On the Teacher", for instance, the translation of the verb *shi* as "to take as a teacher" (in the phrase "wu shi dao ye") suggests a desire for acute precision. Yet at other times the same rigour seems sadly lacking. In "Funerary Message to Nephew No. 12", for example, Han Yu laments that none can know the will of Heaven or the time of one's death, only to shift to a more personal perspective, and to remark that his own death seems all too imminent. Even in Yang & Yang's translation, the connective that marks this contrastive shift ("Sui ran", "Although this is so ..."), is still accounted for, yet Liu's often more pernickety work omits it altogether, thus missing an important nuance. Such instances are perhaps due less to carelessness than to an insensitivity as to what works in English; for elsewhere Liu is at the other extreme, using unnecessary verbiage. In all, though acceptable, this is rather uninspiring work.

SPRING's study of Tang *guwen* [ancient-style prose] (1983) contains a number of useful Han Yu translations, which follow the original texts closely, but far more consistently so than Liu: rarely does one feel that any detail of the Chinese has been overlooked. This is particularly evident in regard to grammatical structure and particles, which are always brought out in the translation, though one does not always agree with Spring's interpretation of the syntax. Spring's thoroughgoing approach, intended to support her discussion of stylistic features, perhaps inevitably produces sometimes unwieldy results (see for instance the end paragraph of "Offering for a Crocodile"); but in general these translations read relatively fluently.

Han Yu's poetry is less well represented in English. While there were occasional earlier translations of individual pieces (e.g. by Giles), there has been little available until comparatively recently.

GRAHAM (1965) often reproduces small details of expression lost in other translations: for "zhong ye", to cite one such case, we find "the crowded leaves", where others translate less literally. Yet a pragmatic approach – evident, for example, in the lively and varied handling of repetition patterns in "The South Mountains" – ensures that this desire for faithfulness is rarely taken to the point of awkwardness. Indeed, these translations show an imaginative use of English which avoids contrivance.

The frequently more colloquial tone of HANSON's work (in Liu & Lo, 1975) achieves sometimes brilliant effects, such as in "Losing One's Teeth", where the comic irony of the original is exploited to the full: "People say when your teeth go / it's certain the end's near. / But seems to me life has / its limits, you die when you die / either with or without teeth." Elsewhere, this relaxed style slightly lacks the fineness of touch of other translators, and one is left wondering if the textual freedom it entails is ultimately worthwhile. As "popular" translations, however, Hanson's works are generally effective.

HARTMAN's free but reliable translations (in Liu & Lo, 1975) are some of the most innovative, particularly in regard to form. Where others present an unbroken whole, Hartman employs a variety of stanzaic breaks within each poem; though this risks diluting the poem's original unity, it serves very effectively to unpack sometimes dense imagery and to make shifts in the poem more accessible to the Western reader. Also stylistically striking is the considerable use of enjambement (the majority of lines in the Chinese are end-stopped). The effect, coupled with frequent alliterative and assonantal techniques, often achieves poetic beauty, though is sometimes too lush for the Chinese, (e.g. "where leaves all dangling dry from the branches / drop, each alone to the empty steps"), creating a sensual lyric flow perhaps more Western in tone.

OWEN's scholarly translations (1975) are less daring, and less innovation is attempted. They tend to follow each line of the Chinese more faithfully than do Hartman's, though the original imagery is not always replicated, e.g. in "Autumn Meditations, IX": compare Owen's "In sorrow and melancholy I wasted fleeting time" with Graham's richer and less paraphrastic "Grief and care have wasted the shadow on the dial". The result is a slightly plainer, more straightforward rendering.

ROBERT J. NEATHER

Further Reading

Hanson, Kenneth O. (translator), *Growing Old Alive: Poems*, by Han Yü, Port Townsend, Washington: Copper Canyon Press, 1978

Hartman, Charles, "Language and Allusion in the Poetry of Han Yu: The 'Autumn Sentiments'" (dissertation), Bloomington: University of Indiana, 1974

Hartman, Charles, *Han Yü and the T'ang Search for Unity*, Princeton, New Jersey: Princeton University Press, 1986

Hightower, J.R., "Han Yü as Humorist", *Harvard Journal of Asiatic Studies*, 44/1 (June 1984) pp. 5–27 (contains 4 translations)

Luo, Liantian, *Han Yu yanjiu* [Researches on Han Yu], Taibei: Taiwan Xuesheng Shuju, 1977

McMullen, D.L., "Han Yü: An Alternative Picture", *Harvard Journal of Asiatic Studies*, 49/2 (December 1989) pp. 603–57 (a lengthy review article which responds to and challenges Hartman's *Han Yü and the T'ang Search for Unity*)

Schmidt, J., "Han Yü and His Ku-Shih Poetry" (MA thesis), Vancouver: University of British Columbia, 1969

Yu-shih, Chen, *Images and Ideas in Classical Chinese Prose: Studies of Four Masters*, Stanford, California: Stanford University Press, 1988 (chapter on Han Yu contains several translations)

Peter Handke 1942–

Austrian novelist, dramatist, poet and translator

Biography

Born in Griffen, Carinthia, near the Austrian border with the former Yugoslavia, 6 December 1942. His father was German, his mother Slovene. He studied law at Graz University, 1961–65. He then lived for brief periods in West Germany and Paris, with visits to the US, before moving to Salzburg. In 1999 he was living in Paris.

Handke began his writing career with fiction, poetry and drama but it was his experimental plays that first won him real attention. His varied and copious work in many genres, including screenplays, mime and radio theatre, uses language as a means to consciousness and reflects a "new subjectivity". It refers often to a symbolic threshold.

The year 1966 brought him fame, with his first novel, *Die Hornissen* [The Hornets], and a volume of three plays, *Publikumsbeschimpfung* (*Offending the Audience*), *Selbstbezichtigung* (*Self-Accusation*), and *Die Weissagung* (*Prophecy*). Handke was awarded the Büchner prize in 1973. Regarded earlier as a leader of the German-speaking left-wing generation of 1968, in 1999, during the war in the former Yugoslavia, Handke aroused controversy, to which he is no stranger, and accusations of fascism, by voicing his long-standing support for the Serbs in the Balkan conflict. As a gesture of protest against what he saw as anti-Serb bias in the international media and in the West's official attitude, he returned the Büchner prize money.

Translations

Novels and Novellas

Die Angst des Tormanns beim Elfmeter, 1970

Roloff, Michael, *The Goalie's Anxiety at the Penalty Kick*, New York: Farrar Straus, and London: Eyre Methuen, 1972

Wunschloses Unglück, 1972
Manheim, Ralph, *A Sorrow beyond Dreams: A Life Story*, New York: Farrar Straus, 1974

Der kurze Brief zum langen Abschied, 1972
Manheim, Ralph, *Short Letter, Long Farewell*, New York: Farrar Straus, and London: Methuen, 1977

Die Stunde der wahren Empfindung, 1975
Manheim, Ralph, *Moment of True Feeling*, New York: Farrar Straus, 1977

Die linkshändige Frau, 1976
Manheim, Ralph, *The Left-Handed Woman*, New York: Farrar Straus, and London: Methuen, 1980

Das Gewicht der Welt, 1977
Manheim, Ralph, *The Weight of the World*, New York: Farrar Straus, and London: Secker and Warburg, 1984

Langsame Heimkehr, 1979; *Die Lehre der Sainte-Victoire*, 1980; *Kindergeschichte*, 1981
Manheim, Ralph, *Slow Homecoming*, New York: Farrar Straus, and London: Methuen, 1985 (contains *The Long Way Around*, *The Lesson of Mont Saint-Victoire*, *Child Story*)

Der Chinese des Schmerzes, 1983
Manheim, Ralph, *Across*, New York: Farrar Straus, and London: Methuen, 1986

Die Wiederholung, 1986
Manheim, Ralph, *Repetition*, New York: Farrar Straus, and London: Methuen, 1988

Die Abwesenheit: Ein Märchen, 1987
Manheim, Ralph, *Absence*, New York: Farrar Straus, 1990; London: Methuen, 1991

Nachmittag eines Schriftstellers, 1987
Manheim, Ralph, *The Afternoon of a Writer*, New York: Farrar Straus, and London: Methuen, 1989

Mein Jahr in der Niemandsbucht, 1994
Winston, Krishna, *My Year in the No-Man's-Bay*, New York: Farrar Straus, 1998

Essays

Versuch über die Müdigkeit, 1989; *Versuch über die Jukebox*, 1990; and *Versuch über den geglückten Tag*, 1991
Manheim, Ralph and Krishna Winston, *The Jukebox and Other Essays on Storytelling*, New York: Farrar Straus, 1994 (contains *Essay on Tiredness*, *Essay on the Jukebox*, *Essay on the Successful Day*)

Selections of Plays

Roloff, Michael, *Kaspar and Other Plays*, New York: Farrar Straus, 1969 (contains *Offending the Audience*, *Self-Accusation*, *Kaspar*)
Roloff, Michael and Karl Weber, *The Ride across Lake Constance and Other Plays*, New York: Farrar Straus, 1976 (contains *Prophecy*, *Calling for Help*, *My Foot My Tutor*, *Quodlibet*, *The Ride across Lake Constance*, *They Are Dying Out*)

Plays

Publikumsbeschimpfung, 1966
Roloff, Michael, *Offending the Audience* in *Kaspar and Other Plays*, translated by Roloff, 1969; with *Self-Accusation*, London: Methuen, 1971

Selbstbezichtigung, 1966
Roloff, Michael, *Self-Accusation* in *Kaspar and Other Plays*, translated by Roloff, 1969; with *Offending the Audience*, London: Methuen, 1971

Die Weissagung, 1966
Roloff, Michael, *Prophecy* in *The Ride across Lake Constance and Other Plays*, translated by Roloff and Weber, 1976

Kaspar, 1967
Roloff, Michael, *Kaspar* in *Kaspar and Other Plays*, translated by Roloff, 1969; published separately London: Eyre Methuen, 1972

Hilferufe, 1967
Roloff, Michael, *Calling for Help* in *The Ride across Lake Constance and Other Plays*, translated by Roloff and Weber, 1976

Das Mündel will Vormund sein, 1968
Roloff, Michael, *My Foot My Tutor* in *The Ride across Lake Constance and Other Plays*, translated by Roloff and Weber, 1976

Quodlibet, 1970
Roloff, Michael, *Quodlibet* in *The Ride across Lake Constance and Other Plays*, translated by Roloff and Weber, 1976

Der Ritt über den Bodensee, 1970
Roloff, Michael, *The Ride across Lake Constance*, London: Eyre Methuen, 1973; also in *The Ride across Lake Constance and Other Plays*, translated by Roloff and Weber, 1976

Die Unvernünftigen sterben aus, 1973
Roloff, Michael, *They Are Dying Out* in *The Ride across Lake Constance and Other Plays*, translated by Roloff and Weber, 1976

Das Spiel vom Fragen oder Die Reise zum sonoren Land, 1989
Honegger, Gitta, *Voyage to the Sonorous Land; or, The Art of Asking*, with *The Hour We Knew Nothing of Each Other*, New Haven, Connecticut: Yale University Press, 1996

Die Stunde da wir nichts voneinander wussten, 1992
Honegger, Gitta, *The Hour We Knew Nothing of Each Other*, with *Voyage to the Sonorous Land; or, The Art of Asking*, New Haven, Connecticut: Yale University Press, 1996

Poetry

Die Innenwelt der Aussenwelt der Innenwelt, 1969
Roloff, Michael, *The Innerworld of the Outerworld of the Innerworld*, New York: Seabury Press, 1974

Als das Wünschen noch geholfen hat, 1974
Roloff, Michael, *Nonsense and Happiness*, New York: Urizen, 1976

Peter Handke began his literary career as a playwright. His *Sprechstücke*, among them *Offending the Audience*, challenged the conventions of traditional theatre and were instrumental in re-attaching German-language drama to the European context. Since their publication in 1966, Handke has experimented with (and deconstructed) many other literary genres. He has published other plays, numerous novels, short stories, prose works, essays, poetry, radio plays, and filmscripts. Further, Handke's work includes a number of translations from various languages into German, among them Walker Percy's *The Moviegoer* and Aeschylus' *Prometheus Bound*.

In an essay on translation (*Vom Übersetzen*, 1992), Handke describes how his own search for matching words, structures, and rhythms made him realize that to translate was not just to reproduce but to create. He is thus well aware of translation as the rewriting of an original for a different culture. Handke is also conscious of literary translation as literary politics, as evidenced by his own efforts to translate Austrian minority literature in Slovenian into German.

This background and Handke's interest in crossing linguistic borders led to his active engagement in establishing a consistent voice for himself in English. The majority of his works have been translated into English, most of them by two translators. Michael ROLOFF did Handke's early plays and some of his poetry. Ralph MANHEIM, highly praised for his translations of European classics ranging from Freud, Jung, and Heidegger to Proust, Brecht, and Grass, translated Handke's prose works.

Handke and MANHEIM (who died in 1992) had a longstanding collaboration and were accustomed to reviewing translations together. In an obituary for "his translator", as Handke proudly calls him, he praises Manheim's skill in taking liberties while remaining faithful to the original thus re-creating his works in authentic English rather than merely translating them. Manheim's translations, writes Handke, made him read his own works anew – as factual accounts cutting through his own searching and detour-filled German.

A Sorrow beyond Dreams, MANHEIM's prize-winning translation (1974) of Handke's *Wunschloses Unglück*, seems to illustrate Handke's own re-reading experience. The book is Handke's attempt to come to terms with his mother's suicide. He does, however, go beyond the purely personal concern by constantly assessing the course of his mother's life in relation to the historical, political, and social influences to which she is exposed. Manheim's translation captures the tone and the atmosphere of the original. At the same time it seems to make Handke's prose more succint, thus adding immediacy to the account of his mother's life and death.

This heightened immediacy also characterizes Manheim's translations of Handke's later works. They do, however, also reflect the shift of Handke's prose towards a more lyrical tone, which began to make itself felt in *Langsame Heimkehr* (1979). Since then Handke has moved away from being an avantgardist who rebelled against the traditional use of form and language towards using a more classically inspired, loftier style of writing that is characterized by a search for harmony. Manheim decided to follow him as a translator, eager to capture exactly that which he found alien about Handke's new voice, as the writer himself put it.

Manheim does indeed capture the essence of Handke's later prose. His translations render the lyrical language and the philosophical searching of Handke's originals. From *The Long Way Around*, Manheim's translation (1985) of *Langsame Heimkehr*, to *Child Story* (1985), *Repetition* (1988), *Absence* (1990), and *The Afternoon of a Writer* (1989), Manheim's English succeeds in reflecting a poetic quality similar to that of Handke's German. The lightness and clarity of Manheim's prose becomes once again apparent in his posthumously published collection *The Jukebox and Other Essays on Storytelling* (Manheim & Winston, 1994) in which his *Essay on Tiredness* and his *Essay on the Successful Day* stand next to Krishna WINSTON's translation of the *Essay on the Jukebox*, which is more faithful to the original, but is also more laboured.

One major difference between Handke's English and his German body of works stems from Manheim's translating only Handke's prose, not his poetry and plays. Thus, the *Heimkehr* tetralogy was published as a trilogy in English, *Slow Homecoming* (MANHEIM, 1985), leaving behind the fourth book, the dramatic poem *Über die Dörfer*.

Through Manheim's successful and continuous work, the English Handke comes across as a prose writer whose experiments with drama and poetry belong to an early phase of his career. This early phase is associated with another translator, Michael ROLOFF, who is as much an alter ego of the young writer as Manheim is of the later Handke.

Roloff translated all of Handke's early plays and some of his poetry. He takes certain liberties with the *Sprechstücke*, which he calls "speak-ins". In *Offending the Audience* (ROLOFF, 1969), for example, Roloff does not translate literally the invective at the end of the play, but rather the principle according to which it is arranged. Translating each epithet literally, he explains, "would only have resulted in completely discordant patterns", and so he "sought to create new acoustic patterns in English" instead.

In the play *Kaspar*, one of Handke's classic analyses of language and power, ROLOFF (1969) adds American truisms to the moral truisms used by the prompters who address Kaspar. He also introduces changes in order to make Kaspar's rhymes half-rhyme in English. Despite these liberties, Roloff insists that his versions of Handke's plays are translations, not adaptations. This is true if one agrees that translations should create the same effect in the target language (which Roloff succeeds in doing) as opposed to literally reproducing the original.

The consistent body of translations by Roloff and Manheim has created a split in Handke's English persona into young playwright and poet versus mature prose writer. Other facets of Handke's later work have only started to cross over into English with HONEGGER's translations (1996) of the plays *Das Spiel vom Fragen* and *Die Stunde da wir nichts voneinander wussten* and WINSTON's translation *My Year in the No-Man's-Bay* (1998), a work that Handke calls a fairy tale from modern times. These translations stand at the beginning of a new chapter in Handke's English life: the post-Manheim era.

CHRISTA GAUG

Further Reading

Firda, Richard Arthur, *Peter Handke*, New York: Twayne, 1993

Handke, Peter, "Vom Übersetzen: Bilder, Bruchstücke, ein paar Namen" in his *Langsam im Schatten: Gesammelte Verzettelungen 1980–1992*, Frankfurt: Suhrkamp, 1992, pp. 96–114

Handke, Peter, "Für Ralph Manheim: Das Summen des Übersetzers", *Die Zeit*, (20 November 1992) p. 76

Hern, Nicholas, *Peter Handke*, London: Woolf, and New York: Ungar, 1972
Klinkowitz, Jerome and James Knowlton, *Peter Handke and the Postmodern Transformation: The Goalie's Journey Home*, Columbia: University of Missouri Press, 1983
Schlueter, June (editor), *The Plays and Novels of Peter Handke*, Pittsburgh: University of Pittsburgh Press, 1981

Hanshan (Han Shan) fl.627–649

Chinese poet

Biography

Little is known of the life of Hanshan ("Cold Mountain"). The name, also known in the form Hanshanzi ("Master of Cold Mountain"), was apparently adopted as an alias. The multivolume *Complete Tang Poetry*, compiled by imperial commission and first printed in 1707, includes more than 300 poems under his name, along with a brief biographical note, and the Hanshan section heads several volumes of works by Buddhist monks. The biographical note, however, describes him only as a recluse, who lived in the scenic Tiantai mountains of northeast Zhejiang and frequented the famous local Buddhist Guoqing Temple. The poems are written in a simple, often colloquial style, mixing vernacular and literary language, which approximates to that of Buddhist religious verse. However, it seems that his poems, along with a corpus of religious texts of the Buddhist Chan (*Zen* in Japanese) school, found their way into Japan during the 12th century. The earliest extant edition of Hanshan's poems, printed by the Guoqing Temple in 1189, is now in the Palace Library of Japan. He has become a cult figure in Japan and is known as *Kanzan* in Japanese.

Translations

Collections

Henricks, Robert G., *The Poetry of Han-Shan: A Complete, Annotated Translation of Cold Mountain*, Albany: State University of New York Press, 1990
Red Pine, *The Collected Songs of Cold Mountain* (parallel texts), with an introduction by John Blofeld, Port Townsend, Washington: Copper Canyon Press, 1983

Selections

Snyder, Gary, "Cold Mountain Poems", *Evergreen Review*, 2/6 (Autumn 1958); reprinted in his *Riprap and Cold Mountain Poems*, San Francisco: Four Seasons Foundation, 1965, and in his *A Range of Poems*, London: Fulcrum, 1966 (24 poems of Hanshan)
Stambler, Peter, *Encounters with Cold Mountain Poems by Han Shan: Modern Versions* (bilingual edition), Beijing: Panda Books, 1996
Tobias, Arthur *et al.*, *The View from Cold Mountain*, Buffalo, New York: White Pine Press, 1982 (34 poems of Hanshan)
Waley, Arthur, "27 Poems by Han-shan", *Encounter*, 3/3 (September 1954); reprinted in *Chinese Poems*, London: Unwin, 1982
Watson, Burton, *Cold Mountain: 100 Poems by the T'ang Poet Han-shan*, New York: Grove Press, 1962; London: Jonathan Cape, 1970

The reception of Hanshan in English is one of those phenomena in the history of literary exchanges, quite puzzling to the Chinese themselves, which make a legitimate subject of study for students of comparative literature. Hanshan has never been included in the canon of Chinese poetry, and is never likely to be. The reason is not complex: to many native Chinese who know English, the present writer included, it is more pleasant to read him in English than in the original. To a very large extent, Hanshan has been discovered by his Japanese admirers (and even there less as a poet than as a Zen master), and reinvented as a legend by his American translators, especially Gary Snyder, and by Snyder's fellow Beat Generation writer Jack Kerouac (1922–69), who dedicated his novel *Dharma Bums* to Hanshan, and included some of Snyder's translation in a dialogue therein.

Still, the credit of being Hanshan's earliest English translator belongs to WALEY (1954). The 27 poems he has translated read as well as the other works of this great master, and they are in general free from errors. The only quibble one may make is that his Hanshan is almost as balanced and melodious as his Bai Juyi (Po Chü-i), and the former's idiosyncratic voice is somehow missing. Hanshan's later success in the United States is due to Waley's authoritative influence.

SNYDER began his translation in 1955 as an assignment in a graduate seminar under Ch'en Shih-hsiang, an eminent scholar at the University of California, Berkeley, with Waley's versions on hand. His translations of 24 Hanshan poems (1958), along with that of a biography written by a Tang official Lüqiu Yin contained in the Guoqing Temple version, were published after he dropped out of graduate school, took up Chinese and Japanese, started a serious association with Japanese Zen Buddhism, and began to establish himself as a poet in his own right. These translations have since become well known and been frequently anthologized. Influenced by Ezra Pound, William Carlos Williams, and Imagism, his texts excel in presenting vivid images through skillful choice of diction. Despite the not infrequent deviation from the original, the fresh and energetic voice of

Snyder's Hanshan has become a part of modern American poetry.

WATSON, like Waley conversant with both Chinese and Japanese, has profited in his translation (1962) from the annotated Japanese translation of Yoshitaka Iriya. Watson's American English, while not as colloquial as (and somehow less visual than) that of Snyder, works well with Hanshan. While Snyder's Hanshan is primarily a wanderer in search of spiritual enlightenment, Watson's more extensive selection of 100 poems also presents Hanshan as a social critic and piquant satirist, with all his human emotional connections.

TOBIAS's translations (1982) of 34 Hanshan poems are included in the same anthology as 19 poems attributed to Hanshan's fellow recluse ("sidekick" in Snyder's terms) Shide (Shih Te), translated by James Sanford and J.P. Seaton. The versions tend to paraphrase, and can hardly match Snyder's vigor and Watson's zest.

RED PINE's bilingual collection (1983) is the first complete English translation of Hanshan's poems, with the Chinese text on the facing page and each of the 307 poems generously annotated. The book includes an introduction by John Blofeld, who has resorted to all kinds of materials, however unreliable, to fabricate an imaginary biography of Hanshan. The translations are mostly quite literal, making little change to the structure of the original lines. As the translator himself acknowledges in his preface, his greatest problem has been that he is not a poet.

Red Pine's insipid version has easily been superseded by HENRICKS's new complete English version (1990). Henricks, a professor of religion at Dartmouth College, has provided an annotated translation that is not only quite readable but also enriched by thorough exegesis of some of the more interesting texts. It starts with a 26-page introduction; the translations are followed by appendices that include discussion of "internal evidence" of dates, a checklist of previous English translations, an index to themes, and notes on Buddhist terms, metaphors, and stories, and it closes with an index and an exhaustive bibliography that includes sources in Chinese and Japanese, and secondary sources on Hanshan in other European languages. This will remain the definitive Hanshan text for scholars and students alike for many years to come.

More recently, STAMBLER (1996) has offered another variation of Hanshan in English. In an arrangement similar to that of Red Pine's version, the Chinese original is printed above each English text. As is divulged in the choice of the term *Encounters* in the title, this is a very free translation, more in the spirit of Robert Lowell's *Imitations*, in which the translator attempts to mediate across time and space and give the Chinese poet who lived probably a millennium ago a contemporary American voice. The poems do read as poems, but can hardly be judged as translations.

Wu's study (1957) includes a discussion of the myth and reality of Hanshan's historical background and his own not very readable translations of 50 poems. Kahn's short unpaginated essay is an informative survey of Hanshan's reception in English.

YANG YE

Further Reading

Kahn, Paul, *Han Shan in English*, Buffalo: White Pine Press, 1989

Wu Chi-yu, "A Study of Han-Shan", *T'oung Pao*, 45 (1957)

See also the introductions to Watson and to Henricks

Yahyā Haqqī 1905–1993

Egyptian novelist, essayist and short-story writer

Biography

Born in Cairo in 1905. Haqqī studied law at the Sultaniyya Law School in Cairo and went on to practise as a lawyer for a short time. He was then posted to Manfalut, a town in Upper Egypt, as an administrative assistant. After leaving Manfalut in 1929 he took up a position with the Egyptian foreign service, and was sent to Jedda, Ankara, Paris and Tripoli in this capacity. Haqqī published only one full-length novel, *Sahh al-nawm*, 1955, which takes as its subject the aftermath of the Free Officers' Revolution in Egypt in 1952. He was reputed more widely for his short stories and novellas, including his best-known work, *Qindīl Umm Hāshim* (*The Saint's Lamp*), 1944, which illustrates the juxtaposition of Eastern spirituality and Western materialism. He completed seven short-story collections and nine books of essays and journal articles. Haqqī also published several books of literary criticism. He wrote an autobiography, *Khallihā 'alā Allāh* [Leave it to God], 1967. Died 1993.

Translations

Novellas and Short Stories

Qindīl Umm Hāshim, 1944

Badawi, M.M., *The Saint's Lamp and Other Stories*, with an introduction, Leiden: E.J. Brill, 1973

Sahh al-nawm, 1955

Cooke, Miriam, *Good Morning! and Other Stories*, with an introduction, Washington, DC: Three Continents Press, 1987

Yahyā Haqqī was a member of the generation of "grand old men" of 20th-century Egyptian writers which includes also

Tawfīq al-Hakīm and Tāhā Husayn. His early training and background certainly bore a similarity to al-Hakīm's. Both men studied law; both entered government service; both served in the Egyptian provinces; and both men's writings were markedly influenced by that experience. From then on, however, their careers and published output diverged strongly – for while Tawfīq al-Hakīm's most significant contributions lie in the development of the Arabic novel and drama, Yahyā Haqqī remained essentially a master of the smaller-scale forms, – the short story and novella.

The volumes of English translations published by BADAWI (1973) and COOKE (1987) each contain one major work, or novella, and a number of accompanying short stories. Yahyā Haqqī was a careful rather than a prolific writer, and although the English volumes are slim in themselves (a mere 200 pages between them), they give the reader a good representative flavour of his writings. Of the two longer works translated, *Qindīl Umm Hāshim* is of major significance in the development of a group of themes in modern Arabic literature that may be crudely described as the East/West theme; while *Sahh al-nawm*, the themes of which relate to the transition from the monarchical to the republican regime in Egypt, remained to the end Yahyā Haqqī's favourite of all his own works.

Qindīl Umm Hāshim revolves around a protagonist, Ismā'īl, who is brought up in a traditional Muslim family in the Sayyida Zaynab quarter of Cairo. Unlike his brothers he receives a modern education, but because his examination results are not good enough he cannot enter medical school in Egypt and is sent to England to study. While there he comes under the influence of Western civilization, most obviously in the guise of Mary, who both liberates him sexually and awakens him to the delights of art and of nature; in the meantime, he has lost his religious faith. Unlike some earlier works such as Tawfīq al-Hakīm's *'Usfūr min al-Sharq*, however, which treat the protagonist's experiences in the West in considerable detail, *Qindīl Umm Hāshim* deals with Ismā'īl's experiences in Europe comparatively briefly – the main portion of the work being devoted to an account of his traditional upbringing and his struggle to resolve his inner conflict between East and West on his return to Egypt. After a series of crises that effectively constitute a personal breakdown, Ismā'?l eventually realizes that "there can be no science without faith"; reconciled again to his roots, he marries his cousin Fatima (by whom he has 11 children), sets up a clinic in the Al-Baghalla district, and devotes his life to helping the poor.

Despite its brevity (no more than 38 pages in BADAWI's translation), *Qindīl Umm Hāshim* remains one of the most eloquent expressions of the East/West theme in modern Arabic literature. Its appeal owes much to the fact that the author's main concern is for the character of Ismā'īl rather than with abstract questions of cultural relativities; like the other characters in the novella, Ismā'īl's development is depicted with both humour and compassion, and the story is rich with the symbolism of darkness and light – figured both in the "Saint's Lamp" of the title and in Ismā'īl's profession as an eye-doctor.

Qindīl Umm Hāshim poses formidable problems for the translator, for the brevity of the work is reflected also in an economy of expression that extends down to the level of the individual word. As in all Haqqī's writing, every sentence of the work gives the impression of having been carefully weighed and considered for its full effect on the reader. On the odd occasion, indeed, Haqqī's precision seems almost contrived, as economy of expression threatens to lead to obscurity; but the number of such lapses is remarkably small. Another challenge to the translator is posed by the odd snatches of Egyptian colloquial – street cries and the like – which the author uses to add local colour to the work.

The themes of *The Saint's Lamp* are recurring ones in modern Arabic literature – as indeed, in Middle Eastern literature more generally. The conflict between tradition and modernity that tears apart Ismā'īl – and echoes the dilemma of a whole nation at the beginning of the 20th century – is reflected also in *Good Morning!* The novella that forms the core of this volume presents us with a series of sketches of village life and folk before and after the arrival of the train – a symbol of development that recurs also in "The First Lesson", one of the short stories included in Cooke's volume of translations. The modernity heralded by the train is, however, ambiguous, for although in some material respects the villagers' lot appears to have improved, at the same time a sense of alienation has entered their lives, as their rural innocence is shattered by their authoritarian, city-trained leader, the "professor". Moreover, the date of publication of the story – a mere three years after the Free Officers' Revolt of 1952 – suggests that, unlike *Qindīl Umm Hāshim*, the work was also intended by its author as a direct comment on political developments in contemporary Egypt.

The problems presented to the translator by this work are not dissimilar from those of *Qindīl Umm Hāshim*. In general, both BADAWI (1973) and COOKE (1987) cope well with the difficulties involved; their words, like those of Haqqī himself, have been chosen with care, and although Cooke has been criticized by reviewers for mistakes and omissions in her translation, these are unlikely to bother the ordinary reader. For the most part, both translations read easily and smoothly, albeit with a certain woodenness of expression in places to remind the reader that what he is reading is not an original text. In general, however, Haqqī has been well served by his English translators; both volumes also include concise but useful introductions, and Cooke's volume contains a valuable bibliography of translations of Haqqī's works into European languages, including (in addition to English) French, German, Romanian and Russian.

PAUL STARKEY

Further Reading

Badawi, M.M., "*The Lamp of Umm Hāshim*: The Egyptian Intellectual Between East and West", *Journal of Arabic Literature*, 1 (1970) pp. 145–61

Cooke, Miriam, *The Anatomy of an Egyptian Intellectual: Yahyā Haqqī*, Washington, DC: Three Continents Press, 1984

Gohlman, Susan A., "Women as Cultural Symbols in Yahyā Haqqī's *Saint's Lamp*", *Journal of Arabic Literature*, 10 (1979) pp. 117–27

McLean, Katrina, "Poetic Themes in Yahyā Haqqī's *Qindīl Umm Hāshim*", *Journal of Arabic Literature*, 11 (1980) pp. 80–87

Siddiq, Muhammad, "'Deconstructing' *The Saint's Lamp*", *Journal of Arabic Literature*, 17 (1986) pp. 126–45

Jaroslav Hašek 1883–1923

Czech novelist and short-story writer

Biography

Born in Prague, 30 April 1883, the son of an alcoholic schoolteacher, Hašek might generally be described as an inveterate hoaxer, drunkard and miscreant, with a strong inclination towards a kind of mischievous anarchism; in short, the sort of character around whom gather more legends than hard facts. After leaving school he went to the Czecho-Slovak Commercial Academy where he showed some flair for technical subjects and story-telling. He left the Academy in 1902, got a job as a bank clerk, which he promptly lost for unreliability, and by 1903–04 had become involved with anarchist circles in Prague. In 1907 he spent a month in prison for assaulting a policeman. In 1909, with the help of a friend, he became editor of *Svět zvířat* [Animal World] and a year later was able to marry Jarmila Mayerová, whom he had been courting since 1905 against the strong opposition of her father. Hašek lost his job the same year after inventing material about animals and animal behaviour, and advertising "thoroughbred werewolves" to the citizens of Prague. He went on to found and campaign for the fictitious "Party for Moderate Progress within the Bounds of the Law" before being sent to the Russian front in 1915. Hašek was captured and taken to Russia where he ended up writing nationalist propaganda for the Czech Legion. By 1918 he had switched allegiance, become a teetotaller and joined the Bolsheviks. There is little information about Hašek's life at this time, but a change seems to have come over him, as he was well-known among the Russians for his diligence and reliability, becoming Deputy Commandant of the town of Bugulma and a Political Commissar. He did, however, marry again, bigamously, in 1920. He returned to Czechoslovakia the same year and began to write *The Good Soldier Švejk*. He quickly resumed his old way of life and drank and ate himself into an early grave. Died in Lipnice, 3 January 1923.

Translations

Novel

Osudy dobrého vojáka Švejka za světové války, 1921–23

Parrott, Cecil, *The Good Soldier Švejk and His Fortunes in the World War*, New York and London: Penguin, 1973; reprinted London: Everyman, 1993

Selver, Paul, *The Good Soldier Schweik*, London: Penguin, 1930; further abridged version 1939; restored version 1951

Selections of Stories

Havlů, I.T., *The Tourist Guide*, Prague: Artia, 1931

Kožíšková, Doris, *Little Stories by a Great Master*, Prague: Orbis Press Agency, 1984

Menhennet, Alan, *The Bachura Scandal and Other Stories and Sketches*, London: Angel Books, 1991; Chester Springs, Pennsylvania: Dufour, 1992

Parrott, Cecil, *The Red Commissar, Including Further Adventures of the Good Soldier Švejk and Other Stories*, London: Abacus, 1981

Jaroslav Hašek is the only Czech writer whose central creation – the Good Soldier Švejk – is almost as much a part of English literary folklore as of Czech. Švejk (and "Švejkism") have become irrevocably associated with the Czech national character, much to the annoyance of some Czechs.

Attempts to define or characterize Švejk seem hopeless from the beginning – his is a character that eludes fixed definition. As he wanders through the Central Europe of World War I, perpetually on his way to the front, Švejk's every act seems to puncture the pretensions of church, state, monarchy and military and reveal them in all their absurdity (although in another sense these same institutions are too obviously caricatures of themselves for any satirical intent to be taken seriously). Švejk himself, with blissful good cheer, seems keen only to demonstrate his good intent towards these same institutions. He is a picaresque hero, a wise fool (who in large part is not a fool at all), sometimes kind and innocent, sometimes crude and brutal, as untroubled by lying as he is by telling the truth. Almost any simple assertion about Švejk can be countered and contradicted, and perhaps all such assertions can only be made if the reader or critic is taking him – and also, perhaps, the ultimate seriousness of the caricaturing satire – just a little too seriously.

The English translator of *Švejk* faces many problems, the first of which is certainly Hašek's particular use of Czech. Broadly speaking there are two linguistic strata in Czech: *spisovná Čeština* (literary Czech) and *obecná Čeština* (Common Czech); some commentators add another layer between the two. Common Czech has its own syntactical elements, lexicon (sometimes showing the influence of German) and morphology that differentiate it from the (in some ways) more archaic, even rather contrived Literary Czech. Hašek was among the first Czech writers not just to employ Common Czech but to use it as an integral part of the text – something that initially met with much criticism. The tension between Common and Literary Czech is a constant feature of *Švejk*, and obviously impossible to reproduce in English. Typical features of Common Czech such as adding *v* before an initial vowel, e.g. *von* - he, instead of the formal *on* seem rather more colourful and evocative than, for example, the hackneyed dropping of *h* in English, as in "'ere, 'ave an apple?" and cannot be translated in this way (see entry on Havel for more on Common Czech).

The influence of Austrian German is also crucial in *Švejk*, as it penetrated the Czech language (and, at that time, mentality) at all levels. Czech bureaucratic language was modelled on Austrian (or, in Robert Musil's term, *Kakanian*), and much play is made with this in *Švejk*. By the same token Czech military slang was filled with mangled Germanisms, e.g. *mašinkvér* from *Maschinengewehr* (machine-gun). German words were also absorbed into Czech low colloquial speech, e.g. *pucovat* from *putzen* – to smarten oneself up, and *mít recht* from *recht haben* – to be right (see Daneš, p. 230). Again there is no way to render this exclusively German-Czech linguistic milieu in English.

A last important point: Czech is especially rich in vulgarisms and terms of abuse, and Hašek uses these liberally in *Švejk*, not just for colour but also for characterization. Czech can draw on the usual language of sex and excretion but it also has a fine repertoire of other words (e.g. those derived from animals) covering all possible degrees of severity. English abuse, on the other hand, tends to be limited to a couple of crude obscenities or some rather anaemic expressions, all of which quickly become monotonous.

Paul SELVER's translation (1930) is problematic in two ways. First, Selver abridges the book by missing out book 4 (which was left uncompleted on Hašek's death). This, in a way, is no bad thing, as book 4 does not obviously enhance the already overlong book, but the modern translator would perhaps prefer to leave the decision on what is to be left out to the reader. The second and much more serious charge is that Selver has sometimes bowdlerized what he has translated, missing out not just words and paragraphs if he feels they might offend, but even whole pages. (It is, of course, possible that some cuts were editorial, but other sources also show that Selver could be quite cavalier with his translations). Selver goes so far as to remove some of the irreligious and anti-monarchical statements that are central to Hašek's writing. The chapter *Nové trápení* in book 2 – literally "New Torments" but entirely adequately translated by Paul Selver as *Fresh Tribulations* – is a case in point, with perhaps three or four pages of Hašek's text missing. Selver omits passages of typical lavatorial humour, a scurrilous ditty and section about the Emperor Franz Josef, and a long and brutal passage about Austro-Hungarian atrocities in Serbia. Selver also chooses the mildest vulgarisms he can; as a result of which Chaplain Katz, for instance, becomes a shadow of his former self: expressions like "You lousy crew" and "You pack of rotters" do not even come close to Katz's epic repertoire of abuse. (In fairness to Selver, he was working in the late 1920s and had to take account of British sensibilities at that time).

In Selver's favour it can be said that he manages to reproduce some of Hašek's stylistic oddities quite well. For example, Selver makes a good effort at preserving the tension between Literary and Common Czech (Hašek has a particular fondness for putting low Prague slang next to elaborate and old-fashioned Czech participial constructions: "having done ...", "doing ...", etc.). Selver also avoids some of the stiffness in colloquial dialogue that afflicts Parrott's translation, although the modern reader may find his 1930s idiom slightly quaint. Selver deserves praise for being so quick to translate such an important book, but his version of *Švejk* should be read with care.

Sir Cecil PARROTT's 1973 translation of *Švejk* seems likely to remain the definitive English version for some time to come. Parrott, former British Ambassador to Czechoslovakia, was a great Hašek enthusiast: he translated *Švejk*, another collection of Hašek's stories (titled in English *The Red Commissar* and including five more Švejk stories), and wrote the only English biography of Hašek. Parrott is a rather literal translator, sometimes unimaginatively so. This literalness and uncertain command of English slang registers sometimes leads Parrott into awkward-sounding English. At one point, for instance, Švejk addresses the appallingly drunk Chaplain Katz as follows: "'Drop it, I tell you,' he said, 'or I'll bash your flipper.'" Similarly, sentences like "His speech was interlarded with the most variegated oaths and was brief in content" seem clumsy, rather than amusing as in the Czech. In short, Parrott translates the words literally but often at the cost of leaving the humour behind. In the case of *Švejk*, which is after all a comic novel, this is a serious criticism. The opening of book 1, chapter 15 ("Catastrophe") illustrates the problem well. It is, admittedly, hard to know how to render Colonel Kraus's hilarious imbecilities into equally hilarious English, but Parrott does not manage it. The passage comes out sounding flat and a bit silly, while the Czech contrives to be delightful, satirical and *very* funny all at the same time.

In his article "On Translating Švejk" Parrott argues the need to break up some of the long, syntactically complex sentences that particularly characterize Švejk's speech, "since otherwise it would be difficult for the reader to follow their thread" (p. 71). He gives no evidence for this and the point is certainly debatable. Švejk speaks in the popular narrative style that presents no difficulties to anyone who, for example, has listened to a story told over a glass or two of beer.

Parrott's version of *Švejk* is readable and adequate, although the lack of humour does make the translation quite tedious after a while. There are, however, plenty of critics and readers who would argue that Hašek's book becomes tedious even in Czech. In general, the main criticism of both translations is that they lack most of the comedy and mischief of Hašek's original.

JAMES PARTRIDGE

Further Reading

Daneš, František, "The Language and Style of Hašek's Novel *The Good Soldier Švejk* from the Viewpoint of Translation", in *Studies in Functional Stylistics*, edited by Jan Chaloupek and Jiří Nekvapil, Amsterdam: Benjamins, 1993, pp. 223–47

Frynta, Emanuel, *Hašek, the Creator of Schweik*, translated by J. Layton and G. Theiner, Prague: Artia, 1965

Parrott, Cecil, "On Translating Švejk", *The Incorporated Linguist* 12/ 4 (1973): 70–72

Parrott, Cecil, *The Bad Bohemian: The Life of Jaroslav Hašek, Creator of "The Good Soldier Švejk"*, London: Bodley Head, 1978

Pynsent, Robert, "Jaroslav Hašek" in *European Writers: The Twentieth Century*, vol. 9: *Pío Baroja to Franz Kafka*, edited by George Stade, New York: Scribner, 1989

Gerhart Hauptmann 1862–1946

German dramatist, novelist and poet

Biography

Born 15 November 1862 in Ober-Salzbrunn, Silesia (now Poland). There he observed the wide disparity in wealth, social prestige and language between the nobility and nouveaux riches who frequented his parent's spa hotel and the peasants, weavers and coal miners who laboured under harsh and exploitative conditions throughout the Silesian countryside. Hauptmann fared poorly in the authoritarian Prussian school system and unsuccessfully attempted various studies in agriculture, sculpture and art before deciding to write professionally at the age of 23. He was an immensely prolific writer, producing 50 plays, 25 novels and shorter prose pieces, half a dozen verse epics, numerous poems, fragments, essays, speeches and diaries. His work has been adapted into television and film in Germany, and translated into more than 30 languages. His dramatic work alone encompasses a wide range of genres, including domestic tragedies: *Lonely Lives* (published in German, 1891) and *Michael Kramer* (1900); social dramas: *The Weavers* (1892), *Drayman Henschel* (1897–98) and *Rose Bernd* (1903); historical dramas: *Florian Geyer* (1896); comedies: *The Beaver Coat* (1893); tragicomedies: *The Red Cock* (1901) and *The Rats* (1911); symbolic dramas: *The Assumption of Hannele* (1893) and *The Sunken Bell* (1896); and poetic dramas: *Winter Ballad* (1917). He was awarded the Nobel Prize for Literature in 1912. In his work Hauptmann reveals an unwavering sympathy for the lower classes, a predilection for unheroic characters, and compassion towards human shortcomings and failures, as well as an interest in the transcendent, metaphysical aspects of the human condition. He died 8 June 1946.

The Weavers

Die Weber, 1892

Naturalistic social drama in five acts. First published as *De Waber*, 1892; modified as *Die Weber*, 1892; first performed in 1893.

Translations

Frenz, Horst and Miles Waggoner, *The Weavers, Hannele, The Beaver Coat*, with an introduction, New York: Rinehart, 1951; also in *Masters of Modern Drama*, edited by Haskell M. Block and Robert G. Shedd, New York: Random House, 1962

Lustig, Theodore, *The Weavers* in *Five Plays by Hauptmann*, translated by Lustig, New York: Bantam, 1961 (contains *The Weavers, The Beaver Coat, Hannele, Drayman Henschel, Rose Bernd*)

Marcus, Frank, *The Weavers*, with an introduction, London: Eyre Methuen, 1980

Morison, Mary, *The Weavers: A Drama of the Forties*, with an introduction, London: Heinemann, 1899; New York: Huebsch, 1911; also in *The Dramatic Works of Gerhart Hauptmann*, edited by Ludwig Lewisohn, 9 vols, New York: Huebsch, 1912–29, and 8 vols, London: Secker, 1913–29

Mueller, Carl Richard, *The Weavers*, San Francisco: Chandler, 1965; also in *Masterpieces of the Modern German Theatre*, edited by Robert W. Corrigan, New York: Collier, 1967

Gerhart Hauptmann, along with Arno Holz and Johannes Schlaf, was one of the leading figures in the German Naturalist movement. The extensive use of dialect to evoke a particular milieu or region are said to make much of his work untranslatable. Hauptmann was widely regarded as Germany's most renowned and important modern author prior to World War II. His popularity began to wane, however, when he moved away from naturalistic techniques to write more symbolic and romantic pieces. His failure to take a strong stand against the Third Reich and his celebration by the Nazis further contributed to his declining national and international reputation. Nevertheless, Hauptmann remains an important figure in literary history, both for his role in the international Naturalist movement and for his influence on other writers such as Anton Chekov, Maxim Gorky, James Joyce, Eugene O'Neill, and Arthur Miller.

In 1912, Hauptmann received the Nobel Prize for Literature for *The Weavers*, considered to be the greatest example of Naturalist drama and first revolutionary "drama of the masses" in German literature, anticipating Brecht's epic theater. The play is based on the 1844 rebellion of Silesian weavers that was crushed by the military. In a series of interconnecting tableaux, Hauptmann depicts the suffering of workers who can barely eke out an existence from their miserly wages. They are physically and emotionally spent by a life that allows the factory owners to thrive while the workers are consumed and dehumanized. As one old weaver caustically puts it: "A weaver is like an apple – everyone takes their bite." Inspired by the angry lyrics of a well-known political folk song, "Bloody Justice", and by the rebellious actions of a few militants, the weavers join together to destroy the homes of their oppressors. Originally scheduled to be performed in 1892, *The Weavers* was banned under the pretext that it would incite acts of civil disobedience in the tense social and political climate that characterized a rapidly industrializing late 19th-century Germany. Defunct censorship laws were revived to prevent the play from being staged. To appease the censors, Hauptmann added a new character in the fifth act who believes that the sacrifices of a violent revolution are too great and that faith will be the weaver's final salvation. For many critics on the left of the political spectrum, this ending undermined the play's revolutionary message. Hauptmann's interest in the weavers' plight was both political and personal. The germ of his play, Hauptmann writes in the dedication to his father, was in the stories passed on to him about his grandfather, a Silesian weaver. It is perhaps this personal connection, reinforced by conversations with eyewitness survivors, that allowed Hauptmann to create characters of depth and credible motivation. By conveying the color, rhythm, and melody of their Silesian vernacular, Hauptmann also hoped to reinvest dialect with dignity.

The Weavers presents a particularly interesting case in the field of translation studies because translators have, in fact, two German versions of the same play at their disposal. In the spirit of Naturalism that seeks to reproduce everyday speech as precisely as possible, Hauptmann wrote the play's first version, *De Waber*, in the thick dialect of his native Silesia. In order to make the play more accessible to a predominantly middle-class German audience, however, he modified the original version into dialect-flavored High German in *Die Weber*. From its very inception, therefore, language was a central theme that posed a practical problem: how does one find a balance between an accurate depiction of local character and the requirements for a broader public reception? This same question resurfaces for translators who are faced with the challenge of transcribing the Silesian speech-patterns and dialectical coloring into the British or American idiom. Lewisohn, editor of the first English-language collection of Hauptmann's dramatic works, summarizes the translator's predicament: if translators choose the easiest solution, that is, if they render the speech of Silesian peasants into an existing English dialect, Hauptmann's characters gain a set of associative values, but these values are radically different from those suggested in the original. Translators of the play have resolved the dialect question in different ways that, in turn, determine the particular character and flavor of each translation.

MORISON's *The Weavers* (1899) conveys the colloquial quality of Hauptmann's play both phonetically ("p'r'aps", "c'n") and grammatically (double negatives), yet the occasional awkward wordiness ("plagueyest web", "fiends in human fashion") distracts and diverges from the play's original character. Considering Hauptmann's precise attention to the weaver's lexicon, it is also inappropriate for Morison to paraphrase the act of winding the cotton as (her quotes) "drawing a long bow". Her translation does nicely render speech nuances to distinguish individual idiosyncrasies, as well as class differences. For present-day readers, however, Morison's language, although contemporaneous with Hauptmann's, will inevitably sound dated.

For the sake of readability, FRENZ & WAGGONER (1951) chose not to substitute the Silesian dialect with a comparable regional dialect from the United States, but rather to draw on speech mannerisms common to the country as a whole. Like Morison, they use eye dialect ("ya", "round"), double negatives, and incorrect subject-verb agreement to convey the dialectical pronunciation and idiomatic formulation of non-standard language. One weakness in their version resides in a translation of the "Bloody Justice" song that, while retaining the syllabic verse of the original, does not rhyme and thereby loses its quality as a popular song. Without this rhyme, the stanzas lack their mnemonic quality and are therefore less compelling and convincing as a rallying cry.

LUSTIG (1961) criticizes his predecessors' attempts to render dialect in their translations as "repellent and rapidly outmoded". His translation is succinct and precise, unobtrusively flavored with slang, while retaining differences in individual and class speech mannerisms. Lustig is the only translator to catch the malapropisms in the cabinetmaker's lofty speech made in Act 3 as the latter tries to ingratiate himself with a well-to-do traveling salesman. For example, he's all for the "respectiveness" (as opposed to the "respectfulness") of children towards their deceased parents. Lustig's translation of the weavers' song is also the closest of all translations to the original in rhyme, meter, and content. Given the pivotal role of this political song in the actual 1844 rebellion and in the play, its careful rendition is crucial to the translation's credibility.

MUELLER (1965) aimed for his translation to be speakable and in the present-day idiom. He did not attempt to find a dialect that would directly correspond to Hauptmann's because, as he writes, "in an American version dialects would be either presumptuous, ludicrous, or both". Mueller's translation unfortunately lacks the linguistic subtlety of the other translations and is least attentive to Hauptmann's precise lexicon related to the weaving industry. For example, Mueller simply omits mention of the tool that removes knots from wool (*Noppzängl*=burling iron or pincer) and translates a very particular part of the loom (its *lathe* or *batten*) into a general term (its "machinery"). One of the defining features of Hauptmann's work and Naturalism in general, namely the attention to minute details, is thereby compromised in Mueller's translation.

MARCUS (1980) translated the play for its first professional British production. Linguistically, this version diverges most radically from Hauptmann's original. As reviewers note, the translation is "spare, deft, clear, and direct, with classical simplicity of utterance", and does not convey any phonetic or grammatical idiosyncrasies of dialect. It retains the colloquial tone through freely translated idiomatic expressions that are contemporary and economical ("I've dealt with bigger fish in my time", "Don't bite my head off"). The liberties Marcus takes as a translator, however, occasionally result in omissions, alterations, and interpretive additions to the original that make explicit what Hauptmann keeps implicit. For example, a euphemistic insult in Act 1, "Your mother must have been ridin' a broomstick with Satan to beget such a devil as you for a son", becomes "She must have slept with Lucifer to produce a devil like you." In another exchange in act 1, Old Baumert says in the original: "That sure deserves a little rest"; Baecker: "Rest is better'n money"; OB: "Money wouldn't be so bad neither". Marcus inserts an ironic edge that completely changes the reader's perception of the characters: OB: "I've earned my rest"; B: "Rest in peace"; OB: "That'll be the day". Marcus also takes liberties in his translation of the "Bloody Justice" song. In order to preserve the rhyme, he introduces allusions to the Inquisition and sharks that stray noticeably from the original.

KAREIN K. GOERTZ

Further Reading

Furst, Lilian R. and Peter N. Skrine, *Naturalism*, London: Methuen, 1971

Marshall, Alan, *The German Naturalists and Gerhart Hauptmann: Reception and Influence*, Frankfurt: Peter Lang, 1982

Maurer, Warren R., *Gerhart Hauptmann*, Boston: Twayne, 1982

Maurer, Warren, *Understanding Gerhart Hauptmann*, Columbia: University of South Carolina Press, 1992

See also the introductions to all of the translations

Václav Havel 1936–

Czech dramatist, essayist and politician

Biography

Born in Prague, 5 October 1936, the son of a wealthy architect and nephew of the founder of the Barrandov film studios. Prevented from entering higher education after 1951 "for class reasons", Havel worked as a laboratory technician while completing his secondary education part-time. From 1955 he began to publish articles in theatrical and literary newspapers. Over the next two years his repeated applications to study at university were turned down, but Havel did study economics at the Prague Higher Institute of Technology; an attempt to gain a place at the Prague Film Academy also failed. He completed his military service in 1959 and joined the Na zábradlí (Balustrade) Theatre as a stagehand. His first play, *Zahradní slavnost* (*The Garden Party*) was performed in 1963.

Havel married Olga Šplíchalová in 1964 and over the next four years became active in opposition to the policies of the regime. By May 1968 he was prominent enough to be singled out for attack by the Soviets (in an article in *Literaturnaia gazeta*) and was banned from working in the theatre in 1969. In 1974 he was employed for a time in a brewery in Trutnov (this inspired his play *Audience*) and he continued the human rights activity that culminated in his being one of the founders of Charter 77, set up to monitor human rights in Czechoslovakia. This led to his arrest and detention without trial for five months and a sustained campaign of harassment, surveillance and interrogation by the secret police. He was arrested again in 1978 and in 1979 sentenced to four and a half years' imprisonment – a period described in his *Letters to Olga*. He was released, ill with pneumonia, in March 1983, after which he immediately resumed his human rights activity. In 1989 he was arrested again, but in November of that year he led the Civic Forum movement that toppled the Communist regime. In December he was elected president, a position he still (2000) holds despite resigning for a time in protest against the division of Czechoslovakia in 1992.

The recipient of numerous international literary and humanitarian awards, Havel is a writer whose work divides neatly into two phases: his plays, many of which were issued in *samizdat* form, and first performed in translation outside Czechoslovakia; and, since 1989, his volumes of letters and essays.

Translations

Selections of Plays

Blackwell, Vera, George Theiner and Jan Novák, *Selected Plays, 1963–83*, London: Faber, 1992; New York: Grove Press, 1993 (includes *The Garden Party*, *The Memorandum*, *The Increased Difficulty of Concentration*, *Conversation*, *Unveiling*, *Protest*, *Mistake*)

Goetz-Stankiewicz, Marketa (editor), *The Vaněk Plays: Four Authors, One Character*, Vancouver: University of British Colombia Press, 1987 (contains *Audience* and *Unveiling* translated by Jan Novák, *Protest* translated by Vera Blackwell, and works by Pavel Kohout, Jiří Dienstbier and Pavel Landovsky)

Novák, Jan and Vera Blackwell, *Three Vaněk Plays*, London and Boston: Faber, 1990 (contains *Audience* and *Unveiling* translated by Novák, and *Protest* translated by Blackwell)

Stoppard, Tom, George Theiner, Marie Winn and James Saunders, *Selected Plays, 1984–87*, London: Faber, 1994 (includes *Largo Desolato*, *Temptation*, *Redevelopment; or, Slum Clearance*)

Plays

Zahradní slavnost, 1963

Blackwell, Vera, *The Garden Party*, London: Jonathan Cape, 1969; in *Selected Plays, 1963–83*, translated by Blackwell, Theiner and Novák, 1992

Vyrozumění, 1965

Blackwell, Vera, *The Memorandum*, London: Jonathan Cape, and New York: Grove Press, 1967; in *Selected Plays, 1963–83*, translated by Blackwell, Theiner and Novák, 1992

Ztížená možnost soustředění, 1968

Blackwell, Vera, *The Increased Difficulty of Concentration*, London: Jonathan Cape, 1972; New York: Samuel French, 1976; in *Selected Plays, 1963–83*, translated by Blackwell, Theiner and Novák, 1992

Audience, 1975

Blackwell, Vera, *Audience*, London: Samuel French, 1978; in *Sorry ... Two Plays: Audience and Private View*, translated by Blackwell, London: Eyre Methuen, 1979

Novák, Jan, *Audience* in *The Vaněk Plays*, edited by Marketa Goetz-Stankiewicz, 1987; in *Three Vaněk Plays*, translated by Novák and Blackwell, 1990

Theiner, George, *Conversation: A One-Act Play*, *Index on Censorship*, 5/3 (Autumn 1976) pp. 41–50; in *Selected Plays, 1963–83*, translated by Blackwell, Theiner and Novák, 1992

Vernisáž, 1975

Blackwell, Vera, *Private View* in *Sorry ... Two Plays: Audience and Private View*, translated by Blackwell, London: Eyre Methuen, 1979

Novák, Jan, *Unveiling* in *Three Vaněk Plays*, translated by Novák and Blackwell, 1990; as *Private View* in *Selected Plays, 1963–83*, translated by Blackwell, Theiner and Novák, 1992

Protest, 1978

Blackwell, Vera, *Protest*, *Antaeus* 66 (Spring 1991) pp. 188–207; in *The Vaněk Plays*, edited by Marketa Goetz-Stankiewicz, 1987; in *Three Vaněk Plays*, translated by Novák and Blackwell, 1990; in *Selected Plays 1963–83*, translated by Blackwell, Theiner and Novák, 1992

Chyba, 1983

Theiner, George, *Mistake*, *Index on Censorship*, 13/1 (February 1984); in *Selected Plays, 1963–83*, translated by Blackwell, Theiner and Novák, 1992

Largo Desolato, 1984
Stoppard, Tom, *Largo Desolato*, London: Faber, and New York: Grove Press, 1987; in *Selected Plays, 1984–87*, translated by Stoppard, Theiner, Winn and Saunders, 1994

Pokoušení, 1985
Theiner, George, *Temptation, Index on Censorship*, 15/10 (1986); published separately London: Faber, 1988; in *Selected Plays, 1984–87*, translated by Stoppard, Theiner, Winn and Saunders, 1994

Asanace, 1988
Winn, Marie and James Saunders, *Redevelopment; or, Slum Clearance*, London: Faber, 1990; in *Selected Plays 1984–87*, translated by Stoppard, Theiner, Winn and Saunders, 1994

Zítra to spustíme, 1988
Day, Barbara, *Tomorrow!* in *Czech Plays: Modern Czech Drama*, edited and with an introduction by Day, London: Nick Hern, 1994

Selections of Prose
Vladislav, Jan (editor), *Living in Truth: Twenty-Two Essays Published on the Occasion of the Award of the Erasmus Prize to Václav Havel*, London: Faber, 1987 (6 texts by Havel, 16 texts by others)
Wilson, Paul (editor), *Open Letters: Selected Prose 1965–1990*, London: Faber, and New York: Knopf, 1991

Essays and Other Writings
Na téma opozice, 1968
Berman, Michael, "On the Subject of Opposition" in *Winter in Prague: Documents on Czechoslovak Communism in Crisis*, edited by R.A. Remington, Cambridge, Massachusetts: MIT Press, 1969

Dopis Dr Gustávu Husákovi, 1975
Wilson, Paul, "Letter to Dr Gustáv Husák, General Secretary of the Czechoslovak Communist Party", *Survey*, 21/3 (Summer 1975); in *Living in Truth*, edited by Jan Vladislav, 1987

Moc bezmocných, 1978
Wilson, Paul, "The Power of the Powerless" in *The Power of the Powerless: Citizens against the State in Central-Eastern Europe*, by Havel *et al.* edited by John Keane, with an introduction by Stephen Lukes, London: Hutchinson, and Armonk, New York: M.E. Sharpe, 1985; in *Living in Truth*, edited by Jan Vladislav, 1987

Dopisy Olze, 1983
Wilson, Paul, *Letters to Olga, June 1979–September 1982*, London: Faber, and New York: Knopf, 1988

Politika a svědomí, 1984
Kohák, Erazim and Roger Scruton, *Politics and Conscience*, Stockholm: Charta 77 Foundation, 1986; in *Living in Truth*, edited by Jan Vladislav, 1987

Anatomie jedné zdrženlivosti, 1985
Kohák, Erazim, *The Anatomy of Reticence: East European Dissidents and the Peace Movement in the West*, Stockholm: Charta 77 Foundation, 1985, revised 1986; in *Living in Truth*, edited by Jan Vladislav, 1987

Šest poznámek o kultuře, 1986
Kohák, Erazim, "Six Asides about Culture" in *A Besieged Culture: Czechoslovakia Ten Years after Helsinki*, edited by A. Heneka *et al.*, Stockholm: Charta 77 Foundation, 1986; in *Living in Truth*, edited by Jan Vladislav, 1987

Dálkový výslech: rozhovor s Karlem Hvížďalem, 1990
Wilson, Paul, *Disturbing the Peace: A Conversation with Karel Hvížďala*, London: Faber, and New York: Knopf, 1990

Letní přemítání, 1991
Wilson, Paul, *Summer Meditations: On Politics, Morality and Civility in a Time of Transition*, London: Faber, and New York: Knopf, 1992

Slovo o slově, 1992
"A Word about Words", *New York Review of Books* (18 January 1990); in *Open Letters*, edited by Paul Wilson, 1991

Václav Havel's work falls into two categories: his dramatic work and the political writings – articles, essays and speeches – which brought him to prominence as one of the leading voices of the so-called "dissident" movement from the mid- to late 1960s. These categories, of course, are not as clear-cut as this suggests. Havel's plays are concerned with the same issues as his political writing: the analysis of a particular type of society and the attitudes of mind that create and sustain that society. Nevertheless the plays do form a distinct and separate body of work.

Generally speaking Havel's political writings are not *too* difficult to translate – their argumentation and language is clear, systematic and analytical. The main danger for the translator is that he or she will produce a less incisive work, and especially that the irony present in Havel's writing will be weakened or lost. The plays are slightly more problematic. On one level the humour of the plays comes from the usual range of possibilities offered by spoken Czech (see also entries on Hašek and Čapek), but Havel is also fascinated by language itself, especially the depersonalized bureaucratic language that characterized Czech communism. The humour and irony (and, indeed, tragedy) of plays like *The Garden Party* or *The Memorandum* come from the depiction of the dehumanizing effects this language can have on the individual or society, and, as with Havel's more overtly political work, it is easy to lose the point in English. Perhaps the most difficult language in Havel's work is that of *Letters to Olga*. These letters from prison are written in a deliberately dense, almost gnomic language, Havel figuring (correctly) that it would be ignored by the prison censors as being too difficult to comprehend and therefore harmless.

Vera Blackwell was the first English translator of Havel's plays and has translated and adapted six of them in total. In translating *Zahradní slavnost* (*The Garden Party*) Blackwell (1969) was faced with the intractable problem of how to render into another language texts in which the words are deliberately divorced from their meaning; Havel's absurdist use of Czech is at times reminiscent of Ionesco's of French. The play opens, for example, with a breathtaking exchange of utterly meaningless proverbs: the form of the words is that of a proverb, but there is no content. Blackwell sometimes translates literally and sometimes, less successfully, invents her own proverbs (the end of act 1 scene 1 is notably weakened). The same principle of words without meaning is repeated throughout the play in several linguistic registers, but Blackwell does not differentiate sufficiently between these. The *Tajemník* and *Tajemnice* (the male and female forms of the same word are not conveyed by Blackwell's "Secretary" and "Clerk") at the beginning of scene 2 should speak in a ludicrous and exaggerated "officialese", but this is toned down in the translation. Similarly when Hugo meets Plzák he should adopt the latter's barely literate low colloquial speech, but again the translation does not reproduce this. Blackwell does better with the circular logic and meaninglessness of Hugo's exchange with the Director in scene 3 but in general her translation is, in Paul Trenský's words, "not too felicitous" (1980).

BLACKWELL's version (1978) of the late one-act play *Audience* is mostly faithful to the original, although there is a little padding in places. The main problem for the translator of *Audience* is reproducing the Maltster or Brewmaster's language, which is *obecná čeština* (Common Czech) at its best (see also essay on Hašek). Havel uses several of the typical features of Common Czech present here, such as the rich vocabulary of swear-words employed by the Maltster, and adjectival endings becoming *-ej* instead of *-ý* (e.g., "je to mùj dobrej známej – nějakej Tonda Mašku" translated by Blackwell as "old friend of mine, see. A Tonda Mašek?"). Unfortunately these features are not really equivalent to Blackwell's "mate", "bloke", "ain't", "stuff 'em" and so forth. Blackwell's Maltster sounds too much like an imitation of a "working-class" accent: "You might even have a little shut-eye in there, if you like. Well, what do you say?" BLACKWELL (1967) does better with *The Memorandum* (*Vyrozumění*), apparently more at home in the linguistic environment of the office than in that of the brewery. Nevertheless, she has a similar problem with the character Helena when, for example, she addresses the new manager as follows: "To seš ty? Musíš se, čoveče, nějak zasadit o ten byfet, fakt!" The joke lies in the details of the lexis: the use of the colloquial second person singular "seš", "čoveče" instead of the correct "člověče" and so on. Blackwell's "Are you, love? Well, you must do something about this snack-bar, I mean it!" is too bland and loses the joke.

Jan NOVÁK (1987) translates *Audience* with gusto: the Brewmaster now sounds like a Los Angeles pimp rather than a Czech brewer ("Man, you're suckin' on it like it was some French Cognac, or somethin'!" or "So why ain't you drinkin'? You'd rather be sippin' a little wine, wouldn'tcha?") and he swears with the usual monotonous obscenities that English is capable of, instead of the rich and varied vulgarities of Czech. The language and phraseology of the translation is fully Americanized: "hick", "semester", "downtown", "you don't understand didley", etc. Novák's translation is virile and entertaining and follows the text closely, yet it is extremely misleading as it lacks the irony of the original and the subtle humour of the language.

George THEINER (1976) has also translated *Audience* (along with two other plays), producing a functional but rather flat version. Once again the Brewmaster (now Foreman) is the source of the problem. His: "I'm telling you, nowadays no one wants to pull anyone else's chestnuts out of the fire, and that's a fact," sounds too wooden to be plausible, and many of the Foreman's speeches are afflicted with the same problem. As ever, the humour and irony are missing, and while Theiner's translation may not mislead to the extent that Novák's does, neither does it entertain.

Barbara DAY (1994) has translated just one of Havel's plays, the rather untypical *Zítra to spustíme* (translated by Day as *Tomorrow!* but more literally it would be "We'll Start it (up) Tomorrow!") – a collaborative effort written with Peter Oslzlý in 1988. The play was written to provide a factual counterbalance to the communist portrayal of events leading to the founding of the first Czechoslovak Republic at the end of 1918. The play is partly a factual and partly an imaginative reconstruction, written in a clear and simple, almost didactic language, and Day translates it as such.

Tom STOPPARD (1987) is perhaps Havel's ideal translator. He brings the obvious advantages of being a pre-eminent playwright to bear on *Largo desolato* (of which he is the dedicatee) and produces a translation that is faithful to Havel's original but is also an excellent play in itself. Stoppard is completely at home with the quickfire verbal repartee of the play, but most impressively he manages to reproduce the rhythm of the Czech perhaps as closely as is possible in English; the opening of scene 4 is a particularly fine example of this. Stoppard's feeling for what works on stage (a feeling evidently not shared by other translators) is evident throughout *Largo desolato*. Finally, and perhaps most remarkably, the translation is as funny as the original – a considerable achievement in translation from any language.

As already noted above, Havel's political and other writings do not pose quite the same difficulties for the translator as his plays. Perhaps Havel's finest and most representative work in this area is the long essay *The Power of the Powerless*, well translated by Paul WILSON (1985). Wilson, in fact, is responsible for most of the translations of Havel's non-dramatic work, and while one could quibble with occasional phrases (such as translating "skutečný vnitřní stav společnosti" – literally "the real internal condition of society" – as "a genuine state of mind in society" in *Letter to Dr Gustav Husák* (WILSON, 1975)) such occasional awkwardnesses do not significantly alter the force of Havel's arguments. The same might also be said about WILSON's admirable efforts in translating (1988) the intentionally difficult *Letters to Olga* – Havel's ethical and philosophical meditations addressed to his wife from prison and written to elude the prison censorship. These can be hard work and confusing to read, but that is a feature as much of the Czech originals as of the translation.

JAMES PARTRIDGE

Further Reading

Blackwell, Vera, "Havel's *Private View*", *Cross Currents*, 3 (1984) pp. 107–19

Gibian, George (editor), "Havel's Letters from Prison", *Cross Currents*, 3 (1984) pp. 188–207

Trensky, Paul I., "Havel's *The Garden Party* Revised" in *Czech Literature since 1956: A Symposium*, edited by William E. Harkins and Paul I. Trensky, New York: Bohemica, 1980, pp. 103–18

Anne Hébert 1916–2000

Canadian poet, novelist, short-story writer and dramatist

Biography

Born 1 August 1916 in Sainte-Catherine-de-Fossambault, near Quebec, and brought up in and near the same city. Her father was a civil servant, a poet and a critic, her maternal grandfather an architect. Her education was interrupted by ill-health and she was much affected by the premature death in 1943 of her cousin, the poet Hector de Saint-Denys Garneau, and by the sudden loss of her sister soon after. Her first collection of poems appeared in 1942, the first volume of stories, sounding a characteristic note of revolt, in 1950. Her first novel, *Les Chambres de bois* (1958; translated 1974 as *The Silent Rooms*), won the Prix France-Canada, presaging other awards. From 1960 Hébert spent much time in Paris, and eventually settled there, though she visited Canada frequently. Best known for the novel *Kamouraska* (1970; translated 1973 with the same title) and *Les Fous de Bassan* (*In the Shadow of the Wind*), 1982, she has also written plays for radio and for the cinema. A dominant theme in her fiction, which is mostly set in Quebec province, is the conflict between the forces of society and the individual's, and especially woman's, drive to freedom. She died 23 January 2000.

Translations

Selection of Poetry

Poulin, A. Jr, *Anne Hébert; Selected Poems*, Brockport, New York; BOA Editions, 1987

Poetry

Le Tombeau des rois, 1953

Miller, Peter, *The Tomb of the Kings*, Toronto; Contact Press, 1967

Poèmes, 1960 (*Le Tombeau des rois*; *Mystère de la parole*, 1960)

Brown, Alan, *Poems*, Don Mills, Ontario: Musson, 1975

Short Stories

Le Torrent, 1950; enlarged edition, 1963

Moore, Gwendolyn, *The Torrent: Novellas and Short Stories*, Montreal: Harvest House, 1973

Novels

Les Chambres de bois, 1958

Mezei, Kathy, *The Silent Rooms*, Don Mills, Ontario: Musson, 1974

Kamouraska, 1970

Shapiro, Norman, *Kamouraska*, Don Mills, Ontario: Musson, and New York: Crown, 1973

Les Enfants du sabbat, 1975

Dunlop-Hébert, Carol, *Children of the Black Sabbath*, Don Mills, Ontario: Musson, and New York: Crown, 1977

Héloïse, 1980

Fischman, Sheila, *Héloise*, Toronto: Stoddart, 1982

Les Fous de Bassan, 1982

Fischman, Sheila, *In the Shadow of the Wind*, Toronto: Stoddart, 1983; London: Dent, 1984

Other Writing

Hébert, Anne, *Dialogue sur la traduction: A propos du Tombeau des rois*, with F.R. Scott, in French and English, edited by Jeanne Lapointe, Montreal: HMH, 1970

Most of Anne Hébert's work has been translated into English, although some works (e.g. Peter MILLER's early translation *The Tomb of the Kings*, 1967) are not easily available. This marks her status as one of French Canada's leading writers, one who has been recognized by the anglophone world as a major author of both prose and poetry. Originally better known as a poet in Quebec, she is now internationally known for her novels.

Hébert's poetry is well served by the English versions. BROWN's translation (1975) contains both *The Tomb of the Kings* and *Mystery of the Word*. The translation of these poems, both concerned with the conflict between the real and the unreal, is extremely accurate and, particularly in *The Tomb of the Kings*, reads like poetry written in English. In *The Mystery of the Word* the translation is most effective in the short poems like "Snow" and "Annunciation"; the longer poems are less successful in English. The preface by Pierre Emmanuel to the French edition is not included in the English translation. The 1967 edition of *Le Tombeau des rois* does not differ from that in *Poèmes* and the Brown *The Tomb of the Kings* is valid for it. POULIN's volume (1987), which was prepared after discussion with the author herself, contains a selection of poems from *Poèmes* and a number of previously unpublished and untranslated poems. The translation is remarkable for its absolute fidelity to the original French, to the extent that it is easy to guess the French word from the choice of the English word. Despite this fidelity and the suggestions of Hébert herself, the translation is not always perfect: "le bouc et l'agneau" (the [billy] goat and the lamb) is translated by the "buck and the ewe" which is neither accurate nor poetic and "Barques amarrées, balancées ..." becomes "Boats moored, balanced ..." where "riding at anchor" would be more appropriate and meaningful. There are occasions when the closeness of the translation renders the English almost meaningless. Usually, however, the poetry of the French is recaptured almost word-for-word in the English translation.

MOORE's 1973 translation of Hébert's haunting, eerie stories at times reads quite awkwardly. Moore has opted to follow the original text very closely, almost word-for-word at points, sometimes using words that, while linked to the French, have a different meaning in English. The style and elegance of the original are not consistently reproduced in the translation.

Hébert's first short novel is a tale of sexual obsession and a struggle for freedom well rendered by MEZEI (1974). Her translation does not include the preface by Samuel de Sacy which precedes the French text. This apart, the translation is complete and largely accurate despite a few minor oddities such as "pures" rendered by "reckless" or "sa face amère" becoming "the bitter lines of his face". The translator has recaptured the simple clarity of the French, and produced a stylish and readable English version. *Kamouraska*, the first of Hébert's novels to achieve fame, depicts a woman on the edge of a nervous breakdown, haunted by her murderous, adulterous past, struggling to retain control of herself and of events. The translation (SHAPIRO, 1973) makes a real effort to capture the breathless, broken style of Hébert with short verbless sentences, exclamations and questions. In doing so it frequently changes the emphasis of the French and occasionally omits words or even clauses and sentences. The English is lively and colloquial, perhaps more colloquial than the French. It does not entirely succeed in reproducing the tone of the French, which reflects the social position of the principal characters. DUNLOP-HÉBERT (1977) has more success with *Children of the Black Sabbath*, a story of black magic and witchcraft within a rural community in Quebec. Despite the occasional omission of a word or a phrase this is an outstandingly good translation. It is accurate and at the same time it captures the different registers in which Hébert writes. The interior monologues, the racy dialogue and the religious musings are all given appropriate translations. The novel reads easily and, just like the original French, makes the reader eager to discover the conclusion. FISCHMAN (1982) succeeds brilliantly with *Héloise*, the gruesome tale of ghosts destroying a young couple in Paris, in a version that captures the breathless, jerky style of the French narrative. There are no inaccuracies, and the translator combines a word-for-word rendering with a lively and convincing English style. She was equally successful in 1983 with Hébert's most acclaimed novel, *In the Shadow of the Wind*, a tale of murder and sexual obsession set in a poor fishing village on the shores of the St Lawrence River. The different styles of the French narrative are expertly captured in a stylish translation that offers all the nuances and subtleties of the French original.

PETER NOBLE

Further Reading

Boak, Denis, "*Kamouraska, Kamouraska*", *Essays in French Literature* 14 (1977) pp. 69–104
Collie, Joanne, "Anne Hébert's *"Ecriture féminine"*, *British Journal of Canadian Studies* 3/2 (1988) pp. 285–92
Godard, Barbara, "My (m)Other, My Self: Strategies for Subversion in Atwood and Hébert", *Essays on Canadian Writing* 26 (1983) pp. 13–44
Godin, Jean Cléo, "Rebirth in the Word", *Yale French Studies* 45 (1970) pp. 137–53
Noble, Peter, *Hébert: Les Fous de Bassan*, Glasgow: Glasgow University French and German Publications, 1995
Pallister, Janis L., "Orphic Elements in Anne Hébert's *Héloïse*", *Quebec Studies* 5 (1987) pp. 125–34
Rea, Annabelle, "The Climate of Viol/Violence and Madness in Anne Hébert's *Les Fous de Bassan*", *Quebec Studies* 4 (1986) pp. 170–83
Sénécal, André J., "*Les Fous de Bassan*: An Eschatology", *Quebec Studies* 7 (1988) pp. 150–60
Russell, Delbert W., *Anne Hébert*, Boston: Twayne, 1983
Winspur, Steven, "Undoing the Novel of Authority with Anne Hébert", *Teaching Language Through Literature* 26/2 (1987) pp. 24–32

Hebrew, Modern

Literary Translation into English

Modern Hebrew emerged as a literary language of Central and Eastern European Jews during the last decades of the 18th century. Although Yiddish was their spoken language, their written language was traditional Hebrew. During the *Haskalah* (the Jewish Enlightenment, 1780–1880), a new form of Hebrew evolved serving as the medium for the propagation of the modernization and Europeanization of Jewry. By 1848 Yiddish and Hebrew were replaced by German as the spoken and literary idiom of Central European Jewry, but in Eastern Europe, because of the different political and social conditions, Hebrew writing continued. Only towards the end of the century was its supremacy challenged by the rise of Yiddish as an alternative Jewish literary language and by Jewish literature written in Russian. As East European Jews despaired of their hope of emancipation, Hebrew writers began rejecting the aspirations of the *Haskalah* and advocating Jewish self-emancipation, and most of them became Zionists after 1881, the year of the outbreak of the Jewish pogroms in Russia. Partially successful attempts were also made to revive Hebrew as a spoken language.

The poetry and fiction produced by the *Haskalah* writers were generally of minor literary significance and nowadays are usually considered as mere exercises and experiments preparing the way for the golden period of European Hebrew literature (1881–1914) whose achievements approached those of European literature. The more important writers of fiction in this golden period were Mendele Mocher Sefarim (1835–1917), Micha Josef Berdiczewski (1865–1921), David Frischmann (1859–1923), Isaac Leib Peretz (1852–1915) and Joseph Hayyim Brenner (1881–1921). Judah Leib Gordon (1831–92), Hayyim Nahman Bialik (1873–1934) and Shaul Chernikhowsky (1875–1943) were its leading poets, and Ahad Haam (1856–1927) its brilliant essayist and editor. Initially many of their works were translated into German or Russian, the dominant European languages in areas where most Jews resided.

As a reaction to pogroms and acts of discrimination, millions of East European Jews began migrating to the United States and other English-speaking countries after 1881. A small but committed number of Zionists also settled in Turkish Palestine, where a Hebrew literary center developed in the early 1900s and attempts to revive Hebrew as a spoken language succeeded.

As the number of Jews living in the English-speaking countries grew, English translations of Hebrew works began to appear and were directed mainly at Jewish audiences. Their publication was often subsidized, if they were not actually printed, by Zionist or Jewish educational organizations.

The earliest novel translated into English was Kalman Schulmann's pot-boiling historical novel *The Fall of Bethar* (Chicago: Jewish Advocate, 1879). It was followed by several translations (often abridged) of Abraham Mapu's biblical romance *Ahavat Zion* (Lore of Zion), the first of them entitled *The Prince and the Peasant* (1887). A later translation in biblical English by Benjamin Schapiro, *The Shepherd Prince* (New York: Broadside [a Protestant religious publishing house]), appeared in 1922.

Between 1890 and 1945 an average of fewer than four translations from Hebrew to English appeared each year (Goell, 1975) These figures exclude non-literary works and may be too small, since it is doubtful whether they include all the many translations appearing in Jewish periodicals. The writers most frequently translated were Bialik, Chernikhowsky and Ahad Haam, the leading Hebrew authors of the European period.

Translators usually resorted to biblical English to render the Hebrew original, and few translators were professional writers. An excellent example of a successful use of biblical English is the translations of Bialik's King Solomon legends by Herbert Danby (Goell, 1975, items 77, 296).

World War I and the Communist Revolution that followed destroyed the Hebrew centers in what became the Soviet Union, where Zionism and the Hebrew language were banned as counter-revolutionary. In Poland, Lithuania and Latvia, however, both Zionism and Hebraism grew in influence, but during World War II these Jewish communities were annihilated.

Even before the founding of Israel, Hebrew became the spoken and literary language of Palestinian Jews. For the first time in more than two millennia, most contemporary Hebrew authors are native speakers of Hebrew and their writing has acquired the freshness and flexibility of a living language. Close contact with the Jews of the United States and the English-speaking world, where the majority of world Jewry reside, led to an increase of translations of Hebrew literature into English. New translations were also directed at the general English-reading public. By 1975 more than 40 per cent of all translations from the Hebrew were into English (Goell, 1975, foreword)

Since 1945 some 30 anthologies and periodicals devoted exclusively to translations of Hebrew into English have appeared (*ibid.*, nos. 43–69, 635); 32 volumes of individual translations of books of verse by Hebrew poets (*ibid.*, nos. 70–98); 13 anthologies of pure fiction (*ibid.*, nos. 101–11); and more than 100 translations of individual volumes of fiction. (*ibid.*, nos. 112–201); and about 25 plays (*ibid.*, nos. 202–16), 20 essays (*ibid.*, nos. 217–36) and 37 children's books (*ibid.*, nos. 237–74). Almost all the leading European Hebrew poets and writers of prose fiction have been entirely or partially translated into English.

According to Robert Alter, by the 1980s Hebrew literature had become the second most visible foreign literature in the United States (Alter, 1991) "Novels by Amos Oz, A.B. Yehoshua, Aharon Appelfeld, Yaacob Shabtai, David Grossman and Yoram Kaniuk appear in English usually within a year or two after their original publication or even appear before their Hebrew edition". Poets like Yehudah Amichai and T. Carmi have been translated by eminent English poets (Ted Hughes, Jon Silkin, Stephen Mitchell, etc.) and almost all of their works have been translated into English, as have parts of the poetry of Dan Pagis, Abba Kovner, Amir Gilboa, Dalya Ravikovitch and other leading poets.

A whole generation of professional translators has usually overcome the inherent difficulties of translating a Semitic language into an Indo-European language. Earlier translators tended to resort to the English phrasing used so skillfully by the authors of the King James version of the Bible. During the European period, many Hebrew authors employed a quasi-biblical style, but even then biblical English gave their works an obsolescent tone. After the 1940s, spoken Hebrew lowered the high diction used by Hebrew writers, easing the task of rendering Hebrew texts into modern English. Yet, to this day, most Hebrew writing still alludes to phrases, personalities and events in classical Hebrew literature, providing a rich sub-text whose resonance is often lost in translation. An outstanding example of this failure are the extant translations of the works of J.S. Agnon (1888–1970) – the most important and innovative writer of Hebrew prose and the only Hebrew writer who has earned a Nobel Prize (1966). His highly textured style appears to be untranslatable.

Hebrew is a Semitic language whose grammar, morphology, syntax and vocabulary are totally unrelated to English, which is an Indo-European language. Modern Hebrew writing has preserved many elements of biblical Hebrew. It is still good Hebrew form to use the conjunctive "*waw*" ("and") with a frequency that would be frowned upon in English. The *waw*, being a single preclitic letter, often opens a line of poetry. It is frequently introduced to balance a particular metrical pattern. Like English "and" it can suggest other meanings, "then, next", for example. While modern Hebrew has diminished the use of parallelisms, they are still acceptable, particularly in poetry (for example *lo nafal davar velo era* – "nothing befell", i.e. happened, "and nothing occurred"). Similarly, modern Hebrew has retained the biblical cognate accusative: *He dreamed a dream.* Like that of other Semitic languages, Modern Hebrew's verbal system has only five finite tenses: the perfect (past), imperfect (future), imperative and participle (present); and Rabbinic Hebrew adds another tense in the form of a compound with the root *haya* (to be) plus the participle, indicating an action that was happening, used to happen or would or could happen. There are two non-finite forms not used in English. Moreover, while the perfect and imperfect forms generally denote respectively past and future tenses, the boundaries separating them are often fluid. English has a more precise verbal tense system and has also developed a subtle series of compound tenses: "He has gone", "he will have gone," "he has been seen," "he will have been seen", etc.

Hebrew is hardly as rich in adjectives as is English. It must rely on verbal forms or compound nouns to express an adjectival sense. Post-biblical Hebrew, including modern Hebrew, often employs a double genitive structure: noun plus an enclitic genitive pronoun and a genitive preposition and noun. Thus *ahiv shel David* means "his brother of David" i.e. "David's brother". Hebrew prefers coordinate clauses joined by a conjunction where English favors subordinate clauses.

Above all, because Hebrew literature extends over more than three millennia, every Hebrew word or phrase has many layers of meaning that cannot be conveyed by translation. Unlike English, which had undergone secularization even before the Elizabethan era, Hebrew had remained a "holy tongue" at least until the mid-19th century. Every contemporary secular Hebrew author must still struggle against or adapt the religious resonance that almost every Hebrew word sets in motion (see Patterson, pp. 12–15).

The translation of Hebrew literature into foreign languages has been encouraged by the Institute for the Translation of Hebrew Literature, which is partially subsidized by the Cultural Authority of the Israel Ministry of Education and Culture.

EZRA SPICEHANDLER

Anthologies of Translations

Alter, Robert (editor), *Modern Hebrew Literature*, New York: Berman House, 1975

Anderson, Elliot (editor), *Contemporary Israeli Literature: An Anthology*, Philadelphia: Jewish Publication Society of America, 1977

Bargad, Warren and Stanley F. Chyet (editors), *Israeli Poetry: A Contemporary Anthology*, Bloomington: Indiana University Press, 1986

Birman, Abraham (editor), *An Anthology of Modern Hebrew Poetry*, New York: Abelard-Schumann, 1968

Blocker, Joel (editor), *Israeli Stories: A Selection of the Best Contemporary Hebrew Writing*, New York: Schocken, 1966

Burnshaw, Stanley, T. Carmi and Ezra Spicehandler (editors), *The Modern Hebrew Poem Itself: From the Beginning to the Present*, New York: Holt Rinehart, 1965; with new afterword, Cambridge, Massachusetts: Harvard University Press, 1989

Carmi, T. (editor), *The Penguin Book of Hebrew Verse*, New York: Viking, and London: Allen Lane, 1981 (best anthology of Hebrew poetry of all eras; modern Hebrew poetry pp. 509–79)

Dor, Moshe and Natan Zach (editors), *The Burning Bush: Poems from Modern Israel*, London: W.H. Allen, 1977

Flantz, Richard (editor), *PEN Israel*, Tel Aviv: PEN Center, 1974

Flantz, Richard and Amos Oz (editors), *Until Daybreak: Stories from the Kibbutz*, Tel Aviv: Kibbutz Meuhad / Institute for the Translation of Hebrew Literature, 1984

Friend, Robert (editor), *Israel*, London: Compton Press, 1974 (Modern Poetry in Translation, 22)

Goldberg, Barbara (editor), *The Stones Remember: Native Israeli Poetry*, Washington, DC: Word Works, 1991

Halkin, Simon (editor), *Modern Hebrew Literature: From the Enlightenment to the Birth of the State of Israel*, new edition, 2 vols, Jerusalem: Office of Oversea Students of Hebrew University 1969–70; New York: Schocken, 1970 (original edition, 1950)

Kahn, Shalom J. (editor), *A Whole Loaf: Stories from Israel*, Tel Aviv: Karni, and New York: Vanguard Press, 1957

Lask, Israel Meir, *Palestine Stories*, Jerusalem: Tarshish, 1957

Lelchuk, Alan and Gershon Shaked (editors), *Eight Great Hebrew Short Novels*, New York: New American Library, 1988

Ma'oz, Rivkah (editor), *The Arab in Twentieth-Century Hebrew Fiction*, Hebrew University of Oversea Students, 1976

Ma'oz, Rivkah (editor), *To Be a Free People in Our Own Land: Trends in Israeli Fiction*, Jerusalem: Akademon / Hebrew University of Oversea Students, 1980

Ma'oz, Rivkah (editor), *In the Lands of the Patriarchs' Desire: The Twentieth-Century Hebrew Short Story*, Jerusalem, Hebrew University of Oversea Students, 1985

Michener, James (editor), *First Fruits*, Philadelphia: Jewish Publication Society, 1976

Nitzan, Shlomo (editor), *A Collection of Recent Writings in Israel*, Tel Aviv: PEN Israel, 1993

Penueli, S.Y. and A. Ukhmani (editors), *Hebrew Short Stories: An Anthology*, Tel Aviv: Institute for the Translation of Hebrew Literature, 1965

Penueli, S.Y. and A. Ukhmani (editors), *An Anthology of Modern Hebrew Poetry*, Jerusalem: Institute for the Translation of Hebrew Literature, 1966

Ravikovitch, Dalia (editor), *The New Israeli Writers: Short Stories of the First Generation*, New York: Funk and Wagnalls, 1969

Schwartz, Harold and Anthony Rudolf (editors), *Voices Within the Ark: The Modern Jewish Poets*, New York: Avon, 1980

Silk, Dennis (editor), *Fourteen Israeli Poets: A Selection of Modern Hebrew Poetry*, London: Deutsch, 1979

Spicehandler, Ezra (editor), *Modern Hebrew Stories* (bilingual edition), New York: Bantam, 1971

Tammuz, Benjamin and Leon Yudkin (editors), *Meetings with the Angel: Seven Stories from Israel*, London: Deutsch, 1973

Periodicals

Ariel: A Quarterly Review of Arts and Letters in Israel (Jerusalem)

Modern Hebrew Literature, published by the Institute for the Translation of Hebrew Literature

Bibliographies

Bibliographies of translations from Hebrew are issued periodically by the Institute for the Translation of Hebrew Literature:

Duchovni, Nava, *Bibliography of Modern Hebrew Literature in Translation*, New Series, issued almost every year by the Institute for the Translation of Hebrew

Goell, Yohai, *Bibliography of Modern Hebrew Literature in Translation*, Tel Aviv: Institute for the Translation of Hebrew Literature, 1975

Goldberg, Isaac and Amnon Zipper, *Bibliography of Modern Hebrew Literature in Translation*, Tel Aviv: Institute for the Translation of Hebrew Literature, 1979–86

See also Index Translationum, New York: Unesco, issued annually to 1986

Further Reading

Alter, Robert, "The Rise and the Rise in the United States",

Modern Hebrew Literature, new series 7 (Fall–Winter 1991), pp. 57
Halkin, Hillel, "On Translating *Sippur Pashut*" in *Agnon: Texts and Contents in English Translation*, edited by Leon I. Yudkin, New York: Marcus Wiener, 1988
Literary Review, special Israel issue, 1/3 (1938)
Patterson, David, "University Teaching of Modern Hebrew in Translation" in *Modern Hebrew Literature in English Translation*, edited by Leon I. Yudkin, New York: Marcus Weiner, 1987
Spicehandler, Ezra, "On Teaching Hebrew Poetry in Translation" in *Modern Hebrew Literature in English Translation*, edited by Leon I. Yudkin, New York: Marcus Weiner, 1987

Heinrich Heine 1797–1856

German poet and essayist

Biography

Born Harry Heine in Düsseldorf, probably 13 December 1797, of Jewish parents. He went to various schools, including one Hebrew and some Catholic, and from 1814–15 to a business school. After he had been an apprentice banker, then an apprentice grocer, in Frankfurt (1815), Heine worked in his uncle Salomon's bank in Hamburg, and in 1818 was set up in a cloth business that went bankrupt in 1819. From then until 1825 he studied law at the universities of Bonn, Berlin and Göttingen, emerging from this last as a doctor of law. In 1825, thinking to facilitate an establishment career, he was baptized a Protestant with the name Christian Johann Heinrich Heine, but his revolutionary opinions hindered professional progress in Germany. From 1825 he travelled and wrote – literary works as well as journalism – in Germany, England and Italy, settling definitively in Paris in 1831 and marrying a Frenchwoman in 1841. In Paris he was a correspondent for French and German journals. He was bed-ridden after 1848 with paralysis resulting from spinal tuberculosis, but continued writing poetry and political and other essays. He died 17 February 1856 in Paris.

The success of Heine's early prose accounts of his travels, *Reisebilder* (*Travel Pictures*), 1826–31, allowed him to give up the law and write for a living. He is best known as a lyric poet, especially for *Das Buch der Lieder* (*Book of Songs*), 1827, poems from which have often been set to music. The troubling image of the Doppelgänger (double) often figures in Heine's poetry. He also wrote autobiographical sketches, essays, memoirs, ballet scenarios and plays. A last trip back to Germany, 1842–43, gave the impulse for two satirical verse epics, *Deutschland: Ein Wintermärchen* (*Germany: A Winter's Tale*) and *Atta Troll* (*Atta Troll*), 1847.

Translations

Collections

Bowring, Edgar Alfred, *The Poems of Heine, Complete: Translated into the Original Metres, with a Sketch of His Life*, London: Bell, 1859
Draper, Hal, *The Complete Poems of Heinrich Heine: A Modern English Version*, Cambridge, Massachusetts: Suhrkamp/Insel, 1982
Leland, Charles Godfrey, *The Works of Heinrich Heine*, 20 vols, New York: Croscup and Sterling, 1900–

Selections of Poetry

Arndt, Walter W., *Songs of Love and Grief: A Bilingual Anthology* (parallel texts), Evanston, Illinois: Northwestern University Press, 1995
Branscombe, Peter, *Heine: Selected Verse* (parallel texts), Harmondsworth: Penguin, 1967
Feise, Ernst, *Heinrich Heine: Lyric Poems and Ballads* (parallel texts), Pittsburgh, Pennsylvania: University of Pittsburgh Press, 1961
Lazarus, Emma, *Poems and Ballads of Heinrich Heine*, New York: Worthington, 1881
Martin, Theodore, *Poems and Ballads*, Edinburgh and London: Blackwood, 1878
Untermeyer, Louis, *Poems of Heinrich Heine*, New York: Heritage Press, 1917; revised edition, New York: Harcourt Brace, and London: Routledge, 1923

Selection of Prose

Robertson, Ritchie, *Heinrich Heine: Selected Prose*, Harmondsworth and New York: Penguin, 1993

ARNDT's translation is a bilingual anthology (1995), with the German and the English texts facing each other. He also tried to translate Heine "in the Verse Forms of the Original", and succeeds rather well in doing so, but at the price of accuracy. As with so many other translators of Heine's poetry, the combined demands of rhyme and meter nudge him farther and farther away from the original, until at times the translation is more like a "free improvisation" on a theme by Heine. Arndt always retains Heine's tone and Heine's wit, though sometimes at the cost of Heine's words. "Frau Ungluck hat im Gegenteile / Dich liebefest ans Herz gedrückt" [Lady Bad Luck has, on the other hand / Pressed you close to her heart in love], for instance, becomes "Misfortune's hug is, *au contraire*, / A snug and matrimonial fit."

More than a century earlier, BOWRING (1859) attempted to do what Arndt did. His is one of the great and unjustly forgotten translations of Heine's complete poems, whereas Arndt offers only a selection of about 150 poems. Bowring's diction may be a little dated at times, but he has really captured the rhythm, the flow, and the wit of the original. He is also less given to improvisation. Where he, for instance, has Heine write "many a score" of "immortal ballads" on his beloved's eyes, Arndt has him "launch an entire fleet of deathless poems" – too reminiscent of Marlowe's Helen in his *Dr. Faustus*.

In keeping with Penguin Books's editorial policy, BRANSCOMBE's selection of verse (1967) consists of a running prose translation in English, at the bottom of the page, to accompany the German text. The translation is meant to be a "crib", and it is a very good and reliable one. It should not be used by readers who do not know German relatively well, since the translation would give them a totally wrong idea of Heine's art. Readers who do know German well will, on the other hand, be grateful for the occasional assistance this translation provides.

DRAPER's translation (1982) provides the reader with the complete poems of Heinrich Heine, one of three to do so, the other two being Bowring and Leland. Draper tries to keep to the rhyme of the original, wherever Heine used rhyme, and his attempts are not always as felicitous as one might have wished. Sometimes he has to resort to relatively heavy padding, even to the extent of adding a whole line, to achieve rhyme. He is at his best when translating Heine's unrhymed poetry, which he renders in an idiomatic English that is able to mirror the sudden, drastic changes of register in the original, as well as Heine's not infrequent play on sounds. Where Heine rhymes, though, Bowring rhymes better than Draper. Draper, however, has excellent notes that enable his readers to supplement his translation with the knowledge they need to understand better all the nuances in the original.

Like Arndt's, FEISE's translation (1961) is a facing page, bilingual anthology of Heine's poems. The selection is not as large as that given by Arndt, but the translation is at least of the same quality. Where he does not have to rhyme, Feise (also unjustly forgotten), manages to catch Heine's tone and wit to perfection, without embroidering his own variations on the original. Where he has to rhyme, though, Feise is nudged even farther away from the original than Arndt, translating lines like "Sie kämmt es mit goldnem Kamme" [she combs it with a golden comb] as "it falls through her comb in a shower".

LAZARUS (1881) offers a selection of Heine's poems and ballads, but the title is somewhat misleading since almost all the poems are taken from Heine's first big collection, the *Buch der Lieder*, or *Book of Songs*, whereas the rest of his oeuvre is either severely under-represented or not represented at all. The translation is very dated now, paradoxically because its diction was so much of its own time. There are too many clichés on the level of diction, and too many elisions on the metrical level, to tempt the contemporary reader.

LELAND (1900–) remains the only complete translation of all of Heine's work, both poetry and prose, into English. As such, it has often been used as the "basis" for other translations, not listed here, in which the diction and the meter were adapted somewhat to the changing tastes of changing times. Unfortunately, Leland's original translation is as dated as Lazarus's, both in diction and in recurrent metrical ineptitudes. Even more unfortunately, he also dated his own work on the morphological level, by insisting on "thou" and the inevitable concomitant "-est"s, or even "-'st"s throughout.

MARTIN's translation (1878) is redolent with the worst affectations of late Romantic/Victorian diction. His Heine "aches to [my] very heart's core", for instance, because that ache has to rhyme with "Sweet, what dost thou wish for more." The desire to rhyme makes Martin lose control of his syntax somewhat too often for his reader's comfort; in addition to this, his work also exhibits the weaknesses of Lazarus's and Leland's, only to a greater extent. He also peppers his revision with French phrases, presumably both to remind the reader of Heine's long exile in Paris, and because they offer convenient rhyme sounds. They add nothing to the translation, however, while detracting from the simple mastery of the original. There is no earthly reason why Heine's "grosses Heer" [big army] should have to become "Grande Armee" in English, nor Heine's "Ehrenkreuz" [cross of honor] "croix d' honneur".

ROBERTSON's selection (1993) is one of the few translations of Heine's prose that are readily available to the general English reading public. In keeping with the fascination of the Heine myth, Robertson has picked out prose texts that can be easily related to Heine's biography, omitting those of more historical, philosophical, or aesthetic importance. The translation, though, is excellent.

UNTERMEYER's translation (1917) offers only a smallish selection of poems, and one that is weighted, once more, toward the *Buch der Lieder / Book of Songs*. He, too, tries to rhyme where Heine does, and he, too, predictably pays the price, even producing such near doggerel as "I've written for many a year" to rhyme with "my dear", and "wrought a bitter torture here". Even though the selection was reprinted after World War II, as was Lazarus's, its appeal to the contemporary reader is limited.

ANDRÉ A. LEFEVERE

Further Reading

Fairley, Barker, *Heinrich Heine: An Interpretation*, Oxford: Clarendon Press, 1954

Hofrichter, Laura, *Heinrich Heine*, translated by Barker Fairley, Oxford: Clarendon Press, 1963

Lefevere, André, "Barbarossa is a Dutchman: Some Observations on the Translation of Poetry Loosely Based on Some Translations of Heinrich Heine", *Linguistica Antverpiensia*, 24 (1991) pp. 107–18

Lefevere, André, "Why the Real Heine Can't Stand Up In / To Translation" in *La Traduction dans le développement des littératures*, edited by José Lambert and Lefevere, Bern and New York: Peter Lang, and Leuven, Belgium: Leuven University Press, 1993

Reeves, Nigel, *Heinrich Heine: Poetry and Politics*, Oxford: Oxford University Press, 1974

Sammons, Jeffrey L., *Heinrich Heine: The Elusive Poet*, New Haven, Connecticut: Yale University Press, 1969

Sammons, Jeffrey L., *Heinrich Heine: A Modern Biography*, Princeton, New Jersey: Princeton University Press, 1979

Zbigniew Herbert 1924–1998

Polish poet

Biography

Born in Lvov, Poland (now Ukraine), 29 October 1924. Herbert's grandfather was English. His father, a bank manager, had fought in the armed struggle for Polish independence. Herbert went to school in Lvov, continuing his education under the German occupation at the King John Casimir University, an underground educational establishment, where he studied Polish literature. Later in World War II he served in the Home Army of the Polish Resistance. In 1944 he moved to Kraków, where he attended the Jagiellonian University, graduating in economics in 1947. He went on to gain an MA in law at Nicholas Copernicus University of Toruń in 1948. He also studied art history in Kraków, at the Academy of Fine Arts, and philosophy, under Henryk Elzenberg, at the University of Warsaw. After finishing his education he rejected the option of becoming a state prosecutor under communist rule, and his early jobs included ill-paid work as a bank teller, a labourer and a journalist, editing the *Przegląd Kupiecki* [Merchant's Digest]. He published articles and reviews in periodicals such as *Dziś i Jutro* [Today and Tomorrow] and *Słowo Powszechne* [Universal Word]. He refused to involve himself in literary life in Poland under communist rule and was expelled from the Writers' Union for his political dissent. He was able to start publishing his poetry publicly only after 1956; he regained official approval after this date, and was readmitted to the Writers' Union. His first collection, *Struna światla* [Chord of Light], published in 1956, immediately established his position in the forefront of the "new wave" of Polish writers that evolved during the political "thaw" of the late 1950s in Eastern Europe. After 1956 he worked as an administrator at the Union of Polish Composers and as an editor at *Twórczość* literary journal, 1955–65. From 1965 to 1968 he edited *Poezja* [Poetry]. He was awarded the Alfred Jurzykowski prize in 1964, and the Austrian Nikolaus Lenau prize in 1965, the first of a number of awards from outside Poland. In 1968 he married Katarzyna Dzieduszycka. During the 1960s his work began to gain a wide readership outside Poland, and he became popular in the English-speaking world after a translation of his poems, *Selected Poems*, appeared in 1968 in the US and England, promoted by the American poet and supporter of Herbert's work, Al Alvarez. Herbert travelled abroad during the 1970s; he was professor of modern European literature at California State College, Los Angeles, 1970–71. He took a post as a visiting professor at Gdańsk University on his return to Poland in 1972. He won the prestigious Herder prize for his work in 1973, and was honoured with the Knight's Cross, Order of Polonia Restituta, in 1974. During the 1980s he was closely involved with the pro-democracy Solidarity movement in Poland. He left Poland in 1986 and settled in Paris. He won the Bruno Schulz prize in 1990 and the Jerusalem Literature prize in 1991. Herbert returned to Poland in 1992. He suffered from ill health for many years, and produced little poetry towards the end of his life: his last poems were published in 1998. Died in Poland, 28 July 1998.

Herbert was one of the most important postwar Polish writers. His poetry was revered in his own country and widely appreciated internationally. He has been referred to as "the conscience of Polish literature" and his poems were acclaimed by both fellow writers and literary critics. He was also an accomplished essayist. His most important collections of poetry, many of which give voice to the protagonist Pan Cogito (Mr Cogito), include *Hermes, pies i gwiazda* [Hermes, a Dog and a Star], 1957; *Studium przedmiotu* [A Study of the Object], 1961; *Pan Cogito* (*Mr Cogito*), 1974; and his 1983 collection of allegorical poems about the difficulties of living under martial law, *Raport z oblężonego miasta* (*Report from the Besieged City*). His last collection of poems is *Epilog burzy* [Storm's Epilogue], published shortly before his death, in 1998. His book of essays resulting from his travels in France and Italy, *Barbarazyńca w ogrodzie* (*Barbarian in the Garden*) appeared in 1962, and a later collection, *Martwa natura z wędzidłem* (*Still Life with a Bridle*) in 1991.

Translations

Selections and Anthologies of Poetry

Barańczak, Stanisław and Clare Cavanagh (editors), *Polish Poetry of the Last Two Decades of Communist Rule: Spoiling Cannibals' Fun*, Evanston, Illinois: Northwestern University Press, 1991 (contains 12 poems by Herbert)

Carpenter, John and Bogdana Carpenter, *Zbigniew Herbert: Selected Poems*, with an introduction and notes, Oxford and New York: Oxford University Press, 1977

Czerniawski, Adam, in his *The Burning Forest*, Newcastle upon Tyne: Bloodaxe Books, 1988 (contains 14 poems by Herbert)

Gillon, Adam and Ludwik Krzyzanowski (editors), *Introduction to Modern Polish Literature*, 2nd expanded edition, New York: Hippocrene, 1982 (contains 7 poems by Herbert)

Miłosz, Czesław and Peter Dale Scott, *Zbigniew Herbert: Selected Poems*, with an introduction by A. Alvarez, Harmondsworth: Penguin, 1968; New York: Ecco Press, 1986

Poetry

Pan Cogito, 1974

Carpenter, John and Bogdana Carpenter, *Mr Cogito*, Oxford: Oxford University Press, and New York: Ecco Press, 1993

Raport z oblężonego miasta, 1983

Carpenter, John and Bogdana Carpenter, *Report from the Besieged City and Other Poems*, with an introduction and notes, New York: Ecco Press, 1985; Oxford: Oxford University Press, 1987

Prose

Carpenter, John and Bogdana Carpenter, *Still Life with a Bridle: Essays and Apocryphas*, New York: Ecco Press, and London: Jonathan Cape, 1991

March, Michael and Jarosław Anders, *Barbarian in the Garden*, Manchester: Carcanet, 1985; San Diego: Harcourt Brace, 1986

As can be deduced from the list above, Zbigniew Herbert has been largely translated into English by a single team: John and Bogdana CARPENTER. Selections of Herbert's poetry appearing in later collections usually draw heavily on these translations, an example being the important collection edited by Stanisław Barańczak and Clare Cavanagh, *Polish Poetry of the Last Two Decades of Communist Rule: Spoiling Cannibals' Fun*, 1991; the 12 poems included here are translated by CARPENTER & CARPENTER – except for "Report from a Besieged City", translated by Czesław MIŁOSZ, and "Buttons", translated by BARAŃCZAK & CAVANAGH. The particular selection in *Spoiling Cannibals' Fun*, however, may be regarded as being especially representative of Herbert's work, Barańczak being the poet's most illuminating critic. It also contains translations of two poems ("Tranformations of Livy" and "The Adventures of Mr. Cogito with Music") from Herbert's latest (1990) collection *Elegia na odejście* [Elegy on Parting], not included in any other of these selections.

The other translators of significance are MIŁOSZ and CZERNIAWSKI. Some of the translations by Miłosz and Peter Dale SCOTT in *Selected Poems* (Penguin, 1968) also appear in the various editions of Miłosz's anthology *Postwar Polish Poetry* (1965, 1970 and 1983); the third expanded edition (1983) also contains a few of the *Mr Cogito* poems translated by the Carpenters. *Polish Writing Today*, edited by Celina Wieniewska (Penguin, 1967) also contains some of Miłosz's translations from the 1965 edition. Many of Czerniawski's translations collected in *The Burning Forest* previously appeared individually in *Encounter* or in other leading literary reviews, as indeed did some of the Carpenters' translations before they were published as collections. There are a few other translations, scattered in general anthologies; worth mentioning is the collection *Introduction to Modern Polish Literature: An Anthology of Fiction and Poetry*, edited by Adam Gillon and Ludwik Krzyzanowski, which, in its second expanded edition (New York: Hippocrene Books, 1982), contains seven poems by Herbert, six translated by Magdalena CZAJKOWSKA and one by Adam GILLON.

The main translators (Miłosz, Czerniawski, the Carpenters) are all competent. It is very difficult to make any fair comparison or judgement as to who is the most successful, since the overlap between the three is very limited and because the Carpenters have now translated so much more than the others, including all the poems from the *Pan Cogito* cycle and from *Raport z oblężonego miasta*. There is an overlap of only three poems between the Carpenters' *Selected Poems* (1977) and the Miłosz & Scott collection (1968). Ten of the poems in Czerniawski's *The Burning Forest* (1988) are also translated by the Carpenters (1977, 1985). All the translators are successful in conveying content and semantic meaning. They wrestle, however, in varying degrees with Herbert's specific use of language.

Miłosz and the Carpenters discuss Herbert's language in some depth and are fully aware of the difficulty of preserving the style of a poet who combines so many complex and even contradictory voices, often employing simultaneously the linguistic formality of high culture, of the moralist and the classicist, with the more intimate, colloquial idioms of everyday speech; they also note such additional problems as his "highly developed sense of metaphor", his creative use or non-use of punctuation, his "tongue-in-cheek persona", his irony, but also his "eminent sanity", "honesty and soberness". Both Miłosz & Scott's translators' note and the Carpenters' introduction observe how his poems "were composed according to patterns of thought" (Miłosz), how often "he follows the movement of thought – the special colloquialness of silent thinking". In their attempt to convey the whole content and effect, the Carpenters decided on a policy of interpretation: "One of the major principles of translation of these poems has been to *interpret* Herbert's meaning as thoroughly as possible". This is a potentially controversial approach but one which the present writer at least believes has worked well; with a poet so deeply immersed in philosophy the translator *must* have a clear idea of the thoughts intended. In order to bring out as much of the linguistic complexity as possible, the Carpenters also decided on the combination of a Polish and English native speaker (as did the main translators of Szymborska). Miłosz and Scott, however, translated their poems not jointly but individually, though they each "examined and corrected" the other's work. Given the supreme challenge of Herbert's poetry, both "teams" are reasonably successful. There are times, of course, when a fresh and critical reader might disagree with the choice of an English equivalent but, when pressed, one would be hard put to it to find an alternative. Meanwhile, the prose translations of MARCH & ANDERS (1985) and of CARPENTER & CARPENTER (1991) are in both cases accurate and readable and successfully convey Herbert's immense sense of curiosity as well as his erudition regarding so many arcana of classical and European culture.

URSULA PHILLIPS

Further Reading

Barańczak, Stanisław, "Zbigniew Herbert and the Critics", *Polish Review*, 30 (1984) pp. 127–48

Barańczak, Stanisław, *A Fugitive from Utopia: The Poetry of Zbigniew Herbert*, Cambridge, Massachusetts: Harvard University Press, 1987

Barańczak, Stanisław, "Zbigniew Herbert and the Notion of Virtue" in *New Perspectives in Twentieth-Century Polish Literature: Flight from Martyrology*, edited by Stanislaw Eile and Ursula Phillips, London: Macmillan, 1992

Carpenter, B., "The Prose Poetry of Zbigniew Herbert: Forging a New Genre", *Slavonic and East European Journal*, 28 (1984) pp. 76–88

Czerniawski, Adam (editor), *The Mature Laurel: Essays on Modern Polish Poetry*, Bridgend, Glamorgan: Seren Books, 1991

Davie, Donald, "Ironies out of Poland: Zbigniew Herbert" in *Slavic Excursions: Essay on Russian and Polish Literature*, Manchester: Carcanet, and Chicago: University of Chicago Press, 1990

José Maria de Heredia 1842–1905

French poet

Biography

Born at La Fortuna, Cuba, 22 September 1842, his father a wealthy Spanish coffee plantation owner, his mother French. The family soon moved to Paris. Heredia went to school at Senlis, north of Paris, and went on to study in the capital at the École des Chartes, where archivists and librarians are trained. Paris was his home from 1861. Heredia was prominent in the group of French poets, led by his friend Leconte de Lisle, that came to be designated "Parnassians" from the title, *Le Parnasse contemporain* [The Contemporary Parnassus], of the three series of brochures published by Alphonse Lemerre in 1866, 1871 and 1876, in which many of their poems appeared. Heredia collected his whole output of 118 sonnets and some longer poems in *Les Trophées* (*The Trophies*), 1893. His poems are admired for the sharp concision and restrained marmoreal perfection of their form and their vivid visual and atmospheric evocation, based on erudition, of the ancient and medieval past and the exotic present. In 1894 he was elected to the Académie Française. He became librarian at the Bibliothèque de l'Arsenal in 1901. Died at Bourdonné, Île-de-France, 3 October 1905.

The Trophies

Les Trophées, 1893

Edition

Poésies complètes, Paris: Lemerre, 1924

Translations

Hill, Brian, *The Trophies: Fifty Sonnets*, with an introduction, London: Hart-Davis, and Philadelphia: Dufour Editions, 1962

Sewall, Frank, *The Trophies: Sonnets by José-Maria de Heredia*, Boston: Small Maynard, 1900

Taylor, Edward Robeson, *Sonnets of José-Maria de Heredia*, San Francisco: W. Doxey, 1897

José-Maria de Heredia, born in Cuba of an Hispano-French family proud to trace its origins back to a conquistador who had served under Cortés, complemented a scholarly life in Paris by giving expression to fervent emotions within a tightly circumscribed form that challenged technique and invited explosive compression. In 1893 Heredia gathered into a volume entitled *Les Trophées* the sonnets that he had written and published separately over the preceding decades. Taken as a whole, the collection may be seen as vivid and precisely observed fresco of privileged moments in myth and legend, history and art, in Ancient Greece and Rome, during the Middle Ages and the Renaissance. The wonder of nature is not forgotten either, and it was most probably the great international exhibitions in Paris that awakened his interest in the newly revealed civilization of Japan. Following the example of Victor Hugo, who in his *Légende des siècles* had accepted his publisher's advice and scaled down epic poetry to make it more acceptable to the reading public, Heredia went a large step further in the same direction when he confined vast events and titanic emotions within the narrow confines of the Petrarchan sonnet. This verse form, which had fallen into disrepute since the Renaissance but been given fresh validity by Romanticism, was particularly cultivated by the French Parnassian group. It was not only by dedicating *Les Trophées* to its leader, Leconte de Lisle, that Heredia declared his allegiance to its principles. As well as adhering to its ideals of impeccable craftsmanship in verse, he also accepted the doctrine that an impersonal, impassive manner of expression was essential in any work of true literary merit.

The translation of sonnets from *Les Trophées* presents a challenge which, though formidable, has proved irresistible to poets and versifiers around the world. Among those who responded early were two Americans, Frank SEWALL (1900), a Swedenborgian pastor, and Edward Robeson TAYLOR (1897), a deft Californian versifier often called upon for occasional poems. Both translators also warmed no doubt to Heredia's evocations of what Theodore Roosevelt, the man of the hour, had taught his countrymen to call the "strenuous life". The publication record of Taylor's translation indicated that it was well received in an age when deft versification was still esteemed, and it remains quite an achievement.

Examination of TAYLOR's version of *Antoine et Cléopâtre*, an acceptably typical touchstone, will reveal strengths as well as weaknesses. Reasonably substituting pentameters for conventional French alexandrines that might be unhandy in English and would certainly feel foreign, Taylor respects the structure of his original. Mirroring the scheme of the original with five rhymes, he matches quatrain with quatrain, tercet with tercet and, indeed, usually works line for line, with even their interrelationships respected, so that the drama of gradual realization is preserved until the final line where "Only a boundless sea where galleys fly" (Touche une mer immense où fuyaient des galères) serves very well as a conclusion, capturing the sense of hopeless and infinite despair. In his choice of words Taylor preserves both Heredia's characteristic use of proper nouns for precise reference and his technique of referring to the same person in various ways so that we see the Roman general and the Egyptian queen in different lights as the poem unfolds. But these undoubted successes are counterbalanced by sacrifices to the need to maintain the metre. "Wistfully" in the first line unwarrantably pre-empts the development of the sonnet. For "le fleuve, à travers le delta noir qu'il fend", "delta-cleaving Nile" is a coinage without parallel in Heredia; "fair tresses" changes the colour of Cleopatra's hair ("ses cheveux bruns") while adding a hackneyed poeticism; "crystalline, fond eyes", like her "yeux" that become "orbs", are also some distance from simple "prunelles claires"; and, least fortunate of all, "l'ardent Imperator", shorn of an adjective charged with meaning, is reduced to a mere "chieftain".

It is instructive to see how the same sonnet is handled by Brian HILL (1962). A poet of some standing in his own right, he had translated a number of French 19th-century poets, including Théophile Gautier and Verlaine before turning to Heredia. He offered versions of only 50 of the sonnets in 1962, by which time the international vogue for Heredia had largely waned and accomplished versification had lost much of its former prestige. In *Antoine et Cléopâtre* Hill, who is also freer than Taylor in his rhythms, does not tie himself to reproducing the rhyme scheme of the original. Yet though the pattern is different in detail, with eight rhymes arranged in a somewhat different scheme, the sense that we are dealing here with a sonnet is maintained, and, like Taylor, he follows Heredia in his articulation of the form. In the second half of the 20th century, that is perhaps enough. Proper nouns are again employed to good effect, and the language, like Heredia's, is concrete and precise. Like Taylor, Hill cannot capture the force of Heredia's initial "tous deux", an ominous insistence on the fact that the two form a pair that we know will soon fall asunder, but no adverbs are needed to fill out the first line, and though the order of the second quatrain has to be altered, three verbs for "ployer et défaillir" is compensation indeed. The second tercet again causes some problems. "Then did the burning Emperor behold" (Et ... l'ardent Imperator vit ...) seems to introduce the old-fashioned poetic verb only because something is needed that will rhyme with "gold", the adjective stubbornly declines to become figurative, and "Emperor" makes a larger claim for Mark Anthony than "Imperator", which Heredia left in its Latin form. Fortunately Hill is able to redeem himself with a good final line: "A whole wide sea where routed galleys fled". This has the unadorned, matter-of-fact despair of the long-drawn-out original.

Neither Taylor nor Hill can quite equal Heredia in his own genre, but it cannot be denied that both translators, using means that may be seen as reflecting to some degree the poetic idiom and verse style of their own ages, manage to convey Heredia's meaning and a good deal of his manner in a form that is notoriously demanding.

CHRISTOPHER SMITH

Further Reading

Harms, Alvin, *José-Maria de Heredia*, Boston: Twayne, 1975
Ibrovac, M., *José-Maria de Heredia: sa vie et son oeuvre*, 2 vols, Paris: Presses Françaises, 1923
Ibrovac, M., *José-Maria de Heredia: Les Sources des "Trophées"*, Paris: Presses Françaises, 1923
Ince, W.N. (editor), *Les Trophées*, London: Athlone Press, 1979

See also the translator's introduction to Hill

José Hernández 1834–1886

Argentine poet, politician and journalist

Biography

Born November 1834 at Pueyrredón, Argentina. From 1841 to 1845 he went to an elementary school in Barracas. Later he worked, and on several occasions fought, on the side of the Federalists of Argentina in their long struggle against the Unitarians or Centralists. In his journalism and his famous epic poem, *Martín Fierro*, he defended the gauchos of the pampas, among whom he had spent time in his youth, against the hostile Unitarian view of them as brutal and backward. As a political journalist Hernández contributed to, founded and edited various newspapers. He died in Buenos Aires 21 October 1886.

Martín Fierro

El gaucho Martín Fierro, 1872 [i.e. 16 January 1873], later sometimes entitled *La ida de Martín Fierro* and translated as *The Departure of Martin Fierro*; and *La vuelta de Martín Fierro*, 1879, translated as *The Return of Martin Fierro*

The first instalment of *Martín Fierro* (1873), a narrative poem in two parts, was published for urgent political reasons, to defend the gaucho, the rural, largely mestizo cowhand of the Argentine pampas. Under the liberal government of Domingo Faustino Sarmiento (1868–74), the gauchos were conscripted to fight the original inhabitants of the pampas, chiefly the Araucanians, who as late as the early 1870s still posed an immediate military threat to the capital Buenos Aires. At the same time, Sarmiento strongly fomented immigration from Europe at the direct expense of the gaucho. These are the ills denounced in Hernández's poem, and their effect is to drive the poem's central character, Martín Fierro, beyond the frontier, where he goes to live with the Indians: "savage" as they are in his eyes, they are still preferable to Argentines. In the late 1870s, governmental policies shifted, while the machine gun tipped the balance in the exterminatory war against the Indians. Accordingly, in part 2 of his poem (*The Return of Martin Fierro*, 1879), Hernández brings his hero back and accommodates him in Argentine society.

Translations

Auslander, Joseph, *A Fragment from Martín Fierro (El gaucho)*, New York: Hispanic Society of America, 1932
Carrino, Frank G., Alberto J. Carlos and Norman Mangouni, *The Gaucho Martín Fierro: A Facsimile Reproduction of the First Edition, 1872* (bilingual edition), with an introduction, Delmar, New York: Scholars' Facsimiles and Reprints, 1974

Holmes, Henry Alfred, *Martin Fierro: The Argentine Gaucho Epic*, with an introduction, New York: Hispanic Institute in the United States, 1948

Luquiens, Frederick Bliss, "Spanish American Literature" (stanzas from *Martín Fierro*), *Yale Review*, 17/3 (April 1928) pp. 553–55

Owen, Walter, *The Gaucho Martin Fierro*, with an introduction, Oxford: Blackwell, 1935; New York: Farrar and Rinehart, 1936

Stanton, Brian Eugene, *Martin Fierro*, Rexburg, Idaho: Madison Books, 1988

Ward, Catherine Elena, *The Gaucho Martin Fierro* (parallel texts), revised by Frank Carrino and Alberto J. Carlos, with an introduction by Carlos Alberto Astiz, Albany: State University of New York Press, 1967

Formally, José Hernández's poem consists mainly of octosyllabic sextains (rhymed abbccb) and as such belongs to the tradition of gauchesque poetry begun earlier in the 19th century, which draws on the idiom of gaucho ballad singers. This idiom involves a special pronunciation of Spanish (e.g. *j* for *f*, *naides* for *nadie*) and includes many words from the Indian languages, chiefly Araucanian, Quechua and Guarani, spoken by the gaucho's maternal ancestors. For this reason, most editions in the original Spanish include a glossary of such gaucho terms, and rendering them into another language requires double translation. The same unorthodoxy lies behind the fondness for wordplay, particularly in the exchanges between Martín Fierro, first with an immigrant sentry and second with a black couple. Of especial interest in part 1 are Martín Fierro's self-description as a poet-singer, and the scenes that display his good gaucho life before Sarmiento, his fight with an Indian, and his move beyond the frontier.

Despite its propagandistic origins, and although it is somewhat uneven and wordy in part 2, *Martín Fierro* stands as a major work, claimed by some to be the epitome of the Spanish American *criollo* (a person of Iberian stock but native born), and by others to be the Argentine epic. It was Che Guevara's favourite poem.

The gaucho and gauchesque literature attracted the attention of English-speaking writers already in the 19th century, W.H. Hudson being a salient case. Yet it was only after World War I that Hernández's poem began to be actually translated into English, which was also the time when versions in other languages began to appear (Italian in 1919, followed by German, French, Catalan, Guarani, Arabic and others).The first examples are the fragmentary versions of LUQUIENS (1928) and AUSLANDER (1932), both published in the US. These were followed by the first full-length translation of both parts, by Walter OWEN, a Scot who spent his life in Argentina. Published in Oxford in 1935 (and republished shortly after in the US), this version marked the graduation of the first cohort of Argentines sent to Oxford as Prince of Wales scholars.

As the first solidly published translator of Hernández's poem, LUQUIENS offers four stanzas from the start and two from the end of part 1. They are chosen to exemplify "the simple, unaffected idiom of the gauchos". In fact they have the patriarchal effect of turning Martín Fierro into a "cottage dweller", who before things went wrong under Sarmiento lived happily with "the wife", "under his own thatched roof".

OWEN's translation has had easily the widest appeal. Rhymed and rhythmic, it has a certain Scots drive. As a singer, Fierro says "let my tongue be glib and sweet, my words be not halt nor few", and he remembers "a dram from the demijohn" in the good old days. The translation also echoes sung poems of Owen's day by Masefield and others, hence "the lilt and the beat of the plainsman's song". For ideological reasons stated in his introduction, Owen strives to bring out Fierro's *criollo* nature, and with that a certain Christian dignity: "I sought no quarrel, nor drew a knife, / save in open fight and to guard my life". The verbal freedom Owen allows himself pays most dividends when Fierro, having just lost his wife and children, taunts the black couple ("you look like an ass ... tute fellow"; "it's a little bit ... chilly tonight").

After World War II and the founding of the United Nations, when cultural interest in Latin America awakened further, another round of translations appeared, all of them published in the United States. First among them were those of HOLMES (1948) and WARD (1967), writers who had each spent time in the River Plate region, the former as a teacher, the latter as daughter of the British Ambassador to Argentina. Ward's translation was revised for publication by CARRINO & CARLOS, scholars who then went on to publish a translation of their own, in collaboration with MANGOUNI (1974), and sponsored by Unesco. More recently, through a small press in Idaho, STANTON (1988) has offered a new reading of the first part, which he calls "a masculine adventure in verse".

HOLMES is primarily interested in the story of Martín Fierro and its ethical significance, and to this end he dispenses with rhyme, metre and line, leaving only the stanza as a subdivision for his prose translation. In the process, wordplay and musicality suffer, while in their stead we get the sententiousness and high tone of the "Psalmodist" cited in Holmes's introduction. This Fierro says of himself as a singer: "[the Eternal Father] dowered me in my mother's womb and sent me hither to sing" (compare WARD's closer "out of my mother's womb I came into this world to sing"). Some touches however are more accurate than anyone else's, for example, the rendering of "ranchito" simply as "home".

Lined but with no metre or rhyme, WARD's version reflects the current English of her day and attends well to rhythm and phrasing. She catches particularly well the distinctive care Fierro feels for his wife when she had no option but to go off with another (so different from the Hispanic point of honour), and Ward senses indigenous echoes in his language. Examples are her renderings of Quechua terms like *achura* ("have my guts", in the fight with the Indian), *chasque* ("special post"), and *rotoso* ("dirty", applied to him as a gaucho, and often wrongly derived from the Spanish roto, "broken").

Of part 1 only, the CARRINO–CARLOS–MANGOUNI translation carries over some of the wording of the WARD version that CARRINO & CARLOS had previously revised, along with the notes, but in general introduces a new and pronounced American accent of its own. This version insistently favours a tough cowboy idiom, in Fierro's account of himself as a singer ("singin' I'm gonna die") and of his agility as a fighter ("there ain't no flies on me"; "I got to the door fast, shoutin': 'Don't nobody try an' stop me"'; "I swung my ass around"). It also homogenizes and domesticates the pampa, making of the *criollo* simply a "man". Though reductive, this down-to-earth reading sometimes gets us closer to Fierro's own perspective, for example when he is on the frontier "that warn't worked yet" (elsewhere "uncultivated", or even "unclaimed"), thinking of "sneakin'" off to join the Indians (OWEN and WARD have "I'm off to the Indians").

GORDON BROTHERSTON

Further Reading

Brotherston, Gordon, *Latin American Poetry: Origins and Presence*, Cambridge and New York: Cambridge University Press, 1975

Holmes, Henry Alfred, *Martín Fierro: An Epic of the Argentine*, New York: Hispanic Institute in the United States, 1923

Hudson, W.H., *Far Away and Long Ago: A History of My Early Life*, London: Dent, and New York: Dutton, 1918

McCaffrey, William Mark, "The Gaucho from Literature to Film: Martín Fierro and Juan Moreira" (dissertation), San Diego: University of California, 1983

Shaw, Bradley A., *Latin American Literature in English Translation: An Annotated Bibliography*, New York: New York University Press, 1976

See also the translators' introductions to Carrino, Holmes and Owen

---

Hesiod lived c.700 BC

Greek poet

Biography

According to the poet himself, he lived in Ascra, in Boeotia (central Greece), where his father had settled after leaving an unsuccessful seafaring life in Cyme, Asia Minor. He tended sheep on Mount Helicon where, he wrote, the Muses appeared, gave him a poet's staff and told him to sing of the gods. He won a tripod for singing a poem, probably his *Theogony*, at the funeral games of Amphidamas in Chalcis. The story of his meeting and contest with Homer was probably fictional. Said to have died in Locris or Orchomenus.

Hesiod was one of the earliest-known classical Greek poets, and his epic poetry is often compared with the writing of Homer. The question of chronology of the two poets' work has been much debated. Two significant poetic works have been definitively attributed to Hesiod. His *Theogony* is a narrative describing the creation of the universe and the history of the gods; the later *Works and Days* is in the form of counsel to the poet's younger brother, advocating an honest and just life and giving practical advice on agricultural and domestic matters. Several other poems were spuriously attributed to Hesiod after his death, in particular the works known as the *Shield of Herakles* and the *Catalogue of Women*.

Translations

Chapman, George, *The Georgicks of Hesiod*, London: H.L. for M. Patrick, 1618

Cooke, Thomas, *The Works of Hesiod*, London: n.p., 1728

Elton, Charles Abraham, *The Remains of Hesiod*, London: Lackington Allen, 1812; revised edition, 1815

Frazer, R.M., *The Poems of Hesiod*, Norman: University of Oklahoma Press, 1983

Lattimore, Richmond, *Hesiod*, Ann Arbor: University of Michigan Press, 1959

Way, Arthur S., *Hesiod*, London: Macmillan, 1934

West, M.L., *Hesiod: Theogony and Works and Days*, Oxford and New York: Oxford University Press, 1988

Two distinct Greek texts, not certainly by the same poet, but attributed by tradition to Hesiod, are covered in this entry: the *Works and Days* (conventional Latin title *Opera et dies*) and *Theogony*. Various sub-sections of these short epics have sometimes been excerpted by translators; they have gone under such titles as "Catalogue of Women", and "Battle of the Gods and Titans". The *Shield of Achilles* (or *Shield of Hercules*) is now generally thought not to be by Hesiod, though it has sometimes been translated in the same volume as works still usually attributed to him.

It is the *Works and Days* that CHAPMAN translated in 1618, called in his version *Georgicks* because the Virgilian title made this then-obscure work appear to be of a familiar type. The translation is divided by Chapman into three parts, which he calls "The First Book", "The Second Book" (on farming lore), and the brief "Hesiod's Book of Days" (on lucky and unlucky days in the calendar; into which is inserted a Hesiodic fragment preserved in Plutarch describing various real and fabulous animals). The disparate impression is registered in Chapman's prefatory note, and turned into an occasion for praise: no other book "do[es] the world so much profit for all humane instruction as this one work", because here there is "no dwelling on any one subject" but instruction in "all humane affairs". Chapman's decasyllabic couplet version constituted for a century the only English Hesiod. His sinewy English is demonstrably that of a poet, though the poet is at times overshadowed by the scholarly interpreter – whose observations obtrude themselves into the margins of every page. The version also interpolates glosses and other extraneous material into the text.

COOKE was a minor 18th-century poet who translated from

Bion, Moschus and Plautus as well as Hesiod. The heroic couplets of his *Works and Days* and *Theogony* (1728) are often limp, and his understanding of the Greek has been called into question. His phraseology can be cliché-ridden and bathos is sometimes effortlessly achieved; yet there are also stretches of surprisingly good writing:

But should he, wretched Man, a nymph embrace,
A stubborn Consort, of a stubborn Race,
Poor hamper'd Slave, how must he drag the Chain!
His Mind, his Breast, his Heart, o'ercharg'd with Pain!
What congregated Woes must he endure!
What Ills on Ills which will admit no Cure!

Cooke's Hesiod was accompanied by notes composed by Theobald.

ELTON (1812) translates the *Works and Days* into competent Augustan couplets, whereas he renders the *Theogony* and *Shield of Achilles* into sub-Miltonic blank verse comparable in manner and quality to Cowper's Homer. His notes draw attention to literary parallels, most frequently with Milton, Homer and the Bible. Elton sees Hesiod as a "sublime" poet of "romantic elegance, or daring grandeur" and "vigorous simplicity". Today, his rendering of the *Theogony*, in particular, is likely to seem cloyingly overdone, as in this sample from the battle of the Gods and Titans:

Nor longer then did Jove
Curb down his force; but sudden in his soul
There grew dilated strength: his whole of might
Broke from him, and the godhead rush'd abroad.
The vaulted sky, the mount Olympus, flash'd
With his continual presence; for he pass'd
Incessant forth, and lighten'd where he trod.

WAY's version of 1934 is self-consciously archaizing in several respects, in a fashion best indicated by quotation:

An thou wilt, I will tell thee in outline another myth from my lore
Wisely and well; and this in thy memory heedfully store,
How Gods and mortal men from the same source sprang of yore.
First came into being of speech-dowered men a race of gold
Created by Gods immortal, the halls of Olympus who hold.

This is, then, a kind of pastiche Renaissance version. The outlandishly foreign is welcomed and retained: we have such epithets for Zeus as "Cloudrack-herder" and "the Aegis-bearer". Way is most tolerable in passages of straightforward narrative.

LATTIMORE's *Works and Days* (1959) has a highly unusual format. The right-hand page contains his translation, the left what he describes as "an extremely concise summary in the form of gnomic scholia". The effect seems eccentric, but the approach has been praised as a "masterful solution" to the difficulty of following the poem's abrupt transitions (Lamberton, 1988). Lattimore's translations themselves veer abruptly in idiom between biblical and modern American English:

Now that the earth has gathered over this generation,
These are called pure and blessed spirits;
they live upon earth,
and are good, they watch over mortal men
and defend them from evil;
they keep watch over lawsuits and hard dealings;
they mantle
themselves in dark mist
and wander all over the country;
they bestow wealth; for this right
as of kings was given them.

In FRAZER's own words, his 1983 Hesiod (*Theogony*, *Works and Days*) "offers an approximation to the dactylic hexameter of the original", attempts line-by-line equivalence but sometimes takes more lines "in order to obtain a clear and idiomatic English", and permits itself to expand the "thought of the original" or to make it "explicit where it was only implicit". But the English has some properties of the garbled non-language classicists often tolerate in translations – "Thus did Zeus, whose plans are unfailing, chidingly speak" – and the metrical structure is often obscure or non-existent:

Baneful Night also bore Nemesis, an avenging plague for
mortal men; and then Deceit and Sexual Love and
baneful Old Age and Eris (Strife), a hard-hearted demon.

Nor, in fact, is the English always clear, if this means "self-explanatory": "For the gods keep hidden the livelihood of men". This translation is very evidently the work of an academic rather than a poet.

WEST (1988) sticks to prose except for a few passages where "formal structure is important". The main intention is to provide a reliable paraphrase that can be used in conjunction with the Greek; the student is also served by full explanatory notes at the back of the volume. This is a readable and accurate rendering of the two works, if prose is all that is required:

So he ordered, and they all obeyed lord Zeus son of Kronos.
At once the renowned Ambidexter moulded from earth the
likeness of a modest maiden by Kronos' son's design, and
the pale-eyed goddess Athene dressed and adorned her.

West acknowledges that he may "sometimes [have] made Hesiod sound a little quaint and stilted", adding only that "he is".

STUART GILLESPIE

Further Reading

Lamberton, Robert, *Hesiod*, New Haven, Connecticut: Yale University Press, 1988

Maclure, Millar, "The Minor Translations of George Chapman", *Modern Philology*, 60 (1962–63) pp. 172–82

Hermann Hesse 1877–1962

German/Swiss novelist and poet

Biography

Born in Calw, Swabia, 2 July 1877, into a family of Protestant ministers and missionaries. His father and maternal grandfather were orientalists. Between 1881 and 1886 the family lived in Basle, and Hesse acquired Swiss citizenship. He was educated at monastery schools in Swabia, then earned a living at various trades. A collection of poems, *Romantische Lieder*, was published in 1899. From 1899 to 1904 he worked in Basle in the book trade. He had his first public success with the novel *Peter Camenzind* (1904) and became a freelance writer. From 1901 he travelled in Italy and in 1911 went to India. He married three times, in 1904, 1924 and 1931. In 1912 he moved to Switzerland, resuming Swiss citizenship in 1923. A one point he underwent Jungian analysis. From 1919 he lived in Montagnola in the Ticino canton of Switzerland. His writings are characterized by support for pacifism and individualism and the novels are preoccupied with complex relationships between conflicting characters. In 1943, the year of the publication of his most famous novel, *Das Glasperlenspiel* (*Magister Ludi*, 1949; *The Glass Bead Game*, 1969), Hesse's name was blacklisted in Germany. The main narrative in this complex work is set in the future, in the imaginary realm of Castalia, where the central character becomes Master of a lofty and mysterious game engaged in by the scholarly community, in the course of which process all aspects of human culture are examined. A prolific writer, producing not only novels and poetry but also essays and letters, Hesse was awarded many Swiss and German literary honours. *The Glass Bead Game* won him the Nobel Prize for Literature in 1946. Died in Montagnola, 9 August 1962.

Translations

Novels

Peter Camenzind, 1904
Strachan, W.J., *Peter Camenzind*, London: Peter Owen, 1970

Unterm Rad, 1906
Strachan, W.J., *The Prodigy*, London: Peter Owen, 1957

Gertrud, 1910
Rosner, Hilda, *Gertrude*, London: Peter Owen, 1955; revised edition, New York: Farrar Straus, 1969

Rosshalde, 1914
Manheim, Ralph, *Rosshalde*, New York: Farrar Straus, 1970; London: Jonathan Cape, 1971

Demian, 1919
Strachan, W.J., *Demian*, London: Peter Owen, 1960

Siddhartha, 1922
Rosner, Hilda, *Siddhartha*, New York: New Directions, 1951; London: Peter Owen, 1954

Der Steppenwolf, 1927
Creighton, Basil, *Steppenwolf*, London: Secker, and New York: Holt, 1929; revised by Walter Sorell, New York: Random House, 1963, Harmondsworth: Penguin, 1965

Narziss und Goldmund, 1930
Dunlop, Geoffrey, *Narziss and Goldmund*, London: Peter Owen, 1959; Harmondsworth: Penguin, 1971

Das Glasperlenspiel: Versuch einer Lebensbeschreibung des Magister Ludi Josef Knecht samt Knechts hinterlassenen Schriften, 1943
Savill, Mervyn, *Magister Ludi*, London: Aldus, and New York: Ungar, 1949
Winston, Richard and Clara Winston, *The Glass Bead Game*, with a foreword by Theodore Ziolkowski, New York: Holt Rinehart, 1969; London: Jonathan Cape, 1970

Hermann Hesse's popularity in the English-speaking world during the 1960s, especially among young hippies in America, owed little to the quality of the available translations which, with the exception of *The Glass Bead Game*, was not high. *Steppenwolf*, for instance, the novel that enjoyed the greatest success, is seriously flawed, even though Basil CREIGHTON's version (1929) was revised by Walter Sorell in 1963. Omissions are frequent here: of whole sentences from the preface, of the subtitle "For Madmen Only" from the Treatise, and – perhaps for prudish reasons – of the inscription from the Magic Theatre sequence: "Oh for a thousand tongues! For gentlemen only." Tenses are inaccurate, particularly in the Treatise, where the original speaks of the hero Harry Haller consistently in the present, as befits a character still alive, but the translation sometimes switches arbitrarily to the past. Careless errors in vocabulary also abound. Thus Haller's gout (Gicht) becomes "poison" (Gift); "professorial" "professional"; and "ascetic" "aesthetic".

Some of the passages on music, so central to the novel, are hopelessly garbled. A basic misreading of the preposition "von", for example, leads to "Transformation *from* Time into Space by means of Music" where "Transformation *of*" is correct. Elsewhere, listening to a concert of early music, Haller is said to glimpse another world "after two or three notes of the piano", whereas the vision actually occurs "between two bars, played *piano* by the woodwind"! The translation is equally inadequate when it comes to other key themes. These include psychology, where "soul" is usually preferred to the more appropriate "mind" for German "Seele"; the notion of fully realized humanity or "Menschwerdung", which gets lost in the heavily gendered "ideal of manhood"; and the critique of Haller's humourless histrionics, where "pathos" and "pathetic" are misleading as equivalents of German "Pathos" and "pathetisch". To their credit, the translators cope well with the novel's recurring images, such as those drawn from cosmology, and their versions of Hesse's interpolated doggerel poems are no worse than the originals, but these virtues hardly outweigh the numerous errors.

Hesse's "Indian" novel *Siddhartha*, also a cult book for American youth in the 1960s, is better served by Hilda ROSNER's translation (1951). Language and style are markedly simpler here than in *Der Steppenwolf*, and the temptation to elaborate on them is rightly resisted by Rosner. Faithful in its attention to detail, this version rarely omits anything. The references to Bhuddist and Hindu lore are well handled, apart from two instances where, through careless retention of the German genitive "s", the god Vishnu becomes "Vishnus". Those passages that, despite the Indian setting, owe more to German Romanticism or Goethe are also nicely rendered, though the occasional allusion to the imagery of Hesse's beloved Nietzsche is missed, as when the wisdom-seeking hero, Siddhartha, contemplating suicide, refers to "das grosse Erbrechen" ("the great vomiting") and not, as the translation has it, "the great deed". Rosner makes the odd slip elsewhere, for instance when the courtesan Kamala is said to rejoice at *her* erotic mastery over Siddhartha rather than his over her, but for the most part the translation is admirably accurate.

The same can not be said of W.J. STRACHAN's translation (1960) of *Demian*, the novel that so appealed to German youth after World War I. Generally adequate in conveying the central theme of a young man's journey to self-realization, this version is however marred by significant omissions, among other things of the novel's subtitle – "The Story of Emil Sinclair's Youth" – and its epigraph. The reader does encounter the latter, as in the original, in the body of chapter 5, but only in a truncated version. More serious are the frequent careless renderings such as "hot" (German "heiss") for "hoarse" ("heiser"); "on the right" for "on the coat-rack" ("am Rechen"); or "orgasm of self-destruction" for "orgy" ("Orgiasmus"). At points, such negligence leads to utter nonsense like "almost fanatical yet passionate absorption", where the original has "passion*less*" ("leidenschaftslos"). Another example concerns young Sinclair's sense of relief when, having secretly raided his savings box, he is reprimanded by his father merely for having dirty shoes. Here, Hesse's analogy with a man guilty of murders who is being questioned about nothing more than the theft of a bread roll results in the absurd version: "a criminal who is being tried for stealing a loaf of bread when he has confessed to murder." If this shows disregard for all logic, other misconstrued passages stem from historical ignorance (e.g. of Bismarck and the Social Democrats) or unfamiliarity with key sources such as Nietzsche ("Flucht in warme Herdennähe" rendered as "flight to cosy firesides" rather than "to the warmth of the herd").

Such errors apart, and despite the occasional false register, especially when rendering the conversations of Sinclair and Demian in typically public-school English, Strachan's *Demian* at least captures the general tone of Hesse's original. In this respect, by comparison, Geoffrey DUNLOP's version (1959) of the 1930 novel *Narziss und Goldmund* must be judged a failure. Presumably because of the medieval setting, Dunlop often employs a quaintly archaic English to render Hesse's for the most part standard modern German. Thus we encounter "hog's flesh" for simple "pork"; "tire-woman" for "chamber-maid"; "leech" for "doctor"; "leman" for "lover", and the like, as well as hybrids such as "stattholder" or German imports like "spielmann". Constantly one detects a desire to improve upon or supplement Hesse's text. This results in considerable distortion, whether by over-writing, as in "the joyous plesaunces of beauty" for the literal "beautiful land of art", or by wilful substitution, as when "schöne Dinge" (beautiful things) become "pleasant toys". Dunlop is also guilty of omissions (an 11-line second paragraph in chapter 13) and careless misreading of words: "Schüssel" (bowl) confused with "Schlüssel" (key), and "Geschichte" (story) with "Gesicht" (face). The translation of the very first paragraph of the novel, a detailed description of the entrance to Mariabronn monastery, contains several serious errors in syntax and vocabulary and, though the accuracy level improves in later chapters, few pages are wholly reliable. *Narziss and Goldmund* may not be Hesse's best novel, indeed it borders at times on the kitschy, but it merits better service than this.

Hesse's last and longest novel *Das Glasperlenspiel*, which he worked on over a 10-year period from 1932 to 1942 and which led to the award of the Nobel Prize for Literature in 1946, makes considerable demands on the translator. The reflections on the "Age of the Feuilleton" with which it begins involve highly sophisticated cultural criticism. Descriptions of the eponymous imaginary game – "a mode of playing with the total contents and values of our culture" – require a range of mathematical, musicological, linguistic, literary and philosophical knowledge. The various stages of the life of the central character Josef Knecht, which constitute the central narrative strand, are interspersed with essayistic reflections and debates on all manner of subjects from the nature of historiography to Chinese thought, from ethics to aesthetics, from politics to religion. In addition to the life itself, the translator also has to cope with the hero's "posthumous" writings (the "hinterlassene Schriften" of the work's subtitle), which include 13 poems in a variety of forms and three imaginary biographies set variously in a primitive matriarchal society, in 3rd-century Gaza, and in ancient India.

Richard and Clara WINSTON's translation (1969) not only improves considerably on the first English version by Mervyn SAVILL (1949); it is by a long way the most reliable rendering into English of any work by Hesse, far superior to the available versions of his earlier and in many respects less demanding novels like *Demian*, *Der Steppenwolf* or *Narziss und Goldmund*. The Winstons excel when it comes to the ramifications of the Glass Bead Game itself, which they rightly restore to prominence in the novel's title. Their account of its history in the introduction, and the later descriptions of the individual games devised by Fritz Tegularius or by Josef Knecht himself, especially that based on the architecture of a traditional Chinese house, are models of accuracy and attention to detail. Even when unable to follow all of Hesse's variations on the word "Spiel" (both "game" and "play"), they manage to remain faithful to the sense, rendering "Spielerei" as "superficiality", for instance, or the character Tegularius's "Hang zur Verspieltheit" as "tendency to fritter away his talents".

A particular virtue of the translation is the way in which it observes and retains key terms and images that recur throughout this finely patterned novel, especially those relating to the contrasting themes of servitude and mastery, *vita activa* and *vita contemplativa*, and a whole cluster of imagery deriving from Nietzsche. Where a key German term has no adequate single equivalent in English, the Winstons usually take pains to bring out the full connotations, opting for "cheerful serenity", for example, to convey the sense of "Heiterkeit", the life-affirming quality Knecht opposes to the sceptical pessimism of his friend and opposite Designori. Their handling of the important long conversation between these two figures in chapter 9 is especially good, as is that of the earlier encounters between Knecht and Father Jacobus, the character based on the historian Jakob Burckhardt. In the latter context, the translators show a sound grasp of the issues involved in the debates on historiography, especially Hesse's critique of German philosophy of history or "Geschichtsphilosophie". It is all the more surprising, then, to find them later mistranslating this term – in a passage clearly aimed at Hegel – as "historical philosophy".

For all their general excellence, the Winstons do make the occasional slip of this nature. Usually it is a matter of choosing the wrong equivalent in a particular context: "scholarship", for example, instead of "science" for "Wissenschaft" where the term is clearly contrasted with the arts; or "seminaries" for "Seminare" where the secular and modern setting points to "university departments". There are, however no really glaring mistakes of the kind often encountered in other Hesse translations. (Unfortunate instances of "God" for "Gold" and of "footpath" for "footbath" must be print errors.) Omissions, too, are rare. A key paragraph from the Statutes of the Order of the Glass Bead Game is translated in a slightly truncated and distorted form on the first occasion it is quoted, but fully and correctly on the second; the wording ought ideally to have been identical in both instances, as in the original.

When it comes to the poems that follow Knecht's biography, the translators, in their attempt to observe metre and rhyme, must be granted more licence. Mostly their efforts are successful, but they unfortunately sacrifice sense to rhyme or rhythm on two occasions in vital final lines. In "Stages" ("Stufen"), a poem also quoted in the body of the narrative, they substitute "bid farewell without end" for the literal sense "bid farewell and regain health", which is crucial to the novel's recurring Goethean theme of self-renewal. And in the last poem, itself entitled "The Glass Bead Game", they give a false impression of the Olympian security of all the Game's initiates who "... cannot be dislodged or misdirected, / Held in the orbit of the Cosmic Soul." The original, by contrast, admits of the possibility of their falling, albeit only to the "sacred centre" ("Und keiner kann aus ihren Kreisen fallen, / Als nach der heiligen Mitte hin.") Here a significant parallel to the main action of the novel gets lost, since the lines are relevant to Knecht's quitting the Order, only to die shortly afterwards when plunging into an ice-cold mountain lake. Otherwise, apart from a rather garbled version of "A Toccata by Bach" – the work of a separate translator, Alex Page – the poems accurately capture the style and contents of the originals. So too do the three appended "Lives", purportedly the work of Knecht in his student days.

Taken as a whole, the translation is, it must be stressed in conclusion, a towering achievement. Unlike some other major 20th-century German novels, Hesse's *magnum opus* is thus, thanks to Richard and Clara Winston, available to English readers in a form its stature merits.

DAVID HORROCKS

Further Reading

Boulby, Mark, *Hermann Hesse: His Mind and His Art*, Ithaca, New York: Cornell University Press, 1967

Freedman, Ralph, *Hermann Hesse, Pilgrim of Crisis: A Biography*, New York: Pantheon, 1978; London: Jonathan Cape, 1979

Mayer, Hans, "Hermann Hesse and the 'Age of the Feuilleton'" in *Hesse: A Collection of Critical Essays*, edited by Theodore Ziolkowski, Englewood Cliffs, New Jersey: Prentice Hall, 1973

Sorell, Walter, *Hermann Hesse: The Man Who Sought and Found Himself*, London: Wolff, 1974

Ziolkowski, Theodore, *The Novels of Hermann Hesse: A Study in Theme and Structure*, Princeton, New Jersey: Princeton University Press, 1965

Ziolkowski, Theodore (editor), *Hesse: A Collection of Critical Essays*, Englewood Cliffs, New Jersey: Prentice Hall, 1973

Thomas Hobbes 1588–1679

English philosopher, political theorist and translator

Biography

Thomas Hobbes was born 5 April 1588 in Malmesbury, Wiltshire. He went to schools in and near Malmesbury, early becoming proficient in Latin and Greek, then in 1602 or 1603 to Oxford. He graduated in 1607 or 1608 and went on to become tutor and later secretary to the second earl of Devonshire. In 1631, three years after the second earl's death, Hobbes was made tutor to William Cavendish, the third earl. He knew Bacon, and travelling in Europe with his patrons he met Mersenne, Descartes, Gassendi and Galileo. The formation of his anti-scholastic philosophical project, to apply geometrical and mechanical principles to political science, was given impetus by the approach of civil war in England. In 1640 he completed *Elements of Law Natural and Politic* (published in1650 in two parts); also in 1640, alarmed by the impeachment of Strafford, Hobbes fled to France, where he stayed for 11 years. In 1647 he became tutor in mathematics to the exiled future Charles II. *De Cive* appeared in 1642. In 1651 came his most important work, *Leviathan; or, The Matter, Form and Power of a Commonwealth Ecclesiastical and Civil*, in which he advocated absolute monarchy. After Cromwell permitted his return to London in 1652, Hobbes produced *De corpore* (1655) and *De homine* (1658). His views, including the necessity of subordinating church to state, aroused hostility and in 1666 he was forbidden to publish in England. *Behemoth*, a history of the

Civil War, was published posthumously in 1682. Hobbes died at Hardwick Hall, one of the Cavendish family seats, 4 December 1679.

As well as his philosophical works Hobbes produced some original works in Latin, of a literary nature, notably *De mirabilibus pecci* (1636; *The Wonders of the Peak*, 1678) and *Historia ecclesiastica* (1688; *A True Ecclesiastical History* ..., 1722); the English versions of these were by anonymous translators. Hobbes translated or part-translated some of his own philosophical texts from Latin to English and vice versa, but also published three major literary translations into English of Greek classic texts. That of Thucydides' *Peloponnesian War*, which had a strong bearing on the evolution of Hobbes's political theory, was published in 1629, and his verse translations of Homer's *Iliad* and *Odyssey* in 1674–75.

De mirabilibus pecci, carmen (*The Wonders of the Peak*) is a poem of approximately 540 Latin hexameters, written 1626–27 or earlier and first published in about 1636 (there seems to be no title page extant), 2nd edition London, 1666, 3rd edition 1675. An English translation by "A Person of Quality" appeared in the 1678 edition.

The poem was given as a 1627 New Year's gift to the second earl of Devonshire but at his death shortly afterwards (1628) it was addressed to his son, the infant William Cavendish, third earl of Devonshire (permission to dedicate it to the infant third earl was requested of Lady Devonshire on 6 November 1628 (see Miriam Reik, *The Golden Lands of Thomas Hobbes*, Detroit: Wayne State University Press, 1977). Since the young recipient was clearly of no age to appreciate the intricacies of the 540 or so lines on a journey through the topography of that part of the the Peak District surrounding the Cavendishes' great house of Chatsworth in Derbyshire, the poem – vastly outsize in comparison with the usual three- to four-stanza New Year's tribute – belongs to the coterie and travel relationship that a much younger Hobbes shared, as tutor, with his contemporary charge, the learned second earl of Devonshire.

While the "Devil's Arse of Peak" was celebrated in vernacular poetry and masque by such artists as Ben Jonson and Michael Drayton, Thomas Hobbes placed its local history and anatomical mythology in the classical context of the seven wonders of the world and the classical Latin language of Virgil, Lucretius, Horace and Ovid among others. Blending the modish genres of the country house poem and the journey poem, Hobbes works scientific propositions about acoustics and the nature of matter and reflections on contemporary politics into an erotic allegorization of the Cavendishes' privileged hold on the political, financial and mineral resources of the region. The showy humanist learning of the piece may have served to introduce Hobbes to the learned circles that he would encounter during his travels with the second earl of Devonshire. For a translator, the principal challenge is how to unfold the many layers of meanings structured in each line so as to produce a translation that does justice to Thomas Hobbes's elaborate design, entertaining wit and political acumen.

The 1678 translation, *The Wonders of the Peak*, by "A Person of Quality", addressed a wider public and pursued aims other than those of the text it communicates. Its frequent misreadings and paraphrases suggest a work of literature challenging in its own right. Based on extensive consultation of the MSS at Chatsworth and in the British Library, a new translation, which sets the poem and earlier translation in context and is accompanied by an extensive historical and literary introduction, is in preparation by the present writers.

Though written earlier, the *Historia ecclesiastica*, according to Molesworth, was first published in 1688, accompanied by the preface in Latin prose by Thomas Rymer. The Molesworth edition also features a one-page glossary where some of Hobbes's witty semantics, often of humanist provenance, are glossed in Latin. A full census of the manuscript sources is still under research.

In the *Historia ecclesiastica*, Thomas Hobbes presents his riposte to contemporary ecclesiastical poetry such as George Herbert's "The Temple", but more profoundly revisits religious history to reflect on the causes of the English Civil War in elegiac couplets (alternating dactylic hexameters and pentameters). A syntax apparently simpler than that of *De mirabilibus pecci* and vocabulary typical of ecclesiastical Latin predominates. But Rymer's well-chosen epigraph affixed to the poem from Ovid, *Metamorphoses*, I, 130-31, signals Hobbes's own lament for the descent of the Golden Age into violence and brutality. Among other classical sources invoked by Hobbes, Horace's satiric use of the fable about the town mouse and the country mouse (*Satires*, II, 6) features prominently. The corruption of the Christian Church, and of its analogue the Roman Empire, by sophisticated charlatans of various pedigrees is traced by Hobbes in a style reminiscent of the snappy dialogue of the Latin comedies. Translation of this witty, yet philosophically serious, work presents the problem of conveying adequately the convergence of classical, ecclesiastical, philosophical and contemporary political references. For the *Historia ecclesiastica* is an extraordinary epitome of Hobbes's more voluminous political and theological writings. No matter how extensive his text, Hobbes shows a consistent preference for epigrammatic statement joined to a highly developed sense of humanity's tragic absurdity.

The 1722 edition of the *Historia ecclesiastica* has an anonymous English translation into English facing the Latin text; under an Australian Research Council grant the present writers are completing a new translation accompanied by extensive introductory material.

The provenance of the clarity and visceral quality of Hobbes's expression in Latin and English can be seen in his idiosyncratic translations of Thucydides' *History of the Peloponnesian War*, his first large-scale publication, and of Homer's *Iliad* and *Odyssey*, among his final labors. During the Renaissance, Greek was considered easier than Latin and therefore linguistically closer to the bucolic golden age. Homer was the rustic bard of epic, while Virgil was the urbane sophisticate of the genre. According to this pedagogic valuation, Greek was often taught first to very young students. Hobbes's choice to translate Thucydides' Greek may also be linked to his advocacy of rural values in the contemporaneous *De mirabilibus pecci, carmen*. The perspicuity of Hobbes's translations proceeds from his commitment to plain speaking, as for instance in his version of the opening of Thucydides' oration of the ambassadors of Corcyra:

> Men of Athens, it is but justice that such as come to implore the aid of their neighbors (as now do we), and cannot

> pretend by any great benefit or league some precedent merit, should, before they go any farther, make it appear, principally, that what they seek conferreth profit, or if not so, yet is not prejudicial, at least to those that are to grant it.
>
> (*The English Works of Thomas Hobbes*, edited Molesworth, vol. 8, p. 38)

Here Hobbes foregrounds the issue of justice, which is indeed the first word in the Greek address, "Dikaion, o Atheinaioi..." A translation in the Loeb series (Charles Forster Smith, *Thucydides: History of the Peloponnesian War*, 4 vols, London: Heinemann, 1952) more carefully keyed to the sequence of the original rambles vaguely:

> It is but fair, citizens of Athens, that those who, without any previous claim on the score of important service rendered or of an existing alliance, come to their neighbours to ask aid, as we do now, should show in the first place, if possible, that what they ask is advantageous, or at least that it is not hurtful.
>
> (Forster Smith, vol. 1, p. 57)

The end of the 17th century saw much general interest in re-translating the great classical epics to express semantic and societal changes. The timing of Hobbes's translations of Homer suggests such an impetus, while the formulaic nature of Homer's language, his pastoral similes and metaphors, his focus on issues of kingship and tyranny, and his privileging of material objects such as Achilles' shield also coincide with Hobbes's own discursive values. Like the shield itself, Hobbes's translation of these great epics uncovers the voice of an orderly, rural society asserting its power to master the forces of war. The terrible and mysterious descent of Apollo Smintheus, Apollo as the Mouse-God of Darkness and Disease, to wreak his vengeance on the Achaeans, in the opening lines of the *Iliad*, is rendered in language typical of Hobbes's appropriation of epic discourse to the English countryside:

> His prayer was granted by the deity;
> Who with his silver bow and arrows keen,
> Descended from Olympus silently
> In likeness of the sable night unseen.
> His bow and quiver do behind him hang,
> The arrows chink as often as he jogs,
> And as he shot the bow was heard to twang,
> And first his arrows flew at mules and dogs.
>
> (*The English Works of Thomas Hobbes*, edited Molesworth, vol. 10, p. 2)

Such an accent is particularly successful at conveying the many rural scenes in the *Odyssey*. For example, Hobbes's vocalization of Circe's dwelling place suggests a scene at an English country house:

> Down in a dale they Circe's palace found,
> Built of square stone; the place was full of shade:
> Lions and wolves about it lay o' th' ground,
> Whom Circe tame with magic arts hath made;
> These flew not at my men, but laid their noses
> Upon them lovingly, and wagg'd their tails
> As dogs salute their masters; Circe's doses
> So much above their natures fierce prevail.
>
> (*ibid.*, vol. 10, p. 398)

PATRICIA SPRINGBORG and PATRICIA HARRIS STÄBLEIN

Translations (from and by Hobbes)

De mirabilibus pecci, carmen, by Hobbes, c.1636

"A Person of Quality", *The Wonders of the Peak*, facing the Latin text in Hobbes's *De mirabilibus pecci: Being the Wonders of the Peak in Darby-shire, Commonly Called the Devil's Arse of Peak; in English and Latin; the Latin Written by Thomas Hobbes, the English by a Person of Quality*, 1678

Historia ecclesiastica, by Hobbes, 1688

Anonymous, *A True Ecclesiastical History from Moses to the Time of Martin Luther, in Verse, by Thomas Hobbes, Made English from the Latin Original* (parallel texts), 1722

Thucydides, *The History of the Grecian War Written by Thucydides*, 1629; *The Peloponnesian War (The Thomas Hobbes Translation)*, edited by David Grene, 1960; *History of the Peloponnesian War: Hobbes's Thucydides*, edited with an introduction by Richard Schlatter, 1975

Homer, *Homer's Iliad*, 1675

Homer, *Homer's Odyssey*, 1674

Further Reading

Beale, Peter, *Index of English Literary Manuscripts*, vol. 2, part 1 (Behn–King), New York and London: Mansell, 1987

Buxton, John (editor), *Charles Cotton: Poems*, London: Routledge and Kegan Paul, 1958

Drayton, Michael, *Poly-Olbion: A Chorographical Description of Great Britain* (1612–22), parts 1–3, New York: Burt Franklin for the Spenser Society, 1889; reprinted 1970

Fowler, Alastair, *The Country House Poem: A Cabinet of Seventeenth-Century Estate Poems and Related Items*, Edinburgh: Edinburgh University Press, 1994

Orgel, Stephen (editor), *Ben Jonson: The Complete Masques*, New Haven: Yale University Press, 1969

Hobbes, Thomas, *Thomae Hobbes Malmesburiensis: Opera Philosophica*, edited by Sir William Molesworth, 5 vols, London: Bohn / Longman Brown Green and Longman, 1839–45, reprinted Aalen: Scientia, 1961 (*De mirabililibus pecci* and *Historia ecclesiastica* in vol. 5)

Hobbes, Thomas, *The English Works of Thomas Hobbes of Malmesbury*, edited by Sir William Molesworth, 11 vols, London: Bohn / Longman Brown Green and Longman, 1839–45, reprinted Aalen: Scientia, 1962 (Thucydides in vols 8–9, Homer in vol. 10)

Parfitt, George (editor), *Ben Jonson: The Complete Poems*, Harmondsworth: Penguin, 1988 (revised edition)

Raylor, Timothy, *Cavaliers, Clubs and Literary Culture*, Cranbury, New Jersey: Associated University Presses, 1994

Report on the MSS and Papers of Thomas Hobbes in the Devonshire Collections, Chatsworth, London: Royal Commission on Historical Manuscripts, 1977

Salgado, Gamini (editor), *Four Jacobean City Comedies*, Harmondsworth: Penguin, 1985 (first published 1975)

Skinner, Quentin, *Reason and Rhetoric in the Philosophy of Hobbes*, Cambridge and New York: Cambridge University Press, 1996

E.T.A. Hoffmann 1776–1822

German short-story writer, novelist, dramatist, critic and composer

Biography

Born Ernst Theodor Amadeus Hoffmann in Königsberg, Germany, 24 January 1776. He was writer, composer, stage designer, theatre director, musical critic and, during his last years, lawyer at the Prussian Supreme Court. Hoffmann was part of the German Romantic period with his fantastic fairytales and historical stories, and at the same time transcended Romanticism with his realistic, psychological depictions of highly gifted and artistic, yet tormented souls. They came to life in characters such as Nathanael in "Der Sandmann" ("The Sandman"), the mad musician Johannes Kreisler in the novel *Kater Murr* and "Kreisleriana", and the obsessed goldsmith Cardillac in "Das Fräulein von Scuderi" ("Mademoiselle de Scudéry"). Hoffmann himself represents the double aspect of the bourgeois citizen and the anti-establishment bohemian artist, which led to him being praised and at the same time misunderstood and condemned by contemporaries and future generations alike. He wrote five novels, three collections of short stories, fairytales, novellas, assorted articles on various contemporary composers (Beethoven among them), several plays and various essays. Offenbach's opera *The Tales of Hoffmann* (1881) is based on three of the stories.

While Hoffmann's complete works have been translated many times in France and proved strongly influential on French writers, particularly in the 1830s and 1840s, only parts of his output are known in the English-speaking world, mainly via translations of individual short stories or collections of stories. In the 19th century the majority of translations appeared in literary periodicals, having been put into English anonymously by amateurs with an enthusiasm for literature. Died in Berlin, 25 June 1822.

Translations

Novels

Die Elixiere des Teufels, 1815–16

Gillies, Robert Pierce, *The Devil's Elixir*, 2 vols, Edinburgh: Blackwood, 1824

Lebensansichten des Katers Murr, 1820–22

Kent, Leonard J. and Elizabeth C. Knight, *The Life and Opinions of Kater Murr* in *Selected Writings of E.T.A. Hoffmann*, vol. 2, translated by Kent and Knight, Chicago: University of Chicago Press, 1969

Selections of Short Stories

Hollingdale, R.J., with Stella and Vernon Humphries and Sally Hayward, *Tales of Hoffmann*, Harmondsworth and New York: Penguin 1982 (contains "Mademoiselle de Scudéry", "The Sandman", "The Artushof", "Councillor Krespel", "The Entail", "Doge and Dogaressa", "The Mines at Falun", "The Choosing of the Bride")

Kent, Leonard J. and Elizabeth C. Knight, *Selected Writings of E.T.A. Hoffmann*, vol. 1, Chicago: University of Chicago Press, 1969 (contains "Ritter Gluck", "The Golden Pot", "The Sandman", "Councillor Krespel", "The Mines of Falun", "Mademoiselle de Scudéri", "The Doubles")

Robertson, Ritchie, *The Golden Pot, and Other Tales*, Oxford and New York: Oxford University Press, 1992 (contains "The Golden Pot", "The Sandman", "Princess Brambilla", "Master Flea", "My Cousin's Corner Window")

Scott, Sir Walter, "On the Supernatural in Fictitious Composition, and in Particular in the Works of E.T.A. Hoffmann", *Foreign Quarterly Review*, 1/1 (July 1827) pp. 60–98 (includes long excerpts and synopses of the plots of "The Entail" ["Das Majorat"] and "The Sandman" ["Der Sandmann"])

Short Stories

"Der goldene Topf" in *Fantasiestücke in Callots Manier*, 1814–15

Carlyle, Thomas, "The Golden Pot", with an introduction, in his *German Romance: Specimens of Its Chief Authors*, with an introduction, Edinburgh: Tait, 1827; reprinted in *Novellas of Ludwig Tieck and E.T.A. Hoffmann*, introduction by Eitel Timm, Columbia, South Carolina: Kamden House, 1991

"Ritter Gluck" in *Fantasiestücke in Callots Manier*, 1814–15

Anonymous, "Gluck", *American Monthly Magazine* (1830)

"Das Majorat" in *Nachtstücke*, vol. 2, 1817

Gillies, Robert Pierce, "Rolandsitten" in *German Stories*, translated by Gillies, vol. 2, Edinburgh: Blackwood, 1826

Die Serapions-Brüder, 4 vols, 1819–21

Ewing, Alexander, *The Serapion Brethren*, 2 vols, London: Bell, 1886–92

"Die Nussknacker und Mausekönig" in *Die Serapions-Brüder*, 4 vols, 1819–21

Bell, Anthea, *The Nutcracker and the Mouse-King*, illustrations by Lisbeth Zwerger, London and Boston: Picture Book Studios, 1983

"Das Fräulein von Scuderi" in *Die Serapions-Brüder*, 4 vols, 1819–21

Gillies, Robert Pierce, "Mademoiselle de Scuderi" in *German Stories*, translated by Gillies, vol. 1, Edinburgh: Blackwood, 1826, pp. 3–168

Holcraft, Richard, "Madame [sic] de Scuderi" in *Tales of Humour and Romance*, translated by Holcraft, New York: Seymour, and London: Longman Rees Orme Brown and Green, 1829

Other Writing

Clarke, Martin, *E.T.A. Hoffmann's Musical Writings: Kreisleriana, The Poet and the Composer, Musical Criticism*, edited by David Charlton, Cambridge and New York: Cambridge University Press, 1989

Letters

Sahlin, Johanna C., *Selected Letters of E.T.A. Hoffmann*, with an introduction by Leonard J. Kent and Sahlin, Chicago: University of Chicago Press, 1977 (concentrates on letters about Hoffmann's various artistic careers, based on the edition of his letters by Friedrich Schnapp, 1970)

In 1824 the Scotsman R.P. GILLIES introduced E.T.A. Hoffmann's work to English readers with *The Devil's Elixir* (a translation of the novel *Die Elixiere des Teufels*, 1815–16). This portrayed the German Romantic as a writer in the tradition of the English Gothic novel. There followed in 1826 Gillies's translations "Mademoiselle de Scuderi" and "Rolandsitten" published in his collection *German Stories*, which was received with enthusiasm, particularly for its brilliant translation. Gillies's stories exemplify the 19th-century notion of the translator as interpreter and textual editor. Despite the changes and editorial additions, they provide a quite accurate transcript of the original text, written in idiomatic English: "One may read Mr. Gillies's three volumes ... without ever suspecting from the style that the whole was not originally conceived and executed in English" (*Blackwood's Magazine*, December 1826, p. 857) or, as a contributor wrote in *Blackwood's Magazine* in 1827: "... he has contrived to prune off all the indelicacy of his German original, without doing the smallest injury to the author's genius".

Gillies's colourful translations show deep understanding, of, for example, the comical situation in the "Irish Anecdote" in *The Devil's Elixir*. Gillies translates the German word for Irishman with "disciple of St Patrick", calls the Scotsman "Scotch Highlander" and the Englishman "English wag". On the other hand, the translator omits references to religious topics and adds descriptions that create a more Gothic style than is to be found in the original German texts, especially as regards *The Devil's Elixir* and "Rolandsitten". He aims to increase the chilling effect of the story, for instance embellishing the text with evocations of Gothic horror whenever the mad monk Medardus is mentioned. Gillies also adds descriptions of typical German habits and domestic circumstances that might be unfamiliar to the average English reader. The most important additions are to be found in the presentation of the protagonist Medardus's frame of mind and motivation. Here, Gillies provides a clearer insight into the character's behaviour than does Hoffmann, but he also changes some of the original meaning.

Gillies's contemporary Thomas CARLYLE translated Hoffmann's tale "The Golden Pot" and included a biographical introduction to its author. His version was published in 1827 as part of his collection of German contemporary writers, *German Romance*. In contrast to Gillies, Carlyle tried to stay as close to the original as possible. He aimed at truthfulness, even at the expense of literary quality or morality. His foremost aim was literary fidelity: " ... to convey the Author's sentiments, as he himself expressed them, to follow the original, in all the variations of his style ... In many points, both literary and moral, I could have wished devoutly that he had not written as he had done; but to alter anything was not in my commission" (quoted in Carr's article "Carlyle's Translations from German"). "The Golden Pot" is almost a literal translation, often preserving even the structure of the German sentences with the verb at the end of a clause. In some cases Carlyle tries to catch and preserve the sound and mood of Hoffmann's text, for instance by translating "das Gelispel und Geflüster und Geklingel" as "the whispering and lisping and tinkling". Rather than translating German compounds into English phrases, when no accepted English compound was available, he imitates the German style, thus creating strange and often artificial sounding words. In other instances the literal translation leaves the English sounding slightly strange and clumsy.

Only very rarely does Carlyle change the original: by omitting short sentences without vital meaning to the text; by adding an explanation; or by slightly changing the phrasing to make them more acceptable for the Victorian readership as when "wurde heisser die Sehnsucht, glühender das Verlangen" is toned down to the luke-warm "his longings grew keener, his desires more warm" and "es helfen Beutigel, die man ... dem Hintern appliziert" becomes less offensive to his more prudish English readership as "leeches are good for it, if applied to the right part".

In all, Carlyle provides a very precise and accurate translation of Hoffmann's "Der goldene Topf", one that catches the atmosphere of the original and its mixture of the mystical and the comical. At the same time the style and language of the translation leave no doubt that this is a story taken from a different country and culture, translated into English and still containing a faint impression of foreignness and otherness.

Throughout the 19th century Carlyle's "The Golden Pot" was to be republished in England and America in various collections of tales of German writers. It was reprinted in 1991 in a collection of novellas by Hoffmann and Ludwig Tieck.

Carlyle's strongly moralizing introduction to his translation "The Golden Pot", together with Sir Walter Scott's portrayal of Hoffmann as the drunken libertine and writer of "Gothic Horrors" in his article in the *Foreign Quarterly*, "On the Supernatural in Fictitious Composition" (1827), resulted in the British developing a liking for Hoffmann's Gothic stories. At the same time the American readership was drawn to the writer's historical and musical tales. The earliest of these American translations were "The Lost Reflection" ("Die Geschichte vom verlornen Spiegelbilde"), a comical tale, translated anonymously and published in 1826 in the Boston *Athenaeum*, Richard HOLCRAFT's translation of "Das Fräulein von Scuderi", published in *Tales of Humour and Romance* in 1829, and "Gluck" ("Ritter Gluck") in the *American Monthly Magazine* in 1830.

There were but a handful of attempts at Hoffmann's *Serapions-Brüder* (*The Serapion Brethren*, translated by Alexander EWING (1886–92) and at the *Fantasie- und Nachtstücke*. Of Hoffmann's later works and major novels, only the fantastic satirical novels and tales, such as *Kater Murr* (*Kater Murr*), *Prinzessin Brambilla* (*Princess Brambilla*), *Klein Zaches gennant Zinnober* (*Kleinzack*) and *Meister Floh* (*Master Flea*), were translated into English. His musical writings, which include musical criticism and short stories about composers and musicians, are for the most part untranslated, although CLARKE (1989) offers a good selection.

Die Elixiere des Teufels had been translated four times in England, but only once in America. On the other hand, "Meister Martin"("Master Martin the Cooper"), "Rat Krespel" ("Councillor Krespel"), "Die Fermate" ("The Fermata"), "Der goldene Topf" ("The Golden Pot"), "Datura Fastuosa" ("Datura Fastuosa"), "Signor Formica" ("Signor Formica"), and "Das öde Haus" ("The Mystery of the Deserted House") became much more popular in America.

Hoffmann's most popular works in the English-speaking world are the novellas "Der goldene Topf" ("The Golden Pot"), "Die Bergwerke zu Falun" ("The Mines of Falun"), "Das Majorat" ("The Entail") and, in particular, the triad "Das Fräulein von Scuderi" ("Mademoiselle de Scudéry"), "Der Sandmann" ("The Sandman"), and the famous children's story "Die Nussknacker und Mausekönig" ("The Nutcracker"). Over the last couple of decades English readers seem to have rediscovered a taste for Hoffmann: there has been an upsurge in translations of his works, and of one work in particular: the fairytale *The Nutcracker*. In the last 10 years alone this popular story has appeared in more than 10 versions by various translators.

PETRA MARIA ANNA BAUER

Further Reading

Ashton, Rosemary D., *The Reception of German Literature in England from the Founding of the "Blackwood Magazine" (1817) to the Time of Carlyle and His Disciples*, dissertation, Cambridge University, 1974

Bauer, Petra, "The Reception of E.T.A. Hoffmann in 19th-Century Britain" (dissertation), Keele University, Staffordshire, 1999

Carr, C.T., "Carlyle's Translations from German", *Modern Language Review*, 42 (1946), pp. 223–32

Gudde, E.G., "E.T.A. Hoffmann's Reception in England", *PMLA* (1926) pp. 1005–10

Segebrecht, Wulf, "E.T.A. Hoffmann and English Literature" in *Deutsche Romantik und English Romanticism*, edited by Theodore Gish and Sandra G. Frieden, Munich: Fink, 1984, pp. 52–66

Zylstra, Henry, "E.T.A. Hoffmann in England and America" (dissertation), Cambridge, Massachusetts: Harvard University, 1940 (contains a detailed analysis of Hoffmann's translation and reception in England and America until 1932)

Hugo von Hofmannsthal 1874–1929

Austrian dramatist, poet and essayist

Biography

Born in Vienna on 1 February 1874, into a family of bankers. He went to school in Vienna; from 1892 he studied law at Vienna University, then Romance languages, specializing in French literature. He had written poetry while still at school and had won early public success with lyrical dramas such as *Death and the Fool* (1900, translated 1914), but in the early 1900s (see the *Chandos Letter*, 1905) he moved away from lyricism to a more stageable dramatic style, making use of modern theatre techniques in plays that explore modern human problems via ancient myths (*Elektra*, produced as a play 1903, as an opera 1909). *Jedermann* (1911) is a re-working of the medieval *Everyman* morality play. Other pieces were based on plays by Molière and Calderón.

Hofmannsthal had become a full-time writer in 1901. From 1909 he collaborated with Richard Strauss, creating libretti, notably for the operas *Der Rosenkavalier*, *Ariadne auf Naxos*, *Die Frau ohne Schatten* and *Arabella*. In 1919, with Strauss and Max Reinhardt, he helped to found the annual Salzburg Festival of Music. He died at Rodaun, Vienna, 15 July 1929.

Translations

Selections

Hottinger, Mary, Tania Stern, James Stern and Michael Hamburger (editors), *Hugo von Hofmannsthal: Selected Writings*, 3 vols, London: Routledge and Kegan Paul, and New York: Pantheon, 1952–64 (vol. 1: *Prose*, edited by Hottinger, T. Stern and J. Stern; vol. 2: *Poems and Verse Plays*, edited by Hamburger; vol. 3: *Selected Plays and Libretti*, edited by Hamburger)

Selections of Plays and Libretti

Hamburger, Michael, *Hugo von Hofmannsthal: Poems and Verse Plays* (bilingual edition), introduction by T.S. Eliot, London: Routledge and Kegan Paul, and New York: Pantheon, 1961

Hamburger, Michael (editor), *Hugo von Hofmannsthal: Selected Writings*, vol. 3: *Selected Plays and Libretti*, New York: Pantheon, 1963; London: Routledge and Kegan Paul, 1964 (contains *Electra*, *The Salzburg Great Theatre of the World*, *The Tower*; *The Cavalier of the Rose*; *Arabella*, *The Difficult Man*)

Schwarz, Alfred, *Hugo von Hofmannsthal: Three Plays*, translated by Schwarz, with an introduction, Detroit: Wayne State University, 1966 (contains *Death and the Fool*, *Electra*, *The Tower*)

Plays and Libretti

Der Tor und der Tod, 1900, produced 1898 (written 1893)

Hamburger, Michael, *Death and the Fool* in *Hugo von Hofmannsthal: Selected Writings*, vol. 2, edited by Hamburger, 1961

Mierow, Herbert, *The Fool and Death: A Metrical Translation*, Colorado Springs: Harvey W. Hewett-Thayer, 1930

Schwarz, Alfred, *Death and the Fool* in *Hugo von*

Hofmannsthal: Three Plays, translated by Schwarz, 1966
Walter, Elisabeth, *Death and the Fool*, Boston: Badger, 1914

Elektra, 1904, produced 1903; revised, with music by Richard Strauss, 1908, produced 1909
Schwarz, Alfred, *Electra* in *Hugo von Hofmannsthal: Selected Writings*, vol. 3, edited by Michael Hamburger, 1963, also in *Hugo von Hofmannsthal: Three Plays*, translated by Schwarz, 1966
Symons, Arthur, *Electra*, New York: Brentano, 1908

Der Rosenkavalier, 1911
Holme, Christopher, *The Cavalier of the Rose* in *Hugo von Hofmannsthal: Selected Writings*, vol. 3, edited by Michael Hamburger, 1963
Kalisch, Alfred, *The Rose-Bearer* (parallel texts), New York: Boosey and Hawkes, 1912; London: Calder, 1981

Jedermann: Das Spiel vom Sterben des reichen Mannes, 1911
Sterling, George, *The Play of Everyman*, San Francisco: Robertson, 1917
Tafler, M.E., *The Salzburg Everyman: The Play of the Rich Man's Death as Acted before the Cathedral at Salzburg*, Salzburg: Mora, 1911, 1929

Ariadne auf Naxos, 1912; revised 1916
Kalisch, Alfred, *Ariadne on Naxos*, New York: Boosey and Hawkes, 1912; new version, 1943

Die Frau ohne Schatten, 1916, produced 1919
Hollander, Jean, *The Woman without a Shadow*, Lewiston, New York: Mellen Press, 1993

Der Turm, 1925, revised 1927, produced 1928
Schwarz, Alfred, *The Tower* in *Hugo von Hofmannsthal: Three Plays*, translated by Schwarz, 1966

Arabella, 1933
Gutman, John, *Arabella*, New York: Boosey and Hawkes, 1955
Wydenbruch, Nora and Christopher Middleton, in *Hugo von Hofmannsthal: Selected Writings*, vol. 3, edited by Michael Hamburger, 1963

Poetry
Hamburger, Michael, *Hugo von Hofmannsthal: Selected Writings*, vol. 2: *Poems and Verse Plays*, London: Routledge and Kegan Paul, 1961
Stork, Charles Wharton, *The Lyrical Poems of Hugo von Hofmannsthal*, New Haven, Connecticut: Yale University Press, 1918

Other Writing
Brief des Lord Chandos an Francis Bacon, 1905
Hofmann, Michael, *The Lord Chandos Letter*, London: Syrens, 1995
Stockman, Russell, *The Lord Chandos Letter* (bilingual edition), Marlboro: Marlboro Press, 1986
Hammelmann, Hans and Ewald Osers, *The Correspondence between Richard Strauss and Hugo von Hofmannsthal*, Cambridge and New York: Cambridge University Press, 1961

Hugo von Hofmannsthal has been unjustly neglected outside Germany and his native Austria. He began his literary career early, at the age of 16, producing some of the finest lyric poems in German literature, but by his mid-twenties he had virtually renounced verse in favour of the more socially involved drama. His lyric verse is of an aesthetic style, opaque and almost mystical. The quality of the verse relies heavily on the sound of German.

Charles Wharton STORK's *The Lyrical Poems of Hugo von Hofmannsthal* (1918) was the earliest translation of a considerable body of Hofmannsthal's poems. It is largely an attempt at a literal rendering. The light and suggestive tone of Hofmannsthal's poems is difficult to translate. Stork's touch is too heavy and too rhetorical. These versions have dated, but they are not helped by Stork's unfortunate use of "thee", "thou", "thy" and "o'er". Stork's language is not contemporary and would probably have sounded a little dated even at the time of composition; it sounds more mid-Victorian than early Modernist. "In Memory of the Actor Mitterwurzer" is Stork's best attempt, but then the original is in a rhetorical as opposed to a lyrical style. Stork should be given credit for his attempts but he is simply too artificial and his use of archaic phrases produces such incongruous lines as "Yet he sayeth much who 'Evening' saith."

Michael HAMBURGER (1961) is by far the best translator of Hofmannsthal's verse. In recent years he has done the most to revive interest in the works of Hofmannsthal. Hamburger never attempts a literal translation but re-creates the poems in the true spirit of the original without so deviating from the text as to make it unrecognizable. Hamburger himself thought it impossible to translate German lyrical verse into English adequately, until he translated Hofmannsthal's poetry. The subtlety and the sound of his versions are as yet unsurpassed.

Der Tor und der Tod is a lyric playlet written when Hofmannsthal was only 19 years old. The work shows Hofmannsthal's growing disenchantment with Aestheticism, through the character of Claudio, who is visited by Death.

MIEROW's *The Fool and Death* (1930) is a rather turgid attempt. On the whole academic and hollow, it strives to sound grave and profound but destroys the complex subtlety of the verse. There are moments where he grasps some of the quality of the original, but too often he produces a bizarre archaic tone: "With glozing words thou mad'st thyself my friend."

Michael HAMBURGER has produced, as with the poems, the most successful version with his *Death and the Fool* (1961). He retains a similar rhyme scheme and metrical rhythm without distorting the content. Hamburger takes a certain freedom with the wording but only as much as is needed when attempting to re-create the quality of Hofmannsthal's play. The result is astounding. It is hard to envisage a translation better than this.

Alfred SCHWARZ's *Death and the Fool* (1966) is more recent but is still disappointing. The language is innocuous and plain, never rising above a common quality of language. Schwarz's translation is too literal to capture the quality of this play. Although it is consequently easy to read, the power and rhythm of Hofmannsthal's verse are totally absent. Schwarz seems torn between paraphrase and verse and ends by producing neither. The translation is set out as verse but has no rhythmic quality to justify it. This would be a disappointing and discouraging translation to read as an introduction to Hofmannsthal's work.

As a dramatist Hofmannsthal is probably best known for his

play *Everyman,* which since 1920 has been performed every year at the Salzburg Festival. The play is written in simple rhyming couplets in the tradition of the medieval morality play. Hofmannsthal used the English *Everyman* (1509) and the play *A Comedy About the Rich Dying Man, Called Hecastus* (1549) by Hans Sachs as the sources for his version.

George STERLING's *Everyman* (1917) is a re-working of the anonymous *Everyman* and Hofmannsthal's play rather than a translation. In place of the source text's rhyming couplets he uses blank verse as it "lends an articulation, flexibility and suspense not readily accessible to one [Hofmannsthal] who would use the other and monotonous form". Furthermore, Sterling adds characters and scenes to the original in an admitted attempt to maximize "the appeal and coherence of the play". With the insertion of the War and Workman figures this version moves away, as regards content, from Hofmannsthal's attempt to create a simile in the medieval tradition. Not only does Sterling add characters but he alters our perception of the existing ones as well. He seems to attempt to update and correct the original rather than translating it.

M.E. TAFLER's *The Salzburg Everyman: The Play of the Rich Man's Death as Acted Before the Cathedral at Salzburg* (1911, 1929) is written in prose but on the whole is true to the original. He keeps the contemporary language Hofmannsthal employs. Probably the only difference, apart from his use of prose, is that in the original God appears on stage whereas in this version only God's voice is heard. Tafler indicates changes made for performances at Salzburg and is therefore an interesting source for the production history of the play.

On the whole Hofmannsthal's work probably deserves new translations. Apart from Hamburger none of the translators has managed to capture the quality of Hofmannsthal's work, especially not of his verse. This is one of the reasons why Hofmannsthal is known for the libretti he wrote for Richard Strauss's operas rather than for his work as a dramatist and poet. Among the libretti as translated by KALISCH (*The Rosebearer*, 1912, *Ariadne on Naxos*, 1912), HOLME (*The Cavalier of the Rose*, 1963); HOLLANDER (*The Woman without a Shadow*, 1993), GUTMAN (*Arabella*, 1955); WYDENBRUCH & MIDDLETON, *Arabella*, 1963) and other named and unnamed translators, some of the early versions continue in use for English-language performances and recordings of the operas, Kalisch being particularly favoured. In the nature of things less easily memorable, the libretti are perhaps less sharply borne in mind by the anglophone public than their famous musical settings. To ensure a continued English existence of Hofmannsthal's work a re-awakening of interest from translators into English is needed.

KEVIN BARTHOLOMEW and KATJA KREBS

Further Reading

Coghlan, Brian, *Hofmannsthal's Festival Dramas: Jedermann, Das Salzburger grosse Welttheater, Der Turm*, London: Cambridge University Press, 1964
Hamburger, Michael, *Hofmannsthal: Three Essays*, Princeton, New Jersey: Princeton University Press, 1972

Friedrich Hölderlin 1770–1843

German poet

Biography

Born at Lauffen, Württemberg, 20 March 1770. He studied theology at Tübingen and philosophy at Jena. He did not become a minister in the church but preferred to earn his living as a private tutor. After an unhappy relationship with the wife of his employer in Frankfurt (she figures as "Diotima" in his poetry), he left Germany in 1798 to work as a tutor in Switzerland and France, but went back to Germany in 1802. He was already physically ill and from 1806 was insane. He died in Tübingen, 7 June 1843.

Hölderlin was religious but not a believer. His difficult poetry, using with virtuoso skill the hexameter and the ode form, was influenced by Schiller and the neoclassical Klopstock, inspired by ancient Greek culture and marked by noble melancholy with regard to love and human destiny. His translations from classical authors, especially Sophocles and Pindar, and his views on translation, have proved important. The late recognition in Germany of the power and beauty of his own work began in the 20th century with his effect on Rilke and Stefan George.

Editions

Hölderlin never saw a book of his poems through the press. The first collection was published in 1826, though he had no hand in preparing it. The texts used by translators are taken principally from the following editions: (1) *Hölderlins Sämtliche Werke*, begun by Norbert von Hellingrath, completed by Friedrich Seebass and Ludwig von Pigenot, 1913–23; (2) *Sämtliche Werke und Briefe Friedrich Hölderlins*, Leipzig: Insel, 1926, edited by Franz Zinkernagel; (3) *Hölderlin: Sämtliche Werke*, Stuttgart: Kohlhammer, 1943–85, edited by Friedrich Beissner; (4) *Hölderlin: Sämtliche Werke*, Frankfurt am Main: Roter Stern, 1975–, edited by Dietrich E. Sattler. The two modern editions, known respectively as the Stuttgart edition (edited by Beissner) and the Frankfurt edition (edited by Sattler), differ in their conception and presentation of the unpublished material. Beissner assumes Hölderlin was working towards a definitive version and so constitutes a text as the closest approximation to the putative final version and gives variants in the apparatus. Sattler regards the later poems as poems-in-process and projects the phases in composition from the photocopied manuscript, establishing a "Lesetext" (reading text) to provide a base from which to negotiate the temporal and spatial disposition of deletions, amendments and expansions. No translation before 1975 used the Frankfurt edition, and no translator so far has attempted to present Hölderlin's later poetry as poetry-in-process, though all three editions of Michael Hamburger's *Poems and Fragments* have both short odes and their later, expanded forms and also hymns in various stages or versions.

Translations

Selections of Poetry

Constantine, David, *Selected Poems*, Newcastle upon Tyne: Bloodaxe, 1990

Gascoyne, David, *Hölderlin's Madness*, London: Dent, 1938

Hamburger, Michael, *Poems of Hölderlin* (bilingual edition), London: Nicholson and Watson, 1943; 2nd edition, enlarged and radically revised, with metrical versions of the odes and elegies, London: Harvill Press, and New York: Pantheon, 1952

Hamburger, Michael, *Hölderlin: Selected Verse* (bilingual edition), with an introduction and prose translations, Harmondsworth: Penguin, 1961; reprinted with an updated bibliography and occasional amendments to the introduction and the text of some translations, London: Anvil Press, 1986

Hamburger, Michael, *Friedrich Hölderlin: Poems and Fragments* (bilingual edition), London: Routledge and Kegan Paul, and Ann Arbor: University of Michigan Press, 1966; 2nd edition, Cambridge: Cambridge University Press, 1980, reprinted 1986; 3rd edition, enlarged, with a new introduction, London: Anvil Press Poetry, 1994

Henderson, Elizabeth, *Alcaic Poems* (bilingual edition), London: Oswald Wolff, 1962; New York: Ungar, 1963

Leishman, J.B., *Selected Poems of Hölderlin* (bilingual edition), London: Hogarth Press, 1944; 2nd edition, 1954; reprinted Westport, Connecticut: Hyperion Press, 1978

Loving, Pierre, *Short Poems by Friedrich Hölderlin*, Girard, Kansas: Haldeman and Julius, 1925

Middleton, Christopher, *Friedrich Hölderlin, Eduard Mörike: Selected Poems* (parallel texts), Chicago: University of Chicago Press, 1972

Prokosch, Frederic, *Some Poems of Hölderlin* (parallel texts), New York: New Directions, 1943

Riley, John and Tim Longville, *In the Arms of the Gods*, Lincoln: Grosseteste Press, 1967

Riley, John and Tim Longville, *Friedrich Hölderlin: What I Own*, Pensnett, Staffordshire: Grosseteste Review, 1973

Riley, John and Tim Longville, *Hölderlin / Mandelstam*, Manchester: Carcanet, 1998 (contains the translations that appeared in Riley & Longville, 1967 and 1973)

Santner, Eric L. (editor), *Hyperion and Selected Poems*, New York: Continuum, 1990

Sieburth, Richard, *Hymns and Fragments* (bilingual edition), Princeton, New Jersey: Princeton University Press, 1984

Novel

Hyperion, vol. 1, 1797; vol. 2, 1799

Santner, Eric L. (editor), *Hyperion and Selected Poems*, 1990

Trask, Willard A., *Hyperion*, New York: Signet, 1965

Theoretical Writings

Burford, William and Christopher Middleton, *The Poet's Vocation: Selections from the Letters of Hölderlin, Rimbaud and Hart Crane*, Austin: University of Texas, 1967

Pfau, Thomas, *Essays and Letters on Theory*, with an introduction, Albany, New York: State University of New York Press, 1988

The first important collection of Hölderlin's poems in English was GASCOYNE's *Hölderlin's Madness* (1938), which is indebted to French surrealism and Pierre-Jean Jouve's *Poèmes de la folie de Hölderlin* (Paris, 1930). Short poems are preferred, including drafts and fragments and some of the haunting, rhymed pieces from Hölderlin's latter years – presented here with a touch of assonance – and four not so short poems by Gascoyne, who says his versions are not translations, "but a free adaptation, introduced and linked together by entirely original poems". Just the same, most of them stay close to the text, with occasional variations. Simple, clear, sometimes beautifully cadenced, they are presented as visions Hölderlin had in his madness, or on its verge, "a world of extraordinary transparency" in which "everything stands out in light and shade, in height and depth". By comparison the 15 poems in PROKOSCH's little book (1943), which are introduced "apologetically, as humble versions of a poetry which uniquely transcends translatability", seem a random selection, metrically correct, though muffling Hölderlin's boldness, turning "der Gott" at the beginning of "Patmos" into "the Almighty", and elsewhere presenting a "saintly Socrates". LEISHMAN (1944) has a much larger selection and matches syllable for syllable, stress for stress, even when translating free verse. Commendable as this is, given that Hölderlin's sense of the just word first found an adequate form in the tight economy of short odes in Greek metres, the emphasis is tilted first one way and then another. Thus, "cloyed at last with sweetest play" ("The Fates") is offered for "vom süssen / Spiele gesättiget", with "cloyed" for "gesättiget" (satisfied, sated), "sweetest" for "süss" (sweet) and "at last" for the sake of the two syllables. HENDERSON (1962) tries her hand at alcaics and captures something of Hölderlin's everyday sublime. There are some fine renderings in this little volume, e.g. "Each Day I Take ... ", but as with other translators, metric fidelity may induce somewhat convoluted syntax and a decorously elevated tone.

The translations offered by RILEY & LONGVILLE (1967, 1973, 1998) – which include the so-called *Thalia Fragment*, a draft fragment of *Hyperion* – cover the range of Hölderin's mature poetry, from odes to elegies to hymns in free verse. These forms are mirrored by way of analogy, rather than with metrical rigour, while the few late poems are transformed into something altogether tauter, more cryptic, and rhymeless, eschewing the complaisance of Hölderlin's feminine rhymes. At their best the versions sound pleasingly natural and idiomatic, though not in the least lax, and if sometimes the plain talk chafes against the exaltedness of vision, this tension appears to be willingly and wittingly accepted, in line with forgoing the exaltation of regularly recurring metre. MIDDLETON (1972) also takes a freer hand with metre, is good at the sublime and with intimate, enrapt epiphanies, and likes an occasional lurch in register, as in "The Farewell", where measured gravity: "But meaning a different fault the world's intent / Practices a different task, hard, different laws" suddenly turns colloquial: "Custom and habit snaffle / Day by day the soul from us". In keeping with this freer approach, the lines in some of the late hymns and fragments are broken down into further spatial and rhythmic units. It is possible to hear distant echoes of Gascoyne's *Hölderlin* in SIEBURTH's selection (1984), which offers versions, based where possible on the reading texts in the Frankfurt edition, of almost all the poems and fragments in free rhythms that were written between 1801 and 1806. Unlike alcaics and asclepiads, these poems immediately sound modern, as though Hölderlin had read Pound. The diction of these versions is lean, close to contemporary speech, and risks flatness, though often enough it echoes Hölderlin's "intricate aural profiles" (Sieburth):

> The clear tempered clouds
> Carry like the blackbird's call, well-
> tuned by the thunder, by God being there.

CONSTANTINE (1990) aims at "equivalence of effect", and this notion might have been extended from metre to tone, which in his versions is more everyday, less ode-like or hymnic – though Hölderlin can be astonishingly informal – and while this often works well:

> once I'll have
> lived like the gods and more I'm not asking
> ("The Fates")

at other points the effect is a touch prosaic:

> Their spirits, kept
> From spoiling in the bud
> Blossom for ever;
> They have a still
> Eternal clarity of gaze.
> ("Hyperion's Song")

Instead of "kept from spoiling in the bud" which sounds too specific – roses, for example, rot (spoil) in the bud – precious, ecstatic-instatic heights are attained in LEISHMAN's phrase (1944), "Chastely sheathed / In retiringest petals" for "Keusch bewahrt / In bescheidener Knospe", whereas it is characteristic of HAMBURGER's approach in his first Hölderlin book (1943) that he translates each word with a lexical equivalent: "Chastely preserved, / In modest bud", and this is still the wording in his 1994 edition. Hamburger set out to avoid any "intrusion of the translator's idiosyncracies into the author's work" and to translate, as he later puts it, "as much as possible of the original's quiddity". Accordingly, the revised edition (1952) of his 1943 selection matches Hölderlin's Greek strophes throughout, often meeting the constraints with the idioms of ordinary speech. For instance "so", in "So we wanted to part? Thought it both good and wise?" ("The Farewell"), arose when the line was adjusted to the metre, and it sounds just right, a natural inflection and a potentially ominous opening. Similarly, the next line, metrically correct, but stiff, in 1952: "Why like murderers awed, did we regret the deed", is later modified to "Why, then, why did the act shock us as murder would", which is closer to the letter and "Why, then, why" provides the required trochee and a breath of spontaneous speech. *Poems and Fragments* (Hamburger, 1966) for the first time offers metrical versions of the two substantive fragments of Hölderlin's unfinished play *Der Tod des Empedokles* (The Death of Empedocles). The third edition (1994) adds a number of poems not included in earlier editions, and the introduction has been re-written, largely in the light of the Frankfurt edition, which also provides the text for some of the late poems. Altogether, Hamburger's work on Hölderlin spans 50 years and documents, a steady process of revising and enlarging, no doubt sustained by Hamburger's faith in the power of translation to mediate something vital and essential contained in the original, its quiddity. These translations, easily the most comprehensive collection of Hölderlin's poetry in English, work quietly and work well. They have been recognized by many as an outstanding achievement, not least by others who have translated Hölderlin's poetry.

Besides *Hyperion* (see below) SANTNER's volume (1990) includes a selection of poems focused on the later work, with English versions taken from SIEBURTH, MIDDLETON and HAMBURGER. Santner's selection is aimed at "reading Hölderlin in the age of difference". He correlates the three translators with poetic values inherent in the original, suggesting that Sieburth tends "to draw out more of the sobriety and Junonian restraint", whereas Middleton has "profiled more the ideal and heroic tonalities", with Hamburger tending "to take more a middle ground ... producing what might be considered 'mimetic' renderings".

TRASK's version (1965) of *Hyperion* reads well, and the sense is rarely missed. If it is true that Hölderlin's epistolary novel has to be "ecstatic Romantic fiction" or it is nothing (Trask), this version has to be rated as very good, even outstanding. Nevertheless, there is a freshness and spontaneity in the original that eludes the translation, crisp as it often is. *Hyperion* is written in language not far removed from Hölderlin's own letters or those of his friends; "möchte" was and is perfectly everyday, there is nothing of "would fain" about it, just as "du" and "ihr", unlike "thou" and "ye", belong to common speech. *Hyperion* in this version is self-consciously historical and decidedly more high-flown than its German model.

This is the version used by Santner in *Hyperion and Selected Poems*, except that it has been adapted by David Schwarz along lines that correspond to Santner's difference-mediating aims. Even so, there are still occasional sentences like the following with its "but"s and "but not"s:

> "For were they but modest, these people, did they but not make themselves a law unto the better among them! did they but revile not what they are not, yet even that could be condoned in them, did they but not mock the divine!"

It is a pity that this was not revised, particularly as the adaptation aimed to preserve "the jarring strangeness of Hölderlin's diction so that it strikes the American reader precisely as strange rather than merely foreign or archaic" (Santner).

PFAU's collection (1988) contains virtually all of Hölderlin's writings on aesthetics and literary theory, including a selection of letters, and is a valuable addition to the corpus of Hölderlin's work available in English in book form (previous translations published in periodicals are listed in Pfau's bibliography). This is a faithful and attentive translation, as close as possible to the sense, the emphases and the syntactical complexities of the original texts. The volume is well annotated and is preceded by a much needed and incisive introduction.

RAYMOND HARGREAVES

Further Reading

Constantine, David, *Hölderlin*, Oxford: Clarendon Press, and New York: Oxford University Press, 1988

Fehervary, Helen, *Hölderlin and the Left: The Search for a Dialectic of Art and Life*, Heidelberg: Winter, 1977

Hammer, John Charles, "Hölderlin in England" (dissertation), Hamburg, 1966

Harrison, R.B., *Hölderlin and Greek Literature*, Oxford: Clarendon Press, 1975

Louth, Charlie, *Hölderlin and the Dynamics of Translation*, Oxford: Oxbow, 1998

Santner, Eric L., *Friedrich Hölderlin: Narrative Vigilance and the Poetic Imagination*, New Brunswick, New Jersey: Rutgers University Press, 1986

Unger, Richard, *Hölderlin's Major Poetry: The Dialectics of Unity*, Bloomington: Indiana University Press, 1975

See also the translators' introductions, notes and comments on translation in Hamburger, Middleton, Pfau, Santner and Sieburth

---

Miroslav Holub 1923–1998

Czech poet and scientist

Biography

Born in Plzeň, western Bohemia, 23 September 1923. He attended the Classical Gymnasium there, receiving a good schooling in Latin and Greek, later adding German and French. From 1942 Holub worked as a labourer at Plzeň railway station. After the end of the war Holub studied medicine at Charles University in Prague, completing his studies in 1953. Between 1954 and 1971 Holub worked at the Microbiology Institute of the Academy of Sciences, specializing in immunology. During this time he was also editor (1951–64) of the popular science journal *Vesmír* [Universe] and in 1955 was one of the founders of the journal *Květen* [May] and a literary discussion circle linked to it (Milan Kundera was also an early member of the group). *Květen* was associated with the "Poetry of the Everyday" movement, which reacted against Stalinist pathos in poetry, and Holub's early poetry was very much in this vein. In April 1956, during the Second Congress of the Writers' Union, Holub was one of several eminent writers (including Jaroslav Seifert and František Hrubín) who denounced Party constraints on literature. In 1958 Holub published his first book of poetry *Denní služba* [Day Service]; he received his doctorate the same year. He continued to publish regularly – poems, essays, *reportage* and feuilletons – throughout the 1960s. In 1967 Holub was one of the two non-communist members of the Central Committee of the Writers' Union, also being "discovered" that year by the English poetry reader after the publication of *Selected Poems* by Penguin. Holub's first work after a long period (1971–82) during which he was not permitted to publish in Czechoslovakia was *Naopak* (*On the Contrary*). During this time his books often came out in translation only – Czech editions were published some years later. After 1982 he continued to write essays and poetry, much of which has been translated into English. Holub is currently recognized both as a leading authority in the field of immunology and as the most successful modern Czech poet in English translation. He died in Prague, 14 July 1998.

Translations

Numerous translations of Holub's poetry have appeared in a wide range of journals in England and America, including: *London Magazine*, *Partisan Review*, *Prairie Schooner*, *Times Literary Supplement*, *The Field*, *American Poetry Review* and many others. Most of these translations have subsequently appeared in book form and are not included in the following bibliography. Apart from Holub's usual translators (listed below), Stuart Freibert, O. Reynolds, L. Tucker and M. Kraus have contributed translations to some of these journals. Holub himself was often actively involved in the work of his translators.

Selections of Poetry

Milner, Ian and George Theiner, *Selected Poems*, with an introduction by A. Alvarez, Harmondsworth and Baltimore: Penguin, 1967

Milner, Ian, Jarmila Milner, Ewald Osers and George Theiner, *Poems Before and After: Collected English Translations*, Newcastle upon Tyne: Bloodaxe Books, 1990

Poetry

Ačkoli, 1969

Milner, Ian and Jarmila Milner, *Although*, London: Jonathan Cape, 1971

Naopak, 1971–82
Milner, Jarmila and Ian Milner, *Notes of a Clay Pigeon*, London: Secker and Warburg, 1977
Osers, Ewald, *On the Contrary and Other Poems*, foreword by A. Alvarez, Newcastle upon Tyne: Bloodaxe Books, 1984

Sagitální řez, 1988
Friebert, Stuart and Dana Hábová, *Sagittal Section: Poems, New and Selected*, Oberlin, Ohio: Oberlin College Press, 1980

Interferon, čili o divadle, 1986
Hábová, Dana and David Young, *Interferon; or, On Theater*, Oberlin, Ohio: Oberlin College Press, 1982
Osers, Ewald, George Theiner, Ian Milner and Jarmila Milner, *The Fly*, Newcastle upon Tyne: Bloodaxe Books, 1987

Syndrom mizející plíce, 1990
Young, David and Dana Hábová, *Vanishing Lung Syndrome*, Oberlin, Ohio: Oberlin College Press, and London: Faber, 1990

Ono se letělo, 1994
Osers, Ewald, *Supposed to Fly: A Sequence from Pilsen, Czechoslovakia*, Newcastle upon Tyne: Bloodaxe Books, 1996

Prose
K principu rolničky 1987
Naughton, James, *The Jingle Bell Principle*, Newcastle upon Tyne: Bloodaxe Books, 1992

O příčinách porušení a zkázy těl lidských, 1992
Young, David (editor), *The Dimension of the Present Moment: Essays*, various translators, London and Boston: Faber, 1990

Science Writing
Anonymous, *Immunology of Nude Mice*, Boca Raton, Florida: CRC Press, 1989

Miroslav Holub's twin professions of scientist and poet come together in his poetry. It is trite just to say that he brings a scientific method to poetry; rather Holub believed the two strive for the same goal, even if by different means: "There is no deep difference between the scientific mind and the artistic mind: both include the maximal creativity with the maximal freedom. Science is both theoretic and experimental. Art is only experimental" (quoted in *Selected Poems*, p. 10).

Holub's approach to poetry is empirical and analytical. His early poems are stripped down, almost skeletal, without a single spare word. They are written in free verse form which is often held together by a tightly controlled rhyme. It is noted elsewhere in the present work (Czech entry) that the high degree of inflexion in Czech allows for greater rhyme resources than in English, and Holub employs these resources to the full.

Another vital element of Holub's poetry is the ironic and mordant wit that underscores so many of his poems. In general this is not difficult to translate from a linguistic point of view, but a successful rendition depends on the translator sensing the irony in the first place, and this does not always happen. The poems from the 1950s and 1960s tend to be more subtle in their irony, concealing it cleverly behind apparently simple poetic structures. The poems from the 1970s are bitterer and more openly caustic, which is quite understandable since Holub could not be published at this time.

Holub's professed aim is for people "... to read poems as naturally as they read the papers, or go to a football game. Not to consider it as anything more difficult, or effeminate, or praiseworthy" (*Selected Poems*, p. 15), and while it is true that he is by far the most popular Czech poet among the English poetry-reading audience, it is not quite clear that this is the audience he originally had in mind. Holub is sometimes called an "unliterary" poet – and he does avoid so-called "poetic language" and the over-use of metaphor – but his use of the sound resources of Czech, of assonance and related consonant groups, is quite definitely "literary". It is also a quality that is rather understressed in translation because of Holub's unliterary (we might add: scientific) reputation. Nevertheless, in Czech terms Holub is, in a sense, anti-poetic establishment. Whether he has the same status in English poetry circles is open to question.

For the poems composed 1956–70, it is the important collection *Selected Poems* (1967) that first brought Holub to the attention of the English audience, with 26 poems translated by George THEINER, 25 by Ian MILNER and one collaborative effort. Whatever the technical faults of the collection it clearly struck a chord with its readership and must take some of the credit for Holub's later success in English.

In general these are some of Holub's tersest and most concentrated poems; Czech inflexion allows Holub this degree of concentration. In "Realita" ("Reality"), for example, the Czech poem contains 47 words and the English translation 71. Holub's lines: "[před] / faktem stolu, / faktem okna, / faktem prostoru, / faktem oceli / sedmiřezené" have been rendered by Ian MILNER with articles and prepositions that could have been avoided: "[before] / the fact of the operating-table / the fact of the window / the fact of space / the fact of steel / with seven blades". The same problem afflicts George THEINER in his translation of "Moucha" ("The Fly"): "řev, / supění, / sténání, / dupoty a pády" becomes: "the shouts, / the gasps, / the groans, / the tramping and the tumbling". Theiner has put articles in and changed the verbal nouns of the Czech into simple nouns. The Czech is also acoustically much richer and subtler than the English. Similar possibilities for assonance and semi-rhyme that inflexion provides can also be seen (or rather heard) in the opening of the poem *Patologie* (*Pathology*), which is based around the masculine genitive plural ending *-ů* and locative plural ending *-ích* / *-ých*; inevitably this is lost in translation.

Many of Milner and Theiner's translations are reprinted in the anthology *Poems Before & After: Collected English Translations* (1990), and Ewald OSERS supplements their work with another 30 or so poems, including a particularly ingenious version of the early poem "O Popelce" ("Cinderella"). Osers obviously does not try to reproduce exactly the basic dactylic metre of the original, nor Holub's clever verbal punning, but he does succeed in giving the poem a clearly defined rhythm while still preserving a pattern of semi-rhymes and rhymes that is not dissimilar to the Czech. He does, however, seem to add a line towards the end of the poem. Similarly in "Poledne" ("Midday") an extra line (" ...that day") seems to have crept in, but otherwise Osers captures the deceptive calm of the poem rather well, and the twist at the end is delivered with just the right amount of irony.

For the poetry written 1971–82, Jarmila and Ian MILNER's version (*Notes of a Clay Pigeon*, 1977) of Holub's *Naopak* contains several inexplicable moments of mistranslation and occasionally misjudges the tone of these most ironical of Holub's poems (although allowance should be made for possible authorial or editorial changes between 1977, when the Milners' translation appeared, and the first Czech edition in 1982). The mistranslations range from slightly pedantic details (such as translating "Stručná úvaha ..." as "Brief Thoughts ..." rather than the more correct and poetically more pleasing "Brief reflection..." used by Osers – see below) to more serious mistakes of sense, as in the poem "Samota Mínótaurova" ("Loneliness of the Minotaur"). Stylistic clumsiness sometimes mars the poems, for example translating "skrze niž se ubírá kamsi historie" as "due to which history is on its way somewhere or other" – surely too ungainly a sentence for Holub's linguistic precision.

In *Poems Before and After*, Ewald OSERS (1987) has retranslated some of the poems from *Naopak*, rather improving on the Milners' earlier work. Osers is more faithful to the word order of the original, insofar as it is possible for English to follow the very free word order of Czech, and he seems more sensitive to the bitter irony of the Czech. Osers's text is also not free of slips, such as turning "vřískající kočky" into "mewing cats", rather than the Milners' "screeching cats" in the poem "Stručná úvaha o kočkách rostoucích na stromech" ("Brief Reflection on Cats Growing in Trees"), but these are not too intrusive.

In his poetry written from 1990, Holub left behind the short free verse forms and the precise irony of his earlier poetry for an often less concise, sometimes self-indulgent free verse form. The assonance ("Někteří, naklíčeni se ve sklenících ...") and related consonant clusters ("tvrdohlavé svrbění smrti ...") familiar from all of Holub's work are still clearly evident, but as ever these are not reproducible in English. David YOUNG and Dana HÁBOVÁ (*Vanishing Lung Syndrome*, 1990) translate literally enough to make the sense and intent of the poems available to the committed poetry lover. Occasionally a phrase or line is left out, but presumably this must have been with the knowledge of the poet as he worked closely with Young and Hábová.

JAMES PARTRIDGE

Further Reading

Alvarez, A., *Under Pressure. The Writer in Society: Eastern Europe and the U.S.A.*, Harmondsworth and Baltimore: Penguin, 1965

Crawford, Robert, "Independent Europe: Czecho-slovakia: The Transnationality of the Czech Immunologist", *Poetry Review*, 80/2, pp. 8–10

Eagle, Herbert, "Syntagmatic Structure in the Free Verse of Miroslav Holub", *Rackham Literary Studies*, 3 (1972) pp. 29–49

Heaney, Seamus, "The Fully Exposed Poem", *Parnassus: Poetry in Review*, 11/1 (Spring–Summer 1983) pp. 1–16

Milner, Ian, "Microscope and Magic: Miroslav Holub and his Poetry", *London Magazine*, 27/12 (1988) pp. 78–82

Osers, Ewald, "Ono se letělo", *Poetry Review*, 85/2 (1995) pp. 26–27

Homer 8th century BC

Greek epic poet

Biography

Nothing is known for certain about the identity or life of Homer, the problematic figure, supposedly blind, to whom is traditionally attributed the oral composition, long after the time of the events described in them, of the two verse epics, the *Iliad*, which tells of the Trojan Wars, and the *Odyssey*, the story of the travels of the Greek hero Odysseus (Ulysses), returning home after those wars to Ithaca. Some features of the language of the epics in their surviving written form suggest that Homer may have lived in Ionia. To the same person are also traditionally ascribed the *Homeric Hymns*.

Iliad

Ilias, 8th century BC

The *Iliad* occupied the place of honor in Greek literature. Along with the *Odyssey*, also attributed to the poet known as Homer, it formed the basis of Greek education and served as the fountain of the Greek literary imagination. Homer's authority remained supreme throughout antiquity. The Roman rhetorician Quintilian reflects this admiration in his famous comparison of Homer to the ocean that encircles the world and flows into every lesser river.

The *Iliad* balances two momentous themes. On the one hand it describes the anger of the Greek hero Achilles, first against Agamemnon and later against Hector, his refusal to continue fighting at Troy and then his return to battle to avenge the death of his friend Patroclus. On the other hand it takes as its subject the courage of Hector, champion of the doomed city of Troy.

For two thousand years, through radical changes in literary fashion, the *Iliad* has remained central to the western literary heritage. The importance of the *Iliad* is reflected not only in the amount and intensity of critical attention that it has attracted but also in the number of translations it has inspired: more than 200 complete or selected translations into English from 1581 to the present. No work of antiquity has been translated more often into English, with the possible exception of its companion epic, the *Odyssey*.

Scholarly interest has addressed most often the inseparable issues of interpretation and origins; for any consideration of the artistry of the *Iliad* must take into account the circumstances of its composition. Scholars now agree with some version of the theory, first proposed in the mid-20th century by Milman Parry, that the *Iliad* is the result of a long, complex tradition of oral narrative, that is, of tales created on the spot and sung by bards to audiences of aristocrats. The bard would improvise on a given theme, creating lines of poetry (traditionally the dactylic hexameter) which develop in the tale. Research has demonstrated that the bard was operating out of a memorized thesaurus not only of themes and specific episodes but also of thousands of lines and partial lines of verse.

Whether himself a bard or the sophisticated adaptor of this tradition, Homer (the name applied in antiquity to the otherwise unknown composer) shaped this mass of tales into a structured narrative that was first written down some time in the mid-8th century BC.

While the importance of the *Iliad* has remained unchallenged and its continuing hold on the western literary imagination cannot be denied, the meaning of Homer's epic is much debated. Readers of the Renaissance, for example, saw the *Iliad* as both a poem and a philosophic allegory. In the 18th and 19th centuries the *Iliad* served as both an enduring model of aesthetic sublimity and a model of statecraft. The 20th century, while finding more reasons to praise the genius of its author, reached different, often conflicting interpretations of the *Iliad*: for some, the concept of heroism that it celebrates is noble and ennobling, its hero Achilles a true model of human excellence. For others, most notably Simone Weil, the *Iliad* is a bleak story of force and brutality that is preserved from utter nihilism only by occasional vignettes of human compassion.

Translations

Chapman, George, *The Iliads of Homer Prince of Poets*, London: Nathaniel Butler, 1611

Dryden, John, in *Fables Ancient and Modern*, London: Jacob Tonson, 1700

Fagles, Robert, *The Iliad*, with an introduction by Bernard Knox, New York: Viking, 1990

Fitzgerald, Robert, *The Iliad*, New York: Doubleday, 1974; London: Collins, 1985

Lang, Andrew, Walter Leaf and Ernest Myers, *The Iliad*, London, Macmillan, 1882; revised edition, 1892

Lattimore, Richmond, *The Iliad of Homer*, Chicago: University of Chicago Press, 1951

Macpherson, James, *The Iliad of Homer*, 2 vols, London: Becket and De Hondt, 1773

Murray, A.T., *The Iliad* (bilingual edition), 2 vols, London: Heineman, and New York: Putnam, 1924–25

Newman, Francis W., *The Iliad of Homer*, London: Walton and Maberley, 1856

Norgate, T.S., *The Iliad*, London: Williams and Norgate, 1864

Pope, Alexander, *The Iliad of Homer*, 6 vols, London: Bernard Lintott, 1715–20

Rieu, E.V., *The Iliad*, Harmondsworth and Baltimore, Penguin, 1950

The challenge of translating the *Iliad* begins with its language, a unique composite Greek fashioned by a succession of oral poets over several centuries. Homeric Greek includes grammatical structures and syntactic forms from different dialects and different centuries that coexist without apparent distinction or discomfort. It is a language of oral presentation that exists only in this context. Its most distinctive feature is the use of the formula (a group of words regularly employed under the same metrical conditions to express an essential idea). A representative example of a formula is the recurring epithet, a descriptive phrase regularly associated with a particular character, such as "swift-footed great Achilles".

While the story of Troy and the *Iliad* itself inspired numerous narratives from the Middle Ages on, the history of the *Iliad* in English translation essentially begins with the publication of George CHAPMAN's partial translation in 1598 and his complete *Iliad* in 1611, with the ambitious title *The Iliads of Homer Prince of Poets. Never Before in any Language Truly Translated.*

Chapman's explicit goal, "with Poesie to open Poesie", seems to presage the modern emphasis on the goal of translation as the creation of a text of equivalent artistic impact. Like every translation, Chapman's is in part an act of interpretation. Much influenced by the Renaissance emphasis on the allegorical aspect of the *Iliad*, Chapman often expands his translation, adding verses of his own invention (in Chapman's words "needful periphrasis") to make Homer's "mysticke meaning clear" to the reader.

Chapman employs 14-syllable rhyming couplets and adopts an elegant, highly ornate style, derived ultimately from Latin and particularly Virgil, that Renaissance theorists emphasized was appropriate for "heroick poesie".

The importance of Chapman lies in large part in his demonstration of the power of a poetic rendering to bring life to an ancient text. His English *Iliad* is characterized by an energy and virtuosity that would inspire John Keats to write that he never breathed the "pure serene" of Homer's art until he "heard Chapman speak out loud and bold".

Like Chapman, John DRYDEN, the next major English poet to translate at least portions of the *Iliad* (in *Fables Ancient and Modern*, 1700) makes explicit the interpretive lens through which he approaches his task. Comparing Homer to Virgil, Dryden declares the Greek poet "more according to [his] genius" and translating Homer a greater pleasure because he is "full of fire" and "rapid in his thoughts".

None the less Dryden, like Chapman, writes in a refined poetic style seemingly more attuned to the literary density of Virgilian epic than to the rapid, fiery narrative of Homer. Dryden's attempts to recreate the "violent, impetuous" nature of the *Iliad* occasionally result in such unfortunate lines as this description of the angry Achilles: "foam betwixt his gnashing grinders churn'd." For the most part, however, Dryden has created a translation that lends elegance to Homer at the expense of simplicity.

Alexander POPE, the next great and perhaps the most influential translator of the *Iliad* (1715–20), shares much of Chapman's interpretative perspective. He too read the poem as an allegory. Pope's Achilles is a flawed hero whose failings are part of the poem's overall philosophic argument "that we should avoid Anger, since it is ever pernicious in the Event".

Pope's published translation was accompanied by an elaborate critical apparatus and voluminous notes. To prepare this he called on numerous scholars. In Samuel Johnson's words, "when he felt himself deficient he sought assistance; and what man of learning would refuse to help him?" The actual translation, though aided by such scholars, was Pope's own.

Pope also had been influenced by theories of heroic poetry that promoted a Latinate style, and he can be described as rendering Homer through Virgil and Milton. His translation suppresses the more barbaric scenes of the original while giving greater emphasis to pictorial descriptions and the moral implications of the characters' actions. His classical echoes enhance the epic grandeur of his translation, but also produce an occasionally inflated rhetoric that betrays the immediacy of Homeric language.

Pope is the first translator, however, to create a poetic language that, like Homer's Greek, is at once artificial and swift-moving. When Achilles rages at Agamemnon, the English has both the elegance and the violence Pope admires in Homer:

Nor yet the rage his broiling breast forsook,
Which thus redoubling on Atrides broke
O Monster, mix'd of Insolence and Fear,
Thou dog in forehead, but in Heart a Deer!

Pope even creates a literary version of Homer's formulaic language, but by creating his own recurring phrases rather than by translating the formulas of Homer with the same English phrase each time.

Though much praised, Pope's translation was not without its detractors. In the 19th century, in his essay *On Translating Homer* (1896), Matthew Arnold rightly criticizes Pope for employing a "literary style ... unfitted to ... the simple naturalness of Homer". And yet the investigations of the 20th century that have dispelled the romanticized notion of the primitive Homer and substituted a sophisticated adapter of his inherited tradition make Pope's translation seem even more powerful and insightful. Like the King James Bible, Pope's *Iliad* is the rare work of translation that survives as a work of art in its own right.

The 19th century produced a large number and wide range of translations of the *Iliad*, in both poetry and prose. The translations of this period are characterized by a deliberate use of archaic English, in an apparent attempt to communicate the foreignness and the antiquity of the Homeric world. In adopting a monumental style redolent of the Bible, particularly the Old Testament, to suggest the antiquity (and perhaps also the authority) of Homer, the 19th-century translators had been anticipated in the prose rendering by James MACPHERSON (1773), who is better known as the creator of *Ossian*.

Typical of this archaizing approach is the poetic translation of F.W. NEWMAN (1856), who imitates the language of Beowulf and the Old English epic tradition, often creating an artificial language difficult to understand ("therefore on him bestow'd he it to gratify the monarch") that unfortunately borders on self-parody.

Matthew Arnold's important essay both inspired and influenced a generation of 19th-century translators. Arnold argued that the translator of Homeric epic should be judged on the ability to re-create four essential qualities of the Greek: rapidity, directness in vocabulary and syntax, plainness in matter and the expression of ideas, and nobility.

Arnold's argument, along with his criticism of the Latinate translations of Pope and others for failure to meet the criterion of plainness, led to numerous translations in less ornate English. Even the best of these efforts, for example the translation of Thomas Starling NORGATE (1864), are betrayed by a reliance on archaic English.

Among this proliferation of poetic translations, it is ironic that perhaps the most widely read translation of the *Iliad* to appear in the 19th century is a prose version by LANG, LEAF & MYERS (1882), which became the preferred edition for use in schools in both Great Britain and the United States. The English is usually stolid, quaintly but not painfully archaic, and generally easy to read.

No survey of the *Iliad* in translation can omit that prepared by A.T. MURRAY (1925) for the Loeb Classical Library, a monumental undertaking designed to make the corpus of Greek and Latin classical literature available to the general public. Typical of the series, Murray's translation, like his version of the *Odyssey*, also for Loeb, is semantically accurate but generally graceless. The translation, printed facing the original Greek, has provided countless students of Greek with an aid to their own efforts at translation.

The 20th-century equivalent of the Lang, Leaf & Myers translation is the prose version of E.V. RIEU (1950), whose translation of the *Iliad* has been widely used in schools ever since its publication. Rieu produced a translation unmatched for clarity and simplicity but generally devoid of verbal play or artistic power. This *Iliad* is not just translated, but also tamed.

In addition to these popular prose versions, the 20th century witnessed a surge of strong poetic translations of the *Iliad*. In part, the interest in Homeric poetry has been sparked by a new appreciation of the *Iliad* as a work of art, new debates concerning its meaning and relevance for the modern world, and a new understanding of the process of its creation.

While 18th-century translators like Pope are more successful with the grandeur of the *Iliad* and less successful with the directness of Homer's oral style, translators in the 20th century are generally more successful with Homer's directness than with his grandeur. Among the poetic translations produced in the 20th century three stand out as exceptional in terms of artistic power and/or popularity.

The verse translation of Richmond LATTIMORE (1951) adopts a free six-beat line in an attempt to reproduce what Arnold called the rapidity of Homer's Greek. Much influenced by Parry, Lattimore declares that his goal is to re-create in his English the formulaic nature of Homeric verse.

By staying close to the original, Lattimore has produced a poetic translation that, like a Greek ship hugging the shore and avoiding the open sea, hovers near the meaning of the Greek text at the expense of avoiding the poetic depth of the original. Despite the persistent lack of elegance of expression that reduces the power of his rendering, Lattimore has created an austere English *Iliad* that powerfully conveys the ritual nature of Homer's style. At its best, Lattimore's version gives a glimpse of the way that Homer arranged words, phrases, and lines while maintaining a stately tone.

Lattimore's style was more suited to the somber *Iliad* than to the playful *Odyssey*, which he also translated. His *Iliad* became a favored school text, preferred to that of his rival in translation, Robert FITZGERALD, although Fitzgerald's translation of the *Odyssey* was often preferred to that of Lattimore.

FITZGERALD's *Iliad* (1974), though it fails to reach the heights of his brilliant translation of the *Odyssey* (1961), is one of the few translations to provide a powerful aesthetic experience. Like Pope, he has been accused of distorting Homer; like Pope's own distortions, Fitzgerald's reflect a poet's effort to recreate the poetry of the *Iliad*.

His poetic resourcefulness, so attuned to the *Odyssey*, seems less suited for the *Iliad*'s extended scenes of carnage and anger. Fitzgerald's *Iliad* is most impressive in the occasional scenes of art and artifice, such as the extended description of Achilles' shield:

> Upon the shield a soft terrain, freshly plowed,
> he pictured: a broad field, and many plowmen
> here and there upon it ...
> and the earth looked black behind them,
> as though turned up by plows. But it was gold,
> all gold – a wonder of the artist's craft.

It is less effective in scenes of war, where Fitzgerald tends to impose his own more lyric sensibility on the harshness of Homeric description.

Translation of Homer involves a delicate balance of scholarship and poetic inspiration. Lattimore's translation is more successful in its scholarly fidelity to the formulaic nature of Homer's Greek, re-creating the strangeness of his poetic language while generally avoiding the creation of a false English. Fitzgerald, while achieving greater success in the more important enterprise of recreating the power of the Greek as poetry and narrative, suppresses the strangeness of Homer.

The translation of Robert FAGLES (1990) manages to combine the strengths while largely avoiding the weaknesses of his two immediate predecessors. His translation was greeted with praise and numerous awards for his ability to produce a poem that re-created both the grandeur and the vitality of the Greek. Denis Donoghue, using Arnold's categories, called the translation "rapid, plain, direct and noble". These qualities are apparent in Fagles's translation of Homeric battle scenes, as in this simile of a warrior:

> Like a lion lighting on some handsome carcass,
> lucky to find an antlered stag or wild goat
> just as hunger strikes – he rips it, bolts it down,
> even with running dogs and lusty hunters rushing *him*.

Less free than Fitzgerald, Fagles follows the Greek far less closely than Lattimore. As Homeric Greek blends dialects, so Fagles manages to blend a formal poetic language with elements of colloquial American English.

Fagles's translation reflects a modern interpretation emphasizing character and psychology. His Achilles, far from the "warning against the dangers of anger" of Chapman and Pope, is both the essence of the aristocratic ideal and the positive forerunner of the Greek tragic hero who is passionately devoted to his own private ideal of conduct; and this translation brings out both aspects of Achilles. Though his battle scenes fall short of the blunt brutality of the *Iliad*, he deftly and sensitively evokes the power and pathos of the original in its scenes of verbal confrontation.

The history of the *Iliad* in English translation reflects both the importance of Homer's epic and the shifting tides of critical response. Allegorical interpretation deeply influenced the initial efforts. In the 19th century Arnold's emphasis on plainness, itself derived from the dominant critical opinion of Homer, influenced a whole generation. The 20th century witnessed several comparative movements: a tendency to read the *Iliad* as a novel, a discomfort with its emphasis on martial force, and a growing appreciation of Homer's creative genius in adapting an oral tradition to new artistic possibilities. Given the evidence of past fascination, it is certain that the number of translations of the *Iliad* will continue to grow.

DENNIS M. KRATZ

Further Reading

Arnold, Matthew, *On Translating Homer*, London: Longman, 1861
Clarke, Howard, *Homer's Readers*, Newark: University of Delaware Press, 1981
Kirk, G.S., *Homer and the Oral Tradition*, Cambridge and New York: Cambridge University Press, 1976
Mueller, Martin, *The Iliad*, London: Allen and Unwin, 1984

Odyssey

Odyssea, 8th century BC

No character from ancient literature has exerted as firm or constant a hold on the Western literary imagination as has Homer's Odysseus. No work has inspired more imitations, transformations or translations than the *Odyssey*. In the *Iliad* Homer had built an epic on the theme of anger of the Achaians' greatest warrior; in the *Odyssey* he fashioned an epic on the return of their cleverest.

Little is known of the circumstances in which the *Odyssey* was composed. It is generally agreed that the *Odyssey* follows the *Iliad*, to which it seems to refer, and therefore could not have been written down before the latter part of the 8th century BC. Although the product of the same oral tradition, and probably the same poet, that created the *Iliad*, the *Odyssey* is a vastly different poem. The ancient world, for the most part, considered the *Iliad* the greater of the two. The critic Longinus, writing in the 1st century AD (in a work entitled *On the Sublime*), expresses the opinion that Homer composed the *Odyssey* in his old age, when his talent was "a setting sun". But Longinus immediately qualifies the implied criticism of the *Odyssey* by pointing out that this was, after all, the old age of *Homer*.

Like the *Iliad*, the *Odyssey* celebrates heroism; but it depicts a different kind of hero for a different world, a man whose essential characteristic is cleverness. Achilles, hero of the *Iliad*, hates lies and deception. Odysseus is a story-teller who brags about his powers to deceive and is not above disguising himself as a ragged beggar to gain victory.

The *Odyssey* extends the depiction of heroic action beyond the confines of war, armed conflict, and men. The action of the *Odyssey* takes place in settings ranging from sophisticated courts to the caves of brutish monsters. In this world brute strength, while valuable, is less valuable than the ability to create, interpret, and keep from being fooled by, convincing fictions.

Translations

Bryant, William Cullen, *The Odyssey of Homer*, Boston: Houghton Mifflin, 1873
Buckley, Theodore A., *The Odyssey of Homer*, London: George Bell, 1874
Butcher, S.H. and Andrew Lang, *The Odyssey of Homer*, London: Macmillan, 1879
Chapman, George, *Homer's Odysses*, London: Nathaniel Butter, 1614(?)
Cook, Albert, *The Odyssey*, New York: Norton, 1967; 2nd edition, 1993
Fagles, Robert, *The Odyssey*, with an introduction and notes by Bernard Knox, New York: Viking, 1996
Fitzgerald, Robert, *The Odyssey*, New York: Doubleday, 1961; New York: Heinemann, 1962
Lattimore, Richmond, *The Odyssey of Homer*, with an introduction, New York: Harper and Row, 1967
Mandelbaum, Allen, *The Odyssey of Homer*, Berkeley: University of California Press, 1990
Murray, A.T., *The Odyssey* (parallel texts), Cambridge, Massachusetts: Harvard University Press, and London: Heinemann, 1919; revised by George E. Dimock, Cambridge Massachuetts: Harvard University Press, 1995 (Loeb Classical Library)
Palmer, George Herbert, *The Odyssey of Homer*, Boston: Houghton Mifflin, 1891
Pope, Alexander, *The Odyssey of Homer*, 5 vols, London: Bernard Lintott, 1725–26
Rieu, E.V., *The Odyssey*, London: Methuen, 1945; Harmondsworth and Baltimore: Penguin, 1946; revised by D.C.H. Rieu with Peter V. Jones, Harmondsworth and New York: Penguin, 1991
Rouse, W.H.D., *The Odyssey*, Edinburgh: Nelson, 1937; New York: New American Library, 1949
Shaw, T.E., *The Odyssey of Homer*, New York: Oxford University Press, 1932; London: Oxford University Press, 1935
Worsley, Philip Stanhope, *The Odyssey of Homer*, 2 vols, Edinburgh: Blackwood, 1861–62

The *Odyssey* presents the same difficulties to the translator as the *Iliad*. Above all, a translation must take into account the nature of the language of Homeric epic: a unique composite Greek fashioned by a succession of oral poets over several centuries. Homeric Greek is an artificial language, not spoken outside the epic tradition; it includes grammatical structures and syntactic forms from different dialects and different centuries that coexist without apparent distinction or discomfort. Its most distinctive feature is the use of the formula (a group of words regularly employed under the same metrical conditions to express an essential idea). A representative example of a formula is the recurring epithet, a descriptive phrase regularly associated with a particular character ("circumspect Penelope") or event (the well-known "rose-red fingers" with which dawn always makes her appearance).

As an epic about art, deception, and a hero whose superiority is based on his skillful use of language, the *Odyssey* presents an additional challenge; for it is suffused with artful language. Homer explores and exploits the possibilities of Greek with countless puns and plays on words.

Typical, and essentially untranslatable, is the famous trick that helps Odysseus escape from the huge but relatively dim-witted Cyclops named Polyphemus, telling him that his name is *outis* (Greek for "nobody"). When Polyphemus is blinded by Odysseus and calls out to the other cyclopes that "nobody" wounded him, naturally they ignore him.

Homer uses the trick as the basis of an elaborate pun later in the episode; for Odysseus, basking in his own cleverness, declares that his *metis* had won the day. In this line the Greek word *metis* has two equally possible meanings: it is an alternate form of *outis* (used in subordinate clauses) and the word for *metis*, or cleverness, the very quality that he demonstrates in both the original trick and the present statement.

The history of the *Odyssey* in English translation begins, as does the corresponding history of the *Iliad*, with a version by George CHAPMAN (1614?). Deeply influenced by a tradition that read the *Odyssey* as an allegory of the human soul, Chapman emphasizes the philosophic implications of Odysseus' journeys. This emphasis is evident in his translation of the opening lines: "The Man, O Muse, informe, that many a way / Wound with his wisedome to his wished stay". "Wisedome" is a profoundly interpretive translation of the Greek *polytropon*, which literally means a man "of many turns", that is, a wily man who always knows which way to turn, a clever man with many ways of thought. This philosophic vision, which lent a somber tone to Chapman's *Iliad*, seems out of place in the *Odyssey*, and has the effect of suppressing the narrative energy of the Greek.

Alexander POPE also turned to the *Odyssey* (1725–26) after translating the *Iliad*. In both efforts he enlisted the assistance of scholars more familiar with Greek and issues of scholarship than he. While the translation of the *Iliad* was clearly Pope's work, however, Pope's *Odyssey* is the work of a team that included Pope and two university-educated churchmen. Elijah FENTON translated books 1, 4, 19 and 20; William BROOME translated books 2, 6, 8, 11, 12, 16 and 23. Pope translated the other books while also organizing, supervising and having the final say over the contributions of his collaborators.

The result is less satisfying than his *Iliad*. Like Chapman, Pope was hampered by a heavily allegorical interpretation of the poem; and his predilection for extended descriptions of setting at the occasional expense of action, coupled with a rather sententious presentation of Odysseus' longer speeches, fails to express the vitality and humor of the original.

While the 18th and early 19th centuries produced numerous translations of the *Odyssey*, Matthew Arnold's influential essay *On Translating Homer* (1861) must be considered the next significant event in the history of the *Odyssey* in English translation. Arnold emphasized "rapidity" and "eminent plainness" as two Homeric qualities essential for the translator to recreate; and he faulted Pope, in particular, for his failure to meet these aesthetic criteria. Other characteristics that Arnold considered essentially Homeric were simplicity of ideas and nobility of manner.

Arnold's essay sparked a group of literary translations that reflected its aesthetic argument. Arnold himself singled out for praise a translation that attempted to reflect the "four principles": composed in Spenserian meter, P.S. WORSLEY's *Odyssey* (1862) does not seem more rapid and elegant than Pope's or Chapman's, and it is far inferior as poetry.

Two translations reflecting radically different approaches appeared, on different sides of the Atlantic, within a year of each other. In 1873 William Cullen BRYANT published the first important translation by an American poet. Its iambic pentameters often create the rapidity and clarity that Arnold emphasized. In 1874 Theodore BUCKLEY published a prose version, faithful on the semantic level but failing to communicate any sense of the *Odyssey's* poetry or verbal dexterity. To give an aura of antiquity, Buckley turned, as would many translators after him, to the language of the King James Bible.

As the novel became the dominant genre of narrative in English, prose versions became more common. Inevitably, these prose versions tended to present the *Odyssey* as a novel of adventure more than an epic poem. The most widely read prose translation of the 19th century was produced by the team of S.H. BUTCHER & Andrew LANG (1879). (Three years later Lang would join with two other translators to create an equally popular version of the *Iliad*.) Lang and Butcher, following the fashion of the time, use the language and cadences of the Old Testament to emphasize the antiquity of the tale. In their version, for example, a serving woman did not mix hot and cold water; rather she "poured in much cold water and next mingled therewith the warm." The stilted language communicates the story but little of the verve of the Homeric narrative.

No survey of the *Odyssey* in translation can omit that prepared by A.T. MURRAY (1919) for the Loeb Classical Library. Murray's translation is, like his version of the *Iliad*, typical of the series: semantically accurate but lacking in elegance. Again, the translation, printed facing the original Greek, has provided countless students of Greek with a minimal aesthetic experience but a valuable aid to their own efforts at translation.

Three other prose versions, of varying success, deserve mention. The least successful of these, by T.E. LAWRENCE ("Lawrence of Arabia", writing under the pseudonym T.E. SHAW), appeared in 1932. Lawrence mirrors the conglomerate nature of Homeric Greek, though unintentionally, since his Greek was limited, by mixing a variety of English dialects. Brusque military speeches are interspersed with archaizing descriptions full of biblical allusion. Unfortunately the components coexist rather than coalesce, and the result is both artless and flat.

Lawrence in fact based much of his translation on another prose translation, by George Herbert PALMER (1891). Palmer's prose reads smoothly but he does not attempt to recreate any of the word-play or the sense of play that permeates the Greek.

Both W.H.D. ROUSE (1937) and E.V. RIEU (1946) adopt the strategy of "novelizing" Homer's epic. Both produced prose *Odysseys* in clear, relatively unadorned English that was aimed at the general reader. Both avoid the archaizing tendency of Lawrence and so many 19th-century translators; neither makes any attempt to recreate the *Odyssey* as a work of verbal art.

In the 20th century three major poetic translations dominate the field, dwarfing other versions for both general readership and use as school texts. Among the translations overshadowed by these three are two of considerable merit.

Albert COOK (1967) provides a line-by-line translation that pays particular attention to the *Odyssey* as a work of sophisticated playfulness. Cook's translation has much in common with the urbane, poetically smooth version of Allen MANDELBAUM (1990). They share the quality of readability and both have numerous felicitous passages; but neither ever rises to heights of poetic excellence, and neither ever captured the attention of a large readership.

The translation that most closely recreates the poetic fecundity and playfulness of the *Odyssey* is unquestionably that of Robert FITZGERALD (1961), after Bryant the first poet of significant reputation to translate the *Odyssey*.

In the struggle of the translator to produce the words and the spirit of the original, Fitzgerald inevitably chooses the spirit. Unfortunately, he has a tendency to substitute his vision and poetry for Homer's. Where the Greek, for example, simply declares that people tend to praise the latest song that they have heard (that is, the latest fad in story-telling), Fitzgerald offers "men like best / a song that rings like morning on the ear". A striking image, but it is not Homer's.

Richmond LATTIMORE (1967), on the other hand, based his translation on the desire to follow as faithfully as possible the literal meaning and formulaic nature of Homeric verse. His version, as a result, gives a superbly faithful but dulled glimpse of the brilliance of the Greek behind Lattimore's English. None the less, Lattimore's translation, with its poetic recreation of the rhythm of Homer's Greek, possesses a quality lacking in every other English version, especially the prose versions (to all of which it is far superior). A dulled glimpse of the verbal art of the *Odyssey* is better than no glimpse at all.

A comparison of one passage reveals the marked difference between the approach of Lattimore and that of Fitzgerald. In book 13, Athena expresses her doubled delight in intellectual acuity. She has been pleased on the one hand by the inventiveness of a false story that Odysseus has told her about himself, on the other by the fact that this cleverest of men has failed to recognize her disguise as a young boy.

Lattimore translates:

> It would be a sharp one, and a stealthy one, who would
> ever get past you
> in any contriving, even if it were a god against you.
> You wretch, so devious, never weary of tricks.

The English has the austere clarity that characterizes Lattimore (and works to much better effect in his translation of the *Iliad*). The meaning is clear, but the tone is flat. Lattimore here, as often, settles for the prosaic equivalent of a Greek word rather than discovering a word of comparable wit. "You wretch" seems far too moral for the Greek word *skhetle*, which in the context expresses affection more than disapproval.

Fitzgerald, on the other hand, recreates the bantering mood of Athena's speech:

> Whoever gets around you must be sharp
> and guileful as a snake; even a god
> might bow to you in ways of dissimulation.
> You! You chameleon!

Fitzgerald has an Odyssean talent with words, but Odysseus is not to be trusted. This passage reflects Fitzgerald's strength while also representing his weakness as a translator. "Guileful" is a better choice than 'stealthy' for the Greek *poikilometes* (a joining of the words for "mind" and "dappled"), and "chameleon" both elaborates on the color image implied by *poikilometes* and effectively evokes Athena's affectionate response to Odysseus' alluring fiction. The comparison of Odysseus to a snake, on the other hand, is purely Fitzgerald's invention. Snakes and guile were not a connection Homer would have recognized. It is specific to the Old Testament. By creating this connection for the modern reader Fitzgerald misleadingly grafts on to Athena's praise a connotation of evil absent from the Greek.

Lattimore's translation is less fluid but provides a more faithful presentation of Homer's words and style; Fitzgerald's poetry is more arresting but his additions to and alterations of the text are often intrusive.

Between the Scylla of Lattimore and the Charybdis of Fitzgerald, Robert FAGLES (1996) steers a clever middle course, preserving the formulaic nature of Homeric verse without lapsing into awkward or prosaic English. He translates Athena's depiction of Odysseus as "foxy, ingenious". As often in his version, he diffuses the meaning of specific words rather than relying on one English word. In this passage, for example, it would take "some champion lying cheat" to rival Odysseus for "all-round craft and guile". Like Fitzgerald, he creates an animal image of cleverness familiar to the modern reader; unlike Fitzgerald, he avoids imbuing this image with an inappropriately critical moral sense.

Fagles translates Odysseus' aforementioned pun on *metis* as " laughter filled my heart to think how nobody's name – my great cunning stroke – had duped them one and all." While not as brilliant as Homer's pun, this translation at least suggests the connection between "nobody's name" (with alliteration for emphasis) and Odysseus' cunning.

This *Odyssey* differs from its predecessors in its attention to the women characters of the *Odyssey*. The years intervening between the versions of Fitzgerald/Lattimore and Fagles witnessed a shift in critical opinion concerning the *Odyssey*. Modern readings give greater emphasis to two aspects of the poem. They stress the role of creating and recognizing artful deception as a heroic quality; moreover, many contemporaries see Penelope as an artful co-hero (who, after all, weaves her own deceptions) rather than merely the patient wife awaiting the return of her long-absent husband.

Fagles comes as close as any translator ever has to fusing speed with dignity in fashioning an English *Odyssey*. His translation of *polytropon* as "the man of twists and turns" reflects the modern fascination with the art (rather than its morality, as in Chapman's "Wisedome") and sets the tone for a translation faithful to the art and the words of the original. Homer's epic, however, shares with its wily hero the qualities of intelligence and elusiveness. Fagles's version merely adds to a centuries-long conversation with Homer's text that surely can be expected to have many more twists and turns.

DENNIS M. KRATZ

Further Reading

Arnold, Matthew, *On Translating Homer*, London: Longman Green Longman and Roberts, 1861

Clarke, Howard, *Homer's Readers: A Historical Introduction to the Iliad and the Odyssey*, Newark: University of Delaware Press, 1981

Felson-Rubin, Nancy, *Regarding Penelope: From Character to Poetics*, Princeton, New Jersey: Princeton University Press, 1994

Schein, Seth (editor), *Reading the Odyssey: Selective Interpretive Essays*, Princeton: Princeton University Press, 1996

Segal, Charles, *Singers, Heroes and Gods in the Odyssey*, Ithaca, New York: Cornell University Press, 1994

Homeric Hymns, c.8th–4th centuries BC

The 33 Homeric hymns are mainly narrative poems dealing with the gods, attributed in antiquity to Homer, but later seen to be of widely varying dates and authorship. Overshadowed by the Homeric epics, the hymns, especially the longer ones (to Demeter, Apollo, Hermes, and Aphrodite, and the fragmentary hymn to Dionysus) are in no way inferior to the *Iliad* and the *Odyssey*. They are masterpieces of storytelling, ranging in tone from objective clarity (Apollo) to deep pathos (Demeter) and playful humour (Hermes).

Translations

Athanassakis, Apostolos N., *The Homeric Hymns*, Baltimore: Johns Hopkins University Press, 1976

Boer, Charles, *The Homeric Hymns*, Chicago: Swallow Press, 1970; revised edition, Irving, Texas: Spring Publications, 1979

Brown, N.O., "The Homeric Hymn to Hermes" in *Classics in Translation*, vol. 1, *Greek Literature*, edited by Paul MacKendrick and Herbert M. Howe, Madison: University of Wisconsin Press, 1952, pp. 81–87

Chapman, George, *The Crowne of all Homer's Works, Batrachomyomachia: or, The Battaile of Frogs and Mise, His Hymnes and Epigrams*, London: John Bill, probably 1624; reprinted in volume 2 of Allardyce Nicoll's edition of Chapman, New York: Pantheon Books, 1956 (Bollingen Foundation); London: Routledge and Kegan Paul, 1957

Congreve, William, "Homer's Hymn to Venus" in *The Works of Mr William Congreve*, vol. 3, London: Jacob Tonson, 1730, pp. 366–82
Edgar, John, *The Homeric Hymns*, Edinburgh: James Thin, 1891
Evelyn-White, H.G., in his *Hesiod, the Homeric Hymns and Homerica* (bilingual edition), London: Heinemann, and New York: Putnam, 1914; revised edition, London: Heinemann, and Cambridge, Massachusetts: Harvard University Press, 1936 (Loeb Classical Library)
Fowler, Barbara Hughes, *Archaic Greek Poetry: An Anthology*, Madison: University of Wisconsin Press, 1992
Hine, Daryl, *The Homeric Hymns, and the Battle of the Frogs and the Mice*, New York: Atheneum, 1972
Lang, Andrew, *The Homeric Hymns: A New Prose Translation and Essays, Literary and Mythological*, London: George Allen, and New York: Longmans Green, 1899
Sargent, Thelma, *The Homeric Hymns*, New York: Norton, 1973
Shelley, P.B., "Hymn to Mercury" (1820), "Homer's Hymn to the Earth, Mother of All" (1818), and others, available in editions of Shelley's works
Shelmerdine, Susan C., *The Homeric Hymns*, with an introduction, Newburyport, Massachusetts: Focus, 1995

Since the Homeric hymns are for the most part narrative, even the most prosaic translation is readable. The storytelling is what matters most here. However, good verse translations are preferable because they make the reader more aware of the poetry.

CHAPMAN (probably 1624), one of the great Elizabethan translators, is valuable for the richness of his English. He uses sprightly heroic couplets. In accordance with the custom of his age, he tends to use Roman names for Greek deities, e.g. Venus instead of Aphrodite, but not consistently: Hermes is not changed into Mercury. His translation does not include the great hymn to Demeter, the only manuscript of which was not discovered until 1777.

The elegance and vigour of CONGREVE's translation (1730) of the hymn to Aphrodite as "Homer's Hymn to Venus", in heroic couplets, reflects his period.

SHELLEY's version of the hymn to Hermes (1820, as "Hymn to Mercury"), in *ottava rima*, is probably the Homeric hymn best known to English readers. It is a masterpiece. Using heroic couplets, Shelley also translated part of the hymn to Aphrodite (as "Homer's Hymn to Venus") and several of the shorter hymns, of which "Homer's Hymn to the Earth, Mother of All" (1818) is outstanding. His translations are not literal yet still quite faithful to the original.

EDGAR's and LANG's translations are close in time (1891; 1899) and in manner. (Lang acknowledges his use of Edgar's version.) The English, characteristic of the period, reads like a combination of the King James Bible and William Morris's romances. Edgar's choice of words is somewhat less ornate than Lang's. Both are charming and enjoyable.

EVELYN-WHITE's literal prose translation (1914) is reliable and quite readable and makes an attempt to convey the dignity of the original texts.

BROWN (1952), author of the important study *Hermes the Thief*, provides a simple and clear translation into idiomatic English prose.

The short lines of BOER's free verse translation (1970) are imaginatively arranged on the page. The effect is one of ease and openness; the poems are accessible to fast reading, and the eye at once grasps larger units of meaning. This kind of reading experience does not even remotely correspond to the originally oral presentation of the hymns, but since we read rather than hear them, there is much to be said in favour of Boer's visually appealing disposition of the texts. (It may be noted that he changes the traditional sequence of the poems.)

HINE (1972) makes the unfortunate attempt to re-create Greek dactylic hexameters in English, a language that does not align itself easily into this kind of metrical pattern. The effect is heavy, and the syntax of Hine's translation frequently sounds forced.

SARGENT (1973), unlike Hine, succeeds in her use of dactyls because she is more flexible: for instance, some of her lines are pentameters, others hexameters. She approximates the dignity, and the length, of the Greek dactylic hexameter. If one reads aloud, the effect of her verse is not entirely natural, but since modern readers tend not to do so but to read in silence, the slight stiffness of this version is not disturbing. On the whole, this is a very good translation.

ATHANASSAKIS's (1976) is the best scholarly translation available. It is in free verse arranged to correspond line by line with the original texts. The accuracy and the readability of this version are unimpeachable, and there are excellent notes.

FOWLER's anthology (1992) includes the hymns to Demeter, Hermes, Aphrodite, Dionysus, and Athena. These renditions, in free rhythmic verse, are clear and elegant and yet do not sacrifice precision.

SHELMERDINE's translation (1995) is in prose that looks like verse on the page because it follows the Greek line by line. This book is valuable to the student because of its painstaking introduction and notes, but accuracy outbalances stylistic beauty in the translation.

ZOJA PAVLOVSKIS-PETIT

Further Reading

Preziosi, P.G., "*The Homeric Hymn to Aphrodite:* An Oral Analysis", *Harvard Studies in Classical Philology*, 71 (1966) pp. 171–204

See also the introduction to Shelmerdine

Horace 65–8 BC

Roman poet

Biography

Born Quintus Horatius Flaccus at Venusia (now Venosa) in Apulia, south Italy, 8 December 65 BC. His father was a propertied freedman. Horace was educated in Rome and Athens. In 44 he joined Brutus' faction and in 42 he fought as an officer at the battle of Philippi, where Brutus was defeated. When Horace returned to Rome in 41 his land had been confiscated. He joined the civil service and, forced by poverty, turned to writing. He became a friend of Virgil and in 38 met Maecenas, who became his patron. Horace rose to be the supreme lyric poet of his time. The emperor Augustus gave him a farm in the Sabine hills. Died 27 November 8 BC.

The works that made of Horace the eternal embodiment of Augustan culture are the *Satires* (book I, c.35; book II, c.30), the *Odes* (books I–III, 23; book IV, 13), the *Epodes* (c.30), and the *Epistles* (book I, 20; book II, c.14). The second book of *Epistles* contains the *Ars poetica*, written between 23 and 14.

Satires

Satirae; book I, c. 35 BC; book II, c.30 BC

Translations

Beaumont, Sir John, the elder, translation of Satire II.6 in *Bosworth-Field*, edited by his son, Sir John Beaumont, London, 1629

Carne-Ross, D.S. and Kenneth Haynes (editors), *Horace in English*, with an introduction by Carne-Ross, London: Penguin, 1996

Conington, John, *Satires, Epistles, and Art of Poetry*, London: Bell and Daldy, 1870

Cowley, Abraham, translation of Satires I.1 and part of II.6 in *The Works of Mr. Abraham Cowley*, London, 1668

Cowper, William, Satires I.5 and I.9 in *The Works of Horace in English Verse*, edited by W. Duncombe, London: B. White, 1767

Creech, Thomas, *The Odes, Satyrs, and Epistles of Horace*, London: Jacob Tonson, 1684

Drant, Thomas, *A Medicinable Morall, that is, the two Bookes of Horace his Satyres, Englyshed accordyng to the prescription of saint Hierome*, London, 1566; also in *Horace His arte of Poetrie, pistles, and Satyrs Englyshed*, London: Thomas Marshe, 1567

Evans, Lewis, [The first two satires or] *poesyes of Horace* [translated into English] *meeter, by Lewis Euans schoolemayster*, London: Thomas Colwell, [1565?]

Fanshawe, Richard, translation of Satires I.6, II.1, and II.6 in *Selected Parts of Horace Prince of Lyricks, and of all Latin poets the fullest fraughte with excellent morality*, London, 1652; also in *The Poems of Horace, Consisting of Odes, Satyres, and Epistles, Rendred in English Verse by Several Persons*, London: Henry Brome, 1666

Francis, Philip, *The Satires of Horace*, London: A. Millar, 1746 [the third volume of Horace's works translated by Francis, following on *The Odes, Epodes, and Carmen Seculare of Horace* (bilingual edition) of 1743–46. In subsequent editions, his translation of the satires is located in Volume III of *A Poetical Translation of the Works of Horace*.]

Fuchs, Jacob, *Horace's Satires and Epistles*, with an introduction by William S. Anderson, New York: Norton, 1977

Howes, Francis, *The Epodes, Satires, and Epistles of Horace*, London: W. Pickering, 1845

Jonson, Ben, translation of Satire II.1 added in 1616 to the end of Act III of *The Poetaster*, London, 1616

Pope, Alexander, *The First Satire of the Second Book of Horace, Imitated*, London, 1733; *The First Satire of the Second Book of Horace, Imitated ... to which is added, the Second Satire of Horace Paraphrased*, London, 1734; imitation of Satire I.2 in *Sober Advice from Horace, to the Young Gentlemen about Town*, London, 1734; *An Imitation of the Sixth Satire of the Second Book of Horace*, London, 1738

Rochester, John Wilmot, earl of, imitation of Satire I.10 ("An allusion to Horace") in his *Poems on Several Occasions* [London, 1680]

Rudd, Niall, *The Satires of Horace and Persius*, with an introduction, London: Penguin, 1973

Smart, Christopher, imitation of Satire I.3 in *The Horatian Canons of Friendship*, London: Newbery, 1750; *The Works of Horace Translated Literally into English Prose*, bilingual edition, London: Oswald, 1756; *The Works of Horace Translated into Verse*, London: W. Flexney, 1767

Swift, Jonathan, imitation of part of Satire II.6 in *Miscellanies in Prose and Verse*, edited by Swift and Pope, London: B. Motte, 1727; imitation of Satire II.1 ("A Dialogue between an eminent Lawyer and DR. SWIFT ...") in *An Essay upon the Life, Writings, and Character of Dr. Jonathan Swift*, London, 1755; imitation of part of Satire I.6 ("On Noisy Tom") in *The Works of Jonathan Swift*, London, 1755–79 [1762].

The two books of Horace's *Satires* are his earliest work, written c.35 BC and c.30 BC respectively. Though sometimes satirical in the modern sense, they may often be read as conversations, *causeries*, on a variety of topics: an account of a trip, the virtue of simple living, the wisdom of modest independence, etc. In Satire I.4 Horace tells us that the tone of his satires is like that of ordinary conversation; only the meter (dactylic hexameter) distinguishes them from prose. Confusion in the Renaissance about the nature of satire (the relation to satyrs and satyr plays; its proper level of diction; its moralizing function) impeded the translation and reception of Horace's *Satires*. Dryden's *Discourse concerning the Original and Progress of Satire* (1692) was influential in clarifying the disputed points for English readers.

Although there is some uncertainty about the date (1565?), EVANS's translation of the first two satires of the first book of Horace's *Satires* appears to be the first translation of any of Horace's works into English. He adopted fourteeners for his translation, as DRANT did in the next year in his complete translation (1566) of the *Satires*. Both translations are clumsy, metrically unwieldy, and insensitive to Horace's Latin. Horace's medieval reputation as a moralist (it is in this guise that *Orazio satiro* appears in the *Inferno)* attracted Drant, and he expurgates and sometimes radically alters the original in the interest of Christian morality.

JONSON's translations from Horace tend toward literal exactitude and literary inelegance. Samuel Johnson may have had him in mind when he judged that "the shackles of verbal interpretation ... debar [literal translations] from elegance." Jonson's translation (1616) of Satire II.1 does however have its importance for the way it presents Horace as an exemplary model for the contemporary literary scene.

Like Jonson, BEAUMONT (1629) translated Horace into pentameter couplets. Beaumont's version of Horace's most famous satire, the story of the country mouse and the city mouse, is fluent and mostly idiomatic. The couplets lead him to expand the original, sometimes redundantly, but at other times he adds lively detail to the scene and action.

Although he had some success in suggesting the diverse meters and the occasionally high style of the *Odes*, FANSHAWE (1652) is less effective at reproducing the conversational tone of the satires. In the three satires he translated, his reliance on parenthesis and abrupt transitions keep him from producing a sense of the flow of conversation.

COWLEY includes two translations (in pentameter couplets) from the *Satires* in *Several Discourses by way of Essays, in Verse and Prose* (1668); Satire II.6 in the essay "On Agriculture" and Satire I.1 in the essay "On Avarice". The congenial and quietly reflective tone of the essays is remote from his earlier rather extravagant verse and translations. His rendering of the story of the city mouse and the country mouse has been claimed as one of his finest works.

ROCHESTER's imitation of Satire I.10 in pentameter couplets, in which Dryden stands in for Lucilius, was the first such imitation of the classics, Samuel Johnson notes; imitating classical satire was subsequently very popular. It was written in the summer of 1675.

CREECH's nearly complete translation of Horace is generally known today only because both Pope and Swift mocked him: "*Creech* murder'd *Horace* in his senseless Rhymes, / But hung himself to expiate his Crimes" (Swift, *Epigrams against Carthy*). His version of the *Satires* in pentameter couplets (1684) is far from fluent, but the anonymously revised edition of his translation was the standard for 50 years, and it has its virtues: a vivid sense of rural life and an understanding of the plain style as a proper medium for translating the *Satires*.

SWIFT (1727) imitates Satire II.1 (in octosyllabic couplets) to defend his own practice of satire. His imitation of part of Satire I.6 in pentameter couplets is very free; it lampoons Sir Thomas Prendergast, a member of the English and Irish parliaments. His most famous imitation is the first part of Satire II.6 in octosyllabic couplets, to which Pope added his own imitation of the second part. Pope explains that while his design was "to sharpen the Satire, and open the Sense of the Poet", Swift's was "to render [Horace's] native Ease and Familiarity yet more easy and familiar".

POPE's imitations (1733, 1734, 1734, 1738) of four satires by Horace (in heroic couplets, except for the continuation of Swift's imitation of Satire II.6 in octosyllabic couplets) are complex re-creations of the original. Frank Stack points to the "lively, endlessly open, play between the texts", adding that "each poetry seems to open up the other and give it new vitality" (Stack, 1985). Pope does not reproduce the humbler passages in the *Satires,* and his level of diction is much higher than Horace's; he offers a poem to stand on its own terms equally with Horace.

FRANCIS's great success with the *Odes* (Johnson: "Francis has done it best; I'll take his, five out of six, against them all") is not repeated in his *Satires* (1746). Although his versions are accomplished pentameter couplets, he seems ill at ease with the rustic quality and the level of diction of the original.

SMART's imitation of Satire I.3, attempted "in the manner of Pope" and in heroic couplets, is far from the level of Pope; however, Smart's colloquial tone does respond to an element of the original. His popular prose translation published in 1756, it has been argued, is more than a crib, and its inversions and occasionally contorted syntax do something to re-create aspects of Horace's poems. The verse translation of 1767 is metrically somewhat monotonous; it suffers from what Byron diagnosed (in a different context) as "the fatal facility of octosyllabic couplets".

COWPER's early translations (1767) of two satires in octosyllabic couplets are fluent and skillful at re-creating Horace's friendly and intimate conversational tone. Some of Cowper's own poetry, such as "An Epistle to Joseph Hill, Esq.", shows an expert mastery of this tone.

Published in the mid-19th century, HOWES's translation of the *Satires* in pentameter couplets recalls an earlier, 18th-century style. Though very little known and never reprinted, his translation (1845) of Horace's hexameter poems may well be the best complete translation in English. Howes refers to Horace's "address and dexterity", his "air of unstudied ease", and his rhythmical variety, which he attempts to reproduce in his translation.

CONINGTON's translation (1870) in pentameter couplets became the standard throughout the later 19th and early 20th century. It is the most literal of the poetic translations of Horace's *Satires,* and it presents a colorless and remote antiquity.

Horace's *Odes* attracted renewed attention from poets in the 20th century, but the *Satires* did not. They have fallen to translators (such as RUDD, 1973, and FUCHS, 1977) who, writing for an academic market, have faced the problem of creating a style closer to the original than verse translation, and yet more poetic than a prose version. Both adopt the meter, if it is meter, that has become popular in modern times, a six-beat line of variable length. Fuchs is more successful in creating a conversational tone, Rudd offers helpful notes, but neither writes poetry.

CARNE-ROSS & HAYNES reprint translations by Jonson, Beaumont, Cowley, Rochester, John Oldham, Creech, Swift and Pope, George Ogle, Francis, Cowper, and Howes.

KENNETH HAYNES

Further Reading

Fraenkel, Eduard, *Horace*, Oxford: Clarendon Press, 1957

Hopkins, David, "Cowley's Horatian Mice", in *Horace Made New*, edited by Charles Martindale and David Hopkins, Cambridge and New York: Cambridge University Press, 1993

Rudd, Niall, *The Satires of Horace*, Cambridge: Cambridge University Press, and Berkeley: University of California Press, 1966

Stack, Frank, *Pope and Horace: Studies in Imitation*, Cambridge and New York: Cambridge University Press, 1985

See also the introduction by Carne-Ross in Carne-Ross & Haynes.

Odes and Epodes

Odes (23–13 BC) and *Epodes* (c.30 BC)

Translations

Ashmore, John, *Certain Selected Odes of Horace Englished*, London: H.L[ownes] for R. Moore, 1621

Brome, Alexander, *The Poems of Horace, Consisting of Odes, Satyres, and Epistles, Rendred in English Verse by Several Persons*, London: Henry Brome, 1666

Conington, John, *The Odes and Carmen Sæculare of Horace, Translated into English Verse*, London: Bell and Daldy, 1863

Creech, Thomas, *The Odes, Satyrs and Epistles of Horace*, London: Jacob Tonson, 1684

Francis, Philip, *The Odes, Epodes and Carmen Seculare of Horace* (bilingual edition), 4 vols, London: A. Millar, 1743–46

Hawkins, Sir Thomas, *Odes of Horace, the Best of Lyrick Poets*, London: A.M[athewes] for W. Lee, 1625

Holyday, Barten, *All Horace His Lyrics, or His Four Bookes of Odes, and His Book of Epodes*, London: H. Herringman, 1653

Lytton, Edward Bulwer, Lord, *The Odes and Epodes of Horace: A Metrical Translation*, Edinburgh: Blackwood, 1869

Marsh, Edward, *The Odes of Horace*, London: Macmillan, 1941

Michie, James, *The Odes of Horace*, New York: Orion Press, 1963; London: Rupert Hart-Davis, 1964

Rider, Henry, *All the Odes and Epodes of Horace, Translated into English Verse*, London: J. Haviland for R. Rider, 1638

Shepherd, W.G., *The Complete Odes and Epodes*, Harmondsworth and New York: Penguin, 1983

Smart, Christopher, *The Works of Horace Translated into Verse, with a Prose Interpretation*, 4 vols, London: W. Flexney, 1767

Few collections of lyrical poetry have exerted a more enduring influence than the odes of Horace. The odes combine formal discipline with sensitivity and imagination. The poet responds to contemporary events, both public and private. Whether discussing the achievement of Augustus or the pleasures of wine, they are characterized by both their lucidity and their density of meaning, and by the remarkable adroitness with which they exploit the flexible word order of Latin.

Individual odes by Horace were early translated by poets such as Sidney and Campion, but the first substantial collection was that of ASHMORE (1621), which offers versions of 15 odes and one epode (II). Using mostly heroic couplets, Ashmore has many moments of flatness, but can on occasion (as in his version of II.14) achieve a certain lapidary dignity. He attempts fidelity of meaning and, largely speaking, resists addition.

Translating more poems than Ashmore (36 odes, 4 epodes), Sir Thomas HAWKINS (1625) concentrates, as he tells us, on "the morall, and serious *Odes*", in preference to Horace's "wanton and looser straines" (Sig.A1 verso). Employing both iambic pentameters and tetrameters, Hawkins is generally doggedly faithful. The demands of metre and rhyme frequently force him into awkwardness and infelicity, however.

The first complete version (save for epodes VIII and XII, omitted on the grounds of their alleged obscenity) of the odes and epodes was that of Henry RIDER (1638). Rider is serious and scholarly (his Dedicatory Letter and Address to the reader are worth reading for his thoughts on the translation of Horace), but no poet. His heroic couplets are often very prosy. Sheer clumsiness of expression is too frequent; there is little sense here of Horace's sophistication.

Nor, indeed, is such sophistication to be found echoed in the work of Barten HOLYDAY (1653) – assuming the collection to be his (there is some doubt as to the authorship). But Holyday's versions do differ in one important respect from those of his predecessors. His is the first serious attempt to imitate Horace's metrical variety (one exception is Ashmore's translation of I.1). Holyday's scholarship was real enough, but successfully to have imitated Horace's own metres would have required poetic gifts far beyond any he possessed. The results are crabbed at best, and almost incomprehensible at worst.

The collection published under the name of BROME (1666) is made up of translations by a number of contemporaries and predecessors (see Brooks and Cameron below), including those of Sir Richard FANSHAWE (first published in 1652). Fanshawe's versions are often somewhat free, and he is prone to elaborate Horace's imagery; but he gives us something of Horace's stylistic and metrical variety, and produces genuine English poems (eg. I.8, I.34, Epode II). Fanshawe was clearly deeply in sympathy with Horace. Brome's collection also includes accomplished versions of IV. 2 and I. 5 by Abraham COWLEY. Much else in his collection is banal.

The version by Thomas CREECH (1684) offers fidelity, and a certain energy of rhythm and diction, but is deficient in tonal variety and elegance.

The 18th century's admiration for Horace generally found more convincing poetic fulfilment in imitation and adaptation than in translation.

The Horace of FRANCIS (1743–46) has poise and assurance, sometimes achieved at the cost of rather florid expansion. Still, Francis convincingly makes Horace speak the poetic language of the 1740s.

The verse translation by SMART (1767) followed his prose version of 1756, which had a considerable commercial success, and remains very readable. In verse, Smart's Horace has a sprightliness of manner and urbanity of tone, to some extent achieved by substantial expansion and addition. Smart is alert to the metrical variety of his original, and his version of I. 38 – described as "in the original metre exactly" – is a remarkable and intriguing piece.

In the 19th century the translation of Horace seems almost to have become a leisure-time activity for dons and clerics, and few of the products are of enduring interest. Two do, though, deserve continuing attention. John CONINGTON (1863), first Corpus Professor of Latin at Oxford, is generally at his best (eg. II.7, II.9) in the political and public poems.

The Horace of Edward Bulwer-Lytton, Lord LYTTON (1869) is unduly neglected, an intelligent and assured performance. In unrhymed approximations to the Sapphic and Alcaic metres, accompanied by interesting annotations, many of his versions offer meticulous fidelity in an idiosyncratic idiom which makes unusually persuasive use of inversion.

Translations of Horace in the 20th century were numerous. An attractive ease and elegance of expression are achieved in the version of the odes by MARSH (1941), though at the cost of many omissions and additions. Marsh's own preface declares his preference for "expressive laxity" over "a forced and wooden correctitude". In a manner now decidedly old-fashioned, but still attractive, Marsh produced a version which is, at any rate, pleasurably readable.

James MICHIE (1963) achieves an attractive lucidity of manner, though the search for rhymes sometimes leads to a certain verbosity which is decidedly un-Horatian.

W.G. SHEPHERD (1983) makes no use of rhyme and is more concise than most English translators of these poems. He also sustains a greater tonal variety than is often found in English Horaces. He creates some striking effects by the juxtaposition of different levels of diction – though it must be said that such effects do not always have specifically Horatian originals.

Many of the best translations of individual poems by Horace are not to be found in these collections, but scattered amongst the pages of numerous other volumes. The reader who wishes to become familiar with the history of English translation of the odes will certainly need to know, for example, Milton's version of I. 5, Ezra Pound's of 1. 31, those by Robert Herrick and Basil Bunting of II. 14, by Ben Jonson of IV.1, among many others. A representative sampling of the range of English translations can be found in *Horace in English*, edited by Carne-Ross and Haynes.

GLYN PURSGLOVE

Further Reading

Brink, C.O., *Horace on Poetry*, Cambridge: Cambridge University Press, 3 vols, 1963–82 (the second volume of this definitive work includes the text of the *Ars poetica* with full commentary)

Brooks, Harold F., "Contributors to Brome's Horace", *Notes and Queries*, 174 (1938) pp. 200–01

Cameron, W.J., "Brome's 'Horace' 1666 and 1671", *Notes and Queries*, 202 (1957) pp. 70–71

Carne-Ross, D.S. and Kenneth Haynes (editors), *Horace in English*, Harmondsworth: Penguin, 1996

Edden, Valerie, "'The Best of Lyrick Poets'" in *Horace*, edited by C.D.N. Costa, London: Routledge and Kegan Paul, 1973

Goad, Caroline, *Horace in the Literature of the Eighteenth Century*, New Haven, Connecticut: Yale University Press, 1918

Pursglove, Glyn, "'But Horace, Sir, was Delicate, was Nice'", *The Many Review*, 5 (1987) pp. 16–23

Sharbo, Arthur (editor), *Christopher Smart's Verse Translation of Horace's "Odes": Text and Introduction*, Victoria, British Columbia: University of Victoria, 1979

Storrs, Sir Ronald (editor), *Ad Pyrrham: A Polyglot Collection of Translations of Horace's Ode to Pyrrha, Book I, Ode 5*, London: Oxford University Press, 1959

The Art of Poetry

Ars poetica, between 23 and 14 BC

Composed by Horace towards the end of his life at some time between 23 and 14 BC, his *Ars poetica*, the third and final poem in his second book of *Epistles* and addressed to the uncertainly identified Piso and his son, has for over two millennia been one of the most frequently read works on poetics surviving from antiquity. Less profound than Aristotle's *Poetics*, but less didactic than the treatises of Donatus that date from the 4th century AD, it discusses, in just 476 lines, the nature of the poet and of poetry. The approach is mainly generic, presenting the rules and conventions of the various sorts of literature. Many of the recommendations are couched in the negative, as injunctions about what to avoid. The first readers of the *Ars poetica* may well have enjoyed Horace's satiric thrusts, as much as the urbane, allusive and epigrammatic style in a work that is in fact only ostensibly addressed to 'prentice poets, though they can certainly learn a lot from it.

Translations

Byron, Lord, *Hints from Horace* (written 1811) in *The Complete Poetical Works*, vol. 1, edited by J.J. McGann, Oxford: Clarendon Press, 1990, pp. 288–318

Carne-Ross, D.S. and Kenneth Haynes (editors), *Horace in English*, with an introduction, Harmondsworth: Penguin, 1996

Conington, John, *Art of Poetry*, in *The Satires, Epistles and the Art of Poetry of Horace*, London: Bell and Daldy, 1870

Creech, Thomas, *Ars poetica*, in his *The Odes, Satyrs and Epistles of Horace*, London: Jacob Tonson, 1684; and many subsequent editions

Drant, Thomas, *Horace, His Arte of Poetrie, Pistles and Satyrs*, London: Thomas Marshe, 1567; facsimile edition, Delmar, New York: Scholars' Facsimiles, 1972

Elizabeth I, Queen of England, (lines 1–178), 1598 manuscript in *The Poems of Queen Elizabeth I*, edited by Leicester Bradley, Providence, Rhode Island: Brown University Press, 1964

Francis, Philip, *The Art of Poetry*, in his *A Poetical Translation of the Works of Horace*, London: A. Millar, 4 vols, 1746

Jonson, Ben, *Horace, His Art of Poetry (1640)*, Amsterdam: Theatrum Orbis Terrarum, 1974

Oldham, John, in his *Works*, 4 vols, London: J. Hindmarsh, 1686, facsimile, Delmar, New York: Scholars' Facsimiles, 1971

Roscommon, Wentworth Dillon, 4th earl of, *Horace's Art of Poetry*, London: Henry Herringman, 1680; reprinted 1684; with *An Essay on Translated Verse*, Menston: Scolar Press, 1971

Sisson, C.H., *The Poetic Art: A Translation of Horace's "Ars poetica"*, Cheadle: Carcanet Press, 1975

In the *Ars poetica* (II, 133–34) Horace touches briefly on translation; like Cicero (in *De optimo genere oratorium*, IV, 14), he speaks out against over-scrupulous word-for-word versions, without, however, indicating what positive steps will lead to better results.

The *Art of Poetry*, like the rest of Horace's work, has regularly tempted and challenged translators in Britain (and the rest of Europe) since the Renaissance, even though most conventionally educated people could, at least until the end of the 19th century, read the relatively short text in the original Latin for themselves. Thomas DRANT, from Lincolnshire, matriculated at St John's College, Cambridge, and composed verses in Greek, Latin and English for Queen Elizabeth's progresses. He followed up his 1566 version of Horace's *Satires* by publishing a year later his translation (1567) of the *Ars poetica*, rendering Horace's hexameters as rhyming fourteeners. Queen ELIZABETH I adopted a similar meter for her partial translation (II, 1–178). This version is perhaps most remarkable as testimony to the humanistic interests that impelled her in 1598 to produce it. It is preserved in an manuscript in her own hand. The fashion had changed by 1605 when Ben JONSON chose pentameter couplets for his translation, which, however, also remained unpublished, until printed after his death in 1640.

The publication in Paris in 1674 of Boileau's *Art poétique*, which, in a key statement of French classical ideals, combined direct imitation of Horace with astringently witty and adroitly versified criticism both of developments in literature in France over the previous century and of contemporary trends, set the tone for a series of versions of the *Ars poetica* that appeared in England. Horace was not only translated, but pressed into service in the literary debates of the day. The translation (1684; first published in 1680) by Wentworth Dillon, 4th Earl of ROSCOMMON, forms part of this well-travelled gentleman's endeavours to found an English literary academy rather like those with which he had become familiar in France; the next step was to be the publication of his *Essay on Translated Verse*. Dillon significantly remarks that he thinks "it could never be more seasonable than now to lay down such rules as, if they be observed, will make men write more correctly and judge more discreetly". Despite his "veneration" for Jonson, he considers that his translation had been spoiled because subject to the twin constraints of literalness and rhyme. Declaring that, for his part, the "chief care has been to write intelligibly", Dillon produced an elegant version in blank verse.

Following close on Dillon's heels, John OLDHAM (1686) paid his respects to him, but preferred heroic couplets. A schoolmaster whose Juvenalian satiric verve was directed against the Jesuits, he discloses in his Advertisement an attitude to translation akin to that of Dryden, who appreciated Oldham's work. Taking Horace's own advice, he remarks that he has not been "over-nice in keeping to the words of the original"; the better course, he considers, has been to "avoid stiffness", for his aim is "to hit (as near as I could) the easy and familiar way of writing which is peculiar to Horace in his *Epistles* and was his proper talent above all mankind". His resolve is, moreover, to put Horace into "modern dress", not only making him speak "as if he were living now", but altering the scene from Rome to London and using English names, places and customs, "where the parallel would decently", he remarks, "give a new air to the poem, and render it more agreeable to the relish of the present day".

As well as dedicating his 1684 version, in couplets, of Horace's *Odes, Satyrs and Epistles* to the "very much esteemed John Dryden", who was said to have encouraged him to embark on an enterprise somewhat ill-suited to his personal literary bent, Thomas CREECH pays tribute to the teaching of Thomas Curgenven, by this time a schoolmaster at Sherborne, and also acknowledges his debts, in comprehension and expression, to Dillon. Best known for his versions of Lucretius, Creech states that he eschews literal translation, thinking it "better to convey down the learning of the Ancients". Though a number of editions were called for, Creech's version was superseded by that of the Revd Philip FRANCIS. He was born about 1708 and educated in Dublin, where the first part of his translation of Horace is said to have been published in 1742, to be followed by a complete version, including the *The Art of Poetry*, in London in 1746. It was reprinted many times in the 18th century and the earlier part of the 19th.

Hints from Horace, described by BYRON as "being an allusion in English verse to the Epistle 'Ad Pisones'" and intended as a sequel to *English Bards and Scotch Reviewers*, was written in spring 1811 but left unpublished for 10 years. Bare-faced cheek and self-confident satire give unexpected life to the classic. Of the numerous further translations that have not ceased to appear throughout the 19th and 20th centuries, though Horace's doctrines no longer command the respect they did in classicising times, the one dating from 1870 by John CONINGTON, the first professor of Latin at Oxford University, was particularly highly rated in its day.

Horace in English, edited by D.S. CARNE-ROSS & Kenneth HAYNES, with an interesting introduction and specimens of translations from the Renaissance to the present, contains a fascinating "version" of the *Ars Poetica* made up of samples from translations from Jonson to C.H. SISSON (1975).

The older versions of the *Art of Poetry* in English are probably more instructive than modern ones, as Horace was a livelier issue at the time of their production.

CHRISTOPHER SMITH

Ödön von Horváth 1901–1938

Austro-Hungarian dramatist and novelist

Biography

Born in Fiume (Rijeka), 9 December 1901, of a Czech-German mother and a Hungarian father. He was a child in Budapest, a young student in Munich, spoke many languages, and had to work to achieve complete proficiency in one. Like many other Austro-Hungarians, he came into his artistic own in Berlin, in the mid-1920s. Here he lived out the artistic and political ferment of the Weimar Republic, revelling in a world of actresses, circus performers and the city's lowlife. His writing of short sketches and plays was constructed from the observation of human types and events. His fame initially resulted from a performance of *Italian Night* (1930), a snapshot of the evils and dangers of the rising Nazi party and of society's blindness to them. *Tales of the Vienna Woods* (1931) attacked the underside of proverbial Viennese charm. For these satires he won a contract with Ullstein, a significant publishing house, and the Kleist Prize for young writers, awarded by their peers. He was taken up by prominent literary circles in Berlin and, because of this and his activities with the League for Human Rights, came to the unfavourable attention of the Nazi party. By 1933, Horváth's plays could no longer be performed in Germany, nor were they accepted by any important theatre in Vienna. Of the nine plays he wrote after this, only one was published before his emigration to Zürich in 1934. In 1936–37, he wrote two novels, *Ein Kind unserer Zeit* (*A Child of Our Time*) and *Jugend ohne Gott* (*Youth Without God*), which enjoyed great success, both in German and in eight other languages, including English. Immediately after Hitler's invasion of Austria on 14 March 1938, Horváth made his way to Amsterdam and then to Paris. In June 1938 he was killed in a storm by the branch of a falling tree.

Translations

Selections of Plays

Ketels, Violet B., Paul Foster and Richard Dixon, and Richard Downey, *Four Plays by Ödön von Horváth*, New York: PAJ Publications, 1986 (contains *Kasimir and Karoline*, *Faith, Hope and Charity*, *Figaro Gets a Divorce*, *Judgment Day*)

Plays

Geschichten aus dem Wiener Wald, 1931

Hampton, Christopher, *Tales from the Vienna Woods*, London: Faber, 1977

Kasimir und Karoline, 1931

Ketels, Violet B., *Kasimir and Karoline* in *Four Plays by Ödön von Horváth*, translated by Ketels *et al.*, 1986

Glaube, Liebe, Hoffnung, 1932

Foster, Paul and Richard Dixon, *Faith, Hope and Charity* in *Four Plays by Ödön von Horváth*, translated by Ketels *et al.*, 1986

Hampton, Christopher, *Faith, Hope and Charity*, London and Boston: Faber, 1989

Don Juan kommt aus dem Krieg, 1936

Hampton, Christopher, *Don Juan Comes Back from the War* in *Don Juan Comes Back from the War / Figaro Gets Divorced: Two Plays by Ödön von Horváth*, translated by Hampton and Ian Huish, Bath: Absolute Press, 1991

Figaro lässt sich scheiden, 1936

Downey, Roger, *Figaro Gets a Divorce* in *Four Plays by Ödön von Horváth*, translated by Ketels *et al.*, 1986

Huish, Ian, *Figaro Gets Divorced* in *Don Juan Comes Back from the War / Figaro Gets Divorced: Two Plays by Ödön von Horváth*, translated by Hampton and Huish, Bath: Absolute Press, 1991

Novels

Zeitalter der Fische, 1953 (*Jugend Ohne Gott*, 1936, and *Ein Kind unserer Zeit*, 1937)

Wills, Thomas R., *The Age of the Fish*, New York: Dial Press, 1939

Most critics and historians rank Ödön von Horváth with Bertolt Brecht; Peter Handke vociferously declared him better. The difference between the two is that where Brecht is ideological and schematic, Horváth is ironic and detailed. In many of his plays, he revived and re-cast the *Volksstück*, an 18th-century theatrical genre practised in Vienna throughout the 19th century. It is a satirical form, aimed at contemporary foibles and fashions of the people, and generally contains a strong musical element. For Schikaneder, this music was Mozart's *Magic Flute*; for Horváth, one might say it was language. His characters are the little people, constantly in danger of losing their toe-hold in society, remarkable chiefly for their stupidity. They speak regional dialects, raddled and vitiated by the semi-educated jargon of pretentious underlings.

Knowledge of Horváth's works survives in roundabout ways. In his lifetime, he was deprived of an audience by political silencing and exile. The war threatened to extinguish the writing entirely, so much of it having gone unpublished. Today, it is available in a collection of four volumes of drama, verse, novels, essays, and letters. Winston gives an illuminating chronology of the rebirth of interest in Horváth after World War II, which demonstrates his importance to 20th-century letters.

Horváth's plays allude to matters as diverse as Asian mythologies, 20th-century laws and 18th-century librettos. The subtext, a densely felted fabric, is contained in lines delivered in provincial dialect or urban argot, adulterated with prefabricated, half-understood political or bureaucratic jargon meant to make the speaker sound educated. Everything means something else, something additional; each sentence stands for a lesson in the decay of a social structure or an oration on the human potential for unteachability. Clearly, all talk of translating Horváth cuts straight to the discussion of language-and-culture that is one of the central topics of today's translation theory.

Existing translations of Horváth's work are not plentiful. The earliest one, from 1939, is of the novels, whose language is more lyrical and less loaded than that of the plays. And yet it is not satisfactory: where the German is spare and almost artificially simple, the English in WILLS (1939), *The Age of the Fish*, is choppy, often bizarre, and shows no responsiveness to the mood and style of the original. This version has gone through eight printings, the most recent one in 1978. For many years it was the only English witness to Horváth's work.

One might expect that Horváth's plays would fare better, as they were often translated with an eye to performance. Some translations call themselves adaptations, but this may be a euphemistic cover for incompetence; errors stemming from failure to understand abound. Others are flat because they are unable to find language for a German that expresses distinctions of class that English-speaking culture does not recognize. Because of this difficulty, many translators have chosen a neutral language to navigate the plays. Christopher Hampton's lively, modern speech is a notable exception, in his *Tales from the Vienna Woods* (1977); *Faith, Hope and Charity* (1989); and *Don Juan Comes Back from the War* (1991). But this reduces the plays to paraphrasable plots; it does not transmit the living works that still influence German writers.

Jarka's analysis of some of Horváth's translations and his account of their reception history makes it clear that work remains to be done. Existing Horváth scholarship in English has nothing to do with an aesthetic response. The gap that prevents English-speaking audiences from experiencing what Horváth created is cultural as much as linguistic. Closing it calls for informed and inspired translation, inspired and knowledgeable acting. Finally, perhaps a great rapprochement could be achieved by staging individual performances in a festival. Thus, one might achieve with film, music, and visual art some of what language strives to attain.

GERTRUD GRAUBART CHAMPE

Further Reading

Huish, Ian, *Horváth: A Study*, London: Heinemann, and Totowa, New Jersey: Rowman and Littlefield, 1980
Jarka, Horst, "Horváth's Work in the United States", *Publications of the Institute of Germanic Studies*, University of London, 43 (1989) pp. 81–94
Winston, Krishna, *Horváth Studies: Close Readings of Six Plays (1926–1931)*, Bern: Peter Lang, 1977
Winston, Krishna, "Ödön von Horváth: A Man for this Season", *Massachusetts Review*, 19 (1978) pp. 169–80

Bohumil Hrabal 1914–1997

Czech novelist and short-story writer

Biography

Born in Brno-Židenice, 28 March 1914; he grew up in the breweries of which his father was manager. He began a law degree in Prague but was prevented from completing it by World War II, working instead at Kostomlaty railway station (near Nymburk).

Hrabal completed his law studies after the war but never practised. After the Communist take-over in 1948 he worked in a series of manual jobs: as a foundry-man in the steel town of Kladno, a waste-paper baler in Prague and a stagehand, among other things. A period of literary success in the 1960s was followed by difficult years after 1968–69 when he could not be published. He began to be published again in heavily edited form after police pressure had led to his making slight concessions to the regime, including a partly bogus avowal of "support" for Socialism and his signature of the so-called "Anti-Charter" opposing the ideas of Charter 77. Nevertheless most of Hrabal's finest work remained in manuscript or was published abroad in the 1970s and 1980s. Hrabal never lost his home readership, however, and gradually his important newer books began to be issued in Prague to great acclaim, e.g., *Obsluhoval jsem anglického krále* (albeit in a restricted edition at that time – 1980). Three volumes of memoirs, written as if from his wife's point of view, were published in the late 1980s, first in Canada, then at home. He was being treated in hospital for arthritis when he died, on 3 February 1997, as the result of a fall from the fifth floor while trying, according to an obituarist, to feed the birds.

Translations

Novels

Taneční hodiny pro starší a pokročilé, 1964
Heim, Michael Henry, *Dancing Lessons for the Advanced in Age*, New York: Harcourt Brace, 1995; London: Harvill, 1997

Ostře sledované vlaky, 1965
Pargeter, Edith, *A Close Watch on the Trains*, London: Jonathan Cape, 1968; as *Closely Watched Trains*, New York: Grove Press, 1968; as *Closely Observed Trains*, London: Sphere, 1990

Postřižiny, 1976, and *Městečko, kde se zastavil čas*, 1978
Naughton, James, *Cutting It Short and The Little Town Where Time Stood Still*, London: Abacus, and New York: Pantheon, 1993

Obsluhoval jsem anglického krále, 1980
Wilson, Paul, *I Served the King of England*, London: Chatto and Windus, and San Diego: Harcourt Brace, 1989

Příliš hlučná samota, 1980
Heim, Michael Henry, *Too Loud a Solitude*, San Diego: Harcourt Brace, 1990; London: André Deutsch, 1991

Collection of Short Stories
Heim, Michael Henry, *The Death of Mr Baltisberger*, New York: Doubleday, 1975; London: Abacus, 1990

Short Stories
Heim, Michael Henry, "Palaverers" in *This Side of Reality: Modern Czech Writing*, edited by Alexandra Büchler, revised by the translator, London: Serpent's Tail, 1996, pp. 58–67
Němcová, Jeanne W., "The World Cafeteria" in *Czech and Slovak Short Stories*, edited by Němcová, London and New York: Oxford University Press, 1967, pp. 136–49
Wilbraham, M., "A Breath of Fresh Air" in *White Stones and Fir Trees: An Anthology of Contemporary Slavic Literature*, edited by Vasa D. Mihailovich, Lewisburg, Pennsylvania: Bucknell University Press, 1977, pp. 558–67

Other Writings (texts from *Dopisy Dubence*, 1989–)
Bohac, Ilya, extracts in *Interference: The Story of Czechoslovakia in the Words of Its Writers*, edited by Peter Spafford, Cheltenham, Gloucestershire: New Clarion, 1992, pp. 141–43
Čulík, Jan and Lesley Čulík, "The Magic Flute", *Scottish Slavonic Review*, 16 (1991) pp. 7–18
Hájek, Igor, "Total Fears" (abridged), *Times Literary Supplement*, (24 May 1991) pp. 5–6
Kussi, Peter, "The Magic Flute" in *Good-Bye Samizdat: Twenty Years of Czechoslovak Underground Writing*, edited by Marketa Goetz-Stankiewicz, Evanston, Illinois: Northwestern University Press, 1992, pp. 130–34
Kussi, Peter, "The Magic Flute" in *Prague: a Traveler's Literary Companion*, San Francisco: Whereabouts Press, 1995, pp. 134–39
Naughton, James, "Meshuga stunde" in *Storm*, edited by Joanna Labon, 1 (1991) pp. 47–59
Naughton, James, "The White Horse" in *Cape 2: America*, edited by Nicholas Pearson, London, 1992(?), pp. 44–48
Naughton, James, *Total Fears: Letters to Dubenka*, Prague: Twisted Spoon Press, 1998 (contains "The Magic Flute", "Public Suicide", "A Few Sentences", "The White Horse", "November Hurricane", "Meshuge Stunde", "A Pity We Didn't Burn to Death Instead", "Total Fears", "The Rosenkavalier")

Screenplay
Ostře sledované vlaky, with Jiří Menzel, 1965
Holzbecher, Josef, *Closely Observed Trains: A Film*, London: Lorimer, 1971

Many of the characters and events in Bohumil Hrabal's prose are drawn from his life, although the reader should be careful not to see his work as too literally autobiographical. Hrabal's mature prose is written in a language so uniquely his own that the Czechs call it "Hrabalese": *hrabalština*. This language is partly derived from Hrabal's literary stance as a spontaneous oral story-teller, or better, 'palaverer' (in Czech *pábitel*) – the common man who has "seen a thing or two" and wishes to impart his experience at exuberant, entertaining length. *Pábitelství* (from the verb *pábit*, first used as a semi-nonsense or nonce word by the late 19th-century poet Vrchlický to describe his excessive smoking) has also come to mean *any* kind of obsessive creative activity, especially that which relieves and liberates the individual from the greyness of life (cf. the story "Pábitelé" ("Palaverers") itself). The English word "palavering" is only the verbal expression of this mad creativity, but *pábitelství* can take many forms.

Hrabal's novels are thus often constructed as continuous blocks of prose made up of greatly extended, digressive sentences, as though the story-teller is only occasionally pausing for breath (apparently this has much to do with the way Hrabal's own Uncle Pepin used to relate his own splendid stories). Hrabal also likes to adopt the voice of the "common man", doing so with at times prodigious use of colloquialisms, slang and dialect. At the same time he is a modernist and uses the devices of modernism: stream of consciousness (in the form of spontaneous narrative flow), elements of surrealism, literary collage and so forth. His prose is unashamedly poetic and carefully (but swiftly) crafted. Naturally, reproducing this linguistic and textual complexity and sense of endlessly flowing, improvised oral spontaneity in English is extremely challenging, and the translators are often more successful where Hrabal is syntactically and lexically least Hrabalesque, in his more plainly composed narratives or sections of text.

In *Dancing Lessons for the Advanced in Age*, Michael Henry HEIM (1995) has, for the most part, produced a remarkably successful translation of a particularly problematic book. The problem lies in the fact that the entire text (about 17,000 words in Czech) is one endless, unbroken sentence – a continuous flow of association and digression (sometimes compared with Molly Bloom's monologue in Joyce's *Ulysses*). That said, the book should not read as a deliberately difficult or consciously literary text for, in a sense, it is the most concentrated expression of Hrabal's *pábitelství*: the Uncle Pepin-like narrator babbles on and on without a break as he tries to impress a young beauty. Heim faithfully reproduces this verbal torrent in his translation without losing the reader, or bewildering him more than the text calls for. Heim's translation does, however, have two important flaws. Firstly, the title in Czech literally means "Dancing Lessons for the Older and more Advanced" which clearly has connotations over and above the English title. Secondly, and perhaps more seriously, there is a complete mistranslation in the very first line of the English edition. Hrabal's "Tak jako za vámi, slečno, tak jsem nejraději chodíval za krásnejma slečnama ke kostelu ..." is rendered as: "Just like I come here to see you, young ladies, I used to go to church to see my beauties ..." The trouble is that the narrator is addressing *one* woman ("slečno" is a vocative singular – roughly "Miss"), not several. Heim (or his editor) repeats the mistake at the end of the book and then compounds it by removing the short (one-page) passage that concludes the work – the passage beginning: "The sun set and Miss Kamila stood on the ladder, ate cherries, and smiled down at the old man who brought her roses every day ..." Hrabal himself has said that this passage is part of the book and it is included in all modern editions, including Hrabal's collected works. Although Heim's translation is in most other respects admirable this is a serious omission and needs both acknowledgement and justification.

In *Closely Observed Trains* (translation first published 1968 as *A Close Watch on the Trains*) Edith PARGETER handles the delicate balance between staying faithful to the original text and rendering it in a natural and convincing English with considerable skill. Her task is perhaps slightly easier than that facing some of the later translators of Hrabal's work, as the novel is generally more conventional in form and language than most of his other works. Nevertheless his typical long, digressive sentences still wind their way through the narrative. Pargeter, as published (and we shall not claim to know the possible role of publishing editors in this process), shares with Wilson and Heim the tendency to break up the sentences and to paragraph the text in a more conventional way, but her shifts of punctuation or of the order of clauses in a sentence are less noticeable because of the book's greater stylistic orthodoxy. In one or two places her rendition of dialogue sounds a little stilted, but on the whole the book is translated with the care that Pargeter brought to all her translations from Czech.

The Death of Mr Baltisberger: Michael Henry HEIM (1975) has produced a translation of these early Hrabal stories with an air of possible haste, unfortunately losing much of their character. In Heim's translation, as with Wilson's, it is precisely the vital quality of *pábitelství* that is missing. For example, Heim will "flatten out" a colourful or unusual metaphor such as "Vona holka byla po sebevraždě jak metař po bagu" ("that girl went after suicide like a street-sweeper after a fag-end") into the ordinary "that girl has suicide on the brain." The opening paragraph of "The Notary" – a description of a stained-glass window – reads like a rather breathless summary of the loving and elaborate description of the window in the Czech. Heim revised the important story "Pábitelé" ("Palaverers") for the 1996 anthology *This Side of Reality*, but the changes are very small and the text is only marginally more free-flowing.

The two novels *Cutting It Short* and *The Little Town Where Time Stood Still* are loosely autobiographical, the second a sequel to the first. The same characters appear in both (at different stages of their lives), although the narrative voice changes from that of Hrabal's mother to that of the young Hrabal himself. Both are written in typical Hrabal style; each chapter, in effect, is one long paragraph. James NAUGHTON (1993) is the only one of Hrabal's translators who exactly reproduces this typical manner: Heim, Wilson and Pargeter all break up their respective texts, significantly altering the texture of Hrabal's prose. On the other hand, the dogged literalness and insistence on close syntactic and lexical tracking of Naughton's approach arguably has its own pitfalls, like any approach to Hrabal translation. Naughton does capture the novels' changes in tone from a lyrical, slightly surreal beauty to low comedy or poignancy and melancholy. The most contentious aspect of Naughton's translation, for reviewers, was his decision to reproduce the effect of Uncle Pepin's own Moravian dialect by giving him a diluted broad Scots accent. Inevitably this raises an old problem of reader perception and translation theory: does Uncle Pepin's Haná dialect have the same connotations for the Czech reader as a Scottish accent does for the English (or, for that matter, Scottish) reader, and how should one deal with non-standard (e.g., regional), and non-neutral, especially colloquial registers when translating?

Paul WILSON (1989) is well known for his fine work on Václav Havel's letters and essays and his translations of Josef Škvorecký's popular novels. Wilson seems much less comfortable with Hrabal's narrative manner, however, and (perhaps with his publishers' encouragement) he appears to have ended up imposing on the novel *I Served the King of England* a style slightly different from that in which it was written. The result is highly readable and enjoyable but not always as faithful to Hrabal as it might be. As usual the most serious structural change is the breaking up of free-flowing prose into normal paragraphs and the forcing of sometimes quite drastic breaks in the sentence flow. As a result the book reads more like a conventional narrative than the imaginative and stylistically unusual prose work it really is. Another silent change, for which Wilson gives no justification, is the omission of the brief formulaic sentences that open and close every chapter in the source text. These sentences ("Listen carefully to what I'm about to tell you" and "Is that enough for you? I'll finish at that for today") are clearly part of Hrabal's story-teller stance and their omission is inexplicable. A number of other small omissions and flattenings of sense weaken the translation, notably the important philosophizing by the narrator on the subject of death and beauty (p. 228) has been simplified and consequently muddled.

Too Loud a Solitude (1990) is the better of HEIM's two earlier translations from Hrabal. The problem of evaluating the translation is complicated by the fact that several slightly different manuscripts of the novel were in circulation for some time before a definitive version was settled upon. Heim's published translation has a different ending from the text now included in Hrabal's collected works. That aside, Heim's translation is certainly enjoyable and does not stray too far from the spirit of Hrabal's original. There are, however, some arguably serious mistakes in the detail, and in one or two places this can be slightly confusing. On the first page of the novel, for example, Heim's "I am a jug filled with water both magic and plain" both is unclear in itself and loses the necessary reference to Czech folklore and religion of the water living and dead (*živá a mrtvá voda*), *both* of which have magic properties; similarly, *Popelčin oříšek* ("Cinderella's nutshell") is definitely not "Aladdin's lamp", and so on. There are also a few points where phrases and short sentences are missing, but this could, in fairness, be a result of manuscript variations.

Plans to publish James Naughton's complete translation of *Letters to Dubenka*, a sequence of texts experimenting further with spontaneous writing and focusing *inter alia* on the events around 1989, have so far not been fulfilled; only a couple of the letters have appeared in periodicals. Short extracts by other translators have also been published in periodicals and anthologies.

JAMES PARTRIDGE

Further Reading

Gibian, George, "The Haircutting" and "I Waited on the King of England" in *Czech Literature since 1956: A Symposium*, edited by William E. Harkins and Paul I. Trensky, New York: Bohemica, 1980

Hrabik-Samal, Mary, "Case Study in the Problem of Czech–English Translation with Special References to the Works of Bohumil Hrabal" in *Varieties of Czech: Studies in Czech Sociolinguistics*, edited by Eva Eckert, Amsterdam: Rodopi, 1993

Roth, Susanne, *Laute Einsamkeit und bitteres Glück: Zur poetischen Welt von Bohumil Hrabals Prosa*, Bern and New York: Peter Lang, 1986 [Czech edition, updated]

Roth, Susanne, "The Reception of Bohumil Hrabal in Czechoslovakia and in the 'West'", *Czechoslovak and Central European Journal*, 1 (1992)

Rothová, Susanne, *Hlučná samota a hořké štěstí Bohumila Hrabala*, Prague: Pražská imaginace, 1993

Hsin Ch'i-chi

See Xin Qiji

Hsueh-Ch'in

See The Dream of the Red Chamber

Peter Huchel 1903–1981

German poet

Biography

Born 3 April 1903 in Lichterfelde, a suburb of Berlin, into a middle-class family, and he lived mainly in rural Brandenburg. He studied philosophy at university in Germany and Austria, and spent some time in France working as a farm labourer and writing poetry. In World War II he served in the German army and was a prisoner-of-war in the USSR. He was an artistic programme director for East Berlin radio until 1948, and from 1949 to 1962 editor of *Sinn und Form*, the foremost GDR literary magazine, maintaining there, however, an independent policy. The poetry collection, *Gedichte*, had appeared in 1948. He lost his editorship in 1962 on account of his liberalism, went to live in Potsdam, and was allowed to leave East Germany in 1971. His second collection, *Chausseen, Chausseen* [Roads, Roads] (1963) had been published only in West Germany, where the third and fourth were also brought out (*Gezählte Tage* [Numbered Days] and *Die neunte Stunde* [The Ninth Hour], 1972 and 1979 respectively) and where he settled finally. Between 1972 and 1977, Huchel travelled in the UK and other countries, giving readings of his poems, until his health failed. His lyric themes are conveyed through description and images drawn in the early poems from nature and religion; later the lyrical register became more modern and topical. He died in Staufen, near Freiburg, 30 April 1981.

Translations

Selections of Poetry

Hamburger, Michael, *Selected Poems*, Cheadle, Cheshire: Carcanet, 1974 (9 poems from *Chausseen, Chausseen* and 22 from *Gezählte Tage*)

Hamburger, Michael, *The Garden of Theophrastus and Other Poems*, Manchester: Carcanet, and Dublin: Raven Arts Press, 1983 (contains 4 poems from *Gedichte*; 22 from *Chausseen, Chausseen*, 23 from *Gezählte Tage*, and all 37 from *Die neunte Stunde*)

Anthologies of Poetry

Hamburger, Michael and Christopher Middleton (translators and editors), *Modern German Poetry 1910–1960: An Anthology with Verse Translations*, London: MacGibbon and Kee, and New York: Grove Press, 1962

Hamburger, Michael (editor), *East German Poetry: An Anthology*, Cheadle, Cheshire: Carcanet, 1972; New York: Dutton, 1973 (includes 16 poems from *Chausseen, Chausseen*, of which 9 are translated by Hamburger, 6 by Christopher Levinson, 1 by Christopher Middleton)

Schwebell, Gertrude Clorius, *Contemporary German Poetry: An Anthology*, New York: New Directions, 1964

Peter Huchel's reputation as one of the truly outstanding German lyric poets in the second half of the 20th century rests essentially on four slim volumes of verse published sparingly over a lifetime of writing. The translating endeavours of Michael HAMBURGER, friend and fellow poet, have ensured that the bulk of Huchel's poetry is available to English-speaking readers. Already back in 1955 the briefest acknowledgement of Huchel's poetic talent had been made in the *Times Literary Supplement*, but critical awareness and appreciation seriously began only in the 1960s. It was fairly late on in his life then, that he came to the attention of the English-speaking world – and arguably as much for political as poetical reasons.

Huchel was 59 when the East German state forced him to resign in 1962 the editorship of the journal *Sinn und Form*, which he had built up from its inception in 1949 into an internationally recognized literary organ, but which had incurred the displeasure of the cultural functionaries for its too liberal stance. Huchel was then placed under virtual house arrest and forbidden to publish in the East, so his second volume of verse, *Chausseen, Chausseen* – his first collection, *Gedichte*, had appeared in both East and West Germany at the end of the 1940s – was brought out in 1963 in West Germany. By then, individual poems were being translated and appearing in anthologies such as *Modern German Poetry 1910–1960* (HAMBURGER & MIDDLETON, 1962), and *Contemporary German Poetry* (SCHWEBELL, 1964), and in journals both sides of the Atlantic.

Not until 1971 was Huchel permitted by the East German authorities to go into exile, first to Italy and then West Germany. He was now able to travel and became known to English audiences through three visits to the British Isles and, more vitally, in terms of wider recognition, through translations. The start of the 1970s records the first substantial critical appreciation in English of the German poet (Flores, 1971), while in 1972 Huchel was represented in Michael HAMBURGER's anthology *East German Poetry*. That volume contained selections from 12 poets and included 16 poems (out of the original 48) from *Chausseen, Chausseen* (only Bobrowski and Kunert were more widely represented). Of the 16, nine were translated by Hamburger himself, six by Christopher LEVINSON and one by Christopher MIDDLETON. Hamburger readily admits to taking "a few small liberties with the sense, toning down epithets whose exact counterparts no longer pull their weight in English poetry". Thus, the (literally) "sublime" brightness in the poem "Behind the Brick Kilns" is transposed simply as "noble". The quality of such poems as "Landscape beyond Warsaw" (Hamburger), "Roads" (Hamburger), "The Pastor Reports on the Downfall of his Parish" (Levinson), reflecting memories of the war, "The Garden of Theophrastus" (Hamburger), mirroring Huchel's parlous position in East Germany at the start of the 1960s, and "Psalm" (Hamburger), dealing with the dangers of living in a nuclear age, shines through into the translations.

Two years later, in 1974, HAMBURGER produced his version of Huchel's *Selected Poems*. It might be seen as a testing of the waters, for the selection is taken from only two of the three volumes of Huchel's verse then published (ignoring *Die Sternenreuse* [The Star-Trap], 1967, which was, fundamentally, a reissue of the collection *Gedichte*), and it contains only 31 poems: nine – the same nine unchanged – from *Chausseen, Chausseen* that had appeared in *East German Poetry*; and 22 (out of the original 63) from *Gezählte Tage*. Worthy of mention – from an English perspective – is Huchel's turning to Shakespeare. Focusing on notable (significantly, tragic) characters, Huchel goes beyond the purely personal dimension of his own predicament to reflect wider topical concerns in respect of the political divisions in Germany (e.g. in "Ophelia", "Macbeth", "Middleham Castle").

As a tribute to Huchel, who died in 1980, HAMBURGER produced, nearly a decade after *Selected Poems*, an expanded collection of the German poet's verse under the title *The Garden of Theophrastus and Other Poems* (1983). Here we find a more rounded presentation of Huchel's work and worth: 86 poems, including four examples, for the first time, from Huchel's volume *Gedichte*. Hamburger felt unable to translate more from it, considering "the rhymed, metrical verse, at once close to a tradition and highly individual, of Huchel's most characteristic early poems" to be less amenable to faithful translation. The problem reveals itself in the very opening poem (and one of Huchel's best known), "The Maid": for once, English seems unable to match the compactness and density of the original German. "Paraffin lamp" becomes "oil lamp", "teats" becomes "udder" (for the sake of the rhythm); half-rhymes have to make do instead of full ones in six of the nine stanzas. But as Huchel's verse increasingly turns from regular stanza forms and rhyme to free verse, so potentially fewer become the difficulties of translation. This collection includes 22 examples from *Chausseen, Chausseen*, incorporating still the same nine translations to be found in the earlier-mentioned volumes, but now too some other excellent examples such as the sombre, contemplative Italian poem "San Michele" (with its theme of temporality) and the political "Dream in the Steel Trap". Hamburger also provides his own version of "Wei Dun and the Old Masters", which had appeared in Christopher Middleton's translation in *East German Poetry*. Similarly "The Trek", "To the Deaf Ears of Generations" and "Swans Rising", translated in *East German Poetry* by Christopher Levinson, now appear in Hamburger's own versions. The variations are slight, but here arguably more telling poetically (certainly in the last example). The *Gezählte Tage* section is the same as appeared in *Selected Poems*, with one addition – "April '63", which poetically celebrates Huchel's 60th birthday and provides, on his part, a rare glimpse of sunshine at a time of growing gloom and dislocation. Hamburger concludes *The Garden of Theophrastus and Other Poems* by translating Huchel's last volume of verse, *Die neunte Stunde* (1979), in its entirety of 37 poems. These final verses had become ever more cryptic as Huchel strove to decipher the coded messages of life to be found in nature, history and myth. Literary allusions still play their part as, in the concluding poems, with death staring him in the face, Huchel draws on the ultimate tragic figures of Lear and Hamlet ("The last word / remains unspoken, / it swims off on the backs of beavers. / Nobody knows the secret.").

The 1970s had finally brought the public recognition that Huchel deserved yet never sought, and various literary prizes were heaped upon him in these years. But Huchel was a poets' poet and a more lasting and telling testimony is the indebtedness to him as poet and inspiration so readily acknowledged by other writers – from Bobrowski to Biermann, Kirsten to Czechowski.

IAN HILTON

Further Reading

Flores, John, *Poetry in East Germany: Adjustments, Visions and Provocations 1945–70*, New Haven, Connecticut: Yale University Press, 1971, pp. 119–204

Hilton, Ian, *Peter Huchel: Plough a Lonely Furrow*, New Alyth, Blairgowrie: Lochee, 1986

Victor Hugo 1802–1885

French poet, novelist and dramatist

Biography

Born Victor-Marie Hugo in Besançon, 26 February 1802, the third son of an officer in Napoleon's army and of his royalist wife, a sea-captain's daughter from Nantes, Brittany. As Victor's father served in the imperial campaigns, his wife and children followed, living in Italy (1805–08), then in Paris for a couple of years, then in Spain (1811–12). When the parents separated in about 1812, Victor settled in Paris with his mother and brothers. He attended schools there and later, irregularly, the law faculty of the university. He began to attract critical attention for his poetry at an early age. He won two poetry prizes in 1818 and in 1819, with his brothers, founded a literary review, the *Conservateur littéraire*. He published his first book of poetry, *Odes et poésies diverses*, in 1822 and was awarded a small pension by Louis XVIII. He married Adèle Foucher in October 1822 (five children). Hugo's first novel, *Han d'Islande* (*Hans of Iceland*), appeared in 1823. He was moving in romantic circles during the 1820s, writing prodigiously and becoming leader of the romantic movement in France; the preface to his unwieldy verse drama *Cromwell* (1827) was a manifesto of the new literature.

Hugo achieved wide success in the 1830s, particularly after the sensational first performances of his iconoclastic and innovative verse drama *Hernani* in 1830 and the publication of his historical novel *Notre-Dame de Paris* (*The Hunchback of Notre-Dame*) in 1831. Hugo wrote several volumes of poems and a number of important plays during this period. It was when she was performing in one of the latter, the prose drama *Lucrèce Borgia*, that in 1833 Hugo met the actress Juliette Drouet and began what was to be a 50-year liaison. He travelled to Germany, Belgium and Switzerland during the late 1830s.

Hugo was elected to the Académie Française in 1841 and ennobled as Vicomte Hugo in 1845. After the death by drowning of his eldest daughter Leopoldine, in September 1843, Hugo had become deeply depressed; in addition, his 1843 play *Les Burgraves* (*The Burgraves*) had not been been a success – the day of romantic drama was past. He published very little for the following decade, involving himself instead in political life. Earlier he had been a legitimist, then a liberal monarchist; now he was on the side of social and political reform. He founded a newspaper, *L'Événement* (later *L'Événement du peuple*), in 1848. Following the Revolution of 1848 he was elected a deputy for Paris in the Constituent Assembly (1849), and later became a member of the Legislative Assembly of the Second Republic. After Louis Napoleon's coup d'état of 1851 and the establishment in 1852 of the Second Empire, which Hugo had opposed, he spent nearly 20 years in exile, first in Belgium, then in Jersey and last in Guernsey, where he lived with Juliette Drouot. Hugo wrote two major collections of poetry in exile: *Les Châtiments,* 1853, a book of satirical verse targeting Napoleon III, and *Les Contemplations* (1856), a volume of lyrics that included an elegy for his dead daughter. In the late 1850s he started work again on his novel *Les Misérables*, begun in the 1840s. It was eventually published in 1862 to critical and popular acclaim and made Hugo a national hero.

Adèle Hugo died in 1868. In 1870, after the fall of the Second Empire, Hugo returned to France. In 1871 he became for a short time a deputy in the National Assembly. He was defeated in the 1872 election because of his sympathy for the supporters of the Paris Commune of 1871. He published his last major work, the novel *Quatre-vingt-treize* (*Ninety-Three*) in 1873. He was elected to the Senate of the Third Republic in 1876 but was not active politically after this time. He divided his last years between Guernsey and Paris, writing very little as his health declined. Juliette Drouet died in 1883. Hugo died in Paris, 22 May 1885. He was given a national funeral and interred in the Pantheon.

Novels

Translations

Han d'Islande, 1823

Alger, A. Langdon, *Hans of Iceland*, London: Routledge, 1897

Anonymous, *Hans of Iceland*, London: J. Robins, 1825

Aungle, K., *Han of Iceland*, London: Ward Lock, 1888

Campbell, Gilbert, *The Outlaw of Iceland*, London: Ward and Downey, 1885

Bug-Jargal, 1826
Anonymous, *The Noble Rival; or, The Prince of Congo*, London: George Peirce, 1845
Wilbour, Charles E., *Jargal*, New York: Carleton, 1866

Le Dernier Jour d'un condamné, 1829
Hesketh-Fleetwood, Sir Peter, *The Last Days of a Condemned*, London: Smith Elder, 1840
Reynolds, George W.M., *The Last Day of a Condemned*, London: George Henderson, 1840
Woollen, Geoff, *The Last Day of a Condemned Man and Other Prison Writings*, Oxford and New York: Oxford University Press, 1992 (includes translations of *Claude Gueux* and 2 items from *Choses Vues*, 1887–1900)

Notre-Dame de Paris, 1831
Alger, A. Langdon, *Notre-Dame de Paris*, 2 vols, London: Sampson Low Marston, 1891
Bair, Lowell, *The Hunchback of Notre Dame*, New York: Bantam, 1956
Beckwith, J. Carroll, *The Hunchback of Notre-Dame*, London and Glasgow: Collins, 1953 (first published in *Victor Hugo, The Novels Complete and Unabridged*, 26 vols, London: Dent, 1899)
Krailsheimer, Alban, *Notre-Dame de Paris*, Oxford and New York: Oxford University Press, 1993
Shoberl, Frederic, *The Hunchback of Notre-Dame*, London: Richard Bentley, 1833
Williams, Henry L., *The Hunchback of Notre-Dame*, New York: Dick and Fitzgerald, 1862

Claude Gueux, 1834
Pyrke, Duncombe, *Capital Punishment ... Claude Gueux*, London: Robert Hardwicke, 1865

Les Misérables, 1862
Anonymous, *Les Misérables*, London: Wordsworth, 1994
Denny, Norman, *Les Misérables*, London: Folio Press, 1976; 2 vols, Harmondsworth: Penguin, 1980
Hapgood, Isabel F., *Les Misérables*, 5 vols, New York: Crowell, 1887
Wilbour, Charles E., *Les Misérables*, London: Routledge, 1887
Wraxall, Sir F.C.L., *Les Misérables*, with an introduction, 3 vols, London: Hurst and Blackett, 1862

Les Travailleurs de la mer, 1866
Anonymous, *The Toilers of the Sea*, Stroud, Gloucestershire: Alan Sutton, 1990
Campbell, Gilbert, *Workers of the Sea*, London: Ward Lock, 1887
Thomas, W. Moy, *Toilers of the Sea*, London: Low Son and Marston, 1866

L'Homme qui rit, 1869
Phillips, Bellina, *The Laughing Man*, in *The Novels, Complete and Unabridged, of Victor Hugo*, London: Dent, 1899
Steele, Mrs A.C., *By Order of the King*, London: Bradbury and Evans, 1870

Quatre-vingt-treize, 1873
Bair, Lowell, *Ninety-Three*, New York: Bantam, 1962
Benedict, F.L. and J.H. Friswell, *Ninety-Three*, London: Sampson Low, 1874
Campbell, Sir G., *Ninety-Three*, London and New York: Ward Lock, 1886

Han d'Islande (1823), Victor Hugo's first novel, presents the translator with the difficult choice of either faithfully reproducing its faults, such as the questionable authenticity of its historical and geographical setting, or of paying them as little attention as possible. In general, translators have chosen the latter course. The ANONYMOUS *Hans of Iceland* (1825) is described in the translator's preface as "a *rifaccimento* of a French romance ... ." Though a fair rendering of the story, it is a rather selective adaptation which omits a number of chapters, replacing them with its own linking text. CAMPBELL's *The Outlaw of Iceland* (1885) presents a careful translation of the integral text, and it is well attuned to the spirit of the original. AUNGLE's *Han of Iceland* (1888) is similarly faithful, though not without some awkwardness of rendering, and ALGER's *Hans of Iceland* (1897) is better.

Bug Jargal (1826) has been translated as the ANONYMOUS *The Noble Rival; or, The Prince of Congo* (1845) and by WILBOUR as *Jargal* (1866). The latter is the more accurate version, both in its grammatical and its lexical rendering of the original, and its style is more natural.

Le Dernier Jour d'un condamné (1829) is a story that presents a powerful argument against capital punishment, and its translation has sometimes been associated with a campaign against the death penalty. HESKETH-FLEETWOOD's *The Last Days of a Condemned* (1840) was published with the translator's "observations on capital punishment". Though it has some rough edges, exhibiting a number of awkward Gallicisms, it conveys Hugo's message with energy and efficiency. The same can be said of REYNOLDS's *The Last Day of a Condemned* (1840). More than a century and a half later, WOOLLEN's *The Last Day of a Condemned Man* (1992) competently conveys the text to the modern reader.

To the English-speaking reader, *Notre-Dame de Paris* (1831) is probably the best known of Hugo's novels. SHOBERL was the first to interpret the title as *The Hunchback of Notre-Dame* (1833). His translation is sound and clear, and there is no doubt that his example influenced subsequent versions. Shoberl attempts, from time to time, to allude to the medieval setting by inserting archaisms. For example, as Frollo is about to fall from the cathedral tower, the timeless remark from the crowd, "Mais il va se rompre le cou..." becomes "By'r Lady, he must break his neck". WILLIAMS's *The Hunchback of Notre-Dame* (1862) reads quite well, though in an attempt to make the language as accessible as possible, the lexical range of the original may have been diminished. ALGER's *Notre-Dame de Paris* (1891) contains a number of variations from the original sense, though they are generally justified in a clear rendering which keeps the spirit of the source. BECKWITH's *The Hunchback of Notre-Dame* (1899, 1953) combines respect for the original with a competence that has justified a number of reprints in more recent times. He observes in a translator's note, "Victor Hugo is one of the masters of literature whose themes are especially difficult to render in a foreign tongue. If translated too literally, the English becomes harsh, disconnected; if rendered into modern, well-rounded phrases, the virility, the peculiar historical accent disappear." BAIR's *The Hunchback of Notre Dame* (1956) tends towards the latter end of this spectrum. The simple and direct language, though generally appropriate, is sometimes strained. This translation displays little or no attempt to convey a period flavour, and it is apt to omit problematic phrases. KRAILSHEIMER's *Notre-Dame de Paris* (1993) is closer to the sense and spirit of the original.

Claude Gueux (1834) is another story that presents an argument against capital punishment. PYRKE's *Claude Gueux* (1865) was published at a time when the abolition of the death penalty was under consideration by the British Parliament. It conveys the force of the original with adequate handling of Hugo's distinctive style.

The length of *Les Misérables* (1862) makes translation a considerable task, and it is remarkable that WRAXALL's *Les Misérables* (1862) was published in the same year. He quotes from a letter written to him by Hugo requesting "the utmost fidelity" and continues, "My chief anxiety has been to keep myself out of sight and give the precise meaning of every word." In concluding his introduction, he observes that it is "no child's play to translate a work like *Les Misérables*". Despite these modest remarks, this is by no means too literal a translation, and the sense is competently handled. WILBOUR's *Les Misérables* (1887) was also the basis of a number of later editions. HAPGOOD's *Les Misérables* (1887) is precise and direct, using language which is easily accessible to the modern reader. It seems that successive translators of the novel in the second half of the 20th century were guided by the work of their predecessors and sought to resolve any difficulties encountered in the past. In the introduction to his *Les Misérables* (1976), DENNY refers to three previous translations, presumably those of Wraxall, Wilbour and Hapgood. One of these, perhaps Wraxall's, "a brave attempt to follow Hugo in the smallest detail, almost literally word for word", is the target of his scorn: "the result is something that is not English, not Hugo and, it seems to me, scarcely readable. It reads, in short, like a translation..." On the other hand, it is by no means evident that Denny's approach is significantly different from that of his predecessors; he continues an evolution that brings the novel more firmly within the grasp of the English-speaking reader. The same may be said of the most recent ANONYMOUS *Les Misérables* (1994).

The first translation of *Les Travailleurs de la Mer* (1866), THOMAS's *Toilers of the Sea* (1866), was still the standard version a century later and has not really been superseded. One may compare CAMPBELL's *Workers of the Sea* (1887). Even a recent ANONYMOUS *The Toilers of the Sea* (1990), despite some modifications, is recognizable as the work of Thomas.

L'Homme qui rit (1869), with its sometimes rather strange portrait of England, is not easily presented to an Anglo-Saxon audience. STEELE's *By Order of the King* (1870) is an adequate version, though prone to awkwardness, giving the impression that the translator is not quite able to cope with Hugo's style. PHILLIPS's *The Laughing Man* (1899) reads more easily, though both render "Gwynplaine fut effrayant" in the final scene as "Gwynplaine became awful".

Hugo's last novel, *Quatre-vingt-treize* (1873) presents the translator with a formidable challenge with the episode of the loose cannon, in chapters 4 and 5 of the first part. Here is the full panoply of Hugolian style, and it is a good measure of a translation to compare how well it is handled. BENEDICT & FRISWELL's *Ninety-Three* (1874) is adequate, despite a number of awkward patches. CAMPBELL's *Ninety-Three* (1886) resolves more of the difficulties. BAIR's *Ninety-Three* (1962), despite some debt to previous versions, is both secure and more accessible to the modern reader.

JOHN R. WHITTAKER

Further Reading

Grossmann, Kathryn M., *The Early Novels of Victor Hugo: Towards a Poetics of Harmony*, Geneva: Droz, 1986

Houston, John Porter, *Victor Hugo*, New York: Twayne, 1974; revised edition 1988

Maurois, André, *Olympio; ou, La Vie de Victor Hugo*, Paris: Hachette, 1954; there is more than one translation, including that by Oliver Bernard, *Victor Hugo and His World*, London: Thames and Hudson, and New York: Viking, 1966

Richardson, Joanna, *Victor Hugo*, London: Weidenfeld and Nicolson, and New York: St Martin's Press, 1976

Poetry

Hugo, who first became known as a poet, wrote verse throughout his life on subjects inspired by his private life and public events and by his opinions on religion and politics. Having attacked poetic stasis in the form of the classical alexandrine and the traditional hierarchy of registers, and ranging in the scale of his poems from the short song to the three-part cycle, Hugo renewed and enriched with unflagging energy and virtuosity the techniques and forms of French poetry: love lyric, meditation on nature, satire, elegy and epic, as well of course as verse drama. The titles of his major collections of poems are: *Odes et ballades* [Odes and Ballades], 1826; *Les Orientales* [On Oriental Themes], 1829; *Les Feuilles d'automne* [Autumn Leaves], 1831; *Les Chants du crépuscule* (*Songs of Twilight*), 1835; *Les Voix intérieures* [Inner Voices], 1837; *Les Rayons et les ombres* [Sunbeams and Shadows], 1840; *Les Châtiments* [The Reckoning], 1853; *Les Contemplations* [Poems of Contemplation], 1856; *La Légende des siècles* (*The Legend of the Centuries*), 3 series, 1859, 1877, 1883; *Les Chansons des rues et des bois* [Songs of Street and Woodland], 1865; *L'Année terrible* [The Terrible Year], 1872; *L'Art d'être grand-père* [The Art of Being a Grandfather], 1877; *Les Quatre Vents de l'esprit* [The Four Winds of the Spirit], 1881; and posthumously: *La Fin de Satan* [The End of Satan], 1886; *Toute la lyre* [The Lyre Entire], 1888–93; *Dieu* [God], 1891.

Editions

Oeuvres poétiques, 3 vols, Paris: Gallimard, 1964–74 (Éditions de la Pléiade)

La Légende des siècles, Paris: Gallimard, 1950 (Éditions de la Pléiade)

Translations

Selections

Guest, Harry, *The Distance, The Shadows: Selected Poems*, London: Anvil Press/Wildwood House, 1981

Hartley, Anthony, in *The Penguin Book of French Verse*, vol. 4, edited by Hartley, London: Penguin, 1959; 1-volume edition, 1975

Rees, William, *French Poetry, 1820–1950, with Prose Translations*, London and New York: Penguin, 1990

The rapid decline in both critical and popular appreciation of Hugo's poetry which came about shortly after his death towards the close of the 19th century has today, more than a century later, scarcely been reversed. This most prolific and grandiose of poets – the dominant voice in French verse throughout most of his exceptionally long and productive life – is still largely relegated to the status of a worthy if distant ancestor of the French literary scene who continues to live on only in the polite world of high school literature classes. This undervaluing in the French literary and academic sphere is duplicated in Anglo-American circles, where very little of his vast corpus of poetry is readily available to the English-speaking reader.

The most substantial selection of Hugo's poetry in translation into English is that of Harry GUEST (1981). His treatment of the earlier poetry is to adopt a very free, more "modern" approach, not reproducing the prosodic features of the original French, often to the complete neglect of matters such as punctuation. "Le Matin" finds the line "Et déjà dans les cieux s'unit avec l'amour" all but left out; elsewhere effects of variation of Hugo's line lengths are lost because there remains little of the contextual regularity. Guest is no doubt well advised not to attempt to force Hugo into the alien voice of *English* Romanticism, but one may wonder whether he has managed to transmit Hugo's voice through other means: there seems to be a distinct lack of passion, replaced by a much more discursive descriptiveness. However, the reticence and (intentional) prosaic qualities of many of the poems are well retained. The poem "Oceano nox" becomes, none the less, completely disfigured by the undue insertion of blanks within the lines (is this an attempt to convey the poem's concern with undulatory nothingness?) such that the structure of the Hugolian alexandrine is utterly destroyed to no obvious purpose. The major work "Tristesse d'Olympio" is included in a very free but convincing version (with fewer omissions than in other poems) displaying fine sensitivity to matters of internal balance. Hugo's most enduring collection, *Les Contemplations*, is represented by works from each of its six books, although one might feel that Guest rather overdoes the "lightness of touch" – praised in the preface – of "Mes deux filles", in which the last (French) line is rather hyperbolically made to stretch over four lines. However, the approach to poems such as "Ce que c'est que l'amour" displays more understanding of Hugo's metrical innovations. From the late verse, the comparatively well-known "Booz endormi" starts badly but quickly recovers, while the curious poem "Rosa fâchée" becomes even stranger in its English guise, displaying little discernible relationship with the original.

HARTLEY (1959) includes five prose renderings of works from the "Puisque j'ai mis ma lèvre" of 1835 to the "À Théophile Gautier" of 1872. The generic constraints of prose make it impossible to convey the surprising effects of enjambement of the French but, despite this, these versions attempt to remain faithful and unfussy, even if they do tend a little excessively to the Hugolian prosaic.

REES (1990) has 11 plain prose renderings, which are similarly close to the original French and inevitably suffer from the same generic drawbacks. For better or worse, these are often punctuated as prose and undergo thereby a slight loss in the impassioned hesitancy of poems such as "Souvenir de la nuit du 4" in which "Sa bouche, / Pâle, s'ouvrait" becomes "his pale mouth hung open", the prose perhaps unable to sustain the fragmentation of the verse.

PAUL RICKETT

Further Reading

Cogman, Peter, *Hugo: Les Contemplations*, London: Grant and Cutler, 1984

Frey, John A., *Les Contemplations of Victor Hugo: The Ash Wednesday Liturgy*, Charlottesville: University Press of Virginia, 1988

Nash, Suzanne, *Les Contemplations of Victor Hugo: An Allegory of the Creative Process*, Princeton, New Jersey: Princeton University Press, 1976

Pruner, Francis, *Le Sens caché des Contemplations de Victor Hugo*, Paris: Tredaniel, 1986

Plays

Translations

Selections

Burnham, I.G., *Dramas*, Philadelphia: George Barrie, and London: H.S. Nichols, 1895

Slous, Frederick and Camilla Newton Crosland, *Dramatic Works of Victor Hugo: Hernani, The King's Diversion, Ruy Blas*, London: Bell, 1887

Plays

Cromwell, 1827

Burnham, I.G., *Oliver Cromwell* in *Dramas*, translated by Burnham, 1895

Hernani, 1830

Burnham, I.G., *Hernani* in *Dramas*, translated by Burnham, 1895

Gower, Lord F. Leveson, *Hernani; or, The Honour of a Castillan*, London: W. Sams, 1830

Kenney, James, *Hernani; or, The Pledge of Honour*, Lacy's Acting Edition of Plays, London: Lacy, 1850

Newton Crosland, Camilla, *Hernani* in *Dramatic Works of Victor Hugo*, translated by Slous and Newton Crosland, 1887

Sharp, R. Farquharson, *Hernani*, London: Grant Richards, 1898

Marion de Lorme, 1831

Burnham, I.G., *Marion de Lorme* in *Dramas*, translated by Burnham, 1895

Le Roi s'amuse, 1832

Slous, Frederick, *Le Roi S'Amuse! ... Translated into English Blank Verse, and Entitled Francis the First; or, The Curse of St Vallier*, London: Stewart and Murray, 1843; revised as *The King's Diversion* in *Dramatic Works of Victor Hugo*, translated by Slous and Newton Crosland, 1887

Lucrèce Borgia, 1833

Young, William, *Lucrezia Borgia*, London: privately printed 1847

Angelo, 1835
Coe, Ernest O., *Angelo*, London: David Stott, 1880
Davidson, G.H., *Angelo and the Actress of Padua*, London: G.H. Davidson, 1855

Ruy Blas, 1838
Alexander, W.D.S., *Ruy Blas*, London: Digby and Long, 1890

By comparison with his novels, few translators have been attracted to Victor Hugo's plays. No doubt this is due, first, to his lesser importance as a dramatist than as a poet and novelist and, second, to the difficulties that his plays present in their performance on stage.

The general view of the verse drama *Cromwell* (1827), Hugo's first play, is that it is unperformable. It was certainly never performed during Hugo's lifetime, and its principal interest lies in a lengthy preface which served as a manifesto of French Romanticism. BURNHAM includes the play in his *Victor Hugo Dramas* (1895), the most complete collection of Hugo's plays in English translation. He translates the preface *in extenso*, and makes an admirable effort to resolve some of the difficulties presented by the text. It cannot be said, though, that this translation would be necessarily more easy to perform than the original.

Of all Hugo's plays, *Hernani* (1830) is the most widely translated and probably the most familiar to an English-speaking audience. During its first two performances, the Comédie Française was the scene of a famous pitched battle between Classical and Romantic factions, marking a crucial point in the development of French Romanticism. The battle began with the enjambement of the first two lines, which represented a break with the traditional rules of French prosody. It is inevitable that such points of style will lose their impact when translated into English verse, where enjambement is comparatively frequent, yet attempts have been made to convey them.

Lord GOWER's *Hernani; or, The Honour of a Castillan* (1830) was published privately before being performed before the queen and royal family at Bridgewater House, the translator's residence, on the 22nd June 1831. It is in verse, in iambic pentameter couplets which are as traditional as the alexandrine, though less perturbed by the enjambement. Perhaps the potent emotions of the final scene are rendered with too much restraint, though the clipped language does not cause them to descend into banality. KENNEY's *Hernani; or, The Pledge of Honour* (1850) was the version that had first been performed at the Theatre Royal, Drury Lane, on 8 April 1831. The translator precedes his version with "remarks" which detail a number of problems arising from the inept management of the first production, such as the night scene of the fifth act taking place in broad daylight. Iambic pentameter blank verse is used, and there is no attempt to reproduce the famous enjambement. NEWTON CROSLAND's *Hernani* (1887) is the work of an established poet. The iambic pentameter is economical and reasonably well contrived, though certain points could be better handled. The gradation of the penultimate line of the play, as Doña Sol turns the face of the dead Hernani to her, "Plus près ..., plus près encor ..." becomes the rather awkward "More near – still closer." BURNHAM's Hernani (1895) is in prose, and he renders the opening line of Don Carlos as "Say two words more and you're a dead duenna!" This conveys the urgency of the threat, though it may not entirely represent the verbal manner of a Spanish nobleman. Nevertheless, it is a translation that is both faithful to the original and accessible to the modern reader. R. Farquharson SHARP was the Keeper of Printed Books at the British Museum, and his *Hernani* (1898) returns to the use of the iambic pentameter. Though the sense is quite secure, the verse is less well handled than that of Newton Crosland, and one suspects that the translator might have enjoyed freedom from the restraint it imposes.

Marion de Lorme (1831) is a verse drama based on a historical character, a 17th-century courtesan, and includes Louis XIII and Richelieu among the *dramatis personae*. It was written in 1829, its first production being delayed by censorship. BURNHAM's *Marion de Lorme* (1895) is, like his *Hernani*, in prose, clear, effective and faithful to the sense of the verse original. It has not yet been superseded in its accessibility to the modern reader, and the language is well chosen to convey the full impact of the story.

Le Roi s'amuse (1832), the tragic story, in verse, of a jester at the court of François I, formed the basis of the plot of Verdi's *Rigoletto*. SLOUS's *Francis the First; or, The Curse of St Vallier* (1843) is a version in blank verse which was printed for private circulation. It is sometimes less concise than the original, but it is a reasonably efficient translation. A revised version entitled *The King's Diversion* was included in the collection *Dramatic Works of Victor Hugo* (1887), jointly produced with Camilla Newton Crosland.

Lucrèce Borgia (1833), in prose, portrays the notorious poisoner gloating over the death of several young victims before being stabbed by one, who turns out to be her son. YOUNG's *Lucrezia Borgia* (1847) is a rather free translation which takes the direction of expediency in view of stage production, and which makes a good number of modifications to the sense and to the structure. It is composed in pentameters which are well handled and have a suitably Shakespearian tone. BURNHAM's *Lucrezia Borgia* (1895) is the modern-dress version, and it is debatable which has the greater impact.

The prose drama *Angelo* (1835) also has passion and poisoning among its ingredients. It seems that translators have tended to shy away from a direct rendering of the final scene, when Rodolpho stabs Tisbe, Angelo's mistress, in the mistaken belief that she has poisoned his paramour Catarina, Angelo's wife. DAVIDSON's *Angelo and the Actress of Padua* (1855) is described by the translator as "a very ingenious and judicious adaptation of the French one. That which might have proved unpalatable to English notions and taste is expunged, and something better substituted." He makes a radical modification to the final scene by having Tisbe stab herself! COE's *Angelo* (1880) offers a different solution. The translator, noting that the strict sense of the original would "inevitably leave a feeling of distaste on English minds, revolting to their sense of propriety and moral justice", has Rodolpho forcing Tisbe to drink the poison in the belief that she had administered it to Catarina. All then proceeds to a suitably tragic conclusion, and a translation of the last scene in its original version is offered in an appendix. As the translator states in his preface, "There are some points on which the French mind and the English mind materially differ".

Ruy Blas (1838) is represented by ALEXANDER's *Ruy Blas* (1890), which attempts "to render into English the form, as well as, if possible, the spirit of the great French drama." Twelve syllable rhyming couplets are used, more cumbersome in English than the French *rimes plates*. A distinctive detail is missing in the final stage direction, when Hugo has the dying Ruy Blas suddenly restored to health and vigour as the Queen says his name. No doubt Alexander found this unrealistic, and he has him say "(with a last effort) Thanks. I die!"

JOHN R. WHITTAKER

Further Reading

Affron, Charles, *A Stage for Poets: Studies in the Theatre of Hugo and Musset*, Princeton, New Jersey: Princeton University Press, 1971

Houston, John Porter, *Victor Hugo*, New York: Twayne, 1974; revised edition 1988

Maurois, André, *Olympio; ou, La Vie de Victor Hugo*, Paris: Hachette, 1954; there is more than one translation, including that by Oliver Bernard, *Victor Hugo and His World*, London: Thames and Hudson, and New York: Viking, 1966

Richardson, Joanna, *Victor Hugo*, London: Weidenfeld and Nicolson, and New York: St Martin's Press, 1976

Wren, Keith, *Hugo: Hernani; Ruy Blas*, London: Grant and Cutler, 1982

See also the translator's preface to each of the plays in *Dramas*, translated by Burnham, 1895

Hungarian

Literary Translation into English

The Hungarian language, also called Magyar, belongs to the Finno-Ugric sub-group of the broader Ural Altaic family of languages. Finnish and Estonian are the two European languages related to Hungarian. Today, Hungarian is spoken by about 16 million people, and ranks 30th in the world according to the number of people who speak it. It is an agglutinative and phonetic language, in which the words are pronounced exactly as written. The stress is always on the first syllable of the word, and because of the harmonization of vowels and the assimilation of consonants, the spoken language sounds very melodious.

After its differentiation from Finno-Ugric, which occurred around the year AD 1000, the evolution of Hungarian is divided into four successive stages: ancient Hungarian, old Hungarian, middle Hungarian and, from the end of the 16th century, new Hungarian. During and after their migratory period, the Hungarians came into contact with many other nations and assimilated from them new ideas, with new words. Thus there are words used in agriculture that have been taken from Turkish and Slavic peoples, religious words taken from Italian and Slavic missionaries, and trade and commerce terms borrowed from German. In spite of the loan words, 80 per cent of the Hungarian vocabulary used today belongs to the original Hungarian and Finno-Ugric language family.

Leslie Könnyü, the Hungarian-American poet and writer, affirms that it is easier to translate into Hungarian than the other way around. To translate Hungarian, especially verse, into English is a lot more complicated. First of all, one cannot translate word-for-word because of the differences in syntax and word order between the two languages. For example, in Hungarian we say, "a ház*ba* megy" (the house-into he goes). The "*ba*" (into) is a suffix. In English the preposition comes before the noun, "*into* the house". Hungarian is a post-positional language (there are 36 post-positions), while English is a prepositional language.

Hungarian is a highly inflected language; English has few inflections. While Hungarian resembles English in having no grammatical indication of noun gender, the complex Hungarian declension system contains more than 20 different case-suffixes for nouns, plus signs for indicating plural and possessive. Though there are only three tenses (present, past, and future, with no auxiliaries), the conjugation of verbs in Hungarian is complex also. There is a developed system of pronouns of address.

The morphology of Hungarian being rigid, with grammatical categories indicated by suffixes, a greater liberty of word order is possible than in the dominant Subject-Verb-Object pattern of English. The language also lends itself readily to word-formation. In all, Hungarian favours both precision and nuance.

Translating Hungarian poetry into English presents special aspects. In Hungarian, vowel harmony enlarges the possibilities for rhyme. The distinction between long and short vowels facilitates the use of classical metres. The natural cadence of English is short-long, the iambic foot. In Hungarian, with the first syllable of the word always receiving the stress, Hungarian's natural cadence is long-short, the trochaic foot. The English translator has therefore, the tendency to change the trochaic into iambic.

Among the most prolific of Hungarian literary critics of all time was József Reményi (1892–1956), a professor of literature from Cleveland, Ohio, who wrote in English. He translated Hungarian poetry into English, though he preferred to write critical essays, especially on the literature of the 19th and 20th centuries. A collection of his works was published by Rutgers University Press under the title *Hungarian Writers and Literature* (1964). One who contributed much in the area of poetic translation into English was József Grósz, an economist from Portland, Oregon. Grósz, a poet and a graduate in business studies of the University of Vienna, concentrated primarily on the poet, Endre Ady. The second edition of Grósz's *Hungarian Anthology*, co-authored with W. Arthur Boggs (1916–66), appeared in 1966, and in 1985 he published a translation of Imre Madách's *The Tragedy of Man*. A more recent translation of Madách's dramatic poem, staged by the translator in Edinburgh, is an adapted version by Iain MacLeod, *The Tragedy of Man* (1993).

The earliest American translations from Hungarian into English are found in the 1853 *Számüzöttek Lapja* [The Exiles' Paper], as well as in *Graham's Magazine*, which published some of Sándor Petőfi's poems in English. The translator of Petőfi's verse was Mihály Heilprin (1822–88) who arrived in America in 1856. In 1881 and in 1889, William N. Loew, a New York lawyer, published an anthology entitled *Magyar Poetry*. In 1906 Frigyes Riedl utilized Loew's translations in his *A History of Hungarian Literature*. E. Delmar and E.B. Pierce also published Petőfi's poetry in English translation in 1948.

The Eastern Kentucky professor, Antal Nyerges, has translated the poetry of Endre Ady, Attila József, and Petőfi, without rhyme. Among more recent translators of Hungarian verse can be found Maxim Tábory, a librarian from Goldsboro, who helped Watson Kirkconnell with *Hungarian Helicon*, and later Leslie Könnyü with *Hungarian Bouquet*, and who published his own volume, *Frost and Fire*. In 1977, Miklós Vajda and Columbia University Press published an anthology, *Modern Hungarian Poetry*, which consists of poems by 41 contemporary Hungarian poets living and writing in the postwar years. To date, it is the most comprehensive treatment of modern Hungarian poetry available in English. Major American, British, and Canadian poet-translators contributed to the effort, which involved working from rough translations. Professor Albert Tezla, of the University of Minnesota, published in 1980 a literary anthology in English, entitled *Ocean at the Window*, which incorporates Hungarian prose and poetry since 1945 and includes translations of works by such notable writers as István Őrkény, János Pilinszky, László Nagy, Ferenc Juhász, István Csurka, and Sándor Csoóri among others. The most ambitious translation project involving Hungarian poetry is the two-volume, *In Quest of the "Miracle Stag": The Poetry of Hungary. An Anthology of Hungarian Poetry from the 13th century to the Present in English Translation*, edited by Adam Makkai, Professor of Linguistics at the University of Illinois at Chicago. Volume 1, published in 1996, is 964 pages and includes the work of Hungary's major deceased poets; it concludes with an essay, "A Nation and Its Poetry", discussing influential literary and artistic trends, from the leading Hungarian essayist, László Cs. Szabó. Volume 2 will present the work of living Hungarian poets from Hungary and the diaspora.

In the field of drama, Clara Györgyey edited, translated and published in 1993, through Forest Books and in co-operation with Corvina Press, *A Mirror to the Cage, Three Contemporary Hungarian Plays*, which includes the works of István Örkény, György Spiró, and Mihály Kornis. In 1991, Paj Publications, New York, as part of its series on contemporary drama, published in English translation five plays by Hungary's newer generation of playwrights, edited and introduced by Eugene Brogyányi. The plays by András Sütő, Géza Páskándi, István Csurka, György Spiró and Mihály Kornis reflect the social realities of Hungarian life, particularly those of identity crisis and the role of the intellectual in society. With the aim of revealing the profound complexity of life in Hungary, Albert Tezla selected and edited the plays of Gábor Czakó, Géza Bereményi, and György Spiró, three contemporary young playwrights, for a co-publication in English by Forest Books and Corvina Books entitled *Three Contemporary Hungarian Plays* (1992). Katharina M. and Christopher C. Wilson have dedicated themselves to familiarizing the English-speaking world with the plays and writings of Árpád Göncz, Hungary's first democratically elected president in four decades and one of Hungary's foremost playwrights and a translator himself (*Voices of Dissent: Two Plays by Árpád Göncz*, 1989, and *Árpád Göncz: Plays and Other Writings*, 1990). A perennial favorite of the English-speaking world is Ferenc Molnár, whose many plays have been translated and performed on the stages of America and Great Britain. His best known work is perhaps *Liliom*, which was adapted and used as the basis for the musical *Carousel*.

Anthologies that concentrate on a single topic have also been produced in English. The most recent is Katherine Gyékényesi Gatto's *Treasury of Hungarian Love Poems, Quotations & Proverbs*, published by Hippocrene Books, New York, in 1996. David Ray's *From the Hungarian Revolution* (1966) treats the theme of the Revolution of 1956. Others devoted to special periods are *The Plough and the Pen: Writings from Hungary 1930–1956*; *Landmark: Hungarian Writers on Thirty Years of History*, edited by Miklós Szabolcsi (Budapest: Corvina, 1965); *The Face of Creation: Contemporary Hungarian Poetry*, translated by Jascha Kessler and others (Minneapolis: Coffee House Press, 1988); *Turmoil in Hungary: an Anthology of Twentieth-Century Hungarian Poetry*, edited and translated by Nicholas Kolumban (St Paul, Minnesota: New Rivers Press; distributed by Small Press Distributors, Berkeley, California, 1982).

Kolumban has also produced a translation of a single poet's work, the selected poems of the contemporary poet Sándor Csoóri, entitled *Memory of Snow* (1983). The *Selected Poems of Sándor Csoóri*, translated by Len Roberts, was published not long ago by Copper Canyon Press (1992). Ferenc Juhász's poetry can be found in two translated editions, Kenneth McRobbie's *The Boy Changed into a Stag* (1970), and in Edwin Morgan's *Ferenc Juhász: Selected Poems*, in the Penguin Modern European Poets series (1970). A selection from János Pilinszky's poems was translated by Ted Hughes and János Csokits in 1976 and published by Carcanet New Press. George Gömöri, Tony Connor, and Kenneth McRobbie produced the first and only English edition of the selected poems of László Nagy: *Love of the Scorching Wind* (1973). Selected poems of Endre Ady were translated by Eugene Bard in 1987. *Birds and Other Relations, Selected Poetry of Dezső Tandori* (1986), was translated by Bruce Berlind, a poet in his own right, who also put into English some of Ágnes Nemes Nagy's poetry. Besides Nemes Nagy, the only woman poet who has merited an English-language edition of her poems is Zsuzsa Rakovszky. Selections from three books of her poems, *Zsuzsa Rakovszky, New Life*, translated and introduced by George Szirtes, were published as part of the Oxford Poets series in 1994.

After Petőfi, Miklós Rádnoti is the Hungarian poet who has been most translated into English. English versions of his poetry appeared in 1972, 1977, 1979, 1980, 1985. Most recently, Zsuzsanna Ozsvath and Frederick Turner have published *Foamy Sky: The Major Poems of Miklós Radnóti* (1992).

The translation of Hungarian poetry into English is not a new phenomenon in Britain. Sir John Bowring published an anthology in 1830, which was followed by the publication of some of Petőfi's poetry in English. A member of the Kossuth emigration (1848), Ferenc Pulszky, also translated Hungarian poetry into English. *Between: Selected Poems of Ágnes Nemes Nagy*, translated by Hugh Maxton, was published by Dedalus in Ireland and in co-operation with the Hungarian publishing house, Corvina, in 1988. Pál Tábory (1908–74) and Tamás Kabdebó published *100 Hungarian Poems* in 1976. In Sydney, Australia, the talented translator Egon Kunz published *Hungarian Poetry* (1955), which includes primarily the works of 19th-century poets.

Hungary has also produced a number of well-done translations. Among the best translators are B. Balogh, N. Vally, Rene Bonnejea, Ilona Kovács, Miklós Vajda (*Modern Hungarian Poetry*, 1977), and especially Dezső Kosztolányi (1885–1936), the cosmopolitan and talented literary translator, who translated from several foreign languages into Hungarian. Corvina, the Hungarian publisher, independently or in co-operation with foreign presses, has sponsored and produced a number of translations, such as J.C.W. Horne's rendering of Imre Madách's *The Tragedy of Man* in 1963, the fourth English translation and the seventh English-language edition of this dramatic masterpiece. In 1985 appeared the first collection of early Hungarian literature in English, edited by Tibor Klaniczay, and published by Corvina Press, *Old Hungarian Literary Reader 11th–18th Centuries*, which allowed the English-speaking reader to get a glimpse of the evolution of Hungarian literature, as well as the historical and social background of the works. Such well-known writers as Keith Bosley, G.F. Cushing, Edwin Morgan, Peter Sherwood, and W.D. Snodgrass provided the translations.

A good introduction to Hungarian prose is the collection of short stories introduced by Alfred Alvarez and published by Corvina as *Twenty-Two Hungarian Short Stories* (1967), and by Oxford University Press as *Hungarian Short Stories*. An anthology of 30 short stories by contemporary Hungarian authors was also translated by Lawrence Wolfe, and published in 1936. This particular volume has an introduction by Alexander Korda. In 1962, *Hungarian Short Stories*, from the 19th and 20th centuries, was published by Corvina. More recently (1998) Ester Molnar translated *Thy Kingdom Come: 19 Short Stories by 11 Hungarian Authors*, published by Palatinus in Budapest.

The novels of Ferenc Móra, Mór Jókai, and Kálmán Mikszáth have also been translated into English. Corvina in the late 1980s published in English two anthologies of short stories incorporating the writings of Hungary's foremost contemporary writers, such as István Örkény, Erzsébet Galgóczi, Péter Nádas, and Péter Esterházy, among others. Géza Csáth's short stories were translated by Jascha Kessler in 1980, and reissued under the title *Opium* by Viking Penguin in 1983. Recently, Oxford University Press initiated a series, Central European Classics, and in co-operation with the Central European University and the Soros Foundation has published *Skylark* (Dezső Kosztolányi) and *Be Faithful Unto Death* (Zsigmond Móricz), translated into English by Richard Aczel (1993) and Stephen Vizinczey (1995) respectively.

Unquestionably the most recognized and prolific literary translator of Hungarian works into English was the former president of Acadia University, the Canadian, Watson Kirkconnell (1895–1957). The most important and probably the best anthology of Hungarian poetry in English is his posthumously published 792-page *Magyar Helikon*. The collection contains around 500 poems from 185 poets, including the entire *Toldi*, and *The Death of King Buda*. Kirkconnell translated from many European languages into English. He learned Hungarian perfectly, and translated the poetry in such a way that he matched the English meter, the rhythm, and rhyme to the original Hungarian. He traveled frequently to Hungary, and taught English at the University of Debrecen Summer Program, from which university he also received an honorary doctorate. He often worked in co-operation with Hungarian translators such as Béla and Lulu Báchkai, Tivadar Edl and Maxim Tábory. He published his first translation, *The Magyar Muse*, an anthology of Hungarian poetry 1400–1932, in 1930. This was followed by *The Death of King Buda* in 1936, and in 1947 *A Little Treasury of Hungarian Verse*, treating authors primarily from the 19th century, with some from the early 20th century. He wrote critical studies on the poet Endre Ady, on the Hungarian language, and on his travels to Hungary, which appeared in the *Hungarian Quarterly*, the *Slavonic and East European Review*, and the *East European Review*; in 1964 and 1968, two English translations of selected works by the poet László Mécs appeared posthumously.

With the eradication of the former political and social barriers between East-Central Europe and the West, there has been a resurgence of interest in the culture and literature of Hungary, as exemplified by the recent establishment of the Central European Classics series by Oxford University Press. In future, the number of literary translations from Hungarian into English will surely increase. Hungary, in the 21st century, by virtue of the new technologies and the importance of the universally accepted "global vision" approach to politics and commerce, appears to be on the brink of finally emerging from her linguistic and cultural isolation.

KATHERINE GYÉKÉNYESI GATTO

Further Reading

Basa, Enikő Molnár (editor), *Hungarian Literature*, New York: Griffon House, 1993

Illés, Lajos (editor), *Nothing's Lost: Twenty-Five Hungarian Short Stories*, Budapest: Corvina, 1988

Kabdebó, Thomas (editor), *Hundred Hungarian Poems*, Manchester: Albion Editions, 1976

Molnár, Ferenc, *Romantic Comedies: Eight Plays*, New York: Crown, 1952

Nagy, Moses M. (editor), *A Journey into History: Essays on Hungarian Literature*, New York: Peter Lang, 1990

Tezla, Albert, *Hungarian Authors: A Bibliographical Handbook*, Cambridge, Massachusetts: Belknap Press, 1970

Tóth, Éva (editor), *Ma / Today: An Anthology of Contemporary Hungarian Literature*, Budapest: Corvina, 1987

Tāhā Husayn 1889–1973

Egyptian autobiographer, novelist, critic and educator

Biography

Tāhā Husayn was born into a farming family at Maghāgha in Upper Egypt and lost his sight in his youth. He married a Frenchwoman. He became professor of Arabic literature in Cairo and later Rector of Alexandria University and he served twice as Egyptian Minister of Education. His world view was broad and his intellect, scholarship and commitment, as teacher and administrator, to the cause of enlightened education won wide recognition. He died in Cairo.

Translations

Autobiography

al-Ayyām, 3 vols, 1926, 1939, 1967

Paxton, E.H., *An Egyptian Childhood: The Autobiography of Taha Hussein*, London: Routledge, 1932; reprinted, with new introduction by P. Cachia, London: Heinemann, and Washington, DC: Three Continents Press, 1981

Wayment, Hilary, *The Stream of Days: A Student at the Azhar*, with an introduction, Cairo: Al-Maaref, 1943; revised edition, London and New York: Longmans Green, 1948

Cragg, Kenneth, *A Passage to France: The Third Volume of the Autobiography of Taha Husain*, Leiden: E.J. Brill, 1976

Novels

Adīb, 1935

El-Zayyat, Mona, *A Man of Letters*, Cairo: American University in Cairo Press, 1994

Du'ā' al-Karawān, 1934

As-Safi, A.B., *The Call of the Curlew*, Leiden: E.J. Brill, 1980

Ahlām Shahrazād, 1944

Wahba, Magdi, *The Dreams of Scheherazade*, Cairo: General Egyptian Book Organization, 1974

Other Writing

Mustaqbal al-Thaqāfa fī Misr, 1938

Glazer, Sidney, *The Future of Culture in Egypt*, Washington, DC: American Council of Learned Societies, 1954

A member of the generation of Egyptian writers that also included Tawfīq al-Hakīm and Yahyā Haqqī, Tāhā Husayn exerted a profound influence on the development of modern Arabic literature – an influence recognized in his unofficial title "Dean of Arabic letters". Much of his influence was as a literary critic and thinker rather than as an imaginative writer; he wrote extensively on Islamic history and society, and was able to put his ideas on the development of Egyptian education into practice as adviser to the Ministry of Education, as the first rector of Alexandria University, and later as Minister of Education himself. His ideas on the place of Egyptian culture in the modern world were expounded at length in *Mustaqbal al-Thaqāfa fī Misr*, the importance of which is confirmed by the existence (unusually for such a work) of an English translation, competently done by GLAZER (1954).

Tāhā Husayn's reputation as an imaginative writer rests largely on his three-volume autobiography *al-Ayyām*, and especially on the first volume, originally serialized in the Egyptian periodical *al-Hilāl*. The work was one of the first pieces of 20th-century Arabic literature to attract attention outside the Middle East and has been translated into many languages; in Egypt itself, it remains one of the best-loved works of modern Arabic literature. Despite its status as autobiography rather than fiction, it figures prominently in many accounts of the development of the Arabic novel, both because of its style and tone – which lend it some of the characteristics of fiction – and because of its appearance at a time when interest in novel-writing was beginning to gain ground in Egypt. Many novels of this period were predominantly autobiographically based, and in this context Tāhā Husayn's work (which is itself written in the third person) may be seen as having made a major contribution to the development of the genre.

Linguistically, the work presents one of the most pronounced examples of the author's characteristic prose style, which owes something – so it has been suggested – to his blindness from an early age: strings of clauses are linked together by simple conjunctions to form seemingly endless sentences in a manner that mirrors, but extends, some of the features of classical Arabic prose style. Essentially inimitable, these features present formidable difficulties for the translator into English. PAXTON (1932), though generally accurate, has a dated air to it, seldom reading like anything but a rather stilted translation. In many places, the translator has fallen into the common trap of attempting to reproduce the structure and pattern of the Arabic sentence too closely; but the author's use of repetition and parallelism, and the stylistic eccentricities which in Arabic serve to give the work its charm, in English often sound merely odd. As a result, although the reader of the English translation may well come away with a vivid impression of the young Tāhā Husayn's boyhood upbringing in Upper Egypt, he or she is unlikely to gain much sense of the mature writer as a stylist.

The second volume of *al-Ayyām* continues Tāhā Husayn's account of his education, covering his life as an Azhar student from 1902 to 1910. The book is of considerable interest not only from a literary point of view but also for its insider's portrait of life in the Azhar during a transitional period in its history. As befits the progress through life of the protagonist, it is less whimsical and more down to earth than the first volume of the autobiography; none the less, most of the features of the style of the earlier volume reappear here. WAYMENT (1943) generally copes better with the eccentricities of Tāhā Husayn's Arabic than does Paxton, perhaps because she is more aware of the choices to be made and accordingly less afraid to face them. In her introduction – and presumably with half an eye on Paxton – she frankly states: "I have tried to avoid literal translation, which only results in a sort of spurious local colour such as hinders genuine comprehension. The graceful assonances and repetitions of the original have also disappeared, though I can only hope that some of its charm remains." A comparison between Paxton's and Wayment's translations suggests that Wayment's translation strategy is indeed a more effective one.

Nearly 30 years separate the publication of the second and third volumes of *al-Ayyām*, and from a literary point of view the third volume is of less interest. By comparison with the first two volumes of *al-Ayyām* also, much of Tāhā Husayn's fiction proper appears somewhat uninspired. Indeed, of the author's novels only *Du'ā' al-Karawān* (1934) and *Shajarat al-Bu's* (1944) can lay claim to an important place in the history of modern Arabic fiction. Of these, *Du'ā' al-Karawān*, which is written in a uniquely lyrical style, presents problems of translation not dissimilar to – though more acute than –those of the first two volumes of *al-Ayyām*. Like Wayment, AS-SAFI (1980) demonstrates a sound grasp of the problems involved, suggesting that the dilemma is "how to bring about an equilibrium whereby the original aesthetic flavour is transferred into English without hindering genuine comprehension" and concluding that "in many cases, only an approximation, rather than a complete translation, is possible in order to present a natural, acceptable rendition". His keen awareness of the poetic qualities of the original is demonstrated by his inclusion in the preface of a short passage reworked in English free verse, and his version generally reads smoothly and easily.

From among Tāhā Husayn's other novels, EL-ZAYYAT (1994), herself a granddaughter of the author, has produced in *A Man of Letters* a polished and eminently readable translation of *Adīb*, a work of interest for its early treatment of the East/West theme also tackled by Tawfiq al-Hakīm and subsequently to become one of the most widespread themes in modern Arabic literature. No amount of care lavished on the English translation, however, can disguise the faults in the author's novelistic technique, in particular his excessive reliance on letters as a means of advancing the narrative. WAHBA's (1974) version of *Ahlām Shahrazād* is of indifferent quality.

As already suggested, Tāhā Husayn's writings have enjoyed rather mixed fortunes in their English versions. It is particularly unfortunate that the English translation of the work on which his literary reputation above all rests – the first volume of *al-Ayyām* – should be less satisfactory than those of some of his other works. Overall, however, the translations available should serve to give the English-speaking reader a reasonable idea of the range of Tāhā Husayn's writing even if, for a full appreciation of his style, there is little alternative but to tackle the original.

PAUL STARKEY

Further Reading

Cachia, Pierre, *Tāhā Husayn: His Place in the Egyptian Literary Renaissance*, London: Luzac, 1956

Hourani, Albert, *Arabic Thought in the Liberal Age, 1798–1939*, London and New York: Oxford University Press, 1962

Kilpatrick, Hilary, *The Modern Egyptian Novel: A Study in Social Criticism*, London: Ithaca Press, 1974

Sakkut, Hamdy, *The Egyptian Novel and Its Main Trends from 1913–1952*, Cairo: General Egyptian Book Organization, 1971

Semah, David, *Four Egyptian Literary Critics*, Leiden: E.J. Brill, 1974

J.-K. Huysmans 1848–1907

French novelist and art critic

Biography

Born Charles-Marie-Georges Huysmans (he used Joris-Karl, the Dutch form of his given names, only to sign his literary works) in Paris, 5 February 1848. He was the only son of a French mother and a struggling Dutch illustrator who had settled in Paris. In 1866 he entered the civil service, remaining at the Ministry of the Interior until his retirement in 1898. During the 1870s, Huysmans forged links with the Naturalist movement, especially with Émile Zola. His first novel – *Marthe, histoire d'une fille*, 1876 (translated 1927) – describes the dismal life of a prostitute in a licensed brothel. This was followed by *Les Soeurs Vatard*, 1879 (translated 1983), a study of the life of two women bookbinders; *En ménage*, 1881 (translated 1971), a pessimistic account of the unsatisfactory existence led by an unsuccessful novelist; and *À vau-l'eau*, 1882 (translated 1927), the story of the misfortunes and disappointments of a struggling civil servant. Huysmans is primarily known today as the author of *À rebours*, 1884 (translated 1922), described by Arthur Symons as "the breviary of the decadence", and *Là-bas*, 1891 (translated 1924), a novel steeped in occultism and Satanism. *En rade*, 1887 (translated 1992), in which Huysmans intercuts powerful naturalistic descriptions of the French countryside with dream sequences, was much appreciated by the Surrealists in the 1920s. During the 16 years of his life remaining after he completed *Là-bas*, Huysmans explored the mystical aspects of Catholicism in a trilogy of barely veiled autobiographical novels: *En route*, 1895 (translated 1896); *La Cathédrale*, 1898 (translated 1898); and *L'Oblat*, 1903 (translated 1924). Huysmans, who was an early champion of Impressionism, also published three substantial collections of art criticism (*L'Art moderne*, 1883; *Certains*, 1889; *Trois Primitifs*, 1904). Died in Paris 12 May 1907.

Translations

Novels

Les Soeurs Vatard, 1879

Babcock, James C., *The Vatard Sisters*, Lexington: University Press of Kentucky, 1983

À rebours, 1884

Anonymous, *Against the Grain*, Paris: Groves and Michaux, 1926; reprinted London: Fortune Press, n.d. [1931]; New York: Dover, 1969

Baldick, Robert, *Against Nature*, Harmondsworth and Baltimore: Penguin, 1959

Howard, John [i.e. Jacob Howard Lewis], *Against the Grain*, New York: Lieber and Lewis, 1922

Mauldon, Margaret, *Against Nature*, with an introduction by Nicholas White, Oxford and New York: Oxford University Press, 1998

En rade, 1887

Ashton, Rachel, *A Haven* in *The Decadent Reader: Fiction, Fantasy, and Perversion from Fin-de-Siècle France*, edited by Asti Hustvedt, New York: Zone, 1998

Hale, Terry, *Becalmed!*, London: Atlas Press, 1992

Là-bas, 1891

Anonymous [i.e. Alfred Allison], *Down There*, Paris: Groves and Michaux, 1928; London: Fortune Press, 1930

Hale, Terry, *The Damned*, Harmondsworth: Penguin, 2001

Wallis, Keene, *Down There*, New York: Boni, 1924; reprinted New York: Dover, 1969; reprinted Sawtry, Cambridgeshire: Dedalus, 1989 (translator unacknowledged)

En route, 1895

Paul, C. Kegan, *En Route*, London: Kegan Paul Trench Trübner 1896; reprinted Sawtry, Cambridgeshire: Dedalus, 1989

La Cathédrale, 1898

Bell, Clara, *The Cathedral*, London: Kegan Paul Trench Trübner, 1898; reprinted Sawtry, Cambridgeshire: Dedalus, 1989

L'Oblat, 1903

Perceval, Edward, *The Oblate*, London: Kegan Paul Trench Trübner, and New York: Dutton, 1924; reprinted New York: H. Fertig, 1978; reprinted Sawtry, Cambridgeshire: Dedalus, 1996

The earliest works by J.-K. Huysmans to be published in translation in English were the largely autobiographical novels describing his conversion to Catholicism. These are *En route* (1895), in which the effect of sacred music, and the assistance it provides in conquering the sensual appetites, is described during a retreat in a Trappist monastery; *La Cathédrale* (1898), where the similar influence of medieval art and architecture is revealed during a sojourn at Chartres Cathedral; and *L'Oblat* (1903), in which Huysmans's hero Durtal is denied the sanctuary of the cloister only by the rise of anticlerical forces in post-Dreyfus France. Kegan PAUL's translation of *En route* appeared in 1896, only a year after the French edition, while BELL's *The Cathedral* came out the same year as the French original (1898). For reasons that are not entirely clear, the concluding volume of what is commonly thought of as Huysmans's Catholic trilogy, *The Oblate*, was not translated until 1924, some 21 years after the novel was published in France. Although PERCEVAL's version of *The Oblate* is the weakest of the three, all are marred by stylistic infelicities and occasional abridgements. The following example, taken from *The Oblate*, is illustrative of this:

> Et quand le moment suprême des noces fut venu, alors que Marie, que Magdeleine, que saint Jean, se tenaient en larmes, au pied de la croix, [elle, comme la Pauvreté dont parle saint François, monta délibérément sur le lit du gibet et, de l'union de ces deux réprouvés de la terre] l'Église naquit; elle sortit en des flots de sang et d'eau du coeur victimal et ce fut fini [...]
>
> (*L'Oblat*, 1903; reprinted Paris: Plon, 1929, p. 301)

> But when the supreme moment had come, when Mary and Magdalene and St John stood weeping at the foot of the Cross, and Christ gave up the ghost, and the Church came forth in floods of blood and water from the heart of the victim, that was the end ...
>
> (*The Oblate*, translated by Edward Perceval, 1924, pp. 242–43)

Given that the passage in question is the author's most complete statement of the Dolorist position he came to assume in the novel, these textual alterations cannot always be considered as minor.

For a writer of such stylistic and intellectual complexity, Huysmans enjoyed reasonably high print runs in France. Michael Issacharoff suggests that the initial print run for *En route* was around 20,000 copies, while Robert Baldick provides documentary evidence that *La Cathédrale* sold a similar number of copies within a month of publication. Between 1908 and 1965, a further 64,000 copies of *En route* and 103,000 copies of *La Cathédrale* (together with a further 65,000 copies in the Livre de Poche collection) were printed by Plon. Huysmans was much less popular in Britain. The first English edition of *En route* enjoyed a print run of only 2,000 copies. Although there was a second edition the same year of a further 1,000 copies, the third, fourth and fith editions (of 1908, 1918 and 1920) were 500 copies each. Likewise, the print runs for the first edition of *The Cathedral* and *The Oblate* were 2,000 copies.

Nowadays, it is *À rebours* (1884) that is generally considered to be Huysmans's most important novel. HOWARD's bowdlerized translation of this work, as *Against the Grain*, was not published until 1922 however. This translation would seem to reflect Anglo-American anxieties concerning the portrayal of human sexual activity. Among many other cuts and changes, chapter 6 (in which des Esseintes seeks to corrupt a 16-year-old boy by taking him to a heterosexual brothel) is entirely omitted, and a description of a brief homosexual liaison is removed from chapter 9 (Banks, 1990). Although a slightly later edition, ANONYMOUS (1926), published in Paris by Groves and Michaux, restores these omissions, doubts must remain about the textual integrity of all subsequent editions (of which there have been at least 15) prior to Baldick's new translation in 1959.

BALDICK's translation, entitled *Against Nature*, is not only complete but also stylistically elegant. (It is reputed to have sold at least 5,000 copies every year since it was first issued.) Additional authority is lent to this translation by the fact that the translator was also responsible for the standard biography of its author. A new version of *À rebours* by Margaret MAULDON (1998) won the 1999 Scott Moncrieff prize for translation from French to English.

Doubts concerning textual integrity must be raised with respect to the translation of *Là-bas* (1891). The first British translation, which contains substantial cuts, was published by the Fortune Press in 1930. This anonymous edition was the work of Alfred ALLISON and had been published uncensored two years earlier by Groves and Michaux in Paris. The second Fortune Press edition of 1946 similarly contains numerous changes and abridgements. As with Howard's translation of *À rebours*, the majority of these omissions concern matters of sexual morality (though some potentially blasphemous passages are also bowdlerized):

> Il empoigna son chapeau et fit claquer la porte. Attends, je vais t'en ficher moi, de l'idéal! et il courut chez une prostituée qu'il connaissait dans le Quartier Latin.
> Je suis depuis trop longtemps sage, murmurait-il en marchant, c'est sans doute pour cela que je divague!
> Il trouva cette femme chez elle [– et ce fut atroce.
> C'était une belle brune qui sortait d'une face avenante des yeux en fête et des dents de loup. Haute en chair, habile, elle effrondrait les moelles, granulait les poumons, démolissait, en quelques tours de baisers, les reins.]
> Elle lui reprocha d'être resté si longtemps sans venir, le cajola, l'embrassa; [mais il se sentait triste et haletant, gêné, sans convoitises authentiques; il finit par s'abattre sur une couche et il subit, énervé jusqu'à crier, le laborieux supplice des échinantes dragues.]
> Jamais il n'avait plus exécré la chair, jamais il ne s'était senti plus répugné, plus las, qu'au sortir de cette chambre!
> (*Là-bas*, 1891; reprinted Paris: Gallimard, 1985, p. 123)

> Seizing his hat, he went out, banging the door behind him. "Just wait, I'm going to have done with you, with the ideal", – and he hurried to a prostitute's, a woman he knew in the Quartier Latin.
> "I have been a good boy over long", he muttered as he walked; "no doubt that is the reason I am all astray!"
> He found the woman at home. She reproached him for not having been to see her for so long, cajoled and kissed him – and the rest.
> Never had he abhorred the flesh more or felt more sick and disgusted as he left the house.
> (*Down There*, translated by Alfred Allison, London: Fortune Press, 1930, p. 120)

The 1946 Fortune Press edition, while clearly based on Allison's translation, shows further signs of censorship:

> Seizing his hat, he went out, banging the door behind him. "I'm going to have done with you, with the ideal", – and he hurried to call on a woman he knew in the Quartier Latin.
> "I have been a good boy too long", he muttered as he walked; "no doubt that is the reason I am all nervy and stupid!"
> He found her at home. She reproached him for not having been to see her for so long, cajoled and kissed him ...
> Never had he felt more sick and disgusted as he left the house.
> (*Down There*, translated by Alfred Allison, London: Fortune Press, 1946, p. 76)

Given the unreliability of the Allison translation, the first American translation of 1924 by WALLIS has established itself as the most authoritative English-language version. The latter has been frequently reprinted in both Britain and the US. Closer inspection, however, reveals a text that is not only dated but riddled with inaccuracies. These inaccuracies reflect the translator's lack of familiarity with quite common French terms relating to such areas as prostitution and hypnotism. Thus, the perplexing remark made by the narrator in the opening chapter that he was considering entering a monastery "somewhat as street girls think of going into a house" is a consequence of the fact that the author was using the word *maison* in the sense of *maison close* (brothel). Likewise, the peculiar business of the powerful magnet sending out its waves from the centre of Paris towards the beginning of chapter 15 proves, on closer inspection, to be a reference to the "magnetic fluids" of a mesmerist. Given that *Là-bas* is a novel that explores sexuality and hypnotism in some detail, the continual uncertainty of this translation creates considerable problems for the reader.

A new translation of *Là-bas* (as *The Damned*), the first for more than 70 years, by HALE is forthcoming in 2001. It is anticipated that this translation will provide a readable contemporary version based on careful scrutiny of the author's work practices and historical sources.

BABCOCK's accurate and intentionally literal version of *The Vatard Sisters* (1983) represents the first translation of this important early work, published in 1879.

HALE's translation of *En rade* (1887) as *Becalmed!* (1992) is generally seen as an atmospheric rendering of the original, though on its appearance one critic found the English title (despite the exclamation mark) insufficiently ironic, while another would have preferred a version syntactically closer to the original (especially with regard to the translation of free indirect speech). ASHTON's 1998 translation provides that closer reading, but is otherwise awkward and undistinguished.

TERRY HALE

Further Reading

Baldick, Robert, *The Life of J.-K. Huysmans*, Oxford: Clarendon Press, 1955

Banks, Brian R., *The Image of Huysmans*, New York: AMS Press, 1990

Beaumont, Barbara (editor and translator), *The Road from Decadence: From Brothel to Cloister: Selected Letters of J.-K. Huysmans*, London: Athlone Press, and Columbus: Ohio State University Press, 1989

Issacharoff, Michael, *J.-K. Huysmans devant la critique en France (1874–1960)*, Paris: Klincksieck, 1970

Hypertext and Translation

With advances in computing, the new hypermedia environment has enabled its users to call up information on the Internet, access virtual libraries via the World Wide Web, and disseminate texts from a home computer connected by modem to any other computer terminal. Given the immediacy of accessing, retrieving and publishing materials globally, the current transition from print to electronic technology signals a period of cultural change analogous to that brought about by the Gutenberg revolution. Computers are not only transforming the ways in which communication takes place but are also beginning to alter the ways in which research and teaching is conducted in the Humanities. From the point of view of Translation Studies, it should be acknowledged that while American English, as the dominant language of computing, has reduced the need for translation in terms of global communication, computer and CD technology are also, however, affording possibilities for practising and studying translation, as well as thinking about it, that have only just begun to be realized.

The term hypertext was first used by Theodor H. Nelson in the 1960s to highlight the new possibilities afforded by electronic text. Unlike text published in book form, hypertexts are virtual texts, which can be cross-referenced and linked to any number of other texts. This allows users to navigate their own pathways through a given text or corpus of material, to create networks with other related texts or images, each link leading to another, ad infinitum. Users are thus given increasing control as to what they read and how they read; and although they cannot change the texts produced by another person, they can interactively engage with, assemble and re-write those texts, which they download and save onto their own hard disk. While this is transforming both our concept of what a text is, and our experience of reading and writing, it is also affecting existent conventions of reading, writing, translating and editing. Here, a text is no longer a unified entity with clearly identifiable borders, but an open network in Roland Barthes's or Umberto Eco's sense; nor is the hypertext bound by the strictures of a single or clear reading text, as is the case in current practices of textual editing, requiring a linear, sequential mode of reading; but, by contrast, what an open hypertextual environment can display is a text's entire history of production and transmission. The vantage point for translation is that multivariant versions can be called up simultaneously, compared, annotated, and therefore also reworked.

So far, the most important projects that have used computer technology to enable the comparison between different textual variants of the same foreign text are: Paul D. Kahn's Chinese Literature web, which allows access to the different versions of Du Fu's poetry, including the Chinese text, transcriptions, varying translations, and other reference and contextual material; and the hypertext system developed by a team at Dallas Theological Seminary, CD Word: The Interactive Bible Library, which stores different versions of the Bible together with the Greek texts, dictionaries and commentaries. Both systems are designed as an aid to the scholar, giving comprehensive access to materials that would otherwise remain scattered in libraries across the globe, and as an aid to students, facilitating ready access to this material. Since hypertexts allow users to sift through various versions as well as requiring them to choose which path to follow through these texts, they positively encourage users to take on an active role in the process of meaning production, to produce a translation of their own from the texts on the screen. As such, hypertexts foster collaborative writing, blurring the very distinction between writer, reader and translator, precisely because each time the user makes a choice, linking one version to another, annotating this or that, the user is adding his or her own "versioning".

Hypertexts are also a visual reminder of the impossibility of putting a stop to the proliferation of meaning; which is to say, the quest to unlock the text's definitive meaning and transfer the original intact to produce an equivalent target text is rendered untenable with the simultaneous presence of a whole series of differently translated versions of ostensibly the "same" source text. Equally, the virtual presence of all the writers, be they the foreign author, the translators, the editors or the commentators, undermines the notion of a univocal authorial voice which might be decoded and then reproduced faithfully by the translator. As such, hypertexts materially embody many of the theories proffered by postmodern thinkers, who have questioned the supremacy of notions such as authorship, originality or uniqueness, and who have sought to deconstruct the hierarchical relations that valorize uniqueness over variation, original over translation, author over reader. In arguing that a text is always an intertext, that is, a trace of other texts, itself a translation of other texts and fragments of language, postmodernists have unthought and unhinged the conceptual difference between original and translation, between what is deemed primary and unique, and what is deemed secondary and second-rate. In practising many of these theoretical tenets, the multi-user format of hypertexts announces a new way then, not only of reading, writing and translating, but also of studying and researching texts, literatures and translations.

KARIN LITTAU

Further Reading

Landow, George P., *Hypertext: The Convergence of Contemporary Critical Theory and Technology*, Baltimore: Johns Hopkins University Press, 1992

Laviosa-Braithwaite, Sara, "Computers and Translators", *The European English Messenger*, 5/1 (1996) pp. 39–41

Littau, Karin, "Translation in the Age of Postmodern Production: From Text to Intertext to Hypertext", *Forum for Modern Language Studies*, special issue on translation, edited by Ian Higgins, 33/1 (1997) pp. 81–96

I

I Ching (Yi Jing) uncertain date BC

The *I Ching* is an ancient Chinese divination classic, which seeks to explain the processes of natural change through the modulation of 64 "hexagrams", or six-line diagrams (said to have originated with the mythical sage-ruler, Fu Xi). The work as we now have it represents less a single text than a complex tradition of accretions, within which a central distinction can be made. The original text, sometimes referred to as the *Chou I* (pinyin: *Zhou Yi*), comprises the hexagrams themselves, the "Judgements" on each hexagram, attributed to King Wen of Zhou (reigned 1099–1050 BC), and the "Line-statements" on the hexagram lines, attributed to his son, Zhou Gong (modern scholarship has now disproved these attributions). In addition to these early portions, there are a later set of 10 archaic commentaries, which themselves became part of the classic and which are known as the "Ten Wings". Traditionally ascribed to Confucius, their dating is uncertain, but most, including the highly important "Xi ci zhuan" ("Commentary on the Appended Verbalizations") are thought to be at least as early as Western Han (began 202 BC).

Editions

Among the considerable number of editions available, the following are of note for the present survey:

Zhou yi gujing jinzhu, by Gao Heng, Shanghai, 1947; reprinted Beijing: Zhonghua Shuju, 1984 (contains the text of the original classic, i.e. minus the Ten Wings, with Gao's own notes, and some important introductory essays on specific problems of textual understanding)

Zhou yi zhezhong, by Li Guangdi (1642–1718, Qing dynasty), *Siku quanshu* edition (text with one of the influential later commentaries, plus collected earlier material)

Zhou yi zhushu, with the commentary of Wang Bi (226–249, Jin dynasty) and subcommentary by Kong Yingda (574–648, Tang) *et al.*, edited by Sibu Beiyao (the complete text plus two of the most influential early commentaries)

Translations

Blofeld, John, *I Ching: The Book of Change*, London: Allen and Unwin, 1965; New York: Dutton, 1968

Kunst, Richard A., *The Original Yijing: A Text, Phonetic Transcription, Translation and Indexes, with Sample Glosses*, dissertation, 2 vols, University of California, Berkeley, 1985

Legge, James, *The Yî King* in *The Sacred Books of China: The Texts of Confucianism*, Oxford: Clarendon Press, 1882; reprinted New York: Dover, 1963; London: New English Library, 1971 (The Sacred Books of the East, edited by F. Max Müller, part 2)

Lynn, Richard John, *The Classic of Changes: A New Translation of the I Ching as Interpreted by Wang Bi*, New York: Columbia University Press, 1994

McClatchie, Rev. Canon Thomas, *A Translation of the Confucian Yi King, or, The Classic of Changes*, Shanghai: American Presbyterian Mission Press, 1876; reprinted Taipei, Taiwan: n.p., 1973

Ritsema, Rudolf, and Stephen Karcher, *I Ching: The Classic Chinese Oracle of Change: The First Complete Translation with Concordance*, Shaftesbury, Dorset, and Rockport, Massachusetts: Element, 1994

Shaughnessy, Edward L., *The Composition of the Zhouyi*, dissertation, Stanford University, California, 1983

Shaughnessy, Edward L., *I Ching: The Classic of Changes*, New York: Ballantine Books, 1996

Sung, Z.D., *The Text of Yi King (and Its Appendices)* (bilingual edition), with an introduction, Shanghai: China Modern Education Corporation, 1935

Wilhelm, Richard and Cary F. Baynes, *The I Ching; or, Book of Changes*, German translation by Wilhelm (1924), rendered into English by Baynes, New York: Pantheon, 1950; London: Routledge and Kegan Paul, 1951; the standard edition on which all reprints are now based is the important 3rd edition, Princeton, New Jersey: Princeton University Press, and London: Routledge and Kegan Paul, 1968; CD-ROM version, Princeton: Princeton University Press, 1996

First made available to an English-speaking public through the works of 19th-century missionaries, the *I Ching* had, by the latter part of the 20th century, become something of a growth industry. While a small but steady trickle of scholarly translations continues to appear, interest in "Eastern mysticism" has led to a flood of more popular recensions, whose status as translations is highly questionable; these latter are not considered in the present survey.

Approaches to the translation of the *I Ching* differ considerably. One consideration is the composite nature of the work, outlined above: while the majority of translations present the complete work, certain scholars interested in its origins as a pre-Confucian mantic text have focused solely on the earliest material, without the Ten Wings. Also of crucial importance is the question of which traditional commentary one follows when trying to make sense of the text's often obscure and elliptical language: a late-imperial understanding of the text will often produce strikingly different results from a translation informed by a pre-Tang commentary. Of further relevance is the translator's personal view of the work's contents: some, such as Lynn, take an explicitly "historicist" approach; others, like Wilhelm, present the work as a "book of wisdom", possessing some deep and universal truth; still others lay greater emphasis on its oracular applications.

Of the two Victorian translations considered here, that of McClatchie (1876) should be used with extreme care. Notwithstanding the relative infancy of *I Ching*-scholarship at the time, there are inexcusable errors that reflect both a flawed understanding and a sometimes slapdash approach. One persistent problem is the confusion of the Judgement and Image statements with their respective Ten Wings commentaries. Thus McClatchie has King Wen speaking the text of the "Commentary on the Judgement" rather than the Judgement itself. Elsewhere, phrases such as "My clan knawing my flesh ..." (at Hexagram 38) suggest a lack of subtlety exacerbated by a muddled reading of the commentaries, while slips such as the reading of "xiong" (Hexagram 61, Top Nine) as "good luck" instead of "bad luck" further undermine the work's credibility.

By comparison, Legge's near-contemporary work (1882), which clearly shows the influence of the later commentarial tradition, is a considerable improvement. Though criticized by some later scholars for taking an unsympathetic approach to the text, it remains a surprisingly thorough piece of early scholarship. While its rather wordy style and heavy use of interpolation sometimes become cumbersome, as the author struggles to give meaning to images of which he is not always certain, this is a work still deserving of consultation.

Sung's work (1935) is essentially Legge's translation printed with a Chinese text. A disingenous introduction suggests that "many changes have been introduced", but these are basically confined to presentation: translations of each hexagram name are added, the Ten Wings are printed in their more usual order (split up amongst the hexagrams), and the original terms "Six" and "Nine" in the line-statements are substituted for Legge's "divided" and "undivided".

Originally published in German (1923), Wilhelm's translation, in its English version by Cary Baynes (1950 and 1968), has long been the best-known and most influential Western presentation of the *I Ching*. Wilhelm's understanding is largely informed by the late commentarial tradition. A subtle example of this occurs early in the "Xi ci zhuan", where the phrase "gang rou duan yi" is translated "firm and yielding lines are differentiated" (cf. Li Guangdi and other Qing commentators); early commentators such as Wang Bi, by contrast, interpret the terms *gang* and *rou* here as broader cosmic principles, making no explicit mention of the lines (cf. Lynn's "hardness and softness"). In general, Wilhelm's work still commands respect, though one should be aware of errors, and of a sometimes idiosyncratic understanding of the text, which as Shchutskii notes (1960, translated 1979), "perhaps makes [it] more interesting to read, but distorts, sometimes significantly", long-accepted interpretations. Wilhelm's style is markedly different from that of earlier translators: he employs a sparse phraseology that attempts to capture the terseness of the original and, with it, a sense of the work's enigmatic imagery; though partially successful in this, Wilhelm is sometimes over-zealous: when considered alone, certain phrases seem excessively obscure.

Blofeld's popular but intelligent *I Ching* (1965) places the emphasis firmly on practical divination. Though purists may complain that it lacks rigour (its sometimes paraphrastic passages seem a far cry from the textual intricacies of e.g. Lynn), its concision achieves an accessibility that comes as welcome relief to those bogged down in Wilhelm's sprawling mass of commentary. Moreover, Blofeld often manages to convey the essential purport of a passage more effectively than Wilhelm. His lively, down-to-earth style provides a strong contrast to the latter's stark Germanic mysticism.

The 1980s saw an increasing interest in the earliest texts of the *I Ching*. Various scholars, in particular Shaughnessy (1983) and Kunst (1985), have sought to reconstruct its original meaning through an archaeological approach, turning to such sources as early bronze and oracle-bone inscriptions, and to the earliest extant texts of the work, from the Mawangdui Tombs (c.163 BC). Such studies produce interesting new textual insights: to cite one well-known example, the phrase "yuan heng li zhen" (found in the Judgement for Hexagram 1, and elsewhere) might indicate not the "four virtues", by which "Confucian" commentators (and translators) understand the term, but rather a statement concerning the beneficial nature of a particular divination.

Lynn's scholarly translation (1994) draws explicitly on the commentary of Wang Bi (itself translated in its entirety, and interspersed with the main text in the manner of a traditional Chinese layout). Whether Lynn ultimately succeeds in fathoming the imagery of the text any more satisfactorily than previous translators is debatable. But the recourse to this earlier commentarial tradition does at least produce fresh interpretations that sometimes get closer to the text's literal meaning, as the "Commentary on the Words of the Text" for Hexagram 2, Top Six, illustrates well. To cite one succinct example from this difficult passage, the reading of "yi" as "equal" in the phrase "*yin* seeks to equal *yang*" is seen to be a later gloss not found in the earlier commentaries; thus Lynn renders *yi* with its normal meaning of "to suspect": "*yin* provokes the suspicions of *yang*". Lynn's style eschews the brevity of Wilhelm: indeed its wordiness sometimes approaches that of the Victorian translators; and though generally far more astute, his interpolations do not always impart the correct nuance, as in the passage from "Xi ci zhuan" cited above at Wilhelm, where the Lynn translation of "duan" as a passive in the phrase "... gang rou duan yi" ("... which *are determined* by whether hardness or softness is involved") seems questionable even in Wang Bi's understanding.

By contrast, such adherence to one interpretive line is anathema to Ritsema & Karcher (1994), whose translation is primarily intended for use as a personal "psychological tool". Since the "quality of the encounter with the Oracle" will differ according to each individual's circumstances, they argue, the translation must attempt to suggest the "multivalence" of interpretive possibilities and nuances present in the original text, at least some of which would inevitably be lost in a conventional translation. Therefore, they try to mirror the Chinese exactly in both word order and vocabulary, employing a single word for each character, and using the same English gloss for that character throughout. The problems inherent in this approach are legion. To begin with, the resultant phrases emerge in a laconic Chinglish that makes even Wilhelm's tersest statements seem elegant. Moreover, it rests on the fundamental methodological flaw of assuming that it is possible to recreate the Chinese reader's experience in English by transposing the effects of a naturally imagistic and syntactically isolating language into one that is highly cohesive. It effectively shuns real questions of textual interpretation in favour of the naive idea that ancient Chinese is a rag-bag of disjointed images from which readers can pick and choose a meaning at will.

ROBERT J. NEATHER

Further Reading

Peterson, Willard, "Making Connections: 'Commentary on the Attached Verbalisations' of the *Book of Changes*", *Harvard Journal of Asiatic Studies*, 42 (1982) pp. 67–116

Shaughnessy, Edward L., "I Ching (Chou I)" in *Early Chinese Texts: A Bibliographical Guide*, edited by Michael Loewe, Berkeley, California: Society for the Study of Early China, Institute of Asian Studies, 1993

Shchutskii, Iulian K., *Researches on the I Ching* [1960], translated from the Russian by William L. MacDonald and Tsuyoshi Hasegawa, with Hellmut Wilhelm, and with a preface by Gerald Swanson, Princeton, New Jersey: Princeton University Press, 1979

Wilhelm, Hellmut, *Change: Eight Lectures on the I Ching*, translated from the German by Cary F. Baynes, New York: Pantheon, 1960; London: Routledge and Kegan Paul, 1961

Wilhelm, Hellmut, *Heaven, Earth, and Man in the Book of Changes: Seven Eranos Lectures*, Seattle: University of Washington Press, 1977

Ibn Hazm 994–1064

Arab prose writer, jurist, historian and theologian

Biography

Ibn Hazm was born in Córdoba in 994 into a family that was of Christian origin – his great-grandfather had converted to Islam. He lived in a turbulent age, and, as a fanatical supporter of the ruling Umayyad dynasty, he found his fortunes ebbing and flowing with theirs. His political career reached its zenith in 1023 when he was appointed chief minister by the caliph 'Abd al-Rahmān V. However, seven weeks later 'Abd al-Rahmān was murdered by his opponents and Ibn Hazm was imprisoned. It is not until 1029 that we hear of him again. By that time he was already in semi-retirement, doing some teaching but mainly writing books. He had developed a radical stance in religious matters, becoming the leading exponent of the Zāhirī school of law. In his writings he launched scathing attacks on the stance of the religious authorities in al-Andalus and on the 'Abbadid dynasty, which had taken control of the province of Seville. In return he was declared a *persona non grata* in most of Muslim Spain and his writings were ceremonially burned in Seville. He ended his days on his family estate near Huelva, dying in Manta Lisham, near Seville, in 1064. In the circumstances it is hardly surprising that few of his many works have survived or that some of these are still in manuscript.

The Ring of the Dove

Tawq al-Hamāma, probably after 1024

Translations

Arberry, A.J., *The Ring of the Dove: A Treatise on the Art and Practice of Arab Love*, London: Luzac, 1953, reprinted 1994; New York: AMS Press, 1981

Nykl, Alois Richard, *A Book Containing the Risāla Known as The Dove's Neck-Ring, about Love and Lovers*, edited by D.K. Pétrof, Paris: Geuthner, 1931.

Abū Muhammad 'Alī ibn Hazm was one of the most notable polymaths produced by medieval Muslim civilization. The traditional Arab view of him was neatly summed up by the noted Syrian biographer Ibn Khallikān (1211–82): "Ibn Hazm was the most eminent of all the natives of al-Andalus (Muslim Spain) by dint of the universality and depth of his learning in Islamic sciences ... and his profound acquaintance with the Arabic language, his abilities as an elegant writer, a poet, a biographer and historian." It has to be said that most of his Andalusian contemporaries had taken a much more jaundiced view of him.

Two books by Ibn Hazm have attracted interest in the West. The first is the *Kitāb al-fical fī l-milal wal-ahwā' wal-nihal*, which may be loosely paraphrased as "The Book on Religious and Philosophical Sects". This was the first attempt in Arabic to cover, at least in part, the study of comparative religion. It is generally agreed to be Ibn Hazm's most important work, in which he shows scholarship of the highest level as a historian of religious ideas. Outside Islam the work's main focus is on Judaism and Christianity, of which Ibn Hazm shows an impressive knowledge; but it also deals with dualism, astral religions and metempsychosis. All are examined from the author's own strict Islamic standpoint; so too are all the Islamic sects and schisms.

However, it is a work of a totally different kind that has been the subject of a number of translations. This is the *Tawq al-Hamāma*, literally *The Dove's Neck-ring*, a treatise on love and lovers. There had been several earlier Arabic works on this subject and there were to be many more. None compares with that of Ibn Hazm, whose autobiographical touches and psychological insight lift his work out of the routine.

The *Tawq al-Hamāma* was probably written in the period immediately following Ibn Hazm's fall from power in 1024, though some would date it earlier, as the latest personal events to which he refers are linked to a period in 1022 when he was also out of favour. The work is conceived as a *risāla*, an epistle, in which the author puts forward his views on a subject as part of an imaginary exchange of letters with a friend. As is usual the epistle is prefaced by an introductory section and rounded off by an *envoi*. Ibn Hazm uses the introduction cleverly, bringing in the first of several comparisons between the vagaries of the civil strife (*fitna*) of the time in which he lived and the vicissitudes of love. When Ibn Hazm moves to the main part of the *risāla*, he adds a further formal element by dividing it into three sections of 10 chapters each, with each section to be thought of as one ring and thus part of a tripartite *tawq*: the beginnings of love; the accidents of love and its satisfaction; and the trials and misfortunes of love. The first two sections flout the conventions of strict Islamic morality both in their general tone and in the anecdotes they contain. The third section redresses the balance, ending with chapters on the "turpitude of sin" and the "merit of abstinence". Some have argued that these last two chapters are a later addition and/or a sop to the moral climate of the time. That seems unlikely, though it is clear from the *envoi* that Ibn Hazm is aware that he will offend zealots. He seems to have written a work for his friends, in which he balances the amoral nostalgia that pervades the earlier parts with some of the moral fastidiousness that is generally found in his writings.

The only serious effort to translate the *Kitāb al-fical fī l-milal wal-ahwā' wal-nihal* is the almost complete Spanish version by M. Asín Palacios (5 vols, Madrid 1927–32) – an invaluable work, with extensive background essays. An English translation is underway, but it is unlikely to be ready until 2001.

The *Tawq al-Hamāma* was lost to sight until an edition of the sole surviving manuscript was published by Pétrof at Leiden in 1914. The work soon attracted the attention of orientalists, and from the 1930s there has been a steady trickle of translations – in English: A.R. NYKL (Paris 1931), A.J. Arberry (London 1953); in French: L. Bercher (Algiers 1949), G. Martinez-Gros (Paris 1992); in German: M. Weisweiler (Leiden 1941); in Italian: F. Gabrieli (Bari 1949); in Russian: A Salie (Moscow/Leningrad 1933); in Spanish: Emilio García Gómez (Madrid 1952), R. Mujica Pinilla (Madrid 1990).

ARBERRY's translation is reasonably adequate, though it is not one of his more sparkling efforts. Best of the others are Martinez-Gros and Mujica Pinilla. The most complete bibliography is provided by García Gómez. Soon after its publication, Carlos Quirós Rodríguez published a critique of García Gómez's translation ("Una reciente traducción de 'El Collar de la Paloma' de Ibn Hazm, de Córdoba"), to which García Gómez replied ("En torno a mi traducción de 'El Collar ... ' ").

In 1990 one of Ibn Hazm's texts on Islamic ethics, *Al akhlak wa'l-siyar*, was translated into English by Muhammad Abu Laylah in his *In Pursuit of Virtue: The Moral Theology and Psychology of Ibn Hazm al-Andalusi* (London: Tatta, 1990).

ALAN JONES

Further Reading

Arnaldez, Roger, Ibn Hazm entry in *Encyclopaedia of Islam*, new edition, Leiden: Brill, 1968

Nicholson, Reynold A., *A Literary History of the Arabs*, London: Unwin, 1907; 2nd edition, Cambridge: Cambridge University Press, 1930, reprinted Richmond, Surrey: Curzon Press, 1993

Nykl, A.R., *Hispano-Arabic Poetry and Its Relations with the Old Provençal Troubadours*, Baltimore: Furst, 1946; reprinted 1970

Henrik Ibsen 1828–1906

Norwegian dramatist and poet

Biography

Born 20 March 1828 into a prosperous family at Skien, Telemark, Norway, and went to school locally. During his childhood the family fortunes failed. After apprenticeship to an apothecary he began to study medicine but was attracted to the writing of drama and published *Catilina* in 1850. From 1851 to 1857, as house dramatist to the Norwegian Theatre at Bergen, he wrote several plays. From 1857 to 1862 he was director of the Norwegian Theatre in Christiania, now Oslo. After this theatre went bankrupt Ibsen travelled in Norway, Italy (where he lived 1864–68 and 1878–85), Egypt, and Germany (living there 1868–78) and 1878–91). He returned to

Norway in 1891. His creative writing ceased after he suffered a stroke in 1900. He died in Christiania, 23 May 1906.

Ibsen's career as a dramatist exactly covers the second half of the 19th century and divides into two periods: romantic (1850–73] and modern (1877–99). His plays of the 1850s are largely apprentice work set typically in an idealized medieval Norway. In 1863 came the first mature drama, *The Pretenders*, a fine historical tragedy in which Ibsen's gift for pungent, realistic dialogue is revealed for the first time. However, his international fame and influence rest on two romantic verse plays, *Brand* (1866) and *Peer Gynt* (1867), and a cycle of 12 realistic prose dramas, from *Pillars of Society* (1877) through such now familiar masterpieces as *A Doll's House* and *Hedda Gabler* to the more forbidding *When We Dead Awaken* (1899), which Ibsen called his "epilogue".

Ibsen was introduced to British readers and audiences in the 1890s, primarily through William Archer's translations, Elizabeth Robins's sensitive performances of such roles as Hedda Gabler and Hilde Wangel in *The Master Builder*, and the determined advocacy of George Bernard Shaw. During the 20th century Ibsen's plays have been re-translated and performed with increasing frequency in the English-speaking world, where readers can choose from numerous collected, selected or individual editions of his plays.

Editions

The standard Norwegian text of Ibsen's works is the Centennial Edition: *Samlede Verker: Hundreårsutgave*, 21 vols, edited by Francis Bull, Halvdan Koht and Didrik Arup Seip, Oslo: Gyldendal, 1928–57. The plays and poems are also available in a paperback edition: *Samlede Verker*, 3 vols, Oslo; Gyldendal, 1962

Translations

Collections of Plays

Archer, William and others, *The Collected Works of Henrik Ibsen*, entirely revised and edited by William Archer, translated by William Archer, Edmund Gosse, Charles Archer, Frances E. Archer, Eleanor Marx-Aveling, Mary Morison, C.H. Herford and A.C. Chater, 13 vols, London: Heinemann, and New York: Scribner, 1906–12 and many reprints; some of the translations had already been, and would be again, published singly or in other collections (vol. 1: *Lady Inger of Östråt*, translated by Charles Archer; *The Feast at Solhoug*, translated by William Archer and Mary Morison; *Love's Comedy*, translated by C.H. Herford; vol. 2: *The Vikings at Helgeland* and *The Pretenders*, both translated by William Archer; vol. 3: *Brand*, translated by C.H. Herford; vol. 4: *Peer Gynt*, translated by William and Charles Archer; vol. 5: *Emperor and Galilean*, translated by William Archer; vol 6: *The League of Youth* and *Pillars of Society*, both translated by William Archer; vol. 7: *A Doll's House* and *Ghosts*, both translated by William Archer; vol. 8: *An Enemy of the People*, translated by Eleanor Marx-Aveling; *The Wild Duck*, translated by Frances E. Archer; vol. 9: *Rosmersholm*, translated by Charles Archer; *The Lady from the Sea*, translated by Frances E. Archer; vol. 10: *Hedda Gabler* and *The Master Builder*, both translated by Edmund Gosse and William Archer; vol. 11: *Little Eyolf*, *John Gabriel Borkman* and *When We Dead Awaken*, all translated by William Archer; vol. 12: *From Ibsen's Workshop; Notes, Scenarios, and Drafts of the Modern Plays*, translated by A.G. Chater; vol. 13: Edmund Gosse, *The Life of Henrik Ibsen*

Fjelde, Rolf, *Ibsen: The Complete Major Prose Plays*, New York: Farrar Straus, 1978 (contains *Pillars of Society*, *A Doll House*, *Ghosts*, *An Enemy of the People*, *The Wild Duck*, *Rosmersholm*, *The Lady from the Sea*, *Hedda Gabler*, *The Master Builder*, *Little Eyolf*, *John Gabriel Borkman*, *When We Dead Awaken*; some of the translations had appeared in earlier Ibsen collections by Fjelde

McFarlane, James Walter, Graham Orton and others, *The Oxford Ibsen*, with introductions, 8 vols, London and New York: Oxford University Press, 1960–77 (vol. 1: *Early Plays*; vol. 2: *The Vikings at Helgeland*, *Love's Comedy*, *The Pretenders*; vol. 3: *Brand*, *Peer Gynt*; vol. 4: *The League of Youth*, *Emperor and Galilean*; vol. 5: *Pillars of Society*, *A Doll's House*, *Ghosts*; vol. 6: *An Enemy of the People*, *The Wild Duck*, *Rosmersholm*; vol. 7: *The Lady from the Sea*, *Hedda Gabler*, *The Master Builder*; vol. 8: *Little Eyolf*, *John Gabriel Borkman*, *When We Dead Awaken*)

Meyer, Michael, *Plays: Henrik Ibsen*, 6 vols, London: Eyre Methuen, 1980 (vol. 1: *Ghosts*, *The Wild Duck*, *The Master Builder*; vol. 2: *A Doll's House*, *An Enemy of the People*, *Hedda Gabler*; vol. 3: *Rosmersholm*, *The Lady from the Sea*, *Little Eyolf*; vol. 4: *Pillars of Society*, *John Gabriel Borkman*, *When We Dead Awaken*; vol. 5: *Brand*, *Emperor and Galilean*; vol. 6: *Peer Gynt*, *The Pretenders*; as *The Plays of Ibsen*, 4 vols, (revised edition), New York: Washington Square Press, 1986 (contains the same 16 titles distributed through 4 volumes and in a different order); most of these translations also appeared singly at earlier dates

Selections of Plays

Ellis-Fermor, Una, *The Master Builder and Other Plays*, Harmondsworth: Penguin, 1958 (contains *The Master Builder*, *Rosmersholm*, *Little Eyolf*, *John Gabriel Borkman*)

Le Gallienne, Eva, *Six Plays by Henrik Ibsen*, New York: Modern Library, 1957 (contains *A Doll's House*, *Ghosts*, *An Enemy of the People*, *Rosmersholm*, *Hedda Gabler*, *The Master Builder*; some of the translations had already been published separately)

Orbeck, Anders, *Ibsen: Early Plays*, New York: American-Scandinavian Foundation, 1921 (contains *Catiline*, *The Warrior's Barrow*, *Olaf Liljekrans*)

Van Laan, Thomas, *Catiline; and The Burial Mound*, New York and London: Garland, 1992

Watts, Peter, *The League of Youth, A Doll's House, The Lady from the Sea*, Harmondsworth: Penguin, 1965

Plays

Brand, 1866

Herford, C.H., *Brand: A Dramatic Poem*, with an introduction and notes, London: Heinemann, 1894

Hill, Geoffrey, *Brand, by Henrik Ibsen: A Version for the English Stage*, London: Heinemann, for the National Theatre, 1978

Meyer, Michael, *Brand*, London: Hart-Davis, 1960

Wilson, William, *Brand: A Dramatic Poem*, London: Methuen, 1891

Peer Gynt, 1867, produced 1876
Green, Paul, *Peer Gynt: American Version*, New York: Samuel French, 1951
See entry on *Peer Gynt*, below

Kejser og Galilaeer, 1873, produced 1896
Ray, Catherine, *Emperor and Galilean: A Drama in Two Parts*, London: Samuel Tinsley, 1876

En Folkefiende, 1882, produced 1883
Miller, Arthur, *An Enemy of the People: An Adaptation*, New York: Viking Press, 1951

Hedda Gabler, 1890, produced 1891
Le Gallienne, Eva, *Hedda Gabler*, London: Faber, 1953

John Gabriel Borkman, 1896, produced 1897
Ewbank, Inga-Stina and Peter Hall, with an introduction, *John Gabriel Borkman*, London: Athlone Press, 1975
Wright, Nicholas and Charlotte Barslund, *John Gabriel Borkman*, London: Nick Hern, 1996

Poetry
Garrett, F.E., *Lyrics and Poems from Ibsen*, London: Dent, and New York: Dutton, 1912
Northam, John, *Ibsen's Poems*, Oslo: Norwegian University Press, and Oxford: Oxford University Press, 1986

Other Writing
Sprinchorn, Evert and others, *Letters and Speeches: Ibsen*, edited by Evert Sprinchorn, New York: Hill and Wang, 1964

Henrik Ibsen's early national-romantic and historical dramas made their way into English only gradually. ARCHER included translations of *Lady Inger*, *The Feast at Solhoug*, *The Vikings at Helgeland*, *Love's Comedy*, and *The Pretenders*, in his edition of the *Collected Works* (1906–12); and in 1921 ORBECK published the first English versions of *Catiline*, *The Burial Mound*, and *Olaf Liljekrans*. The complete early plays were not available until 1970, when MCFARLANE & ORTON added *Norma; or A Politician's Love* (a parody of Bellini's opera), *St John's Night* (a "fairy-tale comedy" disowned by the dramatist), and the alternative versions of *Catiline* and *The Burial Mound*. VAN LAAN's scholarly edition (1992) of *Catiline* and *The Burial Mound* (also with alternative versions) is of equal value. His accurate and readable verse translations are faithful to Ibsen's metres and intermittent use of rhyme, which Van Laan sees as "mandatory to conveying the effect of the original text".

Published in 1866, *Brand* is a large-scale dramatic poem written in rhyming iambic and trochaic verse. Brand is a Lutheran priest whose desire to inspire his congregation with an unconditional faith leads to his own destruction. Arguably the greatest verse tragedy since Racine, it has only recently come into its own in English theatre. Four versions of *Brand* deserve attention.

WILSON's 1891 prose translation remains the most faithful to Ibsen's meaning. HERFORD (1894) is also accurate, and reproduces Ibsen's strong verse lines successfully, albeit without the rhymes; on balance this is the best reading version. MEYER's *Brand*, first published in 1960, employs a kind of free verse which intermittently turns into iambic pentameter or lapses into prose. His rendering seems undistinguished now, though it was used for Michael Elliott's memorable 1959 production with Patrick McGoohan as Brand.

HILL (1978) was uniquely suited to translate *Brand*. His best-known poem "Genesis", whose speaker sets out "To ravage and redeem the world", comes extremely close to Brand's fiercely messianic speeches, in theme, metre, and imagery. To parallel Ibsen's verse, Hill uses an irregular three-beat line and his own rhyme scheme, admitting that this is less a translation than "a version for the English stage". It could be objected that Hill has over-Christianized the play. Brand's last question of God, "Gjelder ej et frelsens fnug / manneviljens quantum satis ...?" (does not the quantum satis of man's will merit one speck of salvation ...?), becomes "Why is salvation / rooted so blindly on your Cross?/ Why is man's own proud will his curse?" Readers, then, should beware, but this is the strongest acting version of *Brand*.

The League of Youth (1869) is a satirical comedy about an opportunistic politician whose liberalism masks, in Haugen's words "ambition for position, power, and wealth through marriage". The best versions are by ARCHER and MCFARLANE.

Emperor and Galilean (1873), Ibsen's two-part "world-historical play" about Julian the Apostate, remains, like Thomas Hardy's *The Dynasts*, a fascinating closet drama, though it has been successfully produced on BBC radio. RAY's version of 1876 (the first translation into English of an Ibsen play; included in Archer's *Ibsen's Prose Dramas*) is described by Miriam Alice Franc as "pale and colourless". ARCHER and ORTON can both be recommended.

Between 1889 when he translated *A Doll's House*, and 1912 when he completed his Ibsen edition, ARCHER worked tirelessly to introduce English-language readers and audiences to Ibsen's modern cycle. As late as 1919, Franc would claim that Archer's "collection has been reprinted again and again in England and America and will undoubtedly remain for many years the standard English edition of Ibsen". By that time, such plays as *A Doll's House*, *Ghosts*, and *Hedda Gabler* had revolutionized the English stage.

The first serious challenge to Archer came from the American actress LE GALLIENNE who in 1928 began to translate, star in, or direct, the modern cycle. Seeking to de-Victorianize Ibsen, she gave *Hedda Gabler* (1953), for example, a 1920s setting, and played Hedda as the elegant, cigarette-smoking woman associated with the comedies of Noel Coward. Le Gallienne's published translations, however, reproduce Ibsen's stage directions and dialogue without any real attempt to modernize or adapt. Though she complained, incorrectly, that, in Archer, Ibsen's "great Viking ship, with its clean ... uncompromising lines, has been muffled under Victorian drapery", her own versions do not make Ibsen's ideas more "savagely alive", as she seemed to think they did.

During the Depression and World War II, Ibsen fell out of favour with American audiences. Robert A. Schanke points out that Ibsen's harsh image of the bourgeois family, and the independent spirit of such heroines as Nora Helmer and Rebekka West, stood little chance in an era that looked back to "traditional American values" even as it "presented women as sexual commodities" in the new beauty pageants and on the silver screen. Those who did venture into Ibsen territory often relied on more or less radical adaptation in the hope of dusting off what one 1935 review dismissed as "sacred relics". The sad results of misguided adaptation can be seen in GREEN's insensitive Americanization (1951) of *Peer Gynt*, and Arthur MILLER's nervous efforts (1951) at disguising the anti-democratic sentiments in *An Enemy of the People*. Unfortunately, Miller's remains the most widely-read version of the play.

During the 1960s and 1970s, FJELDE's responsible and idiomatic translations of the modern cycle found favour with audiences and readers disabused, by bitter experience, of the American dream. Fjelde's promotion of Ibsen's plays and ideas is admirable. The idiom of his translations is, however, distracting for non-American readers, and Van Laan rightly argues that Fjelde substitutes "verbal variation for Ibsen's repetition of identical words".

In England, a dominant line of realistic drama can be traced from Archer's translation of Ibsen's modern cycle, through the work of Harley Granville-Barker, John Galsworthy, and Somerset Maugham, to that of Terence Rattigan. The relatively conservative theatre language of this tradition meant that Archer's style enjoyed a long sunset, despite the anti-Victorianism that flourished between the wars. Even when new translations did appear, like those by WATTS (1965) and ELLIS-FERMOR (1958), they made little significant change to the tone of Ibsen's dialogue. Ellis-Fermor must, however, be given credit for expressing her *debt* to Archer, which she describes as "beyond estimate".

The revolution in English drama, exemplified by John Osborne's *Look Back in Anger* (1956), and Harold Pinter's *The Caretaker* (1960), was most clearly felt in a language new to 20th-century English theatre, alternatively violent, ironic, terse, and evasive. This in turn created a need for new and tougher translations of classic drama. In Ibsen's case this need was to some extent met by MEYER, whose translations, from 1960, enjoyed a success almost as great as Archer's, and contributed to a second golden age of Ibsen productions in the British theatre. Kenneth Tynan, the most influential drama critic of the 1960s, described Meyer's Ibsen as "crisp and cobweb-free, purged of verbal Victoriana"; for George Steiner, "Meyer's translations of Ibsen are a major fact in one's general sense of post-war drama"; and J.C. Trewin claimed: "The plays shine freshly from the page ... This will be our definitive Ibsen." Gratitude for Meyer's revival of Ibsen's plays should not, however, blind us to his faults, or indeed persuade us that *any* translation can be "definitive". Meyer, for example, is too wordy, and like FJELDE (1978) uses idioms and diction that date and localize his versions. He also makes arbitrary cuts and changes, such as the substitution of "Danielle" for "Diana" as the name of Ejlert Løvborg's nemesis in *Hedda Gabler*, which breaks Ibsen's subtle chain of allusions to Greco-Roman myth and tragedy. Van Laan is justified in his opinion that Meyer is "too loose in his rendering of the source text and at times insensitive to stylistic registers".

MCFARLANE & ORTON began publishing the eight-volume *Oxford Ibsen* in 1960. Their translations of the modern plays are more accurate than Meyer's and read well, though they have not had the same theatrical success. The edition itself, the only complete English collection of the plays, is a superb work of dedicated scholarship, with good introductions, translations of Ibsen's drafts and notes, and accounts of contemporary reaction to the plays. SPRINCHORN's careful selection (1964) of Ibsen's letters and speeches makes a valuable supplement.

The rapid dating of Meyer's versions has prompted more and more directors to commission individual translations of the modern plays. Inga-Stina EWBANK & Peter HALL worked closely on *John Gabriel Borkman* for Hall's production in 1975, and in 1996 Nicholas WRIGHT & Charlotte BARSLUND translated the same play for the Royal National Theatre. Both versions, especially the later one, are written with an economy of style that trims the dialogue without damage to its meaning. In Ibsen, for example, when Ella Rentheim complains that an "icy gust" blows from "his kingdom" in the mines, Borkman replies "Det pust virker som livsluft på meg" (That gust works on me like the breath of life); in Wright & Barslund, this becomes "It brings me life". Nothing essential is lost, and the terseness gives the actor something of Norwegian's cold, hard-edged quality, itself a kind of irony in Ibsen's coldest play. It remains to be seen what direction English translations of the modern cycle can take from this point.

The only creative works of Ibsen not included in *The Oxford Ibsen* are his lyric, narrative, and occasional poems. GARRETT's selection of 26 lyrics, with the narrative poems "Pa vidderne" ("On the Moors") and "Terje Vigen", was published in 1912. This was replaced in 1986 by NORTHAM's translations of all the poems Ibsen admitted to two volumes published in 1899 and 1902. Northam's decision to match Ibsen's metre and rhyme works very well in "On the Moors" and "Terje Vigen", perhaps because their narrative drive and popular rhythms seem to come straight out of the Victorian ballad tradition. The short lyrics are another matter. Northam shows how "My white swan" for "Min hvite svane", the first line of "En svane" ("A Swan"), "sounds stiff, dull and stilted – and all because *Hvite* and *svane* are di-syllabic, and 'white' and 'swan' monosyllabic". In the end his imitation of Ibsen's syllable count and rhyme scheme leads Northam too often into quaint diction and an unidiomatic tendency to drop the definite article. In "With a Waterlily", "blomsten med de hvite vinger" (the flower with the white wings) becomes "flower of the whitest winging", where accuracy and idiom are sacrificed to match Ibsen's syllables and provide a rhyme for "bringing" in the previous line. In the same poem, Northam translates "nøkken later som han sover" (the water-troll pretends that he is sleeping) as "water-spirit plays at sleeping", which gives an air of babytalk to what in Ibsen is a serious warning. In this and other lyrics, Northam's fascination with the mechanics of Ibsen's verse obscures its beauty and its strangeness, and he might have done better to prepare a bilingual edition with literal English prose translations printed below the Norwegian. We can, however, be grateful to Northam for his completion of the Ibsen canon in English.

JOHN LINGARD

Further Reading

Akerholt, May B., "Henrik Ibsen in English Translation" in *The Languages of Theatre: Problems in the Translation and Transposition of Drama*, edited by Ortrun Zuber, Oxford: Pergamon Press, 1980

Ewbank, Inga-Stina, "Translating Ibsen for the Contemporary English Stage", *Theatre Research International* (1976), pp. 44–53

Ewbank, Inga-Stina, "Ibsen on the English Stage: The 'Proof of the Pudding is in the Eating'" in *Ibsen and the Theatre: The Dramatist in Production*, edited by Errol Durbach, New York: New York University Press, 1980

Franc, Miriam Alice, *Ibsen in England*, Boston: Four Seas, 1919
Schanke, Robert A., *Ibsen in America: A Century of Change*, Metuchen, New Jersey: Scarecrow Press, 1988
Törnkvist, Egil, "Translating *Et dukkehjem*" in his *Ibsen: A Doll's House*, Cambridge: Cambridge University Press, 1995
Van Laan, Thomas, "English Translations of *A Doll House*" in *Approaches to Teaching Ibsen's "A Doll House"*, edited by Yvonne Schafer, New York: Modern Language Association of America, 1985

Peer Gynt

Peer Gynt: en dramatisk dikt, 1867; first performed, with music by Edvard Grieg, in 1876

Translations

The Norwegian text of *Peer Gynt* has remained unchanged through numerous editions, except that, since 1960, the spelling has been changed to standard modern Norwegian, i.e. *riksmål*, from the Dano-Norwegian spelling used by Ibsen.

Archer, William and Charles Archer, *Peer Gynt: A Dramatic Poem*, with an introduction, London: Walter Scott, 1892; 2nd edition, New York: Scribner, 1906; London: Heinemann, 1907
Fjelde, Rolf, *Peer Gynt*, New York: New American Library, 1964; 2nd edition, Minneapolis: University of Minnesota Press, 1980
Fry, Christopher and Johan Fillinger, *Peer Gynt: A Dramatic Poem*, Oxford and New York: Oxford University Press, 1970; and in *The Oxford Ibsen*, edited by McFarlane, vol. 3, Oxford: Oxford University Press, 1972
Ginsbury, Norman, *Peer Gynt*, London: Hammond, 1945
Green, Paul, *Peer Gynt: American Version*, New York: Samuel French, 1951
McGuinness, Frank and Anne Bamborough, *Peer Gynt*, London: Faber, 1990
McLeish, Kenneth, *Peer Gynt: A Poetic Fantasy*, London: Nick Hern, 1990
Meyer, Michael, *Peer Gynt* in *Plays: Henrik Ibsen*, translated by Meyer, vol. 6, 1980 (originally published separately, 1963)
Northam, John, *Peer Gynt: A Dramatic Poem*, Oslo: Scandinavian University Press, 1993
Rudkin, David, *Peer Gynt*, with an introduction, London: Methuen, 1983
Sharp, R. Farquharson, *Peer Gynt*, London: Dent, 1921; New York: Dutton, 1925
Watts, Peter, *Peer Gynt: A Dramatic Poem*, with an introduction, Harmondsworth: Penguin, 1966

Peer Gynt is a five-act dramatic poem with some formal and thematic resemblance to Byron's *Manfred* and Goethe's *Faust*. Unlike earlier romantic heroes, however, Peer Gynt *evades* self-fulfilment: he goes "round about", in accordance with the "troll ethics of self-sufficiency" (Aarseth), only to discover that his self, like the wild onion he peels in act 5, has nothing at the core. Peer is redeemed by Solveig, the play's Gretchen-figure, but many feel that this ending sits oddly with Ibsen's harsh portrait of a spiritually bankrupt life.

Peer Gynt is an immensely difficult work to translate into English. It is very long: 4302 lines. It is written in a wide variety of regular and irregular metres and rhyme schemes. Ibsen's frequent use of double rhymes – *jente/vente*, *hjemme/glemme*, etc. – is hard to parallel in English, which lacks the Norwegian "abundance of verbal forms ending in unstressed syllables" (Van Laan). Where *Brand* has a uniform tragic intensity, *Peer Gynt* refuses to be pinned down in terms of genre or tone. Translators must find ways to convey comedy, pathos, satire, and elegy. There are strong folk-tale elements in the play, but these are more demonic than "folksy". In the words of Ibsen's poem, "A Verse" (1877), Peer Gynt's life is "a war with trolls" who represent the beast in man (Aarseth) and should not be sentimentalized. Another problem is that it is unusually hard to provide an accurate translation that will also work on stage. The play's exuberant fantasy can tempt translators into their own "freedom", which may lead to interesting theatre but will cheat the audience of Ibsen's play. Only two translators, WATTS and RUDKIN, have come close to balancing accuracy with stage-worthiness.

English translators of *Peer Gynt* can be placed in four categories: (1) Archer and his followers, who imitate Ibsen's metres but do not use rhyme; a method approved by the dramatist; (2) Those who attempt Ibsen's rhyme scheme as well as his metres; (3) Those who use prose throughout, except for songs and hymns; (4) Those who use prose except for songs, hymns, *and* passages like Peer's reindeer story, which seem to demand a lyrical approach. The best translations to date fall into categories 1 and 3. A full rhyming version (2) is almost impossible in English, and the shift from prose to verse (4) has a jarring effect, especially in the theatre.

ARCHER (1892, 1906) sought to convey "some faint conception of the movement and colour, the wit and pathos, of the original", and to provide "a 'crib' to the Norwegian text". The result is an accurate, line-for-line, translation that reproduces Ibsen's metres with considerable skill but makes no attempt at rhyme. Archer's verse flows better in the longer, irregular lines: the wedding dance, for example, or Peer's encounter with the Woman in Green. The decision to match the syllable count of the shorter, regular lines leads, by Archer's own admission, to syllabic padding – "Gun *a*missing" – and inversion – "Swam the buck". Cutting syllables to match Ibsen's count also creates Aase's delightfully Slavic, "You in air were riding reindeer". There *is* now an archaic tone to this pioneering translation, but Archer does capture some of the tough, sinewy quality of the verse, and he remains uniquely faithful to Ibsen's diction and meaning.

SHARP (1921), like Archer, follows Ibsen's metres and abandons rhyme. He avoids, however, "purely verbal literalness" and a "line-for-line rendering" of the text. The result is more idiomatic than Archer but far less reliable as a guide to Ibsen's meaning, and Sharp consistently waters down the demonic elements. His Young Trolls cry out "Now jump on his face", whereas Ibsen's "Now get his sight" (Nu i synet på ham) makes it clear that they wish to blind their victim. Similarly, Sharp's Woman in Green says merely that the devil was her midwife, whereas in Ibsen she says, "When I gave birth, the devil grasped me by the back", a more immediate and a more sinister image. Ironically, Arthur Rackham's fine colour illustrations convey more of the play's essence than this translation does.

GINSBURY (1945) follows Archer in normally avoiding

rhyme and seeking to preserve "the rhythm of each scene". Occasional rhymed sections such as Peer's serenade to Anitra and the "threadballs" scene in act 5, work well. Some of Ibsen's toughness is preserved, but this translation is full of arbitrary changes and misreadings. Ibsen's Peer calls the giant pig he rides into the mountain his "trusty steed" (ganger god), but Ginsbury changes this to "trusty sow", losing the point that Peer now sees the world through "trollish" eyes. Ginsbury also turns the desert cave (*hulen*) from act 4 into a grave, and translates "the norms of beauty" as "a Northern concept of beauty", apparently extracting "Northern" from "*normer*". The edition itself is, however, valuable for its generous supply of photographs from Tyrone Guthrie's famous production with Ralph Richardson as Peer.

GREEN's (1951) American version is a prose adaptation, written in collaboration with Lee Strasberg, that butchers and travesties Ibsen's play. The trolls are required to chant "Hunh!" in unison "*like Negro steel drivers*". In case the Woman in Green's pregnancy should pass us by, a Troll courtier announces: "Your majesty, the princess is suddenly pregnant". Peer Gynt is saved from the Boyg when Solveig appears as "*a radiant vision*" to lead an offstage choir in a biblical psalm. This is Ibsen reduced to the level of a Disney cartoon. Nothing is left to the imagination.

MEYER (1963) chose "a free verse with broken rhythms ... apart from certain passages which demand rhyme". His broken rhythms tend to become prose in many places, and this translation suffers from occasionally quaint diction, as when "draugen" (a kind of sinister water troll) becomes the Shakespearean "flibbertigibbet". Like Fjelde, Meyer also makes sexual innuendo too overt: the second Seter Girl's "do it roughly" is changed to "come and rape me", for example. The square brackets indicating cuts made in the Old Vic production are an unnecessary distraction for the reader.

FJELDE (1964, 1980) attempts to match Ibsen's metre and his rhyme scheme, using for the most part half- or "slant" rhymes: so "truth" rhymes with "wrath", "steel" with "pool", "Fuchs" with "shakes", and so on. These are distracting to the reader, especially when the intermittent use of full rhyme draws attention to the weakness of the half-rhyme technique. Fjelde takes Archer to task for using archaisms and inversions. He is, however, guilty of the occasional inversion himself – "To the wedding I'm off" – as well as padding and arbitrary change, often in the interest of half-rhymes. Ingrid's father is simply "angry" (*arrig*) in Ibsen; in Fjelde he is "angry as a beet". Ibsen's Woman in Green warns Peer that she will demand her share when "you pet" (*degge*) Solveig. Fjelde has, when "you put off your clothes". "It's all over with the rest of you" becomes "The rest of you reeks like a rotting fish", to provide a full rhyme for "wish". Fjelde is more successful in some scenes (Peer's act 2 apostrophe to the mountains, and the Cairo madhouse, for example), but in general this translation reflects the near-impossibility of answering Ibsen rhyme for rhyme.

FRY (1970) follows Archer, except that his lines are often loosely iambic tetrameters and pentameters in the manner of his own verse plays. As in his own writing, Fry both delights and irritates. "Kind little walnut of a mother" is touchingly right for "Little, ugly, kind mother", and "Blue-blooded trolls" is the best rendering of "adelstroll" (Noble-trolls). However, he cannot resist quaint diction, such as "winnicking", "twizzling" and "nousled", and many lines are subject to arbitrary change: "Give you time and you'll be a prince" (Ibsen/Watts) to "Give me time and I'll crow on a dunghill"; "like hair and comb" to "like faggots and peas"; and "asinine friends" to "arse-licking friends". Fry is also too fond of jarring British slang such as "Off her rocker", and "shagged out", and distracting literary allusions: "Black Beauty" and "jug-tereu-tereu" (T.S. Eliot, *The Waste Land*). In the end, Fry is far less successful than Watts in updating the Archer tradition.

RUDKIN (1983) wrote his prose translation of *Peer Gynt* for an RSC production in 1982. Instead of cutting scenes or sections, he aimed at "distillation: compressing each scene, beat, line ... into a minimum number, not of words, but of syllables". A unique feature of Rudkin's version is that the Norwegian characters use "a stylized rural Ulster speech". This works surprisingly well, not least because Rudkin respects Ibsen's meaning. No one, in English verse or prose, has captured the excitement of Peer's reindeer story so successfully as Rudkin, or the mounting violence of the wedding dance. The dialect may limit its production value outside the British Isles, but this remains the best English prose translation of Ibsen's play.

MCGUINNESS (1990) translated *Peer Gynt* for Dublin's Gate Theatre. Finding "a sense of ironic parallels between Ibsen and Ireland's cultural dilemmas", McGuinness gives the dialogue a lightly southern Irish flavour, and cleverly links the Cairo madhouse with Sinn Fein when Begriffenfeldt claims that each lunatic is "Himself alone", an apt translation of Ibsen's "*seg selv*" (himself). By his own acknowledgement, McGuinness moves between translation and adaptation. Aase threatens to "fart" her son from this world, and the trolls and Boyg scenes in act 3 are broken down quite successfully into the "telegraph" style of German expressionist drama. There are lapses of taste – such as Peer's reference to "Arab shagging" – and what seem to be misreadings: Ibsen's Peer Gynt exports idols (*gudebilleder*), not "dirty pictures", to China. Too unreliable for a reading text, this translation none the less captures much of the play's theatrical exuberance and strangeness.

MCLEISH (1990) mixes verse and prose, using verse "at moments of high fantasy or lyricism", which include Peer's reindeer story and his apostrophe to the mountains. Written for the British National Theatre, McLeish's *Peer Gynt* has a tongue-in-cheek tone suiting a production where the older Peer was played as a kind of stand-up comedian. The Seter girls call "cooee" to the trolls; the trolls' motto "to yourself be enough" becomes "be true to your self-ish"; Peer Gynt says "Bottoms up" as he drinks the "Bull-beer"; and in act 5 he blames the "Fucking trolls" for his life's failure. Taking a fashionably populist route, McLeish dilutes the play's demonic quality and blurs its meaning.

NORTHAM (1993) attempts "to provide the reader with a closer account than usual of [Ibsen's] verse forms". This means that he imitates the original rhyme schemes as well as the metres, uses full as opposed to half rhymes, and even tries to match Ibsen's frequent alternation of double and single rhymes. The result is a strong rhyming verse translation of *Peer Gynt* that is clearly superior to Fjelde's. Northam is extremely adept at rhyme and on the whole respectful of Ibsen's meaning. He does, however, use inversions and esoteric words for the sake of rhyme: for example, "judgment extreme"; "in sand is rolling"; "shoat", an obscure word for a young pig, used to rhyme with "goat"; and "bothie" for the Seter Girls' hut (*selet*). As in his valuable translations of Ibsen's poems (Oslo: Norwegian University Press, 1986), Northam's chief fault is an archness of phrasing that can read like pidgin English: "He is supple in the legs" becomes "He's got legs full of feeling" to rhyme with "ceiling"; asked by Begriffenfeldt if he is mad, Northam's Peer says, "save the mention", instead of "God help me" – McGuinness's accurate and idiomatic rendering of "Gud bevares" – which would not rhyme with "attention"; this Peer also asks the Cook to say "the our Father prayer" instead of the Lord's prayer. The sheer cleverness of Northam's double and triple rhymes threatens to become an aesthetic end in itself, rather like solutions to a cryptic crossword puzzle, as in "barded/guarded", "by Jingo/lingo" and "stallion/rapscallion". Nevertheless this translation is a remarkable achievement that would make by far the best English *Peer Gynt* for teaching purposes, were it not for the high present cost of this edition.

WATTS (1966), again in the Archer tradition, uses very little rhyme and conveys a sense of Ibsen's four-stress lines without becoming heavy-handed. Watts admits to being "especially free with Ibsen's metres" in the shorter, trochaic lines which in English are "hard to bear without rhyme". There are no lapses of taste, and only a few blurred or mistranslated lines. Watts's Peer calls women "the weaker sex", where Archer's "worthless crew" is both more accurate and stronger. In Watts's auction scene, we are told that Peer Gynt "hanged himself" years ago, whereas Ibsen writes "he was hanged" – hardly an unimportant difference. This remains, however, the best English verse translation: accurate, readable, and performable.

JOHN LINGARD

Further Reading

Aarseth, Asbjørn, *Peer Gynt and Ghosts: Text and Performance*, London: Macmillan, 1989

Arestad, Sverre, review of Fjelde's translation, *Modern Drama*, 8 (1966) pp. 447–49

Fjelde, Rolf and Sverre Arestad, "Translating *Peer Gynt*", *Modern Drama*, 10 (1967) pp. 104–10

Logeman, Henri, *A Commentary, Critical and Explanatory, on the Norwegian Text of Henrik Ibsen's Peer Gynt*, The Hague: Nijhoff, 1917; reprinted Westport, Connecticut: Greenwood Press, 1970

Van Laan, Thomas (editor and translator), introduction, in *Catiline, and The Burial Mound*, by Ibsen, New York: Garland, 1992 (not on *Peer Gynt* but valuable as a guide to the problems of translating Ibsen's dramatic verse)

See also the introductions by Archer, Rudkin and Watts

Ideology and Translation

Ideology is commonly understood as a systematic set of political beliefs about the world held by a particular, often dominant, group in society and is more often a term of abuse than a key to understanding. If ideology is seen more generally as a set of beliefs or values that inform individuals' or institutions' view of the world and that allow them to analyse or interpret facts, events, history, then it is obvious that translators are like other human beings in having a specific ideological perspective on the world that will shape their work. The existence of ideology raises questions about the supposed "neutrality" of the translator. Do translators faithfully reflect the ideology of the source text? Do translators adapt the text to the ideological outlook of the target audience? Does the translation always reflect the ideological concerns of the translator with his/her specific discursive history and life experiences?

Translation has typically been an important feature of culture and language where there is a process of consolidation of language and national identity. Translation in Elizabethan England, Romantic Germany and 19th-century Ireland performed the important ideological function of establishing the legitimacy or indeed primacy of the vernacular language as a privileged means of expressing a particular *Volksgeist*. The translators were, in a sense, the ideologues of the vernacular. Translation, therefore, does not simply reflect ideology but contributes to ideology formation.

The translation of prestigious texts from antiquity not only bore testimony to the range of the vernacular language but also demonstrated through difference that the vernacular was incomparably superior because it was deemed to be more metaphorical, imaginative, dynamic or flexible. The normalization and standardization of the vernacular that has been the work of translators in many languages is related to the important ideological task of political unity through linguistic homogeneity. Translators are architects of national unity, the evolution of which frequently involves the suppression of minority voices in a culture in the name of the world-view of the dominant class that is close to political power. Ironically, it is often translators who later act in a counter-hegemonic fashion to retrieve, resurrect or revive the suppressed minority culture or language.

Lawrence Venuti has argued in *The Translator's Invisibility* (1995) that translation always occurs in a socio-historical context. Translators of texts are subject to the power relationships that inform their translation strategies. Translators of texts from politically dominated to politically dominant cultures will favour fluent translation strategies where the lexical, syntactic and cultural otherness of the source text will be removed or naturalized in response to the target culture's explicit or implicit desire to conquer and assimilate the other. The rationale had been provided by St Jerome (c.AD 347–420) in *De optimo genere interpretandi*, where he stated, "the translator considers thought content a prisoner which he transplants into his own language with the prerogative of a conqueror". The view is reiterated at the end of the 16th century by Edmund Spenser in his *A View of the Present State of Ireland* (1596). Declaring his hostility to the continued use of Gaelic in Ireland, Spenser claimed, "for it have ever been the use of the conqueror to destroy the language of the conquered and to force him by all means to learn his". Power asymmetry has two consequences. At the level of text, translations are produced that conform to the dominant group's perception of the translated other. Tejaswini Niranjana in her *Siting Translation: History, Post-Structuralism and the Colonial Context* (1992) sees this process at work in orientalism, where the categories of text, genre and discourse are used in such a way as to produce stereotypical representations of the oriental other in Western translations of texts from Indian and other traditions. The second consequence of power differences is the direction of translation activity, with a massive imbalance globally favouring North–South rather than South–North or South–South translation. Thus, translation as an activity contributes to the dissemination of the values and world-view of the powerful northern hemisphere, but the ideological traffic in the opposite direction is minimal. The paucity of South–South translation means that cultures in the southern hemisphere may not always perceive areas of commonality in their experiences of cultural oppression or change. In the northern hemisphere itself, of course, there is widespread divergence between the power and prestige of the various languages and cultures in the hemisphere. The ideological plight of many of Europe's minority languages, for example, is strikingly similar to that of the languages and cultures of the southern hemisphere.

Race and class are factors that shape the construction of ideology in particular circumstances. Gender is another category that will crucially determine a world-view, a thesis that has been articulated by many feminist theoreticians in recent decades. The implications of the feminist critique for the ideology of translation have largely been addressed by Canadian translation scholars who have both the multilingual sensitivities of the Canadian situation and exposure to feminist theory from both the anglophone and the francophone worlds. The feminist theoreticians of translation would argue that ideological neutrality in translation is a patriarchal fiction and that the evidence for this is visible in countless translations where references to women or aspects of their culture are systematically misrepresented by male translators. They advocate a more proactive role for the translator where she makes her gender identity visible through translators' prefaces, translation footnotes, lexical choices, metaphorical selection and alternative discursive practices. The feminist approach to translation does not claim to be ideologically disinterested, but proposes a counter-ideology of translation to contest what is perceived to be the unspoken ideology of patriarchal practice in translation. Feminist theoreticians are committed to the notion of the "translator's signature", in common with many theoreticians who are attracted to the "cultural turn" (see below) in translation studies. The translator does not subscribe to a naturalizing theory of translation, where ideology and the translator are rendered invisible and the character of the translation and the values implied by it are seen as "natural" or "normal". Rather, translators make themselves visible, announce clearly their ideological disposition towards a text (for example, by claiming to make the text familiar or foreign to target culture readers) and make explicit in prefaces the mediating presence of the translator. The signature of the translator is thus visible everywhere in the translation. The active presence of the translator is partly expressed by André Lefevere's notion of translation as "rewriting". Texts are not simply translated. They are rewritten for a target audience and the ideological assumptions made by the target audience about the subject and/or source culture of the translation will have a crucial bearing on the translator's strategies.

One difficulty facing translation theoreticians is where to situate the operation of ideology in translation. Are translators unconsciously and passively subject to the dominant values of their class, gender and culture? Are translators shaped by the larger systems and structures of discourse and language which are articulated through the translation subject who is the effect rather than the cause of these systems and structures? Or are translators fully constituted, autonomous subjects who exist in their own right and whose individual life histories determine their approach to translation in general and specific translations in particular. In other words, is ideology situated at the level of society, language or the individual? Douglas Robinson in *The Translator's Turn* (1991) argues that the "ideosomatics" of language is the voice of social mastery internalized in the body of the translator, and that ideology works at microcosmic, electrochemical levels, thus making resistance to ideological over-determination difficult though not impossible for the translator. Other theoreticians have preferred to consider how ideological concerns affect the interaction between translators and culture in the diachronic and synchronic sense. This was the approach adopted in Susan Bassnett and André Lefevere's *Translation, History and Culture*, which appeared in 1990. The translator's poetics that will in part determine his/her translation strategy are related to ideological presuppositions at individual, linguistic and social levels. The focus on ideology also led to an approach to translation history that went beyond anecdote and description to a more analytical engagement with the role of translation in human history. This new translation historiography is best exemplified in the collective work jointly edited by Jean Delisle and Judith Woodsworth entitled *Translators through History* (1995). The polysystems theorists further stressed the primary importance of ideology in translation theory, most notably Gideon Toury in his *In Search of a Theory of Translation* (1980). Toury's earlier studies of the translation of Hebrew literature into English had led him to the conclusion that ideology rather than linguistics or aesthetics crucially determined the operational choices of translators. Indeed, the fact of translation occupying a primary or secondary position in the polysystem is related to larger ideological crises in the aesthetic and/or social system. Polysystemic theory, by emphasizing the role of social norms and literary conventions in determining translation choices, shifted the emphasis from the individual translator to larger social structures. In the German-speaking world, the work of Katharina Reiss and Hans Vermeer with their *Grundlegung einer allgemeinen Translationstheorie* (1984) and *Translation Studies: An Integrated Approach* (1988) by Mary Snell-Hornby presented translation as primarily an act of cultural rather than linguistic transfer. Translation was not transcoding and was primarily an act of communication. The text to be translated, like the translator, was an integral part of the world. Therefore the 1980s witnessed what has been sometimes referred to as the "cultural" turn in translation studies, which might equally well be called the "ideological turn" in translation studies, as what one theoretician terms "culture", another terms "ideology". This ideological turn was partly a reaction to what was felt as the baleful influence of both Chomskyan and neo-behaviourist linguistics on translation studies, where social contexts were excluded either as irrelevant or as introducing an element of enquiry that was not susceptible to rigorous, scientific, objective analysis.

Of course, ideology is to be found not only in the work of translators but also in the way that translation and translators are studied. Though much has been written about the process of literary translation, the sociology of literary translation has received little attention. To what extent do the material circumstances of literary translators influence their self-perception and aesthetic choices? What is the role of literary translation in the corporation of university teaching and why has literary translation on the whole a weak disciplinary identity? Are distinctions between literary and pragmatic translation based on erroneous notions of difficulty and elitism that are a form of ideological overcompensation for an unsatisfactory economic situation? Many of these questions are related to the issue of power which is distributed across different agencies in society. These agencies may be publishing houses, bookshops, the media, professional translation associations or university language departments. The agencies possess varying degrees of power over who gets translated, when, how and for whom. In the case of translated literature in the English-speaking world, foreign literature may get translated, but, in the absence of a critical infrastructure that responds positively and knowingly to this literature, the translations will attract the attention of few readers and bookshop owners. This in turn makes publishers chary of investing in translation. The distribution of the ideological power to persuade potential readers and influence consumption patterns therefore acts as a real constraint on the development of literary translation. A further level of ideological investigation that is still in an infant state is the exploration of intra-textual literary representations of translators. The purpose of that approach is to examine how translation is itself translated into literature. Thus, travel writing, science fiction, mainstream literary fiction are analysed with a view to establishing how translation is ideologically constructed in texts. The intra-textual approach not only highlights how translators and translations are popularly perceived but it also draws attention to translation as an important locus of contemporary ideological preoccupation with topics such as hybridity, multiculturalism, fragmentation, alterity and nomadism.

Interest in ideological questions in translation shows no signs of abating, and it is undoubtedly an area where the theory and practice of literary translation have much to teach other disciplines.

MICHAEL CRONIN

Further Reading

Bassnett, Susan and André Lefevere (editors), *Translation, History and Culture*, London: Pinter, 1990

Berman, Antoine, *The Experience of the Foreign: Culture and Translation in Romantic Germany*, translated from the French by S. Heyvaert, Albany, New York: State University of New York Press, 1992

Cheyfitz, Eric, *The Poetics of Imperialism: Translation and Colonization from The Tempest to Tarzan*, Oxford and New York: Oxford University Press, 1991

Delisle, Jean and Judith Woodsworth, *Translators Through History*, Amsterdam: Benjamins, 1995

Gentzler, Edwin, *Contemporary Translation Theories*, London and New York: Routledge, 1993

Homel, David and Sherry Simon (editors), *Mapping Literature: The Art and Politics of Translation*, Montreal: Véhicule Press, 1988

Lefevere, André, *Translation, Rewriting, and the Manipulation of Literary Fame*, London and New York, Routledge, 1992

Niranjana, Tejaswini, *Siting Translation: History, Post-Structuralism, and the Colonial Context*, Berkeley: University of California Press, 1992

Rafael, Vicente L., *Contracting Colonialism: Translation and Christian Conversion in Tagalog Society under Early Spanish Rule*, Ithaca, New York: Cornell University Press, 1988

Reiss, Katharina and Hans J. Vermeer, *Grundlegung einer allgemeinen Translationstheorie*, Tübingen: Niemeyer, 1984

Robinson, Douglas, *The Translator's Turn*, Baltimore: Johns Hopkins University Press, 1991

Robinson, Douglas, *Translation and Taboo*, DeKalb: Northern Illinois University Press, 1996

Simon, Sherry, *Gender in Translation: Cultural Identity and the Politics of Transmission*, London and New York: Routledge, 1996

Snell-Hornby, Mary, *Translation Studies: An Integrated Approach*, Amsterdam: Benjamins, 1988

Toury, Gideon, *In Search of a Theory of Translation*, Tel Aviv: Porter Institute for Poetics and Semiotics, Tel Aviv University, 1980

Toury, Gideon, *Descriptive Translation Studies and Beyond*, Amsterdam: Benjamins, 1995

Venuti, Lawrence (editor), *Rethinking Translation: Discourse, Subjectivity, Ideology*, London and New York: Routledge, 1992

Venuti, Lawrence, *The Translator's Invisibility: A History of Translation*, London and New York: Routledge, 1995

Yūsuf Idrīs 1927–1991

Egyptian novelist, short-story writer and dramatist

Biography

Born in 1927, Idrīs spent his childhood in the Nile Delta region. In 1945 he moved to Cairo to study medicine at Cairo University. He began writing short stories while still a student and published several examples in newspapers before his graduation in 1951. He began to practise medicine but continued his involvement in both political causes and fiction; his first collection of short stories, *Arkhas Layālī* (*The Cheapest Nights*), was published to great acclaim in 1954. In the same year he was imprisoned for his political activities. Released in September 1955, he began a career in journalism, writing articles for the newspaper, *Al-Jumhūriyyah*. The period of the late 1950s and 1960s up till the June War of 1967 was to be Idrīs's most productive; in a remarkable outpouring of creativity, he published several short story collections, as well as a number of plays and novels. In 1967 he gave up his medical practice and assumed an administrative post in the Ministry of Culture. As was the case with many Arab authors, the June War of 1967 had a profound effect on his literary career. During the 1970s and 1980s poor health, fits of depression, and the demands and distractions involved in writing a weekly column for the Cairo daily, *Al-Ahrām*, combined to reduce his creative output still further. He died in London in 1991.

Translations

Selections of Short Stories

Allen, Roger (editor), *In the Eye of the Beholder: Tales of Egyptian Life*, Minneapolis: Bibliotheca Islamica, 1978 (contains "A Stare", "The Wallet", "City Dregs", "Playing House", "The Omitted Letter", "The Aorta", "The Concave Mattress", "The Greatest Sin of All", "The Little Bird on the Telephone Wire", "The Chair Carrier", "The Chapter on the Cow", "Lily, Did You Have to Put the Light On?", "In Cellophane Wrapping", "A House of Flesh")

Cobham, Catherine, *Rings of Burnished Brass*, with an introduction, London: Heinemann, and New York: Three Continents Press, 1984 (contains "The Stranger", "The Black Policeman", "The Siren", "Rings of Burnished Brass")

Wassef, Wadida, *The Cheapest Nights*, London: Peter Owen, 1978 (contains "The Cheapest Nights", "You Are Everything to Me", "The Errand", "Hard Up", "The Queue", "The Funeral Ceremony", "All on a Summer's Day", "The Caller in the Night", "The Dregs of the City", "Did You Have to Turn on the Light, Li-li?", "Death from Old Age", "Bringing in the Bride", "The Shame", "Because the Day of Judgement Never Comes", "The Freak")

Novel

al-Haram, 1959

Peterson-Ishaq, Kristin, *The Sinners*, Washington, DC: Three Continents Press, 1984

Plays

al-Fārafīr, 1964

Abdel Wahab, Farouk, "The Farfoors" in *Modern Egyptian Drama: An Anthology*, edited and translated by Abdel Wahab, Minneapolis: Bibliotheca Islamica, 1974, pp. 351–493

Le Gassick, Trevor, "Flipflap and His Master", in *Arabic Writing Today*, vol. 2, *The Drama*, edited by Mahmoud Manzalaoui, Cairo: American Research Center in Egypt, 1977, pp. 335–453

While Yūsuf Idrīs contributed to several literary genres in Arabic, there can be little doubt that his major contributions lie in the realm of the short story, of which he was an acknowledged master. As the studies of Somekh (1975, 1985) make clear, Idrīs's use and manipulation of language – a rich blend of the features of the standard written and the colloquial – constitutes a primary feature of his artistry, and this facet of his creativity presents the translator with significant issues of appropriate discourse. Such is the wealth and creative brilliance of Idrīs's output, however, that problems like these have not stood in the way of translators; indeed translations of individual stories abound in a wide variety of English-language journals, such as the *Journal of Arabic Literature* and *Contemporary Literature in Translation*. However, we shall concentrate here on the three translated anthologies that provide a good sample of his output. The first to appear was *In the Eye of the Beholder* (ALLEN, 1978), edited by the present writer, a selection of stories culled from a number of collections up to 1971 and translated by a number of specialists in modern Arabic literature. One of the aims of this collection is to show through stories from different periods the way in which Idrīs experimented with both structure and style and, above all, the brilliant way in which he involves his readers in the construction of the narrative itself. The translations deliberately verge towards the literal, perhaps too much so in some cases, but, while the results may at times seem somewhat alien to the reader of English literary texts, the features and impact of the Idrisian narrative are preserved: the determination to involve the reader in the creation of the story itself and the frequent manipulation of point-of-view. The selections range from vignettes belonging to his earliest period, through nightmarish visions (as in "The Aorta") from the troubled political period of the 1960s, to sardonic tales such as "The Greatest Sin of All" and contemporary parables such as "The Concave Mattress". In addition to the differences in technique in the stories themselves, the ways in which the different translators represented in this collection deal with the complexities of Idrīs's style and technique – his always colourful blend of different levels of language, for example – ensure that his genius is well represented in all its variety and waywardness.

Wadida WASSEF's collection, *The Cheapest Nights* (1978), is named after one of Idrīs's most famous early stories, in which he makes use of his experience as a medical inspector to explore the linkage of poverty and overpopulation. There is some duplication of contents with *In the Eye of the Beholder* – and most notably in the superb novella, "City Dregs", which contains a depiction of the poorer quarters of Cairo that constitutes one of the most brilliant pieces of language in all of modern Arabic literature – but this collection has a greater concentration on the earlier period in Idrīs's career. While the titles of some of the English versions are faithful renderings of the Arabic originals, the translator has not been afraid to use as titles interpretations of the story's contents; thus, "Abu Sayyid" (a name) becomes "You Are Everything to Me", and "Shaykhūkhah bi-dūn junūn" (Old Age Without Madness) becomes "Death from Old Age". In fact this approach to the translation process pervades the collection as a whole, in that the translations are more in the form of close paraphrases of the original rather than attempts at replicating all of Idrīs's admittedly complex and somewhat alien detail. From this point of view the two collections that have been surveyed can be seen as representing two poles, the more and less literal, of the translation process.

A third and later collection is *Rings of Burnished Brass* (1984) translated by Catherine COBHAM, who has since published a number of accomplished translations of modern Arabic fiction. This collection is a valuable addition to the two noted above, in that it is devoted to somewhat longer narratives, all of them dating from the 1960s. Like many Egyptian writers, Idrīs, initially an enthusiastic supporter of the goals of the 1952 Revolution, had by this time (1961) found himself one of the victims of its policies towards opposition groups. The vision is now much darker, more sinister and symbolic. However, the allusiveness that characterizes Idrīs's shorter fiction during this period is not so evident in these longer narratives; indeed, it has often been suggested that Idrīs, the master of the spontaneous in both inspiration and writing, was less successful at controlling lengthier structures. In her introduction Cobham herself expresses a certain surprise at the relative ease with which she was able to remain close to the syntax of the originals, while needing, of course, to be maximally creative at the level of the individual word.

Turning briefly to other genres, Idrīs is represented here by the novel, *The Sinners*, and the famous and highly successful play, *The Farfoors*. PETERSON-ISHAQ's translation (1984) of the novel comes provided with ample annotation to give the English reader some of the "local colour" with which Idrīs fills this narrative of provincial tensions surrounding the annual arrival of migrant workers to assist peasants at harvest-time. The English style tends to replicate that of the Arabic, with its add-on clauses and asides, but it is nevertheless a faithful rendering of one of Idrīs's less than successful attempts at lengthier fiction. The play comes in two very different versions: the one by ABDEL WAHAB (1974) is considerably more literal, making use of footnotes to explain the plethora of local detail and humorous allusion that is one of the hallmarks of the play; the other, by Trevor LE GASSICK (1977), is entitled "Flipflap and His Master", a piece of interpretation that carries into the translation itself, in that a sizeable portion of the local references is omitted. However, what the resulting version lacks in local colour it certainly makes up for in readability.

ROGER ALLEN

Further Reading

Allen, Roger, "The Artistry of Yūsuf Idrīs", *World Literature Today* (Winter 1981) pp. 43–47

Allen, Roger (editor), *Modern Arabic Literature*, New York: Ungar, 1987

Allen, Roger (editor), *Critical Perspectives on Yūsuf Idrīs*, Washington, DC: Three Continents Press, 1994

Badawi, M.M., *Modern Arabic Drama in Egypt*, Cambridge and New York: Cambridge University Press, 1987

Kurpershoek, P.M., *The Short Stories of Yūsuf Idrīs: A Modern Egyptian Author*, Leiden: E.J. Brill, 1981

Somekh, S., "Language and Theme in the Short Stories of Yūsuf Idrīs", *Journal of Arabic Literature*, 6 (1975) pp. 89–100

Somekh, S., "The Function of Sound in the Stories of Yusuf Idris", *Journal of Arabic Literature*, 16 (1985) pp. 95–104

Gyula Illyés 1902–1983

Hungarian poet, short-story writer, dramatist and essayist

Biography

Born 2 November 1902 into a peasant family in Rácegrespuszta, Western Hungary. He was educated in Budapest and, in the 1920s, at the Sorbonne in Paris. In 1921 he was forced, because of his left-wing political involvement, to leave Hungary, and he lived in Paris until 1926. In Hungary his work was widely disseminated; it won many prizes at home and was honoured abroad (International Grand Prize for Poetry, 1965), particularly in France. His poem "One Sentence on Tyranny" was translated into more than 40 languages. He himself translated French poetry into Hungarian. His was a large and varied output, but his heroic poetry won his greatest fame.

Illyés's early work showed various influences, especially that of French Surrealism, but later his writings affirmed the personal characteristics of form and content that earned him his standing as the foremost Hungarian writer of the century. He was a political writer, fired by a desire for reform at home of the outdated Hungarian class system and for the autonomy of Hungarian minorities abroad. He stood up against the overbearing Communist regimes in his country. His work, which included a cycle of plays written in the 1950s and 1960s on various historical subjects, brought the life and concerns of the peasants into mainstream national literature. He wrote a biography (1936) of his 19th-century compatriot and fellow-poet Sándor Petőfi. Illyés travelled widely. From 1970 he was vice-president of International PEN. He founded the literary periodical *Magyar Csillag* (1941). He died in Budapest, 14 April 1983.

Translations

Selections of Poetry and Prose

Balogh, Barna and Susan Kun, *Once Upon a Time: Forty Hungarian Folk-Tales*, Budapest: Corvina, 1964, 2nd edition, revised by Ruth Sutter, 1970 (a selection from the author's 77 Hungarian folk-tales, *Hetvenhét magyar népmese*)

Kabdebo, Thomas and Paul Tabori (editors), *A Tribute to Gyula Illyés*, Washington, DC: Occidental Press, 1968

Kabdebo, Thomas and Paul Tabori (editors), *Selected Poems by Gyula Illyés*, London: Chatto and Windus, 1971

Smith, William Jay (editor), *What You Have Almost Forgotten: Selected Poems*, with an introduction, Budapest: Kortárs Kiado, and Willimantic, Connecticut: Curbstone Press, 1999

Tabori, Paul, *Matt the Gooseherd*, Harmondsworth: Puffin, 1976 (adaptation of the folk-tale "Matyi Ludas")

Anthologies

Alvarez, A. (introduction), *Twenty-Two Hungarian Short Stories*, Budapest: Corvina, and London: Oxford University Press, 1967

Duczynska, Ilona and Karl Polanyi (editors), *The Plough and the Pen: Writings from Hungary 1930–1956*, London: Peter Owen, 1963; Toronto: McClelland and Stewart, 1968

Gatto, Katherine Gyékényesi (translator and editor), *Treasury of Hungarian Love Poems, Quotations and Proverbs in Hungarian and English*, New York: Hippocrene Books, 1996

Grosz, Joseph and W. Arthur Boggs (editors), *Hungarian Anthology: A Collection of Poems*, Munich: Griff, 1963; revised and enlarged edition, Toronto: Pannonia Books, 1966

Hungarian Poetry; Poésie hongroise: 1848, 1919, 1945, Budapest: Youth Publishing House, 1968

Kabdebo, Thomas (editor), *A Hundred Hungarian Poems*, Manchester: Albion Editions, 1976

Kessler, Jascha *et al.*, *The Face of Creation: Contemporary Hungarian Poetry*, Minneapolis: Coffee House Press, 1988

Literary Review, special Hungarian issue, 9/3 (Spring 1966)

Szabolcsi, Miklos with Zoltán Kenyeres (editors), *Landmark: Hungarian Writers on Thirty Years of History*, Budapest: Corvina, 1965

Tóth Éva (editor), *Today: An Anthology of Contemporary Hungarian Literature*, Budapest: Corvina, 1987

Vajda, Miklós (editor), *Modern Hungarian Poetry*, New York: Columbia University Press, 1977

Other Writing

Puszták népe, 1936

Cushing, G.F., *People of the Puszta*, Budapest: Corvina, 1967; London: Chatto and Windus, 1971

Petőfi Sándor (biography), 1936

Cushing, G.F., *Petőfi*, Budapest: Corvina, 1973

CUSHING's translations (1971, 1973) of Illyés's two major prose works, *Puszták népe* (*People of the Puszta*, 1936) and *Petőfi Sándor* (1936), represent a monumental achievement in familiarizing the English-speaking world with two of the writer's most significant works (forty of his folktales were later translated by BALOGH & KUNS; his folktale, *Matyi hudas*, was adapted into English by TABORI). Although Illyés's reputation as one of the major poets of the century has grown steadily, it was his autobiographical and sociological study of the daily life of the farm worker, *People of the Puszta*, called one of the most outstanding non-fiction works of Hungarian literature by the literary critic and historian Tibor Klaniczay, that reached the average reader, and led to "the discovery of Hungary". Cushing's idiomatic prose reflects the, at times, objective sociological, at times, personal, poetic tone of this document. This was followed by Petőfi which to this day remains the best biography of that poet, whom Illyés saw as the embodiment of his own revolutionary ideals. Cushing's rendering of these works conveys aptly Illyés's artistic and idiomatic prose, and it may be said that Illyés's reputation as a master craftsman of the Hungarian language has not been tarnished by the English versions. The translator also possessed the wisdom of not venturing into the deeper perils of poetic translation of Petőfi's verse, which he calls walking the tightrope between representing the poet as a great artist or as an insipid, banal versifier. Rather he has made a compromise by re-creating the original meters and using unrhymed iambic pentameter. Cushing's purpose in both works was to offer the English-speaking reader something of the original flavor and the mood of Illyés's prose. He has also done great service in his translation of *Petőfi*, which appeared in celebration of the 150th anniversary of the birth of the legendary 19th-century poet, by including an appendix of explanatory cultural notes.

English translations of Illyés's poetry and stories consist of items chosen from his many published volumes and printed, as listed above, in selections and anthologies in the US, the UK, Canada and Hungary.

KABDEBO & TABORI's two editions of Illyés's poetry (1968 and 1971), the second an expanded version of the first, created by a retinue of translators, are an excellent glimpse into the scope and power of Illyés's verse. The translators have tried to stay as close as possible to the original Hungarian in both content and form. The approach of the editors and translators has been to treat the immediate prose or quasi-prose translations as basic rough texts, as opposed to artistic creations, thus forcing themselves to re-create the artistic integrity of the original Hungarian as much as possible. In some cases, for example that of the famous poem "A Sentence on Tyranny", the strong governing idea of the poem could facilitate a freer translation. The editors in their selections and translations have sought to convey the pathos, the self-doubt, the gentle irony and tenderness, along with the frequency of horror, shock, and subsequent contemplation, characteristic of Illyés's work, and reflective of Hungary's cataclysmic 20th-century history. In cases where the original intricate rhyme-syllabic-stress-scheme of the poems posed unsurmountable barriers, the translators chose to sacrifice elements of form for the sake of content.

KESSLER uses collaborative translation in his efforts to create Illyés's poems in English. Working with a word-by-word English version, with the original syntax intact, he re-creates the poem in English, repeating the poet's lines and stanzas. Most of all, in his renderings of Illyés's poems, Kessler seeks to recover the poetry that Robert Frost said gets lost in translation – Illyés's spirit and the genius of his language.

SMITH's collection (1999) incorporates translations that had been done over a period of 30 years, beginning with the pioneering work of Kabdebo and Tabori. Enriched by Smith's own translations and those of other contemporaries, the volume reflects Illyés's struggle against tyranny of any sort, his fight for social justice, and his love for his native land and its peoples – especially the less fortunate, its unsung heroes. The translations evoke Illyés's love of language, of detail, and his poetic craft, reflected in a style that Smith calls lyrical realism.

VAJDA's *Modern Hungarian Poetry* contains 19 Illyés poems in English translation. All of the translations were done by poet-translators, affirming the notion that only poets should translate poets. The anthology's stringent standards, established by Miklós Vajda, the then editor of *The New Hungarian Quarterly*, have resulted in an unusually high quality and an artistic collection.

KATHERINE GYÉKÉNYESI GATTO

Further Reading

Basa, Enikő Molnár (editor), *Hungarian Literature*, Whitestone, New York: Griffin House, 1993

Czigány, Loránt, *The Oxford History of Hungarian Literature*, Oxford: Clarendon Press, and New York: Oxford University Press, 1984

Klaniczay, Tibor (editor), *A History of Hungarian Literature*, translated by József Hatvany and István Farkas, Budapest: Corvina, and London: Collet's, 1964

Reményi, Joseph, *Hungarian Writers and Literature: Modern Novelists, Critics, and Poets*, edited by August J. Molnar, New Brunswick, New Jersey: Rutgers University Press, 1964

Imitation

When Plato calls poetry an imitation of an imitation at two removes from the real world of his eternal transcendental forms (*Republic*, 602), and when Aristotle calls tragedy an imitation of a serious action (*Poetics*, 6), the term imitation in these instances, for which the Greek word is *mimesis* (sometimes translated as "representation"), is being used to relate literature to reality and to life. Literary imitation, which as a general phenomenon must be as old as literature itself, first becomes a topic of critical discourse in Alexandrian times, when imitation of the ancients (*mimesis ton archaion*) became a more conscious practice among poets and artists (the Venus de Milo represents a classicizing tendency in the Hellenistic phase of Greek sculpture). But it was at Rome that the doctrine of literary imitation acquired a central importance, reflecting the actual practice of a Roman culture built upon imitation of the Greeks from the beginning. In his prologues, the comic playwright Terence (fl. 170 BC), defending his practice of amalgamating scenes from different plays of his Greek predecessor Menander, adopts a more liberal attitude to "translation" than contemporary rivals. He is talking about imitation, though he does not use the term. The central Roman authority on poetic imitation is Horace in his *Art of Poetry* (c. 15 BC), where he warns the *imitator*, in dealing with the cultural tradition, which he calls *publica materies*, not to be a *fidus interpres*, a literal interpreter, inhibited either by *pudor*, modesty or a sense of his own inadequacy, or by *lex operis*, the law of genre (131–35); the conservative tendency to assert the validity of generic rules is counterbalanced by a liberal allowance for creative freedom in the imitating poet. Influential too is the extensive discussion of imitation by Quintilian in the 10th book of his *Education of an Orator* (c. AD 95). He ranges widely over the Greek and Roman tradition, identifying and characterizing the best models for the would-be orator. The orator cannot succeed by imitation alone; but it is a necessary technical prerequisite if he is to develop and perfect natural talents. The most inspiring account is to be found in the treatise *On the Sublime*, traditionally attributed to the Greek rhetorician Longinus but probably written in the first century AD; imitation and emulation (Greek *zelosis*, Latin *aemulatio*) of the great writers of the past is the royal route to sublimity. Imitation of this kind could never be confused with theft or plagiarism. Imitators can be inspired with enthusiasm like the Pythian priestess of Apollo; so writers as diverse as Herodotus, Archilochus, Stesichorus and Plato have been inspired to contest the prize with Homer.

The imperative to imitate the ancients is central to the aspirations of Renaissance humanists and one that distinguishes them from their medieval scholastic predecessors. In their desire to revive classical Latin, the Renaissance humanists turned to classical models, especially to Cicero. In their own Latin, extremists refused to use words or expressions which could not be paralleled in the Roman writer even if they were dealing with Christian subjects. Erasmus ridiculed this servile and blinkered form of imitation in his *Ciceronianus* (1527), in which he advocated a return to the broad-based principle of imitation, enshrined in Quintilian, with reference to more than one model. He also believed that fruitful imitation involved absorption of the spirit, not merely the letter, of predecessors, and that it had to serve the needs of the present, which always has new matter to express. In poetry, the humanists saw Virgil as the supreme classical model, who had imitated Theocritus in his *Pastorals*,

Hesiod in his *Georgics* and Homer in his *Aeneid*, successfully transcending the Greeks in the poetry achieved in the process.

Enunciating principles basic to the formation of the incipient poet in his commonplace book *Timber* (published in 1640 after his death), Ben Jonson lists first *ingenium*, "the goodness of natural wit", and *exercitatio*, "practice"; then comes *imitatio*, "to be able to convert the substance, or riches of another poet, to his own use ... to draw forth out of the best and choicest flowers, with the bee, and turn all into honey, work it into one relish and savour: make our imitation sweet: observe how the best writers have imitated and follow them." The simile of the bee, of classical origin (see, for example, Macrobius, *Saturnalia*, 1 praef. 5), is a favourite commonplace to express the imitative process in the Renaissance. This is followed by *lectio*, "the exactness of study and multiplicity of reading which maketh a full man"; finally, art must be added to make all perfect. Here imitation is an integral part of a larger humanist discipline which, imparted to Jonson at his grammar school, laid the foundation of his own career, in which by virtue of his classical training and the judicious use of imitation it promoted, he changed native practice in all the genres in which he worked. This discipline remained central to the educational practice of Latin teachers in grammar schools until very recent times, so that long after imitation had ceased to be recommended by poets and critics it continued to be influential through practice at school.

In the later 17th century, first in France and subsequently in England, writers began to compose formal imitations of the classics. John Oldham, for example, in 1681 published his version of Horace's *Art of Poetry*, explaining that he has put the Roman "into a more modern dress than hitherto he has appeared in, that is, by making him speak as if he were living and writing now. I therefore resolved to alter the scene from Rome to London, and to make use of English names of men, places and customs, where the parallel would decently permit". "It is a kind of middle composition between translation and original design", wrote Dr Johnson in his *Life of Pope*, "which pleases when the thoughts are unexpectedly applicable and the parallels lucky." The most famous examples in English are Pope's *Imitations of Horace*, composed in the 1730s, and Dr Johnson's imitations of Juvenal in "London" (1738) and "The Vanity of Human Wishes" (1748). After the 18th century, when artists no longer desired so consciously to align themselves with classical predecessors, this form of imitation largely died out, but the *Imitations* (1962) of Robert Lowell may be loosely considered to be in this tradition.

With the advent of Romanticism and its over-riding emphasis on the power of the role of the imagination in the theory and practice of art, imitation ceased to be a ruling critical principle. In practice, however, when loosely considered, it continues as a general cultural phenomenon, though operating more widely than in the Renaissance and neo-classical periods. The English poets of the 1890s, for example, imitate the achievements of the French symbolists. Even the modernists could be said to have alternative models; Ezra Pound looks to the troubadours and the Chinese (as well as to Propertius). And so it goes on.

ROBIN SOWERBY

Further Reading

Brooks, Harold F., "The Imitation in English Poetry", *Review of English Studies*, 25 (1949) pp. 124–40

Butt, John (editor), *The Twickenham Edition of the Poems of Alexander Pope*, vol. 4, *The Imitations of Horace*, New Haven, Connecticut: Yale University Press, and London: Methuen, 1968

Gilbert, Allan H., *Literary Criticism: Plato to Dryden*, Detroit: Wayne State University Press, 1940

Martindale, Joanna (editor), *English Humanism: Wyatt to Cowley*, London and Dover, New Hampshire: Croom Helm, 1985, pp. 98–156 ("Classicism and Imitation")

Rudd, Niall (editor), *Johnson's Juvenal: London and The Vanity of Human Wishes*, Bristol: Bristol Classical Press, 1981

Scott, Izora, *Controversies over The Imitation of Cicero as a Model for Style*, New York: Teachers College, Columbia University, 1910; reprinted New York: AMS Press, 1972

Sowerby, Robin, *The Classical Legacy in Renaissance Poetry*, London and New York: Longman, 1994

West, David and Tony Woodman (editors), *Creative Imitation and Latin Literature*, Cambridge and New York: Cambridge University Press, 1979

Improving on the Original

Conscious attempts on the part of the literary translator to improve on the text may be divided into two types: those made on some parts of the text in compensation for losses in other parts, such as adding a joke here for a joke lost there; and those made on the whole text without anything in particular to compensate for, including minor operations such as correcting wrong names and dates or removing obvious discrepancies, and major operations such as adding graphic details or deleting parts regarded as superfluous, inserting puns, and making stylistic or structural changes.

It may be said that attempts of the first type do not really constitute improvement in the strictest sense of the word, because the translator, one may argue, is only trying to "level the score", or to produce a roughly equivalent effect, so that he may remain "faithful" to the author.

But improvements of any kind, whether compensatory or not, are considered illegitimate by theoreticians of the fidelity school, at least where "serious literature" is concerned. As Nida (and

Taber) stipulate, the translator is not to "correct apparent errors", or to improve on the original, "even when he thinks he can do so" (Nida,1964); he is not to "add information derived from other parts" of the text, and may "make explicit in the text only what is *linguistically* implicit in the immediate context of the problematic passage" (Nida and Taber, 1969).

Newmark concedes to the translator the right to try to "write a little better than the original", to "improve the logic" and "correct mistakes of fact and slips", etc., when he is engaged in "communicative translation"; but this approach is to be applied only to the translating of "popular fiction" and so on, whereas for "serious imaginative literature" the "semantic translation" method must be used, where "all such corrections and improvements are usually inadmissible", and the translator, confining himself to "render[ing], as closely as the semantic and syntactic structures of the second language allow, the exact contextual meaning of the original", has to be resigned to a product "always inferior to its original" (1981; 1988).

There is therefore no question of improvement except in the sense of making structural changes that are necessary because of linguistic differences. The literary translator is not supposed to add or subtract, even with the best intention, lest such alteration affect the original meaning and/or style.

The structural changes are considered necessary because even for closely related languages there are significant differences in respect of *obligatory* rules and *optional* rules (Catford, 1965). Whereas obligatory rules are usually matters of grammar which not even the most idiosyncratic author can totally disregard, the optional rules are quite freely manipulated to communicate meaning and mark authorial style.

The literary translator, acting in good faith, may nevertheless be tempted to improve on the text when translating between totally disparate languages. Linguistic rules and discourse strategy tend to be so different between the source language culture and the target language culture that a close semantic translation is ruled out. To ensure that the translation reads as "literature", some literary translators may take it upon themselves to make sometimes controversial changes to the original. Nida's published lectures in China provide useful reference on the considerable restructuring that takes place in the translation between disparate languages such as Chinese and English (Nida, 1982).

In any case, deliberate departure in general from the original text is frowned upon by conservative theoreticians and lay persons alike. One most commonly heard argument against improvement as such is that proper translation must be faithful to the original and that if you do not want to be faithful, you should create your own work instead.

The linguistic factor aside, the attempt to improve on the text may be due to the attitude of the translator towards the source text and his/her translation poetics. The translator's attitude towards the source text is in turn influenced by the status of the source literary polysystem relative to that of the target literary polysystem and at the same time by the position of the work in the source and/or target polysystem(s) (see Lefevere, 1992).

When the source polysystem is weak in relation to the target polysystem, the translator tends not to regard the text he/she is translating as authoritative even if it is so in its own polysystem, and consequently will in all likelihood attempt an *acceptable* rather than an adequate translation, trying to improve on the text in the process. A classic example is Edward FitzGerald, who pronounced quite unabashedly:

> It is an amusement for me to take what Liberties I like with these Persians, who (as I think) are not Poets enough to frighten one from such excursions, and who really do want a little Art to shape them. (quoted from Lefevere, 1992)

But when the source polysystem is strong, even a work semi- or non-canonized in it may enjoy a sacred status in the target polysystem, and thus the translator may feel obligated to keep close to the words of the source text.

In cases where the source and target polysystems are roughly on an equal footing, the attitude of the translator towards a source text depends mainly on its position in the source polysystem (Toury, 1980).

The poetics of individual translators varies considerably, for there are always two opposing archetypes of translators – the "faithful", who work "on the level of the word or the sentence", and the "spirited", who work "on the level of the culture as a whole, and of the functioning of the text in that culture" (Lefevere, 1992) – coexisting in a society, with others somewhere in between. But at any particular time one poetics will be dominant, exerting pressure on all translators, though to different degrees (Toury, 1994).

The question as to which poetics will dominate others is partly determined by the position of translated literature in the literary polysystem. When translated literature occupies a peripheral position, the poetics that emphasizes acceptability is more likely to prevail, and the translator will be more ready to adapt the text to the target culture, and produce what he/she thinks to be an improvement on the source (Even-Zohar, 1990).

This question is ultimately linked to the status of the home literary polysystem relative to foreign ones, for when a literary polysystem is strong and stable, translated literature usually occupies a peripheral position in it (Even-Zohar, 1990).

Take, for example, David Hawkes and John Minford's translation of the Chinese novel *Hong lou meng*. The Anglo-American literary polysystem is strong relative to many others, and self-sufficient. Consequently, translated literature can occupy only a peripheral position, foreign classics do not enjoy the same authoritative status as they do in their respective home polysystems, and the dominant translation poetics in such an "aggressively monolingual" culture naturally values acceptability, to the point that it has become a cause of complaint for some theorists (Venuti, 1995). As it turns out, translators aiming to produce "acceptable" translations are among the most spirited ones who make conscious and consistent attempts to improve systematically on their source text.

Meanwhile, the issue of improvement may also be considered from the perspective of the intended use and audience of the translation. For example, according to Eugene Eoyang, there are surrogate translations, contingent translations and coeval translations (Eoyang, 1993).

Surrogate translations are translations that aim to supplant the original. The assumption is either that the original is inaccessible or that the audience of the translation is interested only in the translator's view of the original anyway. Contingent translations are translations that are characterized by their "impenetrability and cumbersomeness" and are intended more for "the student of the language" than the literature student or the general reading public (Eoyang, 1993).

Contingent translations are always inferior to their originals, to which they defer and which they never attempt to emulate in the first place. In contrast, surrogate translations may succeed or fail on their own merits. *Some* of Ezra Pound's translations of *Shijing* (*Book of Songs*), for example, are considered to be just as inspired as, and may justifiably be said to rival, their Chinese originals (Eoyang, 1993).

Against contingent and surrogate translations Eoyang postulates the concept of coeval translations. They are intended to satisfy the modern discerning reading public who are familiar with the original, if not also capable of reading it in the original language.

Coeval translations, if few and far between, are generally highly successful translations. What is interesting, though, is that a coeval translation done in the dominant language is likely to gain greater currency and win wider critical acclaim and will in due course serve as a *superior* surrogate of the original. The translations of Colombian author García Márquez by Gregory Rabassa, which Eoyang regards as an example of coeval translation, may be an example of coeval translation becoming surrogate translation. García Márquez himself was reportedly more given to reading Rabassa's English translations than to reading his own works in Spanish (*Newsweek*, 1 December 1986).

All in all, the above discussion has examined the various factors that may account for perceived improvements on the text in the practice of literary translation. It must be noted that improvement is always a matter of perception, which may vary quite significantly from person to person. Whether improvements are actually consciously *attempted* or just happen by circumstance, and whether these are *actual* improvements, remain open questions. More often than not, what are regarded as improvements from the point of view of the target culture are violations from that of the source culture; if seen from a neutral ground, they are simply departures made to conform to the dominant ideology and poetics, or the socio-cultural norms in general, of the target culture.

NAM FUNG CHANG and SHING-YUE SHEUNG

Further Reading

Catford, J.C., *Linguistic Theory of Translation: An Essay in Applied Linguistics*, London: Oxford University Press, 1965

Eoyang, Eugene Chen, *The Transparent Eye: Reflections on Translation, Chinese Literature, and Comparative Poetics*, Honolulu: University of Hawaii Press, 1993

Even-Zohar, Itamar, "Polysystem Studies", *Poetics Today*, 11/1 (1990)

Lefevere, André, *Translation, Rewriting, and the Manipulation of Literary Fame*, London and New York: Routledge, 1992

Newmark, Peter, *Approaches to Translation*, Oxford and New York: Pergamon Press, 1981

Newmark, Peter, *A Textbook of Translation*, New York: Prentice Hall, 1988

Nida, Eugene A., *Toward a Science of Translating, with Special Reference to the Principles and Procedures Involved in Bible Translating*, Leiden: E.J. Brill, 1964

Nida, Eugene A. and Charles R. Taber, *The Theory and Practice of Translation*, Leiden: E.J. Brill, 1969

Nida, Eugene A., *Translating Meaning*, San Diego: English Language Institute, 1982

Toury, Gideon, *In Search of a Theory of Translation*, Tel Aviv: Tel Aviv University, 1980

Toury, Gideon, *Descriptive Translation Studies and Beyond*, Amsterdam: Benjamins, 1994

Venuti, Lawrence, *The Translator's Invisibility: A History of Translation*, London and New York: Routledge, 1995

Indian Languages, Ancient

Literary Translation into English

Sanskrit is known to have existed from the second millennium BC, and belongs to the Indo-European family of languages. As Sir William Jones said in his lecture to the Asiatic Society of Bengal in 1786, "The Sanskrit language, whatever be its antiquity, is of wonderful structure, more perfect than the Greek, more copious than the Latin, and more exquisitely refined than either." The discovery in Europe, towards the end of the 18th century, of striking structural resemblances between Sanskrit on the one hand and Latin and ancient Greek on the other helped open the way to the development of comparative philology and thence to modern linguistics.

Sanskrit is a flexional language. For nouns it has three genders, three numbers (singular, dual and plural), and eight cases. Adjectives are declined in concord with their noun. The verb has an active, a passive and a middle voice, and there are three moods: indicative, imperative and optative. In the indicative, the verb has five tenses. One of the features of Sanskrit is a tendency towards the formation of compound words and structures. Sanskrit is generally written in the Devanagari script.

The first translation of an Indian text into English was published in 1785, a version of the *Bhagavadgītā* by Charles Wilkins. The second translation, in 1789, was of the romantic play *Abhijinānasākuntalam* (more commonly known as *Shakuntala* or the *Shakuntalam*) by the greatest of Sanskrit dramatists, Kālidāsa (c.5th century AD). The latter had been translated by Sir William Jones, known in his own times as Oriental Jones for having founded a whole new branch of knowledge called orientalism (which, however, has come to be critiqued, and even debunked recently as wilful misknowledge by Edward Said and others).

The choice of the first two Sanskrit texts to be translated into English could hardly have been more apt, for while the *Gītā*, a short religious and philosophical poem interpolated into the *Mahābhārata*, encapsulates the Indian metaphysical world-view more succinctly and accessibly than almost any other scriptural text, the *Shākuntalam*, which presents the chequered story of the love of a king and a forest maiden, is agreed to be the most excellent of all secular or literary Sanskrit texts. These translations, together with several others that quickly followed (and were in turn promptly translated into other European languages), proved to be a complete revelation to the West, which had known hardly anything of Indian and Eastern philosophy, religion or literature before. Just as translations from Greek and Latin had earlier facilitated the Renaissance, there now followed, according to the French scholar Raymond Schwab, a veritable "Oriental Renaissance". No thinking or creative mind of the West in those times was left untouched by this explosion in knowledge, even though not all might have been equally ecstatic. Coleridge copied into his notebooks a striking Sanskrit simile he had found translated by Jones; Shelley and Keats wrote poems using Indian subject-matter; Byron famously orientalized and so did his friend Thomas Moore, publishing what proved to be the most popular of all the romantic poems of the age, *Lalla Rookh* (1817), narrating the journey of a Kashmiri princess across north India; while the poet laureate Robert Southey, in his mini-epic *The Curse of Kehama* (1810) fulminated violently against Hinduism on behalf of proselytizing Christianity.

Though the enthusiasm for Indian literature waned and was in part subdued by the on-going military conquest of India, through which Indian literature too came to be seen as inferior, a band of devoted British orientalists kept transmitting a larger and larger body of Sanskrit literature through "discovery" and translation. These efforts were consolidated in time into two magnificent series of punctiliously edited and translated volumes: The Sacred Books of the East, edited by F. Max Müller of Oxford, and the Harvard Oriental Series. The translators were all Westerners (with one exception) in contrast with similar series of translations of pretty much the same Sanskrit texts into English produced by some Indian publishing houses, notably the Chowkhambha publishing house, of Benares (now Varanasi), and the Bhandarkar Oriental Research Institute, of Pune, where the editors and translators were nearly all Indian.

The urge on the part of Indians to translate their own literature into English not only fulfilled a pedagogic need, for even Sanskrit was often studied in English in the Indian universities set up by the British, but it also represented a patriotic impulse to show the world the sophisticated literary glories of ancient India, produced at a time, as was often asserted, when the British were still clad in woad and living in caves or forests. (Thus an assertively anti-colonial, if anachronistic, comparison that has run and run over the last 200 years is that Kālidāsa is the Shakespeare of India.) Among the variety of Sanskrit works, besides the literary and the scriptural (e.g. the *Vedas* and the *Upanishads*), that came to be translated during the 19th century were the *Manusmriti* (the digest of ancient Hindu laws), the *Arthashāstra* (partially comparable to *The Prince* of Machiavelli), the *Kāma-Sutra* (a comprehensive, not to say exhaustive, treatise on sexuality comparable to hardly any work in the West), and a number of ostensibly devotional texts, such as the *Gitagovindam*, which were, however, quite poetically erotic at the same time. A favourite kind of work for translation has been anthologies of *subhāshitas*, or epigrams and quotable quotes on subjects ranging from this world to the next, including a famous series of 100 verses each on the themes of love, morality and renunciation by the poet-king Bhartihari. A treatise on Indian poetics, the *Nātyashāstra* has often been compared with Aristotle's *Poetics*.

It was somewhat late in the day that Western scholars realized Sanskrit was not the only ancient language of India. There coexisted with it Prakrit, a more colloquial and less refined variant which was used by women and servants even in Sanskrit plays. The one independent masterpiece in Prakrit, the *Gāthā-saptashati* (in its Sanskritized title) comprises 700 verses on erotic enchantment as well as disenchantment, often in a common rural setting. Another Sanskrit-related language, Pali, in which the Buddha preached and which became by and large the language of Indian Buddhism, was often translated into other European languages before English.

But the ancient language of India that Sanskrit most effectively eclipsed was Tamil. Tamil belonged to quite another family of languages, the Dravidian, and to a part of India, the South, that remained for long relatively uninfluenced by Sanskrit. Tamil had its own poetics, enunciated in the *Tolkāppiam*, its own verse epics, its own anthologies of narrative poems and its own modes of lyric and didactic poetry, and gradually they too came to light through English translation, done often by English civil servants and missionaries as in the North. However, a residual sense of Tamil having been neglected in comparison with Sanskrit still persists in many contemporary translations from the language.

Sanskrit remains the language through translations from which the Western world knows its ancient India. Even now, grand projects are afoot in the West for translating afresh the two foundational epics of India: the *Rāmāyana* at the University of California at Berkeley and the *Mahābhārata* (probably the longest poem in the world, at over 200,000 lines) at the University of Chicago.

The early British fascination for ancient India (at the expense of contemporary India, with which they found themselves in an antagonistic and problematic relationship) ensured that well into the 20th century the great majority of the Indian texts translated into English were from the older Indian languages. During the same period, Sanskrit texts were also being translated or sometimes "transcreated" into all the modern Indian languages by Indian translators, in an endeavour at indigenous renewal and in order to resist Western literary and cultural influence.

Today in India, however, there is a new generation of readers who not only cannot read Sanskrit but also cannot read Sanskrit translated into any of the modern Indian languages. Over the last decade, Indian affiliates of Western publishing houses, such as Penguin India and HarperCollins India, have published English translations of several classic Sanskrit texts, done by and for Indians themselves. When the *Bhagavadgītā* was first published in English translation in 1785, the Governor-General of the day, Warren Hastings, contributed to it a preface in which he declared that "works such as this one will survive when the British dominion in India shall have long ceased to exist". He could not have foreseen the post-colonial turn in Indian history, through which, long after the British dominion has ceased to exist, the *Bhagavadgītā* seems likely to survive and circulate rather better in English translation than in the original language – perhaps even within India in the decades to come.

All the texts mentioned above are available now in more than one translation, often by both Westerners and Indians.

HARISH TRIVEDI

Further Reading

Dimock, Edward C., *The Literature of India*, Chicago: University of Chicago Press, 1974

Gonda, Jan (editor), *History of Indian Literature*, Wiesbaden: Otto Harrassowitz, 10 vols, 1975–

Jesudasan, C. and Hepzibah Jesudasan, *A History of Tamil Literature*, Calcutta: YMCA Publishing House, 1961

Mukherjee, Sujit, *Translation as Discovery, and Other Essays on Indian Literature in English Translation*, New Delhi: Allied, 1981; London: Sangam, 1994

Schwab, Raymond, *La Renaissance orientale*, Paris, 1950; translated by Gene Paterson-Black and Victor Reinking as *The Oriental Renaissance: Europe's Rediscovery of India and the East, 1680–1880*, New York: Columbia University Press, 1984

Indian/South Asian Languages, Modern

Literary Translation into English

In South Asia, questions of language have become synonymous with questions of identity, and translation the site where the region's most heated post-colonial ambivalences and insecurities are playing themselves out.

South Asia comprises seven nations (India, Pakistan, Nepal, Bangladesh, Bhutan, Maldives and Sri Lanka) whose swirl of varied and interrelated languages make multilingualism a necessity, and whose vibrant orality defies attempts at drawing neat linguistic unities. India's constitution officially recognizes 17 indigenous languages, one of which (Bangla) is the national language of Bangladesh, and another of which (Urdu) is the national language of Pakistan. The contentious national borders created in the north by a violent partition of the former British colony of India at Independence in 1947 were fashioned along communal not linguistic lines, thus intensifying the general impression that religion not region was the basis of a community's identity. In post-colonial India, vernaculars are treated in much the same manner as they were treated by the (overwhelmed) British colonists: as an ebullient and chaotic language soup. Language speakers switch registers and dialects so readily that census takers will often instruct citizens as to the official name of their primary language.

During the movement for independence from Britain, freedom fighters championed the use of local vernaculars as a means of bolstering the people's self-respect, and yet, paradoxically, even after Independence in 1947, English continues to reign as the lingua franca in many of these nations. Today on the profusely multilingual Subcontinent, lawmakers, poets and street vendors alike switch readily from local dialect to national language to English to local dialect, in easy gestures so much a part of life that speakers seem unaware of the larger political ramifications. In a sense, then, every South Asian has become a translator, journeying back and forth between linguistic territories, trying to make meaning stable despite the inherent dynamism and contradictions.

The bulk of literature translated from South Asian vernaculars into English is written, published and distributed within the Subcontinent itself, a situation that neatly confounds mercantile associations with the etymology of the word *translation* ("trans-latus", i.e. carried across) and its suggestions of long, cumbersome maritime voyages bearing goods from exotic lands. Nevertheless, more attention is paid on both sides of the world to translations published in the West, and translators like A.K. Ramanujan who establish their careers in the UK or the US enjoy higher status than those working in South Asia. Not coincidentally, though translation has become a prolific industry, there are just as many prominent theorists (Homi Bhabha and Anuradha Dingwaney, for example) who regard translation as a metaphor for the liminal state many South Asians find themselves in, journeying culturally and linguistically between European and Asian ways of conceiving of the world.

Translation into English, then, becomes the focus of extreme ambivalence, since English is seen as the primary language through which writers in South Asia will gain recognition abroad (and, consequently, recognition at home). That means that however powerfully South Asian experiences are expressed in the various indigenous languages, a literary work achieves renown only when rendered into English, and so the indigenous-language literatures are being influenced by what can or cannot be translated easily into English. Works are lauded, unconsciously, for their translatability. At the same time, the more fiercely writers feel the need to assert a typically South Asian identity in literature, the more English has been stretched to accommodate their grammar, word choice, and world view.

South Asian languages are written phonetically, and, with the exception of Urdu and Dhivehi (the national language of the

Maldives), read left to right. Sentences are based on a subject-object-verb word order, but because post-positions (functioning like case endings) rather than word order usually indicate the relation among units in a sentence, there is considerable flexibility in rearranging the units for effect, an opportunity poets take particular advantage of. In addition, the prevalent use of the instrumental-subject construction embues the languages with a vaguely passive quality that is difficult to render as elegantly in English. South Asian languages are also replete with echo words, reduplication and phonesthetic words, which create a lively playfulness in the source language but which sound excessive when transliterated into English. Most significantly, South Asian writers traditionally mix vocabulary and syntax associated with particular regions, classes, castes and religious groups to create a vigorous texture to their poetry and prose, an effect that takes advantage of the widespread multilingualism of South Asia but that is hard not to flatten when moving into English.

Until the 19th century, present-day India did not even conceive of itself as one entity. A jumble of feudal states and territories, India – like the word Hindu – derives from a designation Persian traders used in ancient times for the subcontinental lands east of the Sindhu or Indus River (now in present-day Pakistan.) People's loyalties lay with their caste group more than with king or countrymen, to such an extent that even people of the same geographical region identified themselves as speaking different languages. Over the millennia, battles were fought over territory, but even the few noteworthy empires could claim no more than half the Subcontinent as theirs, and none brought the countless unruly local language groups under control. By the time the British entered the Subcontinent – first not as rulers but as traders – at the end of the 16th century, Moghul emperor Akbar reigned over a vast sweep of territory in the north extending from Kabul to (present-day) Calcutta, and yet maintained his native (and to South Asia, alien) Persian as the language of the court. As British power waxed and Moghul rule waned over the next two centuries, Persian continued to be used as the official language of administration, until the beginning of the 19th century when British colonists realized the time was right to assert their authority using English.

The British followed the Moghul example of using the foreign conquerer's tongue to rule over the diversity of linguistic and political territories in South Asia. And like the Moghuls, the British fostered a less than subtle belief in the superiority of their mother tongue, which soon made the difference between political and artistic power difficult to discern. Thomas Babington Macaulay, in his infamous "Minute on Indian Education", crassly declared that "a single shelf of a good European library is worth the whole native literature of India and Arabia", thus urging an educational strategy for India (later adopted) that would create "a class of persons, Indian in blood and colour, but English in taste, in opinion, in morals and in intellect". India's elite was educated to consider its own vernaculars divisive, impractical and even unworthy, and thus the intellectually ambitious came to identify most closely with the English tradition of letters.

Linguistically, the Subcontinent's dividing line runs across the Deccan plateau at its waist: in the north, languages like Hindi, Urdu, Punjabi, Bengali and Gujarati belong to the Indo-Aryan branch of Indo-European while, in the south, Tamil, Telugu, Malayalam and Kannada are part of the Dravidian language group, another linguistic family entirely. Sinhala in Sri Lanka, however, is Indo-European. Later in the 19th century, when the Nationalist movement began to gather speed, the question of a national language began to politicize these divisions. For example, when an upper-caste movement in northern India succeeded in claiming Indo-Aryan Hindi the national language at Independence, disaffected Dravidian-language speakers strengthened their resolve to make English and not sectarian Hindi the lingua franca of India.

In governmental terms English is claimed as an official language of India and Pakistan, and is recognized for its widespread use in the other three South Asian countries. Even promoters of indigenous literary traditions recognize the necessity of English for literary exchange. The pre-Independence Progressive Writers' Manifesto of 1935, for example, which proclaimed an historical link between literary and civic responsibility, and eventually led to the founding of India's Sahitya Akademi (the Academy of Letters), was written first in English by expatriate writers living in England and later translated into vernaculars by and for those in the various regions of India. The irony, then, is that the struggle for independence in the 19th and 20th centuries has resulted in a self-conscious promotion of the literary possibilities of the many vernaculars, as well as of English as an emerging South Asian language.

The first person to use translation as a means of promoting (and defining) Indian heritage in English was an 18th-century Englishman, Sir William Jones. His controversial interest in the Orient led him to translate several classics from Persian as well as Sanskrit in a manner that literary critic and translator Tejaswini Niranjana claims cast "the natives [as] unreliable interpreters of their own laws and cultures". Throughout the pivotal 19th century and into the 20th his translation methods were held as the model for rendering South Asian texts into English, so that generations of students were encouraged to adopt a writing style that conveyed these same asymmetries and excesses. It was not until 1913, when the Nobel Prize for Literature was awarded to Rabindranath Tagore for his own translation of his *Gitanjali* from Bengali that native translators began to be deemed worthy in the West.

Tagore's success in translating himself resulted in his being claimed by literary traditions in both India and England, two distinct worlds separated by more than seas. Significantly, Tagore translated the *Gitanjali* on board ship while travelling from India to England for the first time, in a dislocated state that would become increasingly familiar to South Asian writers of the later 20th century. Scholars such as Mahasweta Sengupta and Sujit Mukherjee have noted the discrepancy between Tagore's Bengali version and his English version, charging him with overtranslating himself into an English context and allowing himself only those moments of Indianness that pandered to Victorian stereotypes of the mystical East. Tagore's translating methods – with outdated "dost thou" and "speakest not" grammar and a tendency to smooth over specific cultural details with phrases like "chanting and singing and telling of beads" – were indicative of those that became prevalent for most of the 20th century. Many translators responded to the gap in perception between their (South Asian) source language literary outlook and their target language (English) view by over-encumbering the syntax and vocabulary of the target language text, striving and sometimes even straining to convince unconvinced English readers of the worthiness of their literary experience in the source text.

Poet and folklorist A.K. Ramanujan gained fame, from the 1960s onwards, for translations that negotiated this gap somewhat differently, by simplifying rather than embellishing the English syntax and offering substantial footnotes and glossaries to explain untranslatable words and concepts. His spare, elegant renderings of poetry and prose from Tamil, Kannada and Malayalam drew admiration from American and English as well as Indian readers, and influenced new generations of translators in a minimalist and carefully academic approach to translating. His work, however, eventually came under attack most notably by literary critic Tejaswini Niranjana in her book, *Siting Translation* (1992), for "accepting the premises of a universalist history...", trying to show how the works are "always already Christian, or 'modernist', and therefore worthy of the West's attention". Instead, Niranjana advocates a translating method popularized by Gayatri Spivak, that seeks to counter these historical imbalances by calling attention to the differences rather than smoothing them over.

Ironically enough, Spivak achieved her fame originally through translations not from her native Bengali but from French, translating into English deconstructionist philosopher Jacques Derrida's *Of Grammatology*. Even her translations of Bengali writer Mahasweta Devi have a muscular, complicated prose style that disrupts the flow of the narrative. Rather than italicizing South Asian words that may be foreign to an English reader, she italicizes English words that had been adopted in the source Bengali text, thus trying to dramatize with fontwork the multilingualism so prevalent in South Asia.

Since Tagore, however, the most significant nod towards gestures to translate South Asian experiences into English letters was Salman Rushdie's winning of the Booker Prize in 1981 for *Midnight's Children*, a novel written in Indian English about a protagonist born at the exact moment of Independence. Although not a translation in the conventional sense of the word, the prose is written in a hybrid style that offers creative solutions to the problems so many writers face who move between South Asian and English cultures. "Out of think air, baby. Dharrraaammm!" shouts one of Rushdie's characters in *The Satanic Verses* (1988) as he falls – allegorically, one would like to think – from the sky to English soil below, "Wham, na? What an entrance, yaar. I swear: splat."

CHRISTI A. MERRILL

Further Reading

Bhabha, Homi K., *The Location of Culture*, London and New York: Routledge, 1994

Derrida, Jacques, *Of Grammatology*, translated by Gayatri Chakravorty Spivak, Baltimore: Johns Hopkins University Press, 1976; corrected edition 1998

Dingwaney, Anuradha and Carol Maier (editors), *Between Languages and Cultures: Translation and Cross-Cultural Texts*, Pittsburgh: University of Pittsburgh Press, 1995

Jones, Sir William, *The Works of Sir William Jones*, 6 vols, London: G.G. and J. Robinson, 1799; 13 vols, London: Stockdale and Walker, 1807; reprinted 13 vols, Delhi: Pravesh, 1979

Kachru, Braj B., *The Indianization of English: The English Language in India*, Delhi, Oxford and New York: Oxford University Press, 1983

Masica, Colin P., *Defining a Linguistic Area: South Asia*, Chicago: University of Chicago Press, 1976

Mukherjee, Sujit, *Translation as Discovery and Other Essays on Indian Literature in English Translation*, New Delhi: Allied, 1981

Niranjana, Tejaswini, *Siting Translation: History, Post-Structuralism, and the Colonial Context*, Berkeley: University of California Press, 1992

Ramanujan, A.K. (editor and translator), *The Interior Landscape: Love Poems from a Classical Tamil Landscape*, Bloomington: Indiana University Press, 1967; London: Peter Owen, 1970

Ramanujan, A.K. (editor and translator), *Speaking of Siva*, Harmondsworth and Baltimore: Penguin, 1973

Rushdie, Salman, *Midnight's Children*, London: Jonathan Cape, and New York: Knopf, 1980

Rushdie, Salman, *The Satanic Verses*, London: Viking, 1988; New York: Viking, 1989

Rushdie, Salman, *Imaginary Homelands: Essays and Criticism, 1981–1991*, London: Granta, 1991

Sengupta, Mahasweta, "Translation, Colonialism and Poetics: Rabindranath Tagore in Two Worlds" in *Translation, History and Culture*, edited by Susan Bassnett and André Lefevere, London: Pinter, 1990

Shapiro, Michael C. and Harold F. Schiffman, *Language and Society in South Asia*, Delhi: Motilal Banarsidass, and Columbia, Missouri: South Asia Books, 1981

Spivak, Gayatri Chakravorty, *In Other Worlds: Essays in Cultural Politics*, London and New York: Methuen, 1987

Spivak, Gayatri Chakravorty, "The Politics of Translation" in her *Outside in the Teaching Machine*, New York: Routledge, 1993

Trivedi, Harish, *Colonial Transactions: English Literature and India*, Calcutta: Papyrus, 1993; "new" edition, Manchester: Manchester University Press, 1995

Tagore, Rabindranath, *Gitanjali: Song Offerings*, with an introduction by W.B. Yeats, London: Chiswick Press, 1912

Indirect Translation

Indirect translation, within the context of literary translation into English, means the rendering of foreign-language texts into English, the *lingua franca*, through intermediary sources. A tool of multicultural transfer, it has helped to produce, over the centuries, both English literature in translation and world literature in English translation. Kittel & Frank (1991) define indirect translation as "any translation based on a source (or sources) which is itself a translation into a language other than the language of the original, or the target language". Viewed from the perspective broached at the outset, this definition would seem to be narrow and inadequate, since indirect translation can be, pragmatically, based on a source (or more than one source) which is itself a translation into the source language or the target language or any eclectic combination of languages.

Ezra Pound once remarked: "English literature lives on translation, it is fed by translation: every new heave is stimulated by translation, every allegedly quiet age is an age of translations." In the history of English literature, the medieval and Renaissance periods stand out as prime examples of fallow ages "using translators as a means of revitalizing the target (literary) system" (Bassnett, 1993). During burgeoning periods of national literatures, translation has the important function of literary enrichment. From these and the other periods, in which indirect translation plays a significant role in literary fermentation and other functions, emerge many interesting phenomena.

Medieval translation is characterized by, among other things, a lack of interest in the textual sources of originals and by the treating of original texts as sources "for literary exploitation by the devices of amplification proper to the literary tradition and the idiom of the target language" (Burnley, 1989). The origin of textual sources sometimes remains an unknown parameter: as, for instance, when Chaucer, working as compilator, produced "The Clerk's Tale" (an analogous case is his translation of Boethius's *De Consolatione Philosophiae*) by weaving together two versions of the story of patient Griselda – Petrarch's Latin version, and an anonymous French translation of it. In deriving inspiration from different texts, in what Von Stackelberg calls "eclectic translation" (e.g. translation from two source texts), in the production of "The Second Nun's Tale", Chaucer the author has become the very source of his own "translation". And the source text, instead of being a static document, has become an "utterance, evanescent and sonic, that must somehow be made to 'speak' again" (Norton, 1984). Chaucer's compositional method, both as an author and as a mediating translator, is symptomatic of "the situation of translation within the rhetorical tradition of invention" (Machan, 1989), a fact registered by the following observation: "(The) elasticity of medieval translation with regard to sources becomes a norm, as vernacular translation evolves within the tradition of textual commentary, so that a translation may render its original through a sequence of intermediate sources, displacing the original even as it serves a replicative and exegetical function" (Copeland, 1989). Such translated texts, for which no "genuine" source texts exist, are, none the less, called "literary translations" or "pseudotranslations".

The circumstances – surrounding the status of the source texts – under which literary translators worked have other ramifications with a bearing on the state of medieval literary translation. For example, the source text with which the translators were working might be itself a translation, e.g. a French version of a Latin original, its ancestry possibly complicated by the existence or the tradition of Greek or Hebrew sources. In such cases one is uncertain about the exact sources of translation since "the earlier translator's blunders and omissions in describing his source were likely to be perpetuated in the new rendering" (Amos, 1920). Thus, the existence of intermediary sources means that both the translation's subject matter and the comment on that subject matter, for example, might come from the intermediary French or Latin sources.

In the 16th century, translators of the romance and novella, such as Lord Berners and Sir Thomas North, employed the intermediary French rendering instead of going to the original Spanish. Later, instead of rendering straight from the Spanish version of Cervantes's *Don Quixote*, Thomas Shelton, Peter Motteux and Tobias Smollett, for example, translated from the French. It must be noted that the adoption of an intermediary version of a text was sometimes determined simply by the personal preference of the literary translator or the extent of his knowledge of the source language.

In the realm of literary creation, indirect translation is perhaps not such a disadvantage as it might appear, despite a negative report, in Eugene A. Nida's *Toward a Science of Translating* (1964), on its corrupting effect on the source text. The Plutarch of Sir Thomas North, a source of inspiration for Shakespeare's Roman plays, "was translated not from the original Greek, but from the French of Jacques Amyot, and because of this double refraction detail is often blurred that was perfectly clear in the original" (Cohen, 1962). Could it be that the fire of the Muses, fuelled by suggestiveness rather than by determinacy, burns even more ardently through the misty vistas and atmosphere of a rendering at a Platonic second remove from the original? Lord Berners, in the 1530s, knowing no Spanish, translated *The Golden Book of Marcus Aurelius* of the Spaniard Antonio de Guevara from an intermediary French translation, thus providing the germ for the euphuistic style of the early Elizabethans.

Nevertheless, there are potential pitfalls that literary translators working with the indirect approach may fall into. Ezra Pound's *Cathay* poems, made from Ernest Fenollosa's manuscript and cribs to the ideograms of Rihaku (Li Bai / Li Po) are examples of comparatively successful indirect translation, where he is considered to be at his best both as poet and as translator. Rather more suspicious, however, is the case of Witter Bynner's English translation of classical Chinese poetry, from the texts of Kiang Kang-Hu. Bynner's observation (1929) that "(b)ecause of the absence of tenses, of personal pronouns and of connectives generally, the translator of Chinese poetry ... has considerable leeway as to interpretation", given that the relations between propositions are paratactic in Chinese and hypotactic in English, and the fact that Bynner had worked indirectly from his collaborator's notes, might account for some of the errors that crept into his rendering. Still, a whole horde of English language translators who had no Chinese was drawn to Chinese literature: e.g. Stuart Merrill, Helen Waddell, Amy Lowell, Kenneth Rexroth, with their various uses of "prose trots, previous translations, French versions, the word-by-word aid of sinologists" (Steiner, 1975). And despite the derivative nature of their translation methods, "[p]aradoxically, scandalously perhaps, these constitute an ensemble of peculiar coherence and they are, in one or two cases, superior in depth of recapture to translations based on actual knowledge of the original" (Steiner).

The English Bible, particularly the King James Version, forms an important part of the canon of English literature in translation. Both as a source for English literature and as a literary influence, the translated English Bible is inexhaustible. For example, the Bible is one literary source for John Dryden's *Absalom and Achitophel*; as a literary influence, the Bible operates as an anthology of different genres, including historical writings (e.g. Genesis, Joshua), dramatic writings (Job), lyric poetry (the Psalms and the Song of Songs), prose fiction (Ruth, the Apocrypha), etc.

The history of the English translation of the Bible poignantly reveals the derivative nature of indirect translation. The Coverdale version (1537), for example, was not translated from the original Hebrew and Greek but was made with reference to "fyve sundry interpreters", namely Zwingli and Leo Juda's Zurich Swiss-German Bible of 1524–29, Luther's German Bible, Pagninus's Latin Bible of 1528, the Vulgate, and Tyndale's New Testament and Pentateuch.

The title of the King James Version (1611) reads: "The Holy Bible, Conteyning the Old Testament, and the New: Newly Translated out of the Originall tongues: & with the former Translations diligently compared and reuised." The intermediary sources having a direct literary bearing on the history of the so-called Authorized Version (A.V.) come under the rubrics of English versions and of versions in languages other than English. Among the English versions of the Old Testament possibly consulted by A.V. translators, there were portions of Tyndale's Old Testament, Coverdale's Bible, "Matthew's" Bible, the Great Bible, Taverner's Bible, the Geneva Bible, and the Bishops' Bible. Of translations into languages other than English, there were the Complutensian Polyglot, Luther's Bible, the Zurich Bible, the Latin Bible of Pagninus, the Latin Old Testament of Munster, Lefevre's French Bible, Olivetan's French Bible, Leo Juda's Latin Bible, Castalio's Latin Bible, Casiodoro de Reina's Spanish Bible, Arias Montanus's Latin-Hebrew Bible, Tremellius's Latin Old Testament, the revised French Bible of 1588, Cipriano de Valera's Spanish Bible, and Giovanni Diodati's Italian Bible. Such a literary influence, exerted by the Rheims New Testament, even trickled down to the phraseology of the Authorized Version of the New Testament.

The English translations from national literatures have become the basis on which further translation into other national languages has been based. Examples include translation into Indian languages of A.K. Ramanujan's *Speaking of Siva* (1973) and *Hymns for the Drowning* (1981) and translation into Filipino of Antoine de Saint-Exupery's *The Little Prince*. In contemporary India, English translations of literatures written in one of the autochthonous languages will be further rendered into the other indigenous languages. These phenomena may be termed collectively catalytic translation. Sometimes the English rendering has become so famous as to have almost obliterated the source text (for example, Edward FitzGerald's English translation of *The Rubaiyat of Omar Khayyam*, whose origin is in Persian). Through such indirect translation, texts of more obscure national origins have become accessible to an international readership. Many of Ibsen's plays, for example, have been translated not from the original Norwegian but from English, as well as from other intermediary languages such as German and Japanese.

RAYMOND S.C. LIE

Further Reading

Amos, Flora Ross, *Early Theories of Translation*, New York: Columbia University Press, 1920; reprinted New York: Octagon Books, 1973

Bassnett, Susan, *Comparative Literature: A Critical Introduction*, Oxford and Cambridge, Massachusetts: Blackwell, 1993

Benson, Eugene and L.W. Conolly, *Encyclopedia of Post-colonial Literatures in English*, vol. 2, London and New York: Routledge, 1994

Burnley, J.D., "Late Medieval English Translation: Types and Reflections" in *The Medieval Translator: The Theory and Practice of Translation in the Middle Ages*, edited by Roger Ellis, Woodbridge, Suffolk: Brewer, 1989

Bynner, Witter, translations from the texts of Kiang Kang-Hu in their *The Jade Mountain: A Chinese Anthology*, New York: Knopf, 1929

Cohen, J.M., *English Translators and Translations*, London: Longman, 1962

Copeland, "Rhetoric and Vernacular Translation in the Middle Ages" in *The Medieval Translator: The Theory and Practice of Translation in the Middle Ages*, edited by Roger Ellis, Woodbridge, Suffolk: Brewer, 1989

Ellis, Roger and Ruth Evans (editors), *The Medieval Translator*, 4, Exeter: University of Exeter Press, and Binghamton, New York: Medieval and Renaissance Texts and Studies, 1994

Kittel, Harald and Armin Paul Frank (editors), *Interculturality and the Historical Study of Literary Translations*, Berlin: Schmidt, 1991

Lefevere, André, *Translating Literature: Practice and Theory in a Comparative Literature Context*, New York: Modern Language Association of America, 1992

Machan, T.W., "Chaucer as Translator" in *The Medieval Translator: The Theory and Practice of Translation in the Middle Ages*, edited by Roger Ellis, Woodbridge, Suffolk: Brewer, 1989

Newmark, Peter, *A Textbook of Translation*, New York: Prentice Hall, 1988

Niranjana, Tejaaswini, *Siting Translation: History, Post-Structuralism, and the Colonial Context*, Berkeley: University of California Press, 1992

Norton, Glyn P., *The Ideology and Language of Translation in Renaissance France and Their Humanist Antecedents*, Geneva: Droz, 1984

Steiner, George, *After Babel: Aspects of Language and Translation*, Oxford and New York: Oxford University Press, 1975; 3rd edition 1998

Toury, Gideon, "Translating English Literature via German – and Vice Versa: A Symptomatic Reversal in the History of Modern Hebrew Literature" in *Die Literarische Übersetzung: Stand und Perspektiven ihrer Erforschung*, edited by Harald Kittle, Berlin: Schmidt, 1988

Intertextuality: The Function of Literary Translation

One often overlooked vehicle of change or redirection in a national literary tradition is the entry of a foreign text via its translation. It is interesting that countries where there is censorship of incoming materials, either overtly by direct legislation and the banning of titles, or covertly by the policy of translating few foreign books, often manifest deeply embedded literary and literary-critical outlooks. Should a foreign text succeed in entering, the potential force it represents in itself through its translation and then as intertextual generator is vast. Translation therefore plays a multiple role in the tranposition and transformation of linguistic, ideological and cultural exchanges.

The essential intertextual functions and operations of literary translations can be illustrated by scrutiny of French, the basis of a strongly self-contained literary culture that often maintains its identity by means of such bodies as the Académie Française to ensure the purity of grammar, expression and style and to prevent the infiltration of foreign influences and words. Yet when the *Mille et une Nuits* (*The Thousand and One Nights*) appeared as a "translation" (A. Galland, 1704–17) it became immediately, by its exoticism and otherness, an intertext whereby comparative reappraisal of the host cultural tropes could be examined, criticized and often satirized. The social and political hierarchy, the customs and manners, within the source text, were so radically opposed to the unquestioned norms in France that they provided automatically the ground for intertextuality's evaluative functions to operate.

Works in translation can also transform generic or formal parameters of a national literature, even in the case of such relatively unestablished structures as the novel. The translation-intertext as new form serves to regenerate or reorganize old models. An illustration is the translation into French of Scott's novels in the early 19th century and Faulkner's in the early 20th. The former reinstated a strongly historical and rural as opposed to classical or pastoral frame of reference for the novel, and thence for characterization, plot, dialogue and description. In many discussions of the "realist" novel in France, the influence of Scott is forgotten or barely acknowledged. A similar skewed literary history repeats itself in respect of the American influences on the French novel of the 1930s. Different patterns and modes of narration, such as that of Benjyin Faulkner's *The Sound and the Fury*, served to question assumptions about narratorial suitability and coherence, narrative reliability and respectability. Of course, such experimentation had occurred within French literature itself to some degree (for example, in Diderot's *Jacques le Fataliste*), but the foreign text by its translation enables confrontation of acceptability and possibility on a scale that impinges more extensively on genre transformation. The actual original texts, however, will in this instance be remembered less for their individual influence than for their collective contribution to changes in modes of representation.

The ludic dimension of intercultural materials in translation provides a further operation whereby highly self-conscious forms gain resonance via their foreign doubles. Practitioners such as the *nouveaux romanciers* do more than indulge in clever allusion, intellectual or elitist high-cultural play with appeal to the minority audience; they often displace these same artifacts by using foreign intertexts, in translation, that belong both to high and to popular culture. Literary intertexts which contain their translation may of course also add unwittingly to the ludic dimensions of writing when the translation contains errors of idiom, confusions of culture-specific signifiers such as ineptly translated titles or proper names, or social realia that do not exist in the target culture. Yet as Lauren G. Leighton points out, "Despite these and similar blunders, it is still possible to consider a translation excellent and praiseworthy so long as it conveys the most important thing – the artistic individuality of the original author in all the distinctiveness of his style." (*The Art of Translation*, 1984)

Whereas style often counts more than complete accuracy in the literary translation and its intertexts – because it is always contrastive and comparative at some level in accordance with some or all of the functions above, thus achieving a new posterity through its colonization of the new linguistic fibre and fabric – this is not the case for non-literary texts in translation. To quote Leighton again: "The most important thing for business translations is precision of vocabulary" (*ibid.*). Appropriation by translation, however, makes the translated (inter)text an annexation of its original foreign philosophical/critical discourse. Its incorporation into a different linguistic system does not detract from its otherness as argument and its authority as leader-discourse. Indeed, the translation's status as conveyor of accurate communication and disseminator of ideas is heightened. Therefore, where the translation has been too hastily produced, or where the translator mistakes conceptual idiom and terminology, or fails to render nuance or ambiguity, major misrepresentations of the original may occur, or worse, whole schools of subsequent thinking can be built on erroneous foundations because intertexts from the translation are assumed to be "correct" and hence given an authority that can be proved unreliable or discredited only by means of revision or comparison with the original.

The work of Jacques Derrida, Julia Kristeva and Luce Irigaray in translation serves to illustrate this point. Errors and confusions in syntax, semantic distinctions and specialist terminology in the translations have simply been reiterated and "canonized" as such intertexts are circulated as authorities within a body of non-French critics in the fields of critical theory, psychoanalysis or feminist theory. However, to judge these translations according to the literary versus "business language" distinction, making accuracy of vocabulary paramount, is also too limited and limiting when it comes to evaluating these theorists' contributions to academic research and to international communication through translations of their work. Many "business" texts are also highly "literary" in that their style and arguments pivot on allusive, homonymic, at times parodic French with frequent double negatives or other rhetorical devices. Faithful translation also entails a stylistic transposition, so that Kristeva finds a voice in English that neither flattens out the multicultural dimensions of the original nor over-complicates the complexities of her writing. While it is necessary to highlight the dangers of relying on secondary sources as authorities, among which sources translations form a major category, without translations international debate would be severely impoverished. Translating contemporary foreign theorists also serves to underline the complex nature of literary-critical translation itself; stylistic, with generic parameters once deemed "literary", it cannot be the province of hack translation. Neither can the translator of a number of theorists sacrifice the individual author's integrity or range of expression for a "house style" of technical accuracy demanded by a series editor or publishing house.

Translation is then also a creative remake of language, of an order different from but no less important than creative writing. Its demands on the translator – of fluency, linguistic range and facility with words – put paid to notions of the translator as parrot or as artisan in the passive voice.

MARY M. ORR

Further Reading

Gentzler, Edwin, *Contemporary Translation Theories*, London and New York: Routledge, 1993
Hatim, Basil and I. Mason, *Discourse and the Translator*, London and New York: Longman, 1990
Lefevere, André (editor and translator), *Translation / History / Culture: A Sourcebook*, London and New York: Routledge, 1992
Lefevere, André, *Translation, Rewriting, and the Manipulation of Literary Fame*, London and New York: Routledge, 1992
Leighton, Lauren G. (editor and translator), *The Art of Translation: Kornei Chukovsky's A High Art*, Knoxville: University of Tennessee Press, 1984
Leighton, Lauren G., *Two Worlds, One Art: Literary Translation in Russia and America*, DeKalb: Northern Illinois University Press, 1991
Orr, Mary, *Claude Simon: The Intertextual Dimension*, Glasgow: University of Glasgow French and German Publications, 1993
Steiner, George, *After Babel: Aspects of Language and Translation*, Oxford and New York: Oxford University Press, 1975; 3rd edition 1998
Venuti, Lawrence (editor), *Rethinking Translation: Discourse, Subjectivity, Ideology*, London and New York: Routledge, 1992
Venuti, Lawrence, *The Translator's Invisibility: A History of Translation*, London and New York: Routledge, 1995

Eugène Ionesco 1909–1994

Romanian-born French dramatist

Biography

Born in Slatina, Romania, 26 November 1909, to a French mother and a Romanian father, Ionesco spent his childhood partly in France and partly in Romania. He graduated in French literature from Bucharest University in 1933, married in 1936 and in 1939 went with his wife to Paris. He resided in France for most of the rest of his life, writing full-time (with some painting also) from 1945. From 1950, with the one-act sketch *The Bald Prima Donna* (*La Cantatrice chauve*), he exercised a powerful anti-realist influence on European drama, creating with Arthur Adamov, Jean Genet and Samuel Beckett the "theatre of the absurd". His many plays present in comical or grotesque form the paradoxes of verbal communication. They are anarchic and alienated while touching on philosophical and political problems; in many of them there is a strong element of dream, drawn from personal experience. Among his other writings, many of which exist in English translation, are essays, fiction and an autobiography, *La Quête intermittente* (1987; *The Intermittent Quest*, 1988). There are also some screenplays and television scenarios. Ionesco's work was recognized internationally from the late 1950s onwards by the award of prizes and academic honours; in 1970 he was elected to the Académie Française. He died 18 March 1994.

Translations

The French titles of the numerous Ionesco plays translated into English are given below, with dates of the first performance in French:

La Cantatrice chauve (*The Bald Prima Donna*), 1950; *La Leçon* (*The Lesson*), 1951; *Les Chaises* (*The Chairs*), 1952; *Victimes du devoir* (*Victims of Duty*), 1953; *Amédée; ou, Comment s'en débarrasser* (*Amédée; or, How to Get Rid of It*), 1954; *Jacques; ou, La soumission* (*Jacques; or, Obedience*), 1955; *Le Nouveau Locataire* (*The New Tenant*), 1955; *Le Tableau* (*The Picture*), 1955; *L'Impromptu de l'Alma; ou, Le Caméléon du berger* (*Improvisation; or, The Shepherd's Chameleon*), 1956; *L'Avenir est dans les oeufs; ou, Il faut de tout pour faire un monde* (*The Future Is in Eggs; or, It Takes All Sorts to Make a World*), 1957; *La Jeune Fille à marier* (*Maid to Marry*), published 1958; *Le Maître* (*The Leader*), published 1958; *Tueur sans gages* (*The Killer*), 1959; *Rhinocéros* (*Rhinoceros*), 1959; *Scène à quatre* (*Foursome*), 1959; *Apprendre à marcher* (*Learning to Walk*), 1960; *Délire à deux* (*Frenzy for Two*), 1962; *Le Roi se meurt* (*Exit the King*), 1962; *Le Piéton de l'air* (*A Stroll in the Air*), 1962; *La Soif et la faim* (*Hunger and Thirst*), 1964; *La Lacune* (*The Oversight*), 1965; *Le Salon de l'automobile* (*The Motor Show*), published 1966; *L'Oeuf dur* (*The Hard-Boiled Egg*), published 1966; *Les Salutations* (*Salutations*), 1970; *Jeux de massacre* (*Here Comes *a Chopper*), 1970; *The Duel* (*The Duel*), 1971; *Double Act* (*Double Act*), 1971; *Macbett* (*Macbett*), 1972; *Ce formidable bordel!* (*What a Bloody Circus!*), 1973; *La Vase* (*The Mire*), published 1974; *L'Homme aux valises* (*The Man with the Luggage*), 1975; *Voyages chez les morts* (*Journeys among the Dead*), published 1985

Selections of Plays

Allen, Donald M., *Four Plays*, New York: Grove, 1958 (contains *The Bald Soprano*; *The Lesson*; *Jack, or, the Submission*; *The Chairs*)

Watson, Donald (vols 1–3, 5–11), Derek Prouse (vol. 4), Clifford Williams (vol. 11) and Barbara Wright (vol. 12), *Plays*, vols 1–12, London: John Calder / Calder and Boyars, 1958–79 (vols 1–7 also published New York: Grove Press) (contains vol. 1: *The Lesson, The Chairs, The Bald Prima Donna, Jacques; or, Obedience*; vol. 2: *Amédée, or, How to Get Rid of It, The New Tenant, Victims of Duty*; vol. 3: *The Killer, Improvisation, Maid to Marry*; vol. 4, translated by Prouse: *Rhinoceros, The Leader, The Future is in Eggs*; vol. 5: *Exit the King, Foursome, The Motor Show*; vol. 6: *A Stroll in the Air, Frenzy for Two*; vol. 7: *Hunger and Thirst, The Picture, Anger, Salutations*; vol. 8: *Here Comes a Chopper, The Oversight, The Foot of the Wall*; vol. 9: *Macbett, The Mire, Learning to Walk*; vol. 10: *Oh What a Bloody Circus!, The Hard-Boiled Egg*; vol. 11, translated by Watson and Williams: *The Man with the Luggage, The Duel, Double Act*; vol. 12, translated by Wright: *Journeys among the Dead: Themes and Variations*)

Watson, Donald, *Rhinoceros, The Chairs, The Lesson*, London: Penguin, 1962

Plays

La Cantatrice chauve, 1954, produced 1950

Allen, Donald M., *The Bald Soprano*, in *The Makers of Modern Theatre*, edited by Barry Ulanov, New York: McGraw-Hill, 1961

Watson, Donald, *The Bald Prima Donna*, in *Plays: Volume 1*, translated by Watson, 1958

Le Roi se meurt, 1963, produced 1962

Watson, Donald, *Exit the King*, in *Plays: Volume 5*, translated by Watson, 1963

Jeux de massacre, 1970

Bishop, Helen Gary, *Killing Game*, New York: Grove Press, 1974

Watson, Donald, *Here Comes a Chopper*, in *Plays: Volume 8*, translated by Watson, 1971

Voyages chez les morts, 1980

Wright, Barbara, *Journeys among the Dead*, in *Plays: Volume 12*, translated by Wright, 1985

Eugène Ionesco's playwriting went through several distinct phases, beginning with a series of experimental one-act plays, the aim of which was to "empty words of their content, to designify language, to abolish it" (Ionesco, *Un Homme en question*, 1979), and ending with what are essentially dramatic transpositions of recurrent personal dreams. In between came a number of plays written in a more traditional vein, the Bérenger cycle (so called after the main protagonist), which Ionesco would later dismiss as "wordy" (*Entre la vie et le rêve*, 1977), followed by a number of adaptations of his own or borrowed material. In order to take full account of this diversity of styles, a work from each of the four periods in question will be considered, the English translations being compared with their North American rivals, where these exist.

It is unquestionably the early one-acters that cause the biggest headache for translators. In contrast to the creative use of language by normal people, the characters in these plays talk mechanically, not so much *using* language as being used by it. Their utterances thus acquire a momentum of their own, with individualized speech often giving way to proverb or cliché, words disintegrating into isolated syllables or even letters, and meaning being swamped by pure sound. Given the arbitrary relationship between sound and meaning, the translator's task is particularly difficult at those intermediate stages of linguistic decomposition in Ionesco's plays where remnants of meaning still co-exist and interact with sound associations.

A case in point is Mr Smith's assertion in *La Cantatrice chauve* (produced 1950) that "le pape n'a pas de soupape. La soupape a un pape". Here the word-play depends in part on the language-specific homophony of *soupape* and *"sous-pape"* (the arbitrariness of which is highlighted by the English equivalents *valve* and *"sub-pope"*, respectively), in part on the equally arbitrary fact that the French word for *valve* contains as one of its syllables the French word for *pope*. Not surprisingly, perhaps, neither WATSON (1958) nor ALLEN (1961) is very successful in reproducing the effect of the original. Both have preserved its semantic incongruity but have resorted to creating a mainly cacophonous effect, by means of assonance and alliteration. This does, however, have a certain justification, for the line in question begins with "Le pape dérape" (literally, "the pope is slipping"!). The snappier rhythm of Watson's "The pope's eloped! The pope's no soap! Soap is dope" makes it marginally preferable to Allen's "The pope elopes! The pope's got no horoscope. The horoscope's bespoke". Elsewhere in the play, Watson's translation is distinctly superior. Not only is Allen guilty of some elementary mistranslating, he also copes less well with the wordplay of the original. Allen's rendering of the following extract from the Fireman's tirade (where the punning is highlighted for the sake of clarity) is feeble: "... un vitrier plein d'*entrain*, qui avait fait, à la fille d'un *chef de gare*, un enfant qui avait su *faire* son *chemin* dans la vie / Son *chemin* de *fer* / Comme aux *cartes*" becomes "... a glazier who was full of life and who had had, by the daughter of a *station-master*, a child who had burnt his *bridges* His britches? / No, his bridge-game". These verbal *quid pro quos* are a weak alternative to the original puns. WATSON's rendering is much cleverer: "... a *publican* full of *spirit*, who got by child the daughter of a *station-master*, and this child learnt how to play the game of life / *bridge*, for instance / *railway bridge*". Watson has seen fit to preserve the opening pun at the expense of the information value of the passage (which is, of course, nil). Since it is word shape rather than sentence meaning that determines the orientation of the speech, this is entirely legitimate. By the same token, the glazier could equally well have been a market-gardener who was full of beans, an electrician who was a bit of a live wire or a taxi-driver with a big hooter. Admittedly, the disappearance of the railway motif involves some translation loss. This being so, and since the glazier has become a publican anyway, he might just as well have been turned into a laundryman, … who was always *letting off steam*, who gave a *station-master's* daughter a son, who never once *went off the rails* but was *shunted* from foster-home to foster-home, without a motive, without a *locomotive*.

Elements of fantasy and lyricism make *Le Roi se meurt* (*Exit the King*), produced 1962, possibly the most difficult of the Bérenger plays to translate well. WATSON's version (1963) doesn't quite live up to the promise of its skilfully translated title, for as well as failing on occasions to bring out the full implications of Ionesco's text it also contains some uncharacteristic inaccuracies. Both weaknesses are evident in Watson's handling of the following passage: "… les feuilles se sont desséchées, elles se décrochent. Les arbres soupirent et meurent. La terre se fend encore plus que d'habitude". Watson's "… the brittle leaves are peeling off" concertinas the process of decay by reducing the number of finite verbs. The problem is compounded by his second sentence, "the trees are sighing and dying", where the choice of verbs that rhyme dilutes the sense of succession. Given the thematic centrality of the process of decay, this is careless translating. His third sentence, "the earth is quaking rather more than usual", is even less satisfactory: *se fendre* means *to crack* or *to split*, not *to quake*; and *encore plus* means *even more*, indicating a much more critical state of affairs than Watson's "rather more". However, this is not to say that the English text has no redeeming features. "Your winning ways and your firework displays" is, for example, a very neat rendering of "vos artifices et vos feux d'artifices".

Helen BISHOP (1974) has been taken to task by Hela Michot-Dietrich (1980) for having "massacred" *Jeux de massacre*. Valid though the criticisms are, the faults indicated scarcely add up to a massacre, even a figurative one. Of major concern to Michot-Dietrich are Bishop's omission of certain stage directions, her invention of scene titles that have no basis in the original and her failure to preserve the transparency of "hasard objectif" ("deliberate accident" in Bishop) and "mauvaise foi" ("stupidity"), where the original terms are said by Michot-Dietrich to allude to surrealism and existentialism, respectively. The distinctiveness of the former term, which is an important concept in André Breton's work and which is invariably translated by his English-speaking commentators as "objective chance", makes this particular point of Michot-Dietrich's irrefutable. On the other hand, it could hardly be claimed of an expression as widely used as *mauvaise foi* that Sartre enjoyed exclusive rights to it in the sense of "bad faith" (though something better than "stupidity" could have been found). At a more detailed level, Michot-Dietrich points out the inadequacy of rendering "l'âme de l'homme" as "the human spirit", *homme* being ambiguous as between *mankind* and the *male sex*. Clearly, in a scene that segregates the sexes, the critic is right to insist on the importance of this ambiguity (which "a man's soul" would have preserved). Curiously enough, a number of the criticisms apply also to WATSON's version (1971), suggesting that Bishop's renderings are less idiosyncratic than Michot-Dietrich would have us believe. Watson, too, incorporates scene titles, which are, moreover, remarkably similar to Bishop's. And his "the soul of man" is no better than her "human". On the whole, however, Watson is much more respectful of the text than Bishop, who is inclined to modify it needlessly. In spite of this (and the alleged massacre), Bishop's linguistic understanding is at least as sound as Watson's and her dialogue rather more fluent.

Finally, Ionesco has been well served by Barbara WRIGHT's translation (1985) of *Voyages chez les morts*. Her English has an authentic ring to it, with a touch of colour added here and there to the inherently more abstract character of the French. Thus, "c'était pour arranger tes affaires" is nicely rendered as "it was to feather your own nest" and "laisse donc ces choses-là, mortes depuis longtemps" as "Oh, let bygones be bygones, it's all dead and buried, now"; however, it might be felt by some that such renderings are uncomfortably close to the clichés that the playwright is so fond of deriding. Her approach to Ionesco's nonsense-language, which makes a modest comeback in this play with Jean's final monologue, is similarly flexible, though with slightly less satisfying results. For example, whereas "Il paraît qu'il ne faut pas dire cela, lire cela, se rappeler cela, pire cela, ker cela" starts with the eclipse of meaning by sound, degenerates into ungrammaticality with "pire cela" and ends in the total gibberish of "ker cela", Wright decides to stop short of the total breakdown embodied in the nonsense-word "ker". There are also a few perplexingly rough edges to Wright's text, rendered salient by its general smoothness.

The need to focus the present discussion on a limited number of texts has given rise to some glaring omissions. In the case of the early plays, the lack can be made good by reference to the very stimulating article by Richard Takvorian and Michael Spingler (1983). Less excusable, perhaps, is the absence from this survey of Derek Prouse's *Rhinoceros* (1960), for not only does it invite comparison with Watson's versions of the rest of the Bérenger cycle but the editors of the 1962 Penguin volume have already done Prouse the disservice of misattributing his translation to Watson. It must suffice here to point out that, while little separates these two translators in terms of accuracy, the quality of Prouse's English gives him the edge over Watson, whose renderings can occasionally sound too Gallic. Among the adaptations, *Macbett* (1972) would have been an interesting alternative to *Jeux de massacre*, with Watson and Charles Marowitz adopting quite different approaches to the play: although the latter has rightly chosen to give more emphasis to the burlesque dimension of the text than Watson, by way of an earthier idiom, it is the latter's version that is the more linguistically accurate. Finally, although good reasons could be found for taking as an example of the "dream plays" *L'Homme aux valises* (1975) (for not only is there an English and an American version but both are the result of collaborative efforts, the American one having involved the playwright's own daughter), to have concluded with Ionesco's swan song, *Journeys Among the Dead*, is perhaps equally fitting, not least because it introduces a successor to Watson as Ionesco's English translator.

PAUL REED

Further Reading

Michot-Dietrich, Hela, "The Massacre of Ionesco's *Jeux de massacre* or Pitfalls in Translation", *Translation Review*, 6 (1980) pp. 20–24

Takvorian, Richard and Michael Spingler, "Sounding Ionesco: Problems in Translating *La Leçon* and *Jacques; ou, La Soumission*", *Comparative Drama*, 17 (1983) pp. 40–54

Watson, Donald, "Bon esprit, bon sens ou bons mots?", *Palimpsestes*, 1 (1987) pp. 115–37

Irish

See Gaelic: Irish

Italian

Literary Translation into English

The Language

Italian is the closest modern descendant of classical Latin, from which it has evolved directly, albeit through late and mediaeval forms. Its first surviving recorded use in written form dates from the late 12th century, but it was another hundred years before Dante Alighieri (1265–1321), with his *Divina commedia*, firmly established it as a major language distinct from Latin.

However, during the period when Latin was evolving into its successor tongues, Italy experienced successive waves of invasion by Celtic and Germanic peoples, resulting in considerable regional linguistic differences, above all in the spoken language. Italy's subsequent history, initially, as the power of Imperial Rome faded and died, the history of many independent city states, and eventually that of larger regional groupings (Naples, Rome, Genoa, Milan, Turin, Venice), often under foreign domination, with national unification occurring only in the late 19th century and arguably still not wholly assimilated, has preserved this regional diversity. The Accademia della Crusca was founded in 1582 in Florence with the objective of standardizing and purifying the Tuscan language used by Dante, but, in the absence of political centralization, enjoyed only limited success nationally, although Tuscan is indeed today the standard literary form. In 1793, the Accademia temporarily lost its independence, and it was never again as important as were its sister academies in France and Spain. Italian has therefore developed in a fashion closer to that of the Germanic languages of northern Europe, led by the linguistic habits of its colloquial speakers rather than by an educated social and political class expressing its preferences through a formal institution. Nevertheless, the long, unbroken Italian literary tradition, which no other European country possesses in the same degree, has slowed the rate of linguistic change to below what has been experienced elsewhere. Dante is more accessible to a modern reader than is any other writer of his time in any other European language.

The sounds of modern spoken Italian are produced noticeably far forward in the mouth, and its pure, open vowels and the related diphthongs, which have made it the preferred language for much musical performance in the European tradition, retain their phonetic value irrespective of emphasis. These factors help to form the highly mobile facial musculature characteristic of Italian-speakers. The language has a strong tonic stress, and habitually lengthens the stressed vowel, which is usually the long vowel of the word's Latin original and therefore often in the penultimate syllable, but the position of the stressed vowel is subject to many variations. Since these are not normally indicated in the written language they represent a source of difficulty to the foreign speaker. In its evolution from the Latin Italian has dropped or simplified many of the consonants. It avoids consonantal clusters, and has no aspirate or dental fricative, but by preserving the vowel sounds and pronouncing fully the remaining consonants it retains a rhythmic and phonetic variety which can be satisfactorily represented in English.

In particular, the fact that terminal vowels retain their value has meant that the person and number of a verb are fully indicated by its ending, so that the pronoun subject is redundant except for emphasis, and that the referent of an adjective is often made clear, in the spoken as well as in the written language, by its gender, so that the noun itself may be omitted. The effectiveness of these semantic markers also means that word order is relatively flexible, though less so than in classical Latin. In common with most Romance languages, Italian has dropped the original Latin inflectional systems of nouns and adjectives, retaining only some of the pronominal inflections.

The systems of verbs, however, is particularly rich and varied. The simple passive voice has disappeared, but in the active voice five simple indicative tenses and two in the subjunctive mood remain in normal colloquial use, while a considerable number of compound tenses, active and passive, indicative and subjunctive, can also be constructed.

Perhaps because of its strong oral tradition, modern Italian makes great use of a variety of suffixes to indicate niceties of meaning. All the main parts of speech may be modified in this way, which is particularly useful in adapting new formulations to the existing constraints of the language, since a foreign root can be fitted out with a standard Italian inflectional ending, allowing it to be conjugated and made to agree according to the normal rules of syntax. The resultant variety of modificational forms goes some way to make up for the fact that Italian, with its almost exclusively monolingual inheritance, possesses a relatively poor variety of root forms. This relative poverty may also in part explain the tendency of Italian-speakers, so often caricatured, to supplement the formal content of their speech by hand gestures and other body language.

Many of the suffixes indicate different degrees of size or importance, together with an affective component. They frequently represent a difficulty for the translator, since the appropriate equivalent in English, which enjoys a much greater diversity of linguistic roots, will normally be found by exercising a careful choice of vocabulary among this available diversity, and by varying the sentence structure, rather than by applying a modifier – suffixed or not – to a more basic word. Where this fact is not recognized, too precise a rendering of the implications of an Italian suffix by the use of English modifiers may produce a text that is at once childish and heavy, as when the familiar terminations *-ino* and *-etto* are translated by such formulations as "a nice little..."

Italian is spoken only in Italy, southern Switzerland and certain Italian expatriate communities about the world. It therefore remains protected from non-Latin importations, but by virtue of its structure it is able to accommodate such elements with facility – as indeed it accommodates neologisms constructed within its own linguistic heritage. Perhaps for these reasons, in spite of the strong influence of its primary Latin origin, Italian remains a lively and virile modern language, and continues to develop in a healthy fashion.

George S. Miller

Up to the Renaissance

Translation from Italian entered English literature at the highest level. Chaucer (?1340–1400), who visited Italy in the 1370s, drew on the works of Dante (1265–1321), Petrarch (1304–74) and Boccaccio (1313–75) for ideas, phrases and entire stories in *The House of Fame*, *Troilus and Criseyde* and *The Canterbury Tales*. He acknowledged his debt to Dante and Petrarch, but never mentioned Boccaccio. In some cases – as when he based "The Clerk's Tale" not on Boccaccio's original Italian story of Griselda (*Decameron*, 10, 10) but on the Latin version that Petrarch translated from Boccaccio – Chaucer may have been unaware of his source. The medieval concept of *translatio* included appropriation and adaptation to new purposes, and Chaucer often reworked his Italian sources rather than merely translating them, but there are exceptions, as when he inserts in his story of *Troilus and Criseyde*, derived from Boccaccio's *Filostrato*, an expanded 21-line translation of one of Petrarch's most characteristic sonnets of inner conflict (*Canzoniere* 132). Petrarch's first quatrain reads:

S'amor non è, che dunque è quel ch'io sento?
Ma s'egli è amor, perdio, che cosa et quale?
Se bona, ond'è l'effecto aspro mortale?
Se ria, ond'è sì dolce ogni tormento?

The first seven-line stanza of Chaucer's *Canticus Troili* (Book I, 400–06) shows his hero, smitten by Criseyde, reflecting as follows:

If no love is, O god, what fele I so?
And if love is, what thing and which is he?
If love be good, from whennes cometh my woo?
If he be wikke, a wonder thinketh me
When every torment and adversite
That cometh of hym, may to me savory thynke,
For ay thurst I, the more that ich it drynke.

The first three lines are close translation; the last four expand a single line of Petrarch. Another example of direct translation is Chaucer's invocation of God in the very last stanza of *Troilus and Criseyde* (Book V, 1863–69), which quotes Dante's *Paradiso*, Canto 14, 28–30.

Quell'uno e due e tre che sempre vive,
e regna sempre in tre e 'n due e 'n uno
non circunscritto, e tutto circunscrive

is rendered:

Thow oon, and two, and thre, eterne on lyve,
That regnest ay in thre, and two, and oon,
Uncircumscript, and al maist circumscrive.

15th and 16th centuries

In Renaissance England, Italy was seen as the home of civility and learning. English writers drew widely on Italians such as Petrarch, who was the most imitated literary figure in Europe, having built a repertoire of conceits and personae in his love poetry that were easily adaptable at many different levels. His 16th-century English followers included Sir Thomas Wyatt (1503–42), Henry Howard, Earl of Surrey (?1517–47), and Sir Philip Sidney (1554–86). Their use of Petrarch ranged from direct word-for-word translation to free adaptation, based on Petrarch himself and on his "Petrarchist" imitators. Wyatt also used other Italian sources: ironically, his somewhat xenophobic satire "Mine own John Poyntz" in which he rejoices that he is not

where Christ is given in prey
For money, poison and treason in Rome –
a common practice used night and day.
But here I am in Kent and Christendom

is adapted from a satire by the Florentine Luigi Alamanni, rejoicing at being safe in Provence rather than in godless Rome, where only coiners and poisoners can go home unscathed:

Non sono in Roma, ove chi in Cristo creda,
E non sappia falsar nè far veleni,
Convien che a casa con suo danno rieda.
Sono in Provenza ...

Petrarch's other major work in the Italian vernacular, the *Trionfi*, was translated into English by Lord Morley in the mid-16th century.

Modern scholars have suggested that the Elizabethan and

Tudor translators of England regarded translation as a form of national service, similar to sea-exploration and buccaneering, and felt free to adapt imported works to the ideology and phrasing of their native country. The vitality of Elizabethan translation has also been attributed to the fact that translated works were being introduced to a country that was from the literary point of view still backward, but whose language was at its freshest and most vigorous. In this receptive atmosphere, several important Italian prose works found a ready audience. Sir Thomas Hoby's version, published in 1561, of Castiglione's *Book of the Courtier* (1528), although initially not as well known as the Latin versions of the same book, shaped the English notion of a gentleman and exerted a far-reaching influence on English-language literature. Hoby's method of translation was free and expansive: his latest editor, Virginia Cox, notes that he visualized the Italian original and rephrased it in a personal way. Hoby provided a model of dialogue and of rational and argumentative discussion, which was mined by Elizabethan dramatists including Shakespeare. Similar claims have been made for George Pettie's translation of Stefano Guazzo's *The Civile Conversation*, published in 1581. Guazzo's original Italian text had appeared in 1574; two separate French versions were published in 1579, and Pettie worked from those, supplying missing passages from the Italian. Another blueprint for civilized living was Giovanni Della Casa's *Galateo*, written between 1551 and 1555; Robert Peterson's English version of the *Galateo*, thought to be based on an anonymous French version of 1573, was published in 1576, subtitled *A treatise of the manners and behaviours, it behoveth a man to use and eschewe, in his familiar conversation*. The translator states his educational purpose – "I thought his lessons fit for our store, & sought to make him speake English". This he pithily achieves, rendering Della Casa's most memorable piece of advice even more vivid than the original: "And when thou hast blown thy nose, use not to open thy handkercheif, to glare uppon thy snot, as if thou hadst pearles and Rubies fallen from thy braynes".

Some of the writings of Machiavelli (1469–1527) were printed in Italian in 16th-century England. Translations also appeared: *The Art of Warre* was translated by Peter Whitehorne (1563) and dedicated to Queen Elizabeth, while the *Florentine Historie* was translated by Thomas Bedingfield (1593). More dangerous Machiavelli works such as *The Prince* (written in 1513) and the *Discourses* were not licensed for printing in England, even in Italian; the first English translations by Edward Dacres did not appear until 1636 (The *Discourses*) and 1640 (*The Prince*).

Translations from the Italian (often indirect) had a major influence on the Elizabethan drama. The soldier and poet George Gascoigne (c.1534–77) directly translated two Italian plays, *The Supposes* (1566) from Ariosto's *I suppositi* and *Jocasta* (1573) from Ludovico Dolce's *Giocasta* (itself translated from Euripides). Other influences came through the *novella* or short story, one of the great literary forms of the Italian Middle Ages and Renaissance, some of the best examples of which are imported into English through French. Thirteen stories by Matteo Bandello (1485–1561), translated from Belleforest's French version, were included in Geoffrey Fenton's *Certain Tragicall Discourses* (London, 1567). Fenton's immensely successful translation of Guicciardini's history of Italy, published in 1579, was likewise taken from the 1568 French version by Chomedey. (The *Storia d'Italia* had been published posthumously in 1561.) Among the 101 stories in his highly successful *Palace of Pleasure* (1566), which has been called "the storehouse of Elizabethan plot", William Painter translated a number of tales from Boccaccio and Bandello; explaining that he had used a French version of Bandello, because the original, being written by a non-Tuscan, was not proper Italian. The playwrights who drew on the Italian plots made available by Painter included Shakespeare (*All's Well That Ends Well*, *Romeo and Juliet*) and Webster (*The Duchess of Malfi*). Shakespeare took the story of *Measure for Measure* from another Italian tale, in Giraldi Cinthio's *Gli Hecatommithi* (1565), translated into English by George Whetstone in *An Heptameron of Civil Discourses* (1582). *Othello* also came from *Gli Hecatommithi*, but there is no known intermediate English text and Shakespeare may have gone direct to the Italian original or to a French translation published in 1584. Thus, published translations taken directly from Italian were not the only means of assimilation. An "intermediate" translation lay behind Shakespeare's second source for *Romeo and Juliet*: besides Painter's translation, he used Arthur Brooke's verse *Tragicall History of Romeus and Juliet* (1562), adapted from Boaistuau's French version of Matteo Bandello's Italian original. And the story of the Lady of Belmont, which supplies the main plot of *The Merchant of Venice*, is not among the tales translated by Painter from *Il Pecorone*, by the 14th-century Ser Giovanni Fiorentino. No translation of the story is known from Shakespeare's time, so how he got it remains a mystery. Likewise, the first published English translation of Boccaccio's tale of Bernabò and Zinevra (*Decameron* 2.9) which supplies part of the story in Shakespeare's *Cymbeline*, dates from 1620, four years after the playwright's death. Once again, the trail of provenance is unclear.

Selections from Boccaccio had appeared, as we have seen, in the *Palace of Pleasure*. One of the most famous episodes from Boccaccio's *Filocolo* appeared in 1566 as *The Most Pleasant and Delectable Questions of Love*, translated by "H.G.", while his *Amorous Fiammetta*, translated by Bartholomew Yong, was published in 1587. The first full English version of the *Decameron* appeared in 1620. The translator may have been John Florio, translator of Montaigne and compiler of the first Italian–English dictionary. He worked from one of the many censored Italian editions (the book had become a controversial work in Counter-Reformation Italy), and took the opportunity to beef up Boccaccio's style and add extra Protestant flavouring to the depiction of the Church in the *Decameron*.

Great Italian narrative poems were also translated. In 1591 Sir John Harington published his translation of Ariosto's epic *Orlando Furioso* (1532), dedicating it to his godmother Queen Elizabeth; this work, in the words of Barbara Reynolds, "has entwined itself with English literature to a degree exceeded only by Dante's *Divina Commedia* and the love poetry of Petrarch". The Elizabethans were quicker to translate Tasso's epic, *Gerusalemme Liberata*. This first appeared in Italian in 1580, and was still being revised by its author 10 years later. Five cantos translated by Richard Carew appeared in 1594, while Edward Fairfax's complete version, under the title *Godfrey of Bulloigne*, was published in 1600. This version became, in the words of a later translator, an English classic; it influenced both Spenser (who closely imitates Tasso in parts of *The Faerie*

Queene) and Milton, and was frequently reprinted. Tasso's pastoral play, *Aminta* (printed in 1581) appeared in English in 1591, the first of many translations.

17th Century

The influence of Italian culture in England declined considerably during the 17th century, displaced by the growing prestige of France. Although Italy was often perceived as decadent, some significant translations were done. Guarini's *Pastor Fido* (1589), another pastoral play much admired in its day, was first translated in 1602, possibly by Sir John Dymock; *The Faithfull Shepherd* (1647) by Sir Richard Fanshawe (a diplomat who also translated from Latin, Portuguese and Spanish) is the best known among a host of English versions. Giambattista Marino (1569–1625), a Neapolitan poet hugely successful in his day but afterwards regarded as flashy and over-ornate, was among the Italian poets translated by William Drummond of Hawthornden and by Edward Sherburne. The first book of Marino's *Strage degli Innocenti*, a poem about Herod's slaughter of the innocents published posthumously in 1632, was translated by Richard Crashaw (c.1612–1649) as part of his religious collection, *Steps to the Temple* (1646). A translation of the whole *Strage degli Innocenti* by "R.T." appeared in 1675.

Some of the English interest in Italian writing was less literary than scientific or religious. Galileo was translated posthumously by Thomas Salusbury in 1661. The dissident Venetian friar Paolo Sarpi (1552–1623) was a friend of Sir Thomas Wotton, first resident English ambassador to Venice, and of Wotton's chaplain William Bedell (who later promoted the first Irish translation of the complete Bible). Works by Sarpi were printed in Italian in England, and there was a string of English translations. As the *Historie of the Councel of Trent*, translated by Nathanael Brent, his *Historia del Consilio Tridentino* (1619) went through four editions.

John Dryden, the great practitioner and theorist of translation, worked on a collection of *Fables* in verse at the end of his life; the resulting book, which appeared in 1700, included three stories freely adapted from the *Decameron* (4.1, 1.8, 5.1), based both on Boccaccio's original Italian and on the 1620 English translation.

18th Century

The English admiration for Italy, and for its Renaissance classics, revived in the second half of the 18th century, partly through the efforts of Guiseppe Baretti, who lived in London and was admired by Dr Johnson's circle. Baretti helped William Huggins to revise his new translation of the *Orlando Furioso* in *ottava rima* (1755), the first since Harington's version of 1591; Huggins is also believed to have made a full translation of Dante's *Divine Comedy*, but it was never published. Shortly afterwards, the Irishman Philip Doyne produced a fine version of Tasso's *Gerusalemme Liberata*, the first since Fairfax's *Godfrey of Bulloigne*; Doyne's *The Delivery of Jerusalem* was published in Dublin in 1761. His introductory remarks, placing Tasso's poem on the same level as the *Iliad* and *Aeneid*, compare it to "an elegant and well-finished Italian building, that delights the eye at a distance, and improves with nearer view; it has all the graces of the Italian architecture". Doyne's Tasso was, however, quickly eclipsed by another new *Jerusalem Delivered* in rhyming couplets (1763) by James Hoole, with a dedicatory letter by Dr Johnson; this became the standard English Tasso. Hoole also translated the plays and cantatas of the contemporary Pietro Metastasio (1767), and did the *Orlando Furioso* in rhyming couplets (1783). The first complete published *Divine Comedy* in English (1802) belongs to the Irish clergyman Henry Boyd, who had published the *Inferno* in Dublin in 1785 along with a brief unsuccessful sample from his unpublished complete *Orlando Furioso*. Like Doyne with Tasso, Boyd sets Dante among the ancient epics, although he briskly denies this status to Tasso: "The superstition that led the Crusaders to rescue the Holy Land from the infidels; instead of interesting us, appears frigid, if not ridiculous. We cannot be much concerned for the fate of such a crew of fanatics." Boyd's Dante is stodgy, dim and domesticated (the Virgin Mary takes on the quasi-Elizabethan title of the Virgin Queen), but he helped to revive the English interest in Dante, soon crowned by the highly successful Cary translation of 1814.

A readable translation by Thomas Nugent of Benvenuto Cellini's *Vita* appeared in 1771, giving English readers a vivid glimpse into the life of this Renaissance artist (1500–71) and his contemporaries. One of the leading figures in the Italian enlightenment, Cesare Beccaria, also found an influential readership in England; his treatise *Dei delitti e delle pene*, first published in 1764, was anonymously translated from the French version and published as *An Essay on Crimes and Punishments* in 1769. The first translation was followed by several others on both sides of the Atlantic.

19th Century

The revival of interest in Italian literature gathered momentum in 19th-century England, although, as Mario Praz observes, English writers drew inspiration not so much from Italian literature as from the Italian landscape, art and people, and many of their most Italianate creations were not actually translated or adapted from Italian originals. Yet there was an awareness of contemporary Italian writing. The tragedies and memoirs of Alfieri (1749–1803) were enthusiastically received in English. Both versions of Manzoni's *I promessi sposi* (1827 and 1840–42) were translated almost as soon as they appeared. Later in the century the political writings of Giuseppe Mazzini (1805–72), who lived much of his life in London, were translated repeatedly. The poet Giosuè Carducci (1835–1907) was translated by Frank Sewall in 1892, and many times thereafter. The American novelist William Dean Howells (1837–1920), who served as American consul in Venice in the 1860s, produced *Modern Italian Poets: Essays and Versions* (1887).

The older classics were also kept in view. Wordsworth translated some Chiabrera (1552–1638) epitaphs and Michelangelo (1475–1564) sonnets. Byron, who concluded his *Childe Harold* in 1818 with a lengthy poetic tour of Italy and homage to her writers, and who claimed the authority of Ariosto for the changeability of his style in that work, also translated the first canto of the *Morgante Maggiore* by Luigi Pulci (1432–84), a comic forerunner of Ariosto's *Orlando Furioso*. In his Advertisement to the Pulci translation Byron asks the reader's indulgence, pointing out that "the antiquated language of Pulci, however pure, is not easy to the generality of Italians themselves." He compares the Italian language to "a capricious beauty, who accords her smiles to all, her favours to few, and sometimes least to those who have courted her longest." His aim was "to present in an English dress a part at least of a poem never yet rendered into a northern language; at the same time that it had been the original of some of the most celebrated productions on this side of the Alps."

In dealing with older texts Victorian translators tended, in the words of J.M. Cohen, to confer "on all works alike the brown varnish of antiquarianism", aiming "to convey the remoteness both in time and place of the original work". This is true of John Payne's accurate but archaic *Decameron* (1886), but there are exceptions; for example, in 1862 the satirist Thomas Love Peacock published "The Deceived", a lively and readable translation of the anonymous Sienese play *Gl'Ingannati* (1531), although some secondary scenes are merely summarized, and certain passages (e.g. act 4, scene 1, act 5, scene 5) are labelled "untranslatable". When one checks the original, "untranslatable" turns out to mean "extremely indecent"; censorship was of course a major concern during the Victorian era, partly owing to the rise of mass literacy. The first English translator of Giambattista Basile's Neopolitan *Pentamerone* (1634), John Edward Taylor (*The Pentamerone; or, The Story of Stories. Fun for the Little Ones*, London, 1848) cut out many of the author's 50 tales on moral grounds: "The gross license in which Basile allowed his humour to indulge is wholly inadmissible at the present day in a work intended for the general reader; the moral sense of our age is happily too refined and elevated to admit indelicacy." However, the second translator, Sir Richard Burton (1821–90), a prodigious linguist whose other translations included an unexpurgated *Arabian Nights* and *Kama Sutra*, omitted nothing in his readable though sometimes inaccurate translation, published in 1893 in a limited edition.

Dante Gabriel Rossetti (1828–82), son of an Italian exile, combined translation and original poetry to bring Italian culture to the forefront of English literature. His pioneering translation of *The Early Italian Poets, with Dante's Vita nuova* first appeared in 1861. Another influential figure was the Renaissance scholar John Addington Symonds (1840–93), who published translations of Michelangelo (1878) and Poliziano (1879), as well as a new translation of Cellini's *Life* (1887). This tradition of scholarly translation from the distant past was to persist into the following century.

20th Century

Literary translation from Italian in the modern period displays a wide variety of approaches. In the field of poetry translation we have the prose crib, the faithful version, the free adaptation, the partial translation, and even deliberate mistranslation. Take Guido Cavalcanti's heartbreaking Ballata XI: "Perch'io non spero di tornar giammai, / Ballatetta, in Toscana ..." Ezra Pound, one of the most influential proponents of translation as a literary activity, championed Cavalcanti (c.1255–1300) in a language vigorously blending antique language and contemporary rhythms. His translation of *The Sonnets and Ballate* (1912) renders Ballata XI: "Because no hope is left me, Ballatetta, / Of return to Tuscany ...". The word *Ballatetta* (little ballad) is left untranslated until the fourth stanza, and up to then might be assumed by a non-Italian reader to be a female character in the poem. T.S. Eliot recycles Cavalcanti's opening line at the start of his "Ash Wednesday" (1930):

Because I do not hope to turn again
Because I do not hope
Because I do not hope to turn ...

Although one of the meanings of "turn" is "return", that aspect emerges only when one considers Eliot's line in relation to Cavalcanti's. Stanley Burnshaw, in *The Poem Itself*, identified one of the main strands in modern poetry as "the poetry of appropriated effects"; here the appropriation is ambiguous, creating a characteristically modern dazzle of overlaid meanings out of a mixture of half translation and mistranslation.

Another response related to translation, as James Holmes noted, is a poem "about" a poem. An interesting example in the Italian area comes from the "Translations and Imitations" section in Donald Davie's *Collected Poems 1971–1983*, which includes "'Pastor Errante'", partly a selective translation, partly a meditation on the Leopardi poem "Canto notturno di un pastore errante dell'Asia". Starting out from a picture of an unspoiled American West, "a true / Pastoral, sheep-bells ringing", Davie turns ironically to his intertext:

... Asia
Is what Leopardi
Too plangently imagined, that much nearer
The god's faint trace. And
"*Moon*",
He starts out, bald as that, "*what are you doing*
There in the sky? Unspeaking moon,
What are you about? ...

Later, still drawing on Wild West language, Davie translates Leopardi's image of the grave that awaits mortal man, the "Abisso, orrido, immenso / Ov'ei, precipitando, il tutto oblia" as "*the / Hair-raising gulch where he, / Oblivious, pitches in*". He explicitly skips a bit of the Leopardi poem, and offers an irritated comment on Leopardi's acceptance of his personal unhappiness:

"*... whatever may come of*
Good or satisfying is
For some one else. For me, my life is evil."
What sort of a frigid monster would one have to
Be, to derive consolation
From such a confession?"

By his interspersed technique, Davie foregrounds the acts of translation and commentary as a poet's way of confronting the tradition.

While few English-language prose writers have engaged in translation, poets have ventured into many foreign territories. (One reason may be that one can translate a poem quite quickly, and get help with the difficulties, whereas extended prose translation is a slow, solitary craft.) Most poetry translation is more or less unpaid, so the choice of text is an important factor. Seamus Heaney writes in his essay "Dante and the Modern Poet" that "when poets turn to the great masters of the past, they turn to an image of their own creation, one which is likely to be a reflection of their own imaginative needs, their own artistic inclinations and procedures." Heaney himself includes an eloquent version of Dante's Ugolino episode from *Inferno*, cantos 33–34 in his 1979 collection, *Field Work*. The image of bestial violence returns in three lines quoted from the Ugolino translation in Heaney's poem, "The Flight Path" (collected in *The Spirit Level*, 1996), with reference to a contemporary Irish hunger striker.

Translation, then, can meet imaginative needs that cannot be immediately supplied from a poet's personal resources, or from the native tradition, or allows the poet to express deep inner thought without burdening the ego with the demands of authorship. Robert Lowell, interviewed by D.S. Carne-Ross for the first issue of *Delos*, said: "In a way the whole point of translating – of my translation, anyway – is to bring into English something that didn't exist in English before. I don't think I've ever done a translation of a poem I could have written myself." Lowell included a faithful and sober version of the Brunetto Latini passage (from Dante's *Inferno*, Canto 15) in his 1967 collection, *Near the Ocean*; the more extravagant translations in his 1961 collection, *Imitations*, largely done while the poet was in hospital, include Italian poems by Leopardi, Carducci, Ungaretti and Montale. In translating Montale's "La casa dei doganieri", he rewrote the original in an edgy and emphatic style, disdaining accuracy and resorting to etymology rather than surface equivalence: "tu non ricordi" (you don't remember) becomes "you haven't taken it to heart" – *cor* being the Latin for heart. At his English publishers, Faber and Faber, T.S. Eliot insisted on the title "Imitations" (rather than "Versions", which Allen Tate had suggested to Lowell), and warned that the word "translation" would "attract all those meticulous little critics who delight in finding what seem to them mis-translations". In his preface Lowell adopted a Drydenesque position on translation; he had tried to write "live English", as if his original authors were "writing their poems now and in America". He contrasts his appropriative method with the "modest photographic prose translations" provided by George Kay in the *Penguin Book of Italian Verse*.

Prose translations of poetry are not always modest or photographic: one thinks of the highly ambitious prose renderings of Petrarch sonnets by J.M. Synge. And even the most genuinely modest prose translations of poetry, designed merely to aid comprehension, can sometimes achieve a measure of independent, or at least interdependent, artistic success. (Beauty in translation may be thought to arise from the consonance between texts.) While Montale (1896-1981) translations have appeared in books or collections by Edwin Morgan, George Kay, Antonino Mazza, Jeremy Reed, G. Singh and Jonathan Galassi, some of the explanatory versions in scholarly books (by critics such as Jared Becker, Rebecca J. West and Glauco Cambon) can hold their own with the best poetic versions. Scholarly books are in fact a large and sometimes interesting repository of poetry translation. Mention should also be made of distinguished academic translators such as Charles Tomlinson, who has published Italian poets (including Ungaretti and Bertolucci) both in his personal volumes of translations and in *The Oxford Book of Verse in English Translation* (1980). Another expert academic translator, Allen Mandelbaum, has produced justly celebrated versions from Italian, ranging from Dante to Quasimodo (1901–68).

In 20th-century verse translation, the dominant ethic is fidelity to the source. A fine example is the scrupulous and expressive version of Leopardi's *Canti* by John Heath-Stubbs (1946). Edwin Morgan takes a similar approach in *Rites of Passage* (1976): "Despite the forceful exemplars of Ezra Pound, Robert Lowell and Christopher Logue, I have persistently refused myself their freedom of approach, and have tried to work within a sense of close and deep obligation to the other poet." Morgan includes only poems "done directly from the original texts" because "it seemed fairer to present the results of immediate poet-to-poet impact", but he bases that impact on a careful approach to his originals.

Among the reasons that motivate translation may be a perceived affinity of voice or social position. Lawrence Ferlinghetti and Francesca Valente translated *Roman Poems* (1986), a selection from Pier Paolo Pasolini (1922–75), for City Lights Books of San Francisco, of which Ferlinghetti is joint series editor. Personal friendship can also underpin fine translations, as in the superb selection from Franco Fortini's poetry *Summer Is Not All* (1992), done by Paul Lawton (1924–), a retired official of the World Health Organization. Fortini also provided the introduction for Lawton's beautiful Leopardi selections (1996).

Poetry, unlike prose, is often translated more than once. The Roman dialect poet Guiseppe Gioacchino Belli (1791–1863) attracted a wide range of translators. In Victorian times, selections from Belli were translated into prose by Hans William Sotheby (1874) and verse by Frances Eleanor Trollope (1880). His modern translators include Eleanor Clark, Edwin Morgan, Robert Garioch (in Scots), Harold Norse (in New York slang), Desmond O'Grady, Miller Williams (American demotic). Anthony Burgess translated a selection of Belli's Biblical poems, with ingenious rhymes in the Byron/Auden tradition, as part of his novel *ABBA ABBA* (1977).

Twentieth-century theatrical translation presents some special features. As with poetry, many plays were translated by more than one person. This could happen even within single versions of a play, as the translation of theatre texts often involved an uncredited intermediate translator. Many theatrical translations remained unpublished, given the negligible market for theatre scripts, and some fine versions may never have been recorded. Many translations involved some degree of adaptation for specific productions, and the main "translation" was from page to stage rather than from Italian to English. That said, the 20th century saw a large number of translations from the 18th-century Goldoni (1707–93) and from Luigi Pirandello (1867–1936), whose translators included Marta Abba, Frederick May and Eric Bentley.

The volume of literary prose translation from Italian grew enormously in the 20th century. Several contemporary Italian works had a major impact on the English-speaking world. Ignazio Silone's *Fontamara* was translated into English by Eric Mosbacher and Gwenda David (London, 1934), and by Michael Wharf (New York, 1934), almost simultaneously with the first Italian-language edition; in these and later versions *Fontamara* played an important part in shaping the world's response to Fascism in the 1930s and beyond. Similarly, Carlo Levi's *Christ Stopped at Eboli* (1945), translated by Frances Frenaye in 1947, projected an influential image of the perennial problems of southern Italy. Stuart Woolf's translation (1959) of Primo Levi's *If This Is a Man* (1947) introduced English-speaking readers to one of the essential writers of the century. William Weaver's fine English version of Umberto Eco's (1980) international bestseller *The Name of the Rose* appeared in 1983.

When one looks at the profession of prose translation, a striking contrast emerges between Italy and the English-speaking world. In Italy, many leading writers including Montale, Vittorini, Pavese, Calvino, Celati and Eco have translated English and American novels. In the other direction, the "creative" translators are far fewer and sometimes (as in the case of D.H. Lawrence's versions of Verga) considerably less competent. Most of the leading translators from Italian are not well known as creative writers, although they often have other types of literary or scholarly expertise. Archibald Colquhoun wrote a book on Manzoni as well as translating him (he also did some Calvino novels, and Lampedusa's historical novel *The Leopard*). William Weaver (1923–), who has produced convincing versions of authors as diverse as Calvino, Pasolini, Gadda and Eco, is among other things a leading authority on opera. Isobel Quigly is an editor and biographer as well as a translator. Henry Furst ghost wrote some of Montale's literary journalism. And there are notable exceptions on the creative side: Patrick Creagh (1938–), whose translations include Dante, Leopardi, Ungaretti, Calvino, Vassalli, Brancati, Bufalino and Marta Morazzoni, and a classic version of Claudio Magris's *Danube* (1989), is an accomplished poet; Tim Parks (1954–) whose "stable" of Italian authors includes Calvino, Tabucchi and Calasso, is probably better known as an award-winning novelist and non-fiction writer than as a translator.

Many translators are multilingual: for example, Frances Frenaye, who has translated a string of authors including Guareschi, Alvaro, Croce and Vittorini, translates from French as well as Italian. Eric Mosbacher has also worked from French and German. The translators already mentioned have turned their hands to many authors, but there are others who have specialized in one or two: for example, Angus Davidson has done the English version of almost all of Moravia's novels; Svevo is mostly translated by Beryl de Zoete; Dick Kitto and Elspeth Spottiswoode translate Dacia Maraini's novels, investing her prose with real distinction.

Some translators are university teachers propagating their favourite authors to an English-speaking readership. Thus, Robert Lumley is a "gatekeeper" for Gianni Celati both as scholar and translator. Joseph Farrell has translated Leonardo Sciascia and written an important monograph on him. This dual role is not confined to contemporary authors: Thomas G. Bergin, Professor of Italian at Yale and a gifted explicator of Italian literature, made fine translations of Dante, Petrarch, Vico, Quasimodo and others, while Kenelm Foster, O.P., Reader in Italian at Cambridge, translated Manzoni's *Storia della Colonna Infame* and the letters of Saint Catherine of Siena. Nor is the combination of scholarship and translation confined to people with academic appointments: George Bull worked for the Institute of Directors in London and wrote books on Michelangelo, Vatican politics and business topics as well as translating Cellini, Vasari, Machiavelli, Castiglione and Aretino for the Penguin Classics series.

Certain publishing houses, large and small, including Harcourt Brace, Secker and Warburg, CollinsHarvill, Serpent's Tail and Quartet, and poetry publishers such as Carcanet, and Dedalus Press in Ireland, have played an important role in making Italian texts available in English. Penguin Classics has a particularly glorious history; one of the early books in this series was Dante's *Inferno* (1949) translated by Dorothy L. Sayers (an expert on Dante as well as a hugely successful detective story writer); Sayers also did the *Purgatorio*, and after her death her *Paradiso* was completed by Barbara Reynolds, who also did Dante's *Vita Nuova* and a highly readable verse translation of Ariosto's *Orlando Furioso*. G.H. McWilliam's elegant version of the *Decameron* is another highlight of the Penguin imprint. Other publishers such as Oxford University Press (in their World's Classics series) have covered major Italian classics, and in America academic publishers such as Garland have commissioned translations of many medieval works; the American university presses are also active in this area.

At the beginning of the 21st century, the field of translation from Italian to English looks promising. The educational establishment and the media have begun to recognize the importance of translation. Publishers generally remember to pay their translators and mention them on their title-pages (although some examples of miraculous translation can still be found). English-language readers are increasingly open to foreign literatures. Translators may be encouraged by the availability of prizes, and the Italian Government administers a number of prizes and grants to support publication; translators' colleges and professional associations are flourishing. Most of all, however, the future of literary translation from Italian, as from any other language, rests – as it has always rested – on the shoulders of those many modest polymaths who open the channels between writer and reader.

Cormac Ó Cuilleanáin

Further Reading

Cohen, J.M., *English Translators and Translations*, London: Longman, 1962

Fucilla, Joseph, G., "Italian Literature" in *The Literatures of the World in English Translation: A Bibliography*, vol. 3: *The Romance Literatures*, part 1, edited by George Parks and Ruth Z. Temple, New York: Ungar, 1970

Healey, Robin, *Twentieth-Century Italian Literature in English Translation: An Annotated Bibliography, 1929–1997*, Toronto: University of Toronto Press, 1998

Keenoy, Ray *et al.*, *The Babel Guide to Italian Fiction in English Translation*, London: Boulevard, 1995

Kirkpatrick, Robin, *English and Italian Literature from Dante to Shakespeare: A Study of Source, Analogue and Divergence*, London and New York: Longman, 1995

Marshall, Roderick, *Italy in English Literature, 1755–1815: Origins of the Romantic Interest in Italy*, New York: Columbia University Press, 1934

Praz, Mario, *The Flaming Heart: Essays on Crashaw, Machiavelli, and Other Studies in the Relations between Italian and English Literature from Chaucer to T.S. Eliot*, New York: Doubleday, 1958

J

Max Jacob 1876–1944

French poet and artist

Biography

Born in Quimper, Brittany, 11 July 1876, of a Jewish family. He grew up in Brittany and left school in 1894 to try his hand at painting and writing. He moved to Paris in 1896. Once there he barely survived by giving piano lessons, and pursuing various trades and odd jobs while attending art courses. In 1898 he was hired as an art critic for *Le Gaulois*, but quickly resigned to return to Quimper; but he was back in Paris in 1901. Though he continued to move from job to job, in this period he befriended such notable writers as Apollinaire, Reverdy, Cocteau, and Picasso. Picasso eventually served as Jacob's godfather when he converted to Catholicism in 1915. By 1921 Jacob began to live off an on at the Benedictine monastery at Saint-Benoît-sur-Loire, where he found a certain peace of mind, but for short periods of time only. He was arrested, as a Jew, by the Nazis in 1944 and died of pneumonia in Drancy concentration camp, 5 March 1944.

As a modernist poet, he is perhaps best known for his collection of prose poems *Le Cornet à dés* (*The Dice Cup*), 1917. In addition he wrote verse (including *Le Laboratoire central* [The Central Laboratory]), 1921, haunting fiction (e.g. *Le Cabinet noir* [The Darkroom], 1922), religious meditations, correspondence, ballet scenarios and a libretto, and illustrated some of his own works. He was made a member of the French Legion of Honour in 1932.

The Dice Cup

Le Cornet à dés, 1917

Translations

The French text used by most translators is the one published by the author at his own expense in 1917, which then reappeared with Stock in 1923 and thereafter was augmented and reissued with Gallimard in 1945. A second volume, *Le Cornet à dés II*, appeared with Gallimard in 1955.

Ashbery, John *et al.*, *The Dice Cup: Selected Prose Poems*, edited by Michael Brownstein, New York: State University of New York, 1979

Black, Moishe and Maria Green, *Hesitant Fire: Selected Prose of Max Jacob*, Lincoln: University of Nebraska Press, 1991

Bullock, Michael, *Double Life and Other Pieces: Thirty Prose Poems from "Le Cornet à dés"*, London: Oasis, 1989

Schneider, Judith Morganroth, in *The Play of the Text: Max Jacob's "Le Cornet à dés"*, edited by Sydney Lévy, Madison: University of Wisconsin Press, 1981

Not long ago, Richard Howard, the eminent American translator of Baudelaire's *Les Fleurs du Mal*, among other canonical texts, said words to the effect that translations perceived as definitive should probably be redone at least every 30 years. This statement not only goes to the heart of the translator's task in general, regardless of the historical moment, but applies particularly to the modernist texts produced by the protean, kaleidoscopic poet and creative artist Max Jacob.

As the self-proclaimed inventor of the prose poem (and of course he knew the kind of verbal invention he pursued was always already a reinvention), Jacob created what William Carlos Williams would call sometime later "verbal machines", that problematize the direct linkage between the signifiers and the signified, between the sign system (the black type juxtaposed to the white page) and its meanings. Jacob wrote with the express purpose of playing out what had been one of the primary goals of Romanticism in the century preceding his own: to destroy the old (old forms, old expressions, old ideas) and create something new (all the while affecting complete buffoonery, that is, giving the impression it was all just fun).

The paradigmatic shift, that oxymoronic, creatively destructive process or "askesis" necessitated by the objectives of the modern text, found its most complete articulation starting in the 1850s with the works of Baudelaire and thereafter in those who understood his Sisyphean quest of *modernity* (a word he coined himself for an essay on *Le Peintre de la vie moderne*). As Ross Chambers has pointed out, the key to understanding the legacy of Baudelairean poetics revolves around two provocative words found in the essay on the *Exposition universelle 1855*. Those words are: "perpetual abjuration". A system of invention or artistic creation, an approach to innovation or original composition predicated on its own perpetual rejection. The modernist text à la Baudelaire must continue to throw down the gauntlet, or at least give the semblance, to its reader, its critic, but above all its translator. It must defy all efforts to pin down something once and for all, at the very least its genre, but above all its meaning.

When the artistic patron, Jacques Doucet, asked to buy some of Jacob's writings in 1917, which resulted in the publication of a collection under the title *Le Cornet à dés* (in addition to an entirely different kind of text focusing on religious conversion, Jacob's *La Défense de Tartuffe* [The Defense of Tartuffe], in 1924), he hardly realized how this disparate, undefinable series of prose poems paid homage to Baudelaire's legacy, let alone understood the intertext with Mallarmé's *Un Coup de dés* [A Throw of the Dice] whose nose it tweaked (at least with the title), all the while respecting its intent. Breaking old vessels to create new ones, Jacob intended, with what he selected from that large trunk where he kept his manuscripts accumulated from the day of his arrival in Paris in 1896, not just one point of view, one throw of the dice, but a veritable cornucopia of styles, voices, tones, that is potentially contained within a "dice box" as Wallace Fowlie rendered the title in 1969. While a specific meaning is clearly imparted by Fowlie's "dice box", it is no more satisfactory in English than "The Dice Cup" (ASHBERY *et al.*, 1979).

The ASHBERY selection, the first major attempt at Jacob in English, manages at its best, with its multiple translators (John ASHBERY, DAVID BALL, MICHAEL BROWNSTEIN, Ron PADGETT, Zack ROGOW, and Bill ZAVATSKY), to convey the heteroclitie quality of Jacob's textual posturing, permutations, puns, parodies, in brief all his textual tactics to subvert the old to get to something with a glint of newness. The translations run the gamut from *mot à mot* to the creative renderings of Ashbery, Brownstein, and Zavatsky.

Not that a diachronic progression is implied, but Lévy's critical evaluation (1981), accompanying Judith Morganroth SCHNEIDER's selected translations, is a quantum leap forward in terms of re-evaluating Jacob's role in modern art as well as revealing the sophistication of his thought. No longer can this close friend and inspiration of most of the Parisian literati before and after World War I be portrayed merely as an eccentric converted Jew trying to make the adjustment from his provincial home town of Quimper to the "City of Light", only to end up a victim of the Nazi scourge in a detention camp at Drancy in 1944. SCHNEIDER demonstrates a remarkable ability to slip into the linguistic skin of her subject matter, particularly with respect to those small, thinly laced pieces that force the translator of poetic or experimental texts more often than not to deal with the harrowing decision: whether to stay as close as possible to the text or to flesh it out. Of special interest are poems like: "1914", "War", "Capital", "Table Cover", and "The Bibliophile".

BULLOCK (1989), however, eschews a creative approach and gives a close read of approximately 30 of the more than 150 prose poems contained in *Le Cornet à dés*. Although perhaps a little too close to the text sometimes, he none the less provides the essential building blocks in English for conveying the effect of Jacob's myriad verbal improvisations, that seemingly endless metamorphosis or process of transformation so characteristic of his writings.

More recently, as critics and translators have begun to recognize Jacob's essential role not only in the conceptualization of modernist art but in its performance as well, they have begun to turn their attention to his other prose forms: Jacob's novels, short stories, satirical sketches in a classical mode, along with his religious meditations (for an exhaustive analysis of this subject see Christine Van Rogger-Andreucci's 1994 *Poésie et Religion dans l'oeuvre de Max Jacob*) are indeed the focus of new interest and a new generation of readers. As more and more detailed studies like the one just mentioned appear, along with reprintings, and dissertations written and published on Jacobian poetics, translatory efforts will shift to his overall contribution. One can safely assume that the rediscovery has only just begun. In that regard the BLACK & GREEN anthology (1991), which privileges prose offerings, is quite successful, while we await a more complete presentation in English of the enormous contribution of this tortured, mercurial poet.

ROBIN ORR BODKIN

Further Reading

Collier, S.J., "Max Jacob and the 'Poème en Prose'", *Modern Language Review*, 51/4 (October 1956)

Collier, S.J., "Max Jacob's *Le Cornet à dés*", *French Studies*, 11 (April 1957)

Fowlie, Wallace, *Climate of Violence: The French Literary Tradition From Baudelaire to the Present*, New York: Macmillan, 1967; London: Secker and Warburg, 1969

Kamber, Gerald, *Max Jacob and the Poetics of Cubism*, Baltimore: Johns Hopkins Press, 1971

Schneider, Judith Morganroth, *Clown at the Altar: The Religious Poetry of Max Jacob*, Chapel Hill: University of North Carolina Department of Romance Languages, 1978

Thau, Annette, *Poetry and Antipoetry: A Study of Selected Aspects of Max Jacob's Poetic Style*, Chapel Hill: University of North Carolina Department of Romance Languages, 1976

See also translators' introductions and discussions in Ashbery, Black & Green, Bullock, and Lévy (editor)

Jens Peter Jacobsen 1847–1885

Danish novelist, poet and translator

Biography

Born 7 April 1847 in Thisted, a small town in the northwest part of Jutland. From an early age, he showed an almost equal propensity for literature and science. His first literary achievement took the form of lyric poems in the style of Danish Golden Age romanticism, and included *Gurre Songs* (*Gurresange*, written 1868–69, published posthumously in *Digte og Udkast*, 1886), which are best known as the text for Schoenberg's *Gurrelieder*. In 1872, while a student at the University of Copenhagen, he published a novella, "Mogens", and a translation of Charles Darwin's *On the Origin of Species* (1859). A year later he won a gold medal for his dissertation on algae, and in 1874 he published his best-known poem "Arabesque to a Drawing by Michelangelo", and a translation of Darwin's *Descent of Man* (1871). It is not surprising that a thematic tension between symbolism and naturalism should inform much of Jacobsen's creative writing. While "Mogens" brought him some recognition in Denmark, his real national and international fame grew from the novels *Fru Marie Grubbe* (1876) and *Niels Lyhne* (1880). Like his younger Russian contemporary, Chekhov, Jacobsen wrote his best work in the shadow of tuberculosis (which was first diagnosed in 1873). He died 30 April 1885 in Thisted at the early age of 38.

Jacobsen was initially identified with the naturalistic movement, most notably by Georg Brandes, who included Jacobsen in his study entitled *Men of the Modern Breakthrough* (*Det moderne Gjennembruds mænd*, 1883). In the 20th century, however, his symbolist vein has been valued more, especially in Germany and Austria, where he had a strong influence on Hoffmansthal, Rilke and Mann. Jensen records 17 German translations of *Niels Lyhne*. Jacobsen has been much less appreciated in the English-speaking world, though new translations of his prose fiction are now appearing.

Translations

The most recent translations of Jacobsen are based on the Collected Works edited by Jørn Vosmar (Copenhagen: Borgens Forlag, 1986); another valuable edition, with 2 volumes of Jacobsen's letters and numerous illustrations, is the 6-volume set edited by Frederick Nielsen (Copenhagen: Rosenkilde of Bagger, 1972–74)

Selections of Poetry

Billeskov Jansen, F.J. and P.M. Mitchell, "Arabesque II" in *Anthology of Danish Literature: Realism to the Present* (bilingual edition), edited by Billeskov Jansen and Mitchell, Carbondale: Southern Illinois University Press, 1972

Damon, S. Foster and Robert Silliman Hillyer, selected poems in *A Book of Danish Verse*, edited by Oluf Friis, New York: American–Scandinavian Foundation, 1922; reprinted Freeport, New York: Books for Libraries Press, 1968

Jensen, Niels Lyhne, "Monomania" in his *Jens Peter Jacobsen*, Boston: Twayne, 1980

Selver, P., *Poems* (parallel texts), Oxford: Blackwell, 1920

Stork, Charles Wharton, selected poems in *A Second Book of Danish Verse*, edited by Stork, Princeton, New Jersey: Princeton University Press for the American–Scandinavian Foundation, 1947; reprinted Freeport: Books for Libraries Press, 1968

Stories

Mogens, 1872; *Mogens og andre Noveller*, 1882

Grabow, Anna, *Mogens and Other Stories*, New York: Nicholas L. Brown, 1921 (omits "A Shot in the Fog" and "Two Worlds")

Nunnally, Tiina, *Mogens and Other Stories*, Seattle: Fjord Press, 1994

Novels

Fru Marie Grubbe: Interieurer fra det syttende Aarhundrede, 1876

Larsen, Hanna Astrup, *Marie Grubbe: A Lady of the Seventeenth Century*, New York: American-Scandinavian Foundation, 1917; revised edition by Robert Raphael, Boston: Twayne, 1975

Niels Lyhne, 1880

Larsen, Hanna Astrup, *Niels Lyhne*, New York: American-Scandinavian Foundation, 1919; Boston: Twayne, 1967

Nunnally, Tiina, *Niels Lyhne*, Seattle: Fjord Press, 1990; 2nd edition, 1995

Robertson, Ethel F.L., *Siren Voices (Niels Lyhne)*, London: Heinemann, 1896; issued anonymously as *Niels Lyhne*, New York: Collier, 1900

Jens Peter Jacobsen's poems vary in style from the ballad metres of *Gurre Songs* to the free verse of his "Arabesques". They have a high reputation in Denmark but are perhaps too dependent on an atmosphere and music peculiar to Jacobsen's use of Danish to travel well. An English analogy would be the lyrics of Walter de la Mare, which it is hard to imagine in another language; and it comes as no surprise that Jacobsen's stylistic models should have included Poe, Swinburne and Pater (Raphael, 1975).

SELVER (1920) was the first to attempt Jacobsen's verse in English. His attractively printed volume contains 10 lyrics, with the Danish version of each poem facing the English text. He keeps the metre and rhyme scheme of the Danish, but his claim that "my renderings are as close to the originals as could be reconciled with readable English" needs some qualification. In "Genre-Picture", "vredt" (angrily) becomes "featly", and "sweetly" is added to the last line in an attempt to match Jacobsen's rhyme scheme. Similarly, in "Silken Shoe upon Golden Last" Selver adds "I trow" to find a half-rhyme for "snow". In general, archaism and padding limit the value of Selver's work. He is more successful with the unrhymed free verse poems, such as "Arabesque I" and the famous "Arabesque to a Drawing by Michangelo" ("Arabesque II"). Even here, however, quaint diction and inversion blur the focus of Jacobsen's imagery. "Tog bølgen land?" (Did the wave reach land?) becomes "Forged the billow landward?", for example, and "Glødende Nat!" (Glowing night!) the more literary "Glow-laden night!". The best English version of "Arabesque II" can be found in BILLESKOV JANSEN & MITCHELL's bilingual anthology (1972). The brief selections by DAMON & HILLYER (1922) and by STORK (1947) serve mainly to supplement Selver's choice with some of the earlier lyrics, especially two from *Gurre Songs*. These translations too have difficulty in capturing the musical appeal of Jacobsen's verse. Shorn of its rhymes by Stork, the power of "Dream!" is lost, and his version of the lovely song, "Irmelin Rose", which is known to all Danes through Nielsen's setting, seems completely flat. One poem that does cross the language frontier is "Monomania", in JENSEN's translation (1980), perhaps because its stark, expressionist style seems less individual than is usual for Jacobsen. The opening lines "I am mad? / But I know my madness, / Its essence and its cause" – seem distinctively 20th century, though they were written in 1869.

Mogens and Other Stories was first published in 1882. Apart from the title novella (which had been published separately in 1872), it contains two short stories: "A Shot in the Fog" and "Mrs Fønss"; two prose sketches (skitser): "Two Worlds" and "There Should Have Been Roses"; and a sinister parable: "The Plague in Bergamo". The fame of "The Plague in Bergamo" may rest on its anticipation of 20th-century absurdist and existential traditions, but it lacks both Kafka's humour and Camus's political humanism. The contemporary reader will probably respond more sympathetically to the superb parallel evocations of rain and fire in "Mogens", and to the mature craftsmanship of "Mrs Fønss", where Jacobsen employs the "more relaxed" (*roligere*) style he found in *Marie Grubbe*. Mrs Fønss, a widow who defies her children's jealousy to marry a man she had loved and lost in her youth, is one of Jacobsen's finest characters, and her story can hold its own against Chekhov and Joyce.

GRABOW's translation (1921) of this collection is a little dated but still readable. However, she leaves out "A Shot in the Fog" and "Two Worlds", and NUNNALLY's version (1994) is clearly preferable, being complete, idiomatic and more accurate than that of her predecessor. Grabow, for example, confuses the reader of "Mogens" by rendering "et lille pigehoved" as "a little girl's head", and "et lille pigeansigt" as "a little girl's face", which gives the impression that the hero is going to marry a child. Here the translator seems to think that the neuter "et lille" governs the common noun "pige" (girl) instead of "hoved" (head) and "ansigt" (face). In "The Plague in Bergamo", Grabow has the butcher turn his "back" to the altar, but "bagdelen", in this context, mean the more blasphemous "backside". Both mistakes are corrected by Nunnally. Grabow can also be unidiomatic, as in "the fall of the foliage was going on apace" ("Mogens"), where Nunnally's "the falling leaves were at their peak" is accurate and unaffected. Nunnally's versions of all these stories read like English originals while remaining faithful to Jacobsen's style and meaning.

The full title in Danish of Jacobsen's first novel means "Lady Marie Grubbe: Interiors from the Seventeenth Century". Marie Grubbe (1643–1718) was the daughter of a Danish landowner. Her marriage to a natural son of King Frederik III ended in divorce and a second marriage was annulled when Marie began an affair with her husband's stableboy, 20 years her junior. Rejected by aristocracy and gentry alike, she married her lover and kept a ferry inn with him till her death. Jacobsen uses the documents of her life to create the fascinating portrait of a woman who refuses to play by men's rules, who is repeatedly punished for her "wilful" behaviour by father, husband, and king, but who survives, and attains an unexpected degree of contentment after, and to some extent because of, her social fall. In the novel's beautifully written coda, Marie justifies her life to Ludvig Holberg (the meeting did take place and is documented by the dramatist himself). When Holberg asks her if she believes "we shall rise again from the dead", she gives the memorable reply: "How shall I rise? As the young, innocent child I was first among people, or as the honored and envied favorite of the King and the ornament of the court, or as poor old hopeless Ferryman's Marie? And shall I answer for what the others, the child and the woman in the fullness of life, have sinned, or shall one of them answer for me? Can you tell me that, Master Holberg?" (LARSEN).

As this passage might suggest, the main challenge for a translator of *Marie Grubbe* is to find English equivalents of different styles of speech for the large cast of characters, not to mention their letters and interior monologues. The characters speak, write and think according to their age, sex, region, rank, and even – so Jacobsen claimed, at least – according to the way in which Danish changed during Marie Grubbe's lifetime. The novel's narrative and descriptive passages are not as hard to render, being somewhat less breathless than Jacobsen's style in *Niels Lyhne*.

LARSEN (1917) is the only English translation of *Marie Grubbe* to date, though a new version by Nunnally is promised. Larsen's unfortunate omission of "Interiors ..." from the title deprives us of Jacobsen's hint that his work had analogies with the domestic school of Dutch art, which flourished during the heroine's lifetime. There is indeed a Vermeer-like glow to many of the descriptive passages, and Jacobsen tells Marie's story in episodes that tend to remain in the reader's mind rather like pictures in a gallery: the 14-year-old girl bathing her arms in a heap of roses; the young woman at the height of her beauty receiving homage from a kneeling courtier; the lonely wife playing her lute by the fire in Aggershus (Akershus) Castle.

Larsen's version of the novel has inevitably dated since its publication in 1917, though it remains far more readable than the inept 1930 translation of Undset's great saga of medieval Norway *Kristin Lavransdatter*. Where Charles Archer and J.S. Scott turned Undset's dialogue into a grotesque parody of Elizabethan English, Larsen gave the 17th-century language of Jacobsen's characters a lightly archaic touch – "'tis" in place of "it is", for example; similarly, Marie's letters of complaint to her sister have the right epistolary formality. Larsen's attempt to reproduce Jutland dialect (Jysk) is not very good (though Jacobsen's phonetic Jysk is itself problematic). She also allows the inversion natural to Danish, but not English, to govern word order, as in : "Peacefully and quietly the days passed". It is time for a new English version of *Marie Grubbe*, but Larsen has served its purpose well.

The eponymous hero of *Niels Lyhne* is a poet. He grows up on the family estate, Lønborggaard, torn between his mother's dreamy love for romantic poetry and his father's practicality. The adult Niels can never heal the resultant division in his personality, and all his friendships, love affairs, and writings are doomed by his inability to reconcile dream with reality, the idea with the fact. In the novel's penultimate chapter he seems set to achieve integration in a happy marriage, but first his young wife dies, then his baby son. In a despairing gesture Niels volunteers as a soldier in the defence of Schleswig, and he is mortally wounded at the battle of Dybbøl (1864). Here Jacobsen movingly parallels the individual's fate in an indifferent universe with a small nation's vulnerability in a power-hungry world. The well-known last sentence reads (in NUNNALLY's translation): "And then finally he died the death – the difficult death."

If *Niels Lyhne* is harder to translate than *Marie Grubbe* or the short stories, it is because its artistic effect depends on two related factors: a subtle analysis of the way the characters' minds work from moment to moment, which foreshadows the stream-of-consciousness technique of Joyce and Woolf; and a stylistic virtuosity that threatens at times to exist for its own sake. One of the book's first reviewers wrote: "But is it [the style] natural? Is it not astonishingly mannered and in the end as exhausting as it was at the start enticing? And is there always meaning in this bubbling and glittering stream of words?" (*Faedrelandet*, 1881). This is unjust, but there is enough truth in the criticism to make it a useful caveat for English translators and their readers: a translation, however accurate, that does not confront the problems of Jacobsen's style will make the early review *seem* to be just.

There are three English translations of *Niels Lyhne*. ROBERTSON's title, *Siren Voices*, is a bad start, but her version (1896), is much less dated than many translations from the period. She does, however, tend to take short cuts, trimming some of Jacobsen's sentences, especially when repetition is involved. She also makes additions, the clumsiest being a gloss on Holger Danske as "our country's half-mythic national hero", which the reader will assume is Jacobsen's comment, since it is placed in the text and not in a translator's note.

LARSEN (1919) obviously found *Niels Lyhne* more difficult than *Marie Grubbe*. She is more accurate than Robertson, but still comes short of capturing the rhythm of Jacobsen's prose. Like Robertson, she considers the three-word paragraph in chapter 3 ("She was tall") too insignificant to stand on its own, and adds it to the next paragraph, thus spoiling Jacobsen's dramatic introduction to the Pre-Raphaelite beauty of Edele Lyhne. Jacobsen frequently punctuates his long rolling paragraphs with short powerful or ironic ones – "And so they were married"; "She was tall"; "Then he died"; "She rather liked scenes" – an alternation that mirrors the hero's inner conflict between dream and reality. A translation must respect this alternation and face the more formidable task of capturing the wave-like rhythm of Jacobsen's sensuous descriptive passages or internal monologues. Larsen spoils this rhythm, often correcting Jacobsen's comma splices, as in the 110-word single-sentence paragraph describing Bartholine Lyhne's romantic yearning for unattainable beauty. Larsen divides this into three sentences, and the link between style and meaning is lost. The task is formidable, but failure to accomplish it means that the reader will tend to agree with those who find Jacobsen's prose style overblown.

Reading NUNNALLY's translation (1990) of *Niels Lyhne* after those of her predecessors is like watching a blurred slide projection coming into focus. One simple reason for this effect is that her knowledge of Danish is obviously better. Robertson and Larsen, for example, translate the pathetic end to Bigum's declaration of love for Edele – "Saa kunde han gaa" – as "he too might go" (Robertson) and "Then he could go too" (Larsen); but Jacobsen actually writes, "Then he was free to go" (Nunnally). However, the real achievement of this translation is its sensitive re-creation of Jacobsen's elusive style. Where the earlier versions made the novel seem a series of brilliant fragments thinly linked by Niels Lyhne's life, the new one reveals Jacobsen as a master of fictional architecture as well as lyrical virtuosity. Everything now fits into place. Many readers may still prefer *Marie Grubbe*, if only because the heroine is more inspiring than Niels Lyhne, whose hapless drifting around Europe on a private income can seem a little precious today; but even if *Niels Lyhne* is not "undoubtedly Jacobsen's supreme achievement" (Johannesson, 1990), we now have an English version that reveals it to be a hauntingly original work.

JOHN LINGARD

Further Reading

Craft, Robert, "Great Dane" (review of Nunnally's translation of *Niels Lyhne*), *New York Review of Books*, 39/17 (22 October 1992)

Jensen, Niels Lyhne, *Jens Peter Jacobsen*, Boston: Twayne, 1980

Johannesson, Eric O., afterword to *Niels Lyhne*, translated by Tiina Nunnally, Seattle: Fjord Press, 1990

Madsen, Börge Gedsö, introduction to *Niels Lyhne*, translated by Hanna Astrup Larsen, New York: Twayne, 1967

Raphael, Robert, introduction to *Maria Grubbe*, translated by Hanna Astrup Larsen, Boston: Twayne, 1975

Japanese

Literary Translation into English

The Language

The Japanese language is spoken by almost the entire population of Japan – around 126 million people in 1996 – but no other country uses it as either a first or a second language. Nevertheless, as far as the number of native speakers is concerned, Japanese ranks sixth among the languages of the world. It also has a rich literary history going back to at least AD 6, the date of the oldest Japanese books. Undoubtedly, a strong oral culture of songs and stories, if not histories, genealogies and expressions of religious piety, antedated these first works to display the particular Japanese genius. The language that expressed the oral culture of Japan, by this time an established state with at least 200 years of active contact with its neighbours, was Japanese. However, no indigenous writing system had developed within Japan to cope with the native language so, according to tradition, early in the 6th century the arrival of Buddhism from the continent was accompanied by the introduction of Chinese script, which was taught to the Japanese court by Korean scribes. Hence, Chinese characters, used to write in either Chinese or Korean, were first utilized as the instrument of written communication. Soon after, the Chinese script was being used to write Japanese. Needless to say, it was a long, complicated process of adoption and innovation that eventually led to the way in which Chinese characters (two phonetic syllabaries also were eventually derived from Chinese) are used today to represent Japanese. Thus, the Japanese writing system is exceedingly complicated, with four ways now used to represent the same concept: Chinese characters, two types of native syllabary and also the Roman alphabet.

Unlike the languages spoken in Europe or mainland Asia, Japanese is spoken solely on the islands of Japan; thus it is physically isolated from other languages in a way that even English, for example, is not. The physical isolation of Japan is paralleled by the linguistic isolation of Japanese: it is a language-isolate with no known genetic affiliation to other language families (apart from the languages of the Ryūkū islands, which are seen by most Japanese as dialects of Japanese) although many linguists speculate that Korean may well the closest relative of Japanese in linguistic terms.

There is, of course, no shortage of theories as to possible genetic affiliations; older theories often relate Japanese to the languages of North Asia, most often placing Japanese in the Altaic language-group; newer theories view Japanese as a mixed-language with an Altaic superstratum but with an Austronesian or some other substratum. However, no conclusive evidence has yet been presented to validate any of the theories proposed to date. The Japanese language remains an orphan.

Japanese shares a common subject-object-verb (SOV) grammatical word order with most of the worlds' languages, but, again, this contrasts markedly with the English SVO pattern. Phonologically, Japanese is a commonplace language, with five vowels and a simple set of consonants. The syllabic structure is equally straightforward, usually consisting of a consonant plus vowel pattern. Japanese, like English, has many dialects, and virtually all of the Japanese dialects, as with the standard language itself, have tones but they are very different from, for example, Chinese tone patterns.

Japanese is usually classified as an agglutinative language, since verbs and, to a lesser degree, adjectives, are highly inflected. The inflections generally incorporate much stylistic information, reflecting the circumstances in which sentences are used. The grammar of a particular Japanese sentence – inflections, syntactic expressions, word order – can usually tell us whether the sentence was spoken or written, and, if spoken, whether it was uttered in informal or formal circumstances, and often, whether it was uttered by a male or female speaker. So the form of expression in Japanese is affected far more than many other languages by contextual factors: the formality of the setting, the sex and social status of the speech-act participants and so on. Japanese has a highly elaborate honorific system which extends to the use of pronouns (and their avoidance) as well as verbs, vocabulary, etc. This factor, too, reinforces the importance of context, itself a reflection of the nature of Japanese society, which puts great stress on social interdependence.

Undoubtedly the most difficult aspect of the language for non-Japanese to acquire is the writing system. The Japanese writing system has been described as the most complex in the world and its mastery demands an enormous investment of time and effort. It is generally assumed that it takes more than nine years of school education before Japanese children can read a newspaper satisfactorily. Indeed, even in the final years of secondary education the Japanese are still acquiring the final details of their writing system. The three Chinese-derived scripts comprise more than 2000 basic symbols, with Chinese characters accounting for most of these. However, the complexity of the writing system does allow for a high degree of complexity of expression when writing Japanese, and so in some ways enriches the literature.

The chief difficulty of literary translation into English arises from the features of the language summarized above: namely, that the Japanese and English languages have very little in common. Their grammars are completely dissimilar, with word order, inflections and a host of other distinctive elements of both languages fundamentally different. In the area of vocabulary, too, the two languages are far apart. Most European languages are genetically and culturally related to English and share much cognate vocabulary, but, with the exception of loanwords, Japanese words are quite unrelated to English. The sociolinguistic landscape of Japanese is, in the most important areas, quite unlike that of English and other European languages; thus the meanings of Japanese words, the entire semantic context in fact, is more marked by difference from English than by similarity.

The question of semantic incongruity cannot be emphasized enough. The interdependent nature of Japanese society has influenced Japanese literature to the extent that some writers have described it as literature embedded, not merely in a complex matrix of socio-cultural associations, but in a literary tradition of allusion that reflects and deepens that very complexity. Naturally, literary allusion is more commonly found in classical or medieval literature than in literature written in modern times (especially post-war literature) but, as in all languages, though perhaps more so for Japanese, literary and cultural allusion is so tightly interwoven into the semantic field that even contemporary writing has more than its fair share.

Literary Translation from Japanese

Culture often follows the flag, and the same is true of translation. Nineteenth-century translations of Japanese literature into English are mostly the work of the diverse band of diplomats, scholars and adventurers who settled in Japan, or visited it frequently, after its forced opening to the West in July 1853 by Commodore Matthew Perry's heavily armed US naval squadron. (Prior to this time there was practically no contact between English-speaking nations and Japan, and as a result no literary translations from Japanese into English exist.) Paradoxically, most of these pioneer translations were British rather than

American, but this is perhaps a reflection of the commercial and political realities, as well as of the scholarly momentum originating in the older, established tradition of Sinology, which was dominated by the British thanks to their long history of contact with China. Among those pioneers, the following two names stand out: Basil Hall Chamberlain (1850–1935), first professor of Japanese at Tokyo Imperial University and the first translator of the mytho-historical document known as the *Kojiki* (1882, 1906) – regarded by Japanese from long ago as the storehouse of Japanese ancient tradition – as well as translator of a collection of classical poetry (1880); and the diplomat W.G. Aston (1841–1911), translator of another *ur*-text of Japanese tradition and history, the *Nihongi* (1896), and also author of the first history of Japanese literature in English (1889). Chamberlain's translation of *Kojiki* was bowdlerized by the translating of passages relating to coitus between the gods into Latin, but none the less it was a significant scholarly landmark. Among the several fin-de-siècle writers who took Japan as their major theme, the American author Lafcadio Hearn (1850–1904) reigns supreme with his rewriting (not translations) of Japanese tales and legends in collections like *Kokoro* (1896) and *Kwaidan* (1904).

The period prior to World War II was dominated by the legendary English translator, Arthur Waley (1889–1966). Not content with Japanese literature, Waley made a number of major translations from Chinese literature as well. Waley's first complete English version of the classical Japanese masterpiece, *The Tale of the Genji* (6 vols, 1925–33) was hailed in its own time as a literary triumph, a judgement vindicated subsequently by history. Waley is regarded as the first major translator of Japanese genuinely to do justice to the originals as literature. Several commentators have noted that his concern with tone and register so illuminated his rendering of the *Genji* that subsequent translators have been unable to avoid his influence. His painstaking efforts to create a natural English-language voice and tone for the narrative results in a translation of this 11th-century tale that reads like an original text. Naturally, some liberties have been taken in achieving such a stunning success, for instance, inventing "divans" for the court ladies to lie on (in the source text they sit on straw matting) or occasionally embroidering the narrative with passages not in the original, but given the fact that Waley worked from old editions of the *Genji*, without the benefit of modern Japanese commentaries, such blemishes as do exist, in the opinion of most commentators, pale beside the translator's genius. Waley made translations of other classical prose narratives, such as *The Pillow-Book of Sei Shonagon* (1928), and also translated several Noh plays (1921) to great acclaim.

Waley's American contemporary, Ezra Pound (1885–1972), is better known as the author of the *Cantos* (1917–67) than as a translator. Pound's translations of Chinese poetry, based on Ernest Fenollosa's transcriptions and notes, published as *Cathay* (1915) exercised a profound influence over his generation, and, some scholars have argued, influenced Waley's own translation style. But Pound also translated Noh drama (again basing himself on Fenollosa's notebook versions), the final selection of which (published in 1916) reached a large audience and inspired *At the Hawk's Well* (1916), W.B. Yeats's own attempt at an original Noh. Clearly, versions deriving from the notes of an antiquarian ignorant of the Japanese language, and translated by a scholar and poet himself with no Japanese, can hardly be thought of as accurate translations or, even, perhaps, as translations at all. Yet Pound's skill as a poet makes some lines in the "translations" memorable, so memorable that the poet himself uses them as source material in his *Cantos*.

Translations in the pre-World War II period was not restricted to Waley alone. Other translators included several Japanese scholars, notably Torao Taketomo with his *Pawlonia*, a 1918 selection of modern writers including Mori Ōgai (1862–1922) and Nagai Kafū (1879–1959), and also the well-known American scholar Glenn Hughes, who introduced several modern novelists in translation, especially Akutagawa Ryūnosuke (1892–1927), to a Western audience. But none commanded the respect that Waley did, and it is often said that the splendid crop of postwar translators saw only Waley as their predecessor.

At this point it is worth noting the labour of love undertaken by the Dutch scholar, Lodewijk Pierson, in his efforts extending over 40 years to publish the first complete, annotated English translation of the *Man'yōshū*, the oldest collection of Japanese verse (compiled mid-8th century). Pierson's translation, published separately in several volumes (1929–64; selection, 1966) was pursued from "the point of view of the linguist" as Pierson notes, but none the less had some literary merit.

Two complete English translations of the *Man'yōshū* have been completed by native Japanese scholars in the postwar era, and several collections have also been published, both before and after World War II, but Pierson's pioneering efforts deserve mention not only because of his massive scholarship, but also because his prose versions of the verse have a clarity at times lacking in the two postwar translators, who have chosen to pack their translations with rigid metrical structures.

World War II had the effect of producing a large group of Japanese-language specialists – some originally trained for the war effort and some having commenced their studies earlier – but who, after the war, turned their hands to literary translation. Among the outstanding scholars and translators thrown up by the war, two American authors have reached a world-wide audience with their translations and scholarship. Donald Keene and Edward Seidensticker have translated authors both ancient and modern. The two anthologies of Japanese literature edited by Keene, published in 1955 and 1956 respectively, set the tone by publishing new translations of much of the Japanese literary canon. Following in Waley's footsteps, Keene stressed that the translations were "literary and not literal". Keene himself went on to translate such classical works as the 14th-century essay *Tsurezuregusa* (*Essays in Idleness*), 1967 and modern works like Mishima Yukio's contemporary Noh dramas (1957) and Dazai Osamu's finest novel *No Longer Human* (1958). Seidensticker has also worked on many translations of both classical and modern literature: his version of *The Tale of Genji* (1976) being the best-known of his renderings in the former category, while his translations of the fiction of Kawabata Yasunari (1899–1972), the Nobel Laureate in Literature for 1968 (these translations, some argue, played a pivotal role in the awarding of the Nobel Prize to Kawabata), are the most highly regarded in the latter category.

Translations of modern fiction into English by the postwar translators and their successors – including such writers as Ivan Morris, Howard Hibbett, G.W. Sargent, John Bester, Michael Gallagher, Juliet Carpenter, Dennis Keene, Alfred Birnbaum,

Van C. Gessel, Geraldine Harcourt, Ralph McCarthy and Anthony Chambers – have made the modern Japanese novel by authors as diverse as Kawabata, Mishima, Dazai, Ōe Kenzaburō (awarded the Nobel Prize for Literature in 1994), Tsushima Yūko, Murakami Haruki, Abe Kōbō, Tanizaki Jun'ichirō, Endō Shūsaku and Ibuse Masuji available to readers in the English-speaking world. A clear generational bias favouring recent authors appears in the works chosen by the translators who came onto the scene in the 1960s, 1970s and 1980s. Contemporary novelists like Murakami Haruki, with his bestselling novels (translated by Alfred Birnbaum) *Norwegian Wood* (1989) and *Dance Dance Dance* (1994), had English translations of their work appear only a few years after the publication of the originals. Similarly, certain of the younger generation of translators are, like Birnbaum, associated with particular authors: Van C. Gessel with his translations of Endō Shūsaku; Geraldine Harcourt with her renderings of the distinguished female author Tsushima Yūko, and Ann Sherif with her versions of the leading figure in contemporary women's fiction, Yoshimoto Banana. Of course, there are exceptions to this rule: Anthony Chambers has continued translating the works of the master 20th-century novelist Tanizaki Jun'ichirō (1886–1965), following on from the earlier generation of translators who included Seidensticker and his contemporary, Howard Hibbett.

Likewise, the translating style adopted by the current generation of (mostly American) translators favours a strong infusion of American idiom in order to make the contemporary Japanese novel "contemporary" in English. Though originating in Arthur Waley's creation of a Bloomsbury salon for his English-language transposition of *The Tale of Genji*, the contemporary stylistic preference for American English may well reflect the current state of English-language politics, where literary momentum appears to have shifted so as to be directed more towards the US than the UK.

Stylistic experiment is most notable in the work of postwar translators of Japanese poetry. The famous American poet Kenneth Rexroth (1905–82) imitated his predecessor Pound when he rendered his translations of classical Japanese poetry – *One Hundred Poems from the Japanese* (1964) and *One Hundred More Poems from the Japanese* (1976) – in a distinctively modernist mode. His contemporary and equally distinguished American colleague, the poet Gary Snyder, somehow translated the popular Japanese Buddhist poet Miyazawa Kenji (1896–1933) into himself with his renderings of Kenji into English in *The Back Country* (1968). Scholar-translators such as Hiroaki Sato have also worked on single volumes of Kenji (1989) and Sato has also translated other modern poets like Takamura Kōtarō (1883–1956, translation 1992). Robert Epp, another scholar-poet, is single-handedly translating into English the complete poetic works of a number of modern poets, including Hagiwara Sakutarō (1886–1942, translation, 1992), Maruyama Kaoru (1899–1974, translation, 1992) and Tsuboi Shigeji (1897–1975, translation, 1993) but his stylistic model, as with Hiroaki Sato, has clearly been the earlier generation of American poet-translators. Classical poetry translated by such scholars as Edward Cranston in *The Gem-Glistening Cup* (1993), Helen Craig McCullough (*Kokin Wakashū*, 1985) and Steven D. Carter (*Traditional Japanese Poetry: An Anthology*, 1991) follows the precedent of the translations in Earl Miner and Robert Brower's highly acclaimed landmark study *Japanese Court Poetry* (1961), which elaborate and expand the originals as against the sparer, more modernist versions of Rexroth.

Publishers like Allen and Unwin in prewar England for Arthur Waley and Alfred A. Knopf and New Directions in the US played an important role in the postwar "boom" in demand for modern Japanese fiction. Also, the dominance of the "literary" over the "literal" trend in translation style may well owe much to in-house instructions made by editors of these presses. The avalanche of publications of classical Japanese literature from the 1960s onward undoubtedly stems from the proliferation of university courses in Japanese and the university press networks in the US and UK that encouraged and assisted the best of the graduate students to publish their translation work. The publicity generated by extra-literary events like the two Nobel prizes in literature awarded to Kawabata and Ōe, and the sensational suicide of Mishima, also helped to create a market for translations of modern Japanese fiction. In recent years, the emergence of Japan as a leading world power has also sparked interest in the literature that seems likely to continue.

Debates over Japanese literary translation have started to heat up over the past decade or so, and questions about the accuracy and efficacy (in terms of conveying the "Japaneseness" of the originals) of Americanized or Anglicized translations of Japanese literature are beginning to bring into question stylistic modes of translation sacrosanct in the postwar era. The increasing attention paid in Japan to English-language translations is also likely to focus scrutiny on the linguistic process of translation rather than on the tired old arguments about literal versus literary. But that translations will continue to be made, and in ever greater proportions, seems a foregone conclusion. The isolation of the Japanese language is now no barrier to translation, indeed the notion of "isolation" when applied to the vast edifice of Japanese literature in translation appears quaint and curious. Through translation, modern Japan is now as familiar to anglophone readers as any other modern society; surely it is about time too.

LEITH MORTON

Further Reading

Backhouse, A.E., *The Japanese Language: An Introduction*, Melbourne and Oxford: Oxford University Press, 1993

Fowler, Edward, "Rendering Words, Traversing Cultures: On the Art and Politics of Translating Modern Japanese Fiction", *The Journal of Japanese Studies* , 18/1 (1992) pp. 1–45

International House of Japan Library, *Modern Japanese Literature in Translation: A Bibliography*, Tokyo: Kodansha International, 1979

Japan PEN Club, *Japanese Literature in Foreign Languages 1945–1990*, Tokyo: Japan Book Publishers Association, 1990

Keene, Donald, *Dawn to the West: Japanese Literature in the Modern Era*, 2 vols, New York: Holt Rinehart, 1984

Keene, Donald, *Seeds in the Heart: Japanese Literature from Earliest Times to the Late Sixteenth Century*, New York: Holt, 1993

Kodama, Sanehide, *American Poetry and Japanese Culture*, Hamden, Connecticut: Archon, 1984

Miller, Roy Andrew, *The Japanese Language*, Chicago: University of Chicago Press, 1967

Miner, Earl R., *The Japanese Tradition in British and American Literature*, Princeton, New Jersey: Princeton University Press, 1966
Morris, Ivan (editor), *Madly Singing in the Mountains: An Appreciation and Anthology of Arthur Waley*, New York: Walker, and London: Allen and Unwin, 1970
Morton, Leith, "What Went Wrong? Translating Japanese Literature in Australia", *Australian Book Review*, 122 (July 1990) pp. 14–17
Morton, Leith, "Translating Japanese Poetry: Reading as Practice", *Journal of the Association of Teachers of Japanese*, 26/2 (November 1992) pp. 141–81
Paolucci, Anne, *Japan: A Literary Overview*, New York: Griffon House, 1993
Seidensticker, Edward G., *This Country, Japan*, Tokyo: Kodansha, 1979
Shibatani, Masayoshi, *The Languages of Japan*, Cambridge and New York: Cambridge University Press, 1990
Shionozaki, Hiroshi, "The First Translator into English of All the Manyoshu Poetry", *The Transactions of the Asiatic Society of Japan*, 4th series, 9 (1994) pp. 87–111
Shulman, Frank Joseph, *Japan*, Oxford and Santa Barbara, California: Clio Press, 1989 (World Bibliographical series, vol. 103)
Yoshizaki, Yasuhiro (editor), *Studies in Japanese Literature and Language: A Bibliography of English Materials*, Tokyo: Nichigai, 1979

Alfred Jarry 1873–1907

French dramatist, novelist and short-story writer

Biography

Born in Laval, in the northwest of France, 8 September 1873, and went to school in that region and in Paris. He was discharged after a short period of military service because of ill-health. He mingled actively in literary and artistic circles but is best known for his play *Ubu roi* (*Ubu Rex*), first performed in 1896. This comical but brutal and sinister work originated in a puppet play created by the author, when he was at school in Rennes, to make fun of one of the masters. In a short life of exuberant eccentricity Jarry wrote other plays – including further pieces about Ubu – as well as verse, novels and short stories. The most notable of these works is the novel *Les Gestes et opinions du docteur Faustroll, pataphysien* [The Deeds and Creeds of Doctor Faustroll] (written 1898), which led to the establishment in 1948 of the Collège de Pataphysique, "pataphysics" being the anti-rational "science of imaginary solutions". Jarry was a forerunner of Surrealism and of the Theatre of the Absurd. He died in poverty in Paris, 1 November 1907.

Ubu Rex

Ubu Roi, 1896

Ubu Rex is a voluminous and often inconsequential 5-act satirical farce about the greed-driven usurpation of power. The physically and psychologically grotesque Ubu, egged on by his wife, Mère Ubu, murders the king of Poland, seizes the throne and plunders the state, oppressing nobles and peasants alike. Poland is attacked by the Czar of Russia – various farcical scenes of warfare are staged and commented on with inventive coarseness – and Ubu has to retreat, but he and his wife survive and go home.

Translations

Benedikt, Michael and George E. Wellwarth, *King Ubu*, in *Modern French Plays: An Anthology of Plays from Jarry to Ionesco*, edited by Benedikt and Wellwarth, London: Faber, and New York: Dutton, 1964
Connolly, Cyril and Simon Watson Taylor, *Ubu Rex*, in *The Ubu Plays*, edited by Taylor, London: Methuen, 1968; New York: Grove Press, 1969; reprinted London: Methuen, 1991
Edwards, Paul, *Ubu Roi; or, The Poles*, Paris: privately printed, n. d.
Slater, Maya, *Ubu the King*, in *Three Pre-Surrealist Plays*, translated and with an introduction by Slater, Oxford: Oxford University Press, 1997
Wright, Barbara, *Ubu Roi*, London: Gaberbocchus Press, 1951; Norfolk, Connecticut: New Directions, 1961

The premiere of *Ubu Roi* on 10 December 1896 at the actor-director Lugné-Poë's avant-garde Théâtre de l'Oeuvre in Paris has been compared by critics to the first night of Victor Hugo's *Hernani* in 1830. In both cases, critics and general public alike were outraged. W.B. Yeats, for example, who attended the first performance of *Ubu Roi*, was shocked that King Ubu carried a toilet brush in place of a sceptre.

The history of the translation of *Ubu Roi* in English is as much a history of the manner and style of the performance of the play as of the literary quality of the translation. Jarry himself had very precise ideas about the staging of *Ubu Roi*. Indeed, for some critics the play's most significant innovation is its utter rejection of the prevailing discourse of realism in favour of a revolutionary theatricality. Stanley Chapman, who attended the (unpublished) Spike Milligan adaptation at the Cochrane Theatre in London in 1980, in which Charlie Drake played Ubu, has written that many of the jokes and ideas were extremely corny. However, he also claims that Drake's performance was both menacing and hypnotic – powerfully representing the idea of an ignorant, unpleasant man achieving world domination. Yet this version, according to Chapman's analysis, made a number of radical departures from the original text, including relocating the opening scene to Dagenham. The published translations (certainly the versions noted here) tend to represent close readings of the original text and not explorations of the theatrical possibilities of the play.

Alfred Jarry has been well served by his English translators, all of whom are extremely conscious of the importance language held for the author of *Ubu Roi*. TAYLOR (1968), for example, notes that the language in the Ubu plays is an unusual mixture of schoolboy slang, mock-Shakespearean heroic declamation, and rapid repartee. In addition to these problems of pace and register, the inventiveness of any translator will be taxed by Jarry's extensive range of neologisms (not least the infamous *Merdre!* with which the play opens). These remarks are echoed by SLATER (1997), who further asserts that it is important not to "underplay" the difference between elevated discourse and vulgarity.

Given that all five versions listed above are more than competent, preference for one version rather than another is to some extent a matter of personal taste. How can one evaluate, for example, the inventiveness of the five different solutions to the problem of translating *Merdre*? Wright translates the word as *Shittr!*; Connolly & Taylor as *Pschitt!*; Benedikt & Wellwarth opt for a close variant on Wright's approach with *Shitr!*; while Slater prefers *Crrrap!* Inventive though these solutions may be, they all fall far short of the offensive surprise caused by the original. Possibly the Spike Milligan version came close to capturing the spirit of the original by substituting a visual equivalent for the word. Mention must be made of Edwards's ingenious verbal solution to the problem, however: he has Ubu first decline the word *shit* as if it were a Latin noun (*shit, shit, shitam, shitae, shitae, shitarse*) and then conjugate it as a Latin verb. The manner in which the translator lingers over the word *Merdre*, translating it by some 204 dog-Latin variants, is not only extremely funny but also establishes the radical clash between high and low culture that is at the heart of the play at the same time as causing potential offence to those of a conservative turn of mind.

WRIGHT's version (1951) represents a close reading of the original text by a translator who is sympathetic to the aims and intentions of the author. Variation in register is generally well handled, and Jarry's neologisms are inventively translated without recourse to far-fetched solutions.

CONNOLLY & TAYLOR's version (1968) was originally commissioned by the theatre director Peter Brook. Despite the latter's initial enthusiasm for the project, it remained unperformed on the grounds that it had "a literary but not a theatrical energy" (Clive Fisher, *Cyril Connolly: A Nostalgic Life*, London: Macmillan, 1995) This seems an entirely accurate judgement despite the fact that this version incorporates a number of songs from Jarry's own later two-act *guignol* adaptation.

BENEDIKT & WELLWARTH (1964) provide a close reading of the original text, with inventive solutions to the most pressing translation problems. However, this version could be criticized for lacking variation in the register employed.

SLATER (1997) also provides a close but inventive reading of the play. Ubu's favourite expletive, "par ma chandelle verte", for example, is replaced by the equally phallic innuendo of "By the wick of my candle". The translator also seeks to convey the discordance between the high and the low language of the play by the introduction of recognizable phrases from *Macbeth* (a play with which *Ubu Roi* has a number of clear affinities) and by rendering the alexandrines employed at one stage by Mère Ubu as iambic pentameters. As the translator notes, the reader might not notice such a strategy, but an actress playing the part of Mère Ubu would stress them accordingly and so establish a deliberate change in register.

EDWARDS's version (no date), published in a small edition and circulated among Jarry scholars, is the least known of the five translations examined here (though it is regularly performed, being a reconstruction of the 1888 version for puppets, at model theatre exhibitions in the UK). In many respects the most convincing. High and low registers are constantly in collision throughout the translation. After Ubu's opening scatological conjugations, Mère Ubu replies: "O! Language! That's a nice way to talk. Père Ubu, thou art a bloody hooligan" ("Oh! voilà du joli, Père Ubu, vous estes un fort grand voyou"). Possibly because it is privately printed, Edwards's translation stresses (though not unduly) the vulgarity of the original, takes greater risks than commercially available translations, and displays enormous sensitivity to the performance quality of the language. As a commentator, moreover, Edwards looks much further afield than *Macbeth* as the underlying literary influence on the play. This critical judgment also informs the translation. Indeed, he claims that the translator of *Ubu Roi* needs to review – vengefully – the literary tradition of his or her own country as if still under the yoke of school.

TERRY HALE

Further Reading

Chapman, Stanley, "Letter Concerning Productions of Ubu in the UK" in *Xiana*, edited by Alastair Brotchie, London: Atlas Press, 1993

Slater, Maya, "Note on the Translation" in *Three Pre-Surrealist Plays*, translated by Slater, Oxford: Oxford University Press, 1997

Taylor, Simon Watson, introduction to *Ubu Rex* in *The Ubu Plays*, edited by Taylor, London: Methuen, 1968; reprinted 1991

Juan Ramón Jiménez 1881–1958

Spanish poet and prose writer

Biography

Born in Moguer (Huelva) in the south of Spain, 23 December 1881, and possessed from childhood a strong passion for poetry. He published his first poems in the newspapers and magazines of Seville and smaller towns and soon won local fame. The few early poems that have been preserved give no indication of what his mature work would be. From 1912 until 1936 Jiménez lived in Madrid, returning only occasionally to Moguer. In 1916 he married Zenobia Camprubi. The outbreak of the Spanish Civil War forced them to go to America where he lectured in different universities. In 1956 he was awarded the Nobel prize for literature and this brought wide attention to his poetry. Zenobia died only two days after word came from Stockholm. Jiménez did not long survive his loyal companion of 40 years; he died two years later in Puerto Rico, 29 May 1958.

His literary production extends over a period of more than 50 years: *Rimas* [Poems] (1902), *Arias tristes* [Sad Airs] (1903), *Jardines lejanos* [Distant Gardens] (1904), *Pastorales* [Pastorals] (1905), *Sonetos espirituales* [Spiritual Sonnets] (1917), *Platero y yo* (1914, complete edition 1917) (*Platero and I*, 1956), *Diario de un poeta recién casado* [Diary of a Newly-Married Poet] (1917), *Eternidades* [Eternities] (1918), *Piedra y cielo* [Rock and Sky] (1919), *Belleza* [Beauty] (1923), *Poesía* [Poetry] (1923), *Song* [Song] (1936), *Españoles de tres mundos* [Spaniards of Three Worlds] (1942), *La estación total* [The Total Season] (1946), *Romances de Coral Gables* [Coral Gables Ballads] (1948), *Dios deseado y deseante* (1948–49) (*God Desired and Desiring*, 1987), *Animal de fondo* [Enduring Animal] (1949), *Tercera antología poética* [Third Poetry Anthology] (1957)

Edition

The Spanish text used by translators is basically that of the *Tercera antología poética (1898–1953)* (1957), which was revised by the author and his wife

Translations

Prose Poems and Sketches

Platero y yo, 1914; complete edition 1917

Nicolás, Antonio T. de, *Platero and I*, Boulder, Colorado: Shambhala, 1978

Roach, Eloïse, *Platero and I*, Austin: University of Texas Press, 1957

Roberts, William and Mary Roberts, *Platero and I*, Oxford: Dolphin, and New York: Duschnesr, 1956

Selections and Anthologies of Poetry

Burnshaw, Stanley, *The Poem Itself: 45 Modern Poets in a New Presentation*, New York: Holt, 1960 (4 poems by Jiménez)

Hays, H.R., *Selected Writings of Juan Ramón Jiménez*, with an introduction by Eugenio Florit, New York: Farrar Straus, 1957

Kemp, Lysander, Willis Barnstone and Kate Flores, in *An Anthology of Spanish Poetry*, edited by Angel Flores, New York: Anchor, 1961, pp. 273–86

Merwin, W.S., Rachel Frank and Julia Howe, *Poetry*, 82/4 (1953) pp. 184–224

Nicolás, Antonio T. de, *Stories of Life and Death*, New York: Paragon House, 1986 Nicolás, Antonio T. de, *God Desired and Desiring* (bilingual edition), New York: Paragon House, 1987

Nicolás, Antonio T. de, *Invisible Reality* (bilingual edition), New York: Paragon House, 1987

Nicolás, Antonio T. de, *Time and Space: A Poetic Biography*, New York: Paragon House, 1988

Roach, Eloïse, *Three Hundred Poems, 1903–1953*, Austin: University of Texas Press, 1962

Trend, J.B., *Juan Ramón Jiménez: Fifty Spanish Poems*, Oxford: Oxford University Press, 1950; Berkeley: University of California Press, 1951

Turnbull, Eleanor, in her *Ten Centuries of Spanish Poetry* (bilingual edition), Baltimore: Johns Hopkins University Press, 1955, pp. 426–47

What is exceptional about Juan Ramón Jiménez's long career is that there is no decline in the poet's creative enthusiasm, nor in his capacity for renovation. He conceded that literature might attain relative beauty but held that poetry aspires to the attainment of absolute beauty. His devotion to poetry, to beauty, was not so much an aesthetic posture as an ardent religious cult. He saw beauty in nature and he came to identify it with poetry and with God. This sentiment gives his work its unity, gaining intensity as the poet advances in age. Although Jiménez showed a marked preference for free verse, he reverted from time to time to fixed forms, particularly the octosyllabic verse.

After Jiménez received the Nobel Prize for Literature in 1956, English translations of his work began to appear. While his volumes of poetry were published in rapid succession from 1900 to 1923, his prose pieces were not collected and printed in volumes but remained dispersed through magazines, newspapers and notebooks. Not until after his death were most of them made accessible to the public.

The popularity of *Platero and I*, first published in 1914, has been enormous, not only in Spanish-speaking countries but throughout the western world. The many translations into other languages – including French, German, Italian, Portuguese, Swedish, Norwegian, Dutch, Basque, Hebrew and English (various translations) – attest to the universality of its appeal.

Platero is a collection of prose poems and sketches, each of which can be read independently, but which taken together form a unified work. There is no narrative continuity; the unity of the book is achieved through the setting – Moguer and its surroundings – recreated with remarkable concision and sensitivity and through the two characters: the author himself and his donkey, Platero, who appear in nearly all of the prose poems.

ROACH's translation (1957) is the most widely known. She has been one of Jiménez's most devoted translators; her version of *Platero* was very well received when it appeared in 1957. The ROBERTS translation (1956) is a more sensitive and accurate piece of work; it is illustrated by Baltasar Lobo. This version is the one used by Fogelquist for his quotations in *Juan Ramón Jiménez* (1976). NICOLÁS's *Platero* (1978) remains close to the Spanish text, with some very good passages.

Jiménez received more attention for his poetic works than for his prose, and this is reflected in the number of translations. Most of these translations are to be found in anthologies, journals, articles and dissertations; only a few books contain exclusively translations of Jiménez's poetry.

HAYS's (1957) translations reveal occasional inaccuracies. The selection is thoroughly representative, however, and the introduction by Eugenio Florit, one of Jiménez's confidants, provides useful information. The work no doubt suffered from the demand for quick publication created by the award of the Nobel prize.

ROACH's translation of *Three Hundred Poems* (1962) is a representative selection of Jiménez's poems competently translated. Hers is a personal selection from 50 years of Jiménez's poetry; she is certainly sensitive to the poet's purpose but she often overtranslates, and there are occasions when she does not seem to grasp the meaning. The selection also contains occasional lapses. This version has been used by H.T. Young for his quotations of Jiménez in *The Victorious Expression*, and by P.R. Olson in *Circles of Paradox*.

J.B. TREND (1950) offers highly controversial translations of 50 of Jiménez's poems in which many liberties are taken in an attempt to re-create the subtle sensibility of the poetry and the grace of his Spanish. The results are dubious, presenting many deviations from the original.

NICOLÁS's translations (1986–88) are convincingly close to the original Spanish selection of Jiménez's poems; his work is accurate and respects the Spanish text. He is clearly a devoted translator of Jiménez's poetry.

Other translations of Jiménez's poetry in mixed collections are: BURNSHAW's in *The Poem Itself* (1960), which contains four literal translations and commentary by Eugenio Florit; KEMP, BARNSTONE & KATE FLORES's in Angel Flores's *Anthology* (1961), which is too brief but contains some good translating; MERWIN, FRANK & HOWE's *Poetry* (1953), devoted to Jiménez, with very good translations; and TURNBULL's (1955), with various translations in her usual old-fashioned tone.

EVA NÚÑEZ MÉNDEZ

Further Reading

Cardwell, Richard A., *Juan R. Jiménez: The Modernist Apprenticeship 1895–1900*, Berlin: Colloquium, 1977

Fogelquist, Donald F., *Juan Ramón Jiménez*, Boston: Twayne, 1976

Olson, Paul R., *Circles of Paradox: Time and Essence in the Poetry of Juan Ramón Jiménez*, Baltimore: Johns Hopkins Press, 1967

Young, Howard T., *The Victorious Expression: A Study of Four Contemporary Spanish Poets*, Madison: University of Wisconsin Press, 1966, pp. 75–136

Young, Howard T., *Juan Ramón Jiménez*, New York: Columbia University Press, 1967

Jin Ping Mei 16th century

The *Jin Ping Mei* is a novel of 100 chapters with its title derived from the names of three of the protagonist's mistresses. Generally regarded as one of the "Four Masterworks of the Ming Novel", it was of controversial authorship (it passed under the pseudonym of a "Smiling Scholar of Lanling"); it was probably written during the last two decades of the 16th century. Further revisions of the manuscript continued into the early 17th century. From among the several surviving versions of the novel scholars have focused their attention on three texts.

(1) The earliest extant edition, entitled the *Jin Ping Mei cihua*, dates from the last years of the Wanli reign (1573–1619) (with a preface dated in 1618) and is hence known as the "Wanli edition". Extensively interspersed with poems, popular songs, song sequences, fragments of dramatic dialogue, and various types of literary cross-references, which either enrich the description of the action or reveal the state of mind of the main characters, it is generally considered a superior text, though it remained in obscurity for centuries and was rediscovered only in 1932.

(2) The text that dates from the Chungzhen reign (1628–44) and is hence known as the "Chungzhen edition" is considered an inferior version on account of incompetent editorial tampering. This text has not only deleted many of those poems, songs and other quotations and ineptly rewritten the first chapter, but also made numerous tactless alterations throughout the book.

(3) The *Zhang Zhupo ping Jin Ping Mei*, with a preface dated in 1695, does not differ textually in any substantial way from the Chungzhen edition, but it contains the ingenious commentary of an important critic, Zhang Zhupo (1670–98).

Despite its notoriety as pornography – it contains numerous explicit descriptions of sex – the novel, which involves the relationship between the wealthy young merchant Ximen Qing (Hsi-men Ch'ing) and his many wives and mistresses, is primarily a novel of social criticism and, to some extent, may also be regarded as a novel of manners. As Hanan (1961) has observed, the novel is saturated with two issues: money and social status. It is also the first classical Chinese novel (preceding Cao Xueqin's 18th-century novel *Hong Lou Meng*) that focuses on everyday life within the enclosed world of an urban household, rather than on the military exploits of generals and princes, or the heroic deeds of chivalrous outlaws.

Translations

Anonymous, *The Adventures of Hsi-men Ch'ing*, New York: Library of Facetious Lore, 1927 (private printing)

Egerton, Clement, *The Golden Lotus: A Translation, from the Chinese Original, of the Novel Chin P'ing Mei*, 4 vols, London: Routledge and Kegan Paul, 1939; New York: Grove Press, 1954; revised edition, 1972

Miall, Bernard, *Chin P'ing Mei: The Adventurous History of Hsi Men and His Six Wives*, with an introduction by Arthur Waley, London: John Lane, 1939; 2 vols, New York: Putnam, 1940; New York: Capricorn, 1962

Roy, David Tod, *The Plum in the Golden Vase; or, Chin P'ing Mei*, vol. 1: *The Gathering*, with an introduction, Princeton, New Jersey: Princeton University Press, 1993

With its extraordinary multi-level verbal density, its rich allusions and cross-references, the novel presents a great challenge to translators. This, as well as the unabashed descriptions of sex, prompted Herbert A. Giles (1845–1935), author of the first history of Chinese literature in English (1901), to remark that the translation of this novel demands "the nerve of a Burton". It is therefore not incomprehensible that the earliest venture of introducing the novel to Western reader, the ANONYMOUS text (1927), took the form of paraphrase. Privately printed in 750 numbered copies, it condenses the 100-chapter novel into 18 chapters in simple, straightforward English prose. There has been no record of this translation having ever gained much attention from either the reading public or the academy.

MIALL's text (1939), translated into forceful and lively English from the abridged German version of Franz Kuhn (1930), consists of tastefully selected episodes from the novel (rendered into 49 chapters), passing over all the erotic passages. It contains a short but well-composed introduction by Arthur Waley (1889–1966), who in his middle age was already the doyen of Oriental studies in the Western world at the time. Waley recounts the popular legend about the authorship and origin of the novel, and discusses, from then available sources, the early history and subsequent reception of the book.

EGERTON's *Golden Lotus* (1939), titled after the name of the protagonist's most colorful and nymphomaniacal wife, was the first complete translation of the novel in the West. With the "untiring and generously given help" of the famous Chinese novelist Lao She (1899–1966), who taught Chinese at the University of London in the 1920s and to whom the book was dedicated, the translation is not only readable but also relatively free from serious errors and misinterpretation. Unfortunately, like Otto and Artur Kibat, who made the six-volume complete German translation of the novel (*Djin Ping Meh*, Hamburg: Die Waage, 1967–83), Egerton did not use the superior Wanli edition, which was unavailable to him when he undertook the project. Following the Victorian practice, and conforming to the decorum of pre-World War II Britain, Egerton rendered all the explicit passages about sex into Latin. In the revised edition (1972), however, all the Latin passages have been translated into English. It also includes a brief introduction and a list of the main characters.

In the wake of André Lévy's brilliant scholarly French translation (*Fleur en Fiole d'Or*, Paris: Gallimard, 1985), ROY (1993) has based his translation on the superior text of the Wanli edition. Unlike Lévy, who for some reason still deletes some of the longer song sequences and other literary borrowings, either wholly or in part, Roy has decided to render the Wanli edition *in extenso*, including the two prefaces, colophon, and eight song lyric texts that precede the first chapter. Although only one of the projected five volumes has come into print at this time, Roy's translation, a labor of love that leaves no stone unturned, is meant to be, and on its completion will certainly become, the authoritative text that supersedes all previous renditions in English. The first volume contains one-fifth of the original (20 chapters), an introduction, a thoroughly comprehensive cast of characters (in 56 pages), and 40 beautifully reproduced illustrations of Chinese prints, and it is complete with notes, bibliography, and an index. Also included in the appendices are Roy's commentary on the significance of the prologue contained in the first chapter of the Wanli edition, and translations of the complete texts of lyrics or song sequences that are cited only in part in the novel, whenever those are available from other sources. In the annotations Roy has made an admirable attempt to identify the sources of quoted material. In general the translation has kept the "natural color" (*bense*, to use a Chinese critical term), and captured the verbal diversity and liveliness, of the original. Its success with the common reader still remains to be seen, but it will undoubtedly be appreciated by students and scholars of Chinese literature and history for generations to come.

Hanan's articles, with their substantial contributions to scholarship, represent the excellent pioneering research carried out on the novel in the West. Hsia (1968) offers an idiosyncratically negative view: although he calls the work a milestone in the development of classical Chinese fiction, he rates it as a "most disappointing novel" in terms of its style and structure. The crudely printed monograph by Carlitz (1986), which derived from a doctoral dissertation completed at the University of Chicago, follows Roy's thesis of the underlying Confucianism in the novel, and discusses the significance of the novel's extensive use of drama and song. Readers who are interested in the role and variation of sexuality in Chinese culture may want to consult the Dutch sinologist Gulik's study (1961), which makes numerous references to the novel, and is richly decorated with original Chinese illustrations. Last but not least, ROY's introduction (1993) to his translation, based upon the his long-time scholarly research, is updated on scholarship, and frequently illuminates our understanding of the novel (especially by his examination of the rhetoric of the novel in the light of Bakhtin's theory), though his insistence on referring to the philosophy of the ancient Confucian thinker Xunzi (Hsün-tzu) as "a key to the novel" is rather controversial.

YANG YE

Further Reading

Carlitz, Katherine, *The Rhetoric of Chin P'ing Mei*, Bloomington: Indiana University Press, 1986

Gulik, R.H. van, *Sexual Life in Ancient China: A Preliminary*

Survey of Chinese Sex and Society from ca. 1500 BC till AD 1644, Leiden: E.J. Brill, 1961

Hanan, Patrick D., "A Landmark of the Chinese Novel" in *The Far East: China and Japan*, edited by Douglas Grant and Millar MacLure, Toronto: University of Toronto Press, 1961

Hanan, Patrick D., "The Text of the *Chin P'ing Mei*", *Asia Major*, new series, 9/1 (April 1962) pp. 1–57

Hanan, Patrick D., "Sources of the *Chin P'ing Mei*", *Asia Major*, new series, 10/1 (July 1963) pp. 23–67

Hsia, C.T., "Chapter V: *Chin P'ing Mei*" in his *The Classic Chinese Novel: A Critical Introduction*, New York: Columbia University Press, 1968

Plaks, Andrew H., *The Four Masterworks of the Ming Novel: Ssu Ta Ch'i-Shu*, Princeton, New Jersey: Princeton University Press, 1987

St John of the Cross (San Juan de la Cruz) 1542–1591

Spanish poet and mystic

Biography

Born Juan de Yepes y Álvarez, in Fontiveros, Ávila, Spain, 24 June 1542. He was sent to live at an orphanage by his widowed mother, and, financed by a patron, studied at the Jesuit college in Medina del Campo 1559–63. He became a Carmelite monk as Fray Juan de Santo Matía in 1563. He attended the Carmelite College of San Andrés at the University of Salamanca 1564–68, and was ordained a priest in 1567. He helped St Teresa of Avila to establish the austere reformed Discalced (Barefoot) Order of Carmel, whose first convent she had founded in 1562. He was appointed subprior of the first Discalced Carmelite house for men at Duruelo, near Fontiveros, in 1568, and founded another at Mancera in 1570. He was rector of a new Carmelite college at the University of Alcalá 1570–72, and was later appointed chaplain at St Teresa's convent in Ávila, where he stayed 1572–77. His activities in the Carmelite reform movement caused him to be arrested and imprisoned (1577) in an unreformed monastery in Toledo, where he wrote much of his poetry. He escaped in August 1578, and was rector of a new Carmelite college at Baeza from 1579 to 1582. After the division of the orders, he was given a succession of posts among the Discalced: prior at Los Mártires, Granada, 1582–88; vicar provincial of Andalusia 1585–87; and prior at Segovia, 1588–91. He fell out of favour after further disagreement among the Discalced Order in 1591, and withdrew to the monastery of Úbeda, near Jaén, where he lived a solitary life as a simple friar until his death. He died at Úbeda, 14 December 1591. He was beatified in 1675 and canonized in 1726. His feast-day is 14 December; in 1926 he was declared a Doctor of the Church.

St John of the Cross is best known as a Christian mystic and poet. His three most important and influential mystical poems are *Cántico espiritual* (*The Spiritual Canticle*); *Noche oscura del alma* (*Dark Night of the Soul*) and *Llama de amor viva* (*The Living Flame of Love*). All these works take as their theme the spiritual journey of the soul to God. The poems of St John of the Cross were published posthumously in 1618.

The Dark Night of the Soul

La noche oscura del alma, 1618

Translations

Treatise and Poem

Backhouse, Halcyon (editor), *The Dark Night of the Soul*, London: Hodder and Stoughton, 1988

Kavanaugh, Kieran and Otilio Rodríguez in their *The Collected Works of St. John of the Cross*, with an introduction by Kavanaugh, New York: Doubleday, 1964; 2nd edition, Washington, DC: Institute of Carmelite Studies, 1991

Lewis, David, *The Obscure Night of the Soul* in his *The Complete Works of Saint John of the Cross, of the Order of Our Lady of Mount Carmel*, 2 vols, London: Longman Roberts and Green, 1864; revised edition, edited by Benedict Zimmerman, 2 vols, London: Thomas Baker, 1891 (for subsequent editions see Zimmerman)

Peers, E. Allison, in his *The Complete Works of Saint John of the Cross*, 3 vols, London: Burns and Oates, 1934–35; Westminster, Maryland: Newman Bookshop, 1945; revised edition, London: Burns Oates and Washbourne, and Westminster, Maryland: Newman Bookshop, 1953

Zimmerman, Benedict (editor and reviser) *The Dark Night of the Soul*, translated by David Lewis, 3rd edition, London: Thomas Baker, 1908; 4th edition, London: Thomas Baker, 1916; reprinted Greenwood, South Carolina: Attic Press, 1973

Poem only

Barnstone, Willis, in *The Poems of Saint John of the Cross*, (bilingual edition), translated and with an introduction by Barnstone, Bloomington: Indiana University Press, 1968; in English only, New York: New Directions, 1972

Campbell, Roy, in *Poems of St John of the Cross* (bilingual edition), translated by Campbell, London: Harvill Press, 1951; New York: Pantheon, 1953

Nicholson, Lynda, in *St John of the Cross: His Life and Poetry*, by Gerald Brenan, Cambridge: Cambridge University Press, 1973

Nims, John Frederick, in *The Poems of St. John of the Cross* (bilingual edition), translated by Nims, New York: Grove Press, 1959; 3rd edition, Chicago: University of Chicago Press, 1979

Symonds, Arthur, in "The Poetry of Santa Teresa and San Juan de la Cruz", *The Contemporary Review*, 75 (1899) pp. 542–51

The Dark Night of the Soul is the title of an unfinished treatise in two books, cast in the form of a commentary on a poem in eight stanzas which begins "En una noche oscura", "On a dark night". Although St John of the Cross states that the poem contains all the doctrine he expounds in the commentary, his primary interest is in the exposition of the first line, and he leaves the commentary unfinished during the third stanza. The *Dark Night* treatise is the second part of a commentary on the poem, the first part being entitled *Subida del Monte Carmelo* (*Ascent of Mount Carmel*). These two works are always printed together and for practical purposes may be treated, as St John himself implies, as a single work covering the four aspects of the dark night in the scheme he follows (the active night of the senses, the active night of the spirit, the passive night of the senses, the passive night of the spirit).

The history of the *Dark Night* in English is connected with the history of the textual criticism of the original. The first English translation of the *Dark Night* is that of LEWIS (1864), 250 years after the work was originally published (Alcalá, 1618). This long gap was no doubt the result of St John's readership being drawn almost exclusively from the Roman Catholic world and, within that, primarily from members of religious orders. Before 1864, English readers would have been dependent on French and Latin translations (Paris, 1622; Cologne, 1639). Since the middle of the 20th century the works of San Juan have reached a much wider public, thanks largely to the work of Allison PEERS and CAMPBELL, and they have shared in the general increase of interest in works of spirituality that marked its closing decades.

The chief difficulties posed for the translator by St John's prose writings are his use of a technical vocabulary drawn from an Aristotelian-Thomist tradition, and the length and syntactical complexity, so typical of the age, of some of his sentences. Words like "accidental", "essential", "substantial" and "virtual" conserve meanings that may still be familiar to theologians but that otherwise have fallen out of use. The theological framework on which he depends and the biblical imagery he uses are not as familiar as they were. The poem poses other problems. It uses the tightly-constructed metre and rhyme scheme of the five-line verse of the Spanish *lira*, virtually impossible to reproduce in English without sacrificing much of its lyrical beauty.

LEWIS (1864; preface by Cardinal Wiseman) followed the Spanish text of the *Noche oscura* as printed in volume 27 of the *Biblioteca de autores españoles* (1853), itself based on the 1703 edition of the works of St John and far from accurate by the canons of modern editing practice. The second edition of Lewis (1891) was revised by the Carmelite Benedict ZIMMERMAN; the third (1908), which carries Zimmerman's name, was a further revision of this. The fourth edition (1916) marked a significant departure, because Zimmerman was able to use the first critical Spanish edition of the century, that of Gerardo de San Juan de la Cruz (Toledo, 1912–14). In a prefatory note, the publisher explained that he had acquired the rights to its English translation. Zimmerman introduced further corrections but also included material omitted in the earlier editions (usually because it had been considered controversial), giving the original Spanish for all these passages in footnotes.

Lewis's original title had been *The Obscure Night of the Soul*, so that it is to Zimmerman's first revision of 1891 that we owe the expression for which St John is best known, "the dark night of the soul". Zimmerman's translation is certainly more accurate, and, unlike Lewis, who provided marginal summaries to assist the reader, he divides each chapter into numbered paragraphs (though these do not usually correspond to the numeration of editions currently in use). Lewis capitalizes freely, with the result that St John's treatise appears to deal with rigid categories (a view most modern critics would wish to reject). Zimmerman abandons this, though he fails to capitalize "lover" when it refers to the divine protagonist in the poem. Because he omits what he no doubt considered rhetorical flourishes, and because he often divides long periods into shorter sentences, Lewis achieves a more punchy style than Zimmerman in places, and sometimes uses expressions that still communicate well, such as "characteristics" rather than "peculiarities" for "propiedades". Zimmerman is not always consistent: sometimes he translates "sensitiva" as "sensitive", at other times, less misleadingly, as "sensual", for expressions like "la parte sensitiva del alma" ("the sensual part of the soul").

A major step forward came with the work of E. Allison PEERS (1934–35), whose translation was largely responsible for introducing St John to the 20th-century English-speaking world (and for the quotations from his writings in T.S. Eliot's *Four Quartets*). Peers based his translation on the new critical edition of the saint's work edited by Silverio de Santa Teresa (Burgos, 1929–31). He criticizes his predecessors for their omissions, paraphrases and failure to render accurately St John's biblical quotations, which are often versions of passages the saint remembered from the Vulgate, rather than the Vulgate text itself. Suspicion of vernacular translations of the Bible in the Roman Catholic Church until the Second Vatican Council (1962–65) no doubt explains why Lewis and Zimmerman kept to official forms. In his preface, Peers explains that because of the inaccuracy of earlier Spanish editions English readers could never be sure "whether in any particular passage, they are face to face with the Saint's own words, with a translator's free paraphrase of them or with a gloss made by some later copyist or early editor in the supposed interests of orthodoxy". While he occasionally seeks to clarify the meaning, Peers signals any departure from the original (as well as the principal variants) in the footnotes. He prefers accuracy to stylistic elegance "where the two have been in conflict" and tries "to reproduce the atmosphere of a 16th-century text as far as is consistent with clarity". Sometimes he breaks up discursive sentences into shorter units, and he translates biblical (and other) quotations in Spanish "strictly as St. John of the Cross made them". For the first time in an English translation, Peers provides introductory material to guide the reader through the intricacies of the text. Given the age of the translation, it is not surprising that it has a somewhat archaic feel, since the influence of the Prayer Book and the King James Bible still governed forms of expression in religious literature. But Peers's translation is reliable, and remained unchallenged for 30 years.

The KAVANAUGH & RODRÍGUEZ translation, which first appeared in 1964 but which was thoroughly revised to coincide with the quatercentenary of the saint's death (1991), adopts a clearer, more modern style, while remaining faithful to the text (based on two Spanish editions of the 1980s by leading Carmelite scholars). In his foreword, Kavanaugh explains that while he has "preserved John's traditional and biblical ways of speaking about God and Christ" and therefore his masculine nouns and pronouns, he has usually "avoided the masculine generic by recasting the sentence". In this respect, the 1991 translation reflects the ferment in theological language on both sides of the Atlantic (though, paradoxically, the human protagonist of the *Dark Night*, "the soul", is feminine in Spanish). It is likely to remain the standard English version for the foreseeable future. BACKHOUSE (1988) breaks up sentences, omits rhetorical flourishes, adds clarifications where necessary and achieves a readable, plain style, but loses the stylistic feel of the original, like some contemporary versions of the Bible addressed to the supposed average reader. Its merits and faults can be seen where it seeks to iron out difficulties and avoid technical terms: compare Kavanaugh, "We have examples of this ineffability of divine language in Sacred Scripture" with Backhouse, "The Bible has a number of examples of this".

SYMONS (1899) translated some of St John's poems, including "Upon an obscure night". His version is not as literal as he claims, but it is certainly dull, and at some points misunderstands the original. CAMPBELL (1951) was the first and remains the best-known translator of the complete poetic works of St John's poetry. His rendering of the poem, like that of Symons, manages to retain the form and versification of the *lira*, but it is hard to see how it could be bettered, even if the first three stanzas are less successful than the rest: the dark night is "gloomy", while he translates "dichosa" in three different ways, thus failing to mirror the careful gradation of the poem. NICHOLSON (1973) is less satisfactory. The metre of the verse is irregular, occasional assonance replaces regular rhyme, and some of the expressions are not very happy (line two, "In love's anxiety of longing kindled"). NIMS (3rd edition 1979) follows the *lira* and does not substantially alter the sense of the poem, but offers a more poetic reinterpretation of some lines, with one unexplained divergence: in the penultimate stanza "on my neck he wounded" becomes, unaccountably, "and the fire there where they lay!".

COLIN THOMPSON

Further Reading

Alonso, Dámaso, *La poesía de San Juan de la Cruz*, Madrid: Consejo Superior de Investigaciones Científicas, 1942

Balthasar, Hans Urs von, "St John of the Cross" in *The Glory of the Lord: A Theological Aesthetics*, vol. 3, translated by Erasmo Leiva-Merikakis, edited by Joseph Fessio and John Riches, Edinburgh: T. and T. Clark, 1986

Brenan, Gerald, *St John of the Cross*, Cambridge: Cambridge University Press, 1973

Cugno, Alain, *Saint John of the Cross: Reflections on Mystical Experience*, translated by Barbara Wall, New York: Seabury Press, 1982; as *St John of the Cross: The Life and Thought of a Christian Mystic*, London: Burns and Oates, 1982

Peers, E. Allison, *Spirit of Flame: A Study of St John of the Cross*, London: SCM Press, 1943; New York: Morehouse-Gorham, 1944

Thompson, Colin P., *The Poet and the Mystic*, Oxford: Oxford University Press, 1978

Trueman Dicken, E.W., *The Crucible of Love: A Study of the Mysticism of St Teresa of Jesus and St John of the Cross*, London: Darton Longman and Todd, and New York: Sheed and Ward, 1963

Turner, Denys, *The Darkness of God: Negativity in Christian Mysticism*, Cambridge and New York: Cambridge University Press, 1995

Ynduráin, Domingo (editor), *San Juan de la Cruz: Poesía*, Madrid: Cátedra, 1989

Uwe Johnson 1934–1984

German novelist

Biography

Uwe Johnson, the first important creative writer to take as his theme the divided Germany after World War II, was born 20 July 1934 in Cammin, Pomerania, and spent his childhood in Mecklenburg, studying later at the universities of Rostock and Leipzig. When in 1959 his first work, *Ingrid Babendererde*, was rejected by an East German publisher, he moved to West Berlin, and the novel *Mutmassungen über Jakob* (1959, translated 1963 as *Speculations about Jakob*) was published in West Germany, where it won the 1960 Fontane prize. His next novel, *Das dritte Buch über Achim* (1961; *The Third Book about Achim*, 1967), was awarded the 1962 International Publishers' prize, and other works, projects and prizes followed. Using an experimental narrative technique Johnson explored a wide and surprising range of East and West German characters, professions and situations. Johnson continued to live in the Federal Republic until 1974, with a period from 1966 to 1967 in New York, working as editor for German literature for his American publisher, Harcourt Brace. From 1975 he lived in England, where he died, at Sheerness, Kent, 15 March 1984. All his major works have been translated into English.

Translations

Novels

Mutmassungen über Jakob, 1959

Molinaro, Ursule, *Speculations about Jakob*, New York: Grove Press, and London: Jonathan Cape, 1963

Das dritte Buch über Achim, 1961

Molinaro, Ursule, *The Third Book about Achim*, New York: Harcourt Brace, 1967; London: Jonathan Cape, 1968

Zwei Ansichten, 1965

Winston, Richard and Clara Winston, *Two Views*, New York: Harcourt Brace, 1966; London: Cape, 1967

Jahrestage: Aus dem Leben von Gesine Cresspahl, vols 1-3, 1970–71; vol. 4, 1983

Vennewitz, Leila, *Anniversaries: From the Life of Gesine Cresspahl*, New York: Harcourt Brace, 1975 (contains vol. 1 and part of vol. 2)

Vennewitz, Leila and Walter Arndt, *Anniversaries II*, San Diego: Harcourt Brace, 1987 (contains part of vol. 2 and all of vols 3–4)

Short Story

"Eine Reise wegwohin" in *Karsch und andere Prosa*, 1964

Winston, Richard and Clara Winston, *An Absence*, London: Jonathan Cape, 1969

When Uwe Johnson's first work, the novel *Mutmassungen über Jakob*, appeared in 1959 shortly after he had fled to West Berlin from East Germany, it caused something of a sensation. Here was an East German author writing about the division of his country and presenting his viewpoint to the free world. The story's protagonist, Jakob Abs, a railroad dispatcher in an East German city, is morally torn when he is asked to spy for the German Democratic Republic (GDR) and ends up being killed by a locomotive in a mysterious accident/murder/suicide. However, this plot has to be pieced together by the reader through Johnson's unorthodox writing style and language, both of which caused a sensation as great as that produced by the contents of the book. Since then, numerous German critics have tried to analyze Johnson's style, which was at its most radically different stage in his first published novel. According to W.J. Schwarz in *Der Erzähler Uwe Johnson* (1970), the text consists of three separate units that are interwoven throughout and sometimes, but not always, distinguished from each other by different print. Add to that the very colloquial German, the occasional Mecklenburg dialect, the very technical details regarding trains, the erratic punctuation, and what has been designated as parataxis – a peculiarity of the syntax whereby clauses follow each other in an endless chain without conjunctions – and the task of the average German reader, let alone the translator, becomes very difficult.

Considering all this, one has to commend MOLINARO (1963) who translated Johnson's first published work. She gives it the equivalent title *Speculations about Jacob*, since the author makes it clear that both the omniscient narrator and the other characters are only "speculating" and cannot be certain about the events. Molinaro has followed the printing practices of the original, which distinguish the interior monologues from the narrative part and the dialogues by using cursive script, but she has also identified by name the person who is doing the talking. She has transliterated Russian phrases according to English practice and tried to approximate dialect and very colloquial speech (the Mecklenburg dialect "gäms" becomes "gimme"). When necessary, Molinaro has substituted the names of persons for the original pronouns and sought the assistance of the Pennsylvania Railroad with the technical translation. All in all, she has succeeded in providing us with perhaps a more readable text than the author's, by clarifying a lot of lexical ambiguities without losing sight of the overall meaning and purpose of the novel.

MOLINARO also translated (1967) Johnson's second novel, as *The Third Book about Achim*, again a literal translation of the original German title. The story deals with Karsch, a West German journalist, who is invited to the GDR by an old East German girlfriend and tries but fails to write the biography of his former girlfriend's present boyfriend Achim, a champion racing cyclist. The narrative is presented in a series of questions and answers, such as: "Who is this Achim?" and this imitation interview technique results in a clearer plot line than in *Speculations about Jakob*. However, many of the idiosyncrasies of Johnson's style remain, as they do throughout the body of his work; all of his translators have tried to maintain them as long as they do not obscure the text. References have also been clarified here and paragraphs split up so as to be made more digestible.

The WINSTONS' *An Absence* (1969) is actually the translation of only one short story of about 60 pages which in German appeared in the 1964 collection *Karsch und andere Prosa* together with four other short pieces. In essence it tells the same story as *The Third Book about Achim* except that it adds what happens to Karsch after he leaves the GDR and has problems readjusting to West Germany. This is done in a straight narrative manner by a third-person narrator in a much shorter form than in the novel. The Winstons had an easier and shorter text to render into English than did Molinaro and have done so successfully. It should be noted, however, that the original title of this short story is "Eine Reise wegwohin", which might translate literally as "A Trip to Somewhere Far Away", and also that the short biography of the author at the end has the wrong birth date.

The 1965 novel *Zwei Ansichten* was translated, also by the WINSTONS, as *Two Views* (1966). It is obvious that the views of the title are once more those of East and West Germany, the GDR and the Federal Republic of Germany (FRG) as personified by the East German nurse Beate D. and the West German photographer Dietbert B., two young people who meet and fall in love before the Wall goes up in August 1961, making the separation between the two Germanies even more final. This novel is divided into chapters narrated by the two characters alternately and proceeds in a more or less straightforward manner, albeit retaining some of Johnson's peculiarities of syntax and language. However, the translators have clarified obscure references and given the young characters their first names instead of initials.

Although Johnson continued to write and be written about after the late 1960s, most of his energies until his death in 1984 seem to have been devoted to his major work in four volumes, *Jahrestage*, which he began in 1970 and finished in 1983. In this novel, the author returns to one of his first characters from *Speculations*, Gesine Cresspahl, then the title character's girlfriend, who has now become an interpreter, and after living first in West Germany, has moved to New York, only to find out that she really does not fit in anywhere, like so many other characters in modern fiction. The narrative is structured around newspaper entries from the *New York Times*, starting in the late 1960s, and among other things presents a view of the US through East German eyes.

Leila VENNEWITZ was asked to render Johnson's four-volume work into English, albeit in a slightly abridged version, which resulted in an excellent translation (1975, 1987) of the first three German volumes; the last one had to be translated by Walter ARNDT (1987) because of Vennewitz's prior commitments. Perhaps the clearest sign of the merit of this translation is to be found in Johnson's high praise of Vennewitz's contribution, especially since he had lived and taught in the US and had at times thought of translating the novel himself. Vennewitz, an English-born Canadian translator of other contemporary German writers and winner of both the Society of Authors Award (London, 1968) and the American PEN Award (New York, 1979), visited Johnson and carried on an extensive correspondence with him regarding this translation. According to E. Fahlke and J. Gaines's account of their conversations with Johnson, *"Ich überlege mir die Geschichte": Uwe Johnson im Gespräch* ["Thinking Things Over": Conversations with Uwe Johnson], this correspondence is to be found among Johnson's archives. The questions of the translator to the author range in subject from the translation of the title (would the more literal *Days of the Year* be better?) to clarification of references and passages of dialect. As part of this close cooperation between author and translator, Johnson sent Vennewitz the original clippings that he had used from the *New York Times*, as well as maps, sketches, and photographs, and as a result the English-language reader can rely on a masterful translation of the original.

HERA T. LEIGHTON

Further Reading

Enright, D.J., "Make It Hard: Speculations about Jakob", *New Statesman* (6 June 1963)

Fahlke, Eberhard, *"Ich überlege mir die Geschichte": Uwe Johnson im Gespräch*, Frankfurt: Suhrkamp, 1988

Schwarz, Wilhelm Johannes, *Der Erzähler Uwe Johnson*, Bern: Francke, 1970

Sir William Jones 1746–1794

British jurist, oriental scholar, linguist and translator

Biography

Born in Westminster, London, 28 September 1746, to a Welsh family. He was the youngest child of the mathematician William Jones, who died when Jones was three years old. Encouraged in his studies by his late father's scientific colleagues and friends, he went to Harrow School in 1753, where he studied classics and learned French and Italian. He also had himself taught some Arabic and Persian. He attended University College Oxford, from 1765 to 1768, helping to pay his fees by working as a tutor to lord Althorp, the young brother of Georgiana, duchess of Devonshire. He became fluent in a number of languages: by the end of his life he could read 28. His first publication, a translation from Persian to French of the life of Nadir Shah, was published in 1770, followed closely by further translations from Persian and other oriental languages. He was elected a fellow of the Royal Society in 1772. He became acquainted with eminent scholars, including Samuel Johnson, Edward Gibbon and Edmund Burke. He decided on a legal career, for financial reasons, and was called to the Bar at the Middle Temple, London, in 1774; he subsequently wrote a number of essays and treatises on law and became commissioner of bankrupts.

In March 1783 Jones was knighted, and he married Anna Maria Shipley the following month. He went to India later that year to take up an appointment as a judge in the Supreme Court of Judicature in Calcutta, Bengal, where he remained until his death. He founded the Bengal Asiatic Society in 1784 for the study of oriental languages, literature and philosophy, and gave many lectures on Indian anthropology, history and zoology in the course of his presidency of the society. Jones learned Sanskrit in order to translate and publish a major digest of Hindu and Muslim law, which he left incomplete at his death. He made a highly important address in 1786 to the Bengal Asiatic Society, published in *Asiatic Researches*, on the comparative philology of Sanskrit, Greek and Latin. Jones was a close acquaintance of several successive governors-general of India during the 10 years he was in Calcutta; these included Warren Hastings, lord Cornwallis and Sir John Shore (later lord Teignmouth), Jones' biographer, who published an edition of some of Jones's works. Died in Calcutta, 27 April 1794.

Sir William Jones, polymath and minor poet, was a lawyer by profession. His translations were among the first to provide Europe with knowledge of the literature of two distinct oriental civilizations, those of the Islamic world and of classical India. He was educated at Harrow and at University College, Oxford, where he supplemented his classical studies by learning Arabic and Persian from a tutor whom he himself employed. For some time he was more interested in Persian than in Arabic, though by 1768 he was recognized as an expert in both languages. His first seven major publications were all connected with them, though not always with literature, and most of them included translations. The most important were: *Poems, Consisting Chiefly of Translations from the Asiatick Languages* (1772); *Poeseos Asiaticiae commentariorum libri sex, cum appendice* (1774); and *The Moallakat* (1782).

There is a feeling that Jones was at his best as a translator of Persian, but the versions from Arabic are still creditable. There is a liberal scattering of errors in them, and he has a bucolic view of the desert, among other failings; but he displays an empathy with the poetry he is translating, perhaps because of a creative tension between the oriental poetry he studied and his views on poetry in general. These are set out in an essay appended to *Poems ... from the Asiatick Languages*, "On the arts commonly called imitative", and may be regarded as the earliest formulation of the poetics of Romanticism. He was clearly able to give strength and new perspective to these ideas from his knowledge of Arabic and Persian poetry, and in turn the newly formulated ideas further stimulated his interest in the Arabic and Persian material.

There is a considerable dispute about the extent of the influence of Jones and his translations from Arabic and Persian outside the world of scholarship, but it can hardly be classed as negligible: Byron, Southey and Thomas Moore all take up his oriental themes. Moreover, the translations played an indirect role in arousing Goethe's interest in Persian and Arabic poetry. That interest eventually flowered over 30 years later in the *West-östliche Divan* (1819), when it was revived after the publication of a German translation of the poems by the 14th-century Persian poet Hafiz by von Hammer-Purgstall (Vienna 1814).

Jones's work as a translator slowly had to give way to his career as a lawyer. In politics he held radical Whig views and these proved a barrier to legal advancement. He was first promised a judgeship in the Calcutta Supreme Court in 1778, but it was not until 1783 that he was finally appointed and sailed for India. The move to India brought a dramatic change to his interests in translation. Shortly after his arrival he began to learn not only Bengali but also Sanskrit and Prakrit, the language of Sanskrit commentaries; and though he never lost his interest in Arabic and Persian, they fell into the background. The 1780s saw some translations of Sanskrit religious work by Charles Wilkins, but it was Jones who was the first to translate a literary work, the 3rd-century play *?akuntal?* by the great poet and dramatist K?lid?sa. This was first printed in Calcutta in 1789 under the title of: *Sacontala; or, The Fatal Ring*. This was another pioneering translation, and the *?akuntal?* was to catch the interest of many romanticists, both writers and musicians.

From this point until his death Jones was preoccupied with translation of a quite different kind: legal texts of both Hindu and Islamic law. For India, at any rate, these were his most important legacy.

In addition to the translations contained in the works mentioned above, some are also to be found in Jones's *Dissertation sur la Littérature Orientale* (London 1771).

There have been several biographies. Arberry's is quite good and reasonably easily available.

ALAN JONES

Translations

Poems, Consisting Chiefly of Translations from the Asiatick Languages, 1772

Poeseos Asiaticiae commentariorum libri sex, cum appendice, 1774

The Moallakat; or, Seven Arabian Poems Which Were Suspended on the Temple at Mecca, with a Translation, a Preliminary Discourse and Notes, Critical, Philosophical and Explanatory, 1782

Kālidāsa, *Sacontala; or, The Fatal Ring: An Indian Drama, by Calidas, Translated from the Original Sanscrit and Prakrit*, 1789

Further Reading

Arberry, A.J., *Asiatic Jones: The Life and Influence of Sir William Jones, Pioneer of Indian Studies*, London: Longman, 1946

Cannon, Garland, *The Life and Mind of Oriental Jones: Sir William Jones, the Father of Modern Linguistics*, Cambridge and New York: Cambridge University Press, 1990

Cannon, Garland and Kevin R. Brine (editors), *Objects of Enquiry: The Life, Contributions and Influences of Sir William Jones*, New York: New York University Press, 1995

Clark, Steve, "Orient Knowledge Not so Pure", *Times Literary Supplement* (21 March 1997)

Franklin, Michael J., *Sir William Jones*, Cardiff: University of Wales Press, 1995

Jones, Sir William, *The Works of Sir William Jones*, 6 vols, London: G.G. and J. Robinson, 1799; 13 vols, London: Stockdale and Walker, 1807; reprinted 13 vols, Delhi: Pravesh, 1979

Jones, Sir William, *Sir William Jones: A Reader*, edited and with an introduction by Satya S. Pachori, Delhi, Oxford and New York: Oxford University Press, 1993

Jones, Sir William, *Sir William Jones: Selected Poetical and Prose Works*, edited by Michael J. Franklin, Cardiff: University of Wales Press, 1995

Murray, Alexander (editor), *Sir William Jones, 1746–1794: A Commemoration*, Oxford and New York: Oxford University Press, 1998

The Journey to the West

Xijou Ji / Hsi-yu chi, 16th century

The Journey to the West, variously known as *Monkey*, the *Hsi-yu chi*, *Xiyou Ji*, *A Mission to Heaven*, *Record of a Journey to the West*, etc., is the English translation of a famous piece of classical Chinese fiction, attributed to Wu Ch'eng-en (c.1506–81), about whom little is known. In its different English versions, it is a combination of picaresque novel, folk epic, fabliau, Dante's *Divine Comedy* and Bunyan's *Pilgrim's Progress*, mixing satire, religious allegory, hagiography, history and farce into a rollicking tale. Told with tremendous verve and gusto, it is a fictionalized account of the pusillanimous Chinese Buddhist priest Tripitaka's 7th-century pilgrimage to India in search of Buddhist sutras, with his companions the heroic and roguish Monkey, Pigsy and Sandy, and their encounters with spirits, deities, demigods, ogres and monsters along the way.

Translations

Complete Versions

Jenner, W.J.F., *The Journey to the West*, 3 vols, Beijing: Foreign Languages Press, 1982–84; abridged version, with an introduction, Hong Kong: Commercial Press, 1994

Yu, Anthony C., *The Journey to the West*, with an introduction, 4 vols, Chicago: University of Chicago Press, 1977–83

Abridgements, Excerpts and Adaptations

Chai, Ch'u and Winberg Chai, *Hsi-yu Pu* in their *A Treasury of Chinese Literature: A New Prose Anthology*, New York: Appleton Century, 1965 (contains chapter 59, a 17th-century sequel to the *Xiyou Ji*)

Chan, Plato and Christina Chan, *The Magic Monkey, Adapted from an Old Chinese Legend*, New York: McGraw Hill, 1944

Hayes, Helen M., *The Buddhist Pilgrim's Progress: From the Shi Yeu Ki, "The Records of the Journey to the Western Paradise", by Wu Ch'eng-en*, New York: Dutton, and London: John Murray, 1930

Hsia, C.T. and Cyril Birch, "The Temptation of Saint Pigsy" in *An Anthology of Chinese Literature*, vol. 2, edited by Birch, New York: Grove Press, 1972 (contains chapter 23)

Richard, Timothy, *A Journey* [cover title: *Mission*] *to Heaven: A Great Chinese Epic and Allegory*, Shanghai: Christian Literature Society, 1913

Theiner, George, *The Monkey King*, edited by Zdena Novotna, London: Hamlyn, 1964 (abridged, translated from the Czech)

Waley, Arthur, *Monkey*, London: Allen and Unwin, 1942; with an introduction by Hu Shih, New York: Day, 1943; adapted for children as *The Adventures of Monkey*, New York: 1944

Wang, Chi-chen, "The Monkey King" in *Chinese Wit and Humor*, edited by G. Kao, New York: Sterling, 1974 (contains chapters 1–8)

Wang, Hsing-pei, *Monkey Subdues the White-Bone Demon*, Bejiing: Foreign Languages Press, 1958

Ware, James, "The Fairy-Land of China", *East of Asia Magazine*, 4 (1905) pp. 83–89, pp. 120–27

Werner, E.T.C., "How the Monkey Became a God" in his *Myths and Legends of China*, London: Harrap, 1922, pp. 325–69

Wilhelm, Richard (editor), *The Chinese Fairy Book*, New York: Stokes, 1921 (selections translated by Wilhelm from his German version)

Woodbridge, Samuel I., "The Golden-Horned Dragon King; or, The Emperor's Visit to the Spirit World", *North China Herald*, 1895

Yang, Hsien-yi and Gladys Yang, *Excerpts from Three Classical Chinese Novels*, Beijing: Chinese Literature, 1981 (chapters, 27, 59–61)

The history of the English translation of *The Journey to the West* shows a long genealogy of different renderings, in mixed modes, each with its own merits and defects. Best known to the English reader is perhaps Arthur WALEY's *Monkey* (1942). An abridgement that contains 30 chapters (1–15, 18–19, 22, 37–39, 44–49, 98–100) out of the 100 original chapters, it is a scintillating, natural-sounding and reasonably accurate translation of Wu Ch'eng-en's work. Waley says in his preface that those episodes he has retained have been translated almost in full, "leaving out, however, most of the incidental passages in verse, which go very badly into English". Caveats should, perhaps, be issued against Waley's omission of the original profusion of poems, since the poetry functions, among other things, to underscore the novel's structural and textual intent, and therefore any such omissions damage *ipso facto* the integral artistic design of the Chinese classic. This point, however, is controversial, since there exist different measures by which a rendering can be judged to be a legitimate mirroring of the original. Waley's translation also contains occasional minor errors, the most classic and anecdotal of which is perhaps the misrendering as "a red-legged immortal" of the original sense, "a bare-footed immortal".

Waley (1942) was published by Allen and Unwin in London. The American edition (1943) contains a scholarly introduction by Hu Shih, and a "Note on the Translation" in which Hu Shih points out a few passages at which his interpretation differs from Waley's. Waley's *tour de force* has undergone many other editions, including a 1944 adaptation for children.

To Waley's abridged version, W.J.F. JENNER's unabridged, 3-volume translation, *The Journey to the West* (1982–84), provides an alternative reading. Jenner has also provided an abridged version (1994), based on the complete version published by the Foreign Languages Press, Beijing, 1988. This abridgement, containing 34 chapters (about a quarter of the original translation) and a translator's introduction, covers the most entertaining and famous episodes of the story. Like Waley, Jenner has omitted nearly all of the verse passages in the novel.

Also an unabridged version, Anthony C. YU's 4-volume *The Journey to the West* (1977–83) is a scholarly exegesis of the Chinese work. Volume 1 (1977) contains a comprehensive introduction and chapter endnotes with generous citations from primary and secondary sources. It represents the extreme end of the translation spectrum that aims at faithful textual reproduction of the original work, complete with everything from recreation of verse passages, faithful transliterations of Taoist cinnabar alchemical terms and names for famous horses (chapter 4). Unfortunately, in his unswerving attempt at source-text oriented translation, Yu has largely defeated his own purpose of translating. How many English readers can understand such esoteric, reverential treatments as the retention of the lapidary four-syllabic lines, the rhyme scheme, etc. in the translated text? There are, in the source text, other similar cases of untranslatability where, simply, no English equivalents exist for the interplay of phonetic and semantic elements and for terms fraught with arcane Buddhist and alchemical meanings. The English reader, denied an intimate knowledge of such culture-bound elements, will simply fail to grasp the meanings of Yu's translation. Occupying no position in the English target literary polysystem, since it fails to secure the understanding of the target reader, Yu's rendering may thus lose the claim to the status of literary translation.

Waley's and Jenner's smooth-flowing, native English style distinguishes itself from Yu's rather stodgy, sometimes repetitive prose, cluttered with academic annotations, abbreviations, etc. The distinction between the two types can be understood if different criteria and audiences for translation are borne in mind. Waley's and Jenner's idiomatic translations represent an example of "a surrogate translation" that survives by virtue of its impact on the target monolingual readership, whereas Yu's academic rendering is that of "a contingent translation" helping the incipiently bilingual audience to access the original (Eoyang, 1993).

Apart from Waley's abridgement, and Jenner's and Yu's complete versions, there are other mixed modes of rendering the work, e.g. excerpts in translation, adaptations, translations plus summary, mediated translation, and self-translation from other translations of the Oriental classic.

Among the translated excerpts are: HSIA & BIRCH's rendering (1972) of chapter 23 of the original, "The Temptation of Saint Pigsy"; YANG & YANG's complete translation of chapters 27 and 59–61 (1981); James WARE's translated excerpts, "The Fairy-Land of China" (1905); Samuel I. WOODBRIDGE's translated excerpt, "The Golden-Horned Dragon King" (1895), based on S. Wells Williams's Chinese version; Chi-chen WANG's translation of selections, "The Monkey King" (chapters 1–8) (1974); and CHAI & CHAI's edition and translation of chapter 59, *Hsi-yu Pu*, the 17th-century sequel to the *Hsi-yu chi* (1965).

There are also various adaptations in English from the classic vernacular tale: E.T.C. WERNER's adaptation, "How the Monkey Became a God" (1922); Helen M. HAYES's adaptation, *The Buddhist Pilgrim's Progress* (1930); CHAN & CHAN's *The Magic Monkey* (1944); and Hsing-pei WANG's *Monkey Subdues the White-Bone Demon* (1958).

Another type of rendering is provided by Timothy RICHARD's translation of chapters 1–7 and summary of chapters 8–100 of the novel, *A Mission to Heaven* (1913), based on C.C. Qiu's Chinese version. There is also George THEINER's indirect English translation from the Czech, *The Monkey King* (1964). And Richard WILHELM self-translated into English his own German, synoptic renderings from the Oriental novel, and published them in New York in 1921, as chapters 17, 18, 69, and 74 in his *The Chinese Fairy Book*.

The dialectic between full translations and adaptations of *The Journey to the West* raises the controversial question of what constitutes the invariant core of the source text to be transferred in full by the reader-cum-interpreter translator (Bassnett-McGuire, 1980). The adoption of "a hierarchy of 'correction' between these categories" as a criterion by which to judge the relative merits of these renderings would appear to be a hermeneutic fallacy. Full translations and adaptations (as well as other modes of rendering) fulfil, in their own ways, their unique hermeneutic objectives, with the former category generally serving as accurate, critical exegesis of the original work, whereas the latter constitute a remoulding of original ideas for reception by a target readership with different socio-cultural conventions and literary tastes.

RAYMOND S.C. LIE

Further Reading

Anderson, G.L. (editor), *Masterpieces of the Orient*, enlarged edition, New York: Norton, 1977

Csongor, B., "A Comparative Analysis of *Shui-hu Chuan* and *Hsi-yu Chi*: The Bounds of the Classic Chinese Novel", *Acta Orientalia*, 29 (1975) pp. 1–6

Dudbridge, Glen, *The Hsi-yu chi: A Study of Antecedents to the Sixteenth-Century Chinese Novel*, Cambridge: Cambridge University Press, 1970

Dye, Harriet, "Notes for a Comparison of the *Odyssey* and *Monkey*", *Literature East and West*, 8 (1964) pp. 14–18

Eoyang, Eugene Chen, *The Transparent Eye: Reflections on Translation, Chinese Literature, and comparative poetics*, Honolulu: University of Hawaii Press, 1993

Fu, James S., *Mythic and Comic Aspects of the Quest: Hsi-yu Chi as seen through Don Quixote and Huckleberry Finn*, Singapore: Singapore University Press, 1977

Hightower, James R., *Topics in Chinese Literature: Outlines and Bibliographies*, revised edition, Cambridge, Massachusetts: Harvard University Press, 1962, pp. 104–05

Ota Tatsuo, "A New Study on the Formation of the *Hsi-yu chi*", in *Acta Asiatica*, 32 (1977) pp. 96–113

Plaks, Andrew H., "Allegory in *Hsi-yu chi* and *Hung-lou Meng*", *Chinese Narrative: Critical and Theoretical Essays*, edited by Plaks, Princeton, New Jersey: Princeton University Press, 1977

Waley, Arthur, *The Real Tripitaka, and Other Pieces*, London: Allen and Unwin, and New York: Macmillan, 1952

Attila József 1905–1937

Hungarian poet

Biography

Born in Budapest, Hungary, 11 April 1905, to poor working-class parents. His father abandoned the family and emigrated to the US when József was three years old, and his mother worked as a maid and a washerwoman to support the family. She died in 1919, and József tried to commit suicide shortly afterwards. Although desperately poor, he went to high school and later to the University of Szeged to study Hungarian and French literature. At the age of 17 he started writing poetry for the radical Hungarian literary journal *Nyugat* [The West]. When his first collection of poetry, *Szépség koldusa* [Beggar of Beauty], was published, in 1922, he was expelled from the university because of its revolutionary content. He continued his studies in Vienna and Paris. He was influenced there by the philosophy of Hegel and by Marxist political thought. He returned to Budapest and joined the Communist Party, writing poetry for circulation in its illegal broadsheets. He was expelled from the party in 1930 for his opposition to party doctrine. He founded the literary journal *Valosag* in 1932 and in 1936 co-founded the review *Szep Szo*. He was fined by the authorities in Budapest for protesting against the execution of two prominent Hungarian communists. The last years of József's life were dominated by his increasingly schizophrenic condition and his mental instability. He underwent psychoanalysis, which did not improve his situation. He produced much work during this period, however, and began to achieve an international reputation for his proletarian poetry. He stayed in a mental hospital for a short time in 1937 and appeared to recover from his illness. Later that year, however, he committed suicide by throwing himself under a train. Died in Balatonszárszó, Hungary, 3 December 1937.

After József's death his lyrical poetry became popular, particularly during the communist regime in Hungary, and was widely read in the rest of Europe; József came to be considered one of Hungary's major poets of the 20th century. His best-known poems were written towards the end of his life. His later collections include *Nincs bocsánat* [There is No Pardon], 1936–37 and *Utsoló versek* [Last Poems], 1937. His collection *Medvetánc* (*Bear's Dance*), 1934, was a result of his friendship with the composer Béla Bartók.

Translations

Selections

Bátki, John, *Attila József: Selected Poems and Texts*, edited by George Gömöri and James Atlas, with an introduction by Gömöri, Cheadle Hulme, Cheshire: Carcanet, 1973

Hargitai, Peter, *Perched on Nothing's Branch: Selected Poetry of Attila József*, with an introduction by David Kirby, Tallahassee, Florida: Apalachee Press, 1993

Kabdebo, Thomas (editor), *Attila József: Poems*, London: Danubia, 1966 (20 poems translated by Thomas Kabdebo, Michael Beevor, Michael Hamburger, John Szekely, and Vernon Watkins)

Morgan, Edwin, in his *Sweeping Out the Dark*, Manchester: Carcanet, 1994

Nyerges, Anton N., *Poems of Attila József*, with an introduction, Buffalo, New York: Hungarian Cultural Foundation, 1973

Anthologies and Reviews

Gatto, Katherine Gyékényesi (editor and translator), *Treasury of Hungarian Love Poems, Quotations and Proverbs in Hungarian and English*, New York: Hippocrene, 1996

Grosz, Joseph and W. Arthur Boggs (editors), *Hungarian Anthology: A Collection of Poems*, 2nd edition, Toronto: Pannonia, 1966

Kunz, Egon (editor), *Hungarian Poetry*, Sydney: Pannonia, 1955

Morgan, Edwin, in *New Hungarian Quarterly* (Summer 1968)

Novak, M.P. and Béla Királyfalvi, in *Hudson Review*, 20/4 (1967) and in *Kenyon Review*, 3 (1968)

Sutter, Ruth, in *Chicago Review*, 18/1 (1965)

Zion, Matthew and George Gömöri, in *New Writing of East Europe*, edited by Gömöri and Charles Newman, Chicago: Quadrangle, 1968

BÁTKI's 1973 translation, and George Gömöri's introduction to it, attempt to display the totality of the poet Attila József as a writer and human being. The prose translations of "Curriculum Vitae", the sketch "Suicide", and three letters are of particular value in enabling an English-reading public to grasp and appreciate the essence of his work, as a manifesto for the outcast, the marginalized, the underdog. The particularly complicated nature of much of József's political poetry – Marxist philosophy embodied in intricately rhymed and structured stanzas – has made it almost impossible to translate (although it has been attempted by several of the translators listed above) without the translator sharing the linguistic dexterity and intense political posture as that possessed by József himself. So we find a preponderance of personal poetry (such as GATTO's translation) over political poetry in Bátki's translations, much of it conveying the dialectical and innovative nature of József's poetry as a whole. As Bátki states in his introduction, his poetic translations are to be viewed as a bridge, not a betrayal. The translator's knowledge of Hungarian has helped him tremendously to deliver in contemporary English the tone, the essence of a human situation, and the landscape of József's verse. The 50 poems included in this anthology are arranged in something approaching chronological order, starting with 1923 and continuing up to poems from 1937, the year of József's suicide, and reflect the evolution of József's political thought, which culminated in a call for a democratic and humanistic socialism.

NYERGES (1973) chooses to call his translations of József's poems an experiment, based more on instinct than any particular *modus operandi*. He circumvents conventional translation, and at times does violence to József's form, justifying this technique by alluding to József's own unorthodoxy in matters of form. Nyerges's rationale seems to be to familiarize the western reader, in any way possible, with József's ability to capture in verse a specificity and concreteness about social and economic life that was unique and original. At times this specificity in English does stretch our aesthetic tolerance, such as when he uses the word "auricles" to translate the Hungarian word for heart in the poem "Weary Man". In fact, Nyerges, as translator, is criticized by Hargitai for superimposing his own unique poetics over the original aesthetic strategy of the poet himself. Nevertheless, Nyerges's volume is a valuable contribution to educating the English-speaking world about József and his oeuvre. The anthology offers a well-written introduction, and notes explain the poetic references and the circumstances in which the poems were written. The list of selected readings and the English-Hungarian table of contents help make this the most complete work in English about József's poetic output.

HARGITAI's translations (1993) of 40 of József's poems are the most natural and colloquial versions in English. An award-winning translator, and a perfectly bilingual Hungarian-American poet, Hargitai brings to his translations an unsurpassed knowledge of idioms and ear for the diction of the common man. He examines the process of translation, and in particular of translating József's poetry, in a 1983 article (see Further Reading) in which he defines his approach to translation as an attempt to convey the relationships between poetic structure and content. He strives to capture the aesthetic effect – the essence – as well as the aesthetic strategy of József's poetry. A given strategy will produce a given effect, but neither rendering only the structure nor conveying only the content is sufficient. Hargitai places great emphasis on form, and on József's deviation from traditional forms, as indications of his originality. Hargitai's translations reflect a faithfulness above all to József's aesthetic effect, but try to remain as faithful as possible to form, diction, syntactic constructions, and sense of line.

MORGAN's *Sweeping Out the Dark* (1994) contains 25 poetic translations of József's poems, presented in chronological order from the early "Heart-Innocent" to some of the last poems. His translations are as true to form and content as possible and have been criticized for only a few instances of misunderstanding the intent of the original. It is the most recent attempt to further critical interest in one of Hungary's most important 20th-century poets.

KATHERINE GYÉKÉNYESI GATTO

Further Reading

Czigány, Loránt, *The Oxford History of Hungarian Literature*, Oxford: Clarendon Press, and New York: Oxford University Press, 1984

Hargitai, Peter, "Problems of Translating Attila József", *Translation Review*, 12 (1983)

Klaniczay, Tibor (editor), *A History of Hungarian Literature*, translated by József Hatvany and Miklós Szabolesi, Budapest: Corvina Press, 1982

Reményi, Joseph, *Hungarian Writers and Literature: Modern Novelists, Critics, and Poets*, New Brunswick, New Jersey: Rutgers University Press, 1964

Juvenal c.AD 50 to 65–after 130

Roman satirist

Biography

Born Decimus Junius Juvenalis, c.AD 50–65, or perhaps later. He was probably born in Aquinum, in the Volscian country. Few details of his life are known: he may have been a member of a wealthy elite, since he does not mention a patron. Accounts of his army career and exile by Domitian have no foundation. Juvenal is mentioned by the writer Martial, and was acquainted with him; otherwise he was not well known in his own lifetime. Died after AD 130.

Juvenal is known solely for his 16 *Satires*, probably written at the beginning of the 2nd century, during the reigns of the emperors Trajan and Hadrian. Juvenal's *Satires* , written in hexameter verse in a rhetorical style, provide an angry, indignant and later ironically detached commentary on the corruption and vices of contemporary Roman society, and have been much studied and translated by later writers, notably by the English dramatist John Dryden.

Satires

Satirae, AD 110–30

Translations

Creekmore, Hubert, *Satires: A New Translation*, New York: New American Library, 1963

Dryden, John *et al.*, *The Satires of Decimus Junius Juvenalis: Translated into English Verse*, London: printed for Jacob Tonson, 1693

Gifford, William, *The Satires of D.J. Juvenalis*, London, 1802

Green, Peter, *The Sixteen Satires: Juvenal*, Harmondsworth and Baltimore: Penguin, 1967

Holyday, Barten, *D.J. Juvenal and A. Persius Flaccus Translated*, Oxford: W. Downing, 1673

Humphries, Rolfe, *The Satires of Juvenal*, Bloomington: Indiana University Press, 1958

Johnson, Samuel, *London: A Poem in Imitation of the Third Satire of Juvenal*, London: printed for R. Dodsley, 1738

Johnson, Samuel, *The Vanity of Human Wishes: The Tenth Satire of Juvenal*, London: R. Dodsley, 1749

Lowell, Robert, "The Vanity of Human Wishes" in his *Near the Ocean*, New York: Farrar Straus, and London: Faber, 1967

Robinson, Steven, *Juvenal: Sixteen Satires upon the Ancient Harlot*, with an introduction, Manchester: Carcanet New Press, 1983

Rudd, Niall, *The Satires*, introduction and notes by William Barr, Oxford: Clarendon Press, and New York: Oxford University Press, 1991

Stapylton, Sir Robert, *Juvenal's Sixteen Satyrs; or, A Survey of the Manners and Actions of Mankind*, London: Humphrey Moseley, 1647

Juvenal's satires combine moral passion with vivid language. He offers us what is perhaps the most compelling of all surviving evocations of the life of Rome in the first century AD. In his use of naturalistic detail, his controlled sarcasm, his hyperbole, his complex rhetoric, and much else, Juvenal's poetic achievement is one of the triumphs of Roman literature. In its abundance of pointed phrases, its large rhetorical units, and its abundance of topical and historical reference, it confronts a would-be translator with many difficulties. These are compounded by many textual problems.

STAPYLTON's pioneering translation (1647) is always workmanlike, but cannot often rise to an appropriate pitch of intensity. Stapylton's heroic couplets do not fully exploit the rhetorical possibilities of rhyme; the many open couplets are often merely diffuse. The extensive notes provide an interesting insight into Renaissance interpretations of Juvenal.

The posthumously published translation of Barten HOLYDAY (1673) is pedantically faithful, but at a considerable cost. As Dryden wrote in his *Discourse of Satire* prefaced to the translation of 1693: "If rendring the exact Sense ... almost line for line, had been our business, *Barten Holiday* had done it already ... .And, by the help of his Learned Notes and Illustrations, not only *Juvenal*, and *Persius*, but what is yet more obscure, his own Verses might be understood".

Altogether different in quality is the collaborative translation supervised by DRYDEN (1693). Dryden translated Satires I, III, VI, X and XVI. The other translators were Nahum TATE (II, XV), Richard DUKE (IV), William BOWLES (V), Charles DRYDEN (VII), George STEPNEY (VIII), Stephen HERVEY (IX), William CONGREVE (XI), Thomas POWER (XII), Thomas CREECH (XIII) and John DRYDEN, Jr (XIV). Dryden probably "polished" the work of the other contributors. The whole is one of the masterpieces of English verse translation. In variety and control of tone, in witty use of rhyme, in emotional and moral power, in their assured command of the available technical resources, the best of these versions (e.g that of Satire X) more than justify their relative "freedom".

The 1693 Juvenal is "betwixt a Paraphrase and Imitation" (Dryden, *Discourse of Satire*); the versions of Satire III (*London*) and X (*The Vanity of Human Wishes*) made by JOHNSON (1738; 1749) are fully-fledged imitations. With his modernization of references Johnson illuminates parallels; in the process of his metamorphosis of the originals a Christian gravity effectively replaces Juvenal's violence of temper.

GIFFORD (1802) had already shown himself a fierce satirist in poems such as the *Baviad* (1794) and the *Maeviad* (1796) before he came to translation. His couplets lack the sheer vigour of Dryden but are frequently pointed in the precision of their attack. He found in Juvenal "an awful and impressive sublimity" and it is after such effects that his translation strives.

Gifford's long remained the standard version; it is only in relatively recent times that there have appeared several translations in verse deserving serious attention. Rolfe HUMPHRIES (1958) abandons the heroic couplets that had hitherto been the norm, working, rather, in unrhymed dactylic hexameters ("only roughly scannable, with here and there an iamb", as Humphries himself puts it). His idiom is generally lively and attractive (though the absence of notes of any kind will make it difficult to follow for many readers), but anachronisms like a "space ship" or a "strip-tease broad" are distracting. Certainly we are at something of a remove from Gifford's "sublimity".

CREEKMORE (1963) also employs hexameters, rather more strictly than Humphries, but this time in rhyming couplets. Though there are successes (VI works well, for the most part), the form becomes wearing at length. Some of Creekmore's updatings of allusions are less than happy – Steve Reeves is a poor substitute for Corbulo (III.251).

GREEN (1967) also uses hexameters (unrhymed) – with fair freedom – and is unafraid of modern colloquialism. He sometimes sidesteps the difficulties of Juvenal's references by, to use his own terms, substituting the function for the name. So when Juvenal names T. Annius Milo (II), Green omits the name and talks, instead, of "gangsters". Though immediate comprehensibility is certainly enhanced, the texture of Juvenal's verse is crucially changed. Green's is an accomplished, informed and scholarly translation, though it is not poetry of the highest order.

The version – in blank verse – of Satire X by Robert LOWELL (1967) has a bare clarity that is impressive. Much detail is stripped away and the result has an impressive trenchancy.

ROBINSON (1983) is characterized by a crabbed obscurity, presumably designed to "preserve the strangeness", which Robinson's introduction sees as one of the aims of translation. Though there are some intriguing local effects, this is not, one suspects, a version to which many readers will return with any frequency.

RUDD (1991) is altogether more accessible, though not through the kind of populism of which Robinson is suspicious. Rudd is learned, scrupulous and lucid. His hexameters (again unrhymed) are mostly fluent; his annotation is consistently helpful. It is not surprising that Juvenal should have been of particular interest to our times. In Humphries, Green and Rudd we have three thoroughly competent modern versions; we have yet, however, to produce a translation as genuinely poetical as Dryden's.

GLYN PURSGLOVE

Further Reading

Broderson, G.L., "Seventeenth-Century Translations of Juvenal", *The Phoenix: The Journal of the Classical Association of Canada*, 7 (1953) pp. 57–76

Highet, Gilbert, *Juvenal the Satirist: A Study*, Oxford: Clarendon Press, 1954; New York: Oxford University Press, 1961

Rudd, Niall (editor), *Johnson's Juvenal: London and the Vanity of Human Wishes*, Bristol: Bristol Classical Press, 1981

See also the prefatory material to the translations of Dryden, Green, Robinson and Rudd

K

Kabir c.1448–c.1518

Indian mystic and poet

Biography

Born c.1448 in Vārānasī (Benares), Uttar Pradesh, India. Details of his life are conjectural and unreliable. According to legend, he was born to a Brahmin widow who abandoned him at an early age: some authorities report his divine virginal birth after his mother visited a Hindu shrine. Kabir was probably adopted by an impoverished Muslim weaver. Brought up as a Muslim, Kabir later became interested in Hinduism, particularly the teachings of the Vaisnava *bhakti* master Rāmānanda, of whom he became the most famous disciple. Kabir went on to establish his own religious teaching, *sahaja-yoga* ("simple union") which drew on both Hindu and Muslim doctrines, as well as Sufi mysticism. His devotional poetry was sung or spoken, and was apparently unwritten until recorded by others during and after his lifetime. Kabir's poetry was highly influential among the common people of North India, and as a result he was persecuted by both the Brahmins and the Muslim community; he was eventually exiled from Benares by the Muslim emperor, Sikandar Lōdī. Died in Maghar, c.1518.

The major written texts of Kabir's work are the *Bījak* [Account Book], compiled by a disciple some time in the 17th century, and his poems in the sacred book of the Sikhs, the *Ādi Granth*, compiled in 1604.

Translations

Selections

Sethi, V.K., *Kabir: The Weaver of God's Name*, Amritsar, Punjab: Radha Soami Satsang Beas, 1984

Vaudeville, Charlotte, *Kabir*, vol. 1, with an introduction, Oxford: Clarendon Press, 1974

Vaudeville, Charlotte, *A Weaver Named Kabir: Selected Verses*, with an introduction, Delhi and New York: Oxford University Press, 1993

Poetry

Ādi Granth (compiled 1604)

Dass, Nirmal, *Songs of Kabir from the Ādi Granth*, with an introduction, Albany: State University of New York Press, 1991

Bījak (compiled 17th century)

Hess, Linda and Shukdev Singh, *The Bījak of Kabir*, San Francisco: North Point Press, 1983

Hess, Linda and Shukdev Singh, *A Touch of Grace: Songs of Kabir*, Boston: Shambhala, 1994

Shah, Ahmad, *The Bijak of Kabir*, Hamirpur, India: privately printed, 1917

Oral and Popular Traditions

Bly, Robert, *The Kabir Book: Forty-Four of the Ecstatic Poems*, Boston: Beacon Press, 1977

Lorenzen, David N., "Kabir's Most Popular Songs", chapter 5 in *Praises to a Formless God: Nirguni Texts from North India*, Albany: State University of New York Press, 1996

Tagore, Rabindranath with Evelyn Underhill, *One Hundred Poems of Kabir*, with an introduction by Underhill, London: Macmillan, 1915

Kabir was an oral poet-singer who lived in Vārānasī, on the bank of the Ganges River in North India, and who by all accounts never wrote down a word. Tradition has it that he was illiterate, and some of his most frequently repeated couplets satirize pandits who can read and expound on millions of words but are ignorant of the one syllable that could set them free. Before discussing translators of Kabir, we must ask: What were they translating? Where do the texts come from?

We can only surmise that some people started writing down songs and aphorisms of Kabir during his lifetime. Raised in an obscure family of Muslim weavers, Kabir acquired fame and a growing following as he continued to perform his powerful, at once iconoclastic and mystical utterances. Religious poetry in North India conventionally carries the name of the poet in a signature line near the end of each lyric. So songs attributed to Kabir spread swiftly on the currents of oral performance. This kind of dissemination breeds change; memory and creativity play tricks with the received version; whole songs can be fabricated in a voice approximating the poet's and inserted into the tradition with the tag, "Kabir says". This is the exuberant and semi-anonymous nature of oral tradition and has nothing to do with dishonesty.

Written traditions coalesced as sectarian groups created Kabir collections. The earliest confirmed date for such a collection is 1604, the year in which the Sikh sacred scripture *Ādi Granth* reached its final form. The *Ādi Granth* contains poems by Sikh gurus and other revered saints, including hundreds attributed to Kabir. Though the Kabir Panth (sect) claims that its sacred text, the *Bījak*, was recorded in the poet's lifetime, historical evidence supports, at the earliest, a 17th-century compilation. The Dadu Panth of Rajasthan also amassed major manuscript collections of poetry. Anthologies of Kabir verses culled from Dadu Panth manuscripts are often called *Granthavali* but may more properly be designated as Rajasthani traditions. From these sources eventually came printed versions, attempts at critical editions, and translations. The oral tradition is still very much alive. After decades of exclusive interest in traditionally sanctioned written collections, there are signs of fresh scholarly interest in the oral and popular.

With Kabir, then, source texts are in motion. Of the three major written traditions, only the *Ādi Granth* corpus has remained fixed for nearly four centuries. The *Bījak* has two major recensions. The Rajasthani tradition is most fluid of all, based on widely varying manuscripts from which it is very difficult to construct a critical edition. Differences in translations occur not only because of the usual differences between translators and historical periods but also because of the fluidity of the sources. Kabir's style, content, and belief system can vary dramatically, depending on which part of the river of Kabir tradition one dips into for text.

The history of important English translations of Kabir begins with Rabindranath TAGORE, the Bengali poet who in 1913 became the first non-European to win the Nobel Prize. His 1915 renderings of 100 poems were done in consultation with the English writer on mysticism, Evelyn Underhill, who wrote the book's introduction. The originals from which they worked did not come from any old manuscript tradition but rather demonstrate the dynamic nature of oral tradition. Tagore's friend, Bengali scholar K.M. Sen, collected Kabir songs, mostly as sung by wandering ascetics; Hindi transcriptions with Bengali renderings were published in 1910–11. These, along with unpublished English versions by another friend, were the bases of Tagore's *One Hundred Poems*. His translations wear remarkably well, though the style is certainly dated. The selection reflects both popular tradition and Tagore's own mystical and literary taste. This Kabir is less caustic and more constantly ecstatic than the sharp-eyed observer of society who appears in older collections.

About 60 years after *One Hundred Poems*, the American poet Robert BLY (1977) revised 44 of Tagore's versions in his own style. Bly comments: "The English of the Tagore-Underhill translations is hopeless, and I simply put a few of them, whose interiors I had become especially fond of, into more contemporary language ..." Bly made the songs far more alive to the modern ear, taking liberties, of course, as he did so. He made no pretense of having consulted the original language. An example of Tagore's lines and Bly's transformations:

> Within this earthen vessel are bowers and groves, and within it is the Creator:
> Within this vessel are the seven oceans and the unnumbered stars ...
> And within this vessel the Eternal soundeth, and the spring wells up.
> Kabir says: "Listen to me, my friend! My beloved Lord is within."
>
> (Tagore)

> Inside this clay jug there are canyons and pine mountains, and the maker of canyons and pine mountains!
> All seven oceans are inside, and hundreds of millions of stars ...
> And the music from the strings that no one touches, and the source of all water.
> If you want the truth, I will tell you the truth:
> Friend, listen: the God whom I love is inside.
>
> (Bly)

Certainly TAGORE and BLY, both based on the same early 20th-century source, account for the majority of people in the English speaking world who have known and admired Kabir.

Scholars have taken a different approach, seeking the earliest and most reliable texts, carefully documenting and annotating their work. The dean of scholar-translators in the Euro-American world is Charlotte VAUDEVILLE. Her 1974 and 1993 selections represent stages in her effort to translate ever more reliable source texts. The former provides many hundreds of *sakhis*, Kabir's aphoristic couplets. The latter presents many *pads* or song texts, with a much smaller selection of *sakhis* ("witnesses", i.e. pithy sayings). Both volumes include long, masterful introductions on Kabir, his historical period, religious environment, and textual sources (1993 largely reproducing 1974, but with some significant revisions); both provide concordances. The translations have the virtues of Vaudeville's profound learning, with many notes and strenuous efforts to preserve old texts while jettisoning recent additions. They are clear and accessible, though somewhat burdened with archaisms and not literarily exciting.

DASS (1991) for the first time provides a complete English translation, in a single book, of the verses attributed to Kabir in the *Ādi Granth*. This is an important contribution. Dass is a reliable scholar and again offers clear, accessible translations with useful notes, introduction, and other apparatus.

SHAH (1917), while a very poor translation, remains the only complete English version of the *Bījak*.

HESS & SINGH (1983) provides approximately half of the *Bījak* text and includes substantial essays and notes by Hess. Published by a literary press, this translation aims at poetic quality and intensity as well as scholarly reliability. Hess & Singh 1994 is an abridged version of 1983.

A preface to SETHI (1984) says: "The primary aim of the translations has been to bring out the spiritual meaning that is the essence of Kabir's compositions." Published by the Radha Soami sect, which claims Kabir as one of its saints, this collection mingles old manuscript traditions with modern devotional song collections. But it clearly marks the source of each poem.

Vaudeville, Dass, Hess & Singh, and Sethi can be used together by readers who wish to compare translations of numbered poems from the important older collections.

Invaluable for anyone who wishes to look more deeply into the original Hindi sources of Kabir is Callewaert and Op de Beeck (1991). For decades Callewaert has been collecting manuscripts in western India and preparing editions, word indices, and dictionaries of Kabir as well as other important medieval poets. While 1991 is a landmark work, Callewaert has a forthcoming edition of Kabir based on older and more reliable manuscripts.

LINDA HESS

Further Reading

Callewaert, Winand M. and Bart Op de Beeck, *Nirguna bhakti sagara / Devotional Hindi Literature: A Critical Edition of the Panc-Vani, or, Five Works of Dadu, Kabir, Namdev, Raidas, Hardas, with the Hindi Songs of Gorakhnath and Sundardas, and a Complete Word-Index*, 2 vols, New Delhi: Manohar, 1991

Hess, Linda, "Three Kabir Collections: A Comparative Study" in *The Sants: Studies in a Devotional Tradition of India*, edited by Karine Schomer and W.H. McLeod, Berkeley, California: Religious Studies Series, and Delhi: Motilal Banarsidass, 1987

Lorenzen, David N., *Kabir Legends and Ananta-das's Kabir Parachai*, Albany: State University of New York Press, 1991

Franz Kafka 1883–1924

Czech-Austrian German-language novelist and short-story writer

Biography

Born in Prague, in the Austro-Hungarian Empire (now capital of the Czech Republic), 3 July 1883. He was the son of a wealthy Jewish businessman, and attended German-speaking schools in Prague, later studying law, at the insistence of his father, at the German Karl Ferdinand University in Prague, gaining a doctorate in 1906. He worked for an insurance company in Prague from 1908. He was engaged twice to a Berlin woman, Felice Bauer, but they never married. Kafka wrote a number of short stories and longer fiction during this time, including the novella *Die Verwandlung* (*The Metamorphosis*), published in 1915, and the story collections *Ein Landarzt* [A Country Doctor] and *In der Strafkolonie* (*In the Penal Colony*), both published in 1919. He contracted tuberculosis in 1917, and was confined intermittently in a sanatorium 1919–21. In 1922 ill-health eventually forced him to retire from his employment. He moved to Berlin in 1923 to concentrate on writing and get away from his authoritarian family; there he met and lived with a Jewish socialist, Dora Dymant, who accompanied him back to Prague in early 1924 when his health deteriorated. Kafka spent his last months in a sanatorium in Kierling, near Vienna. Died 3 June 1924 in Kierling.

Kafka published relatively little. Of his best-known and most influential works, only *Die Verwandlung* came out during his lifetime. His famous novels, *Der Prozess* (*The Trial*), *Das Schloss* (*The Castle*) and *Amerika* (*America*), were published posthumously in 1925, 1926 and 1927 respectively by his close friend and executor Max Brod, despite Kafka's instructions in his will that his writings be destroyed.

The Trial

Der Prozess, 1925 (written 1914–15)

Translations and Adaptations

Berkoff, Steven, *The Trial and Metamorphosis: Two Theatre Adaptations from Franz Kafka*, Ambergate, Derbyshire: Amber Lane Press, 1981

Berkoff, Steven, *The Trial, Metamorphosis, In the Penal Colony: Three Theatre Adaptations from Franz Kafka*, Oxford: Amber Lane Press, 1988

Mitchell, Breon, *The Trial: A New Translation Based on the Restored Text*, New York: Schocken, 1998

Muir, Willa and Edwin Muir, *The Trial*, London: Gollancz, and New York: Knopf, 1937; definitive edition, Harmondsworth: Penguin, 1953; New York: Schocken, 1968

Muir, Willa and Edwin Muir, *The Trial*, definitive edition, revised, with additional chapters and notes by E.M. Butler, London: Secker and Warburg, 1956; New York: Knopf, 1957

Parry, Idris, *The Trial*, Harmondsworth: Penguin, 1994

Pinter, Harold, *The Trial*, London and Boston: Faber, 1993

Scott, Douglas and Chris Waller, *The Trial*, with an introduction by J.P. Stern, London: Pan, 1977

The MUIRS' translation (1937) is still the classic version of Kafka's novel in English read throughout the world in popular editions. All the later translations are to a certain extent "based" on their version, or at least have to take it into account. No one could deny the quality of the writing – its ability to render Kafka's words so "easily and naturally" – produced by this husband and wife team, Edwin a poet in his own right and Willa a "precisian" (as they call the door-keeper in the parable "Before the Law"). The influence of their Scots Calvinist background has been identified in the text, and parallels have been drawn between the Muirs' "provincial" use of English and the "colonial" purity of Kafka's "Prager Deutsch" as described by Wagenbach. Certainly the interpretation of Kafka's writing in Britain and the United States as "religious allegory" was deeply affected by the introductory note to their translation of *The Castle* (1930), in which Edwin Muir likens K's attempts to grapple with the Castle authorities to Bunyan's *Pilgrim's*

Progress. The Muirs also firmly established the English title of the novel *The Trial*, losing the secondary reference to "process", i.e. development, and replacing it with the element of "trial and tribulation", i.e. suffering.

The early progress of Kafka's novel in its English version, as in the German, was dominated by Max Brod's hand in the editing of the text and his desire to emphasize the "religious humour" of the writing. Indeed all translators since the Muirs have had to take a position on what constitutes the "definitive" text. The Muirs accepted Brod's arrangement of the unfinished novel: the order of the chapters, the chapter headings and the exclusion of the "fragments" and deleted passages. The Muirs' first version in fact included Brod's addition of the last four lines to round off chapter 8. Some later editions of the Muirs' translation carry Brod's admission: "This chapter was never completed." Likewise, most editions of their translation are accompanied by Brod's "postscript to the first edition".

BUTLER's revision of the text (1956) was to be a "new edition with additional material", i.e. an appendix consisting of the unfinished chapters and fragments along with the passages deleted by the author. Uyttersprot's suggestions as to a reordering of the chapters had appeared in a monograph in 1953. They were not, however, persuasive enough, despite his acceptance of this thesis, to cause Butler to reorganize the text by, for example, including of the fragment "Staatsanwalt" ("Public Prosecutor") as a prologue to the story, which would have ruined the effect of the universally known opening to the novel. This is of course understandable given the widespread view that the openings (and endings) in Kafka's writing are the "key" to the interpretation of the texts. Butler's revision tidies up the most glaring eccentricities of the Muirs' version, but Butler's own suggestion of "traduced" in place of the Muirs' "Someone must have *been telling lies about* Joseph K." (my italics) for the memorable opening sentence has fortunately been changed back in most later editions of the Muirs' text.

The 1977 SCOTT & WALLER version amends this to: "spreading lies about Josef K." The spelling of the central character's name in this way is symptomatic of the alienation effect at work in their version. This distancing of the story to an imaginary *Mitteleuropa* is heralded by J.P. Stern's identification, in his introduction, of the popular conception of "the Kafkaesque" as "weird". This tendency of the translation is emphasized by the picture on the front cover of the Picador paperback edition reinforcing the image of oddity, madness even. Unlike the Muirs, these translators were aware of the literary reception and influence of Kafka's writing, particularly in the non-German-speaking world, e.g. parallels with the writing of Beckett and Borges. Their aim is to capture the "flat, colloquial style" and "lustreless informality" of the original, avoiding "the formal and occasionally solemn diction of the previous version". The highlighting of the grotesque and the surrealistic fits in with the reception of Kafka's writing as part of the Yiddish comic tradition, while the presence of masochistic or fetishistic elements supports psychological and psychoanalytic interpretations. Like the popular versions of the Muirs' translation, this version excludes the fragments and emendations, presumably on the grounds that they would only further confuse the already confused casual reader. The breaking up of the text on the page, particularly the dialogue, preempts the adaptations of the novel for the stage and screen by BERKOFF (1981) and PINTER (1993), which naturally play on dramatic elements within the story, turning the fluidity of the novel into a series of static "tableaux". For instance, Berkoff changes the Inspector's inquisitorial request for the newly arrested man to confirm his identity: "Josef K?" into an accusatorial: "VOICE [loudly]: 'Josef K!'".

PARRY's "new translation" of the novel (1994) reinforces this matter-of-fact quality in his rendering of the opening sentence as "Someone must have made a false accusation against Josef K." In general his version makes the details of the story more explicit, "literal" and concrete, in keeping with recent tendencies in Kafka criticism towards treating the text as a literary artefact based on Kafka's recorded despair at the inescapability of metaphor. Thus Josef K.'s acting out his arrest to Fräulein Bürstner ends with him kissing her "on the mouth and then all over her face like a thirsty animal who scours with his tongue the surface of a spring he has found at last". At the "Entscheidung" of Josef K.'s case, when the narrator interprets Kafka's comments on the manner of his death, the moralizing intentionality of the MUIRS' version: "... as if he meant the shame of it to outlive him", made somewhat ambiguous by SCOTT & WALLER with: "... as if the shame of it should outlive him", becomes for Parry almost a statement of fact: "... as if the shame would outlive him". Parry is clearly interested in relating the details of the story to Kafka's life, in keeping with the recent return to a biographical approach to Kafka's writing – his diaries and letters to Felice, Milena Jesenská and his father – which interprets it as a critique of the social situation by a "representative man" of the 20th century.

A new translation by Breon MITCHELL, "based on the restored text" of *The Trial*, was published in 1998.

ANTHONY MATHEWS

Further Reading

Crick, Joyce, "Kafka and the Muirs" in *The World of Franz Kafka*, edited by J.P. Stern, London: Weidenfeld and Nicolson, and New York: Holt Rinehart, 1980, pp. 159–74

Gray, Ronald, "But Kafka Wrote in German" in *The Kafka Debate: New Perspectives for Our Time*, edited by Angel Flores, New York: Gordian Press, 1977

Jakob, Dieter, "Das Kafka-Bild in England, 1928–1966", *Oxford German Studies*, 5 (1970) pp. 90–143

Kafka, Franz, *Der Prozess, in der Fassung der Handschrift: Textband; Kritische Ausgabe*, edited by Malcolm Pasley, Frankfurt: Fischer, 1990

Kafka, Franz, *Der Prozess, in der Fassung der Handschrift: Apparatband; Kritische Ausgabe*, edited by Malcolm Pasley, Frankfurt: Fischer, 1990

Mathews, Anthony, "The Influence of Translation on the Interpretation of Kafka's *The Trial*" (thesis), Norwich: University of East Anglia, 1985

Mellown, Elgin W., "The Development of a Criticism: Edwin Muir and Franz Kafka", *Comparative Literature*, 16 (1964) pp. 310–21

Muir, Edwin, *An Autobiography*, London: Hogarth Press, and New York: Sloane Associates, 1954

Muir, Edwin, "To Franz Kafka" in his *Collected Poems 1921–1958*, London: Faber, 1960

Muir, Edwin and Willa Muir, "Translating from the German"

in *On Translation*, edited by Reuben A. Brower, New York: Oxford University Press, 1966

Pasley, Malcolm, "Kafka's *Der Prozess*: What the Manuscript Can Tell Us", *Oxford German Studies*, 18/19 (1989–90) pp. 122–118

Uyttersprot, H., *Eine neue Ordnung der Werke Kafkas? Zur Struktur von "Der Prozess" und "Amerika"*, Antwerp: C. de Vries-Brouwers, 1957

The Castle and America

Das Schloss, 1926 (written 1921–22)
Amerika, 1927 (*Der Verschollene*, written 1911–14)

Translations

Das Schloss, 1926

Harman, Mark, *The Castle: A New Translation Based on the Restored Text*, New York: Schocken, 1998

Muir, Willa and Edwin Muir, *The Castle*, London: Secker and Warburg, and New York: Knopf, 1930; definitive edition, with additional material translated by Eithne Wilkins and Ernst Kaiser, London: Secker and Warburg, 1953; New York: Knopf, 1957; several reprints

Underwood, J.A., *The Castle*, with an introduction by Idris Parry, Harmondsworth: Penguin, 1997

Amerika, 1927

Hofmann, Michael, *The Man Who Disappeared (Amerika)*, Harmondsworth: Penguin, 1996

Muir, Willa and Edwin Muir, *America*, London: Routledge and Kegan Paul, 1938; New York: New Directions, 1940; definitive edition, London: Secker and Warburg, and New York: Schocken, 1949

Kafka's last novel, *The Castle*, was the first to be translated by the MUIRS (1930) and Edwin Muir's introductory note had a profound influence on the reception of Kafka's writing as a whole in Britain and the United States (see entry on *The Trial* above). It is, however, quite remarkable that until J.A. UNDERWOOD's new translation (1997), a joint winner of the 1998 Schlegel-Tieck Prize for translation from German, there were no significant attempts to retranslate this unfinished work. The situation may be explained by the relatively greater accessibility of *The Trial* and the miniaturistic perfection of the short stories, as opposed to the rambling incompleteness of *The Castle*, its endless turning around and around the same basic situation – K.'s exclusion from access to the Castle authorities – without the slightest prospect of resolution. Its open-endedness is possibly essential to the work's "meaning", so that a parallel has been drawn between Kafka's inability to finish his novels and stories – sometimes signalled by an obviously discordant "false ending" – and the existential situation of his central character as a representative modern man, painfully aware of where he has come from, but totally unable to survey the land ahead of him on a journey without teleological significance.

Apart from the translation by WILKINS & KAISER of the fragments and incomplete sections, provided later by Kafka's friend, the Austrian-Czech writer Max Brod, there has been little concern with revising either Brod's editing of the novel or the Muirs' version of the text. As in the case of the other works by Kafka, literary critics have concentrated on the memorable opening – K.'s arrival in the village and the description of the somewhat unimpressive Castle above – taking the Muirs' admirable version as a basis for commentary. The ending, in Brod's "definitive edition" of the text, includes his reading of the conclusion to chapter 18 as well as his editing of the whole of chapters 19 and 20. In the same way as his postscript to the first edition of *The Trial* affected the reception of that novel, the interpretation of Kafka's last novel – as a quest for admission to a state of grace – was considerably influenced by Brod's epilogue to the first edition, in which he claims his friend once told him how the novel was to end: "The ostensible Land Surveyor was to find partial satisfaction at least."

The search for a stable version of the original texts for future translators to work with has been aided by the publication, based on the manuscripts in the Bodleian Library at Oxford, of Pasley's critical edition of *Das Schloss* in 1983 and by Schillemeit's critical edition of *Der Verschollene* appearing in the same year, and it was completed by Pasley's critical edition of *Der Prozess* in 1990. A new translation of *The Castle*, "based on the restored text", by Mark HARMAN was published in 1998 – paralleling Breon Mitchell's similarly revised version of *The Trial*.

As the title of the critical edition indicates, the novel known as *America* was referred to in Kafka's manuscript as *Der Verschollene* ("The Man Who Disappeared") or the "American novel". The MUIRS' translation (1938) kept Brod's title along with his editing, including his positioning of the unfinished chapter to which he gave the title "The Nature Theatre of Oklahoma" at the end of the novel, following, like his version of *The Castle*, what he claimed was Kafka's intention: that the novel "should end on a note of reconciliation"(see Brod's postscript to the first edition of *America*). Naturally, the translators go along with Brod's correction of Kafka's misspelling "Oklahama" in what has been up until this chapter a novel in almost a "realist" mode. Thus, both in the original and in the translation, the novel has a "happy end", perhaps negating, perhaps fulfilling the central character's pursuit of the "American dream". The nightmarish quality this dream has taken on since the outbreak of the Vietnam War has been reflected in the frequent spelling "Amerika" – literally with a "k" – in English-language publications, critical for example, of the American way of life or US foreign policy. It is all the more surprising therefore to find a lack of attempts at an updated version of this, Kafka's first-written novel, along the lines of Scott & Waller's translation of *The Trial*, highlighting the grotesque and the surrealistic elements of what has often been received in the US as a picaresque novel almost in the home-grown tradition and which has spawned a genre of writing "after Kafka". Likewise, given the concreteness of the world represented in the novel (in which Kafka was still experimenting with the more metaphorical or detached style that was to be employed in *The Trial* and *The Castle*), it is strange that only recently (1996) has there appeared an alternative to the Muirs' version, Michael HOFFMAN's (significantly dual-titled) *The Man Who Disappeared (Amerika)*, which – along the lines of Parry's translation of *The Trial* – emphasizes the down-to-earth physicality of the events witnessed by Karl Rossman, even if *Amerika* was for Kafka purely an act of the imagination, since he never actually experienced the reality of "America".

ANTHONY MATHEWS

Further Reading
Kafka, Franz, *Das Schloss: in der Fassung der Handschrift*, edited by Malcolm Pasley, Frankfurt: Fischer, 1982
Kafka, Franz, *Das Schloss: Roman, in der Fassung der Handschrift*, edited by Malcolm Pasley, Frankfurt: Fischer, 1982
Kafka, Franz, *Der Verschollene*, edited by Jost Schillemeit, 2 vols, Frankfurt: Fischer, 1983
Kafka, Franz, *Der Verschollene: Roman, in der Fassung der Handschrift*, edited by Jost Schillemeit, Frankfurt: Fischer, 1983
Sandbank, Shimon, *After Kafka: The Influence of Kafka's Fiction*, Athens: University of Georgia Press, 1989
White, J.J., "Endings and Non-Endings in Kafka's Fiction", in *On Kafka: Semi-Centenary Perspectives*, edited by Franz Kuna, London: Elek, and New York: Barnes and Noble, 1976, pp. 146–66

Stories

Selections of Stories
Glatzer, Nahum N. (editor), *Franz Kafka: The Complete Stories*, New York: Schocken Books, 1971; as *The Penguin Complete Short Stories of Franz Kafka*, Harmondsworth: Penguin, 1983
Josipovici, Gabriel (editor), *Franz Kafka: Collected Stories*, London: Dent, 1993
Kaiser, Ernst and Eithne Wilkins, *Dearest Father: Stories and Other Writings*, New York: Schocken Books, 1954; as *Wedding Preparations in the Country, and Other Posthumous Prose Writings*, London: Secker and Warburg, 1954
Muir, Willa and Edwin Muir, *The Great Wall of China and Other Pieces*, London: Secker, 1933; revised edition, London: Secker and Warburg, 1946
Muir, Willa and Edwin Muir, *The Great Wall of China: Stories and Reflections*, New York: Schocken Books, 1946
Muir, Willa and Edwin Muir, *The Penal Colony: Stories and Short Pieces*, New York: Schocken, 1948; London: Secker and Warburg, 1949
Muir, Willa and Edwin Muir, *In the Penal Settlement: Tales and Short Prose Works*, London: Secker and Warburg, 1949
Muir, Willa, Edwin Muir, Tania Stern and James Stern, *Description of a Struggle, and The Great Wall of China*, London: Secker and Warburg, 1960
Muir, Willa, Edwin Muir, Ernst Kaiser and Eithne Wilkins, *Wedding Preparations in the Country and Other Stories*, New York: Penguin, 1978
Muir, Willa, Edwin Muir *et al.*, *Description of a Struggle, and Other Stories*, Harmondsworth and New York: Penguin, 1979
Pasley, Malcolm, *Shorter Works*, vol. 1, London: Secker and Warburg, 1973; reprinted as *The Great Wall of China and Other Short Works*, Harmondsworth: Penguin, 1991
Underwood, J.A., *Franz Kafka: Stories, 1904–1924*, with a foreword by Jorge Luis Borges, London: Macdonald, 1981

Stories
Die Verwandlung, 1915
Berkoff, Steven, *Metamorphosis* in *The Trial and Metamorphosis*, translated by Berkoff, 1981
Corngold, Stanley, *The Metamorphosis: A Critical Edition*, New York: Bantam, 1972
Jolas, Eugène, "The Metamorphosis", *Transition* (Paris), 25 (Fall 1936) pp. 27–38; 26 (Winter 1937) pp. 53–72; 27 (April–May 1938) pp. 79–103
Lloyd, A.L., *The Metamorphosis*, London: Parton Press, 1937; as *Metamorphosis*, New York: Vanguard Press, 1946
Muir, Willa and Edwin Muir, "The Transformation" [1933] in *The Penal Colony: Stories and Short Pieces*, translated by Willa Muir and Edwin Muir, 1948; bilingual edition, as *The Metamorphosis / Die Verwandlung*, New York: Schocken, 1961
Pasley, Malcolm, *Franz Kafka: The Transformation and Other Stories*, Harmondsworth and New York: Penguin, 1992
Underwood, J.A., "The Metamorphosis" in *Franz Kafka: Stories, 1904–1924*, translated by Underwood, 1981

Unlike the incomplete and unrevised novels, Kafka's short stories stand perfect in their well-crafted concision. Recently, literary critics have concentrated their attention on the shorter works on the grounds that the novels have been "over-interpreted" and that by comparison the short stories – which Kafka allowed to be published during his lifetime (including the first chapter of the novel *America*, translated as *The Stoker*) – have been neglected by all but a few initiates to the inner mystery of his writing, who see the short stories as providing *in nuce* the solution to the Kafka problem, albeit as an "immanent meaning" to be refined from a close reading of the finely honed original text. In the English-speaking world such a tendency has been well served by the translation of the various stories by the MUIRS, KAISER & WILKINS, and also by Tania and James STERN and Malcolm PASLEY.

Naturally, the story that has generated the greatest amount of critical attention and, perhaps for this reason, prompted the greatest number of (re-)translations is *Die Verwandlung* (1912), first translated by the MUIRS in 1933 as *The Transformation*, though subsequent editions of the Muirs' version have appeared as *The Metamorphosis* and lately as *Metamorphosis*. Whether or not the loss of the everyday register of the German title has been compensated by a gain in the classical reference, one notices that PASLEY's recent English version of the story (1992) has returned to the Muirs' original title. As to the loss of the definite article, the uniqueness of the event recounted in the story would seem to favour its use rather than, in its absence, the generalization of an experience none of us has had to suffer, however metaphorically we might share in the central character's fate.

For the MUIRS (1948), Gregor Samsa awakes one morning from uneasy dreams "transformed" (not "metamorphosed") into "a gigantic insect". CORNGOLD (1972) has him "changed ... into a monstrous vermin" (in an uneasy singular), PASLEY further mutates him into "a monstrous insect" and finally he emerges in UNDERWOOD (1981) as "a giant bug" (while some despairing commentators even refer to him as a "cockroach"). This translational transformation of the central character from a zoological category into a household pest is accompanied by a growth in "monstrosity", an escalation not just in size but in horror – paralleling the development in the interpretation of *The Trial* towards the grotesque and the fantastic – despite the short story's universally acknowledged matter-of-fact tone. Mercifully, the various editions of the translations spare us an illustration of the physicality of the "ungeheueres Ungeziefer" (though Spielberg has yet to tackle the story) since Kafka is recorded to have been opposed to the visual representation of something he considered to be not just a metaphor ("It was no dream").

BERKOFF's dramatic adaptation (1981) of the story has seized on the uncanny nature of the situation, creatively exaggerating its cinematographic and balletic elements, using – among other things – mime and slow motion, as when his "Mr Samsa" throws the deadly apples at Gregor. As regards the names, PASLEY keeps to the Central European locale, calling the protagonists, "Gregor Samsa" and "Herr Samsa", while UNDERWOOD goes beyond Berkoff in anglicizing the central character to "Gregory Samsa", his father being "Mr Samsa" (and Gregory's sister becoming "Meg"), on the debatable grounds that "they are people, not foreigners". In addition, Gregor's attitude to the demands of his job is brought considerably nearer to home in time and place by being changed from PASLEY's "The devil take it all" to UNDERWOOD's "Oh, to hell with the whole thing". Like Scott and Waller with their version of *The Trial*, UNDERWOOD, in his *The Metamorphosis*, is conscious both of changes in English idiom since the Muirs did their classic translations and of the influence Kafka's writing has had on the history of literary modernism as associated with Beckett and Borges (the latter of whom wrote Underwood's foreword).

The ending, with its unmistakable change of tone, opens out the story from the claustrophobia of the Samsas' flat, though none of the translators has chosen to emphasize the exceptional nature of this "false ending" by separating it off, for example, by a line space as in the German original (and the translations) of *In der Strafkolonie* (*In the Penal Colony*). In parallel with the transformation of tone at the end of *The Trial* and the "The Nature Theatre of Oklahoma" at the end of *America*, the "conclusion" of *The Metamorphosis* is presented in the translations as almost "natural" and unproblematic, despite the incompletion of his novels and Kafka's own recorded dissatisfaction with the ending of this particular short story, its return to "normality".

ANTHONY MATHEWS

Further Reading

Berkoff, Steven, *Meditations on Metamorphosis*, London and Boston: Faber, 1995

Corngold, Stanley, *The Commentators' Despair: The Interpretation of Kafka's Metamorphosis*, Port Washington, New York: Kennikat Press, 1973

Pasley, Malcolm, "Kafka's Semi-Private Games", *Oxford German Studies*, 6 (1971–72) pp. 112–31

Georg Kaiser 1878–1945

German dramatist

Biography

Born 25 November 1878 in Magdeburg. He left his Lutheran school in 1895 and followed his father into business, working in Argentina, Spain, Italy and Germany. Throughout his life he was committed to writing, and this commitment, allied to fragile health, led him to abandon his business career. Marriage in 1908 enabled him to indulge his literary, especially his dramatic, ambitions. There were various financial difficulties, however, one of them, in Munich in 1920, involving a period of imprisonment. From 1921 to the early 1930s his plays were very frequently performed, but they were banned and burned by the Nazis from 1933 and, though continuing to write, he lived in increasing isolation and eventually fled to Switzerland, where he lived from 1939 to 1944. He died 4 June 1945 in Ascona, a few weeks after the war in Europe ended.

Translations

Selections of Plays

Kenworthy, B.J. (editor), *Plays*, vol. 2: *Georg Kaiser*, London: John Calder, 1981; New York: Riverrun Press, 1982 (contains *David and Goliath*, *The Flight to Venice*, *The President*, and *One Day in October*, all translated by Kenworthy, and *The Raft of the Medusa*, translated by Garten and Sprigge)

Ritchie, J.M. (editor), *Five Plays*, London: Calder and Boyars, 1971 (contains *The Burghers of Calais* and *From Morning to Midnight*, both translated by Ritchie, and *The Coral*, *Gas 1*, and *Gas 2*, all translated by Kenworthy)

Plays

Grossbürger Möller, 1914, produced 1915

Kenworthy, B.J., *David and Goliath* in *Plays*, vol. 2, edited by Kenworthy, 1981

Die Bürger von Calais, 1914, produced 1917

Ritchie, J.M. and Rex Last, *The Burghers of Calais* in *Five Plays*, edited by Ritchie, 1971

Von morgens bis mitternachts, 1916, produced 1917

Dukes, Ashley, *From Morn to Midnight*, London: Henderson, 1920; New York: Brentano, 1922

Ritchie, J.M., *From Morning to Midnight* in *Five Plays*, edited by Ritchie, 1971
Weisstein, Ulrich, *From Morn to Midnight* in *Plays for the Theatre*, edited by Oscar G. Brockett and Lenyth Brockett, New York: Holt Rinehart, 1967

Die Koralle, 1917
Katzin, Winifred, *The Coral*, New York: Ungar, 1963

Gas 1, 1918
Kenworthy, B.J., *Gas 1* in *Five Plays*, edited by Ritchie, 1971
Scheffauer, Herman, *Gas*, London: Chapman and Dodd, and Boston: Small and Maynard, 1924

Der Brand im Opernhaus, 1919, produced 1918
Katzin, Winifred, *Fire in the Opera House* in *Eight European Plays*, edited by Katzin, New York: Brentano, 1927

Der gerettete Alkibiades, 1920
Morgan, Bayard Quincy, *Alkibiades Saved*, New York: Brentano, 1927

Gas 2, 1920
Katzin, Winifred, *Gas 2*, introduction by Victor Lange, New York: Ungar, 1963
Kenworthy, B.J., *Gas 2* in *Five Plays*, edited by Ritchie, 1971

Der Protagonist, 1921, produced 1922
Garten, Hugo F., *The Protagonist*, *Tulane Drama Review*, 5 (1960)

Die Flucht nach Venedig, 1923
Kenworthy, B.J., *The Flight to Venice* in *Plays*, vol. 2, edited by Kenworthy, 1981

Der Präsident, 1927, produced 1928
Kenworthy, B.J., *The President* in *Plays*, vol. 2, edited by Kenworthy, 1981

Oktobertag, 1928
Bernstein, Herman and Adolph E. Meyer, *The Phantom Lover*, New York: Brentano, 1928
Kenworthy, B.J. *One Day in October* in *Plays*, vol. 2, edited by Kenworthy, 1981

Das Floss der Medusa, 1963, produced 1945
Garten, H.F., and Elizabeth Sprigge, *The Raft of the Medusa* in *Plays*, vol. 2, edited by Kenworthy, 1981
Weisstein, Ulrich, *The Raft of the Medusa*, *First Stage*, 1 (1962)
Wellwarth, George E., *The Raft of the Medusa*, in *Postwar German Theater: An Anthology of Plays*, edited by Michael Benedikt and Wellwarth, New York: Dutton, 1967; London: Macmillan, 1968

The author of more than 70 plays, Kaiser was one of the most important dramatists of the Expressionist period. The early influence of Hauptmann and Wedekind gave way to that of Hofmannsthal's neo-Romanticism, but it was not until the success of *The Burghers of Calais*, performed to enormous acclaim in January 1917, thanks to the support of the socio-anarchist intellectual Gustav Landauer, that Kaiser's literary career was assured. In this play the altruism of the burghers' leader, moved to offer his life to save the besieged town, is depicted as a step on humanity's path to peace and solidarity. *From Morn to Midnight* (about an insignificant bank clerk who, inspired by love, embezzles the means to a frustrated attempt at living by ideals) achieved similar success, and these two productions were followed by the *Gas* trilogy (*Die Koralle*, 1917; *Gas 1*, 1918; *Gas 2*, 1920), in which the destructive forces of industrialization and war are confronted by an ideal of community based on an ultimately unattainable individual transformation. The years between 1917 and 1923 brought a success Kaiser was never quite able to recreate. Adapting once more, to the materialism of the Weimar Republic, he turned to more popular forms, the revue and social comedy, interspersed with anti-militaristic dramas. His unpopularity with the Nazis led to the banning of his work. His last years were devoted both to drama based on classical themes and to further anti-Nazi and pacifist works.

The translation of Georg Kaiser's work into English has followed the same pattern as that of other German Expressionist dramatists. When they were at the peak of their popularity in Germany (in Kaiser's case, between 1917 and 1923), their best received works (in Kaiser's case *Von morgens bis mitternachts* and *Gas 1*, though not, surprisingly enough, *Die Bürger von Calais*) were immediately translated. This initial impetus prompted some later, less well-known, works to be translated (in Kaiser's case *Oktobertag*, *Der Brand im Opernhaus* and *Der gerettete Alkibiades*), only for changing public tastes in the 1930s to consign the authors once more to oblivion. The rediscovery of Expressionism in Germany in the late 1960s, largely a by-product of the politicization of German literature in that decade but also a response to the centenary celebrations of the Expressionist generation, prompted a new German critical edition, which, in due course, encouraged a later wave of translation. The latter stage of this process is, in Kaiser's case, reflected by the two volumes edited by J.M. Ritchie and B.J. Kenworthy.

In his introduction to the *Five Plays* volume, RITCHIE (1971) warns the reader of the "incredible difficulty" of the language of *Die Bürger von Calais* and prepares us for the "incredible height" reached by the level of address. In the event, however, the reader's credulity is never seriously strained, for when the German becomes ambiguous or obscure the translators of this volume tend to amplify and elucidate. Two examples may suffice: "Woge" ("wave") is helpfully explained as "wave of emulation", "Hoffnung" ("hope") as "hope of my escape". Such a method of translation is not without its problems: by making the language more explicit, more accessible to the reader, the translators inevitably forfeit the resonance of the German original, dissipating the intensity that derives from Kaiser's use of the isolated noun and diminishing the very quality of "Pathos" that is Kaiser's hallmark. Such is the insoluble problem facing the translator of Kaiser's most Expressionistic work.

For the most part, RITCHIE's *Five Plays* edition and its companion volume *Plays, Volume Two* (1981), edited and translated for the most part by KENWORTHY, convey the sense of Kaiser's plays accurately, even ingeniously. A comparison with the original German reveals, in the former volume, a disturbing number of discrepancies: three of the five lists of characters are incomplete and on some 20 occasions stage-directions, phrases, sentences, even whole exchanges, are omitted. While it is Kaiser's own predilection for incantatory repetition that possibly induces some of these excisions, the English reader is entitled to have all Kaiser's text. Nevertheless, the reader is well served by the efforts made by the various translators to convey, in as idiomatic a way as is compatible with the stylized language of the originals, the flavour and the meaning of Kaiser's dramas. The volume edited by Kenworthy presented fewer difficulties in the original, Kaiser having abandoned progressively his high-flown, visionary tone. This second volume contains a range of Kaiser's plays from his pre-Expressionist work to his dramas of the 1920s and 1930s. The versions offered are accessible, idiomatic and accurate.

RHYS W. WILLIAMS

Further Reading

Kenworthy, Brian J., *Georg Kaiser*, Oxford: Blackwell, 1957

Schürer, Ernst, *Georg Kaiser*, New York: Twayne, 1971

Shaw, Leroy, *The Playwright and Historical Change: Dramatic Strategies in Brecht, Hauptmann, Kaiser and Wedekind*, Madison: University of Wisconsin Press, 1970

Silva, M. Helena Gonçalves da, *Character, Ideology and Symbolism in the Plays of Wedekind, Sternheim, Kaiser, Toller, and Brecht*, London: Modern Humanities Research Association, 1985

Kālidāsa fl.c.AD 400

Indian poet and dramatist

Nothing is known about Kālidāsa, the greatest poet and dramatist of ancient India, except what little can be deduced from his works. Most probably he worked under the patronage of Candra Gupta II who, from his capital at Ujjain, ruled most of northern India from c.AD 376 to 415. The grace and clarity of his style, together with his outstanding powers of description, put him among the few writers in Sanskrit whose work has a universal appeal. Seven of his works survive: *Raghuvaṃśa* – a lyric narrative in 19 cantos – about the deeds of the hero Rāma, his ancestors and descendants; *Kumārasambhava* – a lyric narrative in eight cantos (continued in a further nine cantos by a later author) – about the events leading up to the birth of a son to Śiva and Pārvatī; *Meghadūta*, "The Cloud Messenger" – a lyric monologue in 110 stanzas, with fine descriptions of landscape; *Rtusamhāra* – a lyric poem describing the cycle of the six Indian seasons; *Mālavikāgnimitra* – a drama of court intrigue surrounding King Agnimitra's love for the princess Mālavikā; *Vikramorvaśī* – a drama based on the legend of the love of a mortal king for the heavenly nymph Urvaśī; and *Śakuntalā*, more properly *Abhijñānaśākuntalam*, "(The Drama) of Śakuntalā and the Token".

Sakuntala

Śakuntalā, c. 4th century

Śakuntalā is a drama in seven acts, in prose and verse. Male characters of high status speak in Sanskrit, all other characters – men, women and children – in Prākrit (conventionalized dialect to suggest colloquial speech). The story is a radical transformation of a minor episode in the *Mahābhārata* (I. 62–69).

Editions

There are two main recensions of the text, neither superior to the other: Bengali (B) and Central Indian, or Devanāgarī (D). Standard editions are: (B) R. Pischel, *Kalidasa's Śakuntalā: An Ancient Hindu Drama*, 2nd edition, with a preface by Carl Cappeller, Cambridge, Massachusetts: Harvard University Press, 1922 (Harvard Oriental Series, vol. 16); and (D) N.R. Acharya, 12th edition, Bombay: Nirnaya Sagar Press, 1958.

Translations

Binyon, Laurence, *Sakuntala by Kalidasa*, prepared for the English stage by Kedar Nath Das Gupta in a new version written by Binyon, with an introductory essay by Rabindranath Tagore, London: Macmillan, 1920 (B/D)

Coulson, Michael, *Śakuntalā* in his *Three Sanskrit Plays*, Harmondsworth and New York: Penguin, 1981; reprinted London: Folio Society, 1992 (includes translations of the *Śakuntalā* episode in the *Mahābhārata* and of a Bengali adaptation by Abanindranith Tagore) (B)

Emeneau, M.B., *Kālidasā's Abhijñāna-Śakuntala*, Berkeley: University of California Press, 1962 (B)

[Jones, William], *Sacontala; or, The Fatal Ring: An Indian Drama by Calidas, Translated from the Original Sanscrit and Prakrit*, Calcutta: Joseph Cooper, 1789 (B)

Miller, Barbara Stoler, *Śakuntalā and the Ring of Recollection* in *Theater of Memory: The Plays of Kālidāsa*, edited by Miller, New York: Columbia University Press, 1984 (D)

Monier-Williams, Monier, *Śakoontalá; or, The Lost Ring: An Indian Drama*, Hertford: Austin, 1855 (D)

Rajan, Chandra, "Abhijñānaśākuntalam" in *Kālidāsa: The Loom of Time: A Selection of His Plays and Poems*, New Delhi: Penguin, and New York: Viking Penguin, 1989 (B)

Ryder, Arthur W., *Shakuntala* in his *Kalidasa: Translations of Shakuntala and Other Works*, London: Dent, and New York: Dutton, 1912 (B)

While out hunting, King Dusyanta comes to a forest hermitage where, in the absence of the sage Kanva, he is received by the sage's foster-daughter Śakuntalā. The king and Śakuntalā fall in love and marry without ceremony. The king returns to his capital, after giving Śakuntalā his signet ring as a keepsake. An irascible holy-man comes to the hermitage and, receiving no welcome from the day-dreaming Śakuntalā, lays a curse on her: the man of whom she dreams will not recognize her unless he also sees the keepsake. Since no word comes from the capital, Kanva decides to send the pregnant Śakuntalā, under escort, to the king to be acknowledged as his wife. Face to face with Śakuntalā, the king remembers nothing. Śakuntalā in desperation feels for her ring, but it is lost. The king repudiates her. In a sudden flash of light she is spirited away. Soon after, a fisherman finds the king's ring inside a fish he has caught at the very pool in which Śakuntalā had bathed on her way to court. The ring is shown to the king and he remembers everything. To Dusyanta, now tortured with remorse and longing, Indra, king of the gods, sends his charioteer, Mātali, with a request for help in subduing some demons. Dusyanta duly conquers the demons, then travels with Mātali through the air to a mountain hermitage inhabited by divine beings. Here he sees a child playing with a lion cub and gradually realizes that it is his son, born to Śakuntalā in the hermitage to which her mother, a heavenly nymph, had carried her. Dusyanta and Śakuntalā are reunited and all is explained.

In the judgement of Indians and non-Indians alike *Śakuntalā* is not only the finest of Kālidāsa's three plays but the outstanding masterpiece of Sanskrit drama. All the greater is the challenge it sets the translator. From the outset he has to acclimatize his readers to a landscape, mental as much as geographical, that will be unfamiliar. He must convincingly re-create the atmosphere of spiritual idealism that pervades the play and preserve the connection Kālidāsa makes between the psychology of his characters and the lives of the plants and animals in the forest hermitage where most of the story unfolds. The dialogue may present few verbal difficulties, but it requires a sensitive ear to achieve exactly the right tone and inflection so that the speech sounds natural yet not too colloquial. Interspersed with the prose of the dialogue are some 200 verses – a sizeable proportion of the play. These can be descriptive or reflective, or else serve to vary the speed and intensity of delivery. Here the challenge to the translator is to reproduce the limpid concision of Kālidāsa's language without losing any of its expressive richness and subtlety. Whatever the degree of his success, he may take some comfort in the knowledge that even in Kālidāsa's day the gulf between text and performance was wide: *Śakuntalā*, like other Sanskrit plays, was a dance drama in which vocal and instrumental music, dance and mime combined to bring out the full meaning of the written text. An acting version for the Western stage, if it is not a pastiche, will require some degree of abridgement and adaptation of the original.

JONES's (1789) translation was one of the earliest to be made from Sanskrit into English, and the first appearance of the play in any European language. Although the text he used was defective and his grasp of its meaning at times imperfect, Jones produced a version in prose that is both clear and elegant. A remarkable achievement in itself, it remains a landmark in cultural, as well as literary, history. To English readers it revealed the existence of a hitherto unknown literature, ancient, exotic and sophisticated. And in various retranslations it created a vogue for India throughout Europe, most notably in Germany, where Georg Forster's version of 1791 inspired Herder and Goethe, and fuelled the fantasy of an idealized India among German Romantics. The interest aroused by Jones's translation prompted his teacher, Charles Wilkins, to translate the episode in the *Mahābhārata* on which Kālidāsa based his play (*The Story of Dooshwanta and Sakoontalā*, London, 1795).

MONIER-WILLIAMS's (1855) free translation follows his own edition of the text, published in 1853. It is in prose, blank verse and, occasionally, rhymed verse. But the prose is cumbersome and there is no evidence in the verse of his attempt "to avoid diluting Kálidása's poetical ideas by paraphrastic circumlocutions or additions".

RYDER's (1912) version is also fairly free, that is, not concerned to reflect every detail and nuance of the original. His prose is clear and straightforward but the rendering in rhymed verse of each of Kālidāsa's verses inevitably compels deviations and omissions from the original. Beside the metrical variety, the concision and the subtlety of the Sanskrit verses, Ryder's can only seem banal: instead of heightening the effect of the play they break its spell.

BINYON's (1920) abridged version for the stage (performed in London, 1919) is a free rendering, mainly in blank verse. Though sensitive to the poetry and the elevated tone of the original, Binyon does not scruple to expand or even to vary Kālidāsa's images – never to good effect. His demure, mildly archaizing verse savours too much of the study and, no less than the other versions under review, it is in the study that it belongs: a version for the contemporary stage could keep far closer to the text and the acting conventions of the original.

EMENEAU (1962) intended his close translation as an aid to students reading Pischel's 1922 edition. It is in prose throughout, with no pretensions to elegance. His attempt to reflect the different shades of colloquial speech, supposedly mirroring the variety of Prākrit in the original, is likely to jar on most English, and some American, ears.

COULSON's (1981) version is close, accurate and true to the tenor of the original. In conveying Kālidāsa's verse he is sensibly, if disappointingly, cautious: the distinction from prose is more apparent in the typography than in any heightening of language. Despite the occasional false note, missed nuance and awkward turn of phrase, this version comes closest to a convincing re-creation of the original.

MILLER (1984) too keeps close to the text and, on the whole, renders it faithfully. Beside Monier-Williams's over-upholstered manner, hers can seem refreshingly spare. But though she successfully matches the concision of the original, it is with some sacrifice of its richness and grace. Some of her verses read like haikai, others, however, like telegrams.

RAJAN (1989) follows the original closely, gives its meaning with fair accuracy, distinguishes verse from prose (without aspiring to the poetic) and occasionally finds the felicitous word or phrase. Yet, for the most part, her translation does not escape the stigma of translationese – and of cliché. This criticism applies equally to other translations into unidiomatic English made by Indian scholars and by the Swede A.H. Edgren (1894), none of which can be read with pleasure.

PETER KHOROCHE

Further Reading

See the introductory essays in Coulson (1981) and in Miller (1984), which also provides an extensive bibliography

Ghassān Kanafānī 1936–1972

Palestinian novelist and short-story writer

Biography

Ghassān Kanafānī was born 9 April 1936 in Acre in Mandatory Palestine, the son of a lawyer. He attended French missionary schools, until his family was forced into exile during the 1948 war in Palestine. His family first stayed in Lebanon, then moved to Damascus; Kanafānī completed his secondary education there. In 1952 he began his studies at the University of Damascus, but was expelled in 1955 because of his involvement in the Movement of Arab Nationalists. He moved to Kuwait to take up a teaching position in 1955, and in 1956 became editor of an Arab nationalist newspaper, *al-Ra'i*. While in Kuwait he began to write short stories. He moved to Beirut in 1960, and worked as a journalist and editor, as well as publishing his first novel, *Rijāl fī al-shams* (*Men in the Sun*), 1963. In 1967 he helped to found the Popular Front for the Liberation of Palestine, the Marxist Palestinian branch of the Movement of Arab Nationalists, and he edited the Front's weekly journal, *al-Hadaf*. He was killed, along with his niece, by a car bomb, 9 July 1972.

Kanafānī represents a unique phenomenon in the history of modern Palestinian culture, combining an original literary talent with a political commitment that took him to the highest reaches of the Popular Front for the Liberation of Palestine and for which he eventually paid the ultimate price of assassination, supposedly by Israeli agents. A man of many gifts, he was a talented amateur artist as well as a leading writer of modern Arabic fiction. In addition to the novels and short stories for which he is best known outside Palestine, he wrote essays, plays and literary criticism, producing studies of Palestinian resistance literature and of Zionist literature. Despite his close involvement with official Palestinian organizations, he always maintained that he was first and foremost a creative artist. As such, he refused to conform to the stereotypes often associated with spokesmen for the Palestinian cause: in *'Ā'id ilā Hayfā'* (*Palestine's Children*), for example, he gives a sympathetic portrayal of an elderly Jewish couple who are refugees from European anti-Semitism.

Translations

Novellas and Short Stories

Rijāl fī al-shams, 1963

Kilpatrick, Hilary, *Men in the Sun, and Other Palestinian Stories*, with an introduction, London: Heinemann, and Washington, DC: Three Continents Press, 1978

Mā tabaqqā lakum, 1966

Jayyusi, May and Jeremy Reed, *All That's Left to You: A Novella and Other Stories*, with an introduction, Austin: Center for Middle Eastern Studies, University of Texas, 1990

'Ā'id ilā Hayfā', 1969

Harlow, Barbara, *Palestine's Children*, London: Heinemann, and Washington, DC: Three Continents Press, 1984

Kanafānī's reputation today depends primarily on his two novellas *Rijāl fī al-shams* and *Mā tabaqqā lakum*. *Rijāl fī al-shams* tells the story of a human smuggling operation that goes horribly wrong: three Palestinians, desperate to build themselves new lives in Kuwait, are trapped in the empty water-tank of a lorry while the driver – himself a Palestinian – hurries to complete the border formalities. But the August sun of the desert has proved too much for the three and they perish of suffocation and heat exhaustion, leaving the driver, Abul Khaizuran, only to wonder why they had not banged on the sides of the tank to attract attention. In a final act of humiliation, their bodies are stripped of valuables and dumped at the nearest garbage dump.

Rijāl fī al-shams is a work that succeeds in encapsulating in a remarkably small number of pages the fate of successive generations of Palestinians, abandoned by the rest of the world and humiliated at every turn as they clutch at the one fragile straw left to them – the impossible dream of material well-being. The work is replete both with symbolism and with irony: Abul Khaizuran, for example, is himself impotent as a result of an earlier war-wound. Moreover, despite the "local" nature of its theme, the work succeeds in transcending the limitations of its immediate subject: as KILPATRICK (1978) notes in her introduction, "Abu Qais's memories of the land he left behind ... could be matched by the stories of thousands of displaced persons who have been uprooted in Europe and elsewhere, while the naïve, barely educated Marwan ... is a brother of the economic refugees from the Caribbean, the Mediterranean and the Indian subcontinent who throng London, Paris and Munich."

Although considerable use is made of "flash-backs" in *Rijāl fī al-shams* as a means of explaining his characters' motives, Kanafānī's technique is never obtrusive and the work moves towards its climax with a directness and inevitability that well reveal the author's mastery of his chosen form. Less interested in words for their own sake than as a vehicle for ideas, his language presents fewer problems for the translator than that of, for example, Idwār al-Kharrāt or Jamāl al-Ghitāni. That is not, of course, to belittle the achievement of the translator, whose prose – like that of the original – moves smoothly and unobtrusively to the inevitable climax. She has also in the same volume given us a useful selection of six of Kanafānī's shorter stories – all again excellently translated – which reveal that, central though the Palestinian cause was to the author, it was not his exclusive concern: while some of the stories have obvious roots in the plight of the Palestinians, "A Hand in the Grave", "The Falcon" and "If You Were a Horse ..." deal with more general themes – love, death, superstition and human frailty.

The "flashback" techniques Kanafānī employed in *Rijāl fī al-shams* were further developed in the later novella *Mā tabaqqā lakum*, whose English version, like that of the earlier work, is published accompanied by a selection of the author's short stories. The work revolves around a period of some 18 hours in the life of a Palestinian family, separated from each other by the Israeli occupation; as Hamid struggles across the desert to rejoin his mother in Jordan, his sister Maryam struggles to free herself from her despicable husband Zakariyya. The experimental nature of Kanafānī's narrative technique is pointed up in the author's short "clarification", where he explains that the work involves five "heroes" – the three main human characters being joined for this purpose by Time and the Desert. Hamid and Maryam also serve as the principal narrators of the story; both first- and third-person narrative is employed, and changes in narrator, time and place are indicated by the use of different typefaces. Although well-established in English and other Western literary traditions, the use of these techniques with such assurance by an Arab author during the 1960s makes *Mā tabaqqā lakum* a notable contribution to the development of Arabic narrative technique.

Kanafānī's use of different intensities of print is reproduced in the translation by JAYYUSI & REED (1990), which employs italics and bold typefaces to replicate the original. As Roger Allen notes in his introduction, differences in the linguistic structure of Arabic and English make it difficult to convey the full range of subtleties of the original text. None the less, this is an accomplished translation which successfully captures both the mood of the Arabic and the heightening of pace and tension as the novella proceeds to its conclusion. The 10 short stories published in the same volume again provide an excellent illustration of the diversity of Kanafānī's concerns, which extend far beyond the narrow confines of the "Palestine question" as such: particularly poignant is "Death of Bed 12", which combines a keen awareness of the frailty of the human condition with an imaginative approach to narrative structure.

HARLOW (1984) continues the same formula as the two other volumes, combining the translation of a novella, "Return to Haifa", with some dozen short stories illustrating different facets of Kanafānī's technique. As the title of the volume indicates, the stories have been selected to provide a "child's-eye" view on the Palestine question – the main story in the collection relating the return of a Palestinian couple to a Haifa they have not seen for nearly 20 years. Other stories in the collection are set between 1936 and 1967 – many focusing on 1948, the date of the creation of the state of Israel.

Through his works of fiction, Ghassān Kanafānī has played an important part in humanizing the plight of the Palestinians and in making their cause accessible to a wider audience. He has been well served by his English translators, who are extending that audience to the non-Arabic-speaking world.

PAUL STARKEY

Further Reading

Allen, Roger, *The Arabic Novel: An Historical and Critical Introduction*, Manchester: University of Manchester Press, and Syracuse, New York: Syracuse University Press, 1982

Kilpatrick, Hilary, "Tradition and Innovation in the Fiction of Ghassān Kanafānī'", *Journal of Arabic Literature*, 7 (1976) pp. 53–64

Siddiq, Muhammad, *Man is a Cause: Political Consciousness and the Fiction of Ghassan Kanafani*, Seattle: University of Washington Press, 1984

Wild, Stefan, *Ghassan Kanafani: The Life of a Palestinian*, Wiesbaden: Harrassowitz, 1975

Nikolai Karamzin 1766–1826

Russian travel and short-story writer, historian and essayist

Biography

Born on his father's estate at Mikhailovka, Simbirsk province, Russia, 12 December 1766. He first attended a private boarding school in Simbirsk, and was at Professor J. Schaden's boarding school in Moscow from 1775 to 1781. From birth he was enlisted in the Preobrazhenskii Guards but served only from 1782 to 1783 in St Petersburg, resigning in 1784. His first literary work was published in 1783. He was admitted to the masonic lodge in Simbirsk in about 1784. The following year he moved to Moscow to join the literary circle of N.I. Novikov, and became a journalist. He travelled to Germany, France, Switzerland and England during the years from 1789 to 90. He maintained an independent career as writer and editor in Moscow from 1791 to 1803. He married Elizaveta Ivanovna Protasova in 1801 and had one daughter. Karamzin was appointed Imperial Historiographer in 1803, and undertook historical research and writing in Moscow from 1804 to 1816. In 1804 he married Ekaterina Andreevna Kolyvanova, the illegitimate daughter of Prince A.I. Viazemskii, with whom he had three sons and two daughters. He composed *Zapiska o drevnei i novoi Rossii* (*A Memoir on Ancient and Modern Russia*) and presented it to tsar Alexander I in March 1811. Following Napoleon's occupation of Moscow, he was evacuated to Nizhnii Novgorod in 1813. He moved to St Petersburg in 1816 and spent his remaining years in St Petersburg and at Tsarskoe Selo. In 1818 he was elected to the Russian Academy. He died in St Petersburg, 2 June 1826.

Karamzin was a historian and prolific writer, who engaged in wide-ranging literary activity, as a poet, prose writer, critic, journalist and editor. He is acknowledged for his influence on the language of Russian literature through his reform of its vocabulary and idiom, and for his introduction of the new sentimentalist style to Russian fiction: this became known as the "new style" (*novyi slog*). He established the literary journal *Moskovskii zhurnal* after his return from European travel in 1791; his influential *Pis'ma russkogo puteshestvennika* (*Letters of a Russian Traveller*) were published in the journal from

1791. His important short stories *Bednaia Liza* (*Poor Liza*), and *Natal'ia, boiarskaia doch* [Natalia, the Boyar's Daughter] were also published in the *Moskovskii zhurnal* in 1792. Karamzin edited the literary journal *Vestnik Europy*, to which he contributed fiction, criticism and poetry, from 1802 to 1803. His major work was a 12-volume history of Russia, *Istoriya gosudarstva rossiyskogo* [History of the Russian State], the first of its kind, published from 1818 to 1829, and unfinished when he died.

Translations

Travel Writing

Pis'ma russkogo puteshestvennika, 6 vols, 1791–1801

[Feldborg, Andreas Anderson], *Travels from Moscow through Prussia, Germany, Switzerland, France and England*, 3 vols, London: J. Badcock, 1803

Jonas, Florence, *Letters of a Russian Traveler 1789–1790*, New York: Columbia University Press, and London: Oxford University Press, 1957

Short Stories

Frol Silin, 1791; *Bednaia Liza*, 1792; *Natal'ia, boiarskaia doch'*, 1792; *Ostrov Borngol'm*, 1793; *Iulia*, 1794

Elrington, John Battersby, *Russian Tales*, London: G. Sidney, 1803 (includes "Lisa", "Frol Silin", "Natalia", "Julia")

[Feldborg, Andreas Andersen], *Tales, from the Russian of Nicolai Karamsin*, London: J. Johnson, 1804 (includes "Lisa", "Frol Silin", "Natalia", "Julia")

Hawkins, William E., "The Island of Bornholm" in *The Literature of Eighteenth-Century Russia: An Anthology*, edited by Harold B. Segel, vol. 2, New York: Dutton, 1967

M., G., "Karamsin's Tales", *The German Museum* (September–October 1800; January–February 1801) (includes "Flor Silin" [*sic*], "Julia", "Poor Lisa")

Nebel, Henry M. Jr, *Selected Prose of N.M. Karamzin*, Evanston, Illinois: Northwestern University Press, 1969 (includes "Poor Liza", "Natalie, the Boyar's Daughter", "The Island of Bornholm", "Julia")

Whittaker, Robert, "Poor Liza" in *The Literature of Eighteenth-Century Russia: An Anthology*, edited by Harold B. Segel, vol. 2, New York: Dutton, 1967

Poetry

Bowring, John, in his *Rossiiskaia antologiia: Specimens of the Russian Poets*, vol. 1, London: for the author, 1821; Boston: Cummings Hilliard, 1822; vol. 2, London: Whittaker, 1823

Essays

[Estaf'ev, A.G.], "Present State of Commerce in Books, with Remarks on the Love of Reading, in the Interior of Russia", *The Literary Panorama*, vol. 1, London: 1807

Nebel, Henry M. Jr, *Selected Prose of N.M. Karamzin*, Evanston, Illinois: Northwestern University Press, 1969

Pelenski, Jaroslaw, in *Russian Intellectual History: An Anthology*, edited by Marc Raeff, New York: Harcourt Brace, 1966

Wiren-Garczynski, Vera von, "The Literary Essay" in *The Literature of Eighteenth-Century Russia: An Anthology*, edited by Harold B. Segel, vol. 1, New York: Dutton, 1967

Nikolai Karamzin is associated with the introduction of an elegant and carefully wrought "new style" (*novyi slog*) into Russian letters in the last decade of the 18th century, and became the first Russian writer of prose to gain an appreciative audience both in his homeland and in Europe through the translations of several of his works into Danish, English, French, German and Italian. Karamzin's name began to appear in British journals at the very beginning of the 19th century, and a series of translations was published both in journals and in book form. The invariable provider of both information and "original" texts was the German man of letters J.G. Richter (1763–1808), whose *Briefe eines reisenden Russen* and *Erzählungen von N. Karamsin* appeared in Leipzig in 1799–1802 and 1800 respectively.

However, although the source was identical, the three stories that appeared in *The German Museum* (M.G., 1800–01) were in every respect superior to the versions published two and three years later in book form (ELRINGTON, 1803, and FELDBORG, 1804): not only were they more faithful to the German, and thereby inevitably having a greater chance of staying nearer to the original Russian, but they were written in a far better English. The strangeness of certain English phrases in FELDBORG's version (1803) of the travel letters, *Pis'ma*, was noted by reviewers and is evident in the stories as well: the most widely read and accessible translations were not from Russian but from German, translated into English by a Dane. At the same time, the distance from the true originals may be gauged from the preface to the first version of *Frol Silin* (M.G., 1800), which declared that "much has been omitted; the beginner, who perhaps may use the translation as a help to understand the original better, must not censure, if he finds many passages different from the Russian", particularly when it is realized that these lines were already Richter's.

This linguistic salmagundi had a reprise with variations in the next translation to appear. On this occasion it was the first version of a Karamzin essay (EVSTAF'EV, 1807) although Karamzin was not named as its author. It was moreover the first translation of a work by Karamzin directly from the Russian, but made by a translator (a member of the Russian embassy in London) whose native tongue was Russian, not English. Nevertheless, it is more accurate and reads better than at least one much more recent version (WIREN-GARCZYNKSI, 1967).

BOWRING (1821, 1823) was English, but he relied on English and French cribs provided by friends in St Petersburg when he produced the first metric versions of poems by Karamzin. An interesting selection of mainly shorter and earlier poems (10 in all), they included, notably, "The Churchyard" (Karamzin's "Kladbischche", itself a re-working of a German poem by L.T. Kozegarten), which became popular in the English-speaking world, particularly in America, where it was included in school anthologies. "The Churchyard" reveals clearly the Bowring method, called by a later critic (Thomas Shaw, 1843) "'the flowery paths of dalliance' so often trodden by the *paraphraser*": the comparative terseness of the original is frequently replaced by a more emotive periphrasis or poetic cliché and the unrhymed dactylo-trochaic lines become rhymed anapaests.

Bowring's anthology marked the second stage in British awareness of Karamzin's work, but it was followed by a century of almost total neglect, certainly with respect to new translations. Only in the 20th century and in the general context of the rise of Russian studies in British and American universities after World War II did Karamzin become again the subject of study and of further translation, now made exclusively from Russian.

It was a university press that published a new translation of *Pis'ma russkogo puteshestvennika* (JONAS, 1957), but the presentation was far from academic (e.g. no indication of either the edition used or of the considerable number of letters and passages excluded for such dubious reasons as their being "repetitious" and "cloying"). The translation itself inspires little confidence, presenting us on the first page with a schoolboy howler ("*scorched* by fits of melancholy" for "*grieving*" ["podgoriunivshis"]) and elsewhere with cultural lapses such as "paintings of Lady Hamilton" for "paintings by [Gavin] Hamilton". It remains, nevertheless, the most accessible introduction to Karamzin's major work for Anglophone readers.

The bicentenary, in 1966, of Karamzin's birth heralded a great surge in translations of his prose, equalled only by the Richter-inspired years at the beginning of the preceding century. Three anthologies or collections, in preparation at more or less the same time, resulted in inevitable duplication. Among the tales, there were two or more versions of *Bednaia Liza* and two of *Ostrov Borngol'm*, the latter appearing for the first time in English. There was a most welcome selection of Karamzin's essays, which included, however, no fewer than three new translations of *O liubvi ko chteniiu*, to add to EVSTAF'EV's (1807). A curiosity is WIREN-GARCZYNSKI's translation (1967) of *Un mot sur la littérature russe* (1797): seemingly unaware that Karamzin wrote in French, she translates from a modern Russian version (Russian as the intermediary language!). While generally accurate, her versions of the essays occasionally suffer from inappropriate register, e.g. "the purpose of moralization" or "the success of intellectuality". WIREN-GARCZYNSKI, PELENSKI in 1966 (reliable translations) and NEBEL (1969) all provide examples of essays not found elsewhere in English.

WHITTAKER's version (1967) of *Bednaia Liza* combines infelicity of expression with a lack of feeling for the connotations of English words and glaring mistranslations. Its inferiority to Nebel's version is evident in almost every respect.

NEBEL (1969) marks a highpoint in translations from Karamzin. He has the distinct advantage of being a Karamzin scholar as well as a sensitive translator. He thus has an awareness of the features it is necessary to attempt to retain in order to do justice to both the content and the style, "as exactly as the syntax and semantics of English will allow". He also makes the crucial decision to follow, as far as English usage will permit, Karamzin's punctuation.

ANTHONY CROSS

Further Reading

Cross, A.G., *N.M. Karamzin: A Study of His Literary Career, 1783–1803*, Carbondale: Southern Illinois University Press, and London: Feffer and Simons, 1971

Kawabata Yasunari 1899–1972

Japanese novelist, short-story writer and critic

Biography

Born in Osaka, 11 June 1899. He was orphaned at the age of three and was raised by his grandparents until their death when, still in his teens, he was left totally on his own. His later writings are permeated by an "orphan complex" engendered by this experience, entailing a feeling of ultimate loneliness, rootlessness and nihilistic inclinations. These features of his writing prompted Mishima Yukio to call him "an eternal wayfarer". Kawabata published several tanka poems and short stories when he was only 16 years old, marking thus the beginning of a long and prolific career. While attending the elite Imperial University, Kawabata pursued his calling both as a novelist and as a literary critic. Though known today primarily as a writer uniquely gifted in capturing the feminine aestheticism of traditional Japan, in his youthful days Kawabata was very much in the vanguard of the modern art scene. Together with Yokomitsu Riichi and Kataoka Teppei, he was at the center of the Neo-Sensualist Movement (Shinkankaku-ha), an avant-garde literary movement heavily influenced by the Futurism, Dadaism, Expressionism and Surrealism that dominated Europe during the 1920s. Kawabata's experiments with language, both narrative and cinematic, exercised a prolonged influence on his later writings. During the war, a self-imposed silence impelled him to turn to the classical works such as *The Tale of Genji* for solace. The post-war period marks the most creative and prolific period of Kawabata's writing career. Novels such as *Snow Country* (1947), *Thousand Cranes* (1949), *The Sound of the Mountain* (1949–54), *The Master of Go* (1951) and *The House of the Sleeping Beauties* (1961) are among the best-known and most representative of his works. He was awarded the Nobel Prize for Literature in 1968. Kawabata committed suicide, 16 April 1972; no note was found.

Translations

Novels

Yukiguni, 1947

Seidensticker, Edward G., *Snow Country*, with an introduction, New York: Knopf, 1956; Tokyo: Tuttle, 1957

Senbazuru, 1949
Seidensticker, Edward G., *Thousand Cranes*, New York: Knopf, 1958; Tokyo: Tuttle, 1969

Yama no oto, 1949–54
Seidensticker, Edward G., *The Sound of the Mountain*, New York: Knopf, 1970

Meijin, 1951
Seidensticker, Edward G., *The Master of Go*, New York: Knopf, 1972; London: Secker and Warburg, 1973

Mizuumi, 1954
Tsukimura, Reiko, *The Lake*, Tokyo and New York: Kodansha, 1974

Koto, 1962
Holman, J. Martin, *The Old Capital*, San Francisco: North Point Press, 1987

Utsukushisa to kanashimi to, 1965
Hibbett, Howard, *Beauty and Sadness*, New York: Knopf, 1975

Collections of Short Stories
Dunlop, Lane and J. Martin Holman, *Palm-of-the-Hand Stories*, San Francisco: North Point Press, 1988
Seidensticker, Edward G. *et al.*, *The Izu Dancer and Other Stories*, annotated by Shonosuke Ishii, Tokyo: Harashobo, 1964; new edition, Tokyo and Rutland, Vermont: Tuttle, 1974
Seidensticker, Edward G., *The House of the Sleeping Beauties and Other Stories*, Tokyo: Kodansha, and London: Quadriga Press, 1969; New York: Ballantine, 1970

Essays
Seidensticker, Edward G., *Japan the Beautiful and Myself: The 1968 Nobel Prize Acceptance Speech* (bilingual edition), Tokyo and Palo Alto, California: Kodansha, 1969
Viglielmo, V.H., *The Existence and Discovery of Beauty*, Tokyo: Mainichi Newspapers, 1969

Kawabata Yasunari ranks with Tanizaki Jun'ichirō and Mishima Yukio as one of the three most widely-read Japanese authors in the Western world. As the first writer in Japan (and only the second in Asia) ever to be awarded a Nobel Prize for Literature (1968), Kawabata's place as a distinguished writer is secure both within Japan and beyond its borders.

The discussion of translations of Kawabata's works can only begin with an expression of profound gratitude to Edward G. SEIDENSTICKER. It is largely due to his tireless effort and superbly rendered translations that the English world came to share the fragile beauty of Kawabata's lyrical prose. Although Seidensticker has sometimes been faulted for misunderstanding the Japanese original, his accomplishment is remarkable because Kawabata's laconic and ephemeral language has often been considered untranslatable. Dubbed as the most "Japanese" of all Japanese writers, Kawabata forsakes tight plot movement and resists prescribed narrative structure. Instead, he employs seemingly casual, random plots and focuses on capturing the elusive sense of beauty in nature. Heavily influenced by the poetic tension resulting from transitory brevity and contrastive imagery of the *haiku* and *renga* (linked verse) tradition, some of his short vignettes, like the *Palm Stories* (DUNLOR & HOLMAN, 1988), reflect the author's stoic aestheticism. On the other hand, Kawabata also wrote for the popular audience through newspaper serializations in the language of rather mundane realism. Between these two polarities are the works that are considered to be his best, such as *Snow Country* and *The Sound of the Mountain*. They walk a fine line, couching the sometimes sentimental, melodramatic plotlines in a highly refined, poignant, artistic language. Considering the author's earlier bold, experimental use of language, the task faced by any translator who tackles Kawabata is daunting. He must determine the proper diction for the multi-layered linguistic textures, explain coherently the technical terms and the cultural context for the cultural icons (tea ceremony, Japanese *go*, etc.) that Kawabata often employs, and penetrate the detached, nonchalant surface language to reach into the deeper interiority of the text.

Seidensticker's labor of love began in the late 1950s and reached full swing in the 1970s, following Kawabata's Nobel Prize in 1968. *The Izu Dancer and Other Stories* (*Izu no odoriko*, 1926; SEIDENSTICKER *et al.*, 1964) contains four early short stories including the famed title story, translated by Seidensticker, and less well-known stories translated by Leon PICON and George SAITO. The title story captures the shy eroticism of adolescence. Seidensticker's rendition, which first appeared in the *Atlantic Monthly* in 1954, though lucid and easy to read, contains many casual omissions. Dialogues, in particular, as well as the names of many towns and hot springs that the translator deemed unimportant, are left out. Although the story is usually interpreted as an odyssey of the young protagonist's encounter with the kindness of strangers, one of the key elements in the narrative is the distinctive diction of the language spoken by people of various classes and professions, which the translation unfortunately fails to convey adequately.

Snow Country (*Yukiguni*, 1947) was the first major work Kawabata published after World War II. Written and partially published from 1935 to 1947, it is Kawabata's quintessential masterpiece, combining an astonishingly perceptive explication of sensuality and, at the same time, a keen awareness of the futility of desire. SEIDENSTICKER's translation (1956), which is credited with aiding the author to garner the Nobel Prize, excels at capturing the evanescent nature of the narrative. As the translator points out in his introduction, the author has chosen a theme that makes a meeting between *haiku* and the novel possible. The translation's generally pensive tone and the competent handling of descriptive scenes of nature and of the famous, elusive segment of twilight in the mirror serve the original well.

The immoral urges of desire and lust are framed within the ritualistic restraint of the tea ceremony skillfully portrayed in *Thousand Cranes* (*Senbazuru*, 1949). With an even more daunting task than *Snow Country*, SEIDENSTICKER (1958) strives to balance the text's exotic elements with the deeper message concerning human experience and desire embodied in institutionalized rituals such as the tea ceremony and the *miai* or pre-arranged marital system.

The Sound of the Mountain (*Yama no oto*, 1949–54) was hailed as one of the best post-war novels to portray the state of old age. Through the vivid and sometimes sentimental observations of the protagonist Shingo, the reader gains insights into a post-war Japanese society in which the old and the new, the past and the present converge and conflict. Approaching death and the diminishing vitality of Shingo serve as a metaphor for the decaying, ruined Japan of the elderly. Ivan Morris praised the translation as a "masterpiece", and it was awarded the 1970 Book of the Year Award in the United States. The translation nevertheless had its detractors. Fukuoka Tôru harshly castigated SEIDENSTICKER's failure (1970) to reflect Kawabata's style faithfully (*Shi to tomo*, vol. 22, no. 1). Roger Thomas criticized the translation's "awkward Hemingway-like style".

The Lake (*Mizuumi*, 1954) is considered one of the less successful novels of this period because of its lack of a definite closure and its being published as a popular novel. The impulsive, obssessed main character Gimpei is a kind of hero very different from the previous pensive, decorous moral beings. Here, Kawabata explored the concept of *makai* (demonic realm) and the dark, perverse side of human deviation. Reiko TSUKIMURA's translation (1974) is generally accurate and readable, but its flat language fails to convey the frenzied, claustrophobic mood of the novel.

The House of Sleeping Beauties and Other Stories includes the title story ("Nemureru bijo", 1961) and famous short stories of the later period such as "One Arm" ("Kataude") and "Beast"("Kinjû"). These later stories provide a glimpse into the more eccentric side of Kawabata's writing, in which disillusionment with human relationships and the incapability of communication manifest in total silence ("Sleeping Beauties") and fragmented limbs ("One Arm").

Translations and the studies of Kawabata tend to focus on the few works that are associated with the Nobel Prize and ignore the bulk of the lesser-known short stories, novels and criticism that he produced during his long and productive career. His lyrical, episodic works, such as *Asakusa Kurenaidan*, popular fiction serialized in newspapers and women's magazines, his critiques on the work of his contemporaries, and his theorical exposition on fiction, *Shôsetsu no hôhô* [The Methodology of Fiction], are logically the next candidates for translation.

Two translated essays, *Japan the Beautiful and Myself* (Kawabata's Nobel Prize acceptance speech; translated SEIDENSTICKER, 1969), and *The Existence and Discovery of Beauty* (VIGLIELMO, 1969), a lecture delivered at the University of Hawaii, are also important for understanding the classical influences and underlying aesthetic principles in Kawabata's creative writings.

FAYE YUAN KLEEMAN

Further Reading

Boardman, Gwenn, "Kawabata Yasunari: A Critical Introduction", *Journal of Modern Literature*, 2 (September 1971) pp. 86–104

Keene, Donald, "Kawabata Yasunari" in his *Dawn to the West: Japanese Literature of the Modern Era*, 2 vols, New York: Holt Rinehart, 1984

Miyoshi, Masao, *The Accomplices of Silence: The Modern Japanese Novel*, Berkeley: University of California Press, 1974, pp. 94–121

Peterson, Gwenn Boardman, *The Moon in the Water: Understanding Tanizaki, Kawabata, and Mishima*, Honolulu: University of Hawaii Press, 1979, pp. 121–200

Swann, Thomas E., "The Master of Go" in *Approaches to the Modern Japanese Novel*, edited by Kinya Tsuruta and Swann, Tokyo: Sophia University Press, 1976

Swann, Thomas E., "Kawabata Yasunari" in *Approaches to the Modern Japanese Short Story*, edited by Swann and Kinya Tsuruta, Tokyo: Waseda University Press, 1982

Tsuruta, Kinya, "The Sound of the Mountain" in *Approaches to the Modern Japanese Novel*, edited by Tsuruta and Thomas E. Swann, Tokyo: Sophia University Press, 1976

Ueda, Makoto, "Kawabata Yasunari" in *Modern Japanese Writers and the Nature of Literature*, by Ueda, Stanford, California: Stanford University Press, 1976

Ueda, Makoto, "Snow Country" in *Approaches to the Modern Japanese Novel*, edited by Kinya Tsuruta and Thomas E. Swann, Tokyo: Sophia University Press, 1976

Vernon, Victoria, "Creating Koharu: The Image of Woman in the Works of Kawabata Yasunari and Tanizaki Jun'ichirō" in her *Daughters of the Moon: Wish, Will, and Social Constraint in Fiction by Modern Japanese Women*, Berkeley: University of California Institute of East Asian Studies, 1988

Nikos Kazantzakis 1883–1957

Greek poet, dramatist, novelist and essayist

Biography

Born in Iraklio (Heraklion), Crete, 18 February 1883, when the island was still part of the Ottoman Empire. His childhood experience of the revolutionary struggle against the Ottomans haunted him throughout his life, as did the larger-than-life figure of his father. He entered the University of Athens in 1902, ostensibly to study law, but his ambitions were already literary. In 1907 he went to Paris, where he wrote a postgraduate dissertation on Nietzsche's theory of the state while attending lectures by Henri Bergson, whose philosophical system became the centre of his own world-view. Back in Greece in 1909, he gained recognition as a playwright but earned his living through translations and children's books. In 1911 he married the novelist Galatea Alexiou (divorced 1926). A sojourn on Mount Athos in 1914 led him to consider "How man becomes eternal" as the central theme of his life and work. In 1917 he went into the mining business with a foreman named Zorba, and in 1919 he was sent by Prime Minister Venizelos to repatriate Greeks being persecuted in the Caucasus. Both experiences richly influenced subsequent novels. In 1920 everything changed with Venizelos's fall from power and then with Greece's defeat by Turkey in Anatolia in 1922. Disillusioned with nationalism and influenced by Galatea's left-wing orientation, Kazantzakis came to view Soviet Russia as the West's saviour. In Berlin in 1923 he completed his "post-communist credo", *The Saviors of God, Spiritual Exercises*, an attempt to amalgamate communism with Buddhism and Bergsonism. This became the guiding philosophy for all his subsequent writings. In 1924 he met Eleni (Helen) Samiou, who was to become his companion and, in 1945, his second wife. In 1925 he began his massive epic, *Odyssey*, meant to flesh out the ideas in *The Saviors of God*. All the while, he was earning his living chiefly by writing travel books. In 1927 he was invited to Moscow for the celebrations of the 10th anniversary of the Russian Revolution – the only Greek so honoured. After travelling extensively in the Soviet Union, he concluded that the ideal of communism was none other than "Americanization" – i.e., total materialism (see *Toda Raba*). The following years were occupied by attempts to escape Greece, where he was being prosecuted for atheism. Unsuccessful in establishing a career in Western Europe, he was forced back to Greece, where in 1933 he secluded himself on the island of Aegina in order to complete the *Odyssey* and write more plays, none of which was produced. When the Germans invaded Greece in 1941 he was confined on the island. He endured the famine following the invasion, composed *Zorba the Greek* during it, and generally overcame his alienation from his homeland. When the Germans left in 1944 he vowed to help Greece by entering politics as head of a small group of democratic socialists devoted to reconciliation. The civil war made this a futile gesture. Kazantzakis's final period (1946–57) was spent in exile, first in England, afterwards in France where he worked (1947–48) for Unesco, heading a programme for the translation of classic texts. During these last years, he obtained worldwide recognition, initially for *Zorba the Greek* after it was translated into French, then for the novels written in exile, some of which were published in translation before they appeared in Greek. Posthumously, the *Odyssey* in Kimon Friar's translation attracted rave reviews, whereas the Greek publication had been largely ignored or ridiculed. In 1956 Kazantzakis was awarded the Lenin Peace Prize and was the leading candidate for the Nobel Prize until the last minute, when the committee awarded it instead to Juan Ramón Jiménez. On 26 October 1957, at the age of 74, he died at Freiburg as a result of an obligatory inoculation against smallpox and cholera. The Greek Church refused to allow his body to lie in state in Athens, but he was buried with honour in his native Crete.

Kazantzakis translated works by Homer, Plato, Dante, Machiavelli, Goethe, Nietzsche, Darwin and Bergson.

Translations

Novella

Ofis kai kríno, 1906

Vasils, Theodora, *Serpent and Lily*, with the manifesto *The Sickness of the Age*, Berkeley: University of California Press, 1980

Novels

Toda-Raba, 1934 (in French), 1946 (in Greek translation)

Mims, Amy, *Toda Raba*, New York: Simon and Schuster, 1964

Le Jardin des rochers, 1939

Howard, Richard, *The Rock Garden*, New York: Simon and Schuster, 1963

Víos kai politeía tou Aléksi Zormpá, 1946

Wildman, Carl, *Zorba the Greek*, London: Lehmann, and New York: Simon and Schuster, 1952

O Kapetán Michális, 1953

Griffin, Jonathan, *Freedom or Death*, New York: Simon and Schuster, 1956; as *Freedom and Death*, Oxford: Cassirer, 1956

O Christós ksanastavrónetai, 1954

Griffin, Jonathan, *The Greek Passion*, New York: Simon and Schuster, 1953; as *Christ Re-crucified*, Oxford: Cassirer, 1954

O teleftaíos peirasmós, 1955

Bien, P.A., *The Last Temptation of Christ*, New York: Simon and Schuster, 1960; as *The Last Temptation*, Oxford: Cassirer, 1961

O ftochoúlis tou Theoú, 1956

Bien, P.A., *Saint Francis*, New York: Simon and Schuster, 1962; as *God's Pauper: St. Francis of Assisi*, Oxford: Cassirer, 1962

Oi adherfofádhes, 1963

Gianakas Dallas, Athena, *The Fratricides*, New York: Simon and Schuster, 1964; Oxford: Cassirer, 1967; London: Faber, 1974

Sta chrónia tou Meghálou Aleksándhrou, 1979 (for children)

Vasils, Theodora, *Alexander the Great: a Novel*, Athens: Ohio University Press, 1981

Sta palátia tis Knosoú, 1981 (for children)

Vasils, Theodora and Themi Vasils, *At the Palaces of Knossos: A Novel*, Athens: Ohio University Press, and London: Peter Owen, 1988

Poetry

Odíssia, 1938

Friar, Kimon, *The Odyssey: A Modern Sequel*, New York: Simon and Schuster, and London: Secker and Warburg, 1958

Selection of Plays

Gianakas Dallas, Athena, *Three Plays*, New York: Simon and Schuster, 1969 (contains *Melissa*, *Kouros*, *Christopher Columbus*)

Plays

Melissa, 1939, produced 1962

Gianakas Dallas, Athena, *Melissa* in *Three Plays*, translated by Gianakas Dallas, 1969

Koúros, 1955, produced 1977

Gianakas Dallas, Athena, *Kouros* in *Three Plays*, translated by Gianakas Dallas, 1969

Christóforos Kolómvos, 1956, produced 1975

Gianakas Dallas, Athena, *Christopher Columbus* in *Three Plays*, translated by Gianakas Dallas, 1969

Sódoma kai Gómora, 1956, produced 1983

Friar, Kimon, *Sodom and Gomorrah* in *Two Plays by Nikos Kazantzakis*, translated by Friar, St Paul, Minnesota: North Central, 1982

Voúdas, 1956, produced 1978

Friar, Kimon and Athena Dallis-Damis, *Buddha*, San Diego, California: Avant, 1983

Komodía, traghodía monóprakti, 1969

Friar, Kimon, *Comedy* in *Two Plays by Nikos Kazantzakis*, translated by Friar, St Paul, Minnesota: North Central, 1982

Travel Writing

Ispanía, 1937

Mims, Amy, *Spain*, New York: Simon and Schuster, 1963

Iaponía-Kína, 1938

Pappageotes, George C., *Japan, China: A Journal of Two Voyages to the Far East, 1935 and 1957*, New York: Simon and Schuster, 1963; as *Travels in China and Japan*, Oxford: Cassirer, 1964

Anglía, 1941

Mims, Amy, *England: A Travel Journal*, New York: Simon and Schuster, 1965; Oxford: Cassirer, 1971

Taksidhévontas: Italía – Aígyptos – Siná – Ierousalím – Kypros – O Moriás, 1961

Vasils, Theodora and Themi Vasils, *Journeying: Travels in Italy, Egypt, Sinai, Jerusalem and Cyprus*, Boston: Little Brown, 1975

O Moriás in *Taksidhévontas*, 1961

Reed, F.A., *Journey to the Morea*, New York: Simon and Schuster, 1965; as *Travels in Greece (Journey to the Morea)*, Oxford: Cassirer, 1966

Letters

Mims, Amy, *Nikos Kazantzakis: A Biography Based on His Letters*, by Helen Kazantzakis, New York: Simon and Schuster, and Oxford: Cassirer, 1968

Ramp, Philip and Katerina Anghelaki-Rooke, *The Suffering God: Selected Letters to Galatea and to Papastephanou*, New Rochelle, New York: Caratzas, 1979

Other Writing

Salvatores Dei. Askitikí, 1927; revised edition as *Askitikí. Salvatores Dei*, 1945

Friar, Kimon, *The Saviors of God; Spiritual Exercises*, New York: Simon and Schuster, 1960

Anaforá ston Gréko, 1961

Bien, P.A., *Report to Greco*, New York: Simon and Schuster, and Oxford: Cassirer, 1965

Sympósion, 1971

Vasils, Themi and Theodora Vasils, *Symposium*, New York: Minerva Press, 1974; New York: Crowell, 1975

Nikos Kazantzakis's career would have been a disaster without translation. He did gain early recognition in Greece as a dramatist but abandoned the stage in disgust after one of his plays was denied production. If Greeks knew him at all in the 1920s and 1930s it was as a journalist, polemicist, and writer of very fine travel books. His study *The Saviors of God, Spiritual Exercises* was largely ignored when it appeared in 1927, and the gargantuan *Odyssey*, longer than Homer's *Iliad* and *Odyssey* combined, was derided as an unreadable monstrosity. He was just beginning to regain access to the Greek stage in the 1940s when political developments forced him into exile. At that point he had published only two novels, both in the first decade of his career. He still thought of the novel as a secondary genre, following poetry and drama; nevertheless, he had written *Zorba* in 1941–42 under pressure from his companion, Eleni Samiou, and a whole new career as a novelist opened up for him when this work was translated into French by Yvonne Gauthier (aided by Galatea's sister, Elli Alexiou), was published under the title *Alexis Zorba; ou, Le Rivage de Crète* (Paris: Editions du Chêne, 1947), and was reviewed in glowing terms – for example, as "une grandiose explosion de lyrisme, une épopée chaleureuse ... Dans notre littérature contemporaine à quel écrivain pourrait-on comparer Kazantsaki?" (*Paru*, July 1948).

Kazantzakis began immediately to translate some of his plays into French; more importantly, he found a devoted translator of his works in Börje Knös, a high official in Sweden's Ministry of National Education. Knös's Swedish rendition of *Zorba* came out in Stockholm in 1949. Meanwhile, *Zorba* had been accepted by publishers in England, the United States, and Czechoslovakia. All the subsequent novels were translated first by Knös. Unfortunately, the English translations of *Zorba*, *The Greek Passion*, and *Freedom or Death* that followed were not done directly from the Greek. Indeed, there seems to have been a sequence going from Swedish to German, from German to French, and finally from French to English! When Helen Kazantzakis discovered this after her husband's death, she forbade her British publisher to commission further translations until they could be done directly from the original Greek. This new (and obviously much better) arrangement started with Peter BIEN's rendition (1960) of *The Last Temptation*.

Along with Knös, the most important figure in the huge "translation industry" that made Kazantzakis's works available in scores of languages was Kimon FRIAR. He and Kazantzakis first met in 1951. Friar undertook to translate the 33,333 lines of Kazantzakis's *Odyssey* and even relinquished a secure teaching position in the United States in order to complete the project. He worked intensively with Kazantzakis, sometimes face-to-face, sometimes by post, finishing a prose version in 1954, then collaborating closely with the author again as he reworked the prose into verse. The immense text was handsomely published by Max Schuster in 1958.

The peculiarities of the Kazantzakis "translation industry"

need to be examined somewhat further. *Toda Raba* is a case in point. Written in French, it was translated into Greek by Yannis Manglis in 1946. The English version by Amy MIMS (1964) is from the Greek, not the French original. This causes problems. Where Kazantzakis writes "tu interviens" (you are intervening, interfering, taking sides), for example, the English has "you're getting involved" – almost the opposite of the true meaning. Why? Not because the translator misunderstood the Greek but because the Greek – *endiaféresai* (you are interested) – is a mistranslation of the French. The moral of the story is: translate from the original.

The second- or third-hand translations of *Zorba* (WILDMAN, 1952), *The Greek Passion* (GRIFFIN, 1953), and *Freedom or Death* (GRIFFIN, 1956) read well enough in English but are sometimes very far from their original texts owing to excisions, additions, and bloopers that can be explained only by this same failure to work from the original. An example in *Zorba* is "Like two wild ducks [sic]" (p. 307) for the Greek's "like two comrades" ("sa dyo syntrófoi").

Translating Kazantzakis (and also many other Greek writers) is a special challenge because Modern Greek can so easily dip into Medieval Greek, the Koine of the New Testament, or Ancient Greek, and nevertheless be readily understood by educated readers in Greece. English certainly cannot dip into Anglo-Saxon or Middle English in the same way; nor can it use the King James version of the Bible when Kazantzakis quotes the Koine Greek of the Gospels, since the former has acquired an "elevated" tone in English whereas Koine Greek was meant for the common people and is still felt to be "ordinary" in Greece today. But these and other difficulties also make translation from Greek an exhilarating game in which the translator attempts to do justice to registers going all the way from peasant speech to Plato. All Greek writers of the late 19th and early 20th centuries were aware that "demotic", the Greek of everyday speech, was being developed in their hands as a literary vehicle; they did not have a Shakespeare or a Dante in their tradition who had accomplished this already. Their experimentation with vocabulary, syntax, and prosody is largely lost in translation; yet the translator must be aware of this added dimension and must try somehow to create an equivalent in the target language. So, although Kazantzakis was extremely beholden to translators, translators in their turn are extremely beholden to Kazantzakis for giving them texts that are so linguistically exciting.

PETER BIEN

Further Reading

Bien, P.A., *Kazantzakis and the Linguistic Revolution in Greek Literature*, Princeton, New Jersey: Princeton University Press, 1972

Bien, P.A., *Kazantzakis: Politics of the Spirit*, Princeton, New Jersey: Princeton University Press, 1989

Bien, Peter, *Nikos Kazantzakis: Novelist*, London: Duckworth, and New Rochelle, New York: Caratzas, 1989

Levitt, Morton P., *The Cretan Glance: The World and Art of Nikos Kazantzakis*, Columbus: Ohio State University Press, 1980

Middleton, Darren J.N. and Peter Bien (editors), *God's Struggler: Religion in the Writings of Nikos Kazantzakis*, Macon, Georgia: Mercer University Press, 1996

Prevelakis, Pandelis, *Nikos Kazantzakis and His "Odyssey": A Study of the Poet and the Poem*, translated by Philip Sherrard, New York: Simon and Schuster, 1961

Idwār (Edwar) al-Kharrāt 1926–

Egyptian novelist and short-story writer

Biography

Born in Alexandria in 1926 and brought up in a Coptic Christian environment. Al-Kharrāt studied law at Alexandria University, and was detained (1948–50) because of his political activities. He worked for an insurance company, and in the 1960s edited a literary magazine.

Al-Kharrāt's writing – even when not autobiographical in the strict sense of the term – is frequently marked by autobiographical elements that reflect his status as a member of a minority community in a predominantly Muslim society. He is generally acknowledged as one of the pioneers of Egyptian "modernism". His first publications were collections of short stories, beginning with *Hītān 'āliya* [High Walls] in 1959. He did not turn to the novel form until comparatively late in his career, publishing his first novel, *Rāma wa-al-Tinnīn* [Rama and the Dragon], in 1979 – since when he has gone on to produce some half-dozen further novels, as well as further collections of short stories, literary criticism and translations from Western languages.

Translations

Novels

Turābuhā Za'farān, 1986
Liardet, Frances, *City of Saffron*, London: Quartet, 1989

Ya Banāt Iskandariyya, 1990
Liardet, Frances, *Girls of Alexandria*, London: Quartet, 1993

In terms of background and experience, al-Kharrāt shares some characteristics with the younger writers belonging to the so-called Egyptian "generation of the sixties", of whom Jamāl al-Ghītānī is perhaps the most talented. Like many of the "generation of the sixties" (though at an earlier date), al-Kharrāt had been imprisoned for his political views. Following the Arab defeat in the 1967 war with Israel, he also edited for a time the literary and cultural magazine *Gallīrī 68* ("Gallery 68"), which brought together members of the new generation of writers to voice their revolt against the establishment, both literary and political. Despite these associations, however, his work remains entirely distinctive, both because of the comparative (though not total) absence of direct political comment, and because his outlook has remained free from the bitterness and cynicism that has characterized the work of many younger Egyptian writers. In al-Kharrāt's writing the individual is still important, capable of asserting himself and seeking fulfilment in a world that he perceives through a subjective kaleidoscope of rapidly shifting senses and feelings.

Equally distinctive, and important, is al-Kharrāt's use of language, marked by long sentences in which new ideas are triggered by a character's perceptions and memories, undermining the logical temporal sequence of events and often producing an effect akin to that of a prose poem. Al-Kharrāt's command of the subtleties of the Arabic language far outstrips that of most of his contemporaries and, although it cannot be said that his style is universally successful, at its best it succeeds in combining precision of description with a powerful sense of the subjectivity of human perception and emotion. Less successful passages result when his fondness for verbal jugglery is allowed to dominate the text, producing a turgid – at times, almost unreadable – effect.

These linguistic difficulties pose a powerful challenge for any translator and it is not surprising that, to date, only two novels and a handful of al-Kharrāt's short stories have been translated into English. Neither *Rāma wa-al-Tinnīn* nor its successor *al-Zaman al-Ākhar* [The Other Time] (1985) yet exists in an English translation, and despite the obvious importance of the theme – a love affair, between the Copt Mīkhā'īl and a Muslim woman, which challenges conventional Islamic attitudes – it is hard to see either book having more than limited appeal for the average English reader. In *Turābuhā Za'farān*, however, al-Kharrāt has produced a more readily accessible work, in which the autobiographical element is more evident. Set in the Alexandria of the 1930s and 1940s, it is linked to the earlier novels in that the protagonist is again called Mīkhā'īl: the story (subtitled in the original Arabic "Alexandrian Texts") tells the story of his progress through childhood and his gradual loss of innocence, culminating in his involvement in the revolutionary movement in its struggle against the British occupying forces. The images encapsulated in the titles of the book's nine chapters – "Billowing White Clouds", "A Small Bar in Bab el-Karasta", "White-Winged Gulls", "The Green Bronze Sword", etc. – provide focal-points around which Mīkhā'īl's memories revolve; as he moves towards adulthood, women play an increasingly important role in his life, but the real heroine of the book remains Alexandria herself, vividly depicted in a finely crafted prose which has aptly been described as Proustian.

Yā Banāt Iskandariyya returns us to the Alexandrian world of Mīkhā'īl through a narrative in which al-Kharrāt's imaginative technique is, if anything, even more skilfully deployed. Again, the protagonist's memories provide the links that bind the book together – memories above all of the women of Alexandria, be they neighbours, schoolgirls or prostitutes. Al-Kharrāt succeeds in depicting a city whose sights, smells and tastes can be almost felt by the reader through the medium of his prose; at the same time, the girls assume an almost mystical character, as symbols of the eternal feminine:

> Girls of Alexandria, sea of Alexandria: constant unending seduction: affection which cannot perish.
> However many she is, she is one: however fleeting, she is eternal.
> How can I resist her?

It goes without saying that al-Kharrāt's prose, which marries Western modernistic techniques with a profound knowledge both of the Arabic language and of the Arabic literary tradition, requires a translator with very special gifts if the end-product is to convey successfully the spirit of the original. Al-Kharrāt is himself a distinguished translator into Arabic, who has published a number of literary translations, including a version (made at second hand, via English and French) of Tolstoi's *War and Peace*. In Frances LIARDET (1989, 1993) he has been fortunate to find a translator able to make his unique vision her own and to express it in an English idiom so finely crafted that the reader is seldom conscious of reading a translation at all; this is no mean feat when the translator is confronted with long, unpunctuated Arabic stream-of-consciousness passages which may at times meander on for a page or more.

In the preface to *City of Saffron* Frances LIARDET acknowledges the generous help and advice she received from al-Kharrāt himself in making her version, and compares the art of translation to building a dry-stone wall: the trick is to "choose the [stone] which fits snugly enough to support the weight of succeeding stones". Her two translations discussed in this essay are generally considered to be among the most successful attempts to render works of modern Arabic literature into English. They deserve to be widely read, both for the brilliance of al-Kharrāt's original text and for the polish and vigour of Frances Liardet's translations.

PAUL STARKEY

Further Reading

Badawi, M.M. (editor), *Modern Arabic Literature*, Cambridge and New York: Cambridge University Press, 1992 (The Cambridge History of Arabic Literature), pp. 267–68, 319–21

Badawi, M.M., *A Short History of Modern Arabic Literature*, Oxford: Clarendon Press, and New York: Oxford University Press, 1993, pp. 174–76

al-Kharrat, Edwar, "The Mashriq" in *Modern Literature in the Near and Middle East 1850–1970*, edited by Robin Ostle, London and New York: Routledge, 1991

al-Nowaihi, M., "Memory and Imagination in Edwar al-Kharrat's *Turābuhā Za'farān*", *Journal of Arabic Literature* 24 (1994) pp. 34–57

Khayyām, Omar

See Omar Khayyām

Danilo Kiš 1935–1989

Serbian novelist, short-story writer and dramatist

Biography

Kiš was born in Subotica, Serbia, 22 February 1935. He lost his parents, who were Jewish, when they were sent to Auschwitz in 1944. He was brought up by another relative and went to school over the border in Hungary and later in Yugoslavia. He graduated from Belgrade University in 1958 and went on to teach Serbo-Croat in various French universities. Kiš lived in Paris from 1979.

His richly-textured fiction drew on his own experiences and those of other Jews, notably in occupied Belgrade. It engaged with human suffering, particularly that generated by war. His first novel *Mansarda* [The Garret] appeared in 1962. As well as producing novels and stories for traditional publication Kiš wrote for the stage, television and radio; he also translated from French (Baudelaire, Verlaine) and other languages. Kiš was awarded literary prizes at home and abroad. He died 15 October 1989.

Translations

Novels

Bašta, pepeo, 1965

Hannaher, William J., *Garden, Ashes*, New York: Harcourt Brace, 1975; London: Faber, 1985

Peščanik, 1972

Manheim, Ralph, *Hourglass*, New York: Farrar Straus, and London: Faber, 1990

Grobnica za Borisa Davidovica, 1976

Mikić-Mitchell, Duška, *A Tomb for Boris Davidovich*, with an introduction by Joseph Brodsky, New York: Harcourt Brace, 1978; Harmondsworth: Penguin, 1980

Enciklopedija mrtvih, 1983

Heim, Michael Henry, *The Encyclopedia of the Dead*, New York: Farrar Straus, and London: Faber, 1989

The four novels that have been translated into English represent the major works of this exceptionally talented, original and important European writer. Danilo Kiš was born in Northern Yugoslavia, near to the Hungarian and Romanian borders. More importantly, he was born in 1935 and his father was a Jew who was taken, with several other family members, to Auschwitz and never returned. Kiš thus experienced the horrors of the Nazi regime at first hand. The theme of his father's disappearance, at an age when those around the child felt a need to protect him from the truth, thus deepening the trauma of his bewilderment, has provided a shaping principle for three of Kiš's novels, including *Garden, Ashes* and *Hourglass*. In an important sense, the age into which Kiš was born is more significant than the place: his work is devoted to an examination of the human potential for brutality unleashed by World War II. At the same time, he acknowledges a particular responsibility as a Jew to treat the other great horror of the 20th century: the Stalinist purges. He felt this imperative keenly as he grew up in the hypocrisy and double-speak of communist Eastern Europe. Kiš studied Comparative Literature at the University of Belgrade, emerging with a wide knowledge of the world's literatures and the demands of creative writing in the late 20th century. In particular he shares a contemporary frustration with invention, in favour of the "document", since no work of the imagination could be either as horrific or as fantastic as "reality". Kiš wrote of writing as "an alchemical process", a transmutation of "matter" into the "perfect metal". The resulting works are deeply serious, in terms of both their content and their commitment to the writer's craft. At once intricate and fragmented, they present a special challenge to the translator.

Garden, Ashes is an intense evocation of growing up into a world of sinister mystery and dark undercurrents, but one also of colour, light and texture, involving all the senses in one compelling and ultimately undecipherable whole. The valiant translation by William HANNAHER (1975) conveys much of this intricate complex. Here an inefficient suicide lives on:

> The next day, she was found unconscious amidst the murderous flowers. Subsequently, as the victim of the

> vengeance of the flower gods, she fell beneath automobiles and streetcars. Peasant carts and swift fiacres ran over her. Yet every time she emerged from under the wheels hurt but alive.

In general Hannaher reads fluently enough until compared with the original. Then it becomes clear that Hannaher has let Kiš down in details of phrasing and above all in terms of rhythm. And, paradoxically perhaps, it is this aspect of Kiš's style that acquires an increasingly crucial role as the content of his works become more superficially documentary.

A Tomb for Boris Davidovich offers a challenge of a particular kind, as the different fragments of which the novel is composed make different stylistic demands. This work is an exploration of the mind of the terrorist and the torturer, focused on the Stalinist age but ranging far in time and space. The English translation (MIKIĆ-MITCHELL, 1978) has served the text well. Brodsky, in his introduction to Mikić-Mitchell, declares this "very dark book" (whose writing he characterizes as much more sparse than in the "gem of lyrical prose" that is *Garden, Ashes*) to have been "splendidly translated into English". The style, dense but agile, of the original is often well caught:

> If the roads of destiny were not so unpredictable in their complex architecture, where the end is never known but only sensed, one might say that, despite his horrible end, Karl Traube was born under a lucky star (provided our thesis is acceptable that, despite everything, the temporary suffering of existence is worth more than the final void of nothingness).

To date this is the work that has had most success in terms of reprintings. The book has wide appeal as an extraordinarily vivid and powerful account of a phenomenon of central importance to an understanding of the present age.

The Encyclopedia of the Dead, described as "a strange and lyrical meditation on the meaning and nature of love and death", is a collection of stories of astounding referential range. It draws on the Bible, the Koran and a wealth of historical and contemporary texts, illustrating a statement Kiš quotes as made in connection with Borges: "Erudition is the modern form of fantasy" ("The Anatomy Lesson", translated by Michael Henry Heim, *Formations*, 2/1, Spring 1985, pp 176–84). *Hourglass* is arguably Kiš's finest work, combining his main themes and technique in a documentary of extraordinary power. It has the textual intricacy and sheer beauty of *Garden, Ashes*, but these are combined with the mature observations of a deeply sceptical and essentially creative mind. The translations of the latter two novels (HEIM, 1989, and MANHEIM, 1990) represents fine examples of the craft; it is clear that both translators have made strenuous efforts to reproduce the complex colours and rhythms of the original and they have succeeded in conveying the particular genius of this remarkable writer.

CELIA HAWKESWORTH

Further Reading

Bankovich-Rosul, Jelena S. "The Awakening of the Sleepers in Danilo Kiš's *Encyclopedia of the Dead*", *Serbian Studies*, 5/3 (1990) pp. 85–89

Birnbaum, M.D. and R. Trager-Verchovsky, "History and Human Relationship in the Fiction of Danilo Kiš" in *History: Another Text*, Ann Arbor: Michigan Studies in the Humanities, 1988, pp. 29–44

Birnbaum, M.D., "The Fiction of Danilo Kiš", *Cross Currents*, 8 (1989) pp. 345–60

Czarny, Norbert, "Imaginary-Real Lives: On Danilo Kiš", *Cross Currents*, 3 (1984) pp. 279–84

Gorjup, Branko, "From 'Enchantment' to 'Documentation'", *Canadian Slavonic Papers*, 29/4 (1987) pp. 387–94

Longinovic, Tomislav Z., "The Improbable Universe: Ideology, Identity and Borderline Poetics in the XX Century Slavic Novel (Kiš)" (dissertation), Iowa City: University of Iowa, 1989

March, Michael, "Danilo Kiš interviewed", *Normal*, 4 (1990) p. 86

Oja, Matt F., "Fictional History and Historical Fiction: Solzhenitsyn and Kiš", *History and Theory*, 27 (1988) pp.111–24

Riley, Carolyn (editor), *Contemporary Literary Criticism*, vol. 57, Detroit: Gale, 1990: Kiš entry, pp: 239–54 (reprints of 15 reviews and articles)

Rosenburg, Karen, "An Interview with Danilo Kiš", *Formations*, 5/2 (1989) pp. 46–51

White, Edmund, "Danilo Kiš: The Obligations of Form", *Southwest Review*, 71 (1986) pp. 363–77

Heinrich von Kleist 1777–1811

German dramatist and short-story writer

Biography

Born in Frankfurt an der Oder 18 October 1777 into a noble Prussian family with military traditions. He entered the army himself, serving in the campaign against the French revolutionary forces. However, he found army life uncongenial and resigned his commission in 1799. In 1800 he became engaged to a general's daughter, Wilhelmine von Zenge, but the engagement was later broken off. Kleist studied at the

University of Frankfurt an der Oder and became interested in philosophy; his reading of Kant in particular encouraged a natural tendency to depression. He travelled widely in Germany and Switzerland, where he wrote his first play, *Die Familie Schroffenstein*, published anonymously. In 1803 he suffered a nervous breakdown and burned the manuscript of his tragedy on the subject of Robert Guiscard, Duke of Normandy; he was later persuaded to rewrite a fragment of this play. Arrested in French-occupied Berlin in 1807 on suspicion of being a spy, he spent several months in a French prison, where he wrote his tragedy *Penthesilea*. His two comedies *Amphitryon* and *Der zerbrochene Krug* were also written in the first decade of the 19th century. His later plays *Das Käthchen von Heilbronn* and *Die Hermannschlacht* took up patriotic German themes in reaction to the Napoleonic wars. Kleist now went into journalism, and was co-founder of a journal called *Phöbus*, which soon failed. However, he became editor of the *Berliner Abendblätter*. Meanwhile he was writing a number of *Novellen*, comprising in all eight stories of varying length, first published in various periodicals and collected into two volumes as *Erzählungen* (1810 and 1811). His last play, *Prinz Friedrich von Homburg*, was completed in 1810. On 21 November 1811 Kleist entered into a suicide pact with a friend, Henriette Vogel, who was ill and wished to escape a painful death; he shot first her and then himself on the banks of the Wannsee near Berlin.

Translations

Selections

Constantine, David (editor and translator), *Selected Writings*, London: Dent, 1997 (contains essays, all the stories, 3 plays, and some letters)

Greenberg, Martin, *Five Plays*, New Haven, Connecticut and London: Yale University Press, 1988 (contains *Amphitryon*; *The Broken Jug*; *Penthesilea*; *Prince Frederick of Homburg*; *A Fragment of the Tragedy of Robert Guiscard*)

Hinderer, Walter (editor), *Plays*, with a foreword by E.L. Doctorow, New York: Continuum, 1982 (contains *The Broken Pitcher*, translated by Swan; *Amphitryon*, translated by Passage; *Penthesilea*, translated by Trevelyan; *Prince Frederick of Homburg*, translated by Sherry)

Plays

Amphitryon, 1807, produced 1899

Greenberg, Martin, *Amphitryon: A Comedy after Molière* in *Five Plays*, translated by Greenberg, 1988

Passage, Charles E., in *Amphitryon: Three Plays in New Verse Translations* [Kleist; Molière; Plantus], translated by Passage and James H. Martinband, Chapel Hill: University of North Carolina Press, 1973; also in *Plays*, edited by Walter Hinderer, 1982

Robert Guiskard, Herzog der Normänner, reconstructed dramatic fragment, 1808

Greenberg, Martin, *A Fragment of The Tragedy of Robert Guiscard, Duke of the Normans* in *Five Plays*, translated by Greenberg, 1988

Penthesilea, 1808, produced 1976

Greenberg, Martin, *Penthesilea* in *Five Plays*, translated by Greenberg, 1988

Lamport, F.J., *Penthesilea* in *Five German Tragedies*, translated by Lamport, Harmondsworth: Penguin, 1969

Trevelyan, Humphrey, *Penthesilea* in *The Classic Theater*, edited by Eric Bentley, New York: Doubleday, 1959; also in *Plays*, edited by Walter Hinderer, 1982

Der zerbrochene Krug, 1811, produced 1808

Greenberg, Martin, *The Broken Jug* in *Five Plays*, translated by Greenberg, 1988

Morgan, Bayard Quincy, *The Broken Pitcher*, Chapel Hill: University of North Carolina Press, 1961

Swan, Jon, *The Broken Pitcher* in *Plays*, edited by Walter Hinderer, 1982

Prinz Friedrich von Homburg, 1821

Greenberg, Martin, *Prince Frederick of Homburg*, in *Five Plays*, translated by Greenberg, 1988

Lloyd, Francis and William Newton, *The Prince of Homburg* in their *Prussia's Representative Man*, London: Trübner, 1875

Sherry, Peggy Meyer, *Prince Frederick of Homburg* in *Plays*, edited by Walter Hinderer, 1982

Stories and *Novellen*

Erzählungen, 1810–11 (contains "Michael Kohlhaas", "Die Marquise von O", "Das Erdbeben in Chili", "Die Verlobung in St. Domingo", "Das Bettelweib von Locarno", "Der Findling", "Die heilige Cäcilie", and "Der Zweikampf")

Greenberg, Martin, *The Marquise of O and Other Stories*, New York: Criterion, 1960; London: Faber, 1963 (contains all 8 stories)

Luke, David and Nigel Reeves, *The Marquise of O and Other Stories*, Harmondsworth and New York: Penguin, 1978 (contains all 8 stories)

Taylor, Ronald, *Six German Romantic Tales*, London: Angel Books, 1985 (contains "The Earthquake in Chile" and "The Betrothal on Santo Domingo")

Single Story

"Michael Kohlhaas", 1810

Kirkup, James, *Michael Kohlhaas*, London and Glasgow: Blackie, 1967

Lloyd, Francis and William Newton, *Michael Kohlhaas* in their *Prussia's Representative Man*, London: Trübner, 1875

Essay

Über das Marionettentheater, 1924

Wilford, Gerti, *On a Theatre of Marionettes*, London: Acorn, 1989

The stage works of Heinrich von Kleist are regarded in Germany as artistically almost on a par with those of Schiller and Goethe, although Goethe was antipathetic to the younger dramatist, not altogether surprisingly, since the turmoil of mind manifested by Kleist himself and his characters was symptomatic of a time when the optimistic rationalism of the Enlightenment was wearing thin. Goethe's own production of Kleist's comedy *Der zerbrochene Krug* at the Weimar court theatre was a failure: the minds of the two dramatists were not in accord. As E.L. Doctorow points out in his preface to the 1982 volume *Plays* (edited by HINDERER) containing translations of four of

Kleist's plays, "Kleistians struggle monumentally with their perceptions; something else than what they expected is happening to them ... No wonder Franz Kafka loved this writer." Ambiguity of intention and action is characteristic of the figures in Kleist's dramas, notably in his most famous play, *Prinz Friedrich von Homburg*, in which the protagonist, facing execution for having anticipated a battle order (although his anticipation of it in fact won the battle), reacts in a way far from the accepted heroic norm and yet appears to redeem his honour, is pardoned and wins the hand of his beloved in a happy ending of a complex and unsettling nature.

This play, and Kleist's comedy *Der zerbrochene Krug* (variously produced in English-language versions as *The Broken Pitcher*, *The Broken Jug* and *The Cracked Pot*, see below), have received rather more attention in the English-speaking world than his other dramas. *Der zerbrochene Krug*, a comedy of rustic naïveté and corruption – naïveté on the part of the young lovers Eve and Ruprecht, corruption personified in the village judge Adam, whose designs on Eve are eventually unveiled and thwarted by the visiting inspector Walter – has struck various theatrical directors in the English-speaking world as being susceptible of adaptation to other localities, periods and dialects. An adaptation of 1956 for stage performance, by Donald Harron, transferred the action to the Canadian province of Western Ontario in 1813; a stage version by Henry Livings produced at the Stratford East Theatre in London in 1986 moved the setting to the Pennines during the Napoleonic wars; and most recently a version by Blake Morrison in Yorkshire dialect and entitled *The Cracked Pot* was produced in the United Kingdom. Of the versions available in print, the translation by MORGAN (1961) is in rather conventional blank verse, with some archaisms, the version by SWAN (1982) is also in blank verse, using a rather freer line, while the best to date is by GREENBERG (1988).

The same can be said of GREENBERG's translations of the other four dramas by Kleist in his volume, the further titles being *Amphitryon*, *Penthesilea*, *Prinz Friedrich von Homburg* and the fragment *Robert Guiskard*, of which he alone provides an English version. Throughout, abandoning the standard iambic pentameter, he employs sinewy free verse with conversational rhythms, in line of descent from the verse drama "revival" of the 1950s as represented by T.S. Eliot and Christopher Fry. His versions of *Amphitryon*, *Penthesilea* and *The Prince of Homburg* all move at a more rapid pace than their predecessors by PASSAGE, TREVELYAN and SHERRY respectively in the 1982 volume edited by Hinderer. *Penthesilea*, as LAMPORT (1969) points out in his preface to the Penguin Classics edition of his *Five German Tragedies*, presents the translator with special problems: "For sheer ferocity and bloodthirstiness, few tragedies can compare with *Penthesilea* ... much of it is written in an extremely distorted syntax ... impossible to imitate in an uninflected language like English. Partly this seems to be a deliberate imitation of classical epic verse." Lamport's own version of Kleist's complex account of the relationship between Penthesilea, the Queen of the Amazons, and the hero Achilles is in any case a good one, in regular iambic pentameters.

Another and considerably earlier version of *Prinz Friedrich von Homburg* well worth a mention is the translation by LLOYD & NEWTON (1875) in their book *Prussia's Representative Man*, with which they set out to introduce Kleist to the British public. Their biographical and critical account is followed by versions of the full text of the play and of one of the stories, indeed the longest, *Michael Kohlhaas*. The choice of these two major works by Kleist is well judged, and so is their rendering into good, unpretentious 19th-century English.

While the English-speaking stage has steered clear of the historical pageantry and patriotism of *Das Käthchen von Heilbronn* (which none the less also contains Kleistian psychological complexity in the figure of the masochistically devoted heroine of the title) and *Die Hermannsschlacht*, and has also left aside the domestic tragedy of *Die Familie Schroffenstein*, Kleist's other plays have had a number of stage performances either in adaptations of existing translations or in new translations for specific productions. Thus a new translation of *Penthesilea* by Neil Curry was made for a production in London at the Tower Theatre in 1961, and TREVELYAN's translation, in an adaptation by Eric Bentley, was given as *The Fall of the Amazons* in Buffalo, New York, in 1979. A specially commissioned version of the work for the BBC by Robert Nye was broadcast in August 1971. Amphitryon, in a translation by Lawrence Wilson, was given a television production in the UK in 1953. Although a French production of *Prinz Friedrich von Homburg* with the actor Gérard Philipe in the title role proved very successful in France at the Avignon Festival of 1951, the play had to wait for a British premiere until 1976, when it was performed in a translation by Jonathan Griffin at the Manchester Royal Exchange Theatre, with Tom Courtenay in the lead. This version was also produced in the US in the same year, and a television version was transmitted there in 1977. The play received another British translation, by John James, for a production on the Cottesloe stage of the National Theatre in 1982.

Kleist's *Novellen* have found rather more popularity in the English-speaking world than his plays. Perhaps the ironies, ambiguities and often violent drama of his plots appear more approachable on the printed page. These works of prose fiction vary in length from the extremely short ghost story "Das Bettelweib von Locarno" ("The Beggar Woman of Locarno"), often regarded as a model of its kind, to the very long "Michael Kohlhaas", a dramatic tale of the eponymous horse-dealer's inexorable pursuit of justice, which equally inexorably brings him to the scaffold. This story, bulked out towards the end by a semi-supernatural sub-plot generally thought to be a flaw, is long enough to stand on its own, both in the 19th-century translation given by LLOYD & NEWTON (see above) as a specimen of Kleist's fiction, and in the good, straightforward translation by KIRKUP (1967). It also appears in the two volumes containing all eight of Kleist's stories translated by GREENBERG (1960) and LUKE & REEVES (1978). Nearly 20 years separate these two translations, the period during which Greenberg was working on the perhaps more difficult task of translating the five plays, and Luke & Reeves write in the preface to their 1978 version: "We have felt that a new attempt was justified: Martin Greenberg's version (... now out of print) was marred by too many errors of comprehension and taste, which we have tried to avoid, while remaining in good measure indebted to its frequent felicities". Their Penguin Classics version is an excellent rendering, conveying the menace and irony found even in the two stories ("The Marquise of O" and "The Duel") that do not end in tragedy. Two of the shorter stories that do culminate in tragic violence, "The Earthquake in Chile" and "The Betrothal on Santo Domingo", are also given fine renderings into easy and readable English prose by TAYLOR (1985) in *Six German Romantic Tales* (the other four stories are two by E.T.A. Hoffmann and two by Ludwig Tieck).

The most famous of Kleist's journalistic pieces, his essay on the marionette theatre, received a translation in a limited edition by WILFORD (1989), with etchings and engravings by Hellmuth Weissenborn. A previous translation was contained in *German Romantic Criticism*, edited by A. Leslie Willson, vol. 21 of The German Library, New York, Continuum, 1982.

It is interesting to note that while Kleist's reputation in the German-speaking countries has not really been matched outside them through the translated versions of his works, they can be said to have "translated" very successfully into other media in the 20th century, notably as opera librettos. Although Richard Strauss described Kleist as *uncomponierbar* ("uncomposable"), composers of the mid-20th century have not agreed with him. *Penthesilea* was set by Othmar Schoeck in his opera of 1927; *Der Zerbrochene Krug* provided the theme for a chamber opera by Fritz Geissler of the former East Germany in 1971; and *Prinz Friedrich von Homburg* was the basis of an opera by Hans Werner Henze (1960). Also worth mentioning is Eric Rohmer's film version (1976) of *Die Marquise von O*, made in German, shown with English sub-titles in the English-speaking countries.

ANTHEA BELL

Further Reading

Maass, Joachim, *Kleist: A Biography*, translated by Ralph Manheim, London: Secker and Warburg, and New York: Farrar Straus, 1983

Reeve, William C., *In Pursuit of Power: Heinrich von Kleist's Machiavellian Protagonists*, Toronto: University of Toronto Press, 1987

Reeve, William C., *Kleist on Stage, 1804–1987*, Montreal: McGill-Queen's University Press, 1993

Stahl, Ernst Ludwig, *Heinrich von Kleist's Dramas*, Oxford: Blackwell, 1948; revised edition, 1961

See also the prefaces by Greenberg to his version of the five plays, and by Luke & Reeves to their translation of all the stories in the Penguin Classics edition.

Kong-zi

See Confucius

The Koran (al-Qur'ān) 7th century

The Koran is the sacred book of Islam. For Muslims it is the word of God as revealed by the archangel Gabriel to the prophet Muhammad and thence to mankind. Some non-Muslims take the view that it is the composition of Muhammad, with the most sympathetic suggesting that brooding by Muhammad eventually induced an involuntary recitation.

The central theme of the Koran/Qur'ān is the belief in one God, the merciful God who is the Creator of Heaven and Earth and all things and beings in them. Along with the passages that tell of God and His signs, there are also stories of people and prophets, in which one finds Arabian, Old Testament and New Testament material and a little from later centuries. Exhortation to belief and rectitude is common from the earliest revelations onwards. There is also much polemic against the unbelievers, often connected with vivid eschatological pictures; an Apocalypse which is the prelude to the Day of Judgement; the Judgement, when each individual will be judged and the righteous conveyed to Heaven and its bliss and the unrighteous to Hell and its miseries. After Muhammad moved from Mecca to Medina in 622 (the *hijra*) one finds guidance on more specific religious and legal matters.

Translations

Muslim

'Ali, Abdullah Yusuf, *The Holy Quran: Text, Translation and Commentary* (parallel texts), Lahore: Ashraf, 1934

'Ali, Muhammad, *The Holy Qur'an: Arabic Text, English Translation and Commentary*, Woking: Islamic Review Office, 1917; 7th edition, Lahore: Ahmadiyyah Anjuman Isha'at Islam, 1991

Asad, Muhammad, *The Message of the Qur'an* (bilingual edition), Gibraltar: Dar al-Andalus, 1980
Irving, Thomas B., *The Noble Qur'an: The First American Translation and Commentary*, Brattlerboro, Vermont: Amana, 1984
Pickthall, Marmaduke, *The Meaning of the Glorious Koran: An Explanatory Translation*, London: Knopf, 1930, New York: New American Library, 1953, and many reprints; bilingual edition, Hyderabad, India: Government Central Press, 1938, often reprinted

Non-Muslim
Arberry, A.J., *The Koran Interpreted*, with an introduction, 2 vols, London: Allen and Unwin, and New York: Macmillan, 1955; in 1 vol., London and New York: Oxford University Press, 1983
Bell, Richard, *The Qur'an*, 2 vols, Edinburgh: T. and T. Clark, 1937–39
Dawood, N.J., *The Koran*, Harmondsworth: Penguin, 1956; 5th edition, London and New York: Penguin, 1990
Palmer, E.H., *The Qur'an*, 2 vols, Oxford: Clarendon Press, 1880 (Sacred Books of the East, vols 6 and 9); with an introduction by R.A. Nicholson, 1 vol., London: Oxford University Press, 1928
Rodwell, Rev. J.M., *The Koran*, London: Williams and Norgate, 1861; with an introduction by G. Margoliouth, London: Dent, and New York: Dutton, 1909; with an introduction by Alan Jones, London: Dent, and Rutland, Vermont: Tuttle, 1994
Sale, George, *The Koran, Commonly Called The Alcoran of Mohammed*, London: C. Ackers for J. Wilcox, 1734, with many later editions; facsimile edition, with introduction by Robert D. Richardson, Jr, New York: Garland, 1984

The text of the Koran was originally revealed in pieces of varying length, most of them apparently relatively short. These basic units then took their place in the working units of the Koran, the *suras* (loosely "chapters"), which in the standard recension number 114. Revelations are believed to have occurred over a period of years from 610 AD to Muhammad's death in June 632 AD. It is traditional to divide the *suras* into four or five periods: Early Meccan, Middle Meccan, Late Meccan and Medinan being the most popular schema. Though there is some justification for this, particularly as far as the Medinan period is concerned, it has two serious drawbacks: many of the *suras* contain material from at least two periods, and the criteria for classification, particularly for the Middle Meccan and Late Meccan periods, are somewhat vague and impressionistic. We have little idea how the process of *sura* formation and revision worked, though occasionally there are passages that point to intuitive grouping.

Though the Koran was originally revealed orally, in quite early passages it refers to itself as The Book, and there is some evidence of pieces being committed to writing whilst Muhammad was still at Mecca. In the later years at Medina he appears to have had a group of "Scribes of the Revelation", each with responsibility for a part of the text. It is not clear what happened to their material after Muhammad's death, but in comparison with other religions the sacred text moved very quickly towards the form in which we have it today. A single version which rendered void a mass of variants that had arisen through widespread oral transmission was declared to be authoritative by the caliph 'Uthman some 20 years after Muhammad's death; and to a very large extent the only changes that have taken place since that time are connected with the improvements in Arabic script that took place in the 8th century AD. This version is essentially Sunni, and Shi'is argue that some verses are missing. The main difference between the two views of the text, however, lies in exegesis (*tafsir*).

Stylistically the Koran calls on four main registers that were current in 7th-century Arabia: the clipped, gnomic style of the soothsayers (*kahins*); the admonitory, exhortative and argumentative style of the orators (*khatibs*); the narrative techniques of the story-tellers (*qass*); while in the Medinan period the verses containing social legislation appear to approximate to the style used in formal agreements. The mixture of registers, with an overall rhetorical flavour, is unique in Arabic.

With the passing of time, feelings about the uniqueness of the Koran gave rise to a doctrine of its inimitability (Arabic *i'jaz*) and this became fixed Muslim dogma; and whilst Quranic exegesis has always been considered laudable, translation has long been a problematical area. A minority of scholars equated inimitability with untranslatability and have gone on to forbid translation. The majority, however, have deemed translation to be a service to non-Arab Muslims, and this view led to early translations into Persian and Turkish, to at least one old Spanish translation after the reconquest and latterly, from the mid-19th century onwards, to a steady trickle of translations in English, largely from the Indian sub-continent. The best of them is by an English convert, PICKTHALL (1930).

Western translations, on the other hand, have until recently shown an anti-Islamic tinge. The first was a Latin version made by Robertus Ketenensis (Robert of Ketton) and others for Peter the Venerable, Abbot of Cluny, in 1143. Five hundred years elapsed before the next full translation, that of Pierre Du Ryer, into French in 1647. The first English translation was made from the French version by Alexander Ross in 1649. The first translation direct from Arabic into English was that of George SALE in 1734. Since then there have been four major ones: RODWELL (1861), PALMER (1880), BELL (1937–39) and ARBERRY (1955). At least one other is in the offing.

This division of translations may seem surprising, but the religious position of the Koran makes it virtually inevitable. There is a real gap, well shown by the first paragraph of Pickthall's foreword:

> The aim of this work is to present to English readers what Muslims the world over hold to be the meaning of the words of the Koran, and the nature of that Book, in not unworthy language and concisely, with a view to the requirements of English Muslims. It may be reasonably claimed that no Holy Scripture can be fairly presented by one who disbelieves its inspiration and its message; and this is the first English translation of the Koran by an Englishman who is a Muslim. Some of the translations include commentation offensive to Muslims, and almost all employ a style of language which Muslims at once recognize as unworthy. The Koran cannot be translated. That is the belief of old-fashioned Sheykhs and the view of the present writer. The Book is here rendered almost literally

> and every effort has been made to choose befitting language. But the result is not the Glorious Koran, that inimitable symphony, the very sounds of which move men to tears and ecstasy. It is only an attempt to present the meaning of the Koran – and peradventure something of the charm – in English. It can never take the place of the Koran in Arabic, nor is it meant to do so. Before publication the work has been scrutinized word by word and thoroughly revised in Egypt with the help of one whose mother-tongue is Arabic, who has studied the Koran and who knows English; and when difficulties were encountered the translator had recourse to perhaps the greatest living authority on the subject. Every care has thus been taken to avoid unwarrantable renderings.

If one accepts this view, which is common amongst Muslims, one is tied; if one does not, one is damned. The damned can at least look at the Koran as an outstanding work of literature as well as a landmark of religion.

English translations of the Koran can be divided into two groups. The first consists of those done by Muslims. These include Muhammad 'ALI (1917), Muhammad Marmaduke PICKTHALL (1930), 'Abdullah Yusuf 'ALI (1934), Muhammad ASAD (1980), and Thomas B. IRVING (1984). This is only a small cross-sample of the numerous Muslim translators available. All show due reverence, but none is as accurate as one might hope and expect. Pickthall is the best, with fewest mistakes, and enjoys some respect among Western scholars.

Of the second group of English translations, those done by non-Muslims, SALE (1734) was very good for its time and very influential. It held sway for a century and a quarter and was used by such figures as Gibbon and Carlyle. Its *Preliminary Discourse* is now very dated, though it covers an impressive background. The translation is fairly accurate, and many of its notes are based on the important Arabic commentaries of al-Zamakhshari and al-Baydawi.

RODWELL was an Anglican clergyman with a good knowledge of Hebrew as well as Arabic. A major feature of his translation (1861) was that he arranged the *suras* in what he believed to be the correct chronological order. In doing this he reflected the scholarship of the time, but it was an error; and in the latest edition of his translation the traditional order has been restored. Rodwell's sound knowledge of Jewish and Christian sources enabled him to furnish cross-references that are still valuable.

PALMER was an excellent scholar, and his version (1880) was the best and most accurate so far. He adopted a paragraph style of translation, which is useful for the longer pieces, but slightly less so for the early material. It is somewhat deficient in its notes.

BELL (1937–39) applied the norms of Biblical criticism to the Koran. Though he retained the traditional *sura* order, he divided each *sura* into various pieces, often re-arranging the order within the *sura*. He operated on the basis that Muhammad had worked to produce a book, but that what we have is incomplete and garbled. Bell's work is of great interest to specialists, though it is now agreed that his ideas about the rearrangement of the text are mistaken. Moreover the scissors-and-paste approach produces an unreadable translation.

DAWOOD (1956) is the least satisfactory of the translations that are widely available. It has a mistaken Rodwell-type re-ordering of the *suras*, and it often uses paraphrase. It has no compensating merit.

ARBERRY's translation (1955) is the most accurate so far and the most sympathetic. He also splits up the long verses in a way that makes the text more readable, though the basis for splitting is intuitive. The real problem with this otherwise good translation is that the introduction is nothing more than a brief survey of some previous translations, and the body of the translation contains not a single note.

ALAN JONES

Further Reading

Binark, Ismet and Halit Eren, *World Bibliography of Translations of the Meanings of the Holy Qur'an: Printed Translations, 1515–1980*, edited by Ekmeleddin Ihsanoğlu, Istanbul: Research Centre for Islamic History, Art and Culture, 1986

Korean

Literary Translation into English

The Language

Research on the origins of the Korean language has been conducted since the late 19th century and can be divided into three phases. In the first phase early researchers on the origins of the Korean language proposed various theories relating Korean to Ural-Altaic languages, Japanese and Chinese, and to Dravidian and Indo-European languages. Among these the theories that related Korean to the Ural-Altaic languages and to Japanese were the most influential. Westerners who wrote about Korea at the end of the 19th century identified similarities between Korean and Ural-Altaic languages. According to these scholars Korean displays the following characteristics typical of Ural-Altaic languages: harmonization of vowels, morphological agglutination, lack of precise grammatical markers for gender and number, and restriction of consonants in prefixes and suffixes. However, this research is limited by the lack of extensive evidence of these connections between Korean and Ural-Altaic languages.

In the second phase G.S. Ramstedt criticized the theory of the Ural-Altaic origins of Korean and instead proposed the theory that Korean belongs to a group of Altaic languages that includes the Turkish, Mongolian and Tungusic groups. Ramstedt felt that the Ural-Altaic theory was too broad. In his work "Remarks on the Korean Language" (1928) Ramstedt offered some evidence that Korean belongs to the Altaic group.

In the 1950s Poppe and many Korean scholars thoroughly investigated the comparisons of Korean and other Altaic languages and developed this approach. According to Poppe, Korean can be traced back as one branch of the Turkish-Mongolian-Tungusic group. His research went a step further than Ramstedt's and firmly established the position of Korean as part of the Altaic group. Poppe, comparing Korean and the Altaic languages, found structural similarities in grammar and some similarities in some suffixes and pronouns and in vocabulary.

In the current phase, debate continues among scholars about the origins of the Korean language. Since the 1960s Korean scholars such as Lee Ki-mun, Kim Bang-han and Ch'oe Hak-geun have refined the theories of the origins of the Korean language proposed by Ramstedt and Poppe. While these scholars admit that there are common points between Korean and the languages of the Altaic group, they have some reservations about including Korean with the Altaic languages in the same way as the Indo-European languages are grouped together. Currently most scholars accept the designation of Korean as an Altaic language but emphasize the need for further research in order to define precisely the relationship between Korean and the other languages of this group.

Lee Ki-mun acknowledges the contributions of Ramstedt and Poppe but points out some weaknesses in their research, such as limiting evidence to modern Korean while ignoring archaic Korean forms, and insufficient exploration of the non-Altaic characteristics of Korean. Kim Bang-han emphasizes that research on the connections between Korean and Altaic languages is still at a relatively elementary stage and much more detailed evidence is needed to support these hypotheses. Ch'oe Hak-geun has examined the connections between language and culture including religious legends and customs and historical records. He concludes that it is most fruitful to compare Korean with languages of Northern peoples.

The following characteristics of the Korean language may affect translation: (1) Modern Korean, unlike some Indo-European languages, does not allow two consonants to come together at the beginning of a word. However, foreign loan words may begin with double consonants. (2) In Korean, as in some other Altaic languages, vowel harmony is stressed with certain terms to show a contrast in meaning. Examples include usage of certain vowels to give contrasting impressions of brightness/darkness, lightness/heaviness, sensitivity/dullness. (3) Korean does not strongly differentiate stress or intonation, but in certain cases there is a distinction between shorter and longer sounds. (4) More than half of Korean vocabulary consists of foreign loan words, particularly words of Chinese origin. (5) In Korean two-syllable words predominate. (6) Korean employs many honorific forms. The distinction between respectful language and plain or informal speech is particularly marked. (7) The distinction between singular and plural is not emphasized in Korean, and many Korean sentences do not clearly indicate number. (8) In Korean there is no grammatical category from the gender of nouns. (9) Korean is considered an agglutinative language, and the root of the word remains the same while the suffix changes. (10) In Korean, to a certain extent, the functions of verbs and adjectives overlap, and both are used in descriptive and predicative forms. (11) In Korean, adjectives do not have comparative and superlative forms. Comparison is shown by using an adverb with the adjective. (12) The basic word order of a Korean sentence is: subject, modifying words or phrases, object, complement + verb, qualifiers. (13) For an interrogative sentence the appropriate suffix is added to the root of the predicate.

Certain aspects of traditional Korean culture and society have resulted in communications styles that differ markedly from those of English. Traditional Korean society was based on agricultural communities where patience and endurance were stressed rather than individualism. Koreans had a naturalistic attitude according to which harmony between humans and nature was ideal and confrontation tended to be avoided. Therefore the following general differences can be observed between Korean and English in terms of communications styles: (1) In many Korean sentences the subject is not stated. While in English the contrast between personal pronouns is decisive, in Korean there may be ambiguity in this aspect. (2) While English tends to require a high level of factual verification, in Korean verification is mostly by situation, including such factors as facial expression. (3) In Korean, expressions that stress a collective spirit are much more frequent than in English. (4) Generalizing expressions are much more common in Korean than in English. (5) Since honorific expressions are common in Korean, there is a corresponding tendency to lower the self. Instances when an unassuming manner is appropriate include references to family members, the presentation of gifts, and the offering of a meal. (6) Korean social encounters employ a higher percentage than English of formal and ritualistic phrases. (7) Koreans tend to avoid conversations with strangers, therefore casual conversational expressions are less common than in English. (8) While in English "yes" and "no" are clearly indicated in conversation, in Korean there is frequently ambiguity in this regard.

Literary Translation from Korean

Until the mid-19th century Korea was almost unknown in the western world. Owing to the closed-door policy of the late Choson period (1392–1910) Korea had very little contact with western countries and only limited contact with certain Asian nations. Therefore Korean literature and culture were almost unknown to the outside world. However, in the late 19th century Korean culture began to be introduced to the rest of the world by western missionaries who came to Korea to promote Christianity. In the late 19th and early 20th century James S. Gale and some other missionaries translated traditional Korean tales and classical works. By the 1950s the translation of Korean literature into English began to expand.

Before 1950, translations of Korean literary works into English were rare. One of the representative early translations was Horace Newton Allen's *Korean Tales, Being a Collection of Stories Translated from Korean Folk Lore* (New York: Putnam, 1889). Among the other translations of traditional Korean tales that appeared during this early period were: William Elliot

Griffis's *The Unmannerly Tiger and Other Korean Tales*, and Berta Metzger's *Tales Told in Korea*, published in New York in 1911 and 1932 (Stokes) respectively. James S. Gale, who had come to Korea in the late 19th century as a missionary, published a translation of the classical Korean novel, *The Cloud Dream of the Nine*, by Kim Man-jung in 1922 (London: O'Connor, and Boston: Small Maynard, 1924). One of the early collections of Korean poetry in translation was Joan S. Grigsby's *The Orchid Door: Ancient Korean Poems*, which appeared in Kobe in 1935 (reprinted, New York: Paragon, 1970). During this time translations tended to be done by missionaries who had lived in Korea for a long time. These early translators attempted to introduce the little-known culture by concentrating on traditional legends, classics, and a limited amount of poetry.

The translation of modern Korean poetry into English began later than the translation of classical works. One of the earliest anthologies of modern Korean poetry in English is Zong In-sob's *An Anthology of Modern Poems in Korea* published in Seoul in 1948. Zong, who was one of the earliest translators of Korean literary works into English after World War II, also published *Folktales from Korea* in 1953 (New York: Grove Press; 3rd edition, New York: Hollym International, 1982) and *Modern Short Stories from Korea* in 1958 (Seoul: Munho-sa). Richard Rutt, an Anglican priest who came to Korea in 1954, began to translate traditional poetic forms like *sijo* in the late 1950s. In addition to traditional poetry, Rutt translated modern poetry and traditional novels.

In the 1960s the number of translations of Korean literary works into English began to increase. The early 1960s saw a rise in poetry translations, and in the late 1960s there was a rise in translations of novels. Ha T'ae-hung was one of the first to translate the works of Shakespeare into Korean and he also translated many Korean literary works into English. Ha's translations include: *Poetry and Music of the Classical Age* (Seoul: Yonsei University Press, 1958; 2nd edition, 1969), *The Korean Nights Entertainments* (Seoul: Yonsei University Press, 1969), and *Tales from the Three Kingdoms* (Seoul: Yonsei University Press, 1969). With Peter Lee's *Anthology of Korean Poetry from the Earliest Era to the Present* (New York: John Day, 1964) Korean literature began to be introduced in the United States. Chung Chong-hwa translated some of the works of the woman novelist Han Mu-suk during the 1960s. Han Mu-suk is noted as an author of historical novels that emphasize the contribution of Christianity to the development of Korean culture and society. In the 1960s Chung Chong-hwa translated two of Han's novels: *In the Depth* and *The Running Water Hermitage* (Seoul: Moonwang, 1967).

In the 1970s there was further expansion of the translation of Korean literature into English. Many collections of short stories in translation appeared. These Korean stories of the postwar period dealt with the devastation and confusion of war (the Korean War lasted from 1950–53), social injustice, the conflict between eastern and western culture, and ideological struggles. Kevin O'Rourke's *Ten Korean Short Stories* (Seoul: Yonsei University Press, 1973) and Hong Myong-hui's *Korean Short Stories* (Seoul: Iljisa, 1975) appeared at this time.

The trend of translating modern poetry which began in the 1960s continued to develop. In 1970 Ko-won published a volume, *Contemporary Korean Poetry*, at the University of Iowa Press (Iowa City). Certain Korean university presses undertook the project of publishing Korean literature in translation. For example, in 1970 Yonsei University Press published Younghill Kang and Frances Keely's *Meditations of the Lover*, a volume of the poetry of the early 20th-century poet, Buddhist leader and patriot, Han Yong-un. It was during this period that Kim Jaihiun embarked on his career as a translator. After attending the Korean University of Foreign Studies Kim went to the United States to pursue further studies. During the 1970s Kim translated many books of Korean poetry, including a volume of the works of the lyric poet of the early 20th century, Kim So-wol, in 1973, and *The Immortal Voice: An Anthology of Modern Korean Poetry* (Seoul: Inmun, 1974). In the 1970s some translations of the poems of the political protestor and dissident, Kim Ji-ha, appeared in the United States and Japan. Some representative poems of Kim Ji-ha, *Cry of the People and Other Poems* (Hayama: Autumn Press, 1974), were published in Japan.

Richard Rutt, who started to translate traditional poetic forms in the late 1950s, continued to bring out volumes of traditional poetry such as *An Anthology of Korean Sijo* (University of California Press, 1971). Rutt demonstrated the diversity of his interests as a translator with a collection on which he collaborated with Kim Jong-un, *Virtuous Women: Three Masterpieces of Traditional Korean Fiction* (Korean National Commission for Unesco, 1974; as *Virtuous Women: Three Classic Korean Novels*, Seoul: Kwang Myong, 1979). Another translator who covered a wide range of genres was Peter Lee, whose contributions during the period include: *Poems from Korea: A Historical Anthology* (revised edition, Honolulu: University of Hawaii Press, and London: Allen and Unwin, 1974), *Flowers of Fire: Twentieth Century Korean Stories* (Honolulu: University of Hawaii Press, 1975), and the traditional poem, *Songs of Flying Dragons* (Cambridge, Massachusetts: Harvard University Press, 1975).

In the 1980s translations of individual works began to appear separately rather than in the anthology form that had previously been the more usual method of publishing translations of Korean literary works. There was a wide range of translations, from the works of newer authors like O Chong-hui, Kim Chi-won, Kang Sok-kyong, Yi Mun-yol, to those of more well-established writers like Kang Sin-jai, Kim Nam-jo, Ko-un, Mo Yun-suk, Hwang Sun-won, So Jong-ju, and Kim Tong-ni. Translations of Korean literary works appeared in various English-speaking areas, including the United States, Australia, Hong Kong, and the United Kingdom. Translators, including both native Koreans and foreigners who had resided in Korea, gave new directions to the translation of Korean literature.

Chung Chong-wha, who began to translate short stories in the 1950s, published several volumes, including *Meetings and Farewells: Modern Korean Short Stories* (St Lucia: University of Queensland Press, and New York: St Martin's Press, 1980) and a collection of classical poems, *Love in Mid-Winter Night: Korean Sijo Poetry* (London and Boston: Kegan Paul International, 1985). Kevin O'Rourke, an Irish Columbian priest and Professor of English at Kyunghee University, has lived in Korea since the 1960s and has produced numerous translations of classical and modern literature. Among his works are *The Cutting Edge: Selection of Korean Poetry, Ancient and Modern* (Seoul: Yonsei University Press, 1982), *Cho Byung Hwa: Selected Poems* (Osang Publishing Company), and

Looking for the Cow: Modern Korean Poems (Dublin: Dedalus Press, 1999). David McCann is a specialist in pre-modern Korean verse forms who resided in Korea for many years. His translations include *Selected Poems of Kim Namjo*, co-translated with Hyunjae Yee Sallee (Ithaca, New York: Cornell University East Asia Program, 1983), *The Middle Hour: Selected Poems of Kim Chi Ha* (Stanfordville, New York: Human Rights Publishing, 1980), and *Unforgettable Things: Poems* by So Chong Ju (Seoul, 1986). Edward Poitras, a long-time resident of Korea, published Hwang Sunwon's *The Stars and Other Korean Short Stories* (Hong Kong: Heinemann Asia, 1980). This volume is dedicated to the work of one of Korea's best-known novelists. Among his many other translations Poitras edited *New Translations from Korea: A Selection of Modern Korean Literature* (Seoul: Korean Culture and Arts Foundation, 1982), which includes poems, short stories, and theatrical works.

One of the newer writers whose works are widely read is novelist Yi Munyol. He writes of the problems of present-day Korean society against a background of traditional thought. Yi Munyol's works have been translated by Sol Sun Bong (*Hail to the Emperor!*, Seoul, 1986), and Kevin O'Rourke (*Our Twisted Hero*, Seoul: Minumsa, 1987). *Words of Farewell* (Seattle: Seal Press, 1989), translated by Bruce and Ju-chan Fulton, includes the short stories of women writers Kang Sok-kyong, Kim Chi-won and O Chong-hui, who treat the conflicts that women face in contemporary Korean society.

One of the growing trends in the 1990s has been the publication of translations of contemporary Korean writers. In 1990 Kim Young Moo and Brother Anthony of Taizé published a volume of the poems of Ch'on Sang Byong, *Back to Heaven: Selected Poems of Ch'on Sang Pyong* (Ithaca, New York: Cornell University East Asia Program). More recently Kim Young Moo and Brother Anthony translated a volume of the works of the poet Ko Un, *The Sound of My Waves: Selected Poems* (Ithaca, New York: Cornell University East Asia Program, 1993). Brother Anthony, Professor of English at Sogang University, has also produced a number of poetry translations on his own including *Wastelands of Fire: Selected Poems of Ku Sang* (London and Boston: Forest Books, 1989), *Infant Splendor: Poems by Ku Sang* (Samseong, 1990), and *Faint Shadows of Love: Poems* by Kwang-kyu Kim (London and Boston: Forest Books, 1991).

Translation of Korean literary works by Korean and western translators continues to expand and is playing a fundamental role in introducing Korean literature and culture internationally. Among the organizations that have been most active in promoting the translation of Korean literature are: the Korean Culture and Arts Foundation, the Korean Center of the International PEN Club, the Korean Poets' Association, the Korean National Commission for UNESCO, and the Korea Branch of the Royal Asiatic Society.

In closing, it should be pointed out that since the 1950s information on literary translation in North Korea has not been readily available. Therefore the sections of this article on literary translation after 1950 are limited to a survey of important trends and representative works of literary translation in South Korea.

THERESA HYUN

Further Reading

Poppe, N.N., *Introduction to Mongolian Comparative Studies*, Helsinki: Suomalais-Ugrilainen Seura, 1955

Ramstedt, G.J., "Remarks on the Korean Language", *Mémoires de la Société Finno-Ougrienne* 58 (1928)

Ramstedt, G.J., *A Korean Grammar*, Helsinki: Suomalais-Ugrilainen Seura, 1939

Ramstedt, G.J., *Studies in Korean Etymology*, 2 vols, Helsinki: Suomalais-Ugrilainen Seura, 1949–53

Seoul National University East Asian Cultural Research Center, *Kuko Kukmunhak Sajon* (Dictionary of Korean Language and Literature), Seoul: Singu Munhwasa, 1989

Translation Bibliographies

Anderson, G.L., *Asian Literature in English: A Guide to Information Sources*, Detroit: Gale, 1981

Bibliography of Asian Studies, Ann Arbor, Michigan: Association for Asian Studies, 1982

Han-Kyo Kim with Hong Kyoo Park (editors), *Studies on Korea: A Scholar's Guide*, Honolulu: University of Hawaii Press, 1980

Korea Journal Index 1961–91, Seoul: Korean National Commission for Unesco

Silberman, Bernard Samuel, *Japan and Korea: A Critical Bibliography*, Tucson: University of Arizona Press, 1962

Zygmunt Krasiński 1812–1859

Polish poet and dramatist

Biography

Born in Paris, 19 February 1812. His family was rich and aristocratic, and his father, count Wincenty Krasiński, was a general in the Congress Kingdom army, who supported the tsar and Russian rule in Poland. Zygmunt grew up and was educated first on the family estate in Opinogóra, Poland. He studied in Warsaw until 1828, and went to read law at Warsaw University, where he suffered on account of his family's unpopular conservative loyalism. He moved to Switzerland in 1829 and studied at Geneva University. He had already completed a Gothic novel by this date, and he continued to write poetry and plays during the 1830s and 1840s, influenced by the writing of the Polish nationalist poet Adam Mickiewicz, whom he had met in Geneva. He published much of his work as "The Nameless Poet of Poland" to avoid causing political difficulty for his family. In 1832 he travelled to St Petersburg with his father, and met tsar Nicholas I. He returned to Poland briefly, and spent most of the following years living in spa towns in France and Italy, rarely returning to his native country. Krasiński married Countess Elżbieta Branicki in 1843. He was seriously ill for much of his life, eventually succumbing in Paris, 23 February 1859.

Krasiński was, along with Adam Mickiewicz and Juliusz Słowacki, one of Poland's most significant Romantic writers of the 19th century. He is remembered particularly for his two important tragic plays, *Nie-Boska komedia* (*The Un-Divine Comedy*), published in Paris in 1835, which concerns the struggle between the aristocracy and revolutionary democratic movements, and *Irydion* (1836), set in 3rd-century Rome. Neither of these plays was staged during Krasiński's lifetime; *Nie-Boska Komedia*, regarded by Mickiewicz as "the highest achievement of the Slavonic theatre", was not produced until the following century. Krasiński's well-known poem *Przedświt* [The Moment before Dawn] 1843, advocated the rejection of revolutionary violence and reconciliation to Poland's partition. He was a prolific letter writer, and left a significant collection of correspondence with his father, his friends and his lovers.

Translations

Plays

Nie-boska komedia, 1835, produced 1902

Cook, Martha Walker, *The Undivine Comedy and Other Poems by the Anonymous Poet of Poland, Count Sigismund Krasinski*, Philadelphia: Lippincott, 1875 (includes *Iridion* and several poems: "The Fragment", "The Last", "Temptation", "Resurrecturis", "In Memoriam")

Kennedy, Harriette E. and Zofia Umińska, *The Un-Divine Comedy*, preface by G.K. Chesterton, introduction by Artur Górski, London: Harrap, 1924; reprinted Westport, Connecticut: Greenwood Press, 1976

Lytton, Robert, *Orval; or, The Fool of Time and Other Imitations and Paraphrases*, London: Chapman and Hall, 1869

Segel, Harold B., *The Un-Divine Comedy*, with an introduction, in his *Polish Romantic Drama: Three Plays in English Translation*, Ithaca, New York: Cornell University Press, 1977

Wickstrom, Gordon W., *The Un-Divine Comedy*, Lancaster, Pennsylvania: published by the translator, 1969; revised edition, 1972

Irydion, 1836, produced 1908

Cook, Martha Walker, *Iridion*, in her *The Undivine Comedy and Other Poems by the Anonymous Poet of Poland, Count Sigmund Krasinski*, Philadelphia: Lippincott, 1875

Noyes, Florence, *Iridion*, with an introduction by George Rapall Noyes, London: Oxford University Press/H. Milford, 1927; reprinted Westport, Connecticut: Greenwood Press, 1975

LYTTON (1869) is clearly a paraphrase, a reworking twice the length of the original play, *Nie-boska komedia*, using blank verse whereas the original is in prose (apart from Orcio's songs). The preface explains how Lytton himself had been planning a poem on revolution and class conflict, inspired by both the ideas and the calamities of the French Revolution; in Krasiński's text he found sympathy for his own pro-aristocratic political views as well as criticism of the power-hungriness of "superior" individuals of this class. Hence he perceived the central character Count Henryk's contradictory role as an aristocrat, but he failed to understand the philosophical and religious dimension to Krasiński's interpretation of historical forces. There is no evidence that Lytton consulted any Polish source; his paraphrase is based on a French prose translation (preface). He refers to this text as *The Infernal Comedy*, thereby missing the essential meaning of *nie-boska* as "human" (as opposed to *boska*, "divine"). Lytton also incorporates elements of his own work, radically changes some of the names (Mąż/Count Henryk becomes Orval, Żona becomes Veronica, Orcio becomes Muriel! though remaining male ...), and simply omits problematic elements such as the role of the Baptized Jews. Many key elements of the original are, however, preserved: the revolutionaries (renamed here as Panurge and the Modern Brutus) reflect, as do Pankracy and Leonard, the relationship between Robespierre and Saint-Juste; also similar are the portrayal of Muriel's blindness, the rejection of Veronica by Orval, Veronica's madness, the contrast shown between spurious and genuine poetry. Yet the text is too wordy and drawn-out and fails to convey the powerful concision of Krasiński's original.

COOK's *The Undivine Comedy* (1875) is translated from French and German translations, not from the original Polish. Although the original is in prose, the text is rendered here in blank verse; this may be the result of translating from other translations, but the text is also sometimes amplified in order to satisfy the demands of the verse, though not significantly. On the other hand nothing is added or taken away from the content; hence Krasiński's ideological intentions are faithfully conveyed. The tone is somewhat over-exalted; although inspired, Krasiński never becomes breathless, whereas this does – there is a superabundance of exclamation marks.

KENNEDY & UMIŃSKA (1924) is very close in meaning to the original, preserving the prose text and adding nothing extra or superfluous. It is faithful to the linguistic style in that it employs shortish statements rich in imagery and associations. The translators also demonstrate a clear understanding of Krasiński's intentions; both the historical/philosophical and the personal/emotional strands are lucidly conveyed. There are some errors in detail: "sklepy" is mistranslated, for example, as the modern "shops" rather than as "vaults"; *Przechrzta* (a converted or baptized Jew), in part 3, is continually translated as plural (SEGEL, in his revision, 1977, irons out most of these inaccuracies). As to atmosphere, this does more to convey it than any of the other translations, though all fail to capture completely the mystery, painful emotionality and eery power of the original. Kennedy & Umińska perhaps succeeds better because of the elevated, slightly antiquated and "other-worldly" tone evident especially in the introductory speeches to all four parts where, for example, the second person singular form of address (thou, thee, thy, with appropriate verb endings) is preserved from the original. (Segel changes all these to "you" which makes the language feel much more flat and mundane.)

WICKSTROM (1969, revised 1972) was never published commercially and was envisaged primarily as a dramatic text to be produced on stage. This probably accounts for the changes made by the translator/producer. Each of the four parts is given its own title (Krasiński assigns no titles) and described puzzlingly as an "Apostrophe"; the prose invocations at the beginning of each part are reduced to short verses of questionable quality, which do very little to convey the content or atmosphere of the original speeches; one can only surmise that Wickstrom felt these relatively short poems would have greater dramatic effect in his own production. Otherwise the translation relies heavily on Kennedy & Umińska. Occasionally scenes are rearranged and speeches omitted, but not with any great detriment to the overall meaning of the play.

SEGEL (1977) also acknowledges his debt to Kennedy & Umińska, but claims that his is a "new translation". The differences, however, are not major. Although it sometimes feels rather lifeless, this is faithful to the original and demonstrates clear understanding of its meaning. It is the only translation with a lengthy and critically sound introduction. It uses a more modern idiom than Kennedy & Umińska, avoiding thereby their more elevated and archaic tone, but such a tone is arguably more appropriate to conveying the atmosphere of the play.

COOK's *Iridion* (1875), like her *Undivine Comedy*, is translated from French and German translations, not from the original Polish, and similar criticisms of the verse apply, though the content is faithfully communicated. In the case of *Iridion*, however, the translator imposes a new structure, dividing the play into acts and scenes, whereas Krasiński simply has four parts, which he divides into scenes without numbering them; the translation creates five acts and divides the action into Scenes roughly corresponding to the logic of the original. Certain changes are introduced to characters' names: the more familiar Domitian is used, for example, for Krasiński's Ulipanus. There are also mistakes, though again this may be the fault of the intermediary translations: Iridion's mother Grimhilda, for example, is consistently referred to as Crimhild.

NOYES's *Iridion* (1927) is a good translation, generally very accurate and faithful to the original. It is fairly literal; it allows a little poetic licence in its linguistic style yet does not feel badly dated. The import of the play, set in Rome in the 3rd century AD, is clearly understood both in its Polish and in its universal dimensions; this is born out by the informative introduction largely based on work by Polish scholars (notably Tadeusz Sinko).

Apart from those listed, no translations have been traced by the present writer, except for one poem ("God has denied me the angelic measure") in Jerzy Peterkiewicz and Burns Singer's, *Five Centuries of Polish Poetry 1450–1970*, second edition, with new poems translated in collaboration with Jon Stallworthy, London: Oxford University Press, 1970.

URSULA PHILLIPS

Further Reading

Gardner, Monica M., *The Anonymous Poet of Poland: Zygmunt Krasinski*, Cambridge: Cambridge University Press, 1919

Lednicki, Wacław (editor), *Zygmunt Krasinski, Romantic Universalist: An International Tribute*, New York: Polish Institute of Arts and Sciences in America, 1964

"*The Un-divine Comedy*: Drama of Art and Revolution", *Educational Theatre Journal*, 24 (1972) pp. 269–83

See also George Rapall Noyes's introduction to Noyes

Karl Kraus 1874–1936

Austrian satirist, poet and and critic

Biography

Born in Gitschin, a small town then in Bohemia, now in the Czech Republic, 28 April 1874. When he was three his Jewish parents moved to Vienna, where he spent most of his life. While still at school he had reviews published in a Viennese literary journal. He went to Vienna University in 1892 to study law but soon left, finding he could earn a living acting and writing satires. He joined the Roman Catholic church in 1899, but left it in 1923. He made it his mission in his satires, aphorisms and plays to attack corruption and hypocrisy in society and its institutions, particularly as they manifested themselves in language, and he was feared as a fierce critic by politicians and the press. In World War I he wrote an anti-war play, *Die letzten Tage der Menschheit* (*The Last Days of Mankind*), partly composed in 1918, finished 1922, and in 1933 an anti-Hitler polemical work *Die dritte Walpurgisnacht* [The Third Walpurgis Night], published 1952. He was a friend of Trakl, wrote in defence of the avant-garde, translated from Shakespeare and revived the reputation of Nestroy. He gave effective lectures and play-readings.

Kraus was the founder, editor and main contributor of the satirical journal *Die Fackel* (*The Torch*), which appeared, with some intervals, from spring 1899 to February 1936. Died Vienna, 12 June 1936.

Translations

The texts used by translators are those reprinted in the 14-volume edition of the works edited by Heinrich Fischer. *Werke*, vols 1–10 were issued in Munich: Kösel, 1952–1962; vols 11–14, in Munich: Arbert Langen-Georg Müller, 1963–67.

Each of the suggestions for Further Reading below also contains a scattering of translations, usually from the prose, aphorisms or letters, chosen as illustrations rather than as translations intended to stand on their own.

Selections of Prose and Poetry

Ungar, Frederick (editor), *No Compromise: Selected Writings of Karl Kraus*, New York: Ungar, 1977 (includes translations by Sheema Z. Buehne, Edward Mornin, Helene Scher, Marcus Bullock, Michael Bullock, Ungar, and D.G. Wright)

Zohn, Harry (editor), *In These Great Times: A Karl Kraus Reader* (bilingual edition), Montreal: Engendra Press, 1976; Manchester: Carcanet, 1984 (includes translations by Joseph Fabry, Max Knight, Karl F. Ross, and Zohn)

Play

Die letzten Tage der Menschheit, 1957

Gode, Alexander and Sue Ellen Wright, *The Last Days of Mankind: A Tragedy in Five Acts*, abridged and edited with an introduction by Frederick Ungar, New York: Ungar, 1974

Knight, Max and Joseph Fabry, *The Last Days of Mankind: Selections* in *In These Great Times*, edited by Harry Zohn, 1976

Aphorisms

Beim Wort Genommen, 1955 (vol. 3 of *Werke*, incorporating *Sprüche und Widersprüche* 1909, *Pro domo et mundo* 1912, and *Nachts* 1918)

Zohn, Harry, *Half-Truths and One-and-a-Half Truths: Selected Aphorisms*, Montreal: Engendra Press, 1976; Manchester: Carcanet, 1986

Poetry

Worte in Versen, 1916–30

Bloch, Albert, *Poems: Authorised English Translation*, Boston: Four Seas, 1930

Most of Karl Kraus's works originally appeared in his journal, *Die Fackel* [*The Torch*], which was founded by him in 1899, and continued until his death; he was sole author of all contributions after 1911. Some of the works were subsequently published in separate collections; others were used as parts of Kraus's own public readings.

Kraus's work is deemed untranslatable. BLOCH (1930) is representative in explaining that he has chosen what he translated "simply to welcome what seemed least unwilling to surrender itself" (p. 20), which all translators seem to have done. Kraus's program associates proper use of language with ethics; his particular target is journalism, which debases language and robs people of truth. He especially used newspapers (all sections, including advertisements) as occasions to satirize the immorality of the popular press. At the same time, he was able to convey the verbal dexterity of Shakespeare's sonnets and Offenbach's operettas in German, to write poetry that combines critique and art (like that of Heinrich Heine) with the linguistic creativity of Lewis Carroll, and to write sketches and aphorisms with the wit of a Dorothy Parker or an Oscar Wilde – often with materials taken from the newspapers.

His most famous work is *The Last Days of Mankind*, a 770-page docudrama about World War I composed (1918–22) as a series of sketches (court documents, newspaper ads, poetry, songs, dialogues, monologues, expressionist "station" scenes, and cabaret sketches), many of which incorporate words heard on the streets or printed in the paper during the war: "The most glaring inventions are quotations", as Kraus's introduction stated. It was not published in its entirety during Kraus's lifetime, but figured prominently as a pacifist gesture both in *Die Fackel* and his public readings. The epilogue resembles Toller's work, or an early newsreel.

GODE & WRIGHT's translation of this work (as *The Last Days of Mankind*, 1974) incorporates less than a third of the whole. They leave out the prologue (which sets the scene for the war by including the murder of Franz Ferdinand, and a bureaucratic phone conversation about his "third class burial"), starting instead with newsboys selling extras. They stress Kraus as critic of newspapers and reporters, sacrificing the "local color" (especially dialect and specialized verbal usages, such as that of the military) and local history. They indicate which scenes they have translated, but not elisions within scenes; while attempting some of the play's poetry, they do not include the epilogue, the "Last Night", but follow the point of view in Franz H. Mautner's afterword. The translation is readable, conveying the panoramic view offered by the whole, but not Kraus's sense of how each individual style of diction contributes unique culpability to the war.

UNGAR (1977) includes a brief selection of scenes from *Die letzten Tage der Menschheit* in *No Compromise*, as part of his introduction to Kraus. BLOCH's rendering (1930) of the apocalyptic epilogue, the "Last Night", stands alone and is ably rendered in the style of expressionist poetry.

The distinguished translation (1976) by KNIGHT & FABRY (Max Eugen Kühnel and josef Epstein, who also used the joint pseudonym Peter Fabrizius) included in *In These Great Times* is an attempt at creating a shorter playable version in three acts (out of the original five with prologue and epilogue). The translators intercut scenes heavily, carefully indicating what they include and omit, and risk taking on the dialect scenes, catching their more cutting, satirical tone, and differentiating sociolects carefully. They avoid poetry but include Kraus's alter ego, the "Grumbler", who closes the work with a scene about the newspapers, a monologue designed to "ask [the people] what they [press and official world] did to you". The result is a successful rendering of the work's panoramic and differentiated tone.

ZOHN's collections of aphorisms, *Half-Truths and One-and-a-Half Truths*, are chosen on the basis of relative translatability, not to represent the three volumes that Kraus reprinted during his lifetime. None the less, Zohn tries for a translation rather than a re-creation, and replicates some of Kraus's signature devices, like syntactic clefts, concept puns, *portmanteau* words, and spoonerisms, to show how the originals tie faulty language to imprecise or damaging thought. His essay, "Krausiana", offers sample critiques of representative aphorisms that demonstrate their verbal difficulties for the translator.

UNGAR (1977) includes 15 pages of the briefest aphorisms in his selection, competently rendered. His choices of essays and satiric short prose partially replicate ZOHN's selection in *In These Great Times*; both include one of the most famous essays, "Beaver Coat". Zohn has a surer command of how Kraus manipulates standard language, vernaculars, and slang to achieve an arch tone, with slightly more British coloring and more annotations. Ungar includes a selection of Kraus's letters, libel suits, and "found" documents that were printed in *Die Fackel* as quotes without comments.

BLOCH's *Poems* (1930) is a partial misnomer; it offers 89 selections, most of which are poems from the published collections, but it also includes poetry from Kraus's dramatic translations and adaptations, from the epigrams, and from *The Last Days of Mankind*. Bloch stresses Kraus as a pacifist; he annotates poems to underscore their references to the war; he also adds footnotes about his own supposed failures, despite being the only "official" translator. Zohn's "Krausiana" indicates that Bloch withdrew the collection soon after publication, making it a rarity; he agrees about its high quality and its success in conveying Kraus's verbal wit and artistry.

UNGAR's selection includes 14 poems, five reprinted from Bloch, and nine by D.G. Wright; ZOHN's selection (notably printed bilingually) offers five of Wright's translations, one of Bloch's, and a total of 24 more split between two translators. They attempt simply to include the major poems, not to give an idea of the range of Kraus's poetic voice.

KATHERINE ARENS

Further Reading

Grimstad, Kari, *Masks of the Prophet: The Theatrical World of Karl Kraus*, Toronto: University of Toronto Press, 1982

Heller, Erich, "Karl Kraus" in his *The Disinherited Mind: Essays in Modern German Literature and Thought*, Cambridge: Bowes and Bowes, and Philadelphia: Dufour and Saifer, 1952

Timms, Edward, *Karl Kraus, Apocalyptic Satirist: Culture and Catastrophe in Habsburg Vienna*, New Haven, Connecticut: Yale University Press, 1986

Zohn, Harry, "Krausiana, 1: Karl Kraus in English Translation", *Modern Austrian Literature*, 3/2 (Summer 1970) pp. 25–30

Zohn, Harry, *Karl Kraus*, New York: Twayne, 1971 (contains details of publication and translation history)

See also the excellent introductions and other commentaries in the translations; *In These Great Times*, edited by Zohn, includes a chronology of Kraus's life and works, with photographs

---

Miroslav Krleža 1893–1981

Croatian dramatist, novelist, essayist and poet

Biography

Born in Zagreb, 7 July 1893. He was trained for a military career and was for a time in the Serbian army, but after World War I, in which he served in the Austrian army, he devoted himself to writing and socialism. In 1919 he founded a left-wing review. The best known of his works in varied genres are the volume of short stories *Hrvatski bog Mars* [The Croatian God Mars] (1922); among his numerous plays, the anti-bourgeois trilogy *Gospoda Glembajevi* [The Glembays] (1928), *U agoniji* [In Agony] (1931) and *Leda* (produced 1930); and the psychological novel *Povratak Filipa Latinovicza* (1932). His creative writing was combined with works of criticism and erudition and with a chequered political career. Died in Zagreb, 29 December 1981.

Translations

Novels

Povratak Filipa Latinovicza, 1932

Depolo, Zora, *The Return of Philip Latinovicz*, New York: Vanguard Press, and London: Lincolns-Prager, 1959

Na rubu pameti, 1938

Depolo, Zora, *On the Edge of Reason*, New York: Vanguard Press, 1976; with an introduction by Jeremy Catto, London: Quartet, 1987

Short Stories

Cvrcak pod vodopadom, i druge novele, 1973

Lenski, Branco (editor), *The Cricket Beneath the Waterfall and Other Stories*, New York: Vanguard Press, 1972

Works in Periodicals

Bowen, Tim, "The Noble Glembays", *Scena*, 9 (1986) pp. 253–91

McConnell-Duff, Alan, "Kraljevo", *Scena*, 7 (1984) pp. 50–64

McConnell-Duff, Alan, "At the Mind's Edge", *Scena*, 12 (1989) pp. 182–200

Numerous other translations of individual stories, poems and extracts from Krleža's works are listed in Mihailovich (1984, 1988, 1994), amounting to 44 items altogether. Nevertheless, this relatively wide coverage of the writer's opus in English represents only a very small fragment of his prolific output in his native Croatian. Krleža was a towering figure in 20th-century Croatian literature, dominating a period of some 40 years from his first published works in the aftermath of World War I. Between the wars he was involved in the debate about the role of literature in socialist politics and emerged as energetically opposed to dogmatism in art, a stance that was of great importance in the first years of communist rule in Yugoslavia, as it helped steer art firmly clear of the socialist-realist mode prevailing in the Soviet Union and its satellites. From his first published work, in all his abundant essays, diaries and polemical writings, Krleža may be seen as a committed writer, fundamentally engaged in the ideas and politics of his age. His work is set in central Europe and particularly his native Croatia, and deals most extensively with the period from the second half of the 19th century up to World War II. Referring usually to Croatia by its archaic Roman name "Pannonia", he is able to be both specific and symbolic: the main focus of his interest is the decline and ultimate collapse of the capitalist, imperialist system exemplified by the Austro-Hungarian monarchy, and specifically the downfall of the bourgeoisie with its origins in violence and exploitation, its hypocrisy and corruption. The main feature of his work is the dramatic clash of irreconcilable ideas and the futile endeavours of individual rebellious spirits to oppose the prevailing mire that tends to drag all Krleža's protagonists down: having themselves grown out of the corrupt system they try to confront, they are themselves tainted and doomed. From this relentlessly negative condemnation of bourgeois society there emerges a powerful commitment to the possibility of a different kind of system and a second, minor but positive strand in his work, praising the defiant resilience of the peasantry through the ages.

There are two main difficulties in translating Krleža into English and one of them is this latter aspect of his writing, which functions as an intermittent spark of light in the general gloom of his world. The positive peasant figures and notably the character of Petrica Kerempuh, the narrator of a volume of ballads, *Balade Petrice Kerempuha* (1936), speak in the dialect of Zagreb and its surroundings, conveying an authenticity that contrasts markedly with the artificial language of the bourgeoisie, abounding in German and Hungarian phrases. The problem of rendering this local dialect with its particular flavour, its archaisms and gallows humour, in a foreign language is insoluble and means that this whole aspect of Krleža's work must be lost. The profusion of foreign words also presents a problem, but its main purpose – of conveying the pretentiousness of the bourgeoisie – can be communicated even when the words and phrases are not themselves readily understood. More serious difficulties are the whole context of Krleža's work and his own distinctive literary style. Deliberately confining himself to both a central European setting and a specific phase of social and political history, Krleža is most easily read in that context. And, although the most frequent target of his criticism, human stupidity, is timeless, the particular manifestations of it that he describes are inevitably dated. But the greatest obstacle of all is Krleža's own style. Tending to build great complex sentences, which can sometimes run to whole paragraphs, this style is powerful and compelling in its original language: the thundering linguistic structures convey both a remarkable, forceful intellect and an exceptional energy. Arguably these qualities can be more satisfactorily rendered in either German or French than in English, which is more naturally understated and accustomed to conveying implicit meaning. Consequently, Krleža presents many difficulties both for potential translators into English and, I believe, for the reading public. This seems to me to explain the relative paucity of English language translations of this major Croatian writer.

The most recognizably West European Krleža novel, seen by some as a precursor of Camus and even Beckett, *The Return of Philip Latinovicz*, is perhaps the work that presents the least obvious problems. In any case, Zora DEPOLO (1959) has made a very readable version, and her rendering of *On the Edge of Reason* (DEPOLO, 1976) is equally creditable. The volume of short stories, *The Cricket Beneath the Waterfall*, offers a fascinating study of the art of translating such intractable material, as it is the work of several different translators: the majority of them have chosen to follow exactly the rhythms of the original, often producing awkward sentence structures as a result. One story in the collection stands out as particularly succesful: "A Funeral in Teresienburg", translated by Ralph BOGERT. The story contains many of Krleža's key ideas and in this excellent translation may be recommended as an admirable introduction to his work.

Other English versions of writings by Krleža have been published in periodicals, notably MCCONNELL-DUFF's renderings of two short stories, "Kraljevo" (1984) and "At the Mind's Edge" (1989) and "The Noble Glembays", translated by Tim BOWEN (1986).

CELIA HAWKESWORTH

Further Reading

Bogert, Ralph, *The Writer as Naysayer: Miroslav Krleža and the Aesthetic of Interwar Central Europe*, Columbus, Ohio: Slavica, 1990

Engelsfeld, Mladen, "Krleža into English", *Studia Romanica et Anglica Zagrebiensia*, 33–36 (1972–73) pp. 279–92

Ferguson, Alan, "A Critical Approach to Miroslav Krleža's *The Return of Philip Latinovicz*", *Journal of Croatian Studies*, 14–15 (1973–74) pp. 134–44

McGregor, Greg, "The Novels of Miroslav Krleža", *BC Review*, 3 (1976) pp. 5–9

Mihailovich, Vasa D., *A Comprehensive Bibliography of Yugoslav Literature in English, 1593–1980*, Columbus, Ohio: Slavica, 1984; *First Supplement 1981–85*, 1988; *Second Supplement, 1986–1990*, 1992

Viskovic, Velimir, "Krleža's Relation to the Corpus of Croatian Literature", *Bulletin Scientifique*, 11/7–9 (1975) p. 234

See also the editor's introduction to Lenski (1972)

Ivan Krylov 1769–1844

Russian fable writer

Biography

Born in Moscow, 13 February 1769. His father, a captain in the army bureaucracy, died when Krylov was 10, and the family led an impoverished life. Krylov had little formal education, and was sent out to work as a clerk at a young age. He composed poetry and played the violin at an early age, and wrote his first opera at the age of 14. From 1783 to 1793 he wrote five comic operas. He became part of a small intellectual and musical circle in St Petersburg. From 1787 he published mainly satirical journalism until this was repressed by the government of Catherine the Great. He left St Petersburg in around 1797, and was tutored at the country estate of a patron. Karamzin lived in Moscow from 1801 to 1806, serving as governor's secretary from 1801 to 1802. He started translating La Fontaine's fables in 1805, and from 1809 began to write fables of his own, which he made his main literary activity until his death. He returned to St Petersburg in 1806, and, as a result of the publication of his first book of fables, received imperial patronage, being given an official post in the St. Petersburg public library in about 1812. He maintained the Russian section of the library until 1843. He died in St Petersburg, 21 November 1844.

Krylov wrote nine books of fables between 1809 and 1843, which remain his best-known and most influential work. They are in the tradition of Aesop and La Fontaine, and have been noted for their trenchant social criticism, colloquial language and literary realism. In the early years of his career, Krylov also became well known as a satirical journalist and dramatist.

Fables

Basni, book 1 appeared in St Petersburg in 1809; the last edition published in the author's lifetime appeared in 1843 in 9 books – 198 fables in all

Translations

Bowring, John, in his *Rossiiskaia antologiia: Specimens of the Russian Poets*, vol. 1, London: for the author, 1821; Boston: Cummings Hilliard, 1822

[Bowring, John], *Westminster Review*, 4 (July 1825)

Coxwell, C. Fillingham, *Kriloff's Fables*, London: Kegan Paul Trench Trübner, and New York: Dutton, 1921; reprinted St Clair Shores, Michigan: Scholarly Press, 1970

Daniels, Guy, *15 Fables of Krylov*, New York: Macmillan, 1965

Edwards, H. Sutherland, in his *The Russians at Home: Unpolitical Sketches*, London: Allen, 1861

Harrison, J. Henry, *Kriloff's Original Fables*, London: Remington, 1883

Jarintzov, N., in her *Russian Poets and Poems*, Oxford: Blackwell, and New York: Longmans Green, 1917

[Leeds, W.H.], in his "Russian Fabulists, with Specimens", *Fraser's Magazine*, 19 (February 1839) and 25 (February 1842)

Long, James, *Krilof's Fables, Illustrating Russian Social Life*, Calcutta: "The Englishman" Press, 1869

Mead, Stella, *Fables from Russia*, London and New York: Oxford University Press, 1943

Pares, Bernard, *Krylov's Fables*, London: Jonathan Cape, 1926; New York: Harcourt, 1927; as *The Russian Fables of Ivan Krylov* (bilingual edition), Harmondsworth and New York: Penguin, 1942; original title reprinted Westport, Connecticut: Hyperion Press, 1977

Ralston, W.R.S., *Krilof and His Fables*, London: Strahan, 1869; 3rd edition, 1871

Saunders, William Henry, *Poetical Translations from the Russian Language*, London: G., J. and J. Neele, 1826, pp. 52–62

During the long decades of the 19th century when Russian literature appeared largely intractable and unappealing to the British public, Ivan Krylov more than any other Russian writer was able to make an impact by his mastery of the traditional and universal form of the fable, his humour, and what has been termed his "un-Russian (I think British) common sense" (William Gerhardie, 1922). While about one third of his fables have their origins in others, for example those of Aesop and La Fontaine, the great majority are original, and all have found an English translator.

BOWRING (1821) produced the first translations, *The Ass and the Nightingale* and *The Swan, the Pike and the Crab*, which were to become two of the four most translated fables in English. Working from literal French versions, Bowring padded and paraphrased and, while preserving the iambic metre, inevitably increased the number of feet. In the second of the fables he omitted Krylov's last line and missed the whole point of the fable. His later versions (1825) of three more fables are more succinct, if still distant from the originals. They were the first versions (unattributed to Bowring) to appear in America (the Philadelphia *National Gazette and Literary Register*, 3 September 1825). SAUNDERS (1826) belongs very much to the Bowring school of paraphrasers, with particular disregard for Krylov's line lengths and rhymes, but achieving something of his humour and liveliness. LEEDS (1839, 1842) illustrates his well-informed articles on the Russian fabulists with 15 verse translations from Krylov, but his orientation on "novelty of subject" rather than "merit of execution" and an acknowledgement of avoiding "cramping ourselves and thereby rendering our copy stiff and lifeless" give him infinite licence.

In the 1860s–70s the verse paraphrase gave way to the prose version, where form was openly sacrificed to content, but without any necessary fidelity to the originals. It was, however, in "a faithful prose rendering" by RALSTON (four editions between 1869 and 1883) that Krylov gained his greatest British following and won an accolade from Lord Tennyson, who found his work "good and pithy beyond the wont of fables". This was the first volume devoted exclusively to Krylov, and the 93 fables in the first edition became 148 in the third. Ralston felt able to exclude

Krylov's moral on occasion, but in the same year in distant Calcutta another Englishman, the Rev. James LONG (1869), stressed both the social and moral application of the fables. Long added an explanatory title to each and every fable (e.g. *The Donkey and the Nightingale; or, The Ill Qualified Judge*) and carefully preserved the moral. On the other hand, he opted for streamlined, abbreviated versions, far from the literalism of Ralston, whose prose frequently has an archness absent from the witty verse of the originals.

The inevitable retort to Ralston came from HARRISON (1883), who believed that "the spirit of Kriloff cannot but evaporate in prose ... Prose may give the bare skeleton, but nothing more". He attempted to retain Krylov's versification, although frequently substituting the more characteristic English iambic pentameter for Krylov's alexandrines and varying too the use of double rhymes. He also faced the eternal problem of when to "universalize" or "anglicize" (for which he was taken to task by JARINTZOV (1917) and when to retain the Russian features as essential to the effect. His translations (of 149 fables) are among the most spirited, as well as faithful in the attempt to reproduce the whole range of effects in the Russian originals.

JARINTSOV, who prided herself on knowing all the elusive nuances of her native Russian, while allowing herself "some of the liberty which the nature itself of the fable permits", was one of a number of translators of Krylov during World War I, when the fabulist enjoyed a new surge of British interest.

COXWELL (1921) translated 85 fables, seeking "to be faithful to Kriloff's spirit and meaning, and observe the length of his lines and use rhyme forms answering to those of the original compositions". He selected the shorter fables and deemed it permissible, like Ralston before him, to omit Krylov's "moral", if he considered it superfluous. Despite his dexterity in imitating Krylov's iambics, Coxwell failed to match his language, sometimes rendered in a completely inappropriate stylistic register.

Coxwell produced a number of fables not previously translated into English, but only because the publication of PARES (1926) was long delayed, providing the first and only complete English translation of the fables. Such a demanding critic as Prince D.S. Mirsky, suggesting that Krylov was "untranslatable" on account of the "inimitable quality of his Russian", was nevertheless prepared to concede that Pares "succeeded in finding wonderfully happy English equivalents for Krylov's raciest idioms". It is a judgement with which most readers of Pares's Krylov would agree: his long labour of love produced a Krylov in English dress, which, unlike Trishka's caftan (in the fable of that name), was neither too long nor too short. In Pares, felicitous and frequently ingenious solutions to Krylov's verbal effects are combined with folksy sayings and proverbs, epigrammatic codas and a skilful use of metre, rhyme and rhythm.

ANTHONY CROSS

Further Reading

Cross, A.G., "The English and Krylov", *Oxford Slavonic Papers*, new series, 16 (1983)

Milan Kundera 1929–

Czech-born novelist, short-story writer, poet, essayist and dramatist

Biography

Born in Brno, Czechoslovakia, 1 April 1929, the son of a celebrated pianist and musicologist. Kundera studied music at the Charles University and the Film Faculty of the Academy of Music and Dramatic Arts in Prague until 1956, where he became professor of film in 1958. He began writing poetry while he was a student, publishing his first book of poems in 1953. He became a member of the Communist party in 1948; he left the party in 1950, rejoining it from 1956 and taking part in the culturally liberal period known as the "Prague Spring", in 1967–68. Kundera wrote a number of books of short stories, including the well-known three-volume collection written in the 1960s and published in 1970, *Smesné lásky* (*Laughable Loves*). His first successful novel, the satirical *Zert* (*The Joke*) was published in 1967, the year in which he married Vera Hrabánková. Publication of his next novel, *Zivot je jinde* (*Life is Elsewhere*), 1969, was not permitted by the Czech authorities, and Kundera's writing was published outside Czechoslovakia from that date onwards. After the Soviet occupation of Czechoslovakia in 1968 Kundera was persecuted by the government, and his books were removed from libraries and bookshops. In 1970 Kundera was dismissed from his lecturing post at the Prague Film Academy and expelled from the Communist party. In 1975 he emigrated to France with his wife and took up a position as professor of comparative literature at Rennes University. He was stripped of his Czech citizenship shortly after this. He moved to a professorship at the École des Hautes Études in Paris in 1980. He became a French citizen in 1985. Kundera was awarded several international prizes for his work, including the Commonwealth award, 1981, the Europa prize, 1982, the Jerusalem prize, 1984, and the Académie Française Critics' prize, 1987. In 1989 the ban on his work in Czechoslovakia was lifted.

Kundera's best-known fiction, which established his international literary reputation, was published in the West after his writing was silenced by the Czech authorities: it includes his novel *Kniha smíchu a zapomnení* (*The Book of Laughter and Forgetting*), 1979, and *Nesnesitelná lehkost bytí* (*The Unbearable Lightness of Being*), 1984. Among Kundera's more recent novels is *Nesmrtelnost* (*Immortality*), published in 1990.

Translations

Novels

Zert, 1967

Hamblyn, David and Oliver Stallybrass, *The Joke*, London: MacDonald, and New York: Coward McCann, 1969

Heim, Michael Henry, *The Joke*, New York: Harper and Row, and London: Faber, 1982

Kundera, Milan and Aaron Asher, *The Joke: Definitive Version*, New York: HarperCollins, 1992

Zivot je Jinde, 1969

Kussi, Peter, *Life is Elsewhere*, New York: Knopf, 1974; with new preface by Kundera, New York: Penguin, 1986

Valcík Na Rozloucenou, 1976

Kussi, Peter, *The Farewell Party*, New York: Knopf, 1976; London: John Murray, 1977

Kniha smíchu a zapomnení, 1979

Heim, Michael Henry, *The Book of Laughter and Forgetting*, New York: Knopf, 1980; Harmondsworth: Penguin, 1981

Nesnesitelná lehkost bytí, 1984

Heim, Michael Henry, *The Unbearable Lightness of Being*, New York: Harper and Row, and London: Faber, 1984

Nesmrtelnost, 1990

Kussi, Peter, *Immortality*, New York: Grove Weidenfeld, and London: Faber, 1991

Short Stories

Smesné lásky, 1970

Rappaport, Suzanne, *Laughable Loves*, with an introduction by Philip Roth, New York: Knopf, 1974; London: John Murray, 1978; revised edition, Harmondsworth and New York: Penguin, 1987 (contains "The Hitchhiking Game", "Let the Old Dead Make Room for the Young Dead", "Nobody Will Laugh", "The Golden Apple of Eternal Desire", "Symposium", "Dr Havel after Ten Years", "Edward and God")

Play

Jacques et son maître, 1981

Heim, Michael Henry, *Jacques and His Master: An Homage to Diderot in Three Acts*, New York: Harper and Row, 1985; London: Faber, 1986

Essays

L'Art du roman, 1986

Asher, Linda, *The Art of the Novel*, New York: Grove Press, and London: Faber, 1988

Les Testaments trahis, 1993

Asher, Linda, *Testaments Betrayed: An Essay in Nine Parts*, New York: HarperCollins, and London: Faber, 1995

Few authors are as aware of the precarious position of the text as Milan Kundera, whose writing has been censored and banned by the country whose language it represents. "For me", Kundera notes in *The Art of the Novel* (ASHER, 1988), "because practically speaking I no longer have the Czech audience, translations are everything". Indeed, most of his novels appear in French and English before they are even published in their original Czech form. Careful to ensure that his translators remain faithful both to the style and to the tone of his prose, Kundera often oversees or participates in the translating process. As a result, his work displays an acute awareness of its word choice. Part 5 of *The Book of Laughter and Forgetting* (HEIM, 1980) is a good example of Kundera's attention to vocabulary; he writes:

> *Litost* is a Czech word with no exact translation into any other language. It designates a feeling as infinite as an open accordion, a feeling that is the synthesis of many others: grief, sympathy, remorse, and an indefinable longing. The first syllable, which is long and stressed, sounds like the wail of an abandoned dog.

In *Testaments Betrayed* (ASHER, 1995) Kundera devotes a whole chapter to an analysis of the existing translations of one sentence in Kafka's *The Castle*: "The entire sentence is one long metaphor", he writes. "Nothing requires more exactness from a translator than the translation of a metaphor. That is where we glimpse the core of an author's poetic originality". Because Kundera's fiction is crafted poetically (he claims in *The Art of the Novel* to "reject the very notion of synonym: each word has its own meaning and is semantically irreplaceable"), his translators are faced with an immense challenge.

"The writer who determines to supervise the translations of his books", Kundera states in *The Art of the Novel*, "finds himself chasing after hordes of words like a shepherd after a flock of wild sheep – a sorry figure to himself, a laughable one to others". An English-reading audience receives all of Kundera's writing through translators – he writes his essays in French and his fiction in Czech. Of Kundera's works, *The Joke* has the most interesting translation history. Published in Prague in 1967, the novel was banned by the Communist government in 1968. Two months after being censored in Czechoslovakia, the book was published in Paris; British and American editions followed shortly after. Unfortunately, the early translators (or publishers, as the case may be) took liberties with Kundera's style, changing the work's punctuation, shortening segments, and rearranging the order of its chapters. Frustrated by the systematic warping of his text, ("I once left a publisher for the sole reason that he tried to change my semicolons to periods", he attests) Kundera assumed responsibility in 1991 for *The Joke*'s definitive English-language translation. "Books have their fates", Kundera observes in the preface to the 1982 edition

> The fate of the book called *The Joke* coincided with a time when the combined inanity of ideological dictatorship (in the Communist countries) and journalistic oversimplification (in the West) was able to prevent a work of art from telling its own truth in its own words.

The HAMBLYN & STALLYBRASS (1969) translation, published by MacDonald in London and Coward McCann in New York, rearranges much of Kundera's novel, shortening and changing the tone of the text in places. Kundera complains in *The Art of the Novel*: "the publisher cut out all the reflective passages, eliminated the musicological chapters, changed the order of the parts, recomposed the novel".

HEIM's (1982) reworking of *The Joke* is lauded on its cover for being "an unabridged, brilliant translation". In the preface, Kundera credits Heim's translation with being the "authentic version" of the book. After allowing it to be published, however, the author discovered problems with Heim's translation that he had not caught earlier. Kundera writes:

> often the words were remote from what I had written; the syntax differed too; there was inaccuracy in all the reflective passages; irony had been transformed to satire; unusual turns of phrase had been obliterated; the distinctive voices of the characters-narrators had been altered to the extent of altering their personalities ... in good conscience [Heim] produced the kind of translation that one might call *translation-adaptation* (adaptation to the taste of the time and of the country for which it is intended, to the taste, in the final analysis, of the translator) ... [It was] unacceptable to me (author's note, 1992 edition of *The Joke*).

Heim is guilty of what Kundera calls in *Testaments Betrayed* "synonymization", the tendency of translators to enrich the language of the original text: "What terror the words 'be' and 'have' strike in all the translators of the world! They'll do anything to replace them with words they consider less routine".

The final, definitive translation produced by KUNDERA & ASHER (1992) is based on the preceding editions of *The Joke*, but in this edition Kundera and his publisher make sure to check every word with the Czech text, correcting the translations where they have strayed. Asher notes on the cover that this edition of the novel "reflects [Kundera's] original as closely as any translation possibly can: reflects it in its fidelity not only to the words and syntax but also to the characteristic dictions and tonalities of the novel's narrators". Here, embellished phrases are replaced with more direct translations. An example of this in the text: Jaroslav describes himself in part four as "veliký, veliký, veliký". Kundera translates this in 1992 as "long and big"; Heim's 1982 version has Jaroslav feeling that he is "a towering hulk".

In each of his works, critical and creative, Kundera addresses the issue of translation and the broader theme of communication that lends translation its significance. In *The Unbearable Lightness of Being* (HEIM, 1984), a chapter entitled "Words Misunderstood" examines the ways in which two of his characters use the same language differently; the narrator remarks

> While people are fairly young and the musical composition of their lives is still in its opening bars, they can go about writing it together and exchange motifs (the way Tomas and Sabina exchanged the motif of the bowler hat), but if they meet when they are older, like Franz and Sabina, their musical compositions are more or less complete, and every motif, every object, every word means something different to each of them.

Kundera's writing style – at the same time playfully questioning and self-reflectively insightful – is inimitable; his precise characterizations and frequent authorial interjections remind us not only of the importance of faithful translation, but also that the possibilities of the novel are far from being exhausted.

SARAH K. FARRANT

Further Reading

Aji, Aron (editor), *Milan Kundera and the Art of Fiction: Critical Essays*, New York and London: Garland, 1992
Banerjee, Maria Nemcova, *Terminal Paradox: The Novels of Milan Kundera*, New York: Grove Weidenfeld, 1990
Boyers, Robert (editor), *Salmagundi*, 73 (Winter 1987): "Milan Kundera: Fictive Lightness, Fictive Weight"
Misurella, Fred, *Understanding Milan Kundera: Public Events, Private Affairs*, Columbia: University of South Carolina Press, 1993
O'Brien, John, "Milan Kundera: Meaning, Play, and the Role of Author", *Critique: Studies in Contemporary Fiction*, 34/1 (Fall 1992) pp. 3–18
Oppenheim, Lois (editor), *Review of Contemporary Fiction*, 9/2 (Summer 1989): special issue on Kundera

L

Louise Labé c.1524–1566

French poet

Biography

Born Louise Charly in Lyon, around 1524. She was the wife, or perhaps the daughter, of a prosperous rope-maker, or *cordier*, for which reason she was known as "la Belle Cordière". She received an extensive education, learning Latin, Spanish and Italian, in addition to music, riding and fencing. She married Ennemond Perrin, 35 years older than herself. After her marriage Labé became part of the circle of humanist poets in Lyon, which included the writers Maurice Scève and Olivier de Magny; Labé is reported variously to have had a liaison with both these poets, and they have both been named as the subject of some of her best-known love poems. Labé's sonnets, her principal work, were published in Lyon in 1555 as *Euvres de Louize Labé lionnoize*. The publication of these passionate compositions and the unusually free lifestyle she enjoyed prompted rumours casting doubt on her moral character. After the publication of her book of sonnets, Labé moved from Lyon to live quietly at her villa at Parcieu-en-Dombes. She died there in April 1566.

Labe's literary reputation rests mainly on her sonnets, which achieved considerable success during her lifetime; they were published in further editions in 1556. Her other principal work is her prose dialogue *Débat de Folie et d'Amour* (*The Debate between Folly and Love*), also published in 1555.

Translations

Collection

Farrell, Edith R., *Louise Labé's Complete Works*, Troy, New York: Whitston, 1986

Poetry

Sonnets, 1555

Cook, Alta Lind, *Sonnets of Louise Labé, "La Belle Cordière"*, Toronto: University of Toronto Press, 1950

Haley, Martin, *Beatrice: Being the Sonnets of Louise Labé (1525–1566)*, Brisbane, Australia: Simpson Halligan, 1963 (also includes translations from G. Pascoli and Dante)

Knapp, Bettina L., *Les Sonnets / The Sonnets*, with an introduction, Paris: Lettres Modernes, 1964

Lobb, Frances, *Louise Labé, La Belle Cordière: The Twenty-four Love Sonnets*, London: Euphorion Books, 1950

Martin, Graham Dunstan, *Louise Labé: Sonnets* (bilingual edition), with an introduction and commentaries by Peter Sharratt, Edinburgh: Edinburgh University Press, 1973

Prokosch, Frederic, *Love Sonnets*, New York: New Directions, 1947

Débat de Folie et d'Amour, 1555

Cox, Edwin Marion, *The Debate between Folly and Cupid*, London: Williams and Norgate, 1925

Farrell, Edith R., *The Debate Between Folly and Love* in *Louise Labé's Complete Works*, Troy, New York: Whitston, 1986

Greene, Robert, *The Debate Betweene Follie and Love* in *Gwydonivs, The Carde of Fancie*, London: Printed by T. East for William Ponsonby, 1584

Louise Labé, given her meagre poetic legacy, only 24 sonnets and three elegies, has enjoyed an extraordinary success. Her poems have attracted scholars and poets and more recently she has become the preoccupation of feminist studies. The compactness of her collection of sonnets accounts for the relatively large number of translations of her work that have appeared. Her prose dialogue, *The Debate of Folly and Love,* was first translated in part in the 16th century by Robert GREENE (1584), who allowed himself great liberties with the text. Edwin COX (1925) rendered it into a clear smooth English which however includes a number of inaccuracies, and he misses the tone of the original. Edith FARRELL (1986) also shows a lack of familiarity with 16th-century French, and a reliable translation of the *Debate* is still awaited.

It is in the second half of the 20th century that Labé's sonnets attracted an international following, with English translations from Australia, Canada, the UK and the United States. They have all approached differently the task of converting the French sonnet into an English one.

Frederic PROKOSCH (1947) is a recognized poet and he has produced effective and resonant renderings. He has been appreciated for his "happy phrases" and "discreet rhymes" although the verse is not without its contradictions and its rhymes are sometimes unusual.

Frances LOBB's version (1950) is by comparison somewhat heavy. The English has at times an awkward ponderousness and can become contrived to maintain the rhyme scheme. The rhyme is good but the decasyllabic line is achieved sometimes at the expense of accuracy. The result is an interesting exercise in literary translation without the pulse of creative transposition.

Alta Lind COOK's publication (1950) has tended to eclipse that of Lobb. She too remains close to the original both in metre and in style. Like Lobb, she maintains the rhyme scheme of the original, which can prove a little overpowering in English. As has been pointed out, too rigid adherence to the rhyming structure can lead to infidelities in the way the rhythm is conveyed as phrases are reorganized to fit in with the rhyme. There are some approximate transpositions but, on the whole, the collection embodies some of the urgency and passion that Louise Labé injects into the French.

Martin HALEY (1963) follows the rhyme and the text of the sonnets closely. The language sounds mildy archaic and, in places, the interpretation of the text can be questioned. The overall impression is that of mild preciosity, and though the spirit of the original is sometimes reproduced the global effect is less convincing.

Bettina L. KNAPP (1964) has opted for free verse in her handy pocketbook edition of the sonnets. There is a useful introduction but no annotations. Her translation tends towards the literal, with the occasional odd inversion of words to match the metre. In spite of the odd clumsy rendering she often succeeds in capturing the tone of the original.

Peter Sharratt has provided the introduction and the erudite commentary to accompany Graham Dunstan MARTIN's translation (1973) of the sonnets. This is the best edition for academic purposes. The translator has "tried to freshen some of Louise's clichés" and has used "a fairly free sonnet-form, in that many ... rhymes are various sorts of approximations". This policy has led to a collection that manages to remain acceptably faithful to the spirit of the original. The vocabulary is modern, with a judicious use of older terms that befits a stylized expression of emotion. The discreet use of rhyme results in a whole perhaps more agreeable to the English ear than the reproduction of a full set of rhyming quatrains and tercets.

When Edith R. FARRELL's edition of the *Complete Works* appeared (1986), one reviewer was prompted to remark, "It is hard to see the point of yet another translation of Louise Labé's sonnets". This edition does have the advantage of including translations of Labé's other work but the disadvantage of not having the original French text. The view of her renderings is that although poetically acceptable they are marred by inaccuracies and mistranslations.

A sample quatrain from four of the translations mentioned will reveal some of the critical points referred to above:

On voit mourir toute chose animée,
Lors que du corps l'âme sutile part:
Je suis le corps, toy la meilleure part:
Où es-tu donq, ô âme bien aymée?
(Louise Labé, Sonnet VII)

We see each living thing on earth decay
When from the corse [sic] the subtle spirit flies.
You are the better part, I but the clay;
Where are you then, O soul that I so prize?
(Frances Lobb)

We see the death of every living thing,
When soul from body leaves in subtle flight:
I am the body, thou, my soul, the light,
The better part. Where art thou loitering?
(Alta Lind Cook)

All things that breathe and move are seen to die
When from their flesh th'informing souls depart:
Our flesh am I and the you the better part,
So where are you, beloved?...
(Martin Haley)

One sees all living things expire
The moment tenuous soul from body soars.
I am the body, thou art the better part.
Where are you then, O my beloved soul?
(Bettina L. Knapp)

When soul from body like fine smoke departs
Then every living thing to death must go:
I am the body, you its better part:
Where are you then, my well-beloved soul?
(Graham Dunstan Martin)

KEITH CAMERON

Further Reading

Cameron, Keith, *Louise Labé: Renaissance Poet and Feminist*, New York: Berg, 1990

Harvey, Lawrence E., *The Aesthetics of the Renaissance Love Sonnet: An Essay on the Art of the Sonnet in the Poetry of Louise Labé*, Geneva: Droz, 1962

Rigolot, François, *Louise Labé Lyonnaise; ou, La Renaissance au féminin*, Paris: Champion, 1997

Jean de La Bruyère 1645–1696

French satirist

Biography

Born 16 or 17 August 1645 in Paris into a family of public officials. He trained and qualified as a lawyer, but spent most of his mature years living and serving in different intellectual capacities in the household of the Prince de Condé – "le grand Condé", one of Louis XIV's great soldiers and a patron of letters – mainly at Chantilly. Though La Bruyère also wrote some dialogues on Quietism, he is now known almost exclusively for his *Characters*, published and revised in 9 editions between 1688 and 1696. In 1693 La Bruyère was elected to the French Academy, an occasion surrounded by some controversy. The orator and controversialist Jacques Bénigne Bossuet was his friend, and he sided with the "anciens" in the literary "querelle des anciens et des modernes". He died at Versailles, 11 May 1696.

The Characters

Les Caractères de Théophraste, traduits du grec, avec Les Caractères; ou, Les Moeurs de ce siècle, 1688 (3 editions), 1689, 1690, 1691, 1692, 1694 and (posthumously) 1696

Published with his translation of the *Characters* of the Greek philosopher Theophrastus (a classification of human characteristics, published 319 BC), La Bruyère's *Characters* contains, in over a thousand sections of varying length, his own penetrating and tart though not unfeeling views on contemporary society. These views are embodied in maxims and reflections, and in word-portraits of psychological and social types, analysed with virtuoso verbal skills and vividly exemplified.

A couple of English translations of the *Characters* were made soon after the publication of the full French text and reprinted several times; since then, in comparison with his fellow French satirists, La Fontaine and La Rochefoucauld, La Bruyère has received only moderate attention from anglophone translators.

Translations

Collection

Rowe, Nicholas, *The Works of Monsieur de la Bruyère: A New Translation from the Last Paris Edition*, 6th edition, 2 vols, London: Curll and Pemberton, 1713, and several further 18th-century editions (contains "A Defence of M. de La Bruyère" by Pierre Coste, translated by John Ozell; *The Moral Characters of Theophrastus*, *The Characters*, and La Bruyère's speech on his reception into the French Academy in 1693, as well as an original chapter by Rowe, "Of the Manner of Living with Great Men", written "after the method of M. Bruyère")

Selections

Anonymous, *The Characters; or, The Manners of the Age*, translated by Several Hands, London: printed for John Bullard, 1699, and several contemporary revised editions

Laun, Henri van, *The Characters of La Bruyère*, London: Nimmo, and New York: Scribner and Welford, 1885; with an introduction by Denys C. Potts, London and New York: Oxford University Press, 1963

Lee, Elizabeth, *La Bruyère and Vauvenargues: Selections from the Characters, Reflexions and Maxims*, with an introduction, London: Constable, 1903

Stewart, Jean, *Characters*, Harmondsworth and Baltimore: Penguin, 1970

Stott, Helen, *The Morals and Manners of the Seventeenth Century, being the Characters of La Bruyère*, London: David Stott, and Chicago: McClurg, 1890

The difficulty in translating Jean de La Bruyère's *Les Caractères* stems directly from the measured irony and controlled bitterness that become apparent to readers, even of the French text only, when they are aware of the authorial experience that unifies the author's point of view. La Bruyère had purchased an official post he could ill afford but which conferred nobility, and he was a timid, ungainly member of the Condé household, which he had entered, recommended by Bossuet, as tutor to the grandson of the "grand" Condé, in 1684. On the grandfather's death, La Bruyère was made librarian. He was the butt of insensitive jokes but, whatever the unpleasantness to which he was subjected, he remained fascinated by the values and behaviour of the aristocracy of whose entourage he formed part. It is likely that in addition to La Bruyère's own observations, *Les Caractères* contains echoes picked up from members of the court being ironic at their own expense.

The text was completely transformed between the 1st edition, which appeared very early in 1688, and the 9th, which appeared posthumously in 1696, but was prepared and signed by La Bruyère. An ANONYMOUS first English translation "by Several Hands" appeared in 1699, offering a key to the pseudonyms used in the French text. The several hands set about translating in very different ways, but tended on the whole towards being literal, even to the point of unintelligibility, at least until the going got stylistically difficult. It is particularly instructive, for instance, to see the translators grapple with Ergaste (section 28 of "Des Biens de fortune" in the Garapon critical edition, Paris: Garnier, 1962).

Ergaste was one of the army of officials whose responsibility it was to "proposer" or advise the Treasury on means of raising taxation, and on persons suitable for appointment to farm the taxes,

> Laissez faire *Ergaste*, et il exigera un droit de tous ceux qui boivent de l'eau de la rivière, ou qui marchent sur terre ferme ... Le Prince ne donne aux autres qu'au dépens d'Ergaste, et ne leur fait de grâces que celles qui lui étaient dues.

The 1699 English version makes no concessions to intelligibility:

> Let *Ergastus* alone, and he will demand a Right over every-thing that dwells in the Water, or marches on dry land. The Prince gives nothing to anyone but at his Expence, parts with no Favours but what are his due ...

Even apart from the misreading of "tous ceux qui boivent " ("all those who drink") as "everything that dwells", it seems unlikely that the translator understood the text, or "right" would have become "tax" or one of its synonyms, and the double "his" in the second sentence would have had clearer correlatives. There is a variant "qu'à ses dépens" from the 1689, 1690, and 1691 editions. The English "at his Expence" suggests that it was one of these editions being used. What the text means is "at Ergastus's expense" and "any favours he [i.e. the Prince] grants them were really due to him" (i.e. Ergaste) (STEWART, 1970).

The several hands of 1699 include one defeated by La Bruyère's single speaker's share in a little piece of ironic dialogue ("De la Société", section 7):

> Que dites-vous? Comment? Je n'y suis pas; vous plairait-il de recommencer? J'y suis encore moins. Je devine enfin: vous voulez, *Acis*, me dire qu'il fait froid; que ne disiez-vous: "Il fait froid"?

The English gives up on the style:

> Prithee *Acis*, for the satisfaction of your friends, endeavour to speak as they may understand you, for my part I do but guess at your meaning: if you would tell 'em 'tis cold ... say " 'tis cold".

The "city-ladies" of "De la Société", section 69, who will mention "Le Louvre" or "La Place royale", but not allude to Les Halles or the Châtelet, "say nothing plainly" according to the 1699 English, except "the Court and the Palace". The translation then domesticates the source: the "city-ladies" will use a whole sentence rather than say "Cheapside", but ought to do as the court ladies do, which is say "the Exchange" or "Guildhall" if they need to.

The Henri van LAUN translation of 1885 was reissued by Oxford University Press in 1963, with an introduction and notes by Denys Potts which satisfactorily clear up the problem of Ergaste, who demands "a duty from all who drink water from the river or walk on *terra firma*". The Acis paragraph is translated quite straightforwardly, and the paragraph on "town ladies" uses the French names in La Bruyère's original text. Laun avoids La Bruyère's repetition of "grande", in "Une grande naissance ou une grande fortune annonce le mérite", and uses "portends" for "annonce". His aphoristic "As favour and riches forsake a man, we discover in him the foolishness they concealed, and which no one perceived before" actually improves on La Bruyère's less succinct original, from which it omits nothing: "À mesure que la faveur et les grands biens se retirent d'un homme, ils laissent voir en lui le ridicule qu'ils couvraient, et qui y était sans que personne s'en aperçût." The characteristic of Laun is simply a tendency to Victorian pomposity, in which words like "progeny" and "lustre" clog up the delicacies of La Bruyère's translucent style, with its perfectly placed ambiguities, ironies and asides.

Of three other translations, STOTT wrote in 1890, at the high-point of the success of the mythologization of the 17th-century French monarchy. La Bruyère's book put him among "that illustrious throng of learned intellects which made the close of the 17th century and the reign of Louis XIV so great and glorious. Racine, Molière, Bossuet, Fénelon enjoyed with him the favour of the King, and La Rochefoucauld, La Fayette, and Mme de Sévigné were also of the Court." After that, the translation is precisely all you might expect: prim, silly and ignorant. The translator says that she is striving for aphoristic brevity, and she does sometimes achieve it. Though the reader feels her prose cranking up:

> Qui peut se promettre d'éviter dans la société des hommes la rencontre de certains esprits vains, légers, familiers, délibérés, qui sont toujours dans une compagnie ceux qui parlent, et qu'il faut que les autres écoutent?
>
> "De la Société", section 8

If we go much into society we cannot avoid

> meeting certain vain persons who are easy, familiar, and assertive; they are the talkers, the others must listen.

The selection published by LEE in 1903, with pieces from Vauvenargues, shows other translation techniques of the same period, this time not so prim, but cumbersome and over-emphatic.

> Je vais, *Clitiphon*, à votre porte; le besoin que j'ai de vous me chasse de mon lit et de ma chambre: plût aux Dieux que je ne fusse ni votre client ni votre fâcheux!
>
> "Des Biens de fortune", section 12

> I go to your door, Clitophon [*sic*]; my need of your interest gets me early out of my bed and my room. Would to heaven I had no occasion to solicit or be troublesome to you!

It is difficult to put into English "Un caractère bien fade est celui de n'en avoir aucun", but in STEWART's translation (1970) the repetition is a misjudgement: "A man without characteristics is a most insipid character". Equally, there is a misjudgement in the translation of the next remark, "C'est le rôle d'un sot d'être importun: un homme habile sent s'il convient ou s'il ennuie". La Bruyère has chosen his words too carefully for them to be rendered "A fool is always an intruder: an intelligent man knows whether he is welcome or unwelcome". The preface, too, gives cause for alarm in its reference to "the purest Classical canon" and to La Bruyère's inheritance "of Preciosity and Burlesque, both strong currents throughout the 17th century". Preciosity was on the contrary a limited movement, confined to a very restricted circle, and as a conspicuous force it lasted less than a mid-century decade. It seems doubtful, too, that a "galant" "generally means a lover in the fullest sense of the word", or that a "femme galante" is "wanton". None the less, "coxcomb" is good for the French "fat" in section 3 of "Des Biens de fortune". In Stewart what Ergaste would charge for drinking river water is a toll, and the verb in "Une grande naissance ou grande fortune annonce le mérite" becomes, more suitably, "proclaim". "Toll" is not quite right, but the Stewart translation is invariably intelligent.

ANTHONY LEVI

Further Reading

Mourgues, Odette de, *Two French Moralists: La Rochefoucauld and La Bruyère*, Cambridge and New York: Cambridge University Press, 1978

Pierre Choderlos de Laclos 1741–1803

French novelist and army officer

Biography

Born in Amiens, 18 October 1741. He attended a military college 1759–63 before serving for most of the rest of his life in the French army. He married in 1759, was a good husband and father, wrote a treatise on the education of women that was in advance of its time, and invented a kind of explosive shell. His only creative literary work was *Dangerous Liaisons* (1782). He died 5 September 1803 at Taranto, on his last campaign, of dysentery caught at the siege of that town.

Dangerous Liaisons

Les Liaisons dangereuses, 1782

This epistolary novel recounts the plottings of the Marquise de Merteuil and the Vicomte de Valmont, a pair of cynical, depraved ex-lovers, still with brittle designs on each other, who combine forces in order to satisfy their sexual vanity and to procure revenge, by indirections, for slights received from third parties. Selected as their victims and instruments are a naive young girl, Cécile de Volanges, and a chaste and pious young married woman, Madame de Tourvel, who are both to be debauched and seduced. The pitiless machinations succeed, but all the participants in this sexual warfare are destroyed by the process. Madame de Tourvel, after a letter of rupture sent to her by Valmont on Merteuil's instructions, dies of grief and shame. Cécile, her child by Valmont miscarried, goes into a convent. The plotters turn against each other. Valmont, fatally wounded in a duel with a youth who loved Cécile, makes public the Marquise's incriminating correspondence with him. Her reputation ruined, a lawsuit lost, she is cast out of Parisian society; disfigured then by smallpox, she too leaves the battlefield defeated in the end, in effect annihilated.

Translations

The French text of the first edition of April 1782 was never modified by the author, except that he incorporated corrections which figure in the errata in subsequent editions. The standard text now used by French specialists is to be found in the Versini edition of the complete works prepared for Gallimard (Pléiade) in 1979.

Aldington, Richard, *Dangerous Acquaintances*, with an introduction, London: Routledge, and New York: Dutton, 1924

Anonymous, *Dangerous Connections; or, Letters Collected in a Society and Published for the Instruction of Other Societies*, 4 vols, London: T. Hookham, 1784

Dowson, Ernest, *Dangerous Acquaintances*, 2 vols, London: privately printed (360 copies), 1898; reprinted London: Nonesuch Press, 1940, with preface by André Gide and illustrations by Chas Laborde

Hampton, Christopher, *Les Liaisons dangereuses: A Play*, London: Faber, 1985, revised 1986

Hampton, Christopher, *Dangerous Liaisons: The Film*, London: Faber, 1989

Parmée, Douglas, *Les Liaisons dangereuses*, with an introduction by David Coward, Oxford and New York: Oxford University Press, 1995

Stone, P.W.K., *Les Liaisons dangereuses*, with an introduction, Harmondsworth and New York: Penguin, 1961

Published for the first time in April 1782, *Les Liaisons dangereuses* was an immediate success. It was condemned at the time of publication as an immoral text, in spite of the author's claims to the contrary. Critics have remained divided about the intentions of the author but there can be little doubt that it is the intimate insight into the minds of the two main protagonists, Valmont and Merteuil, that has guaranteed the survival of the text and that fascinates us still today. Translating a text so long and complex is no easy matter. The language of the original is rich in 18th-century idiom, and translators these days have to decide whether or not to modernize. A modern text becomes accessible to a wider audience, but the flavour of the original is invariably lost. There have been some interesting translations and, perhaps, some even more interesting adaptations. The novel became a play and then a film. Three films of the novel have been made in the last 40 years. This is probably the only French novel of the 18th century that can claim such filmic success.

The ANONYMOUS 1784 translation is, naturally enough, a "literal" one that is perfectly in keeping with the original. It is accurate and complete. It was published with an extract from the "Correspondence on what concerns the happiness of man and society (No. III), The Utility of Novels. The Novel of Dangerous Connections" by the abbé Kentzinger. This is an interesting discussion about the moral tone of the novel, which concludes, finally, that the novel *is* moral.

DOWSON's translation (1898), published with photographic reproductions of the 1796 French edition, is richly elegant, in English of undoubted charm and sensitivity. A "note to the present edition" explains that Laclos "might more justly than Stendhal, be called the father of French realism. His aim was excellent, but in his endeavour to point his moral he painted the vice which he wished to flagellate in colours so glowing that he appears more an advocate than an opponent of immorality".

ALDINGTON (1924) contains an introduction of some length on the author of the novel. It is a literal translation that lacks the elegance of Dowson's. It is still being used by Routledge, the original publisher, today. DOWSON's translation (1898) was used in the Nonesuch Press edition of 1940. Illustrated by Chas Laborde, this edition contains a preface by André Gide. It also includes, in an appendix, letters that are contained in the manuscript of the novel but that were not published during the author's lifetime.

The STONE translation (1961) is workmanlike and accurate. It contains footnotes given by the translator to explain certain difficulties. The translator, on occasions, keeps the French word or expression. While this undoubtedly enhances the flavour, it must be intensely irritating for non-French-speakers. The information given in the introduction must be treated with caution.

HAMPTON's stage adaptation of the novel, first produced by the Royal Shakespeare Company in 1985, is an exciting one. The play is elegant and mannered, in strict accordance with its setting. Hampton's version is not strictly in accordance with the novel. For example, Merteuil is still present at the end of the play and has the last words: "I dare say we should not be wrong to look forward to whatever the nineties may bring. Meanwhile, I suggest our best course is to continue with the game". The play ends with a clear suggestion of impending revolution.

The film adaptations (directed by Stephen Frears, 1989 and Milos Forman, 1991, the latter with the title *Valmont*) are both interesting, for different reasons. Frears's film, with a screenplay by HAMPTON (1989), is more faithful to the original than Forman's, but both films have undoubted qualities. Hampton's screenplay is similar but not identical to his stage adaptation. Obviously, the film allows greater scenic accuracy and more locations. The conclusion too is different. Merteuil is destroyed in the film and is described as "weary, fragile, vulnerable almost".

PARMÉE's translation (1995) is a reliable one which is readable and which seeks to retain an 18th-century flavour. It benefits from an authoritative introduction by David Coward.

MALCOLM COOK

Further Reading

Coward, David, "Laclos Studies, 1968–1982", *Studies on Voltaire and the Eighteenth Century*, 219 (1983) pp. 289–330

Davies, Simon, *Laclos: Les Liaisons dangereuses*, London: Grant and Cutler, 1987

Rosbottom, Ronald C., *Choderlos de Laclos*, Boston: Twayne, 1978

Thody, Philip, *Laclos: Les Liaisons dangereuses*, London: Arnold, 1970; 2nd edition, 1975

Comtesse de La Fayette (or Lafayette) 1634–1693

French novelist

Biography

Born Marie-Madeleine Pioche de La Vergne in Paris in 1634, to wealthy parents attached to the household of the Richelieu family. She was educated well, with the scholar and man of letters Gilles Ménage as her tutor. Not long after her marriage in 1655 to the Comte de La Fayette, she returned without her husband from his estate in Auvergne to live in the capital, where she frequented the royal court and the highest Parisian society. She became a close friend of Madame de Sévigné and of the Duc de La Rochefoucauld, author of the *Maxims*. The delicate but powerful study of character and motivation in her most famous work, *The Princess of Cleves*, became a benchmark for the development of the French psychological novel. Other novels and stories are attributed to her: *La Princesse de Montpensier* (1662; *The Princess Montpensier*, 1992), *Zaïde* (1670; *Zayde, a Spanish History*, 1678), *La Comtesse de Tende* (not published until 1724; *The Comtesse de Tende*, 1992). Died in Paris, 25 May 1693.

The Princess of Clèves

La Princesse de Clèves, 1678

Novel, published anonymously in Paris in 1678, and attributed, together with other fictional works, to Mme de La Fayette. Her name was first mentioned in connection with *La Princesse de Clèves* only in 1719, as part of an authorial team then believed to include La Rochefoucauld (1613–80) and Segrais (1624–1701). It was not until 1780 that an edition of *La Princesse de Clèves* first gave her the status of sole author. This attribution is now generally accepted, though it has never been established with complete certainty, and is sometimes challenged.

The French text used by translators is basically that of the 1678 edition. Minor variations have been proposed in scholarly editions, in particular in those by Émile Magne in the *Textes littéraires français* series (Paris: Droz, 1946), and by Jean Mesnard (Paris: Imprimerie nationale, 1980).

Translations

Anderson, William, *The Princess of Clèves*, London: New English Library, 1962

Anonymous, *The Princess of Cleves. The most famed romance. Written in French by the Greatest wits of France. Rendered into English by a Person of Quality*, London: printed for R. Bentley and Magnes, 1679

Anonymous, *The Princess of Clèves*, in *A Select Collection of Novels*, vol. 2, London: John Watts, 1720

Ashton, Henry, *The Princesse of Clèves*, London: Routledge, and New York: Dutton, 1925

Buss, Robin, *The Princesse de Clèves*, Harmondsworth: Penguin, 1992

Cave, Terence, *The Princesse de Clèves*, with *The Princesse de Montpensier* and *The Comtesse de Tende*, Oxford: Oxford University Press, 1992

Cobb, Walter, *The Princess of Clèves*, New York: New American Library, 1961; revised edition, 1989

Greene, Mildred Sarah, *The Princess of Clèves*, University, Mississippi: Romance Monographs, 1979

Mitford, Nancy, *The Princess of Clèves*, London: Euphorion,

1950; New York: New Directions, 1951; revised edition, edited by Leonard Tancock, Harmondsworth: Penguin, 1978

Perry, Thomas Sergeant, *The Princess of Clèves*, 2 vols, Boston: Little Brown, 1891; London: Osgood McIlvaine, 1892; revised edition, edited by John Lyons, New York: Norton, 1994

La Princesse de Clèves belongs to many genres. It may be seen as "memoirs" or a "historical novel", giving a vivid picture of court life in Renaissance France. It draws also from the tradition of the "romance", famously exemplified in Madeleine de Scudéry's *Clélie*. Though these elements are present, *La Princesse de Clèves* is most commonly viewed as the first great "psychological novel". Most interest has focused on the intense, intimate and equivocal manner in which it narrates a young woman's struggle to repel an overwhelming love both desired and feared.

The difficulties involved in translating *La Princesse de Clèves* into English reflect its many-sided nature, its 17th-century idiom and its redoubtable ambiguities. finding an appropriate register is no easy task: the immediate impression of dignity projected by an aristocratic society comes with the sense that this is also an appearance masking the unceasing strife of violent, poisonous passions. The seemingly formal (and sometimes borrowed) prose of the historical narrative blends uneasily with the more intuitive, idiosyncratic language used to depict labyrinthine emotional states. Though the syntax can be complex, and at times even clumsy, the problems posed by the lexis are the most challenging of all. Seventeenth-century love-vocabulary offers a palette of subtly contrasting colours which are not all available in English, while abstract terms referring to moral qualities have often no simple equivalents in the target language.

The 1679 ANONYMOUS translation is interesting mainly for being the first. A deliberately archaic style and an indulgence in vague, convoluted formulations sometimes engenders sentences verging on the incomprehensible. The impression of linguistic ineptness is not diminished by gratuitous excisions and interpolations.

The 1720 ANONYMOUS translation was clearly composed with this first version to hand, but it is essentially a new and greatly improved work. The tone is even, the language plain, the focus sharp. Though there is a sustained effort to correct previous errors, accuracy and clarity are not purchased at the expense of delicacy and subtlety. One comparative example: the bizarre "for whom he had inclinations not ordinarily passionate" (1679) and the refined "for whom his Regard has been very tender" (1720).

The 1891 PERRY version is based on an 1889 French edition: it contains the same preface by Anatole France and the same illustrations. It is now available in the LYONS revision of 1994. For Lyons, Perry's translation is "undoubtedly the version that has given the English-speaking public the greatest service". Our pleasure at this service is somewhat diminished by the presence of errors, some monumental: "to inspire her with the love of virtue and make her attractive" is Perry's rendering of the heroine's mother's intention to *lui donner de la vertu et la lui rendre aimable* (to instil into her virtue and a love of virtue). His vocabulary is sometimes archaic, and can be misleading even when simple, as when *inclination violente* (powerful attraction) is translated as "deeply interested". Undertranslation is common, while the syntax is not always designed for immediate understanding ("It was impossible for her not to feel sure that she was the woman whose name was unknown"). The Lyons revision sets out to correct only a small number of the more obvious blunders and infelicities.

ASHTON, a fine scholar and biographer of Mme de La Fayette, prefaces his translation (1925) with a set of Tytler-like aims: accuracy counts first and foremost, and then comes the endeavour to reproduce the author's style and make the result read like English. The outcome is a translation of exceptional scrupulousness, written in a manner that, perhaps consequentially, can on occasion seem stiff.

The 1950 MITFORD translation is the polar opposite. With the emphasis on short sentences and an accessible vocabulary, Mitford sought to appeal to a non-specialist public: she sometimes adds phrases, and omits others, to get the "basic" meaning across in an entertaining way. However, the complex syntactic structures and vocabulary of the source text often mirror elusive, ambiguous inner states: simplification can be tantamount to devitalization. In addition, Mitford is not always at home with the vocabulary of 17th-century French. Most of her errors are eliminated in the revision by TANCOCK (1978): in his preface may be found perhaps the sharpest criticism of her work. It is, however, difficult to change the overall tone of the Mitford translation, which transforms *La Princesse de Clèves* into a piece of light romantic fiction from the mid-20th century.

COBB (1961) produces a puzzling mixture. In tone, the jauntily "modern" cohabits with the archaic: for example, the exclamation marks inserted to liven up dialogues coexist with phrases such as "enervation" and "he betook himself". The translation of love-vocabulary is also uneven: *engagements* is sharply rendered as "illicit love-affairs", but *inclination* and *galanterie* are watered down into "infatuation" and "politeness".

ANDERSON's version (1962) is equally aimed at the mass market, which in this case at least seems to have permitted considerable freedom from the despotism of the source text. Thus the famous opening phrase, *La magnificence et la galanterie*, becomes "The arts of life and love". A penchant for short cuts does not prevent syntactic intricacies such as "she wondered no less that her heart was untouched". There are some major errors on crucial phrases: (*Les passions*) *ne sauraient m'aveugler* becomes "can only blind me".

The GREENE version (1979) is an attempt at a modern, approachable rendering for the academic market. Surprisingly, however, it is filled with jangling discords such as "the Duc" and "the Princes of blood", and contains a disconcerting number of paraphrases and even some mistranslations (for example, *elle lui en dit du bien*, "she spoke of his many love-affairs", and a replication of the *vertu aimable* example from Perry, above).

BUSS (1992) presents a clear, idiomatic version that does not bludgeon the reader into one particular interpretation of the novel's complexities. Though generally reliable, it can undertranslate and, on close examination of particular points, seem imprecise, especially in the difficult area of love vocabulary.

CAVE (1992) provides a translation accurate to Ashton standards, while being fluent and pleasant to read. It manages to maintain dignity of tone without recourse to archaism. Exceptional care is taken precisely to render shades of meaning in those linguistically refined and anthropologically remote areas (such as attitudes to love or moral questions) that, as we have seen, cause trouble for most translators. There is an incisive preface, with clear and helpful notes referred to in the text by a possibly obtrusive asterisk.

JOHN CAMPBELL

Further Reading

Kitagaki, Muneharu, *Principles and Problems of Translation in Seventeenth-Century England*, Kyoto: Yamacuchi Shoten, 1981

See also the translators' introductions to Ashton, Mitford, Tancock, Anderson, Greene, Buss and Cave

---

Jean de La Fontaine 1621–1695

French poet

Biography

Born 8 July 1621 in Château-Thierry, Champagne, where his father was a government official, maître des Eaux et Forêts, in charge of the local forests and waterways. He was brought up in the country. The facts about his education are not fully known, but he was well-read in the Greek, Latin, Italian and French literatures. He probably attended the Collège de Château-Thierry and some time in the early 1630s he went to a school in Paris. In 1641–42 he studied theology at the Oratory in Paris. In 1643 he returned to Château-Thierry and, it is thought, began to write poetry. In about 1646 he studied law (he may have qualified to practise) in Paris, where he made friends and moved in literary circles. At the end of 1647 he married Marie Héricart (one son; separated 1658), but he was a negligent husband and father and most of his life was spent in or attached to the household of eminent patrons, who appreciated his literary brilliance and amiable character. He succeeded to his father's post in the Eaux et Forêts, but sold it.

Foremost among La Fontaine's patrons were, from 1659 to 1661, the chancellor Fouquet, to whom he remained loyal in adversity; from 1664 to 1672, the dowager duchess of Orleans; in the 1670s and 1680s, the duchess of Bouillon; and above all Madame de la Sablière, from about 1673 to her death in 1693. La Fontaine was elected to the Académie Française at the second attempt, in 1684.

La Fontaine admired Molière and was a friend of Racine, to whose family his wife was related, but in the Quarrrel of the Ancients and the Moderns he was on the side of the Ancients.

The *Fables* (*Fables*), were published 1668–94. La Fontaine also left behind poems addressed to members of the royal family and to patrons, friends and people of note, as well as various plays, translations and libretti. The lively and licentious *Contes et nouvelles en vers* (1664–75) attracted moral disapproval and La Fontaine repented of them in 1693, when he thought he was on his deathbed. He died in Paris, 13 March 1695.

Fables

Fables, 1668–94

There is no single edition of the *Fables* used by translators. They were originally published in three stages: books I–VI in 1668, books VII–XI in 1678–79 and book XII in 1694. Subsequent editions have sometimes altered the numbering of the fables within each book, so there is inconsistency in the way the fables are numbered by translators. A good modern French edition is *Fables*, edited by Georges Couton, Paris: Garnier, 1962.

Translations

Collections

Marsh, Edward, *The Fables of Jean de La Fontaine*, London: Heinemann, and New York: Random House, 1931

Thomson, Robert, *La Fontaine's Fables, now first translated from the French*, Paris: Chenu, 1806

Selections

Anonymous, *Fables and Tales from La Fontaine: In French and English* (parallel texts), London: printed for A. Bettsworth, C. Hitch and C. Davis, 1734

Mandeville, Bernard de, *Some Fables after the Easie and Familiar Method of Monsieur de la Fontaine*, London, 1703

Michie, James, *La Fontaine: Selected Fables*, with an introduction by Geoffrey Grigson, New York: Viking Press, and London: Allen Lane, 1979; Harmondsworth: Penguin, 1982 (this edition does not have the illustrations)

Moore, Marianne, *The Fables of La Fontaine*, New York: Viking Press 1954; as *Selected Fables of La Fontaine*, London: Faber, 1955

Scarfe, Francis, *100 Fables* (bilingual edition), Paris and London: British Institute in Paris, 1985

Thornbury, Walter, *The Fables of La Fontaine*, London: Cassell, 1867–70; as *The Fables of Jean de La Fontaine*, Philadelphia: National Publishing, n.d.; New York: Hurst, n.d

Wood, Christopher, *Selected Fables*, edited and with an introduction by Maya Slater (parallel texts), Oxford and New York: Oxford University Press, 1995

Wright, Elizier Jr, *The Fables of La Fontaine*, Boston: J. Wright, 1841; London: William Smith, 1842

The *Fables* of La Fontaine have been a target for translators since the early 18th century. A large number of translations have been published since then and they still continue to appear. Any survey, therefore, of these translations must be selective. The text by its very nature invites a wide variety of approaches. Some translators see it as a collection of moral tales based on Aesop's *Fables* for the instruction of children: others as the exact opposite, pointing out that the moral content of the *Fables*, always assuming it can be determined, can be interpreted in many different ways. Whatever the truth may be, the fact remains that these are highly sophisticated poems, written with unique wit and humour and displaying a bewildering variety of verse forms and rhyme schemes which require the greatest delicacy of touch to render into English. The skill of the translator who attempts the task must be measured by his or her ability to convey not only the dancing rhythms but also the sharpness of observation and underlying significance of La Fontaine's text. Not all succeed.

The earliest attempt to make La Fontaine available to the English public was the publication in 1703 of MANDEVILLE's translations of 29 fables. They are written in eight-syllable rhyming couplets and are delightfully done, tripping along merrily with a swing. No effort is made to follow the original rhyme scheme or verse form, but the overall effect reflects well the gaiety of the original, although the very limited number of fables translated does not do justice to La Fontaine's range. This was followed in 1734 by an edition of 100 fables ANONYMOUSLY translated, intended as a work of instruction, with French and English printed side by side. Prose is the vehicle used and while the translation is accurate, inevitably, in prose, much of the charm of La Fontaine is lost.

It is not until 1806 that a translation of the complete *Fables* appears. This is by Robert THOMSON, who gives a very elegant translation with verse forms that follow the original closely with many happy phrases and amusing touches. The versions are apt and witty and the early 19th-century English adds to their attractiveness.

Another 19th-century translation that proved popular, running to many editions, was that of Elizier WRIGHT, which was first published in 1841. It is in verse and the patterns attempt to follow the original, but the translation, in spite of some ingenious things, is not a successful one. The voice of La Fontaine does not come across in the rather formal and stiff style used, in spite of the variety of verse forms and ingenuity of the rhymes.

An interesting 19th-century version is that of Walter THORNBURY, published by Cassell in 37 parts over a period of three years, 1867–70, with the illustrations of Gustave Doré, which were then very recent. These translations are competent and occasionally inspired but do not have the charm of the 1806 version. Rhyme is used skilfully and an attempt is made to vary the length of the lines to give a semblance of similarity to the original.

The first translation of note in the 20th century is that of the scholar and critic Edward MARSH (1931). This is a translation of the complete work and the renderings are excellent. Marsh brings to the task an observant eye and a sensitive ear. He follows the originals accurately, yet the English is not strained or artificial, although sometimes it can appear slightly dated (who now refers to a certain kind of young woman as a "baggage"?). However, on the whole the tone is right. Those fables that used a light touch get it but those that require a graver note are equally well served. His beautiful translation of *The Moghul's Dream* (XI, 4) illustrates this very well.

The American poet Marianne MOORE published her translations of the *Fables* in 1954. This is a poet's La Fontaine. Here is found the wit, the language, the irony of La Fontaine transposed rather than translated into English verse. La Fontaine is a sophisticated poet, as is Marianne Moore. Sometimes the two sophistications do not always match, with the result that the fine poem before us is not quite La Fontaine. However here are also found words used with flair and delicacy, an imagination at work investing the pictures drawn by La Fontaine with a shimmering light, so that things are seen as they are but not quite as they are. This is a translation like no other. Some examples must be given. In *The Fox and the Grapes* (III, 11) the grapes are described thus: "Matured till they glowed with purplish tint / As though there were gems inside"; and note, in the *Tortoise and Two Ducks* (X, 2), the description of the silly tortoise: "Folly had dealt her one of life's mortal blows", or the beginning of *The Head and Tail of the Serpent* (VII, 17): "A serpent has mobility/which can shatter intrepidity". These renderings show the quality of the translations. While some might question their accuracy none can question their originality.

James MICHIE's *Selected Fables* (1979) has the wonderful illustrations of Grandville (originally published in 1838) and is a good selection with fables from all 12 books. The translations do not necessarily follow the verse forms of La Fontaine but mould them as English usage demands. The versions are competent and read easily, although La Fontaine's effects are obtained with such apparent ease and conciseness that the translator has great difficulty in matching them in English.

Francis SCARFE's 1985 translations of 100 fables is in a bilingual edition. This is a polished piece of work. As far as possible La Fontaine's words are given a fair English clothing. The rhyming is neat and unostentatious and every now and then provides a pleasant shock as one comes upon a particularly clever thought rounding off a sentence. This is not La Fontaine for children, but the translation reveals the depth of his sensitivity and the charming philosophy running through all he wrote. The arrangement is by theme – social, political and philosophical – and by this method Scarfe draws our attention to the range of ideas treated by La Fontaine.

The continuing appeal of La Fontaine is shown by the appearance in 1995 of a translation of *Selected Fables* by Christopher WOOD with editorial material by Maya Slater. Once again French and English are given side by side. The translator says that he wants to try and reproduce the "music of [La Fontaine's] "voice" and to this end uses great variety in the length of lines and verses and rhyme schemes, which are handled with great ingenuity, dash and flair. Meaning runs from one line to the next so that the verse moves easily and fluently, with the rhyme interrupting just enough to mark a beat giving the musical effect the translator is seeking. The language used is racy and up-to-date, which is as it should be for a modern translation, but there are times when the modern turn of phrase jars. Such phrases as "make my day" or "forward planning's not for you" are, by their transitory nature, not suitable for La Fontaine, who does not use slang or fashionable jargon. Yet these elements do not mar overmuch these clever translations, which give the flavour of La Fontaine, using a language that no previous translator has used.

There are also a number of translations done specifically with children in mind. These are of variable quality and while they may be suitable for the purpose for which they are intended, they do not merit consideration as serious efforts to make La Fontaine known to the English speaker.

J.P. SHORT

Further Reading

Mourgues, Odette de, *La Fontaine: Fables*, London: Edward Arnold, 1960

Shapiro, Norman R. (translator), *The Fabulists French: Verse Fables of Nine Centuries*, Urbana: University of Illinois Press, 1992

Sweetser, Marie-Odile, *La Fontaine*, Boston: Twayne, 1987

See also Geoffrey Grigson, introduction to Michie, and Maya Slater, introduction to Wood

Jules Laforgue 1860–1887

French poet

Biography

Born in Montevideo, Uruguay, 16 August 1860. He moved to France at an early age, when his parents decided to return with their numerous children to the Béarn. Jules went to school at Tarbes. By his late teens, Laforgue, now living frugally in Paris, was becoming a friend of many of the emerging Symbolist writers. He was already producing some of the remarkable poetry for which he is known. He worked for a time as a secretary to Charles Éphrussi, the director of the *Gazette des Beaux-Arts*. From 1881 to 1886 he was based in Berlin, employed at the German court as reader to the Empress Augusta. He married an English governess in 1886. Died of tuberculosis in Paris, 21 August 1887. Less than a year later his widow died in England of the same disease.

Laforgue's poetry began to appear as collections only at the end of his short life. His earliest poems, *Le Sanglot de la Terre*, date from 1878–82, but Laforgue did not want them published. *Les Complaintes* appeared in 1885, *L'Imitation de Notre-Dame la Lune* in 1886, *Le Concile féerique*, a short verse drama, in 1886. This was re-edited in the *Derniers Vers*, 1890, which also included *Des Fleurs de Bonne Volonté* as well as what are now known as the *Last Poems*. Laforgue wrote a series of prose stories under the title *Moralités légendaires*, 1887, and a novel, *Stéphane Vassiliev*, not published until 1946. The first *Poésies complètes* was published by Vanier in 1894. Others have followed, notably Pascal Pia's edition (Gallimard, 1970), which includes more recently discovered poems, as well as 69 uncollected ones, plus fragments and drafts of poems. The first of L'Âge d'Homme's three-volume *Oeuvres complètes*, edited by J.-L. Debauve, D. Grojnoski, P. Pia and P.-O. Walzer, appeared in 1986. A comprehensive bibliography, up to 1953, is given in Warren Ramsey, *Jules Laforgue and the Ironic Inheritance* (Oxford University Press, 1953).

Translations

Selections

Dale, Peter, *Poems of Jules Laforgue*, London: Anvil Press, 1986

Martin, Graham Dunstan, *Selected Poems* (bilingual edition), with an introduction, Harmondsworth: Penguin, 1998

Smith, William Jay, *Selected Writings of Jules Laforgue*, Westport, Connecticut: Greenwood Press, 1956

Terry, Patricia, *Poems of Jules Laforgue*, Berkeley: University of California Press, 1958

Poetry

Les Complaintes, 1885

Dale, Peter, *Complaint of a Certain Sunday*, *Complaint of the Poor Knight-Errant*, *Another Complaint of My Lord Pierrot*, *Complaints over Certain Ennuis* in *Agenda*, Ezra Pound special issue, 1980

Dale, Peter, *The Complaints* (complete) in *Poems of Jules Laforgue*, translated by Dale, 1986

Mackworth, Cecily, *Complainte de la fin des journées*, *Complainte de l'oubli des morts* in *A Mirror for French Poetry, 1840–1940*, translated by Mackworth, London: Routledge and Kegan Paul, 1947; New York: Books for Libraries Press, 1969

Smith, William Jay, *Complaint of that Lovely Moon*, *Complaint of the Good Dead Girl*, *Complaint of the Moon in the Provinces*, *Complaint of Lord Pierrot*, *Another Complaint of Lord Pierrot*, *Complaint on Certain Trying Occasions*, *Complaint of the King of Thule*, *Complaint on the Oblivion of the Dead* in *Selected Writings of Jules Laforgue*, translated by Smith, 1956

Sorrell, Martin, *Epitaph-lament* in *Interactions*, Exeter, Devon: University of Exeter, 1989

Staniforth, Paul, *Compleynt of Pierrot's Bridale*, *Another Compleynt of Lord Pierrot* in *Modern Poetry in Translation*, 9 (1998)

Terry, Patricia, *Complaint about a Lady Good and Dead*, *Complaint about a Certain Sunday*, *Complaint of the Poet's Foetus*, *Complaint of the Moon in the Country*, *Complaint of Lord Pierrot*, *Complaint about Certain Annoyances*, *Complaint concerning the Poor Human Body*, *Complaint of the King of Thulé*, *Complaint about Forgetting the Dead*, *Complaint concerning a Poor Young Man*, *Complaint of the Outraged Husband*, *Complaint concerning Melancholy and Literary Debates*, *Complaint about a Convalescence in May* in *Poems of Jules Laforgue*, translated by Terry, 1958

L'Imitation de Notre-Dame la Lune, 1886
Crane, Hart, *Locutions des Pierrots I, II, III* in *The Double Dealer* (May 1922)
Dale, Peter, *Pierrots (One Has Principles)*, *Pierrots (Scene Short but Typical)*, *Asides of Pierrots* in *Agenda*, Ezra Pound special issue, 1980
Dale, Peter, *The Imitation of Our Lady the Moon According to Jules Laforgue* (complete) in *Poems of Jules Laforgue*, translated by Dale, 1986
Pound, Ezra, *Pierrots (scène courte mais typique)* in *Little Review*, 4 (May 1917)
Smith, William Jay, *Litanies of the First Quarter of the Moon*, *Clair de Lune*, *The Clowns*, *Asides from the Clowns*, *Litanies of the Last Quarter of the Moon* in *Selected Writings of Jules Laforgue*, translated by Smith, 1956
Staniforth, Paul, *Pierrots, I* in "Three Versions of Jules Laforgue's *Pierrots, I*" by Martin Sorrell, *Journal of European Studies*, 24 (1994)
Staniforth, Paul, *Pierrots(I–V)*, *The Pierrots' Kind of Talk (I, II, III, IX, XIII, XV)* in *Modern Poetry in Translation*, 9 (1996)
Terry, Patricia, *Litanies for the First Quarters of the Moon*, *Pierrots (I–IV)*, *Pierrots (A Short but Typical Scene)*, *Pierrot Phrases (I, IX, X, XVI)*, *Dialogue before Moonrise*, *Litanies for the Last Quarters of the Moon* in *Poems of Jules Laforgue*, translated by Terry, 1958

Le Concile féerique, 1886
Smith, William Jay, *Gentleman*, *Lady* in *Selected Writings of Jules Laforgue*, translated by Smith, 1956
Terry, Patricia, *The Faerie Council* (complete) in *Poems of Jules Laforgue*, translated by Terry, 1958

Des Fleurs de Bonne Volonté, 1890
Dale, Peter, *Romance* in *Agenda*, Ezra Pound special issue, 1980
Dale, Peter, *Flowers of Good Will* (complete) in *Poems of Jules Laforgue*, translated by Dale, 1986
Smith, William Jay, *Foreword*, *Unparalleled Severity*, *Five-minute Water Color*, *Romance*, *Sunday Piece*, *The Flying Dutchman* in *Selected Writings of Jules Laforgue*, translated by Smith, 1956
Staniforth, Paul, *Pierrot's Melancholia* in *Modern Poetry in Translation*, 9 (1996)
Terry, Patricia, *Rigors Like None Other*, *Next-to-the-last Word*, *Sundays (The Sky ...)*, *Sundays (They Decided ...)* in *Poems of Jules Laforgue*, translated by Terry, 1958

Derniers Vers, 1890
Bell, Martin, *Winter Coming On* in his *Collected Poems, 1937–1966*, London: Macmillan, and New York: St Martin's Press, 1967
Betts, Madeleine, *The Last Poems of Jules Laforgue* (complete), Ilfracombe, Devon: Arthur H. Stockwell, 1973
Dale, Peter, *Solo of the Moon* in *Agenda*, Ezra Pound special issue, 1980
Dale, Peter, *The Complaints* (complete) in *Poems of Jules Laforgue*, translated by Dale, 1986
Smith, William Jay, *The Coming of Winter*, *The Mystery of the Three Horns*, *Moon Solo* in *Selected Writings of Jules Laforgue*, translated by Smith, 1956
Sorrell, Martin, *Approaching Winter* in *South West Review*, 15 (1982)
Terry, Patricia, *The Coming Winter*, *The Mystery of the Three Horns*, *Sundays (To give myself ...)*, *Sundays (It's autumn ...)*, *Simple Agony*, *Solo by Moonlight*, *Oh! If One of Them ...*, *About a Defunct Lady*, *Black Wind* in *Poems of Jules Laforgue*, translated by Terry, 1958

Le Sanglot de la Terre, 1901
Smith, William Jay, *Apotheosis*, *Another for the Sun*, *Funeral March for the Death of the Earth*, *Little Chapel*, *The Impossible*, *The First Night*, *The Cigarette* in *Selected Writings of Jules Laforgue*, translated by Smith, 1956
Terry, Patricia, *Funeral March for the Death of the Earth* in *Poems of Jules Laforgue*, translated by Terry, 1958

Poèmes posthumes divers, 1970
Dale, Peter, *Ballade of Returning* in *Agenda*, Ezra Pound special issue, 1980
Dale, Peter, *Ballad of Returning* in his *Narrow Straits: Poems from the French*, Sutton, Surrey: Hippopotamus Press, 1984

Poèmes inédits, 1970
Dale, Peter, *Don't Stand before This Verse of Mine* ... in *Agenda*, Ezra Pound special issue, 1980
Dale, Peter, *Don't Bend before This Verse of Mine* ... in his *Narrow Straits: Poems from the French*, Sutton, Surrey: Hippopotamus Press, 1984

Stories
Moralités légendaires, 1887
Newman, Frances, *Six Moral Tales from Jules Laforgue*, New York: Liveright, 1928
Smith, William Jay, *Hamlet*, *The Miracle of the Roses* in *Selected Writings of Jules Laforgue*, translated by Smith, 1956

Arguably the inventor of the *vers libre*, and the major exponent of an early Modernist ironic and self-deprecating mode, Laforgue has been a constant target for translators. Laforgue's most illustrious translators have been Hart Crane and Ezra Pound, and, while not strictly his translator, T.S. Eliot openly acknowledged a debt to Laforgue, especially in poems such as *Prufrock*. In more recent years, Laforgue's work has continued to fascinate translators. To date, by far the most complete translation is Peter Dale's (Anvil Press, 1986), although that does not contain Laforgue's first work, *Le Sanglot de la Terre*, or *Le Concile féerique*, or the posthumous and uncollected pieces.

The appeal of Jules Laforgue's poetry to translators probably has much to do with its fusion of apparent naivety and fundamental difficulty (David Cooke). No other French poet, perhaps, has combined so indissolubly a "high art" content with a "low art" form. The problems caused for the translator are correspondingly great, especially as so often the philosophically-minded content finds expression in reworked popular ballads, skipping along to mock-simple rhythms, the whole sprinkled with extraordinary neologisms.

The Pierrot poems as well as *The Complaints* have particularly attracted translators. This may well be because here is found the most systematic fusion of all those elements that may be summed up as Laforgue's irony.

The problems facing the translator of Laforgue are the predictable ones, but on a very demanding scale. Given the crucial significance of the forms and techniques chosen – rhyme, stanzaic shaping, metre – is the translator entitled to recast any of them in the interests of more natural-sounding English? For example, if it seems imperative to keep Laforgue's rhyme patterns, then the risk is that the English will be tortured and distorted. Conversely, if the translator opts for harmonious English at any cost, then what happens to Laforgue's formal singularities, such important vehicles of meaning?

T.S. Eliot is notable for the way in which he absorbed and then reformulated the Laforguian idiom. The results do not have to be judged as translations; they are really poems "after" Laforgue. These are discussed by Ramsey (*Jules Laforgue and the Ironic Inheritance*), as are the Hart CRANE (1922) translations of three *Locutions des Pierrots*. Crane has opted for a somewhat free approach, believing that literal translation would be meaningless.

Ezra POUND (1917) famously admired what he termed Laforgue's "logopoeia", the dance of words among the intellect. His lively version of *Pierrots (scène courte mais typique)* reminds us that he is more great poet than disciplined translator. Pound's version is free, inventive, though he does choose an emphatic rhyme scheme. However, some of his lines, perhaps as a result, read ponderously, notably the closing tercet.

William Jay SMITH (1956) settles for a kind of half-way house, in that he uses rhyme considerably, but not as rigorously as Laforgue. He thus reads fairly "naturally", although his rhythms on occasions are long-winded, and Laforgue's sharp notes of irony are not properly heard. For example, *Complaint of the Moon in the Provinces* does not get the tightly rhymed, deliberately rhythmic couplets of the French original, whose deliberate forms surely are crucial. (Smith's selection includes translations of two satirical stories from the 1887 *Moralités légendaires*)

Rather more incisive are the translations of Patricia TERRY (1958). Her approach is to get Laforgue's rhythms and rhyme wherever it is possible to do so without becoming stilted or unintentionally comic. This means that overall she keeps a respectable percentage of Laforgue's rhymes. Furthermore, she makes numerous lexical choices of great felicity. A good demonstration of her qualities is the cleverly and tightly constructed *Litanies for the First Quarters of the Moon*.

The account by Madeleine BETTS (1973) of the *Derniers Vers* seems always unadventurous, at times quaintly archaic. With her frequent use of explanatory footnotes (her *The Coming of Winter* has no fewer than 31), Bett's little volume perhaps is useful as an uncontroversial introduction for the English-speaker who knows nothing of Laforgue's work.

By far the most ambitious translator to date of Laforgue is Peter DALE. Not only has he taken on by far the major part of Laforgue's poetic output, some poems attempted more than once, but he has rendered it according to the French rhyme schemes and, largely, the rhythmic patterns. Dale has thus imposed on himself the greatest difficulties. It is a matter for debate whether the goal of total fidelity is an appropriate one. Dale's book (1986), taken as a whole, is a monumental achievement. Where individual translations do not work too well, it is because the demands of rhyme have over-controlled the choice of vocabulary, syntactical shapes and metre. But then Dale has not allowed himself the luxury of translating only "easy" poems only in an "easy" way, and he very often expertly captures Laforgue's unique mix of poignant subject-matter, complex vocabulary and nursery rhyme – see, for example, *Complaint of the King of Thule*, a poem that depends on lexical eccentricities, mock-clumsy rhythms, over-emphatic rhyme. All of these are adroitly caught by Dale.

The two published translations by Martin SORRELL seek to capture Laforgue's spirit without being either slavish or free. Where appropriate, his points of reference are contemporary and British – for example, the British Medical Association finds its way into *Approaching Winter* (1982).

Paul STANIFORTH (1994, 1996) died tragically young, before he could see into print any of the 25 versions he did of Laforgue, mainly of Pierrot-inspired poems. Staniforth's translations are characterized by an astonishing inventiveness, a playfulness, a taste for neologism to match Laforgue's own. Sorrell (article in *Journal of European Studies*) gives in full Staniforth's version of *Pierrots, I*, which must stand as one of the most dazzling translations of Laforgue ever.

Graham Dunstan MARTIN (1998) gives plain prose translations at the foot of each page in his substantial selection for Penguin Classics. These are clear, accurate and most helpful, especially when read in conjunction with more ambitious, poetic translations. To get plain prose translations of Laforgue is often far from simple, as Martin points out in his very readable introduction.

MARTIN SORRELL

Further Reading

Arkell, David, *Looking for Laforgue: An Informal Biography*, Manchester: Carcanet, 1979

Collie, Michael, *Laforgue*, Edinburgh: Oliver and Boyd, 1963

Cook, David, "The Fascination of What is Difficult: Peter Dale's Translations of Villon and Laforgue", *Agenda*, 26/2 (1988)

Pound, Ezra, "Irony, Laforgue and Some Satire", *Poetry*, 11/2 (1917); reprinted in *Literary Essays of Ezra Pound*, London: Faber, and Norfolk, Connecticut: Laughlin, 1954

Pound, Ezra, "A Study of French Poets", reprinted in his *Make It New*, London: Faber, 1934; New Haven, Connecticut: Yale University Press, 1935

Ramsey, Warren, *Laforgue and the Ironic Inheritance*, New York: Oxford University Press, 1953

Ramsey, Warren (editor), *Jules Laforgue: Essays on a Poet's Life and Works*, Carbondale: Southern Illinois University Press, 1969

Sorrell, Martin, "Three English Versions of Jules Laforgue's *Pierrots, I*", *Journal of European Studies*, 24 (1994)

See also the translators' remarks in Dale, Martin, and Smith; and the foreword in Betts

Selma Lagerlöf 1858–1940

Swedish novelist and short-story writer

Biography

She was born on 20 November 1858 on the small family estate at Mårbacka, and educated at home. She retained a slight limp after an illness in early childhood. When the family lost their money she trained as a schoolteacher (1882–85) and taught at Landskrona until 1895, when she obtained a travelling fellowship and was able to devote herself to writing. She had become famous with the publication in 1891 of her novel *Gösta Berlings saga*, and went on to write further novels as well as short stories, tales for children and autobiographical works. In 1909 she became the first woman to be awarded the Nobel Prize for Literature. During this period she bought back the family home. Member of the Swedish Academy, 1914. Died at Mårbacka, 16 March 1940.

Translations

Novels

Gösta Berlings saga, 1891

Flach, P.B., *The Story of Gosta Berling*, Boston: Little Brown, and London: Gay and Bird, 1898

En herrgårdssägen, 1899

Bröchner, Jessie, *From a Swedish Homestead*, London: Heinemann, and New York: McClure Phillips, 1901

Jerusalem, 2 vols, 1901–02

Bröchner, Jessie, *Jerusalem*, London: Heinemann, 1903; Garden City, New York: Doubleday Page, 1915; as *The Holy City*, Garden City, New York: Doubleday Page, 1918

Herr Arnes penningar, 1904

Chater, Arthur G., *Herr Arne's Hoard*, London: Gyldendal, 1923; as *The Treasure*, Garden City, New York: Doubleday Page, 1925

Kristuslegender, 1904

Howard, Velma Swanston, *Christ Legends*, New York: Holt, 1908; London: Mathews and Marrot, 1930

Nils Holgerssons underbara resa, 2 vols, 1906–07

Howard, Velma Swanston, *The Wonderful Adventures of Nils*, New York: Harper, 1907; London: Bird, 1908

Howard, Velma Swanston, *The Further Adventures of Nils*, Garden City, New York: Doubleday Page, and London: Hodder and Stoughton, 1911

Löwensköldska ringen, 1925

Schenck, Linda, *The Löwensköld Ring*, Norwich: Norvik, 1991

Selma Lagerlöf was Sweden's leading prose writer of the neo-romantic decade of the 1890s and is the only prose writer of that generation still held in both critical and popular regard. Her debut novel, *The Story of Gösta Berling* (1891, translated 1898), brought immediate fame: set a century earlier in her native province of Värmland (as were many of her stories) and partly based on oral traditions, it is the passionate story of a defrocked parson and the "hellfire club", with which he surrounds himself. Together with the children's book *The Wonderful Adventures of Nils* (1906, translated 1907) and with her public biography, it fixed her reputation as an imaginative but ultimately limited "fairy-tale telling aunt". Less recognized were the range of her work, her moral seriousness, her psychological subtlety and narrative ingenuity, especially when dealing with the supernatural – aspects that have been stressed in the critical re-evaluation of her work, particularly by feminist critics, in recent decades.

After August Strindberg, who stands out as a case alone, Lagerlöf is by far the most translated of Swedish authors for English-language readers. A crude entry count of the bibliographies of translations of their works into English between 1900 and the present day gives Strindberg in the region of 140 compared to Lagerlöf's 40 – which still puts her well ahead of her nearest rival, Pär Lagerkvist, with some 30. There is, of course, a major difference in that the Strindberg industry rolls relentlessly on whereas new translations of Lagerlöf are now rarities.

On the whole, translations of the works of Lagerlöf made their appearance in the English-speaking world not long after the source texts first appeared in Swedish: the great period is between 1910 and 1930 and many of them were published simultaneously or nearly so in the United Kingdom and the United States. A number of these translations went through a variety of editions, moving from publisher to publisher over many years. Thus Velma Swanston HOWARD's *The Wonderful Adventures of Nils* and the same translator's *The Further Adventures of Nils* were first published respectively in 1907 and 1911 – the latest editions of the same translations came as recently as 1984; Howard's *Christ Legends* from 1908 re-appeared for the sixth time in 1993. Further evidence of the popularity of Lagerlöf in translation in the first decades of the 20th century is to be seen in the publication of two overlapping uniform editions: the Mårbacka edition in four volumes (1898–1917) and the Northland edition (1916–17) in nine volumes.

The critical reception of Lagerlöf's works in the English-speaking world was, perhaps unsurprisingly, an exaggerated reflection of that accorded her in Sweden. In spite of the quite representative sample of the range of her writing that became available in English in a short time, *The Story of Gösta Berling* remained the measure against which all else was set. Review after review stressed the romantic intuitive storyteller ("she is a novelist only if novel means any work of fiction ... the spirit of the lyric and heroic ballad is the breath of her work"). It is clear that Lagerlöf was perceived as an exotic and that her country was seen in the same light: one reviewer warns of the "hysteria that occasionally makes its appearance in the solitudes of the Swedish woodland". Overall there was a tendency to conflate the whole of Scandinavia and its history and literature and treat them as exemplifying latter-day emanations of the Viking age.

It cannot be said that Lagerlöf presents the translator with any formidable problems. For literary Swedish of her period her lexis is normal, her syntax uncomplicated, her range of registers not wide. Nor are the historical, geographical and cultural contexts in her created world particularly alien – no more so than, say, the fictive Scottish Highlands in Scott or Stevenson. There is thus some archaism, some dialect. The problems of Lagerlöf lie in the area of tone. Her narrative discourse is markedly oral, but it is not a folksy orality – it is well to remember that she was both a member of the gentry and a schoolteacher. And allied to that there is what has been called "a crucial multivocality, a refusal to settle for unambiguous meanings", which subverts the surface certainty of her texts: this shows itself, for instance, in the frequency of negative constructions and in her predilection for those very Swedish modal adverbs (*ju*, *väl*, *nog*) that imply subtle changes in the attitude of the text.

Lagerlöf was not well-served by her most regular early translator, Velma Swanston HOWARD, who produced versions of some 13 works, some of which went through many editions. Her translations are marred by straightforward mistranslations, stilted English, an inappropriate folksiness, and no recognition of ambiguity. A number of early translators were much more competent, and one wishes that they had done more than the occasional volume. P.B. FLACH's *The Story of Gösta Berling* (1898) both introduced Lagerlöf to the English-speaking world and captured the spirit of the original. Jessie BRÖCHNER's *Jerusalem* (1903), whose original is a massive and difficult novel, is excellent, as is her earlier *From a Swedish Homestead* (1901). From the middle period, there is CHATER's *Herr Arne's Hoard* (1925). Of the few recent translations Linda SCHENCK's *The Löwensköld Ring* (1991) brings to this short novel an understanding of the implications for translation of recent academic work on Lagerlöf's oeuvre: Schenck's version is beautifully done, being true to both the detail and the voice of the original.

PETER GRAVES

Further Reading

Edström, Vivi, *Selma Lagerlöf*, translated by Barbara Lido, Boston: Twayne, 1984

Gustafson, Alrik, *Six Scandinavian Novelists: Lie, Jacobsen, Heidenstam, Selma Lagerlöf, Hamsun, Sigrid Undset*, Princeton, New Jersey: Princeton University Press, 1940

St Andrews, Bonnie, *Forbidden Fruit: On the Relationship between Women and Knowledge in Doris Lessing, Selma Lagerlöf, Kate Chopin, Margaret Atwood*, Troy, New York: Whitston, 1986

Wivel, Henrik, *Selma Lagerlöf: Her Life of Works*, Minneapolis: University of Minnesota Press, 1991

Giuseppe Tomasi di Lampedusa 1896–1957

Italian novelist

Biography

Born in Palermo, Sicily, 23 December 1896, into an ancient, noble and once wealthy family. His father was the duke of Parma, his grandfather the prince of Lampedusa (an island in the Mediterranean), and he duly inherited these titles. He served as a lance-corporal in the Italian army in World War I. He married in 1932. After the coming of Fascism he lived as a scholar out of the public eye. Apart from a few articles, he published nothing in his lifetime. The posthumously published novel for which he is known, *Il gattopardo* (1958); translated as *The Leopard* (1960) by Archibald Colquhoun, was written in the two years preceding his death, which took place in Rome on 23 July 1957. There are also two short stories and a memoir of his childhood, published in 1961 (*Racconti*), that have been put into English by the same translator (1962).

The Leopard

Il gattopardo, 1958

Translation

Colquhoun, Archibald, *The Leopard*, London: Collins and Harvill, and New York: Pantheon, 1960, revised 1961; New York: Knopf, 1991; with *A Memory and Two Stories*, by Lampedusa, translated by Colquhoun, London: Collins and Harvill, 1986 (originally published as *Two Stories and a Memory*, Collins and Harvill, 1962)

Il gattopardo (*The Leopard*) was published posthumously in 1958, after having been rejected by two major Italian publishers, and it immediately became a *cause célèbre*. It enjoyed an enormous success with the Italian public and it has been called the first Italian bestseller; its popularity has continued over the years, and in 1985 it was voted the "most loved" novel by Italian readers in a survey by the literary magazine *Tuttolibri*. It is the only novel written by Giuseppe Tomasi, prince of Lampedusa (often referred to simply as "Lampedusa"), whose name remained obscure during his lifetime. fierce critical controversies greeted the popular success of the book during the 1960s: in hundreds of articles in newspapers and periodicals the author was criticized by the Italian radical *intellighenzia* for supposedly conservative or even reactionary views; on the other hand, the novel was praised by French Marxist writer Louis Aragon.

Set in Sicily in the 1860s, the time of Italian national unification, *The Leopard* is generally classified as a historical novel, and the lavish film version made in 1963 by Italian director Luchino Visconti (starring Burt Lancaster and Alain Delon) reinforced such a reading. However, many critics have pointed out that *The Leopard*, with its constant reflections on the themes of death, time, desire, and the transitoriness of human life, lends itself to multiple readings, and the literary influence of Lampedusa's favourite writers, such as Joyce, Woolf, Proust, as well as Stendhal, Dostoevskii, Shakespeare and many others, has often been noted by critics. E.M. Forster, who was very fond of Lampedusa's writing, argued that it is "not a historical novel" but "a novel which happens to take place in history" (Forster, 1960).

The Leopard has gone through more than 100 editions, and has been translated into 23 languages. Today the ideological debate has quieted down, and Lampedusa has joined the canon of Italian "classic" writers. His complete works, including some unpublished material, were recently published in a prestigious hardback edition (*Opere*, edited by G. Lanza Tomasi, Milan: Mondadori, 1995). This comprehensive edition of nearly 2000 pages should also settle the question of the merits of the different versions of the original text. Lampedusa died before seeing his novel published, and no definitive final version was approved by the author; it was the writer Giorgio Bassani who revised the typescript for publication. In 1968, 10 years after the publication of the book, a controversy arose when a Sicilian university professor (Muscetta, 1968) discovered a different version of the text, a manuscript dated 1957. This version was published in 1969 (Milan: Feltrinelli), with Muscetta claiming it as the "real" version and calling for all translations to be done anew. However, the differences between the two texts turned out in fact to be minor, and critics agreed that they are irrelevant to the general effect of the novel.

The translation by COLQUHOUN (1960; revised 1961), the only one available in English, is based on the first Italian edition of 1958, though the translator claims also to have had access to a manuscript version. *The Leopard* was an immediate success in England and was received with nearly unanimous praise by critics. Colquhoun's translation was generally judged satisfactory, indeed more than one English critic judged it "excellent". However, an American reviewer noted that, though on the whole satisfactory, "it does not always render the brilliance and sophistication of the author's style" (Slonim, 1960), and E.M. Forster considered the translation a "good English dress", which, however, "does not flow and glow like the original ... but it is sensitive and scholarly" (Forster, 1960).

A textual analysis of Colquhoun's *The Leopard* carried out by T. Marangoni (1976) shows that the main problems the translator faced were those of lexicon. Sicilian and southern Italian dialect words are numerous in the Italian text, but are mostly isolated terms rather than entire sentences (only in one passage does the Bourbon king speak Neapolitan dialect). The translator, who was helped by Lampedusa's wife and friends, clearly understood the meaning of the Sicilian terms. For the most part, he adopted the strategy of translating them into Standard English, sacrificing certain touches of irony, and in particular the manifestation of local colour and social class differences in linguistic usage, but on the other hand avoiding footnotes and explanations which would have interrupted the necessary fluidity of the translation. There are a number of French words in the Italian text, usually terms concerning cooking, fashion or furnishings, whose foreignness serves to reinforce the refined atmosphere of luxury and decadence. For reasons that remain unclear, a number of these French terms were translated into English by Colquhoun even though they were also currently used in English. At the same time there are a number of English words in the Italian text that show Lampedusa's excellent knowledge of English culture and whose presence has sometimes not been signalled in the translation; such omissions also simplify the resonance of the original text.

STEFANIA ARCARA

Further Reading

Bassani, Giorgio, "Prefazione" in *Il Gattopardo*, Milan: Feltrinelli, 1958

Colquhoun, Archibald, "Lampedusa in Sicily", *London Magazine* (November 1960)

Colquhoun, Archibald, "The Lair of the Leopard", *Atlantic Monthly* (February 1963)

Forster, E.M., "The Prince's Tale", *The Spectator* (13 May 1960)

Forster. E.M., "Introduction", *Two Stories and a Memory* by Lampedusa, translated by Archibald Colquhoun, London: Collins and Harvill, 1962

Gilbert, J., "The Metamorphosis of the Gods in *Il gattopardo*", *Modern Language Notes*, 81 (1967)

Gilmour, David, *The Last Leopard: A Life of Giuseppe di Lampedusa*, London: Quartet, 1988; New York: Pantheon, 1991

Marangoni, T., "*Il gattopardo* e la sua traduzione inglese", *Filologia Moderna*, 1 (1976)

Muscetta, C., "Saggio di correzioni del 'Gattopardo' completo", *Mimesis*, 1 (1968)

Slonim, M., "As New Winds Swept an Old Island", *New York Times Book Review* (1 May 1960)

Trevelyan, Raleigh, *Princes under the Volcano*, London: Macmillan, 1972; New York: Morrow, 1973

Vitello, Andrea, *Giuseppe Tomasi di Lampedusa*, Palermo, Sicily: Sellerio, 1987

Laozi (Lao Tzu) 6th? century BC

Chinese philosopher

Biography

The name Laozi is given to the supposed author of the *Tao Te Ching* (*Daodejing*), one of the Taoist classics. Tradition situates his birth in the state of Ch'u in the 6th century BC, and gives him the family name Li and the personal name Tan. Legend makes Laozi, the "Old Sage", keeper of the archives of the imperial court. It has him, as an old man, about to leave China for Tibet, writing down at the request of a border guard his teachings about the Way, through contemplation of nature, to Virtue, and to tranquillity and peace. The *Tao Te Ching* may in fact date from long after Laozi's supposed lifetime, and may also be a compilation of poems by several Taoists.

Tao Te Ching (Daodejing)

Translations

Over the past centuries, there have appeared more than 100 English translations of *Tao Te Ching*, a fact that compels each new translator to explain why a new translation is needed. The original Chinese text used by most translators is the *Tao Te Ching* first commented on by Wang Pi (AD 226–49), earlier known as the oldest extant. Since the 1973 archaeological discovery of two older texts made at Ma-wang-tui near Changsha, Hunan Province, some translators based their translations upon these silk manuscripts, believed to be half a millennium older than commonly translated versions. Another edition occasionally translated is one with Ho-shang Kung's commentary (often dated to the reign of Emperor Wen of the Han, 179–57 BC but also dated by some to the 3rd or 4th century AD).

Addiss, Stephen and Stanley Lombardo, *Tao Te Ching*, Indianapolis: Hackett, 1993

Bahm, Archie J., *Tao Teh King Interpreted as Nature and Intelligence*, New York: Ungar, 1958

Bynner, Witter, *The Way of Life According to Lao Tzu*, New York: John Day, 1944; London: Editions Poetry, 1946

Carus, Paul, *The Canon of Reason and Virtue*, La Salle, Illinois: Open Court, 1903; 2nd edition, 1909; bilingual edition, revised, with an introduction, 1964

Henricks, Robert G., *Lao-Tzu Te-Tao Ching: A New Translation Based on the Recently Discovered Ma-Wang-Tui Texts*, New York: Ballantine, 1989

Lau, D.C., *Tao Te Ching*, with an introduction, London and Baltimore: Penguin, 1963; revised edition, Hong Kong: Chinese University Press, 1989

Legge, James, *The Tao Te Ching* in his *The Texts of Taoism*, New York: Julian Press, 1959 (first published in *Sacred Books of the East*, edited by Max Müller, London: Oxford University Press, 1891)

Lin Yutang, *The Wisdom of Laotse*, New York: Modern Library, 1948

Mair, Victor H., *Tao Te Ching: The Classic Book of Integrity and the Way*, New York: Bantam, 1990

Waley, Arthur, *The Way and Its Power: A Study of Tao Te Ching and Its Place in Chinese Thought*, London: Allen and Unwin, 1934; Boston: Houghton Mifflin, 1935; New York: Grove Press, 1958

LEGGE is a 19th-century translator, author of numerous influential works and translations. He translated several essential Taoist works, including *Tao Te Ching* (1891), *The Writings of Chuang-Tzu*, and *The Thai-Shang*, collectively published as *The Texts of Taoism*. Without much to rely on except Chinese dictionaries and commentators of reputation, Legge managed to offer a decent translation of *Tao Te Ching*. His translation displays solid learning in the Chinese language and culture, though it also unavoidably incorporates misunderstanding or inaccurate representation of the original's ideas. An example of this is his rendering of the opening line: "The Tao that can be trodden is not the enduring and unchanging Tao." The original term "ke dao", meaning "can be spoken of" or "told of", is twisted to mean "can be trodden". At the end of each chapter, Legge provides erudite notes and explanations that clarify many concepts, ideas, and terms. In preparing his translation Legge consulted six important sources, including "The Complete Works of the Ten Philosophers" and the Text and Commentary of Wang Pi, which all helped him produce a largely reliable translation.

CARUS published two editions of *The Canon of Reason and Virtue*. The 1964 edition is a combination of the larger and the smaller editions; it contains a comprehensive introduction and incorporates the results of his latest labors in revising and reconsidering the many difficult passages of the Chinese text. This translation, accompanied by the original Chinese text printed in the earlier half of the book, appears faithful to the original's ideas. Each chapter is given a heading to reflect its essence. While most translators do not translate the pivotal term "Tao", Carus renders it "Reason". He also provides a useful "Comments and Alternative Reading", where each chapter is given a careful explanation and some analysis to aid the reader's understanding.

WALEY was an influential sinologue and translator whose translation of *Tao Te Ching* (1958) is among the best known. Differentiating between "historical" and "scriptural" translations, Waley praises Richard Wilhelm's effort (See Further Reading) as the best scriptural translation, and next to it, Paul Carus's. In regard to his own version he distinguishes between "literary" and "philosophical" translations: literary translations attach importance to the beauty of a work, so detailed accuracy has to be sacrificed. He calls his own translation "philosophical" as opposed to "literary", for he believes that "the importance of the original lies not in its literary quality but in the things it says".

There are places in Waley's translation where he is very literal. For example, his rendition of the last two lines of chapter 49 reads, "The Hundred Families all the time strain their eyes and ears, / The sage all the time sees and hears no more than an infant sees and hears." "Baixing" (literally "one hundred names") in the original simply refers to the entire population of a country, but Waley handles it in such a way as to suggest, especially with capital "H" and "F", that "Hundred Families", seen as a proper noun here, represents a special group; and the last line, most would agree, may be a misinterpretation of the original text. In other places Waley can be freely creative. For instance, for the highly ambiguous and debatable second sentence of chapter 80, Waley not only offers a creative reading but adds elements: "He could bring it about that the people would be ready to lay down their lives and lay down them again in defence of their homes, rather than emigrate." Whether the original intends "die twice" or "take death gravely" is still a moot point, but no one has even suggested that death is died in defence of their homes as Waley did, because the idea of defence cannot be found in any edition of *Tao Te Ching*. However, generally considered a "brilliant and definitive" translation, Waley's book has been accepted in the Chinese Translations Series of Unesco.

BYNNER (1944) read no Chinese but did many "translations". In making them he relied entirely upon the assistance of a prominent Chinese scholar, Kiang Kang-hu, who provided him with literal versions of Chinese texts. Faced with the most translated Chinese work, Bynner seemed undeterred by his total lack of Chinese knowledge. His translation reads more like an original text because he is not constrained by the original's strengths or limitations. David Lattimore, having considered translations by Arthur Waley and Lin Yutang, observes, "Bynner's alone is the creation of a distinguished original poet in English." The result of Bynner's effort, explains Lattimore, "if it does not always read like Laotzu, also does not read like a translation"; and, because of the creativity Bynner demonstrated, Lattimore asserts that Bynner's is "the most accessible *Laotzu*, if not the one in which Laotzu himself is accessible".

Bynner stands as an interesting translator not only because he is creative, but also because he benefits greatly from his Chinese collaborator. His work truly is a combined effort of two scholars rather than one. However, his handling of the Taoist text is not altogether above criticism. He sometimes renders "Tao" as "existence", other times as the "way". Another key term, "ming" (traditionally translated as "name"), he renders "terms". "Tao" originally appears twice in chapter 40, but his translation, "Life on its way returns into a mist, / Its quickness is its quietness again: / Existence of this world of things and men / Renews their never needing to exist", inconsistently uses both "way" and "existence" for Tao, thereby causing some confusion, and this is not the only instance.

LIN YUTANG's translations of *Tao Te Ching* and Confucius's *The Analects* exerted a considerable influence on English and American scholars of Taoism and Confucianism. His *The Wisdom of Laotse* (1948) includes a comprehensive, useful study of Taoism as well as a praiseworthy translation of *Tao Te Ching*. He divides *Tao Te Ching* into seven books, each with a subtitle and each being followed by annotations and elaborations. What distinguishes Lin from other translators is his original approach to the work. He points out that the correct approach would be to read Taoist works along with interpretations by ancient Chinese Taoist scholars like Han Fei and Huainantse, but that the best approach would be to read Laozi with Chuang Tzu, the other major Taoist thinker and author of *Chuang Tzu*. Therefore after each chapter Lin supplies well-researched annotations, followed by a Taoist parable, authored by himself, which is often entertaining and humorous. Lin is accurate and faithful in grasping and representing the original text. To illustrate, the second sentence of chapter 80, where Laozi projects his utopian state, has cornered many translators: the problem lies with the Chinese word "zhong" or "chong", pronounced differently depending on whether it is a verb or an adjective. While almost all translators render it "Let the people weigh death heavily and have no desire to migrate far", Lin moves away from the idea of death and emphasizes the concept of life, thus producing a more readable and sensible translation: "Let the people value their lives and not migrate far", which shows true creativity and flexibility in dealing with a thorny issue.

BAHM (1958) is more interested in the philosophical ideas than in stylistic and poetic matters. He calls himself an interpreter, and his *Tao Te Ching* is indeed interpreted as "Nature and Intelligence". Bahm finds that no English word can deliver the key term Tao as adequately as "Nature" with a capital "N", with "Existence" as an alternative. Because it is an interpretation rather than a strict translation, he basically ignores the original syntax and structure and creates his own. In places his interpretation reads like poetry, and in other places, like prose. The earlier chapters seem to be wordy: where most translators use a few words or a clause, he has two or more clauses. The opening sentence illustrates this well: "Nature can never be completely described, for such a description would have to duplicate Nature." This interpretation deviates from the original in both meaning and structure. Later chapters, however, seem to be more economically handled and flow more smoothly. Bahm aims to render the spirit rather than the letter, and, perhaps accepting Walter Gorn Old's statement that "it is safe to say that the more literal the translation may be the more obscure its meaning", he makes his translation as non-literal as possible; the result is a blending of prose and poetry that causes the translation to wobble in places.

LAU's translation (1963) is influential. It has often been consulted by other translators and has been anthologized in world literature textbooks in the United States. His neat work starts with a long but none the less valuable introduction treating the scope of Laozi's influence on Chinese thought and life, followed by a thorough analysis of important passages of the *Tao Te Ching*. The translation divides into two books, following the traditional way of arranging the 81 chapters: chapters 1–37 for Book One, and 38–81 for Book Two. Lau's free verse flows smoothly; his choice of words is careful and effective. Ambiguous lines or difficult ideas are often accompanied by well thought out notes in succinct language. Controversial sentences are also handled in a skillful way. For example, the problematic last two lines of chapter 49, widely regarded as ambiguous and hard to translate, Lau renders "The people all have something to occupy their eyes and ears, and the sage treats them all like children." Though the interpretation of the first coordinate sentence seems questionable, the second certainly catches the spirit of the original. The translation is supplemented by two appendices: "The Problem of Authorship" and "The Nature of the Work", both of which provide further assistance to the specialist and the general reader. The glossary he provides is also a valuable reference that introduces a considerable number of texts and authors relevant to *Tao Te Ching*.

HENRICKS's (1989) solid translation was completed after 10

years' study of the Ma-wang-tui texts. Because all other translations of *Tao Te Ching* were based upon what Henricks calls "received" texts, his copies of the earlier texts do not represent the text as it was seen by the commentators whose names they bear. The older texts Henricks used have many variants from "the received texts and make better sense to him. One typical example is the last line of chapter 33, where the traditional text has the word "perish" while the Ma-wang-tui texts use "forget", though the two words are close homophones in Chinese. To Henricks, the Ma-wang-tui texts make clearer sense in saying "To die but not be forgotten – that's true long life", while the other versions – Paul Carus's "One who may die but will not perish, has life everlasting" for example – are hardly intelligible. Another noteworthy aspect of Henricks's work is its new arrangement of the two books: he followed the Ma-wang-tui texts, placing the Book of Te first and the Book of Tao second; i.e., his version begins with chapter 38, which is a discourse on Te, rather than with the conventional chapter 1 that treats Tao.

Part One of Henricks is "The Translation", a straightforward presentation of the entire text with no notes or comments, intended for the general reader. Part Two, "Text, Commentary, and Notes", repeats the translation but is accompanied by notes indicating the differences between Text A and Text B of the Ma-wang-tui manuscripts, and is meant for specialists who want to know more about the difference between the two texts and between them and the received texts.

MAIR's (1990) is another translation based on the recently discovered Ma-wang-tui manuscripts. Like Henricks, Mair was inspired by this important discovery and decided to do a new translation "far more accurate and reliable than any published previously". Most translators do not bother translating the second pivotal term, te, simply rendering it "virtue". Mair, however, spent two full months trying to locate a satisfactory term before finally deciding on "integrity". His aim in the translation is "to create an authentic English version of the *Tao Te Ching* that is both eminently readable and sinologically precise". To Mair the primary duty of a translator is to convey, as closely as possible, a semblance of the original text, including such matters as form, content, style, diction, and sound. In keeping with this spirit, he attempted to translate the various voices he found in the Chinese original: the Taoist mystic, the political strategist, the utopian architect, the anti-Confucian philosopher, the clairvoyant poet, and the meditative Yogin.

Because the Mair translation follows the text arrangement of the Ma-wang-tui manuscripts, the Book of Te, or Integrity as Mair calls it, comes before the Book of Tao. Since the Ma-wang-tui texts are in many places either corrupted or miscopied, some vocabulary appears unintelligible and produces mistranslation. One such case can be found in the last sentence of chapter 49 (chapter 12 in the Ma-wang-tui texts): where the received texts have "child", which is used as a verb in a context meaning "to regard as children", the recently discovered manuscripts have a homophone with a similar ideogram. Mair sticks to his texts and translates, "The common people all rivet their eyes and ears upon him, / And the sage makes them all chuckle like children." While there is nothing absolutely wrong with this rendition, it does not make good sense, either. The whole translation has strong points, however. Concise and clear, it displays poetic beauty while retaining the original's terseness. In almost every case the translator, true to his principles, works hard to represent the original in both style and content, making the reading enjoyable for the most part.

ADDISS & LOMBARDO's *Tao Te Ching* (1993) is a recent translation of the Wang Pi text. The translators offered four reasons to justify their undertaking: (1) they were aiming to translate, not explain, the text; (2) they found earlier translations generally verbose, so they tried to keep "the bare bones of the language" in order to preserve at least some flavor of the original text; (3) their translation is gender neutral because they believe that *Tao Te Ching* often praises the female spirit; and (4) they provide what they call an interactive element in translation: a transliteration of one line in each section, along with the original Chinese characters. In a large measure the translators accomplished their objectives.

The translation, however, in its effort to avoid explanation and to favor Anglo-Saxon monosyllables over Latinate polysyllables, contains sentences that show inaccuracy in understanding. For example, the famous opening sentence through their reworking becomes "Tao called Tao is not Tao." Not only is the original meaning of "ke dao" lost, but a highly meaningful modifier, "chang", is not translated; the meaning of this important line therefore appears distorted. On the other hand, much of the terseness of the original is preserved, and the translation is made to resemble the original's structure. Burton Watson writes of their effort, "It is this poetic force and beauty of the text that the translators ... have been most concerned to bring across in their translation. It seems to me they have succeeded brilliantly."

GUIYOU HUANG

Further Reading

Chen, Ellen M., *The Tao Te Ching: A New Translation with Commentary*, New York: Paragon House, 1989

Feng, Gia-fu and Jane English (translators), *Tao Te Ching*, New York: Vintage, 1972

Hughes, E.R., *Chinese Philosophy in Classical Times*, London: Dent, and New York: Dutton, 1942

Kaltenmark, Karl, *Lao Tzu and Taoism*, translated from the French by Roger Greaves, Stanford, California: Stanford University Press, 1969

LaFargue, Michael (translator), *The Tao of the Tao Te Ching: A Translation and Commentary*, Albany: State University of New York Press, 1992

Lin, Paul J., *A Translation of Lao Tzu's Tao Te Ching and Wang Pi's Commentary*, Ann Arbor: Center for Chinese Studies, the University of Michigan, 1977

McCarroll, Tolbert (translator), *The Tao: The Sacred Way*, New York: Crossroad, 1982

Mitchell, Stephen (translator), *Tao Te Ching: A New English Version*, New York: Harper and Row, 1991

Rump, Ariane with Wing-tsit Chan (translators), *Commentary on the Lao Tzu*, by Wang Pi, Honolulu: The University Press of Hawaii, 1979

Waley, Arthur (translator), *Three Ways of Thought in Ancient China*, London: Allen and Unwin, 1939; New York: Doubleday, 1956

Wilhelm, Richard (translator), *Tao Te Ching: The Book of Meaning and Life*, translated from the German (1911) into English by H.G. Ostwald, London and Boston: Arkana, 1985

Wu, John C.H., *Tao Teh Ching*, Boston: Shambhala, 1989

François, duc de La Rochefoucauld 1613–1680

French moralist and memorialist

Biography

Born in Paris, 15 September 1613; known by the title Prince de Marcillac until the death of his father in 1650, when he became the sixth François in the ancient line of dukes of La Rochefoucauld. He received an informal aristocratic education and already in 1628 was married to Andrée de Vivonne (died 1670), with whom he had eight children. In 1629 he entered military service. He campaigned with Louis XIII's army in Italy and later the Netherlands (1635–36). He was imprisoned by Richelieu for a week in 1637 for his part in the duchesse de Chevreuse's conspiracy against the court, then banished for two years to his château at Verteuil, north of Angoulême. Returning to soldiering, he fought at the battle of Rocroi (1643), the siege of Gravelines (1644) and the battle of Mardick (1646), where he was seriously wounded. He took an active part in the Fronde (1648–53), plotting with the duchesse de Longueville against Mazarin, and was wounded again during fighting in Paris, 1652, then fled to Luxembourg. He went back to Verteuil in 1653 and to Paris in 1656. He now frequented the salons and intellectual circles of the capital, notably those of Madame de Sablé and Madame de Sévigné and especially that of Madame de La Fayette, with whom his liaison lasted until he died. He saw one last spell of military service, in Louis XIV's Flanders campaign of 1667–68. He died in Paris, 17 March 1680.

La Rochefoucauld is famous as the author of the *Réflexions; ou, Sentences et maximes morales* (1665), usually known simply as the *Maximes* (*Maxims*), a collection of finely chiselled prose aphorisms, drily pessimistic in general tone, first published in a pirated edition in 1664. His other major collections of prose are the *Mémoires* [Memoirs] (1662) and the posthumous *Réflexions diverses* [Sundry Reflections].

Maxims

Réflexions; ou, Sentences et Maximes morales, 1665

There is no one single text of the *Maximes* used by translators. The best modern French edition is *Maximes*, edited by Jacques Truchet, Paris: Garnier, 1967.

Translations

Anonymous, *Moral Reflexions and Maxims ... Newly Made English*, London: printed by D. Leach for Andrew Bell, 1706

Anonymous, *Moral Maxims by the Duc de la Roche Foucault*, London: A. Millar, 1749

Anonymous ["N.M.P."], *Maxims and Moral Reflections by the Duc de la Rochefoucauld. A new translation*, London: Griffith and Farran, 1883

FitzGibbon, Constantine, *The Maxims of the Duc de la Rochefoucauld*, with an introduction, London: Allan Wingate, 1957

Kidwelly, J.D., *Epictetus Junior; or, Maxims of Modern Morality*, London: T. Bassett, 1670

Powell, George H., *The Moral Maxims and Reflections of the Duke de la Rochefoucauld*, 2nd edition, London: Methuen, 1912; New York: Frederick Stokes, n.d.

Pratt, Kenneth, *Maxims of La Rochefoucauld*, Halifax, Yorkshire: Haworth Press, 1933

Tancock, Leonard, *Maxims*, with an introduction, Harmondsworth: Penguin, 1959

The *Maxims* of François, duc de La Rochefoucauld, has always been popular with translators and one can see why. It is an attractive text from the point of view of both the subject matter and the manner of presentation. A series of aphorisms, some short, some not so short, beautifully conceived and executed, propound a cynical view of the selfish and corrupt nature of man that immediately strikes a responsive chord. While most readers agree with the accuracy of La Rochefoucauld's pessimistic analysis of human nature in the *Maxims*, they can in fact be read in different ways. One reads and despairs of oneself or one reads and despairs of others. Many translators who have tackled this text seem to fall into the second category and use it as a lesson in morality. The best translators present the text without trying to score moral points. There are six editions of the *Maxims* published in La Rochefoucauld's lifetime, if one counts the pirated edition published in The Hague in 1664 as the first. These differ quite markedly from each other, as La Rochefoucauld altered his text from edition to edition by adding new maxims, suppressing ones already there and altering the wording. Most translators have used the 1678 edition, the last to be published in La Rochefoucauld's lifetime, but this does not mean that the translations are consistent. There can be a wide variation in the order in which the maxims are arranged, depending on how the translator deals with new or suppressed maxims.

Translation started almost as soon as the work was published. The Dutch edition of 1665 was the text used by KIDWELLY, who published a translation in 1670 under the title of *Epictetus Junior: or, Maxims of Modern Morality*. There was no mention of La Rochefoucauld as the author. This is a picturesque version that translates more or less literally but with a turn of phrase that is often arresting. For instance, the following rendering of Maxim no. 12 (1678 edition): "Though a man be ever so industrious in the smothering of his passion under the veil of piety and honour, yet some claw thereof will still be visible". However, this translator is not aware of or does not worry about the problems posed by such words as *honnêteté*, *intérêt* and *honnête homme*, which appear relatively frequently. Here "honesty", "interest" and "honest man" are what is offered and these manifestly do not convey in English the complicated conceptions inherent in the corresponding French.

The 18th century saw at least 17 translations of the *Maxims*, starting in 1706 and finishing in 1799. Most of these content themselves with reproducing their predecessors more or less verbatim. The ANONYMOUS 1706 *Moral Reflections and Maxims* does not specify either the translator or the edition used but the edition is probably the 1678 one. The translator is intent on underlining the bleak picture of human nature painted in the text. The translation is competent, with many enjoyable turns of phrase and an awareness of some of the difficulties that need to be surmounted. For instance, *honnête homme* becomes "accomplished man", which is not a good translation but is better than "honest man". A translation published in 1749, again without mentioning the translator, introduces a new order into the way the maxims are arranged. They are placed under headings arranged in alphabetical order starting with "Ability" and ending with "Youth". This destroys the pattern of La Rochefoucauld's intentions and introduces a quite arbitrary set of judgements concerning the theme of any given maxim. One presumes the intention here (ANONYMOUS, 1749) was to provide a handy reference book for anyone looking for a pithy saying on a certain subject, but as a means of getting to know the thought of La Rochefoucauld it is not to be recommended. Unfortunately this arrangement persists in some translations right into the 20th century.

The 19th century was almost as prolific as the 18th in the production of translations of the *Maxims*. Many simply reproduce the texts of previous editions. In 1883 *Maxims and Moral Reflections* appeared with a Preface signed N.M.P. This is called a new translation and it has many virtues. It is based on the 1678 edition and presents the text in a straightforward way. The problems of translating certain words are clearly understood and an effort is made to come to terms with them. This is a good version for its date.

The *Maxims* remained popular with translators in the 20th century but the translations are of variable value. POWELL's 1912 translation is simply an edition of that of 1706. PRATT's 1933 version uses the "heading" arrangement and the maxims are not numbered. The translator claims that his translation is word for word but the result is often far from satisfactory. An attempt is made to cope with *honnête homme* by using different words to translate it in different contexts. There is much to be said for this as a way round the difficulty but it is open to question when different translations are used within one single maxim.

The 20th century did, however, produce two outstanding translations of this work. FITZGIBBON's 1957 version is intelligent and elegant. The difficulties the text presents have been coped with in a variety of ways. Unfettered by the dogma of word-for-word he has produced many felicitous renderings that give the meaning and at the same time the flavour of the original as, for instance, in "The world is full of pots calling kettles black" – a substitution of an English saying for an equivalent French one, but preserving exactly the tone and meaning of the original. This is something not many translators have achieved. There is an interesting Preface and a useful account of the 17th-century publishing history of the *Maxims*.

The other good 20th-century translation is that of TANCOCK (1959). He sees the sheer baldness of La Rochefoucauld's style as being the most daunting aspect of his language to render into English. A good version, he thinks, would require twice the number of words to give the full meaning. He acknowledges, though, that this would be paraphrasing and not translating, so he forces himself to be concise and simple. The result is sharp and staccato, as is the original. He too admits the difficulty of finding adequate translations for *honnête homme*, *intérêt* and *amour-propre*. He plumps for "gentleman", "self-interest" and "self-love" respectively. These are not, perhaps, as good solutions as FitzGibbon's , but they work well enough. This translation is an excellent tool for getting to know an author whose originality and acuteness of observation have long been acknowledged.

J.P. SHORT

Further Reading

Moore, W.G., *La Rochefoucauld: His Mind and Art*, Oxford: Clarendon Press, 1967

Watts, Derek A., *La Rochefoucauld: Maximes et réflections diverses*, Glasgow: University of Glasgow French and German Publications, 1993

See also the translators' introductions to FitzGibbon and Tancock

---

Latin

Literary Translation into English

The Language

Latin, the language of the city of Rome, developed in periods conventionally distinguished as follows: Early Latin, to about 100 BC; Classical Latin, to the death of Augustus in AD 14; Silver Latin, to about AD 150; Late Latin; Medieval Latin. Latin was a literary language in all these eras, but a simpler form known as "basic" or "vulgar" Latin was spoken by the common people.

Latin was diffused through most of Western Europe as Rome's influence grew. French, Spanish, Italian, Portuguese, Catalan, Provençal and Romanian, as well as a number of dialects such as Corsican, all derive directly from it. The English language ultimately derives from Anglo-Saxon, which is cognate with Latin; many Latin-English connections also result from direct borrowing of words. This process began in earnest in the 7th century, when Pope Gregory sent St Augustine the Lesser to convert the Angles; here the Vulgate Bible had a major role to play. Another important phase comes in the 13th and 14th centuries, when Middle English is being formed as an official and literary language from what remains of Anglo-Saxon. Direct borrowing from Latin, and more extensive borrowing of Latin-derived vocabulary from French and Italian, is responsible for hundreds of new words in this period. The process continued and gathered pace in the Renaissance. Today, much of the abstract vocabulary of English is classically derived, and there is some tendency for the Latin element to become more pervasive in both everyday and formal English.

Latin is a highly inflectional language, but overall its grammatical forms are less varied than those of Greek. It has no article, no dual number, no aorist tense, and only traces of a middle voice and an optative mood. The possibilities of constructing compound words and expressing abstract concepts are more restricted; Latin lacks the great variety of particles and prepositional usages that makes Greek so appropriate for the expression of abstract or philosophical thought. The Romans were not on the whole an imaginative race, and Latin is not naturally suited to verse either: its long, sonorous sounds do not fit readily into metre, especially lyric metres. On the other hand, Latin has great concision and precision. In syntax, the most significant feature is perhaps the elaborate and rigid set of principles governing the sequence of tenses and the forms of indirect quotation.

One of English literature's greatest translators from Latin, the 17th-century poet John Dryden, found the "beauty of that language" to lie in "the turns of the expressions, the figures and connections of words". The effects created by Virgil or Horace through intricate arrangements of everyday words are rocks on which many an English translator has foundered. But Dryden was writing on this occasion about prose, where the "turns of the expressions" are sometimes deceptively easy to translate: Cicero's rhetoric, for example, has often been the template for structurally foreign "English" versions. Dryden registers a complaint familiar from many verse translators when he writes of the "natural succinctness" of Latin – English is far more "compendious", he says, meaning that it will take more words and more syllables to convey the same meaning. Latin metre, based on syllable-length and not (as in English) on stress, is a perennial obstacle for translators, and the best successes in rendering verse have often been achieved, paradoxically, by selecting a completely different English metrical form. Where vocabulary is concerned, it is all too easy for an English translator to coin Latinate words. Dryden writes apropos of his versions of Virgil: "a poet must first be certain that the word he would introduce is beautiful in the Latin, and is to consider in the next place whether it will agree with the English idiom ... let him use this licence sparingly, for if too many foreign words are poured in upon us, it looks as if they were designed not to assist the natives but to conquer them".

Literary Translation from Latin

This discussion has set out as it means to continue. Dryden's voice has been given prominence above; in what follows, the emphasis is on the intersection of Latin literature with the English literary tradition, and hence especially with translations by major English writers. At least as regards literary texts, more Latin-English translation has gone on in the last millennium than from any other language into English, and there is no attempt below to deal with *all* forms of this phenomenon. In this account, not all translations are treated as equal in interest or importance. In particular, translations of Latin religious and philosophical texts, and of neo-Latin writing, go generally undiscussed.

To 1500

The early accessibility of Latin to comparatively many readers in Britain partly accounts for the slow beginning made in translation of it. The first complete direct translation of the *Aeneid*, for example – one of the best-known literary Latin works in the Middle Ages – did not occur until Gavin Douglas's Scots rendering of 1513, published in 1553. Though Chaucer is called a "grant [great] translateur" by his contemporaries, he translated mainly by incorporating into his own poems material from texts in other languages. Classical Latin literature plays a major role in this process in the form of Ovid, Virgil and other writers, but with the exception of Chaucer's version of Boethius' *De Consolatione Philosophiae* his work is not part of the history of formal translation from Latin into English. In fact it is lesser writers who are responsible for the medieval chapter of this history. Their work is almost always inspired principally by a didactic or pedagogical purpose, the sources being seen as *auctores* ("authorities") rather than as individuals. The "moralists" (Seneca, Boethius) find translators fairly readily, while other popular writers (such as Ovid) are conscripted to moralistic purposes when they are translated. Much Latin translation is done via intermediate French versions.

16th Century

This situation changed gradually during the 16th century. Thomas Wyatt (c. 1503–42) is in the vanguard of poetic experiment in the 1530s, and has an inspired translation of the famous Senecan chorus from the *Thyestes* in the lyric "Stand whoso list". But as a direct translation of Latin poetry this is a rarity in Wyatt's work; he was more interested in translation from modern Italian poets (Petrarch, Sannazaro), though the *influence* of the Latin classics, for example Horace's satires, is often felt in his poetry. Wyatt's contemporary Henry Howard, Earl of Surrey (?1517–47), introduced blank verse into English in the course of translating several books of the *Aeneid* (published in the 1550s); his selection is succeeded by those of Thomas Phaer (1558) and Thomas Twyne (1573), neither memorable. But by the latter date a new era is arriving. The Elizabethans and Jacobeans, helped by Ben Jonson (1572–1637) – himself a translator of Horace, Virgil and other Latin poets – to see the classics as "guides, not commanders", are responsible for a rich range of translations in both prose and verse, beginning to embrace the classical Latin canon as a whole. The early Elizabethan translators experiment with Martial, the non-epic Ovid, Apuleius, Virgil, Horace, Plautus, Pliny, Sallust, Livy; Terence, Lucan and the difficult Tacitus come somewhat later in the 16th century. This is a rich and heterogeneous mixture. It is wrong to imagine an English Renaissance devoted to the accepted "classical" Latin works and writers; for one thing there is a pronounced taste for later, and often in today's terms non-standard, texts. The Elizabethan translators worked from an enthusiastic wish to invigorate life with classical values as they understood them, to energize English writing with the sophisticated literary forms and the knowledge displayed in classical texts. With some exceptions they were not scholars; they were often associated not with the universities but with the Inns of Court, as is the case with

Richard Stanyhurst, Timothy Kendall, George Turberville and Thomas Phaer. Sometimes, like their predecessors, they translate Latin books from intermediate versions, often in French.

The Elizabethan-Jacobean period is so rich in translations that a little more detail as to its achievements is in order. The epics of Ovid and Virgil continue to hold attention: Arthur Golding's *Metamorphoses* (1567) is a substantial and enduring Elizabethan translation, partly the cause of the importance of Ovid as a source for Shakespeare and many other contemporaries. Shakespeare is capable of parodying its fourteeners in *A Midsummer Night's Dream*, but Golding's verse has its charm, as in Medea's invocation from book VII, which famously lies behind one of Prospero's soliloquies in *The Tempest*:

> Ye Ayres and windes: ye Elves of Hilles, of Brookes, of Woods alone,
> Of standing Lakes, and of the Night approche ye everychone.
> Through helpe of whom (the crooked bankes much wondring at the thing)
> I have compelled streames to run cleane backward to their spring.
> By charmes I make the calme Seas rough, and make ye rough Seas plaine
> And cover all the Skie with Cloudes, and chase them thence againe.

As for other epic poetry, translations of the *Aeneid* have been mentioned already, but Virgil's translators look well beyond that text. The second half of the 16th century sees the first complete versions of the *Eclogues* (George Turberville, Abraham Fleming), the *Georgics* (Fleming), and some of the shorter poems the Renaissance attributed to Virgil (William Webbe).

This period also sees a flowering of translation from Catullus, with Jonson's famous lyric "Come, My Celia" (in *Volpone*); William Byrd's *La Verginella*, from Catullus' second epithalamium, very influential on the genre in English; and other well-known versions of Catullan poems by Thomas Campion (1567–1620). Catullus is, in fact, the principal Latin lyric poet: there is no English Tibullus or Propertius at this time, and translators of Horace generally avoid the *Odes* until 1621 (John Ashmore). Seneca's importance as a dramatist for the later 16th century should be mentioned: his appeal seems to have been wide, and his tragedies are re-created in grotesquely Elizabethan diction in the version by several hands, *Seneca His Ten Tragedies* (1581). Historical prose, understandably in view of the period's intellectual priorities, could be said to be the single most important field of Latin translation in the European Renaissance as a whole; in Britain the translators include Arthur Golding for Caesar (1565), Henry Savile for Tacitus (1591), Philemon Holland for Livy (1600) and Ammianus (1609). But much popularity still attaches to the older favourites of the moralists, Boethius and Cicero, retranslated many times with affectionate zeal.

17th Century

This is a period of considerable change. Thorough knowledge of Latin has become universal among the lettered classes by the 17th century, so the purposes of translation alter subtly. Old and new worlds intermingle: George Sandys's translation of the *Metamorphoses* (1626–32) constitutes the first literary production by the English settlers in America, written while Sandys worked for the New Virginia Company, but its elaborate interpretative approach to the poem, allegorically based, is distinctly a product of the European Renaissance. More Latin literary territory is opened up to translation – importantly satire, with Barten Holyday's complete Persius of 1616 (reprinted four times) and Robert Stapylton's complete Juvenal of 1644. The major English poets increasingly become the major translators too, so that Abraham Cowley (1618–67) and John Dryden (1631–1700), for example, produce extensive work both in classical translation and otherwise. Shorter poetic forms such as lyric and epigram are notably popular with translators, with a much wider spread of texts now being translated. There is continuing interest in Catullus: translators or imitators – the line is hard to draw – include Richard Lovelace, Abraham Cowley, Robert Herrick and William Crashaw. Lovelace also exemplifies interest in epigram in his *Lucasta* by translating Ausonius and Martial as well as Catullus. A long series of versions of Claudian's *De Sene Veronensi*, linking importantly with Horace's Second Epode in the "Beatus Ille" tradition in English, begins with Sir John Beaumont in 1629 and continues through Thomas Randolph, Mildmay Fane, Cowley and Vaughan, on into the 18th century and beyond. Translators of Horace's odes and epodes even before the Restoration period include Thomas Hawkins (1625), Henry Rider (1638), John Smith (1649), Richard Fanshawe (1652) and Barten Holyday (1653).

But there is also full-scale translation of the most extensive Latin texts, culminating in Dryden's complete *Works of Virgil* (1700) – an achievement of such obvious authority that the following century can muster hardly anyone willing to attempt a replacement. Dryden is at the forefront of a wave of classical translation from 1680 onwards. He is a theorist of translation too, his tripartite division of the field into paraphrase, metaphrase and imitation the basis for much subsequent discussion. His contemporaries – John Oldham, Samuel Garth, Matthew Prior, Edward Sherburne and many others – achieve a consistently high standard in their work of rendering mostly Latin authors, including prose writers such as Tacitus as well as poets. There is a notable surge of interest in Ovid, from a Dryden-sponsored *Epistles* by several hands in 1680 to Samuel Garth's collaborative *Metamorphoses* of 1717, including contributions by Alexander Pope, William Congreve, Joseph Addison, John Gay and Dryden in reprinted form. Some hitherto untranslated, or obscurely translated texts are involved in this burgeoning national enterprise: Dryden's unforgettable excerpts from Lucretius are a striking example. An emerging middle-class audience with a less solid Latin training, or in the case of women readers usually no Latin training, forms part of the impetus – Dryden appeals to such a readership explicitly in some of his prefaces.

18th Century

Dryden and his contemporaries are often described as the first generation of English "Augustans". The term refers to the use English writers and critics made of the Latin poets of the Augustan era, the first century BC, as stylistic models or authorities (Virgil and Horace being the most important). English "Augustanism" continues, in the conventional view, throughout the 18th century. Literary history is full of generalizations, and this one like all others should be distrusted. English writers do not all have the same priorities during this period of a century or more, and many "Augustan" values can be found expressed in quite different eras. If we think that the works chosen for translation by major writers show what models a period has chosen, we find a tendency towards, but not an exclusive concern with, the Augustan classics in this one. There is Dryden's Virgil in 1697, but there is also Pope's Homer in the 1710s and 1720s. Of the six writers at the centre of Pope's Temple of Fame (in his 1715 poem of that name), only three are Roman: Homer comes first and Virgil second; they are followed by Pindar, Horace, Aristotle and Cicero.

Yet Alexander Pope (1688–1744) is responsible for a series of *Imitations of Horace* as well as translations of the Homeric epics, and arguably this work is, indeed, more representative of his age. Matthew Prior, John Gay, Joseph Addison and Jonathan Swift are examples of Pope's contemporaries who translated parts of the witty, urbane Horace, satirist, lyric poet, literary theorist. They join practically every Restoration poet of any note; outstanding are Dryden's Horatian odes and Cowley's *The Country Mouse*, from Horace's Satire II.6. They also join many scores of very minor translators of Horace: the impression may be acquired from the catalogue of a major library that almost all 18th-century English clergymen published versions. Even those 18th-century Horaces singled out for praise by their contemporaries have failed to stand the test of time – Philip Francis's version of 1743–46, lauded by Samuel Johnson and reprinted into the 19th century, is a case in point. With few exceptions, comprehensive enfeeblement eventually overtakes 18th-century Horatianism. This is the case for Latin-based satire in general, as increasing numbers of translators and imitators turn to Persius, Martial, and even Juvenal as well as Horace in order to find or create opportunities for witty reflection on their own times, usually with predictably ephemeral results.

The 18th century shows more self-conscious attitudes than the 17th: a developed literary culture is starting to question and to manipulate Latin material, often ironically. This may have aesthetically positive as well as negative consequences for translations. Christopher Smart's complete Horace (prose and verse) of 1756–70, for instance, is light-hearted enough, especially in the satires, but it is also very readable. Smart's imitation of Satire I.3 shows why he is an exception to the generally uninspiring picture of later 18th-century Horatianism:

> If sick at heart, and heavy at the head,
> My drunken friend should reel betimes to bed;
> And in the morn, with affluent discharge,
> Should sign and seal his residence at large;
> Or should he, in some passionate debate,
> By way of instance, break an earthen plate;
> Would I forsake him for a piece of delph?
> No – not for China's wide domain itself.

The advantages of being able to take for granted in one's audience both a thorough knowledge of the classics and a shared set of aesthetic values (based largely upon them) are reflected clearly enough in Samuel Johnson's two weighty imitations of Juvenal, *London* (1738) and *The Vanity of Human Wishes* (1749). Johnson infuses a grave moralism into Juvenal's rhetorical wit, dramatically altering the tone and spirit of the Latin to produce heroic couplets of conspicuous sonority:

> Unnumber'd suppliants crowd Preferment's gate,
> Athirst for wealth, and burning to be great,
> Delusive Fortune hears th' incessant call,
> They mount, they shine, evaporate and fall.

Arguably, later 18th-century Latin translators are at their best when they are most concerned to leave their originals behind them, or use them for their own purposes.

19th Century

It is to another literature, Greek, that the next phase of English literature owes most allegiance, and though translation of Latin works of course continues, it is the preserve much less of the English writer than of the scholar or pedagogue. The Romantics find in Greek literature the pure and the original, in Latin the debased and derivative. Hence, for example, the marked elevation of Homer over Virgil, Coleridge even asking (a question almost unimaginable in any other era) "if you take from Virgil his diction and his metre, what do you leave him?", while Byron labels the Latin poet a "harmonious plagiary and miserable flatterer". But these are extreme positions. Shelley and Wordsworth translate from the *Aeneid* (the latter in heroic couplets indebted to Dryden), and Landor, a youthful translator of the *Georgics*, finds nothing in Homer "so impassioned, and therefore so sublime, as the last hour of Dido". Still, Landor also takes for granted Virgil's overall secondary status: "we find him incapable of contriving, and more incapable of executing, so magnificent a work as the *Iliad*". Latin translations and adaptations by the English Romantics are, in fact, relatively few; nevertheless their existence should not be overlooked. Their number includes Byron's free version of the *Ars poetica* called *Hints from Horace*, and versions of Catullus by Leigh Hunt, Byron and Wordsworth. A translation of Juvenal VII was carried out by Wordsworth. Lucan was translated by De Quincey, a case of an English Romantic translator finding qualities unavailable in Greek literature: De Quincey writes of a "moral sublime" in Lucan "perfectly distinct from anything known to the Greek poetry". This "sublime" is what Shelley admired in Lucan, in large part ultimately a matter of republican egalitarianism.

The continued dominance of the classical curriculum in school and university education into the Victorian period ensured the continuing cultural centrality of Latin literature. (Tennyson's earliest surviving poem, written between the ages of 11 and 14, is a translation of Claudian's *De raptu Proserpinae*.) Although Greek writers normally tended now to be accorded at least theoretical priority, it was undoubtedly with Latin that many Victorians felt more at home. Full training in the Latin classics is taken for granted; it is, indeed, a criterion of gentility among males.

One reflection of the thoroughness with which the British education system inculcated Latin verse is the impressive level of competence even very minor Victorian versifiers achieve in English prosody – the result of long years spent scanning and composing in Latin metres. It is no coincidence that a large number of Victorian Latin translators experiment with syllabic metres and other unusual metrical forms, making this a notable tendency in the period. Victorian versions of the *Aeneid* may serve to illustrate something of the range of possibilities attempted. James Henry, a classical scholar who had edited the poem in Latin, constructed an unusual blank verse version of books I and II in 1845. Eight years later, Henry published translations of books I–VI in two-stress lines:

Across to be ferried
The foremost were begging,
And in love with the further bank
Stretched their hands out;
But the boatman severe
Now some takes, now others,
And some from the strand
Removes far and keeps off.

Another classical scholar, John Conington, followed with his translation into the octosyllabic metre of *Marmion* in 1866; here is part of the corresponding passage:

Each in pathetic suppliance stands
So may he first be ferried o'er,
And stretches out his helpless hands
In yearning for the further shore.

William Morris's line-by-line version of 1876 is in rhymed fourteeners, harking back to the early translations by Thomas Phaer and Thomas Twyne. But the diction's mixture of the archaic with the prosaic deprives it of dignity and subtlety:

I sing of arms, I sing of him, who from the Trojan land
Thrust forth by Fate, to Italy and that Lavinian strand
first came: all tost about was he on earth and on the deep
By heavenly night for Juno's wrath, that had no mind to
sleep:
And plenteous war he underwent ere he his town might
frame
And set his gods in Latian earth, whence is the Latin
name ...

Charles Bowen, one of the next contenders, argued in the preface to his translation of 1887 that a longer line still, a form of hexameter, was required. One final metrical experiment some way into the 20th century deserves mention: Robert Bridges's line-by-line *Aeneid* in quantitative hexameters (1916). The task was arduous, the result, including symbols to guide pronunciation, curious (the souls on Lethe's banks as a specimen again):

So throng'd they; and each his watery journey demanded,
All to the further bank stretching-out their arms impatient:
But the sullen boatman took now one now other at will,
While some from the river forbade he', an' drave to a
distance.

There is much energy of experiment in 19th-century Latin–English translation, and much variety of achievement. We have glanced at epic, but in many other directions the picture is crowded. If we look at shorter forms, Catullus' translators, for example, include J.H. Frere, George Moore, Aubrey Beardsley, George Meredith and F.T. Palgrave. Catullus' "impurity" is tolerated by the Victorians for the sake of his lyric grace. (Martial and Ovid, on the other hand, are in recession among translators, being thought to offer no such compensations.) Yet, though more translations were produced than at any previous time, very few are still readable today. The explanation seems to lie largely in the Victorian reverence for the classics, the inhibiting sense of modern poetry as a debased version of better stuff. Important as it is to try to emulate them, equality with these immortals is not realistically to be expected; a fatal attitude for the translator, condemning his or her work to secondary status from the start.

20th Century

In some ways the story of 20th-century literary translation in English, especially from Latin, is the story of the impact of one man, even of one work. In the 1910s Ezra Pound (1885–1972) gathered together a number of friends and associates to found a literary movement he called "Imagisme", which was to attempt a revitalization of poetry, notably through the rediscovery of other literatures. One of his most important early translations was from Latin, and it became his most notorious, outraging the classical establishment. Pound's *Homage to Sextus Propertius* (published 1917 onwards), as well as containing the elements of a new aesthetic, turned out to be enormously influential in its bold, unconventional approach to the whole medium of translation. This adaptation does different things at different points. Pound found beneath the surface of Propertius' elegies a vein of political critique, and sometimes this is uppermost in his version:

And my ventricles do not palpate to Caesarial ore
rotundos
Nor to the tune of the Phrygian fathers.
Sailor, of winds; a plowman, concerning his oxen;
Soldier, the enumeration of wounds; the sheep feeder, of
ewes;
We, in our narrow bed, turning aside from battles:
Each man where he can, wearing out the day in his
manner.

Elsewhere, Pound's apparent blunders, inconsistencies and stylistic flamboyance go to suggest a translator unconcerned with making good sense or recapturing the "essence" of Propertius. The strongest impression is of Propertius' strangeness and foreignness:

Persephone and Dis, Dis, have mercy upon her,
There are enough women in hell,
quite enough beautiful women
Iope, and Tyro, and Pasiphae, and the formal girls of
Achaia,
And out of Troad, and the Campania,
Death has its tooth in the lot ...

The importance of this translation (if the term is appropriate) for the rest of the 20th-century encounter with Latin literature can hardly be overstated. So influential were its radical new procedures that within a few years almost any creative translator's work can be identified as "post-*Homage*". Pound's immediate followers included Richard Aldington, translator of Apuleius, and Hilda Doolittle ("H.D."), who translated Sappho and

Euripides. But many other names must be added at one or more removes. Nearer to the present, the Americans Louis and Celia Zukofsky are in a clear line of descent from Pound as translators and some of their work is dedicated to him. Their complete Catullus, which appeared in 1969, "follows the sound, rhythm, and syntax of his Latin – tries, as is said, to breathe the literal meaning with him" (Preface). This is a "homophonic" translation which attempts to convey the effect of the original through English which does indeed sound like the Latin. From their Catullus LI:

Ille mi par esse deo videtur,
ille, si fas est, superare divos,
qui sedens adversus identidem te
spectat et audit

He'll hie me, par is he? the God divide her,
He'll hie, see fastest, superior deity,
quiz – sitting adverse identity – mate, in-
spect it and audit
[The literal meaning of the Catullus is:
He seems to me the equal of a god,
He seems, if it may be, the gods' superior,
Who sits opposite you, again and again
Watching and hearing you.]

Most readers have reacted unfavourably to this immensely difficult and perhaps immensely absurd "phonemic" form of translation – there is a critique of it in Lefevere (1975). One thing is certain: its deliberately disconcerting tactics, nothing like "acceptable" to the scholarly establishment, are conceived in the wake of Pound's experiments.

Two ways of suggesting the range and diversity of 20th-century English-Latin translation are to mention some of the English writers who have published such work, and to summarize what has been done with a single Latin author. With no attempt at exhaustiveness, under the first heading might be listed the following: Thomas Hardy's Catullus, A.E. Housman's Horace, Robert Graves's Lucan and Apuleius, C. Day Lewis's Virgil, Allan Tate's *Pervigilium Veneris*, J.V. Cunningham's Catullus, W.S. Merwin's Persius, Ted Hughes's Seneca, Robert Lowell's Latin elegists and Juvenal, Peter Porter's and Tony Harrison's Martial, and Seamus Heaney's Virgil. Not all these translations are outstanding or even good; this is merely a way of suggesting how many of the modern English-speaking world's literary talents, not including "professional translators", have been involved in such activity. Under the second heading, to summarize what has been done in this century with a single Latin author, we might take translations of Martial's *Epigrams*, a popular source-text in this period. Large selections or complete Martials are published by A.E. Street (1900), Paul Nixon (1911), A.S. West (1912), W.J. Courthope (1914), A.L. Francis and H.F. Tatum (1924), J.A. Pott and F.A. Wright (1924), Dudley Fitts (1956), Rolfe Humphries (1963), Philip Murray (1963), Ralph Marcellino (1966–68), Bariss Mills (1969), Palmer Bovie (1970), Donald Goertz (1971) and James Mitchie (1972). Smaller selections have been translated by Peter Porter, Peter Whigham, J. P. Sullivan, Brian Hill, Tony Harrison, J.V. Cunningham, Harold Morland, Roy Swanson, Dorothea Wender, Alistair Elliot – and many others of less note.

All this seems to suggest that Latin-English translation is a substantial part of 20th-century literary culture. It is worth mentioning that its most successful practitioners often have their roots elsewhere than in England: writers from the US, Scotland and Ireland have done much interesting work in recent years. Economic and social factors have played their part: the American urge to respect tradition coincides with a shortage of expertise in Latin, for example, and publishers have commissioned a significant proportion of post-war classical translation to furnish the campus bookstore with the material to make good the deficit. In Britain, declining enrolments for Latin courses have had the effect, indirectly, of promoting such major series as the Penguin Classics (now so long-established it is offering a second and third translation of some Latin authors to replace outdated earlier ones). Yet, as in the Victorian era, far too much of this translating activity is clearly not in the nature of the "making new" that Ezra Pound prescribed. "What we do not want", Christopher Logue once wrote, "is bad writing hiding behind efficiency in ancient languages". This brief survey set out with John Dryden, who wrote "it is only for a poet to translate a poet". Though the nature of the pressures exerted by readers and by the wider culture has clearly changed since Dryden's time, the kind of translation needed has not. It is to be hoped that many more poets will translate poets as the next millennium gets under way.

STUART GILLESPIE

Further Reading

Bolgar, R.R., *The Classical Heritage and Its Beneficiaries*, Cambridge: Cambridge University Press, 1954

Bolgar, R.R. (editor), *Proceedings of an International Conference on Classical Influences*, 3 vols, Cambridge and New York: Cambridge University Press, 1971–79

Braden, Gordon, *The Classics and English Renaissance Poetry: Three Case Studies*, New Haven, Connecticut: Yale University Press, 1978

Bush, Douglas, *Classical Influences in Renaissance Literature*, Cambridge, Massachusetts: Harvard University Press, 1952

Gillespie, Stuart (editor), *The Poets on the Classics: An Anthology of English Poets' Writings on the Classical Poets and Dramatists from Chaucer to the Present*, London and New York: Routledge, 1988

Greene, Thomas M., *The Light in Troy: Imitation and Discovery in Renaissance Poetry*, New Haven, Connecticut: Yale University Press, 1982

Highet, Gilbert, *The Classical Tradition: Greek and Roman Influences on Western Literature*, Oxford: Clarendon Press, and New York: Oxford University Press, 1949

Hooley, Daniel M., *The Classics in Paraphrase: Ezra Pound and Modern Translators of Latin Poetry*, Selinsgrove, Pennsylvania: Susquehanna University Press, and London: Associated University Presses, 1988

Jenkyns, Richard (editor), *The Legacy of Rome: A New Appraisal*, Oxford and New York: Oxford University Press, 1992

Kallendorf, Craig, *Latin Influences on English Literature from the Middle Ages to the Eighteenth Century: An Annotated Bibliography of Scholarship, 1945–1979*, New York: Garland, 1982

Kupersmith, William, *Roman Satirists in Seventeenth-Century England*, Lincoln: University of Nebraska Press, 1985
Lefevere, André, *Translating Poetry: Seven Strategies and a Blueprint*, Amsterdam: Van Gorcum, 1975
Lord, George de Forest, *Classical Presences in Seventeenth-Century English Poetry*, New Haven, Connecticut: Yale University Press, 1987
Palmer, L.R., *The Latin Language*, London: Faber, 1954
Pfeiffer, Rudolf, *A History of Classical Scholarship from 1300 to 1850*, Oxford: Clarendon Press, 1976
Sowerby, Robin, *The Classical Legacy in Renaissance Poetry*, London and New York: Longman, 1994
Weinbrot, Howard D., *Augustus Caesar in "Augustan" England: The Decline of a Classical Norm*, Princeton, New Jersey: Princeton University Press, 1978

Latin America: Translation Studies

The history of Latin America destined its culture to be envisioned as a metaphor of translation. The complex implications of this metaphor cast much light on certain general translation topics: the pervasiveness of translation in multicultural and multilingual societies, the broadening of the horizons of interlingual translation, the elaboration of interconnections between cultural history and translation theory, the emergence of autonomous bodies of thinking that cater for historical specificities, the expansion of the sources of theorization for translation, the high status and visibility of literary translation in other contexts as a counterpoint to the state of the art in the current anglophone agenda. The rich corpus of Latin American translation theories is making a strong contribution to translation studies in general as pursued in England, the United States, Canada, and India; outstanding is the case of Jorge Luis Borges. The impact of other more recent but no less remarkable Latin American theories of translation has already been acknowledged by scholars such as Susan Bassnett (England), Edwin Gentzler (US), Sherry Simon (Canada), Harish Trivedi (India) and other specialists who have had contact with their exponents in the last few years. Bassnett, for example, has acknowledged the innovative contribution of the anthropophagy-related theory of translation developed by the present writer from 1989 within the framework of postcolonial studies, and has related it to Canadian feminine translators' contribution.

Specifically in relation to the connection between Latin America and the English-speaking world in the 20th century, reference may be made to Argentina: the role played by the journal *Sur*, whose first issue was dedicated to the translation of Shakespeare; the interest and availability in the 1940s and 1950s of translations of Joyce and Eliot; the market interest in the same decades for novels from the English-speaking world, particularly those of Woolf, Dos Passos, Hemingway, Steinbeck, Caldwell, Capote, etc.

Brazil also experienced a translation boom in the 1940s and 1950s, referred to as the Golden Age of Translation in Brazil – one likely explanation for the boom being financial prosperity and the need to produce national books because war had made importation difficult. Anglophone writers translated in that period include Conrad, Chesterton, Joyce, Mansfield, Huxley, Steinbeck, Faulkner, Greene. The role played by the Concretist poets in Brazil from the 1950s is impressive. They developed an autonomous translation theory, besides translating Pound, Joyce, Donne, Herbert, among other English-speaking writers. Another translation boom, this time in poetry, occurred in Brazil from the late 1970s onwards, associated with the easing of the dictatorial regime. The present writer has studied the role of translation from the 1970s, a period that also introduces the postmodern debate and its rewriting of the past. The dense translation movement involved the construction of an alternative past and the rewriting of tradition. Although not exclusive, the presence of anglophone poets is marked in that period, the English Metaphysical poets and the Romantics being outstanding presences; between 1978 and 1992 a total of 24 anthologies of British poets were translated. A decisive role has been that of the poet-translator Augusto de Campos, who has translated Pound, cummings, Joyce, and Donne, among anglophone writers.

Our brief historical overview, with emphasis on the 20th century and Argentina, the Caribbean, and Brazil, highlights the Latin American contribution to translation thinking, stressing its relation to the Anglophone world and its availability in English. It should be mentioned, however, that the focus on such a relation does not necessarily imply a centrality of English; Latin America has intense translation activity in relation to many Western languages and has been known for its construction of an autonomous theoretical framework for translation which, being quite innovative, has contributed to the revitalization of translation thinking throughout the world.

The conceptual approximation between Latin America and translation has been mainly developed by the Cuban Gustavo Pérez Firmat in his study of modern Cuban literature (1989), by the Argentine writer Ricardo Piglia (1991) and by the Brazilian translation theorist Else R.P. Vieira (1992). Firmat has conceptualized the notion of a translation sensibility developed by Cubans throughout history; translation, in his view, is a concept applicable to Cuba and also to the whole of the New World; his argument is that Cuban culture is translational because it has absorbed and integrated foreign models. Piglia makes a similar point; his focus, however, lies on the sense of a dissociated cultural memory metaphorized as a "cross-eyed look" (1991). In his view, Latin America begins as a metaphor of translation; for the Argentines, tradition, as it is read out of context, takes the form of translation; the territory of the writer and, accordingly, of the translator, is that of "ex-tradition", hence the view of Latin America as fiction and translation. Vieira has developed a theory of translation and anthropophagy, while further questioning the parameters of the translator's invisibility and of historical immutability; she pursues the interrelatedness of translation, colonialism and postcolonialism; conceptualizing Brazil and Latin America as metaphors of translation, she goes beyond the theoretical expression of a need grounded on negatives (invisibility, immutability) and presents images of a bilateral flow evident in the metaphors of cannibalism, blood transfusion, communicating vessels, etc. (Vieira, 1994) A similar note is suggested by Sandro Sticca, who claims that translation appears to be a fundamental component of the New World; moreover, the coming together of a dominant and a non-dominant culture, one imposing on the other and the second attempting to liberate itself from the first, is at the origin of the problematic of the "discovery" of the New World and of translation. Alita Kelley, interfacing linguistic and cultural dimensions, claims that Spanish in Peru is impregnated with Quechua culture, so it is *a priori* a cultural translation – an example is the writer José María Arguedas, whose Spanish has a Quechua syntax and world view.

Several of the great names among Latin American authors had much to do with and much to say about the translation of literary works and its relation to culture, history, and criticism. Latin America has in fact developed a poetics of translation, a tradition of translation, an innovative body of thinking that reconceptualizes its main tenets and allows for an experimentalism in its praxes; it has also contributed to the siting of translation in the postmodern era. Yet relatively little has been written in the academy to compare with the response of writers worldwide (e.g. Rushdie, Kundera, Seth, Carter, and a myriad others) to the play on translation and its cultural possibilities embodied in the work of such as Borges, Cortázar, García Márquez, Cabrera Infante, Guimarães Rosa, the de Campos brothers, Silviano Santiago and Lya Luft, for instance. At its best, the academic response has been fascinating and ingenious as in Aníbal González's analysis "Translation and Genealogy: *One Hundred Years of Solitude*". In the famous novel by the Colombian Nobel prize winner Gabriel García Márquez, published 1967 and translated into English in 1970, two views of translation are metaphorically presented. One view textualizes dissemination and the Latin American continent's history of plurality and linguistic cosmopolitanism: the character José Arcadio returns to the town of Macondo speaking a Spanish contaminated with sailor's slang, his body covered in multilingual tattoos – the words in each language spelling out the trajectory of his maritime adventures in his life's history, which duplicates the history of his continent. In the other view, Aureliano Babilonia, albeit named after Babylon, the Hebrew Babel, is always trying to decipher the *Ursprache*, the primordial language (for a study of translation and genealogy in this novel see González 1987. For another Nobel prizewinner, the Mexican Octavio Paz, translation is the basis of communication, as learning to talk equates with learning to translate, in his view, translation within the same language does not differ from translation between two languages, and world history repeats a child's history: even the most isolated tribe needs to cope one day with the language of the other. This ingrained sense of translation and of the encounter with the other finds an echo in other Latin American theorists.

In fact, the pervasiveness and prominence of translation in Latin America, suggested by Marquez, Paz and Piglia, among others, and its importance as an object of theorization invite a look at the post-babelic panorama of Latin American colonial history. The background of colonial multilingualism, evangelization, the improvised training of translators, the role of the university and of the printing press in preserving, or not preserving, the translation archives – all this highlights the importance and pervasiveness of translation in Latin America from the moment of the continent's discovery.

Georges L. Bastin (1998) notes that when Columbus landed in Spanish America he found in use there some 1,000 languages, the natural consequence being that interpreters, who were referred to as *lenguas* (tongues), had to be used from the outset; moreover, even though Spanish monarchs expected the European language to be used, the Indian languages continued to be employed for evangelization and oral contact, whereas Spanish and Latin were used for written documents. Columbus's initial attempt to communicate with the local peoples had been made through a polyglot converted Jew, Luis de Torres, knowledgeable in Castilian, Latin, Arabic, Hebrew, Greek, and Armenian, but he had had also to turn to indigenous translators (Delisle and Woodsworth, 1995). Columbus, Amerigo Vespucci and Cortés captured South American natives in order to teach them Spanish and make them into *lenguas*, the best-known case being La Malinche, Cortés's lover and interpreter (Bastin, 1998) (for an account of La Malinche's controversial role, see "Exploration and Conquest" in Delisle and Woodsworth, 1995). Evangelization also enhanced translation, because the converters could not be expected to learn so many diverse languages, and a minimum of understanding, by converts, of religious texts was necessary for the task. The coming of independence (1816–25) was to give another boost to translation in Spanish-speaking Latin America within the context of cultural interchange with countries other than Spain (Bastin, 1998).

In Brazil, where 102 different language groups were identified, it has been hypothesized that oral translation may have been a form of communication between tribes; it has been further reported that the Portuguese and the indigenous peoples frequently communicated through gestures and that Portuguese deportees and adventurers who remained in Brazil later acted as *línguas*, a phenomenon similar to the Spanish *lenguas*. The Jesuits adopted for evangelizing a lingua franca used by the native peoples along the coast; Father José de Anchieta even became an expert in Indian languages, but with the expulsion of the Jesuits by the Portuguese government (1759), much of this work disappeared. Another important factor is that waves of immigration from Africa brought other languages, among them Yoruba, and Portuguese was consolidated as the hegemonic language only with the arrival in Brazil in 1808 of the Portuguese royal family fleeing Napoleon's troops (Barbosa and Wyler, 1998).

If the histories of the Spanish and the Portuguese blocks of the continent share some similarities, other points reveal sharp distinctions which have a bearing on their respective histories of translation. Printing presses were installed early in the 16th century in Mexico City and Lima, and universities were founded in these two places and in Santo Domingo; yet many of the first translations disappeared (Bastin, 1998). As for Brazil, printing was banned from the time of the discovery, and the ban was lifted only when the first legal printing press was set up in 1808. Many foreign books smuggled into the country by conspirators fighting for Brazilian independence were read in foreign languages with no need for translation. The first university in Brazil was not set up until 1920, even though some schools had existed from the early 19th century; it was only in the 1930s that printing presses began to flourish in Brazil and translation was given an impetus. Paradoxically, publishing and translating boomed in the 20th century in Brazil, and Brazil's output alone nearly equals the total for Spanish-speaking Latin America (Barbosa and Wyler, 1998).

Brazil and Argentina differ in relation to translation in the 19th century. Whereas Argentina favoured the translation of the classics, Brazilians translated more contemporary literature from England, the US, and France. Poe and Dickens are examples of anglophone writers translated by the leading fiction writer Machado de Assis; Byron was a pervasive presence whose impact lasted up to the early 20th century and who re-emerged in contemporary translations in the 1980s. Translations of plays and of feuilletons also played a very important role in the 19th century.

The visibility and the high status of writers-*cum*-translators, the view of translation as recreation, and the predominance of literary translation are features shared by both Spanish- and Portuguese-speaking Americas. Jorge Luis Borges, Julio Cortázar, Pablo Neruda, Octavio Paz, Guillermo Valencia, Haroldo de Campos, Augusto de Campos, Clarice Lispector, Lya Luft, Manuel Bandeira, Rachel de Queiroz, Érico Veríssimo and Monteiro Lobato are examples of the great Latin American writers-*cum*-translators. A great body of high quality literary translation is produced in both larger blocks of Latin America, along with translators' commentaries and theorization. Latin America is a large expanding market for the translator, and even though the profession still lacks official status (as pointed out by Barbosa and Wyler), writers-*cum*-translators enjoy great literary prestige. Their translations are often reviewed in the important newspapers, a site also for the publication of their own views on translation, operational procedures and metalanguage. The Brazilian contribution has been outstanding with regard to translation theory propounded in prefaces and through metaphors (notably by Haroldo de Campos and Augusto de Campos), in special issues of journals, in literary supplements, and in national newspapers.

The Argentine Jorge Luis Borges received international recognition and was awarded the Formentor Prize, with Beckett, in 1961. Not only was he one of the main contributors to the revitalization of translation theory; his name also established a connection with the work of Shakespeare, the English Romantics, Kipling, Yeats, Woolf and American authors such as Hawthorne, Poe, Melville, Whitman, Faulkner; further he introduced Joyce into Argentina, with the publication of his own translation of the last page of *Ulysses* in the journal *Proa* in 1925 and, in collaboration with Norman Thomas di Giovanni, translated into Spanish Faulkner, Woolf, Whitman; he is also associated with translation criticism, through, for example, his famous analysis of Edward FitzGerald's translation of Omar Khayy?m's *Rubaiyat* into English or that of the translations of *1001 Nights* into the main European languages. The recurrent appearance in his writing of characters who are translators or critics of translation highlights the role played by translation since the dawn of Western literature. Borges thought of translation as creation and as a way of enriching the language, since it can draw upon the means of expression of other languages and transmit stylistic procedures, new poetic forms, narrative models and forms; he further approached the problem of tradition from a broad perspective, browsing through Eastern and Western cultures and world literature, having furthermore conceived of the reader as one who generates infinite texts from a single one (Delisle and Woodsworth, 1995).

Borges does not stand alone in Argentina nor in Latin America, the whole of which has often been a fertile soil for the development of translation thinking, more visibly so in the present century. The wealth of neologisms for and concepts of translation advanced by the contemporary Brazilian translator and theorist Haroldo de Campos is evidence of the boom not only in translating but also in theorization in Brazil: translation as "verse making", "reinvention", a "project of recreation", "transilluminations" (stemming from his translation of Dante), as "transtextualization", as "transcreation", as "transluciferation" (stemming from his translation of Goethe's *Faust*), as "transhellenization" (from his translation of the *Iliad*), as "poetic reorchestration" (from his rendering of the Hebrew Bible into Brazilian Portuguese), etc. Further registers, translational procedures and sources of theorization in Latin America have been identified, leading to the claim that these are suggestive of a paradigm shift in translation in Latin America: one that redefines translation as a locus of duality, rather than excluding binaries such as source/target, superior/inferior. Translators' metalanguage, in general, mixes critical discourse with the use of metaphors, in themselves a source of theorization that introduces new registers and sites Translation Studies in Brazil within the postmodern and poststructuralist agenda. These metaphors in translators' metalanguage take on very special meanings in Latin America, conveying senses of bilaterality, distributing power hierarchies, and pointing to new configurations, such as the digestive metaphor, "blood transfusion", "communicating vessels", a "cross-eyed look", etc. Most importantly, they herald innovative theories of translation, such as Haroldo de Campos's poetics of transcreation, or Augusto de Campos's intranslation and Silviano Santiago's double plagiarism; these registers point to praxes that move translation beyond polarizations: in a double trajectory, they interweave texts and poetic diction from the target culture into the original text.

Vieira has further advocated the incorporation by Translation Studies of fictional-theoretical parameters as a step towards "postcriticism"; this move, which she has labelled "the fictional turn in Translation Studies", stems from a distinctive contribution of Latin American literature; for example, Borges's well-known "Pierre Menard" and his other essays, half-way between scientific and fictional discourses, deconstruct many of our inherited assumptions on translation; they are a point of reference in Latin America and throughout the world. Spanish-speaking Latin America, in particular, tends to use fiction as a locus for theorization on translation. Among fiction writers who have reflected upon the processes of translation from a cultural perspective, Jorge Luis Borges, Julio Cortázar, Ricardo Piglia (all Argentina), Cabrera Infante (Cuba), and Gabriel García Márquez (Colombia) are the most significant names. These authors problematize conventional views of translation as a subsidiary practice and reflect upon the historical context in which this task is performed. Moreover, they establish a relationship between translation and literary tradition, working towards a rereading of literary history and national literatures from the perspective of intercultural contacts. Studies started by Suzanne Jill Levine and continued by Cristóbal Pera reveal that the task of translation is one of the most important themes in Cabrera Infante's *Three Trapped Tigers*, which, from beginning to end, is pervaded by the theory and praxis of translation; in fact, the character who opens the text is a translator. Cabrera Infante himself learned English in his youth and worked as a translator in Cuba at a time when the country was enormously influenced by the United States; he has since collaborated with the translators of his own work; his view is that translation is something that is added to the original writing and, by adding or reducing the original, it always betrays.

A notable feature of Translation Studies in Spanish-speaking Latin America is that a good deal of innovative research that does justice to the wealth and originality of translation thought in these countries is carried out and published outside the countries of origin. A few examples are: Susan Jill Levine, in the United States (theorist of translation as subversion, translator of Latin American fiction, she has also been an expositor mostly of Cuban views of translation through fiction); Aníbal González, also based in the United States (working on Gabriel García Márquez's views on translation through fiction); Frances Aparicio, whose work was published in Spanish in the United States (emphasizing mostly Argentine writers such as Cortázar); Else R.P. Vieira, in Brazil (from a Brazilian perspective, she compares Chilean, Argentine, Mexican, and Colombian contributions to translation through fiction and in translators' metalanguage); Adriana Pagano, also in Brazil (work on Argentina with a Brazilian perspective); Alita Kelley, based in the United States (who has been publishing on the question of translation of Peruvian texts into English and its cultural implications).

In a different dimension and incorporating the postmodern style of criticism as creative writing, the UK-based Bernard McGuirk has incorporated Latin American translation theories and praxes into his performative meditations on Borges, Vallejo, Carlos Fuentes, Susana Thénon *et al.* (McGuirk, 1997; see particularly chapter 5, "Poetry, Pedagogy and Untranslatability"). Most recently, in his theoretical and political study "Falklands/Malvinas and/as Excess: On Simultaneous TransNation and the Poetry of War" (1998), he shows how writers such as the Argentines Borges and Susana Thénon, compared with the Welsh Tony Conran and the precursor Wilfred Owen, wage war in poetry by struggling to translate not only between but also within cultures; his claim is that the capacity of these writers to appropriate, and at the same time, to lay bare, the doubts upon which earlier traditions of war poetry often rest can be compared with the intellectual and aesthetic processes of translation.

Translation from English has carried strong political implications, such as its use in Nicaragua in the early 1930s as a weapon against imperialism; the point is made by Steven F. White in his study of José Coronel Utrecho's translation project (White, 1991).

A valuable contribution towards the development of the notion of Latin America as an open text to be translated emerged in the United States in the book *Translating Latin America: Culture as Text* (1991), the sixth in the series *Translation Perspectives* (edited by William Luis and Julio Rodríguez-Luis). The volume contains selected essays from the homonymous Interdisciplinary Conference held in 1990 at the Center for Research in Translation (CRIT), State University of New York at Binghamton. The argument is that Latin American culture has to be "translated", if it is to be understood, especially outside its new environment, but also, depending on the complexity of the issues to be dealt with, inside its own borders. By "translation" is meant the interpretation of, the re-codification of a text into other "languages"; the focus of the conference was the "translation" of Latin American culture into the "language" of those who lived outside it. A broader understanding of the very toponym Latin America, beyond its "Latinness", also informed the conference, which included in its scope not only the Hispanic Unites States, Central and South America and the Caribbean, but also the anglophone, Dutch, francophone and Portuguese cultures of the region (Luis and Rodríguez-Luis, 1991). Among those who contributed to the conference were Gregory Rabassa, Suzanne Jill Levine, and Margaret Sayers Peden, active translators of Latin American literature into English. Rabassa is perhaps the best known and the most active of those translators and is mainly responsible for the challenge of translating such important and difficult writers as García Márquez, Vargas Llosa, Lezama Lima, and Cortázar (Sticca, 1991). Levine is the translator of the Cuban Gabriel Cabrera Infante and the Argentines Julio Cortázar, Adolfo Bioy Casares, and Manuel Puig into English; she has further written valuable articles and an important book on her experience of collaborative translation with these writers and about their contribution to innovative translation thinking (*The Subversive Scribe*, Levine 1991). Peden is the translator of the Mexican Carlos Fuentes into English.

The many interfaces of cultural translation, together with related issues such as the translatability of cultures, are addressed by a joint Latin American and British enterprise, forthcoming in England, *Retranslating Latin America: Dimensions of the Third Term* (edited by Bernard McGuirk and Else R.P Vieira). Hybridity, in-betweenness, displacements, transculturations are some of the terms whose Latin American specificity emerges as contributors interpret the title of the collection as they think appropriate to their respective and different institutions and loci of enunciation. The representation of cultural translation thus emerges both as a project and a plurality. In the shuttle effect aimed at by the volume, identity/alterity is a binary that is problematized. A relational poetics, questions of reading cross-culturally, the redrawing of the relation between local and global cultures are some of the sub-topics of the collection. If not in binaries, how then is the encounter with the other via translation to be represented? Examples of answers emerge from contributors such as Ricardo Piglia, Haroldo de Campos, Augusto de Campos, Silviano Santiago, and Lya Luft. Piglia weaves tradition, identity, and fiction in Latin America and contributes with the above-mentioned metaphor of the cross-eyed look that embodies the tensions of cultural displacement. Augusto de Campos's preface to "Verse Reverse Controverse" contributes with the digestive metaphor ("My way of loving them is translating them. Or devouring them according to Oswald de Andrade's anthropophagic law") that sites translation at a remove from the source/target dichotomy. Similarly beyond polarizations, cast in a third dimension where both original and translation are both donor and receiver, is Silviano Santiagos's project developed in "A Double Plagiarist", originally the preface to his translation of Prévert – a dual trajectory that points to an ambiguous space of absorption collateral with self-expression. A view of translation as transformation and as a locus of duality is conveyed by Haroldo de Campos who, in his "On Translation as Criticism and Recreation", establishes his own relationship with Ezra Pound's project and those of Brazilian precursors such as Odorico Mendes, highlighting further dimensions of translation theorized as a critical operation and as rewriting. Creativity and the power of expression are elements that emerge as Lya Luft explores the dimensions not only of betweenness but also of againstness in her "Countercurrents" meditations as a translator.

A challenge faced today by translators and Translation Studies and that involves both an English and a Spanish dimension is the literature of the Latinos in the United States. In contemporary society, as is argued by Sandro Sticca, Puerto Rican writers born and living in New York are doing the same as the chronicler El Inca Garcilaso (1540–1616) and other marginal people forced to employ another language and translate between cultures. Sticca's example of duality of cultures, textualized in both Spanish and English, raises the issues not only of bilingualism and biculturalism but also of self-awareness and pride (Sticca, 1991). Reyes's consideration of Chicano literature stresses the problem of translating texts written in interlanguage, i.e., in a blend of two separate languages; these bilingual and bicultural texts pose a concrete problem to translation: whether to render the original interlingual text with its English and Spanish segments in an integrally English form, to be read as a monolingual work, or to present the text in its original form with an interlineal translation of the non-English segments (Reyes, 1991). A more recent contribution by Isabel Santaollala examines the insistence of the Latino *barrio*/neighbourhood on being translated not as an undifferentiated locus of enunciation but as a site of thirdness; she examines how the spaces granted to Hispanic women in the US cinema have shifted from the invariably fixed and narrowly defined towards more realistic and empowering portayals (in McGuirk and Vieira, editors, forthcoming).

Another issue that has been addressed by Translation Studies in relation to Latin America is that, in general, there is a visible asymmetry between the into-English publication of Latin American names and the publication in Spanish and Portuguese of texts originally in English. The number of translated books published in the English-speaking world is notoriously low – the 1982 Nobel prizewinner García Márquez being a notable exception, with an enormous commercial success. Even this special case presents problems: the swift succession of publications of this writer's work in English offered readers a false idea of simultaneity and fecundity; moreover, the appropriation of García Márquez, especially in the North American context, reveals an attempt to incorporate him as a modern classic writer into the accepted literary culture of the European and American world that conceals Latin America. García Márquez himself has said that the English translation of his novel *One Hundred Years of Solitude* (by Gregory Rabassa, his translator into English from 1970 to 1982) reads better than the original Spanish.

The translation of García Márquez into English and other languages, however, fits into a larger literary event of the 1960s, when the translation of Latin American literature reached a milestone. The so-called Boom begins with Julio Cortázar's *Hopscotch* (1963, English translation 1966), and continues with Carlos Fuentes's *The Death of Artemio Cruz* (1962, English translation 1964), Mario Vargas Llosa's *The Green House* (1966, English translation 1968), Gabriel García Márquez's *One Hundred Years of Solitude* – the first international bestseller in Latin American history (1967, English translation 1970) – and Roa Bastos's *I, The Supreme* (1974, English translation 1986). According to Sticca, the Boom was a period of literary experimentation and creativity in which Latin American authors received international notoriety, as was the case with Borges; this interacted with political and historical circumstances that helped to promote the translation of Latin American texts. The changing events in Cuba associated with the revolution and the subsequent Cuban missile crisis brought the island, the Caribbean and Latin America to the attention of the world; concomitant events in the United States played an important role in the emergence of the translation of the Boom novels, more specifically the fact that universities established new Latin American Studies programmes and strengthened existing ones to focus attention on the region. Literature in translation evolved as a way of understanding the complexity of thought and cultures of the US's neighbors of the South; an explosion of translations from Spanish to English also promoted the formation of translation centres and programmes in the United States (Sticca, 1991). One issue that still demands further studies by translation scholars is the absence of Brazilian literature from the Boom (for a study of the Latin American boom as a literary event, see "The 'Boom' of the 60s", in Gerald Martin, 1989; for a list of Latin American major writers and works available in English see "Primary Texts" in Gerald Martin, 1989; for a thematic classification of the Latin American "New Novel" see Nunn, 1991).

Another paradox to be addressed is that the Latin American context of 500 years of development of translation sensibility and thinking, as well as the presence of internationally-renowned translation theorists, does not necessarily correlate fully with the formal study of translation, be it *stricto sensu* (the instrumental training of interlingual translators) or *lato sensu* (the development of Translation Studies, involving descriptive studies of interlingual, intercultural, and intersemiotic translation), both relatively new in Spanish-speaking America and in Portuguese-speaking Brazil. In what follows, a brief summary of the state of the art is presented.

In Brazil, the University of São Paulo (USP) started in 1978 a translators' training course that has moved away from an instrumental view of translation towards a functional and cultural orientation; MAs and PhD degrees on Translation Studies are accommodated within the Department of Modern Languages. Among USP's postgraduate research lines, literary translation mainly from English is stressed. USP also publishes regularly a journal on Translation Studies, *Tradterm*.

Translation Studies is one of the majors of the Postgraduate

School of Applied Linguistics of the São Paulo State University of Campinas (UNICAMP) and has produced a large body of research on translation.

Still in Brazil, against the background of a lively debate between these two groups – the so-called pragmatists (the USP group) and the anti-logocentrists (the Campinas group) – a new segment of research was started at the Federal University of Minas Gerais as part of a PhD programme on Comparative Literature. Emphasis is placed on cultural contexts and the construction of translation archives.

The Federal University of Bahia, in Salvador, offers a specialization course on translation; comparative work on different translations of the same text is the outstanding feature of research.

Georges Bastin has suggested that university programmes aimed at the training of translators in Spanish Latin America first started in Argentina in 1945. Of special relevance is the work that has been carried out by the Colegio de Traductores de la Ciudad de Buenos Aires, which regularly publishes a translation journal, *VOCES*.

As for Centres for Training in Translation/Interpretation and Linguistics-oriented Research on Translation in Brazil, mention should be made of the Catholic University of Rio de Janeiro (PUC-Rio) which has had a pioneering role in the training of translators in Brazil, its activities having started in 1969. It offers BA degrees on translation or interpreting (English/Portuguese). The Faculdade Ibero-Americana in São Paulo has run for over two decades a course on translation and interpreting from English and Spanish; a BA degree in Translation (English and/or French) is offered at the São Paulo State University at São José do Rio Preto (UNESP); the MA in Applied Linguistics at the Federal University of Minas Gerais offers research on the discursive and cognitive bases of translation, interpretation, and intralingual translation. The Federal University of Rio de Janeiro carries out graduate research on translation.

Even though it is not always possible to draw a sharp line between linguistics – and literature-orientated courses, one could name other centres in Brazil for the training of translators or for linguistics-based research: the Catholic University of São Paulo (PUC/SP), the Federal University of Santa Catarina in Florianópolis, the University of Brasília, and the Federal University of Ouro Preto.

ELSE R.P VIEIRA

Further Reading

Barbosa, Heloisa Gonçalves and Lia Wyler, "Brazilian Tradition" in *The Routledge Encyclopedia of Translation Studies*, edited by Mona Baker, London and New York: Routledge, 1998

Bastin, Georges L., "Latin American Tradition" in *The Routledge Encyclopedia of Translation Studies*, edited by Mona Baker, London and New York: Routledge, 1998

Delisle, Jean and Judith Woodsworth (editors), *Translators through History*, Amsterdam and Philadelphia: John Benjamins, 1995

González, Aníbal, "Translation and Genealogy: *One Hundred Years of Solitude*" in *Gabriel García Márquez: New Readings*, translated by Bernard McGuirk and Richard Cardwell, Cambridge and New York: Cambridge University Press, 1987, pp. 65–80

Levine, Suzanne Jill, *The Subversive Scribe: Translating Latin American Fiction*, St Paul, Minnesota: Graywolf Press, 1991

Luis, William and Julio Rodríguez-Luis (editors), *Translating Latin America: Culture as Text*, Binghamton: Center for Research in Translation, State University of New York, 1991

McGuirk, Bernard, *Latin American Literature: Symptoms, Risks and Strategies of Post-Structuralist Criticism*, London and New York: Routledge, 1997

McGuirk, Bernard, "Falklands/Malvinas and/as Excess: On Simultaneous TransNation and the Poetry of War" in *Borges and Europe Revisited*, edited by Evelyn Fishburn, London: Institute of Latin American Studies, 1998

McGuirk, Bernard and Else R.P. Vieira (editors), *Retranslating Latin America: Dimensions of the Third Term*, Nottingham: University of Nottingham Press, 2000

Martin, Gerald, *Journeys through the Labyrinth: Latin American Fiction in the Twentieth Century*, London and New York: Verso, 1989

Nunn, Frederick M., " The Latin American 'New Novel' in Translation: Archival Source for the Dialogue between Literature and History" in *Translating Latin America: Culture as Text*, edited by William Luis and Julio Rodríguez-Luis, Binghamton: Center for Research in Translation, State University of New York, 1991

Reyes, Rogelio, "The Translation of Interlingual texts: A Chicano Example" in *Translating Latin America: Culture as Text*, edited by William Luis and Julio Rodríguez-Luis, Binghamton: Center for Research in Translation, State University of New York, 1991

Sticca, Sandro, "Culture as Text: The Cuban / Caribbean Connection" in *Translating Latin America: Culture as Text*, edited by William Luis and Julio Rodríguez-Luis, Binghamton: Center for Research in Translation, State University of New York, 1991

Vieira, Else R.P., "Por Uma Teoria Pós-Moderna da Tradução" (dissertation), Belo Horizonte, Universidade Federal de Minas Gerais, 1992; summary, as "Eine Postmoderne Übersetzungstheorie" in *Übersetzungsswissenchaft in Brasilien: Neue Beiträge zum Status von "Original" und Übersetzung*, edited by Michaela Wolf, Tübingen: Stauffenburg, 1996, pp. 103–116

Vieira, Else R.P., "A Postmodern Translational Aesthetics in Brazil" in *Translation Studies: An Interdiscipline*, edited by Mary Snell-Hornby, Franz Pöchhacker and Klaus Kaindl, Amsterdam: Benjamins, 1994, pp. 65–72

White, Steven F., "Translation in Nicaraguan Poetry as a Literary Weapon against Imperialism" in *Translating Latin America: Culture as Text*, edited by William Luis and Julio Rodríguez-Luis, Binghamton: Center for Research in Translation, State University of New York, 1991

Latvian Writers in English Translation

Latvian folklore goes back to very ancient times, while literature in the proper sense of the word developed only in the second half of the 19th century, in connection with the growth of nationalism and the desire for political independence. The glory and motherlode of Latvian culture and language has always been the folk-song (*daina*), and it has been said that "the chief inner problem ... of Latvian literature is: whether, to what extent and *in what way* a new contact has to be established with the folk-song" (Jānis Andrups and Vitauts Kalve, *Latvian Literature*, Stockholm, 1954, p. 92). Many writers either were and still are firmly rooted in the *daina* or at least have some perceptible connection to it. Attempts at complete independence from this tradition are relatively few.

Typically a *daina* consists of four lines of verse. Thus it is highly compact and economical in its mode of expression, yet a whole universe of observation and feeling is contained in it. The number of collected *dainas* and their variants is approximately one million, and although they directly reflect a traditional rural society, it can be truly said that "nothing human is foreign" to them. A strong feeling for nature, a prominent work ethic, and a whole spectrum of reactions to archetypal human experiences ensure their continued importance and vitality.

A notable characteristic of the *daina* is that it is chiefly the creation of women: it has been estimated that they have composed over 70 per cent of Latvian *dainas*. Indeed, women writers have been consistently prominent in all branches of Latvian literature.

The political vicissitudes endured by Latvia form one of the great tragedies of the 20th century. At the end of World War II a very large number of Latvians chose to go into exile rather than submit once again to Russian domination. Thus there developed two different strains of literature: the Soviet and the exilic. The former to a large extent lost its freedom of expression; the latter, its essential ties to the homeland. However, many writers on both sides continued to produce good work.

Latvian and Lithuanian form a particular group within the Indo-European family of languages. In itself, Latvian is not difficult to translate into English. However, since Latvian is highly inflected, and modern English is not, it is a challenge to the translator to do justice to the more varied syntax of Latvian. On the other hand, Latvian vocabulary is more limited than English, but (not unlike classical Latin) Latvian possesses a lean strength that runs the risk of sounding trite and obvious in translation. This is especially so with the *daina* and with poets who have a strong affinity to the folkloric. Still, Latvian folk-songs attracted the interest of English readers as early as Sir Walter Scott's rather free rendition of some of them (in *The Foreign Quarterly Review*, 8/15 (1831)).

Like other small countries, Latvia tends to be overlooked or ignored, and so does her literature. Although few nations have produced as much literary activity *per capita*, with a large number of works of real excellence, most of Latvia's writers remain untranslated into English. When a translation does come out in the West, it tends to be a labor of love, published by a small, out-of-the-way press and often nearly impossible to locate. In the Soviet bloc, on the other hand, the translation industry formed an important appendage of propaganda and was subsidized by the state. However, writers whose work was chosen for translation were for the most part adherents of the regime and intrinsically not very interesting.

The anthologies considered here give some indication of the variety and scope of Latvian literature. The works listed under particular authors represent a selection of texts available in English. Inclusion in this list is an indication of quality, while omission of authors and works is for the most part due to unavailability.

Anerauds (1967) puts most of his emphasis on Soviet writing, some of which is not very good. Still, there are some interesting items here, done by various translators.

Baumanis's anthology (1946) is for the most part a reprint of Matthews's *The Tricolour Sun* (which was subsequently revised as *A Century of Latvian Poetry*, see below). The additional explanatory material is helpful.

Benjamins (1985) offers admirably creative versions of a number of *dainas*. His work can be viewed as part of the folkloric tradition: he puts together compound poems that synthesize already existing material. He calls his method "agglomeration and selection", and comes up with poetry as fresh and exciting in English as in the prototype. It is difficult to think of a better way of making the *daina* accessible to the English reader.

Cedrins (1984) includes poets writing in exile as well as Soviet poets, among the latter the outstanding Čaklais and Ziedonis (see below). This anthology is the work of many translators, some the poets themselves. The quality of translation varies.

Despite prosy renditions, Katzenelenbogen (1935) is indispensable. Not only is his the first attempt to translate a large variety of *dainas* into English, but the essays that introduce the anthology provide very important information on the background of Latvian folk poetry, and the first part of the book, which deals with the Lithuanian *daina*, furnishes indispensable material for comparison and contrast with the sister culture.

Matthews's *A Century of Latvian Poetry* (1957) is a revised version of his *The Tricolour Sun* (Cambridge, 1936). This is a basic anthology of representative poems. It suffers somewhat from the fact that the translator superimposes his stylistic imprint upon the style of some 71 poets, many extremely different from one another.

Rubulis's anthology (1964) contains samples of some of Latvia's prose classics, by authors such as Jānis Akuraters (1876–1937), whose "The Young Farmhand's Summer" is included here, Kārlis Skalbe (1879–1945), sometimes called "the Latvian Andersen", Edvards Virza (1883–1940), and others. The translations are by various hands and vary in quality. Included is "An Historical Survey of Latvian Literature".

Speirs (1973) is an important translator of Latvian literature, but this anthology is inconvenient to anyone who wants to make use of the parallel text, since translation does not face the original but is placed on the following page. The poets represented do not sound sufficiently different from one another.

Straumanis (1986) translates two Latvian plays: Jānis Rainis's (1865–1929) *Fire and Night* and a more modern work, Mārtiņš Zīverts's *Power*. The former is one of the most famous works in

Latvian literature, a call to freedom based on legendary material and written by Latvia's most important poet. *Power* too is a remarkable play. The quality of the translation is good.

We come now to individual authors. Stahnke (1984) appends her translations of two of Aspazija's (1868–1945) plays to her biographic study of this important poet and dramatist. The translations are highly readable and should be stageworthy as well.

Čaklais is one of the most interesting contemporary poets writing in Latvia. Speirs's version (1987) is of high quality.

The power of Eglītis's indignation over human suffering during and after World War II, as well as his striking imagery, are well served by Fearnley (1984), although there is no attempt to render the poet's forceful use of rhyme.

Perhaps more than any other Latvian poet in this century, Lazda (1902–57) expresses the spirit of the *daina*. Her powerful simplicity is difficult to transfer to another language. Snikere (1986), herself a well-known Latvian poet, manages better than anyone else could.

The chapter (Pavlovskis-Petit, 1996) from Mauriņa's (1897–1978) autobiographic novel is part of a translation in progress. Mauriņa's recollections, written concurrently in a German and a Latvian version, paint a vivid picture of Latvia as part of the Russian Empire, during independence, Soviet takeover, and Nazi occupation.

Skalbe's tales are part of every Latvian child's upbringing, and "Pussy's Water Mill" (perhaps better titled "Little Cat's Mill") is one of the best (Matthews, 1952).

Ziedonis, an important contemporary poet who lives in Latvia, is well translated by Callaghan (1987). Perhaps most interesting in this collection are his parables.

Zīverts's play *The Jester* (Bēziņa-Felsberga, 1964) is of particular interest to English readers because it deals with Shakespeare and the "Dark Lady". Falstaff is one of the characters – a missionary.

ZOJA PAVLOVSKIS-PETIT

Translations

Anthologies

Anerauds, Jānis (editor), *Amberland: Selection from Latvian Poetry and Prose*, Riga: Liesma, 1967

Baumanis, Arturs, *Latvian Poetry: An Anthology of Latvian Lyrics in English Versions*, Augsburg: A. Baumanis, 1946

Benjamins, Eso, *Dearest Goddess: Translations from Latvian Folk Poetry*, Arlington, Virginia: Current Nine, 1985

Cedrins, Inara (editor), *Contemporary Latvian Poetry*, Iowa City: University of Iowa Press, 1984

Katzenelenbogen, Uriah (editor), *The Daina: An Anthology of Lithuanian and Latvian Folk-Songs*, with a critical study and preface, Chicago: Lithuanian News Publishing, 1935

Matthews, W.K. (compiler and translator), *A Century of Latvian Poetry*, London: John Calder, 1957

Rubulis, Aleksis (editor), *Latvian Literature*, Toronto: Daugavas Vanags, 1964

Speirs, Ruth, *Let Us Get Acquainted / Iepazīsimies: Nine Soviet Latvian Poets* (parallel texts), Riga: Zvaigzne, 1973

Straumanis, Alfreds (editor), *Fire and Night: Five Baltic Plays*, Prospect Heights, Illinois: Waveland Press, 1986

Individual Authors

Aspazija, "The Silver Veil" and "The Serpent's Bride", translated by A.B. Stahnke, in *Aspazija: Her Life and Her Drama*, Lanham, Maryland: University Press of America, 1984, pp. 177–253 and 255–348

Čaklais, Māris, *Premonition* (parallel texts), translated by Ruth Speirs, Riga: Liesma, 1987

Eglītis, Andrejs, *Gallows over Europe: Poems* (partly parallel text), translated by Robert Fearnley, London: Calder, and New York: Riverrun Press, 1984

Lazda, Zinaīda, *A Green Leaf*, translated by Velta Snikere and Robert Fearnley, Maidstone, Kent: Woodcutter Press, 1986

Mauriņa, Zenta, "The Cyclops, Dooshecka, and Other Teachers", translated by Zoja Pavlovskis-Petit, *The Antioch Review*, 54/1 (1996), pp. 46–59

Skalbe, Kārlis, *Pussy's Water Mill*, translated by W.K. Matthews, Stockholm: Goppers, 1952

Ziedonis, Imants, *Flowers of Ice*, translated by Barry Callaghan, Toronto: Exile Editions, 1987; Riverdale-on-Hudson, New York: Sheep Meadow Press, 1990

Zīverts, Mārtiņš, *The Jester*, translated by Lucija Bēziņa-Felsberga, Sydney: Sala Press, 1964

Further Reading

Pavlovskis-Petit, Zoja, "The Problem of Diminutives or How to Do Justice to the 'Daina'", *Translation Perspectives*, 3 (1987), pp. 4–14

See also the preface to Benjamins's version of *dainas*

Comte de Lautréamont 1846–1870

French prose poet

Biography

Although there have been a number of fanciful biographical reconstructions, only a bare outline of Lautréamont's life is known to us. He was born Isidore Ducasse in Montevideo, Uruguay, 4 April 1846, the son of a French consular official. From 1859 to 1862, he was a boarder at the Imperial Lycée at Tarbes in the Hautes-Pyrénées, where he was two years behind for his age. In 1863, aged 17, he entered the Lycée at Pau which he left two years later without taking his *baccalauréat*. Following a brief visit to Montevideo in the summer of 1867, Ducasse, with his father's financial assistance, established himself in Paris as a man of letters. He wrote, and published in fragments from 1869, the lyrical, phantasmagorical poetic prose fragments, *Les Chants de Maldoror*, which were to influence the Surrealists. A collection of *Poésies* came out in 1870. He died in Paris, 24 November 1870.

Translations

Les Chants de Maldoror, 1868–69

Knight, Paul, *Maldoror, and Poems*, Harmondsworth: Penguin, 1978

Lykiard, Alexis, *Lautréamont's Maldoror*, London: Allison and Busby, 1970; reprinted in *Maldoror and The Complete Works of the Comte de Lautréamont*, translated by Lykiard, Cambridge, Massachusetts: Exact Change, 1994

Rodker, John, *The Lay of Maldoror*, with an introduction by Rémy de Gourmont, London: privately printed for subscribers of the Casanova Society, 1924

Wernham, Guy, *Maldoror by Lautréamont*, New York: New Directions, 1943; with a preface by James Laughlin, 1965

Poésies, 1870

Knight, Paul, *Maldoror, and Poems*, 1978

Lykiard, Alexis, *Poesies and Complete Miscellanies* (bilingual edition), London: Allison and Busby, 1978; and in *Maldoror and The Complete Works of the Comte de Lautréamont*, translated by Lykiard, 1994

Wernham, Guy, in *Maldoror by Lautréamont*, translated by Wernham, 1943

The first chant of *Les Chants de Maldoror* was privately printed by Balitout Questroy et Cie in 1868 and had no author's name on the title page. It elicited no critical attention except for a brief notice in an obscure periodical. Ducasse presumably entered it for some form of spurious competition organized by a Bordeaux printer who reprinted it the following year in a miscellaneous collection entitled *Parfums de l'âme*. In 1869, Ducasse contracted with the publisher Albert Lacroix to bring out a complete edition of the six chants, partially financed by the author. Lacroix, fearing prosecution, delayed putting the volume on sale until the following year. In the event, *Les Chants de Maldoror* by the "comte de Lautréaumont" attracted then only a single notice. It is commonly thought that this pseudonym derives from a *frénétique* novel published by Eugène Sue in 1838: *Latréaumont*. Although Max Waller, the founder of *La Jeune Belgique*, managed to interest several major writers in Ducasse in the mid-1880s (especially Léon Bloy and J.-K. Huysmans), the turning point for his literary reputation occurred towards the end of the second decade of the 20th century: André Breton published Ducasse's *Poésies* in the surrealist journal *Littérature* in 1919 (these texts had not been reprinted since 1870, when they had been issued in pamphlet form); in 1920 *Poésies* appeared in book form with a preface by Philippe Soupault; and, also in 1920, the publisher La Sirène brought out a new edition of *Les Chants de Maldoror*. Since then, the nightmarish vision of the comte de Lautréamont has established itself as a major work of the 19th-century imagination.

Although LYKIARD (1994 edition of his 1970 translation) is scathing about earlier translations of *Les Chants de Maldoror*, Isidore Ducasse has been better served by his translators than some other authors. However, Lykiard is correct to point out RODKER's (1924) tendency to archaism (still a common tendency in some literary translations of the period), occasional misreadings, and even misprints – e.g. "Vous, dont le calme enviable ne peut pas faire plus que d'embellir le faciès ... " (VI, i) becomes "You whose enviable calm cannot but embellish the faeces ... " for "features, aspect". None the less, given the difficulty of the original text, Rodker's version is not without stylistic interest – which is perhaps only to be expected of a translator who published Ezra Pound, was partly responsible for an edition of Joyce's *Ulysses*, and was a poet in his own right.

Lykiard equally lambasts WERNHAM's version (1943), noting numerous errors and even a "difficulty with the English language". Again, although there is some justification for such a remark, the case is overstated. Wernham's translation generally reads well, largely (though not entirely) eschewing the overwrought archaicism of Rodker. Wernham's edition, moreover, contains the first English translation of the *Poésies*.

LYKIARD's translation (1970), the third to appear, provides a close reading of the original text that is stylistically accomplished (as might be expected of a professional translator who made some mark as a novelist in his own right in the 1960s and 1970s). The 1994 edition is, moreover, the most complete English-language version, providing a translation not only of all Ducasse's major texts but also of some more marginal pieces, and a thorough critical apparatus, including such material as the interview with Paul Lespès, who had attended the lycée at Pau with Ducasse and who described his former schoolfellow as a cheerless and taciturn individual already drawn to extravagances of thought and style.

The weakest of the four versions is perhaps that of KNIGHT (1978), which has a tendency to sacrifice accuracy for easy readability. Not only does this version contain numerous errors and omissions, but it has an inadequate scholarly apparatus – the translator even failing to note which edition of *Les Chants de Maldoror* served as the source text.

TERRY HALE

Further Reading

De Jonge, Alex, *Nightmare Culture: Lautréamont and Les Chants de Maldoror*, London: Secker and Warburg, and New York: St Martin's Press, 1973

Nesselroth, Peter W., *Lautréamont's Imagery: A Stylistic Approach*, Geneva: Droz, 1969

See also the "Introduction: Preface without Memoirs" and "Note on the Text and Translation" in Lykiard, *Maldoror and The Complete Works of the Comte de Lautréamont*, 1994, pp. 1–19, 20–24 (and Lykiard's notes, pp. 289–334)

Lazarillo de Tormes

La vida de Lazarillo de Tormes, published 1554

Anonymous 16th-century Spanish novel. As the opportunist central character, starting out in life as guide to a blind beggar, struggles alongside other rascals to survive harsh treatment and many vicissitudes, the text satirizes Spanish mores and institutions, especially the church and clergy.

Editions

Burgos y Amberes Alcalá de Henares (editor), *La vida de Lazarillo de Tormes y de sus fortunas y adversidades*, 1554

Jones, R.O. (editor), *La vida de Lazarillo de Tormes y sus fortunas y adversidades*, with an introduction and notes, Manchester: Manchester University Press, 1963

Translations

Alpert, Michael, *Lazarillo de Tormes*, with an introduction, in *Two Spanish Picaresque Novels*, translated by Alpert, Harmondsworth: Penguin, 1969

Anonymous, *The Pleasant Adventures of the Witty Spaniard Lazarillo de Tormes*, London: J. Leake, 1688

Anonymous, *The Life and Adventures of Lazarillo de Tormes Written by Himself*, London, 1708

Anonymous, *The Life and Adventures of Lazarillo de Tormes, Written by Himself*, London: R. & J. Bonwick and R. Wilkin, J. Walthoe and T. Ward, 1726

Anonymous, *The Life and Adventures of Lazarillo Gonsales, Surnamed De Tormes, Written by Himself*, London, 1777

Anonymous, *The Life and Adventures of Lazarillo De Tormes*, 2 vols, London: J. Bell, 1789

Cohen, J.M., *Blind Man's Boy*, with *Two Cautionary Tales* by Cervantes, London: New English Library, 1962

How, Louis, *The Life of Lazarillo de Tormes and His Fortunes and Adversities*, with an introduction and notes by Charles Philip Wagner, New York: Kennerley, 1917

Lorente, M.J., *Lazarillo de Tormes, His Life, Fortunes, Misadventures*, Boston, 1924

Markham, Clements, *The Life of Lazarillo de Tormes, His Fortunes and Adversities*, London: A. & C. Black, 1908

Markley, J. Gerald, *The Life of Lazarillo de Tormes: His Fortunes and Adversities*, with an introduction by Allan G. Haladay, New York: Liberal Arts Press, 1954

Merwin, W.S., *The Life of Lazarillo De Tormes: His Fortunes and Adversities*, with an introduction by Leonardo C. de Morelos, New York: Doubleday, 1962

Onís, Harriet de, *The Life of Lazarillo de Tormes, His Fortunes and Adversities*, with an introduction, Great Neck, New York: Barron, 1959

Roscoe, Thomas, *The Life and Adventures of Lazarillo de Tormes* in his *The Spanish Novelists: A Series of Tales from the Earliest Period to the Close of the Seventeenth Century*, London: Bentley, 1832; New York: Warne, 1880

Rowland, David, *The Pleasaunt Historie of Lazarillo de Tormes, a Spaniard, Wherein is Conteined His Marvellous Deeds and Life, with ye Strange Adventures Happened to Him in ye Service of Sundery Masters*, London, 1576; edited by J.E.V. Crofts, Oxford: Blackwell, 1924

Singleton, Mack Hendricks, *Lazarillo de Tormes* in *Masterpieces of the Spanish Golden Age*, edited by Angel Flores, New York: Holt Rinehart, 1957

It is a tribute to the enduring popularity of *Lazarillo de Tormes* that there currently exist some 16 translations and more than 75 full or partial editions in English. The translations are listed above, although only those of particular merit or interest will be discussed.

La vida de Lazarillo de Tormes was the first of the typically Spanish genre of realistic fiction known as the picaresque. It was a great success in Spain, and numerous editions were printed. The first English translation appeared just over 20 years after its publication in Spanish, and quickly became popular in England too. In her book *Antecedents of the English Novel 1400–1600*, Margaret Schlauch notes that much of English literature of the 1570s and 1580s was stimulated by Spanish sources: "Its prime source was the anonymous classic *Lazarillo De Tormes*", whose realism, vivacity and freshness contrasted with classically inspired works.

The first translation was by David ROWLAND of Anglesey in 1576 and was used extensively for a long time. It seems likely that he used the Amberes edition of 1554, plus the French translation *L'histoire plaisante et facetieuse du Lazare de Tormes espagnol* (1561). Rowland selects judiciously from the French version, but does not hesitate to give his own rendering when the French is incorrect or infelicitous, with names and places derived mostly from the Castilian text. The translation benefits from regular explanatory marginal notes, and a certain amount of new material is added, usually for clarification, comment or explanation. In his survey of editions and translations of the work in English, Julio-Cesar Santoyo makes a comprehensive comparison of the Rowland text with the Spanish. Overall Santoyo feels that the English is more verbose than the very concise original, giving the example of "Hideputa!", which Rowland expands to "A whoreson, art thou afraid of thy father?", among others. This verbosity can sometimes be attributed to difficulty in rendering a passage, lack of a good English equivalent, or to an opportunity to embroider the text with witticisms. Rowland frequently injects adjectives and adverbs not in the original – "Vinose a vivir a la ciudad" becomes "He came immediately to this noble Citie", and his style contains characterizing pairs of synonyms such as "like a true and faithful man" for "como leal criado". In general, Rowland preserves the humorous gravity of the subject with a generally accurate rendering, occasionally but not unduly influenced by Spanish grammatical usage.

This translation was not questioned until the publication of an ANONYMOUS English version in 1726. The edition was illustrated with 20 copper cuts. In it the translator speaks contemptuously of Rowland's version: "It was done in English many years ago, but the style is obsolete and the story much mangled." The translation varies considerably from Rowland's text, being written in far more modern English, and J.E.V. Crofts, who produced a 1924 edition of *Lazarillo*, described it as "saucy in style and paraphrastic in method". It is rhythmic and contains many added phrases. As in Rowland's translation, the mock-biblical style of parts of the text is not retained, nor is significant punning, for example, in the analogy between the bull's horns and the devil in the first tractatus. It also includes spurious second parts.

The ANONYMOUS translation published in 1789 by J. Bell differed from its predecessors in omitting an introduction and Lazarillo's prologue, as did the remaining 18th-century editions. This version is considered to be a bad translation, which loses a lot of the humour in its literalness, and is remote from the Spanish in a number of places. Some of the Spanish names are unrecognizable – Gelves becomes the battle of Geleas, and Escalona is Evealona.

Thomas ROSCOE's translation of 1832 lacks the original prologue, although the text is not divided into chapters, but retains the "Tratado" headings of the Spanish. The next translation did not appear until 1908, and was made by Sir Clements MARKHAM. There are extensive notes to the translation, plus marginal guide notes, and in parts the text reads fluidly and naturally. He makes a clumsy attempt to convey the pun on the bull's horn (diablo) and the devil mentioned above: "... and gave me a tremendous blow against the devil of a bull", which has the wrong associations in English, and there is no attempt to mimic the mock-biblical style when it occurs. Many omissions in the translation are for the sake of delicacy, and much of the crude unpleasantness of story is smoothed over and lost.

There were several subsequent translations during the 20th century, including those of HOW (1917), LORENTE (1924), MARKLEY (1954), SINGLETON (1957), ONÍS (1959), COHEN (1962) and MERWIN (1962). The most significant 20th-century translation is the one by ALPERT (1969). He uses R.O. Jones's 1963 edition of the text. The translation is the best-known and most widely-read version today, descibed in a review in the *Times Literary Supplement* as "careful but plain". Alpert identifies translation difficulties in his introduction to the text, principally the colloquial, racy language interspersed with elegant literary mannerisms. He attempts to use current English without adopting archaisms. Much of the punning is lost, and the language is prosaic and commonplace, using the rhythms of speech. The intentional biblical echoes in "oro ni plata no te puedo dar" is rendered dully as "I won't make you a rich man, but I can show you how to make a living." Alpert uses the vocabulary of old Spanish currency in the text, with a prior explanatory note. Quevedo's picaresque novel *El buscon* (*The Swindler*) is published in the same volume, and the translations have done much to bring the Spanish picaresque within the reach of the contemporary reader.

ELIZABETH DRAYSON MACDONALD

Further Reading

Flores, Ángel, *Spanish Literature in English Translation: A Bibliographical Syllabus*, New York: Wilson, 1926

Pane, Remigio Ugo, *English Translations from the Spanish, 1484–1943: A Bibliography*, New Brunswick, New Jersey: Rutgers University Press, 1944

Santoyo, Julio-Cesar, *Ediciones y traducciones inglesas del Lazarillo de Tormes (1568–1977)*, Vitoria: Colegio Universitario de Alava, 1978

Schlauch, Margaret, *Antecedents of the English Novel, 1400–1600: From Chaucer to Deloney*, Warsaw: PWN / Polish Scientific Publishers, and London: Oxford University Press, 1963

Underhill, John Garrett, *Spanish Literature in the England of the Tudors*, New York, Macmillan, 1899; reprinted New York: AMS Press, 1971

Siegfried Lenz 1926–

German novelist, short-story writer, dramatist and essayist

Biography

Born 17 March 1926 in Lyck, at that time in East Prussia, now in Poland. After a short spell towards the end of World War II serving in the German navy, he studied philosophy and literature at Hamburg University from 1945 to 1948. He then became a newspaper reporter and editor, got married in 1949 and turned to freelance writing. His first major piece of fiction was the novel *Es waren Habichte in der Luft* [There Were Hawks in the Sky] (1951). This work, written when Lenz was literary editor of *Die Welt*, gained him the Rene Schickele prize of 1952, the first of many recognitions bestowed on him through the years.

That text was followed by a steady output of novels and stories, as well as several plays for radio and stage. Many of Lenz's works have not yet been translated into English.

Lenz celebrated his 70th birthday in 1996 with the publication of a collection of stories, *Ludmilla*. The appearance of another novel – his 11th – *Die Auflehnung* [The Rebellion] immediately afterwards confirmed his continuing creative urge. Lenz is one of the most popular and successful of German prose writers overall of the second half of the 20th century. He is an author of consistent production and consistent level of performance in a traditionalist realist manner of story-telling, an exponent of the "Heimatroman" (hometown novel, novel of provincial life) in the positive sense (Bullivant, 1987).

Translations

Novels

Stadtgespräch, 1963

Bullock, Michael, *The Survivor*, New York: Hill and Wang, 1965

Deutschstunde, 1968

Kaiser, Ernst and Eithne Wilkins, *The German Lesson*, London: Macdonald, 1971; New York: Hill and Wang, 1972

Das Vorbild, 1973

Parmée, Douglas, *An Exemplary Life*, New York: Hill and Wang, and London: Secker and Warburg, 1976

Heimatmuseum, 1978

Winston, Krishna, *The Heritage*, New York: Hill and Wang, and London: Secker and Warburg, 1981

Der Verlust, 1981

Read, Ralph R., *The Breakdown*, London: Methuen, 1986

Exerzierplatz, 1985

Skelton, Geoffrey, *Training Ground*, London: Methuen, and New York: Holt, 1991

Short Stories

Lukas, sanftmütiger Knecht, 1958

Heller, R.P., *Lucas, Gentle Servant* in *German Narrative Prose*, vol. 3, edited by Werner Rehfeld, London: Wolff, and New York: Dufour, 1968

Das Feuerschiff, 1960

Bullock, Michael, *The Lightship*, London: Heinemann, and New York: Hill and Wang, 1962; London: Methuen, 1986

Die Erzählungen 1949–1984, 1986

Mitchell, Breon, *The Selected Stories of Siegfried Lenz*, New York: New Directions, 1989

Two strong features of Siegfried Lenz's writing are the sense of regional dimension (whether the setting is in his native Masuria, or in the far north of Germany, in Norway, or indeed in Africa), which permits him to depict marginal locations and situations; and a preoccupation with World War II (he had briefly seen service in the navy towards the end before deserting to the woods of Denmark) and its aftermath, which enables him to centre on the thematic problem of overcoming the past: of facing up to the question of personal and collective guilt and to the lessons of history.

This is the essence of Lenz's fifth novel *Stadtgespräch* (literally "Towntalk") (1963), the first to be translated into English, by Michael BULLOCK in 1965 under the title *The Survivor*. The narrator tells of an incident he witnessed in a town in an occupied northern European country during World War II. Forty-four civilian hostages, taken by the enemy after a Resistance attack on a German general, die because Daniel, the Resistance fighters' leader, does not give himself up. To surrender, or not, is the moral dilemma posed in the novel both at the time the events take place and after the war, as different characters relate the incident from their point of view. Lenz makes it clear that such moral issues are ongoing and have no simple answer.

Michael BULLOCK had already translated, as *The Lightship* in 1962, the first of Lenz's writings to appear in English, the title story of a collection that had been published in German in 1960 (*Das Feuerschiff*). In this tale of a lightship taken over by gangsters, the translation conveys faithfully and effectively the element of violence and emotional tension, evoking powerfully the psychological effects of guilt.

It was his sixth novel, *Deutschstunde* (1968), that brought Lenz true international recognition. To date two million copies have been printed in German and it has been translated into 25 foreign languages. The English translation – now by KAISER & WILKINS – appeared in London in 1971 and in New York in 1972, under the nearly literally rendered title of *The German Lesson*. The central character, young Siggi Jepsen, a policeman's son, is serving in the early 1950s a three-year sentence for theft, in a reformatory situated on a symbolically remote island in the river Elbe. He has to compose an essay in German on the pleasures of duty. As he writes, the story of his complex life between 1943 and 1946 is set against the lives of a range of other people who had also lived in the changing Germany of the last part of World War II and afterwards; thus are posed the unresolved problems arising from conflict between individual and collective ties and responsibilities.

Five years later, yet a different translator, Douglas PARMÉE, produced his version of Lenz's next novel *Das Vorbild* (literally, "The Model"; 1973), which appeared on both sides of the Atlantic as *An Exemplary Life* in 1976. Here again, society's shortcomings are exposed alongside introspective reflections, now those of three characters, differentiated by their age, class and politics, trying to find a suitable role model to propose, in a textbook, for emulation.

Another five years. Another novel. Another translator. This time the English version, *The Heritage* (1981), of *Heimatmuseum* (literally "Local History Museum"; 1978), was by Krishna WINSTON. Another story of conflicting motives, of moral choices to be made in changing times, is told in flashback by the museum's curator/destroyer.

The novel *Der Verlust* (literally "Loss" – in this case loss of speech, of the power to communicate; 1981), was translated, as *The Breakdown* (1986), by yet a different person, Ralph R. READ.

Training Ground (1991) duly followed the publication of the original novel *Exerzierplatz* (1985). The English version this time was by Geoffrey SKELTON. The recalling by the narrator, Bruno Messmer, of 30 years working as an employee at a large tree-nursery enables Lenz to introduce memories of World War II as well as pointing up aspects of the contemporary German social scene such as perverse antagonism towards outsiders, and obstructive bureaucracy.

In between Lenz's consistent production of the novels have also come numerous collections of short stories. Subsequent to the appearance of *The Lightship*, other individual stories have been translated sporadically into English over the years. For example, *Lucas, Gentle Servant* was translated by R.P. HELLER in *German Narrative Prose*, published in London and New York in 1968. But the most comprehensive collection of Lenz's short stories in English translation is the US-published *Selected Stories*, edited and translated by Breon MITCHELL (1989).

School texts in Germany and abroad testify to Lenz's popularity at all levels. He is the subject of university dissertations. That six, i.e. half, of his novels have been translated into

English, as well as a selection of his short stories, is testimony to Lenz's ready acceptance by readers in the English-speaking world, who, curiously, must still await the first major biographical and critical study of Lenz in English. Colin Russ (1967), one of the pioneer English Germanists who have been working on Lenz, did much to stimulate interest in him in the UK.

Lenz has remained faithful in general to one German publisher, Hoffmann and Campe. His work has appeared on the English market, however, with a variety of publishers and almost invariably different translators, as market forces dictate the book trade industry. The translators of the major novels have in the main been tried and tested figures of merit who have essentially succeeded in transcribing the meaning and spirit of the original into English. What is noticeable are the omissions from Lenz translations of "bits and pieces" of the German, their absence being due to editorial and publishing demands, so that we read, for example, on the cover of *The Heritage*: "The English Language edition has been shortened with cooperation of the author". The later major novels normally run, in any case, to over 400 pages!

IAN HILTON

Further Reading

Bullivant, Keith (editor), *The Modern German Novel*, Leamington Spa and New York: Berg, 1987
Halverson, Rachel J., *Historiography and Fiction: Siegfried Lenz and the "Historikerstreit"*, New York: Peter Lang, 1990
Murdoch, Brian O. and Malcolm Read, *Siegfried Lenz*, London: Wolff, 1978
Prager, P. (editor), *Zeit der Schuldlosen* (play by Lenz), London: Harrap, 1966
Russ, C.A.H. (editor), *Das Wrack and Other Stories*, London: Heinemann, 1967

Giacomo Leopardi 1798–1837

Italian poet, essayist, and scholar

Biography

Born 29 June 1798 at Recanati, Italy, the eldest son of the Conte Montaldo Leopardi and the Marchesa Adelaide Antici. His early life, up to late 1822, was spent in the socially restricted environs of his parents' household at Recanati. His education was entirely private, based mainly on a self-imposed regimen of study in his father's library, the resources of which, while sometimes romantically exaggerated, were considerable. His programme of study proved physically and psychologically ruinous – from the age of 17 he was an invalid, with damaged eyesight and a hunched back, and a depressive – but it was precociously productive: of editorial and philological work, and of translations. Those efforts brought him the friendship of the literary scholar Pietro Giordani, and the patronage of the great German philologist and historian Niebuhr. Pleading the insecurity of his health, Leopardi refused offers of academic employment at Berlin and Bonn. He experienced three unhappy and improbable infatuations with women. A measure of absolute financial independence was given, from 1825, by commissions from the Milanese publisher Stella. From then until 1828 he lived variously in Bologna, Florence and Pisa, doing scholarly work, adding to the *Canti* [Lyrics], and writing the essays and dialogues that made up for most of the 19th century the basis of his reputation. After a spell at home in Recanati, the charity of friends allowed him to escape to Rome, to Florence, and finally, in the company of the firmest and most charitable of his friends, Antonio Ranieri, to Naples. He died there 14 June 1837, a fortnight before his 39th birthday. The collection of his work was superintended by Ranieri and appeared in Naples in 1845, the basis of modern editions of the poetry and much of the prose.

Translations

Collections (complete or near complete)

Bickersteth, Geoffrey L., *The Poems of Leopardi* (parallel texts), with an introduction, Cambridge: Cambridge University Press, 1923; reprinted New York: Russell and Russell, 1973
Cliffe, Francis Henry, *The Poems of Leopardi*, London: Remington, 1893; 2nd enlarged edition, London: John Macqueen, 1903
Morrison, J.M., *The Poems ("Canti") of Leopardi*, London: Gay and Bird, 1900
Nichols, J.G., *The Canti; with a Selection of His Prose*, Manchester: Carcanet, 1994
Townsend, Frederick, *The Poems of Giacomo Leopardi*, New York and London: Putnam, 1887
Tusiani, Joseph, *Leopardi's Canti*, Fasano: Schena, 1998
Whitfield, John Humphreys, *Canti* (bilingual edition), with an introduction, Naples: Scalabrini, 1962; Manchester: Manchester University Press, 1967

Major Selections

Barricelli, Jean Pierre, *Poems*, New York: Las Américas, 1963
Cloriston, Henry, *Poems in Prose and Verse*, London: Postal Literary Alliance, 1907
Flores, Angel (editor), *Leopardi: Poems and Prose*, Bloomington: Indiana University Press, 1966
Grennan, Eamon, *Selected Poems of Giacomo Leopardi*, with

an introduction, Dublin: Dedalus, 1995; Princeton, New Jersey: Princeton University Press, 1997
Heath-Stubbs, John, *Poems from Giacomo Leopardi*, with an introduction, London: Lehmann 1946; revised version, with Iris Origo, in *Selected Prose and Poetry*, edited, with an introduction, by Origo and Heath-Stubbs, London: Oxford University Press, 1966, New York: New American Library, 1967
Jack, R.D.S., M.L. McLaughlin and C. Whyte, *Leopardi: A Scottis Quair*, Edinburgh: Edinburgh University Press, 1987
Martin, Theodore, *Poems (Canti)*, Edinburgh: Blackwood, 1904
Oliphant, Margaret, *Blackwood's Magazine*, 98 (1865) pp. 459–80, and *Cornhill Magazine*, 34 (1876) pp. 341–57; these version are selectively reprinted in "Margaret Oliphant's Leopardi" by Robert Cummings, *Translation and Literature*, 7/1 (1998) pp. 75–98
Trevelyan, R.C., *Translations from Leopardi*, Cambridge: Cambridge University Press, 1941

Minor Selections
Lawton, Paul, *Canti*, edited and with an introduction by Franco Fortini, Dublin: UCD Foundation for Italian Studies, 1996
Lowell, Robert, "Two Translations from Giacomo Leopardi", *Kenyon Review*, 23 (1961) pp. 571–74; third translation in *Imitations*, New York: Farrar Straus, 1961, London: Faber, 1962
Pound, Ezra, "Leopardi: Her Monument", in *Canzoni of Ezra Pound*, London: Mathews, 1911
Weiss, Theodore (editor), *Quarterly Review*, Leopardi number, 1956
Wrangham, Francis, "To Italy", in *Winter's Wreath*, vol. 5, edited by "A.H.", London, 1832; the text in "Archdeacon Francis Wrangham and a Poem by Giacomo Leopardi" by Frederick May, *Italian Studies*, 19 (1964) pp. 83–90

Ever since G.H. Lewes first wrote about him in 1848 until the present, Giacomo Leopardi has been reckoned unaccessible in English. Brown's 1887 review of Townsend isolates a number of difficulties in the translator's way: that Leopardi is a subjective and abstract poet; and that he is a rhetorical poet, meaning partly that he works selfconsciously in a tradition, partly that he is a "poet of the ear", exploiting aural patterns so intricate as to frustrate replication. In seeming contradiction, Rizzardi (1961), reviewing Lowell's imitations, adds the difficulty of reproducing in English a language poetically so unobvious. Leopardi has been compared with many English poets, but he has no parallel: there is no ready informing model for the translator. Eamon Grennan quotes the observation that the translator of the *Canti* who suspects that his own powers are not of the order of Milton's in *Lycidas* or *Samson Agonistes* "would do well to stick to plain prose".

The first translation into English is of the *All'Italia* by Francis WRANGHAM (1832), still writing when the great ode had a convincing life in English. Significantly, two other 19th-century attempts to translate Leopardi's odes – of the *Inno ai Patriarchi* by the Etonian master Geralomo Picchioni (Eton, 1844); and of the *Sopra il monumento di Dante* by the Hellenist Richard Jebb (Cambridge, 1898) – are into Latin and Greek. After Wrangham, English versions of Leopardi's canzone metres, if observed at all, rely on never fully naturalized variants of them. Margaret OLIPHANT's very unpedantic notions of canzone metre actually supply (1865, 1876) the most convincing English, at least for Leopardi's idylls.

TOWNSEND's version (1887) is generally faithful to the sense but not to the manner. Brown's review rates highest the translation of the minor *Imitazione* for its having "something of the feeling of Blake": it is not much like Leopardi. Townsend's is the first complete Leopardi but, from its inattentiveness to the manner, gives no sense of Leopardi's range. Neither does CLIFFE (1893), who, from a conviction of the irrelevance of Leopardi's rhetoric, presents blandly faithless adaptations. MORRISON (1900) offers a corrective to this standard inattentiveness, advertising a translation "close without being servile"; but its strenuous fidelity leaves the syntax often tangled and the sense obscure. BICKERSTETH's version (1923), still valued after more than 75 years, remains the most ambitious translation and, with its supplementary critical matter, among the most useful accounts of Leopardi. It aims to be faithful "to the form (metre, cadence, rhyme, sound, accent, rhythm, tone, style, etc.) of the original". Its manner has dated, but its ambitions offer more of an insight into Leopardi's enterprise than a rendering faithful to the sense. WHITFIELD's version (1962) is anxiously faithful to the sense, but the manner is unanxiously flat. Singh (1990) comes close to recommending it as a crib. NICHOLS (1994) includes selections from the prose, the dryness of which offsets the dominant *vago* of the verse, played up by delicate assonantal effects. This may be the most intelligent Leopardi in English, and its poetical unevenness is apparent only as a falling away from real incidental achievement. That its ingenuities are not obvious or sustained, as Bickersteth's are, may be a testimony to its naturalness. I have not seen TUSIANI's versions (1998), but they are likely to achieve wider distribution than they presently enjoy.

The monotony of 20th-century selections is almost programmatically emphatic. MARTIN's 22 translations (1904) sacrifice the sense to a generalized, faintly Wordsworthian fluency, but he often quite cunningly imitates Leopardian schemes. CLORISTON (1907) on the other hand, often ponderous and uncertain, is clearly happy only with blank verse. TREVELYAN (1941) translates only those poems he likes, and regards as translatable. He has some success. Iris Origo's *Leopardi: A Study in Solitude* (1953), supplements her own versions of illustratively deployed poems with Trevelyan's versions. ORIGO collaborated (1966) with another poet, John HEATH-STUBBS, when he supplied revised versions of his own 17 earlier translations (1946) for a selection of Leopardi's prose and verse. Eamon Grennan regards these mainly unrhymed, idiomatically easy versions as the best available. Theodore WEISS's aggressive introduction to the Leopardi number of the *Quarterly Review* in 1956 argues for Leopardi's as the first truly modern sensibility. The verse translations, by various hands, are in the main slackly written and colourlessly modish, though the opening version of *All'Italia* by Margaret BOTTRALL presents a strong challenge to the ethos of the volume. Angel FLORES's (1966) selection of 10 years later is better tempered and much richer. Muriel KITTEL (a minor contributor also to Weiss's volume) is well represented here. So is Edwin MORGAN, who features also in R.D.S. JACK *et al.*'s *A Scottis Quair* (1987), which contains 12 poems by various hands in up to three versions: English, Scots and Gaelic. GRENNAN (1995) translates 16 poems, and in an intelligent introduction reasserts the obvious and forgotten point that Leopardi was a Romantic poet. Leopardi's canzone schemes are entirely abandoned, but the lines are energized by often beautiful assonances. Grennan's is perhaps the most convincing translation to date. He acknowledges Morgan and Kittel among his predecessors and also BARRICELLI's "poetic prose" versions (1963) and, along with Ottavio M. Casale's useful *A Leopardi Reader* (Urbana: University of Illinois Press, 1981), Arturo Vivante's selected *Giacomo Leopardi: Poems* (Wellfleet, Massachusetts: Delphinium Press, 1988, 2nd edition). Grennan also contributes to Sonzogni's collections of versions and "responses" (1998). Also from Ireland are selected *Canti* translated, often graciously, by LAWTON (1996). Scattered lyrics are available in general anthologies of Italian poetry, notably and with distinction by ELLIOT (1993). Singh's very rich bibliography (1968) notes incidental translations from the 19th century.

A slender but important contribution to the history of Leopardi translation is made by POUND (*Canzoni*, 1911) in his version of "Sopra il ritratto di una bella donna". This difficult piece of pastiche uniquely mimics Leopardi's conciseness. LOWELL (1961), on the other hand, in his versions of "L'Infinito", "Silvia", "Il Sabato del Villaggio", develops an equivalent of Leopardi's apparent casualness ("If a line scans, this is an accident").

ROBERT CUMMINGS

Further Reading

Anonymous, "Leopardi on the Right Language of Translation", *Translation and Literature*, 1 (1992) pp. 141–50

Barricelli, Gian Piero, "A Poet of a Poet: Comments on Pound's Translation of Leopardi's *Sopra il ritratto di una bella donna*", *Italian Quarterly*, 64 (1973) pp. 68–76

Bibliografia leopardiana, 6 vols, Florence: Olschki, 1931–86

Brown, H.F., review of Frederick Townsend's *Poems of Giacomo Leopardi*, *Academy*, 32 (1887) p. 115

Elliot, Alistair, *Italian Landscape Poems*, Newcastle upon Tyne: Bloodaxe Books, 1993

Lewes, G.H., *Fraser's Magazine*, 38 (1848) pp. 659–69

Origo, Iris, *Leopardi: A Study in Solitude*, 2nd enlarged edition, London: Hamish Hamilton, 1953

Rizzardi, Alfredo, "Il Leopardi tradotto da Robert Lowell", *Studi Americani*, 7 (1961) pp. 443–63

Singh, G., *Leopardi e L'Inghilterra*, Florence: Le Monnier, 1968

Singh, G., *I canti di Giacomo Leopardi nelle traduzioni inglesi: Saggio bibliografico e antologia delle versioni nel mondo anglosassone*, Recanati, Italy: Centro Nazionale di Studi Leopardiani, 1990

Sonzogni, Marco, *Or volge l'anno / At the Year's Turning: An Anthology of Irish Poets Responding to Leopardi*, Dublin: Dedalus, 1998

Traversi, Derek A., "The Development of Modern Italian Poetry," *Scrutiny*, 10 (1941) pp. 143–56

Mikhail Lermontov 1814–1841

Russian novelist, poet and dramatist

Biography

Born in Moscow, 2/3 October 1814, the son of a retired army captain. His mother died when Lermontov was three, and he was brought up mainly by his grandmother on her estate in central Russia. He received an extensive education at home. He moved with his grandmother to Moscow in 1827 and there attended the School for the Nobility, 1828–30: he studied ethics and politics, and wrote poetry. He studied literature at Moscow University 1830–32; he left after disagreeing with a professor at the University, and attended the Junker School, the military cadet school in St Petersburg, until 1834. He was appointed as a cavalry cornet to the Regiment of Life Guards Hussars stationed at Tsarskoye Selo (now Pushkin), near St Petersburg. He continued to write during this period, concentrating mostly on narrative poetry and plays. He was exiled to the Caucasus in 1837 for his lyric poem commemorating Pushkin's death. Pardoned by the authorities, he returned to St Petersburg in early 1838. His novel *Geroi nashego vremeni* (*A Hero of Our Time*) was published in 1840. As a result of a duel with the French ambassador's son, he was exiled again, to the Tenginskii Infantry Regiment on the Black Sea, from 1840–41, and distinguished himself in battle at Valerik River. While staying in Piatigorsk spa, where he was seeking treatment for his health on his return from leave, he became the focus of personal intrigue and animosity, and was killed in Piatigorsk, during a duel with another officer, on 15 July 1841.

Lermontov was one of the most influential romantic writers in 19th-century Russia: he is often referred to as Pushkin's successor. His work achieved wide popularity and critical acclaim both in his lifetime and beyond. His first poem, *Vesna* (*Spring*), was published in 1830, when he was 16. His later poetic work includes the romantic narrative poem *Demon* (*The Demon*), which he worked on from 1830 onwards, in successive versions; *Parus (The Sail)*, 1832, one of his best known lyric poems, and *Mtsyri* (*The Novice / The Circassian Boy*), published in 1840. His elegy on the death of Alexander Pushkin, *Smert' poeta* (*Death of a Poet*), 1837, brought him both fame and controversy, with its denunciation of the Russian aristocracy. Lermontov also wrote satirical verse, such as *Tambovskaya kaznacheysha* (*The Tambov Lady*), 1838 and *Sashka*, published posthumously in 1862. Lermontov's important psychological novel *Geroi nashego vremeni* (*A Hero of Our Time*) was published in 1840. His most significant work for the theatre is his romantic play in verse, *Maskarad* [Masquerade]; this was completed in 1836, but was considered offensive by the Russian authorities and not performed in entirety until 1862, after Lermontov's death.

Editions

The Lermontov canon has been published in full. The most complete edition in the original Russian is *Polnoe sobranie sochinenii v piati tomakh*, edited by Boris Eikhenbaum, 5 vols, Moscow-Leningrad: Academia, 1935–37. Other excellent editions were produced in 1947–48 (4 vols) and 1979–81 (4 vols).

Translations

Selections of Prose and Poetry

Daniels, Guy, *A Lermontov Reader*, with an introduction, New York: Macmillan, 1965

L'Ami, C.E. and Alexander Welikotny, *Michael Lermontov: Biography and Translation*, with an introduction, Winnipeg: University of Manitoba Press, 1967

Pyman, Avril, Irina Zheleznova and Martin Parker, *Mikhail Lermontov: Selected Works*, with an introduction, Moscow: Progress, 1976

Selections of Poetry

Johnston, Charles, *Narrative Poems by Alexander Pushkin and by Mikhail Lermontov*, with an introduction, New York: Random House, 1983; London: Bodley Head, 1984

Kayden, Eugene M., *The Demon and Other Poems*, with an introduction by C.M. Bowra, Yellow Springs, Ohio: Antioch Press, 1965

Liberman, Anatoly, *Major Poetical Works* (parallel texts), with an introduction, Minneapolis: University of Minnesota Press, and London: Croom Helm, 1983

Nabokov, Vladimir, *Pushkin-Lemontov-Tyutchev: Poems*, London: Lindsay Drummond, 1947 (3 of the 10 poems included were originally published in *Three Russian Poets*, translated by Nabokov, Norfolk, Connecticut: New Directions, 1944)

Novel

Geroi nashego vremeni, 1840

Foote, Paul, *A Hero of Our Time*, with an introduction, Harmondsworth: Penguin, 1966

L'Ami, C.E. and Alexander Welikotny, "Taman" and "The Fatalist" in *Michael Lermontov: Biography and Translation*, Winnipeg: University of Manitoba Press, 1967

Nabokov, Vladimir, with Dmitri Nabokov, *A Hero of Our Time*, with a foreword by Vladimir Nabokov, Garden City, New York: Doubleday, 1958

Parker, Martin, *A Hero of Our Time*, in *Mikhail Lermontov: Selected Works*, translated by Avril Pyman, Irina Zheleznova and Martin Parker, Moscow: Progress, 1976

A substantial proportion of Mikhail Lermontov's works has been translated into English, with his novel *A Hero of Our Time* as well as many of his poems available in numerous versions. For a bibliography extending into the 1960s, see Lewanski 1967. The translations reviewed here were produced in the post-World War II period.

DANIELS (1965) offers an eccentric collection, some three-quarters of which is taken up by Lermontov's unfinished novel, *Princess Ligovskaya* (*Kniaginia Ligovskaia*, 1836) and an 1831 play, *The Strange One* (*Strannyi chelovek*), which is classed among the writer's juvenilia. Both of these prose works naturally exhibit certain features characteristic of the mature Lermontov, but remain of interest only to specialists who are by definition unlikely to need a translation. That said, the English versions of these two prose works are highly accurate.

A much more valuable part of this collection is Daniels's translation of poetic texts, although his choice is once again highly capricious. His sample consists of some 20 shorter lyrics, a number of them drawn from Lermontov's early (and uneven) work, two complete narrative poems, and excerpts from two others. A particularly successful translation is his version of "A Song about Tsar Ivan Vasil'yevich ..." ("Pesnia pro tsaria Ivana Vasil'evicha ...", 1837), a narrative poem in which Lermontov imitates the metric and verbal patterns of Russian poetic folklore. The overall effect has been reproduced to an admirable degree, in this case helped by the fact that this genre lacks rhyme, so there is no need to engage in the "padding" and syntactic contortions that are the all-too-familiar products of the attempts to preserve rhyme schemes in poetic translations. Yet Daniels is also successful in some instances where he has retained this feature. Two good examples are "The Prisoner" ("Uznik", 1837) and "I Walk Alone ..." ("Vykhozhu odin ia ...", 1841), where the poet's imagery has been reproduced almost without distortion. In a number of other cases Daniels has chosen either to dispense with Lermontov's rhymes entirely (while preserving the meter) or else to keep them only partially, rhyming every second line. Some, but not all, of these renditions are successful. Daniels has supplied the volume with a bombastic introduction that can only be called unfortunate.

JOHNSTON (1983) offers three major narrative poems by Lermontov in this collection: "The Tambov Lady" ("Tambovskaia kaznacheisha", 1836), "The Novice" ("Mtsyri", 1840), and "The Demon" ("Demon", 1841). In the first of these, Lermontov follows the metrical pattern conceived by Pushkin for *Eugene Onegin*, i.e., the so-called "Onegin stanza", and Johnston, who had earlier translated Pushkin's "novel in verse" in its entirety, has produced an outstandingly effective version of Lermontov's satirical work. No serious mistranslations obtrude, although there are some instances of exceedingly convoluted syntax and a certain amount of "padding" for the sake of rhyme. Though this problem is very modest in scale, it is also present in Johnston's translations of "The Novice" and "The Demon", where it becomes far more damaging because of the unrelieved seriousness of these later works. The tongue-in-cheek tone of "The Tambov Lady" permits the reader to accept some odd constructions and a sprinkling of corny rhymes as a possible part of the intended effect, while the same features in the two later poems risk introducing an inappropriately comic nuance (e.g., " ... dressed / in a habiliment of lowly / hairshirting was that maiden breast"). Johnston acknowledges this danger in his translator's note, and it needs to be stressed that he has successfully avoided bathos in all but a very few instances. In fact,

Johnston's translations of the three narrative poems are the best available English versions of these works.

KAYDEN (1965) offers a generous and well-chosen selection of Lermontov's verse: 17 early poems, 48 from the mature period (including all the best-known lyrics), and four long narrative poems. But the admirably representative nature of Kayden's sample is more than offset by the uneven quality of the translations. Major departures from Lermontov's imagery are characteristic of every poetic text checked against the original. At the same time there are many instances of excellent translation of some greater or lesser part of the original. Yet for some reason Kayden seems incapable of sustaining this level of quality over a whole poetic text. The volume includes an introduction by C.M. Bowra and brief notes on some of the texts by the translator.

L'AMI & WELIKOTNY (1967) present the largest collection of Lermontov's works in English available in one volume. The book contains more than a hundred of the shorter poetic texts, several narrative poems (including "The Demon", "The Novice", "Sashka" and "Izmail Bey"), two stories from *A Hero of Our Time* ("Taman" and "The Fatalist"), and the drama "Two Brothers" ("Dva brata", 1836).

Although, as we learn from the introductory essay, this book represents a labor of love stretching over many decades, it is easily the least professional of the collections considered here. Apart from a multitude of plain mistakes, the frequently stilted phrasing, and the innumerable examples of imagery lost or distorted, the book annoys on a purely technical level by its absence of any recognizable order in presenting the texts, with some poems written by the teenaged Lermontov interspersed with the perfect products of his maturity. There are also more than a scattering of unnecessarily rare English words like "byre" or "gyves", as well as some preposterous literalism (e.g., "red girl" for "deva krasnaia" (beautiful girl), perversely justified in a footnote as being "so vivid that one wishes to retain it"). The translation of prose works is more satisfactory but remains inferior to the versions of Foote and Nabokov.

LIBERMAN (1983) has produced a huge volume of widely varying worth. Part of the book's 635-page bulk is explained by his decision to have his translations face the Russian originals. There is also a compendious, always helpful, and often acute commentary on each poetic text, totaling some 150 pages, and an introduction containing a vigorously worded statement of Liberman's approach to translation. He asserts here that Lermontov's importance as a poet depends far more on the phonetic features of his verse than on "the actual wording", and the translations offered reflect a consistent application of this principle. It appears that by assigning absolute priority to meter, rhyme, and the undefined quality he calls "sound symbolism", Liberman has created a theoretical justification for downgrading the importance of the cognitive meaning and imagery of the original. Examples can be drawn from every single poem included in this collection. In an 1840 poem ("Est' rechi ..."), Lermontov gave eloquent expression to the immense importance that pure sounds held for him, but it is surely significant that he formulated this idea in a clear and intellectually coherent manner. The point is that the informational features of a poem, above all including its system of images, cannot and must not be sacrificed as readily as Liberman is always prepared to do. What Liberman has produced is a collection of "variations on themes by Lermontov", occasionally rather good ones, but nevertheless texts that must be recognized as no more than partial translations of the original Russian.

NABOKOV's 1947 translation of 10 Lermontov poems (three of which constituted the entire Lermontov sample in Nabokov's 1944 collection *Three Russian Poets*), was produced before his conversion to the dogmatic literalism famously represented by his version of *Eugene Onegin*. For that reason one is almost shocked to note the degree to which Lermontov's imagery has been tampered with. In Lermontov's "Dream" ("Son", 1841), for example, the opening lines read as follows: "V poldnevnyi zhar v doline Dagestana / S svintsom v grudi lezhal nedvizhim ia" [In the heat of noon, in a Daghestan valley / I lay motionless with a bullet in my breast]. Nabokov translates: "I dreamt that with a bullet in my side / in a hot gorge of Daghestan I lay." The changes are significant. First, and most important, Nabokov has made dreaming explicit, while the original implies it by the title alone. The location of the wound is different, and Lermontov's references to the time of day and to motionlessness have been dropped. It is the kind of alteration that Nabokov would mock furiously in later years, yet it is typical of all the translations from Lermontov contained in the 1947 volume. One might say that it is a measure of Nabokov's great subsequent influence that we now look upon his own early versions as quite unsatisfactory. In this connection it is interesting to add that a decade later, in the translator's foreword to his 1958 rendition of *A Hero of Our Time*, Nabokov offers a much revised version of the same poem, this time retaining Lermontov's imagery almost exactly. The new translation begins as follows: "In noon's heat, in a dale of Dagestan, / with lead inside my breast, stirless I lay."

On the textual level, NABOKOV's 1958 translation of *A Hero of Our Time* is a painstakingly reliable version of the original (*Geroi nashego vremeni*, 1840), and it seems that the only discrepancy between it and the canonical Russian text is the absence of a division of the novel into parts one and two in the English variant. The problem with this rendition is thus not with the translation in the narrow sense, but with the unusual nature of the foreword and copious notes added by the translator. Nabokov begins his foreword with appreciative comments on the innovative construction of the novel, but the greater part of his text consists of a harsh criticism of Lermontov's style, which is said to be inelegant, dry and drab, filled with hackneyed epithets, and "almost as crude as Stendhal's French". Lermontov is also taken to task for his dependence on such banal devices as eavesdropping. In fact Nabokov sees so many shortcomings in the novel that the praise he unexpectedly dispenses in the last paragraph of his foreword seems almost like a belated recognition of the need to justify anyone's reading this book in the first place.

The endnotes contain more sniping at Lermontov's expense. While Nabokov here offers much genuinely useful information on literary references, Caucasian geography, and historical realia albeit (frequently doing so with the pedantic excess that is his trademark), he also makes numerous comments critical of Lermontov's text. Thus the narrator's passing remark to the effect that unsophisticated individuals are especially responsive to the beauty of nature receives the following rejoinder in Nabokov's endnote: "This is, of course, a romanticist notion. It is completely untrue." The issue here is not whether Nabokov is or is not justified in his criticism, but rather the intrusive manner in which he constantly injects himself into Lermontov's narrative. In similarly annoying fashion, he takes pains to draw attention to minor themes that, in his opinion, are not followed up in the novel, as well as to point out romantic clichés that strike him as unconvincing or preposterous, or both. In an important article, Nicholas A. Warner (1986) argues that Nabokov's ultimate aim was to create a competing "shadow text" that would preempt the reader's perception of the novel. Fascinating as this game might be for the literary sophisticate, it raises an irritating obstacle to the direct and independent appreciation of Lermontov's work.

FOOTE's 1966 version of *A Hero of Our Time* may well have benefited from Nabokov's earlier translation of this novel in terms of accuracy; in any case, there seems to be only an insignificant scattering of minor errors in basic meaning. Lermontov's style is rendered with great fluency, and endowed with unmistakably British overtones ("Poor chap", "give us the price of a drink", etc.). There is a competent introduction, but no other annotations.

PYMAN, ZHELEZNOVA & PARKER (1976) contribute their various translations to a well-produced collection containing 28 shorter lyrics, three long narrative poems (including "The Novice" and "The Demon"), and three prose works, among them the complete *A Hero of Our Time*. The poetic texts were translated by Pyman and Zheleznova, with each responsible for a roughly equal volume of translation. Pyman's versions are generally superior to those of Zheleznova, whose phrasing can often be stilted and unnatural, but neither translator approaches the level of quality achieved by Johnston or by Daniels (in his better moments). *A Hero of Our Time* is presented in the translation of Martin Parker, here somewhat revised from the version he first published in Moscow in 1947. The level of accuracy is quite good, and this may indeed be the reason why Nabokov has not included Parker in his listing of mistranslators of Lermontov's novel. The collection is richly illustrated but has the misfortune of bearing a Soviet-era introduction filled with the predictable bromides.

ALEXIS KLIMOFF

Further Reading

Lewanski, Richard C. (editor), *The Literatures of the World in English Translation*, vol. 2: *The Slavic Literatures*, New York: New York Public Library / Ungar, 1967; revised 1971

Reid, Robert, "The Critical Uses of Translation: Lermontov's *A Hero of Our Time*", *Essays in Poetics*, 11/2 (1986)

Warner, Nicholas, A., "The Footnote as Literary Genre: Nabokov's Commentaries to Lermontov and Pushkin", *Slavic and East European Journal*, 30/2 (1986)

See also the translator's introductory material and notes to Liberman and to Nabokov, and the translator's introduction to Johnston

---

Nikolai Leskov 1831–1895

Russian short-story writer

Biography

Born at Gorokhovo, Orel province, 4 February 1831. He was the eldest of seven children. He received an informal education by tutors, followed by a few years of perfunctory study at the gymnasium in Orel, which he left in 1846. Leskov worked as a clerk in Orel criminal court, but in 1849 was transferred to Kiev as assistant clerk in the army recruiting bureau. Civil service work in Kiev acquainted him with the "cradle of Russian civilization", and it gave him the opportunity to mix with university teachers. In 1853 he married Olga Smirnova (who was later committed to an insane asylum). He resigned from his post in 1857 and worked for the firm of Scott (his British uncle by marriage) and Wilkins in estate management, which gave him the wide experience of provincial village life on which he drew extensively in his stories. Three years later he moved to Moscow and his first articles were published in the same year. In 1861 he settled in St Petersburg to work as journalist and writer. He travelled to Eastern Europe and Paris during 1862 and 1863 and published a series of travel sketches of the trip. He lived with Katerina Bubnova from 1865 to 1877, a relationship that resulted in four step-children and one son (Andrei Leskov, 1866–1953, later to become the writer's biographer). From 1874 to 1883 he served on the Scholarly Committee of the Ministry of Education until his dismissal. He undertook further trips abroad in 1875 and 1884. The publication of his collected works began in 1889. Volume 6, though all contents had previously been published, was banned by the censor.

Most of his early works were written under the pseudonym M. Stebnitskii. His first major works were *Ovtsebyk* (*The Musk-Ox*) and *Ledi Makbet mtsenskogo uezda* (*Lady Macbeth of Mtsensk*). Other shorter works of the 1860s were "Voitel'nitsa" ("The Amazon") 1866 and "Zhitie odnoi baby" [Life of a Peasant Martyress] (1863). His first novel *Nekuda* [No Way Out] (1864) contained a depiction of his circle of acquaintances, which they found far from flattering; together with the reputation he had already earned from an unfortunate article written by him in 1861, he became something of an outcast. However, the next 10 years saw more successful extended works, *Soboriane* (*The Cathedral Folk*), *Zapechatlennyi angel* (*The Sealed Angel*) and

Ocharovannyi strannik (*The Enchanted Wanderer*). The 1870s and 1880s brought many articles and stories on radical non-Orthodox believers, including his study of the English evangelist Lord Radstock, "Velikosvetskii raskol" [Schism in High Society] (1876). Numerous stories about "righteous ones" (*pravedniki*) included "Odnodum" [One Track Mind] (1879) and "Nesmertel'nyi Golovan" [Deathless Golovan] (1880). Stories questioning ecclesiastical assumptions and suggesting a more spiritual and less formalistic religious approach included "Na kraiu sveta" [On the Edge of the World] (1875), "Melochi arkhiereiskoi zhizni" [The Little Things in a Bishop's Life] (1878–80), and "Nekreshchenyi pop" [The Unbaptized Priest] (1877). One of his best-known short stories, "Levsha" ("Lefty"), was published in 1881. By the late 1880s Leskov was having difficulties with the censor in view of his growing dissent. His later works included many treatments of ancient church legends, as well as "Polunoshchniki" [Night Owls] 1891, "Iudol'" ("Vale of Tears") 1892, "Zagon" [The Cattle Pen] 1893, "Zimnii den'" [A Winter's Day] 1894, and "Zaiachii remiz" [The March Hare] (1894, but not published until 1917). He died suddenly in St Petersburg on 21 February 1895.

Translations

Selections of Short Stories

Edgerton, William, B., *Satirical Stories*, New York: Pegasus, 1969

Hanna, George H., *The Enchanted Wanderer and Other Stories*, Moscow: Foreign Languages Publishing House,1958(?); reprinted Moscow: Raduga, 1983

Lantz, K.A., *The Sealed Angel and Other Stories*, Knoxville: University of Tennessee Press, 1984

McDuff, David, *Lady Macbeth of Mtsensk and Other Stories*, with an introduction, Harmondsworth and New York: Penguin, 1987

Magarshack, David, *The Enchanted Pilgrim and Other Stories*, London: Hutchinson, 1946; Westport, Connecticut: Hyperion Press, 1977

Magarshack, David, *The Amazon and Other Stories*, London: Allen and Unwin, 1949; Westport, Connecticut: Hyperion Press, 1977

Magarshack, David, *Selected Tales*, with an introduction by V.S. Pritchett, New York: Farrar Straus, 1961; London: Secker and Warburg, 1962

Norman, R., *The Musk-Ox and Other Tales*, London: Routledge, 1944; Westport, Connecticut: Hyperion Press, 1977

Shotton, Michael, *Five Tales*, with an introduction London: Angel, 1984

Short Stories

Ovtsebyk, 1863

McDuff, David, "Musk-Ox" in *Lady Macbeth of Mtsensk and Other Stories*, translated by McDuff, 1987

Norman, R., "The Musk-Ox" in *The Musk-Ox and Other Tales*, translated by Norman, 1944

Iazvitel'nyi, 1863

Norman, R., "The Stinger" in *The Musk-Ox and Other Tales*, translated by Norman, 1944

Shotton, Michael, "A Spiteful Fellow" in *Five Tales*, translated by Shotton, 1984

Ledi Makbet mtsenskogo uezda, 1865

Hanna, George H., "Lady Macbeth of Mtsensk" in *The Enchanted Wanderer and Other Stories*, translated by Hanna, 1958(?)

McDuff, David, "Lady Macbeth of Mtsensk" in *Lady Macbeth of Mtsensk and Other Stories*, translated by McDuff, 1987

Magarshack, David, "Lady Macbeth of the Mtsensk District" in *Selected Tales*, translated by Magarshack, 1961

Voitel'nitsa, 1866

Magarshack, David, "The Amazon" in *The Amazon and Other Stories*, translated by Magarshack, 1949

Soboriane, 1872

Hapgood, Isabel F., *The Cathedral Folk*, New York: Knopf, and London: Bodley Head, 1924; reprinted Westport, Connecticut: Greenwood Press, 1971

Zapechatlennyi angel, 1873

Lantz, K.A., "The Sealed Angel" in *The Sealed Angel and Other Stories*, translated by Lantz, 1984

McDuff, David, "The Sealed Angel" in *Lady Macbeth of Mtsensk and Other Stories*, translated by McDuff, 1987

Tollemache, Beatrix L., "The Sealed Angel" in *Russian Sketches, Chiefly of Peasant Life*, translated by Tollemache, London: Smith Elder, 1913

Ocharovannyi strannik, 1873

Hanna, George H., "The Enchanted Wanderer" in *The Enchanted Wanderer and Other Stories*, translated by Hanna, 1958(?)

Magarshack, David, "The Enchanted Pilgrim" in *The Enchanted Pilgrim and Other Stories*, translated by Magarshack, 1946; as "The Enchanted Wanderer" in *Selected Tales*, translated by Magarshack, 1961

Paschkoff, A.G., *The Enchanted Wanderer*, with an introduction by Maksim Gor'kii, New York: McBride, 1924; London: Jarrolds, 1926

Na kraiu sveta, 1875

Prokurat, Michael, *On the Edge of the World*, Crestwood, New York: St Vladimir's Seminary Press, 1992

Levsha (Skaz o tul'skom kosom levshe i o stal'noi blokhe), 1881

Deutsch, Babette and Avrahm Yarmolinsky, *The Steel Flea*, New York: Harper, 1943; revised edition, New York: Harper and Row, 1964

Edgerton, William B., "The Steel Flea" in *Satirical Stories*, edited by Edgerton, New York: Pegasus, 1969

Hanna, George H., "Lefty; Being the Tale of Cross-Eyed Lefty of Tula and the Steel Flea" in *The Enchanted Wanderer and Other Stories*, translated by Hanna, 1958(?); published separately Moscow: Foreign Languages Publishing House, 1965

Hapgood, Isabel F., *The Steel Flea*, Boston: Merrymount Press, 1916

Magarshack, David, "The Left-handed Artificer" in *The Enchanted Pilgrim and Other Stories*, translated by Magarshack, 1946; as "The Left-handed Craftsman" in *Selected Tales*, translated by Magarshack, 1961

Iudol', 1892
Muckle, James, "Vale of Tears", with *On Quakeresses*, edited by Muckle, Nottingham: Bramcote Press, 1991

Of all the great Russian prose writers of the 19th century, Nikolai Leskov presents one of the most formidable challenges to the translator. In an age when "transparent", Turgenevesque prose was the norm, Leskov was a deviant. For him language was not simply a medium of communication, but a potential art object in its own right, something to be played with, sculpted into interesting shapes. "He knew the language to the point of performing tricks with it", Lev Tolstoi said about him. Some of Leskov's linguistically creative characters give birth to what the Russians call *slovechki* – amusing neologisms, often based on puns or folk etymologies. Such *slovechki* as *buremetr* for "barometer"'(combining *buria*, "storm", with *metr*) or *kleveton*, for "newspaper column" (combining *kleveta,* "slander", with the French loan-word *feuilleton*) are a Leskovian trademark, known to every literate Russian. But what is a translator to do with them?

Besides tricks, the difficulties of translating Leskov also derive from his enormous sociological range. In his early life he travelled widely through the Russian empire and was exposed to many strata of society, from princesses to peasants. In his works he makes use of many kinds of "marked" language: not only regional dialects of Russian or even related languages, such as Ukrainian, but the specialized vocabulary of particular professions, most of all, the clergy. The translator must hunt for comparable mixtures of non-standard and literary English, but the ingredients are likely to be too locally identifiable – a Petersburg *izvozchik* talking like a Brooklyn taxi-driver. What to do?

A systematic comparison of the many translations of Leskov's numerous works – disregarding publications in magazines, I count 52 translations by 16 translators of 34 works, published in 19 separate books – would occupy a large volume. Analysis here must therefore be limited to a very few characteristic specimens. I particularly regret that space limitations preclude discussion of many interesting translations – those of *Ovtsebyk* ("The Musk-Ox") by R. NORMAN and by David MCDUFF; *Iazvitel'nyi* ("The Stinger" / "A Spiteful Fellow") by Michael SHOTTON and by David MAGARSHACK; *Soboriane* (*The Cathedral Folk*) by Isabel F. HAPGOOD; *Ocharovannyi strannik* ("The Enchanted Wanderer") by several translators; and *Iudol'* ("Vale of Tears") by James MUCKLE.

One of Leskov's most famous stories, "Lady Macbeth of the Mtsensk District" seemingly presents fewer traps for the translator than usual. Here Leskov atypically writes as omniscient author, in standard Russian, and the translations for the most part glide smoothly – until they hit a snag. A single example: invoking a favorite theme, Russian church music, Leskov describes how people crowd a church to hear "how the deep bass rumbles like an organ and the high-flying tenor pours out the most whimsical appogiaturas". The passage is mangled by all three translators (HANNA, 1958(?); MCDUFF, 1987; MAGARSHACK, 1961), since none of them can get away from "octave" as the cognate of *oktava*, not realizing that *oktava* has the secondary meaning of "low bass" (HANNA also unaccountably transforms "appogiaturas" into "fugues"!)

The heroine of "The Amazon" is a vivid example of the motley linguistic results of class displacement. Originally from the Mtsensk artisan class, she has established herself in business in Petersburg (as a procuress). She thus visits upper-class houses and has picked up some elements of upper-class speech, often garbled, which are superimposed on her native dialect. To render without loss in another language this "double-layered" diction is virtually impossible. MAGARSHACK (1949) generally chooses to convey only the semantic content of the heroine's discourse, without much effort to reproduce its bizarre colors. "I had invited such a *grandezvous* to come see her the next day", she relates in the source text, typically melding two "aristocratic" French loan-words, so that a rendezvous with a grand person becomes a *grandezvous*. Magarshack translates only the sense: "I had invited such an important gentleman to come see her the next morning", and a picturesque bit of Leskov is lost.

"The Sealed Angel", like many of Leskov's works, is told as an oral story-within-a-story (*skaz*) by an ex-Old Believer of the artisan class, who employs both archaic ecclesiastical diction and the specialized language of icon-painting. The three existing translations are creditable efforts, though those by MCDUFF (1987) and by LANTZ (1984) are far the more professional. In an exceptionally difficult passage the narrator, with a dazzling display of folk connoisseurship, describes an icon he and his fellow workmen especially revered, the angel of the title. This angel has symbolic "thongs" (*torotsy*) coming out of his ears. They completely baffle TOLLEMACHE (1913), but (with some help from Soviet commentaries) McDuff and Lantz both get them right, and both supply endnotes explicating this and other technicalities of icon painting, Lantz's being somewhat fuller and more accurate than those by McDuff.

The question of annotating translations is of course a vexed one – some regard all notes as distracting and pedantic, while others are grateful for their helpful explanations. Those who appreciate good annotations will admire those supplied by Michael PROKURAT (1992) for "At the Edge of the World". Father Prokurat has made a noble effort to track down allusions and references even natives might miss.

Leskov's most famous short story is *Levsha*, a tour de force of *skaz*, told in the colorful language of an ultra-patriotic old gunsmith. Describing the foreign travels of Tsar Alexander I from the supposed point of view of a xenophobic Cossack general in the emperor's suite, the language is studded with inventively garbled foreign words. One brief illustration must suffice: "In the main hall [of a museum] there were various enormous [*ogromadnye*, combining two synonyms, *gromadnyi* and *ogromnyi*] busts [*biustry*, conflating *biust*, "bust", with *liustra*, "candelabra"], and in the middle under a *valdachin* [b's and v's get mixed up in many foreign loan-words] there stands the *Abolon polvederski* [a marvelous concoction, derived, of course, from Apollo Belvedere, with a suggestion of contamination with *obaldui*, "blockhead", and an unmistakable connection with the word for "half a pail", *pol vedra*, universally familiar as a measure of vodka]." The translators variously struggle to echo this bizarre cacophony. HAPGOOD's "huge busts" and "canopy" (1916) render only sense without form, but she does record "Abolo Polveder" in the text, with a footnote explaining "half-bucket Apollo". MAGARSHACK (1946), as usual, takes the literal route, with "enormous statues" and a "big canopy", but even he makes an effort with Belvedere. Lowering the alcoholic content a bit, he turns it into "Apollo Belvebeery". HANNA (1958(?)) cravenly abandons all effort to reproduce the linguistic oddities and reduces the passage to "big busts", a "canopy", and "a statue of the Apollo Belvedere". The DEUTSCH & YARMOLINSKY version (1943) is not a translation at all, but an "adaptation" retold for children; the "Apollo" passage is deemed beyond their reach and omitted entirely. The boldest and most inventive of the translators is EDGERTON (1969), who dodges no hurdles. He comes up with "tremendulous estuaries" for the big statues, a "canoply" for the valdakhin, and for the Belvedere "Apollo Velvet Ear" – phonetically splendid, though with the vodka connection regrettably sacrificed.

Clearly, a perfect rendering of such a passage – and perhaps of any passage – is beyond human reach, but the struggle for maximal approximation must continue.

HUGH MCLEAN

Further Reading

Lantz, K.A., *Nikolay Leskov*, Boston: Twayne, 1979
McLean, Hugh, *Nikolai Leskov: The Man and His Art*, Cambridge, Massachusetts: Harvard University Press, 1977

Gotthold Ephraïm Lessing 1729–1781

German dramatist, critic, fabulist, and essayist

Biography

Born in Kamenz, Saxony, 22 January 1729, one of the large family of a Lutheran pastor. He attended the Fürstenschule in Meissen and in 1746 went to study theology at the University of Leipzig, where he took an enthusiastic interest in the town's theatre. In 1749 he began a period of activity as scholar, playwright, critic, reviewer and translator, taking an M.A. at Wittenberg in 1752 and coming to public notice in 1754 with his *Vademecum*, a forceful attack on Samuel Gotthold Lange's translation of Horace. Coming after several early comedies, beginning with the performance of *Der junge Gelehrte* in 1747, his *Miss Sara Sampson* (1755), the first German domestic tragedy, was a great success. In 1759 there followed another play, *Philotas*, fables, as well as critical letters on contemporary literature, the 17th of which contained Lessing's *Faust* fragment. In 1766 art theory was the subject of *Laokoön*. Lessing wrote the first serious comedy to be authentically grounded in events arising from the Seven Years' War, *Minna von Barnhelm* (1767). As house critic to the German National Theatre in Hamburg, Lessing produced the seminal *Hamburgische Dramaturgie* (1767–69), re-interpreting the *Poetics* of Aristotle and advocating a change in German drama away from French neo-classical constraints and towards the genius of Shakespeare. He remained just as productive in the last decade of his life. In 1770 he was appointed librarian at the Herzog August Bibliothek in Wolfenbüttel. He completed the prose tragedy of *Emilia Galotti* in 1772, but bereavement after the death of his wife and only child, loneliness and increasing ill-health did not prevent him from engaging in 1778–79 in a sharp theological dispute against dogmatism, and with the dramatic poem *Nathan der Weise* (1778) nobly expounding the case for religious toleration. He died in Brunswick, 15 February 1781.

Translations

Collections and Selections

Barnard, H.H., *Cambridge Free Thoughts and Letters on Bibliolatry: Translated from the German of G. E. Lessing*, London: Trübner, 1862 (includes translations of *Eine Parabel*, *Axiomata* and the *Anti-Goeze*)

Boylan, R. Dillon, *The Dramatic Works of G.E. Lessing*, edited by Ernest Bell, 2 vols, London: G. Bell, 1878, (vol. 1: *Tragedies*: *Miss Sara Sampson*, *Philotas*, *Emilia Galotti*, *Nathan the Wise*; vol. 2: *Comedies*: *Damon; or, True Friendship*, *The Young Scholar*, *The Old Maid*, *The Woman-Hater*, *The Jews*, *The Freethinker*, *The Treasure*, *Minna von Barnhelm*)

Chadwick, Henry (editor and translator), *Lessing's Theological Writings*, London: A. & C. Black, 1956, Stanford, California: Stanford University Press, 1957; selections reprinted in *Nathan the Wise, Minna von Barnhelm, and Other Plays and Writings*, edited by Peter Demetz, 1991

Demetz, Peter (editor), *Nathan the Wise, Minna von Barnhelm, and Other Plays and Writings*, New York: Continuum 1991

Holroyd, Rev. James J., *Three Comedies*, Colchester: W. Totham, 1838 (contains *The Freethinker*, *The Treasure*, *Minna von Barnhelm*)

Rönnfeldt, W.B., *The Laocoön and Other Prose Writings*, London: W. Scott, 1895 (includes extracts from the *Hamburg Dramaturgy* on acting, Voltaire and Shakespeare, historical accuracy in drama, comedy, the dramatic unities, the mingling of comedy and tragedy, Aristotle and tragedy; and a translation of *The Education of the Human Race*)

Comedies

Damon; oder, Die wahre Freundschaft, 1747

Boylan, R. Dillon, *Damon; or, True Friendship* in *The Dramatic Works of G.E. Lessing*, translated by Boylan, vol. 2, 1878

Die alte Jungfer, 1747
Boylan, R. Dillon, *The Old Maid* in *The Dramatic Works of G.E. Lessing*, translated by Boylan, vol. 2, 1878

Der junge Gelehrte, 1747
Boylan, R. Dillon, *The Young Scholar* in *The Dramatic Works of G.E. Lessing*, translated by Boylan, vol. 2, 1878

Der Misogyn, 1748
Boylan, R. Dillon, *The Woman-Hater* in *The Dramatic Works of G.E. Lessing*, translated by Boylan, vol. 2, 1878

Die Juden, 1749
Boylan, R. Dillon, *The Jews* in *The Dramatic Works of G.E. Lessing*, translated by Boylan, vol. 2, 1878
Walsøe-Engel, Ingrid, *The Jews* in *Nathan the Wise, Minna von Barnhelm, and Other Plays and Writings*, edited by Peter Demetz, 1991

Der Freigeist, 1749, produced 1767
Boylan, R. Dillon, *The Freethinker* in *The Dramatic Works of G.E. Lessing*, translated by Boylan, vol. 2, 1878

Der Schatz, 1750
Boylan, R. Dillon, *The Treasure* in *The Dramatic Works of G.E. Lessing*, translated by Boylan, vol. 2, 1878
Holroyd, Rev. James J., *The Treasure* in *Three Comedies*, translated by Holroyd, 1838

Minna von Barnhelm, 1767
Anonymous, *The School for Honor; or, The Chance of War*, London: Vernor and Hood, 1799 (Robert Harvey was probably the translator: Seifert, 1973, 272)
Boylan, R. Dillon, *Minna von Barnhelm* in *The Dramatic Works of G.E. Lessing*, translated by Boylan, vol. 2, 1878
Holroyd, Rev. James J., *Minna von Barnhelm* in *Three Comedies*, translated by Holroyd, 1838
Johnstone, James, *The Disbanded Officer; or, The Baroness of Bruchsal*, London: T. Cadell, 1786
Maxwell, Major-General Patrick, *Minna von Barnhelm; or, A Soldier's Luck*, London: University Press, 1899
Meech, Anthony, *Minna von Barnhelm*, with *Sara* translated by Ernest Bell, Bath: Absolute Press, 1990
Northcott, Kenneth J., *Minna von Barnhelm*, Chicago: University of Chicago Press, 1972
Wrankmore, W.C., *Minna von Barnhelm; or, A Soldier's Fortune*, Leipzig: A. Gumprecht, 1858

Tragedies
Miss Sara Sampson, 1755
Bell, Ernest, *Sara*, with *Minna von Barnhelm*, translated by Anthony Meech, Bath: Absolute Press, 1990
Boylan, R. Dillon, *Miss Sara Sampson* in *The Dramatic Works of G.E. Lessing*, translated by Boylan, vol. 1, 1878

Philotas, 1759, produced 1780
Boylan, R. Dillon, *Philotas* in *The Dramatic Works of G.E. Lessing*, translated by Boylan, vol. 1, 1878

Emilia Galotti, 1772
Aesch, Anna Johanna Gode von, *Emilia Galotti*, Great Neck, New York: Barron's, 1959
Berrington, Rev. Joseph, *Emilia Galotti* (manuscript; first performed Theatre Royal Drury Lane, 28 October 1794), appended to "The Eighteenth-Century Translations of Emilia Galotti" by Edward Dvoretzky, *Rice University Studies*, 52/3 (1966) pp. 1–106
Boylan, R. Dillon, *Emilia Galotti* in *The Dramatic Works of G.E. Lessing*, vol. 1, translated by Boylan, 1878
Lamport, F.J., *Emilia Galotti* in *Five German Tragedies*, translated by Lamport, with an introduction, Harmondsworth and Baltimore: Penguin, 1969
Lewes, Charles Lee, *Emilia Galotti*, London: Sampson Low and Marston, 1867
Thompson, Benjamin, *Emilia Galotti*, London: Vernor and Hood, 1800

Dramatic Poem
Nathan der Weise, 1778, produced 1783
Boylan, R. Dillon, *Nathan the Wise* in *The Dramatic Works of G. E. Lessing*, translated by Boylan, vol. 1, 1878
Jacks, William, *Nathan the Wise: A Dramatic Poem*, with an introduction by Frederick W. Farrar, Glasgow: Maclehose, 1894
Lustig, Theodore H., *Nathan the Wise* in *Classical German Drama*, translated by Lustig, with an introduction by Victor Lange, New York: Bantam, 1963
Morgan, Bayard Quincy, *Nathan the Wise: A Dramatic Poem*, New York: Ungar, 1955; in *Nathan the Wise, Minna von Barnhelm, and Other Plays and Writings*, edited by Peter Demetz, 1991
Raspe, R.E., *Nathan the Wise: A Philosophical Drama*, London: J. Fielding, 1781
Taylor, William, *Nathan the Wise: A Dramatic Poem*, Norwich: Stevenson and Matchett, 1791

Critical Theory
Laokoön; oder, über die Grenzen der Malerei und Poesie, 1766
Beasley, Edward C., *Laokoön* in *Selected Prose Works*, edited by Edward Bell, London: Bell, 1879
McCormick, Edward Allen, *Laocoön: An Essay on the Limits of Painting and Poetry*, Indianapolis: Bobbs Merrill, 1962
Phillimore, Sir Robert, *Laocoön*, London: Macmillan, 1874; New York: Dutton, 1905
Steel, William A., *Laocoön, Nathan the Wise, Minna von Barnhelm*, London: Dent, and New York: Dutton, 1930

Wie die Alten den Tod gebildet, 1769
Zimmern, Helen, *How the Ancients Represented Death* in *Selected Prose Works*, edited by Edward Bell, London: Bell, 1879

Die Hamburgische Dramaturgie, 1767–69
Rönnfeldt, W.B., *Dramatic Notes* (excerpts from *The Hamburg Dramaturgy*) in *The Laocoön and Other Prose Writings*, translated by Rönnfeldt, 1895

Writings on Freemasonry
Ernst und Falk: Gespräche für Freimaurer, 1778–81
Cohen, Abraham, *Lessing's Masonic Dialogues (Ernst und Falk)*, London: Baskerville Press, 1927
Mackenzie, Kenneth R.H., *Ernst and Falk* in *Freemason's Quarterly Magazine* (1854; Dialogues 1–3); in *Freemason*, 5 (1872; Dialogues 1–5)
Zwiebel, William L., *Ernst and Falk* in *Nathan the Wise,*

Minna von Barnhelm, and Other Plays and Writings, edited by Peter Demetz, 1991

Writings on Morality and Religion

Das Christentum der Vernunft, 1750

Chadwick, Henry, *The Christianity of Reason* in *Lessing's Theological Writings*, translated by Chadwick, 1956

Fabeln, 1759, *Abhandlungen über die Fabel*, 1759

Richardson, J., *Fables*, York: C. Etherington, 1773

Über den Beweis des Geistes und der Kraft, 1777

Chadwick, Henry, *On the Proof of the Spirit and the Power* in *Lessing's Theological Writings*, translated by Chadwick, 1956

Das Testament Johannis, 1777

Chadwick, Henry, *The Testament of John* in *Lessing's Theological Writings*, translated by Chadwick, 1956

Eine Parabel, 1778

Barnard, Hermann H., *Eine Parabel* in *Cambridge Free Thoughts and Letters on Bibliolatry*, translated by Barnard, 1862

Axiomata, 1778

Barnard, Hermann H., *Axiomata* in *Cambridge Free Thoughts and Letters on Bibliolatry*, translated by Barnard, 1862

Anti-Goeze, 1778

Barnard, Hermann H., *Anti-Goeze* in *Cambridge Free Thoughts and Letters on Bibliolatry*, translated by Barnard, 1862

Die Erziehung des Menschengeschlechts, 1780

Chadwick, Henry, *The Education of the Human Race* in *Lessing's Theological Writings*, translated by Chadwick, 1956

Robertson, Frederick William, *The Education of the Human Race*, London: Smith Elder, 1858, and later editions and reprints

Die Religion Christi, 1780

Chadwick, Henry, *The Religion of Christ* in *Lessing's Theological Writings*, translated by Chadwick, 1956

Although all Gotthold Ephraïm Lessing's major works have been translated into English, there has been as yet no translation of his collected works. Translation is mostly of single, frequently of multiple works. The range of Lessing's writing and the breadth of its appeal have ensured that since 1773 different selections of his oeuvre have found dedicated and increasingly skilled translators. The translations selected here are divided into groups that reflect the variety of his published work. The lists of original works to have been translated are comprehensive but for the one exception of his unfinished drama of *D. Faust* (1759), the translation of which by Frances Leveson Gower (1823, 1825 and probably 1887) is noted by Seifert, the most comprehensive bibliographical source up to 1973.

The early comedies from *The Young Scholar* up to and including *The Woman-Hater* reflected something of Lessing's experience at school in Meissen but mostly his years as a student in Leipzig, which was then renowned for its commerce, fashion and its university. *The Jews* and *The Freethinker*, his Berlin comedies, were of far more serious purport, the first attacking anti-Semitism and the second highly critical of unthinking atheism. *The Treasure* was not an original work of Lessing's but his translation of Plautus' comedy *Trinummus*. The true merit of the early comedies, their lively dialogue and skilful exploitation of characters and situations, is increasingly acknowledged by scholars, although, with the exception of *The Jews*, the early comedies have been rarely performed since the 18th century and rarely translated. HOLROYD (1838), BOYLAN (1878) and WALSØE-ENGEL (1991) offer accurate translations of different plays. Conceivably, if ironically, a revival of the early comedies is perhaps more likely in translation for specialized productions in England than in their original language.

By far the most successful of Lessing's comedies, in terms of the number of performances and of translations, was the five-act prose drama *Minna von Barnhelm*. The motives for translating vary. JOHNSTONE (1786) was inspired by the play's popularity on the French, Danish, Dutch and Russian stages but opted for nothing more than adaptation on the grounds that: "I should tremble to translate him; his language is neat, pure, and graceful; his humour high coloured and characteristic; and his wit delicate, yet lively." He abridged the play substantially and renamed all the characters. Dedicated to the Queen (presumably Queen Charlotte, wife of George III), Johnstone's adaptation was performed at the Theatre Royal, Haymarket. HOLROYD (1838) was motivated more by Lessing's reputation in Germany, by the reviewers' praise of his comedies generally and by their conformity to Dr Johnson's contention that comedy should render "vice and folly ridiculous". He saw Lessing as a possible antidote to the decline of drama in England at the time. WRANKMORE (1858), writing from Reudnitz near Leipzig, describes *Minna* as the best German comedy of all time. Its dialogue, when translated into English, is, he contends, ideal for teaching the art of English conversation to German pupils educating themselves without a teacher: their translation can be checked against his own. MAXWELL's translation (1899) seeks to "raise the stature of the military in the eyes of a public" and to draw attention away from the wretched caricatures of soldiery, so familiar at the time, to the "high-toned nature" of Tellheim, an officer in the Prussian army, in love with the Saxon heroine, the "genial generosity" of his sergeant Werner and the "rugged fidelity" of Just, Tellheim's batman.

JOHNSTONE (1786) offers a free adaptation, not a translation. HARVEY (probably the "Anonymous" of 1799) is distinguished by an imaginative rendering of character names. Minna becomes Lady Louisa Barnhelm, Just is renamed Trim and the innkeeper's nose for money is reflected in the appellation Shark. The translation is free, with frequent omissions and errors of vocabulary and idiom. Poetic features are largely ignored: Lessing's play on the repeated "Unglück" (V, iv) is first rendered as "disasters" and then as "distress". The translation is occasionally ponderous (e.g. "for with me all is exculpated"), a fault not to be found in the original. Harvey translates "Pudel" as "spaniel", whereas Holroyd simply refers to the poodle as "dog". While Harvey ignores "I climbed down" altogether, Holroyd mistranslates with "I stooped down", and yet, to judge from Holroyd's use of idiom and vocabulary generally, his command of German is comparatively better. WRANKMORE (1858) ignores scenic divisions and thus diminishes theatrical and dramatic appeal. His translation is fastidiously accurate but without always capturing the *mot juste*: "before the door on the threshold" and "he bounds before me" warrant smoother renderings, such as those provided by MAXWELL (1899): "he lay on the threshold just outside my door" and "he frisks about in front of me". Maxwell marks a clear improvement on all earlier translations, although his choice of introspective epithets in Tellheim's short monologue in V, ii is odd: "peevish, purblind, faint-hearted, and torpid". When dealing with male relationships, Maxwell translates intuitively well. MEECH (1990) produces better epithets for the same monologue by Tellheim: "touchy, short-sighted, timid, sluggish", although the last one misleadingly suggests a physical rather than an emotional cause for Tellheim's state of mind. There are odd slips in Meech, but he demonstrates an ability to translate not only accurately, fluently and idiomatically, but also for theatre performance. NORTHCOTT (1972) provides a scholarly translation with a high degree of accuracy, but produces a readable text rather than one destined for the stage. With the evolution of the translator's art and the English translators' increasing sensitivity to the nuances of the German language, the more recent translations are almost without exception the better ones.

The English setting of Lessing's first domestic tragedy, *Miss Sara Sampson* – again in five acts and in prose – and the influence of English Restoration comedy and Samuel Richardson's sentimental novels upon its creation, have not discouraged translators, although it has been translated only rarely, namely, by David Ritterhouse (1789) of Philadelphia, Eleonore H. (1800) and Ernest BELL (1933). In 1990 Bell's version provided the text for the English premiere of the play when it was performed in London by the Cheek by Jowl Company to enthusiastic audiences.

Philotas, a short prose tragedy not divided into acts, was Lessing's neo-classical exploration of the Roman military concept of honour, which ends in the eponymous hero's suicide; the play was first published anonymously in Berlin at a critical time for Frederick the Great's Prussia, but found little success or lasting appeal, important though this exercise in stoicism was for Lessing's development as a dramatist.

Of his tragedies it is undoubtedly the five-act prose *Emilia Galotti*, his second domestic tragedy, that was the most successful, whether in the original German or in English translation. It is still performed today, but more frequently in German than in English. In 1966 Edward Dvoretzky published reprints of two of the earliest translations, the first of 1786 and consisting only of selected contextualized passages by a librarian of the British Museum, Henry Maty; the second, eventually established as translated by Rev. Joseph BERRINGTON, was premiered, though with limited success, on 28 October 1794 in the Theatre Royal Drury Lane. Dvoretzky observes that Berrington retained not more than 70 per cent of the original. He gives the details of Maty's selections and accounts for the several errors in both their versions. THOMPSON (1800) resequences Lessing's hierarchy of the dramatis personae, which gave priority to Emilia and the Galotti family, and produces a rather stilted translation without any divisions into scenes, and in five acts of continuous prose. There are free renderings and, above all, idiomatic inexactitudes in most translations, but Thompson is more sensitive to the task of rendering the original into the sequences and rhythms appropriate for English on stage. The modern translations are generally the more accurate, notably those by AESCH (1959) and LAMPORT (1969), the former, for example, being one of the first to come fairly close to the meaning of the Prince of Guastalla's initial expression of despair about his daily routine ("Die traurigen Geschäfte") with "Oh, these wretched chores". Emilia's famous dying response to her father's instantaneous, rhetorically intended question immediately after sinking Countess Orsina's dagger into his daughter's heart has had various renderings over the ages, not all of them reflecting the gravity and pathos of the situation, nor indeed the gentle beauty of the metaphor with which Lessing chose to evoke the idea that in a self-willed death Emilia was escaping the violation and degradation of her person by the Prince. The dying Emilia replies to her father's anguished "My God! What have I done?" with "Broke off a rose before a storm did blast it" (Maty); "Cut off a Rose before the Storm had shiver'd it" (Berrington); "You have broken a rose before the storm had robbed it of its leaves" (Thompson); "Plucked a rose ere the storm had blighted it" (Lewes); "Broken a rose, ere the storm scattered its petals" (Aesch).

Rudolph Erich RASPE (1781), who translated scientific and mineralogical works into English, wrote about volcanoes and was the creator of Baron Münchausen's narrative of his marvellous travels and campaigns in Russia, was the first translator of *Nathan the Wise*, producing his translation hardly three years after the publication of Lessing's dramatic poem in 1778. His treatment of the dramatis personae and his description of the play as a philosophical drama, where Lessing called it a dramatic poem, stray from the original. Ignoring his own generic attribution of the work, Raspe wrongly states that the original was not written for the stage (a common enough misconception) and he ignores the unrhyming iambic pentameters of the original, and the special kind of punctuation to which Lessing used specifically to direct the actors, by translating into prose. Generally, Raspe is accurate, fluent, readable and declaimable, but from time to time he colours the original. Yet he succeeds in retaining something of the poetic flavour of the original, for example, the poetic symmetries ("his name I know not what – his death I know not where") that recur in all Lessing's works for the theatre. TAYLOR (1791) recaptures these symmetries too. While approving of Schiller's abridged version for the stage, Taylor translates the entire work and keeps closer than Raspe to the style, mood and poetry of the source text. His version is more poetic, occasionally denser as a result, but showing sensitivity towards the enactment and production of speech in performance. Taylor is however more neglectful of the important stage directions than Raspe. JACKS (1894) wrote his translation as a form of relief from his parliamentary duties. In his introduction Frederick W. Farrar notes that by then there had already been various translations and that Jacks's translation was the first by a Scot.

The parable of the three rings and the positive affirmation of the charitable essence of the three monotheistic religions which are at the centre of this dramatic poem have given rise to different readings and considerable controversy. It is therefore important that the quality that the original ring and its two indistinguishable counterfeits possess is accurately translated. Lessing describes the jewel in the ring as an opal reflecting a hundred different colours and having the mysterious power of making pleasing to God and man whoever wore it believing in this power. The implication is that an act of faith is needed in order to be pleasing to God and man. The use by MORGAN (1955) and LUSTIG (1963) of "magic" for "geheim" ("mysterious" or possibly "secret") to describe the opal's power betrays the spirituality of Lessing's intention, but Taylor's "hidden" is quite close and he and Jacks ("secret power") clearly understand both the importance and the meaning of "in dieser Zuversicht" in their albeit more prolix versions, respectively "in this view, and this persuasion", "in this faith and confidence".

Translations of the *Hamburg Dramaturgy* and *How the Ancients Represented Death* are rare. The *Dramaturgy* chronicled productions of plays performed between 1767 and 1769 at Hamburg's German National Theatre, which employed Lessing as theatre critic, and ranged from a practical discussion of acting to discussions on the nature of tragedy. Lessing's essay on the visual representation of death by the Ancients defended the view that the Ancients had not used skeletons to signify death. He referred to Homer, ancient poetry generally, and Bellori's *Admirandis*, among other sources, to demonstrate the Greek tradition of pairing Sleep and Death together, their common denominator being Rest, and argued that the Greeks rarely represented Death as something terrible.

Lessing's *Laocoön* found a far wider readership. It took the statue of Laocoön, now in the Vatican, for its inspiration, reinforced Winckelmann's emphasis on the importance of beauty for Greek art, sculpture and coins, although differing with him on a few counts, and distinguished, according to the materials used and their spatial and temporal functionality, between the primarily co-existential arts of painting and sculpture and the primarily sequential art of poetry. This work has been translated frequently and, despite its length, never in abridgement.

RÖNNFELDT (1895) provides a fluent translation but is occasionally neglectful of the finer points of grammar. He chooses vocabulary for certain key concepts, such as "Zeichen" ("symbols"), "figuren" ("forms"), "bequem" ("suitable"), "eigentlich" ("special"), for which more appropriate terms are available. PHILLIMORE (1874) had done distinctly better. His translation, in easily readable English, was closer to the original and more precise, and used more appropriate terminology for the particular context, eg., "signs" for "Zeichen", "figures" for "figuren", "proper" for "eigentlich". In order to reflect his esteem for Lessing's work, Phillimore prefaced his translation, which is dedicated to W.E. Gladstone, with a motto from Lewes's *Life of Goethe*: "Macaulay told me that the reading of this little book formed an epoch in his mental history, and that he learned more from it than he had ever learned elsewhere." BEASLEY (1879), to whom Rönnfeldt is strikingly close, captures detail more accurately than either Rönnfeldt or Phillimore, e.g., "artikulierte Töne" are "articulated sounds", not "articulate sounds". STEEL (1930) reads awkwardly and although he uses appropriate terminology he seems otherwise not to have benefited from the infelicities of earlier translations. MCCORMICK (1962) is accurate and conveys Lessing's argument well, but he is unnecessarily free, writing for example of co-existing "wholes" (as Beasley and Rönnfeldt also do) when Lessing does not.

Lessing's *Ernst and Falk* consists of five dialogues, the first three of which proceed by a series of cryptic questions and answers to reveal the ideal nature of freemasonry, and the last two of which contain first Ernst's disillusionment with the masonic practice after he has been adopted and finally Lessing's speculative enquiry into freemasonry's origins and its essence. COHEN (1927) came across a reference to MACKENZIE's translation (1854 and 1872) in Mackey's *Encyclopaedia of Freemasonry* only after completing his own. He observed of it: "Conversations, without any explanatory introduction or comments. Certain difficulties in the text have been glossed over, and some phrases, obscure to him, altogether omitted". Cohen is abundantly annotated with comprehensive explanations of the various allusions to masonic issues and practices at the time of Lessing's original, which Cohen considered hardly intelligible without them. Despite his doubts about Lessing's etymology of "Masonry", Cohen was sufficiently moved by the "stirring and so closely reasoned ... exposition of the *raison d'être* of the Order and the place it has to fill in the destiny of the human race" to undertake further investigation of the issue before including it. ZWIEBEL (1991) ends his translation prematurely, with no explanation by translator or editor, before Lessing begins his speculative investigation of the etymology of "massoney" and of Sir Christopher Wren's role in English freemasonry. Zwiebel is idiomatic, fluent, up-to-date and incomplete, his notes are unsystematic and there are occasional errors. Cohen reads easily; it is occasionally stilted, with the odd archaism, but it is accurate on the whole and complete.

Whether reviewing books, writing essays, responding to some harsh theological judgement or other form of intolerance, whether defending the defenceless against their critics or developing his own theses on reason and Christianity, Lessing demonstrates that his religion, though unorthodox at times, is the religion of Christ. It is the importance to him of Christ's message of love that is at the heart of his daring and effective defence of the Jews against the cruel anti-Semitism of the age and of Muslims against the charge of heathendom. Lessing was profoundly attracted to the genre of fable and knew intimately the fables of Aesop, La Fontaine and Phaedrus. He thought the fable a genre par excellence for bringing together poetry and morality, and in 1759 he published a collection of his own, which contained essays he had written on the genre. His fables were translated infrequently, although accurately. Single fables have also been translated occasionally. RICHARDSON (1773) is unique in providing an early, comprehensive and accurate translation of the 1759 edition of Lessing's fables. Lessing's various public letters and his pamphlets, parables and diatribes against religious bigotry and intolerance, often flying in the face of the prevailing orthodoxy, made even his friends anxious for his safety. Morally justified though his line undoubtedly was, being firmly rooted in the doctrine of Christ, Lessing became more antagonistically personal and vindictive than he had ever been before, above all in the *Axiomata* and his campaign against his fulminating adversary, the Protestant Hamburg preacher, Joachim Melchior Goeze, which found expression in the so-called *Anti-Goeze*. Fundamentally Lessing opposed the view that the well-being of Christianity was rooted solely in the Bible. BARNARD (1862) offers clearly expressed and careful translations of these two works, and also of Lessing's *Parable*, a short work that illustrates the irrelevance of arguing acrimoniously about the origins of Christianity when its wondrous presence is already there to behold and far worthier of appreciation. With similar care and concern for detail, CHADWICK (1956) focuses on Lessing's more positive affirmations of the teachings of Christ and of St John as expressed in his reply to Johann Daniel

Schumann in *On the Proof of the Spirit and the Power*, *The Testament of John*, *The Religion of Christ* and, of all Lessing's writings on religion, on the one that succeeded more than the others in rousing sustained controversy, *The Education of the Human Race*.

Lessing's *The Education of the Human Race* consists of 100 paragraphs of poetic prose which explain the Old and New Testaments as stages in the religious education of mankind from Judaism to Christianity, from uncivilized idolatry to monotheism, from belief in the coming of a new kingdom on earth to one in heaven, from the religious education contained in the Bible through to perfection, the final stage of God's revelation. The hypothesis elaborated towards the end of the work, that the process of perfecting the soul so that it grows ever closer to God's absolute state of perfection, or even being taken into it, might be effected through the generations, aroused particular controversy. ROBERTSON (1858) and CHADWICK (1956) both offer close and accurate translations, the latter occasionally free but also more readily comprehensible to the English-language reader. In several passages their translations are indistinguishable. Although both contain minor inaccuracies, and frequently the same ones, they have each run to several new editions and reprints.

EDWARD M. BATLEY

Further Reading

Dvoretzky, Edward, "The Eighteenth-Century Translations of Emilia Galotti", *Rice University Studies*, 52/3 (1966) pp. 1–106 (Appendix A, The Henry Maty Translation of *Emilia Galotti*, pp. 25–42; Appendix B, The Drury Lane Version of *Emilia Galotti*, 1794)

Morgan, Bayard Quincy, *A Critical Bibliography of German Literature in English Translation 1481–1927, with Supplement Embracing the Years 1928–1955*, New York: Scarecrow Press, 1965

Seifert, Siegfried, *Lessing-Bibliographie*, Berlin: Aufbau, 1973

Smith, Murray F., *A Selected Bibliography of German Literature in English Translation 1956–1960*, Metuchen, New Jersey: Scarecrow Press, 1972

Todt, Wilhelm, *Lessing in England, 1767–1850*, Heidelberg: Winter, 1912

Carlo Levi 1902–1975

Italian novelist, essayist and painter

Biography

Born in Turin, 29 November 1902. He studied medicine at the University of Turin and graduated in 1924 but never formally practised. He turned to painting (his work was shown as part of the expressionist Six Painters of Turin exhibition held in 1929), literature and politics. Levi's socialist ideals and Jewish heritage brought him into conflict with Mussolini's fascist regime. He spent extended periods in Paris with the leaders of the Italian Resistance and while in France he helped to found the Giustizia e Libertà underground organization. This activity eventually led to his arrest in 1934 and his subsequent exile to Grassano and later to Gagliano, both in Lucania. Two years later Levi was freed under a general amnesty and he resumed political activity. He was instrumental in the formulation of the left-wing Action Party and edited its journal *L'Italia Libera*. He emigrated to France, but returned to Italy to work with the Resistance. In the 1960s he was elected as senator in the independent list of the Italian Communist Party. Levi is best known for his novel *Christ Stopped at Eboli*, in which he described the social conditions of the village of Gagliano, under the fictitious name of Aliano. Died in Rome, 4 January 1975.

Translations

Documentary Novel

Cristo si è fermato a Eboli, 1945

Frenaye, Frances, *Christ Stopped at Eboli: The Story of a Year*, New York: Farrar Straus, 1947; London: Readers' Union, 1949; with a new introduction by Levi, Farrar Straus, 1963

Novel

L'orologio, 1950

Farrar, John, *The Watch*, New York: Farrar Straus, 1951; London: Cassell, 1952

Essays

Paura della libertà, 1946

Gourevitch, Adolphe, *Of Fear and Freedom*, New York: Farrar Straus, and London: Cassell, 1950

Le parole sono pietre: tre giornate in sicilia, 1955

Davidson, Angus, *Words Are Stones: Impressions of Sicily*, New York: Farrar Straus, 1958; London: Gollancz, 1959

La doppia notte dei tigli, 1959

Bernstein, Joseph M., *The Linden Trees*, New York: Knopf, 1962; as *The Two-Fold Night: A Narrative of Travel in Germany*, London: Cresset Press, 1962

Written in Florence between Christmas 1943 and July 1944, Carlo Levi's first published book, *Christ Stopped at Eboli*, reflects the intensely dramatic months of the clandestine resistance fight against Fascism. It records the central events in his year of political exile in Lucania in 1935, and the everlasting bond that develops between the local peasants and an elusive northerner. This very personal story was an instant success on its publication. The modest jacket of the Einaudi edition was a reproduction of one of Levi's paintings – the image of a boy holding the head of a slaughtered goat. The author himself introduced his literary enterprise as "a book of war" for a New Italy.

This aesthetic and political claim is expressed in a style that is a genuine contribution to a sensitive understanding of southern Italian culture and its harsh socio-economic conditions. Levi writes with vigour, guided by an eye for compelling and humanistic details, and portrays the lives of the peasants and the nature of their historical isolation with colour and analytical incisiveness. His narrative mode relies on simple, poetic language, which enforces his search for the truth. Levi's stylistic choice embraces a complex system of phrases, words, gestures and ancient values, all of which assert the authority of his discovery of a different civilization. By creating history from personal knowledge, he brings into play the contexts and associations that once made this reality comprehensible to him, and also gives value to a lost world, its symbols and empirical truths, including its moral stands on social justice. Levi's language defines a vision of control that challenges the literary traditions of neo-realism, the ethnographical novel, and autobiographical narratives. All of this makes it particularly difficult for a translator.

The first American edition of *Christ Stopped at Eboli* was published by the recently founded Farrar Straus, a company later to retain exclusive rights to all books by Levi in English. FRENAYE's translation set the standard: a number of publishers have faithfully reproduced the 1947 version. Frenaye's work makes an effort to incorporate popular phrases and the cadences of southern Italian speech. The translation is clear and crisp, but, while the shades of meaning and many of the original stylistic variants are maintained, the poetic intonation of Levi's words is inevitably diminished. The English style conforms to Levi's theoretical investigation of language as an instrument to achieve the truth in portraying how ideals may coexist with the coercive abuses of state power. In 1963, Farrar Straus added to its 2nd edition a "Letter" by Levi to the publisher, where the author points to experience, painting and poetry as the fundamental strengths of this novel, which remains his most acclaimed book.

From the early 1950s onward, Levi's works were translated into English unusually quickly after their publication in Italian. The eight short essays in *Of Fear and Freedom* shift the terms of Levi's personal and political investigation to the crisis of civilization. They expose the intellectual weaknesses within the philosophical premises of Nazism and the theory of the State, and seek to identify the fundamental incoherence with which Europe met the death of freedom. Written in 1939, while Levi was in exile at La Baule, the book explores the possibility of a democratic, ethical and political reorientation. It reveals his ability for historical analysis and for identifying emblematic collective phenomena.

GOUREVITCH's translation (1950) relies on a word-for-word rendering. It includes the author's preface to the 1946 edition. Gourevitch's own preface asks whether any translating venture can claim to recognize and fully appreciate the significance of the original work. He posits the inevitable betrayal of the text and admits to his great difficulties in approaching Levi's prose, which he describes as epical and poetically beautiful. For example, the depth given to the original by the use of Latin and ancient Hebrew cannot be matched by a vernacular English. Gourevitch plays with the richness of Levi's language and tries to convey the flavour and sound evoked by his stunning images, which underlie the historical reality of this intensely private and brilliant book.

Levi's novel *The Watch* is crucial to understanding the politics of transition in postwar Italy. It offers a compelling account of what happened on the streets of Rome and Naples during a social crisis. Levi's writing is not easy to classify according to traditional literary genres. The term "novel" may be used to describe his two most structured narrative works. *The Watch* draws on magic, memory and poetry as receptacles of knowledge. It asserts an imaginary, intuitive space through stories of traumatic events, occasional encounters and apparitions. Beginning with a conventional symbolic device (a broken watch), it shows how the narrator, deprived for three days of the Bergsonian direction of time, discovers a sacred, non-linear human structure in his fragmented environment. Without his watch, he has to take refuge in a subjective world, where the flux of time is closer to the natural essence of man. In a prefatory poem, omitted from the English edition, Levi states that the mechanical rhythm of the watch's hands functions as a metaphor of human existence. Levi's approach to storytelling intercuts everyday life with observations on language and politics. Reality, myth, truth and fable coexist in the form of cultural poetics.

FARRAR's English version (1951) oversimplifies the compelling tone of the original work. Only occasionally does it enable us to glimpse Levi's immediate, dense and textured style and its use of contemporary and ancient words to enhance the poetry of sound. Any translation of this work must meet the challenge of re-working the Italian text.

Two more collections of Levi's essays have been translated into English: *Le parole sono pietre* (*Words Are Stones*), 1955, winner of the prestigious Viareggio Prize, and *La doppia notte dei tigli* (*The Linden Trees*), 1959. Analytically brilliant and very moving, the essays offer striking insights into a culture that has shaped the ethos of Western society and politics. They also provide a rare portrait of Levi the man. The first volume includes a number of essays originally published in 1951; these are lucid introductions to the problematic conditions that underlie the world of the Sicilian peasants. The book takes the form of a journal recording three trips to the island, and shows Levi developing a new awareness and redefining the boundaries of existence. DAVIDSON's translation (1958) tries to maintain the personal traits of Levi's language by incorporating some of the Italian words into English. The effect is one of a close encounter with the meaning of the original text.

The Linden Trees, a narrative of travel in Germany, is Levi's account of the harrowing sense of delusion and unrest haunting a country still crippled and divided by guilt. He looks beyond the façade of the economic realities to examine the ambivalent obsessions and preoccupations, which would, after the traumas of war, coalesce into the heart of contemporary Germany. BERNSTEIN's translation (1962) is journalistic, even mechanical, and loses many of the poetic nuances of Levi's text.

GAETANA MARRONE

Further Reading

Catani, R.D., "Structure and Style as Fundamental Expressions: The Works of Carlo Levi and Their Poetic Ideology", *Italica*, 56 (1979) pp. 213–29

See also the translator's preface to Gourevitch

Primo Levi 1919–1987

Italian essayist and fiction writer

Biography

Born into a Jewish family in Turin, 31 July 1919. He was educated at the University of Turin, where he obtained a degree in chemistry, before beginning work as an industrial chemist in Milan. Increasingly subject to anti-Semitic legislation under Mussolini's regime, he eventually joined the Italian Resistance, forming a small guerrilla force, before being captured. Held initially at Fossoli, he was transferred to the Auschwitz concentration camp complex in Poland in 1944, an experience he was one of the few to survive. Returning to Italy in 1945, he began a long career as an industrial chemist with SIVA in Turin, 1945. Two important events occurred in 1947: he was married, to Lucia Morpurgo, and his first book *Se questo è un uomo* (*If This Is a Man*), which described the Auschwitz period, was published. Subsequently Levi combined his writing with his work as a chemist, eventually retiring from the latter to devote himself entirely to writing in 1974. He was awarded a number of prestigious literary awards, including the Strega prize (1979) and the Viareggio prize (1982). He committed suicide in Turin, 11 April 1987.

Almost all of Levi's works have as their mainspring his experiences during World War II as a victim and survivor of the Holocaust. Other major works include the stories and essays of *Il sistemo periodico* (*The Periodic Table*), 1975, the narrative *Se non ora, quando?* (*If Not Now, When?*), 1982, and his final book, the essay collection *I sommersi e i salvati* (*The Drowned and the Saved*), 1986.

Translations

Testimonial Narratives

Se questo è un uomo, 1947, new edition, 1958

Woolf, Stuart, *If This Is a Man*, London and New York: Orion Press, 1959; as *Survival in Auschwitz*, New York: Collier, 1961

La tregua, 1963

Woolf, Stuart, *The Truce: A Survivor's Journey from Auschwitz*, London: Bodley Head, 1965; as *The Reawakening (La Tregua): A Liberated Prisoner's Long March Home through East Europe*, Boston: Little Brown, 1965

I sommersi e i salvati, 1986

Rosenthal, Raymond, *The Drowned and the Saved*, New York: Summit, and London: Michael Joseph, 1988

Short Stories

Storie naturali, 1966 (under the pseudonym Damiano Malabaila), 1979 (republished under the author's name); *Vizio di forma*, 1971

Rosenthal, Raymond, *The Sixth Day and Other Tales* (selection from *Storie naturali* and *Vizio di forma*), New York: Summit, and London: Michael Joseph, 1990

Il sistema periodico, 1975

Rosenthal, Raymond, *The Periodic Table*, New York: Schocken, 1984

Lilít e altri racconti, 1981

Feldman, Ruth, *Moments of Reprieve*, New York: Summit, and London: Michael Joseph, 1986

Racconti e saggi, 1986

Rosenthal, Raymond, *The Mirror Maker: Stories and Essays*, New York: Schocken, 1989

Essays

L'altrui mestiere, 1985

Rosenthal, Raymond, *Other People's Trades*, New York: Summit, and London: Michael Joseph, 1989

Poetry

L'osteria di Brema, 1975; *Ad ora incerta*, 1984; *Opere*, vol. 2, 1988

Feldman, Ruth and Brian Swann, *Shemà: Collected Poems of Primo Levi*, London: Menard Press, 1976; as *Collected Poems*, London and Boston: Faber, 1988; 2nd edition, 1992 (contains previously uncollected or untranslated poems which are translated by Ruth Feldman alone)

Longer Fiction

La chiave a stella, 1978

Weaver, William, *The Monkey's Wrench*, New York: Summit, 1986; as *The Wrench*, London: Michael Joseph, 1987

Se non ora, quando?, 1982
Weaver, William, *If Not Now, When?*, New York: Summit, 1985; London: Michael Joseph, 1986

Other Writing
Levi, Primo and Tullio Regge, *Dialogo*, 1984
Rosenthal, Raymond, *Dialogo*, Princeton, New Jersey: Princeton University Press, 1989; as *Conversations*, London: Tauris, 1989

Primo Levi left a remarkably varied body of work. His reputation as a writer developed mainly during the 1980s and several of his texts are now used in schools in Italy. This reputation, however, relates mainly to his writings about his experience of Nazi persecution. Levi was one of a number of survivors of the concentration camps who felt impelled to record their memories of the offence, but he is, together with Elie Wiesel, perhaps one of the best known among the wider reading public. Levi's effectiveness at communicating his personal experience of Buna-Monowitz (Auschwitz) and the degradation of the individual in the camps is not due simply to the veracity of his account. In *Se questo è un uomo* (*If This Is a Man* / *Survival in Auschwitz*) Levi does not present a chronicled series of events or an itemized account of his suffering. Instead he concentrates upon the particular episodes that epitomize for him the nature of the concentration camp experience; each episode is a powerful image which documents the gradual destruction of individual humanity.

Levi deals with the memory of Holocaust experience in a variety of literary forms: testimonial narrative, extended essays, a novel, numerous short stories, various journalistic essays and poetry. His writings also include collections of futuristic short stories, contemplative essays, and an anthology of writings that have influenced his life.

The nature of the subject matter of *Se questo è un uomo* (1958) makes a faithful translation of the utmost importance if the essence of the author's experience is not to be lost or diluted. WOOLF (1959) is close and handles problematic passages skilfully. The stylistic contrapositioning of the *passato remoto* and the present tense is found on a number of occasions in the source text, depicting firstly the particulars of the ordeal and also the impact of it upon the individual. Woolf respects the use of tenses as far as is reasonable and, on those occasions where such usage is not possible, he aims at an equivalence of effect.

In *Se questo è un uomo*, time is a concept with no relevance within the context of the extermination camps, whereas in Primo Levi's next narrative account, *La tregua*, time is seen more in terms of a series of chronicled events; the passage of time once more has relevance for the survivor seeking to regain consciousness of his humanity. WOOLF (1965) is accurate, successfully capturing the lightness of tone that marks several chapters of the source text.

I sommersi e i salvati is a grave and thought-provoking reflection upon the Nazi concentration camp system as it affected those who came within its domain. The author's ideas are often complex and philosophical, but the intended readership is a general one and thus his thoughts are expressed with great clarity. ROSENTHAL (1988) strenuously attempts to remain true to the original. Levi's thoughts shine through in a translation that is noble in intention and captures the sense of the author's continual struggle to communicate some comprehension of the enormity of events. Too strict an adherence to the syntactic structure of the source text, however, leads to a somewhat unnatural rendition.

The Sixth Day (ROSENTHAL, 1990) comprises selected tales from *Storie naturali* and *Vizio di forma*, both of which are collections of futuristic stories. The title is taken from one of the short stories, an understandable strategy given the difficulty of translating the play on words inherent in the original titles. In attempting to remain true to the source texts Rosenthal sometimes forgets that certain Italian grammatical constructions cannot be translated directly into English. The result is a rather creaky translation, particularly in passages containing dialogue.

Each story of *The Periodic Table* (ROSENTHAL, 1984) has as its motif a chemical element. This presents a challenge for the translator in that technical terms and descriptions of scientific analysis are interspersed in the general narrative. It is, however, Rosenthal's dependency on the word order of the original text, rather than any technical points, that can lead to some curious translations, and even to ambiguity, as in "I made my wife die for the insurance", rather than "I killed my wife for the insurance money".

Moments of Reprieve (FELDMAN, 1986) contains selected stories from *Lilít*, which itself is a collection of selected stories originally published in the newspaper *La Stampa*. The stories chosen for translation concern in some way the author's experience of Nazi persecution. Feldman's translation is fluent and faithful to the original. She successfully communicates Levi's prowess as a story-teller.

Other People's Trades (ROSENTHAL, 1989) comprises 39 of the 51 essays contained in *L'altrui mestiere*, plus four originally published in *Racconti e saggi*. This admixture, together with the reorganization of the contents, is not explained, although the specifically linguistic discussion of several essays that have been excluded might have been considered of limited appeal to an English-speaking readership. Rosenthal's rendering is competent, with occasional nice touches.

The Mirror Maker (ROSENTHAL, 1989) comprises a selection of essays and stories published in *Racconti e saggi*, together with other journalistic essays published in the Italian newspaper *La Stampa*. The English remains close to the meaning of the source, but expression is sometimes stilted because of attempts to reproduce Italian vocabulary and syntax. Of particular interest is the essay "Translating Kafka", in which Levi discusses his motivation for translating Kafka's *The Trial* from German into Italian.

A collection of a few poems that Primo Levi wrote for family and friends was originally translated by FELDMAN & SWANN and published under the title *Shemà* (1976), winning the John Florio prize for best Italian to English translation. These poems were republished in *Collected Poems* (1988), together with additional poems translated by Feldman, taken from *Ad ora incerta*, and also a poem sent by the author to Feldman. Further poems, some of which have been published posthumously in the second volume of the author's collected works, appeared in the 1992 edition. On the whole the translators are faithful to the rhythm and tone of the original, which sometimes involves slight, but acceptable, departures from a literal translation. Some errors and misunderstandings of the Italian present in the 1988 edition are not amended in the 1992 edition, including the omission of a verse in "The first Atlas".

In *La chiave a stella* (1978) the fictionalized Levi and his alter-ego, Libertino Faussone, tell stories of their working lives and the pleasure derived from a job well done. WEAVER (1986, 1987) captures the jauntiness of Faussone's conversational style, finding colourful equivalents for the colloquialisms and proverbs, although some expressions may read more happily to an American reader than to a British one.

Primo Levi's only novel, *Se non ora, quando?* (1982) tells the story of a disparate band of Jewish partisans who fight their way across Eastern Europe towards Italy with the goal of Palestine ever before them. It received a mixed critical response. WEAVER (1985) is close, not attempting to smooth out any apparent awkwardness of expression, and the diversity of cultures and social backgrounds of the various characters is thus reflected. An oddity, however, is the translation of "fare bella figura" as "to cut a finger" instead of "to cut a figure", although this may be a slip in the editing rather than in the translation.

Dialogo / Conversations (ROSENTHAL, 1989) is a rather literal translation that tends to disregard the relaxed nature of the conversation between Primo Levi, the respected writer and chemist, and Tullio Regge, the distinguished academic and physicist. On a number of occasions Rosenthal favours one interpretation of a word despite the availability of a more obvious choice. For example, the adverbial "why" is turned into a noun to express "il perché", instead of using the more straightforward "the reason"; "anche" is frequently translated as "also" when the alternative "even" is evidently required.

JUDITH A. KELLY

Further Reading

Cicioni, Mirna, *Primo Levi: Bridges of Knowledge*, Oxford and Washington, DC: Berg, 1995

Rosenthal, R., "Translating Primo Levi" in *Primo Levi as Witness: Proceedings of a Symposium Held at Princeton University, 30 April–2 May 1989*, edited by Pietro Frassica, Florence: Casalini, 1990

Sodi, Risa B., *A Dante of Our Time: Primo Levi and Auschwitz*, New York: Peter Lang, 1990

Woolf, J., *The Memory of the Offence: Primo Levi's If This Is a Man*, Market Harborough and Hull: University Texts / Hull Italian Texts, 1995

José Lezama Lima 1910 or 1912–1976

Cuban essayist, novelist and poet

Biography

Born in Havana, 19 December 1910 (some sources give his birthdate as 1912). He grew up in the Fortaleza de la Cabaña military camp, where his father, José María Lezama y Rodda, was a senior figure in the military academy, the Academia Militar del Morro. After the father's death in 1919 the family moved to Havana and lived with Lezama Lima's maternal grandmother. The boy developed a severe asthmatic condition which was to cause him difficulty throughout his life. He attended the Instituto de Havana from 1926 until 1928, and then the University of Havana, where he graduated in law in 1938. While at university he was a co-founder of the literary review *Verbum*. He published his first book of poetry, *Muerte de Narciso* (*Death of Narcissus*), in 1937. He worked in private law practice after graduation, and then in the Consejo Superior de Defensa Social (Higher Council for Social Service). He also edited the journal *Espuela de plata* [Silver Spur], and in 1943 established a poetry journal, *Nadie parecía* [No One Appeared]. From the 1940s he lived in Havana with his mother, until her death in 1964. In 1944 he collaborated in the launching of *Orígenes*, which became an influential avant-garde literary review. He remained as editor of *Orígines* until it closed in 1957. From 1945 Lezama Lima worked as director of the Department of Culture in the Ministry of Education. He travelled to Mexico and Jamaica in 1949 and 1950. He published a book of literary criticism, *Algunos tratados en La Habana* [Some Treatises in Havana] in 1958. After the Cuban Revolution of 1959 he became director of literature and publications at the Consejo Nacional de Cultura (National Council for the Arts). He also acted as an adviser at the Cuban Centre for Literary Research. He was one of six vice-presidents of the Union of Cuban Artists and Writers, 1959–62. Lezama Lima married María Luisa Bautista in 1965. Following the publication of his most important and influential work, the semi-autobiographical *Paradiso* (*Paradiso*), in 1966, he lost the approval of fidel Castro and other Cuban revolutionary politicians because of the novel's frank debate about homosexuality, its Catholicism and its understatement of revolutionary ideology. Lezama Lima wrote very little during the 1970s, partly because of his declining health. Died in Havana, 9 August 1976.

Lezama Lima's masterpiece is generally held to be his epic novel *Paradiso*, begun in the 1940s and published in 1966. It gained him international recognition and remains his most famous work. He was working on its sequel, the unfinished *Oppiano Licario*, when he died. His collections of poetry include the hermetic *Enemigo Rumor* [Enemy Murmur], 1941; a collection that also contained prose, *Aventuras sigilosas* [Silent Adventures], 1945; and *La fijeza* [fixity], 1949. His literary credo is explored in an important essay *Las imágenes posibles* [Possible Images] included in his collection of essays on literature, *Analecta del reloj* [Analecta of the Clock], published in 1953. A collection of his lectures, *La expresión americana* (*American Expression*), was published in 1957, and *La cantidad hechizada* [The Bewitched Quantity], another collection of essays, in 1970.

Translations

Novel

Paradiso, 1966

Rabassa, Gregory *Paradiso*, London: Secker and Warburg, and New York: Farrar Straus, 1974

Stories

Los fugados, 1936

Bush, Peter, *The Truants* in *The Voice of the Turtle: An Anthology of Cuban Stories*, edited by Bush, London: Quartet, and New York: Grove Press, 1997

"Juego de las decapitationes", 1941

Levine, Suzanne Jill and Rachel Philips, *Decapitation Games*, special issue of *fictions*, 6/2 (1981) edited by Levine

José Lezama Lima is a Cuban writer of Joycean stature, yet his essays, poetry and fiction remain largely untranslated and when translated unknown beyond a small coterie of writers and enthusiasts. Gregory RABASSA's translation of the first part of his masterpiece, the novel *Paradiso*, was published in 1974, found itself on the extreme fringe of the vogue for Latin American fiction and never entered the Boom marketplace. The University of Texas Press 1988 reissue and an increasing interest in Cuban literature and traditions may augur better times and a wider readership for Lezama in the English-speaking world. However, it is a sad fact that a writer who combined Catholicism and homosexuality, enormous erudition and striking originality, and who edited a Havana literary magazine – *Orígines* – which drew in major writers from the US, UK and Europe, should still be silenced by the raucous press coverage and hype that greets the latest Isabel Allende or Laura Esquivel, or by the canonical status of García Márquez or Carlos Fuentes.

Lezama was not helped by being scorned by the Madrid literary establishment, marginalized for his aesthetics, religion and sexuality by fidel Castro's regime and largely ignored by the academic world of Hispanicists. He has long been championed by writers such as Guillermo Cabrera Infante and Juan Goytisolo, and now is an inspiration to younger Cuban writers like Senel Paz (b. 1950), whose short story *The Wolf, the Woods and the New Man* in its prose, film and dramatic versions brought Lezama to much wider audiences by making him the favourite author in the pantheon of Diego, the gay protagonist. With the new millennium, is Lezama's hour nigh? Joyce, to whom Lezama can be likened, created an industry, is a household name, and a new translation into whatever language becomes a major event in that culture. At least when more translations are made from Lezama's work into English, then it might be recognized in the English-speaking world that there can be no proper understanding of Latin American culture without a reading of his essays, poetry and fiction.

Gregory Rabassa is undoubtedly the doyen of American translators of Latin American fiction. His art of translating long prose works has developed through translation of such modern classics as García Márquez's *A Hundred Years of Solitude* and Cortázar's *Hopscotch*: the techniques for sustaining concentration over 500 pages, the many drafts, the research, the collaboration with and questions to authors, and the final writing of what will be the original text for millions. Legion are the readers who believe that García Márquez is an English writer, as they believe the Bible was written in English. *Paradiso* has not reached, yet alone crossed that threshold. Were it ever to do so, it is likely that chapter 8 would gain the notoriety, as avidly read pages of condensed erotic encounters, of Molly Bloom's soliloquy at the end of *Ulysses*. For whatever reason, it seems from an analysis of sections of this chapter that RABASSA (1974) was not entirely at home with the novel's erotic content and wordplay. The translation falters over challenges that are not met. There are word-games which Lezama weaves through the chapter that evaporate in English. Lezama uses a number of Graeco-Latinate, medical-sounding words which are translated as if following the adage decreeing that Anglo-Saxon English is a non-Latin language and therefore the translator should avoid Latinism and other "learned" features. However, Lezama deliberately alternates Graeco-Latinate neologisms and direct terms in order to heighten both comic and ironic effects. Farrulaque's physical feature is that he is "leptosomático" – rendered by Rabassa as "small-bodied". That is contrasted with "pero dotado de una enorme verga", explained in the English as "but he could count among his few attributes an enormous member", which more literally and frugally could be "but endowed with a huge cock". This consistent patter peaks in the doubly "learned" depiction of penetration by "el aguijón leptosomático macrogenitosoma" – in the English "a large barb of the small-bodied boy", when the translation fails to rise to the leptosomatic, macrogenetic moment. Later, we are told how phallic flaunting was "esa improvisada falarascopia"; the humour of the neologism is lost in "this improvised phallic display", although we do get a glimpse of the possibilities of translation when the "presuntuoso vitalista" becomes a "cocky vitalist". Farrulaque's sexual exploits are matched by Leregas who proceeds to display his phallic capabilities during a boring geography lesson on the Gulf Stream. In the same passage playful comparisons and images are used in the Spanish which for some reason are absent from the translation. This tendency to consistent under-translation is numerically confirmed when in the rendering of certain indelicate acrobatics "tres libros en octavo mayor" become "two octavo books".

LEVINE & PHILIPS's translation (1981) of Lezama's story (1941) of a Chinese court magician, Emperor and intrigue keeps closely to the plastic, visual qualities of the story, which is a narrative labyrinth generally without the linguistic intensity of later Lezama. The scenes seem inspired by tableaux of court pageantry and this more literal translation has the measure of their strangeness:

> Veían figuras que se desplegaban en espirales uniformemente acceleradas. El emperador, con un agujero dejado por el pico del flamengo debajo de la tetilla izquierdo, continuaba con sus brazos alzados, seguía impulsando romanzas.

> They saw figures unfolding in uniformly accelerating

spirals. The Emperor, with the hole left by the flamingo's beak just below his left nipple, still had his arms raised and was still emitting his songs.

A Yeatsian tremor is introduced in a subsequent phrase, as "El halcón, noble dueño de su precipitarse, abría lo circular..." is translated as "The falcon, noble lord of his precipitous descent, broke the gyre..."

Sometimes the translation of Lezama proves difficult because of his ability to load the simplest combination of simple words with tension and ambiguity. There is a meaning, beyond the literal, of which the reader or translator of Spanish cannot be sure. *Los fugados* (1936) opens with a sentence – "No era un aire desligado, no se nadaba en el aire" – that seems straightforward, yet the meaning goes beyond the meteorological message about a sudden wind whipping the water over the Malecón, to the emotional torment of the two adolescent truants. Does "It was no stray breeze, nobody swam on the breeze" (BUSH, 1997) capture the tension? Will the strangeness of the Spanish seem strange in English, or awkward? How does such prose read in Spanish? Lezama maintained that only the difficult was beautiful, and a translator has thus to be familiar with degrees of strangeness in both the Spanish and the English.

The opening paragraph of the story has an enormously long sentence describing a drop of rainwater meandering its way down a shield advertising a jewellery shop. After two pages it finally falls to the ground, "hasta que al fin caía tan rápidament que la absorcíon de la tierra daba un grito". The first part of this affords no problem. It is the second part that transforms Spanish into something new: literally, "until finally it fell so rapidly that the absorption of the earth gave a cry". Because it was so dry and pleased with the moisture? Or pleased because Luis and Armand are off to the beach? Is the prolonged passage of the drop of water a symbol of the long wait before action? Is there a homoerotic implication – is it a seminal passage? Like a literary critic, the translator has to pursue Lezama's patterns, but to come up not with academic discourse but with words to match the precise and infinite possibilities in the resonances released. Is there, for example, a reminiscence of the cry of the mandrake root? Does "finally fell so rapidly that the absorption of the earth cried out" avoid the collapse into what might seem more natural – "the absorbing / absorbent earth cried out"?

When one considers the range and research and demands on a translator's language that the translation of a very short story imposes, one recognizes the enormity of the task undertaken by RABASSA when he took on the 500 pages of the mature Lezama that is *Paradiso*. One wants to ask how long was he given by his publishers, what was the financial reward, was there a proper collaboration with Lezama or in-house editors. As ever, one wonders what is the secret history of a major translation, that can sometimes be revealed by serious research in archives. Eloísa Lezama Lima, the writer's daughter, notes in her comment on the edition of the Spanish text used by her for the Cátedra series that Rabassa corrected some mistakes in the novel "but we don't know whether or not he had the permission of Lezama Lima, with whom he had frequent correspondence while he was doing the translation". She herself respected these errors, as they were made by Lezama when he revised his text for the 1968 Biblioteca Era edition in Mexico, prepared by Carlos Monsiváis and Julio Cortázar, and as Lezama preferred the voluptuousness of memory to accuracy. His translators are in need of the voluptuousness of language.

PETER BUSH

Further Reading

Goytisolo, Juan, "The Erotic Metaphor: Góngora, Joaquín Belda and Lezama Lima" in his *Saracen Chronicles: A Selection of Literary Essays*, translated by Helen Lane, London: Quartet, 1992, pp. 186–211

Lezama Lima, Eloísa (editor), *Paradiso*, by José Lezama Lima, Madrid: Cátedra, 1980

Li Bai 701–762

Chinese poet

Biography

Also known as Li Po, Li Taibo (Li T'ai-Po), Rihaku, etc. Born in Sichuan province in 701. He came from a wealthy family and maintained a profligate and extravagant lifestyle as a youth, as well as reading widely. During his teens he spent some years with a Daoist recluse, and trained as a knight-errant some time before he was 25. He left home to become a wanderer, visiting Daoist priests and temples and exploring various well-known places in China. He then married for the first of four times and went to live with his wife's family north of Han-chou. By this time he had started to write poetry, and after another period of travelling, during which time his literary reputation was established, he was summoned in 742 to the court of the emperor Xuanzong at Chang'an, the capital city. He was employed there as a court poet until 745, when he fell victim to intrigue and left the court in disgrace, taking up his wandering life again. He met the other major Chinese poet of the period, Du Fu, at this time.

In 757 he became unofficial court poet to the military expedition of prince Lin, brother of emperor Suzong. In 758, after prince Lin attempted to usurp the imperial throne and was executed, Li Bai was banished and imprisoned at Chiu-chang. He was subsequently released, but later banished again to Yeh-lang when charges against him were revived. He spent his last years living at a relative's home in eastern China. Died in Anhui province, China, 762.

Along with Du Fu, Li Bai is generally considered China's greatest poet of the classical period. His romantic poems, which stem from the tradition of Chinese folk ballads, often rejoice in the pleasure of drinking wine, as well as revealing his appreciation of nature and the joys and sadness of love and friendship. His work was widely read and imitated and influenced greatly the work of later Chinese writers, earning him the title of "celestial poet". Among Li Bai's best-known poems are "The Road to Shu is Hard", written about 744; "The Waterfall of Lu Shan" and *Ballads of the Four Seasons*.

Translations

For a discussion of the many available editions, see Hanabusa Hideki, *Ri Haku kashi sakuin* (*A Concordance to the Poems of Li Po*), Kyoto: Jimbunkagaku kenkyûjo, 1957, whose companion volume reprints the important Song dynasty edition. For a modern punctuated edition of Li Bo's complete works (poetry and prose), with commentary by Wang Qi (1696–1774), consult *Li Taibo quan ji*, Beijing: Zhonghua Shuju, 1977.

Ayscough, Florence and Amy Lowell, *Fir-flower Tablets*, Boston: Houghton Mifflin, 1921; London: Constable, 1922; reprinted Westport, Connecticut: Hyperion Press, 1973 (contains 83 poems by Li Bai)

Cooper, Arthur, *Li Po and Tu Fu: Poems*, Harmondsworth: Penguin, 1973 (contains 25 poems by Li Bai with explanatory comments)

Eide, Elling, *Poems by Li Po*, 2 vols, Lexington, Kentucky: Anvil Press, 1984 (lavishly produced limited edition of 150 copies; contains 50 poems)

Fletcher, W.J.B., *Gems of Chinese Verse*, Shanghai: Commercial Press, 1919; reprinted New York: Paragon, 1966

Giles, Herbert A., *Chinese Poetry in English Verse*, London: Bernard Quaritch, and Shanghai: Kelly and Walsh, 1898 (all 21 poems by Li Bai were reprinted in Giles's *Gems of Chinese Literature: Verse*, 2nd edition, London: Bernard Quaritch, and Shanghai: Kelly and Walsh, 1923)

Obata, Shigeyoshi, *The Works of Li Po*, New York: Dutton, 1922; London: Dent, 1923 (contains 124 poems by Li Bo, plus some concerning Li Bai by other poets)

Pound, Ezra, *Cathay*, London: Mathews, 1915 (contains 12 poems by Li Bai (or Rihaku, as Pound refers to him; the first, "The River Song" comprises two different poems in the original Chinese)

Seth, Vikram, *Three Chinese Poets: Translations of Poems by Wang Wei, Li Bai and Du Fu*, London: Faber, and New York: Harper, 1992 (12 poems by Li Bai)

Waley, Arthur, *The Poetry and Career of Li Po, 701–762 AD*, London: Allen and Unwin, 1950; New York: Macmillan, 1958 (study containing large number of translations)

Yip, Wai-lim, *Chinese Poetry: Major Modes and Genres*, Berkeley: University of California Press, 1976 (contains 16 poems by Li Bai)

The translation of Li Bai has focused almost exclusively on his poetry. The earliest important English translations date from the late 19th century, when translators of Chinese poetry began to look beyond the archaic and canonically enshrined *Classic of Poetry* (*Shijing*).

Among these translators, GILES (1898) is perhaps the best known. His work is characteristic of the period in its use of scanned, rhymed English verse. While one must give him credit for occasionally well-wrought lines, Giles's approach now seems very dated and most modern readers will find its bouncing metres and Victorian sentimentality too sickly. Moreover, he frequently takes serious liberties with the original text in order to achieve these effects.

The development of new poetic trends such as *vers libre* in the early part of the 20th century led to a move away from such versification (though some, e.g. FLETCHER (1919) persisted in using the format, while Giles re-published his own works in 1923). The Imagist poets' interest in Chinese led to two important Li Bai collections.

POUND's (1915) is controversial. Based on the notes of Ernest Fenollosa and two Japanese professors (note the Japanese transcription of Chinese names), his works are best approached less as "translations" in any literal sense than as free interpretations. The extent to which Pound reworks the original varies considerably. Sometimes he produces striking phrases that keep close to the spirit and language of the text while bringing in new imagistic insights that strengthen our understanding without resorting to amplification. In "The River-Merchant's Wife", for example, an image of yellow butterflies indicates the onset of autumn and leads on to imagery of decay; in Pound's version, the butterflies "are already yellow with August". Elsewhere, however, Pound's readings seriously garble the original, which one senses becomes merely the source of inspiration for his own expressive agenda: the line "The smoke-flowers are blurred over the river" (in "Separation on the River Kiang") all but completely parts company with Li Bai's text. Yet irritating and unacceptable as such instances are to readers of Chinese, one is sometimes forced to acknowledge their intrinsic beauty.

AYSCOUGH's collaboration with the poet Amy LOWELL (1921) produces more satisfactory results, since much greater attention is paid to literal accuracy – though there are still instances of mistranslation. One interesting feature by which the translators seek also to impart "the *perfume* of [the] poem" is the use of what Ayscough calls "split-ups", where the additional nuances suggested by the constituent elements of a given Chinese character are brought out. Though this practice is now questionable, the results nevertheless sometimes add interest to the English. The presentation of the poems in a wholly free verse format is refreshing, though there are some uncomfortably diffuse lines, where greater economy of expression could have been exercised, either by avoiding unnecessarily cumbersome amplification or by supplying less in the way of precise information (to speak of a "table-lute in a cover of green, shot silk" is over-fastidious).

OBATA's (1922) generally solid translations have a rather more traditional feel than those of Ayscough & Lowell. In particular, he avoids excessively lengthy single lines, preferring where necessary to use two lines rather than one. Though this achieves a greater sense of "poetic" control, it equally sometimes obscures the couplet structure of the original. A fair amount of amplification is employed in an attempt to clarify the links between the original images (e.g. in "Taking Leave of a Friend", he writes: "You go ten thousand miles, drifting away / Like an uprooted water-grass", where the original literally reads, "Lonely tumbleweed, journeying ten thousand miles"). This is acceptable to a degree, though there are more serious cases of tampering. For example, in Li's famous quatrain "In the Mountains" Obata inverts lines three and four of the original in an attempt to make their connection with the opening lines more explicit, an approach that entirely fails to replicate the understated effect of a simple juxtaposition of images.

WALEY's study of Li Bai (1950) is well-known for its rather unsympathetic attitude, and his translations sometimes betray a certain lack of enthusiasm. While generally accurate, they are broadly regarded as too cool and methodical to capture the energy of Li Bo – indeed some scholars believe this to be Waley's least successful translation project. "Hard Roads to Shu" (Waley's version of Li's famous "*Shu dao nan*") is one striking example. It lacks the verve of COOPER's brilliant if free translation, and fails to convey fully the dizzying quality of the original imagery, largely because Waley is simply less daring with his use of English and of rhythm; his more measured version is ultimately just too "safe".

Two collections from the 1970s illustrate how scholars following Waley might attempt to improve on his performance by adopting more radical – and divergent – approaches without sacrificing scholarly rigour.

COOPER's invigorating reading of Li Bai (1973) follows a carefully defined set of prosodic rules, which allows him to reproduce something of the original syllabic structure while retaining flexibility. Much of his work is characterized by an imaginative use of English syntax coupled with the highlighting or subtle reconfiguration of elements found in the original, to produce unexpected effects. "In the Mountains" is one example, in which lines such as "Peach petals *float their streams* away in secret" lift the translation above the blandness of a version such as Waley's, whilst keeping the simplicity of the original. Again, in the opening passage of the "The Road to Shu is Steep", the transformation of five lines into one long subordinate clause ("But when ...") creates a sense of energy not present in many, more strictly literal translations. Though some may regard such renderings as too free, Cooper is always in touch with both the language and the tone of the original text.

By contrast, YIP (1976), whose work reflects a broader reawakening of interest in questions raised by the Imagist poets, develops a detailed case for rejecting previous "distorted" methods, in favour of a "*convergence* of languages and poetics". Yip seeks to give a far greater sense of the Chinese linguistic structure, in which syntactic marking is often weak or implicit, and by doing so, hopes to reproduce the "imagistic" immediacy of the original. Although this sometimes works (in "Seeing off a Friend", the line "Lone tumbleweed; a million miles to travel" is altogether preferable to a rendering such as OBATA's, above), the overall results tend to be rather barren, simply because excessive syntactic isolation in English reads badly. Moreover, Yip does not always faithfully reflect the original. One example, from "The Monk of Shu ...", will illustrate. The Chinese literally reads: "[When] for me he first raised [his] hand / It was like listening to ten-thousand ravine pines". Yip reads: "A mere strumming of strings / A million valleys of pines in unison". Here Yip is trying to construct a pseudo-Chinese syntactic isolation and a sense of static image that are simply not present in the text.

EIDE (1984) returns to a less radical approach. He imparts to his translations a keen sense of poetic form and achieves a mellifluous poetic elegance by paying particular attention to the use of carefully matched line-lengths within couplets, while not imposing any very strict system of scansion; he explicitly avoids end-rhyme, which he believes creates an excessive sense of jauntiness in translation where it does not in the Chinese. If his smooth translations sometimes lack the thrill of some of COOPER's best work, they succeed in keeping closer to the original, and – for example in the way he handles difficult allusions – manage to combine meticulous scholarship with accessibility.

SETH's work (1992) is of particular interest because it returns to a rhymed format. Seth's poetic judgement is often acute: his apposite use of enjambement in "The Waterfall of Lu Shan" ("A jutting stream, the cataract hangs in spray / Far off, then plunges down three thousand feet") is but one fine example. At other times, however, his balancing of form and imagery is less satisfactory. Line three of Li Bai's famous quatrain "In the Quiet Night", for example, reads: "I lift my head and watch the moon"; Seth has chosen to omit the adjective "mountain" (or "bright" in some editions) before "moon" in the interests of line-length, and the image is the poorer for it (compare EIDE's more satisfactory use of the same metre: "I look up at the mountain moon"). With specific regard to rhyme, Seth's renderings are far less stilted than earlier attempts, but the problems of an excessively jaunty tone (cf. remarks at Eide, above) still surface. Whilst for poems such as "Bring in the Wine" or "Drinking alone with the Moon", rhyme may function beneficially, it seems inappropriate elsewhere, e.g. in "The Road to Shu is Hard", where it creates an almost folksy tone that detracts from the power of the original.

Further translations of note are: Rewi Alley, *Li Pai: 200 Selected Poems*, Hong Kong: Joint Publishing, 1980; Wu-chi Liu and Irving Yucheng Lo (editors), *Sunflower Splendor: Three Thousand Years of Chinese Poetry*, Bloomington: Indiana University Press, 1975, pp. 101–14; and Yu Sun's *Li Po: A New Translation*, Shanghai: Commercial Press, 1982, which contains around 100 poems, plus discussion of previous translations.

ROBERT J. NEATHER

Further Reading

Eide, Elling, "On Li Po" in *Perspectives on the T'ang*, edited by Arthur F. Wright and Denis Twitchett, New Haven, Connecticut, and London: Yale University Press, 1973

Fung, Sydney S.K. and S.T. Lai, *25 T'ang Poets: Index to English Translations*, Hong Kong: Chinese University Press, 1983

Owen, Stephen, *The Great Age of Chinese Poetry: The High T'ang*, New Haven, Connecticut, and London: Yale University Press, 1981

Wong, Siu-kit, *The Genius of Li Po, AD 701–762*, Hong Kong: Centre of Asian Studies, University of Hong Kong, 1974

Li Po

See Li Bai

Li Qingzhao (Li Ch'ing-chao) 1084–1151

Chinese lyric- or *ci(tz'u)*-poet

Biography

Li Qingzhao was born in Jinan, Shandong (Shantung), into a prominent family of scholar-officials. She was endowed with prodigious memory. After their marriage in 1101 she and her husband (Zhao Mingcheng, 1081–1129) played in their well-stocked library at guessing on what page, in which volume, the mention of a historical event could be located.

The couple's idyllic existence came to an abrupt end when, in 1126, the Jurched people from northeast China – founders of the Jin dynasty – marched into the capital of the Northern Song and took prisoner the reigning emperor and his father. The remnants of the Song court fled, with a new emperor, to establish a capital in the present-day city of Hangzhou. The couple also fled with their cartloads of books and other treasure – only to see them consumed by fire, looted or stolen. Li Qingzhao's husband died en route and she spent the rest of her life in the south. [Evidence exists that she entered into a bad second marriage in 1132 with a minor official who embezzled her money. She willingly went to court to plead for divorce, which was granted, but also carried an automatic penalty of imprisonment for the wife. Loneliness, exile and personal loss dominated the lyrics of Li Qingzhao as major themes.]

In addition to her "epilogue" to a no longer extant work on epigraphy by her husband, Li's surviving works include several prose compositions, among them an essay on the history and characteristics of *ci*-poetry, another essay on some kind of chess game called *dama*, and a number of *shi*-poems (the earlier, traditional poetic genre). She did not fare as well when it came to the lyrics. She was said to have been the author of a small collection of *ci* compositions entitled *Souyu ji*, or "Rinse-Jade Collection", and a manuscript copy, with only 17 lyrics, might have been consulted by an editor named Mao Jin in 1371; but no copy survived. However, her works were popularly anthologized, and work by other poets were sometimes mistakenly attributed to her. The most carefully-authenticated text of her works is offered by the modern scholar Tang Guizhang.

Editions

Li Qingzhao ji [Collected Works of Li Qingzhao], Shanghai: Zhonghua, 1962 (the first modern attempt at a variorum edition, including 44 of Li's lyrics and an additional 3 by attribution only, along with her prose and *shi* compositions); 2nd edition as *Chongji Li Qingzhao ji*, edited by Mogu Huang, Jinan, Shadong: Qilu Shushe, 1981 (more discriminating revision of the 1962 edition, keeping the same format, but including only 45 lyrics of undisputed authorship and, in a separate chapter, 11 others that the editor considers as attributed only traditionally to Li)

Tang, Guizhang (editor), *Quan Song ci* [Complete Lyric Poetry of the Song Dynasty], vol. 2, Beijing: Zhonghua, 1965 (gives the text of 47 complete poems of her undisputed authorship, along with a list of tune-titles for 24 others that are often erroneously attributed to her)

Translations

Collections

Cryer, James, *Plum Blossoms: Poems of Li Ch'ing-chao*, Chapel Hill, North Carolina: Wren Press, 1984

Rexroth, Kenneth and Ling Chung (translators and editors), *Li Ch'ing-chao: Complete Poems*, New York: New Directions, 1979 (translations of 65 selections, including several erroneously attributed to the poet and more than a dozen *shi*-poems by the *ci*-writer)

Wang, Jiaosheng, *The Complete Ci-poems of Li Qingzhao: A New English Translation*, Philadelphia: University of Pennsylvania, Department of Oriental Studies, 1989 (Sino-Platonic Papers, 13)

Anthologies

Ayling, Alan, in *A Collection of Chinese Lyrics*, rendered into verse by Ayling from translations of the Chinese by Duncan Mackintosh, London: Routledge and Kegan Paul, 1965 (2 lyrics of Li Qingzhao)

Birch, Cyril, (editor) *Anthology of Chinese Literature: From Early Times to the 14th Century*, New York: Grove Press, 1965 (7 lyrics, one translated by K.Y. Hsu and the others by C.H. Kwock and Vincent McHugh)

Chang, Kang-i and Haun Saussy (editors), *Women Writers of Traditional China: An Anthology of Poetry and Criticism*, Stanford, California: Stanford University Press, 1999 (24 lyrics all translated by Eugene Chen Eoyang, inclusive of the 13 that appeared in *Sunflower Splendor*, some with slight revisions; but the new translations also include one lyric ["Xing xiang zi", p. 97] that does not belong to the canon since it is included by neither Tang nor Huang [found only in the 1962 edition from Zhonghua])

Eoyang, Eugene Chen, in *Sunflower Splendor: Three Thousand Years of Chinese Poetry*, edited by Wu-Chiu Liu and Irving Yucheng Lo, Bloomington: Indiana University Press, 1975; 3rd edition, 1990 (13 lyrics)

Generally considered China's greatest woman poet, Li Qingzhao achieved her reputation as a writer of *ci*, or "poems in irregular meters", or "song lyrics" – a subgenre of Chinese poetry that owed its origin to music and became popular in the mid-10th century. Like Sappho's, Li's reputation rested on a small corpus of extant works (in Li's case, fewer than 50 poems). Yet her influence as chief exponent of the "delicate and restrained" (*wanyue*) style of poetry was felt by all subsequent generations of lyricists. Also admired were her daring innovations and musical virtuosity, as well as the immediacy and the sensuous appeal of her imagery.

Mirrored in Li Qingzhao's lyrics were the vicissitudes of the poet's life – which included conjugal bliss, separation from her husband and his subsequent death, flight from an invading foreign army, the demise of an empire, the loss of her home and library, remarriage, divorce, and imprisonment (for a brief period, as a result of the divorce).

Much of the subtlety and understatement in Li's verse defies easy or even smooth translation. Especially when the structure of the original Chinese is being either deliberately or unintentionally ignored by the translator, the result can be bewildering or misleading. For example, when the poet says: "Wild geese fly past – / what hurts my heart / Are precisely these old acquaintances" – with "old acquaintances" referring to the geese (since the migratory birds fly in formation, forming in the sky the Chinese character for "man", thus becoming the symbol of the absent friend) – the imagery is entirely lost in the AYLING & MACKINTOSH version (1965) which reads: "Even the flighting geese / have stabbed me to the heart, / Friends that fly past me out of older memories". In the REXROTH & CHUNG version (1979), these lines become three end-stopped lines: "Wild geese fly overhead. / They wrench my heart. / They were our friends in the old days". The strong sense of the "connectedness" between the images is missing.

Whenever a translation process involves the service of a paraphraser, the temptation exists for a "translator" or "translator team" to engage in some rationalization and padding. For example, REXROTH & CHUNG (1979) give us: "Even Heaven shares our joy, / Making the bright moon shine splendid on your curving flesh". But there is no mention of the "curving flesh" in the original. My translation reads: "Our Creator might have been partial to us / By making the moon shine more brightly on the ground." (Here the translator could have been encouraged to take liberties because the two words I translate as "more brightly" are a Chinese alliterative, onomatopoeic binome (*linglung*), which Li borrowed from a famous poem by the Tang poet Li Bai (701–60), where it is used as a pun to refer to the "crystal curtain". But to insist upon seeing the "curving flesh" of a woman behind a Chinese onomatopoeia can only be regarded as a poet-translator's license.) Similarly, two lines of effective juxtaposition from one of Li's lyrics: "Same kind of longing, / An idle sorrow in two places" (*yizhong xiangsi / liangchu xienchou*) appear in Rexroth & Chung as four lines: "Creatures of the same species / Long for each other. But we / Are far apart and I have / Grown learned in sorrow".

Then, as a tour de force, when Li Qingzhao defies all conventions in the use of reduplicatives by piling up seven pairs of words of the same sound and meaning in the first three lines of another lyric, with a high concentration of dental and apical sounds thus: *xunxun mimi / lengleng qingqing / qiqi cancan qiqi* (meaning "search-search, look again, look again / lonely-lonely / chilly-chilly dreary-dreary woeful-woeful") Rexroth & Chung attempt to duplicate this phonemic feat with "s" and "c" sounds as follows: "Search. Search. Seek. Seek. / Cold. Cold. Clear. Clear. / Sorrow. Sorrow. Pain. Pain". But someone else may prefer the following translation by Jiaosheng WANG (1989): "Seeking, searching: / What comes of it but / Coldness and desolation, / A world of dreariness and misery / And stabbing pain!" A cautious paraphrase, this version sacrifices surface fidelity but gains immensely in conveying the sense. This latest translation of Li's lyrics (though not commercially published) always insists on rendering the "prose sense" of every line, but sometimes at the cost of ignoring such things as the form and structure of the original. For example, the line employing the effective juxtaposition of "one kind / two places" and "longing / idle sorrow" quoted above appears in Wang's version as: "Our yearning is the sort / Both sides far apart endure". But following these two lines are three of Li's best-known lines, which are handled by Wang with considerable finesse: "A melancholy feeling there's no resisting. / As soon as it leaves the eyebrows / It surges up in the breast" – keeping intact the colloquial flavour and rhythm of the original lyric. But the latest translation by Eugene EOYANG in Kang-i Chang's *Women Writers of Traditional China* (1999) offers an even more felicitous translation of the last three lines of this lyric as: "No way to dispel these feelings. / For just when they brim the eyes, / They go straight to the heart". Of course, one has to accept the compromise proposed by the translator in sacrificing Li's artful juxtaposition of *meitou* (literally, the tip of the brow) and *xingtou* (literally, the tip of the heart) for a physiologically more defensible solution; i.e., "tears" that "brim the eyes". That the original image makes no mention of "tears" but merely hints at the knitting of the brow as a badge of grief does not detract from the readers' enjoyment of Eoyang's translation as probably the smoothest possible in American English.

Probably the best translation of Chinese poetry must eschew a rigid approach, relying neither on an "exploitation of the exotic" nor on the "naturalization of the foreign", to use the words of Eugene Chen Eoyang, who maintains that "One must demystify the Other even as one defamiliarizes the Self" in his seminal book *The Transparent Eye* (1993). EOYANG's translations of Li in *Sunflower Splendor* (1975) must still be regarded as having achieved the best compromise. Compare, for instance, his translation of four lines from one of Li's lyrics on the experience of an outing at the lake, in which a binome (*cengdu*) is repeated in the middle two lines:

we'd stray off into a spot thick with lotus,
and thrashing through
and thrashing through
startle a shoreful of herons by the lake

with the version offered by REXROTH & CHUNG in eight lines:

By mistake we found ourselves even deeper
In the clusters of lotus blossoms,
And startled the gulls and egrets
From the sand bars.
They crowded into the air
And hastily flapped away
To the opposite shore.

An unbiased reader will agree that only one of the above versions is a translation; the other, though accurate, is but an unexciting paraphrase.

IRVING YUCHENG LO

Further Reading

Basmanov, M., *Li Tsin-Chzhao*, Moscow: Nauka, 1959, 1970
Ching, Julia, "Li Ching-chao" in *Sung Biographies*, edited by Herbert Franke, 4 vols, Wiesbaden: Steiner, 1976
Eoyang, Eugene Chen, *The Transparent Eye: Reflections on Translation, Chinese Literature, and Comparative Poetics*, Honolulu: University of Hawaii Press, 1993
Eoyang, Eugene and Lin Yao-fu (editors), *Translating Chinese Literature*, Bloomington: Indiana University Press, 1995
Hsu, Kai-yu, "The Poems of Li Ch'ing-chao, 1084–1141", *PMLA*, 77 (December 1962) pp. 521–28
Hu, Pin-ching, *Li Ch'ing-chao*, New York: Twayne, 1966
Liang, Paitchin (translator), *Oeuvres poétiques complètes de Li Qingzhao*, Paris: Gallimard, 1977
Nienhauser, William H., Jr (editor), *The Indiana Companion to Traditional Chinese Literature*, vol. 1, Bloomington: Indiana University Press, 1986

Li Shangyin 812?–858

Chinese poet

Biography

Li's life, though short, spanned the reigns of five emperors, all weak and corrupt rulers. These were the times when the court was constantly plagued by factional strife, *coups d'état*, or open rebellions. The poet's literary brilliance notwithstanding (he passed the *jinshi* or "Presented Scholar" examination at the age of 24 or 25 and was immediately picked as a son-in-law by a high-ranking official), he only ever held a few low government posts in outlying districts of the empire. Frustrated and unhappy, he wrote long narrative poems with intense realism, detailing the suffering of the common herd victimized by war or high taxation. He wrote on historical themes and figures, in poems that are superbly charged with wit and sarcasm. He also wrote on things like cicadas, bees, or willows, and turned these "poems on objects" or *yungwu shi* into thinly veiled allegory or satire. Li Shangyin's greatest claim to fame rests on still another category, poems on love.

The source texts may be found in the following collections (select list):

Quan Tangshi [Complete Tang Poetry], 25 vols, Beijing: Zhonghua, 1960, vol. 16, 6144–6258; Congqi Ye (editor), *Li Shangyin shiji shuju* [Li Shangyin's Poetic Work, with Explanation and Commentary], 2 vols, Beijing: Renmin wenxue chubanshe, 1985; Xuekai Liu and Shucheng Yu (editors), *Li Shangyin shige jijie* [Li Shangyin's Poems and songs, with a Compendium of Explanations and Commentaries], 5 vols, Beijing: Zhonghua, 1988; *Tangshi sanbaishou* [Three Hundred Tang Poems] (a popular anthology compiled by an anonymous 18th-century scholar, an equivalent of Palgrave's *Golden Treasury* for English readers; completely rendered into English as *The Jade Mountain* [see Bynner below]; contains 24 items by Li)

Translations

Bynner, Witter, in *The Jade Mountain: A Chinese Anthology*, translated by Bynner from the texts of Kiang Kang-hu, New York: Knopf, 1929 (contains 24 poems by Li)
Fletcher, W.J.B., in *More Gems of Chinese Poetry*, translated by Fletcher, Shanghai: Commercial Press, 1919 (contains 6 poems by Li, pp. 135–46)
Graham, A.C., in *Poems of the Late T'ang*, translated by Graham, with an introduction, Harmondsworth: Penguin, 1965 (new translations of 13 carefully selected poems)
Herdan, Innes, selection, in *Three Hundred T'ang Poems*, Taipei: Far East Book Co., 1973
Liu, James J.Y., *The Poetry of Li Shang-yin, Ninth-Century Baroque Chinese Poet*, Chicago: University of Chicago Press, 1969 (translation of 100 carefully selected poems, each accompanied by gloss and commentary; also a final chapter on the exploration of the "world" and the "language" of Li' Shangyin's poetry)
Liu, Wu-chi and Irving Yucheng Lo (editors), *Sunflower*

Splendor: Three Thousand Years of Chinese Poetry, with an introduction by Lo, Bloomington: Indiana University Press, 1975 (13 poems)

Yip, Wai-lim, in his *Chinese Poetry: Major Modes and Genres*, Berkeley: University of California Press, 1976 (5 poems, pp. 291–304)

Li Shangyin, a native of Henan province, was an iconoclastic and complex poet of the late Tang dynasty, whose verse, especially in the "regulated-verse poetry" or *lushi* subgenre, marked out a new dimension – in both subject-matter and style – for the so-called "recent-style poems" or *jinti shi*, the chief glory of the Tang era (618–907).

As many as 18 poems in Li Shangyin's collected works are given the title of *Wuti* ("without title"); others have only the first two words of the first line as their title. In a majority of these poems, written in the "recent-style poetry" subgenre – i.e., they are either a quatrain or a "regulated-verse" poem – the poet explored an area of human experience, romantic love between man and women, hitherto scrupulously avoided by Chinese poets. Love between man and woman was indeed a major theme in the ancient *Classic of Poetry* (*Shijing*) and in much of the *Yuefu* ("Music Bureau") poetry of later periods. But the theme of love in earlier poetry – outside of elegies or poems addressed to one's wife, or about the unrequited love of courtesans – tended to be centered on one "invented" persona, as if a poet tried to speak in the voice of another person. Li Shangyin, on the other hand, managed to record actual liaisons, enforced partings, or long separations with all the joy, sorrow, or despondency and despair ever experienced by a suffering lover.

However, by not disclosing the object of his affection, Li has caused much ink to be spilled over the next 10 centuries, sending hundreds of commentators to comb through his work and external sources speculating on the identity of his beloved. The more significant question remains: are these poems necessarily autobiographical? Moralist Confucian critics had always interpreted these poems as expressions of the poet's longing for his political patron. Only modern critics such as Sue Xuelin and others brought out the psychological ramifications of Li's poetry and made a credible case for possible clandestine love affairs that the poet might have had in his youth.

Li's chief devices for heightening ambiguity in his love poems are conceits and allusions. Examples are: "spring silkworms' thread only comes to an end at the moment of death / The candle will not dry its tear until it turns to ashes" (James J.Y. LIU, 1969); or, "Do not let the amorous heart vie with the flowers in burgeoning / One inch of longing, one inch of ashes" (*ibid.*). References to names of constellations, goddesses and immortals from the rich store of Chinese mythology and folklore, in addition to historical events and anecdotes from Chinese philosophical writings and literary works are found in abundance, serving as "objective correlatives" to the poet's own situation. Examples are: "Lady Chia peeped through the curtain at young Secretary Han';/Princess Fu left a pillow to the gifted Prince of Wei" (*ibid.*); or, "Young Liu already resented the distance of the P'eng Mountains:/Now ten thousand more Peng Mountains rise" (*ibid.*). It has been estimated that Li used more than 1,200 such allusions in his work, averaging two per poem. Therefore it is hard to understand some of Li's more erudite poems even at a basic level without the aid of copious gloss and scholarly commentaries, let alone to catch all the nuances of the poet's intended meaning even after all the missing pieces have been put together. Still, Li's fame as poet of love remains supreme.

One feature deemed essential to the perfection of form in the writing of the "regulated-verse poems" is the use of parallelism and antithesis. A "regulated" poem is a poem of eight lines, which can be either heptasyllabic or pentasyllabic, but it is *de rigueur* for the two middle couplets (lines 3–6) to show parallelism (in categories of meaning, such as colour-words matched by colour-words, preposition by preposition, etc.) and antithesis, in terms of the tonal contrast between words, a word in the "even" or *ping* tone matched by a word in the "oblique" or *ze* tone. Li's poetry shows a high incidence of nouns, of sensuous details, such as *jin feicui* ("golden phoenix" [hairpin]) matched in the next line by *xiu furong* ("embroidered lotus-flower" [bed-curtain]). Here the image of a pair of ordinary objects from a woman's sleeping-quarters is reinforced by auditory effect, i.e., in the use of a rhymed-compound (called *dieyun* in Chinese, or "piled-up rhyme") in *feicui* or *bhiəi-tsuì* (Middle Chinese pronunciation) and, in *furong* or *bhio-iong* (Middle Chinese pronunciation), also by punning since *furong* is homophonous with a compound meaning "a husband's countenance". At other times, one might just as easily encounter "alliteration" (*shuangsheng*) such as *xiangxin* ("incense's heart"), reduplicatives such as *sasa* (descriptive of "the soughing and sighing of wind"), or simple repetition of strategically-placed words (sometimes even in the same line), or the subtle blending of sensory experience akin to Western synesthesia. Every line of Li's verse, it seems, is loaded with ore.

Li Shangyin's dexterity in these matters did not come to him by chance; he was also an acknowledged master of the so-called "Parallel Prose" (*pienwen*), a genre comparable with euphuistic and allusive prose in English literature.

The most celebrated, and the most widely anthologized, of Li Shangyin's poems is the one entitled *Chinse* or "The Richly Painted Zither" (*se* being an ancient Chinese musical instrument of horizontal design; the term, sometimes loosely translated as "lute", "harp", or "psaltery"; *chin*, "brocade" or "damask", is used adjectivally to mean "lavishly ornamented"). This poem alone has nearly 20 translations.

The title, "The Richly Painted Zither", however, is the least ambiguous aspect of this poem. Ambiguity starts with the very first line when the poet says that this instrument, "for no reason at all", has 50 strings when in reality a Chinese zither has only 25. Here the poet alludes to the story about a mythological god who, upon hearing the instrument being played by a woman called White Maid, and finding the music unbearably melancholy, ordered it stopped and when she refused had the instrument smashed into two. This legend is followed by two other allusions in the next two couplets. First comes the story told by the Daoist philosopher Zuangci about his having been metamorphosed into a butterfly in a dream and, upon waking, speculating if he had only been a butterfly dreaming itself to be the philosopher. The second allusion is made to the myth about the cuckoo bird (sometimes given as a "night-jar"), which is said to sing so mournfully only because this bird had the soul of an ancient king who had debauched a woman while he sent her husband to war and later repented of his deed and yielded his throne to the husband. Then, in the next couplet, two more allusions appear to be derived from Chinese "unnatural natural history". One is the common belief that pearls form in the oyster only when the moon is full (and in the moonlight would appear to have "tears") and oysters are empty when the moon wanes. The other is the legend that the mist from a jade-producing mountain-slope with the name of "Indigo Field" (warmed by the sun) is really the spirit of Princess Jade, who died of a broken heart after she had been forbidden by her father to marry the man she loved. Finally, scholars have identified a piece of poetic criticism in the writings of an earlier Tang poet, Dai Shulun (732–89), who compares poetry to a "jade-producing Indigo Field sending off mist when warmed by the sun, a scene to be gazed at only from a distance, not to be brought close to the eye".

As regards allusions, of course, valid claim can be made only for those sources that were definitely known to the poet. No record exists to prove that Li knew about Dai's poetic metaphor, however close the phrasing and intriguing the parallel. Yet, despite this abundance of allusions (more than a half-dozen in one poem), "The Richly Painted Zither" is so open-ended that it permits various interpretations – as an elegy for the poet's wife, née Wang, after 14 years of marriage; as a poem about a frustrated affair with a concubine of his political patron or with another beauty; as the poet's personal lament for his misfortunes in life; or as an introduction to the poet's collected works, a poem about the creative process of poetry, about the power of imagistic thinking.

Perhaps the complexity of this poem can best be appreciated by comparing four different translations reproduced below. The first, and also the oldest, was done by W.J.B. FLETCHER, an Imagist poet, with the use of rhyme, and included in his *More Gems of Chinese Poetry*, published in 1919:

The inlaid psaltery fifty chords has; and I know no reason why.
And every chord and every nut vibrates like youth's fond memory.
Sedately born, in morning's dream like butterflies we madly fly.
Then passion gazing on our lord yearns with the cuckoo's wailing cry.

When on the sea the moon is bright, hard pearls are born like tears of woe.
On Fertile Fields where shone the Sun, the gem is lost in mists below.
Such thoughts as these had I recalled, my tears had not such cause to flow.
But ah! transported from myself, I then forgot what now I know!

The second translation is by the late A.C. GRAHAM, an eminent British sinologist, nearly half a century later, in his *Poems of the Late T'ang*, first published in 1965:

Mere chance that the patterned lute has fifty strings.
String and fret, one by one, recall the blossoming years.
Chuang-tzu dreams at sunrise that a butterfly lost its way,
Wang-ti bequeathed his spring passion to the nightjar.
The moon is full on the vast sea, a tear on the pearl.
On the Blue Mountain the sun warms, a smoke issues from the jade.
Did it wait, this mood, to mature with hindsight?
In a trance from the beginning, then as now.

The following two translations are by Chinese translators who have been trained in the West and are conversant with Western literature. Wai-lim YIP, author of the first translation, is himself a poet (who publishes poems in the vernacular Chinese), and he attempts to keep to the structure of the original quite closely. Taken from his *Chinese Poetry: Major Modes and Genres* (1976), his translation reads:

How come the inlaid lute has fifty strings?
One string, one peg, surges of flowery years.
Chuangtzu wakes up, charmed by dream of a butterfly.
Wangti, in spring, returns as a nightjar.
Dark sea: bright moon: pearls with tears.
Blue fields: warm sun: jade engenders smoke.
This feeling: does it have to wait to be memory?
This moment as it comes: already lost as in trance.

One last version, as revised by the late Professor James J.Y. LIU, for *Sunflower Splendor* (edited by Wu-chi LIU and I.Y. LO, 1975), from his own book on the poet (1969), tries to accommodate all the allusions in the text of the translation (with footnotes), observing both structure and meaning of the original:

The richly painted zither, for no reason, has fifty strings;
Each string, each bridge, recalls a burgeoning year.
Master Chuang, dreaming at dawn, was confused with a butterfly;
Emperor Wang consigned his amorous heart in spring to the cuckoo.
By the vast sea, the moon brightens pearls' tears;
At Indigo Field, the sun warms jade that engenders smoke.
This feeling might have become a memory to be cherished,
But for that, even then, it already seemed an illusion.

The ultimate test for a translator of Chinese classical poetry is to decide on what to accommodate and what to eliminate from the rich mosaic of the original, and how the accommodation is to be approached and accomplished.

IRVING YUCHENG LO

Further Reading

Fung, Sydney S.K. and S.T. Lai (editors), *25 T'ang Poets: Index to English Translation*, Hong Kong: Chinese University Press, 1984 (an indispensable reference book which lists, according to the first word of the Chinese title, with the use of Wade-Giles romanization, a total of 119 poems of Li's in English translation), pp.143–65

Huang, Shizhong, *Gudai shiren qinggan xintai yenjiu* [A Study of the Emotional and Psychological Aspect of Some Ancient Poets], Wenzhou: Zhejiang daixue chubanshe, 1990

Nienhauser, William H., Jr. (editor), *The Indiana Companion to Traditional Chinese Literature*, Bloomington, Indiana: Indiana University Press, 1986, pp. 551–53

Su, Suelin, *Yuxi shimi* [The Poetic Riddle of Li Shangyin], an expanded study which includes a reprint of her earlier *Li Yishan lianai shiji kao* [1927; Li Shangyin's Love Affairs], Taipei: Taiwan Commercial Press, 1988

Libertarian Translation

The founding myth of total fidelity in translation, traceable to the 3rd century BC, when 72 learned Jews translated the Hebrew Bible into Greek in Alexandria (the so-called *Septuagint*), a comparison of the versions showing an overlap in every point, established the parameter of the W/word as both source and standard of meaning. The history of translation reveals a gradual deconstruction of the myth, moving from the inviolability of the original towards a pluralization/politicization of fidelity.

Still within source-oriented parameters, the dichotomy word versus sense was later introduced into views of fidelity. In such binary frameworks, the foregrounding of one element implies the relative underscoring of the other; fidelity is thus a term that breeds its opposite, infidelity. Around 10 BC, in his *Ars Poetica*, the Roman poet Horace exhorts the "faithful translator" "to render sense for sense" (in Lefevere, 1992), automatically disavowing fidelity to the word. Yet the priorization of sense over word was long deemed a transgression: Dolet (1509–46), who thought that a slavish word-for-word translation was deficient and so translated Plato freely albeit respecting his intention (in Lefevere, editor, 1992), was burned at the stake.

Contemporaneously, an awareness of mediating between two worlds led Bible translators further to subvert word-for-word translation and an exclusive source-orientation by introducing into fidelity the criterion of communicability of message to receptor. Luther (1483–1546), credited with starting the Reformation through his revolutionary translation of the New Testament (begun 1521), shifts from a philological towards a doctrinaire motivation; banished, he sends out the 1530 circular letter on translation (*Sendbrief vom Dolmetschen*), a defense against accusations of heresy; what matters is the message, and the translation of the Bible is destined for "country people, for women in the house and not only for the learned"; translating is thus interpreting so that the common man may read and understand the Bible and incorporate it into his way of life. In England, Thomas More accuses Tyndale of having changed "the common words to make a change in the faith" (in Lefevere, editor, 1992); burnt at the stake, Tyndale nevertheless provided the bases for the 1611 *Authorized Version*, nearly a century later. The translators of this *Version* paradoxically justify their libertarianism in terms of the very Source of the Word: they "could not follow a better pattern of elocution than God himself ... using divers words, in his holy writ" (in Lefevere, editor, 1992; for a discussion of fidelity / heresy in Bible translations, see Barnstone, 1993).

John Dryden (1631–1700) tries to establish a middle ground by advocating fidelity to the author whose sense is "sacred and inviolable", while admitting restricted areas of flexibility, recognizing that translating is "much like dancing on ropes with fettered legs"; his still predominantly source-oriented tripartite categorization of translation includes metaphrase (word-by-word rendering), paraphrase (priority of sense over words) and imitation (liberty to vary from the words and sense or to forsake both) (in Lefevere, editor, 1992).

Later, and with political nuances, in the context of the rise of nationhood in Germany, Goethe (1749–1832), for example, introduces into the discussion a target-oriented element of nationalism, i.e., concern with the effect of the translation on the receiving nation. In his still tripartite categorization, a prosaic translation may cancel poetic art but it is simple and "surprises us with foreign excellence in the midst of our national homeliness"; parodistic methods involve appropriation and reproduction of the foreign context in the translator's own terms; thirdly and ideally, the original is made identical with the translation because if the translator attaches himself too closely to the original, he may abandon the originality of his own nation (in Lefevere, editor, 1992).

Goethe's further perception that the French "for every fruit ... demand a counterfeit grown in their own soil" (in Lefevere, editor, 1992) leads us into the "belles infidèles" (translations that are beautiful but unfaithful), the concept of which again incorporates political nuances, coinciding with the rise of French cultural imperialism. This expression, first used in France for the translations of d'Ablancourt (1606–64), establishes a tradition that incorporates the aesthetics and the axiomatics of the receiving pole. For d'Ablancourt, "different times do not just require different words, but also different thoughts"; by analogy, ambassadors, lest they appear ridiculous in the eyes of the people they try to please, dress in the fashion of the country they are sent to. In this light, a translation must be elegant, and even the best authors contain passages that are to be touched up or clarified; other passages are not to be translated (e.g., passages speaking of the love of boys, "a custom not strange among the Greeks, even though it seems horrible to us") (in Lefevere, editor, 1992). A colonizing dimension in infidelity to the source re-emerges in the 19th-century British Empire when, for example, the English translator and poet Edward FitzGerald (1809–83) in a letter written in 1857 seems to stress the libertine rather than the libertarian. He patronizingly states that "It is an amusement for me to take what liberties I like with these Persians, who (as I think) are not Poets enough to frighten one from such excursions, and who really do want a little Art to shape them" (FitzGerald, in Lefevere, editor, 1992).

Contemporaneously but in contradistinction to FitzGerald, the poet, painter and translator of Dante, D. Gabriel Rossetti (1828–82), impelled by the Pre-Raphaelite commitment to absolute truth coupled with an interest in the medieval, dismisses literality but reintroduces a source-oriented parameter in fidelity, namely archaization of the translation. Believing that the reason for translating poetry is "to endow a fresh nation ... with one more possession of beauty", the translator, like Aladdin, searches for a lamp, but does not exchange the old for a new one, "glittering to the eye, but scarcely of the same virtue" (in Schulte and Biguenet, editors, 1992). The English poet, critic, and translator of Homer, Matthew Arnold (1822–88), subscribes to the reader-oriented view of fidelity as equivalent effect; but, from an elitist stance, he qualifies it not as what the ancient Greeks felt in relation to Homer, something one cannot tell, nor as what the ordinary Englishman thinks of him, which would be "taking the blind for his guide", but as how the work affects "those who both know Greek and can appreciate poetry" (in Lefevere, editor, 1992).

Early in the 20th century, Sigmund Freud (1856–1939), paradoxically, another "learned Jew", strikes the fatal blow to the founding myth of word-for-word fidelity. As one of the major theoreticians of translation, he brings to the concept an unprecedented scope, extension and depth. Through his approximation of translation, metaphor ("false connection") and transference (unconscious translation), word-for-word or sign-for-sign renderings lose any logic, as when hysterical fantasies are translated into the motor sphere and dreams translate into another script or language (Mahony, 1982; for a detailed analysis of the relationship between psychoanalysis and translation see François Peraldi, editor, 1982). Later, the linguist Roman Jakobson, in his tripartite categorization, coins the term intersemiotic translation, i.e., the transmutation of verbal signs by means of non-verbal ones (1971).

The present writer argues that throughout the 20th century, traditional views of fidelity coexist with libertarian ideas on the reconceptualization and re-evaluation of the notion of origin emerging mostly from diasporic and/or dispossessed and hence multicultural individuals or societies. A breakthrough on fidelity to the sense of the original comes in the 1920s with another Jewish exile, Walter Benjamin (1892–1940). Prioritizing form over sense, he defines an inferior translation as the inaccurate transmission of an inessential content; fidelity in reproducing the form prevents the rendering of the sense of the original, the translated text being thus a partial representation of the original (in Schulte and Biguenet, editors, 1992). Through the metaphor of the circle and the tangent Benjamin conveys his libertarian views of translation, according to which the autonomy of the sense lies in the translated text:

> Just as the tangent touches a circle lightly and at but one point, with this touch rather than with the point setting the law according to which it is to continue on its straight path to infinity, a translation touches the original lightly and only at the infinitely small point of the sense, thereupon pursuing its own course according to the laws of fidelity in the freedom of linguistic flux.

The expatriate American poet, critic, and exponent of poetry translation in the 20th-century English-speaking world, Ezra Pound (1885–1972), broke with many Victorian views, including that of fidelity as re-creation of a sense of the original remoteness through archaisms. He argues that Rossetti's translation of Dante's *Vita Nuova* is remarkable, but that "a *robustezza*, a masculinity" are absent; his own translation preserved the *fervour* of the original (in Schulte and Biguenet, editors, 1992). In contrast to Rossetti's source orientation, Pound advocates bilateral movements in history: the translator develops an awareness of the "atmosphere" of the source meanings, by studying the language, the time, the biography, and other texts of both the author and contemporaries, and transporting that mood and sensibility to the present culture. "*Robustezza*", "fervour", "make it new", "blood brought to ghosts", point to Pound's sharing with Benjamin an emphasis on form and, according to Gentzler, to a translation theory based on a concept of energy in language. Like Chinese characters, words, in a network of relations, represent *things in action*; language can be energized in three ways: melopeia (musical property); phanopeia (visual property) and logopeia ("the dance of the intellect among words"), the last term untranslatable; within form, rhythms and diction are more important than syntax (Gentzler, 1993). Moving far away from faithful adherence, Pound places interpretative translation, the making of a new poem, within the domain of original writing (in Schulte and Biguenet, editors, 1992); in fact, like Chaucer and his contemporaries, he borrows, copies, translates, and adapts without providing the references, which approximates his theory and praxis to intertextuality. His well-known translation of the anonymous *The Seafarer* performs not as faithful adherence but as re-creation and re-energizing: he tries to keep the Anglo-Saxon alliteration and rhythm, but recasts it in modern English while stressing the pre-Christian Germanic values of strength and resilience (Bassnett, 1991), emphasis lying less on meaning than on rhythm, diction and movement (Gentzler, 1993).

The present writer further argues that within the Latin American complex of cultural displacement due to colonization, immigration, and borrowed traditions and identities, there emerges through fiction a reconceptualization of origin and a revision of Eurocentric views of translation and fidelity. The problematizing of origins, centre(s) and frontiers, through lived experiences of a babelic history, cosmopolitism, heterogeneity and unstable and shifting boundaries, has subverted notions of purity and inadequate oppositions by theorizing translation towards a pluralization of fidelity. Translation has, thus, often emerged as a poetics. Latin America, a displaced history and culture, begins as a metaphor of translation; the unfoldings of history add further dimensions to Latin America as a metaphor of translation, in that an overemphasis on "Latin" in the toponym should not lead to the half-truth that the making of Latin America was simply a transatlantic transfer of the Mediterranean world. Apart from the native population, all the elements necessary for the enterprise of colonization were imported (Iberian masters and African slaves), and in the post-colonial period there were several waves of immigration from Europe and Asia, in short, a historical unfolding that challenges borders and binary oppositions. This argument is reinforced by Ricardo Piglia, for whom "Argentine tradition takes the form of translation" as it is read out of context and the existence of a double context is erased; thus, "the figure of *ex-tradition* is the homecountry of the writer" who is "compelled to remember a lost tradition, compelled to cross the frontier". Levine, a Jewish scholar of Latin America and a translator, stresses along similar lines the problematic nature of language boundaries, in that "history's perpetual cycling of empires, colonizations, and migrations allow[s] languages to invade one another, as is reflected in polyglot Latin America and its literatures"; the condition of the exile is that of the translator, both sharing an expanded cultural context and an awareness that no language is an island unto itself and that their own language limitations coexist with the elusiveneess of the other language; so how faithful, and faithful to what, can one be? (Piglia, 1991)

Contemporaneously with Benjamin, Brazilian Modernism in the 1920s, later to influence translation thought in post-modernity, through the Anthropophagy Movement, advocates absorption *and* transformation of foreign models; questioning acritical imitation, it subverts specularity and a one-way flow. Subverting the concept of *imitatio* in the novel *Macunaíma* (1928), Mário de Andrade rewrites Eurocentric historiography and translation theory. Parodying colonization and Catechism, whose project was to make the Indian white inside through the white man's religion and customs, Andrade makes the Amazonian protagonist white *outside*, as the critic Souza has observed. Racially transformed, he emerges in the world of progress of São Paulo as Macunaíma the Emperor and, parodying translation, begins writing after the model of the chroniclers of the 16th-century voyages. His intralingual translation subverts both the model, by writing to the *Indians* about the *civilized* world, and views of fidelity, by borrowing the chroniclers' non-contaminated Portuguese language and the rhetorical code while erasing the original content. Also in the 1920s, the Colombian poet and translator of Keats, Guillermo Valencia, supplements his translation of *Ode on a Grecian Urn* with a dedication sonnet. Displacing arguments in terms of fidelity towards a view of translation as re-creation, he says that the urn came to him and, as a result of his "barbaric hands", it lay in fragments at his feet; with "gentle hands" he restores the fragments, which thus emerge as transformation of the original (for a more detailed analysis of Valencia's view of translation as supplement see Vieira 1996b).

In the 1940s, the self-exiled Argentine Jorge Luis Borges, translator of Virginia Woolf, William Faulkner, and Herman Melville, among other English-speaking writers, also mocks fidelity as literalism. His eponymous Pierre Menard ("Author of the Quixote", 1944) attempts to fulfil word by word his ambition of producing pages coinciding in every detail with those of Cervantes, a project of faithful translation that meant the need to "learn Spanish well, save the Catholic faith, fight the Moors or the Turks", and so on; ironically, the project of duplication is too easy and too uninteresting and Menard decides to keep the *Quixote* but erase Cervantes, also excluding the autobiographical prologue. Alternatively, he would get to the text of the *Quixote* through his own experiences, as Menard himself, and not through a borrowed identity and tradition related to the alien context of "gypsies, conspirators, mystics, Philip the Second, 'autos-da-fé'". In an ambiguous gesture, Borges copies the original but erases the origin (for a more detailed analysis see Vieira, 1996b). This "translation" thus emerges as a parody, an imitation with a critical difference (Levine, 1991). Later, Borges verbalizes his view that for translation to work "it must be transgressive; it must hold nothing sacred" (quoted in González, 1987).

In the 1960s, the Colombian Gabriel García Márquez reconceptualizes translation, genealogy and origin through fiction. In *One Hundred Years of Solitude* (1967), Aureliano Babilonia, whose name, after Babylon or "Babel", stresses confusion, commits himself to a translation task that always begins with a return to the origins, i.e., a deciphering of the *Ursprache* or primordial language (González, 1987). In contrast, another character, José Arcádio, moves away from explanation by origin and stresses dissemination, his body emerging as a textualization of history and translation, allegorically asserting the post-babelic history of Latin America. José Arcádio returns to his own Colombian origins in Macondo after his maritime adventures, speaking a Spanish contaminated with sailors' slang, and his body and unusually big phallus are covered in tattoos – words in several languages spelling out the traces of his adventures, a textualizing of the history of pluriculturalism and multilingualism of his own continent and a view of translation not as reproduction but as dissemination of the origin (for a more detailed analysis of the translation theme in *One Hundred Years of Solitude* see González, 1987 and Vieira, 1996b). Also in the 1960s, the Brazilian novelist João Guimarães Rosa, in his correspondence with his Italian translator, moves away from considerations of fidelity to the original towards a view of translation as continuation and supplementation of the original, and further expresses joy in being continued and surpassed; he expects the Italian translation "to have a little more of Bizzari and a little less of Guimarães Rosa" (for an analysis of G. Rosa's thought on translation see Vieira, 1996b).

Levine has studied the poetics of translation as betrayal in the writings of the Argentine Manuel Puig and the Cubans Cabrera Infante and Severo Sarduy, eventually exiled respectively in Brazil, England, and France. Memory, a treacherous translator, is the *motif*, for example, in Cabrera Infante's *Tres Tristes Tigres* (1967, *Three Trapped Tigers*, 1971), a "failed translation" of *The Satyricon*, already a palimpsest, a parchment inherited in fragments in which other texts interweave, translation thus repeating the original's abuse of source material. Cabrera Infante or Caín (an amalgam of *Ca* and *In* from his first and last names), "true to his name, is an abuser, a subversive of language" for whom no name is sacred, including his own. He makes translation an explicit poetics in *Three Trapped Tigers*: the novel's first character is a simultaneous interpreter; then there is the polyglot Bustrófedon, who endlessly transmutes names and refrains, and parodies Cuban writers, "translating" their styles as he imagines what and how they might have written about the assassination of Trotsky. In a chapter on history as (mis)interpretation, the invisible author parodies strategies and mistakes to show that translation betrays and ultimately all writing suffers from betrayal. The novel itself performs translation through a web of English language texts (including those of movies), the language of the exploiter but also the desired language of power, translated into the Cuban idiom. If Sarduy's writing denies mimesis and exposes the artifice of all representation, his characters and settings constantly metamorphosing and referentiality always being deferred, in "Translatio and Religio" (1973), he questions the very presupposition of an original, demythified as an impostor, a "bad" copy. In his essay "La simulación" (1982), simulation inverts not only what is represented but also the "intent to represent"; the original is already a subversion; equating exile and translation (to be Cuban is to be always in exile), he denies the dichotomies "exile/home, translation/original, self/other" (Levine, 1991).

A philosophical expression of the move away from explanation by origin and from the question of fidelity as semantic equivalence is found in Derrida's rearticulation of translation from the 1960s on. A Jew born in a suburb of Algiers, he shares with Latin Americans the early experience of belonging to a marginal and dispossessed culture. Departing from the founding myth of fidelity, he prioritizes that of the Tower of Babel as dispersion and multiplicity, reconceiving translation as transformation and dissemination (1985a). No original ever remains intact; in *Positions* (1972, English translation 1981), Derrida states that

> translation practices the difference between signified and signifier. But, if this difference is never pure, no more so is translation, and for the notion of translation we would

> have to substitute a notion of transformation: a regulated transformation of one language by another, of one text by another. We will never have, and in fact have never had, to do with some "transport" of pure signifieds from one language to another, or within one and the same language, that the signifying instrument would leave virgin and untouched.

Through the play of *différence/différance*, he further designates a spatial and temporal movement of differentiation and deferral. Thus reconceptualizing self-sufficient and stable notions of an origin, he argues that the so-called original has an inherent lack: it is not a plenitude that comes to be translated by accident but is in a situation of demand, being thus indebted *a priori* to the translation, which, in turn, is indebted to the original (1985a, 1985b). Striking another blow at the notion of translation as a transfer of stable meanings, Derrida questions how the translation supplies the original with what it lacks; and the bases of his investigation are complement and supplement rather than presence, difference rather than identity. Meaning can never be fixed, it is always deferred, and as one tries to grasp it, it disseminates and displays polysemy (for illuminating elaborations of the question of difference in translation, including Derrida's own "Des Tours de Babel", see Joseph Graham, editor, *Difference in Translation*, 1985; for a redefinition of fidelity in translation in the light of poststructuralism and reader theory, see Arrojo, 1986; for appraisals of the impact of Derrida on translation thinking, see Arrojo 1993 and Gentzler 1993).

In postmodern Brazil, the brothers Augusto and Haroldo de Campos, relying on Anthropophagy-based notions of absorption and transformation, reject binary oppositions, introduce bilaterality to notions of fidelity and model in translation and, within a political agenda, deconstruct the dichotomic power hierarchies between hegemonic and marginal discourses, be they of the original, established cultures or high literature. For Haroldo de Campos, translation is a satanic enterprise, a "transluciferation", a "parricidal dismemory"; in his project of transtextualization, he introduces a target-oriented parameter into fidelity, that of translating a foreign text into the style and diction of the national writers. Augusto de Campos, in his "intranslation" project, translates Blake's linear poem "The Sick Rose" into a concrete one or inserts passages from Brazilian songs and literary works into his translation of John Donne. Later, Silviano Santiago elaborates the notion of double plagiarism, by means of which he translates the original into the style and diction of a Brazilian author. Fidelity is thus redistributed and pluralized, as a sense of reverence to the source is implicit in the very act of translating, yet, in a double capture, it is equally accommodated into the national literature (for a full study of A. de Campos's, H. de Campos's, Campos brothers' and Santiago's translation projects, see, respectively, Vieira 1998, Vieira 1992, and Vieira, 1996b; for a shorter version see Vieira, 1994).

In tune with Derrida's view of bilateral debt between original and translation and with the Brazilian postmodern translators' cultural and political redistribution of fidelity, Barbara Johnson discusses "transferential bigamy" philosophically, her views of divided (in)fidelity stressing the linguistic. Bringing together marital mores and theories of translation, she argues that the value of fidelity is low in both domains, the respective crises being identical, for participants in both transactions were once bound by contracts to love, honour and obey but inevitably betray; the desirability of a contract that seems deluded and exploitative from the start is thus questioned. The translator ought, by virtue of an oath of fidelity, to be considered "not as a duteous spouse but as a faithful bigamist, with loyalties split between a native language and a foreign tongue". Conversely, the bigamist is necessarily doubly unfaithful, but in such a way that he or she must push to its utmost limit the very capacity for faithfulness (Derrida, 1985).

The Brazilian translator of 19th-century poetry into English, J.L. Grünewald, subscribes to the adage "traduttore traditore", claiming that it is better to sacrifice semantics than rhyme. Relying on Mallarmé's view that poetry is made of words, not ideas, he claims that sometimes, as in the case of the *Rubāyyāt*, betrayal of sense is the way towards fidelity to form, even though in Wordsworth's case "the virtues of infidelity can be dispensed with". Another contemporary Brazilian, Paulo Britto, translator of Wallace Stevens and Byron, going beyond the "belles infidèles", implicitly and ironically compares translation to prostitution and presents a tripartite categorization of betrayal: to the original, to the translator's mother tongue and to the development of the national literature. For another contemporary Brazilian, Nelson Arscher, the area of difference or mistranslation is what gives life to a text; if there were absolute identity between original and translation, the latter would not have an identity and its own history (for an analysis of Grünewald's, Britto and Arscher's translation projects, see Vieira, 1995). The Chilean contemporary poet and translator Diego Maquieira polarizes translation towards infidelity. Transgression, passion and transfusion – in the etymological Latin sense of "fundere", to melt so as to shape differently – are the basic elements for his view of translation as radical recreation, which he calls "montage". For example, he selected three translations into English of a poem by the Greek Cavafy and built them into one single poem in Spanish. "There is no fidelity to the original text ... something totally distinct", he claims (for a more detailed study of Maquieira as a translator, see Vieira, 1996b).

Subversion and self-betrayal are terms that Levine uses to describe authors-cum-translators like Samuel Beckett whose original emerges not necessarily as the first work but rather as the sum of early drafts; the terms are also applied to Cabrera Infante, Severo, and Puig and herself in the context of the co-translation of their works into English. The three Latin Americans, as they "added puns or parodies, as they touched on the gaps between language and meaning, far from the traditional view of translators as servile, nameless 'scribes', are considered 'subversive', dethroning the "author" and making the original an *incomplete* project that continues to be elaborated" (1991). Departing from the sacrality of the original, in her view still to be found in Freud, she argues that translation brings forth a substratum, a version underneath, implied in the concept of subversion. She ponders the feminine and calls herself a self-betrayer for having fallen under the spell of male discourse. Her genderizing of the adage into *traduttora, traditora* (Levine, 1991) points to female translators' increasing politicization of infidelity in the 1990s, which finds a counterpart in peripheral cultures, both phenomena textualizing a break with patriarchal discourses.

In Canada, Lotbinière-Harwood enhances the political agenda of transgression; viewing translation as a rewriting in the feminine, she adds the suffix "re" to "belle" and the reworded "re-belle and infidèle" changes the beauties into rebels, implying repetition with change; realizing she was working from an "androcentric posture", she gave up translating male writers, and called herself a feminist translator whose practice means making the feminine actually visible and heard in the translation, e.g. by using feminine suffixes in French. "Rewriting in the feminine" is twofold: from the source to the target language and from masculine to feminine (Lotbinière-Harwood, 1991).

One of the attractions of translation, "the most intimate act of reading", is that "the translator earns permission to transgress from the trace of the other", argues the Indian post-colonial theorist, femininist, and translator of Derrida into English, Gayatri Spivak. Echoing Benjamin, she qualifies the task of the feminine translator as facilitating love between the original and its shadow, a "love that permits fraying", the metaphor suggesting the subversion of the feminine role of the faithful weaver. Moving away from fidelity towards dissemination, she stresses rather the need for the translator to surrender to the text and carry out a "responsible translation", especially in the case of women within the heritage of imperialism, in that they bear the stigma of a failure of Europeanization (Spivak, 1993).

From a cultural and functional perspective, the translation theorists Bassnett and Lefevere argue that faithfulness does not operate at the level of words and texts, but as functional equivalence, i.e., the attempt to make the translation work in the target culture as the source text functioned in the source culture, which may mean that a translator will substantially adapt a source text. Lefevere further lays "the old adage to rest once and for all", holding that translators "have to be traitors" (Lefevere, editor, 1992). "Translatio", the epitome of the ideal of faithful translation, is for him what those in authority expect, the purveying of the "right" image of a source text in a different language; yet it is impossible for an exchange of signifieds to occur in an intellectual and emotional vacuum, ignoring the cultural, ideological and poetological overtones of the actual signifiers. As a polar opposite, "traductio", designated by a Latin word that never existed, allows equal weight to the linguistic and cultural/ideological components of the translation process (Bassnett and Lefevere, 1990).

Another contemporary, however, the Prague-born and Paris-based writer Milan Kundera, deconstructs the "belles infidèles" tradition and seems to reconstruct author-centred and original meaning-based views of fidelity. Translation is beautiful when it is faithful, he claims; in his defence of translation as the art of fidelity, he argues that a novelist's power lies both in his imagination and in his semantic precision; it is thus with a passion for exactitude that great novels and works should be translated (*Folha de São Paulo*, 5 May 1996).

It remains for the increasingly globalized world and the new millennium to see which of the currently coexisting myths prevails, the founding one of total fidelity to the origin or the babelic myth of deconstruction and dissemination of the origin – and pluralization of fidelity.

ELSE R.P VIEIRA

Further Reading

Arrojo, Rosemary, *Oficina de tradução: A teoria na prática*, São Paulo: Ática, 1986

Arrojo, Rosemary, *Tradução, desconstrução e psicanálise*, Rio de Janeiro: Imago, 1993

Barnstone, Willis, *The Poetics of Translation: History, Theory, Practice*, New Haven, Connecticut and London: Yale University Press, 1993

Bassnett, Susan and André Lefevere, "Introduction: Proust's Grandmother and the Thousand and One Nights: The 'Cultural Turn' in Translation Studies" in *Translation, History and Culture*, edited by Susan Bassnett and André Lefevere, London and New York: Pinter, 1990

Bassnett-McGuire, Susan, *Translation Studies*, London and New York, Methuen, 1980; revised edition, London and New York: Routledge, 1991

Derrida, Jacques, *Positions*, translated and annotated by Alan Bass, London: Athlone Press, and Chicago: University of Chicago Press, 1981

Derrida, Jacques, "Des Tours de Babel" in *Difference in Translation*, edited and translated by Joseph F. Graham, Ithaca, New York: Cornell University Press, 1985a, pp. 165–207

Derrida, Jacques, *The Ear of the Other: Otobiography, Transference, Translation*, edited by Christie V. McDonald, translated by Peggy Kamuf, New York: Schocken, 1985b

Gentzler, Edwin, *Contemporary Translation Theories*, London and New York: Routledge, 1993

González, Aníbal, "Translation and Genealogy: *One Hundred Years of Solitude*" in *Gabriel García Márquez: New Readings*, translated by Bernard McGuirk and Richard Cardwell, Cambridge and New York: Cambridge University Press, 1987

Graham, Joseph F. (editor), *Difference in Translation*, Ithaca, New York: Cornell University Press, 1985, pp. 13–30

Jakobson, Roman, "On Linguistic Aspects of Translation" in *Selected Writings*, vol. 2, The Hague: Mouton, 1971

Johnson, Barbara, "Taking Fidelity Philosophically" in *Difference in Translation*, edited by Joseph F. Graham, Ithaca, New York: Cornell University Press, 1985

Kundera, Milan, "A Tradução como Arte da Fidelidade: Versões Tornam Possível o Sonho da Literatura Universal", translated by José Marcos Macedo, *Folha de São Paulo* (5 May 1996), Caderno 5, p. 3

Lefevere, André, *Translation, Rewriting, and the Manipulation of Literary Fame*, London and New York: Routledge, 1992

Lefevere, André (editor and translator), *Translation/History/Culture: A Sourcebook*, London and New York: Routledge, 1992

Levine, Suzanne Jill, *The Subversive Scribe: Translating Latin American Fiction*, Saint Paul, Minnesota: Graywolf Press, 1991

Lotbinière-Harwood, Susanne de, *Re-belle et infidele: La Traduction comme pratique de reécriture au feminin/The Body Bilingual: Translation as a Rewriting in the Feminine*, Montreal: Editions du Remue-menage, 1991

Mahony, Patrick, "Towards an Understanding of Translation in Psychoanalysis", *Meta, Translators' Journal, Special Issue: Psychanalyse et Traduction*, Org. François Peraldi, 27/1 (1982) pp. 63–71

Peraldi, François (editor), *Meta, Translators' Journal, Special Issue: Psychanalyse et Traduction*, 27/1 (1982)
Piglia, Ricardo, "Memoria y tradición" in *II Congresso Abralic: Literatura e Memória Cultural, Belo Horizonte, 8-10 de agosto de 1990*, 1991, vol. 1, pp. 60–66
Schulte, Rainer and John Biguenet (editors), *Theories of Translation: An Anthology of Essays From Dryden to Derrida*, Chicago: University of Chicago Press, 1992
Spivak, Gayatri Chakravorty, "The Politics of Translation" in her *Outside in the Teaching Machine*, New York and London: Routledge, 1993, pp. 179–201
Vieira, Else R.P., "A Postmodern Translational Aesthetics in Brazil" in *Translation Studies: An Interdiscipline*, edited by Mary Snell-Hornby, Franz Pöchhacker and Klaus Kaindl, Amsterdam: Benjamins, 1994, pp. 65–72
Vieira, Else R.P., "Nudity Versus Royal Robe: Signs in Rotation from Latin American (In)culture to (In)translation" in *Brazil and The Discovery of America: Narrative, History, Fiction 1492–1992*, edited by Bernard McGuirk, *et al.*, Lampeter, Wales: Edwin Mellen Press, 1996a
Vieira, Else R.P., "From Subservience to Subsequence" in *Theoretical Issues and Practical Cases in Portuguese-English Translations*, edited by M. Couthard and P.A. Odber de Baubeta, Lampeter, Wales: Edwin Mellen Press, 1996b
Vieira, Else R.P., "Eine postmoderne Übersetzungstheorie" in *Übersetzungsswissenchaft in Brasilien: Neue Beiträge zum Status von "Original" und Übersetzung*, edited by Michaela Wolf, Int. Hans Vermeer, Tübingen: Stauffenburg, 1996c
Vieira, Else R.P., "New Registers in Translation in Latin America" in *Rimbaud's Rainbow: Literary Translation in Higher Education*, editedby Peter Bush and Kirsten Malmkjær, Amsterdam: Benjamins, 1998
Vieira, Else R.P., "Liberating Calibans: Readings of *Antropofagia* and Haroldo de Campos' Poetics of Transcreation" in *Post-Colonial Translation: Theory and Practice*, edited by Susan Bassnett and Harish Trivedi, London and New York: Routledge, 1999a
Vieira, Else R.P., "'The White Wall': Pre-facing Silviano Santiago" in *Silviano Santiago in Conversation*, edited by Macdonald Daly and Vieira, London: Zoilus Press, 1999b

Linguistics and Literary Translation

In *Translation Studies* (1980, 1991) Bassnett-McGuire traces the influence of linguistics on the study of translation to the early 1960s, which saw a growing influence within literary criticism of linguistics and stylistics, and renewed interest in Russian Formalism and in the Prague Linguistic Circle. In Britain, the best-known proponent of the linguistic approach to translation is Catford who, in *A Linguistic Theory of Translation* (1965), proposes a theory of translation based on structuralism and the early systemic linguistics of Michael Halliday. Catford's book is the first attempt in English to apply a linguistic framework systematically to translation. Baker's *In Other Words* (1992) is an excellent example of what can be achieved when such systematicity is informed by a very much broader view of linguistics than that which was available to Catford.

The linguistically-oriented tradition within translation studies has been dismissed by Snell-Hornby, in *Translation Studies: An Integrated Approach* (1988) as "dated and of mere historical interest". She discusses mainly German translation scholars' adoption and adaptation of the concept of translation equivalence defined by Catford, and one of her objections concerns Catford's suggestion that textual equivalents may be established by asking competent bilinguals or translators to supply them. One problem with this approach, variability of opinion, may be felt to have been somewhat alleviated now that contrastive linguistics can be carried out using large machine-readable corpora of source and target texts. However, as long as the findings of corpus linguistics are presented in the form of generalization and without due regard to the context and co-text for individual examples, they will not serve to counter objections such as that put forward by Hermans in *The Manipulation of Literature* (1985), to the effect that whereas linguistics may help us where the translation of unmarked, non-literary texts are at issue, it is "too restricted in scope to ... serve as a proper basis for the study of literary translation". It is interesting to note, however, that an elaboration of his modification of Catford's definition of translation equivalence "which may be justified according to Catford's own treatment of the concept throughout his book" forms an integral part of Gideon Toury's seminal article, "Translated Literature: System, Norm, Performance: Toward a TT-Oriented Approach to Literary Ttranslation" (1981).

To deal exhaustively with the theory, practice and outcomes of literary translation, it is undoubtedly necessary to take into consideration a large number of factors including translation norms, literary norms, literary critical theory, literary history, attitudes to foreignness, and so on, as these pertain to the cultures in which both source and target text function. Nevertheless, it is difficult to divorce a literary text from the language in which it is realized, and in which a good deal of evidence of influence from the various factors just enumerated is likely to be found. What is at issue is not so much *whether* linguistics is relevant to literary translation; rather, it is what kind of linguistics, and what kinds of use might be made of the discipline's descriptive and theoretical terms and concepts. To begin to answer such questions, it is necessary, first, to distinguish descriptive and theoretical linguistics from prescriptive linguistics.

The purpose of descriptive and theoretical linguistics is to further our understanding of language. This is done through a continual process of testing theoretical assumptions against data, and analysing data in the light of those assumptions which previous analyses have confirmed to such a degree that they form a more or less integral whole that is accepted as the currently preferred theory. Between them, the mutually dependent fields of descriptive and theoretical linguistics provide accounts and explanations of how things seem to be in language, and a terminology for use in discussions. They are, in principle, forward-looking and non-deterministic, because new data and/ or new conceptions of data always have the potential to, and very frequently do, effect changes in theory.

Prescriptive linguistics, on the other hand, generalizes and abstracts from description to produce rules of correct language use. It is backward-looking and deterministic in both essence and practice, since the abstracting process requires an assumption of a system that is static for long enough to allow the process of abstraction and rule formulation to take place; and then rules, once accepted and learned, are hard to relinquish.

The reason it is important to stress this difference in orientation is that there is a related difference between (i) using the descriptive and theoretical notions and concepts employed within linguistic theory when explaining, commenting on, and making judgements about literary translation; and (ii) advocating that the rules of prescriptive linguistics must be followed when translating literature and consulted when judging translations.

It is hard to argue cogently against the former approach. Most literary translators would probably find familiar the experience reported by Lawrence Venuti when he introduces his article "Translation, Heterogeneity, Linguistics" (1996) by saying that he devises and carries out his translation projects "with a distinctive set of theoretical assumptions about language and textuality" in mind. It is useful to be able to explicate one's assumptions using a vocabulary shared by other interested parties, and, although Venuti means by "theoretical assumptions" something rather broader than assumptions about linguistic units and the relationships between them, he demonstrates thorough familiarity with these and with linguistic terminology in those parts of his article where he discusses his translations.

It is difficult to defend the prescriptivist position in the face of the reality of language use in general and literary translational language use in particular. The problem is that theorists, whether appreciators or depreciators of linguistics in literary translation studies, occasionally fail to keep the distinction in mind, with the unfortunate result that Venuti speaks for a considerable number of scholars and practitioners of literary translation when he saddles linguistic-oriented approaches with the "key assumption" that "language is an instrument of communication employed by an individual according to systems of rules".

In fact, very few linguists embrace prescriptivism. And one would be hard pushed to find any linguist, even among prescriptivists, who would not agree wholeheartedly with Venuti that "language is a continuum of dialects, registers, styles, and discourses positioned in a hierarchical arrangement and developing at different speeds and in different ways". An awareness of this truism of modern linguistics is an integral aspect of, though by no means constitutive of, the kind of sensitivity to language that Venuti displays, and that can be employed to great benefit in teaching, doing, and commenting on literary translation.

In my own writing on the language of literary translations I have used linguistic methodology and terminology in ways that I obviously find particularly useful, to carry out "Translational Stylistics". While no one would wish to claim that this approach is in any way *constitutive* of literary translation studies, is does offer insights that may be used in answering questions which might reasonably be asked within that discipline, and in education programmes in translation.

KIRSTEN MALMKJÆR

Further Reading

Baker, Mona, *In Other Words: A Coursebook on Translation*, London and New York: Routledge, 1992

Bassnett-McGuire, Susan, *Translation Studies*, London and New York: Methuen, 1980; revised edition, London and New York: Routledge, 1991

Catford, J.C., *A Linguistic Theory of Translation: An Essay in Applied Linguistics*, London: Oxford University Press, 1965

Hermans, Theo (editor), *The Manipulation of Literature: Studies in Literary Translation*, London: Croom Helm, and New York: St Martin's Press, 1985

Malmkjær, Kirsten, "Stylistics in Translation Teaching", *Perspectives: Studies in Translatology*, 1 (1994) pp. 61–68

Malmkjær, Kirsten, "Translating the Real Story" in *Linguistic Approaches to Literature: Papers in Literary Stylistics*, edited by Jonathan Payne, Birmingham: Birmingham University Press, 1995

Malmkjær, Kirsten, "What's in an Adjective", *Norwich Papers in European Languages, Literatures and Culture*, no. 3: *Hans Christian Andersen, Translation Problems and Perspectives*, 1995

Snell-Hornby, Mary, *Translation Studies: An Integrated Approach*, Amsterdam and Philadelphia: Benjamins, 1988

Toury, Gideon, *In Search of a Theory of Translation*, Tel Aviv: Porter Institute for Poetics and Semiotics, Tel Aviv University, 1980

Toury, Gideon, *Descriptive Translation Studies and Beyond*, Amsterdam and Philadelphia: Benjamins, 1995

Venuti, Lawrence, "Translation, Heterogeneity, Linguistics", *TTR: Traduction, Terminologie, Rédaction*, 9/1 (1996) pp. 93–117

Clarice Lispector 1920?–1977

Brazilian novelist, short-story writer and journalist

Biography

Born in Tchetchelnik, the Ukraine, 10 December 1920(?). She was the youngest of three daughters in a Jewish family looking for a new life away from the newly formed Soviet Union. Having arrived in Brazil only a few months after her birth, Lispector always considered herself thoroughly Brazilian, culturally and linguistically. After first settling in the north of the family's new country, they moved to Rio de Janeiro. Considered part of the Generation of 1945, Lispector is known for her themes and styles of philosophical and feminist interest. After spending 1944 to 1959 in Europe and the United States when she was first married and her children were young, Lispector, on separating from her husband, returned to Brazil a mature and respected novelist. Her weekly columns for the newspaper *Jornal do Brasil* from 1967 to 1973 consolidated her reputation at home in Brazil. Died in Brazil, 9 December 1977.

Translations

Novels

Perto do coração selvagem, 1944
Pontiero, Giovanni, *Near to the Wild Heart*, New York: New Directions, and Manchester: Carcanet, 1990

A maçã no escuro, 1961
Rabassa, Gregory, *The Apple in the Dark*, New York: Knopf, 1967; London: Virago, 1985

A paixão segundo G.H., 1964
Sousa, Ronald W., *The Passion According to G.H.*, Minneapolis: University of Minnesota Press, 1988

Uma aprendizagem; ou, o livro dos prazeres, 1969
Mazzara, Richard A. and Lorri A. Parris, *An Apprenticeship; or, The Book of Delights*, Austin: University of Texas Press, 1986

Agua viva, 1973
Lowe, Elizabeth and Earl E. Fitz, *The Stream of Life*, Minneapolis: University of Minnesota Press, 1989

A hora da estrela, 1977
Pontiero, Giovanni, *The Hour of the Star*, Manchester: Carcanet, 1986; New York: New Directions, 1992

Short Stories

Laços de família, 1960
Pontiero, Giovanni, *Family Ties*, Austin: University of Texas Press, 1972; Manchester: Carcanet, 1985

A legião estrangeira, 1964
Pontiero, Giovanni, *The Foreign Legion: Stories and Chronicles*, Manchester: Carcanet, and New York: New Directions, 1986

A via crucis do corpo, 1974; *Onde estivestes de noite*, 1974
Levitin, Alexis, *Soulstorm: Stories*, New York: New Directions, 1989 (includes both volumes)

A descoberta do mundo, 1984
Pontiero, Giovanni, *Discovering the World*, Manchester: Carcanet, 1992

Story for Children

A mulher que matou os peixes, 1969
Fitz, Earl E., "The Woman Who Killed the Fish", *Latin American Literary Review*, 11/21 (1982) pp. 89–101

Clarice Lispector's writings have been consistently well translated into English, which unfortunately cannot be said of versions of her works in some other languages. Giovanni Pontiero has translated five of her nine extant volumes into British English, and Gregory Rabassa won the National Book Award for Translation in 1967 for *The Apple in the Dark* into American English. These translations have made available her most accessible and popular works: five of her nine novels, at least six collections of short stories, and, most recently, a large volume of her newspaper "chronicles" (very short pieces mixing elements of the short story and journalism). Unfortunately her most experimental works have yet to appear in English.

PONTIERO's translation of Lispector's autobiographical first novel, *Near to the Wild Heart*, can be enjoyed by English readers on both sides of the Atlantic in this New Directions Book published in cooperation with Carcanet of Manchester. When the novel first appeared in Brazil (1944), it had marked a feminine, Modernist departure from the harsh social realism that had dominated Brazilian literature for at least a generation. While the English version (1990) could not have the same historical impact, the lyric originality and marked female perspective of this early work by Lispector have shown through, perhaps because of Pontiero's considerable previous experience as her translator.

By the winner of the 1967 National Book Award for Translation, RABASSA's beautiful rendition (1967) of *The Apple in the Dark* has showcased a remarkable, brooding novel about a man's psychological meditations, the social construction of angst and anger, the importance of sacrifice and salvation, and the nature of male and female. The translator of several classic Latin American novels of the recent period, Rabassa achieves a very close rendering, flexible in rhythms and subtle in nuance.

SOUSA (1988) retains the experimental form and phrasings of Lispector's essayistic novel, *The Passion According to G.H.*, about a woman's quasi-mystical inner journey. Sensuality and asceticism alternately mask a story about art and language, about the animal and the human, about the rich and the poor, and about salvation and damnation. Together these opposites are used to explore the paradoxes of modern life *vis-à-vis* spirituality and materiality. The translation sustains the parody of biblical language in deceptively simple phrasing.

The sexuality of the New Woman is explored in *An Apprenticeship*, a lesser-known novel (1969) from Lispector's middle period. Accurately rendered by MAZZARA & PARRIS (1986), the novel's concerns pertain to questions of female independence and autonomy, the nature of social cohesion, and the meanings of love and sex for male and female. Religious and artistic explorations are relegated to the background here, in comparison with the Brazilian's other novels, but the translators have favored a vocabulary that reinstates somewhat *An Apprenticeship*'s commonalities of theme and form with Lispector's other texts.

Two distinguished critics of Lispector, LOWE & FITZ have done an excellent job at reproducing *Aqua viva*, the fictional journal of a woman sculptor, in *The Stream of Life*. Blocked in her endeavors as a plastic artist, the first-person narrator attempts to maintain her narration in the present moment in her lyrical diary about creation. In her effort to avoid past and future, the narrator reveals much about life, and her life, as a lived process and a work of artistic creation.

Lispector's most socially committed novel, *A hora da estrela*, has been reproduced with less success by her most frequent translator, Giovanni Pontiero. PONTIERO (1986) translates the highly nuanced voices of the male narrator and the female protagonist whose story he tells. Their voices hail from different worlds – male/female, hungry/comfortable, sociable/alone – yet the novel manages to harmonize their contrasts into a portrait of social possibilities and impossibilities, at moments even melding their voices into unison. Subtle linguistic registers of class, educational background, and gender for the writer/narrator and for the indigent young northeasterner, while different in English, are carefully inscribed in the target language.

PONTIERO's (1972) first translation of Lispector was of her *Laços de família* (Family Ties). This collection of Lispector's earliest stories is also one of her most popular and best-known works. The main themes are: female ways of knowing and being; animals and human proximity to them; writing and relating to others. Unlike the Brazilian's more experimental late works, these stories are her most accessible (in Portuguese and English), while still innovating the genre by down-playing plot and by subtly rewriting patriarchal assumptions.

Already a mature writer when she published these gems of the imagination, in *A legião estrangeira* Lispector added to her repertoire of highly successful short narratives. Superficially traditional in some details, most of these stories are configured in forms more experimental than those of previous collections. In addition to narratives, the volume contains cultural commentary about Brazil and travel, personal anecdotes, journalism, and speculative philosophy. PONTIERO (1986) ably renders these new forms and themes into an English that recognizes the need to stretch language to fit new concepts.

LEVITIN (1989) has combined two of Lispector's late short story collections into one volume of translations that he had previously published in little magazines. The juxtaposition of *A via crucis do corpo* and *Onde estuvistes de noite* from the same year, 1974, makes sense because these pieces reflect a common level of mature authorial control over the mirrorings of form/content and reality/art, as well as a similar thematic interest in the body, the literary grotesque, and the socially marginalized. Levitin translates these short works carefully and well, treating them like Gothic prose poems.

Translated masterfully by the experienced PONTIERO, *A descoberta do mundo* contains Lispector's journalism published in Brazil almost weekly for approximately a decade. Some of the individual pieces in this huge volume are "chronicles" with clear literary qualities, others are drafts or bits of stories and novels readers will recognize, while still other texts allow entry into the mind and world of a brilliant and reclusive writer.

A mulher que matou os peixes is a delightful children's story, exploring themes of responsibility and death in the context of animals (pets), without talking down to the younger set. Translated by one of her earliest and best critics in English, Earl FITZ (1982), the brief narrative is a delightful moral quest for adults and children.

DIANE E. MARTING

Further Reading

Cixous, Hélène, *Reading with Clarice Lispector*, Minneapolis: University of Minnesota Press, 1990
Fitz, Earl E., *Clarice Lispector*, Boston: Twayne, 1985
Marting, Diane E. (editor), *Clarice Lispector: A Bio-Bibliography*, Westport, Connecticut: Greenwood Press, 1993
Peixoto, Marta, *Passionate Fictions: Gender, Narrative, and Violence in Clarice Lispector*, Minneapolis: University of Minnesota Press, 1994

Literal Translation: A Practitioner's View

In 1982, in a brief promotional puff for a forthcoming Royal Shakespeare Company (RSC) production of a new translation by British playwright Dusty Hughes of a play by the Russian Mikhail Bulgakov, the percipient but anonymous columnist raised a point about play translation in the theatre, which over the years has become a slow-burning but still neglected issue:

> How many times have we sat in the stalls, crushed and overawed, discovering that among all his or her other talents esteemed dramatist X or Y has now knocked off the translation of some obscure, if searing, family drama from the Steppes. But do they know foreign languages? Not necessarily.

The question of whether a particular playwright has any knowledge of the language of a given text that s/he is adapting is regularly glossed over or ignored, both in press reviews and in promotional literature announcing new productions of foreign plays. And because literal translators have remained almost totally anonymous, often uncredited and badly underpaid, the overwhelming indifference to their contribution continues to prevail, not only among the general theatre-going public but also within the theatrical establishment. What is more, the issue has now affected poetry also, with several well-known contemporary poets treading the same path as our playwrights and offering their own "new versions" of foreign poems, based on the work of literal translators.

The present writer refers mainly to her own experience in the UK as a literal translator of Russian plays. The fact that specific information beyond that field is difficult to come by reinforces the argument for more openness on the subject, in the dual cause of justice to modern literal translators and scholarly insight into translation processes. The situation in the US with regard to phantom or unprofessional translations of plays seems to be fairly similar to that in the UK but perhaps somewhat better; improved practice has been observed there, notably in the area of recent translations of Calderón.

Before the the expansion of the British subsidized theatre thanks to funding from the Arts Council in the early 1960s, the literal translator situation had scarcely arisen. Foreign plays were staged rarely and were looked upon as something of a curiosity. The commercial theatre presented occasional reverential, big-name productions of foreign standard works by, for example, Ibsen or Chekhov (such as the production of Chekhov's *Ivanov* directed by and starring John Gielgud, which played London's West End in 1965 and New York in 1966), but in general was not interested in risking money on experimentation: it clung to the old policy of filling seats. The dynamic of British theatre in the 1960s changed all this. The Royal Court, National and Royal Shakespeare theatres were all keen to promote the vigorous new work of young playwrights and offer them the opportunity of re-evaluating classical foreign texts in their own, modern context. It is at this point that the fine line between "translations", "new versions" and "adaptations" began to get blurred and the roles of "translator" and "literal translator" to be seen confusedly as one and the same thing.

Early examples of new versions or adaptations of foreign plays were offered by the British playwrights John Arden – with an adaptation of Goethe's *Götz von Berlichingen* as *Ironhand* for the Bristol Old Vic in 1963 – and Christopher Hampton, who pioneered this new approach throughout the 1970s, tackling von Horváth, Molière and Ibsen. In 1977 the Marxist playwright Trevor Griffiths followed the trend, initiated with Christopher Hampton's new version of *Uncle Vanya* in 1970, by offering a stimulating new version of *The Cherry Orchard*. Thus the growing cult of up-and-coming playwrights reinterpreting old classics fuelled a new, increasing emphasis on the marketing of *their* names alongside those of the actors starring in a production.

In the midst of this new trend, who were the literal translators providing most playwrights attempting new versions with an insight into the original linguistic nuances of the plays they were now reinterpreting? It is difficult to be certain, because the subject has rarely been raised, except perhaps at the 1997 Hull Conference on Literary Translation, where Colin Chambers, then literary manager of the RSC, chaired a discussion. In the case of Russian plays, apart from a few older-generation Russian émigrés who translated some plays staged up to and during the 1960s, literal translators working with playwrights on new versions would appear to have been, in general, academics or schoolteachers, plus the occasional dilettante. Having a regular salary, these individuals were not taking on such work out of financial necessity but for the kudos of being involved in a prestigious production bringing the work of a little-known foreign playwright to a wider audience. However, with the rapid proliferation of fringe and experimental theatres from the late 1960s, and more and more impecunious companies eager to jump on the bandwagon and produce new versions of foreign-language plays, the task of finding a literal translator was often reduced to a desperate scramble to find someone, anyone, prepared to turn in a quick translation for very little money. The literal translator's role in such cases would end with delivery of the script; his/her collaboration in the production process beyond that would generally be nil. The natural consequence of such a situation has been that the standards of the literal translators employed have never been monitored, their work has rarely been properly credited, and their attempts to improve their fees have been routinely frustrated by the unwillingness of most theatre managements to negotiate.

Thus a vicious circle was created and has since been perpetuated, with literal translation still looked upon, fundamentally, as an old-fashioned, amateur pursuit, with those who undertake it often working for love, or for fun, or, at worst, because they are so hard up that they will accept any fee, however small. Yet literal translators do have professional standards and professional pride. But they have no power. If they are lucky their name may appear on a theatre programme or on the title page of a published translation, in small print somewhere below that of the playwright. A glance through the list of many drama translations in the present work will testify to how very few literal translators are credited in this way. There are, of course, notable exceptions: some appreciative and generous playwrights make a point of acknowledging the contribution made by their translators. These, though, remain exceptions to the general rule. The listings in the back of a standard theatre programme will give the major artistic credits of everyone involved in the production of a play, from the actors, down to the choreographer who devised a minuet in act 1; it will even give credit where due to the local business that supplied the sherry in act 2 – but where is the literal translator, the one person who acts as the essential conduit between the original text and those performing it?

Absence of recognition of literal translation does not imply any intention to deceive. The matter is obvious to all: if, unlike Michael Frayn with regard to Chekhov or Seamus Heaney with regard to *Beowulf*, translators / adaptors are not known to be experienced or learned in the source language concerned, then it will be assumed they must have had assistance with the creation of their English text.

The problem is no doubt partly the making of literal translators themselves. Perhaps some of them, too self-effacing, undervalue their own contribution. This attitude obstructs the efforts of those who do fight for recognition and improved rates of pay. Also, when so many "amateur" literal translators collude in the perpetuation of the current situation, those who try to earn a professional living from literal translation remain hostage to rigid theatrical payment policies. These decree a standard fee for a literal translation from *any* language, irrespective of length, degree of difficulty or any other considerations. Some theatres, such as the RSC, pay above the average and do their best within tight budgets to proportion fees to the obscurity of the language concerned. The difficulty about offering literal translators more is that in some cases their fee may be taken, either in whole or in part, from that awarded the writer who is doing the final translation or adaptation.

All in all, literal translators are faced with the invidious choice of either swallowing their professional pride and accepting a low fee or walking away from a production that they would like to be involved in. If they do decide to accept the work, they cannot hope to gain some small extra financial reward from royalties. Such are the ramifications in terms of cost to theatres, should they find themselves obliged to pay royalties to literal translators, that the translator is obliged to sign over his or her copyright on delivery of the translation, thus relieving the theatre of any further payments. This also, of course, enables the theatre to use that translation in any way it wishes.

One way out of this impasse would be to accord literal translators higher status than is general at present, Additional money could then perhaps be paid to them for contributing in a more all-embracing, consultative capacity to the production. Theatre companies on the Continent have traditionally placed great value on the role of translators, often employing them as dramaturges, as in the case of Botho Strauss, in his work on Shakespeare in Berlin with Peter Stein. The role of dramaturge was accorded the present writer as literal translator of a new version of *Uncle Vanya* by David Lan, directed by Katie Mitchell as an RSC / Young Vic coproduction in 1998. This made possible a detailed analysis of the text, carried out by her in close collaboration with both playwright and director. It also prompted the drawing up of copious notes on the historical, literary and social background of the piece, notes that the director, playwright and actors all found invaluable in practice, and that also afforded moments of profound insight into the text. More importantly from a linguistic point of view, such in-depth discussion of the nuances of translation of Russian words and phrases led in numerous cases to the preservation in the final version of the original *literal* meaning of the text. Such an approach proves that the literal translator has much more to offer than a perfunctory run through the text. Indeed, the task of literal translation is in some respects more challenging than free translation, since literal translators have to be scrupulous in evaluating the true meaning of every single word, or other translation unit, in the source text, and must steadfastly refrain from adding their own embellishments.

This point is well exemplified by the comment in a typically unaware review of the 1998 production of *Uncle Vanya* by Mitchell and Lan. Praising the text, the review concluded: "It is worth changing Constance Garnett's rendering of a dried-up academic career – '25 wasted years' – for Lan's '25 years pouring water from one empty bucket into another'." The metaphor is, in fact, Chekhov's – straight from the literal version.

HELEN RAPPAPORT

Livy 59 BC–c.AD 17

Roman historian

Biography

Born Titus Livius in Patavium (now Padua), northern Italy, in 59 BC. Little is known about his life and there is no surviving record of his early career. He is thought to have had one daughter and one son. He settled in Rome in about 29 in order to concentrate on his historical study of the Roman empire; he met the emperor Augustus, who expressed an interest in his work. Livy encouraged the future emperor Claudius' historical studies. He died in Patavium, c.AD 17.

Livy was one of the most prominent Roman historians. The work for which he is famous, his *Ab urbe condita* (*From the Foundation of the City* or *The History of Rome*) was an enormous project to chronicle the story of Rome from its founding in 753 BC to 9 BC at the death of Drusus the Elder. It was written in 142 books, only 35 of which are extant, these being books 1–10 and 21–45. The content of the rest of the work was summarized subsequently by later writers in surviving works known as *periochae*. Livy's historical approach was essentially literary and dramatic, and based heavily on the work of earlier writers, such as Polybius and Cato. His work on the *History*, with its theme of the decline of Rome, was intended as a patriotic act to inspire pride in the Roman empire.

The History of Rome

Ab urbe condita [From the Foundation of the City], from c.27 BC

Translations

Anonymous (several hands), *The Roman History by Titus Livius, with the Entire Supplement of John Freinsheim*, 6 vols, London: J. Clarke, 1744–45

Baker, George, *The History of Rome*, 6 vols, London: A. Strahan, 1797; Boston: Wells and Lilly, 1823

Bettenson, Henry, *Rome and the Mediterranean: Books XXXI–XLV of The History of Rome from Its Foundation*, with an introduction by A.H. McDonald, Harmondsworth: Penguin, 1976

Foster, B.O., F.G. Moore, E.T. Sage and A.C. Schlesinger, *Livy* (parallel texts), 14 vols, London: Heinemann, 1919–59; as *Livy in Fourteen Volumes*, London: Heinemann, and

Cambridge, Massachusetts: Harvard University Press, 1965–79 (Loeb Classical Library)
Holland, Philemon, *The Romane History*, London: Adam Islip, 1600
Radice, Betty, *Rome and Italy: Books VI–X of The History of Rome from Its Foundation*, introduction by R.M. Ogilvie, Harmondsworth and New York: Penguin, 1982
Roberts, William M., *The History of Rome*, London: Dent, and New York: Dutton, 1912–26
Sélincourt, Aubrey de, *The Early History of Rome: Books I–V of The History of Rome from Its Foundation*, Harmondsworth and Baltimore: Penguin, 1960; with an introduction by R.M. Ogilvie, Harmondsworth and Baltimore: Penguin, 1971
Sélincourt, Aubrey de, *The War with Hannibal: Books XXI–XXX of The History of Rome from Its Foundation*, edited and with an introduction by Betty Radice, Harmondsworth and Baltimore: Penguin, 1965
Walsh, P.G., *Ab urbe condita, Books XXXVI, XXXVII, XXXVIII, XXXIX*, and *XL* (parallel texts), Warminster, Wiltshire: Aris and Phillips, 1990–96

Titus Livius (Livy) encompasses the virtues and vices of both the Roman Republic about which he wrote and Augustus' Roman Empire for which he wrote. His sturdy if unfashionable patriotism comes through in his preface, which has also a surprisingly modern pessimism about it, in that it suggests that the history of Rome is a story of a decline and fall in moral standards. He had intended to take the foundation of Rome in 753 BC as his starting point and to conclude with his own day; in the event he wrote 142 books ending with the death of Drusus the Elder in 9 BC. We are left with only 35 books: 1 to 10 describing the largely legendary early history of Rome and the wars against local enemies such as the Samnites, the best-known books, 21 to 30, involving the struggle against Hannibal, and books 31 to 45 recounting Rome's involvement in the Eastern Mediterranean between 200 and 150 BC. (We miss the difficult and controversial 1st century BC entirely, although there is some evidence to suggest that Livy was not at his best during this period).

Even these fragments have proved too much for modern translators. Both the Loeb and the Penguin versions have needed a team of more than two translators, and the admirable Aris and Phillips series have now taken to issuing editions of single books with both Latin text and translation. More leisured ages found translators able to tackle the whole of Livy's work and capable of appreciating Livy's patriotic imperialism as well as his account of the machinations of an oligarchical society. The 19th century, although not devoid of imperialism or patriotism, was more sceptical about Livy's accuracy, and scholarly editions in the 20th century have been at pains to show his credulity about his sources, as well as his geographical inaccuracy and general unreliability. But Livy is still our main source of information about the early period of Roman history. It is fortunate that in SÉLINCOURT (1960) Livy found the ideal translator, a man acknowledged to share his broad vision, easy narrative style and love of a good story; but unfortunate that he did not live to complete his task.

HOLLAND's translation (1600) of the whole of Livy was only one of the achievements of a long life that included qualifying as a doctor of medicine and serving as headmaster of a school. He translated a number of classical works, but Livy is the author from whom he derived most fame, and his translation was frequently reprinted. By the beginning of the 18th century his garrulous and archaic style had become outmoded, and it is not wholly surprising that Pope puts Holland, under his Christian name of Philemon, into his *Dunciad* as an example of useless learning.

It is equally unfortunate that the ANONYMOUS translation (1744–45) which replaced Holland in popular taste was one written by a variety of hands, and that, though in a slightly less idiosyncratic style, showed its concern for accuracy by including a version of the missing books 11 to 20 inserted by Freinsheim. BAKER's version at the end of the 18th century (1797) is a slight improvement, but this was not a good time for classical scholarship or English letters. It was however the standard translation in the 19th century until the monumental effort of ROBERTS (1912–26) for the Everyman series. A clergyman of old-fashioned learning, Roberts praises in his preface Livy's high moral tone, closely associated with his strong religious sense, and he himself adopts the same high moral tone in narrating the story of Sophonisba. The cadences of the pulpit are heard in the sketch of Hannibal's character; he is said to show "a perfidy worse than Punic, an utter absence of truthfulness, reverence, fear of the gods, respects for oaths, sense of religion".

The multi-authored Loeb edition of FOSTER, MOORE, SAGE and SCHLESINGER (1919–59) translates the same passage by "he had no regard for truth and none for sanctity, no fear of the gods, no reverence for an oath, no religious scruple". This edition, though conscientious and accurate, continues to make Livy rather boring, long-winded instead of chatty, pompous rather than dignified. It is true that Livy is not one for Tacitean brevity, but that is no reason to fill the narrative with words like "abrogated" and "thereupon" and phrases like "unto no small degree".

The Penguin version of SÉLINCOURT, BETTENSON and RADICE (1960–82) is a great improvement, although scholars might worry about the way in which some of the later books translated by Bettenson were cut. Scholarly prefaces written by such experts on Livy as R.M. Ogilvie and A.H. McDonald are reassuring. Sélincourt and Bettenson were both schoolteachers, and while they may miss out, or not care for, the latest minutiae of classical scholarship, they make up for this with the easy flow of their narrative, the memorable phrase, and a vigorous energy designed, as Livy designed, to compel the reader to keep on reading. Radice, the general editor of the Penguin series, pays this tribute to Sélincourt: "Neither De Sélincourt nor Livy would suffer the forward surge of the narrative to be held up by details like the exact spelling of a disputed Spanish place-name." Sélincourt is contemptuous about trying to imitate the style of an author, saying that a translator can write only in his own style; it was lucky that his was so like Livy's, and that his successors were able to imitate him.

WALSH's editions (1990–96) provide sold scholarship and an accurate if unexciting translation.

TOM WINNIFRITH

Further Reading

Walsh, P.G., *Livy: His Historical Aims and Methods*, Cambridge: Cambridge University Press, 1961; 2nd edition, Bristol: Bristol Classical Press, 1989

Ramon Llull 1232–1316

Catalan philosopher, theologian, poet and writer of romances

Biography

Ramon Llull alias Lull or Raimundus Lullius was born in Palma de Majorca in 1232 into a land-owning family from Barcelona. He married young, but left the Majorcan court about the age of 30, when after a series of visions he devoted the rest of his long life to spreading the Gospel. He learned Arabic in order to debate with Muslims and developed a philosophical system, the "Great Universal Art of Finding Truth", intended to make possible access to God by rational means. He travelled to the Christian courts of Aragon, France and the Papacy to enlist support, with small success, and also travelled as a missionary in North Africa and the Eastern Mediterranean. He urged university teaching of Oriental languages and non-Christian theologies. He died in 1316 either at Bejaïa in North Africa or in Palma, and was later beatified by the Roman Catholic Church.

He wrote nearly 300 works, in Catalan, Latin and Arabic. Many of them are devoted to his Art. Others, like *Blanquerna*, are exemplary romances in which the characters spend much of the time in debate and teaching by means of analogies: this was a favoured technique of the medieval preacher, based on the assumption that the mind first grasps concrete things and rises through them to knowledge of God.

Translations

Selections

Bonner, Anthony J., *Selected Works of Ramon Llull*, 2 vols, Princeton, New Jersey: Princeton University Press, 1985 (vol. 1: *The Book of the Gentile and the Three Wise Men*; *Ars Demonstrativa*; *Ars Brevis*; vol. 2: *Felix; or, The Book of Wonders*; *Principles of Medicine*; *Flowers of Love and Flowers of Intelligence*)

Bonner, Anthony J. and Eve Bonner, *Doctor Illuminatus: A Ramon Llull Reader*, Princeton, New Jersey: Princeton University Press, 1993

Peers, Edgar Allison, *Thoughts of Blessed Ramón Lull for Every Day*, London: Burns Oates, 1925

Turner, Robert, *Philosophical and Chymical Experiments of ... Raymund Lully*, in *Paracelsus of the Chymical Transmutation, Genealogy, and Generation of Metals and Minerals*, by Parcelsus, translated by Turner, London: printed for R. Moon and H. Fletcher, 1657

Single Works (arranged alphabetically: only some dates of composition are known)

L'arbre de filosofia de amor, 1290; completed 1298

Peers, Edgar Allison, *The Tree of Love*, London: SPCK, and New York: Macmillan, 1926

L'art de contemplació, 1282 (part of *Blanquerna* and also translated with it)

Peers, Edgar Allison, *The Art of Contemplation*, London: SPCK, and New York: Macmillan, 1925

Blanquerna, 1283

Peers, Edgar Allison, *Blanquerna*, London: Jarrold, 1926; edited by Robert Irwin, London: Dedalus, and New York: Hippocrene, 1986

Clavicula

Anonymous, *Clavicula; or, A Little Key ... which is also called Apertorium (the opener), in which all that is required in the work of Alchymy is plainly declared* in *Aurifontina Chymica*, by J.F. Houpreghts, London: printed for William Cooper, 1680; edited by Allen G. Debus, New York: Johnson, 1967

Hermes' Bird

Cremer, F., *Hermes' Bird* in *Theatrum chemicum Britannicum*, compiled by Elias Ashmole, London: J. Grismond for N. Brooke, 1652

Llibre d'amic i amat (part of *Blanquerna* and also translated with it)

Bonner, Eve, *The Book of the Lover and the Beloved* in *Doctor Illuminatus: A Ramon Llull Reader*, by Bonner and Anthony J. Bonner, Princeton, New Jersey: Princeton University Press, 1993

Johnston, Mark D., *The Book of the Lover and the Beloved* (parallel texts), Warminster, Wiltshire: Aris and Phillips, 1995

Peers, Edgar Allison, *The Book of the Lover and the Beloved*, with an introduction, London: SPCK, and New York: Macmillan, 1923; revised edition, 1946

Llibre de les bèsties (part of *Felix* and also translated with it)

Peers, Edgar Allison, *The Book of the Beasts*, London: Burns Oates and Washbourne, 1927; Westport, Connecticut: Hyperion Press, 1978

Llibre de l'orde de cavalleria, 1275

Caxton, William, *The Book of the Order of Chyualry or Knyghtode*, from a French version, Westminster: William Caxton, c.1484; London: Kelmscott Press, 1892

Haye, Sir Gilbert of the, *The Buke of Knychtede and The Buke of the Governaunce of Princis*, from a French version, in *Gilbert of the Haye's Prose Manuscript (AD 1456)*, vol. 2, edited by J.H. Stevenson, Edinburgh: Scottish Text Society, 1914

Loutfut, Adam, in *The Book of the Ordre of Chyualry, Translated ... by William Caxton ... Together with Adam Loutfut's (1494) Scottish Transcript*, edited by Alfred T.P. Byles, London: Oxford University Press, 1926

Rethorica nova

Johnston, Mark D., *Ramon Llull's New Rhetoric* (parallel texts), Davis, California: Hermagoras Press, 1994

Ramon Llull was one of the first authors to write Catalan prose, and the first to write poetry in Catalan instead of Provençal, which was the traditional language for the lyric in Catalonia. Llull's style presents two main problems to the translator: his art functions by means of an idiosyncratic vocabulary: "So that understanding might have the wherewithal with which to endure in love, lovefulness, lovability and loving endured in love, and understanding endured with them" (*Flowers of Love*, in *Selected Works*, translated by BONNER,vol. 2, p. 1227). In his narrative and more simply didactic works the underlying difficult sense is overlaid by a spare plain style. Like many early prose writers, he uses simple syntactic structures, with little interest in subordination; he repeats words like "do" and "thing" where the modern language would use a variety of terms. He is also rather humourless.

The history of Llull's works in English translation falls into three periods. In the 15th and 16th centuries he was read for his *Book of the Order of Chivalry* (see Yates, *Astraea*, pp. 106–08, for his possible influence on the Elizabethan chivalric revival). In the 17th century he was viewed unjustly as Raymond Lully the alchemist (see the translations by TURNER, 1657, and CREMER, 1652, and the ANONYMOUS 1680 version of the *Clavicula*). Only in the 20th century has Llull been seen as a literary or doctrinal author. The rebirth of interest in Llull in Great Britain can be attributed to the translations of Edgar Allison PEERS of 1923 onwards; since 1985, translations for the scholarly community by the Americans BONNER and JOHNSTON have appeared. Whereas Peers's translations were published by Christian concerns such as the Society for Promoting Christian Knowledge or Burns Oates and Washbourne, "Publishers to the Holy See", those of Bonner and Johnston emanate from academic and university presses.

Llull's first book to appear in English was one of his least typical, the *Llibre de l'orde de cavalleria*, in which a knight-turned-hermit instructs a squire in a religious form of knighthood. Its authorship was not known in England. It came to Britain via the French translation, from which derive the Scots version of Sir Gilbert of the HAYE (1456; first printed 1847) and the English translation of William CAXTON (c. 1484, reprinted by William Morris in 1892). Caxton adds an epilogue calling for a revival of chivalry in England. In 1494 Adam LOUTFUT produced a second Scots version, this time out of Caxton's edition (it was not printed until 1926).

Edgar Allison PEERS (1891–1952) was Gilmour Professor of Spanish at the University of Liverpool from 1920. His principal reputation today is as a popularizer and translator of Spanish and Catalan literature. Peers was also the author of three volumes of *Studies of the Spanish Mystics* (1927–60), and he began his Llull translations with the more mystical works. *The Book of the Lover and the Beloved*, inserted in *Blanquerna* and purporting to be work of Blanquerna himself, is a sequence of 366 aphorisms: "each verse [in the biblical sense] suffices for contemplating God a whole day", as Llull explains (JOHNSTON, 1995). With the exception of the much longer *Blanquerna*, the Peers translations are pocket-sized octavos that lend themselves to devotional use.

The style of his Llull is peppered with archaisms:

> [the ox] said that he had no evil intention whatsoever toward him [the lion], nor had he any mind soever to commit aught that should harm him or his court; for the king had honoured him, the more so, because he was one of the beasts which the king was accustomed to eat, and the king desired not to eat him; wherefore he ought to give to the king all the honour that was his due"
>
> (*Book of the Beasts*).

Peers remained true to his stated intention to "modernise Lull's language only where to do so seemed essential" (*Blanquerna*, introduction): in the passage quoted "soever", "aught" and "wherefore", although they might seem intrusive or even smack of Wardour Street, do genuinely render archaisms in the Catalan; however, "desired not" is Peers's own turn. Peers reads as strangely in English as Llull does for the modern Catalan reader.

Few modern translators would be as accommodating of archaisms. BONNER (1985) renders the same passage thus:

> [the ox apologized to the king], saying that he was not really guilty of anything, nor could he imagine ever doing anything bad against the king or his court, since the king had seen fit to honor him. And since he was an animal that kings found good to eat, and the king did not want to eat him, he therefore felt especially obliged to keep and maintain all the king's honor
>
> (*Selected Works*, vol. 2).

JOHNSTON's two translations (1994, 1995) are printed with the original text facing, and are (seemingly) intended as aids in the comprehension of the Latin or Catalan.

BARRY TAYLOR

Further Reading

Yates, Frances A., *Astraea: The Imperial Theme in the Sixteenth Century*, London and Boston: Routledge and Kegan Paul, 1975; London: Pimlico, 1993

See also the studies in Bonner and Johnston

Lo Kuan-chung

See San Guo Zhi Yan Yi

"Longinus"

Nothing is known of the anonymous 1st-century AD author of the influential critical treatise, long ascribed, in error, to Dionysius Cassius Longinus, a Greek rhetorician of the 3rd century AD.

On the Sublime

Peri hypsous, 1st century AD

Translations

There are 11 known manuscripts of "Longinus' " *On the Sublime*; 10 of these date from the 16th and 17th centuries. By far the oldest surviving manuscript is the 10th-century *Codex Parisinus s. Parisiensis 2036* (known as *P.*), and it is generally assumed that all the later Greek texts are derived from this source. Many modern scholarly texts (Roberts, Russell) are ultimately dependent upon it, though other more accessible translations (Dorsch, Grube) tend, in turn, to rely on one or more of these scholarly texts.

Dorsch, T.S., *On the Sublime* in *Classical Literary Criticism: Aristotle, Horace, Longinus*, Harmondsworth and Baltimore: Penguin, 1965

Grube, G.M.A., *Longinus: On Great Writing*, with an introduction, New York: Liberal Arts Press, 1957

Hall, John, *Dionysius Longinus of the Height of Eloquence*, London, 1652

Prickard, A.O., *Longinus on the Sublime*, Oxford: Clarendon Press, 1906; revised edition, 1946; reprinted Westport, Connecticut: Greenwood Press, 1978

Pulteney, John, *A Treatise of the Loftiness or Elegancy of Speech*, London, 1680

Roberts, W. Rhys, *Longinus on the Sublime* (parallel texts), with an introduction, Cambridge: Cambridge University Press, 1899; reprinted New York: Garland, 1987

Russell, D.A., *Longinus: On Sublimity*, with an introduction, Oxford: Clarendon Press, 1965

Smith, William, *Dionysius Longinus on the Sublime*, London: J. Watts for W. Innys and R. Manby, 1739

The first printed version of the text was produced by Francis Robortello in Basle (1554). His "discovery", the precise source of which is unknown, was followed by a number of editions and translations, including the first one in English (Hall, 1652); but it was Boileau's French version, *Traité du sublime* (1674), that largely fuelled interest in "Longinus".

Few of the translations capture adequately the spirit of the original, which as well as being a book on how to write, itself revels in the possibilities of writing: it makes abundant use of metaphor, and compound and figurative expression. It is also virtually impossible to mimic in English its elaborate and rhythmic sentence structure.

HALL (1652) is the first English translation of Longinus; a clumsy and inaccurate version reliant on Latin texts. However, in its attempts to translate the difficult concept of the sublime in terms of eloquence or grandeur of expression, it arguably comes close to the intentions of the original. It also contains what appear to be original renderings of some of the verse, notably the otherwise unrecorded piece by Sappho known as the *Ode to Anactoria*, discussed by Longinus.

PULTENEY (1680), like Hall, is often inaccurate but does highlight the extent to which Longinus is, at least in part, an orator's manual. The avoidance of the word "sublime", which Johnson later defined in his *Dictionary* as "a Gallicism", is particularly noteworthy, as this translation draws heavily upon Boileau (1674), and as such tends to present Longinus much more dryly than the original.

SMITH (1739) is arguably the first serious English version of Longinus. Like Pulteney, it is based on Boileau, and again reflects the pervasiveness of this translation throughout the 18th century, when there is a spectacular growth of interest in Longinus' ideas. It is one of the first English translations to settle on the use of the word "sublime" (see Monk, 1935, pp. 18ff.). Though clearly second-hand, and not always faithful even to Boileau, it does have an elegance of expression that in some ways comes close to the original.

In the 19th century a number of scholarly translations of Longinus were produced, many of which used Weiske's Latin and Greek variorum edition (1809). The culmination of this work is represented, in some respects, by the editions of Roberts and Prickard, on which many later versions (Dorsch, Grube) rely.

ROBERTS (1899) goes back to *P.* and offers an accurate if at times slightly stilted translation, coupled with a parallel Greek text based on *P.* with some plausible emendation. The notes and apparatus, too, are informative. However, this version lacks the playfulness and inventiveness of the original: for example, in a section that itself deals with the use of figures, it reads "we all know that a richly comparisoned style is pretentious", whereas a rendering truer to the spirit of Longinus might be "Only a sophist has bells on his harness wherever he goes" (Russell). It also relies, in the main, upon A.S. Way's slightly wooden verse translations, and can be a little vague in its translation of some of the Greek author's technical vocabulary. Despite its shortcomings it is still, to some extent, the standard text.

PRICKARD (1906), too, is largely accurate, if, perhaps, a little stilted for modern taste. One notable oddity, which was common among 18th-century readers of Longinus, is the translation of the Greek *bathous* as "bathos", as opposed to the correct sense of "profundity" or "depth". Rather contentiously, given the debate over the authorship of Longinus, it includes some rhetorical fragments attributed to Cassius Longinus.

GRUBE (1957) is based on Prickard, though for *bathous* it reads "depth". It is one of the few modern translations to avoid the use of the term "sublime", preferring instead expressions like "great writing", which recalls earlier English translations (Hall, Pulteney). Its style is enjoyable and approachable, particularly in the choice of verse renderings, and it has brief but informative notes. This unintimidating version should meet the needs of most non-specialists. However, it should be noted that it is alone in reading one of the sections as a criticism of Plato, rather than the usually conjectured favourable comparison between Plato and another writer, Lyius.

RUSSELL (1965), like Roberts, goes back to *P.*, and is perhaps the most authoritative modern translation. It reproduces the section headings supplied by *P.*, and while possibly not as enjoyable a read as Grube it is clearly less contentious in its conjectures. It justifies well its departures from the Greek text, and explains, perhaps most clearly of all, Longinus' technical terminology. The serious student might also be directed to Russell's Greek text of *On the Sublime* (Oxford: Clarendon Press, 1964).

DORSCH (1965) offers a version of Roberts; it can be recommended for its accessibility and because it enables easy comparison with two other major Classical theorists.

Longinus' indirect (often very indirect) influence upon English literature and aesthetics ought, finally, to be mentioned. Some indication of this can be gleaned from Abrams, Henn and Monk.

PAUL WRIGHT

Further Reading

Abrams, M.H., *The Mirror and the Lamp: Romantic Theory and the Classical Tradition*, Oxford and New York: Oxford University Press, 1953
Grube, G.M.A.. "Notes on Peri Hupsous", *American Journal of Philology*, 78 (1957) pp. 355–60
Henn, T.R., *Longinus and English Criticism*, Cambridge: Cambridge University Press, 1934
Monk, Samuel Holt, *The Sublime: A Study of Critical Theories in XVIII-Century England*, New York: MLA, 1935
Weinberg, B., "Translations and Commentaries on Longinus up to 1600", *Modern Philology*, 47 (1950) pp. 145–47

See also the introductions and notes of Roberts (1899) and Russell (1964, and edition of the Greek text, 1965)

Longus 2nd–3rd centuries AD

Greek novelist

Biography

Nothing is known about the author of *Daphnis and Chloe*. Even the name of Longus may be spurious. The story shows good knowledge of Lesbos, where the action takes place; the author is well-read in Greek, and to some extent Latin, literature – such is the extent of our information.

Daphnis and Chloe

Daphnis kai Chloi, 3rd century AD

Daphnis and Chloe stands out among the handful of surviving ancient novels. Goethe's opinion was that one should re-read it every year. *Daphnis and Chloe* is unique as the only pastoral romance from the Classical period and also because it subtly and convincingly describes the development of its characters' feelings. Most of the action is psychological, unlike what predominates in other works of the genre, where shipwrecks, abductions, attacks by brigands, and the like constitute the main interest. In addition to offering a fine delineation of the awakening and growth of erotic love, *Daphnis and Chloe* glorifies the cycle of seasons and life in natural surrounding, albeit idealized.

Translations

Anonymous [James Craggs?], *The Pastoral Amours of Daphnis and Chloe: A Novel*, 4th edition, London: J. Knox, 1763
Anonymous, *Daphnis and Chloe: A Pastoral Novel*, Penzance, Cornwall: Vernor and Hood, 1803
Anonymous, *Longus: Literally and Completely Translated from the Greek* (parallel texts), Athens: Athenian Society, 1896
Daye, Angell, *Daphnis and Chloe: excellently describing the weight of affection, the simplicitie of love, the purport of honest meaning, the resolution of men, and disposition of Fate, finished in a Pastorall and interlaced with the praises of a most peerlesse Princesse, wonderful in Maiestie, and rare in perfection, celebrated within the same Pastorall, and therefore termed by the name of The Shepheards Holidaie*, London: Robert Waldegrave, 1587; in *Daphnis and Chloe: The Elizabethan Version from Amyot's translation by Angel Day, reprinted from the unique original*, edited by Joseph Jacobs, London: D. Nutt, 1890
Edmonds, J.M., *Daphnis and Chloe, with the English Translation of George Thornley, revised and augmented: The Love Romances of Parthenius and Other Fragments, with an English Translation by S. Gaselee* (parallel texts), London: Heinemann, and Cambridge, Massachusetts: Harvard University Press, 1916; reprinted 1979 (Loeb Classical Library)
Gill, Christopher, *Daphnis and Chloe* in *Collected Ancient Greek Novels*, edited by B.P. Reardon, Berkeley: University of California Press, 1989, pp. 285–348
Hadas, Moses, *Three Greek Romances: Longus, Xenophon, Dio Chrysostom*, New York: Doubleday, 1953
Lindsay, Jack, *Daphnis & Chloe*, London: Daimon Press, 1948
Lowe, W.D., *The Story of Daphnis and Chloe: A Greek Pastoral* (parallel texts), with an introduction, Cambridge: Deighton Bell, 1908; reprinted New York: Arno Press, 1979
Moore, George, *The Pastoral Loves of Daphnis and Chloe*, with an introduction, London: Heinemann, 1924
Smith, Rowland, *The Greek Romances of Heliodorus, Longus, and Achilles Tatius, comprising The Ethiopics; or,*

Adventures of Theagenes and Chariclea; The Pastoral Amours of Daphnis and Chloe; and The Loves of Clitopho and Leucippe, London: Bohn, 1855

Thornley, George, *Daphnis and Chloe: A Most Sweet and Pleasant Pastorall Romance for Young Ladies*, London: John Garfield, 1657; frequently reprinted, notably with changes in the Loeb series (see under Edmonds)

Turner, Paul, *Daphnis and Chloe*, with an introduction, Harmondsworth: Penguin, 1956; 2nd edition, 1968; with revised introduction, 1989

The history of English translations of *Daphnis and Chloe* reflects fluctuating attitudes toward eroticism: from the earliest, expurgated versions through the coyly sweet translations of the 18th century, some of them explicit and others chastened, then those of the Victorian period, when the book was regarded as obscene, and finally contemporary versions, which strive after a faithful rendering. Numerous older translations, even when expurgated, appear without the translator's name. A complicating factor is that some of the translations are from French versions rather than the Greek original.

A different kind of anonymity as well has plagued English renditions of *Daphnis and Chloe*. Many versions before the 20th century are adaptations rather than translations and frequently do not even acknowledge Longus as the original author. In addition, one translator may utilize heavily the work of a predecessor without mentioning to whom he is indebted. There have been very many imitations that have influenced, and been influenced by, translations. Among such are Fletcher's *Faithful Shepherdess* (derived from Longus through Guarini's *Il Pastor Fido*) and Ramsay's *Gentle Shepherd*, as well as English works derived from Bernardin de Saint-Pierre's *Paul et Virginie*, which is freely based on *Daphnis and Chloe*. Only a very few of the closer versions of Longus are covered here.

The best translations succeed in expressing the mixture of the simple and the ornate that characterizes this highly poetic work. The worst sound contrived or cloying.

DAYE or Day (1587) based his version on the enormously influential first French translation, that of Jacques Amyot (*Les amours pastourales de Daphnis et de Chloé*, Paris 1559, expurgated and published anonymously). Daye condenses or expands at will; he paraphrases frequently, and inserts a lengthy pastoral poem in honour of Queen Elizabeth. This enchanting bibliographic curiosity, edited by Jacobs (1890) from the only copy he says survived destruction at the hands of Puritans, is interesting as a work of its period rather than a translation of Longus, who is not mentioned on the title page.

Estimates of THORNLEY (1657) have ranged from "free and pleasing" (McCulloh) to "dry and lumpy" (Moore). This translation is expurgated and does not acknowledge Longus on the title page. It is based more on a Latin translation (in Jungermann's 1605 Greek/Latin edition; see EDMONDS, p. xx) than on the original.

The ANONYMOUS version of 1763 is a paraphrase rather than a translation but it is fairly close to the original. Erotic passages are not omitted. It is an odd feature of the preface that the translator apologizes for some ancient customs such as the exposure of infants but not – as older versions tend to do – for the sexual material. The English is pleasing.

The ANONYMOUS version of 1803 is reputed to be by C.V. Le Grice. The translator elaborately disclaims taking any part in the "muddy waters of sensuality" and contrasts "the grossness of the Pagan Religion" with its "impure images" to "the sound of the Sabbath Bells" of his own period. The style of the translation, however, is elegant and enjoyable if one reads it for what the translator does approve: the pastoral elements.

SMITH (1855) exemplifies Bohn translations at their most plodding. However, he omits nothing. When he is embarrassed, he resorts to translating into Latin. His version is based on that of Le Grice although not identical with it. Beginning at this version in the present survey, an important fragment of the text discovered in 1809 by P.L. Courier and incorporated into his French edition becomes part of English translations. (On Courier, see LOWE's introduction; like almost everything else dealing with Longus, the history of this discovery too is ambiguous and involved.)

The ANONYMOUS translation of 1896 is very readable, in the lucid and limpid English that agrees with the ethos of Longus' narrative.

LOWE (1908) expurgates and there is little virtue in what he does translate. His style is rather cumbersome and archaic, but he does provide a good brief introduction to the history of the text and its earlier editions and translations.

EDMONDS's original edition (1916) of Thornley uses Latin for erotic passages. The 1979 edition has the entire text in English. When he corrects some of Thornley's errors, Edmonds adapts Thornley's style, as he also does in the long passage discovered by Courier and unavailable to Thornley.

MOORE (1924), a notable Anglo-Irish writer, sets up as his aim to redeem "the loveliest of stories from bad Greek and bad English". This is a translation not from the Greek but from the French of Courier. Enjoyment of Moore's style is an acquired taste, but if one does take to it one will find it beautiful.

LINDSAY's translation (1948) is slightly euphemistic in erotic passages; otherwise this is an excellent version. Lindsay was attracted to late Classical antiquity and translated a number of works belonging to it, including Apuleius' *The Golden Ass*. A stimulating essay follows his translation of *Daphnis and Chloe*.

HADAS's version (1953) is reliable but does not flow and does not compare favourably with other modern translations of Longus, although it is one of the most widely available.

TURNER (1956) is excellent, reliable and readable; this is one of the best versions, along with Lindsay's and Gill's. The introduction, though brief, is scholarly and packed with valuable information.

Aside from being an excellent translation in its own right, GILL's version (1989) has the advantage of forming part of an omnibus collection of ancient Greek romances in modern translation, which enables the reader to see *Daphnis and Chloe* as part of a genre yet unique.

ZOJA PAVLOVSKIS-PETIT

Further Reading

McCulloh, William E., "Selected Bibliography" in his *Longus*, New York: Twayne 1970, pp. 133–34

MacQueen, Bruce D., "Annotated Bibliography of Editions and Translations of *Daphnis and Chloe*" in his *Myth, Rhetoric, and Fiction: A Reading of Longus's Daphnis and Chloe*, Lincoln: University of Nebraska Press, 1990, pp. 261–67

See also Moore's and Turner's introductions

Pierre Loti 1850–1923

French novelist and travel writer

Biography

Born Louis-Marie-Julien Viaud, the youngest of three children, 14 January 1850, in Rochefort, a former naval port on France's Atlantic coast. He went to school in Rochefort and for a while in Paris. In 1866, when his family had fallen on hard times, he joined the French Navy as a cadet, and in 1869 he went to sea as a midshipman. As a naval officer from 1871 to 1910 Loti travelled the world. His exotic destinations – the Pacific Islands, Turkey, West Africa, Japan – formed the background of his novels of the 1880s. Later, they provided the subject matter of works describing his journeys, impressions and experiences in Morocco, the Middle East, China, India, Persia and the Far East. He married in 1886 (one son). Exactly three-quarters of Loti's 36 works have been translated into English, initially in Britain and then increasingly in the US. His best-known novel, *Pêcheur d'Islande* (*An Icelandic Fisherman*), based on the life of Breton fishermen, has been translated into 14 languages and appeared in more than 40 editions in English. In 1891 Loti was elected to the Académie Française. He died 10 June 1923, in Hendaye.

Translations

Novels

Aziyadé, 1879
Laurie, Marjorie, *Constantinople (Aziyadé)*, London: T. Werner Laurie, 1927

Rarahu; ou, Le Mariage de Loti, 1880
Bell, Clara, *Rarahu; or, The Marriage of Loti*, New York: Gottsburger, 1890; as *The Marriage of Loti (Rarahu)* London: T. Werner Laurie, 1925
Monkshood, G.F., *The Marriage of Loti*, London: Langham Translations, 1908; London: KPI, 1986

Le Roman d'un Spahi, 1881
Monkshood, G.F. and E. Tristan, *The Romance of a Spahi*, London: Greening, 1912; as *Love in the Desert (The Romance of a Spahi)*, London: London Book Co., 1928

Mon Frère Yves, 1883
Baines, W.P., *A Tale of Brittany*, London: T. Werner Laurie, 1923; New York: Stokes, 1924
Fletcher, Mary P., *My Brother Yves*, London: Vizetelly, 1884

Pêcheur d'Islande, 1886
Baines, W.P., *The Iceland Fisherman*, London: T. Werner Laurie, and New York: Stokes, 1924
Cadiot, C., *An Iceland Fisherman*, London: J. and R. Maxwell, 1888; New York: Gottsburger, 1891
Endore, Guy, *An Iceland Fisherman*, Stockholm: Norstedt, 1931; New York: Knopf, 1946
Farwell de Koven, A., *An Iceland Fisherman*, Chicago: McClurg, 1889
Martin, J., *An Iceland Fisherman*, New York: Collier, 1902
Melcon, H.A., *An Iceland Fisherman*, New York: Burt, 1901

Madame Chrysanthème, 1888
Ensor, Laura, *Madame Chrysanthème*, Paris: E. Guillaume, 1889; London: Routledge, 1897; New York: Boni and Liveright, 1921

Fantôme d'Orient, 1892
Gordon, J.E., *A Phantom from the East*, London: T.F. Unwin, 1892

Matelot, 1893
Robins, E.P., *Jean Berny, Sailor*, New York: Cassell, 1893

Ramuntcho, 1897
Baines, W.P., *A Tale of the Pyrenees (Ramuntcho)*, London: T. Werner Laurie, and New York: Stokes, 1923

La Troisième Jeunesse de Madame Prune, 1905
Plimsoll, S.R.C., *Madame Prune*, London: T. Werner Laurie, 1905; New York: Stokes, 1919

Les Désenchantées, 1906
Bell, Clara, *Disenchanted*, London and New York: Macmillan, 1906

Selection of Stories
Hearn, Lafcadio, *Stories from Pierre Loti*, Tokyo: Hokuseido Press, 1933

Autobiographical and Travel Writing

Propos d'exil, 1887
Bell, Clara, *From Lands of Exile*, New York: Gottsburger, 1888

Au Maroc, 1890
Baines, W.P., *Morocco*, London: T. Werner Laurie, and Philadelphia: McKay, 1914
Robins, E.P., *Into Morocco*, New York: Welch, Fracker, 1889

Le Roman d'un enfant, 1890
Bell, Clara, *A Child's Romance*, New York: Gottsburger, 1891
Smith, Caroline F., *The Story of a Child*, Boston: Birchard, 1901

Le Livre de la pitié et de la mort, 1891 (2nd edition)
O'Connor, T.P., *The Book of Pity and Death*, London and New York: Cassell, 1892

L'Exilée, 1893
Rothwell, Fred, *Carmen Sylva, and Sketches from the Orient*, New York: Macmillan, 1912

Jérusalem, 1895
Baines, W.P., *Jerusalem*, London: T. Werner Laurie, 1915; Philadelphia: McKay, 1916

Figures et choses qui passaient, 1898
Anonymous, Introduction by Henry James, *Impressions*, London: Constable, 1898; New York: Brentano, 1900

Reflets sur la sombre route, 1899
Rothwell, Fred, *On Life's By-Ways*, London: Bell, 1914

Les Derniers Jours de Pékin, 1902
Jones, Myrta L., *The Last Days of Pekin*, Boston: Little Brown, 1902

L'Inde (sans les Anglais), 1903
Inman, George A.F., *India*, edited by Robert Harborough Sherard, London: T. Werner Laurie, 1913; New York: Stokes, 1929

La Mort de Philae, 1908
Baines, W.P., *Egypt*, London: T. Werner Laurie, and New York: Duffield, 1909

Un Pèlerin d'Angkor, 1912
Baines, W.P., *Siam*, London: T. Werner Laurie, 1913

Un Jeune Officier pauvre, 1923
Stein, Rose Ellen, *Notes of my Youth*, edited by Samuel Viaud, New York: Doubleday, and London: Heinemann, 1924

Political Writings
Turquie agonisante, 1913
Sands, Bedwin (pseudonym of George Raffalovich), *Turkey in Agony*, London: African Times and Orient Review, 1913

La Grande Barbarie, 1915
Hueffer, Ford Maddox, *The Trail of the Barbarians*, London: Longmans Green, 1917

La Hyène enragée, 1916
Laurie, Marjorie, *War*, London: T. Werner Laurie, and Philadelphia: Lippincott, 1917

Pierre Loti's style is essentially simple. This has not, however, made it any easier for translators to cope with French word order (e.g. "Aunt Berthe, motionless in her chair, whose eyes I felt upon me", C. BELL (1891), *A Child's Romance*); abstract nouns (e.g. "Everywhere there are sadnesses as of the end, mute resignations to the fecund decompositions", W.P. BAINES (1923), *A Tale of the Pyrenees*); or a multiplicity of adjectives (e.g. "her tiny little mobile lively eyes", S.R.C. PLIMSOLL, 1905, *Madame Prune*, p. 166). Nor has it prevented them from committing bad blunders – for example, translating "malaise" as "unhealthy" instead of "Malay" (W.P. BAINES, 1924, *Iceland Fisherman*), "petit-nègre" as "little nigger" (C. BELL, 1890, *The Marriage of Loti*) or "trilles savants as "*scientific* trills" (M. FLETCHER, 1884, *My Brother Yves*). It was nevertheless not too difficult to provide sound translations of Loti's non-fictional, more documentary volumes about his travels, such as *India* by G. INMAN (1913) and *Jerusalem* and *Egypt* by W.P. BAINES (1915, 1909). In Loti's fictional works, however, his narrative may be straightforward but his descriptions, where he wishes to convey a sense of the exotic or a delicately nuanced, momentary impression of a scene, test the skills of his translators. Some – M. LAURIE's version (1927) of *Constantinople* and G. ENDORE's 1931 *An Iceland Fisherman*, for example – have managed to catch the author's aesthetic sensitivity and created a poetic style matching his. Others such as W.P. BAINES translate without proper insight and far too literally; his rendering of some of Loti's non-fictional works is thus far better than his translations of the novels *Mon Frère Yves* (1923) and *Ramuntcho* (1923).

To convey the exotic Loti makes use of non-French words or foreign speech in his novels; this met with different responses from his translators. C. BELL (1890) in her *Rarahu; or, The Marriage of Loti* retains much of the Tahitian of Rarahu's letters and songs but omits actual dialogue and translates Loti's explanation in French of individual Tahitian words. As regards the novels set in Japan, S.R.C. PLIMSOLL (1905) translates in *Madame Prune* the names of the characters (Madame Cherry Blossom, Mr Kangaroo, etc.) while L. ENSOR (1889) in her *Madame Chrysanthème* translates the names of the tea-houses but leaves the characters with their French names. In his version of *Ramuntcho* W.P. BAINES diminishes the exotic effect of Basque local colour by constantly translating "pelota" as "tennis" and "pelotaris" as "players". Loti's descriptions of exotic flora or furnishings can also put a stain on the translator's vocabulary, as in the jungle scenes of *The Romance of a Spahi* or the scenes of local life in *Morocco*. Naval terms and jargon can also pose problems when translating the novels set at sea: what is the right term for Brother Yves's "livret de marin" or for the "chasseurs" boats in *Iceland Fisherman*?

It is mainly, however, Loti's depiction of sea, sky or landscape that needs delicate handling. Take, for example, the sensitivity to sound and mood achieved by Marjorie LAURIE with "the soft splash of oars falling on a slumbering sea" and "Now and then a carpet of spotless snow was spread beneath our feet as we gazed down on old Stamboul deep in repose" (*Constantinople*). Other more impressionistic examples of Loti's descriptions can be found in his masterpiece *Pêcheur d'Islande*.

The majority of the English-language editions of *Pêcheur d'Islande* (*An Iceland Fisherman*) are based on the translations by CADIOT, BAINES, and ENDORE. The first and earliest of these (CADIOT, 1888) has had most of the passages concerning love and sex cut out, combines chapters 1 and 2 of part 5, and makes several blunders (e.g. the phrase about the ships which "ramassent les balais" on their return being translated literally, p. 248!) but does also contain some neatly expressed lines (for example: "a pale, dim light ... bathing all things like the gleams of a setting sun", p. 11). The BAINES translation (1924) is complete but is extremely literal and often inaccurate. Loti's delicate depiction of the sea's shimmering surface ("c'étaient des moires, rien que des moires changeantes qui jouaient sur la mer") being rendered as "there were waterings, nothing but changing waterings, which played over the surface of the sea" (p. 46). ENDORE's translation (1931) is in contrast fluent and sensitive to the mood of the novel and captures beautifully in places the wistful, delicate poetry of Loti's impressionism (for example: "In the sky above them floated shapeless, colourless clouds full of an indefinable, unearthly luminosity ... a lovely dawn trailed its rosy hues over the waves ..."). Equally impressive is his translation of the scenes describing the passing shoals of fish, the sun rising in the mist near Iceland and the storm at sea).

The American translations by FARWELL DE KOVEN (1889), MARTIN (1902), and MELCON (1901) are fairly fluent and clear, though at times this involves a certain looseness in translation and the omission of lines considered too awkward to put into English, superfluous to the main story, or a little bit vulgar. Some of the descriptions of sky and sea (in part 1, chapter 6, for example) in Farwell de Koven and Martin do, however, come close to the sensitivity and poetry of Endore.

MICHAEL G. LERNER

Further Reading

Lerner, Michael G., *Pierre Loti*, New York: Twayne, 1974

Lu Xun (Lu Hsün) 1881–1936

Chinese short-story writer, poet and essayist

Biography

Lu Xun was born and brought up in the scenic town of Shaoxing in Zhejiang province, which provided the background of many of his short stories. In 1902, he went to Japan on a government scholarship. There, while a medical student, he was influenced by the experience of translating European writers, especially Darwin, Nietzsche, and the Russian authors, and switched his interest to literature. After returning to China in 1910, he first taught at local schools and then served in the Ministry of Education of the new Republican government while concurrently teaching part-time at several universities. After the literary revolution of 1917 he began to write in the vernacular language and soon became famous as a short-story writer and essayist. In the mid-1920s he received teaching appointments in two southern universities, but from 1927 until his death of tuberculosis in 1936 he supported himself as a professional writer. Besides his scholarly works and some translation (primarily from Japanese), he published two collections of short stories, a few volumes of miscellaneous writings, and many collections of mostly satirical essays. Although he once announced that he had no intention whatsoever of becoming a poet, his poems, in both classical and vernacular forms, were posthumously collected. Lu Xun has long been canonized in China like a cultural saint. The first edition of his *Complete Works* was published only two years after his death in Shanghai 19 October 1936, and all his works, including his diaries, letters, and translations, are now available in well-edited annotated collections. Even in his lifetime his short stories were already translated into Japanese and various European languages. Academic interest in the man and his writings has continued for many decades.

Translations

Selection

Yang Xianyi and Gladys Yang, *Selected Works of Lu Hsun*, 4 vols, Beijing: Foreign Languages Press, 1956–60; 2nd edition, 1964

Short Stories

Leung, George Kin, *The True Story of Ah Q*, Shanghai: Commercial Press, 1926

Lyell, William A., *Diary of a Madman and Other Stories*, Honolulu: University of Hawaii Press, 1990

Wang, Chi-chen, *Ah Q and Others: Selected Stories of Lusin*, with an introduction, New York: Columbia University Press, 1941; reprinted Westport, Connecticut: Greenwood Press, 1971

Yang Xianyi and Gladys Yang, *The Complete Stories of Lu Xun*, Bloomington: Indiana University Press, and Beijing: Foreign Languages Press, 1981

Anthologies

Isaacs, Harold R. (editor), *Straw Sandals: Chinese Short Stories 1918–1933*, Cambridge, Massachusetts: MIT Press, 1974

Mills, E.H.F., *The Tragedy of Ah Qui, and Other Modern Chinese Stories*, from the French version (1929) by J.B. Kyn Yn Yu, London: Routledge, 1930

Snow, Edgar, *Living China: Modern Chinese Short Stories*, New York: Reynal and Hitchcock, 1937; reprinted Westport, Connecticut: Hyperion Press, 1973

Poetry

Ch'en, David Y., *Lu Hsun: Complete Poems* (parallel texts), Temple: Center for Asian Studies, Arizona State University, 1988

Huang Hsin-chyu, *Poems of Lu Hsün*, Hong Kong: Joint Publishing, 1979

Jenner, W.J.F., *Lu Xun: Selected Poems* (parallel texts), Beijing: Foreign Languages Press, 1982

Other Writing

Lin Yutang, "The Epigrams of Lusin" in *The Wisdom of China and India*, edited by Lin, New York: Random House, 1942, pp. 1083–86

Yang Hsien-yi and Gladys Yang, *A Brief History of Chinese Fiction* (translation of *Zhongguo xiaoshuo shilüe*, 1924), Beijing: Foreign Languages Press, 1959, 2nd edition 1964, 3rd edition 1976; Westport, Connecticut: Hyperion Press, 1973

Yang Hsien-yi and Gladys Yang, *Old Tales Retold*, Beijing: Foreign Languages Press, 1961; 2nd edition, 1972

Yang Hsien-yi and Gladys Yang, *Wild Grass*, Beijing: Foreign Languages Press, 1974

Yang Hsien-yi and Gladys Yang, *Dawn Blossoms Plucked at Dusk*, Beijing: Foreign Languages Press, 1976

Translation of Lu Xun's short stories into English started in the author's lifetime. LEUNG's translation of *The True Story of Ah Q* (1926), the author's longest and best-known story, suffers from its flat and stilted English, but it was memorable as among the earliest renditions of the author's works into a Western language. Lu Xun himself granted Leung the right of English translation and replied to his many inquiries regarding the text.

MILLS's *The Tragedy of Ah Qui* (1930), which includes three of Lu Xun's stories, is from Kyn Yn Yu's slightly bowdlerized French translation (1929), acclaimed by the French writer Romain Rolland (winner of the 1915 Nobel Prize for literature) who said he was moved to tears by reading them.

ISAACS's *Straw Sandals*, a collection of modern Chinese short stories selected with the help of Lu Xun himself (who also wrote a foreword for it) in 1934, could not find a publisher until four decades later (1974). It includes four of Lu Xun's short stories translated by George A. KENNEDY, who in his late years taught at Yale University. Two of them were first published in Isaacs's small English newspaper in Shanghai in 1932 and reprinted in the collection with some revision.

SNOW's *Living China* (1937) includes five short stories and two prose pieces by Lu Xun, preceded by a biography of the author. Snow, a journalist famous for his report on the Chinese Red Army and his personal relations with the Chinese communist leaders, knew only a little Chinese himself. When translating Lu Xun's pieces he found a collaborator in the author's close friend, the young writer Yao Xinnong. The English reads very well, but Snow "candidly emphasized" that it was not offered as a literal translation, that what he did was rather, in his own words, "to convey the spirit of a piece of work, to interpret it rather than to photostat it".

WANG's collection (1941) includes 11 short stories, rendered into facile American English prose, and a critical introduction. While it is still quite readable today, the translation does not fully convey the author's verbal diversity, and its scanty notes are insufficient for the reader to grasp the cultural density between the lines. As a translation in American English it is now superseded by **Lyell** (1990).

LIN YUTANG (1942), famous for his translation of Chinese literature as well as his numerous books in English on China and Chinese culture, has rendered into English 35 memorable short passages carefully selected from the author's essays (entitled "epigrams"), preceded by a short but very illuminating introductory note. Lin's translation, always highly readable though somewhat free, gives us a glimpse of the mood and temper of what he ranked as "one of the most biting satirists of Chinese culture".

Among all translators of Lu Xun, the husband-and-wife team of YANG Xianyi (Hsien-yi) & Gladys YANG has made the most important contribution. The four-volume *Selected Works* (1956–60) is by far the most comprehensive collection of Lu Xun's works in English (one volume of short stories, prose poems and memoir pieces, and three volumes of essays), and it will surely remain invaluable to scholars of modern Chinese literature in the future. Several volumes of Lu Xun's works, put into collections by the author himself, have also been rendered into English by them in their entirety, including *Dawn Blossoms Plucked at Dusk* (memoir pieces; translated 1976), *Old Tales Retold* (fictionalized ancient myths and legends, including a short play; translated 1961), and *Wild Grass* (prose poems; translated 1974). They have also translated (1959) *A Brief History of Chinese Fiction*, which derived from Lu Xun's Beijing University lecture notes between 1920 and 1924. With their long and wide experience in translating classical Chinese literature as well, they are perfectly at ease in this work, which contains numerous excerpts from classical Chinese fiction. In general, the translation of the Yangs, in fluent and smooth British English, is very reliable. Some may find that their translation does not reflect adequately the various idiosyncratic voices of the authors, but such a degree of versatility is difficult to achieve in any translation.

LYELL (1990), also the author of an excellent study (1976) of Lu Xun's life and works, rose to the challenge of providing a new complete version of Lu Xun's short stories in American English. His translation has successfully captured the nuances of stylistic diversity in the original, especially the contrast between the literary and the vernacular. It should also be commended for its abundant scholarly annotations.

Among the several translations of Lu Xun's poetry, HUANG's (1979), which includes 46 classical style poems and four in vernacular form, should henceforth be dismissed on account of its awkward English and numerous errors, let alone the hackneyed and simplistic Marxist interpretation found in its commentaries and notes.

JENNER's selection (1982), which includes 47 poems (39 old-style and 8 vernacular ones), provides the Chinese texts on opposite pages for comparison, with seven reproductions of poems in the author's own calligraphy as frontispieces. The translation, which uses rhyme occasionally (and quite interestingly, more for the vernacular poems than for the more strict classical style verse), is generally faithful to the original, but it often misses its force and verve.

CH'EN (1988) provides the only complete translation of all of Lu Xun's 66 poems, plus miscellaneous fragments and extant poetry titles without text. As in Jenner, the original texts are printed on opposite pages. Ch'en makes a line-by-line conversion of the original (which helps to reflect all the stanzaic forms), and preserves the rhyme (so important in Chinese poetry) remolded in familiar English schemes. He does not assume any poetic meter but resorts to other phonetic means, such as alliteration and assonance, to enhance the musical effects of the translation. The book is further enriched by its scholarly annotations and commentaries, indispensable for the reader in rendering intelligible the author's rich use of allusions and double meaning, and by a useful bibliography. Readers and scholars interested in Lu Xun's poetry should read Ch'en's book in comparison with the study by Kowallis (1995), which concentrates on the classical style poems.

YANG YE

Further Reading

Goldman, Merle (editor), *Modern Chinese Literature in the May Fourth Era*, Cambridge, Massachusetts: Harvard University Press, 1977

Hanan, Patrick D., "The Technique of Lu Hsün's Fiction", *Harvard Journal of Asiatic Studies*, 34 (1974) pp. 53–96

Hsia, T.A., *The Gate of Darkness: Studies on the Leftist Literary Movement in China*, Seattle: University of Washington Press, 1968

Huang, Sung-k'ang, *Lu Hsün and the New Culture Movement of Modern China*, Amsterdam: Djambatan, 1957; Westport, Connecticut: Hyperion Press, 1975

Kowallis, Jon Eugene von, *The Lyrical Lu Xun: A Study of His Classical-Style Verse*, Honolulu: University of Hawaii Press, 1995

Lee, Leo Ou-fan (editor), *Lu Xun and His Legacy*, Berkeley: University of California Press, 1985

Lee, Leo Ou-fan, *Voices from the Iron House: A Study of Lu Xun*, Bloomington: Indiana University Press, 1987

Lyell, William A. Jr, *Lu Hsün's Vision of Reality*, Berkeley: University of California Press, 1976

Průšek, Jaroslav, "Lu Hsün the Revolutionary and the Artist", *Orientalistische Literaturzeitung*, 55/5–6 (May–June 1960) pp. 229–36

Průšek, Jaroslav , "Lu Hsün's 'Huai Chiu': A Precursor of Modern Chinese Literature", *Harvard Journal of Asiatic Studies*, 29 (1969) pp. 169–76

Semanov, V.I., *Lu Hsün and His Predecessors*, translated and edited by Charles J. Alber, White Plains, New York: M.E. Sharpe, 1980

See also the translators' introductions to Ch'en, Lyell and Wang

Lu You (Lu Yu) 1125–1210

Chinese poet

Biography

Born in 1125, he was only one year old when the capital of the Song empire, Kaifeng, fell to invading troops of the northern state of Jurchen Jin (Chin), and his family, along with the imperial court, fled south where the Southern Song state was established. In his youth Lu You studied hard and passed all the civil service examinations with distinction. Thenceforth, however, he served mostly at a number of insignificant provincial positions, and was frequently dismissed from office, probably on account of his uncompromisingly hawkish political views. He spent his late years largely in retirement, on a small government pension and some income from farming. He left behind him a chronologically arranged collection of more than 9,000 poems in the *shi* form, more than 100 lyric songs in the *ci* (*tz'u*) form, as well as a variety of miscellaneous prose writings that include an official history of the regional Southern Tang regime (937–75), and a travel diary.

Translations

Selections and Anthologies

Candlin, Clara M., *The Rapier of Lu: Patriot Poet of China*, with an introduction, London: John Murray, 1946 (contains 43 poems and an essay)

Chang Chun-shu and Joan Smythe, *South China in the Twelfth Century: A Translation of Lu Yu's Travel Diaries, July 3–December 6, 1170*, Hong Kong: Chinese University Press, 1981

Gordon, David M., *The Wild Old Man: Poems of Lu Yu*, San Francisco: North Point Press, 1984 (contains 127 Lu You poems)

Liu, Wu-chi and Irving Yucheng Lo (editors), *Sunflower Splendor: Three Thousand Years of Chinese Poetry*, with an introduction by Lo, Bloomington: Indiana University Press, 1975 (includes 20 Lu You poems translated by Burton Watson, I.Y. Lo, Chiang Yee and James J.L. Liu)

Payne, Robert (editor), *The White Pony: An Anthology of Chinese Poetry from the Earliest Times to the Present Day, Newly Translated*, New York: John Day, 1947; London: Allen and Unwin, 1949 (includes 27 Lu You poems translated by Pai Chwen-yu)

Price, James P., "Ten *Tz'u* by Lu Yu" (parallel texts), in *Song without Music: Chinese Tz'u Poetry*, edited by Stephen C. Soong, Hong Kong: Chinese University Press, 1980

Rexroth, Kenneth, *One Hundred Poems from the Chinese*, New York: New Directions, 1956 (includes 11 poems of Lu You)

Waley, Arthur, *Translations from the Chinese*, New York: Knopf, 1941 (includes 4 poems of Lu You)

Watson, Burton, *The Old Man Who Does as He Pleases: Selections from the Poetry and Prose of Lu Yu*, New York: Columbia University Press, 1973 (contains 63 poems and excerpts from the travel diary)

Lu You, a prolific author, was primarily known as the greatest poet (in the *shi* form) of the Southern Song (Sung) period. Two disparate themes dominate in Lu You's poetry: the patriotic and the idyllic. In the former we feel his indignation at the enemy occupation of north China and read about his dreams of fighting against the barbarian troops; in the latter we hear about the little joys and sorrows of everyday life in his farming village. It is no surprise that most translators have chosen to concentrate on his poems in the latter category, since his patriotic poems are, as Burton Watson has observed, "difficult to translate precisely because of their intensely personal and passionate nature which, if not brought over into just the right language, is likely to sound petulant and bombastic."

Numerous anthologies, not all of which have been listed here, have included selections of Lu You. Among earlier renditions of Lu You's poetry, WALEY's (1941) easily stands out. While he generally avoids using rhymes as he believes "it is impossible to produce in English rhyme-effects at all similar to those in the original", Waley has tried to produce regular rhythmic effects by using a stress in English to represent each character in Chinese. Though only four short poems in celebration of rustic life are included, they are a great pleasure to read, like most of Waley's works.

PAYNE's (1947) anthology includes 27 *shi* poems by Lu You, mostly octaves and quatrains, preceded by a two-page biographical note. Payne regards himself chiefly as the "editor and reviser": the translations are done by a number of Chinese scholars, revised by Payne and submitted back to them until final agreement is reached. The Lu You selection is attributed to PAI CHWEN-YU. Following Waley's example, Payne and his collaborators do not use rhyme, but rather turn the original lines into simple and rhythmic English prose. The translation is generally free from inaccuracies but frequently reads more like the paraphrase of poems than the poems themselves.

The American poet REXROTH (1956) includes 11 poems of Lu You in both the *shi* and the *ci* forms. While they all read very well in English, they are far less *translation* than Ezra Pound's *adaptation* or Robert Lowell's *imitation*. The rendition is extremely free, and in the case of the famous lyric song "Phoenix Hairpins", serious misunderstanding of the original has occurred.

Sunflower Splendor (1975), probably the most comprehensive anthology of traditional Chinese poetry in English to date, includes for the Lu You selection 14 *shi* poems, translated by WATSON, LO and the renowned artist CHIANG YEE, and six lyric songs (*ci*) translated by James J.Y. LIU. The selection, though small, is quite representative: all 20 texts are among the most-anthologized ones of the author, and they provide a glimpse of the variety in form, genre and theme of the original. While the anthology itself sometimes suffers from the great differences in the degree of freedom or faithfulness vis à vis the original found among its numerous collaborators, the Lu You selection is done by translators known for their fidelity and scholarship.

Whereas most translators have focused on Lu You's *shi* poems, SOONG's important volume on the lyric song (*ci*), *Song Without Music*, that contains translations as well as critical essays, includes 10 songs by Lu You translated by PRICE (1980).

Printed side by side with Chinese texts, the translation is commendable in its loyalty to the originals and its pleasing clarity.

Among the works devoted exclusively to Lu You, CANDLIN's little book (1946) begins with an introduction that consists of a miscellany of biographical and critical materials including observations on Lu You by the author's own son and by a Manchu emperor, as well the translation of one of the author's self-revealing essays, and concludes with a chronological Index of Dates. The poems are divided into three groups: seven under the topic of *Patriotism*, 15 under *Travel*, and 21 under *Nature*. Candlin received some help from a number of leading sinologists (including Lionel Giles and Carrington Goodrich) of her time, hence her translation is relatively free from errors, though occasionally she still, quite unintelligibly, skips an entire line. She tends to break her text into very short and broken lines: a quatrain in the original is generally turned into more than a dozen lines. However, her translation has in fact acquired an individual flavor of its own and should not be brusquely dismissed.

WATSON's book (1973) contains 63 *shi* poems and excerpts from the travel diary, which chronicles a trip from Shanyin (in modern Zhejiang), the author's native town, to Sichuan (Szechwan), in the year 1170. One of the leading translators and interpreters of East Asian literature today, Watson has been instrumental in introducing to the English-speaking public the rich variety of the poetry of the Song dynasty, so often overshadowed by that of the Tang dynasty, generally considered as the Golden Age of Chinese poetry. This volume was completed in addition to his previous translations of the works of Su Shi (Su Shih) (1965) and of Yoshikawa's monograph on Song poetry (1967). Like all Watson's other works, the translation is generally accurate and highly readable. In facile and smooth colloquial American English, Watson's translation of prose frequently has an edge over that of verse, but in this case the verse translation works well, especially with Lu You's poems of daily life, which form the core of Watson's selection. The partial translation of Lu You's travel diary is now superseded by CHANG's (1981) fully annotated complete translation (based on SMYTHE's draft), an important work for those interested in Chinese travel literature.

GORDON's volume (1984) contains the largest selection of Lu You's *shi* poems (127), mostly in the regulated verse forms of octaves and quatrains. In his experiment of looking for "an English equivalent" for Lu You's lines, he uses caesura to break the Chinese line into certain rhythmic units, which results in distracting affectedness, and the translation is also marred by frequent errors and misunderstandings due, quite obviously, to the translator's rather superficial knowledge of Chinese.

Duke's (1977) monograph in Twayne's World Authors series remains the only biographical and critical study of the author in English. It should be commended for its scholarship, but the numerous translations of Lu You's poems in the book, while generally accurate, are often (as has been critically noticed) very awkward to read, probably because of the dubious attempt to recreate the syntax of the originals in English. Yoshikawa's sometimes opinionated study (1962), in Watson's graceful translation (1967), provides a general background for students of Song poetry as well as an insightful introduction to Lu You's achievements as a poet in the *shi* form.

YANG YE

Further Reading

Duke, Michael S., *Lu You*, Boston: Twayne, 1977

Yoshikawa, Kōjirō, *An Introduction to Sung Poetry*, translated by Burton Watson, Cambridge, Massachusetts: Harvard University Press, 1967

Lucan AD 39–65

Roman poet

Biography

Born Marcus Annaeus Lucanus in Corduba (now Cordova), Spain, 3 November AD 39, son of a Roman Knight and nephew of the Stoic philosopher and tragedian Seneca the Younger. In 40 he moved with his family to Rome. He studied there and later in Athens. After being a friend and favorite of the emperor Nero, who appointed him to public office, Lucan joined Piso's conspiracy against the emperor. Discovered, he was forced to commit suicide, and died in Rome 30 April 65.

In 62 he had published the first three books of the *Pharsalia*, his epic account of the civil war between Julius Caesar and Pompey. It is thought he intended the work to cover the period from Caesar's crossing of the Rubicon in 49 to Cato's suicide in 46 BC or Caesar's death in 44, but only 10 books in all, the last incomplete, were written. Lucan's narrative ceases in 48, with the death of Pompey. The work takes its traditional name from the subject of book VII, the battle of Pharsalus, in the plain of Pharsalia in Thessaly, where Caesar defeated Pompey in 48.

Pharsalia

De bello civili, from 62 AD

Translations

Gorges, Sir A., *Lucan's Pharsalia: Containing the Civill Warres Betweene Caesar and Pompey*, London: E. Blount, 1614

Graves, Robert, *Pharsalia: Dramatic Episodes of the Civil*

Wars, with an introduction, Harmondsworth: Penguin, 1956; Baltimore: Penguin, 1957
Joyce, Jane Wilson, *Pharsalia*, Ithaca, New York: Cornell University Press, 1993
Marlowe, Christopher, *Lucan's First Booke Translated Line for Line*, 1600; in his *Complete Works*, vol. 1, edited by Roma Gill, Oxford: Clarendon Press, and New York: Oxford University Press, 1987
May, Thomas, *Lucan's Pharsalia; or, The Civil Warres of Rome, betweene Pompey the Great and Julius Caesar: The First Three Bookes*, London: Norton and Mathewes for M. Law, 1626; all 10 books, 1627
Rowe, Nicholas, *Lucan's Pharsalia*, 2 vols, London: Jacob Tonson, 1718
Widdows, P.F., *Lucan's Civil War*, Bloomington: Indiana University Press, 1988

The *Pharsalia*, or *De bello civili*, an epic poem in 10 books telling of the civil war between Julius Caesar and Pompey, is Lucan's only surviving work. It was held in high regard from the Middle Ages right through the 18th century, and is now beginning to recover from two centuries of comparative neglect. Both Barnabe Googe and George Turberville apparently considered translating the *Pharsalia*, the latter claiming to have given up the task so that it might be done by a worthier poet, Thomas Sackville, Lord Buckhurst. However this recommendation was not acted upon and, although allusions to Lucan, and evidence of his considerable influence, may be seen in the works of, for example, Chaucer and Lydgate, the first published translation from his work did not appear until 1600. This was Christopher MARLOWE's blank verse, line-for-line rendition of the first book of the *Pharsalia*. It is hardly surprising that Lucan's portrait of Julius Caesar as an impious and overreaching tyrant should have appealed to the creator of Guise, Dr Faustus, and most particularly Tamburlaine, who is himself aware of the affinity, proclaiming that:

> My camp is like to Julius Caesar's host,
> Nor ever fought but had the victory;
> Nor in Pharsalia was there such hot war ...
> (1 *Tamburlaine* III, iii, 152–54)

The apocalyptic violence of Lucan found an answering voice in Marlowe, as his translation of the comparison between Caesar and thunder demonstrates:

> So thunder which the wind tears from the clouds,
> With crack of riven air and hideous sound
> Filling the world, leaps out and throws forth fire,
> Affrights poor fearful men, and blasts their eyes
> With overthwarting flames, and raging shoots
> Alongst the air, and, nought resisting it,
> Falls, and returns, and shivers where it lights.
> (152–58)

The first complete English translation of the *Pharsalia* was that of Sir Arthur GORGES, published in 1614, and written in clumsy octosyllabic rhyming couplets. David Norbrook notes a telling contradiction in the marginal notes to Gorges's translation which adumbrates the problematic status of a poem about civil insurrection in a century that saw so many political upheavals.

On one reading, the passage is to be dated early in Nero's reign, and Lucan "teacheth NERO how he should gouerne, by an Imagination of what is": this is the familiar humanist strategy of giving advice under a mask of praise. Another note, however, baldly declares that "This is meere Ironicall flattery". (Norbrook, 1993, p. 53)

The English Civil Wars and the fear of Stuart absolutism coloured the way readers responded to Lucan. Although not all modern critics are convinced that the poem should be read as a republican manifesto, the *Pharsalia* has often been associated with a strong distaste for authoritarianism and tyranny. This connection is particularly apparent in the next full-length translation of the *Pharsalia*, that of Thomas MAY, completed in 1627. May was to become a partisan of the Parliamentary cause in 1642, and worked on behalf of Cromwell's regime, as Secretary of Parliament, until his death in 1650. The significance of his decision to translate Lucan's poem of civil war was noted by John Aubrey, who wrote that his "translation of Lucan's excellent poeme made him in love with the republique, which tang stuck by him". May's version was written in rhyming couplets and, although more competent than Gorges's effort, is far less smooth and accomplished than Rowe's later translation. It was the character of Cato who provided the strongest focus for Whiggish enthusiasm. One celebrated episode, Cato's attack on superstition in Book IX, was translated by Robert Wolseley, John Dennis, Nicholas Rowe, George Jeffreys and George Lord Lyttleton. And of course one of the most famous Whig authors, Joseph Addison, took the character of Cato as the subject of his best-known tragedy.

The most important translation of the *Pharsalia* is that of Nicholas ROWE, Shakespeare editor and playwright. Once again we may see the link in his contemporaries' minds between an interest in Lucan and republican political sympathies. His biographer James Wellwood commented that "He had entertained an early inclination for that Author, and I believe it was the darling passion he had for the liberty and constitution of his Country, that first inclin'd him to think of Translating him". Rowe's first essay in translating Lucan was a short passage, II, 232–325, the conversation between Brutus and Cato about civil war, which appeared in Tonson's *Poetical Miscellanies, the Fifth Part*, in 1703, and he later went on to publish further excerpts, VI, 1–262 and the whole of Book IX. It seems that Tonson had projected a complete translation of Lucan by several hands, but this plan never came to fruition. Rowe's complete translation, written in heroic couplets, appeared in 1718. Here is his more leisurely rendition of the lines that appear above in Marlowe's translation.

> Such while earth trembles and heaven thunders loud,
> Darts the swift lightning from the rending cloud,
> Fierce through the day it breaks and in its flight
> The dreadful blast confounds the gazer's sight;
> Resistless in its course delights to rove,
> And cleaves the temples of its master Jove;
> Alike where-e'er it passes or returns,
> With equal rage the fell destroyer burns;
> Then with a whirl full in its strength retires,
> And recollects the force of all its scattered fires.
> (I, 288–98)

Inevitably Rowe's *Pharsalia* is compared with the great translations of the Augustan age: Pope's Homer and Dryden's Virgil. If he cannot be said to match these shining achievements, this is no reason why his very real merits should not be recognized, any more than the superiority of Homer and Virgil need blind readers to the strengths of Lucan. The translation was widely admired, Dr Johnson, in particular, paying it generous tribute. Rowe's is an expansive, even a free, translation in comparison with Marlowe's rigorous metaphrase; at one point in a note he explains that he has departed from his author in describing a corpse gradually returning to life in response to Erictho's magic, because that seems more convincing than Lucan's statement that it was revived all at once. Although he might sometimes seem almost too smooth and elegant a poet to reproduce Lucan's distinctive style, Rowe's translation includes many powerful passages, which do justice to the horror and violence of the original.

Lucan perhaps found his most unsympathetic translator in Robert GRAVES, whose prose translation appeared in 1956. Among the epithets applied to the *Pharsalia* in Graves's very forthright introduction are "clumsy", "monotonous", "degenerate" and "brutally sensational", although he does concede that "his occasional polished epigrams make highly serviceable quotations". He aligns Lucan's appeal with the popularity of the bleak modernist poetry of Pound and Eliot. Graves's own views are engagingly transparent. "Shelley has been taken to task for preferring Lucan to Virgil, but he too lived in a cranky age and showed extreme emotional instability". Graves states that his aim is to make the *Pharsalia* as clear and immediately comprehensible as possible, which perhaps explains why his version reads at times more like a translation of Caesar's prose than of Lucan's highly rhetorical verse.

More recent translations of the *Pharsalia* include those of Jane Wilson JOYCE (1993) and Peter WIDDOWS (1988). Wilson Joyce's translation is based upon a six beat line, with occasional variations, and Widdows's version is written in unrhymed hexameters.

SARAH ANNES BROWN

Further Reading

Dilke, O.A.W., "Lucan and English Literature" in *Neronians and Flavians*, edited by D.R. Dudley, London and Boston: Routledge and Kegan Paul, 1972

Hesse, Alfred William, "Nicholas Rowe's Translation of Lucan's Pharsalia: A Study in Literary History", (dissertation), Philadelphia: University of Pennsylvania, 1950

Norbrook, David, "Lucan, Thomas May, and the Creation of a Republican Literary Culture" in *Culture and Politics in Early Stuart England*, edited by Kevin Sharpe and Peter Lake, Stanford, California: Stanford University Press, 1993; London: Macmillan, 1994

Lucretius c.94–c.55 BC

Roman poet and philosopher

Biography

Lucretius (Titus Lucretius Carus) is one of the greatest Roman writers and belongs to the scant handful of philosopher-poets in world literature. Virtually nothing is known about his life. His apparently unfinished poem *De rerum natura* (*On the Nature of Things*: see below for other translations of the title) illustrates and expounds Epicurean teachings in six books of magnificent hexameter verse that vies with that of Virgil, who was indebted to it. Lucretius' aim is to free human beings from fear, especially fear of death and of the gods. He is passionately committed to this mission. His poetry expresses deep love for the natural world and compassion for the human predicament, and shows excellent intellectual grasp of his subject matter.

On the Nature of Things

De rerum natura, 1st century BC

Translations

Bailey, Cyril, *Lucretius on the Nature of Things*, Oxford: Clarendon Press, 1910; included in *Titi Lucreti Cari de rerum natura libri sex* (parallel texts), edited, with an introduction, by Bailey, 3 vols, Oxford: Oxford University Press, 1947

Bovie, Palmer, *Lucretius*: *On the Nature of Things*, New York: New American Library, 1974

Copley, Frank O., *The Nature of Things*, with an introduction, New York: Norton, 1977

Dryden, John, in *Sylvae; or, The Second Part of Poetical Miscellanies*, London: printed for Jacob Tonson, 1685

Esolen, Anthony M., *On the Nature of Things/ De rerum natura*, Baltimore: Johns Hopkins University Press, 1995

Humphries, Rolfe, *The Way Things Are: The De rerum natura of Titus Lucretius Carus*, Bloomington: Indiana University Press, 1968

Jackson, Thomas, *Titus Lucretius Carus on the Nature of Things*, Oxford: Blackwell, 1929

Latham, Ronald, *Lucretius on the Nature of the Universe*, Harmondsworth and New York: Penguin, 1951

Mantinband, James H., *On the Nature of the Universe: A New Verse Translation*, New York: Ungar, 1965

Munro, H.A.J., *De rerum natura* (translation), London: Bell, 1886; as *On the Nature of Things*, 1908
Winspear, Alban Dewes, *De rerum natura*, New York: S.A. Russell, 1956
Wooby, Philip F., *Lucretius: About Reality*, New York: Philosophical Library, 1973

Editions of the text of Lucretius vary widely, not only in wording but in the sequence of lines and passages as well. Thus translations can often be out of step with one another. Modern interest in Lucretius favors the poet over the philosopher: consequently, the main job of the translator is to convey a sense of Lucretius' "fiery temper" and the "torrent of his verse" (to use Dryden's description) without, however, underplaying or misrepresenting Lucretius' philosophical references and terms. Many of the latter are neologisms Lucretius introduced into Latin; translators wisely refrain from undertaking similar manipulation of English. Prose translations usually convey Lucretius' meaning quite well but one must bear in mind that this is a great poet, second only to Virgil in Latin literature. Hence, verse translations are preferable in principle, although very few approximate the impact of the original.

DRYDEN (1685) included several excerpts from Lucretius in his *Sylvae*: "Lucretius. The Beginning of the First Book", "Lucretius. The Beginning of the Second Book", "Translation of the Latter Part of the Third Book of Lucretius. *Against the Fear of Death*", "Lucretius. The Fourth Book. *Concerning the Nature of Love*", and "From Lucretius. Book the Fifth" Dryden's renderings of Lucretius' dactylic hexameters, in rhymed iambic pentameters, are noteworthy not because they are likely to satisfy the modern reader of Lucretius but because they are excellent samples of Dryden's poetry and of his era's taste in classics.

MUNRO's reliable and readable prose rendering (1886), frequently reprinted, is basically a scholar's translation but is surpassed by Bailey's in that category. Munro is somewhat archaic, but not intrusively so.

BAILEY's edition and commentary (1910) are basic and indispensable. His "Prolegomena" of 171 pages give an excellent introduction to Lucretius. This is the best prose translation of the great poem – one cannot imagine a better, since not only is Bailey absolutely reliable but he also manages to convey the sense that we are dealing with poetry. The reader may balk at occasional archaisms such as the use of the second person singular personal pronoun ("thou") and locutions such as "'tis" – features avoided by the best contemporary translators.

JACKSON's rhythmic prose (1929) reads well, giving the effect of iambic verse. He is somewhat dependent on Munro's version, yet his translation is his own. It would have been an advantage to print it as iambic free verse, which it essentially is: more space on the page would make the reading flow more easily. As it is, anyone with an ear for poetry will recognize the rhythm but will be slowed down by its prose-like presentation in print.

LATHAM's prose rendering (1951) is simple, reliable, and idiomatic, with no pretense to poetic merit. A helpful outline of Lucretius' very complex poem precedes the translation.

WINSPEAR's version (1956) is in free rhythmical verse. He soundly makes no attempt to observe correspondence of lines and helpfully puts headings over groups of verses to steer the reader through the intricacies of Lucretius' argument. His verse looks good on the page: there is a good deal of space, which facilitates reading, and at the same time the uneven length of his lines is analogous to the nervous quality of the original. He uses archaic forms such as "thou".

MANTINBAND's rhythmic free verse (1965) reads like prose, quite the opposite to Jackson's prose that sounds like verse. This is not one of the best translations but it does have some helpful footnotes.

HUMPHRIES (1968), a very notable translator of the classics, uses free verse for his rather free translation. The line-for-line correspondence is wisely given up here: where sense demands, Humphries adds lines. Along with Bovie's this is the best version of Lucretius in English. The verse is vigorous but light, Lucretius' tone comes across better than in other translations, and there can be no doubt in the reader's mind that this is a poem. It takes a poet to translate one.

WOOBY's verse (1973) is notable as one of the very few attempts to approximate the hexameter in English. This is an interesting and very challenging undertaking, but ultimately doomed to failure. The sound is inferior to iambic English or even to prose, and the enormous length of the lines makes reading irksome. Prose is actually easier on the eye, and the mind, because it is unbroken. On the other hand, a good verse rendering will break up the text at just the right points and pace it properly – something Wooby does not accomplish. This translation is neither literal enough nor free enough.

BOVIE (1974), a notable translator of several classics, uses blank verse as the nearest equivalent in English to the Latin dactylic hexameter. His rendering is excellent in all regards. An occasional roughness in his use of meter subtly corresponds to Lucretius' ruggedness.

COPLEY (1977) also uses blank verse, but in his attempt to translate line by line he unfortunately sometimes abridges the text (since English blank verse lines are shorter than Latin hexameters), and on other occasions pads his lines to preserve the correspondence. Because of this, although his feeling for Lucretius' language is excellent, other renderings are preferable. He offers a good, concise introduction dealing with Epicurean philosophy.

ESOLEN (1995) uses blank verse and shows considerable inventiveness in trying to produce a close line-by-line translation, but the result is somewhat awkward because of this self-imposed limitation. Still, this is a very readable version.

ZOJA PAVLOVSKIS-PETIT

Further Reading

See the translators' prefaces in Esolen, Humphries and Latham

Ramon Lull

See Ramon Llull

Luo Guanzhon

See San Guo Zhi Yan Yi

Lusophone African Writers in English Translation

Literary activity in former Portuguese Africa began during the second half of the 19th century and accompanied the development of the press in those areas where the presence of a colonial administration and a mixed creole population were most firmly established: the Cape Verde Islands, Luanda and to a lesser extent Benguela in Angola, and Mozambique Island and Quelimane, near the mouth of the Zambezi, in Mozambique.

After the partition of Africa by the European colonial powers at the Conference of Berlin in 1885, and the more robust implementation of colonial rule, literary activity in Portuguese Africa was curtailed, and after the imposition of the Salazar dictatorship in 1934 it was subject to the ever increasing vigilance of the censors. By the late 1930s, however, and particularly after the end of World War II, literature became a force that reflected and in turn nourished the aspiration for political independence. This was eventually achieved after a sustained guerrilla campaign in 1975.

If one discounts the early ethnographic translations of Héli Chatelain in Angola at the end of the 19th century, and of Elsie Clews Parsons in the 1920s in the Cape Verdes, on the grounds that their translations were from folktales expressed in the local vernacular, translation of Lusophone African texts and authors really dates only from the 1960s. This coincided with the growth of interest in African literature generally, as well as with the international publicity being given to the independence wars in Portuguese Africa.

The first anthology of African poetry in Portuguese was published in Paris in 1958, modelled on Léopold Senghor's earlier *Anthologie de la nouvelle poésie nègre et malgache de langue française* (1948), which had merited a preface by Jean-Paul Sartre. The Angolan exile Mário de Andrade's *Antologia da poesia negra de expressão portuguesa* (1958) brought together poems by writers from Angola, Mozambique and São Tomé, who would later become seminal figures in the development of modern Lusophone African literature. The sudden, albeit limited, availability of African poems in Portuguese undoubtedly explains the inclusion of translations from Andrade's collection in Gerald Moore and Ulli Beier's pioneer anthology *Modern Poetry from Africa* (1963). This was followed by Ezekiel Mphahlele's *African Writing Today* (1967), which included translations of poems by, among others, the Angolan poet and political leader Agostinho Neto and the Mozambican poet and journalist José Craveirinha. By the early 1970s, armed struggle against Portuguese colonial rule was claiming more international attention, and this was reflected in Margaret Dickinson's anthology, *When Bullets Begin to Flower: Poems of Resistance from Angola, Mozambique and Guiné* (1972).

Then, in 1974, Marga Holness's translation of Agostinho Neto's poems was published under the title of *Sacred Hope*. By the 1980s, resistance had become revolution, a change amply reflected in Chris Searle's anthology, *Sunflower of Hope: Poems of the Mozambican Revolution* (1982).

The first prose work in English translation by a Lusophone African writer was Luís Bernado Honwana's *We Killed Mangy-*

Dog and Other Stories (1969). First published in Portuguese in 1964 and subsequently banned, these short stories by a writer and journalist who spent time in a colonial jail for political activities were translated by Dorothy Guedes, the English wife of a Portuguese architect resident in Mozambique.

Translations of prose works by single authors became more frequent after the mid-1970s. By this time, novels and collections of short stories were widely available either in Portuguese editions or in those of the newly created writers' associations and unions in the now independent Lusophone countries. At the same period, "co-operators" (a revolutionary euphemism for aid workers) entered the countries and became familiar with the work of local writers. In this way, the work of Luandino Vieira, then Angola's most widely known fiction writer, came to be published in English. Vieira's novella, *The Real Life of Domingos Xavier* (1978), set during the anti-colonial uprising, had been published in French translation as early as 1971, before the appearance of any Portuguese edition. The year 1980 also saw the translation of Vieira's most famous work, *Luuanda*, a controversial collection of stories which had won a prestigious literary prize in Portugal in 1965, while the author was in prison. Also published in 1983 was the translation of *Mayombe*, a novel by another Angolan author, Pepetela, who was to become his country's most prolific fiction writer. *Mayombe*, which had sold widely in Angola when first published in 1980, is set during the colonial war in the enclave of Cabinda, but is also a treatise on the problems of nation building in the context of the modern state in Africa. Such was the honesty with which it discussed issues like tribalism and revolutionary dogma that it came to be studied on cultural studies courses in a number of African universities.

The years between 1988 and 1996 witnessed the translations of further Lusophone African prose works. Uanhenga Xitu's *The World of "Mestre" Tamoda* (translated 1988) is the comic account of the antics of one of Portuguese-speaking Africa's favourite literary characters, a bush lawyer whose self-taught flowery Portuguese leads him unwittingly into conflict with the colonial authorities. The Mozambican author Mia Couto's short stories, *Voices Made Night* (translated 1990) and *Every Man is a Race* (translated 1994), similarly evoke the cultural dualism of a society in transition between tradition and modernity, between ancestral forms of culture associated with rural life and imported urban values. Pepetela's *Yaka* (translated 1996) is the saga of a colonial family over three generations. At the same time, anthologies or special issues of journals (*Passport to Portugal; The Literary Review*) have continued to bring to the attention of an English-speaking readership the variety of literature being produced in Lusophone Africa.

The challenges facing the translator of Lusophone African literature are similar to those that face translators of other African literatures in European languages. Portuguese interrelates in a variety of ways with the indigenous languages of Angola and Mozambique. For most speakers it is a second language and has therefore been infiltrated by the influences of local mother tongues. For others, particularly those living in the big cities, it has become the main instrument of communication, while at the same time taking on an expressiveness different from that of its European matrix. Writers like Luandino Vieira and Mia Couto have exploited local lexical and syntactical characteristics in an attempt to give their Portuguese a truly national flavour. This is particularly the case with Vieira,who uses Kimbundu (the vernacular of the Luanda area) in some of his dialogues as well as creating Portuguese verbs out of Kimbundu words. Literal translation would, in the words of one of Vieira's translators, "have made the English incomprehensible". This means that stylistic liberties have to be taken with the English rendering, and where possible, unorthodox word order or sentence construction introduced in order to preserve the flavour of the original.

DAVID BROOKSHAW

Anthologies

Dickinson, Margaret (editor and translator), *When Bullets Begin to Flower: Poems of Resistance from Angola, Mozambique and Guiné*, Nairobi: East African Publishing House, 1972

Gerrard, Mike and Thomas McCarthy (editors), *Passport to Portugal*, London: Serpent's Tail, 1994

Literary Review, Madison, New Jersey: Farleigh Dickinson University, vol. 38/4 (1995)

Moore, Gerald and Ulli Beier (editors), *Modern Poetry from Africa*, Harmondsworth: Penguin, 1963; revised edition, 1966

Mphahlele, Ezekiel, *African Writing Today*, Harmondsworth: Penguin, 1967

Searle, Chris, *Sunflower of Hope: Poems of the Mozambican Revolution*, London: Allison and Busby, 1982

Translated Authors

Couto, Mia, *Voices Made Night*, translated by David Brookshaw, Oxford: Heinemann, 1990

Couto, Mia, *Every Man is a Race*, translated by David Brookshaw, Oxford: Heinemann, 1994

Honwana, Luís Bernardo, *We Killed Mangy-Dog and Other Stories*, translated by Dorothy Guedes, London: Heinemann, 1969

Neto, Agostinho, *Sacred Hope*, translated by Marga Holness, Dar-es-Salaam: Tanzania Publishing House, 1974; London: Journeyman Press, 1988

Pepetela, *Mayombe*, translated by Michael Wolfers, London: Heinemann, 1983

Pepetela, *Yaka*, translated by Marga Holness, Oxford: Heinemann, 1996

Vieira, Luandino, *The Real Life of Domingos Xavier*, translated by Michael Wolfers, London: Heinemann, 1978

Vieira, Luandino, *Luuanda*, translated by Tamara L. Bender, with Donna S. Hill, London: Heinemann, 1980

Xitu, Uanhenga, *The World of "Mestre" Tamoda*, translated by Annella McDermott, London: Readers International, 1988

Further Reading

Chabal, Patrick (editor), *The Post-Colonial Literature of Lusophone Africa*, Evanston, Illinois: Northwestern University Press, and London: Hurst, 1996

Hamilton, Russell G., *Voices from an Empire: A History of Afro-Portuguese Literature*, Minneapolis: University of Minnesota Press, 1975

Keenoy, Ray *et al.*, *The Babel Guide to the Fiction of Portugal, Brazil and Africa in English Translation*, London: Boulevard, 1995